Other offerings from funsub books:

love, actually,
realizing the universal loving ideal.

The New York Saturday Press,
Omnibus, digital, and unabridged editions.

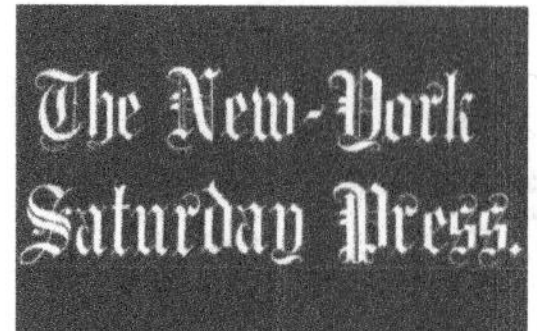

AI go BOOM!

A practical guide to the old-world apocalypse.

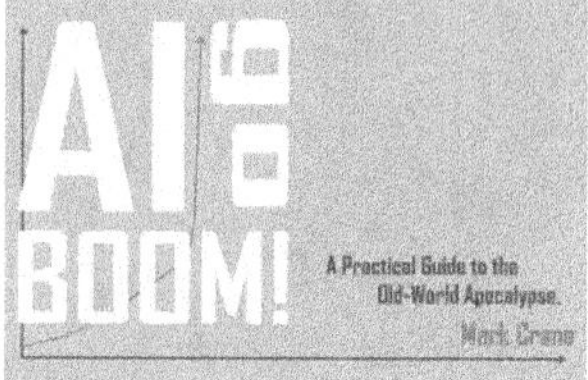

American Slavery: As It Is.

A wonderful hand-crafted, limited edition facsimile edition of the most influential abolition book.

Browse my eBay store of iconic first editions, antique toys, and rare artworks, in addition to original source materials related to the New York Saturday Press and Bohemian NYC.

BONUS! For a FREE pdf of the 1870 "Fast Man's Directory and Lover's Guide to New York City," what was essentially a printed guide to prostitution in NYC, please sign up for my email list by scanning the QR code at right.

The New-York Saturday Press.

1858 ★ ★ ★ *Omnibus Edition* ★ ★ ★ 1866

Henry Clapp, Jr., founder and editor.

The New-York Saturday Press.

1858 ★★★ *Omnibus Edition* ★★★ 1866

Edited by

Mark Crane

FUNSUB BOOKS

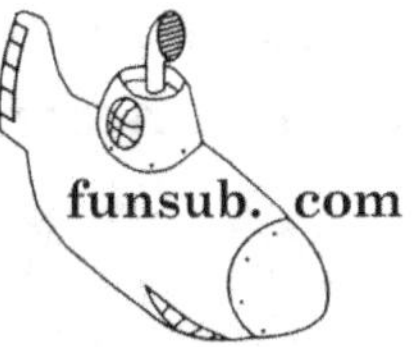

New York Saturday Press Omnibus Edition, 2025.

from an 1857 Paul Girardet woodcut from Hippolyte Sebron
looking south on Broadway at the Spring Street intersection.

ISBN 978-1-967987-03-0 KDP Paperback
ISBN 9781967987016 Kindle
ISBN 9781967987009 IngramSpark Softcover
ISBN 9781967987023 IngramSpark Hardcover
Library of Congress Control Number: 2025911566

Funsub Books can bring authors to your live event. For more information or to book a live event, contact mail@funsub.com.
Manufactured in the United States of America.

First Edition

ACKNOWLEDGEMENTS

This project would not have been possible without the archives provided by the Historical Society of Pennsylvania and their fabulous staff. Thank you!

Lehigh University maintains a wonderful archival program focussing on the literary milieu at Pfaff's, offering a wonderful array of online resources under the title: The Vault at Pfaff's, An Archive of Art and Literature by the Bohemians of Antebellum New York. Thank you!

New York Saturday Press Omnibus Edition consists of carefully selected articles from the entirety of each of the journal's two separate runs, an introduction, glossary, and other complimentary material.

CONTENTS

funsub books links 2
Introduction 9

October 23, 1858 12
October 30, 1858 22
November 6, 1858 24
November 13, 1858 27
November 20, 1859 29
November 27, 1858 33
December 4, 1858 36
December 11, 1858 40
December 18, 1858 44
December 25, 1858 45
January 1, 1859 53
January 8, 1859 57
January 15, 1859 59
January 22, 1859 60
January 29, 1859 63
February 5, 1859 64
February 12, 1859 69
February 19, 1859 70
February 26, 1859 72
March 5, 1859 74
March 12, 1859 78
March 19, 1859 84
March 26, 1859 87
April 2, 1859 88
April 9, 1859 89
April 16, 1859 93
April 23, 1859 96
April 30, 1859 100
May 7, 1859 103
May 14, 1859 105
May 21, 1859 107
May 28, 1859 109
June 4, 1859 111
June 11, 1859 118
June 18, 1859 120
June 25, 1859 123
July 2, 1859 125
July 9, 1859 128
July 16, 1859 129
July 23, 1859 131
July 30, 1859 136
August 6, 1859 139
August 13, 1859 141
August 20, 1859 146
August 27, 1859 149
September 3, 1859 153
September 10, 1859 157
September 17, 1859 161
September 24, 1859 166
October 1, 1859 169
October 8, 1859 174
October 15, 1859 177
October 22, 1859 182
October 29, 1859 185
November 5, 1859 188
November 12, 1859 194
November 19, 1859 198
November 26, 1859 206
December 3, 1859 210
December 10, 1859 214
December 17, 1859 221
December 24, 1859 226
December 31, 1859 235
January 7, 1860 243
January 14, 1860 252
January 21, 1860 256
January 28, 1860 262
February 4, 1860 266
February 11, 1860 274
February 18, 1860 281
February 25, 1860 284
March 3, 1860 291
March 10, 1860 298
March 17, 1860 301
March 24, 1860 296
March 31, 1860 309
April 7, 1860 313
April 14, 1860 318
April 21, 1860 321
April 28, 1860 323
May 5, 1860 331
May 12, 1860 333
May 19, 1860 336
May 26, 1860 340
June 2, 1860 342
June 9, 1860 344
June 16, 1860 345
June 23, 1860 351
June 30, 1860 355
July 7, 1860 359
July 14, 1860 361
July 21, 1860 361
July 28, 1860 363
August 4, 1860 364
August 11, 1860 368
August 18, 1860 370
August 25, 1860 370
September 1, 1860 373
September 8, 1860 378
September 15, 1860 379
September 22, 1860 381
September 29, 1860 383
October 6, 1860 384
October 13, 1860 385
October 20, 1860 386
October 27, 1860 387
November 3, 1860 390
November 10, 1860 392
November 17, 1860 395
November 24, 1860 396
December 1, 1860 399
December 8, 1860 403
December 15, 1860 404
August 5, 1865 408
August 12, 1865 412
August 19, 1865 413
August 26, 1865 415
September 2, 1865 416
September 9, 1865 420
September 16, 1865 421
September 23, 1865 422
September 30, 1865 423
October 7, 1865 425
October 14, 1865 428
October 21, 1865 430
October 28, 1865 431
November 4, 1865 432
November 11, 1865 432
November 18, 1865 436
November 25, 1865 439
December 2, 1865 440
December 9, 1865 442
December 16, 1865 442
December 23, 1865 445
December 30, 1865 448
January 6, 1866 451
January 13, 1866 452
January 20, 1866 454
January 27, 1866 457
February 3, 1866 457
February 10, 1866 459
February 17, 1866 460
February 24, 1866 465
March 3, 1866 467
March 10, 1866 472
March 17, 1866 474
March 24, 1866 474
March 31, 1866 475
April 7, 1866 478
April 14, 1866 479
April 21, 1866 481
April 28, 1866 482
May 5, 1866 484
May 12, 1866 485
May 19, 1866 487
May 26, 1866 490
June 2, 1866 491

Glossary 494
Nota Bene: My Visit to Pfaff's 526
Maps Descending Broadway 527
About the Editor 531

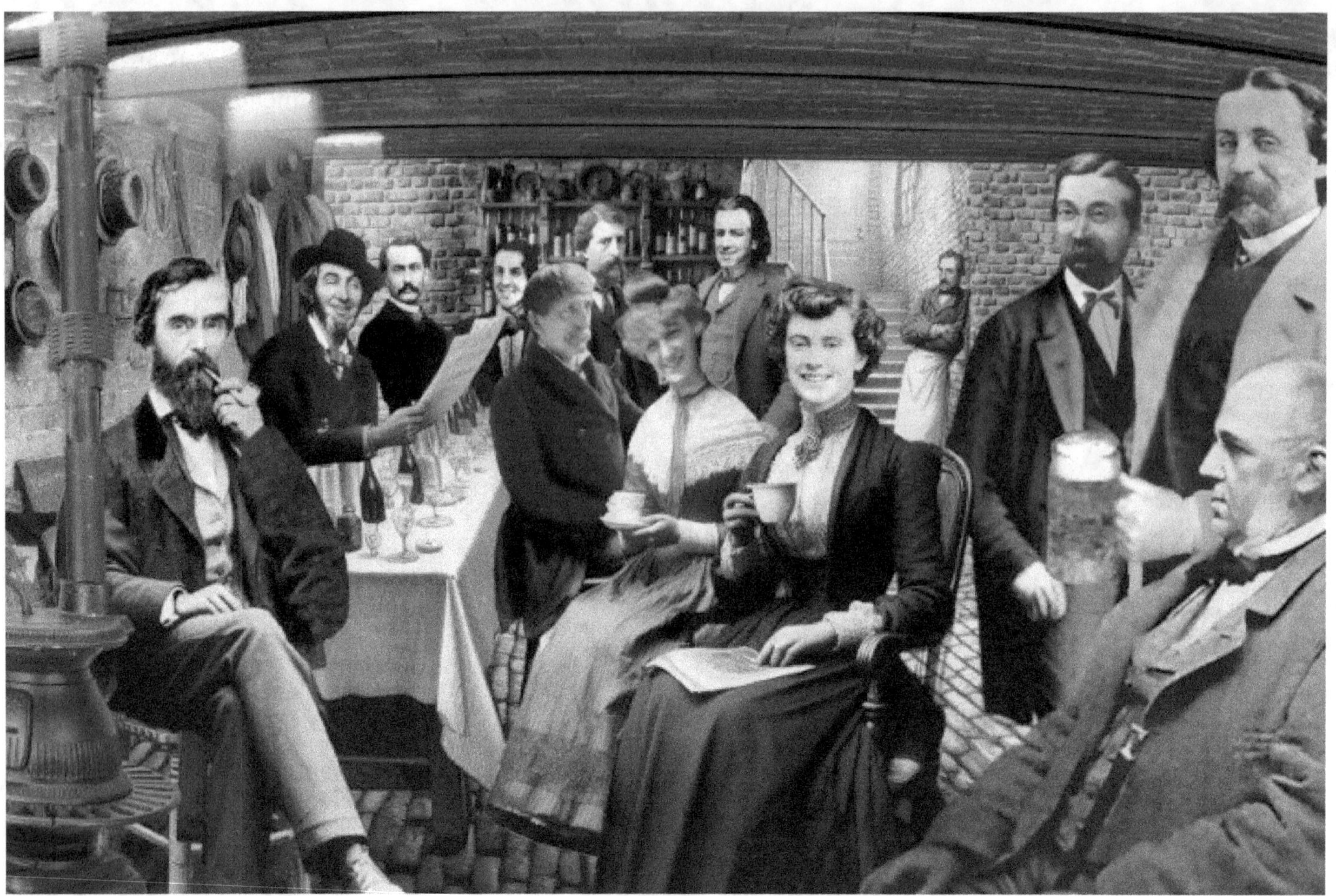

"Under the Sidewalk at Pfaff's"
Left to Right: Clapp, Whitman, Arnold, House, Winter, Homer, Campbell, Burroughs, Clare, O'Brien, Wilkins, and Gurowski.

Introduction.

And now, to tread on lower ground. I like enthusiasm. I like its manifestations. I like a good roar. It is electric. For that reason I recently went to the opening of the New Bowery Theatre, and simply to hear some Bowery cheers. We do not understand roars on this side of the town. We are out of practice too. We roared a little at Macready, years ago, and at points of Webster's, when the "sleeping lion" raised his mane; we might have roared for Fremont, and hope to do so for Seward, but we are a child's cry to the Bowery. Think of youth, spirits uncontrolled, reddest health, and lungs of all conceivable metals, practised nightly at a fire! There were four thousand pair, and Niagara was a joke to them. There were cheers for everything—for the house, for the curtain, for the paint, for Brougham in a side box, for the orchestra-leader, for each fiddler as he entered; and when the curtain rose upon the company, assembled in their best clothes for the opening address, George Washington, the Goddess of Liberty, and old Shakespeare, visibly changed countenance, and shook in the agony of an anticipated tumble.

A joyous sight is that young untutored feeling, bursting forth in its own tongue, giving sound to its sensations, untrammelled by forethought, unrepressed by care.

And now, adieu !

Nessuno.

--*The Saturday Press, 9/24/1859*

The Bohemians of Broadway: Resurrecting the New York Saturday Press.

Take a trip with me to the late 1850's; the steep faces of Broadway's theaters and fashionable hotels echo with the clatter of carriage wheels and hoofbeats against the pebblestone paving. There is a hustle, as today--deliveries, urgent matters, and just as well routine trade conducted; out-of-towners promenading; love affairs being arranged. Tobacco odors, manure, fresh butchery, perfume direct from Paris, roasting oysters, newsprint,... and oily coal smoke floating above has you catching a mote in your eye.

We stand at number 647, just north of Bleecker Street, on the west side of the thoroughfare, the Coleman House Hotel; not to enter, but to step down, where a restaurant proprietor's name is painted dimly on the brick, "Chas Pfaff," the odors of coffee and sweet breads wafting up. Down these steps, Charles Pfaff, a good-natured German, keeps a store of fine wines and barrels of pilsner against the walls of a wide space with a fourfold vaulted ceiling. Boisterous argument, caustic laughter, glad greetings vie for your ear, if the time of day is right. Plates of beefsteak and German pancakes, boiled mutton with potatoes, and spring chicken, are raised above the bobbing crowd as serving women find their way.

Among these mostly young and enthusiastic "Pfaffians" (the "P" is silent) are the writers who contribute to *The New York Saturday Press*, the first American Bohemian journal. Their Bohemianism is a fresh import from Paris, spurred by the popularity of Henri Murger's 1845 *Scènes de la vie de bohème* (Scenes of Bohemian Life). The nascent idea is for a non-traditional lifestyle embraced by artists, writers, and performers, and marked by anti-establishment views, free love, and idleness, or, put another way, intentional poverty. Their writing is intelligent and witty; idealistic and headstrong; brazenly opinionated and at times just so very erroneous.

The gigantic single sheet, folded once to form four 24 x 19-inch pages, means to stir the pot where art and culture are concerned.

At the head of a long table presides the editor of the *Saturday Press,* Henry Clapp, in his mid-forties, an elder to the rest; puffing away at a clay pipe, his expression is obscured behind a long, dark beard. There are no rivals to this "King of Bohemians" as only a fool would envy his continual struggle to keep the business end of this maybe-2,000-circulation journal aloft through the end of the month. He is the kind of a man who makes very close friends quickly, but loses them soon after they've been foolish enough to invest.

William Winter, a poet and editor, is the young man with the droopy mustache. He is engaged in conversation with his sweetheart, Scottish novelist and poet for the *Saturday Press*, Elizabeth Campbell, and her dear friend, Ada Clare, (not her real name), a self-invented Charleston girl, who struck out for Paris when her father died. Ada returned to New York as an unapologetic single-mother, where she tried, and failed, at a theatrical career, before finding her voice as "cricket" for the *Saturday Press.* Not a stranger to Pfaff's, she is known as the "Queen of Bohemia."

That's Ned Wilkins, leaning against the counter, with the flashy attire and the cat-that-ate-the-canary smirk. He pens the "Dramatic Feuilleton," using a French term for a critical commentary on art and literature. In his weekly column, Ned has founded the American style of (as William Winter will one day phrase it) "writing about the stage and society in a facetious, satirical vein, striving to lighten heavy or barren themes with playful banter, and to gild the dreariness of criticism with the glitter of wit."

Walt Whitman, a Brooklyn journalist closer to Clapp's generation than most of the others, is seated quietly in the shadows. Though he is not known for standing for drinks, he has recently won hearts, delivering a sensation to the journal with his convention-defying poetry. Without even an attempt at rhyming, he writes verse that appeals to the 'lowest' instincts of the reader: sensual, primitive, and obscene!

One example of the intensity of the response: Clapp sends Whitman's poetry collection *Leaves of Grass* to the reviewer Juliette H. Beach, way upstate near Niagara Falls. Her husband, a newspaper editor himself, intercepts the package, scratches out a scathing review of his own that goes so far as to encourage Whitman to kill himself, and returns the review in his wife's name. Clapp prints the review supposedly without reading it, stoking controversy, which both he and Whitman are pioneers in seeing as good for business.

There are few as manipulative as Whitman. Whitman is childlike in his innocence yet independent, forthright, and demanding in inventiveness. Reading Whitman is to engage with an artistic focus that at first seems trivial, juvenile, and painstakingly kind; and then to have that understanding usurped—to be led about by this new friendly child at his whim, with no ability to deny the artist's authority. It is the shock of surrender of authority to the weak, to the sensual, to the attentive observer.

It may seem counterintuitive to a Modern that Whitman's poetry should have been vilified as obscene but that he was nonetheless respected and accepted in his genteel and straight-laced day. The idea is he was a homosexual, so he must have been an outcast, no? When Moderns talk of Whitman and the Bohemians, it isn't long before the subject of homosexuality comes up, as several of the writers have been rumored to have had secret, maybe even organized, homosexual encounters. Some modern online articles even (absurdly) refer to Pfaff's as the "first gay bar." Still, there is little in the *Saturday Press* that seems homoerotic in nature.

In 1858, the term "homosexuality" does not exist. The idea of sexual identity, as we understand it today, wouldn't emerge for another fifty years. The truth is that in 1858 people are seen as separate from their sexual behaviors. If a man is noticed to be unusually affectionate towards other men, the issue is behavioral and implies no identity. This can be difficult for modern readers to grasp. Whitman, for instance, finds himself welcomed with open arms by people who regard his poetry as obscene, because society–before easy transportation, long-distance communication, moving pictures, mass media, our overall default sense of security; let alone television, computers, and iPhones–that now long-antiquated society is just too vital to life in the 1850's to willingly destroy for the sake of condemning a person's behavior. People need society to flow smoothly, without conflict.

Abolition radically changes all that. Abolition introduces an idea that is all at once more important than social cohesion.

The best example of this revolutionary shift is seen in the case of the Grimké sisters, Angelina and Sarah, daughters of a South Carolina slaveholding family, who, inspired by Quaker teachings, abandoned their Episcopal training, moved north, and became editors for the American Anti-Slavery Society. In 1839, this society operated a printing press out of the back of Brick Presbyterian Church, directly across from New York City Hall, where the Grimkés collected material and printed anti-slavery pamphlets and books that they would send unprompted to Southern slaveholding families like their own. The printed materials served as accusatory instruments, meticulously documenting the names, dates, and locations associated with morally reprehensible acts committed by respected Southerners against enslaved individuals.

This sudden reversal of societal norms–the assertion of morality over social amity–is seen by Southerners as an acute disrespect, and a heinous injury to Southern honor. The tip of the spear of Southern reaction to the abolition movement is hatred, arson, and murder.

For his own reasons, Clapp, whose social circle and financial backing come largely from the South, quietly shares Southerners' disdain for the abolitionist movement. He would prefer not to say why, and he discourages editorial discussion of the issue.

Abolitionists align themselves with other progressive causes: women's rights, temperance, free love--a movement advocating for women's liberation from marriage's legal constraints--and Spiritualism—a wildly popular new religion combining spirit communication with Christianity. While Clapp supports free love, he opposes the zeal of other reform movements. He derides the "noisy, unmeaning howls" of women, African Americans, and their allies as preachy, meddlesome, and fanatical—a reaction that echoes how modern right-wing critics view political correctness. Clapp's version of the epithet is "Grundyism," after a priggish theatrical character of the 1840's, "Mrs. Grundy," who spares no one her wagging finger.

Just months before the outbreak of the Civil War, Clapp reprints an editorial from a Black newspaper, *The Weekly Anglo-African,* condemning the *Saturday Press* for its silence on slavery. Clapp's decision to print just this criticism without rebuttal or comment serves as a petulantly tacit acknowledgment of the accusation.

Clapp's intolerance extends to nearly every group outside his own small circle--Blacks, Jewish, Irish, Quakers, even Bostonians. It is vital to him to maintain the higher moral ground, so he couches much of his intolerance in a distaste for factions. With inspiration, he professes that the *Saturday Press's* motto is "Humanity first and everything else afterward." Unexamined, the sentiment seems reasonable, but in the case of a country roiling with division over the issue of slavery, it is an argument against moralism and division and in support of a wicked status quo.

I think of him as a curmudgeon. A moralistic cumudgeon, at that! And, so, the word hypocritical fits in there somewhere also. Just hear him go on about fellow publishers as unscrupulous opportunists who sell their souls for the advertising revenue his *Saturday Press* would kill for. He is not the type of character a Modern would expect to find marshalling Bohemians to write about art and culture.

The legacy of the *Saturday Press* does not belong to Clapp, however. Most of its writers are young, enthusiastic, and idealistic. They embrace the spirit of change, even if it threatens the old social cohesion. The women are usually married, contributing via correspondence. The men live in boarding houses in Greenwich Village (known only as the 9th Ward in those first 50 years after it was incorporated into the city.) Each morning, they hike downtown to the numerous newspaper editorial offices located across Park Row from City Hall. More often as independents than contracted staffers, they submit articles, stories, or illustrations; negotiate terms for new assignments; and try to collect on past debts. The pay is maybe $4 per article; a little more for a woodcut illustration; an extra $7 a week to serve as editor.

1851 Currier lithograph of City Hall Park, while Brick Church is still standing at right. We are looking north from where Park Row meets Broadway.

Around lunchtime, they gather at Crook and Duff's, a restaurant on Newspaper Row serving the publishing crowd. Drinking in antebellum New York is spirited, and there are more than a few of these men who are pickled before the horse-drawn omnibus trip back uptown. Maybe they return to their garrets to nap or work; maybe they end up at a raucous saloon or brothel, or maybe they bring a bottle and friends back to the boarding house. After dinner, it is common to walk and hail friends on the street or in the park, or to visit homes of family friends, where they may socialize late into the night.

The *Saturday Press* always lives in the shadow of Damocles' sword, whether the editorial columns boast of success or warn of possible failure. After 103 issues, Clapp's finances run dry, and the journal folds. In a few months, American bloodlust sparks a Civil War that results in more US deaths than all other American wars combined.

A few months after the end of the war, Clapp finds the financing for a new version of the *Saturday Press*. In its second iteration, other young writers will go on to success after cutting their teeth under Clapp's editorship--Mark Twain and Artemus Ward, among them.

After 44 additional issues, the *Saturday Press* fails again financially and ceases publication for good.

Such a brief period, such a small circulation; but the reputation earned by the *Saturday Press* scaled far higher. The public interest in these Bohemian heroes—several who died romantically young, leaving just their *Saturday Press* contributions as their life's legacy—saw a nostalgic resurgence a few decades later, and popular books recounted their sprightly tales.

The writing from the *Saturday Press,* itself, though, saw its last light of day in 1866. Since that time, only scholars have made the trip to a few scant library collections to browse the tattered, flaking bound broadsheets. At some point, they were photographed for microfiche, but the images were poor, maybe only 75 percent legible. In digitizing and republishing them, I have not only resurrected all sorts of treasures, but the collection really brings this period of New York City's history to life. I have learned so much about these people who lived and thrived on our same city's streets. I can't go anywhere in the city without thinking of them.

- Henry B. Jenkins, teller of the Phœnix bank on Wall Street, described as "a man past middle-age", is persuaded by the wiles of an attractive young "waiter-girl" to embezzle hundreds of thousands of dollars for the benefit of her extortionist conspirators.
- Daniel Dunglas Home (pronounced "Hume") popular Scottish spiritual medium, according to devotees, regularly levitates to the ceiling during seance.
- NYC teenager, Frances Amelia Bartlett, is wooed at her home on 14th Street by one of the world's richest men, 55-year-old Cuban planter, Don Esteban Santa Cruz de Oviedo. He showers her with Tiffany jewelry and carloads of French fashions suited to be the envy of any court of Europe. Dubbed "The Diamond Wedding," thousands jam Mulberry Street to witness as the two are married at St. Patrick's Cathedral in the most ostentatious celebration the city has yet witnessed.
- Nixon's Circus at Niblo's Garden Theatre features the Hanlon Brothers: an acrobatic act with a grand-finale involving an audience-frightening 40-foot fall.
- Former US Senator, Preston King, after being appointed as Collector of the Port of New York, reportedly becomes

so overwhelmed with the corruption he is assigned to eradicate that he ties a bag of bullets around his neck and leaps to his death off a NYC ferry.

- British actress-become-theater-manager, Laura Keene, conquers New York with Tom Taylor's popular farce, "Our American Cousin." The play is such a success that she is still touring it six years later, before a Washington D.C. audience at Ford's Theatre, when President Lincoln is assassinated in a box above the stage.
- Circus performer, Omar Kingsley, known as Mademoiselle Ella Zoyara, disguises as a girl to increase interest in his act of "graceful" dangerous riding tricks. Though he is eventually exposed and abandons the popular character, he will return as Zoyara for benefits.
- "Tommy" (Tateishi Onojiro,) a 17-year-old interpreter and one of the youngest members of Japan's first diplomatic mission, quickly becomes immensely popular. His wit, cheerful nature, and youthful good looks especially charm American ladies.
- A 16-year-old immigrant, raised in the Bronx, Adelina Patti, steps into the limelight on the stage of the Academy of Music on 14th Street, and in one evening establishes herself as the world's greatest soprano.

As a Modern, reading these sheets now, I find Americans on the verge of an apocalypse; going through rapid changes; struggling with maintaining that authentic humanity; as young people always do; as we do on the verge of being overcome by our own invention; we seek touch with the idealized value of aestheticism against a world that threatens to create knowledge that will trivialize those aspirations.

The *Saturday Press* captures a moment in history that will not recur. People will never again stand in such awe at the sight of oil paintings, to marvel with such open receptivity. Never again will they be the first to publicly express ideas, carving new paths for themselves and their society toward unknown, seemingly endless horizons—all while disease and war rage around them, smothering their children, elders, and lovers.

We see the past incorrectly. As if artistic expression was disconnected from its moment, but emerged from the individuality of the artist. There is no artist until the moment creates the artist. The moment is the spirit of the artistic revelation. When we find ways to imagine the full nature of a past moment, only then are we able to truly share in the joy, the loss, the fortitude, and the yearning.

I've presented all of the best of the writing here and many of the advertisements. I've excluded the *Saturday Press's* much-publicized lists of new books, as they are just postings, not reviews.

About two-thirds of the writing pieces in the *Saturday Press* were extracts, "contributed by a pair of scissors." At the time, post office franking privileges allowed editors to exchange issues with one another without paying postage. Additionally, there were no legal copyright restrictions, so editors could freely reprint material from any source they found. While it was customary to credit the original source, it wasn't legally required. Fortunately, Henry Clapp was conscientious about attribution; thus, while much of the *Press's* original content was either uncredited or published under pseudonyms, sources were typically identified when material was borrowed from other journals. Most of these reprinted extracts are excluded from this Omnibus Edition, which focuses on assembling the most entertaining original pieces from *Saturday Press* contributors into a single, cohesive volume.

I've included an extensive glossary of archaic or time-contingent terms, places, and people, along with brief biographies (when available) of *Saturday Press* contributors and a 4-page scrolling map of Broadway. Lean on this resource, and you will surely enrich your enjoyment. The *Saturday Press* did not feature illustrations (save for a single line drawing of a nose,) but I've been able to furnish lots of fascinating photographs and period woodcut engravings.

And so, take a trip with me to October, 1858. New York City bustles with transformation: the ambitious Central Park project has just broken ground. At Fashion Race Course in Flushing, baseball history unfolds as the New York All-Stars defeat the Brooklyn All-Stars in the first baseball game to charge admission (fifty-cents). The city streets are changing too—the first mailboxes appear on corners, and R.H. Macy prepares to open his pioneering store on 6th Avenue at 14th Street. Just down the way, at Broadway and 14th Street, the Roosevelt household welcomes a newborn who will one day become President: Teddy.

President James Buchanan inaugurates the new trans-Atlantic telegraph cable by exchanging greetings with Queen Victoria—only to have the cable fail soon after. The city's celebration of the cable's initial success turns catastrophic when fireworks ignite a blaze that severely damages New York City Hall.

Then comes another spectacular fire. At the Crystal Palace—a grand exhibition hall and beer garden on 42nd Street where Bryant Park now stands—two thousand patrons flee as flames engulf the structure. Despite its vaunted "fireproof" design of glass and cast iron, modeled after its namesake in England, the building burns to the ground in just 21 minutes. Yet remarkably, amid the chaos, not a single person is injured...

Mark Crane, September, 2025.

THE SATURDAY PRESS.

VOL. I.—NO. 1. NEW YORK, OCTOBER 23, 1858. PRICE, 5 CENTS.

PUBLISHER'S NOTICE.

THE SATURDAY PRESS is published at No. 9 Spruce Street, New York.

Terms.—$2.00 per year; Five Cents per single number.

Advertisements, Ten Cents per line for each insertion.

Specimen Copies will be sent to any part of the Union on the receipt of three cents to pre-pay postage.

The Saturday Press.

[For the Saturday Press.]

THE SHADOW ON THE WALL.

I passed her way as the dying day
Was trembling to its fall,
Humming a song as I strolled along
When a shadow on the wall,
A shadow dark and tall,
A shadow on her chamber wall,
Silenced my step and song.

Like a spectral maid, or an aspen shade,
That shadow dark and tall,
Reluctant strayed as the moon beams played
Upon the chamber wall,
That shadow like a pall,
Trembling upon the chamber wall,
Trembling as if afraid.

That seraph shade which trembling strayed
Upon the chamber wall,
Like a timid maid who strays afraid
Within a haunted hall,
That shadow dark and tall,
Quivering upon the chamber wall,
Was my sweet Adelaide.

* * * * * * *

The evening sped, and the angels fled
With the beauteous form and all,
And humming a song I strolled along
When that shadow on the wall,
That shadow like a pall,
That shadow on her chamber-wall,
Haunted my step and song.

And now each night, when the moon beams bright,
Or the star beams softly fall,
Her shadow so pale, no more afraid,
Dances upon the wall,
Her shadow dark and tall,
Dances upon my chamber wall,
Dances, no more afraid.

That joyous air, that face so rare,
The beauteous form and all,
The golden hair now glittering there
With the moonbeams, on the wall,
That shadow dark and tall,
Dancing upon my chamber-wall,—
Naught but herself so fair!

Yes, beauteous maid, sweet Adelaide,
Thy shadow on the wall,
Like a sylvan maid, or a seraph shade
At a merry moonlight ball,
Thy shadow dark and tall,
Dances upon my chamber-wall,
Dances, though thou art dead!

THE LIVING CORPSE.

BY WILLIAM NORTH.

Why the fancy has seized me to write the strange history which follows, is to me inexplicable. My utter indifference to human sympathy, human praise, or human opinion, which will soon be seen to be no vain affectation, would seem to render such art superfluous. Perhaps the necessity for some species of action, which even the inert granite is supposed to be imbued with by the progressive spirit of Nature, may account for the proceeding. Since, however, I intend to write, I propose to write intelligibly. It is difficult to describe sensations where memory alone must furnish their corresponding ideas. Were I a human being, in the strict sense of the word, I should, if I may judge by what I see others do, apologize for the imperfection of my narrative. As it is, I shall reproduce the images of the past with the fidelity, as also with the indifference, of an echo. It is perhaps the first time that a DEAD MAN has spoken in the language of the living, though approximations to the phenomenon are to be found in many writers of the day, whose works, I, being absolutely destitude of passions, can alone dispassionately criticize. Weak minds will either fail to comprehend, or recoil with horror from my revelations. To the thinking few, they will be a curiosity, which I affirm gravely to be unparalleled in the annals of literature, or the records of history.

I was not always a living corpse. I am not a natural monster. I was born alive, in the full sense of the word. Nay, I was the result of an unbridled passion, and gifted with all the fiery vitality which such lawless indulgences not unfrequently produce. My mother was an Italian Princess, my father a private soldier in the Prussian cavalry. My birth took place in secrecy, and with all the precautions of pride and shameful terror. I was brought up in an atmosphere of mystery, and though invisibly protected, was, from my earliest recollection, an utterly isolated being. At the age of one-and-twenty, after completing, as they say, my studies at the University of ———, I was placed in possession of a fortune of one hundred thousand dollars invested in the English funds, and informed that henceforth I was my own master; whilst I was supplied with a plain and probable legend to serve as a convenient substitute for a more authentic pedigree. It was under these circumstances that I set out on my travels, in the prime of youth and love of enjoyment. My form was tall and powerful, my face of a rare and marked beauty, and my talents of that order which make the great heroes, poets, and criminals of this imperfect world. My destiny was in my own hands, and I became, if not the greatest, at least the most extraordinary of earth's children. I state these facts in their naked simplicity, because what is termed vanity, is so utterly impossible to a being of my unique nature, that I can waive all common forms, and introduce myself at once in my true colors to the reader.

I shall commence by a brief account of my youth and education, or rather of the early movements of my mind, which led me to adopt a course so singular in its audacity, both of conception and execution.

My two dominant passions, before the extraordinary events which it is the main purpose of this tale to record, were an intense longing for exalted sensations of pleasure, and as a means to this end, a burning thirst for knowledge. Having renounced all religious creeds, and set at defiance all social prejudices, I resolved to make the aim of my existence the attainment by study and experiment, of the most certain methods of scientific enjoyment.

It was naturally what the world calls preeminently selfish; as if one man could be more or less selfish than another; as, if in obeying the laws of his organization, any one could act other wise than yield invariably to the strongest motive, as if any motive could be sought else than a certain amount of *force* acting upon an individual being!

But I will not philosophize. My human and living readers would not understand me if I did. Their perceptions are clogged by passions and prejudices. Hence truth is strange to them, and even terrible. There are some few, eagle-eyed, who can gaze upon the sun, undazzled. To these my philosophy would be impertinent; to the mass it is incomprehensible.

I will tell my story without obscurity. I will use the plainest language, and speak to popular acceptations.

I was, then, a voluptuary, but not a common voluptuary. I saw that the ordinary mines of enjoyment were too exhausted, or only to be worked more deeply by labor that defeated its object. I perceived that the most crowded paths of pleasure turned back, by circuitous courses, in never-ending circles.

I resolved to abandon these pastures of gregarious man. But before abandoning them, I tested them by experience. I plunged into all the dissipations of my age. I sought all the distractions that youth, a strong well-nerved body, and an active mind could hope to obtain. I bought all the diversion that gold could buy. I lived with my generation; I surpassed them; I led them. I practised a systematized moderation. I essayed unbridled excesses. And—I was disappointed.

I did not, as the cant phrase goes, awake from my illusions. I had read, seen, and thought too much. I was too clear-headed to have any illusions. Where others saw misty prospects, I saw naked facts. I summed up, and found the balance on the wrong side. My experiment was a failure.

I had travelled, I had seen the wonders of art, and the beauties of nature. I had had access to the best, and the worst of society. I had labored, and been rewarded by fame. The book which I wrote, won the applause of a nation. I foresaw that it would obtain new triumphs in foreign lands; and my foresight has been confirmed by fact. Lastly, I was united to the woman I loved; who brought me thrice the fortune I expected, and a mind cultivated beyond my hopes. And with all this—I was dissatisfied. I craved for intenser pleasure; more exalted excitement, and I could not disguise from myself that it was so. I reflected deeply.

"What," said I, "is happiness? Is it a monotony of sensations, which are taken to be pleasurable on the faith of popular opinion, whilst the inward voice still whispers languor and tedium, whilst half the day is passed in a dreary vacuity of mind, which is, at best, merely the bare negative of pain? Is it a feverish working and striving for objects which on attainment invariably become insipid and indifferent?

"Certainly not. Reasonably regarded, it is surely a positive, appreciable state of consciousness, in which we can say without hesitation to the moment, in the words of Goethe, 'O linger yet, thou art so fair!' It is a certain condition of the nervous system, and without that condition—misery."

I fell to watching myself studiously at different times, and under various circumstances.

I observed that, at a certain stage, wine produced sensations of extreme delight. But I also observed that these sensations soon gave way to other and more sombre feelings; that, in fact, there was a happy crisis in alcoholic stimulus, which, when once past, could not be recalled on one and the same occasion. Indulgence, too, in wine, was, I perceived, followed by a vague dreary despondency, that lasted incomparably longer than the brief passing moments of delicious exhilaration it produced.

On the whole, it was better to leave the mind to nature and mere mental excitements, than to attempt to light the sacred fire at the now neglected altars of Bacchus.

I need not say, that to become vulgarly intoxicated, was, with me, out of the question. There are some strong brains that defy the utmost possibilities of wine. I could have poisoned myself, but I could not render myself an unreasoning animal, by any amount of spirituous liquors. Often I persevered to the last, and when all my wild companions had sunk, I may say in many cases fallen beneath their potent draughts, I alone sat erect, and at worst discovered that my stomach was a weaker organ than my head. In such cases a feeling of awful and gloomy sadness would possess me, and after sitting long in silent and strangely lucid meditations, I would walk home calmly in the gray of the morning with little outward indication of the debauch from which I had emerged.

It was evident that no cascades of wine—even though they beggared Niagara in their ruby or topaz-like curves—could overarch for me that enchanted palace, in which I desired to spend my days, and defy the adversary—Pain, Evil, Devil, Typhon, Ariman, or Sathanas, in a word, the dread foe, named or nameless, described or indescribable, of human happiness and its continuance.

Apart from all more palpable causes of suffering, man sits between Memory and Desire, between the Past and the Future, as between two rival mistresses, each dragging him toward her by turns with uneasy passion; whilst before him, and as it were balanced on the eternal and invisible tight-rope, sways the only nymph that can bless him with her love, the only goddess he can really and truly possess, if indeed he can possess anything, the divine Present—and he dares not clasp the radiant virgin to his heart, dares not drive to the East nor to the West, along the interminable roads of space, the furies that torment him, madden him, and devour him, now, then, and evermore!

For my part, I said to the sad and pale brunette, the angel Præterita, and to the blonde seductive blue-eyed spirit Future, a like farewell. The genii of Past and Future ruled the race of man—the Earth-God. But one was a rebel and an outlaw; and that one was I.

I said to the Universe, "Let me *feel* happiness, not merely dream it." And everlasting echoes from all the depths of Kosmos, even from the farthest bounds where creation, ever encroaching, borders upon awful chaos, everlasting echoes answered "DREAM!"

And I replied to the spirits of the Infinite, and demanded proudly, "Ye blind legions of monitors! where in nature is your unclouded happiness? where is your *perfection?*"

And the echoes laughed back in mockery, "*perfection!*"

Then I ceased to ask counsel of my men or spirits. For I was determined to be my own guide, and my own teacher, since all the wisdom of the world had not led to happiness. Therefore I scorned its pretensions, and derided its impotence with justice.

I became a great smoker. I purchased the rarest tobaccos and the costliest pipes. I had a perfect museum of meerschaums, narguilés, chibouques, and tubes and bowls of all sorts of shape, size, and contrivance, for the inhalation of the fragrant weed. I purchased, at extravagant prices, the choicest boxes of cigars. I smoked grandly, incessantly, infernally. The atmosphere grew dark with my smoking; at least to my imagination. I wrapped my soul in the incense of tobacco. I created worlds of fancies out of its wreathing vapors. I began to think I had found the resource I wanted, and I often exclaimed in dreamy ecstacy—"Divine Nicotiana!"* I doubted whether the vapors which inspired the Pythoness did not arise from the hookahs of the priests smoking in solemn divan in the subterranean halls of Delphi. And I gave them high credit for having so well preserved the secret they had discovered.

At the same time, like a true Turk, I took care to have the finest coffee of Mocha prepared by the most perfect machinery. I found that, after fasting, the effect of coffee upon the nerves was almost supernatural; but combined with tobacco, it was Elysian. It produced an intense state of enjoyment, during which, I would discourse with a marvellous eloquence to my adoring Mira, who was never weary of following the train of my prolific and far-stretching fantasies. How easily in this period of my madness (as I have since learned to deem it), did I unravel knots in science and philosophy, that puzzled the wise men of ages. How intuitively did I seize on combinations, whose results, in the hands of practical men, might have rendered them the acknowledged benefactors of the world, and enriched whole nations of workers! But with me, all was a reverie of selfish recreation. I created glorious plans, I foreshadowed mighty inventions, as a voluptuous exercise of the mind; I played as it were grand symphonies on the most intellectual themes, and the compositions perished with the dying sounds, like the fantasias of musicians, which are never to be repeated.

But this could not last. My powerful organization resisted for a time the exaggerated abuse of drugs, which, common though they be, are in excess, like all other substances, the deadliest poisons. Smoking destroys the appetite, and ruins the digestive powers. Its effect upon the nerves then becomes tremendous. I soon made this discovery. A neuralgic irritation attacked me, which, as I still pursued my diabolical fumigations, went on with a fearfully *crescendo* movement. Deadly sickness, of a peculiar inactive character; fits of the horrors, in which all things became repugnant, wearisome, and nauseating; ideas of suicide, and awful despondencies, descended upon me like a flight of vultures on a dying antelope. I abandoned the poisons. My prostration was complete and unbearable. I partially resumed them, and tried change of air and scene. I just recovered sufficiently to be able to suffer more acutely. I had evidently, at least temporarily, undermined my constitution. It was at this period, that, like a demon watching his occasion, *opium* became my comforter.

For the first time a book fell into my hands, a dangerous book, which has made many wretched; I mean "The Confessions of an English Opium-Eater." This work, as all the world knows, was written by Thomas de Quincey, an Englishman of letters, who is still living. And with regard to this De Quincey, I will mention one thing that is curious. He is intimately persuaded that he is a fragmentary poet, imbued with considerable transcendentalism. His book is extremely amusing, but the reverse of philosophical, for it arrives at no conclusion. It is an opium book in more senses than the writer would have you believe. Such as it is, however, this book was the immediate cause of my taking to opium.

Its first effects were delightful. It tranquillized my irritated nerves, and I entered, as it were, a new world of dreamy speculation. An invisible barrier seemed raised between me and the external world. Nothing troubled me, nothing annoyed me. I was on the verge of being utterly impoverished by a dispute as to the title of my wife's property. But it gave me no uneasiness. The danger passed away as it came—like a fleeting fancy. The only thing that slightly interfered with my peaceful ecstacy of indolent reverie, was the apprehensions of my wife. She had heard that opium-eating was a shocking thing, and she could not at once get reconciled to the idea. Nor would any thing induce her, personally, to taste the talismanic liquid—the *happiness in bottles*, as De Quincey has aptly termed it.

The effect of opium in producing dreams, so forcibly dwelt upon and splendidly illustrated by that writer, I need not enlarge upon. Enough to state that the number and variety of my visions were infinite. Ages were crowded into nights. The most monstrous and gigantic images were familiar things. Time and space were extended beyond all conception, except that of an opium-eater. Nevertheless, opium palled upon me, and the opium-dream-world became almost tedious. I had, too, an excessive dislike to the taste of laudanum, which, strange to say, increased rather than diminished. One day I returned home with a small vial of bright green liquid in my pocket. It's very color had a mystic poisonous fascination. How much more potent and cabalistic was its spell than the dark, thick, brown, drowsy-looking laudanum! It was Haschisch. Haschisch is a sort of Indian hemp (Cannabis Indicus). The liquid in the vial was an extract from its stalks. This Indian poison is mentioned in Lamartine's Vision of the Future, and in Alexander Dumas' Monte-Cristo. Their exaggerated, or rather apparently exaggerated descriptions of its effects have, no doubt, caused the majority of their readers to consider this marvellous drug as a mere figment of the poet and novelist's brains. It has, however, a real existence, and is in extensive demand amongst the initiated. In effect it resembles opium, but is more exhilarating, and less narcotic. I continued for a whole year to increase my doses of this new elixir of happiness, and did not find myself assaulted by any of the horrible fancies which De Quincey complains of, as the after results of opium. Like King Mithridates, I was becoming familiar with poisons, and they began to respect their master. But, though I lived as much in another world from that of ordinary mortals, as if my habitation had been in the planet Uranus, I could not escape a more terrible poison than even the Hydrocianic, commonly called Prussic acid, in which, as an antidote to certain effects of the *Cannabis Indicus*, I freely indulged. *Ennui*, the spleen, that mysterious and tyrannical malady, pursued me, even into my poison-guarded dream-world. I grew accustomed to the life; the old dreams and fancies recurred, and became tiresome. Already I meditated a deeper plunge in *Venoméry*. I fell on, accidentally, in some review, with an account of the *Arsenic-eaters* of Styria, and of the results of that mania, in heightening the personal beauty of its devotees. Certainly the pure delicacy of Mira's clear, fair complexion, left no room for improvement, except in the fancy of a madman. Nevertheless, I long'd to try the effect of an arsenic varnish—if I may express myself—upon both her and my own countenance. Who could tell whether seeming more beautiful to one another, our love might not acquire new strength, and develope new sources of delight. I was in the midst of a profound reverie, or rather Haschisch dream on this subject, when I received a letter from a scientific friend, announcing the discovery of the effects of inhaling *ether*, in destroying sensation, and rendering surgical operations painless.

I thought that new light burst upon my soul. In one instant, I became a convert to an entirely new system of nervous influence. I rushed out to buy some *rectified sulphuric ether*, and a machine for inhalation. The latter consisted of a bottle, to which was attached a flexible tube, about two feet long, and two inches in diameter. I eagerly poured in some ether, and applied the funnel-like mouth-piece to my lips. After a few inspirations of the vaporized ether, I felt a most marvellous and delicious effect. I felt a stream of joyous expansion steal rapidly through my veins, even to the tips of my toes, which tingled with delight. I at once felt the vast superiority of inhaling the stimulant over swallowing it. Instead of going through the tedious process of digestion, whose functions is disturbed and impeded, as is the case of wine, the purified and refined spirit (for ether is but rectified alcohol) entered at once into the lungs, thence into the aurated blood, and thus through every part of the body with the crimson flood of impatient arteries, and so back with the blue current of the veins, to evaporate harmlessly, leaving nothing but its memory behind it!

"Hence!" I exclaimed, "wine, coffee, tobacco, opium, haschisch! away henbane, arsenic, hydrociana! Course and noxious stimulants, narcotics, and nerve-swindlers, who wrap the soul in cumbrous veils, that, like the robe of Dejanira, invades the life of your votaries. I am no De Quincey, I, to mock myself with vain, half realized fantasies, to stand up to the middle in Styx, and murmur vaguely—*Suspiria de profundis!*"

And now a new field opened to my researches. The world of *gas* spread temptingly before me. Little do the vain mob understand the import of that word—to them the emblem of emptiness. "It is all gas!" they cry. Yes, truly, every thing is gas, is, was, and ever shall be gas. The most solid and material things resolve themselves into mere gaseous combinations. A little more of one gas, a little less of another, and, lo! all the varieties in nature are produced. All was originally gas. Chaos was the confusion of gases. All must resolve itself ultimately into gas. You and I are gas, and gas is every thing.

I became a man of gas, a maker and an experimentalist of gaseous mixtures. I remembered the exhibitions which in my youth I had witnessed of the effects of *laughing gas*, the inhalation of which causes the wildest intoxication, or rather exaltation of the brain, and causes those who breathe it to exhibit the most fantastic feats, illustrative of their predominant passions. If there is truth in wine, in gas there is revelation. Yet the man in whom reason is the ruling faculty, will subdue all outward indications of the mighty *afflatus*. There is a supreme gas, a gas of all gases, and its particles are souls. All other gases exist by numerical arrangement, as Pythagoras well conjectured, when he prefigured the atomic theories of modern days. But there is an ultimate atom, a gas which is the basis of all others, and without which all is vacuum.

I knew that in an atmosphere of pure oxygen, the gas essential to life, and, at the same time, the agent of all decay, the sour stuff (*sauer stoff*) as the Germans call it, an animal could live, and live with a wondrous acceleration of all the physical processes. In man this rapid consumption of matter was accompanied by an equal intensifying exultation of the mental faculties. On this fact I founded my experiments, and the result was, at length, the combination of oxygen with other gases, in an artificial atmosphere of the most astounding and admirable qualities.

To breathe this air, was to breathe positive enjoyment. It was vaporized nectar and ambrosia. Its respiration was the life of a God. But it was also the embodied *Sansar*—"the icy wind of death." No mortal could live more than a few months even in its partially diluted perfection. It was the short life and merry of the reckless popular adage, reduced to palpable embodiment.

On the other hand, this rapidity of life was only apparent. For we measure time by sensations; and the exalted powers of sensation, confirmed by breathing the wondrous gas, gave time a supernatural extension similar to the life of dreams, but free from all their shadowy indistinctness.

My resolution at once was taken. I would live and die in this glorified atmosphere. I would bid farewell to all that was earthly, without hesitation. I bought a magnificent chateau in the South of France. I furnished it by the expenditure of one-third of my fortune, in a few days, with all the luxury that imagination could suggest. I fitted up my apparatus for the production of the gas, and engaged, at the rate of some thousands of francs monthly, a young chemist of first-rate education, and superior energy and abilities. To him, I confided all the management and regulation of the apparatus, and also the absolute control of the servants, and of the whole establishment. One suite of rooms, the most splendid, and with the finest prospect in the chateau, were to be my own enchanted habitation. Into these apartments, except at certain times and with due precautions, no servants were to enter. Every thing that I required was to be sent up through the floor, by means of tables that screwed up and down, by noiseless machinery. No one was to disturb me on any pretext; no letters were to be given me, and as the chemist was poor, almost starving when I first patronized him, I knew that so long as every month brought him a little fortune in itself, I might count on his absolute devotion. Beside, I deceived him as to my intention. There was only one room—the largest and most splendidly furnished in the house—which was to be actually filled with the life-accelerating gas. It communicated with other apartments by carefully constructed double doors, and of course it never entered the mind of the chemist that I intended to live and die in the deadly atmosphere which he was to create, or that, after so carefully ordering these hermetically closing double doors, I should purpose fixing them wide open, the moment I was shut up within my mysterious domicile, and thus causing the whole suite of apartments to fill with the same ethereal poison.

In other respects, the chemist was just the person I wanted; he was patient, faithful, and industrious. At the same time, he was a cold, stern man, well fitted to repress any insubordination or curiosity on the part of the household. And now all was prepared for the experiment. It only remained to persuade Mira to be my companion. For I confess that without her, even the potence of the marvellous gas must have failed in its action on my nerves. Her love had become a habit, a part of my being, I could not live or die without her.

And here let me for the first time say a few words about Mira.

She was an entirely exceptional woman. When I married her, some three years before the date of my final experiment, she was only sixteen years of age. Her beauty (I can find no newer or more intelligible image) was of the order which the finest painters strive to impart to their embodiments of angels, and beings superior to man. Its supreme loveliness was not in its delicate regularity of feature, dazzling whiteness and purity of skin, and majestic symmetry of form. All these seemed merely indispensable conditions of such an individuality. What made her irresistibly pleasing to the perceptions of an imaginative and thoughtful man, was a certain calm unalterable dignity and noble gentleness, that placed her above even the possibility of any of the meannesses and pettinesses of her sex. She had the strong mind of a man, with all the purity and softness of an exquisitely delicate female organization. In temperament she was my opposite, although intellectually, there existed between us a perfect sympathy. She was as calm and serenely contented, as I was feverishly dissatisfied and eager for excitement. Yet she understood and entered into all my wild speculations, as into an interesting drama, of which she was the sympathizing spectator. She was my only confidant, my only friend, my only real companion. With all my restless cravings for greater intensity of enjoyment, her love was my world, my treasure, and my hope—the more so that I might almost be said to mistrust its possession.

That Mira loved me, was indeed indubitable, yet there was a calmness, a purity, and passive even tenor in her love, that could not be called coldness, and which yet in a manner disappointed the fiery adoration with which I loved her. I would not have lost one of her kisses for all the embraces of all the beauties of the earth; and yet, to my fierce and impassioned nature, there seemed more snow upon her bosom, than a poet's simile implies, more than perchance would ever melt beneath my lips ecstatic pressure.

In the delusion of my wild, tempest-tost soul, which, after all, was but that of a mad poet's, astray in the deserts and primeval forests of thought, I knew not that the crown of her glorious beauty and of my delicious, because never satiated, passion, lay in the very qualities which I regretted, and which I insanely hoped to conquer by my infernal and pitiless inventions.

To my surprise, I had no difficulty in persuading Mira to enter the enchanted atmosphere. A first trial of its virtues was of course decisive. We gave ourselves up to the intense joy of life, to which pain, care, and sorrow, regret for the past or apprehension for the future, were necessarily strange. The outer world became nothing to us. Love, exalted to a degree of power which to the breathers of common air is inconceivable, appreciation of beauty and delights which are alike inexplicable and incomprehensible, made up the sum of our existence. I pass over, therefore, the seven times seven days of our ethereal life, a period which in ideas and sensations was equivalent to the ordinary lapse of ages, and hasten onward to the extraordinary catastrophe which left me what I am—a monster, more rare and wonderful than the sphinxes and chimeras of old, my fabulous prototypes.

Nor let the reader foolishly imagine that, because memory or science give me the power of describing passion, and thereby exciting *his* sympathies, that *I* personally do or can feel any echoing vibration of the wild chords which I cause to resound. Unearthly is the music—unearthly the musician.

Opening from the grand saloon of the chateau, was a superb conservatory of more than ordinary dimensions, commanding a view of one of the most splendid landscapes in the world. In the foreground, yet not sufficiently near to intercept the view, rose from the side of the hill, on which stood the chateau, the mingled foliage of an old and primitive forest, while beyond was visible the shining stream of the Rhone, lying, like the crooked sabre of some gigantic Paladin, upon the greensward; and far, far beyond rose the bluish shadowy outlines of mountains behind which the sun would set in golden glory, that made each snow-crowned peak a throne worthy of Sathanas—"the Emperor of the furnace."

Round this conservatory were arranged a collection of strange exotic and tropical plants, so as to leave the centre unoccupied, save by a few couches, chairs, and tables, on which lay volumes of poetry and philosophy, and portfolios of exquisite engravings and drawings. This was our favorite sitting-room. It was only necessary to open the glass doors between it and the saloon, to fill it with the same enchanted air; and I may mention as a curious example of the effects of this atmosphere on vegetation, that the grapes which were quite green and hard on its first introduction, ripened perfectly in a few days, and were the largest and most luscious fruit I had ever tasted or seen. It was one of Mira's greatest enjoyments to call me to watch the camelias budding and flowering actually before our eyes! Were I in the humor, I could write a hundred pages on the wonders of vegetation with which my residence in this gas-world made me acquainted. But I refrain without difficulty. To me, no science is worth a thought.

In the centre of this hall of crystal stood a white marble statue of Minerva, the only statue in which that goddess has ever been represented entirely without drapery. The figure was Mira's. I myself modelled it during the first year of our marriage, and it was carved by one of the most eminent French sculptors, who afterward died mad from a hopeless passion for the original. The fountain sprang from and formed the foliage of a glass tree stem, against which she leant, whilst the point of her spear drooped earthward from her arm, as if languid with the warfare against folly. Her head alone was covered with a helmet, which imparted a singular charm to the divine beauty of Mira's countenance.

At length, one day, toward evening, after seven weeks of solitude and happiness, which no Paradise could more than realize, a fatal accident destroyed at once our enjoyment, our experiment in science, and our lives. Yes—I learned it afterward—we were killed by the merest accident. My chemist, who managed the gas-generating apparatus, forgot to examine the metre at the proper time. The gas continued to enter in unprecedented volumes, and its effects were speedily perceptible.

We were seated in our favorite place in the conservatory, our eyes turned toward the setting sun, listening to the swelling and harmonious cadences of Weber, produced by a self-playing instrument of the rarest workmanship, which I had purchased at Paris for an enormous sum, of its inventor, when a more than usual ecstacy seemed to possess us. Our arms, entwined round one another's forms, seemed to contract almost convulsively, our eyes, our lips, met with deli-

* Nicotiana is the scientific name for tobacco. It is derived from a Frenchman of the name of Jean Nicot, who first imported it to France.

(For the Saturday Press.)

THE SHADOW ON THE WALL.

I passed her as the dying day
Was trembling to its fall,
Humming a song as I strolled along,
When a shadow on the wall,
A shadow dark and tall,
A shadow on her chamber-wall,
Silenced my step and song.

Like a spectral maid, or an aspen shade,
That shadow dark and tall,
Reluctant strayed as the moon-beams played
Upon the chamber-wall ;
That shadow like a pall,
Trembling upon the chamber-wall,
Trembling as if afraid.

That seraph-shade which trembling strayed
Upon the chamber wall,
Like a timid maid who stays afraid
Within a haunted hall,
That shadow dark and tall,
Quivering upon the chamber-wall,
Was my sweet Adelaide.

* * * * * *

The evening sped, and the angels fled
With the beauteous form and all,
And humming a song I strolled along,
When that shadow on the wall,
That shadow like a pall,
That shadow on her chamber-wall,
Haunted my step and song.

And now each night, when the moon beams bright,
Or the star-beams softly fall,
Her angel-shade, no more afraid,
Dances upon the wall,
Her shadow dark and tall,
Dances upon my chamber-wall,
Dances, no more afraid.

That joyous air, that face so rare,
The beauteous form and all,
The golden hair now glittering there
With the moonbeams, on the wall,
That shadow dark and tall,
Dancing upon my chamber-wall—
Nought but herself so fair !

Yes, beauteous maid, sweet Adelaide !
Thy shadow on the wall,
Like a sylvan maid, or a seraph-shade
At a merry moonlight ball,
Thy shadow, dark and tall,
Dances upon my chamber-wall,
Dances, though thou art dead !

THE LIVING CORPSE

BY WILLIAM NORTH.

Why the fancy has seized me to write the strange history which follows, is to me inexplicable. My utter indifference to human sympathy, human praise, or human opinion, which will soon be seen to be no vain affectation would seem to render such art superfluous. Perhaps the necessity for some species of action, which even the inert granite is supposed to be imbued with by the progressive spirit of Nature, may account for the proceeding. Since, however, I intend to write, I propose to write intelligibly. It is difficult to describe sensations where memory alone must furnish their corresponding ideas. Were I a human being, in the strict sense of the word, I should, if I may judge by what I see others do, apologize for the imperfection of my narrative. As it is, I shall reproduce the images of the past with the fidelity, as also with the indifference, of an echo. It is perhaps the first time that a DEAD MAN has spoken in the language of the living, though approximations to the phenomenon are to be found in many writers of the day, whose works, I being absolutely destitute of passions, can alone dispassionately criticize. Weak minds will either fail to comprehend, or recoil with horror from my revelations. To the thinking few, they will be a curiosity, which I affirm gravely to be unparalleled in the annals of literature, or the records of history.

I was not always a living corpse. I am not a natural monster. I was born alive, in the full sense of the word. Nay, I was the result of an unbridled passion, and gifted with all the fiery vitality which such lawless indulgences not unfrequently produce. My mother was an Italian Princess, my father a private soldier in the Prussian cavalry. My birth took place in secrecy, and with all the precautions of pride and shameful terror. I was brought up in an atmosphere of mystery, and though invisibly protected, was, from my earliest recollection, an utterly isolated being. At the age of one-and-twenty, after completing, as they say, my studies at the University of ——, I was placed in possession of a fortune of one hundred thousand dollars invested in the English funds, and informed that henceforth I was my own master ; whilst I was supplied with a plain and probable legend to serve as a convenient substitute for a more authentic pedigree. It was under these circumstances that I set out on my travels, in the prime of youth and love of enjoyment. My form was tall and powerful, my face of a rare and marked beauty, and my talents of that order which make the great heroes, poets, and criminals of this imperfect world. My destiny was in my own hands, and I became, if not the greatest, at least the most extraordinary of earth's children. I state these facts in their naked simplicity, because what is termed vanity, is so utterly impossible to a being of my unique nature, that I can waive all common forms, and introduce myself at once in my true colors to the reader.

I shall commence by a brief account of my youth and education, or rather of the early movements of my mind, which led me to adopt a course so singular in its audacity, both of conception and execution.

My two dominant passions, before the extraordinary events which it is the main purpose of this tale to record, were an intense longing for exalted sensations of pleasure, and as a means to this end, a burning thirst for knowledge. Having renounced all religious creeds, and set at defiance all social prejudices, I resolved to make the aim of my existence the attainment by study and experiment, of the most certain methods of scientific enjoyment.

I was naturally what the world calls pre-eminently selfish ; as if one man could be more or less selfish than another ; as if, in obeying the laws of his organization, any one could act otherwise than yield invariably to the strongest motive, as if any motive could be aught else than a certain amount of force acting upon an individual being!

But I will not philosophize. My human and living readers would not understand me if I did. Their perceptions are clogged by passions and prejudices. Hence truth is strange to them, and even terrible. There are some few, eagle-eyed, who can gaze upon the sun, undazzled. To these my philosophy would be impertinent ; to the mass it is incomprehensible.

I will tell my story without obscurity. I will use the plainest language, and speak to popular acceptations.

I was then, a voluptuary, but not a common voluptuary. I saw that the ordinary mines of enjoyment were soon exhausted, or only to be worked more deeply by labor that defeated its object. I perceived that the most crowded paths of pleasure turned back, by circuitous courses, in never-ending circles.

I resolved to abandon these pastures of gregarious man. But before abandoning them, I tested them by experience. I plunged into all the dissipations of my age. I sought all the distractions that youth, a strong well-nerved body, and an active mind could hope to obtain. I bought all the diversion that gold could buy. I lived with my generation ; I surpassed them ; I led them. I practised systematized moderation. I essayed unbridled excesses. And — I was disappointed.

I did not, as the cant phrase goes, awake from my illusions. I had read, seen, and thought too much. I was too clear-headed to have any illusions. Where others saw misty prospects, I saw naked facts. I summed up, and found the balance on the wrong side. My experiment was a failure.

I had travelled, I had seen the wonders of art and the beauties of nature. I had had access to the best and to the worst of society. I had labored, and been rewarded by fame. The book which I wrote, won the applause of a nation. I foresaw that it would obtain new triumphs in foreign lands ; and my foresight has been confirmed by fact. Lastly, I was united to the woman I loved ; who brought me thrice the fortune I expected, and a mind cultivated beyond my hopes. And with all this — I was dissatisfied. I craved for intenser pleasure ; more exalted excitement ; and I could not disguise from myself that it was so. I reflected deeply.

"What," said I, "is happiness? Is it a monotony of sensations, which are taken to be pleasurable on the faith of popular opinion, whilst the inward voice still whispers languor and tedium, whilst half the day is passed in a dreary vacuity of mind, which is, at best, merely the bare negative of pain? Is it a feverish working and striving for objects which on attainment invariably become insipid and indifferent?"

"Certainly not. Reasonably regarded, it is surely a positive, appreciable state of consciousness, in which we can say without hesitation to the moment, in the words of Goethe,

"O linger yet, thou art so fair!' It is a certain condition of the nervous system, and without that condition — misery."

I fell to watching myself studiously at different times, and under various circumstances.

I observed that, at a certain stage, wine produced sensations of extreme delight. But I also observed that these sensations soon gave way to other and more sombre feelings ; that, in fact, there was a happy crisis in alcoholic stimulus, which, when once past, could not be recalled on one and the same occasion. Indulgence, too, in wine was, I perceived, followed by a vague, dreary despondency, that lasted incomparably longer than the brief passing moments of delicious exhilaration it produced.

On the whole, it was better to leave the mind to nature and mere mental excitements, than to attempt to light the sacred fire at the now neglected altars of Bacchus.

I need not say, that to become vulgarly intoxicated, was, with me, out of the question. There are some strong brains that defy the utmost possibilities of wine. I could have poisoned myself ; but I could not render myself an unreasoning animal, by any amount of spirituous liquors. Often I persevered to the last, and when all my wild companions had sunk, I may say in many cases fallen beneath their potent draughts, I alone sat erect, and at worst discovered that my stomach was a weaker organ than my head. In such cases a feeling of awful and gloomy sadness would possess me, and after sitting long in silent and strangely lucid meditations, I would walk home calmly in the gray of the morning with little outward indication of the debauch from which I had emerged.

It was evident that no cascades of wine — even though they beggared Niagara in their ruby or topaz-like curves — could overarch for me that enchanted palace, in which I desired to spend my days, and defy the adversary — Pain, Evil, Devil, Typhon, Ariman or Sathanas, in a word, the dread foe, named or nameless, described or indescribable, of human happiness and its continuance.

Apart from all more palpable causes of suffering, man sits between Memory and Desire, between the Past and the Future as between two rival mistresses, each dragging him towards her by turns with uneasy passion ; whilst before him, and as it were balanced on an eternal and invisible tight-rope, sways the only nymph that can bless him with her love, the only goddess he can really and truly possess, if indeed he can possess anything, the divine Present — and he — dares not clasp the radiant virgin to his heart, dares not drive to the East nor to the West, along the interminable roads of space, the furies that torment him, madden him, and devour him, now, then, and evermore!

For my part, I said to the sad and pale brunette, the angel Præterita, and to the blonde seductive blue-eyed spirit Futura, a like farewell. The genii of Past and Future ruled the race of man — the Earth-God. But one was a rebel and an outlaw ; and that one was I.

I said to the Universe, "Let me *feel* happiness, not merely dream it." And everlasting echoes from all the depths of Kosmos, even from the farthest bounds where creation, ever encroaching, borders upon awful chaos, everlasting echoes answered "DREAM!"

And I replied to the spirits of the Infinite, and demanded proudly, "Ye blind legions of monitors ! where in nature is your unclouded happiness ? where is your *perfection ?*"

And the echoes laughed back in mockery, "*perfection !*"

Then I ceased to ask counsel of any men or spirits. For I was determined to be my own guide, and my own teacher, since all the wisdom of the world had not yet led to happiness. Therefore I scorned its pretensions, and derided its impotence with justice.

* * * * * *

I became a great smoker. I purchased the rarest tobaccos and the costliest pipes. I had a perfect museum of meerschaums, nargulés, chibouques, and tubes and bowls of all sorts of shape, size, and contrivance for the inhalation of the fragrant weed. I purchased, at extravagant prices, the choicest boxes of cigars. I smoked grandly, incessantly, infernally. The atmosphere grew dark with my smoking ; at least to my imagination. I wrapped my soul in the incense of tobacco. I created worlds of fancies out of its wreathing vapors. I began to think I had found the resource I wanted, and I often exclaimed in dreamy ecstasy — "Divine Nicotiana!" [*Nicotiana is the scientific name for tobacco. It is derived from Frenchman of the name of Jean Nicot, who first imported it to France.*] I doubted whether the vapors which inspired the Pythoness did not arise from the hookahs of the priests smoking in solemn divan in the subterranean halls of Delphi. And I gave them high credit for having so well preserved the secret they had discovered.

At the same time, like a true Turk, I took care to have the finest coffee of Mocha prepared by the most perfect machinery. I found that, after fasting, the effect of coffee upon the nerves was almost supernatural ; but combined with tobacco, it was Elysian. It produced an intense state of enjoyment, during which, I would discourse with a marvellous eloquence to my adoring Mira, who was never weary of following the train of my prolific and far-stretching fantasies. How easily in this period of my madness (as I have since learned to deem it) did I unravel knots in science and philosophy, that had puzzled the wise men of ages. How intuitively did I seize on combinations, whose results, in the hands of practical men, might have rendered them the acknowledged benefactors of the world and enriched whole nations of workers! But with me, all was a reverie of selfish recreation. I created glorious plans, I foreshadowed mighty inventions, as a voluptuous exercise of the mind ; I played as it were grand symphonies on the most intellectual themes, and the compositions perished with the dying sounds, like the fantasias of musicians, which are never to be repeated.

But this could not last. My powerful organization resisted for a time the exaggerated abuse of drugs, which, common though they be, are in excess like all other substances, the deadliest poisons. Smoking destroys the appetite, and ruins the digestive powers. Its effect upon the nerves then becomes tremendous. I soon made this discovery. A neuralgic irritation attacked me, which, as I still pursued my diabolical fumigations went on with a fearfully *crescendo* movement. Deadly sickness of a peculiar inactive character, fits of the horrors, in which all things became repugnant, wearisome, and nauseating ; ideas of suicide, and awful despondencies, descended upon me like a flight of vultures on a dying antelope. I abandoned the poisons. My prostration was complete and unbearable. I partially resumed them, and tried change of air and scene. I just recovered sufficiently to be able to suffer more acutely. I had evidently, at least temporarily, undermined my constitution. It was at this period, that, like a demon watching his occasion, *opium* became my comforter.

For the first time a book fell into my hands, a dangerous book, which has made many wretched : I mean "The Confessions of an English Opium-Eater." This work, as all the world knows, was written by Thomas de Quincy, an Englishman of letters, who is still living. And with regard to this De Quincy, I will mention one thing that is curious. He is intimately persuaded that he is a great philosopher. In reality he is a fragmentary poet, imbued with considerable transcendentalism. His book is extremely amusing, but the reverse of philosophical, for it arrives at no conclusion. It is an opium book in more senses than the writer would have you believe. Such as it is, however, this book was the immediate cause of my taking to opium.

Its first effects were delightful. It tranquillized my irritated nerves, and I entered, as it were, a new world of dreamy speculation. An invisible barrier seemed raised between me and the external world. Nothing troubled me, nothing annoyed me. I was on the verge of being utterly inpoverished by a dispute as to the title of my wife's property. But it gave me no uneasiness. The danger passed away as it came — like a fleeting fancy. The only thing that slightly interfered with my peaceful ecstasy of indolent reverie, was the apprehensions of my wife. She had heard that opium-eating was a shocking thing, and she could not at once get reconciled to the idea. Nor would any thing induce her personally to taste the talismanic liquid — the *happiness in bottles,* as De Quincy has aptly termed it.

The effect of opium in producing dreams, so forcibly dwelt upon and splendidly illustrated by that writer, I need not enlarge upon. Enough to state that the number and variety of my visions were infinite. Ages were crowded into nights. The most monstrous and gigantic images were familiar things. Time and space were extended beyond all conception, except that of an opium-eater. Nevertheless, opium palled upon me, and the opium-dream-world became almost tedious. I had, too : an excessive dislike to the taste of laudanum, which, strange to say, increased rather than diminished. One day I returned home with a small vial of bright green liquid in my pocket. It's very color had a mystic poisonous fascination. How much more potent and cabalistic was its spell than the dark, thick, brown, drowsy-looking laudanum! It was Haschisch. Haschisch is a sort of Indian hemp (Canabis Indicus). The liquid in the vial was an extract from its stalks. This Indian poison is mentioned in Lamartine's Vision of the Future, and in Alexander Dumas's Monte-Cristo. Their exaggerated, or rather apparently exaggerated descriptions of its effects have no doubt caused the majority of their readers to consider this marvellous drug as a mere figment of the poet and novelist's brains. It has, however, a real existence, and is in extensive demand amongst the initiated. In effect it resembles opium, but is more exhilarating, and less narcotic. I continued for a whole year to increase my doses of this new elixir of happiness, and did not find myself assaulted by any of the horrible fancies which De Quincy complains of as the after results of opium. Like King Mithridates, I was becoming familiar with poisons, and they began to respect their master. But, though I lived as much in another world from that of ordinary mortals, as if my habitation had been in the planet Uranus, I could not escape a more terrible poison than even the Hydrocianic, commonly called Prussic acid, in which, as an antidote to certain effects of the *Canabis Indicus,* I freely indulged. *Ennui*, the spleen, that mysterious and tyrannical malady, pursued me, even into my poison-guarded dream-world. I grew accustomed to the life, the old dreams and fancies recurred, and became tiresome. Already I meditated a deeper plunge in *Venemum*. I fell in, accidentally, in some review, with an account of the *Arsenic-eaters* of Styria, and of the results of that mania, in heightening the personal beauty of its devotees. Certainly the pure delicacy of Mira's clear fair complexion left no room for improvement except in the fancy of a madman. Nevertheless, I longed to try the effect of an arsenic varnish — if I may so express myself — upon both her and my own countenance. Who could tell whether seeming more beautiful to one another, our love might not acquire new strength, and develope new sources of delight. I was in the midst of a profound reverie or rather Haschisch dream on this subject, when I received a letter from a scientific friend, announcing the discovery of the effects of inhaling ether, in destroying sensation and rendering surgical operations painless.

I thought that new light burst upon my soul. In one instant I became a convert to an entirely new system of nervous influence. I rushed out to buy some *rectified sulphuric ether,* and a machine for inhalation. The latter consisted of a bottle to which was attached a flexible tube, about two feet long, and two inches in diameter. I eagerly poured in some ether and applied the funnel-like mouth-piece to my lips. After a few inspirations of the vaporized ether I felt a most marvellous and delicious effect. I felt a stream of joyous expansion steal rapidly through my veins, even to the tips of my toes, which tingled with delight. I at once felt the vast superiority of inhaling the stimulant over swallowing it. Instead of going through the tedious process of digestion, whose functions it disturbed and impeded, as in the case of wine, the purified and refined spirit (for ether is but rectified alcohol) entered at once into the lungs, thence into the aerated blood, and thus through every part of the body with the crimson flood of impatient arteries, and so back with the blue current of the veins, to evaporate harmlessly, leaving nothing but its memory behind it!

"Hence !" I exclaimed, "wine, coffee, tobacco, opium, haschisch ! away henbane, arsenic, hydrociana! Coarse and noxious stimulants, narcotics, and nerve-swindlers, who wrap the soul in cumbrous veils that, like the robe of Dejanira, invades the life of your votaries. I am no De Quincy, I, to mock myself with vain half realized fantasies, to stand up to the middle in Styx, and murmur vaguely — *Suspiria de profundis!"*

And now a new field opened to my researches. The world of gas spread temptingly before me. Little do the vain mob understand the import of that word — to them the emblem of emptiness. "It is all gas!" they cry. Yes, truly every thing is gas, is, was, and ever shall be gas. The most solid and material things resolve themselves into mere gaseous combinations. A little more of one gas, a little less of another, and lo! all the varieties in nature are produced. All was originally gas. Chaos was the confusion of gases. All must resolve itself ultimately into gas. You and I are gas, and gas is every thing.

I became a man of gas, a maker and an experimentalist of gaseous mixtures. I remembered the exhibitions which in my youth I had witnessed of the effects of *laughing gas,* the inhalation of which causes the wildest intoxication, or rather, exaltation of the brain, and causes those who breathe it to exhibit the most fantastic feats, illustrative of their predominant passions. If there is truth in wine, in gas there is revelation. Yet the man in whom reason is the ruling faculty, will subdue all outward indications of the mighty *afflatus*. There is a supreme gas, a gas of gases, and its particles are souls. All other gases exist by numerical arrangement, as Pythagoras well conjectured, when he prefigured the atomic theories of modern days. But there is an ultimate atom, a gas which is the basis of all others, and without which all is vacuum.

I knew that in an atmosphere of pure oxygen, the gas essential to life, and at the same time the agent of all decay, the sour stuff *(sauer stoff)* as the Germans call it, an animal could live, and live with a wondrous acceleration of all the physical processes. In man this rapid consumption of matter was accompanied by an equal intensifying exaltation of the mental faculties. On this fact I founded my experiments, and the result was at length, the combination of oxygen with other gases, in an artificial atmosphere of the most astounding and admirable qualities.

To breathe this air, was to breathe positive enjoyment. It was vaporized nectar and ambrosia. Its respiration was the life of a God. But it was also the embodied *Sansar* — "the icy wind of death." No mortal could live more than a few months even in its partially diluted perfection. It was the short life and merry of the reckless popular adage, reduced to palpable embodiment.

On the other hand, this rapidity of life was only apparent. For we measure time by sensations ; and the exalted powers of sensation, confirmed by breathing the wondrous gas, gave time a supernatural extension similar to the life of dreams but free from all their shadowy indistinctness.

My resolution at once was taken. I would live and die in this glorified atmosphere. I would bid farewell to all that was earthly, without hesitation. I bought a magnificent chateau in the South of France. I furnished it by the expenditure of one-third of my fortune, in a few days, with all the luxury that imagination could suggest. I fitted up my apparatus for the production of the gas, and engaged, at the rate of some thousands of francs, monthly, a young chemist of first-rate education, and superior energy and abilities. To him I confided all the management and regulation of the apparatus, and also the absolute control of the servants and of the whole establishment. One suite of rooms, the most splendid, and with the finest prospect in the chateau, were to be my own enchanted habitation. Into these apartments, except at certain times and with due precautions, no servants were to enter. Every thing that I required was to be sent up through the floor, by means of tables that screwed up and down, by noiseless machinery. No one was to disturb me on any pretext ; no letters were to be given me, and, as the chemist was poor, almost starving when I first patronized him, I knew that so long as every month brought him a little fortune in itself ; I might count on his absolute devotion. Besides, I deceived him as to my intentions. There was only one room — the largest and most splendidly furnished in the house — which was to be actually filled with the life-accelerating gas. It communicated with the other apartments by carefully constructed double doors, and of course it never entered the mind of the chemist that I intended to live and die in the deadly atmosphere which he was to create, or that, after so carefully ordering these hermetically closing double doors, I should purpose fixing them wide open, the moment I was shut up within my mysterious domicile, and thus causing the whole suite of apartments to fill with the same ethereal poison.

In other respects, the chemist was just the person I wanted ; he was patient; faithful, and industrious. At the same time, he was a cold stern man, well fitted to repress any insubordination or curiosity on the part of the household. And now all was prepared for the experiment. It only remained to persuade Mira to be my companion. For I confess that without her, even the potence of the marvellous gas must have failed in its action on my nerves. Her love had become a habit, a part of my being, I could not live or die without her.

And here let me for the first time say a few words about Mira.

She was an entirely exceptional woman. When I married her, some three years before the date of my final experiment, she was only sixteen years of age. Her beauty (I can find no newer or more intelligible image) was of the order which the finest painters strive to impart to their embodiments of angels, and beings superior to man. Its supreme loveliness was not in its delicate regularity of feature, dazzling whiteness and purity of skin, and majestic symmetry of form. All these seemed merely indispensable conditions of such an individuality. What made her irresistibly pleasing to the perceptions of an imaginative and thoughtful man, was a certain calm, unalterable dignity and noble gentleness, that placed her above even the possibility of any of the meannesses and pettinesses of her sex. She had the strong mind of a man with all the purity and softness of an exquisitely delicate female organization. In temperament, she was my opposite, although intellectually, there existed between us a perfect sympathy. She was as calm and serenely contented, as I was feverishly dissatisfied and eager for excitement. Yet she understood and entered into all my wild speculations, as into an interesting drama, of which she was the sympathizing spectator. She was my only confidant, my only friend, my only real companion. With all my restless cravings for greater intensity of enjoyment her love was my world, my treasure, and my hope — the more so that I might almost be said to mistrust its possession.

That Mira loved me, was indeed indubitable, yet there was a calmness, a purity, and passive even tenor in her love that could not be called coldness, and which yet in a manner disappointed the fiery adoration with which I loved her. I would not have lost one of her kisses for all the embraces of all the beauties of the earth and yet, to my fierce and impassioned nature there seemed more snow upon her bosom, than a poet's simile implies, more than perchance would ever melt beneath my lip's ecstatic pressure.

In the delusion of my wild tempest-tost soul, which, after all, was but that of a mad poet's, astray in the deserts and primeval forests of thought, I knew not that the crown of her glorious beauty and of my delicious, because never satiated, passion, lay in the very qualities which I regretted, and which I insanely hoped to conquer by my infernal and pitiless inventions.

To my surprise, I had no difficulty in persuading Mira to enter the enchanted atmosphere. A first trial of its virtues was of course decisive. We gave ourselves up to the intense joy of a life, to which pain, care, and sorrow, regret for the past or apprehension for the future, were necessarily strange. The outer world became nothing to us. Love, exalted to a degree of power which to the breathers of common air is inconceivable, appreciation of beauty and delights which are alike inexplicable and incomprehensible, made up the sum of our existence. I pass over, therefore the seven times seven days of our ethereal life, a period which in ideas and sensations was equivalent to the ordinary lapse of ages, and hasten onward to the extraordinary catastrophe which left me what I am — a monster more rare and wonderful than the sphinxes and chimeras of old, my fabulous prototypes.

Nor let the reader foolishly imagine that, because memory or science give me the power of describing passion, and thereby exciting his sympathies, that I personally do or can feel any echoing vibration of the wild chords which I cause to resound. Unearthly is the music — unearthly the musician.

Opening from the grand saloon of the chateau, was a superb conservatory of more than ordinary dimensions, commanding a view of one of the most splendid landscapes in the world. In the foreground, yet not sufficiently near to intercept the view, rose from the side of the hill, on which stood the chateau the mingled foliage of an old and primitive forest, while beyond was visible the shining stream of the Rhone, lying, like the crooked sabre of some gigantic Paladin, upon the greensward ; and far, far beyond rose the bluish shadowy outlines of mountains behind which the sun would set in golden glory, that made each snow-crowned peak a throne worthy of Sathanas — "the Emperor of the furnace."

Round this conservatory were arranged a collection of strange exotic and tropical plants, so as to leave the centre unoccupied, save by a few couches, chairs and tables, on which lay volumes of poetry and philosophy, and portfolios of exquisite engravings and drawings. This was our favorite sitting-room. It was only necessary to open the glass doors between it and the saloon, to fill it with the same enchanted air ; and I may mention as a curious example of the effects of this atmosphere on vegetation, that the grapes which were quite green and hard on its first introduction, ripened perfectly in a few days, and were the largest and most luscious fruit I had ever tasted or seen. It was one of Mira's greatest enjoyments to call me to watch the camelias budding and flowering actually before our eyes! Were I in the humor I could write a hundred pages on the wonders of vegetation with which my residence in this gas-world made me acquainted. But I refrain without difficulty. To me no science is worth a thought.

In the centre of this hall of crystal stood a white marble statue of Minerva, the only statue in which that goddess has ever been represented entirely without drapery. The figure was Mira's. I myself modelled it during the first year of our marriage, and it was carved by one of the most eminent French sculptors, who afterwards died mad from a hopeless passion for the original. The fountain sprang from and formed the foliage of a glass tree stem, against which she leant, whilst the point of her spear drooped earthward from her arm, as if languid with the warfare against folly. Her head alone was covered with a helmet, which imparted a singular charm to the divine beauty of Mira's countenance.

At length, one day, towards evening, after seven weeks of solitude and happiness, which no Paradise could more than realize, a fatal accident destroyed at once our enjoyment, our experiment in science, and our lives. Yes — I learned it afterwards — we were killed by the merest accident. My chemist who managed the gas-generating apparatus, forgot to examine the metre at the proper time. The gas continued to enter in unprecedented volumes, and its effects were speedily perceptible.

We were seated in our favorite place in the conservatory, our eyes turned towards the setting sun, listening to the swelling and harmonious cadences of Weber, produced by a self-playing instrument of the rarest workmanship, which I had purchased at Paris for an enormous sum, of its inventor, when a more than usual ecstasy seemed to possess us. Our arms, entwined round one another's forms, seemed to contract almost convulsively, our eyes, our lips met with delirious love, and — I remember no more. When I recovered possession, not of my senses, but of my consciousness, I was still seated upon the sofa on which the angel of death had surprised us, whilst on the marble pavement, at full length, her face turned upwards with an expression of supernatural felicity, lay Mira — Mira, my wife, friend, and goddess — the fairest and noblest of women. She was dead.

Mira was dead. That was evident. But what was I ? I rose, and regarded curiously the culpable chemist, who, having discovered his oversight, had hurried too late to our rescue. He had thrown wide open the windows of the conservatory. I inhaled the common air of the sky. But, though I breathed and moved, however incredible may appear the statement of a fact hitherto unknown to science, I was to all intents and purposes as much a dead person as Mira herself. That is to say. I was dead to all sensation, emotion, passion, or by whatever other phrase may be described the action of the external world upon the sensitive being. It is true, I could hear, see, feel, taste, and smell but such sensations had no longer any influence upon me either in causing dissatisfaction or satisfaction. My sensations were mere facts to my consciousness and no more. Mira was dead, that was a fact. She lay there, pale and beautiful, before me — a fact. I myself had lost the half of my life — a fact. The chemist who was the author of these hideous calamities, as men would say, stood trembling before me — another fact. In a word, I was a *living corpse*. One class of nerves, the nerves of sympathetic sensation, appeared either paralyzed or exhausted of their circulating fluid. Love and anger were no longer my attributes. I had reached, truly, and at one stride, the centre of indifference told of by some philosophers. But it was a *centre* of *indifference* which they talk of without understanding. I did not understand it — *I was in it.*

The chemist stood pallid and trembling before me. He was a cold, unimpassioned, little impressionable man. But in the presence of my dead eye and marble rigidity of feature he trembled involuntarily. No doubt he mistook my absence of emotion for sonic tremendous effect of internal passion. He evidently dreaded an explosion of a terrible nature. But I merely said —

"She is dead — you are no longer wanted — go."

For one moment he looked at me with a most extraordinary expression, then, overwhelmed by the icy look with which I covered him, he departed in silence.

I remembered that his salary from the beginning was unpaid. Nor had he ever the courage to ask for it. Of course I could have no motive in sending it to him. The happiness of others was to me no longer a possible subject of interest. A man takes no interest in others, who can take none in himself. The chemist, driven to despair by poverty, committed suicide in the course of the same year.

At the end of a week, the body of Mira was buried. In the mean time, from physical habit, as it appeared, I one day took up a book — a volume of poetry. It was no longer poetry to me, but a collection of signs representing certain phenomena. A book of arithmetic was to me of precisely equal interest.

I had eaten and drunk nothing since the great catastrophe, though I had been urged to do so by people to whose entreaties and pity I was alike indifferent. But, remarking that my body was wasting away, I ate a measured quantity, which I continued to do regularly afterwards, though without any appetite or enjoyment.

I had reason and power of command over my body as much as ever. But those operations which formerly were the result of impulse, I had now to perform as pure acts of will. The only reason why I did not quietly await death, was a clear intellectual consciousness of the fact that I was in an abnormal state, and that it was also possible that I should return to the natural conditions of humanity.

Without being a desire, the discovery of the means of effecting this change became my only object ; and in order to attain what, in reality, I cared nothing about (the contradiction is only apparent), I spent years in trying the most extraordinary experiments in natural science ever imagined. Perfectly indifferent to the success or non-success of my experiments, I yet worked on. If I might be said to have any thing left resembling a desire, it was a passionless inclination towards abstract truth, which seemed to be a sort of mechanico-spiritual law of my being. But to compare this mere gravitation towards an abstract centre to the ardent enthusiasm of ordinary men of science, would be absurd. And here, I recognize the impossibility of conveying to a living man the impressions of a corpse. Therefore I abandon further attempt at illustration.

Perhaps one fact may explain more than much analysis. After some years, during which time I made numerous scientific discoveries of the most remarkable character, I lighted upon the secret. I had it in my power at any moment to return to life, to rise again from the dead and once more to share the passions and cares of men. But I had no motive to change my condition. I remained a corpse. The discovery was to me — a fact.

Why should I again inhale the gas of happiness and destruction, why revive to an existence that would be a type of the fabled hells of legendary lore? Mira is dead. I am a living corpse ; and I am the only being bearing the shape of man who could ever honestly declare himself to be *perfectly contented with his lot.*

EDITORIAL.

If anybody has a right to say "We," it is the occupant of our editorial chair ; for when, in the pride of our heart, we ordered that solemn piece of furniture, and detailed the various mysterious attributes it must possess, our worthy and simple-minded cabinetmaker, observing that we always addressed him in the first person plural, so constructed the machine (for it really is a machine) that it should accommodate not merely our own editorial corpus, which of itself is rather bulky, but our whole editorial corps.

For this, then, if for no other reason, we assume at once the prescriptive "We ," and use it not as a signifying, according to Webster, "men in general, including the speaker," but the speaker alone excluding men in general.

And while doing, we may as well reply in advance to all inquiries as to the editorship of the SATURDAY PRESS, by the simple if not satisfactory statement, that it is edited solely and exclusively by "Us."

And now a word as to our mode of editing.

Not long since we heard a distinguished lawyer of this city remark that he thought it would be a great improvement in our city newspapers if they would abolish their editorial department entirely, and devote the space it occupies to useful information or to the lucubrations of sensible men. The remark was rather a startling one, but on being explained it struck us that our friend was more than half right. At any rate, we are indebted to him for a very valuable hint, acting upon which we will here inform the readers of the SATURDAY PRESS, that while it will doubtless contain as much valuable matter as any other journal, it will not give up its editorial columns on the one hand to lengthy political articles (in which nobody that we know of takes any interest), nor, on the other, to pedantic disquisitions on subjects—European politics and the like—concerning which our editors and the public at large are, and might as well remain, wholly ignorant.

The one aim of the paper will be to furnish its readers with as great a variety of possible of interesting facts, leaving him the privilege of making his own comments.

With political matters, we shall have very little to do. The common supposition that the reading public are chiefly interested in the squabbles of politicians, is as unfounded as that in matters of fiction they have no taste except for flash stories. The truth is that they have been bored to death with both. Most of our newspapers, filled as they are with such trash, would appear to be edited for the exclusive benefit of hack politicians and servant girls ; two very numerous classes of people, no doubt, and one of them (the second) sufficiently intelligent ; but whatever their deserts they hardly deserve so much attention from the press, for there still remains a large portion of the community who at least have some claims to consideration, though they happen to care nothing about "Bleeding Kansas," and have never read a line of "The Pirates Revenge."

Among this class, there is demand especially for a more complete report of what is doing in the world of letters. This demand we shall do our best to meet, and by this means, and the publication of well-written stories, such as appear in the best English Reviews, and laterally in the "Atlantic Monthly" and "Harper's Magazine," we hope to make at least a readable paper.

MACKAY ON SPITTOONS.

Mr. Charles Mackay, who has our readers like ourselves had probably forgotten, made a flying trip through this country, some time since, in charge of a distinguished Dead Head, is out in a late number of the *Illustrated London News,* with a jeremiad on the American custom of chewing and spitting. The only redeeming thing about the article, is that it is not written in verse. In other respects, it is characterized by the author's usual feebleness. But the man really deserves pity. Throughout all of his travels, from Maine toGeorgia, he seems to have seen nothing but spittoons. Spittoons in the hall, spittoons in the parlor, spittoons in church, spittoons in Congress, spittoons in court, spittoons

Up-stairs, down-stairs,
In my lady's chamber,

and when the distinguished man lectured on the poetry of England, Scotland, and Charles Mackay, nothing but Col. Fuller and a congenial collection of spittoons to welcome him. What with this, and the universal red hot stove, the poor fellow was literally roasted and spitted. His sufferings like those of General Jackson, were intolerable. He had seen his own countrymen filthy beyond expression in the use of snuff, taking it with a spoon instead of the finger and thumb, and slobbering themselves all over with it ; but this he had got used to. Possibly he had the habit himself. He had lived most of his life (until he came to America), in the neighborhood of streets the stench from which would instantly suffocate any body but a Scotchman ; but to this, he had got acclimated. The one thing he couldn't stand, was tobacco-chewing. This so shocked his nerves, that for a time he could neither rhyme nor reason. His moral system became (and at last accounts remained) completely prostrated.

How he ever got back to the old country, nobody knows, and, which is more, nobody cares. The only people who sympathized with him here, were the ladies, who did everything for him except attend his lectures ; they went so far as to promise him to have nothing to do with tobacco chewers hereafter (beyond marrying them), and to aid him in all other ways in his crusade against the spittoon. They evidently looked upon him as the most begrimed and bespit-upon man in the country, and therefore helped him in every way to return home as soon as might be, like Dickens, and get cleaned. But Alas ! he is still in a suffering condition, and in his dear old Glasgow (the dirtiest city in the world), and on the banks of the dear old Thames (the dirtiest river), pours out night and day his dismal lamentations, crying out, like the leper of old, *"Unclean ! Unclean !"*

—The Hon. Horace Mann, in his recent lecture on the "Relation between Colleges and the People," says, among other equally felicitous things, that he regards every young man who can control his appetite, and who obeys all the laws of longevity, as already *"half gentlemen, half hero, and half Christian* ;" from which it would seem that the youth who has fulfilled these simple conditions, though he is neither an entire gentleman, an entire hero, nor an entire Christian, is nevertheless, by a miraculous combination of these characters, not only an entire man, *but a man and a half.*

—It is proposed to create two new officials in the Fire Department, one of whom shall have a thousand dollars a year for overseeing repairs, and the other two thousand dollars for repairing overseers. Verily, we live in strange and circumlocutionary times.

[For the Saturday Press.]

SIXES AND SEVENS.

It was Saturday evening. I had just dined at Delmonico's. Meanwhile the city had undergone such a change that it didn't know me. I hardly knew myself.

Union Square, tired of gazing at the statue of Washington, had coolly walked down Broadway and relieved the Battery, which was only too glad to exchange places with it, and which proceeded to consort with the pretty nursery maids of the quarter, as it had kept such company all its life.

Distracted omnibuses, turned upside down, with their wheels whizzing in the air, were dragging their reversed and refractory horses in every direction in search of the old localities.

An endless file of men and women, most of them standing on their heads, were dancing up and down the sidewalks, and leaping over, under, and through each other in inextricable confusion.

Fire engine No. 9 was winging its way through the heavens like a flying machine, with two hundred men and boys in red shirts streaming behind it like the tail of a comet.

Taylor's saloon was standing, roof down, in the middle of the street, and an infuriated policeman was ordering it to get on its legs and go home.

This spectacle making me hungry, I walked into the chimney of the building, and was drawn up by suction to the gilded eating room, where I at once ordered hard boiled potatoes and mashed eggs, which were immediately brought to me by a ballet girl, whom I had seen the night before at Laura Keene's, smoking a horn-pipe. The room was full of people eating the daily newspapers and reading dried toast and mutton-chops. Mr. Taylor was standing behind the counter near the door, distributing money to all the customers as they passed out. Having requested a napkin, the ballet girl offered me her handkerchief, on declining which and explaining concisely what I wanted, she brought me an umbrella. I then ordered coffee, when, with incredible despatch, an extremely civil waiter laid before me the neatest of all possible coffeepots, containing the most delicious mocha ever drank out of Turkey, a silver pitcher filled with the purest country milk, boiling hot, and an ample supply of rolls and butter, which would do credit to Paris, though no credit can be got for them in New York.

In a word, I was drunk.

On leaving Taylor's, and receiving from that liberal gentleman my share of the money he was so lavishly distributing, I proceeded, as directly as I could under the circumstances, to Burton's theater, where I saw Rev. Dr. Bellows performing the part of Toodles in The Serious Family, after which he danced a Highland fling with Mademoiselle L'Amoreux. Both performances were received with immense delight by a crowded house composed of the cream of society, which, strange to say, stood the heat of the atmosphere without curdling. I noticed that Rev. Mr. Tyng and Capt. de Riviera occupied one of the private boxes, while another was devoted to Henry Ward Beecher and Patrick Hearn. The newspaper critics, headed by Mr Fry, were located at the back of the stage, and spent the evening smoking champagne and drinking real cigars, in which they were joined from time to time by the actors and actresses, who were summoned in a shrill voice by Deacon Hallock, the famous call-boy.

At the close of the entertainment, there was a loud call for Mr. Beecher, who came forward and sung a comic song.

To sum up, everything throughout the evening was conducted on the most liberal and approved principles, and (Mr Bellows being a Unitarian) without a single violation of the "Unities."

In a word, I was very drunk.

From the theater I started for my room, No. 896 Atlantic street, Brooklyn, and being in haste took the Staten Island ferry boat, which, owing to some confusion on the part of the pilot, deposited me at quarantine landing, where, in company with George W. Curtis, whom I met in the ladies cabin, I was arrested on the charge of having aided and abetted in the burning of the hospital. My own participation in that event, however, having been disproved by the fact, of which I had evidence about me, that when it occurred I was in an Insane Asylum (which ought also to be burnt), I was promptly liberated the next morning and sent up to the city in charge of a benevolent fruit-woman, whom I fell furiously in love with, and was only prevented from marrying on the spot (wherever that was) by the fact that she had a husband and six full grown children, all alive and flourishing—on Blackwell's Island.

In other words, I was not yet sober.

On tearing myself away from the fruit-woman, having first accepted her whole stock of apples, and given my watch in exchange, I received to go straight home, but having taken the Fourth Avenue cars at the park found myself in a few moments, owing to the treachery of the conductor, who never touched at Brooklyn at all, in front of Dr. Bellows' church, which looked so much like a theater that I entered it at once, and found Burton in the pulpit holding forth to a congregation of clergymen in defence of the Church. On looking about me, I found that nearly every clergyman in the city was present, and was told by the one who sat next to me (Dr. Osgood) that their respective pulpits were occupied for this day only by leading metropolitan actors, Dr. Tyng's by Jordan, Dr. Hawks's by Jefferson, Dr. Springs by Walcott, Dr. Potts' by Laura Keene, Doctor Osgood's by Blake, etc.; the only theatrical stars who had declined, being Tom Placide, the older Wallack,—these gentlemen having plotted other engagements,—and Dion Boucicault who refused to preach without being paid for it.

I regretted not having been able to hear Jefferson (called, since his clerical performance, Awful Jefferson) and Blake, who are said to have been very solemn on the occasion ; but it was something to have heard Burton, who treated his subject with a skill and pathos worthy of his great ancestor, the author of "The Anatomy of Melancholy."

The eloquent comedian commenced his performance with the remark that the common prejudice against the Church, was to a great extent unfounded. It was his opinion that despite its faults, it had been of great use to mankind. Church-going might, indeed, like anything else, be carried to excess, though he knew several persons who had indulged in it four or five times a week for many years, and were nevertheless very good citizens. He considered that although pulpit performances were sometimes of a questionable character, still it was not to be denied on the other hand that they often had a high moral tendency. Moreover, he had observed that although the usual modes of applause were forbidden in churches, still the audience always contrived to manifest their delight at the expression of any noble or generous sentiment. This was an encouraging sign, which, in his opinion, preachers would do well to profit by. The charge that clergymen were inferior to other men in manliness and purity of character, he considered to be somewhat exaggerated. It was true that they were brought before the courts for criminal conduct oftener than the members of his own profession, but then we should consider their peculiar education and the temptations to which they were exposed, and judge them with more lenity. Besides, in this respect, there had been considerable improvement in late years, although he regretted to observe, that when any of them had fallen by the way, there was always a diseased curiosity on the part of the public to hear them preach. This he considered to be a direct encouragement to vice, as a preacher often acquired a popularity by committing a faux pas which he never could have acquired in the more direct line of his duty. Mr Burton wound up his very sensible discourse by suggesting that if men and women of the world—actors, actresses, ballet girls, prize-fighters, editors, Bohemians, etc.,—would only attend church now and then (and they would soon get used to it), the effect would be to liberalize the character of sermons, to improve the quality of pulpit oratory, and to elevate and ennoble the clerical character.

The services having been concluded with a Doxology, Mr Burton descended from the pulpit, and was immediately surrounded by a large number of eminent clergyman, who congratulated him on the success of his effort, promised him to do what they could in the way of reform, expressed the hope that he and his associates would encourage them and their good resolutions by attending church oftener, and finally invited him to a public dinner to be given at an early day at Tammany Hall, in celebration of the union between Church and Stage. Mr Burton accepted the invitation—getting leave to extend it to his friends, Jefferson, Blake, etc.,—and then went home to dine with Doctor Potts, who at once despatched a note to James Gordon Bennett, and Horace Greeley, inviting their presence at a small card party, in the evening.

Determined now to find my way home as soon as possible, I put myself under the protection of Dolly Davenport, whom I found in a back pew of the church, reading the Bible, and the next day at five P.M., woke up and found myself in—Jersey City.

This completely sobered me, whereupon I instantly resolved not to go to Delmonico's again for a year ; a resolution which I kept until yesterday, when I took another dinner there, immediately after which (to show that I was in a perfectly clear state of mind), I wrote the above authentic narrative, now offered, the compliments of the occasion, for insertion in the first number of the SATURDAY PRESS.

Yours as much as anybody's,

A BOHEMIAN.

DRAMATIC FEUILLETON.

LAURA KEENE'S.—THE NEW COMEDY.

I declare, that someday or other—when I have found a manager of weak mind who will produce it—I will write a comedy of modern life which shall be constructed on the following principles :—I will have my nobleman a virtuous honest person, who has never been a seducer or a fop, and who is not the victim of any impending disclosure relative to his past life. My lawyer shall be a decent man, whose enjoyment in life does not altogether consist of absorbing the nobleman's property and enveloping him in a network of mortgages and promissory notes. I will construct a Yankee who shall be a well-conducted, well-spoken young man, dressing like other people, behaving himself properly in a drawing room, not spitting on the carpet—a Yankee who is not preternaturally "cute," who does not expose all the bad people, and reward all the good, and who on no occasion alludes to himself as "a tarnation critter," or, "this child." My mother—with marriageable daughters—will not be "a manager" or "a campaigner," and will treat the deserving young lover in moderate circumstances with courtesy. One of her daughters shall marry the rich man whom her family wishes her to marry, and, what is more, marry him willingly. The other shall refuse to elope with the ruthless villain who plans her destruction. The young fashionable man of the piece shall speak without a lisp. The soubrette shall be civil and incorruptible. I will have no lost wills turning up in the last act. The people who are rich in the first act shall keep their wealth, and remain wealthy at the fall of this curtain. In short, I will write a piece so natural, so unstrained, so correct in its delineation of what concurs is everyday life, that I am certain unless I find a manager of unusually weak intellect, the public will never have an opportunity of knowing how I succeed.

I am driven to this desperate resolve—he who becomes a dramatic author in New York must, indeed, be desperate—by having witnessed, for these last few years, a succession of comedies and dramas all founded upon the same model. Everything going wrong in the first act, everything going right in the last. I am weary of the nobleman in difficulties, weary of the fashionable mother who is always match-making, of the sleek attorney always cheating, of the young swell always lisping. It is continual partridge on the stage. By way of a change, give me even a piece of ostrich.

Miss Laura Keene produced at her theater, on last Monday evening, a comedy in three acts, said on the bills to be

"By Mister Tom Taylor, of Londor, in Middlesex, England,"

As this statement would run, when placed in that agreeable hexameter measure in which Mr. Longfellow versifies that portion of the Directory of the period, where the address of Mr. Miles Standish's ancestor is given. This latest and most astonishing production of the English dramatist, might have been turned out of a machine. Mr. Babbage exhibited, in London, an apparatus, which, on the twisting of a crank, ground out very tolerable Latin verses, no two exactly alike. Can it be possible, that the author of "Still Waters," has such a machine adapted to comedy, with which he intends to supply the American market ?

Mr. Taylor's Comedy is entitled, "Our American Cousin," the following is my general impression of the plot :—

We find Sir Edward Trenchard—"a Hampshire baronet" the bills call him, just as one would say "a Newtown Pippin"—residing, naturally enough, at Trenchard Manor, where, at the time of the rising of the curtain, the people necessary to carry the piece on are assembled. The principal personages when ticked off may be presented thus,—

SIR EDWARD TRENCHARD,—melancholy baronet with sprightly daughter. Supposed to be rich, but is in reality embarrassed.—Property heavily mortgaged to one Coyle, a lawyer.—Manners funereal.—Dress solemn and substantial.

FLORENCE TRENCHARD. —Sprightly daughter, who does the skip, the merry laugh, and the shaking curls business. In love with a penniless Lieutenant in the Navy. Dress—white tarletane.

LIEUT. VERNON. Penniless lieutenant in a midshipman's jacket : color, ultramarine. Is particularly anxious for a ship in the first act. I was in hopes he'd get it in that act, and go away in it, and be drowned, Gets it in the second act, and doesn't go away in it at all. Manners nautical in the highest degree. He throws out his grappling irons when he embraces Florence. Runs across the bows of several persons. Is always within hail when a female gives the signal of distress, and makes his exit with that step peculiar to theatrical mariners when they retire after the horn-pipe.

LORD DUNDREARY. Foolish English aristocrat, who speaks with a lisp, dresses preposterously, and is laughed at and snubbed by everybody. Perfect picture of the English Lord. They are all fools, all lisp, and are always made butts of.

COYLE—The villainous attorney. The usual black designs and Gators.

ABEL MURCOTT (Coyle's clerk).—Has seen better days. Been once in love with the sprightly daughter. Kicked out of Trenchard manor when the passion was discovered. Took to drink. Became Coyle's factotum. Knows all Coyle's secrets. Dress, dilapidated ; nose, red.

ASA TRENCHARD.—The live yankee. One of those persons that one meets with at every step in Massachusetts or Vermont. Conversation runs continually on eels, snakes, alligators, stone fences, mint juleps, hoss flies, punkin pies, chowder, and such like national institutions. Makes himself at home in strange mansions by insulting all the guests, abusing the food, and talking familiarly to the servants. Gets the better of everybody in conversation. Will be at once recognized as the perfect type of a Vermont gentleman of fortune traveling in Europe.

MARY MEREDITH. Poor relation of the Trenchards. Keeps a dairy. Milk and modesty, butter and beauty, candor and cream cheese.

Fashionable matchmaking Mother, fashionable heartless Daughters, funny Servants, etc.

EVENTS.—Sir Edward Trenchard's brother emigrates to America in consequence of his sister having married one Meredith, a man beneath her in rank, against his consent ; and finding in that country a branch of the Trenchard family settled in Vermont, leaves, in dying, his property in England to his young American relative Asa—thus disinheriting his sister's child, Mary Meredith, who, in consequence, makes butter. Asa arrives at Trenchard manor, being invited to stay there while he is arranging the business of his inheritance. One of his first proceedings on entering the house, is, when luncheon is served, to rush to the table before any of the guests, take the covers off the dishes, tell his hosts that it's "a dreadful mean set out," send the butler to gather mint in the garden, despatch Miss Florence to the housekeeper's room for sugar and brandy, and then and there, in the presence of ladies, and in the best drawing-room of Trenchard manor, he proceeds to make mint juleps. Having, by these proceedings, instructed his hosts in the manners and habits of an American gentleman, he commences instantly to poke his nose into everybody's business. Discovers that Sir Edward is hard up, and in the power of Coyle, who threatens him with ruin if he does not give him the hand of his daughter, the sprightly Florence ; finds out that the penniless lieutenant in the ultramarine jacket wants most desperately to marry Florence and get a ship ; fathoms the various hypocrisies of the fashionable mother and the heartless daughters ; rummages out the fact that Sir Edward is not, after all, in Coyle's power, but only apparently so—Coyle having concealed a document which reinstates the baronet in his wealth ; falls in love with Mary Meredith, the right heir to the property he inherited, and is captivated with such a divinity of dairies. Apparently contented with having done everything that he ought not to have done, he suddenly makes amends by commencing to do everything which he could not, by any possibility, be expected to do. He gets the penniless lieutenant the much-longed for ship ; he burns old Trenchard's will, and thus constitutes Mary Meredith an heiress ; he makes Coyle drunk in the wine-cellar of Trenchard manor ; robs him of his private keys, discovers the important paper, and restores Sir Edward Trenchard to Hampshire and to himself ; he gets Murcott the drunkard, Coyle's place as agent to the Trenchard estate ; he exposes and defeats the managing mother and heartless daughters ; and having arranged the entire company in couples around the stage, after the supposed way in which Noah arranges his guests in the ark, the curtain falls on everybody being engaged to be married to everybody.

It is giving Mr Jefferson the highest praise to say, that he made so utterly worthless and conventional a piece pleasing to the audience. On his shoulders the entire fate of the comedy rested, and he succeeded in bringing it through beyond all anticipation. Exaggerated as the type of character which he sustained—that of Asa—undoubtedly was, there was a praiseworthy effort on his part to soften the glaring coloring and infuse a little nature into the distorted picture. His costume, instead of being the odious conventional dress of the stage yankee, had about it a mere indication of that character. In one or two scenes of a serious nature, Mr Jefferson gave indications of a pathetic quality for which I had not given him credit.

Mr Sothern, as Lord Dundreary, was, perhaps, all that the author intended. He talked as no one ever talked ; dressed as no one ever dressed ; and bore with insults that few would have borne with. I would assure Mr Sothern that there is no part so profitless to the actor as such parts as that of Lord Dundreary. Any one can play them : nor is there any scope for one actor proving himself better than another.

With the exception of Mr. Couldock's rendering of the sketchy part of Abel Murcott, which was forcible and well conceived, I have nothing pleasant to say about the rest of the characters. Miss Keene's performance of the part of Florence was vapid in the extreme. Miss Wells, as Mrs. Mountchessington, the fashionable mother, pitched her naturally high voice so very high, that it was painful to listen to her : she seemed to be penetrated, in fact, vocally with the lesson inculcated in Mr Longfellow's "Excelsior."

I would respectfully remark to the gentleman who sustained the part of Lieut. Vernon, that the uniform of an English lieutenant in the Navy does not consist of a short jacket of ultramarine merino, and a nondescript cap with a gold band. Ten minutes search at any print shop on Broadway would have furnished him with a colored design of the proper uniform, and saved him from presenting himself in an attire which was not alone incorrect but ridiculous.

"Our American Cousin," in spite of all these drawbacks, was greatly relished by the audience, and may be pronounced successful : a result, however, which I persist in attributing entirely to Mr. Jefferson's exceedingly quaint performance.

WALLACK'S THEATRE. DANCE'S COMEDY.

This charming little theater resembles those cabinet pictures which artists tell you, you can admire through a microscope, the execution is so fine, the details so minutely carried out, the art so well concealed. Fitfully brilliant as was Mr. Stuart's management of this pleasant place of amusement, during the past season, yet I felt on Mr Wallack's reopening a sense of security in the hands that held the reins, which no other manager in the city could inspire. The drill of the company is so perfect, the dramatic machinery moves so smoothly. There is elegance, but there is also strength. A touch of dandyism, but, under the dandyism, there is muscle. So, in the emotionless lounger, in Hyde Park, all the exterior is perfumed and carefully tailored, yet, on occasion, he can ride over a six foot wall, lead a charge up the heights of the Alma, or hit from the shoulder like Cribb or Molyneux. It is with no feeling of ingratitude to the out-going lessee, that I express my pleasure at seeing Mr. Wallack once more in the managerial chair at the corner of Broome Street. To Mr. Stuart the public is indebted for much delightful entertainment, and he bore himself with extraordinary liberality and gallantry during a season of unexampled melancholy and distaste. Generous to dramatic authors, and unusually amiable to artists, he certainly leaves none but pleasant memories behind him.

But, somehow, Mr Wallack belongs to that theatre. He rescued it from rapid decay and made it a theater, which, in its peculiar line, had no rival in the city. The completeness of his little companies, the excellence of the stage management, which, if never daring, was always satisfactory and elegant, the certainty of a perfect propriety reigning on the stage, all rendered it a necessity with such of our people as relished polite comedy and unobjectionable melodrama.

One of those elegant trifles, which Mr. Charles Dance constructs better than any other author, was produced there on Monday night. I saw it on Tuesday. It is entitled "Marriage a Lottery," and is in two acts. It is one of those petite drawing-room comedies, the spirit of which depends entirely on easy and epigrammatic dialogue, of which the author, in such works as "a Morning Call," and "Delicate Ground," has already shown his mastery. Both acts pass in a very charmingly painted interior. The critic of the *Times* thus epitomizes the plot: "The hero is a gentleman of undecided habits, who falls into the clutches of an ambitious matron with a marriageable daughter, and conceives, by some impossible train of reasoning, that he is bound to be tormented by the one, and wedded by the other. He is relieved from his predicament by the usual expedients. An assistant lover steps in and relieves his principal of the young lady, whilst compensatory cheques for prosperous amounts appease the old one." The machinery of the piece is slight and improbable, but the dialogue is brilliant, and what may be called the conversational situations, extremely amusing. The hero, one Mr. Wilful Waverly, a wealthy bachelor, was played by Mr. Lester, with exceeding ease and graceful humor. One or two points of his acting, such as allowing his hat to remain on his head in the absurd position in which Mrs. Pointer (Mrs. Vernon) placed it, merely for the sake of raising a laugh, were farcical; and out of tone with the well-bred character of the comedy. Mrs. Vernon's interpretation of the tyrannical would-be mother-in law was absolutely faultless, and Mr. Sloan's dogmatic Grimsby, the valet, full of quiet excellence. Mr. Brougham's very amusing burlesque of "Neptune's defeat," helped by his very amusing singing and acting, and Miss Mary Gannon's dashing assumption of the "Gay Young Spark," *Electros*, still continues to attract good audiences.

PICCOLOMINI AT THE ACADEMY OF MUSIC.

The fair young princess, who as Mr. Ullman insists, does not care about being a princess; the Cardinal's niece, who, we are bound to believe, has inherited all the Cardinal virtues, made her debut on Wednesday night, at the 14th street Opera House. The house was crowded. It was one of the best toilletted assemblages I have ever seen. Beauty and Tiffany were in the ascendant, and the boxes, dress circle, and parquette were *parterres* of floral and female bloom.

It is difficult to form a correct judgment of Mademoiselle Piccolomini's vocal powers in an Opera like the Traviata. It is an Opera of expression, and does not abound in those florid passages, which, in some of Rossini's works, are such infallible tests of the executive powers of a singer. All that the music of La Traviata required, Piccolomini, I think, performed. She was intensely dramatic, moving, and sympathetic. The quality of her voice is eminently suitable for the rendering of that intense story of domestic woe which Verdi has set to music. That terrible third act, with its broken utterances of despair, and its wild death song of passionate joy at the end, was given by Piccolomini with wonderful pathos and electric force. Her acting in all, even the most minor details, is a study, and is seemingly spontaneous. It remains for us, however, to hear Mademoiselle Piccolomini in Grand Opera, where she will become the rival of such singers as Grisi and Cruvelli, before the public can determine her rank as a vocalist.

Her debut, on Wednesday night was, however, in all respects, a perfect triumph, and her many recalls vehemently enthusiastic.

THE TRIBUNE CRITIC.

It is well known to students of human nature, that no person is so ruthless to an erring woman as a woman who has erred. Some time since, the *Tribune*, a paper of the most abandoned grammatical morals, severely reprehended a gentleman named Hazeltine, for looseness of conduct with his nouns and verbs. The *Tribune* was inexorable to its fellow sinner. Hazeltine has, I trust, reformed, but the *Tribune* still holds on to its vicious courses. Its musical critic thus insanely discourses of the concert of Mlle. Emma Wellis,—

"She (the lady) performs on the Alexandre organ—a new style of chamber organ, about the size of a cabinet piano. *In this capacity* she has no rival for excellence."

In what capacity ? That of chamber organ ? If so, what in the name of Calliope *is* this Mademoiselle Wellis ? Is she an automaton, full of pipes, and stops, and keys ? Does she wear crinoline, or is she dressed in rosewood ? I pause for a reply.

Here is a bewildering statement,—

"She performed a fantasia on the Trovatore, two melodies by Miolan, the organist, a duo on the organ and piano, playing on an instrument with two sets of keys, the one giving the organ, the other the piano, and a Christmas hymn by Adam.'

I wonder how the Trovatore liked the fantasia that was performed on him ? What wonderful sets of keys must these be, "one of which gives the organ, while the other munificently contributes a piano, and a Christmas hymn by Adam."

The idiot eulogizes the Alexandre organ. "The tone," he says, "is adequate to sustain a small choir." What a heavy swell that organ must have ! What sort of support does it give a small choir ? Does it merely suspend the youthful vocalists in mid air, or give them board and lodging ? Marvelous instrument !

Go on, Critic of the *Tribune*, give us some more of your astonishing English composition. Clever and learned as Mr. Fry's criticisms frequently are, I prefer yours. There is an unconscious humor about them, that is inimitable.

DRAMATIC ON DITS.

Mr. Bourcicault has in rehearsal at Niblo's, and will produce there on Tuesday, a new piece with the mysterious title of "The Pope of Rome." The cast is to embrace the entire strength of the company; but whether Mr Bourcicault is to play the Pope himself, I have not learned. He wears the turban so well in Nana Sahib, that it is not improbable he may be ambitious to assume the tiara.

Mr. Frank Goodrich, one of the authors of "Fascination" and of the "Poor of New York," has just completed an original five set comedy of modern social life in New York, of which report speaks favorably. I am not at liberty to mention the title.

It is rumored that Mr. J.W. Wallack will appear this spring in an original five act drama written expressly for the company.

Doctor Palmer, the author of "Miss Wimple's Hoop," in the last two numbers of the *Atlantic Monthly*, is engaged in dramatizing that interesting story.

DODO.

TREMENDOUS FIGHT !

COMBAT BETWEEN PATRICK AND BRIDGET O'FLANNAGAN.
BRIDGET THE VICTOR !

(Reported exclusively for the Saturday Press.)

Five Points, Saturday, October 23, 3.10 A.M.

The Great Fight, which has long been looked forward to in select Irish circles, between Patrick O'Flannagan and Bridget, his wife, came off yesterday, at the Five Points, there being an attendance of over three thousand persons, mostly Dead Rabbits. There had long been domestic strife in the bosom of the O'Flanagan family, and the great question now was, *to which the mastery* ? both parties having consented to abide by the result of a free fight.

Persons from all the neighboring quarter, and from all the purlieus of the Fourth and Sixth Wards were present, including a brilliant attendance of the Fancy from all parts of the city.

Patrick had for second a well known common councilman, while Bridget was ably seconded by an ex-alderman.

DETAILS OF THE FIGHT.

FIRST ROUND.

At twenty-two minutes six seconds past two precisely, the fight began. O'Flannagan was slightly drunk, but looked defiant. Bridget's form was beautiful, and, from the appearance of her nails, was evidently ready to come up to the scratch. They both put themselves at once, in fine positions, O'Flannagan turning like a top on one leg, and his wife standing squarely on her pegs, with her arms akimbo. After jawing a moment, O'Flannagan made two leaps at Bridget, but jumped over her head, and thus changed their relative positions. They then got to work, Bridget putting in her nails several times, and closing one of Patrick's peepers, which, however, didn't prevent him from seeing with the other, and pulling out all the hair on the right side of her head. They then closed and fought desperately, both doing their worst. Here bite followed bite, very rapidly, till one of Bridget's ears dropping off, she screamed and got away, receiving a severe kick as she ran. In this round, Bridget, having outscratched Patrick, got the best of it.

SECOND ROUND.

Both came up bleeding from the last round, which was one of the severest ever fought in the Five Points. It was said, by competent judges, to be equal to anything which ever took place in Washington. Bridget's loss of an ear made her very desperate, while Patrick was equally wrathy at the loss of an eye. The bystanders screamed with delight, and several Dead Rabbits had a private bout on their own hook. This however, lasted but a moment, the scamps having been routed by one of the board of Aldermen present. The combatants then went at it again, Bridget receiving, at first, condine punishment, but never flinching a foot. The chief feature of this round, was a sudden movement of Patrick, by which, taking a bottle filled with whiskey out of his pocket, he danced a kind of Irish jig round Bridget, ending by breaking the bottle over her head. Bridget, however, seizing a fragment of the bottle, gouged Patrick so severely with it, that at the end of the round, she came off with a decided advantage.

THIRD ROUND.

The fighting now began in earnest, as the boys said, the previous rounds being looked upon as only an airy and graceful beginning. Bridget led off by seizing Patrick's nose and literally turning it upside down, so that it will be good for nothing in the future except for taking snuff. Patrick responded by running at her, head down like a bull, and pitching her about four feet against the ropes, where they had a struggle, at the end of which both came to the ground, and Bridget lost her crinoline (to the great amusement of the crowd), and broke one of her fingers. Patrick now fought well, and his friends were encouraged. His remaining eye brightened up at the sight of the fallen crinoline, but a well-planted blow from his antagonist shut it right up like a knife. Still, at the end of this round, the bets were in favor of Patrick.

FOURTH ROUND.

Bridget came to the scratch somewhat down-spirited on account of her dress; but she soon spunked up at the sight of Patrick, and making a fearful lunge at him with her left, seized his head, at the same time, with her right, and nearly twisted it off. Patrick then took a glass of whiskey from a bystander, and having got his head slewed back again, rushed at Bridget with great fury, when they both went to the ground, Bridget being on top, where she remained five minutes, and beat her man's head to a jelly. The bets were now two to one in favor of the woman.

FIFTH ROUND.

Patrick looked like a victim of eternal punishment. His eyes were both cut, and his features were smashed into indistinguishable pulp. Still he came up boldly to the scratch, and, uttering a savage whoop, went at Bridget, pell mell, and, by mere force, threw her six feet in the air, when she came down on her head, making a hole in the ground like a cannon-ball. Patrick, however, couldn't see well enough to take advantage of this maneuvre, but allowed Bridget to get on her pegs again. The work then became very lively, and resulted in Patrick's having his neck badly excoriated, and all his teeth knocked in.

SIXTH ROUND.

Bridget came up remarkably strong, while Patrick was growing weaker and weaker, and showed evident signs of defeat. Bridget led off with her left nails, reaching Patrick's nose (what there was left of it), he returning with a kick which staggered Bridget, when they both stopped fighting and tried to look at each other, but not seeing anybody, began to fight again with renewed energy, O'Flannagan planting both arms round Bridget's neck as if he meant to kiss her, and then biting about three-fourths of an inch off the end of her nose. This made Bridget mad, and she bit the brute all to pieces.

SEVENTH ROUND.

Patrick again took the initiative, and gave Bridget a sharp bite on the right ear, which she returned, by biting off his scalp, and slapping it in his face. They then began to kick each other in the kidneys, in which play, Bridget's eyes being but partially closed, she had the best of it, getting her kicks home in nearly every case. Patrick was now nearly used up.

EIGHTH ROUND.

Patrick came up to time, but showed no disposition to fight. He was aroused only by Bridget's calling him a spalpine, and giving him a box on the ear. He then showed more signs for life and asked for a bottle, which Bridget at once handed to him over the head. He then tried to put in a blow with his right foot, but it was caught by Bridget, who then seized the other and trotted him round the course five minutes, *a la wheelbarrow*, when he fainted from exhaustion.

NINTH ROUND.

Patrick was all abroad. He waited for Bridget to come up, and success had now made her too good natured to keep him waiting, so she walked up and spit in his face. Indignant at this, Patrick made a lunge at her and fell, whereupon Bridget pulled all the hair off of his head and left him for dead.

TENTH ROUND.

The hitting, and biting, and scratching, in this round, was all on one side. Finally, Bridget came in with a blow on Patrick's jugular, which knocked him into a cocked-up hat.

ELEVENTH AND LAST ROUND.

Patrick came up staggering and whining, and looked pitiful, the fight, and nearly every thing else, being taken out of him. He made one last attempt, however, with both feet, when down he came, ka-chunk, to the ground, the most pitiful looking spectacle imaginable. Being unable, after this, to come up to time, or, in fact, to come up at all, it was decided by the arbiter (one of the city judges), that he was down, and thus ended the fight for the mastery of the ancient house of O'Flannagan.

Patrick says it is his last fight, and he looks as though it was.

N. B. By merely changing the names, the above report will answer as well as any other for a report of the fight between Morrissey and Heenan, for the championship of America.

NEW YORK OCTOBER 30, 1858

THE COURTSHIP OF MILES STANDISH.

We cannot for the life of us see any reason why this story should have been written in verse. It was bad enough to spin it out into a book, for if, as the really brilliant author has elsewhere assured us,—

"Life is real, life is earnest,"

it is far too much so to be spent in perusing a work, however brief, which besides not being poetry as it pretends to be, is neither instructive nor agreeable prose. If the little anecdote upon which the whole thing is founded were worth telling at all (which, speaking, unlike John Alden, for ourselves, we beg leave to doubt), it was worth telling in a simple straightforward manner, in the ordinary style of a juvenile narrative. Why Mr. Longfellow should have provoked the Athenæum's most obvious and odious pun upon his name, and in far more serious ways put his literary reputation in jeopardy by pursuing the opposite course, it is impossible to conjecture.

We don't know when we have read a work which affected us more unpleasantly. There is, indeed, no want of melody in the versification, but then throughout the poem (if poem it must be called) sense is so uniformly sacrificed to sound, that we feel at last as if a more suitable title for it would have been "Nothing! set to music." Moreover, to see so slender and superficial a story erected into a poem, is like seeing a beggar stalking on golden stilts, or a thin watery landscape set in a magnificent frame.

We have not the time now to go into a dissertation as to what subjects are adapted to poetic treatment, much less to discuss the long mooted question as to wherein true poetry consists. Nor is this necessary; for we have only to open the book under notice, at random, to find passages which would justify any criticism which the worst enemy of Mr. Longfellow (and we are among his warmest admirers) would be disposed to make.

Henry Wadsworth Longfellow

Take, for instance, the following Priscillian extract, which we print, as it ought to have been printed in the original, in prose:—

"If the great Captain of Plymouth is so very eager to wed me, why does he not come himself, and take the trouble to woo me? If I am not worth the wooing, I surely am not worth the winning!" Then John Alden began explaining and smoothing the matter, making it worse as he went, by saying the Captain was busy, had no time for such things;—such things! the words grating harshly fell on the ear of Priscilla; and swift as a flash she made answer: "Has he no time for such things, as you call it, before he is married, would he be likely to find it, or make it, after the wedding? That is the way with you men; you don't understand us, you cannot. When you have made up your minds, after thinking of this one and that one, choosing, selecting, rejecting, comparing one with another, then you make known your desire, with abrupt and sudden avowal; and are offended and hurt, and indignant, perhaps, that a woman does not respond at once to a love that she never suspected, does not attain at a bound the height to which you have been climbing. This is not right nor just; for surely a woman's affection is not a thing to be asked for, and had for only the asking. When one is truly in love, one not only says it, but shows it. Had he but waited awhile, had he only showed that he loved me, even this Captain of yours—who knows?—at last might have won me, old and rough as he is; but now it never can happen."

Now, we submit that this is the merest prose and is not very brilliant at that. We could select extracts much choicer, and, for that matter much more musical, from the commonest novel of the day.

Then, again, what could be more unpoetical, more utterly common-place than the following, which is also in chief from Miss Priscilla, and which the sensitive reader will of course thank us for not printing as verse:—

"Are you so much offended, you will not speak to me?" said she. "Am I so much to blame, that yesterday, when you were pleading warmly the cause of another, my heart, impulsive and wayward, pleaded your own, and spake out, forgetful perhaps of decorum? Certainly you can forgive me for speaking so frankly, for saying what I ought not to have said, yet now I can never unsay it; for there are moments in life, when the heart is so full of emotion, that if by chance it be shaken, or into its depths like a pebble drops some careless word, it overflows, and its secret, spilt on the ground like water, can never be gathered together. Yesterday I was shocked, when I heard you speak of Miles Standish, praising his virtues, transforming his very defects into virtues, praising his courage and strength, and even his fighting in Flanders, as if by fighting alone you could win the heart of a woman, quite overlooking yourself and the rest, in exalting your hero. Therefore, I spake as I did, by an irresistible impulse. You will forgive me, I hope, for the sake of the friendship between us, which is too true and too sacred to be so easily broken!" Thereupon answered John Alden, the scholar, the friend of Miles Standish: "I was not angry with you, with myself alone I was angry, seeing how badly I managed the matter I had in my keeping." "No!" interrupted the maiden, with answer prompt and decisive: "no; you were angry with me, for speaking so frankly and freely. It was wrong, I acknowledge; for it is the fate of a woman long to be patient and silent, to wait like a ghost that is speechless, till some questioning voice dissolves the spell of its silence. Hence is the inner life of so many suffering women sunless, and silent, and deep, like subterranean rivers, running through caverns of darkness, unheard, unseen, and unfruitful, chafing their channels of stone, with endless and profitless murmurs." Thereupon answered John Alden, the young man, the lover of women: "Heaven forbid it, Priscilla."

And so say we; and Mr. Longfellow ought to have known better than to allow Priscilla, or any body else to say such things.

To those who say it is hardly fair to judge of an author by detached passages, we have only to add that when the author is a poet, and the passages detached are self-evidently not poetry, we think that it is not only fair, but that when the sense is preserved, it is the very thing to do. And perhaps we cannot conclude our article better than by a quotation bearing on this very point, from Pope, who says in the introduction to one of the earlier editions of his works:

"I would not be like those authors who forgive themselves some particular lines for the sake of a whole poem and, vice versa, a whole poem for the sake of some particular lines. I believe no one qualification is so likely to make a good writer as the power of rejecting his own thoughts, and it must be this, if anything, that can give me a chance to be one. For what I have published, I can only hope to be pardoned, but for what I have burned I deserve to be praised."

We think it a pity that Mr. Longfellow did not burn "The Courtship of Miles Standish," especially as the poems which he has cruelly printed in the same volume, are enough of themselves to establish his fame as one of the greatest of living poets.

(For the Saturday Press.)

MY NORTH AND SOUTH.

I am very, very fond
Of a blonde,
Mistress Maud; and so come here:
And yet, and yet, and yet
I like a gay brunette,
Therese, dear !

O, what can a body do
With you two !
Sunny hair and rosy mouth !
Black hair and eyes of jet!
You blonde, and you brunette !
You North and South !

Now, I love you, eyes and curls,
Little girls !
Give me each a dainty hand ;
New England's hand shall lie
On my heart, and yours near by-
You understand !

T. B. ALDRICH.

—MR. CHARLES FRANCIS ADAMS, of Boston, Massachusetts, says that "although not inclined to solicit office [who, except Gerritt Smith, ever was?], yet, if it should be the wish of the people of his district that he should serve them in the National Councils at Washington," they may be assured that "there will be no trifling obstacles that shall prevent him from *taking his place there* at the proper time!" He trusts, moreover, "that through the liberal and comprehensive character of the combination forming to counteract the pernicious policy and to expose the odious doctrines of the National Administration, that all who harmonize in spirit may by their united exertions concentrate their power for the accomplishment of useful ends." And, "if it be the opinion of his fellow citizens that an instrument *so feeble as himself* can be made in any way effective in promoting those ends, all he can promise in return is that whatever of strength God has given him [and he admits that God has not given him any] shall be faithfully devoted to that service."
When will candidates for office stop writing such twaddle?

—Mr. P. T. Barnum, not having succeeded in his operatic scheme, has been lecturing in Manchester, England, on the shortest and surest way of making a fortune. He instanced Shakespeare as a clever and thrifty showman, Chaucer and Scott, Bancroft and Irving, Marlboro and Wellington, Washington and Barnum, as instances of men who have made or might have made their own fortunes. His rules for fortune-making were the following:—Be honest, prompt, exact, adroit, persevering, advertise, mind your own business, don't talk much, and subscribe to a newspaper. His rules are not as good as old McDonough's, the New Orleans miser. The epitome of his experience was to truckle to the rich, grind the poor, and pray for success at the commencement of every undertaking. Ebenezer Francis' rule was to spend nothing and shave paper at the highest rates, while John Jacob Astor's was the Quaker's advice to his son,

"Keep all you have,
Get all you can,
Dishonestly if you must,
Honestly if you can."

—Knowing, as Parson Wilbur says, that "the desire to poetize is one of the diseases naturally incident to adolescence, which, if the fitting remedies be not at once and with a bold hand applied, may become chronic and render one, who might else have become in due time an ornament of the social circle, a painful object even to the nearest friends and relatives," we have felt obliged to suppress several poetic communications which have been sent to us this week, and that, too, without being able to offer the probably well-meaning authors, the least encouragement for the future.

FROM DAY TO DAY.

THE PHILHARMONIC CONCERTS.—The agreeable rehearsals of this Society have begun again. It has been a source of congratulation to many attending them, that they as yet have not been much annoyed with the incessant whispering of the ill-bred young people who attended in such numbers, last Winter, for the purpose of carrying on their flirtations. We would suggest to the managers, that should the same annoyance exist this Winter, they should take some decided steps to put an end to it. Broadway is a place much better calculated, and more appropriate, for those young women to frequent, whose sole aim in life is to be seen of men.

CHEAP LOCOMOTION.—Year after year we complain about the crowded state of Broadway, and yet nothing is ever done officially about it. Who can be foolish enough to expect that anything ever would be? The action will have to come from the City Council; and when did the City Council ever do anything for the convenience of the city? Meanwhile, the steam machine is every now and then to be seen, puffing along, and exciting its usual attention. We saw the other day a genuine Hansom cab, going quietly by. Between these two new projects we ought soon to have means of locomotion which, if offered at a reasonable rate, will become very popular. Some of the omnibus lines have put their fare down to five cents. This is more in accordance with our currency than the old Spanish Sixpence. We may look forward to the time when the hurrying man of business can take the steam engine down to his office for—say three cents, and the man of leisure can take an airing up Broadway, in a Hansom cab, at twenty-five cents, or through the Central Park for fifty. The fact is, that we are the most expensive people in the world. Economy is considered, in a measure, disreputable; a foolish extravagance is thought to be a sign of refinement, instead of being, as it is, a proof of vulgarity. Let anyone look at the dresses draggled in the dirt and mud of the sidewalk on Broadway. In Paris, a man can have his boots blacked in a handsomely furnished room, with the chance of reading the morning papers, for three sous; here, the same operation, *al fresco*, by a small boy, costs twice the money. Can take a cab for one shilling (25 cents); here, let anyone beware how he trusts himself to the tender mercies of a hack driver. But with time, we hope, will come experience, and a better way of managing these things.

Central Park Under Construction, looking south from the Armory (the Crystal Palace dome at upper right) from 1859 Valentine's Manual;

THE CENTRAL PARK.—The work on the Central Park is progressing finely. A very large body of men are kept constantly at work, and though the ground appears from its preparation rather raw, still, there is enough to attract a great many people. They are now engaged in setting out trees. They select from all around the country only such as are of good size and shape, and have grown by themselves, so that they can stand their insulation in their new situations We expect that as early as next Summer, the Park will be a very interesting place of resort. A cave has fortunately been discovered in the ledge of rocks by the Reservoir, and most judiciously improved. A party of laborers are engaged in enlarging it. We would suggest as a motto, to serve as a warning to those who may use it for their picnics, not Dante's "who enter here leave hope behind," but "cavete felices." We may as well say here, that our own generous rule in respect to such matters is, never to look a cave in the mouth.

An Architectural Outrage.—Some one has had influence enough to induce the owners of the good old-fashioned church at the corner of Second avenue and Tenth street, to put a cast iron sort of a portico, of a cast iron order of architecture, upon the front of their church. This is too bad. The anomalous church on the opposite side, and the unhappy Heroditus on the front of the Historical Society building, were enough specimens of bad taste for that locality. The old Stuyvesant church, with its green around it, was a positive oasis. What had it done, that it should be tricked out with cheap, new-fangled, cast iron frippery? Have the congregation altered their religious creed? We believe not. What did they want with a sham portico? Are they going to add some new-fashioned opinion to the thirty-nine articles, and try to make us believe that they were originally forty? Are they going to add to the fine old English of their liturgy, any of the hollow, meaningless jargon of reform? Why then have they treated the church with such disrespect?

SUNDAY RESORTS.—The various gardens around the city, are still full on Sundays. The weather is not yet cold enough to render lager beer and cigars in the open air uncomfortable. The church-goers may complain, but the churches are not open all day, and to those whose means do not afford a comfortable home, in an eligible situation, it is an immense relief to leave their week-day work and poverty, to enjoy the cheap luxury of plenty of fresh air. It is proposed, by the Society for the better observance of Sunday to try and stop the running of the Sunday cars. Do any of those advocating it ever ride in their carriages to church? It is not by telling people that they sha'n't be amused, that they will go to church. Improve the character of the places of resort. Why not open the libraries, at least, on Sunday afternoon? In the respectable city of Boston, the reading room of that most respectable institution, the Athaeneum, is open at that time.

The steeple of St. Mark's Church , upper center, as viewed from Cooper Union, 1856

NEW YORK NOVEMBER 6, 1858

For the SATURDAY PRESS.

AN EVENING WITH MYSELF.

NO. 1.

I have a most interesting experience to record, namely, that of an evening spent with—myself. And strange to say it was a very agreeable experience—so much so, that I have resolved hereafter to cultivate my own society with the same assiduity with which I have hitherto cultivated that of other, and, to me at least, less interesting persons.

In fact, the little that I saw of myself during that memorable evening, was of a nature to excite all my curiosity. I had no idea before what manner of man I was. I had treated myself uniformly as a disagreeable fellow, to be on all occasions coolly received, and when necessary, promptly snubbed. Nevertheless, for men in general, made so far as I could see in the same image, and having, as nearly as I could judge, the same emotions and passions with myself, I had a good deal of respect. None so mean but had some point of interest for me. Indeed, in this respect, at any rate, I was peculiar. It was my favorite occupation to find out new types of character and compare them, not—as I now feel would have been more wise—with myself, but with each other. Hence I became acquainted with a large number of very eccentric people—people of the class commonly called originals. These were my favorites. Yet few of them were very brilliant, fewer still either well-to-do, or well-to-have done, and none of them "respectable." There was only this to say in their favor; they were themselves. There was no hypocrisy about them; no paint, no powder, no extraneous perfume. Moreover, no one of them all was a reformer, a philanthropist, or in any respect whatever a bore. At least not to me. Some of them were "poor devils," others rich devils, others again sadly deficient in any kind of diabolic element, but they all stood for what they were, and I always knew where to find them.

With such like folk I had been accustomed to spend most of my time. One such I had, and still have, for my wife. I didn't marry her, but she married me, and though we have never been "One," but must always, in the nature of things, remain "Two" (except that just now there is a dangerous prospect of our being Three), we love each other very much, and let each other for the most part very humanely alone. She has her "set," and I have mine, and they don't agree together at all; for hers are all women, and mine are not only men, but men who—as is the case with most eccentric people—have had difficulties with the opposite sex, and are in a state of permanent warfare with it. Probably they have been crossed in love. Not a very serious calamity in my opinion, but in the opinion of most men, the calamity of calamities, making a calamity of dear life itself.

This is not a digression, for it was the character of the persons I have just described, which led me to ask, one day :—"Am I too, like these cherished comrades of mine, and this odd wife of mine, an eccentric, or am I but an ordinary mortal, counting one in the census of population, and there an end?" Now this was a very perplexing problem which I had been diligently engaged in not solving for some weeks, when, one afternoon, as I was walking home in an unusually abstract and insoluble mood, I tripped over a log of wood, which the fates or some stupid Irishman had laid across my path, and hurt my foot so badly that I was compelled to spend that evening in my room.

And that was the evening I spent with myself.

My wife was out, somewhere, with *her*-self, my dog with *him*-self, and my house in some sort out with itself, so that I was absolutely alone! I and my problem all alone!

I bound up my wounded foot like the good Samaritan I am, lit my pipe like a good smoker, and proceeded to make other and most hospitable arrangements for my entertainment. With the most scrupulous care I put everything in my room in perfect order. Papers that had been accumulating for weeks were carefully filed. Pictures hung out of square on the wall were nicely adjusted. Books scattered all over the floor were restored to their vacant places in the bookcase. Clothes hanging helter-skelter over the backs of the chairs, " were neatly folded and put away. Finally the carpet was carefully swept—the table, sofa, mantlepiece, étagère, and "whatnot," well dusted—and then, with an ineffable sense of comfort, enhanced by a mild glass of brandy and water, "I" (as Walt. Whitman would say), "I loafed and invited my soul."

Yes, and my soul accepted the invitation, and we loafed together; *I*, quietly engaged in the work of self-examination, and my soul (or "Self") passively submit ting to the operation as something quite original and by no means disagreeable. And I then and there, for the first time became acquainted with myself. Hitherto we had been such strangers that now there was need almost of a formal introduction. For the first time I felt the wisdom of the old injunction "Know Thyself." There were many others, doubtless, who knew me, but I was in a state of deplorable self-ignorance. I need not say how delighted I was to make my acquaintance, nor how anxious I was to be at once and forever on good terms with myself. I felt, moreover, that nothing less than this was due to both of us; that, in a word, we had social claims on each other, which must not on any account longer be neglected. And pacing up and down the room, I said this to myself over and over again, and in each instance met with an affirmative response. It was time—I went on to say as I became more and more familiar and at home with myself—that we ceased to be Two, and became in unity or at One with each other for it was plain to me, as I reflected on the subject, that discord with oneself was the most fatal of all discords, and the most prolific source of unhappiness. It suddenly occurred to me, too, that nearly everybody, however brave he might be in respect to others, was arrantly afraid of himself, and that the few who had finally overcome this terror, were after all the chosen few—the *élite* or elect of God. And what cowardice, I asked, so great as this? Fear, arrant fear, of one's self! Could anything be more ignominious? and with this feeling strong upon me, I literally wooed, courted, and caressed myself, examining the subject of my new interest—or, rather, the poor shell of it—in the mirror, and applying to it all kinds of endearing names.

Now before the reader denounces all this as mere affectation, let him reflect on the ecstatic condition I was in at having for the first time conceived the idea of forming intimate and friendly relations with myself. Or if this thought fails to mollify him (for there is no so wrathy man as the indignant reader), let him suspend his judgment, if he have any, until I have finished my story.

Thus far, I have given only my first emotions, growing out of the stark novelty of my position. I was evidently entering upon a new era of existence, and, without knowing what was to be its character, I was naturally in a state of great excitement. I was about making the acquaintance of a person—and had as it were just shaken hands and taken a social drink with him—whom it would have been well worth my while to travel thousands of miles to see, and yet whom I might almost be said to have travelled thousands of miles to avoid. He had always been near to me,—nearer than my shadow, nearer even than my skin—but I had never before seen him. He had started up before me like a ghost in all the great emergencies of life, but like a ghost had also passed away, unrecognized and almost unnoticed. And now here I was, face to face with him, or some dim shadow of him, and no more afraid of the creature (nor indeed so much), than as if he were my better half, which in one sense, and that a very good one, it just occurs to me that he is. Why then shouldn't I coax and caress him, now that for the first time we were about spending a cozy evening together? At any rate I repeat that I did so, and in this way broke the ice which long years had built up as a cold and impassable bridge between us

Spriggs.

For the Saturday Press.

MY EAST AND WEST

I.

I'm jealous as a churl
Of a girl
Down East, and so here's to her!
And yet I can't forget
Another girl I met
Out in Iowa.

II.

O! which, dears, shall I woo
Of you two?
One the brightest, one the best,
One tall, one short and sweet,
One dull, one hard to beat,
One East, one West.

III.

Now I love you both, dear girls,
Precious pearls;
Then give me each a shake!

You East shall cheer my life:
You West shall be my wife,
And no mistake!

A. B. T.

From Day to Day.

Election Is Over. —A feeling of thankfulness that the election is over, is the feeling in the mind of every man unhappy enough to live near a candidate. What with enthusiastic friends, whose spontaneous enthusiasm bursts out in serenades at the candidates' suggestion and expense, and the crowd of dirty loafers and political hangers-on, who are always on hand on such occasions, ready and eager for a drink, the comfort and quiet of a neighborhood is destroyed . Think of having one's harmonious dreams rudely disturbed by the discord of a half tipsy and ill-assorted brass band, varied with a solo performance on a cannon, as has actually been done.

A New Building.–Just above Grand street, in Broadway, Messrs. Lord & Taylor are putting up a large marble store. We commend the grand arch in the front, which serves admirably to give a fine open effect to the building. We are also glad to see that the architect has carried his stone down to the foundation, instead of using cast iron supports, thus giving an actual strength to the building. The lesson of the insecurity of cast iron buildings, taught in the speedy destruction of the Crystal Palace, should not be forgotten. Many of the most showy stores on Broadway are mere painted man-traps, as will be fearfully shown should they ever catch fire. There has been no more pernicious and dangerous innovation in our modern building, than the use of cast iron as supports for the upper stories, or as a building material for the entire front. Every housekeeper knows how liable her pressed glass articles–if she uses such–are to sudden and almost unaccountable fracture; cast iron has the same property. While under the influence of such heat as would be caused by a fire in any store in Broadway, cast iron pillars are as unreliable as pipe stems, and a cast iron building, as seen in the Crystal Palace, would have the rivets drawn out by the expansion, and fall down like a house of cards. A stop should be put to the erection of such buildings before the truth is taught by a sad destruction of human life. And here we will say that we hope the new store will be built with a stone cornice, instead of a wooden sham one. Many a building has been burnt by having its cornice fired by sparks from a neighboring fire, and most of the buildings in Broadway which are liable to this accident, are too high to be reached by a stream of water from any engine we have in the city.

Steam Fire Engines. —One of these useful machines made a display of its powers some weeks ago, in Wall street. But the recent elections show the folly of attempting their introduction. They cannot vote.

Political Banners.—Are the police aware that it is illegal to suspend any banner across the street. We presume that they don't enforce the ordinance, because they themselves are instituted for the good of a political body, instead of the body politic.

The Sidewalks On Broadway.—Who do they belong to? Anyone who is going to build has no scruples to claim them as his own by tearing them up, and turning all the immense stream of foot passengers out into the street or oblige them to pick their way among the "*disjecta membre*" of the sidewalk as best they may. No more excuse for this than there is for filling up the street with building materials. The lot affords ample room for the storage of the last, until they are wanted for use, while the sidewalk should never be disturbed without giving the public an ample and safe substitute.

NEW YORK NOVEMBER 13, 1858

Literary Intelligence.

—Mr. Hawthorn has been passing the Summer in a pleasant villa near Florence. The public will probably not be disappointed in its expectations of a fresh volume from his pen.

—M. de Paravey has written a paper on the names given to the Torpedo in various languages, with a view to show that there existed in the remotest ages a vague notion that the shocks of that animal were produced by an agency similar to that which caused lightning.

— It is the design of the Burn's Club of New York to celebrate the Poet's birthday by a festival dinner at the Astor House, by telegraphic exchanges with the principal cities of Scotland and other parts of Great Britain, if practicable, and by such other ceremonies as may be deemed appropriate and judicious. The participation in cooperation of the clubs of this country and of the Canadas, and also of such other associations as may feel an interest in the occasion, are earnestly desired, either by written communication, telegraphic dispatches, or delegations, the preliminaries of which may be arranged by previous correspondence.

A NEW PORTRAIT OF PARIS: PAINTED FROM LIFE.

"Paint me as I am".—Cromwell.

"Now being from Paris recently.
This fine young man would show his skill."
Holmes.

BY HENRY CLAPP, JR.

CHAPTER I.

The author smokes, speculates, and becomes philosophical—Looks out of the window and sees a "tide in the affairs of men"—Is spirited back to Paris, and then stranded in London—Thinks these are "great times," and seizes his pen and says so—Gets lost among barriers, barricades, oceans. friths, ferries, steam shuttles, continents, hemispheres, telegraphs, poor women, North and South Poles, newspapers, Greeks, steam, "Manifest Destiny," corn, coal, iron, silk, literature, religion, and fancy goods—Comes out at the end hopeful and cosmopolitan—Gives his idea of a "United Happy Family"—Gets elated, and quotes Nursery Rhymes—Grows zoological and ornithological, poetical and sentimental, till his pipe goes out.

Smoking quietly in my room, the day after my arrival from the Old World, and experiencing that ineffable sense of comfort which is permitted only to a man who has just enjoyed a night's peaceful sleep, after being tossed

"For weary weeks upon a wintry sea,"

I found myself presently in a strange speculative mood as to the rage prevalent in these fast times for travel. My window looked upon Broadway. The immense tide of people surging through that thoroughfare was composed of tributary streams from every quarter of the globe. The scene carried me back to Paris, where, during the previous three years, I had so often been amazed with the variegated current of human life coursing down the broad beautiful Boulevards, and spreading itself in phosphorescent waves over the Elysian Fields. It reminded me also of London, upon whose crowded Strand I had for years seen break and foam the gathered surf of all nations. Surely, thought I—and seizing my pen, surely wrote I—these are great times. The world is at last awake. Mankind is huddling together. The masses unite and crystallize. The half of the world said not to know how the other half lives, is growing wiser. The right hand imparts its cunning to the left. Barriers and barricades disappear. Oceans narrow into friths; friths into ferries. Steam-shuttles fly from continent to continent, and weave the hemispheres together. The electric telegraph transforms the globe into a whispering gallery. Secrets are no longer possible. The poor woman out West exclaims: "They've gone and put a cussed paragraph in front of my door, so that now I can't so much as spank a baby without its being known over all creation." It is pretty much so. Everything is blabbed. The North Pole bobs to the South, and the stars wink at each other all over the firmament. Nothing is sacred. Newspapers come to us at every meal, and expose everything. This sets all the world on the jog, all mankind in a jumble. The earth twirls on its axis, and the remotest dwellers upon its surface join and jostle each other. Greek meets Greek in New York; Brother Jonathan clinks glasses with Johnny Crapeau in Paris, the Chinese cottons to the Cockney in London; strange tongues touch each other and run together; and the word "foreigner" becomes invidious or obsolete. Steam is at work and sweats us out of all our prejudices. Manifest Destiny becomes a religion. Old England annexes the Indies, and Young America stretches out her bony arms and gives the grip to Japan. Thus nations come to know each other; come to embrace each other. They group together in families; cultivate corn and good neighborhood together; see that the balance of power is the balance of trade; and learn to play our American game of swap. They swap corn, coal, iron, silk, literature, religion, and fancy goods, as unsuspecting young people swap hearts, jackets, and jackknives.

All this is hopeful, and out of it may some day grow cosmopolitan nations composed of the elect of the people, and uniting the gaiety of the French, the beauty of the Italian, the dignity of the Spaniard, the simplicity of the Swiss, the subtlety of the German, the solidity and pluck of the English, the gumption and grit of the Yankee. This reminds me of a popular street exhibition in London called "The United Happy Family." The juvenile exhibitor, a bright lad of sixteen, seemed anxious to anticipate the time when "the wolf shall dwell with the lamb; and the leopard shall lie down with the kid, and the calf, and the young fatling together; and a little child shall lead them." With a certain poetic instinct he had located his little theatre in front of the National Gallery, where are grouped together the paintings of all schools—Roman, Venetian, German, Dutch, Flemish, French, Spanish, and English. The scene of our Happy Family was laid in a cage. The *dramatis personae* consisted of dogs that no longer

"Delight to bark and bite,"

though

" 'Tis their nature to;"

genuine cats purring over equally authentic mice; hawks that might have been falcons, roosting side by side with motherly hens; doves, cooing and billing in the presence of slimy serpents; ring-tailed monkeys cracking undisputed nuts and unresented jokes; and fishes swimming in their crystal spheres amid the mewing of cats, the chattering of parrots, and the hissing of geese; while over all this scene of brutal harmony and piscatorial comfort presided a round-eyed owl, with as much dignity as the moon presides over the waves of the sea.

By what happy or unhappy process so many antagonistic elements were brought together without producing a perfect zoological and ornithological chaos, I am neither naturalist nor Christian enough to determine. I merely state the fact as I saw it, adding that never before—had I seen so striking an illustration of the doctrine that

"All nature's difference makes all nature's peace"

Now, there is certainly as great a difference among the tribes of men that inhabit the earth. as among the tribes of animals. The Englishman is as unlike the Frenchman as the bull is unlike the butterfly. The German differs as much from the Spaniard as the beaver from the sloth. A Russian no more resembles an Italian than a bear resembles a bulfinch; while the Yankee is as distinct from the Chinese as the eagle from the mockingbird. And yet who knows but what—as has already been intimated—each of these differing races may one day so blend together the best characteristics of all, as to make of every nation a beautiful Mosaic, and of the world at large a United Happy Family. When that day dawns,

"All lands the ocean laves,
All tribes beneath the sun,
Though separate like the waves,
Will, like the seas, be one;
And warlike emblems change to those of love,
The lion to the lamb, the eagle to the dove."

The writer had proceeded thus far, and was growing more and more sentimental, when, as usual upon such occasions, his pipe went out.

CHAPTER II.

The author replenishes his pipe, becomes confidential, and explains his intentions.

"Patrick, my good fellow, run over to Mrs. Newcomb's and get me a paper of *caporal*" "*Caporal*, did ye say? And will yer honor just tell me what that is ?"

"Certainly, Pat; it's French smoking tobacco. They call it *caporal*, because caporal means corporal, and French corporals smoke nothing else. I shouldn't wonder if the Little Corporal used to smoke it."

"Who's the Little Corporal, yer honor ?"

"Ask the Iron Duke, who, by the way, Pat, never smoked but one pipe in his life, and that made him sick. There's an example for you !"

"Thank yer honor—and it was corporal you said?"

"No, Pat, *caporal;* it's done up in blue paper, and is two shillings a packet; cut!"

Pat having done the errand in an Irish minute—starting at 10 A. M., and getting back at noon—I fill my pipe, light up, and taking my old friend General Reader button-wise, give him my confidence thus:

"The Spirit of the Age said unto me, some years ago: 'Travel!' I travelled. The same Spirit said unto me: 'What thou seest, write in a book.' I write; and, selecting what is freshest in my memory, write about Paris."

"But Paris has been written to death, my friend."

"True, General, but I propose to revive it."

"What presumption !"

"But if the presumption is in my favor?"

"A truce to puns, and explain yourself."

"Well, then, General, if I write what nobody has written, I shall write what somebody will read."

"That's what you call putting the matter in a nutshell, I suppose."

"Just so; but don't interrupt me. Did you ever have your portrait taken, General ?"

"Yes, a dozen times. But what has that to do with it?"

"Listen. Didn't your wife always say it was too serious?"

"Come to think of it, she did. But who told you ?"

"Nobody, General. It's the universal criticism; 'good, but too serious.' Just so with all the portraits of Paris; they are like, but too sober. It's time we had a livelier one. I propose to paint it. What say you?"

"Good, my dear fellow. I'll buy it. Bless me, how full your room is of smoke. I must go.

Good day, and good luck to you !"

And as the General sneezed himself down stairs, I said to myself, "The man who called the General Reader an ass, was too severe."

CHAPTER III.

LONDON—What the author saw and ate, and did there—How he refused to drink 'alf and 'alf, and denied that his countrymen drank hail—quotes Horace Greeley, and establishes his (not Greeley's, but the author's) claim to common humanity—How he found the cozy side of John Bull, and then cut his acquaintance—How he yields to temptation, and visits the land of cutlets and *coups d'état*—How he purchased a benediction, and took up his carpetbag and walked—How he got into a box—How his fellow travellers were armed, and what use an "unprotected female" made of her muff—how he experiences a "touch of Nature"—How he accuses the Tribune of imitating Agassiz—How he gets acquainted with a Commercial Traveller who had seen Mr. Hemerson, and heard his lectures on Reprehensible Men—How he is gratified to learn that the Queen of England is the best little woman in the world, and wouldn't 'arm a flea.

I spent three years in London. I know the dear old fogie metropolis by heart. The plump dome of St. Paul's, swelling over the proud capital like a plumpudding over a Christmas dinner, is as familiar to me as the Old South Steeple rising like a ghost over the City of Notions. Christ's Hospital, with its play-ground filled with little yellow-legged philosophers in long blue frocks and short breeches, (imagine Coleridge or Lamb in such a costume !) is as real in my mind as the Spare-the-Rod-spoil-the-Child Academy of my boyhood. I went to Oxford, to Cambridge, to Windsor, to Brighton, to Coventry, and—to Bungay. I saw Punch and Judy, the Queen, the Hippopotamus, Day & Martin, the incidental Albert, Martin Farquahar Tupper, Gog and Magog, the Lord Mayor, Albert Smith—(Alexander was then in the shell) and, or a Cockney deceived me, the "Prince of Whales." I supped at Evan's, bowled at Kilpack's, heard "Sam Hall" at the Cider Cellars, played chess at the Cigar Divan, and attended the Court of Judge Nicholson at the "Judge and Jury." Moreover, I bolted rump-steaks at Dr. Johnson's Tavern (in Bolt Court); transparent sandwiches at Vauxhall; white bait at Greenwich; and, though no cannibal, "Maids of Honor" at Richmond. If I have not also quaffed "Barclay & Perkins' Entire" in their own Brewery, it is something at least to have seen the blinded premises, especially as I saw at the same time the enlightened drayman who on being asked why he had helped to pull the moustaches of Haynau, replied, "'Cause he's is a bloody Hungarian Refugee, darn him."

"Don't you drink hail in your country?" asked one of the brewers, as I was leaving the establishment.

"No, my good fellow," I replied, "we drink thunder and lightning in America ;" and if the fellow ever gets a draught of New England Rum, he will probably find the statement correct. My not drinking so much as a pot of 'alf- and-'alf while in England, was everywhere a mystery. Horace Greeley tells of one of his compositors, who on being asked to "take something," replied: "No, I thank you; I never drink; but I chew and swear:" and it was only by indulging in a few such weaknesses myself, that I established my claim to common humanity. But to return. Having acquired more than a Cockney's familiarity with London, (for I have met more than one man born within the sound of Bow-Bells, who had never seen the interior of St. Paul's Cathedral—though it ought to be added, in mitigation, that the price of admission is "tuppence,") and having found the cozy side of John Bull, and learned to look upon him as a man and a brother, I was tempted, on one of those sunny mornings which so often belie the stereotyped nonsense parroted abroad by travellers as to the English sky, to make a visit to the land of cutlets and *coups d'état*, and get a peep at the "Nephew of his Uncle." Accordingly, with umbrella in one hand, and personal estate in the other, and after purchasing a cheap benediction of half-a-score of waiters who were imploring my honor not to forget them, (as if any traveller could forget a London waiter,) I footed my way to the railroad station and booked myself for Paris. As there is a saying in those parts to the effect that " only lords, ladies, and loafers, travel by the first-class," and not flattering myself that I belonged to either of those categories, I modestly seated myself in the second, though instead of a car (carriage is the word in England) I found myself in a box—a square box, made of the hardest kind of oak, and having neither arm, leg, (it had knees,) cushion, rug, stove, lantern, nor as much as a peg to hang myself on. Box Brown, running from the Peculiar Institution in a 7x9 packing case, wrong side up, was not less at his ease. My fellow-passengers, more provident than myself, had supplied themselves with warm horse-blankets, and were all rolled up, "snug as a bug in a rug"—like so many cocoons. Each of the males moreover was armed with a "pocket-pistol," loaded to the muzzle with the best cognac, while an unprotected female in the right-hand corner, with a red nose and a blue bonnet, had converted her muff into a portable restaurant, stocked with eel-pies, ginger-beer, and indiscriminate pastry, enough for a three months' cruise. Opposite me sat a commercial traveller, whose long legs annoyed me so much that I had at last to come to a dove-tail compromise with them. This served as an introduction.

"One touch of Nature makes the whole world kin."

The long-limbed genius was a rough customer, like most commercial travellers, (though I remember having once seen a Quaker specimen who was smooth as an eel,) and had been on the road for twenty years. Before railroads were invented he drove a tandem, carried a horse-pistol in each pocket, and was king of the highway. Then there was some romance in his life. He knew every pretty girl on the route, and had two guineas a day for expenses. He has but a guinea now, and travels so fast that he can't tell a girl from a cow. The cars were no sooner under way than he changed his hat for a fur cap, blew up an air-cushion and slid it under him, adjusted his blanket, "wet his whistle," and, pulling out the *Times*, commenced reading it with the desperate air of a man who never skips so much as the pathetic advertisement calling on A. B. to "return to his disconsolate family and be forgiven." Imitating this unsocial procedure, I took a late number of the N. Y. *Tribune* from my pocket, and was soon lost in a scientific disquisition on Political Conchology explaining the difference between hard-shell and soft-shell democrats. Each of us having finished his task, and Legs having looked at his watch, examined the priming of his pistol, tucked up his blanket, and ventured an original remark about the weather, addressed me thus: "Excuse me, sir, but is that an American newspaper ?"

"Yes, sir; would you like to look at it?"

"Thankee, I should, if you've done with it. Never saw one before--by the by, I saw one of your countrymen the other day, Mr. Hemerson. He was a perfect gentleman. If he 'adn't been so thin, I shouldn't have known 'im from an Hinglishman."

"Indeed! I fear you are disposed to flatter."

"Not at all. He was very well dressed, and spoke Hinglish as well as I do. I saw him in London. I heard his lectures on Reprehensible Men. By the way, how d'ye like London, sir?"

"Very much. It's a fine town."

"Nothing like it in America, eh ?"

'Nothing."

"Pray, 'ave you hever been in New York?"

"Often, it's our principal city."

"Ah! You don't say so. I suppose I could go all hover it in a day?"

"Certainly if you went in a balloon."

"Then you 'ave balloons in America. But p'raps you'd like to read the *Times,* sir. It's the leading journal o' Hurope. You'll find a harticle in it to-day on Mrs.—Mrs.—what's-a- name, in America."

"Mrs. Grundy, perhaps?"

"No, no, Mrs.—I forget it; it begins with S."

"Mrs Sigourney, probably."

"Dear me, no; but its something like that—its the name of a State, like Boston and Saratoga."

"Oh, yes, Mississippi you mean."

"That's the name. It's a capital harticle, written probably by Lord Pummice-stone. He's rather hard on you, but you won't mind that."

"Not in the least. But he shouldn't be cruel. I hope the Queen isn't against us."

"Dear me, no. She's the best little woman in the world. She isn't agin nobody. You've nothing to fear from 'er, sir. She wouldn't 'arm a flea."

"I'm glad to hear it, sir; it's a relief."

—We have received several very mysterious communications, every line of which, for some inexplicable reason, begins with a capital letter. In some instances, and for reasons equally unintelligible, the concluding word of each line is made to rhyme with the concluding word of some other line. Moreover, the matter is measured out with a certain curious regularity not unlike that sometimes found in the writings of Poets. What the object of this arrangement was, we have not the least idea: and we are equally puzzled to know why articles thus made up, and otherwise having no interest, should be sent to The Saturday Press. In fact, the whole affair is involved in mystery. Will the eccentric writers be good enough to explain? It is true that we have seen similarly constructed communications printed (capital letters and all) in other journals, but until they were actually offered to us, and we were obliged, therefore, to read them in MS., and to seek to find some sense in them, and to discover the theory of their composition, we had no idea—though they always affected us singularly—how ineffably stupid they were. We hope the next production of the kind that is sent to us will be accompanied by a daguerreotype of the author.

We may as well state here, that in addition to these literary curiosities we have received several original poems, which are now under consideration.

One Thing and Another.

—Why is the air of our court-rooms foul? The police speak of being on the scent of a crime, Do the perpetrators when caught give that disagreeable scent which is always found in a court room? Certain it is that the odor there prevalent is not the odor of sanctity. The actions brought there must have an unjust man as either plaintiff or defendant, since "only the actions of the just smell sweet and blossom in the dust." The offences tried there would seem to be only such as are "rank and smell to heaven." These explanations are more poetical than practical. But the fact remains the same, that our court rooms are the most horribly ill-ventilated places—so much so that a person unused to the consumption of foul air, is sure to pay with a headache for his attendance on the "honorable the court." How the judges can stand it we cannot understand. Perhaps we may account in this way for the corruption of justice we hear so much of.

— Who owns Union Park?—Somebody has usurped the right to close this pleasant little place of resort, at nine in the evening. The excuse given is that it was used as a place of meeting for classes of persons displeasing to the "rigidly righteous," or rigidly respectable. Why not then close Broadway? We believe the tax-payers pay for keeping Union Place in order, and they ought to have the chance to use it. Were they ever consulted about closing it?

—The Evening Post of last Wednesday says: "We were favored this morning with a call from M. Groux, the congenital fissure of whose sternum created such interest at the Medical College to-day. His case is a most remarkable one, and is a rare opportunity for studying, ex visu, the actions of the heart, great vessels, and lungs."

—The resolutions of the Miami Conference of the Church of United Brethren, declaring the wearing of crinoline incompatible with a true Christian's profession, seems to be rigidly enforced by the authorities of that denomination. At a camp-meeting of the Brethren Church, recently held near West Baltimore, Montgomery county, Ohio, Bishop Russell forbade any one with hoops on to partake of the Sacrament, affirming that they would not be welcome at the table of the Lord. The good Bishop is evidently opposed to "enlarging the sphere of woman."

—The following is from the same Journal: Why are sheep the most dissipated and unfortunate of animals? Because they gambol in their youth, frequent the turf, are very often blacklegs, and are universally fleeced.

—The modern woman's rights movement seems to have as one of its objects the changing Aphrodite into Hermaphrodite.

—The most attractive feature of the Cooper Institute is the elegant suite of rooms occupied by the "New York School of Design for Women."

—"Amelia" suggests that we have a department in our paper entitled "Cinnamon Drops in the Candy Store of Thought." We incline to think that our correspondent made a mistake in addressing her letter.

—The latest novelty from Germany is a musical bed, which receives the weary body and immediately "laps it into Elysium." It is an invention of a machinist of Bohemia, and is so constructed that by means of a hidden mechanism, a pressure upon the bed soft causes a soft and gentle air of Auber to be played, which continues long enough to lull the most wakeful to sleep. At the bead is a clock, the hand of which being placed at the hour the sleeper wishes to rise: when the time arrives the bed plays a march of Spoutant, with drums and cymbals, and, in short, with noise enough to rouse the seven sleepers.

Notices of Books.

BITTER-SWEET. *A Poem.* By J. G. Holland, author of "The Bay Path," "Titcomb's Letters," etc. New York: Charles Scribner. pp. 220. Price 75 cents.

"Bitter Sweet" is a remarkable poem, if it is a poem—remarkably whimsical, remarkably American, and remarkably unlike anything we ever read. Its plot, which is not precisely a plot, is not its least remarkable feature. We had no idea that there was any story whatever, until it leaped out upon us at the *denouement*. Then we began to understand why a number of eccentric people were assembled, on a certain Thanksgiving night, in a certain "old red farm-house" in New England: we began to understand why "Ruth" made very naughty speeches, and "David" very long ones; why "David" and "Ruth" went down cellar, and "Grace" and "Mary" up stairs; why "Edward" went up in a balloon with an improper young woman, and why he came down again—in short, we discovered that we had been reading a strange novel of modern life rather quaintly done up in excellent blank-verse, with here and there a patch of rhyme by no means excellent. The plot of the poem is like one of those curious Chinese boxes which you innocently suppose to be solid ivory, until it suddenly opens in your hands to your unspeakable astonishment. We shall not betray the key-note of the poem to our reader, but refer him to the volume, while we make a protest against the form of Mr. Holland's metaphysical enemy—for it is nothing else.

Now, it is very amiable and considerate of Mr. Brandeth to give his pills a coating of silver or an aromatic surface, to render them palatable; but metaphysics are not the kind of physics to be administered in rhyme and rhythm. Mere morality, mere argument, and mere sense, are a thousand times more effective in clear, straightforward prose, than in the most intricate and artistic rhythms. We protest against sermons in verse, and *vice versa*—if we must say it. It should be a poet's aim to create Beauty, which, as Emerson has said, is its own excuse for being. Morality is not poetry, but beauty always is. "Bitter-Sweet" is rich in lines and passages of exquisite poetry, but they are things entirely aside from the great moral lesson Mr. Holland would teach us. We do not object to the lesson. It is admirable. But we like not the sweet Virtues when they come to us in fantastic dresses. A tract should not go wandering about clad in colors like a harlequin.

We think Mr. Holland was somewhat unfortunate in selecting a dramatic form for his story. His characters, as a certain satirist has said of women, have no characters at all, or are possessed of such slight individuality that it would be difficult to tell one speaker from another, if the "lengths" were not labelled. The concluding scene, indeed, is quite effective, and seems almost dramatic when compared with the preceding dialogues. On the whole, we do not think that "Bitter-Sweet" can rank among books as a poem, though it proves Mr. Holland to be a poet; and we must say of it as Leigh Hunt said of "Pomfret's Choice." it is—

"A pretty kind of—sort of—kind of thing.
Not much a verse, and poem none at all,
Yet, as they say, extremely natural.
And yet I know not. There's an art in pies,
In raising crusts, as well as galleries,
And he's the poet, more or less, who knows
The charm that hallows the least truth from prose,
And dresses it in its mild singing clothes.
Not oaks alone are trees, nor roses flowers;
Much humble wealth makes rich this world of ours:
Nature from some sweet energy throws up
Alike the pine-mount and the butter-cup;
And Truth she makes so precious, that to paint
Either, shall shine an artist like a saint,
And bring him in his turn the crowds that press
Round Guido's saints, or Titian's goddesses."

—A number of gentlemen have given to the Boston Mercantile Library Association, a fine cast from the original of the statue, of the Venus de Milo.

—For the first time for three years (says a London contemporary), a number of Punch has appeared in which there is neither wood-cut nor paragraph about crinoline. Hoop deferred maketh the heart glad!

NEW YORK NOVEMBER 20, 1858

Odds and Ends.

WOMEN AT THE OPERA.

A correspondent of the Evening Post is anxious to know if there is not some way by which women can be prevented from making too free a use of their "unruly member" at the Opera; we can think of no process which would accomplish this humane end, short of amputation.

—Alfred Tennyson has returned to his home on the Isle of Wight, from a tour of some months duration in Germany.

—Alexander Dumas, having recovered from his late illness, has left St. Petersburgh on a tour through Siberia.

—The Middlesex Teachers' Association, at their meeting in Malden a few days since, adopted resolutions expressing the opinion that the children of our primary schools should not be confined to study in their seats more than three hours per day. It is a sensible suggestion, and one that should be acted upon in our municipal schools.

—While at Lake George this last Summer, we met with an English traveller who entertained us occasionally with his comments on American peculiarities of language, and, among others, that of saying *at* instead of *in*, as, for example, "I spent the Summer at Nahant," instead of in Nahant. He was making himself quite merry one day over this Yankeeism as he called it, when suddenly one of the company asked him if he had written to his friends in England that he had just spent three days *in* Lake George, and if so whether they wouldn't wonder how it happened that we had no Humane Society in America to rescue him from such a fate. The man, shortly after this, disappeared, and for aught we know, is now recreating himself in Mount Vesuvius.

—*The Photograph News*—a new periodical taking photographic views of things—has a lively correspondent somewhere in Africa who states with great gusto that he has succeeded in photographing the flashing blade of the guillotine in its descent, as well as of figuring the culprit's head during the instantaneous fall from the machine into the basket. The occasion was that of the execution of six Arabs for a cold-blooded murder. The criminals were not brought on the scaffold together, but led up one at a time. The first was the sheikh, who seemed perfectly indifferent to his fate. So rapidly was he bound to the plank and thrust under the axe that the artist had barely time to insert the plate-holder, and get the instantaneous movement in order, before the sharp edge descended, and his head rolled into the basket. This picture was quite successful, and so was the second, but the third and fourth were wholly invisible. How to account for this he doesn't know unless the atmosphere around the scaffold became in some way affected by the blood, the odor of which was distinctly perceptible.

A NEW PORTRAIT OF PARIS: PAINTED FROM LIFE.

"Paint me as I am".—Cromwell.

"Now being from Paris recently.
This fine young man would show his skill."
Holmes.

BY HENRY CLAPP, JR.

CHAPTER IV.

How the author might have been cheated—How he reaches Dover, sees a petrified Niagara, and embarks on a snub-nosed little steamer which he catches whistling under false pretences—How his personal estate is seized by the strong-minded women of Calais—How he is taken to a Den of Thieves, and his invaluables and unmentionables are publicly exposed—How he experiences several "deliverances "not laid down in the Litany—How his passport betrays what manner of man he is—How he peeps through a pigeon-hole and sees a duck—How he meets Legs emerging from the Den of Thieves partially dismantled— And how he wonders that travellers are not more like eels.

In about three hours, each of which might have passed itself off upon me as a good day, we were in Dover, whose white cliffs, a perfect Niagara of chalk, made the Channel look like a broad river of milk and water. Here we found a snub-nosed little boat, smoking a short pipe, wheezing through the nose as if she had the asthma, and blowing a penny whistle under the ludicrous pretense of letting off superfluous steam. About two hundred of us contrived to pack ourselves edgewise on the narrow deck; and after two hours' struggle with a squadron of spiteful little waves trooping over from the French coast, like so many *grisettes* in smart white caps, and no end of flounces, we had crossed the Milky Way and were in the hands of the tri-colored authorities at Calais. I had no sooner landed, than my innocent carpetbag was seized by one of the strong-minded women who seem to have secured their rights in that advanced seaport, and, despite the protests of my gallant American nature, the brisk porteress, rattling her wooden shoes over the pavement like castanettes, and setting her tongue in motion like a cotton-mill, conducted me, with mischievous delight, to that Den of Thieves, the Custom-House. My effects-consisting of little more than three dickeys, a portable boot-jack, a pipe, the daguerreotype of my grandmother, a pair of straps, the American Constitution, a sandwich, a bottle of Cologne, and my other shirt— having been found all right, the bag was marked with what I presume was French for "O. K.," and the proprietor was delivered over to a porter, who delivered him over to a gendarme, who delivered him over to another, who delivered him over to the Pass-bureau. The gendarme was a long, ill-to-have-done looking fellow, encased in a semi-military blue-coat, with semi-circular skirts dangling against his supposed calves, and sporting an awkward long sword, hid away in a patent leather sheath, and appearing to be on the worst possible terms with his legs. His moustaches were waxed to a point, a la Napoleon the Little, and were evidently the pride of his life. His chin was decorated with a fanciful goatee. His whiskers were mown. The use of soap I should say had never been revealed to him. The solemn creature was topped off with a jaunty three-cornered hat, a la Napoleon the Great, which gave a triangular look to the whole concern.

"I know it is a sin
For me to sit and grin
At him here;
But the old three-cornered hat,
And the breeches, and all that,
Were so queer!"

The passport official was a club-headed fellow in spectacles, with a sole-leather complexion, and a crop of coarse hair standing stiff on end, brush fashion, and looking like a seven days' growth of rank grass. He was as grouty as a clerk in a post-office.

My passport evidently puzzled him. He contrived, however, at last, to buzz through it, getting it all wrong, of course, though peering at me all the while over his spectacles to be sure it was "all right," and at last pronouncing that it *was*, albeit, if he read correctly, I have (or had)—"Hair, blue; eye-brows, red; nose, oval; complexion, spare; whiskers, 5 feet 8 inches; age, pointed; height, 25 years;" etc. The reading of the passport finished, and Chubbhead being satisfied that it answered to me in every particular, and that my presence in France would not prevent the Prince President from becoming Emperor, the document was endorsed "Johnny Crapeau," or words to that effect, when I was again delivered over to the three-cornered gentleman, who took me round a fourth corner, and delivered me over to the Railroad office.

A cocky blue cap, a gold-embroidered coat, and a pair of blue trowsers with gold lace running down one leg and crawling up the other, now approached me, while a voice from the blue cap directed me to the Weighing Room. My persecuted carpetbag was then thrown into a huge balance, but not being heavy enough to turn the scales, it was declared, after some consultation, to be within the prescribed weight, and I was directed to a little pigeon-hole on the left to get myself finally booked for Paris. Through this pigeon-hole gleamed a black-eyed Susan, wonderfully done up in roses and ribbons, and fragrant as a scent-bag; while at my approach forth came, like a dove, a pretty white hand, into which I instinctively placed-my ticket. While gazing abstractedly through the oval aperture, and wondering as I gazed, whether all French women had such black eyes and white hands, a tinkling little voice, such as surely never man heard from any other bureau said to me: "Monsieur, here is your billet, if you please;" and folding the now precious document in my wallet, I returned to black-eyed Susan my Frenchiest thanks, and strolled back to enjoy the confusion of my fellow-travellers at the Custom-House. I met Legs striding away from the den like an ostrich.

"The wobbers have stolen my plaid shawl," said he.

"Stolen it! How's that?"

"Why, confound the scoundrels, they said it a was a harticle of female happarel, and that I meant to smuggle it. I told 'em I'd worn it for six-month, and then one of 'em hasked me if I passed for a *femme* in Hingland. Now, sir, do I look like a *femme*? Rather not," said he, answering himself, and looking more like an ostrich than ever. "Rather not. Oh, I should like to catch them fellows on the road in Yorkshire— any dozen of them. I'd show 'em whether I passed for a *femme* or not, the brutes !"

"But why don't you pay the duty ?"

"Pay the devil! I'd see 'em in —! I beg your pardon, sir—I'd see 'em 'anged first! Besides," said he, getting funny, "Hingland expects every man to *do* his duty—not to pay it. And I'll 'ave my revenge," he added, getting savage again—"if I do every frog of a Frenchman I meet with out of his high-teeth. Besides, I'll go to our Hambassador and tell him that the liberty of a British subject 'as been hinwaded, and that this hinfernal republic, like every other —I beg your pardon again—but I'll 'ave my shawl again if it costs a waw !" and he stalked on to the Passport Office as fierce as a Fejee cannibal, while I pursued my way to the Custom-House. The scene there was indescribable. Fussy little women, with an indefinite number of trunks, carpetbags, hampers, muffs, bandboxes, rugs, shawls, fans, bonnet-cases, work-boxes, umbrellas, parasols, poodle-dogs, smelling-bottles and children were rushing frantically about, bribing porters, besieging bureaus, scolding cabmen, and grumbling at everybody. Fashionable young ladies, out on their first continental tour, were practising boarding-school French upon ungallant inspectors in the act of examining the most unmentionable articles of their wardrobe. Fine old English gentlemen were venting their fine old English spleen upon officials who had the audacity to ask if they "had anything concealed upon their persons liable to pay duty." Free and independent young Americans were protesting, with great waste of energy, against anybody's claiming to exercise the right of search upon free-born citizens of the United States. Very Red Republicans were cursing Louis Napoleon for not abolishing a system which the Provisional Government itself did not have the courage to reform. In fine, the whole scene was one of unmixed confusion, the only cool-blooded persons in the crowd being the hardened officials, who seemed to think, with me, that travellers ought by this time to have become reconciled to being plundered as eels have to being skinned.

CHAPTER V.

The author arrives in Paris—Receives a revelation from Legs— Finds himself in a British Inn—Sees a Queen and her Consort hung between two Prize Fighters—Exposes the backward civilization of the Continent—Which gives him the cramp—Sees a Beer Nymph—Learns why he hasn't any cheek—Refuses a Dram—Overcomes a Scruple—Disgusts the Landlord—Makes peace by the aid of Legs—Learns something about his Family—Sees a new Species of Hare "standing on end"—Is introduced to a Baptist—Is ordered to "Circulate "—Circulates—Breaks up a Love Scene—Fees the Nymph—Moves on—And (for further particulars, see next chapter).

I arrived in Paris at midnight. Recommended by Legs, who walked up with me from the dépôt —and who revealed to me, coming along, that he had a brother-in-law in America by the name of Tapeworm, asking at the same time, if by chance I had met him in the street—I went directly to an English Inn in Amsterdam street. That the place was English, was evident at a glance; evident from the dark, dank, dreary atmosphere of the bar-room; from the yellow-sanded floor; from the scent of last night's beer and tobacco from the narrow wooden benches surrounding the room, and giving it an air of a police office; from the array of red-tipped pipes and pewter pots ; from the portraits of "Prince Halbert and Little Wic" ignominiously hung between the portraits of Ben Caunt and Bendigo in the utmost attitude of pugilism ; from a set of lurid pictures representing red-coated British Lords in the patriotic act of breaking their necks over ditches, hurdles, and five-bar fences, for the benefit of humanity, if not of horseflesh; from the straggling set of limp, lear-eyed topers "lying round loose" about the premises, and looking as if they were imported from a kindred house in London as a necessary part of the furniture and live-stock of the establishment; and from a host of other attractions which the backward civilization of the Continent has failed to appreciate hitherto, probably on account of its hatred of "perfidious Albion."

The landlord, a dumpy little Briton, with a knobby pumpkin of a face, and a huge promontory of a nose, was looking out for customers. His ruddy cheeks shone through the glass door, like a pair of red globes through an apothecary's window.

"Do you speak English ?" asked I—though every knob on his face was speaking English at that moment.

"Who, *I* speak Hinglish," said he, pulling out a huge snuff-box, and feeding his nose from an ivory spoon.

"Yes, that was my question."

"Bless your soul, (take a pinch, Sir, it's Mother Miller's best, and none of your scented French powder,) bless your soul, I don't speak anything else; I've lived in this country hever since the battle o' Waterloo—weren't that a rum fight, eh ?—and haven't learnt ten words o' their confounded lingo yet."

"Delighted to hear it, my good fellow—you're a brick; give me your hand," reaching out my own, which he clutched like a lobster.

"Isn't he a stunner?" said Legs, looking down on him like a pair of tongs on a dog-iron.

"He-is-is-so," stuttered I, writhing beneath his grasp, "and a sq-sq-squeezer too. Now, then, landlord, show me a room, if you please. Hang it, man, you've given me the cramp."

"I beg your pardon, Sir; I'm so glad to meet a countryman. Jane!" (to a red-eyed beer nymph at the bar,) "Have clean sheets put on No. 1. And now, Sir, what'll you 'ave to drink? 'Ave a bottle of good Stout. You can't get the like in all Paris."

"Come !" said Legs, "I'll stand."

"Thank you, gentlemen, I don't drink."

"Don't drink! Nonsense, man! Surely say you'll take something. Try a pot of 'alf-an'-half. That won't 'art you."

"Excuse me, landlord, I'm a teetotaler."

"A tee-what ?"

"A teetotaler."

"Come, now, that won't do in this country. A teetotaler in Paris? Why you might as well be a teetotum. You don't mean to drink Paris water, do you? If you do, I'll just order your coffin at once. Do you like pine or mahogany? A teetotaler, eh? That's why you haint no cheeks. Look at mine? There's flesh for you, and I drinks a gallon o' beer a day. Look at Legs. True he haint no calves; but look at his chest. No wadding there. Come, now, let me give you a pint of something; that's a good fellow. In a month I'll make a man o' you. You won't know yourself."

Resisting this cheeky argument, I ordered a pot of black tea, and broke my fast over a hard egg. The next move, after a sound night's rest, was to establish myself in French lodgings. I wanted to know something of the "confounded lingo." So consulting Legs on this subject, he advised me to go to the hotel Corneille, Corneille street, opposite the Odeon Theatre. So, after breakfast, to the great disgust of Cheeks, (who looked like one of Mr. St. John's "Purple Tints of Paris,") I ordered my bill, and sent Boots to No. 1 for my luggage. Legs walked in just at that moment, and made peace with the landlord by forging a story to the effect that his American friend belonged to one of the oldest families in the States, was a medical student, had come all the way to Paris to finish his studies, and of course must live in the Latin Quarter, near Prado and the Hospitals. This being conclusive, especially the old family part of it, Cheeks suddenly becomes reconciled, and continues to do the agreeable. Indeed, he hardly thought it proper to present the member of a family "as old as the hills, and much more respectable," with a bill. I overcame this scruple, however for its the most yielding of all scruples to which flesh is heir—by arranging the matter with my red-eyed friend, the beer-nymph (who had a red nose, too, by the way, though I should not dare to say it except parenthetically), and just as I received my change, down came Backs, with my collapsed carpetbag and umbrella, which he somehow contrived to handle in such a manner as to give them all the importance of a cockney's solid-leather portmanteau and "Shall I send for a Commission-hare to take your luggage?" said Cheeks. "The 'Otel Cornhill is a long way off, but you'll find it a pleasant walk, and the Commission-hare'll show you the sights."

What's a Commission-hare, landlord ?"

"Master means *Commissionaire*," creaked Boots.

"That's what I said, leather-head—Commission-hare."

"He's a man, Doctor, what does everything. They are smartish-looking chaps, in velveteen jacket and trowsers. They all wears jackets. Tails ain't no use. They stand at all the corners close-by the wine-shops. They knows what's good, they does. They aint teetotalers. There's one on 'em over the way. Look at 'im. He's sitting on that rack there, which looks like a skeleton wheelbarrow, only it haint got no wheel. That's what he carries things on. He slings that wooden machine on his back, tail-board down, and trots off with a load of twenty stone like a 'orse. They all comes from the country, where lots on 'em has a bit of hearth about big enough to bury 'em in, which they calls a farm. Darn my eyes if that fellow aint asleep. They always sleeps when they's nothing else to do, cause they don't like to be hidle. That fellow'd sleep till Chris'mas if you'd let 'im alone. But they're clever chaps for all that, and there's nothing they don't know. That one knows a little Hinglish. He was my Boots for a month or two, and I kicked it into him. So he's just the chap for you. You see that brass plate on his jacket? That's his number—11,-456. Everybody's numbered in this country, sir, even to the 'airs of your 'ead. He has to pay a sight for his'n. The police sells it to him. But if he hadn't a good kracter he couldn't buy one at no price. I'd trust them boys with anything. I'd trust 'em with gold if I had any. I've seen 'em moon through the streets with bags of money, as easy about it as a donkey with a load of meal."

"Thank you; that'll do, landlord, I must be moving."

"Stop! I'll call that Commission-hare at once. Baptiste, you rascal, come over here and go with this gent."

Baptiste, whose ears were probably accustomed to the endearments of Cheeks, rushes across the street, waking himself up on the way, and asks: "Vot duz de Monsieur desire ?"

"The Moss-shoer, as you call him," said Cheeks, "desires you to take his baggage to the 'Otel Cornhill, hopposite the Hodeon The-*a*-tre,"

"Oui, Monsieur; yes, sare; tank you. De Hotel Corneille, opposite de Theatre Odeon. I dare vill go vid de Monsieur immediatement."

So Baptiste rushes back to the wine-shop, drinks himself good luck, winks to the bar-maid that he has caught an *Anglais*, and returns, rack in hand, ready to carry anything, from a portmanteau to a feather-bed. Finding no such articles, but only a wan carpetbag and a cotton umbrella, he leaves his rack at the hotel (evidently not without fear that Cheeks will put a wheel to it), mounts the carpetbag on his head as carefully as if it (either the head or the bag, as you please) were filled with eggs, folds the tender umbrella softly under his left wing, and says:

"Now, sare, if de Monsieur is ready, ve vill—"

Circulez! Circulez! Messieurs," interrupts a gendarme, seeing us block up the sidewalk.

"Oui, Monsieur, *circulate,*" interprets Baptiste; "ve shall circulate to de Hotel Corneille."

"Go ahead!" said I. "Good bye, Cheeks—farewell! Legs. Thanks to you both, gentlemen—but stop, there's my card—come and see me. Now, then, Boots, what are you about with Jane? No matter—France will be France —but come along. Here, Jane, is a franc for No. 1 and the clean sheets. Good luck to you."

"*Au revoir*! Monsieur, *au revoir*!"

And so we moved steadily on till we got to the end of the street, when on looking round, there we saw Cheeks watching us from the stoop, and Legs standing on the shady side of him and peering over his shoulders like a mower peeping over a haycock.

[To be continued next week.]

For the Saturday Press.

DREAM-BUILT.

I own a palace by the sea,
Where creamy billows idly curl
O'er sighing shells of rosy tinge,
And stones of sardonyx and pearl.
'Tis seen by no one save myself,—
Its walls are fashioned from the mist,
While through its star-lit corridors
Dim shadows wander as they list.
A phantom-bark, with silken sail,
Transports me o'er the twilight sea,
Unto that far ideal strand,
Where roams the spirit ever free.
I dwelt there in midsummer hours,
And ate the golden lotos-stem,
While spirit hands place on my brow,
Joy's airy, jewelled diadem!
And no one can dissolve the spell,
Save Duty with her iron band,
Who dissipates at will, each dream,
With haughty gesture of command.
But when returned to real life,
The dream still sheds a halo round.
And still the billows lull the soul
To peace, with their remembered sound!

Frederick A. Parmenter.

NEW YORK NOVEMBER 27, 1858

A NEW PORTRAIT OF PARIS: PAINTED FROM LIFE.

"Paint me as I am".—Cromwell.

"Now being from Paris recently.
This fine young man would show his skill."
Holmes.

BY HENRY CLAPP, JR.

CHAPTER VI.

The author philosophizes on Distances—Visits the Holy Fathers—Finds the French language expensive—Meets with an Adventure—and a Beggar—shows the advantage of a prosperous wen—Explains to Baptiste "Why the Yankee spikes the English"—Quotes Secretary Marcy—Learns that Paris is about to become a Seaport—Tires out the Reader—And finishes the chapter.

From Amsterdam street to Cornielle street is, according to the Surveyors, about a mile and a-half, or, according to ordinary pedestrians, half-an-hour's walk; but according to the writer, who scorns all "mean calculations," the distance between any two places, and the time requisite to travel it, depends upon who you are, who you are with, where you are from, and what you are about. Time and Space are no more to me, than Gog and Magog; Day and Night as indifferent as Day and Martin. The ground I was about to travel, then, could not be measured. I was taking my first daylight view of Paris, and meant to enjoy it at my ease. Baptiste kept by my side to answer questions. His knowledge of English was not very profound, but it was deeper than mine of French. I knew the coy language by sight, but had no speaking acquaintance with it. I could say *oui*, but couldn't give the native squeal even to that. Moreover, the first time I drafted the little monosyllable into service—which occurred during our walk—it cost me a shilling; and it was evident that if I got even a tolerable vocabulary on duty at the same rate, it would soon ruin me. The incident occurred on the "Bridge of the Holy Fathers"—an elegant bridge crossing the Seine from the Place du Carrousel, near the Tuileries, to the Quai Voltaire, which quay, by the way, changes its name in disgust at the approach of the Holy Fathers, and suddenly becomes Quai Malaquais. A well-dressed Frenchman, who it seems was stationed on the bridge, and could distinguish a foreigner half a mile off with the naked eye, approached me politely the moment we had set foot upon his premises, and asked what sounded to me like a peculiarly civil question. Baptiste nudged me to go on; but for fear of being rude in the "politest city of the world," I turned round and replied to the gentleman with a double discharge of my best *ouis*. Whereupon the Monsieur took me quietly by the coat, which I had noticed him eyeing all the while as if it had a snake coiled round it, turned down the collar carefully, (as if for fear of getting bitten,) rubbed a soft sponge over it two or three times, then nicely adjusted it again, gave me a self-satisfied look, (as if he had scotched the snake,) inclined himself to the ground, and finished with a soft-spoken remark which I had interpreted to mean "Good day, Sir, I am only too happy to have been enabled to render milor a service." I accordingly touched my hat in return for so much civility, thanked the Monsieur in bad English—the American's usual substitute for French—and continued my walk. But the fellow (how soon some men sink from gentlemen to fellows!) followed me up, and repeated his remark, which I had evidently misinterpreted, with more and more vivacity at every step. I turned to Baptiste, who had been looking on all the while with great glee, for an explanation, which was given to me thus:—"De Monsieur, vich you call him, hab clean your paletot from the grease, and demands—spreading out his two hands like fans, that I might count the fingers—ten sous. Gib to him—withdrawing one fan altogether, and shutting up three parts of the other—gib to him two."

But the coat-cleaner was not to be fanned out of his pay so easily. In fact he protested so violently, and shrugged so desperately, and moreover seemed so bent on following us to the end of the world, (we were already at the end of the Holy Fathers,) that to rid myself of his company, and prevent him from foreshortening himself into a humpback, I threw him ten sous, whereat he gave a final shrug, like a toad, and hopped out of my way. *Moral.*—Never say *oui* to a Frenchman, unless you know what he is talking about.

It was on the Bridge of the Holy Fathers, also, that I got my first view of a French beggar. Thomas Hood used to say that he never knew what the English beggars did with their cast-off clothes till he saw the beggars of Ireland; from which I infer that the Irish beggar is the antipode of the French one. But to our Paris friend; one thing at a time, or, at any rate, one beggar at a time is as much as we can manage. The Beggar of the Holy Fathers, then, like the Bridge of the Holy Fathers, is an institution. He is licensed by the Government. He is seventy years of age, and is blind. He has a wife and a dog. The wife brings him his meals; the dog-helps eat them. He has a chair, which has a cushion. His back is protected from the draft by a board attached to the iron railing. He wears cowhide shoes, and yarn stockings. His head is covered with a fur cap, and his legs are enveloped in a blanket. Moreover, he has a cane, an umbrella, and a foot-stove. He doesn't smoke—the blind rarely do—but he takes snuff, and drinks half a bottle of claret per day. His money-box, which looks like a coffee-mill, is securely made, and rests upon his knees. He attracts customers to it, by playing lively airs on a fiddle. His chief supporters are poor folks, women, and children. The first coin of the day is touched to his lips, and consecrated with the sign of the cross. The last one furnishes him with tobacco. His post is near the North end of the bridge. When tired, he gropes his way to the South end, and makes a visit to a professional brother without legs. He has sat on the Holy Fathers ever since they first became a bridge in 1834. He rejoices that the Revolutionists of 1848 abolished the toll, as the State's loss has been his gain. He regrets that he cannot see the marble statues of Industry and Abundance seated as comfortably as himself (save that their iron chairs have no cushions) at the North end of the bridge, and wonders if other people think, as he does sometimes, that Industry and Abundance are not always found so near together. I added my mite to this comfortable beggar's treasury, and having thus cast a crumb upon the waters, made a *mem.* in my sketch-book, which I have since extended into the following note :—

The French nature is tender; the English tough. The fact that a man is old and blind moves the sympathies of a Frenchman at once; but to move an Englishman's, he must also be ragged and have sore legs. The various persons who appeal to your compassion in Paris are all tidy. The strolling singers are all neat and well-dressed; so are the mountebanks; so are the "nine small children and one at the breast" drawn up in graduated line on the Boulevards; so are the organ-grinders; the man who blows "Home, sweet Home," through a German flute; the flower-girls who thrust violets into your button-hole; the infant-Genin who sweeps the streets on his own hook; the poor mechanic who has been "out o' work, Sir, this six month, and hasn't eaten a meal for a fortnight;" and the old lady who walks into your pocket on two wooden legs, and fiddles you out of sixpence. Rags, and dirt, and bruises, and sores, wouldn't help their case in the least; but in London they are the beggar's stock in trade. A good thriving boil on the leg, or a prosperous wen in the neck, is capital to him; a flourishing fungus is fortune.

Baptiste began to think we should never get to Corneille street. I had stopped him at every turn, and queried him out of all patience.

"I did never see one such *anglais* for to ask questions," he exclaimed, shrugging up his ears. "But, I am not a an *anglais,* Baptiste. I'm a Yankee."

"But, Monsieur, the Yankee spikes the English. Why for he no spike the Yankee ?"

"There is no Yankee language, yet, Baptiste, but we are getting one up fast."*

I then explained to the astonished Commissionaire that the inhabitants of the United States spoke English (to say nothing of spiking them) for the same reason that the inhabitants of Algiers spoke French.

"Vell, Sare," he replied patronizingly, "after all I likes de English very much; it is a very *comfortable* tongue."

Our word comfortable, by the way, has smuggled itself into the French vocabulary with a slight change in orthography, but doesn't know what to do with itself there. We passed one shop where "comfortable pastry" was advertised, and another which rejoiced in having a fresh supply of comfortable ink. Madame Busque, Michodiere street (of whom more anon), has comfortable pumpkin pie.

I lingered on the Bridge of the Holy Fathers at least half an hour, working on Baptiste all the while like a suction-pump. The observing schoolboy who described a bridge as "a thing for boats to sail under" must have got his idea from the bridges on the Thames; for take your stand on any one that spans that busiest of rivers, and the number of steamboats racing up and down its turbid waters—each ducking its jointed funnel as it passes under the arched thoroughfare, and coolly puffing a pipeful of smoke into your eyes, is incredible. But a steamboat on the Seine would surprise the people like a sea-serpent; still such things have been seen on the river, for, in fact, Baptiste informed me that he had seen one "with his own eyes" (placing an emphasis on the words as if he generally used the eyes of other people), and that in the Summer, persons had been known to travel on it as far as Montereau—fifty miles up the river—and back. On Sundays, too, in fair weather, it seems there is something not unlike a steamboat which runs between Paris and St. Cloud, stopping to take breath at Meudon and Sevres; and we have it on the authority of Galignani that "a whole steamboat" may be hired for the day for a hundred and fifty francs." The price of a fragment of a steamboat—a paddle, a boiler, or a shaft, for instance, the usually But the fact that a "whole steamboat" can be procured in Paris at any price or for any service, is what none but the most observing tourist would ever have discovered. Were the Seine an English or American river, it would be alive with steamers from Montereau to Havre. I ventured to say as much to Baptiste, who replied with an air of ludicrous importance :—"But, sare, ve shall soon hab one steamboat from Marseilles, and den," he added, giving a fine instance of the Frenchman's hundred-horse power of induction, "and den Paris will be one grand seaport more big nor London."

And, sure enough, about two years after this conversation, I saw in the Seine an exhausted propeller, which had just screwed all the way from Marseilles, and lay gasping by the river side, after the ten days' labor, like a dying whale. Excepting the new Empress, and the patent ship balloon which was to

> "Put a girdle round the earth
> In forty minutes,"

this wonderful steamer, so "very like a whale," was the greatest curiosity of the season. She was moored in front of the Tuileries, directly under the droppings of the imperial palace; and the official newspapers—which all came out with flaming articles, that would have done credit to Baptiste, pompously headed, "Paris a Seaport"—announced that "His Imperial Majesty had graciously condescended to look at her, exhibiting, in this touching manner, his lively interest in all that concerned the welfare of his people, or the commerce of France." As for his "people," they flocked down to the craft with as much curiosity as so many Loo Choo Islanders swimming out to a steamer from America.

But I see that the reader is getting as impatient as Baptiste, and wishes to be conducted to the Hotel Corneille. Behold us, then, full in sight; and as the house is to form an important feature of our New Portrait of Paris, it shall have the honor of commencing a new chapter.

CHAPTER VII.

Hotel Corneille—The Author dismisses his Guide—Imitates a Duke —Becomes mystified—Fears that the Spirit Rappers have invaded France—Shows his practical turn of mind—Becomes embarrassed —Is relieved by an Englishman—Gets up in the world—Meets a man having a brush on the stairs—Explains the matter—Arrives at the Seventh Heavens —Surveys his new quarters —Hears strange Rappings—Has a Visitor—Smokes a pipe with him—And winds up with a Discourse on Tobacco.

The Hotel Corneille, like most French hotels, is in the form of a very hollow square. It is built of no-colored bricks, stuccoed over in innocent imitation of white marble. It is about a hundred feet through, and has an indefinite number of stories. Each story has ten or twelve folding windows in front, coming down to the floor. The attic consists of an independent wooden story, looking as if it had fallen from some other planet, and didn't feel quite at home. Crowning the edifice are numerous tile-chimneys scattered promiscuously over the roof, and looking like stacks of retired and disconsolate flower- pots. The building is of no particular style, but appears to have been put up before architecture was invented. It has a hospitable, walk-in-and- make-yourself-at-home kind of look, however, which is worth all the architecture in the world." The chief entrance is by a massive double-gate with a small door cut in one wing, reminding one of Newton, or some other philosopher, who had a big hole and a little hole in his door, one for the cats and the other for the kittens. The gate leads through a spacious carriage-way to the court-yard. On the sides of this carriageway are private entrances leading respectively to two large coffee-rooms which occupy the whole of the front ground floor, and have their chief entrances on the street. In the centre of the court-yard is a pretty little fountain enclosed in a circular garden plot.

Corneille street, on the East side of which the hotel is situated, is a narrow thoroughfare, about two hundred feet long, separated by the magnificent Odeon Theatre from a parallel street of the same length, name after Moliere. Near the South end of these streets, and in rear of the theatre, are the elegant palace and gardens of the Luxembourg. The front of the theatre opens on a spacious square, surrounded by showy cafes and cheap restaurants. As I gazed attentively at the frank good-natured face of the hotel; at the commanding theatre in front, with its dark cloister-like piazzas, crowded with curious old book-stalls; and the storied palace with its beautiful garden enlivening the whole scene the fascination of the place to every student was no longer a mystery.

I dismissed the impatient Baptiste at the door of the hotel, and saw him a moment after fraternizing with a brother-commissionaire, No. 1,001, whom he found smoking a pipe on one the stone gate posts, and to whom he no doubt gave an embroidered account of our long walk and a picturesque portrait of the unaccountable Yankee. Acting under the delusion that France as in England, a visitant's status would be calculated by the number and violence of his raps, I thundered half-a-dozen times with great energy, Duke-fashion, upon the resounding gate, which, after giving a sharp click, flew back on its hinges like magic. I looked round the passage to see who had so promptly answered my noisy open sesame, but no one was to be seen. A spirit-rapper could not have managed the thing more dextrously. It was evident that the portals had been thrown open by some unseen hand; but being of a practical turn of mind, I presumed that it was connected in some way with the ministry of the interior. I had no time, however, to solve mysteries. With my carpetbag under my arm, therefore, like a bag-pipe, and shouldering my umbrella as if it were a musket, I marched through the carriage-way into the court-yard, and seeing an office to the right with the word *concièrge* (meaning porter) over the door, entered it at once, and found myself in the presence of a dark-eyed, downy-lipped young lady, in a pinkish cap and white apron, who was engaged in hemming a pillow-case. Dark-eyes having examined me with a glance from head to foot, (taking in the umbrella and carpetbag on the way down,) and not appearing particularly pleased with the survey, fixed upon me an inquiring gaze as who should say: "If you want anything of me, why in name of Babel don't you speak?" I had purposely abstained from taking Baptiste in with me, being resolved to find out at once how an uninitiated foreigner could get along under such circumstances without an interpreter. It was evident that he couldn't get along at all. I pointed to my

* *In an official letter, issued by the late Mr. Marcy, that worthy Secretary called upon our European Consuls to transmit to him certain documents translated into American.*

carpetbag, looked up toward the chambers, and made innumerable signs, for which I received in exchange only a much larger number of shrugs that left me no wiser than before, and a series of pouts from the downy little lip which only increased my embarrassment. Of course Dark-eyes saw at once what I wanted, but it was of some importance, to her as well as myself, that before being shown to a room we should enter into some disagreeable little details as to terms. In this emergency the young lady at last dropped her pillowcase, cast a furtive glance at the mirror, and tripped over to the opposite side of the court-yard to the bureau of the landlady. Meanwhile, as I stood leaning against a huge white porcelain stove in the middle of the floor (an admirable French contrivance for preventing the diffusion of heat), I had a chance to look about me. The office of the concierge, or porter, was a small room say 15x20. Three sides of it were furnished with a wooden frame-work, some eight inches deep, divided into about a hundred and fifty little alcoves, over each of which hung a common house-key, while within stood a tall brass candlestick like a sentinel on guard. Each separate alcove, key, and candlestick, bore a corresponding number, representing a room. In many of the compartments I noticed letters, and neatly folded slips of paper, giving the place the air of a post-office. Hanging at the back of the room was a large card, in a mahogany frame, containing the names of all the lodgers in the house with their respective numbers. Near this card was a printed list of regulations and prices. In one of the front corners was what looked like a bell rope. As I was examining this, and wondering where it led to, a knock was heard at the great gate, whereupon Dark-eyes suddenly reäppeared, looked me out of her way, and gave the rope a sharp pull, which was answered by a sharper click. It seemed that this rope was connected with a spring bolt on the gate, and was called the *cordon.* The mysterious manner in which I had been admitted was now explained, and it was no small relief to find that it had no connection with spirit-rapping. Dark-eyes had no sooner "pulled the cordon" than a bland young gentleman in a flash hat, and with the jaunty air of a student, sauntered up the court-yard, entered the office I had been so minutely surveying, and going directly to his alcove, seemed not a little disgusted to find there one of the abovementioned slips of paper. As he cast a rapid glance over the document, and then crumpled it into his waistcoat pocket, it was evident to me at once that he had been looking at his hotel-bill, and that it was about as welcome to him as an unholy writ. He hardly put the thing out of sight, when over came a large bunch of keys with a smiling old lady attached to them, at whom the student cast a furtive glance, and then headed for the door. This was evidently the landlady. She immediately stopped the young gentleman with what I presumed to be a request to "settle that small bill," but which turned out to be the less embarrassing question whether he would have the kindness to serve as interpreter for "one of his countrymen."

It seemed that he was an Englishman. His profuse beard, and especially the little bed of curled hair coquettishly laid out on his upper lip led me to think that he was a Frenchman. On looking at him more closely, however, and remarking his clear blue eyes, soft brown hair, and rich mellow complexion, his English origin was plain enough. I shall not soon forget, either, the pleasant change which came over his fine countenance when he found he was not to be dunned, nor yet the kind manner in which he at once relieved me of all embarrassment. After a few explanations, such as that I was not "one of his countrymen," but a green and ungallicized Yankee (which, by the way, he saw at a glance); that I had just come from Cheeks' Hotel, in Amsterdam street; and that I proposed to try the experiment of French lodgings; the young man—whose name we will call Books—stated to me briefly the system of the hotel, and told me there were rooms at from fifteen to a hundred francs (three to twenty dollars) per month, and that I could "feed" in the house at the rate of about three francs per day, "exclusive, of course," he added, with a sly wink of the eye, "of lush, or what you call grog." I proposed trying the cheapest room I could get which was comfortable.

"Then," said he, "you can have the room opposite mine; it is rather high up, but the nearer the garret, nearer the gods. I am No. 53, you can be No. 53 *bis.*"

"*Bis*? What does that mean?" asked I.

"In this connection it means *repeated*; and it is the word generally used by Frenchmen, where we, in our ignorance of their language, use the word *encore* at theatres and concerts, for instance, when we wish to recall a favorite performer ?"

"Exactly. They don't *encore* in Paris; they *bis*."

[To be continued next week.]

THE HAUNTED HOUSE IN ASTORIA.

A correspondent of the *New Jerusalem Messenger* (Swedenborgian) of the 20th, says:—

In the village of Astoria, in a rather sequestered spot, there stands a house which is most unprofitable property to its owner, because he cannot retain a tenant in it, in consequence of its reputation of being haunted. The story is that its former proprietor was burnt to death in it, and that ever since, his ghost, having no better occupation, passes his time in nightly visits to his house, producing unearthly sounds, opening and shutting locked doors, while they still remained locked, opening windows and throwing out the plates on the grass, though the plates still remained in the closets, and alarming the watchdog by sights and sounds which would drive him from his post to the protection of his master. These tales, and others of the same sort, we heard gravely related by a brave military gentleman who had been a tenant of the house, but had been forced to leave it in consequence of the impossibility of retaining servants who were willing to encounter those ghostly sounds! The house, for the whole Summer, stood vacant. We then, in company with one or two others, took occasion to visit this haunted house, and examined it from cellar to garret, but without seeing or hearing anything remarkable, though possibly, as in many other houses, strange sounds might be heard there at night, produced by rats. The proprietor, despairing of renting his house, then induced a poor family to occupy it rent free. The housekeeper gladly accepted the offer, and at first declared there was no ghost in the house; but latterly she one morning called on a neighbor, in a perturbed state of mind, and assured her that "Sure enough there is a ghost in the house." Then she related the evidence of the fact; she had fastened a strong black thread to a large needle, and sewed it to the pincushion on the table, and both the needle and thread had most mysteriously disappeared. While looking for them, what was her amazement to behold, high up, the needle still fastened to the thread, but suspended and hanging downwards, while the rest of the thread was most curiously woven together, and adhered to the shutter, without anything to hold it. This supernatural work could not, of course, be done by any one but a ghost. Ellen Green, an intelligent young woman, after attentively listening to her neighbor, went with her to the haunted house, to examine this mysterious thread and needle. Sure enough there were the thread and needle as described. But, anxious to solve the mystery, she picked the thread from the shutter, and perceived that it had adhered by means of a spider's web, and just above she beheld the ghost in the shape of a hideous large black SPIDER—a most fitting representative of all ghost stories, as spiders' webs correspond to falseness and treachery.

THE PALACE AND PRINCES OF THE PRESS.

The Boston *Saturday Evening Gazette* has the following subdued notice of THE SATURDAY PRESS:—

A NEW SENSATION WEEKLY.—Mr. Henry Clapp, Jr., a writer of ability, and Mr. T. H. Aldrich, a young poet of promise, have started a weekly paper in New York called "The Saturday Press.". . . . . The editorials have been so strongly tinged with self conceit that one might presume that the editors live in the Fifth Avenue and come to their place of business in balloons. Their threats of independence are the most humorous bits in their journal, and the North River is in imminent danger of being dried up unless these champions break their necks in throwing sixty consecutive literary summersaults in as many issues. They solicit as on favor that newspapers will pitch into the "Press." At least one publisher per week will be seized on Broadway and carried to their sanctum, where he will be broiled on the gridiron until he shouts "Vive Clapp! Hurrah for Aldrich!" Their afternoons they will devote to stopping papers addressed to subscribers who have complimented them by sending remittances to their "valuable paper," as they dislike compliments, and in the evening they will sit down and congratulate themselves upon the great good the "Press" will do society.

If the *Evening Gazette* had not been a Boston paper it would have long since known that the Editors of THE SATURDAY PRESS have inaugurated a style of editorial life, which, combining Eastern splendor with Oriental magnificence, is appropriate enough for them, however beyond the reach of the fraternity in general.

It is a well-known fact in New York, that the editorial corps of THE SATURDAY PRESS, prefer the balloon to all other modes of conveyance in effecting the journey from their residences in Fifth Avenue, to their office in Spruce Street. Hence, the airiness of their styles of composition. Twice a week, they order out their State Balloon, a splendid vehicle built of the finest Indian silk, and inflated with the rarest American gas, in which they make short excursions into the neighboring provinces, having sent on in advance a portable country-seat, which can be erected in a few hours, together with servants, cooks, and a wine-cellar, so that when they choose to descend at the point agreed upon, they find an elegant chateau, a luxurious dinner, and the most tempting wines, to the last two of which they do the fullest justice, balloon-travelling being a great promoter of the appetite.

The splendors of the office of THE SATURDAY PRESS are known only to the Editors themselves, their most cherished contributors, and their office-boy, a young Nubian Prince, whom the chief Editor rescued from captivity while travelling in Abyssinia, and who out of gratitude has ever since followed the fortunes of his benefactor.

The press-room and composing rooms are on a corresponding scale of magnificence. Twelve Georgian slaves of surpassing beauty, unceasingly swing silver censers, in which burn the woods of cedar and aloe, to and fro in the press-room, so that the disagreeable odor, usual in such establishments, is drowned in ever-rolling vapors pregnant with delicious aromas. The printers' galleys are far more splendid than that famous one in which Cleopatra floated down the Cyduus to meet Antony, and of which Shakespeare has left so gorgeous a picture. The various employés of the paper are remunerated so magnificently, that—disdaining to receive their salaries in notes, and the equivalent in specie being too cumbrous—it is found expedient to pay them in diamonds, in which elegant and portable material all demands on the office are satisfied.

Our carriers deliver THE SATURDAY PRESS in straw-colored kid gloves. Each mailbag containing the country edition, also encloses a *sachet de millefleurs*, so that our rustic subscribers on opening their papers are greeted with agreeable floral odors.

Of Editors there are three: one literary, one dramatic, and—THE EDITOR-IN-CHIEF! These personages reside in contiguous mansions on the Fifth Avenue. The architectural decorations of their abodes vie in splendor and fertility of invention with the Albambra of Old Spain. Here the seven colors of the chromatic scale are to be found combining, like the notes of the musical gamut, and forming visual harmonies that ravish the eye. Great masses of mingling hues, flung by windows of stained glass upon the floors, entrance the sight, as the harmonious chords of a grand orchestra entrance the hearing, and seem to be the painted music of the sun. The walls blush with soft neutral blooms. The ceilings are aerial, and yet warm in tone as the skies of a Syrian midnight.

Throughout those spacious chambers, where light and shade are ever-varying, and breaking the gorgeous chromatic combinations into rich and strange novelties of effect, numberless luxurious couches, and wonderfully constructed chairs, are scattered. Indolence nestles in their drowsy cushions. With wide, inviting arms, and deep recesses of down, they seem the consecrated shrines of Repose. The sleeping apartments are at night filled with an atmosphere slumberous as the breadth of the Blue Lotus, while, through the hours of rest, concealed orchestras play sweet melodies; melodies so faint that they seem like memories of music. In the morning, airs invigorant as those snuffed by the chamois of Chamounix, rush through the opened casements across each sleeper's face, and chase the God of Dreams.

These luxurious features are common to all the residences of the Editors of THE SATURDAY PRESS, but there exist in the mansion of each one, certain architectural peculiarities which mark the idiosyncracies of its owner. For example, the Dramatic Editor has attached to his residence a private theatre, on the stage of which a select company of artists perform his own plays, with a vivacity and *esprit*, an accuracy of detail and costume, and a magnificence of scenic decoration, which have hitherto been unknown in histrionic annals. The Dramatic Editor has been driven to seek refuge in these solitary theatric consolations, from the fact, that it would have been otherwise impossible to keep his mind up to its proper critical level, as an unvaried course of New York dramatic performances would have made him an idiot in the flower of his youth. The *Literary Editor*, a youth beautiful as Hylas, learned as Magliabecchi, and poetic as the dolphin-charming Arion, loves the etherealised luxuries of the poets. Gardens glowing with fruits and flowers surround his abode. Bees, imported expressly from Mount Hybia, busily hoard for him in crystal hives, the honey that made Plato's tongue mellifluous. Athenian girls, with golden grasshoppers gleaming in their black hair, and forms that are living songs of beauty, minister to him Capuan and Levantine wines. Flower-crowned, he sinks to sleep in a chamber, the tapestries of which are wrought with choice sentences from the daintiest authors, blazoned in illuminated characters, so that his large blue eyes, unclosing with the early dawn, drink in the wedded sunlight of Heaven and of Man.

Of the EDITOR-IN-CHIEF it is scarcely becoming in us to speak at any length. This majestic and ineffable Being, though frequently condescending enough to share the society, and even the revels, of his associates, is nevertheless a creature of such lofty and solitary nature, that it would be in vain for the weak pen that travels over this page to depict his attributes. A pigmy hand endeavoring to grasp a gigantic globe would not be more impotent than any attempt of ours to compass this miracle of intellectual grandeur.

There is, in addition, a vague and awful Power connected by mysterious ties with THE SATURDAY PRESS, to whom we are accustomed to allude as

The Unrevealed.

Dwelling ever in the serenity of conscious might, He watches over, counsels, protects us. He is to us the veiled source of beneficence and fertility. The embodied Nilus who, inaccessible and lonely, pours upon our sheet the flood that sustains and fructifies. To ordinary minds He would appear merely as the Proprietor of this Journal. The "Princely Proprietor" perhaps, in the cant phraseology of the day. To us He is an august Intelligence, passionless but bountiful.

We have never seen Him! Seated behind a screen of perforated gold, after the fashion of the Emperors of Japan, He delivers to us his Oracles. We hear and obey. His invisible Hand pours the wealth with which we sustain our enterprise into the respectful laps of His subjects.

With regard to our treatment of publishers, we beg to assure the *Evening Gazette* that its theory of our cruelties to that race are unfounded. Certain reckless members of the profession, stimulated by a fatal curiosity, have sought to penetrate our mysteries, and perished miserably on the threshold. When Doctor Livingston brought with him to France a poor African of the desert, the overwhelmed savage, thunderstruck at the splendors of Civilization, expired in a paroxysm of wonder.

Let this be a warning to future aspirants, lest in striving to lift the veil that falls between our marvels and the world, they expiate their rashness in Death.

THE AUTOCRAT OF THE BREAKFAST- TABLE.

Oliver Wendell Holmes is, indisputably, our greatest humorist, and "The Autocrat of the Breakfast-table," the most brilliant series of magazine papers ever written in this country. Since the first number of the Atlantic Monthly, the wit, poetry, pathos, and idiosyncrasies of the "Autocrat" have been the delight of everybody. Dr. Holmes's views of men and things are not always vast or comprehensive, but they are always individually quaint and most admirably put. Messrs. Phillips, Sampson and Company have brought out the "Autocrat" in a solid 12mo. volume, illustrated by Mr. Hoppin. The book, as a piece of workmanship, is not a fair specimen of the publishers taste and skill— we except the title-page, which is exquisitely arranged. There is little or no margin to the pages, and the binding is neither elegant nor substantial. The "Autocrat" is the hit of the season, and should have been a marvel of book-craft. We regret to say that Mr. Hoppin is not at all at home with "the Landlady's Daughter" or "the young fellow called John," or, in brief, with any of the peculiar and amusing people who figure at the immortal "Breakfast-table." Notwithstanding the sharp outlines which the author gave him, the artist has entirely misconceived their characters. The picture on page 154 is a charming drawing, but we do not think that it is the "Autocrat's" idea of " B. F." Mr. Hoppin can sketch the Hoppin family to the life; but he is seldom or never successful with less familiar subjects. But in spite of all this, the "Autocrat" will say his wise and pleasant things for many a long year to come; "the young fellow called John " will always be young; "Benjamin Franklin" will never improve in French, and the damask roses on the cheeks of "The Schoolmistress" will be fresh and dainty until all the Beatrices have made husbands of all the Benedicks, and possibly a century after that!

Oliver Wendell Holmes.

Notices of Books.

The Four Sisters —A Tale Of Social And Domestic Life In Sweden. By Fredrika Bremer. Translated by Mary Hewitt. Philadelphia: T.B. Peterson & Brothers.

If memory is not playing us a trick, Mr George P. Putnam published the above work, some two years since, with the title of "Hertha," the heroine of the story. That which we call a rose, by any other name would smell as sweet; but the importance of floral nomenclature, and the value we place on the title of a book which has become dear to us through its merits or associations, are very different things. The custom of publishing old books as new ones and, unhappily, it is a custom in this city and elsewhere—cannot be too severely denounced. "The four Sisters," or "Hertha," is a charming book. Frederika Bremer is fortunate in having so admirable a translator as Mary Hewitt.

Dust And Foam; Or, Three Oceans And Two Continents. By T. Robinson Warren. New York: Charles Scribner. Pp. 397. 8vo.

The author has led a wild, roving life, going in pursuit of either fortune or pleasure, to South America, California, Australia, the Sandwich Islands, China, and some of the islands in the China Sea. The record of his adventures and observations is pleasant and interesting. His style is not of the best, but he takes a practical, business view of the manners and customs of the people he meets. His contrast of the stability of society in Australia with the disorganization of California, leads us to find the cause in the settled character of the Englishman as compared with the roving American, a class whose disposition the author's own story illustrates. He gives an account of the leader of the recent Chinese rebellion, representing him in the character of a religious enthusiast. He attempts to justify the Coolie trade, that it is for or the Coolie's final benefit, notwithstanding the numbers that die on the passage. He gives the view of the man of the world, on the effect of Christianity and civilization upon the Sandwich Islanders. The book closes with the prospectus of a scheme for steams communication with South America.

NEW YORK DECEMBER 4, 1858

A NEW PORTRAIT OF PARIS: PAINTED FROM LIFE.

"Paint me as I am".—Cromwell.

"Now being from Paris recently.
This fine young man would show his skill."
Holmes.

BY HENRY CLAPP, JR.

CHAPTER VII.

Concluded.

Books now introduced me formally to the landlady, Madame Foucher, who was, of course, delighted to have the honor of my acquaintance, *etc., etc.*, as in such cases made and provided. After a word or two of consultation with the *anglais*, who informed her that I was an American; that I had come, I forget how many thousand miles, to see her great and beautiful country; and that I had often heard of her famous and excellent hotel as one of the lions of the capital; (here the Madame made a profound courtesy, which tickled Books like a receipt-in-full)—Dark-eyes was ordered to produce the register of the house, in which I was requested to record my name, age, profession, country, the last place I was from, etc., "in accordance," said the polite hostess, apologetically, "with the instructions of the Government, who will transfer the record to the books of the police."

Books made the entry for me, and when he came to the "profession," wrote the word *rentier,* which he afterward told me meant capitalist, or gentleman living on the interest of his money. Before closing the register, the landlady asked Books to tell her what the meaning of the word *loafer* was; saying that another American in the house, Col. Somebody, from Virginia, had written that against his name. Books had to refer to me. I told him that Col. Somebody was evidently as much of a wag as a colonel, and that loafer meant idler, or vagrant, or vagabond, according to circumstances. Remarking that there was many a true word written in jest, Books gave the old lady a liberal interpretation of my reply, by saying that a loafer was a very fine gentleman. My passport was now deposited with Dark-eyes, and Books being evidently a pet with that young lady, (for he had found it good policy to fee all the eyes in the house,) she began to look upon me with favor, and to "hope I should find a room to suit." Madame Foucher hurried over to her bureau, to get a fresh supply of keys, saying that she would meet us at No. 53 *bis,* which she had no doubt Monsieur the American would find very genteel.

The ascent to the chambers of the hotel was by three separate staircases, viz: one on each side of the courtyard, leading to the North, South, and West sections of the house, and the third, at the back of the yard, appropriated exclusively to the East section, which being comparatively retired, was occupied chiefly by families, and was called by the students the "Quarter of the Respectables." We ascended the South staircase, while the Madame was to rejoin us by the North. Going up the first flight we met a servant who appeared to be skating his way down on one leg; but on close observation I found that he had a brush fastened to his shoe instead of a skate, and that he was sliding along the wooden stairs lengthwise, and sidling his way down for the purpose of polishing them. On the first landing we saw a thick oaken stick, about three feet long, looking like a handspike, and having a wide slit in one end which was furnished with a large piece of yellow beeswax. It appeared that this instrument was used first, and then followed up with the brush which served to "put on the shine."

No. 53 *bis* was on the seventh story. Madame Foucher, who notwithstanding her bulk, was a woman of considerable activity, had arrived there before us, and was just unlocking the door. I engaged the room immediately. The price was about four dollars a month without meals, or eighteen dollars with breakfast and dinner. Preferring to graze at large, I agreed to pay the four. I then offered to settle for the first month in advance, (much to the astonishment of Books,) but the proposition was promptly declined as being contrary to the rule of the house, which was to pay regularly at the end of each thirty days. I fancied that the just-slight-enough-not-to-be-impolite emphasis placed on the word "regularly," made my companion wince a little. The terms thus agreed upon, I was left in full possession of the room, with instructions always to leave the key with the *Concierge*, and the suggestion that if I had any valuables with me, (I had none save my umbrella,) to deposit them at the bureau of the hotel for safe keeping.

"I have deposited mine," said Books, as the landlady rustled down stairs, "with my aunt."

"Then you have relatives in Paris ?"

"No—not so much as a relative pronoun; but you'll be a lucky fellow if you don't find out who my 'aunt' is before you leave town."

"I see; she's probably a relative of your 'uncle' in London—a blood-relative, I should say—sign of the ⁂."

"Just so, and a dear good woman she is."

I now proceeded to survey my new quarters. The room was about twenty feet square, and eight in height. The floor was composed of octangular red tiles, relieved here and there by strips of carpet. The paper hangings represented an original species of a bluebird fluttering through a pale yellow sky towards the ceiling. There was a folding window opening inward and looking into the courtyard. It was closed by a perpendicular bolt running the whole length of the sash, in the centre, and worked by an iron crosspiece which screwed the bolt half-round, and hooked each end of it into a socket. The fireplace was small, and furnished with two common dogirons without legs, an iron backlog cast to resemble a log of wood, a small iron fire-stick, an ingenious blower working up and down like a window, by means of weights and pulleys, and a pair of tongs, made without joints, sugar-tong fashion, straddling at ease in the corner. On a broad marble mantlepiece were two fluted brass candlesticks, a pair of fancy porcelain vases, radiant with calico roses and violets, and a crazy timepiece perched on four gilt columns, and confined for safe keeping in a glass case. The bedstead was spacious, and of the usual French model. It was supplied with a wool bed resting upon several straw mattresses, a scant assortment of sheets and blankets, a diamond figured counterpane looking like an immense diaper, and, over all, a blue sack of eider-down serving as a comforter." By the head of the bed was a *cabinet de nuit*, containing—no matter what. The rest of the inventory—all the articles being made of black walnut—consisted of a marble-topped bureau with four drawers; a marble-topped secretary with a drop-leaf; a marble-topped washstand with a large decanter and tumbler in the first story, and a small pitcher and bowl in the second; a marble-topped centre-table; half-a-dozen red-bottomed armchairs; and a dark bay towelhorse. Everything that had an arm, a leg, a knee, a foot, or a back to it, was more or less dislocated; the green baize of the secretary and the marble-top of the centre-table were discolored in such a manner as to show that the previous occupants of the chamber had lived anything but stainless lives; the crayon portraits of young women sketched up the walls were far too life-like to have been done from memory; while numerous caricatures of the landlady in the act of presenting her "small bill," showed that even when absent in the body the worthy hostess was present in the spirit. The room seemed spectral with the ghosts of departed tenants. Presently, hearing strange rappings, I began to hum

"Who's dat a knocking at de door?"

when in walked Books, with a clay pipe running out from his figurehead like a bowsprit with its staysail set, and looking, truth to say, anything but like a spectre. (I believe it may be laid down as a principle that ghosts never smoke.) How unkind of him to disturb an illusion which else might have united me to the world of spirits, and thus turned the tables of my unbelieving heart!

"I hope I don't intrude," said he, laughing at my air of surprise, and hauling down his staysails.

"Not at all. I was merely admiring my room and trying to get the hang of it. Wait a moment till my bag comes up, and I'll take a whiff with you."

"You probably smoke nothing but cigars."

"You're right—when I can get nothing but cigars."

"You don't mean to say that you smoke pipes?"

"Try me, my dear sir."

"Come over to No. 53 then."

Behold me, then, within an hour after my arrival at the hotel, comfortably seated in the room of a man whom I had never seen before, and actually smoking a pipe with him. A clay pipe (not an absurd meerschaum, but an honest clay pipe, made, like ourselves, out of the dust of the earth) is the best conductor of that subtle fluid we call sympathy, in the world. It bridges over the gulf which separates man from man. It is a universal token of fellowship. It precludes all vain words and ceremonies, and establishes a mysterious communion between soul and soul. Your first pipe with a man is an event. It transforms him into a friend. The blue currents, as they unite gracefully over your head, form, as it were, a new heaven peopled with good angels. The true symbol of peace (as Noah would have known had there been a smoking room in the ark) is not the olive-branch, but the tobacco-plant. The introduction of this

"Plant divine, of rarest virtue,"

into general use, is the greatest blessing conferred on man by the discovery of America. How gladly it crossed every sea, and how welcome it was beneath every sky! "In Europe," says a sensible writer in *Blackwood*, "from the plains of the sunny Castile to the frozen Archangel, the pipe and the cigar are a common solace among all ranks and conditions." And yet, like all the pioneers and missionaries of Civilization, tobacco has had to work its way into the hearts and homes of the people through abuse, persecution, and martyrdom. "But in vain," to quote from *Blackwood* again, "in vain was the use of it prohibited in Russia, and the knout threatened for the first offence, and death for the second. In vain Pope Urban VIII. thundered out his bull against it. In vain James I. wrote "In Counterblaste to Tobacco.'" . . . . "In the East the priests and sultans of Turkey declared smoking a sin against their holy religion, causing its votaries to be strangled; yet nevertheless the Turks and Persians became the greatest smokers in the world. In China the practice is so universal that every female from the age of eight or nine years wears as an appendage to her dress [the dear girls!] a small silken pocket to hold tobacco, and a pipe." In fine, the consumption of tobacco in the world is now about two millions of tons per year, and all sensible men are fast becoming confirmed Tobacchanalians.

"Now, then, how do you like the looks of our hotel?" asked Books, setting his staysail again, and filling it with a fresh puff.

"Well, Sir, except that it gives me the foot-ache getting up those slippery stairs, the place seems to me very comfortable."

"So it is; and when you come to get your French legs on, you will run up and down the waxed thoroughfare as nimbly as Boots. But why didn't you go to Meurice's? That's where most English and Americans put up."

"For two good reasons; first, because I didn't want to get fleeced, the novelty of that operation having worn off in my case some years ago; and, second, because I haven't come three thousand miles from home to see either Yankees or (begging your pardon) Cockneys.

"Judging from most of my countrymen whom I have met on this side of the Atlantic, the chief object of their travels, (next to their being able to say that they have been abroad,") is to meet with and glorify—each other. In Liverpool, they pass by every true British hotel, and go to the Waterloo; in London they do the same, and rush to Morley's; in Paris they avoid a Frenchman as they would a frog, and drive to Meurice's; for fear, it would seem, that in Liverpool they might meet with Lancashiremen, in London with Cockneys, and in Paris with Frenchmen, and thus learn something about the respective peculiarities of these persons, to study which, it appears, was not "in the bond." I have seen New Yorkers who have been in London a year without being able to tell a Cockney from a countryman, and in Paris two years without learning enough French to prevent their asking for a boot-jack when they meant to order a turbot."

"Yes," replied Books, "and the wonder is that the waiters didn't in every instance take them at their word; for the French look upon the English and the Americans an original, omnipotent, and omniverous race of mortals, who would be as likely to eat (and digest) live oak as anything else. But how do you account for your countrymen going to such hotels ?"

"Because the American is eminently a gregarious animal. He likes to go in herds. A Yankee by himself, in any part of the world, is as melancholy a spectacle as an ungleaned stock in a harvested corn-field. He hates solitude, and foreigners are no company to him. The Englishman is too serious for him; the Frenchman is too frivolous; and *neither of them chew*."

"What does he travel for, then ?" "God only knows."

"But you are an American; why do *you* travel?"

"Not to hunt up stray Yankees, as you see." What then?"

"Well, God only knows *that* too. I certainly have no great thirst for information, and dislike moving about as much as a cat. But somehow I like to see all sorts of folks, and can't very well do it without considerable locomotion. I don't much care where I am; and I've no prejudices: I don't think a man is ever good for much without them, but that is my misfortune."

"You are probably married?"

"Probably not, and probably never shall be. It's not in my line. I look upon marriage as the upshot and catastrophe of civilization; and I'm no civilizationist. I don't care to have my likes and dislikes circumscribed."

"But if it wasn't for marriage, the world couldn't be kept a-going."

"I don't care for that, either."

"But what do you care for ?"

"Nothing."

"Come, now, you are joking."

"Be it so. That is in my line. A woman said to me the other day (for I do see a woman now and then) that she didn't believe I ever spoke a serious word in my life. I wish it had been true. The world is too serious by half. What is there so stupid and solemn as man in all God's creation? What is there here on the earth, or up yonder in the skies, to be so mighty solemn about? Nature herself is half the time on the broad grin. She laughs at us even through her tears. But the world is like

"A rogue in grain,
Veneered with sanctimonious theory"

At this point in the conversation, I observed Books staring at me with the fixed, desperate look of a man making superhuman efforts to keep awake; so to prevent his dropping asleep, I dropped the subject, and set his eyelids in motion again by proposing a fresh pipe.

(To be continued in our next.)

For the NEW YORK SATURDAY PRESS

IN THE WOODS.

I walked alone in depths of Autumn woods;
The ruthless winds had left the maple bare.
The fern was withered, and the sweet brier's breath
No longer gave its fragrance to the air.

The barberry strung its coral beads no more.
The thistle-down on gauzy wings had flown,
And myriad leaves, on which the Summer wrote
Her blushing farewell, at my feet were strown.

A loneliness pervaded every spot;
A gloom of which my musing soul partook,—
All Nature mourns, I said: November wild
Hath torn the fairest pages from her book.

But suddenly a wild bird overhead,
Poured forth a strain so strangely clear and sweet.
It seemed to bring me back the skies of May.
And wake the sleeping violets at my feet.

Then long I pondered o'er the poet's words;
"The loss of beauty is not always loss."
Till like the voice of love they soothed my pain,
And gave me strength to bear again my cross.

O murmuring heart thy pleasures may decay;
Thy faith grow cold, thy golden dreams take wing.
Still in the realm of faded youth and joy,
Heaven kindly leaves some bird of hope to sing.

ALBERT LAIGHTON.

Portsmouth, N. H

Dramatic Feuilleton.

THE PROSPECTS OF THE SEASON.

With the first snow the theatrical season may be said to have set in. One scarcely realizes the long nights until the ground is whitened, and the trees of the parks are leafless. Christmas—time of holiday to Tom, Dick, and Harry, emancipated from school—is a time of toil to those ladies and gentlemen who, inhabiting that mysterious region bounded by the green curtain, furnish the youngsters with themes for endless talk after their return to Greek Grammar and the *Pons Asinorum*. Then the still dormitories are illumined with memories of the Ravels, their spangles and wondrous disparitions; of Mr. Lester, his splendid uniforms and more magnificent assurance when he enacts those comedy heroes whom no circumstances can abash, and who after dispensing various patrimonies with needless profusion, terminate by marrying an innocent heroine in white muslin, with ten thousand pounds a year in her own right. I can never look upon the theatrical season as fairly commenced until I see the dress circle and *parquet* chubby with young holiday faces, and gleaming with those juvenile uniforms in which American pedagogues see fit to encase their youthful charges.

Ido not think that my little friends will have what they themselves term a "high old time" at the theatre this season. I hear nothing of tremendous *spectacles* or uproarious burlesques on the *tapis*. The pen of Brougham rests upon the triumph of Pocahontas and Columbus. Laura Keene is about to give us, to be sure, that wonderful fairy poem, the Midsummer Night's Dream, with Puck and Bottom, and Oberon and Titania. There we will, of course have gigantic mushrooms appearing through square trapdoors cut in the midst of sylvan scenes; fairies clearing the clouds on obvious wires, an ass's head displaying the usual profound zoological knowledge of the proper man, and Mendelssohn's wonderful music doubtless admirably performed by Mr. Baker and his orchestra.

It is a hazardous experiment for Miss Keene to undertake the production of such a piece as the Midsummer Night's Dream. This extraordinary fantasy—perhaps the most thoroughly original dramatic performance in all of Shakespeare's works—deals with such wild, quaint elements, that its realization on the stage requires a subtlety of manipulation rarely met with in New York theatres. Its exquisite poetry and wonderful humor charm us in the closet, because there Imagination is the scene-painter, and Fancy the machinist. The fairies float through ether, shapely as the old gods, prismatic as the rainbow. The forest is dewy with the liquid pearls sown by Night; Titania is radiant with a supernatural beauty. Bottom assumes his asinine head-piece without the aid of a dresser, and it seems to belong to him as naturally as the stag's legs do to the satyrs and fawns. The scene shifts from Athens to the Palace of Theseus without prompter's whistle, and in noiseless grooves. Hippolyta puts on no paint, and Lysander does not wear false calves. The utter unreality becomes real, and the grotesque and beautiful figures embroidered on this strange tapestry, fall into harmonious relations in the solitude of the study. But when presented to us in flesh and blood, and calico and gimp, and yellow ochre and canvass, how difficult it is to preserve the mystic beauty of the poem. A course slip of the scene-painter's brush, an accidental glimpse of the carpenter's hand at the wings, the slightest instability in Bottom's head-dress, and lo! instead of being in a wood near Athens, encompassed with whispering oaks and phosphoric fairies, we find ourselves suddenly landed in the dress-circle of a New York theatre, and remember that we paid fifty cents at the door.

O'Brien, by Gunn.

Miss Laura Keene will, doubtless, do her best in the production of the Midsummer Night's Dream. She will certainly have room for a display of managerial talent and industry. But if, as is too often the case, she is not going to work in that loving and artistic spirit in which such works should only be produced, it were much better that she confined herself to the production of comedies like "Our American Cousin," which, without drawing largely on the intelligence of the audience, draw large sums of money to the treasury.

Mr. Wallack is, like Miss Laura Keene, also busy with a Shakespearian revival. Sometime before Christmas we are to be favored at this theatre with the Merchant of Venice, Mr. Wallack, of course, filling his time-honored *role* of Shylock. This is without any exception the most striking of all Mr. Wallack's Shakespearian performances, and supported, as rumor says he is about to be, by new scenic illustration, and magnificent costumes, it will, doubtless, attract large audiences, a feature for which this theatre has not been as yet remarkable during the season.

Probably the most attractive theatrical event of this season will be an amateur performance, in aid of the Dramatic Fund Association, undertaken on a scale of unusual splendor, at the Academy of Music. It is understood that the chief attraction at this performance will be an original drama, constructed expressly for the occasion, by three gentlemen of literary repute, and produced with an attention to scenic detail, and to costume, seldom witnessed in this city. A large number of gentlemen and ladies in this city, possessing marked talents for the stage, will for the first time, on this occasion, give the public an opportunity of judging their concealed ability, and the direction of the performances being confided to a professial gentleman, whose genius, as an actor, is not second to his talent as an author, it is predicted that this attempt will, at least, be free from those executive crudities for which amateur performances are generally distinguished.

MR. RANGER AT WALLACK'S THEATRE.

A gentleman bearing the name of Ranger, and who, it is stated in the bills, is of American and English celebrity, has been resuscitated by the management of this theatre from what must have been a considerably long interment. Mr. Ranger is an actor of the school of Fanen, and much resembles that great actor after he had lost his teeth. I saw him play Sir Peter Teazle in Mr. Sheridan's wonderful comedy. It is a part altogether too large for him. The extraordinary geniality of that well-bred, hen-peeked gentleman, is broader than Mr. Ranger's shoulders. He was pleasant, and sometimes laughable, but far inferior to Mr. Blake in the same character—that is when Mr. Blake was sufficiently condescending to know his part. The majority of the characters were so wretchedly sustained in this performance that I have scarcely patience to speak of them. Lady Sneerwell, Sir Benjamin Backbite, Maria, and Joseph Surface, were all as bad as they well could be. Miss Henrarde is a *danseuse*, and has no business to play high comedy; Mr. Wheatleigh as Sir Benjamin, did not seem to have the remotest conception of the tittle-tattling "Maccaroni" of the period; Mr. Sloan —an excellent actor—was altogether out of his line in Crabtree, and I must say, that however correct Mr. Dyott may be as an elocutionist—doubting nevertheless his correctness in that department of his art—I am certain that the author never intended Joseph Surface to be presented as a whining, transpicuous villain, but rather as a well-bred and elegant double-dealer, who is at length unmasked by force of circumstances. Mr. Dyott's Joseph Surface would not deceive even a New York detective policeman.

FITZ-JAMES O'BRIEN.

Notices of Books.

THE WITCHES OF NEW YORK as encountered by Q. K. Philander Doesticks, P.B. New York: Rudd & Carleton. 1859.

The lovers of Montaigne, Charles Lamb, and our own polished humorist, the "Autocrat," will find but little to delight them in the exaggeration which characterizes Mr. Thompson's books. In the essays of Elia, delicate and subtle thought is wrapped up in the quaintest prose: with Mr. Thompson, all the quaintness is generally in the wrapper. He has a funny way of saying things, but not always a way of saying funny things. Nothing is so satiating as mere style. It is the skeleton and not the soul of prose.

Doesticks by Bellew.

Mr. Thompson's "Witches of New York" deserves a kind of praise which could not well be awarded to his previous productions. Not that the author has neglected to pile up the adjectives, or ceased to be striking at the expense of human nature and the English language—but because he has really done the public a service in calling attention to an evil the extent and influence of which are bitter satires on the laws of this city. That there exists among us a class of people, who, under the mask of Astrology, Necromancy, and other absurd professions, have reduced theft, seduction, and every imaginable crime to a system, is simply a frightful fact. In exploring the dens of these creatures and laying bare their revolting operations, Mr. Thompson has performed a good act, the serious importance of which he does seem to understand, since he treats the whole affair (excepting in his preface) as he would a dog-fight, or "Doesticks on a Bender." Mr. Thompson is a man of peculiar genius, but he has not written his best things.

NEW YORK DECEMBER 11, 1858

A NEW PORTRAIT OF PARIS: PAINTED FROM LIFE.

"Paint me as I am".—Cromwell.

"Now being from Paris recently.
This fine young man would show his skill."
Holmes.

BY HENRY CLAPP, JR.

CHAPTER VIII.

Books—Balzac—Thackeray—American Snobs—What the Author thought of his Crib—New light on the subject of Gates—The Art of pie-making in France—What it is to be comfortable—How an individual becomes a number—Great men and small Dames—Preparation for dinner—Soap—English pigs—Books' *Cabinet de Toilette*—A fast set—The trough—A difficult problem—The student as a financier—The dinner—The Author anticipating the course of Nature—A real French scene—What is beauty?

Books was a man of letters. He had come to Paris to graze in French pastures. The works of Balzac, Hugo, Lamartine, Beranger, Soulié, Dumas, and George Sand, were scattered about his room in every direction. Not an English book was to be seen, except Thackeray's Vanity Fair. Balzac and Thackeray were his gods. "Love me, love them," said he. It was easy enough to love him, and not difficult to love Balzac; but to love Thackeray, whose

"—meddling intellect
Misshapes the beauteous forms of things,
And murders to dissect,"

and who has a clique of imitators in America who lounge in the ante-chambers of fashion, and give us keyhole observations of society, required some effort.

"Balzac," said Books, taking up his *Père Goriot*, and growing enthusiastic, "Balzac is the Shakespeare of novelists. He lays the heart of French society open before you till you hear it throb. He not only analyzes but exhausts it. Nothing escapes his eye, and everything has significance to him. Fashionable, commercial, literary, aristocratic, official, and common life, are all the same to him. He has surveyed and fathomed them all, and you have only to read him to know their depth and bearings. He is neither overawed by kings nor repulsed by beggars.

'A man's a man for a' that.'

His versatility is miraculous; his knowledge is universal. He is equally at home in the parlor and in the kitchen, the palace and the pothouse, the castle and the cot, and he has not merely described but daguerreotyped them all. He states a principle more clearly than Cousin, generalizes better than Lamennais, details better than Dickens or Dumas. He has a healthier imagination than Hugo, more male vigor than Proudhon, more eloquence than Lamartine, more observation than even Thackeray. His works unite every charm. The pictures of Claude have not a more brilliant atmosphere; Rembrandt does not manage light and shade with more effect; Rubens is not a more gorgeous colorist; Raphael is not more exquisitely delicate; Turner, of our own times, is not more original and startling. In a word, as I said, Balzac is the Shakespeare of novelists."

"And Thackeray ?"

"Well, you may call him the Molière. But all this is tedious. Some day you shall tell me about your gods. I have a deity or two myself in America. But tell me, how do you like your crib? I call this my nest. Stiff, No. 54, calls his a den; while Hogg, No. 30, next floor below, I was disgusted to find chalked on his door one morning, with an appropriate illustration, 'The Sty!' The *cafés* down stairs go by the name of Billiard Traps, and No. 30 calls the *table d'hote* the Trough."

"You appear to be a fast set, here."

"Rather; but tell me, what do you think of your crib? You'll find it rather cold with that brick floor, and they sell fuel in this town by the pound, like bread and potatoes."

"I like my crib as you call it, or my sanctuary as I mean to make it, first rate. It looks cosy. Not so cozy as yours, though, with its carpeting of French novels, its clutter of newspapers, and the glorious confusion which seems to reign here. By-the-way, what a curious coal fire you have there! Why don't you have a grate?"

"I don't want one. Grates are not much used in this country, except in the houses of the grate—if you'll excuse a small pun. And I've got so used to the French system of fire-making, that I shouldn't know what to do with such a machine if I had it."

"What is that system, pray?"

"I'll tell you. You notice that my fireplace, which is small and deep like yours, is nearly full of ashes. These serve to throw out the heat. Isidore (that's the servant on this floor, for each floor has its servant who 'does the rooms') threw in about a bushel of ashes the morning I came here. You must get him to do the same for you. The plan is, then, first to make a small wood fire, then put on a good lot of bituminous coal, which is the only kind except charcoal used in this country —"

"By-the-by, lest I forget it, what do wood and coal cost in Paris? You say they are sold by the pound."

"I pay three francs per hundred weight. Wood and coal are the same price. You can get supplied in the house. They generally bring you a hundred weight at a time, and, which is the best of all, put it down in the bill. Isidore 'll manage that for you."

"Thanks; and now go on with the fire, if you please."

"Well, the wood and coal make a very hot fire, and soon heat the room. When the wood
burns out, the coal settles down upon the ashes, and being supported in its place by the iron-dogs and firestick, simmers slowly away, and, with a little feeding, keeps up a good temperature all day. It doesn't make the tidiest fire in the world, but what does a bachelor care about that, when there are no women about? Who wants a fireplace to look like a boudoir? Think of our polished grates in England, hemmed in with an iron fence, and having a gawky poker and shovel by the side, looking like a couple of armed sentinels, in brass caps and steel breast-plates, standing there to keep you at your distance! And fancy those infernal subterranean furnaces over which the women stand by the hour, getting themselves puffed out with hot air, like balloons, as if the dear creatures weren't aerial enough by nature? For my part, I want a fire that I can get at, and poke, and 'put my foot in' if I wish; but if I try that at home, I raise the house about my ears. Look at that pile of hot ashes! Doesn't it do your soul good? Isn't it hearty, and hospitable, and homely? I tell you what it is, Sir, I never knew what it was to be comfortable till I got perched up in this nest. And yet my folks are everlastingly writing me to come home! And now, confound 'em, they've cut off supplies, and mean to starve me out! They little know the resources of the *Hotel Corneille*, when they try that game. Why, I could stand a two years' embargo here !"

At this point in the conversation in walked Isidore, who informed Monsieur 53 that he had just brought up the *sac de nuit* of Monsieur 53 *bis*. Here Books revealed to me that when a man entered his name on the register of the hotel, he left it there, and degenerated at once into a number. "I, for instance," he added, "am no longer Mr. Books here, except among my intimate friends, but am Monsieur 53 at your service—and you may consider yourself henceforth as Monsieur No. 58 *bis*, thus having a longish name after the manner of your countrymen."

"What do you mean by after the manner of my countrymen ?"

"Why I mean that nine out of ten Americans whom I have known have at least one middle name, while we English as a rule—except among the nobility, whom I never count—have none. Thus, our good old Saxon name John Brown becomes John Washington Brown or John Adams Brown with you, while John Smith becomes J. V. C. Smith, perhaps; for among your other peculiarities, you often mention a person's first names by initials, which we never do; hence we hear you speak of N. P. Willis, R. W. Emerson, G. P. Morris, W. H. Prescott, etc., and are left to guess what the initials stand for. Still I have observed that most of your great men have no middle names, as for instance, George Washington, John Adams, James Madison, Patrick Henry, Daniel Webster, Henry Clay, Edward Everett, Washington Irving, George Bancroft."

"Yes, and you might add, though I never thought of it before, Benjamin Franklin, Thomas Jefferson, James Monroe, Andrew Jackson, Zachary Taylor, Millard Fillmore, Franklin Pierce, Washington Allston, Hiram Powers, Rufus Choate, Richard Hildreth, Davy Crockett, and so on down to Sam Houston, and your humble servant !"

I now retired to my sanctuary, to perform the simple operation of unpacking, and preparing for dinner. My first disappointment was in finding a short supply of water and learning that the article soap was not in the bond, which, by-the-way, reminded me of a circular issued in 1848 by the Paris Congress of Peace, calling upon every member to "bring his own soap." Revisiting No. 52 to make up the deficiencies of the moment, I was told by Books that nothing surprised a Frenchman more than an English man's consumption of soap and water. "Why," said he, "the idea of a man's washing himself more than once a day seems to the people here preposterous. The other day Isidore rushed to my room in a great rage, exclaiming, 'Good heavens! what a dirty people you English are! There's No. 54 and No. 66 wash themselves three times a day, the pigs, as if a garcon had nothing to do but to fetch water.' And yet," continued Books, "Frenchmen bathe much oftener than we do, and you'll find a cheap bath-house in almost every street, with accommodations for both sexes, and every convenience except—"

"Soap!"

"Just so; and by the way, till you get set up, anything in my *cabinet de toilette*, except the toothbrush, is at your service; and, if I were you, I should lock up all my combs and brushes, for Isidore, who is a bit of a dandy in his way, and is soft just now on the dark-haired young lady with the downy lip whom you saw at the bureau, treats mine as if they were common property, like umbrellas and tobacco."

Examining what my friend called his *cabinet de toilette*, I found it to be a three-cornered deal washstand, standing like a schoolboy in disgrace, in the remotest corner of the room, and furnished with a toothbrush irregularly worn down to the ivory; a hairbrush, with the veneer curling off the back, and exposing the wire seams; half a bar of yellow soap; several black hairpins; three bottles of *pomade hongroise* for the moustache; besides numerous articles not strictly belonging to the establishment, such as a paper of tobacco, a blackingbrush, two or three pipes, a volume of Balzac, a new dicky, a bottle of ink, etc. Slicing off a piece of the soap with the dicky string, I returned to my room, and had just finished my hasty toilette, when I was startled by the clanging of the dinner-bell, and the sudden entrance of Books armed to the ears with an enormous shirt-collar, and having a miraculous bow to his cravat, which he had learned to execute that morning, for two cents, of a lad who was a professor of the art, and practised it in the next street round his right calf.

Arriving at the diningroom, which was on the ground floor at the North side of the courtyard, I found a seat prepared for me among the English at the East end of the table. Books forthwith introduced me to his circle of friends, consisting of Stiff, a Pre-Raphaelian artist; Hogg, a gentleman at large; Squills, a comic writer; Hope, a young gentleman with expectations; and Brick, a "writer of tragedies and comic almanacs." Hogg took the head of the trough, as he called it, and commenced the exercises not with a grace, which the gravity of his countenance led me to expect, but with the remark, evidently not impromptu, that he ought to have been named Cow, since he was always being called on to carve. Our dinner consisted of six courses, viz: lentile-soup, boiled beef, fried potatoes, roast mutton, green salad, and preserved prunes, each being brought on with such a parade of crockery and cutlery as to give the really moderate meal the air of a sumptuous repast. By the side of each plate was a napkin, folded tent-wise, a bottle of red wine, and about three inches of bread sliced from a ten-foot roll standing in a corner of the room, like the literal staff of life. I was told this might be considered a fair specimen of a thirty cent *table d'hote* dinner; and, as Hogg characteristically remarked, it was certainly "filling at the price." Most of the persons at the table were medical students. Their general appearance was that of earnest young gentlemen engaged, not so much in the study of medicine, as in this great question of student life, viz: if *a* represents income, and *b* expenses, while *b* stands for double the quanity of *a*, how can *a* and *b* be brought to reasonable terms? An ugly question this, refusing in any way to be solved here below skies, and causing such trouble in the world by its eternal non-solution as one does not care in cool blood to contemplate.

I know not why it is, but the French student is generally hard-up. Debt seems to be a necessity of his nature. He is, therefore, a man of expedients, and though often without a shirt, is never without a shift. His precocity in fiscal attainments borders on the miraculous.

"At eighteen years he copes with men,"

Compared with him, the shrewdest financiers in Wall street are bunglers. His skill is displayed, not so much in raising the wind, as in dispensing with it. How he trims his sails, the gods only know, but he stems the tide like a clipper, and tacks in the wind like a yacht. He winds himself up every morning, and goes through the day on tick. His mainspring is the credit system. Keeping this in order is his science. The most experienced tradesmen, with all his army of bankers, brokers, and shavers, is a child to him. His peculiar institution is the pawnbroker's. His capital is the "substance of things hoped for;" his credit, the "evidence of things not seen;" his currency, promises to pay. He is a happy combination of Micawber, Skimpole, and Mr. Biddle, and lives like John Bull on the interest of his debts. Writs serve only to light his pipe, bailiffs to arrest his ennui. The only "summons to court" he recognizes are billets-doux from his sweetheart. Let me haste to add that the compensating fact in his character is, that when he has outwitted all the sharks of the capital, he retires to the country, remits to the creatures each his pound of flesh, and devotes the rest of his life to duty, drugs, and dominoes.

(To be continued in our next.)

NUMERICAL RELATIONS OF NATURE.

Every one has observed that the leaves of some plants stand in pairs opposite each other on opposite sides of the stem. In other plants the leaves are scattered over the stem, but in these cases, also, we find them arranged in the most regular manner. Commencing with any given leaf, for instance, we shall find the next leave above this one-third of the way round the stem; the next another third, and the next another third, so as to stand exactly over the first. The series is therefore arranged in a spiral, which may be designated by the fraction 1-3. Taking another plant we shall find the next leaf above any given one two-fifths of the distance around the stem. The next will be four-fifths, the next six-fifths, and so on, each leaf moving two-fifths of the circumference further around the stem. Here is a spiral, therefore, which may be expressed by the fraction two-fifths. In precisely the same way we discover in other plants spirals which may be expressed by the fractions 3-8, 5-13, 8-21, &c. If in the case of opposite leaves first mentioned we consider each leaf as separated from the preceding by one-half the interval around the stem, we shall obtain the series of fractions 1-2, 1-3, 2-5, 3-8, 5-13, 8-21, &c. It must be kept in mind that these fractions are ascertained by actual observation. But notice the relation which exists between them. Each numerator is equal to the sum of the two preceding numerators, and each denominator to the sum of the two preceding denominators. Knowing this law, we may continue the series to any extent; and it has been so continued and fraction obtained to which plants have subsequently been found to correspond. Is all this the result of chance? Is it not rather mathematics? law? intelligence?

But the most wonderful coincidence is yet to be noticed. Neptune, the remotest planet, revolves around the san in 60,000 days: Uranus, the next, in 30,000 days, which is one-half the preceding number, Saturn, the next, in 10,000 days, which is one-third of the period of Uranus; Jupiter revolves in 4,000 days, which is two-fifths of the period of Saturn. And so we go on through the system, and find a law regulating the revolutions of the planets, which is identical with that which determines the arrangement of leaves upon the humble stem of a plant. This wonderful law is so exact and uniform in its application that, before the discovery of the planet Neptune, the botanist in his garden could have predicted its existence and place in the heavens with greater precision than the French astronomer in his observatory. Moreover, an examination of this series of fractions renders it impossible that any planet should exist exterior to Neptune, though more may exist within the orbit of Mercury. Astronomers will therefore please take notice and not be found planet hunting in the deserts of space beyond the orbit of Neptune—*Prof. A. Winchell.*

ON THE DEATH OF THE TEMPERANCE MOVEMENT.

The Temperance Movement is dead. During its life it accomplished at least one good thing. It secured for us all the right *not* to drink. Meanwhile it left the right to drink intact. In other words, it failed to accomplish a very foolish thing which it proposed, and accomplished a very wise thing which it did not propose. Its famous axiom that wines and distilled spirits are slow poisons, turned out to be so true, that they were found to be the slowest poisons in the world, and, therefore, not fit articles for legislative proscription. Its attempt to have everybody excommunicated from the Church who drank or sold intoxicating liquors was, of course, unsuccessful. The Church never cared anything about the matter, and never did anything about it till it was compelled to, and then it did it badly, and at once repented of it.

The Movement finally went into politics, where, of course, it made a fool of itself, besides making fools of a great many people who ought to have known better, and knaves of a great many more who did know better.

It then, after a protracted and painful illness, died a violent though not unnatural death, and went to its grave unattended and unnoticed, if not

"Unwept, unbonored, and unsung."

Probably all the other" Movements" will soon follow. Somehow, the age seems pretty much resolved to do its own moving. It is more and more inclined to look upon all organized and official attempts to move it, with suspicion. When what Carlyle calls "the Spouting Wretches" order it to "move on," it refuses, like the mule of an age it is, to budge an inch. Or, if it budge at all, it budges in disgust round a corner, out-o'-sight, and when the spouters have spouted themselves hoarse, they find it leagues and leagues ahead of them. What the law of its progress is, no one has been able, as yet, to define.

Now it goes up, up, up,

and

Now it goes down, down, down,

but, on the whole, it goes up oftener, or further, than it goes down, and nobody can possibly tell how or why. *Tant mieux.*

The worst of Movements is that, when they move at all, they move in such funny little circles that it makes one dizzy to look at them. The Movers themselves don't think so, for they imagine that they are traversing and moving the universe. This, however, we like, for it makes them amusing, at least. This, with their tragic aspect when they get excited (presenting one of the most moving spectacles we can think of), is one of their redeeming features.

But, to return to the late Temperance Movement. One of the greatest mistakes it made was that of supposing that because three-fourths of the men who commit crime drink spirits, that therefore three-fourths of the men who drink spirits must some day or other commit crime. We had this dinged into our ears so often that at one time we really believed it. It sounded so plausible. We got rid of the delusion, not by observing that three-fourths of the spirit-drinkers did not commit crime (for this fact might, perhaps, have been plausibly disposed of), but by observing that three-fourths of those who *did* commit crime were also in the habit of drinking tea, and not only that but coffee, and in some exceptional and melancholy cases, *water,*—a little statistic which seemed to us to knock the logic of the Movement square in the head; for if three-fourths of all the criminals in the world were in the habit of drinking tea, or coffee, or water, it followed, of course (reasoning Movement-wise), that it was this fact which made them criminals; and yet not even the Movers themselves would venture on such an assertion.

Another and more serious mistake the Movement made, was in assuming that the most natural drink of man was cold water. Or, was it hot water? We forget for the moment, but the matter is not important. It was water at any rate.

Now, the argument against such a theory, like the argument against Grahamism, is simply and conclusively this: *The human palate thinks otherwise*; and the human palate being a divine and not a human institution, has as much right to be gratified as the human ear or the human eye. Man was not made to live by bread alone, nor by bread and water alone. His palate, which, in its natural state, is the only competent judge in the matter, calls for an immense variety of food, and an immense variety of drinks, while the earth on which we live is so well adapted to the palate as to supply in abundance everything that it desires. In fact a scientific analysis of the eatable products of the earth would be a scientific analysis of the human palate, and *vice versa.*

This settles the matter. The objection that the palate may crave bad liquor, or bad food, amounts to nothing. The only point is, that the universal human palate demands something else besides bread and water; and that since the beginning of the world it has had a longing for the juice of the grape, for the flesh of birds and animals, and for countless other varieties of food which simple Nature, unaided by Art, could never provide, any more than she could provide painting and sculpture for the eye, or decent music for the ear. For Nature, after all, is a small affair without Man.

To limit the human palate, then, to two or three articles of food or drink, would be to deny the wisdom of the Creator, and scout at His whole scheme of creation. The truth is that He designed forman—for man here upon the earth, and for man *now,* and at all times,—an amount and an intensity of happiness which gloomy ascetics, and gloomier theologians, reasoning from their own narrowness and stinginess of soul, have never been able to conceive. And a large part of this happiness—not the largest part, perhaps, nor the most important, but still a large and a very important part—it was intended we should receive through the medium of the much-abused, though God-created senses. Through the sense of hearing we were to have music with all its exquisite delights; through the sense of sight, we were to have the varied beauties of nature and of art; through the sense of smell the most delicious perfumes, natural and artificial; through the sense of taste the richest and most delicate fruits, wines, viands, etc.:—the evident intention being that the senses, like all the other faculties of man, should be not only *useful* but *pleasurable*; in other words, that they should be a constant source of enjoyment to him. Nature, herself, teaches us this beautiful lesson by ministering to them in a thousand delicate, though for the most part unappreciated ways. She does this, especially, for the sense of taste, though she takes the whole sisterhood of the senses under her charge, and encourages them by her example to revel in beauty and in luxury, and thus accomplish their legitimate and beneficent destiny.

Dramatic Feuilleton.

BURTON'S THEATRE.—MISS VANDENHOFF AND HER PLAY.

I went to Burton's theatre one cold night this week, and saw a corpse. A dramatic Lazarus risen from the dead, clothed in the cerements of the grave, and galvanised by some occult power of stage-magnetism into a spasmodic life. This solemn and funereal resuscitation was performed to an appropriately mournful audience of some three or four hundred citizens, none of whom seemed quite certain whether they had obtained admission to a sarcophagus or a theatre. The remains which were exhumed on this occasion, consisted of a five-act play, entitled, in the language of the flesh, "Woman's Heart," and said to be by Miss Vandenhoff. I had hoped never again to see any such galvanized monster. I had hoped that the five-act play in blank verse had been safely deposited in the tomb of the Capulets, and the door of the sepulchre sealed and shut down on it forever and ever. I was unhappily mistaken. "Woman's Heart" is as colorless, as bloodless, as stiff and as corpse-like as any of its long deceased kindred that used to afford our correct grandmothers that decorous and emotionless amusement in which alone it was in those times genteel to indulge. The following plot of the piece I extract from the Daily Times, promising that the poetic fervor of the youthful critic of that journal has induced him to paint the cheeks of the mummy until he fancies it a living being.

On the rising of the curtain we are introduced to a sculptor's studio; statues are placed round the room; on a table is a block of marble just beginning to feel the breath of genius, and flush into life; and on a sofa, reclining in a graceful drapery, and watched by the intense eyes of the enraptured artist, we see a tall, poetic-looking girl, with an expression on her countenance as if she listened with her heart as well as with her ears. That is Isolina, a foster-sister of Angiolo, the artist—his model, his all—in-all, his bride. Their language is charming, from its purity and affection; her voice is soft and low—an excellent thing in woman—but her motions have a strange constraint. She puts out her arms uncertainly: she stretches forth her feet searchingly; and, with a full, winning trustiness, places her hand on Angiolo's shoulder, for she is blind. But all other senses are sharpened to a painful degree. She feels his coldness in a single tone of his voice, detects the waning of this sympathy that once existed between them in the slightest motion of his form, and inquires with those sightless eyes, and scarcely in articulate words, what can be the reason of the change? He offers the affection of a brother—ambition has entered his heart, and he has cast her off, selfishly, at the instigation of his pride. One interview she resolves to have, and finds her way to the magnificent palace, in which the sculptor now pursues his art. Fatigued by her walk, she lies down upon the sofa and falls asleep. Angiolo comes in; his great friends visit him; the beautiful girl is discovered, and makes an impression on the sovereign. Two years now pass. Her father, the Marquis Albrezzi, has recognized her. The touch of science has removed the cloud from her sight, and she is now the noblest heiress in the land. Her hand is petitioned for by the Prince. She rejects his suit, but agrees, at her father's request, to sit for her portrait. She has never seen Angiolo. The Marquis makes it imperative on the part of the painter not to speak, and a very pretty scene in dumb-show takes place. Envy has been at work against the painter; he is arrested and hurried off to prison. She follows him to his dungeon, obtains his pardon from the Duke, and the Marquis is reconciled to the nuptials.

It is with regret that I have to point out the exaggerations of this generally excellent critic, but I find it to be about the shortest way of criticizing Miss Vandenhoff's play, to invert the picture furnished by the *Daily Times*. In the first place, when the curtain rises on the sculptor's studio, we do not see upon his table "a block of marble just beginning to feel the breath of genius, and flush into life." We see a two-shilling plaster cast, half concealed with what seems to be a strip of bed-ticking, and presenting no indication whatever of "flushing into life"

That the two persons discovered are *Angiolo* and *Isolina,* I admit, but that she is his (*Angiolo's)* "all-in-all, his bride," I respectfully beg leave to deny, for they are not married until the fifth act, and we are as yet in the first. As to what an "all-in-all" is, intrinsically, I have not the remotest idea.

Can it be possible that the critic of the *Daily Times* is a Londoner, and when he wrote "all-in-all," meant "half-and-half?"

Without pursuing any further what may seem to be a vein of hypercriticism, I will come at once to the performance. Miss Vandenhoff played the character of Isolina, the blind girl, and Mr. Swinbourne (a gentleman fresh to the New York boards) that of Angiolo, the sculptor. The rest of the characters are of no interest, and demand no notice.

Miss Vandenhoff is a lady with a classically-turned head, and an uneven voice, in which the low notes are hoarse, and the remainder vary between breaks and lisps. She acts with a certain intelligence which is not without its effect; but whether it arose from the slimness of the audience, and consequent lack of magnetic support, or whether her histronic powers were really limited, I only know one thing and that is, that her performance was feeble, and resembled rather the effort of a tolerable amateur, rather than that of an artist. This young lady in the first place has very evidently never studied the blind people as a class, or, if she has studied them, has failed to learn that placidity and not pain, is the normal expression of a human being addicted with loss of sight. The blind do not suffer from the deprivation of which they are the victims. They are alive to outward impressions, because impression is, so to speak, their life, but that eagerness which they manifest to catch those subtle physical manifestations does not embody itself in contractions of the facial muscles to such an extent as that practiced by Miss Vandenhoff. During the continuance of the misfortune with which she is supposed to be afflicted, she presents the appearance of a person who is suffering from the effects of some powerful medicine, rather than of one who has supplied the loss of one sense by the extension of the others. The success of "Woman's Heart" as a play might be secured if the delicate and difficult interpretation necessary to its elimination were fulfilled. The play as a play has no action. People in tunics and feathers, who call one another "Prince" and "Marquis" without any apparent reason, for they do not resemble in any way princes or marquises; these people, in feathers and tunics, come in in a lugubrious manner, with an invisible speech each, which they pull out of invisible pockets, and deliver in an abstracted manner, as if they couldn't help it. Having done this, they severally retire in turn to the back of the stage, or retire altogether. The latter proceeding, I regret to say, being the least frequent. This speechifying without any approaches to action, lasts through three acts of the piece, and the fourth act commences where the second should begin.

The sculptor Angiolo is apparently a most insane individual. A couple of seedy-looking courtiers enter his studio, and give him a few orders for statues, whereupon he immediately commences to tear hair, to expand his chest, to look wildly at the gallery, perform those other antics which are consecrated to violent emotion on the stage. Do Mr. Palmer, of Albany, and Mr. Powers, at Florence, behave so when they receive an order from Mr. Peter Cooper, or Mr. William B. Astor? Do they strike attitudes, and swear in language composed entirely of words of six syllables, that they will never forsake art, but that she will always be their mistress? I have known some sculptors, since eminent, in their poorer days, and I am certain that the first thing they would have done on being the recipient of such piece of good fortune as Mr. Angiolo, would be to immediately ask an advance of $100 from their patron, and go and give a supper with the money to their friends.

But I cannot spare the space to be funny or critical any longer, that is, always supposing I have been either. "Woman's Heart" is a stupid play of a *genre* long since deceased. Miss Vandenhoff has nothing striking or original as an actress about her, and her assistant, Mr. Swinbourne, is as conventional as the play.

WALLACK'S THEATRE.—THE REVIVAL

I witnessed an evening rehearsal of the Merchant of Venice at this theatre, on Wednesday evening. As it will have been produced before this article is published, I cannot, of course, offer any criticism on the performance, a logical deduction that even Bunsby would appreciate. I cannot, however, refrain from saying that I was delighted and surprised by the extraordinary efforts made by the management in the getting up of this piece. The walls of this little theatre seemed, on a sudden, to have crumbled away, and long, dark canals, of Venetian aspect, to usurp Mercer street. The scenery, so far as I saw it, was admirable; in particular, I may mention the place of the Lions, which does Mr. Isherwood infinite credit. The Carnival scene was wild and picturesque, the *toku-boku* tone of which was enhanced by the very characteristic music of Mr.
Cooke.

Mr. Wallack, himself, in the few passages in which he at all let himself out, proved that he has still retained, through so many months of sickness, that marvellous voice, which even now has no equal on the stage. I purpose next week to treat at length of this Shakespearian revival, which promises to be one of the most important dramatic productions of the season, both as regards historical research, and excellence of *mis en scene.*

"UNA VOCE PORKO FA."

The following extract is given intact from the Paris *Figaro*; but whether it is a pigment or a figment, I cannot undertake to say. There is, it seems to me, an excellent opportunity for Mr. Ullman to accuse the editors of the lively French paper from which I quote, of not living luxuriously:

Autre inscription. Ce n'est pas, cette fois, sur une pierre tumulaire, elle est tracée au—des—sus d'une boutique, à Rome, la ville des papes et de M. Edmond About.

PICCOLOMINI PIZZICAGNOLO

Padre della celebre cantante

C'est-à-dire Piccolomini, charcutier, père de la célèbre cantatrice.

Cette inscription; relevée par un de nos amis, M. G..., termine à tout jamais la discussion pendante sur l'origine de la Dame aux Camellias.—Les uns la faisaient descendre d'un pape, d'autres la faisaient remonter à un charcutier,—Les charcutiéristes avaient raison.

RICHMOND IN THE FIELD.

They keep a poet, it seems, at the South. I had thought that Mr. Ricbard B. Yeadon, of South Carolina, had monopolized all the Austral bunkum, but the literary gentleman of the Richmond Theatre, Virginia, uses up that eloquent lackey of the Bonnerian and Ledgerian Everett. Observe in the following bill—which is a programme of performance at Richmond, on an evening during the present month—with what luscious eloquence he ushers in the star of the night. *Voila!*

ENGAGEMENT OF THE FAR-FAMED AND GIFTED TRAGEDIAN,

MR. J. W. WALLACK,

Who will have the honor of making his first appearance, in two years, on

MONDAY EVENING, NOV. 2,

IN HIS EXTRAORDINARY AND FORCIBLE IMPERSONATION OF THE

Iron Mask!

A performance, so made up of emotion, so vital with the sentiment and action of awful suffering, expressed with a power so vivid, that from the hidden

ARCANA OF NATURE!

MR. WALLACK appears to have wrested the knowledge of rendering

GRIEF INCARNATE

Amid the varying standards of histrionic excellence, the safest and most reliable is that erected upon the ever truthful

Impulse of Sympathy

By which Mr. WALLACK'S personation has been decreed all over the country, a power and truthfulness,

NEVER EXCELLED!

Attested in the thrills of horror, the exclamations of grief, swelling frequently into audible sobs; the irrepressible tear suffusing the eyes alike of "brave-hearted men," and

MERCY-CREATED WOMEN,

And the marked sympathetic sensation of sorrow, which, night after night, his masterly performance awakens, will be presented this evening, after careful rehearsals, and with a powerful distribution of characters. This great Play has been received in

EVERY CITY

With the greatest applause, and performed in London, when first produced, by Mr. WALLACK, at his Theatre, upwards of &c., &c., &c.,

Of what nature can be the private life of the man who composed such a bill? Supposing his name to be Jones—which is as good a name as any other—does he of mornings, when shaving is necessary, demand of Mrs. Jones 'the saponaceous material wherewith to perform his matutinal tensorial operations?" Is a coat with him anything less than a garment, and are boots anything humbler in phrase than "cordovan encasements for the pedal extremities?" I should like to hear the author of the above document demand nutriment of an Irish waiter at a restaurant. Would not that functionary look aghast? What would a porterhouse steak become in the mouth of so polysyllabic a person? The college of medicine would shiver at the scientific accuracy with which he would demand the anatomical dissection of the bovine animal.

Whoever the author of the bill that I quote may be, I strongly advise the enterprising Mr. Bonner, of the *Ledger,* to engage him. With so strongly-marked and picturesque a style of literary composition to assist, I think there would be no fear of Mr. Everett's creating any decline in the circulation of that profitable sheet.

I may as well mention before concluding, that which the gentleman of the Richmond Theater forgot to mention, viz: that it is not Mr. J. Wallack whom they announce in such grandiloquent style, but Mr J. W. Wallack, *junior.*

Fitz James O'Brien.

NEW YORK DECEMBER 18, 1858

A NEW PORTRAIT OF PARIS: PAINTED FROM LIFE.

"Paint me as I am".—Cromwell.

"Now being from Paris recently.
This fine young man would show his skill."
Holmes.

BY HENRY CLAPP, JR.

CHAPTER VIII.

Concluded.

The young gentlemen of the Hotel Corneille were evidently philosophers, who had one and all arrived at the conclusion that if the old enemy, Two and Two, wouldn't yield and make Five, it was no fault of theirs. In the

"—Good time coming, boys,"

when, according to the philosophy of Josiah Warren, (who is in no way connected with "Ten Thousand a Year,") everything shall be had for nothing, while cost shall be the limit of price, and all trade shall increase and multiply *pro rata,* the old multiplication table will, doubtless, be revised to meet the new emergency, and Two and Two doing business on a larger scale will make Five or Fifty as easily as they now make Four.

But while I have been digressing in this way, Course No. 1 of our dinner has been served, and Fejux (a comic waiter) is at my elbow, wondering if the new Monsieur will ever finish his potage. Now, as the said Monsieur, being no Esau, never could see the philosophy of drenching a famished stomach in a hot bath of lentiles and water, he condescends to enlighten Master Fejux on this point, and gladly exchanges the bath in question for a cubic inch or so of boiled beef. Moreover, if it would not be too gross a violation of the rules of the house, he thanks the said Fejux, in a particularly silver tone of voice, to so far anticipate course No. 3, as to serve him with a—small potato. The comic servant complies with the request as if he were anticipating the course of nature, and laying out the poor vegetable before its time, stares at the Monsieur as if he had ordered a boiled sausage.

The dinner passed off, as a Frenchman would say, "without incident." But a stranger would have inferred that the students, when they arrived at the dessert, were either in hot blood, in hot water, or in-sane. Above the music of knives and forks, resounding like a chorus of "bones" through the hall; above even the cymbalesque accompaniment of a thousand clattering plates; were heard a hundred shrill voices yelling, now in discordant unison, anon in terrific solos, as if some question of overwhelming importance had suddenly sprung up, and it was a matter of life and death; 1st, that every man present should lay out his utmost nature upon it; 2d, that no one should on any account agree with his neighbor; and, finally, that every one should treat it as a matter involving his everlasting *parole d'honneur*. What the apparent *emoute* was about, I had no idea, and to my surprise Books and his companions, who were earnestly engaged discussing the matters immediately upon the table, paid no attention to it. At last, however, when a long cadaverous young gentleman, sporting a snub-nose, a split upper lip, and cracked spectacles, flew up from his seat like a rocket, and throwing his arms about as if they were signal boards, delivered a violent harangue that threatened to split his other lip, and make a shipwreck of his whole countenance, I ventured to ask my right-hand man, the Chairman, what all the fuss was about. Hogg suspended his more congenial functions for a moment, and turning his attention to the speaker, (who had just carried away his spectacles,) informed me presently that the tremendous subject under discussion was, which of two singers neighboring Cafe Concert, M'lle Blanche or M'lle Sainte was the more beautiful.

I breathed more freely.

"Apropos of the *Cafe Concert,*" said Hogg, finishing his second *supplement* of apricots, "suppose we take your friend there this evening, and show him the lions."

"Capital idea,"cried the Pre-Raphaelite Stiff. "I intended to go there this evening to see M'lle Blanche. I mean to use her as a Madonna in my new picture for the exhibition."

"The devil you do," exclaimed Briggs, "she's got a face like an owl."

"That's why I like it," rejoined Stiff, "this painting all women as birds of Paradise is ridiculous. I go in for nature, and the best women I know of in the world are the most ugly. The charm of a woman, under favor of Mahomet, is in her soul, not in her face. Her beauty is not a nose and lip affair, but a matter of expression. Regular features are all humbug. Look at George Sand: look at Miss Martineau: look at Miss Cushman: look at Mrs. Stowe."

"I never knew an ugly man nor an ugly woman in my life," said Books, "who didn't have that argument by heart. There's my cousin Sally Pamphlet, who had the small-pox two years ago, and has been pitied for it ever since—she raves about beauty of expression from morning to night. I don't blame her for it, poor woman, for there's a method in her madness. And I don't blame Stiff, either, for the same reason. But they both know better; and depend upon it when a woman compliments anybody—any man I should say, for women don't compliment each other—on his 'fine expression,' or his 'interesting looks,' or his 'intelligent face,' she is either satirizing him for his ugliness, or making a special plea for her own. That horrid old maid, Miss Gratacaps, who has a box over there in the 'Quarter of the Respectables,' said to me that she liked Hogg, 'because his features were so picturesque.' As for you, Stiff, I don't like your system. It may be Pre-Raphaelian for ought I know, but it is certainly preposterous. As for being true to Nature, excuse me, but that's all bosh. Nature is always true to herself. She has her whims like other folks, and at times is a great wag, but she is always consistent, and never puts a jewel of gold in a pig's snout."

"That may be," interrupted Hogg, "but she puts pearls in oysters."

"I know, but she doesn't cast them before swine, nor suffer even oysters to wear them. As for the notion that good women are generally ugly, it hasn't been my experience. The best women I have known have been the most beautiful. Homely women are generally bad-tempered. Ugliness curdles the heart. Strong-minded women, whom Stiff admires so much, are ugly enough, no doubt. They make capital of their ugliness. They seek to make up in eccentricity what they lack in grace, and despise personal charms as a vagabond despises personal property. Lacking womanly delicacy, they affect manly energy, and even manly apparel. Denied the crown of beauty, they covet the breeches of authority. Deliver me from strong-minded women !"

Here Squills interposed, exclaiming, "Come, a truce to discussion, gentlemen. You are all right and all wrong. As for me, I'm neither a Pre-Raphaelite nor a Post-Raphaelite, but a kind of cross between the two, an Ideal-Realist, just as my expectant friend Hope is a real Idealist. My theory is, that beauty is a matter of moral organization. Fine soil, fine flowers. Even the features are subject to this law, and change both form and expression with the development of the mind. It isn't the shape of the head which determines true character, as Professor Feeler would have you believe, but the character which determines the shape of the head. The idea that

'From the body soul to form doth take,'

is sheer absurdity. If you come to features, the finest in man or woman is the mouth, the proper line of which is the true line of beauty; and the mouth being the most susceptible of organs, is as true to the movements of the soul as the aspen leaf to the breath of heaven. No woman of character will fail to have this charm, and every woman of superior refinement, true genius, or lofty devotion, will have it in great perfection. Moreover, there is a certain atmosphere of beauty constantly exhaling from a pure character, which invests the other features with a halo of loveliness, and makes the whole face irresistibly fascinating. I might add that all the features are more or less susceptible to change, and that, not only from internal development, but from external circumstances. A husband and wife, for instance, often come to resemble each other strikingly, and so do intimate friends."

"Enough of your long-winded theories, for the present," squealed Hogg, who was getting impatient for his coffee, "but some day, Stiff, we'll all go to your study and see your Twelve knock-knee'd Apostles. I saw your St. John the other day, by the way, on the sly. Where was the fun, my dear fellow, in making him bandy-legged like yourself?"

"Why, confound it, Hogg, most men are bandy-legged. You can't argue a dog's hind leg straight, as the proverb says.

'I take folks as I find 'em,
And paints 'em as they are.'"

"Come along," said Books, "there's no arguing with Stiff. He's so infernally true to Nature that I wonder if he don't cut Art entirely. Why he can't paint a tree that hasn't got a fungus on it as thick as his head."

"True," said Brick, "he's put a rosebush in his Garden of Eden, every leaf of which is worm-eaten. But let's be off to the Concert. I want to see M'lle Sainte. I intend to introduce her in the character of a Cheap Model in my new tragedy, *The Artist in Distress*, of which, by the way, Stiff is to be the hero.

"I should think you, too, had the Pre-Raphaelite fever," said Hogg, "judging from your selections of characters. If you don't look out, Stiff, I'll paint you for Judas."

"Don't be alarmed," rejoined Stiff, "I have taken you for that character, and used Brick in my Descent from the Cross, as the repentant thief."

Here Squills insisted upon our immediate adjournment, saying that he intended to write a fancy sketch of the Concert and its characters for the *Household Words*.

"The more fool you," remarked Brick, "for you'll never get the credit of it. Nine people out of ten suppose that Dickens himself writes everything that appears there, and, for an apostle of author's rights, he is about the coolest swindler I know of. As for you Americans," he added, turning to me, "you deliberately collect the best articles of his contributors, and publish them in book form as 'Works by Charles Dickens.'"

I had to plead guilty to the charge, but endeavored to offset it with the fact that the English had recently acted even more dishonestly, in publishing a series of books by Peter Farley, which Peter had never seen.

"True," cried the Englishmen, in chorus, "but two wrongs never made a right," and continuing the discussion through all the phases of Copy-right and Copy-wrong, we rose from the dinner-table, and, on Squills' motion, adjourned to the *Cafe Concert*, to finish the matter over our mocha and music.

HOLIDAY GIFTS,

At the Old Established Bookstore,

757 BROADWAY (LATE OF 645),

Where may be purchased

CHILDREN'S PICTURE BOOKS,

Story Books for Boys and Girls, Indestructible, Moveable Pictures, and every variety of Toy Books;

HANDSOMELY BOUND GIFT BOOKS,

Standard Works and Illustrated Editions of the Poets;

BIBLES AND PRAYER BOOKS;

Writing Desks of superior make, Chessmen, Boards, &c., &c.; Children's Games, Backgammon, &c., &c.;

ALL AT LOW PRICES.

Card Engraving and Printing;

VERY SUPERIOR STATIONERY.

Subscriptions received for all the Magazines and THE SATURDAY PRESS.

MILLER, MATHEWS & CLASBACK,

757 BROADWAY, corner of Clinton Place.

[To be continued next week.]

NEW YORK DECEMBER 25, 1858

THREE OF A TRADE,

OR, RED LITTLE KRISS KRINGLE

The city was muffled in snow, and looked as calm, and pale, and stately, as a queen in her ermine robes.

It was night, and the tinkling of innumerable sleigh-bells made the frosty air musical. The sleighs themselves sped silently through the streets, painted blackly against the white snow as they passed, like so many phantoms winging their way to a festival on the Brocken mountain.

It was late, for the corner groceries were shut. The last draught of poison had been drained over the counter. The last victim had staggered home to his trembling wife. The red, unwholesome light that flared over the door had been extinguished, and the bar-keeper was snoring in his bed behind the flour barrels.

In the bleak shelter afforded by the projecting wooden awning of one of the corner-groceries in Greenwich street, close to where that thoroughfare nears the river, and huddled up against the side of the large coal-bin that stood hasped and padlocked on one side of the entrance, two little figures were visible in the dim glimmer of the night. Two little children they were, sitting with their cold arms embracing each other, their chill cheeks pressed together, and their large weary eyes looking out hungrily into the blank street.

Down by the wharves they saw the tall slender masts of ships piercing the sky like the serried lances of some band of gigantic Cossacks. Among the black halls a few late lights still shone, and the air rang occasionally with the voice of a drunken sailor, who from some friendly doorstep, where he had involuntarily cast anchor, chanted his experiences of a young West Indian lady of color, who rejoiced in the horticultural name

"Santa Claus paying his usual Christmas visit to his young friends," ~ Winslow Homer for Harper's Weekly, 1858

of Nancy Banana.

Presently, a mystic music seemed to fall from the arched skies upon the city. It was the chimes of old Trinity ringing the Old Year out and the New Year in. The thrilling notes of the changes following each other in measured flow, vibrated through the air like music made by the feet of marching angels. They jubilantly seemed to scale the slope of Heaven. The wild melodious clangor floated over the great silent city. Myriads of aerial Moors, clashing their cymbals, seemed to march over the house-tops. The clock was trembling on the stroke of twelve, and Time had one foot already in the territories of the New Year.

"Tip, listen to the bells," said one of the two children, that were huddled beneath the grocery-awning, speaking in a faint though clear voice, like a bell heard in a fog, "listen. It is time for Kriss Kringle to come."

Tip's cold little lips opened and nothing issued therefrom but a low, plaintive "I'm hungry, Binnie."

"So am I," said Binnie, with a sort of far-off cheeriness, as if his heart was at a considerable distance, and could communicate only very faintly. "But, let as wait. Perhaps Kriss Kringle will bring us something nice. What would you like most Tip?"

"Coffee and cakes wouldn't be bad," said Tip, hesitatingly, as if rather afraid of the consequences if he allowed his imagination to run away with him.

"Or a plate of roast beef rare, with potatoes and peach pie," suggested the more reckless Binnie, "just such as mother used to give us on Sunday. Poor mother !"

"What are we going to do to-morrow, Binnie, to get some money?"

"Shovel snow off the stoops," answered Binnie, resolutely. "We'll go into Union Square early and ask all around at the houses whether they want the side-walk cleared. Some of 'em are sure to give us a quarter; we might make fifty cents, and then wouldn't we have a time!"

"When we were living in the country with mother what fun we used to have on New Year's," said poor little Tip, creeping up closer to Binnie, with a shiver, for the night was getting very cold, and a few large snow-flakes commenced falling straight down from the fleecy sky, white as the manna that fell in the desert, but alas! not so nutritious.

"O golly! yes. What a good mother she was to us, and what things we used to find in the old stocking that she gave us to hang up! Kriss Kringle don't come to us any more now that she's dead. I wonder if he really used to come down the chimney Tip, or if 'twas only make believe."

"I don't know," said Tip. "I watched ever so many nights, but somehow I always fell asleep just before he came, and then the things got into the stocking. I used to dream, though, that I saw him. A little man with a red coat all covered with gold lace, and a long feather in his cap, and a little sword by his side. And he used to smile at me, and say, 'Tip, will you be a good boy if I put something into the stocking for you?' and then I used to promise, and when I had promised I used to hear music sounding all through the house, a great deal finer than the music we heard when we went to the circus, Binnie; and then Kriss Kringle would take off his hat to me, and make a jump, and go clean up the chimney out of sight, like a red cricket. Ah! how cold it is Binnie, and how hungry I am. Tell us a story."

The wind arose in the North, and came down upon the city with a savage howl. The heavy snow-flakes fled before him into every angle and nook, like terrified white birds trying to hide themselves from some vast-winged, screaming falcon. They thrust themselves into the crevices of the windows, and between the slats of the green window-blinds; they got under the sills of the doors. They left the centre of the streets, and flew madly into the gutters; they huddled themselves into the dark corner where Tip and Binnie were cowering, ran up the legs of their ragged trowsers, and slid down between their frail shirt-collars and their cold little necks. It was a fierce, biting, scratching wind of prey, and poor Binnie and Tip felt his talons digging into their flesh.

Just as the pair of vagrants had drawn closer together, and Binnie was trying to stop his teeth—which began to chatter—from biting in two the thread of the story that the patient little fellow was about tell his brother, they heard a faint cry, something between a moan and a whistle, sounding close to them. Looking out into the dim twilight they beheld a dwarfish figure standing on the sidewalk, moaning and waving its arms. It seemed to be a little man about two feet high, clad in a red coat, covered with gold lace, and wearing a little cap, in which was stack a long feather, that was bent nearly horizontal by the wind. A tiny sword, about the length of a lead-pencil, dangled at his side.

"Oh! Binnie," whispered Tip, "Its Kris Kringle come again. I know him. He used to look exactly like that in my dream. I ain't afraid of him. Are you?"

"Not a bit," answered Binnie. "He looks a nice little chap. I hope he has brought us some thing."

The little man on the sidewalk seemed very uneasy. He waved his long arms continually, took off his little cap every now and then with a quick jerk, as if he were making a series of abbreviated bows to the two little vagrants, and then hopped about, moaning the same shrill and extraordinary moan.

"Blanie, I think he's cold; let us ask him to come and lie down with us and warm himself," said Tip. "You know, in all the fairy books, if you treat a fairy well, he's sure to give you three wishes."

Whatever Binnie may have thought of the suggestion of warming anything by putting it close to icicles as himself and his brother, the latter part of the speech seemed to strike him as containing a felicitious idea. So, bracing his chattering teeth as well as he could, he said:—

"Kriss Kringle, will you come and lie down with us, and we will warm you ?"

The little red-coated man made no reply to this hospitable invitation, but danced, and shivered, and moaned, and doffed his tiny cap many times in succession.

"Come, Kriss Kringle," continued Binnie, beckoning to the dwarf, "come in out of the
snow."

"Maybe he don't speak English, Binnie," suggested the imaginative Tip.

This was a new view of the case, and Binnie began to consider within himself whether, by some inspiration of the moment, he might not suddenly master the particular foreign tongue with which their new friend was acquainted, when, suddenly, the little man made a swift leap and landed right in Tip's lap.

"Why, Binnie !" cried Tip, "it's not Kriss Kringle after all; it's only a monkey!"

Sure enough it was a monkey: a poor shivering little Brazilian, with pleading eyes and soft, silky hands, and a countenance that seemed to tell of a life of sorrow. A bit of broken chain dangling from a belt round his waist told his story. The eternal organ in the street; the black-bearded, heartless Italian; the little switch that scored his back at home; the cruel pinches to induce politeness, when wondering schoolboys proffered their hoarded coppers; the melancholy pantomime of sprightly gratitude which was taught with blows, and performed in fear and trembling. Poor little runaway! Poor little vagrant! He seemed to know that he had found brothers in misfortune when he thrust his timid, silky paw in Binnie's hand, and laid his little hairy face against Tip's cold bosom.

The ohildren vied with each other in attentions to the poor little wanderer. I do believe that if Tip had an apple or a chestnut at that moment, hungry as he was, he would have given it to his red little Kriss Kringle. The boys placed him between them, and tried to snuggle him up in their tattered clothes. He clung to them as if he really loved them. His little hand found its way into Tip's shirt-bosom—if that collection of discolored tatters which he wore beneath his jacket could be called a shirt—and laid just over his heart. The poor vagrants kissed and fondled their pet; and, God help them! were almost happy for the time.

Meanwhile the snow drifted and drifted right under the shed where the vagrants lay. It began to pile itself up about them on all sides, and it clung to every projection of their persons. The air grew colder and older. The wind swooped at them under the shed—still, like the wide-winged, shrieking falcon—as if it would take them up in its talons and bear them away to its bleak nest to feed its unfledged tempests. Closer and closer the three houseless creatures drew together, until a great drowsyness fell upon them, and the sough of the storm sounded farther and farther off, and sleep and snow covered them.

Then a dream came to Binnie and Tip. Red little Kriss Kringle jumped up suddenly from his rest in their bosom, clad in the brightest finery. A wondrous white egret's plume waved in his cap, and he wore a breastplate of diamonds. His red coat was redder than the blossoms of the wild Lobelia, and his sword was hilted with gold. Then he said to the boys, "Boys, ye have been very kind to me, and sheltered me when it was cold, so now ye shall come with me to the sweet land of the South, where ye shall idle in the sunshine forever and ever !"

Then he led them down to the wharf near by, where, moored among the black hulls of the ships, they found a beautiful golden boat, so bright with many-colored flags that it seemed as if her tall masts had swept the rainbows from the sky. Fairy music sounded as the sails were set, and they sailed and sailed and sailed until they landed on the sweet Southern shore. There they found strange trees with leaves of satin and fruits of gold. Wonderful birds shot like stars from bough to bough. The rivers sang like musical instruments. From the limbs of the trees trailed brilliant tapestries of orchideous flowers, which, with their roots in the air, sucked the sunlight into their secret veins, until their blossoms were covered with the splendor of Day. Here red little Kriss Kringle led them to the foot of a huge tree covered with white flowers, and made them lie down while he fed them with fruits of a magical flavor. The sun shone cheerfully on their heads. The birds sang their pleasant songs. The huge tree rained its white blossoms on them, as they dropped off to sleep weary with delight, until they reposed beneath a coverlet of scented snow.

When the first day of the New Year dawned, and the grocer's boy came from his bed behind the flour barrels to take down the shutters, he saw a mound of snow close by the side of the coal-bin. He brought the shovel to take it away and the first stroke disclosed the three little vagrants lying stark and stiff, enfolded in each others' arms.

Fitz James O'Brien.

A NEW PORTRAIT OF PARIS: PAINTED FROM LIFE.

"Paint me as I am".—Cromwell.

"Now being from Paris recently.
This fine young man would show his skill."
Holmes.

BY HENRY CLAPP, JR.

CHAPTER IX.

THE Author Confesses to a Weakness—Grows Presumptive—Culti vates a Passion—Apologizes for being Alive—Exposes the Selfishness of Mankind—Proves himself to be a Tobacchanalian—Makes the amende honorable to the Ologists—Dismisses a Delicate Question—Describes a Coffee Concert—Finds out all about Lorettes, Grisettes, étudiantes et id etc., to the end of the Chapter.

As "most men are mortal," it may, perhaps, be safely asserted that every man has his weaknesses. I flatter myself, at any rate, to have mine, and among them is a passionate love of coffee. Presuming that a few years hence, if the world progresses at its present rapid rate, I shall be unable to procure the article except in "original packages," I am cultivating my passion for it in order that a "bag" may seem no more to me then than a pound does *now*. And if other coffee-bibbers do likewise, the blessed tribe of long faces will have the pleasure of seeing the growth of our dear berry increase under their care as fast as the profane grape, which was never before in such good hands.

I admit that the delicious Mocha is a "slow poison"—perhaps one of the slowest poisons in the world—but that is one of its charms. It is so pleasant to be poisoned without knowing it! To see whole nations slowly dying out while increasing every day in population and strength. To see men of only six mortal feet unconsciously "dying by inches," for sixty years! To be "undermining one's constitution" every hour, and yet at the end of half a century be as straight and stiff as a Norway pine!

I ask pardon of the whole physiological crew, while I confess that according to all their most orthodox doctrines, and in obedience to their most infallible calculations I ought to have died a quarter of a century ago at least; and if I had had sufficient reverence for their melancholy science, I should have done so, if only for the "good of the cause." The man who wouldn't willingly die that such a noble race might live, is as bad as the reprobate who didn't relish the idea of being damned that other folk might be saved. But mankind is so selfish!

Tobacco alone, my dear reader, killed me, according to the physiologists, before I was one-and-twenty. According to the same authority I have, for an indefinite period, "died daily," as St. Paul would say, of strong tea. In fact, most of my acquaintances, in company with myself, have figured in the indisputable statistics of mortality, and had our "funeral-baked meats" served up at Hope Chapel and the Tabernacle, (for the edification and nutrimentation of the moral statisticians wont there to assemble,) a hundred times. How to excuse oneself under such circumstances for being alive, (in the vulgar, unscientific sense of the word,) and thus to make the *amende honorable* to the numerous class of mortally offended 'ologists, is rather a delicate question, which I therefore dismiss without further notice, and return to what was to have been the theme of this chapter, namely, the Coffee Concert.

Though there were at least fifty coffee concerts in Paris, the one already alluded to was considered by my companions as the only one worth mentioning. This favorite place of amusement was about ten minutes walk from our hotel, in the direction of the river. The Concert Room was a queer multangular-shaped hall, abounding in mysterious alcoves and corners, and capable of holding from four to five hundred persons. At one end was a small stage, illuminated by a world of side-lights and foot-lights, and having a fanciful drop-curtain on which was printed:

On est pris de renouveller sa consommation a chaque entr' acts.

I saw the same notice at another place of the kind, some months afterward, which was translated into English thus:

One is requested to renew his consumption between all the acts.

There was another announcement to the effect that "all calls for repetition and all rapturous applause were expressly forbidden, and that any person violating either of these rules would be arrested by the authorities." A corp of *sergens de ville* was stationed in the room to enforce order, and also, in view of the republican tendencies of students, to officiate as Napoleonic spies.

The stage was brilliantly decorated with curious ornaments, (in the style of Louis Something,) gilded mirrors, etc. Lolling in comfortable armchairs, were half-a-score of preternatural young women, dressed and painted very much in the fashion of ballet-girls. These were the singers. Their names, in company with those of three or four performers of the less attractive sex, who were kept in the background, figured in a written programme of the evening's entertainment, hung over the door in suggestive proximity to an inviting bill of fare. Among these songtresses were—

M'lle Sainte, the "first comic," a monumental young lady in red hair and pink eyes, dressed in white, and looking in the distance like a new lighthouse;

M'lle Blanche, "second comic," a long-faced damsel

"With a fierce gray eye, and a bending beak,"

who was encased in a stiff copper-colored dress, and had the look and swing of a diving-bell;

M'lle Pauvrette, a soprano, the modestest of little women, done up in blue-figured muslin, and looking like a stack of violets;

M'lle Marie, a sentimental melodist, with roses in her hair, roses in her neck, roses in her bosom, roses round her waist, roses everywhere but on her cheeks;

M'lle Brunette, a wild aboriginal creature, with streaming black hair, and dangerous black eyes, who did the heavy tragedy, and had a deep melancholy voice, which had evidently been to sea;

M'lle Louise, a treble genius, who had seen better times, and had not quite forgotten how they looked, and who, in her white plaster-of-Paris complexion and ruby cheeks, looked like an overgrown doll; etc, etc., etc.

In front of the stage was the orchestra, consisting of a veteran performer on a very base viol, a particularly grand pianist, and a chartered corporation of fiddlers. The room was filled with about a hundred deal-wood tables, each calculated for four persons. The company consisted chiefly of students and their sweethearts, clubbed together in picturesque groups. Nearly all the men were smoking pipes, while their more fastidious companions were indulging in the milder luxury of cigarettes. After our company had secured a nice little nook of observation, and ordered each his little cup of coffee or what not; and while a suspiciously blooming young lady was trilling a melancholy song about her virtues, (*Que je juis sage*, etc.,) I asked Squills, who appeared to be specially posted up in such matters, to inform me whether the young ladies about us were the *grisettes* I had heard so much of. Delighted at such a chance to discourse upon his favorite theme (his *specialite*), he replied—

"By no means, though they are often represented to be. Their technical name is *étudiantes*, a word which is untranslatable into English, except by the term *studentesses*."

"Incipient doctresses ?" I suggested.

"Not at all. Doctresses are an American invention."

"I beg your pardon, Sir, but I am told that one branch of the medical profession here in Paris is pretty much monopolized by women."

"You mean midwifery."

"Yes. Am I right ?"

"You are; but the midwives are not called doctresses, nor do any of them practice medicine, strictly speaking. The studentesses we were talking of, are so called, not because of their devotion to study, but because of their devotion to students."

"A distinction with a difference, I should say."

"Decidedly. But let me describe the studentess: In the first place, she is what she looks to be—a fast woman. As you see, she dresses in the shabby-genteel style; hangs her bonnet over the chair, and makes herself at home; burns brandy in her coffee; (look at that one over yonder with the blue-black eyes; see her firing up the cogniac as it swims on the surface of the unctuous mocha? and flies about the room from table to table, like a bee, sipping sweets from every cup. She is a harum-scarum kind of creature—"

Harem-scarum, you mean," interpunned Hogg.

"Well, *harem*-scarum, if you prefer, though I don't think much of your joke. I cannot better describe her than by saying she is the counterpart of the fast student. The *Cafe Concert* is her Paradise."

"I should say that Prado was her Paradise," said Brick.

"You are wrong," resumed Squills, "Prado is her Exchange."

"Pray what is Prado?" I asked.

"Prado, Sir, is the fast ball of the quarter; but to go on with the *étudiante*. She has no visible means of support, and spends her mornings in bed, her afternoons at cards and billiards, her evenings here or at a ball, her nights—promiscuously. Don't call her a *femme publique,* for if she should chance to hear you, she'd box your ears, and though that might confirm you in the opinion, you would still be wrong. The *femme publique* is on the lowest round of the ladder; the *étudiante* is only half-way down. She lives in private lodgings, for which she (or some one) pays from fifteen to twenty francs per month, and she changes her quarters as often as the moon."

"I see now; she's nothing more nor less, to speak plainly, than the student's mistress."

"Not at all. The student seldom can afford such luxuries. She is the student's 'friend,' his *bonne amie*. She sews on his shirt buttons for him, ties his cravat, combs his hair, etc. He pays for her coffee and cigarettes, dances with her at Prado, and keeps her—in gloves. She is a friend to him, more or less faithful according to circumstances, as long as he is a friend to her. She is your true Mormonite, only that she makes the plurality rule 'work both ways.' The student calls her his little one, his angel, his adored, or his pig, according to the state of his brain ; and she calls him *her* little one, her deary, her cat, or her monkey, (the last term being at once the most endearing and descriptive,) according to the state of her purse. She has no claim upon him, nor he upon her; and there is no excuse on either hand, though abundance of occasion, for jealousy or recrimination. It sometimes happens that she becomes his mistress, and, in very rare instances, his wife; while cases occur once or twice a year, that when he quits Paris and returns home, she jumps into the Seiene or suffocates herself with charcoal."

"Rather a melancholy life all that, I should say."

"It would be melancholy in most any other country but this; but you see these girls have no appearance of sadness, and though there is a certain recklessness in their air, they are by no means desperate. In England or America, where society is differently constituted—chastity being the corner store, etc.—they would take to drinking and become worse than brutes. But in Paris, where chastity fills at best but a secondary place in the social edifice, they remain sober, are treated with more or less civility, and preserve a certain degree of self-respect."

"That's what most astonishes me."

"It astonished me at first; but consider who these girls are. They are the daughters of poor laborers or mechanics, and have no chance of marriage except with the prospect of certain misery, and no chance of a tolerable livelihood except by pursuing their present course, or living as *grisettes, lorettes, femmes publiques*. Most of them commenced as *ouvrieres*, then become *grisettes,* and finally *étudiantes*."

"Pray what are *grisettes* ?"

Books interposed here, and said he had that day read a little pamphlet which depicted the *grisette* to the life. "The *grisette*," he continued, "differs from the *étudiante* chiefly in this, that she earns her living. Her argument is the same. She would only aggravate her condition by marrying, and she can't support herself alone. Still she is 'cursed with a heart,' as one of them once said to me, through her tears, and has affections like other people. If she contracts a permanent union with a man, 'for better or worse,' she contracts a permanent union with 'poverty, hunger, and dirt,' and becomes in the end an object of compassion and charity. The mass of working-men are in all respects her inferiors; while the most intelligent of them adopt her own mode of reasoning, and remain bachelors. She does, therefore, the best she can. She is a maiden, and single life, with that heart of hers, would be double death; she must *love*. Then again she is an animal, and has an appetite; she must eat. Moreover, she is a woman, and has tastes; she must dress. Finally, she is human, and must do something besides work; she must play. Now as a franc a day, which is more than her average earnings, is hardly enough to pay for rent and fuel, she must either give up all idea of loving, eating, dressing, or playing, or she must have a lover who will feed, dress, amuse—in a word, 'keep' her. If she has children, why, like the *femme publique*, the *étudiante*, the *lorette*, and not a few married women, she must send them to the Foundling Hospital.

"Often this dangerous life leads to a distaste for work, and a diseased love of excitement, in which case, if the *grisette* is good-looking, adroit, and of a romantic turn of mind, she flowers into a *lorette*; if smart, fast, and of a Bohemian turn, becomes an *étudiante*; or if sensual and reckless, degenerates into a *femme publique, i. e*., a licensed prostitute.

"Horrible! But what are the characteristics of the *lorette* ?"

"The *lorette* belongs to the *Aristocracy of Easy Virtue*. Generally handsome, intelligent, intriguing, ambitions, and fascinating; and having a tolerable knowledge of human nature; she contrives by her conquests among fashionable young men to live in considerable luxury, and often to have her carriage, her opera-box, and a retinue of servants. She now and then finds some rich old fool (sometimes an Excellency from Russia or an ex-deacon from New England) who furnishes her with plenty of money, while she indulges in what she calls her caprices with younger and more attractive men (sometimes called *lorets*) to her heart's content. She is the finest-dressed woman you meet on the Boulevards, and looks down upon the *étudiante* in her straw bonnet and cheap finery, and the *grisette* in her plain cap and sixpenny calico, with haughty disdain. She resides in the quarter which takes its name, like herself, from the church of Notre Dame de Lorette, where she usually worships. She lives a dashing life, and reigns supreme at *Mabille,* the *Chateau des Fleurs,* and *Ranelagh*, which are her three favorite balls."

The conversation was here interrupted by a smart business-like woman, in the cap-and-shawl costume of an *ouvriere*, who placed upon our table a fragrant pile of bouquets, and a handful of dirty tickets, while she discharged at us a volume of bad French, (so Books called it; it was Greek to me,) which Squills translated thus: "Come, my lords, now is your time, only two sous each, and what a chance to draw the prettiest bouquet in all Paris !"

We each purchased three or four tickets; and a coral-haired young lady, at the next table, in a coral necklace, coral bracelets, coral brooch, coral ring, and coral nose, having drawn the raffle at Squills' particular request, the prize fell to that young gentleman—who described it in *Household Words*-style as "a stunning flower-garden, with a big dahlia like a *lorette* in the centre, an outside circle of violets blue as so many *grisettes*, and a brilliant parterre of roses, daisies, and pinks, as flashy as so many *étudiantes*."

"Well, Brother Squills," said Brick, who had been making a sketch of Mademoiselle Coraline in the act of drawing the raffle, with a view to his next Comic Almanac, "you are lucky at last. It's a good omen for you. But what do you mean to do with that huge nursery-bed? Do you mean to sleep on it to-night in the hope of pleasant dreams? I'll lay an egg you'll dream of Coraline, there, who is turning up her coral nose because she didn't draw it herself."

"Not I. I know her of yore. You don't catch old birds with coral. She's got a coral heart as well as a coral nose. I invited her to dine with me at Dagneaux's one day—she had a *marble* nose then—and she stuck me for a dinner of fifty francs, eating everything on the bill of fare, and drinking two bottles of wine. The capacity of these girls in the way of eating and drinking is something miraculous. I see she expects me to send the bouquet to her; but she'll be sold. Here, waiter, take these flowers to Mlle. Blanche, on the platform, with my compliments."

"Ask her, at the same time," said Stiff, blushing up to his Pre-Raphaellan eyes, "if she will honor me by accepting an ice."

"Come, now," interposed Brick, "what's the use of tormenting that poor girl? Blanche don't care a button for either of you. She's dead in love with Greenheart, the tall student from Virginia. He rooms next door to me at the Corneille, and has sent her already three *billets-doux*, and a dozen pair of gloves. There he is near the orchestra. He sits there every night. I saw her smile upon him just now. If he sees you sending bouquets to her, you'll have a chance to take pistols with your coffee to-morrow night."

"The duece I shall. Here, waiter—"

But the waiter has just returned with the message that Blanche is grateful for the bouquet, will be proud to accept the ice, presents her respectful compliments to the gallant donors, etc., etc. What could be more condescending? In a short time the fair cantatrice had an opportunity to make her acknowledgments in person; for, one by one, during the evening, the musical lady-birds flattered through the hall on a collecting tour, inviting the guests to deposit their spare coppers in a crimson velvet bag, which in France is the elegant substitute for our mahogany contribution box. Blanche, as she flew by, inclined her little head, by way of thanks, to Squills, who stroked his mustache for an hour after, with as much complacency as if he had been recognized by a queen.

The most humorous part of the evening's entertainment—aside from these episodes—was a comic song by the buffoon of the company, the object of which was to take off the peculiarities, and especially the pronunciation of the English —a song which was rendered doubly amusing by the ludicrous attempts of the singer to embroider his performance with a little Anglo-Saxon. Ridiculing John Bull is, by the way, a favorite amusement with his neighbor Crapeau—the two parties detesting each other with a heartiness which is in itself more amusing than any comedy.

But the concert is over, and we will retire; observing that, with the exception of little Pauvrette, who was neither young nor pretty, and possessed nothing to recommend her to the establishment but a sweet voice, every singer on the stage had received, in turn, her tribute of ices and flowers—to say nothing of oranges and grog—and when the lights were extinguished, was invited to a neighboring restaurant to partake of a hot supper. The neglected Pauvrette went home with her poor old mother, who was waiting for her at the door; and as the mother and child shivered their way into the cold street, the air rung with shouts of dissipation and mirth.

I should add, also, that none of the singers on leaving carried away anything more than a small nosegay; and I learned, going out, that the flower-woman generally repurchased her wares at half-price, and made them serve from evening to evening till they faded away.

As we wended our way homewards, commencing on this fact, chaffing Squills about it, and suggesting that he should introduce it into his proposed sketch for the *Household Words*, this comic young gentleman expressed his disgust by humming to an impromptu air of his own composition:

"Fol-de-rol, fol-de-rid-di-ty,
Cupid is nothing compared to cupidity."

I cannot help stating, here, that Pauvrette finally went to America by the advice of a New York resident in Paris, who told her that as soon as she learned a little English, she could make a fortune in that city as a shop-girl. The disappointment she experienced may be judged of by the following letter written to that gentleman a year and a half after her arrival:

"New York, No.— Grand-st., de 15 July, 1852.

"My Dear Monsieur: It is now 8-teen muns dat i am here in dis barbarous citè. I cannot say you vat a villain place I find it. dare is no existence here for me. De peapel is savarge. De pulpart ov de habitans is dutchmans and irishmans vit de little pox, and one duz not comprend you at orl. i placed myself in a magazine of artifisharl flour, but de dames americains has no gout, and duz not not how to lib. Dare bonnets is monstrous, and dare robes is vorn down to dare feete vich are always long and boony. da is neerla orl six feete high, dare ize is orl gra, and da orl vare specktakels, and has no boosoms. Da has de air to be rich and kommilfo, but da looks kommon orl de same, only de gentlemens has de good looks, but da orl eats tobac and drinks nottin but jew-lips. De street vich appels itself broad-way is very narrow. It is not at orl like de jolie boulevards as you did racont to me, but is very oogly and malproper. De store is in de most bad taste possible, only de hotels is very charmant. de saint neekolarse is more buteelfool dan de tulleries in Paris, but de messieurs who lib dare poots dare enorme legs up on de vindos as if dare boots, vich is nevare clean, vare for to sell. De street is orivaze fool of de omnibus vich galop orl de long ov it vid horses ov de race. it makes vary hot now, and de poor vorkmen and de orses forls doun ded on de pave like de dogs. Yesterda I found myself malade vid de heat tree times. you told me, sare, dat dare vuz no poor peaple in dis corntra, but o ! I cannot tell you how mennee i hab see in de misére. Rooms and every ting is vary deer, and de vages of de femelles is no-tin. One cannot live in his own furniture, but must go at a boredang house vare dare is no potage, nor salade, and de café is not good for de peegs. I am gorn to de tea-hater too or tree times for to distract myself, but de pieces vos not spirituel at orl, and de decorations vos orl dat is in bad gout. I dare nevare shall go again wunse moer. dare is no bals in New York, and no arcades, and no passages, and no jardins, and no barrières, and no cabinets d'aisance, and no nortin for de peapel. Orl de vorld is orkupide vid dare own affairs, dat vich I find vary sad and ègoist. One duz not find, not moar, no café concerts, and in the summaire evenings i no can imagine vot de messieurs and dames duz for to distract each oddare. de Sundays here is horrible. Orl de worl goze to meeting, and iz astonished dat i desire to pla de cards and dominoes, and fume de cigarettes. O! my deer sare, I suffare to return in Paris. I luv better die dare dan liv in dis frightful corntray. I pra you, den, sare, be generouse and envoy me a little money dat i may wunse more see my dear moddare, and i vill tank you tousan and tousan times.

"I have de honneur, monsieur, to salute you, respects eusement, vid de vatare running out of my ize.

Adieu ! Pauvrette."

[To be continued next week].

IN THE CITY.

The country is indisputably a charming place to those who like it; but it has its disadvantages to those who don't. The country is rainy and muddy in Spring, hot and insect-y in Summer, and unendurable in Winter. It is true, there is a bit of Indian Summer, run in parenthetically, at the close of the year. And this is pleasant, providing you have bright company, picturesque scenery, a *cocinero bueno*, and the prospect of returning to town before Nature begins her sensual world-cleaning and white-washing. When the autumnal pageant has passed; when ochre, and crimson, and chocolate-colored leaves are rotting under fall boughs and the trees about the house shiver and moan in the twilight, like old witches; when the wind whistles down the chimney, and upper coat sleeves; when you can no longer walk with Madamoiselle Sylvia in the moonlight; when, in short, the Indian summer has gone off in a whiff, then it is time for you to be out of the country, or into it some six feet. Don't ice-olate yourself in the arctic regions. Don't linger there for Winter to tuck you up under its white coverlid.

But the Town!

Ay, that is the place not for a day, but for all time. That we have rain and mud in Spring is not to be denied; but then we have sidewalks, and Amaryllis is particularly tempting during this period. The grace, care, and coquettishness with which she keeps her snowy drapery immaculate, are marvellous. A single glimpse of Amaryllis, as she crosses over to Stewart's, more than pays one for the moist inconveniences of bad weather. Spring in the city! You get such delicate hints of Spring! The dried up old crone of a geranium, on your window-sill, has put forth a tiny green leaf. It is not one of Nature's diminutive prodigies, and do you not pet it with sun and water? You discover a single blade of grass shooting sharply up from between two bricks in your back-yard. Would a dozen acres of meadow-land delight you more? Amaryllis has hung her canaries at the window. What shrill music they make! They wake you early in the morning, and you see Amaryllis in a distracting *robe de chambre*. And has sky-blue rosettes up and down in front and is tightened at the waist with a silk girdle. You see the five, cunning, white birds of Amarillis's right-hand feeding the noisy yellow idiots in the villa-like cages. The air is full of sweet messages from the South. You select a neck-tie of gorgeous colors. You go down town without your overcoat. You smile genially on Jones. You don't generally smile on Jones, for he lives next door to Amarillis. You are good natured; you cannot tell why. You kick a strip of lemon-peel off the curb stone. You are philanthropic, also, but you don't know why. You don't know why, indeed, until you read Miriam's meteorological observations in the *Journal of Commerce.* Miriam says the springtime has commenced. You are grateful to Miriam.

After several weeks of torturing suspicion, you conclude that Amaryllis must have gone to Nahant. She has. The fair Capulet does not take her "cue" now, and the window-scene is a failure. Biddy feeds the canaries. You are not entirely miserable, though. It is mid-summer. There is a shady side to the street; there are parks and fountains *pro bono publico;* there are Roman punches and orange ices at Maillard's, and a promenade concert at the Academy. You like music, and you spend your evenings, when you are not some- where else, at the Academy. You hear Agnes Robertson sing. She captivates you with her woman's eyes and her boy's costume. You immediately hate her husband. You do more—you forget Amaryllis. There is a maritime view from the Battery, and a salt sea-breeze at Coney Island, and certain leafy nooks over the river, where you can sip *maraschino*, or discuss your *omelette soufflée* within hearing of the rich bass voice of the City Hall bell, when it talks to the fire-men. You can hire a boat at Whitehall and float down the Narrows, or you can sweep by the Palisades in the "Thomas Powell," and catch a glimpse of the wrong side of Fred Cozzens' house, at Yonkers, and, little further up, the quaint, cocked-hat gables of Washington Irving's "Sunnyside." You can drink lager beer, and devour switzer kase, at Hoboken. You can purchase a knot of flowers at the Sibyl's Cave. What an epitome of sweet things is a bouquet! You have the grace and the goodness, the perfumes and the tints of Summer-time, for a shilling. You have the delights of meadow and woodland bound together by an ell of cherry-colored ribbon. You have a fragment of the sky, and a tangle of grass with merry red buds, such as Coleman and Shattuck like to paint; you have dews, and stars, and sunset things! You have a portable flower-garden. You can put it into your waistcoat pocket. You can give it Chloe, who has'nt gone to Nahant. Or, better still, keep it, though it fade, for Amaryllis.

The Summer solstice is over, and the temptation has returned to town. She does not, indeed, hang her canaries at the open window, and your eyes are seldom ravished by a sight of that morning robe, with the blue rosetts in front; but, now and then, when you come home rather late at night, you see the shadow of Amaryllis on the white window-curtain, and you are not entirely unhappy. Your existence becomes worth cultivating. You lounge in your lazy easy-chair, you fill your meerschaum with fragrant Oranoko, and picture to yourself the paradise that lies just the other side of that provoking curtain. Amaryllis has been to the Opera, and is robbing her heavy brown tresses of their brilliant ornaments. You can see the shadow on the curtain lifting its arms. It appears and disappears, and tantalizes you. It is unlacing something, you dont know what, but you mustn't look any more. You remember Keats's description of Madeline, as she disrobes on St. Agnes' Eve? Ten to one you repeat the lines half aloud:

"Of all its wreathéd pearls her hair she trees;
Unclasps her warmed jewels one by one;
Loosens her fragrant bodice; by degrees
Her rich attire creeps rustling to her knees:
Half-hidden, like a mermaid in sea-weed,
Pensive awhile she dreams."

You will paint some such picture. Of course you should not. But the probability is you will.

The time has come when you have to examine the thermometer to ascertain how cold you are. You are very cold when you find the quicksilver some ten degrees below zero; in fact, just twice as cold as you were before you obtained that knowledge. Your pitcher of water says *click* in the middle of the night, and you are tempted to throw your boot at it. It is something mysterious and awful to have your pitcher of water express its opinion of the weather. When you get up in the morning, you discover some very exquisite pictures on your window-panes. They are chiefly representations of polar scenery—weird, terrible, Icelandic pictures. You look at them as you dress yourself, and think of Dr. Kane.

It is Christmas time. Merry Christmas! Ah, but it used to be some twenty years ago. It was fine, then, to loiter through the crowded streets, gazing into the shop-windows—the El Dorados of fancy articles and the Australian lands of bon-bons and rock-candy. What visions you had of St. Nick., with his reindeer equipage on the house-top. You could hear the pawing of the silver hoofs! Something of the old pleasure in Christmas, something of the old faith in Santa Claus, warms in your heart as you stroll down Broadway with the chilly stars sparkling overhead and the white spangles under your feet. The street is illuminated with lights of a hundred colors. It is one long bazaar where you may feast your eyes with the riches of all nations. Turkish looms have been busy for you. Quarries have been opened and streams searched that you might look on clusters of precious jewels. The patient Chinaman has carved his dreamy fantasies in ivory, and the oily Esquimaux has fashioned seal-skin snow-shoes for you. Here you have curious instruments, of brass, and wood, and pearl, within whose tubes and under whose keys lurks passionate music—the spirits of joy and woe. There you have fantastic pipes from Tuscany, wines from Germany, sweetmeats from the Indies, and confections from Paris; Malaga grapes, and creamy bananas, and oranges that turned to gold in the warm air of Cuba. Your slaves in the East have sent you ottars, and gums and scented woods. What is there in all the climes, from

"Lucent syrups tinct with cinnamon,"

to a marble mosque or a Chinese pagoda, that does not lie within your reach? You are Haroun al Raschid in Bagdad, you are Haitalnefous, you are anybody you please, with the world's wealth heaped about you. Have the kindness to help yourself!

You wander through the street in a mid-winter- night's dream. What do you care for the bleak wind, or the snowflakes, or the people who jostle you? You stare at the brilliant shops; you do not know which to enter, for each one is more beautiful than the other, like the Khaleef's forty wives. You pause at Tiffany's. Tiffany's windows are on fire with diamonds. All the water in the underground pipes, which, like huge arteries, traverse the city, could not quench the fire that burns in these stones. This fact is so well known, that the Insurance offices have refused to issue a policy on the building which contains such dangerous merchandise. You flatten your nose on the plate-glass. You see a necklace which you would like to clasp on Amaryllis's perfect throat. He would also like to manacle her white wrists with those turquoise bracelets; you would like—

Listen! High up in the belfry, in the rain, and the sleet, and the dark night, there is a nest of merry birds. They have quiet little hymns which they chirp on Summer evenings. But how clamorous and jubilant they are this Winter night! Why are their happiest, wildest songs kept for the snow and the sleet? Why are they so merry when

—"The sage is withered from the lake,
And no birds sing?"

Why, indeed, let us think of that.

If we should ever move into the country, (and we probably shall, as we have made up our mind not to,) it will be on one condition—that we take the Town with us.

ELEGANT EXTRACT.

We have read with great care the first of Mr. Everett's Verno-Ledgerian papers, and hasten to present our readers with the following concise summary of its brilliant points:

"

"

If we can spare the space, we shall do equal justice the rest of the Series.

Dramatic Feuilleton.

THE DRAMA MADE EASY.

In the court-yard of the Dramatic Poet's house, in Pompeii, there is a picture of a dog in the attitude of attack, executed in mosaic, while over the picture, or over the door—I forget which—is inscribed the usual caution, "*Cave canem*" (beware of the dog). As this Pompeiian dramatic author must, from the style of his abode, have been in very flourishing circumstances—he perhaps had been fortunate enough to write a "*Dame aux Camelids*" or an "American Cousin," and took fifteen per cent on the gross receipts—I am inclined to think that the caution is not intended to be general, but rather to apply to a class of persons which doubtless existed in those antique times as well as in our modern days. I mean would-be dramatic authors. I am sure that the door of the Pompeiian gentleman was besieged by persons with five act comedies, done up in brown paper, under their arms, which they beseeched the successful dramatist to read and present to the manager of the period. Being a man of humane disposition, he kept a painted dog in his court-yard to warn the nuisances off, just as certain proprietors in England placard their parks with notices that "man-traps and spring-guns are set here," while the said forests and hillsides are entirely innocent of any such engines of destruction.

Be that as it may, it is astonishing with what recklessness people in this country attempt dramatic composition—indeed, I may add, every style of literary composition. A young gentleman, who circulates in fashionable society in this city, and who is entirely dependent on his tailor and his knowledge of "the German" for any success which he may achieve, came to me one day and announced that he was going to write a novel. "I don't see," he said, "why I cannot write a novel as well as any one else." I answered, that I did not see it either, and recommended him to commence forthwith. People seem to believe that skill in authorship is a sort of instinct that may develope itself at any moment. That all that is necessary to become famous are pens, ink, and paper, and the resolution to cover a certain quantity of pages. The persons that labor under this delusion would not dream of attempting to make a watch at an hour's notice; they would feel that to be a skilful watchmaker, one must spend years in learning the trade. The mere mechanical knowledge necessary for the construction of a play, can only be acquired by years of study. Yet the amount of plays, ranging from one to five acts, which are manufactured in these "more or less United States" in the course of a year, is positively appalling. I had a peep, the other day, into a manager's secretary. What a night! No chamber in the pyramids, filled with papyrus rolls, ever presented such a spectacle. Piles of white, blue, ruled, unruled, ribboned, twined, legible, illegible, comic, romantic, bloody, and awe-inspiring manuscripts loaded down the shelves. Comedies from Illinois, tragedies from New Jersey, life-dramas from the South, broad farces from the West, and every species of dramatic composition from New York city. I looked at the manager. He seemed healthy, and in his right mind. I came, therefore, to the conclusion that he had not read one of those contributions towards an American theatre. If they had been sent to me I know what I would have done with them. I would have put them all into a large bag, and then gone out for a walk and lost them.

People are astonished that we have not what is called "a national drama." There is no food for a national drama. Washington has nothing romantic about him, and does not become the stage. Marion is picturesque, so is Putnam. But the events are too recent to take any hold of the public mind in dramatic form. Neither will the Indian ever hold the stage. He is passing away from before the footlights, as he is passing away from the American continent.

In domestic life we have no food for comedy,—that is, for sustained comedy. There is a lack of types of character here. A monotony of pursuits produces a monotony of character. We are all running after the dollar, and we all consequently think and act and look "dollar." A people that never have any leisure, never have any salient points of character. Continual motion rubs them smooth. We work in this country till we can work no more. In Europe things are different. There, things settle down; and character-types are the sedimental deposit of life. When men have made a little money in Europe, they are apt to retire from business, and cultivate their hobbies. Twickenham, Hammersmith, Richmond, Passy, Anteull, Asnières, are all inhabited by people who have marked characteristics. One man cultivates flowers, and is botanically branded. Another spends his days in the study of æronautics. Another thinks only of fishing. A fourth is a meteorologist, or a chemist, or an amateur doctor. The different types are inexhaustible, and from these fertile sources the English and French dramatists have no difficulty in populating their dramas with characters which are not only droll, but real. In this country we have no such people. We are all to a certain extent cut out on the same model. We all ride the same hobbies, frequent the same bar-rooms, live the same life at the same hotels, and should have for our national motto, "Ditto, ditto, ditto."

It is not wonderful that with such a national sameness dramatists should be driven to copying from worn-out types long since condemned by our brethren over the water. The New York fireman is a type, but one as disagreeable on the stage as in real life. The boarding-house keeper is another. The flirting young lady in society differs from the unmarried woman of every other nation. Young New York has certain stupid characteristics. The loafer is a tolerably distinct character, and—that is about all.

With care and discretion in the use thereof, there is here about material sufficient for two or three American comedies. Then the supply would be exhausted. So far even, it is astonishing with what persistence our native dramatists have avoided seizing upon the little material they have. They import their characters from England and France, call them Livingston, or Otis, and they forthwith are supposed to play American comedies.

I would advise all budding dramatists to give up the idea of writing what are called "national dramas." Let them eschew comedies of American life, and melodramas of Revolutionary periods. There *is* a field in which it is possible to make a success. It is the domestic drama, which does not depend on character-painting for success, but rather on the reality and sustained interest of its plots. There are many quiet and moving little plays being played every day out in the new settlements, in New England villages, in our cities, and on our farms. Madame Girardin's play of "Sunshine through the Clouds" is an example of this charming style of dramatic composition. Let somebody try his hand at a series of such simple plays, and let us have done with odious platitudes in three or five acts, which are foisted upon us as "American comedies."

INDISPOSITION OF A PUBLIC FAVORITE.

I suffered the other evening from a dramatic disappointment. I went to see the Industrious Fleas, at their theatre, No. 599 Broadway, under the management of Professor Bartoleti. On the evening in question, myself and friend found our way to the theatre through a horrible rain. The audience was slim, consisting, in fact, of my friend and myself. We heard our respective quarters rattle with a melancholy sound into an empty cash-box. The man who took our money looked out of spirits. The lights of the theatre burned blue. Professor Bartolet!—who was needlessly attired in evening costume—seemed to be oppressed by the influences of the weather. There was a general gloom over the establishment. I was not astonished, therefore, when Professor Bartolett advanced to the footlights—we receiving him with great applause—and said, "Ladies and gentlemen, it give me much grief that I tell to you, that the principal artist of our troup is so much disengaged with a cold of great severity, that it will be impossible for us to make a performance on this tonight." The Professor bowed, we renewed our applause; took our tickets for another night—we had not the heart to deprive that melancholy till of our fifty cents—and departed. It is expected that next week the principal flea will so far have recovered from his indisposition as once more to fill his accustomed role. There is a rumor in theatrical circles that his illness was caused by his having escaped the night before and gone on a spree on the body of a particularly sanguine baby, who slept on the premises.

WHAT SANTA CLAUS BROUGHT ME.

The pale moon shimmered through the blind ;
Heart-broken moaned the homeless wind,
As if the whole world was unkind.

The chimes with wild harmonic din,
From turrets, rang the New Year in—
The infant born without a sin.

Amid a heap of ashes hoar,
Like heart that ruin bravely bore,
Still glowed the pine-log's dull-red core.

"There is," thought I (as ærial mirth
From belfries, tingled to my hearth),
"No sadder heart than mine on earth!

"It is the solemn midnight hour,
When Santa Claus, with fairy power,
On sleeping youth bestows his dower.

"And many a curly head to-night,
That dreams upon the pillow white,
Beholds rare visions of delight.

"Each urchin, true to magic laws,
His head beneath the bed-clothes draws,
And lists for fairy Santa Claus.

"Through nursery-rooms the whispers run
Of wonder if the deed is done,
And longings for the morning's sun.

"And all will wake with seeking eyes,
And all will meet with sweet surprise;
For me alone no joy will rise.

"There is but one gift prized by me,
But one pure pearl in Life's dark sea;
And none will bring me Bertha Lee.

"For I am poor, if young and bold,
And though her fondest vows I hold,
I can not clasp the links with gold.

"With bitter words and insults sore
Her father chased me from his door,
Yet Bertha loved me all the more.

"And when we met in secret, said,
'The dying year shall not be dead
Ere this great sorrow shall have fled.'

"Ah! women's vows, when skies are free,
Like summer boats will tempt the sea,
But at the first cloud turn and flee.

"And Bertha since that last sweet tryst,
When Hope from off her lips I kissed,
Has given no sign that I am missed.

"Though I have haunted every place
Where I may hope to see her face,
I find no token, or no trace.

"Bells, ring your triumph through the sky!
I joy not that the year should die :
None mourn his burial more than I."

While thus I conned my sorrow o'er,
And learned a pain unknown before,
There came a tapping at my door.

A gentle tap—and then a pause.
"Who's there?"—
"For me each bolt withdraws;
I am a gift from Santa Claus !"

Oh, Heaven! that voice! It scarce could be!
With one quick leap the door was free,
And on my breast lay Bertha Lee.

She lay and sobbed all white—all cold.
I kissed the dew from her hair of gold.
I held her as Love alone could hold!

Still rang the chimes from belfries brown,
But through the vast triumphant town
There was no joy that mine could crown!

The midnight heard my joyous cry.
"Bells, greet the New Year in the sky!
None welcome his coming so much as I!"

FITZ JAMES O'BRIEN

The New-York Saturday Press.

VOL. II.—NO. 1. NEW YORK, JANUARY 1, 1859. PRICE, 5 CENTS.

The New York Saturday Press,
A JOURNAL OF THE TIMES,
IS PUBLISHED
Every Saturday Morning,
AT NO. 9 SPRUCE STREET, NEW YORK.

HENRY CLAPP, Jr., } Editors.
T. B. ALDRICH, }

TERMS—$2 00 a year; Five Cents a single number.

ADVERTISEMENTS,
10 Cents a line for 1 insertion.
25 " " " 4 insertions.
75 " " " 12 insertions.

SPECIMEN COPIES will be sent to any part of the Union on the receipt of five cents in postage stamps.

DECEMBER XXXI.

There goes an old Gaffer over the hill,
Thieving, and old, and gray;
He walks the green world his wallet to fill,
And carries good spoil away.

Into his bag he popped a king,
After him went a friar;
Many a lady with gay gold ring,
Many a knight and squire.

He carried my true-love far away,
He stole the dog at my door;
The vile old Gaffer, thieving and gray,
He'll never come back any more.

My little darling, white and fair,
Sat in the door and spun;
He caught her fast by her silken hair,
Before the child could run.

He stole the florins out of my purse,
The sunshine out of mine eyes;
He stole my roses; and what is worse,
The gray old Gaffer told lies.

He promised fair when he came by,
And laughed as he slipped away,
For every promise turned out a lie;
But his hole is over to-day.

Good-bye, old Gaffer! you'll come no more,
You've done you worst for me;
The next gray robber will pass my door;
There's nothing to steal or see!

—*Tribune.*

THE CAPTURE OF SCHAMYL BY ALEXANDRE DUMAS.

Translated from "Figaro," for THE NEW YORK SATURDAY PRESS.

Our own Kasan correspondent—the "own correspondents" of *Figaro* are every where—sends us glorious news! Schamyl, the invincible Schamyl, who has gained so many victories over the Russians, and such a brilliant one at the *Porte St. Martin*, has just been captured! and by Alexandre Dumas, alone, very alone—without the faintest collaborator.

Imagine the rejoicing throughout all the Russias. A surtout of honor, lined with the richest furs, has, it is said, been awarded to our great novelist. But, let our own Kasan correspondent relate, in his own terms, the details of this immense event:

Sir:—You have doubtless seen the letter which M. Alexandre Dumas recently communicated to the *Siècle*, and are familiar with the new project of this great man, whose facility and aplomb excite our undying admiration. His letter, if my memory serve me, contained something of this sort: "I intend approaching Schamyl, as near as possible, with the advance-guards of Prince Darejlatinski."

I know not whether you seized the precise sense of this important phrase. You may have imagined that the word *approach*, had reference merely to an insignificant promenade. The characteristic modesty of M. Dumas, forbade his entering into a detailed explanation.

Whatever may have been your impressions concerning the sentence in question, Schamyl, on the other hand, was not to be deceived. It is stated, on the best of authority, that the very morning on which his porter handed him the *Siècle*, the great chief of the Caucasus turned pale, and seemed deeply affected.

Schamyl had the advantage of knowing something about M. Dumas, from M. Paul Meurice. He felt that though he might easily oppose a vigorous resistance to all the Russias, M. Dumas on the other hand was irresistible, and that to this great man, all nations that have learnt to read, abjectly bow the knee. Therefore, he felt it incumbent upon him to keep his weather-eye open. All the military posts of Caucasus were doubled. Notice was given to all the Caucasian custom-houses, that the entrance of negroes was strictly prohibited, and that no traveller could be received without a proper certificate of whiteness. Mr. Dumas, however, undeterred by these stringent measures, advanced by forced marches, steadily upon Schamyl. And here, let me be permitted to chronicle day by day, the movements of this general, without an army, and all the incidents of this eventful campaign.

FIRST DAY.

Departure of M. Dumas. He harangues the army of Prince Darejlatinski, in the following terse language:

"Cossacks, I cannot embrace you all, neither individually, nor still less collectively. I therefore embrace your general!"

Prince Darejlatinski flung himself into the arms of M. Dumas, who held him long upon his bosom. The entire army wept.

The Prince attempts to dissuade the great novelist. "Have a care, dear master. The roads of Caucasus are not safe. I never undertake to travel them without an escort of 50 or 60,000 men."

M. Dumas replied with the politeness that characterizes him:—

"You are perhaps in the right, Prince, but I would not have you to incommode your army for me. However, I am fully capable of capturing Schamyl, all alone. When one has got up a revolution, as I have——"

"A revolution! What one?" inquired the Prince, surprised.

"That of 1848. I alone did it, with my song of the *Girondins*. Read my Memoirs."

"True," replied the Prince; "I had forgotten it, dear master."

"And, besides," continued M. Dumas, "let me allay your apprehension, by stating that I shall not go unaccompanied. I, also, have my army."

The Prince was, at first, at a loss to understand him. The only battalion he could perceive by the side of M. Dumas, was the faithful Rusconi. M. Dumas beckoned, and the faithful Rusconi stepped aside, and the army of which M. Dumas spoke, appeared suddenly behind the faithful Rusconi.

It was the legion of all the novels of M. Dumas, each a fifty-volume story, at least.

Prince Darejlatinski retired to his tent. The faithful Rusconi sounded a warlike flourish. M. Alexandre Dumas placed himself at the head of his innumerable novels. The campaign against Schamyl was opened!

SECOND DAY.

On arriving within sight of Schamyl, M. Dumas and his novels made a halt. The faithful Rusconi was sent forward, garnished with a flag of truce, and the following ultimatum for Schamyl:

"*Article I.* Schamyl shall agree to acknowledge M. Dumas, senior, as the most prolific of all novelists.

"*Article II.* Schamyl shall call M. Dumas, senior, "dear master."

"*Article III.* Schamyl shall deliver up to said Dumas his father, mother, brothers, sisters, and mistresses, if he have any—in order that the said Dumas may make what use of them he may see fit, in the manufacture of his novels.

"*Article IV.* All the secrets, adventures, and private history of Schamyl shall belong to the said Dumas, who shall have the free and exclusive right to them, with the power to convert them into feuilletons for the *Siècle*, *Constitutionnel*, *Moniteur*, *Monte Christo*, or to use them in any other form, large or small, that he may think proper to select."

The faithful Rusconi departed "with a timid but firm step,"—being the style of locomotion usually adopted by the heroes of M. Ponson du Terrail—and returned, five minutes later, with the reply of Schamyl.

Schamyl refused.

He had at first consented to call M. Dumas "dear master," because, he said, it was the custom. But he revolted at the idea of being pressed into a novel; he, his father, his mother, his brothers, his sisters, and his mistresses. "He would not stand," he replied, with some tartness, "being treated like a simple Knight of Harmental."

"The die is cast!" said M. Dumas. "He shall have war! He must have known, that if I came here, it was simply because I was out of copy. Be it so, then! he shall have war." May all the ink shed here be upon his own head! And you, Rusconi, remember that from the height of these snowy peaks of Caucasus, forty odd centuries look down upon you!

THIRD DAY.

The sun, as it rose, was recognized by M. Dumas to be the Sun of Austerlitz, which assertion, the sun taking no pains to refute, the fact will undoubtedly be handed down to posterity.

At the point of day M. Dumas addressed these memorable words to the faithful Rusconi:

"In me, the great novelist, is but the preface to the great captain!" And, in fact, a couple of hours later, he had laid his plan of attack.

The following is the outline of his principal strategic dispositions:

The most difficult part of the undertaking being to penetrate the narrow passes of the Caucasus, M. Dumas resolved to lead forward his light artillery, otherwise called his plays in not more than one act, such as the *Invitation to the Waltz*, *Honor is satisfied*, and *Romulus*.

His 48—or 1848—pounders, *Urban Grandier*, *Hamlet*, etc., were to escort this movement.

The enemy would then observe with a certain degree of apprehension, the advance of the serried columns of the *Constitutionnel*, in which was published *Isaac Laquedem*. The said *Isaac* to be reinforced, at need, by the *Mohicans of Paris*.

Finally, the overthrow of the enemy was to be accomplished by setting on the *Three Musketeers*.

I do not enlarge upon the *Thousand and One Phantoms*, which formed the reserve, in case the battle should be prolonged after night-fall, nor upon the *Forty Five*, which comprised the staff of M. Dumas. All these dramas and novels, teeming with so many thousand lives of Schamyl.

These plans were hardly drawn up, and the signal for the fight was not yet given, when a cry of triumph from the camp of Schamyl startled, for an instant, M. Dumas. He would have been still more surprised had he known the cause of the outcry. A negro, of prepossessing appearance, plump, and well-groomed, with white teeth, and a merry laugh, had just been seized at one of the custom-houses of Caucasus. On being interrogated, he acknowledged that he issued from the *Mousquetaire*. This reply gave the soldiers of Schamyl to believe that they had laid hands on M. Dumas himself. Unhappily, the joy of these mountaineers was of short duration. The letter of a Duchess, found upon the person of the amiable and chocolate-colored captive, established the fact, that his name was Cochinat (Victor). This young author had gone astray, it appears, on quitting the *Café des Variétés*, at an advanced hour of the night. On learning this fact, Schamyl was obliging enough to send him in safety to his Lares and Penates.

FOURTH DAY.

The grand decisive day! The Sun of Austerlitz, alluded to above, could not make up his mind to quit the horizon, so curious was he to be present at the great battle about to take place.

M. Dumas, having aimed the faithful Rusconi straight at the enemy, loaded him up to the muzzle with novels and plays.

At the given signal, Rusconi went off with a great bang. The complete works of M. Dumas exploded, one after the other, and made great havoc with the army of Schamyl.

I am obliged, by the austere impartiality which characterizes the historian, to acknowledge that certain works of M. Dumas produced no effect, and that others entirely flashed in the pan, so to speak.

The *Viscount of Bragelonne*, for example, notwithstanding it fell with its one hundred and odd volumes right into the tent of Schamyl, failed to produce the slightest effect upon that illustrious chieftain.

"That is the fault of Maquet," said M. Dumas, with disappointment.

The *Knight of Harmental* equally failed in all his endeavors to approach Schamyl. The warrior invariably kept him at a distance.

"That is the fault of Maquet, again," cried M. Dumas, despairingly.

Finally, another Knight, named *Red House*, made an attempt, but was also repulsed by Schamyl.

"That's Maquet's doing," groaned M. Dumas, discouraged.

It would appear that this M. Maquet, who is, without doubt, the foreman in M. Dumas's literary foundry, must have surreptitiously added too much alloy to the brass, of which the great novelist's big guns are generally cast.

Another accident occurred, which for a moment, led the faithful Rusconi to believe that all was lost.

Rusconi was out of ammunition. There only remained *The Companions of Jehu*. He made an attempt to crush Schamyl with them; but they failed, all through the fault of M. Gabet, and the faithful Rusconi was at the end of his resources.

Happily, M. Dumas preserved his entire presence of mind! Seizing pen, ink, and paper, at the end of an hour he had a new legion of novels and dramas, fit for the—fire.

The bombardment continued thus during several hours. Suddenly, all was hushed in the hostile camp. *Antony*, *Monte Christo*, and *the Three Musketeers*, fired at an early stage of the battle, had not reappeared. Had they succeeded, or had they been cut up? M. Dumas, unable to bear any longer the horrible anxiety of suspense, marched himself upon Schamyl to learn their fate.

Fancy his private satisfaction when, on penetrating into the enemy's camp, he learned that the victory had been his for upwards of an hour. The mountaineers of the Caucasus had easily resisted the *Viscount of Bragelonne*, a weak little man, without any consistency; but they had been gained over effectually by the millions of the *Count of Monte Christo!*

As to Schamyl, he had been arrested by *d'Artagnand* in the same manner in which the latter arrested the Man with the Iron Mask in days of yore. *Joseph Balsamo* had bejuggled him, and the *Forty-Five Guardsmen* had so completely enthralled him, that M. Dumas found the handcuffs with which he had provided himself, totally unnecessary.

POSTSCRIPT.—What shall I add to this epic page in the life of Alexander Dumas the Great? You will doubtless all see Schamyl appear ere long from the presses of Charlieu, or Cadot; and all the Russias are far more satisfied with him there than in the fastnesses in Mt. Caucasus.

All the histories of Schamyl, all his adventures in war, or in love, all his political or caudle secrets have fallen into the hands of M. Dumas—an immense mine from which the great romancer will draw the wherewithal to live like a prince all the days of his life.

As to the mountaineers of Caucasus, they have not had the same luck with M. Dumas. The only thing they obtained from him, was one subscription to his journal, the *Monte Christo*. JEAN ROUSSEAU.

ANTIPHON.

BY GEORGE HERBERT.

Cho. Let all the world in every corner sing,
MY GOD, AND KING!

Ver. The heavens are not too high,
His praise may thither fly.
The earth is not too low,
His praises there may grow.

Cho. Let all the world in every corner sing,
MY GOD, AND KING!

Ver. The church with psalms must shout,
No door can keep them out,
But, above all, the heart
Must bear the longest part.

Cho. Let all the world in every corner sing,
MY GOD, AND KING!

A NEW PORTRAIT OF PARIS:

PAINTED FROM LIFE.

"Paint me as I am."—CROMWELL.

"Now being from Paris recently,
This fine young man would show his skill."
—HOLMES.

BY HENRY CLAPP, JR.

CHAPTER X.

The Coffee-Concert—The Men and Women who Frequented it—How Familiarity with Them did not Breed Contempt—How we Came to Know the Waiters—The First Class English Servant—How Solemn He is—The First Class French Servant—How Different—The Coffee-Concert Again—The Author's Acquaintances There—Difference Between the French, English, Germans, and Americans, as Talkers—A Frenchman's Mind like a Battery—Students and Studentesses—The Latter not to be Despised—Octavie and Rosalie.

The Coffee-Concert, sketched in the preceding chapter, was my favorite resort for years. Every Summer it was transferred to a large lattice-work inclosure in Madame street, at the northwest corner of the Garden of the Luxembourg. The place became a necessity to me. The men and women who frequented it became as familiar to me as the daily loungers on the Boulevards; and the "familiarity" did not "breed contempt." Night after night I would sit at my little table (for I had selected one as far as possible from the orchestra, which I generally contrived to secure), and while tranquilly sipping my little cup of *café noir* and smoking my clay pipe, observed the curious people by whom I was surrounded, and, at last, nearly every individual had unwittingly revealed to me something of his (or her) secret history. All the waiters got to know me, and one of them—whose scarred face told more touchingly than the pages of Lamartine or Louis Blanc of the revolution through which he had passed, would bring my invariable cup of coffee without my even ordering it. It would often be placed on my table before I had seen him. There was no servility about the man, but he was the most assiduous, the most sprightly, the most sensible servant I had ever seen.

The first-class English servant is something appalling. He is the most solemn creature in the world. I never could get rid of the idea that he was dedicated and set apart by some awful and mysterious ritual, the memory of which haunted him like a guilty conscience. He seems like the relic of the shadow of death. I remember a corps of these solemnities at Furnival's Inn, London, who affected me like a brotherhood of Black Friars. I would as soon have been served by ghosts. When one of them had received an order, he would disappear so stealthily, and return so mysteriously, that it was difficult not to believe that he had immediately sunk through a crack in the door and risen up again through the same place, like a new and uncomfortable species of Dumb Waiter. The creatures would linger about your table, and pick up any crumbs which, in the trepidation of the moment, you might have dropped, like so many ravens. The fellows were all dressed in black, and presided over your meal as over a funeral, looking as glum as demons on half-pay. The idea of offering one of them the customary fee of "thrippence," would no more occur to you than of offering pennies to a parson for a burial service. But I remember that when I omitted the little ceremony, in the first instance, the friar suddenly became human for a moment, and showed that

"The devil a monk was he"

by asking for his pittance as humbly as if he had been no more than top Boots at the Goose and Gridiron.

I had a similar experience at the Clarendon Hotel, where the solemn flunkeys—all six feet high and solemn as magnates—made me feel as if I were being waited upon by Her Majesty's most Noble Knights of the Garter. To put anything into their royal palms but gold, would have been a kind of sacrilege. I recollect mistaking one of them, as he stood along his calves on the front stoop, for "that cypher at the left hand of a royal digit—the incidental Albert," for knowing in what good training the Prince is kept by his Royal Mistress, I was soon convinced of my mistake, by seeing the gartered flunkey in treasonable relations with an indisputable chambermaid.

The first-class French servant, though quite as prompt as his Cockney brother, instead of being as solemn as a cow, is as cheerful as a bird. He is lively without being fussy, civil without being servile, neat without being prim, sociable without being impertinent, and dignified without being solemn. He neither neglects you nor annoys you, and though never hovering about like a demon, is always at hand when wanted, and at the end of the meal receives his little gratuity with as much grace as if it were the Cross of the Legion of Honor.

But to return to the Coffee-Concert. Of course, I made some acquaintances there; for the French are a sociable race, and more than any other addicted to talk. They are the only great talkers I have met with who were not great bores. The reason is, that they don't talk of you like the English, the American, the German, but with you. They are not so humorous as the English, however, nor so grave as the German, nor so 'cute as the Yankee; but they are more ready, more genial, and more witty than either. Their weakness is a passion for generalization and paradox. But even this is a charm. A Frenchman's mind is like a highly charged electric battery, from which you are constantly receiving the most agreeable shocks.

The acquaintances I made at the concert were generally students and studentesses. Most of the former were from the country. This was evident at a glance. They lacked the city touch. They were Frenchmen in the rough, and had been sent to Paris to get a little "shine." But the country ore is difficult to polish. There is something wrong in the grain. It is too soft. You might as well try to polish pudding-stone or putty. This, however, was no objection to me. I was seeking for character, not lustre. I had seen patent-leather heads enough in London and New York. Besides, too much polish destroys the natural enamel, which no artificial brightness can replace. Not that I am an admirer of rusticity. The gods forbid! Your country clown is a very good creature, no doubt, and so is a donkey, or a duck, but not for companionship. He "works up" well in pastorals, and adorns a tale fitly enough, but he doesn't bear inspection. Your country wench, too, has her attractions, like a hen, or a cow, but as a woman—well, even as a woman she is not without a certain charm, and as a figure in a landscape she is invaluable.

"She sails round 'neath the pear, or tree,
A pretty picture is to see,
But nothing more."

My student friends were generally "countrified" without being clownish. Some of them, among the new-comers, were in a rather crude state, like so much raw material, but this made them all the more interesting, for to watch them as they were being manufactured, was like watching the process of crystallization—or dock-making.

The studentesses, whom I came to know, may be judged of, in general, by the description already given. Contact with students had made some of them very bright. They seemed to have been educated by friction. They were not so remarkable for their knowledge as for their smartness. They were like our Western orators—smart in inverse proportion to their learning. They were educated, but not cultivated. What they knew had been learned, not from books, but from experience. Some of them had rather superior minds. I remember two, in particular, Mademoiselles Octavie and Rosalie—who were among the most intelligent persons of my acquaintance. Neither of them could read or write; but

"They knew what's what; and that's as high
As metaphysic wit can fly."

Statisticians, who go about classifying men and women, as if they were minerals, would have placed them in the category of "*Persons with no instruction.*" But neither Octavie or Rosalie could be made into a statistic. They would be as much out of place in a tabular statement as a figure of rhetoric. I was not likely myself to commit the statistician's blunder as to their instruction, for the most ignorant persons I knew were graduates from our first colleges; M. D.'s, A. B.'s, B. A.'s, D. D.'s, etc., who were

"Small by degrees"—

with the natural impossibility of ever becoming

Octavie and Rosalie had graduated at the school of Nature. They had each summered about twenty Winters. Their chief educational defect, as the world would call it, was a refreshing ignorance of literature. But though they knew little about books, and nothing about authors, they had more good sense than could be distilled out of a dozen libraries. Your mere scholar was a fool to them.

Octavie had a natural genius for drawing faces. Still used to say she was a prodigy. She never bothered herself much about accuracy of detail, but would seize at once upon a man's characteristic trait of body or mind, and with a touch of her pencil make it speak to you like a confession.

"She saw the nonsense in the face,
And drew the shameful forms of grace."

I remember her drawing the head of a poor student, who had lost one of his legs in the revolution of 1848. Still told her she had given a one-legged expression to the face itself; and so she had—the features were correct, but they limped. One of her portraits was better than a biography; for she could read character if she couldn't read books. Her mind was not lumbered with other people's thoughts, there was "ample scope and verge enough" for her own. The mysterious sanscrit of the human countenance was the only scripture she could understand. "Silence," said she to me one day, as I was trying to evade one of her questions, by seeming to read her mind, "is much more dangerous for you than speech. When your tongue stops talking, your lip commences and tells the whole story. The tongue is a natural liar, and therefore keeps out of sight. But the treacherous lip, though a servant of the tongue, is always ready to betray its master. So if you wish to deceive me, keep your tongue swinging like a bell, and my ears may lead me astray. But when my ears are asleep, depend upon it my eyes more than fill their place."

The keenness of such a woman was not to be eluded. Her room was always a confessional to me. It was so to every one. Hence her criticisms of society were almost as good as her caricatures of individuals. After being bored by some student with an insipid hash of commonplace literature, or after skimming pert articles in some literary review, to meet with such a mind as hers, which gave everything at first hand, was like getting into a ripe orchard after skimming all Summer on poor preserves.

Rosalie was not so merry as Octavie, but was much more introspective. She studied her own nature, and generalized from that as to the nature of others. She was silent as a star, and therein differed as much from Octavie as a sundial from a townclock. She would sit a whole evening without saying more than ten words, but those ten words were as authoritative as the ten commandments.

Her serenity amid the confused scenes about her was like the calm still water amid the chaos of a great city. The confusion was reflected, but not echoed. Why and how she became what she was, I never asked. It was none of my business. The student to whom she was attached, was an enthusiastic young fellow "in the law." Their love for each other was a religion. Their demeanor to each other—to superficial eyes—was cold almost to indifference; but they were always together, and were evidently more than happy. Their society was agreeable to me beyond that of all other persons. But the enjoyment of it was of short duration. The young man was summoned home, and, ere he departed, the young woman died. I have not looked upon her like since; and but for her should never, perhaps, have known how vastly superior is a nature developed by experience and having all its instincts and emotions quickened into life under the influence of love, to a nature educated in artificial schools, with all its instincts and emotions deadened and depraved by conventional morality and heartless gentility. She was "a very honorable and sincere woman;" and though no stone marks the place of her burial—alas! there were enough thrown at her to make her a monument—I find it always green, and never without a tribute of fresh flowers.

Of course Octavie and Rosalie are not given as types. Poor girls, they were more like shadows. I have introduced them to the reader because they were introduced to me. The ordinary studentess requires no introduction. It is enough to see her. And, to be frank, she had no attraction for me. I didn't like her "make." There are some people, moreover, who should be kept at a good focal distance. I wouldn't have them destroyed, for doubtless they have their uses, like mole and vermin, which we only attack when they annoy us. They are certainly useful in the way of variety. Wanting them, or any other creatures, the great world-scape would be deficient in some element of beauty. Shade is as necessary to a picture as light, and variety is not only the "spice," but the condition of life. Nothing is uniform but death.

[To be continued in our next.]

GUROWSKI.

The Count de Gurowski has honored us with a letter, couched of course, in an aristocratic style of high-breeding, of which the following is a precise copy:

To the Editor or director of personalities in the Tribune:

As you published in to-day's *Tribune* only half the story concerning me and Mr. Herzen, *if you are a gentleman* you will publish my answer to Herzen inserted in the *Evening Post* yesterday, December 23, 1858.

Friday. GUROWSKI.

As we desire nothing in the world so ardently as to prove that we are a gentleman, and as, in the eyes of so eminent a judge of what constitutes a gentleman as the Count de Gurowski, the only thing necessary to establish our claim to that distinction is to copy his letter from the *Evening Post*, we hasten to perform the duty:

Sir: I am gratified to learn from your solemn declaration, contained in a recent number of *La Cloche*, that my statement in *The New York Evening Post* of the 22d of October, to the effect that you had sold your serfs, was erroneous.

The opportunity must therefore be still open to you (and I may be allowed to express the hope that you will lose no time in embracing it) to illustrate by your own example, the splendid philanthropy of which you are so distinguished an advocate; and by forthwith emancipating your serfs, distributing among them in just proportions, the lands they have hitherto cultivated, together with such other privileges as may be within your power, at once vindicate the sincerity of your own professions, and carry the idea of emancipation to a point which the Emperor, in his benevolent designs, never dreamed of reaching.

New York, Dec. 22, 1858. GUROWSKI.

To Alexander Herzen, London.

Having thus placed our character as a gentleman beyond the possibility of question, we are probably competent to make one or two observations. First, then, it is our impression that this letter does not exhibit the Count de Gurowski in a perfectly creditable light. He had made certain positive public allegations respecting Mr. Herzen which that gentleman pronounced false and calumnious. Now, as it seems that these allegations were made without any ground, and as in fact, we submit that it would have been appropriate for him to make for his calumny a very different apology from the insolent epistle which he has so pompously summoned us to copy. Still, we offer this suggestion with diffidence; we have been a gentleman so short a time that we may have no great confidence in our own opinion on such delicate matters. But, as a second point, we are bound to withdraw an intimation contained in our paragraph of yesterday, that probably but for the intervention of the ocean there would be a duel between the parties. We are convinced from the above letter that this was unjust to the Count de Gurowski, and we retract it accordingly.—*Tribune.*

ODE TO A TOBACCO PIPE.

BY JAMES HAMMOND.

Little tube of mighty power,
Charmer of an idle hour,
Object of my warm desire,
Lip of wax, and eye of fire;
And thy snowy, taper waist,
With my gentle finger braced;
And thy pretty swelling crest,
With my little stopper prest;
And the sweetest bliss of blisses
Breathing from thy balmy kisses.
Happy thrice, and thrice again,
Happiest he of happy men;
Who, when again the night returns,
When again the taper burns,
When again the cricket's gay
(Little cricket, full of play),
Can afford his tube to feed
With the fragrant Indian weed;
Pleasure for a nose divine,
Incense of the god of wine;
Happy thrice, and thrice again,
Happiest he of happy men.

JAPAN AND ITS PEOPLE.

The Japanese are fine fellows, and altogether a superior race to the Chinese. They are strictly honorable in all their dealings, and possess all those essential qualities which make men honest, generous, and brave. We were but a week there, and were most courteously treated the whole time; cutting about everywhere both in the town (Nagasaki) and the country. The country was most beautiful and picturesque, and cultivated with the most elaborate care, even to the highest peaks of the hills.

The Japanese are highly civilized and fully alive to the superiority of Europeans in science. They have already made themselves masters of steam, and understand the electric telegraph. In Jeddo, where they had never seen an European ship, they had built vessels from European plans, but although the workmanship was exquisite, the vessels themselves when constructed were, as you may imagine, rather curious than useful. The town of Nagasaki contained upwards of 70,000 inhabitants, but the streets were so quiet and so few people were to be seen moving about that you might have supposed there was not a tithe of that number; but one corroborative fact that to my opinion proves the extent of the population is the number of tea gardens in the vicinity; of which, according to the most moderate computation, there cannot be less than seven hundred. All these gardens were laid out in the most tasteful manner, half garden and half wilderness. Within doors, the house is divided into a number of small rooms, scrupulously well kept with clean mats, but with very little other furniture. A principal attraction of these gardens, however, consists doubtless in the troops of "neat handed Phyllises" that attend upon them. After taking off your shoes you go up-stairs and recline on the softest of all conceivable mats, and presently in comes a most delicious repast, composed of all sorts of Japanese luxuries, of which commend me, before all the rest, to a Japanese salad. The genius of Alexis Soyer never conceived aught to equal this luxury. But as the best of feasts would be insipid without female society, numbers of fair girls lend their presence to the scene, help you to the daintiest morsels with the most delicate attention, and when you then throw yourself back to enjoy your "weed," they call for their instruments, and with lute, harp, and glittering, lull you to the land of dreams with the softest and most plaintive music I ever heard. "Think of that, Master Brook!" All these girls are intelligent, well dressed, and graceful in the extreme, and as such are held in high estimation by the Japanese, who have no qualms or squeamishness about bringing their families into these gardens to take lessons in "deportment" from the attendant houris I have mentioned; whose "frailties" do by no means interfere with their subsequent fortunes, since they marry and are given in marriage without scruple or discredit. All the married women blacken their teeth and cut off their eyebrows, which makes them look hideous. On the whole, I need not tell you that we were very sorry to leave Japan.—*English paper.*

For The Saturday Press.

THE N. Y. TRIBUNE AT FAULT.

The N. Y. Tribune of December 24th, contains a leader describing the artistic destitution of the White House, in which allusion is made to a portrait of Washington, *artist unknown*.

While admiring the piquant style of the writer, I cannot but deplore that he is not better acquainted with facts—the portrait in question being an original by Stuart, and one of his master-pieces.

I send you the following interesting account of this portrait prepared by Jacob Barker, Esq., who, as will be seen, assisted in saving the picture when Washington was occupied by the British in 1814. ARTIST.

THE PORTRAIT OF GENERAL WASHINGTON

WHICH ADORNS THE PRESIDENT'S HOUSE.

The invading army of the British had landed at Patuxent about the 20th of August, 1814, and took up their march for the capital, in the direction of the Wood-yards, twelve miles distant, where the American forces, under the command of General Winder, were concentrating.

President Madison, accompanied by General Armstrong, Secretary of War, visited the Wood-yards on the 23d, for the purpose of conferring with General Winder. He was not there. The troops appeared to be much fatigued by the marches and counter-marches to which they had been subjected. The President and Secretary returned to Washington.

George Washington Campbell, Secretary of the Treasury, and Wm. Jones, Secretary of the Navy, called on General Armstrong for information. He informed them that, from the absence of the General and the appearance of the troops, he apprehended that the British would be in possession of the city the next day. They queried why he, a Revolutionary officer, did not put himself at the head of the army and defend the city. He replied that the Secretary of War was a chamber officer, without authority to assume the command. They inquired if he would do so if the President authorized it? His reply was, Certainly. They immediately repaired to the White House, when the President deferred the decision, saying he would convene a Cabinet council the next morning at seven o'clock, at the navy-yard, when the subject should be considered and decided. The Cabinet, with the exception of Mr. Monroe, who repaired to Bladensburg very early, to which place our troops were retreating, met at the appointed hour. At eight o'clock General Armstrong, being clothed with authority to put himself at the head of the army and defend the city, left for Bladensburg, accompanied by Mr. Campbell. The President remained, and left at nine o'clock, accompanied by Mr. Rush, the Attorney-General, for Bladensburg, to recall General Armstrong. On reaching that place, a few minutes before the fight began, he said to General Armstrong, it is too late to make any change—come with me, and leave the defence with the military authorities, where it belongs; then turned to Mr. Monroe, and other civil officials who were on the ground, and said the same thing to them. They all bowed assent, General Armstrong remarking, if the President would wait a moment, he would see the effect of the Congreve rockets; that the enemy were then preparing to let them off. To which the President had scarce time to reply, before the rockets came whistling their way, which caused an instantaneous flight of the troops, with the exception of one or two regiments of Maryland militia. The 5th and 9th made fight, and distinguished themselves. To these regiments which made good battle were attached General Sansbury and Colonel Pinckney.

After the retreat, about one mile and a half from Bladensburg, towards the capital, the President met Commodore Barney and his brave men, remaining with them until they encountered the enemy, dealing out death and destruction with tremendous effect, until the Commodore was shot down at his gun, for the want of having his flank protected. The writer had the relation of this affair from the President, at the White House, on the day of its occurrence. He remarked that he never would have believed in the difference between regular troops and militia, if he had not witnessed the scenes of that day.

As soon as our troops broke and retreated, the President sent his servant express to warn his good lady of her danger, with directions to leave immediately. This messenger reached the White House about two o'clock. Mrs. Madison, Mr. and Mrs. Cutts, with two servants, left immediately thereafter. Mrs. Madison's last words were, Save the portrait of General Washington, if possible; if you cannot save it, destroy it—under no circumstances allow it to fall into the hands of the British; it is the original, by Stuart; all others are copies. Soon after this the President returned, remained about an hour, described the battle, the flight of the militia, and the havoc on the columns of the British by the fire from Commodore Barney's guns, it making perfect lanes through the ranks, which were immediately filled up without turning their heads to see what had become of their companions. He then left to join Mrs. Madison. About this time the retreating army halted for a few minutes before the President's house. The weather was oppressively hot, and the soldiers greatly fatigued. After supplying them with wine from the White House, Mr. Jacob Barker and Mr. Robert G. L. Depeyster, of New York, aided by two colored boys, took the portrait from the floor where Mrs. Madison had left it, and fell into the trail of the army, and continued with it until nightfall, when they turned off to a farm-house near the margin of the Tiber, where they passed the night, and left the portrait with the farmer's wife for safe keeping. The army encamped two miles further on, and the following day retreated to Montgomery court-house.

After the lapse of a month or two, Mr. Barker visited the farm-house, reclaimed the portrait, and restored it to Mrs. Madison.

The accuracy of a statement made by Mr. Barker and Mr. Depeyster was publicly questioned by Mr. Daniel P. Carroll.

On the publication of Mr. Carroll's letter, Mr. Depeyster applied to Mrs. Madison for her version of the story. Her reply appeared in the *New York Express*, with a copy of a record made by myself on the memorable day of its occurrence:

"WASHINGTON, February 11th, 1848.

"*Dear Sir:* I did not receive your favor containing the newspapers, and therefore is my impatience to assure you of my gratitude for the interest you take in my defence in the little narrative of the picture rescue.

"You will see by the enclosed what was said at the time. The impression that Mr. Carroll saved Stuart's portrait of Washington is erroneous. The paper which was to accompany your letter has not reached me, but I have heard that his family believed he removed it. On the contrary, Mr. Carroll had left me to join Mr. Madison, when I directed my servants in what manner to remove it from the wall, remaining with them until it was done. I saw Mr. Barker and yourself (the two gentlemen alluded to) passing, and accepted your offer to assist me, in any way, by taking you to the two gentlemen to preserve this portrait, which you kindly carried between you, to the humble but safe roof which sheltered it awhile. I admit these evidences of my respect for General Washington—but that I felt a desire to gain laurels in danger of life and liberty to save the likeness of anything; the merit in this belongs to me.

"Accept my respect and best wishes.

"D. P. MADISON.

"To Robert G. L. Depeyster, Westport, Connecticut."

"Extract from a letter to my sister, published in the sketch of my life, written for the National Portrait Gallery:

"WASHINGTON, 24th of August, 1814.

"*Dear Sister:* Our kind friend, Mr. Carroll, has come to hasten my departure, and is in a very bad humor with me because I insist on waiting until the large picture of General Washington is secured, and it requires to be unscrewed from the wall. This process was found too tedious for these perilous moments. I have ordered the frame to be broken, and the canvas taken out; it is done, and the precious portrait placed in the hands of two gentlemen from New York for safe keeping. And now, dear sister, I must leave this house, or the retreating army will make me a prisoner in it, by filling up the road I am directed to take. When I shall again write to you, or where I shall be to-morrow, I cannot tell!

"D. P. MADISON."

"New Years Calls," from New York-Illustrated News, January 16, 1864

NEW YORK JANUARY 1, 1859

A NEW PORTRAIT OF PARIS: PAINTED FROM LIFE.

"Paint me as I am".—Cromwell.

"Now being from Paris recently.
This fine young man would show his skill."
Holmes.

BY HENRY CLAPP, JR.

CHAPTER X.

THE Coffee-Concert—The Men and Women who Frequented it—How Familiarity with Them did *not* Breed Contempt—How we came to Know the Waiters—The First Class English Servant—How Solemn He is—The First Class French Servant—How Cheerful He is—The Coffee Concert Again—The Author's Acquaintances There—Difference Between the French, English, Germans, and Americans, as Talkers—A Frenchman's Mind like a Battery—Students and Studentesses—The Latter not to be Damped—Octavio and Rosalie.

The Coffee-Concert, sketched in the preceding chapter, was my favorite resort for years. Every Summer it was transferred to a large lattice-work inclosure in Madame street, at the northwest corner of the Garden of the Luxembourg. The place became a necessity to me. The men and women who frequented it became as familiar to me as the daily loungers on the Boulevards; and the "familiarity" did not "breed contempt." Night after night I would sit at my little table (for I had selected one as far as possible from the orchestra, which I generally contrived to secure), and while tranquilly sipping my little cup of cafe noir, and smoking my clay pipe, observed the curious people by whom I was surrounded, until, at last, nearly every individual had unwittingly revealed to me something of his (or her) secret history. All the waiters got to know me, and one of them—whose scarred face told more touchingly than the pages of Lamartine or Louis Blanc of the revolutions through which he had passed, would bring my invariable cup of coffee without my even ordering it. It would often be placed on my table before I had seen him. There was no servility about the man, but he was the most assiduous, the most sprightly, the most sensible servant I had ever seen.

The first-class English servant is something appalling. He is the most solemn creature in the world. I never could get rid of the idea that he was dedicated and set apart by some awful and mysterious ritual, the memory of which haunted him like a guilty conscience. He seems like the *valet* "of the Shadow of death." I remember a corps of these solemnities at Furnival's Inn, London, who affected me like a brotherhood of Black Friars. I would as soon have been served by ghosts. When one of them had received an order, he would disappear so stealthily, and return so mysteriously, that it was difficult not to believe that he had immediately sunk through a crack in the floor and risen up again through the same place, like a new and uncomfortable species of Dumb Waiter. The creatures would linger about your table, and pick up any crumbs which, in the trepidation of the moment, you might have dropped, like so many ravens. The fellows were all dressed in black, and presided over your meal as over a funeral, looking as glum as demons on half-pay. The idea of offering one of them the customary fee of "thrippence," would no more occur to you than of offering pennies to a parson for a burial service. But I remember that when I omitted this little ceremony, in the first instance, the friar suddenly became human for a moment, and showed that

"The devil of a monk was he,"

by asking for his pittance as humbly as if he had been no more than top Boots at the Goose and Gridiron.

I had a similar experience at the Clarendon Hotel, where the solemn flunkeys—all six feet high and solemn as magnates—made me feel as if I were being waited upon by Her Majesty's Most Noble Knights of the Garter. To put anything into their royal palms but gold, would have been a kind of sacrilege. I recollect mistaking one of them, as he stood airing his calves on the front stoop, for "that cypher at the left hand of a royal digit—the incidental Albert;" but knowing in what good training the Prince is kept by his Royal Mistress, I was soon convinced of my mistake, by seeing the gartered flunkey in treasonable relations with an indisputable chambermaid.

The first-class French servant, though quite as prompt as his Cockney brother, instead of being as solemn as a cow, is as cheerful as a bird. He is lively without being fussy, civil without being servile, neat without being prim, sociable without being impertinent, and dignified without being solemn. He neither neglects you nor annoys you, and though never hovering about like a demon, is always at hand when wanted, and at the end of the meal receives his little gratuity with as much grace as if it were the Cross of the Legion of Honor.

But to return to the Coffee-Concert. Of course I made some acquaintances there; for the French are a sociable race, and more than any other addicted to talk. They are the only great talkers I have met with who were not great bores. The reason is, that they don't talk at you like the English, the American, the German, but with you. They are not so humorous as the English, however, nor so grave as the German, nor so 'cute as the Yankee; but they are more ready, more genial, and more witty than either. Their weakness is a passion for generalization and paradox. But even this is a charm. A Frenchman's mind is like a lightly charged electric battery, from which you are constantly receiving the most agreeable shocks.

The acquaintances I made at the concert were generally students and studentesses. Most of the former were from the country. This was evident at a glance. They lacked the city touch. They were Frenchmen in the rough, and had been sent to Paris to get a little "shine." But the country ore is difficult to polish. There is something wrong in the grain. It is too soft. You might as well try to polish pudding-stone or putty. This, however, was no objection to me. I was seeking for character, not lustre. I had seen patent-leather-heads enough in London and New York. Besides, too much polish destroys the natural enamel, which no artificial brightness can replace. Not that I am an admirer of rusticity. The gods forbid! Your country clown is a very good creature, no doubt, and so is a donkey, or a duck, but not for companionship. He "works up" well in pastorals, and adorns a tale fitly enough, but he doesn't bear inspection. Your country wench, too, has her attractions, like a hen, or a cow, but as a woman—well, even as a woman she is not without a certain charm, and as a figure in a landscape she is invaluable.

The milk-maid 'neath the cow, or tree,
A pretty picture is to see,
But nothing more.

My student friends were generally "countrified" without being clownish. Some of them, among the new-comers, were in a rather crude state, like so much raw material, but this made them all the more interesting; for to watch them as they were being manufactured, was like watching the process of crystalization —or dock-making.

The studentesses, whom I came to know, may be judged of, in general, by the description already given. Contact with students had made some of them very bright. They seemed to have been educated by friction. They were not so remarkable for their knowledge as for their smartness. They were like our Western orators—smart in inverse proportion to their learning. They were educated, but not cultivated. What they knew had been learned, not from books, but from experience. Some of them had rather superior minds. I remember two, in particular, Mademoiselles Octavie and Rosalie—who who were among the most intelligent persons of my acquaintance. Neither of them could read or write; but

"They knew what's what; and that's as high
As metaphysic wit can fly."

Statisticians, who go about classifying men and women, as if they were minerals, would have placed them in the category of "Persons with no instruction." But neither Octavie or Rosalie could be made into a statistic. They would be as much out of place in a tabular statement as a figure of rhetoric. I was not likely myself to commit the statistician's blunder as to their instruction, for the most ignorant persons I knew were graduates from our first colleges: M.D.'s, A.B.'s, B.A.'s, D.D.'s, etc., who were

"Small by degrees—"

with the natural impossibility of ever becoming

"—beautifully less."

Octavie and Rosalie had graduated at the school of Nature. They had each summered about twenty Winters. Their chief educational defect, as the world would call it, was a refreshing ignorance of literature. But though they know little about books, and nothing about authors, they had more good sense than could be distilled out of a dozen libraries. Your mere scholar was a fool to them.

Octavie had a natural genius for drawing faces. Stiff used to say she was a prodigy. She never bothered herself much about accuracy of detail, but would seize at once upon a man's characteristic trait of body or mind, and with a touch of her pencil make it speak to you like a confession.

"She saw the manners in the face,
And drew the essential forms of grace."

I remember her drawing the head of a poor student, who had lost one of his legs in the revolution of 1848. Stiff told her she had given a one-legged expression to the face itself; and so she had—the features were correct, but they limped. One of her portraits was better than a biography; for she could read character if she couldn't read books. Her mind was not lumbered with other people's thoughts, there was "ample scope and verge enough" for her own. The mysterious Sanscrit of the human countenance was the only scripture she could understand. "Silence," said she to me one day, as I was trying to evade one of her questions, by seeming not to have heard it, "is much more dangerous for you than speech. When your tongue stops talking, your lip commences and tells the whole story. The tongue is a natural liar, and therefore keeps out of sight. But the treacherous lip, though a servant of the tongue, is always ready to betray its master. So if you wish to deceive me, keep your tongue swinging like a bell, and my ears may lead me astray. But when my ears are asleep, depend upon it my eyes more than fill their place."

The keenness of such a woman was not to be eluded. Her room was always a confessional to me. It was so to every one. Hence her criticisms of society were almost as good as her caricatures of individuals. After being bored by some student with an insipid hash of commonplace literature, or after skimming pert articles in some literary review, to meet with such a mind as hers, which gave everything at first hand, was like getting into a ripe orchard after sickening all Summer on poor preserves.

Rosalie was not so merry as Octavie, but was much more introspective. She studied her own nature, and generalized from that as to the nature of others. She was silent as a star, and therein differed as much from Octavie as a sundial from a townclock. She would sit a whole evening without saying more than ten words, but these ten words were as authoritative as the ten commandments.

Her serenity amid the confused scenes about her was like the calm still water amid the chaos of a great city. The confusion was reflected, but not echoed. Why and how she became what she was, I never asked. It was none of my business. The student to whom she was attached, was an enthusiastic young fellow "in the law." Their love for each other was a religion. Their demeanor to each other—to superficial eyes—was cold almost to indifference; but they were always together, and were evidently more than happy. Their society was agreeable to me beyond that of all other persons. But the enjoyment of it was of short duration. The young man was summoned home, and, ere he departed, the young woman died. I have not looked upon her like since; and but for her should never, perhaps, have known how vastly superior is a nature developed by experience and having all its instincts and emotions quickened into life under the influence of love, to a nature educated in artificial schools, with all its instincts and emotions deadened and depraved by conventional morality and heartless gentility. She was "a very honorable and sincere woman ;" and though no stone marks the place of her burial—alas! there were enough thrown at her to make her a monument—I find it always green, and never without a tribute of fresh flowers.

Of course Octavie and Rosalie are not given as types. Poor girls, they were more like shadows. I have introduced them to the reader because they were introduced to me. The ordinary studentess requires no introduction. It is enough to see her. And, to be frank, she had no attraction for me. I didn't like her "make." There are some people, moreover, who should be kept at a good focal distance. I wouldn't have them destroyed, for doubtless they have their uses, like snobs and vermin, which we only attack when they annoy us. They are certainly useful in the way of variety. Wanting them, or any other creatures, the great world-scape would be deficient in some element of beauty. Shade is as necessary to a picture as light, and variety is not only the "spice," but the condition of life. Nothing is uniform but death.

[To be continued our next.]

For the Saturday Press.

TRANSITION.

Just now my frame felt full of fire,
As if a poet's soul possess'd it,
And every nerve was thrilled, like wire
Of harp, when minstrel's hand has press'd it;
My heart felt happy, free, and strong,
Just ready to gush forth in song!

But, suddenly, to gloom was turned
The gladness which so late had thrill'd me;.
Those thoughts of flame no longer burned,
A speechless sense of sorrow chill'd me!
Poor soul, be patient! Thou, ere long
Shalt burst thy chains and sing thy song!

ANNA MARY FRESAN.

THE OLD AND THE NEW.

It is half-past eleven P. M.

The last day of December is about to make its exit. In thirty minutes, by the clock, there will be a death and a birth in the family—in Time's family, we mean. The Old Year will be buried, decently and with some thought, we trust; and the New Year will rule the world, heir to the royal robes of the seasons—the white robe for its youth, the green for its prime, and the mantle of sere and yellow leaves for its old age.

We cling to time as we get older; we part with it reluctantly. Our old friends are dearer; and when the Year, which has made merry and sorrowful music for us, is dying, we would keep it with us yet awhile longer; we have things to say and do, things to undo and unsay; and the cry rises to our heart, if not always to our lips:

"Old Year, you shall not die;
We did so laugh and cry with you,
We've half a mind to die with you,
Old Year, if you must die ?"

Ah! if we could conjure back the poor ghost! Would it be well?

It lacks twenty-five minutes of twelve.

There is restless life in the streets. The brilliant lights in the shop-windows on Broadway flare on a wonderful panorama of faces—some as fresh as beauty and youth can make them, and some old, and wan, and pitiful. The horses, with their girdles of silver bells, have gone mad with melody. The sleighs dart to and fro like huge ground-swallows. Now you catch a glimpse of a lovely face peering from the silky buffalo robes, now a little white hand arranging the furs—you see a diamond sparkling on the dainty third finger. Peals of laughter break from Miss Sweetlips, as the dashes by, and the ragged beggar pauses and listens. A band of music passes through the street playing gay airs. The music grows fainter and fainter, and is lost in the night, the solemn, cold, starry night that hangs over the great city.

A quarter to twelve, says the clock.

There is snow on the long streets of the city, snow on the melancholy leafless trees which shiver in the parks, as if they were waiting for somebody; snow on the house-tops, and up in the dizzy belfry, where certain metallic little birds are nestled. They are silent and stiff with cold; they tremble as the wind shrieks among the beams and rafters overhead, and when a sudden gust sprinkles them with snow, they shake off the flakes petulantly. They will sing anon. Mysterious airs circle around the belfry: there are half audible voices—voices of sorrow and complaint—voices that breathe words of hope, and trust, and love; there is a rustling of frosty wings, and snow-stars fall when the pinions brush against each other in the darkness. But no human eye can see these things. You see only the dismal grey church, the massive carven door-way, the Gothic windows, the square belfry, and the sharp spire which pierces the gloomy atmosphere, and seems to prick a star here and there on the lowering clouds. But, nevertheless, there are weird people out to-night, and the air about the steeple is thick with them. It is ghost-time. The phantoms of Long Ago hover near our firesides, and sit in vacant chairs. Old voices haunt us as we pass into unlighted rooms—faces of children, and gentle women, and we forget for a moment that

"The mossy marbles rest
On the lips that we have pressed
In their bloom."

There are familiar footfalls on the stair-way, and voices of other days.

"O for the touch of a vanished hand,
And the sound of a voice that in still!"

We stare in the grate, and the book we have been reading closes on our finger.

It is twelve o'clock.

Was he a friend of yours, that Old Year? Did he bring you sorrow in many shapes? Did he give you a restless heart and a tired brain? Let him go, then! But if he were kind, if he filled your cup with sweet wines, and bade Love to wait upon your life—why, weep for him, for he is dead. The New Year may not be as kind. If the Old wronged you, the New shall right you. It shall bring you many and precious things. It shall lead you in pleasanter ways; and, ere it grow old and ripe, and ready to drop into the grave, you shall (if you are a lover) touch hands with —let us call her Youth—and Beauty and Goodness, for she ought to be all these!

Listen! the city bells toll for the Old Year.
"His face is growing sharp and thin.
A'ack! our friend is gone.
Close up his eyes: tie up his chin:
Step from the corpse, and let him in
That standeth there alone,
And waiteth at the door.
There's a new foot on the floor, my friend,
And a new face at the door, my friend,
A new face at the door."

And for all good Christian souls we pray—God be wi' you!

For the Saturday Press.

THE CHRISTMAS HYMN I HEARD.

I had heard the Christmas bells, and had ceased awhile to weep,
And was pausing on the threshold of the mystic door of sleep,
When my soul was called to earth again by music soft and sweet,—
The sound of some one singing Christmas carols in the street.

She sang the Saviour's story—his lowly, humble birth,
His youth, his holy manhood, his sufferings on earth,
His death upon the Cross, his triumph in the skies—
And drops of tender sorrow overflowed my aching eyes.

Then he sang of Christmas memories and the influence they shed,
Making dearer still the living, making dearer still the dead;
Of little ones rejoicing in their parents' tender love,
And of greater far rejoicings in the home of God above.

"There," sang she, "round the golden throne the spotless spirits stand,
All clad in robes of purity—a happy shining band;
And their hymn is, 'Glory! glory to the Lord of earth and sky!
Oh! blessed are the innocent—the good who early die!'"

Then I raised me from my pillow, smoothed back my tangled hair,
Hushed the sobs within my bosom, and clasped my hands in prayer;
And when I sank to sleep again the sweetest dreams were given,
For I heard, all night, dear Anna singing Christmas hymns in heaven!

M. E.

Brooklyn, Dec. 26, 1858.

NEW YORK JANUARY 8, 1859

JANUARY.

The woods are bare,
And here and there
The grey moss hangs its mournful hair;
The leaves sun-burned,
By fierce winds spurned,
Lie smoldering 'mid the soil inurned.

The leafless lines
Of trailing vines
Stretch harp-like through the sounding pines;
From their festoons
Ring solemn tunes,
As weird as any Northern runes.

Cold wind, white snow,
Sweeps fast, falls slow,
And chills the landscape's Autumn glow;
The ice-bolts freeze
The naked trees,
And seal the old Year's obsequies.

The days are cold,
The earth is old,
And mourns its Summer's squandered gold;
The birds are dumb,
The springs are numb,
And Winter in his might has come.

FITZ JAMES O'BRIEN.

A NEW PORTRAIT OF PARIS: PAINTED FROM LIFE.

"Paint me as I am".—Cromwell.
"Now being from Paris recently.
This fine young man would show his skill."
Holmes.

BY HENRY CLAPP, JR.

CHAPTER XI.

THE Author's First Five Days in Paris—How in London he was Amazed and in Paris Delighted—The Effect of Paris upon him in the Morning—His First Breakfast and How Famous it Was—How he Astonished a Native and Received a Gratuitous Lesson From Him—How, when in Cowes, he Does as Cows Do—How he was Anxious Not to Pass for a Foreigner—What he Thinks of the Plasticity and Distinguishability of Americans—How he got a Glimpse of Louis Napoleon—His Portrait of Him—What he would Think if he Saw Such a Looking Man in New York.

I have thus far described only a few incidents of my first day in Paris. And what a day it was! I shall not soon forget it. As before stated, I had just come from London.

That vast metropolis had bewildered me with its immensity, and oppressed me with its magnificence. It loomed up in the background of my memory like a gloomy old picture by Salvata Rosa. Paris, on the other hand, as it lay out before me in all its Summer glory, encircled by a double wreath of trees; reclining upon the banks of the sweet-flowing Seine; and basking beneath a sky of more than Italian purity and softness, painted itself upon my mind with all the transparent beauty of a city by Canaletti, and the atmospheric brilliance of a landsdape by Claude.

In London, you are amazed; in Paris you are delighted. Looking out upon the former from the proud dome of St. Paul's Cathedral, you exclaim, instinctively, "How grand!" Gazing down upon the latter from the turreted heights of Notre Dame, you cry out, enthusiastically, "How beautiful!" The English capital oppresses you like a primeval forest; the French fascinates you like a perennial garden. London commands your reverence like a potentate; Paris wins your admiration like a coquette. With the one you deliberate, with the other you flirt. Upon London you make a formal call, with Paris you spend the afternoon and take tea. To the British cockney you touch your hat and "move on;" with the Gallic cockney you shake hands and smoke a cigar. The American traveller spends a week in London and a month in Paris, and returns home thinking of the one and dreaming of the other, resolved all the while to revisit France before he dies, but to go by the way of England.

There was a charm about the beautiful city which was inconceivable. I put up at a curious and venerable hotel, the air of which was so familiar, that a strange home-feeling took possession of me, as if I had stopped there before. Who knows but what, in some pre-existent state I had; for the multangular old house had such an ancient look that Nature seemed to have adopted it as her own,

"And granted it an equal date
With Andes and with Ararat."

Every object about me seemed like an old acquaintance. The narrow street and spacious courtyard reminded me of Havana. The vernacular of the place recalled New Orleans. The Englishmen about reminded me of London. There was an Irishman there whom I had known in Dublin, and a Scotchman with whom I had taken snuff in Edinburgh and at Loch Lomond. Even the landlord seemed like an old friend, for he reminded me of a favorite host in Rio Grande, while a merchant from Canada carried me back to Quebec and the falls of Montmorency. And it was perhaps the combination of these facts, that made me feel as if my little barque of life had suddenly backed water, and glided stern first into an old familiar port.

When I awoke from my first night's sleep, instead of being startled by the novelty of the things about me, and by the strange noises in the street, the very chairs seemed to open their arms to me, my umbrella seemed absolutely to fraternize with the poker in the corner, and the plaintive cry of the milkmaid echoing through the streets sounded as familiar to me as "Home, sweet Home." The sensation was delightful. I hurried on my clothes and rushed down stairs. Save now and then a sonorous snore, serving as a melodious bass to the tinkling fountain in the courtyard, the house was still as the grave. I found the outer gate bolted. I tapped at the door of the concierge, (portress) and in a minute the bolt was sprung, the gate flew open, and I was in the street.

Day had just cracked; in a few moments it broke. I walked instinctively toward the river. The great city was just opening one eye, and beginning to yawn. It had "slept soundly," like a certain great statesman, who now sleeps more soundly than ever, though he "still lives." Newsmen were abroad, with papers still moist with the sweat of the editor's brow. I bought the *Constitutionnel*, and was relieved to learn from Dr. Veron, that the Prince President, (now an Imperial Majesty,) who at the last accounts had a boil on his left thigh, was as well as could be expected. Presently I encountered a postman in stiff glazed hat and crimson-collared coat, (two sizes too small,) assorting his letters in a patent leather box swung around his neck, and serving also as a portable writing-desk, to which his right ear served as a convenient pen-carrier. The butchers, bakers, and wine-dealers, were just opening their shops. I noticed that these were all fronted with ornamental iron railings, and that the butcher's shops had neither door nor window-sash, the strong iron-work answering for both. I attributed the fortified state of these establishments to the fact that revolutions being of such common occurrence in France—being in fact a kind of necessity to the people, like wine and tobacco—such precautions are absolutely indispensable. When "liberty, equality, and fraternity" are rampant, provisions, it would seem, are in rather brisk demand. Eating and drinking are about the only permanent institutions in the land: Grub and Grog are everywhere great facts, like Gog and Magog.

While making these reflections, I ought to have been looking out for my eyes; for a dwarfish little lad, bearing on his shoulders anything but a dwarfish ladder, came near running me through without so much as offering me a Jacob's ascent to heaven. I looked down on the fellow, and found he was a mural advertiser. Curiosity having overcome anger, I watched his movements for a while, and was amused to see him plant his infernal machine against every dead wall he could find, and, running up the half dislocated rounds like an imp, cover the blank space, by means of stencil-boards and fancy colors, with immense advertisements for the million, announcing every species of article from the latest electro-magnetic panacea, to the hundred and fiftieth volume (just out) of Alexandre Dumas' autobiography. This explained to me the scarcity of job-printers in Paris, and the almost entire absence of advertisements in its newspapers. I could not help observing also, that the placards of the innumerable theatres were all of a uniform and diminutive size, and of the most modest appearance; and I learned subsequently that their uniform dimension was not a matter of choice, but was ordered by the all-powerful and all-meddling government —another impediment to the art of printing. The omnibuses now beginning to pass at the slow jog-trot which I presume is also prescribed by law (for the French animal, from the horse to the high-priest, is a poor law-stricken creature), I had a chance to peep into the comfortable, arm-chaired interior of these spacious vehicles, and to notice that every spare inch of space, from the broad-arched ceiling down, was covered with showy advertisements.

The city had by this time opened its other eye, and begun to wink with excitement. Market carts from the country were groaning by, drawn by stout-legged horses in outlandish harness, and driven often by buxom young women, whose rosy cheeks would seem to have been pecked into dimples by the birds. Handcarts, also laden with produce, cracked along the flinty thoroughfares, dragged by stout hucksters, assisted by their bareheaded, wooden-shod wives, sometimes yoked by their side (in typical significance of wedlock), sometimes pushing on behind. Mustached young counter-jumpers lounge to their stores as if still dreaming of last night's adventures. Flashy young women, with mysterious bundles under their arms, trip homeward in suspicious haste. Black-eyed work-girls, whose pretty white caps were but little paler than the care-worn faces they strove to enliven with ribbons and flowers, stroll, basket in hand, to their workshops. Long lines of diminutive policemen (*sergents de ville*) hustle the passersby, and march in bad time and worse temper to their several posts. Water-carriers, men and women, wheel mounted hogsheads of *l'eau fraiche* to their customers, stopping from house to house, drawing the cool liquid from the tap in streams which it is difficult to believe are not solid crystal, and carrying it in braces of iron-bound buckets, yoked to the neck, up never so many stories. Bakers' women trudge alone with huge baskets of bread, leaving *here* immense rolls from three to ten feet in length, *there* family loaves as large as the family-chair bottom. Fuel-dealers, bent double with bags of coal or racks of wood, cheerfully carry their heavy loads up a hundred or more slippery stairs. Outcast Jews, whose heritage in Sartor Resartus-dom appears to be its cast-off garments, weary you with their husky cry of "old clothes! old clothes!!" *Chiffoniers* and *chiffoniéres* (the distinction is sexual) grope along the gutters, and stirring every dirt heap on their beat with iron-tipped sticks or hookers, seize upon every morsel of rag, paper, bone, vegetable or bread, they can find, and toss it with marvellous dexterity over their shoulders into a long-backed conical basket, which they wear slung behind like an immense bustle. And finally—for my morning walk is about finished—crowds of working people of both sexes flock to cheap wine-shops, eating-houses, and milkeries, (*laiteries*,) to take their morning bite. The example is worth following, if only to change the scene, so I take an omnibus back to the hotel, and having made vain attempts during the ride to decipher the posters with which roof and sides were covered, feel, on getting out, as if my eye-lids had suddenly been changed into water-power printing presses, and for the last hour had been hard at work transferring to my poor retina an upside-down advertisement of every article for sale within the city.

The next thing was to get breakfast. Here now was a chance to try the famous French coffee, and still more famous bread. I had no sooner ordered a supply of these delicacies, than a lively waiter, glorying in the name of Fejux, spread a chalk-white cloth upon a little square table, arranged the necessary cutlery and crockery with military precision, and in a few moments placed before me a miniature coffee-pot (which looked as if it had just been borrowed from the nursery, and turned up its nose as if it didn't like to come), an immense pitcher, evidently stolen from "Rachael at the Well" (see somebody's picture at the Academy), a round silver plate, about the size of a dollar, containing a little pyramid of sugar cubes, and a gilt-edged cup and saucer about an inch thick, and much better adapted to the thick-lipped sons of Africa, than to the fine labial proportions of a Yankee. The tiny pot was filled with coffee of a consistency between a liquid and a paste (Day and Martin! what a dose !), while the huge pitcher held, as well as it could, about a gallon of boiling milk. I at once poured all the coffee into the cup—though with difficulty, for it ran like molasses in the winter—and then, American fashion, added a spoonful or two of milk, and (demolishing the pyramid) sweetened it to my taste. The compound duly mixed, I smiled a benediction upon it, and while moisting a slice of bread which I had just cut from a roll over three yards long, sipped it down as if instead of being Mocha it had been nectar. But the strength of the beverage was such that, after a few sips, I had to own up that it was beyond the strength of my poor nerves. Meanwhile a native, sitting at the next table, had been gazing at me with astonishment. He kept silent as long as his French nature could stand it, and then, violently shrugging his shoulders at the risk of dislocating them, and drawing in his round head (the French all have round heads) like a turtle, he sifted a mon Dieu! through his mustaches, and, evidently for the purpose of giving me a lesson, ordered coffee for himself.

Presently he was served; but instead of turning all the coffee into his cup, he poured in about two spoonsful, and then filled it up with the boiling milk, and added four or five pieces of sugar. This done, he cut his bread longitudinally into four pieces, and, taking them in turn, dipped each into the foaming mixture, and sopped away till his cup was dry; moreover, by dint of jerking open his jaws at each mouthful, like a shark, he conducted the operation without so much as dampening his luxurious beard; his shirt bosom was protected by a large napkin or bib, tucked carefully round his neck, *a la baby*. I observed also that the remains of the sugar were at once and unblushingly transferred to his trowsers pocket—a practice, as I afterward learned, which so far from being contrary to French jurisprudence, was only a nice exhibition of French economy and justice. In fact, to deny to a Frenchman the privilege of pocketing his extra sugar, would be an invasion of his domestic rights, sooner than submit to which he would swallow all he could lay his hands on, at the risk of sweetening himself into a preserve, and dying ignominiously of dyspepsia.

The next time I took coffee, I pocketed the extra sugar myself, though not, I confess, without the feeling that I was guilty of petty larceny. But I adhere to the good old injunction: "When in Cowes, do as cows do." Moreover, I was especially anxious not to pass for a foreigner, and I so far succeeded, that after a year's residence, I had to take a freshly arrived American with me to certify that though I neither chewed, shaved, bragged, spoke through my nose, wore black trousers, whistled, nor whittled, I was nevertheless a genuine and incorruptible Yankee.

I have often observed, however, that Americans lose their nationality sooner than any other people. They assimilate easily—much more so, for instance, than the English. I can

"Smell the blood of an Englishman"—

anywhere. You can no more transfigure one of them into a Frenchman, than you can transform a bull into a butterfly. Let him disguise himself as he will, and often does, with the most savage mustache and imperial; feed him for a twelvemonth on frogs and *fricandeaus*; let him live for a lifetime in the *Quartier Latin*, among students and grisettes, yet he will never lose his identity, but will always remain the same stolid sulky old Briton.

I have recently (to anticipate my story) seen Paris alive with Englishmen. They had come over with the Lord Mayor and his Aldermen, to be feted and fed by the portly Prefect. They amused the good people for a fortnight. They were to be found everywhere, and had John Bull (horns and all) been branded on every forehead, they would not have been a whit more easy to recognize. I could distinguish them with the naked eye at the top of the Pantheon—especially the Aldermen. Their big round faces, "fragrant with the mince pies of half a century," and flanked with huge collars rising from their short Durham necks like bulwarks; their plain, pulpy, yet neat "highly washed" appearance, together with their self-satisfied mein and sturdy gait, made them as conspicuous among the light-built, dapper Frenchmen, as a herd of elephants tramping through a bird-market.

Americans are not to be distinguished so easily; they are more dissolvent, and unite more readily with the mass. They are not so afraid, to borrow an old Quaker expression, of "getting into the mixture." They are more sympathetic and genial. A young, not to say a green people, are naturally so. Perhaps, when our national character becomes better formed, when it shall have become hardened and enameled by time, we shall be as stubborn and unyielding as the English. We are certainly not so now, and it is scarcely worth one's while to trouble himself about a distant and facetious posterity.

But to return. I had just finished my breakfast, when suddenly every one in the coffee-room rushed to the door, and my next-table neighbor, dragging me by the arm, informed me that "that scoundrel (*scelerat*) of a Napoleon was passing by." Anxious to see the princely adventurer, I joined the crowd, and was lucky enough to get a good look at him.

I should have known the rogue, even from the caricatures I had seen of him in *Punch*. He had a face of bronze. It told no tales. It hadn't blushed for twenty years. The eyes were small, dark, and partially eclipsed. The forehead, of average height, and neither concave nor convex, seemed, like the rest of the face, to be in the act of retiring from observation. The mouth was fortified by an impenetrable moustache. The nose was long (such as his uncle liked), and served to steady the whole face—like a flying-jib.

The ears, also, were long, and so was the head—long and narrow, like an Irish mile. The general characteristic of the face was want of expression, and a certain demure, ruminating air, like that of a cow.

He is a man of middling height, and neither lean nor fat. He has an upright carriage, a firm step, and a look of unconcerned security, as if he were over-insured Moreover, he is a sumptuous liver, a free-lover, a fast rider, a good whip, and a dead shot.

If I should see such a looking man in New York, he would probably attract my attention by his swarthy complexion, his luxuriant moustache, curled up like a crescent, his small discreet eyes, and his long arched nose, setting the seal upon his countenance, and giving it the expression of an "Israelite indeed, in whom there is" much "guile."

CHAPTER XII.

How the Reader is to be Initiated.—How the French are as much a Mystery to the Author as ever—His Failure for Three Years to form any Idea of them.—What would have happened if he had been an Ambassador, or a Consul, or a Dyspeptic Clergyman.—The Author proceeds with his Work—How he got Settled. —His Color at this Time.—His Philosophy of First Impressions.—A few Words more about the Hotel Corneille.—The Author's Notions about Landlords.—What Solemn Creatures they are in America, etc., etc.

It is well to inform the untravelled reader that he is to be initiated into a knowledge of Paris (so far as he depends upon this work for the ceremony), exactly as fast and as far as I myself was; and, truth to say, that was neither very fast nor very far.

The French are as much a mystery to me now, as they were before I crossed the little but imperious channel which, despite the cunning intervention of steam, and the cunninger *sub*-vention of electricity, separates France forever and ever from old England.

During the three years that I spent among them, all my attempts to form a general and comprehensive idea of their national character (so that I might compare it with our own, if peradventure we have one, which, under favor of the stars and stripes, may be doubted) were completely futile.

They seemed to me alternately the gayest and the saddest, the most profound and the most superficial, the most religious and the most sceptical, the most humane and the most unfeeling, the bravest and the most cowardly, the most polished and the most vulgar, the cleanest, and the dirtiest, the best and the worst of all civilized people. Moreover, I found my judgment in these respects varying according to the state of the weather, the state of my digestion, the state of the funds (generally low), etc., etc. But, in the end, I came to the conclusion that I was neither a philosopher nor a sage, and, therefore, that for me to attempt to be critical or profound, or to see anything more than the veriest outside of Paris, would be utter folly. Happy indeed shall I be, thought I, if I come at last, like the great Balzac, to have a profound knowledge even of the surface of things.

A very comfortable and comforting state of mind this, which saved me a world of trouble; for thenceforth I held it to be my mission (think of having a mission !) not to fathom nor explain, not to reconcile nor even to understand things, but merely to glance at them as they went by (for everything seems to be going by in Paris), and to submit my observations to an indiscriminate and happily indiscriminating public, without further concern.

Had I been an Ambassador stationed *"near"* Paris to present properly endorsed young ladies and gentlemen at Court, and settle the solemn diplomatic question of Breeches; or a Consul sent *"to"* Paris (a distinction which the vulgar, unofficial mind will not appreciate, but which, doubtless, has some awful significance at the "Circumlocution Office" at Washington) to complicate commercial relations and embarrass small tradespeople; or a clergyman sent abroad by his tender-hearted congregation, to get cured of a dyspepsia in French restaurants; or a "regular correspondent," commissioned to frequent Paris *salons*, and worm out the state policy and family secrets of Prince Napoleon; in either of these cases, I should doubtless have acquired, at once, 1st, a perfect knowledge of the French language; 2d, a perfect knowledge of French institutions (eleemosynary and other); and 3d, a perfect knowledge of the French character. But, unfortunately, I was only a private individual, *pure et simple*, and, therefore, could hope for no such success. Wait till I am a Plenipotentiary.

But to proceed with my work. At the last accounts, the author was uncomfortably settled in the higher latitude of a Student's Hotel; had made several peculiar acquaintances, visited one or two peculiar institutions, got an inkling of student-life (apart from its studies), and was gradually making—or, in default of this, wishing—himself at home.

NEW YORK JANUARY 15, 1859

Dramatic Feuilleton.

Dolce far Niente.

How delightful is idleness! Mr. Tennyson, when he wrote "there is no joy but calm," fully interpreted that delicious sensation, when one feels suspended like Mahomet's coffin, between heaven and earth; not all angelic, and yet not entirely mortal. I never could blame Rinaldo when he played truant in Armida's gardens, and sympathize entirely with that hard-working man Ulysses, who, when he got a chance to idle with Calypso, went into the indolent business with enthusiasm. The dramatic critics of the city have it in their power now to be all Rinaldos if they so choose. Some with whom I am acquainted appear to have the most singular ideas of enjoying the holiday with which the beneficence of Mr. Wallack and Miss Keene has blessed them. They go sleighing and come home with inflexible noses. One of them proposed seriously to me to go up to the Central Park to skate. I told him that I would have had the greatest pleasure in accompanying him, if it were not for the frost. But, he remonstrated, you can't have ice without frost. I settled the question by stating that I made it a rule never to skate in frosty weather. Another seduced me over to New Jersey on foot, under the pretence of seeing Nature. I cannot say that Nature received us hospitably. She drenched us, and froze us, and laid slippery traps in our path, whereon we tumbled, and in short behaved in so brutal a manner that I shall never speak well of her again. After this adventure, I took to sofas and cigars, to which, please Brahma, I will stick until next Monday evening, when the spell will be broken, and Mr. Lester Wallack will produce his grand five-act melo-com- ic drama, with new scenery, dresses, music, and a super-abundance of supers. Then will be seen in the orchestra stalls that imposing array of noble countenances belonging to the gang of critics; and judicial brows will contract, or solemn lips will smile according as the verdict is favorable or unfavorable. From what I know of the piece, I am inclined to think that it will be highly interesting. The plot is exciting and ingeniously constructed; the characters are well defined, and Mr. Wallack himself sustains a rile in it so utterly opposed to the character he has been so splendidly impersonating for the last five weeks, that it will be a matter of real interest to witness his performance. The scenery, dresses, and all that sort of thing, are exceedingly fine, and—well, I think I have said enough upon the subject. On Monday night we shall know all about it. Until then—I was going to say adieu, but find that I have still a few remarks more to make. Here they are:

"Comparisons are Odorous."

I have received the following note, and from the complimentary tone in which it is couched, feel that I cannot do less than endeavor to afford as much satisfaction to the writer as lies in my power:

New York, January 11, 1869.

To Fitz James O'Brien, Esq.:

Dear Sir:—Having read your very able and talented theatrical criticisms, and knowing your high ability as a judge of dramatic acting, I would ask you whom you consider best actor, critically speaking, James W. Wallack or Edwin Forrest?

Yours respectfully, C. W. Daly.

Mr. Daly—I presume my correspondent in the well known Shakesperian scholar and legal luminary—must be aware that nothing is more difficult than a comparison between eminent actors, except perhaps a separate analysis of their styles. Nevertheless, regardless of the many difficulties which the subject presents, I have no hesitation in presenting an opinion which I trust will be profitable to my correspondent.

I think it was fortunate that Mr. Daly should have applied to me in this case, rather than to any of my brother-critics, as from never having seen Mr. Forrest perform, I am enabled to present my views of his acting in a more impartial manner than if I had been a frequent witness of his artistic efforts.

Mr. James W. Wallack and Mr. Edwin Forrest are both tragedians. To be a gifted tragedian, requires a sure combination of vocal and physical advantages which are rarely found united in any one actor. I think I may say, without any hesitation, that in the requirements for the stage, Mr. Forrest is as little excelled by Mr. Wallack as Mr. Wallack is by Mr. Forrest. Both these artists have, at various times, played a great variety of parts, and it may not be too much to say that they have been frequently, not to say uniformly, successful. It is in a comparison of their styles that the critic encounters the main difficulty, for excellence is so nearly allied to excellence, that the distinction sought after, subtly evades the grasp of the analyst.

If Mr. Forrest in distinguished for a certain impressive vigor, neither is Mr. Wallack lacking in dramatic force, and although, in some of the lighter shades of human character, the latter gentleman may be said to be almost without a rival, there are those who maintain Mr. Forrest's supremacy in the subtleties of his art. Mr. Forrest is manly and picturesque. Mr. Wallack is picturesque and manly. Mr. Wallack's effects are sudden, yet majestic. Mr. Forrest's are startling, but dignified. Mr. Wallack's voice is musical and forcible; Mr. Forrest's tones are full of melodious strength. In the exhibition of the sterner passions, such as hate, revenge, Mr. Wallack cannot be surpassed; while in the delineation of the stronger emotions, such as animosity and rancor, Mr. Forrest is without a rival. On the whole, I think it may be said with truth, that while the American stage could but ill spare no admirable an artist as J. W. Wallack, the drama would sustain an irreparable loss, if deprived of so eminent a tragedian as Edwin Forrest.

I trust that my well known partiality for one of the gentlemen in question, has not betrayed me into any injustice towards his estimable rival.

Fitz James O'Brien.

RELIGION AT A PREMIUM.

We copy the following businesslike statement from *The Independent*, by which it appears that Religion, in Brooklyn, is at a premium; if the same were only true of Christianity, what a Paradise the "City of Churches" would be to live in!

Pew-Renting in Plymouth Church.— The annual renting of the pews on Tuesday evening at Plymouth Church, Brooklyn, realized the round sum of *thirty-five thousand dollars*! This amount, it will be remembered, results, not from the permanent sale of the pews, but merely from their hiring for one year. The total amount for the last year was fifteen thousand dollars. The increase experienced on Tuesday evening is owing to the large additions made to the membership of the church during the past year, and to the number of those who desire to attend its public services.

In renting, all pews throughout the house (except the pastor's, and three or four others reserved) have a fixed valuation, specified on a printed diagram. The choice of pews is sold at auction to the bidder who pays for each successive choice the highest premium. When we mention that not only every pew was let, but let at a premium, and that the premiums amounted in many instances to three or four times the fixed valuation, the renting on Tuesday evening will be regarded by our readers, as one of the daily papers has remarked, "probably the most spirited sale of church pews which ever took place in this country."

The summary statement of the result is as follows:

Number of pews in house	298
Reserved	5
Pews rented—*all at premiums*	293
Amount of pew-rents, as assessed	12,054
Amount of premiums offered	12,000
Aisle seats assessments	826
Aisle seats premiums	70
Total income	24,950
In round figures, total income	25,000

In addition to these figures, we may mention that a large number of members of the church (to say nothing of a still larger number of the congregation) have been entirely unable to secure sittings. A friend who has made a rough estimate says that nearly *four hundred* church members (or nearly one-third of the entire membership) are left unprovided for!

NEW YORK JANUARY 22, 1859

JOY IN WRITING.

A Railroad Meditation.

You owe this article to an incident to me personally disagreeable. After several week's absence in the West, I had got as far on my return as Trenton, New Jersey. Being heated in the cars, anxious for fresh air, and hearing that there were five minutes to stay, I ventured out, but hardly had I taken a few paces when I heard the train start away behind me. In vain I shouted; the locomotive shouted more loudly than I could—and not only do time and steam wait for no man, but time and steam return to no man. So here I am, at the railroad station, without books, newspapers, magazines; without novel, romance, poem, or biography. A biography I have, indeed, within, but to escape going over *that*, as much as from any other motive, I sit down to scribble, and to fill up some of the duration, which lies between this hour of noon—January the 15th, 1859—and the day of doom—or 8 o'clock in the evening, when the next train comes along. I have pen, ink, and paper, however, as these presents bear witness. Such are grand instruments for amusing one's self, although they may also be instruments for annoying others. And yet what an insult it would have been had any one told the biggest of book-makers, that, as to any practical purpose, he was merely amusing himself in the mighty folios he was with such labor building up. What would great old Ockham have thought of you had you told him this? What would the writer of "The Book of Sentences" have thought? What would Flavell, who made a massive folio on the Human Soul, have thought? What would any of these giants, these men who did the *heavy* business in letters, have thought had you insinuated even in the most delicate manner, that in packing their minds into bulky tomes, which would sleep in the dust of centuries, their impulse was not very different from that which works in the mind of a traveller stopped on his journey, and seeking for some manner to pass time? But then, again, what gladsome and glorious blessings are these instruments of the Mind! Even if what they do may be neglected, or only serve to vex, what comfort they give to those who use them! "Samivel Veller," when he squared his elbows to write his first love letter, and licked his lips at every syllable, was doubly a man—first, because he was in love, and secondly, because he could, in however rude a fashion, write out the love he felt. Had the poor fellow not been able to write, how that love must have scalded his heart, and how the absence which forbade all vocal utterance must have tormented him! But Poetry in his soul, which tortured the "King's English" as he put it upon paper, was relieving music to his heart; it was rapturous song to her who received it—who probably could read as imperfectly as Samivel could write it. Pope says that writing was invented for the sake of lovers. Poor Pope! He knew such passion well—but not for passion as it agonized in such as he, did love ever invent writing. There is a joy in writing which none but writers know, and for the joy it gives I am willing to bear any sort of nonsense in which I think that joy has been felt,—sincerely felt. What a number of writers in our literature have all their real title to esteem from this geniality and joy of utterance! In this, in truth, they have their genius. The remark will apply particularly to the essayists. Evidently, Montaigne wrote in the mere love of writing. He had no public before him. When people accuse him, therefore, of being a corrupt and gross man, they make a very false judgment. If he wrote in our day as he did in his, the accusation might be felt. But there was no public in the time of Montaigne as there is in ours. He had no idea of corrupting men: as little had he an idea of improving them. He was a gentleman at ease, and he loved to write. He contemplated neither the good nor the evil of humanity. And all that he has written is not only in the manner, but in the *spirit* of a Monologue. Perhaps when he wrote those strange and very *un-readable-aloud* thinkings, he did not imagine Print or Publication. Yet take even cultivated men as they are, and you find that Montaigne does but express what most of them feel, but which from altered situations they would not dare to express, and which in these altered situations, they ought *not* to express. Montaigne was a man who had a passion for expression—writing was his medium, and therefore he took to writing. He was not a talker, and if he had been, he had none to whom he could talk. But that he did not care to talk, or care for that mode of self-utterance, may be inferred from the description of his house, and the position of his library. Addison evidently loved to write and found a joy in writing. It is this joy in writing which gives to the compositions of Addison their wealth, and music, and beauty. He does not instruct—he enchants. You do not look to him for new truths, but you are sure to find in him fresh emotions. They well up from his nature in all its senses, affections, and passions. Yet had not Addison loved to write, the world would have lost all that Addison has given it.

Then, there is Charles Lamb; we should have had nothing from him in letters but for his love of writing. For years he was stuck upon the stool of his clerkship; but ledgers could not satisfy him. He was no machine that could be regulated by the debt and credit sides of a balance-sheet. He longed for another life, which only the pen of free thought and free excitement could give him. Through this passionate desire, Charles Lamb, instead of being what Kossuth would call an "unnamed demigod" of "The India-House," has become the "Elia Of The World." We all know him now through his immortal quaintness of tragedy and comedy; but if there were nothing of him but what he did for the India-House, he would have been to the world as the remotest of the Pharaohs. And then Hazlitt, what a joy he had in writing! The fact is, no one can do writing well who has not this joy. Without it, the style is mechanical and artificial. The lyric flow of inspiration is never in it. Without joy, style is merely rhetoric, and there is nothing so remote from eloquence as rhetoric; there is nothing so remote from a truth as a truism, and a universally accepted common-place is the surest to be a universally accepted falsehood. This is what people will *not* see, and so come cant, conventionalism, and imitation.

I have delighted in the reading of Hazlitt, because I felt that he had delight in what he wrote. Joyless as the man was to the world, and to his friends, he had often real ecstacy in himself—in the memories of his childhood, youth, and early manhood. With what sad and solemn eloquence he often refers to those days—those days of dreams and beauty, which, as I have said elsewhere, "come *once* to the most wretched, and never come *twice* to the most blessed." With luxurious delight, I have read his reflec tions written in a country inn, as he looked out on the garden landscape of an English rural district, and while I read, I remembered rural inns, and rural landscapes, in Ireland, which surpassed all that he described. Now, at this bare, vulgar, and barren railway station, his pictures loom up to my mental vision, and the melancholy music of his words lingers in my ear. I care not much for Hazlitt's criticism; but for the *spirit* in which he wrote, his strong personality, his lyrical individualism, for *that* I care a great deal; I care for it with love, because of its vitality, its force, and its independence. I am no artist, not even an æsthetic connoisseur, but if any person enjoys in looking at a picture by Titian one-tenth as much as I do in reading a description of it by Hazlitt, he has indeed an exceeding satisfaction. His words penetrate me, as the picture seemed to penetrate him: the picture seemed to penetrate him from the eye-ball to the marrow; his description penetrates me from the eye-ball to the soul. I wish I had seen Mrs. Siddons in Lady Macbeth; I wish I had seen Edmund Kean in Shylock; I wish I had heard Sebastian Bache upon the organ; I wish I had heard Paganini on the violin; I wish I had heard Catalani sing; yet hardly inferior to the pleasure which these great individuals could have given me, is that which I have derived from reading Hazlitt's commentaries on art. He *lived into* his subject, and as he lived into it, he wrote.—But somewhat too much of this. The next train will soon be on. Yet now that I have got my tools at work —I kindle to my toil, and my toil has already become pleasure. If such pleasure it is with a proser like myself—what must writing have been to the gods? Oh! it is no wonder that ancient sages and singers thought it inspiration. Glorious it is, beyond all other arts. What can any other artist do—compared with the writer! The architect, grandest of all artists in his conception, is the most limited and dependent as to opportunity of impression. His work is fixed; it is local. People must come too see it; and when they do come too see it, they may little understand it. The sculptor can have larger influence. His statue can be removed, or it can be felt through copies, or from casts: the painter can, better than any of these, explain himself—but more extensively than all, more clearly, more distinctly, more spiritually, the *writer* can reproduce his ideas, and circulate them through the millions.

Speaking thus, I am speaking of writing which delights the reader.

What writing does not delight the writer? What Parson or Priest does not write his sermon, and feel while he writes it, as if it might be that of a Bossuet, a Maillon, a Chalmers or a Robert Hall—a Channing or a Martinean? I feel with every such preacher, and however small may be the measure of his intellect, I shall the more enjoy his sermon the more he has had joy in the writing of it. Tracts, pamphlets, orations, speeches, occasional poems, (God bless the mark !) are given to me by the score; I do not read them; it would be sad labor to me, if I did:—but, like Paley, when he saw the tadpoles sport in the warm frog-pond, I rejoice in the happy life which the authors must have had while they were in the rapture of conception and gestation. It is a mistake to suppose that only great writers have enthusiasm. Every creature has pleasure in the measure of its being. The dunce who scribbles a small essay, doats over it, as the genius who brings forth a great idea: for the cat as maternally licks her kitten, as the tigress licks her whelp. When I look abroad into the wilds of nature—where no human consciousness has place—I find pleasure in the thought that some other consciousness is there; at least, in this small planet of our own. So when I look through the dead spaces of a great library, I rejoice that there had been a vast mass of consciousness in the creation of it, though into real vitality it will never come again. I look on a set of stately folios, which some man has spent his life in composing, with a feeling hesitant between grief and gladness: grieved that so much work of mind should be now encircled by dust and tenanted by worms; glad to think how abundant the joy was to him who wrote them —while in writing them he lived in the life of thought and was immersed in the immortal. Whether read or not, his works made life to himself a great activity, a glorious dream, a sublime vision; and though his folios are clad in cobweb, ever and anon some kindred soul will take them down, breathe into them the breath of life, and give them, in transmutation, a new resurrection to humanity. If the writing of them served no better purpose, it kept the author from doing worse; and in putting together even these careless words, I think I have been better employed than if I had been chewing tobacco, smoking cigars, drinking at the bar, or talking with the old local loafer about the degeneracy of morals and the terrible want of practical religion. I have at least got over some vacant hours, and kept my soul from wrong; for that profound poet and divine—Doctor Watts—says that

"Satan finds some mischief still for idle hands to do."

But with all reverence to the Reverend Doctor Watts, that most ancient of sinners, to whom we have given the respectable name of Nicholas, begins with the idle heart, and not with the idle hand. I have kept both heart and hand busy: I now wait for the whistle of the steam-engine, as all of us, indeed, may listen for the trumpet of our doom.

And so ends this Railroad Meditation.

Henry Giles

Art Items.

Art Treasures.

Probably the best collection of portraits in this State is to be found in the Governor's Room of the New York City Hall. This gallery possesses specimens of the best American artists for the last fifty years. Before this period there was scarcely anything painted possessing artistic merit. Though the idea of building up a gallery was conceived after the best days of Stewart and Alston, still the great names of Sally, Morne, Inman, Page, Elliott, Jarvis, Trumbull, and others of eminence, are amply represented. From time to time the city has been presented with portraits and pictures by individuals and governments, and these are included in the collection. If the policy of employing the best artists to paint three or four pictures a year is persisted in, a very valuable historical gallery will be the result.

The gallery commenced with a portrait of Columbus, presented to the city by the Grand Duke of Tuscany some thirty-five years ago. It is an old dilapidated portrait, sombre and rich enough in tone to delight the most fastidious lover of the antique, and negative enough in character to pass for Colombus or any other man. At the time of its presentation, which was made with appropriate deference to the olden time and the illustrious name of the great discoverer, in presence of mayors, governors, and invited guests; it was considered authentic, and valued accordingly, but latterly its claims have been neglected, and it has been hung by some ignorant keeper high above the heads of forgotten mayors and city constables. It is, nevertheless, worthy the study of the art student and the antiquary. Near it used to be hung (not now, for since the fire everything in the room has been in confusion,) a mallow, peaked, long nosed, and intolerably ugly head, stiffly supported in quaint regimentals, which passed in the catalogue, and in the memory of old men, as a portrait of General Bolivar, the South American hero. The picture was presented to the city at the time when the General and his cause were uppermost in the minds of the American people. It was afterwards reported that the city had been cheated in its purchase, as it was the likeness of some other man. It is a poor painting.

There is a portrait here, such a picture as might have been painted in Colonial times, which professes to be a likeness of Governor Stuyvesant. Its authentication seems to be lost, though it is believed to be genuine. The costume is that worn in Stuyvesant's time.

A fine old picture, painted by a master, purporting to be a portrait of Hendrick Hudson, hangs high up among the neglected and distrusted. All these old pictures have received a severe shock from the late fire, and if not soon cared for, will, as generally happens after some smoking and heat, flake to pieces.

A large number of the portraits in this collection are full-lengths. Several of them rank as the best pictures of their class that have been painted by Americans. That of Commodore Decatur, by Sully, is an exceedingly happy composition, and is a fine example of color and drawing.

The excellences of Jarvis are here very apparent in numerous full-length portraits. The city employed him to paint the Commodores, retaining the originals of Bainbridge, Perry, and Swift, and presenting duplicates to other cities.

Elliott, who is, it would seem, the city painter, has here the heads of some ten people, including Governors Hunt and Seymour, and Mayors Varick, Livingston, Clinton, and Wood.

Trumbull has portraits of Presidents Monroe and Taylor, and Governor Clinton, Collins, Lewis, and others. They would hardly rank as first rate portraits in a modern exhibition of the National Academy.

Inman's pictures of Van Buren and Seward hang in this collection. The Seward is esteemed one of his best pictures. By no means the best portrait here, claims in the catalogue to be the joint effort of Inman and Huntington.

A full-length portrait of Governor Marcy, by Wm. Page, is, to our mind, the gem of the collection. Unfortunately, from some cause, the flesh tints have changed a little, but they are still eminently true and beautiful, while the modeling of the features, and the look of life, and resemblance about them, are marvelous. There is a manly force and a vigor about the picture that stamps it as the work of a master. Morse, now best known as the telegraph inventor, has here a head of Gen. Lafayette, which, though well painted, makes of the patriot a very ugly man.

There is hardly, amongst the 14 governors, 24 mayors, and numerous other pictures in the collection, a single one that is not interesting and valuable as a work of art. They can be seen at any time by application to the keeper of the City Hall.

In the Aldermen's Chamber there is Trumbull's full-length portrait of Gen. Washington, together with portraits of Alexander Hamilton, Gov. Clinton, and John Jay. In the Councilman's Chamber there is Vanderlyn's Gen. Jackson, and Com. Hull and Henry Clay by Jarvis. Besides these, there are busts of Chief Justice Marshall, by Fraser, and Clevenger's great bust of Chancellor Kent.

—We are requested to state that Miss Freeman, the artist, who (see advertisement) is to give the second of her series of Readings next Saturday, has no idea of giving up her regular profession, but, on the contrary, is more actively engaged in it than ever, and has just taken a new and elegant studio at No. 726 Broadway, where may be seen several highly finished specimens of her art. By the way, we may as well insert here a hitherto unpublished Poem, addressed to Miss Freeman (herself a Poet), some years ago, by her friend, the late John Howard Payne, and for a copy of which, with liberty to print, we are indebted to an intimate friend of the parties:

To Miss Anna Mary Freeman, on her birthday.

[A LAME APOLOGY FOR THE WANT OF A BOUQUET.]

Forever dear and gifted one,
Whose life a new year has begun,
I have not power to send thee, sweet,
Off'ring for such occasion meet.
I have not need of words to tell
My feelings now—you know them well—
But I have prayers that every year
May see a blemish disappear,
And beautifully fix the grace
Of some new virtue in its place,
Till angels welcome you at last,
Pure with the teachings of the past!
If God this benison bestow,
Unwarp'd by worldly weal or woe,
Let trials dark or bright befall,
Tow'ring, Heaven-balanc'd, o'er them all,
Each birthday which may then succeed,
Will prove a festival indeed
To you, for victories obtained,—
To us, that Providence has deign'd
Still to continue to us here
The gifted one, forever dear!

John Howard Payne

Sunday morning, June 10, 1849.

—Mr. Gignoux has in his room, in the Tenth street studio building, a moonlight view of Niagara Falls, painted for Mr. Belmont. The moon, struggling through the driving clouds, is seen sharply rippling upon the rapids, and casting into broad shadow the masses of falling water, relieved here and there by flashes of spray, which serve to rescue from gloom the grander outlines of form. The Falls under ordinary circumstances are not picturesque, but Mr. Gignoux, with the resources of his art, has contrived to invest them with great pictorial beauty. The large size of the canvas, which is four feet by eight, better enables the painter to give some idea of the magnitude of the scene.

—The first Reception of the artists of the Tenth street studios took place on Tuesday evening last. It was attended by a large crowd of people, the larger number of whom were ladies. Besides the principal gallery, which was hung with pictures painted exclusively by the artists of the studio building, several of the studios themselves were thrown open, and the guests courteously received by their occupants. Visiting these studios constituted a very pleasant feature of the entertainment, and gave those desirous of seeing pictures, their only chance, for the gallery was so crowded as to completely hide its contents from view.

In the rooms of Gifford, Hubbard, Nichols, and Boughton, the landscapists, and Philip Jackson, the sculptor, the guests found ample amusement in the sketches and works of art which they contained. Mr Suydam's room proved particularly interesting, for besides his own sketches, he possesses many fine pictures of the modern French school. His own landscape, a crimson twilight, was a favorite in the gallery.

The gallery was so crowded as to preclude the possibility of seeing the pictures to advantage. We had the good fortune to see a very poetical view of Windsor Castle, with a rainbow effect, by Gifford. Mrs. McEntee had several pleasing landscapes; Mr. Hodgkiss one or two; Hubbard one; Hart several; Gignoux one, particularly good; and many others, which we care not to enumerate. Altogether the evening passed off pleasantly, and we predict great usefulness to both the artists and the public, as the consequence of this and those which are to follow.

—A large painting, by T. Buchanan Read, called the "Spirit Bride," is on exhibition at the shop of Williams & Stevens, Broadway. It represents three finely drawn mortals rather hurriedly slipping down a green waterfall. The Bride is fleshy and natural enough, but the waterfall is undoubtedly supernatural. The picture is effective, and handled with skill and poetic feeling.

NEW YORK JANUARY 29, 1859

ON THE SANDS.

I.

I met Jessie Leigh
   On the sands;
Sweetly she smiled on me,
While breezes from the sea
   Brought dreamy odors as from distant lands,
And the warm sunshine fell
O'er weed, and pebble, and shell,
   Upon the sands.

II.

I sat with Jessie Leigh
   On the sands;
Very fair was she,
And very kind to me;
   I kissed her forehead, and her dainty hands,
While the white moon above
Witnessed our vows of love,
   Upon the sands.

III.

I saw Jessie Leigh
   On the sands;
Cold and still lay she,
Drowned in the cruel sea,
   Her fair hair floating in dishevelled strands.
Would God I too had died,
And slept there by her side,
   Upon the sands!

George Arnold.

Dramatic Feuilleton.

The Question d'Argent.

A Dramatic Author's Association has become necessary. Let us have it. It will promote a good class of dramatic writing, by ensuring adequate remuneration to the authors of plays, and thereby inducing men, who, from their abilities, command their own prices in other quarters, to devote their talents to the stage. A man who lives by his pen cannot, at the present rates of payment, afford to write for the stage. Alexander Dumas, *fils*, takes a year to write a five-act comedy. If it is successful, he makes fifteen or twenty thousand dollars, getting eight or ten per cent on the gross receipts of the theatre every night it is performed, besides obtaining payment, at certain fixed rates, for every performance in the provinces. He can, therefore, afford to spend the time necessary to produce a perfect work of art. Contrast this with the payment an author would get in this city for a similar work. Five dollars an act is the usual rate of payment for a five-act play at a first class theatre. We will suppose the play to be a great success. The expenses of the theatre, nightly, including everything, we will fix at three hundred dollars, that being about an average drawn between the expenses of the three principal theatres of New York. If the play is a great success, it will run, say thirty nights, during which the receipts will be on an average six hundred dollars a night. This leaves a profit of three hundred dollars a night, out of which the author gets twenty-five dollars a night, leaving a balance in favor of the manager of two hundred and seventy-five dollars a night. At the end of the thirty nights, the manager will have made eight thousand two hundred and fifty dollars, while the author will have received seven hundred and fifty dollars. If the dramatic author says that this is a disproportionate profit, the manager will, perhaps, reply that he has run great risks, and, consequently, is entitled to large returns. That (as a prominent manager once said to me, when negotiating for one of my plays,) he can get plenty of plays of the theatrical publisher, for sixpence. That were it not for him (the manager) the author could not get his piece played, and that, in short, having devoted his time, money, and energies to the production of said piece, he is entitled to eight times as much money as the author.

To all this the author, if he has considered the subject, will answer, that if the manager has run risks, he also has done the same. That he has spent months in writing a piece, while the manager has spent weeks in producing it. That if the manager is convinced that sixpenny plays imported from England will fill the theatre, why does he desire original dramas? That so far as the argument of authors being dependent on managers is concerned, the obligations are perfectly reciprocal, for, although if there were no theatres there would be no pieces performed, still, if there were no dramatic authors, there certainly would be no managers nor actors.

EFFECT OF THE DRAMATIC COPYRIGHT LAW.

Frank Bellew's 1856 NY Picayune cartoon depicting playwrights, Benjamin Baker, Cornelius Matthew, Dion Boucicault, Fitz-James O'Brien, Charles Gayler, Edward G.P. Wilkins, and John Brougham, rushing to the court clerk's office to take advantage of the new copyright law.

A well worn argument on the managerial side of the question is, that as theatres do not charge European prices of admission, so they cannot afford to pay European prices for authorship. Let this be granted at once. But the London and Paris theatres do not charge eight times as much for a ticket of admission to the play, as the New York theatres; while the New York manager makes eight times as much out of a piece an the man who wrote it.

These are some of the reasons why a Dramatic Author's Society is necessary. Most professions have their combinations. The printer's society regulates the price to be paid for composition. Physicians have an understanding as to fees. Why should the dramatic authors of this country not combine for self-protection? I do not mean to accuse the liberality of managers. In a business transaction every man has a right to make the best bargain he can, but if a fair and equitable scale of payment for dramatic writing were established, it would conduce, I think, to much more harmonious relations between author and manager, would tend to improve the state of the American drama, and prevent many disagreeable controversies about the remuneration of authors, which frequently results from the present very loose system.

Again, dramatic authors require protection from the unscrupulous provincial manager. This voracious being is without conscience. When we had no dramatic copyright, he was a lawless robber, who took to the theatre as the highwayman of old took to the road, and violently confiscated dramatic property. A Philadelphia manager—may his bones know no rest, and may innumerable jackasses bray around the tomb of his ancestors!—absolutely hired a stenographic writer to take down in short-hand a play of mine that was then performing at Wallack's Theatre, and performed it in my teeth at his robber's den, assisted by his associate brigands. Now, when the copyright hangs over his iniquitous head he goes more slyly to work. He gets a published copy of the play, casts it for his theatre, alters the title, and produces it. The author, having no means of correspondence with the various cities in which there are theatres, remains in blissful ignorance of the fact, that somewhere out in

Wisconsin, or Iowa, the managerial bandit is growing fat upon his brains. The establishment of a Dramatic Author's Society would regulate all this; one of its most important pieces of machinery would be a secretary, whose duty it should be to hold correspondence with every theatrical city in the Union; who would keep the run of every piece performed through the country; would detect, by means of his emissaries, any such trick as

I have described; would collect the author's fees, and hand them over, deducting the fixed commission, and, in short, strike terror and consternation into the ranks of the bandits.

I would suggest to gentlemen prominent in dramatic literature, to make a move in this matter. There is plenty of material, and every necessity for establishing an American Dramatic Author's Association.

FITZ-JAMES O'BRIEN.

NEW YORK FEBRUARY 5, 1859

"JANE EYRE."

The statement now going the rounds of the papers,—and which was inadvertently copied into THE SATURDAY PRESS—to the effect that the novel of "JANE EYRE" was turned away from the publishing doors of almost every respectable house in London, and was pulled by accident out of a publisher's iron safe, where it had begun to grow mouldy, by the daughter of the bookseller, who had himself forgotten it, is wholly incorrect. The facts of the case are that the manuscript of "JANE EYRE" was sent by Miss Brontë on the 24th of August, 1847, to publishers Smith, Elder, and Co., London, who accepted it with such promptness that in fifty-three days of that date,—namely, on the 16th of October,—it was published. It should be stated, however, that the same firm had just previously—some time in July—declined "THE PROFESSOR," but in such terms that Miss Brontë, in a letter written on the 2d of August, thanked them for their considerateness, and about three weeks,—to wit, as we have said, on the 24th of August, 1847,—sent to them her immortal "JANE EYRE," of which "THE PROFESSOR," may be said to have been, in some sort, the germ. We state these facts as an act of justice, alike to the memory of Miss Brontë, and to the repudiation of her publishers.

WATCHING.

BY MRS. M. J. M. SWEAT.

Far out into the twilight
 I gaze with throbbing heart;
At every sound I tremble,
 At every footstep start.

Faster the darkness deepens,
 Faster the night comes on,
And through the long, long hours
 I sit and weep alone.

The neighbors' lamps are lighted,
 And from each window shine
Bright beams of friendly welcome—
 There is no light in mine!

Their households are assembled,
 Their homes are full of glee,
Their shadows flitting swiftly
 Across the light I see.

But there is one whose coming
 Would make my home more light
Than those which glow the brightest,
 This dark and dreary night.

And though my heart grows heavy,
 I still must watch and wait,
For surely he will enter
 Some night within my gate.

TWO PLACES OF AMUSEMENT.

A few evenings since, two individuals might have been seen approaching the portals of the Academy of Music. One of them was a young man of fashionable exterior, whom we will call George Augustus. His companion was the beautiful and accomplished Gunhilda. They enter, arm-in-arm, and are escorted by the bland usher to their appointed place, the fair Gunhilda proceeding with that peculiar step—a sort of "quiddle"—only to be seen in ladies as they enter a theatre. After the customary rustling of her plumes, she finds herself comfortably seated, her ample and costly drapery covering George Augustus, with the exception of two important points—to wit, his own head, and that of his cane,—which latter is of ivory, artfully fashioned into the semblance of a human leg. The lady's gloves are of course of virgin white, gleaming like tooth of Ethiop. George Augustus was *ganté* in a faint purplish rose-color. His face does not denote great intellectual powers, but it is mild and benevolent, with a faint dash of despair. His whiskers are resplendent, and form the great charm of his *personnel*: the style thereof being pointed, gothic, and flamboyant, while the color is a subdued straw. In such a position as this in the midst of a brilliant throng, with a lovely girl beside him, listening (or being supposed to listen) to the noble music of Don Giovanni,—and with such whiskers, what more could the heart of man desire?

Alas! George Augustus was *blasé*. He had exhausted all earthly pleasures; he had quaffed the cup of mortal experience to the dregs. In vain for him were the flashing eyes of Gunhilda veiled with the soft film of affection; in vain for him had Mozart written, Ullman catered, and Piccolomoni flirted with her divine elbows. His soul was dark; his spirit craved excitement.

George Augustus never conversed. His remarks were confined to simple ejaculations, emphatic, but not discriminating. He was silent even during "*Il mio tesoro.*" He smiled faintly when the statue bowed its hat off, revealing a chevelure of astounding nigritude, and still more decidedly, when Mr. Formes jumped over the prompter's box. He gave little heed to the grand harmonics of the last act, but he paid marked attention to the commendatore delivering his awful warning, with one eye upon his feet, in order to see that he was in the middle of the trap, and to insure his comfortable descent; and his gentle eye lighted up with emotion as he saw the irreverent Leperello eating maccaroni, and choking himself withal. He imagined himself in a circus (excuse him, his libations had been numerous and potent)—and he was prepared to see the great Formes with a bunch of fireworks at his rear, or scattering flour upon the bystanders. He is disappointed in his hopes, however; the somewhat inactive demons come in to point the moral and bear off the unhappy Don to his lurid future residence, and the audience take their departure.

George Augustus (I grieve to say it) resigns the fair Gunhilda to a friend, and pursues his devious course down Broadway in quest of other adventure. He made the "facile descent" at several corners, and at last found himself in a side street, at the door of a "café chantant" (or, to speak more properly, as there is no coffee on the premises), a "Free and Easy." He entered, and sat him down a pensive hour to spend. He found himself in a long narrow room with a bar at one end and a small stage at the other. It was filled with gentlemen who I am inclined to think were not distinguished for aesthetic culture, as they were easily pleased, and encored everything indiscriminately. The saloon was so skilfully arranged that the "management" was enabled to mix fancy drinks at the bar in its shirtsleeves, and at the same time ring the bell for the orchestra and vocalists. The room was filled with little tables, each with three matches upon it, at which the audience sat, every man with his lager bier, or other fluid, before him. The walls were covered with placards, stating the price of the liquors, or setting forth the transcendant merits of that world-renowned comedian, Mr. William Doolan, whose benefit I take pleasure in informing the public will take place some Tuesday evening.

This institution differs in several respects from the Academy of Music. The most remarkable feature is the *entente cordiale* which exists between the performers and the audience. The latter, if not enlightened critics, are at least frank in the expression of their opinions, and make various suggestions to the singers, which are received with the utmost good-nature. It is even allowable to wink at the prima donna, who is not averse to returning the compliment. This lady has a voice of such peculiar timbre that it makes your blood run cold, and causes you to shut your teeth very firmly together. She sings "Beautiful Venice," "We met by chance," and other songs of that ilk, together with that ineffably sweet ditty, "Rosalie

Carousing in a concert saloon, by Frank Beard for the Illustrated News, 1862.

the Prairie Flower," which has a great effect upon the untutored minds of her hearers. The male ballad singer is, I think, the greatest bore of this establishment. He favors the audience with the "Bay of Biscay" (o!), "The White Squall," "Woodman, Spare that Tree," etc. But the great attraction is Mr. William Doolan, the unrivalled comic vocalist. This gentleman has great "breadth of style," tremendous action, and an extraordinary development of muscle. His ideas in regard to costume are simple and grand. A very ragged coat, any kind of a stick in his hand, and some pigment of a violent red on the end of his nose, are all that he requires for any emergency. With a noble disdain for all cramping formalities, he sets at defiance the narrow-minded precepts of Mr. Lindley Murray, and adopts his own peculiar views with regard to grammatical construction. As the metre of his songs is of a rather ragged and limping description, he is frequently obliged to resort to suspended cadences, after which he gets more or less out of tune, but that is a small matter in this locality. The humor of these performances is of a somewhat dreary nature; in fact, they may be said to have no point at all, but he fully atones for this defect by a solemn allusion to the memory of Washington in the last verse, during which he takes off his hat and looks reverently up to the ceiling. There is also a danseuse in the troupe, who is somewhat ponderous, and whose motions forcibly remind you of a kangaroo. She makes a queer mixture of her performances, mingling an Irish fling and a Highland jig with a Yankee Polonaise, all to the music of the Star Spangled Banner, and she aids herself in posturing by bracing her toe against the beard of Shakespeare depicted on the back scene. The ministering angels of this institution are affable and unreserved in their manners, not in the least shackled by the cold conventionalities of fashionable life. The remarks interchanged between them and their male friends are easy and familiar, if not sprightly. Their dresses are distended by some occult contrivance, which, as they brush through the narrow passages, is sometimes horizontal, and sometimes nearly vertical. As it batters against your legs, you are led to believe that it is made from the rim of an omnibus wheel.

I am told that in this place they sometimes give sacred concerts, and that the distinction between the sacred and the secular music is exceedingly nice, only apparent to the acute perception of the management, which with an exquisite sense of propriety has affixed to the walls a notice requesting the audience not to applaud on Sunday night.

Our friend George Augustus is at last roused from his apathy. The united energies of Mr. Doolan and John Barleycorn have accomplished that which Mozart failed to perform. He is drunk and enthusiastic. He applauds everything with "effusion," bringing down his hand upon a ring of lager left upon the table, to the great detriment of his delicately tinted gloves, He orders a bottle of champagne, and insists upon treating the beauteous Hebe who bears to him this rather doubtful nectar. He orders another bottle, and becomes affectionate. The capacity of his fair companion is by no means small, but at last the champagne begins to tell upon her, and she too becomes affectionate. The effect is now extremely fine: all eyes are turned upon the reckless youth who orders champagne; and so he demands another bottle, and still another. The waiters hover over him from all parts of the room with astonishing celerity whenever a cork is drawn, like so many vultures. He treats the orchestra and the singers: the ladies and gentlemen of the stage sing with one eye upon the sparkling glasses waiting for them at the footlights; the pianist sacrifices a large portion of his harmony as he uses one hand to raise the tumbler to his lips; the portly double bass glares stolidly at his portion over the top of his spectacles, and the horn is exalted.

But such happiness is too bright to last. George Augustus begins to succumb; he orders no more champagne, and his lovely friends of course leave him. His whiskers are frightfully disarranged, his head sinks upon his manly breast, and this wicked world is shut out from his vision. He sleeps. Let us respect his slumbers.

W. H. F.

Dramatic Feuilleton.

Mr. Gayler's Female Cousin—The Horses at Niblo's—Awful Disclosures respecting Mr. Lester—The Opera and the Theatres Elsewhere.

Did the reader ever know a job *litterateur* ? They are of many varieties. Printing House Square knows them, sometimes to its joy—oftener to its sorrow. The job *litterateur* will get up for you a play, a novel, a romance for the *Weekly Blazer*, an essay for the *North American*, or a poem for the Yankee Soap Man, at the shortest possible notice, and on the most reasonable terms. The writer hereof, who is nobody at all—that is, nobody of any consequence cannot say whether or not the author of "Our [Female] American Cousin" is a jobber. But the play is odorous of that peculiar Hard-Up perfume so familiar to those who have frequented the *coulisses*. A house "over the way" has made a lucky hit. Some one in England has written a fairish play, which, thanks to Mr. Joseph Jefferson, the New England man, is not made entirely repulsive to common humanity. The public crowds the house over the way for no end of nights, and the refined, amiable, agreeable, and accomplished *financiere* of the establishment smiles in her blandest way over the plethoric receipts. The other house, meantime, hath languished. It is like a battered belle that hath had many lovers and in her old age is forsaken. The first sincere affection that the theatre now called Burton's experienced, was that of Miss Laura Keene, who went into it with a degree of freshness and ardor that surprised the public. Then came another lover, uglier, older, but richer, and Mr. Burton reigned in Laura's stead. His shifts, and toils, and troubles, and tribulations, are well enough known. Early in the present season, he made an engagement with an English Opera Company for three months. There were good artists in this Company, but still it was not a good Opera Company. The public would not have it at any price. After three or four miserable performances, the "Opera season" was suspended. The manager, much disgusted, packed up Captain Cattle's hook, spoons, silver watch, and other "wallybles," and, sheltered by Mr. Sleek's umbrella, as well as protected by Lady Sowerby Creamby, made his way to the South. At last accounts he had sailed for Havana, probably to make arrangements for the performance of the last new farce, "The Purchase of Cuba."

While the cat has been away the mice have been playing to awfully thin houses. Sundry astonishing tragedians and melancholy comedians were summoned from the interior to perform before a "metropolitan" audience, but the metropolitan audience did not appear. At last, in humble remembrance of the advice of Mrs. Chick, the new amateur managers resolved to "make an effort," and hence, "Our [Female] American Cousin," who bears a very strong resemblance to our Cousin over the way, and which was, to use the mildest expression that happens to come in our way just now, suggested by it.

In other words, Mr. Gayler's Cousin is Mr. Taylor's Cousin, with a slight difference in attire. A Yankee girl, in Mr. Gayler's play, visits England to pay her respects to her uncle, a wealthy baronet, in an extraordinary *robe de chambre* and a shirt of suspicious integrity. She is received with honor by the ladies of the family, who are supposed to be aristocrats, but who have the manner and dress of sewing girls "fixed up" for a picnic. The Yankee is, after all, rather better fed than the others. Her uncle, of course, turns out to be a great rascal—all English noblemen are, according to the opinion of the theatre-going public. His machinations, however, are thwarted by the young lady from New England and her attorney, who is dressed like a plow-boy on Sunday, precisely the costume which is affected by the leaders of the Suffolk bar. The dialogue has evidently been written in a great hurry. There are, however, good things in it, and it is "patriotic" enough to satisfy the most *exigeant* upholder of the Star Spangled Banner. The author is surely a clever man, who can do better. The play has had a moderate success, the glory of which belongs chiefly to Miss Julia Daly, who plays the "Yankee Gal" with real comic vim. She has a cynical, quizzical, expression which is rare in women, and which is perfectly irresistible. In this play, when she is supposed to be hoaxing the "Britishers" till just before the falling of the curtain, when she appears as a well-bred and accomplished woman, the idiosyncracy I have mentioned has full play. My Anna Maria, who is a terrible critic, says that Miss Daly is a crinoline Jefferson, and I think the beloved one is right. Finally, although there is too much slang, and several situations which are not in good taste, Mr. Gayler's 'Female Cousin' (we should like to hear him call a New England "lady" a "female," *once*,) is rather a nice sort of person, and worth the trouble of a visit.

Mr. Rice, called with that familiarity which, as Mr. Mantilini says, "breeds despisens," "Dan" Rice, has, with the Philharmonic Society, alternate possession of Mr. Niblo's theatre, which, by an excess of poetic imagination common to managers, is denominated a "Garden." Mr. Rice belongs to the aristocracy of circus clowns. He rarely indulges in familiarity with the ringmaster, and never says "'ere we har." That announcement is unnecessary. Rice pervades the entertainment. It is all Rice, and not curried at that. There are some good riders, such as Melville, the astonishing Australian, and a little girl named Alice. Then there are the "Comic Mules" that no one can ride, and a horse called *Excelsior*, though he is no higher than ordinary horses, except when he is on the top of a ladder, which he ascends with evident reluctance. Yet Rice is always present. Rice with jokes which are not all good nor new. In fact the majority are bad and old. There is too much Rice; and, to put it bluntly, may we ask Mr. Niblo to give us more Mule and less Rice?

Apropos to Niblo's, they say that its days are numbered, and that on the first of May next, when Mr. Niblo's lease expires, the Metropolitan Hotel will be extended over the scene of so many pleasant things in the past. Niblo's was splendid once. I remember when Fanny was younger than she is now, and I had something very, *very*, VERY particular to say to her, and nowhere to say it, that the brilliant idea struck us of going to Niblo's. There was only a pantomime, and we could talk without disturbing anybody. We did it, and that is all that is necessary to be told to you. However, there is a balm in Gilead, perhaps. They say that Mr. Niblo has been buying land in the Fourth avenue, corner of Twenty-third street, and that if he can get lots enough he will build a theatre there. The location is a capital one.

I have been inundated with communications in relation to Mr. Lester's whiskers, which he lately sacrificed to Art. The general opinion of the crinoline world is, that he looks "awful." But this is not all. The eminent comedian is accused, by a correspondent, evidently a disappointed Thespian, of parricide. It is declared that he deliberately kills his own father by taking the most prominent place in the fifth tableau, and that he unnecessarily exposes Miss Mary Gannon to danger from the falling ruins of the Sultan's palace. "How funny it is," remarked the Brightest, "to see all those people scrambling to get near a wall that is tumbling down, when usually everybody runs away from such things." There is a *bon mot* of a distinguished tragedian, anent *The Veteran*, that is worth giving. "I saw it," said Metamora, "good piece: believe it is in six acts: saw five: end of fifth everything fell down or thought it ought to be end of the piece, went away."

However, in spite of, and perhaps in consequence of all the jokes, *The Veteran* brings crowded houses every night, and the greenness of the author's laurels will make up for the sacrifice even of his whiskers.

I intend, next week perhaps, to make incursions into the other theatres. They are a little dull just now, but no matter. For those who are interested in such matters, I may just mention that the pretty sisters Western are drawing crowded houses to the Bowery; that Mr. Eddy has reappeared at the Broadway, much to the delight of his audiences; that Mr. Chanfrau is at the National, where he intends to bring out the Silsbee version of Our "American Cousin," which remarkable work of art, although advertised to death, does not attract very full houses at Laura Keene's.

In the musical world, the principal topic is Mr. Stoepel's "Hiawatha," the score of which has received much praise from competent critics. Just now it is the cause of a great war between the Boston *Courier* and *Dwight's Journal of Music*. The articles are technically mysterious, but doubtless both critics are right. There is another row about the same work nearer home. The composer desired to combine the Liederkranz Society and Mendelssohn Union in the choruses. The Liederkranz have good tenors and basses; the Mendelssohn Union good sopranos. What the one has, the other lacks; so by combining them a perfect *ensemble* could be had. But it can't be done, as each society thinks itself capable of doing the work alone. It strikes me that Art will rather get the worse in this very pretty quarrel. However, Mr. Stoepel will give us Hiawatha at the Academy in about a fortnight. Mrs. Heron-Stoepel, who is now at Chicago, will return in season to perform her portion of the work, to wit, the illustrative readings.

Things that Everybody Knows.

There will be a little more Opera here next week. The enterprising Ullman brings back his brief but expensive prima donna, Piccolomini, for the performance, on Friday evening and Saturday morning, of Don Pasquale. I think she will be a capital Norma—don't you? After that eventful Saturday, there will be no more opera until April. More's the pity, remarks Anna Maria, to which I respond Amen! The short opera season in Philadelphia, two weeks, has resulted, on *dit,* in a profit of six thousand dollars.

While Mr. Brignoli has been having a sore throat at the Clarendon, or singing the Don Pasquale serenade for the delectation of Lord Napier's guests at Washington, Mr. Henry Squires, who is a *rara avis*, an American with a tenor voice, has been singing Brignoli's roles al Louisville, and has had a great success. Anna Maria told me when he sung at Burton's, that he would do. She knows. She said, "he sings well, and has a good pure voice. To be sure (continued the dear one) his legs are not very straight, but still he is a good actor, and will be a much nicer Edgardo than Brignoli." Well, Anna Maria is justified in her opinion by the editor of the Louisville *Democrat*, who, in writing about the performance of Traviata, gets into ecstasies about Mr. Squires. *Voila!*

"Of Mr. Squires we can speak only favorably. True, his voice is not of great power; nor would we have it so, for the presence of great power would take from the elegance of tone, and be an absolute loss. We should like to have one little fault to find with his style, just to temper the admiration he has excited, but no. In listening to his tones, as they float through the house in wavelets of melody, one loses all thought of time and place—sees only him—hears only him—thinks of him only. His tones are pure, fresh, true, and warm—filled with the spirit of that inner melody which the mortal organs are too imperfect fully to express—filled with that life and feeling which conquers all hearts."

The Violetta of the night was Mme. de Wilhorst who, it is said, sung and acted the role with so much *verve* as to astonish everybody. She is another of Anna Maria's pets; Anna Maria has a strong belief in the the future of De Wilhorst.

As for the future movements of these nightingales —Strakosch intends to open, "on or about" the middle of March, Mr. Pike's new opera house at Cincinnati. I find in the papers of the porcine city a call for a public meeting of its citizens, "friends of art and enterprise" to take action "with regard to the Inauguration Festival" on the 22d February. The theatres of Cincinnati are just now in a bad way. Wood's new concern has just been sold out under the hammer. The National has reverted from the hands of Mr. Baker, who attempted to set the Ohio River on fire and did not do it, to those of its owner, Mr. Bates. It is stated that Mr. Ullman has hired the last named theatre, and will open it with Piccolomini on the same night that the operatic performances are commenced at the other house.

The Howard Athenæum at Boston is a very unfortunate theatre. Some fine day, when I have nothing else to write about, I intend to give a sketch of its history. Very recently Mr. Sothern, the same who plays Lord Dundreary so well, undertook to resuscitate in fallen fortunes with Mrs. Sinclair-Forrest, a lady who has literally had her trials. But all in vain. Mrs. Sinclair played in a new piece and a good one, Mr. Falconer's "Extremes," to extremely thin houses. On the occasion of her benefit performance the lady lost her temper; or at least we should judge so from the following remarks made by her to the audience:—

"I shall only thank you for the kindness I have received at your hands, despite the powerful exertions used to prevent me from pursuing a profession which I adopted seven years ago from the necessity which then arose, and which still exists, of earning my daily bread. * * * * * Before leaving England I was warned that strong influences would be exerted, and that calumnies too dreadful to mention had been carefully circulated against me—but I felt confident that it is not consistent with the American character to aid in crushing a poor woman, who has neither father nor brother to defend her, and who only seeks to be allowed to labor for her living, and asks but a small share of that support so liberally bestowed on others."

After Mrs. Sinclair came the Bourcicaults, who only played two nights, and then returned to New York. Mrs. Bourcicault was one of the most brilliant stars of the Light Guard, eclipsing even "the Generals."

Anna Maria thinks the lady is "too big to crush."

Miss Teresa Esmonde, who was recently snubbed by Mistress Fanny Kemble, has heaped coals of fire on that person's head by sending her tickets to the Esmond readings, and suggesting that the Kemble may there learn "manners." Rather bad taste on both sides.

The American Academy of Music, Philadelphia, will be offered for rent by the year, commencing on the 8th of March. Ullman will probably be the new lessee, and will then have the chief theatres of New York, Philadelphia, and Boston, under his control.

PERSONNE

LEAVES FROM A LADY'S PORTFOLIO.

Embroidery.

Flosa silk is used to embroider on either silk, satin, merino, or any fine material which does not require washing. To embroider on cloth, fine flannel, or merino, that is to be washed, it is necessary to use three-corded or saddler's silk. Chenille is sometimes employed in canvas-work, but, being one of the richest materials used in embroidery, it shows to the greatest advantage on velvet, silk, or satin. Worsted is used chiefly for embroidery on canvas, but on fine merino, brown holland, and even white muslin, it is equally beautiful. The colors of German worsted do not fade when washed with soap.

A light and simple frame is the most convenient for the abovementioned species of embroidery. The frame may consist merely of four smooth pieces of light wood, half or three-fourths of a yard in length, and one-fourth of an inch in thickness, neatly joined together. The frame should then be covered with ribbon or muslin wound tightly around it. To this muslin the material designed to be embroidered is to be sewed. Square frames are preferable. After the frame has been prepared, the pattern to be embroidered should be drawn. If the material used is silk, or satin, or muslin, or any transparent substance, the pattern may be fastened on the wrong side, hung over a window-pane, and traced upon the material with a lead pencil. When velvet, or cloth, or any dark-colored silk, is to be embroidered, the pattern may be drawn on white tissue, or blottingpaper, and the paper lightly tacked on the right side of the velvet. The embroidery is to be executed over the paper, and when the work is completed, the paper is carefully torn away. Sometimes patterns are drawn on dark materials by means of chalk, but the chalk is apt to rub off.

After the pattern is drawn, the work should be sewed into the frame in such a manner as to be perfectly smooth and even. It is not necessary that the frame. should be of the same size as the materials to be embroidered. If the stuff is longer or wider than the frame, the portion over may be rolled up and covered with—white. When the article is smaller than the frame, a piece of muslin may be sewed on so as to make the stuff of the necessary size. Entire cleanliness in handling is of course essential.

Woman and Matrimony.

Some one has said that "matrimony is with women the great business of life, whereas with men it is only an incident"—an important one, to be sure, but only one among many to which their attention is directed, and often kept entirely out of view during several years of their early life. This difference gives the male sex a great advantage over women; and, therefore, the best way for them to equalize their lot, is to think as little about it as the men do. Young women ought to be in no haste to accept a lover. Let them know him a sufficient time to judge of his qualities of mind, temper, and habits, before they allow themselves to take so important a step. In general, young women are much too anxious to involve themselves in this respect. The less a woman's mind dwells upon lovers and matrimony, the more agreeable and profitable will be her intercourse with gentlemen. If ladies would regard gentlemen more in the light of intellectual beings, who have access to certain sources of knowledge of which they are deprived, and seek to derive all the benefit they might from their peculiar attainments and experience in the school of busy life,—if they would converse with them as one rational being should with another, and not be reminding them that they are candidates for matrimony, they would doubtless enjoy far more than by regarding them under the exclusive aspect of possible future admirers and lovers. When the latter is the ruling and absorbing thought, ladies may be said not to have the proper use of their faculties; their manners are constrained and unnatural; they are not unfrequently embarrassed, and inclined to say what is ill-judged and out of place,—thus oftentimes appearing to great disadvantage, and defeating their own purposes.

The Wardrobe.

At this season of the year, every lady who has the means, should have her wardrobe well stocked with flannel apparel. In procuring this article, it should also be borne in mind that the best and finest flannel is always the cheapest in the end. It should be soaked for a night in cold water to strengthen the fibre before it is cut out. For a petticoat, a good pattern is three breadths of flannel, each a yard and a quarter in length, though a less quantity is often used. The blue selvage should be cut off, and the two edges laid one over the other, and first run together neatly along the middle, and then herring-boned down at each edge, to make the seam flat. A tuck is usually run in the garment at first, which may be let out if the flannel shrinks in washing; the bottom should be finished with flannel binding, the top gathered, not plaited, and set into a linen band. Also, in the skirts of dresses, sleeves, etc., and in all articles to be washed, the fulness should be gathered, not plaited, as it is thus less liable to be torn with the point of the iron. It is a most important economy in clothing to have every article of dress made to fit well, though easily.

In all cases, too, where a woman is called upon to perform household duties, her dress should be simple and suited to her occupations; the hair and feet neatly and perfectly dressed always marks good taste; and a plain printed dress, that will look fresh when it is washed, is the proper morning dress for domestic occupations; nothing is so contrary to the fitness of things as wearing an old silk dress when making pastry or nursing a baby. When a mother has daughters grown up, it is affectation and folly to dress them like herself; the silks and sober colored materials that are becoming to her mature years, are as unsuitable to her daughters as the pretty muslins or baréges which they wear would be to her. It is not advisable to buy many dresses at once, since fashion in these days is so capricious; and though it is weak and imprudent in any one to follow fashion after the reckless manner of some, yet is most becoming to avoid all singularity, and to dress like the rest of the world.

Articles for the Hair.

The importance of the hair in point of ornament is very great, and on this account it should receive the most careful treatment; and, considering the peculiarity of its structure, It is no wonder that, when badly treated, hair becomes rapidly injured in quality and color. Unless the skin is kept in a healthy state, and its epidermis or covering is removed by friction or washing, the hair can with difficulty grow, and as a consequence it is dwarfed, or even deformed, by being twisted on itself as it lies confined in its course through the skin. Grease, in all its varieties, is no stimulant, though it aids the growth by allowing the hair to escape from its glands: whatever is a stimulant to the skin has a similar effect upon the hair, the vessels of the skin itself and of the hair-glands being closely connected. Soap is generally injurious, from its removal of the oily matter of the hair; but in some cases, when there is a quantity of old and tough epidermis accumulated, and obstructing the growth of the hair, nothing else will bring it into a proper condition. With proper cleanliness, the hair need never be touched with soap, egg, or any other solvent of oil. Nevertheless, if daily washing is not practised—which in the case of the long hair of ladies can scarcely be expected —an occasional washing with the yolk of egg is found beneficial.

Next to washing comes friction, which acts in the same way, and when not too violent, is very efficacious. But when employed through the medium of a sharp-toothed comb, or a very penetrating brush, which is improperly used, it is mechanically injurious by leaving the true skin bare of its covering, and causing it to become inflamed. Few people use a brush in a proper manner. The first thing they do is to drive it into the skin in a perpendicular direction, which necessarily causes injury when followed by a rough thrust in a lateral direction. But if carefully used, the brush ought to be pushed into the hair at an angle with the surface of the skin, and as soon as it reaches that surface, it should be kept from irritating it more than enough to raise any loose particles there may be. It is of no use to attempt to prevent this abuse of the brush, by allowing the use only of one having soft bristles, because the latter cannot be made to enter hair that is stiff or curly, and is, therefore, quite inefficient.

"ARABELLA."

NEW YORK FEBRUARY 12, 1859

DAMNED.

BY H. L. FLASH.

You told me love is sweet,
But you lie ;
There is a sting
Hid beneath his downy wing,
And his feet
Trample down the human heart,
Till the burning blood-drops start,
And you die.

I will tell you-she was fair,
Very fair;
Her eyes were soft and meek,
Yet prodigal of light;
And her hair
Hung in wavy masses low,
On a brow as pure as snow;
And her cheek,
Soft and white,
Had been tinged with rosy light,
By the spirit of a sunset
That had died for love of night.
I had worshipped—I was weak—
I lost my self-control—
I clasped her jewelled hand—
And—but you cannot understand
How the waves of feeling roll
Till they overwhelm the whole;
How our passions are the daggers
Stabbing reckless at the soul.

She is dead—so am I.
I cannot find her here.
There's no light, nor air, nor sky,
Only fear.
Time has ceased—'Tis forever.
We will never meet again.
All my dark, despairing pain
Will leave me never, never.
And she, who cursed me with deceit,
Even while I kissed her feet,
Is—can you tell me where?
She is in some other sphere,
And it may be she can hear
Thrilling wildly on her ear,
My despair.

She will shudder in the dark—
She will crave but for a spark
To light her suffering soul on the darksome track to me.
But she cannot find me here—
She must keep within her sphere,
And shudder on forever in her dark eternity.

THE BEAUTIFUL SNOW.

O! the snow, the beautiful snow,
Filling the sky and the earth below;
Over the housetops, over the street,
Over the heads of the people you meet;
Dancing,
Flirting,
Skimming along,
Beautiful snow! it can do nothing wrong,
Flying to kiss a fair lady's cheek;
Clinging to lips in a frolicsome freak;
Beautiful snow from the heavens above,
Pure as an angel, and fickle as love!

O! the snow, the beautiful snow!
How the flakes gather and laugh as they go!
Whirling about in its maddening fun,
It plays in its glee with every one.
Chasing,
Laughing,
Hurrying by,
It lights up the face, and it sparkles the eye;
And even the dogs, with a bark and a bound,
Snap at the crystals that eddy around;
The town is alive, and its heart in a glow,
To welcome the coming of beautiful snow.

How the wild crowd goes swaying along,
Hailing each other with humor and song!
How the gay sledges, like meteors flash by,
Bright for the moment, then lost to the eye;
Ringing,
Swinging,
Dashing they go
Over the crust of the beautiful snow;
Snow so pure when it falls from the sky,
To be trampled in mud by the crowd rushing by;
To be trampled and tracked by thousands of feet,
Till it blends with the filth in the horrible street.

Once I was pure as the snow-but I fell:
Fell, like the snow-flakes, from Heaven-to hell;
Fell, to be trampled as filth of the street;
Fell, to be scoffed, to be spit on, and beat.
Pleading,
Cursing,
Dreading to die,
Selling my soul to whoever would buy,
Dealing in shame for a morsel of bread,
Hating the living and fearing the dead:
Merciful God! have I fallen so low?
And yet I was once like this beautiful snow!

Once I was fair as the beautiful snow,
With an eye like its crystals, a heart like its glow:
Once I was loved for my innocent grace—
Flattered and sought for the charm of my face.
Father,
Mother,
Sister, all,
God, and myself, I have lost by my fall.
The veriest wretch that goes shivering by
Will take a wide sweep lest I wander too nigh:
For all that is on or about me, I know
There is nothing that's pure but the beautiful snow.

How strange it should be that this beautiful snow
Should fall on a sinner with nowhere to go!
How strange it would be, when the night comes again,
If the snow and the ice struck my desperate brain!
Fainting,
Freezing,
Dying alone!
Too wicked for prayer, too weak for my moan
To be heard in the crash of the crazy town,
Gone mad in their joy at the snow's coming down;
To lie and to die in my terrible woe,
With a bed and a shroud of the beautiful snow!

—Harper's Weekly

UNREST.

BY HESTER S. DE GROVE.

Beat on, thou great world-heart! beat on,
Though each pulsation, born in pain,
Sighs for the golden ages gone,
Or, fainting, grasps for future gain.

O, ill, that human heart must bear!
O, grief, that rolls its anthems deep!
O, joy, that fades to anxious care,
Or nestles in an infant's sleep!

Is there no rest, thou wondrous sea,
Thus panting on the breast of time?
Chanting unrest tumultuously,
'Till heaven and earth responsive chime.

The eye may weary of the light,
The ear, of music's softest tone;
But sleep will clasp its brother night,
And sound and sight alike are gone.

The tired eagle seeks his nest,
The beast lies down in shaded lair,
But human souls, life's cross once pressed,
'Tis toiling onward everywhere.

NEW YORK FEBRUARY 19, 1859

"Ella Burns," The American Phrenology Journal, Jan., 1859.

LITTLE ELLA.

Following the chivalric lead of the *Tribune*, several of the dramatic oracles of the city press are down on the mother of Ella Burns for allowing that brilliant little creature to give public readings. The argument (or the assumption, rather) is—1st, That Ella could not, by any possibility, have been brought to her present degree of perfection as a reader, without previously undergoing a series of mental and physical tortures which none but the most cruel of mothers could have had the heart to inflict; and, 2d, That any mother who allows herself to be supported by so young a child, proves herself, by that fact, to be an indolent, vicious, and unnatural parent.

Now in reply to the first of these assumptions,

it is only necessary to say that every one who has seen little Ella Burns at home, knows perfectly well that so far from being the unhappy victim of maternal avarice, the relations between her and her mother are of the most affectionate and beautiful nature; that so far from being compelled to read in public, she takes immense delight in it; that, in fact, recitation, whether in public or private, is a source of perpetual enjoyment to her; that she has the same taste for it that other children have for music, or dancing, or drawing, or dressing, or mischief; and that, finally, if there is any compulsion in the matter, it is on the side of Ella herself, who, if her mother were to quit her to-morrow, and she were left to follow her own bent, would, we verily believe, take the Academy of Music at once, and give a series of public entertainments on her own hook.

As for the second assumption, that it is disgraceful for a mother to be supported by so young a child, we should say, with all due deference to the oracles aforesaid, that that depended very much on circumstances. If the child had decided gifts, which, by being properly cultivated and developed, could enable it to earn ten or twenty times as much as the mother could earn by any of the half-paid callings that man has condescended to leave open to woman; and if the public use of these gifts involved no cruelty toward the child, we think that the mother would not only be justified in allowing herself and her child to be supported in this way, but that it would be the most sensible thing that she could do. The idea that the child would become corrupted in any way by pursuing such a career is sheer nonsense. It is based on the common prejudice that public performers are, as a rule, an immoral set of people; whereas, the fact is, that they compare favorably in respect of character with any class in the community—not excepting our moral and religious teachers, who, for that matter, are themselves public performers, and are exposed (with what result it is not worth while to discuss here) to all the temptations which beset actors, singers, readers, dancers, equestrians, acrobats, or any other caterers for the public.

Dramatic Feuilleton.

Personal.

According to the Code of Honor (Galway edition), it would be proper for me to send this week to the Editor of The Saturday Press, a hostile message rather than my few loose leaves anent plays and players. "There is nothing, sir," said young Whiskers to me, after having had his nose pulled by a man who would not fight, "there is nothing," remarked the festive Whiskers, "like notoriety for a man." And I tacitly agreed with Whiskers, partially because I never dissent from statements of an abstract character, and partially because Whiskers was in an excited state of mind and dangerous, being bigger than I. Now I have an opportunity for notoriety. The editor of this journal has wilfully and wantonly compared the Brightest and Best of her Sex, *videlicit* my Anna Maria, to governments, hobbyhorses, lap-dogs, and things of that sort. *He* would not deprive *me* of HER! He, *Corpo di Bacco*! Of all things in the world, as the dear one would the idea is absurd. Whiskers *jeune*, could do it better, and she detests him, because his legs are too long for the German.

However, I am magnanimous. The race may be benefited by the Editor, and I will not sacrifice him. Go! Be happy. Anna Maria don't mind. She has managed two breakfasts, three dinners, one *bal costumé*, one *soirée* with *tableaux vivants*, and appeared as the "Bandit's Bride" at the Ferrero fancy hops. All this since last Saturday. She is light and gay. Why should I be sanguinary? I am not. I say go, Editor, in peace. Bless you!

I have correspondents, too. Several wish me to answer all sorts of impossible questions. Briefly—

I won't.

Another desires to know who I am?

Let him or her understand that I am a citizen, sheltered by the American Eagle, likewise a householder, and furthermore, I have been drawn (and quartered) on the Grand Jury. In view of the last named circumstance, let him or her tremble and beware!

An Operatic Lunch.

Piccolomini has come and gone. Here on Friday night singing to no end of opera-cloaks and myriads of white cravats; here on Saturday for the delectation of oceans of crinoline; gone on Monday to the provinces, Nor'-nor'-west and Sou'-sou'-west." What a time we had with our *soirée* and our single *matinée*! To be sure the Don Pasquale was not great, according to the critics. Not so good with Piccolomini, Maggiorotti, Florenza, and Lorini, at two dollars, as with Bosio, Marini, Badiali, and Salvi, at fifty cents; but while the latter sung to empty houses, the former, according to all accounts, brought seven thousand dollars to the manager's till, with a mediocre performance of an unpopular opera. Certainly, the Academy was full on last Friday and Saturday. On the last named day, Anna Maria rose at an early hour, and stationed herself in Irving Place before 12 o'clock, noon. In vain : the Brightest was hustled and elbowed into a corner by an inundation of crinoline roughs; and, as she said, was obliged to stand up from noon until after 4 o'clock. Some person of a practical turn of mind suggested that she might have gone away. The absurdity of the idea precluded the possibility of a reply. The unfortunate Gradgrind was withered by a glance.

As for the opera itself, I never could see why it should be abused. *Don Pasquale*, it seems to me, will compare favorably with any of Rossini's repertory. If not so elaborate as the Barber, it is certainly quite as amusing, and, indeed, not half so tiresome. Norina is a charming role, and most charmingly is it expressed by Piccolomini. The way in which she abused her antique lover was glorious to behold. I have suffered the same sort of thing, and I speak by the card. As for the others, Maggiorotti (where on earth did he get that name?) was a terrible bore, about as artistic as a town-pump in dry weather; of Florenza, I can remember nothing but a dress-coat and a pair of legs like John Gray's compasses; Lorini managed the serenade pretty well, but sung too loud; the chorus was wretched, while the orchestra was picked up like Falstaff's forces, here, there, and everywhere.

However, let us, like Honest Sancho Panza, be thankful for what we have, and never look an opera manager in the mouth.

The Philadelphians made a great time over their benefit to Piccolomini, on Thursday week. It was not a benefit to her, exactly, but rather to an extensive pair of mutton-chop whiskers sent here by Lumley, to see that the dimes were forthcoming. However, the intention was good, and who cares for names? Not the Philadelphians, surely; not the ornament of New York society, who, in humble imitation of the Italians, sent a pair of doves from the boxes. The doves, stupid things, came to anchor half-way between the divinity and her adorer. The people laughed cruelly, and absolutely shouted, when a carpenter was sent out to "poke" the messengers of affection from their roosting place. The course of true love never did run smooth, once!

"In the Days we went a-Gipseying."

Redolent of the old country is Mr. Harvey Pearson (I came near dropping that h), who is the last star at the Broadway Theatre. Thoroughly British is Mr. Pearson. Altogether rural. Distinctly pastoral. Odorous of the Hawthorne hedge. A realization of Herring, with quite as much poetry. He, Pearson, plays that peculiar phase of the yeoman, which libraries, lyceums, lectures, and, more than all, railways, have nearly extinguished in England. Time was, when many a well-to-do farmer, or country squire, within two hundred miles of London, lived and died, without visiting the metropolis, but low fares and express trains have broken down the barrier between the country and the town, and the Yorkshireman, and he of Lancashire, and the burly son of Somerset gradually approximate the Cockney. The time may come when the middle and lower classes of England will speak the English language universally. They don't do it now.

But let us return to our South Down, which is Pearson. *Imprimis*, I am glad he did not play *Bob Tyke*. Every Yorkshireman thinks it to be his religious duty to play *Bob Tyke*. Now, although *Bob Tyke* is a good part, there are several other good parts in "The School of Reform." I should like to see an actor in America who can play *Ferment* or *Lord Avondale*. No, Pearson was right. He appeared in an impossible two-act drama, called "The Villagers. There is a villain with very red cheeks, very black moustache, and a resplendent hat; his accomplice is a limp young man, with bushy hair, suggestive of Phalon; the limp young man has likewise a fine complexion, a shiny black frock coat, and an immense Californian diamond brooch. The limp young man wants confidence, and generally leans pensively against the wing, or looks as if he expected to be photographed, with the flat as a back ground. They talk much these villains—in a gothic room, with no furniture whatsoever. They conspire to ruin, and do ruin a virtuous young man in a turn-down shirt collar, and no further indication of linen. The virtuous young man looks like a medical student of a serious turn of mind. He shouts in the most awful way, and tells his wife to "unhand" him a great many times. The poor thing is thrown about in the cruelest way. Just then along comes the good Samaritan in the shape of our country friend. As a matter of course he discomfits the villains; the first goes off unregenerated, but the limp one avows penitence in a weak way; the ruined man relinquishes his latch-key, and the lady "smiles again," which is all very nice and amusing, if not altogether new.

I shall not quarrel with a play, however bad, which gives me such a clever artist as Mr. Pearson. I see that some of the daily critics compare him to the late Lysander Thompson. I think he is neater and smoother in his style than Mr. Thompson; fresher, rounder, and more unctuous. In appearance he is much like Mr. Burton. He has the jolliest laugh in the world, and can sing a ballad with the best of them. I hope that Mr. Pearson will join a regular metropolitan company. He will find it more to his profit in every way than starring. He would be a very great addition to Mr. Wallack's company.

Mere Mention.

The American Cousins at Laura Keene's and Burton's, are still attractive. At the first named house, Mr. Jefferson's benefit occurs to-night; it was announced for last week, by mistake. The Western sisters are engaged at the Broadway, and Mr. Joseph Proctor is playing at the Bowery.

Hear it, O Belgravia, and May Fair! There's a man at Burton's, who plays a London Swell inbedticking trowsers!

Things that Everybody Knows.

Mr. Stoepel's "Hiawatha" is announced to be given positively on next Monday at the Academy of Music. With a fine Orchestra, good vocalists, such as Mrs. Long and Mrs. Harwood, the affair ought to be a great go.

"Our American Cousin" is announced at the National Theatre, Cincinnati. I have been requested by a large number of colonels, judges, honorables, and things of that kind, to "add by (my) presence to the brilliancy" of the ball to be given to Mr. Pike in inaugurating the Opera House, next Tuesday. Can't go so far to be brilliant for other people.

The *Evening Post* says, that, at the next Philharmonic Concert a symphony by Mr. George Bristow will be produced, and that he is to be honored with a Grand Testimonial Concert, to take place at the Academy of Music on the evening of March 8. Several choral societies will assist the Harmonic on this occasion.

Clapisson's "Fauchonette," written in '56 for Miolan-Carvalho, is to be produced at New Orleans for Cordier. Piccolomini will sing at the Orleans in March, and Musard will conduct the carnival masquerades.

Mr. Hackett has been stranded at Philadelphia, and "persuaded" to play "for one night only" (of course).

Miss J. M. Davenport is playing at Baltimore.

Somebody at the Boston Theatre tried to snub the "young ladies of the ballet," whereupon Mr. and Mrs. E. L. Davenport took sides with the *coryphées*. The grateful angels have presented their patrons with silver napkin rings, and there has been some pretty correspondence.

Mme. Celeste has dissolved all partnership with Webster, and if she does not take the Lyceum where she is now acting, she may visit us again. She was always popular in every way in this country.

The country papers are full of blunders anent the Amateur Performance for the Dramatic Fund. The fact is that it is purposed to give at the Academy of Music on or about the anniversary of the Association, April 10th, a performance of comedy and opera by amateurs moving in Japonica circles. The comedy will be written for the occasion. The opera will probably be Don Pasquale. I hear the name of Mr. Schemerhorn mentioned as the director of the comedians, and that of Mr. Van Zandt *impressario* of the opera. Probably Miss S—r will sing Norina. It was originally purposed to give Dr. Ward's opera, "The Gipsey's Frolic," but it is too long, and the Doctor would not have a demi-semi-quaver cut out for all the wealth of "either Ind."

Mme. de Wilhorst has made a great sensation at St. Louis by her singing and acting in the Traviata. Brignoli had joined the troupe, and was to make his debut in the Puritani.

Mme. Elise Biscaccianti is giving concerts in Canada. She intends soon to leave for Australia and the East Indies.

Miss Avonia Jones, daughter of the Count, Chevalier, and so on, sailed from New Orleans for San Francisco on the 5th February, without once rushing into the embrace of her *pére noble*.

Mr. Thomas Barry, of the Boston Theatre, has had a benefit there, when numerous *cadeaux* were offered to him by his *employés*. Mr. Barry is a worthy old gentleman, just like the new piece in which he acted "The Last of the Pigtails;" in these days of volcanic eruptions, it is really refreshing to find a splendid fossil.

The Handel and Hayden Society of Boston commenced their 43d season on Sunday last, with "Israel in Egypt." The solo singers were Mesdames Harwood and Long; MM. Adams, Wetherbee, and Powers.

The Philharmonic Society of this city intend to build a music hall immediately. Niblo's is not large enough, and they can't agree with the Academy people. Mr. Gibson, a prominent decorator and glass stainer of this city, has, *on dit*, possession of the lots on Broadway, Thirteenth street and Fourth avenue, whereupon he purposes to erect a theatre or a music hall. If a theatre, Mr. Joseph Jefferson is mentioned as the probable manager.

William Warren was in town last week with a new Salisbury. That Bohemian had again changed his lodgings. A pecuniary difference of opinion between lodger and landlord. "He left," said S., "my small account on the table, and I found it at night. He showed me that he had an eye to heed, and I immediately proved to him that I had a foot to speed. (Lady of the Lake.) Fearing accidents, I gave my Tobias to Mrs. S., saying: Hold *you* the *watch* to-night." (Hamlet).

Penco will be our next operatic sensation. She is at the Italiens, Paris, and has the best soprano voice in the world.

The theatrical statistics of the last year are interesting. The theatres of Paris received at their doors 13,878,499f. Pieces were played by 215 dramatic writers and 50 composers; in 1857 there were only 199 dramatic authors and 39 composers. The French Comedy played 78 different pieces, of which nine were new; of these 78 different pieces, eleven of Molieres were played 129 times, and nine of M. Scribe's were played 143 times. The most successful pieces of the year at this theatre were Le Bourgeois Gentilhomme, which was played 36 times, and M. Scribe's Les Doigts de Fee, which was played 55 times. A good story is told of M. Louis Lurine, the new manager of the Vaudeville Theatre. As soon as he was fairly in possession of his place, an actress came tripping into his room. "My dear fellow," said she, "I am delighted to see you have this place. Come, get out pen, ink, and paper, and draw up my engagement." "Your engagement?" "Why, yes; you certainly are going to engage me?" "Indeed I am not." "You are not? Why you went to your predecessor ten times to get him to engage me, and now—" "I took care of your interests then; I take care of *mine* now."

The latest Parisian novelties are *Saint Hubert*, drama in one act (verse), by M. Boisseaux, at the Odeon; *Anguille Sous Roche*, vaudeville, in one act, by M. Jacques Lambert; *L'Avocat d'un Grec*, vaudeville, by M.M. Labriche and Lefranc.

Personne.

P. S.

Domestic Affairs.

On Monday night, M'lle Jeannette Essler, announced in the bills as "the most remarkable, elegant, graceful, expert, and daring tight-rope artist in the world"—as everything, in fact, except the daughter of Fanny—makes her first appearance at the Niblo-Circus in the gallant company of "the most distinguished London clown," Mr. (the idea of mistering a clown!) Nat. Austin.

Mrs. Kemble's last reading from Shakespeare, in New York, previous to her retirement from public life (from which, if we are not mistaken, she has retired once or twice before, having an evident distaste for it), took place last evening at Dodworth's.

The French Theatre is about completed, and is said to be a very artistic and Frenchy little affair. The subscribers are to meet there this afternoon to select their seats.

Mr. A. W. Fenno has abandoned his profession of actor for the present, and is about to give a series of lectures here and "elsewhere," on Spiritualism. A provincial editor (in Boston, we think) says that this piece of intelligence will be interesting to Mr. Fenno's many friends, though what he deals with is *immaterial*! Not bad, that, for the country.

A Mobile paper tells how an audience in that city was entertained to the verge of a charm," by Edwin Booth's performance of Richelieu in that city. The "verge of a charm" is great.

Somebody advertises in the Boston papers, with great show of capitals, that "Mrs. Macready Is Coming!" Who is Mrs. Macready?

Mr. Barrow and Mr. and Mrs. E. L. Davenport give a "selection of Dramatic and Poetic Readings" this evening at the Tremont Temple, Boston.

Stephen Massett has just had a complimentary benefit in Charleston, S. C., which must have been very disagreeable to all parties, as according to the newspapers, the hall in which it took place was "crowded to suffocation." Moreover, sixty young gentlemen of the Collegiate School recited Edgar A. Poe's "Chime of the Bells" with "killing effect."

Owing to the sudden indisposition of Miss Keene the other evening, the character of Florence Trenchard,' in the 'American Cousin,' was assumed by Miss Marian Macarthy, who acted the part so much to the satisfaction of the audience that she was complimented by a call, before the curtain"—which, in fact, was never called at all!

At McVicker's Theatre, Chicago, a company of amateurs have been playing (or working) "The Rivals." The stage-lorn young gentlemen were announced in the bills as a "Water Street Merchant," a "Distinguished Counsellor," an "Eminent Barrister," a "Gentleman from Racine," a "Bookkeeper," etc. The performance culminated in a fancy-dance by a lady amateur, who, according to the papers, was what the *Evening Post* would call a "beautiful girl."

A correspondent of the *Tribune* writes in high terms of commendation of a Shakesperian reading, lately given in West Lebanon, N. H., by Mr. Hampden Cutts, of Hartland, Vt.

Mrs. Lesdernier will give the third of a course of readings on Tuesday evening next, at Dodworth's Hall. It will be recollected that her readings were interrupted some weeks ago by the death of her two sons.

Foreign Affairs.

A letter from Riga speaks of a manuscript, in Haydn's handwriting, of a comic opera, entitled "L'Incontro Improviso," presented to the library of that town by Prince Esterhazy, when he visited it on his way to the coronation of the Emperer in 1856. Haydn was 25 years chapel-master in the Prince's family, and many of his productions still remain in manuscript in its archives.

Grisi, walking out one day in St. Petersburg with her children (for Grisi has children), encountered the Emperor, who after a gracious salute asked her, facetiously, "Are these your little *Grisettes*?" "No, Sire," was the reply. "They are my *Mario-nettes*." And *àpropos* of Mario. The papers are just now gossiping about the distinguished tenor in this style:

The tenor Mario owns a villa about a mile distant from Florence, filled with all luxuries, and above all with objects of vertu and art. Though he occupies it but a few months in the year, it is generously open to visitors when he is not there, as to his numerous friends when he is; for then he lives verily like a prince, with Grisi (falsely called his wife, since her husband is still living), and their four children. Mario travels like a prince—as recently, on going thence with Grisi, to meet their Paris engagement, when his suite comprised no less than fourteen carriages. Children, nurses, governess, and servants, go with them. They are as proud of their unfortunate (?) daughters, as *Mademoiselle* Rachel was of her sons.

Taglioni also owns, or did own, a Florentine villa, where, in earlier days, her "light fantastic toe" found rest, at intervals, among poetic hills.

Robert Brough, the dramatic author, has been compelled to appear on the boards of the Lyceum Theatre. Mrs. Keeley, who played Hector, in Brough's comic "Siege of Troy," was taken ill. No one capable of taking her place; none willing to risk it; none up in the words; manager in despair; treasurer in agony; author in a puzzle; cabinet council held, and a bottle of wine called in to assist in the conference; wine vanishes, difficulties vanish; prospects brighten; Brough finishes the bottle with, "By Jove! I shall go on in the part myself." Went on and was applauded. If he chooses to remain on the stage he seems likely to become a capital actor.

A new drama has just been successfully produced at the Lyceum, London, founded on Lamartine's Geneviève, and taken from a French piece entitled Les Orphelines de Valneige. Madame Celeste has the principal part, which is that of a seamstress.

Mr. Basil Baker, one of the last remaining actors of the old school, died somewhat suddenly, about a fortnight ago, at his residence in Grove-street, Liverpool, at the age of fifty-four.

A proposition to convert the garden of the Palais Royal into a Winter garden, by means of a glass roof, has been made to the French government by M. de Bernage, and is likely to be adopted.

Ristori is at Naples. A correspondent says that her representations are thinly attended. "In addition," he observes," to the many topics now occupying the public mind, and the general anxiety and trouble, the celebrated tragedienne has against her the party of Sadowski, her rival, who, living at Naples, is supported out of local pride."

Civilization is invading Stamboul! According to late letters, the magnificent theatre of the Sultan has just been inaugurated in presence of his majesty, his family, and the principal dignitaries of the empire, and orders were given for the performance, on the 14th, of the comic opera of the "Scaramucia," at which time the ladies of the harem, for the first time in their lives, were to be present in the different boxes. Shouldn't we like to have been there?

A new two-act drama, "The Borgia King," by Mr. Slous, author of "The Templars," etc., has been produced at the Adelphi, London, and it is understood that an engagement is pending with Mr. and Mrs. Charles Matthews to appear at the same theatre.

Cardinal Wiseman's drama, entitled "The Hidden Gem," has been performed at Liverpool with great success. Why wont Archbishop Hughes write one for Laura Keene's? It would certainly meet with a catholic reception.

The last dramatic novelty in England is a new comic actress, Miss Henrietta Sims. She made her debut in Tartuffe, playing the part of Elmira, which, according to the papers, she rendered with a good deal of spirit. But judging by the following item from the London *Athenæum*, the papers are not always to be relied on in such matters:

That we are not over-suspicious in declining to accept foreign vouchers in print for great successes, was anew proved to us the other day, by a letter from Paris, from a writer to be relied on,—stating that the Semiramide of Madame Penco is, what her Norma was, bad, however showy.

Signor Mongini, a tenor of foreign repute, is said to be engaged at Drury Lane for the coming Opera season.

Quelq'un.

NEW YORK FEBRUARY 26, 1859

Everett House Hotel, 1860, northwest corner of Fourth Avenue and East 17th Street

PATRIOTISM.

Mr. Everett is advertised to repeat his Oration on the character of Washington, at the Academy of Music, next Friday evening. The 71st Regiment will escort Mr. Everett from the Everett House to the Academy and back, attended by Dodworth's band and a crowd of small boys. The Cards of Admission are beautifully got up, being printed in glowing colors, and presenting artistic likenesses of Washington and Mr. Everett. These Cards need not be given up at the door. The number of persons admitted will be limited to the capacity of the house. At Laura Keene's, the farce of "Our American Cousin" is followed by "A series of Pictures, simple and unpretending in their nature, and designed as a slight illustration of the Life of Washington, and consisting of the following: Washington as a Surveyor—Washington as a Farmer—Washington as a Son—Washington as a General."

AN APOLOGY FOR THE EXCELLENCE OF THIS WEEK'S SATURDAY PRESS.

If our paper for this week were filled up with politics, religion, love, murder, rape, seduction, prize-fights, personal quarrels, etc., etc., we should have no occasion to apologize for it. It is more likely that in that case we should have to print two or three extra editions. But as a large portion of our limited space is given up to a record of what is going on here and abroad in the World of Thought—in other words, to the most complete and interesting list of new and forthcoming publications which can be found in the world, we do humbly apologise, and, though we can make no promises of future amendment, do earnestly crave our readers' kind indulgence.

It is our misfortune, however, to believe that authors and authoresses are quite as important a class of people as tradesmen, politicians, stock-jobbers, prizefighters, murderers, thieves, etc., whose proceedings, to the all but total exclusion of everything else, fill up most of our journals.

Dramatic Feuilleton.

ACADEMY OF MUSIC. HIAWATHA. *A Romantic Symphony, in Two Parts. Composed by* ROBERT STOEPEL *The words from* LONGFELLOW'S *Poem. The vocal solo music sung by Mrs.* HARWOOD *(soprano); Mr.* MILLARD *(tenor); Mr.* GUILMETTE *(baritone). The choruses sung by the* MENDELSSOHN UNION.

I always thought that the ancient Athenians were quite right in ostracizing Mr. Erastus Brooks's friend Aristides. There is such a thing as being too good. For this reason, I cannot agree with my musical friend of the *Times*, or the galvano-electrical critic of the *Tribune*, in abusing the Modern Athenians because they declined to hear Mr. Stoepel's HIAWATHA. They are clever, those Bostonians. They communed, one with another, in this wise: "Readings are bores; symphonies, sleepy; oratorios, awful. The latter we must sustain, because the Handel and Haydn people belong to us, like the Frog Pond, and the Parker House, and then it is a nice place to go to on Sunday evenings, when the theatres are shut. Now here is this young man Stoepel, who wants us to listen to his Symphony of Hiawatha, which remarkable, and astonishing, and altogether Bostonian poem has been served up to us like as Mr. Higgins's oysters have been served up to us, in every style. There is certainly no law against Mr. Stoepel's doing his Symphony here; likewise there is no provision in the Revised Statutes to compel us to go and hear. If such a law existed," remarks young Mr. Coke, who is a wit in his small way, "it might be declared null, under that section of the Constitution which provides that no cruel or unusual punishments shall be inflicted." So no one except Mr. Longfellow and the critic of the *Courier* troubled himself about Hiawatha in Boston. Famine fell on Hiawatha, and Minnehaha was, to use a familiar expression, down in the mouth. Defeated in the provinces, the composer fell back upon the metropolis, which sustained him, moderately. I say moderately, for a great part of the audience at the Academy of Music, on Monday, had the peculiar air of persons who get their amusement as they obtain religion at a prayer-meeting, without money and without price. I don't mean that they were amateurs, professors, or *dilettanti*, but rather persons picked up as they found the wedding guests in the parable—gentlemen whose waking hours are spent in the practice of the ennobling science of selling dry goods, and ladies whose devotion to art depends materially upon whether Mrs. Brown over the way, will let her little girl mount guard over the baby. The newspapers were fully represented—the men had generally had a look at the score—and here and there I could see a scout from the fashionable world, sent to report as to whether or not the thing was worth going to hear. I don't believe that people staid away because the work was written here, as the *Times* and *Tribune* argue. I don't believe that Felicien David's *Desert* would bring so many people together, even with free tickets. For, be it remembered, that, strictly speaking, symphonies are bores: They are written almost always to gratify the egotism or heighten the reputation of the composer. No money ever comes from them. Of course I refer now to symphonies which take up the whole of an evening in their performance. They are generally so elaborate as to keep one's mental faculties upon a constant strain, and that is not nice. Paterfamilias goes to sleep, and Madame counts up the cost of the bonnets in her vicinity. Anna Maria cannot flirt with young Whiskers, because there is a fanatic behind her who beats time with his toes, and says hush! whenever the Dear One opens the ruby gates.

Having now relieved my mind upon the question as to why people did not go to hear Mr. Stoepel's music, let me examine the further question, as to what he had provided for them.

Hiawatha is an Indian Symphony. The Indians had a great many, as Dr. Hawks will tell you in his next ethnological paper. There is one very much like Hiawatha. It is a touching narrative of one Brown,—John Brown. The introduction has the grand simplicity which deifies common things. The person, Brown, "had," says the poet, "a little Indian, had a little Indian, had a little Indian, had a little Indian boy." The poem is written in the style introduced by the author of the Battle of the Nile, successfully imitated by Bonner in his advertisements, and by Mr. Longfellow in Hiawatha. Thus we are told many times that John Brown had a little Indian; in the nautical poem, the bard is never done saying "I was there all the while." The *Herald* informs us that "everybody reads it," four hundred times, and the endless repetitions in Hiawatha must have been as wearisome to the printer as they are tiresome to the reader.

The music of John Brown is simple, but vigorous. It commences with an andante movement expressive of the youth of the Indian and the joy of Brown at his possession, and after a few bars comes to a sharp close on "boy," a square specimen of contrapuntal writing, descriptive of the brevity of the youthful savage and the bounding elasticity of the morning of existence. In the elaboration of the esthetic effects, it is superior to the Battle of the Nile itself. Perhaps you don't like this style of criticism. It is the real thing, I can tell you. But, as comparisons are odoriferous, I shall not institute one between John Brown and Hiawatha. The latter is really a very creditable work. The instrumental music is admirably done. No. 5, "The Fight with Mudjeeweekis," commencing with a war song, which is more Scotch than Indian, and culminating with a tremendous row among all the instruments, is very fine. The orchestral part of No. 13, the transition of the seasons, is very pretty, though not quite new. In fact, the writing for the orchestra was an agreeable surprise to everybody. It was admirably played, too, the composer conducting in person and keeping the fiddlers well in hand. As for the vocal score, I am not able to commend it, neither can I condemn it. The tenor has two solos; the soprano, two; the baritone, one; there is a trio for these voices, and there are six choruses. I believe that the vocal score is weak, but the singers were not good enough to justify an opinion of that kind. The Mendelssohn Union, if not on positively bad terms with some of the choruses, had only a slight acquaintance with them, and the performance suffered from a cause which I pointed out three weeks ago. The Mendelssohn people are strong in sopranos, but weak in tenors and basses. It was almost impossible to hear the male voices. The best chorus, however, the Harvest, was well sung, and got an *encore*, which was fully deserved. I hope no one will think I undervalue the labors of the Union. They are now far ahead of the older societies, and have learned the real secret of chorus singing, exact time. Voice and ear come by nature, but time only by severe practice.

The solo singers are pretty well known. I was disappointed in Mrs. Harwood, who has a great Boston reputation. She has a good choir voice, and sings in tune. Her executive resources are only moderate, and her musical enunciation is very indistinct and slovenly. She had that peculiarly animated expression of countenance which is so eminently Bostonian, and which makes one think of the granite pillars in front of the Court House. I don't say that Mrs. Harwood thought it was a bore, but she looked exactly as I would have felt if I had thought so. Millard was amusing. He has all the airs of a fine tenor, without the voice or education. Anna Maria says he's not to part his hair in the middle, because he's not a bit like Mario. Dr. Guilmette was a good deal like Dr. Guilmette, and Dr. Guilmette is careful that the public shall not forget what Dr. Guilmette is like. He knew the music, however, and sung it very well.

The musical summing up of this Court would be that Mr. Stoepel has written a fine work, with here and there a souvenir, of course; that his orchestra was excellent, his chorus better than usual, and his singers moderate. Altogether, that several more rehearsals are needed before the next performance.

I am not naturally an enthusiastic person; it is not my custom to rush into people's arms, but I think if I had room enough I could get up a little burst for Mrs. Heron-Stoepel's reading of the bits of the poem, which came in like silver bars in the golden tracery of the music. The lady mastered the trochaics, and gave the lines with exquisite clearness, delicious vocal modulation, and profound simplicity. When she laughed with Min-ne-ha-ha, it was really the music of the falling waters; flirting with Hiawatha was a combination of the tender tremulousness and Eve-like archness which the poet gives the rustic maiden. But she don't have it. I suppose it is the railways, but at any rate the rustic maiden is not simple. Give the rustic maiden genius without a bank account, and a stock broker with one, and she takes the latter. So she is not simple; she is clever. But to go back a block or two. The Heron was splendid, in every way; proud, happy, handsome, and much applauded. It was *Camille* cured by Dr. Green's probang, converted by Doctor Cheever, and *Armand* making a grand *coup* for fame. She wore, says A. M., a brown *moire antique*, with a point lace collar, a diamond cross, and a wrapper of real point lace, lined with blue silk. Mrs. Harwood wore a white *moire* evening dress. The Editor thought there might have been a little *more* of it about the shoulders, but A. M. couldn't see the joke.

The performance was long, but not a bore, by any means. I am very glad to hear that it is to be given on Wednesday of next week. I shall certainly hear it again.

Washington in a Blaze of Glory.

The *Pater Patria* has suffered a great deal lately, but the crowning act of Martyrdom was when he fell into the hands of Miss Laura Keene, who dished him up in a series of *tableaux* on Monday. Whiskers, who had been dining out, remonstrated with me upon this and other matters connected with Washington. "You know," said the lively youth, "whatever they may say, that he was a gentleman, and he really wouldn't like this sort of thing;" as for the *tableaux*, they were well enough, except the third, "Washington as a son." The rigid expression of the grandmother of her country, combined with a sudden uplifting of her hand, and a change in the position of George, gives one the idea that he is going to be spanked, but he is only blessed, which is a relief. They had another *tableau* about him at the Broadway, and Mr. Brougham has put him in a drama for the Bowery. It is just barely possible to have too much of this sort of thing.

Mere Mention.

Burton has sent word from Cuba, to his ever faithful Moore, to close the "most magnificent temple in the universe," and closed it is. "Our Female American Cousin" will, doubtless, proceed to astonish the provinces. Burton denies the rumor that he was driving a volante and flirting with the signoritas on the Alameda.

The Western Sisters have been playing at the Broadway. Mr. Eddy announces his Shakesperian play without naming the title. It is said to be Antony and Cleopatra. Mr. H. Pearson is reëngaged here.

They tried the American Cousin at the National, and it did not draw. Miss Keene brought a suit against Purdy, in the Common Pleas, to try the question of property in the MS.; as neat an absurdity as the copyright dodge. The piece was withdrawn and the defence abandoned. How Miss Keene could get an injunction against Mrs. Silsbee's property, passes my comprehension.

They are still having a good time with *The Veteran* at Wallack's. Mr. Wallack will shortly be presented with a piece of plate by the artists of the company. Mr. Couldock, who plays *Abel Murcot* so well, is to have his benefit at Laura Keene's this evening.

Mr. Burnett, the stage manager at Laura Keene's, has been very ill of rheumatism, and his part is played by Mr. Varrey.

The Editor of this paper has seen "Our American Cousin." He is convalescing, but is cautioned against any similar imprudence in future.

Things that "Nobody" Knows.

That retiring person, Mistress Frances Anne Kemble, has again disappeared from public life, so far as Dodworth's Rooms represent it. She made a very pathetic speech about some flowers which had been sent to her anonymously, and the *Home Journal* says there was scarcely a dry eye in the house. Not enjoying the felicity of being among the mourners on the melancholy occasion, may I request the privilege of a little private cry on my own account?

Mr. Jacob Barrow, the rotund spouse of the eminent actress and agreeable woman, Mrs. Barrow, intends to reopen the Howard Athenæum, Boston, very soon. He has engaged one of our very best artists, Mr. Charles Walcot.

The amateur performance in aid of the Dramatic Fund Association has been definitely fixed for the 20th April, at the Academy of Music. The programme will include a comedy in three acts, "The Dark Hour before the Dawn," which is, *on dit*, taken from *La Main de Fer et le Gant de Velour*. The work in its present shape is from the skilful hands of Messrs. John Brougham and F. B. Goodrich. *Don Pasquale* will also be sung; the leading female *roles*, in the comedy and the opera, will be sustained by two ladies who rotate in the upper circles, somewhere about Murray Hill. Their names are kept a profound secret—that is, no more than five hundred young women have been entrusted with it.

There is a report of Piccolomini's speech in response to the serenaders in front of the Troy House, as follows: "Shentlemen—I am veer mooch obligee for dis complimentz. I am veer poore speak Anglish, unt I feels sleepy." Quite like it, no doubt.

Piccolomini arrived at Cincinnati on the 22d, and had a peep at the "gorgeous" ball which inaugurated Pike's Opera House; it appears, by the description, to be a great deal like our Academy, only "more so" in the extreme elaboration of the decorations.

An enterprising person has advertised a new skirt, "The Piccolomini," which "can be taken to pieces." Is that intended as a hit at the critics of the fair prima donna?

Mr. Carl Gärtner is giving classical concerts in the *foyer* of the Philadelphia Academy. Who is Carl?

Brignoli has published an Album of his own composition, and all the young ladies are in raptures about it, except A. M., who has never got over a weakness for Tiberini. The Album is the finest work in the way of music printing I have ever seen. The composer was lately singing at St. Louis, with Mme. De Wilhorst, and others of the Strakosch troupe. The houses were full, and the manager in a state of bliss supreme. The season closed on Saturday last.

The provincial papers that appropriated my item about Mme. Stoltz will be kind enough to correct an error of the types, which made me talk about the Carlo Felice at *Geneva* instead of Genoa.

Mayor Tiemann, Governor Morgan, General Sandford, Deacon Harper, Peter Cooper, and several other celebrated musical amateurs, are going to give Mr. George Bristow a complimentary benefit at the Academy of Music next Thursday evening.

Mrs. Julia Dean Hayne must be a very good actress. A Savannah paper remarks that "her personation of *Lady Gay Spanker* was above criticism, which is all we need say about it." Quite a sensible idea that!

Mr. Strakosch's English is not so pure as his musical style. In announcing the opera at Chicago (22d) he says: "Mr. Strakosch regrets exceedingly of informing the public, that in consequence of a serious indisposition of Madame Cora de Wilhorst and Mr. Squires, caused by the fatigue of the voyage, *and in order to produce the opera with greater perfection*, the opening night announced for last evening, had to be unavoidably postponed."

PERSONNE.

NEW YORK MARCH 5, 1859

Domestic Art Gossip.

Leutze's return to this country enables us to welcome his presence as well as to chronicle his latest productions. The first in order is a sketch showing Washington in the battle at Princeton at the moment of victory. The British troops are indicated in the background; Washington, on a rearing horse, occupies the central position on the canvas, and is waving his hat, in the act of huzzaing to his followers that the "day is ours." Mr. Leutze proposes to paint the subject on a large scale. His second work is a story without a name, for the picture has no specific title; there are figures, light, and color, to denote pictorial melody, as there are sequences of tone and modulation in music to excite our thought—it is a pictorial "song without words." We see a cardinal, accompanied by a few attendants, advancing towards us, down a broad stair case, at the foot of which is a kneeling female presenting a petition, while half concealed behind a stone abutment of the steps is an elderly personage, evidently awaiting the result of her application. The scene is in the open air. A happy combination of flowers, costumes, and architecture, all bound together by a warm glow of sunlight and harmonious color, arouse in our minds all the associations we have connected with historical incidents of this class. The remaining pictures are a fine portrait of a Prussian officer, and a group in full-length representing the artist's children. Added to the above, we would mention another work, lately completed, but which has been forwarded to Baltimore to W. T. Walters, Esq., for whom it was painted, illustrating a passage in Paradise and the Peri, from Moore's poem of Lalla Rookh. The sketch of Washington at Princeton has been purchased by N. B. Collins, Esq.; the story without a name, by Shepherd Gandy, Esq. Since Mr. Leutze's return, he has painted an admirable portrait of Mr. Lang.

—Among late productions in our city that we have to chronicle, one of the most noticeable is Hicks' portrait of Dr. Kane. This picture—for it is a picture, something more than a portrait—is treated differently from the same subject painted by Mr. Hicks a few months ago. We see the intrepid navigator, his legs wrapped in a wolf's skin, seated in his cabin, engaged in writing up his journal; two of his companions appear in the background asleep, and around upon the walls hang guns, pouches, and scientific instruments; on one peg is suspended a red tippet on account of its color, red acting as a stimulus in these colorless latitudes, while on another peg is an engraving of Sir John Franklin, half concealed by a broken sword suspended over the print. The whole is illuminated by a single lamp on the left, its light falling strongest upon the head of Dr. Kane, which is the point of interest in the picture.

—Rossiter and Mignot's Mount Vernon picture—or rather a finished study for it—is drawing near to completion. It will prove an attractive work. The mansion at Mount Vernon is represented with a group on the piazza, into which we look lengthwise; the group consists of Mrs. Washington and her daughter-in-law, who are sewing, and Washington and Lafayette, who are engaged in conversation. On the grass in the foreground are a servant and the two Custis children. Leaving the mansion, the eye wanders over the lawn to the trees, through which we catch glimpses of the Potomac river. The likenesses of Lafayette and the two children are from original pictures procured at Arlington; that of Lafayette represents him at the age of twenty-seven, which was his age at the time the picture now at Arlington was painted, and which Lafayette presented to Washington.

—Kensett is painting a composition for R. L. Stuart, Esq. The picture is an upright: The scenery which suggested the picture is a view in New Hampshire, taking in the Saco and White Mountains. Large trees rise from a wooded bank in the foreground, and relieve upon a serene sky; we look over a ravine in the middle distance, and a plain which stretches to the distant mountains, all enlivened by that delicate play of light and shade, which renders Mr. Kensett's pictures so attractive.

—Durand is engaged upon a large upright composition, representing scenery suggestive of the Plaaterkill Clove, Catskill Mountains. Two large trees—a black-birch and a sycamore—in the immediate foreground, are the principal "figures" of the scene; they stand near the brink of a fall, over which are hanging rocks and trees, forming an opening, so that we see the sky and ravine below, and the stream coursing along a huge mountainside to the sunny plain in the distance.

—An International Art exhibition is about to open in this city, on the corner of Broadway and Fourth street. Its attractions—and they will be very great—are to consist of fine contributions from the schools of Berlin, Munich, Dresden, and Düsseldorf. A portrait of Humboldt, by Professor Schader, contributed by the venerable *savan* himself, will be in the collection.

—

Foreign Art Gossip.

—Signor Eugenio Agneni, the Roman fresco painter, who during his brief residence in England, has already acquired much distinction by the graceful and picturesque manner in which he has decorated the Queen's retiring room in the Italian Opera House, Covent Garden, has recently submitted to the notice of the Society of Arts a new invention. This unique style of pictorial decoration, for which the name of mirror-painting is probably the simplest and most appropriate designation, consists of imaging upon the inner surface of a mirror, from which the quicksilver has been previously removed, groups of aerial figures so daintily tinted, and arranged with such delicate skill, that they have the appearance of flying or floating through the Summer air. The mirror represents a bright, cloudless atmosphere, and the figures seem to be gliding through it with the sportive, buoyant, and elastic motion which distinguishes the "gay creatures of the elements."

—The Memoirs of Thomas Uwins furnishes the following anecdote of Turner. A young merchant travelling towards Bologna, who knew nothing of Art and nothing of the reputation of artists, relates it to Uwins, who transcribes it in one of his letters from Italy: "I have fortunately met with a good-tempered, funny little elderly gentleman, who will probably be my travelling companion throughout the journey. He is continually popping his head out of the window to sketch whatever strikes his fancy, and became quite angry because the conductor would not wait for him while he took a sunrise view of Macerata. 'D—n the fellow!' says he, 'he has no feeling.' He speaks but a few words of Italian, about as much of French, which two languages he jumbles together amusingly. His good temper, however, carries him through all his troubles. I am sure you would love him for his indefatigability in his favorite pursuit. From his conversation he is evidently *near kin to*, if not *absolutely,* an artist. Probably you may know something of him. The name on his trunk is J. W., or J. M. W. Turner!"

—Dr. Plumer, in an address delivered at, the opening of a Female Seminary in Wheeling, Va., made the following very sensible remarks: "I hope, sir, you will not teach poetry here—I mean what some people call the science of composing poetry. If it will come from some of these youths, let it come, but don't force it. I feel about like the Methodist preacher, who was giving a charge at a class meeting about some regulations. While in the midst of his charge a lady uttered a shout. 'Now,' says he, 'brethren and sisters, since the subject of shouting has come up, I'll give you my views on the subject. Never shout from a sense of duty. If you feel that you can't hold in—why then shout, but not otherwise.' I hope, then, that no one will ever write poetry from a sense of duty. Poetry is despicable, unless it is first class. Poor poetry is about the meanest of all things. As the Latin satirist has said, 'neither gods nor men can endure it.'"

Original Poetry.

A FRAGMENT.

BY ABBY H. PRICE.

There comes a soft and rosy light
From mystic chambers of the past,
Of glowing love and friendship bright,
That erst their sacred halos cast.

We know fond hearts were once our own—
Sweet wanderers from celestial bowers—
And brilliant hopes were gaily strown,
Like dewdrops o'er fragrant flowers.

We see afar their bright wings gleam
As radiant birds in distant sky;
We see them scattered on life's streams
As faded leaves in Autumn lie.

Are all these gone? Our treasures lost!
Our joys but visions of the past;
Our bark on billowy waters tost,
To be on deserts wrecked at last!

Faith answers no! for passing scenes
Are shadows only of the true;
The vail of doubt that intervenes
Hides the bright real from our view.

Within the darkest pools of crime
The richest blooms have deepest root;
Through Wintry blast—o'er stinging time—
Love learns to tread with lightest foot.

Though forms we love may pass away,
Friends seem to change and hope to die;
Though darkness ends the brightest day,
And happiest moments soonest fly.

Darkness is good to vail the light,
Change shows us God in higher forms;
Blindness gives birth to inner sight,
And virtue strengthens 'mid the storms.

"SO NEAR, AND YET SO FAR!"

BY MRS. M. J. M. SWEAT.

Why comest thou in dreams to paint anew
Thine image on my heart;
To gild afresh each worn and faded hue
With thine own magic art?

Why give the glory of old days to Night,
When, at the touch of Morn,
My prayers are powerless to delay thy flight,
In vain I curse the dawn.

Why bless the hours, when I am wrapt in sleep,
To make the day more lone,—
Why seem such tears of penitence to weep,
To turn again to stone?

Could'st thou but know the welcome my heart gives,
In spite of all my wrongs,
And see the yearning love that in me lives,
And still to thee belongs!

One word of tender pleading from thy lips,
Would rend these clouds away;
Would clear the heavens—break the long eclipse,
And give us back the day.

If I must shut thee from my heart and life,
O haunt my dreams no more!
Why seek forever to renew the strife
For a reward so poor?

But if thou lovest, as in days of old,
Come in the noon's broad light:
Let all the treason of thy past be told,
Nor stoop again to flight.

Come not thus stealthily to mock my rest
With promise sweet and fair,
Or be once more my heart's most honored guest,
And thine old glory wear!

Such nights of joy, such bitter days as this,
Would make a hell of heaven:
Bring me no tempting prophecy of bliss,
Or—yield and be forgiven!

THE SICKLES-TRAGEDY.

The "Dishonored Husband" has always been a favorite subject of popular sympathy. Whatever he may do to avenge his wounded honor,—especially if it is something horrible,—he is sure to be upheld in. In the case of Mr. Sickles, if he had murdered his wife as well as her lover, he would have been not only justified, but applauded. The act would have been in accordance with all our modes of thought. "Down with the vile woman! Trample her under foot! Kick her into the dirt! Blast her! Curse her! If possible, kill her—the infamous creature!" That's the feeling.

And we are all Christians.

But how about the Dishonored Wife? The term doesn't exist. Why should it? Who, especially in gallant America, ever heard of a husband dishonoring his wife? No one. We men are "all, all honorable," of course. But suppose we are not? Suppose we do dishonor our wives? Suppose hundreds of us—thousands of us—do so, and do so pretty openly, too; and talk about it—boast of it, even? What then? Is that anything to make a row about? What is woman that we are mindful of her, or the daughter of woman that we regard her? Isn't she our toy, our plaything, our slave; made to minister to our caprices, and subject herself to our tyranny? Hasn't that been her destiny from the beginning? And in pay for all this, don't we support her? Or, failing to do that, allow her the honor of supporting us? What, then, has she to complain of?

Suppose that an anonymous letter had been sent to Mrs. Sickles, informing her that her husband had a secret *liaison* with another woman? And suppose she had found out, on investigation, that he had? Is it so uncommon an occurrence that she should go into fits about it, and cry her beautiful eyes out? Read Dr. Sanger's *History of Prostitution*, and see! Besides, is a *man* to answer to a *woman* for his conduct? A pretty state of things that would be! Isn't he lord of creation? Hasn't he a right to do as he pleases, without question? Ought not his wife to be everlastingly grateful that he condescended to marry her, and to give her his name,—without making any impertinent inquiries into his private character? Why didn't she inquire into it before marriage? "Because she didn't dare to?" Why did she marry him, then? Would he have married her if he had had any doubts as to her character?

"But the cases are different." Of course they are. He is a *man*, and she is nothing but a *woman*. What business has a woman to pry into a man's secrets? It is the duty of a woman to be delicate—discreet—lady-like; in a word, blind. Isn't love always blind—especially woman's love?

We confess that in the present state of public sentiment on this whole subject, we hardly know how to write a serious word about it.

Think a moment. A husband who dishonors his wife doesn't even weaken his social position; he is received by what is called good society, quite as favorably as before. Some say, more so. In a word, he is indulged with perfect impunity. Any inquiry by his wife as to his conduct out of the house, is treated as the last degree of indelicacy and impertinence. He may absent himself from her for weeks—for months—on business, or on pleasure, without his wife having the shadow of a right to question him as to his behaviour; whereas if she absent herself from him for a single night, without being able to give him a full and circumstantial account of where she has been, and what she has being doing, she is at once subjected to the most horrible suspicions. And the moment a woman is suspected, she is lost.

Again. When a man commits a great crime—greater even than adultery, which is not in the eye of the law a capital one, nor a very grave one, even—and his wife adheres to him through all his disgrace and dishonor, her praises are in the mouth of everybody. But when a woman commits a crime, a crime at all serious—and above all, the crime of adultery—the husband who cleaves to her in her shame, becomes the laughing stock of the whole community.

Suppose that every wife in America, who had proofs of her husband's infidelity, should at once leave his bed and board, and then proceed to murder his paramour? What a scene of desolation and carnage would our land present! What trains, what caravans of human corpses—corpses, often, of young and beautiful women—would fill up all our roads, and darken all our streets! In less than a week every burying-ground in the country would be full.

Let us be careful, then, how we justify Mr. Sickles in killing Mr. Key. It is a poor rule that won't work both ways. If a husband has a right to murder the man who causes his dishonor, certainly a wife has a right to murder the woman who causes *her* dishonor: although, as we have intimated, there will be a time of terrible havoc and bloodshed if women ever come to think so.

But this murdering is always a bad business, whether done by the individual or by the State. We advise both husbands and wives to give up the idea of it. If they can't get along without dishonoring each other, they had better separate. And it would be well if we men got some new notions about honor; that we should learn, at least, that a wife may be dishonored as well as a husband; and that a woman has as much right to avenge herself, as a man to avenge himself. It will be seen from the above that we have no very deep sympathy with Mr. Sickles. His whole conduct in the matter has been disgraceful. Think of his extorting from his wife a written confession of her shame in the presence of witnesses—the brute—and then allowing it to be bandied about the house! Fancy *her* trying to get a written confession of the same kind out of *him*! And just fancy him giving it to her! We can imagine the scene. Sickles, full of virtuous indignation, insists that his young wife shall, then and there, in the presence of witnesses, make a full and detailed confession of her guilt. With fear and trembling, the unhappy woman consents to do so. But, just before signing the document, a brilliant thought occurs to her: "My dear husband, I have now done what you commanded me. Here is my confession; but, before signing it, I have to request that you, in your turn, prepare in the presence of these same witnesses, a written confession of *your* infidelities—stating when, where, with whom, and how often, *you* have dishonored *me*. Do this, and then, my dear, we will exchange confessions, and, if you wish, they shall both go before the public, who will then be able to judge between thee and me."

What a thunderbolt this would have been to the outraged husband! And what consternation there would have been among the discomfited witnesses! Why on earth didn't it occur to the Dishonored Wife to pursue some such course? Why? Simply because it had never occurred to the poor woman that a dishonored wife had any right to complain. Dishonored wives rarely do complain. It wouldn't do any good if they did. All the sympathy the world can spare is laid out on dishonored husbands. The dishonored wife is simply laughed at. Hence she keeps her dishonor to herself, only too proud to have, on any terms, an honored (even though unfaithful) husband. This may be all right enough, only it strikes us as queer. That's all.

And now, just one word in defence of Mrs. Sickles. When she married, she was a young, beautiful, and affectionate girl, and was, no doubt, devoted to her husband. It was a necessity of her nature to be loved and admired, and he loved and admired her. As long as this continued, we have no doubt she was faithful. But when his love cooled, and his admiration died out, and she found that she was no longer "all-in-all" to him, she was exactly in a condition to throw herself into the arms of the first man who would be to her the loving, caressing, idolizing person, that her husband once was. She found such a man, it seems, in Mr. Key: and—we know the result.

Of course she is ruined for life. Far, far better would it have been for her had she been shot; for every day's life she now lives is made worse to her than a thousand deaths. The few who are "without guilt" will perhaps let her alone; but the rest will eventually stone her into the grave.

O, that instead of the young and thoughtless creature she still is, she were a noble and gifted woman, who would take this occasion to avenge the wrongs of her sex, by exposing the horrible state of public opinion, which, for the same offence, brands the wife with infamy, and leaves the husband untainted even in reputation!

Dramatic Feuilleton.

In the Desert.

When there is really nothing to do, perhaps the best thing that a man can do is to do it, that is nothing, as well as nothing possibly can be done. In this position stand that agreeable class of persons who are called by individuals of a lively imagination, dramatic critics. There is literally nothing going on, and yet a man is expected to write an article. It is Sahara with the world of the theatre. The chief theatres make of Our American Cousin a Veteran-attraction. The critics browse in *cafés chantants*, sulk in their own dens, or wander hopelessly to where some person, in a suspicious shirt and dingy smalls, throws butcher-knives at another person, who is a great fool for allowing any one to do it at the price. Even the Circus has lost its charm. A man could go there and be bored by Rice, but there came a time when there was too much Rice. It was, as I said once before, all Rice, and having arrived at the point beyond which, etc., Rice had his congé, for which, seriously, all thanks. Now, at the Circus, they have Cinderella, performed by a large number of females, of various sizes. It is very curious, and quite amusing for the children. Anna Maria convoyed nearly the whole juvenile population of the Fifteenth Ward, on Wednesday last, and the Beloved One really had a matronly air that was quite killing.

The adventurous young gentleman of the *Tribune* has, however, found an oasis. It is in the shape of a person named Menken, who has made her début at the National Theatre. Menken is female. Menken plays soubrettes. By all accounts she is a sort of prairie Lola Montez. I first heard of her at Dayton, a highly interesting town in Ohio. There she played in some one of the numerous pieces wherein young women, in a short allowance of clothing, go through with certain evolutions that are supposed to be military. The Dayton Light Guards, or Light Infantry, or Light some thing or other, were so much charmed, as men and as Guards, that they chose Mistress Menken as their ruler, and she wears the title of Captain to this day. Such a thing could not happen anywhere except in America, and here it is especially Western. When we add that the Guard paraded at the theatre under the command of their actress-captain, the thing is complete. She has now come, sword in hand, to conquer the metropolis, and the *Tribune*-critic, albeit a man of peace, has been to see the crinoline warrior. I have not yet ventured. The critical office daily proves more and more dangerous. If a man writes that a *prima donna* can't sing, or wont sing, or kicks up rows, he runs the risk of having his life bullied out of him. If, with only the natural female weapons, I am to be put down, what should I do against the Menken, who could, no doubt, bring a light artillery battery in the field against me, and serve the pieces herself.

So I leave the lady to the *Tribune*, and I rescue the notice from the obscurity of the City Items. *Voila*!

National Theatre.—Ada Isaacs Menken, an amateur of some fame in the West, is playing at this house. She has talent, but it is like the gold in quartz veins all in the rough: and she must undergo the refining process of intelligent and critical audiences before she can hope to become an actress. She must correct another grave error at once, and that is her style of dressing in Protean pieces. When people go to the ballet, they expect to see a peculiar and questionable freedom in the toilet; but that style ought never to be misstated, much less outstripped, upon the legitimate style—not even on the Eastern side of the city. There is a hearty earnestness and dashing style about Miss or Mrs. Menken, which, under proper training, gives promise of better things; but, like most Western mental products, she wants taming down.

A short experience in Printing-House-Square might do her some good.

Mills.

About two or three Sundays ago, Mr. Carl Bergmann, with the assistance of Caradori and several other Pompæian relics, gave a concert at the City Assembly Rooms—which we say *en passant*, are the very worst rooms in which to give a concert on the face of the earth. At this concert, there were some two or three hundred Germans; other people prefer to stay at home on Sunday evenings. There was a new name in the programme. The name of Mills. Mills who would play something on the piano. Nobody ever heard of Mills. But everybody in the musical world here had heard of him next day. He is a most admirable pianist of the school of Liszt, but with more delicacy and finish than is usual with the followers of that distinguished artist. His touch has that divine sympathy which the world calls genius. He plays rather like an earnest enthusiastic German than an Englishman, and is indeed fresh from the conservatory of Leipsic. Without doubt, Mr. Mills has a fine career open before him.

Theatre Francais.

Before the issuing of the next Saturday Press, the French Theatre will have been opened to the public. It will be, at first, the most fashionable and agreeable place of amusement in the city. The opening is fixed for Tuesday next. The following is a full list of the artists engaged :

M. Paul Laba, artiste du Théatre Français, de Paris, jeune premier rôle.
M'lle Eugénie Sen, de l'Odéon, soubrette et Déjazet.
M'lle Lau'e Chevalier, des Variétes, jeune première.
M'lle Jane Montheaux, ingénue.
M'me Pauline Dupont, grande coquette et 1st rôle.
M'me Alexandrine Daire, 1st duègne et mére noble.
M'me Tallot, grande utilité.
M'me Louise, utilité.
Mr. Bertrand, premier comique.
Mr. Edgard, jeune comique.
Mr. Tallot, pére noble et premier rôle masqué.
Mr. Charrier Delalain, fort second amoureux.
Mr. Thiery, comique grime.
Mr. Sage, troisième rôle (au besoin).
Mr. Henry W., second amoureux comique.
Mr. Leon, utilité.

Dramatic Fund Benefit.

The editor has received the following note, to which we recommend the especial attention of Mr. John Brougham, *et id.*

February 28th, 1859.

Dear Sir:—In your paper of the 26th inst. you state that the amateur performance in aid of the Dramatic Fund is definitely fixed for the 20th April next. If it could be put off until after the 24th April, the Committee would oblige a number of ladies, and no doubt add to the receipts of the evening, as many people will not attend a dramatic performance on Holy Week. Please make the suggestion to the Powers that be, and oblige. A Wellwisher to the Fund.

Mere Mention.

Lord Dundreary (Mr. Sothern), whom someone called an outrageous *plagiarism* on the English nobility, has his benefit at Laura Keene's this evening. American Cousin, of course. The awful effects of excessive avarice have been seen in the conduct of the management of this house, with regard to Mr. Taylor's play. When it first appeared they could have sold plenty of copies at a fair price, but the amount asked was so inordinate to the value of the trash, that is, if it has any value, that the managers hesitated. One or two employed stenographers, who were at first ordered to desist from taking down the actor's words. But they were not to be bullied like hungry actors, and the play was taken down. Now it is being played at two theatres in Boston, and in various other parts of the country. Any one could play it here with impunity.

The *Veteran* is still a good card at Wallack's, and will be continued for the present.

Antony and Cleopatra is to be done at the Broadway next week. The Mise en scene will be very fine. In about six weeks the Broadway Theatre will be pulled down, when Mr. Eddy intends to build a new one up town. Nothing is yet settled about Niblo's Garden. Mr. Burton will be in town next week to make arrangements for the reopening of his theatre.

Things that "Nobody" Knows.

Some person, feminine evidently, writes to the Cincinnati *Commercial* in the following "rich style" about Piccolomini:—

And have I nothing to say about her *singing*? That I have. The sounds of her voice linger with me now, and melodize my soul as I think of her. Nothing can exceed the sweetness and clearness of her medium tones, and that gentle dying away of her falsettos. But she is not, as yet, a true *artiste*. Her voice is like her character—as all voices are—fresh, unsullied, flexible, but unformed—lacking depth and earnestness. To gain this, she needs those four years of sorrow and discipline that developed the depth and fervor of Jenny Lind's character. When, after having devoted years to study, and her triumphs had just begun—when she had just tasted the sweets of human adulation, and the pure happiness flowing from the divine gift of pouring out her naturally earnest soul in song, she was suddenly deprived of her voice. The silver notes had fled, and before an expecting audience she stood mute and palsied with despair. And for four long anguished years the hope of her life was taken away! This it was that afterwards gave *soul* to the natural tones of her voice. She then sung with an *humble* heart, and her tones were earnest and *womanly*—appealing to the inmost sorrow of every human soul, and winning sympathy from the universal heart of nature.

What folly then to compare Piccolomini with Jenny Lind. She is just now where the Lind was when the cloud came over her life. She knows not what disappointment or defeat is. Success and adulation have followed her steps from childhood. She but lives in the bliss of this success, and sings out the joy of her young childish heart.

A little spoilt too, she is—a little girl vanity mingles with her artless manner, and comes too truly from her woman's heart. I longed to take her in my arms and say, "Dear little Piccy, you are just as sweet as you can be—but don't let them spoil you. Keep your pure girl heart devoted to your art, and one of these days you may be good enough for some good man's dear little wifey!"

But then it would be a pity for her to do that, wouldn't it? Such a voice as hers does not belong to herself to give away as a *part* of herself. It is a God gift to the *world.* Oh! that she could feel this with a fervor that will enable her to immolate her heart's best treasures upon the shrine of her noble art! Who shall say that she would not be thrice blessed?

That is splendid. A *prima donna* successful and not spoiled, would be the ninth (Bonner is the eighth) wonder of the world!

They are doing "Our American Cousin" at the Howard Athenæum and the Boston Museum. F. S. Chanfrau and W. Warren are the Trenchards; E. L. Davenport and J. A. Smith the Dundrearys. There are cheap concerts at the Music Hall and Boston Theatre, where there was to be a Mount Vernon Ball, on the 4th March. The affair is under the patronage of innumerable honorables, colonels, and things of that sort.

Mr. Barry Sullivan is playing at Cincinnati.

Mme. Cora de Wilhorst has returned to town after a series of brilliant successes in the West. She was one of the particular stars of the Charity Ball, at the Academy, on Thursday. Mme. de Wilhorst will rejoin the Strakosch Company at the Cincinnati Opera House, where the first Opera season will be commenced on Monday week.

Piccolomini will be at St. Louis next week.

Mario was singing recently at a private soiree at the residence of Rossini, a number of musical and artistical notabilities being present. As they were parting, Mme. Taglioni approached Mario to compliment him, and said, "I'm sure you do not recognize me." "Ah, Madame," answered the tenor, in a tone of amiable reproach, "Indeed I do." "But you sing," said Taglioni, "as in your youthful days, while I can dance no more." "Yes, but you have carried away the dance with you," gallantly answered the singer. Very neat.

A letter from Naples says: "Signor Verdi left us a few days since for Rome, where he will bring out his new opera, entitled 'La Vendetta dei Domino.'" It was intended for Naples, but was prohibited.

M. Meyerbeer's "Dinorah" has entered into another stage of preparatory progress, its orchestral rehearsals having commenced. The opera may, therefore, be looked for some time after Easter.

PERSONNE.

NEW YORK MARCH 12, 1859

For the NEW-YORK SATURDAY PRESS.

ON THE TOWN.

The lamps are lighted, the streets are full,
For, coming and going, like waves of the sea,
Thousands are out this beautiful night;
They jostle each other, but shrink from me!
Men hurry by with a stealthy glance,
Women pass with their eyes cast down;
Even the children seem to know
The shameless girl of the town!

Hated and shunned I walk the street,
Hunting—for what? For my prey, 'tis said;
I look at it though in a different light,
For this nightly shame is my daily bread!
My food, my shelter, the clothes I wear!
Only for this I might starve, or drown;
The world has disowned me, what can I do,
But live and die on the town?

The world is cruel. It may be right
To crush the harlot, but grant it so,
What made her the guilty thing she is?
For she was innocent once, you know:
"Twas love! that terrible word tells all!
She loved a man and blindly believed
His vows, his kisses, his crocodile tears;
Of course the fool was deceived!

What had I to gain by a moment's sin,
To weigh in the scale with my innocent years,
My womanly shame, my ruined name,
My father's curses, my mother's tears?
The love of a man! It was something to give,
Was it worth it? The price was a soul paid down;
Did I get a soul, his soul in exchange?
Behold me here on the town!

"Your guilt was heavy," the world will say,
"And heavy, heavy your doom must be;
For to pity and pardon woman's fall,
Is to set no value on chastity!
You undervalue the virgin's crown,
The spotless honor that makes her dear."
But I ought to know what the bauble is worth,
When the loss of it brings me here!

But pity and pardon? Who are you
To talk of pardon, pity to me?
What I ask is justice, justice, sir!
Let both be punished, or both go free.
If it be in woman a shameful thing,
What is it in man, now? Come, be just:
(Remember, she falls through her love for him,
He, through his selfish lust!)

Tell me what is done to the wretch
Who tempts, and riots in woman's fall?
His father curses, and casts him off?
His friends forsake? He is scorned of all?
Not he: his judges are men like himself,
Or thoughtless women, who humor their whim:
"Young blood,"—" Wild oats"—" Better hush it up:
They soon forget it—in him!

Even his mother, who ought to know
The woman-nature, and how it is won,
Frames a thousand excuses for him,
Because, forsooth, the man is her son!
You have daughters, Madam (he told me so),
Fair innocent daughters—" Woman, what then?"
Some mother may have a son like yours,
Bid them beware of men!

I saw his coach in the street to-day.
    Dashing along on the sunny side,
With a liveried driver on the box;
    Lolling back in her listless pride,
The wife of his bosom took the air:
    She was bought in the mart where hearts are sold:
I gave myself away for his love,
    She sold herself for his gold!

He lives, they say, in a princely way,
    Flattered and feasted. One dark night
Some devil led me to pass his house:
    I saw the windows a blaze of light;
The music whirled in a maddening round,
    I heard the fall of the dancers' feet:
Bitter, bitter, the thoughts I had
    Standing there in the street!

Back to my gaudy den I went,
    Marched to my room in grim despair,
Dried my eyes, painted my cheeks,
    And fixed a flower or two in my hair!
Corks were popping, wine was flowing,
    I seized a bumper, and tossed it down:
One must do something to kill the time.
    And fit one's self for the town!

I meet his boy in the park sometimes,
    And my heart runs over towards the child:
A frank little fellow with fearless eyes,
    He smiles at me as his father smiled!
I hate the man, but I love the boy,
    For I think what my own, had he lived, would be:
Perhaps it is *he*, come back from the dead—
    To his father, alas! not me!

But I stand too long in the shadow here,
    Let me out in the light again.
Now for insult, blows perhaps,
    And, bitterer still, my own disdain!
I take my place in the crowd of men,
    Not like the simple women I see :
You may cheat them, men, as much as you please,
    You wear no masks with me!

I know ye! Under your honeyed words
    There lurks a serpent: your oaths are lies;
There's a lustful fire in your hungry hearts,
    I see it flaming up in your eyes!
Cling to them, ladies, and shrink from me,
    Or rail at my boldness—Well, have you done?
Madam, your husband knows me well;
    Mother, I know your son!

But go your ways, and I'll go mine:
    Call me opprobious names, if you will:
The truth is bitter, think I have lied:
    "A harlot ?" Yes! But a woman still!
God said of old to a woman like me,
    "Go; sin no more," or your Bibles lie:
But you, you mangle His merciful words
    To—"Go, and sin till you die!"

Die! the word has a pleasant sound,
    The sweetest I've heard this many a year:
It seems to promise an end to pain,
    Anyway it will end it—here!
Suppose I throw myself in the street?
    Before the horses could trample me down,
Some would-be friend might snatch me up,
    And thrust me back on the town!

But look, the river! From where I stand
    I see it, I almost hear it flow:
Down on the dark and lonely pier—
    It is but a step—I can end my wo!
A plunge, a splash, and all will be o'er,
    The death-black waters will drag me down;
God knows where! But no matter where,
    So I am off the town!

R. H. STODDARD.

S TEINFELD'S BITTERS.

STEINFELD'S BITTERS.
STEINFELD'S BITTERS.
STEINFELD'S BITTERS.
STEINFELD'S BITTERS.
STEINFELD'S BITTERS.
STEINFELD'S BITTERS.
STEINFELD'S BITTERS.
STEINFELD'S BITTERS.
STEINFELD'S BITTERS.
STEINFELD'S BITTERS.
STEINFELD'S BITTERS.
STEINFELD'S BITTERS.
70 NASSAU ST.
70 NASSAU ST.
70 NASSAU ST.
70 NASSAU ST.
70 NASSAU ST.
70 NASSAU ST.
70 NASSAU ST.
70 NASSAU ST.
70 NASSAU ST.

WHAT IS THE REASON
That Bowel Complaints, Bilious attacks,
Fevers and Diarrhoea, are not wholly
eradicated from our midst? Simply
because the unfailing remedy for those
complaints is not kept on hand in every
household in these
UNITED STATES, as in EUROPE!
This remedy acts immediately on the part
affected; it goes directly to the seat of the
disease, and when its healing mission is
complete, the body is left in the full glow
of health, and free from the invariable
costiveness which succeeds the use of drugs
and patent medicine poisons. This heaven-
sent benefaction to the human race is the
discovery of that
GREAT FRENCH CHEMIST, LEROUX.

After many years' study and research, he,
by accident mainly, met with a certain essence
which possesses extraordinary healing powers
in ailments consequent on deranged digestive organs; this he compounded with
the purest and most delicious brandy, and named it
THE CORDIAL COGNAC BITTERS.
These Bitters have an agreeable taste, as thousands in the States can now testify, using them
rather as an ordinary drink than as a medicine. Their healing properties exert themselves
within five minutes, and speedily eradicate the complaint. They are of infallible efficacy in all
and every of the following diseases:

DIARRHEA.
CHOLERA.
FEVERS.
AGUE.
COLIC.
BILIOUS ATTACKS.
BLUES.

Large consignments have been forwarded during the past year into the Western States, and
their healing virtues were found to be
triumphantly successful, in withstanding the
ravages of Yellow Fever in the cities of
NORFOLK AND PORTSMOUTH.
The Cholera Cordial Cognac Bitters may be obtained of the Sole Agent and Importer,
S. STEINFELD, No. 70 Nassau street, N. Y. City, both wholesale and Retail. Also, of all
respectable Druggists throughout the States.

NO FAMILY SHOULD BE WITHOUT THEM!

SYRACUSE, Nov. 14, 1858.

DEAR PIERSON: You are aware I have been for a long time severely afflicted with a deranged stomach, and have received no benefit from the counsel of my doctors, or the use of
various quack medicines. By your advice, I brought home with me a bottle of STEINFELD'S
COGNAC BITTERS, and in consequence of its operating so charmingly upon my digestive
organs, I am anxious to have more of it at once. Won't you stop into No. 70 Nassau st., and
direct the agent to pack up five or six bottles securely, and send at once by American Express?
Let the bill follow to pay on receipt. If the agent has any objection to do so, you will be kind
enough to pay, and draw on me for the amount.
    If he sells cheaper by the dozen, see that I have the benefit of it. Yours truly,   M.
BALLARD.

SOLE AGENT
SOLE AGENT
SOLE AGENT
SOLE AGENT
SOLE AGENT
SOLE AGENT
SOLE AGENT
SOLE AGENT
SOLE AGENT
SOLE AGENT
SOLE AGENT
SOLE AGENT
FOR M. LEROUX'S
FOR M. LEROUX'S
FOR M. LEROUX'S
FOR M. LEROUX'S
FOR M. LEROUX'S
FOR M. LEROUX'S
FOR M. LEROUX'S
FOR M. LEROUX'S
COGNAC BITTERS,
COGNAC BITTERS,
COGNAC BITTERS,
COGNAC BITTERS,
COGNAC BITTERS,
COGNAC BITTERS,
COGNAC BITTERS
70 NASSAU ST
70 NASSAU ST
70 NASSAU ST.
70 NASSAU ST.
70 NASSAU ST.

SOLE AGENT FOR M. LEROUX'S COGNAC BITTERS

POEMS*

BY FRANCES ANN KEMBLE.

The writings and sayings of certain individuals seem in the eyes of their admirers to be privileged above those of less favored humanity; to be sublimated far beyond the reach of ordinary criticism, to be entitled to an approbation that cannot be disputed, and to a merit that should not be questioned. A book, however, written by a person of mature years, with his or her name, in full, appended to the titlepage, is a fair subject of legitimate criticism; and, in fact, being promulgated to the public, challenges its scrutiny and opinion. Such a work may be fairly commented on, in its literary and intellectual aspect, without any extraordinary obligations of deference to the views of social circles, and without properly subjecting the critic, as a consequence of the omission of such deference, to a charge of personal prejudice or of professional severity.

Mrs. Kemble, not contented with prominence in the dramatic world, has, in the book above noted, entered the poetic lists, and contributed her quota to the many specimens of versification, often the offspring of misdirected or insufficient talent, that are daily offered up to the voracity of a never satiated and generally not over fastidious literary community.

Whatever may have been the object of the fair authoress in issuing this production to the public,—whether it was a desire to add to an already enviable reputation, or a motive of a more material character,—it is to be hoped that it has been attained. If increased literary reputation, however, was the object, there is, perhaps, some room for doubt as to whether results have been obtained adequate to meet the requirements of self-complacency or the partiality of friendship.

"*Ne sutor ultra crepidam*" is a motto of old but universal application, and seems, in the present case, far from inapplicable.

Long practised and ably experienced as Mrs. Kemble may be in interpreting, to the satisfaction of general audiences, the vivid imagery, poetic fervor, and philosophic profundity of the "Bard of Avon," but little of those brilliant qualities seem to have come down to his interpreter.

The former flies from earth, in his burning chariot, far into the glowing realms of immortality; but unfortunately, he has carried his mantle with him: it certainly has not descended upon our authoress; and although, in the volume before us there is an imitative longing after the great original, manifested in an affected quaintness of expression, an antiquity of inversion, and a struggling after far-conceived and dimly illuminated metaphors, the ambition of the attempt seems mainly to illustrate the unsatisfactory nature of the result.

The following extracts may serve as specimens of this feature in the style of the volume before us :

What is my lady like? thou fain would'st know—
A rosy chaplet of fresh apple-bloom,
Bound with blue ribbon, lying on the snow;
What is my lady like? *the violet gloom*
Of evening, with deep *orange-light below*?
She's *like the noonday smell of a pine wood*;
She's like *the sounding of a stormy flood;*
She's *like a mountain-top high in the skies,*
To which the day its earliest light doth lend.

—and so on, with a half dozen or more similes, equally forced and incongruous, constructing a composite female that would be an invaluable addition to Barnum's collection, and who would have certainly made quite an *eligible match* for Frankenstein's sympathy-seeking monster.

The following is also full of strained and incongruous metaphor:

Phoebus his golden hand
Hath laid upon the *white mane of the sea,*
And springing from the fresh brine gloriously,
He glances keen o'er the long level strand.
Now comes his horses up, all snorting fire, etc.

The following is a comical *mélange* of dolor and housewifery—

If I believed in death, how sweet a *bed*
For such a blessed slumber could I find
Beneath the *blue and sparkling coverlid*
Of that smooth sea, stirred by no breath of wind.

Mrs. Kemble had evidently just such a comfortable "blue coverlid" in her house, the souvenir of which suggested the above simile. She speaks of the stars—

That now shine forth
Winking the slumberer's destinies,—

The sleepy rascals—dozing on their watch—forsooth!

In a "Sonnet" she speaks of a

Maiden you might scarce think fair
The first time that across your path she past;
And, suddenly, you would be fettered fast
In the *thick meshes of her chestnut hair!*

The "floating motions, gay and glad," of this hirsute maiden, who must have spread out her hair to catch her beaux, as our fishermen do their shad-nets, are subsequently compared

To Summer rain showers twinkling to the earth,
When all the shrubberies rock in rustling glee.

This latter is certainly a comical figure, if not very inappreciable.

It is somewhat difficult to imagine, for example, a series of blackberry, hawthorn, elder, huckleberry, and other favorite "shrubberies," rocking about in "rustling glee," enjoying a good joke, if you please, or pleasant thing among themselves.

In her originality Mrs. Kemble is hardly more successful than in her imitations. Her style is exaggerated, somewhat affected, and rarely, if ever, forcible. She shows, too, a singular deficiency in all ordinary knowledge of versification; crudities, and discords of rhyme and measure, as well as thought, occur as frequently as they might in the first muse gushings of female-boarding-schooldom, blushing semi-weekly in the hospitable columns of a provincial newspaper. In apostrophizing Shakespeare, Mrs. Kemble finds no more forcible and emphatic way of addressing that distinguished individual than as

——Spirit *strong and bland*!
Lord of the speech of my dear native land!

In which latter qualification, apart from his "blandness," he was quite equalled, perhaps, if not excelled, by such lesser luminaries as Johnson, Walker, and Lindley Murray, Esqrs.

The following commencement of lines "To the Picture of a Lady," are very mawkish, and one would think hardly worth publication by a female out of her "teens"—

Lady, sweet lady, I behold thee yet
With thy pale brow, brown eyes and solemn air,
And *billowy* tresses of thy golden *hair*;
Which *once to see, is never to forget*!
But for short space I gazed with soul intent
Upon thee;—and the limner's art divine,
Meantime, poured all thy spirit into mine.

The feebleness of thought and infelicity of expression of this specimen are hardly inferior to the explanatory and eulogistic platitudes, whilom introduced as accessory to the portraits of titled fashionables, collected into so-called "Books of Beauty."

The lines, "Written on Cramond Beach," begin as follows, and are as feeble as the above:

Farewell, old playmate! on thy sandy shore
My lingering feet will leave their print no more;
To thy loved side I never may return, etc.

The syntax of the following extract would hardly pass muster in a district school:

Death and I,
On a hill *so* high,
Stood side by side;
And we saw below,
Running to and fro,
All things that *be* in the world *so* wide.

Here we have a description of waves very much after the "*rimbomba*" school:

Rising and rounding,
Rolling, rebounding,
Echoing, resounding,
And running into curves of creamy spray.

From a piece called a "Fragment," written on a hot day, we have a specimen of Mrs. Kemble's *comic* poetic power:

For me my mind is solely wrought

Boston: Ticknor & Fields.

To this one wish; O! in a pond
Would I were over head and ears!
(Of a cold ducking I've no fears,)
Or any where, where I am not,
For, bless the heat, it is too hot!

In an "Epistle," Mrs. Kemble speaks of

Princes and *counties* Palatine,
Who ruled and revelled on the Rhine.

Can anybody imagine a "county" Palatine, or otherwise, *ruling and revelling*!

Some of the rhymes adopted by our authoress would have made even Sternhold and Hopkins, those reverend versifiers of Gothic memory, pause and consider. "Deliver" and "forever"—"head" and "sheltered "—"way" and "away"—"woes" and "allows"—"still" and "dwell"—"chorister" and "theatre"—"light" and "freight"—make but sorry couples.

In a piece called an "Impromptu," we have the following queer piece of rhyming:

My fount of song, dear friend, 's a bitter *well*,
And when the numbers freely from it flow,
"Tis that my heart and eyes o'erflow as *well*.

The ideas and subject-matter which form the basis of these poetic effusions are often singularly deficient in force, sentiment, and imagery—in fact, they are at times peculiarly *jejune*.

We sincerely believe that Mrs. Kemble is actually forcing nature when she writes poetry—that she is deficient in the divine gift or *afflatus* that constitutes the essential element of poetic character—in the grace, sensibility, and delicacy of thought and emotion that enable one to receive and impart refined poetic impressions. Like all poets, and particularly poetesses, Mrs. Kemble seems to have had, or fancies she has had a melancholy experience of life, in fact that she is a special target for the sports of those disagreeable old ladies, the "*Fates*" and "*Eumenides*." Judging also, from the major part of the contents of the book before us, she is very anxious that the world should know all about this lacerated state of her feelings, and the lugubrious aspect of her mundane contemplations. Hence doomed she is continually writing of "the path she is doomed to tread"—her "spirit worn and weary"—her "dawn overcast"—her "throbbing heart"—the "phantom" that "haunts" her life—her "sinking lonely bark launched upon the sea"—the story of her "shipwreck"—the "horrible despair of ope and love forever overthrown," and so on *ad nauseum*.

The subjects treated of, however, are in the main very diverse, and in heterogeneous contrast. We have, among a multitude of others, the following original topics: "Lines on being blessed by a child,"—"Lines on a Young Woman,"—"Lines on reading with difficulty some of Schiller's early love Poems,"—"To—–,who fell from a precipice into a mountain torrent,"—"Epistle from the Rhine to Y—, with a bowl of Bohemian glass,"—"Scraps,"—"The prayer of a lonely heart,"—"To Mrs. —,"––"To my guardian angel,"— "On a musical box,"—"Lines written at night,"—"Lines written after a walk,"—"Lines written after a ball," etc., etc.

The composition of this volume, made up as it appears, at different times, during an extended period, seems to us to bear a funny analogy to a scrap-bag kept by some old dame in the country, wherein, from the time that she was a young miss, she has been wont to stow away all her little remnants and remainders—now a piece of silk, now of fustian, now a scrap of calico, now of satin—until a great collection has been obtained, and then, after a long time elapsed, old and new, fresh and rusty, faded and fantastic, are carefully gathered together and made up, mayhap, into a gigantic "counterpane," and exhibited at some rural fair to gaping admirers, and woe be to the individual who does not say *Amen*! to their eulogistic ejaculations.

There is one selection, however, that we will make with pleasure, and with a greater satisfaction, from its contrast with its predecessors. It is the most striking, if not the only piece of original thought and good writing in the book:

FAITH.

Better trust all, and be deceived,
 And weep that trust, and that deceiving;
Than doubt one heart, that, if believed,
 Had blessed one's life with true believing.

Oh, in this mocking world, too fast
 The doubting fiend o'ertakes our youth!
Better be cheated to the last,
 Than lose the blessed hope of truth.

The antithesis of the first verse is striking, the sentiment beautiful, and the rhythm faultless. If Mrs. Kemble had written a book of such poetry as this, instead of the careless and common-place compositions which she now asks the public to patronize, she would have received a high meed of praise and admiration.

For the New York Saturday Press.

DRIFT-WEED,

Or, Common Thoughts rendered into Words.

—

BY MRS. M. J. M. SWEAT.

I.

One important office of the past is to teach us what we may expect in the future; and a vast increase of personal power is often the result of a keen analysis and thorough comprehension of our relationships in our bygone experiences. The amount of progression discoverable in our past, may be taken as the ratio of movement in the coming time. Also from such analysis and self-study do we learn to distinguish the ephemeral from the permanent influences of our lives, which, in the passing, are often indistinguishable. The passions and emotions which stand firm under the searching examination we are able to give them when they are removed from the immediate present, may be declared realities for us forever. Standing on this ground the heart is able to look calmly on as the memory summons up each past emotion, and the intellect passes an impartial judgment upon it; while from those which it condemns, as well as from those which it sanctions, material for a correct prophecy for the future may be drawn. The best preparation for a new life may be made by obtaining, in the first place, a thorough knowledge of the old life, and he who shrinks from confronting the past, can hardly prove a wise or even a brave combatant with the future.

For this self-knowledge to be valuable, it needs not that the life should be very full of external vanity or startling incident; the thought-life of most persons furnishes rich material when it is brought fairly into light. Outward actions are but the manifestation of the response which the inner nature gives to the forces which are brought to bear upon it, and it is not always those which seem most violent at first, which prove in the end, most important as agents of interior development. It is through experiences quite within the range of ordinary life, that the richest natures often unfold themselves and attain to an inner harmony, of which only their own hearts are aware till some sudden lightningflash gleams upon them, reveals them to the crowd and shows them to be really far up in the calm serenity of self-possessed souls.

II.

The man who rushes off upon a tangent, makes a great show when looked at from the little portion of the circumference which can see him at all, but viewed from the centre, which commands the whole plain of the horizon, and takes in the full and finished beauty of the circle—he is but a poor, spent ball, on which all motive force will soon cease to act.

III.

Oddity almost always involves a certain weakness of character, an incompleteness of development—we had almost said, a lack of talent, for it is comparatively easy to become conspicuous through doing things in a *different* way from that in which others do them,—but to do them in the *same* way, and attain to preeminent success with apparently ordinary means that is indeed something! Oddity encouraged in its possessor, though it attracts attention, and has sometimes a quaint charm while in its freshness, often degenerates into disease and tyrannizes as remorselessly over the patient as he does over those about him. The lane which leads into this region of country, has no turning, and the pedestrian upon it is almost always ashamed to retrace his steps in the sight of those who unsuccessfully endeavored to persuade him to remain with them upon the high-road. Many a man with an established reputation as "an odd genius," feels the contempt implied when others pass unnoticed in him what they would resent in others, and would gladly rid himself of his self-originated isolation from ordinary rules, if he could do so without the shame of a public recantation, and amid the mortification of seeing others astonished at his assuming the responsibilities of ordinary social courtesy. People are as much surprised to see an oddity become reasonable, as to see a miser become generous.

IV.

How much of our time is taken up in merely supplying omissions, or in making reparation for injuries which ought never to have been committed! We say an unkind word, or do a thoughtless deed—perhaps we only omit an opportunity for kindness—and the little monitor within us will not let us rest till we leave our business or our pleasure, and go forth to soothe the hurt, or efface its remembrance by some new impression or some friendly service. We all recognize, in the main, the claim which others have upon us for something more than the cold legality of an undisturbed independence, and however we may at times fancy that we are nothing to others, as they are nothing to us, it takes but some slight change of outward circumstance, or some involuntary variation of inward emotion, to bring clearly before us the actuality of our dependence, and the reality of our responsibility. Few of us can sit down contentedly, when we discover that we have inadvertently pained another, and even our pride is interested, to urge us to a frank apology for wrong done in ignorance or haste. Pity that our experience in this way does not teach us a quicker discretion in new emergencies.

THE CODE OF HONOR.

SICKLES killed poor KEY from a sense of honor. The act was required of him by the Code. What we should do without the Code, Beelzebub only knows. Do without it, perhaps. Its chief function is to regulate the killing of people, and make it respectable. Not only respectable to kill, but respectable to be killed. A man who is killed according to the Code has no right to complain. He can tell of it as he crosses the Styx without blushing.

Had Sickles followed his instincts, his victim might still have been alive. But the Code wouldn't let him follow his instincts. It don't believe in instincts. They are vulgar. And, moreover, are apt to be manly. It deals,—the Code does,—in nothing but honor. Wounded honor! This is its staple. Sickles's feelings were all right; they were not wounded, in the least; but his honor had been touched. So the Code had its back up at once, and insisted that he should become a murderer, and then all would be well. His honor would be satisfied, and Mrs. Sickles, but no! Mrs. Sickles wasn't taken into the account. She was only a woman. She might go home and die. What could she know about honor?

Sickles didn't want to murder Key, but the Code made him do it; wrote him anonymous letters, and insisted on his doing it; in fact, stood by and saw him do it. And Mrs. Grundy, who believes in the Code,—in fact, believes in nothing else,—says it's all just as it should be, and that if Key didn't want to be killed, he had no business to be found out. The Code never troubles people till they are found out. It has no objection to seduction, to adultery, to treachery, or to any other crime, till they are publicly exposed. Then the Code is wide awake, and on its mettle.

But for the Code, Mr. Sickles would be hung. Hung by the opposition Code. As it is, he will go unpunished. He stuck to the Code, and the Code will stick to him. If he behaves himself, the Code will allow him to return to Mrs. Sickles. He wants to, now, we are told, but the Code wont let him. If he stays away a little longer, *she* wont let him. And she would be right though the Code don't think so. The Code made Sickles perform the little farce of taking away his wife's wedding-ring. It was very Codish, that. And Sickles did it with great éclat. "Well done!" everybody said "Bravo!" He didn't return *his* ring—the Code would have been shocked at *that*—he only took back *her's*. Took it back indignantly, and made up a great virtuous face about it, as if he had done something sublime, and the gods were applauding him for it. Poor, Code-striken Sickles! The next day he wanted to send the ring back to his wife. But the Code wouldn't let him, unless he first broke it in twain. So he broke it and sent her the pieces. Another farce. There's nothing pleases the Code like a good farce. Any thing simple, straitforward, honest, offends it. It is contrary, in fact, to its principles. That is, if it have any principles. But the great difficulty with the Code is, that it hasn't any. It simply represents *the lowest state of public sentiment for the time being*. Hence its popularity in Washington, which is the moral cesspool of the nation.

Whatever a man does spontaneously, from the promptings of his nature, even from the activity or vehemency of his passions, is entitled to a certain degree of respect. It is at least honest. But whatever he does in obedience to a Code, or from fear of public ridicule, is entitled to nothing but contempt.

And the same with woman; for she, too, has her Code. The Code-Grundy. All her life-time, and down to her very grave, she stands in mortal fear of Mrs. Grundy. It is Mrs. Grundy, just now, who makes her persecute Mrs. Sickles. Her natural instincts would lead her to fly to her sister's rescue. But Mrs. Grundy won't let her. Mrs. Grundy insists that she shall shrug her pretty shoulders, pout her pretty lips, lift up her pretty hands, denounce Mrs. Sickles as the vilest of creatures, and thus do what she can to break her heart, and send her, crushed and bleeding, to the tomb.

But we have no patience to pursue the subject. If men and women will allow themselves to be made fools of by society, and its miserable Codes, we suppose there is no help for the matter. It may be well, however, to call attention to the fact.

POOR CAP-MAKERS, AND CYCLOPÆDIA-WRITERS.

The *N. Y. Tribune* publishes an affecting article entitled "TWO CENTS A-PIECE FOR MAKING MEN'S CAPS." We are pleased to have the editors of so influential a journal expose the low price paid for labor, and wait with some anxiety for another article from them on the same subject, entitled "TWO DOLLARS A-PAGE FOR MAKING CYCLOPEDIAS." Allow us to make a suggestion as to the mode of treatment.

In the article on the CAP-MAKERS occurs the following passage, referring to one Mrs. G., No. 10 Mulberry street:

> "We found her," said the visitor, "hard at work, making boys' black cloth caps, trimmed with braid, and bow, and buttons, lined with glazed muslin, and wash-leather, and with patent-leather front; for the making and pressing of which she received two shillings per dozen, or two cents a-piece. I did not believe it, and asked to see her passbook. It was true. 'In good times,' she said, 'I used to get three and sixpence a dozen, but now the price is reduced !'
>
> "Save us from such grasping tradesmen, and from the necessity that makes families dependent upon them!"

Now in the article on the CYCLOPÆDIA-MAKERS, the same style might be adopted, as thus:

> "We found him (the Cyclopædia-maker) hard at work, composing elaborate articles, full of figures, statistics, etc., which had cost him months of study and research, and for the collecting and preparing of which he received from the Messrs. Appleton two dollars a-page, or less than is paid by the Tribune for articles requiring no study or research whatever. We did not believe it, and asked to see his accounts. It was true. 'In other times,'" he said, 'I used to earn five and ten dollars a-page for much lighter work, but now the price is reduced.'
>
> "Save us from such grasping publishers, and from the necessity that makes authors dependent upon them."

—The colored people of Boston and vicinity met on Monday evening last in commemoration of the martyrdom of CRISPUS ATTUCKS, the colored American who was shot by the British in State street, in 1770. Speeches were made by Rev. John B. Smith (colored), Charles L. Remond (colored), and Wm. Lloyd Garrison (white). A quadrille band and volunteer glee clubs were in attendance. After the speaking, the remainder of the evening was passed in dancing.

—Officer Buckman, of the 7th Ward Police, arrested three little boys last Sunday for selling newspapers. Nothing seems to delight the heart of a policeman so much as arresting little boys.

Dramatic Feuilleton.

The French Theatre.

"Curious fellows, those French authors," said young Whiskers to me, in front of Anna Maria's *loge*, on Tuesday. [Most charming *loge* in the house, of course; all the opera-glasses levelled at it, like the Lancaster guns at the Malakoff. *She* didn't know it, bless your soul, of course not!] I assented, calmly, to the remark of the hirsute youth. He went on: "I saw this play "a great while ago, ten years at least, at Mitchell's Olympic, a little concern about the size of this. Mary Taylor played in it, and so did Walcot and "George Holland. You remember Mary Taylor, miss." [The

Beloved One frowned. She doesn't go back ten years. She is doing the infantile just now.] "Well, they called it *The Lioness of the North*, then, and I remember that it was very nice. And they played it at Wallack's too, calling it *Prison and Palace*." The Brightest remembered this circumstance, and told us how awfully the ladies were costumed, and how sweet Mr. Wallack Lester was as a Russian officer, shut up in prison. Whiskers, when he got an opportunity, which was not at an early period, the conversational powers of A. M. being fluvious, went on to remark upon the awful conduct of Messrs. Bayard and Lafont, in stealing *Un Changement de Main* from *The Lioness of the North*, by Mr. Selby, and *Prison and Palace*, by Mr. Palgrave Simpson, two English authors, who have suffered almost as much from Parisian piracy as Mr. Dion Bourcicault. Whiskers could not deny that the play was better in French, but that did not excuse the theft. I quite agree with Whiskers, and I think that when our Government sends a Minister who can speak French, to Paris, and they get that little affair of the musical pitch settled, something will be done about it. Why, at the *Porte Saint Martin*, three years ago, they absolutely had the impudence to steal *The Phantom* from Mr. Bourcicault, and *Jocko* from the Ravels. And then added insult to injury, by calling them "revivals." What does the religious press say to that?

So much for the origin of this comedy. The theatre and the artists have received many praises from mouths of wisest censure. The critics and men about town rejoice that at last there is something besides Miss Laura Keene's eternal American Cousin and stiff "Washington tableaux" [O Liberty! etc.]; and Mr. Lester Wallack's inevitable shell-jacket. Like Honest Sancho Panza, they look not the gift-horse in the mouth. And really, my Editor, the theatre is quite pleasant. It will remind you a little bit of the *Palais Royal*, slightly of the *Variétés*, but more of the *Beaumarchais* or *Folies Nouvelles*. The répertoire, I understand, is to include the best selections from all sources, the best comedies chiefly, and perhaps, by-and-bye, some comic opera. For the first performance, the house overflowed with an essentially metropolitan audience. No Cape Cod; no Orange county; no Chicago; no provincials of any sort. Frenchmen in great numbers, clean and dirty; a few with pure linen and beards new reaped. A minority, however, were they. Considering the quantity of soap they make, Frenchmen are the dirtiest people in the world.

The play is a good comedy of the kind, and has plenty of sharp dialogue. It is written to display, chiefly, the qualities of the first young man, who is to the modern French comedy what the Ellistons and Kembles were to the Doricourts, Rapids, Young Marlows, and so on, of eighteenth century dramatists. I may be pardoned, then, for saying that the modern style requires better actors than those demanded by the era of lace, and velvet, and buckles, and ruffles, and powdered wigs, and all the bravery of old time gentlemen. In the United States there never has been a man who had the gaiety and manner to perform the leading comedy parts. I refer to native actors. Mr. George Jordan, the best we have, looks well, costumes gorgeously, and has a good stage-presence, but no gaiety. In serious roles (modern), where there is a dash of cynicism, he is superb. Mr. Lester Wallack is an elegant man, but his acting is too demonstrative, and frequently sinks into positive vulgarity. He mistakes bustle for gaiety, acts at his audience, and persistently fills the stage to the exclusion of every one else. He is the best, however, that we have, and has the superior advantage of knowing that we must recognize him. In England, there is no one, I believe, except Mr. Charles Mathews, a most admirable mimic, superb in some one-part pieces, arranged for himself. He has gaiety and manner, but not the artistic power of sinking the man Mathews in the character which Mathews assumes. So you never forget Mathews, and you do not say I have been to the theatre and have seen a charming comedy, but I have been to see Mathews, and I am—disappointed.

When I see a man who can come upon the stage in modern morning or evening costume, and interest the audience without having to descend to gag or local slang, then I will change my opinions.

Now I stick to the French.

And the success of M. Laba, the Alexis of Tuesday, quite fortifies my opinion. M. Laba is not handsome. He is rather stout, his legs are short, and his nose of colossal proportions. He has, however, a clear, fine eye, a good mouth, and a pleasant smile. He would not be considered, in a first rate Parisian theatre, say the *Gymnase*, as good enough for the first parts. He is so much better, however, than anything we have had, that he made a reputation at once. He can act without looking at the audience; he can bring down the house in roars of laughter for a good line, without throwing it over the souffleur as if it were a cannon ball instead of a bon mot. He does not grimace, nor jam his hands in his pockets, nor kick about the stage. He is gay and joyous enough, has sufficient assurance, but it is of that order of impudence which does not make one think that such a fellow would be kicked out of any gentleman's house.

And don't you often have that idea?

So much for Laba. He is a great treat, and, as such, give him a fair chance.

I must apologize to the ladies for not giving them the precedence. But that is the fault of the author chiefly. Neither the Empress (M'lle Chevalier) nor the ingenuous Feodora (M'lle Montheaux) have so much opportunity as the Alexis. Good, they are, however. Pretty, and well dressed, the latter of course. Chevalier has hardly presence enough for grand rôles like that of the Empress; she was sweet, elegant, and dignified, but did not mark the contrasts between the promptings of the woman's heart and the sovereign's pride of place, with sufficient clearness. The Feodora was deliciously *naive*. I like simplicity—in the classic poets, and on the stage. The French *ingénue* is a national type; no one ever saw an American *ingénue*. I rather think not.

Of course there was one awkward fellow. Who ever saw a first representation without one? Alexandre, officier des gardes, was not a bit like a guard nor an officer, not even of the police. He was a limp young man, standing in a melancholy way, like a half-melted ice; lost in a pair of long boots was Alexandre; much bothered with a sword, which seemed ten feet long, was Alexandre. Poor Alexandre! He was unobtrusive, and I pitied him.

I pitied him. Wretched youth—how terrible his condition!

The afterpiece was a vaudeville, in one act, *Un Monsieur qui prend la mouche*, in which Bertrand, another clever comedian (eccentric), made his *début* in the hero, a young man who takes to heart all sorts of imaginary offences, and resents them as deliberate insults. He also made a success, and I ought not to forget our old friends, Thiery and Tallot, who played well in both pieces. The title of the farce bothered a good many beginners, unfortunate persons wandering in the mazes of irregular verbs. One young gentleman informed A. M. that he understood the language perfectly, and when asked for a translation of *Un Monsieur qui prend la mouche,* said, "Ah! 'm! yes! I know; it's the man that stole the handkerchiefs." Pretty good for a savant, eh?

Now I shall not bore you any more about the French theatre, but close with a quotation from the esthetic Fry. It is a little after the style of Mr. Bunsby, but is, nevertheless, apropos. He says: "The pieces are well put on the stage, and the directors seem desirous to command approval. In proportion as this enterprise is sustained, will greater variety and excellence be forthcoming; and the probabilities favor its continuance and extension."

Mere Mention.

They have brought out another "Cousin "—English this time—at the Bowery. He is the most stupid of all. When is this run upon Cousins going to cease? And when it is over, will the authors—horrible thought —take up our other relations,—aunts, uncles, grandmothers, and so on? Don't, please. Bless 'em, let'em rest.

Miss Laura Keene has had only four lawsuits since last week. Her Cousin has reached his 124th night, and Jefferson has some new gags. The Veteran is up to his 50th performance at Wallack's, and holds on gallantly. Mistress Menken, or le Capitaine Menken, has left town, and the *Tribune* office still stands erect. The effect of keeping the door of a theatre is nearly as disastrous to the finer feelings as writing for Appletons' Cyclopædia. A *ci-devant* check-taker has just been appointed on the police!

The papers say there are to be four new theatres built this Spring. One for Bourcicault, on the site of Mozart Hall; one by Gibson, corner of Thirteenth street and Broadway; one for Eddy, near Houston street and in Broadway; and one by Mr. Haswell, in the Bowery, near Canal street. The inevitable Trimble has already commenced work on the last-named site, I am told; but the others are still on paper only.

Antony and Cleopatra.

I intended to be very Egyptian and, of course, very profound; very classical and, of course, very unintelligible, in speaking of the performance of *Antony and Cleopatra*, which was done in a gorgeous kind of style, at the Broadway theatre on last Monday. But I wont. I'll spare you, though you don't deserve it. I'll give you only a little, after the style of the introductory remarks in the new edition of Shakspere. Cleopatra was a colored person, of good family; came from the Ptolemies, who built the Tombs. She fell in love with an army-man from Rome, one Antony, and ruined him, as a great many army-men have been ruined before, and will be again. While he was philandering at Alexandria, he aroused the indignation of his brother-in-arms, afterwards his brother-in-law, Colonel Cæsar, and, in the end, the Antony forces were soundly thrashed by the opposition. Out of these circumstances, several good-intentioned persons have attempted to make a play. That pleasant scapegrace, Sir Charles Sedley, who used to fight two duels of a morning, and write a comedy before dinner, tried it; so did old Dryden, and one Will Shakespeare, an actor and a disreputable tavern-lounger, who wouldn't be asked out to dinner nowadays, and to whom Mr. Richard Grant White would not speak in Broadway. The play produced by Mr. Eddy is partly Shakespeare's and partly Dryden's. The best acting scene—the concluding one of the third act—is all from Dryden. Next to Titus Andronicus, Antony and Cleopatra is the heaviest and most disagreeable of Shakespeare's historical tragedies. Loosely written and badly constructed, with only shreds of character here and there, no modern manager would accept it. He would say that the speeches put in the mouth of Cleopatra displayed rare poetic genius, depth of passionate description, wonderfully beautiful similes, and so on, and that really he should be very glad, but the public, you know, etc., and hadn't the young man better try again, and so on.

I have seen Antony and Cleopatra. Where duty calls, in the terse language of the Firemen's motto, there you will find me. And there I was. It was an awful bore. Acting generally bad. fair, though too slow. Cleopatra a very large person. Antony pretty fair, though too slow. Cleopatra a very large person dressed in crimson velvet: bad idea for Egypt, if the temperature is as high as Sir G. Wilkinson represents it. Bad for large women anywhere; crimson velvet makes them look like the Pyramids. The scenery was splendid, and the costumes, with exception noted , handsome, and I have no doubt, correct. I can't say positively, for obvious reasons. If the acting could have been omitted, except Mr. Eddy's scene in the third act, and the bacchanalian chorus in the second, the performance would have been better. I particularly object to Cæsar, who was a short man with hair à la plaster, and those peculiar legs which one sees underneath the curtain before the minor theatre opens its glories to the humble gaze. Short, stubby legs. Legs that seem always to say "D—nation foiled again!" Legs which shout "What ho! without there——bring in the banquet!" Legs which suggest unclean shirts, beer, and bad hats, in private life. You can always detect a gentleman by his finger nails, and I can give you an actor's status by inspecting his legs.

I don't know whether it is worth while to go and see Antony and Cleopatra or not. On the whole, I think the scenic beauties in the second and third acts will pay for the trouble. There is some ballet too, in which Ducy-Barre is charming.

PERSONNE.

NEW YORK MARCH 19, 1859

DIVORCE EPIDEMIC IN PITTSBURG.

The Pittsburg *Gazette* says: "Judge M'Clure took occasion on Saturday to refer to the increasing number of applications for divorce that come before him. He says there is hardly a Saturday, at least, when he does not carry home a pocket full of depositions in cases which are absolutely too outrageous and disgusting to be called up before the Court. The detail of all these scandalous matters the Judge is obliged to wade through with, and oftentimes proof is so overwhelming that the Court is forced by a sense of duty to grant a decree of divorce. The very worst of it is, too, that either one or the other or both of the parties enter again into a new marriage contract, within a week after they are off with the old, and one which, in nine out of ten cases, will result as the former one did. Thus *two* prospective divorces are begotten of the former *one*. This is outrageous. One gentleman of the Bar stated to us that in a case that came under his own notice, the woman, who had procured the decree on Saturday, was married again on the very next day. This has become an evil so crying that Judge M'Clure gave out his intention to refuse the decree in any and every case where there was a technical or other possible and legal excuse.

SOMETHING BEYOND.

BY MARY CLEMMER AMES.

Something beyond, beyond this wintry day!
Kiss me, sweet Love, nor thus so sadly sigh;
Light dawns above this hour, so drear and gray,
And gilds the sky.

Something beyond! Though now—thy joy unfound—
The life-task falleth from thy trembling hand,
Be brave, be patient! In the fair Beyond
Thou'lt understand.

Thou'lt understand why our most royal hours
Couch, sorrowful slaves, bound by low nature's greed,–
Why the celestial soul's a minion made
To narrowest need.

In this pent sphere of being incomplete,
The imperfect fragment of a beauteous whole,
For yon rare region where the Perfect meet,
Sighs the lorn soul;—

Sighs for the Perfect! Far and fair it lies;
It hath no half-fed friendships, perishing, fleet,—
No partial insight, no averted eyes,
No loves unmeet.

Beyond, beyond, no pitiless fate shall e'er be stilled
Of love; for love, that makes the weak heart pant
The soul—the fountain of its yearning filled—
Will have no want.

Something beyond! I shall have ceased to pine—
Life's weary work, its wearier waiting done—
To see my soul's divine ideal shine
In the eyes of One.

Something beyond! Ah, if it were not so,
Darker would be thy brow, O dark to-day!
Earthward I'd bow beneath life's smiting woe,
Too sad to pray.

Something beyond! The immortal Morning stands
High o'er the Night; calm shines her prescient brow;
The pendulous star, in her transfigured hands,
Lights up the Now.

One Thing and Another.

—Mr. Fitz James O'Brien has taken up his residence in Cambridge, Mass., near the University.

—An actor in Georgia, in the course of a play, kissed the wife of a brother actor once oftener than the authorized version of the play required, and was thereupon severely whipped by the outraged husband. Having been a "star" before, says the *Tribune*, and now being provided with the "stripes," he thinks he is entitled to represent the flag of his country.

—The Rev. Mr. Jenkins, whose recent headache inspired some alarm among his friends, has so far recovered, that on Tuesday last he walked twice round Union Square, and on Wednesday morning was enabled to eat the white of an egg, and half of a buckwheat cake.

—The introduction of sewing machines into the boot and shoe manufacture has led to strikes at Northampton and Stafford (Eng.). We read in the local papers that some hundreds of shoemakers have left Northampton on tramp, and it appears to be the determination of large numbers of the men to persist in a course which shall make the use of the machine impossible.

—The Providence *Journal* copies the following from an Athens paper of Feb. 5:

"Other ancient monuments have been found in the course of excavations between the Erecthenum and the Parthenon. They are as follows:

"A pedestal of Pentilican marble, on which is sculptured the figure of a warrior, with helmet and shield; above it is the inscription, 'Xenocles,' the father, probably, of the tragic poet Carcinus. Although mutilated, the work exhibits much artistic merit. The pedestal was found built into the side of the door of a small chapel, the ruins of which were thrown out in the excavations. Within this chapel are Christian tombs, as the manner of burying intimates. They belong to the Byzantine period, and underneath them there are foundations from still earlier times.

"Here also, were discovered broken pieces of a colossal statue (perhaps of Minerva) draped to the feet.

"Not far from the same spot they have found an anaglyph of four men standing, and beneath them an inscription, obliterated except the last syllable. It belongs to the best period of the art. It was one of the votive offerings that stood in front of the Parthenon.

"Some important inscriptions have also been found and published in the archæological paper. One of them is very interesting, both for the matter of it and for the beauty of the characters. It is written in Attic letters.

"It is worthy of notice that the precincts of the Parthenon and the Erectheum are discovered to be floored with overlapping rows of stones, from the rock of the Acropolis. This work was probably done when the Acropolis was leveled off.

—A San Francisco letter, describing the fortnightly departure of the steamer, says, "Then comes a great time, and the hugging and kissing begin—such awkward kissing, too: random shots, an outrageous waste of the good things of this life. Sometimes a kiss lights on the nose, eye, ear, or is lost in a head of mussed-up hair. A bonnet stands no kind of a chance—it gets smashed on the first movement, and by the time a woman has got through and been passed from hand to hand, or rather arms to arms, of brothers, cousins, friends, and acquaintances, she is a pitiable object, and presents the appearance of having gone through an Irish row—red eyes, hair down, bonnet smashed and knocked around on one side of the head, shawl askew, and the general symmetry of her figure destroyed by pockets stuffed full of donations from friends—apples, cakes, ginger snaps, letters, a little good brandy, magazines, novels, and a bottle of milk for the baby."

Dramatic Feuilleton.

A Clear Intrusion.

The Editor of The Saturday Press has some remarkable things. He calls them ideas.

I have my private opinion on the subject, and I hold the Editor in the utterest contempt.

I believe the public joins me in these sentiments. I appeal, then, confidently, to the public, and I ask seriously, what it thinks of an Editor who wishes to write in his own paper?

Right! It *is* insanity, and it must be humored. I will permit him to air his little ideas in these sacred leaves. I am magnanimous.

Two objects will be gained. He will be satisfied, and the public will not have so much of me. Mashallah! It is good.

Still another intrusion. It appears that my remarks of last week upon the French Theatre have stirred up some of the English actors to exceeding wrath. All the greenrooms said, there's a fellow writing a lot of nonsense on a subject of which he knows nothing.

And the greenrooms had a champion.

Sir Dion de Bourcicault, armed capapie, bristling with points, spurs gallantly into the columns of the lively *Tribune,* and in a clever article contradicts, altogether, the statements of the esthetic Fry, which were printed in the same columns a few days before. Uses the sovereign "we," does Sir Dion, and appends the magic initials of his name to the article as well.

Now I really don't intend to reply to the man who writes that there is "more than one company" in this city better than the French. There is no such thing as a good company here, and has not been for several seasons, because managers, to satisfy private prejudices, exile the best artists to the provinces, and this Mr. Bourcicault knows well enough.

But the *Courrier des Etats Unis* has taken up the glove, and in a very Frenchy and untranslatable way, as follows:

Un article remarquable—où nous avons cru reconnaître la touche du critique d'un de nos plus grandes feuilles quotidiennes—a notamment paru dans le *Saturday Press.* Prenant la question de haut, l'écrivain fait ressortir l'influence heureuse que notre scène est appelée à exercer sur les habitudes exagérées et mal réglés de la scène américaine. Il ne nous appartient pas d'insister sur cette thèse, qu'ont d'ailleurs épousée la plupart des autres critiques; mais l'article dont nous parlons nous a particulièrement frappé par la vivacité de la forme en même temps que par le valeur du fonds.

L'opinion ainsi exprimée parait toutefois avoir offensé certains amour-propres, si nous en jugeons par une curieuse épître qui s'est glissée dans la *Tribune* d'hier matin. Pourquoi M. Wm. H. Fry a-t-il cédé à un étranger sa plume ou tout au moins sa place? Nous l'ignorons; mais il eût assurément mieux fait de la tenir lui même. Le critique de circonstance se livre en effet à des excentricités d'appréciation d'autant plus bizarres qu'ells sont émises sur le ton pédantesque. Il avance successivement les énormites suivantes:

1. Que M'lle Sen n'est pas une Déjazet, mais bien une soubrette INGENUE !!!
2. Que Miss Agnès Robertson est le vrai type de la Déjazet !
3. Que les costumes des *Premières armes de Richelieu* étaient un contre-sens historique !
4. Que la pièce était mal mise en scène !

Certes, nous ne nous attendions pas à celles-la. Mais il faut passer quelque chose à l'amour-propre, surtout quand il est doublé d'amour conjugal. Alors même que cette petite sortie aigre-douce ne serait pas signée des initiales D. B., il est aisé d'y reconnaitre la plume d'un des plus illustres plagiaires de la scène française, qui cumule avec cette qualité la profession de comédien et le titre d'époux d'une des étoiles de première grandeur de la scène américaine. Vous étes orfèvre, M. *Dion Bourcicault*—et de plus vous étes mari.

I am going to let these pundits settle the matter among themselves.

The performance of *Les Premieres Armes de Richelieu*, upon which Mr. Bourcicault's article was founded, was not equal to that of *Un Changement de Main*, but was still fair. The new soubrette, Sen, has the misfortune to be fat. Think of the Marshal Duke of Richelieu being fat! Why, he would have killed himself if he had ever turned one hundred and twenty pounds avoirdupois. I have seen the rôle played with more gayety and its idosyncracies more strongly marked than by M'lle Sen, but I still believe that M'lle Sen is a good artist, although not a soubrette-Dejazet, an article which is not very plenty even in France, where there is any given quantity of all sorts of women—except pretty ones.

The name of Dejazet alone, raises one's expectations to a dangerous pitch. It recalls reminiscences of the most mischievous, the most gallant, the most naive, in fact, everything the most French in the world. Dejazet was and now is the incarnation and the type of Parisian deviltry, of all the fascinations of that wicked capital which the Reverend Cream Cheese preaches so prettily against at home, and enjoys so much when he goes abroad.

But I forget the Editor. There, go ahead.

The Editor's "Ideas."

[Instigated by the —, no, that would be profane, but by our dramatic critic, which is about the same thing—we went the other night to the French Theatre. The play was *Les Premières Armes de Richlieeu*; the youthful duke being represented (incarnated, would perhaps be the better word,) by M'lle Sen, who made her début on the occasion. To the best of our poor judgment, the performance was a failure, though Personne, who ought to know (though he don't), says it was "fair." If he had said "from fair to middling," we should have had more latitude of interpretation, and might have agreed with him. But then we had a bad seat, and couldn't hear ten words that were spoken. All vocal effects were, in consequence, wasted upon us. We had to hear with our eyes, and the gas being very fitful and spasmodic all the evening, even that was not easy. It wasn't our fault that we had a bad seat, for the parquette being full, and all the pews (pews take the place of boxes at the Theatre Français) being taken for weeks ahead—according to the pew-openers' story—we had to put up with a place in the common four-shilling part of the house provided for the vile multitude, and by some acoustic feat, so arranged that nothing can be heard there except disputes at the door, which, though they may be dramatic (as everything French is), are not particularly entertaining,

We had, therefore, to rely for our enjoyment, upon the use of our eyes, and according to their judgment,—which may have been perverted by the flickering of the lights,—the play was not only badly acted, but indifferently "mounted." In fact, everything pertaining strictly to the stage-business was such as in any theatre in Paris would be promptly put down; was such, in fact, as would not be tolerated in any respectable theatre even in New York. This is all we have to say, and if Personne differs with us in opinion, so much the worse for him. The chief amusement we got in return for our money was the spectacle offered by the various grades of ushers (or pew-openers), each one *fraichement decoré*, and all rushing frantically about the house as if the existence of the world (to wit, France) depended on their keeping in swift and perpetual motion. The various styles of spangles, rosettes, etc., worn by these worthy officers (who form, it seems, a rigidly constituted hierarchy), was in itself an entertaining study, while their alacrity and success in keeping the people from finding their seats, was superior, in its way, to any feat at Niblo's.

In conclusion, it is no more than fair to say that the actors and actresses seemed to be very clever, but to be suffering under the disadvantage of an arbitrary and mysterious rule of the house (enforced "for this time only"), that no one should be cast in a part which he or she could possibly perform.

One more explanation. We may have got out of temper from having been located not only in a bad seat, but next to two Alsatians who, in addition to being very garrulous, were offensively redolent of garlic. Under such circumstances, we could hardly have enjoyed Rachel. But, after we *did* enjoy the Ushers; moreover, did also enjoy the pew-arrangement; and, furthermore, when (at last!) the play was over, did *very much* enjoy the rush of the "foreign element" toward a free lunch in the adjoining fruit store, where the rapidity with which pyramids of ham, herring, and pickles, were annihilated, was something to be remembered by a well-fed man for life. Reader, if you wish ten seconds of real mirth, go to that fruit store (if it has not been eaten out) any evening at the close of the theatre, and see the effect of gratuitous feed upon newly arrived and voracious foreigners. If Louis Napoleon should establish a free lunch in France, he would in two years time be made Dictator of all Europe. May he never try the experiment !]

The Monarch of the Forest.

Since the departure of the lamented, and I may say lamentable Rice, from Niblo's Garden, various novelties have been introduced to the public without brilliant success. To speak mildly, too much circus is a bore. There was a man named Thayer, called "Doctor" in the bills (and he *did* cut up the English language terribly). He was an humorist of course. In these days of philological progress, we have no such things as clowns. Indeed words of less than three syllables are out of date. Well, Thayer was an imitation of Rice. Rice in a weak way. Rice talking continuously about our flag star-spangled, our Union "galorious," and so on *ad nauseam*. Thayer soon got what Miss Laura Keene calls a Southern *congé*, and after him came the Van Amburgh animals; with an elephant who does no end of astonishing things, and looks at the bass viol as if he would like to take it out of him, as the boys say.

Then there is the tiger, who has a passion for small Philadelphian children after the manner of the Fijis (that's the latest orthography, vide the *Atlantic Monthly*; between Harvard College and Noah Webster, one will not know how to spell any thing pretty soon),

and the old lion who sneered at the critical majesty in me represented, and absolutely had the impudence to yawn in my face. The lion is a veteran artist, and knows, as a coryphée du ballet told me once, that the less one has to do with newspaper people the more one gets out of them. There is a bad boy in the menagerie, a leopard, whose residence adjoins that of the lion. He makes rows, the leopard does, and lately entered the lion's apartment and behaved impertinently, whereupon the actual resident knocked the interleopard down, shook him a little, and then sat himself quietly down in his favorite corner, as if scorning to use his superior strength even over his tormentor.

So much for the private life of the artists at Niblo's.

It is a model for the opera people, prime donne particularly. Publicly they—the animals—don't amount to much. The lion, the *père* noble of the party, evidently looks upon the whole thing as an immense bore, and is as blasé as any lion could be. He is the monarch of the forest deposed by insurrection, and deprived of his bank account.

Brown.

Summoned by Brown, I went one night last week to the Academy of Music. Brown was to have a complimentary benefit. That generally means that one has to pay out a great deal of money, and get in a very little. But Brown, I hear, was more fortunate. Sundry enthusiastic individuals absolutely paid the rent of the house for that evening for Brown, and so to the trowsers of Brown came much gold and silver, and city notes.

Did I understand some one to ask, who's Brown? Did you ever see in Broadway a lithograph of a rather good-looking fellow with a great deal of hair flying about in a loose way, a large amount of shirt-collar, and a bow like the running-noose of a two-inch cable? Below is written J. B. Brown, and appended is a certificate as to Mr. Brown's elocutionary qualifications, signed by various editors of defunct *Mirrors* and other literary reflectors of the same calibre.

That is the portrait of Brown. And it was my privilege to see the actuality of my dreams. (That's a bit of Anna Maria's diary. Where on earth she ever

got it, I don't see.) Well, Brown is an elocutionist of

the Old School, with gestures like the signals of the Semaphoric telegraph, and nearly as far out of date as that institution. Brown is a good enough elocutionist of his class; has a good voice and impressive manner. But people now-a-days don't do this sort of thing, even on the stage, and in private life it is absurd. Teach children to read slowly, enunciate clearly, pronounce properly, and to understand thoroughly the meaning of what is read, and that is all we can ask for. Gestures spring naturally from the peculiar passion or sentiment portrayed, but the elocutionist teaches the gesture first, and the thing of which it is a sign afterwards. Thus thirty "young ladies" (not girls) of Mr. Brown's corps, recited something or other in concert, and their dear, delicious, thirty sinister arms went up like thirty pump-handles before they opened their charming mouths. It is very amusing, for once, but I hear that it is done very often in respectable houses. Heavens! how much has Brown to answer for!

There was "a lady from private life" who read a scene from Macbeth, of course the most difficult one in the play. Not to be ungallant, I trust that the ties of society will not be recklessly sundered in this instance. Art really does not demand the sacrifice.

I felt something like an intruder at this Brown soirée. The audience, composed, I should judge, in good degree of the friends of the elocutionists, thought it was grand, and applauded continuously. Well, perhaps they were right, and I am wrong, as they generally are.

The Amateur Play.

Society has heard the new play (by Brougham and Goodrich) read. Society, I am told, rather likes it. It is "The Dark Hour before the Dawn," comedy-drama, in five acts. The report that the Editor of the *Sunday Courier* was asked to the reading and did not go because there wasn't to be lunch, is a base fabrication. Whiskers thinks he will play in the new piece, and

Anna Maria intends to come out in a new hat for the occasion.

Nothing in Particular.

They say that the public's lively friend, Max Maretzek, has been detained in Havana, on account of some little pecuniary difficulties. He is one of those men who are continually being ruined, but who still have plenty of money. If the Havanese succeed in making him pay up, there is still some hope for the success of the Atlantic Telegraph. Meantime, we hear of a benefit to Mme. Gassier, which brought in, presents and all, about twenty thousand dollars. Gazzaniga's was likewise very lucrative. Nearly all the artists will shortly astonish Broadway, and things look like an artists' opera season at Burton's, the corpulent manager of which temple hath returned to town with Captain Cuttle and Mr. Aminidab Sleek. The opening of Burton's with the opera would complete the good work already commenced by the French Theatre, and give the coup de grace to the *Veteran* and *Our American Cousin*; the houses at Laura Keene's and Wallack's having fallen off materially within the last week. The public wants a little novelty once in a while, though the managers seem oblivious to the fact.

The papers are full of rumors in regard to new theatres. So far as I can learn, only one is assured, and that is on the site of the National Garden, in the Bowery. Offers for that have been made by Messrs. Fox and Lingard, the present managers of the Bowery Theatre, and it is probable that they will be the lessees. Mr. Bourcicault has made an offer of one hundred thousand dollars for the Mozart Hall property, and the tender has been conditionally accepted.

Niblo's Garden, I am told, will positively remain as it is. The new theatre site for Mr. Eddy will be above Niblo's. A new theatre is much wanted in New York.

The Opera at Cincinnati opened on Tuesday with "Martha," Colson, Brignoli, etc. The *Commercial* says it is bound to succeed in spite of the "Sneers of our Eastern cotemporaries." Who, for goodness sake, has been sneering at it? The Augusta *Age*, or the Kennebec *Journal*, or the Skunkville *Clarion*? Why not let the child have his toy in peace, and without making fun of him?

Mme. Cora de Wilhorst, who has been in town for the past fortnight, and seriously ill, is rapidly convalescing.

Mme. d'Angri has sung Azucena in the Trovatore, at Madrid, and made a furore, according to the French papers.

A friend, who arrived on the *Arabia*, informs me that the second and third representations of the Christy Minstrels (Raynor, Pierce & Co.,) at Paris, were greatly successful. So we may expect some curious feuilletons from Fiorentino, Jarin, and others,—some bon mots in *Figaro*, and caricatures in the *Charivari* all of which will pull in the five-franc pieces amazingly.

Messrs. Mason & Thomas, at their *matinee*, this week, introduced a new mezzo soprano, Mrs. Mozart, who is well spoken of by the dailies. I didn't hear her.

PERSONNE.

NEW YORK MARCH 26, 1859

The Special Committee of Aldermen appointed by the Common Council, of Brooklyn, to make suitable arrangements to celebrate the introduction of water, are determined that the celebration, which is to take place on the 27th of April next, shall be on a scale commensurate with the importance of the event it is intended to commemorate. The general plan for the observance of the day will be as follows: National salutes will be fired in the Eastern and Western Districts; the bells throughout the city will be rung morning, noon, and night, and while the procession is in motion; there will be one fountain in operation in the Eastern District, and another in the Western District, all day; fire-works in the evening, in different parts of the city—the public buildings to be illuminated, and all citizens will be requested to illuminate their residences. During the day there will be a procession, composed of all the civil and military organizations, and societies of all kinds, which will pass through some of the principal thoroughfares to City Hall square, where there will be addresses and an original ode, written for the occasion. On the route of the procession it is expected that the residents thereon will decorate their dwellings and erect suitable emblems. The Sabbath Schools and Public Schools will be invited to participate in the proceedings; and, in fact, it is proposed to make it a general holiday.

NEW YORK APRIL 2, 1859

Literary Notes.

—Mr. Fayette Robinson, who died on Saturday, the second victim of the 14th street poisoning case, was the author of "Mexico and her Military Chieftains," published in Philadelphia in 1847; "Organization of the United States Army," in two volumes, published in 1848; and "California and its Gold Regions," published in this city in 1849. He was a native of Virginia, and some years ago was employed in the *Herald* and *Tribune* offices as translator. Latterly he has been engaged in other pursuits.

—Charles Dickens's new periodical is to appear on the 30th of April, with the singular title, "All Round the Year." A new serial tale by Mr. Dickens will be commenced in the first number. The last number of *Household Words* will appear on the last Saturday in May.

—The Russian Ministry of Education has devoted the sum of 300,000 roubles for the support (so say the papers) of *successful* authors. The great unsuccessful are left to shift for themselves.

—Some one blamed Dr. Marsh for changing his mind. "Well," said he, "that is the difference between a man and a jackass; the jackass can't change his mind, and the man can—it's a human privilege."

—Mr. Everett has been invited by a number of our prominent citizens to re-re-re-deliver his oration on Washington, and will do so in May, at the season of the religious anniversaries. It is understood that he intends to make an addition to this production, setting forth his views upon Washington's emancipation of his slaves, to which the distinguished orator has never before alluded.

—Verdi's new opera, "*Un ballo in Maschera*," has been produced at the Apollo Theatre, Rome. The duet in the second act, and the whole of the third act, met with great applause, and the maestro was called for on the stage, to receive the congratulations of the audience, not fewer than twenty-three times.

—Great preparations are making at the Crystal Palace, London, for the Handel Festival. The orchestra is to be extended for the accommodation of four thousand performers, vocal and instrumental, and experiments are making with the object of concentrating and increasing the sound. The works given two years ago are to be repeated, with the addition of the Dettingen Te Deum.

Original Poetry.

TRAILING ARBUTUS.

BY GEORGE ARNOLD.

I.

Wandering over the breezy slopes
Where the trailing arbutus grows,
(That little flower that timidly opes,
While the wind of March still blows,
Its delicate buds of the palest rose,
And blossoms white as eternal snows),
O, Love, we walked, and cheerily talked,
That breezy, blustering day,
Where the March winds blow, and the pink buds grow,
Wet with the morning's crystalline dew,
And far below us, stretching away
'Neath the sky with its Spring-time azure hue,
The heaving, flashing, glittering bay
In solemn breadth and beauty lay!

II.

Sitting under the cedar trees,
Inhaling their odor rare,
With the swaying, swinging, dallying breeze
Playing among thy hair,
Ah, still my fancy thy image sees—
The chequered shadow and shine on thy face,
Lighting the place with a holy grace,
While thy voice was lifted in ballads old
Of maids who were fair, and men who were bold—
Ah, heaven! thou too wert fair!

III.

The wind is blowing and blustering still
On the lofty cedared slopes,
And still on the southerly face of the hill
The trailing arbutus opes;
But alone I sit 'neath the cedar trees—
Alone with the boisterous blustering breeze,
The flowers, and my own sad memories,
While the murmur that comes from the flashing seas
Whispers to me, all solemnly,
That love is only a vanity!
Well, it has flown, as the winds have blown
Last Autumn's dead leaves rustling down;
Each Spring, the trailing arbutus grows
When the March wind blows, but love, when it goes,
Alas, is forever gone!

Dramatic Feuilleton.

Le Roi est Mort! Vive le Roi!

There is a good deal of difference between the present century and the last; and, as a general thing, I think we are rather in advance of the old fogies; but this does not prevent me from rejoicing, with three times three, and one more, at the removal of *Our American Cousin* from the bills of Laura Keene's Theatre, and the substitution of *She Stoops to Conquer*, a comedy by that poor, shiftless, Bohemian-like scribbler, Oliver Goldsmith. Rascal that he was, too! A wretch whose note of hand would not be worth, to-day, the paper upon which it was written, and to whom you, sir, would not loan five dollars without fear and trembling. Still he wrote *She Stoops to Conquer*; he created old Mr. Hardcastle, the beefiest of English squires; young Mr. Marlow, type of the *jeunesse dorée* of to-day, as of an hundred years ago; Miss Hardcastle, the plus belle des belles, who Stooped to Conquer something that was hardly worth it; and Tony Lumpkin, whose education and manners were quite equal to that of some of the astonishing young men that Anna Maria receives on New Year's Day.

Now, mark you, that I do not praise *She Stoops to Conquer*; but *Our American Cousin* was, to use a mild term, getting to be a nuisance, and, as it is sometimes convenient to go into this theatre to meet a friend, or to get out of the wet, I welcome even Goldsmith, Miss Keene welcomes him, too, and thinks highly of him, because he is dead, and she is not obliged to pay him. The comedy itself is only admirable as a vivid picture of the English country life in Goldsmith's day. In our day, continental travel has humanized the Saxon, he breakfasts à la Française, he dines à la Russe, and sups not at all. So with us in the United States. He who would have a picture of English or American manners, sub tegmine fagi, may as well translate *Les Bourgeois Gentilhommes*, or some other play from the repertoire of the Gymnase Dramatique.

Still, it may be well enough to look back at those old hard drinking, and hard riding, and hard-feeding days, when gentlemen married their cooks, and my lady intrigued with John, master of the horse. But where shall we find actors to embody the types? Where, Sir Roger de Coverley? Where, Belinda? Where, Will Honeycomb? Mr. Blake, who was accidentally born during this century, but who really belongs to the era of powdered wigs, is the only representative of the queer old fathers who are continually threatening to cut off their sons with a shilling, and not doing it. So Mr. Blake was admirable in old Hardcastle. As the play wore on, it was evident that he was the central figure in the group; the others did not belong to the period nor to the play. Miss Keene was not a bit like the character she undertook. No man could ever have mistaken her for a bar-maid—A lady's maid, or a meek "genteel" governess, perhaps, but even that would be stretch of the imagination. She was a great deal like Miss Laura Keene. Mr. Jefferson was good enough, and funny enough, in Tony Lumpkin, but Mr. Jefferson, to my mind, belongs, as well as Miss Keene, to the present day, the day of Conjugal Lessons, and things of that sort. Mr. Sothern was in my bill for Young Marlow. I remember to have seen a heavily dyed moustache and a pair of cavalry boots, and presume that the rest was Mr. Sothern's corporeality. I saw no Young Marlow, however. Think of one of Goldsmith's bucks in a moustache, under his tie-wig. O! G. Jordan and J. Lester, how many errors are committed in your names! Shall I ever see a young American actor without moustaches?

Two of the ladies pleased me much. Mrs. Blake looked as if she had walked out of a frame in some old family portrait gallery, and she played well, too. Miss Stevens was charmingly dressed, and looked, as A. M. hath it, "sweet." The character she played belongs to any period since the Deluge, perhaps before, as well. She had only to be very like a silly girl, and was so. Miss Stevens is very good—unpretentious, refined, and prepossessing. I don't know of so well bred a woman as Miss Stevens on the American stage. And I hear, too, that she is a Michigander! *Mirabile dictu*!

Finally, the comedy was well costumed and carefully played. At the end, Mr. Blake made a curious speech in front of the curtain. It was a good deal like Conway's great effort at the Broadway, when Mathews was called and would'nt come. Mr. Blake said Art was a good thing; Fame was a good thing; but still—Money was better. What he meant, exactly, no one knew, but I think he intended to suit his remarks to the place, and to present the views of the controlling powers of the Theatre, who are said to have a lively sense of the superiority of the Golden Calf over all other properties.

They have been doing here also, a piece called "The Rival Pages," a stupid thing, gotten up, I should imagine, for the special purpose of showing how bad are the legs of two of the actresses. Such displays ought to be encouraged by all friends of reform. They have a powerful moral effect.

I hear that "A Midsummer Night's Dream," which receives a very nice puff in the bills, is to be given on Monday, the 11th. Meantime, to-night, Miss Keene gives herself a benefit, and plays "The School for Scandal."

The Crown of Martyrdom.

I respectfully tender my resignation.

I will not suffer tortures worse than death.

What's the matter? A great deal is the matter. Have you read that valuable advertising medium, the *Herald*? And have you seen there the awful announcements, that within the coming fortnight, two distinguished tragedians, both the greatest that ever lived, will appear at two theatres, up town, in two new plays, in five acts each? Ten mortal acts of "American" authors! I won't stand it. No, not for Golconda, nor Rio de Janeiro, nor the Palais Royal, nor Tiffany's, nor any other place, say Spruce street, where gems and valuable considerations generally abound.

There is Mr. Burton, who, to say the truth, never was a bore, announces "with pleasure" that he has given up the theatre which has been called by his name, and here comes Miss Jean Margaret Davenport, who has lived long enough at Lynn, in Massachusetts, to know better than to manage a theatre, rushes in and will rush out the veteran Leland's (Oliver S., of Waltham,) translation of the weakest of Scribe's plays, La Czarine. Whatever Oliver has done with it I don't know, but I hope for the best. He is a brilliant man, and I don't know any boots equal to his. Miss Davenport has not played here for five years, which is assigned as a reason for her doing so now. Logically, I don't see it. I remember her as a good actress, a little conventional, or so, but still artistic in everything but her costumes, which were not the Parmesan, or even an imitation of it.

However, as the *Express* critic said of Maggioroti (who is a hundred and nineteen), "let this young artist go on. We will watch such budding talent with tearful and anxious eyes."

The artists, I see, are to be "under the *immediate* direction of F. B. Conway." I trust he will not, therefore, be quite so slow as usual.

Miss Davenport's rival across the way—at Niblo's Garden, I mean—will be Mrs. Julia Dean Hayne, who has been engaged by Mr. Eddy. He closes the Broadway to-night, and opens Niblo's on the 11th. Mrs. Hayne has a play by a dramatist who is very popular with managers and actors, because he writes for nothing. [The elegant Leland likewise declines pecuniary compensation, and gives dinners to the actors.] Mrs. Hayne's Shakespeare, or rather, Sir Charles Sedley (the divine Williams was not above lucre), is Mr. Miles, of Baltimore, who has written a five act Comedy called "Senor Valiente." Miles is not a bad writer, but is terribly verbose. He is one of the sweet poets, and much affected by Anna Maria.

Now, sir, I have my election of two things: either to resign—and I would rather not desert you while you have a dollar—or to imitate the critics of the heavy dailies, who, smelling the battle afar off, always dodge suspicious first nights. They—the critics—either get sick, or go on a journey, or have the gout; in fact, they plead as many excuses as the guests in the parable.

I will give you till next week to think the matter over.

Our French Friends Again.

"D. B." has not yet floored Widdows et Sage. In fact, they are hauling in no end of dimes. There has been nothing of great importance presented since the night that QUELQ 'UN went to sleep. They have stolen one of Miss Laura Keene's pieces, *Je dine chez ma mère*, and I hear she will "injunc" Widdows et Sage, as soon as she gets that thousand out of Moses Kimball for playing "Our American Cousin" in Boston. What's the use of a copyright law, if these Frenchmen can steal our pieces? What's the use of Congress, and the star-spangled banner? Sage thinks there is something in the extradition treaty about it. There ought to be, at any rate. D. B.'s friend, Sen, has played in *La Fille de Dominique*, in which she assumes several characters, much after the fashion of Miss Agnes Robertson in *The Young Actress*, with the exception that Miss Robertson was charming, and Sen is not. She was better, however, than in the Richelieu piece, which, as a country editor remarks, she "cannot play with Mr. Forrest." One thing strikes me singularly at the French Theatre, and I should like Carnochan, or some other great surgeon, to explain it, and that is the remarkable weakness of vision among the auditors. This weakness is confined to the upper classes, and must be the effect of the awful debauchery which the stories in the Sunday papers tell me reigns in the gilded saloons of the aristocracy. I go to the Bowery, which is three times as large as the French Theatre, and every one sees with his natural eyes, but at the little shop of Widdows et Sage, almost every customer has his eye glass. If this sort of thing goes on, the up-town people will not be able to see at all. Perhaps some one will bring it up in the Academy of Medicine.

Mere Mention.

The Veteran has nearly run out at Wallack's; tonight is announced as the very last of it, for which, all thanks. It is just possible—and we say it with all respect to have too much of Mr. Lester and Miss Mary Gannon. Next week, Mr. Wallack will play in some of his special parts. Wouldn't he play for me, and many more of his worshippers, in a piece called I think, The Violet? At any rate, the character is that of an old jeweller, named Andre, who gets into an awful scrape about some diamonds. Well, Mr. Wallack is superb in it, and I hope he'll do it, when you'll see that I am right.

Trimble, the inevitable, is going ahead with the New Bowery, which is to hold five thousand persons. Fox and Lingard will be the managers. There's going to be more Rice at the Circus, I suppose for the especial benefit of the *Tribune*, which abused the clown (as he says) for cutting into Doestick's business. I never read Doesticks much, and I never, Providence permitting, intend to hear any more of Rice. Much more to my liking was Madame Tourniaire, who rides as only Frenchwomen of the first order can. She reminds me of lots of pleasant things, too; of the Hippodrome and the Circus in the Champs Elysées, and the wonderful fellows, Jockey Club men, who stand on each side of the entrance for the artists, and penetrate the sacred mysteries beyond. Those days, as I remarked to Anna Maria, will come no more (quotation from the Sonnambula); but sentiment not being in the dear child's way, she didn't seem to mind it much. Apropos of circuses, there is a noticeable article in *Porter's Spirit* of this week, upon the treatment and training of children, horses, and animals generally for the ring. It has made some stir in the fraternity, who don't, I am told, like it.

They have had the first rehearsal of the Amateur play at the Academy. The date of performance is now fixed for the 27th of April. The gentleman who borrowed my copy of the French original is requested to return it to this office, and "save further trouble, as he is known."

We are soon to have some opera with Gazzaniga, who, they say, is married to little Albites. I sympathize with them if it is true. Very likely Ulmann and Maretzek will unite their scattered forces and open the Academy in about a week. The Southern campaign with Piccolomini has not been splendid. The little one is still "down in Alabama," singing to the Crackers and so on. She may be back here to operate on Easter Monday, but I can't say positively. I shall not cry, for I would rather hear one Gazzaniga than an ocean of Piccolominis.

I hear the opera is going on splendidly at Cincinnati. Think of a crowded house to hear Parodi, Mme. Strakosch and Squires in Norma! Heavens and earth! are there any educational facilities in the Provinces ?

About Boston I find nothing except a rumor, which I am slow to believe. It is said that that respectable naturalized citizen, and late British grenadier, Mr. Barry, intends to raise the d—l at the Boston Theatre, on next Monday. Faust and Marguerite (whoever they are) have put up the old gentleman to it, and some of the most respectable people in Boston countenance it. Where's Cotton Mather?

PERSONNE.

NEW YORK APRIL 9, 1859

FANNY FERN.

Don't accuse me of a want of variety to-day. Now you shall have a sketch of Fanny Fern—a woman so independent, that if her picture did not suit her, I think that she would not demur to strike me in the face with her parasol. Fanny is one of the moving institutions of Broadway. Every day that is decent, she may be seen, as regularly as the walking advertisements of the "Destruction of Jerusalem;" sometimes arm in arm with her husband, sometimes arm in arm with her daughter, sometimes alone, taking "peeps from under her parasol." She has an imperial tread, carries her head as if she owned the whole of New York, with an hundred possessions beyond; and if what I read of her long ago is true, she *does* "take nine eyes out of ten." Not that she is so handsome, but she is striking. Neither is she homely; the worst thing that can be said of her looks is, that she bears a slight resemblance to her brother, N. P. Willis, the immortal hyacinth, who is not now, whatever he may once have been, an agreeable looking man. Fanny

Fanny Fern.

is about five feet four, with a graceful form and springy step; she must be forty; sports a profusion of light brown curls, which have just escaped the appellation "sandy.' They cluster over her forehead, making it look both high and narrow. She has light blue eyes, prominent, but well cut nose, shining teeth, and a complexion florid, without being vulgarly so. Her bearing is haughty rather than brazen. It says: "Gentlemen and ladies, attend to your own concerns—I am equal to taking care of mine." Her habitual expression indicates that there is more of good than of evil in her composition, but she could be ugly if necessary. Nature endowed her with very fine sensibilities, and if these have been rendered too sharp by the hard friction of life, it is her misfortune, rather than her sin. Before we condemn people for being thus, or thus, we should follow back the tenuous line of circumstances, which made them what they are. "Fanny" dresses in good taste, generally with black flounced dress, grey cloak, and drab hat, with plumes, and deep black veil; sometimes she wears a sky blue hat, and sometimes she appears clad in black velvet, with a pink bonnet, blossoming with roses.

—New York Correspondence of the Springfield Republican.

CORRESPONDENCE.

HARTFORD, Conn., April 6, 1859.

Mr. Editor:—While you pace the hard pavements, shut in by walls of brick, that bloom not with the Summer, that never bud in Spring, nor bear other fruit than a breaking out of "signs" and similar devices for the entrapping of customers; while you pen those independent, and sometimes savage, leading articles, for which The Saturday Press is noted, or drop down in pungent paragraphs upon the sins and follies of the times; while you review and criticise new books, and cause to be printed almost endless lists of publications just out, or about to appear; while, in fact, you circulate about your office in New York, doing well the work you have in hand, and building up the best, most original, most sincere and worthy weekly literary paper published, I verily believe, in the United States, does it never occur to you that outside of your city border—your surroundings of brick and mortar—your piles of folios, quartos, and duodecimos there lies the broad, smiling, ever fresh and blooming country, with forest, hill, plain, and river, in the midst whereof dwell many of your readers, who love the sounds, and sights, and scents of their surroundings, and who may, perchance, welcome a letter, now and then, from that wilderness—other than of brick walls—wherein they dwell?

A long sentence, that! "It is the first step that costs!"

We have had great floods this Spring in all the Connecticut River valley; that stream and its tributaries, being immensely swollen by the melting of the snows of Vermont and New Hampshire, and the rains that fell almost constantly for one or two weeks. As a weather-fact worth remembering by the curious, I will state that during the months of December, January, February, and March, just past, more water has fallen—as snow and rain—by over four inches, than has ever before been chronicled in some time in the valley.

But floods are of small interest, save when illustrated by horrible, cold-blooded woodcuts, in "Frank Leslie's Newspaper."

The dreary rain to-day, the recent flood in our streets, the soaken aspect of all out-o'-doors, remind me of an incident in my "younger youth," which made upon my mind so deep an impression, that no length of years can ever erase it. The season of the year was not the same, for it was in mid-summer that the event took place; neither was the weather like the present, for the sky was clear, and the sun hot and high; but there had been a flood a few days previous, and for other reasons than that, I am reminded, in dreary weather, of the scene.

I had been alone among the hills of Western Massachusetts, trout fishing, with but indifferent "luck," for the rains which had fallen only a few days previously had so raised all the mountain streams—washing in great quantities of food for the hungry trout—that there were few bites, and the sport was dull.

So about noon I took my rod in pieces, tied it together, lighted a segar, and started saunteringly for home. My road led me down a gorge or narrow valley in the hills, through which a stream—more than brook but not quite river—flowed, and over this stream, by rustic wooden bridges, I was obliged to cross and recross on my way. Completely shut in by the mountains through most of its rough course, there were yet spots here and there, where, through gaps in the dense foliage, glimpses could be had of the broad and smiling meadows spread up and down the valley below me. At one of these points, upon a rough bridge mainly composed of unhewn logs, I paused to take a long look at the beautiful panorama spread out before me.

There was a sleepy, golden haze over the landscape; a look of laziness, and heat, and exhaustion, that heightened by contrast the delicious coolness and shadow of the spot where I stood, and at the same time, the slight chilliness of the mountain-gorge into whose depths the sun never penetrated, rendered the mellow warmth of the prospect a beauty rather than a defect.

I stood for some little time looking out between the tree-tops which parted below me, at this charming scene of quiet and repose, when I became aware of the breaking in upon my peaceful contemplation of some feeling rather than sound—the stream so noisily leaped among the rocks as to drown all other sounds—some feeling of human woe and pain. Below me, down the stream somewhere, there was mortal agony and despair.

I looked hastily in that direction, but my vision was limited, at a few rods distance, by a sudden curve in the little valley, and I only saw the dark, still water, lying shadowless because itself all shade, which formed the upper extremity of an old sawmill pond.

I knew that around this old sawmill, the valley widened, and that one or two small cabins were there inhabited. Towards this spot I instantly bent my steps.

Turning the angle in the stream and road which had intercepted my view of the mill, I found myself advancing upon a group of rough men who ran the mill, and who now stood gathered upon the shore on a point of land a little above the old dam. One man was on the dam itself, clinging to projecting beams and whatever he could lay hold of, and desperately buffeting the rushing stream in an attempt to cross it.

With wild hair and eyes, and a face terrible in its fierce whiteness, a woman ran up and down the bank, uttering quick, sharp cries of agony and despair.

The group of men were in motionless consultation. Doubtless as to what it was best to do, they did nothing. I saw the great, the terrible calamity at once: "There is a child drowned!" I said.

"Oh! my God! my child! my child!" cried the woman, never ceasing her running up and down. "I told you not to let him; I told him not to go; he's drowned! he's drowned! he's drowned!"

"He went in swimming," said one of the men to me; "them's his clothes, there, on the log; that's his father out there on the dam."

The water was deep, dark, unfathomable to the eye; stained, almost to a cherry red, by the decaying leaves in the swamps where it took its rise, all things were hidden that lay in its deeper pools.

A shallow, dusky sheet poured over portions of the dam—which many "freshets" had worn and eaten away in places—while here and there a slowly revolving "whirlpool," which sucked under whatever floated within its devouring reach, showed that there were holes in the sub-structure of the work through which large quantities of water found their way.

The child had last been noticed carelessly venturing within the influence of one of these "whirlpools," and a boat that was fastened near the spot was soon rowed to it. The boat, containing three of the men, floated slowly around and around. They thrust a long pole, armed with a spike, and commonly used amongst the logs, down to the bottom of the pond; they probed with it amongst the half-buried timbers the dam; they peered into the dark depths of the water, but with no result.

All this time the woman ran moaning and bewailing up and down the bank; and the father, upon the dam, struggled with the stream in the insane agony of despair.

They had not given up the search, but the task seemed hopeless.

Presently the door of one of the small cabins opened, and an old—a very old—man came forth.

"It's his grandfather," said one of the men to me. "What good can Crazy John' do?" said another. "Johnny's drowned! Your Johnny's drowned!" cried the woman, "and these men do nothing to get me out my child! He's drowned! He's drowned!" One of the men dived from the boat, and presently rose with his hands full of weeds and water-grasses from the bottom of the pond.

The man upon the dam, with another long, spiked pole, was thrusting wildly about in the depths of the water above where he clung.

"He went in swimming, hey?" said the old man, "and you've none of you thought to throw in his shirt! Throw in my Johnny's shirt, and it will find him!"

"Go into the house, old man, and don't bother here," said one of the men.

"The last thing he wore, if he is drowned, will find him! Throw in his shirt!" said "Crazy John." "Throw it in, and it will find him!"

The woman ceased her running up and down, and silently took the little shirt from where it lay on the log, and threw it in. Then all stood still gazing at the garment, save only the father upon the dam; he continued his wild and useless efforts.

The shirt slowly approached the whirlpool, into which after many revolutions nearer and nearer the centre, and each one more rapid than the last—it was presently sucked.

Then it whirled rapidly 'round and 'round, and disappeared.

But one man, in the boat, who had kept his face near the surface, shading it with his broad hands and peering downwards, made a sudden, nervous gesture, for the pole. It was handed him, and, with a slow, cautious motion, he thrust it downwards.

"He sees the white shirt shining through the water," said the old man," and he has found my Johnny!" The man thrust downwards with the pole, twisted it once or twice, and drew it slowly up. At its lower end there was a white, sad body, with long, dank, and tangled hair streaming about the cheeks, and clinging about it was the little shirt, which had done its errand well."

I never fished in that stream again. When I see nature in a flood of wet, and all out-of-doors drowned, I think of that day.

WARREN.

Dramatic Feuilleton.

The Czarina.

If I wanted a new illustration of the aphorism that fools rush in where angels fear to tread (which I don't), I should seize upon Mr. Oliver S. Leland's translation of Scribe's *Czarine*. It is precisely the style of drama in which the great play-maker had achieved his best successes, in every point of view. It was written in 1853-4; studied during the latter year by Mademoiselle Rachel, and produced at the Français, with all due solemnity, in January, 1855. As a rule, M'lle Rachel was not brilliant on first nights. Few great artists are. There is the double sense of responsibility to author and audience, which distracts the mind, and prevents that degree of absorption in the rôle, which is indispensable to success. But in the *Czarine*, Rachel failed, altogether failed, on account of the utter stupidity of the play. "The Czarine," says a French critic, and a good one, "has not one great quality, one marked characteristic, one attractive point, to raise her above the common level; the author could not have written a more insignificant, pointless, colorless rôle for Mademoiselle Rachel. There is not, from the beginning to the end, a fine passage, an energetic speech." As to its treatment in Paris, the fact that it was acted only two or three times, and then dropped, is a pregnant one. On the day after the first performance, the famous Doctor Véron gave a dinner to Rachel, and M. Scribe was among the guests. The affair had been predicated, of course, upon expectations of success, but as the contrary had been the case, a cloud seemed to hang over the scene. To give herself a fictitious gayety, Rachel, who was always very abstemious, drank two glasses of Champagne, "which," says her biographer, "produced no effect, beyond a headache. As soon as the dinner was over, she withdrew into another room, and gave way to a flood of tears, after which she slipped away home."

I have given this account of the French play, rather for the purpose of preserving the history of the last rôle created by Rachel, than for the introduction to any extended remarks upon Mr. Leland's translation, with which, probably upon the hydropathic principle, Miss Davenport opened the Metropolitan Theatre on Monday, and which has had the usual courtesy-run of four nights. That horrid fourth night! Little Pee-wit, who has written no end of brilliant pieces, never can get over it. It is the stumbling block where genius continually breaks its shins.

What Mr. Leland's idea was in translating such a piece of trash (that is, if he ever had an idea), I cannot see. I can see why Miss Davenport should play it. It answers several managerial conditions: First, it is cheap—in fact, it costs nothing whatever; second, it has but one good rôle, and that, in this instance, for the manager; third, it is a new piece, and about Peter the Great, who, although he has been served up in every sort of dramatic plât, is still good for several more operas, plays, and so on. For these reasons, Miss Davenport produced the play, and bored a very large and respectable metropolitan audience during four, long, mortal hours. The story, though terribly involved, may be summed up in a few words. A young nobleman, handsome and comme il faut, has succeeded in engaging the affections of the Czarina. Detected in a nocturnal meeting with her, and the question of identity being raised, one Olga, a gushing young thing, who also loves him, assumes the responsibility of the royal intrigue, and the marriage of the Count and Olga is commanded by the Czar. But the intrigue with the Czarina still proceeds, and the Czar resolves to make short work of the Count—that is, by making him a head shorter. The Czarina saves him, and in the mean time the ungrateful rascal has fallen in love with his own wife, much to the disgust of the Czarina. Between two fires, the fate of the Count appears to be fixed, when Peter dies from the effects of too much liquor and sperm oil; the Czarina does the magnanimous by the lovers, and there is a tableau of happiness which is very touching.

Miss Davenport's acting in the Czarina was a little slow, but she marked the phases of the character as well as any one could in such a wilderness of words. In a general way, I think Miss Davenport a fine actress of her school, but that is the mathematical school, which is just now out of fashion. She works out her effects on the algebraic principle, thus: given a certain quantity χ a certain other quantity = a certain unknown quantity, which she proceeds to develop with the most painful elaboration and detail. The worst of this school, is that you can always tell when the effect is coming before it comes, and so the artist never has command of the audience.

But notwithstanding all this, Miss Davenport is the truest and the best actress I have seen in New York for many a day. She speaks the English language clearly and well, without the Cockneyisms or affectations of some resident artists. Her enunciation and diction are fastidiously nice, and her voice as sweet as the murmurs of the running brooks. Above all she is faithful, never for a moment forgetting her duty, while she covers up the stupidities of one and the blunders of another, with the most charming, artistic grace. Beyond the Czarina, the other characters are very weak. The actors made them likewise very disagreeable. Mr. Conway's Peter the Great, reminded me of an enraged blacksmith with a cotton mill in his thorax, and Mr. Fisher, generally a clever artist, made terrible work of a bad part, a caricature of the Menschikoff of 1853. Mr. Reynolds was better in the Count than the others in their rôles, but Mr. Reynolds was not the Courtier of Versailles and the Oeil de Boeuf. Mrs. Conway was moderately good in Olga, with the difference that the lady is supposed to be a jeune ingénue, while Mrs. Conway did not look like the one or talk like the other. And I may say here, that the gentlemen in this company are all sadly in need of razors, while the ladies, by appearances, dress their own hair.

The Czarina was a failure, of course. Leland is a brilliant man, but even he cannot expect to succeed where Scribe failed. I think, however, that Leland will eventually get over the fourth night. Unblushing audacity is one of the chief requisites for theatrical successes, and this he has. After the play was over and proper honor had been done to Miss Davenport, some boys, who ought to have been in bed hours before, called for "the author." Scribe did not come, of course, but lo! in front of the footlights was the translator; you or I might have been there with as much propriety. Was it not enough to transfer good French into bad English, without claiming the credit of authorship? The audience thought so, for, with the exception of the boys aforesaid, they quietly walked out.

Anna Maria desires to say that she don't think the moral of this play is very good. I tell her that I could see no moral at all in it, but it is too stupid to do any harm.

I am inclined to think that Miss Davenport's season will survive this attack of Leland, and that is saying a great deal. She is playing now in her own version of the *Dame aux Camélias*. It is the first, and, except Miss Heron's, the most faithful I have seen. Next week a new piece, *The*

Mésalliance, is to be brought forward.

Operatic Operations.

On Monday a large number of our most respectable German fellow citizens had a quiet nap in the Stadt Theatre, Bowery, over Richard Wagner's Tannhauser, which was performed for the first time in this country. Whiskers, who went as a sort of moral duty, says that if it is going to have any run, they ought to provide sleeping arrangements, such as they have on the railways. The best criticism of Tannhauser that I can give you is a *mot* of the late Mme. Sontag, who said that Wagner ought to put the singers in the orchestra, and the orchestra on the stage. An enthusiastic admirer of Wagner told me that the performance of Tannhauser occupied four hours. I mildly suggested that it must be something of a bore. Oh! that was nothing at all; he had written one that occupied four days in its performance. And the man, I understand, is still at large.

P. S. Anna Maria has been very anxious to find out what Tannhauser means. She applied to a thin young man with spectacles, who writes for *Appletons' Cyclopædia*. He reported *Tann*, a poplar tree, and *hauser* house—poplar tree house, and has immediately commenced a paper on that basis, to illuminate the dear one's mind, and to give the young man an idea, I will say just here that Mr. Tannhauser was a German troubadour who lived and bored people by singing his own songs somewhere about the twelfth century. Wagner has resuscitated him with all the modern improvements.

Gazzaniga has come back from Havana, with a new stock of bijoux, and several millions of doubloons. As I thought, she denies altogether the story about her marriage, and the *Eco d'Italia* has some remarks about editors poking their noses into the private life of artists, which I advise the *Evening Post* people to read, if they can. Gazzaniga will sing in the Traviata at the Academy next Monday, in honor of which occasion, Anna Maria will appear in her new Spring hat, for which the Governor suffers to the tune of thirty-five, and as the Beloved One says, "cheap at that." Who the rest of the artists are, I have not heard, but there are plenty of them, such as they are, floating about town. After Gazzaniga's début, which will be a great sensation—people having just begun to find out what a great artist she really is—Alaimo, a prima donna brought over by Maretzek, will sing for the first time in New York. Both singers are going to Europe toute suite, and only stay to oblige, etc., etc., of course.

From Cincinnati, I hear the opera hardly pays, and that there has been no excitement about it, except in the papers, the writers for which were quarrelling over their own blunders. M'me de Wilhorst has sung Lucia, and would close the season with La Figlia del Reggimento for her benefit. Robert le Diable was to be done with Colson, De Wilhorst, Brignoli, Junca, etc. After that achievement, the company was to astonish the Pittsburghers. I presume that Strakosch will stick to the small towns for the present.

A friend, who is quite old enough to know better, thinks he could write musical feuilletons as well as any body, or nobody, because he plays on the "double bass." It is quite an absurdity to suppose that a knowledge of the theory or practice of music is a necessary qualification for a critic. Indeed, it is rather an embarrassment. The less a man knows of music, the better he writes about it. Regard, if you please, our Cincinnati cotemporaries, who can hardly tell the basso from the tenor. Their articles are infinitely more amusing than those of Mr. Dwight or Mr. Fry, or any of the other critics who are acquainted with the subject. Are you answered?

The Amateur Play.

I have a copy of "The Dark Hour Before Dawn: A Play in Five Acts: by John Brougham and Frank B. Goodrich. First performed by Amateurs for the benefit of the American Dramatic Fund." It is dedicated to "Colonel (in what regiment?) Henry G. Stebbins, formerly President of the Fund Association." By way of a refresher, the authors say that the piece "owes its origin to no play, novel, story, or any other more important source than the invention—such as it may be—of the individuals whose names are appended to it as the authors."

From a cursory glance at the copy before me, I am inclined to think that the announcement above quoted is altogether superfluous. However, it is supposed that we are all to deal very tenderly with both authors and actors, and so I shall not review it in advance. The story is of a French wife—a paysanne who has married one of the noblesse, much to the disgust of a great rascal, the heir-presumptive of the husband, and the plot turns on the efforts of this scoundrel to tarnish the wife's ante-nuptial character, so that she may be put away on some high shelf. Two or three of the characters are well drawn, and on the whole I think the play will more than answer the purpose for which it was written. It will be, however, exceedingly difficult for amateurs to perform, and I will give the outside public a guarantee that the first representation will give them fun enough to last a moderate life time. The prices are, to say the least, slightly steep, but I think it will be worth double the money.

Mere Mention.

Miss Laura Keene has produced The Road to Ruin, and rendered criticism unnecessary by doing it in the bills beforehand. Notwithstanding, however, the fact that all hands are acknowledged, according to the bills, to be the greatest, and most powerful, and most magnificent representatives of the several characters, that ever have been, or ever will be seen, here or elsewhere, the public did not rush to the theatre with that spontaneity that might have been expected. In fact, to drop metaphor, the house was very thinly attended, until Our American Cousin was restored for the delectation of Orange County, Cape Cod, Chicago, Nantucket, and so forth.

At Wallack's, As You Like It is the latest production. It was chiefly interesting from the rentrée of that admirable artist, Mr. Walcot, who played Touchstone, and is the only man who ever gave me what I believe to be the author's idea of it. It is a capital performance. Beyond that, and Mr. Wallack's Jaques, which is good, there is nothing particular to say, one way or the other, about the performance, and so consider it said.

The Broadway is coming down apace; the Circus leaves Niblo's this week, for good, and Mr. Eddy, with Mrs. Hayne, opens there on the 18th. If he gets a fair company, he can do the best business in the city. I hope everybody will go to Eisfeld's "welcome concert," at the Academy this evening. His sufferings during the burning of the Austria, his lengthened illness at Fayal, added to his real modest merit, and amiability of character, make his return an object of special gratulation.

Mr. Burton is at Glen Cove looking after his radishes and things.

PERSONNE.

NEW YORK APRIL 16, 1859

A correspondent of the New York Times, writing from Rome under date of Feb. 26, says:

Hawthorne I frequently see in the street, swinging along with a sort of land-measuring pace, smoking, and occasionally looking out from under his shaggy brow and otherwise timorous face. He avoids all society, and is said to be engaged on some new work, the subject of which is not even known by his wife. Motley, who is conceded to be by many English critics, the greatest living historian, I occasionally meet in society gatherings. He is rather tall, has an earnest American expression, and wears his hair parted in the centre. He is still engaged on his historical work. The famous manuscripts of the Vatican, so difficult of serviceable access, have afforded him additional material for his labors. Miss Cushman has taken a house here for five years. She gives most agreeable entertainments, and adds to them a most interesting feature in her own spirited musical recitations. The eccentric Miss Hosmer, the sculptor, lives with her.

—A small work on electric telegraphs is to be published shortly, in Persian.

—Edward H. Benedict, a resident of this city, stabbed his wife in a fit of jealousy last Monday, killing her almost instantly. He afterwards attempted to hang himself, but unfortunately, with less success.

NATIONAL ACADEMY OF DESIGN.

The thirty-fourth annual exhibition of the National Academy of Design, was thrown open on last Monday night to a large number of invited guests. The gallery has since been visited by an unprecedented number. The collection embraces over eight hundred pictures, an increase of over two hundred over any former year. Opinions differ very much as to the excellence of the collection, compared with that of last year, but all agree that it is exceedingly interesting and that the number of positively bad paintings is happily diminishing. There is a large number of new exhibitors. Many of these evince great talent and promise. A new feature is a large increase of female exhibitors; and we hope that the fashion now set may turn the ladies aside from superficial piano-drumming, and lead them into pursuits that will abundantly reward them for their labor.

We shall notice more or less briefly very nearly all the pictures at the collection. We hope to be just, we certainly shall be independent, and we pretend to be somewhat knowing.

No. 7. Making Acquaintance, by W. H. Beard, is a first interview between a grey squirrel and a field-mouse. It is an amicable meeting, the wary parties investigating each other with the curiosity of genuine naturalists, and with a progress that seems to indicate a peaceful separation. The contrast between the brisk air of the squirrel and the meek and timid anxiety of the little mouse, is admirably depicted. The subtle power of expression with the playful sentiment of this unassuming little picture is to our mind far superior to the pretentious animal pictures in this collection, in which the easy trick of glaring colors, and conventional aspects is cunningly substituted for more subtle and more profound knowledge of the habits and characteristics of animals. From the innumerable game books and pictures of the dog loving Englishman, the animal painter can, and almost exclusively does, draw his lazy inspirations, but the wild squirrel must be studied from the life, and in the climate where every American painter should study, at home, and then his success will be a real triumph.

Mr. Beard has done himself greater wrong, by covering his picture with a glass, than the ingenuity of the most malicious hanging committee could have done. It is distressing to look at this picture.

210. Wreck at Start Point, by F. F. Beaulieu; a large and imposing coast scene, with vividly painted cliffs—a type of a numerous class of marine pictures in this exhibition, which though painted with a certain taking cleverness of execution, are nevertheless excessively flimsy, conventional, and false; painted without industry, without study of nature, without knowledge of philosophy—in fact, caricatures, but cunningly leavened with gross and palpable plagiarisms from Stanfield and others of the present eminent school of English marine artists. The water in this picture is produced by a wretched trick, no more deserving the name of art, than does the vile work made by theorem patterns. The house-painter, in his imitations of wood, aims and reaches higher. The beautiful laws that govern water in motion, so lovingly interpreted by the reverent mind of Turner and his honest followers, are here ignored, and a muddy swash stiffened in a dead perception, or worse, by a lawless indifference, is palmed upon (we grieve to say it) a public, too indifferent to truth, or beauty.

227. The Abandoned Ship, coast of Cuba. No ship could possibly so far ignore the laws of gravity as to get so high out of water as this; no shipbuilder could possibly build such a model; no water could possibly behave so absurdly; no rays of light could possibly unite in such colors; and but one mind in the wide world, let us hope, could misname this a scene on the coast of Cuba, or anywhere else.

610. Off Sandy Hook: by E. Moran, a Philadelphia artist, whose only motive, we do believe, in painting Sandy Hook waters, in such fearful agitation of its chalky bottom (see English pictures of chalk-shore water), and strown with such a fearful array of wrecks and fragments of wrecks, must have been to slyly fasten discredit upon our most well behaved and safe harbor. But this is a very clever picture, and bating its conventionality, is full of motion, atmosphere, and pictorial effect. And by the way, we believe there is not a single marine in this gallery which does not float a wrecked mast with clinging ropes and sails, after the distinguished sin of Stanfield. We asked an ancient mariner who stood by, if he had ever seen one, and he said that many hundred thousand miles of sea travel had not revealed one to him.

620. Ex-Governor Throop, a portrait by C. L. Elliott, a head full of character, with a splendid characterization of age, endowed with a freshness and truth of color which will tone down, in years, to a beautiful richness. The portraits of this artist this year are unusually successful in their rendering of character and expression.

647. The Doubtful Bill, an old man prying into the qualities of a bank note, while the indignant woman who has found it, awaits the verdict. This is a decided improvement upon the works of this artist formerly exhibited, and is a very meritorious picture. It evinces a power which with further cultivation, promises very fine things in years to come.

655. Sea Coast of England, by J. F. Cropsey. This is a coast scene under an effect of a thunder storm, painted with a great deal of vigor and knowledge of pictorial effect. But it is hurried and slurred; noble chances for artistic elaboration are neglected, and a picture probably painted in a day, which with more labor, would have been a truly splendid work of art. We have no patience with artists who do not always do their best. It is due to the public for whose approval they are put upon exhibition, and to the artist himself, that they should truly represent his whole capacity. And it is due our readers that we should characterize this and other pictures as they deserve.

693. A very excellent portrait of Mr. Ehninger, by W. O. Stone. We deem this one of the best portraits in the collection.

471. Fog at Narragansett, by T. A. Suydam, a very faithful study from nature, a gem of sincerity and truth. The artist might have decorated his subject with the blandishments of the palette, but he has bravely forborne.

732. A Landscape, by J. B. Bristol, painted in a low, quiet tone, a happy contrast to the somewhat unquiet and forced style that now pervades our landscape art. The aerial perspective of this picture is extraordinary. The fields slope away to the horizon in most perfect gradation. The sky is not in harmony, or is in some other way out of joint. The repose of this picture is very beautiful.

760. Woodcock Shooting, by A. F. Tait. This picture is painted with great skill, and will undoubtedly become a great favorite. The landscape is unusually good, and the expression of the dogs, and their action, is very happy.

No. 28. is a miniature *Alto Relievo*, in marble, of a child's head, very prettily modelled and arranged.

No. 33. Pleasant Valley, by W. R. Miller, is raw in tone and not altogether agreeable, but possesses the great merit of careful drawing and conscientious treatment. Mr. Miller modestly contents himself with not trying to improve nature.

No. 34. The Nun, by E. Johnson, is a most beautiful crayon drawing, full of delightful sentiment and suggestion.

No. 45. A Child's Head, by S. W. Rowse, is perhaps a little flimsey, but it is tenderly drawn, and is a very child, and perhaps all the more delightful for being so slightly outlined since it leaves so much to the imagination.

185. Ex-President Tyler (ordered by Congress). A portrait worthy of the subject, and of Congress.

401. The Witching Time of Night, by G. H. Boughton. A picture which though exquisitely conceived and executed, a superstitious person would hardly care to have about him after dark.

66. A striking crayon portrait of Nichols, the artist, by Miss Elma M. Gove, whose works exhibit more and more finish every year.

59. Crayon head of Hildreth, the historian, marked by all the purity of tone we are accustomed to find in the works of Mrs. Hildreth.

114. A crayon portrait of Dr. Bellows, conventional as a drawing, and elaborately bad as a likeness.

133—134—135. Three miniatures, painted with exquisite grace and feeling by Miss Anna Mary Freeman.

32. A Case of Cameos, by Mr. Launt Thompson. Nothing so delicate and beautiful in the way of cameo-cutting has ever before been executed in this country.

784. A Small Boy of remarkable color, and in an advanced stage of the mumps.

754. A melancholy old man, with a human skull by his side, to enliven him, and a big book in his hand, which he evidently can't read, in consequence of which, as a dodge, he rolls his eye up to heaven, and looks deeply affected,—which he is.

383. A remarkably elegant oval frame (artist unknown), topped off with a crown, and enclosing a rather nice looking lady, in a high state of petrifaction.

108. A sentimental youth, with fiery hair and fancy colored wings, thrumming on what appears to be a battle-door, but may have been meant for a "harp of thousand strings."

778. A partially clad young lady, sitting on the bank of a rivulet, and reflecting on the coldness of water, and the mutability of human raiment.

690. A tropical scene in the Arctic regions, with a mummy-caricature of Dr. Kane, supported by two dead men, one in a sitting posture, and the other recumbent. The accessories of the picture show how badly an artist can draw and paint, when he sets fairly about it. On the whole, Mr. Hicks deserves great credit for giving this brilliant example of how a picture

ought not to be executed.

PICTORIAL ART.

During the last ten or twelve years the most noticeable improvement in the manufacture of books by American publishers, has been the application of Pictorial Art.

The success of Messrs. Carey and Hart, of Philadelphia, who were among the first publishers in this country to employ artists of the highest grade, furnished an example that has since been followed up in a creditable manner by others. And in many instances, our publishers have equalled—in some, perhaps, surpassed—the most meritorious productions of European publishers, with all their advantage of long experience.

Ichabod Crane flees toward Tarrytown, by F.O.C. Darley.

Of the artists in America who have been employed to illustrate books, Mr. F. O. C. Darley stands at the head. For spirited expression and force of character in representation, we believe he has no superior.

He is a sort of citizen of the world in his vocation, if the term may be applied to a man who has never left his native country,—portraying with equal fidelity the Bedouin with his steed and the North American Indian with his shaggy pony; the comical Irishman and the cute Yankee; the droll negro and the mercurial Frenchman. In fact, every type of character is depicted in his productions so truthfully that a stranger might imagine Mr. Darley to be not only a close observer but an experienced traveller.

His delineations of animals deserve particular notice for their lifelike expression and variation of manner. It is said that a shepherd can recognize the individual members of his flock by their different expression of feature alone. Mr. Darley seems to be inspired with this perception; thus, in each ox, horse, dog, sheep, or other animal of his, you may observe a portrait expressing repose or action, as the circumstances may require, instead of being formed on a stereotyped model.

A specimen of Mr. Darley's power of change in expression, may be found in his illustrations of the New England story, "Margaret,"—the party at the "Husking Bee." In the first picture we find several distinct groups, each absorbed in a particular interest. The next scene shows a complete transition; the horror-stricken company startled; every eye strained, regarding the tragic circumstance of the murder. In the *Legend of Sleepy Hollow*, also, where "Ichabod Crane" meets the headless horseman, while "Ichabod" is shaking with terror, "Gunpowder' draws back from the goblin with every nerve,—what force is given !

Both the last named work and *Rip Van Winkle* were republished abroad—*Sleepy Hollow* at Paris, in the *Magazin Pittoresque*, under the title of *Le Val Dormant*, and *Rip Van Winkle* in a neat volume at London.

If we should judge from a collection of Mr. Darley's drawings, we should say he has no *specialité*. A group of Indians engaged in battle or in sport, bending age with silvery locks, a rustic scene with cattle, and a charming landscape in the background, a set of merry-makers, a party of children, backwoodsmen, trappers, or sailors, are rendered with equal care and grouped with uniform beauty.

But if he has no *specialité*, he has a preference in selecting his subjects, as we may learn from his *Buffalo Hunts*, his *Trappers*, and *Indians*, with their characteristic accompaniments, most frequently given.

Several years ago, when the American Art Union flourished, Mr. Darley made four illustrations in outline, depicting scenes from Cooper's novels. These were published in the *Bulletin*, and the announcement of an extended series was made, when, unfortunately the project was cut short by the sudden termination of the Art Union.

We have heard many persons regret that this series, so congenial to Mr. Darley's taste, should have been so abruptly broken off.

The admirers of Mr. Darley's talent were therefore surprised and delighted when Mr. Townsend announced a new edition of Cooper's novels, with two steel engravings from designs by Mr. Darley, and numerous vignettes on wood from the same hand, embellishing each volume. And the several volumes already issued have certainly answered the highest expectation. All the expression of the original drawings is carefully preserved in these fine line engravings, which are finished with great delicacy by masterly hands.

F.O.C. Darley

Mr. Darley's delineations of these characters must give general satisfaction, and add to the interest of this most popular series of American stories, charm of elegant embellishment.

The characters are all well conceived. The "hissing laugh" of "Natty Bumpo" described by Cooper, is easily imagined, as we see him portrayed in the very act, leaning upon his rifle, while the "Judge' eagerly bends over the buck. The spirited and life-like scene on the deck of the *Red Rover*, succeeded by the picture opposite, the solemn moment of death and the preparation for execution, form tableaux, each of which might be considered as a master-piece.

The group forming the frontispiece of the "Mohicans." How exquisitely that is rendered! With the spirited black horse and portly bearing of the rider in contrast to the motherly looking animal bestrided by awkward "David Gannet." The nonchalance of the Scout and the indifference of the Indian.

Then in the illustration to the Headsman. The party descending the mountain in a snow storm preceded by the great dogs, coupled with a leash, scenting the way. The shrinking maiden and the old man, the whole scene softened by the falling snow flakes, forms a beautiful picture.

When the publication of the whole series is completed, we think that the enterprising publisher will have no reason to regret his formidable undertaking, but will find in his success a ten-fold reward.

Dramatic Feuilleton.

In Irving Place.

In one of those curious "Cards" that distinguish the Manager of the Academy of Music, the public has been called to assist at four farewell performances by Mme. Gazzaniga. According to the "Card," she is exceedingly sorry for the death of her husband, exceedingly obliged to the people of the United States (Provincetown and Peoria counted in), and exceedingly anxious to go to Europe. The soirées d'adieux are thus put in the light of a public boon, and so hailed by numerous press-writers, including that daintiest of feminine scribblers who makes epigrammes d'agneau for the Sunday *Atlas*.

Well, I who care as little for the Opera out of season as I would for salmon at Christmas; I who have no new bonnet to display, and no small flirtations to work up, I am obliged to Mme. Gazzaniga for not going to Europe before she gave us *La Traviata*, once more. Then there's no denying that the Academy is a nice sort of a place to go to, always abounding with astonishing young men; always sparkling with pretty women; always gay with brave apparel; always resonant with a Babel of tongues; always piquant with chevaliers d'industrie and artists of society ready to pick the governor's pocket, or to run away with Anna Maria—they don't mind much which. If any one wants a perfect photograph of life in Upper New York, the Academy is the place to find it.

On Monday, when the season commenced with *La Traviata*, there was a very curious audience. I asked Anna Maria if she would show on the occasion, and she was very sorry, but she couldn't. It was the private view night at the Academy of Design, and ma had taken a fancy to those men that paint things. The Beloved One couldn't see any reason for the maternal's sudden devotion to Art, but one must let ma have her own way once in a while, which I think is no more than right. I adored A. M. previously. Now, after this instance of filial affection, so touching and so rare, I worship her.

Well, the Beau Monde went to the private view, and left the Opera to the Demi Monde, who always come out strong for the *Traviata*. Like the boys in the Bowery pit, who applaud when the actors talk about poverty and virtue going hand-in-hand (which they don't), the Demi Monde women flatter themselves that they are like Violetta. The boys have no money and the women no virtue—there the resemblance ceases.

Now I am not going to write a criticism upon the *Traviata*, although it is well worth it. It is the best emotional opera that I have ever heard; and in depth, and fulness, and dramatic expression, Gazzaniga's performance is grand. In the refined coqueting of the earlier scenes Colson is better than Gazzaniga, and Piccolomini is more wickedly salacious in the Brindisi than either of them. Bacchus peeps over her shoulders and little Cupids play round her exquisite mouth. No wonder that, after her first night, Whiskers declined billiards and refused to look at some new trowsers which a fellow at the Clarendon had got out from Paris! But Gazzaniga's last act is a great thing. It positively gives a man a sensation. When I say a man, I mean a man that don't have sensations often, and enjoys them as a gourmet does some triumph of the cuisinier. The way in which she clasps her truant lover transforms him from a stumpy Italian, suggestive of garlic, insurrection, and maccaroni, into the God of War and Love. And as he commences the *Parigi O Cara*, and Violetta, overcome with her emotions, lies half swooning in his arms, you have the most passionate and sensuous of living tableaux. It is the history of two stormy lives compressed into half a minute. And the *Gran Dio*, and the death—ah! you should see that, and watch it closely, some of you actresses who affect to turn up your noses at the Opera, as a dog barks at that which he don't understand.

But I am getting enthusiastic; so, to cool off, I'll think about Tamaro, one of the cheap tenors, and no doubt very good for the money. He is a young man with a "still, small voice," and it was very amusing to hear him try to fill the Academy. Florenza, who was his pa for the night, was below par. He had an immense pair of bucket-boots, and I think that his voice must have gone down into them. One of the daily critics once said of him, that his acting was too prononcé ; I should pronounce it very bad. He acted all the time, and all over the stage at the same time.

But the best part of the performance, for me, was the scene in Irving Place, when the opera had concluded, and the "brilliant throng" were about departing for their "palatial mansions" (dinner at six, and references exchanged). There is a sweet little cherub that sits up aloft to keep a look-out for the hackmen. That cherub made it rain "like all creation" (as a lady from Cape Cod observed), just at the moment that the *Traviata* uttered her final wail. And so, on the steps and under the portico in Irving Place, stood several hundred, more or less, of badly protected, chilly, and moist-looking females, some with crinoline pulled awry, some with dresses drawn over their heads, displaying skirts not like Cæsar's wife's; some with pretty feet and nice ankles, but the majority otherwise; all getting what they called their "death-a-cold," and all in horridly bad tempers. The trowsers community was in an awful state of mind. They couldn't ask the dear (literally) creatures to walk, and hacks would cost a small fortune. One case of especial hardship is worth the attention of the benevolent. Augustus (his first name is Joshua, but he drops that) has only six hundred a year, which is not enough for his board and clothes, and he is continually hard up. Rashly, he conducted Araminta to Irving Place. They came from Araminta's pa's, in Thirty-fifth street, in a stage. Gorgeous was Araminta. Her bonnet was exactly (so Lewson said) like the one that the Empress wore when she laid the cornerstone of the Tuileries. That bonnet must not be sacrificed. Augustus rushed madly out, and seized a hack.

There is desolation in No.—, Pearl street. When the lunch hour comes, and all the other fellows are regaling the inner man, a melancholy wreck may be seen sitting in Byronic attitude on a dry-goods-box. 'Tis Joshua Augustus. Instead of Allsopp's pale, he drinks desolation; in place of sandwiches, he chews the cud of sweet and bitter fancies.

The bonnet was saved: but at what a price!

Until the first of June, there will be no lunch for Augustus. . . . .

Having nothing on my hands but a cigar, I rather enjoyed this exterior scene. It is a solemn warning to youth with limited salaries.

I did not hear the Trovatore, but A. M. says that Tamaro was better (the papers having stirred him up), and that Miss Phillips would have been fine in Azucena if she had had voice enough to sing the music, which she hasn't, and more's the pity, because she is a good artist.

On Friday, *Lucrezia Borgia* was to be given: on today there is to be a Matinée, and on Monday, I hear that *La Favorita* is to be given.

Mere Mention.

They have an opera house in the second story of a building in Cincinnati, which building is owned by Mr. Pike. Mr. Strakosch, an artist of lively imagination, having been tendered a benefit by Mr. Pike, writes to that person to say that he will take the benefit (of course), and further, that the aforesaid "two pair back' is the most splendid opera house in the world, utterly smashing those of London, Paris, Vienna, Jeddo Pekin, New York, Boston, Northampton (where they have been Town Halling the Trovatore in English, by amateurs), Philadelphia, Bangkok, etc., etc. Strakosch ought to have a good house.

On dit, that Mme. Gazzaniga will lay the first stone of the Brooklyn opera house, which is to be commenced on May 11th.

Mr. Wallack is playing some of his old rôles, such as Martin Heywood, in "The Rent Day," and Erasmus, in "The Scholar," to crowded houses. Go and see him.

They have done *Le Mari á la Campagne* at Widdows et Sage's French Theatre, and made an awful mess of it. It was much better at Burton's as "The Serious Family."

At New Orleans, Mr. George Jordan has made a great hit as Jaques in "As You Like It." By some miraculous attack of common sense (miraculous because actors almost always sacrifice everything for "points"), he speaks the famous soliloquy "All the world's a stage," to the Duke and Count, instead of to the audience, as is usual. I am afraid something will happen to that young man yet.

I don't interfere much with governments, or things of that sort; my idea of the civil power, in all its grandeur, being taken from the policeman who pilots Anna Maria over to Stuart's, after she has sailed by Delmonico's, to get a sly peep at the jeunesse dorée ; but I wish now to warn Mr. Buchanan, or the Mayor, or somebody, of a plot, which, I am informed, has been gotten up in the French Consulate, and the Bureau of the *Courrier des Etats-Unis*. Its object is no more nor less than the abstraction of the two works of art that Mr. Wood has just placed in front of his temple, devoted to burnt cork, and bad jokes. The French intend to steal them for the adornment of the Place de la Concorde, which has already been enriched with spoils more or less bloody. Everybody knows what a lot of things old Napoleon cribbed in Italy and Germany, and how the Congress of Vienna obliged him to return them. Now they are after our virtue. If the thing isn't stopped, they will carry off the Father of his Country, from Union Square, and perhaps the Worth Monument.

Miss Laura Keene says that she will positively trot out "A Midsummer Night's Dream" on Monday, and I'm sure, I'm very glad; gracious knows, she's been holding it long enough in terrorem over our heads. If I ever recover from the dazzling splendor of it, I will devote a feuilleton to the performance. The "cast' will include Miss Keene, as *Puck*; Miss Macarthy, as *Oberon*; Miss Couldock, as *Titania*; Misses Stevens and Ada Clifton, as *Helena* and *Hermia*; Mr. Couldock, as *Theseus*; and Mr. Blake, as *Bottom*. There's to be no end of ballet-angels, new scenes, "historically" correct costumes, (if there is any history about the fairies, who wore no costumes whatever, which would be nice, though illegal). I hear that a severe accident which has happened to Mr. Blake, through a fall, may prevent him from playing on Monday, in which case, Mr.

Burnett will act the part of *Bollom*.

I strenuously recommend to the persons who are rehearsing "The Dark Hour Before Dawn," a careful study of the performance of the "doleful tragedy of Pyramus and Thisbe," the cleverest satire upon amateur-acting, that has ever been written.

They have run out the opera in Cincinnati with a grand benefit to Madame de Wilhorst, who seems to have been the only real success of the season. The Strakosch nightingales are now at Pittsburgh.

The Boston *Evening Gazette* says of Mr. Miles's play, Senor Valiente, which is to be acted at Niblo's on next Monday, if "it acts as well as it reads," etc., etc. It reads? What reads? They have a queer style of grammar in the rural districts. The same paper has a model criticism upon *Faust* and *Marguerite* at Mr. Barry's Theatre. It opens with a puff for Mr. Barry, (all right, there's an act of the Legislature to compel that); next paragraph, another puff for the skilful director; next a puff for Mistress Blank's "charming vocalization." Three more puffs follow. *Voici !*

The machinery worked to a charm under the experienced supervision of Mr Tompkins; Mr. Simpkins excellent knowledge of, and correct taste in costume were fully apparent; nor should the property-maker, Mr. Jenkins, be allowed to pass without credit. The auxiliaries were well drilled, and no unlucky *contretems* occurred to create a laugh or mar the success of the play.

Mr. Catgut's music was appropriate, pleasing, and at times, full of melody. To praise him in *extenso*, however, would be like gilding refined gold.

Messrs. Pound Brush and Dutch Metal, merit all commendation for the scenery of Faust and Marguerite.

The actors "left nothing to be desired:" or were "in all respects excellent;" or were "feeling and natural" or, "very acceptable," or "had no equals," or "contributed materially to the play's success." Could Eatanswill do better than this? There is not a word as to what the play is about, who wrote it, or how it is written, or how it was received by the public.

The Mésalliance.

Mr. Leland's Czarina had at the Metropolitan Theatre a short and not very lively reign.

It was succeeded by a translation of the *Dame aux Camelias,* which drew immensely.

Miss Davenport played the heroine very well, but dressed in the worst possible taste.

The lorettes, she ought to know, are the best dressed of the Parisiennes. If she don't know it, let her read Jules Janin's preface to Dumas's history of Marguerite Gautier.

And then the others. Such coats, such trowsers, such boots—and for Paris!

It seemed as if the Temple had been ransacked for dress coats of every period, from the first Consulate up to '48; certainly none of them were built during the last decade.

The acting was on the high pressure principle throughout. Had any young man in Paris kicked up such a row as that made by Mr. Conway on the Metropolitan stage, he would have been turned out of doors, or sent to a maison de santé.

It was very amusing to me.

Anna Maria cried.

It is she who represents the public.

The public has a heart.

I have none.

The exigencies of my profession (I think that's rather good) called me again to the same theatre on Wednesday.

There was to be a new piece.

Miss Davenport had been very wicked during eight nights.

She resolved to treat her admirers to a little goodness, a little patience under affliction, a little constancy in spite of contempt—in fact, a little of all the moral, womanly virtues.

Virtue is a good thing; so is North River shad; but there is such a thing as having too much virtue on the stage.

I submit, with all humility, that four hours of virtue are too much.

If the Baron had been in town I think I should have become disreputable after the performance.

But I went home moral and dull. Thursday sees me bound to the wheel of Ixion, and no oil on hand.

The Feuilleton must be written.

I have forgotten what the Mésalliance (that's the name of the play) is all about.

But perhaps some of the heavy dailies may have accomplished it.

Two cents invested in the *Times* is as good as a fortune.

The critic of that enterprising paper—erudite philosopher—friend of Champollion—has found out what I had forgotten, or never knew.

And here is the plot, very cleverly sketched, too:

The heroine is a book-muslin heroine, violently addicted to pocket handkerchiefs and with a constitutional tendency to hysterics. The hero is a dark, uneasy jealous creature, who will, we are quite certain, appear in a cloak and sombrero, before the end of the play, and who, whenever he is peculiarly brutal towards the heroine, always winds up with a bronchial gurgle and the exclamation, "I love thee still." It may have been an object to the dramatist to secure this gentle man's affections, but how any sensible female could have aspired to the task is at least extraordinary. The young man is wretched from the moment he makes his appearance, and a little sulky. He is generous, and offers to bestow on his sister all his fortune, in return for a very sensible suggestion on her part that he shall retire for the rest of his cheerful days to a monastery. He promises all this, like a very soft person, as he is, and without knowing that he has suddenly become possessed of a large fortune. When the knowledge of this windfall comes to him he indulges in a matrimonial diversion, and to the regret of every one refuses to go to a monastery. He marries a portrait-painter's daughter, and being himself of high, not to say monumental or sepulchral descent, a mésalliance is the result. The sister, haughty considerations of family pride, and perhaps from a feeling that she has been chiseled out of a fortune, conceives an undying hatred to the heroine, whom she proceeds to persecute in five acts and four hours. In the end, virtue is triumphant; the machinations of the wicked sister are exposed, and book-muslin experiences a rise.

The acting, barring that there was too much of it, was good. Why people on the stage will not learn to keep still and speak like rational human beings, I never could see; but they won't. I like Miss Davenport very much, book-muslin and all. The audience seemed perfectly delighted, and the play made a success.

I advise people to go and see it as they pay up stock subscriptions—by instalments. PERSONNE.

NEW YORK APRIL 23, 1859

THE GREAT FARCE.

THE SICKLES FARCE at Washington is becoming more absurd than ever. The persistent efforts on the part of the dramatis personæ, to make the world think they are in earnest, and that Sickles is in real danger of receiving his deserts (though the hangman knows better), have positively deceived quite a number of people, some of whom manifest undue mirth thereat, and wonder if the culprit will make a Dying Confession.

We have no desire to see the man hung,—though we would sooner have half a dozen such men hung than one Mrs. Hartung,—but if the prospect of such an event, or its actual occurrence, would wring a confession out of him, we should certainly like to see the experiment tried.

The confession of *Mrs.* Sickles we have all read; and whoever will read it again, as arranged on our fourth page, will see at once how it was got up, and how little, in fact, she had to do with it.

No woman in the world ever conceived of such a document, though any woman, perhaps, in certain extreme emergencies, might be compelled to pen and to sign it.

A woman can be compelled to do anything.

But why isn't Mr. Sickles man enough to make his confession? Why isn't he impelled to do it by a humane desire to share the load of blame, which, borne now by his wife alone, is crushing her to the earth?

Doesn't he know better than any one else, that however guilty his wife may be, she is an angel by the side of him? And if so, why should she be banished from society, and he be allowed, so far as his conjugal relations are concerned, to go all but uncriticized?

What right has he to compel her to confess to an offence which he himself has doubtless committed more times than he can remember?

And why don't the whole community demand of him, that since he has wrung such a confession out of Mrs. Sickles, that, as an act of common decency, he offset that confession, by as publicly making his own.

If anything can be done to get it out of him—anything short of thumbscrews, and we don't know that, under the circumstances, we would stop there—we wish to heaven it might be done.

The contrast between the moral position of Mr. and Mrs. Sickles at this moment is so unnatural, so infamously unjust, that an effort of some kind ought to be made to set the matter right.

To pretend that her character is worse than his,—or a millionth part as bad,—is, as everbody knows, an outrage on common sense.

Why, then, should he be held up as a martyr, and she condemned as a criminal?

Let him give us an honest confession of his conduct as a husband, and then let the community compare it with her confession as a wife, and judge between them.

As it is, the course pursued towards Mrs. Sickles when contrasted with the tolerance extended to her husband, exhibits a degree of injustice and depravity in the public mind which it is impossible to exaggerate.

For the New-York Saturday Press.

"UNTO THE PURE ALL THINGS ARE PURE."

All the toil of day was over,
Night was coming on apace,
Through the street a woman sauntered
With a bold, defiant face;
On her cheek glowed painted roses,
True ones faded in her hair,
Round about her mouth there clustered
Lines of hard and stern despair.

Pretty girls went by, and quickly
Drew their dresses from her side,
As though if she brushed against them,
Something evil *must* betide;
Haughty ladies swept on frowning,
With a look of scorn and dread;
Could a glance to kill have power,
Surely that poor wretch were dead.

Men met her with bitter mocking,
Careless laughter, heartless jest,
And she answered them all smiling,
While *Hate* raged within her breast;
When a woman stepped before her,
In her arms a little child,
And the baby, looking at her,
Held out both its hands and smiled.

Pretty girls, will you believe me,
Haughty dames who stately swept
By the sin-stained, men who jeered her,—
Will you trust me that she wept?
Shed great tears of love and sorrow,
Tears of passion, strong and deep,
Tears as beautiful and holy
As an angel's eyes might weep?

She could bear the scorn and frowning,
She could heartless jests endure,
But the baby's smiles o'ercame her,
To the pure one she was pure!
Bending o'er the child she kissed it,
When the youthful mother turned,
Anger from her eyes was flashing,
With her hand the girl she spurned.

In a moment fled the tear-drops,
Back returned the brazen stare,
And the people paused and wondered,
Shud'ring as they heard her swear;
Proudly onward sped the mother,
She a Christian deed had done,
Closed the heavenly gates her baby
Opened for that fallen one!

M. E.

Brooklyn, April 13, 1859.

Dramatic Feuilleton.

The Works of Laura Keene and Shakspeare.

The new Hypatia produced, on Monday, a play called *A Midsummer Night's Dream.*

"A Midsummer Night's Dream; a comedy in five acts. By Laura Keene, Richard Grant White, 'Professor H——, of Harvard College,' Genio C. Scott, and William Shakspeare."

I have examined several authorities, and I think I am justified in adding the last name, although it does not appear in full on the titlepage of Miss Keene's book.

I will briefly append the authorities:—

In the *Biographica Dramatica* (Vol. 1, part 2, page 644, et seq.) there is some notice of Shakspeare, and a list of his plays. *A Midsummer Night's Dream*, 1595, is No. 10. In the same work (vol. 3, p. 42) is catalogued No. 294, "A Midsummer Night's Dream, Comedy by W. Shakspeare. Acted by the Lord Chamberlain's servants. 4to., 1600. By James Roberts." The same (295), Drury Lane edition, 8vo., 1768. Charles Knight (London) thinks Shakspeare wrote it all, and I have before me a well printed edition of the works of Richard Grant White, interspersed with Shakspeare's plays (Boston: Little, Brown & Co., 1858), and as nearly as I can ascertain by a notice (Vol, 4, p. 6 to 19), Mr. White believes that Shakspeare was the sole author. Indeed, he says so (p. 15). In no place, except the edition printed for Miss Keene's theatre, can I find her name mentioned as a collaborateur with the divine William S. Mr. Scott, undoubtedly, gave him some ideas of costume. At one and probably some very remote period, Mr. Scott must have had some ideas, and for obvious reasons, must have given them, or sold them to some one.

As to the identity of the plays of Shakspeare and Genio C. Scott & Co., there is little doubt. I have examined the Laura Keene edition and compared it with "Mr. William Shakespeare's Comedies, Histories, and Tragedies, published according to the true original copies. 1 vol., folio. London, 1628," and essentially the works are the same.*

So you see Miss Keene has *intended* to produce Shakespeare's play with the distinguished aid of Genio C.

She has produced a bewildering affair, which crowds the house every night.

So, if she has the money, she will not refuse to let the poet's name be known.

He would not claim the notes. To save his life, he could not define geographically and topographically the situation of Athens. Neither would he put the fabulous accounts of Hippolyta and Hercules, Pyramus and Thisbe, etc., as "*historical*" notes.

But it may be set up as a counter-plea, that as the actors speak very little of Shakspeare's words, and as neither of them resemble, in the remotest way, the creations of his imagination; as, in fact, the play is a thing of the stage-carpenter, and the tailor, and the milliner, that it really is Laura Keene's, and that Shakspeare had nothing or very little to do with it.

That plea I am more willing to admit, after having been jammed in with a good deal of Chicago, and inodorous Chicago, too, for three mortal hours. The affiche says truly that the theatre is crowded to suffocation. I was very nearly suffocated myself. And here I want to appeal to the humanity of the management, and ask them not to block up the aisles with boards. The parquet is choked with a solid mass of men and women. I shudder to think of the slaughter which a sudden stampede would cause.

And now to the play: Perhaps Miss Keene has done wisely in ignoring the Shaksperian comedy. She has gotten up a pretty spectacle, with all the usual surroundings. Her play has, like Shakspeare's, three several actions—three sets of characters. Theseus and Hippolyta, with the four lovers and the Athenian working men, Bottom & Co. The aristocratic lot is of no particular account, only that Hermia and Helena did not give you

* I desire to acknowledge my indebtedness to the Librarian of the Astor Library, who allowed me to look at the folio. I shouldn't be half so grateful if Mr. Astor had not laid a posthumous obligation upon him to do so. Also, I am penetrated with gratitude to Mr. W. E. B*r*on for offering me the same privilege, and to various persons who kindly told me how I ought to write this feuilleton.

the idea of that reckless affection which would induce young women to run the risk of catarrh by making a practice of lying about on faint primrose beds. Then come Puck and the Fairies. These you never can put on the stage. Your Oberon will have thick ankles, and will dress her hair in the Bowery-gals-ain't-you-comin'-out-to-night style; your Titania will be scraggy; your Puck, if a boy, will not understand his part, and if a woman, as in this case, will look for all the world like Dick Swiveller's Marchioness. Then you spangle your other fairies, and they will look with a six-dollars-a-week-and-forfeit-you-three-if-you-are-a-minute-late-air. They are not a bit like fairies, only ballet-girls, and very clumsy ones, with padded legs. They can hardly deceive Chicago unless Chicago is very breezy.

So it is with Miss Keene's fairies. But perhaps Bottom, according to Schlegel and Blake, will save it. I am sorry, but Bottom is very bad. Bottom is not funny. He is not even grotesque. In the words, he is not Shaksperian, nor Keeneian, nor Scottian. He is eminently Blakeian. Peters is good in Thisbe; he has some nice touches of real humor—the only good acting I saw. Blake was vulgar and unpleasant.

I have waited till the last moment to see what my superiors of the heavy dailies would say about this performance of Miss Keene's play. When Burton produced Shakespeare's at Chambers street, three years ago, there were lengthy, elaborate, and well done critiques in the leading journals of the morning after the performance. It is understood that the writers of those articles still wield the critical pens for the same journals. But the *Courier* has nothing; the *Times* nothing; the *Herald* very little; the *Tribune*, a curious paragraph, evidently written by a reporter. It is not at all critical, and the only points I remember are that some of the actresses "looked as beautiful as ever," which may or may not be a compliment, and an attack upon the audience, for the cool way in which they took the scenic beauties of the play. The writer made the error of supposing it to be a "metropolitan" audience. One rarely sees a theatrical metropolitan audience, except for a first night at Wallack's.

I am forced to the conclusion that only as a display of scenery and stage appointments the play has been a succés de curiosité.

The last scene, which is well spoken of, is one of those curious affairs where every thing slides on, or sinks down, or whirls round, and where people are supposed to be in the clouds and yet going up higher, and supernumerary fairies are standing on impossible pillars and one leg a piece. If it would only stop once and make a picture it would be pretty, but now it sets one's head in a whirl.

I ought to say that Mr. Baker's band, strengthened with some brass, which is much too loud, plays Mendelssohn's music fairly. Cooke did it just as well at Burton's with half Baker's force.

And if Miss Keene should at any time hereafter produce one of Shakspeare's plays, I trust she will not over-load her book with notes. My old friends of the folio of 1623, address their model preface "to the great variety of readers, from the most able, to him that can but spell." That's Shakspeare's audience. Let them have him as he is, from the "true original copies," without note or comment, and be sure they will find out his beauties.

A Companion for Leland.

I have found something to bind up with Czarina.

I have discovered a confrère for Leland.

The pendant to the Czarina is Senor Valiente.

The partner of Leland's toils is Miles. Miles of Baltimore, called by the journalists of the Plug Ugly city, "Maryland's gifted son."

The first time I ever heard of Miles was at Laura Keene's. She played an interminable three-act arrangement, about somebody's birthday (one of the longest days I ever experienced). At the end, there was some desire to see the perpetrator of about nine miles of dialogue, but Miles didn't come. Miss Laura Keene did, however, and called the play a "sweet" one, and said she should be glad to cultivate such budding genius as that of Miles.

Other people also "encouraged" Miles, who, like Leland, writes for the fun of it (and with no fun in it), and the ungrateful wretch has now deserted his early patron. He has written a play even longer than the Birthday (there are three days in the last work), and bestowed it all upon Mrs. Hayne—Julia Deane Hayne. She, with Mr. Eddy and others, has given it to the confiding public at Niblo's.

But the public knows a limit to confidence, and objects to being bored more than once by the same person. So they staid away from Miles, and Senor Valiente was a failure in every way.

It is a curious thing. There is an awful scoundrel, named Flintleigh, who marries a widow named Clinton for her money, and snubs the widow's son, who goes away to uphold the star-spangled in Mexico. He is the fifth man that I have heard of who pulled down the Mexican flag from the Castle of Chapultepec (I know four personally,) and run up the flag of the free and home of the brave, and so on. I begin to doubt now whether anybody ever did it. Well, this adventurous youth has had a flirtation with Nell Caverly—that is, Mrs. Hayne—and has been snubbed by her, too. He gets lots of money in Mexico, and comes back as a regular greaser. Everybody talks about him as a terrible cynic, but I couldn't discover it in anything he said. I should put him down as a mild bore talking elaborate nonsense. In the end he circumvents the ancient Flintleigh, who desires to marry Nell, and takes five acts and four hours to do what might have been accomplished by any sensible person in three minutes. He keeps Mrs. Flintleigh stowed away in some corner, and puts Nell to a great deal of mental agony for no purpose whatsoever. When will people learn that the mere involving of a number of circumstances does not make a plot. Without a motive a plot is like a wagon without springs. There is no motive for Valiente's intrigues. The audience know it, and they are not interested. They go to sleep, or go out.

Indeed, some were reduced to reading the *Programme*.

After that I shall say little.

The characters in Senor Valiente are supposed to belong to New York society. There is a fashionable woman in ringlets, who drinks wine in the morning and marries a man who writes poetry: a half broad Indian, who looks and acts more like an insane Chinaman, and an old General, who looks like Webb. Everybody was in Bowery full dress all the time, shiny black frockcoats, white waistcoats, *et. seq.* Flintleigh, according to the conventional rule, was not over clean, and ignored the razor. He was a short man, and much crushed by the way in which he was bullied by Mr. Eddy and Mrs. Hayne, who are both lengthy. The acting was fair. Mr. Eddy and Mrs. Hayne more so than the others. Some of them ought to learn how to go in and out of a drawingroom, but that, perhaps, is asking *too* much.

Senor Valiente is now dead. I presume that his old comrades, the Scott Life Guard, who stood the whole of him on Monday like brave men, as they are, will give him a soldier's burial.

It would be a grand solemnity for the noble army of the unappreciated.

Nothing in Particular.

At Wallack's, they have been doing the Stranger, the Wife, and other exhilarating things of that sort. Mr. Lester Wallack is cultivating his Spring whiskers, and Mr. Brougham, and Mr. Walcot, have been engaged in a pretty piece of business, the details of which I suppress, although it is not the first offence. The enterprising young men who are going to do the "Dark Hour Before Dawn," next Thursday, are hammering away at it, gallantly. The agony will be all over before the next Saturday Press. The attendance promises to be great, and the Athenian youth will be stirred up to merriments; in point of fact, the pert and nimble spirit of mirth will be wide awake (arranged quotation from Genio Scott's works).

La Grace de Dieu.

Widdows et Sage gave us, at the Theatre Français, on Monday and Tuesday, a capital drama, *La Grace de Dieu*. Overcome with the effort, and afflicted with a severe, and very encouraging attack of piety, they then closed the theatre till next Monday. The distribution of *La Grace de Dieu*, was, as usual, very unequal. Chevalier played the poor peasant girl (who goes away and gets ruined, much to the disgust of her Governor); Chevalier was very good in it, and in her utter and entire simplicity, offers a good school for the other actresses here (I mean in the other theatres). The comedians, Bertrand as the Commander, and Edgard as Pierrot, were both capital. The last named performance was one of the best I ever enjoyed. Tallot was a very bad papa, and Sage's Marquis was a very cheap affair, a good deal like the lobby nobility in Irving Place.

The impending sensation here is La Dame aux Camélias for Laba's benefit,—when, I don't know.

Daniel Sickles, Teresa Bagioli, and Philip Key II.

Operatic.

There was nothing particularly astonishing at the Academy this week. On Wednesday, the Favorita was announced, and I had my mouth made up, as the Beloved One says, for a sensation, and was awfully disappointed when they didn't do it, but screamed through Lucrezia. Stefani was good, however, singing Gennaro better than I have heard any one else since Mario. Brignoli must look after his laurels.

Alaimo makes her début on Monday, in *Norma*. I hear conflicting accounts about her.

There is still another début impending, that of Cortésa, who is said to be a better Traviata than Gazzaniga. Coming from Mexico City to Vera Cruz, she was stopped by bandits (curious idea they have, never stop anybody but opera singers, last persons to rob in the world).

Piccolomini will probably sing at the Academy with the Strakosch company, about the 9th of May.

P. S. In answer to numerous inquiries, I will say that the health of Anna Maria is robust. I have not given her opinions this week, for the very good (except for professional critics) reason that she has not seen any of the plays, being engaged in the sackcloth and ashes business. She will come out on Easter Monday, in a state of printemps wonderful to behold.

PERSONNE.

THE CONFESSION OF MRS. SICKLES, AND HOW IT WAS EXTORTED FROM HER.

The disgust felt by the grossness of Mrs. Sickles's acknowledgment of her guilt has been almost universal, and the publication of her confession has been damaging to herself and husband. Her confession was the result of a cross-examination, and for the purpose of showing how it might have been obtained, let us suppose Sickles at a table, his wife seated on the floor overcome with anguish, Bridget Duffy, the nurse, standing within the bedroom; and Miss Ridgely just outside the door; when the following dialogue took place:

S.—Were you ever in a house in Fifteenth street, with Mr. Key?

Mrs. S.—I have been in a house in Fifteenth street with Mr. Key.

S.—How often?

Mrs. S.—How many times I don't know.

S.—Whose house was it?

Mrs. S.—I believe the house belonged to a colored man.

S.—Who lived there?

Mrs. S.—The house is unoccupied.

S.—When did you first visit it?

Mrs. S.—Commenced going there last January.

S. Did you go alone?

Mrs. S.—I have been in alone and with Mr. Key.

S.—How long did you stay there?

Mrs. S.—Usually stayed an hour or more.

S.—Was there a bed in the house?

Mrs. S.—There was a bed on the second story.

S.—What did you do there?

Mrs. S.—I did what is usual for a wicked woman to do.

S.—When did this intimacy commence?

Mrs. S.—The intimacy commenced this Winter, when I came from New York, in that house—an intimacy of an improper kind.

S.—How often have you met?

Mrs. S.—Have met a half-a-dozen times or more, at different hours of the day.

S.—Have you meet this week?

Mrs. S—On Monday of this week, and Wednesday also.

S.—How did you arrange to meet?

Mrs. S.—Would arrange meetings when we met in the street and at parties.

S.—Why did you not speak to him before me?

Mrs. S.—Never would speak to him when Mr. Sickles was at home, because I knew he did not like me to speak to him.

S.—When did he tell you he had hired the house?

Mrs. S.—Did not see Mr. Key for some days after I got here. He then told me he had hired the house as a place where he and I could meet.

S.—Did you agree to it?

Mrs. S.—I agreed to it.

S. Did you have anything to eat or drink there?

Mrs. S.—Had nothing to eat or drink there.

S.—How was the room warmed?

Mrs. S.—The room is warmed by a wood fire.

S. —What arrangement did you make to visit the house?

Mrs. S.—Mr. Key generally goes first.

S. Did you ever go together?

Mrs. S.—Have walked there together say four times, I do not think more.

S—When was you there last?

Mrs. S.—Was there on Wednesday last, between two and three.

S. Did you go alone?

Mrs. S.—I went there alone.

S.—Where was Laura?

Mrs. S.—Laura was at Mrs. Hoover's. Mr. Key took and left her there at my request.

S.—Where did you go from there?

Mrs. S.—From there I went to Fifteenth street to meet Mr. Key; from there to the milk woman's.

S.—How soon after did you meet him?

Mrs. S.—Immediately after Mr. Key left Laura at Mrs. Hoover's, I met him in Fifteenth street.

S.—How did you go in?

Mrs. S.—Went in by the back gate.

S. Did you go in the bedroom, and if so what occurred?

Mrs. S.—Went into the same bedroom and there an improper interview was had.

S. Did you undress?

Mrs. S.—I undressed myself.

S.—Did Mr. Key do so?

Mrs. S.—Mr. Key undressed also.

S.—When did this occur?

Mrs. S.—This occurred on Wednesday, the 23d of February, 1859.

S.—Has Key taken any liberties with you in this house.

Mrs. S.—Mr. Key has kissed me in this house a number of times.

S.—Do you deny any criminal intimacy between you in this house?

Mrs. S.—I do not deny that we have had connection in this house last Spring a year ago, in the parlor on the sofa.

S.—Was I at home during your meetings with Key?

Mrs. S.—Mr. Sickles was sometimes out of town, and sometimes in the Capitol.

S.—When did the intimacy commence?

Mrs. S.—I think the intimacy commenced in April or May, 1858.

S.—Why did you not meet him here?

Mrs. S.—I did not think it safe to meet him in this house, because there are servants who might suspect something.

S.—How did you generally dress?

Mrs. S.—As a general thing, have worn a black and white woollen plaid silk dress, and beaver hat, trimmed with black velvet.

S.—Have you worn any other dresses there?

Mrs. S.—Have worn a black silk dress there also, also a plaid silk dress, black velvet cloak, trimmed with lace, and black velvet shawl, trimmed with fringe.

S.—What dress did you wear on your last visit?

Mrs. S.—On Wednesday, I either had on my brown dress or black, and white woollen dress, beaver hat, shawl.

and velved

S.—Did you arrange with Mr. Key to go in the back way?

Mrs. S.—I arranged with Mr. Key to go in the back way, after leaving Laura at Mrs. Hoover's.

S.—Where did he meet you?

Mrs. S.—He met me at Mr. Douglas's.

S.—Did you make the arrangement to go in the back way at Mr. Douglas's?

Mrs. S.—The arrangement to go in the back way was either made in the street or at Mr. Douglas's, as we would be less likely to be seen.

S.—Where is the house?

Mrs. S.—The house is in Fifteenth street, between K and L streets, on the left hand side of the way.

S.—When did you arrange for the interview of Wednesday, and where?

Mrs. S.—Arranged the interview for Wednesday, in the street, I think on Monday.

S.—How did you get in the house on that occasion?

Mrs. S.—I went in the front door.

S—Was it open?

Mrs. S.—It was open.

S.—Did you occupy the same room?

Mrs. S.—Occupied the same room.

S.—Did you both undress?

Mrs. S—Undressed myself, and he also.

S.—Did you go to bed together?

Mrs. S.—Went to bed together.

S.—Has Key ever rode in my carriage?

Mrs. S.—Mr. Key has ridden in Mr. Sickles's carriage, and has called at his house without Mr. Sickles's knowledge.

S.—After I forbid you to invite him?

Mrs. S.—And after my being told not to invite him to do so, and against Mr. Sickles's repeated request.

By omitting the queries the reader has Mrs Sickles's confession, word for word, as published. The surprise that was felt at the freedom with which she entered into the disgusting details of her criminality, was very natural; but, if our conjecture is correct, and we hope for the sake of decency it is, she will be relieved from much of the condemnation that has been heaped upon the head of the unfortunate woman. —*Sunday Courier*.

NEW YORK APRIL 30, 1859

Dramatic Feuilleton.

The Massacre of Ala(i)mo.

An artist who was born at Palermo, and who has, therefore an hereditary right to sing Norma, undertook that light and agreeable task at the Academy of Music on Monday.

The artist was Alaimo.

The performance was a Massacre.

Hence a pun; see "Life of General Houston," by Lester-Glory-and-Shame-Democratic-Age-Lester, not J. Wallack.

There had been a good deal said about Alaimo, one way and another. Chiefly another. She was imported by Maretzek.

He is the cleverest man in the way of bringing out fiascos, that ever existed.

Alaimo had a brother, who came here some time ago. He had a voice, but didn't know how to sing. She knows how to sing, but has no voice.

I leave it for the public to say which is the more disagreeable.

Alaimo sung at the Havana last Winter, and failed, but that was no reason why she should not succeed here. I put it as a reason to my friend Don Jose de Santarem de Bazan y Bungo, who is the color of café au lait, and has acres of doubloons, whereby A. M.'s ma rather affects him, and he said: "Ah, yes! but you see, in the Havana much things makes many "differs in artists." And, I'm sure, I quite agree with him.

But Alaimo did fail, and she has been put on the retired list, without pay.

So much the worse for Tiffany.

The audience amused me more than the performance disgusted me. Cubans in large numbers, suggestive of Partagas brevas; Orange county, in swarms, come to town to see the Odd Fellows; a clique of coiffeurs, tailors, and children of Israel; critics and amateurs in profusion. The professor of the double bass, radiant. Anna Maria, with her new bonnet, sweeter than Spring lamb, and Chateau Yquem.

And then how everybody recognized the sweet old airs! How everybody hung upon the prima donna as she tremoloed through the Casta Diva, half frightened to death, poor thing! How Orange county beat time with their feet to the Druid's March! It was grand to see so much real enjoyment.

I love Norma for a good many reasons (though one of the Cincinnati critics says it is "the weakest of Bellini's works'). It makes one think of pleasant people in the old days, when I was just entering upon the enjoyment of one of the sweetest of sensuous enjoyments, the Italian Opera.

I became sentimental like the rest. I told the brightest, that it carried me back twenty years, and, forgetting that she was doing the child-like, asked her if she remembered Truffi.

I was immediately snubbed, and Whiskers placed in sunshine for the rest of the evening.

I had my Favorita sensation on Wednesday. Gazzaniga was more than grand in the last scene. It is worth half an acre of land in the middle of the Central Park, that last scene. Stefaní was not on such intimate terms with the music as he might have been, and in the best aspect could not sing this role with Brignoli. People only find out how good that lazy Neapolitan is by comparison with others.

Next week we are to have Pic. back again. Pic.'s card, which is pretty good, is in another, and a less important, part of the paper. (Ten cents a line.)

Pic. will sing, on dit, Alice in *Robert le Diable*, and the gallant firemen (all heart and no toothbrushes), who once gave her an escort, will lend her one of their largest ladders to get up to the music. Then, I am afraid, there will have to be a splice."

However, Pic. is nice, and if she does tackle Alice, she will make a good thing of it. Witness the way she went at Lucrezia Borgia, which wasn't so bad. She reminds me of John Brougham in the variety of her talents. I wouldn't be at all surprised to hear her in Norma, and to see him in Othello, and I have no doubt they would make good things of both of them.

The Opera will be commenced on Wednesday. Ullmann retreats to the Provinces, opening in Boston on the 16th of May. It isn't true that Burton is engaged for the tenor parts.

Trifles.

Miss Laura Keene has been doing a lively business with "A Midsummer Night's Dream." Crowded houses, lots of nice puffs in the papers—the News was positively stunning—extra performances, and so on. Undoubtedly, the piece will run to the end of the season.

I hear and read conflicting accounts about Meyerbeer's new opera, *Le Pardon de Ploermel*, which was produced at the Opera Comique (nice theatre it is too) three weeks ago. A clever amateur analysis of it in the London *Post* gives the general idea that as a comic opera, it is a failure, but acknowledges that it is full of beautiful melodies and graceful writing for the orchestra. The Paris feuilletonists are all loud in its praise. It is to be produced at Covent Garden immediately, and I hope we shall have it here in the Fall. It is quite time we had a new opera.

"Different people," says a popular poet, "has different opinions. Some likes leeks and some likes inions." I am forcibly reminded of the distich by the manner in which an allusion of mine to the second-story Opera House, in Cincinnati, has been taken up by the papers of that city, and of Chicago. You must know that all the towns in the West are as jealous of each other as Anna Maria is of other women's new clothes. She would cut Araminta's throat for her new Cashmere, if she did not fear the Sessions, and yet A. M. and Araminta went to school together, and always kiss each other. Well, the Chicago man says, that "'Personne,' who does the 'Dramatic Feuilleton' of The New York Saturday Press (a most capital feature of a most excellent paper), touches up Strakosch and the Bunsbiacal musical critics of Porkopolis, in the following happy style."

But the Cincinnati journalist calls me a "genius," and says that my allusion to Pike's concern is "foolish as well as spiteful." He says, "in lieu of getting mad and calling names, we advise the Gothamites to hunt up an enterprising New Yorker, who will expend, as Mr. Pike did, half a million for a musical temple; but then, the 'Metropolitans' have such vile taste, that Bulwer's puzzling problem of 'What will he do with it?' would be the next question."

Now, I feel a deep reverence for Pike, just the same as for the Bank of Commerce, and I didn't intend to hurt his feelings. As Mlle. Piccolomini says in her Card, I don't pretend to be a genius, but I can't have these Cincinnati fellows humbugging us. Pike has not only put his Opera House up in the second story, but he has put shops for the sale of whiskey, pork, potatoes, hats, boots, bonnets, and notions generally, on the first floor, so that he gets more than a fair return on his investment, and much credit for enterprise and liberality, which is all bosh. It is a trade-speculation, and doubtless, if the Opera don't prove lucrative, Pike will give the artists "store-truck" instead of coin. But if he really desires to do a great, philanthropic work, let him start an Opera House at Pike's Peak and take all the singers with him. It would be such a boon to suffering humanity that the names of Pike, Howard, and Wilberforce would go down to posterity together.

Mr. Wallack has been playing *Don Caesar de Bazan* this week to crowded houses. He calls it his "original" part. I had a faint Idea that a Frenchman, not of the Wallack family, but still a fair actor, one Lemaitre, was the original. However it isn't much matter. Brougham and Walcot have brought out a new farce, "Box and Cox," but I haven't had time to read the official edition, which is profusely annotated á la Laura Keene.

At Niblo's they have revived (I use the term in its conventional sense) *Antony and Cleopatra*. Nothing new in it except Mrs. Hayne's Cleopatra, which is weak as

Taunton water.

Miss Davenport has been playing Peg Woffington in *Masks and Faces*, at the Metropolitan. It is a capital performance on her part, and the play was generally well done.

Here's a bit of Western musical criticism, which is rather nice than otherwise:

"Of Karl Formes we would simply say, that his voice is a wonder in compass and strength, going down *clear out of sight* in the lower notes; but in regard to the musical part of it, we agree with Brown that if Karl Formes should come in our back-yard at night, and sing in that style, we should feel justified in *stoning him off the premises*. We don't know but that we are alone in our opinion, and don't care if we are."

That man lives in Buffalo—not Cincinnati.

Personne

The Dark Hour Before Dawn.

The "Dramatic Fund" afforded us on Thursday evening, four hours of dramatic fun, which at 50 cents an hour was not dear. We forget whether the play was a tragedy or a comedy. All that we remember is that we laughed all through it, and that when the curtain dropped, our exhilaration,—like that of the audience,—had no bounds.

We always had a partiality for amateurs. Whether it is that they never know (nor let anybody else know) what they are about, and thus excite our sense of the ridiculous; or that being verdant beyond all other human products they minister to our love of "green and growing things," we cannot say. All we can state is that our partiality in this line is such that it embraces even amateur *writers*—though not to the extent of making us print their productions.

Cross-grained people—like Ruskin, for example—are down on amateurs, and see no good in them.

But we are *not* cross-grained. On the contrary, as every one who reads The Saturday Press must know, our most striking characteristic is good nature. Hence to us the amateur is a most delicious invention. The histrionic-amateur (if that is the right word) especially.

And why not? He is so satisfied with himself—in this respect having a decided advantage over the mere professional genius—that not to share in his happiness would be cruel. We *do* share in it. And last Thursday we more than shared in it; for we verily believe we enjoyed "The Dark Hour before Dawn" more than the dear amateurs themselves. And that is saying a good deal: for a more jubilant body of performers, in a certain original and melancholy kind of way, we never saw on any stage. The enjoyment they derived from their costumes alone, was enough to stir the soul (if he only had one) of our Dramatic Critic himself. And no wonder: for a more brilliant display of dry goods was never exhibited even at the Academy of Music.

One young man was so enchanted with his share that we should not be at all surprised to see him airing them, in course of the week, on Broadway. In fact, we are not quite sure but he was a lady in disguise. At all events, he deported himself throughout in a very ladylike manner. Tapeworm (one of Stewart's head men), who sat next to us, said that the young man wore and spoiled during the evening, at least two hundred dollars worth of silks, to say nothing of ribbons.

The young ladies were more modest, and—we may as well say now, lest we forget it—exhibited all the other virtues (except the dramatic, and one or two of these even) in great perfection. Miss B. especially. In fact, this young lady, who had a way of shaking her curls and flashing her eyes which would make the fortune of a professional actress, was more than charming. So, in fact, though in another style, was Miss E., who, with a little less dignity, and one, at least, of her own eyes (she had evidently borrowed those of some obliging neighbor), would have produced a great effect. But it is not fair to criticize amateurs; though the Dark-Hour-Before-Dawn corps would bear criticism better than any we have ever seen. But then, it is the first amateur performance we have had the honor of attending.

About the piece itself, there is little to be said. Moreover, as the *Tribune* very justly observes, "it would certainly be unfair to judge of the merits of a new play when only new professional talent is invoked to bring it through the critical ordeal of its "first representation "—or, in plain language, which the *Tribune* has an emphatic objection to, when it is performed by amateurs.

It struck us that there was a good deal of very sparkling dialogue in the play, and that, in the hands of a good company,—Wallack's or Laura Keene's, for instance, with the addition of Mr. Curtis, as Baron de Trop, and Miss B. as Muscodine,—parts of it, the serious parts especially, would be found very amusing.

In fact, this was more or less the case on Thursday evening, though the house never saw fit to manifest its delight until Mr. W. came forward and recited with his usual vim, two lines from the Epilogue; and then, truth to say, the assembled élite made amends for their previous lukewarmness by breaking out into a fearful storm of applause, which even Baron de Trop himself, spectacles and all, found it difficult to lull. The lines that produced this marvellous effect, and threw us all into a fit of enthusiasm, were as follows:

> You must be wearied by so many rhymes,
> To bore you now would be the worst of crimes.

And, curiously enough, the applause at this point was evidently not expected.

Prologue to The Dark Hour Before Dawn.

BY N. P. WILLIS.

Ladies and gentlemen! I come to say
A word about the Moral of our Play.

The Play itself—(I've read it)—goes to prove
The terrible uncertainty of love.
You smile! Perhaps you think that's nothing new;
And yet, what lovers love alike? No two!
Say what you will of human multiplicity,
Two never yet had just the same felicity!
So let us, if you please, blow one more bubble,
To show you one more kind of love and trouble.

A gentleman gets married, one fine day,
And takes his wife home with him—("all O. K. :")
She of the two was most in love—not funny,
Considering she was poor and he had money;
For woman's justice comes from Heaven above—
When she's no tin, she makes it up in love.
Our bride was therefore fond, and something over—
A balance, mind you! that she gave no lover!
Though not so thought her lord! and there's the bother:
She had been seen by chance to kiss her brother!
Frantic the husband! for the story ran,
His lady had been seen to kiss a man!
On this hook hangs the plot. But I'll not stay
To tell you all the workings of the play.
Suffice it that the story goes to show
To doubt your wife you'd best be rather slow!
You, sir, have chanced, as everybody knows,
Of all the bush to get the sweetest rose;
But, till of that sweet cup you hide the lip,
Don't think the butterflies won't try to sip!
Where honey is, the silly things *will* be,
They're in the habit of it—("Yes, sir-ee!")

This, then, our moral—hotter than perdition
Is that rehearsal of a hell, suspicion!
And, though an angel sometimes turns out human,
Be true yourself, and you may trust in woman!

A CARD.

MLLE. PICCOLOMINI TO THE PUBLIC.

Before saying adieu to the public which has treated me with proverbial generosity, I beg permission to express, in the best way offered me, the promptings of my heart.

I came to this country—so grand, so free, and so charming in its youth and freshness—with high hopes, which have been more than realized.

An artist, who is satisfied, is a miracle. I am a miracle, then.

But, perhaps, the public, or a portion of it, has been disappointed. That is not my fault. Perhaps the announcements on one side were too rose-colored, while the denunciations on the other were too severe.

I never pretended to divine genius. I am simply an artist, who does the best she can in her humble way, and is proud to stoop for the smallest flower that may be thrown at her feet.

There may be others who have the divine spark. Perhaps many others approximate it nearer than I.

I love my art, and devote my whole soul to it. I only ask the public to be fair; you have been more. You have been generous, and whatever success I may have hereafter, the reminiscences of my American tour will be among the sweetest of my little souvenirs.

I would rather stay here than go to Europe. But one—even a spoiled girl, and a prima donna as well—cannot always have her own way; so I must go on the 1st of June.

And, therefore, I have written this in advance of my farewell performances, to thank the public of the whole country (and of New York especially) for the favor that has been lavished upon me.

More than all this. I shall endeavor in the rôles which I am to undertake for the first time here, to show that this previous favor has not been thrown away; but has encouraged me to new exertions.

And so I salute you all. I would be charmed to do it personally, but the country is so large, and the population so immense, that I really fear the time would not be sufficient.

The public's devoted

MARIA PICCOLOMINI.

PERDITA.

BY N. G. SHEPHERD.

Last night the moon shone full and bright,
The wet leaves glistened in its light;
The fountain, overgrown with weeds,
Shone like a bed of silver beads.
'Twas there I saw Perdita stand,
Like some fair ghost—her trembling hand
Plucked wildly at her streaming hair,
And on the thickly scented air
She poured complaint, while shook with sighs
Her gleaming bosom's snows, and tears rained from her eyes.

The faint flowers drooped with odors sweet;
The dank grass, 'neath her naked feet,
Made soft the old, neglected walk.
I thought: "How strange she seems to talk."
Then sank the moon beneath a cloud,
And darkness, with her sable shroud,
Dropped down upon the garden ground;
And hushed was every living sound,
As paled the East with cheerless gray;
And like a lovely dream Perdita fled away.

I lingered where the tall trees made
A sightless mass of deepest shade,
"Till grim Night hid her face in shame,
And Morning dawned with rings of flame.
At noon they told me she was dead,
Spoke pitying words, and kindly led
The way to where she lay at rest—
Her white hands folded on her breast.
Two lives had perished when her breath
Left its poor, ruined shrine—and she had chosen death!

NEW YORK MAY 7, 1859

WHAT NEXT?

We are waiting, with some interest, to see what kind of an ovation is to be offered by our virtue-loving citizens to Mr. Sickles. He has rid the earth of a vile seducer, and is entitled to his reward.

A chaste and grateful public will not, we trust, be backward in bestowing it.

The greatest ovation that has hitherto been witnessed in New York was the one on the occasion of the funeral of Bill Poole. The enthusiasm exhibited by the community in burying that young man was something marvelous. A distinguished foreigner mistook the celebration for a national jubilee, and thought he had never seen so joyous a crowd of people in his life. And as he was an Englishman, he probably never had.

But that wonderful festivity must now be eclipsed. The occasion (if not the man) is a much greater one, and it should be met in a becoming spirit.

Fortunately, Sickles is alive, and will enjoy it. Alas! poor Poole was dead, and probably knew nothing of what was going on.

We must, at least, have a grand procession in Broadway. Not of Dishonored Wives, for Broadway wouldn't hold the half of them; but of Dishonored Husbands, assembled together to pay tribute to their great champion and chief.

The Dishonored Wives can stay at home, and wave their handkerchiefs as the procession passes by.

Or, as being eminently appropriate one of them might improve the occasion, and add materially to its éclat, by going out into the street and killing some woman who had dishonored her, and then a counter celebration might be got up in her honor in another quarter of the city. Say in Central Park.

At all events something must be done, and done, if possible, by both sexes, and on a grand scale.

Mr. Stanton has told us to "go it," and we ought to do so. In fact the cause of conjugal fidelity requires that we should "go it."

A man who bravely comes forth and sacrifices himself (and his neighbor) in the interest of female purity and domestic happiness, certainly deserves well of his kind, and we have no doubt his kind will come out on the appointed day and show that however immoral our city may be it is ready at all times to pay honor to distinguished worth.

If the occasion is allowed to pass without some appropriate celebration, the lesson of the great trial at Washington, with all its touching and reporting incidents, will be wholly lost, while the solemn charge of counsel, urging us all to "go it," might as well never have been spoken !

Let us "go it" then. Let us get up a festival worthy of the day and of the man. The honor and peace of our households—as well as the general interests of religion and good order—demands this of us. If we do not go it now, we shall never go it.

And then what would become of our wives and daughters?

We should like to treat the matter more seriously, but it is wholly out of our power. That farce at Washington, facetiously called a "Trial," has completely upset us. We see no use in hereafter treating anything seriously. If an unarmed citizen can be assassinated in cool blood, under any pretence whatever, by a man like Dan Sickles, and a jury be found to acquit the assassin almost without leaving their seats, why we may as well treat society itself as a farce, and all its laws.

THE HEART OF THE ANDES.

This picture we consider the best that Mr. Church has exhibited. It is not so daring in conception as his Sunset in South America, nor as astonishing as his Niagara; but there is the quiet power and simplicity of truth in it which we did not find so entirely in the others. Charmed as we were with the first view, every visit brings more satisfaction and new beauties to admire. First we would call attention to the careful and accurate truth of the drawing and coloring. There is the conscientious work in the foreground, which shows the study so indispensible to success. There is nothing slighted, nothing done carelessly, nothing "struck in" which ought to be struck out. In this age of hurry and steam, of reputations quickly made and as quickly lost, a great picture which teaches so earnestly the necessity of accurate study and careful work, forms an era in our art history. "What God hath made that call not thou common," is one of the last recorded injunctions which comes to us directly from Heaven.

Mr. Church has felt this and followed it; the little flowers in the foreground are minutely accurate, the moss on the trees is such as we see in the woods, the stones are not ideal stones. Compare this picture with almost any landscape in the Academy exhibition. Nor does this accuracy destroy the poetry of the picture. It is full of the true love of Nature, which cannot misrepresent, which feels the quiet beauty that slumbers on that mountain side, the changing shadows thrown along the peaceful valleys by the restless clouds, the still repose of the tangled foliage, the gay colored flowers that dance under the hot sun, the ceaseless dashing of the waterfall, the eternal repose of the snow-capped mountain peaks, the moist clouds almost breaking into rainbows, and a thousand other natural charms.

We hope that this picture will not be sold abroad; we can illy afford to part with it. It should be kept in the city, and exhibited free. The Corporation could well afford to sell the Common Council to buy such a picture as this. In fact, they might throw the Aldermen into the bargain, and be gainers.

There is some difference of opinion about the framing. There is an advantage in gilt, which first led to its adoption. It harmonizes better with pictures in a bright light than any other frame, and we think that the effect of this framing would be greatly improved by having a gilt beading to divide the picture from the dull tone of the black walnut.

Dramatic Feuilleton.

Charlotte Corday.

I had an a Miss Davenport has been regaling us with an episode of the Reign of Terror.

It is the dramatic version of the story of Marie-Anne Charlotte Corday, aged twenty-four, single woman, of Caen. Everybody knows how she made a journey to Paris, arriving in the sanguineous July of 1793; that she killed the "Friend of the People," Marat, and was herself guillotined, all within a week.

"This," says Carlisle, "was the history of Charlotte Corday: most definite; most complete; angelic-demonic; like a star! Adam Lux goes home, half delirious, to pour out his Apotheosis of her in paper and print—to propose that she have a statue with this inscription: *Greater than Brutus*. Friends represent his danger; Lux is reckless; thinks it were beautiful to die with her."

Now, I am not naturally of a patriotic turn of mind. I should view it as the height of absurdity to ride in a diligence from Caen to Paris for the purpose of killing some one to whom I had never been presented. Learning, says Voltaire, is rarely attractive in a man, never in a woman. When a young woman talks about Carlyle and metaphysics, I always take my hat. The American Daughters of Liberty are bores in a milder way, and let off their patriotism in flags for Number Fifteen Engine, or mottoes in which we are warned against the "insidious wiles of foreign influence," to which the Daughters themselves are often willing victims.

But there is something infinitely interesting and powerfully dramatic in the events of that yellow July evening when the Citoyenne Corday, "noble when nobility was," killed the Citoyen Marat, almost under the nose of his washerwoman and chère amie. That inn in the rue des Vieux Augustins, where she slept all the afternoon and night, and the lodgings of the "Friend of the People," in the rue de l'Ecole de Médicine, are not the least interesting spots in old Paris, even to me.

But the subject, although dramatic in its essence, is not a good one for a play. Paris in that terrible ninety-three could not be put on the stage. Bourcicault tried it once, and clever as he is at such things, made only a succès d'estime. Again the incidents are so strong in themselves that no stage effects can equal them.

Besides all this "Charlotte Corday" at the Metropolitan is as a drama badly constructed, and meanly put upon the stage.

Barbaroux, the grave Girondin, the Deputy of Caen, is made the lover of Charlotte, because he gave her a letter of introduction to Marat. Poor

Barbaroux ! But this was not enough, he was barked through by an actor who was dressed like a Captain in the Navy of the Queen of Great Britain and Ireland, bless her soul.

Poor Barbaroux!

Danton and Robespierre were mildly sanguinary, Fisher was something like Marat both in manner and appearance, and played with becoming ferocity.

And Charlotte, what was she like? Well, she was something like Charlotte Russe, which is nice, and a good deal like Miss Davenport, who however manages to sink a good deal of her conventionality in this role. I suppose that if it is necessary that Charlotte Corday should be played at all, that Miss Davenport can play it better than any one else hereabouts.

As it did not attract very full houses, I apprehend that the public don't think it absolutely necessary to be done at all.

The last scene of the second act is devoted to the performance (I can't call it reciting or singing) of the much abused Marseilles Hymn. The scene is chiefly filled up with two tri-colored flags, which Dawson, in a red gown and a powdered wig, is blessing, or doing something or other to, at the back. Then Miss Davenport has a little flag for her own use, and so it is pretty nearly all flag and Miss Davenport. Away goes the orchestra, Mollenhauer in a terrific state of excitement, and the big drum absolutely thrilling with enthusiasm. Miss Davenport sings the first verse, and then, thinking better of it, recites the others. The singing is not first rate, and the recitation would be better if the words were not exploded in a way that is suggestive of fire-crackers on the Fourth of July.

However, it was quite exciting. The audience went into ecstacies over it. Those who couldn't understand French, which Miss Davenport pronounces well, were thrilled with delight.

So there was more of it, and Miss Davenport was obliged to wade through the blood of tyrants until her voice was exhausted, and her feet must have been very wet.

The effect on Anna Maria, who is not naturally of a sanguinary turn of mind, was so strong that she thinks of killing an Alderman at once.

Miss Davenport will close her campaign at the Metropolitan next week. Although I have sometimes made fun of her and her plays, I do really hope that she will return to us next season. Old fashioned as she is, and at times too conventional, we have no actress here that can be compared with her for a moment, and I am quite sure that the opinion of the public coincides with mine "in this connection,"

Pic.

Whiskers is in a state of beatitude beyond description.

Pic. has returned. Returned from the embraces of the Crackers, the Dodgers, and the Wolverines. Be turned from the "bootiful" prairies and "noice" hotels of the West. Returned to gladden the heart of the Editor and of Young New York generally. Returned to torment the men and annoy the women. Returned to sing badly and to act charmingly. Returned to bag as many metropolitan dollars as possible before the fourth of next month, when she goes to Europe on what the boys call the "Wanderbilt."

At Niagara on Tuesday; singing at the Academy on Wednesday. Pretty good work that. But little Pic has pluck. Travelling in the Provinces, she jumps out of bed at some impossible hour in the morning, gets into her boots, and away she goes r-r-r-sh-sh-sh, all day, singing in the evening, and away again the next day.

It was the Traviata on Monday; of course the Traviata; keep giving us the Traviata, please, until it is entirely worn out, and then go back to the Trovatore. One of these days I shall die of too much Verdi, but not yet.

The audience was "numerous and respectable." Few Japonicas (too much German and paté de foies gras at the Bachelor's Ball the night before), a good deal of Barkhampstead, numerous victims of Spanish tyranny (they don't seem to mind it much) and some Jerusalem. All the susceptible young critics—the Adonis of the *Express*, the Sheridan of the *News*, the sweet singer of the *Sunday Times*. Likewise Whiskers in lavender, and A. M. with that Spring hat, upon which Araminta glances with murderous eye.

The public is a little cool to Pic. The public is afraid of the critics. The critics say that she is a humbug—that is, the majority of them say so. So while the public pays Pic. its money, the public is afraid to display its "feelinks" for fear that it will make itself ridiculous.

The public is an ass of colossal proportions. [Style Gurowski].

I don't know that my opinion about this artist in the *Traviata* is of much consequence now, if it ever would have been, which is doubtful. I think, however, that with the single exception that she is younger and prettier than the others, she has been excelled in every point by her predecessors here. Colson played the character with more finish and grace; La Grange sung the music better; and Gazziniga's last act has never been approximated by any of them.

It is in comic opera that Pic. excels, and here she has the whole field to herself. But, unfortunately for them, few of our people can appreciate comic opera. They must have music which they can whistle. The number of persons who really understand what the opera is, is not large enough to support it, and the curious public must be drawn in to swell the receipt. So a really fine artist like Pic. is injured by being forced into operas which she can neither sing nor act.

I rather enjoyed the opera on Monday. There was a better orchestra than usual, which is a great thing. Then there was Brignoli. Brignoli with all his grace, his impetuosity, his elegance, his utter self-abnegation, his delicious abandon. Once or twice I really thought he would get interested in the scene. That calamity was happily averted. Brignoli's voice is really a treat, after the bad lot of tenors we have had lately. When Brignoli likes to sing (which is not quite often enough), I know of few voices purer, sweeter, or more sympathetic. Beyond that, he is a good artist, thoroughly understanding how to use his great natural gifts with safety to himself, and gratification to the public. A tenor voice is not an iron safe, nor an Indian rubber ball.

Amodio has a grand baritone voice, which he must handle more carefully. It has already lost some of its rotundity of tone, its great beauty.

I was astonished at the number of avocations that are pursued in the Academy by tow-headed boys. There are "books of the a-a-pera," fans, bouquets, and various other articles, thrust under one's nose continually. In the middle of the opera, these young gentlemen have an unpleasant habit of standing so as to obstruct the view of the stage, and sometimes settling their pecuniary differences while the prima donna is going through with her pièce de resistance. I should like, if I can't be allowed to kill one of these traders, to be permitted to smoke; and as I found, by inquiry, that they do not sell matches, I would humbly suggest that they should do so.

Of course everybody will go to the Pic.-Matinée today. She will sing in Lucia, and La Serva Padrona.

Mere Mention.

Mr. Wallack will conclude his performances for the season, about one hundred and fifty in number, next week, and retire like Cincinnatus (no offence to Pike) to Long Branch. The Veteran has had a fine campaign of it and has fought it gallantly. May his crops flourish as his years increase. Peace to the Hut and protection from the musquitos to its gallant proprietor.

The French Theatre has given *Les Memoires du Diable* pretty well. Laba was excellent as usual. Next week Wednesday he has his benefit in *La Dame aux Camélias,* and Mme. Gassier sings for him. I don't think Widdows et Sage are making their eternal fortunes. Perhaps they'll do it in Montreal.

Miss Keene is still doing *A Midsummer Night's Dream*, every evening, every evening, every evening, crowded "houses, crowded houses, crowded houses."

At Niblo's Garden things have not been prosperous, but there is to be made a grand effort with Rob Roy, which is to be done next week with "all the original music." Two very good artists, Lucy Escott and Miranda, have been specially engaged for the vocal department. The idea is an excellent one, and if properly carried out will command success.

The opera, at Philadelphia, commenced on Monday with Gazzaniga. The *Traviata*, of course. Immense enthusiasm of course. Gazzaniga is to be elected president of a fire company and to have a new stage named for her. One of these days she will be as popular as Mrs. Bowers or Peter Richings.

Personne

NEW YORK MAY 14, 1859

Dramatic Feuilleton.

Rob Roy Macgregor—Oh!

More history.

Last week I gave you some entertaining particulars about Miss Davenport's friend, the original Mary Ann, called Charlotte Corday.

This week a short biography of Mr. Rob Roy, alias Macgregor, alias Campbell.

You see I am getting profound.

Training, I may say, for the Appletons.

Becoming a regular "Cyclop."

Well, the subject of this sketch belonged to an amiable family, who had been in the habit of amusing themselves by cutting out their cousins' eyes and sending them to the female relatives of the victims. Robert was of a more peaceable turn of mind, and with the Duke of Argyll (precious lot they were, too; the present one, however, wears a white cravat, has sandy hair, and snuffles for the slave at Exeter Hall,) went into the business of swindling small farmers in cattle-trades. Argyll and the Macgregor had a difference of opinion, probably about the division of the spoils, and the Duke accused his partner of theft. Robert was outlawed and took up cattle-stealing as a light and agreeable means of livelihood. It was he, and not the Sunday papers, that originated the term black mail. He received, from the graziers, tribute of so many cattle per annum, on condition that neither he nor his men should molest the remainder of the herds. He was arrested and tried at Edinburgh, but, I believe, escaped the halter he deserved. He was a sneak, as well as a thief, was Robert. In "the forty-five" he promised to bring his clan into the field of Culloden to help Prince Charles Edward, but kept them at a safe distance until he saw the way things were going, and then went himself, probably stealing a spoon or two by the way.

Those, I believe, gentle public (what a nice creature you are, and how amiably you do submit to be bored), are the principal facts (new idea that, facts in an article about theatres) concerning the friend of Sir Walter Scott and Mr. Eddy. Between them, they make out of a cattle-swindler, a hero; out of a sneaking coward, a chivalric chieftain.

But, as the Boston *Post* said the other day, about a rather ancient joke, thank heaven there's a rising generation.

I can remember, and I am twenty-four, when I thought Rob Roy was much finer than Macbeth. Now, to my mind, Macbeth, unless Laura Keene or Mr. White edits it, is much better.

Rob Roy, however, is amusing, and that is saying a great deal. It is full of action. The scene never stops for a moment. Everybody is doing something all the time. To be sure, they go up a great many terrible crags, some as much as ten feet high in the clear, and there is no special reason for so doing, unless it is for the express purpose of coming down again, but if you want a reason for everything, you can have no melodramas. The whole race of bluefire and patent trap writers, from Pecocke down to Fitzball, Morford, and Gayler, are, theatrically speaking, anything but reasonable beings.

Whenever you are afraid that Rob Roy is going to be a bore, there comes in a song. Now a song, good or bad, is always a relief.

For example: There is in this play an estimable old Jacobite, Sir F. Vernon, who has been green enough to get on the wrong side in politics and religion, and who is obliged to live in a picture-frame with a secret spring, which by the way would not be a secret to my smallest boy, whose years are too tender for trowsers. Now politicians, at best, are bores, but an unsuccessful one is the worst of all. So Sir F. Vernon is not lively, but is choked off in his story of his wrongs, which he is telling to Miss Lucy Escott in full ball dress, white satin slippers, and a circus of crinoline, by a music-cue, after which the lady, rejoicing that she has finally got rid of the Governor, breaks out into a song to the effect that her love was born a Highland lad, when in fact he was a Lowlander, which is a matter of slight (musical) consequence.

Then Mr. D. Miranda, a powerful tenor who would have had a narrow escape from being a good artist had he ever learned how to sing, plays the part of a young gentleman who is continually in trouble; always chased up by a villain with a corrugated larynx and bucket-boots. Yet he warbles away bravely about his love being like the red, red rose, which by the way she's not; more like a white one late in the season. And the whole affair winds up with a chorus "pardon now the bold outlaw," in which various officers who bear the King's commission, as we are frequently informed during the play, are vocally guilty of high treason.

Of course it is pleasant to hear the old airs, makes me think of old times, old flirtations, and other queer old things. But it would be nicer if Miss Escott could sing a ballad with simplicity, and didn't shake the music or her head so much. Did she ever hear of the awful fate of a young lady in Pittsburgh, the sole port of a widowed mother and no end of brothers and sisters, who shook her head off amidst the plaudits of a crowded and delighted audience? Pic. might take warning from the terrible occurrence, too.

The acting of Rob Roy was rather good, although there was no one in it a bit like a Scotchman, except, perhaps, Mr. Bland, who was the "Dougal creature" and not bad. Mr. Eddy's Rob Roy was intoned after the Puseyite fashion, the terminations ending in *ng* or *n* or *m* sounding like those horse-hair things the boys whirl over their heads to resemble a mosquito's gentle lay. Mrs. Macgregor, the original chairman of the first Woman's Rights Convention, was powerfully acted on the principle of the energetic preacher that A. M.'s ma "set" under in New England, and who used to smash the reading-desk sometimes.

Mr. Pearson was in the bill for the Bailie. He was vara amusin, but nae ackit nair talkit like ye Scottish mon, as a friend late frae "Glasgoo" informed me. The others were good, I suppose. I really don't remember. I noticed they nearly all wore moustaches,— curious thing for a century ago.

On the whole, Rob Roy is not bad, and I advise everybody to see it once.

The Opera.

Pic. has had a dart at the Trovatore, but with only moderate success. In the wedding-scene she looked like a pot of Orange county butter, and in the Miserere reminded me of a carpet tack. She was better in L'Elisir, though horridly (A. M.) dressed. Brignoli distinguished himself in a *pas seul*, unequalled for its battiments, aplomb, and so on. I suggest to the director an incidental ballet to be danced by Brignoli, Junca, and Amodio.

Pic's Farewell Matinée to-day. Opera, Don Pasquale.

On Monday, Mme. de Wilhorst sings in the Puritani, in which she is very good.

If brevity is the soul of wit (and I can't see it), then Strakosch's prime ladies ought to say, as well as to sing, good things sometimes.

The Fellow on the Opposite Side of the Way.

The inevitable Maretzek, the indomitable Maximilian, who flourishes in the midst of ruin, thrives upon defeat, and who would go without his maccaroni rather than his opposition, if he couldn't have both, is about to commence operations at the Metropolitan. Maretzek has Cortesi.

Who is Cortesi?

The dailies, and they know nothing about it, say she has a good reputation; where, they neglect to mention, simply because they don't know. (Not generally a reason for withholding information of some sorts.)

Now *I* don't know much about Cortesi, and I am supposed to know everything.

The camp-followers about the Academy, say she is a greater Traviata than Gazzaniga. Figaro-Célestin, who is to the prime ladies, as Fry calls them, what Oliver le Dain was to Louis Onze, says she is handsome, and has a magnificent head of hair.

This is authentic-semi-official.

I would sooner have Célestin's word than those of a college of critics.

With Anna Maria, he makes the people, and the voice of the people admonishes kings! (Cheers.)

So let Cortesi have a chance. And if she is a fiasco, we have Mme. Gassier, who, if not so handsome as Hebe, can sing, I am willing to bet and give heavy odds, an hundred times better than Saint Cecilia, inspiration and all.

Wallack—"Extremes."

Mr. Wallack has survived the tremendous shower of adjectives and adverbs of praise which were showered upon him by the *News*, last Monday, but in his present condition it will not be safe to do it again. The novelty of the week has been Planche's drama, Charles XII., a clever piece, in which the Lion of Sweden is rather more lamb-like in his deeds, and wolfish in his words than Voltaire makes him out. However I prefer Planché to Voltaire, and so does Anna Maria, who was quite charmed with Mr. Wallack's Adam Brock, and said that Mr. Brougham was lovely as King Charles. I don't think the adverb appropriate, but the Beloved One is not particular about such small affairs.

Next Monday they will bring out Falconer's Extremes, a three-act Comedy, very British in its tone, but clever withal. Mr. Lester Wallack plays the part of the hero, a young man who is too good for this world, and who is willing to sacrifice a million rather than lead Mrs. Hoey to the altar, if she does not absolutely insist upon it, which she does in the end. The other characters are aristocrats without money, and democrats with it, so all the questions of the heart are submitted to the question of £, s., d. . I think the piece will be amusing. Brougham, Walcot, and Miss Gannon play in it.

Theatre Francais.

Widdows et Sage are going to Philadelphia next week. I nearly died laughing over the Folies Dramatiques. It is a mock performance of an Opera seria, a tragedy in verse, a modern humanitarian drama, and a ballet, by what is supposed to be the portion of a company of artists engaged in Paris for the Provinces. Edgard is the great artist who can play everything, and Sen the leading actress—Rachel, Rose Cheri, Grisi, and Taglioni, all rolled into one. Both Sen and Edgard were capital, and I "dono' when I've enjoyed anything so much as these Folies, which I advise Mr. John Brougham to put into English "right off."

La Dame aux Camélias, for the benefit of Laba, brought a crowded house on Wednesday. Performance altogether fine; Chevalier superb; better, the Editor says, than Madame Doche, whom I never saw (the only man or woman that has ever been to Paris without seeing her). Laba was gotten up like the Dome of St. Peters, and "calculated to strike the beholder" with mingled admiration and awe." (Murray). I don't know that the Dome knows it, but Laba does. Distinct from the clothes, he was not brilliant. Edgard was irresistibly funny, and the audience very enthusiastic. The play will be repeated this evening.

The Conway Theatre.

Miss Davenport has wound up her season at the Metropolitan, which, as we learn from the bills, is "under" the Lafarge House, without much pecuniary profit, but with an improved reputation, which will tell well in the provinces. For whatever they may say (and they do wince awfully, especially the Porkopolitans, about that second-story Opera House), they will not have any thing which has not first been tried in New York.

I hear now that Mr. F. B. Conway, whose managerial career has not been of dazzling brilliance, has some sort of arrangement with young Mr. Lafarge, who has, on dit, a slight attack of footlight fever, under which there is to be a Summer season with a good company. Mr. John Brougham is engaged, and several other good names are mentioned. Go it!

Upper-Ten Theatres.

Two new theatres near Union Square. Mrs. Bourcicault's fire-proof, iron affair, directly under the bronze nose of the Father of his Country, and Mr. Wallack's on Thirteenth street and the Fourth Avenue. The Bourcicault-affair promises well, with the facile, clever, and popular Stuart, as business-manager; Bourcicault as the stage-director, and Mrs. Bourcicault as a sort of guardian angel, generally. It is an Arcadian tableau.

Summer Luxuries.

The admirers of the baked beans, hasty pudding, and hod-carrier order of dramatic architecture will be overjoyed to learn that Mr. and Mrs. W. J. Florence have taken Wallack's for a Summer season. Mrs. Florence's imitation of a "Boston lady" is Pre-Raphaelite in its exactness and elaboration of detail.

Crinoline and the Coulisses.

Somehow it seems that the people don't appreciate the works of Laura Keene, G. C. Scott, R. G. White, and W. Shakspeare to the extent of as many half dollars as they might. In fact, the audiences have fallen off disagreeably. However, "A Midsummer Night's Dream" will probably run through the season, which will close in about a fortnight. After all, it is only an exchange of one invoice of crinoline for another. When Miss Keene lays down the Sceptre, or, I might say, club of Management—two other divinities with the euphonious name of Gougenheim will reign in the stead of the new Hypatia. The coming managers have lately returned from extensive wanderings in California, and other barbarous regions, where they were kindly treated by the natives, and brought home gold, silver, and precious stones in great quantities. In only one case did the simple-minded savages act with rudeness toward the ladies, and that was when a barbarian absolutely insisted upon being master of his own ship. He was duly snubbed for his pains. During their journeyings, however, the Misses Gougenheim must have committed some awful crime, or they would never have been tempted to open a Summer theatre in New York.

What the —— Do You Mean?

The young man of the *Sunday Times*, who does violence upon the Muses in a feeble way, talks about my being compelled to do something by the "conditions of (my) mythical existence." Would be much obliged for accurate information as to what is meant by "mythical existence."

Collins vs. Wood.

Paddy Collins and "the beautiful Mrs. Wood" have been having a shindy in California. Plenty of cards, miles of attack, replies, and rejoinders; may be all summed up in a single sentence—struggle of egotism against self-conceit. It is difficult to say which is the finer, the sublime impudence of the lady, or the magnificent assurance of the gentleman.

PERSONNE.

Mr. Bigelow, of the New York *Evening Post*, writes the following sad intelligence from Rome, under date of April 7th:

I am sorry to inform you that Mr. and Mrs. Hawthorne, who have been spending the Winter here, are in great affliction. Their daughter Una, an interesting girl of some fifteen Summers, lies at the point of death. Soon after they reached Rome she had a severe chill, while sketching one day in the baths of Caracalla, gastric fever and inflammation of the lungs ensued, which have continued to prey upon her health, with occasional intervals of convalescence, all Winter. Day before yesterday her case took a more serious turn, if possible, and last evening I heard that she was in the last stages of a rapid consumption.

The friends of Mr. Hawthorne will be gratified to learn that letters from Rome, under date of April 16, speak of the improved health and probable recovery of Miss Hawthorne, whose dangerous illness was recently reported.

GRAND HORTICULTURAL FESTIVAL AND SOIREE DANSANTE.—A series of elegant entertainments, to be continued until the 16th, will be given at the Palace Garden (now greatly improved), and in the new and spacious Hall on the West side of the grounds, in aid of a contemplated Horticultural School for Females. Oratory, Music, Flowers, and Birds will be brought into requisition to make this the most interesting, intellectual, and attractive festival ever given in New-York.

The Grand Horticultural Festival at the Palace Gardens has been seriously affected by the rain. We are a free and philanthrophic people, but we are awfully tyrannized over by the weather. We like well enough to assist poor orphan girls, but we don't like to get wet. There is a limit to all things—even to benevolence. However, the weather is clearing up now, and we can afford to be charitable. So the Palace will probably be crowded to-day and Monday (when the Festival closes), and the hearts of the orphans will be made glad. The entertainments offered are of the most charming description, including music, oratory (you should have heard Caroline Fry the other night), dancing, fireworks, etc., etc.

Mr. George Filer, of Belchertown, Mass., writes to the *Springfield Republican* that he and his family have not eaten any flesh during the last twenty-two years, fifteen of which they have abstained from fish, fowl, tea, and coffee, and that through the whole they have enjoyed an unusual degree of health. His weight is, and has been for several years, about two hundred pounds.

Phantom-Wooing.

BY WM. P. BRANNAN.

The mystic twilight welcomed us amain,
Adown a shady vale of pleasing gloom,—
O'erhung with vines, and many a fragrant bloom–
'Till we were lost in love's delicious pain.

The wayside streamlet, sang a vesper near—
In dreamlike cadence, to our utterance low—
A heart-song, gushing with resistless flow,
Of rippling music to the eager ear.

The wanton breath of warm, voluptuous Spring,
Encompassed us with a celestial bliss ;
Each earnest dalliance seemed a lover's kiss—
With so much fondness did each zephyr cling.

Upon this calm and peerless eventide,
My lips found language such as hearts express,
When overburdened with love's sweet excess—
That won for me a soul-enchanting bride.

Was it a vision of my wayward brain,
That led me down beneath those Eden-skies,
With one who made this vale a paradise
Of angel-rapture and elysian pain?

Alas, the scene has changed! my fairy bride
Was but a phantom-love; the dream is o'er—
The magic spell dissolved forever more,
Which charmed my soul on that blest eventide.

Louisville, Ky.

NEW YORK MAY 21, 1859

ONE OF THE DAYS OF MY LIFE.

BY MRS. R. H. STODDARD.

To-day I prefer this silent and sombre room. The idle hills around look greener than ever; the trees twinkle in the sunshine, and the sea laps the beach lovingly, but I will stay here, for my heart is touched with the anguish of memory.

In my duties and enjoyments I too often forget the days of trouble endured by me and mine.

When some association recalls the past, I undergo agonies of remorse, because, like all the rest of the world, I have eaten and drunken, as though it had never been. I suffer my thoughts to dwell on it as an expiation for my indifference, and forgetfulness, till I am exhausted, and time brings round its healing power again.

I have come back to my native town, to visit the relative who occupies the house where my mother lived and died, and where we children were born. Some of us died in infancy. Two of the boys, when grown to manhood, went from us to live in foreign parts. My sister and I were left, and here we lived until she went from the old house, never to return.

This was her room. My aunt, who is a lonely woman, and who possesses the trait of veneration common to women, has kept, not only this room but several others, in the same state in which she found them, when, by my father's will, she took possession of the house. The room fronts the North. The horizon is edged with a belt of woods. Here and there a tree has strayed into the fields which slope down to the low orchard, that lies under the window. The old fir-tree in yonder field where the crows lighted, on their way to the sea shore, still stretches out its ragged, dusty boughs, and the great rock behind it looks as grim and mysterious as it did when I used to clamber over it years ago. The white clouds are boiling up above the woods in the serene blue sky. The rows of stone wall half hidden with shining vines, glisten in the sun. The grain nods and trembles in the shadows that play over it. Birds are flying to and fro, piping to their mates in the distant wood. It was the same when I looked from this window many a Summer ago. It is beautiful, but to me it is sad as death.

The deserted air of the room harmonizes with my sadness; though the furniture is the same, and the pictures and books remain as Lily arranged them, a stranger would know that its animating spirit had left it forever. The little French bed is uncovered, and the curtains and carpet are faded; "a dwelling place, and yet no habitation."

Opening the drawer in her writing table I find a rusty ink-stained pen; a little box of seals with the mottoes I so well remember; a bunch of flower-stalks tied with ribbon, and some letter-envelopes addressed in her name. How strange they look! There is the very one that came that day,—the day that I am now to speak of.

It was an October morning. I awoke at daybreak, and saw the light, ray by ray, look into the windows of the large guest-chamber where I had slept. My sister Lily was in the next room. She had been ill three weeks, and I had taken care of her. She felt better, she said, the night before, and she wanted me to leave her, and take the rest I so much needed. I went, and it seemed to me that I had just fallen asleep when the whole house was startled by a shriek from Lily's chamber. In a moment we were by her bedside. She was not in her bed, but under it, crying, and talking inarticulately. We coaxed her back to the bed; she said she had been pursued by some one who wished to take her away, and she hid from him. It was then about midnight; we went to rest again, and left my aunt to take care of her for the remainder of the night. Early as it was, I rose, dressed, and went down stairs. My mother was astir, and had given orders for breakfast. She said the fright we had, had spoiled her sleep, but that Lily was better, and was then sleeping soundly. I went into the kitchen and talked about Lily, with old Hannah, who was baking cakes. It was always busy and noisy there, and I felt enlivened. Breakfast was served in the family-room. There were but three at the table, my father, mother, and myself. A wood fire burned on the hearth; the cheery hiss of the oak sticks, the aromatic smell of the coffee, and the taste of Hannah's cakes,––I remember them as perfectly as I remember everything connected with that strange day. From the windows of this room we had a prospect of the bay; the beach was the Southern boundary of our place. The day was calm; the sun, half veiled in haze, glimmered through it, more like the moon than himself. The long lines of shimmering water, seemed to roll backward as well as forward, as if the sea were waiting for some sign to fall on either shore. In its movement it was silent. I left my father and mother chatting over the table, and went up to Lily's room, whose windows commanded the prospect I have just spoken of. She was sitting up in bed; the window curtain was drawn aside, and she was staring at the sea. Her long brown hair fell down her pale narrow face, and she held in her hand a cup of untasted drink. I asked her if I should comb her hair, and arrange her bed. "Not yet," she answered; "I will rest awhile." She gave me the cup, and laid back on the pillow. Her illness was a capricious one. She had been moved from chamber to chamber as her fancy dictated, and the one she now occupied was my own. She had been alone much of the time, while I sat in the next room, within her call. She was regaining her health slowly, the doctor told us, and would soon be about, but she was so weak and fragile that we indulged her in all her caprices. One of them had been that I should be her nurse. I was her patient rather; she ordered me as if I were a child; made me perform the most trivial things over and over again. She scolded me, and accused me, and yet I could see that she wanted me near her.

Lily was eighteen, and I was twenty-three. We were different in character and person. Although we were the only children at home, we sympathized less with each other than with any members of our family. We dressed differently, chose different friends, and had always occupied different rooms. When we were away from home, we never wrote each other, and at home, we were seldom together. Lily had musical talent, and occasionally, when I begged her, she would play for me the music that she knew I loved, and in the way I liked, piece after piece, without any interval between them. At such times we talked amicably together, but never confidentially. She liked to make me laugh, by telling me what she called her adventures. But I could never feel that she was related to me, and I cannot remember having felt any gladness when we met each other after a separation. I thought her unfeeling. She bore pain like an Indian, and we should not have known her suffering, had she not been so fragile in strength. She fainted often, and her convulsive tremblings betrayed her, when she would not allow herself to utter a groan. With all her power of endurance, she was so sensitive that the touch of silk or velvet made her nerves crawl, and the sight of a worm made her turn pale.

Terrible words sometimes passed between us. Once I struck her—lifted my hand and smote her delicate cheek. I, a grown woman, did it!

Domestic tragedies are everywhere. No day passes wherein a portion of one is not enacted. But they are hidden till death not only reveals many an infernal secret, but renders justice to the departed soul, who lived and died misunderstood, and wronged. It is almost universally true, that parents and children, brothers and sisters, are ignorant of each others' inner lives. Why is it, that for twenty years of ignorance, one must live twenty more of remorse, repentance, and expiation?

Lily laid back on her pillow, and I took up my sewing. It was a white muslin morning gown, finished except the hem. I sewed in silence. A fire brand broke now and then, and fell on the hearth, and a solitary fly buzzed in the pane. I looked up at Lily, and I met her eye. She smiled faintly, and said: "You and I have become a little better acquainted lately, I think."

I threw down my now completed work, but made no reply.

"Will you," she said, "get from my portfolio that letter which came last week, and read it? It is from B.'s sister; he was buried the other day, and she wrote me about it. B. loved me; did you know it?"

I found the letter and read it; I had seen B. a hundred times, but never with Lily.

"When I get well," she continued, "I mean we shall be happier together. I have been thinking about it since I was first taken ill. You wondered, all of you, at my restlessness. As you moved me from room to room, I seemed to emerge from the clouds that had so long hid us from each other, and when I came here I felt still clearer. It will all be settled between us soon, I am sure. I used to think your room quite an Eden. I suppose because you never asked me into it. I have always admired you. I could not tell you so before, but you will know me some day. And mother, too,—why does mother laugh when I tell her I shall write a poem yet? Well, I have hated you, too; hated you the most when I thought you were loved by some man. I have imitated you, and that has made you despise me. When you went away from home, I used to come in here, and look at your pictures, and turn over the books you liked best. I thought I might find a key that would unlock the door of knowledge and teach me what you really were. Do you remember the day you found me here with your journal in my hand? I did not care for your secrets, but I wanted to keep a journal, and I did not know how. I have kept one since, and you may see it. And do you remember, long ago, how you shook me one day for breaking a bottle of precious perfume, that L. had given you? What made you so fierce? But I bit you."

"Yes," I answered, "I have the scar on my and still—a keepsake I shall always wear."

"Let me kiss it," begged Lily.

I went to the bed, and she took my hand and held it to her lips. I pushed away her tangled hair and kissed her forehead, and went and sat down by the hearth, where we could not see each other. I did not feel like talking, but Lily began again. "I have been engaged to Charley F. a year. I think he must be dead, too. It is three months since I heard from him."

"Why," I said, "you do not love him, do you?"'

"No, not much. I love one of your admirers. I cannot give away my heart twice, can I? Are you aware of your cruelty?" she continued, raising her voice to a loud, steady pitch. "None but your victims tell you of your coquetries, do they? Will you think me romantic if I say I am one? It is over now; my fury and despair have died away, or I could not say what I am saying without cursing. Go back in thought to that first year, when A. came here. Do you imagine that I suffered much when I saw him with you, day after day, month after month? What a weak man he was! How nicely his nature allowed you to prolong my torture! For I knew well that you kept him at arm's length, and at no greater distance either. It was a long time before I could find out whether he loved you, or whether he played a game, too. Do you recall the evenings when your imperious eyes forced me to go, and leave you with him? Do you think that I slept through the long still hours, while you coiled round him with looks of fire, and touched him with hot hands? Oh, no! I waited patiently in the little chamber over the hall, till he left you, and then I went after him. You could not hear my steps. I took off my shoes and walked, many a night in the dew and damp, without them. And we stood under your window, too; the lamp behind your curtain was the light by which we saw each others' faces. Why did you walk about sometimes? We counted the turns your shadow took? You were ever too proud to look about you, and you have been blind, blind. The man must have been afraid of me, must he not? I have seen his face grow white, and his eyes dilate, when we three were together, and I have made him a sign that I should wait for him. I despised him as much as I loved him. What's the reason why I said I would marry Charley F.? Admire the worldly forethought which convinced me that it would be better to have a good husband, than a wicked lover!"

Lily ceased talking. I looked into the fire a long time; what I saw there employed my attention. It was a grotesque city, and my eyes followed a procession that was threading its crooked streets. Red trees grew there, with white fruit; elephants tramped along, and tore them down; and hearses went by, whose palls blackened as they passed. The balconies of the houses were continually falling off, and the towers of castles toppling over. All was as strange and beautiful as the grown-up stories I read when I was a child, and could not understand.

The silence was broken by a slight cough from Lily. There was something so strange in it, that I started to my feet, and looked over the foot-board at her. She did not speak, nor look at me. I ran down stairs to find my mother. She was in the kitchen; her lap was full of golden-skinned peaches, which she was preparing to preserve. "Mother, I wish you would go up to Lily; she looks strangely." She went up quickly, and, an instant after, I heard her voice calling to some one to go for the doctor. I staid below, and from that moment remained in a strange condition, which those who have passed through a crisis will understand. My perceptions were sharp, but my sensibilities were completely deadened. When the doctor came, he said nothing; how, indeed, could he? He knew no more than we did. I wandered about the house, in and out of every room and chamber, looking out of the windows; looking over drawers, books, reading the newspapers, or watching whatever any person was doing near me. There was confusion in the house; not a room was put in order that day. The servants lolled out of the windows, and hung about the kitchen-fire, and talked together with low voices. I saw some of our neighbors creeping to and fro in the passages. The opening and shutting of the doors had a distant, muffled sound. The great clock ticked so loudly in the diningroom, that I heard it up stairs; it seemed to be coming up, step by step.

It was afternoon when my father drove furiously into the yard. He had been away since breakfast, and must have been sent for. He came in, with his whip in his hand, and passed up stairs. A moment after, I heard the street-door shut. He took no dinner; none of us sat down to dinner. About three o'clock the post came in; there were letters for Lily. One was in the handwriting of the man she had last spoken of. I carried them up to her. She took them in her hand; the child's eyes were too dim to read the outside. She held them a moment without attempting to break their seals, and then returned them to me, and said, in a nonchalant tone, "Throw them in my drawer." Mother followed me to the door, and whispered that Lily would not have her hair touched, nor be stirred in any way. She looked at me inquiringly, but spoke as if she were merely telling me an ordinary fact, and I received it as such; but I rushed away. But once (it was in Lily's own chamber) I came to my senses. I wrung my hands till they ached. I caught sight of Lily's little slippers on the floor, and I stared at them till I could see nothing but dizzy specks in the air.

The long day dragged to a close. At six o'clock, the servants huddled away the dinner, and laid the table for supper. Mother came down and poured the tea for us hurriedly. As she did so, I noticed on her finger the slender ring which Lily had always worn. The scene was the same as in the morning, except that candles were on the table. The windows were still open. The sea was as silent as it had been all day, and I saw the shimmering water roll backward and forward in the rays of light that streamed across it from the lighthouse on the opposite point. The sky had merely darkened; no moon nor stars were visible. Not a word was spoken, and mother soon went back to Lily. I took my seat in mother's easy chair, and watched the smoke from my father's cigar; its ashes fell on his clothes unheeded, and he moved it about in his mouth. As fast as one was consumed he lighted another, and I still watched him. There was a continual passing through the room, for it was midway between the kitchen and the hall, but my father never moved, nor turned his head toward the persons that came and went.

Late in the evening I went to see Lily. The lamp was on the floor, and it threw heavy shadows on the ceiling. Two women sat in one corner of the room. I knew them, but I did not speak. Mother was there; she looked pale and sorrowful. Lily was motionless; her hand was twisted in her hair, and she looked at the shadows on the wall. Her nightgown was open on her bosom—how marble white it was! How lovely! I pressed forward between mother and the bed, and looked at her with my face close to hers. She made no sign, and I passed out, and never saw Lily again. I went into the guest-chamber where I had slept the night before, slowly undressed, folded my clothes piece by piece, and went to sleep without the thought that Lily was dying.

A lamp shone in the room, and some one said, "Come, if you would see her." I sprang from the bed, and flew to the door. A long gentle sigh arrested me on the threshold. It was answered by the sea, which gathered itself up, and fell on the shore with a sharp wail. Lily died then. It was the same hour that we rushed to her door the night before.

My eyes fell on mother. She stood within the room, her hand raised as if to avert a blow; her eyes were wild and tearless. Her doom was spoken that night. The death-angel brushed against her as he bore Lily's spirit away.

They wrapped Lily in the muslin gown I had finished that morning, and buried her in a storm.

One of the women, whom I saw sitting in the corner of the room that night, brought me a heavy tress of Lily's hair. She would have spoken to me, but I waved my hand to her, and she turned away. For a long time afterward that woman interested me painfully. She had been alone with Lily several hours the night she died; for my mother, overcome with fatigue, had gone to her own room. This woman was the one who had called me in Lily's last moments; and I never ceased to ask myself, and to ponder over this question, "What did Lily say to her?" I never asked the woman, and I never shall now. But it is still a thought of mingled pain and satisfaction, that there lives one who might reveal the mystery of Lily's death.

I went to her grave yesterday, and pulled up some long yellow grass by the roots; I shall take it with me when I return.

—The "Professor" in *The Atlantic* is constantly, through himself or his friends, iterating and reiterating the claims of Boston to be considered the brain of these United States, or, as a second-hand bookseller in Nassau street described his little store upon his sign: "The moral centre of the intellectual world." Has Boston been so mute and inglorious, that her trumpeters must bray out her claims to honor so persistently? The whole world knows, or ought to know, that the *North American Review* is printed there, and so is *The Line of Battle Ship;* and that Burnham keeps a shop for the sale of old books there, and that the *Dial* died there for want of support. Can these things be, and the world not know of them? Of course not. Besides, Harvard College is there, with its large library, and its ingenious obstructions to its free use by the students. And then, there is Beacon street, and Mount Vernon street, and Bunker Hill Monument. With all these advantages, no wonder Boston is the brain it is, and that her citizens are so proud of her that they treat with their proverbial rudeness the unenlightened residents of the rest of the country. It is well for the residents of other cities to be civil and urbane. Bostonians must be Bostonians. Some people call it provincialism, but that only shows that they have no proper conception of the true function of a brain.

— Whoever walks through the streets of Japan, town or village, will be surprised to notice the number of books exposed for sale in almost every shop. On looking inside he will probably find one or more of the attendants, if otherwise disengaged, busily reading, or listening to something being read by one of the company. In walking through the outskirts of the town, it is not unlikely he will come suddenly on a knot of children, seated in a snug corner out of the sun, all intently engaged in looking through some story book or other they have just bought at a neighboring stall, and laughing right heartily at the comical pictures which adorn the narrative. The conviction is thus brought home to a man's mind that the Japanese are a reading people.

—*The Cincinnati Enquirer* of the 8th, is assured by a gentleman from New York, that Teresa Bagioli (Mrs. Sickles) is preparing for the stage, and will appear on the boards next Autumn. (?)

—The initiative Committee in this city for collecting funds in aid of the families of the soldiers called to fight in the cause of Italian independence, is composed for the present, of the following persons:

Prof. Vincenzo Botta, President, No. 31 West 37th street; Ottavio Fabericotti, Treasurer, merchant, No. 34 Beaver street; G. Albinola, merchant, No.—Murray street; Dr. Giovanni Ceccavini, physician, No. 57 Bleecker street; E. P. Tabbri, merchant, No. 66 Broadway; Gugliet-mo Gajani, lawyer, No. 43 Wall street; Michele Pastacaldi, merchant, No. 57 Pearl street; Vicenzo Squarza, merchant, No. 75 Fulton street.

NEW YORK MAY 28, 1859

Original Poetry.

THE HUMAN HEART.

BY N. G. SHEPHERD.

I.

By anguish wrung, with many cares oppressed,
Weak, erring, sinful, tempted, and betrayed,
Shaken by fears, borne on in wild unrest—
Longing for death, and yet of death afraid.

II.

How many untold crimes and dark deceits
Lark in its secret chambers, earth-defiled?
What skeletons of virtue—vain conceits—
Unhallowed lusts, with Christ's creed reconciled.

III.

What palsied trust, frail Faith in her decline—
What selfish aims—what foolish, fond desires,
And yet, what God-born love, and how divine
The heavenward flight to which its thought aspires

IV.

What patient, meek endurance has it shown—
What silent suffering, and what speechless grief—
To what sublime proportions has it grown,
Carved by Affliction, God's great sculptor-chief.

V.

Yes every form of evil and of good
Has known it, helped to shape its lot:
Christ-like forgiveness and the crime of blood—
Good born of good, and evil self-begot.

VI.

Peace! let it rest—it cannot long outbrave
Life's stormy sea, the adverse winds of fate;
Lifted, at last, on Death's great mountain-wave,
It stands in living light at Heaven's broad gate.

—Wallack's Theatre was the recipient of distinguished honors last Thursday week. In one of the private boxes were seated the well-known actress Mrs. John Wood, Agnes Robertson, W. Stuart, and the Honorable Daniel E. Sickles! It is refreshing to know that the honorable gentleman has at last recovered from his state of temporary insanity.

—Mr. T. Stewart has bought Powers' Greek Slave of Miss Coleman, of Cincinnati, and will place it in his dry goods store, to attract the slaves of Fashion. What a splendid model it will make, to try shawls and things on? Art is looking up. Why don't Douglas & Sherwood purchase "The Heart of the Andes?

—The Prince of Wales has ordered Miss Hosmer's spirited little statue representing "Puck on a Mushroom." Our gifted countrywoman will now be all the rage. Think of purchasing a picture painted by an artist patronized by a Prince!

—Mr. Stephen Massett, who has been visiting the Mammoth Cave, in company with Lord R. Grosvenor, is making quite a sensation in Louisville, in his "Song and Chit-chat of Travel." He will be in New York next week.

—GIFFORD'S Mansfield Mountain, on exhibition at the Academy, has been sold to a gentleman of this city, for $600.

—The receipts from the exhibition of Church's "Heart of the Andes"—now embalmed, and on its way to Europe—were over $3,000; and the artist has refused an offer of $15,000 for it.

—A Zouave, on stepping on board of a vessel at Marseilles, bound for the seat of war, was stopped by the Colonel of the regiment, who recognized, in the soldier's dress, a young girl, who had assumed the uniform in order not to be separated from her lover.

Dramatic Feuilleton.

The New Opera.

If you can bring your mind to comprehend music that makes Brignoli enthusiastic, and gives the Brightest and Best, the original and only Jacobs, Anna Maria, sole and only, "cold chills down the back," then you can have some idea of "Il Poliuto" at the first representation of which I, the Editor, Whiskers, A. M. (in what Fry calls all the provoking finery of opera toilet), and various other distinguished persons, including Piccolomini, Brignoli, and Amodio, assisted on Monday.

I am not going to bore you with anything critical, analytical, or any other cal, about this work. [Arn't you glad?]

I am going to say this, however, that it has, like the *Favorita*, passages which thrill you; passages which display genius; passages which make you say this man had the divine afflatus; the key to the inner recesses of the human soul. That key which neither Meyerbeer, nor Wagner, nor any other living master, except Verdi, will ever find if they live an hundred years.

The finale of the second act of the Poliuto, the duett in the third, and the march in the first, are magnificent. The rest of the opera is common-place. It is quite evident that some hands other than Donizetti's have been at work on the score. Muzio claims a Cavatina for Pic. in the first act. It is good for her voice, but not a bit like Donizetti. It is like what Brown, or Smith, or anybody could do.

The libretto bothered the dear public a good deal. Some of the words were changed; others omitted, and new lines added. The analysis of the plot given in the programme, helped the monster a little, but that is not exactly the plot of the *Poliuto*, but rather that of the *Martiri*, which works are essentially but not precisely the same.

I am going to let you find out the difference for yourself.

I see that the critics are all elaborate, not to say mysterious, in their articles. As nearly as I can make them out, and I am going through a course of study, in cyphers and hieroglyphics, the opera was a good opera, well sung, and successful.

I thought Brignoli was superb. The honors of the night belong to him, chiefly. Pic., however, was very fine. Amodio rather clumsy in a bad rôle.

The mis en scène might have been worse and better. There were our old vestal friends, in white muslin,* likewise, S. P. Q. R.; also Amodio, as a warrior on a car (he looked like a gentleman from Centre Market, in a section of a soft soap barrel); further, we had a real brass band on the stage, which I like; and altogether, Strakosch must have spent as much as—well, say any fabulous amount, five hundred dollars (if there is so much money in the world), and verily he will have his reward.

En avant! Strakosch. The path of glory is strewed with town lots and Chemical Bank notes.

To-day, there's to be a Matinée, and on Monday, Pic. makes her adieux, and intends to orate to the public in English.

That's a good look-out for some fun.

There will be a Matinée on Tuesday, and the début on Wednesday of Cortesi in Sappho, which will be given on Friday, of course.

The season will go on till nearly the end of June.

Mme. de Wilhorst has made her début (the daily papers say successfully) in Oratorio, for the benefit of the "Young Men's Christian Association." Was this by way of penance to the memory of the young men in whose manly breasts she has excited anything but a Christian frame of mind?

Too Gross.

The most stupid canard of the season was that invented by the *Leader* about Pic. having been presented with a carriage and horses by Whiskers. Curiously enough, that youth was the only person in town that believed it, and has quite worn out a copy of our cotemporary by showing it in mysterious corners to sympathizing friends.

A. M. thinks his ma ought to spank him and put him to bed. Et moi aussi.

About Brignoli.

I have not been behind other people in stirring up Brignoli. In fact I have been after him with the sharpest kind of a stick. But I think that even a tenor ought to have fair play. The *Evening Post* don't agree with me. In Tuesday's issue it states that "Mr. Squires took the tenor part in *La Traviata* in consequence of the indisposition of Brignoli. The lazy tenor was out riding an hour before the curtain rose!" Now the *Post*, if so well informed as to the busy B.'s movements, ought to know the fact that his voice was so far fatigued by frequent rehearsals of the new opera that the manager thought it prudent to save it for the more important effort of Wednesday, so that Brignoli had nothing to do with the matter. I quite agree with the *Post* when it says that if Squires had a voice "he might become a popular tenor."

Just Out.

A new edition of the works of Mr. Dion Bourcicault, in duodecimo, gilt edges, bound in linen cambric, with lace corners, appeared on Monday. Only one copy of this edition will be issued.

Mrs. Thomas Barry and Mme. Colson have simultaneously made their debuts in *La Mére et Sa Fille.*

Facilis descensus Averni.

The dissolute and abandoned course of life pursued by Mr. J—n B—gham and C—les W—l—ot culminated on last Tuesday; when, in company with two convicted felons, they went to the Penitentiary, dined in the Alms House, and spoke on terms of equality with some Aldermen.

What an awful evidence of the evil tendencies of the play house! Where's Bellows?

Just Imported.

I was doing better" on last Monday, so I didn't go to see Captain Price and Miss Lucette.

I put them in the order in which the Captain places them.

He evidently belongs to the "dog-and-I-and-father" school.

I hear, however, that he made his début before Mr. BROUGH and a number of other persons connected with the British army and the peerage.

Louis the Nineteenth (I have found a Bourbon) says that when the Metropolitan curtain rose to unfold the glories of Captain Price to an admiring multitude, that the multitude wasn't there. Even the free list didn't come.

The free list was looking at the National Guard, or some Guard or other producing blue lights in Broadway.

But the free list came for the second piece—came in a solid phalanx, like the Light Brigade at Bunker Hill (Balaklava was it, well it's all the same—begun with B, I knew).

The first piece was the elegant little comedy, Delicate Ground, in which Miss Lucette was Madame (you see I am more polite than the Captain), and her attendant Mars, Monsieur. The second piece was the Captain's magnum opus, All's Fair in Love or War.

It is one of the great works of the period. Equal to the new bell-tower in the Park or Appleton's Cyclopædia.

There is a young lady in a French camp. The young lady is loved by a non-commissioned officer (that's Captain Price) and by the Colonel of the Regiment. The Colonel, like all field-officers, is the most absurdly opinionated person in the world, and makes, what Mr. George Christy calls "difficults" for the Corporal. In the end we see the triumph of the Corporal, who leads the lady to the altar, with the regiment in line, open order, officers and colors to the front, full salute for a General of Division.

That's what I call a *nice* play, remarks Anna Maria, and the Pearl of

*Mem. from an antique MS. in the British Museum, supposed to have been written by a Roman Priest, to a friend in the Provinces. The right of translation reserved.
Since these Zouaves of that infernal Tenth Legion returned from Carthage, we have run short of Vestals.
Please send over by return mail, 50, warranted, for the Feast of Saturn.

P. S. We'll find the muslin.

Manhattan was, as unusual, right.

Plays are literary exotics. They are only good in the exact ratio of their absurdity, and their contrariety to everything in life. Now in this every-day world the lady would never have so much as looked at the noncom., or if she had, the Colonel would have simply sent him to Kamschatka, or somewhere else, without the slightest hesitation.

As to the acting of the new stars, the least said, etc.—the proverb's somewhat musty. The Captain, like his distinguished relative, "the noble lord at the head of her Majesty's government," has appealed to the country, gone to Boston, where I really hope they'll like him. He reminds one a good deal of the distinguished amateur, who, with a mirror and a comb, played in the great work at the Academy the other day. His voice has the same exquisite softness, his manner the same high-toned (127th street) elegance; in fact he is a leaf torn out of the same page; a drop from the same bucket.

The lady is a sunny blonde, suggestive of those British: beauties whom you see on the landing-stages as you take your penny worth of Father Thames, or who parade in all the glory of flats and parasols by Albion's chalky cliffs at Dover, or breathe the South Downy breezes of Brighton, or await their attendant swells as the Saturday night boat steams into the harbor of Margate.

Good to look upon is ye English girl. Fair are her locks, blue are her eyes, snowy her hands, saith my old friend Byron, who knew.

Fair is this particular Saxon, la Lucette. Young to the stage I should judge, but still easy and unaffected. With a good singing voice, too, a clear, full, vibrating mezzo-soprano; a thoroughly English voice trained in the English manner. Miss Lucette knows how to sing very well now. In a year or two she will be very fine. I hope she will come back to the metropolis next season. She's too good for Chicago or Orange county. As for the Captain, let him have a dash at the Austrians. If he only acts at them one night, the war will be ended the next day.

The audiences were very select, including the cream of the free list and artists from the provinces. The public didn't come.

What next at the Metropolitan I don't know.

There are plenty of magnificent creatures in town dying to astonish the public, so we may have some of them next week.

Theatre Francais.

Sen had a fine benefit on Saturday. The play was Le Vicomte de Latourières. I went, but it was so awfully hot that I couldn't stay. I'm willing to suffer a good deal for art, but the bouquet of the perspiring Gaul is too much.

Bertrand's benefit to-night.

Trifles.

A Midsummer Night's Dream has been altogether a failure at Laura Keene's. At first it failed to comply with certain artistic conditions required by the promises of the Director, and at the same time was hardly intelligible to the general public. Even the annotations of Miss Laura Keene, Mr. Genio C. Scott, and Mr. Richard Grant White, failed to illuminate the vulgar mind. The consequence was a succés de curiosité, as I predicted some weeks ago. Amongst other out and injured people through Miss Keene's (vide *Daily News*) sortie heavenward, was that eminent naturalized Prussic acid American, Citizen Graumann, who furnished the sunlight, moon's rays, and other celestial things, all for ten dollars, which, according to a document addressed to Miss Laura Keene, she has neglected or declined to pay. The awful majesty of the law represented by Mr. Justice Dusenbery was to settle the affair yesterday. It is shocking to think of people who don't pay tailors and other terrestrial bodies, but the idea of refusing to settle for your sun, moon, and stars, and "spacious firmament on high" (Watts), why, it's absolutely un-Christianlike. I have a horrid suspicion that, if they go to work in this way at the secrets of the Coulisses, we shall have some awful disclosures. Who knows whether Puck paid for his legs, or that Titania is square with Dibblee, or that Bottom has anted for those Saddle Rocks and Bass's Pales for the long wait between the acts?

Ponder, my masters, before you stir up that dangerous wild fowl, the law. Miss Laura Keene, however, is quite used to it. Like Burton, she would die without her summonses, citations, answers, replications, and demurrers. To her eyes the words "In re Brown v. Jones," are like the letters from the Koran which flashed on the scimetar of the faithful.

Chacun (not Charles, H. C. M.'s Vice Consul), à son goût!

Miss Keene has announced a play by Palgrave Simpson, called "The World and the Stage." It is a rechauffée of the various plays which have been written to show that actresses are all as chaste as Diana, and as pure as real Orange county milk. They have all suffered, however, at the hands of a wicked and scandalous world. In England, the injured innocent ones have been Mistress Ellen Gwynn, sometime attached to the Cabinet of Charles the Second; Mistress Margaret Woffington, Kitty Clive, Bracegridle, and Jordan, and Madame Vestris. Literature has come forward, as they say in the theatre bills, "in the handsomest manner" to the defence of these much abused divinities. Simpson, like his namesake of Israeltish faith, has gathered all the old clothes of the other writers together, and made of them a Joseph's coat, perhaps a Mrs. Potiphar's jupon would be nearer the mark, for Miss Amy Sedgwick. Miss Keene will produce it under the special patronage of Doctor B——.

The Misses Gougenheim (shockingly ugly name) commence their Summer season here on 4th of June.

Mr. Jefferson will have a Summer season at the Theatre Francais. He is engaged for next year by Mr. Stuart, for the new theatre up town.

"How much," asks the *Daily News*, "do we not owe to Italy !" and then the rapt youth goes on in this terrible way:

"Beautiful land—cradle of modern civilization—mother and nurse of redeemed literature, of the sciences, and the fine arts Christendom is deeply thy debtor. When the captive Athenians chanted the dramas of Euripides in the quarries of Syracuse, the Muse achieved for them that ransom which gold could not purchase. And thy poetry and music alone should inspire Europe to cut in twain the chains wherewith thou art bound, and set free thy beautiful form again."

Very sweet, of course. But how much does Italy owe to other people? And why leave out the Maccaroni, the best of all the institutions of the land of song?

PERSONNE.

NEW YORK JUNE 4, 1859

Written for the NEW-YORK SATURDAY PRESS.

JAPAN AS SEEN BY A KENTUCKIAN.

BY F. H. B., U.S.N.

On the 13th of May, 185-, after a run of six days from Ousima, the U. S. ship *Vincennes* anchored in the harbor of Simoda. The pilot who, according to the port regulations, should have directed us to the anchorage, soon after came alongside with an excuse for his neglect, and a demand for a fee. His claim had scarcely been satisfied when we were boarded by numerous Japanese officers who desired to learn the object of our visit. Their boats were gaily decorated with flags and banners, on which were painted the armorial bearings of the Prince of Idzu, and were well supplied with weapons of various and singular shapes. After receiving satisfactory answers to their questions, they rambled over the vessel, taking notes and making sketches of the different articles that excited their curiosity or attracted their attention. They remained with us until nightfall, and only took their leave when they had accurately measured the length, breadth, and depth of the ship, and counted and examined every gun in our battery.

On the 14th we had a gale from the N. N. W., and could not leave the vessel, the sea running too high to admit of our landing.

On the next day the wind had in a great measure abated, and as many of us as were not on duty we seized the opportunity of a visit to the shore. A short pull brought us to the landing place, and we were with a people whose exclusive policy had long rendered their country a kind of terra incognita to the civilized world. The devastations of an earthquake which had lately visited the island were plainly visible. On every side we saw where houses had been thrown down or washed away. From the Goyoski, or police station near the landing place, we strolled leisurely up the road towards the town, followed by a large concourse of people, who stared at us as though we were some strange *lusi naturæ* escaped from a travelling museum.

We found the town unlike any other we had ever seen. Its name

Simoda, signifying in the Japanese language "the lower field," is very expressive of its situation. It is bounded on the East and West by mountainous hills; the sea washes its Southern limits, while from the Northern extremity a pleasant valley, that follows the windings of the Inodza-gawa, extends as far as the eye can reach. The town is compactly built, and contains about 7,000 inhabitants. The streets do not exceed fifteen feet in width, and cross at right angles. The houses are generally but one story high, and are built of pine or fir, plastered on the outside with lime and clay. They are occasionally tiled, but are most frequently thatched with a species of Arundo, which grows on the uncultivated lands near the sea. It is in the interior arrangement of the houses that the traveller observes the greatest departure from the European styles. Sliding partitions covered with oiled paper, separate the rooms, which may be enlarged or diminished at the pleasure of the occupants. Straw mats of uniform thickness cover the floors, and serve as a substitute for chairs, which are never used by the Japanese. A few folding screens ornamented with paintings of cities, mountains, men, and animals, with lacquered cabinets and stands, dishes and drinking vessels, and in the centre of the room a box containing burning charcoal and a spittoon for those who smoke, constitutes nearly all the furniture. The males and females are not separated as in China, but occupy indiscriminately the same apartments and eat from the same table. Over "the place of honor" in the principal room of every house is a small gilded temple containing the household gods; and, standing near it, the "ancestral tablet," a slab of lacquered wood, on which are inscribed in gilded characters the names of the different members of the family who have gone to their long homes.

In the city and its vicinity there are numerous temples dedicated to the worship of the Japanese divinities. In the location of their religious houses, the people have exhibited much taste. Groves of funereal cypress and fir trees, and time-mouldered monuments and gravestones, mark their position. The adjacent grounds are decorated in the highest style of Japanese art. Miniature lakes and waterfalls are distributed through the gardens, and every artificial combination of nature is used to enhance the beauty of the place.

In the outskirts of the city we visited the Dai-an-zhi, or Great Quiet Monastery, located on a steep hill-side. A long flight of steps hewn from the solid rock, and winding among monuments and graves, led to the main entrance, where we were received by an inquisitive bondze, who asked innumerable questions, but did not object to our entering and examining the building. A large bell hung immediately in front of the door, and was used to attract the attention of the god, when his good offices were solicited by his pious worshippers. The interior of the temple presented an appearance of neatness and cleanliness which, judging from its exterior, we had not expected to find. Several gilded idols, the size of life, were seated on a platform or dais, at the farthest extremity of the room. The altar, which was carved and profusely gilded, was covered with musical instruments and copper and bronze vases and braziers. Shelves and boxes containing books, were ranged around the sides of the room at intervals of six or eight feet, and oiled paper lanterns were suspended from the roof. We could have remained here hours examining the strange objects by which we were surrounded, but an overpowering smell of burning jossticks and perfumes compelled us to beat a hasty retreat.

There are other larger and finer temples in the city that are filled with idols, and pictures, and priests, and all the gorgeous furniture of Japanese idolatry. Every two or three hundred yards one sees the evidences of idol worship. Temples, shrines, and altars, meet the eye on every side. Stone or wooden images of the principal gods are as frequently found in the centre of a forest, or on the summit of a high mountain, as in the most crowded thoroughfares. Porcelain cups filled with tea, or saki, and bunches of flowers and joss-sticks, the propitiatory offering of some devout worshipper, are tastefully arranged in front of all the shrines.

On the East side of the bay we visited a very small Buddhist temple, standing a few paces from the road side, in a grove of magnificent firs. A fine-looking old bondze, the sole tenant of the place, led us through the building, and exhibited all that was worthy of being seen. In the rear of the temple we found a fine garden, and a beautiful fish-pond, with banks shaded by the *Camellia Japonica*, which here grows in rich luxuriance on every hill side. The priest gave us pipes and tobacco, and seating ourselves under the trees, we smoked and watched the gold and silver fishes sporting in the clear water at our feet. The garden was one mass of bloom. The plants were so completely covered with flowers that the foliage could scarcely be seen. Arborvitæ and pine trees were cut and trained into the most fanciful shapes, showing a skill in the Topiarian art never reached in Europe. Some of them resembled houses, with doors, windows, and steps, formed of the boughs and foliage; others took the forms of animals. Everything was in complete order and in excellent taste, and here, in an air redolent with the finest perfumes, and with delighted eyes gazing on nature in her gayest dress, this old man spends his days, shut out from the great noisy world, but living in a quiet little world of his own, that furnishes every sense with enjoyment. The garden was an earthly paradise, an Eden of happiness, and we only wondered that the priest had no companion to share its pleasures.

The Japanese religion promotes a love for all that is sublime and beautiful in nature. Nearly every temple has its garden and artificial scenery. The poorest altar is decorated with flowers. The love for the beautiful is carried even beyond death, and a common offering at the graves of relatives and friends, is a bunch of flowers, which, when withered, is carefully renewed.

The scenery about Simoda is of a quiet, negative kind of beauty, that does not at first sight give much pleasure. Steep hills shut out the view to the East and West, and the angular lines of the fan-shaped bay present little that is interesting in the South. But far away over the rice-fields that skirt the Northern boundaries of the city, a stone causeway extends its winding length through pleasant valleys and along the little river that empties itself into the bay. Following its irregular course, we pass through villages embowered in groves of bamboo, and tall forest-trees that shade the quiet streets and huckster's stalls, spread out beneath the sheltering boughs. Scantily-clothed fishermen, with heads protected from the sun by broad-brimmed bamboo hats, are seen turning the stones in the stream searching for shrimps, or reclining on the grassy banks lazily watching their floats as they move with the current, or rest quietly on the surface of the deep pools. On the neighboring hill-tops are the quaint shrines and altars erected by the zealous devotee for the honor and worship of his numberless gods. Fields of rice waving in the breeze like the water in the bay, show that the rich harvests of Japan yield an abundant return for the husbandman's labor.

In another direction an object of a different kind and degree of beauty, meets the gaze, its grandeur and majesty contrasting actively with the quiet, passive beauty of the valley scenery. Fusi Yama, 13,000 feet higher than the level of the sea, rears its snow-capped summit high above the clouds that float about its storm-beaten sides and base. Drifts of snow that fill the ravines and diverge in long lines from its highest point, glitter in the bright sunlight like burnished silver. A thick haze envelopes the base, so that only the summit is seen away up in the heavens, its splendor undimmed by a single cloud. Fusi Yama is visible at a distance of 120 miles from the coast, and when first seen looks like a fleecy cloud floating nearly overhead.

In color, in dress, and in manners, the Japanese differed from every people we had ever seen. They are somewhat shorter than Europeans but are stout and well-formed. Their color, a dark yellow, tinged with brown, is clear and bright, and their faces are generally open and expressive. The men wear no beard, and shave the crown of the head, combing the long hair from the neck and temples to the back of the forehead, where it is confined in a single lock. They use pomatum very freely, and take great pride in keeping their fine black hair neat and even. With the exception of the bondzes, who shave their heads, all classes cut their hair after the same fashion. The dress of the men is very simple. It consists of a loose robe with wide sleeves, and is fastened at the waist by a girdle. A cloak with sleeves, having the arms of the wearer embroidered on the breast, back, and shoulders, is usually worn over the long gown. On State occasions wide pantaloons sewn together within a few inches of the knee, are also worn. The Japanese wear hats only in bad weather or while travelling. Their faces are protected from the sun by their fans, an article of dress without which a Japanese of the better class never goes abroad. Straw sandals, such as are worn in Loo Choo, are used as a substitute for shoes.

During the Summer months the servants and laborers are very scantily clothed. We frequently saw porters and field-hands with no other covering than a cotton cloth two or three inches wide fastened about the loins.

The women generally have good features, black eyes, and, when unmarried, very pretty teeth. After marriage they are compelled to blacken their teeth, so that they may be readily distinguished from those who are still in a state of single blessedness. When they are but little exposed to the sun, their complexion is light and fresh, and their cheeks rosy. Their dress is graceful and easy, fitting more closely to the person than that worn by the men. It is loose to the waist, where it is confined by a broad girdle, with the end spread out and hanging down. From the waist to the feet it fits close and somewhat impedes their motions, so that they are obliged to take very short steps. We frequently saw ladies of rank with girdles not less than fifteen inches wide. As an additional indication of their condition, the married women have their girdles knotted in front; those of the unmarried females are fastened behind. Their manner of dressing the hair is very pretty; it is combed to the top of the head and fastened in a loose knot with two or three folds of red parti-colored crape, and is sometimes further decorated with silver pins joined by a miniature chain, which falls in festoons over the hair, giving a jaunty piquant air to the wearer, that is very pleasing.

Many bad customs common to more civilized countries have been introduced here, and the Japanese ladies, like those of Europe and America, endeavor to improve their really handsome faces with paints and cosmetics.

Crows and hawks infest the streets and fill the air with their hoarse cawings and discordant screams. Excellent scavengers are these same noisy birds, and to their selfish care must be attributed the cleanly appearance of the narrow thoroughfares.

Dogs, too, are congregated together in such numbers as to rival the famed canine gatherings of Constantinople. The latter city, however, can urge a better claim for the maintenance of her dogs than can Simoda. The reason which is here assigned for the kind treatment and rapid increase of the miserable curs that "make the night hideous with their howls," is, to say the least, a strange one. Once upon a time, so runs the legend, there lived and reigned in Japan an emperor who, unfortunately for his people, was born under the sign of the dog, that corresponds to—I do not know which of the twelve signs of our zodiac. This wise emperor, to propitiate the gods, or for some other equally sensible reason, promulgated throughout the land an edict directing and enforcing the maintenance and protection of all the curs then living within his dominions, and since his time they have grown in numbers and insolence until they may safely be pronounced the greatest pests that infest the country.

The cats also, scarcely less numerous than the dogs, deserve a notice here. To account for their numbers, Japanese history furnishes no legend. Possibly, like our cats, they have nine lives, and thus their longevity makes amends for their slow propagation. Their resemblance may be further traced in their various sizes and colors, and mousing propensities. They differ however, in one remarkable peculiarity: their tails are less useful than ornamental, for —mirabile dictu! they are not more than two or three inches in length, are in form like a corkscrew—and have a veritable twist from the root to the outer extremity.

In the numerous private houses which we visited, we were hospitably received and kindly treated. The few Loo Chooan words with which I was acquainted, enabled me to make known my most simple wants, and with the aid of the universal language of signs, I managed to sustain a conversation in a strange kind of jargon, about as remarkable for its obscurity as for being intelligible. In many of the houses we were presented with tea and tobacco and cakes. The Japanese are inveterate smokers, and their pipes and tobacco pouches, constantly worn in their girdles, form a necessary portion of their dress. The metal bowl of their pipes is not more than half the size of a thimble, but as it is frequently filled, they manage to consume great quantities of tobacco. When they entertain their friends, the pipes are invariably produced, and after the salutations have been exchanged, they sit together upon the mats and blow a friendly cloud. Their tobacco is of excellent quality, mild, and finely flavored, and is cultivated throughout the whole empire.

While visiting the Japanese in their houses, we had frequent opportunities to examine their beautiful swords, which they always refused to unsheath in the streets. These weapons are admirably tempered, and would compare favorably with the famed blades of Toledo and Damascus. From guard to point they are slightly curved, and are broad, heavy, and highly polished. The hilts are covered with shagrein, and are ornamented with gold and silver, and copper amulets, in the combination called *syakfdo*. My own sword, a plain cut-and-thrust English blade, with regulation—hilt and scabbard, was frequently examined by the Japanese. It was of an excellent temper, thin, and very flexible, while their blades were thick and would not bend. At my request they went through the sword exercise, handling their weapons with great skill and dexterity. Their postures were easy and graceful, and their thrusts, feints, and guards, made with astonishing rapidity and force. The Japanese sword is a badge of rank, and is only worn by certain privileged classes. Every gentleman, and soldiers generally, are entitled to carry two swords of unequal lengths. The short sword is the instrument with which they perform the *Harri-Karri*, "happy dispatch," or, in still plainer English, bellyripping. In this form of suicide, they are taught from earliest infancy consists the happiest and best mode of ending life's cares and ills. "To be or not to be," is a question of moral philosophy frequently agitated in Japan.

In our intercourse with the women we found them friendly and sociable. They evinced none of the shyness and timidity which characterized the women of Loo Choo. Indeed they were invariably kind and polite, and appeared gratified when we noticed or spoke to them. During our stay in Simoda, I made several pleasant acquaintances among the fair sex. One of these, a lively and very pretty damsel, never failed to welcome me in the European fashion, extending her hand when we met, and showing her pretty teeth, which were not disfigured with the black stain used by the married females. My regulation-buttons were in her eyes the most desirable of earthly treasures, and I established myself in her good graces at the expense of two or three of these glittering ornaments which I cut from my coat. After so valuable a present we became excellent friends, and seated upon the clean mats of her apartment, contrived to spend many pleasant hours together.

The Japanese cannot be sufficiently commended for their politeness. Even the poorest peasant had their words of greeting when we met, and their salutation, "*Ohio*," was heard at every corner, and in every crowd. They soon learned that with us Ohio had a different signification, and after a while answered our hail of Kentucky with equal readiness and good humor. They pay great deference to old age, and in their private intercourse are even more observant of the conventionalities of society than we.

Directly after the arrival of the *Vincennes*, the Japanese opened a bazaar in a large frame building near the central portion of the city, and here we spent the greatest part of our time while on shore. At this bazaar we saw specimens of Japanese manufactures collected from every part of the empire. Tier above tier, and pile above pile of beautiful articles, that might have decorated a palace, were ranged in rich profusion throughout the whole building. The wares so temptingly displayed were miracles of art; rich silks, splendid boxes, trays, tables, writing-desks, and drinking cups, the most beautiful combinations of genius and mechanism; objects both useful and ornamental, were offered for sale. Silks wrought by the fingers of high-born criminals; the coarser fabrics of the Northern islands; grotesque images from the toy-shops; paper umbrellas, and handkerchiefs, and silk fans; wares of the most dissimilar kinds and shapes, were spread out to our view. The salesmen were anxious to sell their goods, and recommended them to every passer-by.

All business was transacted in conformity with a prescribed system. A small room separated from the main building was covered with mats, and here were seated the officers who received our money and marked our purchases. The salesmen merely showing us the goods and telling their prices. When we decided on purchasing an article, they wrapped it in a paper, placed it in a box, and carried it to the officers; here they would fall upon their knees and describe the circumstances of the sale, when we would make our payments and be at liberty to remove our purchases. If, after making a purchase, we were entitled to any change, we received payment in foreign coin, or if this could not be procured we were obliged to take some article of equal value with the sum we required. The Japanese invariably refused to give their coin in exchange for ours. We found their porcelain much finer than that manufactured by the Chinese. It is very white and clear, and is ornamented with gold and silver raised-work, and landscapes, and views, in brilliant enamel. I bought here several colored prints, illustrative of Japanese scenery, and manners, and customs. The Japanese drawings exhibit more genius and a greater attention to nature, than are ever seen in the works of the Chinese artists, who show an utter disregard for all rules of proportion and perspective. The representations of the human figure were rather grotesque and misshapen, though they served to give an idea of Japanese features and costume. The landscapes were tolerably well executed, but of course would not bear comparison with the works of more civilized countries.

On the occasion of a ceremonial visit by the Commodore to the Governor of Simoda, we had an exhibition of Japanese hospitality that was novel and pleasing. The procession of officers, sailors, and marines, that accompanied the Commodore, were well armed and presented a very military appearance. The Commodore and his officers were received in a room of the building occupied as a bazaar. The walls were festooned with curtains on which were painted the armorial bearings of the Governor. The courtyard and entrance way were lined with Japanese soldiers bearing pikes and swords to keep back the people who had gathered around in great numbers, attracted by our glittering uniforms and the martial strains of Yankee-doodle as performed on the drum and fife by the infantile musicians of our marine guard. The Governor was a modern Chesterfield, and a model for the imitation of his dependants, so that the hall of audience, as the apartment had been called, was the scene of numerous bowing and bending officers, each vieing with the other in the width of his grin and in the depth of his bow. The Governor was a handsome man, about the middle height, with fine features and form. He is of the blood royal, and in addition to his title of Governor holds the rank of Prince of Idzu. After the exchange of salutations the Japanese offered refreshments of tea, cakes, boiled lobsters, candied sugar, seaweed, rice, snake soup, sweetmeats of various kinds, saki, &c. They played the part of hosts to admiration, helping us bountifully to the different viands spread upon the tables, and frequently replenishing our tiny cups with the finest saki, a liquor distilled from rice. Instead of deprecating their food, as is the custom in many countries, they were continually vaunting its good qualities and recommending it as palatable and easily digested. At the risk of offending our entertainers, I refused several of the dishes offered me, as I had not the most remote conception of what substance, whether fish, flesh, or fowl, they were composed; some of them bore a striking resemblance to boiled shark, and no doubt whatever existed as to the identity of the snakes. While we were feasting with the Japanese officers, the sailors and marines were plentifully supplied with food in the court. Our hosts were kind and attentive, but when any subject was brought forward which they did not care to discuss, they contrived to change the conversation, either indirectly, or by abruptly asking some irrelevant question.

On the 26th, the Governor, with a large retinue of officers and servants, visited the Commodore on board the *Vincennes*, and was received with a salute from our great guns.

Among the strangest of the strange sights presented in Simoda to the eyes of the traveller, are the public bath houses. In one of these houses we saw men, women, and children, mingle indiscriminately in the water. Females of nearly every age, from sixteen to sixty, perfectly naked and without shame, for it was a familiar custom, and common to the whole country, plunged into a large tank of warm water, already crowded with men, and leisurely proceeded in their work of cleaning. I counted on one occasion no less than fourteen naked girls, between the ages of sixteen and twenty, washing themselves before as many men. But little notice was taken of my presence, and they continued their occupation without any attempt at concealment. My astonishment was exhibited in my countenance and uplifted hands, and drew from the laughing girls a few comments which I did not understand, but in a moment they were again polishing their shapely limbs, already clean and white, as though I were not an amazed and admiring spectator. It was indeed a strange sight! Beautiful girls that might fill a Mohammedan's heaven, or his harem, were grouped together about the room; some were removing their clothing preparatory to taking a plunge into the tepid water; others were seated upon the stone floor, before small tubs, bathing their symmetrical limbs, as faultless in their proportions as the voluptuous roundings of the Grecian Venus. What a study for a sculptor! What a lounging place for a libertine! I entered the bathhouse expecting to be astonished, but the scenes I witnessed there beggar description, and I came away fully satisfied that bathing, however necessary it may be, as practised by the Japanese, is not at all conducive to morality.

The habit of bathing in public, is not confined to the poorer classes. On more than one occasion I met at this place, a lively, pretty girl, the daughter of a wealthy shop-keeper, and she mingled with the others apparently without derogating from her superior position and dignity.

Large scars disfigured the bodies of some of the men, and a few among the women exhibited the same unsightly seams. They were produced by the Moxa, a caustic in general use throughout Japan as a cure for nearly every disease.

At 10.40 on the morning of the 28th, I sailed in company with the launch, bound to Hakodadi, in Matsmai. At sunset Simoda was no longer in sight, and the launch was barely visible coasting along the distant shores of the island.

Original Poetry.

THE LOST HEART.

BY HORATIO ALGER, JR.

One golden Summer day,
Along the forest-way
Young Colin passed with blithesome steps alert.

His locks with careless grace
Rimmed round his handsome face
And drifted outward on the airy surge.

So blithe of heart was he,
He hummed a melody,
And all the birds were hushed to hear him sing.

Across his shoulders flung,
His bow and baldric hung:
So, in true huntsman's guise, he threads the wood.

The sun mounts up the sky,
The air moves sluggishly,
And reeks with Summer-heat in every pore.

His limbs begin to tire,
Slumbers his youthful fire,
He sinks upon a violet-bed to rest.

The soft winds go and come,
With mild susurrons hum,
And ope for him the ivory gate of dreams.

Beneath the forest-shade,
There trips a woodland-maid
And marks with startled eye the sleeping youth.

At first she thought to fly,
Then timid, drawing nigh,
She gazed in wonder on his fair young face.

Now swiftly stooping down,
Upon his locks so brown
She lightly pressed her lips, and blushing fled.

When Colin woke from sleep,
From slumber calm and deep,
He felt—he knew not how—his heart had flown.

And so with anxious care
He wandered here and there,
But could not find his lost heart anywhere.

Then he with air distraught,
And brow of anxious thought,
Went out into the world beyond the wood.

Of each that passed him by,
He queried anxiously,
"I prithee, hast thou seen a heart astray?"

Some stared and hurried on,
While others said in scorn,
"Your heart has gone in search of your lost wits."

The day is wearing fast:
Young Colin comes at last
To where a cottage stands embowered in trees.

He looks within, and there
He sees a maiden fair,
Who sings low songs the while she plies her wheel.

"I prithee, maiden bright,"
She turns as quick as light,
And straight a warm flush crimsons all her face.

She, much abashed, looks down,
For on his locks so brown
She seems to see the marks her lips have made.

Whereby she stands confest:
What need to tell the rest?
He said: "I think, fair maid, you have my heart;

"Nay, do not give it back,
I shall not feel the lack,
If thou wilt give to me thine own therefor."

—The Columbia College Commencement will take place on Tuesday next, at 10 A. M., at Niblo's; the annual examination of the classes will begin on Monday at 9½ A. M.

Invocation to the Summer Rain.

BY W. C. BENNETT.

O, gentle, gentle Summer rain,
Let not the silver lily pine,
The drooping lily pine in vain
To feel that dewy touch of thine—
To drink thy freshness once again,
O, gentle, gentle Summer rain.

In heat, the landscape quivering lies,
The cattle pant beneath the tree;
Through parching air and purple skies
The earth looks up in vain for thee:
For thee, for thee, it looks in vain,
O, gentle, gentle Summer rain.

Come thou, and brim the meadow streams,
And soften all the hills with mist;
O, falling dew, from burning dreams
By thee shall herb and flower be kissed:
And earth shall bless thee yet again,
O, gentle, gentle Summer rain.

Dramatic Feuilleton.

EXTRA
DE LA RUE.

Correspondence.

A. M.

Mon cher Rédacteur:

I beg you will *particularly* oblige me by making that *horrid* "PERSONNE" stop making me say things in THE SATURDAY PRESS, which I think, and ma thinks, is the best paper *in the world [*Beauteous Being! how in thy character are blended youth, taste and genius.—ED.], but pa says the men in the bank don't see it—whatever he means, *I* don't know. Well, where was I? Oh, yes! I know, about "PERSONNE.' Ma thinks he is just making fun of me. I would just like to catch him at it. But ma says that you can stop him, because you are the Head One, and you can tell the printers not to put in what he writes, and Charles Henry—that's the young man pa just got into the bank, and he's been to Paris,—he says that it ought to be like it here, and when there is anything in the paper about a person in society, they can just take up the editors and all the writers, and send them to a convent, or some place where they work with a ball and chain round their necks, or somewhere. And Charles Henry (oh, he is so delightful), he says it ought to be the same here, and I think so, too, don't you? Now I have got almost to the end of my sheet, and have not told you what I wanted to. But, oh! if you won't take and put it in your paper, I'll tell you something that PERSONNE nor none of those men know, because Charles Henry says that literary people ain't asked out anywhere of any consequence. Well, it's about Miss T——n that was, and the Countess Blank she is now. Don't you know she was maid of honor—no, dame d'honneur, that's it—to the Empress, and was the handsomest of all of them, so they say; and her picture is in the one that what's his name—something about Winter—painted. Well, she is going to sing at the Academy in the Puritani, for the thing they are going to have for the French, or the Austrians, or somebody that's going to war, or been, or something. And it's going to be real nice, and all the people in society are in it, and the men that write for the papers ain't to have *anything* to do with it. How will Mr. PERSONNE like *that,* I'd *like* to know?

Now I must stop, because here comes that awful Manzocchi, and he asks two dollars a lesson, and Ma says I can't do anything in music, because I talk all the time, and don't get the money's worth. And I guess that's all. And you won't forget about PERSONNE, will you? Please not; that's a dear.

Votre bien dévouée,
Tout-á-vous,
1001 Fifth Avenue, ANNA MARIA.
Thursday.

P. S.—Oh, I forgot! It's about the man he calls WHISKERS I wanted to tell you. They torment him to death, and it isn't right—keep putting him in the *Leader*, which C. H. says, only think, is published in the Sixth Ward by somebody who's done something awful and been made an Alderman for it. I didn't say he ought to be what ma does to the children, because it ain't pretty. And I think it's *a sin and a shame* to take and go and make fun of him. Charles Henry says that all the men at the Club say that *something* ought to be done about it, and so it ought. I am done now.

Forever and ever, A. M.

P. P. S.—Oh, there's something else! You're not to allow PERSONNE to talk about me having cold chills down my back. Ma says it isn't proper for young ladies to have them. Always,
A. M.

THE IVY GREEN,
May the 31st.

Mr. Editor.

I never see your paper in the Bowery, but a man that works in the Ware-house says that you say that the Young Men's Democratic Club is giving concerts into the Academy with them Italians and Dutchmen. Now, I just tell you it aint so. The Club won't go back on the boys that way. It will always sustain the Administration of James Buchanan, which has nothing to do with no kind of music nor harmony. I want you to put this in your paper, because some of the boys say they wont pay red cent (it's ten per cent. on men in the Custom House) to the Club if it is going to buy maccaroni for yellow-skinned loafers.

Yours, respectfully,
J. SMITH, Junior.

NEW YORK, May 31.

Sir:

I beg you will make, on my authority, a formal contradiction of the statement in one of your recent issues, to the effect that the Metropolitan Musical Society is connected with the Young Men's Democratic Club. The Society does not deserve to be dragged down into the dirty pool of politics. It has been founded by a number of connoisseurs, some of whom are engaged in the service of their country, for the purpose of elevating and refining humanity, through the gentle influences of the divine art. They will spare no expense to provide good programmes, and, in proof of that, I may point to the engagement of Dodworth's Band and the Sacred Harmonic Society, both of which organizations, as I am informed by their conductors, are unequalled in the world.

I have been told that the statement in the SATURDAY PRESS was intended for a joke. If such is the fact, I fail to see its point; and I am astonished that a respectable editor should permit his columns to be made the vehicle for silly jests at the expense of an important aid in the spread of civilization and refinement. I have been a subscriber to your valuable paper since its inception, and beg to congratulate you on its success.

At our next concert, it is our intention to play four of Beethoven's longest symphonies, and I trust that you will honor us with your presence on the occasion.

Very respectfully,

A Member Of The Society.

——

——Club, 31st May.

To the Editor of the Saturday Press :

Sir: I am requested by my friend, Mr. Whiskers, to inform you that, in consequence of a libellous attack upon him in your paper, he intends to commence an action at law against you, wherein the damages are laid at fifty thousand dollars. It is my special duty, however, to demand from you the name of the author of the article in which it is stated, inferentially, that it is the duty of my friend's maternal parent to inflict upon him chastisement a posteriori, and to place him vi et arm á coucher.

It is considered by all the men in the Club to be a case clearly within the Code; and that the usual objection to the social status of a newspaper-writer might be waived.

You will do me a favor by sending me an answer by the bearer.

I have the honor to remain,

Your ob't servant,

Fitz-Adolphus Ambulance,

Late of H. B. M.'s Lt. Drag's, with the Crimean medal (three clasps), Chevalier of the Legion of Honor of the Sardinian order of St. Michael, and of the Turkish Medijee, etc., etc..

——

Cortesi.

I said, sometime ago, that nobody knew who Cortesi was.

Before another Saturday Press is printed, she will make every body pretty well acquainted with her.

Critics who heard her at rehearsal were astonished, and it takes a good deal to astonish a critic in the morning. If he really is critical, he has few of those bounding impulses that poets give to people who rise early in the day.

I know that everybody is dying to know whether Cortesi is handsome, but I shall not satisfy their curiosity. Artists, in the morning, are never handsome. Even Whiskers isn't handsome when he first awakes, and Whiskers is the Apollo of Wiedenfeldt.

I believe that Cortesi will be fine in Sappho. Whether so fine as Gazzinaga, who is great, remains to be seen and heard. The Opera has plenty of fine things in it, as certain composers have ascertained and duly cribbed the best. Everybody knows the plot. The prima goes and throws herself into the Sea "all along of" Brignoli, who prefers the contralto, and, as a general thing, I quite agree with him. There is something about the soprano voice that tends to acidulate the temper, and my weak point is caramels. I never can get by Maillard's, that is if I have any money—which is a rare occurrence—or Madame has confidence, which is still more so.

However, Cortesi is going to have success. That's settled. Then there is to be "Robert le Diable," with Colson (Alice), De Wilhorst (Isabella), Brignoli, (Robert, in which, on dit, he is fine), and Junca as Bertram. A very fine distribution. There will be two weeks more of Opera at least.

The Shu-shu-gar Returned.

My special favorite sometimes, the public's (comparatively unimportant body) always, Miss Heron, has returned to town, and of course began by doing a kind thing for an old friend. She played Ingomar for the benefit which Tiemann gave Eddy at Niblo's Garden. Tiemann's lieges attended in great numbers, and sans doute the heart of the manager was made glad with much Chemical and Dry Dock.

Miss Heron (I prefer to adhere to her early name) played Parthenia sweetly, gracefully, and altogether most agreeably. It is not often that I say sweet things, but it is not because I would rather be bitter. It is because either the thing is bad or I'm stupid, or both. But it seemed to be that the simplicity dodge by which Parthenia captures the savage Ingomar (Eddy was properly rumbunctious and cantankerous) is precisely Miss Heron's fate, and that therefore she does it perfectly well. There's wisdom for you.

Relache.

Wallack's and Laura Keene's, which are really the only regular theatres here at present, have closed seasons which were unusually prosperous. Miss Laura Keene has purchased about half the State of Pennsylvania, and Mr. Wallack is in treaty for the rest of Jersey. What in the world he'll do with it I don't know.

But some new hands take the place of the old ones, who are doing the pastoral in flats and crooks of gentle shepherds.

The Misses Gougenheim commence at Laura Keene's with one of the most stupid plays that has been written of late years. It is the King's Rival, written by Charles Reade to give Mrs. Stirling a chance to play Nell Gwynne, a favorite role for stage ladies who have been badly matched. Mistress Nelly, it will be recollected, had several lovers before Old Rowley gave her that sweet house at Richmond, where the Baron's friend, Pepys, always found a pleasant halting-place. But we will talk more about Mistress Nelly next week. The title of the play has been changed by the Gougenheims to "Court and Stage." Cool proceeding, that, but very characteristic of the stage. They steal a man's property, and then mutilate it.

At Wallack's Mr. and Mrs. W. J. Florence will produce, on the 13th, some of those great literary works about the authorship of which there has been so much dispute. Mrs. Florence is une jolie femme, and makes me laugh. So I like her.

Odds and Ends.

The New York correspondent of the *Springfield Republican* writes: "I met Piccolomini in the street yesterday, walking slowly and alone towards the Academy of Music. She wore a plain violet silk dress, with a black silk mantle, a simple straw hat, trimmed with white, and a gossamer black veil. It was a charming picture—this passing glimpse of the sweet-faced little prima

donna, who has won so many hearts with her ingenuous loveliness. If she was thinking of herself, or her dress, she did not show it, which is more than most self-conscious Broadway beauties can say.

The Variétés Theatre, New Orleans, has been closed and Mr. Placide's company, the best in the United States, is to play at Cincinnati en route for New York. They are having great times at Pike's second story opera-house in Cincinnati. Read the following sweetly worded editorial from the *Commercial*:

Pike's Opera House.—The programme at this *magnificent temple* during next week, will be a Musical and Floral novelty of the *most beautiful character*—being no *less* than a Grand Romantic Operetta, entitled "The Forest Festival, or Scenes in Fairy Land," in which not *less* than *three hundred* and *fifty* young ladies appear as sylvan spirits and goddesses. The *entire* vast stage is to be *converted* for the occasion into a picturesque dell with real forest-trees, flowers, birds, etc., amid which are formed beautiful illuminated tableaus. The *ancient* and *classic ceremonials* of crowning the queens of May and Beauty, form a part of the Operetta. The entertainment is very highly spoken of by the press elsewhere as being strictly of a *chaste* and highly interesting character.

Mme. Biscaccianti gave, on Friday, a grand farewell concert at the commercial and poetical metropolis of New Hampshire, Portsmouth. I hope she did better than old Braham, who sung there once, in the early days of the republic, and received the enormous sum of nine shillings, Boston currency.

The French libretto of *Il Poliuto* is thus announced in the *Bibliographie de la France*:

Cammarano.—Polyeucte, tragédie lyrique en trois actes de Salvator Cammarano, musique de Donizetti. Texte italien. Traduction française en regard. In-8o, 51 p. Paris, impr. Morris et Ce; libr. Michel Lévy fréres. 2 fr.

Representé pour la première fois, à Paris, le 14 avril 1859.

At Palermo, the tenor Salviani, who sung some time since at New York, in the *Prophet*, has been singing in *Trovatore* and *Traviata*.

At St. Petersburg, the favorite basso Marini, so well known here, has contracted a fourth engagement. At Parma, Rosa de Vries has been singing with more success than at Palermo.

Mirate, the tenor, has signed an engagement for Rio Janeiro.

Personne.

FOUNTAIN OF NATURAL GAS.

The *Detroit Advertiser* of the 23d ult., has the following communication:

"During a late tour through Western Canada, I visited some curious wells, which had been dug during the past season. They are in the township of Howard, about 15 miles Southeasterly from Chatham, and two of them are about 200 yards apart. They were dug of the ordinary size, about 30 feet, and then bored about 50 feet more, when a stream of gas rushed up suddenly, with a roaring sound that could be heard a furlong distant. A man ventured into one of the wells, but was suffocated with the vapor and fell to the bottom. Another man was lowered to save him, but was obliged to withdraw twice before he succeeded in fastening a rope to the body of the first, who was dead when withdrawn.

"A tube long enough to reach above the top of the ground, was made and driven into the hole, and the well bricked up. It soon filled with water to within about ten feet of the top, the gas escaping through the tube, and the water clear and without any bad taste. But in a short time the gas commenced rising through the water, which it keeps in a constant state of ebullition as in a kettle over a brisk fire; the water rising near one side of the well, and rolling towards the other side and having very much the appearance of dirty soapsuds. No smell is apparent at the top of the well, and the water when drawn from it soon settles, and becomes clear and pleasant to the taste.

"The other well exhibited nearly the same phenomena, and as they were unwilling to risk life in it, has been filled with earth, but the gas still rises through the mud, and has formed for itself three apertures, or craters, at the surface, the largest being of oval shape, 10 by 18 inches in diameter, the bottom being mud, about the consistence of thick batter, and the gas rises through it in bubbles with such force as to throw blotches of mud upwards and outwards a distance full four feet. I saw it only in the daytime, but was told that it could be ignited with a match, and that it would burn for a long time.

"A friend who has since visited it writes thus: 'I think it the grandest sight I ever saw. We visited it about midnight. We saw the light some time before we reached the house, and were informed that the gas had ignited of itself or by means unknown to the family. There are three openings in the top of the well, the largest about the size of a pail. From the largest ascends a flame about three feet high, which burns very clear, and as bright as a heap of shavings. From the other apertures the flame was smaller, but equally bright, and all over the surface of the well are cracks through which issues a flame resembling burning sulphur.'

"About seven miles from Chatham there is another well dug in the same manner as the above described, which exhibits nearly the same phenomena, and in which, although the water in and above the clay is very hard, the water is as soft as rain water, and is drawn to quite a distance in Summer, by the neighbors, for washing purposes. The gas in this well has been on fire several weeks at a time."

—Greeley being out West, and Raymond out East, the subs of the *Tribune* and *Times* are pitching into each other in regular Bowery style. When the cat's away," etc.

—The Chess Monthly gives a table showing Mr. Morphy's scores in Europe. Out of 149 even games he won 117, lost 19, and 13 were drawn. Of 33 blindfold games he won 20, lost 1, and 12 were drawn. Of 35 consultation games he won 17, lost 2, and 16 were drawn. Giving the pawn and move he won 18 games, lost 2, and 5 were drawn. Giving the pawn and two moves he won 14 games, lost 2, and 1 was drawn.

—Mrs. Rosanna Underwood has just been divorced from her husband in Boston. One reason urged, was neglect to provide properly for her support. She also proved that, during the first year of their marriage, they had resided in nine different houses, and during the second, in eleven. The court is said to have been of opinion that the last consideration was clearly a justifiable cause for granting the bill.

—A Dress Reform Convention is to be held on the 22d instant, at Auburn, New York. Ladies without bloomers will be admitted; also gentlemen without curls, turn-down collars, or short capes. In fact, the Convention will be conducted on the most liberal principles. Go.

—An English missionary now in Sumatra lately wrote home that he had "had the melancholy satisfaction of examining the oven in which his predecessor was cooked."

—A singing society in Paris, a short time ago, offered a price for a sacred composition. Amongst other works two were sent in which were pronounced by the society to be unworthy. When the letters which had accompanied the compositions were opened, the name of Carl Maria von Weber was found to be the author of them. The German papers on this occasion display much merriment and irony.

—The Buffalo Express hopes that the title of Mr. Swinton's new work, "Rambles Among Words," is not copyrighted, since it belongs, in justice, to half the books written now-a-days. True.

AMUSEMENTS.

Bible House (extreme left,) Cooper Institute, and Tompkins Market (right.)

NEW YORK JUNE 11, 1859

IMPORTANT QUESTIONS.

To the Editor of the Saturday Press:—

Do our physicians, or do they not, know how to ascertain whether a body found in the water was drowned or thrown into the water after death?

Have they, or have they not, observed the different appearances of such bodies sufficiently to verify the cause of death? If not, let them study the

Chinese medico-legal work called Si-yuen, published in the tenth century, and continually revised and republished by the Government to this day. The following, which I translate from "*L'Empire Chinois*," by Huc, a French missionary (vol. 1, page 303), shows that they claim that there *are invariable* signs betraying these different modes of death:

"Tho Si-yen reviews all imaginable modes of death, and it explains the method to discover these from the bodies of the dead. In speaking of persons drowned it says, their bodies are very different from those which are thrown into the water after death. The first have *the belly much bloated, the hair stuck close to the head, froth in the mouth, the feet and hands stiff, and the soles of the feet extremely white. These signs are never found on those bodies which have been thrown into the water after having been strangled, poisoned, or slain in any other manner.* As it frequently happens in China, that an assassin seeks to hide his crime by a conflagration, the Si-yuen, under the chapter devoted to *the burned,* shows the manner of learning, by inspection of the corpse, whether it was slain before the burning or suffocated by the fire. Among other things it says, that in the first case neither ashes "or vestiges of the fire are found in the mouth or in the nose, whilst they are always found in those of persons suffocated."

Now, Sir, are the observations for two hundred years on these subjects, of a nation of three hundred millions, entitled to no weight? If incorrect, let the learned faculty of this country show what are the signs in the respective cases, for the guidance of coroners in their investigations. There must be a difference of appearance in a wound made in a body when living and when dead; and another chapter in the same work gives the mode of detecting it, and with such certainty it claims that even the bones alone will give an unerring report as to a blow or wound which causes death.

I hope by this communication simply to awaken an interest in the community sufficient to have all the light, which can be brought to bear on it, find its way into the press.

G

THE COOPER UNION.

The indentures by which Mr. Peter Cooper and Sarah, his wife, convey to "The Cooper Union for the Advancement of Science and Art," the property known as the Cooper Institute, have been recorded. By the terms of the indentures the Board of Trustees is composed of the following persons: Peter Cooper, Edward Cooper, Abram C. Hewitt, Daniel F. Tiemann, Wilson G. Hunt, and John E. Parsons.

In case of the death of one of the Trustees, the vacancy is not to be filled, but the Board of Trustees will consist of five members. Every succeeding vacancy to be filled by the remaining Trustees by ballot. Trustees hold office for life, but may be removed by order of the Supreme Court, or may resign. The oldest lineal male descendant of Peter Cooper is to be a Trustee ex gratia, unless he be a Trustee by virtue of original appointment, or by election as provided. If the oldest lineal, male descendant of Peter Cooper be a Trustee by virtue of original appointment, or by election, the number of Trustees constituting said Board of Trustees to be five; if the oldest lineal male descendant of Peter Cooper be not a Trustee by virtue of appointment or election, then until another vacancy occur in the said Board of Trustees by the death or removal of a Trustee, other than such oldest lineal male descendant of Peter Cooper, the number of such Trustees to be six.

The rents, issues, income, and profits of the estate, are to be forever devoted to the instruction and improvement of the inhabitants of the United States in practical science and art.

1. To regular courses of instruction at night, *free to all* who shall attend the same under the general regulations of the trustees, on the application to the useful occupations of life, on social and political science, meaning thereby not merely the science of political economy, but the science and philosophy of a just and equitable form of government, based upon the great fundamental law that nations and men shall do unto each other as they would be done by, and on such other branches of knowledge as, in the opinion of the Board of Trustees, will tend to improve and elevate the working classes in the city of New York.

2. The support and maintenance of a *free reading room*, of *galleries of art*, and of *scientific collections*, designed, in the opinion of the Board of Trustees, to improve and instruct those classes of the inhabitants of

the city of New York whose occupations are such as to be calculated, in the opinion of the said Board of Trustees, to deprive them of proper recreation and instruction.

3. To provide and maintain a school for the instruction of respectable females in the arts of design, and, in the discretion of the Board of Trustees, to afford the respectable females instruction in such other arts or trade as will tend to furnish them suitable employment.

4. As soon as, in the opinion of the Board of Trustees, the funds, which shall, from time to time, be at their disposal, will warrant such an expenditure, such funds shall be appropriated to the establishment and maintenance of a thorough *Polytechnic School*, the requirements to admission to which shall be left to the discretion of the said Board of Trustees, and shall be specifically determined by them, from time to time.

Dramatic Feuilleton.

"Adelaide and Joey."

I wish that the Baron, who gravitates towards elegant wickedness, could have seen the lords and ladies attached to the Court of his most blessed majesty, King Charles the Second of England, and of lapdog memory. Would that he could have seen the Richmonds, the Ethereges, and all the rest of the gallant train! Would that Anna Maria, who has taken to billiards, and is now my bitterest foe, could be compelled to sit and see the whole of "Court and Stage!"

No! I retract the last expression. I would not inflict tortures upon my direst enemy.

I suppose that everybody knows pretty nearly what "Court and Stage" is about. It is a very stupid version of the intrigues between Charles the Second, la belle Stewart, and the Duke of Richmond. By a wonderful exercise of dramatic ingenuity, Mistress Ellen Gwyn is made to play a prominent part in this imbroglio. In fact, Mistress Gwyn is the central figure in the charming group. She is made to do all sorts of kind things, and to attempt to prove the rather illogical assumption of the Demi-Monde, that a lack of chastity—the sex's chiefest ornament—may be made up for by an excess of what is called good heartedness.

Now Mistress Gwyn had a good heart, an open disposition, a generous soul (except when some one else made a success in one of her pet rôles). To show how kind she was, it is only necessary to go over the list of her regular gallants. There were Hart and Lacey, the players; Lord Bucklehurst, Lord Dorset, and another whose name I have forgotten, besides the King. At the period of this play, she had been detected in an intrigue with Lord Dorset, who was attached to the King's person. Then again, the King was terribly in love with la belle Stewart, and to prove it, he sent away all the Gwyns, and the Davises, and the "joyous train of singers and dancers in his Majesty's theatre." "He discarded," says Grammont, "without any exception, all the other mistresses which he had in various parts of the town." Even this does not seem to have touched the fair Stewart, who, after tormenting old Rowley almost to death, married the Duke of Richmond.

The King went back to Mistress Gwyn, who made him pay roundly for placing her on the retired list. She could afford to be good to the poor. Her house was a freehold, her current expenses were borne out of the privy purse, and in addition, she got out of the King as much as sixty thousand pounds in one year. That sixty thousand pounds would account up in Wall street, to-day, at least half a million of dollars.

The only thing that can be said in Nelly's favor, is that she was not vindictive like the Duchess of Portsmouth, nor a scold like her fellow-player, Moll Davis. She was witty after the coarse fashion of her day, and (invaluable quality in woman), generally in a good humor.

In fact, Mistress Gwyn was superior to her class, she was born a courtesan, while the ladies of quality, her rivals, took up the trade en amateur.

I gave last week the reason why Reade wrote this play, probably the worst thing he ever did. I can admire a wicked, witty thing, though I think that it is better to be good than to be bad, other things being equal. But the tendency of this play would be very bad if it was not so exceedingly slow and so dreadfully long that everybody gets tired to death before it is over, and it leaves no impression except one of extreme weariness.

As for the actresses who have so chivalrously taken Laura Keene's Theatre "for the Summer Season," I cannot help thinking they have been a little spoiled by their travels in savage lands. I remember the Misses Gougenheim playing in the farces at the Broadway Theatre, and they were pleasant actresses enough in those days.

But these days are not those. The standard of metropolitan excellence advances every year.

Actresses, on the contrary, do not improve by age. The vintage of ten years ago, if not very well corked, loses its flavor. "Joey," I am sorry to say it, "Joey" was younger once than she is now. "Joey," too, was more natural, more jolly, more soubrettish. "Joey" is now affected, her laugh seems forced, not to say hysterical, and she shakes her curls more than ever.

"Joey" ought to remember the difference between Grass Valley and New York.

Her sister is about the same—a calm, quiet, correct actress, who frequently has a narrow escape from being elegant.

The others are not worth talking about, if we except C. Wheatleigh and Mr. Daly. The manners of the Restoration were very faintly imitated; it was more like the Bowery than Hampton Court.

Theatre Francais.

They have been doing Murger's play, *La Vie de Bohéme*, here, but the French traders couldn't see it. They haven't the faintest idea of what a Bohemian is, and can't imagine that a man may be as jolly with one franc as with one million. The play therefore was not successful, although very well acted. Laba and Edgard were particularly good.

The theatre will be closed till the 14th, when Mr. Sage will have a benefit. La Vie de Bohéme will be repeated.

La Comtesse de Ferussac.

Room for another coronet in the coulisses! The Countess will sing in the Puritani next Tuesday, not for the Italians, as A. M. wrote you last week (the dear child has a wonderful contempt for facts of all kinds), but for the Woman's Hospital. If the Countess succeeds, she intends to remain on the stage.

The Japonica world will come out strong. Anna Maria is in such a state of excitement about it that Carnochan thinks of shaving her head and frappéing it like champagne.

La Comtesse de Ferussac was Miss Thorn, and that's the reason why society is stirred up about it.

La Comtesse de Ferussac has my permission to go ahead.

But she would do well to keep a look-out for the Sunday papers.

A nod, etc., to a blind horse, etc., etc.

Mr. Wallack Orates.

The Veteran took an affectionate farewell of his adherents on Monday. They came out strong for the benefit of Prince John. The Prince made the first speech, and then Mr. Wallack addressed the audience. The speeches were pretty nearly all about the Wallacks, and what remained after that subject was exhausted, was about Moss, the treasurer, who seems to have been engrafted on the house.

However, Mr. Wallack has had a good season, and I hope he'll live to enjoy many more of them. He is a splendid old fellow, and, as they say in the West, long may he wave.

The New Prima Donna.

As I said last week, Cortesi has made everybody hear of her. In the Poliuto she was magnificent, and that is all I can say. She was so good as to seriously affect Brignoli's composure, and to "worry" all the other prime ladies awfully. Her success in Havana, where they appreciate good things in the artistic way, will be something immense. I should write more about her, but I am going out in the country, which is a great deal better than writing for newspapers. Ask the piquant editress of the Sunday *Atlas* if it isn't.

PERSONNE.

NEW YORK JUNE 18, 1859

For the NEW YORK SATURDAY PRESS.

LOST.

BY BARRY GRAY.

'Tis years since I parted from Barbara—
The woman I loved so well—
And every hour has been to me
More bitter than tongue can tell.
I have sought the darkness, and fled the light,
And wept in my deep despair:
I have cursed the day that she crossed my path—
That creature—so frail! so fair!

I met her poor daughter again to-day,—
Her daughter, but not my child—
Who, though she possesses her mother's looks,
Has another's, which drive me wild.
I know it is so—don't tell me I err—
That fancy distorts the truth—
That 'twas babe of mine whom I cast aside,
With the wife I'd wed in youth—

That I was a simple and jealous brute,
And gave my ears to a lie!
Oh! if this were true (but it cannot be),
What a fiendish man am I!
Was he not ever, I ask, at her side?
Did he live, save in her sight?
His words were so smooth, and his voice so low,
He could m make the wrong seem right.

And she—frail woman! was thoughtless and young,
Young as the daughter is now—
And was followed, flattered, and courted, until
She dishonored her marriage-vow.
I'd terrible proof of the truth of this,
In letters that I received:
I know they might have been cruel lies—
But I read, and I believed.

And he—the destroyer! fled from me,
Alone, with cowardly fears—
Perhaps I had found, had he taken her,
Slight comfort amidst my tears,
In thinking the love that he bore the girl,
Might brighten her darkened life,
And prove a solace, however slight,
For the ruin wrought the wife.

But no, he must leave her to me; and I—
Though it nearly broke my heart—
Bade her go from the home made desolate,
For our ways thenceforth must part.
But whither, alas ! should she go? she cried;
She had neither mother nor friends,
And the world was bitter to such as she,
It assails but never defends.

Child that she was! could I send her away,
Though crushed to earth through her shame!
I could not—God knows! I went—she remained,
Despoiled of my love and my name.
Years fled: and I found the laurel of fame;
My coffers ran over with gold;
But all I'd resign for the vanished love
Which was mine in the days of old.

Sometimes I go, under cover of night,
And look on my ruined hearth:
The house is there—and the woman is there,
But my home is not on earth.
Her shadow I've seen on the window-shade—
God help me!—my heart is weak!—
And I felt that I'd like to hear her voice,
And look on her faded cheek.

Her face was the fairest I ever have seen—
Her forehead was white as snow,
And her hair was brown, and her eyes were bright,
In the days of long ago.
It is said that her life since then has been
One of repentance and tears:
That her brow has wrinkled, her hair turned grey,
Through sorrowing more than years.

Should this be so—and I question it not
Great has her punishment been:
But, doubtless, ere now in mercy and love,
God's pardon has cancelled her sin.
Shall I any longer forgiveness withhold,
From one who still is my wife—
Has sinned but repents? No! Christ is my guide—
My prayers Shall be for her through life.

—The N. Y. Young Men's Christian Association have recently opened their new rooms on Broadway, corner of Twelfth street. The reading-room is well supplied with current newspaper and magazine literature, both secular and religious, and valuable additions to the library are constantly being made.

WHERE SHALL I GO?

13 Cottage Place,
New York, June 8th.

Mr. Editor:

Where shall I go this Summer? To Newport, Saratoga, or Long Branch? I can't make up my mind. And it's so perplexing! One has so many particular friends going everywhere. Pa says I had better go to the White Mountains, and get some good, wholesome, fresh air. But, you know, that is away North, almost among the savages, and I don't want to go there a bit. Then one can't dress there much. You have to wear all sorts of common dresses and flats, and great thick, stout gaiters. By the way, I don't see how men can wear such boots as they do. Fred's weigh ever so much, and it is as much as I can do to lift them. But he laughs at me, and pulls them on as if they were as light as a feather, and then jumps and runs about everywhere, to show me how little he cares for them.

But I was talking about something else,—about the White Mountains. I think it would be real stupid up there among the mountains. Don't you? Nothing but climbing hills all day long, and sleeping all night. Fred, my brother, says that there are nice walks up there, and plenty of strawberries. Now, I should like the strawberries, and the walks, especially if Mr.———.

Oh, there, I didn't mean to say anything about him. I don't care much for him, anyhow; only he is so good natured; you can't make him cross.

Then there's Saratoga. I am sick of those springs and that horrid salt water. Pa let's me go there if I promise to drink the stuff three times every day. He says that it is very beneficial. But I don't think so. It tastes like the water from the Dead Sea. I have got some of that, which some "dear, good minister," as she calls him, brought home to Aunt Livingston. It is horrid stuff. She says that it was the metymorphysis of Lot's wife that made the water so salt and brackish. I don't know what that great long word means, and perhaps I haven't got it spelt right; but you editors know all these big words. As I said before, I think the waters are horrid, and I don't believe anybody goes there for them. I know I don't. Last Summer I went there, and, oh, such splendid times we had! You men don't know anything about it. There was Mary Boulere, and Lucy Diggs, she's a sweet thing, only she's got such a horrid name,—and lots of others. And what a flirtation Mary had with George de la Vergne. I thought they were engaged, but Mary told me, last week, that it was only a harmless flirtation. I never liked him much, only he does drive such splendid horses. Fred says he "handles the ribbons better than any other man on the road." What does that mean, I wonder? I can't see what ribbons have to do with horses, unless he means those blue rosettes on the sides of the horses' heads.

Then there is Newport. I like Newport best of all; only I am afraid that Pa won't let me go there. He says it is so expensive, "great outlay and no profit," to use his words. There's none of that horrid water to drink every day there, that's why I like it, though there's plenty of it to bathe in. And then they have dancing there that does one good. I am sure it is a great deal more beneficial to me than the waters. Oh, I think it perfectly lovely. I only hope Pa will let me go there this season. Mary Boulere is going next week and she has got some of the loveliest dresses I ever saw. She is only going to take five trunks. I can't imagine how a girl like Mary can get along with five trunks. I shall have to take at least a dozen, exclusive of bandboxes. Fred laughs at me about my trunks. You know he never takes more than one. But, I guess if he gets many more pairs of pants, like those that came home from the tailor's last night, he will have to increase his travelling accommodations. I measured them this morning—the pants not the accommodations—and they were almost a yard wide across the tops; great, big horrid things. I don't like them a bit, and so I told Fred. The impudent fellow replied that I didn't know anything about gentlemen's fashions, and told me to "leave matters of high import alone, and go to my dolls." The idea of my having dolls! But it's just like Fred.

But I must close this chatter. If you like, you may publish this, but I don't suppose you will think it good enough. Truly yours,

P. R. S.

P.S.—I should have commenced this "Dear Mr. Editor," instead of simple, "Mr. Editor," only Ma was looking over my shoulder, and she wouldn't have thought it proper. She is very particular, you know.

P. R. S.

MR. DICKENS.

About a year ago there was a report that Mr. Dickens had some domestic trouble. It was a matter in which the public was not particularly interested. Mr. Dickens has the right that every man has, to arrange his private matters as best suits his ideas of right. If the press had so misrepresented the trouble, that he conceived it his duty to correct their statements, it might have been done simply and concisely—the more so, the better. A chivalrous man would have sought, in such an explanation, to defend the conduct of his wife, whatever it might have been, from public comment. Such a man could not forget that however he might feel towards her now, he had once loved her, and had taken her to protect through good and through evil report. Even Mr. Dombey hated that his wife should become towns-talk, and David Copperfield strove hard that Dora should not learn that he had become tired of her. But Mr. Dickens writes a letter to a friend, which "he is at liberty to publish," in which the testimony of a servant is brought forward, to prove that his wife had so shocking a temper, he could not live with her. This may be, or may not be true, but a gentleman would hardly have made such a charge, so substantiated. If a man and his wife find their tempers so incompatible that they cannot live together, they had better quietly separate, anything is better than to live a lie. But from Adam all men seem to have inherited the tendency to say "the woman whom Thou gavest me she tempted me." The public, however, showed signs of increasing wisdom in this matter of domestic troubles, and took very little notice of Mr. Dickens' matrimonial jar. The public is accustomed to such things. It has come to the conclusion that a man and his wife had better settle such matters between themselves, and the public shows that it is wiser and better bred than Mr. Dickens.

But, our author was not satisfied here. Messrs Bradbury and Evans did not publish his letter in *Punch.* No sensible men would have done so. Mr. Dickens, therefore, resolves to withdraw from *Household Words*, a work in which they had an interest. He does so, commences a new serial, and advertises that *Household Words* will be discontinued. This was hardly acting like a man of honor. It was only not dishonest enough to be a legal offence. Here, again, the public showed its good sense. Mr. Dickens, whatever he may be in private life, writes good stories, makes a good and interesting serial, and the public supports it to the extent, it is said, of 130,000 already. We do not look on this support as an endorsement of Mr. Dickens' conduct in either of the affairs above alluded to. We think it is simply a recognition of the fact that a man's private character is of no concern to the public, in a matter where its interests are not affected, and further, that the public takes no interest in the details of private scandal, where only private interests are involved. To free the public from the annoyance of an immense amount of unsolicited, and undesired confidence, it only remains that the large class of persons who desire publicity, on any terms, should become well aware of this fact, and act upon it.

LETTER FROM OWEGO.

OWEGO, June 13, 1859.

My Dear Editor:—Thinking that a few lines from this section might not be uninteresting to your numerous readers, I have embarked on an unknown sea of ink to give you some notion of the country, people, and customs, that are to be found on the shores of the Susquehanna, in the quiet vale of Ahwaga.

Owego or Ahwaga (the more melodious Indian name)—is situated at the confluence of the Ahwaga River and the Susquehanna. It is not a deep vale, shut out by "Alpine hills from the rude world," nor is it "margined by fruits of gold, and whispering myrtles," but it will compare favorably with the far-famed vale of Como, in diversity and changing beauty of scenery. Standing in the cemetery, which is picturesquely situated on a high knoll near the confluence of the streams, you command a view of the village, and of the valleys of the two rivers for several miles. Four miles to the East, you catch a view of the waters of the Susquehanna, as they first enter the Ahwaga valley, glimmering like broken pieces of silver among the foliage. On the Northern side, a tongue of rolling high land slopes away heavenward. It is highly cultivated, and with its young, springing herbage, and its velvet carpet of vivid greensward, makes up a lovely pastoral picture. Not four hundred feet over to the Southern side of the stream, the scene is entirely changed. The mountain comes down, almost perpendicularly, to the water, and its sides are grim with black hemlocks and gloomy pines. On one side you behold gushing springs and velvet lawns, and you hear the rippling of pleasant waters, and the joyous carol of birds; on the other you see fallen hemlocks, and shrubless craigs, and you hear the melancholy pipe of some misanthropic thrush, the cry of a solitary loon, and the dull, leaden sound of water dripping from some more covered crevice in the granite.

Leaving this, the river sweeps on toward the setting sun, now curving into graceful lines, now laving the base of some rocky knoll, now laughing among joyous meadows, now almost cut in two by some protruding tongue of richly cultivated high land, now glancing among the hedge rows, trellised vines, and neat cottages of the Hamlet of Fir Croft,

> Sweet Fir Croft, nestling at the feet
> Of uplands ever green,"

now looped to the hilltops by the silver cord of a bright tributary, and now bursting through a mountain, and chafing and roaring between walls of granite. Far to the West, it rolls on among the blue hilltops, ever beautiful, and ever changing in its beauty.

At the confluence of the two rivers, a small island is set in the bosom of the waters, with a few trees upon it, reminding one of those lines in the Prisoner of Chillon :

"And there was a little isle,
Which in my very face did smile,
The only one in view;
A small green isle, it seemed no more,
Scarce broader than my dungeon floor;
But in it there were three tall trees,
And o'er it blew the mountain breeze,
And by it there were waters flowing,
And on it there were young flowers growing,
Of gentle breath and hue!"

Every inch of the Ahwaga Valley is historically sacred. It was here that Tayandanaga, or Brant, the war-chief of the Mohawks, marshalled his warriors, preparatory to his descent on Wyoming. There is an old sycamore still standing, much hacked and cut, around which they performed their war-dance, previous to the massacre. Up and down the valley he raged like a tiger at bay, when Sullivan came up with his army to revenge Wyoming. He disputed every inch of ground, and only yielded when the junction was formed between Sullivan and Clinton. The manner in which this junction was made is worthy of note. Sullivan, as you will recollect, came up the river from the bay, and Clinton was sent across to Otsego Lake, the head of the Susquehanna. Clinton arrived there in a dry time, and found the river so low that he was unable to navigate it in his bateaux, as he had intended. He therefore dammed up the river near where it issues from the lake, and having obtained sufficient head of water, tore away his dam, and came down on an artificial freshet. You can imagine the astonishment and dismay of the poor Indians when they saw the river rising without rain, and beheld the bateaux full of armed white men, and heard the stirring notes of Yankee Doodle.

In regard to the inhabitants of Ahwaga, what can be said that will be believed, coming from a person as partial and interested as the subscriber? Their hospitality is beyond a question, for they once put up with an English Count for two weeks, without tar and feathering him. Their religion has got the true ring, for their ministers are not skeletons; and their intelligence is beyond a question, for they take some hundred copies of The New York Saturday Press. If any of you Spruce street Traglodites do not believe all this, we ask of you to wash the ink from off your middle fingers, shake the editorial dust off your shoes, in-car-cerate your pen-worn carcases on the Erie Railroad, and come and see us. You will find that the word "stranger," in the Ahwaga Valley, "is a holy name."

With a country beautiful beyond comparison; with a climate renowned for health and long life; with inhabitants hospitable and refined; with streams full of trout, and woods of game; with a hotel the best in Western New York, fit even for a Fifth avenuer, and with a host and hostess that can do that wonderful thing, "keep a hotel," why should not Ahwaga become a rival to Saratoga and the Adirondacks, in the estimation of your careworn overtaxed Gothamite! In my next, I will give you some account of the ravages of the great frost, and some account and statistics in regard to a remarkable person called the great Euchre King.

For the present, good-by. A.

Love Matters.

—"The course of true love never did run smooth."—Shakespeare.

—Mrs. Gibbs. of Richmond county, Ga., hanged her husband on the 6th inst., and thinks she did well. He was drunk, and she says he should be treated as a beast while he was drunk. We are not told the way she hanged him.

—A man by the name of Cole has been arrested at Montague, N. J., on the charge of having poisoned his wife to death during her confinement to child-bed. Facts have transpired which, it is alleged, show that Cole and his family physician, Doctor Wickham, had conspired to commit a horrible crime, and an insurance of four thousand dollars having been first obtained on the life of Mrs. Cole. Cole is in custody, but Dr. Wickham managed to escape.

—No little excitement has been created in Vermont by the elopement of a young miss, of Brandon, from the seminary, with a tin pedlar, who hailed from Rutland.

—Some time since the wife of Mr. Poulin, a merchant of St. Joseph, Mo., ran away with her husband's clerk, taking along a little daughter. The following letter, written by the woman to her husband, is published in the St. Joseph *Journal*. The girl Lucy, mentioned in the letter, is a servant belonging to Mr. Poulin, worth about $900, and the child which she proposes to exchange is her own, about four years of age.

Cincinnati, May 23, 1859.

Mr. Isadore Poulin :—Dear Sir,—I wish to write to you a few lines to give you some news of us, and to tell you that Eugenie speaks of you every day, and that she wants to go and see her Papa in the store, and she cries for her good Honorine and her black Lucy, every day. I hope you are not mad at me because I went away with Mr. Augusta. I am very happy with him; he treats me like a wife. I do not regret what I have done, for I am happy with him. I will tell you one thing, if you will give me Lucy, I will give you up Eugenie; if not, you cannot get her. If you are willing to do so, you can come yourself and get her. We will be glad to see you. I want you to write right away as soon as you get this letter; 'cause we might be gone from here if you wait too long. Direct your letter to Eugenie Poulin, Cincinnati, Ohio. Write right off. I cannot wait no longer than ten days. Mr. Augusta will write to you when we receive an answer from you. We are all well, and wish you the same. Kiss the children for me.

Mary.

—Mrs. Sophronia Randle, a married woman, eloped from a small town in Michigan, recently, with a young man named William Wightman. They stopped at a village near Chatham, C. W., where the young man was taken with brain fever, and died. The woman, possessing herself of what money the young man had left (which amounted to some few hundred dollars), returned to her husband and was forgiven by him. He proposes to open a grocery-store with the money secured by his wife!

—The Kansas correspondent of the Boston *Journal* writes:

"A resident of Kansas recently received a letter of inquiry from a citizen of Massachusetts, in regard to his (the latter's) absent wife. The lady had left her lord and master some months previous, and he knew her to be now residing in Kansas with her relatives; but he wished to ascertain whether she passed by her maiden or wedded name, and whether she had instituted proceedings for a divorce. The party to whom the inquiries were addressed investigated the matter, and a few day's since informed the astonished husband that she is now known in Kansas as Miss ———, and that for more than three months he has been *nolens volens* a divorced man! The recent Territorial Legislature passed a special act absolving both parties from the bonds of matrimony. At this rate, Kansas will soon become more popular than Indiana, as a refuge for those who find the ties of Hymen chains of iron, instead of silken cords."

—A mass Convention of Spiritualists is to be held at Berlin Heights (of Free Love notoriety) on the first, second, and third days of next month. Among the speakers announced are S. J. Finney, Mrs. H. F. M. Brown, Warren Chase, B. P. Barnum, and Mrs. S. E. Warner.

—Dr. A. Bastian, who has just published a book in Bremen on his visit in 1857 to San Salvador, the capital of Congo, says that the princesses of the Royal family enjoy remarkable privileges. They may make their selections of husbands from the nobles of the realm, and the happy men have to prepare themselves for their duties and their honors by several months of solitude. To insure conjugal fidelity—not on the part of the wife, who enjoys the greatest freedom—but on the part of the husband, whenever he leaves the house tamtams are beaten before him, and at the sound of them all women must hasten out of the way.

—Letters received from Mr. Hawthorn, state that his daughter, Miss Una Hawthorn, has so far recovered from her late severe illness, that the family expected to leave Rome on the 25th of May.

—Colonel Fuller, in one of his Paris letters to the New York Express, says that "if Americans are some "times harshly judged by men of high intelligence and refinement abroad, let us remember the hard specimens we send them, and be charitable." Pretty good for the Colonel; but he should bear in mind that accomplished gentlemen (like himself and Chevalier Wickoff, for instance)! are necessarily rare in a new country.

The Difference.

"Saratoga and Newport—you've seen them,"
Said Charley, one morning, to Joe;
"Pray tell me the difference between them,—
For bother my wig if I know!"
Quoth Joe, "'Tis the easiest matter
At once to distinguish the two—
At one you go into the water;
At the other, it goes into you?"

—*Boston Post.*

A SKETCH.

BY JULIETTE H. BEACH.

The late March afternoon is wierd and gray,
The crazy wind, in monotone most dreary,
Whispers its half-told tale, and dies away
As if aweary.

Low rifts of snow lie cowering in the lane,
Where yesterday Spring's golden feet were dancing,
And from the skies that wooed her gentle reign
Black clouds are glancing.

I sit within my sewing chair, and dream–
My work, the while, falls idly from my fingers,
And where the firelight drops its mellowest beam
My gaze long lingers.

My little boy lies sleeping. Stirless now
Are the bare feet, so quick and restless lately;
And the blue eyes beneath his thoughtful brow
Are closed sedately.

One hand lies hid among the locks that float,
In careless grace, upon the yielding pillows;
The other on his breast rides like a boat
On Summer billows.

About the couch, where they his waking bide,
His whilom playthings lie in rare confusion;
And underneath, the shoes he thought to hide
In safe seclusion.

He calmly sleeps. The wind moans at the door,
And in the room the firelights' fitful gleaming
Makes pleasant shadows on the crimson floor—
I sit a-dreaming.

I see afar the veiled, uncertain land,
That in the future waits his manhood's coming,
And strive to dissipate, with love's strong hand,
Its mists benumbing.

And is he of that race of laureled kings,
The wearers of the purple of the Poet?
Or like the heroes whom the Poet sings?
His life will show it.

And if he be a soul from falsehood free,
Though he should wear no laurel, sing no story,
To bear his part with honest men shall be
Enough of glory.

The dusky twilight round the casement clings,
The wind lifts up its voice in louder wailing,
And dreary eve folds in her sombre wings
The daylight failing.

Familiar footsteps linger at the door,
And in the room the last faint day-beams quiver;
My dreams glide silently toward the shore
Of Lethe's river.

—At the last meeting of the Sanitary Association the following remarkable facts were adduced:

"Three years since the whole number of buildings of all descriptions in New York was some 53,000. The city is divided into twenty-two wards. In 1856, nineteen of these wards contained a population of 535,027 inhabitants, divided into 112,833 families, averaging a little less than five souls in each family. For the accommodation of these 112,833 families residing in nineteen wards, there were 36,088 dwellings averaging about three and one-half families occupying an entire house. There are but 12,717 of these families occupying an entire house, 7,148 of these dwellings contain two families, 4,600 contain each three families. Thus, while 24,465 of these dwellings shelter but 36,213 families, the remaining 13,623 houses have to cover 76,620 families, averaging nearly six families to each house, showing that about three fourths of the whole population of New York live, averaging but a fraction less than six families in a house, while only about one family in ten occupy a whole house."

—A Western editor thinks that Hiram Powers is a swindler, because he chiselled a Greek girl out of a block of marble.

—The Commissioners of the Central Park give notice that a portion of the Park is now complete and available to persons desiring a short ramble among rocks, grass, and foliage, without going beyond the limits of the city. This finished ground, known as "The Ramble," situated immediately South of the old Receiving Reservoir, is accessible by either the Third, Sixth, or Eighth avenue railroad, at an expense not exceeding six cents. From the termini, at Fifty-ninth street, of the railroads of the Sixth and Eighth avenues it is reached by a walk through the unfinished portion of the Park. At the entrance on Fifth avenue, opposite Seventy-second street, a gravelled walk commences, leading directly to "The Ramble." Access to this entrance can best be had by the Third avenue railroad, leaving the cars at Seventy-first street.

NEW YORK JUNE 25, 1859

Love Matters.

—A young lady in Cincinnati was to be led to the altar on Monday evening, by one to whom she had given her heart's affections. Friends and acquaintances had been invited to the marriage ceremony, and a large number had convened. The hour arrived, yet the bridegroom came not. The bride and guests were in waiting, and the hour passed by, and still the bridegroom delayed in making his appearance. At length the postman called at the house with a letter for the intended bride. It was from her betrothed, and containing the cards of himself and bride—he having been married the night previous to another.

—The Supreme Court of Michigan has affirmed the decision of an inferior Court, that a woman has a perfect right to control, in all respects, all property acquired by her before or after marriage, that belongs to her, independent of her husband.

—A poor servant girl named Rosanna Hogan, 18 years of age, employed at No. 91 Stanton street, while in a very distressed state of mind, took four ounces of arsenic Thursday morning. As soon as her situation was known, she was removed to the City Hospital, where she arrived in a state of collapse. Stimulants and remedies were freely applied by Dr. Cameron, but in the course of two hours death put a period to her sufferings. During a lucid interval, just prior to her dissolution, she informed the nurse that while at a house in Christie street, as a domestic, she was seduced, and intimated that she committed self-destruction to escape the consequences of her disgrace.

—Lady Mary Wortly Montague used to say that the only thing which reconciled her to being a woman, was that she would never be obliged to *marry* one.

—At Baltimore, a few days since, Annie B. Herring sued James Baughen for breach of promise of marriage, laying her damages at $5,000 a moderate amount compared with Miss Effie Carstang's demand of $100,000. The principal evidence offered was documentary. The defendant had committed himself in writing, and the jury gave the plaintiff an award of $3,500. Defendant's letters were written in 1854 and 1855. The second one, dated Baltimore, September 6, 1855, and addressed to Miss Herring, states that it made his heart "leap with joy upon receiving the last letter from her. It carried his mind back to Mechanicstown, and filled him with pleasant recollections of those days and evenings when they sat side by side in their recitals of love, and whether they were absent or present, in sadness or in joy, his heart would ever turn to her; that his pa was not much opposed to the match, and he hoped soon to succeed in bringing his mother over. They would then take a farm near Flintstone, and live happily together."

In his third letter, dated Baltimore, September 8, 1854, he advised her to "take good care of herself, and not to go out at night any more than she could help, as the dew was very heavy, and a great deal of sickness was prevailing. While in Baltimore he had mingled with the rich and gay, but all of their charms fell to the ground like darts against the Tarpian rocks, when compared with the sweet smiles of the girl he left in Frederick county. He hoped to go on in loving and being loved, and trusted that God would watch over and protect her."

In his letter dated Baltimore, September 9, 1855, he says: "I sometimes feel that I would give the world for one hour with my dear Anna, but I hope soon to see the day that we will be one and inseparable."

His fifth letter was written from Deep Creek, Oct. 18, 1854. In this letter, speaking of a lady who had been married only two weeks, he says she has improved wonderfully, and he hoped marriage life would prove so in all cases. He wished soon to be able to clasp her in his arms, never to separate until death, with its relentless grasp, shall lay them in the narrow tomb. In concluding, he said, "Keep up your spirits, and may God watch over and protect you, is the sincere wish of your devoted lover."

Three other letters were received, dated Deep Creek, Nov. 4, 1854; Atherwood, June, 1855; Atherwood, Aug. 22, 1855. The last letter breaks the promise, on account of his mother's opposition to the marriage. He said he believed it would kill her, if he were to marry contrary to her wishes. Verdict for the lady.

AFTER THE RAIN.*

BY T. B. ALDRICH.

The rain has ceased, and in the room
  The sunshine falls an orange flood,
And high upon the village spire
  The sacred cross is bathed in blood.

From out the dripping ivy-leaves,
  Antiquely-carven, old and gray,
A dormer, facing Westward, looks
  Upon the village like an eye.

And now it glimmers in the sun,
  A globe of gold, a disc, a speck;
And in the belfry sits a dove,
  With purple ripples on her neck.

———

The following obvious plagiarism on the above Poem is coolly sent to us by Mr. N. G. Shepherd, as an original contribution to THE SATURDAY PRESS. It is unnecessary to say that, after this, Mr. Shepherd need not trouble us with any further communications.

AFTER THE RAIN.

The rain has ceased, and the sunlight falls
  In a golden flood on the jewelled sod,
It glints on the spire, and rests on the walls
  Of the village-church like a smile of God.

The rain has ceased, and the spent clouds seen
  In the sun's bright path seem to glow with shame,
While the plain below, and the hills between,
  Lie drowned in a mist of yellow flame.

The rain has ceased, and the dark night falls,
  Like a widowed wife, on the earth's cold breast;
In the gloom of the wood the lone bird calls
  Her wandering mate to his home and rest.

———

—A young lady in Cincinnati was to be led to the altar on Monday evening, by one to whom she had given her heart's affections. Friends and acquaintances had been invited to the marriage ceremony, and a large number had convened. The hour arrived, yet the bridegroom came not. The bride and guests were in waiting, and the hour passed by, and still the bridegroom delayed in making his appearance. At length the postman called at the house with a letter for the intended bride. It was from her betrothed, and containing the cards of himself and bride—he having been married the night previous to another.

*See "Babie Bell and other Poems."

ON VIEW AT THE GALLERIES

OF

WILLIAMS, STEVENS & WILLIAMS,

353 BROADWAY,

Church's Celebrated Painting

OF THE

GREAT FALL NIAGARA.

ALSO,

Gignoux's

EXCEEDINGLY PICTURESQUE AND INTERESTING PICTURE,

(Now exhibited for the first time) being a

Winter View of the Great Cataract

FROM GOAT ISLAND,'

Including the TOWER and TERRAPIN BRIDGE, both splendidly shown, for the FIRST TIME, by DAYLIGHT, and affording to the public

AN OPPORTUNITY NEVER BEFORE ENJOYED,

of witnessing, at the same time, the successful treatment of the great subject, by two of the leading members of the rapidly advancing

SCHOOL OF AMERICAN ART.

Admission 25 cents

—At Baltimore, a few days since, Annie B. Herring sued James Baughen for breach of promise of marriage, laying her damages at $5,000 a moderate amount compared with Miss Effie Carstang's demand of $100,000. The principal evidence offered was documentary. The defendant had committed himself in writing, and the jury gave the plaintiff an award of $3,500. Defendant's letters were written in 1854 and 1855. The second one, dated Baltimore, September 6, 1855, and addressed to Miss Herring, states that it made his heart "leap with joy upon receiving the last letter from her. It carried his mind back to Mechanicstown, and filled him with pleasant recollections of those days and evenings when they sat side by side in their recitals of love, and whether they were absent or present, in sadness or in joy, his heart would ever turn to her; that his pa was not much opposed to the match, and he hoped soon to succeed in bringing his mother over. They would then take a farm near Flintstone, and live happily together."

In his third letter, dated Baltimore, September 8, 1854, he advised her to "take good care of herself, and not to go out at night any more than she could help, as the dew was very heavy, and a great deal of sickness was prevailing. While in Baltimore he had mingled with the rich and gay, but all of their charms fell to the ground like darts against the Tarpian rocks, when compared with the sweet smiles of the girl he left in Frederick county. He hoped to go on in loving and being loved, and trusted that God would watch over and protect her."

In his letter dated Baltimore, September 9, 1855, he says: "I sometimes feel that I would give the world for one hour with my dear Anna, but I hope soon to see the day that we will be one and inseparable."

His fifth letter was written from Deep Creek, Oct. 18, 1854. In this letter, speaking of a lady who had been married only two weeks, he says she has improved wonderfully, and he hoped marriage life would prove so in all cases. He wished soon to be able to clasp her in his arms, never to separate until death, with its relentless grasp, shall lay them in the narrow tomb. In concluding, he said, "Keep up your spirits, and may God watch over and protect you, is the sincere wish of your devoted lover."

Three other letters were received, dated Deep Creek, Nov. 4, 1854; Atherwood, June, 1855; Atherwood, Aug. 22, 1855. The last letter breaks the promise, on account of his mother's opposition to the marriage. He said he believed it would kill her, if he were to marry contrary to her wishes. Verdict for the lady.

Fireworks at Brooklyn City Hall to celebrate the first piped water (from Ridgewood), April 28 1859

NEW YORK JULY 2, 1859

A TRIP TO CUBA,

BY THE OVERLAND ROUTE; OR, ALL THE WAY FROM SPRUCE STREET TO CUBA, WITH SUNDRY EXPERIENCES, LIKEWISE A VIEW OF THE PRISON IN WHICH GREELEY, THE MARTYR, WAS INCARCERATED ON HIS JOURNEY TO PIKE'S PEAK.

Yes, the overland-route I took, simply because it was more convenient—the steamer not plying this season. Let me disabuse you at once. I am too patriotic, directly under the forecast light of the Fourth of July, to indite a word about that little, foreign, Spanish-ridden island, which is regarded so avariciously by fillibusters. It is of *our own* Cuba I speak, which is at present all contained within the heart of Alleghany county and from which our Gotham has the misfortune to be two or three hundred miles removed. An inland city,—unless the liberality of modern and progressive geography will allow us to call it an island—sundered from earth on three sides by the New York and Erie Railroad, and on the other by the Genesee Valley canal. Happy man! if you are caught up from this Babel by the cars, some morning, and dropped there at nightfall. I seemed to take Nature and the Cubans alike by surprise. The sun hurriedly gathered up her skirts of light which she had been flaunting all day (the Germans, you know, insist upon our masculine sun's being feminine and wearing crinoline, and it suits my convenience to be Teutonic, just now), and courtesied the usual good night so coquettishly as to shake every spangle in her gorgeous garment, and retired. Fate decreed me to the hotel and a goodly host, and the villagers (as is their wont) came out to sympathize with me with eye and tongue, as though I had been a waif cast upon their shores. Oh, divine country! Oh, simple-hearted, simple-mannered yeomen! My muse fails me to describe their picturesque sports—to sing the innocent pleasures of the Cubans. A motley mass of the hearty villagers is summon'd by the twilight (a gentle bugle) before the stoop of the inn. The inevitable man with one leg was out (every country-village has its inevitable men), and the muscular three cubits of rheumatism was hobbling on his crutches, and he of the mighty watch-fob; also the ordinary villagers, each carrying some emblem of his calling on his countenance. The honest cobbler, with his leather and findings, and, last of awl, his wax threaded on his features so distinctly that I could read "Boot and Shoe Maker' in his face as though it stood there in the big black letters of his sign. And the tailor clipt around so sharply among the crowd that any one would have called him the knight of the shears. And the merchant, who measured each face as though it were a yard of calico, and weighed each word as though it were a pound of allspice. Happy Cubans, out with pipes (Cuba and no Havanas! Clay pipes! Oh, shade of the wicked weed!) to engage in provincial pastimes. "Jim" and "Bill" were to run a foot-race—were to run, had run several, and were running—match after match came off, many papers of tobacco changed hands, and that inland island was shaken to its centre by the shouting and the fun. This is ruralizing, thought I. But now for the balmy sleep of the country—for some Pan to bring a zephyr from the coolest hill-top and woo the ache from my temples and fan me to repose.

Third story, rather steep! Feather bed, rather soft! A band of music on the floor above. Now, if all this goodly island had been molten brass, and poured into Mt. Vesuvius as a musical lining to its hollowness, and this same Vesuvius had been horizontalized in Cuba as a French horn, and blown through by a "Nor-Easter," it wouldn't have been unearthlier, nor harsher to "*all out-doors*" than this brazen-mouthed thunder was, on that eventful night, to *one* indoors. Well, I am easily flattered by attentions—have a good-humored way of construing an insult often into a compliment—and that I—So ho! A serenade! Innocent and appreciative country people! Not so dulcet as Dodworth would render "Yankee Doodle," yet *laborious, loud,* and *long*. "Kind friends," thought I—for I had an extempore speech at tongue's end, anticipatory of being called out. "Kind friends—no more of that exquisite melody on my account—you have proven that your wind is sound. I thank"—but they didn't call me out. I felt like a bottle of sparkling catawba, fermenting and effervescing furiously within, and each additional tune was a cork-screw to unstop my foaming ire.

"The most melodious hours will close," saith the poet. Melodious bands in rehearsal for Independence day, will do ditto—that is, close; eyes and several other things, likewise. Doors won't, however, unless they are fortunate enough to have either lock, bolt, or latch, which my door seemed to have shaken off as an incumbrance. I have heard of an Irish woman who locked a cotton trunk with a pin; I locked my door with a chair-back. Honest Cubans! They can't have designs upon my lean purse! Feather beds are warm! One, two, three doors opening out of my room! That isn't a robber's boot rasping on the stairs? No, it is an honest snore which has set down upon the conscience of an ex-member of assembly, whom, I was told, I was honored to be near. Well, sleep is a flirt, a vixen; court her, coax her, and she spurns you. A quiet snooze must have ensued about here, for bang! slam! I am brought to my perpendicular by the tumbling of the chair, and a man at the head of my bed, skulking, actually. Heigh ho! "Gold and silver have I none, but such as I have give I unto thee." "Your boots, Mister; want *your boots blacked*?"

How I ever survived that night, I know not; but I did, unharmed. My host, in the morning, came as solemnly to my room to escort me down to breakfast, as though I had been a first class funeral, and he an accomplished undertaker. That man has certainly mistaken his calling. Such obvious accomplishments for the coffin and hearse business, would gain him high professional grade in our city. He discourseth so measuredly also. "There," saith he, "within those identical four walls was *Greeley* incarcerated, on his way to Pike's Peak." Upon those identical feathers he snoozed. The brave reformer was not held "in durance vile" by a mob of revolutionary Cubans: was not martyrized for opinion's sake, and the *Tribune's*, but (so mine host veritably relates), the great man had a breech in his breeches, and was confined to the feathers until the sun had passed the meridian. Contemplate the august Greeley thus imprisoned—forgotten by the hostess, who had mislaid his unmentionables—soliloquizing on the goal of greatness. Think of his wardrobe. I understand now what he means when he writes: "I was not much encumbered by my luggage." The landlady is said to hold her soiled hands sacred from henceforth. The needle is triumphantly stuck through the wing of a pasteboard American eagle, ornamenting the dining-room—an honor yielding to it for having wrought in its country's service.

How can I write more? How could I have written less? Time faileth me to poetize the scenery; to sing the many virtues of the people. Visit them if you can. You will come in contact with much that is refreshing and green. Still, if you are called to heaven before you are to take the "overland route" to Cuba, smile sweet acquiescence, for what might be their loss, would doubtless be your everlasting gain.

N.

A GENTLEMAN OF THE OLD SCHOOL.

A New York correspondent of the Charleston *Mercury* says of a well-known physician who walks Broadway in knee-breeches :

"The only surviving eccentric worth mentioning is Dr. Boyle, who dresses in knee-breeches, buckled shoes, shad-bellied coat, huge lappetted vest, cocked hat, ruffles, and flowing wig of last century. It is a mere whim of the M.D., who is a very sensible person otherwise. When he was a boy he had a strange hankering for that costume, and determined to indulge in it when he was rich enough, for the suit is about ten times as expensive as an ordinary civilian's. An increasing medical practice enabled him to gratify his cherished wish eight or ten years ago, and since then he has played the antique very creditably. He is about fifty-five, and jovial by nature; but as he stalks through Broadway, his cast-iron face never reveals the slightest consciousness that he is stared, pointed, and laughed at, by all the passers-by. Unruffled (except in his shirt bosoms and wristlets,) he strides on with a majesty worthy of General Washington."

The gentleman in question, it must be acknowledged, is a character in his way, and has achieved quite an eccentric career. In 1830, at the time of the great revival excitement, he was a distinguished evangelist belonging to the Oneida Presbytery; and many awakenings in this State and New England are due to his labors. In 1833 he became pastor of the Free Church in New Haven. The next year perfectionism broke out in the divinity school, and the reverend gentleman became a convert. He afterward was an editor of the *Perfectionist* and of the *New Covenant Record*. He emigrated to Ohio, in 1837, entered the anti-slavery field, was an eloquent lecturer, etc., etc.

He returned eastward in 1842, and resided at the Northampton Fourierite Community. In 1843, he travelled through several States in company with Doctor E. D. Hudson, lecturing on anti-slavery. This was the conclusion of his anti-slavery labors. He became interested in the doctrines of Emanuel Swedenbourg, though he could never be induced to become formally a member of any New Jerusalem Society, probably regarding the organization as being but another form of the "Old Church." Shortly afterward he commenced the practice of medicine, for which he had been educated before commencing his ministerial career, and has since enjoyed a comfortable degree of prosperity. His unique dress, which effectually advertises him, but which was adopted to no such purpose, enables our citizens to recognize him in his daily pedestrian tour on Broadway and Chambers street; and those who enjoy his acquaintance unanimously testify, despite what he regards his anti-church and non-resistant heresies, to his uniform courtesy, affability, and agreeable conversational powers. Such is the history of a man who, thirty years ago, was one of the most popular and promising preachers of the New School Presbyterian Church.—*N. Y. Eve. Post.*

Correspondence.

ALMOST A PANTHER-HUNT.

HARTFORD, CONN., June 27, 1859.

Mr. Editor:—In the southwestern corner of the State of Vermont, in the heart of a rough, mountainous country, where the Green Mountains begin to lose their loftiness, but are rendered none the less rough and rugged thereby, about five miles above the small village of Reedsboro, stands, or stood, a rambling, old-fashioned hostelry, kept for more than a generation by a family named Canada. I understand that within a few years past other buildings have grown up about the "tavern ;" that there are, a mill of some sort, several private residences, a "store," and—last and saddest innovation of all, speaking, as it does, of death to the wilderness about there—a schoolhouse. I believe, too, that a party of engineers, making surveys in connection with the great "Hoosac Tunnel" road, have passed through there with transit, level, and chain. (What doers away with romance those railroad men are!)

Years ago—which means about fifteen—when I was quite a lad, I made my first visit to the place in company with my father, an uncle, and cousin. We went for trout. Five streams and a pond within a mile of the house—one of the former runs through the inn yard—rendered the locality at that time one of the best in New England for the sport beloved by "contemplative men, and we caught great quantities of fish. There I took the first lesson in throwing the fly—a lesson that has cost thousands of trout their lives since then.

The principal items of remembrance connected with that visit, in my mind, are an immense bear-trap, with great spikes for teeth, that overlapped each other several inches when it was closed; the fact that we performed our daily toilets by the aid of a commodious horse-trough in the yard; the horror of my Cousin George on discovering, one evening, long, red, *female* hairs in his comb; and the falling of my father through a rather wide interstice in a "corduroy railroad" while we were returning, one very dark night, from a day's sport at the "Scotch Settlement"—a collection of deserted log huts, some eight miles away. On that memorable occasion, we actually fished through the length, if not the breadth, of "Texas"—the name of a town with no inhabitants, that we could discover, save a venerable bald eagle and a few "chipmunks."

In 1852, I visited the place again with a fellow-student, who with me, was following a course of mathematical study at the Lawrence Scientific School in Cambridge. Some sign of the changes of which I have spoken above were then manifest, but there was yet no store, nor any schoolhouse there.

We drove our weary horses to the inn door, and alighted. It was the same old bar, with the red counter and the wide fire-place. The old man, Canada, was dead and gone, but a burly son supplied his place amongst the black bottles and broken glasses; in the uncouth young man, with faded, whitey-brown hair, who acted as hostler, I recognized the boy Canada, hired, at a dollar per day, as "guide, philosopher, and friend," upon my former visit, and who then excited my boyish admiration by catching half pound trout with a bit of his red woolen "comforter," in place of the more artistic hackle.

He came in shortly, and amused himself with a comfortable stare at the strangers.

"I see you have forgotten me, Dwight; I remember you, and our crossing the hill, one dark night, from the Scotch Settlement, when my father got into a hole!"

"I swan !" said Dwight.

He said nothing further for the moment, but going behind the bar, opened a drawer filled with all sorts of small odds and ends, from which he presently produced a white-handled pocket-knife. There was a dimly familiar look about it that I could not explain till he spoke.

"I've kep it for you going on to eight years, now!" I looked at my Cambridge friend. He was lighting a cigar, and merely muttered something about "lack of civilization."

"Why did you not use it yourself?"

"Do you suppose I'd borry a feller's property, an' then steal it? I've felt mean lots o' times, for fear you'd think I did it a purpose."

I gave Dwight the handsomest book of flies he ever set eyes on, when we left.

We found that we had come three weeks too early for trout. While Massachusetts was warm and lovely in the full flush of May, this little corner of the world was cold with piled snow in the mountain gorges. The trout would not bite. We satisfied ourselves of that in a full day's "practice" at them.

So the second evening we sat, weary and forlorn, in the dingy bar-room; weary and forlorn, till we had gone deeply into the gin and water—which, with New England rum, and a vile compound they called "brandy," constituted all the tipple known to the place and burly John Canada, on whom had fallen the mantle of his father, had opened his budget of rare bear and panther stories.

I cannot pass the allusion to gin and water, above, without relating an anecdote which actually took place in Saratoga county, New York, four or five years ago. I was one of a party of ten or a dozen, running the location lines for the Sacketts Harbor and Saratoga Railroad humbug. We stopped at a country-tavern, where we were put to sleep in the ball-room, and were looked upon with great awe and respect. It was one rainy day that we were all kept inside" by stress of weather," and were sorely troubled to find means for idling away the hours. Eucre and seven-up were voted bores, and the only man in the party who could sing, or tell a decent story, was down with an attack of low fever. A lucky thought in some one, suggested" a little something to take." We called the landlord.

"Landlord," said I, "we'll have some milk punch." "Yes sir!" with an air of hesitation. "Perhaps, gentlemen, you would like to mix it yourselves?"

We assented, and he departed.

We presently heard an altercation below. His wife, who "rode the grey mare," was berating him. I think she called him "a cussed fool."

It was full fifteen minutes before he appeared, flushed and embarrassed, at the door.

He bore in his arms a large tray; upon it were a bottle of gin, a pitcher of milk, and the dinner-castors, containing pepper, vinegar, mustard, etc.

"*There,* gentlemen," said he, "I *believe* them's the ingregencies."

Burly John's stories at the old Canada-tavern, wiled away the evening pleasantly. Without them, being strangers to the place, without neither books nor newspapers, the evening would have been rather stupid, although there was a certain grandeur in the dimly visible mountain-scenery, that would have kept one quiet at a window for hours.

The moon looked down serenely upon the narrow valley, and the bleak undulations of dark hills; the broad and shallow stream, murmuring over pebbles, flashed faintly here and there with a pale glimmer that was, immediately beyond, lost beneath overhanging boughs; on a distant hill-side gleamed a hundred fiery mounds where a clearing was being burned over; nearer at hand, by the road-side, slept a half-dozen unsheltered kine. Altogether, the look-out from the window, was one not to be soon forgotton.

Within, the scene was equally striking to a denizen of towns. A bright fire burned upon the hearth, casting flickering shadows about the room; dried meats, and vegetables hung from the ceiling; John Canada sat upon his box, smoking a short clay pipe, between the whiffs interjecting his stories, in small fragments; two or three neighbors, in their shirt sleeves sat listlessly about, each with his pipe. In one corner, a very thin, dried-up, crusty-appearing old fellow, with moist, red eyes, and a continually hungry look, muddled himself, in a quiet way, with rum and sugar. The rest all called him "Uncle Paul," and seemed rather to look up to him. So we sat listening to burley John's stories.

He had concluded one, wherein he detailed his narrow escape when pursued by a female bear, whose cub he had stolen, and who finally "overcame" him by knocking him "end over end" over a fallen log, after which, she made off with the cub in her mouth, without so much as injuring him by a scratch, when "Uncle Paul," who had hitherto kept mum, spake :

"You, all on you, that lives here, remember that bear I trapped for, over to Jake Bean's cornfield?"

The men waked up from their indolent postures, and looked at each other, as who should say, "Now we'll get a story!"

"No," said one of them, "never heerd on't."

"That's a leetle curous," said Uncle Paul,' "he was a dreffle great fellow; must have hefted five hundred-weight, easy. Well, I'll tell ye 'bout it. You see, the bear had been philandering 'round some considerably, and had eat up nigh onto the heft of Jake's corn, so, one day Jake came over to my house, an' says he to me, 'lend me your trap,' says he.

"Bear?' says I.

"Bear!" says he.

"Now there's a blamed many ways to ketch a bear. Some folks baits 'em with meat an' sets 'em down a'most anywhere in a corn-field. A bear aint agoin' to come up and put his paws into no such trap as that! He'll spring that trap, easy like, an' carry that bait right off, afterwards!

"Some fellers'll drive a stake in the ground, and stock corn all around it, an' set the trap-hitched onto the stake, jest outside the stack; but if a bear was such a blamed fool as to put his foot in that trap, when he came up to the stack to feed, he'd snake it right straight from the mark, an' there wouldn't be much *trap* left by mornin'.

"You want to fasten a heavy clog to the trap, an' let the bear drag it. He wont go *far* 'fore he'll get tired, an' stop to rest, an' he's easy enough come up with the next day. He leaves his marks where he travels with that are trap hitched onto him.

"When Jake came over to borry my trap I had a kinder idea he wouldn't get it sot right.

"'Jake,' says I, 'how are you goin' to sot that trap?'

"'Sot it?' says Jake, 'why same as any other man would,' says he.

"'How's that?' says I.

"'Stake,' says Jake.

"'Jake,' says I, 'I've trapped *some*,' says I; 'now take my advice, an' don t you do it.'

"'I shall sot the trap to suit myself!' says Jake. 'Do!' says I, gettin' a leetle wrathy, he was so blamed obstinate,·but you wont never sot no trap o' mine, *that* way!' says I.

"'Well,' say Jake, says he, 'sot the trap yourself, if you're so blamed particular!'

"'Well Jake,' says I, 'I don't care if I do go over, an' then that bear 'll get ketched *sure*!

"So I took down the old trap, straightened out all the spikes, hitched on a piece of log-chain that couldn't break, no ways, and went over with him. I looked over the piece o' corn a bit, an' I soon see where the bear had come in, night after night, till he had trod a path as hard an' smooth as the top of that bar, yender. (Don't care if I *do* take a drop more rum!) Soon's I clapped eyes on it I see my way clear.

"'I shall ketch that bear,' said I, 'right in that are path; that's *so*, now!'

"So we hunted up and down till we found a place where the critter had stepped the same foot over a log every time he come, till he'd made a hard, round spot, about the size of a hat.

"'Jake,' says I, '*there's the spot*!'

"'You won't never get no bear there,' says Jake.

"But I knowed bear *some*! 'There's the spot,' says I.

Jake didn't say nothin', but he put his hands in his breeches pockets, and kinder whistled, *con*temptuous like.

"'Jake,' says I, '*you don't know nothing*,' says I.

"'Mebbe I don't,' says Jake, 'an' then, agin, mebbe I do,' says he.

"I see he wasn't in a fit state o' mind to arger with, so I went to work fixin' my trap.

"I got a piece of board an' run it under the track, an' lifted the whole thing up, as slick as a pin. Then I dug a hole underneath, an' sot the trap. Then I took a strip of hemlock-bark an' put the track on it, as smooth as a feather, and sot the whole concern down, so's it looked as nateral as life. Nobody'd a thought nothin' 'd been nigh it. I *knowed* 'twould ketch the critter.

"'Now, Jake,' says I, 'we'll go home to supper, an' to-morrow we'll tickle that bear's ribs !'

"'Mebbe we will!' says Jake.

"'Now look a here, Jake,' says I, 'dont you go to puttin' in none o' your *mebbes*. Jest you go home, an' that bear's ours, sure!'"'

Here "Uncle Paul" ceased speaking, and took a small pull at his rum. Then he quietly relapsed into entire silence.

Not a word was spoken in the room.

"Well?" said I, at length.

"Well !" said "Uncle Paul."

NEW YORK JULY 9, 1859

EXPLANATION.

We incline to think that the charge of intentional plagiarism made in THE SATURDAY PRESS of June 25th against Mr. N. G. Shepherd, was entirely unfounded. The similitude between the poem he sent us, and a poem of the same title by Mr. T. B. Aldrich, may have been—and probably was—purely accidental.

Our only apology for making the charge is, that plagiarism has got to be so common of late that we had resolved to make the first instance of it that came under our notice the occasion of prompt exposure. But the fact is we were much too hasty, since, after all, the similitude between Mr. Shepherd's poem and that of Mr. Aldrich was only in the first verse, and, moreover, was one that might easily have been explained without reflecting in any way upon the author.

We have only to add, in mitigation of our offence, that having published both the poems in reference, the intelligent reader had a chance to judge for himself as to the correctness of our judgment.

Correspondence.

MY FIRST AND LAST PANTHER HUNT.

HARTFORD, CONN., July 4, 1859.

Mr. Editor:—I ended my last letter with the conclusion of "Uncle Paul's" bear story, at the close whereof the bar-room inmates at the old Canada tavern imbibed largely at the expense of the two strangers, my friend and myself.

(I must remark here, in parenthesis, that I am sure I did not write, in my last, "*without neither* books nor newspapers," though the Devil prompted a compositor in your office so to make me say, and the same Evil One influenced your proof-reader to overlook the error. I gnashed my teeth at the sight of it.)

After we had "smiled, and smiled," we again seated ourselves about the room, and an ominous silence fell upon all.

Burly John Canada piled more wood upon the fire, and then sauntered to the door, which he opened to gaze forth upon the weather. A thick blackness had overspread the sky while Uncle Paul was speaking, and a chill gust of wind burst in at the half open door, shaking the bottles and glasses behind the bar till they jingled again, and throwing great puffs of smoke out of the broad fireplace.

Burly John closed the door again, and retired to his seat upon the bar, and presently the rain began to fall, and, being driven against the windows by the fierce wind, beat thereon the Devil's tattoo with a vengeance.

Far down the valley the mounds of fire burning on the "clearing," gleamed with a dull and sombre red, till they became quenched and dead beneath the pelting storm. Then the wind increased and the old house shook and trembled beneath its fury.

"It's a bad night for Pete," quoth John Canada, knocking the ashes from his pipe, and preparing for a fresh smoke.

"A bad night it is," assented the others. "He's ben through badder," soliloquized Uncle Paul, from behind his rum and water.

"Who is Pete?"

"He runs an express," John Canada explained, "from here to North Adams and back, twice a week; takes out fresh meat and so on, and fetches in groceries and store stuff. He's a dark road to go, 'specially through the long holler.'"

The men about the room assented with many ejaculations. Then all fell into silence again, while the tempest without rather increased than diminished in its fury.

There was no lull in the storm, which made too much disturbance about the little hostelry to enable any other outside sounds to be distinguishable, when the door was suddenly burst in, as though by the combined force of the wind and the rushing rain, and a man was precipitated violently into the middle of the apartment.

He was a tall, bony fellow, clad throughout in butternut colored woolen, and bearing a broken, unlighted lantern in one hand and a whip in the other. From every portion of his angular frame ran streams of water. From his old felt hat, from his nose, from his hands, knees, shoulders, elbows, from the skirts of his coat, and the heavy lappels upon his old-fashioned vest, the water ran in pattering streams upon the floor, forming about him a mimic lake, in the centre whereof he stood, like a grim, butternut-colored river-god.

"Give us some gin!" gasped the river-god. The rain had got into his throat, and he gurgled in his speech."Give us some gin, an' look after m' 'orse."

Whilst Burly John poured out a glass of liquor for the soaked expressman, Dwight thrust his long arms into a heavy coat, put a glazed hat over his whity-brown locks, lighted a lantern, and struggled out into the storm.

"Ah!" gasped the new comer, striding towards the fire—the slush! slush! of his feet in the heavy boots he wore spoke of a good two quarts of water within their expansive cowhide—"Ah! that goes to the right spot! What a night 'tis !" He shivered from head to foot, as he spoke, and it was only with considerable effort that he succeeded in getting off his wet boots and his coat and vest.

Then, as he stood in his shirt-sleeves, with his back to the fire, drying himself as best he might, he said suddenly:

"That blamed *cat* followed me through the 'long holler' again! Damn her ugly body! I had my gun this time, but 'twas too dark to fire with any certainty. She must be hard up to chase a man's wagon sech a night as this! Ah! I'm down on her sometime, sure! I saw her eyes like two coals in the darkness behind me, and I swear! I think she jumped into my wagon once!"

Dwight rushed in, with a tempest of rain, through the door, which he closed behind him and bolted. "Where's the codfish you were going to fetch us?" he said.

"In the wagon," said the river-god.

"That's a lie!"

The expressman seemed to take this remark in perfect good part, as though it were only a common form of denial amongst the class he associated with.

"'Tisn't there, eh?"

"Nary codfish!"

"That cat *was* in my wagon!" shouted the stranger, swinging his long arms about. "She's followed me for three year, blame her ugly countenance! Eleven cubs I've killed for her, and still she keeps on runnin' in that confounded holler, an' I can't get a shot at her, blame her picter! What's a feller goin' to do? She'll be luggin' *me* out o' the wagon some o' these nights, see if she don't, an' *then* I'd like to know where you'll get your codfish an' store-duds! D—n the cat! John—blame you, 'tisn't no laughing matter!—give us some more gin!"

The expressman stood in the centre of the room, a cloud of steam rising from his wet clothing, and swallowed his second glass of gin.

I enquired where the "long hollow" was.

About two miles from the tavern, they said. It was a long, narrow gorge in the mountains, through which ran a small stream, and was infested by a certain female panther of fabulous size, that was known to have made her abode there for at least ten years past, and managed always to escape from those who went in pursuit of her. She brought forth a litter of young every year, which were easily killed, but, for herself, she was so cunning and active no man had yet succeeded in slaying her, and she was the terror of all the dogs in the neighborhood. They all agreed that Pete, the expressman, was right, and that the chances were that some dark night he would become "cat's meat" before his time.

My Cambridge friend and I—I may as well call him Jones, for want of a better name whereby to distinguish him—retired to rest full of the panther! I presume we dreamed of it through the night. We awoke early and found a clear and pleasant sun shining over the strips of meadow-land that formed the narrow valley, and, looking out thereat, Jones spake :

"I say, *we'll kill that panther!*"

"We will, or perish in the attempt!"

Jones fervently grasped my hand and I returned the pressure.

Enquiring more about the beast, we learned that it kept itself hidden during the day, but frequented the road through the "long hollow" after nightfall, and that from ten o'clock in the evening to midnight was the best time to get a chance at it.

We procured two guns. Mine was a heavy, long barrelled rifle, carrying a large ball, while the weapon procured by Jones was a very ancient musket, whose old flint-lock had been supplanted by a more modern and efficient percussion-arrangement. Full of ardor, we passed the day in anticipation of our midnight hunt. . . . . .

The hands of my venerable pocket time-piece—inherited from a deceased grandfather—pointed to thirty minutes past nine as we stepped from the clear moonlight into the pine-shadowed portal of the "long hollow."

The thick woods upon either hand stood darkly on the steep hillsides, and the overhanging branches met above the narrow roadway, leaving only an indistinct glimmering of sky through their interlacing ends to mark where the winding path crept up into the heart of the mountain. A small stream, swollen by the previous night's rain, foamed and roared down the narrow gorge, now rushing beneath a rude bridge of unhewn logs, and anon tumbling and plashing down the steep at our side.

There was no sound save that of the water and an occasional gutteral cry from some swift-gliding owl, as he slid through the air on downy and noiseless wing; passing like a night-spirit, seen and gone with a weird, swift silence of passage.

It was well for us that there was no foliage upon the trees, as yet, for, otherwise, we should have been in the midst of a darkness so dense as to have precluded any possibility of hunting. As it was, there was a faint light from just overhead, that struggled down to the foot of the glen where we stood.

We sauntered slowly up the road till we came to a place where the valley widened, and we could hear, by the silver running of the brook, that it was spread into a more shallow and less fiercely rushing stream, and ran over pebbles. Here there was a sort of pause in the ascent; a short, narrow plateau, where the sides of the gorge curved inly, leaving a broader stream and the winding road. Thick bushes, principally young birch and alder, grew at either side of the path, and at about the centre of the level a tall, bare, and fearfully gnarled oak towered high above, throwing one knotty and crooked limb entirely across the road.

At this place we paused. It was the only spot we had found where we could keep within sight of each other and still be some little distance apart.

Jones stationed himself at the lower end of the level, while I took my place above him, just at the point where a sudden curve and ascent hid the road beyond from sight.

Our eyes had become accustomed to the darkness and our ears to the gurgle and plash of the waters. We could see each the other's outline, and could hear each other's steps when we occasionally changed place.

Here we stood or sauntered while the night grew older.

At length I took out my watch. By dint of a long scrutiny I had made the time to be fifteen minutes past eleven.

I was putting it up when I heard a low "Hish!" from Jones.

"What do you hear?" I whispered, clutching my rifle.

"I hear a rustling in the bushes just beside me!" I was not frightened, but a chill ran through me, and I felt myself shivering from head to foot.

"Do you see anything?

"I see the brush bending and swaying—some animal is creeping past me on its belly!" Jones retreated across the road, facing a dense patch of brush, and raising his gun.

"For God's sake, don't fire till you see the creature plainly!"

Jones put down his gun, and I stole towards him.

I paused. I could hear it now, gliding through the brush, and breaking an occasional dead twig. Very little noise though.

Now I saw it; a dark body slowly approaching the spot where I stood, but never in plain view, from the thick underbrush about it.

There was a heavy plunge through the brush, followed by a plash in the brook.

Jones had thrown a large stone at the slow moving shadow.

We had not noticed till that instant that we had followed the movement in the bushes to the foot of the gnarled oak—but we were aware of it then.

For, with a fearful cry between a growl and the hissing snarl of a cat, a large animal glided up the tree and out upon the branch just over us! Daylight could not have made it plainer. It crouched upon the limb with flashing eyes and white fangs gleaming from the distended mouth. Its short, thick tail waving from side to side; its back humped, with each particular hair standing on end with rage, and its ever-changing, savage face, glancing from one to the other.

We both stepped back, and, at the motion, a cry the most savage I ever heard came from the terrible creature above us.

I believe it had determined to spring upon me!

It drew its legs up under it, and turned its hideous countenance full upon me.

Still stepping back I raised my rifle, and at the instant Jones fired.

The beast slid around the branch and hung by its forepaws, uttering cry after cry of pain.

It hung for a half-moment, dropped into the road, and turned with indescribable fury upon me. But it was too late. It had scarcely touched the ground when I had a bullet through its brain, and the terror of the " long hollow' was no more!

WARREN

—The wing of the Spiritualists led by Rev. John M. Spear, claim that a congress of Spirits has been formed, of which Mr. Spear is a medium. They tell us that this congress" has formed seven subsidiary co-ordinate associations, whose province may be guessed from their titles, viz: The Association of Beneficents, of Electricizers, of Element-izers, of Education-izers, of Healthful-izers, of Agricultural-izers, and Government-izers." The first document put forth by this Spiritual Congress, through the mediumship of Mr. Spear, is entitled *The Educator*, "for the Association of Government-izers," of which it is claimed Robert Rantoul is President. According to this manifesto there is soon to be a new Republic in the United States, with a new religion.

—Peter Verdine, a convict in the State Prison of Michigan, the other day coolly and deliberately laid his finger on a block, took an axe and cut it off close to the hand; rolling the finger up in a paper, he gave it to his keeper, saying to him, "Send it to the Governor as an evidence of the truth." He has been endeavoring to get pardoned, and, being fearful the Governor would not believe all that was set forth in his petition, offered this strange evidence of veracity.—*Jackson (Mich.) Citizen, June* 16.

NEW YORK JULY 16, 1859

[For the N. Y. SATURDAY PRESS.]

HASCHEESH;

OR,

HOW DORA AND I SPENT THE FOURTH.

BY MARIE STEVENS CASE.

It promised to be a gloomy day to us; all our friends were out of town, and we had nothing to interest us in the wide city round. So Dora came to me, the evening before, and begged me to spend the Fourth with her.

"But I shall weary you, Dora, before the day is over," I said. "How can we amuse ourselves all alone?"

"I don't know," returned she, half sadly, and her large, dark eyes drooped; but she raised them again quickly, as though a happy thought had struck her. "We can both go to sleep till evening, when we will go to my friend Nettie's, in Fourteenth street, to see the fireworks from the roof; she invited me yesterday."

"But you forget the crackers and guns, Dora. Can one sleep in Pandemonium ?"

"Truly, I forgot that; but," said she, laughing, "we'll take a dose of opium."

"Hascheesh!" I suggested.

"Good!" exclaimed Dora. "Where can we get it? I've heard of that; it gives one exquisite dreams and fantastic visions—the real becomes the unreal, and the dream is the actual—every moment seems an age of ecstacy."

And so she continued, for some minutes, exaggerating the mystic power of this Oriental drug, and finally we resolved to spend our day in dreamland, if we could but find this key to its golden gates.

Fortune favored us, or perhaps our evil genii; for before 10 A. M. a gentleman called, and though Dora had firmly determined to deny herself to every one who might come, the reflection, as she glanced at the card, that the visitor was a man who had travelled in the East, and might possibly aid us in our hascheesh scheme induced her to see him.

Dora questioned him upon the matter at once. He discoursed eloquently upon the hascheesh fantasia, and at length, told us that he had some of the drug in his possession, and if we *really* wished to make the experiment he would send us some. Of course we *really* did, and about an hour after, the mysterious hascheesh came—a strange-looking, green powder, made apparently from leaves or flowers. We examined it with great interest, and took a dose very carefully, according to direction. This was at 11 o'clock, but as the hour of 12 came, and we felt in every respect the same, Dora doubled, and I tripled the dose. One o'clock came. We had watched in vain during the hour for the slightest influence of the hascheesh, and had concluded that her good friend had sent us pulverized catnip or something equally innocent, and was probably at that moment, laughing at our expense.

Presently we went down to dinner, where Dora facetiously asked an old M. D. who sat opposite, what was the precise effect of catnip on the human system, and if it increased the appetite as a general rule. He remarked gravely and with the learned and peculiarly definite air of his profession, that what was commonly denominated catnip, was a plant of the genus Nepeta, and in some conditions of the membranous receptacle of aliment, it might, or might not, in conjunction with the fluids there, form a highly odoriferous and pungent essential oil which would variously affect different people.

During the delivery of this very satisfactory opinion, Dora looked slyly at me, and when we retired from the dining room we amused ourselves over the perilous situation which we might or might not be in, according to the learned Doctor.

Dora, who is always witty, was especially happy on this occasion, and we remained convulsed until laughter seemed the most boundless and exquisite pleasure in the world.

Just then some one tapped at the door for Dora, and I went to excuse her. I remember I did not open the door, but stood with my face close to it, and answered the questioner. A painful sense at length came over me. This person seemed to question me forever. I answered mechanically—in fact I was fast becoming a sphynx—my head expanded to the size of the room, and I thought I was an oracle doomed to respond through all Eternity.

The wicked laugh of Dora, and her soft arms about me, recalled me partially to the fact that I was answering imaginary questions; but the phantasy would not leave me, and I implored my friend to spare me from laughing "Do you not see," I cried, "that I am stone." A terrible fear seized me, lest she should not heed my prayer. I continued in the most impressive manner I could command, "Dora, you know that the expansive powers of stone are very inconsiderable, and if you make me laugh, I shall be scattered to the four winds." My words had no effect: she laughed, and instantly I felt a convulsion in my frame—a deafening explosion followed and I flew asunder in all directions. Then I heard the explosion of the fragments—a myriad of sounds succeeded each other, until I was reduced to a most impalpable powder, and caught by the breeze I was wafted away into space.

Still was my consciousness preserved, and a circum-folding sense of joy and perfect peace possessed me. Amid this delicious dream, the voice of Dora, which seemed all too mortal, bade me return. "Why do you leave me?" she asked. "You do not love me—I am weary, sick." The fear that Dora was suffering roused me, and I made a great effort to dispel my hallucinations. We discussed at great length the problems of birth, life, and death. How unfortunate, I thought, that we had alluded to the last; for now I perceived that Dora's face grew black, and a sense that she was dying made me shudder. I sought to turn the course of our conversation. At that moment my eye rested on some Egyptian vases in the room, and I led Dora to the place where they stood. Over them hung a picture of Cleopatra dying, and we remained transfixed before it. The diadem of Egypt sat proudly upon the brow of the Queen, and there seemed a living agony in her face. She moved, breathed, and spoke. As we looked upon her in her gorgeous robes of State, the whole scene changed, and we were in Egypt. We passed through all the suffering of the unfortunate Queen—the poison of the asp curdled our blood also, and our difficult and painful breathing died on the air with hers. After a while, we returned to life, and Dora, shutting her eyes, turned the picture to the wall—no longer a picture to us, but the place, the time, the living reality.

"Let us shut out this terrible Egyptian world," said Dora, trembling; but we could not—the vases still remained, and the fearful scene we had passed was fresh upon our minds.

"We shall die!" cried Dora. "The poison of the asp is still here," and she clasped her hands over her heart. A bewildering fear came upon us, and just at this moment a clear, strange voice rang out from the air—

"Mortals, you have tampered with forbidden things! How have you dared to return to the land of the Pharoahs? Verily 'ye have sown the wind, and ye shall reap the whirlwind.'"

The voice ceased amid a sound like the roar and crash of arms, and I turned anxiously to my friend.

"Did you hear our sentence?" she asked. Her face was horrible to behold, and I crossed the room to examine my own in a glass. Like her, I was livid, and my limbs were stiff and cold.

"*We are poisoned! We are poisoned!*" cried Dora, throwing her arms out wildly, and tearing her long black hair. "That was the voice of our evil genius. O, God! we are lost forever! The poison of the asp is withering and blackening my heart!"

A terrible sense of the damp, narrow grave came upon us, and struggling in vain for a breath of air, we cried aloud: "God! God help us!"

Dora fell at my feet, and stooping to raise her, I heard strange sounds about us, and stranger beings glided silently by. Were we in the land of spirits? Never shall I forget that dreadful hour. Hour, did I say? It seemed a century, and at that moment, as I looked back to our unfortunate meeting with the Queen, it seemed a vista of eternity. After a while I breathed more freely, and I gazed at these beings, who ran hither and thither, and filled our room. The scene was still Egyptian, and as these mysterious nurses lifted me to the bed and chafed my limbs, I plainly perceived that they were mummies! Yes, veritable, brown, dry mummies, wrapped in the mouldy linen of four thousand years! They did not terrify me in the least; but presently I perceived that they had left Dora on the sofa, and were attending only to me. I felt indignant, but concealing my wrath, I cried out:

"Dear good mummies, don't let my Dora suffer? Go to her—chafe her limbs; she is worse than I am."

I thought they went to her only to please me; but as she turned, after a few minutes and spoke to me, I concluded that I had been unjust to the mummies, and I earnestly begged their pardon. I overwhelmed them with gratitude for their kindness, and as I grew better, I began to study them more attentively. One, a woman, moved about as methodically and cautiously as though she were walking on eggs, and she never turned her head or her eyes, but she turned her whole body. She was dressed in sombre grey, with a straight white cap on her head, and a white kerchief on her neck. She moved always in right lines, and I soon perceived that her course around the room marked regular polygons. "Surely," I said to myself, "she must have been once some great mathematical genius." I longed to ask her, but dared not be so bold. Just then she wheeled about from my bed, faced the mantlepiece, and started towards it in a line which was, I felt convinced, the shortest distance between the two points. She seized a cup thence, turned her head and body and started towards the door; but when she reached the point exactly opposite the foot of the bed, she turned again in the same manner and came directly to the point whence she had started. "What a perfect isosceles triangle!" I exclaimed, looking at the lines which her course to and from the mantlepiece had marked.

She stirred the black mixture in the cup, and now for the first time spoke, in a musty, creaky voice:

"How much did thee take?"

Shocked at this murdering of my mother-tongue, and without stopping to answer her question, I ejaculated in the most respectful language I could command:

"O thou most venerable mummy! do not mind addressing me in English; I shall comprehend your Egyptian just as well!"

A sickly smile passed over her ancient features as I saw her moving in the same direct and circumscribed manner toward the door. I waited for this kind mummy to return,—I enquired for her but she came no more.

"Most sensitive mummy," I murmured, "I have wounded you in that matter of the English, but I shall never be able to repay your kindness."

Two other mummies now entered—tall and stern-looking, wearing moustaches. They conversed in low tones in one corner of the room, sent for the hascheesh cup, examined its contents, muttered something about "Cannabis Indica," and then came again to me. They poured most dreadful mixtures down my throat, rubbed and shook me, fearing I should go to sleep. They placed Dora beside me and gradually all the mummies disappeared. Then I think I slept. The next thing I remember, was Dora's merry laugh, as she turned her large eyes towards me, demanding what all this meant.

"I don't know," I returned, "I am perfectly well! Are not you?"

"Perfectly. Have we been dreaming?"

"No," I said. "Look at our room! These medicines, bath-tubs, hot flat-irons, and wet blankets mean *something*," and we laughed at the comicality of our position.

Suddenly the thought occurred that we had broken our engagement to see the fireworks, and we began to lament it.

"Why, Dora," I suggested, "this is certainly the Fourth of July,—don't you hear the guns?"

"Surely, and the sun has not yet set; I thought whole years had passed."

I looked at my watch—'twas just half past five, and all this terrible scene had occupied only two hours! We were dressed, and at the place to see the fireworks in due season. The effect of the hascheesh was still upon us a little, and the rockets seemed the most astonishing and gorgeous things in the universe. We watched them with intense delight, and, but for our friends, I suppose we should have staid on the roof till the last rocket went up.

Our friends never suspected that we were not perfectly sane, though during the evening, some one remarked that Dora was a little more grave than usual.

I went to see her the next day, fearing to find her sick. She was perfectly well, and anxious to talk over our hascheesh experiment.

"But were we not really nursed by mummies?" I queried.

"Mummies! you simpleton! My good old Quaker friend will never forgive you; you drove her from the room by your ridiculous appellation of *Most venerable mummy* !"

"And those two tall, stern-looking fellows. Were they real flesh and blood ?"

"We shall see," said Dora, laughing, "when they send us their bills."

NO DRAMATIC FEUILLETON.

A correspondent suggested, some time since, that Personne—our virtuous and valiant Dramatic Critic be "suppressed." Now the task of suppressing so much virtue and valor, in this hot weather, struck us as being rather too formidable, and we accordingly invited our correspondent to come down to the office and do his own suppressing. But, strange to say, Personne has, meanwhile, gone and suppressed himself, without anybody's help. What has become of him, it is impossible for us to say. We have written to all the "Anna Marias" we could think of, to get the latest news of him, but thus far without the least result. The rumor that he went up in a fire-balloon from the Palace Garden, the other night, and didn't come back again, is probably apocryphal. But however this may be, he has gone to parts unknown, and it is not likely that he will turn up (or come down) again till the close of the season. Meanwhile, great wailing and gnashing of teeth among our readers (always saving the amiable correspondent aforesaid), as also in the theatrical world, which threatens, unless Personne returns at once to his post, to come to a dramatic and untimely end—which, on the whole, wouldn't be a bad idea.

A man who goes to the theatre in such weather as this must be a very hopeless character, or at any rate, not one likely to reform and "flee from the wrath to come" from any of the incendiary motives usually presented to such people.

The only comfortable place to go to during the heated term is the "Palace Garden"—so-called, we presume, because there is no Palace there, and no Garden. But what of that? Surely no American hankers after Palaces (see "*Home, Sweet Home*," which our folks are so fond of singing—when they are *abroad*), and as for Gardens, your true metropolitan thinks nothing of them except as places which furnish him with his perennial supply of vegetables, wherewith to pelt his favorite prima donna, during the opera-season.

However, in the absence of both Garden and Palace, the P. G. abounds in cozy seats (only they have no backs to them), in cheap fireworks, in paper balloons, in all kinds of good-natured people, and in Mr. Thomas Baker—and a man or woman who can't find enough enjoyment in them, on a hot Summer evening, must be hard to please.

We might add, among the attractions of the place, a large and well-ventilated ballroom, but unfortunately this doesn't appear to be an attraction. Somehow, the frequenters and frequentresses of the P. G. don't think it genteel to dance there. They will dance in all kinds of assembly-rooms, and at all kinds of watering-places, but Mrs. Grundy, dear woman, has not yet decided that it is proper to dance at a P. G., and so, though the aforesaid frequenters and frequentresses are dying to dance—every mother's son and daughter of them—no one has the courage to take the initiative.

The manager's elegant explanation in the papers, that "the impression has obtained to some extent in the city that the soirées dansantes are conducted on the principles of great exclusiveness," is all bosh. If he wants people to dance at his soirées, he must get some twenty or thirty presentable young men and women to set the example. Indeed it won't matter much—judging from what we saw the other evening—if they are not very presentable. The spectacle presented on that same evening was very curious. There was the hall, there was the music (Baker's best), and there were some five or six hundred pairs of uneasy and tolerably well-shod feet; but despite all these "necessary elements," and despite a most touching appeal of the manager and a corps of brilliantly beribbonned and embroidered young floor-officials, it was next to impossible to induce anybody to "rise in dance."

If our own private and exclusive A. M. had been present, we would have been on the floor in a twinkling, or else then and there had a domestic quarrel which not even Mr. C. V. DeForest himself could have quelled. And apropos of this same Mr. C. V. DeForest, we beg to suggest to him that his idea of making the P. G. as silent and solemn as a Quaker meeting, is simply absurd. The P. Geeans won't stand it. Think of that punctilious official having crept up to a group of gentlemen, the other evening, and requested them not to laugh so boisterously! We heard him do it, with our own ears. Why, he might as well have asked the birds not to sing so boisterously. Who ever heard before of regulating the scale of laughter by any fixed rules?

Then, again, while another group was discussing the war, Mr. DeForest coolly requested them to "moderate their tones a little." And all this, not in a private room—not even in the spacious ballroom—but in the open air!

Doubtless the Manager's motive was a good one. But if he expects to convert a gay company of pleasure-seekers into a grim, glum company of ascetics, he slightly mistakes both his functions and his powers: this, indeed, was made sufficiently evident on the occasion alluded to, by the gentlemen continuing their laughter and their discussion, and sending him off to reflect upon their obstreperousness, in the seclusion and silence of his private office.

Making the above allowances, the P. G. is just the pleasantest place to spend an evening at that can be found in the city. The music might, indeed, be of a higher order and still be within the comprehension of the auditors; the fireworks might be a shade more brilliant and varied; but, on the whole, the appointments are very good, and, which is quite remarkable, the refreshments are both excellent in quality and reasonable in price.

NEW YORK JULY 23, 1859

PISCATAQUARIA.

Being a Familiar Letter from Poetas, on the banks of Piscataqua River, to his Friend, the Able Editor in town.

Portsmouth, N. H., July 18, 1859.

My Dear Boy:—I have just lighted a meerschaum-full of Mrs. Newcomb's "May-blossom" with a very picturesque and poetical description of this pleasant old seaport town, which I wrote for The Saturday Press "according to agreement." I couldn't bring my mind to the mailing of that precious document. The fact is, I always make a dash at the *last* tip-top cork that floats upon, the waters of my fancy ("water on the brain," my child !)—a tide that waits for no man; and having had a fresh experience to-day, the manuscript of yesterday seemed as antique as the gambrel-roofed houses it described, and as tiresome as a poem by Shillaber.

So, while the smoke floats from my argillaceous pipe, and an impish robin bobs at the black-hearts close by the open window; while the sun shines, the flowers cut their teeth, the birds sing, and the river does its best to be musical; while, in short, Nature turns the invisible crank that produces a perfect Summer afternoon, I sit in a one-hundred-and-twenty-year old mansion, and stain the virginity of a new sheet, without one tender recollection of yesterday's epistolary platitudes:

"It is good to be merry and wise,
It is good to be honest and true;
It is good to be off with the old love
Before you be on with the new."

To begin :

If there is one thing more distasteful to me than another (and I am happy to say there isn't), it is to go a-gunning. I have several friends, residents here, who are passionately given to this kind of pastime, and as there is not the slightest wild bird or beast within a hundred miles of the town, these facetious fellows are, of course, magnificently provided with shooting-jackets and shot-guns—jackets that are never used, and guns that never go off. This fact, coupled with my distinguished horror of anything so like work, immediately created in me an intense desire to go a-gunning.

To tramp off alone was, of course, out of the question. I know how *that* would have ended. I should have peppered all the guide-boards until they looked like hopeless cases of small-pox: then I should have gone to sleep, gun and I, under a tree, and caught my death-of-cold. And then—bitterest thought of all!—this letter would not have reached you.

Not being tired of life, or at least I wasn't yesterday for two or three hours in the forenoon, I dared not ask any of the "crack shots' to accompany me. Your Crack Shot is so devilishly skillful that he never invites you to get out of the way when you chance to stand between him and the game. If you express the ghostliest doubt as to his ability to shoot around you, he incontinently offers to wager five dollars to one that he can, at fifty yards, shoot off your longest pet eyelash without disturbing the rest. Now you don't want your longest pet eyelash shot off at any price. This strikes him as being unreasonable and unfriendly. You observe a coldness in his demeanor toward you, and you make it a point to keep close by his side the remainder of the day.

While twisting on the horns of my dilemma, I fortunately thought of Tibbs. You know Tibbs? You *did* once. Tibbs is married now, poor fellow! Some men never have any luck! He was always unfortunate, was Tibbs; but genial. He is twice as unfortunate as he used to be, and not half so cheerful. You remember him with his beamy face and nankeen pants. His very neckerchief used to smile. He is changed now. Mrs. Tibbs was a widow, with a perpetual cold in her head and some property. He met her and she married him. That was a bad day's work for Tibbs. You ought to hear her say, *Mr. Tibbs!* once. It sounds just like swearing.

Mrs. and Mr. Tibbs are on a visit to the lady's relations here. I see him quite frequently—she takes him out to air every morning. When she leaves him at home, I am convinced that she puts a spare hoop over him, and poor Tibbs goes to sleep with his weary head resting upon the bars.

Having the honor of not being afraid of anything that lives, and moves, and has its being, I waited until I saw Mrs. Tibbs down town *alone*, then I rushed up to H——'s, where the happy pair are staying, and startled Tibbs. He was ever and never so glad to see me. I shot out my invitation. Would he go a-gunning with me to-morrow? Blue heaven, green woods, yellow water—Sagamore—birds—snap—rip—bang—devil,—dead! heaps of game—large cart to take it home in! Small black flask and large white sandwich under the trees at Sagamore. Would he go?

Mr. Tibbs hesitated.

"The fact is," said Tibbs slowly, "I'd like to; and if Mrs. Tibbs goes to the picnic tomorrow (and she certainly will, because she says she won't), I'll meet you somewhere, and we *will* make a day of it." And a smile, something like the smile of other days, glimmered for a second on the care-worn features of poor Tibbs.

Time and place were agreed upon, and I left Tibbs to borrow a brace of guns from Laighton, the poet, whose volume of pleasant poems, by-the-by, you haven't noticed, more's the pity!

Mr. Tibbs and ten o'clock the next day came at the same time—

"Her heart and morning broke together"
[Gen. Morris.]

I had a most nobby outfit for Tibbs—grey velvet skull-cap, small jacket with gigantic buttons, coriaceous breeches, and—as I knew there was no marshy ground anywhere about—a huge pair of fisherman's boots, perfectly water-proof, too keep his dear little feet dry. Selfishness forms no part of my admirable nature, as I allowed Mr. Tibbs to do all the ornamental on this occasion, and contented myself with plain clothes. And off we went—Tibbs carrying his gun as if it were a baby "nine days old."

Now for a dash of description in the most approved style.

Like a thousand and eighty-nine golden lances, the morning sun bristled up behind the hill-tops, lighting the hayaline and umbrageous depths of Sagamore woods, and twinkling on the spires of the town in the distance, as two solitary travellers might have been seen carefully wending their way down a perilous declivity, the end of which wedded itself to an inexpensive wooden bridge, probably built by the ancient Norman Barons, when they inhabited this part of the country. This bridge extended—very naturally—to the other side of the creek. The travellers have now reached the foot of the descent, and as they pause involuntarily to survey the wild scene which expands, regardless of expanse, before them, we will introduce these personages more particularly to the reader. [Ha! J. P. R. A. B. C. James !]

The slighter, and evidently the elder of these two gentlemen was arrayed in the gorgeous shooting-costume of the period. His air was that of a man who had supped on honors—*a vinculo matrimonii*. He clutched his rifle as if he struggled with a foe, who, if released, would turn and annihilate him. His eye (heroes and heroines never have but one eye worth mentioning) was deeply, darkly, beautifully blue. The companion of this singular and mysterious man was barely in his twenty-second year, a being made for love [that's me!] and beautiful as Apollo Belvidere. No one could behold that commanding form, those Hyperion locks, those soul-subduing eyes, and that crepusculous *moustache*, without feeling in the presence of a superior intellect. Resting gracefully in the hollow of his left arm lay an exquisitely-shaped fowling-piece. The heart of Orpheus! the arm of Hercules! the front of Jove! O, Youth! O, Gun! O, Ten-o'clock-in-the-morning! How thou smilest in the superiority of unconscious strength and beauty, O Youth! How thou glimmerest in the ambient sunlight, O, Gun! And thou, Celestial Hour, how thou passest away, away, never to return the same as thou wert! O, Orpheus, the living; 0, Hercules, the mighty; Jove, the majestic! O, Anacyndaraxes!—But cease, fond Philosophy! Pisistratus Caxton, for that is the name of our hero, suddenly clutches his comrade's arm, and fixes his eyes intently on a ferocious pelican, which clings convulsively to the branches of a blasted banana-tree, and now—"What will he Do with It?"

But to get off the stilts and come back to you, Henry!

Tibbs and I crossed the bridge at Sagamore—which is really a very lovely spot, in spite of all the hyperbole that has been written about it—and plunged into the pine woods on the other side of the creek. "I know a bank whereon the wild thyme blows," and many a wild time I have had the there in those old days when I went to picnics with Laura—she's married now, and snubs her liege-lord to my heart's content. On this bank there are always cool air and shade, caused chiefly by the blowing of the wind and the thickness of the foliage, which renders it impossible for the sun to rest there. To this place I proceeded to lead the gentle Tibbs, who was already tired to death with the two miles walk and his heavy fowling-piece.

"I guess the air here agrees with my gun," said Tibbs in a bird-like manner, and trying to look as if he enjoyed himself.

"The air agrees with your gun? How? Don't see it."

"O," said Tibbs, who always blushes when he brings a *mot* into the world, "it seems to gain a pound every minute."

That fellow Tibbs would be really witty if he were not surrounded by circumstances, or rather *a* circumstance, "over which he has no control."

We jogged on very carefully for fear of frightening the game which abounds in these woods, and which is of so dangerous a nature that the hunter has been known to expiate his rashness in death. I told Tibbs of a woman who was devoured by a black bear only a month before, and showed him the mound which had been placed over (because I suppose they couldn't get it under) her remains. Tibbs was very much affected, and finally wept—brushing away a tear as if he were ashamed of his emotion, just as Mr. Davenport does in the drama of "Black-Eyed Susan." My story made such an impression on Tibbs that he drew his first fire on an unsuspicious calf, which was quietly nosing the sweet-fern within six yards of us; and as Tibbs is a deadly marksman (he told me confidentially that he was "bang up"), the poor animal kept on nosing the fern, and wondered what in the devil made that noise.

"Look here, Tibbs !" said I, as he fired, "*fratricide* is a hanging matter in this State." That delighted Tibbs. He declared he would "get that off" on *you* some day. The idea of getting off such a thing on an Able Editor. It's altogether unnecessary!

We then went on *sans* episode, except that Tibbs's gun went off unexpectedly and unpleasantly over his shoulder, and I brought down two or three imaginary plover, which my amiable companion insisted on finding, and couldn't.

"I say," said Tibbs, "is that thymey bank much further?"

"We're almost there, Tibbs. Here's the split oak, and here's where the path isn't, by Jove! I've lost the way. But never mind, my dear Ramrod," seeing Tibbs's face drawing out like an accordeon, "never mind, I know the way back."

With this I lifted up a curtain of honeysuckle-vines, and lo! we stood in the midst of a party of fifteen or twenty ladies and gentlemen, who were quietly and industriously feasting from a table without any legs—a large white cloth spread rurally on the mossy rocks. Just then, *bang!* went Tibbs's diabolical gun. The gentlemen started and the ladies shrieked—

And, O, my prophetic Soul,—Mrs. Tibbs!

Mrs. Tibbs rose, not like the mythological bird from ashes, nor like Venus from the sea-foam, but from the green sward of Sagamore she rose, and confronted her unhappy consort.

"*Mr. Tibbs!*" that was all she said. Language could go no further.

I shall not prolong this painful scene by indulging in details. The last I saw of my friend, Mrs. Tibbs had him by one hand and his gun in the other, and was frantically marching the pair of them down the road towards town, to the undisguised amusement of the assembled spectators. It was very comical—even to me, who never look at the ludicrous side of things.

I don't know what will become of Tibbs. She will probably stretch him on the rack of her corsets, or break him on the wheel of her hoop.

I shall go up this evening to the H——'s, and remonstrate with Mrs. Tibbs, though I know it is a delicate thing to put one's head into a family jar, for the conflicting elements immediately coalesce, and you find yourself, as it were, in a pickle; but when a man feels the spread-eagle of American Independence fluttering in his left bosom [Hear! hear !], martyrdom becomes an agreeable recreation, and death a thing worth living for.

I got Tibbs into trouble, I must get Tibbs out, "though I perish in the attempt"—to quote from our greatest American novelist, Mr. Cobb.

If you never hear from me again, my dear fellow, keep my memory green as S——'s gloves, and "write me as one who loved his fellow men"—male and female!

Yours, etc., etc.,

E.

Special Notices.

OCEAN MAIL STEAMERS.—The European mails, by the steamship A R A G O, hence for Southampton, will close at the New York Postoffice, to-day, July 23, at 10 1-2 o'clock, A. M.

NOTICE.

We take pleasure in announcing that G. H. Avery Esq., of Owego, N. Y., is associated in the proprietorship and business management of the New York Saturday Press.

Correspondence.

LETTER FROM SARATOGA.

July 19th, 1859.

Dear "Press."—Does not the very name "Saratoga" conjure up to your becitied mind a faëry scene vision of gossamer-clad crinoline in all the freshness of youth and the radiancy of beauty? If your fancy be poetical, you will imagine the fair ones as they appear when promenading in dulcet converse, on the moonlit piazza, or walking, under the same lunar influence, with the fond occupant of all their thoughts, through the romantic grounds of the United States Hotel, with Munck's delicious music-strains to complete the charm. If your poetical susceptibility be not superior to your keen sense of the humorous, you may behold them seated in balloon-rows along the three hundred feet diningroom, and trying to eat as if all-unconscious of masculine gazing eyes; or, you may smile a sourire of good-natured fun, when you perceive them encircling the iron railing of Congress Spring, with a tumbler of the sparkling cathartic, and a wry face at its saltness, as they swallow it in gulps. "It's so horridly salt, mamma!" as an apology for the grimace. "But it does you so much good, you know, dear !" To those who drink it for the first time, every subsequent change of feeling, from ill to well, or from well to ill, is ascribed to "those waters!" But though the change is usually for the better, no one seems to think of the benefits naturally resulting from pure air and early hours; for who, on leaving our "West End" with all its window-shutters still carefully closed as late as nine or ten o'clock in the morning, would here expect to see the belles who keep them so, come "trooping down" to the springs at 6 A. M.! and this, rain or shine, sometimes in a deluge, which in New York would retain them in-doors for a week. Of course there are notabilities here without number. Gazzaniga, one of them, gives us a concert to-morrow night (just previous to her departure for Newport), assisted by Philip Mayer ("baritone," it says on the bills, but he was "bass" at the last concert I heard him), and with that charming fellow, "Albites," to conduct. Sr. Brignoli is here too, en passant, but does not lend, nor even sell, his sweet voice to the concert, which, if he did, would greatly increase its pecuniary, and, still more so, its artistic success. Our illustrious "tenore" "spreads himself" here considerably—drives the very fastest horses in the very fastest manner, eats the best dinners, and commits other indiscretions just as carelessly as if he had never had a voice, or expected never again to experience the need of one. He is actually growing *thin* again, too. (It's those waters, you see!) But over, above, and beyond all, whom do you think we have amongst us? No less than he whose absence you have been lamenting, whose whereabouts you have endeavored to discover, whose latitudinal and longitudinal position all the Anna Marias of your acquaintance could not reveal to you! Yes, "Personne" himself—not quite so "large as life," perhaps (pump-shoes reduce the heels an half inch or more), but "quite as natural;" his moustache having gained in length, he strokes it most complacently with those supernatural, ghostly hands of his, which, I trust, he will soon employ to inform you, and through you, the world at large, of the situation of his A. M. (who is unaccountably invisible, if with him), and of the equally mysterious absence of "Whiskers." A few days ago, the Young Men's Christian Association ("embracing over 100 ladies !" a local paper says), made an excursion from Troy to this place, and "put up "at Congress Hall, where they were given so good a dinner, that the Saratoga *News* published the bill of fare. The large party walked about to see the shows, notwithstanding a dismal rain, the usual accompaniment to picnics. Another smaller party, which came hither yesterday from Troy, not having a storm from overhead, got up one amongst themselves, and nearly killed a youth, who was not of their party. However, one murder more would not matter much, and the act must be becoming rather a title to esteem, since Mr. Sickles not only "walks abroad in the face of day," but has set up a "livery "of his own, to drive out with. Verily! does the man's ostentation court still greater notoriety? By the way, the very few articles you have chosen to devote to this subject, are really the only sound ones that have been written. But "basta!" When I meet "Personne" shall I scold him for you?

Yours, truly, DOLLOPE.

Dramatic Feuilleton.

Personne Redivivus.

I really did not imagine that I was of so much consequence. I had imagined when I suppressed myself—I use your rather inelegant expression—it might be better to say when I cut myself out, I say I had supposed that the heart of ye printer-man would be filled with exceeding great joy; that he would smile with grim satisfaction as he thought of no more feuilletons, no more recondite researches in cypherology, no more Champollion, no more foreign tongues, and eccentric orthography of the Connecticut vernacular,—in fact, no more PERSONNE.

And lo! here he is.

Here is his illuminated MS. engrossed like the Declaration of Independence, or the compliments of one fire company to another.

Monsieur Tonson is arrived once more. He is here actuellement. Salve! oh, Printer-man, Salve! Embrassez moi, mon cher. Baissez-moi. Bien!

Like the Pericles of the Third Congressional District, and Aspasia of Bloomingdale road, we will never, never, never part again (till next time).

Perhaps you, O Editor, Effendi of the Piazza, may have some natural curiosity to learn of my wanderings and their cause.

The first was the weather, and the second was A. M. And here let me say that though the Brightest and the Best has taken to a different line of country, where she undoubtedly thinks she can do better, I cannot permit her sacred name to be taken in vain as it was by one "Growler," in the Sunday *Times* (he don't growl nearly so much as the people who slumber over his platitudes). No, A. M., for literary purposes is mine, copyrighted, patented, entered according to, etc., U. S. A. Office, price one dollar, and I will defend my property at all hazards.

Well, as it was hot, and as I was driven to the brink of despair by A. M., and by hack 126 to the foot of Jay street, I took the *Thomas Powell*, bound for West Point, and other points on the Hudson. You wouldn't think it from her name, but the *T. P.* is a clean, swift, reliable, and altogether excellent boat. I took an inventory of the passengers, and as they all looked as if they were thinking of what they had bought, or sold, or some one who had been circumvented in some kind of a trade, I thought I would let them go their ways; and as I don't care for views, I went to sleep, awaking just as we were entering the Highlands. If one likes scenery, I don't know where he can do better than hereabouts. I think it finer than the Rhine at Drachenfels, but prefer the Rhine on account of the Rudesheimer, and the dinners.

West Point, you know, is a place where they teach young persons who have fathers in Congress, the art of killing Indians and drinking whiskey out in Utah. I think the teaching must be good. The buildings look big enough, the tents white enough, the cadets stiff enough, and their trowsers tight to the verge of rupture.

It is vacation or something, now, and the valiant youth are under canvas. Some of the seniors have the run of the West Point Hotel, which is terrifically military. I am not a man of war, and I was tremulous at the association, so I went to Cozzens's, which is a peaceful place. No soldier there except General Scott, who, like all the really great military men that I have ever seen, has not a trace of that pesky, sabre-jingling, moustache-twirling air of the inevitable sous-lieutenant.

But as the sous-lieutenant amuses me, I drove over from Cozzens's to see him "in society." Under the soothing influence of the moon, and a Gazzaniga cigar (they are better than the Figaro Brittanicas), I forgot most of my troubles, and about A. M. I said: Is there no balm? Are there no more trout in the brooks? And there are.

There was the pleasant hotel, with the fair river spread before it. There the cadet playing upon the piano; there Sophonisba, gazing in rapt admiration at his brief coat-tails; there more cadets, strapped and chevroned, and buttoned up within an inch of their lives—all doing the demnition agreeable. There was PERSONNE, with the Gazzaniga cigar. Superb tableau ! Insensibly I was enchanted, and I quoted these beautiful words of Wainwright:

"Oh, youth! youth! what a treasure thou art. Trifle not with it, ye who possess it, for once gone, it is lost forever! Such is life."

But, seriously, sir, I should like to know, as a sovereign, if we pay these sucking McMahons and adolescent Clam-Gallases thirty dollars per month, give them quarters, medical attendance, and religious instruction, French, mathematics, and stationery, to flirt with our Anna Marias and Sophonisbas. It is shameful.

If the *Tribune's* friend, J. B., has finished up the naturalization question, I wish he would look after the unnatural goings-on up the river.

I left the Editor of the Baptist *Watchman* at Cozzens's (he had been careful to write the name of the paper on his residence), and I hope he has done the Cadets some good before this time.

Leaving the Point bright and early, I crossed the river, and packed myself on board the express-train going North.

And it went North pretty rapidly. The conductor was a "driver." Now I don't know which is the worst, a railway conductor who is too slow, or one who is too fast. This one, however, seems to have hit the golden mean, and his train is as punctual as the sun. Arrived at Albany, he stirred up the baggage-men awfully, and in less than five minutes we heard his "all aboard," sharp as the locomotive whistle. "There's some folks on the boat," suggested a mild baggage-man to the driver, "there's some folks on the boat wants to go to Saratoga." "Why," was the natural reply, "why ain't they here, then ?" "Their things is here, and they're comin' right along." "They've"—was the rejoinder—"got to come in about ten seconds if they're goin' on this train," and he said it as if he meant it, and then sarcastically, "What are they doin', I wonder, gittin' married, or playin' onto the pianer, or lookin' at the ingine, or readin' a novel?" And now appeared, struggling up the landing-stage, from the ferry-boat, *the late party*. I've seen them, sir, everywhere, by Albion's chalky cliffs, in the paternal charge of the douane at Calais, at Ostend, at Versailles, in the tops of the Alps, everywhere, the same red-faced woman, with the same child (sometimes it is a "dorg"), the same thin and apparently much-bullied young man, the same boxes, shawls, and umbrellas. The driver knew them well, and threw them into the carriage like so many bundles of a flash newspaper.

Saratoga, at one o'clock. The same little whitewashed pen at the States. The same journeys to the Springs. The same walks "between drinks." The same dusty drive to the Lake. The same fried potatoes and juleps. But not the same society. Where are the belles and matrons, well-dressed and well-preserved? Where those gauzy angels, who used to float about the Temple of Hygeia, and sport those wonderful French shoes, á la Marquise, along the gravelled walks of the pleasant Park? Where the Anna Marias, with suites of Whiskerses, and pyramids of luggage? Gone!

And, in their places, came wonderfully ugly and awfully old women, from the provinces, with big feet and drab gaiters, last year's silk dresses, turned and made over for the meshing. With surprising things on their heads, and nothing on their hands. It makes one shudder to look at them.

And the young ones! Some might be pretty if they had any one to tell them what to wear, and how to wear it, and in what manner to dress their hair, but now they look like demi-barbarians.

Some few habitués, an invoice of Cubans, of all colors, from dark brown up to light drab. Brignoli (who, oh, horror! was called by a fat lady from Attica, a "fleshy man"), Gazzaniga, adorned with the wealth of "either Ind," make the exceptions, grains of wheat in several barns full of chaff.

And it is for this that one gives up the common necessaries of life; has no Delmonico's, nor even Crooks's, no Bordeaux fit to drink, no bell in his room, no gas, no dinner worth eating, and no coffee afterwards.

I see that a number of Christian young men and women have been at Saratoga; that they dined there, and seemed to like it. But I am not a young Christian, and therefore do not believe in the mortification of the flesh, which is enjoined as an article of the faith. Went to Lake George, and it rained, of course. Lake very wet. Ormsbee at the Lake House, did give us a good dinner, good wine, and coffee, in a civilized way after.

Returning, I had my choice between Saratoga, Sunday and suicide, or a run with the "driver" to New York.

I embraced the driver. He put me down at Thirty-first street at nine hours to a minute.

I could have embraced the gas-lamps, the types of civilization.

I pitied Anna Maria, condemned to stay in the country.

That's my eventful history. Will it do?

In the Wood of Jones.

I have tried a bit more of the campagne this week, and have journeyed to the Bois de Jones, or Joannes, I ought to say. There the indomitable Maretzek, and the indefatigable Anschutz, with various other persons, are giving a fête, musical, pyrotechnical, terpsichorean, equine, in fact they have almost everything going on, and all at once. It is rather bewildering than otherwise, and one comes away with a confused recollection of Rhine wine, Madame Tournaire, fiddles, drums, sausages, shop girls, German fraus and frauleins, jackasses, demi-monde, pipes, policemen, and rosettes.

However, it is impossible to be énnuyé. There is something going on all the time, and that is a great comfort, as the old lady said when she found that though her son-in-law had gone below with the sharks, Abigail Jane had got his "chist."

The Florence-Brough Burlesque.

I don't think it exactly the thing to take a piece written for a London audience, and hash it up for another market, with stale local jests.

To speak mildly, it is an outrageous insult to the author of the original play, and one that no literary man with an idea above coppers, would think of for a moment.

It is stated that Mr. Florence cut, hashed, and as they say, localized Mr. Brough's burlesque himself, and if so, he verifies the old adage of the bar, that a man who is his own lawyer has a fool for a client. The piece, smart enough for the actress (Miss Woolgar) and the audience for which it was written, has been spoiled for this market.

The dailies—or at least two of them—pronounced it a decided success. It was, on the first night, a decided failure.

The *Tribune* objects to the "brevity of the ballet-girls' skirts." I think the tendency of the exhibition is eminently moral. Not one of the girls is in any way tempting, or seducing, or inflaming in any way.

The acting was not brilliant enough to require especial music. The scenery fair to middling, and the music very cleverly arranged by Cooke. Since the first night, the piece has been cut a great deal, but it is still too long.

Stuart.

Stuart, as I said, has taken the Metropolitan, and is making a new interior for it. It will be opened on the 20th of August, there or thereabouts.

Burton

Is still doing Cuttle, Sleek and Company, for the delectation of Orange county and Chicago, at Niblo's.

Jefferson.

I recommend everybody to go to Niblo's Garden tonight and assist at Jefferson's benefit. Next to the Declaration, written by his namesake, Thomas, Awful Jefferson is the most popular of American institutions. Lord Dundreary will appear with A. Trenchard on this occasion, and the bill is light, funny, and, like cold lamb salad and chablis, just the thing for the weather.

Personalities.

Mr. Strakosch sailed for Europe in the Asia on Wednesday, and will bring out something great, if he can get it, for the next Opera season. Grisi and Mario, perhaps. His letter of credit furnished by the Academy stockholders is close on $20,000.

Mme. Gazzaniga is at Saratoga, but goes soon to Newport; where, the papers say, Madame de Wilhorst is shooting snipes en garçon. Having some acquaintance with the topography, icthology, and ornithology of the enchanted isle, and never having seen a snipe there, I look upon the statement with caution, but as the dailies say, I should be false to my duty as a public journalist if I hesitated to place it before my readers.

With regard to "that fleshy man," Brignoli, I perceive that he has been doing something in the gymnastic way, that wipes Blondin out: The *Herald's* Saratoga correspondence says he is driving four horses there, and Gurowski's friend, "the editor of Personalities in the *n. y. tribune*," states that "Brignoli is in Newport, where he is making a great sensation among the belles and beaux by the manner in which he manages a dashing team of superb horses."

Where's "Napoleon W. Johnson" with his four-horse act now? Where Blondin? Where balloon Wise ? Brignoli might make a good thing of it in the opera rélâche by driving at the same time four horses at Saratoga, and two at Newport, two hundred miles apart.

The actual facts are, I believe, that Brignoli is just now suffering from an attack of horse jockeys, previous to his departure for Newport, where he intends to sensationize people.

Brougham is at Boston, and the *Post* has been asinine enough to report a series of disconnected sentences, which it calls a speech, though that impeachment was disclaimed by J. B.

Apology.

I am quite well aware that this is not a Dramatic Feuilleton, though so entitled, but one of the great improvements in newspaper literature, consists in the fact that it is no longer necessary that a man's caption should refer directly or indirectly to the subject-matter of his article.

Vide the *Times* and *Tribune* any day.

So I don't apologize, and leave the caption "Apology" as it stands. So I prove, logically and practically, the theory I have stated.

However, if any one really desires to read about the theatres in this season, I recommend the effusions of the new hand on the *Daily Times*. The æsthetic Seymour, who knew when not to write, as well as when to do so (and that is a great secret in journalism), has taken a congé, and his remplaçant reminds me of the London reporter who was sent to describe a pantomime, and finding that *The Stranger* was the first piece, gave a lengthened analysis of the plot, and an extended criticism of the literary execution of that remarkably able, though somewhat familiar dramatic work.

Personne.

Are these pure canaries?" asked a gentleman of a bird-dealer, with whom he was negotiating for a "gift for his fair." "Yes, sir," said the dealer, confidentially, "I raised them 'ere birds from canary seed." It was deemed sufficient proof of their purity.

GO IT WHILE YOU'RE YOUNG.

"Tis pleasant on a Summer eve,
To join the social throng,
And laugh ha! ha! our cares away,
And sing a merry song:
Youth cannot always last, you know,
As many a bard hath sung;
Then laugh ha! ha! your cares away,
And go it while you're young.

The world may scoff at boyhood's bliss,
And rail at ranting mirth,
If joy admits no outward sign,
Then what is pleasure worth?
The flowers of youth full soon will fade,
As many a bard hath sung;
Then laugh ha! ha! your cares away,
And go it while you're young!

Old age will soon with feeble step,
Come tottering o'er life's way,
And silvery hair and furrowed brow,
Will tell the heart's decay;
Then catch at pleasure as it flies,
Nor heed the bigot's tongue;
And laugh ha! ha! your cares away,
And go it while you're young!

NEW YORK JULY 30, 1859

AN OLD BACHELOR'S LAST LOVE.

BY HENRY CLAPP, JR.

I.

I have no faith in the idea that we mortals can love but once. Nature is not so stingy. Every one is liable to have as many loves, at least, as he has phases in life. That young man of twenty, whom I remember to have called myself, alias Jenkins, twenty years ago, was as different in love matters, as in all others, from the present writer, as twenty years hence, perhaps, will be the old man of sixty, calling himself (if he sees fit) by the same name.

It is one of the caprices of young gentlemen in their teens—and a very sensible caprice it is, too—to like women of mature years, women riper than themselves, married women even; and the liking, within proper limits, is apt to be reciprocated. For mere girls they have a kind of contempt, borrowed from the contempt they have for their late boyhood, and what of it still lingers about them. They have that greenest of all horrors, the horror of being thought green. They stroke their chins impatiently in search of the much-coveted beard, and as soon as its first down appears—that soft, delicious, prophetic fuzz—they purchase a razor, hoist up their collars, proclaim themselves men, and fall in love with women of thirty.

Is this the first and only love about which we hear so much? Judging from my own experience, which was like that of most others, I should incline to hope not. The seraphic being upon whom I laid out my rising affections (Miss Anna Condor) was an old maid of thirty-five, who coiled herself about my heart, like the cunning serpent that she was, and then unreeled herself, at a day's notice, to encircle and wed a rich widower of fifty (Squire Lemon), whom she squeezed to death in less than six months, and from whom she inherited a widow's pile of half a million. And yet I loved her dearly, and gave her the "firstlings of my heart!" Others may have been more fortunate in their first love, but few are disposed to immortalize it.

An old friend of mine, now at Saratoga spending his sixth honeymoon, declares that the intensity of his love has increased in every instance in "arithmetical proportion" (whatever that is, and I believe it is something tremendous), each of his wives seeming to him so much more lovely than her immediate predecessor, who was nevertheless, in her day, the paragon of women, that he wondered how he could ever have dreamed of any body else. But if this is so, what becomes of our theories of first love?

Now I have not only to confess my heresies on this subject to the reader, who is proverbially "indulgent," but am dreading the day when I must make a clean breast of them to Clara Vernon, which will be a much more formidable matter—the said Clara being my last love. How shall I have the courage to declare my passion to her—if passion it is—seeing that she will at once curl up her pretty lips (I think pretty lips may always be assumed), and ask me impertinently whether I am making my thirtieth or fortieth declaration, to which I must needs reply—though I have kept no tally that it is at least my twentieth. Imagine the face she will make up!

But if I don't look out, some young gallant will get the start of me, and be at her feet with his first declaration, which will be as agreeable to her as the first rose of Summer. Well, whoever he is, I hope that she will accept him, for if he doesn't sicken her of first love in less than a fortnight, she is not the dear flirt I take her for. He is sure to be some man who has met her at a ball, and who has danced with her all the evening without once losing step or treading on her dress. As for me, I never danced with her but once, and then I lost not only my step but my footing, and brought her with me to the floor. But a man may be a very good partner for a dance, and yet a very sorry one for life, which is a trifle more serious than a cotillon or even a polka, as I shall take the liberty, in some disinterested moment, of telling her. And yet what does she care about that now? "The world," said she to me the other evening, "is too serious by half. *Nature* is not so terribly glum. She is on the broad grin half the time, and laughs even through her tears. Look at the stars up yonder, winking at each other for very fun all the night long, and laughing at the sober-faced moon."

Still, Clara is more serious than she chooses to appear. It is not always, nor generally, the persons of the most solemn exterior who are the most serious; solemnity is often a mask for stupidity. Clara's jubilant face is honest enough, but it reflects only the surface of her nature. I don't know that she can be called thoughtful, for thoughtfulness implies deliberate and sustained mental action, whereas the movement of her mind, like that of her body, is unpremeditated. She never reasons, and it would seem, therefore, never thinks; but she has that kind of instinct which may be called spontaneous reason, and which dives straight into the heart of things at once. Moreover, she has such a lively imagination that her mind appears to be all of a blaze, except in certain emergencies, when the fire suddenly goes out, leaving her brain, as it were, in a white heat. Such natures are always extremely sensitive, and, gay as they appear, feel and suffer very keenly.

Clara is not a very complete type of this character, for she inherits a certain amount of common sense from her father (a shrewd business man, with a profound knowledge of the surface of things), which tempers her character, and, to my seeming, derogates not a little from its beauty; for, if there is a person less interesting to me than any other, it is what is called a practical, common-sense woman—a woman "with no nonsense about her." Of this sort is Clara's friend, Sally Maunder; a very square and proper person, square-headed, square-faced, square-footed, her head set squarely on her body, and her heart squarely and securely in its place; a prim, prudish person, adhering to all known laws; eating, drinking, dressing, dancing, talking by rule; keeping a diary of all her acts, and a tally of all her expenses; owing no man, eying no man; reading no books not recommended by her preceptors, and playing the whole game of life according to Hoyle.

But it is not of Miss Maunder I wish to speak, but Miss Vernon, who, by-the-way, strangely enough, insists that her friend is the very counterpart of myself, and wonders I don't fall in love with her at once. Sally Maunder my counterpart! Not bad, that.

But it is time to say a word about Clara's *personnel*, or, in plain English, about her looks. (Thus far I have not even stated her age, which may as well be put down at once at seventeen, the old bachelor's ideal.)

I confess that, to the ordinary eye, she might seem a very ordinary girl, and she is not an angel even to mine. In fact, I don't believe in angels; the few creatures of that sort I have met with in novels and plays (they are never met with elsewhere) were not at all to my taste. I may be foolish enough to call Clara by some celestial title, and to attribute to her sundry celestial qualities, when the time comes for filing my declaration, but meanwhile I find her a vain, restless, fickle, capricious, sinful mortal (as sin goes), having a pair of very wicked gray eyes, set in a low, though decidedly unclassical forehead, which retreats behind a tangled mass of straw-colored hair, straggling over her cranium like a species of wild vine. She is too short and slight for her form to be called elegant, and, but for a smallish hand and foot, a haughty little mouth, and a perfect gem of a neck, I am not sure that her person would excite the least attention. But I confess that, until this moment, I never attempted to analyze her charms, and I have a feeling that the work is an indelicate one, something like dissection. Think, for example, of examining her teeth like a dentist, especially as, now I think of it, they happen, like a certain improper kind of verb, to be both irregular and defective, and to be as unlike pearls as her pale lips are unlike rubies, and her freckled bulb of a forehead unlike alabaster. How should I like to be taken to pieces in this way, as if I were a manikin, and held up before the public? A lady of enormous proboscis asked me, a few evenings since, if I didn't think Clara Vernon had a pug nose. I was rude enough to reply, "No more, madam, than you have a trunk." The idea of a large nose smelling out a small one, and pouncing upon it because of its size! It was like a big boy picking upon a little one. And then Clara's nose, though diminutive, and coming to rather an abrupt conclusion, is by no means a pug, as any man of reasonable nasal proportions would perceive in a moment; besides, its delicate flexile little nostrils are beautiful enough to atone for any kind of a nose except a Roman one, which is bad enough on a man, but on a woman is worse than a wen.

Let me add, in the way of description, that Clara has that rarest of charms, a small and well-formed ear—two of them, in fact—which I would as soon kiss (rather, sometimes, on account of whispering privileges) as her defiant lips.

One word now about her movement, and I have done. It can not be called dignified, for it is too spontaneous, too impetuous: but it must be graceful, for as I see her flitting about—lighting, in the course of ten minutes, upon every chair, sofa, lounge, divan, *brioche*, footstool, in the room—she always reminds me of a bird—a bird just escaped from a cage and in no hurry to go back to it, though having half a mind to (a whole mind to, if it *dared*), were it only for the deviltry of the thing.

Now if the reader can't understand, after this, why I am in love with Clara Vernon, and why the one rash aim of my life is to possess her, the fault is not mine. But I can seem to hear some veteran spinster exclaim, "Well, Sir, though I don't think much of your belle, after all, and fancy she would run you a pretty rig (and serve you right) if you should happen to get her, still I should like to know by what right you, a confirmed old bachelor of forty, lay siege to a young heart of seventeen. I wonder how many other women you have been after, how many mittens there are in your wardrobe," etc., etc.

Now, my dear critic, listen!

A venerable aunt of mine, now haply defunct, and, it is to be hoped, in Paradise, used to say, in the decline of her life, that "nobody was old but the devil;" and I hold (and have held for some years) to the same opinion. Genius, good-nature, wit, worth, etc., are always young like the stars; with these no one is old, and without them youth is not worth having. Now, what a girl like Clara wants in the way of a husband—and of course she wants something in that way—is a man possessing these qualities, and whose mind and heart are fresh enough to understand and appreciate hers; and since I am about the only man of her acquaintance who, in her estimation (and she is the only competent judge in the matter), does possess them, why should I not labor to convince her—as I have already, without labor, convinced myself—that they are the qualities which should decide her choice? A regular old bachelor's question, I admit, but how are you going to answer it?

II.

The above was written more than a year ago. The last line of it was hardly dry when I received the following note, which speaks for itself:

"My Dear Friend,—A little bird flew in my window last night, and whispered to me that you and I had frolicked together long enough. Mamma says 'it's a shame;' and Sally Maunder, the cold-hearted thing, (and yet how good she is!) says I ought to ask you to 'explain your intentions.' Now the idea of your having any intentions struck me as so absurd that I laughed in her face. But finally, after a long talk, and especially after the visit of that little bird—which must have been a mockingbird, for it repeated all that mamma and Sally had said, and a great deal more—I concluded to drop you a line, and tell you just what people said about us. The fact is, they call me a coquette, and you a flirt, and say that the way we go on together is ridiculous. In reply, I tell them that ever since that funny love affair of yours with Miss Condor (Anna, I think, her name was), you had been a kind of a woman-hater, and that you took notice of me only because I was a mere bit of a girl, who never had a serious thought in her life. Now, my dear O. B. [short for Old Bachelor], they tell me this is all nonsense, and that hereafter we mustn't be so intimate together.

"I couldn't bear to tell you this to your face, so I thought I would write you a little note about it, that you might not misconstrue any change in my demeanor. In my heart there is no change, for I still think you the best *friend* I have in the world, and can never thank you enough for all your kindness to me.

"I am half ashamed to think I have paid any attention to the gossip of old maids and busybodies; but mamma says that as long as we live in the world we must conform to its ways, and I suppose she is right—though what a stupid world it is after all!

"Yours as ever,

"Clara,

"N. B.—Don't fail to come in this evening as usual; Miss Maunder and Mr. Linton will be here, and we'll have a good game of whist. If you don't come I shall have to play 'dummy.'"

Now what could be said to such a note as this? I wrote no less than six different answers: one pathetic, another remonstrative, a third humorous, a fourth argumentative—and finally tore them all up in disgust. Jealousy took possession of me, and made me believe a rumor that Clara was engaged to Mr. Harry Linton (a briefless young lawyer imported from Wall Street by her father), and that *that* was the secret of the whole affair. As for Miss Maunder, I wished she would mind her own business, and was half disposed to tell her so. What business was it to her whether I had any "intentions" or not? But what was I to do in the matter—give up the ship? "Never!" said I. "Suppose I send her a formal declaration, and try to reason her into accepting me!" I did so, though not for any number of dollars a column would I consent to have that stupidest of documents printed. It was a *chef d'oeuvre* of inanity; and I received in return the most affectionate of notes, in which Clara took all the blame of my delusion and disappointment upon herself, assured me of her sisterly regard, begged of me to continue my visits as before, hinted that I could do much better than marry such a volatile young minx as herself, recommended me to her sex generally as the best and most considerate of men, and in fact sent me exactly the kind of instrument for such cases made and provided.

III.

How nicely that "old, common arbitrator, Time," settles the most difficult of questions!

Within six months after the date of the above note I found a portentous piece of pasteboard on my table, announcing to me in the most official and unquestionable manner Clara's intended marriage with a young Methodist clergyman, from Damariscotta, Lincoln county, Maine, and inviting me to the wedding. Clara Vernon to be married to a down-east parson! "Good for the cloth!" said I; "three cheers for the Yankees!" and the fun of the thing had such an effect upon me that I, too, became preposterous, and in less than six weeks (forgetting my horror of practical, common-sense women) was married in the squarest sort of manner to my square-built, square-minded, square-rigged friend, Miss Sally Maunder, who is at this moment at my elbow, asking me how it is that I can't or won't learn to dot my i's and cross my t's.

—*Harper's Monthly.*

Love Matters.

—The great social event of the day, says the *Tribune*, the marriage (or we should say, the alliance, since it is to be conducted on a royal scale of magnificence) between the Cuban millionaire, Senor O., and the fair Americaine, Miss B., is to be celebrated on about the middle of next month; first in Grace church, to conciliate the Protestant prejudices of the bride, and afterward, with impressive display, at one of the Roman Catholic cathedrals. This golden wedding has been postponed on account of the recent severe illness of the bridegroom, as well as to await the arrival of a one-hundred-thousand-dollar bridal present from Cuba, to be sent by the gentleman's sister to her prospective sister-in-law. So brilliant a *partie*, with his sixty years and his four millions of dollars, has been for more than a year the end and aim of many Fifth avenue matrons on behalf of their budding daughters, and of many Fifth avenue heiresses on their own behalf; but the ambitious hopes of these dowagers and belles have been sadly crushed by a young lady outside of their "set"—portionless, perhaps, but rich in her 17 years, her Eugenie-like features, and her tall, graceful figure, to say nothing of virgin affections.

The auspicious blending of these kindred hearts dates from last New Year's day, when, under the genial influence of the season, generous fortune led his prancing steeds, his yellow interpreter, and his golden self to the house irradiated by her presence; since which time, after a speedy and successful courtship, the ardent lover has plied the curiosity shops of Broadway for gifts worthy of his "golden-tressed Adelaide."

A famous jeweller has, at an unmentionable cost, furnished "one set of diamonds and pearls, consisting "of a necklace, bracelets, brooch, earrings, and head *parure*; one set opals and diamonds; one set emeralds and diamonds; four superb fans, dazzling with diamonds; six exquisite diamond hair-pins; a watch and Chatelaine, wonderful with enamel and diamonds; rings of fabulous splendor, and *et ceteras* too brilliant to enumerate or imagine."

The bridal jewels par *excellence*, now being manufactured in Paris, are to be of pearls of rare size, and diamonds of pure water; and the wreath, which will confine the one-thousand-dollar miracle of a nuptial veil, is to be composed of orange blossoms in jewels, emerald leaves, diamond and sapphire flowers, set in gold:

> The gold doth show her blessedness,
> The sapphires mark her true;

and we may wind up with the Elizabethan item of forty elaborate dresses, to be "composed" in lavish style. After the wedding, and one week of reception succeeding it, instead of the usual tour, the happy pair will retire to honeymoon it in a "palatial" Fourteenth street residence, in which, with love's impatience, the fair fiancée is already installed, under the protection of her delighted parents.

In the Autumn, Senor O. will introduce his bride to his own sunny land; after which the gay capitals of Europe will be made brighter by her advent—and her diamonds. So they say.

Correspondence.

Boston, July 26, 1859.

My Dear Press:—I know you would like to hear something from the Hub of Creation. You don't know how the place is increasing. Any one who had a feeling for the crooked streets with their old houses, would be inclined to weep should he see how the Vandals of trade have attacked, captured, and destroyed the old strongholds of Boston gentility. Franklin street is full of tall, ugly granite stores, Summer street is invaded, while Chauncey Place is already in the hands of the enemy.

Meanwhile, the routed citizens have established a series of horse-railroads running into all the country towns around, and settled themselves there; if they are more ambitious, they can buy a lot on the extended mill-dam, and build in imitation of a New York house. For the Bostonians have given up building "swelled fronts," and their doors are no longer carefully designed to look each like a hole in the wall. In their public buildings, they make also great architectural attempts: the only trouble is the buildings show rather an attempt than a result. The architect wanted to produce something striking for its novelty, forgetting, if he ever knew, that a building which carried in every square foot of its surface the proof that its architect understood and made the best use of his material, would of necessity strike every one as the most original and perfect building he had ever seen.

Let us take one of the last Boston improvements as a sample. They have erected a Free Library building at a cost of four hundred thousand dollars, a piece of wasteful extravagance and abuse of trust almost as bad as the waste in building the Erie Railroad. The front is brick, trimmed with brown stone,—and very foolishly trimmed. You enter the hall and see a small staircase running up on either side, and hereby hangs a tale.

Everybody knows how fine is the effect of an appropriate entrance, and how necessary it is to give dignity to a public building. The architect is said to have introduced in his drawings a grand flight, rising from the junction of the two present ones, into the great public hall. The stairs are there, but are so hidden from view by a screen of stone, that they cannot be seen from below, so that instead of one fine effect, there are two little mean ones. Two explanations are given for the foolish introduction of the stone screen. One is, that on coming to construct the stairs, it was found necessary to introduce the screen to support them; the other is, that Mr. R. C. Winthrop, who was one of the expensive committee, objected to having a long staircase open to view from below, because, in going up, the ladies would be so apt to expose their ankles. I give both stories; they are the only explanations I have heard, and certainly neither of them reflects any credit on either the architect or the committee. But of course, we must expect in a Hub, that the spokesmen will be most prominent in filling all offices of trust. The lower part of the building is devoted to reading-rooms, the decoration of which is tawdry and vulgar to a frightful degree. It is in the *sartor resartus* style, out-tayloring Taylor's, your El Dorado for Irish servant girls. Yet, with all the money squandered, even now, before the books are arranged, the paint on the walls is peeling off, and the gaudy effect here and there discolored by damp and mildew. It is a shame that a library so generous as this, so nobly begun, and so carefully carried on, should not be perfectly enshrined. But this is the way that all committees do their work. Somehow men cannot seem to retain any sense of moral responsibility when they have other people's money to spend.

One of the great changes in Bostonians is their recent belief in their mercantile superiority. In order to be up with the requirements of their new granite palaces, they have made a vigorous attempt to get up a series of immense trade sales. One little anecdote will show how thoroughly they are imbued with mercantile principles of so elevated an order that we may expect to see Boston soon assume the same rank at the head of the mercantile interests of the country, that she has held so long, and so creditably, as the moral centre of the intellectual world.

On the fourth of July, Mr. George Sumner delivered an oration, in which he expressed his opinion that freedom was antagonistic to bondage, both in Europe and in this country. On a motion before the City Council that a vote of thanks be presented to the orator for his oration, it was settled that as the Southern merchants had been invited to attend the trade sales, the vote of thanks had better be postponed until the city of Boston had got as much money out of the aforesaid Southern merchants, as they could be induced to spend. This course is an evidence of a fair and open dealing which must eventually result in obtaining for Boston the position which she deserves. I have not seen anywhere this explanation of the tardy action of the City Council with their vote of thanks; the elevated mercantile principles which governed them in that matter, prevented the papers from stating the true reason of the delay.

The city has lately been in grief for Mr. Choate. Dr. Nehemiah Adaras had the boldness to proclaim in Unitarian Boston, the logical conclusion of the Orthodox belief in the eternal punishment which must result from a neglect of regeneration. He could not assure the friends of Mr. Choate about his present condition, though the Rev. Nehemiah Adams does not seem to feel any doubt about his own future. The inevitable Mr. Everett, of course, found occasion to pronounce a eulogy. Has he missed any occasion for the last ten years? It has become one of the disadvantages of Boston greatness that should the aspirant for local honors die, in congratulating himself at a fortunate escape from the ills of life, his last moments must be soured by the conviction that he exposes himself to a eulogy from Mr. Everett.

Non omnis moriar—Mr. Everett lives after me.

X.

A FEMALE IN MALE CLOTHING.

On Friday of last week two individuals, calling themselves Jack and Charlie, made their appearance in Chambersburg, Pa., and while sauntering through that town the latter attracted much attention—appearance, voice, and manner seeming to indicate that he could not justly claim to be of the sterner sex. His companion, Jack, had drank very freely, and became uproarious in a saloon, incurring the displeasure of the barkeeper, who compelled him to leave. Charlie immediately followed, having been advised by some one that "Sis" had better leave too, and, as he retreated, declaring that he was no "Sis." Shortly afterwards Jack was arrested on the street for swearing. Charlie became indignant at this, declared a "knockdown" would be the consequence, and that he would "stay" with Jack under any circumstances. Both Jack and Charlie were arrested, and complaint having been made by a constable, the magistrate was about to commit them to prison. Charlie became boisterous, threatened all sorts of violence with different kinds of weapons, and was finally searched. Nothing dangerous was found on his person, or with which he could execute his threats." Jack and Charlie went to prison, and there being some doubts of the sex of Charlie, the jailor considered it his duty to make an investigation. The regalia of the Daughters of Malta was found in her possession, and the fact was disclosed that he was a woman. She gave a history of herself. It would appear that she was born and raised in the town of Somerset, in this State. Her name is Matilda Rushenberger, and she is about 24 years of age. About seven years ago, Dan Rice's circus was in Somerset. Her father, who is a blacksmith, did considerable horseshoeing for the circus, and from the visits of Dan Rice to the shop, she became acquainted with him. Rice endeavored to get her brother to travel with him, but he refused. He then, she alleges, persuaded her to accompany him, and up to a short period she has been in his employ. She donned male attire from the time she started, and has been wearing it ever since. Her occupation in the circus was equestrianism and vaulting, and no doubt she figured among Rice's "stars" as "the celebrated Equestrian, Signor Somers as the body, from Franconi's in Paris, and Astley's in London." She says she is not the only female in male attire travelling with circuses in this country. Of course she is rough in speech, and from her degrading and brutal associations seems to have lost all respect for the proprieties of her sex.

—Crinoline was originally the name of a Parisian *modiste*—one Madame Crinoline, who kept a set of dressmaking rooms in the Rue de la Paix. It eventually came into use to denote the article most in repute at her establishment. She it was who, by the invention of horse-hair woven into a sort of cloth and manufactured into petticoats, enabled the fair sex to dispense with that clumsy abomination which always placed them, if not in a headlong hurry, certainly in—a bustle. The name of the petticoat was given from that of the inventor, as has frequently happened; the crinoline, the petticoat, was derived from Crinoline, the dressmaker.

NEW YORK AUGUST 6, 1859

United States Hotel, Saratoga, NY.

LETTER FROM SARATOGA.

Amiable Press:—After the *Herald's* sarcastic criticism of "watering-place literature," who will dare to date a letter from mineral-spring or fashionable sea-side? But though it seems an unavoidable recurrence that "Our Own Correspondent" should describe all the least interesting incidents of his journey at full length, and with the evident purpose of "filling out"—and though it is true that his letters seldom convey news, and always announce that "this is the fullest season ever known, the hotels never having been so crowded," etc., yet there is a better reason for his writing the usual catalogue of repetitions than the *Herald* gives for printing it: it is, not only that "really a great many people" want to know what is thought about them, but because there is a large number of persons who like to "read, ponder, and inwardly digest" just such correspondence, preparatory to choosing their "Villegiatura." The ladies, particularly, read every item with never-flagging interest, especially so when something piquant is said of Miss A——b, or Miss C——d, which vulgar proceeding is, happily, becoming less frequent. What, for instance, can be more indelicate than the Newport letter in *Harper's* of last week. After speaking of Mrs. P——l as "always graceful, pretty, and well-dressed," it mentions where "*nestle* the lovely B——ds," and adds, to a young lady whose appearance as an equestrienne it is pleased to praise : "Graceful, lightsome lady, we must have more than this brief glance at you!" Now, complimentary as the unexpressed thought might have been, what person of refinement could be pleased to hear it spoken of herself, to the public at large? And it promises that "all shall have their turn in these pages." How considerate! But to return to the *Herald:* It supposes that the motive of "such flocks of wealthy families" in visiting the fashionable Summer resorts, cannot be love of enjoyment, because, it thinks, "nothing can be more vapid, tiresome, or fatiguing, than the lives which they lead there." This can be true of those only who lead no other life anywhere else: he who does so here acts from choice.

To be sure, "Personne" (who seems to be "suppressed" again this week) fled the place for fear of being driven to suicide; and Brignoli has gone to Newport, because the climate is so favorable to his "ut." Gazzaniga preceded him there a day or two, after defraying her expenses here by the successful concert she gave at the St. Nicholas Hall. Herr Mayer displayed a pronunciation equally correct in Italian, French, and German songs, and in response to a well-merited encore, accompanied his own song on the piano, having proven himself a good linguist and an excellent musician. The comic airs of Sr. Albites were unpretentious and amusing. Mme. Gazzaniga was rather nervous at first, though the signs of her modesty were less perceptible in her voice than in her blushing cheeks. She sang Donizetti's dramatic piece, "The Mother and her Dying Child," with such thrilling emphasis, and her whole soul seemed so completely absorbed in the fearful situation, that as she sang the last note, an old lady murmured, " My, that's awful!" and several seconds elapsed before the audience recovered from its abstraction to applaud; but *then*, what a "storm" it was! Saturday evening, at the United States Hotel, an entertainment was given of some twelve or fifteen tableaux vivants, the first this season, —"Love at First Sight," "Taking the Veil," "Life Among the Quakers," "Three Phases of Country Life," etc. "Life Among the Quakers' was very funny; the "males" and "females" were first seen sitting apart, eyes bent down, hands demurely crossed—then the gradual approach, the shy sheep's eyes and hovering smile, until the final walking off arm-in-arm, all so quaker-like, were most amusingly contrived. Munck and his band were to have had a benefit, Monday evening; but one night last week, during a German cotillon, the clock struck eleven, and as they are not bound, it seems, to play after that hour, they stopped the music in the midst of the dance. The requests of the animated dancers for a figure or two more being disregarded by the independent band, or its usually good-humored leader, not a name was subscribed for their benefit night, except by *two*, and they "outsiders." Consequently the only *benefit* they receive is that derived from the lesson. If they profit by it, it will be notwithstanding the high price they pay for it. Having pointed a moral, I remain,

Yours, religiously, DOLLOPE.

SARATOGA, August 3, 1859.

MATRIMONIAL PHILOSOPHICS.

BY A. F. BANKS.

When Mr. Smuggins married, he had fondly hoped to insure domestic bliss. Three months after that important event, he expressed his conviction, with savage earnestness, to Mrs. Smuggins—that he hadn't. If he had expected nothing (*vide* an ancient volume), he might have been a blessed individual; as it was, he was a wofully disappointed one.

Mrs. Smuggins quietly delivered a similar opinion respecting herself, and went on with her knitting with an aggravating calmness.

Mr. Smuggins walked about the room evidently under the impression that the law for "assault and battery" was both unhallowed and unconstitutional.

Suddenly he stopped. "Mrs. Smuggins—Mrs. Smuggins!" he roared, as he received no reply.

"Well, well, I hear you, man, I hear you," said that amiable lady; and she took up another loop. "What is it?"

"Am I to have a pudding for my dinner, or *not?*"

Perhaps you may, and may be you mayn't," was his rib's unsatisfactory reply.

"Well, we'll see about that," snarled Mr. Smuggins, stamping round, and making his coat tails fly about. "Well, my dear, you had perhaps best go and *see* about it; Sukey's in the kitchen." And then she dropped a stitch.

"You'd aggravate a saint, Madam," exclaimed Mr. Smuggins.

"Do saints upset chairs in that way?" was the meek inquiry.

"Mrs. Smuggins," said the male proprieter of that euphonious name, confronting his sleeping partner.

"Well."

"Will you go and make me a pudding or not?"

"No."

"You wont ?"

"Don't bother me; I've told you once."

"I fancy, Mrs. Smuggins, that you entered into a compact to obey me," said her shamefully deceived lord, beating the "devil's tattoo" on his best carpet.

"I won't be ordered," was the reply. And the lady, with a great deal of dignity, picked up her traps, and flounced out of the room.

In another minute the outraged gentleman was in the kitchen. "Sukey," he said furiously, "make me a currant dumpling for dinner—plenty of currants."

"Why, sir!" replied that young lady, "here's one a 'bilin."

Mr. Smuggins was in the same dreadful position that we could imagine a certain Editor would be in, deprived of a "grievance." He was fairly flabbergasted—idealess, wordless, with the exception of "nonsense," which came feebly forth.

"Well, look, sir, for yourself," said Susan. "Missus made it with her own two hands an hour ago." And there, sure enough, bobbing up and down, was a glorious sized dumpling—*the* species of dumpling on which he doated.

Considerably mollified, yet filled with the sense of a wronged husband, he proceeded to his wife's room. "Well, madam," he began, "so it seems there is a pudding after all.'

"Is there ?" was the echo,

"Yes, madam, and it is lucky for you that there *is*."

"Is it really?" was the provocative response.

"Yes, madam, *it*—is. In fact, you dared not, no, Mrs. Smuggins, dared not have disobeyed me. You knew that it was made, and wanted to give me a specimen of your infernal cantancourousness."

"In-deed!" replied Mrs. Smuggins with a suspicious emphasis. "Now, if you don't leave the room, *I* will; all that I've got to say is, that I won't be *ordered*." And she went to another room, slammed the door, and locked it. Mr. Smuggins, boiling over with indignation, consoled himself as he went down-town with the fact that he had gained his point, and that his pudding was boiling too.

Dinner-time came, and so did our injured husband. (Dinner's the thing to bring 'em home.) He sat down, said nothing, looked daggers, and pretended to quarrel with the tenderest of tenderloins. The fact was, however, that he was preserving an enormous corner for the dumpling.

The dumpling came. Mr. Smuggins undid the lower button, drew himself half a foot nearer to his work, and handed his plate, saying gruffly—"Give me some of that."

"You can have it all, my dear," was the mild acquiescence of his wife, as she pushed the dish towards him.

Mr. Smuggins took off the cover. He turned pale. "What's this?" he shouted.

"The pudding, my dear,' was the reply. "What the ——have you been doing to it?" he frantically demanded.

"I rolled it in the ashes, my sweet love. You know you said this morning that I dared not disobey you. No more I have, dear. There's your pudding—eat it." The specimen of conjugal obedience disappeared suddenly out of the room, with a hearty laugh. It was lucky for her that the door was on her side, and had been left ajar expressly for a prompt exit.

Mr. Smuggins said many a highly immoral thing on the impulse of the moment; however, he was too much of a philosopher to let his pudding cool; so he cut it open, and scooped out the middle.

He then went down town, and gave a little boy a lick on the head for presuming to slip down against him. He didn't go home to supper. He got that at Thompson's, and then went to the theatre. About ten o'clock, something in the play seemed to tickle his fancy amazingly, for he scratched his head as though an idea had suddenly taken root there, and smiled. Hamlet touched the conscience of a king with a play; had a play touched the conscience of Thomas Smuggins? It looked like it, to judge from analogy; for the king alluded to didn't depart quicker than he did. The main difference between Mr. Smuggins and the crowned blackguard was, that the former made his exit with a grin on his phiz, and the latter didn't.

Mr. Smuggins carried his smile home with him, and up to his bedroom, where Mrs. Smuggins was making paradoxical preparations (by debarrassing herself of her luggage) for a trip to Blanket Bay.

"Deuce take it," said he, a few minutes afterwards, with an "Olive-branch" creak in his tone. "I say, Mary, do you know where my nightcap is? If you do, I wish you'd get it for me, that's a good girl."

"To be sure I will, Thomas," was the hearty response. "Ah! here it is."

"Thank you, thank you."

"Look here, Thomas," said Mary, laying her hand gently on his arm, "we had words to-day; I hope they will never happen again. We haven't been together very long, and we may as well just make up our minds to start straight, or we shall be coming in some day or other most confoundedly crooked. I promised to love you; and I do, dearly. I promised to honor you; well, I do. I also promised to obey you; now, Thomas, ask me to do anything in my power, in reason, or almost out of reason, as you asked me to get your nightcap, and I'll do it, gladly and unmurmuringly. But, if you ask me to do anything as you asked me to make that pudding—*Go!* and make a pudding!' I won't do it. I will obey you, Tom, but I won't be *ordered*."

"There, now! keep still! nuff 'ced," came merrily from Tom's lips, as he closed hers with a thrilling kiss. He put on his nightcap, blew out the light, jumped into bed, and, overcome by the contending emotions of that eventful day, both were almost immediately heard to snore in blissful unison.

MORAL.

Wives.—Let Mrs. Smuggins be your model.

Husbands.—It is no disgrace to be ruled on certain points by a Mrs. Smuggins.

CATSKILL.

Like some huge ruminant in sleep,
Catskill, thou towerest dim;
Thy cedars comb the fleecy clouds
That round thy summit swim;
And sometimes, when the storm-cloud wreathes
Thy form with vapory zone,
The tempest gildeth thee with fire
And calleth thee his throne.

O brother of the sunset-cloud!
Unlock thy treasuries—
Full of strange sights as was the realm
Of the fair Hesperides!
And from the cataract and glen
Upraise the misty veil:
And guide my steps aright, ye nymphs,
Awhile the craig I scale.

A living, pouring galaxy!
The Catterskill I see,—
White, and, in falling, turned to spray,
Then 'lighting laughingly;
Dark gallery over gallery rings
With rock the gorge half round,
And from the edge, far, far on high
The dizzy pines looks down.

Catskill, I stood upon thy cliffs,
And from the swimming height
Beheld thy forests downward slant
Like giant hosts in flight;
And my dilated eyes explored
A boundless reach of view,
With towns that seemed but daisy-clusters
Twinkling in the dew.
And the great landscape seemed, like me,
In reverence to gaze on thee.

J. W. C.

NEW YORK AUGUST 13, 1859

A CITY SKETCH.

—

BY GETTY GAY.

—

"Such soft flowers
From such rough roots? The people under there
Can sin so, curse so, smell so,... faugh!
Yet have such daughters."—*Aurora Leigh.*

—

Aunt Rachel.

My aunt Rachel has not moved for forty years. Her principles are, I am told, just what they were a half a century ago. Her language is as quaint as old English text. Her formal dress is of the same sober hue and cut that it was before I came into existence. And, although all New York moved up-town years ago, she occupies the same house in which she was born. Her neighborhood was in former days very fashionable and pleasant, but in the lapse of time, it has become one of the worst in the city. But aunt Rachel seems to be unconscious of the fact, and nothing offends her so much as to declare it. The transitions in her house have taken place so gradually as to pass unheeded by its mistress, and her attachment for the old homestead has, no doubt, contributed not a little to blind her eyes to the disgrace of its surroundings. She occasionally invites her young relatives and friends, of whom she is very fond, to pay her a visit of a day or two, and much as they dislike her residence, aunt Rachel is too good, too rich, and too generous, to be refused, even by young folks, who are not generally so observant of policy as they learn to be in riper years.

I cannot tell whether aunt Rachel likes me much or not, for, being wayward and outspoken, I have often offended her prejudices, and incurred her displeasure; but I was nevertheless honored with an invitation to spend a day or two at her domicile. I did not dream of declining it, for "anything for a change" has always been my motto—one I have adhered to constantly, practically, and not seldom to my cost.

The next day after being invited, I dressed myself in my best, and started for aunt Rachel's. An omnibus took me near her street, and the remaining distance, the only perilous part of the journey, I performed on foot. I passed through a narrow, filthy thoroughfare, between uncouth, tumble-down shanties, and tall tenement houses, and was saluted at every step with smells which Falstaff appropriately designated as a "villainous compound." The sun was declining; the weather was so warm that the houses seemed to have boiled over, and deposited their scum, or inhabitants, on the sidewalks, which were crowded with old and young, male and female, all sitting or lounging, half naked, smoking, bawling, squealing, or sleeping, in the most contented state of beastliness. The children were covered with a thin coat of filth, which concealed their natural complexions, and their elders, who had charge of them, did not appear much more cleanly. The smallest and dirtiest urchins sprawled in my way, so that I found it hard to avoid treading on them, and the women stared at me with a glaring brazenness that was difficult to sustain.

I had almost reached aunt Rachel's when a drunken woman reeled up against me, and in escaping from her clutches, I was compelled to step into the muddy street. The creature seemed to regard me as the assailant, and, saluting me with a volley of coarse epithets, and waxing furious as she lashed about her with blasphemous vituperations, started toward me, stumbled, and fell into the gutter. A shout of laughter from a hundred gazers greeted her fall; and when she had scrambled to her feet, covered with mud, the shouts of derision that hailed her on all sides exasperated her to madness, and she flew after me like a tigress. I had just reached my aunt's stoop as the frenzied wretch overtook me, and, as I thought, was about to tear my clothes, and myself, perhaps, into pieces, when a large woman thrust herself between us, exclaiming—

"No ye don't, Nance, I tell ye; Mrs. Gray's wisitors is sacred!"

My assailant did not heed this remonstrance, and as the next moment flung off by my protectress, with much violence as to prostrate her upon the pavement. I ran up the stoop in a fright, and was overjoyed to see the door open before I could ring the bell. A very pretty girl, plainly dressed, who seemed to consider my adventure with the utmost coolness, received me kindly, thanked my preserver in the sweetest tones, and, regarding my defeated foe with a look of pity, observed, quietly:

"Poor woman! she was one of the most industrious and careful wives in the world till her husband took drink and politics; but now there is little choice between them; they are the greatest drunkards and bullies in the neighborhood."

I found aunt knitting, as she had been daily, Sundays excepted, for the last forty or fifty years. She accorded me a placid, but cordial welcome, and entertained me during the afternoon, by exhibiting to my admiring gaze a thousand carefully-preserved relics of the past, the value of which she enhanced in her own eyes, and in mine, by recounting the circumstances connected with their origin and possession, with religious fidelity and minuteness. She made me several presents, and insisted upon my playing on an old rickety piano, doubtless one of the first ever made, whose tones were about as musical as the voice of an old crone of seventy attempting to sing. She listened to the diabolical squeaking I forced out of the instrument as if it were celestial harmony, and complimented me upon my skill as a musician. After partaking of an old-fashioned meal called *tea*, which included a great many good things, I read, at my aunt's request, a whole discourse to her from the works of her favorite divine, and a long chapter in the Bible, which rendered me insufferably sleepy. A tedious story she told me about my great-grandmother, in spite of my utmost attempts at wakefulness, lulled me at last into oblivion, from which I was not aroused till my aunt was herself about to retire for the night, and her servant-girl stood ready to show me to the bed-room assigned me. I refused peremptorily to sleep alone, and insisted upon having Lucy, the girl, as a bedfellow. Aunt rebuked my foolish fears, but allowed me to have my way. I now did not feel a whit inclined to sleep; and when alone with Lucy, whose loveliness surprised and interested me more and more, I begged that she would tell me her history. She seemed to regard my curiosity as a compliment, and complied with my request with obliging simplicity and ingenuousness.

Lucy.

"I have been told," said Lucy, "that my parents were both very handsome; but I cannot recollect my mother, for she died when I was an infant; and my father, after her death, caused, in a great measure by his own neglect and cruelty, married for money a woman much older than himself, and grew so great a drunkard and gambler, that his vices soon marred his good looks, as well as his health and fortune. After he had spent his second wife's money, he neglected even the appearance of regard for her, and used her most shamefully. He was at times kind to me, which made my mother-in-law jealous, and she retaliated his unkindness upon me. She was not, however, altogether heartless; for, having, perhaps more than my father once, owed her life to my entreaties while my father was beating her, on one of which occasions I received a blow from his hand, intended for her, which stunned me,—she afterward began to treat me with some appearance of affection, which was cordially reciprocated by me, for I always wanted to love somebody, and I had always pitied her from my soul. As my father grew poorer, he became more morose, desperate, and abusive. One night he beat my mother-in-law senseless. I told him he had murdered her; he believed my words true, and fled to escape the punishment due to his guilt. After a while, however, I succeeded in bringing her back to life, but my father never returned. I learned, some months after, that he had immediately shipped before the mast in a clipper bound for California. There, I have heard, after making some money, he married again, and was at last killed in a desperate street fight.

"We were left in great poverty, and suffered very much, but we fought bravely with our hardships: my mother-in-law worked very hard, and exerted herself to her utmost to educate and bring me up properly, till she heard of my father's marriage two years after, when both her strength and will to do gave way, and she resigned herself to despair. She had always loved my father with all her heart, and this blow was worse than death to her. She sought consolation in drink, and was never sober when she could get liquor. By degrees, she parted with everything to buy it—with trinkets, furniture, and clothes—till our room was bare, and we had only a few rags, which would not bring a cent, or else they, too, would have been sold. The pangs of cold and hunger pinched me cruelly, and I suffered more than words can tell. How many nights I lay awake shivering, starving, and crying bitterly! Sometimes I used to pray, and ask God to take me out of the world.

"At times my mother-in-law used to look at me so strangely, and mutter what I could not understand. I thought she was going mad, and so she was, no doubt. One day she brought a large dashing woman, very showily dressed, into our room, who examined me closely, as you would an article of sale, and said:

"'She might have done well enough, but you have waited too long. She won't pay; she's nothing but skin and bone.'

"'I can't help that,' replied my mother-in-law, hoarsely,' I am no more myself.'

"'Well, I don't mind doing a kindness, even where it does cost too much,' said the woman. 'I will give you what you ask, for you seem to need it bad enough. What's her name?'

"'Lucy.'

"'Come here, Lucy. Would you like to have everything nice to eat and drink, plenty of beautiful clothes, and nothing to do?'

"I told her I was very hungry, but did not mind work. She put money into my mother-in-law's hand, and told me to get ready and go with her. My arrangements were simple, and quickly made. I went up to my mother-in-law to kiss her good-by, but she repulsed me with a shudder.

"'No!' she said wildly. 'I am bad enough, but no Judas-no, no!'

"I burst into tears, and asked what I had done to offend her, but the strange woman seized me by the hand, and observed, coldly:

"'You have done nothing, child, but she's a little crusty, you know. Never mind; come with me, and you shall have kisses enough and to spare.'

"As my captor was leading me away, my mother-in-law sprang after me, for what purpose I could not then think, though I doubt not, now, it was to rescue me, but the other pushed her back, assured me she was crazy (she really looked so), and dragged me off in triumph. As we were going out of the passage, a woman stared at us, and exclaimed:

"So the old woman has sold you to the devil for drink at last? I thought it was coming to that!'

"My captor cursed the speaker, who cursed her in turn, and called her names that frightened me. I wondered whether my mother-in-law had really sold me to the prince of darkness, for I had heard of such things, and believed them possible. I began to cry more bitterly than ever, and the flames and horrors of the deep rose up before me, and filled my mind with unspeakable terror. I forgot my want and starvation in the agony of fear, and hung back, and struggled to release myself, but my purchaser was as strong as I was weak, and dragged me on in spite of my resistance.

"'Where is thee taking that child?' asked an old lady. 'Is she thy daughter?'

"'Mind your own business, old square hood,' said my captor, but I cried, in despair, 'I aint her daughter, ma'am, but mother sold me to her for money to buy drink with.'

"'What does thee intend to do with the child?' demanded the lady.

"'Go to!' said the other, trying to push by her.

"'I am afraid that is where thee is taking this little one, and I withstand thee in the name of the Lord.'

"This dispute quickly attracted the notice of the bystanders, and people passing, who clustered around us in a moment, to enjoy the contest. Something told me that I had arrived at the turning-point of my life, and that I should then be saved or lost forever. The woman, who had me in her grasp, told a plausible story, and would certainly have triumphed over the old lady who withstood her, had I not opposed her lies with a piteous earnestness of tone it was impossible to doubt. My tears and prayers for deliverance excited the wrath of the crowd against my captor, till they began to threaten her with violence.

"'Lynch her!' shouted several voices.

"'Hang her to the lamppost!' bellowed others.

"'Flee from the wrath to come!' said the old lady to the gayly dressed creature, who now turned as pale as her rouge would allow, and let me go. She acted upon the advice offered, and was saluted with hisses and groans as she hurried away in a flutter of fear and anger.

"My rescuer, who was no other than your aunt, took charge of me, and, after giving me such a meal as I had not had for years, and clothing me decently, went with me to find my mother-in-law. She knocked at her door without getting any answer. At last I ventured in, and beheld the object of our search lying on the floor. There was a bottle near her; the room smelt strong of liquor, and she seemed fast asleep. I tried to rouse her in vain, and your aunt put on her spectacles, knelt by her side, and after gazing at her a while, said solemnly:

"'She is dead. We have come too late, and she has drank herself to death. Poor thing! God be merciful to her soul, and to us all!'

"Since that hour your aunt has treated me as if I were her daughter, and I have loved her as though she were my own mother."

Lucy fell asleep at the conclusion of her story, and I sank into slumber soon after.

The Neighborhood.

I was awakened several times during the night by screams and cries that made me shudder, and in the morning by a Babel of sounds, of which I can give no adequate description. They proceeded from the street, and were deafening and distracting, like Vanity Fair in full blast. I sprang from the bed, rushed to the window, and drew up the curtain to ascertain whether or not the world was ending, or chaos returning. I perceived at once that nothing of the kind was taking place, but that all this clamor was only a proof that the world was exceedingly well cared for. Within the length of the block, two vendors of fruit and vegetables, with a cart, and a vociferous boy each, were not only rivaling one another in selling, but in loud and louder bawling for custom. This quartette (the men had both dreadful colds, and the boys steam whistle-pipes of their own) would have sufficed to make the street sufficiently resonant, but it was wonderfully sustained. There was a man who sold straw, bellowing like a bull of Bashan; milkmen whooping like wild Indians; a rag-and-bottle, and an old clothes buyer; an umbrella vender; a dealer in tins; a scissors-grinder; and a "glass-putty" man, with their respective cries, or bells, great and small, besides charcoal and various other vendors, some of whom shouted with a bass as terrible as that of Carl Formes; and others, with a tone as shrill and tremulous as a cracked soprano. A seller of crockery clattered two plates together, by way of cymbals; and a fishmonger, whose trumpet I had mistook for Gabriel's, blew a blast so harsh, that it seemed to have come through a hundred sore throats. There was an organ-grinder busy on the corner, and a German brass-band serenading the lager-bier saloon opposite. Everybody was trying to outdo everybody else, and the aggregate result was outrageous and tremendous. The anvil-chorus was beat into a whisper, a stage alarm into a watch-tick, in comparison. A big fire, with all the New York fire-engines in full play, would resemble it; and I thought of Jerico and the ram's horns in full blast, and wondered why the street did not reel, and the walls tumble into it.

I know the reader expects me to apologize for exaggeration. I shall do nothing of the sort. If he were an Oriental, he would know better than to ask me to do it. The tranquil "West-enders" know no more of certain localities in this metropolis than they do of the heart of Pekin. Let such visit —— street, between —— and —— streets (I give the names in full; if the editor is afraid of libel, and doesn't, don't blame me), in the Spring, rather early, on a fine forenoon, and he will confess that my picture, instead of being overcharged, is mildly drawn.

When I went down stairs, I found that the breakfast had been kept waiting for me. My aunt said she did not wonder at my lateness, for it was a quiet old neighborhood, and induced sleep, but how people could find rest in business-streets, was more than she could understand. Lucy's eye smiled on me with humorous good nature, and I suppressed the mischievous reply that was rising to my lips, for Lucy's story had greatly enhanced my love and respect for the old lady. I could have hugged her for her kindness to that beautiful orphan, but being bred a Quaker, though by no means a professed or rigid one, she would, I knew, have been more alarmed than gratified by such a demonstration, and consequently I subdued the impulse.

After being sufficiently disgusted with the street-clamor, I retired to the back parlor, threw myself upon the sofa, and courted sleep. In the rear of the house, I heard the crying of babies innumerable; but this noise, I fondly imagined, would soon be stilled, and I enjoy a quiet nap, which would compensate for the sleep I had been deprived of during the night. Vain hope! Little was I acquainted with the resources of the neighborhood. The infantine wailing continued. Sometimes it subsided for a moment in a dying strain, inexpressibly plaintive and touching, but only to receive an accession of fresh voices, which would swell its volume to a howl worthy of the lost. Still shriller and more piercing it grew, till the imagination beheld a troop of savage Indians turned among the innocents to work upon them their cruel and murderous purposes. Wilder howling and yelling still! Surely the barbarians are hacking their victims to pieces, roasting them alive, tearing them limb from limb, and subjecting them to tortures too hideous to think of. It can all be heard distinctly in the heart-rending outcry. One cry rises suddenly and far above the rest—keen, agonizing, and excruciatingly pitiful. The Sepoys have got that baby, or ought to have, for what but their ingenious mercilessness could evoke such intolerable and unutterable woe?

I rush to the window and gaze forth. Not an Indian nor Sepoy is in sight, but behold a dismal array of dirty yards, rotting sheds, and rears of houses ten times more unsightly than their fronts! Lines are stretched from tenement to tenement, upon which is suspended linen, and much else fresh from the washtub, the only things clean, except the sky in sight. The dirty yards are filled with dirty women, and dirtier children. In one adjoining aunt's are a mother and six juveniles, including an infant, sprawling and squalling in the arms of the oldest of the half dozen. The young ones play in the dirt, quarrel and fight with each other, unheeded by their maternal parent, who is engaged at the washtub, till their mélée and outcries arrive at an intolerable pitch, when she dives into the midst of them, deals her favors about indiscriminately, a few telling blows invariably hitting the most innocent, when the clamor is carried to the utmost power of lungs. As this chorus is commonly assisted by one in every other yard in hearing in the way of noise and dissonance, nothing is left to be desired; and when, as is mostly the case with the vocal infantine anguish and general hue-and-cry, are "mixed up," and sung simultaneously, such popular airs as, "Annie Lawrie," "Gentle Annie," and "Willie We Have Missed You," at the top of voices cracked all the way up, the introduction of bedlam itself could not have heightened the effect.

Washing seemed to be the steady employment of the women, and baby-spanking their diversion.. They washed every one's clothes but their own—everything else, save themselves and children. The application of a little soap and water to the countenances of their offspring would have wrought miracles, but then, perhaps it would have prevented the mothers from recognizing their own children, and thus create sad confusion.

He must be worse than an infidel who would deny woman the sacred prerogative of "spanking" her own babes, but this does not include the right to extend such favors to the offspring of others. In the yard to the left of us, Mrs. O'Flaherty has usurped the privilege Nature has bestowed exclusively on Mrs. O'Brien.

"Mrs. O'Flaherty," said the latter, in a lofty tone, "by your lave, if ye'd lave my childer alone and kape yer own dacint, ye would be afther acting more like a lady nor yez do at prisent."

"By yer lave, Mrs. O'Brien, as it's all the same to yea," responded the other, in the same key, "what right had your Barney to hit my Pat over the sconce?"

[Here the youthful and ardent Barney broke in—

"What right had Pat to say I was christen'd Barney Madison 'cause my father was cracked?"

"What right had you," retorted Pat, "to say I was christened Patrick Washington 'cause my mither is a washerwoman?"

"Patrick Washington O'Flaherty and Barney Madison O'Brien! Ha, ha ha!" laughed Mrs. O'Donnelly. "Sich grand names for the likes of yez. 'Tis a judgmnt on yer vanity that ye quarrel like cats and dogs about 'em." The O'Brien and the O'Flaherty at once tuned upon the moralist.

"Didn't the O'Briens"—

"And the O'Flahertys too"—

"Go straight from the Garden of Aden into Ireland, which was then Paradise itself, and reign kings over the whole counthry before the O'Donnells had come into this blessed world at all to disgrace it, bad luck to them?"

"Kings of Ireland, indade!" exclaimed Mrs. O'Donnelly in disgust. "I suppose ye will be afther telling me next that yer relations are kings of Blackwell's Island, where they are sint to be supported at public expinse!"

At this insulting insinuation, words being inadequate to express the indignation of the O'Brien and the O'Flaherty, they resorted to blows. Mrs. O'Donnelly stood like Austria pitted against France and Sardinia, one to two, but she was the largest, and the contest seemed doubtful. Had not the public been so lately surfeited with the battles of Magenta, Solferino, etc., I would indulge its appetite for sanguinary description,—for honor, name, glory, inflamed the participants in this struggle, as they have done in many other fierce contests.

> "Though few their numbers, theirs the strife
> That neither spares nor speaks for life."

But I spare the reader the thrilling details, and drop the curtain on this tableau of horror, concluding thus effectively my Pandemoniac "City Sketch."

Aquatic Feuilleton.

"Personne" at Newport.

THE CRIB, Wednesday.

Mon cher rédacteur:

After my Saratoga experience, I had resolved to live only for Fame and your Printer, who loves me, as I rejoice to learn, with an affection passing that of Anna Maria.

But the indifference, not to say the absolute cruelty, of the Brightest and the Best,—for whatever may have happened or not happened, she is still B. B.,—preyed a good deal on my mind, and reduced me almost to a skeleton.

I thought of strychnine, but succumbed to my doctors, who said salt water.

So I went to Newport. First by the Shore Line, through New Haven, New London, East Greenwich, and to the Enchanted Isle, arriving just in time for a drive to the Tea-House, where my shattered breast was somewhat repaired by the cheering influences of tea, tobacco, and the society of the Fair.

Not so fair as A. M., but still, I may say nice, and would do if a man was cast away on some island at the South Pole.

Like Mr. Sumner, I think my health will soon be restored, so that I can renew my labors with the opening of the next Theatrical Session, but it is not quite certain.

If not, I don't envy A. M. her feelings.

She is flying about as if she had nothing "onto her mind." Flirting with extraordinary youths—delegates from Guilford Court House, Old Tar River, Attakapas, and other barbarous districts—men with coats of the last century (not McElrath's), and cravats of the size and texture of a bath-towel.

However, if she likes it, I don't so much mind. I intend to send her fifty copies of your "Adieux," printed last week. I think that is a good way to do it.

But let's to gayer measures.

Would you like to know something about Newport? Odd town. Queer people. Pretty good place though, at the top of the season, which is just about now.

They are doing all sorts of things,—hopping and driving, eating, drinking, flirting, playing on piano and the faro-table, and getting through the time somehow.

Fuller and Burkhardt are here.

So is Page, the illustrious.

After that, it is quite unnecessary to say that we are fashionable up to an absolutely distracting point.

Not all of us are within the charmed circle over which these three graces (F., B., and P.) rule with such despotic sway.

There is the desolate Father of a Family, who has been brought down here by the neck, and "don't see it." The Old Lady thought it would be a good thing for the girls, and in one way or another, it is.

The Old Gentleman would prefer to be in the "store," blowing up the clerks, or eating his chop at Clark & Brown's—sweeter far than all the delicacies of the Ocean House table d'hôte, where I may say I got the other day as bad a dinner, considering the pretension of the house, as I ever ate anywhere, and my experience in the dinner-way is extensive for "a youth to fortune and to fame unknown" (that's from Gray; I didn't know it till lately, and so I quote it continually).

However, the Ocean House is full, so full that they make up cots in the Concert-Hall, where they take in miserable bachelors, who are consigned to the tender mercies of a Celt who thinks towels superfluities, and soap an invention gotten up by bloated aristocrats, to make trouble for servants.

The other morning, when Her Solfeggio Majesty, Queen Frezzolini, wished to try a cadenza or two in this barrack, where she was to give a Concert, a gentleman from Pike county, California (who lives on brandy cocktails and cayenne pepper, and who had taken Cot 19 at four in the morning), after a hard fight with the Tiger, was astounded by a rustle of crinoline (he had already thrown a Deringer and two boots at the Celt), and it turned out to be this same Frez., with her suite. Pike county wouldn't get up. Pike resisted attractions before which, in ancient times, the Marshals of the First Napoleon bowed, the Jockey Club trembled, and the Moutards went insane. Pike was insensible to beauty which, even in these later days, has fascinated the most brilliant of American journalists, the friend of Cranston, the historian of the New York Hotel, the man over all men that the Baron clasps to his heart of hearts.

No, Pike couldn't see it, and Frez. was obliged to forego her rehearsal.

It was Venus and Adonis over again.

We have a pretty strong invoice of Italians here just now. Garibaldi might make a good haul with a scoop-net on the piazza of the Ocean House. They all mustered in force for the Frezzolini Concert, on the 8th. It was a nice affair for a small party, but the piece was rather heavy. There was what they called an orchestra of about seven enterprising persons, who scraped through two overtures; a man named Strini, a one-horse basso, who informed the people that "we" (meaning "some parties unknown to the jury") "met by chance, the usual way" (curious contradiction, people generally meet by appointment), and sung, in a confidential manner, a romance from "Ernani." Then there was a good deal of Frezzolini; more than her voice will stand now. She sung the "Qui la voce" from Puritani, "Home, Sweet Home," with the Venzano valse finale, the Cavatina from Linda, "O luce di quest anima," and the "Ah! non guinge," from the Sonnambula. I am told by the Professor of the double bass (his opinion is not good for much after that fuss about the Figaro Brittanicas), that she was very fine in the Puritani Cavatina, which I didn't hear, but in the others she displayed only some facility of execution, and the relics of a fine voice.

Whiskers said she was "Ah—yes—well, what you call a fine old antique-sort of a wuin, you know" (he meant ruin).

There were lots of people at the concert—the noble army of martyrs who have free tickets, and therefore must go, being fully represented. The men went to sleep or talked to the women, and the women criticised each other's clothes. Albites sent them home in the best of humor with one of his pleasant chansons comiques.

As for the question d'argent, the concert netted just forty-seven dollars, no cents.

That's all we have had, except Hops, where there were a few pretty and well-dressed women—a dispensation of divine providence, for which no one is more grateful than myself. But the majority are dowagers, who are continually abusing their sisters for talking scandal, and yet always doing it themselves. Now, scandal from the lips of a pretty woman isn't bad. There's generally no malevolence in it—only a wish to be amusing; but from retired colonels and captains on half pay, tanned by the smoke and dried in the fire of a hundred tea-fights, it is excessively disagreeable. I forgot to tell you, up above, how I got here, last time. I came in a yacht, and I am, I may say, nautical, I feel an irresistible inclination to get under way, instead of to go out; to bring myself to an anchor, instead of sitting down; to speak in the language of mariners to A. M., who don't see it; and generally I feel a saline thirst, which manifests itself in a terrific consumption of Bordeaux. Dr. Dixon, I know, says it don't quench thirst; but it allays mine wonderfully. I think of doing a nautical drama, and believe that if I say a young woman whose husband had gone "to follow the sea," and was pursued by a scoundrel of a landlord, a villain of a gas-collector, or a curmudgeon of a water-renter, all of whom, struck with her beauty, would make insulting proposals, I'd give her order on you for the "demnition total," and never think about repayment.

Seriously, though, we look pretty well, I can tell you, lying in the pretty harbor, with our colors all set, all our crews in clean clothes, and twenty-five such fine vessels, with a hundred or more splendid fellows in immaculate sailor rig. It isn't often that the ladies get such a treat, I can tell you.

As for the subscriber, his health improves, and his appetite is fair to middling. He is a good deal browner than he was; somewhat broiled behind the ears, and your Saratoga correspondent could no longer complain of the whiteness of his hands. His broken heart is gradually uniting, and he believes he will be able to bear up with tolerable fortitude under the cruelty of A. M. and four meals per diem.

Bless you. Be happy. Adieu.

Personne.

Correspondence.

A LETTER FROM 'LONG-SHORE.

Portland Heights, N. J.

My Dear Press: I don't know as you remember that fine Saturday in June last when I made your sanctum brilliant with my presence, and exhibiting shawl and travelling-bag, announced my immediate departure from your finite corner of the world to this boundless space of land and water—*yclept* New Jersey.

I don't know as you recollect how the Saturday Press and its friends went around the corner of Printing-House Square, to Crook & Duff's, for a farewell libation to two of us—one going to face a Vermont University, with a poem in his pocket, and the other going to face a Jersey Universe, with nothing in his pocket.

If, however, your memory is so obliging as to have retained these eras in the world's history, perhaps it also clings to the fact that I threatened, on that occasion, to write you a letter—or several—which threat you received with the bland dignity becoming your position.

And this epistle is the offspring of that threat.

FITZ-DIAMOND O'LENS, Bart., once avowed, with a charming frankness, in my hearing, that he "didn't like Nature." In that particular, I must confess, I disagree very materially with him. I am very fond of Nature "in every style," as the oyster-shops sign say. I love birds, on the trees as well as on toast; and, as a general thing, greatly prefer the greens of a wooded landscape to those served with corned-beef at the cheap eating-houses. Nature is a capital place to loaf in—that is, if New Jersey is Nature—and I have every reason to believe it is.

Portland Heights consist of a range of steep hills, lying on the southern shore of Sandy Hook Bay. They are the first land visible from inward-bound vessels, and may also be seen from the Narrows, from Staten Island, and, I think, from several other places. The scenery, as viewed from my window, is varied and beautiful, comprising the following "objects of interest :"

1. Water (Sandy Hook Bay).
2. Staten Island (very fine, full-length view).
3. Water (Raritan Bay).
4. Long Island (beautiful distance, showing Rockaway).
5. Water (the Narrows).
6. Sandy Hook (picturesque, with lighthouse, etc.).
7. Water (entrance to the harbor).
8. The Atlantic (the Ocean, not the Magazine).
9. More water.

These ingredients, as you may easily imagine, form a most unexceptionable marine view, surpassed by none that ornamented the walls of the National Academy of Design during the last exhibition. Portland Heights is not a watering place, but it is an exceedingly watery place.

If, perchance, I desire the sights and sounds of fashionable rustication, there is THOMSON's Pavilion (why "Pavilion ?"), two and a half miles away, and as there are two bar-rooms on the premises, I have visited the establishment a number of times. It looks pleasant, with the sailboats scudding up and down the river, the bathing parties on the beach, and the plenitude of young ladies—some of them quite prettywith a plenitude of crinoline, sitting about, in the shade, on the grass plots, and in the gardens, with fans, and flats, and guitars, and things. The scene reminded me, on fine afternoons, of ALDRICH's description—at least, I think it is his; it sounds like him—of the

Orient garden sweet,
Where the crimson violets broadly blow,
And the golden-tawny hyacinths grow,
That October breezes fan;
And where, on a dainty rustic seat,
Sit several dainty little girls
With bronze-brown eyes and languid curls,
Touching, with taper fingers fleet,
The silvery chords of the yataghan!

But, notwithstanding the beauty of the picture thus presented, I most enjoy the freedom of my airy East chamber, where my library (a dictionary, "MAUD," "WILSON's Human Anatomy," and a volume of DE BALZAC), my pipes, my Aeolian harp, and myself, preserve an equitable and harmonious condition of existence together.

Amid these surroundings, my labors are light. To be sure, work is only an amusement, in a place where one has nothing else to do where there are no boats suitable for fancy rowing, no roads suitable for fancy driving, no water warm enough (generally) for fancy swimming, and no society prone to fancy conversation but I do not approve of amusements, so I do not work.

But there are many pleasant, retired places about, where the trees make a goodly shade, and the grass makes a goodly couch. As my invariable costume is that of the native 'long-shoremen—a scarlet flannel shirt, and a pair of canvas pantaloons—I am not afraid to lie down anywhere, at ease, to read, or smoke, or write. Oftenest, though, I like to meditate, to rest, and to gather strength from the "magnetism of the forces" that my host—a philosophical gentleman—says may be absorbed by lying upon the earth. When the wind is a little easterly, it brings a long-drawn, breezy monotone with it; a resonant rumble, rising, falling, and sweeping by with inexpressible dreaminess. That is the surf on Sandy Hook, and it makes divine music to go to sleep by.

When I am too lazy to lie beneath the trees, I go a-fishing. There is a certain old wreck near here—the remains of a marl schooner, sunk on the flats some years ago—and it is a sort of gathering-place for the finny tribe. At low tide, the ancient ribs and timbers, that have "suffered a sea-change, into something rich and strange," poke their green and weedy heads above the surface, and are wonderfully suggestive of submarine scenery. Knots of dark purple mussels, and streamers of dulces, cling to them; the water swirls and ripples around them; the checquered reflections of sunlit waves dance upon their greenish-black shadows, and down, far down beneath, mysteriously dim in the semi-translucent brine, lie vague hints of other beams and braces, that never see the light.

About these the sea-bass, blackfish, and porgies, love to linger. I don't wonder at it. It looks delightfully cool and refreshing down there. The wonder is that the blessed little ignoramuses ever allow themselves to be drawn out of such a loitering place, for the paltry consideration of a fragment of clam—and that with clams at only a shilling a hundred! Were I a fish, I would go clam-bereft all my days, rather than exchange the bars of the Navesink for those of a grid-iron!

I wish, my dear PRESS, that you could entrust all your duties to JOHN, sometime, and take a week of vacation here. I don't think you are quite so inveterate a lotus-eater as myself, but I could guarantee you a period of first-class laziness. I would offer you my spandiest red shirt,—the one with brass buttons,—my best pipe, and lay in an extra supply of fish-hooks. As I know you can't come, I feel perfectly safe in inviting you.

Seriously, however, I do not see why you might not leave your valuable journal some Saturday, and sojourn here until Monday—just long enough to taste the joys of 'long-shore existence—to "loaf and enjoy your soul," as the Kosmos saith, or, if you felt energetic, to climb the rugged mountain's brow, and chase the bounding clam. Can't you?

Hoping that you can, I remain, with the best of wishes for both paper and editor, G. A.

Love Matters.

—Frederick Hotaff, a Cincinnati German, wrote his will on a cellar door, cut his throat from ear to ear, and jumped into the river, because a neighbor charged him with improper intimacy with his wife.

—Among the divorce cases of the last week was that of James and Alice Hampton. This is one of those cases in which the wife is the guilty party. The parties were married thirteen years ago in Philadelphia, and have five children. The husband complained that after their removal to this State his wife commenced to disregard her marriage vows, and in Brooklyn about a year ago, had illicit intercourse with a man named Dempsey and various other parties. The wife made no answer and the matter was referred to a referee, who reported in favor of the husband. The Court granted a decree of divorce against the wife.

—A free negro fortune-teller, Elisha Malone, was whipped to death in Dinwiddie county, Va., last week, by a negro man, slave of Mr. D. Roney. The sable seer had been visiting the wife of the slave for some time previous, on the pretext of telling her fortune, which excited the jealousy of her husband, who, watching his opportunity, seized the offender in the woods, tied him to a tree, and whipped him to death with switches.

—The Mormon saints are persecuted in New York by a perverse generation of heathenish magistrates, who do not appreciate the revelations of the Prophet Smith. A day or two since, Daniel Lee, an Englishman, and a full believer in polygamy, was brought before Alderman Smith, at the lower Police Court, on a charge of bigamy. Honora Towers, of No. 14 Desbrosses street, deposed that she was married to the defendant on the 25th of January, 1857, by the Rev. Father Brennan of the James street Catholic church. Anne Shannon, of No. 180 Orchard street, alleged that she was present at the marriage of her sister Mary to the defendant, at St. Luke's church, London, England, on the 25th of March, 1855, and that the said Mary is still alive and undivorced from her husband. The case for the people was very short, but it was to the point and conclusive against the prisoner. The two wives were in court during the examination, and appeared quite pleased when the magistrate ordered the prisoner to be committed.

—The August number of *The Hearthstone* (a magazine devoted to domestic economy and the welfare of woman) says:

> Disguise it as we may, men now buy their wives. Love-matches are far less numerous than money-matches. And even in cases where love may influence some, money does more. Even in cases where love may have been the controlling motive for the union, it is soon weakened by the feeling of power on the one hand and that of pecuniary dependence on the other. The wife feels degraded, and how can she love him who degrades her? The feeling of pecuniary dependence is the most galling ill that wives now suffer. To be subject to the whims, caprices, and passions of a mean and tyrannical nature for the supply of the common necessities of life, wars upon love. They feel life and energy sapped by it. They must be free to love truly. Who wonders that they become extravagant, or indifferent to their husband's interests when they are allowed no direct power in the matter? Emancipation from this condition will be a great step towards the elevation of woman.

—The N. Y. *Evening Post* says that Mr. Choate was so true and perfect a husband and father that no thought of his being a great man ever entered the household.

—Longfellow describes a flirt as a young lady of more beauty than sense, more accomplishment than learning, more charm of person than grace of mind, more admirers than friends, more fools than wise men for attendants.

—The Detroit papers report the following case: "A man named Robert Edwards, who lives in the town of Greenfield, about five miles from Detroit, was arrested on Sunday evening by officer Gunning. The charge against him is of quite a serious nature, the facts being as follows: Several years ago, the wife of Edwards took a young girl by the name of Dougherty, whose mother resides in this city, for the purpose of bringing her up. After a time, Mrs. Edwards died, and her husband representing that the girl was quite necessary to him as a housekeeper, and that he would clothe and treat her well and pay a certain sum for her services, she was allowed to remain with him. Edwards, by his wiles, soon managed to seduce her, and about two years since she became a mother. The seduction and birth remained unknown to Mrs. Dougherty until a few days ago, who, as soon as she became cognizant of the way matters had progressed, through her son-in-law, a Mr. Foster, endeavored to have Edwards make all the reparation in his power, viz: marry the mother of his child. He refused, saying it would be all right; when Mr. Foster, learning that he was about to bring about a marriage between his victim and a half-witted fellow employed by him as a farm hand, a warrant was issued and placed in the hands of officer Gunning, who, after a long chase, apprehended him on Sunday morning. The officer visited the farm, but Edwards was secreted and could not be found, but was discovered soon after on the ferryboat, on his way from Windsor to Detroit. The prisoner is now in jail."

—At the Convention of Spiritualists, held at Plymouth, Mass., on the 5th, 6th, and 7th of August, the novel feature of a marriage between two Spiritualists was introduced among the exercises. It is thus described:

The declaration of sentiments having been got rid of, the next matter in order was the solemnization of marriage between Mr. Nathan C. Lewis and Mrs. Eunice A. Babbitt, of Boston. The lady was dressed in loose, flowing robes of white, deeply trimmed in blue, and wore blue satin shoes. The two girls, her daughters by a former marriage, were dressed in exactly the same style, and followed her to the platform. The bridegroom placed himself beside her. He is a physician. Both had been married before, and each is about 35 years of age.

Mr. Loveland, who was formerly a Methodist minister, though he does not now appreciate the title of "reverend," addressing the congregation, said: "Although Spiritualists in general do not accept, but are opposed to the regulations that exist legally in regard to the subjugation of woman in the marriage relations, still they do generally, if not universally, admit the propriety of making a public acknowledgment of their relations."

Then, turning to the interested parties, he said: "My brother and sister, I ask you to make no promise, I impose upon you no obligation. All the obligations you have, you have yourselves assumed in your own spirits. I know your hearts. You have already in your spirits consummated the union as far as it could possibly be. I stand not here to marry you. This congregation are not witnesses, and are not called upon to be witnesses of your marriage. But I stand here to affirm legally the fact, and to ask this congregation to join with me in pronouncing a benediction and blessing on the union into which you have entered, which you here acknowledge, and which you here formally before the world complete. In token, then, of this union, which you have cemented in your souls—and which you now confess before the world, please join your right hands."

The happy couple complied with the request. Then Mr. Loveland placed a hand on each of their heads, and blessed them in this form:

"And now, on behalf of this audience, and on behalf of the attending spirits that are around us and with us, I bless this union; I bless you in their behalf, as you start together in the journey of life."

This was the whole ceremony. The bridegroom made a formal bow to the audience. The bride, who had been quietly fanning herself throughout the performance, dropped a courtesy. The pair, with their little attendants in white and blue, stepped off the platform, and the audience applauded so long that it seemed as if they wished the last scene encored.

Then Mr. Wright was called upon to say something on the subject of marriage and paternity. He spoke for a few moments, and ended by presenting to the couple a copy of one of his works, probably "The Unwelcome Child." Shortly afterward the Chairman was made the medium of handing to the bridegroom a bouquet, which he termed a volume of natural theology. Dr. Lewis accepted the gift, and promised to study it. Thus ended the marriage scene.

NEW YORK AUGUST 20, 1859

THE NEW AMERICAN TRAGEDY AT WALLACK'S.

The reader's special attention is called to the fact that on Monday next, Matilda Heron will appear at Wallack's Theatre in a new American Tragedy, entitled "Geraldine, or Love's Victory," written expressly for her by a lady of this city.

Without wishing to anticipate the verdict of the public, we may be permitted to say that after what we have heard of the play from competent sources, and from what we all know of the gifted actress who is to play the leading part, there can be little doubt of its triumphant success.

At any rate, its production will be the great dramatic event of the week, and there will, of course, be the usual crowd of literary and other celebrities present, to enjoy the excitement of a first representation. For the cast of the play the reader is referred to Mr. Bateman's announcement in another column.

The Chicago Leader, of the 3d inst., has the following: "Mr. George Star, of this city, has returned from Pike's Peak. He was with the very Chicago company alluded to in Horace Greeley's statement, and pronounces that statement a humbug. Mr. Star was in the mines nearly a month, and he neither saw nor heard of any man or company of men who had obtained $1 50 a-day as the result of their labor. Mr. Star's opinion is worth that of a dozen Horace Greeleys, and ought to be regarded as a timely warning."

Skepticism run Mad.

Our Skeptical Man (whose opinions we should be sorry to endorse) writes us as follows:

I. I do not believe that Sunday, as understood by the Sabbatarians, is a divinely-ordained institution, for the simple reason that if it were so, the Ordainer would have prohibited rainy Sabbaths, if only to enable people to reach the church. I, however—who am no Sabbatarian—bless the Sabbath-rain and its Creator, seeing in it the workings of his wonderful chemistry in the production of "our daily bread." No churchman can preach to me so rapt a sermon as the cornstalk.

II. I do not believe in spirit-rappings feeling convinced that, were it feasible, our immortal Washington would have availed himself of the very first chance to commence an action for libel against some hundreds of portrait-painters, engravers, and orators.

Original Poetry.

MES ILLUSIONS.

I.

Peace! skeptic, peace! Your heartless words
Fall on my soul like ice;
Why will men at all sacred things
Nibble and gnaw like mice?
Grant it, my life is but a dream;
But if the dream be fair,
Why cloud it? Seek some other theme,
And my illusions spare.

II.

I know that I'm no longer young,
Why, then, disturb my past?
Why taunt me with the stale old song,
That pleasures never last?
Why preach to me the grave's the goal
Of joy as well as care?
My heart says not; then go, my friend,
And my illusions spare.

III.

The world, you say, the same old round
Has gone since it was young,
That bad men thrive, and good men fail,
And saints are often hung;
What then? You are not hung as yet,
So hope for better fare,
And while you still the gallows cheat,
Pray my illusions spare.

IV.

You think mankind no wiser now
Than centuries ago;
Perhaps; but must we reason, then,
That you no wiser grow?
If so, then vent your scornful wrath,
And at your fortune swear,
But leave me to my simple faith,
And my Illusions spare.

V.

I see around me nought but growth,
And yonder wakening sky
Looks down upon the teeming earth
With sweet approving eye.
Your curse, you'll learn the truth one day,—
Is but inverted prayer:
You damn yourself; well, damn away,
But my Illusions spare.

H. C., Jr.

[For the N. Y, SATURDAY PRESS]

PILLSBURY'S HYMN.

(As sung by him to the tune of "We won't go home till Morning.")

In the good old days of the Dungeon and Stake;
When the glorious old curfew made folks betake
To their beds at nine in the evening,
To their beds at nine in the evening;
When the jolly old priest, with his reverend sword,
Poked up vile heretics, until they roared
Under the holy chastening,
Under the holy chastening;
When the Lord's chosen chums did merrily sing,
While the chink in their coffers did jovially ring,
You must go to church on Sunday,
You must go to church on Sunday,
You must go to church on Sunday,
Or pay for staying away.
etc., etc,, etc

A. F. B.

THE SEWING MACHINE.

BY A CONNECTICIT YANKEE.

"Good one! Don't say so! Which did you get?
One of the kind to open and shet?
Own it, or hire it? How much did you pay?
Does it go with a crank or a treadle? Say,
I'm a single man, and somewhat green,
Tell me about your sewing-machine."

"Listen, my boy, and hear all about it—
I don't know what I should do without it,
I've owned one now for more than a year,
And like it so well I call it 'my dear.'
'Tis the cleverest thing that ever was seen,
This wonderful family sewing-machine.

It's none of your angular Singer things,
With steel-shod beak and cast-iron wings;
Its work would bother a hundred of his,
And is worth a thousand! Indeed it is;
And has a way—you needn't stare—
Of combing and braiding its own black hair!

Mine is not one of those stupid affairs
That stands in a corner with what-nots and chairs,
And makes that dismal headachy noise,
Which all the comfort of sewing destroys,
No rigid contrivance of lumber and steel,
But one with a natural spring in the heel.

Mine is one of the kind to love,
And wear a shawl and a soft kid glove;
Has the merriest eyes and a dainty foot,
And sports the charmingest gaiter-boot,
And a bonnet with feathers, and ribbons, and loops,
With an indefinite number of hoops.

None of your patent machines for me,
Unless Dame Nature's the patentee !
I like the sort that can laugh and talk,
And take my arm for an evening walk;
That will do whatever the owner may choose,
With the slightest perceptible turn of screws!

One that can dance, and—possibly—flirt;
And make a pudding as well as a shirt—
One that can sing without dropping a stitch,
And play the housewife, lady, or witch—
Ready to give the sagest advice,
Or do up your collar and things so nice.

What do you think of my machine ?!
Aint it the best that ever was seen?
'Tisn't a clumsy, mechanical toy,
But flesh and blood! Hear that, my boy,
With a turn for gossip, and household affairs,
Which include, you know, the sewing of tears.

Tut, tut—don't talk. I see it all—
You needn't keep winking so hard at the wall;
I know what your fidgety fumblings mean,
Would you like, yourself, a sewing-machine?
Well, get one, then—of the same design—
There was plenty left when I got mine."

THE BALLAD OF THREE LITTLE SOULS.

BY JULIETTE H. BEACH.

Three children played one Summer day,
At sunset, by the ebbing sea,
And moored within the shining bay,
A painted boat rocked lazily.

With prattle full of baby-lore,
And bits of song that told their glee,
They clambered in, and from the shore
The boat went drifting out to sea.

"Mother!" the cry came faint and far—
Beneath the swiftly darkening skies,
They saw the home-light, like a star,
And shoreward gazed with wistful eyes.

Their mother, on the toy-strewn shore
Stood, 'mid the prints of little feet,
And with white lips, but weak no more,
Sent words of peace, and blessings sweet,

"Pray, darlings!" and with clasped hands,
And fear and faith blent in her tones,
She knelt upon the foot-marked sands,
Whispering "Dear Christ! Thy little ones!"

Three little heads, together bent,
Strove on her form their eyes to keep ;—
She knew their voices, softly blent,
Said "Now I lay me down to sleep"—

And so they passed from mortal sight—
But in the billows faintly borne,
She heard "O mother sweet! good night!"
From the dear lips of her first born.

Then rising, wan and tearless-eyed,
She said, "Lord, praises be to Thee!
For these white souls shall never ride,
Storm-tossed and vext, life's treacherous sea!"

And when at midnight came the sound
Of searchers rowing mournfully,
And pale lips said "the boat is found,
And this, that floated on the sea!",

She took the little well-worn hat,
Kissed it, and laid it on her breast,
And when her silence fears begat,
Friends softly said, "she is at rest."

Albion, N. Y.

Correspondence.

Dear Press:—I am a sucking author—sucking authors are sometimes ashamed of their productions, and send them to Editors anonymously. I do so too.

Press, I am without an object in life, and am bothered by a woman. I feel like blowing my brains out. I have lost her love through my own fault, and though I feel that her mental constitution is unsuitable to me, I have loved her three years, and hate to give her up. Love is often laziness. One rests his heart upon a woman, and, though he feels that fifty others would answer as well, he is too idle to lift it off. Press, insert my letters, and give me something to do. I have read you often lately, and drank inspiration from your style. It must be read. When it treats of nothing, its bubbles rise to the surface, sparkling so rosily that we must look at them. I will eschew "*Constellation*" and "*Century*" ponderosity, and be terse. I will model myself upon you, or on "Personne." "Personne" is an institution. Anna Maria is delicious. The wide-awake eyes and parted lips of the Beloved One, as she watches the play with her bored admirer, are ever present to me. Press, pardon my dullness. Writing for you is no easy matter. I pondered what to write about, and concluded to say what came uppermost. I had a sensation recently. Last Fall there appeared in the *Herald* a die-away matrimonial advertisement of a young lady for a sympathizing heart, adding that money was no object, as she had plenty. I suspected it as a piece of school-girl fun, and feeling on that gloomy afternoon as if an adventure would be welcome, wrote her my opinion on the subject, offering my services. I received a reply in six months. It came the other day. I was right. She was a school-girl, and did want fun.

She received *five hundred answers*. They all responded to her wish for a sympathizing heart, "and said nothing about the money." She says she fancied my letter, put it in her desk, and burnt the rest. She soon after left the school. In a fit of ennui or disenchantment, she last week disinterred my epistle and replied to it. Hence my sensation. I have had a second letter from her. I'll send her the Saturday Press. How can I better express my gratitude? Saturday Press! Modest name! who would buy it for its title? who would say the dull stone enclosed such glistening ore? One might think it a diluted Journal of Commerce. Adieu. I will hunt up something for my next. I am at fault to-day. An office-desk engenders no coruscations. Nessuno.

North Conway House, August 15, 1859.

My Dear Editor:—The Saturday Press hasn't come yet. The barbarian postmen wont forward papers as they do letters, so we must wait for the next mail.

I got here Friday night, at 11 o'clock, being the only passenger. A fresh breeze was blowing when we took the steamer *Dover* at Alton Bay, and sailed up Lake Winnipisiogee to Centre Harbor. From Centre Harbor to Conway, thirty miles, we came in a stage, which was nearly full of gentlemen and ladies, but the landlord of the principal hotel there frightened them all into stopping with him, by asserting that there wasn't the slightest chance of getting a room anywhere in North Conway. The rest thought me foolhardy to start, and even urged me to stay after I had got into the stage; but remembering the Spanish proverb—"Never believe a landlord's account of his neighbor's inn "—I rode off without any very serious apprehensions. What an interesting drive I had all to myself! Cool breeze, mountains to the right, to the left, before and behind me, and the full red moon rising, according to my locality, exactly in the North.

When our stage got within a mile of the North Conway Hotel, it was hailed by five ladies, who ordered the driver to stop at a certain place farther above. They were in high glee, and I soon learned by their conversation that they were about to play a joke upon the keeper of some little hotel, which they knew to be entirely full; but their difficulty was to determine who should speak for them, as the landlord knew them all, and would detect their voices. Of course, I came to the rescue, and offered, much to their delight, to speak for them. The stage stopped. The piazza was full, and as the landlord advanced a few steps, I put my head out of the window and asked if he could accommodate us with rooms?

"No, no!—all full!—no place for another soul."

Then I gave him a pitiful account of our weariness, of the other hotels turning us away—six women all alone —no gentleman with us, and begged the privilege of lodging on the parlor floor. By this time, the guests, deeply interested, began to crowd around and to intercede with the host for us, when, according to the direction of one of the ladies, I opened the door of the stage, and the ladies poured out, one by one. As we drove off we heard the most vociferous laughs ring out on the air, mingled with the words, "Sold, sold!"

As we drove up to the hotel, we heard music and the jar of dancing; Mr. Mason had treated his guests to a "Hop."

I find that the people here are mostly from the "Hub of Creation," and they all seem to be well acquainted. We have a "bowling alley," which is patronized very considerably by the ladies of this and the Keersage House. One of our boarders, a young bride of two or three months, is one of the best players. She astonishes us by her "ten strikes," which she accomplishes frequently with the biggest ball. We have also a prodigy in chess—a miniature Paul Morphy—Master H., of Portland, Me., who plays a good deal, and generally leaves the field victorious. I like the ladies of the house—they are certainly very agreeable; some are quite young, and three or four are very handsome.

Visitors are delighted with Echo Lake, situated upon the side of a mountain, and Diana's Baths; the latter, they say, are most wonderfully numerous and elegantly polished basins made in the solid granite by the action of the water. I shall see them very soon for myself.

Mt. Keersage we see from our house, and "White Horse Ledge." I do not distinguish the "White Horse" so clearly as some do; like most things of this sort it can only be approached by a very fruitful imagination.

The thing which most charm me here, is the entire absence of the Fitz-Noodle race, which I learn is in Newport this season. Here is no absurd fashion. Ladies dress when and as they please, and if they choose to go to dinner in morning-wrappers, it is not remarked. The fact is, everybody feels well, and nothing so dissipates ill-humor, human smallness, and human meanness, like fresh mountain air and a healthy digestion.

Yours truly, M. S. C.

NEW YORK A GREAT SPA.

Our special reporter, sent to examine into the Croton-matter, reports that the streams which feed the grand reservoir have worn away their beds down to a mineral rock, a peculiar salt in which has impregnated the water, and given to it the peculiar taste of which we hear so much complaint.

We haste to add, however, that our reporter further states that the waters, by being thus impregnated, have acquired certain medicinal properties, which render them more salubrious than the waters of Saratoga, or any other Spring or Spa in the world. In fact, it is notorious that whenever waters, from being fresh and sweet, become stale, and even nauseous, it is because of their having acquired some sanitary virtue, which makes them more beneficial (if taken in sufficient quantities) than the waters of the clearest mountain-spring.

We cannot, therefore, rejoice sufficiently, that at last our dear Croton water, after having been clear and delicious to the taste (and as a consequence, deleterious to the health) for so many years, has at last become so muddy, and so offensive to the palate, that it may be taken (when well shaken) in any quantity—and that not only with impunity, but with positive advantage to the health.

What the results of this miraculous and beneficial change will be, no one can fully determine. One thing, however, seems to be certain, to wit, that if the fact can only be clearly established that the Croton water is twice as disagreeable (and by consequence, as the medico-mathematical mind will at once perceive, four times as salubrious) as the waters of our fashionable Springs, *one* result will be, that this magnificent metropolis will at once take rank as the greatest and most wonderful Spa in the world, casting the best of them—even Baden—Baden itself—completely into the shade.

And this is a consummation devoutly to be wished; for leaving the beautiful city every Summer, and rushing into the hideous country, has got to be a most intolerable and expensive bore—the only redeeming fact in the case being that we enjoy the city so much more when, at the close of the dismal season (provided, meanwhile, we don't die of ennui or indigestion), we are permitted to return to it. What enthusiasm we then feel at being in a place where we can procure fresh fruits and vegetables, where we can have abundance of light and shade, where we can have immunity from troublesome insects (excepting only Croton-bugs, which are now being killed off by the new properties of the water, which are favorable only to the human species), where we can walk out in the evening without risk of life and limb, where we can have spacious and well-ventilated rooms, and finally, where we can have all the privileges of divine worship, and (henceforth) all the blessings of foetid water.

But so far as this last item is concerned, let us not be too hasty. Dr. Chilton may not finish his promised analysis of the Croton waters for five or ten years to come, and then he may knock our reporter's theory in the head by proving that they have become infected by the introduction of "dead men's bones and all manner of uncleanness." Meanwhile, if any large number of our people die off in consequence of too free libations, we can console ourselves (as in such cases made and provided) by taking all responsibility from the shoulders of the Croton managers, and charging the whole mischief to "the inscrutable providence of God."

But we have no great fear of any increase in our tables of mortality. The human constitution is very strong. Moreover, nothing, unless it be wholesome food, seems to affect it so unfavorably as fresh water and pure air. Anything nauseous—high game for instance, or mineral water, or cod-liver oil (which young men take to increase their bulk, and young ladies to improve their complexion)—is eagerly taken, as if the fact of its nauseousness were an argument in its favor. This accords with our general view of Man and Providence. In all time, "mortifying the flesh" (happily an impossible operation in our individual case) has been looked upon as a most beneficial thing, both for the body and the soul. Hence our love of repulsive medicines (which the wicked homeopathists are so much opposed to); and, hence, also, the opposition on the part of the unco good (who have a cheerful faith in human torture, here and hereafter), to the use of chloroform in surgical operations, and to any form of religion that doesn't provide for the endless torment of nine-tenths of their fellow-creatures.

Well, after all, such notions may be right, since they evidently spring from the consciousness, on the part of those who entertain them, that nothing, however terrible, can surpass their deserts. And in this view of the case, it is possible that our own dislike for tormenting, and even for disagreeable things, may result from an incorrect self-appreciation, and from consequently incorrect ideas of God, whom we look upon as a Being who desires nothing so much as the happiness of the human race, and its entire freedom from pain.

NEW YORK AUGUST 27, 1859

FREE PUBLIC GALLERY OF ART.

New York Historical Society Building,
Second avenue, corner of Eleventh street. Open daily from
9 A. M. till 5 P. M.

[For the N. Y, SATURDAY PRESS.]

SHAKESPEARE'S "JULIUS CAESAR."

The great poet of English literature had a genius, that, like the highways centering at Rome, branched off into every quarter of the empire of mind, and found channels for the treasures of every province of character. Each of his plays has a special characteristic distinguishing it from the rest. In one he paints the workings of the human mind possessed with the devil of ambition; in another, he lays bare the mind in its secret chambers, and exhibits its workings and writhings under the tyranny of parental grief, its bewilderment and its loneliness gradually urging it into an eddy from which it circles down into the vortex of insanity. In another he pictures the honorable sorrow of Hamlet, exhibiting the human mind in a still different channel; and with still another he envelops us in an ethereal, translucent atmosphere of enchantment, truly like a Midsummer Night's Dream. He has dramas of love, of grief, of wrath, of ambition, of retribution, or of jealousy. For every experience in a man's inner history, he appears ready to put forth a counterpart.

But Julius Cæsar is essentially a drama of empire. It rather aims to exhibit a "tide in the *affairs* of men" than a current of the human heart. It announces a great political fact; that individual ambition blinds mankind to the redeeming aspirations of its possessor, creates envy among his equals, and fear among his inferiors, alarms the good, and fills the unprincipled with hatred. It inculcates an admirable political virtue; the subserviency of individual affections to the common good. And it also teaches the short-sightedness of man, and shows how in every one's life there is a critical moment when the highway to prosperity and the road to ruin divide before him, and his fate hangs upon the choice.

"Men at some time are masters of their fates."

We do not wish to be understood as treating this play as a production of Shakespeare's fancy; but, though a historical story, he has framed its detail to ideas of his own. His character of Brutus is an original and a masterpiece. We know not where is to be found another delineation of character so delicate. The great conspirator, the noble Roman, the selfless man, the generous sacrificer of his dearest affections, are blended beautifully with the unflinching soldier of his country. Here is the history. Marcus Junius Brutus is a nobleman of Rome, loved by all, and respected by all, for his generosity and high-mindedness. For the good of the State he is a close observer of the times, and, though he loves Cæsar for Cæsar's self, he remarks his high ambition with sorrow and alarm. The idea of equality and liberty seemed to be closely linked with his standard of the Roman dignity. To be a man and a Roman, and not to be politically free, seemed preposterous. The poet implies a conflict in the mind of Brutus, between his love for Cæsar and his dread of Cæsar's ambition. Into this balance the hot-headed republican Caius Cassius throws the weight of his insidious logic, and Brutus consents to join in a conspiracy already formed against Cæsar's life.

And here also we have Cæsar's ambitious aspirations hinted at. He has refused the crown three times at the hand of Mark Antony (refusing it, however, with manifest reluctance), but the Senate has purposed offering it again, upon a certain day. On this day the conspirators have resolved to assassinate him on his way to the Senate-house. But the conqueror, ignorant of the intention of the Senators, has yielded to the entreaties of his wife, and resolved not to appear that day out-of-doors. Decius Brutus, a conspirator, comes to escort him to the Senate, and thus plays upon his ambition to induce him to alter his determination:

—"The senate have concluded
To give this day a crown to mighty Cæsar;
If you shall send them word you will not come,
Their minds may change."

* * * * * * * * * * *

Cæs.—"How foolish do your fears seem now, Calphurnia!
I am ashamed I did yield to them.
Give me my robe, for I will go."

Here begins a series of errors, continued to the end of the play. Cæsar commits an error in going forth, which costs his life. The conspirators commit an error in sparing the life of Mark Antony and in permitting him to address the people, which costs them the sympathy of the Roman populace, and a flight from the city. They err in giving battle to Antony and Octavius at Phillipi, which error causes the annihilation of their army. Through an erroneous belief that his friend is captured, Cassius destroys himself, and through an accumulation of errors the cause of the conspirators is overthrown and ruined. It is, in fact, a tragedy of errors. "Julius Cæsar" well repays a careful study. It is an intricate network of human characters, all finely drawn, so that the whole forms one of the noblest of Shakespeare's productions. There is another consideration not to be overlooked, since it illustrates one of the finest traits of this great dramatist. It is the high tribute he pays to the nobility and beauty of the character of woman. Shakespeare loved to portray a true woman, and never did he do more justice to that character than in Portia, the wife of Brutus. It is a truthful passage, that containing Portia's idea of a wife's position relative to her husband, and the liberality of the sentiment that must have pervaded the poet's mind when he penned that scene, appears to us to be in advance of the times in which he wrote.

In conclusion let us give Mark Antony's brief eulogy over the dead Brutus, which describes the character of Cæsar's friend and slayer, in a manner we cannot imitate in our own words:

"He was the noblest Roman of them all;
All the conspirators, save only he,
Did that they did in envy of great Cæsar;
He, only, in a generous honest thought
Of common good to all, made one of them.
His life was gentle; and the elements
So mixed in him, that Nature might stand up,
And say to all the world, 'This was a man!'"

The greatest men have their enemies. Even this hero of our literature is contemned by some. But we think we are warranted in saying, that could the great magician see how his fame rolled down the sounding corridors of time, and then look upon the prudish contemners of his genius, he would felicitate himself on not having to number these unenlightened and illiberal minds among his admirers. When other history shall have been forgotten, that of Cæsar will still be read in the immortal measure of William Shakespeare.

J. W. C.

THE SARATOGA PLATFORM.

The following are the resolves passed at the Women's Rights Convention at Saratoga Springs, last week:

Resolved, That women, like men, have a right to do anything and everything which is in itself morally right.

Resolved, That if anything is morally right, but is nevertheless unfeminine, that when Deity creates any woman with the ability and desire to do these things, we must lay the responsibility upon Him, and wholly exonerate the woman.

Resolved, That we will encourage every woman to do every honorable and good thing which she can do; and that we especially enjoin it upon her, in addition to her already admitted womanly duties, to break down the prejudices against her independent action, by seeing to it, that she pursues some noble and important calling in life which the world has hitherto pronounced unfeminine.

Resolved, That we assert the complete and entire equality, though not the identity, of the sexes.

Resolved, That we recommend courtesy, civility, gentleness, delicacy, and propriety, to both men and women.

Resolved, That the amount of education which any rational being can acquire is the only measure of the amount which it is his right to acquire; and, therefore, that no woman should be satisfied till she has disciplined all her powers—physical, intellectual, and moral—to the utmost of their capacity.

Resolved, That a great motive is the only great educator; and, therefore, that it is not enough for girls and boys to study the same books in the same great institutions of learning; but they must look forward to the use of knowledge in the same grand callings and pursuits of life, in order to find the only stimulus which can promote a thorough and effective education.

Resolved, That the substance of our petition to the Legislature may all be summed up in the one demand for entire legal equality to men and women.

Resolved, therefore, That it is only one easy and plain application of the golden rule, "Do as you would be done by."

Resolved, That the right of suffrage contains in itself the germ of all other rights, public and private; and that it is the only guaranty of their inviolability.

Resolved, therefore, the great work of this Convention is to discuss the right of woman to vote and to be voted for. Now is the especial time for this work, as the citizens of the Empire State must be awakened to this subject before the calling of the next Constitutional Convention.

Correspondence.

August 20, 1859.

Dear Press:—I wrote you (when was it? three months ago, by George !) that I was a "Sucking Author,"—that I mildly sent you my anonymous lucubrations—that I was bored—that I wished to air my genius in your sheet, to cure a love-fit,—and that I wanted encouragement.

I am a subscriber.

I called the following Saturday for my paper.

Editor-in-chief sat with extraordinary portentous brow, like an overhanging cliff.

Had it fallen and crushed my venture?

If it had, it suddenly picked itself up again, and shone in the smiling majesty of reputation, of witty stories, witty speeches, and innumerable jokes, unconscious of my outrage, innocent of all knowledge that I ever wrote a line.

I did not open the paper before him—oh no—he might have suspected my guilt. I unconcernedly put it in my pocket, and opened it in the street.

My letter was nowhere!

Ah well! I am a modest youth. If an editor refuses my article, the fault is in my writing, not in his judgment. I resigned myself to give up authorship, and rushed about to watering-places that my love might expire in the flame of a new devotion.

I followed Mercutio's advice, too:

Took a new infection to mine eye.
That the rank poison of the old might die.

I felt better.

Charles Reade remarks, that to cool a love where the lady is restive, there is nothing like doing a good action everyday. Next to that, have an object in life, or make love to somebody else. It is a good specific, if the right lady is found. There are always a hundred around similar to, and better than, the one we have lost, but—how to know them! We meet them in the street; we turn and gaze; we'd marry that girl on the spot and take her for granted! But no; she fades in the distance, exists but as a waif in memory, and we fall back on the old ache.

I often think that, questionable as it may seem, society would be far happier if men and women could speak, without introduction, to those who attracted them. The range of each one's acquaintance would then be great; each would have a wide circle to select a partner from, and unions would be more congenial. Unhappy marriages often result from the limited acquaintance possessed by the parties, leading them to adopt each other—for want of better.

What makes gamblers, seducers, or vagabonds of any kind? Disappointed, or unsatisfied love, and no new object in whom to find consolation, or no means of knowing the object, if found.

Bah, what a world!

I started with a friend this afternoon to hear the music in the Central Park, and scale the rocks—like Arnold (not Benedict, but George) at Neversink, to "climb the rugged mountain-top and chase the bounding clam" (funny dorg !), when another friend entered the car with the Saturday Press in hand (sensible dorg). I looked for "Personne," and found "Nessuno! My letter of three months' back!

Eureka!

I sent my love to the devil, and decided on another. Here it is; and with it an evening's experience.

After Central Park, dined with a friend at the Upper Taylor's.

Fellow near by with a very pretty girl.

It's an immense luxury to feed a girl one's in love with. It seems like keeping house.

Michelet, in his new book on Love, says: "A very profound communion is this of the table, especially where there are but two in the family. Man nourishes woman, and daily brings the food to his lone love. She prepares and cooks it. Part of herself goes with it, and with each morsel is mingled the perfume of her beloved hand. As face to face they sit, who shall say that their natures are not more blended by this calm and gentle communion? Of this law of the stomach, which we consider low and base, nature has made one of the gentlest bonds, a high poesy of the heart, wherein union becomes unity."

Funny fellow is Michelet.

He tells the young husband, if his wife falls in love with some one else, he must not abandon her. If she has fallen, she has so much the more need of him: She is still his, whatever she may have done. He must fold the sweet lamb to his breast, and treat her as one sorely stricken.

Ha! ha!

Topped off at Niblo's. I have been well round the world, my dear Press, and have found nothing of the kind, as a whole, equal to the Ravels and their troupe. At the Grand Opera in Paris, the accredited climax of ballet, individual dancers may excel them, but I by no means saw there the same precision of movement among the mass. Lines of girls would caper in single file down the stage at irregular distances from each other, and the head of one line would often be uneven with her neighbor.

Hennecart is charming and magnetic. She has the bold energetic nose of Cora Mowatt, who placed ice to her temples as she drooped in sleepiness over study. She has also her blue spiritual eye and fair hair. She is Cora Mowatt rejuvenated, and boiled down to a reasonable roundness. Delightful creature! How well, in stage parlance, she "knows her business!" How perfect her pantomime, how devoid of all angularity the motions of her limbs and arms! She is German, and promises one day to be stout. Like other dancers, she will then subside into an actress, or keep a dancing school. May she make hay while the sun shines!

I have been to the Palace Garden lately, where they applauded a young lady singer because she was youthful and pretty, and gave the go-by to an accomplished artiste because she was married. The airs were only so-so that evening, but I'll forgive Baker—he didn't play Yankee Doodle! The great American people had no chance for ecstacy.

What a tune to represent a nation!

I have been to Wallack's, too. I have heard the classical Mrs. Florence, as Columbia, say: "Do ut stoopud!" I have heard her song, too, of "Troubadour how could you do so?" Quite funny, by-the-bye.

Do you want anything more? Here it is, and of theatrical savor.

I was once in a far off town, and made my bow to the sisters Lucille and Helen. Helen is a pretty girl, no more; but Lucille is a great creature—off the stage and on. The amatory letters they receive are legion. One youth wrote to Lucille during her first engagement in New York, that he had seen her every night for three months in Boston—that he had followed her to New York—had seen her every night here—that he adored her—and wouldn't she send him a little money to pay his board and go home with?

Other youths, in the absence of replies, often send their daguerreotypes. These are to be crushers, and of course irresistible. Ha! ha!

Good bye. Do you know what "Good bye" is derived from? It is a corruption of the old "God be wi' ye." NESSUNO.

Special Notices.

MATILDA HERON IN "GERALDINE."

To the Editor of THE SATURDAY PRESS :—

Contrary to your prophecies, all human and supernatural circumstances were avoidable on Monday last, and the new play unfolded itself to the footlights, as announced for that evening. Strange to relate, the piece told more upon me from the pages of its MS., than when draped in senatorial robes. Mayhap it is that in reading, one lingers over each potent passage, and slips lightly through the necessary, though ofttimes tedious, circumstantial detail, with which the play is knitted and woven together. I think I can safely state that the piece was a distinct success. For my own part, whatever be its merit, I know no other native Drama that is equal to it. Yet it seems to me that the field of romantic, baronial drama has long since been reaped, and left bare of seed for new fruit, while in the humble phenomena of the soul's economy lies a fair and waving harvest, whose simple glory far outshines the purple robes and pride of State, upon which our poets seek to build the temples of their fame. Witness the play "*La dame aux Camélias*." Does it seem strange that the plain, unvarnished tale of a woman who knew how to love and to grieve, already eagerly embodied into four great languages, has struck one of the key-notes of the world's heart, while many a cunningly-wrought tragedy, set fast on the solid foundations of history and the proud names of story, has sunk and been buried up beneath the very ponderousness of its pomp and circumstance?

If the author of *Love's Victory* would but close the dusky annals of earl and earldom, of war and warrior, and transcribe for us some of those fresh and simple characters, through which nature is ever throbbing her story of life and love,—

You remember that I had not seen Matilda Heron since that I h my return from France. I may truly say I was one of her wonder-wounded hearers. I thought her then an actress of surpassing capacity, but now indeed has she grown to be the foremost artist who speaks the Anglo-Saxon tongue. If we have no true American Drama, we have at least a supremely-endowed American Tragedian. Yet when this great woman comes to us after years of infinite toiling of soul and body, in the plenitude of fiery force and inspiration, the effulgent impersonation of tragic truth, the sole star-splendor in the vast night-void of American art, the critical gentlemen discover that she promises good things, and fall to comparing her with Eliza Logan and Julia Dean. Alas! do but think of it.

For my part, I care not for the so-called careful, correct actress,—she who is never less than a lady, never more than one. The mission of art is to lift us above ourselves; there the weights of doubt and weakness are stripped away from all noble action and brave speech, there love hangs close about the neck of life. Let the artist beware, then, that she lead us into no puny, conventional circle of art; let her give us no portable passion, convenient for measuring in the hollow of the white-gloved hand; let her not show us the bound eagle, dim of eye, and broken of wing, cowering in the dust before the dogs of fate and fortune, but the strong-winged bird, whose eye is set fast on the sun. She must lead us to the brink of those fiery deeps which underlie the cold crust of human existence, and give us to list to the faint echoes of speechless hopes and longings, whose full-toned harmonies we might not hear and live. Not in the little concave mirror of society, shall she show us the wrong and the misery, the joy and the sorrow of life, dwarfing them to the insect-proportions of the law and the Church; rather in the convex mirror shall they be shown, whose fixed fact revolves upon a moveless centre, while its outgoing rays strike through the utmost disc of vision.

Pardon my egotism in saying this is what a woman of genius should do; rather let me say this is what Matilda Heron has done, and for this do we owe her a national debt, for this shall the question of her life be enrolled in the capitol of our history.

I cannot express strongly enough my respect for Matilda Heron's dramatic conscience, never for a moment relaxing the severe truthfulness of her by-play; when she spoke, it was needless to hear the words, you could read them better in the white quiver of her lips, the glow of her lustrous eye, in each fold and line of her stately robe, in every motion and silence of her proud and passionate form.

I am told that Miss Orton is pretty; truly testimony of a thing is good, but the sight thereof is also comforting. This I say, because many of the finest situations in the play, turn upon the superior beauty of the younger to her elder sister; this we are obliged to take on pure faith, for there is no evidence of sight. If Hubert could have preferred that Edith to such a Geraldine, good taste would have exacted that he perished in the wars. The part of Edith was exceedingly well played, but she ought to be as pretty as Mrs. Allen or Emily Thorne.

I suffered from an intolerable nuisance, during the performance, embodied in a party behind me, who came within the strict province of the constable; all through the play they were engaged in loud talking, and vulgar laughing and chuckling. Such conduct would have ensured their expulsion from a church, and the same protection which is awarded to the worshippers in the temple of the priest, should be given to the devout in the temple of the soul.

Among the distinguished persons present, I noticed Fry, and Seymour, and Stuart, Fanny Fern, Getty Gay, and Ninon of the *Atlas*, together with Doesticks, Dick Tinto, and Personne.

Before I close this already too lengthy letter, I am going to take the liberty to speak of the few faults I noticed in the great artist whose genius and triumphs I have feebly depicted to you: they were an occasional unfortunate management of the voice, causing indistinctness in important passages, and a tendency (though rare) to violence without power. I do not use the term overacting, because it has no meaning for me,—one might as well tell me, that a singer oversings her rôle,— but of a certain falling into mere rampant and ravenous demonstration. Last and worst of all, she is tainted with some of the virtues of the American stage, in voice, pronunciation, etc.; let her keep her own faults if she will, but in the name of the gods, let her wipe the stain of such virtues from the white robes of her genius. But indeed, for her faults I can say with the Poet—

> "True she errs, but in her own grand way,
> Being herself three times more noble
> Than three score of men."

Ada Clare.

Personal Recollections of the American Revolution. Edited by Sidney Barclay. Rudd and Carleton 1859.

It is pleasing to find the interest in our local history which this volume evinces. As a nation we seem in a measure afraid or ashamed of our beginning. In the course of study adopted in most of our colleges and seminaries, the histories of almost every other nation but our own are considered necessary. We have not yet lived long enough to have the charm of antiquity add its interest to the study of our early national history. Our national sensitiveness to criticism shows our want of enlightened self respect. Any thing which tends to call attention to our early history and to the importance of preserving the unpublished records of our revolutionary war, which have hitherto escaped the accidents of time, deserves a hearty greeting. For these reasons we are glad to notice the advent of the Diary of the Revolution: Though it is not written with sufficient art to conceal its art, though the editor shows her sex by the introduction of a love-story which is not good enough to justify its irrelevancy, though she has even a poorer idea of an editor's duties than Mrs. Gaskill, or any of the number of men and women who have been and are ready to assume lightly the duties of that responsible situation, though the entire last half of the book has no other than the more than doubtful merit of increasing the size of the volume, yet with all these faults, which are more those of execution than of spirit, the book deserves credit for its design and for the object with which it was written. It has beside the positive merit of being interesting.

Love Matters.

—The following amusing incident took place on one of the Ohio river steamboats. While the boat was lying at Cincinnati, just ready to start for Louisville, a young man came on board, leading a blushing damsel by the hand, and approaching the polite clerk, spoke in a suppressed voice: "I say," he exclaimed, "me and my wife have just got married, and I'm looking for accommodations." "Looking for a berth?" hastily inquired the clerk, passing tickets out to another passenger."A birth! thunder and lightning, no!" gasped the astonished man, "we haint but just got married!"

—The *Providence Journal* says, a-propos, of Señor Oviedo's approaching nuptials, that it is an "old-fashioned idea that marriage is an exclusive affair of the parties to it, and that when a young lady chooses to marry a man older than herself, it really concerns nobody except the young lady and the man whom she condescends to make happy."

—Ours is a practical age, preeminently a practical age. Ten to one, if when in a very sentimental mood, you ask some dear girl to share your lot for life, that she will beg to be informed how many acres your lot contains!

—"I can't bear children," said Miss Prim, disdainfully. Ms. Partington looked over her spectacles mildly, and replied: "Perhaps if you could, you would like them better."

—A few nights since, a male child, about three months old, was left on a doorstep in Philadelphia, with the following note pinned on its clothing: "Give this child to Bill Davis. He is the father of it. I have kept it as long as I can." Bill has not been found.

—A fellow named Albert Davis was recently tarred and feathered in the village of Croton, Pa. He was called from his house by the representation that a cow was in his garden. When he came out he was seized by several individuals, who gave him a coat of tar and feathers, rode him on a rail, and afterwards egged him out of town. He has not been heard of since. It is said that all this was done by ladies, in male apparel, who were indignant at him for some violation of the love-code.

—At a fancy Fair a sailor was strolling past a stall presided over by a lovely woman. Jack stopped, looked for a moment in breathless admiration, then took a sovereign from his pocket, laid it on the table, and was passing on. "My good friend," said the lady, "won't you take something for your money?" "I thank you, madame," replied the tar, with another look. "I've had more than my money's worth already."

—The following is from the *Schenectedy News*: "An interesting topic of conversation in Newburyport, Massachusetts, at present, is the recent development of free-love principles in spiritualistic circles there. Two couples have already separated, and if rumor be true, there are others in a fair way to become so. One pair who have dissolved partnership, had been united but a few months, and the gentleman is well known in that vicinity as the former husband of a distinguished literary lady, whose writings are familar to those acquainted with the current literature of the day."

NEW YORK SEPTEMBER 3, 1859

[For the NEW-YORK SATURDAY PRESS.]

THE LAST LETTER.

BY FLORENCE PERCY.

Best beloved, beyond your sight,
Where the hills rise bleak and white,
One whose faint and faltering feet,
Walk where light and shadow meet—
One whose true heart never knew
Any other love but you,
Murmurs, on her death-bed lying,
"Love me, love, for I am dying!

"Though the smiling angels wait,
Leaning from the shining gate,—
Though their white hands, reaching down,
Offer me life's fadeless crown,
I would yield it, even now,
For your kiss upon my brow!
Crush me not with cold denying—
Love me, love, for I am dying!

"Many a league of hill and plain
Stretches wide between us twain,
Traversed only by my thought,
Out of love and anguish wrought;
Yet my voice shall tremble through
All dividing space to you,
Like an echo's low replying—
Love me, love, for I am dying!

"Though sweet voices call me o'er
Softly to the other shore,
Where all sorrowing hearts find peace,
And their weary achings cease.
Still my soul, which will not view
Any heaven away from you,
Will not cease its anguished crying—
Love me, love, for I am dying!"

The Little Grave.

"It's only a little grave," they said,
"Only just a child that's dead;"
And so they carelessly turned away
From the mound the spade had made that day.
Ah, they did not know how deep a shade
That little grave in our home had made.

I know the coffin was narrow and small,
One yard would have served for an ample pall;
And one man in his arms could have borne away
The rosebud and its freight of clay.
But I know that darling hopes were hid
Beneath that coffin-lid.

I knew that a mother had stood that day
With folded hands by that form of clay;
I know that burning tears were hid,
"'Neath the drooping lash and aching lid;"
And I knew her lip, and cheek and brow,
Were almost as white as her baby's, now.

I knew that some things were hid away,
The crimson frock, and wrappings gay;
The little sock and the half-worn shoe,
The cap with its plumes and tassels blue;
And an empty crib with its covers spread,
As white as the face of the sinless dead.

'Tis a little grave, but, oh! beware!
For world-wide hopes are buried there,
And ye, perhaps, in coming years,
May see, like her, through blinding tears,
How much of light, how much of joy,
Is buried up with an only boy!

The Worn Wedding-Ring.

I.

Your wedding-ring wears thin, dear wife; ah, summers not a few,
Since I put it on your finger first, have passed o'er me and you;
And, love, what changes we have seen—what cares and pleasures too—
Since you became my own dear wife, when this old ring was new.

II.

O blessings on that happy day, the happiest of my life,
When, thanks to God, your low sweet "Yes" made you my loving wife;
Your heart will say the same, I know; that day's as dear to you,
That day that made me yours, dear wife, when this old ring was new.

III.

How well do I remember now, your young sweet face that day:
How fair you were—how dear you were—my tongue could hardly say;
Nor how I doted on you; ah, how proud I was of you;
But did I love you more than now, when this old ring was new?

IV.

No—no; no fairer were you then than at this hour to me,
And dear as life to me this day, how could you dearer be?
As sweet your face might be that day as now it is, 'tis true,
But did I know your heart as well when this old ring was new?

V.

O partner of my gladness, wife, what care, what grief is there,
For me you would not bravely face—with me you would not share?
O what a weary want had every day, it wanting you,
Wanting the love that God made mine when this old ring was new.

VI.

Years bring fresh links to bind us, wife—small voices that are here,
Small faces round our fire that make their mother's yet more dear,
Small, loving hearts your care each day makes yet more like to you,
More like the loving heart made mine when this old ring was new.

VII.

And, blessed be God, all He has given are with us yet; around
Our table, every little life lent to us, still is found;
Though cares we've known, with hopeful hearts the worst we've struggled through:
Blessed be His name for all His love since this old ring was new.

VIII.

The past is dear; its sweetness still our memories treasure yet;
The griefs we've borne, together borne, we would not now forget;
Whatever, wife, the future brings, heart unto heart still true,
We'll share as we have shared all else since this old ring was new.

IX.

And if God spare us 'mongst our sons and daughters to grow old,
We know His goodness will not let your heart or mine grow cold;
Your aged eyes will see in mine all they've still shown to you,
And mine in yours all they have seen since this old ring was new.

X.

And oh, when death shall come at last to bid me to my rest,
May I die looking in those eyes, and resting on that breast;
O may my parting gaze be blessed with the dear sight of you,
Of those fond eyes—fond as they were when this old ring was new.

OCEAN MAILS.

The European mails by the steamship BREMEN, hence for Southampton, will close at the New York Postoffice today, Sept. 3, at 10 1-2 o'clock, A. M.

—According to the Keokuk Journal, Louis Paulsen, the celebrated chess-player, is about taking his departure from that city to New York, to challenge Morphy to a match game of chess.

Dramatic Feuilleton.

The Black Flag Nailed to the Mast.

Mr. Tom Taylor has been to Paris again.

Mr. Tom Taylor goes to Paris very often, now-adays. He is like that mysterious Old Lady who once had a husband who had something to do with the Customs, so that the Old Lady was able to offer you some tremendous bargains in lace. Mr. Taylor never comes back from Paris without a new play or novel in his boots. Since last Spring he has "run in" no less than three invoices, one of which is Octave Feuillet's "*Périls dans la Demeure*," which Mr. Taylor re-Christened "The House; or the Home," and produced last April at the Adelphi.

Miss Laura Keene, who has that intense affection for Tom Taylor which only managers can feel towards an author whose pieces they get for nothing, selected his last two-act larceny for the plat de resistance of the feast which she offered up to her lieges when she commenced her regular season, on last Monday evening.

The lieges came in large numbers—the house being packed to its utmost capacity. Peoria, Tar River, Attakapas, and Barkhampstead in the majority, of course, but still the metropolis was fairly represented. The subscriber and A. M. were "among the distinguished persons." There was not such a brigade of artists, demi-monde, and small litterateurs, as that which assisted at the first night of "Geraldine," but the dear public, the masses of "matineers," were out in full force.

Orpheus, represented by Mr. Thomas Baker, had the honors of the evening. It is not a great compliment to the artists that they are overshadowed by the fiddlers. The public, however, reasons in this way: We have seen bad actors and bad plays on this stage; but the orchestra has been uniformly good. So vive Baker!

And I say vive Baker! too.

To the play:

I should think it would be very good in French. It is levelled, of course, at that much abused tribe, the husbands. All the French plays, and all the French books pitch into Monsieur Cocardeau. Even in this country the husband has literally no rights: or, if he has them, only keeps them by eternal vigilance. I, as a bachelor, will give my assistance to a movement for the amelioration of the condition of the husbands. *That* I call magnanimous.

The theory of this play is, that if the husband has so much buying and selling, or electioneering, or business of any sort to do, that he cannot find time to do double post duty over Madame, she is entitled to take some nice young man, some Edouard or Alphonse, for what the French call "distraction." In the French books and plays the husband is made the bearer of signals to Alphonse, and is the go-between for the lover and the wife. This sort of thing has been happily hit off by Gavarni in that capital series of sketches, the *Fourberies de Femmes*. One picture is especially clever. Madame and Alphonse are sitting together in earnest conversation, under the Colonel's portrait. She says: "Entends-moi bien: demain matin, il ira t'engager à diner; si tu lui vois son parapluie c'est qu'il n'aura pas sa stalle Francais, alors tu n'accepteras pas; s'il n'a pas de parapluie, tu viendras diner.-Mais (il faut penser du tout) s'il pleut demain matin ?S'il pleut, il sera mouillé, voila tout! Si je ne veux pas qu'il ait un parapluie, moi, il n'en aura pas ! Tu es donc bête ?"

In "The House; or, The Home," we have for the hero a rising young politician, continually up to his nose in blue books, and always in the House of Commons. He loves Madame, but neglects her, a paradox which one never finds except in books and plays. For "distraction," she has taken a very young man, who is terribly infatuated with her, so much so that he won't go off to Kamschatka, or some place, where Her Brittanic Majesty is supposed to need his services in a diplomatic capacity. The affair has reached its ultimating point, when the play commences. Madame has promised to send the friend of her soul a signal by her husband. If things are generally comfortable, the British Senator will not wear an emerald ring; if the fond youth is to go to Kamschatka, or the d—–l, or anywhere else he likes, Monsieur will wear the ring. At this point, the flirtation is discovered by the mother of the young man, who makes a mistake as to the meaning of the signal, and believes, when she sees the ring, that it is a sign of assent, whereas it conveys sentence of banishment. The old mother, who is an "old soldier," and up to all sorts of games, manages to get the ring before the boy sees it, on the Senator's hand, and then commences a series of situations, puerile enough in themselves, but well put together, and worked up to a strong climax, where the husband finds a billet doux, and gets very bilious over it, but finally takes his "erring, but repentant wife back to his forgiving bosom." She takes him back, too, and there is a general taking back all round. The lover takes the back track, after being handsomely snubbed by the injured husband, who says he couldn't think of going out with him, not believing in the Code of Honor, and of Obadiah Wise.

As a dramatic critic I have no morals to speak of. I simply deal with things as they are. But I don't believe in half-way measures. I don't believe in putting a thin varnish of English respectability over a piquant French superstructure. It gives a play a hushed-up air which is very unsatisfying. This piece, now, is well written and carefully constructed, but there is no body to it. It is like a good Bordeaux watered down to the thinnest point. The first act has a narrow escape from being a farce. It went off without laughter or applause. The second is better, and there is a very good scene between the husband and the old lady, but the dénouement is not liked. For my part I don't see how it could be changed. The Brightest and Best of her sex thought it was stupid. She wants another *Veteran,* Mr. Wallack, and I put this in by special order.

As for the acting, it might have been better and worse. Miss Keene, who changed the part of the mother so as to make it the sister of the lover, has much improved in appearance since I last saw her. She acted earnestly, elegantly, and artistically, and was dressed charmingly. Miss Clifton played the naughty wife, and has been generally snubbed by the critics. I am not among the especial admirers of this actress, but I have seen her play much worse than on this occasion, and that when she was roundly praised, too. Her dress was rather loud, A. M. said "perfectly awful," but beyond that question of clothes, to which I have already directed Miss Clifton's prayerful consideration, I don't think she deserved the censure visited upon her head by the *Tribune.* However, she has probably before this time engraved upon her seal, a charge á révanche !

Mr. George Jordan found a moderately good part in the rôle of the husband. His first act would have been better had he imitated the icy English manner. I can see that his idea was to show the amiable side of the statesman's character, and to impress upon the audience the feeling that when out of the House this special Englisher was a jolly good fellow. The idea is artistic, but unfortunately not correct. The Englisher goes to a soirée as a grave matter, and has a solid, severe way of doing it. To this man a wedding, a christening, a ball, or a burying, would have been alike. In the second act, Mr. Jordan played admirably, and recalled to my mind some of the French actors, who are especially good in such rolês as this.

Mr. Daly was the lover. He has a bad manner for a dresscoat; a great test is that same terrible garment. About all that Mr. Daly had to do was to seem sweet and interesting, and he didn't do it.

The play was on the whole well treated, but made only a succes d'éstime.

Something or other called "Our Clerks," was produced on the same night. The author, whoever he is (the affair is British), evidently intended to be funny, and is only vulgar and dismal. The oldest man in the audience couldn't tell what the plot was; indeed, it would puzzle that venerable individual (he is past one hundred and ten, and still enjoys good health) to discover any plot whatever. This terrible infliction nearly swamped the comedian, Mr. F. A. Vincent, whom I remember at Wallack's as a very clever man. I shall say no more about him until I see him in something else.

Miss Keene's preliminary essay is not considered to be very strong, but she is good for a long race, however slow she may appear at the start. The next piece to be done here is Palgrave Simpson's comedy, written on the Masks and Faces model, for Amy Sedgwick. It is called "The World and the Stage."

I forgot to mention, last week, that that excellent artist and popular gentlemen, Mr. Mark Smith, was among the new members of Laura Keene's company. He is worth his weight in hot-house grapes and truffles, about the dearest things I know of.

Operatic.

The season, which is announced in rather Teutonic-English as "One Week's Opera," is to commence on next Wednesday, with Cortesi in the Poliuto. Everybody, I think, will be glad to hear the Poliuto again.

Brignoli, who has been very ill in consequence of drinking too much Congress water (so they say), did not wish to sing just now, preferring to save himself for for the rôle (a fine one) which he is to have in the *Vepres Siciliennes*, which is to be done in October. But it is now understood he will sing, so that the cast will be the same as that of last Summer.

Madame Anna Bishop has arrived here, and will give concerts through the country.

Things Generally.

Melpomene isn't to have a ghost of a chance in the New York theatres this Winter. There will not be a "tragedy company" in town. Mel. must pack up her cold pisen, get her bowie knife ground, and go on a visit to Pike's Opera House or Pike's Peak. I can't say that I am sorry or glad. Thalia is a nice sort of a Muse, and I like her; but sometimes the comedies are not funny to me, while the tragedies always are. It is good for Anna Maria, though, and so I ought to be delighted.

Mr. E. Forrest, tragedian, don't like it. He and Melpomene took the same train together. It is a long time since Edwin travelled with a lady. He, like the Apostles, has shaken the dust of the metropolis from off his feet and avows that he will never come within its gates again. We may survive it, but I trust he'll think better of it. Come Edwin, dearest, be a good boy, and have a look at the *Great Eastern*.

Melpomene was lastly a permanent resident at Niblo's, where Mr. Eddy lost money by her, and when Thalia came from the South with Burton, Mel. left between two days, saying she never could bear that horrid giggling thing. The discontented Muse has found a temporary lodgment with Mr. Bateman, at Wallack's, but she must soon give way to her old enemy. Mr. Eddy won't have her. He commences in October with Burton, who is followed by Barney Williams and wife, and so on.

Poor Melpomene!

"Geraldine" is still drawing good houses at Wallack's, and will be continued through this short season.

The Ravels crowd Niblo's every night. The company does not seem so good as usual, to me, but that's the case with molasses candy, of which I was once very fond. Hennecart, the new danseuse, is pretty, well-shaped, and has had a good school. I suspect she has come over here for practice; when she gets it, she'll be too high for this market. A handsome blonde danseuse would command no end of salary, to say nothing of presents and things, in Paris.

A Pair of Sweet Announcements.

The new hand on the *Times* and the manager of the Metropolitan Theatre are "brave stringers of fine words." Desiring simply to announce the name of the manager, the *Times* says, "Mr. Stuart, the genial Amphitryon and the hero of intellectual successes elsewhere, *will sway the public*, presiding over the feast of reason and *dispensing, with liberal hand, the flow of soul*." The manager calls the theatre. "The Winter Garden, a Conservatory of the Arts, dedicated to the Culture of Comedy, Music, and Ballet, by Agnes Robertson."

If all the announcements are to be in this ornate style, Laura Keene's bill-editor had better patronise Graumann for half a pound of prussic acid at once. Stuart will drive him crazy.

However, let them do it. Anything that is new, these horrid times, when one is bored with the same thing over and over again, is refreshing. I welcome Stuart's ample brow and expansive waistcoat with the same gladness as a weary mariner beholds a Fresnellight, of the first order, flashing over the apparently boundless ocean.

The theatre, on dit, is charming. It will be opened before you hear again from the subscriber. Let us wait THE EVENT with composure.

PERSONNE.

Correspondence.

NORTH CONWAY HOUSE, N. H.,
August 27, 1859.

My Dear Editor:—The rain of yesterday has "scoured" the "White Horse" over on the ledge, and this morning he appears unusually distinct—only the central portion of the head, all the legs, and the lower half of the body are wanting to make it look as much like a "white horse" as anything else.

A party have just left for the Ledges and Thompson's Falls, the ladies in "flats" and sans crinoline, and all with long staffs. They carried their dinner in bags and tin kettles, and had very much the air of pilgrims as they passed under my window. Think of tugging and scrambling up perpendicular ledges all the morning for the sake of taking your cold fare on the highest point! I wouldn't do it if they'd dine me there at the expense of their whole stock of doughnuts and apple-sauce.

Certainly the prospect is glorious this morning. The air is intoxicating. Every mountain is clearly defined against the perfect blue, and the soft white clouds take elfish shapes as they dance over their summits. That will do for a sober New Yorker, I guess. Besides, I don't like to infringe upon the rights of the tall spiritual gentleman, from Boston (of course). He "*does*" the mountains and the clouds. You ought to witness a frequent scene on our piazza. We are all sitting there quietly—gentlemen smoking (the gentleman from Boston doesn't smoke), ladies "*crocheting*," chatting, or reading, when suddenly some one rushes to the end of the piazza exclaiming: "Mr. C.! Mr. C.! *here's a cloud!*" Mr. C. springs from his seat and disappears cloud-like round the corner, his long light hair falling back from his "faultlessly chiseled" countenance. The next breeze from round the corner wafts back the music of his voice, something in this style—

"By Jove! Yes, fine! singular !" Boston people don't go into ecstasies, you know. It's "improper :" they search unceasingly for the beauties and wonders of nature, but you cannot catch one of them in an enthusiasm. I have not heard a strong adjective but once since I've been here, that was a few mornings since, when as usual we were on the piazza. A fine-looking young lady passing by stopped to converse a moment with one of our boarders—by the way quite a distinguished individual, even the late representative of his Majesty of the two Sicilies. morning," she said. How my heart yearned towards "It is a *glorious* morning," she said. How my heart yearned towards that pretty lady. How did she dare to say "glorious?" Was she from Boston? I made industrious inquiry, and ascertained that she was born and bred in New York.

We had a visitation two days since of an organ-grinder who "struck up"

"Fra poco a me,"

from Lucia di Lammermoor. What do you suppose we did? Gave him a sixpence to "move on?" No, sir. We gave him instantly all the pennies and three-cent pieces we had about us. I think the "Fra poco," etc., would have been more appropriate after he had pocketed the change than before. Just then a messenger was despatched from our rival hotel to secure his services. We were disgusted. The honor of our house was at stake. Were those —— (I won't mention the name of their house till they send pay to the SATURDAY PRESS for the advertisement) boarders going to luxuriate in a hand-organ, while we heard the music afar off? Not for "all the kingdoms by the sea." I was immediately commissioned to appeal to this wandering Apollo, in French, and the gentleman from Boston, do. in Italian, for his services during the entire evening in the dancing hall. Between us both we succeeded, invited him to supper, and when the hall was lighted he was escorted there and placed perpendicularly against the upper wall. He commenced to grind and we commenced to dance. Polka, Mazourka, Varsoviana, Waltz, and the Lancers. Saint Polycarp! who shall say hereafter that organ-grinders are not a dispensation? The next morning I went down to breakfast rather late (by accident), and had the honor of a seat by the side of our musical hero.

I forgot to say that during that memorable evening we were treated regally to champagne, by another gentleman from Boston—an Alderman—and, by the way, an exception to the general rule that Aldermen are a half-starved race. I don't believe he'll like that remark; but I shall be in New York before he sees it; besides, I like him, so does everybody else—except the "golden headed cherubim" who set up the "ten pins"—and that ought to satisfy him.

Yesterday we had a reading in the grove. Another gentleman from Boston (you see their name is legion) selected the Autocrat's article in the August *Atlantic Monthly*, and gave the Professor's opinions on Phrenology with a savage delight, which suggested to me the probability that some Phrenologist had publicly given him due credit for his enormous "bump" of self-esteem. *Pia mater!* How that part of his head "looms up!" Human antipathies are usually accounted for in a very significant way. I am acquainted with a man who makes the sweeping assertion that the Scotch are a deceptive, lying people. I learned lately that he was once jilted by a "bonnie lassie." Another person thinks Chess a silly, time-destroying game. He doesn't know a pawn from a rook. Set that down as a fact. Another thinks dancing stupid, and horseback-riding a disgusting amusement. Look at him! He weighs 250 lbs. avoirdupois, and his flesh hangs on him like the old coats and pants on a scarecrow.

After all I'm homesick. I long to get back—even to the dirty streets of New York. "We *are* a one-horse people, *perhaps*," said Boston gentleman No. 4, to me the other day, "but we manage to keep *clean*!" "Small trouble that," I answered, " one Irishman with a good broom can sweep you all out before break-fast." Don't imagine that I dislike all Boston people or that I dislike them generally—very far from it; for by the way the sweetest woman, and one of the most perfect ladies I ever saw, is among us now, and she is Boston born and bred, I believe. Sensible enough to read Michelet's *L'Amour*—admire some parts, and be "shocked" at none. I see that the Boston Mercantile Library Association has ruled it out as immoral. That Association ought to have a weak dose of "peppermint tea," and be sent to bed.

How cool and delightful it is up here! I shall leave these old mountains with a sigh of real regret, though anxious to get home. Next Summer I shall recommend this place to my friends, and if we can make up a "jolly crew" I will join them. Mr. Mason is the polite, kind, gracious host that one does not sooner forget, than the excellent doughnuts and Indian puddings of his wife. She seems a gentle spirit

"Born to bless unseen,"

for though I have been here two weeks, I have scarcely caught a glimpse of her as many times. Addio.

Yours, always truly, M. S. C.

August 27, 1859.

Dear Press:—Do you want my opinion of the new play of "Geraldine ?" My dear fellow, consider: five acts—a jam—August! The air was alive with fans, my shirt-collar in utter collapse. Notices of this production appeared in the dailies. The *Herald* swallowed it unqualifiedly—one might think it the best since Shakespeare; the *Tribune* was severely jocose, and utterly contemptuous; the *Times* preserved an amiable medium. I'll spare you a story of the plot. You can find it in papers of 23rd.

The strength of the piece lies in the fierce and crooked heroine's husband loving his wife's sister Edith, and being loved in return. After several intimations of this fact, assurance comes to the disturbed lady thus: the knight is wounded in a combat, and anticipating an exit, sends his bloodstained scarf and dying words to Edith. To his wife—nothing. He had no thought for her. His fleeting soul was wrapt in the one he loved. Climax: struggle of the imperious Geraldine between tenderness for her gentle sister, and fury at her wrong. Tenderness triumphs. Kissings and clasping. Tableau—very good! Soon a revengeful monk, hating Geraldine, tells her that her husband, now convalescent, and Edith, both sneer at her deformity. Dagger for Edith. Scene. Edith proves the falsehood. More kissing and clasping.

Geraldine, finally concluding that what can't be cured must not be endured, takes poison and gives the lovers a chance.

The play, as lately curtailed, is far from being a bore, the immense personality and fine acting of both Miss Heron and Couldock, keep attention riveted; yet the piece lacks pathos. The known cruelty of Geraldine in the first act, destroys sympathy for her. All eyes were enchained, but few moistened. We gazed on a fine work of art, but we kept cool. And it's as well we did, considering the weather.

The piece, beyond a mediocre banquet-scene in the first act, lacks spectacle. The period lies in the time of Edward the First. The actors are costumed with tolerable accuracy, but the ladies' heads are dressed in the style of the present day. Why is this? Because an American theatre finds wardrobe for actors, but none for actresses? New grievance for the Woman's Rights ladies! This is not the case in Europe. There, both sexes in the profession are equally costumed, and afford a most interesting study of history. But what does the great American people know or care about the past? It has none of its own, and lives in the present and the future. It crowds theatres, let costumes be as they will, and managers are content.

A word upon the actors. Mr. Couldock is an artist of great power in all parts where diabolism is the essential; and here also Miss Heron shines. Will she oblige us by Lady Macbeth and Margaret of Burgundy before she leaves? How splendidly Couldock would second her in both!

Sothern, in this new play, the immortal Lord Dundreary, is a nonentity. He is a very bad tragedian, and a poor reader, at all times, and here has no chance for effective points.

Miss Orton is a quite pretty acquisition to the stage. Her face is good, and figure perfect. She shows knowledge of her art, and powers of no common order. A year since we saw her in the nebulæ of the ballet; she has absented herself, and returns to us a lovely moon.

And Walcot's fool! How little to say, and how well said! Ah, he is an actor, that man!

That will do, will it not? Who wants the plot? Who wants an intellectual analysis? And besides, as I look in this morning's Press, doth not the Able Editor himself discourse commendation? Doth not a fair lady with a poetic name discourse with learned art? And doth not the all-convulsing *Personne* give intimations of an intended descent upon Wallack's, in his salutation of to-day, fresh and sparkling from his country tour?

Personne was my luxury. I have lost him for a month. In despair, I took to four-cent peaches. He has returned, and I can laugh again. We shall have enough of Geraldine. Not too much.

The *Herald's* watering-place correspondence discourseth of a literary doctor who has published six works, the publication being effected at his own expense, and the books being disposed of gratis to his friends, who indulges daily every Summer, in a *ground bath*. Only think! The mode is this: He selects a spot where the ladies do not walk, digs a hole five feet deep, undresses, gets in, sits for an hour in the "bosom of his mother earth," and with mouldy savor returns to the bosom of society. I met him. He came to said watering-place to enjoy the converse of a lady whom he had met a few days before in town. The lady was startled from her sleep in the early morning, by a servant with a pail of water at her door, fresh from the 'pure spring," and adorned with garlands, accompanied by a request from the gentleman that she should wash in it. He had theories about pure spring water. Convulsion, of course, of the lady and her friends.

Such men are philanthropists. They give spice to life. I know one who painted his room-floor green, like grass; ceiling blue, like the sky; and walls, fog color, like the air, thereby getting close to nature in his hourly surroundings.

My dear Press, as my talk is of froth, and I say what comes uppermost, I'll descant upon a heavy Swell whom I have just met, fresh from a European tour. In London, heavy Swell needed a coat. Poole, Louis Napoleon's late tailor, of course—Burlington street, frescoed walls,—flunkeys in powder and plush breeches, to open the glass doors. Swell was impressed; Swell suggested a blue. Grand tailor frowned. "Don't make blue coats now, sir. Nothing but black, now, sir." "Well, I'll see the cloth." "No occasion to see the cloth, sir; we'll suit you, sir."

Swell was meek, and mildly suffered the measure.

Swell was a stranger, yet coat was sent home without a question, and tick given with magnificent indifference. Swell, of course, called and paid the bill (15 per cent. less than a New York tailor's), and shows the coat admiringly to his friends.

Ah, let me see—Hennecart! I thought I had forgotten something—charming Hennecart! whom I descanted on in my last! I lately sought a few words from her. One must have something to write about, you know.

The fair creature was announced as an Italian, she had never heard of the announcement, and turns out to be French-German as she looks. She said she had not "du tout le type Italien," she was "entierement Francaise." She agreed with me that the Ravel Company was the best of its kind in the world, and said, "la troupe est très bien montée."

There were the same blue eyes and fair hair that had kindled poetry in my heart the night before; the cheek was thinned, and pared of its roundness, by excessive exercise, but the whole vision was modest, gentle, and good.

Strange, to look on the lovely creature, and think what astonishing things she can do with her legs!

Rehearsal from ten till two. Dinner—a little walk—a little shopping—sleep—performance—supper-bed. Such is the life of a Ravel dancer. Such is the life of many others.

"Nessuno."

A MORAL TALE.

[In which a great deal is left to the imagination of the very moral reader.]

BY A. F. BANKS.

—

On, on she sped, with fearful look,
  Along the living street,
Until she reached a darksome nook,
  Where roaring waters meet;
And there, apart from human eyes,
  An erring mother kissed her child—
A frowning cloud obscured the skies,
  As though the sight defiled.

O! God! what agony on that brow,
  She prays, and, praying, reels,—
Poor girl! no use in praying now,
  "The world" is at your heels;
On, on it presses with its sneer,
  Its hoot and execration,
Religion owns for thee no tear—
  Its tear were desecration.

Affrighted Nature cries, "Hold! hold!
  Brave, brave the world!
Fiend, is your mother heart *all* cold?"
  Her brain in frenzy whirled.
"Cold?" That mother's heart was boiling,
  O'ersurging with affection,
As her infant, round her coiling,
  Sipped its sweet refection;
O! how her eye did fondly beam,
  Upon her beauteous babe—
Horror! she started as from a dream,
  And with despairing rave,
She hurled it headlong in the stream,
  Warm from its first repast,
Better "Fiend!" "Infanticide,"
  Then Society's Outcast.

One palsied look, away she flew,
  Spurred on by that deep bell,
Another hour, too well she knew,
  Were Reputation's knell.

Unnoticed she had gained her room;
  The morning saw her at her work;
By strategy she 'scaped Love's doom—
  Her life was safe from moral dirk.

—

In the far, far West, a happy mother
  Smiles fondly on guileless faces,
And a fair girl nurses her little brother,
  Whilst pussy her own tail chases.
The kettle's boiling, the cakes all hot,
  Tea's ready—Tom wants to begin it,
But they're waiting for daddy to fill up the pot,
  And dad will be in in a minute.

A knock at the door. The mother went ;
  God! what horror is this?
What sight the blood from her cherry cheek sent?
  What clenches her teeth with a hiss?
She held the door with a desperate hand,
  To keep the children within,
Then, in trembling tone, for she scarce could stand,
  She made assignation of Sin.
She stole forth from her happy home that night,
  But returned in a half an hour;
Tho' her eye flashed strange, her step was light,—
  Like one who had baffled Fate's power.

—

When Time has rolled on, perchance some day
  Some newspaper item may tell,
Of a fossil skeleton found, as it lay
  In a far, far Western dell;
Science may guess (and may be correct),
  That here once lay a deep river's bed,
And curious surmise may haunt those who inspect
  The cramped limbs and the battered head.
But they never may know (for in that far time
  Love's flaws may have kindlier name),
That to silence a secret, a fearful crime
  Had rescued a wife's fair fame.

NEW YORK SEPTEMBER 10, 1859

Original Poetry.

DRIFTING AWAY.

BY W. D. HOWELLS.

As one whom seaward winds beat from the shore,
    Sees all the land go from him out of sight,
    And waits with doubtful heart the stooping night,
In some trail shallop without sail or oar,
      Drifting away!

I ride forlorn upon the sea of life,
    Far out and farther unto unknown deeps,
    Down the dark gulfs and up the dizzy steeps,
Whirled in the tumult of the ocean strife,
      Drifting away!

Like faint, faint lights, I see my old beliefs
    Fade from me one by one, and shine no more;
    Old loves, old hopes lie dead upon the shore,
Wept all about by ghosts of childhood griefs,
      Drifting away!

O never more the happy land shall glow,
    With the fair light of morning on mine eyes;
    Upon its loftiest peak the sunset dies,
And night is in the peaceful vales below,
      Drifting away!

I rise and stretch my longing arms in vain,
    And fold in void embraces on my breast
    The nothing claspt, and with great fear opprest,
Cry to the shores I shall not see again,
      Drifting away!

AURORA BOREALIS.
BY FRED. A. PARMENTER.

I.

The weird Aurora Borealis hurls
Its javelins of opalescent light,
Amid the starry-hearted spheres that brood
Above the shadow-shrouded form of Night!

II.

They redly dart among the pearly clouds
That dot the sky, in white battalions broke,
Ascending o'er the mountain's purple rim,
Like some huge caldron's airy woven smoke!

III.

Then back they dimly fall behind the hills,
As fountain-jets of silver-netted spray,
And lo! for crystal drops of moisture leave
The beadlike stars that gem the milky way!

Owego, Tioga Co., N.Y.

All you that want a mate,
  And to marriage do incline,
If you have slid through '58,
  Now don't through '59.

"SUMMER IS DEAD."

BY MRS. H. J. LEWIS.

Hush! tell it not to the flowers and trees,
Whisper it not to the birds and the breeze;
Let not the blossoms of crimson and blue,
Hear the sad tale, though its burden be true!
      Summer is dead!

Hush! for the sea hath suspended its breath,
Fearing to catch the first summons of death;
And the bright clouds that are passing away,
Fain must drop tears could they hear what you say,
      Summer is dead!

Aye! though her mantle of glory is still
Spread over garden and meadow and hill,
Though the rich bloom hath no touch of decay,
And the bee toils through the long sunny day,
      Summer is dead!

Aye! it is ended! From forest and glen,
From cities alive with the conflict of men,
From the grass at our feet, from the now silent bird,
From earth, sea, and sky, in our spirits is heard,
      Summer is dead!

So much of her glory and gladness is left,
We sigh not as those of her presence bereft ;
Her crown and her garlands unfaded are hung,
Where they dropped when aside they were carelessly flung;
      Summer is dead!

September 1, 1859.

DEATH OF OUR DAUGHTER, LAURA.

[From the Weekly Free South, Aug. 5.]

During the last few days of her illness (her case has been twice before spoken of,) the rest of our children were so absorbed in her interest that but very little work was done in the printing-office, and consequently no paper was issued last week.

Laura was our youngest daughter, a most interesting and affectionate girl, twelve years, eleven months, and six days old. The day before she died (Monday, July 25th, 1859), she sang one verse of the song, "Do they miss me at home?" in a delicate, but sweet and trembling voice. The dear creature knew she would be missed at home; her active fingers at the printing-case, and nimble feet to go an errand, are already (and in the deepest sorrow) "missed at home."

She bore her sufferings beyond a parallel, often inquiring about her sister, Nancy, now in Kansas; the rest of the family all being present, to soothe her pain.

She was a lovely girl, and will long be remembered by her companions, who owe the like debt she has so early and so resignedly settled. Peace to the ashes of Laura, and to her spirit eternal bliss.

WM. S. AND CAROLINE A. BAILEY.

Dramatic Feuilleton.

The Oldest Man in the Newest Bowery.

The other day—I may as well be particular, last Monday,—the Old Gentleman and I dined together, and subsequently promenaded down the Bowery to assist at the opening of the new theatre, which Rhadamanthus-Croesus-Whiting has just completed for George Washington Lafayette Fox and James Lingard, two lucky dogs who are going to make an immense fortune, and have whole rows of high-stoop four-story brownstone fronts.

"Ah," said the Old Gentleman, who had put away a comfortable quantity of Bordeaux, "there used to be a time when we did not go down the Bowery."

"O, yes," I replied, "when everybody lived downtown at the Battery."

The Old Gentleman never heeded this interruption, but went on talking about the time when the Astor House was up-town, and all the swells lived about Beekman street, and "the old Park pit" was in its glory, whatever that was.

The veteran was very bitter against the German element in the Bowery. It startled and shocked him to find all the old-fashioned public-houses turned into lager-bier gardens. We stood a little South of the Old Theatre, when he waved his cane, with a Marius-in-the-ruins-of-Carthage air, and indulged in a "flood of recollections." Where were the "boys" who once made this spot classic ground? Where the crimson-shirted, drab-coated, short-footed, rolled-trowsered, fellows, all heart and no waistcoat, who gave to the term Bowery-Boy a world-wide fame? The type is extinct. We have no more Bowery-Boys, but in their place rowdies and pugilists, who travel armed to the teeth, and find their chiefest pleasure in beating some inoffensive man to death.

And then public-houses. There was the Branch, much frequented by circus-managers, and a favorite resort of the first showman in the country, James Raymond, who made a great fortune, of which the Broadway Theatre represented only a small part. And the North American Hotel, on the corner of Bayard street, where Charley Burke was wont to tie his legs into hard knots, and tell quaint stories by the hour together. And John Worden's, on the other corner, where every body went, actors, managers, editors, tradesmen, boys and all. Along the sidewalk were refreshment and fruit stands, and many a man whose name is strong in the street, and whose daughters are finishing at M'me Chegary's or Mrs. Mears-Burkhardt's, has been glad to breakfast here in an al fresco style, for a very moderate sum, say three cents, though that would be a little dear in those days. And then the stewed oyster and whiskey punches at Rea's, under the North American! Will there ever again be any such stews, or such punches? Never! It can't be.

And the jokes and the sprees, the fun! That we can never have again, nor anything like it.

And they are all gone. All except the good things that were first said here, and which I find now running through the rural press.

And the theatre: The old Bowery when Jackson, L Noir, and Hamblin had it. Here Malibran sung, and all the great artists of those days acted. There were good actors in the stock-companies, too, and Hamblin was sure to have one or two pretty women.

But now the audience is changed. The foreign element predominates, and the mental status of the public is very low. Once Macbeth was the most popular piece that could be offered to a Bowery-audience. Now the taste runs to miserable things called *Ledger*-dramas, and pantomimes stolen or poorly imitated from the novels.

And the Old Gentleman couldn't see it.

But I do not suppose that his opinion is of much consequence to G. W. Lafayette Fox & Co. They have got in the New Bowery a chance to make a fortune, and they evidently intend to do it.

Like the proprietor of Warren's Blacking, they keep a poet in the person of one Pilgrim who will undoubtedly do his best to assist the downward progress of the drama in the Oriental Districts.

The new theatre was disagreeably full, and the bouquet of the public was something wonderful to smell. The front rows of the pit presented a series of heads which, if there is anything in physiognomy, formed as pretty a gallery of rascals as could be found outside of a jail, and with the fairest prospects of getting inside before cold weather sets in. The boxes looked better, and many of the ladies were adorned in the highest Division-street style.

The play, not by Pilgrim, was a splendid thing in its way. It relates to the adventures of a young person of the better sex, who, it appears, has been engaged in the Venetian orange-trade, whether wholesale or retail it does not clearly appear. In other days, when a lady or a gentleman in the Bowery assumed airs of superiority, he or she was satirically informed to this effect, "I know'd you when your mother sold lemons,' which was supposed to be a crusher.

But it is very evident from this play, that trade in tropical fruits was not considered as disgraceful in Venice as in the Bowery. This dealer was an important personage in the State, generally mixed up in all political affairs, and a sort of bear-leader for a young nobleman who is continually talking about liberty for Venice, and his father's grave.

The Governor, it seems, has been deposited in one of those astonishing stage-vaults where one has to go up a flight of steps for no other apparent purpose than to come down another flight. The nobleman makes a good deal of row over the grave, and is about to be forcibly ejected from the premises by a colored person who has the care of them. The mourner and the man in mourning fight, and Ethiopia is overthrown. It may truly be said of this sable delineator that nothing in his life became it so well as his leaving it. He died well. Not so his master, who had a similar difficulty directly afterwards with the same person. He died ingloriously, going to pieces in a heap like a wet towel. A play that has two murders in the first act is not, I may say, cheerful. The catastrophe, I presume, must be a general massacre. The Oldest Man couldn't see the whole of it.

The actors are not much more brilliant than the play. The lady, Miss Cappell, is good-looking, but rather too demonstrative in her style. Belongs, I should judge, to the prairie-school. Extreme prairie, where they locate the old soldiers' warrants. The leader of the republican party in Venice is a little man named Nagle, who acts in an up-hill way that is very distressing. I am always afraid for a man's arteries when I see him acting in the conventional way, which Mr. Nagle has brought back to town after a long and welcome absence. I mean the "way," not Nagle.

But the lady who did the inevitable soubrette, who has the inevitable flirtation with the inevitable low-comedy man (Fox, very good), who is, by a bold and original thought, made a fisherman,—Sir, I have gazed upon charms, and revelled in fascinations, rolled, I may say, in allurements. So has the Old Gentleman. But neither he nor I ever saw anything so stunning as this glorious creature. She made up her head and her mind to hit the audience, and she did it. I had her name in the tablets of my memory, but it has, I am sorry to say, got rubbed out.

Such is man's constancy and lovely woman's inevitable fate.

The New Bowery is very big and handsome enough. The plays, I presume, will be bad enough to be successful, and so long as the audience is satisfied I have no right to growl.

And I don't.

Nine Points of the Law.

A pretty little comedy, which no one can find any fault with.

Given a young widow, Miss Ada Clifton; given an eccentric lover, F. A. Vincent; given a middle-aged, port-winey Britisher, Mark Smith; given a young woman who does not know how to dress her hair, and who is always ready to sing a song on the very slightest provocation, Miss McCarthy; given two other people of no great consequence just here; and there are your characters.

The widow has possession of a house which belongs to the middle-aged Britisher, who desires to get his rights, which he does not get, of course. He gets the widow, who is an actuality, while rights are generally imaginary things which one never appreciates when he does get them.

In this play, Mr. Tom Taylor has shown what can be done by skilful hands with a single incident, and that not remarkably strong. Except the song, which was introduced in defiance of all propriety and good taste, one might imagine—so easy is the dialogue, so natural the situations, and so complete, to the minutest detail, the furniture and surroundings of the scene—that he had been taken into a family confidence, and spent the hour in a real drawingroom.

I thought Miss Clifton played the widow remarkably well. She has naturally a good manner, is graceful, though a little affected, in her carriage and bearing. She is rapidly finding out, however, that the secret of drawingroom acting is like good breeding—a refined courtesy, perfect repose, and a savoir faire, with which people can do nothing in particular in a way to make it exceedingly charming. Mr. Mark Smith played the Englisher in a manner which suggested the *Times* newspaper, London porter, and hot joints, at every step. His dress, however, is a little behind the age. Breeches and top boots have gone out with the mail coaches. Mr. Vincent played well, but was outrageously costumed. Think of even a "gent" making love to a lady, in large check trowsers, red flannel shirt, a bobtailed jacket, and no waistcoat. Why, a Camanche Indian would not do it. The Oldest Man said it was an unheard-of atrocity.

Nine points of the Law," with the "House or the Home," has been played every night this week at Laura Keene's, to crowded houses. I advise every one to see them. So does the Oldest Man.

Things Generally.

"The Brightest and Best" will come out very strong at the Opera, on Monday, when they give the "Poliuto" for the Provincials. Apropos to the Opera, I see that Mrs. James, a New Yorker, who has been waiting a long time for a *début*, has at last made it at Cincinnati. She sung in Rigoletto (Parodi troupe) and made a success. The papers say she has a good voice, knows how to sing, is pretty, and acts well. I am sure I hope it is true, though I don't put much dependence upon the rural press. I take the following, which tastes like my old friend N. G. G., from the Boston *Post*:

The Arts are languishing in Cincinnati. Pork is again and most wretchedly in the ascendant. "The School for Scandal" drew "but a slim audience" to the theatre a few nights since, and at Pike's Opera House "Lucia" was presented to a beggarly account of empty boxes. One of the "crickets" pertinently remarks: "What is the matter? Is music of a high order to languish in our midst for want of proper support from our citizens, and that, too, with a temple reared for its exaltation, with a princely lavishness and luxurious elegance unsurpassed by any other establishment in the world? We trust not."

Perhaps if they could move the Opera House down from the second floor it would pay.

Madame Bishop is going to sing to-night, at the Palace Garden Hall. She is really a great artist, and I would walk any distance, say two blocks, to hear her sing an English ballad. Who else can do it? Any of the Italians? Echo answers "Nary." Go and hear Bishop, all of you.

There is an immense number of entertaining people about now. I mean people whose business it is to give what they call entertainments, though sometimes the public don't see it. There is the immortal Massett, and then there is Hawker, who is as yet unknown to fame in these parts. Pretty soon we shall have Mr. and Mrs. Henry Drayton, who give drawing-room operas, with only two parts, a pleasant thing, I should judge. G. K. Dickinson has just arrived, with three ladies, English singers, and he is going into the entertaining business. Then there is Cowell, known to the fun-loving world by the familiar pre-nomen of "Sam." Sam composes his own songs, and acts them in a way which is exceedingly funny and never vulgar.

So, we run no risk of "entertainments" this Winter, though, in reading some announcements, the doubt of Touchstone as to whether a woman be a good or no, will recur to me.

Geraldine is still drawing full houses at Wallack's. It will be switched off next Wednesday, so people who have not seen it had better "vote early."

The Winter Garden

Will be opened, they say, this evening, but the time may be changed till Monday. I have taken a critical, and altogether dispassionate, view of it. It is a success. Clear, positive, undeniable success. The place has been entirely metamorphosed, and the interior looks something like Wallack's, but more Frenchy. The proscenium is the prettiest and airiest thing in the world, almost a copy of that in the Opera Comique, and the line of sight is perfect from all parts of the house. The decorations are toned down so that they will be an agreeable relief to the stage picture, but not be too loud for the canons of taste. There is so much that is unique and odd about the place that it will at first have a success of curiosity, but I believe it will finally be the unanimous verdict of the public that the Winter Garden is the prettiest and most agreeable theatre in town. As papa Ritchie would remark, nous verrons.

PERSONNE

Correspondence.

THE UNITARY HOUSEHOLD, etc.

DEAR PRESS—Have you ever been to Underhill's Unitary Household? I have dined there several times, and through a friend staying there, who says he never was better off in his life, have been made acquainted with its workings. It includes a row of brown stone fronted buildings on Fourteenth street, opposite the Academy of Music, and though the rent of each narrow house is at the extravagant rate of $1750 a-year, yet by the system of "living at cost" which is here practised, the expense of each individual is less than half what it would be in the neighboring hotels, and about three dollars a week less than it would be in the upper class of boarding-houses.

Now for the term "Unitary." It was translated from the French some seventeen years ago, by the *Tribune*, and used in connection with the improved modes of living which that journal then advocated. It means a unity of material interests, and operates thus: each individual pays rent for his room exactly in proportion to the rent of the whole building, without any profit being made by the head of the house. If any rooms become vacant, however, the rent is divided among all the inmates, who find thereby an increase in their week's expenses. It is therefore the interest of all to procure new inmates among their acquaintances.

The head of the establishment pays himself a salary, and this, together with salaries of clerks, wages of servants, fuel, rent of parlors, kitchens, laundry, and other items, is summed up each week and divided also among the residents. Each room, in addition to its rent, has, if unoccupied, to bear a portion of this charge, which, too, is shared by the inmates. All this is called the General Expense.

The food is charged for exactly at cost of the raw article only, as cooking, waiting, etc., has already been included in the General Expense. People eat at small tables, in the restaurant style: a bill of fare is furnished, and also slips of paper on which the inmates write their names, the date, and articles wished for. The servant takes this, files it, and the clerk after each meal charges it in the books.

Meats thus cost 4 and 5 cents per plate; vegetables, puddings, preserves, pies, fruit, etc., 2 and 3 cents. Coffee, tea, or cocoa, 2 cents. Bread of any kind, 1 cent. Butter or cheese, 1 cent. A great variety is offered, and all at these low rates. No strong liquors are sold in the house, but light wines and champagne are in plenty at the wholesale cost prices. You can thus call for your bottle of red table wine, and pay 25 cents, or your bottle of champagne, and pay 75 cents, instead of $2, which you pay everywhere else.

The system has been in practice seventeen months, and though defective at first, now works admirably. When neighboring establishments, in the heat of Summer, had half of their rooms empty, here there were but half a dozen vacancies. At all other times the establishment has been full to overflowing—the proprietor has no pecuniary care, but fobs his salary and relieves his surplus spirits by comic songs on the piano. A very jolly fellow is he, who has seen many ups and downs of life—studied much and thought much. His experiment of living at cost has well succeeded. He is now one of those nice individuals who can "keep a hotel." Much praise to him. Of all material reforms this appears to me the most vital. It has, so far, succeeded only in reducing the expenses of the mercantile and legal class. Persons who formerly boarded for eight and ten dollars per week, now live here for five. The buildings are at an immense rent and accommodate but a hundred persons. The greater the number of inmates the greater the economy. It is calculated that in an establishment as large as the St. Nicholas, the expense to each, including washing, would not exceed $2 50 per week. It would thus remove mechanics and sewing girls from greasy boarding places and dirty garrets, into regions of silver forks, French cooking, rich carpets and furniture, mirrors, pianos, and high class periodicals; thereby increasing their self-respect, widening their esthetic taste, and enabling them to economize far more than at present. The world moves! This time is not far off. Other persons talk of imitating Underhill on a larger scale, and capitalists stand ready to guarantee the rent and purchase furniture.

My friend is much pleased with his residence at Underhill's. There are people there of fine mental acquirements, and persons of good musical ability. Song, dance, and profitable conversation enliven the evening for those who attend the parlors.

The house, owing to the number of its inmates, has also the advantage of a hotel, in that although society can constantly be had, perfect privacy can be maintained. Families can eat at separate tables, remain in their own apartments, and have no communication with any one.

And now, to the winds with statistics and reform! My pen is dipped in oats, and wants a fling.

Being bound lately to a semi-barbarous district of Jersey, I met a quantity of negroes on the boat, destined to a campmeeting. As a foretaste they indulged in a hymn:

"With singing and shouting, we'll make Jordan roar ;
We'll reach fair Canaan, and stand on the shore."

An artist-friend I met, advised me to attend the meeting. He grew enthusiastic upon its picturesqueness at night, when the lights scattered through the grove, are playing upon the negroes' dusky forms, and their voices ring in the harmony that their untutored, but naturally musical ears, dictate, taking bass, tenor, and alto by instinct.

The negro is a creature of the gorgeous tropics. Their setting sun, their spicy gales, and myriad flowers are implanted in his being. When touched by the wand of civilization, he decks himself in brilliant colors, and as latent visions of beauty fill his soul with their language, so does he with marvellous truth, render it in song, or with instrument of string or wind, revolve the fitful breezes into melody.

The air around us is music, and needs but attuning. Who does not feel that, when enchanted by the echoes of a brass band?

We will then love the air. We will love, too, our fellow-man, for the beauty that is in him, which no cloud of sin can wholly darken. We will believe, that as the air evolves music when marshalled into order, so will man's soul ring wondrous harmonies, when freed from its present chaos.

I showed, my dear PRESS, a sad inappreciation of poetry in my last. I spoke with jest of an enraptured individual, who on a very short acquaintance, followed a blooming being to a watering-place, and sent her one early morning a pail, enwreathed with garlands, of purest spring water, to wash her lovely form. The unresponding lady and her friends were convulsed, and so was I. The idea was too rich! We did not look at its abstract beauty. To a young and gentle wife, fancy the tribute of crystal water embosomed in roses! What fresher, purer, and brighter type could be poured upon, and blended with, her sweet being !

Or, in future ages of purity, when costume will be thrown off or on, as caprice or temperature may dictate;—then even to a maiden—well and good! But to dare to hint at the form of a fair lady of the present day. Oh! oh! It is a face and a dress. It is like the Queen of Spain's legs; not only never to be imagined, but not to be supposed to exist.

Evidently our poet blundered. He is a creature of the future, rather than the present.

NESSUNO.

DIVORCED BY MISTAKE.

One Winter there came to Trenton, New Jersey, two men, named Smith and Jones, who had both of them designs on the Legislature. Jones had a bad wife and was in love with a pretty woman—he wished to be divorced from his bad wife, so that he might marry the pretty woman, who, by the way, was a widow, with black eyes, and such a form! Therefore Jones came to Trenton for a divorce.

Smith had a good wife, good as an angel, and the mother of ten children, and Smith did not want to be divorced, but did want to get a charter for a turnpike or plankroad, to extend from Pig's Run to Terrapin Hollow.

Well, they, with these different errands, came to Trenton, and addressed the assembled wisdom with the usual arguments. First, suppers mainly composed of oysters with rich background of venison; second, liquors in great plenty, from "Jersey lightning," which is a kind of locomotive at full speed, reduced to liquor shape, to Newark champagne.

To speak in plain prose, the divorce man gave a supper, and Smith, the turnpike man, followed with a champagne breakfast, under the mollifying influence of which the assembled wisdom passed both the divorce and turnpike bills; and Jones and Smith—a copy of each bill in their pockets—went rejoicing home, over miles of sand, and through the tribulation of many stage coaches.

Smith arrived home in the evening, and as he sat down in his parlor, his pretty wife beside him—how pretty she did look!—and five of her children overhearing the other five studying their lessons in the corner of the room, Smith was induced to expatiate upon the good results of his mission to Trenton.

"A turnpike my dear; I am one of the directors and will be President. It will set me up, love; we can send our children to the boarding-school, and live in style out of the toll. Here is the charter, honey."

"Let me see it," said the pretty little wife, who was one of the nicest of wives, with plumpness and goodness dimpling all over her face, "let me see it," as she leaned over Mr. Smith's shoulder.

But all at once Smith's visage grew long; Smith's wife's visage grew black. Smith was not profane, but now he ripped out an awful oath.

"Blast us, wife, those infernal scoundrels at Trenton have gone and divorced us !"'

It was too true; the parchment which he held was a bill of divorce, in which the names of Smith and Smith's wife appeared in frightfully legible letters.

Mrs. Smith wiped her eyes with the corner of her apron,

"Here's a turnpike," she said sadly, "and with the whole of our ten children staring me in the face, I aint your wife! Here's a turnpike."

"Blast the pike and the Legislature and—"

Well, the fact is that Smith, reduced to single blessedness, enacted into a stranger to his own wife, swore awfully. Although the night was dark, and most of the denizens of Smith's town had gone to bed, Smith bid his late wife to put on her bonnet, and arm in arm they proceeded to the clergymen of their church.

"Goodness, bless me !" exclaimed the good man as he saw them enter. Smith looking like the last of June shad, Smith's wife wiping her eyes with the corner of her apron—"Goodness bless me, what's the matter?"

"The matter is, I want you to marry us two right off," replied Smith.

"Marry you!" ejaculated the clergyman with expanded fingers and awful eyes; "are you drunk, or what is the matter with you?"

However, he finally married them over straightway and would not take a fee; the fact is, grave as he was, he was dying to be alone that he might give vent to a suppressed laugh that was shaking him all over; and Smith and Smith's wife went joyfully home and kissed every one of their children. The little Smiths never knew that their father and mother had ever been made strangers to each other by legislative enactment.

Meanwhile, and on the same night, Jones returned to his native town—Burlington, I believe—and sought at once the fine black eyes which he had hoped shortly to call his own. The pretty widow sat on the sofa, a white kerchief tied carelessly about her round white throat, her black hair laid in silky waves against each rosy cheek.

"Divorce, is the word," cried Jones, playfully patting her double chin; "the fact is, Eliza, I'm rid of that cursed woman, and you and I'll be married tonight. I knew how to manage those scoundrels at Trenton. A champagne supper—or was it breakfast? did the business for them. Put on your bonnet and let us go to the preacher's at once, dearest."

The widow, who was among widows as peaches among apples, put on her bonnet and took Jones's arm, and—

"Just look how handsome it is put on parchment!" cried Jones, pulling out the document before her; "here's the law that says that Jacob Jones and Ann Caroline Jones are two."

Putting her plump gloved hand on his shoulder she did look at it.

"O dear!" she said, with her rosy lips, and sank back, half fainting on the sofa.

"O blazes!" cried Jones, and sank beside her, rustling the fatal parchment in his hand; "here's a lot of happiness and champagne gone to ruin."

It was a hard case. Instead of being divorced, and at liberty to marry the widow, Jacob Jones was simply, by the Legislature of New Jersey, incorporated into a turnpike company, and what made it worse, authorized to run from Burlington to Bristol! When you reflect that Burlington and Bristol are located just a mile apart, on opposite sides of the Delaware river, you will observe the extreme hopelessness of Jones's case.

"It's all the fault of that turnpike man who gave them the champagne supper—or was it the breakfast?" cried Jones in agony. "If they'd chartered me to a turnpike from Pig's Run to Terrapin Hollow, I might have borne it; but the very idea of building a turnpike from Burlington to Bristol bears an absurdity on the face of it."

So it did.

"And you aint divorced," said Eliza, a tear running down each cheek.

"No!" thundered Jones, crushing his hat between his knees, "and what is worse, the legislature is adjourned, and gone home drunk, and won't be back to Trenton till next year!"

It was a hard case.

The mistake (?) had occurred on the last day of the session, when legislators and transcribing clerks were laboring under a champagne breakfast. Smith's name had been put where Jones's ought to have been, and "wisey wersey," as the Latin poet has it.

NEW YORK SEPTEMBER 17, 1859

THE BORE.

—

Written for the NEW YORK SATURDAY PRESS,

BY GETTY GAY.

—

Oh, he's as tedious
As a tired horse, a railing wife,
Werse than a smoky house; I had rather live
With cheese and garlic, in a windmill, far,
Than feed on cates, and have him talk to me
In any Summer-house in Christendom.
—King Henry IV., Act III., Scene I.

He is the greatest sinner who causes the most unhappiness.
The Bore causes the most unhappiness,
Argal,—the Bore is the greatest sinner.

Boring is the greatest sin. Commit any other. Who steals my purse, steals trash; who steals my good name, much good may it do him; but he who steals my time, robs me of that which no police, law, money, nor power can restore to me, for it is lost, like the Dutchman's kettle, in the sea of oblivion, never more to reappear.

Murder is a horrid crime, but killing time is worse than murder, for we are told that the latter often opens to the victim the gates of Paradise, and introduces him to eternal beatitude, but the destruction of time is total and irremediable. If you feel revengeful, and long to wreak your malice on an enemy, do not plunder him, for he will talk of his losses till he has paid himself for them with interest, simple and compound; do not slander him, for not only may the slander not stick, but its disproval may afterward shield him from condemnation for actual faults, by placing all accusations against him under the same category as your calumnies; do not murder him, for not only may you consequently elevate him to heaven, but yourself to the gallows. No, do nothing of the kind, but bore him, sir, bore him to death.

There is no punishment for boring to death; nothing whatever, judging from the zeal with which so many persevere in it, but unspeakable satisfaction. It is said that a friend cleaveth to one closer than a brother; but a Bore sticks faster than either. The last embrace of foes is nothing in comparison to it. He can only be choked off, and death is sometimes the only power able to release one from his persecution.

The Bore enjoys a happy immunity. A liar may be challenged, posted, kicked, exposed, prosecuted, shot; and a thief, a cheat, a ruffian, may be served in the same way; but the Bore is unassailable, invulnerable. Dulness, in the weakest and worst, is sacred, and forms an adamantine panoply. The Bore is a privileged character, and does with impunity what would hang you or me. His temerity is consequently prodigious. For hours, days, weeks, years, lives, he plagues and tortures men able and willing to kick him into limbo, but who do not, they hardly know why—withheld, perhaps, by the awfulness of stupidity.

The art of boring is simple. Idiots may excel in it. It may be explained in a few words, for it does not consist so much in saying and doing things intrinsically stupid, as in saying and doing things at the wrong time and in the wrong place. A grace may be proper enough; but a long-winded one, when the guests are hungry and the meat is getting cold, is a bore. Music is delightful, but an elaborate performance on the piano, with infinite variations, is, when the polite listeners are lively people and longing to chat, another bore; and so always is an ornate operatic air, sung in Italian by a thin-strained voice, to people who do not understand a word of it.

"Muffing" is one of the most efficacious means and methods of boring. To make myself clear, say, for instance, that a sprightly young fellow or a lively girl, in the full exuberance of health and spirits, is enjoying himself or herself excessively; all the "Muff" has to do is, under some friendly, considerate, or plausible pretext, to suggest moderation, propriety, decency, or the likelihood of misrepresentation, before there is really any occasion for it, and thus bring down the jubilant one at once into the dust and ashes, as the fowler the singing-bird from the tree. It is so gratifying to some to see the face, laughing all over a moment ago, cloud up like a murky sky, and change all its sunshine for glum propriety and sour self-defence. Then the mentor, whoever he may be, feels so vastly moral and righteous! He turns up the whites of his eyes and involuntarily asks God to thank and reward him for the good he has done. The vain fool! It is true that in the midst of life we are in death, and he therefore concludes that we ought always to have a death's head thrust under our noses. Yea, verily,—Amen!

What boring advantages some people enjoy! Think—only think of, and gloat over them, for a few seconds! Of fathers, for instance, disappointed in business during the day, who, finding a pack of rollicking youngsters at home, can vent their accumulated acerbity, and relieve themseves so holily by checking the players' sports, and reading them dismal homilies as long as your leg,—no, that's not the simile, your arm, I mean. Would you not like to commit sins six days in the week, and on Sunday revel in the special prerogative of railing from the pulpit at the very crimes of which you are guilty, and at sinners no worse than yourself? By lashing others you might atone for yourself, and, if so, why should you not lay on unmercifully? Dwell on the thought of being allowed to bore hundreds at your own ease, and of being paid for it, and praised in proportion to the unsparing completeness of your inflictions! Surely, dulness is holy, and her prophets likewise, or how could these things be? Tender mothers, aunts, and elder sisters, are generally lenient at heart, but I know too many who would deem it a dereliction of their duty if they omitted to check every ebullition of juvenile gladness on the part of the children in their charge, and thus embitter the sweetness of their fresh lives with the dregs of sad experience or gloomy conventionality. Thousands have by these means been driven prematurely from the asylum of home into the world and its worst excesses, and have there perished, because the young soul has an appetite for light and joy which will be, must be fed, even though it be with the glimmer of the Jack-o'-lantern, the glittering tinsel and poisonous trash that betray and ruin it. Let it take its full of healthy sunlight and gladness, and fear not, for it is society, not nature, that makes man a captive, a coward, and a wretch. O, fathers, mothers, uncles, aunts, ministers, teachers, and mortals dressed in brief authority, were our Heavenly Father like you, what a sunless, flowerless, joyless, glum, half-frozen world this would be!

But I had almost forgotten the Bores in the Muffs. They are mostly identical, but not necessarily so. Men of science and learning are often great bores. At an hilarious party, when delicious nonsense is flying from one to another, like a sparkling cup full of bubbling nectar; when wit is darted playfully, lambently, like shooting stars, from brain to brain; your scientific wise acre, with his whys and wherefores, and dry profundities; your solid-pudding and cold-dumpling man comes down upon this brilliant volatility like a primitive rock upon a hummingbird or a butterfly, crushing all beneath with its ponderosity, and putting out the sparkle, the airiness, and a careless freedom which was the charm of the circle.

A professional man who carries his profession out of his laboratory, study, office, or proper place of exercise, is too frequently a bore. A tradesman who does the like is ditto. Think of a discourse on theology in a quadrille; pathology at the breakfast table; law over a game of cards; or anatomy in a pleasure-boat! Charming subjects for such occasions would they be, but I have known them to be dragged in still more out of place. I once dined with a doctor who orally analyzed the food as I ate it, resolving it all into poisons and gases, till I thought I must either explode or turn into green corruption before he had ceased his discourse. His favorite subject had rendered his complexion a greenish yellow; but what it had done to the internal man is too dreadful even to surmise, for his breath was like a doctor's shop, and his sphere like that of the grave. Worse than he, is an aged relative of mine, who is never so happy, as when, for my soul's salvation, he is stifling me with the flames and deafening me with the screams of a region unmentionable to ears polite; and, to make the lesson the more telling, he always enforces it at the moment I have the presumption to enjoy myself. I did not mind a little tailor, with whom I danced once upon a time (quel honneur !), who, though he talked of little but the cutting and setting of gent's vests and pants (vile word cabbaging, this), also informed me that it took nine men to make a good tailor, and that no one could cut a dash unless he was cut out for it by such an artist. The tailor was perhaps only the ninth part of a bore; but most tradesmen, whose souls, like the tanner's hide, are impregnated with their business, are full grown bores, and much to be dreaded. If the shoemaker ought to stick to his last, let him do so by all means, the closer the better, but if he will come into society; let it not be his sole topic of conversation. . . . . . .

There is the partial Bore and the unmitigated Bore; the heavy Bore and the flippant one, with

"A brain of feathers and a heart of lead."

But of the entire genus, the species called the crotchety bore, is the most remarkable and various. They are such as ride hobbies to death, and are seldom satisfied unless they can ride them over you. A relation of mine is afflicted with the water-cure, and, though he has killed off several of his children and reduced himself and wife to skeletons by this panacea, he cannot carry on a conversation of any length without plunging into cold water and drenching his interlocutors thoroughly with it. I believe he would revive the deluge every year, if he had his way. That is his crotchet; what is yours, dear reader? Is it fast horses, politics, spiritualism, slavery, anti-slavery, dress, respectability, the french-horn, dogs, singing, fighting, the fire-engine, furniture-auctions, flirting, eating, drinking, sporting, sentiment, poetry, chess, yachting, entomology, or some peculiar religious dogma? What is it? Well, no matter what, so that you do not insist that others ought to think, act, and feel with respect to it just as you do. If you do thus insist, you are a Bore, albeit otherwise an angel, but if you do, with all your heart, allow others the privileges you covet or assume yourself, then give me your hand; you are a jolly good fellow, and deserve my benediction.

A genius in every department of art and industry is sure to arise, master it, and carry it to the utmost degree of perfection. What Paganini was among fiddlers, Shakspeare among dramatists, Columbus among discoverers, Napoleon among generals, or Washington among patriots, was and is Daniel D—lt among Bores. Dan is king among them, and, much as other individuals may excel in any particular branch of boring, he surpasses them all in all.

"Laborious, heavy, busy, bold, and blind,"

there is no subject upon which, no place in which, no persons with whom, he is not an intolerable and incomparable bore. He is wonderfully compounded, being a perfect admixture of conceit and contradiction, impudence and stupidity, pedantry and ignorance, servility and dogmatism, blindness and obstinacy, brutality, rigmarole, insensibility, officiousness, formality, and other similar virtues and excellences I cannot think of at this moment. Dan's prosing is more depressing than the rainiest day in November, and his mind denser than a London fog. His common-places (and he never uttered anything else) are antediluvian, having each, during the last thousand years, begotten more yawns than the longest chapter in the Bible. Dan is ever prone to talk, and has only to join in any conversation to render its subject as flat and stale as an old woman's reiterated morality. He is always ready to give needless advice, and to tell the news that everybody knows. Hackneyed quotations, and jokes with not the ghost of a laugh left in them, sentiments and truisms as familiar and undoubted as the multiplication-table, songs just as soon as they begin to weary and disgust the ear, novelties (that were) when publicity has long tainted them—such materials form the charm of his discourse, and constitute his life and delight.

Dan's art of sinking is so irresistible that he never fails to make the merry sad and the sad desperate. Job's comforters were jolly fellows in comparison to him, and had it been Dan's office to cheer that afflicted ancient, patience would never have been coupled as it is with the patriarch's name. Dan would have driven him wild. Three marriageable sisters had Dan, and how many artifices they were fain to employ to rid the parlor of his presence! But his obtuseness foiled them all, and kept the ladies single, for what young fellow, or old one either, much as he might admire them, could withstand Dan? His heavy artillery, worked by "forty-parson power," swept the field ere the wiles of Venus or Cupid's archery could achieve a single conquest.

Yet he thought himself his sister's ablest ally. No enemy could, however, have done them half so much mischief, for he always managed to say or do the thing fatal to their hopes, and his obvious officiousness and intolerable boring disgusted every suitor, and made him as glad to get away from him as is a schoolboy to escape from his teacher, or a captive from the dreariness of his dungeon. The three sisters became old maids, and Dan blamed them for it, for he was sure he had done his utmost to get them good husbands.

He had two brothers, younger than himself, who were also his special care. How wearily and unremittingly he persecuted them for their good! Edward, the elder of the two, dreaded him more than long prayers, sickness, or an empty purse, and Charlie, the younger, would rather be kept over-time alone in school than endure his company. Being strictly and dismally moral, without the vitality, impulse, or courage to commit the smallest crime, he was entrenched behind his own impeccability, and prized by his parents as a pattern to youth and an example to all. He grew supreme at home, where he stuck like a log too heavy to be removed. He bore down upon the life of the house like an incubus, and Ned, to escape his boring, spent his evenings abroad, and unfortunately fell into evil habits and into company the very reverse of his brother's, but equally bad. He was enticed by gamblers into unfair play, and lost so much that he was reduced to an extremity which led him to commit forgery, in order to obtain means to retrieve his losses. Of course these means only served to sink him deeper, and, being at last discovered and afraid to meet the world's scorn, and much more, his parents' agony, in a moment of despair he committed suicide. Dan moralized over his brother's destruction, and attributed it mainly to the neglect of his advice and contempt of his companionship.

The business which Ned had managed with considerable tact and judgment, was now conducted by Dan; Mr. D—lt being rendered incompetent to fulfil its duties, not so much by age as by affliction, of which the disgrace and untimely death of his favorite son were the cause. Dan, who had first aimed at a profession, possessed now an enlarged sphere for boring. He bored his clerks, his creditors, his customers, his competitors, and everybody who came near enough to be held by the button. His clerks and employés consequently drowsed and shirked their duties; his creditors put on an extra profit for complaisance and time lost in listening; his competitors made a jest and byword of him and all that dealt with him; and such of his customers as meant to pay, left disgusted with his long stories and bungling old fogyism, while those who meditated bankruptcy, humored him to the top of his bent, and, after they had failed, compelled him to follow suit. Dan was somewhat ingenious in imputing his disaster to the discredit and odium which he alleged his deceased brother had brought upon the concern, instead of ascribing it to his own incompetency, to which it was rightly attributable. Dan had not only succeeded in breaking a good and long established business, but his father's heart also. This last blow was more than he could sustain, and he did not long survive his mercantile credit.

Dan, as if he thought it incumbent upon him to make amends for his relatives, grew now more methodically, constantly, and religiously a Bore than ever, and a black cloud of dust is the only thing to which, as a nuisance, he could have justly been compared. Charlie, not having a taste for martyrdom, ran away from home; but Mrs. D—lt, whom Dan condoled with continually, became so oppressed and despairing under the process, that she would surely have died, had not the loss of reason afforded her a dreadful relief, and an asylum from her son in the madhouse. Dan blamed his brothers, dead and living, for this horrible calamity, and thanked his God devoutly that he was not as they.

The three Miss D—lts had now not only to endure this self-righteous nightmare, but the pangs of want and poverty. Dan, however, at last obtained a position in school, and made it at once his duty and pleasure to bore fifty or sixty young hearts for about six hours daily. His sisters, who were employed by the religious society to which he belonged, in tract distribution, nursing, and other charitable offices, became accidentally acquainted with a Mormon missionary, whom they attempted to convert, but who, having more speciousness, fallacy, and zeal than they, succeeded in converting, or perverting, them to his own persuasion. Whether it was the fascination of his wild fanaticism, or their irresistible longing to escape by any method from their brother Dan, who devoted his mornings and evenings to their leaden, gloomy torture, I cannot say, but is only too certain that the polygamist induced the three sisters to leave their relative and join the followers of Brigham Young in Utah. Of course they have each been sealed to some saint long ere this, some say all to the same individual, the missionary who entrapped them, but this it is to be hoped is gross exaggeration.

In this matter Dan blamed himself a little for what he could hardly help, attributing the success of his sisters' seducer to his compulsory absence from home during the greater part of the day. He deems it a remarkable and melancholy fact that he alone of a large and respectable family should turn out well, and has consequently been immoveably confirmed in his musty opinions, formal habits, and snobbish practices. He is now a greater Bore than ever. I hear that he intends to commit matrimony-murder, if done quickly, would in him be a more venial offence. I pity his conjugal victim from my heart of hearts, for what was the most lingering and fatal torture of the inquisition to the agony of being bored to death?

I have lately learned that little Charlie D—It is prospering in the West, having already accumulated quite a little fortune. Dan ascribes his success to the prayers he has sent after him. What do you think, reader?

I could write a volume on Bores, but suspect I have bored you with them enough already. Without them this world would be a paradise, and were it as clear of them as they say Ireland is of snakes, I might consent, if endowed with perpetual youth, to live in it forever.

MADAME BISHOP AT PALACE GARDEN.

The name of Anna Bishop seems to me like a far-off strain of music. Perhaps it is that she was the first artist my childhood's eyes and ears greeted in this planetary sphere. She seemed to me, then, an embodied story from the Arabian Nights, like some Eastern fairy who had charmed all the myriad singing birds of the forest into pouring forth their whole choral melody through her bright lips, leaving wood and grove desolate, sorrowful, silent. So she seems to me now, seems an enchantress; it was wisely kind to remove the canaries hitherto suspended throughout the hall; had they listened to her flute-song, they had hung their little heads in despair, and been mute forever after.

Madame Bishop's success, apart from its being a gratification to her friends and admirers, was a consolation to those who grieve for the fickleness of all things: it proves that the public taste is more stable than fashion. She was the queen of ballad-singers ten years ago; she is still their fair sovereign. Her voice is of that pure and tender type, unhappily so rare in these days; her face one of the finest and most noble I have ever had the fortune to see.

The innumerable audience demonstrated the sincerest delight in her performance. I thought there was even a loving tone in their enthusiasm; perhaps the sound of her sweet voice awakened for them, as it did for me, the angel-memory, to throw a halo around her and lift her out of the puny reach of criticism.

Each time she sang she was earnestly recalled, and gallantly compelled to repeat her songs, with that unbroken accord of applause which the most resolute clacquers never succeeded in raising. Her flute-song, in which the flute-ah! vain flute-strove to imitate her voice, and could not, drew forth cries of rapture from all lips. She is now a renewed fame, and as all must see her, we may hope to keep her for some time to come.

In strict justice to a wonderful and illustrious young artist, I mean Arthur Napoleon, I must say that he divided the honors of the evening with the Prima Donna. He played Liszt's *Midsummer Night Dream,* in a manner to reduce the dillettanti to despair. Although announced to play only twice, the tribunal of the public wish happily doubled that number. As I watched the play of his varying face, following ever the flight of his aerial fingers, whose tide of melody flung the combined efforts of the orchestra away upon the dim shores of insignificance, I could not wonder that he had been the stronghold of public attraction in this temple of art, having for its pure roof the most excellent canopy of the air. He is young, graceful, ardent, with a certain spirituality of manner which belongs only to those whom the gods have created poets in the highest Olympian sense of that word, Moreover he has a face whose intellectual features and lucent eyes blend well with the pure bay leaves with which the Muses have crowned him.

Of all branches of musical art, the piano-sphere is the most intelligent and elevated. A great pianist, is very much in danger of being a great man. The young artist of whom I have been speaking is one of those rare natural marvels, a pianist of genius, whose whole performance is colored with that sincere and spontaneous passion which no amount of mere facility can imitate. All the practice in the world will not bring the faintest tinge of it. It is very annoying for the mechanics of music, but it lies in the inevitable nature of things. Thus all lovers of music, all those who follow ardently its progress towards perfection, will feel a close sympathy and interest for the young virtuoso in question.

The audience on Saturday night consisted of the queerest admixture of nationalities, such as John Brougham, Stephen Masset, Henry Drayton, etc., with a perfect shoal of old-fashioned, well-bred concert lovers. There were family-parties present, who had changed their dinner hour for fear of arriving too late for a good seat, and were to be found composedly arrayed on the front benches, when the gas-man came to light the hall. There were old ladies, former admirers of Madame Bishop, who had apparently not been to a concert since she left New York, and who evidently wore the same articles of toilet, in which they graced her last appearance. There were neat maiden ladies who coughed behind the fingers of their kid gloves, too long for them of course, and kept fanning themselves audibly, with wheezy little fans. Then there was the pious family, who look ominous and black if you do but speak of the Opera, seated also in the front ranks, and handing about among themselves little twisted papers, from which issued an odor of mint and wintergreen, the contents of which created a gentle crunching and munching, whose low monotone insisted upon uniting itself to the efforts of the prima donna, refusing hospitably to take no for an answer. There is a morality even in sugar-plums. I have known persons too virtuous to eat chocolate or pistache, who cannot be pious without a pocket full of peppermint lozenges.

Before I close, I must not omit to pay my compliments of respect to that most excellent gentleman and admirable artist, Carl Anschutz. He was engaged that his name might add to the attraction of the evening, if such a thing was possible. I heard Madame Bishop say she had never known a superior leader. The words of the Diva must not be disputed.

Ada Clare

SPIRITUALISM.

Dear Press :—Last Sunday morning and evening, spiritualistic discourses were delivered at Dodworth's Hall by Judge Edmonds, accompanied at intervals by music. This latter feature attracted me, knowing the exquisite musical taste possessed by the Judge, and in the evening I attended. Unlike at other religious meetings, the congregation conversed unrestrainedly in whispers till the service commenced. Its character was "country New England," and most markedly so. Few young men, fewer young women—all had a mature, married look. Spiritualist meetings, setting aside the notional, unsettled, male faces that are observed, contain among their shrewd business men, a class nowhere else seen. These are inventors, improvers on inventions, and practical men who carry these inventions into use, in advance of society at large. There are plenty of hooped skirt and patent corset manufacturers, sewing machine dealers, originators of queer modes of commercial business that no one else ever thought of and that are dropped after a few month's practice, proprietors of manipulating hospitals, watercure establishments, vegetarian boarding-houses, homœopathic pharmacies, etc., all wide awake on the dollar question, and devoting their wandering moments to metaphysics, unverified science, and theoretic philanthropy.

A few stray every-day faces might be seen on this occasion, but the above type largely prevailed.

Among the women were a few "medium" faces, a few medical faces, and many indicating nothing in particular. The dear creatures are apt to be general, and concentrated on nothing especially. They like men that are general. Let a man's thoughts cover superficially a wide range of subjects, his wife thinks him the greatest individual living, poor and practically useless as he may be; but once let his mind become absorbed upon a single topic, to the exclusion of others, she loses interest in him. Application in that one direction may bring him fortune, reputation, and her, luxury, yet his charm is gone. Her heart sighs, its tendrils wander forth, and often cluster round a new image.

Husbands with preoccupied minds, if you still retain love for your wives, neglect not its manifestations. They are the food and drink of her soul; they cost little of your valued time, and preserve your hearths inviolate. Wives, be jealous only where your husband loves another. His devotion to politics, to science, or to art, not a whit interferes with his love for you. Riches for you—your exaltation—are often the fond goal of his efforts. Overlook, then, his apparent forgettings, and remember, that his love, like the placid true steel, contains the elements of endless fire. Go all of you, and see the "House and Home," at Laura Keene's. Listen to her fine artists on their jewelled stage, and read a lesson in letters of gold on whitest satin.

The Judge took his seat. Courtly gentleman as he is, he blends with these plain good people like a statue of high art among rough hewn images; but, like him, they are of marble, though less happy in their sculptors. Want of finish is often found among reformers; vulgarity, rarely, or never. They leave that attribute to the so-called "higher class," who look sarcastically down upon them, and whose often innately vulgar natures, are thinly veiled by a gloss of dress and conventionality.

The Judge had stationed a portion of Dodworth's Band in an adjoining room. As he sat, delicious spirit music streamed through the air, and steeped the soul in happy tears. There were no tunes; there were long drawn chords. Each chord was a spirit voice. One could dream himself disembodied, and launched on the dim unknown. Heavenly calls of love salute the ear; they are all varied, but they are all love. Each call seemed kindled by a sweet smile; each was a loving welcome. Calls of a fond mother to her erring son, voice of a pure sister, unconscious of his guile; joyous sounds of cherubs; distant, ineffable harmonies; calls of white-robed angel's yearning pity, uncounted calls of all embracing love.

Tearful eyes dwelt upwards, welling with memories sad and sweet, with rapturous hope, or brimming sense of an especial care. All were silent, still, and deeply wrapt.

The Judge rose and read a short exhortation. Again music. He then read the vision of one in a trance, the gist and concluding words of which, were, that "death is, in the eye of wisdom, a phenomenon to be investigated, not a bugbear to alarm." More music. He then again rose for the discourse of the evening. It was upon Death. It was no sermon, no essay, no lecture. It was a series of spirit visits he had received. Many, strange to say, had been for months or years, unconscious in the other life, and as reason dawned, sought him as a medium through whom their earthly friends might know of their existence. One young girl, in an English ballroom, with a disease of the heart, had been stricken in a dance on a date she stated, and had dwelt unconscious for four months. A sailor drowned at sea, swam in spirit to the ship, was taken on board by his dim messmates, and carried—where? He had just awoke from his stupor. Darling sins are taken with us to the other life, and long oppress us with their fearful weight. Old daily habits, and modes of thought, cling likewise with tenacity. One man, who had been a strict Methodist, was conscious only on Sunday mornings, when he heard church bells; another, who on earth, had firmly believed the dead were wakened only by the "last trump," sat idly waiting for its sound. Spirits who wish themselves personally known, assume their costume and expression of earth. Otherwise they might not be recognized. Their faces, though preserving a lingering trace of earthly form, beam with an ideal beauty strange to mortal sense.

The Judge spoke also of a cotemporary on the Bench, who, on reaching the spirit-land was surrounded reproachfully by those whom he had condemned to the butchery of the halter; and of Isaac T. Hopper, who was at once embraced by the myriads he had here succored.

As the discourse closed, again rose the wondrous spells of spirit music, while with recognition glad, and smiling words, the happy hearers parted for their homes.

NESSUNO.

Dramatic Feuilleton.

THE EVENT has eventuated.

The Winter Garden is open.

Le Chauve absolutely radiates with triumph.

The Oldest Man likes it.

I like it.

It is a success. Grand, veritable, extraordinary success.

Without doubt, the dollar-crop in the Winter Garden will be equal to the cotton-crop in Texas.

There was a terrific rush the first night. The Oldest Man never saw anything like it, except at Tammany Hall, when the Faithful come together for a grand powwow about the principles of the Democracy. The subscriber's struggles to reach his stall were worthy of Hercules. I don't think he could have done it. After a series of pushings, and crowdings, and other unpleasant ings, I was precipitated upon an African brother, who guarded the gates to a small Paradise, with nice chairs to sit upon, pretty women to look at, numerous critics looking more or less terribly responsible and distressingly impartial, Cupids over in the corner, fountains and fiddlers in front, beauty, light, flowers, gold, violet, pink, crimson, belles, bankers, heavy swells, artists, and all sorts of nice things all around.

That was the coup d'œil. A charming theatre, all fresh and new. A packed audience. New York. Very light representation from the provinces, and that Southern, which for art-purposes is decidedly the best. Your Northerner is always calculating what it costs, and your Westerner has no eye for anything but ballet-girls, no taste for anything but Bourbon whiskey. But give our Southern brethren a good thing, that don't tread on their corns, which are numerous and terribly sensitive, and they appreciate it.

More than that, they pay for it.

I make that a special paragraph, because the liberal way in which the theatre has been fitted, furnished, and the heavy expense of its personnel, make the question d'argent a very important one. I believe, however, that this will be the New York Theatre, dividing the cream with Wallack's.

The artists are especially well selected to command metropolitan favor. There are no less than four crinolinities, who are universally admired. Each has a special individuality, and is strong in it. Miss Agnes Robertson, delicate, graceful, elegant, and undemonstrative, but still effective. Mrs. John Wood is one of the few actresses that I have ever seen, who know what fun is. Fun, I mean, in its fullest sense—humor and wit combined. K. N. Pepper says, "how hard it is to write good," and many a funny man and woman produce, in the minds of their audiences, an impression similar to that of the eminent American poet. Then there is Sarah Stevens, who is handsome, has a good style, and a natural way of getting on and off and about the stage, which is exceedingly refreshing. For the afflicted, interesting young woman, Mrs. Allen is precisely the Parmesan, imported to special order, and always to be relied upon.

The men, Jefferson, Pearson, Johnston, Davenport, are all New York favorites, and they deserve the hearty greetings they received on the opening night.

As for the play, Mr. Bourcicault's version of "A Cricket on the Hearth," it answered the purpose of displaying the idiosyncracies of the artists, probably, better than any other selection that could have been made. Still, the story is rather descriptive than dramatic. The events are suggested by the characters rather than the characters by the events. Thus the latter are made of secondary importance, and double duty is thrown upon the artists. Then, again, almost every person in the audience has his ideal of the character represented before he comes to the Theatre, and that ideal no artist, however clever, can entirely convey. Thus Miss Robertson's Dot, through a fine theatrical personation, and perfect in conception, was uneven in execution. In the last act she was charming. Here the character is positive; before it was negative. A good, brisk, bustling wife, however agreeable she may be at home, is not a stage-character which affords a large artistic opportunity.

Miss Stevens gave some individuality to Bertha, and Mrs. Allen was terribly heart-broken, as she ought to be. There is an immense amount of affection floating about in the last act, and these young ladies were quite uncomfortably lavish of it.

Distinctly the grand honors of the evening belong to Mrs. Wood and Jefferson. Mrs. Wood's Tilly Slowboy seems to me exactly the thing; that is a matter of opinion. It carried away the audience; that is a matter of fact. Mr. Jefferson was admirable in Caleb Plummer. His costume, and making-up, as it is called, were artistic in the highest degree, and his recognition of his Son, in the last scene, a bit of "business" which places him several feet higher in my estimation.

But I don't intend to go into particulars about this performance, in which every character was well done. The scenery and every appointment of the stage were worthy of a first-rate French theatre.

The fact is, that everything is so carefully done that one has nothing to complain of. And that makes me unhappy.

However, we shall see by-and-by.

Something for Dr. Bellows.

The papers have been very savage upon Miss Laura Keene's friend, Palgrave Simpson, who steals a good deal from the French, but rarely improves what he touches. One of his latest efforts is a three-act play called "The World and the Stage." This play is one of that order of productions by which it is intended to show that poor actresses are savagely virtuous because they are actresses, the coulisses being the nurseries of morality of the most rigid order, and that rich aristocrats are continually getting into scrapes, and would be utterly ruined if the virtuous actress did not come to help them out. This is precisely what Miss Keene does in *The World and the Stage*, and it is very encouraging to know, that in the end "the barrier of prejudice is destroyed," and "no other piece will be performed."

That is certainly enough for one night.

Still, though the piece is absurd and very improbable, as well as a réchauffée of half a dozen others, good and bad, it is so admirably acted and well placed upon the stage, that it has had a money success. The house has been full every night, and the critics are supposed to be crushed. Perhaps like Truth, a lady for whom some of them have so high a respect that they never approach her, they will rise again.

Miss Keene's acting in this play would save a much worse one. The other parts are sketches more or less filled up, and in one or two cases run over.

Operatic.

There was a tremendous rush of our Southern brethren and sisters (*aint* they nice ?) at the Academy on Monday, when the Operatic campaign was commenced with an encouraging house. What I said about the *Poliuto* and Cortesi, last season, has come to pass. The opera is the best card that the management will have this year, unless the *Vépres Siciliennes* should have an unprecedented success.

The artists, on Monday, were about as usual. Cortesi and Brignoli were both superb in the last act. Amodio must be more careful. He was more than once out of tune. What is it? Maccaroni or luxurious ease, or matrimony, or what?

Mme. Gassier sung Somnambula on Wednesday, to a fair house, and Cortesi gave Norma, Thursday, to a crowd.

The season is announced to close next Wednesday.

Bishop.

The concerts of *La Sfogato*, as the late lamented Bochsa used to call Madame Anna Bishop, opened brilliantly, but were swamped by the opera. It is generally conceded, by musical people, that Bishop sings with more sympathy and true feeling than she did ten years ago, but it is nonsense to say that a singer's voice improves with age after she rises thirty. That may answer for London, where the people swallow everything in the papers as a man-of-war's-man tosses off his grog, but it won't do here, and Bishop's voice is pronounced a little usée. She is a fine artist, however, and has no equal in ballad singing, an innocent diversion which is still agreeable to a very large and respectable class of the community.

They are having the Fair of the Institute now at the Palace Garden, and have sent me a "Family Ticket," which A. M. construes in the liberal sense adopted by some politicians in relation to the Constitution. She heads parties which include a large portion of the female population of the —th Ward.

Wallack.

Mr. Wallack will open his theatre next Monday, and the rehearsals of Brougham's new comedy, (Mrs. Hoey, Miss Gannon, Mr. Lester Wallack, Mr. Brougham, and Mr. Walcot in the cast,) are now going on. Green-room gossip speaks well of the immortal John's latest effort. I saw Mr. Lester Wallack at the Winter Garden, tanned a beautiful brown, and looking decidedly agricultural. Mrs. Hoey likewise appeared on the same occasion, and is not so rustic as a Summer residence in Connecticut might be expected to make her. Altogether I should judge that the Veteran's forces were in the best fighting condition. Anna Maria vows and declares that there is no place so nice as Wallack's, while Araminta stands out for the Winter Garden. It is a very pretty quarrel as it stands.

Things Generally.

The Athenian public have been soldiering so much of late, that Art has languished a little. The Boston Theatre is not to be opened until the opera season commences, which will be, probably, about the 26th of this month. The Howard Athenæum audiences have been regaled with a new translation of Mme. de Girardin's "Lady Tartuffe." The *Evening Gazette*, which has a high opinion of its opinion, says that Mrs. Farren's Virginie de Blossac was "a consummate piece of acting;" the critic considers it "a master-piece of the Histrionic Art." The phrases are not quite new, but the *Gazette* was, like Fanny, younger once than it is now. I am charmed to know that Miss Fanny Fitz Farren (why Fitz?) "has it in her power to become, like her mother, one of the first of living actresses." It is to be hoped that the young lady will not keep *it* (whatever it is) in her power, but let out a little of *it*.

Mr. and Mrs. W. J. Florence have succeeded the Farrens, and next week comes Mrs. Bateman's tragedy, "Geraldine."

The Boston people, it occurs to me, are distinguished for what is called their American sentiments. I am a great deal like the man in the play, who as one of a number that were called upon to show their "magnanimity," said to his friend: "I havn't any idea what it is, but if you have any show it." So with the sentiment above alluded to. If you have any, Bostonians, show it for the new play which Miss Heron will act for you next week. Quoting the South street merchant's opinion of Clark's *Knickerbocker*, "it is a good article."

And, by the way, the story invented by the *Tribune*, that there was a serious misunderstanding between ye Heron and ye Bateman (the two most amiable people in the world), is completely put at rest by the following:

Correction.

To the Editor of The N. Y. Tribune:

Sir:—From a statement in your paper of this morning, I perceive you are in error in regard to the relations which exist between Mr. Bateman and myself, and the terms on which we close our contract with each other at the end of the approaching Boston engagement. Instead of our positions being hostile, or our interests in any way at war, I am happy to state that they are entirely amicable, and in all respects what they should be, after three weeks of such triumph and profit as we have both reaped equally from the tragedy of "Geraldine."

I have only to add, that the claims of the highly-gifted authoress of "Geraldine" to dramatic eminence need no word from me to strengthen the verdict of the highly successful engagement which has just been closed; and I am at a loss to know how any one could have conceived the idea that the just reward which she achieved should not have been entirely acceptable to me.

Matilda Heron Stopel,

No. 234 *Sixth avenue*, Sept. 15th, 1859.

The other theatres are running towards the infantile, little Mary M'Vicker, "endorsed by John Brougham" (the Oldest Man never endorses anybody), being at the Museum, and Cordelia Howard at the Museum. Let the effulgent Gayler keep an eye on Willard. "The Son of the Night" is underlined at the National. M. D'Ennery, who cribbed this play of Gayler's, and put it in French for the Porte St. Martin, Paris, has just been made an officer of the Legion of Honor. Gayler ought to be turned into a Colonel of Militia, toute suite.

Verdi is coming over here to write an opera about Niagara Falls. There's inspiration in the idea, and the introduction of Blondin's feet will make a peculiarly happy effect, and quite in the composer's style.

Personne

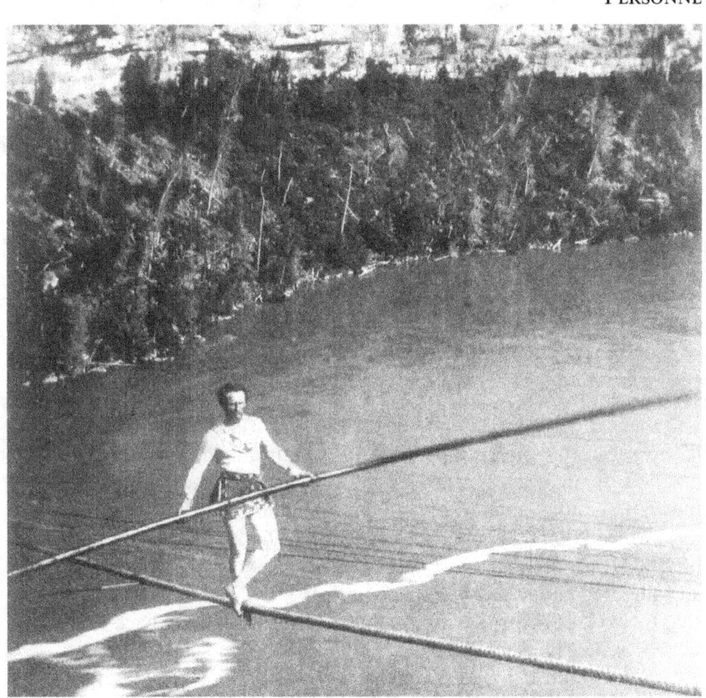

Blondin crossing the Niagara River on June 30, 1859.

LAURA KEENE'S THEATRE.

GREAT SUCCESS

OF THE

NEW ORIGINAL COMEDY

CALLED

WORLD AND STAGE,

WHICH WILL BE

REPEATED NIGHTLY TILL FURTHER NOTICE,

With a cast comprising the names of the following excellent artists:

MISS LAURA KEENE, ADA CLIFTON, MARION MACARTHY, MARY WELLS, FLORENCE BELL, and Mrs. MARK SMITH, and Messrs. G. JORDAN, H. F. DALY, W. H. STEPHENS, F. A. VINCENT, C. WHEATLEIGH, C. PETERS, S. A. SMITH, etc.

NO OTHER PIACE WILL BE PERFORMED.

Door open at 7—to commence at 8 o'clock.

NEW YORK SEPTEMBER 24, 1859

PRESIDENTIAL CANDIDATES.

Prominent among the persons having more or less chance of nomination for the next Presidency, may be mentioned: W. H. Seward, Capt. Rynders, Horace Greeley, E. Meriam, James Gordon Bennett, Lucy Stone, S. A. Douglas, John C. Heenan, S. P. Chase, Henry Ward Beecher, E. Bates, William E. Burton, D. S. Dickinson, Stephen H. Branch, John Bell, G. W. F. Mellen, John P. Hale, Lord Dundreary, A. H. Stephens, Sylvanus Cobb, Jr., Gerrit Smith, N. P. Banks, A. J. H. Duganne, S. P. Hanscom, Henry A. Wise, Awful Gardner, Judge McLean, Andrew Jackson Davis, Jefferson Ditto, Abby Folsom, R. M. T. Hunter, Tom Hyer, J. H. Hammond, Col. Fuller, J. C. Fremont, Chevalier Wickoff, J. C. Breckenridge, Personne of the SATURDAY PRESS, James Buchanan, Peter Cooper, Jane G. Swisshelm, Ned Buntline, Joseph Lane, J. Augustus Page, Henry J. Raymond, Thomas Thumb, P. T. Barnum, Mrs. Bloomer, Parson Brownlow, Deacon Hallock, and Mr. Yeadon's "Orator, Patriot, Sage, Cicero of America, Laudator of Washington, Apostle of Charity, High Priest of the Union, and Friend of Mankind."

MAPLE ISLAND.

Written for the NEW YORK SATURDAY PRESS.

BY AUGUSTUS WATTERS.

Foreshadowing the dissolution of man, the crisp and yellow leaves of the forest were rapidly dropping to earth, while such as were left by the insidious hand of decay were being swept from the creaking boughs by the wailing, boisterous winds of mellow Autumn. The merry mocking-bird had fled to a warmer playground, with many of his little tuneful brothers. Less fortunate than these, the quail, the robin, and the partridge still lingered amid their Summer haunts, while the quacking duck and the long-necked goose, collecting in flocks, came screaming back to the cold waters of the rivers and lakes.

On one of those delightful, mysterious Autumn days, when the soul seems wooed from the body, and floats imperceptibly from earth and its groveling race into the angelic purity of the Spirit-land, two youths pushed out into the lovely Illinois river and proceeded down stream. The red and golden leaves of the dense timber which lined the river banks on either side, were at this time rendered doubly brilliant, as the departing sunbeams lingered about the banks and tinged them with changing hues. Not a sound marred the witching stillness, save the light and measured dipping of the oars, and the occasional hammering of some lonely woodpecker on the trunk of a hollow tree. A gentle breeze just ruffled the surface of the water, and whispered among the crisp leaves, while not one defiling speck was to be seen throughout the broad expanse that stretched above them.

Cheerily and steadily they plied the dripping paddles, and rapidly they glided along the lovely stream. Suddenly an object caught the eye of Martin, and turning to his companion so eagerly as to nearly upset the boat, he exclaimed,

"Do you see that?" at the same instant pointing to an animal that was swimming across the river some distance in their wake.

"What the deuce can it be?"

"As I live, it's a wolf!"

"No, its a young bear!"

"Silence! I'll shoot it, whatever it is," said Martin, catching up his piece and taking aim.

"Stop!" cried his companion, seizing his arm and preventing him; "now I bethink me, it's the dog!" "What!"

"We actually shoved off without taking him in!" And now they laughed heartily, as Milo neared the boat, and Martin proceeded to hoist him aboard. Again the oars dipped into the glassy water and the skiff sped on. None but those who have breathed the fragrant air of a prairie stream, and have viewed an Autumn sunset from its limpid surface, can fully appreciate the feelings of our western sportsmen as they now watched the lengthening shadows of the woods.

A mile had been traversed, and now they hove in sight of famous Maple Island. Grandly loomed its tall oaks and spreading maples from the bed of the foliage with the pure wavelets that played upon its beach. At length they had snugly stranded their skiff and conveyed the contents of the lockers to the shore.

And now we will unfold to the reader what they purposed doing. Upon that end of the island whereon they had landed, towered a huge oak whose base was entirely hollowed out. The extreme size of the cavity, and the remarkable smoothness of its interior had caused the tree to become quite celebrated about the region, and the cavern was generally known as "Maple Island Lodge." It was sufficiently capacious to afford sleeping accommodations for about three persons. Into this receptacle, then, it was the intention of our heroes to deposit their blankets and coats, presently to enter themselves, and therein pass the night. My sporting friends will at once divine the object of this manœuvre, while, for the edification of those unhappy enough to be without the pale of that fraternity, I will remark that early dawn is the aptest time for bagging ducks and geese. And about the shores of this lovely island, these species of the airy tribe were wont to collect at this season of the year in great numbers. While our adventurers are engaged in reconnoitering, I will endeavor to acquaint my reader with its quiet beauty. Maple, walnut, and oak trees here flourished in great abundance. About their giant limbs the grapevine wound its tough and wiry stems, while between their sturdy trunks the hazel-bush and pawpaw tree found room for a less dignified growth. Owing to the majority being maples, and the convenience with which the place could be reached, certain enterprising individuals in the sap and sugar line had made it the scene of their annual Spring labors. Consequently, a cabin built of massive logs, notched at either end, and provided with a huge trough, will not be deemed entirely fabulous, when I assert that such was placed directly in the centre of the island. Winter's snow and Summer's rain, however, had begun to make sad havoc among the logs, one or two of them having entirely rotted through, while half of the less ponderous ones had slidden from the roof and remained leaning against the outer side.

It was quite dark when Martin and his comrade returned to the oak, and they now hurriedly proceeded to build a liberal fire. Having collected a great heap of dead leaves and branches, they soon had a blaze that roared and crackled to a most exhilarating degree, and soon all the warmth and cheerfulness that was before diffused throughout the region seemed now to collect and condense within six feet of the blaze! And in this our hunters reveled to their hearts' content, while they dispatched their frugal supper. Thus far no geese had been heard to alight near the island, though the loud clamoring of many a populous flock ever and anon broke up the silence, as they sped like arrows through the dense gloom.

Presently our heroes ceased to pile on the faggots, and then creeping into their primitive lodging, were soon buried, in spite of the unearthly shrieks of moping screechowls, and the wild sobbing of the wind, in the arms of the drowsy god. . . . .

With the first streak of dawn, they stealthily crept from the oak and prepared for slaughter. A dense volume of mist hung along the river, which rendered objects invisible at a short distance. Nevertheless, our hunters now cautiously proceeded to post themselves in favorable positions along the beach. Presently, the feeble sunbeams worked their way into the mist, and began dispelling it from the placid stream. Then was a sight presented that would have filled the heart of an Eastern sportsman with a surprise paralyzing and ecstatic. Scores of stately geese were slowly gliding about within twenty rods of the shore, some with heads proudly erect, as if bidding defiance to every foe, while others buried their long necks in the water and remained a tempting mark for the hunter's fatal aim. As far as the eye could peer through the fog, shadowy forms were to be seen moving in all directions, while the harsh "honk! honk!" resounded from every part of the island. Martin had remained concealed in a clump of willows for about twenty minutes, when something like two dozen geese sailed within ten yards of him. Carefully raising his piece—bang! went an ounce of shot among the proud little squadron. Honk! honk! honk!" screamed all but two, as they clattered with a great uproar from the water and frantically soared away. "Honk! honk! honk!" echoed a flock from the right. Bang! went a charge from the other hiding-place, and then the din of a general raising of flocks and squads became exciting in the extreme. Away dashed Milo into the river to drag ashore the struggling prizes. One he quickly landed, but the other proved a tougher job. Furiously turning, the gander whacked its heavy beak upon the head of that devoted animal in a manner anything but mollifying to the canine recipient. Like a high-spirited dog, he let forth a series of enraged howls, not at all calculated to pacify a gander, and then at it they went again like two aquatic furies. At length, however, making a desperate snap, Milo buried his teeth in the neck of the vanquished bird and struggled to the shore. Then answering the impatient whistle of the other hunter, who had hit but one, a third goose was deposited on the beach. Again separating, our sportsmen now cautiously stole to the other side of the island, creeping on hands and knees, and trailing their guns through the cold, wet grass, beside them. Only a "few more of the same sort" were left, and these glided so warily about, at a snug distance from shore, that it was only after much skillful manoeuvring Martin succeeded in getting within gunshot. Stretched at full length upon the grass, and concealed by a clump of willows, he waited for the little fleet to consolidate, and then—*bang!* went another ounce of shot among the feathery bulwarks. "Honk! honk! honk!" shrieked the geese, in great terror, floundering from the water, and making off as fast as their heavy bodies would allow them.

"Halloa!" shouted George, hurrying in despair from his hiding-place toward his more fortunate companion.

Splash! went Milo into the stream, and round and round kicked two more unlucky bipeds, disabled but not dispatched. Snap! went the dog's teeth into two more vanquished necks, and soon two more trophies were added to the heap.

They then proceeded to rebuild their fire, and having warmed their chilled limbs, prepared to dispatch a breakfast of crackers and cheese. This finished, and considering their game sufficient, blankets, guns, etc., were then collected and conveyed to the landing-place. And now judge of our hunters' astonishment upon discovering that their skiff had floated from the beach. The oars were still in the same position they had been thrown the night before, but not a sign of the boat was to be seen in any direction.

"Fire and fury," cried Martin, "what shall we do now?"

"Scour the island—or, if need be, swim for it," was the brief response.

"Why, we'd freeze before we reached the middle of the stream!"

"Never mind, let's search for the boat first, and consider that afterwards."

Having examined the beach for the whole length of skiff, they returned once more to the oak, there to hold further counsel as to the manner in which they might gain the opposite shore.

"At any rate, there's no need of anxiety," commenced George, "for though we should find it impossible to cross ourselves, there will certainly be some boats along here in the course of the day to help us off."

Vain would be any attempt of mine to describe the delightful freedom which these two sanguine, thoughtless youths enjoyed throughout that long, delicious, dreamy, Autumn day. Ever and anon they were roused from some most comfortable resting-place of soft, dry leaves, where the warm, genial sunbeams played full upon them, by the loud whirring of a startled quail; and as they clambered about the vine-clad limbs of gnarled oaks, in pursuit of the tempting grapes, now rendered delicious by a touch of frost, they laughed at the nimble pranks of the great fox-squirrels and wished they had brought up their guns that they might occasionally cut one off in "the flower of his youth and beauty." Then they gathered great heaps of butternuts and walnuts, and while seated upon the ground, cracking and feasting to their hearts' content, they regaled each other with moving tales of taciturn ghosts and loquacious desperadoes. And when midday arrived, having proceeded to roast one of their geese on a hickory skewer, they devoured huge slices of the same with great gusto, notwithstanding the absence of a bread accompaniment.

About three in the afternoon, as the youths were reclining on the eastern bank of the island, watching the stealthy movements of a trio of muskrats in the water beneath, a rabbit sprang from behind them and made off in the direction of the old cabin. Up sprang our hunters and followed in hot pursuit. Arriving at the cabin, into which the animal had fled, they then lost sight of it. Rooting in every corner, they could regain no trace of it, but were surprised to find the ground in a certain part lying as if recently dug up and then thrown in again. Casting about for a stout twig with which to continue his explorations, George was still further amazed to find a shovel secreted amidst some brush within a few yards of the spot. Seizing this and plunging it into the loose earth, he quickly displayed the top of a rude but massive box. Eagerly proceeding to raise the cover, a whole store of small bundles were displayed, which, upon examination, proved to be nothing less than neatly done up rings bracelets, breastpins, silver and gold watches, eyeglasses, earrings, and costly plate of various descriptions.

The amazement of our hunters was only equalled by their blank dismay, when the startling truth flashed upon their minds that they were confined upon an island which formed a very rendezvous for thieves. They rushed to the river's brink, but alas! the water was too cold—they'd freeze! Dashing back, they endeavored to arrange everything as they had found it. Then flying to the oak, they proceeded to erase every appearance of their visit. They scattered the ashes of their fire, hid the two oars, and condensed all their baggage into the smallest possible compass. Darkness then gradually stole upon them, and our youths prepared to pass a wretched night—verily, "in fear and trembling."

. . . .

It is uncertain how many hours they had slept, but about midnight they were roused by the grating of oars, as they were plied in low and measured strokes by some invisible oarsman, who glided within a stone's throw of the shore. Listening attentively, they heard the sounds continue until the boat had arrived at what seemed to be the centre of the island. Hereupon, there was a sudden cessation, and then a noise like the rattling of a chain painter gave them to understand that the nocturnal visitors had landed. Soon a fire was seen gleaming through the many chinks of the old log hut; and then, with a great effort calming his own and his companion's nervousness, Martin's resolution was taken. Leaving everything but their guns behind, the two proceeded (after Martin had unfolded his quickly devised plan) toward the beach. Arriving there, they crept along at a snail's pace until they had gained what they judged to be the landing-place of the robbers. By a stroke of good luck, at length

> "Their feeble hands and helpless,
> Groping blindly in the darkness,"

rested in safety upon the gunwale of the boat. Cocking his piece, George stole into the stern, while Martin cautiously gathered up the painter, link by link. Then breathlessly, and by almost imperceptible degrees, shoving the boat from the sand, he stepped in himself, and seizing an oar, pushed vigorously into the stream. Nearly the whole of that long, dark, dreary night, with limbs chilled and eye-lids drooping, did our young adventurers row through the black waters. Ever and anon their little barque would dash heavily against the rocks, threatening them with a bed, if not a grave, in the cold stream, and then a flock of ducks would flounder from their path, and with shrill screams rush away through the inky gloom.

The first faint streak of dawn was tinging the eastern sky with silvery hues, when their boat was stranded near the spot, whence, two days before, they had so merrily set out on their expedition.

Proceeding at once into town, they roused the solitary constable from his bed, and related to him what they had seen. At first he was inclined to laugh at their story, but on its being solemnly reiterated again and again, he at length so earnestly bestirred himself as soon to have collected four stout fellows, besides himself, with whom he at once proceeded to a spot on the shore where the few boats were generally stranded. Quickly shoving one from the beach, the five sprang aboard, and after some vigorous paddling soon found themselves nearing the island. And now, with every eye and ear alert, they cautiously steered for shore. No sign, however, of any human being could they perceive in any direction. After sailing entirely round the island, with the same result, they at last ran their boat ashore. Still no token of the presence of a solitary man was to be observed. They then made their way through a clump of paw paw trees to the hut. Stepping inside, the constable ran his club into the loose earth which he at once perceived in a corner, but without touching the faintest shadow of a box.

"The boys were evidently dreaming, or mad!" burst out the disappointed Dogberry.

"There are signs here which distinctly indicate that *something* has been removed," seriously replied one of the men.

"True enough," returned the other; "let us examine the rest of the island."

They had not gone more than a dozen yards from the cabin when, with a great exclamation, one of the party pointed to a neighboring tree. Dangling from the limb of a huge, gnarled oak, and perfectly rigid, was the body of a man. With arms tied behind his back, and a strong cord about his neck, the unfortunate wretch had now become food for a score of crows that screamed and hovered above his head.

Instantly discharging his piece, the foremost man killed two of the vile birds, and then, with the assistance of his companions, climbed the tree, and cut down the mangled corpse. They buried it in the very spot whence the chest had been taken, and then with a combined expression of horror and amazement on each of their faces, retraced their steps to the boat. According to the request of the boys, one of the men removed the geese, blankets, etc., etc., which were left in the hollow oak, and then the party pulled away from the island. The astonishment of our heroes may be better imagined than described, when they heard the strange conclusion of their strange adventure.

. . . .

Ten years after the foregoing occurrence, a desperate character was captured and executed in Indiana. During his imprisonment, he wrote the memoirs of his life. Among the rest of his misdeeds, he gave a detailed account of the very tragedy which I have just narrated as taking place on the romantic little island. It seems that another boat arrived there after the boys' departure, with a further addition of the gang (which was no less than a branch of the fearful organization known as the Banditti of the Prairies). The poor wretch who was hung had long been looked upon with suspicion by his bloody comrades, and when they discovered that the chest had been opened, and that their boat had been dragged from the beach, they eyed him with ominous glances. When the rest of the gang arrived, they detailed their suspicions, and together proceeded to murder him.

Correspondence.

Dear Press—I was much interested lately in a visit to the Fourth Ward Coffee and Reading Room, in the New Bowery near James street. To those of your readers, who have not heard of it through the dailies, I may remark that it was established by a number of benevolent individuals for the purpose of drawing Bowery boys from low liquor saloons, and their concomitant extravagance, idle and filthy conversation, swearing, drunkenness and fighting, and affording them the gratis entertainment of a neat hall with books, newspapers, periodical, illustrated and non-illustrated, and refreshments at the lowest rates, if they choose to call for it.

I found the hall about 60 feet long, 25 wide and whitewashed. At one end was a small cooking arrangement, hidden by a curtain. Before this was a counter, at which, together with several neighboring small tables, visitors eat; the rest of the room was occupied by a bookcase, and a number of tables upon which laid the various journals, sent in most cases without subscription. The supply was very varied, embracing those of England and Scotland, as well as of America. Many of their titles were entirely new to me. I was agreeably impressed with the two superintendents, who were the only employers visible. They had an eminently respectable and church-going look; one in fact had on a white choker, and looked clerical. From them, I gathered the following facts:

The enterprise was commenced in June last. Owing to the heat of the Summer evenings, the attendance has averaged only about thirty, the class of young men aimed at, preferring in hot weather to stand and sit at street corners, rather than be confined to a room. It is thought that as the season grows colder they will avail themselves more fully of the advantages offered. As the establishment is small, its sphere of usefulness is confined. It is availed of more by studious mechanics, who if they could not attend there would read at home, than by the regular "roughs" whom it is proposed to reform. Still, a fair number of these gentry, round-capped, and wide-awake, drop in, look at the illustrated papers, and always behave themselves with marked decorum. The reform has more vitality than many a foreign mission. I met once an American Missionary who had been twelve years in Turkey, and acknowledged that he had never converted a single Turk. Several, he said, had however, come to "enquire." This gentleman had, during that period, supported a considerable family upon the salary afforded him by the Society at home. I do not wish to decry foreign missions. Some benefit is effected by them, and Providence implants instincts in certain individuals, which impel them to various paths of good, and among others, that of infusing the spirit of Jesus into barbarians; but I would merely suggest to those whose impulses do not lead them irresistibly in that direction, that there are other, and more effective fields of good, at home.

The Fourth Ward Coffee and Reading Room is on the second story. The superintendents remark that had the first floor been hired as a dining-room, the attendance would have been great, and a far larger number would have frequented the reading-room above. On the opening, hundreds applied for dinner, and finding but a trifling refreshment of cold meat, cakes, and coffee, departed. This hint will perhaps be acted on by those who established the place, and I would here suggest to Messrs. Sweeny, Crook and other large dining saloon proprietors in the Bowery, that they devote a room in connection with their establishments to a library and periodicals, charging one cent admission, or a dollar per annum subscription, to defray expenses. Many, after a meal, would enjoy half-an-hour's reading, and the good these gentlemen might effect in that direction would be immense.

And now, to tread on lower ground. I like enthusiasm. I like its manifestations. I like a good roar. It is electric. For that reason I recently went to the opening of the New Bowery Theatre, and simply to hear some Bowery cheers. We do not understand roars on this side of the town. We are out of practice too. We roared a little at Macready, years ago, and at points of Webster's, when the "sleeping lion" raised his mane; we might have roared for Fremont, and hope to do so for Seward, but we are a child's cry to the Bowery. Think of youth, spirits uncontrolled, reddest health, and lungs of all conceivable metals, practised nightly at a fire! There were four thousand pair, and Niagara was a joke to them. There were cheers for everything—for the house, for the curtain, for the paint, for Brougham in a side box, for the orchestra-leader, for each fiddler as he entered; and when the curtain rose upon the company, assembled in their best clothes for the opening address, George Washington, the Goddess of Liberty, and old Shakespeare, visibly changed countenance, and shook in the agony of an anticipated tumble.

A joyous sight is that young untutored feeling, bursting forth in its own tongue, giving sound to its sensations, untrammelled by forethought, unrepressed by care.

And now, adieu ! Nessuno.

WAITING IN THE RAIN.

BY LUCY LARCOM.

A light flashed up in her clear blue eye
Like a ray through a break in the cloudy sky,
As she leaned at the showered pane.
"Thank Heaven, he's come!"—but the train shrieked "Nay!"
And crashed o'er her dying hopes away.
Still she waited on, till the day was gone—
Waited alone in the rain.

Ever, now and again, the cloud-rack through,
There peeped a bud of the heavenly blue
Blue, without speck or stain.
Then the young corn shook in its jewelled mist,
And the violets twinkled like amethyst,
And her eye grew bright with a dewy light,
Waiting alone in the rain.

But the soft blue flower of the sky shut up
Behind the tempest its hollow cup;
The meadows were dim again;
And the warm light faded out of her eyes
While she paced and gazed on the restless skies,
While she tried to keep her wild heart asleep,
Waiting alone in the rain.

It streamed and poured from the shelving bank;
It sprinkled mire on the sedges rank;
It beat on the springing grain.
"Come home!" called the horn from behind the hill.

She heard, but she waited and listened still,
Still gazing back down the iron track,
Waited alone in the rain.

The hours dragged by; it was dark and late.
The cars rushed on with their throbbing freight,
Screaming a laugh at her pain.
But the West uncurtained a wide, clear space,
And the sunset lighted a laggard face,
And the wild, wet day stole in smiles away,
While two hurried home in the rain.

NEW YORK OCTOBER 1, 1859

FALLING LEAVES.

BY JOHN BROUGHAM.

When Winter winds are wailing,
And death rides on the breeze,
With icy breath assailing
The stark and sapless trees,—

It grieves us not to see,
For 'tis their time to die,
And with all nature wither
The leaves that round us lie.

But when the day is teeming
With life, and love, and light,
And in our path is beaming,
The sun-ray of delight;

It saddens us to see,
—Oh! 'tis a mournful thing,
They should untimely perish,
The leaves that fall in Spring!

What though young life has parted
From earth ere Spring has past!
Or old and weary-hearted,
It yields to Winter's blast!

Grieve not, but humbly bend
Submissive to the call;
Nor scorn their simple teaching,
The leaves that around us fall.

[APROPOS OF MICHELET'S "LOVE."]

L'AMOUR.

Que qu' e' est q' ça?

—OR—

LOVE, WHAT IS IT?

BY A POOR YOUNG MAN.

With a Preface which has nothing to do with Fanny.

Done into English, for the NEW-YORK SATURDAY PRESS,

BY FRANK WOOD.

To Madame MARIE-LOUISE-ROSE FORTIN, *Milkmaid at Gonesse*:

MY DEAR MADAME FORTIN:

While selling me, yesterday morning, my usual two-pence worth of milk, you kindly said to me:

"Please tell me, sir, of some nice little book, cheap, and not long, that I can read by myself at home, evenings, after having washed our youngster's face, and heard his prayers, before my man returns from his work."

And I answered you:

"Rest assured, my good Madame Fortin, that I will find it for you."

Whereupon I went out to look for it, and I have found it.

After having served your milk in the Faubourg Saint Germain, go into a bookstore, and ask for

L'AMOUR QU'EST CE QUE C'EST QUE CA?
PAR UN JEUNE HOMME PAUVRE.

It is just the thing you want.

I know very well you will object to me that love, at our age, is mere folly.

But I will reply by two songs of the day:

"C'est l'amour, l'amour, l'amour,
Qui fait le monde.
A la ronde
Et chaque jour,
A son tour,
Le monde fait l'amour."

That's one; and here is the other:

"Ah! que l'amour est agréable!
Il est de toutes les saisons.
Un bon bourgeois, dans sa maison,
Le dos au feu, le veutre à table."

And so on. The rest you must remember as well as I.

Yes, love, Madame Fortin, love is life.

At Rome, a gentleman, a poet—Ovid—courted the Princess Julia, own daughter of the Emperor Augustus —think of that!

And the Emperor Augustus, as was his right to do, exiled Ovid to a far-off country—to Moldavia, or Wallachia, or some such place.

Ovid had written *The Art of Love* in Latin verses. In France, in the time of Voltaire, another poet, Gentil Bernard, composed an *Art of Love* in French verse.

But, as he didn't court princesses, but only ordinary women, what could I you expect? *He* was not sent into exile.

Among us, too, though much later, a physician, Dr. Venette, published in prose a book entitled *Conjugal Love*, which has gone through thousands of editions, and is much sought after, now-a-days, by schoolboys in vacation time.

Finally, quite recently, a gray-haired professor, much loved by these same school-boys, after having given them, in prose, *L'Oiseau* and *L'Insecte*—two charming works—offers them a third, also in prose—*L'Amour*.

This, too, is nothing more nor less than *Conjugal Love*.

But M. Michelet, like a clever man, did not care to steal his title from Dr. Venette.

So at last, a perfect little jewel of a book has just appeared, with the name:

L'Amour qu'est-ce que c'est que ca?
Par un Jeune Homme Pauvre.

This miniature volume sums up and eclipses the four other chefs-d'œuvres.

And for several reasons:

To begin with—like the first, it is not written in Latin—a language which you cannot understand any more than I, Madame Fortin, though, to make an impression upon the vulgar, I pretend to have it at my fingers' ends.

Next, like the second and the first, it is not in poetry.

And you have told me fifty times that poetry was a bore.

And I have no trouble in believing you, when it is not that of Victor Hugo's or Lamartine's, or when it is M. Ponsard's.

Finally, if it is in prose, like the third and the fourth, it has the advantage over them of being infinitely shorter—that is to say, much less tedious. . . .

I had reached this point in my letter, my dear Madame Fortin, when a neighboring clock striking eight—I saw that I had no time to finish it, and that if I did not hurry to buy my daily two-pence worth of milk of you, you would have started for Gonesse.

But what was my joy in hearing you exclaim, the moment you saw me:

"Thank you, thank you, sir! I don't want that nice, little, cheap book, now. I have found a delightful one, namely:

L'Amour qu'est-ce que c'est que ca?
Par un Jeune Homme Pauvre.

And you praised it so that I blushed for the author, who is something of a relation, and a good deal of a friend, of mine.

However, I hadn't the courage to tear up my letter.

Que voulez-vous? Every one has his little spark of vanity.

And so, not being able to send it to you, I address it to the Public.

It is such a good child, that poor Public!

A Fat Critic.

L'AMOUR, QUE QU C'EST QU' CA?

I. Woman.

I.—"Sir, what is it that people love?"

A Gentleman.—"Why, woman to be sure. How stupid you are?"

Now since this gentleman was alone with me I conclude that I was stupid in asking him this question, since, after all, there is not a little truth in his answer.

I was by no means certain that it was woman that we love. Papa Feuillet maintains that the thing we should love best of all is a situation. He himself aspires to a nice little one at the hospital opposite the Pont des Arts. Meanwhile he carries on his little business in the Place de la Bourse, where he is one of the doorkeepers to the catacombs.

Between ourselves, he owes the public favor in which he is held to the prodigious dimensions of his shirt-collar.

But to go back to woman.

I don't know why, but I have imagined that women were all lunatics.

I have been assured that, like the moon, they renew themselves every month. To tell the truth I never could understand a word of it.

Woman does not talk much. Perhaps you think I am joking? Not at all! Woman gossips, tittle-tattles, but does not talk. She sighs, her bosom heaves, her eyelashes are drawn down that she may see the better and be the better seen; and if she, by accident, says anything, her voice is intermingled with sighs.

And "our hearts are at once moved by this ?" . . . Why, there is my portress, a woman who talks a great deal, and she has never produced any such effect upon me.

Woman is always an invalid, after the fashion of a barometer. Anything that makes us furious or sad, asserts itself in her by fever or languor.

My candor prevents my going into families, and yet it seems to me that I can divine the tasks falling respectively to husband and wife:

The husband has the preoccupation, the worriment and cares for the future.

The wife has the house to take care of, the family to care for.

If the man has any troubles, he is troubled, and that is all.

If the woman has troubles,—she is an invalid.

These reflections call up others, and I perceive that to become pedantic in these matters, it is only necessary to examine one's self.

The man should work for both,—more than that even, *he should earn enough for both.*

It would seem to me more rational to put it thus, for example: M. Clément Robert is a great novelist, who has written *The Four Sergeants of La Rochelle*, and Mme. Clémence Robert is a famous good cook, who, solely to retain the love of her husband, invented *les filets à la Châteaubriand.*

Suppose that I am in ordinary circumstances, and that I wish to get married. Before setting out in search of the woman to marry, I naturally ask myself this question:

Shall my beloved be rich or poor?

Since I am poor, I should prefer to have her rich—if fortune does not contribute happiness, it goes a great way towards it, but good sense, your great good sense, now says to you:

She should be gentle, trusting, willing to be guided, and, above all, fresh in heart.

All the rest is of secondary importance.

You must be a colonel on half-pay, a Polish refugee, a broken-down lawyer, or inventor of an exploded humbug to think otherwise.

If my papa Feuillet is not of my opinion, if all his poor children want to marry princesses, it is probably because that is the condition of mind necessary to enable him to get a place in the hospital before mentioned.

I pardon you, O my papa!

Of what nation shall my bride be?

It is perfectly understood that I am addressing myself to Frenchmen.

English women have such a decided passion for beef that a man who marries one of them must expect to see a *primo soprano*, who might have sung in the Sixtine Chapel, preferred, by assimilation, to himself.

The German women are faithful enough, but they speak a language which is very disagreeable to us Frenchmen. If I can judge by the Baden soldier, who mounts guard at the bridge of Kelh, the Germans have a way of asking you the time which sounds remarkably as if they were calling you "old rascal." Besides, I question if the love of sour-krout does not exclude sentiment.

The women of Spain treated Francis I. altogether too badly—for *la belle* Feronierè was as innocent as a white dove—for us not to be convinced of the antipathy of our temperaments.

If you have not Mario's voice, and marry an Italian woman, you are sure to find, some day or other, your conjugal security invaded by a *C* sharp.

The women of Turkey, Greece, Egypt, and all the Orientals generally—including the Algerians, who are of the South—do not know how to make the pot boil, and this might inconvenience a man who is not a millionaire.

I might tell you a great many bad things about the Russian and Chinese women,—the latter cannot maintain their equilibrium owing to the smallness of their feet—about the women of Holland, Belgium, and India, but I am obliged to confess that the limited education I have received compels me to abstain.

Papa Feuillet would marry Siamese sisters to a Mohamedan. He has married a certain M. Roswein, a German, to a certain Italian princess, whom he found in M. Théodore Barrière's "Marble Hearts," where she was known as *Marco.*

Although I have the most profound respect for my papa, I sent him off with a wasp in his ear the other day when he wanted to marry me to a Creole, who had played in comedy at the Odéon, who bore an English name, and who had learned to speak in the Arab tongue at the Porte-St-Martin.

Papa Feuillet is such a distinguished person that he is denied common sense.

I am sure that the author of the book, which I so desire, thinks as I do.

I will now sum up:

Should a Frenchman marry a Frenchwoman?

Yes.

To this question I add another, which the author, of whom I have just spoken, could not have thought of. Of what religion should the woman of your choice be?

For, in spite of any unsophisticatedness, I know that the choosing of a wife is more important than the choosing of a pair of boots or of a hat.

How annoying for a Protestant husband to hear his wife say: "I am going to confession."

How disagreeable for a Catholic wife, at the very moment that she is talking fondly with her husband, to see him escape from her and seek the farthest corner of his apartment, to meditate over some one hundred and seventy-five verses of the Bible!

And the Jews! good gracious!

Just imagine a Saturday, and a Catholic or Protestant wife, as her husband is about departing for the synagogue, saying in her most affectionate tones:

"My dear, I should so like to have some nice pork-chops for dinner!"

Think of the sufferings of a Turk whose wife should be addicted to blue colors!

Suppose that instead of being the son of M. Octave Feuillet, I am an earnest man, and tell me if I do not—jestingly—put my finger in one of the bloodiest wounds of the poor social body.

My answer is this:

Husband and wife must be of the same religion!

And the political opinion of the spouse?

No jesting here, if you please.

Madame de Girardin was a glorious woman.

But she is dead.

Madame Dudevant calls herself George Sand.

Then she is no longer marriageable.

While I am making these reflections, which may betray me, I meet a villager.

"Good day to you, sir," says a little old man to me. "You are very polite."

"There is no occasion to thank me, sir. But don't you know me? I am the shepherd of one of your papa's flocks."

"Ah! delighted to make your acquaintance. You haven't a small situation you could offer me, have you?"

"Not just at present, but——"

Here my papa's candid villager slips these words in my ear:

"*You* know how to read. Now, just give me a taste of this little book here."

And the old man inserts an old book, between the *Proverbs* and *Dalilah* that I have in my pocket.

Blush, chaste works of my father, that until now have grown yellow on the bookseller's shelves, at the neighborhood you are in!

It is a copy of a work which, formerly, was sold at the toy-shops: "The Tableau of Conjugal Love," by Doctor Venette.

Let us doubt Providence henceforth and pin our faith upon the candor of villagers.

You would hardly recognize me now. I have almost a mind to destroy the innocent reflections I made a little while ago. And spite of all, I yet ask myself:

What is love?

On the other hand I need no longer address this question to myself: What is pleasure?

O woman, thee whom we should adore, do not descend from thy pedestal. Remain yet a longer while to me a point of interrogation.

Woman is as she is made.

You must then create your wife.

The wife desires nothing better than to become the complement of the man. She wishes to belong to the man; she wants to be one with him; she does not want to walk, see, think, but through him; she wants to be entirely his.

This is her greatest desire, stronger in her than all the sentiment, all the joys, and all the passions.

She will forget, in order to assimilate herself to him, to submit to him, that she has a mind, a soul, that she has a higher calling, that she has a religion, a father, a God.

Because, when she shall have submitted herself, abased herself—when she shall have crawled at the feet of the man, then she will rise, proudly, and the mistress, she "will haughtily hold out her foot or her hand to the kisses which, but a moment ago, she begged for."

In your turn, man, you beg, because you are subjugated.

Have you not discovered, in six thousand years, what a ridiculous part you play?

You drag the purple of the rulers upon the floor of the temple of your pride.

You are the strongest—physically—and you consign your wife to the kitchen.

When you eat, you make her wait on you.

Beware of the apple of old mother Eve.

She prays you to accept . . . . You consent.

Then she bursts out laughing.

And the woman is right.

She has a right to mock at you in the hour of her triumph—she whom you have steeped in humiliation and neglect;

She, whom you regard as an article of merchandise;

She, whose looks are sold by traffickers to serve man purposes;

She, whom we force to descend into life's realities and who, through some outlandish inclination, is sometimes metamorphosed into a blue-stocking;

She, whom we associate with our whole lives and whom we ought to deify;

She, whom we force to sweep the streets;

She, whom we place unguarded in a large city, and whom we abandon to her fate;

She, to whom we owe a temple and whom we let perish in abodes of wretchedness;

She, whom we strike down by brute force and then throw into a chasm;

She, whom we scoff at, whom we despise, whom we put a price upon, and whom, finally, we murder.

Ah! yes! she has a good right to reject us with disdain when she is tired of our embraces;

She, who gives us life;

She, who gives us that which alone renders life supportable or possible.

But again I ask: What is love?

———

II. Reciprocal Love.

Let us agree to one thing.

You have forgotten, madame, while touching with your ruby lips a glass of *eau sucrée*—you, sir, while smoking your cigar—that but a short time ago a poor young man did some very romantic things apropos of pleasure.

You will leave the young man to his transports, I suppose, with a great deal of satisfaction, in order to chat quietly with the man of the world, who has your mutual confidence.

What influence can you have over a woman in society? None at all. In solitude? Every Influence.

These are two complete truths, since we take as the basis of all our reasoning what we have the foolish vanity to call social order.

Now, solitude is a myth, in these times.

Though fifty leagues away, you can hear the echoes of Paris.

One way remains to you, sir, to have a wife :

Marry one.

Here is a young girl, and a pretty one, notwithstanding that her waist is pinched by a corset.

She is *spirituelle*, although she does play on the piano.

You know how much money her father has got.

Everything goes well, and she is handed over to you.

Mark, in passing, that she is, as usual, but the bonus of the bargain entered into by her father and yourself.

The marriage ceremony takes place. The guests utter their congratulations, and depart. The door is closed upon you. And now, if not boors, you both feel very silly. You are embarrassed, and your wife begins to cry. If you take her to be in earnest, you are an ass.

For the first time the young girl is in a nuptial chamber. She at once becomes conscious of her power, and makes you appear ridiculous.

Why does it always happen thus?

Because, in both of you, something is wanting. I do not know in what you are deficient, because no one has yet answered my question: What is love?

If you are what I suppose you to be—a high-minded person, you will spare the woman whom society has confided to you.

She will be grateful for this kind act. She will thank you when she awakens. This is what is called *the morning gift*. And your wife will, moreover, esteem you.

Dine at home as much as possible. *Narrow the home circle. The wife's presence does not distract the husband from his work.*

A kiss will repose your mind. If you are in want of a word to finish a letter, give your wife a kiss, and the word will flow at once from your pen.

Only, do not initiate her in the details of your labor or your profession. If you have a beginning of poetic aspiration, and are no more than a quarter of an inch above M. Joseph Prud'homme, do not descend from that elevation.

It is the hour of your daily repast.

Your wife has divined your taste. You find everything excellent.

Here is her favorite dish. She tastes it and expresses her satisfaction.

"Eat this, my dear, for I have tasted it."

If you do not think the dish delicious, you deserve to be set at breaking stones in the road at sixpence the yard.

You have no need of servants in your home. Do as if you had none.

You should wait on each other.

If you have a servant girl, and if during the conjugal téte-à-téte at table, you look at that servant girl, your wife has a right to be jealous.

She sees that you are so ugly when you eat that she has a right to think herself ugly also.

And she is perfectly right in thinking so.

The other day I saw one of the prettiest women of Paris. She was eating sausages. And at that moment I would have preferred all the blue-stockings in the capital to her.

Do not talk while eating, because in the first place, you will soil your napkin, and then it hinders digestion.

You cannot imagine how serious I am in writing down this reflection. A good digestion is much more important, in married life, than one thinks.

The wife must read light authors, like Alexandre Dumas, for instance.

Not Paul de Kock nor Balzac.

Above all, not books written by women, even Mme. de Girardin's. The disease may be catching.

It is best that the wife should read but little. *She must preserve the velvet-down of her soul.*

There! I think that happiness has been pretty well planned in this chapter, and yet I do not find here any more than elsewhere, the answer to my question: What is love?

III. Papa and Mamma.

The time comes when the spouse say to themselves: "What will it be?"

And conjecture follows conjecture.

It is for the wife a joy mingled with fear, for she foresees what she must one day suffer.

She also foresees the pleasantness, the sublime, the divine joys of that holy thing which we call maternity!

And the husband?

He feels that he is good for something, entirely distinct from social order. Something which atones for many shortcomings of education, talent, and experience.

He has cooperated in the great work; he has endowed the infinite with something more.

He has procreated his kind!

Let me take you aside; vulgar man,

You, who represent nine-tenths of your species,

You, who are the slave of circumstances,

You, enthusiastic in your greed, which you transform into a virtue by calling it economy,

You, the selfish man, who married a woman because she had more money than you,

You, who foresee that with an increase of family the expenses of the household will increase,

Listen to me, and tell me if I do not speak the truth:

If it were not for *the law*, the only thing that is great, because it intimidates,

Or if you did not fear that your neighbor would find it out and denounce you,

If you had not a religion, dragging after it its hell,

If you did not tremble, finally, ...

You are going to say, "I should like to have *one*."

Very well, it will be reserved for the second, then.

. . . .

Your poignard is dulled, the poison is weak, and the powder is damp.

You have not succeeded.

You are like an assassin, who finds his victim absent.

Is he any the less an assassin?

But you are either a whole-souled man, or you wish to have your first child live.

How beautiful your wife is, and how kind, too; how frankly she caresses you; what a profound friendship you have for each other! There is more than habit in this. The months roll on, fly past, and the fifth arrives. Your wife is not so affectionate now.

She seems to divide her affections, and give that which is habitual alone to you.

You have a rival!

Soon she becomes fitful and waspish. Her wishes run counter to your own.

Do not resist. She is no longer playing a part, she is not now the woman who was testing you, she is the woman who loves some one more than you. Nature has given her the faculty of loving the child that she bears—without this, she would die when her time of suffering came.

Have pity on her, and yield to her. It is not her yoke that you bear, it is that of Nature.

If you submit, she will resign herself to you.

The child is born.

She has had her share of the pain, of intense, incalculable, unheard of pain: take, then, your share of annoyance and trouble.

I shall descend even further into the reality. Do not think that you can demean yourself at this supreme moment.

Disdain nothing; the most ridiculous details are now no longer such.

Do not say "I am going for assistance." No. Act for yourself. Do not assist at everything, but do everything.

Do you not know that on such occasions one makes blunders which are sublime?

And if you should make her laugh a little, where would be the harm? Her laugh is not of derision, it is of joy.

But you are going to say to me: "Come, who are you? By what right do you give me advice?"

"I am a poor young man, and I do not know anything. I made myself a man of proper feeling for an instant, because I did not know before what pleasure was, and now I do know what it is, and what are its consequences.

Nature says this also, as well as I. As for the book in question, it ought to say so, too.

But if I know what pleasure is, and what its consequences are, I do not yet know what Love is.

So I still ask myself that everlasting question :

What is Love?

(To be continued next week.)

444 **BROADWAY.**

MR. HENRY WOOD

has great satisfaction in announcing that he has

AT IMMENSE EXPENSE

effected an engagement wtth the

MOST WONDERFUL

COMIC VOCALIST

OF THE AGE.

MR. SAM. COWELL,

whose extraordinary impersonations of character have been received with

ACCLAMATIONS OF DELIGHT

by the press and public of

NEW YORK,

and who has been pronounced the

GREATEST BUFFO SINGER

IN THE WORLD.

He will appear

TUESDAY,

THURSDAY, and

SATURDAY EVENINGS,

and will discourse, in his

INIMITABLE STYLE,

MUSICALLY AND DRAMATICALLY, UPON

THE GENERAL TOPICS OF THE DAY.

This sterling combination,

THE UNITED TALENT

OF THE

GREATEST COMIC VOCALIST

WITH THE

MOST UNRIVALLED

BAND OF MINSTRELS

IN THE CITY,

offers a variety of attractions

AS UNAPPROACHABLE AS IT IS DELIGHTFUL.

MR. SAM. COWELL'S

POPULAR COMIC CONCERTS

will be continued every

MONDAY,

WEDNESDAY, and

FRIDAY,

AT THE FRENCH THEATRE.

ADELAIDE CORTESI.

"Oh, Music! how in every charm supreme,
  Thy votaries feast on raptures ever new;
Oh! for the voice and fire of seraphim,
  To sing thy glories, with devotion due !"

Six months ago Adelaide Cortesi was an unknown name to me; now she seems a part of the world's patrimony. Six months ago, a few modest lines in the daily papers, announced that Mr. Strakosch had made an engagement with the lyric tragédienne Cortesi. One then asked of another, who and what she was, but none knew, no eye had seen, no ear heard her. Perhaps this very fact helped to fill the house on the occasion of her début; at any rate a vast and curious assemblage sat before the curtain, awaiting the appearance of the unknown artiste behind it.

No one who was present at that moment, will easily forget the explosion of applause which greeted her; even as Juno, she was known by the roseate curve of her neck, before she turned her regal eyes, for the queen of men and the gods. Then she sang, and how all the recollections of the little, the flimsey, the worn out, the artificial voices, we have been fed upon recently, faded away before the full flood-tide of her vast and exuberant voice.

The Opera was *Sappho*, that melancholy story, which Nature is ever repeating, and Cortesi enacted the heroine. This indeed was that Sappho, before the eloquence of whose clarion voice, the wills of the multitude were stricken down, as the high corn is driven earthward before the breath of the fiery South wind. From first to last, the living Sappho, the unhappy love-poet walked, and spoke, and breathed before us. The whole orbit of the passion was trodden through before our eyes. From the first triumphant entry of one whose hands are filled with the palms of victory, and whose pathway is paved with the world's worship, to the trembling pathos of love, in which music floated from her lips soft and low, as though she sang not, but breathed it off like perfume from the tropical langour of her red lips. From the first sickening pangs of doubt and jealousy, to the last cries of tortured hope, and of a stricken but unutterably longing love. From the blackest fury of revenge and hate, to the calm of resignation and death. Who could forget the unhappy Sappho in the last sad scene, as all pale and chill she advances trembling and slow, bearing in her hand the lyre whose chords her hands were never more to touch. First the low, shivering notes on which the heart hung mute and panting; then the sudden kindling of the eye, as it seemed to catch sight of some heavenly vision, the mild and eager notes which followed her eyes to the gods, the voice that seemed to throb with the crimson heart-beats of love, as it strained for the last time, the darling desire to the soul, then leaped with one great gasp upon its dissolution. The eyes, fast growing wide and vacant, fixed themselves on awful space, the stiffening hands refused to hold the lyre, though the fingers went on groping for music-chords in the silent air, while the white lips gave out its notes like moans. Then the soul, breaking suddenly through the anguish of death, sprang up with immortality on its lips, to roll out its grand, triumphant anthem, the echo of whose magnificent mass of sound seemed to rock the building on its foundation, even as it rocked the hearts of men in their breasts, till the whole house was shaken, as by an earthquake of applause.

It may be that I am speaking wildly of the great cantatrice, but there will be too many to speak of the faults in her vocalization, flexibility, style, etc. For my own poor and unlettered part, I will judge of music as it speaks to the heart; I will not ask science to prove it for me. It needs no mathematical demonstration, to be truly felt, unless music, the highest among high arts, is a mere combination of scientific and mechanical sounds, reducible to rule like Custom House business and Algebra. If so, farewell Rossini, and welcome Babbage's calculating machine.

I will dare to avow that for force and earnestness, for passionate vigor and intensity, for large and all-embracing musical conception, for divine abandon of effort and feeling, I know not with whom this artiste can be matched. She is head and shoulders above them all. With this infinite breadth of power, how should her faults be compared with those of others? The line may be the arc of a circle, but we must also estimate the size of the circle it describes. Its curve may descend only to span the entire world of art.

Madame Cortesi, strictly speaking, is not handsome; but her face is easily moulded to the emotion it would express. Her form, and arm, and neck, could not be improved, neither could her eye be brightened. She is apparently young, in full physical health, which, together with her great voice, enthusiasm, and fine intelligence, ensures her a career of triumph, which cannot be limited. Her voice is of the true declamatory style; eloquence, action, creation, are the natural pulses of her life. The folds of her robe flow after her in the measures of stately verse; there is rythm in the droop of her eyelids, and the swelling of her breast beats time to the cadences of unheard music.

The wondrous successes she has achieved in this country, are more than a personal fame; they are a vindication of truth. Unknown, unheralded, she has stormed that fortress of the public, which transatlantic reputation, ushered in with the blowing of trumpets, and the roar of journalistic drums, has so often vainly assailed. Like Medea, she alone has done it, she has planted her colors on the bulwarks of universal praise; long, long may they wave there, as the immortal blue of heaven.

Truth, after all, alone triumphs; evil and error have in themselves the essential seeds of failure; however long that seed may be hidden and lifeless, it is sure in the end to germinate and grow into a noxious and fatal plant.

No senseless rumors of princess and cardinal, of title and royal favor, for this Adelaide Cortesi; they would glare like guilty tinsel on the crown which none can tear off from her brow. We *must* reverence her. We all love, venerate, and bow down submissively before great women; nay, we cannot honestly bow down to anything else. For such great women, nature keeps a stamp, which will not let us mistake them. If we see them not, we look into our hearts only, and we see a cherub that sees them.

Fortunately for the very existence of this haggard world, there exists between true genius—the divine *spiritus*—and all spurious imitations of it, however cunningly devised and assiduously persisted in, a differential calculus, diverging at a geometrical ratio too vast for human arithmetic to compute. Yes, the profane vulgar *can* set their feet upon the threshhold of the temple, *can* creep into the outer courts, but *cannot* enter the innermost sanctuary; erelong there is a fire in the way, in which would explode their volume of gas, and their waxen wings be melted away, but genius wrapped in the Olympic *asbestos*, treads unscathed through the flames.

Genius, thou only glorious image on this dusky globe!—thou true statue of Memnon, in whose choral melody we read the rising of every new sun of hope for the world!—we the true hero-worshippers, and the world's recognized fools, clasping thy feet, make offering to thee of all that we have—our living hearts! Perchance, in the ears of the Gods, these tributary heart-cries sound like voices of thunders, compared with which, the clamorous acclamations of ten thousand heartless lips, nay, even the very artillery of heaven, may seem like the silence of planets extinct!

ADA CLARE.

NEW YORK OCTOBER 8, 1859

THE BORE OF THE SANCTUM.

BY JOHN G. SAXE.

Again I hear that creaking step!
He's rapping at the door!
Too well I know the boding sound
That ushes in a bore.
I do not tremble when I meet
The stoutest of my foes,
But Heaven defend me from the friend
Who comes but never goes.

He drops into my easy-chair,
And asks about the news;
He peers into my manuscript,
And gives his candid views;
He tells me where he likes the line,
And where he's forced to grieve;
He takes the strangest liberties—
But never takes his leave!

He reads my daily paper through
Before I've seen a word;
He scans the lyric (that I wrote),
And thinks it quite absurd;
He calmly smokes my last cigar,
And coolly asks for more;
He opens everything he sees—
Except the entry-door.

He talks about his fragile health,
And tells me of the pains
He suffers from a score of ills,
Of which he ne'er complains;
And how he struggled once with death
To keep the fiend at bay;
On themes like those away he goes—
But never goes away!

He tells me of the carping words
Some shallow critic wrote,
And every precious paragraph
Familiarly can quote.
He thinks the writer did me wrong,
He'd like to run him through!
He says a thousand pleasant things—
But never says "*Adieu* !"

Whene'er he comes—that dreadful man—
Disguise it as I may,
I know that like an Autumn rain,
He'll last throughout the day.
In vain I speak of urgent tasks;
In vain I scowl and pout;
A frown is no extinguisher—
It does not put him out!

I mean to take the knocker off;
Put crape upon the door;
Or hint to John that I am gone
To stay a month or more.
I do not tremble when I meet
The stoutest of my foes;
But Heaven defend me from the friend
Who never, never goes!

LABOR

BY N. P. ROGERS.

I deny that Labor ought to be degraded, or ought to starve. I am bold to deny it. I hazard the startling assertion, that Work ought not to go hungry, or naked, but have something to eat, and to wear. I say nobody, that earns a living by labor, ought to go without it, and I might venture further—that nobody, able to labor, but who does not labor, ought to have a living. I would give them one for the honor of the race, or as God sends rain on the unjust, but they do not deserve it. No laborer should want, and no idler should enjoy, and no man has a right to be idle. He may be for all *me*, but not for all himself. He owes it to himself, to earn his bread at the least,—and to earn it by useful labor, and not useless—much less mischievous labor,—as too many earn, or get it by now. Further, as no man has a right to be idle, and live on the earnings of others, so no man ought to be obliged to support the idle, or to labor much (if any) beyond support of himself. There ought, of course, to be labor enough done on the earth, to support all its inhabitants, richly and if it were properly shared, no one would need do more, and none would do less. Men have no right to overwork themselves, if they can help it. They owe it to their nature and to God, who is dishonored (if that is possible) in its degradation. It is in derogation of glorious human nature, to overwork it, and more grossly so, to have it slothful and idle, and basely live on the unrequited toil of others.

Every one owes it to himself, as well as to his otherwise overburdened and injured neighbor, to do manual labor enough, to earn the bread he consumes, and all his support. He must earn it for himself, or somebody else must earn it for him, which is clearly wrong. He may say he pays for his support, but he ought to consider that he pays money that is not his own,—for he did not earn it—and social combinations that cast it upon him, are vicious, and in violation of human welfare and right. I would not disturb them violently —but I think they are wrong, and will say so.

If everybody worked as much as they ought to, nobody would be obliged to work more than they ought to, which would be a mighty amelioration of human condition and character. A people broken down with labor, whether free labor (so called) or slave, must be morally degraded. It is easy for a Priesthood to ride such a people. They have not the leisure, nor the elasticity of soul to appreciate or assert their own freedom. Their backs are bowed down, like a kneeling camel's, and the Priest mounts them easily, and rides all their miserable lives long.

Everybody ought to earn his own living by manual labor, and if practicable, had better earn thus much, by cultivating the face of the ground. To say nothing of the healthfulness of such labor and the enjoyment of it,—which everybody needs—there is an independence about it, a certainty of remuneration, that human injustice or folly cannot defeat. And then it is due the face of our mother earth. The glorious old mother, her children (for they all repose in her motherly lap) owe it to her, to keep her whole face, where there is terra firma for the noble plow, dressed to her taste and their own. They ought to deck her "universal face in pleasant green." And labor enough done by all, to earn their living, would do it. There need not a man overtoil himself, to turn all earth into a paradise,—a fit abode for gods—and godlike creatures would then inhabit it. Mechanical labor is useful, necessary, honorable. But prosecuted constantly and uninterruptedly, it is not so healthful or pleasant as when mingled with the cultivation and adornment of the earth, nor so sure of requital. He who vests his labor in the faithful ground is dealing directly with God, and human fraud or weakness does not intervene between him and his requital. He is very apt to get his reward. The mechanic is quite apt to fail of his. No mechanic has a set of customers equally trustworthy as God and the elements,—or so unfailingly able, as well as willing to pay. No savings bank even is so sure as the old earth, to restore all its deposits, and with overflowing and gushing usury. Every mechanic knows his own condition best, perhaps. But am I extravagant in saying it would be well for every one to cultivate the earth enough to raise his own support? There is enough earth for all—provided humanity could be allowed to come on to it and dig.

The earth is as fine a one as God could furnish us. I don't believe the Clergy or the Legislature could better it or our honester friends who are looking for the Prince of Peace to come with the torch of the incendiary and set it a-fire. I tell our conflagration friends, by the way, if Christ touches match to this glorious earth of ours (which if He be God, He made to the best of His Almighty skill) and burns it up—or burns a single human creature that sins and suffers on its surface, He is not the "Son of Man" revealed in the New Testament. There is not a trait of character of Him, delineated in the Gospel, that such an act would not violate and outrage. No, let no such inflammatory scenes be anticipated. Would we burn the earth, and our miserable neighbors, if we felt right towards them? No—nor if we felt right, should we ever expect God would do any such thing. It is only when we are wrong and wicked, ourselves, that we clothe our God with such an incendiary and revengeful disposition. Nero set Rome a-fire and played on the fiddle at sight of the conflagration—Nero would most naturally attribute to God the disposition he was then manifesting.

But the earth is as beautiful as God could make it. They complain of its being cursed. The only curse now resting on it, it seems to me, is the curse of an indolent, idle tyranny, and the curse of down-trodden, back-broken labor. No wonder the earth is cursed and blasted. See war let loose upon it, under the sanction of religion, to devastate what poor, desponding Labor has done towards its adornment. See how it drives its harnessed horses through the harvest field, and ruts it with its accursed cannon-wheels, and tears the sweet green sward with its murderous shot. And how it mows down the laborers, manuring the earth with their bones. That is all war ever does for agriculture. It manures the ground with the blood and the bones of the cultivator. Waterloo, they say, was made fat in this way, by that darling system of Kings and Clergy. They rained blood on that field, and the plaster of Paris they spread on for manure, was the bleached and powdered bones of the soldiery.

THE NEW LIFE OF HUMBOLDT.

THE LIFE, TRAVELS, AND BOOKS OF ALEXANDER VON HUMBOLDT: *With an Introduction by* BAYARD TAYLOR, *New York*: RUDD & CARLETON. 1859.

The Life and Travels of Humboldt, recently published by Rudd & Carleton, is the best popular biography we have ever read.

But to us, personally, popular biographies are very unattractive objects.

They generally contain a vast array of what are supposed, by the imaginative, to be facts. These facts are usually awkwardly arranged and grimly uninteresting. It would seem as if the compiler attempted to put all the stupidity of two or three hundred volumes into one.

And he generally succeeds.

Every lover of books does not, unfortunately, have access to libraries. He must depend upon the taste and assiduity of compilers for the cream of literature; and to him, much in little, condensed biographies, compendiums, and cyclopædias (when they are worth anything) are invaluable. To such a reader we commend the present work as a carefully prepared biography of the great modern traveller, "the greatest man since the Deluge," as Alexander I. of Russia, was pleased to term him. This volume is probably the most complete life of Humboldt that has appeared up to the present time, whether in German or English; indeed, it is the best that can be written until the personal friends or relations of Humboldt furnish the world with fresh material.

Mr. Stoddard—we believe it is generally understood that Mr. R. H. Stoddard is the author of the volume, though his name is wanting on the title-page—has evidently spared no pains to produce an accurate and readable book; he has availed himself judiciously of the labors of those who have preceeded him, and prepared from a bewildering mass of rambling facts, a connected, succinct, and readable history. Parts of the narrative are given in Humboldt's own words, and none could be more picturesque; but wherever the author himself has taken up the thread of the story, he is sensible, untechnical, and inviting. His style is particularly clear and fluent.

As the social life of Von Humboldt does not appear to lie within the scope of Mr. Stoddard's plan, we cannot, of course, complain at finding no record of the many years which the savant passed in Paris—no record save a mention of the works which he there prepared for the press.

Mr. Taylor's Introduction contains a pleasant description of Humboldt's personal appearance, and a warm tribute to his memory, but aside from that—with all due respect—it is hardly a valuable addition to the book. The merit of the work itself is its best recommendation.

Taking into consideration the fact that Mr. Stoddard is a man of genius, his success in biographical writing is somewhat noticeable.

Men of genius should seldom or never write biographies, for they seldom if ever succeed. They become enamored of their biographé; they wrap his failings in elegant periods; they magnify his virtues with a double convex lens; they celestialise and etherealise him,—in short, they create such an ideal man that his own mother wouldn't know him from a plaster-of-Paris bust of Apollo.

If this does not happen, it is because the biographer rushes to the other extreme, and sits on the pedestal himself.

Carlyle's "Life of Sterling," for instance.

Sterling was a—well, he was one of those extraordinary persons who are always on the point of doing something splendid, and never do. Carlyle is a man with imagination enough to mistake a pebble-stone for a kho-i-noor. The result was, he made Sterling seem like a genius, when, in truth, Sterling wasn't much of anything in particular.

Mr. Stoddard has had the good sense not to be carried away by his subject; and was too modest to be carried away by himself.

A Sweet Man.

A Council of Ministers of the Christian Baptist persuasion was held at Warren, Mass, on Wednesday, to investigate the following charges made against the Rev. S. K. Sweetman, of Boston, Mass.: the publication of an unclerical pamphlet; making false representations to a Bristol church, in order to hurry it into a bargain; borrowing a shirt and not returning it; sermon-stealing, and advertising for a wife while his third one was still living.

Dramatic Feuilleton.

All About Nothing.

Nary Feuilleton.

Who, pray, can construct such a thing (whatever it is) out of Nothing?

Not Personne with all his esprit;

Nor the Baron;

Nor the Brightest and Best;

Nor the Youngest and Loveliest ;

Nor even the Oldest Man himself;

Much less the Undersigned.

The age of miracles and things has passed, and a Feuilleton can no more be made out of such material than a fish can be made out of water, or a novel out of the depths.

And there is absolutely no other material at hand; for as for "Dot," and the "Sea of Ice," and "Paul Pry," and the Rivals,' and the "Road to

Ruin " (over the left)—they are as useless, just now, for all feuilletonic purposes, as a last year's almanac.

Wherefore, Personne, weary and disgusted, casteth down his great pen as who should say: "Let who will take it up, I'll have none of it."

And lo! I,—I Quelqu' un,—who am ready to take up anything, except a note, at a moment's warning and without grace, have just the requisite amount of audacity for the act ("Fools rush in" etc.) and am in truth, at this instant, grappling with the aforesaid pen as fearlessly and flippantly as if I were a veteran Feuilletonist like Jules Janin, or Burkhardt,—I, who hardly know what a Feuilleton is, and if I did, couldn't probably write one to save my life—least of all a Dramatic Feuilleton, which, though I have been a diligent and delighted reader of Personne from the beginning—is a greater mystery to me now than ever.

All I know of it is that it is something more or less droll about theatres and things, written in a saucy, nondescript, "you're another" sort o' style, and leaving actors, actresses, managers, play-wrights, play-goers, and ye general reader, in a state of utter despair,—refusing, like M'lle Rachel, to be comforted.

It is the same thing in France,—where, I am told, the Feuilleton originated,—and it is ditto here, where (no offence to Baron de Trop) Personne has introduced it, and where (no offence to the wit of the *Dispatch*) he reigns supreme, with no one free to carp at him but Anna Maria, and no one privileged to approach him but the Undersigned.

Lucky Personne !

Luckier Anna Maria!

Luckiest Undersigned!

And now that I have had the audacity to seize upon our dear Feuilletonist's pen, and for topics have the town before me where to choose, what in the name of Jenkins shall I feuilletonize about?

I began with the startling assertion that a Feuilleton could not be made out of Nothing.

Why not?

Especially since Nothing can be made out of a Feuilleton.

The world itself was made out of Nothing, and a very good world, my sirs, it is. The Legislature itself could hardly make a better, with Meriam to help it.

Again, don't you know, reader, that poetry itself is made out of Nothing?

"Nary Nothing," exclaims Parmenter.

And echo answers: "Airy Nothing."

If you doubt it, buy the last new poetry-book [*EarthSongs; or Pomes de Terre*], and see.

Nothing set to rhyme, and sliced up into verses, makes the most charming nonsense in the world; and but for nonsense—dear, delicious nonsense!—we should all go rank crazy.

Your sensible man—to whom a "subject" is as necessary as to a dissecter—is always a bore; while as for sensible women—why, under favor of the sex, I never saw but one in my life, and Page's "Wenus" forbid that I should ever see another.

Sense, in fact, is good for nothing except to aid us in grubbing after what Branch calls the "insensate mineral."

And what do Feuilletonists and Poets care about that?

Ask Personne.

Ask Aldrich.

Ask the Undersigned.

I know that the Oldest Man can't see this; but the Oldest Man can't see anything. He is *all* can't; or rather, he is what Shakspere calls

—a purblind Argus,
All eyes and no sight.

He can't see Cortesi.

He can't see Geraldine.

He can't see (or didn't) the Aurora Borealis.

He can't see the Great Eastern.

He can't see (who but Yeadon can ?) the great "Orator, Patriot, Sage, Cicero of America, Laudator of Washington, Apostle of Charity, High Priest of the Union, and Friend of Mankind,"

And now he is preparing not to see Speranza and Sam Cowell!

Pauvre Aveugle!

He sees nothing but the American Eagle, the Star-Spangled Banner (not Bonner), and THE SATURDAY PRESS.

Perhaps the latter has, at last, made him.

Blind from excess of light!

But, after all, "there are none so blind" (I wonder, though, if this hasn't been said before) "as those who won't see."

And the Old Man won't even go to see—the old land-lubber!

But I am right, in this matter of sense, whether the Old Man sees it or not.

The world is too sensible by half. This "rush of brains to the head" will be the death of it.

John Brougham ruined his last comedy simply by putting too much sense in it.

As though you could make a Ruling Passion out of sense.

Nonsense!

Sense never did rule in this world (" since gentlemen came up "), and never will again.

If it should, we should all become idiots in the flower of our youth.

Some of us have, as it is.

Why did people run after "Our American Cousin,' and after "The Veteran ?" And why do they run after "Dot," and "Garibaldi," and the "Sea of Ice ?" Because there is no sense in them—that is, what the world calls sense.

Tilly Slowboy is as nonsensical a person as there is out; and, for that matter, so is John Peerybingle, and Dot his wife, and Bertha, and Caleb Plummer (awfully nonsensical he is), and Edward Plummer his son, and Tackelton, and, in fact, the whole crowd of 'em.

But how charming they all are, to be sure, and how they make us all in love (within the statutes) with Mrs. Wood, and Agnes Robertson, and Sarah Stevens, and Awful Jefferson, and Harry Pearson, and (though not quite so much) Mr. T. B. Johnson, and the latter-day Fairies!

I have seen them (Dot bless 'em!) now four times, and each time went home in the most nonsensical state of mind possible. The next day I didn't know the multiplication table from the breakfast table, and a jolly Briton who went with me the last time was reduced to such a condition that he couldn't distinguish between the British Lion and the American Eagle (dear bird!), and mistook McWatters, the policeman, for one—or the whole—of the "All-England Eleven."

And half a dozen lagers taken at Pfaff's immediately after, didn't help him in the least.

Nor me either.

We loafed there, and talked over the piece and its nonsensicalities, for over an hour, and then as my friend lives near the Battery and I near the Reservoir, we separated,—he going due North (like Sala) and I due South,—so that neither of us reached home, as you may imagine, till the hard-hearted old clock had done striking its little ones, and—but this sentence is long enough already.

Now if "Dot" had been a "good, old-fashioned, sensible play," we should both have been bored half to death by it, and then should have gone straight home like a couple of well-regulated automata without night-keys.

All which, being interpreted, means that the Undersigned, having nothing whatever to write about, and feeling, in consequence, much more like a fool than a feuilletonist (if the distinction is to be kept up), was driven to pitch into sensible folks and things generally, as the only dodge left to him

And having gone and done it, he now makes his humblest apology and bow, exclaiming at the top of his lungs, and from the bottom of his heart:

Long live THE SATURDAY PRESS !
Long live Personne !
Long live the Brightest and Best!
Long live the Youngest and Loveliest !
Long live the Undersigned!

GREEN SEAL.

QUELQ'UN.

"GERALDINE."

Mrs. Bateman's "Geraldine, or Love's Victory," continues to draw immense houses in Boston. The *Post* of October 3, has the following upon it :—

"Geraldine" is a blossom of literature the full beauties of which are not revealed at the first glance. But as the sun of popular favor shines upon it, and as the spectator returns periodically to inspect it, it slowly unfolds itself and displays by degrees the secrets of beauty hidden in its bosom. This general revealment of the interior genius we have witnessed, and in this reluctance of disclosure we think we see the secret which night after night attracts the same persons to the boxes of the Howard, and binds them there as if with a spell. Seriously, and without exaggeration, we say we think it impossible to find in the range of the modern drama a grander conclusion than that with which the first act of "Geraldine" terminates. In the midst of a scene of splendid revelry, when the head of the wild boar smokes on the ample board, and the red wine has gone round, and the smiles of the high-born ladies of the Castle have blessed with their sunshine the purple libations, the grey-haired, mysterious minstrel enters. He brings with him a presentment of evil. There is death and danger in the air. The fires of prophecy sparkle in his eyes. The antique Nemesis seems to have come again, and a thrill, silent but visible, runs through the gay throng—the chill of impending disaster. His chant commences. To wild sweeps of the harp he recites his tragical allegory. As in each succeeding verse the hidden sense of the fable dawns on the mind of the guilty baron, and on the obtuse brains of the retainers, the dark truth impresses itself, the sensation that stirs the throng deepens, and murmurs of indignation creep from lip to lip like the sounds of the sea when storms approach. At last the fierce old singer launches his final bolt. The conscience-stricken lord leaps to his feet wild with rage. The sounds of strife and imprecations ring throughout the hall. The daughter of the House, pale, trembling, but amazed, rises in terror at this unwonted tumult. She strives to interfere, and most unexpectedly upon her head pours the awful curse from the lips of the minstrel. In vain she pleads for mercy. The relentless tongue speaks on, and the curtain falls on a situation which for dramatic force has never been excelled. Nor are the succeeding scenes much less effective. That wild, terrible entrance of the poor girl when, for the first time hearing whispers of her deformity, with the quick utterance of acute anguish she questions the crafty Prior. The scene of the intended murder reveals one of the most beautiful speeches in the piece. The Prior, who has been inciting murderous thoughts in Geraldine's brain, by suggesting the criminal love of her sister, asks her what she intends doing with the guilty Edith. With poetic subtlety she explains her murderous plan—she will "recall the wandering angel back that watched her childhood's hours." This is an exquisite figurative method of stating an unpleasant and repulsive resolve. Then the serious equivoque with which Geraldine answers the Prior, who, believing that she has assassinated Edith, questions her with thirsty malice, while she who has only killed herself replies that "the life which stood twixt Hubert and long years of wedded love is ebbing fast away." This ambiguous answer leads to one of the great situations of the play, when Edith alive and uninjured enters, summoned by the wild cry of her penitent and heroic sister, and confounds the baffled ecclesiastic with her presence. It is this rare mixture of effective dramatic situation and sterling mellifluous poetry that constitutes the merit and secures the success of "Geraldine." It is various in its character, well constructed in all the essentials of the drama, and written with an ease and fire that will forever render it a conspicuous production of the times.

Theatrical, Musical, etc.

—The Boston *Post* furnishes the following list of salaries paid by the opera management per month: Mme. Cortesi, $2,500; Mme. Gassier, $2,400; Mme. Strakosch, $600; Signors Amodio $800, Brignoli $1,500, Junca $800, Gassier $1,200, Stefani $1,200, Squires Then $400, Rocco $400, Maretzek $1,000, Muzio $800. Then there are fifty musicians in the orchestra—the first violinist being paid $50 a week, and the flutist an equal sum. Beside all this, there are advertising expenses, rent, salaries of an army of property men, doorkeepers, etc., and many "incidentals." The aggregate, for a month, foots up very near $30,000.

—A Philadelphia paper describes Miss Maggie Mitchell as "a fascinating young actress, who bids fair to take a very high stand in her profession, and that at no distant day;" while at the same time it takes occasion to announce that "the fact of filling a popular theatre for a fortnight does not constitute success."

—It is understood in musical circles that the new pitch recommended by the French commission will be adopted in England and the United States. The Messrs. Chickering have declared their intention to use it in their instruments. The pitch is one-third of a tone lower than that heretofore accepted. Whoever teaches any other pitch is sure to be defiled.

—A desperate piece of extravagance, under the title of "The Goose with the Golden Eggs," has just been brought out at the Strand Theatre, London. The author is Mr. Augustus Mayhew—one of the famed Mayhew Brothers. The London *Era* says that "It is a farce of the most ludicrous construction, and of the most outrageous description, but during the forty minutes it occupied, so much laughter was produced, that even had the audience at the end felt disposed to have quarrelled with the trivial means that had excited their mirth, they had not breath enough remaining to express indignation, through an unfavorable verdict." It takes a London critic to write that sort of thing.

—Signor Verdi, the celebrated musical composer, was one of the deputation from Parma who proceeded to Turin to ask Victor Emanuel to accept the annexation of Parma and Piedmont. When the carriages of the deputies were proceeding to the royal palace, the population of Turin singled out that of Signor Verdi for especial notice; and cries of *Viva Verdi* were heard along the line of procession. It will be recollected that it was under this cry of *Viva Verdi* that the people of Italy, before the war, expressed their wish to have Victor Emanuel as their King, the letters of the word Verdi composing the initial letters of *Victor Emmanuele re d'Italia.*

— The following remarkable announcement is from the Philadelphia *Press*:

"We have a Theatrical Item, which will interest thousands of our readers, and it is this: Mr. Lemuel C. White, the renowned teacher of Forrest, Murdoch, Roberts, and thousands of others, at the Bar, in the Pulpit, and on the Stump, will, to oblige many friends, shortly re-appear, for a few nights, at one of our theatres. No doubt hundreds will eagerly avail themselves of this opportunity to obtain a knowledge of Mr. White's style. For more than half a century Mr. White has made Elocution his study, and he is an enthusiast in his art. He will play Macbeth, Othello, Zanga, Pierre, Shylock, etc." It would appear that Mr. Lemuel G. White, the renowned teacher of everybody, was something such a character as Stephen H. Branch, at whose feet have sat all the political apostles (and aldermen) of the day.

—The London *Critic* announces positively that Mr. and Mrs. Charles Mathews are about to return to the United States, by the *Great Eastern*. Mlle. Piccolomini was starring, at last accounts, in Yorkshire and Lancashire, crowded audiences being attracted by her performance of *Violetta* in "La Traviata." A concert was announced for Saturday, September 10th, at the Crystal Palace, supported by the talents of Mlles. Piccolomini, Titiens, and Borchardt, Signor Giuglini, and other artistes of the Royal Italian Opera, Drury Lane, who were to return from their provincial tour expressly for the occasion.

—Signorina Felicita Vestvali—whose too, too solid flesh refuses to melt—has just made a somewhat equivocal success at the Paris Academy, as Romeo, and is engaged for the season at the Grand Opera as first contralto. Mayerbeer has declared his intention to bring out for her his long promised "Africaine," an event to which the musical world looks forward with eager anticipation.

NEW YORK OCTOBER 15, 1859

POETICAL JUSTICE.

It is so rare a thing for men to get their dues in this life, and even after death the world takes so long a time to balance her book, and fulfil her duties as moral executor, that there has been conceived, in men's minds, the idea of a system of rewards and punishments so delicately adjusted and so minutely administered,—arranged, in short, in so imaginative and dramatic a manner, wholly without the aid, and beyond the control, of human agents,—that it has received the title of "Poetical Justice." The propriety of the title may be questioned; perhaps "Divine Justice" might better suit the exquisite fitness of some of its displays, but, after all, there is a sort of grim grotesqueness in many of its revenges, almost too German to be allowed Divine.

History and private experience are rich in illustrations of the workings of this principle of Poetical Justice. Some of them are amusing, some sublime, and some simply grotesque. We heard of a little incident which occurred the other day in Boston, and which is almost too good to be believed, but we may now offer it to our readers to be enjoyed without the drawback of incredulity which troubled us. They may believe it, for it is true.

Our Boston friends have recently been called on to sustain a severe affliction in the shape of a statue of the late Daniel Webster, executed by Mr. Hiram Powers. Mr. Powers is a sculptor whose work has been very much overrated by his countrymen and by himself, and the present statue would seem to be the very worst thing he has made. To be sure, it has one excellence: it has been the cause of a great deal of very good wit in others, and moreover, but we are doubtful if this may be considered a recommendation, it has given opportunity to Mr. Edward Everett to air another of his cheap and glittering orations before an admiring Boston audience. In this oration Mr. Everett informs us that on occasion this statue can come down from its pedestal and walk about. This we take the liberty of doubting. No figure with such legs, that is, if the shabby pantaloons do not belie the limbs they cover, could, by any effort, exercise the function of walking. But, if Mr. Everett speak truth, and the statue can move, we wonder it has not slunk away, long ago, rather than brave the shower of jeers and ridicule with which it is pelted, day after day, by its pitiless visitors. In truth, we doubt if Mr. Everett knows as much about the statue as he thinks, but whether it can come down or not, it certainly had some trouble in getting up, as our readers may gather from what we are about to relate.

A few mornings before the one on which the statue was to be inaugurated—early in the morning, before the little city was well awake—one of the most respectable citizens, an ardent admirer of the living Daniel, and a worshipper of his brazen image, grudging the time lost in sleep from the contemplation of those sublime features and sublimer pantaloons, left his bed, and stole out to enjoy the double luxury of a walk in Boston Common, and a look at his beloved Daniel, his face smitten by

Webster statue on Boston Common.

the beams of the new risen sun. Cheered by the drizzly morning, and the grating East wind,—your only atmosphere for a genuine Bostonian,—our respectable friend walked along the Mall—tiptoe with expectation—until, at length, mounting the terrace before the State House, that venerable pile from which, as every Boston boy with one drop of true blood in his veins firmly believes, Michael Angelo drew the idea of St. Peter's, he lifted the mild lustre of his respectable eyes, and saw—but the sight was too terrible, that we should lightly reveal it. His cheek grew pale, his hair stood as much on end as its native sense of propriety admitted, his knees knocked together, and, with as much haste as, under the terrible circumstances, a well-bred Bostonian, and a resident of Beacon street, was capable of employing, he proceeded toward the house of a friend, and violently rang the bell.

Alarmed by the vehement sound, the window was thrown up, a night-capped head was protruded, and an extremely anxious, and slightly testy voice, demanded the cause of so untimely a summons. But, to reveal so dreadful a secret in so public a manner, to shout it out from the street to an upper story, and so run the chance of having the fearful scandal bruited about the neighborhood, was too much for our excited, but still respectable Bostonian. He beckoned and whispered his sleepy friend to descend. Alarmed by the manner of the summons, filled with undefined doubts and fears, that worthy person proceeded, with all the haste his trembling hands allowed, to array himself decently, and descended to the door. No sooner had he reached it than he was seized nervously by the arm, hurried into a corner, and begged to dress himself at once. "Good Heavens, B. !" he said, "what is the matter? You are as pale as death!"

"Come away," replied the other, "don't stop to talk, get off your night-gown, put on your coat, something dreadful has happened: they have got the statue of our dear Daniel hung by the neck, and he looks so much like *the other Webster*, its horrible."

Shocked by this announcement, and feeling that the fate of Boston, and consequently of the universe, of which, as is well known, Boston is the hub, depended upon their early action, the two friends hurried off to the State House, and there saw, half veiled by the morning mist, half revealed by the sickly gleam of a befogged Boston sun, the ghastly spectacle. There hung, from the great Derrick, dismally, like a gallows, suspended by a chain about his neck, the grim figure of "the Great Expounder," his baggy pantaloons looking as if the legs they covered were withered and twisted with agony, and the whole arrangement, coupled with the identity of the names, recalling, only too vividly, the ghastly end to the terrible tragedy that, only a few years ago, shook Boston respectability, and all Beacon street to its very centre.

There had the whimsical spirit of Poetical Justice been amusing herself, through twelve long hours, with the spectacle of this great man, whose friends, with a zeal that would be almost praiseworthy, if it did not savor too strongly of political chicanery and wirepulling, have exalted to the position of a demi-god, until the mass of men are doubtful whether Daniel did not, somehow, have a Divine, as well as a New Hampshire, origin,—this great man, we say, actually hung in chains like the worst sort of malefactor, and only the restless devotion of his over-zealous admirers hindered that all Boston, in one hour more, might have seen a sight that would have sent unparalleled dismay into every loyal bosom, albeit there are wicked ones who would only have smiled at this odd occurrence, brought about, apparently, by the inability of the workmen to finish the pedestal before sunset so as to allow of the statue being fairly placed until the next day.

We say "apparently" brought about in this way, but, in truth, Nature, Fate, Poetical Justice, call it by what name you will, contrived this grim touch of humor! Perhaps she half repented of her trick, as she withdrew her hand, and veiled it with night and the obscurity of the morning, so that only those two might see it, remembering what streaks of goodness there were in the man, and, for his mere humanity, ashamed to have him seen in such a foolish plight. But, thinking of how much absurdity has been spoken, written, sung, and preached about her far from perfect creature, remembering the long oration to be said on the morrow, in which she was sure to find a great deal of superfluous discourse and many fine words, remembering all the chaff, and bombast, and Choatitude, and "windy suspiration of forced breath" of which the good "boon companion," but third-rate "Man," had been the subject in times past; remembering, also, how this man had been, every way, a corrupt example, far from a steady light of clear integrity and loyal purpose to his countrymen, and how, at the last, he turned his back upon all his highest principles, betraying them with a kiss for silver—she left him where he hung.

Now, if—as Mr. Everett says—the statue can come down, why did it consent to hang twelve hours in chains? Did it feel a secret consciousness that statue and man deserved the sly, sarcastic touch?

TEN YEARS BETWEEN DRINKS.

BY JOHN W. WATSON.

Did I start?
Well! the clink has waked my heart
Do you know,
What has passed of weal or woe,
Since in other days we drank
Just as careless as to-day?
Can you call the span of years
That have hurried on their way?

Is it Ten?
Little thought we there, and then,
While unseen,
Of the void to go between,
While the blood danced madly through
Every beating youthful vein,—
Of the half a score of years
Ere we'd meet and drink again.

Yes; 'tis true!
Time has lain his hand on you.
Look at me :
Full a score of years you see
Dashed in broad unerring lines
Down my face, and in my hair:
Years, and wringing of the heart
Leave their certain tokens there.

In those years
Have been crowded hopes and fears,
Dreams of gold,
Fancies young and memories old.
Life has waked to glad my soul,
Bloomed and blossomed, drooped and died;
What I sought not, given me ;
What I coveted, denied.

Where is she
Who once loved, and lived for me?
She is dead;
Sod has knitted o'er her head;
Hands that once were warm in mine,
Moulder in the greedy ground;
Limbs I clasped in love's embrace,
In the clods of earth are bound.

There has been
One that you have never seen,
One whose whole
Grew into my secret soul.
Half those years I worshipped her;
Then, she kissed my trembling hand,
Spread the pinions of her soul,
And fled into the silent land.

This my child,
Came into my heart, and smiled,—
Still that smile
In my memory comes awhile,
Like the Summer lightning flash
Skimmering on the blackened skies,
Making earth awhile seem bright,
Where the darkest shadow lies.

Where are those
Through whose hearts our memory flows?
Do you know
Of the friends of years ago?
Those we drank with, those we loved,
Where on all the earth they lie?
If on earth they still remain,
Do they think of you, and I?

Touch my glass:
Let those thoughts as quickly pass
As the wine
Loses all its sparkles fine;
Let the Winters come and go,
Summer always comes between,—
Let us think the years can bring
Nothing worse than what has been.

FINE ARTS.

Correspondence.

FROM THE ADIRONDACS.

Adirondac Woods, Oct. 8th.

My Dear Press :—Do you know where the Castle of Indolence is? I presume you think you do, and imagine you have had many a revel in it, but I assure you that unless you have lived at least a fortnight in a bark camp in the woods, you have never found it. It's the most marvellous place to be lazy in, man ever saw. Nothing around but the grand, gloomy, silent woods, nothing to excite thought or action beyond the daily physical necessities of the physical life, no news, no newspapers, no books but old ones (brought with you). You wake and sleep undisturbed and unexcited by anything of human interest; you forget that there is such a thing as business or trouble, debts or debtors, profit or loss.

Well, I have been living in that castle for two months and better, in a kind of conscious Rip Van Winkleism. It was bright green Summer when I came, the Summer became old and faded, and gala Autumn came in scarlet and gold; the scarlet and gold grew crimson and purple, and the sad Autumn put on the sere and yellow leaf, and to-day, Oct. 8th, the bare boughs of birch and buck lace over a gray sky from which the dreamy flakes of snow are falling softly, to melt as they touch the dried leaves that make the earth yellow and brown.

My castle isn't exactly the residence one would choose for Winter. It is only a castle against care; it is built of spruce bark on a foundation of logs, is 12 feet long by 11 deep, and at the back about 4 high, rising to a front of about 3 feet, which front is window, door, and register; it gives me light, air, and heat. In defiance of the threat which the sky sends down to me so still and so stern, a huge pile of birch logs blazes and crackles a challenge to snow or rain to extinguish its ardor in human service.

To a man who has no special human obligations, or who, having them, can forget them, this is the most marvellous place of recreation and recruiting the wide world can offer. It is a veritable dream-life—not a sight or sound in it reminds one of the actual social existence he has been leading, he soon forgets the want of the usual social stimuli—the daily paper, the new books, the special evenings, are all passed over in the steady current of mere physical sensations—the savage life and its wants seem to come back on humanity with all the power of a natural condition hardly escaped from. The body and its wants absorb all the care one can have here.

Some New Englander, whose name I can never remember, built himself a log cabin, or some other kind of cabin, in the woods near Concord, to try what solitude (!) was, and I suppose to see how cheaply he could live. Why didn't he make a whole thing of it, and push into the wilderness where there should not be a hard road made by the people who came to see what solitude looked like, and how nearly it resembled insanity, and where he couldn't be receiving baskets of notions from home by way of alleviation to the savage condition of his larder! It were worth while to try the experiment here where a human face don't intrude thrice a year, and whence it is a days' journey to the nearest home and habitation, and that only a backwoodman's log cabin. I kill my deer, and catch my trout in the lake which lies "at my door," as you say in civilization; these with a grouse shot now and then near my camp, furnish my viands, but I have no cornfield, so I must draw on the settlements for all gramineal supplies. I am not trying to see what I can do in the way of playing solitary, so I make no sacrifice of comfort to consistency; I have a hired man stay with me most of the time to cut wood and cook when I don't feel so disposed; but he spends part of every week at home, and so there are many days in which I can measure my powers against the imperative demands of nature and enjoy an absolute solitude. It is a grand sensation, that of being entirely alone in a wild world like this—to feel like an Atlas bearing on your own shoulders all there is of human value in your system. I hear strange footsteps of wild beasts around my camp at night, and in the morning find the tracks of the panther just outside the circle of heat of my fire, and the shyest and most timorous of the animals come around me at times, so still is it here. Deer have walked up at night to see the blaze of the camp-fire, and wonder perhaps, at something new; my hound at times whines and trembles as he comes to me for safety, for something he scents in the darkness outside, for a hound you must know, my dear PRESS, is a timid beast so far as panthers and bears are concerned. Everything in brief centres on *me*.

This is what some men call the natural way of living —if it is more natural to eat than to think, I grant it; but if not, not. I'll give you by-and-by some notions I have got here—acquired by the experimentum crucis—of the relation between the savage and civilized lives, the brute and the human in other words: *now* I am talking of the bare fact of physical life. It don't cost much here and it is easily footed up. Not including my man's wages (and I could do without him), the account is as follows: Venison—interest, wear and tear, etc., of; 1st day, $20 (at 20 per cent. for the day will only last about five years), $4; 2d, gun, $35 (lasts 10 years), $3 50; 3d, boat (lasts 4 years), $7 50; 4th, powder, lead, caps, $2 50; total, $17 50, for a years' venison. Trout, by a similar summing up, about $5. Then of the importations we allow 1 lb. of flour, ½ lb. of butter or pork per day, worth, here, about 14 cents; sugar, tea, coffee, etc., 10 cents per diem, making, if my meagre arithmetic avails, somewhere in the neighborhood of 25 cents a day for living, or $90 a year. Add to this the reasonable allowance of $50 for clothing, $15 for boots and shoes, and we have $165 as the cost of a man's maintenance. Now per contra, let us see what a man can earn in the same way of living. The skins of his deer will bring him an average of $50 a year, furs that he might catch in the Autumn, $150 (a good allowance for the Adirondac now), and if he could salt his fish down and send them to the settlements, he might realize $40 or $50 more, making a total of $250 to pay expenses, and replace dogs, guns, boats, etc., etc. I remember that the *Tribune* made a great fuss about that Concord man's living so cheaply, and held it up as an example to some young men living in the city; but like some other of the *Tribune's* theories it don't allow for contingencies and human imperfections. To go through the programme I have laid down a man must work hard all the time, live like a savage, and be, at the end of it, quite as much of a brute as his hound. A man may live here six months and give his intellect a thorough rusting, and afterward think better and work more energetically; but to continue it would destroy all intellectual power as certainly as it would establish physical. On this topic more anon.

It is a charming thing to act savage amateur for a few weeks, to be your own servant and master at once, to feel dependent on no one for bed or board, for stick or steak, to have no calls on you, from society or family (i. e. *also* if you haven't *promised* to write some letters to the SATURDAY PRESS), to swing your own axe, pull your own oar, and cook your own dinner—but to live so! Thank God for society even badly organized as it is with thieves and bullies and politicians, and chief priests, scribes, and pharisees. There is a certain delight in all these self-rendered services, which bears repetition quite a time, to feel the swing of a sharp, heavy axe, and see the clean, white, birch chips fly, and hear the trees crash and thunder down; but its a beggarly thing to *have* to go and chop wood to keep warm whether you want to or no, and to be obliged to go out to hunt some raw rainy day, when you've got a great hole in your boot and no cobbler within twenty miles. But I doubt not there is a certain good even in this. One thing I have found out my dear PRESS, which I will add by way of moral to my fable, there is more fire in the axe than in the wood-pile.

ANTAEUS.

Dramatic Feuilleton.

My Pre-Raphaelite Drama.

I have a play founded upon fact, to which I desire to direct the attention of our enterprising managers. The theatre is in the square bounded by Houston, Prince, Mott, and Mulberry streets.

The centre of the stage is a grand cathedral, not so handsome as Notre Dame, but putting that religious edifice's nose out of joint as to the squalidity of its surroundings.

Within the cathedral are the principal actors in the play. The Primate of the church with a real mitre on his head and a real crozier in his hand is assisting at the dénouement of the plot.

It is not new. It is, in fact, the old story.

The heroine, a lovely blonde of the Eastern (State of Maine) type, tall and straight as the cedars of Lebanon; a lily of the valley; yea, a rose of Sharon, one which this humble pen cannot paint, nor Lubin throw a perfume upon.

The bridegroom is brief in stature, and well stricken in years. Distinctly not a blonde. On the contrary a dark brunette.

Color, that of coffee with a very little milk.

But he has what you, sir, youthful, handsome, strong, clever though you may be, have not.

He has four millions of qualifications for matrimony *à la mode* which you do not possess.

And the ceremony proceeds: May, bright, blushing, rosy Aurora, is joined with short, cold, dark December.

They do these things better in the other theatres, so far as plots are concerned, I know. There, we should have had the ceremony proceed up to a certain point, when a stranger who had gained admittance to the church by
bribing the officers on guard at the cerulean entrance, would suddenly appear, throw off a cloak, and say:

"I outbid yon brief Cuban, for your priceless jewel; there is a certified cheque for eight millions."

Whereupon there would be, naturally, a terrible row, but finally it would be ascertained that the young lady loved the young man when he drove a butcher wagon "in other days;" that he resolved to make a fortune for the express purpose of laying it at her feet. That he went out to Arizona with Lieutenant Mowry, and after being scalped, and generally knocked about by the Camanches, he saved the life of a big Indian, who, out of gratitude, the genuine article is only found in a crude state, showed him a silver mine, richer than Tiffany's and Ball & Black's put together.

And so he comes back to claim his bride.

And he gets her. The ancient Corydon retires in the handsomest manner to dominoes and cigarettes.

The primate joins the hands of the young people, there is slow music by the orchestra, and the curtain descends reluctantly upon a tableau of happiness.

But in my pre-Raphaelite drama we have things as they absolutely and positively exist. There's no mistaking the reality of the scene. Not even the Baron's friend, the manager of the Porte St. Martin Theatre, would spend so much money on a play as has been laid out for the costumes, properties, etc., for the first performance of this piece. A hundred thousand dollars, no less. Look at the principal actors, and the astonishing young ladies and gentlemen, who act as supernumeraries on this occasion. Did you ever see such lace, such muslin, such flowers, such ravissant head-dresses, such coats, such cravats, such trowsers, such diamonds, such everything that's nice at Wallack's, or Laura Keene's, or the Winter Garden?

I should think not.

And then the populace, the street scenes, the pre-Raphaelite tenant houses, the three-cent groggery on the one corner, the coffin shop on the other, the women nursing their infants on the sidewalk, the actual boys with real holes in the seats of their trowsers, the positive thieves and rowdies; the faces on which disease, and shame, and want, and hunger, had written their mark as plain as the brand of the galley-slave. Then, intermixed with the lower orders, we have some shipwrecked ladies and gentlemen, the hem of whose garments must not touch the apparel of the poor wretches whose domain has been invaded.

Then there must be some real policemen, always making blunders, and trying to conceal them by shouting in a very loud voice, and driving the populace into impossible corners; and flunkeys, all in new liveries, who look down upon the mob with that lofty contempt which a man in a good coat always feels for an old friend who is seedy.

That will make up my play, and I claim that it is a good one.

It has plenty of action; it delineates the effect of the master passions, except Love, which is out of fashion, except in middle-aged tragedies, like Geraldine, and it affords the finest opportunity for stage effects. It is very short, this play of mine. No long-drawn agony, no wading from act to act through four mortal hours, no utter weariness, no drowsy speeches-it is all packed into an hour's time.

Very likely the original costumes and properties may be hired for the theatre which reproduces this play. The daily press may be relied upon as unanimous in its favor

What do you say Messieurs the Managers to the pre-Raphaelite drama?

The Draytons.

I am sorry that artists like Mr. and Mrs. Drayton should not have attracted more public attention than they have received.

At their first performance the little French Theatre was not over half filled, and I could see but few people beyond the brigade of dead-heads, who are always on hand to manufacture public opinion by boring people to death with their opinions, as if any one in the world cared about them.

But I am afraid that the metropolis won't be able to see the Drayton entertainment. It is all Drayton, and toujours perdrix is not good.

Drayton sings a good song with a good voice, and a capital school. He is a pretty good actor, with the exception that he chants colloquial dialogue in the Andersonian style. Mrs. Drayton is a good artiste with a bad voice. Her costumes are scarcely the thing for this locality, though doubtless considered very fine in the provinces of Albion.

But there is, as I said before, too much of Drayton. Nothing but Drayton for a matter of two hours and a-half. Even the Brightest and Best would become tiresome within that period.

What I advise Mr. Drayton to do is to organize an English opera company, take to the rural districts and come back to the metropolis in the early Summer when any of the theatres will be glad to give him achance.

The Oldest Man can't see the Parlor Opera.

The Opera.

I suppose every one has read Ullmann's pathetic proclamation about the opera season which is to commence next Monday, with Speranza in the Traviata. Of course there will be a great house to hear the new prima donna, who will be all the more kindly received because she makes no pretensions. The main attraction of the season, however, is to be the *Vépres Sicilifor* the *mise en scene* of which fifteen or a hundred and fifty thousand dollars, I forget which, have been, or are to be, expended.

Meantime, the artists have been singing for the delectation of the Bostonians, who have not rushed to the opera with that ardor which they exhibit when there is going to be a horse race or a prize fight. The "crickets" are, as usual, muddy. Cortesi is patronized, Gassier pooh-poohed at, Brignoli snubbed, Amodio and Junca puffed mildly. It is really laughable to see the awful passion that one of the weekly papers, the *Express*, I think it is, works itself into about Brignoli, who, it seems, don't see Boston. What, O! Editor, is Boston to Brignoli? Dost know that he is one of the three best tenors in the world, and while his voice is preserved, is perfectly independent of all mundane influences, Boston editors included? Dost know that Strakosch has been trying, for two years, to find a tenor to supplant Brignoli, and as yet without success. I have heard only two better—Mario and Guiglini; Piccolomini puts Brignoli before Guiglini.

Everybody will be glad to hear of Maretzek's good fortune in obtaining the Theatre Tacon, at the Havana. Its a sure fortune for the indomitable impresario.

Post-Raphaelite Theatres.

Nothing new yet. Theatres are doing well, of course. Otherwise they would change the bills. Everybody is living in hope that the people from Peoria, Boston, and other country towns will go home, so that we can have a new piece or two. Miss Laura Keene announced last week that she would revive the *A Midsummer Night's Dream,* "with all its bewilderingly beautiful scenery," on Wednesday. Mr. Mark Smith was to play Bottom. But on Tuesday there was such a terrific rural rush for *The Sea of Ice*, that it was kept in the bills for the week. At Wallack's they are still hammering away at the old comedies, which no earthly power can compel the subscriber to see. The piece of "interest, fun, and history," which Mr. Wallack underlines, is Moncrieff's "Rochester." Queer historical authority, Moncrieff, but since Genio C. Scott and Miss Laura Keene have entered the field of Minerva, we are not surprised that Mr. Wallack should quote the author of "The Cataract of the Ganges." They have also at this Theatre, an adaptation of the French vaudeville *Les Deux Aveugles,* to be played by Brougham and Walcot. Mr. Bourcicault has a new piece ready for the Winter Garden. I hear that *Dot* is to be rubbed out this week, after a run of thirty nights.

There are rumors of crinoline rows in the coulisses. Miss Ada Clifton has retired from Laura Keene's company, as I predicted. I presume that Miss Clifton will replace Miss Stevens at the Winter Garden,—the latter being engaged at New Orleans. I hear also that a very great feminine favorite with the metropolitan public has been tempted by a splendid offer from the New Orleans Varietes, and intends to deprive us of the light of her countenance, which I had relied upon to sustain life through the Winter.

Happy Orleanois! Miserable New Yorkaise!

I am so cut up by this intelligence that I can scarcely compose myself so far as to say, like Mr. Webster, I ain't dead yet, and to subscribe myself, à la Anna Maria,

Votre bien devoué,

Tout-à-vous,

PERSONNE.

NEW YORK OCTOBER 22, 1859

MODESTY MILITANT.

Mr. Washington Bartlett having sown the wind of notoriety in the matter of his daughter's marriage with Don Esteban Sancta Cruz de Oviedo, begins to reap the whirlwind; this, however, does not satisfy him. To him a whirlwind is the merest puff. He yearns for a tornado. He is resolved to secure it. The method he adopts has ingenuity, if not novelty, to recommend it. He institutes a series of "Corrections" of unimportant details, and clothing them in the language of injured dignity, sends them forth to the world through the columns of the public journals. But unfortunately Mr. Bartlett's ambition vaults too high. It o'erleaps itself. The motive is too clearly apparent to be for an instant misapprehended. Even were it not too late at this day to assume the virtue of humility and modesty, Mr. Bartlett's manner of doing it would at once convict him.

The fact appears to be that this gentleman's appetite for fashionable fame is unappeasable. That his daughter should be glorified as she has been by the resonant rhetoric of a dozen reportorial pens, is not enough. He considers that his claim to the position of *père noble* in the recent social comedy has not been recognized with sufficient distinctness. He purposes to correct this. He therefore fulminates defiant manifestoes, in which he imparts to the community the intelligence that he has "been twenty-five years in the public service, and been associate proprietor and editor of journals on both sides of our continent;" that "he himself wrote the first editorial ever printed in the now famous city of San Francisco, *and with his own hands*, when Chief Magistrate there, pulled the press for the first printed sheet ever printed in that city;" that "his daughter has spoken and written the Spanish and French languages fluently from childhood;" and other items of equal public importance, set forth with all the intensity of italics and small capitals. Now this is not the language of a man who shrinks from notoriety. It is evidently an ill-concealed attempt to fan into a lasting flame the already fading spark of public interest which his indelicately-ventilated private eccentricities had awakened. It is an effort to prolong the agony of excitement, which for a brief hour dragged him and his from their domestic seclusion to stand in immodest exposure before the staring scrutiny of the world.

We confess to no such Pharisaical faith as that avowed by some journals which, while reviling the alleged indecency of open comment upon an occurrence like this, gloat with particular affection over its minutest features. With the Philadelphia *Press*, for instance, which republishes the entire report of one of the New York papers in one column, and devotes another to wreakages of typographical wrath upon the spirit of journalism which justifies such narrations, we have no sympathy. We feel that this Oviedo wedding, from beginning to end, was a subject eminently suited to newspaper discussion. We believe that it was so intended by its projectors; that mines were carefully laid, to be sprung at the proper moment for the benefit of the general curiosity; that plans were deftly devised for insuring the largest share of publicity. For a month New York was effervescent upon this matter. To deny it newspaper consideration would have disappointed everybody, and no persons more, we believe, than those most immediately concerned. But with the culmination of the event, the public would naturally have paused, and suffered the parties to return to the obscurity in which Mr. Bartlett, it seems, will not permit them to repose. Our community is easy to forget, and Mr. Bartlett's wounds, if he had received any, would have healed the quicker, had he not thus invited renewed irritation. A disturbed paternal sense of wrong does not seek relief in newspaper proclamations as to a daughter's lingual capabilities, nor in the protrusion of additional and quite irrelevant personal information. Mr. Bartlett says of himself and his household; "We "claim to be a strictly private family." Why, then, these new revelations of his own antecedents, which nobody ever heard of and nobody cares for? He says that on the first intimation of his daughter's engagement, "people hurried to the shops for news, or waylaid his servants with inquisitive questions." This is certainly an avowal calculated to inspire belief in the writer's sensitiveness! It is quite a new bit of intelligence, piquant and odorous. He moreover asks with some show of feeling, "Is it a crime to have a large circle of acquaintances, and to write to them to witness a marriage ceremony? Is it any fault of ours that thousands surrounded the church who had not been invited?" Hardly, we should judge; but allowing these questions to be put in good faith, and restraining all inquiry in the matter of the thousands of invitation cards printed—not written—with accurate directions as to the course to be adopted by holders, and variously tinted to secure precedence of certain colors—whence emanated the tickets possessed by the myriad strangers, none of whom had ever heard the name of Bartlett, and who wondered at the glare of impertinence which sought to include them in so vain a pageant? Perhaps Mr. Bartlett will say, as he has said of the orders to view the bridal gifts while in course of preparation at the warehouses, that they were "forged." This, indeed, is not unlikely, as he has intimated his design, in case of necessity, to continue his contributions to the current literature of the day. He will, perhaps, explain the mystery of those subtle allusions to reportorial hostility caused by his refusal to confer invitations in certain cases. He will possibly reiterate his ideas, respecting the beauty of Don Esteban's presents. He will again assure us of his former journalistic distinctions in terms showing that, according to his notion, a correct use of English language is not an essential point of editorial eminence. He may, indeed, relate closer particulars of his daughter's earlier education and of her course during the progress of her courtship, than he has yet vouchsafed. After this he will no doubt arise in all the rectitude of insulted pride, and say, "Behold, how temperate I am! Emulate my reticence, O Editor, and cease to scatter broadcast the vulgar vanities which I would not for the world encourage. Respect the sanctity of retiring privacy, and let oblivion's balm, for which I clamor day by day, fall soothingly upon me." But, Mr. Bartlett, we think the public will not see it.

JOVE'S GREATEST BLESSING.

BY A. F. BANKS.

If I from great Jove had the choice of a boon,
Best fitted to keep Life's strained fiddle in tune,
I'd choose—Money-Grubbers, don't sneer so and start!—
I'd choose, by the gods! I would choose a Young Heart.

'Tis a glorious gift, with a magical power,
To brighten the bright, or to cheer the dark hour;
Though from Fortune's fair face the glad smile should depart,
What matter? so long as you've got a Young Heart.

Oh! blest is the mortal whose course has been such,
From the wild boyhood's hoop to the old age's crutch,
To ensure the best blessing that Jove can impart,
The head of a man, and a child's Merry Heart,

So come, let us see if we can't shape our ways,
To live loving and loved for the rest of our days;
Life, at best, is up hill, and old Care is the cart,
But the load is made light by a merry Young Heart.

Thoughts and Things.

BY ADA CLARE.

No. I.

By some extraordinary coincidence, nearly all the serial stories which recently animated the pages of magazine literature have suddenly come to a close. Perhaps it is that the mind bursts into immediate maturity under the ripening influences of the full Autumn, and feels that the time for bringing in the harvest-sheaves is come.

Of the serials none can dispute the incalculable superiority of Mrs. Stowe's "Minister's Wooing." the most powerful work of fiction which has sprung from the American Press. It is a religious work, all about religious subjects, yet I pity the staunch old Presbyterian who reads its pages, unless he be proof and bulwark 'gainst all reasoning. What keen, resolute, disastrous onslaughts upon the Calvanistic beliefs. What ripping up of the body and soul of the old Puritanic faith! It would be impossible to conceive of a more horrid and ghastly mental picture, than that she shows us induced in a whole community by the prevalence of hideous dogmas which men have dared to call the religion of Christ. There are passages in this "Minister's Wooing," whose stately and superb command of language, whose deep pathos, whose indescribable eloquence, I know not how to compare with aught in the prose literature of the English language. It is a book which will not be forgotten. The limpid blue eyes of Mary, full of infinite sorrowings, shine tender and sad, into the innermost recesses of the memory.

But the inevitable discovery, the ignominious penny, has turned up again, before the eyes of the all-beholding critics. Perchance they say, a woman may have gathered the materials for this work, but ah! certainly a man has tinkered them together. This scene is too vigorous, too bold, too learned, it comes upon us with too much force, we feel that it is a man's fist, that is taking our minds under the ribs. Keep, keep your soft fingers, madame, for stitching together the minor, unessential parts of your story; your brother the preacher, who is never truly great except when he is writing surreptitiously under your name, shall work out for you all the vital and essential details of the same.

Oh! that I were wise, like these critics, from whom the hands of their brothers are never hidden. I too, know occasionally the hands of my sisters, but it is generally by the whiteness of their sweet little fingers, and the exceeding softness of the skin. But when it is dabbled in printer's ink, I have lost my wisdom, I care not what sex it wears, I am only ambitious that it's force be not demonstrated about the region of my ears. But for these noble martyr men who make immortal reputations for women, and are themselves forever unknown and mute! Why is it that their works do not betray them for themselves, when the naked handprint of their power is never to be mistaken on the lights and of a woman's thoughts? No palms have they, not even the inverted triumph of the thorn-crown. Nothing but dark silence for these invisible Titans of literature, these dumb Atlases, who lift up immortalities on their shoulders, and are forever hidden and speechless beneath them. . . . .

Trumps has continually increased in interest. Evidently Trumps were not drawn in the beginning, and all the interest hangs on the last suit. It is from the most excellent hand of G. W. Curtis. At first I feared it promised to be dry and prosing, but it has steadily gathered interest, and blossomed forth in great glory at last. Taking it as a whole, it is a most spirited and graphic story, and will compare most bravely with any of the serial stories we have just had from the great English masters.

Charles Reade's *Good Fight* is written in his usual fascinating style, but he does not seem at home in the antique. He is a prophet of the modern. It was very cunning in him to place Margaret in a delicate situation near the end,—it was his only chance of warming our hearts towards her.

Thackeray's *Virginians* must create a profound interest in all who are accustomed to his style, but it is less animated than the *Newcomes.*

He cannot make George Washington an entertaining character; that great man wants a pedestal to stand on, or a brazen horse upon which to sit. When stepping down from his greatness, he leaves his carpet-bag in our hall, enters our back parlor, and announces his intention of joining us in a saintly horn of lager, we cannot help feeling our spirits dismally dashed, and almost dare to think he is a little, just a little of a bore. Heaven forgive me for speaking thus of the Father of my country, but I should wish he had not distinguished me so highly; I should wish he had selected Pfaff's, as the place worthy to furnish lager for heroes.

Dickens is not so entertaining as usual, but then, my children, what would you have? *All the Year Round* needed a commencement from the hand of Dickens, and he had many and other important works to do. If the simultaneous action of too many cooks will prove fatal to a single broth, so also will the simultaneous manufacture of too many broths prove fatal to a single cook.

I have just read *Out of the Depths*. It is very well written, in the main, but full of the most wearisome cant. The religious reflections of the work are introduced on St. Paul's ingenious suggestion, in season and out of season. I even went to see it dramatized at the Museum. There it reminded me of the famous silk stocking of metaphysical notoriety, which had been darned so often, that not an atom of the original texture of it remained. The great topic of dialectical skirmishing, as to whether the same essence which collected around it form color, texture, etc., in the original silk, was still here, though expressed in cotton thread, might easily be adapted to this play. The story of *Out of the Depths* has been accommodated with so many patches, of such miscellaneous cut and shape, and color, that it seems as if all of the exploded stage effects, the renounced conventional characters, the departed dramatic conversations and costumes, had foisted themselves upon it, and swarmed in a horrid little population beneath its loose and unclaimed roof.

Yet both book and play have elements of success in their intention, which is good. The rehabilitation of the unfortunate woman will ever be a subject of deep interest to all earnest and just minds, even as it ever has been since the time when of all the world, the only one without sin refused to cast a stone at her.

Dramatic Feuilleton.

Hazlitt Redivivus.

I have not performed the whole duty of a Dramatic Critic this week.

I have neglected, refused, and omitted to go to Laura Keene's Theatre, where *A Midsummer Night's Dream* has been revived in a way which has bewildered the savant who "does up" the Amusements for the *Daily News*. He calls the play, which I think I proved last season to be Shakespeare's, "Laura Keene's Midsummer Night's Dream." Immediately afterwards, however, I am startled by the announcement that "This beautiful creation of *Shakespeare* is certainly one of the most fructuous for absorbing interest and for *bewilderingly amazing* an audience which can be placed in any manager's hands, and in all candor we must say that Miss Keene does wonders here."

That's pretty good, but there is something much better a little further on, where our ungrammatical cotemporary becomes ecstatic over a young woman who plays Oberon. "Always" (the young woman) "devoting much attention to her toilet, she has now by a thorough change of costume added largely to her gorgeous beauty, *while her acting of this part is rendered far superior by her to that which could be accomplished by any other actress we know*."

That's delightfully muddy. Peoria or Biloxi couldn't do better.

Our "Cricket" also tells us that "Mr. Mark Smith read and acted the part of Bottom entirely too chaste for Nick the Weaver—we have no doubt he will work easier in a few nights."

Perhaps it would better if he should play easier.

"Mr. Vincent" (more *News*) "went through the part of *Quince* rough shod." [Goodness gracious! where's Pacalin ?] "He was entirely too boisterous and loud mouthed. We would suggest that *Quince* was an humble, quiet carpenter" (you'd better not say that over again in the Bowery or near the *Tribune* office), "and was entirely ignorant of the low comedy gag."

What's "gag"? And how do you know?

I don't know whether the *News*, or Laura Keene, or Genio C. Scott, or Mark Smith, or Richard Grant White, or Shakespeare, or the "gorgeous" beauty of *Oberon*, has "injured" *A Midsummer Night's Dream*, but the public don't seem to see it, and we are to have in its place a capital play, *The Wife's Secret,* first produced here by the Charles Keans, and never acted by any one else.

Before that, however, Tom Taylor's *Contested Election*.

I am told also that Mrs. John Wood has been engaged by Miss Keene, and I am sure I am very glad of it. Mrs. Wood makes everybody laugh; and is a good sort of an actress to have about here, where everybody is so infernally respectable and awfully dull.

That's pretty strong, but you can skip it *s. v. p.*

Theatre Français.

My finer feelings were so much cut up last week by the great wedding, that I forgot all about our French friends, whom Mr. Sage has imported for the abonnés.

The abonnés, I believe, don't see it.

The say they did better last season, without half so much fuss. The prime young man, Mannstein, is pretty good, and the *soubrette* M'lle Darcy, is good and not pretty. The only piece worth seeing has been a charming little thing of Alfred De Musset's, *Un Caprice*. If they do it again I advise you to go. It's a good thing to do.

Lester Rochester Wilmot, Earl of Wallack.

A play intended to illustrate the adventures of this famous nobleman was produced at Wallack's Theatre, on Tuesday.

It is a remarkable thing, this play, because the hero has some reputation for wit (vide, Pepys' Diary, State Poems, the Grammont Memoirs, *Two to One*, St. Evremond's Letters, and *The Veteran*), but, nevertheless, he does not say one good thing from the beginning to the end of the piece.

I don't believe in Pepys, nor in Anna Maria, who was in love with the *Veteran*, any more.

He is a "fast man," too. A fast man who is continually going to do something awful, and never doing it. A fast man who is making love to a rustic beauty, who certainly does not give one the idea of rigid virtue, yet he never advances one step with her from the beginning to the end of the play,—"fast man," too, who never takes a sign! Bah!

The only fast thing I could see about the affair was the changes of dress, which were not disguises by any means, though probably so intended.

Given a heavy black moustache, light dragoon whiskers, with other capillary attractions and disguise, is, to say the least, a joke of colossal proportions.

No, Mr. Rochester looked exactly like Mr. Lester at a fancy ball. Not a bit like an actor.

Still the thing is amusing. Positively funny at times. The songs in the ancient copy have been cut out, but Mr. Rochester sings "Simon the Cellarer" in such a superb way, that I advise Brignoli to look to his laurels.

The only difficulty in Mr. Lester's way arises from the fact that I saw two or three professional critics applauding him.

The other characters are things for Mr. Rochester to knock about. The more that is done, the more amusing to the audience they become.

That is unpleasant for the actors, but their troubles are of no consequence to you or I.

Art demands personal sacrifices; butchers have no esthetic aspirations, grocers no confidence worth speaking of.

As usual with this house, certain people came out very strongly on the question of clothes. Mrs. Hoey was 'gorgeous,"' Miss Gannon "resplendent," Mrs. Sloan "superb," Mr. Lester "grand," Mr. Brougham "sublime."

There, isn't that a nice puff? Who says I never say anything good about any one?

The sheperdesses and things in the last act—which they finish, as usual, when in a scrape, by a dance—look as if they had been cut out of a picture by Watteau. The tableau is really pretty, and the costumes, trés bon goût.

John Brougham, as a gentle shepherd, is nice likewise. Why can't we have Blake in a chip hat, brief tunic, and silk tights?

Horticultural Disturbance.

Some how or other, Gardens can't get on without rows.

I don't know what there is in horticultural pursuits which should stir up people's biliary secretions and make them do and say wicked, uncharitable, and awful things. But it always happens so.

Look at the Garden of Eden for example.

No horticultural enterprise ever promised better than that, according to all accounts, but in a short time the whole affair was broken up, and very respectable people, descendants of the original proprietors, have been obliged to write Feuilletons and resort to other extraordinary means of gaining a livelihood.

I am aware that the classic poets, Virgil especially, were very fond of singing the praises of people who were engaged in horticulture, and that the late Mr. Webster used to write pretty letters about it to his farmer at Franklin.

But Virgil never had a watermelon of his own, and Mr. Webster's favorite estate at Marshfield was only good to shoot over, and make chowders on.

So we can't depend on the poets, nor the orators. We must come to facts; and the fact is that there has been a row in the Winter Garden, whereby Mrs. Wood has seceded from those bowers.

Then I am informed that a German gentleman, who plays on the kettle-drum, has received his congé. Likewise three other sons of harmony—likewise from fair Germania.

What is a Winter Garden without Wood ?

What is an orchestra without kettle-drums?

One can't realize it.

And yet they are going on.

Bourcicault has been subsoiling and using quick fertilizers with such success as to have raised a novelty. Not a pure novelty, but a reproduction of a French graft.

The Pacha and his Bears is the French piece.

So the Jardin d'Hiver is changed to the Jardin des Plantes.

Vive Bourcicault.

Not that Mr. Bourcicault's *Chamouni III.* is a remarkably entertaining work. On the contrary, it has the narrowest escape in the world from actual stupidity.

There is a Pasha with a red nose, who tries to sing, and fails; first, because he don't know the air, and second, because he has no voice worth mentioning. Then there are two American travellers, Mr. Jefferson and Mr. Johnston,—who are evidently intended as funny people, but who are not at all amusing,—and Mr. Holland, a Mandarin, who is not so bad.

The feminine department comes out strong. Such an array of splendid creatures, in such ravishing costumes, with such extraordinary things that they sit around upon, ought to set the Jeunesse dorée wild.

It's the fashion now to be blasé, and generally not to see it.

That's very bad for the ballet, who have to rely on Peoria and Biloxi.

Miss Agnes Robertson is the favorite Sultana of the Pasha who can't sing. Miss Robertson was very near being placed in a similar predicament; while poor Mollenhauer was "bothered intirely." I never saw a leader who managed to mix up things in such a horribleness as M.

Miss Robertson's costume was faultless of course. Still she did not altogether become it, if I may use a feminine expression. She rather gave me the idea of Whiskers caught in Broadway, without his trousers, that is if such a horrid catastrophe could be taken in, all at once, by the finite mind.

The scenery was exceedingly pretty, and there were several "breakdowns," with one of which the play ended.

Ill-natured people might say "appropriately ended," but I'm lamb-like and don't.

Altogether, I'm afraid that Chamouni won't do.

Shocking Accident in Irving Place.

Did you read about the awful stirring up which the passengers by the *Quaker City* received coming from Havana the other day. Some pin or other gave way, when something fell on something else, and the whole engine was smashed beyond redemption.

That was the case at the Academy last Monday. Speranza, the new prima donna, was the crank-pin. She gave way. Then Amodio had too much of our gallant Firemen, and lost his voice cheering "forty's fellers." Then Crescimano, the new prima donna, was as rough as one of those gentleman of meteorological pursuits who come all the way from Grass Valley to be plucked by hotel-touters, owl-line hackmen, and slop-shop drummers. Crescimano is hardly good enough for Chicago, and that is saying a great deal.

Brignoli had a chance and improved it. The *rôl* (*Manrico* in the *Trovatore*) is one of his best; but he surpassed himself in it on Monday.

Wednesday things improved. The house was pretty well packed. The children of Israel came out very strong in more ways than one.

The Opera was Ernani, with new tenor (Stigelli), new baritone (Ferri), and Crescimano. The prima donna was rougher than ever. The tenor is a good artist. His voice is nothing to brag of. The upper notes in it are excellent, but the lower and middle ones come from the throat, and therefore lack volume. He looks like a candidate for the Assembly in the Fourth Ward.

The baritone, Ferri, is a capital artist. His voice is not so strong as Badiali's, nor so sweet as Amodio's, but his method is better than either of them, and he is an admirable actor. His cast of countenance is Oriental, and the Hebrew claque came near spoiling his début through over enthusiasm.

So far good. But where is the prima donna ?

Rosencrantz and Guildenstern are splendid, but where, if you please, are we to look for Hamlet?

The Barney Williamses

have commenced at Niblo's Garden in grand style. I have not yet seen them, but hear all good things about them.

Nous verrons, next week.

PERSONNE.

NEW YORK OCTOBER 29, 1859

Written for the NEW YORK SATURDAY PRESS.

WAITING FOR THE WHISTLE.

Many are the tribulations of those who travel by railroad, and not the least among them is the delay upon the less frequented routes, occasioned by the want of connection between different roads. I am well aware that in comparison with the horrors caused by defective bridges and culverts, this is a trifle light as air; but nevertheless, considered per se, it is sufficiently annoying.

A short time since, I found myself deposited at a dreary New England station, with the information that the next train would pass in six hours. I was totally unprepared for such an emergency, for I had no books, no friends, and, as our neighbors of the thirty-million island express it, with a tropical luxuriance of negative, "no nada." I employ myself at first in pacing the platform and meditating upon the flight of time, and then look at the clock in the station-house, which informs me that I have still five hours and forty-five minutes to wait. I observe that there is another victim, a placid old lady, with great round spectacles and very blue fingers, who is already engaged in knitting with what appear to be small crowbars. Her stocking is violent in color, tremendously ribbed, not to say corrugated, or fluted like an Ionic column, and is the largest I ever beheld. I admire the philosophy of the old lady, and the colossal proportions of the stocking, and wonder what son of Anak will ever wear it.

I proceed to examine the walls of the room, which are covered with placards, announcing the merits of patent medicines. I read them all carefully, and discover that an astonishing number of clergymen are benefitted thereby. I flatter myself that I am now thoroughly informed in the matter of labels, and am in a position to detect instantly the counterfeit from the genuine. I find some names that are deeply mysterious, such as "Brown's Bronchial Troches," and "Pomade Philocome." I observe "Jones's Instant Exterminator," and am in doubt whether to exterminate myself or somebody else. I ask myself if I am in want of vermifuge, and decide immediately in the negative. After I have taken in all the medicines (mentally), I look at certain railroad maps, and perplex my mind with the various advantages of rival routes to the West, and then I look at the clock. Alas! I have only gained twenty minutes.

I wander about in a disconsolate way for some moments, when I am relieved by a "distraction." A locomotive has suddenly appeared, and I go out to look at the monster. I find him taking a huge, but frugal, repast of wood and water, interspersed with large doses of bark, while a good Samaritan is pouring oil into his joints. I admire his great capacity and high state of polish, and observe that his name is "Hercules," and that he has a small plaster cast of the infant Samuel on his front. I cannot quite see the connection between that young divinity student and the demigod, but I suppose it is all correct. The monster finishes his dinner, and places himself upon the platform, where he is being turned around by Milesian power at the crank. Now the infant Samuel is praying like a young Gheber, with his face to the East, and now he faces due North. But here Hercules puzzles me, for he seems utterly wanting in dignity. He starts furiously away, as if nothing short of a hundred miles would satisfy him, but after going a few yards, he stops suddenly, and comes back on another track; then he seizes hold of a quiet baggage-car and carries it madly on a third track, where he leaves it, and comes back again, and then rushes in the opposite direction and returns; and altogether acts in such an imbecile and vacillating way, that I am quite ashamed of him, and transfer my admiration to the switcher, or switchman, or whatever he is called, who seems to fully comprehend all this intricate maze. I look at this man with infinite respect, and think he must possess considerable mathematical powers. I firmly believe that he can even understand a wind and current chart.

At length my friend Hercules is quiet, and I return to the house, where there is a new attraction. I observe that a species of trap-door has been opened, disclosing a counter with refreshments, over which presides a youthful maiden, who possesses a sort of "beauté du Diable," combined with an utter want of sweetness of expression, which is a very common type of face in Yankee land. Her features are thin, but well formed, and strongly marked—not exactly "chiselled "—(I believe no features of mere flesh and blood ever are, or could be "chiselled," without the most disastrous results.) Her hair is a warm, not to say hot auburn, twisted into ringlets of a most rigid and pertinacious spiral, and her face expresses that contempt for her species, which is sometimes observable in railroad officials of every grade. She favors me with a song, wherein I am informed that she is "Queen of a fair-hairy band."

Her voice does not altogether please me. It combines the sweetness of the parrot, with the grace and flexibility of the owl; but to use a forcible, if not elegant expression, it is "squawky." I retire from the presence until the song is finished, and then I return and purchase some refreshments for the sake of beguiling a few moments. I find a glass jar of octogenarian apples, which I decline, and select some fossiliferous gingerbread, some candy, and an extremely flexible cigar. I tender the necessary copper, which the maiden accepts scornfully, and then retire to a remote corner to examine my treasure. I commence with the candy, which appears to be coated with something of an earthy nature; but as I progress into the interior, it becomes more salubrious. In the next place, I attack the gingerbread; but as I have some regard for my teeth, I immediately desist, and go out and place it upon the rail in front of the locomotive, as a new labor for Hercules—not without some fear lest he should be thrown from the track. My apprehensions are unfounded—the gingerbread is crushed, and I am inspired with a new respect for Hercules. Then I proceed, with some difficulty, to light my flexible cigar and after one whiff, I throw it away, with as near an approach to profanity as my gentle nature and careful moral training will permit.

I look mournfully at the clock, and discover that I have still four hours more upon my hands. I find that my opinions of men and things are fast altering, for I now recall, with tender emotion, certain individuals of my acquaintance, whom, in happier moments, I was wont to designate as bores. I am fast getting desperate, and ready for anything. I think I could read, with complacency, an American comic journal. I am not sure that I could not even sit and listen to the whole of Pizarro. I pick up a scrap of newspaper, and find it contains, as I expected, a description of the Oviedo jewels. I think I will write something, and hesitate whether to commence a life of Jefferson, or like most of the poets, to make an attack upon that helpless young gentleman upon his back, known as Prometheus; but I can find no paper for either purpose, and the world suffers a loss.

Then I reflect upon the erroneous views of the hours—entertained by Guido and others. Instead of rather heavy-footed damsels, dancing blythesomely upon nothing in particular, they should have been depicted as snails or farm-horses, and other creeping things.

I feel it necessary to renew my stock of patience, so I go and look again at the placid old lady, who is still at work upon the mighty stocking; and then I take a walk, but as it has not pleased heaven to make me either a botanist, or a mineralogist, I grow weary of the desolate country, and return to the station, where, upon the platform, I find a pile of luggage, which I proceed to examine. Most of it is commonplace and uninteresting, but I observe a quaint old hair trunk, with mediæval handles, and a barbaric expanse of keyhole, which undoubtedly belongs to our lady of the blue fingers. There is a bald spot upon it, where the hair on the side of the horse who furnished the covering has been worn away by chain traces; and I meditate upon the career of this unfortunate animal until the subject is exhausted—which is not long. I discover a sea-chest, with a certain air of circumnavigation about it, together with a neat man-o'-war clothes-bag, and a hammock, skilfully rolled, so as to display the clews coquettishly. I am interested in this, and enter the house, where, by the freemasonry of the craft, I at once recognize the owner, a quiet young man, probably a second mate, with no outward indication of his trade except a certain carelessness of attire, and a very heavy overcoat, which all second mates wear at all times, and in all places. This man has perhaps visited almost every port in the world, and his whole life may have been a tissue of romance; yet he is shy and unobtrusive, and, unlike the hero of a late novel by Mr. Charles Read, he neither shivers his topsails or his timbers. In fact, I doubt if in the whole course of his life (apart from his professional duties) he has ever uttered as much nautical lingo as Mr. David Dodd contrives to introduce into an hour's conversation with two young ladies.

In striking contrast to this silent son of Neptune, there is an individual arrayed in the highest style of sartorial embellishment, and wearing earrings, who is narrating his adventures to a party of admiring and open-mouthed rustics. I listen to his ultramarine and rather Munchausen-ish "yarns," from which I learn that he is attached to a coasting schooner upon Long Island Sound. Like all tyros in the profession he is dreadfully "salt," and seasons his discourse with the combined beauties of Commodore Trunnion, Admiral Benbow, and the whole of Chelsea hospital. One would think he belonged to the old pigtail school, and had fed upon tar from his youth upward.

I grow weary of his tremendous epithets, and go out into the air, where danger awaits me. I see a train of carriages approaching, and in a moment I am surrounded by any number of country girls. I learn that they are attending a newly-married pair upon an extensive bridal tour of ten miles to the next station. The bride is white and gauzy and interesting, and the other party is uneasy and painfully well-dressed, as I suppose is customary upon such occasions. It so happens that the blissful swain is an acquaintance of mine, and I proceed to congratulate him, not exactly as they do in farces, by wishing him many happy returns of the day, but I have no doubt in some equally inappropriate manner. During the next quarter of an hour I am being presented to a succession of blooming damsels. I count thirteen of them, and then my senses fail me, and I "hold my breath for a time."

When I recover, I attempt to converse with some of them, but with indifferent success; and at last I ignominiously retreat to the "gentleman's room," so called. Here I find several natives who appear to frequent this place with an insane idea of amusement. I examine them, but find little to interest me. I fancy I can discover the effect of the railroad upon them; they are all more or less contaminated by city influences; every man of them wears an Oak Hall coat; and they do not even designate the time in the good old way, by guessing it is about two hours afore sundown; but state in a precise and official manner that it is 4.25. I observe one of them who wears very short pantaloons, which I have found to be generally the sign of an inquisitive disposition. I am not mistaken in my theory; he begins to question me, and I resign myself to him, body and soul. I am fascinated by him, and submit to be cross-examined like a witness until he has pumped me dry. I have no longer any family secrets; he is in possession of my past career, my present condition, and my future prospects. At last there is a lull, and I flatter myself that he has "asked all the questions there are;" but I am mistaken. He only pauses to bite off a chew of tobacco, as the sailors say, "as big as a horse's lip from his eye down." I avail myself of the opportunity and begin to question him, but I can derive but little satisfaction. His life seems to have been a blank; I can only learn that the old vampire comes to this place every day to fatten upon unfortunate travellers. Heaven knows how he spent his time before the station-house was built. He recommences in full vigor, and I despair of release. But here a rosy round-faced boy comes in, bringing a great gush of vitality with him, who proves to be the son of my grand inquisitor; and while his attention is diverted I effect my escape.

At last the hour of my deliverance is at hand; there are cheering indications; officials are bustling about; the ticket-office is opened, and a conductor suddenly springs into being, who is eagerly questioned, and makes answer,—"short, sharp, and decisive." Every face brightens and looks eagerly expectant. Presently the sweet tones of the whistle are heard; my friend Hercules appears, and at last, oh rapturous moment! I am seated in the cars, and he is rushing with me into the busy world.

W. H. F.

THE INDIVIDUALITY OF GENIUS.

Poetry, Painting, and Sculpture, form a kind of Trinity of Imagination, and are the offspring of inspired genius. Imagination is one of those eccentric nymphs that degenerate if forced to follow systematic and mathematical paths; and she exhibits most grace when allowed to dance her own spontaneous measures. The worst foe of literature and art is hero-worship,—that enthusiasm concerning certain kings of thought, which, in its veneration for the old, almost proscribes true originality in the new. From this tyranny, Poetry and Sculpture are, perhaps, the greatest sufferers. All absorbed in admiration for Homer, Milton, and Dante, Phidias, Angelo, and Giotto, our modern poets and sculptors seek first for a Homeric or a Phidian basis for their structures, rather than following inspiration in all its freedom.

This fact is most distinctly to be remarked in modern ARCHITECTURE. Originality seems to have nothing to do with the designing of our finest buildings. We pay a blind homage to all that is classical; and what is classical is imagined to be from necessity great and noble. A poor imitation of the Parthenon gains more admiration than an original design would, though it were more beautiful than the Parthenon itself. So long as we keep this exclusive respect for the ancients, we are only prolonging the existence of one of our favorite subjects of lamentation, viz, the inferiority of the modern. In fact, the modern always will be inferior to the ancient while its endeavors to equal it are confined to mere servile imitation. The error lies in our adulation of the production, rather than the conception. When we see a statue of rare merit, we confine our admiration to the beauties and graces of the face and figure, instead of bestowing it upon the splendid thought, the fine inspiration, that carved that statue in the mind of the sculptor. Thus, in architecture, it is the temple or the citadel we are enraptured with, and therefore it is that which we strive to imitate. This thirst for successful plagiarism naturally tends to fetter the workings of inspiration, and turn the eyes of ambition from the future to the past. Hence, Ruskin says, our architects are no architects, but only builders.

When the great heart of humanity throbs in symphony with poetic strains, it would seem strange that an old and primitive age should dictate poetry to all ages, yet such is almost the case, and is the result of our unscrupulous homage of the classical. True, this does not so well apply to the poetry of words and thoughts, as to the poetry of the marble; yet the imitative impulse is equally alive in both. Young poets, or young aspirants for that name, are far more apt to endeavor to model their style upon that of acknowledged classics than to electrotype their own fancies. Their error consists in ascribing all the glory to the ideas and the style of the great writers, rather than to the genius that embodied them. It is, in fact, this faculty of embodying one's own emotions, this vivid electrotyping power, that constitutes the great property of genius. Every enlightened man feels within him the gush of poetic rapture, and if every man had the power of putting this rapture into articulate language, we should all be great poets. It is but few who receive this gift, and they are recognized as poets by the test of that unutterable something in the breasts of the rest of mankind. We feel that they have translated the language of the heart into the language of the tongue.

It is, then, genius that makes a poet, but a poem is the offspring of genius inspired. The poem itself is only admirable because it is in the universal language of the heart. Therefore, let the modern poet speak this language as his own heart dictates, and let it be free from the brogue of imitation. There is something startling, something of awe in a new idea, but nothing very admirable in a thousand poems whose merit consists in being written in the Homeric or the Byronic style.

A. WATTERS.

Thoughts and Things.

BY ADA CLARE.

No. II.

I have seen Page's Venus, and I do not think it immodest. I know that many people differ with me in opinion, considering it to be too immoral for the human eye to gaze on, without colored spectacles, or through a black gingham veil. But how could a form so fragile, so delicate, be in anywise unchaste? Yet I will frankly admit that the Venus was quite as immodest as the white doves who drew her chariot.

There are many persons who think the human form a crime. It is only by forgetting that that form is capable of being divested of its clothes that they are able to think it other than a monster. If they could once fully realize that under their own clothes they themselves are naked, they would at once become hopeless residents of Bedlam.

I was much amused by the behavior of the ladies with whom the Dusseldorf Gallery was crowded on the occasion of my visit. Of course they did not go there to see the Venus! A sudden appreciation of the Dusseldorf Gallery had seized them simultaneously—a gallery to which, as every one knows, hundreds of new and fine pictures are added every year. Probably it was the picture of "Diana and her Nymphs," that attracted them all; else why should they have been crowded around it? I will not be so malicious as to draw conclusions from the fact that they admired that picture through the backs of their heads, and that it was placed exactly opposite the Venus.

I watched the ladies, too, as they entered. The younger ones gave it a furtive, not indignant glance over their shoulders, as they passed. The good-natured matrons trusted themselves to look at it with one eye, while others did penance for looking at it by gazing, afterwards, on some strictly religious picture. But your severe, antique maidens, whose age and Spartan virtue might have been supposed to put them beyond the danger of corrupting thoughts, glared at the opposite side of the room, with that slaughtering look in their eyes that convinced me that they would have gladly undertaken to stone Page with their own hands, for the unpardonable sin of suggesting that a woman may be young, handsome, and seductive.

But I cannot think this Venus, with the exception of the extreme purity of the form, a work of high art. The face is not even pretty. It is a face that indicates to me bad grammar, and an antipathy to bathing, which, in Venus, to say the least, would be very inconvenient. If that hair is golden, what do the storywriters mean when they speak of carrotty locks?

While I gazed upon this picture, a question of deep moment suggested itself to my mind, and I have not yet been able to solve it. It is this: If the *Herald's* suggestion, that the Venus on exhibition outstepped the lines of modesty, caused such an influx of ladies to the Gallery, what multitudes would have flown there, in case there had been a hint that an immodest Apollo was to be seen? This is not a conundrum, but a subject for serious scientific consideration.

o°o

I have had my thoughts on the late notorious wedding. I fear Miss Bartlett is not very shrewd, though the papers call her so. As if it took any shrewdness for a handsome, intelligent young woman, to captivate any elderly gentleman! I am not intending to censure her conduct. Eighty per cent. of women, and ninety-five of men, would have acted in the same way, under the same circumstances. A trap baited with four millions would catch a good shoal of souls any day, let alone bodies. Editors and Poets need not complain of it. They do what they can, with the rest of us, to set up money in the holiest places, crying "Glory be to thee in the highest!" As the world goes, four millions was a legal, proper, conventionally religious object, if not an honest and noble one. The bride's want of shrewdness consisted in parading the Oviedo man before the eyes of the public—a ceremony legally necessary to the contract, perhaps, but in reality a tedious encumbrance on the Oviedo estate. As it did not seem possible utterly to remove this incumbrance, the most sensible proceeding, it seems to me, would have been to conceal it as much as possible. The young lady might easily have married in private, sailed for Europe, and spent the Winter in Paris, after which she might have returned to America, in four-million-fold glory, completely and forever obscuring, by her fair and intellectual presence, the disparity between herself and her husband.

o°o

"Hope deferred maketh the heart sick." We have that on the authority of the prophets; therefore we have a right to be weary of the deferment of the Speranza.

Marie Cruvelli has not yet arrived. With regard to that artiste, I have noticed a story going the round of the journals, to the effect that she had been accustomed to star with her sister, and claiming excellence for her on that score. I was in Paris when she made her supposed début, in one of the provincial towns of France. This was some time after the marriage of her sister, and her consequent retirement from the stage. I remember that the Parisian journals spoke of her as having so fine a voice, that her sister, the illustrious Sophie, fearing her rivalry, had prevented her appearing upon the stage during her own career. Thus Marie is truly a novice, and that should only the more interest the public in her fresh and beautiful voice.

But for me the Opera is no longer a temple to worship in; its glory hath departed. They have let go by the chief among ten thousand, and altogether the grandest of them all. Of course I mean Cortesi. She, upon whom every Muse has seemed to set her seal, to give the world assurance of a genius. I can hear none other sing after her, without an emotion of passionate regret. To me, she has plucked the very soul out of music, and left it dead and colorless without her. Like Rachel, I am refusing to be comforted.

o°o

What an amount of brass it must require in the elementary constitution of the body, to plagiarize as people do in these days. The *Knickerbocker* publishes this month a story called the "White Queen," which is founded identically on a story in the *Atlantic Monthly* last Winter, supposed to be written by Miss Caroline Cheesebro', called the "Queen of the Red Chessmen." Did the author suppose the theft could pass unnoticed? What artlessness indeed!

Think of "Henry St. John, Gentleman," for a title in these days! The author has never heard of Miss Muloch's "John Halifax, Gentleman;" oh! certainly not.

MARY MORROW.

I.

Yes! the scene is all unaltered;
Scarce a tree is hewn or blighted,
Since our ardent faith we plighted
In our morning—in the springtime of our lives.
I see the river gently stealing—
The tireless swallows still are wheeling
Around the barn,
Methinks the self-same frogs are croaking
In yonder tarn!

II.

O'er pine-clad peaks, and painted meads,
And mountain rocks and marshy reeds,
The same supernal waves of light
Yet seem to flow,
That laved the feet of Mary Morrow,
Ten years ago.

III.

I've wandered by Italian streams,
And toiled among Tyrolean passes,
And felt the heart-bewitching gleams
Of Alpine and Italian lasses,
But never, in the gaudy day,
Nor by the moonlight's softened ray,
Have I beheld such spirit eyes
As those of Mary,
When o'er yon painted mead she tripped
So like a fairy?

IV.

Oftimes from Arden's hallowed realms,
Where joy makes vocal every glade,
Bright spirits seek this vale of tears,
To tell us of what heaven is made!
Too well my boyish heart divined
That this was Mary's work with me—
To point me out the way to Heaven,
Then sink into the daisied lea!

V.

Far up the mountain craggy side,
Upon a flat rock, huge and hoary,
Where oft, amid the crumpled leaves,
When Autumn filled the woods with glory,
Young Mary rested while she told
Some passage in the Saviour's story,
I writhe in bitter pain
To think that forty years may pass
Ere we may meet again!

VI.

The Summer sun in splendor gleams—
The fish are sporting in the streams,
The birds their merriest carols sing,
And echo makes the woodland ring
With harmony and joy:
But ah, my heart is rent in twain,
And never shall it thrill again
When Spring dispels fell Winter's gloom,
Or Summer buds in splendor bloom,
As when I was a boy.

VII.

What serves it when the bard is dead,
And hands that wrought are stiff and cold,
To heap up stones above his head,
And wet with tears insensate mold!
In yonder grave where daisies bloom,
And Winter spreads his winding sheet,
My hopes, my aims, my heart, are dead
To Winter cold or Summer heat.

A VOICE FROM OWEGO.

MR. EDITOR: Although my subscription to the SATURDAY PRESS has not yet expired, I take great pleasure in remitting you two dollars, to show that your appeal in the last number is responded to by at least one of your readers.

You may not know it, dear Editor, but in Owego, the SATURDAY PRESS is an institution—indeed, I may say a peculiar institution.

Ask G. H. A. if it isn't.

And, by the way, I wish you would send it more regularly. Why can't we have it on Saturday? for one of the ministers here says it's a capital preparation for Sunday. Don't flatter yourself, though; for two of them—two regular solemns, set apart by all sorts of ceremonies from the rest of mankind, and set over very decent kind of congregations—say, with the *Recorder*, that you ought to be promptly put down. One of them would hang you, if he could—and, for that matter, quarter you. At any rate, he wouldn't quarter you before you were hung—though I know more than one good fellow who would, and give you good quarters at that. For don't imagine that because this is a little provincial town, that it is a town of bigots. Far from it. There isn't a more liberal place in the State; and if we have a bigoted divine or so, and one or two not over charitable deacons, that is no more than are found everywhere. You have such people even in the metropolis—or used to have, when I lived there. The fact that you have a hundred or so subscribers here, is something to our credit—isn't it?

But what was I going to say? Oh! this—that you musn't, on any account, let the SATURDAY PRESS go down. We can't spare it.

Daniel Webster once said, in one of his exalted moments, that if the national debt couldn't be paid in any other way, he'd pay it himself. He didn't do it—debt-paying not being one of his gifts—but doubtless he would have done it if he had had the means. So with me and the SATURDAY PRESS: if it couldn't be saved in any other way, I'd save it myself, if I could. But you see I can't—though I am good for two dollars more, if you want it, if not two and a-half. So keep up a good heart, and believe me, though I never saw you "in the flesh" (they say nobody else ever did),

Your friend and well wisher,

A SATURDAY PRESS-BYTERIAN.

Owego, Oct. 25, 1859.

ART-ATTRACTIONS.

"The French and English Exhibition" at the Academy of Design, and the exhibition of Page's "Venus" at the Dusseldorf Gallery, will positively close to-day (Saturday). Church's "Heart of the Andes" will be on exhibition at the Studio Building for a short time longer. These, Waugh's "Italy" at Hope Chapel, and the exhibition of Rosa Bonheur's "Muleteers and "Morning in the Highlands" at Goupil's new gallery, 772 Broadway, are the principal art-attractions now on view.

NEW YORK NOVEMBER 5, 1859

Original Poetry.

AN IDYL OF OCTOBER.

BY GEORGE ARNOLD.

I.

JULIE, MARY, BILLY, and I,
Walked down the cedar-lane one day,
When the sun was bright in an Autumn sky,
And the trees with their Autumn tints were gay;
Down to the bridge our way we took,
Past the chestnuts that crown the hill—
Down to the bridge that crosses the brook,
On the road to the cider-mill.

II.

A year before, we had trod the lane,
And then, half-jesting, ourselves we bound
To take the self-same walk again,
When another year had rolled around ;—
So, when another October glowed
On shrubby hollow and wooded ridge,
It found us threading the cedar-road,
And loitering on the bridge.

III.

The water swirled 'mong the oaken posts,
In long, dark currents, eddying by,
And floating leaves, like shadowy ghosts,
Were borne on its bosom silently.
The breezes dallied with JULIE's hair,
Where mingling gold and umber played—
Fair MARY's face seemed still more fair
In the flickering shine and shade.

IV.

We feasted our eyes on the pleasant scene,
We gathered leaves of a thousand dyes—
Speckled with crimson, spotted with green,
And shaded with hues from Paradise—
We sang and shouted, we laughed and talked,
Till the woods were loud with our echoed glee–
O, never a merrier party walked
In a place more fair to see!

V.

Last year, when under the Autumn sky,
Through these bright Autumn woods we strolled,
We met a lassie, pretty and shy,
Mayhap some seventeen summers old;
A blue-eyed, bashful country-maid,
Who passed us, timidly glancing down,
Her blue eyes taking a deeper shade
From their lashes long and brown.

VI.

I, who have ever been *farceur*—
Loving a merry word always—
Feigned to have fallen in love with her—
A new-found passion, to last for aye.
So, when we spoke of the cedar-lane,
And plans for this year's ramble laid,
We wondered if we should meet again
With the blue-eyed, bashful maid.

VII.

Then, I said that if we should meet
With the country-lassie, modest and fair,
There on the bridge would I kneel at her feet,
And all my passion for her declare:
Well, as we came to the foot of the hill,
Where the maples glow like a colored flame,
Down the road from the cider-mill,
The blue-eyed damsel came!

VIII.

But, alas, for the ways of destiny!
I spied some leaves so gorgeously hued,
Decking the boughs of a maple-tree,
By a fence between the road and the wood,
That I vowed to have them whether or no—
Coveting beauty as some covert pelf—
And, venturing where the ground was low,
In a swamp I found myself.

IX.

There I gathered the prettiest leaves,
Standing, the while, on treacherous ground—
Such fair chaplets as Nature weaves
When Autumn, King of the Year, is crowned—
And there, alone, long after its time,
I found a heaven-blue violet,

Gleaming up from the ooze and slime
Like a jewel, foully set.

X.

Many a leaf of orange and red,
Gold and purple, scarlet and brown,
I found on the branches overhead,
Or where the wind had rustled them down;
Gathering these, no heed I paid
To anything save my leafy load,
And the blue-eyed, bashful, country-maid
Had gone, when I gained the road!

XI.

But JULIE and MARY both were there—
Better than bashful maids are they—
The blue-eyed lassie is not more fair,
And not more modest, as I dare say;
I felt some pride, as surely I might,
When I showed my leaves and my violet—
Those Autumn colors were wondrous bright,
But those faces were brighter yet!

XII.

Whenever I see those leaves again,
Pressed and varnished by JULIE's skill,
I shall think of our walk in the cedar-lane,
And the bridge on the road to the cider-mill;
And if e'er for the bashful lassie I sigh—
I, who have ever been *farceur*—
I will see that she does not pass me by—
I'll wait on the bridge for her!

WAKING FROM ILLUSIONS.

Written for the NEW YORK SATURDAY PRESS,

BY GETTY GAY.

"Too flattering sweet to be substantial."—ROMEO AND JULIET, Act II. Scene 2.

One by one have my most beautiful illusions vanished, and yet so far am I from despair, that I smile with mingled pleasure and sadness as I remember their verdant loveliness. How fresh and sunny they were in childhood, almost angelic, till the touchstone of actual experience, like the disenchanter's wand, exploded them forever, and left nothing but stony reality in their place!

I love my mother fondly still; but the beautiful illusion which hallowed her presence, imparting to my mind at once a heart-joy and a sense of perfect security, is gone, and I behold in her a woman almost as imperfect and fallible as myself. My affection is now measured, rational, and lives on the past; but it was then implicit and unbounded, the main stay of my confidence and of my daily delight. And what I say of my mother is in a degree applicable to my father, though he died years ago, before the excess of my filial affection had been tempered by a knowledge of the world. My heart is as warm as ever, but my head cooler; and the halo that surrounded every beloved object has disappeared, leaving it in cold clear light, which allows neither faith nor imagination to exaggerate its idol. Even things unseen, once as assured as things present and palpable, have, through statements of doubts, evidences, and discussions, partially lost their charm, and that nearness which filled my dreams, the rainbow, and the sunset, with angels, golden portals, and vistas leading up to heaven.

My father was a gentle and noble-hearted man, and I thought him perfection; but I longed for a brother who could share my juvenile feelings, sports, and pleasures. My only brother died in infancy. When I was about five years of age, I was sent to a school for little ones, and there became acquainted with a boy, almost twice as old as myself, who then seemed to me the most beautiful being I had ever beheld. He was "my wish exactly to my heart's desire" for a brother, and I almost looked upon him as such, for he made a pet of me,—perhaps because I was the smallest girl in the school, and, being also very delicate, involuntarily attracted his sympathy. He soon grew to be the hero of my day and nocturnal dreams, and I loved him more than I did either of my sisters, or even the baby.

He allowed me to stand or sit on the bench beside him, to play with his soft, curling, glossy brown hair, laughed on me with his beautiful blue eyes, and sometimes kissed me and gave me fruit and candy. But my love for him was not selfish, and the candy, fruit, and kisses might have been withheld, without causing any perceptible diminution in my regard for him. His partiality was remarked, and my schoolmates used to call him my beau. The import of the word was more than I could fully comprehend, but it conveyed to me meaning enough to gratify my pride, and fill my little heart with delicious confusion.

At home I was much flattered. I was very observant, and my sayings were considered remarkable in so small a child. But must I confess the truth? I was anything but an apt scholar, for I lacked that parroty faculty which enables children to learn their lessons without understanding a word of them. I was slow in committing to memory, and, being so fragile, my teacher was cautioned against urging too arduous application on my part. At the time I speak of, I had made less advance than any of my fellow-pupils; and, on one occasion, when the old maid who kept the school had been too busy all day to attend to me, I was turned over to my favorite boy, a very apt scholar, who undertook to hear me read my lesson. I was much excited by this event, and blushed as I approached him, and stood demurely by his side. My thoughts were constantly wandering from the page upon which I was gazing, and were too much occupied with him to allow me to do justice to myself. I gave him, no doubt, a deal of trouble, which disturbed the sweetness of his temper and disgusted him not a little with his employment. Becoming conscious of his displeasure, I grew more embarrassed and made more blunders than ever. Among others, I persisted in mistaking capital B for capital R, which letters seemed to me exactly alike, with the exception of their tails, one of which turned in while the other turned out; but which curl made the character B, and which R, was more than I could, for the life of me, recollect. My boy-teacher got out of all patience with me at last, and exclaimed:

"Well, I didn't think you so stupid! You are the biggest dunce in school!"

This to her who at home was esteemed so "smart" and before the very girls who had envied me so much on account of the preference the speaker had previously shown for me above them all! I heard them titter with delight at my disgrace. I can recollect the sensations I experienced then, perfectly, as if they had been awakened within the passing hour. The harsh words of one I had looked up to with so much esteem and affection, shocked me like blows, and my blood seemed to become suddenly heated, rising and filling my neck and face till sense grew dim,—as if my head had been wrapped in a veil. I had often heard my mother speak of feeling as if she would have sunk through the ground, and I said to myself, I feel like mamma now. I knew that all eyes were upon me, and I would gladly have vanished, but my limbs felt like lead. Something began swelling up from my bosom into my throat, and would certainly have choked me, had I not burst into tears.

What took place immediately after this I cannot say, but I believe I was very much convulsed, and remember, as I was recovering, hearing the governess ask my juvenile tutor :

"What have you been doing to this poor little thing?"

"I only called her a dunce," said he.

"That cannot be the cause, I am sure," rejoined the other, "for I must have called her so myself a dozen times. What did he do, Getty?"

I was a thousand times too proud to confess the truth, and replied, "Nothing—I am sick."

I was immediately put on the sick list, and soon afterwards sent home. I cried myself asleep that night, but I never after spoke to the boy who had offended me, and hardly deigned to look at him again. My excessive sensitiveness was morbid, no doubt; but in this instance, it taught me a useful lesson—not to long for a brother, nor to expect either great patience or constant gentleness from the rougher sex. My childish ideal was destroyed, and I censed to look for perfection, which was one step gained in wisdom that many adults obstinately refuse to take.

There was another of my schoolmates who dazzled my eyes—Minnie Melton—a girl wearing flesh-colored stockings, sleeves looped up with ribbons, and a shorter dress than any of us. She was lively, bold, and dashing, the daughter of an actress, and bought my friendship cheap—with copper lace and spangles. She told me such wonders of the theatre, and her mother's performances, that I allowed my father no respite from my coaxings, till he took me to see the play called "Cherry and Fair Star," in which "Fair Star was personated by Rosa Melton, parent to the girl with the flesh-colored stockings. Words are too dry and cold to paint my rapture at the sight of fairyland and Mrs. Rosa Melton, with vapory skirts, magic silver wand, and emblematic star. I was completely carried away by them, and filled to overflowing with their beauty and enchantment. The gorgeous magnificence, the thrilling life, the dazzling charms of the stage, made it appear a heaven to me, and I had, for weeks after, no room in my mind for anything else. I could not look upon Mrs. Melton as a mere mortal, but rather as a bright spirit, who had put on a visible form out of benevolence and condescension to humanity.

I did not, of course, reflect upon my own childish ideas, and hardly knew what I thought at the time, but gave free scope to the delicious new life with which they inspired me. I courted intimacy with Miss Minnie Melton, and coaxed her to accompany me to Sunday-school. She consented, and I called for her at the hotel at which her mother was stopping. I had dressed myself with unusual care, and wore a beautiful little quilted blue satin hood, lined with white silk, and trimmed with swan's-down, which set off my face to the utmost advantage. Even Mrs. Melton, herself, who was peeping through the blinds, honored me with a look and a compliment, which made me as proud and happy as a queen.

One Monday, during intermission at school, Miss Minnie took me aside, and told me that her mother had fallen in love with my hood, and wanted to wear it on her benefit night, in a new piece which was to be presented on that occasion. "If," said she, "I would lend it to her for a couple of days, she would return it to me uninjured, and repay me for the loan with any quantity of spangles, tinsel, and other glittering things." I was flattered immensely, and promised to let her have the hood. I was as good as my word, but had to steal the article out of my mother's bureau, and give it slyly into Miss Melton's possession, for fear my sisters should report proceedings at home, where they might fail to obtain general approval.

That my hood, however, should be hallowed, as it were, by being worn by so celestial a being as "Fair Star," the ravishing Rosa Melton, was a source of delicious exultation to me. "It would," Minnie told me, "appear upon her golden locks as she came down from the clouds, and win a share of the applause that would greet her descent." The thought set my lively imagination all aglow, and I half expected that some virtue would accrue to the hood, from the exalted experience through which it was passing. If, when I next put it on, it should make me look like a fairy, and enable me to become invisible at will; if I should find its quilting stuffed with diamonds, or its swan's-down set off with a double row of emeralds and rubies, I felt how happy and proud I should be to display my triumph to my prosaic relatives; but not that I should be taken at all by surprise.

I was nevertheless rather anxious to get my hood back, for I was afraid that mother, and grandmother, too, who held theatrical people in great contempt, would have no mercy on me, if they found out what I had been doing. After several days had passed without the fulfilment of the borrower's promise, I began to entreat Miss Minnie rather urgently not to postpone it any longer. Morning after morning she put me off with the excuse of forgetfulness, and flattering promises, and Sunday came round at last; but as it rained hard I had fortunately no occasion for the hood, and did not go out all that day. Another six days elapsed, on every morning of which I was played with as before; but when the next Sunday arrived, which proved very fine, I knew I must get the hood or take the consequences, more than I had the courage to face.

I rose early that morning and went to Mrs. Melton's hotel. Nobody was stirring in the place, and I walked about it like one lost. I tried to attract attention, but without avail. I felt a kind of pleasing awe in anticipating my interview with the "Fair Star" of my imagination, and half expected to behold her suddenly spring up through a trap-door, arrayed in snowy muslin, fleshings, and dazzling jewelry, or to see her descend through the ceiling, partially hidden in cloudy radiance, with a brilliant star on her spotless brow, standing on a floral throne, and presenting me with my hood on the end of her silver wand, with the addition of a pair of flexible glass slippers, or some such present equally elegant.

But nothing of the kind occurred; and seeing a waiter gliding about, I had to muster the courage to acquaint him with my business, but was told that it was no time to think of disturbing Mrs. Melton, and that I must come later. I had to go home without my hood, to breakfast, and after dressing for Sunday school, I managed to slip away again and return to the hotel. This visit was more successful, for I found Minnie, who again tried to put me off; but I told her plainly that I could not go back without what I came for, as I should be whipped if I did, and that I thought she had no right to expose me to punishment for doing her a kindness. She hesitated to usher me into her mother's room, but as she could not find the hood herself, she had no alternative, and in I went. I entered hesitatingly, expecting to be overpowered by a blaze of light, for my mind was prepared for a scene of fairy elegance and luxury, but not for what I actually beheld.

Never had I seen a picture of confusion equal to the appearance presented by that apartment. Everything it contained seemed tumbled, huddled, and "mixed up generally," in a manner best calculated to shock my Quakerish sense of order, cleanliness, and propriety. Costumery, made into what my grandmother would call "wads," was scattered here and there, and though there was a sufficient number of chairs and tables in the room, there was not a seat or spot clear of encumbrances. The floor was littered over with Mrs. Melton's dress, lying just as she had stepped out of it, with dirty clothes, empty bottles, odd shoes, soiled stockings, theatrical properties, and other miscellaneous articles. Upon the table stood empty glasses, bottles, and plates, sprinkled with fragments of segars, bread and cheese, and fish-bones. Above a marble wash-stand I saw the beautiful golden hair hanging, which I had imagined to be the natural growth of Mrs. Melton's head, and beneath it lay a set of false teeth grinning in frightful mockery. The walls were ornamented with two or three pictures of dogs and race-horses, and the mantel with small heaps of stage jewelry, that I had mistaken by gas-light for genuine, but the glass, wax, and coarse setting of which appeared common and lustreless in the light of day. Instead of the delicate perfume I had anticipated, the strong smell of stale liquor filled the room; and in lieu of the soft music I had expected, I heard the heavy breathing of the sleeper, in the bed occupying the corner of the room.

I was all eyes for the moment, and took in everything almost at a glance. I should now have to study a room half an hour to get it daguerreotyped in my mind as that was in less time than it has taken me to describe it. I began, as fine writers say, to experience a revulsion; but there was something stronger in store for me. The sleeper—that sallow, freckled, thin-haired, sunken-mouthed little woman—could it be Mrs. Rosa Melton herself? I should never have recognized her, had not Minnie in answer to my blank stare of astonishment said:

"That's my mother."

I had never dreamed of such a transformation, and would willingly have attributed it to some fell enchanter. She looked ghastly in her sleep. As we met with no success in our endeavors to find my hood, Mrs. Melton had to be awakened and made to understand the case. I see her now rolling over in bed, yawning lazily, half opening her big black eyes, disfigured underneath by blue shades and bagginess, demanding with an oath, in a tone as harsh as a rough man's, what was the matter. Her daughter explained. She honored me with a drowsy glance, and cursed me for disturbing her about such a trifle. She cursed my hood, too, and said she did not know where it was, though Minnie might look for it in the dirty clothes bag; but if we disturbed her again, she would skin us both alive. Having uttered this threat in a theatrical tone, she rolled over again, and swore herself to sleep.

The dirty clothes bag was hauled from under the bed, and soiled linen, dirty stockings, and towels were pulled out of it, and at last my unfortunate hood. At first I positively refused to recognize it; but it was mine, alas! and the transformation it had undergone was as deplorable as Mrs. Melton's from "Fair Star" to herself. Crushed, torn, soiled, and stained inside and out, it had lost all definite shape and color, and was no longer fit to be worn in the rain, much less suited for "Sunday best." By one string I held up my lately beautiful hood, now a limp, draggled, rent, spotted, disgusting thing, from which the swan's-down dropped in discolored particles, and against which my sense of smell and of vision revolted; the sight was too much for my feelings, and I burst into tears. The lame apology and consolation Minnie offered were unheeded and unheard, and I went home, weeping as I went.

There was no hope for it—wear it I must. I wiped it; tried to smooth and coax it into shape; bedewed it with my tears; but was wholly unable to get rid of a single stain, its sickly smell, or to bring it into any form whatever. I carried the loathed thing in my hand till we were outside of the door, and waited till the old folks had gone in front before I put it on. Vain stratagem! It proved as unavailing as it was shallow. My sisters' keen eyes discerned my disgrace in a moment, and hailed it with a simultaneous shout. Concealment was idle, and I had to confess the truth to them. Jennie, my elder, contented herself with a bitter "It serves you right, you little fool!" and walked stately on, paying no more heed to me; but Addy, my younger sister, who enjoyed a great flow of spirits, and had much of the monkey in her disposition, did not fail to improve the occasion to the utmost. She allowed herself to fall into the rear in order to view my hood from that point, declaring, as she returned to my side, "that she never saw anything so awful in her life: that she was sure Mrs. Melton had borrowed it for her dog's bed, and kept it till it was too dirty for him to sleep in." Then she shot ahead and took a look from the front, entreating me when I came up, to change hoods with the next beggar-girl that came along, if I could find one so foolish as to do it. When we arrived at Sunday school, she collected all the girls about me, told the story of my misfortune with mock sympathy, and insisted upon showing them the hood, which she said I was so proud of because it had been worn over Mrs. Melton's wig, and had slept a week next to her dirty stockings in the old clothes-bag.

But it was at home that I suffered most severely for my folly. There is no reason, however, why I should put the reader through the terrible ordeal I was compelled to endure. Let him drop a tear of genuine sympathy, and I consent to spare his feelings and pass on. The poetry and romance of my nature,—which had misled me in the matter of the hood,—had to sustain a severe shock and many a shaft of ridicule; but my father reproved me as gently as wisely.

"It is rather early for you to have such a lesson, Getty," said he; "but it comes better too soon than too late. If you live to be a woman, you will learn that the finery of this world, like the show on the stage, has much that is mean and disgusting behind it. You cannot help admiring the glittering and the beautiful, my child, but it is only safe to trust the good and the true."

"Ah! handsome is as handsome does," ejaculated my grandmother, who the next morning, as Minnie was calling for me on her way to school, bounced out and fired such a volley of stinging reproaches at her, that I doubt much if the little Thespian (a celebrated actress now) ventured within gun-shot of the house for years afterward.

Thoughts and Things.

BY ADA CLARE.

No. III.

I have just returned from a visit to a neighboring town, not many miles distant from New York, whither I went to witness the theatrical performance of a friend, notwithstanding her entreaties that I should not see her under such exasperating circumstances as she was surrounded with there,—notwithstanding her assurance that "the *stock* company, though having their heads on, had nothing in them, and ran round the stage like sick pismires on uncertain legs." But knowing the lady's personal attractions, and having heard her talents commended as most fine and rare, I determined to risk the surroundings.

The evening I had chosen was the occasion of the lady's benefit. I concluded to walk there, and on my way asked for directions from a very small boy. He declared his own steps to be bent in that way, and gallantly offered to conduct us, which escort we joyously accepted. What wonderment was mine, when he led me down a dark lane, into which the pigs would not have entered without the most masterly driving. Groping my way after him, and treading with much tribulation on the inconsistent paving-stones, I was suddenly stopped before a building, the door of which looked like the small cork of a dwindling little bottle, labelled "Theatre."

o o o

I was then ushered into the smallest temple, I may safely state, in which the Muses were ever throned. Sitting in the front rank of the box-circle, I was seized with an anatomical curiosity to measure the length of my arm, by stretching it over the parquette to shake hands with the gentleman who commanded the more momentous fiddle. The parquette seated thirty-two full-grown creatures; and though I am not prepared to substantiate the fact by oath, I am confident that the entire theatre would have seated three hundred, or even three hundred and nineteen people. At last the curtain rolled up and displayed a stage of the size of a Baptist pulpit, and bearing in its appointments a general resemblance to the same. The play commenced, and I saw a drama represented, to whose language I listened in astonishment. Had I then never seen the "Lady of Lyons," that the words of those who spoke with the tongues of men and actors, were strange and unintelligible to me? Did I hear the fair Pauline called Mamselle *Dish of Pills*, and no avenger near to force them down the libelling throat? What are these allusions to cabbages and turnips? Whence comes this whole kitchen-garden of vegetable metaphors? I know, I know that my lord the baronet did not soil his white-gloved fingers in bowling turnips through his dainty play.

I hear "What a coward is a man who has lost his *virtue* !" I had thought the word used was honor, but hearing it to be *virtue*, I am awfully staggered at the assertion. I think, while my blood freezes in my veins, what if my beloved country should be subjected to an invasion of foreign foes? In my trembling hands, the string which binds my roll of peppermint lozenges, breaks, and down they clatter one by one, in dismal succession, sounding like the hollow echo of my last hopes, rolling into the parquette of disappointment.

I brace my nerves, to sympathise with the unfortunate Pauline, whose efforts are at every step foiled and undone. Finally I turn to make a general survey of the audience. One thing above others strikes me—every other man has a toothpick in his mouth. The swain next to me is leaning forwards on his elbows, aggravating his dental members with a very large, very black jackknife, which is varied ever and anon, by snapping the blade in and out, wantonly regardless of the fact that knife-hinges were not constructed for the demonstration of perpetual motion.

The *Lady of Lyons* is finally dispatched in cold blood, and the curtain rises on a farce. The star of the evening sings charmingly, and with toothpicks waved aloft in air, the house screams with delight. Now a scene comes on, in which a number of students are presenting the lady with a tobaccobox. The presentation being over, the leader of the band, suddenly remembers that it is cue to kneel. All of the others stand irresolute whether to follow their leader or not, and finally settle the difference, by bending one knee and stiffening the other. The chief begins to bellow his love to the lady, when the uncertain followers are suddenly smitten with an idea, and cry "hear, hear !" The lady turns upon them with a wrath upon her brows, which plainly indicates that she is not deaf, which even indignantly protests against the insinuation touching the sensibility of her auric nerves. Suddenly a spectral arm, whose body is hidden in the side scenes, swoops across the stage. Each finger, bristling with separate meaning, writhes in violent contortions. Not Hamlet's father clothed in blasts from hell, nor Banquo shaking his gory locks, did so rack and fright the disposition of beholding men. It blows off the irresolute followers from the stage, as though it were a volley from a cannon's mouth. Even the ardent love-maker dropped his love, and flew before it. Not so the lady; she captured bodily the frightened swain, and brought him back to his vows and her feet.

The play, at last, is over; I rise as one in a dream—while the cold drops fall from my brow. I am sensible that I am about to be led behind the scenes; my limbs refuse to bear me—the arena swims around me. My companion gives me a supporting hand. I pass through galleries, through private boxes. I leap out of a window, upon a three-legged chair. I climb over the stage, cutting my way through dismantled cottages, over prostrate mountains, under inanimate windmills. By turns, I leap, I plunge, I crawl, I fly, I swim! Down stairs whose steps have a mad desire to personate inclined plains, and hopelessly acute angles; up stairs whose Alpine steeps would fright the pregnant hinges of the knee, though planned on Brobdinagian scale.

The smallness of the space is amended by the hugeness of the confusion. The turtle of impediment rests on the serpent of difficulty—that again on the elephant of impossibility. Up and down, down and up, I go—over and under, through and above, below and around, until I am at last thrust into a cell, where I fall, lifeless, into the arms of the star-lady.

The following criticism of the performance appeared, the next morning, in one of the daily papers:

THEATRE.—The —— brought out a new star last evening, Miss——. She appeared as Pauline—a character that she sustains with marked ability. Miss—— is a young lady of decided talent. She has a glorious figure, and is, by all odds, the best-looking actress we have had at the Gayety Theatre this season. Miss—— is a very spirited actress, and is full of all those stage movements so necessary to the success of a first class *artiste*. Miss—— is never still. She is continually doing something to give employment to the eyes and admiration of the audience. Miss—— made a decided hit last evening, and we expect to see her create a perfect furore among our good-looking young men. This evening she appears as Parthinia, in Ingomar the Barbarian. We expect to see the house crowded with yellow kids and lavender-flavored handkerchiefs.

°°°

I think the happiest days are far from being the quickest to pass away, notwithstanding the popular belief to the contrary. When we suffer, the days wear themselves out with dragging against the sharp corners of our griefs. In a long, weary voyage at sea, the eye, ever gazing on a vague waste of waters, loses its estimate of distance, while the mind equally lets go all measurement of time. But the blue shore at last breaks upon the sight, starred with its thronging cities. To the yearning ear ripples a murmur of sweet words and voices. An earth-mother, too, smiles up a welcome from her deep heart, through her beamy eyes of hill, and stream, and town, and forest—and lo! time and distance are again born in the mind, and all that uncounted, timeless water-path hangs dim and spectral in space. So, indeed, the heart takes no count of days or years, in the sullen, trackless ways of doubt and despair; but let some new hope and happiness sweep shining up before it—then it weighs and strives to hold back each moment for the sake of its own joy, and all that vast void of grief which it has toiled through, blackens in the distance, with its eternity contracted to a breath-spasm, and its world-disc shrivelled to a pinpoint of space. If it were not so, if pain worked the same intensity in its endurance, that pleasure does in its enjoyment, in the present grievous dispensation of life, half the existing hearts would crack and break up, like glass vials under exhausted receivers.

I have discovered another instance of plagiarism. *All the Year Round* publishes a story called "Lois the Witch," of which the plot and circumstances are wrenched boldly and unblushingly from Miss Cheesbro's "Victoria."

I understand that the story, "The Queen of the Red Chessmen," attributed to that lady, is really from the pen of Miss Hale, of Boston.

Dramatic Feuilleton.

Operatic.

Two sensations:

1. *Maria di Rohan*: Gazzaniga, Stigelli, Ferri, Mme. Strakosch.
2. *La Favorita*: Gazzaniga, Beaucarde, Amodio, Junca.

Maria di Rohan is not very frequently done here, and it is not generally well treated when it is done.

The story is pretty good, though hardly the thing for the domestic fireside of a New-Connection Methodist family.

Probably everybody knows all about Maria. She was a very well bred person, with a weakness for flirtation.

That was in the time of Louis something (not Delmonico's), or the Regency, I forget which.

In such matters, one can't be particular about dates, —the number of women of Maria's order having been very large, in France and elsewhere, at all known periods.

I am told that there are several in New York, now.

They are good things to make plays and operas of.

In point of fact, I don't know what the composers and dramatic authors would do without them.

In this opera, Maria gets into a great deal of trouble through her flirtations, first with the contralto, a sort of Page of the last century, and then with the tenor, the *Count de Chalais*, a man about town, and not a proper person to ask to dinner, if there are grown-up young ladies in the family. The baritone, the *Duke de Chevreuse*, who has a proprietory right over Maria, don't see all this in an agreeable light; and after terrific row, and several fights and propositions to fight, he (the baritone) takes the tenor into a little closet on the left hand side of the stage, and then and there, with a deadly weapon—to wit, a pistol, charged with powder and a leaden bullet—does him to death. Returning, the triumphant baritone strikes an attitude in the centre, and the unfortunate Maria flops down in one corner, like a discarded bath towel.

As I said, it is a very pretty story.

The music is considered as among the finest that Donizetti has written,—passionate, powerful, sensuous, —it belongs to the thorough Italian school, which I believe no one except Donizetti, Verdi, and Mercadante ever expressed.

It is unfortunate for us, however, that the artists will take liberties with the score of *Maria di Rohan*, cutting and slashing it as furiously as if it were a *Ledger* drama, or a five-act tragedy by "a distinguished American author." Stigelli, the tenor, had very hard work with his rôle, and sung what he could manage of it, as if he was in great pain. He may truly be called a painstaking artist. [That expression is original with the critic of the *Spirit*.] Gazzaniga got herself up very well for Maria, and looked like the fascinating feminine whom she intended to represent. She sang the Cavatina of the first act,—a favorite concert-piece with her—admirably; and although overshadowed, not to say bullied by the baritone, was still very fine in the last act.

Ferri won the honors of the night, as Badiali did before him, and as every decent baritone always will in this opera. People always like to see the tenor pitched into when it is done strong, and Ferri is absolutely ferruginous. I am very fond of this baritone's style of singing; his mezzo-voce is the best I have ever heard, and his execution remarkably fine. He nearly set an enthusiastic foreign friend of mine crazy, and created a real furore.

Mme. Strakosch looks too prim, proper, and matronly en garçon, and was not equal to the musical requirements of the rôle of di Gondi. Who can ever forget the slashing way in which Vestvali acted it? She suggested rope ladders, assignations, duels, and billet doux in every movement.

That'll do for *Maria*.

Now about Beaucardé.

I think young Coupon expressed the opinion of the audience that assisted at the *Favorita* on Wednesday.

Young Coupon's Governor is cashier, or something, in a bank, and the juvenile looks at everything from a Wall-street point of view.

So he said to me: "I say, do you know what I think?"

Never having suspected him of any exercise of his mental faculties, if he has any, I, of course, replied in the negative:

"Well, I'll tell you: Brignoli's stock goes up ten per cent. every time they take and trot out a new tenor. I'd like five shares in it now."

Now I don't intend to compare Brignoli and Beaucardé together. But the comparison is irresistibly forced upon a public which has become accustomed to the first-named artist in a rôle, the music of which is admirably suited to his powers. So this public says Beaucardé may have been a great singer; he certainly sings well now; he is a fair actor, though not young enough nor handsome enough for the Leonoras to go crazy about; but he has evidently, in some inspired moment, sung himself out of voice.

Like all the artists, Beaucardé has been a warm political partizan in Italy. In '48 he was a most ardent Republican—one of the reddest of the red. A friend, who was at Florence during that exciting period, tells me that Beaucardé went, personally, day after day, among the insurgents, singing the songs of Liberty, and teaching them to the young men. At night he would go to the theatre, and sing in the opera. The next day would find him again in the ranks. His voice was then in its prime, but he has absolutely almost worn it out.

Such an artist as Beaucardé really is, even now, cannot fail with our public. This is quite as certain as Coupon's idea, that Brignoli will not be supplanted. It is a good idea, also, to have an artist like Beaucardé, to keep Brignoli up to his work.

Gazzaniga's *Leonora* is a truly great performance. In the last act, she gives you a sensation equal to the shock of a galvanic battery. There are occasional flashes in Gazzaniga's acting which are worthy of Ristori.

The Matinées are coming up again—the manager having pledged his word that the programmes shall be given as announced, without mutilation.

They used to cut an act here and there, to oblige some artist who was hungry and wanted his maccaroni at half-past three.

The public, crinoline, said it was a shame, and kept its dollar for marrons glacés.

Now the public is mollified. So every one will go to-day, when the programme is immense. There is a good deal of good Italian opera, and the Draytons in *Don't Judge by Appearances*—very appropriate motto for the Academy, just now.

Apropos to the Draytons: They open at Hope Chapel on Tuesday, and will do very well, I believe. They ought, however, to pray to be delivered from the insane partisanship of certain asinine friends, who are laboring zealously to secure for the Parlor Opera the hostility of the entire press.

Rows and Things.

My little affair with the jokers of the *News* and the old *Spirit* is going on famously.

Next to the diptheria, it is the greatest thing of the season.

The *News* man takes my advice and keeps his temper.

He is a good boy. I accept his apology. I forgive him freely. Let him consider himself embraced,— French fashion.

There, we are friends again!

The other is not so philosophical. He does let his angry passions rise; he *does* wish to tear out the subscriber's eyes, and writes sundry wicked things about the subscriber, which lacerate the subscriber's tender susceptibilities in the most agonizing way.

Evidently belligerent is the friend of Virtue, and of the Draytons.

I don't see it.

But I warn him to beware of one thing. Let him say what he pleases about the wicked, the corrupt, the malicious, the ill-looking, the ignorant, the stupid PERSONNE, but let him beware how he speaks of the Brightest and Best of her sex,—the favorite female child of the Eagle, the most angelic creature that was ever sheltered by the Flag of the Free, or any other drapeau,—need I say, ANNA MARIA !

One word against her, and I shall be changed from a Feuilletonist to a Fiend, and shall send the Last of the Barons after the heaviest of the critics, at once.

So, rash youth, be warned in time. There is a step, beyond which, etc., etc.

Laura Keene's.

The Election wouldn't do here, and it has been temporarily replaced by *The Marble Heart* (Les Filles de Marbre), in which Jordan is splendid as *Raphael*, Wheatleigh very good in *Volage,* and Miss Keene clever, though occasionally jerky and spasmodic, as *Marco*. It is a very entertaining style of play, *The Marble Heart,* and I recommend Dr. Bellows to see it before it gives place to the *Wife's Secret* which is up for next Monday.

The Barney Williamses

Are still doing a rousing business at Niblo's Garden, which is crowded every night by the nobility of the Oriental districts, the gentry from Peoria and Pike county, and ordinary people from the Fifth Avenue and other parts of the world. The last thing is a lively piece, called *Ireland as It Was,* in which persons who have been so unfortunate as to own estates in Ireland and expected to get any rent from their tenants, are abused as they richly deserve. The incidents of the play, as may be imagined, are of a particularly exhilarating character, and Mr. Barney Williams relieves my mind very much by the announcement in the bills that things in Ireland look much better now than when this play was written.

A. M. inquires, in the simplicity of her heart, why do the play then.

Bless your dear little soul,—isn't Barney Williams an Irishman?

George Christy

Has commenced a burnt-cork campaign at Niblo's Saloon. Just think of it,—where they have the Bachelor's Ball! Facilis descensus Africanius. To oblige "a literary friend," (crinoline) who adores G. C. I shall see him half an hour and report progress.

Theatre Français.

They have been stealing another of our pieces here; *Les Crochets de Père Martin,* is nothing more nor less than a three act drama, written by "a distinguished American author," for Mr. and Mrs. W. J. Florence, and produced at Wallack's last Summer, under the title of "There's many a slip twixt the Cup and the Lip." People say, however (you know people will say all sorts of absurd things), that the French piece is a great deal the best. It is quite certain that it has made a veritable success, a fact which is owing, with out the slightest doubt, to its American origin.

Novelties.

At the Winter Garden, *Nicholas Nickelby*.

At Wallack's a Walcotized version of *Les Deux Aveugles*. They are both cleverly done, and have had a due measure of success. In the *Nicholas Nickelby* the honors belong to Miss Agnes Robertson as Smike, Jefferson as Newman Noggs, and T. B. Johnston as Squeers. T. B. has toned down a little and is much better for it. His performance was decidedly one of the very best order. The acting throughout was very good. If you want to have a real good laugh you ought to see Holland as the Specimen Boy at D., the Boy's Hall.

The other piece, "Going it Blind," is an affair between Brougham and Walcot, and between them they manage to make a good thing out of it.

Miss Walcot has done the work of translation very cleverly; and I hope to hear before a great while that she has employed her pen in some dramatic work of greater intrinsic merit than *Les Deux Aveugles*, which does not amount to much at the best.

N. B. If any one is disgusted with this Feuilleton, let not the subscriber be blamed.

It is the diptheria.

Now don't ask me what the diptheria is? Never mind, please; it is something very disagreeable, and I have got it awfully.

The only thing that consoles me, is that everybody has got it more or less, and that it is considered quite the correct sort of thing to do. After all it is not so bad as being bored to death by a veteran proser, like the "musical cricket" of the old *Spirit*.

PERSONNE.

VENUS AND THE DUSSELDORF GALLERY.

To the Editor of the Herald:—

DUSSELDORF GALLERY, Nov. 1, 1859.

To-day's *Herald* says:—"We see that Page's Venus has been transferred to the gallery of the National Academy of Design, Tenth street, with the view, we presume, of giving its beauties the advantage of a better light;" and goes on to say—"It was pretended by connoisseurs in these matters that it was badly placed and badly lighted in the Dusseldorf Gallery." The real reason for its withdrawal was, that during its stay (owing, perhaps, to your *critiques* thereon) a class of visitors attended the gallery who evidently came not to view a work of art, but a picture of that character which would pander to their baser passions; though they were doomed to disappointment, as they pretty plainly expressed by their manner on leaving, grumbling out some such sentence as—"Why, there is nothing immodest in that picture; it's a take in," &c., &c. This, coupled with the fact the daily journals announced that at a drinking saloon in Broadway "The Venus on a half shell, with other unsophisticated pictures," &c., &c., were on free exhibition; and out of respect to the feelings of the artist (who, though a stranger to me, is, I believe, a gentleman of refined and most sensitive nature—one who would not wish the agent employed by him for its exhibition to thus gain money at the sacrifice of name, pride and self-love), we determined to close the exhibition. As to the amount received at the doors, perhaps a faulty caligraphy has caused the three to be taken for a five—the correct figures being $3,010 12. You will be pleased to understand we could have retained the picture for another month, but had the privilege to conclude our agreement at the end of four weeks, which we did for the reasons stated above, and though, perchance, at a pecuniary loss to ourselves. It has been replaced by Mr. William L. Sontag's "Dream of Italy," a work we trust, which will command the attention of your pen.

THE DIRECTOR of the Dusseldorf Gallery.

Inauguratory Concert.

Mr. Robert Goldbeck, assisted by Messrs. Perring and Aptommas, advertises an attractive Concert for this (Saturday) evening, for the inauguration of "Goldbeck's Music Hall""—which, by the way, is the handsomest hall of its size in the city, and admirably adapted in all respects for lectures, readings, musical entertainments, and the like. For particulars of this evening's concert, see advertisment.

Tit for Tat.

Apropos of Dubufe's portrait of Rosa Bonheur, now on exhibition at Goupil's, Jo. Cose (whose French is at least doubtful) says that as Rosa painted des boeufs, it was no more than fair that Dubufe should paint Rosa.

The Great Eastern.

An idea of the size of this mammoth steamship may be inferred from the fact that persons occupying her forward berths are to be charged double price, on account of the advantage they will have of arriving in port in advance of their fellow-passengers.

NEW YORK NOVEMBER 12, 1859

Dramatic Feuilleton.

Various Things.

The Teutonic population has been in a high state of excitement, apropos to the celebration of the one hundredth anniversary of the birthday of F. von Schiller, who was a great poet, and who therefore belongs as much to you and me, Able Editor, as to Burkhardt, or Belmont, or any other Germanian. But this Festival has been made distinctly German, and therefore it is of no more consequence to us than if it had taken place at Stuttgart or Berlin, instead of at the City Assembly Rooms and the Academy of Music, in New York.

At the City Assembly Rooms, some seventy fiddlers, in several rows, had a severe difficulty with that terrible Ninth Symphony of Beethoven, which I believe no one, out of Boston, has any right to play. They say the Symphony was well played, but the singers were bad. At the Academy there were tableaux vivants, illustrative of Schiller's works, and a short drama, "Wallenstein's Camp." It is a pity that one of his good pieces, the *Robbers*, or *Mary Stuart*, or the *Maid of Orleans*, or *William Tell*, could not have been given.

Instead of that, however, Judge Daly made a speech!

Mr. Wallack has brought out, with what is technically called "a powerful cast," Buckstone's drama, *The Wreck Ashore*.

Mr. Bourcicault is preparing for the Winter Garden a five-act play, the scene of which is laid in the Southwestern part of the United States. It may be expected at the Winter Garden in about three weeks from this time. Just now Smike is drawing fine houses, and therefore remains in the bills.

You have heard of the art-discussion between the members of No.— Fire Engine Company, in relation to the proper decoration of their machine, and of the final result in the passage of a resolution moved by the Foreman, to the effect, "that the tub be painted blood-red, and adorned with the figure of the Goddess of Liberty chained to a rock."

That story was told about a late lamented Senator, who "met with an accident" in California the other day. After he died, your amiable neighbor, the *Tribune*, described us what a friend of mine would call a "d——d elegant gentleman"; and it seems that his example has a refining effect upon several other persons, connected with various other "tubs." For one, Plunkett, a lineal descendant of Brian Boru, having written for that especial haunt of the Muses, namely, ye Theatre de Bowery, a drama called "Three Eras in a Fireman's Life," and said piece having been accepted, and Boniface being announced to play the part of "the Hon. D. C. Broderick," there came a gentle message to the management, to the effect that if the play was performed they would tear the house down. The managers referred the matter to the notice of pious Pillsbury, who, it seems, was not equal to dealing with it, and the play has not yet been presented.

That's the beauty of Republican Government and Metropolitan Policemen !

The *Express* and some other journals have printed a long story about Mario having married a Spanish Marchesa, and then deserted her, and have endeavored to connect it with the recent occurrences at the Madrid Opera-House, where Grisi was twice hissed in Norma. It is all bosh. Grisi was hissed because the Madrid people did not wish to hear her. She has remained on the stage long after the period when she should have retired.

The Draytons have commenced Parlor Operations at Hope Chapel, which they have fitted up with a neat stage and theatrical accessories. Notwithstanding the earnest efforts of the critic of the old *Spirit* to injure the Draytons, they have yet a fair prospect of permanent success.

Genius, sir, rises triumphant above the fulsome flattery of its friends.

They had a great bill at the Bowery the other night, when the powerful moral drama, *Jack Sheppard*, was announced, with "three ladies" as *Jack*, one for each act. I made up my mouth for a new sensation, but was prevented from having it by another engagement. I haven't been the same man since.

The pretty actresses are going off rapidly. Lucille Western is married. [Eheu! M le Baron] so is Josephine Gougenheim; Adelaide has sailed for Europe, and Miss Ada Clifton has gone to Havana.

The Wife's Secret.

Did you ever go to the old Park Pit?

No? Well, then, you know nothing about plays. You may talk about Brown and Jones, but you ought to have seen Robinson! There was an actor for you—rather!

Ask the editor of the *Programme* about it.

He was one of the old Park Pit fellows, and that is the reason why he writes such sweet articles in his paper.

They had good plays at the old Park, in spite of the Pit, and the *Programme*. One of them was *The Wife's Secret*, drama in five acts, by Lovell, author of *Love's Sacrifice*, and other good plays.

The incident upon which the plot is founded is not new. It has been used in a piece called St. Mary's Eve, which was played by Celeste, but not at the old Park. There, the Charles Keans did *The Wife's Secret*, and it had a deserved success.

It is the beau ideal of the sentimental, emotional drama. You have a lovely English country-house, in the middle of the Seventeenth Century. The master, a Colonel in the Parliamentary forces, is about to return to his home. The adherents of the man, Charles Stuart, are scattered in every direction, hunted by the spies of the Protector. Among these unfortunate gentlemen is Lord Arden, whose sister is married to the Parliamentary Colonel aforesaid. Arden takes refuge in the house of his sister. Of course he has the most thorough contempt for his Cromwellian brother-in-law, who, on his part, is resolved to maintain the existing government at any hazard, and would give a malignant to the block as coolly as he would eat a sausage.

The Wife, who dearly loves her husband, and has the most devoted affection for her brother, is compelled by the latter to swear to keep the secret of his hiding-place intact from everyone. The point of the play, then, is in the struggle between the Wife's devotion to her husband, and her desire to keep her oath to her brother. This is put before the audience in the plainest, clearest, and most compact way, and the plot is easily and naturally evolved.

The play has no "poetical beauties," for which, all thanks. You are not bored continually with fine speeches which are written to show off the "gifted writer," who, properly, should have been confined to the corner of some village newspaper.

The acting was very good. Miss Keene depicted all the varying phases of the character with remarkable skill. Her performance of the fifth act was truly admirable.

For the others: Mr. Jordan acted gracefully and well; sacrificed, likewise, his side-whiskers, but wore "curly hair," which the Cromwellians did abominate and put away from them, as a wicked device of harlots and swash-bucklers. In gallant bearing and elegance of costume, trés bon gout from shoe-buckle to collar, Mr. Jordan was far more like a cavileer than the representative of Lord Arden, who looked and acted as if he had just escaped from some Amateur Histrionic Lunatic Asylum. However, there is some consolation in the fact that he had very little to do. Mr. Burnett played the Steward very well, but acted a little too much. Some bits—especially his exultation at the end of the third act, where the Colonel through a window sees his wife embracing her brother, then supposed to be her lover—were very fine. Miss M'Carthy plays a Page, who should be more soberly dressed; and Miss Wells the waiting-maid of the lady of the house, a part which should be acted by a younger and more comely woman.

Altogether, however, the play was well done. Two things I noticed especially—the tasteful arrangement of the stage, the surroundings, furniture, costumes, etc., correct to the smallest detail; and the rigid administration which must have been brought to bear upon the production of a five-act play, with the first performance of which no one could pick a flaw. The performance passed off as smoothly as if the actors had been playing in the same piece together for twenty nights.

I sat through the whole five acts, and I am going to do it again. The only thing I fear is, that the play is too good for our people, whose dramatic digestion has been spoiled by red-pepper and Worcestershire-sauce dramas.

The Sicilian Vespers.

There seems to be a lively difference of opinion among the musically-disposed portion of the community, as to the merits of what a foreign friend of mine calls "Werdi's Wapers."

If I remember rightly, the opera did not have such an astounding success in Paris, where it was produced at L. N.'s own theatre, and as Ullmann says, "written at the Emperor's express command";—although how he could "command" Verdi, who is not a French subject, does not seem clear to the subscriber.

So far, the Vespers has not been so successful with this public as the *Trovatore* or the *Traviata*. But an opera which I consider much better than either of the two last-named, to wit, *Rigoletto*, made a dead failure on the first night. Now it is the most popular of the composer's works. The Vespers is not so wealthy in popular melodies as Verdi's other operas. It runs more to morceaux d'ensemble, and elaborate combinations, which remind you of Meyerbeer. The music of the third act is all good, but it is rather a study for a connoisseur than a treat for the popular ear. Strictly speaking there are only two melodies which one can carry away in his head. These are the light chorus in the first act, and the Bolero in the last. They are both quite familiar; the first sounds like twenty other things, and the second is a vehicle for ambitious young ladies, who think they are ready to come out at the Academy when they can manage to sing a scale.

As for the drama distinct from the music, it has not been helped by being done into choice Italian. It is not a lucky subject, and although often used, has always proved a delusion and a snare to the dramatist. I can remember but one instance where the contrary was the case. When I was a small boy (only a few years ago), one of my theatrical idols was Mr. Charles R. Thorne, an actor who has circulated pretty generally all over the world, and is just now at Pike's Peak; in those days he was a handsome man, and a powerful actor in the old fashioned d—nation-foiled-again school. When he had a benefit Mr. Thorne always played a drama called sometimes *Di Procida*, alias John di Procida, alias *The Avenger*, alias *The Moor of Sicily*. This was successful, because it carefully avoided all the historical facts in the case, if there are any. *John* was a Moor, who had a daughter, *Stella*, a good-looking young woman, much affected by the Viceroy of Palermo, a double-dyed scoundrel, who bullied all the men and seduced all the women—except Stella, who didn't see it; and when the Viceroy was about to "use force to accomplish his base purposes," *John* arrived in a suit of brass clothes and a great hurry, and polished off the Viceroy in a hand-to-hand combat. Everything fell to pieces then, and the play closed with an eruption of Mount Vesuvius.

That's what I call a good play. When they shouted "Sicily was free," I always felt glad; but now when I find that Sicily only stays free a day or two, I've lost my interest in its political affairs.

Brignoli and Colson seemed quite as indifferent as myself. Colson plays the rôle of a young lady who is mixed up in politics to a tremendous extent;—she is also "dead in love" with Brignoli, and thinks seriously of killing his father (which in that country, I suppose, would not be considered in the light of an unget-over-able "obstacle to their union"); first she *is* going to be married, and then she isn't; and then she is going, in all the glory of black Lyons velvet (Anna Maria said it could *never* have cost less than eight dollars a-yard), to have her head cut off; and then the Viceroy thinks better of it; and then she is going to be married, when the Sicilians come down, at the signal of a general fire-alarm, and massacre the whole lot. There's no eruption—at which I was disappointed; but there is a valuable architectural study in the scenery of the last act, all the orders being combined in a novel way.

Colson went through all her little difficulties with the most charming equanimity, and took all the ills of life and the prospect of immediate death with the calmness of a true philosopher. She sung the music correctly; but, in a thoroughly emotional rôle, the public demands something more. It is not Colson's fault that she is not a lyric tragedienne. She's the best singer of French comic opera we have ever had here, and is rapidly improving in Italian; but she has little or no sympathy,—having been cut out and polished from a hard French model.

I hear it whispered that the cast of the Vespers is to be changed, and that Gazzaniga and Beaucardé are to take Colson and Brignoli's rôles.

It has been objected to Gazzaniga that she cannot sing the Bolero so well as Colson; but that is of no consequence. There is no earthly reason why the prima donna should sing a Bolero in that situation.

All the daily critics praise the mise en scene, and I agree in what they say. The concluding scenes of the first and second acts are the most brilliant ever seen at the Academy.

There has been a good deal of fine writing, too, about the opera, and I close with the following sample: "The persistent *ictus* of the light-footed, delirious, Mediterranean terpsichoreanism."

Quite unnecessary to say that that is one of Fry's sentences.

Correspondence.

To the Editor of the SATURDAY PRESS:

DEAR SIR—I have no objection to being pitched into critically. I don't mind having a saw run on me, and can stand a good rasping as well as any one you know; but I do object to being accused of writing original comedies from the French.

When *Personne*—whom I admire quite as much as he admires the angelic "A. M."—states that the comedy by CORMAN *et* LE GRANGE, entitled *Le Crochets du Pere Martin* is the original of a comedy written by me, and played at Wallack's Theatre, last Summer, entitled "Many a Slip 'Twixt the Cup and the Lip," he simply states that which is not true, for these reasons:

Firstly—I have never seen the French comedy in question, either in print or on the stage.

Secondly—I never heard of it until I saw it announced at the French Theatre.

Thirdly—I had never seen a translation of it, neither did I know that a translation had been made, until after I had written my comedy.

Fourthly—The comedy of "Many a Slip 'Twixt the Cup and the Lip" was written nearly, if not quite, four years ago. And

Fifthly—As far as I can learn, there is no similarity between my comedy and the French play in question. Yours very truly, CHARLES GAYLER.

Brooklyn, Nov. 8th, 1859.

If Mr. Gayler will read the analysis of the plot of *Les Crochets*, printed the other day in the *Evening Post*, he will see that the rascally Gauls have stolen his main idea—as I stated.

PERSONNE.

Thoughts and Things.

BY ADA CLARE.

No. IV.

I have finished reading "Beulah." Let the fact be recorded as a proof of my extreme pertinacity of purpose. "Beulah" is another inane copy of "Jane Eyre." But it is a waxen, corky, wooden-jointed, leather-and-findings imitation of it. Authors too often imagine that when they have succeeded in portraying an unnatural character, and stuck it all over with ridiculous traits, like porcupine-quills, that they succeed in creating a type. They never seem to imagine what lumbering and foolish monsters they erect.

"Jane Eyre" was a breathing, blood-warmed being, whose vitality might have been uncommon,—but it was still life. In her wrists, you felt the beatings of purple pulses; and troops of passionate longings, visible though veiled, swarmed in her sober eyes. But "Beulah" is a wearisome, artificial piece of paste-board, in whose troubles you cannot sympathize, whose pride is obstinacy,—whose grief, sentimentalism of the flabbiest sort,—and whose whole life, too appallingly stupid to be reflected upon.

o o o

I saw the "Marble Heart," last week. Three years ago, I saw it so often that every line was familiar to me. It gave me a curious twitch at the heart to see it again. It was like coming unexpectedly upon a dead friend's letters.

Laura Keene is one of the few actresses I have seen, adapted, both by nature and art, for her profession. I think the true secret of effective stage delivery is neither accent nor action; it is tone. Tone is the sole medium of communicating a feeling so that the hearer may sensate that feeling. Without it, it is vain to master the art of elocution;—it is a mere dead and flat outline, destitute of form and life.

Laura Keene's emancipation from the conventional tyranny of the stage in gesticulation, manner, etc., is, to me, her greatest charm,—and we all know that her charms could, without forgery, sign themselves legion. Her rendition of Marco was refreshingly different from the stage-puppets we generally see. She seems to have judiciously determined how a woman like Marco would have acted under given circumstances; not how any other would have rendered it on the stage. Acting admits of—nay, demands—exaggeration; but only in the direction of truth.

I have also seen Smike, and have seen it to my great satisfaction. Of course it is well put on the stage. Mr. Stuart is one of thc few managers who have an æsthetic idea of the dramatic art and its auxiliaries. For instance, he attaches as much importance to youth and beauty, as he does to chairs and tables. If a rôle includes beauty among its properties, he insists that she who plays it shall not be ugly and misshapen. He will not expect an audience to see beauty where it is not, any more than he would ask them to believe that a trombone is a pair of spectacles. The cast iron actress, who knows her business so well that she makes all others know it is a business, is not in his view a candidate for parts in which youth and loveliness are the prominent features. He would not have assigned the part of Madame Mantilini to a plain woman, nor expected, after the manner of a rival theatre, an elderly and broken-voiced soubrette to enact the part of a child. Perhaps that is the reason why there is an indefinable charm of taste and refinement about his theatre, as well as about the dramatic performances therein.

Miss Agnes Robertson's Smike was a most touching and heart-finding picture. She had but one fault, she was too pretty for an idiot. Jefferson however was the mainspring of the piece. When I see him personating such parts, to such artistic perfection, I regret deeply ever to have seen him disgrace himself as Asa Trenchard. Yet even as Newman Noggs, I was sorry to see him relying at times for applause upon mere overdrawn awkwardness. He might spare himself some of his gyrations in the first scene. Lame and deformed people seek generally to disguise their misfortune, not to be continually exposing it. Mrs. Allen was charmingly attired as Madame Mantilini, and altogether I never saw her look so well before. Mr. Johnson was almost too real as Squeers. Miss Agnes Clinton, who took the part of Miss Jones, a most lengthy and remarkable part, of one line, was to me the real surprise of the piece. Her insolent giggling and pert indignation when remonstrated with, were of so admirable a naturalness, that it brought a round of applause and a burst of laughter from the whole house. When a young lady unacquainted with stage business, and cast in a part of a single line, can force out of that single, meaningless line, a recognition of herself, from a not over-ardent audience, she need not fear to miss success in her career. Mr. Stuart, who is the most appreciative of managers, will be sure to employ her talent to better advantage ere long.

o o o

I have entered, too, the cage of the biggest of all the elephants,—of course I mean the balloon. I have seen the great frowsy, floundering thing, and have not been able to take in its size yet. One thing struck me particularly, —the smallness of the car in which the passengers are to be confined. Toothbrushes, hand-towels, and all the machinery of ablution will, of course, be out of the question, and not in the car. With this idea in my mind I lost sight of the heroic, daring, glaring deeds to be done by those bold enough to embark in it for a long journey. I could only think that before becoming heroes they were destined to become as dirty as rascals.

o o o

Last week a sketch appeared in this paper entitled "Waking from Illusions," which has been read, or ought to be read, by every one. I read it, and its perusal suggested to me the fact, that while Getty Gay is wakening from her illusions I am getting more and more wrapped up in mine. I had intended to devote a part of this column to the confessions of an enthusiast, but as my space is limited I will leave it for another week.

o o o

Oh vain men! when will you learn that there is no such thing as despising love? You cannot respond to it, cannot appreciate it, cannot understand it; but as for despising it, you might as well fling your scorn up against the silent but shining night. You can despise love, even as you can tread out the heavenly lights. You trample upon the image of love in your own thought, believing that you trample on love itself. The reflection of the stars falls upon the stream of your own minds, and you with rude feet tread upon their image, but you have not crushed them. Look up! look up! and there they are shining above you, mute, sad, and wandering, but never, never to be under your feet.

Art Items.

—Church's "Heart of thc Andes" is still on exhibition at the Studio-Building in Fourth street, and attracts a large number of visitors. It will be sent, shortly, to the provinces—Boston, Philadelphia, etc. The subscriptions for the proof-engravings have been nearly all taken up. The painting itself is said to have been sold to a gentleman in this country for $15,000.

—The admirers of Rosa Bonheur's works should visit the two fine compositions by her, which are now on exhibition at Goupil's, 772 Broadway. In *Los Borriqueros* they will find an episode of Pyrennean life which, whether regarded in its landscape aspects or in its figure and animal delineations, is equally characteristic and striking. "Morning in the Highlands," by the same artist, is softer and soberer composition, but yet characterized by the same richness of coloring and fidelity to nature, which are the prominent features of her other works. Both pictures were sold from the easel, and belong to foreign collectors.

—Mariette, the celebrated French archæologist, has engaged 3,000 persons to work at excavations in the principal historical sites of Upper Egypt.

—The New York correspondent of the Philadelphia *Press* writes:

> Leutze has returned to town from West Point, where he has been passing the Summer, painting "Washington at Princeton." He has taken one of the large rooms in the Artists' Building, in Tenth street, a large and handsomely-furnished edifice, constructed with especial reference to the requirements and convenience of artists. Every room in the building is now engaged. Among those who have recently taken rooms is one of the Philadelphia artists—Hazeltine; and Whitridge Lamdin, it is said, intends making New York his future residence.

—The Hon. Hamilton Fish has confided Palmer's exquisite statue of the "White Captive" to Mr. Schaus, who is making arrangements for its public exhibition.

—A splendid photograph of Governor Wise is to be seen at Brady's Gallery, No. 643 Broadway, next door but one to Pfaff's.

[For The Saturday Press.]

MADELEINE.

BY AUGUSTUS B. KNOWLTON.

I.

A mystic beam is the cold moonshine,
As it streams o'er the face of Madeleine,
And the stars shine dim, and the wind blows drear,
With a sound of woe, and a sound of fear—
Now, why is the lady sleeping?

II.

And a gust of wind from the North-east falls
On the scutcheoned flag o'er the castle-walls,
And it dashes it deep in the moat below—
Then the wind blows on with a sound of woe;
Ah, why is the lady sleeping?

III.

The blind old owl in the castle tower
Gives a shriek of pain, as the fearful hour
Of twelve from the castle-clock slowly is tolled,
And forth on the night is mournfully rolled.
Now, why is the lady sleeping?

IV.

And hark! through the wailing clouds—oh, hark!
The night-birds swirl in the growing dark;
Then a death-like stillness swarmeth around—
A stillness that seemeth almost a sound.
Ah, why is the lady sleeping?

V.

And the white moon wrappeth herself in a cloud,
As ghastly and gloomy and cold as a shroud,
And the stars shine dimmer and seem to die,
Till the last has dropped from the dismal sky.
And still is the lady sleeping!

VI.

Colder the moon grows, gloomier still,
Strange shadows creep o'er the convent hill,
And murky and drear do the mists hang low,
As the night-wind floateth them to and fro;
Still, still is the lady sleeping!

VII.

Still Madeleine sleeps; so passeth the night,
Till the narrowest ray of crimson light
Steals up from the sea, oh! far away,
And it waxeth and weaveth a crown for the day;
Still, still is the lady sleeping!

VIII.

Up mounteth the red sun higher and higher,
And the moon grows pale in the morning's fire,
And Madeleine wakes, but the clouds remain—
Ah! would to God it were night again,
And would that the lady were sleeping!

IX.

For over the meadows and over the sands,
Through Christian countries, from Pagan lands,
There speedeth a knight on a steed of black,
And he spurreth amain—alack! alack!
That the lady is not sleeping!

X.

And his steed was black, and his sable plume
Throws a shadow as black as the day of doom;
But it gaily tossed o'er his drooping head,
For though he rode madly, the knight was dead.
Ah, would that the lady were sleeping!

XI.

Swift rode the knight, and the sands and the mire
Burned 'neath the horse's hoofs of fire;
Wildly he rode in the morning's sun—
Ah, would to God it had never shone!
Would, would that the lady were sleeping!

XII.

And lo! as he neareth the castle-gate,
The hoary old seneschal, ever at wait,
As he flung to the portal, shuddered and fell:
"Jesu Maria! 'tis a fiend from hell!"
Ah, would that the lady were sleeping!

XIII.

The dead rider staid not to wind his horn.
But dashed through the portcullis, on, madly on,
Ne'er stopping a whit for bolt or bar,
He came like a shaft from the heavens afar:
Ah, would that the lady were sleeping!

XIV.

Into the courtyard, into the hall,
As though he came at the lady's call,
Right into the chamber of Madeleine;
He spoke not a word, and he made not a sign:
Would, would that the lady were sleeping!

XV.

And now he halts, and his mantle drops
From the festering bones of a living corpse,
And the jaws drop down, and the bandage white
Falls from the face—oh God, such a sight!
Would, would that the lady were sleeping!

XVI.

Oh! cross thee, fair, sweet Madeleine!
Now cross thee once more at Our Lady's shrine;
For lo! on his finger, that fleshless bone,
The ring of her plight to the Lord of Lorn!
Would, would that the lady were sleeping!

XVII.

Now the rider lifts his swaying arm,
And the blue lips murmur some heathenish charm,
Then he shrieks in a voice too fearful to tell,
"Last night, last night as the clock struck twelve!
Would, would that the lady were sleeping!

XVIII.

I cursed the Christ and the true eleven,
I cursed my God and the hosts of heaven,
And I died, as I cursed, as the clock struck twelve !"
Then he vanished in air, this vision of hell.
Would, would that the lady were sleeping!

XIX.

A white stone shivers the moon's pale beam,
And the stars look sad in the silvery stream;
But they still gleam forth in the cold moonshine,
And they smile on the grave of Madeleine.
Now, now is the lady sleeping!

[For the N. Y. SATURDAY PRESS.]

HELIOTROPE.

BY EDMUND C. STEDMAN.

I walk in the orange twilight,
Along a garden-slope,
To the shield of moss encircling
My beautiful Heliotrope.

Oh sweetest of all the flowerets
That bloom where angels tread!
But never such marvellous odor
From Heliotrope was shed,

As the passionate exhalation,
The dew of celestial wine,
That floats in tremulous languor
Around this darling of mine.

For, only yester-even,
I saw the dearest scene!
I heard the delicate footfall—
The steps of my love, my queen.

Along the walk she glided:
I made no sound nor sign,
But ever, at the turning
Of her star-white neck divine,

I shrunk in the shade of the cypress
And crouched in the swooning grass
Like some Arcadian shepherd
To see an Oread pass.

But when she came to the border
At the end of the garden-slope,
She bent, like a rose-tree, over
That beautiful Heliotrope.

The cloud of its subtle fragrance
Entwined her in its wreath,
And all the while commingled
With the incense of her breath.

And so she glistened onward—
Far down the long parterre,
Beside the statue of Hesper,
And a hundred times more fair.

But ah! her breath had added
The perfume that I find
In this, the sweetest of flowerets,
And the paragon of its kind.

I drink deep draughts of its nectar;
I faint with love and hope!
Oh, what did she whisper to you,
My beautiful Heliotrope?

EDGAR A. POE.

The following paragraph is from the N. Y. *Tribune:*

"Edgar A. Poe and His Critics" will shortly be published by Messrs. Rudd & Carleton. It is written by a lady whose prospective relation with the poet was interrupted by his death. It is a plea in favor of a man of genius *whom every one steps out of the way to kick at, from the Edinburgh Reviewers downward.*

In illustration of the words we have italicized, we may remark that soon after the death of Poe, the editor of the *Tribune* received a letter running thus:

Dear Sir: In your extensive correspondence, you have undoubtedly secured several autographs of the late distinguished American poet, Edgar A. Poe. If so, will you please favor me with one, and oblige
Yours respectfully, A. B.

To which A. B. received the following reply:

DEAR SIR: I happen to have in my possession but one autograph of the late distinguished American poet, Edgar A. Poe. It consists of an I. O. U., with my name on the back of it. It cost me just $50, and you can have it for half price.
Yours,

Horace Greeley.

Comment is unnecessary.

A Lucky Friday.

Yesterday, the 11th of November, by a wonderful coincidence, was the birthday anniversary of Personne the cricket, Aldrich the poick, and H. C., Jr., ye oldest man.—Donations thankfully received.

Capital Discovery.

The originator of the American motto "Go-a-head," is said to have been Dr. Guillotin.

NEW YORK NOVEMBER 19, 1859

For the Saturday Press.

THE STRAW HAT.

A Picture at the Doctor's.

—

BY W. D. HOWELLS.

—

The sweet shade falls athwart her face,
And leaves half shadow and half light
Dimples and lips in open day,
And dreamy brow and eyes in night.

So low the languid eyelids fall,
They rest their silk upon her cheek,
And give delicious laziness
To glances arch and cunning meek.

It cannot frown, the placid brow!
Hidden in rare obscurity,
They cannot hate, the indolent eyes!
The sins they do not strive to see.

And are the sunshine of her cheeks,
The wanton dimples, a real play,
So frolic—earnest in their sport,
They do not care to look away?

And oh, if Love, kiss-winged should come,
And light on such a rose as this,
Could brow, or eyes, or dimples blame
Such lips for giving back a kiss?

TWO HOURS WITH A MADMAN.

Written for the New York Saturday Press,

BY LIZZIE CAMPBELL.

It happened one time that in travelling across a tract of country where I had business, I got benighted, and about eight o'clock, my horse and myself being tired and pretty nearly worn out, I drew rein before the door of a comfortable-looking farmhouse, and dismounting, knocked at the door with the handle of my whip. It was opened by a little girl, who stood in the doorway, holding a candle in one hand and keeping back her thick curly hair with the other, while she looked at me half-shy as if demanding my business.

"My dear," I answered to that questioning look, "is there any one in the house besides yourself?"

"Yes, there is," she answered; "father and mother and the boys."

"Well, ask your father to come here a moment—I want to speak to him."

She retreated and entered the room behind her, and in about half-a-minute the farmer came out. I made known my business, explained that I had been overtaken by the night, that my destination was several miles distant, and that both my horse and myself were unfit for further travelling till we had procured food and rest.

With the hospitality common to all farmers, especially American ones, my host for the night bade me welcome, conducted me into a large kitchen, with a floor so white that you involuntarily pitied the hands and arms that had brought it into such a state of cleanliness, and bade me seat myself before the blazing fire while supper was being got ready; and then, not forgetting my horse, he told one of the "boys" to feed him and take him to the stable.

After supper, as I felt unusually tired, I asked to be shown the place where I was to pass the night, and was conducted to a comfortable room with a downy bed, white counterpane and curtains, upon the second floor, by my host himself, who, after bidding me "good night," left the candle with me and departed, closing the door after him.

Tired and sleepy as I was, I hurriedly undressed, went to bed, and in five minutes was, soundly sleeping. A grinding, grating sound awoke me, at what time I don't know, but the moon, which did not rise till very late, was fully up, its bright rays streaming in through the window, from which I had purposely looped back the curtain, that the first streak of daylight might wake me, as I was anxious to proceed upon my way. There, sitting full in the moonlight, was a man with a long carving-knife in his hand, which he was leisurely sharpening upon a piece of grindstone, and which I now perceived made the sound that had awakened me. I thought surely I was dreaming; or, if I was awake, what in the name of Heaven meant what I saw? and still the man leisurely ground the blade of the knife, and in a perfect stupor of amazement I lay perfectly quiet with wide-open eyes looking at him.

In a few minutes he stopped grinding, and passing his finger carefully along the edge of the knife he nodded and shook his head knowingly, to intimate to himself that he had brought the blade to a proper degree of sharpness. My blood ran cold; a kind of panic seized me when I saw that action, and the cool, calculating smile with which he held the knife up between him and the full moonlight, looking at it with the air of a connoisseur. Then he leisurely got up, stepped over to the table where I left the candlestick, and began looking around for something,—a match, I conjectured!

While his back was turned, the idea of slipping from the bed and bolting out at the door suggested itself to me; but before I had time to act upon it the match was found, and holding the candle in one hand, the match in the other, and the handle of the knife between his long wolfish-teeth, he came over towards the bed. Even then I might have attempted to escape by rushing at him, wrenching the knife from between his teeth, and so getting the advantage; but even that I was not capable of, so overcome was I by the surprise and horror of my situation, and, through all, such an insatiable curiosity possessed me to know what he was about to do, for as yet I could only conjecture that his purpose was to murder me.

He struck the match against the wall and lit the candle, and then took the knife from between his teeth, and took firm hold of the handle in his hand. I felt faint and sick, when I fully realized then that my last chance of escape was gone. He bent over me, flashed the light full upon my eyes, and perceiving that I was awake, exclaimed with a wild laugh:

"Ha! ha! Awake, eh? Ha! ha! Glad of it, sir; I meant to wake you if you hadn't done it yourself. I consider it cowardly to kill a sleeping man."

And he laughed at me again, and peered into my face with his red, hot, burning eyes.

I could see at once that he was mad, and I saw that the horror of my situation was increased. At first I had thought him a robber, or I hardly know what I thought—but now I *knew* that he was a madman; from his own words, too, I knew that it was his intention to murder me, and I felt that little short of a miracle could save me.

After he had taken a good look at me, he sat down upon the bed, and to my intense horror began slowly running his finger, with great care, along the edge of the knife,—evidently he had no intention of suffering by the experiment,—and then he said:

"I don't intend to kill you just now. Perhaps not for half-an-hour,—perhaps not for an hour. But I guess that's about the longest you have to live. First, I mean to have a talk with you. Do you know where I come from?"

I did not, indeed, and I told him so, wishing within myself with my whole heart that he would take it into his crazy brain to find his way back there and leave me to sleep in peace.

"You don't know, eh? Well, I don't mind telling you. Don't you see that church-spire away there to the left?"

No, I didn't see the church-spire, nor anything else in the world at that moment but the burning eyes of the maniac; so I told him I didn't see the object he spoke of.

"Don't see it, eh? How blind! Why, see there!" and to aid me in discerning this imaginary object, he rose and went toward the window and looped the blind still farther back. "There see it now?"

"No," I said, "I didn't see it yet;" and I hoped he would try to pull the curtain still further back, or pull it down, or something,—anything to divert his attention from me a moment longer, that I might leap from the bed and bolt out of the room.

I was already sitting up, and to glide down upon the floor was the work of an instant; but at that moment the madman, annoyed that I couldn't see the church-spire, dropped the blind, turned round quickly, muttering, "blind, blind;" and instantly comprehending my intention to escape, bounded toward me with a spring like a wild-cat, and catching hold of me with his bony hand, waved the gleaming knife over me in such close proximity to my face as to be anything in the world but pleasant.

"Oh, you will, will you? Just lie down there; still, now, still, or I'll kill you before ever the half-hour is up. Lie down ;" and with herculean strength he lifted me up with his, one hand, and I was no feather in weight, I can tell you, and bounced me down with a force that shook the whole bed.

I did lie down, and seeing that I was inclined to obedience, he directed my attention to the window again by inquiring, "Do you see the church-spire now?"

I didn't see it any clearer than before, it being slightly impossible, as no church-spire existed within ten miles; but I saw that the maniac was getting irritated at my want of capability to see what did not exist; so I thought it might be as well to keep upon good terms with him, and to his question this time I admitted I did see the spire.

"Ah, good, good. Well, under that spire is a church, and around the church is a graveyard. There I live, and there I came from. It's very lonesome sleeping there in the damp cold ground, and the grave-worms ugh! to feel them creeping along over one's skin, so slimy, and slippery, and cold, banqueting upon the warm flesh of the dead. They say the dead are cold; it's a lie, sir, a lie! Feel my flesh; is it cold?"

He bared his skinny arm and forced me to lay my hands upon it.

"There, is that cold?"

I told him no.

"Is it warm?"

I replied that it was, and he continued:

"They make it cold, the grave-worms do. They make it cold and slimy as they crawl over it. Did you ever feel the grave-worms on your flesh?"

I shuddered with disgust as I told him "No."

"You didn't, eh? Lucky dog! But you're not dead yet; wait awhile and you'll feel them, just as I do. Pretty soon ;" and he whirled the carving-knife round and round his head, and then brought it down with a sudden swoop till he grazed my throat.

With a groan of agony, not for the slight scratch, but the horror of mind under which I was, I recoiled from the glittering blade, shuddering as if I would have sunk down through the bed,—down, down, through the floor. How I wished in my soul that I could have done so,—down anywhere out of that horrible presence. With a loud laugh the maniac observed my terror, and then he said:

"Frightened, eh? frightened! I won't kill you, for half-an-hour yet. I'm going to experiment upon you. I think I'll bleed you to death, just to try how long it will take you to die. Eh? what do you think of it?'

What did I think of it? My God! I thought nothing—only that I would soon be dead, or as mad as my companion, if some deliverance was not soon opened up. I never prayed much,—God forgive me!—but just then I breathed something, I scarcely know what, for aid, for help, for deliverance. I know that I dared not attempt to escape. My first movement would have been the signal for my death-blow; and if I called aloud, I might not awaken any or one in the house, but merely infuriate the madman to such an extent that he might immediately butcher me. What under Heaven to do I knew not, and if the maniac in his desire to "experiment" should open a vein, I must inevitably bleed to death. Meantime he was waiting for an answer to his question, which he repeated rather angrily:

"What did I think of his proposal to bleed me to death?"

I was about answering something desperate, and giving myself up for lost, when a bright idea flashed across my troubled brain. Oh, how devoutly I thanked Heaven that I had read the "Arabian Nights" in my boyhood! There was my idea, which as yet only Heaven knew whether it would be successful or not; I would tell him stories and beguile his fancy till morning, and then surely I would have some means of escape. I answered his question by another.

"Suppose I tell you a story about bleeding to death—or rather about a man who supposed he was being bled to death, and died from the fright?"

"Died from the fright, eh? Well, let's hear it."

Very gladly I began, making it long, and adding as much as I possibly could to the original, which was something I recollected long ago to have heard about some one who wished to "experiment," and had a man blindfolded, his arm bandaged, and gently pricked, but not sufficiently to bring the blood, and then heard the regular drop, drop of blood,—or what he supposed to be his own blood, though in reality only water, till he died from the mere supposition that he was being bled to death. I forget the story now, but it is familiar to every one. When I concluded, I suggested to the maniac that he should try this model experimenting, and see how long I would take to be frightened to death.

"Yes, yes," he answered, with a sly, cunning laugh; "very good, very good," and seeing through the device, with the cunning of madness, he laughed again as he said: "Very good, sir, very good. And you would take till morning to die; and meanwhile I want a companion in the churchyard, yonder, down among the grave-worms. Come, bare your arm, and let me do as I said. I'll bleed you. I intended to have taken your head off first; but I've changed my mind, because I wouldn't like to have a headless companion. Bare your arm."

God! what was I to do? I felt my brain seethe and whirl, as though I too were going mad. With a desperate effort to be calm, I said:

"Suppose I tell you another story first?"

"Oh, no, you can tell while you bleed "

"But I shall want to watch the blood flow, too," I said, with an effort to refrain from shuddering.

"True, true," he answered. "Well, let's hear your story—quick, begin."

I waited for no urging; I was too glad to find him in the humor to listen; so I began and related every story I could think of,—as soon as one was done, beginning another,—and in this manner, nearly two hours passed. As I was about to begin another story, he stopped me, peremptorily:

No, no; no more! I won't listen! I've listened too long already, and I've no time to bleed you, either! I may take your head off, as I first intended, disagreeable as it is to have a headless companion!"

Around and around his head again went the glittering knife, coming down in a direct line with my throat; and then, as the edge, sharp as a razor, touched my skin, I forgot the prudent considerations that had hitherto kept me silent, and gave vent to my horror and terror in a cry so loud and long, so shrill and ear-piercing, that the maniac started back in affright, and actually trembled at the unearthly sound. No wonder! I tremble this moment, myself, when I think what an awful cry it was; and I almost fancy I can still hear the sound of it, when I close my eyes, and shudderingly look back to the hour.

The effect upon the madman was not of long duration. A third time he waved the knife around his head, and was just preparing for a spring forward, when the farmer and his eldest son burst into the room. The effect that these new actors upon the scene produced upon the madman, was strange and almost incredible. The knife remained uplifted, and the hand in which it was held seemed suddenly petrified and unable to move. He cowered beneath the gaze of the farmer, as a child might do under the eye of a master, and without the slightest resistance, allowed the knife to be taken from his hand, and himself quietly led from the room by the farmer and his son.

Then, when I was left alone, the reaction after all my terror, horror, and excitement, overpowered me, and I sank back upon the bed, almost insensible. I thanked God for my escape, and hardly conscious of my own feelings or actions, I lay quite still, awaiting what was to follow. I felt that there was no farther cause for alarm, and in a dreamy sort of way, I tried to account for the adventure. I looked around upon the room, and all seemed so like a dream, that I could almost have persuaded myself that I was the victim of an unpleasant illusion; but then, to bring me back to the reality of all that had transpired, there was still the light burning upon the table, and I knew I had put out the light before retiring; and another proof that I was awake, and had been for a couple of hours past, was the scratch upon my throat, where the knife had grazed it, and I shuddered to think how nearly my thread of life had been cut in two.

Presently the farmer and his son returned, and I was informed that my terrible and most unwelcome visitant was an unfortunate brother-in-law of the farmer's who had been crazed for some years past; that during certain seasons, especially at that phase in which the moon then was, he was quite mad and dangerous, though at other times harmless. Unfortunately for me, his door had been neglected that night, and instead of being locked, had been left open. I listened to all these explanations, and received my host's apologies and expressions of regret for my disturbance and peril, by making a mental vow never to sleep with my door unlocked in a strange house, and if ever placed so that I should be obliged to crave the hospitality of strangers, to make particular inquiry whether any mad person, brother-in-law or other, dwelt in the house.

THE FIRE-FIEND.

A Nightmare.

FROM AN UNPUBLISHED MS. OF
THE LATE EDGAR A. POE.
IN THE POSSESSION OF CHARLES D. GARDETTE.

I.

In the deepest dearth of Midnight, while the sad and solemn swell
Still was floating, faintly echoed from the Forest Chapel Bell–
Faintly, falteringly floating o'er the sable waves of air
That were thro' the Midnight rolling, chafed and billowy with the tolling—
In my chamber I lay dreaming by the fire-light's fitful gleaming,
And my dreams were dreams foreshadowed on a heart foredoomed to
Care!

II.

As the last long lingering echo of the Midnight's mystic chime,
Lifting thro' the sable billows to the Thither Shore of Time—
Leaving on the starless silence not a token nor a trace—
In a quivering sigh departed; from my couch in fear I started:—
Started to my feet in terror, for my Dream's phantasmal Error
Painted in the fitful fire a frightful, fiendish, flaming face!

III.

On the red hearth's reddest centre, from a blazing knot of oak,
Seemed to gibe and grin this Phantom, when in terror I awoke,
And my slumberous eyelids straining, as I staggered to the floor,
Still in that dread Vision seeming, turned my gaze toward the gleaming
Hearth, and—there!—oh! God! I saw It! and from out Its flaming jaw It
Spat a ceaseless, seething, hissing, bubbling, gurgling stream of gore!

IV.

Speechless, struck with stony silence, frozen to the floor I stood;
Till methought my brain was hissing with that hissing, bubbling blood:—
Till I felt my life-stream oozing, oozing from those lambent lips :—
Till the Demon seem'd to name me: then a wondrous calm o'ercame me,
And my brow grew cold and dewy, with a death-damp stiff and gluey,
And I fell back on my pillow in apparent soul-eclipse!

V.

Then, as in Death's seeming shadow, in the icy fall of Fear
I lay, stricken, came a hoarse and hideous murmur to my ear:—
Came a murmur like the murmur of assassins in their sleep:—
Muttering, "Higher! higher! higher! I am Demon of the Fire!
I am Arch-Fiend of the Fire! and each blazing roof's my pyre,
And my sweetest incense is the blood and tears my victims weep!"

VI.

"How I revel on the Prairie! How I roar among the Pines!
How I laugh when from the village o'er the snow the red flame shines,
And I hear the shrieks of terror, with a Life in every breath!
How I scream with lambent laughter, as I hurl each crackling rafter
Down the fell abyss of Fire, until higher, higher, higher
Leap the High-Priests of my Altar in their merry Dance of Death!"

VII.

"I am Monarch of the Fire! I am Vassal-King of Death!
World encircling, with the shadow of its Doom upon my breath!
With the symbol of Hereafter flaming from my fatal face!
I command the Eternal Fire! Higher, higher, higher, higher
Leap my ministering Demons, like Phantasmagoric lemans
Hugging Universal Nature in their hideous embrace!"

VIII.

Then a sombre silence shut me in a solemn, shrouded sleep,
And I slumbered like an infant in the "Cradle of the Deep,"
Till the Belfry in the Forest quivered with the matin stroke,
And the martins, from the edges of its lichen-lidded ledges,
Shimmered thro' the russet arches where the Light in torn files marches,
Like a routed army, struggling thro' the serried ranks of oak.

IX.

Thro' my ivy-fretted casements filtered in a tremulous note
From the tall and stately linden where a Robin swell'd his throat:—
Querulous, quaker-breasted Robin, calling quaintly for his mate!
Then I started up, unbidden, from my slumber Nightmare-ridden,
With the memory of that Dire Demon in my central Fire
On my eye's interior mirror like the shadow of a Fate!

X.

Ah! the fiendish Fire had smouldered to a white and formless heap,
And no knot of oak was flaming as it flamed upon my sleep;
But around its very centre, where the Demon Face had shone,
Forked Shadows seem'd to linger, pointing as with spectral finger
To a Bible, massive, golden, on a table carved and olden
And I bowed, and said, "All Power is of God, of God alone!"

LETTER FROM THE WOODS.

In the Woods, Oct. 20th.

My dear Press:—I take it for granted that you and most, if not all, of your readers, know nothing of this absolute solitude,—probably care to know as little by personal experience. It is one thing to spend a period of time alone where we see on every side the evidence of human consociation—where you may be assured that some one has been, perhaps an hour before, and may be an hour hence,—and where the evidence of that personal presence is gathered by every sense of the five named, and as well by the one unnamed; for something of us all lingers in places we leave, long after we have consciously departed;—but to be alone in the wilds, where no axe was ever struck but your own, where no human sign-manual meets your eye, and where you might signalize and call forever, and—all your means of communication exhausted—be as far from human intercourse as ever, this *is* solitude.

In this absolute isolation, one becomes conscious of mental phenomena, like those physical ones we see in cases of mutilation or deprivation of certain senses—the faculties which we disuse seeming to turn all their vitality towards those which continue their functions. In the absence of social intercourse, the imagination is quickened, until one lives in the midst of sights and sounds which it requires all the vigilance of the remaining active senses to keep from making us captive to their illusions. The hearing becomes so acute that it seems to hear silence; and every nucleus of sound becomes articulate, and often, catching the tone of familiar voices, calls to you from hundreds of miles away,—till at times, your heart will leap up, with beat suspended, to hear the call repeated,—half persuaded of a physical presence. I have stopped, I know not how many times, midway in some action, to listen to the murmur of approaching voices, convinced, for the instant, that some visitors had arrived. I have even rowed across our ferry in hottest haste, to meet some one whose call I heard on the opposite side, and found all silent and solitary,—until, now, I never go until I hear the signal twice, distinctly.

Sitting by the camp-fire at night, dreaming away the evening, I hear the baying of distant hounds so clearly, that if the owl in yonder hemlock did not hoot, I should hardly know that the sound was not actual. I have ceased to wonder at fairy stories and haunted houses,—half expect, indeed, to see fairies tripping out from the huge, hollow birch, and feel almost hunted by the wehr-wolf. But I have ceased to believe in Robinson Crusoe, and am convinced that Simeon Stylites would have left his column before his toes stiffened, if he had not had visitors. In fact, the alternatives—one or other of which seems to me the inevitable consequence of this absolute solitude—are insanity, or an utter reactive lethargy of the whole intellect, and a gradual assimilation to brute life. The only two instances of this life I know, in this country, are of the latter kind, and in this way I should suppose most rough, vigorous natures would go, since the indispensable physical activity and simplicity of life, by keeping the body in complete health, would prevent insanity where there was greater inclination to physical than mental action; but in the other case, where there was a tendency to imaginative and spiritual life, I should regard insanity as the natural consequence of solitude. The rationale of it seems to me simple, logical. This nature of ours has a spiritual gravitation;—up or down is a question of specific gravity. We are held in mid-air by the thousand cords of social affinities,—severing which, we soar into thin space and asphyxia, or we sink and grovel, bemired and earth-smothered.

But moderate the dose—temper solitude to the endurable point, and, oh marvel! you have found the elixir of health. The myth of Antaeus and Hercules is true every day. The demigod, who seems to have been the incarnate spirit of work, indefatigably personified, finds it impossible to destroy the earthborn so long as he can return to his mother earth; but once cut him off from his terrene recreation, and he is lost. I wonder if Antaeus was not some old reformer, who pitched battle with the Puritanism of his time, and taught that it was only another form of sin; that to starve and outrage the animal element of the human nature, was just as absolute a disfigurement of the Divine image as to neglect the religious element; that we were just as certain to get into the wrong place if we cut our earth-ties, as if we cut the stays by which the heavens hold us up. If he *was,* we may well be sure that the priests of the day made him a monster, a rebel against the powers of Olympus, and declared war against him; and in the controversies that followed, they worked the poor fellow so hard that he never found time or heart to get back to the woods and green fields, and so finally succumbed to overwork, and was canonized—over the left. Or perhaps they put him in prison walls, where—shut out from the sources of his intellectual strength and health, from the inspiration of books and green leaves—the life of his life died in madness. I say nothing of the more literal interpretation: that they gave him a position where his understanding was unavailing, and all earthly communication was reduced to a single line, pending which he succumbed, etc., etc.

"Served him right," says our neighbor of the *Christian Tranquillizer*, "for disturbing the status quo of the religious world with new and strange doctrines." Patience, moderation, faithful friend; Antaeus is wiser to-day than yesterday, and you may not find it so easy to get his heels clear of the sod as you did in those old times.

Don't you think my interpretation of the fable at least plausible? The moral is to me clear, at any rate. We are triune—(leave that sentence out, if you think our orthodox neighbors will take offense at it; you know they like to insist on their own explanation of the likeness of man to God): the physical nature, with all its enjoyments, sensations, and attributes, is as needful to the integrity of a man as a heart of prayer. *Integer vitæ* can never be said of a man who neglects the proper use of his muscles, any more than it can be said of the most profane and sensual prizefighter. The end of life is perfection;—and that poor, starveling priest, who confounds spiritual ecstasy with divine Life, and wastes, day by day, into a shadow of humanity, reason yielding to his superstitions, as his body to his misguided fervor,—is as much a sinner as the gourmand who thinks, when his breakfast is done, only how he may pass the time to dinner. One is just as far as the other from obeying the command, Be ye perfect.

The fact is, all Christendom wants recreation, not recreating. The world is well enough, if the plan were filled out; but between the priest and the schoolteachers, we have all grown so one-sided (or two-sided) that the third leg of the tripod is, in many cases, only in embryo. Hercules has almost got us supended, and the only resource we have, is to get back to our mother earth without delay, and with abandon.

And here, in the wild, weird woods, my dear PRESS, Antaeus has a lodge. I cannot invite you to visit me now in it ;— the woods are snowed up, and the streams froze up, and you can't get here until the lakes freeze up; but I'll tell you (in the course of time) what you will find here, if you will come another Summer.

Yours truly,

ANTAEUS.

[For the NEW YORK SATURDAY PRESS.]

NEW YORK SOCIETY.

Truly the most amusing thing in the world, from a philosophical point of view, is New York society. Were it not for its cosmopolitan character, and the large admixture of foreigners, it would be intolerable for its snobbishness.

Being a mercantile aristocracy, it swings its different castes entirely upon the pivot of Wholesale and Retail.

The wife of a wholesaler rigorously excludes the wife of a retailer from her circle of acquaintance.

Sugar and Molasses by the hogshead quite ignore the same articles by the pound or gallon. Bales of cotton are oblivious to cotton by the yard.

Now, some of these same individuals in the wholesale way are dull, illiterate persons, not well-bred, nor very well-born; and yet they expect to be received with distinction, in preference to agreeable, talented, well-educated mortals, whose unlucky destiny has decreed that they should operate in a smaller way, for want of larger capital perhaps, but who are infinitely more entertaining to an unprejudiced person, who compounds for the amount of mental enjoyment in society in preference to wholesale stupidity.

The very best society in New York, besides the purely literary, is derived from the families of those who were honorable, prudent merchants fifty or eighty years since. Many of these left sufficient property for the maintenance of their families at the present day without business. Therefore, in a community where the majority are merchants in different degrees, there should be a sliding-scale of the amount of intellectual and social qualifications each one can contribute for the benefit of society.

Then, again, beside the self-constituted aristocracy of wholesale and retail, there is a vast amount of snobbishness shown in locality. Some dreadful vulgarian residing in Fifth avenue—and, dear reader, improbable as you may think it, there are a few such, some whose antecedents are better forgotten than remembered,— will fairly roll over the claims of an infinitely superior denizen of one of the tabood avenues or localities. This is the aristocracy of bricks and mortar, and brown-stone. Instances are constantly to be seen of some of the non-elect of society straining every nerve, and making immense sacrifices, to obtain a residence in Fifth avenue, under the impression that the fact of living there would alone procure them the entrée of the charmed circles to be found in some of the palatial mansions therein. Such stress is laid upon locality by many who have yet to achieve an escutcheon to display upon their banner in the bloodless, but bitter contest incessantly waged, called the Battle of Society.

Oh! dear reader, how I have sifted all these shams and humbugs with the independence and observation of one who can do without all of them, if necessary, or who will select those who wear nature's insignia of nobility. The descendants of many of the *useful* as well as ornamental professions, jostle each other with great dignity in the Halls of our *Resumers*.

If Mrs. Baker wears the most point-lace, she is queen of the occasion. What inanity and selfishness pervade these brilliant assemblies! What heart-burnings flutter under their brocades! What a chaos is self-constituted aristocracy! What a baseless fabric!

The consequence of all this fustian is, that men of intellect now seek the smaller literary circles, and withdraw themselves from the stupidity of grand parties, and general society, leaving the field open to Brown's young men who dance, and to whom the feminine rivalries of who shall outvie and outstrip her neighbor, are a matter completely suited to their calibre.

All the Americans who can now live abroad, where society is more sensibly constituted, and where for the trouble of getting one's self up for a soirée, one receives a certain amount of spiritual and mental enjoyment, which amply compensates for the exertion. In the best circles abroad they would laugh at the claims of those who cannot bring one idea to a reunion, but are invited for the clothes they wear and the houses they live in, the cultivation and improvement of point-lace and brown-stone !

This is the general effect, on a stranger, of New York society taken from a salient point of view. But who shall dare decry the tone and polish of the many small circles revolving in their own orbits in the great social firmament, forming the most delightful assemblies,— where the cultivation and grace of the host and hostess draw around them all that is desirable and enjoyable of society in its highest sense?

There is a vast amount of material among the New Yorkers, to produce a more brilliant combination than any other city in the world, if they only knew how to evoke it. The very cosmopolitan character of New York is one of the greatest points in favor of the highest cultivation and variety. Here we have the best elements of other nations mingling in our social life. The robust health and reliability of the English; the high cultivation and mental gifts of the Germans; the grace, style, and elegance of the French; the dignity, intelligence, and fascination of the Spanish and Italians;—all these mixing and intermarrying with our beautiful and graceful, but fragile and superficial Americans, improve both us and themselves, by giving us the qualities we have not, and receiving from us the modification of their intensities. If a Madame Recamier, a de Stael, or some of those interesting spirituelle Precieuses of the last century, who so perfectly understood the necessary ingredients and arrangement of the social mystery, could arise in our midst and remodel the present indescribable structure of our society, it would soon become the social Paradise of the world.

Citoyenne.

BOOKS OF THE DAY.

I may as well say here at once, that the books which I shall mention in this article are all published by the Harpers. The majority of them are novels, as witness the following list:

1. John Halifax, Gentleman, by Miss Muloch.
2. A Life for a Life, by the same.
3. Henry St. John, Gentleman, a Tale of 1774-75, by John Esten Cooke.
4. My Third Book, by Mrs. Moulton.
5. Walter Thornley: or, a Peep at the Past, by the author of Allen Prescott.
6. The Bertrams, by Anthony Trollope.
7. A Good Fight, and other Tales, by Charles Reade.

"Everybody," observed a friend of mine recently, "writes novels." That may be, but does everybody read them? I trow not. Still it is a safe calculation to estimate, that there are as many, or nearly as many novel-readers as there are novel-writers. For if there are some who have got beyond the spellingbook, that do *not* read novels, there are some who have got beyond the copybook who do *not* write them. What state of mind would Henry Fielding be in, were he to come back now, and make a short sojourn in London? I say in London, because *there* he could see, at one view, the state of his own art among the whole English-speaking race. It would in the beginning, I suppose, be surprise at the number of its workers. There might be something of perturbed vexation mixed up with the surprise. His feeling may be illustrated by a story which I once heard of an eminent tragedian. He had a sword made, which, by a secret cunning of contrivance, made when he shook it quite a fearful sound. In some of his performances, especially in Richard, at a certain point, this had immense effect: it was a pinnacle—as we may figuratively express it—a pinnacle of astonishment to the audience, and of glory to the actor. One night he went to see the Richard of another actor. On his return home where a confidential friend awaited him, he was silent, moody, and disturbed. Dark thunder-clouds rested on his brows; sleeping lightning smouldered in his eyes; and he strode up and down the room with the tread of angry Jupiter. His friend ventured at last to inquire the cause of his excitement? No answer. The inquiry was repeated with respectful sympathy, and with affectionate urgency. "O! dash it, Sir," exclaimed the great tragedian,—"dash it, Sir, *they're all now shaking swords.*" So might the great master of the prose Epic exclaim, "Dash it Sir, *they're all now writing novels.*" Yet why should the tragedian have been annoyed? Could he not have said, "Ay, the rascals can shake swords, but can they act Richard?" and so might Fielding have said, "Ay, any thousand of them can write novels, but I alone could write Tom Jones."

Another impression which he would be likely to receive, would be, that most of the writers were wonderfully virtuous—that they would give the world abundantly of cakes, but deprive it of ale. He would notice that Fiction was full of religion, and of philanthropy, and of reform. He might from this suppose that most of its writers become saints, martyrs, and apostles. They must have given up the world for the sake of their race, and be as indignant at the offer of payment from publishers, as St. Peter was at that from Simon Magus. "I," he might whisper to himself, "was not over-fond of money, but I took what the trade would give me, though to tell the truth that was not overmuch; but to people like these, of such godly inspiration, the mammon of unrighteousness must be vile abomination." But suddenly another thought would strike him : "The world is converted. If it were not, such wonderfully excellent preachers—beings so pure and disinterested, would be read only to be roasted." But in looking again he would see by the names—if he did not by the style—that most of the authors were women. "Ah, ah!" he would murmur, "go to, go to; that makes different matter of it. Women are so good themselves they fancy all the world good, or that it can easily be made so. I who know the wickedness of the world well, had always faith in the sanctity of woman, always believed that the inward and divine beauty which was hers in Paradise, was never wholly lost to her. The feminine is that side of the world which needs the least conversion; but I observe that as it is women who mostly write novels, so it is women who mostly read them. If men read what women write, they do not greatly heed it; so after all *the world is not converted.*" Had he stepped across to Paris there would have been no danger of his being misled by fiction as to the righteousness of the world, in writers or readers, in men or women; on either side of the channel he would have found, if truth were known, no enormous amount of difference in the reality. He would not return, however, from his earthly visit, without the consciousness that he had successors in his art—in women as well as men—who, clear of his errors, were kindred with his genius.

As to myself, I do not read novels. I read too many of them in my youth; and I now can understand that abstinence in mind as well as in body, while we are young, is good for the whole life.

Fiction is the *wine* of imagination; and as the wine which cheers the body is most appropriate to festively rare occasions—or to as rarely despondent ones—or to the decline of years,—so is the *wine* which cheers the mind. Besides, I have not leisure, and the reading of Fiction is a luxury which I cannot now afford. But if I do not read in person, I do by proxy. I have tried all the above list on my deputies, and I aver on the word of a close observer, and of a conscientious critic, that I have never seen them flag; I inferred that the task was pleasurable, for they had nothing for the work but the doing of it.

I did read "The Bertrams," but as it has been many weeks since, I only remember that it interested me peculiarly, as displaying a keen faculty in the morbid anatomy of certain diseased orders of human character. This novel was made the occasion of an able disquisition in *The National Review* (England), on the Ethics of the Legal Profession, squinting aside at those of the Clerical. But this is no place to argue systems of casuistry. There is no man who is not a capital casuist when the decision does not touch his own *case*. The cleric is clear on the duty of the advocate; the advocate is no less clear on the duty of the cleric; and so it is through all possible relations of humanity.

"A Good Fight," by Charles Reade, I have also read. Reade has one excellent quality of a story-teller, the power of arresting and keeping attention; if you listen when he begins, you must listen till he ends. What other qualities he may have or want, judged by the higher forms of power, there is here neither occasion nor space for adequate examination. The present story turns a quiet and deep domestic tragedy into a lively and exciting melodrama. The real incidents are as follows: A certain citizen of Tergou (or Gouda), in Holland, had ten sons. One of them was named "Gerard,' and from his childhood had been destined for the Priesthood. But in Siebenbergen or Sevenhills, a village near at hand, lived an old physician; and he had a handsome daughter, the which young Gerard loved, loved her secretly and passing well. When his family would press him into orders, he fled, and made his way to Rome. He earned his living by transcribing; for the art of printing, though invented, had not come fully into use. In the meantime, the unwed girl retired to Rotterdam, and became a mother. Her child was a son, and that son was the illustrious Erasmus. The fugitive father having heard that the young woman had died, entered immediately into the Priesthood. He returned to his native country, and learned how fatally he was deceived. But he was faithful to his vows; the mother of his child lived, according to the best authorities, virtuously. She, however, died, while her boy was yet young; the father soon followed; the orphan was educated for the priesthood, entered it as unwillingly as his father had done, and had as little true vocation for it. Erasmus himself admits that his birth was illegitimate—but his father was no priest at the time. His enemies asserted that he was. His mother was virtuous ever after; but there are those who affirm that Erasmus had an elder brother. Bayle, as he always does, goes learnedly into the particulars; and in his work, those who care may study them. A writer in the "Quarterly Review" accuses Bayle of being "malicious," as well as of being "unsatisfactory;" but it seems to me that Bayle endeavors to be on the side of Erasmus; and relating to the circumstances connected with the birth of Erasmus, the Reviewer makes no substantial additions to Bayle's investigations. Mr. Reade turns this into a romance. Gerard is an amiable and learned youth; as he goes to Rotterdam to contest a prize for writing, he meets Margaret and her old father. He does them kindness. There is love; then, naturally and romantically, trouble; all sorts of adventures and persecutions; escapes from terrible imprisonment; flight to Italy; has carried from his prison a valuable parchment—a deed of the old doctor's property, out of which a villain cheated him; does not receive the lying letter; does not become a priest; has found out the worth of the parchment; hastens home; produces the deed; old doctor is made rich; old villain kills himself; Gerard marries Margaret; the ancients die, ripe in years; the young people fill a big house with children; and everybody is as happy as the day is long. There is a large amount of sentiment, of suffering, and of danger; and the style, as distinctively as ever, is all the author's own. The plot is active with bustle and incident; the situations are striking, and the changes startling. Put it on the stage in pantomime, and it would make an effective ballet of the serious kind.

I ought to have added to the above list "Harry Lee; or, Hope for the Poor." It is a story for children, and all alive with the soul of goodness. Charity and childhood come well together; and to young hearts the tale affords a twofold delight, which not only interests their curiosity, but their sympathy, when it shows them the deeds of blessed charity in the salvation of neglected childhood. There are little hearers who are listening to the story read aloud while I write, and judging by their manifestations of enjoyment, earnestness of attention, and raptures of applause, the writer has achieved a great and enviable success. And why should not the young public have its ideal pleasures? And how gracious, too, it is in genius, not only to amuse innocence, but also to help it on to virtue!

There are two kinds of fiction—the explicit and the implicit: novels and romances are the one; history, commonly so called, is the other. A good novel is fact in the guise of fiction: a brilliant history is fiction in the guise of fact. I think this last position might be proved almost à priori, and from the nature of the case. A history that rivets the attention, that gives sustained and exciting mental pleasure, must have a plan—unity—sequences—a *predominating idea*,—and must be the work of a single mind. It must, in short, be an epic; and the epic of the historian differs only from that of the poet in this: the epic of the poet is written in verse, that of the historian in prose; in the epic of the poet the idea is selected for the facts, in the epic of the historian, the facts are selected for the ideas. I could say much on this point, but space forbids. The position might be proved by examples; and it could be shown that from Herodotus to Macaulay every history, which mankind has not been willing "to let die," has been an epic, and because of being an epic it has lived. For this, also, good reasons could be given. Gibbon's Rome is a magnificent example, and Hume's England is another. A large library of works exists on the Life of England, in all its stages, relations, and conditions; and that library the few will study, but the many will read the story of it in the pages of Hume,— and possibly, for all time, they will continue there to read it. This, in itself, shows what a wonderful genius was in the man. "The Student's Hume," a copy of which is before me, has suggested these remarks. It is not a mere manual or abridgment, but an excellent condensation, with corrective notes, and a good continuation to the present time. As I looked through it I remembered the days of my youth—when the good time came not, or the school-books drew nigh—of which one might say, "I find instruction in them." I then read the History of England in Goldsmith's Abridgment of his own abridgment. My idea of idea of a King, formed from the wood-cut at the beginning of each reign, was that of a terribly grim personage sitting on a throne, with a crown on his head, and a sword or sceptre in his hand. It was on a par with what I saw in Mother Goose,—where "the King is in the parlor counting out his money,"—while "the Queen is in the kitchen eating bread and honey." But enough of this.

"The French Revolution of 1789, as viewed in the light of Republican Institutions," by John S. C. Abbott, is on my table; but I have not yet had time to read it, and I will not assume the privilege of an impartial critic, to give an opinion on that which I have not read. The title of the book is suggestive rather than satisfactory. A book of most pregnant import might be written on "Republican Institutions, viewed in the light of The French Revolution." "Republican Institutions" are, at present, on sad and sore trial among ourselves; and they do not seem so much to give us light, at least for this moment, as to hold us in suspense. Despotism is not that alone of an individual; and liberty in relation to polity or person, it is not easy to define. Political existence is very like personal consciousness. Men of different nations can no more judge for each other politically than individuals can personally; for as the beggar would not exchange his personality for that of the noble who gives him charity, neither would the people exchange their nationality with those who call them slaves, and boast of their own freedom. In all such matters there are mystic relations of mind to locality and life, which cannot be explained or reached. But the mystery of this French Revolution no one has yet approached. It has been contemplated in all directions, outside and from within, by thinkers and writers of all varieties of theory and culture; but not one of them alone, nor the whole of them together have plucked out the heart of its mystery. In the French Revolution men supposed that the problem of modern Europe had come to its solution; but instead of that it was only enunciated in the hurricane of slaughter and of terror: the enigma is as dark as ever, and it will not be solved, until it solves itself. The French Revolution still continues. But even of the supposed beginning we get no intelligible view, by bringing separately into notice certain classes, upon whom is to be laid all the burden and all the guilt. May not a peasant, in his place, be as great a rascal as a Prince, and according to his degree, contribute his share to the general iniquity? It is time to be done with the talk of popular innocency. *All men*, for the wrong or misery which comes upon their country or their race, are guilty in their order; and therefore, when ruin or calamity falls upon a country, every class has justly its portion of the blame. In any critical epoch of a nation's history, we have the culmination of a certain era in its life—and of life in relation, not to its separable divisions, but to its collective existence.

Such an epoch was the French Revolution,—only it was more than French; it was properly a revolution of social Christendom, and throughout social Christendom it is still working. It has been ascribed to the evils of the French aristocracy; to the evils of the French Church—or to all of them in unity.

The great philosophical politician, De Tocqueville, had recently begun to review all the conventional errors as to the condition of France, with respect to the antecedents and consequents of its revolution, in his work on the "Old Regime;" and I most heartily regretted his early death—not alone because a noble so was lost to the world, where such souls are always wanted, but also because he had entered on a line of enquiry, which was a deep historical desire, and which perhaps he, of all men, could best satisfy. He would have shown us fully, what of the Past produced the Revolution, and what of the Past survived it. The French Church has been the most blamed as the cause of it—and here is what De Tocqueville the whole, says of the French Church: "I doubt whether, on even taking into account the startling vices of some of its own members, the world ever saw a more remarkable body than the Catholic clergy at the time the Revolution broke out. They were enlightened; they were national; their private virtues were not more striking than their public qualities: and yet they were largely endowed with faith, sufficient to bear them up against persecution. I began to study the old regime—full of prejudice against the clergy; I have ended my task, and feel nothing but respect for them."

Henry Giles

[For The Saturday Press.]

MATER DOLOROSA.

BY FRED A. PARMENTER.

I.

The gay saloon is lighted,
And the maskers dance within
To the merry sound of viols,
And the tinkling mandolin.

II.

But list! a sudden silence
Creeps over the crowded room,
As Lillian proudly enters,
In a robe of purple bloom.

III.

Her forehead is crowned with diamonds,
Outshining her ebon eyes,
As calmly she gazes about her
In a daintily feigned surprise.

IV.

A dancer of knightly bearing
Offers his jewelled hand,
And away they circle, followed
By all the white-robed band;

V.

While the Mater Dolorosa
Of Raphael, on the wall,
Looks down in tearful sorrow
On the merry maskers' ball.

VI.

But see! its quivering features
Have something of Lillian's look,
As of one who has read too deeply
In Destiny's mystic book.

VII.

Oh, Lillian, queen of beauty,
With statuesque, regal air,
Will you ever taste of anguish
More than your soul can bear?

VIII.

Will the crown of starry diamonds
Be changed to points of fire,
Fretting your marble forehead
In silver-sparkling ire?

IX.

Will Raphael's dolorous Mater
Truly be like your face,
When further your feet have hastened
In Life's laborious race?

X.

Ah me! I am not a prophet,
And I will not seek to tell;
But whatsoever befalls you,
Lillian, I wish you well!

Dramatic Feuilleton.

"Aux Italiens."

Thus sings the poet of dress-coats, white cravats, and "real valenciennes," Owen Meredith, and so say I:

> Of all the operas that Verdi wrote,
> The best, to my taste, is the "Trovatore ;"
> And Mario can soothe, with a tenor note,
> The souls in Purgatory.
>
> The moon on the tower slept soft as snow;
> And who has not thrill'd in the strangest way,
> As we heard him sing, while the gas burn'd low,
> *"Non ti scordar di me?"*

And we had the Trovatore, on Thursday, for Albertini, and Beaucardé, the inspired.

They had a very good success so far as the audience was concerned, but the critics don't seem to see it.

The *Tribune* and *Times* say nothing about the Prima Donna; the *Herald* praises her method and school, but is silent about her voice, which was under a cloud, or a cold.

I think Albertini is a very fine artist, and I have never seen so much real excitement as the fourth act, and particularly the "*Non ti scordar di me*," created.

The Brightest and Best solemnly declares that Brignoli is fairly beaten by Beaucardé, who has really made a terrible fluttering among the crinoline true-tenor believers.

Beaucardé was very fine in the last act, but, as a gentleman from Nantucket said, he "hollers too much"; you always think that he is going to put his hand on his mouth, and hail the maintop-gallant yard, or some other impossible part of the ship. Beaucardé doesn't wear tin trowsers in this part, but appears as a private gentleman of the fourteenth century.

Altogether, the Trovatore performance was a very interesting one. Beaucardé made a sensation, as I said before, among the crinolines; and the general opinion was highly favorable to Albertini.

Amodio slipped and fell over a high note, which he attempted in the Il Balen, his pet song. The effect was ludicrous, and I don't much wonder that everybody tittered.

I was sorry for my rotund friend, and I advise him to forswear sack, live cleanly, and take care of his voice.

Small Matters.

It would be highly gratifying to some people if they could find out from the papers whether or not the *Sicilian Vespers* is successful.

The *Times* says it is a failure, and pitches into the people because they do not see it.

The *Tribune* claims it as a positive triumph, the esthetic Fry being in raptures with it; and the *Herald* says it has not made the sensation which was expected.

It is quite certain that the Vespers is an attractive opera. The Academy was quite crowded on Wednesday, and there will, undoubtedly, be a great rush to the Matinée to-day, when it is to be given for the very last time.

Next week our Teutonic fellow citizens will be expected to go into ecstasies over Mozart's "Magic Flute," which is quite new here, I believe.

At the French Theatre, they have given the *Demi-Monde* and *Le Medecin des Enfants*—the former very good, and very immoral; and the latter very dull, and very moral.

That is too often the case with other things, as well as plays.

I see it stated that Laura Keene has employed "a distinguished American author" to do the *Demi-Monde* into English. I trust he will have an easy time of it, and that the play will be allowed to slide quietly into the same infantile grave where the *Question d'Argent* sleeps, with its baby fingers encircling the manuscript of *White Lies*.

Norma, as done at Laura Keene's, has a good deal of fun in it, and although I don't like to see men in womens' clothes, (nor women in boy's clothes) I was much amused with Mr. Mark Smith's performance of injured Priestess. The duet with *Adalgisa* (Vincent) is the best thing in the piece.

All the critics agree in praising Adalina Patti, and I hope that her debut will be arranged before the present opera season is over.

The *Wreck Ashore* is, I regret to say, a total loss. It was a pity that people couldn't see it, for Dyott had a splendid death-scene, in which he was sure of two two-shilling rounds of applause. Lester Wallack died well, too, but not in the good old Park Pit style, like Dyott. Mrs. Hoey was very good, considering she keeps a coupé. I think aristocracy interferes with art; don't you? They do John Brougham's comedy, *Romance and Reality,* at Wallack's on Saturday. The gay and gallant author has been laid up in the dry-dock for some days with the gout, but is about again like a young partridge.

I don't hear of anything new under way at the theatres, except Bourcicault's five-act play. They say that Laura Keene is preparing a piece called *The Dead Heart*—a cheerful title.

"Right of Translation Reserved."

I take the following from the London *Court Journal*, October 22d:

Apropos of art, here is something curious—a bulletin of the British drama this week:

PRINCESS'S—

Ivy Hall……………………………Un Roman d'un Jeune Homme Pauvre.
Puss……………………………………………… La Femme Chatte.
Love's Telegraph…………… …………………. Les Gants et l'Eventail.

OLYMPIC—

A Husband to Order…………………………Un Mariage sous l'Empire.
The Porter's Knot……………………………. Les Crochets du Père Martin.
Retained for the Defence…………………………………Les Avocats.

NEW ADELPHI—

Willow Copse……………………………………La Closerie des Genets.
Love and Hunger……………………………………… La Tour d'Ugolin.
Ici on Parle Français……………………………… English Spoken Here.

SAINT JAMES'S—

Magic Toys………………………………………Les Pantins de Violette.

STRAND—

The Goose with the Golden Eggs……………La Poule aux [Œufs d'Or.

SURREY—

The Bridal of Beatriz…………………Emilie Galotti. (From the German.)

SADLER'S WELLS—

A Fool's Revenge……………………………Le Roi s'Amuse. (Rigoletto.)

More Chances for the British Dramatist.

The following named are the newest pieces in the hands of the Paris Managers:

La Jeunesse du Goethe, opera in five acts, by M. Meyer-beer. The drama by M. Henri Blaze de Bivry, for the Grand Opera.

At the Français, a proverb by Augustine Brohan, and *La Comédie à Ferney*, by MM. Louis Lurine and Albéric Second.

Edward About furnishes a five-act comedy, *Le Mauvais Œil*; a one-act comedy, *l'Education d'un Prince*. M. Th. Barriere has written a one-act piece, *Le Feu au Convent*; and M. Ernest Legouvé gives us *Un jeune homme qui ne fait rien*, comedy in one act, in verse.

Fast Women a la New Bowery.

I don't believe, O Effendi of the Piazza, that you ever heard of Moncrieff.

He was a Bohemian of the severest type, lived in London "during the last war," and wrote for the theatres.

Sad trash his plays were, as you may see by his "Rochester," which Mr. Lester Wallack has reedited, and called "Fast Men of the Olden Time."

Another piece by Moncrieff was called "Tom and Jerry"; and you may have seen the extensive Mr. George Barrett play "Corinthian Tom," a weakness in which he used to indulge on his benefit nights.

Then there was another brilliant production, likewise by Moncrieff, and called "The Cataract of the Ganges," in which principal character was the Rajah of Delhi, a very immoral ruler, who used to give petit soupers to the corps de ballet in the Temple of Brahma.

These plays have filled many a managerial coffer when the works of the "divine Williams" wouldn't draw sixpence.

It is not surprising, then, that the managers of the New Bowery were obliged to put aside, for the moment, even the resplendent genius of "J. Pilgrim, Esq.," and to present a new version of "Tom and Jerry" and "Rochester" combined.

They call this lively salad "Fast Women of the Modern Time."

The idea of the play is entirely fresh, and the language is of that terse and elegant character which finds favor in the Oriental districts.

The fast women are three in number, thus:

No. 1. The Soubrette—Dejazet, a young woman with a slight obliquity of vision, a long nose, and her hair in the approved Bowery-gals-a'n't-you-comin'-out-to-night style. As a piece of information to A. M., I may say that this charming young lady wore false braids, the ends of which were fastened in a thing like a bouquet-holder and tipped with silk tassels. This gorgeous creature burst upon my astonished gaze in a magnificent morning costume, and she seemed like a radiant angel on the New Canal street plan. She had the first rôle in the play. She spoke nearly all the sensation-speeches, appeared en garçon, danced a hornpipe, sung various songs, and was the ostensible commander of the everlasting "fifty beautiful young ladies who appear on the stage and go through with most elaborate military manœuvres."

No. 2 was a somewhat slower and heavier fast woman than the fairy above mentioned. No. 2 was not distinguished for personal attractions, but had a voice which reminded of the good old days of melo-drama, when art depended entirely upon a copper-fastened larynx. The lady in question has to rescue her lover from "fearful peril" (he is shut up in a garret in Little Water street), and the row she makes about it is worth double the price of admission.

No. 3 is a mild type of the "Yankee gal." I came to this conclusion through the presumptive evidence afforded by a yellow wig and a white apron, the national feminine costume of New England, according to the dramatists who hold the mirror up to nature, occasionally.

Take the three artists I have described as well as my feeble powers will permit (no pen, however eloquent, could do full justice to their multifarious charms), get them into all sorts of rows, end every act and almost every scene with a knock-down, throw in a song or two, and you have the latest effort of the metropolitan dramatic muse.

The dialogue is delightful. It is drawn from some well of undefiled English in the vicinity of Rutgers street. It breathes a pure and lofty spirit of patriotism, and of deep reverence for that charming institution, the Fire Department.

The following tabular statement will give an approximate idea of the diction of this noble work:

Distinct puffs for the American Eagle……………..25
Incidental allusions to the Bird…………………….....50
Remarks upon the duty of a true American………..40
  do. do. our gallant Firemen…………………...35
Puffs for our flag, direct and incidental…………....60

This summary includes only the first act.

Who says, after this, that we have no dramatic literature?

If the true end and aim of the drama is to depict the manners of the time according to the ideas of the audience before which it is acted, then the Bowery Theatres are the best in town, and the "Fast Women" one of the most magnificent plays since the time of the Baron's "old Greeks."

Ireland as it Isn't.

They have produced at Niblo's Garden another of those peculiar impossibilities called Irish dramas. The present affair is called "All Hallow's Eve," and is supposed to be founded upon the popular Irish superstition, that if a young woman performed certain cereal incantations on "Snap Apple Night," she would see the figure of that interesting personage her future husband.

There are two Hibernian ladies who are afflicted with this terrible mania. One is sentimental and goes by the sweet name of Ida Vernon (which I think beats Ada Clare); of course Mrs. Williams is the comic feminine.

There is a ruined spendthrift in top-boots, who goes about talking to himself and saying that he "don't care a straw" for the sentimental young lady; all he wants "is her money," and various other stereotyped stage Irish characters.

In the first act, while the ladies are at their matrimonial conjurings, an attempt is made by the immoral and sordid person in the top-boots to abduct the sentimental young lady; but through an entirely original incident,—the change of cloaks,—the volatile feminine is carried off instead.

Now this delightful person is fiancée to one "Rody O'Connor," the same Irishman with the same many-caped overcoat, the same stick, the same red wig, the same dances, and the same songs, and by the same token, the same jokes that I have seen on the stage, and nowhere else, ever since I was born,—five-and-twenty years ago, last Friday, of blessed memory.

After this explanation, the acute reader will divine, that after numerous difficulties of an easily surmountable nature, the villain is foiled by the comic Irishman, and that the latter is comfortably married to the lively young woman, whose virtue has been, by his efforts, preserved from the profane touch of the spoiler. When I have said that Mr. and Mrs. Williams have capital parts, and that they make the most of them; that the villain was a very mild type of a scoundrel; and the sentimental lady, quite sentimental enough for the money, I shall have finished with All Hallows' Eve, which has at least the merit of brevity.

Hope Deferred.

The Fireman's drama, at the Bowery, is again postponed.

The "tubs" have a little affair of their own, which they intend to exhibit in our streets next Sunday, and the Bowery Theatre people are kind enough to say that they will not interfere with the "outside show."

Correspondence.

New York, Nov. 12th, 1859.

Dear Personne:—In your opinion, what Opera is productive of the sweetest melody?

Very respectfully, Charles.

Reply.—I dono.

Personne.

NEW YORK NOVEMBER 26, 1859

Literary Notes.

—We learn by an advertisement in the *Tribune*, that "Mr. Bayard Taylor has just returned from his California tour in behalf of the N. Y. *Mercury*." How kind o' him.

—The London *Publishers' Circular* says, it is reported that the author of "A Good Fight,"—which was somewhat abruptly concluded in *Once a Week*,—will publish it in a separate form, considerably altered and extended.

—Rev. W. H. Channing, of Liverpool, it is said, has reconsidered his acceptance of the call to the Thirteenth Congregational Church of Boston, and will remain in England.

—Henry Ward Beecher charges that in the American edition of Spurgeon's Sermons, his sentiments on Slavery, contained in the English editions, have been suppressed. The *Independent* says: "A friend who has Compared the English and American editions, assures us that it is true."

—The London correspondent of the Manchester *Times*, says:

Those in the secret are anticipating with considerable curiosity the renewal of the controversy as to the antiquity of Mr. Collier's famous amended folio of Shakespeare. This time the matter will be dealt with, not by the mere cursory treatment it could alone receive from letters in the *Times*. A huge pamphlet is in preparation, going minutely into the authencity, not merely of this, but of other important documents used by Mr. Collier in his editions of the poet's works; and, without prejudging the case, it is evident, from the men who are united in questioning them, that the learned editor will be put upon his mettle in defence of his authorities.

—It is said that the new monthly about to be issued in London, under the editorial charge of Mr. Thackeray, is to be entitled The Cornhill Magazine. His chief collaborateurs are to be James Hannay, Sala, H. Sutherland, Edwards, and Mr. Dallas. Mr. Sala is to commence with a series of papers on "Hogarth and his Times."

'BEULAH' AGAIN.

I, too, have read 'Beulah,' oh, Ada Clare! and it does not add up for me as it does for you, yet do I not altogether like it. It is an earnest, un-everyday book, full of thought, if not thoughts, and it seems to me more suggestive of power, than powerful.

Some one has said with unjust sarcasm, that it is easier to find out the faults of a good book, than to write a better one. That this is so, is surely no reason why those who cannot write the book should overlook its defects.

To the person of cultivation and average intellect, who reads a book of this kind at one or two sittings, it becomes in some sort a picture, in which he beholds at once all the beauties and blemishes. In this he has the advantage of the author, who works out his characters bit by bit, by the labor of many days, subject in heart and brain to influences physical and mental, which lend daily a coloring of their own to the work of his hands, resulting, perhaps, in faults and inconsistencies unperceived by himself, but plain to his readers.

I used sometimes, in idle moods of my school-days, to amuse myself by poring over a page of English print, in a patient but vain effort to give it the aspect of a strange language—to see it with the eyes of a foreigner. It is an impossibility. We read a foreign language word by word from the surface, as it were. Every word stands out clear and distinct by itself, destitute of that careless, unconscious blending of phrase with phrase, sentence with sentence, with which we dream over a page of our native tongue.

An author's book is his dialect; and to impartially examine and criticize it in detail, becomes a task more difficult to him than to the least gifted of his readers. Perhaps not one in a thousand of those who have read the book, could have written 'Beulah.'

But we all see that some of its personations are crude and inharmonious to the last degree.

It seems incredible that one who writes as some portions of 'Beulah' are written, could have limned a character so tame, and weak, and wanting in truth to its original conception, as Eugene Graham. One feels that to carry out that conception he should have sinned, if at all, splendidly, retaining in his fall some traces of a fine nature and unusual abilities. But he is the merest commonplace "dissipated young man," with the narrowest possible social opinions, expressed in the tritest of stereotyped terms. From first to last the only proof we have of Eugene Graham's boasted talents is the word of our author; and when the book is closed, we leave the man as we found the boy—a being of splendid *promises*.

Beulah herself is vexation of spirit; one of that class of heroines no longer new, the prototype of Jane Eyre,—yet mark! Ada Clare, not to be disposed of as an "imitation." A strong, self-reliant, and one feels obliged to add, *good* character, as grim and downright as her name, with a sort of brusque honesty closely verging on ill-breeding, and a defiant way of upholding her own opinions, one cannot help thinking Beulah Benton the most unprepossessing of characters. Intellectually, she is the superior of Miss Brontë's heroine; but personally, she never excites in us a tithe of the interest which makes us eagerly follow the fortunes of Jane Eyre, and draw a long breath of satisfaction when she at last becomes Rochester's.

I question, indeed, if the majority of Beulah's readers experience any pleasurable sympathy in the scene which reunites her to her long-absent guardian. She appears always too cold-hearted, too devoid of those attributes with which we instinctively invest youth, to arouse in us any warmth of emotion.

Even in these days of female authorship, when almost every woman has ventured—if ever so little way, still ventured—within the charmed borders of Bohemia, this young lady, to whose literary aspirations everything else must give way, who selfishly sacrifices to a passion for fame, years of a man's life,—accepting him at last, only when the incense of that fame is no longer fresh, excites in us nearly the same degree of awesome repugnance, with which the dames and men of forty years ago regarded a genuine specimen of the bluestocking.

Yet however unattractive the portraiture of Beulah may be, it cannot be charged with inconsistency. I incline to the belief that this character, and that of Dr. Hartwell—fine but unfinished—are the only prominent ones in the volume which are true to the author's evident idea. Dr. Asbury cannot be called original; he is the "good old gentleman" of novels. Pauline is rather a sketch than a character; and Cornelia Graham is a mystery. From the first appearance of the latter in the schoolroom of Madame St. Cymon, to the very last scene of her life, one is constantly expecting to read the riddle, and as constantly disappointed.

'Beulah' belongs to that class of books which take up a single question, and make it their prime object, bringing all their powers to bear upon its elucidation.

The author has chosen a theme interesting to all, and right earnestly has she taken hold of her work. Yet her process is scarcely new. It is doubtful if the course of reasoning which Beulah pursues, and which leaves her at last with no belief, only a faith, has not been followed almost in detail, by most of the thinking men and women of this age, with various results. And this is where the book touches the sympathies of its readers. In its metaphysical character lies the power of 'Beulah'; and the deep and well-conned reading, and the masterly handling of abstruse and perplexing subjects displayed by its author, will give and hold for it a place in the mind, which it will never occupy in the heart.

JULIETTE H. BEACH.

Albion, N. Y., Nov. 21st.

Thoughts and Things.

BY ADA CLARE.

No. V.

Attracted by its very original title, I have been tempted to read "Henry St. John, *Gentleman*." It has not been hard reading, for the style is graceful and unpresuming. The plot of the story is of the ancient, wormeaten type, turning upon intercepted letters and Italian tiring-women. It is a dreary mode for to-day: one might as well try to resuscitate the gored dresses and powdered wigs of the past. The book seems to me to be in a fluid state; it wants consistency; it is what children call sloshy. It is too much like literature on tap—the chapters suggest the division into pints and quarts. Yet there are many charming, graceful little bits of description sown through the work. Further, I suppose it contains a fund of useful and interesting information concerning the early revolutionary history of Virginia, which if I do not appreciate, the writer is certainly not at fault. I have never shown a proper interest in my revolutionary ancestors; to me they have ever been dismal and lorn beings. Patriots, as a class, I know are noble creatures, but they are seldom interesting. Yet I never passed, on the Champs Elysées, the statue of the sublime Maid of Orleans, without the involuntary reverence of a bowed head. To me there was something awful in the simplicity of that kneeling form, with its upturned, utterly tragic face. I have sometimes thought that I heard a thrill break through the grief-stricken mouth, and saw a light burst out from the grand, sad eyes, 'gainst which the sun's light shone drear and dim.

"Henry St. John, Gentleman," shows the evident impress of a woman's hand. Nay, there are many passages in the work that it would grieve me to the heart to believe any but a woman could write. I cannot, oh! I will not believe that our men have become so depraved, as to acquaint themselves with the mysteries of a woman's hairdressing, or the arrangements of the rosettes on her shoes. The knowledge that she wears hoops can only be given over to the most abandoned of men.

°°°

There is a rumor afloat that the Harpers offered a prize for the most inane story that should be sent them during the last month. Rumor goes on to say that nineteen hundred stories competed for the prize, but the "*Armistice*" carried the day triumphantly. And matchless indeed is the inanity of that story; it is the very marrow of stupidity, the Jove among dunces. Nothing I know of could be compared to it for idiocy, but a story published a few months ago, called the "Rainy-Day." The Messrs. Harpers, who are certainly the keenest-witted publishers in the country, must have some sly reasons for publishing such stories. I feel personally abused when this Magazine becomes dull, because I have taken a peculiar interest in it hitherto for its entertaining matter, and because the Easy Chair once published an anonymous letter from me. "Regular Habits," and "Veni, Vide, Vici," are good opiates; they would cure the ear-ache, and the patient may be assured that the remedy is not much worse than the disease. Miss Cheesebro' has a story also in the last number. I felt little interest in the plot, but whatever that lady's hands find to do, she does in an interesting manner. She has never visited the realm of the commonplace even in her dreams. For which four or five times, beloved virtue let her name be forever blessed!

°°°

People talk of being surprised because the "Sicilian Vespers," of which everybody admires the music, has not met with the very great success it merited. It has perhaps been owing to the fact, that the Prima Donna could not interest her audiences. Cortesi or Cruvelli would have insured its success, because they would have been able to magnetize the audience. No one could accuse our poor little Colson of doing that. Either the audience or the Prima Donna must command. They will either give her their admiration as a natural tribute, or as a simple patronage. The first never palls; it is like the light of the sun by which we live; while the other is the glimmer of the streetlamps, trimmed and lighted for a consideration. We all of us worship the sun as naturally as we breathe, while amateur lamplighters are certainly rare.

°°°

A reply to my remarks on "Beulah," appeared in the last number of the SATURDAY PRESS. Only one line of it struck me. That was the author's desire to present Miss Evans with "a pair of white elephants." It would be a very unsafe thing to be admired, if admiration could call forth not only the desire, but the power to bestow such weighty tribute. Different minds of course would express themselves by different beasts. Mrs. Stowe, for instance, the morning after the issue of the "Minister's Wooing," might have found the silence of her back-garden broken by the brays of a pair of zebras united to the howlings of a small family of hippopotami. What would Laura Keene think, if she were forced to accept as a tribute to her talents, an unsophisticated Bengal tiger, and a nice, fat, enterprising boa constrictor? Imagine the emotions that would swell the beautiful breast of the Cortesi, if her rendition of Sappho should call forth a mastodon and a pair of sperm whales! If the idea were properly carried out the occupation of bouquets were gone. Every theatre and opera-house would be provided with a menagerie on its ground-floor, for the accommodation of the enthusiastic young men who might wish to compliment the Prima Donna with a beast. In the very moments of his frenzy he might rush forth and purchase a eulogistic rhinoceros, or an adulatory crocodile. Mechanical contrivances of ropes and pulleys could then be managed for letting the beasts down from the roof. This invention would not only avoid the necessity of marching the beasts through the audience, but would afford a sweet and cheerful surprise to the artist, who should find herself suddenly crowned with a chaplet, not of bays, but of bears.

°°°

"Sword and Gown" is truly an entertaining book. It is quite refreshing after the apotheosis of the rigmarole which our Press now seems to be. The writer has risen so far above his last production, that he must have gone up in a balloon from "Guy Livingston" to this. It is full of genial wit, and delightful, saucy, racy writing of every style. The tragedy at the end was totally unnecessary; it was wilful murder.

I confess that though I often admire the writings of men, it always pains me to see a man exposing himself to general remark and to the gaze of women, by thus coming publicly forward. The sacred precinct of home is the true sphere of man. Modesty, obedience, sobriety, are the true male virtues. We love to see the sweet male violet hidden under domestic greens. I mean not to say that men have never succeeded in writing; but compare them with the great mistresses of art, and where are they? Echo answers, "Gone out for a horn; in case of fire, keys may be found next door." There is something effeminate in the literary or artist man, that our sex repudiates. We do not want man to be too highly educated; we want him sweet, gentle, and thick-skulled. There are many things he can learn with impunity. He should learn the multiplication-table, for instance. He should learn to read, also, because the works of Mrs. Sherwood, T. S. Arthur, and the publications of the American Tract Society, should sometimes beguile his gentle hours; but above all things in his education, let not the sacred dumpling be neglected. Do not suppose I would keep the man in ignorance; but why puzzle his brain, built for the cultivation of the moral sense, with such abstruse sciences as geography, history, grammar, spelling, gauging, etc.

It must not be supposed we do not love men; in their proper sphere we are willing to love, cherish, and protect them. But we do not want them as rivals—we wish to be able to unbend to them. Their strength must lie in their weakness. When we take them under the wings of our love, let them not take to crowing.

Let no profane woman suggest that men have a right to enter the arena of the arts, in proportion as they exhibit a capacity for them. I will indignantly ask what capacity has to do with sphere? I will brand her as a dangerous radical, if she say that whatever nature has fitted him to do she exacts of him. I will ask her if she means to say that these things are to be managed on so low a scale as that of nature and truth? We want all our men alike to the least atom, and all of them steeped in the kitchen to the very lips.

Let puddings be made, though the heavens fall!

Vain will it be to enumerate to me, the great things men have done. In the first place I will intemperately deny the existence of those things. If you corner me so that I am forced to acknowledge them, I will retreat to my great stronghold, that we don't want intelligent men, that our choice is only the angelic dunce.

On the other hand we wish their moral and social virtues to be developed to the utmost. The moral sense of the man, the perception of the man is too sweet to be trusted to the companionship of mental ability. Don't tell me about the great, dignified, free-willed, God-stamped soul, with its birthright of immortality and the possession of itself, which cannot be traded away for a mess of society's cold pottage. All such illogical arguments I will answer by saying, that if you let the soul get out of its cage for one minute, you will undermine all the foundations of society. Besides the question is not what the man is, but what we women wish him to be. It is radical to call things by their right names. If I choose to call a bootjack a spoon, and use it for sipping my tea, you would be doing a bad thing for society by telling me it would not act in that capacity. For morality must always be indulged at the expense of virtue. Physical force cannot take into consideration any such little matters as justice and truth. When did souls show any muscles; can *they* hit out from the shoulder? As we are brutally the stronger sex, we wish to use men's natures as conveniences. We want to make parlor-ornaments of those natures, by covering them over with conventional putty, stuccoing them according to taste with little virtue-shells, then enclosing the whole within the glass-case of immaculate propriety. Every one has seen and admired those lovely ornaments of shell-work, made in the above manner, looking like sentimental dog-kennels or over-grown pepper-castors just returned from a marine spree.

If through means of this article one intellectual man becomes silly, or one large mind renounces its mental sphere, and devotes itself to erecting the noble homemade shirt, this article will have accomplished its prayerful work, and the writer will not have lived in vain.

THE EAGLE AND THE TURKEY.

In our national aviary the Turkey has an honorable place. His sphere is lowlier than that of the Emblematic Bird. Proudly conscious of the responsibility of his office, jealous of the confidence reposed by more than twenty millions of freemen in his potential pinions and conservative claws, the Eagle beats against the azure gates of heaven, looks with unblinking eye into the splendid heart of the sun—disdainful of earth, save when, lighting majestic on some lofty peak (Pike's, for example), he shrieks the glory of the nation he has the honor to represent to the farthest pole. The Turkey's ambition has a much narrower horizon. In his vainest moments, a conspicuous strut to a lively gobbling accompaniment is ample satisfaction to his soul. He desires far more to pleasantly pick his way through life in the poultry-yard, than to soar in the sunshine, or count kindred with the stars. He spreads his wings only for the protection of some oppressed and sorrowing fellow-fowl, or to shake their damped plumage dry. His tastes and habits are all domestic. He regards with equanimity the more brilliant exploits of his lordly brother. The Eagle's constantly increasing reputation gives him no jealous pang. He is contented to stand apart, and share none of the honors which accumulate at the end of that superb beak, and in the corners of those burning eyes.

But homely virtues are still pretty certain to receive a fair share of public appreciation. Brilliant gifts or attainments may dazzle for a time; but after a time, we know it is lack-lustre they are. Great reputations are the favorite carrion of the cruel vulture Society. The "belle of the season" is the shining mark for detraction and ridicule; and perhaps, all embosomed in the flowery compliment that flutters to her ear through perfume, there is a sting that will inflict a rankling wound. We criticize unsparingly our great men. Washington has felt the scalpel. His memory is not let alone; and it is one of the favorite amusements of the day severely to punch the head of Daniel Webster, low-lying many years. Our Eagle does not escape the common lot. We all take pride and comfort in the brave bird. We have him in commemorative brass on our buttons and over our shop-doors. He is let loose in our conversation. Perhaps no people are more thoroughly at home in ornithology than we. But we sometimes make merry, too, at the expense of the winged defender of our stars and stripes; and say things that would cause a depression of his crest, if it were not such a very stiffly stuck-up crest; and freely indulge in equivocal pleasantries directed at each and all of the members of the bird's corporeal frame.

But the shrinking humility of the Turkey is his sure defence. He has no bright fame to be tarnished. Like the very quiet people that are always stealing gently, almost timidly, across our path of life, and are loved by us most dearly, the unassuming bird of Thanksgiving enjoys our undivided affection. Forever insensible to the delights of oyster-sauce, and callous to the touch of "Boned," be the tongue that wags in contempt or ridicule of the favorite fowl!

This general confidence, however, this universal pride, is not to be thus negatively accounted for. The lives of myriad Turkeys that have gone before demand an honest tribute to the exalted heroism which, after all, is the peculiar attribute of this species of the feathered tribe. The Eagle will drown the combined voices of nature, shrieking in our behalf. For us he will flap mightily his wings. He will clutch our colors, and then they cannot grovel in the dust. What foe shall tear them from him in the fight? But—will he quietly lie down and die for us? When was our Eagle known to offer himself up a willing sacrifice upon the shrine of patriotism? The annals of Turkeydom tell of immemorial oblations to the divinity of Freedom. The Turkey is the universal John Brown of the animal creation. His paths of glory lead but to the gravy.

These are our only reflections upon the Thanksgiving of 1859.

Dramatic Feuilleton.

Little Patti.

A début on Thursday. An off-night. People full of turkey and champagne. A bit sleepy, and not a bit enthusiastic.

Little Patti stirred them up with an exceedingly long pole, sharpened at both ends.

The Oldest Man saw it, and forgot his gout in his wild excitement. (He'll remember, to-morrow.)

I saw it.

Anna Maria saw it to an immense extent.

People saw it who are not in the habit of seeing anything, having already seen almost everything, and found nothing in anything.

She is a fresh petite Pate de Foies Gras, with Truffes of Perigord, and a great many more in a given quantity than you generally get.

If she had made her début at Solferino, or any other place in Italy, the people would have gone wild, and broken things all to pieces.

Here is a young girl, only sixteen, who sings like a thorough artist, doesn't scream, takes E flat as if she had plenty more of it, and has the sweetest, freshest voice in the world.

She has a fine future. I enroll her among my protegés. She is the best operatic stock going, and like Panama, is bound to have a sudden rise.

The managers of the Academy have got a splendid sensation in this brown little girl, with the magnificent black hair; the fine, large, Italian eyes, and the most charming mouth in the world.

She is not unlike Piccolomini, so far as having the material for a popular pet is concerned, but sings a hundred times better than that delicious little humbug.

En avant, little Patti! Go forward in your flowery career! The next few years of your life will be crowded with the triumphs, which wealth, taste, and culture, award to art in one of its most delightful forms.

I can promise you, between the managers, and the other prime donne, and your lovers (I beg you to understand that I don't mean people whom you love), and other things too numerous to mention, you'll have a delightful time of it.

Room there, you veterans of the coulisses, you heroines of an hundred fights, with more scars than decorations, and more airs in your heads than in your throats, room for little Patti!

La Reine de l'Opéra !

Vive la Reine!

I don't mind confessing that I went to sleep over the *Magic Flute, Die Zauberfloete,* or *Il Flauto Magico*, for the management with its customary liberality don't mind what they call it. So did almost everybody else.

Everybody else, in point of fact, except Bergmann, Burkhardt, and the Teutonic cricket, who never washes his face, always wears long hair, and a dirty shirt, and thinks he looks like Schiller.

The Oldest Man came out strong for the *Magic Flute*. It seems he heard it in Europe, or somebody else heard it, and told him it was a splendid thing.

So he patronized the subscriber about it. He said now you will hear something fine—a great work, sir; none of your modern trash, gotten up for the music shops; but a grand thing, an immortal thing, a magnificent thing.

Mozart, sir, remarked the old gentleman, taking another glass of sherry (City Hotel stock), Mozart was a great man; but you new school, Music of the Future fellows, can't see it.

No, I remarked mildly, we can't.

And I say, continued the Venerable, I say that the Music of the Future ought to be played by-and-bye, when, perhaps, they may understand it; though I'm – —if I believe they *ever* can.

More sherry.

I replied, briefly, that perhaps it might be as well if the Music of the Past had been buried with its composers.

The old gentleman laughed, but he hasn't asked me to dine since.

A harmless mot cut me out of '48 Lafitte, and Duff Gordon sherry.

Be warned, ye youths, etc.

However, the Oldest Man could only stand the first act, and then kept himself awake by taking snuff and looking at Butt.

As for A. M., who is quicker at slang than at her irregular verbs, she says that the *Magic Flute* is a good opera, "if a man don't care what he says."

She has, however, recommended to my notice a young man from Boston, who is looked upon, in his boarding-house, as a great musical amateur, and a gentleman of fine literary talents.

This opinion has been arrived at from the most conclusive evidence. Thus :

He came from Boston.

He has yellow hair, green eyes, and a chalky complexion.

He wears spectacles.

He plays the piano.

He always appears in black clothes.

He has only one lung.

His general health is "poor."

He writes for the *Ledger*.

He never pays the landlady until he has been driven into a corner.

He goes to Pfaff's.

This rising young man has written for me a splendid highfalutin criticism upon the *Magic Flute*.

I can only give a brief extract, and intend to send the balance of the MS. to the *New American Cyclopædia.*

Here:

"In the art-warm metropolis of down-trodden Austria, seventy years ago, arose one of the mightiest genii of modern times,

"Col. WOLFGANG MOZART!

"Born of poor, but respectable parents, he never kept a coupé, like Brignoli and Mrs. Hoey, but he did better.

"He composed the *Magic Flute*, and gave the MS. to his friend Stigelli, to be produced by his admirer, Ullmann.

"' Let,' said Mozart to Ullmann, 'let the Star Spangled Banner wave over one of my scores and I shall die content.'

"At that moment, there entered a mysterious stranger, who saluted the composer with profound respect. 'I am commanded,' he said, 'by a person of rank to'—

[See American First Class Book for the yarn about the Requiem.]

"'I am confident,' continued Mozart, after the stranger had made his deposit and retired, 'that I shall never survive *The Magic Flute* and *The Requiem* together.'

"'I shall die bequeathing my fame to Carl Formes, for whom I wrote nearly all my operas. I hope he will produce them in Boston.'

"Such are the romantic and touching circumstances under which this great work has been presented. It is one of the liveliest efforts of a refined and tender sensibility, and will, therefore, have a great success in Boston.

"It commences with an overture, which is written for all the instruments, and played by most of them. The overture is a noted specimen of the idiosyncratical developments, and the manipulative skill of the composer. The tender tones of the clarionets, alternate in pastoral harmony with the pizzicato movements of the violins, while the effect of the sub-dominant fifths in four extra basses, with the ensemble of the scintillating kettle-drums, make up a corps d'œil which is rarely experienced anywhere except in Boston.

"In the vocal score, we find a superfluity of melodic gems, all distinguished for their contrapuntal execution and fugacious harmoniousness.

"There is a choral of grand resonancing, in various kinds of time, according to the relations of the conductor and the chorus-master; this is the finest thing I ever heard anywhere except in Boston.

"The singers were not so good as those of the Handel and Haydn Society. Madame Colson has an elaborate bravura which contains a high note (F in alt.), and she did not sing it. All the Handel and Haydn soprani sing F in alt.,—continually carry it about, in fact, in their reticules and things."'

[Here the cultivated youth (the finest critic in the country, sir), begins to grow exceedingly transcendental, and consequently a little mysterious; so I reserve him for the *Cyclopædia.* Look out when they get to M——. It is a very good thing for the Appletons, who, as I understand, pay for manuscript as people in Wall street buy their libraries—by the lineal foot.]

Small Matters.

Lord Dundreary (Mr. Sothern) has been suing Miss Laura Keene for a breach of contract. The latter has a verdict for some rent which is owed to her, not by Sothern, but by another person, to whom she (Miss Keene) had sub-let her theatre.

The affair reminds me very forcibly of the mot of an old lawyer, who used to say that there were two things utterly inscrutable: one, the decrees of Divine Providence; the other, the verdict of a petit jury!

Mr. Lester Wallack is preparing an English of *Le Roman d'un Jeune Homme Pauvre.*

The play will be in six tableaux, and the distribution will include all the prominent artists of the theatre.

The Wife's Secret is still attractive at Laura Keene's. Next week, at the French Theatre, there is to be a benefit for Mannstein, the jeune premier. M'lle Dupont has volunteered, and the piece de resistance of the evening will be *La Closerie des Genets,* a drama by Frederic Soulie. It has been adapted in English, under the title of *The Willow Copse.*

The immortal T. Placide has returned to town, as handsome as ever.

Mr. Brougham's comedy, *Romance and Reality*, has been revived at Wallack's, and has been found very attractive. Mr. Brougham has a benefit this evening, and plays *D. Brulgruddery* in *J. Bull*.

Mr. Walcot is to have a benefit at Wallack's, next week. He will play, for the first time, *Lord Ogleby* in *The Clandestine Marriage*.

Edwin Booth, a tragedian of some cleverness, and a great deal of notoriety, has been playing an engagement at Boston, and if we may judge by certain publications in the *Sunday Times* of this city, has made many conquests among the ladies of the modern Athens. Actors always have one ardent admirer. One man who flatters and toadies them. One man who swears by them. One man who puts himself in a pose before them, and says, like Captain Edward Cuttle, "there's a head." The "Vagabond" of the *Sunday Times* is the special and exclusive admirer of E. Booth.

And to show what a great man E. Booth is, the Vagabond prints the letters which "Roscius" receives from bread-and-butter school-girls, who write the same things to Snooks, the walking gentleman at the Museum, the Lord Fitz-Clarence Foozle in all the farces, only that Snooks has no Vagabond so stupid as to print them for him.

Why don't Mr. Jordan and Mr. Lester Wallack print their correspondence, edited by the Vagabond? It would make a splendid holiday souvenir. The ladies might not feel flattered, but that's no matter.

The HERON plays on Monday, at the Winter Garden, for the benefit of Mrs. Bourcicault. The sensation drama, *Pauline*, is to be acted. The rehearsals of Mr. Bourcicault's new piece have commenced. Mr. G. W. Consuelo Jamison, and Mrs. G. C. Howard, the original Topsey, have been specially engaged for the colored elements in it.

S. Cowell commences operations at the Theatre Français on next Monday night. The advertisements say that S. C. is "excruciatingly" funny.

According to the best lexicographical authority, excruciate is from the Latin excrucio, from crux, a cross, and means to torture, to torment, to agonize, to put to severe pain.

If S. C. intends to do this it is wrong, and pious Pillsbury ought to interfere.

I see no reason why I should not dine on Thanksgiving Day as well the protegés of the Five Points Mission.

This alimentive tendency on my part, will abbreviate the Feuilleton, a fact which will, without doubt, be especially agreeable to your readers, who perhaps will wish that some one would give me a good dinner every Thursday.

So will the subscriber ever pray.

PERSONNE

NEW YORK DECEMBER 3, 1859

Thoughts and Things.

BY ADA CLARE.

I will not trust myself to comment upon "Avolio, and other Poems," by Paul H. Hayne. My judgment could not be set at a pin's fee if I did. When I was a child I thought him a greater poet than Tennyson, and childish impressions are not easily worn off. Being myself a native of the same State and city with the author, and one of his earliest acquaintances, it would seem even a little indelicate for me to sing his praises. I copy here one of the many sonnets contained in the little volume, and leave it to justify itself.

LIFE.

Suffering!—and yet magnificent in pain!
Mysterious!—yet like Spring-showers in the sun,
Veiling the light with their melodious rain
Life from the worlds beyond hath radiance won;
Its gloomiest phase is as the clouds that mourn
'Neath the majestic brightness of the Arch,
Where nobler orbs in deathless daylight burn,
And God's great pulses beat their music-march:
The Heaven we worship dimly, girt with tears
The spirit Heaven! what is it but a Life,
Lifting its soul beyond our mortal years
That oft begin, and ever end in strife—
Strife we must pass to win a happier Height;
Nature but travails to reveal us—light.

°°°

Did any one discover the plot, the merest outline of the plot of the Magic Flute, without assistance from the libretto? If so, he or she ought to have lived in the time when the Sphinx's riddle was propounded. That mind would have defeated an Almanac of Sphinxes.

The plot however might have been constructed on this ingenious plan. The author takes a punch-bowl (if not convenient, his hat will do as well), writes a number of anecdotes, and puts them into the bowl miscellaneously. He then puts on a pair of green spectacles, and drawing them out one after the other places them side by side. He then begins at the first one, follows it accurately, so on to the next, without regard to sentiment or circumstance, until he comes to the end. It is then ready to be set to music, and it is apt in time to become classic.

°°°

The appearance of "la petite Patti" brings lack to life a type of voice that seemed to be disappearing out of the world—the utterly melodious. Her voice has no dramatic accent, no dramatic power at all. Music through her accomplishes its simplest and highest purpose—the production of sweet sounds. For the eye she has nothing; but her voice is the ear's paradise.

°°°

Dickens's story is finished at last, and we are none of us satisfied. I can't help feeling that the hero acted like a fanatical muff. On the mere possible chance of saving the life of some old steward or other, he risks his own life, his wife's, her friend's, her father's, their child's, and actually sacrifices, though unwittingly, his friend's. If a man takes upon himself to intrude uninvited into a den of lions, under the belief that he is called upon to teach those self-willed creatures the laws of propriety and morals, ten to one they prefer to study gastronomy without his assistance, and eat him, as we do radishes of a Summer morning. Every one need not expect such luck with beasts as our friend the gentle Daniel had.

°°°

In these days, when philanthropy is so followed, a new invention added to her stock of trades is a blessing. Temperance, anti-lunatic asylumism, anti-slavery, anti-capital punishments, are getting to be very tedious insects. I offer to any reformer, as a gift, my new branch of philanthropy—a crusade against the fatal pie. I enroll myself as the first anti-pietist.

By the pie, I mean that dense, leaden-hued concavity of dough, into which a certain damp, lumpy substance is introduced, called by compliment after various respectable fruits. This awful thing has found its way into most private dwellings, and into all public houses. Its use in many places supersedes that of brandy, but the two horrible drugs are oftener consumed together. The outer walls of the fatal pie are composed of musty and incapable flour, united to the lard of hogs, grown too rabid even for the consumption of that animal. Into these domestic coffins are placed masses of superannuated preserves, doctored with any or many of the acid family, and the whole hermetically sealed with a cover of the coffin-mass.

Ada Clare

I have seen fathers of family preaching against the horrors of spirituous liquors, while they were building up dyspeptic mountains on the plates of their children, in the shape of the demoniac pie. Last week I visited one of those pie cellars, in which the clerks of the business city come down to swallow a hasty lunch of the pie. Innocent young men with blue eyes and corn-like hair, entrusted with banking business, with brokerage, with speculations in stocks, with commission business, with flour and grains, with book-publishing, etc., all, all sucked into this whirlpool, all standing in their spotless innocence and glowing faith to feed on the accursed food. One fair young man demanded a pumpkin pie, a blear, circular thing, apparently moist from the breaking out of a horrid perspiration through its ghastly pores, and covered with a light-yellow glue, born it seemed of the union of soft soap and sugar, through which ran intersecting streaks of dark-orange, swelling out like angry veins. Into the innocent mouth this thing is thrust, jammed, nay, crammed, and lo, in a moment it has joined the invisibles. The glass of cheap brandy which follows the pie, seemed to me in comparison to it a most harmless fluid, a most mild form of madness.

While travelling in England a fearful accident occurred to me, while on the train for Oxford. Even now I tremble and turn pale in relating it. It was near dusk; it was raining slightly, and the wind moaned drearily through the screams of the engine. In the midst of a short nap, I was awakened by the cry, "ten minutes for refreshments." In a few minutes, one of the gentlemen who had occupied the same car with me returned, and begged me to eat a certain something which it was too dark for me to see. Supposing it to be a respectable cake or roll, I bit into one side of it, and instantly felt as if my teeth were those of the Dragon of Cadmus, and were about to rise up to slay me, through outraged personality. Reader, I had bitten an *Eel-Pie*. Years may snow their whiteness upon this head, this hand may become palsied, this heart may lose the faculty of admiration,—but never will I forget the emotion of that moment.

You have all of you tasted the eel, and you have all of you remarked that, alas! too many of them suggest the unmitigated whale-blubber. These are the ones usually devoted to the pie, after having been served up as a fish and refused by the imploring palate. They are then shut up in opaque and air-tight walls of dough, and left to intensify and aggravate their own implacable spermoiliness. When these have remained on the counter two or three days, imagine the emotion of one who opens them. The feeling of the Fisherman who opened the casket and let the tallest of the Genii out of it, was mild in comparison.

I am going to close this article with the melancholy confessions of a pie-eater. 'Twas in a private and select circle that he rose up, suddenly, and spoke. "Oh! my friends," he cried, "I have had youth, and strength, and friends, and hopes like you—but where are they all? buried under the fatal pie. Avoid the pie, for it leadeth to death; it seemeth brilliant and fair, but it leads to ruin and death. My father was a noble soapboiler, and I was the pride of his heart. One miserable day, I met with evil companions who persuaded me to eat of oyster-pie,— a pie peopled with oysters in their dotage, delivered over in their second childhood to the tender mercies of dough. Oh, wretched pie! thou wast the rock upon which the bark of my hopes struck and went down. From that moment I became a slave to pie. My wife entreated, my child held up its little hands, my friends reasoned, the pastor prayed for me; but the demon had entered my soul, and would not be dispossessed. I went on eating, eating to my own ruin. Day after day, night after night, I haunted the pie-cellar, with staring eyes and dishevelled hair, eating, eating, until the friendly policeman conveyed me to my abode. Oh, that abode! how had the loveliness of its walls fallen away! Pie was written on every fragment of my broken hearthstone,—pie, on the haggard face of my wife,—pie, on the starving raggedness of my children! I had now eaten up all my substance; through the medium of pie I had masticated whole acres of landed estate and thirteen brick houses. Finally, the last sad act of the stern drama remains to be told. One night I returned home in a state of madness, and, unable to sleep, ordered one of my children forth to purchase more pie. Heedless of her entreaties, I forced her forth. She returned with the pie in her trembling hands. While I devoured it, I heard the sounds of sobs and cries proceeding from my wife and children, who now slept on the floor, their bed having been parted with the preceding week. A fiendish thought suddenly swirled into my mind. Enraged by their grief, I determined to make them eat of the pie. I seized my wife by the hair, and dragged her to the middle of the room. 'Wretch,' I cried, 'eat, eat!' Vain were her tears, her entreaties, her anguish. By force, she ate of the pie; by force the children devoured it. Suddenly smitten by remorse and terror, I left them swooning on the floor, and fled forever from the wretched hovel. I know not whether death claimed them as its victims; but from that hour I was a changed man, and pie hath not since passed my lips.

"Oh! my friends, my young friends, take solemn warning by me; and remember that the feet of the pie-eater are planted on dough, and oceans of tartaremetic roll around him. On one side yawns the pumpkin-Charybdis; on the other towers blackly the cold-meat Scylla!"—Here the voice stopped, and I was about to burst into tears, when one of the inmates of the room cut off the floodgates of my emotion. He said, "Pay no attention to that stupid old dyspeptic! He gets the nightmare occasionally, and talks in that way. To-night he has over-eaten—nay, he has gorged himself with mince-pie, and this is the result!"

This, indeed, staggered me; for everybody knows that none of the reformed drunkards ever preach eloquent temperance under the sunset glow which the human anatomy receives from Jamaica rum. Ah, no; never!

WASHINGTON IRVING.

BORN, APRIL 3, 1783

DIED, NOVEMBER 28, 1859

DEATH OF WASHINGTON IRVING.

The hand which now essays this eulogy, has often handled the pages of WASHINGTON IRVING. When we began first to read, we read *The Sketch Book*; we read *Salmagundi*; we read *Tales of a Traveller*. How great must have been our love of him—a love fostered by the old family tradition! We feel it now to have been strong, great, and decided. Whatever Mr. WASHINGTON IRVING did, he did well. There is no better, purer, sweeter English prose than his. There is no American writer who has made such an Anglo-American reputation. He came at an early period—comparatively early, we mean—into the field of letters. His *History of New York* is the finest satire since those of Swift. His *Salmagundi* compared favorably with *The Spectator*. The charms of Bracebridge Hall, and of *Tales of a Traveller*, seduced the sternest of the English critics, and obtained the patronage of Mr. Murray, a great English publisher. As a literary man, he was not afraid either of hard work or of hack-work. He could have had no particular temptation to undertake either *The Life of Columbus, The Alhambra, Abbottsford,* or *Newstead Abbey;* but he worked upon all these with a will, —just as he worked, afterwards, upon his great serious work, *The Life of Washington*. He had the true feeling of a literary man—that proper sense of his own importance, and of the importance of his own proper productions, which sustained him in poverty, and afterwards brought him wealth. He was the most eminent instance, we believe, in this country, of a gentleman rising from mediocrity to competency of fortune by the labors of his pen. If his last works were not excellent, his first were extraordinary. Since Addison, no man in the literature of our English language has been so loved. He made no enemies. He made only friends, and these friends were made for life. Those who read him in their infancy, shed tears, yesterday, over the report of his death; remembered his generosity, his geniality, and his goodness; recollected how kind, just, and manly he had been. His works pass into English literature. His memory passes into English and American hearts. He has put his creations into New York history, as Shakespeare has put his into English history. Dutch governors are as immortal as Falstaff. This was much to do, but Mr. IRVING has done it thoroughly and charmingly. No man of literary pursuits will be so remembered. No man taking to pen and ink will be so beloved. It was by a fine dispensation of Providence, that this excellent person was saved the mortification, the pain, and the distraction of poverty, and was enabled to devote himself to literary pursuits thoroughly and honestly. No man of letters will suffer a pang, to know that he was more fortunate than most of us can hope to be; that there was about his latter days the charm of affluence; that he escaped the old griefs, and ancient tortures, and chronic sorrows of the literary career. At seventy-seven years of age, he goes to his grave more thoroughly beloved than any writer in the country. May we hope that he will sleep as quietly as Rip Van Winkle, and rise to a morning more glorious than that which burst upon the old Dutchman! Of all American writers who have lived, published, and died, no one is so sure of fame as WASHINGTON IRVING.

AMUSEMENTS.

ACADEMY OF MUSIC—
FAREWELL PERFORMANCE.

CLOSE OF THE SEASON.

LAST APPEARANCE OF ADELINA PATTI.

This (Saturday) Morning, at 1 o'clock,
A GRAND ADELINA PATTI MATINEE,
which will most positively be the last for the next two months,
At which
MLLE. ADELINA PATTI
will appear in the entire Opera of

LA SOMNAMBULA.

Mlle. ADELINA PATTI..........as...................... Amina.
Sig. BRIGNOLI.................as...................... Elvino.
Sig. AMODIO...................as...................... Rudolfo.

Price of Admission, $1.
N. B.—The season opens in Philadelphia next Monday.

WINTER GARDEN. FRIDAY AND SATURDAY
THE LAST NIGHTS OF
DOT,
AND
SMIKE.

Ere these beautiful pictures of Home are withdrawn from the Winter Garden,
THOSE FAMILIES AND CHILDREN
who have not yet seen them, are informed that
THE PRESENT WEEK
will close these genial entertainments.
Therefore,
FATHERS AND MOTHERS,
BRING THE CHILDREN,
BRING THE CHILDREN,
BRING THE CHILDREN,
BRING THE CHILDREN,
BRING THE CHILDREN,
TO SPEND
AN EVENING
WITH
CHARLES DICKENS.
BRING THEM
TO SEE
LITTLE DOT
AND
POOR SMIKE.
Entertainments commence at seven, to end early.

Dramatic Feuilleton.

A Prima Donna upon the most Reasonable Terms.

Once upon a time, of course a great many years ago, and a great way off from here, there was a theatre, chartered as an institution for the encouragement of the art of Music, and called the Academy thereof.

Directly after the charter had been obtained and the building erected, the Muses came to take possession and were courteously entertained.

But they are very extravagant, these Muses. They, like all clever ladies, spend a terrible lot of other people's money. They ruined several managers, and were finally obliged to leave the premises.

The Academy passed into other hands. Into the hands of men who supplied the places of good singers with their own sweet voices, expressed in elaborate newspaper "cards." They attempted the old theatrical dodge of "hundreds of auxiliaries," "splendid scenery," a corps du ballet composed of the loveliest creatures in the universe, costumes manufactured by the distinguished Snooks, tailleur to the Emperor of New Jersey, and armors constructed originally in Connecticut, and especially for the John Brown insurrection.

It was Mr. Crummles's and Nicholas Nickleby's piece over again.

"We'll have a new show-piece out directly," remarked Mr. Crummles. "Let me see—peculiar resources of the establishment—new and splendid scenery—you must manage to introduce a real pump and two washing-tubs. It'll look very well in the bills, in separate lines—real pump! splendid tubs!"

In addition to the "real pump," there were always a good number of artists who had been triumphant or inspired, somewhere or sometime or another. No prima donna under fifty was to be looked at for a moment. At that age the voice is seasoned. These old moustaches were paid or promised immense sums. The pump and the tubs duly arrived from New Jersey, and were passed through the Custom House; some of the stockholders were so delighted that they let off some poor devils in Wall street with an easy shave, and the season began under the most magnificent auspices.

But the public didn't somehow see it. It is a wicked public, and it had no respect for the pumps. It asked for a voice.

All the prime donne put together couldn't contribute the article, and they received amongst them four or five thousand dollars per month, kept coupés, gave dinners, wore two-button gloves, and disported themselves right regally.

Thereupon one of the managers said to him of the tubs and the numerous auxiliaries ("vomited," as Bourcicault says on the stage), "I have a little girl at home, who has a voice, and who wishes to sing. She is so unfortunate as to be my sister-in-law, and therefore does not expect that she will be paid a great deal, or have any tubs, or armors, or new clothes built for the operas in which she may appear."

That was the modest proposition of a little thing of sixteen, one Patti, never heard of, never inspired.

It is scarcely necessary to say that Crummles did not see it, until the tubs refused to stand on their own bottoms, tumbled to pieces in fact.

Then the little girl came out; she had a contract to sing six times in each month, for

TWO HUNDRED DOLLARS PER MONTH!

That was cheaper than the real tubs, was it not?

Thirty-three dollars and thirty-three-and-one-third cents plus, for singing like a Malibran, a Lind, or a Sontag !

Thirty-three dollars and thirty-three-and-one-third cents plus, for attracting to the Somnambula and Lucia people who would not have the tubs or the inspired veterans on any terms.

Figuratively thus:

	Gross Receipts
Poliuto (inspired veterans) ($2,200 per month.)	$275
Huguenots (great tub piece)	1400
Lucia (new prima donna) ($200 per month.)	1500
Somnambula (ditto)	2500

And this very reasonable prima donna, let me tell you, sings the *Somnambula*, as no one has sung it here; in the finale she was equal to, and I think better than Lind.

This a fancy sketch, of course; but if all my fair readers—and I hope I have a good many—will go to the Matinée to-day, they may experience something like it.

The Antiquarian Researches of Mr. Walcot.

Mr. Charles Walcot, whom I adore religiously, has reached up as we say in New England "on to a high shelf," and taken down a splendid antique.

Did I hear anybody say Olympic?

You are mistaken, sir, it is older than the Olympic. It is the comedy of the last century. An affair of that entertaining period when our venerated forefathers were getting ready to hammer away at the forces of King George. When people wore silk coats, satin breeches, point-lace ruffles, and kept on hand a stock of choice compliments for the especial delectation of the fair.

Mr. Walcot had a benefit on Wednesday, and brought out *"The Clandestine Marriage*. Com. by George Colman and David Garrick. Acted at Drury Lane. 8vo, 1766."

The gifted writer from whose work I quote the above title, states further, that "this is indisputably one of the best comedies produced in the present age."

I think I may as well quote the whole of this notice (written about half a century ago) as a model for the critics of the day, who, to say the truth (a luxury in which I occasionally indulge), are a very slip-slop order of fellows:

The hint of it came from Hogarth's *Marriage Alamode*, as the Prologue confesses. It was received at first with very great applause, and still deservedly continues to be a favorite performance. We have usually heard that Garrick's share of this piece was Lord Ogleby and the courtly family, and Colman's, Sterling and the city family. But the following was related to us by a gentleman, who declared that it was from the mouth of Mr. Colman himself: "Garrick composed two acts, which he sent to me, desiring me to put them together, or do what I would with them. I did *put them together*, for I put them into the fire, and wrote the play myself." Garrick, however, wrote both the Prologue and Epilogue to it, the latter of which is a little drama in itself. The incomparable acting of the late Mr. King, in the part of Lord Ogleby, could not be too highly praised, nor will it ever be forgotten by those who have seen it. A female critic (Mrs. Inchbald) says, "Lord Ogleby, once the most admired part in this comedy, is an evidence of the fluctuation of manners, modes, and opinions;—forty years ago it was reckoned so natural a representation of a man of fashion, that several noblemen were said to have been in the author's thoughts when he designed the character; now, no part is so little understood in the play; and his foibles seem so discordant with the manly faults of the present time, that his good qualities cannot atone for them." To this it has been well replied, that, "considered merely as a delineation of manners, Lord Ogleby is, no doubt, a fleeting and fugacious being; but the foundation of his artificial character is so noble, so generous, and so kindly, that, whenever it can find a proper representative, it must continue to excite our sympathies." But we must observe, that the part of Canton, however amusing to the galleries, is an illiberal caricature of the Swiss nation, and therefore disgraceful to the English stage.

My ideas about the *C. M.* may be briefly summed up.

Mr. Walcot is a beau of the very old school, a Frank Waddell of the other century. Very well done. Pre-Raphaelite, absolutely photographic in its exactness.

But why do it?

If my friend, the veteran of 1812, couldn't see it, how can I?

It is the old, very old story again. The good, sentimental white muslin and pink ribbon heroine, the nice young man in a bob-tailed claret-colored coat, tight breeches, and a chapeau bras. The lively girl, who runs to coupés and bracelets, and says, very sensibly, that she would rather have a coach-and-six with indifference, than a stage-ride with a true lover. A vulgar old woman, ditto man, a valet of the most ponderous order, a Swiss, and a chambermaid of the purest antique type, make up the characters, who are rather ingeniously mixed up in a very weak plot.

I have read the play throughout, and have not found a single bon mot, and nothing which I call an epigram.

I am afraid that our great grandfathers were more easily moved to laughter than the perverse people of the present day.

Now, we should write after this comedy some lines composed by Churchill, a friend of Colman's, upon Hogarth :

With curious art the brain, too finely wrought,
Preys on herself, and is destroyed by thought;
Constant attention wears the active mind,
Blots out her powers, and leaves a blank behind!"

Let "J. Pilgrim, Esq.," look out.

Colman wrote altogether over thirty plays, and I think it would be hard for any theatre-goer of to-day to remember the name of any one of them except *The Clandestine Marriage*, which was revived in London for Mr. Farren. Now it has drawn a good house for Mr. Walcot, afforded several people a fine chance to display nice costumes (Brougham's, for Canton, was exceedingly artistic), and I advise Mr. Lester Wallack to gather together all the copies, and send them to the Stuyvesant Institute, there to slumber quietly with the Abbott Museum and the Velasquez picture of C. Stuart No. 1.

Something New at Last!

Now that opera season is over, we may expect something new from the theatres.

Mr. Bourcicault's play, to which I have already alluded, is in active rehearsal, and is announced for Monday. The heroine is the child of a Louisiana planter, by a quadroon mistress, and hence the name of the play—*The Octoroon*.

I give this piece of information for the especial benefit of the Sunday papers, and so let us have no blundering about it.

The play, which is a serio-comic drama, in five acts, is pronounced by greenroom report, the best of the author's productions.

The scene is laid entirely in Louisiana, and the characters are all American. Mr. Bourcicault plays an Indian; Mr. Johnston, a bad overseer; Mr. Jefferson, a Yankee of an inventive turn of mind; Mr. G. W. Consuelo Jamison, an old negro; Mr. A. H. Davenport, a young Southerner, of the type which you see flying about the New York Hotel, and the foyer of the Opera. Pearson is a planter. The heroine will be played by Agnes Robertson.

Among other effects in the play, there will be an exact representation of a sale of slaves at auction. That is all I am going to tell you about the piece, although I know some more.

It will make a powerful excitement, this play, or I'm no prophet.

There will be no performance at the Winter Garden to-night.

I suppose that Mr. Lester Wallack will bring out his romance of a *Poor Young Man* (I wish somebody would write the romance of the Subscriber, and make it lucrative) sometime next week. Mr. Lester is clever at the arrangement of such material as that which Feuillet offers him in this work, and I have no doubt that the piece will do.

I hear that Miss Laura Keene has in preparation a melo-drama, called *The Dead Heart*. It has been produced at the Adelphi, London, and is said to be a thrilling affair of the Ambigu School. As *The Wife's Secret* is no longer very attractive, I presume we will have the *D. H.* (why not *Dead Head*?) very soon.

Mr. Brougham will write the holiday piece for Wallack's. The subject is, I believe, *Rip Van Winkle*, often attempted, but never well treated.

Various Matters.

People in the Provinces and elsewhere, who steal from this department of The Saturday Press, are respectfully informed, that the announcements herein rest only upon the personal veracity of the Subscriber, which is not, when he is in a hurry, of the Sunday-school standard.

I never use anything from any newspaper without mentioning its name.

That is not because I am good and honest.

It is because I don't believe anything that any ofyou say.

And as I may take a fancy to make an item or two "out of my own head," able journalists will do well to affix the unusual credit when they honor me by copying my matter.

Cortesi has been making a great row among the susceptible Cubanos. The *Diary of the Marines*, and all the other Havana papers, are "tickled to death" with her, and one joker (*Old Spirit*) gets off (*Daily News*) the following poem, which reminds one of K. N. Pepper's "Oad to a Turkle":—

ADELAIDA CORTESI
EN LA
LUCRECIA.

No como Safo, de su amor cautiva
con lágrimas de fuego te alimentas,
que un indomable corazon alientas
que el vicio enciende y la venganza aviva,
Al que te adora ó tu pasion esquiva
con bárbaras augustias atormentas,
y anunciando la muerte te presentas
con duro corazon y faz altiva.
Mas no esperes que el ánimo se espante;
no dolores agudos nos oprimen :
al ver en ti á Lucrecia agonizante
De divino places las almas gimen ;
que en tu frente Adelaida, en tu semblante,
aun hermoso aparace el mismo crimen.

Matilda Heron commenced an engagement at Niblo's Garden on Monday, and played *Camille* "for the 520th time," which I think quite enough.

The programme of the play contained the following extraordinary announcement:

> It was in the impersonation of Camille she *first clutched with a bound* her dramatic diadem—with it her name will ever be identified, and descend in the annals of the stage.

If she doesn't play something else, that "diadem," which she has obtained in such a remarkable way, will slip off from her head, and perhaps go the way of all collateral—to Simpson's.

By the way, she and Eddy are going to play in *Bertram*; or, *The Castle Spectre.*

I wont miss that, you may be sure.

Mrs. Hoey, who keeps a coupé, and Mr. Jordan, who don't, announce their benefits this evening. Mrs. Hoey plays in *The Soldier's Daughter*, and in Mr. Hurlbut's very clever comedy, *Americans in Paris*.

Barring the coupé, Mrs. Hoey is a promising young actress who deserves to succeed.

Jordan likewise is a clever actor, and ought to be encouraged.

Mr. Sam Cowell, the long-expected and much talked about singer, has made his début in America, at the French Theatre.

Mr. Sam Cowell has sung several comic songs in a way which I have never heard equalled.

Mr. Sam Cowell has made a great many people, including the subscriber, who is naturally of a melancholy turn of mind, laugh very heartily indeed.

Mr. Sam Cowell, according to my narrow and bigoted view of things, is a public benefactor. There are people, however, who don't see Sam Cowell.

There are people who say that a man who, in this age of enlightenment, in these days of telegraphs and railways and so on, sings such splendid antiques as the "Cork Leg," ought to be severely punished.

These grumblers are gentlemen of the old school, bucks of Washington Hall, fellows who can tell you, sir, of the time when New York did not extend "above Bleecker."

Happily for myself, and doubly fortunate for my readers, Ido not remember those halcyon days. "The Cork Leg" is quite new to me, and I enjoy it immensely.

The fact of the matter is, that Sam Cowell is exceedingly clever; he sings very well, and his songs are admirably acted. I never saw a man who could sing the London street-ballad so well as this same Sam Cowell.

PERSONNE.

FOR THE SATURDAY PRESS.

PFAFF'S.

[From the N. Y. correspondence of the Boston *Saturday Express*.]

On the shore of that sea which is always troubled, and tossing in a madness of omnibuses and target-shooters, and men, women, and children who are too late for something—Broadway—but far enough removed to catch only the hoarse echoes of its multitudinous thunder; seldom penetrated by the waifs, the organ-grinders' poor girls, that want pennies, and, I fancy, pity, sometimes, or the wretches that have stranded on the stony shore—under the pavement, and the pretty petticoats and illimitable legs, and all the melancholy faces in their pride and paint, and pretence of expensive dinners which have never been eaten, and reputations which have never been won there is a saloon. The sign to the sea is a modest one, and mariners in the yeast only discern faintly the words "PFAFF" and "RESTAURATION," neither of which has a light-house alluring significance.

Cut off from the main apartment, and nestling, like some coral home of happy mermaids, right below the distracted main; unattainable by the chance applicants for the nebulous glories of a glass of very excellent beer, or the consolations of a dinner worthy of a more celebrated cuisine, a small, casual room, undefined in proportions, embracing a round table and some chairs, and a gallant row of wine-casks, prepared, all of them, for any bibulous emergency, attracts the querulous attention of the uninitiated, who do things at bars in the common way.

This is the capital of BOHEMIA; this little room is the rallying-place of the subjects of King Devilmaycare; this is the anvil from which fly the brightest scintillations of the hour; this is the womb of the best things that society has heard for many-a-day; this is the trysting-place of the most careless, witty, and jovial spirits of New York,—journalists, artists, and poets.

Bohemia centralizes here at PFAFF's about five o'clock in the dimming day. The splendors of aristocracy are wanting. It is a plain place in tone and appointment —unmirrored, unhung with the pictures of masters, unsoftened by carpet or cushion, breathing no soft perfume or superior music.

But when the throne is set, and the king is on it; when the brilliant fellows who give the dish of life its condiment, and recklessly sprinkle themselves like pulverized diamond into the floating literature of the day, are unreverentially gathered around; when, breathlessly rapid, a German Mercury deposits favorite food and gobblets foaming full, and hoary-headed pipes upon the uncovered board; when the text of the moment is announced, and the mouths open all about the table for hap-hazard emissions of quip, and quirk, and queer conceit, of melancholy mirth and laughing sadness; when the shuttlecock of soul is in the air, and every battledore of sympathy is striking at it, then, dearly beloved, who count your sphere a very much higher and nobler and more respectable one than this, there is lustre in the atmosphere, and celestial cymbals make melody, and clay is turned to shining gold!

Adelina Patti.

Still on the margin of the Sea of Life,
Which all in vain her wondrous eyes would scan,
She raised her voice—and o'er its waters ran
A sudden thrill, with joy and beauty rife.
The restless waves kept measure with her song,
The listening hills sent back a glad refrain,
And every billow of the swelling main,
From crest to crest, passed the sweet sound along.
Each little bark upon the bounding sea,
Danced to the cadence of her tuneful voice,
While pitti-patti went each pulse with glee,
And hearts long joyless could not but rejoice;
For not a bird by flowery lawn or lea,
E'er filled the sky with such sweet minstrelsy.

H. C. JR.

NEW YORK DECEMBER 10, 1859

For the NEW YORK SATURDAY PRESS.

A HUNTING STORY.

WE were resting in camp after the morning's hunt, some reclining at ease, and some half erect, puffing away at pipe or cigar, and discussing the incidents of the hunt. Two or three of the guides, who were always glad to listen to the conversation of the party, sat at the entrance of the shanty in profound attention, broken now and then by a hearty guffaw as some mishap was told of, or an exclamation which denoted that some other bit of bad luck had happened before in their knowledge. The dogs had driven two deer, and one of them had come down to water within a few rods of where a boat was stationed. C——, whose boat it was, had fired deliberately from that distance, as the deer stood still to reconnoitre, previous to taking to the lake, and had not touched him.

"I can't understand it," said C——. "I had a dead sight, and was sure I had put the ball through him; but he only raised his head a little higher and looked all about him leisurely, and finding nothing to excite especial alarm, raised his white tail, and cantering a few rods along the beach, went back into the bushes."

"It was the biggest buck I've seen this year, anyhow," said C——'s guide, a staid, quiet fellow, who was at the moment lighting his pipe at the camp-fire. "Steve, you remember the big buck you killed on the big mash down on the Raquette, two years ago?"

"Guess I do," said Steve, "I sold his *horns* to a New York fellow for five dollars."

"Well, he was jest the mate to that."

"What kind of horns did he have?" rejoined Steve. "Jest like an arm-chair, only the upper fork was kinder crossways."spam Jam

"I know him d——d well," said Steve; "the devil couldn't hit *him*." Then, after a moment's pause, he went on: "But I'd like to have *another* try at him: if I didn't draw blood on him, I wouldn't still-hunt next Fall; *I'd* go to diggin' taters."

We all turned to Steve, curiously, knowing him to be one of the best shots in the woods, whether at flying or standing mark, it being nothing unusual for him to kill a duck on the wing with a rifle-ball.

"Why," said he, speaking to one of the party, who had been out with him the year before," why, Mr. Snapshot, that's the same fellow we tried so many times last year, he feeds right over here, jest in back from the head of the pond." Then to the rest of the party: "I went in there last Fall, when Mr. Snapshot was hunting here, to put out. I see some almighty big tracks where a deer had been down in the night on the beach, and I tracked him back about half a mile, and started him out of his bed. He wa'n't more'n ten rods from me when he jumped up, and he run kinder slantin' towards me. I drew right on him as he went past, but never touched a hair. I had Carlo's rope round my arm, and I guess he started and pulled my hand down so I shot under. But I let Carlo go after him, and I never see a dog go as *he* did. The deer run straight for the lake, and I don't believe Carlo was a rod behind him when he got to the water. I never see such a tearing in all my life as that buck and dog made."

"Yes," said Snapshot, to whom Steve looked at the end of his short yarn, as if to ask him to take up the thread, "I heard the shot and then heard the dog open, and was sure that the dog was coming straight to the lake; but, not dreaming of the deer's watering so soon, didn't watch very closely; but when I heard the dog give the bark that shows that the deer has watered, I jumped into the boat to go after him. I was watching on Robin's Rock, a mile down the lake, and the deer came in at the very head and coasted, as I found by the dog's running along shore and going into the woods on the opposite side; so that before I was within good seeing distance he had gone out again. I heard the dog go down the lake, and pulled back to the rock. My first look showed me the deer a third of the way across the lake, and making down for the bold point beyond Agassiz Bay. The wind was heavy up the lake, with occasional white-caps, and I found it a hard pull; but the wind prevented him from either hearing or scenting me, and while he was coasting along the bold shore to find a good place to land, I slipped in and cut him off before he had any suspicion of being hunted. He wheeled from the land and reared out of water half the size of his body, and dashed off like a horse for the opposite side of the lake. I had had a hard pull of more than a mile, and found it all I could do to manage him going against the wind. I had a withe to throw over his head; but as often as I approached to put it on, he would double with such quickness, that before I could get my boat around and follow him on the new tack he would have swam several rods. When I kept cautiously behind him, so as to be ready to follow on either tack, he would turn a summersault in the water and swim directly past me. I dared not shoot him, for he would sink and the weight of his antlers would not let him rise again. I followed him so half an hour, when I finally succeeded in getting the withe over his horns, and waited for his plunges to cease before shooting him; when with a vigorous surge he parted the withe. I dropped it to take to my oars again, and found that one of them had fallen out in some way and was floating at some distance behind me. I hesitated a moment whether to *paddle* after the deer, or to go after the oar and then row after him; but exhausted as I was I feared to give him so much vantage, and I took the stern seat and paddled after him. I caught him, but found the boat so difficult to manage in the heavy wind, that I soon grew tired and unable to keep up with him. I concluded to risk sinking him, and fired; but though within two rods I missed him, and then fired three barrels of a revolver with like effect. I had the pleasure of seeing him walk leisurely up the beach and dash into the woods. I went after the dog and put him on the track again, but the buck led off to Raquette Falls and there lost the dog, who came back late in the day, showing signs of a hard pace. We knew the deer would be back again on the next night to his old feeding-ground; So after breakfast on the next day Steve went back where he had put out before, and found his track again fresh as though made but a few minutes. It was easily distinguishable, Steve said, from its immense size. This time my companion, who had watched in Osprey Bay the day before, wished to try the head of the lake so I took his post of the day before."

Steve laughed out here and ejaculated, "You know a deer don't run to the same place two days together, and I guess you didn't object much to going down into West bay, (for so the guides persisted in calling it, though *we* had changed the name to Osprey Bay); I guess you thought he'd run there."

Snapshot laughed in turn, and without replying to the implication went on: "The deer generally come in either at the end of the beach, at the bottom of the bay, or else on the rocky point in the middle of it. I drew my boat on a rock that lies opposite the point and commands the shore. I waited two hours, and finally heard the dog coming along the foot of the mountain. He lost the scent at the big brook that comes in at the beach; and while I was waiting for him to find it again, and watching the mouth of the brook expecting to see the deer come there, I heard the limbs crack on the point, and the next moment he stalked out. The wind, though gentle, blew from me to him, and he scented me and stopped. I had a fair sight, at not more than thirty rods distance, and was tolerably sure of him. Still, I waited to see if he would water, for I was a little anxious to try our yesterday's game again. He snuffed and looked, but as I lay quite motionless he could determine nothing, but, thinking it on the whole suspicious, turned round very deliberately and stepped towards the covert. I bleated like a fawn, and he stopped, when I fired. He pricked up his ears but did not move. I had my Sharp's rifle, and slipped in another cartridge; but the second shot was as harmless as the first. Before I could give him the third he had walked into the woods. Shortly after, the dog came down to the shore, evidently entirely off the scent,—which however he found after a time, as he soon took the back track, and not long after was baying towards the narrows, along the point which lies between Agassiz and Osprey Bays. Long before I could get there, both deer and dog had crossed and gone off in the same direction as the day before, whence Carlo returned towards evening, lame, and completely used up, so that we would not run him the next day."

Here Steve broke in again, with, "Yes, sir; Carlo had that buck in the river all day; he drove him in at the falls, and over to Ampersand Creek, and he crossed the creek twice, and then run back to the *Raquette*, and took to the river up by the big rock. Bill Johnson—*Raquette* Bill, you know—was out in front of his house, and saw him swim past; and he chased him down the river two miles, and got sight at him three times; but every time the cap snapped, and then he went out for good. I believe the d——d old cuss knows a thing or two that a deer oughtn't to. But I'd like to try a fair open shot at him ;—I'd know if a bullet wouldn't go through his d——d hide."

Steve, irate, chewed the cud of mortifying memories. Snapshot resumed: "That day there came up to camp a New York gentleman, Mr. H——, whose guide, Scott Peck, had a dog that I never knew a match for, for sticking to a scent, though he was very slow; and we arranged for a hunt with both dogs and three boats the next morning. But we were out of venison, and that night I concluded to try night-hunting. We had a capital jack, which threw light enough to see a deer at eight or ten rods, and almost count the prongs on his antlers. The moon set at about eleven, and as soon as it was down we started, and made directly for the beach where Steve had seen the big buck's track. Steve paddles as still as death" (here Steve looked down, smiling sheepishly, and picked at something on the bosom of his hunting-shirt); "and before we had got within thirty rods of the beach, we heard the familiar splash of the deer's feet in the water.

I lit up, and Steve pushed for the sound. We found the deer standing broadside to us, and looking over his shoulder at the lamp. I fired when we got within four or five rods, and the deer floundered heavily back into the bushes at the edge of the marsh, and fell. Steve turned the boat to go after him, when, just beyond where he had stood, we saw another, looming immense in the dim light. He was facing us, and I could see distinctly the white stripe on his breast, and a mingled confusion of antlers; but Steve, whose sight was better from the stern of the boat, where the glare of the jack does not disturb the eyes, exclaimed, in a very low, but very distinct whisper, The big buck, by G—!' As quick as possible, he turned the full light of the jack on him, while I slipped another cartridge in my rifle. The deer even took a step or two towards us, and then, as if satisfied, turned his head towards shore, when, as he gave me his broadside, I fired. He stopped an instant, turned his head towards us, and then started like a racehorse for the woods. We heard him plunging through the alders until he reached the open woods, when he stopped, whistling like a trumpet, and then started again for the mountain. We heard his gallop die away in the distance, when Steve broke the silence with, 'Hell and d—n,' and we went after the deer we *had* killed.

The next morning we got started early, and one boat was sent down into Osprey Bay, one to the narrows, while one kept the head of the lake. I took Osprey Bay as before. It was nearly two hours before I heard the dog, running along the flank of the mountain, quite a mile from the shore of the lake. He followed the high land back toward Simon's pond—you know that lies over toward Tupper's lake, West of Osprey bay about three miles—and went out of hearing entirely. It was twelve o'clock and past before I heard anything more of him, and then he came in hearing, running straight for me. I was lying on a rock in the sun, watching the minnows playing around its foot, and pushed off into the lake to fasten to a fishing-buoy a hundred rods from shore, so that he wouldn't scent me. I recognized old Drive's voice, and knowing that he was never within half a mile of the deer, I began to look sharp for him. You know that the water grows quite shoal in the bay down about half to the outlet, and there it grows deep for a little way, and then comes the long beach at the outlet. Presently I saw him dash in at the shallow place. It was splendid: he threw the spray up in front of him full six feet high, and galloped along the water bellydeep, until he came to the high rocks just beyond the Osprey's nest"—

Here L— nodded to Preston, his guide, and whispered, "That's where I shot the Osprey the other day?"

Preston nodded assent.

"When he went out and took to the woods, I started immediately as hard as I could pull for the beach; but before I was half-way there he emerged from the forest again,—the old buck,—and galloping the whole length of the sand beach in full sight, went into the woods at the other side. H—, who had been stationed at the narrows, came in sight just as the deer disappeared, as Scott, knowing from the direction the dog had taken that the deer would run for the outlet, had started to cut him off. We rowed up to the beach to see the tracks, and they were certainly a quarter larger than any I had ever seen before. Scott caught Spot as he came by, and we pulled back to dinner. I had to go out of the woods the next day, and that was my last hunt after 'the big buck.'"

"Oh well," said Steve, "'twan't the last time he was hunted that Fall; they had him in two or three times after that. Uncle Silas Arnold come up, 'most still-hunting time, with a party; and they drove up to Raquette Falls, and put out in between the Falls and Follingsby Pond. They drove the big buck into the falls just where Uncle Silas was watching. There arn't many men around here can beat him shooting; he always shoots at a deer's head whether he's running or not, and he 'most always brings 'em, too; but he see this buck swimming right to him in the still water under the falls, and he had a dead sight not more'n six rods off, and didn't touch him. I 'spect he had the buck fever, them horns was so all fired big. Uncle Silas said he'd give ten dollars just to have shot the horns off, and let the buck go. He said they was the biggest horns *he* ever *see*."

"But, Steve," said Snapshot," you said that you were going to still-hunt him after the leaves were all off; did you try it?"

"Yes," said Steve, half reluctantly, "I still-hunted there three days, Jess Corey and me; and one day I come up to that big buck. I'd been following his track all morning, and all to once something moved in some bushes not more'n two rods off. The bush was so thick I couldn't make out what it was; but I was jest going to shoot, and thinks I, maybe it's Jess—it was blue, and Jess had a blue shirt on—and the more I looked, the more it was like him. I could see the arms, and shoulders, and all, and by'm-by I sung out, Jess, you d—d fool! why don't you speak? Do you want to get shot?' But I hadn't no more'n spoke when he jumped, and I'm blest if it wasn't the big buck—and I'd been standing not two rods from him five minutes. He went by me so quick, I didn't see nothing but a blue streak; I let have as well as I could, but the devil could hit a deer with such a sight. If I'd only known it was him before I spoke, I guess he'd 'a found what it was to have a hole in his jacket, d—d sudden. I don't believe he's a common deer, but I don't know about any deer's having a hide that'll turn a rifle-ball."

We made simultaneous movements towards breaking up, and Preston asking who wished to go and examine the lines, Land the Judge filed off with him, and the rest of us to whatever came to hand.

W. J. S.

MOUNT VERNON, N. Y., Dec. 2, 1859.

[For THE SATURDAY PRESS.]

MORTUAVIVA.

BY W. D. HOWELLS.

I.

She sang, and I heard the singing,
Far out of the wretched Past,
Of meadow-larks in the meadow,
In a breathing of the blast.

Cold through the clouds of sunset
The thin red sunlight shone,
Staining the gloom of the woodland
Where I walked and dreamed alone;

And glintining with chilly splendor
The meadow under the hill,
Where the lingering larks were lurking
In the sere grass hid and still.

Out they burst with their singing,
Their singing so loud and gay;
They made in the heart of October
A sudden ghastly May,

That faded and ceased with their singing.
The thin red sunlight paled,
And through the boughs above me
The wind of evening wailed;—

Wailed, and the light of evening
Out of the heaven died;
And from the marsh by the river
The lonesome killdee cried.

II.

One night of Indian Summer,
The smell of the dying leaves
Was sweet, beneath the maples,
That darkened the cottage-eaves.

In the dark there is nonsense uttered
Where two are quite alone—
A young girl and her lover
Talking in undertone.

O life! that I thought so earnest !
O love! that I thought so strong!
Ah me! for the tender promise
Long kept and broken long!

III.

For one, I hate the remembrance
Of most things past away;
If I could, I would chain my fancy
Down to the dust of to-day.

But ever my fancy rises
With wild, unfettered flight.
The windows are brilliantly lighted,
And there is a party to-night.

I linger before I enter
The hot and shining room?
She stands in the window's recess,
Half-hid by the curtain's gloom;

Half-turned away from the talkers,
With her lips half-oped to speak,
And the sweeping silk of the eyelash
At rest on the perfect cheek.

I long (but I act like the actors,
And play my stupid part)
To clasp her and keep her forever
Upon my hungry heart—

To tell her that I remember
All that I seem to forget—
That in my soul's dim silence
The perfumed lamp burns yet.

So we talk of the weather and parties,
And she makes play with her eyes;
The talk is rather insipid,
The talkers not over-wise.

The talk is rather insipid;
Ah! why should it be so?
Somehow in my darling's sunshine
The perfumed lamp burns low!

IV.

The songs of sorrow are many,
But this is the saddest thing
That ever in all my lifetime
I heard a poet sing:

To love and to outlive it—
In the hollow heart inurned,
To have but a handful of ashes
Where the fires of passion burned;

To hate for the fault of the present
The fulness of pure delight,
To keep love's recollection
In scorn and self-despite.

My darling! if you were buried,
Believe me that I would bring
To deck the place of your slumbers
The sweetest flowers of Spring.

I would sing your virtues and graces,
And grieve with such constancy,
That people should credit your tombstone,
And even believe in me.

V.

The song is done, but a phantom
Of music haunts the chords,
That thrill with its subtle presence,
And grieve for the dying words.

And in the years that are perished,
Far back in the wretched Past,
I see on the May-green meadows
The white snow falling fast ;—

Falling, and falling, and falling,
As still and cold as death,
On the bloom of the odorous orchard,
On the small meek flowers beneath;

On the roofs of the village-houses,
On the long, silenced street,
Where its plumes are soiled and broken
Under the passing feet;

On the green crest of the woodland,
On the cornfields far apart;
On the cowering birds in the gable,
And on my desolate heart.

PALMER'S STATUE.

The White Captive.

Of the comparatively few subjects selected by American Artists from our own History, which though young is so prolific, we think Palmer's "White Captive" the most remarkable illustration of its wealth of material, and its perfect adaptability to the high requirements of Sculpture.

The true Artist is evinced, perhaps, as well in the selection as in the treatment of a subject.

The moment chosen to represent the White Captive is one of the highest pathos,—not the instant that she has been made a prisoner, which would be too painful, nor the time when her fate is decided, which would leave nothing to be suggested; but the transition from the one to the other, when an expression of moral grandeur pervades the figure, an elevation of character above all ordinary passions or emotions, and when beauty is most exalted, yet how tender, sensitive and lovely!

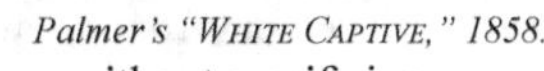

Palmer's "White Captive," 1858.

The statue is nude, thus affording the sculptor an opportunity of carrying expression to its highest point toward perfection, with the most beautiful and susceptible of created forms as a means, without sacrificing an historical to an artistic or poetic truth. She stands confronting her savage captors, her form averted, her face turned toward them; the wrists are bound to each other, the left arm behind the back, the hand closed; the right arm is drawn backward in a gentle curve, the hand holding with delicacy and firmness the tree by her side, corresponding with the face in vitality of expression, and leaving the outlines of the torso uninterrupted. The head, *unlike* the most famous of the ancient statues, is large enough to be intelligent; the face is one that we could love; it is beautiful in form, but *not of the conventional rigidly classic type*, and its expression touches our inmost soul. The physique is fine, healthful, elastic; it is *truthful*, but not *literal*; every member and fibre seem to throb with the life and emotion that is centred in the face, and are realized with a delicacy of manipulation almost beyond comprehension. It is nature refined and exalted.

It is worthy of remark, perhaps, that in ancient sculpture, the age of immaturity and decline was distinguished by an attention to costume that was not practised when art had reached its highest expression; —then, flesh was considered the chief object of imitation, and everything else treated as accessory. It was also under a republican form of government that ancient art reached its culminating point, and produced works that have been imitated by Europe ever since. It now remains to be seen whether the Republic of the West will maintain the originality and independence already inaugurated in sculpture and landscape.

"ANNA MARIA" OUT OF TOWN.

Dear Mr. Editor:—I am out of patience! And you cannot wonder at it, when I tell you the reason. Here has my name been used publicly, for the past three years or more, *bon gré, mal gré*, without ever in reality a word from myself appearing in print. All my ideas privately expressed, every opinion I may have offered or careless remark I may have chanced to let fall, have been snatched up with lightning-like rapidity and inserted in the columns of some journal, without even so much as asking my consent or begging my pardon. Now, is it not enough to stir up all the wrath which it is possible to awake in my woman's heart? Henceforth "Anna Maria" shall speak for herself, and I would warn all readers in future to guard against whatever PERSONNE or any other mischievous critic may write, when, to shield himself from comment or blame, he throws all the burden upon the shoulders of poor "Anna Maria." It is astonishing what liberties the world in general seems disposed to take with some members of our distinguished family. There is poor cousin Flora, *née* McFlimsey, *now* the stately Mad. ——; what a tumultuous uproar she created not long since amidst our fashionable circles, and all because a certain *jeune homme pauvre*, to immortalize his name, employed his muse to reveal the secrets of poor Flora's heart. Not, by-the-bye, Mr. Editor, that either I or her husband ever supposed she had such an article among all her possessions—oh, no! only, although Flora never was exactly a favorite of mine, yet, in vindicating her rights, I am endeavoring to defend those of the family. As for Flora herself, I don't think all that was said disturbed her equanimity in the least, so absorbed was she with displaying

"Her latest and dearest imports from Paris,
To that hateful old ogre—*her dear Mrs. Harris !"*

And now, dear Mr. Editor, after all this preamble, you and I will have a confidential little chat, in which, of course, all the confidence will have to be on my side. *Mais que signifie cela?* Do not wonder, or enlarge your beautiful eyes, by opening them too widely at learning that "Anna Maria" is *out of town.* True it is not the season when one is apt to seek retirement in the country, neither am I weary of city-life—of the opera—the charming matinées or the promenade. Ah, no! my heart is too faithful to the memory of past loves to forget all these but you know that "blessings *brighten* as they take their flight," and thus I am trying an experiment to find whether *I* am a blessing or not, and whether my memory will brighten in the hearts of my friends, now that I have taken my flight! To-night I have been turning over the pages of Dickens's Little Dorrit, and thinking meanwhile of Ullmann's Little Patti. Not that there is the least connection between the two; but, in this quiet little place, where I am now writing, Little Patti, who has burst like a star of the first magnitude suddenly upon the operatic horizon, has her home. I can look out from my window and see, in the white moonlight, the old schoolhouse where she and I in other days sat conning our dry lessons; and I cannot help wondering if, amidst her brilliant triumphs, she will ever think of those days now past, and of the old schoolmates who used to listen enraptured to her sweet voice, little dreaming in their innocent hearts that in the little dark Italian girl who stood before them they would one day behold the brilliancy of a *musical star*. I should not have said Italian girl—for Little Patti is a native of our own free land—although of Italian parentage. Dear little Adelina! How plainly do I see her now before me—even as I used a few months ago so often to see her! How pretty she was, with her large dark eyes looking softly through the deep fall of lace that shaded her broad-brimmed hat! I would not have thought to ever see in the little girl playing with her tiny dog (for Little Patti, like all other *interesting* young ladies, possesses the whitest of little poodles) the real impassioned Lucia or hapless Leonora. But time worketh wonders; and Little Patti has left her girlish home to form the sparkling centre of a new circle. Perhaps she may forget "Anna Maria"—yet here I would offer my humble tribute as a tiny leaf to twine in the bright garland weaving for her youthful brow. . . . . This is a quiet little village, but once in awhile they are lively up here. Doubtless, the question is not exactly *àpropos* just now; but, Mr. Editor, did you ever keep Hallowe'en? During November I was visiting here for a few days. And here I must express my wish that all Anna Marias and Flora McFlimseys had a few such dear "country cousins" as I have. It would do them good to visit these same cousins once in awhile. 'Twould reveal to them human nature, ungloved by artificiality. But about Hallowe'en, which I spent with some friends fresh from the land of Robbie Burns, who had brought with them all the dear old traditions and beautiful superstitions of their native land. And what a merry time we had! And how strange it seemed to "Anna Maria," to be there amidst the merry group that gathered around the great kitchen fire!—no formality there I can assure you. What a witchery lurks in the hours of Hallowe'en! Even the moon that night, as she looked softly down through the mist, had a wierd, unwonted look in her silvery rays; and in the air itself one seemed to feel almost an invisible presence like to the elves and sprites of ancient lore. Numerous were the tricks, the spells, and mysterious incantations performed. First was the melting of the lead, which melting was done in a great iron spoon, after which the lead was poured by some fair one into a glass of cold water. The lead immediately assumes a variety of shapes, which are believed to resemble the instruments or tools belonging to the profession of the fair experimentres's future husband. This is tried three times. One young lady had each time a host of little nails! As for "Anna Maria," a variety of little things resembling surgical instruments fell to her lot; from which it is augured that some day a disciple of Esculapius will successfully sue for her favor. Of course, she will in future keep a sharp lookout upon all young physicians. Next came the burning of the nuts, the paring of apples, and the trial of Destiny's cups. For this last, three cups were placed in a row upon a table, into one of which was put clear water, into another foul, while the third was left empty. One was blindfolded, and put her hand into a cup. If she by chance placed her hand in the clear water, this denoted a youthful husband; if in the foul, a *widower;* and if in the empty cup, she was doomed, alas, to single blessedness! This is tried, of course, three times, the cups being changed each time. "Anna Maria's" lucky hand found the cup of clear water, from which she knew the physician to be both young and handsome. The evening waxed late; and now came the last trial, which was to go alone into a room, holding a light in one hand and an apple in the other. The light is to be placed upon a table before a mirror. When the clock strikes twelve, over the mirror a shadow will glide which shall resemble the being unknown, who one day will claim our heart-worship. This, all hesitating and trembling, did foolish "Anna Maria." The clock struck the mystic hour: "Anna Maria" lifted her eyes slowly to the glass before her, and started with surprise to behold—her own smiling face! By this she thinks that, *possibly,* the handsome young doctor may resemble *her.* Long will the frolics of this evening be remembered. For a true picture of these festivities, one has only to read the poem, entitled "Hallowe'en," by poor Robbie Burns.

But my letter grows long. The clock strikes twelve, and though this is no charmed eve, yet, mayhap, some obliging invisible sprite will waft to the hearts of absent friends the adieu of

"ANNA MARIA."

Thoughts and Things.

BY ADA CLARE.

VII.

I saw the tragedy of "Bertram" last night. It was like coming beneath the shade of some great, dark, majestic oak, after having travelled leagues through pleasing but unimpressive shrubs. MATILDA HERON was well calculated in her native majesty to carry out this illusion. Her Imogen was of the lofty though gloomy type. Something like an atmosphere of grandeur seemed to exhale itself from her every stately motion. Her attitudes and tones set themselves on the highest summit of dramatic dignity; but her voice is hardly powerful enough for Niblo's Theatre,—a Theatre which despises acoustics, and looks with scorn upon the auric nerves. So much for the Queen of our Drama.

Mr. Eddy, as Bertram, was an infinitesimal Forest. The ninety-ninth trituration for instance.

°₀°

It may not be out of place for me to say a few words here with regard to my remarks on "Beulah," in a former number of THE SATURDAY PRESS. The few lines which referred to that book were simply an expression of my honest and unbiased opinion. Unbiased, because my preconceived opinions were all strictly in favor of Miss Evans. I was more astonished than I could easily describe, the following week, when I learned that Derby & Jackson had withdrawn their advertisements from THE SATURDAY PRESS, for the reason that my article had attacked one of their publications. It is astonishing that publishers will persist in viewing the public as a lumbering, idiotic animal, led by the nose by mere puff and balderdash. As if the reading public could not distinguish between sickly, unmeaning sycophancy, and the sincere convictions of the heart. Besides, when the columns of the paper are equally open to the other side of the question, the whole case becomes exaggerated. It is taking the cube-root of the ridiculous. Nay, it does not quite agree with the logical habits of mind, which I am told the members of the sex so superior to my own invariably possess.

I will also take the liberty of saying here, that this series of articles commenced with a view of stating my honest convictions about the passing events of the day, and that in the same course I shall strive to continue. The opinions they express will sometimes be diametrically opposed to those of the Editor, and of Personne. Not that either of them is in danger of breaking his heart, or losing his appetite on that account.

If I call a book good, when I believe it to be bad, I am sinning against truth and my own heart. Besides, the lie is the most unprofitable of investments. It is a snare to the feet, and confusion to the heart. It crawleth for a season and dieth like the worm. Truth was twinned at its birth with Immortality, and knoweth not the name of Death."

o o o

I have read the "Queen of Hearts," by Wilkie Collins. I was aggrieved to find that the plot of the book was a mere thread upon which to string together a number of previously-published stories. I had read all but three of them. The same author is contributing at present a very exciting and entertaining serial to *Harper's Weekly*. Wilkie Collins seems to me to have somewhere in his being, a single fatal atom. He misses greatness by a hair-line only. He evidently prides himself upon the minuteness of his descriptions. But a thing is not always graphic because it is minute. Minuteness only conduces to the graphic where it consists of a number of living facts in the most condensed form. If a single fact is hammered into great ductility, so as to stretch along a telegraphic line, that accomplishes nothing more than the rigmarole.

"The Woman in White" is thus far to me a very interesting story; I even dare to hope it may be great.

o o o

Once upon a time, I am told, the Blue-Stocking was a living fact; now she exists only in the minds of the fogy-men old enough to remember her. Some of these curious old fossil-fellows are still extant. Through means of these eye-witnesses and the copious analyses of various male writers, I am able to conceive of her exact picture. The minds and works of such kindly retain an unfailing fund of the noxious scales from this fish, in order that we may know how the horrid creature sported herself in the slimy waters of her existence.

Thus to my eyes is she painted. The Blue-Stocking is an intellectual woman. She is a female who possesseth mental gifts. These mental gifts, of whatever nature they be, she weareth in the manner the porcupine doth his quills, and with the same intention. She hath wrenched the curves from her form, and her body is now bounded by square lines, with the occasional diversion of a wildly acute angle. Her hair calleth brush and comb its direst foes. A threatening pen gapes at each ear. Her claw-like hands are long, scraggy, and immortally ink-spotted. Her feet are clothed in maimed stockings, and forlorn slippers flap their wings about her heels as she walketh. Such is the seediness of her attire, that the Scavenger claimeth her for his own, the sympathetic ash-barrel singeth to her "come rest in this bosom," and the scare-crow waggeth at her the cornstalk of scorn as she passeth.

Doubly an Amazon, she hath seared her two breasts, in order to plant upon them the iron muskets of literature; yea, and lest the blueness of their veins should draw to her the softening influence of the blue-eyed angel of love.

She hath been known to bear children, but there is no record that she hath known the maternal sentiment. She cannot rank so high as the weazle in the treatment of her offspring. She feedeth them on sour meal and musty bread—for the pen dried up the source of milk in her breasts, ere they were seared. She delivereth them over to the devouring elements. Naked are they thrust forth to the biting winds. She maketh their bath a watery grave. Hungry dogs attack them before her eyes, and she waiteth to close her sentence ere she rescueth their mangled remains. She seeth them creep into the fire, crisp themselves into toast before her eyes, and deposit themselves in her own gown in black blotches of carbon; but her emotion venteth itself in a "hum," and a nib of the impatient pen.

She feedeth on strange flesh and mysterious bread. Her food cannot attract caloric; it is cold and clammy even during the process of cooking. A needle causeth her to foam at the mouth. All that is hard, and harsh, and graceless in nature clustereth around her. Even the blue-bottle fly she calleth a coquette, and crusheth with ireful heel. Her eyes are optical Gorgons, whose glance turneth the heart into stone.

But with the male sex lies the chief terror of her coming. When she beholdeth the male, she mocketh at him in her wrath. Her mane is erect, her eyes vomit flames, her feet are pawing the ground, and her mouth snorting tempest-making words. Tall, thunderous and terrible, she driveth the male shrieking before her.

Now, alas! how painful the contrast. The literary woman is hardly to be distinguished from the rest of her sex, except in the small matter of being a trifle more amusing. Grace and beauty cling to her form, and she loveth to drape herself in luxurious garments. She feedeth on savory food. The needle is a magic wand in her hands. She beareth lovely children, and holdeth them fast to her soul, in the purest of pure loves. She feedeth them from the living stream in her breast, the drops of which are nature's most precious and sacred pearls. The whiteness of her breast shines like stars, and the most limpid blue of heaven courses itself in veins thereon, giving sweet entertainment to the holy angel of love.

She is full of warm aspirations, deep longings, kindly sentiments, entertaining thoughts, and above all others proveth the glory of the master-passion. The male feareth her no longer; he knoweth how prone she is to love him. Her lips are like the crimson heart of the fragrant tropical rose, and breathe out ardent words to him, that the shallow and ignorant were not born to speak.

Alas me! how degenerate hath the age become! for in these modern days, the truly great woman hath her heart so fused into her head, that all the fires of hate, and envy, and calumny, and persecution, cannot unlock that God-sealed embrace.

Dramatic Feuilleton.

Personal.

It may be refreshing to repeat a remark which I made at the commencement of the season, that these leaves are not written for the glorification of any manager, actor, or actress; but entirely for the entertainment of the public. People who have formerly imagined that they had a divine right to be puffed continually, cannot exactly see this, but they will by-and-bye. In the meantime, the Able Editor has mounted a six-pound howitzer, which commands the entrance to his sumptuous bureau, and the subscriber has bought a new pair of shoes with very thick soles. Prenez garde!

Mr. Bourcicault's "Octoroon."

I gave you, last week, the plot of the new piece at the Winter Garden. That is, I gave as much of it as there is any necessity for. People who want the rest may read the dailies, or the Sunday papers, which always steal the plots, errors and all, from the *Times*, *Herald*, or *Tribune*.

And they are so mean, too, that they steal sometimes from an infant like The Saturday Press.

That's worse than sacrilege!

Mr. Bourcicault's *Octoroon* is an inconvenient piece of property. She bothers me a great deal. The author has written an anti-slavery play and he hasn't. I can say with him, that to me Trojans and Tyrians are exactly alike; that my friend Smith, whose governor works a hundred hands on the Red River, is as good a man to live with as my other friend Brown, who does the abolition dodge in Vermont, and hopes to get into Congress by it. Still I have an objection to plays which deal with delicate social questions, not because they may interfere with my views upon the question at issue, for I have no views upon any question; but because when I go to theatre I don't like to have any strain upon my mental faculties. Heaven knows they are not over and above strong. Then I don't see why my feelings, which are exceedingly susceptible, should be worked upon unnecessarily. I object to seeing the Octoroon put up on the table and sold to the wicked overseer (I don't believe the gentlemen of the South would permit a young lady like Zoe to be sold under any circumstances), and if so, I don't think it is exactly the thing to judge the peculiar institution by an exceptional case, which after all is entirely an imaginative one. I quite agree, too, with a great many people who object to the dénouement. The idea of the author is good enough. He desires to punish crime in the person of the bad overseer, and in the case of the Octoroon, to show that when the father hath eaten of sour grasses, the teeth of his children are set upon edge. But the Octoroon's life might have been saved, and her lover given to her rival. Disappointed love is a terrible thing. I know a lot of fellows who have been troubled with it, and have suffered "dreffully,' so they tell me. Packing Box, who delivers parcels all over the world, and who is a great critic upon art and literature, and can tell you, without knowing a word of French, nor English, from which Paris Feuilletonist I take my bon mots, had it so badly once that he could not go to the office for three days, and the affairs of the country were completely knocked up in consequence.

But if I go on this way, I shall never get through with the Octoroon, and to tell you the truth, I don't intend to, this week. I was saying, however, what I didn't like, and I may as well finish with that branch of the subject. I don't like the physiological lecture which the young lady gives to her lover. And besides, a young man madly in love would care very little about the color of his mistress' finger nails, or for the circumstance that the roots of her hair were off color. If all the young people who get sweet upon each other should enter upon such minute physical analyses, there would be few opportunities for the illustrious Brown to appear in wedding favors. I don't like to see the Octoroon sold any more than I would be pleased to learn that some stock-broker, with a wig and dyed whiskers had paid down forty thousand cash, and taken Anna Maria off her ma's hands, although I think the old lady would be glad to get rid of her, and have a son-in-law to bully, for half the money.

There are as many Octoroons on this island as there are in the Attakapas.

There are Zoes sold in New York every day, Effendi; the only difference is that there are no Doras nor Georges to save them. The motto of the Knickerbocker Octoroons is a charge à révanche, and they get it, generally, I can tell you.

That's what I don't like. Now I'm coming to something which I do like.

I like the admirable way in which the author has constructed his play. It is a model which I advise all the adolescent dramatists to study. The same talent displayed upon an unobjectionable subject would have gained unanimous applause even for Mr. Bourcicault who is too clever to be popular.

But the truth is we are all a little tender upon the subject of our great National Sin, and would rather have it kept out of sight.

I like several of the characters very much. It was a happy idea of the author, the friendship between the Indian and the slave-boy, the union of the representatives of the two despised, bullied, snubbed, and spat upon races. The Southern belle, Dora, is also capital. She would answer for the type of an American belle in the North as well as the South. I know the animal a little bit, and speak from experience. Scudder is a good character; and in fact all the artists have strong parts. The best acting was that of Mr. Bourcicault, Miss Robertson, Jamieson, Jefferson, and Mrs. Allen. The latter caught the idea of her rôle exactly, and expressed it faithfully. I liked Miss Burke, too, in little Paul; and must not forget to say something about Miss Secor, whose representation of a Southern-gilded youth was superb. It was Juleps, faro, navy-revolvers at ten paces if you like, St. Charles and New York hotels all over. It was one of those little artistic opportunities which Bourcicault knows so well how to create, and which, when realized, help the vraisemblance of a play immensely.

That's pretty nearly all I have to say about the Octoroon, just now, except that it has so far drawn crammed houses, and promises to nett several brown stone fronts for the author and Le Chauve. Next to myself I would rather he should have them than any one else.

"Everybody's Friend."

A pleasant comedy under this title has been done at Wallack's.

It is an English piece done from the French by an industrious literary thief, named Stirling Coyne, for Mr. and Mrs. Charles Mathews. There was not a good house for the first night, and I was glad of it. The time was when a crowded audience might have been counted upon at this theatre for any English play, but now they attract no attention except in isolated cases. The most attractive thing that managers can do is to put up the works of native or resident dramatists. They always command attention. If they are bad they go to the dogs at once, but if they are only moderately good they are sure of success.

I am quite free to speak my mind upon this subject because I don't write plays.

That's a relief, is it not?

Everybody's Friend is not worth much time. The plot is very slight, and has been used twenty times before. The dialogue, however, is smart, and some of the situations are ludicrous. Mr. Lester Wallack succeeded moderately with a rôle which is too brisk for him, Brougham and Walcot were capital, and the crinolinities, Mrs. Hoey and Miss Gannon, had nothing to do, and tried to do something, and didn't do it. I went with a young gentleman who is commissioned by J. B. to uphold the flag of our country on the ocean wave. He is a blonde, my officer, and not to put too fine a point upon it, has red hair; he is a thorough barbe rouge, and rather likes it. I am not a brunette, exactly, and I quite sympathize with my maritime friend, when he wants to know why they always play the spooney young men in yellow, and the snobs in red wigs. Why is it that everybody falls in love with young men that have black curly hair? They always do. A. M., who is not quite a fool, though she tries as hard as ever she can to make people think so, went wild about Jordan's raven tresses in *The Wife's Secret*. Even Ada Clare, a blonde of the blondes, couldn't refrain from a slur at youths with corn-colored locks.

Its altogether wrong, and we, Palinurus and myself, protest against it. If it wasn't against the rules of the service, he'd have Walcot out. I'll take care of Brougham when his new piece is produced.

One Thing and Another.

Mr. Mark Smith, who is both an artist and a gentleman (there are not many people on the stage of whom I could say as much), has a benefit at Laura Keene's Theatre to-night, when *Still Water Runs Deep* will be acted. Everybody ought to go.

Mark Smith.

Apropos to benefits, one of my young men said rather a neat thing about Mrs. Hoey's the other day. Some one at the Club asked young Dimes, where he was on Saturday? "Oh," remarked the youth. "I went to Wallack's, and saw Mrs. Hoey in two pieces." "Bon Dieu," said my young man, who is proud of his French, "that's awful, she was coupée en deux, n'cest pas?" That is considered one of the finest things of the season, and the airs that the young fellow puts on, are insufferable.

The Philadelphians are having a rather good time of it, than otherwise, with things that belong to the metropolis. The opera opened on Monday, with the *Poliuto*. The ruthless critic of the *Press* touches the artist on the very sorest point. Listen:

> Virtually, there are only three performers of any note required for this opera. On the present occasion, these were Madame Gazzaniga, Signor Brignoli, and Signor Amodio. They looked in excellent condition and rude health,—Madame Gazzaniga nearly as stout as Brignoli was when we saw him first; Brignoli rapidly approaching the original rotundity of Amodio; and Amodio about one-half larger than he was two years ago. These be the degrees of comparison stout, stouter, stoutest. We will not be so unkind to this pinguidity as to breathe the Oriental prayer, "May their shadows never be less."

The *Press* rather likes the opera, and has discovered that the finale of the second act is a quintett. They are very clever in the right-angled village "over yonder." We ignorant metropolitans always thought that it was a sestett and chorus.

Thursday was assigned for the début of Adelina Patti in *Lucia*. Chestnut street had been invaded with an army of Spaniards, devotees of the young prima donna.

Mrs. John Wood has produced at the Arch street Theatre a romantic drama, "*The Daughter's Vow; or Love's Disguises*." Mrs. Wood plays the part of a young woman disguised as a boy ;—her "ma" is the author of the deception, which is committed in order that the estate of the Governor, a French baron of the ancien regime, may not go out of the direct line. Sometimes the young lady indulges in the luxury of crinoline; and once, while doing so, she captivates one *Hyppolite*, a man of war. This youth gets very melancholy because he cannot find his *Phillis* again, but finally meets her at the house of the Baron, as a young man. A sort of camaraderie springs up between them, and *Hyppolite* makes *Amadis* his confidant, as young men will do, as I know by awful experience. When Hyppolite's health is getting "poor," instead of suggesting, as I do, temperance, cold baths, and all the other moral virtues, *Amadis* appears to the forlorn one as a female. Of course, he gets wilder than ever, and the play ends with a wedding, of course.

The *Press* critic says:

> Of Mrs. Wood, we can say with justice that she made a most favorable impression. She is a beautiful woman, sings with taste and skill, and dances very gracefully. Her voice is singularly sweet, soft, and expressive. She does not rant, but preserves all through the piece that naturalness of manner so necessary to a good piece, but so unpopular with Western audiences. This piece, however, while it develops Mrs. Wood's accomplishments, affords no field for that peculiar humor with which report has clothed her. The bills announce her, with theatrical modesty, "as the queen of comedy and song," and our people are no doubt anxious to see her in a part calculated to develop all these powers. We remember her as *Tilly Slowboy*, in New York, where she played Miss Agnes Robertson (metaphysically speaking) into a "cocked hat"; and while we want no better representative of Dickens's charity-girl than Mr. Clarke, nothing would please us better than to see *her* in the same character before a Philadelphia audience.

Max Maretzek has been having a grand row with the Havana "crickets." The Prensa man having pitched into the Opera in a white-wine vinegar style, Max stopped his tickets, whereupon all the other editors, with a degree of esprit du corps, which is worthy of imitation, immediately declined to use the privilege of free admissions. They are all comparing Cortesi with Gazzaniga, and in the *Traviata*, they say the latter will never be replaced by the former, so far as Havana is concerned.

I hope, for the sake of Ada Clare, that Adelaide's constitution (which is apparently vigorous) will bear up under this blow, and that she will come back from the "ever faithful island" safe and sound.

There have been some rumpuses in the coulisses during the past week. "Awful" Jefferson seceded from the W. G., on account of the old difficulty about big type with Richelieu Bourcicault. Awful was reëngaged, however. Miss Laura Keene having taken a fancy to play *Hester Grazebrook* in Tom Taylor's rather stupid play, *An Unequal Match*, the part of Sir Charles Somebody—an unhappy fellow, who has nothing to do but heavy laying around in a dressing-gown, and smoking a meerschaum—was sent to Mr. Jordan, who refused it, and virtually resigned his situation. Probably the affair will blow over.

Here is the plot of *The Dead Heart*, the piece which Miss Laura Keene is preparing. It was written by Mr. Watts, for the Adelphi, London, and produced there about a month ago:

> Mr. Phillips prefaces the play with an acted prologue. In these premonitory scenes the pride, frivolity, and profligacy by which the patrician orders were so infamously distinguished in the reign of Louis XV. are portrayed; while now and then, amid the wassail and revelry, the sullen murmurs of popular discontent break ominously on the ear. Prominent among the leading characters is the *Abbé Latour* (Mr. David Fisher), an insidious and dissolute churchman, who, beneath a polished and persuasive manner, conceals a corrupt heart and a spirit savagely vindictive. He prevails upon the *Count St. Valerie* (Mr. Billington) to carry off *Catherine Duval* (Mrs. A. Mellon), the affianced bride of *Robert Landry* (Mr. B. Webster), a young artist, who is regarded with bitter aversion at Court as being the leader of an intrepid and enthusiastic band of students, whose eloquent harangues have awakened in the people love of liberty and scorn of their oppressors. The *Count* manages to effect an entrance into *Catherine's* chamber at night; her cries for help bring *Landry* to her aid; but the *Abbé*, armed with a *lettre-de-cachet*, and backed by a party of musqueteers, appears suddenly on the scene, and carries the ill-fated artist to the Bastille. In this frightful dungeon he remains for eighteen years. His friends believe him to be dead, and under this conviction *Catherine* gives her hand to his rival and becomes *Countess St. Valerie*. Time wears on and the *Count* dies, leaving his only son *Arthur* (Mr. Billington) in the guardianship of the *Abbé Latour*, who perfidiously resolves to work his ruin, being urged thereto by a double motive-hatred of the lad's father, and a dishonorable passion for his mother, whom he hopes to mould more easily to his purpose when she is removed from the influence of her son. The heartbroken mother indignantly rejects *Latour's* overtures, but how shall she rescue her boy from the subtle villain who is luring him to destruction? The smouldering fires of the Revolution have now, in 1789, burst out in furious flames, and Paris is a scene of anarchy and bloodshed. The Bastille is taken by the mob, and among the prisoners whom they restore to liberty is *Robert Landry*, a poor emaciated creature, apparently in the last state of mental and physical prostration, who, however, slowly recovers his consciousness, and, in the invigorating sense of freedom, gradually resumes his native energy of intellect. On learning that *Catherine Duval* has been married to *St. Valerie*, he resolves on a cruel and desperate revenge, and this object he pursues with stern inflexibility of purpose. In the second act we find him an influential member of the Convention, and among his proscribed victims are the young *Count* and the *Abbé*, both of whom have been imprisoned in the Conciergerie, and are to be consigned to the guillotine the following morning at daybreak. In vain had the *Countess* sued for mercy on behalf of her son. The dead heart" of the prisoner of the Bastille is insensible to the appeals of pity, and with cold disdain rejects the mother's prayer. But with a refinement of vengeance he resolves that *Latour* shall die by his hand alone. The *Abbé* is summoned by his order to his private apartment in the prison, where, after reproaching him with his crimes, and the bitter wrongs he has endured at his hands, he places a sword in his hand, and tells him he must fight him on the spot until one of them be slain. This interview concludes with a duel, in which the *Abbé* is slain. The young *Count* is to be the next victim of *Landry's* vengeance; but discovering from certain papers found in *Latour's* pocketbook that the late *Count St. Valerie* was not a party to his imprisonment, and that *Catherine* had married the *Count*, believing *Landry* to be dead, the cold heart warms, *Landry's* love for *Catherine* returns, and, resolving to save her son's life, he mingles among the prisoners who are destined for execution, answers to the young man's number, and is borne to the place de Gréve, where he is about to be bound to the guillotine, when the curtain descends.

A. M., to whom I have shown this plot, thinks it is "sweet."

Mr. Brougham is not doing *Rip Van Winkle*. So all the chiffoniers who stole that item can go to work and correct it. What did I tell you, brigands, last week? The Brougham piece is a purely imaginative affair, and is called *The Winter King*.

Sam Cowell has thoroughly ingratiated himself with his audience, who certainly seem to be the happiest people in town. Not afflicted with any dangerous amount of gayety, there is still nothing more pleasant to me than the sight of a lot of people forgetting in the presence of a good artist, their toils and troubles and grievances and all their little cares, and have a jolly good laugh, not at, but with the artist. This is a great power, and this Sam Cowell seems, in my poor judgment, to have.

The French Theatre, proper, has been in rather a bad way. Les abonnés don't come down with that celerity which might be expected from the proverbial generosity of the Gaul, and were it not for the outside patronage, American, Spanish, and German, there would have been a smash long ago. Mannstein, the jeune premier, had a good benefit on Tuesday, and played in *La Closérie des Genets*.

Cheap opera by the Invalides at Niblo's, next week.

PERSONNE.

NEW YORK DECEMBER 17, 1859

FROM THE WOODS.

MY DEAR PRESS :—If, as it seems to me is the case, a good, firm, complete humanity,—animality I might say, —is the indispensable basis to anything like a perfect attainment of spiritual completion, how far are they from hope who build a spiritual edifice on the impoverishing of the physical foundations! If the body be *only* of use as the vessel on which the immortal voyager shall cross seas of trial, how shall they be pardoned who venture afloat, heedless of stability of timber or security of seam, and so are drowned out of a shattered, sinking craft, their voyage half done? Yet, systematically and persistently, modern puritanism teaches and practices the subjugation of the whole animal nature, passes the senses over to the devil as his proper province, and looks askance at one who values his appetites as one who stands in especial danger of being damned. The mighty cords of supreme law are spun into such fine threads of injunction and restraint, that they may be made to enmesh the whole soul in bondage, to reticulate doctrines so that motion must be followed by a breaking of the meshes, exercise of freewill by infraction of ordinances.

I have no intention of discussing the matter in full,— at present I am thinking of what seems to me one of the most splendidly and healthily animalizing influences; yet one which the puritanism of the day has stamped barbarous, inhuman (as if murder were not as peculiarly *human* as forgiveness), and to be done away with by divine command,—I mean hunting. There is many a man in my own knowledge, who, from morbid refinement of sentiment and superstitious regard of animal life, keeps his blood cold and tranquil in his veins, when it would bound into an undreamed-of life with the excitement of the chase,—into the white and chilly purity of whose life a Summer's hunting would send a rosy glow and vital warmth he would never know without the taste of blood. No exercise, no pursuit, no amusement, compares with it for invigorating and intensifying all the physical attributes. I do not care whether it be the shooting of quail or the chasing of buffaloes, the little hunt or the great, the effect is all one. It is not that it brings men into contact with nature, though it does that for many who would never see her face unveiled without it; but that, in the very exercise of those faculties of combativeness and destructiveness, there is involved the development, by healthy stimulus, of mental as well as physical qualities essential to a complete and well-balanced life. I might be deeply and mysteriously metaphysical, but I abstain. I know from personal experience, that, to a constitution depraved by puritanical excesses and enfeebled by superstitious observances, Hygeia has no remedial agent like gunpowder and fishhooks. I esteem of no weight the consideration of the lives of the animals; they were given for the service of man, and any way in which they can be employed to further his well-being is *entirely* justifiable. I think that the good my hunt this morning did me was worth the existences of a thousand deer (if others did not need them more) like the buck I brought home after the drive. It was glorious! a complete and magnificent day;—the sun, when we left the camp, blazing along the mountain sides, lighting peaks and ridges; while out of the blue ravines rose the mists, as if the snow, which lay soft in the woods, were rising to kinship with the clouds that hung and clung to the summits of the highest peaks. There was just a silvering of snow over everything, just a bracing cold in the still morning air, and the mirror-lake was just dimmed by the thinnest mist which rose from the water, as though it were glass breathed on. My man went into the woods to "put the dog out," and I rowed to a rocky point which overlooks the whole South side of the lake for more than a mile. Half an hour elapsed, as it generally does, before the dog found a deer's track, and then his deep rich baying woke the echoes all round the still, snowy hills. Sometimes the half-hour is an hour and a half, and then patience is the first virtue cultivated, and one listens with intense eagerness for the first bay indicating that the deer is afoot; but when the snow lies on the ground, a good hound makes quick work of disturbing his morning nap. And then commences the excitement: the deer doubles and turns; back, back he goes to the very foot of the far-off mountains, and the bay of the hound dies away, and is lost so long that we are sure that he has driven the deer into some other lake; when, faintly, as he comes over some intervening ridge, the rapid incessant yelp, denoting that the scent is strong and that he is close to the deer, quickens the ear, which has been making of every bird-cry and uncertain sound a bark of dog. Nearer and nearer, coming in a straight line for the lake, we mark the deer's flight by the dog's pursuit, until it seems as if he must be in the water the next instant; when all is still the deer has thrown the dog off from the scent by taking refuge in a stream which flows into the lake. It is only for a few minutes, however, and then, with an energy that makes every nerve thrill with sympathetic excitement, he opens again on the new-found track. Now he comes, a noble buck, and bursting through the trees that marge the lake, stands still a moment to be sure that the dog is following, and then dashes in. The water is shoal for a few rods, and he gallops through the water, sheeted in spray; only his haunches and white tail erect are seen behind that flying water; deeper, deeper, and his galloping becomes laborious, and then he loses footing of dry land, never to touch it with his black hoof again. Rapidly he swims along, taking a direction parallel with the shore, and as near it as he can swim easily, turning his antlered head to and fro to catch the bay now so near. Then comes the good hound in the buck's very footsteps, and howls in token of watering the deer; next he sees him, and plunges in to follow. It becomes time to interfere. The water is cold, and the dog, chilled, will drown before he reaches the farther shore to which the deer turns his way.

You might call it unsportsmanlike to catch a deer in the water, and kill him at your own terms; but row your own boat, catch your deer before you kill him, and see if you have not done a manly thing. Our deer is to leeward, and we must come in behind him, and get where the wind will not blow the scent to him, or he would touch shore again, and be off before we could get within shot of him. Still, still, as the oars of Charon. The deer is so far off already, that we can see his antlers no longer; but a few minutes' pulling gives us at once the wind of him, and a place between him and the shore; and then the pull comes! It is not very difficult to overtake him, as a man can row a good boat three feet while he swims one; but he has a long start, and it will try every nerve to catch him before he reaches the further shore, where is a sandbar he has tried before, and knows well. At last the boat heads him; and he, for the first time, so still was the approach, sees the proximity of a new danger, and turns for a rocky shore, to which we intend to drive him. He rears out of the water, like a horse, and springs forward, as though his feet had again touched firm ground. We follow at a short rifle-shot; and watching the moment when his forefeet touch the bottom, and his shoulders emerge from the water, the ball cuts his spinal cord, and he wilts into pliant death. *"Cruel ?"* Bah! what was life to him more than to the fly which, in Summer, I should kill as it lighted on my hand? Is he not mine by bequest from Adam? and is he not mine for all my needs and uses? Well, there he floats, dead-still. Must go and pick up poor Carlo, who is swimming still, and with half-stifled yelp, declaring his opinion of the uses of the oar. *"Emulating brutes ?"* Well, why not? Am I not the sum of all brutes? Is not all the brute-life concentrated in mine? and have they any gift denied to me, who am a man—the microcosm —the reunion of all the divine attributes—before scattered through the animal universe? *Au revoir !*

Antaeus.

For the NEW YORK SATURDAY PRESS.

HOW WINTER COMETH

To Palace and Hovel.

BY CHARLES D. GARDETTE.

He comes! The tardy Winter comes!
I hear his footsteps through the Nights!
I hear his vanguard from the heights
March through the pines with muffled drums!

His naked feet are on the mead :
The grass-blades stiffen in his path,
No tear for child of Earth he hath!
No pity for her tender seed!

The bare oaks shudder at his breath:
A moment by the stream he stays—
Its melody is mute! A glaze
Creeps o'er its dimples, as of death!

From fettered stream, and blackened moor,
The city's walls he silent nears:
The mansions of the Rich he fears!
He storms the cabins of the Poor!

The curtained couch, the glowing hearth,
The frost-rimed Greybeard's power defy:
He curses as he hurries by—
And strikes the Beggar, dead, to Earth!

For every gleaming hall he spares,
A hundred heartless hovels hold
Hearts pulseless, crisp with ice and cold,
Watched by a hundred grim Despairs!

The Forests grow by His command,
Who saith, "He lendeth to the Lord
Who giveth to the Poor!" Your hoard
Is His! Ye stewards of the land!

Here is your Mission! Ye who feed
Your lavish fires! Not afar,
But at your doors, your Heathen are!
God's Poor—your creditors! Take heed!

The path is long to Pagan shores;
Their skies are sunny: God o'er all!
The Winter's deadly harvests fall
Around you! Deal your Master's stores!

Philadelphia, Dec. 3, 1859.

[For The Saturday Press.]

BYGONES.

BY N. G. SHEPHERD.

The old house stands in the silent street,
The same as in other days;
But the many friends I was used to meet
Are gone on their different ways.

The button-wood trees are there, as of yore,
But their limbs are leafless and bare;
I glance, as I pass, through the open door,
And I mark the winding stair,

And the place where Minnie was wont to hide,
In her childish, innocent glee;
And I wonder if, where the dead abide,
She can ever think of me.

Ah! little I dreamt, when a careless boy,
That those days could ever fly,—
That Minnie dear, with her smile of joy,
Would once fold her hands and die,—

That low in the churchyard's grassy mould
They would make for her a bed:
Though I sometimes likened her hair's warm gold
To a glory round her head.

But time has softened the grief since then,
And God has been wondrous good;
And I wait with patience the moment when
I shall join her beyond the flood.

UNION-SAVERS.

When this now great overgrown Union was still in its cradle, down there in Boston or whereever; when it required no end of dry-nursing and rocking to keep it quiet; ere a baker's dozen stars had condescended to light upon its little banneret; when the dear bird that presided over its destinies was but an insignificant little eaglet trying to grow a beak ;—even at that distant and facetious period of its history, although it gave every sign of health, and was altogether a robust, obstreperous, and provokingly healthful infant, the Croakers began to croak about it, and the Howlers to howl about it, as if its precious life were every moment in danger, and nothing short of a pungent and patriotic set of Union-Savers could possibly rescue it from an early and disagreeable tomb.

And these Croakers and Howlers have been at their dismal work ever since, until Union-Saving, like undertaking and grave-digging, has come to be a profession, and the creatures engaged in it are seen swarming about the Confederation like birds of ill-omen, cawing and jawing worse than so many crows in a cornfield.

If these Croakers are to be believed, the Union is always on the eve of immediate and violent dissolution, and can be saved from such a catastrophe only by their joint and discordant lamentations.

At one time, it was to be destroyed by the Right of Search; at another by the United States Bank; then again by the Tariff; until finally its doom was irrevocably sealed, the other day, by the late John Brown,

Meanwhile, the Union increases in health and strength every hour, and belying prophecy after prophecy, ought, long before this, to have put every Croaker in the land to the blush. But no. Were the nation one vast frog-pond, the air would hardly be more resonant with their melancholy croakings, than it is at the present moment.

North and South, East and West, wherever the Union-Savers are found, their senseless and stupefying wail is heard, as if the globe itself were about to be unhitched from its axis and left, like an insane and inscrutable comet, to flounder its frantic way through space.

We presume it is of little use to complain of this state of things, since what has been must be, and since, moreover, the Croaker or Union-Saver is an order of being as necessary to the world as the buzzard, the screech-owl, or the wild locust.

So we should rather like to have it understood that we don't complain, more especially as if we did we should be open to the accusation of croaking against the Croakers, who are really not worth the music.

What we want particularly to do, is to call attention to them just at this crisis, when they are out in unusual force, and are making altogether too much noise. Moreover, we would like to warn simple and unsuspecting persons against believing a word they say, by showing that they and their predecessors have been repeating the same stupid things, or things nearly as stupid, ever since the Union existed, and that it is foolish therefore to pay any heed to them.

For our own part we do utterly loathe and abhor the croaking animal of every species—whether political, commercial, social, or religious. Croaking enough is done by the frog to answer for the whole animal kingdom. When men take to the business it is only to accomplish some dark and mischievous purpose. As for the Union-saving Croaker, he belongs to the worst possible species of the reptile, and ought to be promptly exterminated; the more so as just now he has got possession of the Capitol, and is retarding the business of the country at a cost to the people which is incalculable.

For The Saturday Press.

REQUIESCAM.

BY GEORGE ARNOLD.

I.

Give me, when I die,
A grave among the corn and clover;
Let me peaceful lie
In some field, with forests nigh,
Where the blossoms, bending over,
Mingle sigh for sigh,
With ever-rustling leaves
Whispering to the rustling sheaves.

II.

Let the tall trees wave
High above my grave,
And strew, each Fall, their treasures o'er me,
Leaves of gold and brown,
Softly floating down,
Or driven wildly onward when 'tis stormy.

III.

O, give me not a tomb—
White, and marble-cold, and dreary—
In the church-yard's gloom!
Rather, when I'm weary
Let me lie at rest
'Neath the clover, growing fair
In the warm sunshiny air,
With its thready tendrils twining round my breast.

IV.

So, tranquil be my sleep,
When the hazy, slanting beams
Rest on forest, vale, and steep,
Through long Summer afternoons,—
Be my slumber still and deep—
Let the new and waning moons
Come, and go, and bring me dreams!

Thoughts and Things.

BY ADA CLARE.

VIII.

I have been re-reading "My Lady Ludlow," by Mrs. Gaskell. I had the pleasure of reading it serially, as it appeared in the "Household Words." It is my ideal of style in narrative-writing. The eloquent simplicity with which the heart-wounding story of Virginia is told, is enough honor for one life. The style, I confess, is my model in writing. Ah me! am I not standing on the very earth, and aiming up at the heaven-set cloud!

°°°

I have fathomed the reason why "Harper's Monthly" was so dull and inane last month; it was with a view of surprising us with the brilliancy of this.

"The Atoms of Chladni," is a most able and thrilling story.

"How the Snow Melted on Mount Washington," is a charming, graceful sketch, as pure and delicate in style as the snow it treats of, though far from being so cold.

"Behave Yourself," seems to me to be written by a man recently married. But there is no seeming about the fact that the author knows how to write well, and does it.

°°°

I saw the first representation of "The Unequal Match," and I confess,—without the rack, this time,— that it was just a little dreary—that is, when the unfailing Laura was out of sight of the audience. A quaint idea hovered about my brain while listening to her voice. I was reflecting upon its extraordinary power and sweetness, and I thought what a pity it could not be planted as a germ, and made to bear a harvest of similar voices, with which to endow those actresses—alas, how many !—who squeak their way through the drama in indistinct and feeble trebles. Oh! Priestess of distinct speaking, of natural and potent elocution, receive here the homage of one of your most honest admirers!

°°°

Yesterday I happened to be visiting a gentleman's office situated near the East River, in a narrow, squalid by-street. One of those impractical streets, so resorted to by practical men of business. As I sat at the window, a scene daguerreotyped itself on my mind—a scene in which misery and ludicrousness were locked together like a pair of moral Siamese twins.

At the corner stands the grandest and most pompous mansion in the street. It is a triangular, two-story house, rounded over in its upper construction like a madly exaggerated, apple-dumpling. Its color is that of a neglected teaspoon, while the windows are of that wild and emphatic yellow seen only in the eyes of patients afflicted with the jaundice. At the main-door stands a large coal-box, containing coal for the retail trade, which box, for some mysterious reason, is decorated with two long frowsy rags. The retail principle is acted upon most rigidly, for I observe that a woman purchases her coal and carries it off in a dismantled soup-tureen.

The second house drops immediately into the one-story-and-caller type. The cellar is occupied by a meek cobbler. The broken panes of glass are tastefully tapestried with old boots and shoes, and from the window streams a gigantic and flaunting piece of leather, which with great delicacy advertises the trade within.

The other floor shelters a washerwoman; and the roof, provided with various fishing-lines, presents a lively display of marine trowsers standing on their heads, and desperate shirts holding fast to the line by one limber arm.

The third house is a fantastic boarding-house, kept by an exiled French baron or barber. As the Baron is also a fabricator of boots, the lower windows are garnished with musty specimens of the same, of which the toes are protruding through the windows like horny elbows through the classical drapery which beggars so often assume. The main door is surmounted by a bull's eye, long ago blind through the assaults of street mud. The door being open, it displays a tall, lean staircase, down which a black stream of water is continually crawling, brawling bashfully, as though it were a mortified serpent suddenly conscious of its own failure in legs.

The area-fence runs half-way out upon the sidewalk, and over it is leaning a wilderness of lank children, clothed for the most part in a wild profusion of irregular woollen wings, confined to the neck with a piece of colored pack-thread. These children are leaning over the area-fence, exasperating the illustrious boot-maker within, by crowing like cocks, barking like foxes, snorting like wild hogs, croaking like vultures, howling like panthers.

Just before the door stands what I suppose to be a cart, though it would require a workman deeply versed in that article to tell what could have been its possible use, unless indeed it were for the express accommodation of philosophical fowls, judging by the great number of them seated on its rim, mild but resolute, looking with firm eyes into the bottom of the cart, and probably awaiting some scientific phenomenon in it. Two children are standing before the door of the second house, recently weaned by their appearance, who are watching with eagle-gaze the arrival of a wagon before a warehouse in the vicinity. As soon as the vehicle stops, they swoop upon it, and contrive with rash dexterity to pilfer a pound or two of loose cotton. Then they fly on the wings of the wind, to trade it at the corner-grocer's for gingerbread, turtles, and dragons.

By-and-by a strange miscellaneous muttering and roaring issues from the second story of the fantastic boarding-house. As the windows are open, I look in and see that it arises from a general family-fight. This civil war includes an old man, his wife, three sons, and their uncle.

The affair seems to be managed on the plan of miscellaneous action, each individual against all the rest; motto—*Any head that comes up, hit it.*

After a while one of the sons drives the uncle into the street. The old woman also drives her husband before her, by means of considering his head a door-lock and continually thrusting a vicious brass key into it. He rushes down the street, thoroughly impermeated with the warlike spirit, determined to fight somebody, and snuffing the battle with wrathful nostril from afar. After running twenty yards, he tears off his coat, makes another short run, and tears off his vest; similar run, and rolls up his sleeves. All the while he sputters out oaths, not under the dominion of the English grammar. Too excited for a display of syntax, he makes impracticable modifications of the Anglo-Saxon, such as "by dam," "go to dam," etc.

In the meanwhile the whole population of the neighborhood are hanging out of the windows to witness the skirmish between the uncle and his loving nephew. The children in the corner house are suspended to the windowsill, as if they were bell-glasses, with the air exhausted within. The man in the shop below comes to the door with a rusty lock in one hand, and is cleaning it with a hair-brush dipped in lamp oil. His attire is probably intended to imitate the graceful, toga-system of the Romans. It consists of wide spotted pantaloons, the monotony of whose design is occasionally diversified with a sportive and lively caterpillar. He has a long flowing apron confined at the waist with a woollen girdle which has formerly been a woman's tippet. Just above his ears is bound a turban made of an old red cloth, splashed with yellow, the lambient ends of which dangle down as far as his knees. On perceiving the children at the windowsill, who are illustrating the upward pressure of the atmosphere, he suddenly rushes back into the house, a howling and uncontrollable maniac.

All at once the uncle is capsized in the mud, and the dutiful nephew jumps upon his head. One leg of the uncle's trowsers becomes disconnected, and that leg dyed by the mud to a graceful and subdued mouse-color, he brandishes in the air, crying out, "would your murther your uncle, Rufus ?"

The dutiful nephew betrays no compunction of conscience about slaughtering any number of uncles Rufus. But the father, who has finished distributing his garments on the highway, suddenly appears. Seizing hold of the undressed leg of the prostrate Rufus, he drags him out from under the feet of the dutiful nephew, who is cheerfully engaged in treading his head down into the paving-stones.

°°°

I forgot to mention Rose Terry's story, "Mrs. Anthon's Christmas Present," in speaking of *Harper's Monthly*. The story, like all stories from her hand, opens well, and gives promise of exceeding great excellence. But before it is finished, there is some moral iron supposed to be hot, and therefore to be eternally struck. She seems to imagine herself in the pulpit, and to be industriously preaching at us. No, dear Rose of the bright field of letters, thy mission is a higher one; to charm the head, and touch the heart is thine.

"VANITY FAIR."

A new and original Fair, of a comic character, is to be opened at No. 113 Nassau street, next Wednesday! under the management of Mr. Frank J. Thompson, assisted by a brilliant corps of interesting and accomplished young people, chosen by the sharp-eyed capitalist of the concern from the literary jeunesse dorée of the country.

The name of the enterprise is to be *Vanity Fair*; and instead of being established for a season, and for the benefit of a class—like the fair at the Academy of Music, for instance—it is to be carried on for all time, and for the benefit of the whole human race, like Wild's candy and THE

Saturday Press.

We have been favored with a prospectus of the institution, and also with a sight of the wares to be on exhibition for the first week, which consist of such a display of caricatures, bon mots, epigrams, jeux d'esprit, etc. (for who does not know that we are speaking of the new comic paper?), as has never before been offered to the American public.

The object of *Vanity Fair* will be *not* to "shoot Folly as it flies" (for the leaden-winged creature, unfortunately, never will fly, else there would be no need of shooting it), but to daguerreotype Folly as it exists and flourishes in our midst, and then do what it can toward making it ridiculous.

The object is a good one, and the parties engaged in it, so far as we are informed, are admirably qualified for their work.

We postpone further notice until the fruits of the first week are before the public, and meanwhile refer the reader to the advertisement of the manager in another column.

Dramatic Feuilleton.

The Irrepressible Conflict in the Coulisses.

What did I say a little while ago, when Mrs. Wood nullified, and seceded from the Winter Garden, about the effect that horticultural pursuits have in stirring up the angry passions of man and womankind?

I don't remember just now exactly what it was, or I should repeat it. N'importe.

There have been more rows at the Garden of Eden. This time it is Adam and Eve that have voluntarily gone out into the wilderness.

In other words, Mr. Bourcicault wanted more money for his Octoroon than even M' Clusky would be willing to pay, and Le Chauve, animated by that good genius that always comes to help clever people out of tight places, made, on Wednesday night, a splendid coup d'état, worthy of LN himself.

It was decreed:

I.

The Union heretofore existing between Bourcicault and Stuart, is dissolved.

II.

Awful Jefferson, with the proviso that he is not to get up *The Naiad Queen* or *The Sea of Ice,* is appointed Stage-Director, vice Bourcicault removed, and will be obeyed and respected accordingly.

III.

The Superintendent of the Entrée des Artistes—*i. e.* the Back-Door-Keeper—will inform Mr. Bourcicault if he shows, that his services are not needed. [That's the approved Custom House way of doing it.]

IV.

In consideration of the fact that Mrs. Allen is descended from one of the First Families of Virginia, to her is awarded the rôle of the *Octoroon*, with an earnest request that she will do the best she can with it at the price. Mr. Pearson, an Englishman who never saw an Indian, is undoubtedly the most fitting person to embody the Stage-idea of the aborigine. It was intended by the direction, that Miss Clinton should illuminate the part of *Dora Sunnyside*, but out of regard to Mrs. Allen's feelings, which are fine, and must be conciliated for political reasons, that part is assigned to Mrs. Stoddart.

V.

One hour is allowed for the study of the parts by the new artists. The usual penalties for imperfections in the text will not be enforced.

VI.

Lieutenant-Colonel A. H. Davenport is detailed to make the announcement to the public, embodying the above facts.

Le Roi est Mort!
Vive le Roi!

The Colonel, and all the others, obeyed the decree—the *Octoroon* was enacted as usual, and there was no earthquake, nor other extraordinary phenomena.

It is not so clear to my mind that the King is dead. It appears that he demanded an increased compensation for the play, on the ground of the danger which he incurred as its author. To this was opposed a contract, which both author and manager had signed, but which the latter refuses to be bound by. Whether or not the threats that have been made against Mr. Bourcicault, by people who don't see slavery exactly in his light, form a sufficient excuse for annulling this contract, is matter for the lawyers.

The hurried performance of Wednesday showed what a little pluck will do on special occasions. The rôles were not given to the new artists till an hour before the performance commenced, yet they were all ready. Mrs. Allen has had many compliments for her performance of Zoe, which I have not yet had the pleasure of seeing. There were two Doras (they are very plenty, these animals); Miss Clinton and Mrs. Stoddart were both ready for it when the curtain rose. Le Chauve was obliged to play Paris for one night only, and the apple was awarded to Mrs. Stoddard.

I think almost every theatre habitué will be glad to see in Mr. Jefferson the artistic head of affairs at the Winter Garden. He will have a fine opportunity to affirm as a manager the high position which the unanimous voice of the public has awarded him as an artist.

The Half-shell Opera.

The General-in-Chief of the Invalides, Frezzolini, did not come to time, and so the forces at Niblo's Garden included only the gushing Albertini, the inspired Beaucardé, the handsome Ardavani, the fascinating D'Ormy,—whose voice has probably gone to look after her legs, which are nothing at all, compared to what they used to be,—and the unappreciated Maccaferri.

The artists have given, so far, the *Lucrezia* and the *Trovatore*.

In the *Lucrezia*, Albertini was good, though she sung excessively sharp. The *Trovatore* was nothing to brag of, Beaucardé having given up Manrico to Maccaferri, who gets out his notes in the same way that they break stone up at Sing Sing.

I am afraid that the half-shell opera will not last long enough for Mr. Eddy to complete his studies in the language of Dante, Alfieri, and Mancini.

One Thing and Another.

This has been a dry week at the theatres. Nothing new or fresh has been done anywhere. Laura Keene was to play a new piece on Friday evening, a local comedy, called *Distant Relations*, said to be by the subscriber, which assertion, like several others which have been made lately concerning the same unworthy person, is a sheer fabrication. I believe that the play is by the extensive Gayler. Mr. George Jordan has been a bad boy, refused to play in *An Unequal Match*, and has therefore been set out in the cold. If he will promise to be good, and not to do so any more, perhaps he may come back.

We are to have little Patti over here from Philadelphia next week, Wednesday and Thursday. Apropos to that, if you haven't read the letter of the President of the Academy, a fine old fossil named Davis, to the Union-Savers, you have lost a laugh. I found it in the *Express*, which is strong on the Union-saving business, because it don't cost anything, and brings in advertisements. Charles Augustus says in his letter, that the Trustees of the Academy, when he informed them that it was wanted for the Union meeting, could hardly be restrained from manifesting their joy in some public way. Their motto is E Pluribus Unum (quite correct about their *prime donne*), and they immediately give the Academy for nothing! It is a curious habit some people have—that of giving away things which don't belong to them. However, in the next paragraph we are assured that Ulmann himself has become troubled about the Union, and that he is so much interested about the meeting, that he will give up a night which he otherwise could not use, which I call "uncommon handsome" on his part. In the end of his letter, Mr. Davis cautions the Union-Savers against breaking things about the Academy, which strikes me as being a little absurd.

At any rate, when the opera managers turn Union-Savers, our institutions must be in a bad way.

Mrs. John Wood, as I hear from a man who got in from Philadelphia the other day, and may be seen at the New York Hotel, has been drawing crowded houses at the Arch. As the illustrious Wheatley has been ornamenting Broadway this week, I presume that Mrs. Wood's engagement will be continued.

The management of Wallack's Theatre does not seem so active as usual. A. M. wants to know when *The Romance of a Poor Young Man* is coming out, and I am to tell Mr. Lester Wallack to hurry it up as rapidly as possible.

Talking of A. M., I must tell you that she, the Brightest and the Best, the real, genuine, original article, the Venus around whose fairy form revolve all other crinoline systems as satellites, is not well pleased that some one hath taken her name in vain, and in The Saturday Press. She don't write for the papers. She considers it low, and not the sort of thing for a young lady whose ma keeps a coupé and visits in Madison avenue.

She, Anna Maria, is satisfied with a little. All she wants is peace and harmony, with two operas, two new flirtations, three parties, and a thé dansant or so every week. She begs me to present her compliments to you, and would be obliged if you would "desist the use of her name" in conjunction with any young ladies who go to Jersey in December.

I think the dear child is right.

The French Theatre is smashed on the question d'argent. The artists give themselves a benefit tonight, when everybody ought to go. Mr. Bateman has engaged Mlle. Darcy, the soubrette, to sing some of those nice little French chansonnettes at Sam Cowell's concerts, which wax strong with the public day by day.

Miss Patti has made a terrific sensation at Philadelphia. When she sung the *Sonnambula* last Wednesday, the Academy was crowded, and the Quakers worked themselves up to a degree of enthusiasm without a parallel in the memory of the Oldest Man, who has gone over to condole with his friend Forrest on the award of the referee in the great case.

And finally, my beloved brethren, to conclude my discourse with you this week, and to see fair all round, I have asked the Able Editor to append hereunto the letter of Mrs. Bourcicault on the great question of the day.

It may reasonably be doubted whether or not the public will ever get at the whole truth about the émeute at the Winter Garden.

For my own part I don't believe there is any such thing as truth in the world, so I am not at all anxious about this particular dispute, which may be, after all, only a dodge to help *The Octoroon* along. Meantime I hear that it is to be produced at the New Bowery.

Miss Hattie Andem's concert at the Cooper Institute, next Tuesday, will be worth looking after. Lots of good artists will assist the bénéficière.

Personne.

—

Letter from Mrs. Agnes Robertson Bourcicault.

To The Editor Of The Herald: Sir, I have withdrawn from the Winter Garden; but my reasons for doing so have been incorrectly stated in your journal of this morning. Yesterday I wrote to the management as follows:

> To W. Stuart, Esq :—*Sir*,—I decline to appear any more in the "Octoroon." I regret to find that the piece has given offence to a portion of the public, and my part in it especially. I receive continually letters threatening me with violence, and when I go on the stage I do so in fear of some outrage to myself or to my husband. Therefore, I beg to withdraw the play. Yours truly,
>
> Agnes Robertson Bourcicault.

The Press had pointed out the political tendency of the "Octoroon," and your journal especially had blamed its production at this unhappy crisis. Oppressed by the sense that many of the public regarded the play as you did; that I was the object of just censure, having received letters from many families in this city urging the withdrawal or alteration of the play; intimidated by letters threatening us with violence,—as woman, I could not hold the position which the management desired to compel me to endure. I felt that I was unconsciously made the instrument to wound the feelings of one part of the public to gratify the other. In every sense my position was a painful one. I will not permit my name (or my husband's if I can help it), to be associated with any scheme to make money out of a political excitement—especially on such a subject as slavery and at such a moment as this. The "Octoroon" was not intended to succeed on such merits. In your notice this morning you state that it has produced me over over thirteen hundred dollars for six performances. It is true; but I cannot consent to sell my own self-esteem and the good opinion of my friends at that or any price.

In reply to the above letter, the following was handed to my husband at four o'clock yesterday afternoon. It is written by Mr. Thomas C. Fields, the Public Administrator, to whom Mr. Stuart states that he has assigned the Winter Garden—of which Mr. Fields claims to be the manager:

> Wednesday, Dec. 14, 1859.
>
> My Dear Sir,—Mr. Stuart has handed me your note, the contents of which surprise me. You have entered into an engagement with me to give the services of your wife, yourself, and pieces on certain terms, which, by your acceptance of those terms, you have to-day under your hand ratified. I now require Mrs. Bourcicault and yourself to perform in said piece, the "Octoroon," this evening, and shall await your answer till six o'clock, when, if no satisfactory answer be received, I shall proceed to make such arrangements as may become necessary by reason of your refusal.
>
> Yours, etc., Thomas C. Fields, Trustee of the Winter Garden.

On consultation, it was thought it might be better that I should perform last night, rather than cause any public inconvenience. Accordingly, at a few minutes before six o'clock, I went to the Winter Garden, and was refused admission by the stage-porter, who informed me that he had received orders from Mr. Fields not to admit me. I am, sir, your obliged servant,

Agnes Robertson Bourcicault.

December 15, 1859.

NEW YORK DECEMBER 24, 1859

WALT WHITMAN'S POEM.

Our readers may, if they choose, consider as our Christmas or New Year's present to them, the curious warble, by Walt Whitman, of "A Child's Reminiscence," on our First Page. Like the "Leaves of Grass," the purport of this wild and plaintive song, well-enveloped, and eluding definition, is positive and unquestionable, like the effect of music.

The piece will bear reading many times—perhaps, indeed, only comes forth, as from recesses, by many repetitions.

[For The Saturday Press.

CHRISTMAS EVE.

—

BY CHARLES GAYLER.

—

Fill the cup! Fill it up!
I'm sad, to-night.
Let it sparkle, clear and bright!
In it let me drown my pain;
Fill it up! again! again!
I'm sad, to-night. Heigho!

Fill the cup! Fill it up!
I'm gay, to-night.
Circle it with flowers of light!
Let me drink deep the witching draught;
My soul 'twill to Elysium waft.
I'm gay, to-night! Ha! ha!

Fill the cup! Fill it up!
I love, to-night.
Wine to love adds double might.
To Her! to Her of the Melting Eyes!
My Life! my Joy! my Paradise!
I love, to-night. Heigho!

Fill the cup! Fill it up!
I weep, to-night.
My tears shall flow by its ruby light,
O'er the daisied sod, above the breast
Of my darling, where she lays at rest.
I weep, to-night. Heigho!

Fill the cup! Fill it up!
I die, to-night.
Pledge me once more the goblet bright.
I come, Bright Spirit! O joy divine!
Ye conquer Death, O Love and Wine!
I die, to-night. Ha! ha!

A Child's Reminiscence.

PRE-VERSE.

Out of the rocked cradle,
Out of the mocking-bird's throat, the musical shuttle,
Out of the boys's mother's womb, and from the nipples of her breasts,
Out of the Ninth-Month midnight,
Over the sterile sea-sands, and the fields beyond, where the child, leaving his bed, wandered alone, bareheaded, barefoot,
Down from the showered halo and the moonbeams,
Up from the mystic play of shadows twining and twisting as if they were alive,
Out from the patches of briars and blackberries,
From the memories of the bird that chanted to me,
From your memories, sad brother—from the fitful risings and fallings I heard,
From that night, infantile, under the yellow half-moon, late-risen, and swollen as if with tears,
From those beginning notes of sickness and love, there in the mist,
From the thousand responses in my heart, never to cease,
From the myriad thence-aroused words,
From the word stronger and more delicious than any,
From such, as now they start, the scene revisiting,
As a flock, twittering, rising, or overhead passing,
Borne hither—ere all eludes me, hurriedly,
A man—yet by these tears a little boy again,
Throwing myself on the sand, I,
Confronting the waves, sing.

REMINISCENCE.

I.

Once, Paumanok,
Up this sea-shore, in some briars,
Two guests from Alabama—two together,
And their nest, and four light-green eggs, spotted with brown,
And every day the he-bird, to and fro, near at hand,
And every day the she-bird, crouched on her nest, silent, with bright eyes,
And every day I, a curious boy, never too close, never disturbing them,
Cautiously peering, absorbing, translating.

II.

Shine! Shine!
Pour down your warmth, Summer sun!
We bask—we two together.

III.

Two together!
Winds blow South, or winds blow North,
Day come white, or night come black,
Home, or rivers and mountains from home,
Singing all time, minding no time,
If we two but keep together.

IV.

Till all of a sudden,
May-be killed, unknown to her mate,
One forenoon the she-bird crouched not on the nest,
Nor returned that day or night, nor the next,
Nor ever appeared again.

V.

And thenceforward, all that Spring,
And all that Summer, in the sound of the sea,
And at night, under the full of the moon, in calmer weather,
Over the hoarse surging of the sea,
Or flitting from briar to briar by day,
I saw, I heard at intervals the remaining one, the he- bird,
The solitary guest from Alabama.

VI.

Blow! Blow!
Blow up sea-winds along Paumanok's shore!
I wait and I wait,
Till you blow my mate to me.

VII.

Yes, when the stars glistened,
All night long, on the prong of a moss-scallop'd stake,
Down, close by the shore, almost amid the slapping waves,
Sat the lone singer, wonderful, causing tears.

VIII.

He called on his mate,
He poured forth the meanings which now I, of all men, know.

IX.

Yes, my brother, I know,
The rest might not—but I have treasured every note,
For every night, dimly, down to the beach gliding,
Silent, avoiding the moonbeams, blending myself with the shadows,
Recalling now the obscure shapes, the echoes, the sounds and sights after their sort,
The white arms out in the breakers tirelessly tossing,
I, with bare feet, a child, the wind wafting my hair,
Listened long and long.

X.

Which now I too sing,
Repeating, translating the notes,
Following you, my brother.

XI.

Soothe! Soothe!
Close on its wave soothes the wave behind,
And again another behind, embracing and lapping, every one close.
But my love soothes not me.

XII.

Low hangs the moon—it rose late,
O it is lagging—O I think it is heavy with love.

XIII.

O madly the sea pushes upon the land,
With love—with love.

XIV.

O night!
O do I not see my love fluttering out there among the breakers?
What is that little black thing I see there in the white?

XV.

Loud! Loud!
Loud I call to you my love!
High and clear I shoot my voice over the waves,
Surely you must know who is here,
You must know who I am, my love.

XVI.

Low-hanging moon!
What is that dusky spot in your brown yellow?
O it is the shape of my mate!
O moon do not keep her from me any longer.

XVII.

Land! O land!
Whichever way I turn, O I think you could give me my mate back again, if you would,
For I am almost sure I see her dimly whichever way I look.

XVIII.

O rising stars!
Perhaps the one I want so much will rise with some of you.

XIX.

O throat!
Sound clearer through the atmosphere!
Pierce the woods—the earth,
Somewhere listening to catch you must be the one I want.

XX.

Shake out, carols!
Solitary here—the night's carols!
Carols of lonesome love! Death's carols!
Carols under that lagging, yellow, waning moon!
O, under that moon, where she droops almost down into the sea! O reckless, despairing carols!

XXI.

But soft!
Sink low—soft!
Soft! Let me just murmur,
And do you hush and wait a moment, you sea,
For somewhere I believe I heard my mate responding to me,
So faint—I must be still to listen,
But not altogether still, for then she might not come immediately to me.

XXII.

Hither, my love!
Here I am! Here!
With this just-sustained note I announce myself to you,
This gentle call is for you, my love.

XXIII.

Do not be decoyed elsewhere!
That is the whistle of the wind—it is not my voice,
That is the fluttering of the spray,
Those are the shadows of leaves.

XXIV.

O darkness! O in vain!
O I am very sick and sorrowful!

XXV.

O brown halo in the sky, near the moon, drooping upon the sea!
O troubled reflection in the sea!
O throat! O throbbing heart!
O all—and I singing uselessly all the night.

XXVI.

Murmur! Murmur on!
O murmurs—you yourselves make me continue to sing, I know not why.

XXVII.

O past! O joy!
In the air—in the woods—over fields,
Loved! Loved! Loved! Loved! Loved!
Loved—but no more with me,
We two together no more.

XXVIII.

The aria sinking,
All else continuing—the stars shining,
The winds blowing—the notes of the wondrous bird echoing,
With angry moans the fierce old mother yet, as ever, incessantly moaning,
On the sands of Paumanok's shore gray and rustling,
The yellow half-moon, enlarged, sagging down, drooping, the face of the sea almost touching,
The boy ecstatic—with his bare feet the waves, with his hair the atmosphere dallying,
The love in the heart pent, now loose, now at last tumultuously bursting,
The aria's meaning the ears, the soul, swiftly depositing,
The strange tears down the cheeks coursing,
The colloquy there—the trio each uttering,
The undertone—the savage old mother, incessantly crying,
To the boy's soul's questions sullenly timing—some drowned secret hissing,
To the outsetting bard of love.

XXIX.

Bird! (said the boy's soul),
Is it indeed toward your mate you sing? Or is it mostly to me?
For I that was a child, my tongue's use sleeping,
Now that I have heard you,
Now in a moment I know what I am for—I awake,
And already a thousand singers—a thousand songs, clearer, louder, more sorrowful than yours,
A thousand warbling echoes have started to life within me,
Never to die.

XXX.

O throes!
O you demon, singing by yourself! Projecting me!
O solitary me, listening—never more shall I cease imitating, perpetuating you,
Never more shall I escape,
Never more shall the reverberations,
Never more the cries of unsatisfied love be absent from me,
Never again leave me to be the peaceful child I was before what there, in the night,
By the sea, under the yellow and sagging moon,
The dusky demon aroused, the fire, the sweet hell within,
The unknown want, the destiny of me.

XXXI.

O give me some clue!
O if I am to have so much, let me have more!
O a word! O what is my destination?
OI fear it is henceforth chaos!
O how joys, dreads, convolutions, human shapes, and all shapes, spring as from graves around me!
O phantoms! You cover all the land and all the sea!
O I cannot see in the dimness whether you smile or frown upon me!
O vapor, a look, a word! O well-beloved!
O you dear women's and men's phantoms !

XXXII.

A word then,
The word final, superior to all,
Subtle, sent up—what is it?—I listen;
Are you whispering it, and have been all the time, you sea-waves?
Is that it from your liquid rims and wet sands?

XXXIII.

Answering, the sea,
Delaying not, hurrying not,
Whispered me through the night, and very plainly before daybreak,
Lisped to me constantly the low and delicious word Death,
And again Death—ever Death, Death, Death,
Hissing melodious, neither like the bird, nor like my aroused child's heart,
But edging near, as privately for me, rustling at my feet,
And creeping thence steadily up to my ears,
Death, Death, Death, Death, Death.

XXXIV.

Which I do not forget
But fuse the song of *Two Together*,
That was sung to me in the moonlight on Paumanok's gray beach,
With the thousand responsive songs, at random,
My own songs, awaked from that hour,
And with them the key, the word of the sweetest song, and all songs,
That strong and delicious word which, creeping to my feet,
The sea whispered me.

Walt Whitman.

[For The Saturday Press.

CHRISTMAS.

I.

Hail Christmas! blessed, holy time,
To pious souls in every clime,
Who celebrate with joy and love
The advent of the Sacred Dove—
The Word made flesh, sent down from heaven,
God's priceless boon to mortals given,
The virgin mother's sinless babe
All lowly in a manger laid—
While o'er his head, with radiance bright,
The Star of Bethlehem cheered the night,
And led the wise men to his shrine,
To worship Him, the Child divine.

II.

O blessed *happy* Christmas day!
To hearts with youth and pleasure gay—
When friends and kindred joyful meet,
To pass the hours in converse sweet,
And frolic glee, and festal mirth,
Surround the happy household hearth.

III.

O holy, *saddened*, Christmas hours!
To homes where sorrow darkly lowers—
Where fond hearts weep, their idols dead,
Their cherished hopes forever fled,
Love's fairest flowers crushed in their bloom,
And laid within the silent tomb,
To stricken hearts, O Holy Dove—
Send peace and comfort from above.
Our Father God! our risen Lord!
Support, and strengthen, by Thy Word—
And grant to Faith's ecstatic sight,
The Star of Bethlehem's hallowed light,
To shed its radiance o'er the gloom,
And lead to joys beyond the tomb.

W.

For THE NEW YORK SATURDAY PRESS.

BORN.

BY SALLIE BRIDGES.

A requiem and a jubilee!
An infant born, a mother dead!
A storm without, a wail within!
A starless heaven overhead!
A father's half-averted eye!
Hot tears above a white robe shed!
A flickering firelight in the room,
Strange shadows swaying 'mid the gloom,
A broken flower, a bud's fresh bloom,
A life that wrought its giver's doom!

Thus welcomed in an ominous hour,
A new soul wakened on the earth;
With snow and hail on striving winds,
With death and sorrow in the hearth!
What fate is hid in coming years,
Thus heralded by such a birth?
A loveless childhood, wild and lone;
A youth of yearnings, crushed, unknown;
A heart with idols overthrown;
A woman's lot! moan, baby, moan!

THE LOVE OF A PUPPET!

A Christmas Story.

Written for The New York Saturday Press

BY T. B. ALDRICH.

I.

Long ago, long before General Washington snubbed a King, and set up a coat-of-arms on his own account; long before the stars and stripes waved over this happy land; long before the Genius of America rose up sublimely under the crepusculous pinions of the Spread-Eagle; in short, long before anything in particular had happened to this great and glorious Continent, there stood a narrow-windowed, gambrel-roofed, well-to-do mansion, on the spot now known as the Four-Corners. The four roads meet there to this day; but the old house is gone forever and ever—faded out like a shilling ambrotype; more's the pity, for it was a fine edifice, in its glory, and sported a cupola (there were only three in the colony), from which you could see the garrison-house at Portsmouth, and beyond, the white-caps of the Atlantic, breaking in silver and azure on Newcastle Light.

At the period of which I write, there dwelt between the walls of this prepossessing piece of architecture the following more or less interesting personages:

1. Worshipful Godfry Pynchon (the Heavy Father of our little drama).
2. Madam Hepzibah Pynchon (the Mercenary Mother).
3. Kathie Pynchon (the Heroine coming to grief).

The worshipful Godfry Pynchon had once been a man of great wealth; but a series of disasters, including a scalping-frolic on the part of the neighboring Womponsags, had reduced his fortune to about forty acres of good land, the Pynchon mansion, and the Pynchon family. In the last was his sweetest wealth, though he did not know it. I refer to Kathie Pynchon, who, as I have intimated, is the Juliet of our melodrama. She must suffer the penalty of heroines. She must be described.

Never, since gentlemen were invented; never, since the first author wet the first goosequill in the first ink-horn, preparatory to dashing off his first chapter, was there ever a heroine so hard to describe as Kathie Pynchon, nor a scribbler less able to describe her than myself. I might, indeed, tell you something about the trimmest little figure, and the sauciest blue eyes, that ever fell to the lot of a Puritan maiden; but I hate to catalogue the charms of a lovely woman. That Kathie was lovely, there can be no doubt in the mind of man. The lads of the village were distracted about her; the old men looked at her sunny face, and immediately remembered their courting-days; and even her rivals forgave her beauty, she was such a warm-hearted, blithesome little wretch.

It would take me all day to draw up merely a list of the masculine hearts which this playful Lamb split in two, at divers times, from the moment she put on long dresses until her seventeenth year. So I shall not do it. But at last Kathie herself came to grief, and it is at this momentous epoch that our curtain rises, and the play begins.

It was snowing, as it can snow only in New England. Great white feathers came floating down from the cold gray clouds, darkening the whole atmosphere: Stone-walls, and roads, and barns, and fat comfortable farmhouses, appeared to sink gradually into the earth, threatening to leave everything level.

At one of the diamond-shaped windows of the Pynchon house stood Kathie, looking at the snow—no she wasn't. She was weeping and trying not to weep. The instant a tear came, she nipped it in the bud with a pocket-handkerchief, small enough to be the personal property of a fairy; but scarcely was one tear wiped away, when another sprung up to take its place, just like Indians in a skirmish. Now, as a general thing, I am not fond of Niobe. Women are not pretty when they cry. But Kathie was not a common woman, and she never looked lovelier than she did at that identical moment. Her sweet face was shrined like a saint's, in her rich blonde hair; her lips were red and pouty; and her soft white bosom rose and fell with a certain sort of archness, in spite of her sorrow. Altogether, she was very charming as she stood there at the window of the quaint old mansion, weeping. Imagine one of Hoppin's almond-eyed women looking out of a Gothic window by Vaux, upon one of young Boughton's Winter scenes.

The frost steals steadily over the pane, and the fair face is lost.

In the same room with Kathie Pynchon was her mother, an oldish lady with sharp features, who sat by the wide-mouthed fireplace, toasting her feet in the face and eyes of two grotesque andirons. This personage, austere and severe to look at, as she sat in the red shadows of the blazing hemlock-logs, was by no means a woman not to be respected. She had her weak side, like the most immaculate of us; and it is our especial fault if she comes to the reader wrong-side up. At present she does not appear in an amiable light; for what plaintiff can appear amiable while arguing that money and age are sweeter things than love and youth?

The defendant stood by the deep-set casement, tearful and vexed, though the plaintiff, thus far, had got the worst of it.

There had been a lengthy and spirited conversation going on between these two while we stood outside, like a pair of cold-blooded monsters, admiring Kathie's troubled face from an art-point of view. It was one of those lip-contests in which women are such gladiators. Heavens! what wounds they give and take, and never flinch a bit! Now and then an awful thrust will bring the tears—but that's only a pleasant kind of bleeding.

Kathie laid her hot face against the cool window-glass; the enemy folded her hands over her knees; and it was a truce between them. But it was not of long duration, for the enemy in retreating wished to fire a parting shot. Presently Madam Pynchon looked up.

"Davie Howe's grandfather came over in the *Mayflower*. A proper good family is Davie Howe's, and very, very old."

"So is he," said the Lamb at the window.

There are none so deaf as those who won't hear.

"He owns the new wheat-houses. He is a man of mark. He is as rich as——"

As he can be, Madam Pynchon was going to say.

As he is ugly, Kathie was going to say.

But neither finished the sentence. It was cut short by an interruption, and the interruption proceeded from Kathie herself.

While Madam Pynchon was exploiting Davie Howe's pedigree, Kathie had been unconsciously tracing something on the window-pane with one of her taper fingers. When Kathie's tearful eyes fell upon her handiwork, she broke out in a silvery ringing laugh, and pointed to the window.

"What's that, child?" cried Madam Pynchon, startled.

"Only see!" said Kathie laughing through her tears. [I shall not afflict the reader with a venerable allusion to April.] "Only see! it is for all the world just like it!"

"Like what, Kathie ?" said the enemy, perplexed and interested.

And this is what the Lamb's pearl of a nail had traced in the frosty glass:

"Why, Davie Howe's NOSE!" shrieked Kathie.

The enemy held up her hands in horror.

At this moment Edward Pynchon came in from the barn. As he brushed the snow off his long peruke, he looked at his wife, and the following silent dialogue took place:

His eyes. Have you told her?

Her eyes. Yes.

His eyes. What does she say?

Her eyes. NO!

II.

WHILE Kathie, feverish and sick at heart, throws herself on a two-story bed hung with stiff, white dimity, and Mr. Pynchon and his wife sit by the fireplace, down stairs, occupied with no pleasant thoughts, I will let the reader into the secret of Kathie's tears.

Next to the Pynchon estate was Squire Howe's farm—the best tilled and most valuable tract of land in the township. This fact had frequently impressed itself on old Pynchon's mind, but never so forcibly as when Davie Howe's son, who had been educated by his father's relatives in England, returned to the homestead to assist Davie in managing the establishment, and, ultimately, to be its sole proprietor. Mr. Pynchon looked at Kathie, and then at Richard Howe, and said,

"They were made for each other."

And when the old gentleman saw his roguish daughter flirting just a little with his rich neighbor's son, his heart was glad within him. But at the very moment when his hopes were brightest, and his heart was lightest, an event took place which rather interfered with his plans.

Richard Howe died.

Kathie was sorry, as anybody is when anybody dies. Then old Pynchon, like the philosopher he was, said to himself:

"If Kathie can't wed Davie Howe's son—and she can't, he being dead—she can wed Richard Howe's father."

It was a brilliant idea.

But Kathie failed to see it. In fact, at that time Kathie did not see much of anything, save Walter Brandt. It is not quite plain to me how this came about; but one day as young Brandt stood looking at Kathie with all his eyes, there was a tumult among the rose-leaves on Kathie's cheek; and Kathie's heart went beating against Kathie's corsets in a manner marvellous to think of. It was all over with the Lamb as quick as that. The Lamb flirted no more. The village lads and lassies knew what that meant. So it came to pass that Kathie did not weep so much for Richard Howe as she might have done under different circumstances.

When Mr. Pynchon was informed of these things by an officious neighbor, that gentleman was wroth overmuch.

"Walter Brandt," he said, "hath not land enough for a crow to stand on. I'll hear no more of it!" Then there was trouble in the family. The doors of the Pynchon house were closed against Walter, and Kathie was forbidden to hold converse with the Outcast.

"I cannot get rich here," said Walter Brandt. "I'll seek fortune elsewhere. Will you be true to me, Kathie? Will you marry me, if I come back within three years, Kathie ?"

"Ay, if you come back within fifty years!" said the brave little Puritan maiden.

So they kissed, and cried, and parted, as many a pair has done before and since.

Walter had been gone over two years. One, only one letter—which Kathie wore right next to her warm heart was all the tidings that had reached her from the wanderer. In those days, however, people seldom got more than three or four letters during their entire lives. Kathie made the most of one, and waited patiently for the happy day; and would not have been utterly wretched if Davie Howe's name had not become a familiar word in her family. Then Davie Howe himself, under favor of Mr. Pynchon's sanction, pressed his suit with Kathie, and made himself very disagreeable. In the meanwhile, Kathie had been treated with great tenderness by her parents, who used all their gentle eloquence to persuade the Lamb to drink at the same stream with the old wolf. But she wouldn't.

One day things took an unpleasant color.

"Widow Brandt's son is coming back to the settlement," said neighbor Goodman to neighbor Pynchon.

Mr. Pynchon wheeled about on one heel.

"How d'ye know?" he asked, sharply.

"My brother has writ it to me from Holland," said neighbor Goodman proudly. And he drew out the letter.

"Have you told this to any one?"

"Nay, I have this moment received the document."

"John, you shall have that strip of hay-land at your offer."

"Thank you, neighbor Pynchon, heartily."

And Mr. Pynchon made a feint of hurrying off; he walked two paces, paused, and said, in a nervous manner:

"And, John, you'll not need to mention that affair—the letter—you know. And, John, how long would it take to go to Holland?"

He meant how long would it take to come from there.

"Three months or more," said John.

Mr. Pynchon went home.

"Kathie shall marry Davie Howe this Christmas," said he.

"But I won't!" said Kathie, when Madame Pynchon broke the subject to her; and then ensued that combat which ended in headache and inglorious tears. As the old folks sat by the fire that night, and as the coffin-like clock on the staircase doled out eight, old Mr. Pynchon started abruptly, and looked up at his wife.

"Four years ago to-night"

Then she too remembered.

Four years ago that day, their son Will was lost off Newcastle Light. Four years ago that night, the waves threw his body, scornfully, on the rocks.

It was a sorry anniversary for the Pynchon family.

III.

In a smoky, dingy inn, in one of the zigzag streets of a Dutch sea-port-town, three sailors sat at a stained-oak table, smoking clay-pipes and drinking from huge pewter tankards. There was a clinking of glasses and a clashing of low Dutch at the back end of the room, where the innkeeper stood behind a rough counter receiving the small change. At round squat-tables, in various parts of the room, sat knots of obese burghers, playing with greasy cards and soiled dominoes. They all wore long, ferocious-looking beards, and might have been taken for malignant goblins in the dense smoke which filled and clouded the apartment-smoke from thirty industrious pipes, smoke from the sputtering garlic and potatoes which were being fried in the next room.

As the three foreign sailors leaned over the table, taking tempestous draughts of the frothy beer, an old woman, who appeared to grow out of the stifled atmosphere, suddenly stood beside them. She was gaunt and shaky like a skeleton, and her white hair hung wildly about her face.

It was Margaret Van Eyck, the fortune-teller.

"Would ye know your destinies, mynheers?" said a creaking voice.

One of the men, a giant of a fellow, with bushy black hair, held out a brawny hand to the woman, and winked a small sunken eye at his companions.

The crone looked at the lines in his palm, and shook her head.

"You will die before a twelvemonth."

"Gramercy!" cried the other two sailors.

"You lie, I shan't!" said the man, withdrawing his hand quickly. "Up sail and be off, or I'll dash this grog over your ugly cut-water."

And the man raised the heavy tankard menacingly. A strong hand was laid on his arm.

"Jack, I should forget we were messmates if you did that."

"There, Walter, boy," said the man, putting down the tankard; "I can't stand them phantom-ships. Tell her to sheer off."

"What's your name?" asked the crone, stooping over the sailor whose interference had saved her a wetting.

"Walter Brandt," said the man, who was so good and brave, that he would have told his name to the devil himself.

"Come here, Walter Brandt," said old Margaret, moving slowly toward the door.

The sailor rose from his seat, and followed her good-naturedly.

"Have ye wife, or child, or sweetheart, across the ocean?"

"Ay," said Walter Brandt.

"A sweetheart! I see her in your eyes!"

It is likely enough, for Kathie was always there.

"Would it make her heart leap to hear from you this night?"

"Like a rabbit," said Walter Brandt.

"Then, here, take this," and the old woman handed Walter a small phial, filled with a dull greenish liquid. "To-night, at twelve o'clock, never a moment sooner nor later, uncork the bottle, and before you can wink thrice, there will be a sweet whisper at your sweetheart's ear."

"Bless my eyes!" cried Walter Brandt.

You could have counted every one of the honest fellow's handsome teeth while old Margaret was telling him this. He took the phial mechanically, placed it in the pocket of his sou'wester, and went back wondering and doubtfully to his pipe.

The old crone vanished, as she came, in the smoke.

That afternoon, the big awkward bark, "Kathie Pynchon," Captain Brandt, put out to sea in a spanking wind. Soon the bleak gray coast faded away like a line of mist.

Then the sky darkened.

Then the sea boiled and hissed.

Then the wind blew great guns, and the waves lashed the sturdy bark, which rolled and floundered about in the trough of the sea, like a safe, comfortable old tub, as it was, and never once thought of swamping. On and on she went, under bare poles. When the sun went down the gale increased in fury. The sea broke clean over her deck. At midnight a man was washed overboard. Walter was lashed to the helm, and as the sailor was swept by him, he heard the poor wretch cry out—

"A curse on that old witch!"

Then a great wave dashed Walter against the helm, and the bottle in his pocket snapped. Wizz! went something through the air.

"Bless my eyes!" said Walter Brandt.

IV.

I AM certain that my lady readers are seasick by this time, and would like to be put on shore. You see I have been out in the yacht "Zinga" with the gentle creatures, and know all about it.

We are once more in New England.

The people of the Colonies, like modern and sinful folk, had their amusements; and among the diversions which most delighted the Puritan mind were—I blush to say it—Puppet-Shows.

Now, about this time there strolled into the village of Portsmouth an eminent professor of Puppetism, whose name is so long and unpronouncable, that I shall call him Hans Von Meerschaum de Spuyten Duyvel, for brevity. This H. V. M. de S. D. was, in many respects, a remarkable man—remarkably old, remarkably plain, and remarkably insane on the subject of manikins. He had given his whole life to the manufacturing of modern men and women on a small scale, and had brought the art to such perfection, that it was absolutely startling to see his gimcranks strut about the stage, and hear them chatter in the choicest fractured German, for Von Meerschaum was a very clever ventriloquist withal. He got up a sort of comic-tragedy in which his little people played with great *esprit*. Some of his love-scenes were quite as neat and pathetic as anything you could see at the Winter Garden, or the Volks' Garten, as to that matter. In fact, when the puppet Corydon kissed the puppetess Chloe, in the second act, the Puritan maidens on the front seats actually blushed, and more than one lugubrious elder was observed to assume a look of severity.

Christmas was coming (I don't say this in a satirical sense), and Von Meerschaum was devoting his energies to the preparation of a show that should astonish the natives. Early in the morning, and late at night, the professor worked at his manikins with such success, that every now and then he fancied that he had accomplished the one desire of his life, *videlicet,* to create a real living, walking, talking, eating, digesting, pigmy monster.

"Dat would be one astonishment," said Yon Meerschaum, chuckling.

So it would.

But just as Mynheer thought he had got everything all right, imagined that the toy was about to draw a preliminary breath, fancied that he felt it palpitate between his fingers—just at that critical moment he discovered that the wretched puppet was only wood and paint, and glue and things, and not the genuine article at all. Then Mynheer was in despair, for half an hour, at the end of which time he commenced the construction of another human being on new principles, and never for a second doubted his success, until the dratted thing wouldn't walk nor talk, but only lie flat on its back, and stare at him with its unwinking lobster eyes.

I have ventured into this slight episode, because I think there is a moral in it—and morals are the most useful things we can put into our two stockings during Christmas-times. Like poor Von Meerschaum, the very best of us—especially us miserable story-writers—do little or nothing all our lives but make dead puppets. The statesman makes his; the merchant his; the philosopher his; in short, there is no man so foolish, or so wise, but he contributes one manikin, at least, to that great puppet-show, the World.

And now—*en route*.

Von Meerschaum's workshop was in the loft of a tall block-house which, in war-times, was used as a lookout, to watch the operations of the redskins. The Indians, of late, had been engaged in a friendly home-traffic in scalps, and the watchtower had fallen into disuse, until Von Meerschaum moved into it with his nicknacks, one day, after having paid a month's rent in advance to the treasury of the commonwealth.

Hans Von Meerschaum sat in his curiosity-shop late one night, as usual, putting the finishing touches to a manikin on which he had lavished all the resources of his ingenuity,—a sailor-boy, one foot high, carved and jointed in a most wonderful manner, and dressed to the life in blue jacket, and flowing white duck trousers, tight at the hips. The little imp all but breathed, as he lay across the puppet-maker's knees, grinning atrociously, and waiting patiently for Von Meerschaum to put on the upper part of his skull. There was something terrible in the toy, as it lay there, minus the top of its cranium. The head was a shell of wood, into which the artful professor had stuffed a ball of cotton batting sprinkled with red pepper, to represent brains. Two blue glass beads composed the eyes; the lips were touched with vermillion; the nose and brow were full of expression; and indeed the whole figure, face and body, was a marvel of workmanship.

With a fine camel's-hair brush, Von Meerschaum was carefully applying a thin coating of glue to the edges of a curly wig, which was to fit over the cavity in the sailor-boy's head, and render him attractive.

"Twelve o'clock, and all's well," droned out the village watchman.

A sudden gust of wind blew back the wooden shutter, and nearly extinguished the professor's candle. Whizz! went something through the air, and flop! went something into the cotton and pepper brain of the puppet on his knee. Von Meerschaum, who had not noticed this, carefully fitted the curly wig on the doll's head.

Then the sailor-boy rolled off the old man's knee, fell plump on the floor, and sprung on its feet in a jiffy. "Bless my eyes!" cried the manikin, giving a nautical hitch to his little trousers.

Von Meerschaum nearly dropped out of his chair with astonishment.

"Ter tyfle!" exclaimed Von Meerschaum.

"Bless my eyes!" cried the manikin, surveying himself.

"Ter tyfle! ter tyfle! ter tyfle !" cried the old puppet-maker, dancing round the room in delight. "I made him mit my own hands! O, ter tyfle! ter tyfle!"

Then he laughed, then he cried; then he stopped and looked at the Wonder; then he was off again, forty horse-power, shouting that name which is never heard in polite society without a shudder.

"Let me out, you lubber!" shrieked the manikin.

"You lubber!" shouted Von Meerschaum, in ecstacy; "and I made him mit my own hands!"

And away he went round the room like mad.

Two bright sparks flew from the manikin's eyes.

"I'll jump out this window, you old fool!" cried the imp, and he ran to the casement.

Von Meerschaum stood aghast; then he made one dash at the manikin and caught him by the leg just as he was disappearing.

O, you will, will you!" cried the exasperated professor, and he administered such a spanking to the puppet as no urchin in the settlement could have lived through.

O, how mad the manikin was!

He gritted his little teeth, he clenched his fists, he nearly strangled with rage. Then he thrust his hand into his pocket for a plug of pigtail to chew his wrath on.

When Von Meerschaum beheld that he was off again.

"I'll make my fortune mit him!" cried Von Meerschaum, bursting with happiness.

"No you won't," said the manikin, who appeared to understand everything perfectly. "I won't play. I'll knock all your wooden puppets into splinters, blast their eyes!"

This threat fell like a thunderbolt on Von Meerschaum. He saw at a glance that all depended on the will of the manikin, and here he had been beating him the first thing! Beating him, just as Mrs. Jones beats little Jones when he falls overboard and neglects to drown himself!

Then the old puppet-maker took the manikin on his knee and begged his pardon, and kissed him, and cried over him, like an old idiot. And from that moment Von Meerschaum was the unhappy slave of his manikin. He cringed before him, he worshipped him; he fed him on sea-biscuit and pigtail incessantly, and even starved his own poor stomach to buy grog for the awful little monster. He did everything in the world for the brat but give him his freedom, which, of course, was the only thing in the world that it wanted. He had an immense tub of water, and built miniature corvettes for Captain Jack to launch and amuse himself with. He erected a splendid mansion for Captain Jack, and locked him up in it carefully every night. And then Captain Jack would knock over the tables, and break the chairs, and kick out the fireplace, and damage things generally. Then he would swing himself in his yarn hammock, strung across the best parlor, and bob up his funny little head every once in awhile, and abuse poor old Von Meerschaum like a pickpocket!

To record the conversations which took place between the old man and the manikin, would be to fill up twenty quarto volumes; but the gist of all was:

Manikin—"Let me out! let me out!"

Von M.—"What for, mine little man?"

Manikin—"To see her, HER, HER!"

Von M.—"To see who, mine darling little man?"

But the manikin refused to explain.

Day after day went by, and poor Von Meerschaum was driven to the verge of distraction by the goings on of that wretched little beggar.

"You're no shentleman," said Von Meerschaum to him one day, severely.

"Bless my eyes!" cried the manikin, walking lame like Von Meerschaum.

Weeks flew on, and matters became worse. The manikin appeared to be suffering agonies. It refused to eat, and the professor was in despair. He had to take a reef in the waistband of Captain Jack's trousers; and the puppet grew thinner and thinner every day. One morning Von Meerschaum walked into his shop, troubled and perplexed in the extreme, like that respectable colored person in the play of Othello. He opened the door of Captain Jack's house and begged him to come out.

The manikin lay in his hammock, and refused to stir a foot.

"O mine heart, mine little man, come out! Help me in mine troubles; I will do all what you wishes."

On hearing this the manikin bolted out of the hammock.

The old man took him on his knee, and smoothed his curly hair fondly, like a woman.

"To-morrow will be Christmas eve," said Von Meerschaum, rather confusedly, "and the good Mynheer Pynchon has sent for my puppets for to play at his fräulein's wedding, mine pearl."

The manikin gave a start.

"Now mine good little man, mine brave little man, will you not do your little tricks for the good peoples? And then," added the old man sorrowfully, "you may go where you will please."

"Here's my flipper, old fel'!" said the puppet, stretching out his absurd fist.

Then old Hans brightened up directly, and never was so happy.

"My fortune will be made!" said Von Meerschaum. "And I shall see *her*, HER, HER!" shrieked the manikin.

V.

And Kathie Pynchon all this time?

The Lamb had been used badly. Hitherto Mr. Pynchon had tried by dint of patient argument to convince Kathie that she loved Davie Howe; but when he found that Walter Brandt would probably come to the relief of the distressed garrison before many months, he changed his tactics. One day he would expostulate with Kathie solemnly, then he would take no notice of the poor child for a week. This was hard to bear. It was cruel not to be spoken to; it made Kathie feel like a poor relation at her father's table. But even that was not so heartbreaking as to have him coax her, and plead with his eyes—the eyes which used to look so lovingly on her. That was bitter almonds.

"I wish I were lying in the churchyard!" said Kathie, white as death.

"You must marry Davie Howe!" cried Mr. Pynchon, out of patience.

In the meantime the color went out of Kathie's cheeks; her eyes wore a lack-lustre look; she went about the house like somebody's unhappy shadow; and the lips that used to bud and blossom into laughter, had forgotten how to smile. Heartache was "the grim chamberlain that lighted her to bed."

A fort cannot always be a fort if there are no ready hands to repair the breaches. Kathie had not a soul to help her in this unequal bombarding. Now and then she scattered the old people with a gun loaded to the muzzle with feminine grape and canister, but not often. The enemy saw that she was weakened, and plied their shot unmercifully. Kathie's guns hung fire now. The small sarcastic shells which she threw at allies' outworks broke weakly in the air, and did no damage. She had parted company with Hope, and the enemy's lines came down on her. What could Kathie do? She tried to die; but I have observed that people never die when they want to. At last she threw herself on her mother's bosom, and said:

"I don't care what becomes of me—sell me, if will. But," added Kathie, with a show of her old spirit," isn't there anybody who will give more for me than Davie Howe offers ?"

This somewhat dashed the old folks.

Then they sent for Davie Howe. Davie Howe leered, and kissed Kathie's hand, and Kathie shrunk back, as if an asp had stung her.

VI.

It was Christmas Eve. It was freezing cold, and the snow had commenced falling shortly after twilight; flake after flake lighted on the ragged trees and the stiff fences, like millions of magical white birds.

It was Christmas Eve. There were bright lights in the Pynchon mansion. The windows glared out on the darkness like great sinister eyes. Kathie was to be married.

The preparations for this event were on an extensive scale. There was to be music; and young ladies in powder, and crimson farthingales, and high-heeled shoes, were to float languidly through monotonous minuets;

there was to be a feast, and a charade, and a puppet-show, and heaven knows what not.

The ceremony was to take place at eight. At seven o'clock the rooms were already crowded.

Garmented and garlanded for the sacrifice, Kathie Pynchon sat in the parlor of the Pynchon house, surrounded by a bevy of fair young girls, who, for the first time in their lives, did not envy the belle of the settlement. Kathie's pallid face and faded lips told rather a terrible story. But she looked enchantingly, from the highest wave of blonde tresses down to the diamond-studded buckles on her white satin slippers. Her costume, ladies? Silk, and things.

As she sat in the large, heavy-carven oak chair, two pretty feet were just visible underneath her tremendous hoop—two elastic ankles crossed coquettishly. The young men of the village beheld them, and grieved. [Picture !]

It was a quarter after seven, and expectation was on tiptoe for the arrival of the bridegroom.

Love, if I understand it, is a state of things, bordering on a state of mind. For several days prior to the time appointed for saying the lifelong words, that ancient gentleman, Davie Howe, was in a fever with regard to his bridal costume, which was intended to go a trifle beyond anything that had been seen in the Colonies. It was to be a gorgeous affair, gotten up without regard to expense, or anything else. The village under— I mean tailor, sent it home piecemeal. First, the coat, blazing scarlet, richly trimmed with gold braid, and faced with watered-silk. Next, the long-waisted waistcoat of maroon-colored cloth. Then the white silk hose. Then the faint-blue satin choker. But the small-clothes, the grand, elaborate, black velvet knee-breeches, that marvel of human art, there had been some mistake in them. First they were too tight, and a seam was let out. Then they were too large, and a seam was taken in. And then they didn't fit at all. In the meantime, the happy day had dawned, and Davie Howe's small-clothes were not finished. Twenty times that day did Davie send a messenger to the distracted artist; and twenty times was the messenger sent back with the assurance that the garment should be ready in season.

Six o'clock arrived, and the knee-breeches didn't. In a fit of phrenzy, Davie Howe mounted his horse, and dashed over the glaring ice to the village, three miles off, with the unalterable determination to scalp the luckless tailor. Half-past seven came, and the elder Pynchons grew uneasy. What could have occurred? And then a quarter of eight dropped in naturally enough, like a bore to dinner. The guests looked perplexed and amused; eight o'clock struck satirically, and a half-suppressed titter went round the room. There was an awful pause.

"'My dear," whispered Madam Pynchon to her husband, "let the man, Von Meerschaum, show his puppets, and divert the people, while Japhet rides over to Davie Howe's—something must have happened."

At the end of a long, narrow room, adjoining the library, our friend Von Meerschaum had placed his mimic theatre. He had spent half the day in arranging the stage, and the other half in keeping Captain Jack from knocking everything to splinters. That young salt was in a state of mind neither to be imagined nor described. He had quietly allowed himself to be brought to the house with the other traps; but he was no sooner under the roof, than he conducted himself in a most unbecoming manner. He upset the professor's pet street-scene, tore down the green curtain, punched out the left eye of King George (the gallant Yankee tar!), and maimed for life the inoffensive automaton, whose humble ambition was confined to the tight-rope business.

Poor Von Meerschaum was in great grief.

"Then let me see her!" shouted the manikin.

"See who, my heart?" cried the professor, ready to turn into tears.

"Kathie Pynchon, you old idiot!" yelled the manikin.

But Von Meerschaum dared do nothing of the sort. He attempted in vain to pacify the little demon. In the middle of all this, the clock sounded eight, and Madam Pynchon summoned him to exhibit his wonders some three hours before the time agreed. Von Meerschaum's face drew out like an accordeon. His stage was in dire confusion, owing to Captain Jack's passion; and it would take him at least an hour to set chaos in order. His countenance was such a picture of comical misery, that the sailor-imp fairly shrieked with delight.

"Look here, old fel'!" he said, suddenly; "let me see Kathie Pynchon for one moment alone, and I'll not only help you mend matters, but I'll act like a good boy with the rest of the blockheads. If you don't, shiver my timbers but I'll blow a breeze in that infernal old box of yours!"

"My child," said Madam Pynchon, bending over Kathie, "the—the puppet-player says he must speak with you a moment."

Kathie rose mechanically and followed the servant, and Madam Pynchon smiled in a helpless and ghastly manner on the company.

As Kathie entered the room, Von Meerschaum glided out, and closed the door after him, holding on to the latch like grim death.

"Don't you know me, my dove?" said a voice that caused Kathie's heart to leap up in her throat.

She started like one from a dream, and stared around the room. Then she glanced at her feet, and beheld the manikin, with his tiny arms stretched out towards her. She gave a quick little scream, and jumped up in a chair, holding her dress closely about her.

"Bless my eyes!" cried the manikin.

Ah! that was Walter Brandt's own "Bless my eyes," tone, accent and all. Kathie was struck dumb. "I am demented," thought Kathie; "too much sorrow has turned my brain."

"Kathie," said the manikin tenderly, "I have been true to you."

"Yes," said Kathie dreamily.

"True by day and night, Kathie, in storm and sunshine."

"Yes," replied Kathie, sobbing.

"And to night you wed Davie Howe!"

Kathie had thrown herself into the chair, and was weeping in her two hands, the tears glittering between her fingers like diamonds. The manikin was evidently affected. He brought a small box from the corner, placed it at Kathie's feet, and, mounting this, climbed upon her lap.

"Kathie, dear," he whispered into that pink shell, her ear. "I know how they forced you to this. I love you, Kathie !"

The poor girl, scarcely knowing what she did, folded the puppet in her arms, and held him against her bosom, and rained down kisses on the little villian's mouth.

The door of the room was suddenly broken open, and Von Meerschaum, followed by Mr. and Madam Pynchon and half the guests, rushed madly into the apartment.

"O Kathie, my child!" cried Madam Pynchon. "How can I tell her, good people? how can I tell her? O! O!! Somebody break the news to her gently—you, good neighbor Pynne.'

"Davie Howe hath broken his neck or something on the ice," said the frank Puritan.

Madame Pynchon was going to faint—fourth time. Nobody caught her. *Mem.* Concluded not to faint.

Kathie turned pale, and dropped the manikin. It fell with a crash to the floor.

Whizz! went something through the air and out the door.

There lay the manikin, the cotton protruding through a crack in the skull, and one green glass bead of an eye glistening hideous on the floor: right leg broken—compound-fracture of the spine. There it lay.

Then Hans Von Meerschaum de Spuyten Duyvel set up a howl.

In the midst of this, a light, agile foot bounded up the stairs, and somebody threw his arms around Kathie Pynchon. It was—I don't wish to shock the sensitive nerves of the reader by being too dramatic—it was Walter Brandt. Who else should hold The Lamb?

Kathie's recent experience with the bewitched puppet had prepared her to undergo any supernatural or preternatural arrangement without a shudder. That is the only way I can account for Kathie's extraordinary behavior on this occasion. She put her soft round arms about Walter Brandt's neck, and laid her blushing velvet cheek close to his honest, bronzed face. That Kathie Pynchon!

"Monster!" shrieked Madam, her mother. Her meaning remained a profound mystery. Whether she alluded to Walter, or Kathie, or poor Davie Howe himself, never transpired.

"Don't be a fool, my dear," said Mr. Pynchon in persuasive tones to his wife. It is clear that Providence hath been against us in this matter. I have nothing to say. The girl may wed whom she likes."

I trust this remark was disinterested on Mr. Pynchon's part; but I shrewdly suspect that neighbor Goodman had something to do with it.

"He's made a mint o' money," remarked Goodman, sotto voce, to Mr. Pynchon, while Kathie was misbehaving herself with Walter.

There was no wedding that night in the Pynchon mansion; but as there was a bride waiting, a banquet spread, a charade to be solved, and a minuet to be danced, the affair was not long delayed. Walter and Kathie were wed on Christmas night—and Davie Howe forgotten.

Kathie never breathed a word concerning the puppet to Walter; she believed that she was insane that time, and deemed silence wisdom, as it generally is. It was not many years after this, that Kathie Brandt held a manikin of her own in her arms; and it looked so like Von Meerschaum's manikin, that you would have died with laughter if you could have seen it!

And poor Von Meerschaum. I wish I could say something cheerful about him; but the fact is, he was never the same man after Captain Jack's fall. He never manufactured any more manikins. He had no heart to.

"Ah!" he used to say, confidentially, "dat vas a puppet as vas a puppet, and I made him mit mine own hands!"

It would be an anachronism for me to wish Kathie a merry Christmas at this late day; for the Lamb was taken tenderly to the fold ages and ages ago. It would be superfluous, too; for I believe that Kathie and Walter, and all true lovers who have died, are enjoying perpetual Christmas somewhere. But I may wish the reader a joyous New Year, may I not? while I hang out this literary stocking for the brittle sugar-candy of his good will. *Dei gratia!*

[For The Saturday Press.

CHRISTMAS.

BY ALLEN D. VORCE.

I.

To-night a thousand hearts beat glad,
In honor of old Christmas-time;
And ringing round the earth there goes
The music of a Christmas-chime;
And merrily through the air there floats
The rhyme of the minstrel's Christmas-tune,
Who stands beneath my cottage-eaves,
Singing a ballad to the moon.

II.

Light are hearts that dance, to-night,
Beneath the holly and mistletoe;
Many the kisses given and taken,
As the merry dancers come and go.
Decked is the boar's-head with ivy buds,
And a vine runs round the wassail-bowl,
And Summer sits high in many a heart,
And loud is the laugh of many a soul.

III.

Brightly blazes the old yule-log,
And the flowers of the fire wreath 'round,
As many a mug of old brown ale
With its drinker hath sanction found;
And Mirth sits high 'neath the cottage walls,
And the poorest are rich for a day,
For there reign within the cotter's heart,
Feelings that are akin to May.

IV.

But with us are passed those customs old,—
Few care for the days that were:
Forgotten is the vine-wreathed bowl,
And Christmas old armchair.
And soon in the poet's rhyme alone
Shall these customs refuge find;
For the holly and the mistletoe
Have long been left behind.

OUR GOOD WISHES.

A Merry Christmas!

With a few choice exceptions, we wish everybody a Merry Christmas.

If we were more Christian,—by which we mean if we were more noble, more manly,—we should make no exceptions, but extend our good wishes, especially as they cost nothing, to the entire human race.

But, then, it is such a raving and incomprehensible race, and includes such queer kind of people!

Fancy, for instance, our wishing a Merry Christmas to the creatures who, having failed in the attempt to bribe The Saturday Press into puffing their wares, are now gloating over the possibility of starving it to death!

We couldn't think of such a thing.

Besides, people of that sort are sure of a Merry Christmas anyway.

The turkeys and things (when dead and senseless) gravitate toward their spacious kitchens as though impelled by some mysterious law of Nature.

So, wishing them a Merry Christmas would not be very meritorious in us after all, except as a piece of superlative magnanimity,—and magnanimity, truth to say, is a virtue we are not over-prone to win in its minor degrees.

We extend the compliments of the season, then, first to our friends and, after, to that far more numerous class, the friendless, who are grateful even for a wish.

May Christmas bring merriness to them all, and cheer their hearts not only with bright pictures of the past, but with the more substantial joys of the present, and something like a comfortable look-out for the future.

A barrenish sort of wish, we fear; but, at any rate, a hearty one.

Not so barren, though, after all,—though we may never see the fruit of it.

No good wish is ever lost. It is written in the eternal nature of things that nothing good shall ever wholly fail of its purpose.

Blessed, then, be the day that transforms us all, in word at least, into good-wishers! and thrice blessed that its wishes are associated with him who, though he knew not where to lay his head, yet conferred on the world that wealth without which we are all poor indeed!

This concentration of the thoughts of millions at a given moment, on one event, and making the memory of that event the occasion of kindly words and deeds all the earth round, is one of the greatest and most cheering facts in human experience.

How utterly it obliterates, for a time, all feelings of caste, and proves that the human heart, once moved to its centre, is bound by no petty restrictions, but heaves upward everywhere, like the sea to God, and outward to the uttermost parts of the earth.

Yet what a little place it is, after all, this earth, as compared with the Universe!—and how foolish for the handful of mortals scattered over its surface to wrangle with each other in perpetual discord, when, by rallying round one common name,—the name that resounds, to-day, from so many lips,—they might become one in spirit even as they are one in form, and be fitted to realize the great truth, that all created intelligences emanate from and tend toward the same source, where eventually they will meet, not only nation with nation, but planet with planet, system with system, until the vast circle of human and other existences shall, after ages of growth and development, be complete, and a fiat shall go forth as in the beginning, pronouncing all to be "Good," and proclaiming that "there shall be no more death, neither sorrow, nor crying, neither shall there be any more pain; for the former things are passed away."

Thoughts and Things.

BY ADA CLARE.

IX.

"A Wife's Trials and Triumphs" is not an interesting book, though it is by no means a badly written one. Great art should be used in order to interest the mind in the unvaried miseries of the creations of romance. It should appear that these miseries are unavoidable, by being born not only of their own acts, but of the accidents of fate and fortune. As soon as they seem to spring methodically from an obstinate succession of foolish acts, as soon as certain causes produce them as effects with severe scientific certainty, the reader regards them as ineffable bores. The imagination is very ductile, but only in the warm region of passionate, heart-convulsing story. In the cold atmosphere of bare and barren assertion, it becomes a dense and unimpressible metal again. It is so in real life. When a man by habitual drunkeness, or any other persistent vice, involves himself in a succession of miseries, his friends desert him, not so much because of their want of charity and kindness towards the erring ones, as because they have rendered themselves too terribly tiresome to be borne. Even pity goes down in that yawning whirlpool of unutterable weariness.

Against the main incident of the book, I am going to enter my firm protest. It is the old story of the mother's leaving her only child to die while she is flaunting at a ball. I do not say the circumstance has never happened in real life, but it is too unnatural and too repulsive to be again related, unless with some splendid and powerful purpose in view.

I appeal to the maternal imagination whether it can conceive of the statement of a mother's leaving her only child, in a dangerous state, hovering on the brink of convulsions which must necessarily end in death, to visit an entertainment where she strongly dislikes to go. Add to it the facts that the mother is a woman of deep feeling, that she loves her child, that she is the only person who can soothe its paroxysms, that she recalls to her mind that it may cry "mama," with piteous wail while she is away,—and the maternal imagination rises up in indignation, and flings its challenge in to the face of the narrator. A confirmed lunatic might have so acted, but then the author should have stated that the scene was laid in Bedlam, and respectable medical testimony should have attested the statements.

° ° °

Whenever I hear men or women speak in bitter satire of infants, I feel convinced that in the mechanism of their souls there is some false principle. It becomes doubly repulsive when they are themselves the parents of children. To those who watch closely the developments of a baby, it is very plain that for every annoying capacity it has, there are a dozen winning and endearing ones. The trial it is to the patience is a million-fold rewarded in the treasure it pours out to the heart.

How soon it forgives us when we have thwarted its wishes, and perhaps given it pain for the committal of some innocent error! How soon the beloved eyes, still drowned in tears, smile out their pardon, and the sweet lips entreat a kiss, that baby-kiss compared to whose purity, all others how selfish and sullied!

The highest imagination of the painter has never been able to picture the angel of heaven, other than in the form of a young child. A simple copy of its innocent, guileless face, of its perfect and graceful form, is at once the loftiest type of seraphic impersonation. It is a fortunate fact that with a few exceptions all mothers are kind and loving to their infants. Alas! that they do not carry this sentiment through the lives of their children. Some mothers, who were most tender to their young children, allow this love to grow cold and neglectful as they grow up to maturity.

The bond of connection between the mother and babe both before and after birth is too sacred a mystery to be lightly dealt with. It is Nature's most solemn and touching secret, which the deep maternal heart alone is permitted to share. For woman alone, suffering and despised, borne down with her own griefs and the scorns of men, with all the burdens and ills of humanity, Nature draws away the veil from the whiteness of this glorified mystery, and lets her feel these divine pulsations that throb through the heart of life. Let not the man tread upon this holy ground. The burning of a sacred fire hath hallowed it from the impure touch of his feet. Let him turn aside in silence and in awe.

o°o

I have seen Laura Keene's new play "Distant Relations," and in one sense like it. Not in a literary sense, of course, but I think that any play that fosters the Union-loving sentiment in the breasts of the multitude should be respected and encouraged.

Miss Laura Keene was admirable of course; it is a rare thing to see her otherwise. She is so much the best actress we have in her line, that to find fault with her would be what is familiarly termed, "quarrelling with one's bread and butter."

Mr. Burnett's enactment of the negro was so good, that the first sight of him brought tears to my eyes, it carried me back so forcibly to the scenes and associations of my early Southern life. There was a certain "Uncle Exeter" looking very much like the Uncle Toby of the play, who was the oracle of my childhood. I and my little cousins held the statements of Uncle Exeter to be invulnerable; the absolute proofs of science and mathematics could nothing against them. Dear old black slave! I know thou hadst no wrongs; but if the book of thy memory had been black with them, the tender cherishing with which young children encircled thy life, and the pure tears with which they bedewed thy grave, had abundantly blotted them out.

o°o

I was present at the Drayton-Matinée last Saturday. I think Mr. Drayton the most finished and elegant comedian I have ever seen. What a triumph it is to make people laugh in that dreary tomb called, in cruel satire. "Hope Chapel "! The very atmosphere of the place elongates the countenance as though it were stretching it on the rack. But Mr. Drayton soon burst for us the cerements of the tomb. He is a fine singer, capital general artist, inimitable comedian, and handsome man. If that is not a partie-carrée of brilliant excellencies, I know not what brilliancy is, and for me the bat differs not from the nightingale.

o°o

The story of "Apelles and his Contemporaries given me great entertainment. All the characters in the book are characteristically, some of them exquisitely drawn. Besides, every one loves to read an interesting account of the grand old masters of art. There is much, much more than cant and pedantry in a devotion to the classics. The fame of these glorious ones of the Greek and Roman past is a pure fame, because it is a fame shorn of all the unspiritualities of circumstance. It is set far away like still stars beyond us—so far, so high, that the little voices of rivalry, and detraction, and envy, are dumb below it. Its immortality looks to us like eternity.

o°o

Miss Jane Austen, the shrewdest and most humorous delineator of character who ever has lived, or perhaps ever will live, thus defends the art of novel-writing, which in her own peculiar style, she carried to such perfection:

> I will not adopt that ungenerous and impolitic custom, so common with novel-writers, of joining with their greatest enemies in bestowing the harshest epithets on novels, and scarcely ever permitting them to be read by their own heroine, who, if she accidentally take up a novel, is sure to turn over its insipid pages with disgust. Alas! if the heroine of one novel be not patronized by the heroine of another, from whom can she expect affection and regard? I cannot approve of it. Let us not desert one another—we are an injured body. Although our productions have afforded more extensive and unaffected pleasure than those of any, other literary corporation in the world, no species of composition has been so decried. From pride, ignorance, or fashion, our foes are almost as numerous as our readers; and while the abilities of the nine-hundredth abridgement of the History of England, or of the man who collects and publishes in a volume some dozen lines of Milton, Pope, and Prior, with a paper from the Spectator, and a chapter from Sterne, are eulogized by a thousand pens, there seems almost a general wish of decrying the capacity and undervaluing the labor of the novelist, and of slighting the performances which have only genius, wit, and taste to recommend them.
>
> "It is really very well for a novel,"—such is the common cant. "What are you reading Miss——?" "O, it is only a novel," while she lays down the book with affected indifference, or momentary shame. It is "only," in short, some work in which the greatest powers of the mind are displayed, in which the most thorough knowledge of human nature, the happiest delineation of its varieties, the liveliest effusions of wit and humor, are conveyed to the world in the best chosen language.

Dramatic Feuilleton.

Philadelphia Etiquette.

There is a great row going on over yonder, on the banks of the Delaware.

It is not about the Union, nor the medical students, nor Mr. George William Curtis.

It is apropos to Brignoli, and all about etiquette.

Here is the story:

The Philadelphians see Patti to an immense extent. She is a good girl, and does not hesitate to say that Philadelphia is charming; that the reed-birds are "nice," and the butter "sweet."

Certainly she has had quite enough of the butter.

The Philadelphians, on the other hand, don't see Brignoli. He is a méchant, a bad boy, who pooh-poohs Broad street, which is eight miles long and sixteen miles wide, and makes love to the prettiest girls in the place, directly under the noses of the peg-top youths.

In New York, he is not over popular, personally; in Philadelphia, his insouciance is quite proportionate to the colossal rage of the villagers against him.

Last Saturday night Patti sung for the custodians of the Mint and Independence Hall.

Chestnut street emptied its young men into the Academy, Broad street, and bouquets flourished in the stockholders' pen. [They corral them, like cattle in California.]

Patti was called out. The stage was covered with bouquets.

The warblers, Brignoli and Patti, appeared. Excitement among the Broad-street youths. Brignoli picks up one bouquet and hands it to Patti. The other five-and-forty floral offerings to the shrine of Genius remain upon the stage. Great indignation among the Broad Street youths.

Patti must be had out again.

She appears, led by Brignoli. More vegetables.

He picks up one bouquet, and leads the Siren off.

There is a hiss from a Chestnut-street counter-irritant, and Brignoli, in his best Italian and sweetest demi-voce, says "Bless you, my child, bless you!"

Patti's eyes get larger than ever, and I am afraid that she is laughing.

The fury of the infants now rises to the boiling point.

Patti must appear again. The old scene is repeated.

Brignoli picks up ONE bouquet.

And there was much wailing, and cursing, and gnashing of teeth, over the bars of the Girard House. The bouquet-brigade had the pleasure to see their offerings picked up by a "super," and as the odor of flowers isn't nice for the voice, it is more than probable that none of the bouquets ever approximated the angelic nose, or were even touched by the divine hands of the prima donna.

Of course this is a great thing for the local papers.

For the moment, it has diverted attention from that mad dog who is shot every day by Officer Simpkins in Moyamensing, or the new dry-goods shop of Snip & Co., in Chestnut street.

The *Dispatch* pitches into Brignoli, and says he is a no gentleman.

Mon dieu! And he keeps a coupé!

But look! who is this preux chevalier, this Bayard, this Chesterfield, this Amadis de Gaul, this Count d'Orsay, this Frank Waddell, who comes to the rescue of the gentle Neapolitan?

It is that "d——d elegant gentleman" (excuse the expletive), that sweet-scented, suave, agreeable, and, next to Gurowski, the cleanest, the most delicate, and the most refined of savants, philosophers, and critics, the Solon of the Philadelphia *Press*, the bosom friend of Lord Brougham and the late Doctor Maginn—R. Shelton MacKenzie, Esquire, D.C.L.

Hear the learned Doctor:

> The European custom, to which Brignoli strictly adhered, is for the gentleman who hands on a cantatrice to pick up one bouquet, and leave the servitore di scena, a theatrical footman, to pick up the remainder. And, indeed, he had done so, we noticed, on previous nights. A tenor is not expected to be a servant. Brignoli fulfilled the requirements of the situation by exercising towards Signorina Patti what ordinary politesse demanded.

There, don't you feel better now? I do.

As for the bouquet-business, I never could see it; and, if I were a prime lady, I should prefer the cost of them in cash.

About Brignoli, however, the Doctor was half right; and when the tenor came on the stage on Monday, he was astonished by some applause. So it does the Philadelphians good to be snubbed occasionally.

Faits Divers.

The French Theatre has come to an untimely end. Sage wasn't so wise as he believed himself to be, and the subscribers, all but forty, "caved in."

The artists have been exiled to the Bowery (Hoym's Theatre), where they announce *La Dame aux Camélias* for Thursday and Saturday of this week.

Meantime, Sam Cowell keeps things going at a lively rate at the French Theatre.

Bourcicault is to be stage-manager at Laura Keene's Theatre, where he proposes to bring out *The Heart of Mid-Lothian*, Misses Keene and Robertson as *Jeanie and Effie Deans.* They can quote this pretty thing out of the divine Williams (edited by Miss Keene and Genio C. Scott):

> So we grew together,
> Like to a double cherry seeming parted;
> But yet a union in partition,
> Two lovely berries moulded on one stem.

There now, who says I can't say nice things about people?

Mrs. Wood, who has finished fascinating the Philadelphians, will probably return to the Winter Garden.

Something for the New York Bar.

There have been two new theatres opened down-town this week—one in the Superior Court, and the other in the Circuit Court of the United States. *The Great Divorce Case*, a very long, if not very clever drama, was revived in the Superior, with the old cast: Mr. O'Conor as *Mrs. Forrest,* and Mr. John Van Buren as *Mr. Forrest*. Van Buren, finding his rôle a little heavy, called in a clever young man named Brady, an Irish comedian, to help him out with it. They had got as far as the fourth act at the last accounts.

In the Circuit Court, the old farce, *Diamond Cut Diamond*, has been revived, under the, title of *The Sale of the Octoroon*, incessament. Mr. Green C. Bronson, one of the best heavy old men in the country (and lately engaged to do the Notary at the Municipal Theatre), appears as *Mr. Stuart and Mr. Fields* (Corsican Brothers), and Mr. Cram, who has had some experience in eccentric comedy under Mr. Burton's management, plays *Mr. Bourcicault.* The manuscript has been handed to the stage-manager, Ingersoll, who being engaged in getting up a nautical drama, postponed the reading of the new play till to-day.

One of the oldest performers in this theatre wants to know how it is that Mr. Fields comes to administer on the effects of the Winter Garden before its decease.

That's considered a good thing about the Courts.

They have also in rehearsal at the Marine Court a lively little comedietta for Laura Keene and George Jordan, called, *Wanted, a Week's Salary.*

Hache à la Laura Keene.

For a clever woman, Miss Laura Keene is certainly a very bad critic of plays.

Now I don't say that as the result of rejected addresses, for Miss Keene never refused any play of mine. Indeed, she ought to be the heaven-born goddess for authors, for she has given a chance to things that any one else would have thrown out of the window.

The hash which she calls a comedy is precisely one of those things.

I don't think it ever had an author. It seems like one of those interesting works cooked up between the box-office and the green-room, and resembling, for all the world, the mess which they get up in the cheap eating and boarding houses—a vile olla podrida, composed of the leavings of yesterday's dinner. My friend the Bohemian can tell you all about it.

The fact is, that *Distant Relations* has not the remotest connection with comedy. There is no plot, no intrigue, no epigrammatic dialogue; and the characters, especially those supposed to represent high life, are not quite so artistically done as the first drawings of a schoolboy with a piece of chalk, on a board fence.

There are some coarse jokes (generally fine old antiques), and a great deal of cheap patriotism.

People laugh at the one, and applaud the other; but that don't make the piece a good one, nor does it redeem Miss Keene's artistic reputation, which, as they say, she has no longer the excuse of impecuniosity for debasing.

And then the saving of the Union! Bah! Isn't there enough of that humbug in the papers, that we must be bored with it on the stage?

And then the taking of the name of Anna Maria in vain!

Mille de tonnerres!

She, the Pearl of Manhattan; the Brightest and the Best; a work wherein Nature in her gentlest mood, and Art in its highest development, have joined to produce one entire and perfect crysolite";—she the coarse, loud-voiced, slangy daughter of a cheap boarding-house keeper!—she, who looks upon "all those people" with abhorrence!—she, who wears nothing but two-button gloves, has her own maid, and has walked on nothing but roses, read nothing but Aldrich's poems, eaten nothing less expensive than paté de foies gras all her life!

It's "dreffful," now, isn't it? And don't you think I could have Miss Keene up in the Circuit Court for infringement of copyright?

What a shame!

The *Express* says:

"Mr. C. Jerome Hopkins has been the unexpected recipient of a letter from Dr. Franz Liszt, the eminent Hungarian pianist and composer, expressive of his approbation of his late efforts for the advancement of native musical artists, *and urging a prosecution of the same*."

Liszt is too harsh. I know as well as he that our artists have done some awful things, but their intentions have always been good, and they don't deserve prosecution.

Jam Redit Virgo.

A capital house for *Lucia* on Wednesday. Fashionable, dorée, brilliant, including lots of people whom one really wouldn't expect to go to hear Lucia who (to tell the truth) has been younger once than she is now.

The Sonnambula is somewhat familiar. Everybody has heard *Count Rodolpho* express how ravished he is by the charming scenes of his boyhood, how charmed he is with the town-pump, and how *Amina* reminds him of his Anna Maria première, who was too good for this world, and was "took away," all along of which he went to the wars, and came back with a red stripe down to his trowsers, and a gold hoop around his head. Likewise familiar to the Oldest Man as well as to the Youngest Poick, is the awful grief of Brignoli over Amina's supposed faux pas, her terrible anguish at the end of the second act, her remarkable gymnastic feats in the third, and the extraordinary vocal flights in which she expresses her satisfaction at the happy termination of affairs, and tells everybody not to mingle one human feeling, say the question of Honiton, bridesmaids, and breakfasts, with the bliss which is being revealed to her through the medium of the Tenor, who is very happy and very much ashamed of himself, as I'm sure every man (Anna Maria speaks) that goes and makes such a fool of himself as that ought to be.

Still, though familiar as the *Adventures of R. Crusoe*, and as hacknied as *Pilgrim's Progress,* people now crowd the Academy for *Sonnambula* and *Lucia* when Patti sings. They get interested, too. Blasé fellows, who only go to the opera on duty with Madame or Mademoiselle, are touched by the sweet, sympathetic, birdlike notes of this enfant charmant, who walks upon rose beds, and goes to sleep among the violets.

Eheu, Effendi! What a splendid thing it is to be young and famous. To have even Philadelphia excited about you, and to recall souvenirs of long ago in the hearts of old rascals like you and me. Hinc illae lachrymae; but no more of it.

We are to have more opera next week. Patti will sing three times, twice in *Don Giovanni*. The Directors of the Academy are going to get up a great benefit for her as benefit for the savior of the Opera. That is great deal better than talking about saving the Union and not doing it.Then there will be a night for the *Sicilian Vespers* (with the real tubs), and an *Ernani* (for Susini, ex-Major under Garibaldi). Gazzaniga will sing in the *Don Giovanni* and *Ernani,* and altogether it will be a fine week. A. M. intends to go every night or die in the attempt. So does your slave.

Personne.

NEW YORK DECEMBER 31, 1859

A Story for New Year's Eve.

Written for The New York Saturday Press,

BY JOHN W. WATSON.

How gloriously it snowed!

None of your sleety, wet, sloppy snows, at which every flake comes down like a great lump of lead, and only lies a minute upon the pavement before it goes to swell the mass of slosh and drabble. No! it was a light, feathery, jovial snow. A snow where the flakes came whirling and whirling down, always uncertain where they would stop, and at last dropping themselves on the pure white couch, in an easy, careless way, like a beautiful little lady gliding out of the waltz into the luxurious folds of a satin sofa.

Down they came, the glad and laughing flakes, filling all the air, covering the housetops, tipping the sills, and clinging all around the crevices, the lampposts, and the railings. Paying no respect to persons, dressing up the hat-rims, putting epaulettes on the shoulders, and piling up on the breasts of the well-buttoned overcoats, until they tumbled off in heaps. Filling up the carts and wagons, and sending them home with unpaid loads. Giving the horses a white woolly fleece, and stealing stealthily into every nook, cranny, and broken window.

How those that went to and fro enjoyed the snow! Their faces glowed all over with crimson. They ran and shouted, sometimes to themselves, sometimes to those they met but did not know. They sung, and made short condensed jokes to each other across the pavement, or across the street. They looked in shopwindows, and talked to each, as though all the world was acquainted with all the world, and then ran on laughing at nothing, and thought nothing—the very drollest thing that ever was known.

For oh! it was New Year's Eve, and a clear, cold, dry snow, that bade fair to make good sleighing on the morrow; and then the great city would be all alive, and the streets would swarm with callers, dashing about from house to house, saying good things, renewing old recollections, sipping sparkling wines, and doing a thousand things, each one more hearty and jovial than the other.

It was the New Year's Eve, and all the world seemed wild with delight. The sorrow, the sin, the shame were not lessened; they were all there upon the streets, looking at the New Year's Eve, but the gay ones had it upon this night, and the town was laughing aloud. Up Broadway, there came a handsome, dark-eyed, dark-haired fellow. It was easy to see by the glare of the gas that his eyes were bright, as well as dark, and those who chose to look deep into them might see there plenty of wild, laughing humor, even through the heavy frown that sat upon his face. Stephen Price marched stolidly on amid the crowd; there was no smile about him, no answering to the shout and the joke, no response on his lip or in his heart. He was going home,—to the house he called his home, a lonely home for a New Year's Eve,—a quiet, humble room in a boarding-house. He had but just left the office, where he had staid later than usual, making excuses to prolong the time of his departure,—excuses which Stephen hardly dared confess to his pride, but which, when the waiting failed to bring forth a response, sent Stephen Price homeward with a heavy frown and a heavy heart.

While he is trudging wearily home, through the glad crowd, the story must be told.

Three years before, Stephen Price came from a town two hours distant from New York, to enter as a junior clerk in the house of John Greenwell & Co. Stephen had lost father and mother at an early age, and had been consigned to the unwilling care of his Uncle Hampton, his mother's only brother, a stern, quiet, business man, who knew nothing but business and duty. Mr. Hampton was a bachelor, and Stephen, as a necessity, fell solely into the charge of his uncle's housekeeper, an easy-going, kind-hearted woman, who allowed the already spoiled boy to do as he pleased, and know no will but his own. It will be making no strange sequel to such a line of treatment, to say that Stephen Price, as he sprung from boy to manhood, sprung correspondingly into vices and careless habits. While no act showing a badness of purpose could be charged to Stephen Price, he was yet held up in the town as the head and leader of all aggression and recklessness, feared by staid, steady-going people, and solemnly winked at by those who declare that it requires a mischievous boy to make a smart man. If a hard practical joke had been perpetrated, or an unpopular person punished by any boyish revenge, the sufferers always declared that it was unnecessary to hold an inquisition to discover the culprit. They could see Stephen Price's hand as originator and abettor, and Stephen Price accordingly bore the responsibility.

As the boy was growing into the man, at that very critical period that the change comes for better or for worse, Stephen felt the inconvenience of his character, and was disposed to change for the better. The townspeople, however, did not join him in the resolve. It was too convenient for them to have a scapegoat, and the secret sins of the place still came home to the young man as they had to the boy. Stephen was idle, they argued, and it followed, as an impossibility, that he could keep from mischief. He was idle; this was true, but it was through no choice of the young man. His uncle, while looking with stern displeasure on the follies of the boy, and the gathering dissipations of the man, took no means of turning the really strong energies into a channel of usefulness. A frown or a sneer was all the answer Stephen ever received to his application that some chance might be opened to him in life; and the uncle made no secret of his belief that the boy was a ne'er-do-well, and would never reach any useful end. He had, through his prejudices, convicted and condemned him without a trial.

Stephen was popular with his associates, He never flinched from punishment to save another. He never betrayed his comrade to save himself. He was the hero of his peers. One, a slight, delicate boy, Warren Grey, loved Stephen Price the scapegrace, as he did his life. Stephen had once thrown himself between Warren and severe punishment, and Warren Grey never forgot it. He looked up to Stephen as to a superior being, one possessing that physical power which he so lacked, and—as Warren knew, whatever others might say—the nobleness to understand how to use it rightly. While the flaxen-haired boy clung, almost to worship, to the older and stronger, Stephen, in his turn, bent with more than a boyish passion to Leonie, Warren's only sister. A fair-skinned, blue-eyed, childish creature, was Leonie Grey; soft, yielding, and dreamy, and yet over Stephen Price she held the sway that no imperious beauty could have commanded, no physical force could have compelled. A word from Leonie, and the headstrong boy would forego his wildest plots; a tear trembling in her eye, and Stephen Price turned his revenges into services. Leonie was the guiding-star that bore the untrained boy through many perilous places, and lighted the growing man to better things than his own heart, unguided, knew.

Stephen was nineteen—a strong, healthy, handsome fellow. He had been quick at school; and though his teachers declared him the most troublesome boy in the town, a creator of anarchy and confusion, they also gave him credit for quickness of comprehension and great ability. There was no complaint against Stephen Price for want of industry or quickness in learning. One morning the young man awakened to this. It broke upon him in an instant—as though the knowledge had heretofore been a sealed book—that he was capable of serving himself, if his uncle would not serve him. With the natural energy of his character, he lost no time. He only wondered how he could have so long waited. He would wait no longer. He would hew out his own path in life. He would make a name and a position, and Leonie should share it with him. It was all revolved in his brain in an hour; the plans laid, and even worked to completion in theory. In an hour he stood upon the pinnacle of fortune, chafing under the thought of how many years must come between its birth and its consummation.

"Leonie, I am going to leave you. I am going to New York."

The girl stared wildly at the boy who had grown all at once into a man—who had, in one single day, added five years to the expression of his face, to the words from his tongue. She stared, and grew paler as she looked in his feverish eyes.

"To New York !'

The words fell upon Leonie's ear, and were repeated by her in a vague way, as though conveying no meaning.

"To New York. *This* is no place for me. I wonder how I have ever borne it until now. I am going to New York, Leonie, to seek my fortune and—yours."

Stephen ended his sentence in a low tone, and took Leonie's hand between both his own. She understood him well enough now—and Stephen caught her quickly in his arms, or Leonie would have fallen. There was no color in her lips, as he pressed them to his, and whispered to her:

"It is best, Leonie—much the best. I have a life to make for both of us, and a wasted past to redeem. You must help me. It is for your sake, Leonie."

The blood flew back from Leonie's heart, and the two faces that were pressed so closely together glowed with crimson; but the speech had not yet come to her. She only wound her arms about his neck and kissed him on the cheeks and on the forehead—kissed him as a darling sister would have done, without passion, but with an all-abiding, all-confiding love.

"I have marked out my course, Leonie, and if my reading has not taught me falsely, I shall certainly succeed. In years I shall return here, and show those who have predicted evil for me, that I am better than they. I hate them all. I hate my Uncle Hampton."

"O no, Stephen," and Leonie put her fingers on his lips, "do not begin wrong. You must not hate any one. You must not go away from your uncle with harsh words on your tongue."

"I shall not trouble myself about him at all; he has troubled himself little about me. I am going this very day; and when I am gone, he can do as he likes."

The young man looked down, and held the little white fingers listlessly in his own. The other hand slid gradually up until it rested his shoulder.

"Stephen, you must not go away without your uncle's permission. Whatever his coldness to you, I feel sure that he loves you. You will not go away without his permission. No good fortune will follow you if you do."

Stephen knew that Leonie was right. He had steeled his heart against his uncle, but he could not harden it against Leonie; and half an hour later, he stood before his uncle's desk with the same words he had just spoken to Leonie.

"Uncle, I am going to New York."

The old man raised his eyes from the paper on the desk, and fixed them with an astonished gaze on Stephen's face. Whatever he saw there, it altered his usual mode of action in an instant. Stephen expected only a sneer, or a harsh command to abandon his intention—instead of which, after Mr. Hampton had looked at his nephew, without speaking a word, he dropped his eyes back to the desk, and said,

"Well?"

"I am tired of this life, and intend doing something for myself."

"What?"

Stephen had created in his own mind a fabric for the future; but when the stern, practical question came from the stern, practical man, he was silent. Gradually he unfolded before the cold, unsympathizing old man, his life-secret. He told him what he hoped, and what he dreamed, and finally told him all—all but his love for Leonie.

The next day Stephen Price left his native place for New York. A cold shake of the hand, a present of fifty dollars, and a letter introducing him to the firm of John Greenwell & Co., with an intimation that nothing farther need be expected, was his parting from his Uncle Hampton. There was something more powerful to send him on his life-journey from Leonie Grey. Only a few words from the fair girl, but they rang in his ears louder than the thunder of the train that bore him away—louder than the hum and crash of the city —louder than the cry of temptation, and stronger than the years that bridged the river of Time.

Leonie had said, with her arms twined about his neck, that she loved him—loved him in life and in death—him, and him only, forever. They had sealed their love with one long pressure of heart to heart. And Stephen went away, firm in the belief that the day would come when he would claim Leonie, and that Leonie would keep his dream unsullied.

The hand of Warren Grey was the last that Stephen grasped, and he drew the boy, to whom he felt more than a brother, with a quick, convulsive embrace, to him, as the cars rolled out of the dépôt, and then he sprang back to the platform, and was whirled away to the great city.

Three years, with Leonie Grey ever before him, the young man had worked away at the desk for Messrs. John Greenwell & Co.; three years, brave in heart, he had denied himself even the sight of Leonie; three years, since he had first stepped into the city, Stephen Price had studied and wrought with the one great end before him—Leonie! He must show those who had prophesied for him that he was worthy of her. He scorned to droop by the way; and so it was that each new difficulty that sprang up before his lance went down with a gallant thrust. He conceived that his boy-reputation had followed him into the house of John Greenwell & Co.,—and a greater gravity and attention to business were the result. He saw that his education was not suited to business-exigencies, and a good part of his spare salary of five hundred dollars per annum went to fulfil the necessity. None so early, none so late, none so watchful as Stephen Price. His attention and self-sacrificing manner had met with great commendation from the heads of the firm, but not with advancement. Three years had now gone over, and Stephen stood no nearer his great end than on the day he came to New York. He would not complain, nor suffer any word of despondency to pass his lips—nothing even that bordered upon it, save only once in awhile in his letters to Leonie. She, with a true woman's courage, bade him hope on; they could both wait, she said,—when at last the fruit was ripe, it would be fuller and richer.

But this was New Year's Eve, and Stephen Price was walking homeward with a heavy heart. It had been the custom of Messrs. John Greenwell & Co. to present each of their employés with something substantial as a New Year present. The first year of Stephen's service, they had given him the very neat watch which he then wore; the second year the gift was fifty dollars; and this third year, Stephen had looked anxiously, though he feared to confess it, for the same gift. He had for many months been thinking over an intention to visit his old home;—to see Leonie ;—to be once more a week with her for whom he had so struggled for three years. It was with this intention that, for the first time since he had been with them, he asked from his employers a week's holiday. It had been granted, but the gift to which he had looked for the means of accomplishing his great thought came not. He had seen each of his fellow-clerks receive their presents, and depart with the happiest faces, while he, last of all, went away unrewarded. There were some bitter thoughts circling through Stephen Price's brain that night on his way home. He thought of how much he had striven, not perhaps for Messrs. John Greenwell & Co., but for Leonie; and where was his reward? And then, many instances of his watchful devotion to his employer's interests, came up in his mind. One in particular within a few months, the acknowledgment of which he held in his pocket, in the shape of a letter from Mr. Greenwell himself, praising his foresight, and declaring that his premature attention to a certain matter of insurance had saved the firm an almost irretrievable loss. And yet he was going to his lonely home, on this New Year's Eve, when everybody else was so happy, a poor clerk on five hundred a-year, and only a few shillings in his pocket, which he rattled sarcastically as he felt for his night-key to let himself in.

"For the love of Heaven, young gentleman, give me something to buy me some food."

Stephen turned with a start—the voice had awakened him from his unquiet dream. There stood a man, or what had once been one. His clothes thin and squalid. His outstretched hands gaunt and claw-like, his face pinched and grey, and his eyes burning with a fire that spoke of agony and insanity. Stephen did not look long to take all this in. Utter, terrible, starving poverty, spoke out from every line; and the young man gathered up the stray coins in his pocket, and put them in the beggar's hand.

"And this is my New Year's Eve," thought Stephen, when he had got his coat off and his slippered feet resting on the fender. "And here is the property I have amassed by three years' labor." He looked around sneeringly at the few books and prints, the clothes, and what trifles lay about the room. "The wealth of three years;—what nonsense it is for the world to talk of honesty and perseverance; what nonsense to assert that 'money is the root of all evil.' The world is a fool. Give me money, and I would not be spending this New Year Eve sulking over my solitary fire; I would be in the streets; I would look for misery and wretchedness; I would make happiness and be happy myself. Give me wealth, and to-morrow I would be the happiest fellow alive. To-morrow, I would have those who years ago consigned me in their own minds to a bad end, acknowledge me their superior. To-morrow, I would see Leonie. To-morrow, I would have her name the day she would be my wife. Warren should be rich. My uncle should regret his hardness. I would be great, and respected."

Stephen pondered over it all, and contrasted his theory of three years ago with his present. He listened to the noise in the street, to the hundred sounds that told of the wild hilarity of the crowd, and then he came back to his own cheerless loneliness. Even in the very house there were gay times, but nobody asked him to join. The quiet young man, who always spent his evenings over his books, or in his room writing, had no companions in the house. He could hear the sound of music from below, and dancing. Then he could hear them laugh. Then came a ring, a silence, he heard his name, a step upon the stairs, a tap at his door. "Come in!" The door was opened and his landlady appeared, ushering in the gaunt beggar to whom, an hour before, he had given his last cent upon the doorsteps. Stephen started to his feet, but was too much astonished to speak. In a moment the man closed the door, and they were alone. There was an air of self-possession about the beggar, that seemed totally at variance with his position; and Stephen, as he looked at the wild ghostly eyes of the man, could not conceal from himself that they carried with their gaze something that sent a chill, nightmare sensation over him.

"This visit takes you a little by surprise," were the man's first words as he drew a chair to the fire, after turning the key in the door.

"Yes!"

Well, sit still, you will be satisfied with it," he went on, "if you will listen patiently to what I have to say, without believing me either mad or drunk." Stephen did not speak.

"Did you ever wish to be rich ?"

Stephen started.

Could the man read his thought with those eyes of fire?

"It will be useless for you to say 'yes.' Asking the question is a mere matter of form. Who is there would not be rich? Who is there that, while suffering with a plethora of wealth, a glut that wears out both soul and body, would relinquish the curse? What will you do to possess boundless wealth?"

"Anything, everything!"

"Well answered," was the man's response, rubbing his dry, skinny hands together until they grated like a coffee-mill. "Will you give up the one you love best in all the world?"

"No !'

"No?" And the man laughed a little fearful laugh that sounded far away up the chimney. "No? Then there is one thing that you will not do. Will you consent never to do an unselfish action?"

"No!"

"No!" The man was delighted, the coffee-mill went harder than ever, and the laugh went out on the top of the house. "Then that's another thing you won't do. Will you kill your dearest friend?"

"No!" and Stephen jerked about on his seat fearfully, and scowled at the man.

"No, again! O dear! this is beautiful. Three things you will not do." The man drummed petulantly with his foot, rested his chin on his hand, and looked at Stephen. "Well! well! we must find you something more pleasant. Will you consent that, as long as its results meet with your desires, you will follow no occupation or business to increase your wealth?"

Stephen thought a moment, and answered, "Yes!"

"It is a bargain," said the man. "You shall be the richest in all the world. See, my friend, I did not need the pittance you bestowed upon me this evening; I am rich beyond conception." And the beggar drew from his pocket a handful of gold mixed loosely with gems of rare beauty and size.

Stephen involuntarily stretched forth his hand. "Not this, not this," the man said, "this will be nothing to what you shall have before the night is over. I have told you to listen patiently, without believing me either mad or drunk."

Stephen promised.

"I possess the secret of transmutation of metals, and must part with it before midnight."

The man hissed this into Stephen's ear; and despite of his promise, the young man sprang to his feet, and looked upon his companion as a madman, blaming himself for listening so long to one who so outraged probability.

"Sit down, sit down," he continued, and Stephen yielded to the command. "I repeat what I have said. I have the power to turn the baser metals into gold. Before this night is over, you shall be convinced. I am the alchemist, Alexander Sethon."

Again Stephen sprang from his chair.

"Speak truth, man, or something that sounds like it. Is there anything in my face that led you to believe that I am a fool?" and the blood rushed up in Stephen's forehead and cheeks, "Alexander Sethon the alchemist has been dead some centuries."

The man laughed again, until the echo ran all about the house, and came in shivering through every opening, no matter how small.

"Yes, so I have been told," he chuckled out. "I died, they said, at Cracow, in Poland, in 1604. I ought to know best about that; I died to save my life. Ah! that false scoundrel, Sendigovius, who rescued me from my prison and the rack, only to consign me to a worse fate. Had he left me to the Elector of Saxony, who sought to wring my secret from me by the torture of fire and starvation, I could not have fared worse. No! I did not die. I feigned death to escape the hands of Sendigovius. We are allowed, by virtue of the great medicine, to live five hundred years; and to possess the secret of transmutation half that time. My term for the last ends this night at twelve. To live for the balance of the time, I am obliged to impart my secret, and I have selected you as my heir."

"Selected me! Why?" and Stephen still gazed doubtingly on the man.

"Why? For the very simple reason that I have only a few moments ago told you: that he who has the curse of gold, would never relinquish it by his own will. I have always known that, before midnight of this year, I must surrender the secret and the power that it confers, to another, and still I have clung to it with a passion that has deterred me from day to day, and from year to year, in the selection of the recipient. I have fallen upon hundreds, and rejected them, until, when the night came down upon this, my last day, I had made no choice. I came into the streets dressed as a beggar, with the resolve to bestow the great gift on whoever gave the first alms, in the hope that by so doing, I would confer it on one who would use it better than I have done. You were that one, and on you has fallen the gift of gold."

Stephen was stupefied. He looked long and earnestly at the man. He was not mad; every word he uttered came clear and coherent. He would—

"Speak quick, do you accept?" The man rose to his feet, and made one step toward the door. "There is no time to lose; it wants now but two hours of midnight. There must be no trifling. Do you accept? If so, follow me."

He opened the door, and stood in the hall. Stephen drew on his boots with a quick jerk, and threw his coat over his arm. The man slipped along with a noiseless eel-like shuffle into the street. On he went, never looking behind. On through the crowded streets touching nobody. On by glaring gas-lit windows without looking. Down a dark, weary-looking lane,—up a crazy staircase,—there was the rattle of a key in the lock, a dull, dreamy light coming through an open door, and Stephen Price stood beside the man in a small room, where just enough light glowed from a furnace to show the contents. There were jars and retorts, crucibles and pipes, scales, strange instruments, and moulds. But that to which the young man's eye clung with greedy tenacity, was the heaps and piles of yellow gold, lying everywhere, loose and careless, as though it were but the meanest dross. He was wild with excitement, and for the first few moments the words of the Alchemist fell on unheeding ears.

An hour passed away, and Stephen Price was the possessor of the secret of transmutation, the embryo-monarch of the wealth of the world. The Alchemist stood watching the trembling successor of his greatness.

"That wisdom," he said, "for which I toiled so long, you have in a single hour. When I pass from this place, the power will be gone from me. I have yet to live, should I so choose, two centuries and a half. The gold which I have spent these last years in making, and which now lies in this room, is my own. To-night I shall remove but little of it; to you I leave the task of sending it to me at such places as these letters direct."

The Alchemist placed some documents in Stephen's hand, and took from the shelves a few ingots of the gold, which he placed in his pockets.

"The powder of projection is also the medicine of life. Use it cautiously, and remember that it is powerless on all save yourself. One thing only more. In this phial"—he held a colorless fluid to the light—" is a liquid which may yet serve you; it is no transmitted knowledge, it is a discovery of my own. If at any time you should weary of this secret, or weary of your invulnerable life, drop a single atom from it, and the perfume will reach me wherever I may be, and I will teach you how to relieve yourself of the burden. Farewell! Remember your oaths, remember your promises !'"

The Alchemist was gone.

All night long Stephen Price sat in the dim, smoky room, melting and casting. All night long he went on adding heaps and piles to the heaps and piles of gold. He saw the daylight come through the little prison-like window, but still he worked on. Ingot after ingot rolled out of the moulds. The clocks of the city rang out the midday strokes, and the sun was shining merrily. Once in awhile the far-distant tinkle of the sleigh-bells and the hum of the crowded street would come up to him; but still he worked on. Gold, gold! more gold! The night fell down, and hunger drove him forth. He ate with ravenous celerity, and hurried back, lest somebody should discover the spot of his wealth. More gold! Deep into the night his fire glowed, until he sank exhausted beside it, and slept until the sun streamed in the window. The first sight that met Stephen's eye as he awakened, were the documents given him by the Alchemist, telling him where to send the gold. He looked at them with a shiver of dread, and about on the heaps of glittering metal with desiring eyes. He gave the treadle of the bellows a few motions, and the fire burned fiercely up. The letters were in his hand. The gold danced and shimmered in his eyes. There was a groan, a chatter of the teeth, a licking tongue of flame, and the papers lay a mass of cinders in the furnace.

More gold. Day after day, night after night, Stephen Price sat before the furnace. He brought food, and remained within the room, slept beside his wealth. He smelted and cast, piled, and heaped, and thought. He thought of Leonie. He loved Leonie ; but now, O! now he was rich,—and would be great. He loved Leonie ; The fire blazed up with a fierce forked tongue of flame. But now, he could not marry her. He must marry a proud, a queen-like woman, one whose connections were great in the land. One who could do honor to his wealth. Yes! he loved Leonie; he would make her rich. He would make Warren rich. They should all be rich; but he must know them no more. More gold. The days and the nights were rolling away, and the wealth lay in millions in the dusky room. Some place of greater security must be found. By night, he took the treasure away, and by day placed it in safety. In banks, in the mint, in the hands of the assayers and refiners. Rich men and officials bowed to him, and talked of great investments. Bankers and brokers questioned cautiously, and wondered from whence had arisen this sudden millionaire. Haggard men with eager eyes offered brilliant schemes of speculation. Beautiful women smiled and fluttered about the man of gold. No more love. He loved Leonie. He must see Leonie. The furnace fire should be dark for awhile, and Stephen Price would see Leonie.

Once more he stood in the town where he was born. Once more he clasped Leonie in his arms. Leonie, so beautiful, but not proud. Leonie, more childlike, more sisterly, more confiding than ever. So beautiful, but not proud. So angel-like, but not great. Warren, too, had grown to be a man. A mild, gentle, blue-eyed, brotherly man. Everything, everybody was improved. Even his harsh uncle Hampton had grown kind, and grasped his hand with a fervor he had not known in the olden time. Once more Stephen Price was a boy. The years were lost, and his life was gained.

Days went by, and the great memory of the gold came back. He was wasting time. He must return to his furnace-fires. He loved Leonie. O! yes, with all his soul; but—Leonie could never be his wife. He must look higher. He must go back to his gold, and he must tell Leonie that she was free.

One bright, snowy, moonlight night, by the cheerful blaze of the snug parlor of Leonie's home, Stephen Price told her of his great wealth. He pictured it in its immensity to the listening girl, who sat silent and grave. He spoke of their altered positions, of his aspirations and ambitions; and then, while he told Leonie that he still loved her, he bade her relinquish all hope of becoming his wife, and said that from then she was free.

Leonie rose slowly to her feet, and looked wildly at the man who was speaking so coldly, so fearfully. She looked with one long steadfast gaze, and a great shrill cry went through the house, and Leonie lay cold and lifeless upon the floor. They took her from Stephen Price's arms, and bore her away to her room, and the next morning the man of gold was flying toward the city.

Days and weeks passed by, and the furnace-fires glowed incessantly. Stephen Price was courted and flattered, and grew greater every hour. One day there came to him, in the very midst of his splendor, a wild-eyed, pale, and trembling man. He looked long at Stephen Price, and spoke, before the millionaire knew his old schoolmate, his brother, Warren Grey. "Leonie is dead!" were his words.

Stephen Price started, but gold inspires confidence. He stared fearlessly on the ghostly man, and leaned well back in the luxurious chair.

"You are her murderer!"

Stephen Price stretched forth his hand to the bell-rope, that the lackeys who would spring to the summons might thrust the impudent intruder into the street. He was not quick enough; the trembling man had his hand on the rich one's throat, and clung there with the hold of a tiger. They struggled and held each grimly for life. As the door flung open, and the servants, alarmed by the noise, rushed into the room; the rich man had thrown off the trembler with a great curse, and he lay with his face upward on the floor. The lackeys sprang to hold down the prostrate man. There was no need; he would never rise more without aid. The man was dead, they told their master, and the command was to bear him away to the nearest stationhouse, he was a robber, and had justly met his fate.

The dispensers of justice came up to the man of gold, and took his deposition. They were sorry to trouble him. A mere matter of form. A desperate villain, no doubt. Had been already recognized as a bad character. Fortunate escape. Must be more careful. Good citizens are scarce. The city swarms with these fellows.

Stephen Price was congratulated on his escape from the robber, by all his great friends. They cautioned him about the lavish display of wealth that tempted the attack. They commended his bravery. They said everything; and everything they said, burnt and seared like a branding-iron into the heart and brain of the millionaire.

The days and the months went on, and the great friends of Stephen Price whispered among themselves. The millionaire never made any investments, never made any speculations, never gave to great charities, or doled out his wealth in small ones. It was very strange, they said, the man of gold never gave great parties, or courted society. Stranger still, he never formed intimacies, and looked suspiciously on all who approached him. Most strange and wonderful, nobody gained anything by his wealth,—they said it was all lavished on himself. Still more strange and wonderful and so, those who were rich and powerful dropped away, but the poor, the parasites, the hopers against hope, still clung on, and sought, without success, to bleed the rich man. They came back with fresh vigor to the attack, until Stephen Price lashed about him with blind fury, like a great worm crawling and twisting amid an army of termites. The world, he said, was one mass of vampyres, who wanted only his gold, and they should not have it. He thought no more of the proud beauty with high-born connections. He looked upon every woman's smile as a pitfall for his wealth; on every man's fair word, as a lure. He grew so very old in worldly lore and selfish wisdom, that the hard furrows deepened on his face, and the silver came freely in his dark hair. He sat in the midst of his hired servitors, and dreamed that he had buried the past,—the past that was so beautiful once, but now struggled up through all the surroundings of his gold, like a great grim ghost, withering and blasting whatever it touched.

Once again, it was the New Year's Eve. Stephen Price sat alone in his gorgeous, gilded home. The streets were filled with music: the music of the pattering feet; the music of the tinkling bells; and the music of the human voice in gladness; and the prayer that arose to God, from a million of happy hearts. Stephen Price, surrounded by every appliance of ease, and every splendor of wealth, cursed the music of the streets. He looked in the mirrors that hung on every side, and saw only himself. No longer the Stephen Price of old, but changed, so changed from the hale, handsome fellow of the past. He must be old, now. It seems such a weary while since the great burden first came. One year! O! gracious heavens! but one year to turn the heart to stone; to furrow the face; to dim the eyes, and silver the hair. All in one year!

A Happy New Year!
A Happy New Year!!
A Happy New Year!!!

Stephen Price crouched down in the silk-lined chair, and scowled toward

"Only one year! What will another bring? I cannot die. Ah! there I am safe. Gold can be won by the world, but not life. Only—one—year."

A Happy New Year!
A Happy New Year!!
A Happy New Year!!!

The rich man crouched deeper and deeper. The room was growing very chill. Where came those shadows from, that flitted along the frescoed wall? Not from the street; the blinds were closed and the curtains were drawn. Again—Leonie—Warren. Oh! how terribly chill the room is.

Stephen Price is fumbling, clumsily, in a secret pocket. He has become a trembler. There is a sound all through that beautiful room as of a shivering, chattering man. The night is very cold. He holds a small phial of colorless liquid in his hand, and tries hard with shaking fingers to draw the cork.

A Happy New Year!
A Happy New Year!!
A Happy New Year!!!

"Oh! dear me, Mr. Price, excuse me. I thought you said 'come in,' when I knocked. I really didn't know you were asleep. How can you sleep on New Year's Eve? This gentleman wanted to see you. That bundle does so look as though it was a present for you, that I showed him right up. Dear me, Mr. Price, I do hope you'll come down stairs this evening, and help us make egg-nogg. Do make yourself sociable on New Year's Eve. We're all plain folks, but we'll be right glad to see you."

And off the landlady bustled.

"A package for you, Mr. Price, and I wish you a Happy New Year, sir!"

Stephen took the package; it was very heavy for its size. The man was gone.

"A package for me?"

He stripped away the envelopes. Was he awake? There was gold! More gold! all in rolls. No ingots; but good, sound, solid coin. Two letters. Who from? The handwriting of Uncle Hampton, and of Mr. Greenwell. What mystery is this?

Sir,—Enclosed please find One Thousand Dollars ($1000), as a partial acknowledgment of the firm of John Greenwell & Co., that your services have been acceptable to them. You will also please take notice, that from this date, the desk formerly occupied by our respected bookkeeper, Mr. Nicholas Gorse, who has become one of the house of Humdrum, Sloe & Co., will be your position. Your salary will be Two Thousand Dollars ($2000) per annum.

Your obedient servants,

JOHN GREENWELL & Co.

New York, Dec. 31, 18—

A Happy New Year!
A Happy New Year!!
A Happy New Year!!!

Stephen thought the music of the streets was beautiful.

—Dec. 31, 18—.

My Dear Boy,—I earnestly wish you A Happy New Year. How much real pleasure it gives me to greet you so, when I know how well you deserve it! I have to confess to you my agreeable disappointment in your altered life, but I know that you will not insist on apologies from an old man. I know who your good angel has been, and believe me that I love her more dearly than a daughter. I have been in correspondence with Messrs. John Greenwell & Co., and their praise of you has been the most agreeable business intelligence I have ever received. There is some talk on their side of a partnership. When they have concluded about this, the money shall not be wanting. From them I hear that you have leave of absence. To-morrow, then, I shall see you; and if I am not mistaken, somebody will call back his young days, and dance at a wedding before the month of January is gone.

With the renewed affection of your Uncle,

James Hampton.

A Happy New Year!
A Happy New Year!!
A Happy New Year!!!

[For THE SATURDAY PRESS.

NEW YEAR'S EVE.

I.

With a bottle and a friend—
Friend is Tom, and bottle Sherry—
I shall now begin and end
This brief space where two years blend,
Wondrous wise and merry.

II.

Never yet was there a woe
That had not a pleasure pressing
Close upon its heels; and so
Through the Old and New we go,
Each at some time blessing.

III.

Though the Old Year brought to me
Little joy and much of sorrow,
In the New I hope to be
Happier; my joys, you see,
Always come—to-morrow.

IV.

So, when Fifty-Nine shall end,
Tom, and I, and Golden Sherry
—Finest wine and oldest friend—
Kill the space where two years blend,
Making wondrous merry.

GEORGE ARNOLD.

THE ROYAL BOHEMIAN SUPPER.

[Reported by Getty Gay.]

Her Majesty the Queen of Bohemia on Christmas-night received her most distinguished subjects at supper, in her palace fronting on 42d street. Though suffering from a cold and hoarseness, Her Majesty graciously presided at the royal board in person, showered her smiles with sunlike impartiality, and made everybody happy.

Among her most illustrious guests were her royal Captive, the Grand Seignor of Turkey; Count Wilkinski, Minister Plenipotentiary from the Court of Empress Anna Maria; the Countess of Peoria; Lady Gay; Baron Clapper; Sir Peter Porter, Knight of Malta; Sir Archibald Hooper; and Lord Pierceall, Troubadour to Her Majesty.

Whether the Queen intended to remind her Oriental Captive of his native land, or to display the greatness of her glory by humiliating so exalted a personage as the Grand Seignor, we know not; but she ordered him to carve the turkey. He bowed his head submissively to the royal mandate, and disappeared from the room with downcast looks, following in solemn procession after the bird. Ere long, he returned with the skeleton of the same, and placed it before the Queen. A thousand swords flashed in the gas-light, and the sanguinary stream of the Sublime Porte would have been spilt on the instant but for the command of the Queen, who calmly demanded an explanation of the audacious potentate.

He opened not his mouth.

"Did you mean, sir," put in Baron Clapper, who could not keep his tongue quiet—"did you mean, sir, by this to intimate that you have 'boned' the turkey, or that you make no bones' of our Royal Mistress ?"

The G. T. drew himself up to his full height, some seven feet, and said,

"Precisely—just so! I deposited the skeleton of the turkey before you all, that you might derive great moral, if not material, nutriment from it. A moment ago, what gobbler among you was so fat as this? And now even G. G. is no leaner! Once upon a time I was the greatest of Turkeys;—behold me now! The Queen turned pale; the lights burned blue; there was an awful pause. After several baskets of champagne had been emptied, the company recovered its spirits.

The G. T. was not slaughtered, but the havoc made in the viands was terrible. The mirth grew fast and furious, but not faster than Baron Clapper's tongue. He rattled away, getting off a great many good things, and some very bad. He toasted every one, but first of all proposed the health of the Youngest and Loveliest—the Queen of Bohemia.

Her Majesty replied by giving "The Oldest Man."

The Baron took it to himself, declaring that the title belonged to him, not on account of the length of his years or beard, but by reason of the sagacity of his counsel, and his inability to remember when he was born. He retaliated by giving the First of Her Majesty's subjects—the infant Prince of Bohemia—which was responded to with immense enthusiasm.

The Queen was much gratified, and proposed to drink to the long life and prosperity of THE SATURDAY PRESS, the independent organ of Bohemia.

Baron Clapper sprang to his feet, and burst into a torrent of eloquence which rolled on till it gave out. He declared that the success of his darling paper was owing to Her Majesty's and others' contributions, and gave "The army of contributors to THE SATURDAY PRESS." Count Wilkinski, in replying, answered that the Baron was not only a brick, but a tower, as no other man living could have carried the PRESS through a week, under banks of jokes more ponderous than bullion.

The Queen of Bohemia drank to Cortesi, queen of Song; "The Oldest Man" to Patti, Queen of Melody, and then the health of her majesty's Troubadour was purposed in due order. He, in reply, sang a song the words of which were composed by the Queen herself. It deserved an encore, and won it. "The Flower of Peoria" was next given, and obtained from the Countess a musical response of such delicious sweetness as fairly to entrance all hearers. Her beauty, melody, and vivacity quite overthrew the Baron, and he fell at her feet. Even Count Wilkinski with all his vaunted indifference, after trying hard "not to see it," had to melt, like snow in the sunlight, beneath her radiant power. In jealousy the Baron rose and proposed the health of the Empress Anna Maria, casting dark insinuations at the same time, which roused the Count like a lion from his lair.

"Anna Maria is not a myth!" he thundered.

"Do you lisp, sir?" asked the Countess.

"No, madame," said he blushing. "Anna Maria is a miss and not a myth. She was born of rich but respectable parents and "—

"That's why you are banished, I fear," said the Baron.

The Count retorted; swords were drawn; but the Queen soon brought the heated noblemen to a sense of propriety, and, to give them an example of magnanimity, proposed the health of the captive Oriental Monarch. The G. T. answered in the choicest Arabic, but, on account of the confusion, could not obtain a fair audience. Sir Archibald Hooper, so tenderly attached to the Countess, was also drank to, and much complimented by the ladies, for no one can get round them like Hooper. Lady Gay, who flirted (with the Baron and the Count) in a scarlet dress, embroidered, was last toasted on account of the inflammatory nature of her costume, and was drank to by all except Turkey, who had taken offence at her high color.

The champagne baskets and bottles now growing empty, and the Bohemians full, each member of the company gave way to his wildest inspiration. The Baron challenged the Troubadour to a singing bout, and, before he broke down, he managed to get through three bars of "Old Hundred." Lady Gay tried to talk sentiment; the Grand Turk to joke; the Countess to repeat her own poetry, and relate her early inducements; but the Troubadour poured forth lay on lay; the Knight of Malta drank freely to his own health; the Queen of Bohemia looked more than ever like the Goddess of Love and Beauty; and Count Wilkinski, thorougly dissolved for the first time in his life, fell at Her Majesty's feet, renounced his fealty to Anna Maria, and swore eternal allegiance to the Bohemian Queen!

Dramatic Feuilleton.

Sir Walter Scott in the Coulisses.

Miss Laura Keene announces, officially, the engagement of Mr. Bourcicault and Miss Agnes Robertson, whose irrepressible conflict with Le Chauve promises to be a nice thing for the lawyers.

Mr. Bourcicault, as I stated last week, is at work upon *The Heart of Mid-Lothian*, a novel by Sir Walter Scott; and I believe a "good work," though I never read it.

I had however a sort of shadowy idea that Sir W. Scott aforesaid had died some time ago.

I was wrong it seems.

Miss Keene's advertisement announces that this beautiful and popular tale will be produced "under the supervision and control of the author, at whose disposition Miss Keene has placed all the resources of the theatre."

Which I am sure is very kind on the part of Miss Keene, and Sir Walter will make, no doubt, a very fine stage-manager.

It is further announced that the new play will be produced "as soon as the new scenery and rehearsals will permit."

I trust that the scenery and rehearsals will permit as soon as ever they can, for goodness gracious knows (Anna Maria) that it is high time (Anna Maria's ma) that something new was done at some of the theatres.

What are they Doing?

Well, at Wallack's, they have got a very good run out of *Everybody's Friend*, a great triumph for the artists, as the play has no merit of its own to speak of. It is harmless, however, and is therefore much liked at this theatre, which is frequented by thin-skinned people, those called conservatives, because they always conserve their own interest at the expense of any principle that may be going.

They have also revived for Mr. Blake a fine old antique, which Mr. Lester Wallack, who is getting philologically fine lately, calls a "Fairy Folly." Its positive title, "Knocks and Noses," is more suggestive, and it might be a good thing for the Baron to modernize. As it is, it is quite oldfashioned—reminds you of Ned Windust and Tom Placide; but it is good as affording a fair part for Mr. Blake.

I remember once being present in a café (and cakes) to which the lower order of Bohemia, to wit, the newsboys, did invariably resort for festive purposes.

On the particular occasion to which I allude, some of the city boys were entertaining a youth to fortune and to fame unknown, who sold papers at Poughkeepsie.

[If you are anxious to read anything about the theatres, you had better skip this, and wait for the Sunday papers.]

The boy from Poughkeepsie was not a Bohemian.

He lived "with his folks."

He gave all of his money to his mother.

He never went to the theatre, but occasionally had a shy at the circus.

Immense disgust among the other boys greeted this short and simple annal of poor Poughkeepsie.

They looked upon the Mercury of Orange County, as you would regard a newly-arrived Esquimaux, a fresh Bostonian, or a recently-imported Philadelphian.

Poughkeepsie was sound upon one question, however. When he was interrogated as to which paper sold the best, he promptly responded, The *Herald*. All the other boys adhered to the same opinion, and several of them declared that if by any extraordinary convulsion of Nature the *Herald* should ever die, there never could be such another paper—*for the boys.*

That's the case with Mr. Blake.

When he leaves the stage, and may the good gods postpone that event for many years yet, there will be no such actor left. And how fine a holiday-artist he is! Listen to his laugh, drink in his bonhommie, which exhales from him as naturally as the perfume from Oscanyan's otto of rose. At this season, when people go to the theatre to be entertained, not to be instructed, which is a synonym for bored, Mr. Blake shines in his best sphere, and is the best actor now speaking the English language.

That's what I have been dying to say about William Rufus for a long time.

And now I've said it, and I feel better.

Here's a health to thee, O rotund comedian! May no sorrow, nor tribulation, nor tailor's bills, nor poor relations, nor no manner of disagreeable things come to thee! May thy life-road be lined with flowery hedges in continuous bloom!

The *Distant Relations*-stuff at Laura Keene's would not go down, although covered with a sugar-coating of sixpenny patriotism. The theatres would do much better to leave vexed political questions alone. Look at Mr. Wallack! You don't catch him with any chaff of that sort, and he is right. The *Green Bushes* was announced here for Friday, and *on dit* Bourcicault's play produced under Sir Walter Scott's direction, for Monday week. Mr. Bourcicault will find that he has not the Winter Garden artists at the house across the way. Miss Keene's company is, on the whole, utterly wretched, considering the reputation of the house.

Over at the Winter Garden, the *Octoroon* is getting along comfortably. I like Mrs. Allen's *Zoe* pretty well (pretty and well), all excepting that in the last scene she puts about a pound and a half of India ink around her eyes, and it makes her look as if she had just been having a fight with some of "40's fellers."

I may say, for the benefit of the jeunesse dorée, that Mrs. John Wood, who passed through town last week, en route to Rochester and Toronto (don't that make you shiver?), is definitely engaged at the Winter Garden. Wood is a good thing to do, and I'm glad she's coming back.

Operatic Dissolving Views.

The opera-people came over from Philadelphia this week, and will to Boston this afternoon.

The programme for the week here was knocked into a cocked hat by the terrible "No opera to-night," which was hung out in front of the Academy on Monday. *Ernani* was to have been done for Major Susini, but Stigelli kept his mouth open while riding on the rail through Jersey, and couldn't sing; Colson was not pretty well, either; Gazzaniga was quite sure she was sick; Brignoli couldn't be found, and little Patti was entering the Philadelphian additions on her roll of victims.

So the first night was Tuesday, *Don Giovanni*. An immense bore. Ten-inch, at least, and would kill at four miles off. Why don't some one, say Burkhardt, edit *Don Giovanni,* and put the *La ci darem*, the *Batti! batti!* and the *Vedrai carino,* all in the first act? Then people could go away comfortably at half-past nine, instead of having to wait till eleven, and then to go home in a disagreeable state of mind.

Patti's *Zerlina* was a pleasant, naive performance. Next to Piccolomini, Patti is the most charming Zerlina that I remember.

She however had the audacity to introduce in the *Batti! batti!* a cadenza which cannot be found in the score.

That's sacrilege, and the Mozartists were furious.

I suggest that the prima donna shall be compelled to undergo the following course of German :

First to hear the whole of the *Tannhauser;* second to study Schlegel on the old Greeks; third to commit to memory and repeat the *Dispatch* criticism on the *Magic Flute*; and lastly to embrace the critic of the *Staats Zeitung.*

I think after that, if she survived, she would not dare to take any liberties with Mozart's score.

It is painful to reflect, however, upon so striking an instance of the degeneracy of the age, or the youth, rather, and still more dreadful to notice that the public uphold the criminal as they did on Thursday, when Patti had her benefit, and was bouqueted, and caressed, and applauded, almost to death.

The "Little One," as the amiable Strakosch calls her, is going now to Boston.

Going to Boston! just as if it was not cold enough here.

But let us give to Cæsar the things that are Cæsar's, provided we don't want them ourselves.

Boston is a good place for the Opera.

Boston is, next to New York, the most catholic city in the Union when the question of art comes to be considered.

And I conjure my fellow-townsmen (sum civis Atheniensis), by

Faneuil Hall, by the State House, by the Common, by Everett, and Holmes, and Lowell, and Longfellow, by Ticknor & Fields, by the Parker House, and by Cambridge, to receive Patti handsomely. She is prime commercial paper, with first rate collateral security, and does not absolutely need your endorsement, but would be grateful for it.

And O! ye Juniors which are the salt of the University, see to it, that Patti has the adoration which Alma Mater hath always accorded to artistic triumphs. And thou Pater Familias, who, as a Senior in 1849, went wild about Amalia Patti, be now discreetly enthusiastic about Adelina, who has make the Oldest Man a raving and incomprehensible idiot, and brought on such an attack of the gout, that Carnochan says he must never have any more Burgundy or Green Seal.

Bless you, my child, bless you; and run along to Boston.

And now, Effendi, as I shall not address the readers of The Saturday Press again until next year, I will take this opportunity to offer the usual compliments of the season to all the people who "see" the Feuilleton, and to wish speedy reformation to those who don't.

To the youths I would recommend the practice of the moral virtues, and particularly that of modesty, during the festive season. To the medieval philosophers I have nothing to say; they will do well enough by themselves.

And to Bohemia, all hail!

It is your Carnival. You are wanted at dinners and suppers, and receptions without end. You are the crême de la crême when there is any fun going on. To the men I will suggest the propriety of preserving a proper dignity when associating with people in trade, and never look at a man under a hundred thousand. You will be careful to impress upon the mind of such a person the littleness of all earthly possessions, and to let him know, while you drink his Lafitte and eat his pâté de foies gras, that there are some things which money cannot buy.

And as for the Bohémiennes, I will leave them to the Queen of that land, the only free community on the face of the earth. Free, because released from the shackles of conventionality; free, because recognizing no divine right, except that of mental superiority, which is really divine; free, on account of a variety of other things which I haven't time to mention.

Vive Bohemia !
Vive la Reine!

Tres devoué,

Personne.

For the New York Saturday Press.

THE FEAST NIGHT OF THE TWO QUEENS.

BY CHARLES DESMARAIS.

I.

Last night was a Queen's Feast-night,
The Queen of the timid stars
That tremble in legions of scintillant light
Around the red pennon of Mars!

II.

Yes! last night the Moon-Queen won
Her maidenhood's richest prime;
And her radiant face snatched a kiss from the Sun,
To illumine the night-march of Time!

I.

Last night was a Queen's Feast-night,
The Queen of my Life—my Love!
The planet that thrills me with throbbing delight,
As the Moon thrills the ether above!

II.

Yes! last night my Heart-Queen won
Her maidenhood's furthest goal;
And her kisses still glow, like a central Sun
Through the innermost night of my soul!

Dec. 12th, 1859.

For The Saturday Press.

ALONE BY THE HEARTH.

BY GEORGE ARNOLD.

I.

Here, in my snug little fire-lit chamber,
Sit I alone;
And, as I gaze in the coals, I remember
Days long agone.

II.

Saddening it is when the night has descended,
Thus to sit here,
Pensively musing on episodes, ended
Many a year.

III.

Still in my visions a golden-haired glory
Flits to and fro;
She whom I loved—but 'tis just the old story—
Dead, long ago!

IV.

'Tis but the wraith of a love; yet I linger
(Thus passion errs),
Foolishly kissing the ring on my finger—
Once it was hers.

V.

Nothing has changed since her spirit departed,
Here in this room—
Save I, who, weary, and half broken-hearted,
Sit in the gloom.

VI.

Loud 'gainst the window the Winter-rain dashes,
Dreary and cold;
Over the floor the red fire-light flashes
Just as of old.

VII.

Just as of old—but the embers are scattered,
Whose ruddy blaze
Flashed o'er the floor where her fairy feet pattered
In other days!

VIII.

Then, her dear voice, like a silver-chime ringing,
Melted away;
Often these walls have reëchoed her singing,
Now hushed for aye!

IX.

Why should love bring nought but sorrow, I wonder?
Everything dies!
Time and Death sooner or later must sunder
Holiest ties.

X.

Years have rolled by; I am wiser and older—
Wiser, but yet
Not till my heart and its feelings grow colder,
Can I forget.

XI.

So, in my snug little fire-lit chamber,
Sit I, alone,
And, as I gaze in the coals, I remember
Joys long agone!

[For The Saturday Press.

LEAVES FROM NATURE.

'Tis Winter, and Nature sleeps. Strong trees stand stripped of their foliage; weak plants are withered and dead. Birds cease to gladden the day with their song; sweet flowers no longer perfume the air with their fragrance. Ice, formed by chill Winter's air, impedes the flowing of the little streams; and the grass that once made the meadows green and beautiful, has hid its tall head, and left them bare and naked. Every sign has gone that could remind us that once Nature was full of life and freshness—save the blooming Evergreen, which, notwithstanding the freezing cold, always stands bright and cheerful amid the surrounding gloom, like a smile of the Comforter to a troubled soul.

But Nature is talking to us in her sleep.

Listen to what she says:

All men have sorrows. There are times when they are sad and disheartened; and as the trees and plants are now stripped of their foliage, so do men sometimes seem to lose all their earthly comforts. Friends desert them, like the birds who go away in Winter; and cease to comfort or aid them, like the flowers that no longer perfume the air. Without friends, and with scarcely any hope, their time slowly passes on, like the icebound streams. Life seems sad and dreary, like the meadows that were once beautiful. Yet there is always left to them one bright, happy thought—*Right!* Consciousness of Right—*the blooming Evergreen.*

R. W. P.

[For The Saturday Press.

TO THE WATER-LILY.

BY N. G. SHEPHERD.

Queen of the lake, where, mirror'd in the tide,
Thy modest image views the pictured sky,
How gently past thy matchless form I glide,
Flower of the snowflake leaf and golden eye.

Emblem of what is pure, I look on thee
As something holy, shaped by hand divine;
Thou piece of rarest sculpture, made to be
Bride of the waters, bowing at thy shrine.

From out the womb of yonder cloud afar,
That rears its billowy breast against the blue,
Thou seem'st to have fallen, like a silver star,
Let loose from God's right hand, then fixed anew.

This lesson do I learn from thee, fair flower,
That I, while journeying toward my destined end,
May point some thoughts to that celestial bower,
Whence we are come, and whither we all tend.

NEW YORK JANUARY 7, 1860

WALT WHITMAN'S NEW POEM.

[From the Cincinnati Commercial.]

The author of "Leaves of Grass" has perpetrated another "poem." The N. Y. Saturday Press, in whose columns, we regret to say, it appears, calls it "a curious warble." Curious, it may be; but warble it is not, in any sense of that mellifluous word. It is a shade less heavy and vulgar than the "Leaves of Grass," whose unmitigated badness seemed to cap the climax of poetic nuisances. But the present performance has all the emptiness, without half the grossness, of the author's former efforts.

How in the name of all the Muses this so-called "poem" ever got into the columns of the Saturday Press, passes our poor comprehension. We had come to look upon that journal as the prince of literary weeklies, the *arbiter elegantiarum* of dramatic and poetic taste, into whose well-filled columns nothing stupid or inferior could intrude. The numerous delicious poems; the sparkling *bons mots*; the puns, juicy and classical, which almost redeemed that vicious practice, and raised it to the rank of a fine art; the crisp criticisms, and delicate dramatic humors of "Personne," and the charming piquancies of the *spirituelle* Ada Clare—all united to make up a paper of rare excellence. And it is into this gentle garden of the Muses that that unclean cub of the wilderness, Walt Whitman, has been suffered to intrude, trampling with his vulgar and profane hoofs among the delicate flowers which bloom there, and soiling the spotless white of its fair columns with lines of stupid and meaningless twaddle.

The numerous delicious poems; the sparkling *bons mots*; the puns, juicy and classical, which almost redeemed that vicious practice, and raised it to the rank of a fine art; the crisp criticisms, and delicate dramatic humors of "Personne," and the charming piquancies of the *spirituelle* Ada Clare—all united to make up a paper of rare excellence. And it is into this gentle garden of the Muses that that unclean cub of the wilderness, Walt Whitman, has been suffered to intrude, trampling with his vulgar and profane hoofs among the delicate flowers which bloom there, and soiling the spotless white of its fair columns with lines of stupid and meaningless twaddle.

Perhaps our readers are blissfully ignorant of the history and achievements of Mr. Walt Whitman. Be it known, then, that he is a native and resident of Brooklyn, Long Island, born and bred in an obscurity from which it were well that he never had emerged. A person of coarse nature, and strong, rude passions, he has passed his life in cultivating, not the amenities, but the rudenesses of character; and instead of tempering his native ferocity with the delicate influences of art and refined literature, he has studied to exaggerate his deformities, and to thrust into his composition all the brute force he could muster from a capacity not naturally sterile in the elements of strength. He has undertaken to be an artist, without learning the first principle of art, and has presumed to put forth "poems," without possessing a spark of the poetic faculty. He affects swagger and independence, and blurts out his vulgar impertinence under a full assurance of "originality."

In his very first performance, this truculent tone was manifested. He exaggerated every sentiment, and piled up with endless repetition every epithet, till the reader grew weary, even to nausea, of his unmeaning rant. He announced himself to the world as a new and striking thinker, who had something to reveal. His "Leaves of Grass" were a revelation from the Kingdom of Nature. Thus he screams to a gaping universe:

"I, Walt Whitman, an American, one of the roughs, a Cosmos; I shout my voice high and clear over the waves; I send my barbaric yawp over the roofs of the world !"

Such was the style of his performance, only it was disfigured by far worse sins of morality than of taste. Never, since the days of Rabelais was there such literature of uncleanness as some portions of this volume exhibited. All that is beautiful and sacred in love was dragged down to the brutal plane of animal passion, and the writer appeared to revel in language fit only for the lips of the Priapus of the old mythology.

We had hoped that the small reception accorded to his first performance had deterred Mr. Whitman from fresh trespasses in the realms of literature. Several years had passed away, his worse than worthless book had been
forgotten, and we hoped that this Apollo of the Brooklyn marshes had returned to his native mud. But we grieve to say he revived last week, and although somewhat changed, changed very little for the better. We do not find so much that is offensive, but we do find a vast amount of irreclaimable drivel and inexplicable nonsense.

We have searched this "poem" through with the serious and deliberate endeavor to find out the reason of its being written; to discover some clue to the mystery of so vast an expenditure of words. But we honestly confess our utter inability to solve the problem. It is destitute of all the elements which are commonly desiderated in poetical composition; it has neither rhythm nor melody, rhyme nor reason, metre nor sense. We do solemnly assert, that there is not to be discovered, throughout the whole performance, so much as the glimmering ghost of an idea. Here is the poem, which the author, out of his characteristic perversity, insists upon calling the Pre-verse:

"Out of the rocked cradle,
Out of the mocking-bird's throat, the musical shuttle,
Out of the boys's mother's womb, and from the nipples of her breasts,
Out of the Ninth-Month midnight,
Over the sterile sea-sands, and the fields beyond, where the child, leaving his bed, wandered alone, bareheaded, barefoot,
Down from the showered halo and the moonbeams,
Up from the mystic play of shadows twining and twisting as if they were alive,
Out from the patches of briars and blackberries,
From the memories of the bird that chanted to me,
From your memories, sad brother—from the fitful risings and fallings I heard,
From that night, infantile, under the yellow half-moon, late-risen, and swollen as if with tears,
From those beginning notes of sickness and love, there in the mist,
From the thousand responses in my heart, never to cease,
From the myriad thence-aroused words,
From the word stronger and more delicious than any,
From such, as now they start, the scene revisiting,
As a flock, twittering, rising, or overhead passing,
Borne hither—ere all eludes me, hurriedly,
A man—yet by these tears a little boy again,
Throwing myself on the sand, I,
Confronting the waves, sing."

This is like nothing we ever heard of in literature, unless it be the following lucid and entertaining composition:

"Once there was an old woman went into the garden to get some cabbage to make an apple pie. Just then a great she-bear comes up and pops his head into the shop, 'What, no soap !' So he died, and she married the barber; and there was present at the wedding the Jicaninies and the Piccaninies, and the Grand Panjandrum himself, with the little round button at the top; and they all fell to playing the game of catch as catch can, till the gunpowder ran out of the heels of their boots."

The "poem" goes on, after the same maudlin manner, for a hundred lines or more, in which the interjection "O" is employed about five-and-thirty times, until we reach the following gem :

> "Never again leave me to be the peaceful child I was before; what there, in the night,
> By the sea, under the yellow and sagging moon,
> The dusky demon aroused, the fire, the sweet hell within
> The unknown want, the destiny of me."
>
> O, but this is bitter bad!
>
> "O give me some clue!
> O if I am to have so much, let me have more!
> O a word! O what is my destination?
> O I fear it is henceforth chaos !"

There is not a doubt of it, we do assure you! And, what is more, it never was anything else. Now, what earthly object can there be in writing and printing such unmixed and hopeless drivel as that? If there were any relief to the unmeaning monotony, some glimpse of fine fancy, some oasis of sense, some spark of "the vision and the faculty divine," we would not say a word. But we do protest, in the name of the sanity of the human intellect, against being invited to read such stuff as this, by its publication in the columns of a highly respectable literary journal. What is the comment of the Saturday Press itself on the "poem'? It says:

> "Like the 'Leaves of Grass,' the purport of this wild and plaintive song, well enveloped, and eluding definition, is positive and unquestionable, like the effect of music. The piece will bear reading many times—perhaps, indeed, only comes forth, as from recesses, by many repetitions."

Well, Heaven help us, then, for as we are a living man, we would not read that poem "many times" for all the poetry that was ever perpetrated since the morning stars sang together. "Well enveloped, and eluding definition." Indeed! We should think so. For our part, we hope it will remain "well enveloped till doomsday; and as for "definition," all we can do in that direction is to declare that either that "poem" is nonsense, or we are a lunatic.

If any of the tuneful Nine have ever descended upon Mr. Walt Whitman, it must have been long before that gentleman reached the present sphere of existence. His amorphous productions clearly belong to that school which it said that neither gods nor men can endure. There is no meaning discoverable in his writings, and if there were, it would most certainly not be worth the finding out. He is the laureate of the empty deep of the incomprehensible; over that immortal limbo described by Milton, he has stretched the drag-net of his genius; and as he has no precedent and no rival, so we venture to hope that he will never have an imitator.

THE QUARTETTE.

BY ORTHRON.

Kingsley Gerald loved music! If Riverside had been nearer to New York, or New York nearer to Riverside, Mr. Ullmann had been a richer man. But Kingsley lived out of town. Otherwise, his twenty-five cents would have enriched the treasury every Opera night. Twenty-five cents, because in our Academy of Music the third circle is far the best place for hearing; and so Kingsley would have sacrificed his feelings to the cause of High Art, and at the same time treated his pocket with that kind consideration which it demanded. But stern Fate spared him this sacrifice, and demanded a still greater one. Therefore he lived out of town, where good music was heard only semi-occasionally.

It happened one night, however, that Kingsley was invited out to meet some friends. Musical friends, with other musical friends, come down from the city to spend the holidays. The party met, and Kingsley's heart—a warm, eager, fiery, soft, melting heart, under a cold exterior—was in a state of delicious preparation. For, lo! and behold! one of the singers was a young and beautiful woman! That was not all. He had met her once before; and that under the same circumstances, a few years ago, when she was a blushing, unmarried girl. Music and beauty on that former occasion had stirred his heart; but it had all been forgotten since. Now it came back to him with double force.

Kingsley talked to everybody, took it upon himself to answer every remark of the fair one, and followed her warmly with his eyes.

They sang! But somehow or other, he only thought of the fair Soprano. The deep Bass seemed to be doing its best to uphold and support the beautiful young spirit that was taking its flight in song! The rich Alto followed closely, and seemed murmuring words of sisterly counsel and encouragement. While the Tenor seemed to hover about it fondly, in sad, complaining, loving adoration!

Altogether, the music sank into their hearts, and Kingsley only kept the tears out of his eyes by applauding vehemently, and talking vigorously to the Soprano, during the pauses.

What business had he to fall in love? Who said he fell in love? He didn't!

She was a married woman. When he saw her before, she was a blushing maiden; now she was wedded, and had a little babe, of a few months old, sleeping safely in its cradle, utterly unconscious of its mother's musical tendencies. What business had he to fall in love? Yes! But she was young, now! Not childish, not too dignified, not brilliant, but young, and sweet, and lively, with a beautiful face and form,—a mother, —and altogether the dearest, most wifely little creature possible!

They sang all the evening. They went away. She put her soft, warm, ungloved hand in his, Kingsley thought, in a way that was earnest and tender.

He walked home in a sort of musical, poetical, loving, longing, sad, somnambulistic revery. The house was shut up,—people gone to bed. He sat down in the sittingroom by the fire, with only one light burning. If it had been Summer, and moonlight, he would have gone down to the beach, and watched the sky. It was too cold for poetizing outdoors, so he sat by the fire.

There he did fall in love! Imagined himself taking a last farewell—whispering in her ear that he wished the music could last forever—the quartette being changed to a duett, and they two the performers! Then he did fall in love, and got jealous of the Tenor (her husband), who played the piano, had very dirty hands and finger-nails, and a very black, dirty shirtcollar! Then he thought it might be the music; but dropped that thought, and fell in love again; when the idea popped into his brain that the Tenor looked very thin and pale, and perhaps he might die some day! Who knows? But he couldn't bear the idea of having that first child sickly through hereditary succession, so he abandoned that idea. Then he fancied that the Tenor, having a very sensitive nature, had realized so fully his utter unworthiness of the love of the Soprano, and felt so deeply the complete absurdity of any attempt to appreciate or return her love, that he was languishing away in despair. This made him sad a little; but he soon revived, and wished that in mercy he might be saved from the pain and grief of such a languishing, lingering illness, by a sudden death!

Then he bemoaned his own desolate condition, his lonely room; pictured to himself fireside-scenes, domestic happiness, conjugal bliss, etc., etc. (Sure signs throughout, that he wasn't in love with any person, but only with married life!) Then he worked himself into a fever, and shed a few tears! Thinking, before his eyes were dry, that "tears" rhymed with " years,' and then going through a series of curious intellectual gymnastics, beginning somewhat as follows: "Tears! Tears! These idle tears! Years! Years! These long, sad years! I love! I long! I faint!"

All this time his eyes were getting dryer; and having fortified himself against getting faint, by going down in the cellar, and eating a big piece of apple-pie, he came back, and once more went through the same intellectual gymnastics. (All of this being a sure sign that he wasn't in love!) Finally (surest sign of all!) he rushed into the library, seized pen and paper, and wrote:

Was it the Song or the Singer?

I.

Was it the Song or the Singer,
That filled my heart with pain?
Was it she, or her sweet music,
Her beauty, or the strain ?

II.

Wildly my heart is still throbbing
With love or deep delight!
And my soul has been moved deeply,
By magic power this night !

III.

Was it the beautiful Singer?
I must not see her more!
She was found by one more happy,—
Would we had met before !

IV.

Was it that musical sweetness?
Alas! if that were right,
I would set my heart to music,
And sing it through the night!

V.

Was it the beautiful Singer?
Ah! then I cannot rest
Till she shares this soft, sweet sadness,
And nestles on my breast !

VI.

Was it the musical chiming
Of voices sweet and low?
If her voice should say "*I love you* !"
'Twould be more sweet, I know!

VII.

Was it that tenderest Music?
Ah! no! my heart is deep!
It was she! the beauteous Singer,
That roused my soul from sleep!

VIII.

She is personified Music!
That low, soft, cooing Dove!
She will coo to me sweet, some day yet,
"Darling! I love! I love !"

Years—long years rolled around, and the Poet and she—No! they didn't do anything of the kind!

I suppose you would like to have me tell now, how for many a long year the Poet cherished her image in his breast, and didn't see her. How he moved about strangely and sadly for a time, as if some mystery enshrouded him, and then suddenly disappeared. How a mysterious stranger appeared in Rome—rich as Croesus or John Jacob Astor,—patronized all the Artists, and helped the American ones,—was a painter, sculptor, poet, etc., etc., etc., himself,—joined Garibaldi, and received a sabre-cut upon his bronzed cheek, and finally disappeared as mysteriously as he came. How the same individual, with slouched hat, big whiskers, and sabre-cut upon his bronzed cheek, dropped down in New York. How one day, as he walked down a dark and narrow street, he heard a familiar voice singing an old song, long out of date, called: "Was it the Song or the Singer?"—How gazing upward he saw a pale, thin face, sweet in its thinness, looking out from an attic window, where a single rose-tree was growing in a flowerpot on a shelf. How he enquired of the old woman in the cellar, who told him that the lady had come there long ago—how she grew thinner and thinner, and was so poor that she worked on a patent Fifteen-Dollar Sewing-Machine!

Then, how delicately he relieved her condition, and substituted (unknown to her!) a splendid Wheeler & Wilson for the Patent cheap Sewing-Machine! How finally he made himself known to her; and like that dear, good soul in Vanity Fair (not the new comic paper, but Thackeray's Vanity Fair!) Col. Sugar Plums, otherwise called Dobbin, clasped the children to his arms (there were more than one, now!) the widow to his heart, and was happy ever afterward!

No! We don't intend even to hint at such a thing!

It wasn't so!

Kingsley went to bed, and tossed to and fro throughout the night upon his weary couch. (He had eaten another piece of apple-pie after finishing the Poem!) The fit lasted for two or three days, and he moved about in an abstracted, dreamy way; turning around, however, to look at every woman he saw in the street with a small child in her arms. Then the idea seized him, and he made a practical application of his love, by going to one of the popular Musicians, and engaging him to compose a tune expressly for this new Poem called: "Was it the Song or the Singer?" The popular Musician hunted through his store of German music till he found a tune which fitted the words, and which was so old and poor that he thought it must be unknown, and thereupon composed it expressly for the new Poem. It was published! And Kingsley gave out the words were by Gen. Geo. P. somebody or other, the famous Poet who wrote "Scribbler! Spare thy Rhymes!" The popular Musician, Rudolph Heinfetter Steelaleetle (who was only a poor little, miserable, American, Musical Bohemian, with a false German name!) had his name printed upon it in the biggest letters. The music, itself, was of the poorest, shallowest, dullest description.

All these things taken in connection, made the Song sell, of course! Soon it became the most popular song of the day, and was transplanted to foreign soil in the pages of an English Song-Book, where it was made to exemplify the musical genius of America, and became fashionable in the London drawingrooms.

Kingsley had it conveyed to the fair Soprano, anonymously, taking good care that she knew where it came from. He called to see her husband on business shortly after, at the house,—in the evening, and she sung it for him with so much feeling, that he nearly went down on his knees before them both. He didn't though!

He went away. Yes! he was called off suddenly to California, or Oregon, or Kansas—some place or other where there wasn't any women.

He came back. Stayed at home two days, and finding that the Soprano had moved out of town, on the line of some Railroad, resolved deliberately to go and visit her. It was Winter. There was a Freight-Train off the track, and about twenty miles from the city, Kingsley Gerald, and the Railroad cars came to a stand still. They waited there two hours,—only. Kingsley had read in a newspaper, while away, that there had been an addition of four at one birth to the family of T. Singer, Esq. Somehow or other that thought occupied pretty much all of the two hours. He had not seen the statement in next day's paper, that this was a hoax. That four kittens only were added to the family. Still he thought of what he had heard. He reached Bleak Hill about 11 P.M., half frozen. The fair Soprano was up, the youngest child being sick, (teething maybe!) She called her husband, who let him in. The kitchen-range was slightly warm yet, so he thawed out there as much as possible, and then went to bed. It was a small room. There was a window at the head of his bed—a window at one side a window at the foot—and at the other side, a window, opening into a bleak garret, where the wind howled.

That night the mercury went down to fourteen below zero!

The cover was thin. Kingsley thought of the newspaper paragraph—remembered that it was the anniversary of the famous Quartette night—remembered and thought of pretty much everything, in fact; as he wasn't at all troubled with sleep. He came downstairs next morning with his hair very rough, and his hands unwashed; having demolished the hair-brush in his attempts to break through the ice in the pitcher.

The fair Soprano appeared in the morning, as bright as could be expected after a sleepless night. (Sick child-teething maybe!) But they had to breakfast by candlelight—the train started before sunrise—and the cars were just reached by the most unceremonious departure, and the hardest scrabbling.

Kingsley Gerald's love for the fair Soprano froze solid that night. It never thawed out again! His reflections we cannot describe. Suffice it to say, there was one question under a thousand forms: "What is Love? Is it impulse, or feeling, or association, or passion, or admiration, or heat? Which?"

One thing we can say. Kingsley repented of his sin in misleading the hearts of thousands by his false and foolish song, and did his best to atone for that crime. He wrote:

Beware! Youth! Beware!

I.

There's a charm and a joy in her lips of rose,
In her ringlets, soft and light;
In her eye that one moment with passion glows,
And then softens, sadly bright!
But beware! Youth! Beware!
It is Music hath charmed thy sober thought!
Feel as you may—but think as you ought!
Beware! Youth! Beware!

II.

There's a charm and a joy in her youthful face,
Where the blushes make their nest!
In the lines and the curvings of dainty grace,
And the heaving of her breast!
But beware! Youth! Beware! etc.

III.

There's a charm and a joy in the female form!
There's a charm in Music, too!
You may give to the maiden your thoughts most warm,
But give Music all its due!
And beware! Youth! Beware! etc.

IV.

You've a thought and a dream of some maiden fair,
Who shall all you most love be!
But look out! it is Music hath laid a snare !
And look close! this is not she!
So beware! Youth! Beware! etc.

V.

There's a magical charm in the tender dream
Of a maiden, dear and true!
But all maidens like visions of true love seem,
When sweet Music thrills you through!
So beware! Youth! Beware! etc.

VI.

There's a magical charm to the tender heart
In a maiden, fair and young!
But O! think not the Singer had all the art!
"Twas the song that you heard sung!
So beware! Youth! Beware!
It is Music hath charmed thy sober thought!
Feel as you may—but think as you ought!
Beware! Youth! Beware!

Kingsley determined that this recantation should be more widely read than his first false song. So he deserted entirely the popular Musician, Rudolph Henifetter Steelaleetle,—wrote the Music for it himself, published, and advertised it widely.

As the tune was really a fine one, and as the poem contained a truth and a moral, of course it fell flat and cold upon the public ear. Kingsley paid for his advertising in advance, read all the puffs (duly paid for) in the papers, and one day walked up to the publishers to get the proceeds of his new and popular song. When he came out, he walked hastily down Broadway, turned into a side street, and finally, reaching the river, rushed frantically—upon the boat for Riverside!

Kingsley Gerald astonished his mother and sisters for the next week, by his ghastly, harrowing countenance and the quantity of dinner he made way with.

He published no more songs!

○ ○ ○ ○ ○ ○ ○

Moral.—Never imagine yourself in love, or propose while under the influence of Music!

Moral No. 2.—Poetic inspiration is the Music of the soul. If you write Poetry in the full swell of this poetic inspiration, don't publish till it has had time to cool, and you have had time to read it coolly, under usual, commonplace circumstances.

Beware! Youth! Beware!
It is Music hath charmed thy sober thought!
Feel what you may—but think what you ought!
Beware! Youth! Beware!

Thoughts and Things.

BY ADA CLARE.

The *Atlantic Monthly* publishes the first number of a serial story by Miss Preston, entitled "The Amber Gods." I am so dazzled by a reading of the first number, that I hardly dare express my opinion of it. So much splendor gives rise to distrust in my mind. Is there no redundance in all this blaze of glowing rhetoric, in this passionate outpouring of wildering words, in this sensuous eloquence of poetic fervor? I hope not; I hope all the glory of light in this un-metred poem radiates from the illimitable sun-star. But the author must not blind us with unshadowed radiance. Masses of lustrous blue, heaped upon the passionate eagerness of crimson, and that again upon the majesty of proud purple, floating tremulous upon the radiate pulses of pure light, through whose fiery gaps and golden chasms sound in the heavenly distance stops of planetary music. But the eye and the heart grow sick and languid with ravishment, and turn towards the distant grey, through whose solemn monotone shines the faint tremor of stars.

Thus far the "Amber Gods" is worthy of being set beside Madame George Sand's "Lelia," to my mind the most wonderful book in the French language.

°°°

Last night I was present at Arthur Napoleon's benefit. No true lover of music can afford to be indifferent to this young artist. He has done much to ennoble the noblest of instruments. I do not envy the cold impassibility of that man or woman who could listen unmoved to the sweeps of melody that drop pearl-like from his fingers.

How high he stands above many of those engineer-pianists, whom the Press loveth to honor; the perfect execution of Mills, for instance, seems to me, to be many fathoms below his pure spirituality of harmony. His school of performance is that of that matchless poet-musician, that very Apollo of the piano,—Gottschalk.

Closing my eyes last night, I could often imagine that the music was wrought by the sacred and illustrious hands of Gottschalk himself. In saying that, have I not drained the cup of praise to its utmost deeps? I think so.

I liked the Comedy of "Everybody's Friend," at Wallack's. The critics are inexorable; so, they say, are the best judges. But I think the first province of a comedy is to be comic, which that, to my mind, illimitably is. It has given me more cause for laughter, than any play I have seen since the "Faux Bonshommes" in Paris. Mr. Brougham played the part of a highbred gentleman, of a bashful turn, which is the only part, leaving out the bashfulness, that I think he is fitted to play. The part of low, ragged, roaring Irishmen, I hate to see him enact. It is putting himself on a level with such fellows as Florence.

Mr. Brougham can neither look nor act the ill-bred man. That handsome, manly face, that rich, sweet voice, that fine figure, ere given to him with a different view. He is the most influential man on the stage in New York, and his is the power to exalt and refine his art. Then why waste himself in farces and jigs?

°°°

I am often accused of mistaking wit for humor. I wonder if I am not a slandered being.

I think two indispensable qualities of humor are tact and good-nature. Whenever a thing becomes bitter, I cannot think it humorous. It becomes satire or perhaps wit.

The true humorist takes not only the comic but the good-natured view of his subject. In all his pleasantry he is sure to wound no feeling. His tact is an instinct to teach him in what direction and how far he shall go.

I have heard men wonder that humor and pathos should be found united in the same mind. I not only think that where humor is found there is pathos, but I think the former cannot exist without the latter. Humor floats and swims joyously about on the winds of lightness and pleasure; its green leaves and its twinkling flowers riot in the sun; but their stems run deeply down and strike themselves upon a grave, earnest root, from which pours up the bright sap of their life.

He who stumbles clumsily in his sport-making on the deep sensibilities of those with whom he sports, wounding and irritating those sensibilities, displays in so doing, not humor, but the total ignorance even of what humor is. He who plays upon the physical or mental deformities, the misfortunes or errors of early life, the beliefs, aspirations, or heart-wounds of his companions, may play upon a pipe; but though he may fret Humor, he cannot play upon *her.* Comedy has no kiss for the chill, white lips of cruelty and pain. A single drop of blood drowns the laughter in every eye.

We are told that the cruel bull-fights of Spain were much patronized by women. We are told, also, that on them waited the signal of relief to the wretched human victim, over whom the infuriate animal had gained the victory. There is no record, however, that my sex displayed much merriment at this entertainment. Nay, I know they held up no calm hands to arrest the cruel proceeding; their white and shivering fingers sprang nervously up, with blue and blood-suppressed nails, more in entreaty than in fashion.

Humor is the true "reduction to the absurd," of the false social problem. When the foolish human throat wears itself out with shrieking its pitiful platitudes about talent, and love, and women, and religion, humor takes pride in displaying the ludicrous side of the argument.

When that pompous little frog-convention strives to swell itself out into the majestic proportions of truth, humor loves to paint its funny little strut of ceremony, its grotesque affectation of puny dignity and command. It even leads heavy-footed truth to the spot where that poor reptile is crawling. Truth, the all-crushing, puts its foot down upon it, there is a gurgling sound, the reptile convention turns over, its horrid little legs writhe for a moment, then hang damp and limber, and it is given over to decay.

When men argue about the incapacity of women, with the works of George Sand and Elizabeth Browning and Charlotte Bronté and Jane Austen and Rosa Bonheur under their eyes, of what avail will it be to argue with them? If a man insists that the sun shines not when he is at the very moment blinded by striving to look at it, there will be no logic strong enough to convince him. But in either of the two cases it would be easy to convey to him a ludicrous view of his unbelief. You might ask him, who refuses to acknowledge the shining of the sun, to illume a farthing dip, and with that to throw the sun into shadow. Or you might ask him, who refuses to believe in woman's genius, to set his own little tattling powers in comparison with the vast abilities of the women I have mentioned.

I heard a linen-draper's clerk, all side-whiskers and simper, declare that the woman and man together were a whole, but the woman was one-fourth and the man three-fourths of the whole. While he made this remark his eyes were fixed on the superb form of the Cortesi. It was at the moment of one of her finest tragic efforts; her face blazed with latent passions, while along the thunder of her voice, her lambient eyes shook their fires like lightnings.

I thought of the long dapper gentleman, whisker, simper, and all, weighed in the balance against the grand prima donna, and the idea was adorably comic. It was like putting Mount Etna in one balance, and a good, fat pumpkin in the other. If he could have seen himself in this humorous light, I am sure he could never have made such a comic remark again.

The true humorist must be a gentleman by nature. The vulgar and illbred man can have a coarse wit, but he cannot be a humorist. Delicacy and refinement, I believe, are necessary to the vitality of humor. Whatever fund of comicality a story may have in itself, it may be undone by coarse words or vulgar allusions in telling it. From being funny it immediately sinks into disgusting harshness. Humor, in taking hold of coarse subjects, must refine and take the corrupting principle from them, else she had better keep her hands pure from their contact. When the jokes become "broad" around the convivial table, good feeling and real enjoyment go out, and all truly sensitive hearts are smitten with sadness. All genial minds abhor the vulgar and obscene in whatever light they choose to present themselves; they know them to undermine, wherever they are, the illumined foundation of amusement.

If every mind were delicate and refined, could the passion of love know any satiety? I believe not. This humor, which I for my own poor part love to honor, is not the harlequin's art, not the mere laughter of fools. I have called it the glittering flower, whose root strikes deep into the earth, but its eye is fixed upward. Even while it plays in the sweet airs, it yearns towards the sun. So humor is seldom without an earnest aim. Tears often glisten beneath its laughter. It not only sports with the follies of life, but it aims to inscribe its solemn memorial of right and good on the pages of the world's melancholy history.

[For The Saturday Press.

THE NEW-BORN.

The sky was arching over me to-day,
    This Sunday morn,
As deep and clear as it will be, I pray,
To that dear little one, who, yet unborn,
    Struggled to find his way
Into the life the preachers call forlorn.

I paced my little garden, built around
    With city walls,
But so protected by them, I have found,
Even in Winter, that the sunlight calls
From the damp, chilly, and unwilling ground,
    As here at noon it falls,
The same sweet flowers that in June abound.

The distant chimes rang out upon the air,
    Their Sunday hymn,
Of faith and hope in His protecting care,
    Whose eye is never dim,—
Who lovingly has placed his children here,
And comforts them if they will trust in Him.

The swelling tones from out the distant spire,
    Now loud, now low—
Sinking to silence, and then rising higher,
Seemed to my anxious heart as though
    They sang the strong desire
And need we feel for love, while here below.

While musing thus, the church across the way—
    Where one can hear
Only the terrors of the judgment day,
The wrath of God, the cause we have to fear
His cruel power, which for his vengeance may
    Condemn my infant there
To the hell-fire, which nothing can allay—

Commenced to toll its harsh, discordant bell,
    Marring the song
Of faith, of hope, of love, the chimes would tell,
Of God's sweet mercy, suffering so long,
As though persistently it cried, "In hell
    It is that we belong,
Not where our Saviour and his Father dwell."

The jarring discord caused a bitter doubt,
    Whether or no
It was my heart that made the chimes ring out
Their trustful praise, so needed here below,
Or but the distance made them seem devout;
    While sadly doubting so,
About the world and life, I heard a shout:

"Come, sir, and see your new-born infant son,"
    The old nurse cried;
"O! may his life, this New Year's day begun,"
I said to the pale mother at his side—
"Be governed by the song the chimes have rung,"—
    She smiled with trustful pride—
"And when it ends, an angel song be sung!"

The Richest Woman in England Elopes with her Footman.—The London correspondent of the Manchester *Guardian* gives the following information in regard to the elopement of Mrs. J. H. Gurney with her footman:

The lady in question was the daughter of the late Richard Gurney, by whom she had a fortune of nearly £25,000 a-year, absolutely secured to herself. She was considered the richest married woman in England. All this fortune she is now free to dispose of as she likes—in enriching, if she chooses, the fortunate flunkey whom she has chosen for the partner of her flight. Her injured husband has already taken the first steps for obtaining a divorce, but such is the pressure of divorce business before Mr. Justice Cresswell's Court, that his solicitor has been informed, I am told, that fourteen months are likely to elapse before the case can be brought to issue.

Meanwhile, the affair is a great blow to the large and respectable Gurney connection—so well and widely known for its philanthropic activity, as well as its wealth.

[For The Saturday Press.

ROYAL AND RUSTIC.

BY HIRAM RICH.

I.

Your queen sits arrayed in imperial purple,
While flatterers fawn at her indolent feet;
Yet mine is as fair in her unadorned raiment
Her heart is as warm and her presence as sweet.

II.

Your queen hath her castles for Spring-time and Autumn,
Her gardens, where slave-tended daffodils bloom;
But mine rears the vine with the tenderest fingers—
Ah! the daintiest roses are those in her room.

III.

Your queen hath the fleetest and proudest of navies,
Silk-pennoned, but steeled in the might of their pride;
Mine hath but a shallop, though light as a lily,
Or dream-painted blossom, it graces the tide.

IV.

I doubt not your queen hath inherited glory,
Anon it will fall to one regal as she ;—
Some will deepen the purple that darkens the chancel,
While some will declare whose her sceptre shall be.

V.

My queen hath her own uninherited glory,
Ah! ne'er to be worn by one regal as she ;—
Fair maidens will meet, in the blush of the sunset,
Too sad to think—"Whose will her diadem be?'

Dramatic Feuilleton.

Sahara.

A dull week in the theatres. Dry times in the coulisses. A week for heavy dinners, jovial visits, much Bordeaux, and many pipes. A week for Anna Maria, rather than for Personne.

Ah, Effendi! you should see the Pearl of Manhattan's clothes, about these times. Mr. Butler's friend, Flora McFlimsey, wasn't a circumstance to her, this week.

There was a lovely, pearl-colored silk, with real Valenciennes flowers, the invoice of which (it came plumb from the Boulevart des Italiens) nearly set the governor wild; and ma thinks, between that and the cold weather, he's sure to have the gout, which will be still more expensive, as he won't allow anybody but A. M. to come near him then; and perhaps he won't have to pay for that,—oh, no! not at all, by no means, as Mr. Weller would say.

"What is that you say? Never mind A. M.! Tell us about the theatres!" Just tell *her* that, once.

I insist that the subject of A. M. is quite apropos to the theatres.

What would they do without the demoiselles charmantes, and the jeunesse dorée ?

And what are these ornamental classes of the community doing this week?

Do they see the theatres, compared with boned turkey, mayonnaise de volaille, Honiton, loto, flirtation, Russian quadrilles, the German cotillon, and vingt-et-un? No, indeed, and so the playhouse is given over to the children and the Peorians, who have to put up with Ravels, *Green Bushes*, and *The Octoroon*.

Apropos to *Green Bushes*, Celeste once told me a very good story about its performance in London. I will try to repeat it in her peculiar French-English.

Ah, oui, Monsieur, he is vara good play; I makes much moneys wiz him at ze Adelphi. Every night, before I go to my dressingroom, I tell my cab he stop before ze pit door, and I see up ze avis "pit" full. Zen I go to dress, bien satisfy because I know ze house good. Mais! I have one what you call skelton in my house. Ze two comiques was Misser Wright and Misser Bedford. Zey was bien amis, and haves all jokes to each oder. Ah, zey was so funny toujours. At ze repetitions, zey make me laugh to kill myself.

Well zey have vara short scene in quatrième act, where I comes down from ze rock, and have to lie as I was dead upon ze stage. I must arrest myself zare till zey have finished, and zen zey discouvere me. Bien ze first night zey behave ver vell, and discouvere me in two three minute. I zank Misser Wright, mais! helas! he wink wid his eye to Misser Bedford, and zen I know zere is cabal, and I was terrify. Ze second night zey have few gags, things you know vich is not in ze play, but vich make much the house to laugh. Ze next night zey have more gags, and pretty soon zey extend ze scene from two tree minutes to one half hour, and I must lie perdue all zat time. I become enragée! I command Misser Wright he no gag. He laugh and wink wid his eye to Misser Bedford. I beg him, and he cry, and he say it is Bedford, and zat Bedford is one méchant who lead him away, and zen he scold Bedford and zen zey go way wid their fingers on zeir nose.

Aprés ze piece was run two hundred nights, I take him off and go play him en province. Aprés some times I revive him in London, and on Thursday I put up ze notice for ze répétition générale on Saturday; ze performance on Monday.

Misser Wright he come to me in ze foyer, and he speaks wid me so :

"You are not, Madame, to do ze Green Bush next Monday."

"Oui, certainment, Misser Wright," I reply. "It is not possible, Madame," he say.

Why not?" I say.

"Simply because Misser Bedford and I have forgot to remember all ze gags."

Zen I say wiz ze grande air: "I do him," and I go home delighted, parfaitement. Zey forgot ze gags. I no have to stay on my back on ze stage while zey talk. We have two répétitions and no gags. O! I was joy ver much! Ze night come; and Mon Dieu! zey speak all ze gags which zey have before, and some ones new. I almost die wiz rage. I send for Misser Wright. I say to him, "Misser Wright, you tell me you forget ze gag for ze Green Bush, and mille de tonneres! you come on ze stage and speak zem all, while I am fatigued excessive."

"C'est vrai! Madame, repond le drôle. I did forget ze gag, but ze potboy he remembare zem all, and we learns zem from him."

It was one dam leetle pot-boy who brings ze biere to ze artiste, and who had tresor ze gag. I was so enragée I cry; and when I go to dress aprés, Misser Wright he send de salute pour Madame, and advise if she feel ver bad she put some more Cognac in her water before she go to bed, and take him warm.

Ze brigand!

A Husband to Order

Will have only a very brief existence at Wallack's, or any where else, for the matter of that.

I have seen something about one hundred nights in London; but that if true is not important. London runs don't amount to anything here, nowa-days.

A Husband to Order is a two-act comedy, *Un Mariage sous l'Empire*, clever but not brilliant. The public goes away from the performance only remembering that Mr. Lester's buckskins were irreproachable, and Mrs. Hoey's laces and diamonds the real thing.

The critics tell the public that Mrs. Hoey is an aristocratic French female, who has been compelled by the Emperor to marry a splendid looking fellow like Lester, who is parbleu! one of the middle class, but a Colonel in the Grand Army.

Now the fact is, a Colonel in the Army, in those days, condescended, when he married a broken down aristocrat.

But the contrary is the case with this Colonel. He is snubbed by his new wife, and resolves to leave her forever and ever.

But, like the subscriber, who has often swore a great oath never to see A. M., any more, and altered his mind when half a block away from her house, the Colonel comes back disguised in plain clothes, pumps the lady, ascertains that he is rated A. in her affections and retakes her to his bosom.

This is all very fine until you come to look at it closely. The quarrellings over the mésalliance is natural, perhaps inevitable. It occurs to-day as well in the Fifth avenue as in the Rue des Champs Elysées. But the form of the reconciliation is absurd. Mr. Lester was not disguised in any way, and would not have deceived any woman for a moment. Instead of dissolving she would have tormented him without mercy. There are two very well drawn minor characters in this piece, a jolly Brittany farmer admirably acted by Mr. Blake, and a Baron of the ancient régime, fairly played by Mr. Sloan.

Faits Divers.

The French artists have resumed possession of the theatre in Broadway, and have performed during the week *Les Lionnes Pauvres* and *Les Crochets du Pére Martin.*

Mr. Lester Wallack's new play, *The Romance of a Poor Young Man*, will be produced next Wednesday or Thursday.

It is understood that *The Octoroon* will be withdrawn from the Winter Garden in about a fortnight, to make room for a new piece.

A correspondent, who makes an inquiry as to why Mr. George Jordan is not at present acting in the city, is informed that since his irrepressible conflict with Laura Keene, LL.D. (in which Portia lost her case), he has received many offers, both here and in the Provinces, but pending the decision in his suit, he could not accept any of them. I presume that Mr. Stuart will, in good time, secure the services of so finished, able, and popular artist as Mr. Jordan, and that he will make his rentrée at the Winter Garden.

Mr. Bourcicault's new version of *The Heart of Mid-Lothian* is announced to be produced at Laura Keene's Theatre next Monday night. I don't see anything more about Sir Walter Scott in the avis, and I'm afraid that we shall have to put up with Bourcicault as stage-manager. Perhaps Sir Walter might be better, but not much.

The Webb Sisters are going to play over in the Bowery. Are you not delighted? I am. I never saw them, but the "entire California press pronounces them to be the best artists of the day."

I await the débuts of the Webb Sisters with feverish anxiety.

En Province.

The Heron has been doing a new play in Boston.

Lesbia is the title, and the Shu-shu-ga has conveyed it herself from the Gaul.

The Athenian crickets are in their usual non-lucendo condition of mind about it.

One joker (the *Courier*) commences his article by saying that "if the man lives who, after spending an entire evening in a theatre, witnessing the first representation of a five-act play, can then at eleven o'clock sit down and at once give an intelligent opinion upon the piece, he is a rare bird," and then goes on to prove the veracity of his statement as far as he is individually concerned, by giving a quadrilateral account of the leading incidents in the plot.

I gather, however, from it a few items here and there.

The scene is laid in Venice. Of course, Toujours Venise. Well, it is a nice place, but why not in Oswego sometimes?

However, to get on: Lesbia is a gushing young Venetian who has made a faux pas. "The partner of her guilt" grows tired of her, and throws her over for another. This is the delightful state of things with which the play commences, and then there goes on during four hours what our cricket calls "merely a conflict between love and jealousy," ending with the suicide of Lesbia.

There are, it appears, two good male characters, which were played by J. W. Wallack, Jr., and E. L. Davenport. A part called Raspo was appropriately cast to Mr. Hatchet.

I should go more minutely into the details of this play, but as I hear it is to be done in the metropolis, and as no one has any great respect for rural criticism, I refrain. Apropos to the general subject, I may make a most important literary and dramatic announcement, one that will create an intense excitement in the "gilded saloons of the aristocracy."

Listen:

My new five-act tragedy, *Anna Maria*, is nearly ready for the stage, and it is probable that a young lady of rare accomplishments, brilliant personal attractions, rare and aristocratic conjunctions, will make her first appearance upon any stage, etc., etc.

Where, I ask, where will the *Octoroon, Jeanie Deans, Geraldine, Lesbia*, Mr. Bateman, Walt Whitman, Miss Agnes Robertson, and the Shu-shu-ga, be, after that?

They have the Opera in Boston this week, and don't seem to know exactly what to do with it.

Generally they don't see Ullmann's pumps and real tubs, and object as the metropolitan critics did to the stupid cast of the *Vespers*. Then they talk about "an unwieldy barge, hideously improbable in its mechanism," and even make fun of Granger, armorer to their Imperial Majesties, L. N. and B. U.

All the articles commence with puffs for the new chandelier. The *Post* says it "created a sensation."

The *Courier* declares that "it is really a splendid thing, "and that the chorus paid more attention to it than to the conductor." Again, after pitching into the people all round, "the chandelier is very fine."

That's what they call satire in the provinces.

Patti was seen and heard to an immense extent. The *Atlas* critic don't like the *edge* of her voice, whatever that is; but it will probably be ground down for him. The poor *Vespers* gets another bat in the eye. The *Lucia* "is worth all the *Vespers* that ever blotted paper." Brignoli, we are told, seemed to "move as though under the shadow of an iceberg."

He was in a colder place.

He was singing to a Boston audience.

Kane couldn't have done that without shivering.

PERSONNE.

[For THE SATURDAY PRESS.

THE STANDARD OF DEFEAT.

—

My young friend, Mr. T. B. Aldrich, had in the THE SATURDAY PRESS, a week or two ago, a delightful story, enlivened by woodcuts.

That may be very well for Aldrich, but it must be understood that this article is not to be illustrated.

The reason is, that I entertain enmity toward artists.

Listen.

The narration will perhaps bring upon me the scorn of society and the pitiless sarcasms of friends. But at present I am insensible to objurgation. I know, at least, that I shall find a gloomy satisfaction in revealing the circumstances of the most touching incident of my life.

When I first saw Miss Egglesbyn, not many months ago, she was standing, artistically absorbed, before Mr. Fred. Church's last and greatest painting. Her lips were slightly parted, and one of her eyes was closed. The other was shaded by her delicate right hand, which she had twisted into an extemporaneous lorgnette, for purposes of optical concentration. Her face glowed with admiration, and the flutterings of the pink parasol in her left hand betrayed the tremulous excitement which animated her. She was a stranger to me, yet I yearned toward her. When I said to Bowden, my companion, that she was very beautiful, he blandly acquiesced, and turned his attention to the production of Mr. Church. His coolness made me shudder, and I betook myself to the warmth of fascination which the fair stranger diffused.

Presently her lips were agitated. "Ah! what soul," she murmured, addressing nobody in particular; whereupon I felt emboldened to answer.

"Pardon me," I said, "it is The Heart, and not Soul, that you are gazing upon."

The reader will observe the subtle delicacy of this jest. The young lady at once appreciated it, for she permitted a rosy flush to suffuse her cheeks, and her eyes to turn approvingly in my direction. But the natural restraints of modesty checked her hilarious impulses, and repelled the rising smile, ere it had fully illumined her countenance.

I sought the proprietor of the establishment. "Colonel Stevens," said I, "were you ever in love?"

The Colonel made an interrogation-mark of his eyebrows.

"Because," I continued, "if you never have been in love, you cannot understand the peculiarities of my present position, and I should prefer that you would not undertake to try, for the human mind ought never to be subjected to vain struggles. But if, Colonel, you have been in love—Colonel, do you know the young lady within, who honors Art generally, and Mr. Church specifically at this moment?"

The Colonel beamed upon me, and admitted something of the sort. I think his remark was that he didn't know anybody else; which struck me as forcible and appropriate, inasmuch as it would have been difficult for any person, enjoying this lady's acquaintance, to take the least thought of the outside feminine world.

"Colonel," said I, "hitherto I have known you only as a soldier and a gallant hero; but now war thoughts must leave their places vacant, for in my breast come thronging soft and amorous desires."

"That's 's Shakespeare," said the Colonel.

"True," said I, "it is."

"Mr. Gamples," said the Colonel, "what can I do for you, sir?"

"Colonel," said I, "you can make me acquainted with the goddess yonder, who wields the pink parasol."

The Colonel uttered benevolent words of assent, and led me to the object of my anxieties. In an audible voice he pronounced our two names, hers first, waited until the dignity of formal preliminaries was over, and after turning conversation into the pleasant channels of the weather and its prospects, left us.

When I say that since that moment my mind has only known a broken peace, I sufficiently indicate the importance of the occasion.

I unguardedly extended the happiness I had just experienced to my companion, Bowden. Limitless generosity, and a too credulous confidence in the integrity of friends, have been my bane from childhood.

I mean to be just. Bowden, though a cruel deceiver, and an agonizing thorn in the side of my happiness—though the heartless spiller of my cup of bliss and the hard-soled trampler upon my affections—is an accomplished creature. Moreover he is an artist, and knows all about touches and tints and middle-grounds and things, which to me are Eleusinian in their nature. At the time when I presented him to Miss Egglesbyn, without regarding my feelings, he said something to her. She answered. Then he said some more, then she answered again. I think the subject was Mr. Church's picture; and I know that when I ventured an occasional opinion, I was ignominiously put down and crushed by Bowden, from whom I had a right to expect more considerate treatment.

But as soon as we went forth into Broadway, I felt myself upon safer ground, and capable of competition with my companion upon more equal terms. I competed, and, I think, with credit to myself.

For many weeks thereafter, I was occupied with Miss Egglesbyn. I studied her tastes, and purchased Ruskin, and went into a course of æsthetic reading, with a special view to counteraction of the artist who maintained acquaintance with the lady whom I adored, as if to spite me.

I never told my love, but let concealment, like a bug in a rug, prey on. Once I intimated a remonstrance in the matter of Bowden, but I do not think it was kindly received. It was after this manner that it came about:

"Miss Egglesbyn," said I one day, "do all New York beauties have as many followers as you?"

"Dear me," said she, quite confused, "what a question'!"

"Well," said I," do they?"

"Followers?" said she inquiringly.

"Yes," said I.

"O, I have my little suite," she answered innocently.

"Suites to the sweet, of course," said I; "but might I assume to advise that several thousand artists at least should have no place among your chosen friends?"

"You might, sir," she answered, "but it would be very presumptuous. Let us not talk of it."

This was depressing, but my spirits are naturally recuperative. So I besought the favor of conducting Miss Egglesbyn to the English and French Exhibition on the next day, and after gaining her favorable answer, withdrew. We were to meet at one o'clock, P. M., at Twenty-sixth street.

I considered myself sound on the English and French question. I had been immersed in the morasses of Pre-Raphaelism for several days and felt able to discuss Turner and the rest of those people with vigor. Still there were some points upon which I desired a more exact understanding. So the next morning I took Ruskin under my arm, and went off in search of Bowden, in the Studio Building.

"How are you, my boy?" said Bowden.

"Festive," said I.

Bowden and I affected good-will toward one another. I hid my undercurrent of contumely by an uppercrust of frankness. I suppose he did the same by me, although I never asked him.

"What's up?" said I.

"New picture," said he; "see,—Standard Bearer. Come, I'm glad you're here. Be my model; I want a model."

I thought he did, but restrained my first impulse to tell him in what way.

"Can we talk?" said I.

"To be sure," said he.

"Very well," said I; "I want to consult with you upon certain questions of Art Principles—something abstract and metaphysical."

"Good," said he.

Under his guidance, then, I submitted myself to the arrangements he proposed. The long stick of his sketching umbrella, with its corroded spear, was thrust into hand. A stray shirt, fished from some recess of his wardrobe, was wound around it. This was the Standard. I was then horizontalized upon a sofa, and distorted into strange postures. My legs were wreathed in wondrous sinuosities. My arms were tossed aloft. My head was twisted sharply and stiffly to the right.

"Can you stand it?" asked Bowden.

"Of course," said I.

"Most people think so," said he, "but it isn't easy, after the first two minutes."

I laughed him to scorn. "I can do this forever," I said.

At the end of five minutes, perspiration enveloped me. My limbs lost their vitality. My pulses throbbed. Two more, and various aches assailed me. But how could I show weakness at this time? With heroic fortitude, I held to my position for ten other minutes, talking lightly all the while. Then my voice failed me, and my strained nerves yielded.

"Hold up, Bowden," I said, a little faintly; "it is rather hard."

"I thought so," said Bowden; "You can't do it, I guess."

Then the Gamples blood rose. "Do it!" said I, "nonsense. I want to pull off my boot, that's all." The boot was discarded, and, outwardly firm, though inwardly insecure, I resumed the rack.

For nearly half an hour, I sat quiet. At last all was over. Bowden was gratefully profuse. He assisted me to rise. He seemed concerned to find that I was cramped. As I endeavored to pooh-pooh him, I found, to my horror, that I could not turn my head.

When I revealed this state of things, Bowden laughed. At that, I offered to quarrel with him, but he excused himself. Finding he was not to be irritated, I had no hesitation in uttering many splenetic things to his disadvantage.

In the midst of my wrath, I remembered my engagement. My watch told me the hour had passed. I am afraid that I bestowed profanities upon Bowden, who became inhumanly boisterous over my wry-necked efforts to settle my choler.

I left him in anger, and shook much dust from my feet upon the mat outside his door. I walked rapidly up Tenth street, encountering inquisitive glances from respectable passengers, and derisive allusions to the misfortune of my neck from rude and ragged children. I burned with shame.

Just after turning up Fifth avenue, I met Miss Egglesbyn. As I advanced, she looked ominously at me. I adroitly placed myself at her left side, that my horrible incapacity to turn might not be too abruptly exposed.

"You have missed your appointment, Mr. Gamples," she said, sternly.

"Pardon me," I said, endeavoring to conceal my embarrasment; "there were causes which I may explain."

"The engagement was your own, sir; not mine," she said.

We were walking down the avenue. I kept the inside, for reasons before mentioned. Miss Egglesbyn expressed anxiety to change positions with me. I protested, with some degree of pathos, I think. She insisted. What could a man do?

This change was my great reversal. I strove in vain to move my unwilling muscles. I know that, facially, I deepened into an unhealthy purple. Miss Egglesbyn asked me, in a tone of wonder, what could be the matter. I was unable to look upon her. A steady glare in an opposite direction was all I could accomplish. But something must be done. I must speak to her, excuse myself, retire, and hope for her lenience. How to do this? Only one way was clear.

I turned slowly round, until my eyes met hers, and walking backward, began to utter phrases which I now believe may have been incoherent. Miss Egglesbyn recoiled in alarm. My hesitating sentences, my ruddy hue, my marvellous retrogressive eccentricity of motion, all seemed to appal her.

"Mr. Gamples," said she, "what have you been doing?"

"Miss Egglesbyn," said I, "I have been Standard-Bearing."

"Sir," she said, before I could offer another explanatory word, "that I regret to see you thus, I need not tell you. But so public an affront ought not to pass unrebuked. You will leave me now, and you will understand me when I say that it is proper our acquaintance should here terminate."

I was dumbstruck. Her horrid suspicions were evident to me. My lips refused their office. I looked appealingly at her, but she moved away in stately silence. Could any sharper pang remain for me? Yes, one. For just below me, at the corner, I saw my evil worker, my Quei-shin (Chinese mythology), approach her smilingly, and after little affabilities, walk pleasantly away with her up Tenth street in the direction of the English and French Exhibition. Need you wonder, now, that I claim for this article immunity from illustration?

E. H. H.

[For The Saturday Press.]

THE DIAMOND-HUNTER.

Inscribed to C. A.

I.

Sages told me, snowy-bearded,
  That the diamonds Love and Truth,
Though deep hidden, still rewarded
  All who sought for them in youth.
From my childhood I went searching
  O'er each varied earthly lot—
In the mountains, in the valleys,
In the palace, and the cot.

II.

Long my pilgrimage had lasted—
  Long my spirit yearned in vain;
Pride had jostled, Hate defied me,
  Sin had jeered, with all her train.
Many a hope had bloomed and perished,
  Many a year had come and gone,
Still I trusted in the sages,
  And I was not all forlorn.

III.

"Surely," said I, "surely somewhere,
  Truth and Love I yet will find,
While there's incense in the flowers,
  Truth there must be in mankind."
Instant, then, from out her bower,
  Stepped the fay named Caroline,
And, behold, those priceless jewels
  Sparkled in her azure eyne!

A. WATTERS.

[2025 Editor's note: The following article, signed merely with an asterisk, was actually written by the ever-self-promoting Walt Whitman.]

ALL ABOUT A MOCKING-BIRD.

What is the reason-why of Walt Whitman's lyric utterances, as soon as any of them is heard, rousing up such vehement intellectual censures and contumely from some persons, and then equally determined bravos from other persons?

Passing by certain of the latter, the complimentary sort, with which the journals, welcoming Walt's reappearance and recovery of his singing-voice after an obstinate three years' dumbness, have accepted that Mocking-Bird Chant printed by us in the Saturday Press, of Dec. 24, preceding, we seize upon and give to our readers, in another part of the paper, a specimen of the sort of censure alluded to—a tip-top cutting-and-slashing criticism from the *Cincinnati Daily Commercial*, which we have conned with unfeigned pleasure. All of which is respectfully submitted as outset for something else made way to be said, namely:

We feel authorized to announce, for certain, that the Mocking-Bird, having come to his throat again, his cantabile, is not going to give cause to his admirers for complaining that he idles, mute, any more, up and down the world. His songs, in one and another direction, will, he promises us, after this date, profusely appear.

We are able to declare that there will also soon crop out the true "Leaves of Grass," the fuller-grown work of which the former two issues were the inchoates—this forthcoming one, far, very far ahead of them in quality, quantity, and in supple lyric exuberance.

Those former issues, published by the author himself in little pittance-editions, on trial, have just dropped the book enough to ripple the inner first-circles of literary agitation, in immediate contact with it. The outer, vast, extending, and ever-wider-extending circles, of the general supply, perusal, and discussion of such a work, have still to come. The market needs to-day to be supplied—the great West especially—with copious thousands of copies.

Indeed, " Leaves of Grass " has not yet been really published at all. Walt Whitman, for his own purposes, slowly trying his hand at the edifice, the structure he has undertaken, has lazily loafed on, letting each part have time to *set*,—evidently building not so much with reference to any part itself, considered alone, but more with reference to the ensemble,—always bearing in mind the combination of the whole, to fully justify the parts when finished.

Of course the ordinary critic, even of good eye, high intellectual calibre, and well accomplished, grasps not, sees not, any such ideal ensemble—likely sees not the only valuable part of these mystic leaves, namely, not what they state, but what they infer—scornfully wants to know what the Mocking-Bird means, who can tell? —gives credit only for what is proved to the surface ear—and makes up a very fine criticism, not out of the soul, to which these poems altogether appeal, and by which only they can be interpreted, but out of the intellect, to which Walt Whitman has not, as far as we remember, addressed one single word in the whole course of his writings.

Then the workmanship, the art-statement and argument of the question. Is this man really any artist at all? Or not plainly a sort of naked and hairy savage, come among us, with yelps and howls, disregarding all our lovely metrical laws? How can it be that he offends so many and so much?

Quite after the same token as the Italian Opera, to most bold Americans, and all new persons, even of latent proclivities that very way, only accustomed to tunes, piano-noises and the performances of the negro bands—satisfied, (or rather fancying they are satisfied), with each and several thereof, from association and habit, until they pass utterly beyond them—which comes in good time, and cannot be deferred much longer, either, in such a race as yours, O bold American of the West!

Walt Whitman's method in the construction of his songs is strictly the method of the Italian Opera, which, when heard, confounds the new person aforesaid, and, as far as he can then see, showing no purport for him, nor on the surface, nor any analogy to his previous-accustomed tunes, impresses him as if all the sounds of earth and hell were tumbled promiscuously together. Whereupon he says what he candidly thinks (or supposes he thinks), and is very likely a first-rate fellow—with room to grow, in certain directions.

Then, in view of the latter words, bold American! in the ardor of youth, commit not yourself, too irretrievably, that there is nothing in the Italian composers, and nothing in the Mocking-Bird's chants. But pursue them awhile—listen—yield yourself—persevere. Strange as the shape of the suggestion may be, perhaps such free strains are to give to these United States, or commence giving them, the especial nourishments which, though all solid and mental and moral things are in boundless profusion provided, have hardly yet begun to be provided for them—hardly yet the idea of that kind of nourishment thought of, or the need of it suspected. Though it is the sweetest, strongest meat-pabulum of a race of giants—true pabulum of the children of the prairies.

You, bold American! and ye future two hundred millions of bold Americans, can surely never live, for instance, entirely satisfied and grow to your full stature, on what the importations hither of foreign bards, dead or alive, provide—nor on what is echoing here the letter and the spirit of the foreign bards. No, bold American! not even on what is provided, printed from Shakespeare or Milton—not even of the Hebrew canticles—certainly not of Pope, Byron, or Wordsworth,— nor of any German or French singer, nor any foreigner at all.

We are to accept those and every other literary and poetic thing from beyond the seas, thankfully, as studies, exercises. We go back—we pause long with the old, ever-modern one, the Homer, the only chanting mouth that approaches our case near enough to raise a vibration, an echo. We then listen with accumulated eagerness for those mouths that can make the vaults of America ring here to-day—those who will not only touch our case, but embody it and all that belongs to it—sing it with varied and powerful idioms, and in the modern spirit, at least as capable, as loud and proud as the best spirit that has ever preceded us.

Our own song, free, joyous, and masterful. Our own music, raised on the soil, carrying with it all the subtle analogies of our own associations—broad with the broad continental scale of the New World, and full of the varied products of its varied soils—composite—comprehensively Religious—Democratic—the red life-blood of Love, warming, running through every line, every word. Ah, if this Walt Whitman, as he keeps on, should ever succeed in presenting such music, such a poem, an identity, emblematic, in the regions of creative art, of the wondrous all-America, material and moral, he would indeed do something.

And if he don't, the Mocking-Bird may at least have the satisfaction of dying in a good cause. But then again he looks so little like dying, anyhow.

D. D.

NEW YORK JANUARY 14, 1860

[ORIGINAL]

You and Me and To-Day.

1. With antecedents,
With my fathers and mothers, and the accumulations of past ages,
With all which, had it not been, I would not now be here, as I am,
With Egypt, India, Phenicia, Greece, and Rome, With the Celt, the Scandinavian, the Alb, and the Saxon,
With antique maritime ventures,—With laws, artisanship, wars, journeys,
With the poet, the skald, the saga, the myth, and the oracle,
With the sale of slaves,—with enthusiasts,—with the troubadour, the crusader, and the monk,
With those old continents whence we have come to this new continent,
With the fading kingdoms and kings over there,
With the fading religions and priests,
With the small shores we look back to, from our own large and present shores,
With countless years drawing themselves onward, and arrived at these years,
You and Me arrived,—America arrived, and making this year,
This year! sending itself ahead countless years to come.

2. O but it is not the years,—it is I,—it is You,
We touch all laws, and tally all antecedents,
We are the skald, the oracle, the monk, and the knight,—we easily include them, and more,
We stand amid time, beginningless and endless—we stand amid evil and good,
All swings around us—There is as much darkness as light,
The very sun swings itself and its system of planets around us,
Its sun, and its again, all swing around us.

3. As for me,
I have the idea of all, and am all, and believe in all,
I believe materialism is true, and spiritualism is true—I reject no part.

4. Have I forgotten any part?
Come to me, whoever and whatever, till I give you recognition.

5. I respect Assyria, China, Teutonia, and the Hebrews,
I adopt each theory, myth, god, and demi-god,
I see that the old accounts, bibles, genealogies, are true, without exception,
I assert that all past days were what they should have been,
And that they could no-how have been better than they were,
And that to-day is what it should be—and that America is,
And that to-day and America could no-how be better than they are.

6. In the name of These States, and in your and my name—the Past!
And in the name of These States, and in your and my name—the Present!

7. I know that the past was great, and the future will be great,
And I know that both curiously conjoint in the present time, in myself and yourself,
And that where I am, or you are, this present day, there is the centre of all days, all races,
And there is the meaning, to us, of all that has ever come of races and days, or ever will come.

WALT WHITMAN.

[ORIGINAL]

LEAVES FROM NATURE.

What a beautiful day! As I threw open my blinds, the Winter's sun poured in its rays almost as warm as the Summer's sunbeam. The snow had melted from the earth, and dead leaves (vegetation's tribute to chill Winter's blast) seemed dressed in diamonds, so brightly did the raindrops resting upon them sparkle in the sunlight. Did I not miss the cheerful notes of the little birds, or the sweet perfume of blooming flowers, I could fancy it a bright Spring morning. Sitting by my open casement, though basking in the sun's warm rays, I soon felt so cold that I was forced to close the window. Gazing on this scene of beauty, thus protected from the chilly air, I could scarcely realize that the cold drear face of Winter could wreathe itself in such sunny smiles. Soon the wind began to blow, and black clouds hid heaven's blue canopy; ere long it began to rain; and as the drops fell upon my cottage roof, they told me in their pattering language that, "As the morning had been beautiful, so did the tempter always clothe himself in enticing colors, and by his pleasant smiles and winning ways seek to lead the good astray, as you were led to think the air warm and balmy by the Spring—like warmth of a Winter's sun. The dead leaves are those who follow evil paths, and the diamond raindrops resting on them are angel's tears who weep for those who no more follow their heart's promptings, as the earth no longer retains its garb of innocence, the pure white snow. In all your actions, if you hear not conscience (the notes of the little birds) prompting you to act, or feel not the calm satisfaction (perfume of blooming flowers) arising from a pure heart, you may be sure you are not doing right—it is not a Spring morning. As the bright rays of a Winter's sun failed to keep you warm, so will a path of error, brightened with pleasure and excitement, fail to make you happy. Guilt and remorse will keep from your heart all feelings of contentment, as the black clouds to-day cover the blue curtain of the sky. Troubles and sorrows will constantly descend upon your head like the continual droppings of the rain. Your life will be rendered wretched by a feeling toward all men of suspiciousness and doubt, which drive away all thoughts of trusting confidence, just as the mist and fog of to-day render the earth impenetrable to a sunny ray."

R. W. P.

Thoughts and Things.

BY ADA CLARE.

Women's dress is one of the most agitated, if not one of the most agitating subjects I know of. Every one has read the vituperation of the hooped skirt, long dress, small bonnet, etc., with approval or contempt, as the sex may be. Every one, too, must have noticed how utterly ineffective the newspaper attacks upon such fashions have been. Crinoline, for instance, has held its calm and haughty ground, with denouncers to right of it, denouncers to left of it, denouncers before it, denouncers behind it, without contracting a square inch of its circumference.

I think one strong reason for this lies in the fact, that my sex keenly saw that the way to win the sneers of the other sex was to accept their amendments in the way of dress. Most of us have noticed the amiable reports in different journals of the Woman's Rights Conventions, and that the ire of the reporters is mostly excited by the fact that the female pleaders are attired in the manner they are perennially advising to us. The absence of crinoline is generally the great moral defect that raises the reporters up to their appalling pinnacle of cant. I would be pleased to see the young man who would walk the length of Broadway with a female, reasonably dressed, according to the male standard—which reasonable costume may be briefly described as a heavy, unsupported skirt, hanging lank and limber about the forlorn figure, a huge bonnet, projecting like melancholy eaves over the brow, with a view of protecting it from the wind and sun, and a pair of heavy thumping shoes, whose heels show grim and savage behind,— for the skirt of the dress must be short enough to display the demoniac shoe. I should like to see the reasonable male who would champion it.

On the other hand, how devoutly he admires the much-abused fashion.

The woman with her dress floating gracefully off from her figure, supported by the light and easy hoop-skirt, below which it falls to sweep the ground in the natural flow of beauty; with one of Laurent's most lovely French bonnets, receding daintily from the brow, so as to give the woman a chance to show the beauty of her hair, and to make some practical use of her eyes and ears; with her fine little feet encased in well-made, well-soled patent-leather boots, of which the toes alone are visible. O! I can paint to myself the philosopher at the feet of this divinity.

The truth is, that the fashion of dress the male sex are urging, in theory, upon our acceptance, is not only a disfiguring, but a cruel and unhealthy one.

Take, for instance, that much-slandered article, the hoop-skirt. As long as the public modesty is such that even the most indistinct symptoms of limbs in a woman is considered a dangerous and demoralizing thing, the hoop-skirt will remain a beauty and a blessing. The attempt to disguise the shape of the woman by hanging innumerable heavy skirts about her hips, has ever been disastrous to her health and spirits. All women remember with horror the weight they were expected to suspend from their hips and shoulders, a few years ago,—such weight seeming to devitalize those delicate organs, without which the world could not exist.

Around 1860, Sporting the Bloomer.

Just as that barbarous weight was increased by the quilt, the rope-skirt, the corded-skirt, the flounced-skirt, and woman's burden had become greater than she could bear, an angel came lightly up to her, and in expanding its wings, snatched from her the grievous burden, and bade her go and suffer no more. This angel was in the shape of numerous rows of light and well-covered steel, all linked together with narrow tape, and so nicely adjusted with bands, etc., that the hips, the waist, and the shoulders were equally entrusted with carrying it, commonly called the hoop-skirt. At this angelic approach, away fled the savage garments, so long the torture of my sex; and in Summer, all that was necessary to the elegance of her toilet was a simple white over-skirt, that a baby might have carried.

Now that the womb of the woman ceased to be dragged and torn out of its place, there seemed some hope that the human race to come might reap some benefit in a new physical energy, etc. Now forsooth the male sex, finding how extremely sanitary and agreeable it is for mine, have taken to abusing it with all their power.

As for the long dress, sweeping the ground, it cannot and will not be done away with, until the costume of the woman becomes exceedingly short. The neither long nor short dress is a thing hideous to behold. Venus herself could not look graceful, if her heels alone were exhibited to the public gaze. The human race have inherited vulnerability of heel from Achilles, and therein can beauty and grace be stricken.

No woman, I think, would object to the short dress, if it would reveal the whole of the foot and ankle.

One thing above others pleases me: it is to see men annoyed by the prevailing fashion. Not out of malice am I pleased, but out of a sense of justice. When I see the supposed lords of creation in a car, of a hot Summer's day, with their indignant heads only appearing above the pyramid of light dry-goods, which swell up to their chins, I laugh and am satisfied. Because, when women proposed to wear a truly sensible and beautiful dress, men opposed it, not only by argument, but by brute force. The Bloomer is the costume to which I refer. Of course, when I mention it, men will have in their minds a picture of the Bloomer as they have seen her. They must try to remember, if the superiority of their minds will allow them, that the Bloomer has been worn only by old and ugly women, who exhibited the most hideous taste in its combinations. Let the young and lovely have a chance at it for a month or so, and I would like to see where male logic would be at the end of it.

Fancy a beautiful young woman, of a June evening, in a white sprigged muslin dress, coming just down to her knees, and finished off at its termination with a puff of pink ribbon and white lace. Her pantalettes, made of sprigged blonde lace, very full, Turkish style, are gathered up with a knot of rose ribbons at the knee, and from thence hang half-way down her lovely leg. The foot, encased in a bronze gaiter with brass heels, is exhibited to the human eye, together with the ankle, and eight inches above it. Her dress is made full in the waist, and as it approaches the white shoulders and neck, it is gathered in loose folds, with a band of pink ribbons, which terminates in a knot of the same on the breast. A string of pearls is clasped about her fair throat, and the same gathers up her short sleeves. Add to this picture the health which so comfortable a dress, conducing to open-air exercise, would bring—that health expressed in the soft bloom of her cheeks, the kindly brightness of her eyes, and the crimson on her lips, that would make the roses feel they were no longer subjects of poetry—and men can hardly help melting before this vision of loveliness, unless they are men of stone.

As the case stands now, even with the blessing of the hoop-skirt, the woman's costume entirely indisposes her for outdoor exercise. For before she can go forth, she must go through with a series of manœuvres as tedious as a military drill. The number of things she is obliged to put on and take off involves a sacrifice of time and patience to which the martyrs were utterly strangers. The consequence is, regular exercise is very rare among women, and no wonder that men, their offspring, have such weak digestions and such selfish habits.

If the Bloomer dress ever comes into sway, carried out in an elegant, tasteful, coquettish manner, I fancy that it will bring with it a freedom for women from conventional lies, from deceit and much uncharitableness, and from their intense desire for money. The dress would be so much less expensive than the present one, and would require taste so much more than extravagance, that one great motive for mercenary marriages were gone. Woman, relieved from the continual burden and fretfulness of an unnatural attire, would grow in good sense and in kindly feeling; childbearing would become easier, and the physical education of children might become an art instead of an accident.

But until that time comes, may the hoop-skirt reign triumphant, and men be buried 'neath its expanses, and expenses!

o o o

I hear Winter's "Song of the Ruined Man" much eulogized. I cannot admire it. With the text he begins with, a practised versifier might go on rhyming until the seas were dry. All you have to do is to conjure up all the things that one should not laugh at, and then laugh at them, and there's your poem. On the contrary, Walt Whitman's "Child's Reminiscence" could only have been written by a poet, and versifying would not help it. I love the poem.

[ORIGINAL]

FEUERBILDER.—GERMANESQUE.

BY W. D. HOWELLS.

The children sit by the fireside
With their little faces in bloom;
And behind, the lily-pale mother,
Looking out of the gloom,

Flushes as if a rosebud
Were bursting in her heart;
But the father sits there silent,
From the firelight apart.

"Now, what dost thou see in the embers?
Tell it to me, my child,"
Whispers the lily-pale mother
To her daughter sweet and mild.

"O, I see a sky and a moon
In the coals and ashes there,
And under, two are walking
In a garden of owers so fair.

"A lady so gay, and her lover,
Talking with low-voiced words,
Not to waken the dreaming flowers,
And the sleepy little birds."

Back in the gloom the mother
Shrinks with a sudden sigh.
"Now, what dost thou see in the embers?"
Cries the father to the boy.

"O, I see a wedding-procession
Go in at the church's door,—
Ladies in silks, and knights in steel,—
A hundred of them, and more.

"The bride's face is white as a lily,
And the groom's head is white as snow;
And without, with plumes and tapers,
A funeral paces slow."

Loudly then laughed the father,
And shouted again for cheer,
And called to the drowsy housemaid
To fetch him a pipe and beer.

[ORIGINAL]

MY TAILOR AND I IN THE LATE PANIC.

Sartor, quoth I, the suit is well enough,—
I find no fault with stitching, style, or stuff;
But as for this marsupial display,
What crotchet could have led you so astray?
Are you such Rip Van Winkle of a goose
As still to dream that pockets are in use,
When Astor scarcely can with truth be said
To have the handling of "a single red"?
Pockets in times like these! Sir, 'tis no less
Than wasteful and ridiculous excess;
As who should build a many-chambered bin,
In a great dearth, to garner nothings in?
Out with your shears! Come, man alive! don't shrink,
But off with these lean sarcasms in a twink,
Whose presence, like the spendthrift's empty purse,
But serves to make the "aching void" still worse.
Well done! And now, with no more fret or fuss,
That patient little bill I'll honor—thus:
"Cashier of Hades' Bank, at blind man's sight,
Pay bearer's ghost, and debit mine.

ALL RIGHT.

Oct. 19, 1859.

Dramatic Feuilleton.

Up with the Tartan!

What was it that I said a little while ago, when the Bourcicaults seceded from the Garden of Eden, and went out into the wilderness, about its not being quite so clear that the king was really dead, notwithstanding that the whole greenroom, from Awful Jefferson, who assumed the Speaker's Mace, down to la belle Clinton, who didn't play *Dora Sunnyside*, shouted le Roi est mort?

And the Sunday papers cried with one voice, le Roi est mort! For, be it remembered, that the young and talented critics of the Sunday papers are authors who are endeavoring to create an American drama. They have all sorts of splendid things on hand, such as five-act tragedies in verse, dramas in prose, comedies, farces, and so on, in all sorts of shapes, except the proper and the right ones.

These pieces are often done in the provinces, and occasionally in the metropolis, when some one is jobbing a theatre.

They always fail; they never get beyond that horrible fourth night, the pons asinorum of adolescent dramatists.

Curiously enough, this asinine public wont go to see a stupid play because it is written by the illustrious Brown, the editor of the *Blazer*. They wont have *Kerjunca; or, the Demon of the Inquisition*—a beautiful thing in five acts, blank verse, exactly like Beaumont and Fletcher on any terms.

Yet Brown is popular. About the City Hall and the Custom House he is considered an immense fellow. He has written some very sweet things in Anna Maria's album, and the Dear Child thinks he is much nicer than the subscriber, who writes only prose, and not sweet prose at that.

Mais! this stupid public, this dolt of a public, what does it mean by withholding its half-dollars from the popular Brown, and showering them upon the villainous Bourcicault, who has already attempted to dissolve the Union and ruin the dry goods trade?

More than all, he don't see the American press ! And the wretch lives! Has Jove no bolt left? Some absurdly practical person may say that the public pays Bourcicault because he is clever and entertaining, and wont have Brown because *Kerjunca* is a bore.

In that case, what is to become of the American drama? Where are the purists and the legitimists? Where the Bourbons? Let us hear from them.

In the meantime, apropos to *The Heart of Mid-Lothian.*

I was right about Sir Walter Scott, Bart. He *is* dead, and so he did not get up the play. Perhaps Bourcicault did it better than the author of *Waverly* could have done it.

The latter might possibly have over or under-estimated Miss Laura Keene's resources, "whatever they may be."

I have an indistinct remembrance of having read *The Heart of Mid-Lothian* in my green and salad days, when I was good, like Aldrich, and ate pie; so I can say little of the story, which I suppose every one of my readers knows better than myself.

Walt Whitman, and various other competent critics, declare that the beauty, the force, and the power of the delightful romance cannot be expressed dramatically; and they may be, possibly are, quite right.

I know, however, that Mr. Bourcicault has made a very affecting and interesting play out of it, and perhaps I can't do better than to quote the expression which Charles Reade puts in the mouth of Quin, the actor, during a dispute about the merits of Mistresses Woffington and Bracegirdle. "All I know is," said he, "that one of 'em makes me laugh, and t'other makes me cry, and that's enough!"

That is the case with this play of Bourcicault's. Its construction, from the nature of the case, is not so artistic as some of his previous plays,—*Jessie Brown*, for example; but for skilful treatment, the trial-scene, the murder of *Madge Wildfire*, and the attack upon the tolbooth, will all rank highly in the acting-drama.

It may be that some one has done all this much better before. I do not deal with traditions. I belong to this day, this week, and this hour. I, in point of fact, pooh-pooh the old Park-pit. There!

In the first act of *Jeanie Deans* (that is what they call it, I believe,) there is a good deal of going about the stage and looking carefully into corners for people that you know are not and could not be there by any possible or impossible chance, and the ending of the act where Deans père "cusses" Effie, may be just a little too Bowery. It is not the less so on account of Miss Keene's hysterical and extra-spasmodic action, when she ought to be stunned and utterly overwhelmed by the blow that has fallen upon her, nor by Mr. Charles Fisher, who gave the curse savagely, as if he liked it, which, I opine, was not the author's idea. On the contrary, I think that D.D. is exercised in his mind a good deal, and has to relieve himself by a swear. My respected progenitor used to do it occasionally, and we took it as a matter of course.

The second act is given to the trial-scene, which was admirably managed.

The arrangement of the stage was very good; and I noticed but two little points which need reformation. There was a superfluity of cotton-headed supernumeraries at the barrister's table, and the intelligent jury might have been cleaner. I don't think that the Scottish yeomanry wore moustaches and dyed them a hundred years ago. I hope not.

Mr. Bourcicault's performance of the Counsel for the Defence was a great hit. He made it a sort of Lincoln's-Inn Dick Busteed. His short, dry ahem! his peculiar twitch of his gown, and handling of his brief, reminded me of a heavy leader before the Court of Queen's Bench, while the manner in which he bullied the Counsel for the Crown, recalled to the mind some souvenirs of that brilliant, American, forensic light, the late Counsel to the Corporation.

Miss Robertson began to act in this scene, and her behavior on the witness-stand was admirable. The struggle between her sisterly affection, and the stern regard for the Sunday-school truth in which she had been educated, was a real triumph of art.

I have fine feelings and delicate sensibilities. I was on the point of gushing. The strain on the lachrymal glands was severe. All the women who had nice pocket-handkerchiefs had gushed long before this time. Young Coupon, who had been doing a heavy amount of dining at home, and had punished an immense deal of the governor's Burgundy, gushed palpably. He said afterwards, at the Club, that he didn't do it, but A. M. vows and declares that she saw him with her own eyes, and I needn't say that any one who doubts those eyes, etc., I shall be obliged, etc., etc.

Miss Keene's best scene was that directly after the trial. The interview with Jeanie was earnestly, carefully, and artistically acted.

The next point of interest was the murder in Meg's cottage. Miss Wells modelled *Meg* after Cushman, and might have done worse. Miss Wells has received many well-deserved compliments for her performance of a most repulsive part.

Following the course of the drama, we come to Jeanie's interviews with the Duke of Argyll and the Queen. Royalty and nobility were represented by Miss Deland and Mr. Mark Smith. The latter was gotten up without regard to expense, and had a manner which may have been like that of the Macallum More, but I think was a little too ponderous and precise.

He is supposed to be at breakfast, this Duke, and he poured out his own chocolate!

Heavens! a Duke of the ruffle-and powder period pouring out his own chocolate! Here is the way in which the thing was really done. It was written by Dickens for France, but the manners of the nobility were the same in both countries:

> Monseigneur was about to take his chocolate. Monseigneur could swallow a great many things with ease, and was by some few sullen minds supposed to be rather rapidly swallowing France; but his morning's chocolate could not so much as get into the throat of Monseigneur, without the aid of four strong men besides the Cook.
>
> Yes. It took four men, all four ablaze with gorgeous decoration. And the Chief of them, unable to exist with fewer than two gold watches in his pocket, emulative of the noble and chaste fashion set by Monseigneur, to conduct the happy chocolate to Monseigneur's lips. One lacquey carried the chocolate-pot into the sacred presence; a second milled and frothed the chocolate with the little instrument he bore for that function; a third presented the favored napkin; a fourth (he of the two gold watches) poured the chocolate out. It was impossible for Monseigneur to dispense with one of these attendants on the chocolate and hold his high place under the admiring Heavens. Deep would have been the blot upon his escutcheon if his chocolate had been ignobly waited on by only three men; he must have died of two.

Peters was admirable as the chief of the four strong men, but where were the other three?

Miss Robertson acted charmingly in the scene with the Queen, and almost everybody dissolved again. Now came the most delicate portion of the play. There was a mob to be represented. Now a stage-mob is a difficult thing to do. The men make mobs of your groups, and groups of your mobs. When they should rush, they linger or pose; when they should stand still, they run off. But here was a mob which seemed like the real thing. It was fierce, turbulent, noisy, and picturesque. It groaned at the guard, con amore. It pitched into the Tolbooth with a will. It was a good mob, suggesting riot-acts and trials without end.

The tableau finale is very fine. The Tolbooth in ruins, the mob and soldiers fraternizing, the sisters clasped in each other's arms, not to forget the red fire and the nice pocket-handkerchiefs, made up a charming ensemble.

There was a hurricane of applause, and a terrific call for the destroyer of the Union, the subverter of the Constitution, the defyer of the laws, the trampler upon the Eagle, the snubber of the Genius of Liberty, and the sneerer at the Sunday papers.

Curiously enough, Bourcicault was received not only with favor, but with positive enthusiasm. He had the first and the only call from the house, although Misses Keene and Robertson appeared. Ladies waved those moistened pocket-handkerchiefs, men threw up their hats, and several stout colonels from Peoria came very near to apoplexy. Bourcicault seemed quite surprised at being the Pet of the Public, and I don't wonder.

I am sorry, because if Bourcicault gets to be popular he will be no longer interesting.

But let us cheer up, stand by, and hope for the best. The public, after all, is as capricious as you, Madame, when you pet Monsieur one day, and snub him the next.

As it is, the King has come to something more than his own again.

The tartan is elevated to the highest possible point. Miss Robertson's royal Stuart-plaid is talked of in the clubs as a nice thing for waistcoats; and Keene's is seriously thought of for trowsers. I am going through a heavy course of Gaelic, and think strongly of mounting the Cameronian tartan. I knew a man in the Fifty-ninth (I think that is the Regiment) and dined at the mess. So I think I am entitled to the plaid, don't you?

I came very near forgetting Mr. Baker's arrangement of the music. The Scotch airs are as delightful as the Scotch whiskey when the Baron makes the punch, and the Youngest and the Loveliest smiles over the decoction. But the whiskey splits your head, while the music sometimes, if you have souvenirs, only makes your heart ache. I can get over the latter without ammonia, and with Anna Maria (Oh!), and so I like it best. As to Baker's orchestra it is capital, and I repeat what I have said before that sometimes the play here is stupid, but the music is always good. In this music the utricularis tibia plays a most important part, and it is done by a professor.

I say again, up with the tartan!

All the blue bonnets over to Bourcicault!

And special homage from Scotia to Miss Agnes Robertson! She exudes the perfume of the heather, her eyes drop mountain-dew, her mouth says haggis every time she opens it. She is the bonniest lassie that ever captivated a Hieland lad. [Remark of a gentleman recently from Glasgow, done into English by the subscriber; copyright secured, and right of translation reserved.]

Faits Divers.

Mr. Wallack publishes a card, in which he says that *A Husband to Order* is doing so well, that he finds it to his interest to continue it for the present. So Anna Maria and others who are on the qui vive for the *Roman d'un Jeune Homme Pauvre,* can get off and make their minds easy for the present.

Awful Jefferson has given out the parts for Miss Heron's *Lesbia*, and that young lady will be trotted out at the Winter Garden, if Hayes can get the scenery done, on Monday week. Heron will play Lesbia; young Wallack the heavy Venetian, who has a prejudice against the Falieri family, and "cusses" them through five acts, more or less. Jordan has been specially engaged for the jeune premier; so that the cast will be a good one.

Cook's Circus will be opened at Niblo's Garden next Monday. Cook is a Briton of some note in the sawdust world, and will introduce some entirely new wrinkles into the Cirque, which I like very much when it is well done.

I hear from the modern Athens that the people are still enthusiastic about little Patti, and there is therefore an irrepressible row between the managers, Ullmann sticking to the real tubs, and Strakosch sticking to his crinoline. Meantime, Gazzaniga has made a sensation in Saffo.

The Habaneros are wild about the *Do* of the new tenor Musiani. He sings it in the *Di quella pira* at the end of the third act of the *Trovatore*. It was the singing of this note by Tamberlik which made him such a favorite with the Parisians.

Some of your non-æsthetic readers may be in the dark as to what the *Do* is. It is the French *Ut*, generally called the *Ut de poitrine.* And if anybody wants to know what that is, here you are: "It is the first of the monosyllables adopted by Guido, and still used by the French in solmization. The Italians deeming this syllable too hard for free and easy pronunciation, substitute in its place that of *Do*. *Ut* and *Do* are always the tonic or key-note of the major mode, and the mediant or third of the minor mode."

I hope that's quite clear, now, and beg to offer my profoundest salaam.

PERSONNE

NEW YORK JANUARY 21, 1860

[For the Saturday Press.]

Yourn and Mine, and Any-Day.

[A Yawp, after Walt Whitman.]

1. With antecedents and consequents,
With our Fathers, Mothers, Aunts, Uncles, and the family at large accumulated by past ages,
With all which would have been nothing if anything were not something which everything is,
With Europe, Asia, Africa, America, Peoria, and New Jersey,
With the Pre-Adamite, the Yarab, the Guebre, the Hottentot, the Esquimaux, the Gorilla, and the Nondescriptian,
With antique powwowing,—with laws, jaws, wars, and three-tailed bashaws,
With the butcher, the baker, the candle-stick-maker, and Ralph Waldo Carlyle,
With the sale of Long Island Railway stock,—with spiritualists, with the yawper, with the organ-grinder and monkey,
With everybody and everything in general and nothing and nobody in particular, besides otherbodies and things too numerous to mention,
Yourn and Mine arrived,—The Arrival arrove, and making this Nonsense:
This Nonsense! sending itself ahead of any sane comprehension this side of Jordan.

2. O, but it is not the Nonsense,—it is Mine,—it is Yourn,
We touch all effects,' and tally all bread-sticks,
We are the Etceteras and Soforths,— we easily include them, and more;
All obfusticates around us,—there is as much as possible of a muchness;
The entire system of the universe discomboborates around us with a perfect looseness.

3. As for Mine,
Mine has the idea of my own, and what's Mine is my own and my own is all Mine and believes in it all,
Mine believes meum is true, and rejects nix.

4. Has Mine forgotten to grab any part?
Fork over then whoever and whatever is worth having, till Mine gives a receipt in full.

5. Mine respects Brahma, Vishnu, Mumbo-Jumbo, and the great Panjandrum,
Mine adopts things generally which are claimed by Yourn,
Mine asserts that these should have been my own in all past days,
And that they could not no how have been nobody else's,
And that to-day is neither yesterday nor to-morrow, and that I-S is is.

6. In the name of Dogberry,—and in Mine and Yourn, —Bosh!
And in the name of Bombastes Furioso,—and in Yourn and Mine,—Gas!

7. Mine knows that Dogberry was an Ass, and Bombastes Furioso a likewise,
And that both curiously conjoint in the present time, in Yourn and Mine,
And that where Mine is, or Yourn is, this present day, there is the centre of all Asininities,
And there is the meaning to us, of all that has ever come of Yourn and Mine, or ever will come.

SAERASMID.

Philadelphia.

[For the Saturday Press.]

All about Drummers.

BY J. W. WATSON.

Drumming! When I mention this word to my friend Hyacinth Jones, he says, "Of course, my dear boy, I know all about it. Drumming, certainly, it is performed by manipulating two pieces of wood on a bit of sheepskin. A very pretty accomplishment, by the by. Nothing finer than to hear that band of drums in our regiment, the 7th, my boy. You should hear them." I am obliged to admit that Jones takes the popular view of the question.

But, should I, making a speciality of the case, call upon Serge, of the firm of Serge, De Laine & Co., to explain to an intelligent public, what his house understands by the term "Drumming," Serge would say,

"Drumming, sir, is the latest and most approved method of opening connections, and of keeping them open, both with cash-men and time-men. Four-months men, six-months men, and twelve-months men, require, sir, to be Drummed and properly Drummed."

Mr. Serge, you can retire.

Drumming, ladies and gentlemen, is only another phrase for what in England was once termed "the occupation of a bagman," or more recently, that of "a commercial traveller." To properly fill the post of Drummer, calls for many great requisites, the first and most important of which is a knowledge of human nature.

A Drummer goes out from a large wholesale house or manufacturer in the city, for the avowed purpose of selling goods, either at the time of visiting the customer in a distant city or part of the country, or of cultivating that customer for a prospective sale, at such time as that person may visit the city from whence Mr. Drummer originates.

The duties of the Drummer are multifarous, his grades ditto. He ranges from salary $500 to salary $5,000 per annum, and—perquisites. He goes out with his trunk or valise stuffed with the goods he is expected to sell, partaking largely of the genus pedlar, or he starts with an assuming array of baggage well filled with the most stunning marvels of the tailor, hatter, and bootmaker, wherewith to astonish the provincials. In the recesses of that baggage, can be found many sweet little articles of novelty and cost, such articles as cannot be found in a country-town, and would be held in high estimation by Mrs. Smith, the spouse of that identical Smith, who, every Fall and Spring, makes quite a considerable bill with "Our House." Drummer has an elegantly careless way of managing all this. He does not go to Smithtown to sell goods. O! no. He is far above this. He is only out to keep up the connection. He tells Smith that he has taken Smithtown on his way to some distant place, thought of Smith, and felt as if he would like the pleasure of shaking hands with him, and of renewing old times. Drummer has a lively recollection of the last visit of Smith to New York, when Drummer shewed him around and they had a general good time. Smith is a little frightened at first, to see Drummer, not from any fear of enquiry into his stability, but Smith is a strong man at home, a good family-man, and a Church-member. He sees at a glance, that if Drummer should stay a day at Smithtown, it would be necessary to reciprocate; and a terrible shadow of Mrs. Smith and the naturally inquisitive way of woman, flashes across him. He does not know how fallible Drummer may be, and Smith trembles at the revelations he could make concerning that general good time in New York.

Drummer, however, as a man of the world, does not leave Smith long in doubt on this point; and that gentleman's mind once easy, he dines with Drummer at the Smithtown Hotel. A capital dinner, one glass of brandy-and-water, no champagne. "Thank you! Thank you! Mrs. Smith, you see, is rather queer about those things. You'll spend the evening with us, of course; a few friends, make you acquainted. Yes! I was noticing it, a very beautiful thing. Scissors, thimbles, spools, all ivory. Very odd indeed! Japan work, eh? Never saw one like it. 'Pon my word, I couldn't think of it. Don't insist. Mrs. Smith won't know what to say. Yes! rather funny idea, that of yours. Say that a friend in New York, wishes not to be known. She'll be puzzled to death, and wont sleep for a week. Now you'll be up by five, time enough for tea. The first brick house as you get up the hill. Not a drop more, for the world. Mrs. Smith, you see. Ha! ha! ha!"

And away goes Smith with that Japan workbox under his arm, which he is pledged to represent as coming from some unknown friend; and which pledge Smith will assuredly break within ten minutes of getting the box home, and Drummer knows it well.

Drummer goes up that evening, time enough for tea, and is received with great empressement. Smith has put on a standing collar for the occasion. Mrs. Smith and Miss Evelina Smith are got up lavishly. Mrs. does the tea, and Miss the piano. The company drops in,— among them, several pretty girls; but Drummer can see none but Miss Evelina, through whose head visions of being transplanted to New York, and of Drummer's commercial greatness, chase each other.

And thus Drummer floats away from Smithtown, leaving behind him an aroma of courtesy, off-hand nonchalance, and pleasant dreams, that will endure for a long time to come, and be likely to bear fruit, in the shape of a visit of Miss Evelina to New York the next season, when Smith comes to buy goods; in which case, the general good time will be repeated in a more limited way, counting Miss Evelina as in. While Drummer at his next stopping-place will write home to Serge, De Laine, & Co., that he has done Smith, and finds him all right, sound, wind and limb, and "as good as wheat." After which "the house" knows it can continue to sell goods to Smith on six months' credit, or longer, and enlarge his account, should he wish it.

In all this visit to Smithtown, not one word is *spoken* of business.

This is a type of the drummer magnificent, who scorns the selling of goods while on his travelling excursions. He is an enthusiast in his profession, and writes himself "Salesman." He only travels "to keep up his connection," that is, to see the customers to whom he sells goods in the Spring and Fall, at their own homes in the Summer. He drops in on them, accidentally, of course, merely in a friendly way. He is not like the man who is sent out by a second or third rate establishment, with his samples, to sell goods on the spot, or the agent who is sent down with a power-of-attorney "to secure that little account." Our first-class drummer luxuriates on a salary of perhaps $5000, with a carte blanche from the house, to draw upon them for any farther amount necessary to cultivate business. It could hardly be expected that he should "do" New York and other places, on so paltry a salary. The salary is paid for his connection already formed, and his ability to handle it. Or, in other words, for the acquaintance he may have through the country with people who are buyers of goods in his line, and for his particular tact in keeping those customers from year to year, and not letting them carry their custom to others in that line. To do this well an excellent memory is requisite, that he may recall faces and names, and when a customer makes his appearance immediately address him, "Ah! Mr. Smith, glad to see you, how are all the folks at Smithtown?" This clinches the matter at once. If, argues Smith, Mr. Drummer, through whose brain calculations for thousands daily find ventilation, and whose customers are legion, can so readily recollect me, and Smithtown, it stands to reason that Mr. Drummer must hold me in great personal esteem. And, if Mr. Drummer takes the trouble to turn out of his way to visit me at Smithtown, it is very conclusive that Mr. Drummer must find a charm in my society. It is very plain that Smith could not have heard of the inquiries that were made by Drummer on the occasion of that visit to Smithtown. Of the quiet yet searching questions regarding his accumulation of real estate, and of his personal habits.

An illustration of Drummer's wonderful powers of memory, will not be bad. I met him one day dodging about the parlors and passages of one of the large hotels. He stopped uneasily for a few moments to talk with me, and then, as though with a divided duty, dashed away. He was back instantly and said, "wait for me here one minute, I'll come directly back," and pulling a small memorandum-book from his pocket, he ran rapidly over its leaves until he settled on one and read, "Ephraim Brown, Detroit, small man, greyish hair, lame of left leg, walks with cane, mole on right cheek, very quiet, widower, three daughters, Sarah, Josephine, and Mary." All this he read off sotto voce, pocketed the book, and took another walk through. Suddenly I saw Drummer swoop down on an elderly gentleman, whom I knew in a moment for Ephraim Brown of Detroit. The affectionate manner with which he approached Brown, was really gratifying to me, and must have been equally so to that gentleman, when once he knew his man, though it struck me he rather shied from Drummer at first, as he would have done from a confidence-man, pocketbook-dropper, or some other equally hospitable professional. In less than five minutes Drummer trotted Brown up to me with an introduction, and affecting enquiries after the Misses Sarah, Josephine, and Mary. It is quite needless to add that Drummer after "doing" New York to the entire satisfaction of Brown, sold him "a stiff bill," and sent him back to Detroit rejoicing.

Brown was emphatically a six months man.

The effect to which this system of Drumming is carried, would have rather astonished our steady forefathers in trade, who sat quietly in their cobwebby countingrooms and awaited the coming of their customers. They were content in turning their capital once in two years, making a sturdy profit and hating "close buyers." They slept securely on their pillows irregardless of a panic, and troubling themselves little with country-paper which they could not get through bank. They did not toss uneasily in the morning at the recollection that they were so many thousands short that day, while its representatives were upon the books in the shape of dues by Southern men, and Western men, sold upon four-months, and running to fourteen. In these days, when three partners make a firm, high-sounding, on a capital of ten thousand dollars each, or thirty thousand in all, and each of these gentlemen must have a stylish house, and belongings at the rate of ten thousand per annum, there must be some wonderful sharp work to make the books balance, and the capital must be turned a little oftener than once in two years.

The land swarms with Drummers. They people the hotels and crowd the cars. If you mark a traveller whose *blazé* air is painfully apparent, be sure he is a Drummer. His hat will wear the glossiest sheen, his boots the patentest of patent-leather, his watchguard and charms beyond criticism, and a diamond ring of no mean value to grace the little finger of the right hand. You will talk with him—he babbles with information, he has been everywhere, seen everybody, can tell you the proper hotels to stop at through the length and breadth of the land. He has cultivated courtesy and never forgets it. After you have left him, you will mentally weigh your man, and conclude that you have crossed the path of some millionaire, travelling to brush away the dim spectre of *ennui.*

After all I have said, I stand much in the position of a certain honorable Member of Congress from Pennsylvania, who a few years since fought valiantly for the abolition of a body of officials, whom he denominated "the greatest set of rascals unhung." A defender declared the honorable gentleman spoke unknowingly.

"Not know! not know, gentlemen!" shouted the indignant Pennsylvanian, "Wasn't I one of 'em myself for seven years."

And, wasn't I one of 'em myself?

At Pfaff's.

In spite of pride, in erring reason's spite,
One thing is sure, whoever is is tight.

[For the Saturday Press.]

A RATHER COOL TIME.

New Haven, Jan. 16th, 1860.

It is pleasant to sit in a warm room, with slippered feet, wadded dressing-gown, a stuffed armchair, every appliance, in fact, of comfort and ease—to sit and look back at some old time, when accident or misfortune had placed one in a position the very reverse of what is now so much enjoyed. All good is only so by comparison, and present pleasure is enhanced tenfold by recollections of past pain.

So I sit to-night, and 'enjoy myself' the more by recalling some dismal Winter scenes through which I have passed at one time and another, and contrasting therewith the pleasing sensations of warmth and security that now surround me. One of these little episodes was this:

It was on that very Green River whereof Bryant wrote,

'When breezes are soft, and skies are fair,'

that there occurred to me, one cold, moonlit night, a most dismal, disagreeable adventure, the which I can never look back upon without a shudder at the possibilities of catastrophe then opened to my immediate view.

It was, as I have said, a cold night; it was more, it was a *very* cold night; one of the first in the early Winter, and all the more chilly that we had as yet experienced so few of them. We had before us a long perspective of sleighing-parties and frolics on the ice; for the Winter in Greenfield, Massachusetts, brings seven or eight weeks of sleighing with it as a matter of course, with a likelihood of twelve or fourteen. In saying 'we,' I intended to indicate the more elderly inhabitants of the village, for I was at that time a boy of about twelve years of age, and sleighing-parties and matters of that sort were the last things I thought of or cared for. They necessitated females, and females I, at that time, held in much the same estimation that I did the mumps, or any other disagreeable institution. I have considerably modified my views since then. All of which is by the way, and wholly unnecessary.

It was a very cold night in early Winter, and Green River was frozen over with the first ice of the season. As a natural consequence, all the boys were out with their skates. There is, or was, a piece of water called "The Bend," once a portion of the channel of the river, which at that point had curved in the shape of a large ox-bow. There had come a "freshet," in some Spring, years ago, and the river had cut through the narrow neck of land where its stream above and below had approached within a few hundred feet; had cut through, leaving its old channel to become gradually a long, narrow, irregularly curved pond, filled with eels, horn-pouts, perch, and other small fry. In the Winter this pond was great skating-ground, there being no current to disturb its early freezing, and very little depth in most parts of it. So the boys all congregated on "The Bend" for an evening of grand sport.

Fires were quickly lighted on the banks, and soon dozens of light young figures might be seen skimming the surface around the long sweep of the pond, bearing flaming brands on high, or joining in some game upon the smooth ice. Exercise kept us warm, and the sport and exhilaration were immense. The scene was not a little wild and romantic, shut in as we were on every side by hills, with thickly-wooded slopes coming down from the South to the very brink of the river, whose dark, frozen surface glittered in the moonlight only a few feet from us; only separated by a narrow belt of sand thrown up by the current from year to year.

Presently a friend of mine—he is at present a successful young merchant in New York—whom I will call Tom, proposed that we two should steal away from the others and try the river. We knew it was unsafe, and for that very reason we determined to risk it. We crossed the narrow boundary between and launched off, up stream.

Ah! how glare' the ice was, and how merrily we glided over its surface! How the ring of our resounding skates sped on before us up the river! How free and wild it was shooting away from the bonfires and the torch out into the silent night!

Those of your readers who have been *boys*—and I trust that most of the male portion of them have been —will understand me.

Past small sandy beach, and thicket, and willow copse, we sped up the river. Up to the bridge, and above it, where in the perpendicular banks we were wont to dig out, in Summers past, the nests of the sand-swallows,—up till we came to gleaming, rushing water, and turned suddenly in shore to save ourselves from a wetting.

Then, after waiting a little, and wondering what 'the boys' would think when they missed us, we were off down the river again.

Tom was much the best skater of the two, and after we passed the bridge he led me in the race down by two or three hundred feet, and was very apparently increasing the advantage. I was straining every muscle to keep my distance, and was listening with chagrin to the deeper and sharper ring and roar that accompanied his passage down the stream, showing with every stride that he was getting yet further from me. For there is this peculiarity in the noise made by skates upon the ice, that it is more apparent at three hundred yards distance than at twenty.

I was straining and fretting my way down behind him, listening to the music of his going, as it swept along the banks and round the curves of the little river, and was watching his swift gliding 'with all my ayes,' when suddenly the music was broken, cracked into a thousand little fragments of sound, and at the same instant Tom threw up his arms and went down!

The thin ice, which nearly the entire length of our swift course had sunk beneath us, rising again as we passed on, had at length given way, and Tom was in the river!

There was no doubt about that. As I swept past him the instant after, I caught one sickening glimpse of his struggling form tossed by the swift current. It was terrible. He had never before appeared to me so fine and generous and noble a fellow as he did then, when I felt certain that I was about to lose him. The river ran swift, and on the cheerless, snow-covered banks were no friends to whom we might call for aid.

At all events I could not bear the thought of leaving him to drown *alone,* and so I skated back towards him; for I had first passed down the river some little distance from the spot where he had broken through. I came back cautiously and he called to me not to approach him. I believe that most, if not all, young lads are generous and chivalric in their natures, and the feeling that prompted him to warn me against coming towards his place of imminent peril, urged me to go on from a feeling that I *might* save him, and that it would be cowardly to desert him whether I were able to rescue him or no.

I skated back cautiously, I noticed that the ice just about here was very smooth and black, showing it to be both new and thin, and I also noticed that when I went with more than usual slowness it sunk beneath me, placing me for a moment in a sort of hollow.

It was only by constant and regular motion that even my light weight was borne up by it, and I do not believe it was over an inch in thickness.

Then I knew that there was no help for it. I had got up within a few feet of where he still bravely struggled in the water, and I could hear the rush and gurgle of the stream he buffeted with.

It was a very dreadful thought that we might float down under the ice till we sank in the still depths of the grist-mill pond.

Would our friends miss us very particularly? Would there be a funeral in case they did not find our bodies? If so, would there necessarily be coffins? and what could they inscribe upon our tombstones?

No one within hearing but we two, how was it ever to be known to any one what had become of us? Might they not reasonably think that we had gone away to join a band of pirates or a circus company, and so continue to look for us whenever the stage came in on future Summer evenings with a load of strange passengers?

Above all—to leave our friends and come down to the horrible present—how would it *feel* to be drowned ? All these thoughts, as kneeling and stretching my hand forward to reach Tom's, within two minutes of the time he had broken through, I felt the ice give way around me, and then sank quietly down into the cold water.

I came up in a second, breaking the ice as I rose, a few feet below the spot where I had gone in. Tom was immediately beside me, keeping his head still above the water, and thrashing about him at a tremendous rate.

I swam while I could, as he had done, our heavy woollen clothing soon becoming saturated, and too heavy for that, however. Then I tried if I could touch bottom, and found that I could keep my toes on the sand and my mouth above the surface, and no more. I communicated the fact to Tom, who thereupon quit the thrashing upon the ice with his arms, which had hitherto kept him up, and settled down for an instant's breathing spell.

There was no time for more, for the fierce current tore us from our feet, and hurried us down stream; cold, terrible, and resistless, it took from us all life and animation by the indescribable numbness it sent through every fibre.

This could not last long, evidently. We were getting utterly chilled through and powerless. For myself, I know that while I was in the water I lost all fear of dying, and pretty much all care to live, and I presume it was the same with my friend. But there was still an instinct of self-preservation left, and that prompted us to break the ice before us towards the shore.

We were both apparently seized with the same idea at the same time, and both put it in practice, although we knew that between ourselves and the land lay a deep, still pool, where we were in the habit of bathing in quite another fashion in the Summer.

Unless we could break the entire distance across this, and reach the willows on the bank, keeping our heads meanwhile above water, we were as surely drowned as ever were any two lads shipwrecked a hundred miles from the nearest land, or cast on a terrible, rocky shore in a fierce gale. Of course we knew this, and I presume we both thought of it.

But just as we had reached the boundary of this pool, we found ourselves simultaneously upon our hands and knees upon the ice, which here, over the still water, was strong enough to bear us.

There was no doubt about it! Chilled, stiff, aching to the innermost core of our beings, we were yet alive and saved!

It seemed hardly possible after the certainties of three minutes before—after the absolute standing face to face with Death—when hope had gone out, and we only wondered how long and how painful it would be to die. We had never supposed that any one could be so stupid and thankless over such an escape.

In fact we stood upon the shore, looking back at the great, open place our struggles had made in the river, where the black water rushed, whirling and terrible, as at some strange and unpleasant thing with which we had little to do.

We had been more comfortable during our five or six minutes in the water, than we were now we were out of it, with every cold blast, every icy breath, piercing our wet garments and slowly encasing us in an armor of ice.

So Tom said, "I guess we had better go home." I thought so too.

WARREN.

[For the Saturday Press.]

LEAVES FROM NATURE.

NO. IV.

As I sit by my cottage hearth, I hear the rain beating sullenly without. Though enjoying the warmth of a large fire, and surrounded by all things from which to gain comfort, I cannot help sorrowing for the loss of Summer. It seems only yesterday since joyous Spring came and washed up the flowers; when the barks of the trees were cracking with green buds, and the yellow bees were busy sucking sweets from the climbing honeysuckle. Now all is dark and dismal. The wind whistles drearily around the hills; insects that used with gay life to fill the grass, are housed; even the snakes avoid the chilling scene, and have hid themselves. I can see no planet throbbing through the dark that sends me comfort;—I only see the wild boughs as they blow against my window. I watch the day fade into twilight, and see the shadows grow into darkness.

As night's black curtain shuts all objects from my vision, I seem to be in a dream of love, conjuring up those things on which I joy to dwell—recall scenes that once gave me pleasure. I go back to childhood's days, when my youthful brain formed bright pictures, but to be rubbed out almost as soon as made, and think them like flowers washed up by joyous Spring, and stricken down by Winter's blast. I look back to my young manhood, when each pulse beat with an ambition for success, and imagine it a tree in springtime, cracking with green buds. I think of the time when from each episode in life I drew but pleasant thoughts, and liken it to the climbing honeysuckle, from which the yellow bees cull their sweetened food.

Now these times are past! Why do I long for that which I know I cannot have? Old age cannot possess the youthful mind, nor can a Winter's air be perfumed by Summer's flowers. By advanced years my eyes are dimmed and my form is bent. My pleasures now are the realities of the past. My fire burns dimly; I throw on some sticks of wood; the flames leap cheerfully up the chimney, and throw a pleasant, homelike light about the room. A cricket from under my kitchen cupboard begins to sing its cheerful notes, and in its chirping language tells me not to mourn for what is past—that a "whistling March will plant again the April meadows"; wheat-fields will grow bright in their own time; in their own day the king-cups will come through the grass; and somewhere there is light, if your weak thought can strike upon the way.

R. W. P.

Thoughts and Things.

BY ADA CLARE.

"Sir Rohan's Ghost," by Miss Prescott, is a book that almost disconcerts one by its brilliant originality. The Press gives us so many inanities, so many literary platitudes, that our minds are almost unprepared to face such dazzling books as this one. Who is Miss Prescott, is a question that every American story-writer can afford to ask with anxiety. It is astonishing how Nature elects some upon which to stamp her seal of 'finished,' ere they have worked, while others must toil and struggle weary year upon year to acquire the ability which they were born with. This young, and I am told beautiful lady, seems to be equally acquainted with all the fine arts, that is, as far as my poor judgment can determine, for I am not a judge of anything but laces and French bonnets.

I am awaiting the developments of her story, the "Amber Gods," with some agitation, chiefly because I am cherishing a tender, let us hope not fatal passion, for its hero, which is the cause of that melancholy and lorn state of mind into which my friends have remarked that I have fallen lately. If some Northriver fishing-man draw up in his net, so that it be broken with the weight thereof, a wet and lifeless female form, with white, distorted face and tangled hair, whose fingers must yield to the embrace of the surgeon's knife ere the *Atlantic Monthly* can be unlocked from her grasp, let no coroner's inquest cavil over her. What do those dreadful beings know of the *all-devouring*? Lay her nameless in the earth; and O, ye readers of *Thoughts and Things*, drop a tear upon this column which shall ever more be mute. Then let a mandate go forth that all heroes of romance be the fashionable fictitious hero, of the pompous, church-going, temperance society order. Let the elderly family-physician, that frizzled perfection of respectability, fat and consistent, asthmatic and deeply religious, have the lovely Medora. Let him who gave her calomel when she was a confiding infant, and in whose presence her mother never dared to sit alone, take off the lovely creature—the moral of the story demands it. Let Miss Prescott beware how she introduces as heroes into her romances, those ravishing darlings of reality, whom men must always sneer at, and women ever adore, since in loving these only, can she learn the vast and self-sustaining resources of her own deep heart.

°°°

Misrepresentation," by Mrs. Drury, is a powerful novel, its construction is always dramatic, and sometimes intensely so, but it is full of weary windings and turnings. All the characters are marked, and full of nervous vitality, but they are most of them chained to the Tarpean rock of diffusiveness, and quite buried under the weight of insignificant circumstantialness, and teasing, tedious detail.

°°°

The February number of *Harper's Magazine* publishes a story by Fitz James O'Brien, which attracts much notice. The story "Mother of Pearl," opens with an exquisitely beautiful chapter on pearl-fishing, but it seems to me that the crisis of the story is a little uninteresting. The drug called hasheesh has become too well domesticated to assist in a crisis now. It is on too good terms with the digestion. Let us have some drug more awful and mystic to round off our harrowing climaxes—buckwheat for instance; it is time that the buckwheat-cake-eater should come forth and soliloquize.

°°°

Every one has seen "The heart of Mid Lothian" at Laura Keene's theatre, and every one has admired the exquisite and heart-rending portrayal of the heroine by Laura Keene; but I did not write these lines with a view to eulogize that unrivalled artiste, it was to consider a subject which that play set strongly before my heart's eye, and caused me to ponder much upon,— the Lie. The play more than the book sets the truth before one in such a monstrous and loathsome light, that it would almost make one in love with the Lie. The Lie is not a matter of assertion, but of feeling. Some of the falsest people in the world never misstate facts; they only inoculate them with such a sentiment, that they outstrip mere untruths as the arrow does the wheelbarrow.

Liars are generally heartless persons; they are generally cold, selfish, and malignant. I have seen persona who misrepresented everything, in whose lips every statement was colored and changed from the original fact by the imagination; but these are by no means Liars, they are often endowed with the truest and most honest hearts, and in all their wanderings from exactitude make no mischief, do no real wrong. But the malignant Liars, those that go about seeking whom they may injure and annoy, sullying the pure, slandering the honorable, separating friends and acquaintances, staining affections, careering madly against every virtue that makes human nature divine, O! these are the ones that the gods abhor, and for whose sake famine and pestilence have been sent into this world.

I believe that the Liars harm and annoy themselves more than they do others. They fret and sting the true hearted, but they seldom seriously injure them. But for themselves I can imagine that their feet are as it were set on quicksands, that nothing is solid, nothing reverent, nothing lovely to them. That corrupt and hideous words and voices hiss in their ears, and loathsome faces swarm through their dreams. Can the confirmed Liar love or honor or believe anything?

For my own poor part I cannot understand why brilliant men and women of this day should affect to despise the true and admire the false. What has the false, that strutting little pedlar, about him, haggling around his imitated wares, to make him so courtly and fashionable?

Truth never looks so lovely and desirable to me, as when I have for a moment deviated from her. O! how can men and women be estranged forever from her sweet approval and presence!

But why should the clever and brilliant affect often to despise her? The scientific man, the mathematician, the romancist, the artist, the poet, and the musician, all feel that their acts are dead without her,—how then can the human heart and soul afford to say hither thou canst not come! If there were no truth there could be no dependence placed on nature. The sun might splash the midnight with its fires, and the new moon and darkness seize upon and devour the noonday. Winter and its snows might tumble headlong upon the riot of the June roses, and burning passionate Autumn, with its fiery eyes, wither the sweet, pale faces of the Spring flowers. The orbit of our planet might be wrenched away from its integrity, and this globe be sent to wander on the unknown ways of accident. If truth were not the ruler of life and the universe, arts and seasons and sciences and loves and laws and rights and realities might all dash themselves into blind chaos, and sweep round us in a melancholy waste of horror.

If I could get into the secrets of the persistent Liar, what an anatomical study were that! Can the liar love, can it be a friend to anybody, can it cherish children, can it sport in the wild, exhilarating waves, can it weep for tragedy, can it listen to the music of Cortesi? But ah me! what does the Liar think of itself? does not its logic of the false persuade it that all life and inanimate form, and all feeling, are dreams and illusions, rough phosphoric outlines traced upon a wall, and waiting for a resolute hand to rub them out?

It is to me a question whether the soul can be false, whether the false does not prevent the existence of a soul.

My questions are infinite: Does the liar ever yearn after the palm-shores of futurity? Can it ever long to have the wings of a dove to fly away and be at rest! Has it remorse? Does it mourn over its errors, and imperfections, and temptations? Does it ever yearn to lighten the burdens of others, to sorrow with their sorrowing and rejoice with their rejoicings?

One thing I will refer to here, that is, the belief of men that there is sex in lying; that is, that when speaking of my sex, truth is of no consequence. To hear some sensible men speaking of women, you might suppose them (the men) to be hopeless lunatics. What confusion of tongues is there, what moral impossibilities, what social extravagancies, what literary blindness, what oratorical deafness, what stupendously illogical conclusions! You may hear a man stating facts, and uniting causes and effects, in speaking of the characters and abilities or women, with a looseness of reasoning that, if introduced into the lowest scientific or artistic consideration, would cause the dead philosopher to grow livid with dismay even in his ashes. Read, for instance, a male criticism on female productions. Does he not insist that the woman's efforts are weak, when the one he is criticizing rises up into the heavens for very strength? Does he not stop to state that the queen of the poultry-yard, the divine muffin-maker, is his divinity? Does he not waste our time with discourses about his domestic proclivities, and the strictures upon the silly buttons of his ridiculous shirt?

Of course we all feel grieved when Peter the cook serves us with muddy coffee,—but do we immediately turn to maligning Carlyle, and assail his ears with our guilty cups?

O, fie my brothers, my dear, much-loved brothers; is this the logic, the sound philosophy, the manly honor, you are forever shrieking of, from the housetops of your conventions!

The man should exalt and assist the woman, even as she should exalt and assist him. The two sexes need have no jealousies, no injustice, no hatred between them in the abstract. Nature divided them into two sexes, that they might the better love each other.

But once more I am going back to my melancholy subject, the horrible Type-liar. I am firmly convinced it cannot really believe in the immortality of the human soul; for who could wilfully mar and poison their own natures, if they could trust in that grand, and life-giving doctrine? Its whole life has been a lie, and that lie is undone; all its hypocricies, selfisms, cant, deceits, stripped away from it, and it is set face to face with the unalterably true. Perhaps the feeble existence of the Liar will fade out there, as the lamp ceases to burn when the external atmosphere is torn away from it. Truth may be to it an exhausted receiver, under which it shall shrivel up and become a shapeless and inanimate mass. Who can tell? None but the gods!

Dramatic Feuilleton.

The Circus from the Coulisses.

"If there is anything I love," remarked the Brightest and Best in a moment of weakness, "it is olives. I *like* you," she kindly continued, "but I *love* olives." That is the æsthetic distinction between my passion for the theatres and the circus. The theatres furnish the solid everyday dinner, the potaufeu, the roti, and the mince-pie (for Aldrich); but the circus is the Roman punch, which according to Wikoff (and I should like to find a better authority on the dinner-question), refreshes the palate and quickens the almost jaded appetite.

I can't express to you, O Effendi, the joy that I felt when I read in the daily papers that Cook's Circus was going to be opened at Mr. Niblo's Garden, which has brought forth in its day some rare specimens of horticulture.

Cook is from Astley's Amphitheatre, London. Cook's father had either been here or seen a man who knew another man who was interested in the circus-business— I beg pardon, equestrian profession—ever so long ago, about the time of the great fire, before Anna Maria was born, and when her Ma was just a mere child. Cook published a card, in which he said something nice about his Governor, and likewise informed an anxious and an expectant public that he had brought over all his traps from Albion's chalky cliffs "in several successive steamers," and happily without damage, either to the steamers or the traps.

Bien! We shall go to this tremendous affair. Anna Maria is to get herself in marching-order in good season, for between the tickets they really sell, and those they give away to get up enthusiasm, the first night of the Circus is always a jam. We were, however, a little late, the Dear Child not being able to make up her mind exactly what to wear. [If her pa could be reduced to such a state of abject destitution as not to allow her over a thousand dollars per annum for her dry-goods, I should be delighted.]

When we arrived at Mr. Niblo's Garden, the admirers of that very popular, entertaining, and elegant young man, and the adherents of the Circus proper and improper, had filled every part of the building with what the reporters of the Union-meetings call "a dense and solid mass of humanity."

We had orchestra-places, but between us and the fiddle-bow of the illustrious Cooke (F. V. of the Flirt-harmonic) there was an impassable wall of butchers and arrangements of that sort, from before which I shrunk aghast.

Now A. M. has been tenderly reared; her Ma has often assured me that she never thought she would succeed in bringing her up; and in one sense she was quite right, as it is Ma whom the Brightest and Best has brought up, instead of being brought up by her.

[What does the philologist of the *Evening Post* think of that sentence?]

About A. M., however, I have noticed two things. At parties she out-Germans the strongest dancers uptown, she is powerful on chicken-salad and green-seal, and when there is a question of any kind of a show or lark on hand she can go through anything. So she might have managed the butchers; but I happily lighted upon a friend of mine who is a "Cricket" for one of the great dailies. Apart from his avocation, he is quite a respectable person, and I have met him here and there at good houses. I do not always agree with him in matters of art. In point of fact I quite agree with the artists whom he does not praise, and the litterateurs who want his place, when they say he is not a good "Cricket," and ought to be crushed out peremptorily.

However, he was very useful to us on this occasion, and induced Mr. Nixon, whom A. M. thinks a very nice person, to give us chairs in the coulisses.

At the circus the coulisses are very good places, because the scenes are never changed, and you can see the whole of the Ring before you; while behind and all about, there are the performers divested of their spangles and things, and walking and talking just like ordinary people—you and me for example. Then you can talk and laugh as much as you please, and for a first night they always have refreshments wherewith the "Crickets" are subsidized.

So we saw the circus from the coulisses. Men came and offered their devoirs to A. M. just the same as if she had been in Pa's box at the Academy; the Queens of the Arena fell in love with her bonnet; and she is nearly dead from an irrepressible affection which she took for a pony.

The Hanlon Brothers.

I am just reminded of a horrid conventionality which was introduced into journalism during the dark ages, and which cannot exist under the sunlight of progress and reform. Some people, however, still cling to the absurd idea that when a man commences to write about a special subject, he ought to adhere to it, and not sail off into the quagmires of digression. These old fogies may expect a description of the circus-performances at my hands. I only wish they may get it, that's all.

A few words, however.

My first and last love in the circus is the Clown. I am naturally of a saturnine, melancholy, atra-bilious temperament, and the Clown's jokes are generally so awfully bad that I take a sardonic pleasure in bearing them. Then I enjoy overmuch the dialogues between the Riding Master and Mr. Merryman. It is not always a clever man who makes you laugh most. The hero of the two bottles of Chartreuse to finish a dinner with, was one of the funniest men I ever knew, and never intentionally made a joke or anything like one in his life.

So I looked sharply after this Clown. I had had a canon of criticism laid down for me by a fair writer, who, with the acute perception and wonderful analytical power for which the sex hath in all ages been distinguished, has discovered that the main merit in a comedy is to have it comic. Putting that with Awful Jefferson's mot, that it's no joke to write a comedy, and so it's very difficult to find any jokes in one, I watched the clown.

Who could tell? Perhaps I might get something from him for the Feuilleton.

But no, he wasn't comic, and had a black moustache. So the evil communications of light comedians corrupt the good manners even of clowns.

I soon tired of the Clown. What else have we? Ponies, pretty and well trained. The same thing has been done better. A boy named Barclay, who rides a "dashing pony act." A. M. declares that he is immense, and wants to steal him. Extraordinary gymnastic feats by two brothers of the name of Hanlon. One of them has a sort of cage up at the top of the proscenium; he goes to it by an immense bell-pull, and after doing all sorts of extraordinary things, forty feet above the Ring, makes a leap of at least twenty feet over to another bell-pull, and then descends, to the relief of everybody. Then they do some wonderful things together, these brothers. I wonder if they carry it out in real life. I should not like to have my brother standing on my head while I was dining, it seems to me. But I suppose one gets accustomed to all these things, after a while.

Meanwhile, the Chevalier de Gant-Rouge goes every night with the view of seeing Thor as Hanlan break his neck.

As for the horses and the riders, we have first a "brilliant equestrienne, Mlle. Ella Zoyara, who is pronounced by her profession, even her rivals (!), to be the most accomplished, daring, and fascinating rider that ever appeared in the arena." This Gorgeous Creature, having fascinated all the princes and nobility of Europe, including F. Joseph, at Vienna, and V. Emmanuel, at Turin, has come over here to conquer the Western world.

Mlle. Ella Zoyara.

Mlle. Ella is not beautiful. Mlle. Ella has a frame more like that of a man than a woman. Mlle. Ella has high cheek-bones, and is generally muscular. I shouldn't like to have any violent personal difference with Mlle. Ella. She rides well, but takes up an immense deal of valuable time in doing nothing particular, "waiting," as a friend of mine from the Bowery remarked, "for her second wind." Robinson, the leading male rider, is very good; he rides after the fashion of Eaton Stone, and Melville.

The circus itself is a very nice, clean, bright affair, the attendants being adorned with fresh liveries and real top boots.

The Brightest and Best, whom I have long suspected of a weakness for a passed-midshipman in the Navy, objects to their turning summersets and leaping horses over the star-spangled banner, which is represented as large as life on the flags used in the Ring. The budding patriot was quite violent for a moment, but yielded to the blandishments of marrons glacés, forgetting alike the mariner and the flag he has been commissioned to defend.

On the whole I advise everybody to do the circus at least once. It is nicer than the theatre, because if you get bored you can go away and cut a piece out of the programme without its ever being missed.

Faits Divers.

The *Octoroon* goes home this week, and her place at the Winter Garden will be filled by a young lady from Venice, by name *Lesbia*, a protégée of Matilda Heron. There is a good deal of talk about the new play which will have a full house the first night. Mr. Wallack, jeune, and G. Jordan, are into it,' as well as Heron.

Mrs. John Wood has returned to town from Canada. She will play in Boston next month, and afterwards at the W. G.

"Standing Room Only," is the invariable sign in front of Laura Keene's Theatre now-of-nights. Bourcicault is making a fine thing of Sir W. Scott, and Miss Keene is in receipt of a sufficient nightly sum to keep her from actual starvation. One thing I am going to suggest to V. R., Queen of Great Britain, etc., etc., and that is that she ought to do something nice to Miss Deland, who makes V. R.'s ancestress, G. R. No. 2's Queen, infinitely handsomer than she really was. Will the British Consul attend to this, or shall I have to send directly to Pam?

They have adopted my suggestion in Boston about Adelina Patti, and gone 'e'enamost crazy' about the linnet of Twenty-second street. She made a great hit in the *Barber of Seville*, on Tuesday, when no places could be had at night for love nor money. She will sing this opera and the *Elisir d'Amore*, with others, in this city next month.

The Octoroon draws very well at the Howard Athenæum, Boston. On the first night, some rabid Union-savers, probably in the shoe-trade, hissed the allusion to Mason & Dixon's line (almost the only epigram in the play), and the slave-sale, which *is a* little tough from a Milk street point of view.

The Webb sisters have opened the Wood Minstrel Hall, in Broadway, as a theatre. It is called by the nonsensical name of the Broadway Boudoir. The sisters are clever, but coarse and provincial. The younger divinity is quite pretty, and I have high crinoline-authority for saying that she has the prettiest neck in the world.

Nothing new yet at Wallack's. Do, Mr. Lester Wallack, hurry up your *Poor Young Man.* He has had time enough to get old, grey, rich, and gouty, since you have been at work upon him.

The Webb Sisters.

Personne.

[For the Saturday Press.]

A VOICE FROM THE LOST.

Once the hills were crowned as kings of morning,
Youth was flowing in a crystal stream,
And the flowers of faith the banks adorning,
Drifted with me like an Eden dream.
Far on high, through joy's untroubled places,
Sang I merry songs to life's great sea,
And the nights but showed me starry faces,
Lovers happy from eternity.

But I gave that Past with all the Heaven
Of its hearts for love I bore to *him*,
He who kissed, then left me to be driven
Where the sharks of crime expectant swim.
From that day I hear my mother calling
Faintly through the jasmine-shaded door;
On her face the golden rain is falling,
There I see her shining evermore!

O! the music of those rosy hours,
When *his* heart was beating close to mine,
All the days we walked through myrtle bowers,
Where the sweetest orange-blossoms twine!
But the Summer faded, and he left me
Withered flowers and an icy sky,
To the Winter's cruel kisses, left me
In a garret with my babe to die!

In the freezing moonbeams I was clinging
To my smiling babe's unheeding clasp,
Hoping that the morn was swiftly bringing
My release from life's relentless grasp.
Hope was dead, I found, as light was breaking,
For a corpse upon my bosom lay,—
God had led the babe, without awaking,
Out of night, to His eternal Day!

Listen! how the bells are wildly ringing
Through the driving tempest's moaning gloom;
And the great cathedral-choir is singing
Happy hymns that mock my silent doom!
All my years are dark and old with sinning,
New years never flush my sky with light;
Thirst, and coldest want, and death beginning,
Lead my bleeding feet through endless night.

Maidens far within the sanctuary,
Over whom the clouds of incense sweep,
Tell me, do you think the sainted Mary
Sees the jewelled shames your bosoms keep?
Narrow souls like yours can hold no passion,
All your thoughts are stamped with Custom's mould;
Whitest sins you do to suit the fashion,
And you buy forgiveness with your gold!

See before the gleaming altar kneeling,
Sneering crimes in fair Religion's dress,
Priests whose lives to God's fierce wrath appealing,
Walk the earth in masks of holiness.
Men draw back from me with looks of loathing,
Like a tainting pestilence I go;
For the badge of wrong is ragged clothing,
And they see it through the falling snow.

God will right Creation at its ending,
When these palace-tombs shall fall to dust,
Into darkest graves of sorrow sending
Resurrection-beams of spirit-trust.
Death has come! the gates of the Hereafter
Glimmer redly through the trembling air!
Hark! who shriek around me horrid laughter?
Fiery fingers braid my tangled hair!

God of mercy, I expect no pity!
I must sink beneath thy vengeance-glare,
But I shall not miss thy shining city
If *his soul*, my Clarence, be not there!
I forgave him, Thou hast not forgiven;
Grant me what my dying moments pray :
Let his guilty soul and mine, unshriven,
Close together meet thy Judgment Day!

EASTBURN BENJAMIN.

January, 1860.

NEW YORK JANUARY 28, 1860

[For the Saturday Press]

Poemet.

Of him I love day and night, I dreamed I heard he was dead,
And I dreamed I went where they had buried him I love—but he was not in that place,
And I dreamed I wandered, searching among burial-places, to find him,
And I found that every place was a burial-place,
The houses full of life were equally full of death, (This house is now,)
The streets, the shipping, the places of amusement, the Chicago, Philadelphia, the Mannahatta, Boston, were as full of the dead as of the living,
And fuller, O vastly fuller, of the dead than of the living;
—And what I dreamed I will henceforth tell to every person and age,
And I stand henceforth bound to what I dreamed;
And now I am willing to disregard burial-places, and dispense with them,
And if the memorials of the dead were put up indifferently everywhere, even in the room where I eat or sleep, I should be satisfied,
And if the corpse of any one I love, or if my own corpse, be duly rendered to powder, and poured in the sea, I shall be satisfied,
Or if it be distributed to the winds, I shall be satisfied.

WALT WHITMAN.

Thoughts and Things.

BY ADA CLARE.

Miss Harriett Prescott has finished her story of the "AMBER GODS" in the *Atlantic Monthly.* For me it is a superb story. I felt while reading it as I did when I saw Ristori for the first time, as if all my faculties were locked in a trance, and I was alive only through speechless admiration. For me this is eloquence, this is poetry, this is action. I rejoice with myself, I wring my own hands laughing, I throw my self with tears of pleasure on my own breast,—a new admiration is born to me, my life is enlarged, my soul has another pulse.

Rose Terry writes (also in the *Atlantic*) a humorous sketch, entitled "MATILDA MUFFIN." It has a nice comic originality, and, like everything that lady does, is well done; but the idea is sadly old-fashioned. How very quaint it must be to live in Connecticut, catching only the far-off echoes of the world's life as it rolls onward in metropolitan places! A thing has passed away here, long before it ceases to be visible in Connecticut, just as any of the fixed stars could die out of heaven, and its last light travel many years ere reaching this planet, so that to us it would be an existence, long after it was forgotten in space.

In metropolitan cities the literary woman is no longer accused of sternness toward the other sex; fraility is what they accuse her of now. The male, who is always the protector of virtue, follows vindictive in her footsteps, to dry the tears no longer of the betrayed mutton-chop, but of injured propriety; her crime he says is no longer a domestic, but a moral one. That's a relief to my soft feelings, for I should grieve to see confiding victuals betrayed and then cast aside to perish of shame and repentance, while their remorseless betrayers floated gayly through the proud columns of the *Atlantic*.

Perhaps I am signing my death-warrant in making this confession, but if a man wants to chastise literary pretention in me, if he wishes to wring my bosom and agonize my soul, let him treat me as the highly intelligent being without any weaknesses; let him have no topics in speaking with me but solemn ones; let him weigh me down with wit, with puns, with deep remarks of any kind, with scientific and logical statements; let him, refusing to listen to my naturally stupid little conversation, insist on my being sarcastic and brilliant; let him deny me all sorts of nonsensical caprices for all sorts of ridiculous people and things; let him deny my right to be a fool with the foolishest of follies, and the hoop-skirt will become a burden to me, and the next Spring flowers will blush over my grave.

o o o

I know not what connection there is between my grave in particular, and human fathers in the abstract, yet the latter have stepped out of the former into my thoughts.

The father is the ludicrous and therefore the mournful figure in the comedy of life.

His offspring brings for him much care, much work, and some pride, but very little heart-pleasure. What a melancholy object is the father during the most trying period of his wife's experience! Does she not treat him with contumely, with contempt, with indignation? He is a wretch in her eyes; he stands up a huge target for all the arrows that come from her suffering and irritable mind and body to aim at. But why need I say more: the abject and down-trodden creature which the father of the unborn child becomes, has been the subject of wittier pens than mine.

But the summit of his nervous wretchedness is only reached when the time of her trial comes. He wanders about, a clumsy and aggravated creature in everybody's eyes—secretly considered a brute. All the vials of his wife's reproaches and despairs are poured out on his devoted head; not a lock on it but is drenched with them. Nurses, doctors, aunts, housemaids, walk over him as though he were a worm, and trample upon him until he is no longer remembered. His house is turned into a hospital, and he is therefore couched upon a straw bed in the garret. Dread things are served up to him in the kitchen as food. All his habits are treated as crimes; he is not even allowed a glass to shave with; so when he slinks meekly into his wife's chamber, she protests, with tears in her eyes, that the ugliness of his countenance had well-nigh thrown her into convulsions. He approaches guiltily the cradle where the little one lies, furtively drops a kiss on its sweet face, upon which it instantly gives forth a piercing wail, thereby entering the universal protest against him. He starts back cowed and humbled, while the pale mother in her bed sobs out that she is resigned to suffering herself, but prays that he will spare her innocent child.

As time goes on, and his son advances to maturity, he has nothing but a forlorn pride to console him. The little fellow that has been a part of his mother's body, that has drawn his life for months from her breast, that has slept in her arms, and known no Providence but her, as he grows, still thinks his mother an angel, while his father appears to him an inexorable judge, put in authority in order to thwart all his plans, and nip all his pleasures in the bud.

The father takes upon himself the chastisement of his son's transgressions, and the boy goes forth from the assumed sternness of the father, revenge and rebellion rankling in his heart towards that parent while he throws himself upon the tender bosom of his mother, who mingles her tears with his, to soothe away the passion of his grief and anger.

All through life it is so: the father pays the young man's bills; but his manner of doing it takes away from the kindness of it. The father refuses to sympathize with the youthful follies and extravagancies and tastes of the young man. He exercises a domestic tyranny over him, he remonstrates sternly with him, he sneers at, irritates, threatens him. The consequence is, the son loses his respect for him; he fears, avoids, and deceives his father, but he cannot love him.

On the contrary, the mother keeps an immortal youth for her child. She sympathizes with his caprices, rejoices and sorrows with him, and to her he is never ridiculous nor bad. The mother and son must be depraved indeed ere they can become indifferent to each other. She thinks her child the man among men, chief among ten thousand and altogether lovely; he thinks his mother the only perfect woman in the world. But the name of his father is seldom tenderly on his lips; about him the son preserves an ominous silence.

I commenced these remarks with a view to deploring the forlorn position of the father, but I know that it is in a great measure his own fault. He begins wrong. He regards the mother of his child as a mere childbearing creature, and her offspring resents it ere it is born.

O, if he could learn that child-bearing was as much a matter of the soul as of the body; if he could look into the mother's heart, and read the deep disquiets, the passionate doubts, the dim yearnings, the fears, the sorrowings, the anguish of love, that make the travail of the soul harder than that of the body! How much he could lighten that burden if he were not blinded with pride and materiality! for, indeed, the heaviest weight of all to her is the conviction that she struggles alone. She feels that he in a measure despises her, that he regards her patience, her suffering, her sadness, as an unnecessary folly which she was born to suffer. Even his pity has the air of condescension, and his love that of convenience.

O, fathers, can you wonder that the life growing out of hers, colored with her hopes, and fears, and emotions, so often comes into the world to consider you its enemy, to treat you with fear and deceit ?

I believe there are three parties to the birth of a child, the mother, the father, and God. When the father refuses to acknowledge that high spiritual element in conception, he loses only himself, and the child belongs to God and its mother.

All through life the foolish pride of the father appears; he treats the child as a mere tool in his hands, to inherit his name and work out his wishes. He deprives him of his pleasures when he is a child, without condescending to explain to him that his own welfare is alone considered. All his love and interest and anxiety goes for nothing; the son believes only in what he sees, his harshness, his coldness, his unfamiliarity. He loses one of the most lovely of Heaven's blessings, filial affection. But why should he lose it? The boy is not so horrid a monster that he cannot be treated as a friend by his father. He is subject to persuasion, to kindness, to good sense; he need not feel that he is forced to do things by being bullied by one bigger than himself.

The father is not incapable of inspiring affection, as the devotion of the daughter to him often proves. He is better than he seems.

Dramatic Feuilleton.

Faits Divers.

They have two "Octoroons" over in the Bowery; and, as I see by the dailies, they are both doing very well. I have not yet had the time required for an Oriental trip. Meanwhile, the horn of the Bourcicault is exalted, and there is no chance for *Kerjunca*.

When the House gets organized, Brown intends to lobby through two bills,—one for the peremptory crushing of Bourcicault, and the other to make the production of *Kerjunca* obligatory upon the managers.

The Patti-wing of the Opera company will return to Irving-Place next week, and open on Thursday. Little Patti has made such a hit in Boston, that she has, on dit, grown two inches in height, and enlarged her crinoline. The Athenians think that, next to the Old Greeks and Mount Auburn, she is the best thing out. One of the country-members of the Legislature 'cal-klates' it would be a good 'idee' to set up her 'stat-oo' between those of Webster and Horace Mann.

A most remarkable instance of pure affection for art was afforded the other day in the Court of the Marines (so called because they tell the most awful stories there), by Mr. John S. Mæcenas Lutz, who swore that he had no interest in the profits or losses of Miss Laura Keene's Theatre, and received no salary for his services as Treasurer. I have been so far penetrated with admiration at Mr. Lutz's magnanimity, that my digestion has been seriously impaired.

I have seen a letter from my young friend, Mr. Jack Pouce, who was believed at one time to have died of too much PERSONNE.

Master Pouce was a young man, born of rich but respectable parents, and lived in a four-story brownfront house, in a street where there are no stables nor butcher's shops.

He loved—not wisely, but too well—the Brightest and the Best. She, after a brief period, said he was too short for the German, and set him out in the cold, with a number of other ineligible youths.

Pale melancholy and Dark Hennessey marked him for their own. He shunned the haunts of men, and took to the East side of the town.

Finally his Governor exiled him to the rural districts, where he pursues the festive trout, and slays, once in a long while, the bounding deer.

He corresponds with Sophonisba to whom he told his love, and in his last letter encloses a printed programme, with the following remarks:

"This is a gay place; the young ladies wear freckles on their faces, but no hoops, and the young men indulge in blue overalls, chew gum, and anathematize 'by goll.' You will please hand the enclosed to PERSONNE, and tell him that the Academy of Music is too near —— to amount to much, and that he had better sell out his stock in the Irving-Place property, and invest his money in our Town Hall."

The bill which accompanies the letter is headed "The Cantidores are Coming. Fun without Vulgarity." It proceeds to state that,

Professor Nichols has the honor of announcing to the Ladies and Gentlemen of this place and vicinity, that he will give one of his chaste and pleasing Entertainments at Halsted's Hall, on Wednesday evening. All that is pleasing, yet chaste in Wit and Humor, will be portrayed, forming in all a luscious Feast of Mirth and Music, which in the above Hall presents extraordinary inducements to the Lovers of Fun and Elegant Amusements.

The performance commences with the "inimitable comedy, entitled *The Swiss Cottage*, or *Why don't She Marry? O! Liberty for Me! No Man's Wife I'd be."* Professor Nichols plays "Natz Tick the Witty Lover." Mrs. Nichols is the *Lisette*, and Miss Emma Sanders, the *Corporal Max.* In part second Professor Nichols is announced for three comic songs; Mrs. Nichols dances a Highland fling, an Irish jig, and a Jordan breakdown, plays a violin solo, and sings two or three songs. The whole concludes with "the very laughable French pantomime entitled, *The Clown Outwitted; or, Who "Stole the Liquor?"* with Professor and Mrs. Nichols in the leading rôles. Admission fifteen cents. No halfprice. "Music for dancing after the entertainment, if desired. Tickets ken be had at Swinard's grocery."

I have written to Jack to send the Professor and his troupe down to the metropolis. I would give anything to have a dash at them, and Gayler has a piece, *not* from the French, already for their début.

Mrs. Bateman has made a drama out of Longfellow's *Evangeline*, in which Miss Kate Bateman will make her début at the Winter Garden, about the middle of March.

"Marino Faliero Beheaded for his Crimes."

The Winter Garden presented a very curious ensemble, last Monday night.

Matilda Heron, the Shu-shu-gar, had returned to the metropolis, and was to play in a new piece which had been rehearsed in the provinces, and much admired by the pundits of Philadelphia and the modern Athens, The house was packed with the most knowing audience I have ever seen in a New York theatre.

It was a profound 'sell,' this *Lesbia;* an immense hoax, this Heron-version of *Les Noces Venitiennes*. I have seen a good deal of trouble in my time. Anna Maria has moments when she is very disagreeable. I always get a bad partner at whist, and rarely hold over three honors. I have corns. Men whom I detest always insist on shaking me by the hand, and women, whom I adore, as a rule, wont have me at any price. All these are minor miseries compared to the sufferings which I endured during the first performance of *Lesbia.*

I know that I can't tell you, O! Effendi of the Effendi Piazza, what a bore it is, but I'll try:

Les Noces Venitiennes is a drama by Victor Séjour. It is announced by the Shu-shu-gar as a "Sensation Play." It is all about Venice, the Falieri family, the Council of Ten, the Bridge of Sighs, and so forth.

Lesbia, who might as well have been in Kamschatka as in Venice, so far as the plot is concerned, is a courtesan and a spy, in a short white silk dress with blue stripes, and gold fringe around the tops of her boots. When you are first introduced to this splendid creature, she is paying a visit to *Orceola*, an unamiable old rascal, in a black and red robe de chambre, and a beard of many colors, for which I would suggest Mancini. He presents her with a slight token of his regard in the shape of a purse, which she stows away in her pocket. Before she leaves the trysting-place (the palace of the Doge), Lesbia is deeply affected by the arrival of Colonel *Galieno*, the fascinating young man of the drama. Like all army-men, he is powerful with the beau sexe. Even when his dug-out—they call it a gondola, but it isn't—appears afar off, Lesbia falls terribly in love with him and rejects the old gentleman's purse "with scorn."

In real life this would be considered the most wonderful case of conscience on record.

Simultaneously with the appearance of the conquering hero, comes the Doge and the Council of Ten, all very mild, pacific, and not over clean persons in appearance. *Galieno* makes a long speech to them, in which he talks a great deal about himself, a prevailing complaint with army men, from Julius Cæsar down to Jefferson Davis. He finally sees what every one else has discovered some time before, namely, a panel which formerly contained the portrait of an unsuccessful politician, Marino Faliero. The panel is covered with a black pall, lettered "Marino Faliero, beheaded for his crimes." *Galieno*, being the grandson of the beheaded, is naturally exercised in his mind by this inscription, and tears it down. *Orceola*, a political enemy of the Falieri family, immediately pitches into *Galieno*, and appeals to the Council of Ten.

That respectable body acts according to the usual senatorial practice,—one which is summed up in the remark of a Scotch member of Parliament, who said that he had heard a great many speeches that changed his mind, but never one that altered his vote. So the C. O. T. pronounce, unanimously, against Colonel *Galieno*, who goes off to a mountain pass, puts on a short-tailed coat, with a great many small buttons in front, wears black velvet breeches, sports two watches and a Vandyk hat, carries a carbine, and is, in short, a brigand. *Lesbia,* still in her gold-fringed gaiters (she ought to exchange them, in that line of country, for Balmorals), has become Mrs. Galieno, a la main gauche, and things are going on quite comfortably, when Mademoiselle *Viola,* the granddaughter of *Orceola*, goes out for a walk, as one might go to see Uncle Jemmy at Clover Hill, and is nipped by the brigands. Being pretty,—and Mrs. Allen is very pretty,—the brigands engage in some athletic game, like matching pennies, for her. When the result is announced, she don't see it, and is protected by one *Spalatro*, between whom and some of the other rascals, an irrepressible conflict springs up. At the critical moment, *Galieno* appears, and shields the maiden. Aprés, he falls in love with her, as a matter of course.

Now commences a terrible state of things. *Lesbia* has been the chere amie of *Galieno* during five years, and distinctly objects to his new affinity. *Orceola* don't see him at all. Gets, in fact, in an ungentlemanly state of indignation about it: Springs the Council of Ten upon *Galieno*, and intends to put him through a course of thumb-screws, and things of that sort. *Viola* sticks to *Galieno*, and they agree to take a cup of cold poison together; when the Governor relents, and, as it seemed to me, very considerately dies, although they all take a long time to do it. *Lesbia* thinks she will go into a convent, and so ends the play. By the way, I am requested to inquire as to the fate of *Spalatro*, who mysteriously disappears after the third act.

Now, in the first place, as far as I am concerned, I object to this continual pitching into Venice. It is really one of the nicest places in Europe. Not dark, nor bloody, nor gloomy, nor disagreeable, as the dramatists make it, but gay, lively, and á giorno in the extreme. I tell you, Effendi, that, next to Paris and Rome, Venice is the most delightful city on the Continent. And as for the Bridge of Sighs, bah! There is, or was a place at the end of it, where you can get a Milanese cutlet and a Maccaroni such as the Trois Fréres cannot approach.

And this special play, what is it? It is a dull melodrama, which neither interests, nor entertains, nor thrills you in any way. Here and there a good situation, or a fine tableau, but between all these a succession of dreary wastes without a single oasis. The actors speak the most utter balderdash, our American expression "highfalutin" gives the best idea of it, and there is not one natural bit in the whole of the play. It is cheap, theatrical trash, from the beginning to the end.

I do not speak of the moral of the play, although it teaches nothing. I am not one of those persons who advocate the Sunday-school drama; but I think that art does not require a sacrifice of all the proprieties. I believe, as a rule of art, as well as of moral ethics, that whatever is not essentially good and true, and is so recommended by itself to one's natural instincts, is wrong and false, and no matter how carefully and elaborately it may be done, must be inevitably damned.

But, in the matter under present consideration, we are not required to go very deeply. *Lesbia* is a very bad play in French, and is still worse in English, or what is called English in the coulisses.

As for the acting: Miss Heron has not made a success in her new rôle. It is said that she has fallen off since her great success in *La Dame aux Camélias*. For one, I do not see it. It appears to me that she is *Marguerite Gautier* in everything, no better and no worse than when she first played at Wallack's.

True, she moans and howls a little more in *Lesbia* than in *Camille*; true, her costumes are in the worst taste and make her look much heavier than she is; true that the little touch of nature, which was the chiefest of her charms, has disappeared: but the mistake you have all made in the case of Matilda Heron, as in that of Laura Keene, is in the supposition that a clever woman with some stage tact is an artist. It is a very grave error. Rachel was a clever woman when she played the soubrettes in a Boulevart theatre, but she never was an artist until Samson took her in hand; and, after all, she was never satisfied with her own work. We have not on the American stage a woman-artist in the tragic way, and only Miss Robertson, and Mrs. Wood, and Miss Gannon in comedy. This is the fault of the public, which runs to pretty faces and nice wardrobes.

I don't object to them any more than any one else; I only protest against the cant of criticism which exalts shams and humbugs to places where they do not belong. In the case of Heron she has artistic perceptions and instincts, but she has been spoiled, like Laura Keene and Mrs. Hoey, by outrageous puffing.

I have been led into such a long essay that I see I have but a little space to give to the other artists at the Winter Garden.

Mr. Wallack, not an especial favorite of mine heretofore, surprised me with a most vigorous and vividly artistic performance. I do not think that Macready himself could have played the part better or even as well. Every pose was effective, and considering that the *Orceola* is a purely conventional rôle, the acting was eminently natural. Mr. Wallack saved the play from utter failure. I liked Mr. Jordan in *Galieno* very much, and Anna Maria says that Mrs. Allen was very sweet as *Viola*. She acted exceedingly well, and displayed more real sympathy and dramatic passion than I have ever seen in her before.

I have taken up a great deal of valuable time in saying what I might have put more directly thus: *Lesbia* is a bore; and, were it not for Mr. Wallack's acting, a fiasco. The managers of the Winter Garden were very stupid in spending so much money to give so bad a play so fine a mise en scéne. Awful Jefferson must give us something better than *Les Noces Venitiennes*; as my friend the Duke would say, "it won't wash."

Mr. Lester Wallack's Poor Young Man.

On Tuesday, at Wallack's, *The Romance of a Poor Young Man* was produced. The audience was quite as numerous, but not so distingué as that at the W. G. on Monday.

Every one, I presume has read the novel or the play. The former has been very well translated, and the drama does not differ from it in any essential point. The Wallack version is a literal translation from the French play, made by Mr. Pierrepont Edwards, and arranged for the stage by Mr. Lester Wallack.

It is, in the main, a good play, although it is too long, and there is a little, just a little too much of Mr. Lester Wallack in it.

There are five acts and a prologue. The prologue introduces the Poor Young Man (Mr. Lester Wallack), starving in a Parisian garret. He has here two friends, a man of medicine (Mr. Brougham), who represents the advocate and the doctor of the novel, and an old female servant, who has taken to letting lodgings. The doctor sends the Poor Young Man into the Laroque family, with the intention of marrying him to M'lle. Marguerite, a very interesting young person who is afflicted with a disagreeable impression that every man who looks sweetly at her is after her bank account, which is plethoric. The Poor Young Man is as proud as he is impecunious. He is a Marquis (I notice that no one on the stage pronounces the word properly) turned Steward, and is occasionally snubbed, which treatment he resents in such a manner that in the usual course of things he would have been kicked out of the house. Au contraire, the women, including the governess, fall in love with him, and after doing all sorts of impossible and extraordinary things, he ascertains that he is the real owner of the estate; upon which Mademoiselle thinks that marrying him is the very best thing she can do. Then, according to the bill," the peasants enter in their picturesque Breton costumes," and there is a general tableau of rejoicing. A state of things which I, for one, would not disturb for the world.

I must, however, tell the people who have read the charming novel that if they go to the theatre expecting to see the characters reproduced on the stage, they will be disappointed.

The actors and actresses couldn't do it if they tried, and perhaps it is better that they don't try. Take the men to begin with. There is a fine contrast between the characters of the poor Marquis and the wealthy insouciant man of the world, whom you dislike at first, but who in the end turns out to be a trump. Mr. Lester Wallack's pride is offensive. It is not the outward sign of the innate dignity of a nobleman who has been placed in a trying and delicate position; it is only the stage gentleman, trying to accommodate himself to the peculiarities of a new character. Mr. Walcot did not play well, because he played too much. There is nothing so difficult to represent on the stage as the well-bred man of the present day, and it is not decrying Mr. Walcot's real artistic merit, to say that he cannot or does not do it. Of course he is not vulgar, but at the same time he has not the requisite savoir faire. Mr. Brougham's character is clumsily written. He gives it a certain vraisemblance, more than could be expected from the materials placed in his hands.

As for the women, Mrs. Hoey is not a bit like Mademoiselle Marguerite, the cold proud beauty whom Feuillet describes so finely. Nearer to the author's idea is Miss Morant, who gave a piquant flavor to the governess in the earlier scenes, but very nearly spoiled it all by a melo-dramatic exit, which was laughably absurd in a play of this kind. Miss Gannon, with her hair á la Josephine, was delicious in the lachrymose dame. I don't think that this capital actress is properly appreciated. I owe her a great deal. She always puts me in a good humor, and next to Wood has more real fun than any other actress on our stage.

Now as I fear that I am getting to be a bore, I will take my hat and go after a very few words. Mr. Wallack has made a very fair play out of *The Romance of a Poor Young Man*. People who have not read the novel will think that the drama is exceedingly good. The weakest point is that which should be strongest, the tower scene. This is made purely Bowery. After a great deal of talk about his honor, the Poor Young Man makes a terrific leap from the highest point of the tower, to the great injury of a large number of mattrasses. The audience liked Mr. Lester's jump so much that he came before the curtain after doing it, and like *Snug the Joiner*, allowed the ladies to see that he was uninjured. Was ever anything so absurd?

The Romance of a Poor Young Man was more successful than *Lesbia*, although the former cannot be set down as a positive triumph. Like all of Feuillet's plays, not excepting his greatest and best, *Dalila,* it is too purely narrative and descriptive, and throws a burthen on the artists to which they are not equal.

The public, however, did not seem bored, and called Mr. Lester Wallack out, or rather some people made a noise, and he came out, and delivered a characteristically modest speech, taking a good deal of credit to himself, giving some to Mr. Edwards, and a little to the artists.

He neglected to mention M. Octave Feuillet, who had, it is generally supposed, something to do with the authorship of *Le Roman d'un Jeune Homme Pauvre.* For a foreigner and a Frenchman, he is a fair writer; and

Messrs. Lester Wallack and Pierrepont Edwards ought to be magnanimous, and give the young man a chance.

Sweetly, O Editor, your own

Personne.

P. S.—A. M. wants to say that though she isn't a "Cricket," she don't see the new pieces at Wallack's and the W. G., and as for her give her Laura Keene's and the Circus. I am afraid the Dear Child is more than half right.

P.

LEAVES FROM NATURE.

Yesterday I was looking at a beautiful horse. He seemed the personification of gentleness. As I approached him, to obtain a nearer view, he put down his head as if he would be caressed; when I was about to stroke his neck, he bit at and nearly succeeded in wounding me. (He did tear my coat.) The gentle appearance of that animal is like the weather we have enjoyed for the past week. For although the warm air don't bite, it gives severe colds by tempting one, with its mildness, to cast off the usual Winter protection of thick clothing.

On every side, from every person I hear but the same remark, "What charming weather!" "Tis true the air is mild, the sun is warm, but I cannot enjoy this unseasonable atmosphere. With me, each season has its own peculiar characteristics: Spring is hopeful; Summer, sweet content; Autumn, dissatisfaction, sorrow, whose winds are but sighs of the dying trees; Winter, bold victory. There is something so like the great conqueror in "Old Winter," as he makes earth bow in nakedness to him, and forces all live things to run from his path, and seek shelter from his chilling blasts, that it seems a pity he should be interrupted in so victorious a career. Perhaps I would not think so much of this, did I not know that Winter was sure to win in the long run. (I am but human and always prefer being on the stronger side). I know that from some unforeseen cause the cold has allowed itself to be surprised by a power from the South which is much stronger than was anticipated, and thought it prudent under the circumstances for the present to quit the field; but shortly there will arrive a strong reinforcement from the North Pole, and the Southern visitor will disappear with much greater celerity than he arrived. Another serious objection that I have to the warring of the seasons, is the wretched walking to which we are all subjected until the quarrel is settled one way or the other. Did ever anybody see such riding, walking, or getting about in any style, as we've experienced for ten days? The streets and roads now are beginning to be in a passably good condition, the sun having been victor long enough to remove part of the dead and dying bodies of the enemy from the battle field. Is it not indeed a sad prospect when we think all this war will have to be reenacted, our streets once more will be blocked with the decaying remnants of Winter, and the air will be filled will horrid shrieks emanating from the lungs of the stage-drivers, who vainly endeavor to enforce their horses to pull the omnibuses, when the nags with astonishing pertinacity insist upon tumbling down. And the crossings for pedestrians who cannot like Mons. Blasé, afford to have a "coupé." How they will encase their lower limbs in gutta-percha, vainly hoping thus to wade through the deep and gory stream without becoming covered with a dark substance closely resembling mud. Even the proposed improvement in dress made in the SATURDAY PRESS two weeks since, would be useless, unless very high boots were added to the costume. Singular as it may appear, I see quite a lesson founded on this mud. One much more lucid than its opaque origin would lead one to suppose. Others have "seen it," indeed, who had a decided advantages of the lilies of the field. In significance it is extraordinary and illimitable. And certainly, if I turn away from my own hurried and careless expression to announce this immense truth in the memorable words of another, I may hope to be forgiven. And this is the lesson of the mud; which I trust somebody with the biggest pair of spectacles on record will be able to see:

"Truth crushed to *earth* will rise again,
The eternal years of God are hers;
But error wounded writhes in pain,
And dies amid her worshippers."

R. W. P.

NEW YORK FEBRUARY 4, 1860

The Oasis in the Desert.

Written for The New York Saturday Press

BY LIZZIE CAMPBELL.

I.

I was left an orphan at an early age, when I became the charge of an aunt, my father's sister, who, although she was never unkind to me, would, I have no doubt, have been as well pleased if I had never come into the world, as she had a large family of her own. I remember I used to think when I was a child that no one was half so well supplied with cousins as myself. There were five boys and six girls in the family besides myself, a quiet, dark-complexioned, strange-looking child, of whom no one took any farther notice than to say when I was first observed, "What a strange little girl!"

As far back as I can carry my memories of childhood, I see that remark looming out from every corner of the past, from the time when, at the age of seven, I first took up my abode in my aunt's, and seated myself in the chimney-corner, so eaten up by grief that I had not a tear to shed; and then, as my good-hearted but commonplace aunt looked at me, I remember she turned away to her eldest daughter, a buxom, bouncing, red-cheeked girl, with the simple remark, "What a strange little girl!" Till ten years later, I heard the same often-repeated words, "What a strange girl!"

My childhood was so uninteresting, so dry and commonplace, that I have no desire to weary the reader with any details of it, or to carry my own mind back to that period generally so fraught with pleasing recollections, but which for me does not contain one single star to brighten the dark and cheerless sky. I will pass on to my seventeenth year.

It was a bright, beautiful evening late in Summer, and I was seated under a large elm-tree, beside the road, and at some distance from the house, reading.

I was much interested in the book, and I did not hear approaching footsteps, nor, although a shadow was cast across the spot where I was seated, did I become conscious of the presence of any one, till a voice said:

"What a strange girl!"

Then I looked up quietly, neither embarrassed nor much surprised. A pair of dark eyes—I don't know what color, and in after years I never found out—were looking at me with an expression of blended interest and surprise.

When I looked up and met the look, the owner of the eyes smiled a little, and then asked in a full, rich voice, modulated to a tender gentleness.

"Will you be good enough to direct me to Haworth?"

I rose, and with my hand pointed out the road that led in the direction of Haworth parsonage, which was about two miles distant. The stranger thanked me, and passed his way.

I looked after him till he was out of sight, and then recurred to me the words he had spoken to himself, and which had awakened me from the absorption of my book, and for the first time in my life I asked myself what was there about me to elicit the same remark from every one.

I was sorry that man had said it, for there seemed a sort of disgrace in the fact of my being so 'strange,' and I was ashamed of it without knowing why. It had never given me a thought before, but then I felt that I would have given all I possessed, which was *very* little, if that man had not thought the same of me, and made the same remark that every one else made.

I threw down my book angrily, and felt the first feeling of real annoyance that had ever troubled me; and then I crossed the road, and went a little farther on, till I came to a small, deep pond, the dark surface of which made a sort of mirror. I looked in and surveyed myself.

I did look strange, and I didn't wonder any longer that any one seeing me for the first time should think.

What a queer-looking face I had, and what wild eyes—what a large mouth, and what a hook-billed nose, and a quantity of black hair all matted and tangled, as though it had never known either brush or comb, although I was careful to dress it each morning. And then I tried to think how in the world it could be in such a state of barbarous dishevelment; and in trying to solve the mystery I became aware of a fact that had not struck me before.

When reading, I had a ridiculous fashion of running my fingers through my hair, knotting, tangling, and matting it, quite unconscious of what I was doing.

I suppose I had been thus employed when the stranger pronounced me a strange girl; and then, as the great probability of this being the case forced itself upon me, I stamped my foot with impatience. I made many discoveries that Summer evening: till then I did not know that I was impetuous, hot-tempered, and easily excited to anger; for in the humdrum existence I had hitherto led, nothing had aroused my passions, of any kind; but as I continued to look in the glassy mirror, and saw how soiled and torn my dress was, I ground my teeth with anger.

I am ashamed to remember, though it is so long ago, and I was an untutored, uncivilized girl, the sinful feelings to which I gave way, that Summer aftermoon.

Then I went back to the spot where I had left my book, and sat down, taking it listlessly in my hand. My first impulse was to return to my aunt's as speedily as possible, wash myself, comb and brush my hair, and exchange my dress for one of a better appearance; but more suddenly than my angry feelings, even, came a reaction. What did I care for the stranger? Who was *he*? What was he to me? I had never seen him before—probably would never see him again. What did it matter what he thought of me, or how I had appeared in his eyes?

By this time he had reached the parsonage, and quite forgotten that such a being as Catherine Livingston lived, and moved, and had her being in the same world as himself.

I addressed myself to my book again, and tried with all my might to become interested in it.

Quite impossible! Nothing but a pair of strange-looking, dark eyes, with a very gentle light shining deep down in them, was to be seen upon the open page.

I threw aside the book in disgust, and in spite of myself my thoughts returned to the stranger.

Why had that single look such power over me? And why did the sound of that voice linger on my ear? I had seen handsomer men, gayer men, more elegant, more gentlemanly—but there I stopped suddenly. No, I had *never* seen a more gentlemanly man, nor have I ever since seen one more so. Yet what was there about him that so fascinated me, so interested me? What was there in the simple thought of him that so thrilled me? Perhaps it was because he had spoken so very gently to me, and that was something quite new and strange. I don't mean that my aunt, or uncle, or cousins addressed me unkindly; but it was in the rough manner habitual to them, not with the gentle tenderness that so won my heart.

Then I wondered who the stranger was, and where he came from, and what he wanted at Haworth, and why he had asked for Haworth when he was in it. And then I remembered that when strangers inquired for Haworth, they always meant the parsonage. And I wondered what in the world he wanted at that quiet place, where the advent of a stranger was food enough for conversation among the Haworth people for weeks. Perhaps he wished to see Mr. Bronté, or perhaps he was a London friend of Mr. Brantwell's, or probably he had business of some kind with the Miss Brontés.

I can't tell what a strange, painful feeling I had when I thought of the possibility of his business being with any of the young ladies. None of them were handsome, but they were all three almost miraculously clever; and though not beautiful, I knew, for I had seen and spoken a few words to her, what a great charm, all unknown to herself, was about the eldest.

O what eyes she had! And what fairy hands, so white and delicate; and such smooth, glossy, hazel hair! I have sat for hours in the little Haworth church, looking into the ever-varying eyes of Charlotte Bronté, in which shone such a living light from her pure and lofty soul. I should have been listening to the preaching of her father, but those eyes were a sermon in themselves. No wonder that thoughts emanated from the mind shining through them that have since thrilled the whole world!

I awoke from my reverie to the fact that the twilight was so slowly gathering in that I could hardly observe the imperceptible change from broad day, till night came, quietly trailing her sable robes along the warm green earth, and then I raised the book I had impatiently cast aside, and took my way slowly homeward.

That was Tuesday, and on Sunday, having passed the intervening days in a sort of dream, I made the most careful toilet I could, and took the way to Haworth church.

There were present a very few when I arrived, and having taken my seat, with a strange flutter and embarrassment quite new to me, I ventured to look around the church.

Seated directly in front of me, two seats forward, was the object of my thoughts for the past four days. My heart stood still for a moment, and then began to flutter and palpitate in a manner that almost choked me.

I glanced over to the pew occupied by the minister's family. It was empty, and the minister himself had not yet ascended the pulpit.

In a few moments a gentle rustle, almost inaudible in the aisle, made me look around, and I saw the three Miss Brontés pause before their pew. The stranger rose very quietly, bent over, and opening the pew door, held it so till they passed in, and then Miss Bronté thanked him with a beautiful smile that lit up her whole pale face like a ray of sunshine—and I—indeed I don't know how I felt.

When I looked toward the pulpit again, Mr. Bronté had risen and was about to begin the service.

Once, near the end of the sermon, I glanced toward the Bronté pew.

There sat the wonderfully-gifted Charlotte, and her scarcely less gifted sisters, the former looking very much as her own Jane Eyre must have looked when sitting with Mr. Rochester, listening to the conversation of that extraordinary character,—but I think looking gentler and sweeter and lovelier than ever the little governess, the greatest creation of her splendid fancy, looked.

I didn't look away from the minister again the whole time during the service, and at the close I rose the first almost, and glided out of the church.

I think I was about halfway home when a voice close beside me asked: "Are you trying to hurry away from me, my little oddity?" I turned to the speaker with indignation, and instead of replying, I demanded:

"Why do you call me an oddity, sir?"

"Because really I think you are, my little friend," he said, laughing pleasantly; but instead of being disarmed of my wrath by that sweet-sounding laugh, I said, very foolishly I suppose:

"It may be a subject for laughter for you, sir, but it isn't over pleasant to me to be laughed at."

"My dear child, I didn't mean to hurt your feelings, I'm sure. Pray forgive me," he said so kindly, and looking so sorry that my eyes filled with tears.

"Come—are we friends?" and he held out his beautiful hand.

"The very best," I answered, as I shook his hand heartily.

He laughed, and continued, addressing me as he would have done a little child.

"What is your name?"

"Catharine Livingston—but they call me Cathie at at home."

"And may I call you Cathie?"

"Yes, sir."

"I suppose you are going home now, Cathie?"

"Yes, sir."

"Were you at church—I think I saw you there?"

"Yes, sir."

"Can't you say anything but yes, sir?"'' he said, laughing.

"O yes, sir."

"Then why don't you?"

"I haven't anything else to say, just now."

"And don't you say anything except just what you've got to say?"

"Why no, sir," and I looked at him so wonderingly that he laughed outright, loud and merrily, so that the pleasant, cheerful sounds rang out on the still quiet air.

"You don't know what I mean," he said, when he had finished laughing. "Don't you ever converse—do you never express your own thoughts and feelings, to aid to keep up a conversation?"

"No, never;" I said so solemnly, that he laughed again.

"Well you *are* a strange little girl," and he looked fixedly at me.

I felt my cheeks burning, and my eyes caught the fire and literally blazed with anger.

He looked at me in astonishment, and then he said: "What is the matter? Why do you get so red, and what makes you look so angry?"

"I don't thank you for saying that I am a strange girl—you said so the first time you ever saw me—everybody says so. I don't see what makes me so very strange."

"Why, my child, you are angry at nothing—it is nothing wrong, nor disgraceful, or to be ashamed of."

"Is it not?" I asked eagerly.

"Not at all, Cathie. It only means that you are singular, peculiar, unlike other girls. Nothing more—no harm."

"Is that all?" I asked, with a sigh of relief.

"That is all. But here you are home. I must bid you good-bye, and perhaps I may soon see you again. I leave Haworth now. Be a good girl. Good-bye." He took my hand, pressed it between his, and was gone.

The life I had led for seventeen years was bearable no longer. I longed for change—for action—for something to do. Something to occupy my mind as well as my hands. My very heart cried out for something more than the monotony that had hitherto characterized my life. So I began to cast about in my mind what I could do. That I must and would do something, was settled, but *what?*

I had but a very slight education—it all consisted in the ability to read well, spell correctly, and write a good hand, with a little general information which I had gleaned from books. But notwithstanding the meagre supply of knowledge which I possessed, I concluded, after spending the greater portion of a week in determining what I should do, to teach school.

I made known my plan to my aunt, and was rewarded by such a look of incredulous amazement and surprise, that I began to think I had proposed some very preposterous and out-of-the-way thing. However, as soon as a portion of my good aunt's surprise evaporated, she said:

"Where are you going to get scholars, Cathie?"

I met this inquiry with the reply,

"Not in Haworth, aunt. I intend to open a small school for little children in A——;" which was about fifteen miles from Haworth.

My aunt took a few moments to think over this answer, and then she went to an old stocking-foot in the cupboard, and taking out a guinea, she put it in my hand without a single word.

I was affected by her simple kindness, for I knew she could afford me but very little pecuniary assistance, and the silent tears that slowly followed each other down my cheek were my only answer.

My aunt did not ask me whether I considered myself competent for the undertaking I spoke of. Small as were my claims to be considered learned, in her sight I was a scholar.

So it was settled that I should pursue the course I had marked out for myself, and a week later saw me in A——, domesticated in a family that, though then occupying a very humble position, gave me the idea that they "had seen better days."

I opened my little school with a class of five small children, which slowly increased to thirteen, and there stopped; but I was content. In teaching them I improved myself, and I was also enabled to gratify my taste for reading, which was great.

My time passed pleasantly enough, and a year had almost flown away, when again I began to experience new longings for change. Something more, something higher I wanted. I was beginning to discover that there was more in me than mere ability for teaching children; I wished to test my powers; I wished to go forth and battle with the world and return conqueror: but how to do it?

Ah! that was the question that troubled me.

I was returning from school one evening, (which school was in a very small house, containing a single room), thinking, as I had so often done of late, that I must try something else, and endeavoring in vain to conjure up some idea that would be of assistance to me, and clear the way, which was dark, with a ray of light; but I reached the house without making the desired discovery.

What could I do? There were so few things that I could do. And then I entered the house and sat down with a weary sigh.

A moment after, Maria Ritchie, the daughter of my landlady, entered, with the joyous exclamation: "What do you think, Miss Livingston—an old friend of mamma's and mine, Mr. Gordon, from London, is here in A—— and will spend the evening with us. Is it not delightful?" And her handsome face was radiant with happiness.

"Indeed," I said wearily. I took no interest in what she was saying, and would hardly have expressed surprise if she had told me that Prince Albert was coming.

"I am sure you will like him, Miss Livingston. I assure you he can be quite charming when he pleases, and besides, he has written a book, and by the literary world is considered very talented. For my own part, I detest your excruciating, clever people—they are terrible bores. But Mr. Gordon is never such. You would not imagine that all London is in love with his splendid novel, merely to see him and converse with him, although he is very distingué in appearance, and excessively clever in conversation—quite a genius indeed. She said a great deal more, but I don't remember it. Indeed, at the time I hardly understood a word she said, I was so preoccupied; but to-day, as much as I have written comes back to my mind.

When she had tired herself out, and completely exhausted her subject, she declared she "must go and dress," and then left me.

And there I sat, buried in thought as I often was, quite forgetting that my hat and shawl were yet upon me, and that I had not gone to my own little room. Unconscious of everything in the world, till some time afterwards—it must have been an hour—a hand was laid upon my shoulder, and a gay voice exclaimed,

"Dreaming still, Miss Livingston !"

I looked up quickly and saw Miss Ritchie, radiantly beautiful, in a pale-blue Cashmere dress, a relic of former days, a delicate lace collar, and pale pink roses wound among her golden curls.

Before I could speak a word, she continued, turning to the gentleman beside her:

"Miss Livingstone, Mr. Gordon—Mr. Gordon, Miss Livingston."

When she first spoke I thought she was alone, but now I looked toward her companion, and rose to bow, and then pale and almost fainting, I would have sank back again, if he had not sprung forward, and catching my hand said:

"Is it possible—my little friend Cathie !"

Yes, it was the stranger whom I had seen in Haworth a year ago, and who had never been absent from my mind a single day, nay, a single hour since. Miss Ritchie looked surprised, and then as she ran her eye over my by no means elegant costume, she smiled maliciously, and I could not help thinking how exceedingly pretty she was, and mentally contrasting her with my own ill-favored looks.

I excused myself and went to my room. Why did my heart beat so tumultuously?—What was Mr. Gordon to me? Nothing, nothing! And never would be; but yet that thought turned me sick and giddy, and sent every drop of blood to my heart, till my brain whirled, and I sank upon a chair, only half conscious.

I knew then what I suppose the reader has all along known, though it took me a year to discover it, that I loved the man whose very name had been unknown to me till within the past five minutes, and I loved him from the first.

I felt that it must be hopeless. I even fancied I had detected the signs of a reciprocal attachment between the man I loved and the beautiful Maria Ritchie; and then I remembered her wicked, malicious smile, and in my heart I determined she should not triumph over me, and that neither should ever know my secret.

When the hour for tea came, I left my room, and went into the diningroom.

Maria and her lover, as I mentally designated him, were already seated, but he immediately rose, placed a chair for me, and handed me to the table.

Maria colored, with anger, I think.

In the evening, after tea, she proposed a walk.

Mr. Gordon assented, and invited me to join them. I declined, at which Maria smiled and looked pleased, and they both sallied forth.

The moon was high up, and shining brilliantly clear when they returned, Maria leaning upon his arm, and he carrying her hat, swinging by its white strings in his disengaged hand.

I was seated beside the front window, looking out, and they passed as they neared the house, directly in front of the window. So that I was compelled to see all, a sort of fascination kept me chained to the spot. I could not hear what passed—I did not wish to. It was sufficient to be a spy, and I could not remove from that spot, but I was thankful that I was spared the temptation of becoming an eavesdropper also. They were admiring the moon, I think, for they looked from time to time toward the pale chaste Queen, that was just then looking down upon a thousand similar scenes, and then Maria looked up at him, and the moon smiled down upon the beautiful upturned face.

He smiled down, too, and though I think now it was one of his usual kind, gentle smiles, I fancied then that I could detect all the signs of a passionate love in that one glance.

My throat and mouth grew dry and parched, as though the scorching wind of a desert had passed over me, and I know that I was fearfully pale, because I *felt* that my face was as white as it was clammy and cold.

They came toward the house—another moment and they would be in, and *she*, perhaps *both*, would see my agony and read my secret. I felt that I would peril my life before I would give her the triumph of looking in my pallid face then, and reading all that was so legibly traced upon it, so I looked round with painful eagerness for a means of escape. The window at the other side of the room was open, and in a single moment I had reached it, my feet were on the sill, and just as I heard the rustle of her dress in the hall, I was safe upon the ground without. And then I rushed on like a whirlwind, round toward the front of the house, and in my headlong speed I ran against something that caught me, and exclaimed:

"Cathie !"

"Sir!" and I tried to wrench myself from his grasp, but he held me fast, and turned me round so that the moon shone full in my face.

"What's the matter? Where are you going? Why are you so pale?"

I answered him with a fierce look, which melted away when I met the glance of his eyes; and then my own fell to the ground, while a burning blush mounted to my very temples.

Without a single word he put his arm around me, gathered me so closely to his bosom that I could hardly breathe, and then bent down and kissed me.

"God bless you, my little darling! I love you too," he said then, and releasing me, he drew my arm through his, and we walked slowly round toward the front door.

I never thought then whether he loved Maria or not. I forgot my late fierce jealousy; I forgot that the person who had caused it lived; and then I only remembered it when, taking my hands in his, at the door, he stooped forward and kissed my brow, saying, "Goodnight, dear one. I had already said adieu to Miss Ritchie, and was leaving the house when you ran into my arms."

"Leaving without saying 'good-night' to me?" I said, reproachfully.

"Mrs. Ritchie, whom we met at the door, said that you complained of a headache, and had retired."

"O!" I answered, and laughed, and then we parted. . . .

How like a dream, beautiful, too beautiful for waking reality, it seemed to me when I awoke upon the following morning! How could it be? I could not, dared not realize that I was beloved, and by such a man, lest I should awake from the delusion, and die with grief to find my vision of happiness fled.

I said so to Mr. Gordon that same evening, as he sat upon a bench near the same spot where Maria had stood with him upon the previous evening.

For answer, he kissed me, and told me that "he had loved me for my wild eyes when I first looked up at him, and said that he knew that a great soul, and a great mind, only needing cultivation, *which it should have*, were looking out of them," and then he concluded with:

"I once fancied that I loved before, Cathie. Some time I will tell you all about it. But *now* I *know* that

I love, really love."

"Indeed, William Gordon ?"

With a sharp cry of pain Mr. Gordon turned in the direction whence came those words, in a voice of such cutting irony that it hewed right into my heart, and seemed to turn him to stone.

There stood a tall, dark, fearfully beautiful woman, her arms crossed upon her broad full chest, regarding him with a demoniac light in her wicked eyes, and smiling like the fiend she was.

In the name of Heaven what meant it all? was my mental inquiry, which that woman answered by turning to me, and asking:

"And may I inquire why you are here seated, young woman, with MY HUSBAND?"

I heard no more. Like a weight of marble, and quite as insensible and cold, I fell forward upon my face on the ground. . . .

It afterward appeared that when I returned to consciousness, having been carried into the house by Mr. Gordon, and given in charge to Mrs. Ritchie without a word of explanation, I had sunk into a kind of stupor, from which I did not recover entirely for some days.

When I again became quite conscious, and my senses were quite clear, I awoke to the knowledge that I had seen William Gordon for the last time. I felt that it was so and from that hour, when I last saw him, when my senses were leaving me, I have never beheld him.

A letter lay upon the stand awaiting my perusal, and with the calmness, and cold terrible courage of despair, I took it up, broke the seal, and read it. A smaller letter was enclosed, which I quietly laid aside, till I had perused the first.

Here it is:

CATHIE,—

I dare not call you dear or beloved, for one whom I supposed dead *should* have a right to those terms; but though God knows I cannot speak of her as dear to me, I may not dare to speak of another as being so.

Ten years ago, Cathie, I was beguiled into a marriage with one whom my soul loathes and my heart abhors. I will say no more. The enclosed note will prove to you that I am no villain, and have not wantonly trifled with you. Farewell,
GORDON.

I laid it down and took up the other. It was dated four years back, and read thus:

MY DEAR GORDON,—

It is my painful task to inform you that your wife, my sister Anne, lost her life in the vessel that was wrecked upon its return from Europe, last week. You are now, as you so often wished to be, free. Anne was a strange girl, but let the grave hide her faults, say I. Yours truly, HENRY BENNETT.

No further explanations—I wanted no more. That was enough. Enough to know that my idol was another's. Enough to know that great as had been my sin in worshipping it as I had done, it would be still greater to continue that worship. Enough to know that the green and fertile oasis I had discovered in the desert of my life, and on which I had hoped to live forevermore in peace and joy, was swept away forever, poisoned by the scorching simoon, and covered from my sight forevermore by the burning sands. Enough, enough, to know all this—enough, enough!

[For the Saturday Press.]

"LIFE IN SPAIN."

Life in Spain: Past and Present. By Walter Thornbury, author of Every Man his own Trumpeter, Art and Nature, Songs of the Cavaliers and Roundheads, etc. With illustrations. 12mo, pp. 188. New York: Harper & Brothers. 1860.

All of us love Spain; but it is the Spain of fancy, not of fact. It is a lovely vision, winning our hearts away from the weary commonplaces of ordinary life. It is a land of enchantment, a mystical land of dreams and phantoms, over which, beautiful afar off, a strange splendor broods, and the diamond light of eternal morning. Thither our hopes depart, in the inexorable course of destiny. There are garnered up all our lost loves, all our beautiful, impossible ideals. Our Castles are there, our Palaces, waiting for us, our gardens of immortal bloom and verdure, our sweet days of idleness, our nights of passionate joy, wild and voluptuous, the imagined splendors of ideal life,—all are there! It is not wonderful we all love Spain.

Were it possible—because we dislike that our ideals should be disturbed in any way at all—we would, for ourselves, avoid all knowledge of any other Spain than this same beautiful Spain of fancy. But that is not possible. That there shall be a thorn for every rose, seems to be the condition of life everywhere and always. All around us are iron facts. Constantly that sturdy and impecunious old cynic, whom the poet Lowell describes as "the Present, poor and bare," persists in making his "sneering comment." Scarcely in the most sacred temple of the soul can we preserve our pure ideals from sacreligious violation. It were vain to expect exemption for the land of our dreams. The Spain of fact makes its comment on the Spain of fancy; nor is that comment made in vain.

But perhaps it may be well for some persons that the vagary of fancy is so constantly rebuked by the inexorable truth of fact. Anyway, historians and travellers have taken care to do for Spain the very correct thing which they love to do for the rest of the world. Respecting the past and present of that nation, histories and books of travel give ample opportunities of knowledge for those who care to read. Truly the Spain of fancy is not the Spain of fact. But let us not, for the gratification of any private prejudice, deny to Spain those privileges of historic commemoration which are enjoyed by all the nations. We should respect the ponderous dignity of history. We should appreciate the worth of accurate information.

Such is our thought after reading a new book entitled "Life in Spain: Past and Present," which has recently been published by Messrs. Harper and Brothers. The author of this book is Walter Thornbury, an English writer both of prose and verse, who enjoys considerable popularity as an author, alike in this country and in his own.

We gather from this volume that Mr. Thornbury visited, at divers times and under circumstances more or less extraordinary, the most interesting localities in Spain and Portugal,—including Lisbon, Cadiz, Seville, Cordova, Malaga, Madrid, Alhama, Grenada, and Gibraltar. From Gibraltar he passed over into Africa, whence returning he came to England. His book, which is divided into twenty-seven chapters, is principally occupied with the narrative of his observations of manners, customs, and incidents in these and other places. But among these twenty-seven chapters are several which to a certain extent have, or are intended to have, a literary or artistic interest, peculiar and unusual. These chapters relate to "Spanish Proverbs," "Spanish Ballads," "Murillo and his Picture Children," "A Day in the Alhambra," "The Spain of Cervantes and the Spain of Gil Blas."

The style of this narrative is smooth, flowing, conversational. It is unpleasantly diffuse at times, and is marred by some affectations of phrase and manner. There is rarely an attempt at fine writing; yet the book contains several passages of singular beauty, sweet in music and brilliant in color. Of those passages the beauty is enhanced by contrast with certain others, which the author's visible and painful effort at smartness entirely fails to relieve.

As a rule we do not like books of travel. The reason is that, as a rule, they do not deserve to be liked. To read them with anything like critical care is generally labor of the most painful sort. But it is a kind of labor we seldom perform. In the present instance, however, we make an exception to our practice. We have read Mr. Thornbury's "Life in Spain," and we think, not only that it deserves reading with critical care, but also that it deserves commendation as a very successful book of travels.

It is the sweetest charm of a traveller's reminiscences that they preserve and impart to the reader of his written narrative, something of that gay freedom of heart and mind, that charming vivacity of animal spirits, by which he was himself inspired in the delightful contact of novelty, and in some unwonted atmosphere of romance. If he gather violets in the depths of some peaceful valley, where always the sunshine sleeps, and the Summer silence is broken only by the muffled music of the brooks,—let him give us the enchantment, the music, and the perfume, too. If with him we climb mountains, with him let us breathe the mountain air. Whether into the dim solitude of forests, or the populous haunts of men; into the arid desert, amid the ruins of forgotten cities, or far out upon the wild and wandering sea,—wherever he would lead us as his companions, let him take care so to picture whatever he has seen and felt, that we his readers can realize and enjoy it together. In no other way will he give vigor and spirit to his narrative. In no other way can he achieve sympathy, admiration, success.

It is in this view that we think Mr. Thornbury's book may be accounted successful. It is not the writer only who travels in Spain. The reader goes with him there; even the critic goes with him. Together we survey the blue and rose colored buildings of Lisbon; the grave of Harry Fielding on the hill of the Estrella; the yellow domes of Cadiz. Together we drink the wine of Don Sanchez Montilla, and look into the twilight eyes of lovely Spanish ladies. We talk proverbs with John di Coco, and traverse the beautiful Giralda at Seville. By Don Sanchez Balthazar we are rather cruelly bored, in the tenth chapter, with prosy, irrelevant stories, and snatches of indifferent Spanish Ballads. In the Merced at Seville,—formerly a convent, now a picture-museum,—we gaze delightedly at the picture children of Murillo. We see the brown Guadalquivir, the distant mountain peaks. We see leather-appareled shepherds, and women in short, colored, picturesque petticoats. We see beggars crouching at the church-doors, and gipsy women fighting with their knives. We are spectators of bull-fights at Malaga. We are amazed at the lumbering Galera, the intolerable Spanish diligence. We are no less amazed —not to say disgusted—at the sight of filthy, perspiring negroes trampling the Malaga raisins. In the Alhambra we are poetical of course.

> "A thousand years their cloudy wings expand
> Around us, and a dying glory smiles."

We pass into Africa—obedient to our Prospero's will. But Africa we neither see nor care to see. We enjoy that parting dinner at Gibraltar. We make the little voyage to London.

We see the pleasant author safely deposited in the bosom of his family. Then—carefully omitting to read the Appendix—we close the book with a feeling of satisfaction in our quiet but rapid journey; we think Thornbury an entertaining fellow, and good to travel with, and mentally we thank him for the pleasure we have enjoyed.

Thoughts and Things.

BY ADA CLARE.

Fashion dictates three rules for the man of the world, the literary man, and the artist to begin with,—to praise nothing, to admire nothing, to love nothing. The lips must be moulded into an adamantine sneer ere the face can be called manly and forcible. Nothing is brilliant except it be founded on satire. Intellectual surgery has immediate amputation as its one remedy for all things. If a man do but chill his fingers in a sleigh-ride, the only brilliant thing for a friend to do is to cut off his arms at the shoulders.

The critic's art is built up on fault-finding. When a great artist stands before him, he transforms his mind into a microscope with which to discover the infirmity that mingles faintly, often imperceptibly, with genius. When he beholds the precious fault, his heart pants with rapture, he can sympathize with Herschel when he discovered an unknown star. His mind is no longer a microscope, it has become suddenly a crucible, in which he has placed the genius, while industriously melting away all the wealth of gold, to find and hold fast the treasured atom of dross. O! I can imagine the feelings of the man who can first prove to others that Miss Patti has not a fine voice. His heart may even break with joy.

Criticism I believe was never intended to foist itself upon heartlessness. It is as much a matter of perception as of judgment, and the perceptive faculties draw their life from the heart. Alas me! what a sorrowful being the critic must be in this latitude! However bright the wine that sparkles in the cup, he sees death at its bottom. All his life must pass in gathering thorns; he will have none of the myriad roses that stain the air with their crimsons.

One indeed must be brave to be enthusiastic now: he must be brave to run against the thick bosses of the *Negative's* buckler, since the world's speech resolves itself into an *everlasting No.*

All ardent admiration and love pass for sheer craziness. Even the morning stars which we are told sang for joy at the creation of the world, would be remanded by the modern critic to a sidereal asylum for maniacs.

I have always been hopelessly insane myself, in this view, even from earliest childhood. When I was a very little girl, I read "Oliver Twist." I crept up into a garret to be unmolested, and there, as the saying goes, devoured its pages. One day the whole house was alarmed by the moans and sobs of a child. Frantic steps pressed to my garret, and there I was discovered with "Oliver Twist" in my lap, having just gone with the little hero into painful misfortunes, and being thus in the midst of giving way to my sympathies. In those days, when the heroine in the five-act tragedy suffered from unrequited love and fell weeping on the stage, I often became so hysterical as to excite the ire of the politer audience.

Now I no longer suffer for tragedy or despairing story. I weep and throb with them, but they are tears and pulses of enjoyment. I have learned to seek my happiness in the mere action of my emotional nature. I have no need of critically understanding music or the drama. They are simply altars to me where I worship blindly, but with a full soul.

I have always found it a much deeper joy to love than to be loved, to admire than to be admired. The pangs of unrequited love, as soon as they have struggled through the agonies of jealousy and desire, have as much pleasure as pain in them. To have had and to keep one grand, unconquerable, immortal passion, is good for every life. It is the tumultuous undercurrent that keeps the sluggish water pure. For the soul which lives in the world's close atmosphere of calculation and selfishness, it is a window from which it can lean forth to drink in the pure airs from heaven, and to look up with yearning eye after the tender brightness of the stars.

Passionate admiration follows immediately in the divine footsteps of passionate love. The rapture the former brings is not so supernal as that of the latter, but it is not torn with the pangs which at first agonize love.

At present I have three idols in the temple of my admiration,—Ristori, Gottschalk, and Cortesi. Whoso would teach me how to cease to admire these three, would insure my enmity for life.

Ristori played Corinna in a manner to make the heavenly lights her wonder-wounded hearers. I found it impossible to keep my feet fixed on the respectable rocks of materiality and the commonplace. The splendor of her genius came up like a great wave to bear me down to the divine sea of dreams. This is the kind of intoxication which material substance never gave, and which knows no satiety. To deliver oneself over riotously to a boundless admiration, to feel the very air we breathe throbbing with it in radiate pulses, to adore Genius so much that we possess it both actively and passively a thousand-fold intensified, to lose our souls with all their doubts and despairs in it, to feel ourselves transformed into one eternal sense of life, and that panting with the delirium of satisfied adoration,— O, this is the passion of divine joy that holds immortality in the hollow of its hand!

I am happily not one who can wake from my illusions. Time only seemed to press them deeper into my heart. I know not indeed how we of the world's recognized fools could live without such madness. There is so little to us in social lies, and the world's hollow cruel creeds, that our hearts would faint to death without such heavenly food as this.

Is not an inability to love, to admire, a want of certain faculties? Then is it not extraordinary that mental diseases should be less humbling than bodily ones?

A man who is blind points not the finger of scorn at him who can see, boasts not that all skies are shut away from him, nor have I seen the dumb man believing himself qualified to despise him who had the gift of speech. But he who is cold and loveless looks with contempt upon the enthusiast, so that they must be brave who dare to avow an ardent, unquestioning love for anything but cognac, scrip, and bullion.

As for the admiration of love—but for the moment I will be silent on that topic, for too many of my readers have, ere this, mentally struck me on the mouth, crying like Agrippa of old, Much loving hath made thee mad.

But when Ada Clare ceases to tremble, and melt, and glow, before the royal ones of Art, when their voices are not to her voices from Olympus, when her knees refuse to bend in the temple of most high and mighty Genius, when the foot of love is no longer set on the neck of her life, be ready, Gods, with all your thunderbolts, dash her to pieces!

Dramatic Feuilleton.

Personal.

Being somewhat 'friz up' this week, my naturally gushing disposition and gas and water pipes being congealed, I may say dammed, and the theatres being barren of novelty, and as you had last week a good deal more of the subscriber than many important (in their own estimation) people liked, and—well I might go on with that awkward conjunction interminably, but I won't. All I desire to say is that, owing to all the above-mentioned circumstances and some more, I shall give a little space to my correspondence, which is rather a good thing to do, I think.

Correspondence.

To Personne :

I have never been so much disgusted with anything in *the whole course of my life* as your last what-do-you-call-it Feuilleton (just as if you couldn't get an English heading or signature!) Why don't you take and read the beautiful critiques in the Boston and Philadelphia papers, and write like them? What do you go to the theatre for nothing for, unless it is to say sweet and pretty things about the actresses and actors, that is, I mean the star-ones, such as Matilda Heron, and Laura Keene, and Mrs. Hoey? Do You think *you* can play the parts better? Why don't you just take and *try* it, that's all.

There's Matilda Heron, now. I wish you had just written about her like that, in San Francisco, that's all. Actresses' lovers, protectors, and so on, go out gunning every morning after critics who say a single word against them on the stage, though, to do the paper-men justice, they very rarely do say a word that isn't favorable, nice and proper.

And then you must go to work and make fun of *Lesbia*. You can't appreciate it. My cousin Henrietta-Jane, who writes for the *Ledger* a good deal, says it is a high and holy work, dealing with and arousing the best, noblest, and loftiest impulses of our nature. It deals with Love—the divine passion, the religion of Woman—from a grand stand-point. Henrietta-Jane said a great deal more about her sympathies being worked up, and how grand Matilda Heron was when she travelled around the stage in them boots you talk about, and stood in attitudes with all sorts of scarfs and things around her head, and talked with the dear, delightful, melting tears in the voice, which you don't know from moaning and whining.

Besides, don't women moan and whine in real life? I guess they do. My aunt Sarah-Elizabeth, who lives three miles back of Edgartown, on the Cape, kept company with a young man who followed the sea. And they were published, and everything was set for the day, when he took and married a widow-woman in Nantucket, because she was well off. And my ma says that she went and took on just like Matilda Heron does, and you might take and shut your eyes and think it was her. (?)

Then you go and find fault with her dress. What do *you* know about it. And if she wanted to look as if she weighed a ton, is that any of *your* business?

It aint much matter after all, there! The people in Boston—and I guess *they* know—said *Lesbia* was great, and Matilda Heron a divine artist, a priestess of the inner sanctuary of the soul, and so on, and I guess that's enough.

I forgot one thing that Henrietta-Jane said, she said one place after Mr. Wallack had been going around and around the stage saying all sorts of wicked things to everybody for two hours and more, he got exhausted and said to Jordan, "Come! let us cuss together." Henrietta-Jane thinks Cobb never equalled that. And you say it's trash! Who are you?

Then about Laura Keene. A young man in our house who is in a store now, but who has fine literary talents, and plays on the German flute, says he knows all about the Theatre and you don't. Laura Keene (he says and I say) is a delightful actress; unaffectedness, grace, and naiveté mark all her movements. Her facial outline is classic, her figure round with the first bloom of youth, her eyes beam with maiden freshness, and her elocution is like the music of the lutes. [We did that together, *aint* it nice?] And then that dear Mrs. Hoey! Why I have seen her wear real diamonds, and her laces are perfectly lovely on the stage. How anybody but a brute, which you must be, could write against so precious an artist, is beyond my comprehension.

I think the proprietors of The Saturday Press ought to take and get some one else to write. We don't want so much French, nor making fun of everything. We want a real American Feuilleton such as they have in the Sunday papers. I am sure there's the *Dispatch* is funny enough when it don't try to be, and the Sunday *Times* is poetic and delightful.

And if you don't like our actresses, you better go off to Paris at once, and see your French artists (nasty things). Indignantly,

Nancy Scudder.

[No relation to Salem.]

Good Personne !

A capital Feuilleton last week. I always knew you would come round to our side, and told my friend, First-Mortgage, so at the Club many a time. You haven't any actresses now. In my day actresses were only actresses. You never read any stuff in the papers about their religion, or their morals, or their social position, or any nonsense of that sort. Then they all stood fair and square on their own legs. [Now, I understand, there's no telling about the reality of anything.] Those were the days of the old Park, and Mr. Wallack's fine theatre in Leonard street, and Hamblin up the Bowery had some actresses who for beauty and talent would make your hair curl, my boy.

I am glad, Personne, to see you have pluck enough to speak out. It will do them good. The public accepts certain things, not because it is satisfied with them, but because it cannot get anything else. But for those things to claim superiority on account of a forced recognition, is laughably absurd.

I have some English mutton for you, on ——, if you like, and you may have Lafitte if you don't go and upset everything you've done between now and that time, which you generally do; and come at six sharp. None of your nonsense. Unpunctuality at dinner is the meanest of crimes. Yours patronizingly,

The Oldest Man.

Club, Tuesday.

A. M.

I don't know anything about art, or æsthetics, or things of that kind. When I was in the convent I used to get some of the clever girls to do all the hard things for me, and I used to help them smuggle letters for it. Ma says I don't know anything now, but I know I know the German and the Russian quadrille, and crochet, and lots of nice things. When I went to Jeanie Deans I cried and I laughed a good deal, and I wasn't a bit tired. And the Circus too was nice, and I laughed a good deal there and wished there was more of it; and when the man jumped, O, I don't know how far, my heart came right up in my mouth. Now I don't know like a critic, but *Lesbia* made me very tired, and if it hadn't been for chocolates and some young men I should have gone to sleep several times. And I think Mr. Lester's *Poor Young Man* was a great fool, and if I had been the Rich Young Woman I should have taken and married the other man that Mr. Walcot took, and I think Mrs. Hoey was dressed in the best taste, and Miss Gannon made me laugh, and the other woman that played the governess was funny too, and there were more chocolates and young men, and you never saw such a fright as that Miss ——, and I guess that's all. Tout-à-vous,

Anna Maria.

Extracts.

"Very good about Heron, but all wrong about Keene."

"Capital about Heron and Keene, but all nonsense about Mrs. Hoey."

"How can you put Heron in the same category with Miss Keene and Mrs. Hoey. She is a grand artist, they only hacks."

Faits Divers.

Lesbia has gone down to an early grave. "One more unfortunate rashly importunate," etc. There let her rest, and as the lonely stranger plods his homeward way through the Rue de Mercer, near the classic pump on the corner of Amity, let him not, if he can make it convenient, refuse the tribute of a sigh. The boots with the gold fringe around the tops were worth as much as that.

The cool weather has thinned out the attendance at the Theatres. At Laura Keene's, *Jeanie Deans* is found quite as attractive as ever. I suppose it will run along till Spring.

I have seen the *Octoroon* at the New Bowery, and on the whole think the performance a good one. Mr. Boniface, who played the Indian, has all the prerequisites of a first-rate artist. His performance of Wahno-tee was the perfect poetic realization of the character. Another noticeable point was afforded by an exact copy of Mrs. Allen's *Zoe*, at the hand of Mrs. W. G. Jones. La belle Allen has a style at last. She has been honored with an imitation. Let her persevere and she may arrive at the dignity of being cut up in the papers.

I may say here that the New Bowery is a very comfortable, well-ordered theatre, and quite a good thing to do once in a while. It already attracts a portion of the Broadway audience. The company is fair, but there ought to be at least one pretty woman in it.

MM. Lester Wallack, Pierrepont Edwards, and Octave Feuillet's *Romance of a Poor Young Man*, has made a clear and well-defined success at Wallack's. The play has many good points, not the least of which is the intense struggle between the actresses on the question of clothes. It is a first-rate thing for the dry-goods trade, upon which, I am told, rests the foundation of the Union. What a delightful thought it is that the Constitution is supported by crinoline, defended by moire antique, shielded by Lyons velvet, and guaranteed by hoops of steel. Let Louisiana and Maine be united with Berlin wool, let Carolina and Rhode Island meet and kiss each other over a skein of floss silk. It is a great deal nicer than the old stuff about the principles of some party or other. I say let crinoline be exalted. Let the Ada Clares flourish and reign supreme forever and ever.

Our mercurial friends the Gauls are going on with the French theatre, after a fashion. The company is very fair. Laurent, beyond all doubt, the best actress in New York. The stage is well cared for by Mannstein, but a good business manager is needed.

Operatic.

Much to the delight of the Brightest and the Best, we are to have another opera season, to commence at Irving Place next Monday.

The *Puritani* will be sung by Patti, Brignoli, Susini, and Amodio. Anna Maria, who has been at Boston, helping young woman to get married (the most delightful employment of the sex, next to being actually bonded themselves), writes thus to Sophonisba :

"I went to the opera on Wednesday. They sung "the *Puritani.* Patti was delightful, as she always is. Brignoli was not so good as usual. He seemed as if he was mad about something."

He will please recover his senses next Monday. I am afraid the ecstasies of the Athenian critics over his acting in the *Barber* have reduced him to a state of idiocy. It will be very interesting to see Brignoli with his new dramatic laurels. Hear the *Times*:

> The Bostonians have been very good-natured to our wanderers. They have received their operas all the week through with decorous approbation, and have vehemently applauded their oratorios on Sunday nights, although they have been obliged to confess that "Beethoven's symphony in C minor did not *sound natural* away from the Music Hall." They think Patti a pleasing young lady of fine promise, and they have discovered that Brignoli is a person of decided dramatic genius. This discovery alone was well worth the price we have paid for it in giving up our opera so long to the wise men of the East. Our opera-world will have the goodness to prepare itself immediately for a new sensation. We have long heard our accomplished tenor emulating the "pearl-showering" voice of Rubini. To see him grasping at the laurels of Talma will be rapture thrice-refined.

Meantime there have been great rows at Boston. Patti has had a sore throat. Gazzaniga refused to sing unless she was paid, and the funds not appearing, went to law with Strakosch, and as a foreign friend of mine writes, "they are all under their bails." "An editor of a newspaper," as Seward called Greeley, pitched into Strakosch, and there was a personal rencounter with damage, on dit, to the manager. Colson, le mari, had a row with the *Evening Gazette* people about Madame. No list of killed and wounded has yet been received; but as A. M. is on the spot, full particulars may be looked for next week. Queer people these operatic jokers, any way; almost as bad as Congressmen.

Oliver Twist.

Lesbia was replaced, on Thursday, at the Winter Garden, by a new version of Oliver Twist.

A new version, which varied only from that which has been heretofore familiar to the public in two particular incidents,—one the killing of *Nancy Sykes* off the stage, and the other an attempt to give an exact representation of the death of *Bill Sykes*, with his wonderful escape after the murder of *Nancy*—an effect which is altogether beyond the reach of the actor, the stage carpenter, and the machinist.

Matilda Heron was the *Nancy Sykes*, Mr. Wallack played *Fagan*, and Mr. George Jordan essayed the part of the house-breaker. The Shu-shugar makes a good *Nancy Sykes*. She is redolent of White-Chapel and the gin-palace. She made a success, clear and decided. Everybody acted as well as they could, but the play was spoiled by the carpenters. The last act was, through a series of contretemps, an utter failure. This, however, may be remedied, in future performances.

As it is, in spite of a fine cast and splendid mise en scène, Oliver Twist must be set down as only a succès d'estime, which is the polite French manner of killing a play.

Personne.

"The Sleighing Season-The Upset" - Winslow Homer, Harper's Weekly, January 14, 1860

THE SLEIGH-RIDE.

BY EDMUND C. STEDMAN.

Hark! the jingle
Of the sleigh-bell's song!
Earth and air in snowy sheen commingle;
Swiftly throng,
Norseland fancies as we sail along.

Like the maiden
Of some fairy-tale,
Lying, spell-bound, in her diamond-laden
Bridal veil,
Sleeps the Earth beneath a garment pale.

High above us
Gleams the ancient moon—
Gleam the eyes of shining ones that love us
O Could their tune
Only fill our ears at Heaven's noon,

You and I, love,
With a wild delight,
Hearing that seraphic strain would die, love,
This same night,
Straight to join them in their starry height!

Closer nestle,
Dearest, to my side:
What enchantment, in one magic vessel
Thus to glide,
Making music, on a silver tide.

Jingle! jingle!
How the fields go by!
Earth and air in snowy sheen commingle
Far and nigh;
Is the ground beneath us, or the sky?

Heavenward yonder,
In the lurid North,
From Valhalla's gates that roll asunder,
Red and wroth,
Balder's funeral flames are blazing forth.

O, what splendor;
How the hues expire!
All the elves of light their tribute render
To the pyre!
Clad in robes of gold and crimson fire.

Softly fusing,
Every color rare,
Half its own prismatic brilliance losing
Grows more fair,
Blending with the lunar glory there;

Even so, love,
All my yearning heart
In etherial passion is a-glow, love,
And thine art
To its hues new lustre shall impart.

Jingle! jingle!
Let the Earth go by!
With a wilder thrill our pulses tingle;
You and I
Will shout our loves, but aye forget to sigh.

[For the Saturday Press.]

Poemet.

That shadow, my likeness, that goes to and fro, seeking a livelihood,
chattering, chaffering,
How often I find myself standing and looking at it where it flits,
How often I question and doubt whether that is really me;
But in these, and among my lovers, and carolling my songs,
O I never doubt whether that is really me.

WALT WHITMAN.

[For the Saturday Press.]

EPITHALAMIUM.

I.
Let the chimes ring
Their loudest, happiest peal,
For they,
With us, shall sing,
This happy, happy day,
A song of praise
To that sweet love which shall reveal
Life's mysteries.
II.
Not tolling now,
For a departed soul
From earth,
But singing how
The glorious birth
Of perfect love,
A throb of joy above control,
Shall call one from above.
III.
O favored pair—
Ye who this day shall try
So plain
To make appear
The meaning of your pain—
That lesson keep;
Your slumbers then will typify
Your endless sleep.

D. D.

—The fifth and concluding volume of Mr. Ruskin's "Modern Painters" is in preparation. Sir James Prior, the biographer of Burke and Goldsmith, has in the press a life, with selections from the manuscript anecdotes, of Edmund Malone, the Shakespeare commentator.

[For the Saturday Press.]

THE EMPTY FLASK.

[The poet apostrophizeth—chiefly for his own pleasure, but also for that of the Bohemians—a little perfume-flask which they all know something about.]

I.

With something of a sweet regret
Because I know you will not do
The thing I ask you, little pet,
Here in the night I talk with you.
Of you a hundred things I ask:
From mood to mood my fancy slips:
While thus, dear little empty flask,
You breathe the fragrance of her lips.

II.

Now by the sunshine of her eyes,
The love-light of her gentle brow,
The tender music of her sighs,
The dreams that she is dreaming now,—
Give me your secret, good or ill!
Give me her thought—for I will know :—
My little pet, you're very still
And faithful—I can read you, though!

III.

The lingering scent of withered flowers;
The thought how lovely things depart;
The sweet regret for sweeter hours;
The memory of a happier heart;
Love—which the soul no longer keeps ;
Smiles when the face is but a mask ;—
Such meaning in your sweetness sleeps!
These are your secrets, little flask!

IV.

Dear lady, have I read aright
The serious meaning hidden here?
No matter! In my pure delight
Your little gift is just as dear!
Dear—and the moral goes for naught.
I find my sweet content in this :—
You gave it with a gentle thought,
Because you gave it with a kiss!

V.

And so my song is not a task,
'Tis all my ardent joy in you;
I win from out this little flask
The sweetness and the music too!
From where those pretty lips did kiss,
I kiss the rose of orient climes;
And through a splendid dream of bliss,
I fold its sweetness in my rhymes.

WILL WINTER.

Night of January 30th.

[For the Saturday Press.]

THE DEATH-WATCH.

BY FREDK. A. PARMENTER.

I.

I heard the Death-Watch ticking
In the silence of the night,
And its voice, so mournful, ceased not
With the dawn of morning light.

II.

I searched my narrow chamber
In every nook and part,
But found it not, for, ah me!
It was my own sad heart!

Jan. 15th, 1860.

[For the Saturday Press.]

LEAVES FROM NATURE.

I hear that some of my friends are wearied by these conversations with Nature. I am not surprised. For she will not flatter them—and they love to be flattered. Those who commune with her freely, she takes away from themselves. She has no food for vanity, and the egotist famishes on such nourishment. So they are getting very thin. In the country, upon the immeasurable lap of Nature, man reposes like a tired child, and as he looks about him, and at the blue infinity on high, he feels (if he be susceptible of anything more than animal feeling) his own littleness; but in the pentup streets and chambers of the city, where live the scoffers at Nature's teachings, surrounded with luxurious appliances of his own creating, man is lifted into self-importance and grows forgetful of Nature and her Author. The politeness and urbanities of convention, and to the strong mind the struggle with and triumph over the duller and weaker of his kind, flatters self, till in fancy at least man becomes deity. Nature's sunlight laughs in the face of the wit, but not at his jest. She dazzles him with her light, but does not applaud his eloquence, or defer to his cunning. Her voices and her silence are more eloquent than an angel's tongue, and the hopelessness of rivalry with them saddens the proud. Nature's votaries are humble, and draw nigh to her, worshipping the "cause of the effect." To the vain she is ever a stranger; but to the adorer of her mysteries, she opens inexhaustible stores, and imparts perennial joys forever. To them she becomes a living, breathing, speaking goddess. Her vital colors carry home thoughts and feelings to the heart; her fragrance and forms breathe joy into the soul, and her meanings become as clear as the familiar words of those we love. The birds sing, the brooks murmur, the breezes sigh;—the heart listens. The trees wave, the waters sparkle and play, the birds circle, the beasts gambol, in harmony with one's own consciousness, and the sun, instead of being a mere source of material heat, warms one with love.

The senses are often destroyed by disease. Inactivity more often than overwork causes the death of the highest faculties. Unnatural glare and artificial stimuli dull the sight, taste, smell, and hearing, and Nature's sweetness and healthful force cease to be felt or relished. The foul atmosphere, the filthy street, the discordant rattle, the moiling and parasitical life of the city, become the elements of existence with those who have lost a zest for Nature, and they would perish away from them.

To such the earth beyond their bounds is one vast market-garden or pasturage, and the sea a fish-pond. They remind me of the wife of Sir Walter Scott, who, while walking in the country with the great novelist, was requested by him to observe the lambs playing in the Spring clover. "Are they not," demanded the baronet, "well chosen as emblems of innocence and love?" "They are indeed charming creatures," replied her ladyship, "especially with mint sauce." Many entertain sentiments similar to those of Lady Scott, and some have the ingenuousness to avow them. But what a view of Nature is this! Shall it be conceded, that to be rendered acceptable she must die? Or worse, shall it be admitted that our love for her is like the canibal's regard for a human creature, whom he likes best after he has cooked him?

Who prefers a fragrant extract to living floral perfume? Logs to a green and waving tree? The dead splash of an artificial fountain to the gush of the mountain cataract? Or the singing of the caged bird to the joy-inspired notes of the songster of the grove?

If we have sacrificed our zest for Nature, we have lost a sense hardly less valuable than any of the ordinary five. It is a misfortune, and no true theory can be based on it.

A sincere and profound love of Nature's beauties preserves the mind always young and fresh. No man can become truly great and good without it. He may be witty, ingenuous, talented, successful, but with such a deficiency he cannot be a genius or a hero in life, or even in art.

Who loves not his mother is generally a wretch. Nature is our mother in a full and lofty sense. From her breast we derive not only the necessities of life, but immediately or indirectly all that delights the senses—all that supports life and makes it endurable; all that is beautiful in color, ravishing in sweetness and form, enchanting in sound; every relic, indeed, of the lost paradise.

R. W. P.

[For the Saturday Press.]

GONE.

BY GEORGE ARNOLD.

I.

The Summer was long and sweet,
The roses blossomed for me
Over a porch where fairy feet
Went pattering merrily.

II.

All Summer the roses smiled,
Hiding their thorns from sight;
All Summer my passionate heart beat wild
With a feverish love and delight.

III.

Now, Autumn's rain-drops beat
On the casement, drearily ;—
The Summer I found so long and sweet
Has faded forever from me!

IV.

Under each thorny bough
The roses are withering fast,
And my passionate heart beats slower, now,
For the fever of love is past!

NEW YORK FEBRUARY 11, 1860

[For the Saturday Press.]

THE BOBOLINKS ARE SINGING.

BY W. D. HOWELLS.

Out of a fragrant heart of bloom—
The bobolinks are singing!
Out of its fragrant heart of bloom,
The apple-tree whispers to the room,
"Why art thou but a nest of gloom,
While the bobolinks are singing?"

The two wan ghosts of the chamber there—

The bobolinks are singing!
The two wan ghosts of the chamber there
Cease in the breath of the honeyed air,
Sweep from the room and leave it bare,
While the bobolinks are singing.

Then with a breath so chill and slow—
The bobolinks are singing!
Then with a breath so chill and slow,
It freezes the blossoms into snow,
The haunted room makes answer low,
While the bobolinks are singing:

"I know that in the meadow-land—
The bobolinks are singing!
I know that in the meadow-land
The sorrowful, slender elm-trees stand,
And the brook goes by on the other hand,
While the bobolinks are singing.

"But ever I see, in the brawling stream—
The bobolinks are singing!
But ever I see in the brawling stream
A maiden drowned and floating dim,
Under the water, like a dream,
While the bobolinks are singing.

"Buried, she lies in the meadow-land!
The bobolinks are singing!
Buried, she lies in the meadow-land,
Under the sorrowful elms where they stand;
Wind, blow over her soft and bland,
While the bobolinks are singing.

"O blow, but stir not the ghastly thing—
The bobolinks are singing!
O blow, but stir not the ghastly thing
The farmer saw so heavily swing
From the elm, one merry morn of Spring,
While the bobolinks were singing.

"O blow, and blow away the bloom—
The bobolinks are singing!
O blow, and blow away the bloom
That sickens me in my heart of gloom,
That sweetly sickens the haunted room,
While the bobolinks are singing!"

[For the Saturday Press.]

"POEMET."—(AFTER WALT WHITMAN.)

WITH PARENTHESES, ANALYTICAL, STHETICAL, PHILOSOPHICAL, AND EXPLANATORY.

—

BY SAERASMID.

—

Of an individual I or some one or any one loved day (i. e. some day) and night (i. e. ditto) I dreamed I heard some one told me he was dead, (which, considering the perishable nature of humanity, was not, perhaps, unprecedented)
And I dreamed I went where (I dreamed) they had buried him and he was not in that place, (having probably been removed)
And I dreamed I wandered promiscuously round among burial places to find him,
And I found that every place (of burial) was a burial place,
The houses full of life were equally full of death. This house is now (a house).
The streets, courts, etc., etc., etc., (especially since the new city cleaning contracts) of New York, Philadelphia, et al, were as full of dead (vegetable and animal matter) as of living,
And fuller, O vastly fuller of the previous than of the subsequent.
And what I dreamed I have no hesitation in saying and I say it boldly now and for all time, (being the veritable Wandering Jew and Methuselah an infant to me)
And I stand henceforth bound to what I dreamed, (speaking, of course, in a Pickwickian and Congressional sense)
And now I am willing to disregard burial places and to dispense with them, (being the Wandering Jew, as aforesaid, and ergo not bury-able)
And if the memorials of the dead (i. e. posthumous biographies, etc.) were put up indifferently, (i. e. not well bound) everywhere, even in the room where I eat or sleep, I should be satisfied, (i. e. to accept 'em as additions to my library)
And if the corpse of any one loved by anybody (i. e. all corpses in general, none in particular) or if my own corpse should be "brayed in a mortar" and poured in the sea I shall be satisfied, not being able to help it, (and so would everybody else!)
Or if anything else should happen (as something probably will sometime or other in spite of W. W.) I shall be satisfied.

My Angel--Once!

I.

An angel she was, I haven't a doubt,
Though I never discerned her wings;
But it's fair to presume there are angels about
Unencumbered with any such things;
It is pleasant besides; and, wherever we go,
Though our hearts may be ever so cold,
Of all things, to be witched by sweet women, you know,
Is the green of our life—and its gold!

II.

She had eyes of a pure and brilliant blue,
And of course she had golden hair;
And the pearls of her pretty mouth shone through
The murmuring roses there:
You would love the snow of her gentle breast,
And the light of her gentle brow,
And her little hands—and all the rest
That I cannot mention now!

III.

In the innocent days that are wasted and gone
She was gentle and true to me;
And still in my soul that love burns on—
A star on a rainy sea,
But the angel had wings, after all, and she flew
Far away o'er the pitiless tide:
Old Death loved her better than I, and he knew
The true way to make her his bride.

[For the Saturday Press.]

Leaves.

—

By Walt Whitman.

—

1.

The music always round me, unceasing, unbeginning—yet long untaught I did not hear,
But now the chorus I hear, and am elated,
A tenor, strong, ascending, with power and health, with glad notes of day-break I hear,
A soprano, at intervals, sailing buoyantly over the tops of immense waves,
A transparent base, shuddering lusciously under and through the universe,
The triumphant tutti—the funeral wailings, with sweet flutes and violins—All these I fill myself with;
I hear not the volumes of sound merely—I am moved by the exquisite meanings,
I listen to the different voices winding in and out, striving, contending with fiery vehemence to excel each other in emotion,
I do not think the performers know themselves—but now I think I begin to know them,

2.

A Leaf for hand in hand!
You natural persons old and young! You on the Eastern Sea, and you on the Western!
You on the Mississippi, and on all the branches and bayous of the Mississippi!
You friendly boatmen and mechanics! You roughs!
You twain! And all processions moving along the streets!
I wish to infuse myself among you till I see it common for you to walk hand in hand.

3.

Early in the morning,
Walking forth from the bower, refreshed with sleep,
Behold me where I pass—hear my voice—approach,
Touch me—touch the palm of your hand to my body as I pass,
Be not afraid of my body.

[For the Saturday Press.]

PICKINGS.

The play of "Jeanie Deans," at Laura Keene's Theatre, created a profound impression on my mind. Perhaps I'm wrong to say the play, for it was the fine lifelike personification of Miss Keene in the part of Effie Deans, that so wrought upon my sympathies.

Woman is the subject of my thoughts—not as God imaged her, pure, confiding, unaffected,—but as society forces her to be. Society! A miserable state of uncomfortable being. An existence where the greatest liar is the most adept and polite member,—where man is the personification of selfishness, and woman, who should be the type of loveliness and innocence, is made the beau ideal of vanity and deceit,—where the noble promptings of the heart are silenced, —the perfect image God implanted on man's soul washed out.

The story of Effie Deans is brief. Its truthfulness frequently exemplified in common life. A young girl sacrifices at love's altar all that which the maiden most highly prizes. Time rolls on; she is cursed by her parent, condemned by her friends. Eventually she is accused of infanticide (a crime the poor woman is strongly tempted to commit by the lamb-like and forgiving laws of society, and the charitable doctrines of its most respected members). She is tried for a crime, the punishment for which is death, and when she is asked who her betrayer was, refuses to give the name of him she loves. The man who has separated her from her family, ruined her good name, robbed her of all earthly joy, and perhaps brought her to an ignominous death, she refuses to betray, because she loves. This noble woman is denounced by Christians, contemned by Society. I think that if the gates of heaven were wide as the universe, her soul could scarcely enter, 'twould be so big with goodness.

Do not let me be misunderstood. I stand not crime's defender. I am the supporter of the oppressed. Society is too ready to cry unclean, unclean! too willing to crush the unfortunate, thereby to gain the approving smile of its most revered members. For Conscience, the heart's dictates never said, Crush the unfortunate.

R. W. P.

FINE ARTS.

A Great Work of Art, by Crawford.

"DANCING JENNY."

Now on Exhibition at the Dusseldorf Gallery. Also, Barbee's *FISHER GIRL*, and Acker's *DEAD PEARL DIVER.*

Admission 25 cents. Open day and Evening. **548** Broadway.

A Zoological Collection For The Central Park.

—A number of gentlemen of this city, among whom are August Belmont, W. H. Aspinwall, Hamilton Fish, Benjamin R. Winthrop, Benjamin H. Field, Judge Bonney, Alexander W. Bradford, Frank Moore, R. L. Stuart, George Folsom, W. A. Mayo, Henry Delafield, W. P. Lee, have organized an association for the establishment and completion of an extensive Zoological and Botanical Garden in our Central Park. The preliminary meeting was held on Monday afternoon, at which a Committee was appointed to prepare a charter and take other necessary measures for the completion of the object.

Thoughts and Things.

BY ADA CLARE

I hear much and very confusing talk about the Bohemian, at present. I had my idea of what this term implied, but I find it very different from the received definition here.

I thought the Bohemian was by nature, if not by habit, a Cosmopolite, with a general sympathy for the fine arts, and for all things above and beyond convention. The Bohemian is not, like the creature of society, a victim of rules and customs; he steps over them all with an easy, graceful, joyous unconsciousness, guided by the principles of good taste and feeling. Above all others, essentially, the Bohemian must not be narrow-minded; if he be, he is degraded back to the position of a mere worldling.

When I was in Paris I saw a woman who appeared to me to be the incarnation and the highest type of a *Bohémienne*. She had been left a widow with two children and a very large fortune. Instead of chaining herself to the wheels of society and following its prescription for disposing of her income, she determined to spend it in her own way. She gave up the large and gloomy house in which she had lived, and took instead a smaller and much gayer one. Half of her servants she immediately dismissed, retaining those who were the least calculated to make a display.

She thought silver but a bait for midnight robbers, and declining to make her house a trap, she deliberately and without a blush sold the immense accumulation of uncouth family silver, and installed in its place the most beautiful and dainty china and glass that Paris could furnish.

In opening the door of her house you felt that you breathed the love-sphere; everything seemed wrapped in its rosy beam. Entering the parlors, no chill splendor struck you with its utter uselessness; you hardly noticed the furniture at all, everything seemed so living and natural; but as you took the trouble to examine it, you became aware that the most luxurious taste had been indulged to its utmost extent. Nothing was too gorgeous to be used, all this inanimate luxury was merely the slave of the human body, which Madame held to be far above them all.

She was extremely hospitable, and entertained much company, but selected them with utter disregard to the mandates of society. Any entertaining person capable of giving and receiving pleasure in such social intercourse, no matter whether he were artist, poet, banker, statesman, or man of leisure, was equally welcome. There, all social distinctions of rank and wealth fell down, and the human man stood up for himself. Whoever tried to stand upon his bank-account found himself soon tacitly dismissed from the circle. In her presence, all men and women felt that the world's masks dropped from their faces, the world's hollow words died on their tongues, and the soul vindicated its right to the body.

In these entertainments, sometimes dinners and sometimes suppers, the viands were always of such a ravishing description that they might have brought the dead epicure back to life; but they were never served with any *useless* ceremony. No grim, mirth-destroying waiters and butlers stood behind the chairs, turning the guests into stone with their Gorgon scrutiny: servants were only present in the room when their service was required, and then they consisted of a couple of smiling French bonnes, with their jaunty embroidered caps and aprons.

Madame never entertained more than twelve persons at a time; it was one of her principles that large and troublesome parties should be given in the vast and convenient saloons of restaurants, where all care was removed from the mind, and everything was simply represented in money. She often laughed at those people who inhabited immense houses, and toiled all their lives long in taking care of them, with a view to having large rooms for the reception of company. To make one's self a slave every day, in order to be provided for an accidental emergency, she held to be very absurd.

In her toilet was developed the most ecstatic perfection of French taste in dress, which all the world knows is the only standard of taste, yet she was never afraid to be seen unadorned. She would receive the proudest and wealthiest peers of France in a calico robe, whose cost might have been twenty cents a yard, and receive him not only without an apology, but with more stateliness than when attired in her most superb garments. In high dress, her desire seemed to be to draw attention away from her toilet. She was never out of the fashion, and yet never ridiculously in it. If ever a thing became the mode which was unbecoming to her face or form, she was sure to modify it in some slight way, so as to make it the perfection of grace and beauty.

Her chief delight was in impromptu suppers, where a few choice spirits happened to be gathered together at her house. Often she would dismiss her servants to bed, and serve the company herself. She did not make her guests feel that sensation of discomfort which arises from putting the hostess to trouble; on the contrary you felt as if she were a goddess, and annoyance could not approach her. Everything moved around her by magic as if smitten with the deep, full harmony of her nature, and before the heaven of her violet eye, discord sickened and fell dead.

She would descend into the wine-cellar, and bring up with her own hands, covered with jewels whose value could not be estimated, bottles of dusty wine that were worth their weight in gold,—performing with her own splendid hands offices that a lady's maid would have scorned, and with a simple dignity that made them majestic from her touch.

She kept her own hours, despised mere convention, neither paid nor received formal visits, and in everything followed the dictates of high taste and kindly feeling with an utter defiance of established forms. She laughed at and despised the so-called public opinion, and was so much above it in purity, sincerity, and every noble quality that makes man almost on a level with angels, that it either would not or dared not censure her.

She did not go out to seek objects of charity among unknown creatures, with ostentatious purpose and action, but to those who came in her immediate sphere, she was an angel of love and mercy. She had not the vanity to suppose she was called upon to cultivate the desert ferns of Africa; she was content to care for and cherish the flowers that grew in her own garden.

With a natural taste, even a thirst for luxury, she was able to deprive herself of it without a murmur. When she travelled, no one bore the discomforts of travelling with the smiling cheerfulness that she did. No road was too rough for her, no ship's cabin too confined, no wretched roadside inn too squalid. Her own waiting-maid suffered more from the inconvenience of voyaging than she did. Everything that was romantic, instructive, amusing, seized upon her mind in foreign countries; the disagreeable had no chance with her at all.

All her pleasures, however, she enjoyed with the simplicity of a child, whether at home or abroad. Her passion for music was extreme. Although she had held a box in the Italian Opera for ten years, the first pathetic scene would bring warm tears to her eyes sooner than to those of the most sentimental young girl in the house.

No one could approach this woman without an emotion; her presence thrilled the room where she was, and dissolved the hidden selfishness and meanness from the heart, ere one was aware. Her face was perfectly beautiful, her form would have reduced Venus to despair, and her fervent good sense, quick perception, and wondrous natural intelligence, made her a fit companion for the largest minds of the age.

Having in my mind's eye such a type as this, it is no wonder that I cannot appreciate the definition of the Bohemian with which our Sunday papers ring.

They lead us to suppose that the Bohemian must be poor. That he must take pleasure in keeping his boots and his cheese in the same drawer. That he delights in cooking upon his shovel and tongs, and in eating out of the coal-scuttle. That he essentially drinks very much, and becomes affected by liquor. That he must go about, making himself ridiculous, by exposing his private views and feelings to the public, which cannot understand him. That he must shock people's religious and social sentiments by all sorts of harsh, anathematizing onslaughts upon such sentiments. That he should prefer to spend his money on bad liquor, instead of defraying the just debts which he necessarily contracts. That he should speak sneeringly of women; and that he should wilfully let go the true paradise of the body, by sinking himself into a mere slough of carnalism, turning a blind eye to the strong food that Heaven is forever dropping abundantly down to those who choose to receive it, and preferring, like unclean birds, to feed upon the garbage in the gutters.

I will not accept this definition of the Bohemian. I will not believe it, I will not listen to it.

And thou, loveliest image of womanly grace, if thou art not the type of the Bohemian, thou shalt be to me the type of all that is noble among women; for thou hast taught me, that in the midst of every narrow thought, and unvirtuous morality, and uncharitable harshness of code, one woman can spread forth the white wings of an angel, and rising above them all, draw up to her own ardent height those who assemble around her; for thou hast taught me how near beauty, and truth, and purity, and passion, are to God!

[2025 editor's note: It may be noted Ada Clare's son was named Aubrey, and Robert Pearsall, the author of the following piece, was rumored to have a romantic link to Ada for a time.]

[For the Saturday Press.]

THE CHILD'S FIRST LESSON.

A Shooting Star.

'Twas a Summer evening. A mother sat by an open window with a young child resting on her lap. She had been kindly chiding him for absenting himself from her all day; endeavoring to instil a lesson in the young mind by carefully handling the feelings of the heart.

The little one gazed in its mother's face, and encircling her neck with its tiny arms, said, in the sweet accents of affection, that comes only from the infant voice, "Aubrey do love mamma very much!" "O, no," the mother said, "Aubrey cannot love mamma very much, because he does not stay by mamma's side; and all good little boys, when they see their mammas, run to them, but Aubrey never runs to me." The child was silent for a moment, then, pressing his fair cheek against his mother's brow, sobbed, 'Aubrey never do so any more."

Bedtime came. The boy, still resting on his mother's lap, clasped his little hands together, raised his eyes toward the sky, and began sweetly lisping the child's first prayer. Suddenly he stopped, and pointing with his finger, said, "O, see how very fast that little star runs! How much it must love its dear mamma!"

R. W. P.

[For the Saturday Press.]

St. Valentine Victorious.

BY EDWARD H. HOUSE.

On Monday evening, the evening of the 13th of February, the well-ordered mansion of Mrs. Jenkinson Sparkes exhibited a gay confusion. Fashion and taste and beauty had contributed the best they could afford to the success of this popularly respected lady's most brilliant social effort of the season. All artistic, bibulous, and gastronomic resources, had been invoked to magnify the splendor of the occasion. Differing in no definite respect from the multitude of similar convocations which every New York Winter witnesses, it was yet proclaimed, with much extravagance of emphasis—especially within hearing of Mrs. Jenkinson Sparkes—to be the most delightful assemblage ever at any time known, and probably ever to be known. Joyous flutterings of Mrs. Jenkinson Sparkes's jewelled fan revealed the ecstasy each repetition of this flattering phrase imparted to her.

The usual proportions of human brightness and dulness were there. The shadowy gloom of the preponderating element was to a certain extent relieved by the radiance of the few, whose brilliancy did not all proceed from Tiffany and Genin. They, of course, found their advantage in their isolation. The weakness of their numbers aided the strength of their position. It is perfectly in order to say, that as the lightning always performs with best effect in the murkiest atmosphere, so this lively minority—which, after a gradual and sympathetic cohesion, refused to mingle with the baser crowd—gleamed more resplendent by reason of the surrounding obscurity. And the manner in which it flashed its perpetual superiority, was one of the most cheerful things in the world to contemplate.

Just after the hour sacred to pink champagne, pâté de foie gras, mayonnaise, creamy congelations, and kindred glories, when the invasion of the drawing-rooms had recommenced, when the music was silent, and the dainty langour of appetite appeased precluded all idea of brisk activity, the clever congeries took unto itself a corner, and flickered conversationally.

"We are close upon the Fourteenth," suggested Mr. Dudleigh Purl.

"The fourteenth what?" asked Mrs. Vincent Brookes.

"Of February, to be sure," said Mr. Purl.

"Dear me, " said Mrs. Brookes, "what a memory for dates! I thought it was the fourteenth ball of the season, or the fourteenth epigram of to-night, or something important."

"I call it important," said Mr. Purl.

"And so do I," said Mr. Tompkins Tetherly, a sprightly youth of rising fifty, whose pathetic tone just now made everybody laugh.

"Why important?" asked two or three.

"A touching anniversary," said Mr. Tompkins Tetherly.

"A day consecrated to bleeding hearts," said Mr. Dudleigh Purl.

"O, yes," said one lady, "the day when tattered affections are sewed up."

"When Cupid turns tinker," said another, "and solders divided sympa-

Woodcut from Harper's Weekly, 1860.

thies."

"When very red things are served by the brace, and on queer skewers, in every shop window," said a third.

"The day of strong adjectives and weak ideas," said Mrs. Vincent Brookes.

"When everybody is heart-broken except Boyd and his carriers," said the last gentle cynic.

"What do you think, Mr. Bashford?" said Mrs. Brookes.

"I think," answered that gentleman, "that you are all burning with impatience to get scores of Valentines."

"O, for shame. Mr. Bashford !" said many feminine voices, simultaneously reproachful.

"Very likely," said Mr. Bashford.

"To be sure," said Miss Grace Dymonde, "I should never refuse to receive one of those things, you know, if it were very neat, and pretty, and all that."

"And expensive," said Mr. Bashford.

"Certainly," said Miss Dymonde.

"Now what do you think, Julia?" asked Mrs. Brookes of a young lady who had ventured no opinion.

"I object to them," said Miss Julia Larcher. "Be warned, gentlemen, send me no such soft messengers. I wont be adored by rule. I protest against manufactured devotion, and as for sentimental stationary, it is detestable.'

"Now stop, Miss Larcher," said Mr. Tompkins Tetherly, "stop, before matters grow serious. If this is your state of mind, what is to become of the elaborate compositions I have prepared with a view to your particular acceptance."

"I am very sorry, sir; I think you must transfer them to some worthier object. I am relentless."

"But I can't transfer them, you know. I spent two hours detecting a rhyme for Julia. At last I hit it—Julia, peculiar; peculiar, Julia. I don't know any other Julia. Besides I can't make my verses hang becomingly, like a ready-made coat, upon any person that comes along. Consider, Miss Larcher."

"Mr. Tetherly, you fill me with grief; but I don't see how I can make an exception. You see I am going to be absolute and unconditional."

"Mrs. Brookes," demanded Mr. Tetherly, "do you know any available young person whose name is Julia, and whose attributes are particularly heavenly? Because I can't have my verses lost, on any terms."

"Miss Larcher is jesting," said Mr. Bashford.

"No, sir; I am not jesting. I am not horribly serious, but still I am sufficiently in earnest to beg not to be molested to-morrow. I have satisfied myself that of all follies of custom, the Valentine folly is worst. So any of you who value my wish will send me no gilt-paged and perfumed nonsense."

"Miss Larcher assumes that her danger is imminent," said Mr. Bashford.

Miss Larcher's keen eyes flashed in a manner signifiant of dissatisfaction at this thrust; but she answered very quietly, "I seek simply to protect myself, sir."

Then other subjects arose.

The next morning, while Mr. Frank Bashford wrote insincere endearments on imposing sheets of dazzlingly decorated note-paper, Mr. Tompkins Tetherly came upon him.

"All right, my boy," said Mr. Tetherly; "now I am comfortable. I found a Julia, last evening, who fits my verses tolerably well. Her hair is red, to be sure, and I hint at glossy blackness; but that is not my affair. Do you think that is my affair ?"

"Not particularly."

"No, not to speak of. Well, my verses are going to make a sensation. You see Julia Larcher did the wrong thing. Any woman ought to be glad to get those verses. Wait and see the effect when she finds out. It'll be a moral study, sir, that's just what it'll be."

"Ah, Julia Larcher. An odd idea that was. But no matter"—and Mr. Bashford folded together his missives, and began to write their addresses.

"Not much, not much," said Mr. Tetherly, "it's quite unimportant. Apropos of unimportant things, shall you be at Tarlington's to-night?"

"Who else goes?"

"All our party of last night are expected. O, go and see Julia Larcher when she hears about my verses! I tell you, sir, there's an opening for a psychologist."

"Tetherly, will you dispose of these things?"

"Mail-box? Valentine business, evidently. Let me look at the addresses?"

"Of course."

"Why, see here, Bashford. Well, Bashford, you are a bold man."

"Bold?"

"Bold! why, you're a gladiator. No matter; you can take care of yourself. You can rely upon me. Good-day."

And Mr. Tetherly dashed away with that vigor which is characteristic of experienced and determined youthfulness.

When Mr. Frank Bashford crossed the threshold of Mrs. Dedenham Tarlington's drawing-room, the first person that assailed him was Mr. Tompkins Tetherly.

"By Jove, Bashford!" began that elastic gentleman, "you're in trouble. I thought it would be so, and you know I warned you against it. I did all I could, but somehow you never will take counsel from any of us young fellows."

"What's the matter, Tetherly?" said Mr. Bashford.

"Matter!—well, you may call it what you like; matter, if you choose. Only remember that I warned you."

"Well, disclose."

"Julia Larcher, don't you see—stop, is anybody listening? no—Julia Larcher is in a temper that will frighten you, sir."

"That's appalling."

"Well, you may laugh, but it's all owing to the valentine you sent her. I tell you, sir, when she spoke to me about it the fire came out of her eyes like roman candles, and each word snapped like a percussion-cap."

"The valentine I sent her?"

"To be sure."

"But I sent her none."

"Oh, come now, Bashford, this is too bad. Consider, my dear fellow, I mailed it myself."

"My poor Tetherly, go and put straws in your hair; you're growing insane."

"It won't do a bit. I took it myself; and you remember I said to you, 'Now, Bashford, be cautious, and don't send this, because there'll be a difficulty.' Don't you remember that?"

"Tetherly, age is weakening your mind."

"Bashford, what the devil do you mean? I never heard you talk such nonsense in my life!" and Mr. Tetherly strode away in a dignified huff.

This conversation set Mr. Bashford to thinking with unusual earnestness. It presently occurred to him that he might, after all, have committed the extraordinary error of misdirecting some one of his tender testimonials, as Mr. Tetherly had hinted. This certainly must be investigated; so he turned about and sought Miss Larcher.

Presently he caught a distant view of her; it was clear that she saw him, too. He aimed a salutation at her, but it reached her without effect. She showed color in her cheeks, but made no other sign.

As he drew very near, a faint buzzing as of malicious curiosity arose. Mr. Tetherly, it appeared, had not been idle in heralding the entertainment of the evening.

Miss Larcher stood firm and rather unnecessarily erect as he accosted her. Little groups gathered as close as appearances would allow, and turned eager ears in the direction of the rencontrants.

"Miss Larcher, good evening."

Miss Larcher's eyes rested upon him like the reflection of a sunbeam from an icicle. The feeblest acknowledgment that courtesy would admit of was all she vouchsafed.

"Are you ill, Miss Larcher ?"

"No, sir."

"I have interrupted you, perhaps."

"Not at all, sir."

"Possibly you are annoyed at something."

"Possibly."

"I understand you. Then Mr. Tetherly must have been right. In two words, Miss Larcher, I can remove your indignation, if you will permit me."

"I think sir, that silence would be better than excuses."

"But I have no excuses to make, only a misapprehension to correct. The objectionable note," said he, letting his voice fall, to the distraction of the feminine listeners near by, was not intended for you at all."

"This is absurd, sir," said Miss Larcher, in a voice the least bit changed.

"It is absurd, indeed," said he, "but still accidental."

"I am fatigued;" said Miss Larcher; "let me sit in this window "—and she withdrew a few steps to a partially secluded corner, drawing Bashford after her with her eyes.

"Now, sir," she continued, with a small forced laugh, "do not try to deceive me. The matter was better as it was before."

"You may be sure, Miss Larcher, that I tell you exactly the fact. It was a mistake, natural, perhaps, but unintended."

"Why, what is this?" suddenly broke in Mrs. Vincent Brookes, who had been suffering inexpressible agonies since the conversation failed to reach her, and who adopted a bold coup de société to master the position of affairs. "What is the subject that makes you both so solemn ?"

"Nothing that interests you, my dear," said Miss Larcher calmly.

"Do you know," added Mrs. Brookes, struggling to retain a foothold, "that Grace Dymonde is here, just arrived, with the most superb wreath of jewels anybody ever saw?"

Even at this, Miss Larcher showed no weakness. Whatever may have been the tumult within her, she preserved an outward composure, and Mrs. Brookes, quite baffled, went away in anger.

"Miss Dymonde, now," said Bashford—"I did send to her. Or, perhaps, dear me, I wonder, then—" and he began to laugh.

"What, Mr. Bashford! do you mean to tell me that the verses I received were meant for Grace Dymonde ?" asked Miss Larcher, with deeper flushes in her cheeks.

"How can I know," answered he; "what were they about?"

Miss Larcher repeated the first two lines.

"Ah, you remember them, then. Well, yes, they should have gone to her. Are you satisfied at last?"

If Miss Larcher were satisfied, nothing could be more singular than her manner of expressing it. First she seemed covered with confusion. Then she grew a bit paler, and finally said, half sternly:

"And those were written for Grace Dymonde?"

"Why not?"

"Mr. Bashford, how could you write such things to Grace Dymonde?"

"O, easily! Sentimental stationary, you know, is of little account, and manufactured devotion is nothing at all."

"Do you assure me, then sir, that you—"

"Well, I am waiting, Miss Larcher."

"Nothing, sir."

"O!"

But Frank Bashford was no bête. A few seconds of rapid reflection brought convictions to him that were probably of no unpleasant nature, as he smiled quite radiantly.

"Miss Larcher," said he, after a little pause, "I think your displeasure is directed especially against fourteenth of February protestations."

"The reason is, sir, that they all fail in sincerity and truth."

"And if they did not?"

"I should be glad to see the one that did not."

"Miss Larcher, the fourteenth still lasts. It is now nine o'clock. Will you dance with me soon after ten ?"

"Yes, indeed, sir."

"Where shall I look for you?"

"Come here."

For half an hour Frank Bashford was unseen. Glowing, impatient, half doubting, half assured, Miss Julia Larcher awaited him, never moving from her rendezvous. Assaults from Mrs. Vincent Brookes and others were repelled with elegant success.

I know that the bit of paper he brought with him, when he came, was not despised, but read with timid consciousness of all its sincerity and truth, and in brief time enshrined where none but the good letters go. I know too, that the dancing appointment was all forgotten.

The rest that I know, the reader also knows, I am sure.

For the Saturday Press.]

LEAVES FROM NATURE.

Human nature! Isn't it a puzzle? Inanimate nature is direct and simple, even in its mysteries; but human nature is as tortuous as a serpent, coiling a thousand ways, to avoid a thousand enemies. How hard it is to divine the aims or objects of any man or woman one meets! They are not manifest in what he or she says or openly does, but most probably hidden both by manner and speech. The hero of romance, walking through a realm of magic, was not exposed more continually to deception than we are among our fellow-creatures.

What wonder, then, that I prefer to talk with inanimate nature, whose illusions arrive from the imperfections of my senses, and who does not attempt to cheat and deceive me at every turn? How often every day, am I forced to smile at men (who deem themselves, and perhaps are, my superiors in intellect) for inconsistencies and vanities worthy of a child. They think I have no right to publish, because I do not understand the grand art of authorship. Thank Heaven, I do not! They sneer at the writer of the "Leaves from Nature," because in his earnestness he betrays his simplicity, and forgets to say what he does not mean nor feel. Of course it is very stupid in me to allow my language to be simply the vehicle to convey my impressions, but I cannot help it.

Let me speak my heart then—for I relinquish all claim to authorship.

It is amusing even to laughter, to see and hear men who have lived all their lives upon the brains of others, whose craniums are so crammed with the "army of good words the fool hath planted in his memory," as to be incapable of entertaining an original thought, attempt to ridicule me, for the want of some new and salient characteristics. They speak what they do not believe, one thing to-day and another to-morrow. They get their authorship from art and reading, as the fountain its water from the living brook, to play and splash from mechanical force in an endless round without vitality. From works in English, they seem to have acquired a perfect right to steal; and, when they translate from the French and christen afresh, they consider him hypocritical who questions their originality—in which, indeed, they almost persuade themselves to believe. Such is the potency of human vanity, which has made me turn aside from the contemplation of man, to the study of that Nature in which God alone lives and moves, and from which, without perversion, his love and benevolence breathe forever. So many illustrious pilgrims have preceded me in their worship at the shrine of Nature, that what I can say must necessarily appear meagre and commonplace, after hearing the language of their inspiration.

Yet I know my words are not valueless, for they are heartfelt and therefore true to Nature; and I hold that the waving of a leaf, being a natural action, is more truly admirable than the most exquisite bow of a French dancing-master, which is really meaningless.

Nature is always constant, but man is a cluster of inconsistencies. Well it is that poetic impersonations are not real. If the sun, for instance, were a man or woman, to-day he might rise in the East, to-morrow in the West, and the day after, perhaps, not at all. The moon, were she human, might this month fill her horn most copiously, and at some other, during a temperance revival, or something of the kind, repent that she had ever done it at any time, and deny her silver radiance to the night. If the stars were the ladies, whose eyes they resemble, they would at some period find it vulgar and unfashionable to twinkle in the blue vault of heaven, and be shooting and gadding about in every direction. Indeed, if they were females, I am afraid they would be very apt to fall! The Polar Star, disgusted with the North Pole, would try the Equator, by way of a change, and wreck half the shipping on the sea. If the ocean were under the government of such a human god as Neptune, and he in a passion, just think of the consequences.

No! we don't want the sylph-like flowers to paint and perfume themselves anew, the sun to stand still or go back, or the moon and stars to forget 'their proper spheres'; but to obey the laws of Nature, which man refuses to, because he imagines that he knows better than she does, although he pays the penalty of his conceit and wilfulness in a thousand diseases, in pain and suffering, in premature old age and death.

R. W. P.

DEATH OF BURTON.

As this paper is going to press, I hear of the death of the finest comedian of the age. Mr. William Evans Burton expired at his residence in Hudson street, on Friday morning, 10th inst., at the age of fifty-six.

The name and fame of Mr. Burton render eulogiums upon his life superfluous. As Johnson said of Garrick, "his death eclipsed the gaiety of nations." Combining in one and the same person the splendid artist, the eminent belles lettres scholar, the polished and graceful writer, the most genial of hosts, and the most delightful of raconteurs on ship or shore, by the social hearth or the festive board, in every relation Mr. Burton left his impress upon the "very age and body of the time."

He leaves no one to fill his place upon the stage in his peculiar vein.

Weep Thalia! Mourn all ye rosy-dimpled gods of Mirth! Momus himself is dead!

E. W.

Dramatic Feuilleton.

Nil Admirari.

A great many very nice persons of both sexes—persons who are ° very good, very clever, and very philanthropically inclined—persons, in fact, who have tender hearts, fine sensibilities, artistic inspirations, and many more delightful things which I can only, alas! admire, and not share—have lately been much exercised in their minds at the rapid increase of élèves in the Nil Admirari School,—an educational institution where, in one way and another, one has to pay pretty well for his learning.

Mille de tonnerres! What a long sentence !

Do not alarm yourself, I am not going to preach a sermon.

I am afraid that my style has been corrupted by reading "Leaves from Nature." Nature is a good thing to do, but guide-books are never entertaining. We are, however, talking about art, which, in this line of country, is not at all like nature.

I do not purpose to defend the Nil Admirari School. I do not hold my chair in it for that purpose. To the purist of this delightful sect, all things are the same,— weakness and strength, right and wrong, praise or blame; the only question is, To what does it lead, what is it all worth? It is nothing that comes from nothing, and there remains nothing but nothing.

The whole public, with here and there an exception, the personal friend of an actor or actress, or some persons whose taste, or want of it, makes them incline to the coulisses, belongs to the Nil Admirari School.

The public is not such a fool as you may imagine.

The public doesn't think that, so far as theatres go, there is such a wonderful amount of genius floating about, even in the metropolis.

Actors and actresses snugly rolled up in the blanket of egotism, fancy themselves admired of gods and esteemed of men and women. The public laughs and says nothing.

The public don't consider itself bound to be bored to death during four mortal hours for the sake of one good scene which may last five minutes.

The public is not a wet-nurse, either.

It will not go about to seek adolescent artists, feed them with pap, put purple and fine linen upon them, and then bow down and worship them.

Not exactly.

Yet this hard-hearted public can have its little excitements as well as another. See how it hailed Patti, who sprung, like Minerva, a full-fledged artist from the brain of Jove. Mark how it dissolves for *Jeannie Deans*. Regard the real enjoyment which it has at the Circus!

As for art, in its real sense, if we leave out the opera, we are in the desert. The public knows that as well as you or I, and shrugs its shoulders at the pretences of quacks and humbugs.

And the Subscriber, having no fixed rules of thought or action, no settled principles or ideas, no friends to reward, nor enemies to punish—and looking with mild compassion on people who have—belongs to, sides with, and, as nearly as may be, represents the views of the public. That is, like the public, he don't think it worth while having any views about art when there isn't any art to have them about.

Some of these thoughts occurred to me the other night, when I saw *Oliver Twist* for the second time. The piece, since its first performance, has been much improved, but it is still unsatisfactory. Its comedy is generally serious, and its seriousness is painfully comic. According to the profound definition of the Youngest and Loveliest, it must be a pure comedy. She is good as well as young and passing fair, but the manager must not be permitted to hide behind her crinoline. Read his modest announcement:

The character of Nancy Sykes, then played by Charlotte Cushman, being the character in which she first clutched her dramatic crown, will be sustained by Matilda Heron; Fagin the Jew, and Bill Sykes, will find representatives in J. W. Wallack, Jr., and Geo. Jordan, and never, perhaps, as a whole, did characters fall into the hands of artists better fitted to them than those who will constitute the dramatic picture to-night.

Why the Heron should play Nancy, because the Cushman "clutched her dramatic crown" in it (which she didn't, by the way), passes my comprehension. In fact, to use a phrase which I perceive has obtained a somewhat extended popularity, I don't see it.

It seems that Matilda "condescends" to play *Nancy Sykes*. Who is this person to whose "condescension" we are indebted for a mediocre performance? Never mind!

It is not however of Matilda Heron that I speak, particularly.

It is of the Winter Garden, the only theatre in the United States, so far as I know, that is conducted under the supervision of a gentleman by birth, education, culture, and association.° It is here that we should look for dramatic art, if anywhere. Let us take a scene of *Oliver Twist* and see how near they come to the proper standard.

First, as to the murder of *Nancy Sykes*:

In order to be clearly understood, I quote the author's description:

> The robber sat regarding her for a few seconds with dilated nostrils and heaving breast, and then grasping her by the head and throat, dragged her into the middle of the room, and looking once towards the door, placed his heavy hand upon her mouth.
>
> "Bill, Bill," gasped the girl, wrestling with the strength of mortal fear, "I—I—won't scream or cry—not once—hear me—speak to me—tell me what I have done."
>
> "You know, you she-devil," returned the robber, suppressing his breath. "You were watched to-night; and every word you said was heard."
>
> "Then spare my life, for the love of Heaven, as I spared yours," rejoined the girl, clinging to him. "Bill, dear Bill, you cannot have the heart to kill me. O! think of all I have given up this one night for you. You *shall* have time to think and save yourself this crime; I will not loose my hold, you cannot throw me off. Bill, Bill, for dear God's sake, for your own, for mine, stop before you spill my blood. I have been true to you, upon my guilty soul I have."
>
> The man struggled violently to release his arms, but those of the girl were clasped round his, and tear as he would, he could not tear them away.
>
> "Bill," cried the girl, striving to lay her head upon his breast, "the gentleman and that dear lady told me to-night of a home in some foreign country, where I could end my days in solitude and peace. Let me see them again, and beg them on my knees to show the same mercy and goodness to you, and let us both leave this dreadful place, and, far apart, lead better lives, and forget how we have lived, except in prayers, and never see each other more. It is never too late to repent. They told me so; I feel it now; but we must have time—a little, little time !"
>
> The housebreaker freed one arm, and grasped his pistol. The certainty of immediate detection if he fired, flashed across his mind, even in the midst of his fury, and he beat it twice with all the force he could summon, upon the upturned face that almost touched his own.
>
> She staggered and fell, nearly blinded with the blood that rained down from a deep gash in her forehead, but raising herself with difficulty on her knees, drew from her bosom a white handkerchief—Rose Maylie's own—and holding it up in her folded hands as high towards heaven as her feeble strength would let her, breathed one prayer for mercy to her Maker.
>
> It was a ghastly figure to look upon. The murderer, staggering backward to the wall, and shutting out the sight with his hand, seized a heavy club and struck her down.

This terrible scene is so clumsily rendered on the stage as to make every one laugh. After struggling in the approved stage-fashion for ten seconds, during which Nancy repeats some incoherent expressions, Bill drags her off as is supposed into another room, when they had none other, and is there presumed to kill her. Returning, he goes across the stage, à la Bowery, looking at his paws incarnadined, and saying "There's blood upon my hands, she's dead! she's dead!" goes into another impossible apartment. The public grins audibly. It really can't help it. And that is art!

Take Wallack's, as well, with the *Poor Young Man* leaping from the tower, which feat must inevitably have resulted in the breaking of his neck. It is equally as absurd as the hanging of Bill Sykes by a hook in his coat collar.

I am afraid that if these things are permitted to go on, our School will have more pupils than we can well accommodate.

Faits Divers.

That piquant actress and pretty woman, Fanny Morant, who has broken the hearts of all the poor young men and jeunesse dorée about Wallack's, has 'gone and been and done and got married' to a person of the name of Smith. They all do it. I remember that the original A. M., or one of 'em, took out her bonded certificate in the name of one of the Smith family. He was 'in a store,' and had a governor with large amounts of brown-stone fronts, corner-lots, and things of that kind.

° *Mr. Bourcicault might be an exception to this statement, but he is only temporarily the manager of Laura Keene's Theatre. He is almost the only person connected with the American stage who understands the requirements of the drama of to-day.*

So she couldn't see genius and the moral virtues in the person of the Subscriber. However, I had my revenge on this particular Smith: years passed on and I met him not. At last, at last he came.

Time had only deepened the sense of injury in my breast.

My vengeance was terrible; but, considering my wrongs just, I induced Le Chauve to send Smith aforesaid a private box, and he had to stand the whole of *Lesbia*.

The next evening he was on his way to Utica. . .

The men at the Club object to Smith, Fanny Morant's Smith; they think of calling him out, in the following order: Joseph Balsamo, 1; Edward the Blonde, 2; the last of the Stewarts, 3; the Baron, 4; Pagé, 5; Whiskers, 6; Personne, 7. Probably that will finish off Smith, but if it don't, the Virginian Colonel and the Orleanian apostle can have a matinée with him next Summer.

The French *Courier*, which makes, jokes, sometimes, alluding to the marriage of a negro-minstrel with a rich young woman whose parents didn't see it, thinks that the father-in-law of the happy man ought to have chanted *Leave that girl alone*. The subscriber, with deference, suggests that there may be an opportunity of a private performance of the pretty little French comedy, *Otez votre fille*, s. v. p.

The father of the little girl who was burned to death last year at Macon, Georgia, has erected an expensive monument to her memory, with, as an epitaph, some nonsense about the sighs of love not bringing her back to life again. When it is understood that the child's life might have been saved by the expenditure of a few shillings for lamp-screens, it is evident that the monument is a bad financial speculation, unless it is intended as an advertising dodge.

The Christy Minstrels at Niblo's Saloon are worth doing occasionally.

The Boston *Courier* says that the Wood-season opened at the Theatre of that village, on Monday, to a "dismally thin house, and the voices of the actors resounded in lugubrious hollowness." Come back, O Queen of the Soubrettes! and I'll engage that the W. G. shall not display one vacant stall. What, as I have before remarked, what is a Garden, Winter or Summer, without Wood? Likewise bring with you the serious Jefferson, and the fascinating Davenport. We have had sensations enough. We are bored to death. We want to laugh.

The Philadelphia *Dispatch* has a notice of a distinguished young American actress, which 'critique' I recommend to the young man of the Sunday *Times*. The advice I reprint (omitting the lady's name), as it is very good for some people hereabouts :

> Her style of elocution is absurdly unnatural, and miserably weak in its affectation. When she does not drawl like a Quaker preacher, she gasps like a Methodist exhorter at a camp-meeting. The interjection *ah* is tacked on to some of her words as a prefix, and tagged on as a suffix. For instance—"Ah that ah voice! It is, ah: it is, ah—ah my ah husband!"

The city theatres are doing a moderate business, Laura Keene's and Niblo's keeping the lead.

In Irving Place.

Back to Irving Place on Monday came the Linnet of Twenty-second street, with all her suite; the graceful, elegant Brignoli, decked with histrionic laurels cultivated on Boston Common; the rotund Amodio; the square, solid, Major Susini; the handsome Ferri, with his mezzo voce; and so on.

It was the *Puritani,* with Patti, and everybody came. There was Anna Maria in all the glory of a new bonnet with a projecting crown exactly like the bow of a clipper-ship (awfully in the way these things are sometimes; I don't know after all but that I like the little hats better); then there were Les Trois Mousquetaires just returned from arranging the Terpsichorean affairs of the Nation at Washington (they managed twenty-three parties in ten days which isn't so bad for an off-hand); likewise all the children of Israel, masculine and feminine; all the subscribers, including the patriots who furnished the 'demnition cash' to bring out Esperanza, Crescimano and Albertini ; all the pretty women and ugly critics; the entire free list which always growls at the performance; a small deputation from Orange county; a lady and gentleman from Attica on a bridal tour; and a good deal of Peoria.

Patti was delightful in the first act of the Puritani. The polacca, with which I have some slight acquaintance, and the finale, were charmingly rendered. The gem of the night, however, was the *A te o cara*, which has never been so well sung here since Mario. I don't notice any very remarkable improvement in Brignoli's manner of getting on and off and around the stage; but he certainly sings better than before. Patti's acting is more graceful, and considering her very brief experience before the lamps, is remarkably good.

On Wednesday, the *Barber* drew famously. There was a better house than that which greeted La Grange when she made her début in the same opera. The first act I enjoyed very much. Acting and singing very good. Patti's *Rosina* very fresh and charming after the elderly prime ladies who have preceded her in the rôle; it was really refreshing. As a gentleman from the Jerseys remarked, she "looked pretty enough to eat."

In the music lesson, she shocked the weak nerves of numerous legitimate people by introducing "Comin' through the Rye," in the sentiment of which ballad I quite agree, but it is a little old. Why not give us "Wait for the Wagon," or "A little more Cider for Miss Dinah," or something equally good in the touching and sentimental way?

However, badinage apart (I don't do it often since I have been disappointed in love), it was generally voted, like Mancini, a good *Barber*, and it will bear doing again.

The Opera prospects are very bright, all owing to little Patti. The managers will have those corner-lots after all.

The irrepressible conflict with Gazzaniga has been settled, and she will sing in *Safo*, next week.

I hear that negotiations are pending between an agent of Madame Cortesi and Ullmann, by which she will sing at the Academy in April. She will bring out the new tenor Musiani, *ut* and all.

Personne.

NEW YORK FEBRUARY 18, 1860

Thoughts and Things.

BY ADA CLARE

I know not whether it be a more melancholy or ludicrous sight, the little and unnecessary jealousies of artists. How strange that any one should think of enhancing one's own value by depressing that of another! Perhaps this is the reason why the dramatic art, which should be the highest of them all when music is excepted, has something now of coarseness and inferiority clinging to it.

With a very few exceptions, the leading artists on the stage have but one way of disposing of their rivals for fame—with thick, unflinching anathema. Yet nothing sounds so hideously in the mouth of any artist as abuse of his own art and the exponents thereof.

Without a sincere reverence and an earnest enthusiasm for his art, no artist can ever become truly great. And petty jealousy, perhaps, saps the strength of talent more rapidly than any thing else.

Artists should hold each other's hands in mutual bonds of protection and sympathy, and so form a strong flank with which to breast the world's foolish prejudices against them. They will have onslaughts enough from the critics and the blasé public, who have been to Paris, where nobody is ashamed of madly admiring, and have returned with the receipt for impeccability in their pockets. Paris is the last place to go to learn coldness.

All the young Americans I know are more blasé than the most inveterate Parisians. Paris is a place that never exempts you from emotion, so that they who travel with a view to starve out their emotional natures had better sneer at that city and pass it by.

But to return to my subject: why should artists strive to undo each other's fame? Can any actress gain anything by seeking to prove that Matilda Heron and Laura Keene are without talent? A critic might gain thereby, for he should have a wonderful cunning of rhetoric to make a respectable case out of it; but an artist may lose, but cannot gain.

When young poets insist that Tennyson and Mrs. Browning and Shelley cannot write poetry, our opinion of their own powers is not enhanced; we even have a secret suspicion that they are muffs. Can artists take the hint?

All arts must have suns forming planetary systems around them. The litterateur, the musician, the painter, the sculptor knows it and acts therefrom, and it is vain for dramatic artists to seek to discharge the suns, and set up their own little planetary establishments.

Musicians have jealousies enough, but not so many as the stars of the stage. Because a great singer will allow himself sometimes to be utterly carried away by the talent of a rival who is singing before him, and he gives his applause without an attempt to patronize, in speaking of each other, they are, alas! too apt to degrade with a vain view to their own aggrandizement. Gottschalk had, however, a splendid peculiarity in this matter. His appreciation was equal to his power. He had the loftiest intellectual perception of those who were great in his own art. He was utterly above all small rivalries and jealousies; he was unacquainted with the name of malice. O! if all artists were like this splendid one, how long could the snobs of society talk about patronizing music?

Yet, after all, these small jealousies are only excrescences on the characters of artists; they are not the character itself. No class of persons are so generous to each other in cases of real distress as they are. Then they band together, and strain every nerve to lift any one of them out of poverty and illness. The merchants and bankers do not so.

I wish the critics could remember that the artists are under no especial obligation to them for dilating upon them; the benefit is mutual. The critic lives by criticism—that's his bread and beer.

I hope no one will imagine that I am writing thus with a personal view, for I am not. I am particularly averse either to attacking individuals or answering their attacks on me. They need not put R. S. V. P. at the bottom of their satires upon me, because I won't answer them, whatever they may say.

Dramatic Feuilleton.

Faits Divers.

The theatres give us nothing new this week. I am in the desert waiting for Wood, who will be along presently.

Over at the New Bowery they have the very astonishing, I may say stunning, sisters Western, whose claims to artistic eminence rest altogether upon their physical attractions, which are of the loudest and most powerful character. They remind me very strongly of the remark of an English critic about the reviews at the Paris theatres, that they owed their popularity chiefly to the introduction of a number of ladies "whose dresses began very low down, and finished very high up." A new piece nominally, but really a variation of the old theme, has been done for the sisters by Mr. W. B. English. Polly Jordan is the title, and the affiche bears a picture of the lowest and most vulgar character. Where's pious Pillsbury's powerful police?

There are plenty of Poor Young Men about town now—I mean in the theatres. There's Mr. Lester Wallack's Poor Young Man at Wallack's; there's Der Roman Eines Armen Junger Mannes, which has had an immense run of six nights at the Stadt Theatre; and to-night, at the Theatre Français, Mr. Mannstein will produce *Le Roman d'un Jeune Homme Pauvre*. The pieces played at the Stadt Theatre and the Francais are announced as having been written by M. Octave Feiullet; but I sincerely trust they will be as entertaining as the work of Mr. Lester Wallack.

Miss Laura Keene has renewed for *Jeannie Deans* the *Ledger* style of advertising, which pushed *Our American Cousin* over the dull months. I see that there is already a good deal of Peoria and Attakapas in town, so *Jeanie* is good for another month.

The prettiest thing in the way of an imitation that I have seen for many a day, was the "Growler's" paper in the last *Sunday Times*. It was immediately recognized as an exact copy of the style of Mr. S. Wallace Cone, one of the best writers in the Custom House.

Among the large number of kind friends whose minds are exercised about the subscriber's style, is one who conceals himself under the modest mantle of anonymity, and sends me some extracts from a Rochester paper, upon the performance of Mr. ——, as *Sir John Falstaff*. This actor's "reputation," according to your rural contemporary, "stands firmly on the highest round of dramatic fame." His performance of Shakespeare's "beautiful effusion" is a "great rendition;" he "has contested the palm of greatness with the most distinguished actors of the age;" he "stands forth in bold relief;" he is "immeasurably great." The other paper says that "he stands upon the topmost round of dramatic fame," and talks about his "rendition." I am afraid that the actor was, like Garrick, his own critic. He finished his engagement with the very suggestive and appropriate rôle of *Nicholas Flam*.

Last Saturday there was a great time for all the Anna Marias who are in the musical way, the fashionable thing to do, now-a-days. In the morning, at ten, the Flirt-Harmonic Society had a rehearsal. No end of crinoline, and but few trowsers. At one o'clock there was a Patti Matinée, and another tremendous feminine convention, with the attendant Jeunesse Dorées and shopmen who try to set themselves for the gilded youth, and look as if they had been galvanized. The Brightest and the Best was there, of course. She misses Vespers sometimes, but never a Matinée. In the evening there was the third concert of the Flirt-Harmonic, when there was another very large audience to hear a programme which was somewhat too scientific to be generally understood. Colson was to sing the aria from the *Magic Flute,* but got sick at the last moment, and didn't come. Search was made for the inevitable Stigelli, who was found resigning himself to the blandishments of lager bier and sweitzer kaisse, with a friend. Like Anna Maria when she has a design on the Governor's cheque-book, Stigelli had his 'Tear' already, and delighted everybody with it.

Certainly the "Academy" was "one of Music" on that day and evening.

Madame Gazzaniga leaves town immediately. After a concert-tour in the West, she is to sing at the New Orleans Opera House, at the moderate salary of two hundred dollars per night.

The London *Critic* (Jan. 27) says that Tom Taylor's dramatized version of Dickens's "Tale of Two Cities," "has been even more unsuccessful than similar attempts to convert a novel into a dramatic piece." The Critic was immediately picked up and snubbed by Celeste, who writes to the Post that the play had not been produced when the article was published. Queer error for a careful paper like the *Critic* to make.

The piece was done on the 31st, and does not seem to have been very successful. Mme. Celeste played the wife of Defarge, and made a great hit in it, according to the London *News*.

The New Orleans *True Delta* has the following description of a *Dundreary* episode at the Varieties Theatre:

> "Our American Cousin" shows much bottom for a theatrical race. Crowded and brilliant audiences have waited upon Lord Dundreary nightly.
>
> "A somewhat droll event took place at the Varieties on Friday evening. Somebody wrote a witty letter to a member of the company, requesting him to summon all the artists of the greenroom, previous to reading an address to Mr. Sothern, after which he requested that gentleman should be crowned by Mr. Wallack, with the appropriate wreath he took the liberty of presenting for the purpose. The imposing ceremony was performed as directed, and repeated again on the stage during the last act of "Our American Cousin," when Mr. John Owens, the manager, gracefully stepped forward and crowned the immortal Dundreary with a chaste wreath of *Woathled Chethnuthz*, beautifully relieved by small *Oythter Thellz*, and *Shwimp Thkinz*! 'My Lord' made a brilliant acknowledgement, replete with stammering, hops, etc., which ended this somewhat odd presentation, the audience and artists evidently enjoying the joke intensely.
>
> "This was doubtless intended as a 'take off.' On the last night of 'Dot' some enthusiastic admirer threw a wreath to Miss Thompson. It was pretty well understood, so it is said, that the excessively fascinating leader of the orchestra was to pitch the fiddle aside, frantically rush upon the stage, and crown the pleasant little lady. But the manager, who can look stern when he chooses to chase the devil from his eyes, demurred. The consequence was no wreath-crowning that night, 'Dot' contenting herself with coming down to the stage boxes with the floral gift upon her arm. The chestnut present was a stunner, and will put an end to the jump-up-and-kiss-me enthusiasm of susceptible admirers.
>
> "'Everybody's Friend' comes after 'Our American Cousin,' when the public chooses to dismiss Dundreary and the Vermonter."

Mr. Wallack is getting mercenary. He announces that in order to accommodate "the paying public," he is obliged to shut down the gates upon the illustrious brigade of dead-heads. I never imagined that any one except myself ever thought that the people who paid for going to theatres had any rights which managers were bound to respect.

The Webb Sisters are still at the Broadway Boudoir.

The Chevalier de Gant-Rouge went there, the other night, and estimates the gross receipts at $7 50. No brown-stone fronts to come out of that speculation, evidently.

There is a band of bogus Christy Minstrels travelling about in the rural districts. The only pure original Jacobs is that conducted by the fascinating George, at the elegant Mr. Niblo's Saloon.

In Irving Place.

The only thing worth mentioning in the Operatic way,—because the only thing that could claim the merit of novelty (a great merit in these latter days, when everybody is continually doing the same thing over and over again, except Walt Whitman, who does nothing as nobody ever did it before),— is the presentation of *Der Freischutz*, Opera by Carl Von Weber, beloved by Teutonia above all her composers except Mozart.

Carl Von Weber, most excellent master, esteemed by the gods and beloved of Burkhardt and Bergmann!

In Germany, Von Weber is adored. Fanaticism in India is nothing to it.

Let me tell you a story in point. It is not a "story" in your sense, Miss, because it happens to be true.

About fifteen years ago, the manager of one of the German theatres was surprised and delighted with a visit from a college comrade. They embraced; they kissed each other on either cheek. They ate of much sour-krout; they drank stoutly of much bier; they poured down bottle after bottle of the dry wine of the Rhine, and then drifted into a dispute about art, the last argument holden by a drunken man previous to his final appeal to the memory of his mother.

The manager was a devoted admirer of Carl Von Weber. He saw C. V. W. to the farthest possible extent. He was continually engaged in getting up *Der Freischutz,* with all sorts of new sceneries and decorations. His great point of interest was the incantation scene, when the magic bullets are cast, and he excelled all others in arranging demoniacal tableaux. On the day of the final rehearsal, the director invited his friend to visit the theatre, and hear the repetition generale of the "finest Opera ever written."

They went; but mark the stupidity of the guest! He couldn't see *Der Freischutz.* He pooh-poohed Carl Von Weber. That was worse than sacrilege. The friends separated in anger.

Some years passed. The revolution of '48 had broken out. All Germany was in a state of chronic inflammation. The manager and his quondam guest met in the insurgent ranks, and fought side by side at the barricades. The infidel who wouldn't believe in Carl Von Weber fell at the first fire, and died in the arms of the true believer.

The manager, in telling the story, stopped at this point to shed some natural tears, and then proceeded to detail the circumstances that attended the burial of his friend. He had been a medical student, and his body was taken to the College by his comrades, who could not resist so fine an opportunity for a postmortem.

And, said the manager in conclusion, "mark the working of the eternal law of compensation. It was my pleasure to produce *Der Freischutz* with the skull of my old friend as one of the properties for the incantation scene, I doing *Caspar*."

That story includes pretty nearly all I know about *Der Freischutz*. I have a frantic German friend who says that Colson sung remarkably well; that Stigelli was good; although the music was rather too low for his voice, and the voice was very fine. Bergmann's orchestra, fair, but not in so good order as to justify the reputation of the conductor.

The German population did not come out very strongly for this opera—having no great confidence, I apprehend, in the artists. It has been sung twice: the first house was fair, and the second 'shy.'

Adelina Patti has repeated *Rosina*, in the *Barber*—which the young man of the *Sunday Times* calls "another chaplet in the wreath that encircles the brow of the young prima donna"(I don't know what he means, but it sounds sweetly)—and *Amina*. Next week, she will make her début in *Martha*, in which rôle I think she will be very fine. To-day, for the matinée, she will sing *Rosina*, to a Piccolomini house, or I am quite mistaken as to the temper of the public.

Personne.

—Florence Nightingale, in her new work entitled "Notes on Nursing: what it is, and what it is not," says:–

"It is, I think, alarming, peculiarly at this time, when the female ink-bottles are perpetually impressing upon us 'woman's particular worth and general missionariness,' to see that the dress of women is daily more and more unfitting them for any 'mission' or usefulness at all. It is equally unfitted for all poetic and all domestic purposes. A man is now a more handy and far less objectionable being in a sick-room than a woman. Compelled by her dress, every woman now either shuffles or waddles; only a man can cross the floor of a sick-room without shaking it. What is become of a woman's light step—the firm, light, quick step we have been asking for?"

[For the Saturday Press.]

DEATH AT THE DOOR.

Crouching on the marble steps
That led into a house of prayer,
Sat a girl with face half hidden
'Neath a vail of tangled hair,
Looking like a fallen angel
Come to find a shelter there.

Loudly blew the winds around her,
Coldly fell the heartless rain,
Quickly flew the feet bound homeward;
No one saw poor houseless Jane
No one, 'neath his woollen garments,
Felt the blast that gave her pain.

Open wide, great church, your portals—
For this stranger open wide;
Cold and wet she kneels before you,
Let her 'neath your arches glide—
Let her, in your lonely chancel
Safely from the tempest hide.

See! she shudders, growing paler
With each colder, keener blast,
Like a lily late in Autumn
By the careless gardener past—
Past, and left to be by whirlwinds
On the cold earth rudely cast.

Six long days hast thou been bolted,
Sheltering only dust and gloom,
Giving, to thy dumb, dead cushions,
Sumptuous seats, and ample room;
Whilst for poor and houseless strangers,
Sinless, spotless, waits the tomb.

Wealthy men have poured upon you
Golden showers, that you might rise,
Carrying up your fretted columns,
Babel-like, to meet the skies,
Filling dome, and towering belfry,
With the tumult of their cries,

Save us, Lord! we've sinned against thee,
Give us room in Heaven to dwell;
Look! how much we've done to praise thee,
Hear our loud-tongued Sabbath bell;
Louder than all other churches
Doth its Christian music swell.

Soft—she sleeps, poor child, how quiet—
The wind is sighing—now it shrieks—
The night grows dark, the dim-lit lantern
In its rusty socket creaks
While a poor and weakly woman
To the gentle sleeper speaks.

'Tis too late—the words, though loving,
Cannot touch the sacred dead;
Bear her gently, ere the morning
Brings the pious ones to tread
O'er the marble where the dying
Stranger made her painful bed.

Wrap her closely in the flimsy
Rags that hang about her form;
Grandly sounds the dirge that sweepeth
Through the arches of the storm,
Bravely rings the bell that screameth
On the opening Sabbath morn.

Fluttering silks, and dainty laces,
Perfumed robes, and costly fur,
Whispering lovers, sparkling jewels,
Belles and beaux are all astir;
And the pastor in the pulpit,
Prays that man may never err.

ALICE GILL.

For the Saturday Press.]

LEAVES FROM NATURE.

I saw two children, the other day, playing in the checkered sunlight. Between the shadows, the golden rays danced in the air and upon the ground. One of the little ones tried to catch them with his tiny hands. His young companion snatched at the same rays, and the couple came into collision, quarreled and nearly fought over their right to catch the rays in question. A treaty of peace was, however, made between them, and they combined their forces, using all their hands to prevent the escape, and capture the beautiful beams. Still they eluded their grasp, and the bright patch of light waved to and fro, impalpable to them, and in defiance of their efforts. They grew angry at last because they could not secure it for themselves, and stamped upon it in order to crush it out of existence.

The analogy between their conduct and that of men seemed to me at once so complete and comical, that I could not restrain my laughter. The little fellows, however, were not more absurd than their elders. The greatest, the mightiest, and too often the wisest, try for years, and sometimes even for life, to grasp their impalpable sunshine ;—call it glory, power, earthly happiness, contentment, or what you will. It seems ever within their reach, and melts into thin air or nothingness as they clutch it.

While struggling to seize the unreal, how jealous they become of all who attempt to do the same! Some men spend all their days in fighting off others from what they themselves covet, but cannot obtain. Such are disappointed authors, soured—like "wine turned into vinegar"—into critics.

The more politic unite their strength to that of others in the hope of making use of them as instruments to effect their purpose. Such, if success be possible, achieve it.

But man never, in this world at least, obtains the happiness and contentment he promised himself. Fame, power, wealth, or what not, when possessed, turns to dust, air—nothing. The sunlight that was to bring joy to the heart is still uncaught. Man is selfish, and if he cannot have all, is satisfied with nothing. If he had all, would he be better content? Most probably not in the least.

Disgusted on account of his unavailing efforts to grasp the rays of glory, the baffled poet will tell you that the public is a fool, and its delight in trash unaccountable. The unappreciated painter will show you that the prevailing taste is perverted, and true genius extinct. "Music," says the unheard composer, "is, some pretend, extinct; and I think myself, if it receives no better encouragement, it will soon die out." The expelled clergyman exposes the hypocrisy of his sect; the politician, the corruption of government; the bankrupt, the tricks of his trade; and the man whose zest for enjoyment and delicacy of the senses are dead, rails at pleasure as a sinful thing.

I have read to-day, a leaf from Human Nature's book. I would have much rather read twenty from the volume of inanimate creation, in which the God of love alone works, and is everywhere and ever supreme. But, observing last week, that the writer of the "Dramatic Feuilleton," in whose welfare I feel great interest, had become sad, because he could but admire, and not share the sentiments of the previous "Leaves from Nature," I have foregone this week my own pleasure, and hope by so doing to have furnished some sentiment that we can share together.

R. W. P.

NEW YORK FEBRUARY 25, 1860

DARWIN'S "ORIGIN OF SPECIES."

On the Origin of Species, by Means of Natural Selection, or the Preservation of Favored Races in the Struggle for Life. By Charles Darwin, M.A. 1 vol., 12mo, pp. 432, $1 25. New York: D. Appleton & Co.

The problem of creation, it seems, is to be argued over again. It is no longer the question of ancient pagan speculation whether something could be made out of nothing, whether chaotic matter be not eternal, and only the cosmos or beautiful order of the world, be a created thing. It is no longer the dreamy question of the Orient, how an illusive world went forth in a series of emanations from the Divine mind and filled infinite space with its shadowy semblances. It is no longer the Zoroastrian and

Charles Darwin

Gnostic question of the moral character of the universe, and as to whether its demiurgic artificer belonged to the order of angels or of demons.

These high problems of ancient and mediæval metaphysics are wholly ignored by the positive science of our day. Since Hegelianism ceased to be rampant, the race of metaphysicians has become almost extinct; à priori demonstrations of absolute truth are suspected by most thinkers to be specimens of splendid charlatanry; the most active savants of our age ground their speculations on indubitable physics; and the disciples of Auguste Comte boast that his sceptre is swayed over the tomb of all the philosophies.

It may be well for these very admirable and confident positive philosophers (Buckle, Lewes, John Stuart Mill, Darwin, etc.) to remember that only thirty years ago the wisest heads believed that the universe was perfectly explained by Hegel's cabalistic phrase of absolute idealism. History, æsthetics, and theology then received far greater services from the enthusiastic labors of young Hegelians than have yet been rendered by all the positivists to the physical sciences. Without, therefore, admitting that the reign of Comte and his more or less avowed disciples is to be eternal, we may accept with gratitude the valuable results which are certainly proceeding from his school of thinkers at the present time.

Charles Darwin, a savant of established reputation, has published a work on the "Origin of Species" in natural history (absurdly advertised in the newspapers as the "Origin of *the* Species.") His aim is to show that the species of plants and animals are not immutable, and each a special creation, but that by slight variations, perpetuated through long periods of time, species may have been developed from genera, as varieties have grown from species, and sub-varieties from varieties. His argument is akin to that of Lamarck, and the author of the "Vestiges of Creation," but is much more elaborate and minute. He writes with scientific caution and modesty, in a style so accurate and detailed as to be formidably heavy, employing throughout the volume only one single metaphor or rhetorical figure of any kind, and that one utterly unintelligible.

His first point is to show that species are in many cases not well defined, and that the whole order of natural history seems to be in a state of mutation, by reason of constant variations. Thus, even under domestication, important changes may be introduced by intercrossing, by selection of the best individuals for propagation, by choosing parents marked by however slight but favorable peculiarities.

His second point is what he terms the universal and necessary struggle for existence. This follows from the high geometrical ratio of increase common to all beings. If there were no catastrophes, any one of the existing species would be sufficiently numerous in a few thousand years, to cover the whole earth, to the exclusion of everything else. Even slow-breeding man doubles his number in twenty-five years; and if this rate continued, without interruption, for several decades of centuries, there would literally not be standing-room for his progeny. The elephant is the slowest of all breeders, producing only three pairs of young in ninety years; yet even at this rate, there would be, at the end of five milleniums, fifteen millions of elephants on the earth, descended from each pair. Thus between the almost innumerable species there exists the severest competition. Beneath the palpable and fatal fact that the germs of the great majority of plants and animals must be destined to premature destruction, every organic being seems to be struggling to its utmost to increase in numbers. Battle within battle, between nicely adjusted forces, in which universal defeat is the law, and occasional triumph the exception, is the formula which regulates the propagation of all organic life. Those individuals only succeed which have some advantage, either by exceeding strength, or by some slight variation over their fellows. Myriads are born that cannot possibly survive; and a grain in the balance in the severe conflict will give the chance of life to the most favored.

Such is Mr. Darwin's universal struggle for life.

His third point is to prove that this struggle is directed by the law of natural selection. Even the races of domestic animals may be constantly improved and modified by choosing the best individuals for propagation. Nature brings the same discipline to bear upon the whole domain of animal and vegetable life. She seizes at once upon any slight variation that is favorable, and perpetuates it; in the universal pressure, any variation that is injurious is immediately extinguished. In the divergencies of character which appear through the long geological periods, the less improved forms of life fail; they are crushed out by superior and victorious races, which in their turn yield to still more highly improved organisms, selected by Nature through long ages from the multitudinous slight variations offered to her choice in every generation.

An example will illustrate the principle. The wolf secures its prey sometimes by strength, sometimes by fleetness. Suppose that for a period, from the failure of other prey, the wolves in a particular region were obliged to rely for food chiefly upon the deer. During that period, the fleetest, and not the strongest, would stand the best chance of surviving; and in due time the species would become considerably modified, being more fleet and less strong. Thus there are said actually to be two varieties of wolf inhabiting the Catskill mountains,—one with a light, greyhound-like frame, which pursues deer; and the other more bulky, and with shorter legs, which more frequently attacks flocks.

This example illustrates the difference between Darwin and his predecessors. Lamarck would have said that a special desire and effort on the part of the wolf to pursue deer would gradually have produced the requisite organization,—as a fish may, after having desired an atmospheric existence through long generations, at length become a bird. The author of the "Vestiges" would have said that, in the interminable order of consecutive development, a single wolf was at some time produced from a dog, and thus a new species was inaugurated. Darwin claims that amid constant and innumerable variations, natural selection seizes upon those that are favorable, and extinguishes the rest.

Natural selection proceeds by certain laws. Long-continued, excessive use or disease of any part of an organization, modifies it. Climate and habit have their effects. But the most curious law is that of correlation of growth, according to which any variation in one part is followed by variations in other parts. One instance of this kind is that long limbs are almost always accompanied by an elongated head. Others are more whimsical, as, that blue-eyed cats are invariably deaf, and that white sheep may eat with impunity certain vegetable poisons which are dangerous to black sheep. An occasional intercrossing hastens the usual slow process of introducing new species. Dominant groups tend to give birth to new and dominant forms, and the more dominant beat the less dominant, increase and variation into richer and more powerful forms entailing extinction upon those that are inferior.

Natural selection, by accumulating very slight inherited modifications, can act only with extreme slowness. Mr. Darwin's fourth point is to consider the relation of his theory to the geological record. He accepts the vastly increased lapse of time which the most recent geologists have announced. Three hundred millions of years is the smallest number that is now assigned to the period since the secondary formation. Mr. Horner's researches have almost proved that even men sufficiently civilized to manufacture pottery, lived in the valley of the Nile about fourteen thousand years ago. How long antecedent to this ancient period may savages, like those of Patagonia, have roamed through Egypt!

This immense duration of the natural history of the earth favors the theory by allowing ample time for the innumerable species to have been produced from a few parents. But if every step had been taken slowly from a few simple forms, should not the relics of all the intervening species be found in the crust of the earth? And should not the geologist be able to trace back through the more and more ancient formations all those unfortunate species which have perished in the struggle for life, and which would complete the links in the chain of being?

Mr. Darwin demonstrates in answer, the imperfection of the geological record, the extreme poorness of our palæontological collections. Geology has but imperfectly written the history of the world; the earlier volumes of its record are lost, since fossils are not found below the Silurian stratum; and even of its latest volumes we possess only imperfect chapters, relating to two or three countries. The missing volumes and chapters would all be necessary to prove his theory geologically, to trace the series of slight variations from our present species back to the primitive parents.

Such is the argument by which a revolutionary conclusion is attained. Prosecuting his theory to its ultimate results, Mr. Darwin hardly hesitates to affirm the origin of animals and vegetables from one single initiative germ. "I believe," he says, "that animals have descended from at most only four or five progenitors, and plants from an equal or lesser number. Analogy would lead me one step further. . . I should infer from analogy that probably all the organic beings which have ever lived on this earth have descended from some one primordial form, into which life was first breathed."

This theory, supported by a formidable array of learning, and challenging attention by a sort of inherent sublimity, gives a result not only to science but to ethics. It suggests that the processes not only of nature but of man must always be slow, that every new power and capacity must be acquired by gradation, and that a victorious character can be achieved only by mortal struggle.

VICTORIA; or, the World Overcome. By Caroline Cheesbro'. Derby & Jackson.

It is natural that the scene of this book should be laid in New England—a land which presented itself to the imagination of its first settlers as one that would be given up wholly to the Lord, and where what they termed religion, would be the rule of every man's conduct, and the government of the commonwealth. Of course the experiment failed. "Naturam expellas furca tamen usque recurret." Nature is stronger than man, though the world has not yet found it out as fully as it is destined to.

"I pray you not to take them out of the world, but to keep them from the evil." This is the prayer of wisdom.

Not isolation but society is man's fitting position. A freedom in society that the world has never yet known. A happy and glorious communion that it has as yet but dreamed of. The communion of men made in God's image. Men to whom what is now hidden, shall then be revealed.

Miss Cheesbro' and Mr. Judd, in that strange book "Margaret," have both attempted to portray a womanly character developed in entire isolation from the world's conventions,—a sort of female Casper Hauser, exchanging, however, the four walls of the prison for a wide range of nature. It is as impossible to say whether they have succeeded as to judge of the feasibility of the various Utopias that have been written.

Such a character is an impossibility. The perfect man or woman cannot grow up in solitude. Nor does the ignorance that comes from isolation imply purity and innocence in their highest manifestations. Innocence is the child of knowledge, not of ignorance. Purity is gained by action, not by stagnation. It was perhaps well enough for contracted paganism, seeking to obscure rather than discover truth, to glorify the Virgin, making her the priestess to the temple, and making her virginity the test of her innocence and sanctity. With us, under our dispensation, with the promise of freedom through the truth, the type of purity and innocence is the mother.

The flesh is as divine as the spirit. The breath of life that makes man a living soul enters equally into all our members, and only by the free exercise of every faculty is the perfect man developed as the crowning glory of creation.

We pray to be delivered from "the world, the flesh, and the devil." The first two are of divine creation, and it is only he who denies their divinity and tries to shut himself out from their influences that finds the third, the work of his own invention, created in his soul. The results of asceticism, of a narrowing puritanical dogmatism either in religion, morals, or intelligence, is well portrayed in Miss Cheesbro's Victoria. But the love and faith that should overcome the world are not fully shown there. The world is not overcome by death, but by life. To die fighting, even, is not to gain the victory. The tale of a treacherous murder is not the story of a contest. By cutting down the fresh young grass, we cannot learn the richness of the harvest. The rising sap of the maple we can crystallize into sugar; but only by living in the sunshine and the rain can the tree, by its own wondrous secret, evolve from that sap the fresh green leaves of Spring, the luxuriant foliage of Summer, and the gorgeous glories of Autumn.

We have chosen to consider "Victoria" in this light, rather than as a simple story of the times; more as a novel claiming notice as a sincere study of life and nature, and therefore true in all time, than as what is called an historical novel. As a correct portraiture of the period in which the scene is laid, Victoria is worthy of high commendation. But the interest of the work is for us lessened rather than increased by this fact. Puritanism is too small and contracted a sphere for the free development of a character like Maud. It is not of the seventeenth but of the nineteenth century that Miss Cheesbro' should write. It is the woman of today she should describe; the spirit that is in motion all about us, seeking to evolve for woman the innocence and purity of principle and experience, which her divine instincts prompt her to aspire to and attain.

UNCLE ZEB.

WRITTEN FOR THE NEW YORK SATURDAY PRESS,

BY

MRS. R. H. STODDARD.

Uncle Zeb's monument is under my window in the yard,—its top in a rosebush, and its base on a bed of pinks. The stone-cutter brought it on a truck, and with an air of irreverence launched it into its present position. Uncle Zeb ordered the monument the day after he made his will, and left the duty of paying for it to his executors, although he lived long enough afterward to pay for a dozen of the most elaborate workmanship. This monument is a deceptive affair, like most tombstones; a wreath of heart's ease is carved round an open book on the square of the pedestal, and a column runs up from it, ornamented with the long stems and flowers of the white water-lily. As I hang over the window-ledge, my recollections of Uncle Zeb assume the shape of imps which grin at me through the meshes of the lily-stems, and they slide their elfish fingers over the stony leaves of the book, as if they were writing the true story of a life that I alone can read.

My first remembrance of Uncle Zeb dates from an early period of childhood. One day, while I was at my Grandfather's, I heard a bustle in the front entry, and a noise like that of the dropping of trunks. Old Lizzy Bowles, an ancient hanger-on of the establishment, told me that my Uncle Zeb had "come in from a vy'ge," and that I must go into the East room and shake hands with him. I went into the room quietly, and looked out of the window first, where I saw Uncle Zeb's ship, the *Dryad*, swinging at anchor, a mile down the harbor. I then turned and looked at Uncle Zeb, who was toasting himself by a roaring fire which burned in a Franklin-stove. He was in that condition of Toasted helplessness, which a wood fire always engenders in one on a wet, damp day. He strove to mitigate the smart of his shins by continually changing one leg over the other, and he held his baked hands between his crimson face and the fire. He looked at me from behind them a moment, and then reached up to the mantle, and took from it a present which he brought from Liverpool. It was a red and white cow and calf of earthenware, the like of which had never been seen by any juvenile in our primeval village. As he gave it to me, he called me a trollop, and said I looked like my mother. Grandmother, who was knitting a blue stocking in a corner remote from the fire, said, "Sho, Zeb!"

This was my first interview with my relative, and my last present. I retired to the kitchen, and to old Lizzy, who told me about the cargo of crockery which she said Uncle Zeb was going to sell in New York, and make a fortune by.

Uncle Zeb was then about thirty; he had made several voyages previous to the one I spoke of, and was already well to do. My father was some years younger, and at the beginning of Uncle Zeb's sea-life, was a stripling, lounging about home in a round jacket. It sometimes happens in a well-regulated family, that one of its members is overlooked; he is never especially noticed by the rest, and his future is not thought of.

My father happened to be the ignored one in his family, and to that fact I ascribe the difference between him and his relations. His idiosyncracy got no twist from their sympathy. But my father was in love; boy as he was, he thought of marriage, and the way to live afterward. The girl he loved was a poor tailoress; in fact, she made his homespun jackets. She was older than her lover, and had made his jackets with equanimity, while he wore them in a tempestuous state of mind. Grandmother was the Squire's wife; she felt above the poor tailoress. An impartial mind would perhaps have found it difficult to establish the lines of superiority, for Grandmother herself sold milk from her kitchen every day, and did not disdain to keep the milk-score with chalk on her yellow buttery door. The tailoress was very handsome, and very resolute. She would wear feathers in her bonnet; and every Sunday she went to church dressed in better taste than anybody beside, the handsomest Presbyterian of them all. Most of all, Grandmother disliked her because my father loved her. And Uncle Zeb had a weakness in that direction; but it was obscured by selfishness, and died out in moral laziness.

Uncle Zeb went his voyages, and my father, who did not know what else to do, went to sea also; not having any help from Grandfather, he was obliged, of course, to ship before the mast, and went under the command of Captain Southerd, a neighboring farmer, who planted turnips, and carted wood and hay to market, in the intervals between his voyages. Nearly all the inhabitants of our little town were amphibious. The boys took to the water like spaniels; their first toys were punts, and skiffs, and rafts. The men, when they were not sailors, were ship-carpenters. The landowners put their savings into small vessels, which coasted from Maine to Florida, and even went on six months' trips into the Atlantic for whales.

Uncle Zeb and his brother did not meet often. When one was at home the other was generally away. Uncle Zeb bought up the *Dryad*, piece by piece, and went in her to all the trading ports in the world, from St. Petersburg to Calcutta. The merchants from whom he purchased his cargoes, or to whom they were consigned, invited him to their houses, and in this way he picked up bits of eccentricity, which he grafted upon his ordinary manners, and made a very strange compound of himself. At home he travestied foreign ways, and introduced unheard of fashions in Grandfather's house. He swore beautifully in all languages; but his native damns never left him, any more than his appetite forsook him for salt junk and grog, after he had learned to like what he called foreign kickshaws.

Father plodded along on small wages, and had a remote hope of reaching the cabin. When ashore, he lounged in his round jacket, and kept on loving my mother, who waited in patience for a turn in the long lane of their courtship. She snubbed Uncle Zeb whenever she had a chance, and always inquired about Father, of him, by the name of Esau. Grandfather, as well as Uncle Zeb, grew comfortably rich. His investments in sloops and schooners were fortunate ones, and he talked of buying a ship to fit out for a whaler. Feeling the need of a helper, for the first time in his life he turned his attention toward his youngest son, who was then at home, waiting for Captain Southerd to harvest his turnips. A proposal of partnership was made to father, which he accepted; and thus his sea life ended. He was married at once, and he and Mother took to housekeeping with one feather-bed, six small silver spoons, and a hearty affection for each other. Father applied himself to business, and the house that was thus founded became in a few years one of the richest and most influential in our part of the country. Grandfather very soon saw that it would only be necessary for him to take his share of the profits, and that he could safely give up all business matters to his partner.

In a year from the date of their marriage I was born, and at the time of Uncle Zeb's arrival from Liverpool with my cow and calf, I was five years old. That voyage was the last one that Uncle Zeb made. Finding us prosperous, he concluded to retire from business. He invested his money outside of the family-interest, but considerately took up his abode with Grandfather, and indulged Grandmother with the care of him. He occupied himself with watching the domestic and business transactions of the house of A. G. & Son, and banking his money as fast as it came in.

For a few years I cannot remember much concerning Uncle Zeb; the traits I recall belong to my present knowledge of him. When I went to school, it was one of my recreations to go to Grandfather's to dinner at mid-day, and one of my miseries to sit next to Uncle Zeb at the table. His dog, "Die," squatted on the other side of him. We had to wait till Uncle Zeb was carefully helped, by himself, to all the best bits on the table. Then he would give Die a titbit, making her snap her jaws for it, and then one to me. A snarling was kept up between him and the dog through the whole meal.

He would not have the potatoes on the table, they must be kept hot on the kitchen fire; so Grandmother sat, fork in hand, watching him; when he wanted one she fished it from the kettle, and he ate it scalding hot, with noise. Grandmother occupied a child's high chair, and wore a black satin hood over her high-crowned cap. She never dined or supped till after Uncle Zeb; and I had the best of times after he and Die had retired from the table. Grandmother took excellent care of her graceless son. He wore ruffled cambric shirts; and many an afternoon when the sun's rays slanted through the narrow kitchen windows, and made her resemble, in her shining spectacles, an owl, have I seen her laboriously plait his ruffles with a case-knife. On Sundays she combed his hair; it was fine and straight, and of the color of wet sand. It was unchanged to the day of his death. On Sunday afternoon he went to church in a great camlet cloak, and carried a cane with leather tassels. He listened to the sermon with an air of respect, and broke Grandmother's heart with deriding it after he got home.

Now and then he had a visitor, some piratical looking captain, or foreign merchant; the visitor was never introduced to any of the household, but was entertained in the parlor with tumblers of red wine and equivocal stories. As he never minded whether I came or went, I sometimes had the benefit of the latter. His laughter always arrested me; it contradicted him, it was so racy and hearty. His teeth glittered in his sardonic face, and lighted it up; they were long, white, and regular, and like his hair they never changed.

Two visits per diem were Uncle Zeb's allowance for our house. The first was made an hour or so after dinner, when he loitered in the kitchen, and tickled the servant girls, or poked them with his cane. Afterward, with his hat in his hand, he sought mother, and, however long his stay, he held his cane and hat as if on a visit of ceremony. He talked well; he was sarcastic and witty, and never bored anybody. The second visit was made after supper, when father was at home. There was no confidence between the brothers, and no sympathy; but they passed cigars to each other, and enveloped themselves in clouds of smoke, and discoursed through it on commonplace subjects.

As soon as I was fledged, I was sent to boarding-school. My vacations were short, and I did not observe what went on at home; things seemed to run smoothly in the grooves of habit. I accepted appearances for realities. The business of A. G. & Son had greatly increased. All the year through, their ships were arriving in port, or were fitting for sea. Our household was a gay one, and Grandfather's house was full of comers and goers. He knew little of the private affairs of the concern, but smoked his pipe, and burnt holes with its falling ashes in his fine blue pantaloons, in peace and tranquillity. Uncle Zeb had given up ruffled shirts, and had taken to Marryatt's novels. He neither bought nor sold; he never gave advice, or asked an opinion. He had a habit of going to funerals, but he went in a cheerful state of mind, as if the deceased had done him a favor by dying. He was respected as a moneyed man. The world admires what it dare not be a consistent, selfish skeptic; and our little world gave its admiration to my hard-headed Uncle Zeb. He was cautious, because he was cold,—prudent, because he was indifferent. As a token of the respect of his townsmen, he was elected Representative, and had a seat in the State House for several years. He brought home a great many volumes of Revised Statutes, which Grandmother stored in the garret, with the dried herbs. What he did as a member of the honorable body of Representatives nobody knew. He only spoke of the toughness of the pie-crust, and the hardness of his bed at his boarding-house.

When I was eighteen I left school and came home for good. I was the only young woman in the family connexion, and was considered worthy of much attention. Uncle Zeb, however, did not like me. He had his way of exasperating me. He always talked as if he knew that I must know that virtue was only a pretence. It was a game we were all playing. It was becoming in a woman to affect modesty; it was her capital. He gave me credit for shrewdness, and he had no doubt but that I should play my cards admirably. If I grew enraged at him, he laughed at me; but sometimes I made his cold blue eyes gleam with anger by telling him one or two unpleasant truths. His manner was usually deferential to women; but his ribaldry would break out now and then, and I have known him to be as coarse as Rabelais in a room full of ladies. It was done with an air, as if he were obliging us with his candid wit.

It was not long after my return from school when I perceived that something weighed on father's mind. When I accompanied him on his many drives from one business-place to another, I saw the mask of cheerfulness drop from his face; he was absent-minded and silent. One day when we were alone, I begged him to tell me what troubled him, and then he owned to me that his business affairs were vexing him; that things had been going behindhand for a year; but I must say nothing of this, for he had hopes of being able to overcome his difficulties. Independent of his business perplexities, the keeping it secret was a trouble; he dared not retrench any expense, and he feared the effect of the truth on Grandfather, who was becoming childish. We went on this way for two years; plan after plan of salvation failed; but father's energy and good temper never left him. One day I thought of Uncle Zeb. "Why wont he," I said to myself, "put some of his thousands to the wheel ?" I determined to tell him the state of affairs: I did not expect much from his generosity, but something from his pride; and thought, too, that his shrewdness might enable him to make something eventually out of any loan he might offer. So I sought him, and found him lying on the floor in the East Room asleep. I roused him, and did not wait for him to open his eyes before I began my tale. When I had finished, he eyed me for a moment, and said:

"So, you'll have to come down. Your devil's pride will be broken."

I stared mutely at him, but inwardly called myself a fool.

"I'll see," he said, "about buying up the family acres when the crash comes; but as for piling my money on the ruins of your father's speculations—that I wont do. Go home; if your father knew this he would pull your ears, though he is idiot enough not to do it."

I rose from my chair, looking, no doubt, just as I felt, for he laughed, and said, "Kick me if you like."

I went home thoroughly miserable, and did not report my interview, while Uncle Zeb on his part was silent also; but I did much mischief that day, and Uncle Zeb did a good stroke of business out of the capital which I had furnished him.

About this time Grandmother was persuaded to take an assistant—one who should unite in herself the qualities of companion and housekeeper. As there exists such a race of females, one was easily found. She was a remote cousin (this race is apt to be distantly related), and lived forty miles away, in Grandmother's native place. Her name was Nancy Goring, her age thirty-five. She was poor, intelligent, proud, and adroit. She had pretty, delicate hands, a large nose, and wore her hair parted at the side of her head. Her wardrobe was neat, but scanty; and Grandmother, who believed in making people happy as far as good clothes and food went, bought material for dresses and petticoats, and the companion's first duty was to make them up. After the dresses were made, she was allowed to knit and to sweep a little; but Grandmother's pride was still too great to allow herself to be supplanted in housekeeping.

Uncle Zeb proposed the position of hair-comber to Nancy, as Grandmother's eyesight was failing, and whenever she combed his hair now she fell asleep, and made an irregular thing of it. Nancy accepted; and from that time she began to pay him all sorts of delicate attentions, from cutting his finger-nails and tying his cravat, to mixing his grog and looking over his accounts. Uncle Zeb understood Nancy's devotion to him; but Nancy was very uncertain as to the nature of his feelings for her. She was desperately bent on turning Uncle Zeb from the errors of a bachelor, into the merits of a husband. She watched him, and followed him, and grovelled about him; but all in vain. Uncle Zeb never gave way. One day Grandmother's eyes were opened. She found Nancy, with a red silk handkerchief of Uncle Zeb's in her hand, which she had rolled into a tight ball, imprecating its owner hysterically.

The next day Nancy returned to her native place.

Our evil days drew near. A ship,—the one father depended on as his last hope,—made a broken voyage, and he was obliged to succumb. The house of A. G. & Son failed. A few days before the public announcement of the failure, he told it to his family. Then Uncle Zeb played his part. He behaved as if he had received an insult from father; he glowered with rage, and cursed him for his duplicity and foolishness. How dared he disgrace the name with failure and poverty? Had he given up all his property to his creditors? He, himself, had taken what measures he could to save some little from the wreck; and then it came out that he had obtained from Grandfather every cent of his private property: deeds had been signed by Grandfather in Uncle Zeb's favor, merely, as Uncle Zeb had told him, to make him safe if ever a rainy day came along. He had not made any nice distinctions between personal property and that which belonged to the firm, but had clawed into his possession all he could, and left the reputation of it to rest on father, if possible, if the creditors should discover it, and make allowance for it in the settlement.

The failure came out, and our house was beseiged from morning till night by creditors. They were the more angry for its being unexpected. They not only wanted their money, but an explanation. Father had his office closed, and staid at home to receive them. The parlor was full of Ledgers, and councils were held over them, during which his character and conduct were discussed as if he had not been present. Not being a creditor, Uncle Zeb was denied the pleasure of being a member of the council; but he came and went a dozen times a day, without speaking to one of us. He went about the shipyards poking the timber with his cane, as if he would like to hurt it, and I saw him on the wharf studying the spars of the vessels. He was taking much more exercise than he had been accustomed to, and it evidently did not agree with him. His ownership in certain properties was denied by the creditors; but they could not prove that the large homestead which had been Grandfather's belonged to the firm; so it passed into Uncle Zeb's keeping. But the creditors increased the percentage of what father was to pay on his debts, in consequence.

So we were ruined. Father made some arrangement by which his parents were not disturbed in their way of living; but mother, and the rest of us, gave up our purple and fine linen. Although Uncle Zeb lived in his own house now, the expenses of living were not defrayed by him, but by A. G. & Son. But if he did not complain, who should? He felt contempt for father; at the same time, I believe he had some admiration for his dignity and patience. Uncle Zeb was too clear-minded not to understand himself. He began to hate himself, and this self-hatred made him reckless; from this time he gave rein to his evil nature, and his pace was awful.

The next year Grandfather died, and was buried with his fathers, who slept under the mossy slate-stones of the Puritan times. Meanwhile father had prospered; he had paid within a twelvemonth the demands of his creditors, and had something left to begin the world again.

Another female cousin had come to reside with Grandmother, who dozed perpetually, or bemoaned Grandfather piteously. The cousin's name was Sally Packer, a middle-aged woman, who lived on patent medicine, took snuff, and believed in signs. She was wonderfully ignorant, but full of that low cunning which serves such people instead of knowledge. She had a faculty for mending broadcloth, and she was always at Uncle Zeb's clothes. Her waxed thread was whizzing through them from morning till night. She did not profess to know much, she said, but she would like to see the woman who understood tailoring better. She called Uncle Zeb a "superior being," and talked to him about property;—her respect for money was immense. Her manner toward him was full of humility, and if he came near her, she made a feint of retreating, at the same time casting her small eyes upward with an adoring expression. She meekly offered her snuffbox to him whenever she took a pinch, and after a little he fell into the habit of snuffing with her. He employed a portion of his time in experimenting with alcohol. Cloudy tumblers stood on the shelves with curious mixtures in them,—a sediment of rhubarb overlaid with brandy, or gin and senna, or pounded Brandreth's pills in Jamaica rum. He had a theory that if physic was taken with a dram it could have no deleterious effect. Night and day he drank his compounds. He set his bed on fire; he fell on the dining-table and crashed the dishes; he rolled off his horse with his feet in the stirup; he laid in the street. But Sally Packer was his providence; she kept harm away from him. She dragged him to bed; she washed him; she dressed him, and she fed him ;—and he cursed her.

The consequence of his theories was, that one morning he woke up with a paralysis, and father was obliged to take charge of him. Tenderly and mercifully he cared for him, for he was speechless and helpless. Sally Packer hustled him about as if he were a baby. How he wanted to rail at her! His eyes glared and burned with rage, whenever he saw Father come into his room. One night his watcher was startled from a nap, by the sight of Uncle Zeb in the middle of the floor.

"My cursed tongue is loose," he said, "and I can walk. Get out of the way!"

He wrapped the counterpane round his gaunt form, and tottered downstairs into the street. He leaned against the fence and looked up to the sky, and chafed his feeble hands, and then crept back to bed; but from that night he was better, and soon became well.

Grandmother soon followed Grandfather, and slept near him in the same narrow bed. Sally Packer asked leave to remain long enough after the funeral to put the house in order. It was granted, and it took her years to do it—in fact, the house was never in order afterward; and so she staid. She convinced Uncle Zeb that no one could take care of him better than she could. She told him that the selfish world might say she expected to be remembered in his will; but it was not so. She had a good home of her own in Swampscot; a house, which, although it was not plastered, did not leak a drop, and there was as good a well of water close to it as ever was. She was willing to stay just to keep him from being imposed on, although she didn't know but that his relations were as honest as anybody's relations.

No one imposed upon either Uncle Zeb or Sally. The Lares and Penates of the ancient household were broken; its former friends deserted it. It did not agree with Sally Packer's principles to have company; her moral constitution was averse to anything like hospitality. Uncle Zeb was indifferent whether anybody came or went. So Sally kept her ground, and had her own way. Uncle Zeb cursed and ridiculed her every day of her life. She cajoled, and wrangled, and worried, and petted him. Now she complained of being worn out with hard work, and now, that it was a place her betters would be glad to be in.

Both were to be found, usually, in the kitchen of the old mansion, a low-ceiled, dingy room, with a great brick hearth, on which Sally had ranged for convenience a row of pots and kettles. A fire burned, Summer and Winter, on the great iron dogs. Sally's chair was in one corner of the hearth, where she could poke the fire, or stir the contents of the pots and kettles; her snuff-box, and comb, and an almanac, were on the shelf above the fire. Her hair was thick and gray, and she was fond of combing it when she had a leisure moment. She wore short dresses of black bombazine, which never required washing, and went barelegged; her shoes were made of coarse carpet, on account of her corns. Uncle Zeb generally reclined on a wooden settee under the window; an old woollen cloak, rolled up, served him for a pillow. At the foot of the settee, whenever Uncle Zeb reposed on it, lay an ugly dog, which was Sally's property, by name 'Spot." Picked bones, the remains of Spot's feasts, were strewed under the table, and under the settee. Spot had a habit of howling in his sleep, and Uncle Zeb had a habit of kicking him for it. As he declined the trouble of taking off his hat when he laid down, it suffered in looks and resembled a pair of windless bellows. He took snuff lying down; the result to his nails, and beard, and clothes, was deplorable. After Grandmother's death he resumed the habit of dram-drinking, minus the drugs, in the full expectation of killing himself. He began then to fling his money into wild schemes; he would amuse himself with using up as much as he could of his property, he said, before he was summoned to move off for good. He had some trouble, for he would not give it away; so he built and rebuilt inconvenient houses, and drained barren fields, and planted in the sand, and blasted rocks, and made roads that led to nowhere.

Everybody now knew Uncle Zeb's character, and he and Sally were the curiosity and aversion of the neighborhood. The old house grew darker and more dismal every day. He was continually cutting doors and passages through the walls; he seemed to have an idea that they would enable him to elude some enemies that might come upon him. Sally had all the carpets taken up and put away, and all the beds stripped. She slept on a stuffed bench outside Uncle Zeb's door. All the furniture was piled away; the looking-glasses were covered, and the shutters of every room were fastened. All she wanted for daily use was congregated in the kitchen, and there she staid as if she were waiting for some event to happen.

Once in a while I lifted the latch of the porch door. Sometimes the inmates noticed me, and sometimes not. Now and then Uncle Zeb would sit up in his crumpled hat, and revive with me his recollections of his voyages, and tell me many a piquant and picturesque anecdote. Sally would also forget herself a moment, and listen with admiring "Laws, Capen Zeb." But oftener I was the silent witness of angry disputes, when she stunned me with her foolishness, and he pained me with his profanity. His common salutation to her was, "You lying jade," whereat she whimpered, or scolded, according to the mood of the moment.

Father remonstrated with him once, but Uncle Zeb drove him away. He made his will soon afterward, and ordered the monument of which I have spoken; but his constitution was an iron one, and it bore much before he had a second stroke of paralysis. When he did, his case was at once hopeless, and father again took the post of an only friend. Sally was at her wit's end. She threw the medicine out of the window, and whispered about poison. She shook Uncle Zeb to make him speak. She talked and cried over him, till father was obliged to turn her from the room

The night he died father staid by his bedside. About one o'clock Uncle Zeb turned over, the first time he had moved since the stroke. His fingers trembled toward father's. The first kindly look he ever gave his brother, beamed in his wild eyes then. Faint broken words struggled on his lips; but it was too late for speech—"Your wife, Mary," was all he said, so he went out of this world, an unhappy mutilated spirit.

The homestead reverted to father; but it stands empty. The doors and passages which Uncle Zeb cut are open; and the beds that Sally stripped, still stand bare. No one has been there since the day of the funeral.

"EDGAR POE AND HIS CRITICS."

These words form the title of a book written by Sarah Helen Whitman, of Providence, R. I., and published in this city by Messrs. Rudd & Carleton.

The little book commends itself to the notice of the public by the importance of its subject, the reputation of its author, and the elegance of its mechanical style.

It has long been known that Mrs. Whitman intended to publish a defence of Poe. For certain sufficient reasons, it was expected that her statement would possess the authentic value of intimate knowledge. This book has therefore been eagerly anticipated, and is now pleasantly received by a large number of readers interested in the subject to which it relates.

It is well known that, subsequently to the death of Poe, Mr. Rufus Wilmot Griswold became his literary executor, and wrote his Memoir. And it is equally well known that, in the way of literary biography, there are few things more amusing or more contemptible than the Memoir that Dr. Griswold wrote. Of the Doctor himself we have nothing to say. We remember, as Mrs. Whitman counsels us to do, "that the memorialist now claims from us that tender grace of charity that he was unwilling or unable to accord to the man who trusted him as a friend."

Of the charges against Poe which are set down in that Memoir, many are entirely trivial, some are undoubtedly false, and some probably are true. They are, in substance, that he was dissipated in youth, and never became respectable; that he was frequently inebriated; that he was neither diligent nor honest in business; that he was irregular and extravagant; that he was poor; that he married a woman unfit to be his wife; that he assumed to be insane, and was full of affectations; that he printed contradictory judgments of men and books; that he was a plagiarist; and, finally, that he exhibited scarcely any virtue in either his life or his writings.

In regard to all this, Mrs. Whitman's design is thus set forth in the Preface to her book: "Dr. Griswold's Memoir of Poe has been extensively read and circulated; its perverted facts and baseless assumptions have been adopted into every subsequent memoir and notice of the poet, and have been translated into many languages. For ten years this great wrong to the dead has passed unchallenged and unrebuked.

"It has been assumed by a recent English critic that 'Edgar Poe had no friends.' As an index to a more equitable and intelligible theory of the idiosyncrasies of his life, and as an earnest protest against the spirit of Dr. Griswold's unjust memoir, these pages are submitted to his more candid readers and critics by One of his Friends."

As a defence of Poe against the specific charges of Dr. Griswold, this book disappoints its preface and amounts to nothing. As regarding certain unimportant calumnies of certain obscure people, it amounts to a complete refutation.

One critic is mentioned who is not obscure. That is the gentle George Gilfillan, of whom it has been felicitously remarked that he thinks himself a great painter because he paints with a big brush. This critic has stated that Poe caused the death of his wife in order that he might have a fitting theme for the Raven: "A serious objection to this ingenious theory," retorts Mrs. Whitman, "may perhaps be found in the refractory fact that the poem was published more than a year before the event which it was intended to commemorate."

For ourselves we confess a weariness of critical discussions relating to Edgar Allan Poe. To view this man aright the world is not yet far enough away from him. The grass has not withered on his grave.

Time will inaugurate a broader and truer custom of criticism than any which prevails in the present. When the test of small morality is no longer applied to genius and to art; when impertinent curiosity, rebuked by the sanctity of private life, ceases to unveil the errors and infirmities of the private man; when works of art are judged as works of art, and genius is analyzed without reference to the petty chances and accidents of physical or social life, then will criticism cease to be gossip; then will genius, intellect, and art imperially command and reverentially receive the recognition, the sympathy, the justice of mankind.

Dramatic Feuilleton.

Dust and Ashes.

I am afraid that you, Effendi of the Piazza, are not as reverent as you are venerable. I much fear that you very often fail to hear the voice of the muezzin from the minaret, and that you miss one if not all the diurnal prostrations towards the East, prescribed for all true believers. I am afraid that you are not so constant at Vespers as is the Brightest and the Best, and that when there you put up never an Ave nor a Pater for the Subscriber.

I am afraid, in point of fact, that it will be news to you when I tell you that it is Lent!

Were you in Paris you could not mistake it. There would have been Mardi-Gras and the Bal Masqué at the Opera; and débardeurs, and Dianas from the Quartier Bréda; and Calypsos from the Closérie des Lilas; and bad champagne and worse filets Chateaubriands; and a headache and a matter of an hundred francs out of your pocket, when you intended only to spend twenty-five; and so on. Dost remember, Effendi, the charming description of the Carnival in "Beppo"? It may be absurd; but I adhere to Byron above all the new lights. The Brightest and the Best likewise leans lovingly to the poet-peer, and her copy of his works, which she had in the convent, is covered with the killed and wounded,—for be it known that the American demoiselle begins to flirt long before she is emancipated from short frocks. The Youths may say I'm absurd and old fogy. True. They are clever,—that adolescent crew over whose fair temples career the rosy-fingered Hours, weaving the first garlands of sweet success; they know a great deal, but there are somethings, Effendi, that you and I know which they don't know, and one of them is the value of old things, old books, old wine, old friends. So I adhere to Byron, 'see' Byron in point of fact; and to prove it, ask you to quote this out of the poem I have referred to:

> "'Tis known, at least it should be, that throughout
> All countries of the Catholic persuasion,
> Some weeks before Shrove Tuesday comes about,
> The people take their fill of recreation,
> And buy repentance ere they grow devout,
> However, high their rank or low their station,
> With fiddling, feasting, dancing, drinking, masquing,
> And other things which may be had for asking,"

I have taken up all this time to tell you what even Burkhardt, who is not noted for his talent at condensation, would have put in half a minute and half a line, thus:

It is Lent. Lent marks a division in the theatrical season. In all strictly Catholic countries they shut up the Opera in Lent. I don't include France among the Catholic countries, for L. N. isn't a bit better than a heathen.

It didn't use to be so in the good old times when Louis Quinze was king, when there was a Dubarry and a Petit Trianon, and when men wore silk coats and honiton, and went out three times a week regularly to keep their wrists in play. Then the Opera was rigorously closed in Lent. Then all the prime ladies exiled themselves to the Convent of the Capucines from Mardi-Gras to Easter-Monday, and went through an immense amount of moral and religious blue-pill. How magnificently they must have sung the Misérérés. What wouldn't Archbishop Hughes give for such a choir, when he gets his new Cathedral done!

But we have changed all that.

We have no more Chevaliers, no more Kings, no more Dubarrys. We are good and virtuous. We have aldermen who always wear new hats, and the Mayor goes to meeting' twice every Sunday. I am good, too, and read the Sunday papers religiously. If that isn't penance, I don't understand the meaning of the word.

What am I coming at? Never mind. You shall see presently.

I am looking at the beginning of Lent from a theatrical point of view. It is the half-way house in the season, the station which marks the top of the tide which flows between September and June. If a play is produced in January and runs up to the first of March comfortably, it may be set down for another four or six weeks. Peoria and Attakapas begin to come to town now, as one may see by the Saint Nicholas Hotel porch. It is quite true that Attakapas is a little riled, and has sworn a big oath that he will take his cayenne pepper and cocktails in some place other than Manhattan, but he can't keep away. If New York were really a foreign city, in government I mean, Attakapas would like it much better, and spend more money in it. As it is, however, he does pretty well. He must keep cool, and if he feel his angry passions rising, let him walk as far as Union Square, and gaze upon the statue of the Father of his country, the Academy of Music, and the Unitary Home.

During the next forty days, then, we shall have dusty times in the theatres.

At Keene's, *Effie Deans* will continue to frantically ask to be permitted to go 'to her feyther' every night, every night, every night; and at Wallack's the *Poor Young Man* will not cease to make his terrific gymnastic sacrifice for the hand of his Anna Maria. "Bless him!" remarked the veritable Pearl of Manhattan, "how good "he is! I don't know any one who would do that for me."

I think she was right.

The Opera goes off to Peoria, after next week. Early in April, l'on dit there will be a Maratzek-season at the Winter Garden, with the new prima donna Fabri, who has just arrived from South America. Fabri, I am assured, is a good article. No fabrication about her. They say she has all the passion and intensity and tragic power of the Cortesi school, and her execution is equal to that of the most exquisite singers of cantabile operas. Cortesi and the tenor, Musiani, will not arrive till April.

Le Chauve may give us something new at the Winter Garden. There are half a dozen very clever English burlesques which have never been done here, and in which Mrs. Wood could shine. Without Wood I really don't know what we should do.

As it is, we can manage to get along until the micarême, when things may look brighter.

Gottschalk.

I am very glad to hear that Maretzek has engaged Gottschalk, who has had a great success in Havana. His return to Manhattan will bring joy to the hearts of all the Anna Marias, and carry grief to all the pianists who, so far as popularity goes, at least, cannot stand against him.

Operatic.

Nothing new yet in Irving Place. Gazzaniga was to sing in Sappho last week, but an irrepressible row broke out between Brignoli and the managers, and the tenor refused to appear. Sappho always was an unfortunate young woman, and threw herself off from the top of a high rock because the object of her affections fell in love with the contralto, a good-looking young woman, whereas Sappho was only clever and 'literary, not mercantile,' wrote for the *Ledger*, and so on.

Patti has sung *Lucia*, the *Puritani*, and *Sonnambula*, over again. Her voice. improves in volume, and she shows signs of marked dramatic talent. On Monday they did a chorus by Muzio, in honor of Garibaldi. There was the Italian play, supported by Major Susini; there was Gazzaniga, so full of patriotism that I was afraid she would sing the top of her head off; there was Brignoli, glowing with love of country, in Elvino's bob-tailed jacket and abbreviated trowsers, all the choristers shouting away as if for dear life.

The chorus was pretty good, but I suspect Muzio, who is young, single, and not bad looking, of some improper intimacy with a young lady from Germany named *Martha*. Muzio is certainly on such familiar terms with her, that her proprietor, Herr von Flotow, would be justified in asking him his intentions, or going after him with a shot-gun. It is the most desperate flirtation, except one or two, that I have seen lately.

Martha will be at the Academy in person next week. Patti does her, of course. Then we shall see what we shall see.

Theatre Francais.

M. Feuillet's *Poor Young Man* has been the grand success of the season at the French Theatre. On Thursday the second representation attracted a very large audience, in which the American element predominated. The Gaul, curiously enough, refuses to sustain his own theatre. Art is, to him, good; money is better. So the theatre languishes unless there is some special attraction for the American savage.

Le Roman d'un Jeune Homme Pauvre had an excellent distribution. Voici!

M. F. MANNSTEIN remplira le rôle de............Maxime Odiot
" JUIGNET celui de. ....Laubébin
" BERTRAND ....Bévallan
" BARRY. ....G. de Lussac
" LOIRET.. .... Alain
" EDGARD... Champlain
" ALPHONSE. .... Desmarets
" TALLOT. .... Laroque
" LEON.. Vauberger
" CHARLES
" GASTON..2 domestiques
Mme. LAURETTI remplira le rôle de. .... Marguerite
Mme. ADOLPHE celui de. ....Mme. Laroque
Mlle. DUPONT. .... Mlle. Héloin
Mme. CECILE. .... Aubry
Mlle. ANTOINETTE, ... Christine
Mme. TALLOT...Mme. Vauberger
Une jeune fille. ....Mlle. Ines

I wish you to print the whole cast, because every part was artistically acted, and the performance therefore a very fine one.

When you see Mr. Lester Wallack's *Poor Young Man,* you go away from the theatre remembering only that you have seen the young man go up to the top of a tower for the purpose of jumping down again. At the French theatre, you see a capital play charmingly rendered, and tastefully decorated. All this in a house which has only been kept open by the most heroic efforts on the part of the manager, who has succeeded, without great outlay, in mounting the piece as well as it is done at Wallack's, and without making any fuss about it.

The great charm about the French play, however, lies in the exact balance of the characters. In the English version, the parts are cut, trimmed, altered, and worked over.

While this is all well for the interests of the theatre, and while it redounds to the glory and profit of the manager, one can't help thinking, in seeing the French play, that in the English version it has been terribly slaughtered. The character of M. Bévallan is a case in point. Mr. Wallack destroys his individuality, and makes him little more than a stick. At the French theatre he is as important as the hero himself, and is presented as a broad full type of character which forms the strongest contrast with the idiosyncrasies of *Maxime*. Bertrand was admirable in Bévallan. He was a sort of French Chevalier Wikoff, always about, always saying something clever, always keeping things going, and taking reverses or successes with the light, easy philosophy of a true man of the world.

Mannstein's *Maxime* was a careful, well-studied, and altogether excellent performance. He acted the part with elegant and refreshing simplicity. I wish some of our actors knew the meaning of that word. The French ladies did not have so much advantage over their Wallack sisters in appearance as in manner,—that delightful manner which no one but a French woman has, and which comes to them all, high and low, by intuition. The female characters in the French play are somewhat altered in the English version, Mrs. Vernon's being cut down, and Miss Gannon's written up.

I have written much more than I intended about the *Roman d'un Jeune Homme Pauvre.*

I might have summed it all up in a simple sentence, and told you the next time it appeared in the French bills to do it, if only as a matter of curiosity.

W. G.

Thalia has come back to the Winter Garden, and has gathered about her throne a goodly number of her admirers. In other words, Mrs. John Wood, one of the very few actresses in this country who has an individuality and a speciality of her own, has returned to town, and although she has not yet appeared in any new piece, has attracted very large, and constantly-increasing audiences. On Thursday, not a seat was to be had in the theatre after the performance commenced. I shall not bore you with any remarks about the fine old antiques such as *The Governor's Wife, An Object of Interest,* and *Jenny Lind*, in which Mrs. Wood has acted. Where in the world such things come from I can't imagine. *The Governor's Wife* I remember as an old play the very first time I attempted to dye my tender and budding moustache. Let me tell you, that is not yesterday. In *Jenny Lind*, Mrs. Wood's imitations of the larks and linnets of Irving Place are capital. That of Lagrange is the only good musical imitation that I remember to have ever heard. Of course the town is delighted with Mrs. Wood, and she, I suppose, reciprocates the feeling.

Personne.

[For The Saturday Press.]

A WINTER SUNRISE.

BY JOSEPH BARBER.

Up through the gray—drowning the starry host
In the red deluge of its spreading waves—
Flows the auroral tide; and shapes of cloud
That wandered, ghost-like, through the cold blue night,
Wear on their cheeks the life-bloom of the dawn.
Snow-crested peaks, where, scarce an hour ago,
The star-light shimmered—and the tent-like firs,
Draped with the silver fringe-work of the storm,
Have caught the rosy glory. On the plain,
The drifted ridges, winnows of the blast,
Are touched with flame; and see! in yonder glen,
Upon its front the silenced waterfall
Wears the same hues that arched its Summer spray.

NEW YORK MARCH 3, 1860

[For the New York Saturday Press.]

PARTING.

BY GEORGE ARNOLD.

I.

White and small was the hand I pressed
Behind the rose-covered cottage door,
While the moon rode low in the azure West
And the tremulous vines, by the wind caressed,
Cast flickering shadows over the floor—
Swinging, swaying, and sighing lowly,
"Perfect love is the one thing holy !"

II.

Rosy and ripe were the lips I pressed
Behind the rose-covered cottage door.
While the orioles slept in their downy nest
That swung in the vines by the wind caressed,
Casting weird shadows over the floor—
But the wind in the tremulous vines sang ever
"Love must perish and hearts must sever!"

PFAFF'S.

In reply to numerous communications,—some of them from distant parts of the country (Peoria, etc.), —it may be well to say that PFAFF's is simply a modest Restaurant and Lager Beer Saloon, at 647 Broadway, which, owing to the fact that PFAFF is a 'jolly good fellow,' and has an excellent bill of fare at moderate prices, is extensively patronized by young literary men, artists, and that large class of people called Germans.

BOHEMIANS.

There is a class of highly cultivated persons in Paris, —mostly literary men and artists,—who, owing in part, perhaps, to their somewhat Nomadic habits, have come to be called Bohemians,—just as a much larger and much less interesting class of people in this country have come to be called, with an equal disregard of the original meaning of the word, Yankees.

The name is in both cases un-translatable and untransferable.

To speak of a French Yankee would not be more absurd than to speak of an American Bohemian. Any one, therefore, who assumes the name of Bohemian in this country makes himself ridiculous.

Aside from the affectation of the thing, there is no sense in it.

The elements of Bohemianism do not exist here. The very state of society excludes it.

We are ruled in this country by Mrs. Grundy, and scarcely one of us has a tether longer than her apron-string.

The Bohemian, on the contrary, wouldn't know Mrs. Grundy if he should see her. Herein is his chief peculiarity and his greatest charm.

An American may quarrel with Mrs. Grundy, as he may quarrel with his mother, but he never ignores her. He would as soon think of ignoring the atmosphere.

For this reason, if for no other, the Bohemian cannot exist in America.

But there are more potent reasons, and among them this, that to be a Bohemian requires a peculiar kind of esprit, not to say of culture, which is found with us only in the case of those few individuals who by extensive travel, or by natural good sense, have become in the best sense of the word, cosmopolitans.

It will be seen from this very general statement, that the assumption of the name Bohemian in this country, is indicative either of great ignorance or of gross arrogance.

We incline, on the whole, to attribute it to the former; since, if we may judge by a few indications, the prevalent idea of a Bohemian, especially in New York, is that of a man who, from circumstances beyond his control, doesn't happen to move in what is called 'society.'

Now in Paris, on the contrary, the Bohemian is courted by society; for he possesses preeminently those charms of character which among cultivated people in France are mostly in demand.

In fact, as we have intimated, it requires the peculiar state of society that exists in France to create the Bohemian—a state of society where wealth, as such, and even learning, as such, goes for nothing, while birth, as such, goes for very little; in a word, a state of society in which that peculiar intelligence and esprit, and that elegant refinement and good taste which come only from generous culture and gentlemanly instincts, go for everything.

If in the progress of things there shall ever be formed in this country a distinct national character—and we are far enough from it, as yet—it is not impossible that out of it will grow a condition of society equal in independence, in self-respect, and in real culture, to any that has ever existed in the old world; and then, but not till then, we may have among us a type of character as fine in temper and as elevated in tone as that which in Paris goes by the name of Bohemian.

[For The New York Saturday Press.]

STORM AND SUN.

BY CHARLES D. GARDETTE.

"You think there will be a storm,' you say?
So do I!
In my soul it hath lower'd all day! All day
A canopy, storm-glutted, sullen, and grey,
But cloven, at times, by the lightning's play,
Hath hung o'er my spirit-sky!

'O! you only spoke of the gathering gloom
Overhead?'
Aye! a ripple of rain-drops, a flash, a boom!—
And the sun-gold again in your curtained room;
And the air all steeped in a misty perfume
From the grateful earth-throats shed!

But I—I speak of a deadlier cloud—
Do you heed?
Its thunders mayhap will not be so loud,
But its bolt will strike!—and a crimson'd shroud
May reek in its track! Is your hard heart cow'd?
Dare you taunt me to the deed?

Ha! ha! Do you think I have not seen?
If he creep,
But once more, my heart and its sunlight between—
My heart and its sunlight; you know what I mean—
The sod that he tramples shall not be green
With all the tears you can weep!

. . . .

The storm came, and found us silent—and sped!
Then, she spake :
'Love is not all woven of one bright thread;
There is steel with its gold, you have often said:
I *was* hard! And you? Let it pass! Overhead
All is gold! Will not *your* sun break?'

[2025 editor's note: The following notice is for a benefit to be given for George Wilkins, brother to Ned Wilkins, aka Personne. Ned lived with George, George's wife, and 3 children. George's sudden death left Ned as the family's support.]

BENEFIT PERFORMANCE AT THE ACADEMY OF MUSIC.

The public has already been informed that a benefit performance is about to be given, on a grand scale, at the Academy of Music, in behalf of the family of one of its principal and most respected agents, who died a few days since in Boston, while there in discharge of his duties.

We are not permitted to refer more particularly to the beneficiaries, but we cannot allow the occasion to pass without saying that he whose sudden demise has thus brought them so sadly before the public, was a gentleman with whose personal acquaintance we were favored, for several years, and whom, alike in his private and in his professional life, we, in common with all who knew him, held in the highest esteem. We understand that the time fixed for the benefit (to consist of a morning and evening performance) is Saturday, March 10th, and that among the distinguished artists who, with the cheerful consent of their respective managers, have already volunteered their services, are Madame Alberti-ni, Mrs. Barney Williams, Mrs. John Wood, Miss Agnes Robertson, Mrs. Hoey, Miss Mary Gannon, Sigmor Beaucard é, Mr. Ernest Perring, Mr. Dion Bourcicault, Mr. Lester Wallack, Mr. George Jordan, Mr. Joseph Jefferson, Mr. Brougham, Mr. Walcot, and Mr. A. H. Davenport.

NEW YORK MARCH 10, 1860

[For The New York Saturday Press.]

THE SONG OF THE BACCHANAL.

In Vino Veritas.

Fill the goblet to the brim;
Life is full of little cares—
Youth is fleeting—Hope grows dim—
Age comes on us unawares.
Let us drink while life is young;
Drink, till every eye doth shine!
Drink, till Wisdom moves the tongue!
Truth lives nowhere but in wine!

Love is but a cheat, a dream;
Vows are made to disregard,
Little is as it doth seem,
Human hearts are cold and hard.
Drink till morning touch the East,
Quaff the honey of the vine!
Fool is he who drinks the least,
There is truth in ruby wine!

Woman's words are falsehood's self,
Meant but to beguile the soul;
Lay such bait upon the shelf,
Drown them in the rosy bowl.
Drink till reels the brain with mirth—
Till the stars shall cease to shine!
Truth dwells nowhere on the earth,
Love within the spirit's shrine!

N. G. SHEPHERD.

[Written for The New York Saturday Press.]

AUNT ELLEN'S CHARGE.

BY J. W. WATSON.

I remember, when I was a little girl, once writing a letter to my grandmother, and taking it myself, that I might in person explain some points that I was conscious were rather obscure.

Carrying out this principle, I am about to write the story of two lives, in respect to which I have been forced to stand as a silent spectator, and bring it myself, that I may explain away the obscurities.

I am all alone to-night,—alone in the great old house that within my recollection swarmed with noisy, happy people. When I say alone, I mean that I—Ellen Sybrandt—am the only one left, of the once large family within its walls. I am left with the servants, and my own thoughts. To-day my nephew George has left me for school. It is the first day we have been separated since his birth. He was fifteen, and a fine good boy, and I knew, in spite of my fondness and my egotism, that it was time, long since, that he went where he could learn something more than could be taught by his old maiden Aunt Ellen. And yet though I say it who perhaps shouldn't, the old maid had not been neglectful in imparting what she herself knew. Under all the reflections generated by my loneliness, and the retrospection it has brought, it will not sound strange if I should confess that I have been crying, and in spite of a usually recuperative disposition, I am very sad.

Twenty years is long, very long to look forward to, but as a backward view it is but a span of time, over which the mind goes almost at a jump. With me it is but a spiritless jump. Twenty years ago, I was then counted as an old maid, having reached thirty. I could sit in this very room and number eight brothers and sisters, myself as the oldest, making nine children. Our darling mother and father were both living, and our family, all counted, including Aunts Mary and Margaret, were thirteen as happy people as one would meet in a month's travel.

Only twenty years, and I am the only one left, and this strange thing has come so gradually after the first shock, that it seems now as though it was an expected occurrence. It seems as though it was a known fact, ever since my very earliest years, that one after the other of the dearly loved should pass away, and at last I, wrinkled, white-haired, and alone, should be sitting in the old homestead parlor, looking into the flickering blaze this November night.

My mother was the first to leave us. Just twenty years ago come the thirtieth of this month, she died, and I, as the eldest girl, strove my best to supply her place with the dear little ones. If she has the privilege of looking down upon me, I feel sure of her conviction that my heart has been in my task through all the terrible chastenings, and clung to each of those loved ones, as devotedly as her own could have done.

I had two brothers a few years younger than myself, who, when manhood came to them, went out into the world and fought their life-battle. It was one of but few years. George, my own, my nearest, and dearest, lies mouldering at Valparaiso, where he was called on business, and stricken down with fever. Only six months before, we had intelligence of the death of my brother Walter, who had been killed in a duel at New Orleans. Walter was wild and reckless, but O how dearly was he loved! And I think it was the news of his death which struck the first chill to my father's spirit. He would never forgive himself for having sent Walter away from home, in hope that it would have a good effect. I have always thought that he failed from that time, and when there came the second shock, announcing that George had passed to his long sleep, he could not rally himself under the blow, and within the year we laid our father in the quiet spot in Preston churchyard, where one by one all but I have joined him.

It was of my sisters Josie and Ettie that I was about to write, and the tale by itself is a sad one enough, without telling all the sad events that preceded and followed it. Since the death of my brothers, next to myself, they were the eldest. Josie, tall, dark, beautiful, and proud, was nineteen. Ettie was tall, and as perfect a specimen of the blonde, as Josie was of the brunette. I was really proud of my sisters, perhaps more so from the fact that I was never the possessor of beauty. Ettie was two years the younger of the two, and as gentle as her sister was proud. I admired Josie, but I loved Ettie most. There was that in her childlike face, her clear, bright blue eyes, that insensibly led one to love her, and pet her, as they would have petted a child. As opposite as they were in all things, there could be no firmer love than that which existed between my sisters Josie and Ettie.

Three years my brother George had been at Valparaiso previous to his death. Most of his letters spoke of a friend he had made there, whom he called Warren Martelle. It was rarely that George's letters did not speak in the most extravagant terms of this friend. The name became as familiar to us all at home, as one of our own, and after George's announcement, that when it pleased fate to allow him once more to join us, that Warren was to come with him, we would each, —my two sisters, and myself—lay claim to our brother's friend, and jokingly declare that when he came, each should try her powers of fascination, to catch the wealthy young Englishman in her nets. Even I, who had never been an expert at winning an admirer, threatened my beautiful sisters with my rivalry, declaring that I would on that occasion spend all my pin-money in new ringlets and rouge.

They were to have been with us the following Summer, but when Spring came, it brought letters from Warren Martelle that told us our brother would come no more. Had he been of our own blood, he could not have written more fully from the heart, or spoken more feelingly. He had been with George, the letters said, when he died, and to him had been breathed all the words that would have gone to brothers, sisters, and all, had he been at home. He would come, he said, and bear verbally all he had not written. He was to settle George's business, and his own, which would cause a delay of some months, when we should see him at Preston, where he would resign into our father's hands, George's property.

The Summer passed away, and Autumn was verging very far toward Winter, before Martelle came, and then he came to find us fatherless. There was something very pleasant about him at first sight. He was very handsome. The brown hair fell carelessly over his bronzed face, and there was an air of case and abandon about him, that could hardly fail at a glance to please any woman,—especially if she dwelt so quietly as we, and was so little versed in the world. It was more than a year since Warren Martelle's name had passed our lips in the joking way that we once had spoken of him; but I feel sure that each of my sisters thought many times within that first hour, when he came into our home, of the frequent mock threats they had made each other, to appropriate him who was now in our midst.

From the moment I saw Warren Martelle, Ifelt that he had come for the place in my heart, made vacant by the death of George; I felt that I could love him, very dearly; but let me be well understood when I say, that I could never have loved him as a husband, and had such an unlikely thing occurred as an offer from him to that effect, it would have met refusal upon my part, without a moment's hesitation. There must have been something of that in my eyes, or in my manner, the moment we met, for as he took my hand, he drew me toward him, and kissed me on the cheek, but he kissed neither of my sisters.

I have said that at this time I was little more than thirty, but in my own mind I was quite as old as I am this night with twenty more years on my head. I had always been accustomed to assume the air matronly, and though we were but three women alone, and open subjects for neighborly remark, yet this matronly position led me to overrule all thought else, as I insisted that Warren Martelle should make his stay at our house, while he was in Preston.

For the first few days our talks were all very sad. They were of George, and many time Martelle won a step farther into my heart, as I would watch the tears trickle down his cheeks, while he was speaking of him; but gradually the sadness wore away, and we came back to our old manner, somewhat subdued. Warren was with us, as with those whom he had known for many years, and all things were as unconstrained. Somehow it had never been a question of doubt in my mind, that it was the destiny of Martelle to marry one of my sisters. It was only a problem, and I had no warrant for this conclusion, not even the slightest basis, unless I built upon the jesting remarks made between us after reading in my brother's letters the praise he bestowed on his to us as yet mythical friend. And yet, many times through that Spring and Summer, when we were looking forward to his arrival, I caught myself gravely speculating as to which of those beautiful ones he would choose for a wife. And now, while he was with us, I watched curiously to see the first and earliest dawning of the hundred little nameless nothings that should say to one of them, "I love you."

I had not to wait or watch long. It was Ettie, darling Ettie, that had won the first love-glances of Warren Martelle; bright-eyed, child-like Ettie. Why I should have been more happy when I knew that his love had fallen upon Ettie, I cannot tell, but such was the truth, and upon its foundation, I built many fine fabrics of the future. At first I fancied that as his preference was more strongly displayed, Josie yielded to her sister, and showed a carelessness for the society of Martelle, but I was soon to see my mistake, and find that she had not been so close an observer as myself; that perhaps she did not see or feel that she was not on an equality with Ettie in the heart of Warren Martelle.

It seems strange how I can sit here to-night and write of all this, very much as though I had been a mere spectator, but so it is, and time must bear the blame, if there is any. The question of love is merely one of transfer, and I am obliged to believe that I have centered all the love that ever glowed in my bosom for all created things, upon my last hold in life, my nephew George.

Month after month passed away, and Martelle was still our guest. All that he had come to do as a matter of business, which was the delivering of George's property, was long since done. There was nothing now to detain him with us but his own will, and well I knew how strong this was, for no mother ever watched her children, as I watched my sisters with Martelle. I could see plainly that there was only an affectation of submission on the part of Josie. There was a flash of her great dark eyes, and a compression of her lips, when Martelle seemed to seek the society of Ettie alone, when he walked with her unattended, when he talked with her in earnest whispers, that sent a chill through me, and left an unpleasant depression not easily shaken away. But it was not until one certain day that I knew the real meaning of this. Martelle, and, as I supposed, both my sisters were away upon the river, while I was busy about some household work. That I might obtain some necessary trifle, I went to my sister Josie's room. Not knowing that she was there, I opened the door without knocking, and as I stepped quickly into the room, was astounded to see her come hastily toward me, with her hands outstretched, and say harshly,—

"What do you want?"

I was too much taken by surprise to speak, not only at finding her there, when I supposed her away, but to find her with hair dishevelled, eyes swollen with weeping, and bloodshot, and with an appearance of entire prostration not reconcilable with anything with which I had become cognizant. What I answered I forget, but I do not forget her next words, they were spoken in such a sharp, earnest tone; she said: "Go out, go away; you have no business here," and at the same time she laid her hand upon my breast, as though she would push me away.

O, what a rush of thought came to me at that moment! Years and time passed through my brain like meteors. These were the first unkind words she had ever spoken to me, and they brought the blood bubbling up in my heart, and the tears in a flood to my eyes. I caught the hand that touched my breast in my own, and pressed it to my lips. I was too much excited for speech; all I could say was,—

"Josie, darling, sister!"

But this was enough to loosen the founts of both, and for many minutes we wept heartily in each other's arms, without a word. What strange mental communication there is in physical contact! I learned more in those few minutes, while I held that weeping head upon my bosom, without a word spoken on either side, than I had learned in all those long months that I had watched. I had no need to ask questions, I knew, and when I could find words I said to her,

"Be proud, and submit."

The tears ceased in an instant, and she answered,—

"I have been proud, I have submitted, until it is eating away my soul."

"Better die," I said, "than the world should know."

"Better die," she echoed vacantly, "yes, better die," and her hands clenched, and her lips whitened, as she walked hastily through the room. There were no tears now from her; I shed them though, plentifully. In a little time she came to me and took my hand.

"Why do *you* cry?" she said. "It is all alike to you, Ellen, where Warren Martelle bestows his love, more especially when it is given to your own sister. Why should you cry, when Ettie is to be his wife? But"—and she looked at me with her brows lowered—"she cannot love him satisfyingly. He will bear no undemonstrative love. The woman who is to be Warren Martelle's wife must be made of something less yielding than Ettie Sybrandt." She drew a long breath, and then, as though speaking into some far distance, she whispered,—

"Baby-face!"

"O, sister!"

"It is true," she continued, passionately. "Ettie is weak, and they never can be happy together."

"O, Josie !"

"If I think so, shall I not speak it? She is blind, he is blind, and I—O! I, Ellen," and then with one great burst of passionate tears, she threw herself upon the bed, and wept aloud. I went gently to her side, and tried to raise her in my arms, but she buried her face in the pillows. In a few moments she raised herself, and kissed me, and then said,—

"Will you leave me now, darling? You can do nothing to aid me, and why should you suffer with me? I have not willingly made you a partner in my —shame, I will call it. And so, sister, you will forget, for my sake, all that has passed to-day. Will you forget it?". I promised her that I would try, and once more I bade her be strong, and suffer, and then I left her. In a few hours Warren and Ettie had returned, and Josie came from her room. There was a strange alteration in that few hours. Those to whom I looked for lightness and gaity, had suddenly become sad and heavy, while Josie was never more apparently careless and happy. I, alone, knew how untrue it was, in her case, but I had no theory in my mind to account for the subdued quietness of Ettie, or the momentary forced pleasantness of Martelle. A shadow had fallen that blackened all things, but I looked in vain for the object that stood before the sunshine.

From this day it seemed a change had come over our house. There was no longer the quiet tranquillity of happiness that once reigned. On the face of Josie, when Martelle was present, there was always a smile, and upon her lips a pleasant word. I fancied that he knew the deceit equally with myself. There was always a strange, sideway glance in his eyes toward her, and a flashing of his dark face when she gave way to more than ordinary flow of spirits. But Ettie rarely, or never smiled. It could not be that the love she bore Martelle, should effect her to such a depth of sadness. I could see her drooping eyes often raised to her sister's, a blush settle upon her face, and again they would be cast to the ground. It was then I thought that she was in possession of Josie's secret, and that it was this, pressing upon her that made all the change. What blindness is it falls upon us, during the most important moments of our lives, and which in the double blindness of retrospection we imagine we could remove the next time, always the next time, only to fall back in the same groping way.

Poor Ettie, as the weeks went by, she was more and more sad, her cheek grew paler every day. What could I do to bring back its color? This thought came to me every hour, and every hour it went away unanswered, and still Ettie drooped, and I, blind and silent, knew not how to stretch forth my hand to her aid. I had no solution to the mystery but that to which I had already the key. I had no expression for it by the voice, only by my eyes, as I looked from one to the other of my sisters, and from them to Martelle. I was dumb, as well as blind. O! that I had those years to reenact. Perhaps! to be blind, and dumb again?

In the midst of my agony, I can use no other word, it came to me from Ettie, that Martelle would leave us in a few days, for the city, and that on his return they were to be married. It was the first word I had heard definitely, of the time fixed for their union, though I had looked forward to such an end daily. He would go, Ettie said to New York, and in one month he would be with us again. There was a strange whiteness over Ettie's face when she said this, and her eye failed to meet mine. How I wished for her confidence, that I might know, and judge for myself whether he who was now going away, would ever return, or whether he had only won my child-sister's heart for pastime, to be flung from him, as carelessly as he had already perhaps, flung a score in the past. In all this I forgot Josie, I felt sure that she would conquer, that whatever her struggle, it would die with her. But Ettie was not equal to so great a task, she would not come forth conquerer, but would surely fall in this battle of the heart. It was only for Ettie I trembled.

It was the night before the day of his departure, Martelle was to be away by daylight next morning, and we were to bid him farewell that evening. He and Ettie had been sitting upon the porch since twilight,

Josie had been with me in the sitting-room, looking steadily with a vacant unoccupied air through the window at the moon. I could hear from where I sat, the dull hum of the voices of the pair who were upon the porch, but I could distinguish no words, though every few moments I started, as I thought the sound of a sob came to my ears. So certain did this now become to me, that I could bear it no longer, and I arose, and went to the hall and called Ettie. There was a hush for a moment, and then her answer in a choked voice. She came, and as I thought, had been crying. Poor child! I laid her head upon my bosom, and kissed away the tears rapidly, and then I bade her say farewell to Martelle, and come to her chamber. I stood there, and awaited her re-coming. Something there was working its way up into my heart, about Warren Martelle, and at that moment I had my first harsh thought of him. But O! how quickly I crushed it down. My brother George's friend, he who had acted so faithfully and honorably, in obeying his last wishes, he could do no wrong. And I hated myself almost for the false thought that sprang to my heart that moment. I could see their shadows from where I stood, and I could see that he held Ettie in his arms, with his head bent down over her. They parted, and Ettie stood in the door, looking more like a ghost in the moonlight, than anything human. He held both her hands in his, pressing them to his breast, until she sprang quickly away from him, and said, "May God be just to you, Warren, as you are to me." The words sounded strange to me, and for many a day I pondered over them. She did not know that I still stood in the hall, where she had left me, for she started when I stepped forward to meet her, but in an instant threw herself into my arms, with a long choking sob. It was almost like carrying Ettie, when I took her to her chamber. It was almost like undressing a helpless child. There were no words spoken, but I laid her in the bed, and sat there holding her hand, and putting back the tearwetted hair from her pale forehead, until she fell asleep, sobbing, and starting, like a troubled child.

It was more than an hour after when I went down stairs. I had some faint hope that Martelle would have retired, and that I should have been spared bidding him farewell. I do not know why I should have wished to avoid this, beyond the fact that I always believed in abrupt partings, without the formality, or tears, as the case might be. But my hope was not realized, and I was startled when I came back to the room to find him and Josie sitting closely together upon a sofa, and speaking so earnestly as not to perceive my entrance, until I stood before them. What did this mean? I was about to ask the question as the thought bubbled up to my mouth, but I strangled it, and waited. The time was but a few minutes until he retired, but to me it seemed hours. That misgiving which had crossed me as I stood in the hall, came back with tenfold force, and I sat there speechless. Even when he rose, and came with outstretched hand to bid me 'Good-night,' I could not conquer the chill that passed over me as I took his hand and saw him leave the room. He did not kiss me at his departure as he did at his coming, nor was there a word spoken between myself and Josie after he had left the room. I thought there seemed rather an anxiety on her part to hasten away, and avoid conversation. I felt, as I went to my room, that the shadow was still deepening about me, and that night, as I laid my head upon my pillow, I almost wished that my fears of Martelle's non-return might be realized.

There was a spiritless, silent way with Ettie all the month that she waited for the days and weeks to go over, until Martelle's return. Every week came a letter from him, which she never opened in our presence, or allowed me to see the contents of, but upon the moment of its reception Ettie wandered away with it to her room, and was seen no more that day. The month passed over, and Martelle came not, but before another week had been added to it, there was another letter. This time, from her eagerness, Ettie broke the seal the moment it came to hand; I alone was in the room with her. I watched her eagerly for a little space. There came a flush over her pale face, and an unnatural brightness in her eyes, but they were gone as quickly as they came, and a deathly color set, even upon her lips. I stepped hastily to her side, but too late to save her from falling. The letter dropped from her hand, and as I bent straining to lift her from the floor, I heard her whisper, as though she were speaking from a dream, "Ellen, I am dying." O, how full my heart was, as I raised my baby-sister from the floor, and laid her upon the sofa. How I feared even to look upon the letter that lay there open, that I might learn what I already knew. I could only say in a voice of terror, as I knelt beside her, and covered her cold, listless hand with kisses,—

"O no, darling, O no."

I picked up the letter, it read:

Ettie Dearest,—Do not blame me that I do not come. I am forced to leave New York for the South. I shall be gone perhaps a month, perhaps longer. Learn to be happy until such time as I can see you again.

Warren.

And this was all, a score or two of words to break a heart! A letter that bore upon its every line, coldblooded abandonment. A coward who feared to tell her, whom he had been toying with to amuse his leisure, that he had never loved her. O! that my brother George were living, I thought, to strike the life from this false friend. No! there was none to avenge the wrecked love, from which the sea of life was ebbing away.

That evening we carried Ettie to her room, that room which she never left again alive. If tenderness and tears would have saved her to us, if prayers and love would have purchased her life, Ettie would have lived; but one sultry day in September, we laid our darling by her mother's side, and came back silent and crushed to the old home, that home that was never again to be what it had been.

From the day of the last letter, the name of Martelle had never passed our lips. To me, he seemed dead, as much so as the darling one we had but just laid in the grave. It was therefore with a shiver of terror, that I one day, about a month after her death, took from the hands of one of the servants, a letter in Martelle's handwriting, directed to Ettie. I held it irresolutely a while, and then stepped toward the fire to cast it in the flames. Josie had been watching me intently, I knew this, and as I raised my hand for that purpose, she put up her own and caught the letter from my grasp.

"Do not destroy it," she said, "how can you tell what it may communicate."

"Can it communicate life?" I asked.

"It may," was her response.

I did not understand, I could only think. Did she still love Martelle? Could she love the man who was the murderer of her sister? O! no, I would not let such base thoughts enter my brain. To her, though, I relinquished the letter. There was something frightful in the cold, impassive way, she broke the seal, and read the contents, and then handed it to me, saying, 'Read.' As well as I could through my tears, I read :

My Own Ettie,—All is right, and I come to ask your forgiveness. I have been neglectful, dearest, but your love will forgive me all. I have tested absence, Ettie, and I come to you again with four-fold love. Ettie, in one week after you have received this, I will be with you, never to part again on earth.

Warren.

"What does this wretch mean?" I said, crushing the letter in my hand.

"Let us hear him," she answered.

"Hear him! hear him justify his desertion and villany, sister! have you loved this man so blindly that you can see him, and hear him justify himself for his baseness and cruelty? Can you look upon him, and justify yourself to your angel-sister, who is now looking down upon you?"

She spoke again as coldly as though she was discussing a matter connected with another.

"Yes! I can confess that my love for Warren Martelle carries me so far that I would wish to hear him justify himself in acts that otherwise will be great crimes. I have really loved him, Ellen, I do really love him, until I know that his conduct has been base toward my sister. Real love, Ellen, trusts,—trusts through ill fame and dark report, through neglect and absence."

I felt the same terrible chill creep over me, that I felt upon the night I bade Martelle farewell, in that very room.

"Sister," I said, "I cannot hear this, I feel that the spirit of Ettie rises up to rebuke me. I have listened to every prompting of my heart toward Martelle, but they have all expired, there is no light for him, nothing but darkness and dread."

"I am no longer a child, Ellen, I am as able to judge and act for myself as you are. I have said that I love Martelle. Love like mine, was not to be crushed away in a moment. I knew that his love for Ettie would be a struggle to its fulfilment. I knew the hearts of both, and I knew the result. To you I spoke warningly. It was you who should have stepped between, in the birth of the passion,—not me, I was powerless. Can you blame me now, when I feel that Warren Martelle yielded only to the momentary desire to shake off the chain that was about him, and now, realizing that he is forfeiting honor, and his own esteem, hastens back, too late to redeem his rash promises? Can you blame me, that I still love him, even though it be a hopeless, fruitless love, until I hear from his own lips his defence."

Ah! this was too dreadful to hear; I was too horrified to believe, to realize. That Josie could openly declare her love for him who had caused her sister's death; that she could declare her intention to hear him in defence, and as I felt certain, forgive him, for how surely would he make his defence right, before such a tribunal.

I had not long to think. Before the week had expired a carriage rolled to the door, and Warren Martelle sprang from it. I rose to my feet, and stood cold and stone-like, as he entered the room. What a change had passed over the man in the five months he had been absent! He was wild and haggard, and the tones of his voice had changed. He looked about the room, and before advancing to myself or my sister, he said in quick, harsh way,—

"Where is Ettie?"

"Dead !" I answered.

"Dead!" he repeated looking at us each with a gaze that seemed to lack understanding. "Dead! O yes! I knew it, I felt it. Yes, dead," and then pressing his hands hard upon his temples, he staggered forward, and before we could reach him fell upon his face.

I will pass over some weeks, during which Martelle lay in our house struggling between life and death. It was a sore struggle of the physical power, while the mental lay dormant. Could I help it, that my heart softened toward this self-broken and ruined man. Not so much, that I could forgive the past, and see him take once more the place he had forfeited; but enough, that I could say "Go, and sin no more."

Why should I dwell on those terrible days, those days that now seem like a dark nightmare. Those days when I knew the great evil that was coming upon me, and was powerless to avert it. When I knew that I was about to lose another sister; but O! how much rather would I have lost her by death, than to have known, that by the blindness of love and passion, the past should be obliterated, and womanly pride smothered. Why should I recount, how one day, when his mind again dawned, Josie drew me unwillingly to his bedside to hear his defence, which was no defence to any save herself. It was sophistry, base sophistry. O! that same blinding passion that hurried her on. We all know what is a natural sequence to my story. They were married one year after the death of Ettie; they stood together before the altar, with her memory in their hearts, and sacred oaths upon their lips. And then they went away to travel. I was glad that they left me. I could not have come to see them in their wedded state, in the same spots that now were consecrated by me to the memory of Ettie. They went away, and though I had frequent letters from Josie, yet to me she seemed like one dead. Her letters read to me constrained, as though she were writing what would be read by other eyes than our own, or as though she were addressing me after an ill-adjusted quarrel. She never made mention of her husband, or gave way to any of those pleasant trifles that sparkle like jewels on the young bride's path. I knew that my sister was not happy, but how could I know the dreadful poison that was eating away her heart? It was almost a year since their marriage, when the letters I had been receiving from my sister ceased, and for some weeks I did not hear from her, nor did I know in consequence of their rapid changes, where to address her. While in this uncertain state of anxiety, one day a package came to me; I broke it hastily open, and found two letters addressed to myself, one from Martelle, the other from my sister. I do not know why I selected his first, but upon doing so, a few lines gave me the benumbing intelligence of my sister's death. She had died while giving birth to a child, which was still living, and which with her latest breath, she had consigned to my care, making her husband solemnly pledge himself to respect that wish. For the purpose, he wrote, of carrying out this end, he had addressed me. The child for whom he had made ample provision by settlement, as the accompanying papers would testify, would soon be despatched to me by the hands of its nurse. Accompanying this was the jewels, and the will of my sister.

One only thing more. I would that my story could be told without, but though every word and letter burn through my heart in writing, it must be told. The letter from my sister:

ELLEN,—As when a child, I came and laid my head upon your bosom, sobbing out all my sorrows, or pleading for forgiveness, so come I to you now, Ellen. I am writing this in health and strength, but I pray you to read every line as though it were written upon the bed of death. I have the warning, Ellen, something that tells me surely, that I shall never see you again, and that in this land, so far distant from my home, I shall soon die. This letter will come to you when I am dead. Let my death be the atonement for my great sin. How shall I tell you the depth of disgrace and wickedness into which I have allowed my passion to lead me. How shall I plead with God for mercy, that I may be allowed to join that sister in heaven whom I have so wronged. No! I know it is hopeless, there is no forgiveness.

Ellen, to me only upon her deathbed, Ettie confided the terrible secret that sapped away her life. Warren Martelle was her seducer, her destroyer; he fled from her basely, but he could not fly from his own conscience, and his fears. It was this brought him back, and it was this that made him wed the sister. This, and his passions. With the fading of this came the realization of our union.

It is useless to give more of the letter. I am an old gray-haired woman, but I would not be young again, even if I had no other day of pain to relive but that one, and it was balanced by all the pleasures of a lifetime. It is too terrible to remember.

In due time came Josie's child. Thank God! he looks like his mother, with no memory of the father's face about him. I have called him George Sybrandt, and sometimes I fancy he is very like my dear brother George. Of Martelle since the day of that letter, I have only had one intelligence. It was authentic, and may God forgive me for saying it was gratifying. It came as an official document from the United States Consul at Valparaiso, saying that he had been killed in the street, supposed from jealousy. This was five years after I first saw him.

"God moves in a mysterious way."

Thoughts and Things.

BY ADA CLARE

A new romance by HAWTHORNE is an epic-event in literature. HAWTHORNE is, with one exception, the best prose-writer in America. His language and the characters he creates bear a close resemblance to each other; they both have a high nervous temperament and a vital color.

The "Marble Faun" is not equal in energy and dramatic vigor to most of his earlier works. The characters seem more faintly defined—probably from the fact that the narrative rambles loosely through a wide field of art-life. The scene is laid in the Halcyonland of story—Italy—which the author has wisely studied in reality, before attempting to weave it into fiction.

There is a double plot in this story; there are two women who are supposed to contrast two great female types, and two men created with the same view. Hilda, whom the author creates as the type of all that is soft and tender, of the dove-nature in woman, utterly falls short of his object. Her gentleness seems like affectation; her purity, a want of feeling; her angelic horror of sin, a ridiculous and impertinent exaggeration of her own virtues. Miriam, the stronger character in the story, is one day her dearest and most devoted friend, while the next she forbids her even to touch her dress, because the deeper-hearted woman has not been able to lie with her eyes. O fie! they slander us heartily, these men. This is no woman; 'tis a piece of pale Italian marble, that cheats us with the semblance of life. The truly angelic woman would be the last of her sex to cast off her best-loved friend, in such a scene as this book pictures. Crime is at times indistinct—its boundary lines intermingle often indistinguishably with those of necessity; but sorrow is never to be mistaken; grief clothes itself with an awful scientific certainty.

Miriam, the unangelic, is the more womanly and lovable of the two. Nothing could be more touching and beautiful than her love for Donatello. These two characters have caught a glow from the warm Italian sky, while the other two have still the dust of Salem on their hearts—a drop of that blood in their veins, which burned young women at the stake as witches.

The story is full of interesting details of Italian life and scenery; and the treatment of art-life in Rome will probably prove of vast interest to many.

I subjoin the following extract from the most powerful scene in the book:

THE FAUN'S TRANSFORMATION.

Miriam and Donatello were now alone. She clasped her hands, and looked wildly at the young man, whose form seemed to have dilated, and whose eyes blazed with the fierce energy that had suddenly inspired him. It had kindled him into a man; it had developed within him an intelligence which was no native characteristic of the Donatello whom we have heretofore known. But that simple and joyous creature was gone forever.

"What have you done?" said Miriam, in a horror-stricken whisper.

The glow of rage was still lurid on Donatello's face, and now flashed out again from his eyes.

"I did what ought to be done to a traitor!" he replied. "I did what your eyes bade me do, when I asked them with mine, as I held the wretch over the precipice!"

These last words struck Miriam like a bullet. Could it be so? Had her eyes provoked or assented to this deed? She had not known it. But, alas! looking back into the frenzy and turmoil of the scene just acted, she could not deny—she was not sure whether it might be so, or no—that a wild joy had flamed up in her heart, when she beheld her persecutor in his mortal peril. Was it horror? —or ecstasy?—or both in one? Be the emotion what it might, it had blazed up more madly, when Donatello flung his victim off the cliff, and more and more, while his shriek went quivering downward. With the dead thump upon the stones below had come an unutterable horror,

"And my eyes bade you do it ?" repeated she.

They both leaned over the parapet, and gazed downward as earnestly as if some inestimable treasure had fallen over, and were yet recoverable. On the pavement, below, was a dark mass, lying in a heap, with little or nothing human in its appearance, except that the hands were stretched out, as if they might have clutched, for a moment, at the small square stones. But there was no motion in them, now. Miriam watched the heap of mortality while she could count a hundred, which she took pains to do. No stir; not a finger moved!

"You have killed him, Donatello! He is quite dead!" said she. "Stone dead! Would I were so, too!"

"Did you not mean that he should die ?" sternly asked Donatello, still in the glow of that intelligence which passion had developed in him. There was short time to weigh the matter; but he had his trial in that breath or two while I held him over the cliff, and his sentence in that one glance, when your eyes responded to mine! Say that I have slain him against your will—say that he died without your whole consent—and, in another breath, you shall see me lying beside him."

"Oh, never !" cried Miriam. "My one, own friend! Never, never, never !"

She turned to him—the guilty, blood-stained, lonely woman—she turned to her fellow-criminal, the youth, so lately innocent, whom she had drawn into her doom. She pressed him close, close to her bosom, with a clinging embrace that brought their two hearts together, till the horror and agony of each was combined into one emotion, and that, a kind of rapture.

"Yes, Donatello, you speak the truth!" said she; "my heart consented to what you did. We two slew yonder wretch. The deed knots us together for time and eternity, like the coil of a serpent !"

o o o

Last week I was casually present at the *French Theatre,* during the performance of a play called *Marie-Jeanne ou la Femme du Peuple*. I was astonished to see that so touching a piece, and so admirably acted, should attract little or no attention from the Press and the Public. If *Jeannie Deans* and *The Octoroon* can draw a crowded house for a single night, *Marie-Jeanne* ought to be played to crowds for a whole season.

The play is a domestic melodrama, which the natural extravagance of the French language both in words and gesticulation, renders it peculiarly suited for. Madame Laurett, who played the heroine, is by several degrees the best actress in New York. The inexpressibly beautiful and touching pathos which she throws into the part of the heart-broken mother, could scarcely be too much praised; it won for her two such genuine recalls before the audience after expressive scenes, as none but the highest talent ever receives.

It is much to be wondered at, that the 'French Theatre' is not overcrowded at every representation. It should be considered as a school for the acquirement of the French language. Many persons are attempting to acquire that language in the dreary ways of private tuition, who would find attendance upon French Dramatic performances, not only the most rapid manner, but infinitely the most agreeable one of accomplishing the same. When the imagination and the heart assist in the efforts of the intellect, they seem to sandal its feet with wings.

LEAVES FROM NATURE.

On a beautiful mild day in early Spring, I met a blind old man led by a boy. The latter was ruddy, bright-eyed, and joyous with healthy life, but the blind old fellow wore the look of extreme acerbity and decrepitude. The contrast between them was striking as complete, and I wondered whether the disparity of their minds was equally great.

"Are you not glad Spring has come?" I asked the old man. "No," said he, in querulous tones, "I am not glad of anything. Spring comes back to the earth, but never more to me. Can Spring restore my sight, or make me young again? I hate the Spring."

"I should think you would like it," I replied, "for the sake of others; for the pleasure it affords your little companion, for instance."

"What does he care for the Spring, or her flowers and blossoms? He is longing for Spring to make way for Summer, that brings fruits and berries, of which he hopes to steal and eat his full. He is going to consume his life as I and others have done: waste the Spring of it in idlemess; scratch up its Summer in the indulgence of passion; and squander its Autumn in attempts to recall what is gone forever. I have reached Winter, and, like a blasted tree, shall wear its bleak barrenness in all seasons."

"You have the wisdom of experience," I remarked.

"Of what use is that to me, I cannot go over the ground again. It comes too late, and cannot revive a single pleasure or zest I have lost. It teaches me regret, and you know the old rhyme,

"'If wisdom be but sorrow's spy
'Twere better not to know.'"

"Why, I have an uncle older than you are," said I, "and he, is happier and jollier than I am."

"Then he has not 'rushed the seasons' as I have done," answered the old man frankly.

"Perhaps not. Neither Spring nor Summer have left him yet; for he is as merry as the one, and warm-hearted as the other. He is as full of ripe goodness as Autumn. I verily believe 'There is no Winter in his year;' and die when he may, he will leave behind him no kindlier heart, or more genial companion. When he drops, like mellow fruit from the bow, 'twill only be because he is ripe for heaven."

I often afterward reflected upon this conversation with the blind old misanthrope, and found a great deal in his remark about 'rushing the seasons.'

Much as we deprecate the appearance and concomitants of age, we are all in desperate haste to make ourselves old. Americans more than any other people are guilty of this superlative folly.

Our boys cannot wait even for their teens, ere they assume the garb, airs, confidence, habits, and vices of men. No practice can tend more than this, to enervate or even destroy the intellect and the body. The evil is still growing, and there seems to be no help for it.

Our young men rush the seasons, incontinently. They have not the patience to await the regular rotation of Summer, Autumn, and Winter. No, they insist upon growing prematurely old, jaded with life, *blasé,* and 'used up' before their powers are really half developed. To become supremely indifferent to everything, and incapable of simple enjoyment, admiration or esteem, seems to them to be a mark of superiority and depth; they study in fact to become as much like my blind friend as possible.

Just as if life were not short enough, and as if age was too slow in coming. Just as if the world did not roll through the seasons at the rate of thousands of miles an hour, and needed hurrying up.'

To keep away, or smooth out the wrinkles of age, the heart must be kept young, by loving one's fellowmen, looking on the bright side of things, eschewing the Nil Admirari school, and courting contentment.

Old Age's bills-payable are duly presented by Time; but the possessor of a cheerful mind, which infallibly expresses itself in the countenance, may often get them renewed indefinitely; for a smile is as winning as gold, and a laugh as healthy as fresh air and exercise.

I conclude, therefore, that it is rash and foolish to 'rush the seasons,' and infinitely better to make the most of them as they arrive in their order and fulness.

Yet how frequently Young America jumbles all the seasons together, commingling the youthful age of Spring with vices ripe as Autumn, and philosophy as cold and barren as Winter.

If the march of progress can be no better conducted, let chaos reign again! R. W. P.

NEW YORK MARCH 17, 1860

"THE MARBLE FAUN."

Previous to the publication of "The Scarlet Letter," no American author was so little known as Hawthorne. Such a remark he used sometimes to make of himself. But that book bore him at once to the summit of renown as a romancist, and amply justified the verdict which gave him a high place among the prose-writers of this country. His literary career since then has lain in the sunshine of illustrious success. His position in literature is positive and immutable. Unlike those authors who, as Johnson once said, "make themselves public without making themselves known," he is a celebrated without being a popular writer. As Dr. Channing has felicitously remarked, they have not the largest audience who speak to the largest number of people.

The sympathetic readers of Hawthorne, the most cultivated of his own countrymen and of Europeans, welcome with enthusiasm and delight his new romance of "The Marble Faun.' It is published in two elegant volumes,—not too elegant though, for the treasure which it is their happy fortune to preserve,—by Messrs. Ticknor & Fields.

Few readers are very grateful to the critic who prematurely destroys for them the novelty of a romance, by unveiling in dry analysis the secrets of its plot. We intend our readers no gratuitous unkindness in this respect. There seems to be no reason why we should do more than indicate in general language our general impressions of this book.

The romance of "The Marble Faun" is comprised in fifty chapters. Its principal action is in Rome, though there are scenes in Perugia and in a castellated retreat among the Apennines. Its prominent characters are four in number; namely, Donatello, Count di Monte Beni,—a young Italian nobleman, whose wonderful resemblance to the Faun of Praxiteles forms the key-note of the narrative; Kenyon, a young American sculptor, located in Rome; Miriam, the heroine and the mystery of the drama;—and lastly, Hilda, an American girl, and like Miriam herself, a painter, but in whom the cardinal virtues and all the saintlike attributes of woman are harmonized in a lovely though somewhat frigid union.

These four persons are at first presented as occupying towards each other the relations of friends. Ultimately, however, at different times and under different circumstances they assume relations more tender and interesting. Donatello loves Miriam, and Kenyon loves Hilda; and, as it is refreshing to know, the affection is in both cases returned,—though not with spontaneous reciprocity. For Donatello and Miriam there is crime, remorse, penitential sacrifice,—all the tragedy of passion and of life: for Kenyon and Hilda, there is pure love, made altogether charming by every accessory of romance, and at last fulfilled by marriage and 'wedded bliss."

Our promise to refrain from analysis of the plot will not preclude us from commenting on the characters in this story, which are artfully peculiar and representative.

Hilda is a young girl who dresses in white and lives in a tower. She has brown ringlets, a delicate healthful complexion,—probably 'sea-shell pink,'—an intelligent, sensitive face, pretty hands, and a graceful figure. Her character is well indicated by a remark of her own, describing herself as "a poor lonely girl, whom God has set here in an evil world, and given her only a white robe, and bid her wear it back to Him, as white as when she put it on." This young lady is a good painter in oils and water-colors, and has an ardent affection for multitudinous doves. She is at one period somewhat pointedly addressed by the guilty but magnificent Miriam, who tells her she would not be acting as an angel, but as a human creature, and a woman, among earthly men and women, she needs a sin to soften her. The character is finely drawn. All of us know it exceedingly well. But, as Tom Moore once observed,

> "Be an angel, my love, in the morning—
> But O be a *woman* to-night!

Kenyon is one of those commonplace persons who have 'high promise' and 'increasing celebrity.' He is learned in Art, moral to a degree, rather talkative and very fond of Hilda. Altogether he is not interesting, and we neither wonder nor grieve at his consignment to the secluded paradise of matrimony. Donatello is the hero. He is of the lineage of Monte Beni, descended from a progenitor not altogether human, a sylvan creature who long ago wooed and won a mortal maiden, and whose characteristics, affecting his whole progeny through many generations, are sometimes vividly illustrated in some individual of the race. Donatello realizes in nature the mythical Faun of antiquity. He is breezy and beautiful as morning; strong, ardent, and tender, though not intellectually developed till sublimated by his love for Miriam, his crime for her sake, his awful remorse and penitence. The author remarks, somewhere in the second volume, that the contemplation of an imperfect portrait bust of Donatello, made by Kenyon, originally inspired him with the idea and design of this romance.

But the grand creation of the story is Miriam. She is described as springing from English parentage, on the mother's side, but with a vein, likewise, of Jewish blood; yet connected, through her father, with a princely family of Southern Italy. A creation we say, though the author seems to intimate that he has taken a hint at least for the character, from real life. His mysterious remark is that "the reader—if he think it worth while to recall some of the strange incidents which have been talked of, and forgotten, within no long time past—will remember Miriam's name."

Very early in the progress of the story, Donatello visits the studio of Miriam, who shows him her own portrait painted by herself. This felicitous occasion is thus improved by the author for a description of his heroine: "She was youthful, and had what was usually thought to be a Jewish aspect; a complexion in which there was no roseate bloom, yet neither was it pale; dark eyes into which you might look as deeply as your glance would go, and still be conscious of a depth that you had not sounded, though it lay open to the day. She had black, abundant hair, with none of the vulgar glossiness of other women's sable locks; if she were really of Jewish blood, then this was Jewish hair, and a dark glory such as crowns no Christian maiden's head. Gazing at this portrait, you saw what Rachel might have been, when Jacob deemed her worth the wooing seven years and seven more; or perchance she might ripen to be what Judith was when she vanquished Holofernes with her beauty, and slew him for too much adoring it."

The character of Miriam combines all that is proud and majestic with all that is passionate and tender in the nature of woman. In depicting her subtle and varied emotional experiences,—the slow pursuit of a haunting and deadly horror; the dim presentiment of impending evil; the struggle of hatred and fear; the triumph of crime; the bliss and the agony of love; the long, moonless desolation of remorse,—in this Hawthorne has richly displayed that power of subtle, introspective analysis for which he is preeminent among the writers of the age.

In this romance of "The Marble Faun," considering it as a work of art, it is not possible to discover many faults. It is compact and symmetrical. Excepting the odd and pleasing phantasy of the Faun, its plot is marked by no peculiar originality; but that plot is developed and managed with unerring skill and with perfect grace. There are several scenes in the story thrilled with the fervor of a wild imagination, and awful in their mystery and gloom; so that it will not be surprising if those critics who discovered, in other and greater of Hawthorne's works, a tendency towards what they call the unnatural and the tragic, should augment their violence in outcries against the present.

It is sufficient to express a belief that there are more things in heaven and earth—and literature—than are dreamt of in the philosophy of commonplace people; and to add that, laugh we ever so gaily, human nature has its tragic side, and human experience its tragic aspect,—which perhaps it might not be altogether vain sometimes to contemplate.

There is one intensely disagreeable feature in this romance, which we shall mention without comment : that is, its incidental, labored, and inelegant puffery of certain American artists, now or formerly located in Rome. The reader will notice this distasteful nonsense alike in the preface and the body of the work.

In his preface the author explains that "Italy, as the site of his romance, was chiefly valuable to him as affording a sort of poetic or fairy precinct, where actualities would not be so terribly insisted upon as they are and must needs be in America. . . . Romance and poetry," he adds, "ivy, lichens, and wall flowers, need ruin to make them grow."

The questions here raised might well stimulate discussion. It is our own opinion that Hawthorne is never so truly himself as when on his native soil and with an American theme. He is thoroughly an American, and peculiarly a New Englander. His romance of "The Scarlet Letter" expresses his nature, and is his greatest work; and to that, the romance of "The Marble Faun" is inferior in all essential respects.

But, waiving the choice between that hallowing sanctity of poetic sentiment which haunts "the mouldering lodges of the past," and that fiery breath of song which glows with the living action of the present, and is instinct with the vitality of a progressive age,—one thing is certainly true and certainly charming in this romance, that it realizes and reflects all the majesty and pathos of venerable antiquity and of desolated empire. All is here that is romantic in old, deserted ruins, gray with the storms of age, and green with the benediction of ivy. The subterranean horror of the Catacombs, the dim superstition of vast Cathedrals, the varied charms of historic association, the poetry of storied scenes,—all unite to enhance the power and the splendor of this romance. It is youthful with the youth of Nature, and glorious with the golden lustre of Art.

Evangeline, by Louisa Lander, 1858. "Creative Commons Evangeline" https://commons.m.wikimedia.org/wiki/File:Louisa_Lander_-_Evangeline_(PEM_202.12.1.1)_02.jpg by Crawdad Blues licensed under CC BY 4.0; http://creativecommons.org/licenses/by/4.0/

Thoughts and Things.

BY ADA CLARE

I can well understand how Hawthorne could create two characters like Hilda and Kenyon, believing them to be lovable, after seeing his bust at the Dusseldorf Gallery. It has been done by Louisa Lander, a young New England lady, whose talent is said to threaten a serious rivalry to that of the celebrated Harriet Hosmer. Hawthorne's bust witnesses for itself as a good likeness; it is evidently copied from a stern, strong original; the imagination has not been allowed to enter there. The very beautiful statue of Evangeline is by the hand of the same young lady. The heroine of the pastoral poem is represented to be asleep; her sleep is so natural that you are constrained, while near her, to speak in whispers for the fear of awakening her from her slumbers.

The Dusseldorf Gallery is the only place in town where a lady, in the toils of shopping, can at the same time rest from her labors and amuse her mind. In that respect it is invaluable.

Women and men,—I mean to say those without any very deep sentiment or profound thought,—are apt to have very vague and eccentric notions about morals. With them, every minor variation from an inflexible routine of life is recorded under the head of problematic morals. Their diagnosis of the supposed virtuous malady is a wondrous one, for the given symptoms of that disease embrace every development natural to the unchained mind. An acquaintance with general literature, a frankness of speech and manner with men, a disposition to dress becomingly, a sensitiveness to dramatic pathos, a good appetite, a cheerful expression of countenance, an inability to worship ministers, a liking for sugar-plums, a love for piano-music, an occasional acquaintance with Lubin's powder *rouge,* an aversion to lying, an ability to think for one's self, the power in case of extreme thirst of drinking from a pump, are all set down as sure symptoms of an invalid moral system.

This arises from the fact that men, above all the professionally moral ones, suppose women to be virtuous only because they are slaves to custom. They imagine the female mind to dwell in the kingdom of virtue only when they are fast locked in with a padlock, and that the least chance of getting out of their prison is made the opportunity of rushing headlong into promiscuousness.

Virtue, on the contrary, only exists where there is freedom of action. So necessary is this element of freedom, that the constrained woman can never be said to be virtuous, however pure she may be. The laws of society, the social and religious code, may construct a quality called morality, but they have no acquaintance with virtue. For it is as much an inherent, self-sustaining quality as courage, generosity, truthfulness, or any of the attributes that go to make up the human soul.

Virtue is that quality that keeps a woman pure and incorrupt through whatever scenes in life she may pass, whatever knowledge she may acquire, whatever she may do. The virtuous woman knows nothing of worldly temptations, nor social lies; her instincts come directly from nature and from God. In her soul there lives a bright flame that burns away corruption, and leaves all subjects clean and pure before her eyes. She avoids vice as she does pestilence, because it is a horror to her; all prurient views of things disgust and sicken her; a defamation of her own body she regards as though one should blot the stars with mud.

To bind her with the shackles of convention and the terror of public opinion, were as superfluous as to prevent the populace by law, from walking into the mouths of hyenas, or from thrusting themselves into blazing furnaces.

The freer the mind of the virtuous woman is, the less chance there is of her degrading herself. Nothing is more easy than to cheat the tribunal of society, but where the only tribunal is one's own heart, who can deceive that?

A woman can hardly be said to be virtuous, in the active sense of the word, before she has fully loved, just as a man is brave only in the passive sense of the word, until that quality has led him to face danger. A young maiden can be called chaste; the term virtuous does not apply to her.

Virtue is begotten of love and freedom. It seems to be very hard for men to understand this. Perhaps it is that the miserable errors into which the precepts and example of their own sex lead them ere they are able to judge for themselves, render them incapable of comprehending incorruptible purity in woman. As it is, the great body of men persist in believing, against all record and the witness of their own eyes, that the woman who can accept one man can accept all men. The least unit of the collective body is made to stand for the whole. Such atrociously illogical deductions would not be allowed to stand for an instant in any other reasoning but that of a metaphysical character.

How would it sound to argue that because we can eat strawberries with impunity, therefore we can with pleasure devour any of the objects included in the vegetable kingdom, strychnia and sulphuric acid for example? Is it strictly logical to state that because a lady can train a lap-dog into a legitimate pet, that she could therefore teach a hippopotamus to run before her by a silken string, sleep upon her pillow, and drink from a baby's spoon?

One strong love, and a physical looseness of character, are the two things farthest apart in this globe. They are the two poles; you can only approach the one by steadfastly leaving the other behind you. The difference between the moral and the virtuous woman, is that the one reverences the law, and the other reverences God; the one takes harsh, self-righteous views of everything, the other treats all subjects widely and with brave charity; the one wishes to crush and ruin the erring ones of her own sex, the other desires to bring them back to nature and truth; the one makes chastity a matter of show, the other a divine feature of the soul.

Above all things I desire to express here the vast gulf that lies between one love and miscellaneous attraction. In all metaphysical sciences,—love above them all,— what is gained in intensity is lost in universality.

There are women, I know, daily trading themselves away at the very noble price of esteem, worldly prudence, an establishment, a good name, male protection. For these I cannot answer. I know no standard for judging of them. But those who have not weighed themselves in the balances against sand, who have followed in full faith the dictates of the divine law of love, may not stoop to profane the temple of the body, without falling millions of leagues below themselves.

These women love, and therein they save their souls alive. That sublime fire utterly consumes their unchaste thoughts, their false theories, their canting falseness, their envious and uncharitable feelings toward their own sex. The bright fires that have reverently fed on heavenly food, will not stoop to feed on baser prey; they turn their pure flames hungering upon their hearts, and burn them up to virtue.

o o o

The brilliant Editor of the *Sunday Courier* wishes to know in whose favor I make the exception with regard to Hawthorne's position in American literature. I don't mind answering the question to him, as, though he may not agree with me, he will certainly understand me. I mean Miss Harriet Prescott. If the respected Editor has read 'The Amber-Gods,' he will not be astonished to hear me say, that in my mind, its style for superabundant power and eloquence, stands above all American prose-writing. Hawthorne never did, never can equal it.

[For The New York Saturday Press.]

"ADRIFT!"

There's a body adrift—a ship aground!
And the cold rain falls with a sobbing sound,
While my weary feet pace the damping ground,
George, darling!

My brown curls are washed by the dreary rain,
And my tears flow down with a grievous pain,
As I seek for thee through the mist in vain,
George, darling!

The clouds scowl upon me with dark'ning hate;
The wind, mocking, murmurs" too late, too late!"
O Love is stronger than tempest or fate,
George, darling!

We two are adrift on a pitiless tide,
Where the mist and storm have sundered us wide,
Yet death's surge will wash us up, side by side,
George, darling!

The night closes round me chilly and gray;
My sad eyes are blinded by tears and spray,
But I've seen the shore where we'll meet one day,
George, darling!

SYBELLE.

[From The N. Y. Evening Post.]

THE ASTOR LIBRARY VISITED BY A GHOST.

For several days past there has been a bit of personal gossip afloat up-town, which, as in all similar instances, has been highly exaggerated. Yet even allowing for these exaggerations, the facts or the suppositions—whichever they be—as related by one of the principal actors, are of themselves strange enough to satisfy the most inveterate admirer of the marvellous; and as the story has been solemnly asseverated before a mixed company of some twenty persons, and afterwards retailed and repeated so much as to be almost the town-talk, we are committing no impropriety, we trust, in stating the circumstances, as far as we have been able to discover them.

The numerous literary persons and others who frequent the spacious halls of the Astor Library will be interested, therefore, in learning that their favorite retreat is haunted. Of course on seeing the comfortable well-lighted rooms in the day time, when filled with careful readers, and enlivened often by the presence of a gaily-dressed lady and other visitors, nothing seems more preposterous than the idea of ghosts. But let the reader imagine these wide halls as they are at night, swathed in darkness, the gloomy alcoves casting yet deeper and gloomier shadows—when a foot-fall reverberates through the wide expanse with mysterious echoes, and when the lamp borne by the startled explorer along tortuous passages and among musty tomes sends but a feeble ray, that scarcely serves to make the darkness visible, and the aspect is very different. At this time the Astor Library—and, for that matter, all large libraries at such a time is a rather dismal place, and suggests, unpleasantly enough, to any one who may be there alone, Hood's lines:

"O'er all there hung a shadow and a fear,
A sense of mystery the spirited daunted,
Which said, as plain as whisper in the ear,
The place is haunted."

It was at such a time, in such a place, and to one lonely explorer, that the ghost of the Astor Library appeared.

To understand the circumstances of this remarkable apparition the more fully, the reader should remember that Dr. Cogswell, the efficient librarian, has been for some time engaged in the compilation of a complete catalogue of the library. Although over a year since it was commenced, the work has only reached to the letter P. Dr. Cogswell is an unmarried man, and occupies a sleeping apartment in the upper part of the library, the janitor residing in the basement. It is the rule of the library to dismiss visitors at sunset, and during the evening and night no individual besides Dr. Cogswell and the janitor and his family remain in the building.

Against the advice of his friends, Dr. Cogswell devotes hours of night that should be given to repose, to the pursuance of his work on the catalogue. Naturally anxious to hasten forward its completion, and fired with all the enthusiasm of a professed bibliopole, his labors in this tedious and difficult task are almost incredible. At the same time the work is of that dry, statistical character, which is by no means suggestive of fanciful apparitions, nor is the indefatigable compiler a man easily swayed by the passing delusions of the eye or brain.

Some two weeks ago Dr. Cogswell was at work as usual on the catalogue. It was about eleven o'clock at night, and having occasion to refer to some books in a distant part of the library, he left his desk, took his candle, and, as he had often done before, pursued his course among the winding passages toward the desired spot. But before reaching it, while in an alcove in the southwest part of the older portion of the building, he was startled by seeing a man respectably dressed in citizen's clothes, surveying a shelf of books. The doctor supposed it to be a robber who had secreted himself for the purpose of abstracting some of the valuable works in the library; after stepping back behind a partition for a moment, he again moved cautiously forward, to catch a glimpse of the individual's face, when to his surprise he recognized in the supposed robber the features of a physician (whose name we forbear giving) who had lived in the immediate vicinity of the library, and who had died some six weeks ago! It should be borne in mind that this deceased person was a mere casual acquaintance of Dr. Cogswell, not an intimate friend, and since his death Dr. Cogswell had not thought of him.

But the apparition was in the presence of a man not easily scared. The librarian, so far from fainting or shrieking, as might reasonably be expected, calmly addressed the ghost:

"Dr.——," said he," you seldom, if ever, visited this Library while living. Why do you trouble us now when dead?"

Perhaps the ghost did not like the sound of the human voice; anyway it gave no answer, but disappeared.

The next day Mr. Cogswell thought over the matter, attributed it to some optical delusion, and in the evening proceeded with his work as usual. Again he wished to refer to some books, and again visited the southwestern alcove. There again, as large as life, was the ghost, very calmly and placidly surveying the shelves. Mr. Cogswell again spoke to it:

"Dr. ," said he, "again I ask you, why you who never visited the Library while living, trouble it now when dead?"

Again the ghost vanished, and the undaunted librarian pursued his task without interruption. The next day he examined the shelves before which the apparition had been standing, and by a singular coincidence found that they were filled with books devoted to demonology, witchcraft, magic, spiritualism, etc. Some of these books are rare tomes, several centuries old, written in Latin, illustrated with quaint diagrams, and redolent of mysticism; while on the next shelves are their younger brethren, the neat spruce works of modern spiritualists, of Brittan, Davis, Edmonds, and others. The very titles on these mystic books are suggestive. There are the Prophecies or Prognostications of Michael Nostrademus, a folio published in London in 1672; Albamasar de Conjectionibus; Kerner's Majikon; Godwin's Lives of the Necromancers; Glanvil on Witches and Apparitions; Cornelius Agrippa; Bodin's Demonomania; Lilly's Astrology, and others, a perusal of any of which would effectually murder the sleep of a person of ordinary nerve for at least half a dozen nights. It was these volumes that appeared to attract the apparition.

The third night, Mr. Cogswell, still determined that the shade, spirit, delusion, or effect of indigestion—whatever it might be—should not interfere with his duties, again visited the various books to which he wished to refer, and when occasion demanded, did not fail to approach the mystic alcove. There again was the apparition, dressed precisely as before, in a gentleman's usual costume, as natural as life, and with a hand raised, as if about to take down a book. Mr. Cogswell again spoke—

"Dr.——," he said boldly. "This is the third time I have met you. Tell me if any of this class of books now disturb you? If they do, I will have them removed."

But the ungrateful ghost, without acknowledging this accommodating spirit on the part of its interrogator, disappeared. Nor has it been seen since, and the librarian has continued his nightly researches since without interruption.

A few days ago, at a dinner party at the house of a well-known wealthy gentleman, Mr. Cogswell related the circumstances as above recorded, as nearly as we can learn. As some eighteen or twenty people were present, the remarkable story of course was soon spread about. A number of literary men, including an eminent historian and others, heard the recital, and though they attribute Mr. Cogswell's ghost-seeing to the strain and tension of his nerves during his too protracted labors at the catalogue, they yet confess that the story has its remarkable phases. Both Mr. Cogswell and the deceased physician were persons of a practical turn of mind, and always treated the marvellous ghost-stories sometimes set afloat with deserved contempt. And, as they were not at all intimate, it will be at least a curious question for the psychologist to determine, why the idea of this deceased gentleman should come to Mr. Cogswell's brain and resolve itself into an apparition, when engaged in dry, statistical labors, which should effectually banish all thoughts of the marvellous.

Acting on the advice of several friends, Mr. Cogswell is now absent on a short trip to Charleston, to recuperate his energies. His indefatigable industry, his devotion to the interests of the Library, and his great efficiency as a librarian, render it highly desirable that he should enjoy recreation and repose, and not endanger his health by a too close application to his duties. In regard to the apparition we will make no comments, but give the story as related, by Dr. Cogswell, as we are credibly informed, and as it has already been talked about in various literary and domestic circles in this city.

The N. Y. Saturday Press.

HENRY CLAPP, Jr., Editor.

NEW YORK MARCH 24, 1860

[For The New York Saturday Press.]

A FATAL LOVE.

BY ADA CLARE.

Henri Ernstein had been a resident of Paris but a few weeks, so it was not singular that the day on which our story opens, he should have lost his way in that great and universal metropolis. Henri's residence was in the Rue de Berri, and after walking all day, and wearying himself more than he cared to acknowledge, he arrived by a description of the most extraordinary circles, at the Church of 'Notre Dame de Lorette.' He had that repugnance to asking his way, which all persons feel in a strange town. Moreover, being far from an adept in the French language, he shrank from encountering that insulting pity which the Frenchman always wears in his face when a question is addressed to him in imperfect French. He did not know where a carriage could be obtained, and though omnibuses were continually passing him, he had no clue to their destinations. One of them, in dull red letters made the direful proposition of whirling him to the 'Barrière de l'Enfer,' while another, in cheerful green, assured him an immediate passage to Mont Parnasse. As Henri was not a poet, neither of these offers tempted him; besides, the arresting of a French omnibus is a matter of great boldness, perseverance, address.

Just as he was nearing the church, he became aware of the fact that some ceremonial was taking place within, so he concluded to enter, as much with a view of witnessing that ceremonial, as of resting himself after his weary walk.

He soon perceived that a number of young girls and boys were receiving their first communion. He had hardly taken his seat before his attention was arrested by a face whose extreme loveliness was heightened by the freshness of extreme youth. It was sometime ere he began to notice her dress, but when he did, he perceived that though very neat and very tasteful, it denoted respectable poverty.

While he was thus intently gazing at her, she turned her face suddenly, and their eyes met. A look of curiosity, of surprise, deepened the expression of her face, while his was suffused with a blush of confusion.

Just at the moment that the full beauty of her face was turned upon him, a sudden sensation as of memory struck sharp against a foreknowledge of the future, smote across his soul with a thrill of undertoned and mysterious pain. In the events of his after life, he had cause to look back upon that sensation, with most bitter remembering.

When the ceremony of the communion was over, Henri followed mechanically in the steps of those who were leaving the church, and began to walk listlessly down the 'Rue Laffitte.' As he was thus walking and musing, he came into violent contact with the slight figure of a woman, who was leading by the hand a little girl, clothed in white, who had evidently been one of the juvenile communicants. To Henri's entreaties for forgiveness a face was turned, and it was the face that had caught his attention in the church.

After a dozen assurances on his part that it was accidental, and on hers that Monsieur would do her a favor not to speak of it, it occurred to Henri that he might prolong the conversation by inquiring his way. "Would Mademoiselle have the kindness to inform me in which direction lies the 'Rue de Berri?'

"O, Monsieur is very far from it, very far, indeed."

"Of whom, then, should I ask my way, or how best should I get home without being laughed at ?"

"Monsieur is afraid of being laughed at! Well, it is hardly so far, after all, and if Monsieur will accept my guidance, I will offer to conduct him, as I am going in that direction myself."

Henri, though astonished at this confidence in a stranger, so rare in a French girl, accepted her escort with delight.

As they walked slowly along, Henri's admiration for her beauty was vastly heightened by the charm of her easy, simple, and modest conversation. She informed him that the young communicant was her little sister Julie, that her intelligence was of that rare and wondrous kind which every child has been supposed to possess. That her own name was Hortense Desiré, and that her mother and herself, though in receipt of a small income, added to it by embroidering for a fancy store. That they lived in the Rue de Fauburg St. Honoré,' on the fourth floor, and that they cultivated two roses and a honeysuckle, which were placed in that window where the sun shone in the morning.

As they approached the neighborhood in which Mademoiselle Hortense lived, the young lady was suddenly seized with the fear that her mamma would upbraid her for allowing a strange gentleman to walk home with her. After much discussion it was agreed that Henri should go home with her, and plead his own cause with the terrible mamma. At any rate Miss Hortense remarked, with the loveliest glow of kindness on her innocent face, that she should have the satisfaction of having been of service to a gentleman in distress, even if her mother refused to be appeased.

When on reaching the very door of the young lady's apartment, and the sound of footsteps announced that it was about to be opened, Henri's heart began to beat heavily in expectation of beholding a very formidable personage. To his surprise a still young woman appeared, whose personal beauty was very rare indeed, and whose dainty little person was set off to the best advantage by that exquisite French taste which beautifies everything it touches. Henri scarcely knew which to admire most, the mature beauty of the mother, or the half-blown loveliness of the daughter.

As soon as they had entered into the little parlor, Henri began to make an elaborate explanation. But what with nervousness, confusion, and very unsteady French, he had a melancholy time of it, for after the anguish of much speaking, Madame did not understand that he had been lost, but supposed him to be discoursing in a remarkable manner on partridges. Here Hortense came to his aid, and explained the adventure to her mother. Madame did not seem inexorable; in fact she did not seem offended at all. Indeed such was the courtesy with which Henri was treated, that he soon found himself sufficiently assured to ask as an extreme favor that Madame would allow him to conduct herself and daughters to the theatre the following night.

At this proposition, Mademoiselle Julie went off into convulsions of rapture, and Mademoiselle Hortense was artless enough to clasp her arms about her mother's neck, and press two warm kisses on her fair cheek. This silent appeal seemed to set at rest the mother's uncertainty, and she accepted his invitation with great graciousness.

Henri, on rising to go, was about to hand his card to Madame, but on a second and an evil thought, he concluded to give her an assumed name. So he took out a blank card, wrote Carl Sontag upon it, and handed it to her. She received it with a smile, and after making the most respectful adieu, and assuring her that he would find his way home from that neighborhood, he descended into the street below.

His first emotion on leaving the house was self-congratulation at having encountered so charming a family. After this he had time to think over the personal beauty of Hortense. He remembered with a troubled heart the mass of her light brown hair, thrown off from her white brow, the graceful turn of the fair throat, and the tender earnestness of her large brown eyes, which seemed to have far down beneath their surface a deep and changeless melancholy. Her voice, too, he thought was destitute of that levity generally found in young French girls; nay, when she spoke it seemed to have a refrain, which echoed its way far down into the deeps of a yearning and ardent heart. Henri mentally determined to make any self-sacrifice, rather than disturb the peace of such a loving and gentle creature.

The next evening he was faithful to his appointment, and found the three ladies in the wildest flutter of expectation. The theatre he had chosen was the 'Vaudeville,' and the play that drama of adorable comicality 'Les Faux Bonshommes.' Henri thought that one set of human beings had never given another such extreme entertainment, as the enactors of that piece did to the members of his little party.

Julie could hardly be persuaded to leave the theatre until Henri promised her the pleasure of seeing another play at no distant time.

During the course of that evening he engaged the services of Hortense as an instructor in French, and it was settled that he should go every day at a certain hour, to receive her instructions. Henri had come to Paris with the ostensible purpose of studying medicine, but his conscience was easily persuaded that he must first study French.

Several weeks passed away and his improvement in the language was so wonderful, that he was enabled without much suffering to converse for hours with Hortense. In the meanwhile he continued most profusely in his civilities to the family, until the heart of mother and sister were completely won.

One night, about five weeks after the commencement of his acquaintance, he obtained a stage-box at the 'Ambigu-Comique,' and invited Madame and her daughters to go there with him to see the play of 'Benvenuto Cellina.' His invitation was of course accepted, and great joy was expressed that they were to be refreshed with pathos instead of comedy that night.

Henri thought he detected in Hortense a look of languor if not of suffering; that she was sad he was certain, for at every plaintive strain in the drama, he saw a heavy tear gather on her eyelash, ere she brushed it hastily away. There is a heart-rending scene in this play, where the heroine grieves over a disappointed love. At this point our poor little Hortense immediately dropped her head in her hands, and broke into piteous sobbings. It was some minutes ere her agitation could be soothed; then she calmed the anxious solicitations of her mother by assuring her that it was the heat, the closeness of the theatre, the interest of the play, a headache, etc. But Henri was not so easily convinced. A joyous suspicion of the real cause of her emotion flashed across his mind. "I am loved," he said as he watched the trembling of her mouth, and saw the eyes, still filled with tears, avoiding his own. He dropped his hand at his side to seek for hers, and when he found it, it just fluttered for a moment in his, then was still.

The following day he called upon her at an hour when he knew her mother and sister would be absent, determined to offer her his hand and heart. Hortense was alone looking very pale, but to his surprise her eyes met his with pure confidence, without a trace of embarrassment, and the roses in her cheek did not gather the faintest blush upon their whiteness. That their faith was plighted the one to the other each of them felt, as also that the time was come for mutual vows of love, yet neither of them evinced the least shadow of agitation.

When he had told her of his love, of his desire to unite his fate with her for all time, her lips and eyelids just trembled a little, then she came frankly to him, sat close beside him on the sofa, and dropped her white face on his shoulder. He put his arm very softly about her, and gazed gently down into the still, sad eyes that looked so calmly and honestly up into his. They say that the drowning man in those few moments in which the soul is toiling out of the body, sees the whole record of his past, blazing in fiery characters before him. So in this moment when Henri's former levity of character was being drowned out of him, he saw all the sad and emotional events of his life irradiated with the melancholy light of pathos, shining clear before him. Troubled with these emotions he bent over and pressed the first kiss of love on her lips—the kiss without passion of a love that knew no tumult.

From that day all gaiety dropped like a veil from the face and heart of Hortense, leaving them shrouded in a dead, grave calm. She moved about the house a still spirit, performing every duty, ever ready to minister to each want and desire of mother and sister, but the resigned, sober look never brightened in her eyes, the fixed trouble never melted into smiles on her mouth. Mamma at first teazed, then remonstrated, then grieved, but all in vain. Finally she concluded that nothing would restore her to herself, but union with the man who held her heart, and for that she must patiently wait.

As soon as Hortense's approval was obtained, Henri wrote to his father, stating the case simply and truly, and entreating his consent to marry, at the same time fully determined to do so, whatever answer he might receive.

Ten days passed away without a word from his father, until one morning just as he was about to go out for his breakfast, a heavy knock came on the door, which proved to be from the hand of that gentleman himself.

Henri's father did not appear to have seen thirty-five Winters, but the fact was that forty-two Summers had offered him their shining fruits and flowers. His type was different, in fact antagonistic to that of Henri, for he had large black eyes, and a bright, dark complexion. Altogether, most persons would have considered him the perfection of mature, manly beauty. The first glance at him convinced Henri that his consent was granted, that he had come to make it the more sure by giving it in person, so he greeted him with a long, affectionate embrace.

As soon as they had breakfasted together, Ernstein senior proposed going at once to the residence of his future daughter. As they walked along, Henri told his father how fearful he had been that the marriage would have been forbidden him on account of the lady's inferiority in point of station and fortune. Then his father told him that as soon as the opportunity offered itself, he would relate to him a story of his own early life, which would prove the folly and the madness of such worldly pride.

"I came here in person, my son," he said, "in order to prove to thee how much I honored thy manly and unselfish conduct. I am proud of thee, that thou couldst not win and then throw aside a loving and innocent heart. Ah! if thy father had been so wise—but I will tell thee all to-night. Now I must think of happier things, in order to welcome most heartily thy fair bride.

It occurred to Henri only as they were ascending the stairs, that his father was unacquainted with the name of his love. At this additional proof of confidence in himself, he only felt the more happy and grateful. The bell was answered by Julie, and her they followed into the parlor. In a few minutes Madame entered, with her violet eyes drowned in smiles, and her glowing cheeks seeming to stain the air about her with rich color.

As soon as she perceived Henri's father, the violets in her eyes and the roses on her cheeks seemed smitten with a deadly, blasting frost. He was equally changed and agitated by her presence, and 'Vivienne!' and 'Henri !' broke mutually from their lips. In another moment he was holding her close in his arms, and she was clinging passionately to his breast.

Henri was only aroused from the overwhelming astonishment into which this scene had thrown him, by hearing in a heart-rending voice––'O my God, I have loved my brother.' She knew it all, the supernal instinct of despair laid the whole story at once naked before her eyes. None had noticed that she had followed her mother immediately into the room.

Henri turned and saw her standing there rigid and motionless like death wrought out in the whiteness of marble. At a glance he took in the dreadful pallor of her face, the infinite grief in her wide eyes, the throes of her white and shapeless lips. He would have caught her in his arms, but she shudderingly waved him off, then said in measured, low voice, "My father, why have you mercilessly abandoned your child, and left her to die thus of grief and shame?"

"O my daughter, my little Hortense, can you not forgive your father? Believe he has expiated his crime in much suffering. But now that he has found you, he will cherish you as the chief treasure of life. If you have lost a husband, you have found a father and a brother, I a wife and a daughter. Will you not come to these arms, where as a tender, lisping infant you have so often been hushed to sleep. Will you not come to my heart?"

"Nay, nay," she said; "I have nought to do with living hearts, for mine is fainting away to death. Not in thine either, mother; nor in thine, Henri : you three have combined to ruin and kill me;—are you satisfied? Why, my mother, did you not confide to me the history of my birth, and of my father! And why, Henri, have you given me a name that cannot have been your own!

Henri hung his head in shame, and knew not what to reply.

"Three of you united in deception to break my heart! O, why had I not instinct to know you were my brother? Now I cannot be your sister—I am bowed with shame. Come hither, little Julie; thou hast never wronged me: come hither, and let thy sister look on one loving face ere she drops into the dark gulf of death."

Her whole body fell back in a heap on the chair; the agonistic struggling of remorse and despair seemed to have broken up the central point on which turned vital power of resistance, and blotted her pure and perfect face into a white and shapeless mass.

At the entreaty of her mother, Henri was led away by the elder Ernstein, in the belief that her agitation could never be soothed in his presence.

As they rode home, his father related to him the story of his own youth. How after the death of Henri's mother, he had sought distraction in the gay metropolis of Paris; how he had there loved and wedded Vivienne Desiré; how he had feared to acknowledge the unequal marriage to his father; how he had abandoned Vivienne when Hortense, or Henriette as she was then called, was a yearling baby; and how he had so arranged his affairs that a small income should fall annually into the hands of the mother—enough at least to secure her from want.

Henri told his father how, in the mutual love of Hortense and himself, there had never been any affection that might not have subsisted between brother and sister, upon which purity of affection he grounded his hope that Hortense world soon be able to see in him a dear brother, in which light he was already able to view her.

That evening Henri, at the request of his father, remained at home, while the latter went to ascertain the state of the daughter's health and the mother's mind. Vivienne Desiré received him with frigidity, did not even offer him her hand, and remained standing while she spoke to him.

"I have come to ask of your—of our daughter, Vivienne, how is she?"

"My daughter, sir, is very faint and ill, and needs at the moment my care."

"Vivienne, there was a time when you did not call me sir. Will you not listen to me kindly for a few moments?"

She bowed her head. "Vivienne, you know that I did once love you, that I left you with regret; but you do not know what I have suffered for the crime of deserting you. You do not know that your image has ever been at the inmost core of my heart. That I vainly sought for you several years past, when you were probably not in this city. That at any moment, in those long, weary years since we parted, I fondly desired to acknowledge you as my honored wife. Learn, then, that I love you still; that I now humbly implore you to take that place in my heart and home which you have so long been denied." She bowed her head lower still. "I know, dearest Vivienne, that while I have been growing an older and a graver man, you have been only perfecting your mature and glowing beauty. But for the sake of our old love, of our child, will you not strive to restore me the heart I so little merit ?"

By this time her head drooped heavily on her breast, and he heard the faint sound of sobs growing thicker as he listened. Is it necessary to say that these two hearts closed together in one life again? Could any woman that remembers, and loves, and is entreated, be inexorable? I think not; nay, I know not.

Hour after hour flew by, while these two, folded in each other's arms, exchanged their mutual loves and Vows, wandered in sorrowful tenderness to the distant past, and planned a faithful and inseparable future. It was near midnight before he thought of the son he had left at home, or she of the heart-wounded daughter who lay hushed in grief so near her. Her memory returned to her with the sound of a deep moan, at which she started, and immediately disappeared from the room. In a moment she returned to say that her daughter was nervous and suffering, and begged that he would leave her for the night.

The following day the father and son arrived early at the apartment of Madame Desiré, who from that day, was to assume the name of Ernstein, which legally belonged to her. They found Hortense reclining upon a sofa, with her mother seated beside her. At their entrance the latter greeted them with bright smiles, but the former, lying motionless on her sofa, answered their anxious inquiries after her health, with mournful face and subdued voice. All their efforts to interest and distract her mind were equally futile. The same dry eyes and white face were hers at last as at first. She had formerly been very fond of flowers, but now the rare and fragrant cluster of them that Henri placed in her hand, was pressed for a moment to her sighing lips, then it fluttered down from her wan fingers and was forgotten.

Day after day they strove to break the toils of this deep dejection in which her soul was caught, but that soul was torn with the pangs of remorse, and utterly refused to be comforted. She said she desired only to lapse into the sleep of death. She prayed that they would make her a grave far away from Paris, in the quiet, peaceful earth, where the sound of the world's storm-tost life would to her be mute, where nature would wrap her in its green mantle of peacefulness, and those perennial wild flowers that smile up in the austere eye of Winter would flush over her the glory of their crimson immortality.

As hour after hour dropped slowly and blankly off into the past, her heart grew sadder and heavier. No eloquence of appeal or cunningness of logic could convince her that she had not sinned. Her heart wore itself away with weeping for the guilt, which she believed to be equal to her woe. This pure and divine creature persisted ever in stripping off the white robes of an angel, in which heaven and the goodness of her own heart had clothed her, to shroud herself in the solemn blackness of despair and death.

Vivienne Ernstein and her husband finally became convinced that the heart of her life was stricken, and that its life-blood was ebbing away drop by drop, pang by pang, grief by grief. They then concluded that the only chance of life she had, was in being removed from the presence of familiar scenes and faces, as well as from the presence of Henri. It was arranged between them that they should secretly prepare to leave for Germany, without the knowledge of Henri, lest he should insist upon accompanying them. The day for their departure was fixed for one on which the young man should necessarily be absent from Paris.

On that day accordingly, the three set forth in a capacious travelling carriage, as it was proposed to take the journey in short and easy stages. Hortense neither resisted nor questioned when she was made ready for the journey, but submitted with a patient and touching listlessness. When they placed her in the carriage she neither spoke of, nor appeared to remember Henri. She seemed locked in the jaws of a ghastly and treacherous calm, and gave no sign of vitality except the stertorous breathing and slow pulsations of sick life.

That evening, Henri having accomplished his business sooner than he intended, returned to the city at once. On arriving at his lodgings he was astounded to find a note from his father, announcing his departure with his wife and daughter. Henri flew to the residence of Hortense, and learned from the concierge that they had left in a carriage some hours before; that is to say, Madame and her daughter had been taken away in the carriage,—Julie had been placed in a school that very day. Fortunately she was able to inform him exactly of the road they had taken, and with this information he determined to follow them.

He was able to find a horse at a neighboring stable, and deeming that to be the quickest manner of overtaking them, he mounted it and rode forth without delay.

It was now about dusk of a sombre evening in Autumn. The leaves swam and tottered about on the waves of a heavy, rolling wind. There was an oppressiveness in the air that betokens the coming of a storm, and it seemed to intensify the presentiment of evil within him. A sense of loneliness hung dull about him, and with it a host of thronging thoughts and memories rushed to his mind, mixed with great bitterness and pain. He was torn with regrets, troubled with the melancholy storm-atmosphere, as he listened to the heavy beatings of his sick heart, each little pulse rolling heavily off from it, and leaving it the sadder for its flight. Faster and thicker the leaves swirled about him, and plainer and deeper grew the evil foreboding within.

After several hour's hard riding, Henri thought he distinguished the dark outline of a carriage in the road before him. At this sight he urged his horse on to its utmost speed, and in a few moments he found that he was gaining fast upon it. At last he was near enough to cry out to them to stop, and in another moment he was at the window of the carriage, and could plainly see by the wan, cold light of the moon, his father and Vivienne sitting close and lovingly together, while Hortense was supported with pillows on the front seat. In another moment he had sprang into the carriage. "Hortense," he whispered, but there was no answer.

"I think," said his father, "that she sleeps; it is now several hours since she has spoken. My Vivienne and I have whispered in order not to disturb her."

"How was she, sir, when you left Paris?"

"She was very calm and silent, and has not spoken at all except in faint replies to her mother. Since that time she has sighed many times, but for the last two hours has been quite still. So we sat very close, and whispered softly in order not to awaken her."

"Has she seemed more ill to-day than usual?"

"Yes, much weaker, but we must not despond; time and new scenes will renew her strength and life. Nothing that love or wealth can do shall be spared in brightening her future. Her wishes shall be germs out of which full-timed fruit shall ever grow. I know the red roses will blush and blow again in her sweet lips and cheeks, and her eyes, like the pure heaven, shall show shining stars in their deeps. My sweet little daughter has done with sorrow and trial now."

"She seems to lie stiffly, sir; had I not better place her head gently on my shoulder? O father, O my father! I cannot bend her form—It is stiff and cold like marble." Both mother and fathers now sprang forward and caught her hands in theirs, the mother with an awfully tragic cry of grief and fear.

"O father, O mother! her throat, her face, her lips are cold and still. No breath comes from her mouth. Quick! a light; we may revive her. O Hortense ! O my sweet sister! O my soul !"

The elder Ernstein struck a light with much difficulty, his agitation causing his hands to tremble and quiver so. Finally he succeeded in lighting a carriage-lamp and holding it before the face of the girl.

Alas me! what a sight it shone upon! Closed eyes, and white lips, and ashen face, and drooping, patient palms! Vain the chafing of the poor hands, vain, vain the cherishing of the pale cheek, vain the agonized breathing into the still lips. No warmth, no motion, no life there. Vain the cries of the mother, the remorse of the father, the pleadings for forgiveness of the brother. All calm, and pure, and silent there. Yet all that look of pain and doubt had faded from her features. No more self-torture, no more breaking of heart, every fixed lineament of her pure and placid face spoke eloquently of peace, and hope, and joy. The shadow of light had fallen upon her face, lifting it to the saint's look of glorified calm; Death had branded it in forever.

HAWTHORNE.

The senile editor of *The Sunday Courier* is after us with solicitude and a sharp stick. Being troubled in his mind with the belief that we have made a blunder, he comes to our rescue with the following benevolent paragraph:

> A Slight Mistake.—Our youthful and inexperienced cotemporary, the Saturday Press, says, in speaking of the Marble Faun :
>
> "Previous to the publication of The Scarlet Letter,' no American author was so little known as Hawthorne."
>
> Such a singular error as this would have been made only by one so young. Previous to the publication of the Scarlet Letter there was hardly an American author more widely known, at least among American readers, than Hawthorne. He had been an active and popular contributor to the magazines, before the publication of the Scarlet Letter, some twenty years, and his 'Mosses from an Old Manse,' had rendered his name almost as familiar in England as that of Washington Irving.

It is rather a trivial matter to discuss, but, out of kindness for the senile person aforesaid, we will endeavor to soothe his troubled spirit by showing that we have made no mistake at all.

The character of Hawthorne's writings,—which address themselves peculiarly and exclusively to imaginative and cultivated minds, —Is such as arbitrarily precludes their popularity. Accordingly Hawthorne never was, is not now, and probably never will be a popular writer. This is rather creditable than otherwise to him. When Cobb stars are in the ascendant, it is "better to err with Pope than shine with Pye."

'The Scarlet Letter' it was that first made the name of Hawthorne a golden word. From the time when that book appeared, his audience has been increasing. But the established facts regarding his literary career, amply prove that he was scarcely known at all prior to its publication. His first book was a romance, published anonymously, at Boston, in 1832. The first series of "Twice-Told Tales' appeared in 1837. They were collected from Magazines. It was five years before the second series appeared, in 1842. In 1845 was published the 'Journal of an African Cruiser,' which Hawthorne edited from the MSS. of Lieutenant Bridge. In 1846, he made and issued a third collection of Magazine papers, entitled 'Mosses from an Old Manse.' The book was attractive to a few cultivated people, but it did not pass to a second edition till eight years after its first publication. It was in 1846, also, that Hawthorne accepted the office of Surveyor in the Custom House at Salem. In 1850 he published 'The Scarlet Letter,' and immediately his books began to be more widely sold, circulated, and read. 'The House of Seven Gables' appeared in 1851, and in 1852 'The Blithedale Romance.' It does not seem, however, that his literary success was very satisfactory, for in the same year he wrote the Life of Pierce,—between which performance and his subsequent appointment to the Consulship of Liverpool, the connection cannot be altogether obscure, even to the logical perception of the senile editor.

[For The New York Saturday Press.]

A MEMORY.

Black rains of March, that fall and sob
  All the long night, upon my roof,
Fall soft, sob low, where thy drops throb
  Over the heart that lies aloof
From Time, that every living heart doth rob.

How many times, O muttering rains
  That haunt the Spring's returning feet,—
How many times have your refrains
  Wakened my heart to memories sweet,
Since hers was shut, to all Life's loves and pains?

I would not count the years. New Springs
  Have laughed, and wept, and died, like her,
Since I last saw the amber rings
  Of her long hair, or felt the stir
Of her warm breath, like Summer's balm-bathed wings.

And the Spring comes again; I know
  That all the paths we trod of old
Are slowly growing green, where blow
  The southland winds, and from the mould
In woods still bare, some hardy violets grow;

The robin folds his wings of dun,
  And doubtful, trills his happy notes;
And glittering in the noonday sun,
  The bee, impatient, hums and floats,
And the tall lilac's buds swell one by one.

But in the black March night, the rain
  Lies on my threshold, and on hers;
And with a weird and ghastly pain
  That holds my heart, and sleep defers,
Shivering I watch for dawn to come again.

Juliette H. Beach.

Albion, N. Y.

Thoughts and Things.

BY ADA CLARE

'Against Wind and Tide' will be indeed valuable to the genuine novel-reader—the gentle old maid of village locality for instance, devoted to charity and the circulating library. The plot is so complicated and involves so many little interplots, that it is impossible to keep any lookout for the coming sea, or rather, event. Modern novels are so transparent in plot and character, that it is often easy from the first chapter to look straight through to the harbor attained in the last. There is much vigor of treatment as well as ingeniousness of plot, in this book.

°°°

Friendship is a scandalously ill-used term and sentiment. Most people of a canting turn, when annoying and injuring those in any way placed in their power, do it under the name of friendship. Most of us remember when our aunts, guardians, or teachers, marred our most innocent pleasure under the proclamation that they were our best friends. In those moments, I, for one, would gladly have exchanged them for enemies.

Friendship, according to the notion of some people, consists in seizing hold upon human beings, prying into their affairs, teazing them with advice, undoing their surest plans for happiness, insulting them with censure, and then at the slightest revolt from this detestable impertinence, turning upon them with the worst malignity.

Friendship for any being is not a system of espionage and dictation: it is the acceptance of the individual through whatever errors he may fall into. The false, pompous friend, insists that his views be adopted by his friend; any dissention in feeling he regards as ingratitude; while the true one loves to see him treading freely in the ways of his own nature, knowing that the bond of friendship is not to be broken by the swayings of an opposing wind. If friendship—the purest of human sentiments—can make no sacrifices to differences of opinion, of belief, of action, it had better resign its high estate; for the exigences of trade, of society, of mere animal life, even, can make such sacrifices easy.

I am not in favor of much self-sacrifice in this world; that is not what I demand in friendship. For those who wilfully, continually, and usefully sacrifice themselves for others, I feel a sincere respect, but I always avoid them; they are doomed beings, and no good can come of them. It is a sort of contemptuous respect, too, that we feel for them; the only dignified self-sacrifice is that for those who are dearer than ourselves.

If friendship is a censorship, an inquisitorial tribune, let it be reduced to a legal system at once, where at least it will be restrained within the bounds of ordinary decency.

It is a sad illustration of how far prejudice and selfishness can go, to see those who have been bound together by the nearest ties of blood and interest, turning with cold maliciousness upon one of them who has slid away from their routine of thinking, even. These, as friends, feel themselves justified in persecuting the apostate in a manner that enemies would blush to employ. Perhaps this is the reason why most persons of deep thought and marked character find it impossible to assimilate with their own relatives, not distinguished for those qualities. These friends have the means, as well as the faculty, of wounding your feelings and violating your belief to an extent of which the scandal-loving heartless public fall far short. This is not much to be wondered at, it is the effect of an inverted interest. With the world success always succeeds; one's relations are always most bitter when one succeeds in a way they disapprove of.

But this is not friendship; to a friend we should feel the power to tear off the mask which the world forces us to wear; to untie our hearts and let them loose in the friend's heart; to confess there all our deep disquiet, our doubts, our scorn of ourselves, our slipping down from our ideals, and there to receive the sweet absolution of sympathy.

This, it seems to me, is something higher than the friendship which is founded upon living in the same street, having the same tailor, holding the same notions, eating the same victuals.

[For The New York Saturday Press.]

VAGARY.

BY W. D. HOWELLS.

Up and down the dusty street,
I hurry with my burning feet—
Against my face the weird waves beat,
Fierce from the city-sea of heat.
Deep in my heart the vision is,
Of meadow grass and meadow trees,
Blown silver in the Summer breeze—
And ripe red hillside strawberries.

My sense the city tumult fills,—
The tumult that about me reels
Of strokes and cries, and feet and wheels.
Deep in my dream I list, and, hark!
From out the maple's leafy dark,
The fluttering of the meadow lark!

About the thronged street I go—
There is no face here that I know;
Of all that pass me to and fro
There is no face here that I know.
Deep in my soul's most sacred place
With a sweet pain I look and trace
The features of a tender face,
All lit with love and girlish grace.

Some spell is on me, for I seem
A memory of the past, a dream
Of happiness remembered dim,
Unto myself that walk the street
Scathed with the city's noontide heat,
With puzzled brain and burning feet.

Dramatic Feuilleton.

Faits Divers.

Your entertaining contemporary the *Courrier des Etats Unis* annihilates the Subscriber because he did not appreciate *Diane de Lys*. I called it one of the adulterated plays, mourning that it was a specimen of those lively Gallic concoctions which depend for their interest upon the breach of the Seventh Commandment. *The Courrier* translates adulterate literally, thus, *falsifiée*, and declares that I have charged the author with falsifying French manners and morals. No such thing. It is all right. No more exact picture of French life could be given than in plays like *Diane*. There, now, will that do? And won't you take back all the hard things you have said about me? I really am not used to sulphuric acid, and it hurts my feelings awfully.

Mrs. John Thalia Wood and Colonel A. H. Davenport sailed for Savannah, en route for New Orleans, on Tuesday. The jeunesse dorée were out in full force, and the artists went off under hearty salutes from cheers and Champagne corks. The lady looked as charmingly as ever.

I have been and gone and done C. Gayler's *Poor Young Man*, so I hope that that distinguished American author will smooth his wrinkled front. The burlesque is cleverly put together, and some of the characters are exceedingly well acted. Mr. Nagle, who did the *Young Man,* had a capital make-up for Lester, but his performance reminded me more of James Wallack jeune, than of his cousin.

It was exceedingly good. Then Miss Kate Singleton was a fair copy of the irresistible Mary Gannon, though not so funny. It is very hard to burlesque a caricature. Mrs. C. Howard played *Marguerite* with some dash, but was a little hard at times. Mrs. Eckhardt (who is she?) was *Helouin*; she is a fair actress, and an exceedingly good singer. The weak point in the affair was a swell young man, who looked like an ex 'Ethiopian delineator,' gotten up for a bal paré by the M'Gillicuddy Musketeers. The play went off trippingly, and is certainly very entertaining. Audience limited, chiefly Peoria and Orange.

Two of the Broadway Theatres will be wearing the green next week. Why this sudden outbreak of Hi bernianism I know not. Once when there was a great dinner at Stratford-upon-Avon, in honor of the divine Williams's birthday, Archy was called upon, at a very late hour, for a toast. He had been in the Vice-Chair, and had sent three county magistrates, two clergymen, and half a dozen ensigns of militia to bed. Getting on his feet with some difficulty, the Commodore gave 'The Bards of Ireland.' Very good, said everybody, but why? 'Never mind,' was the reply. 'I don't know; settle it among yourselves.' So we will have Archy's toast next week. Mr. Boucicault announces his work thus "An entirely new Irish Drama, in three acts, written by Dion Boucicault, illustrative of Irish Character, Irish Hearts, and Irish Homes, entitled the Colleen Bawn; or, The Brides of Garryowen, is in active preparation. New music, introducing Irish melodies, by Thomas Baker. of Killarney, MacGillicuddy's Reeks,, Limerick City, The Shores of the Shannon."

Mr. Barney Williams, who evidently thinks that D. B. is poaching on his private manor, announces at Niblo's, "a beautiful Irish Drama, entitled Willie Riley, or Not Guilty, a Tale of Munster, etc. Among the local scenery of this piece, will be represented a truthful picture of the Cork River, and Blackrock Castle, above the Glenmire Road; the Cove of Cork, above Queenstown; Carlisle Bridge and Sackville street, Dublin."

The Williams piece was 'originally written by the author of *The Painter of Brienne'* (whoever he was), and has been re-written by H. G. Plunkett, who is lineally descended from several of the Kings of Munster, and wrote the whole of *Punch* for a number of years. He is first cousin to Dr. Mackenzie, and distantly connected with Burke, generally called the Sublime. If any man can write an Irish play, he can.

The *Sonneur de St. Paul* was announced at the French Theatre, for Thursday of this week. As I always attend to pleasure before business, I went to dine with the St. George's Cricket Club, and let the Gauls slide.

Doctor Schute & Co. have opened a German Theatre on the off nights of the Français. They have Fallenbach, who is a very good actor, and the Fraulein Grahn, who slays Teutonic hearts by the score, and they expect to make a good thing out of it. Very doubtful. of it. Very doubtful.

The Teuton keeps a mighty sharp look-out for his tin. Give him his beer and his bretzel, his pantomime, or his dancer, or his farce, ever so badly played, in a beer saloon, where he can smoke likewise, and all for less than two shillings, and he is contented. Why not?

None of the theatres have done immense business this week. I have not seen a really full house since Mrs. Wood's farewell benefit at the Winter Garden. The managers must stir themselves.

Mrs. Farren and her daughter Fanny are at the New Bowery, playing in a five-act drama with the singularly disagreeable title, *Love's Venom*. The play is a high-pressure affair, with an old lady in purple velvet and ermine, who interferes with the playful dalliance of the customary young woman in white muslin, and the usual adolescent cavalier in silk tights and a velvet doublet. I didn't stay for the result. It was too harrowing. Miss Farren does not lack vigor, whatever else may be said about her. She piles on the steam to a most dangerous extent. I should say that she carried as much as a hundred pounds to the square inch. The life-boats ought to be always on the guards when she is about.

The Broadway Boudoir announces an 'afternoon matinée.' Since 'the last début of old George Kensett,' afternoon-matinée' is as good a thing, as I have heard, 'for off-hand.'

The opera folks seem to be getting on fairly in the city of magnificent swindles. The Washington *Star* keeps a powerful 'cricket.' Right merrily chirps he upon the début of Patti in *Lucia*. He is descriptive. He "can't call to mind who wasn't there. Miss Juliana May was there in a private box; so was an undoubted quorum of both Houses." Then again, he is eloquent: "Patti, warming up to her work, sings divinely, throws out lavish stores of pearly notes, runs up to the extremest height of the soprano register *without effort or contortion of face*, and ends the first act in a blaze of glory. Patti 'will do'." "She is going to be the marvel of the world." It is very encouraging to know that the third act "brings out the fine capabilities of Signor Muller as 'Raymond,' and of Signor Quinto as 'Arthur'."

There is a still more esthetical criticism upon *Ernani*, which was given for Colson on Tuesday. *Ernani* is set down as the 'chef-d'œuvre of musical compositions.' "It brought down the house a dozen times—at times most provokingly, indeed; insomuch as, carried away by their enthusiasm, the portion of the audience not familiar with the score, let loose their hands, canes, and throats, at moments when, in so doing, they prevented their more phlegmatic neighbors, as well as themselves, from enjoying the rendition of passages equally as fine following immediately thereafter." Colson was exquisite, and "Susini's rich, graceful, harmonious, and sonorous heavy notes, came floating from his throat apparently as naturally as the warbling of a mockingbird." Stigelli 'is ranked as a finer tenor than Brignoli,' and the fact that he did not sing a single false note, is called 'a remarkable achievement for any tenor.' Why more remarkable for a tenor than a baritone, soprano, contralto, or basso? Let us know, Capitoline Pundit.

The P. R. in the Coulisses.

The Benicia Girl, whose chief claims to public recognition seem to be founded upon her alleged matrimonial connection with the Boy who has gone over to England with the laudable intention of punching the head of Mr. Thomas Sayers, has been at the old Bowery this week.

Not feeling equal to the task of passing upon Mrs. Heenan's peculiar claims (I am not much in the shoulder way), I procured the services of a distinguished fancy litterateur, who does the athletic business for the dailies. I gave him two Welch rarebits, three English chops, half a pound of cheese, and as much beer as he could drink, and started him for the Bowery.

Next day, I received a greasy note marked with very suspicious stains. The ungrateful wretch had sold me out, said he had to do a dog-fight and a rat conflict for the *Clipper*.

I am informed, however, by a well-known amateur of the P. R. that the Girl has had several pitched battles with the old-fashioned melodramas, and a number of friendly contests with changing farces and lightweights of the *Is He Jealous* school. She is about five feet high, and fights about nine stone seven pounds. She puts up her hands like a green one, and makes play very widely, giving her adversary splendid opportunities to counter on her. Just now, the Girl is not in the best training, and is a little shaky on her pins, and queer about the eyes. If she went into half training, cut off three-fourths of her hair, reduced her stock of pearl powder, and did a little hydropathy, my informant thinks she would be a tip-topper.

The Bowery people have not run after the Girl in any great numbers, having more interest probably in the Boy, who certainly does know how to put his hands up. That's another instance of the depraved taste of the public, which is as absurd in the Oriental districts as in Broadway. They say, 'over across town,' that the Girl can't act, but is that any reason why she shouldn't draw?

The Girl has been in the Metropolitan ring before, however, appearing as a military individual, and I extract the subjoined from the Feuilleton of THE SATURDAY PRESS, March 5, 1859:

The adventurous young gentleman of the *Tribune* has, however, found an oasis. It is in the shape of a person named Menken, who has made her debut at the National Theatre. Menken is female. Menken plays soubrettes. By all accounts she is a sort of prairie Lola Montez. I first heard of her at Dayton, a highly interesting town in Ohio. There she played in some one of the numerous pieces wherein young women, in a short allowance of clothing, go through with certain evolutions that are supposed to be military. The Dayton Light Guards, or Light Infantry, or Light something or other, were so much charmed, as men and as Guards, that they chose Mistress Menken as their ruler, and she wears the title of Captain to this day. Such a thing could not happen anywhere except in America, and here it is especially Western. When we add that the Guard paraded at the theatre under the command of their actress-captain, the thing is complete. She has now come, sword in hand, to conquer the metropolis, and the *Tribune*-critic, albeit a man of peace, has been to see the crinoline warrior. I have not yet ventured. The critical office daily proves more and more dangerous. If a man writes that a prima donna can't sing, or wont sing, or kicks up rows, he runs the risk of having his life bullied out of him. If, with only the natural female weapons, I am to be put down, what should I do against the Menken, who could, no doubt, bring a light artillery battery in the field against me, and serve the pieces herself.

So I leave the lady to the *Tribune*, and I rescue the notice from the obscurity of the City Items. *Voila!*

National Theatre.—Ada Isaacs Menken, an amateur of some fame in the West, is playing at this house. She has talent, but it is like the gold in quartz veins—all in the rough; and she must undergo the refining process of intelligent and critical audiences before she can hope to become an actress. She must correct another grave error at once, and that is her style of dressing in Protean pieces. When people go to the ballet, they expect to see a peculiar and questionable freedom in the toilet; but that style ought never to be misstated, much less outstripped, upon the legitimate style—not even on the Eastern side of the city. There is a hearty earnestness and dashing style about Miss or Mrs. Menken, which, under proper training, gives promise of better things; but, like most Western mental products, she wants taming down.

Personne.

BOOKS, ETC.

[Written for The New York Saturday Press.]

THE MIZZABLE MAN.

BY MARY ORME.

My Uncle was a very miserable invalid. He had dyspepsia, or spinal complaint, or disease of the heart, or softening of the brain, or something or other, I never quite understood what, and he was equally in the dark about his ailments, as were all his friends, and also the doctors, of whom he had a very large number. Nobody quite understood what the trouble was, and yet it seemed plain enough one day, for he had a dreadful burning in the stomach, and so it must be dyspepsia, and the next day he had a ponderous pain in the head, and a confusion of intellect, which showed that his brain was affected, and then it was settled that he had softening of the brain, only to have the fact unsettled the next day, when there was a regiment of gnawing pains in his back, and great weakness of his limbs. These symptoms decided the doctor of the day that he had spinal disease, but that night his heart fluttered, and finally whopped over, like a frightened bird, and the doctors were forced to decide that he had disease of the heart.

One symptom never failed to be present; all the rest were inconstant, coy, and fickle, and not at all to be relied upon. For instance, when the doctor came whose speciality was spinal disease, behold! the only trouble was that his stomach was a vinegar factory; and when the dyspepsia doctor came, then the spine was an extended misery; and so on of all his terrible troubles.

But his nerves never deserted him; that is, he was always conscious of their weakness, pains, and miseries. Never was a more threadbare, out-at-elbows, and decidedly ill-feeling set of nerves than my poor Uncle possessed for his penance in this pitiable world of sick folks.

When he came down in the morning, which hard exertion he generally accomplished about nine or ten o'clock, he went to the window as soon as he entered the drawing-room, and probably there were not three days in a year when he did not exclaim, "Mizzable weather! mizzable, mizzable!" If it did not rain, it was too cold, or too warm; if it were not misty, it was too dry; if the streets were not muddy, they were dusty. It was too close and oppressive, or the house would be blown over by such winds. Altogether the world was not made to live in; it was only intended as a sort of hospital-prison, where the only enviable people were the doctors.

The only inmates of my Uncle's family were himself, his daughter, and myself. His widowed daughter, Mrs. Inflatio Jenkins, honored her father's home by making it her own. I believe her given name was Susannah, but on account of her literary aspirations or successes, she had changed it to Stellita, so that she now styled herself Mrs. Inflatio Stellita Jenkins.

The only comforts that my Uncle had, were the complaints he made, and the pleasure and honor of having a distinguished literary woman at the head of his house. One might suppose that the overwhelming sense of this honor, that my Uncle certainly felt, would have hindered all complaints of my Aunt. There is an old saying that no man is a hero to his valet de chambre, so no woman may be a heroine to her father, but in this case my Aunt seemed 'to be and not to be' at the same time.

I was a very bashful child, and very ugly besides; that is my eyes squinted, and my hair might have been called flaxen, by courtesy, but I was painfully aware that it was towy. And yet I am afraid that neither of these epithets is very significant to my readers, for what do millions in the world know of flax or tow? They may know that they use linen handkerchiefs, and wear linen under-garments, when they are wealthy enough to buy them, but of the raw material of which these are made, the flax that my Grandfather raised on his farm, they know nothing, unless it be the traditionary knowledge preserved in the terms 'flaxen locks' and tow head.'

Well, I was a poor, little, squint-eyed, tow-headed, or flaxen-haired orphan; that last characterization is better, more like my elegant Aunt's ways of speaking, than the more truthful compound adjective tow-headed.

It was not surprising that my Aunt should object to my being known as one of the family. I certainly was no credit to anybody. I was neither ornamental, nor useful, and I was sometimes a very unwilling intruder when my Aunt had company.

I was always an unlucky child. When I was very small, I was what is called un enfant terrible, and now I was thirteen, I had such an awful candor, and such a sense of justice at the back of it, that only 'the just made perfect,' could abide me. I occupied a strange position in my Uncle's house. He was my mother's brother, and his daughter Susy, I beg pardon, Stellita, had married my father's brother. So that my name was the same as my Aunt's. Another reason why she did not wish to have me in sight of her friends. They might hear my name, and they might see a likeness between us, and so conclude that I was her daughter. This last probability I think could have occurred to no one but my Aunt, for she was built on the model of an ancient boiled pudding, boiled in a bag which was not quite so thick as it was long, then her cheeks or face were, or was, very red, and her hair, which was dyed with a solution of lunar caustic, distilled water, and alcohol (I went to the druggists for it), had a burned and bloody look. Now I was pale and sallow, and thin as a shad when the season is over, and my hair I have distinctly stated was towy. In one respect I was like my Aunt Susy. I have a provoking habit of forgetting her new name, and this is another reason why I should be kept out of the parlor. I love to write. I was always reading, or scribbling, and I saved all my odds and ends of literature, and the few letters I had received, as a miser saves gold. Uncle was very kind to me. He loved my mother, for she lived before he was 'mizzable,' and was therefore a pleasant association. He loved me, and reverenced his gifted daughter, and he contrived to have me about him a good deal. I read to him, and I got his dressing-gown and slippers, and put away his coat when he came home from down-town, where he went every day, though ever so 'mizzable.' Some sick folks nurse their nerves and keep them quiet; they muffle the bell, and put sand-dust in the street, and on the sidewalk in front of their houses, to deaden the sounds made by passers-by. Others expose their nerves continually, and, though as fretful as a porcupine, they never soothe themselves, and, and thus save other people from suffering; and again there is a third class who unite both modes. Now my Uncle went out, went down-town, went on change, went everywhere that business called him, and aside from being what is called an irritable man, and having a multitude of doctors, nobody would have thought him sick. He even went journeying to distant cities, but wherever he was, when the day's work was done, he put off his boots and coat, and put on his mizzable mood, and found fault with everything this side Paradise.

My Uncle had his friends, and my Aunt had hers. I did not like either very much. My Aunt did not allow me to get acquainted with her friends, and their long hair and broad shirt-collars did not impress me favorably. Uncle's friends were mostly business-men. A few dropped in of an evening to play whist with him. The three parlors opened into each other, and Uncle occupied the back parlor, and my Aunt the middle one, ordinarily, and I understood that my place was beside uncle's great grey cat in the back parlor.

I remember one evening that cost me a great deal of trouble. Uncle had come home, worse than usual, for he was so sometimes, though one could hardly see how he could be. Professor Saccharini was with my Aunt. She was anxious to impress him favorably, as he was the critic for —— Magazine. She had been reading her poems to him, before Uncle came home, and securing his kind attentions to her forthcoming volume. She wished to be brought before the public as a gentlewoman and a genius, and Professor Saccharini was the man to do this, provided he were pleased.

Mr. Benson, a young lawyer, who did the legal part of Uncle's business, came home with him. Uncle was the most particular man alive about his dinner; he wanted it at the moment, and everything that came on the table had to be found fault with. His daughter was as fond of her dinner as less etherial mortals, but to-day she had food of a more exalted character than roast goose, game pie, and brawn—she was reading her poems to Professor Saccharini.

My Uncle came in, with an extra amount of impatience, as it was late dinner time already, and he heard the drowsy hum of his daughter's voice in the next room. He had experience of her neglecting material for intellectual pleasures, and he spoke very sharply to me. "Lizzie," said he, "go and tell your Aunt that I want to see her. Don't say anything about dinner, for I don't want that mizzable fellow at table, that she is reading to. He would spoil my appetite."

I did not wish to risk the result of opening the folding-doors, near which the Professor might be sitting, and thus expose my Uncle and him to each other, and so I went through the front parlor. As I entered the room, I heard my Aunt say, "This poem being my brightest gem, I wish particularly to have it illustrated." "A happy idea, Madam," said Professor Saccharini in his sweetest tones, and she went on reading to my intense amazement, from a poem by my father. It had come into my possession with some other manuscripts of his, and was literally one of my sacred things.

I waited to hear more. I could not believe it possible that she had stolen this dear remembrance of my father, this beautiful fruit of his genius. Again she paused, and said, "You agree with me, Professor, that this is my chef d'œuvre."

"Most emphatically, Madam. It is a poem worth more than gold. It will stamp your genius at once."

I could contain myself no longer. I rushed forward and tore the poem from her hands, exclaiming "That is my poor, dead father's poem, and you know it. You have stolen it, and you shall not have it." The moment I had the paper in my hands, and had uttered my dreadful fact, I ran back to my Uncle, and regardless of Mr. Benson's presence, I exclaimed, "Aunt Susy took my poem from me."

"You little simpleton, have you told your Aunt to come here?" said my Uncle. "I will tell her, if you will keep this for me," said I to Mr. Benson, feeling that my treasure never would be safe under my Uncle's roof.

Mr. Benson kindly took the paper, and I ran back and told my Aunt she was wanted. She was abusing me to Professor Saccharini, and calling me 'that imp,' and other names not pleasant to hear.

The gentleman was administering emollients, such as, "My dear Madam, no one can doubt you; who would listen to such a perverse thing as that?"

When I returned to the back parlor, Mr. Benson had finished the perusal of the poem, and I had the satisfaction to see him put it in his pocketbook. I heard my Uncle say to him, "She is right. It is her father's writing, and the verses are his, but why she should make such an ado because my daughter chose to read them to somebody, I can't see. Am I to have my dinner to-night?" he exclaimed as he saw me. "If Susy don't choose to come, we will have dinner. Such mizzable ways, and such irregularity, and such a wretched day as I have had! A man without his dinner is a helpless, good-for-nothing being, Mr. Benson."

My Aunt came at this juncture. She looked daggers at me, and I made my escape to the kitchen, where I always found a friend in scraggy Mary the cook, who, though she always had a horseshoe in her forehead, was nevertheless kind to me. I had been here but a moment, before a servant came to seek me. It was my Uncle's pleasure that I should come to dinner. I very seldom sat at table with the family, never unless my Uncle chose to punish his daughter for something, or when some relative was present. I saw now that he must be in a very ill humor, and my heart started on an extra amount of exertion that was hard to bear. If my Uncle had had such a fit, he would have called in some American Corvisart in all haste, and have submitted to his treatment till he wanted to make some speculation, enough to give up quiet and the doctor at the same time.

As I entered the dining-room, my Aunt shot sharp needles from her eyes at me, but she said nothing. My Uncle was saying, "If poor Lizzy's child can't be allowed to eat such a mizzable dinner as this with her mizzable uncle, then I'll send her away to school, where she will be treated like a human being, and I will board out, where I can be treated like one. Give the child some of that bird-pie, Suzy,"—Uncle always called Mrs. Stellita Suzy when he was angry, or too mizzable.

Mrs. Jenkins handed me a neck and a wing of some little bird from the pie, and a minute piece of crust. My Uncle's blood was up. My Aunt had just filled her own plate, but had not yet touched it. My Uncle took the well-filled plate and exchanged it for mine in a twinkling, setting the neck and wing, and the dry bit of crust before his daughter, and his look said, "You mizzable woman."

Mrs. Inflatio Stellita Jenkins was afraid of her father. She was poor, and he was rich. He would probably make a will one of these days. She did not therefore rise and leave the table, but she made some very considerable additions to the moiety of a dinner on her plate, and ate, but I must confess rather gloomily, or sulkily. Mr. Benson was cheerfully inattentive to the disagreeable facts at the table. I looked down and ate my dinner with a consciousness that somebody would have looked arsenic into my plate, if it had been possible. I was badly frightened, and hardly know how I managed to eat through the several courses. I believe I was afraid to do otherwise, for my Uncle uniformly gave me the plate filled for my Aunt, and our stomachs were not of the same pattern; but today mine had its elasticity tested.

My Uncle was as happy at seeing me eat Mrs. Suzy's dinner as a mizzable man could be.

But this was my last dinner with my invalid Uncle, for a long time. The next day Mr. Benson came early to our house. He had been closeted with Uncle in the parlor alone, the night of the dinner, when I and pussy were with Mary the cook below stairs.

When he came in the morning, I had not seen Mrs. Jenkins, and my Uncle told me to go up stairs with the chambermaid, and put into a new trunk, that had just arrived, everything that I wished to take to school with me. "O Uncle," said I, "I can't take you and Ratter."

"I can't spare the cat," said he in alarm; "don't think of taking Ratter with you, Lizzy. I should be too mizzable. It is bad enough to lose you, you poor, wretched child. I don't believe you ever saw a well day in your life, or ever will. You are too much like your poor, mizzable Uncle."

I was more rejoiced than I can tell to get away from my Aunt. I was very much afraid of her since I had plucked her laurel, and my remembrance of her then, is to this day a compound of a hyena's mouth with dreadfully decayed teeth, sanguinary face and hair, and a degree of enbonpoint that only made me think the more the worse. I was, doubtless, a very bad child, and had not any charity, and very little of the milk of human kindness. But with my maturity there still remains a great horror of a literary woman, who could steal poems, and especially the unpublished gems of a dead genius. But how much of blame was due to such acts as these, and how much should be transferred to acts anterior, I must leave for the moralist and the physician to decide, for my Aunt ultimately became an inmate of a lunatic asylum, from the use of opium and hasheesh. I have known several men and women of reputed genius, who took these narcotics, and I never knew one of them who would not lie and steal, and they acquired these accomplishments, whatever their moral character had previously been, in a short time after the narcotic demoralization began.

Alas for poor Mrs. Inflatio Stellita Jenkins. My father's poem stands first in her volume, and how many minor thefts there were, I can only "guess and fear."

Well, I went to school. I was not happy, and my poor Uncle wrote me mizzable letters from every point of the compass, for he became a habitual traveller, because, he said he did not hear the buzzing in his ears when he was in the cars, and his heart did not beat so terribly after dinner, when he had had nothing fit to eat. And then he said he was too mizzable to stay at home after I was gone, "and, what was worse," wrote my Uncle, and then crossed it out and continued, "a very sad thing happened soon after you left; Ratter was poisoned and died, and now your poor Uncle is too mizzable to stay at home, only when he can't avoid it."

When I was terribly tired of school, I began to get attached to everybody about me, I believe a good deal from the force of habit; and when my Uncle came to see me, looking a very bundle of nerves, and offered to take me home, I would not consent to go. I staid three years in the Seminary, and there was a great change in my appearance. My hair had grown dark, and curled easily; my eyes had ceased to squint, and that without the operation for strabismus; and my height was a good deal increased, and I was plump, and no longer of the "Scrag of mutton order of architecture."

One day some one came to the class-room for me, saying that a gentleman wished to see me. I ran down, expecting to see my Uncle, but there was Mr. Benson. He had always seemed near to me since the time that he protected my father's manuscripts. I exclaimed, "Mr. Benson! how glad I am to see you! I hope Uncle is well."

"I have some sad news for you," said he, and I cried out in sorrowful fear, "Uncle is dead."

"No, Miss Lizzie, he is as well as usual."

I was thankful to hear this, and also that Mr. Benson did not call me Jenkins—I dislike the name desperately. "Your Aunt,"—he hesitated—"What is it," said I—fearing some dishonor.

"She is insane, and has been taken to the asylum, and your Uncle has no housekeeper; and he says if you will come home, he will not travel any more; and he said I must be sure to tell you that he would get another grey cat, and do his best to keep you from being as mizzable as he is"—Mr. Benson pronounced my Uncle's pet word so naturally, that we both laughed.

"I am afraid," said he, "it will be a great sacrifice for you to leave school."

"Not a bit of it," said I. "I will like of all things to take care of Uncle, and have you to dine with us, and the grey cat for company."

When I arrived at my Uncle's home in Bleecker street he was there to meet me. I had never seen him look so happy in my life. He had not seen me for a year. He met me at the door, and he exclaimed, "How handsome you have grown, Lizzy! Come right in and see Ratter."

I went into the back parlor, and there on the same rug lay coiled a magnificent tiger cat. Such a great, grand fellow! Such a fine grey, and such broad black stripes! His coat was smooth and shining, and his countenance a very pleasant one; for cats have all manner of countenances, like other folks.

"Is Mary here?" said I.

"Busy with the dinner, I dare say," said my Uncle. "I would not allow her to leave it, as I did not want to welcome you home to a mizzable dinner."

The word mizzable reminded me that I had only said how do you do? to Uncle, but had made no inquiry about his health. I looked at him. He looked better, unmistakably better.

I went up to him, and took both his hands, and said, "Is your health better than it used to be, dear Uncle?"

"I really believe I am not so mizzable as I used to be," said he.

"I am most thankful," said I, and then I ran down to see Mary. The way she blessed me would take herself or another genuine Irish tongue to tell.

I became my Uncle's housekeeper, and he became more and more cheerful and healthy. Mr. Benson dined with us often, and as I disliked the name of Jenkins so much, I was persuaded to change it for that of Benson, on my eighteenth birthday.

My poor Aunt died in the asylum, and my Uncle mourned for her very sincerely, and had her poems, bound in blue and gold, on a stand in his room, but I think he never opened the book. He was not a reader, and so he was not as mizzable as he might have been.

My Uncle does not use his pet word as much so formerly, and he never finds fault with anything at table, because when he complained at first I cried, and he said he could not bear to see me cry, and so he made peace with his dinner from that day. And now, in the bosom of our happy family, with our magnificent cat, I do not think my Uncle is a very mizzable man.

LEAVES OF GRASS.

Messrs. Thayer & Eldridge, an enterprising young publishing firm in Boston, have in press a new and revised edition of Walt Whitman's 'Leaves of Grass.' The book is to be brought out in the most elegant style of print and binding, and will be enriched with many new Poems not before published. The two original editions of the work have long been out of print, and judging from the new demand for it excited by Mr. Whitman's more recent and finished productions (published in the *Atlantic Monthly* and The Saturday Press), we have no doubt that the superb issue now contemplated will meet with deserved success.

NEW YORK MARCH 31, 1860

Thoughts and Things.

BY ADA CLARE

The aesthetics of eating is an art too little cultivated in Anglo-Saxon countries. In France it has already been niched in the temple of fame, and poetry and history have combined to render it ornamental.

In England and America the art of eating is treated entirely in the Pre-Raphaelite school, with an utter scorn of sentiment, and an awful fidelity to nature. The Saxon breast swells with respect for his dinner in proportion as the meat measures for size. His desire is to have the piece large enough to suggest the *whole* animal of which it was a part. He is never better pleased than when the colossal round of beef before you, can portray to your mind the green-bottle eyes, the impatient tail, the muddy legs, the hideous bulkiness, of the animal whom it went to make up in life.

The Gallic mind on the contrary abhors hugeness in meat; he aims to throw an air of refinement and daintiness over all that comes into the magic domains of victuals. The mind, he holds, must lose sight of the original beast, ere it can truly enjoy eating.

It is a mistake to suppose that dining is a universal acquirement or accomplishment; on the contrary diners, like poets, are born, not made. I do not mean to say that the faculty of dining may not be, with perseverance and in a good school, more or less cultivated; but cultivation can never make a diner in the most majestic sense of that word.

As the poet, the great orator, often springs up in the far wilds of the forest, from parents whose unlettered state vies with the ignorance of the caterpillar, so the genuine diner often sees the light for the first time in some New England town, and is forced by fate to steer the feeble bark of his talent through the treacherous waves of corned pork, of cabbage, and of the fatal pumpkin-pie. These indeed are abominable waters, which have worked the destruction of many an epicurean capacity; in them many a digestion floundered, agonized, and sank down; there many a right mind groping blindly after soupe à la bisque, has been swept down by baked beans, and forever given over to oblivion and the tomb.

Paris is the great Mecca of the gastronome; thither must he travel, to do right homage to Epicurus. When the Parisian sits down to his dinner, he does it in the same manner that he goes to the Opera, that he opens a new novel by George Sand, that he beholds a great painting or statue, or any work of art. His food is a song which he is about to sing. To make it for him a true dinner, he wants a congenial companion; he wants a cheerful light; a tasteful room; a graceful table gracefully served; he wants his meats, vegetables, fish, prepared in the most elegant, the most voluptuous manner, with the special care that the remembrance of the original source be extinguished in the rosy mantle of dainty skill; above all, he wants his food to be baptized in the crimson blood of the grape.

Over here in America they consider it an immorality to take pleasure in eating; any amount of victuals may be gorged with virtue if you only devour them under a protest. Clarets or the amber-hued wines, you may not drink at a clean table and with genial conversation, if you would keep your reputation pure; but the worst brandy may be swallowed on foot with a gloomy countenance, from a soiled and reeking bar, and your morality is in no danger of impeachment.

The highly moral American sits down to a solemn dinner just as daylight is becoming blear and ghastly, and just before gas can take the place of the sun. His table is unnecessarily large; it is square; the severe corners seem to jut out with a desire to stab you, and it is so supported that you must meekly resign yourself to sacrifice your own sad legs to the triumphant legs of the table.

Every thing is put sternly upon the board before the awful bell tears through the silence of the house. By the time the family have assembled, the potatoes have resigned themselves to the chill embraces of the ague, the other vegetables have begun to cling to their platters in a manner to infringe on the patent of Spalding's glue, and the beef has grown gigantic white whiskers of gravy. But what of that if the beef is so large that properly hollowed out, it would make a Calvinistic pulpit, and the vegetable-dishes resemble infantile gas-meters; so the family, with lugubrious faces and voices of gloom, fall like so many harpies upon the beef and despatch it with true moral sternness. Wine is not here! Not the harmless, rose-lipped claret, the darling of the genial dinner. Away, away with thee, thou dangerous fiend! Here are towering banks of cold, white water; let the family comfort themselves with flagons of that.

There is a morality even in confectionery. The strictly religious person will always eat ice-cream with the flavor of lemon, and the reputation of the eater always demands that it be consumed with the greatest amount of speed; the conscience is only appeased by the making of quick time. In bon-bons otherwise known as sugar-plums, there is also an individual and personal morality. When you see a demure, pious looking party at a concert, handing about briskly little twisted papers, you may be sure that the odor of mint and wintergreen will issue from them.

I have known persons too virtuous to eat chocolate, pistache or caramels, who cannot be religious without a pocket-full of peppermint lozenges.

o o o

The lovers of good paintings will find much to interest them in the great painting of 'The Pilgrim Fathers,' by Schwartz. It is on exhibition at Goupil's.

o o o

How is it, Mr. Editor, that you have not yet copied the following delicious lyric by Miss Prescott? I find it in Sir Rohan's Ghost:

In the Summer even
    While yet the dew was hoar,
I went plucking purple pansies
    Till my love should come to shore.
The fishing lights their dances
    Were keeping out at sea,
And come, I sung, my true love!
    Come hasten home to me.

But the sea it fell a-moaning,
    And the white gulls rocked thereon,
And the young moon dropt from heaven,
    And the lights hid one by one.
All silently their glances
    Slipt down the cruel sea,
And wait! cried the night and wind and storm,
    Wait, till I come to thee !

Dramatic Feuilleton.

'Personne.'

A delighted foreign correspondent writes thus :—

Qu'est ce que cette 'Personne'? Quel esprit malin! Je gage que c'est une Française, ou plutôt un Français. Gare aux coulisses!

Which being put into English, means—but no, I will not flatter *Personne* by translating it.

Let him do it his-self.

Suffice it to say that the writer evidently doubts not only our great Feuilletonist's nationality—being quite certain that he is French—but even his sex, which he half intimates is feminine!

O, Anna Maria!

For my own part, though I might answer my correspondent's question, I positively refuse to do so, since in consequence of Personne's duty having devolved upon me this week, I am in so unamiable a state of mind that sooner than make the slightest explanation, I will leave him under the fearful imputation (fancy how he will writhe under it!) of being both a Gaul and a Woman.

Zounds and Zoyara, what a joke!

Moi-même.

I do not often flock to the theatre, and when I do I generally scatter before the play is out.

I like the atmosphere of the place, and the people who go there, and about all that is done there (except the music and the gymnastics), but not being a 'genius,' according to Buffon's definition, and therefore having no 'patience,' I invariable get played out after the third act, in which case I either go to sleep and have bad dreams, or rush to the refreshment-room and make myself miserable on bad liquor.

Hence, so far as I am concerned, the theatre has a decidedly immoral tendency—as Dr. Bellows himself will admit—and accordingly, as I said, I rarely flock to it. The reader may not see it, but for this reason I incline to think myself peculiarly qualified to be a Dramatic Feuilletonist.

No offence, however, to *Personne*, who, though he does flock to the theatre continually,—having the fear of Thespis, Thalia and all those people constantly before his eyes—always contrives, as the reader of The Saturday Press need not be told, to bring away with him a golden fleece.

But then *Personne* is an exception to all rules,— which according to a doubtful axiom, is so much the better for the rules, and, in any case, is so much the better for *Personne.*

Whoever can go to the theatre, or anywhere else (except Pfaff's) more than once a moon, and see anything in it, is doubtless a very cheerful bird, but he is not one of my feather. The old proverb is right in saying there may be too much even of a good thing,— the divine partridge itself not excepted. 'Linked sweetness long drawn out' is always a bore.

Indeed I never quite fancied an eternity of anything —not even of happiness; certainly not of the other thing.

And I especially dislike all kinds of eternal people. As for the eternal theatre-goer, or the eternal churchgoer, or the eternal picture-goer, I fear me he must ever be an eternal nuisance. The freshness of his nature soon gets washed away, and nothing whatever is capable of producing a clean impression upon it.

It is for this reason, among others, that I have as great a horror for that class of people called connoisseurs, as Ruskin has for that equally dismal class called amateurs. The opinion of any man of ordinary common-sense is superior to that of such persons, even in regard to their own specialities.

The funniest thing is to hear them talk about 'laws'—especially the laws of the Drama, which is the most capricious and lawless thing in the world, and, from the beginning, has steadily refused to be analyzed or to be subjected to any æsthetic discipline.

It would have been a good thing for the world if the sister arts had been equally independent.

With this feeling, the reader will readily understand how it is that I throw up my hat with joy whenever I see any play or player ride over the heads of the gay connoisseurs, and take captive the hearts of the people.

I have seen it done many times, and I verily believe it has added to my length of days.

The idea that the success of any work of literature or art depends to any measurable extent upon the dicta of critics and quidnuncs is utterly absurd; and it is time that all men and women of genius found this out, if only to prevent their truculence to the Press, which can do nothing *for* them until their success is achieved, and after that can do nothing *against* them.

If this view were generally taken, all truculence and sycophancy would soon be on the side of the Press, which at present plays the master and the tyrant to an extent that has got to be slightly ridiculous.

Nearly every success which has been achieved in any department of art—and especially in dramatic art—has been achieved in the very teeth of the connoisseurs.

As a rule, the only criticism worth having is the instinctive criticism of the people, which, in the last analysis, is all that any of us care anything about.

Some people, I know, pretend to despise it; but I never yet have known anybody who was not as sensitive to it as to an East wind.

This sounds very much like demagogueism, perhaps, but I don't mind that, because every word of it is true.

What right it has in a Dramatic Feuilleton is another matter.

Evangeline.

If I were—as I hasten to assure the inquisitive reader I am not—a sensitive young lady about to make my débût on the stage, and being so situated, had the choice whom I should immediately succeed, it is my firm opinion—though there is no telling what I might do as a young lady—that my choice would *not* fall upon Mrs. John Wood. For, although I have a high opinion of that most exuberant and gushing of actresses, and have in fact several times invested four shillings (and, in one rash instance eight) in her behalf, I do not think her exactly the person, whatever may be her natural benevolence, to prepare the way and make it smooth for any other member of her profession.

And I may furthermore say, that if I were a young lady about to try my fortunes on the stage, and had my choice of a play, I should not select one written by my mother (no disrespect to mothers as an institution), nor one of such an elaborate order that my part in it would require the experience of years to render it with justice to myself and the author.

Nor if the play were of a very high tone, should I choose the middle of Lent as precisely the best time for bringing it out.

But in all this I am probably wrong; for Miss Kate Bateman has gone and done all these things, and done them, everything considered, with remarkable success. Not that she is received with any such boisterous manifestations as those which nightly greeted and inspired her illustrious and irrepressible predecessor (*that*, it would have been unreasonable to expect), but considering her youth, the difficulty of her rôle, and the violence of the contrast she presents not only to Mrs. Wood, but to all the sensation-actresses of the day, she certainly accomplishes wonders.

Mrs. Bateman's play no doubt possesses very great merit; but the central figure in it,—Evangeline,—is such a delicate creation; has, so to speak, so little color, that however well acted, it must appeal chiefly to a class of emotions which by no means predominate among our theatre-goers.

From a popular point of view, I look upon this as a serious defect in the play. At any rate, it presents the greatest difficulty with which Miss Bateman has to contend; and the difficulty is greatly increased by the fact that nearly all the other characters in the play are so strongly drawn as to make the part of the heroine seem even more shadowy and unsubstantial than it really is.

And yet from the time she trips on to the stage with a somewhat forced sprightliness and rushes to the arms of her father—through all the intervening scenes of alternate grief and joy—to the time when she wakes up from a horrible dream and finds herself by the side of her beloved Gabriel, she enlists the sympathies of the entire audience, who throughout give her the noiseless but touching applause of their smiles and tears.

I cannot better finish my say about this subject than by giving the subjoined extract from the *Home Journal*, which I am happy to endorse word for word:

> 'Evangeline' is not like 'Geraldine'—a torrent of passion. It is rather a calm stream of love and sentiment, broken here and there by a rock and an eddy; but on the whole imbued with the serene beauty of the woodland and the meadows through which it winds its way. Mrs. Bateman has constructed from Mr. Longfellow's poem a charming dramatic pastoral, which is full of the fresh odors of the forest. To those whose appetites are vitiated by a systematic course of highly spiced dramatic food, and whose plays must be peppered with murders, and stuffed with mysteries, Evangeline' will seem tame. It appeals mostly to the higher and more refined qualities of the mind. Its tone is subdued, but rich, and pleases the cultivated critic as the rich brown tones of Couture delight the experienced eye more than the vivid reds of Horace Vernet. It has running through it, and surrounding it like an atmosphere, a poetic calm like that of an October day. It is sweet and sober vestured, like a beautiful nun wrapped in religious peace. It is this charming creation of a gifted mother that Miss Bateman has undertaken to interpret at the Winter Garden. We confess to having a weak and unphilosophical theory to the effect that it is a vast improvement to an actress to be young and beautiful. These conditions Miss Bateman amply fulfils, and to them must be added the possession of rare dramatic abilities. Indeed, her performance of 'Evangeline' is a triumph of sweet and natural acting. She is truly the tender, suffering maiden, whose grief, though never wild, is always touching. In certain emotional passages Miss Bateman was singularly unconstrained and free from conventional vocal efforts; and her singing of a little French chanson in the first, and an Ave Maria in the fourth act, gave evidence of an exceedingly sweet voice and purity of style. We hope sincerely that Miss Bateman will resolve to fix herself permanently among our New York stars. We gladly welcome this young queen, who advances so smilingly from the crowd of dramatic skeletons that fill our stage annals. We cannot conclude without saying how charmed we were with Mr. George Jordan's *Gabriel*. It was simple, natural, and manly, and at times the artist imbued it with a quiet strength which was infinitely effective.

Chamber Concert Union.

The second concert of this young but thriving society was given on Tuesday evening, at Goldbeck's Music Hall. Messrs. Guilmette (one of the 'Eternals'), Goldbeck, Saar, Dohler, and Brames, were announced in the programme, and all but the second-named gentleman, who was 'indisposed,' came up to the score. The soirée opened with Schumann's Trio in F Major—a composition full of that rocky solidity and manly passion (not bad that, eh?) which usually characterizes this composer. It was finely rendered by Messrs. Goldbeck, Dohler, and Brames, who claim the credit of having introduced this difficult composition to the New York public. Mr. Saar, a young pianist of promise, played several concerted pieces by Schuberth, with much effect. The success of the evening, however, was a scherzo by Chopin, executed by Mr. Goldbeck. The ardor and spirit with which he interpreted it, brought down such a shower of applause that he had to play another morceau, which, consisting of a 'warbling chain of purled trilles,' contrasted happily with the fiery energy of the former piece.

These chamber-concerts, sustained as they are by some of the most distinguished of our younger artists, deserve the hearty support of the music loving public. There are to be four more soirées, which will be given on succesive Tuesdays.

The Irishry.

I never contrived to get up much interest in the festive Irishman; for although,—Mr. Dion O'Boucicault to the contrary notwithstanding,—I have often seen him on the stage, and have faint recollections of having met with him 'elsewhere,' he has always been to me a very dreary creature. I am willing to admit with Mr. D. O'B. that he is the most industrious fellow in the world (melo-dramatically speaking), and that, in the same sense, he has all those tender, mirthful, impulsive, gushing qualities attributed to him in novels and other romances; but, for all that, his brogue is almost as wearisome to me as that of the Scotchman, and his fun the dismalest thing this side the Bowery.

For this reason I have not been to Niblo's to see *Willie O'Reilly*, nor to Laura Keene's to see *Colleen Bawn*.

From all I can learn, however, I have no doubt that they are both very excellent pieces, and that no one can see them without being convinced that, by an equitable and charming arrangement of Providence and the Playwrights, the poor of this world monopolize all the virtues, and the rich all the vices; and that when the rich and the poor come into conflict, in any matter except that of rent, the poor always get the best of it,—and also that the Celt crushed to earth will rise again, while the Saxon, if only wounded, immediately throws up his cap and asks to be buried in peace under a sweet-appletree.

And what more could a body ask?

The only really funny things, to me, connected with Colleen Bawn, are the following epistolary and oratorical productions of the distinguished 'author' :–

Mr. Boucicault's Epistle to Miss Laura Keene.

39 East Fifteenth Street, New York.

My Dear Madame:

Here is another Drama—my last for this season. It was written in five days, and the labor has rather overtaxed me, as this makes the seventh I have written within the space of twenty-eight weeks —one five-act play, five three-act dramas, and a burlesque. This piece is called 'The Colleen Bawn,' and is Irish to the backbone. It is the first time I have taken a subject from my native country, and, quickly as the work has been executed, I am not the less satisfied with it. 'Twill be found to be, I think, the best constructed of any of my works. Whatever demerits it may have, it is my happiest effort in that particular. The public must determine the rest.

Yours, very truly, Dion Boucicault.

Mr. Bouicault's Oration to the Public.

Ladies and Gentlemen:

I thank you all for your very kind reception of our drama this evening. I think it will be admitted by you all that Irishmen do most of the hard work in this country—I mean real, hard, manual labor. I myself have worked very hard for the past seven months, and I don't believe that for the next three months you could get another idea out of me with a derrick, I have written an Irish drama for the first time in my life. The field of Irish history and romance is so rich in dramatic suggestions that I am surprised that the mine has never been regularly opened before. I had long thought of writing a play from material gathered from my native country, but this is the first time I ever tried it. The story of the piece is founded on a fact which, as you all know, was selected by one of the greatest of Ireland's geniuses, Gerald Griffin, as the foundation for a novel. I am encouraged to hope that our little drama of to-night, though perhaps not much in itself, may prove the small door to let others into a big house, and that other greater men, of finer genius and abilities than I possess, may hereafter give you plenty of Irish plays, which, I am certain, will be appreciated by you, from my experience of your intelligence as American citizens, and of the hearty welcome you have ever extended to everything Irish since the country has been a country.

So much for the Irishry—as Macaulay always called them.

Musical.

Here is an interesting notice of Lurline, from this week's *Musical World*:

Lurline.—Wallace's new opera 'Lurline' has achieved a success in London quite equal to that of any opera ever before put upon the English stage. The notices from the Press of London place it in the highest rank as a most successful lyric work, and are very enthusiastic in its praises.

It differs from most other English operas, as it has no spoken dialogue, the recitatives being arranged as in the later school of Italian operas.

Mr. Wallace is so well known here, and his music so universally popular, that every one was prepared for a work of great merit, but such an unequivocal success could hardly have been anticipated even by his most ardent admirers.

The plot of the opera gives a fine opportunity for scenic effects, and careful attention appears to have been given to this portion of the performance, which is one of its attractions.

We understand that Mr. Wallace will soon be able to bring out the opera in New York, with able assistants, and we predict for it a success equal to that already achieved in London.

The legend of Lorely, on which the story is founded, has been slightly changed to adapt it to the stage.

ACT I.

Represents an antique castle on the banks of the Rhine—Count Rudolph, an extravagant young nobleman, having dissipated his patrimony among his graceless followers, proposes marriage with Ghiva, the daughter of a neighboring Baron, thinking thereby to replenish his coffers. The young lady's father, however, is nearly as poor as the Count, and hopes that the union between Ghiva and this young nobleman will the better enable him to support his own estate. An explanation soon puts an end to the treaty and the hand of the suitor is rejected.

Previous to this rupture, Lurline, the nymph of the Rhine, who, by her enchanted harp and song, lures vessels to destruction in the whirlpool of the river, has seen Count Rudolph in his barque, and fallen desperately in love with him. Accordingly she presents herself to the Count at a wild banquet (the last that he and his companions have determined to hold in the old castle), and, surrounding him by spells, places a magic ring on his finger and disappears. On recovering his reason, the Count has become enamored of the beautiful water-queen; the notes of her bewildering voice and harp attract him to the Rhine; he embarks, despite all interference, is engulfed, and supposed to perish.

ACT II.

Opens in the coral caves, under the waters, inhabited by Lurline and her nymphs, in which, by virtue of the talismanic ring, Rudolph is enabled to exist. His followers are seen in a boat, singing a requiem for the loss of their chief, by which he is so affected, that he urgently desires to return to them for a short time. Lurline consents to his departure for three days, and agrees to await his return on the summit of the Lurlei Berg, at the rising of the moon on the third evening. To augment his happiness, she prevails on her father, the Rhine King, to grant him a cargo of wealth, with which he embarks in a fairy skiff, leaving Lurline in dread of the non-fulfilment of his promise.

ACT III.

On returning to his companions Rudolph discloses to them, and to the Baron and his daughter, the secret of his almost inexhaustible wealth. This produces a great change in the disposition of the latter. The Baron once more courts the Count's alliance, while Ghiva, finding his heart engaged to Lurline, and fearing to lose her now wealthy former suitor, contrives to steal Lurline's enchanted ring from his finger, and cast it into the Rhine.

In the meantime, Lurline, inconsolable in the absence of the young Count, sits singing her laments to the chords of her harp, nightly, on the edge of the Lurlei Berg, where a gnome, in the service of the Rhine King, brings her the plighted ring, in token of her lover's infidelity. Distracted with grief, Lurline resolves to upbraid him for his perfidy and visit him with her vengeance. The old mansion on the Rhine is now the scene of great festivity; but in this gay and gorgeous revel the rich Count is the least happy of his numerous and joyous guests. His heart is away on the Lurlei Berg, with his lovely and faithful Lurline, but he dares not present himself before her without his lost ring. Lurline appears to him when alone and demands the ring. A scene of reproach here takes place, ending by her denouncing the treachery of the companions in whom he most confides. They, grown envious of Rudolph's wealth, plotted to destroy him and to plunder the castle. Their plan is overheard and hastily communicated to the Count by the ever-listening Ghiva and her father, who importune him to instant flight. The assassins are at hand, Rudolph prefers death at the feet of Lurline. The assassins approach, when, Lurline's affection returning in full force, she seizes her harp, and, by the spell of music, causes their destruction, and effects the preservation of her penitent lover.

And here endeth this Feuilleton.

Quelq'un.

[From The New York Traveller.]

ADA CLARE.

Awake upon a couch of pain,
I see a star betwixt the trees;
Across yon darkening field of cane
Comes soft and slow the evening breeze;
My curtain's folds are faintly stirred,
And, moving lightly in her rest,
I hear the chirrup of a bird
That dreameth in some neighboring nest.

Last night I took no note of these;
How it was passed I dread to say—
'Twas not in prayers to Heaven for ease,
'Twas not in wishes for the day.
Impatient tears, and stormy sighs
Enhanced my woe, increased my pain—
I cursed, and cursed, the wildering eyes
That burned this fever in my brain.

O, blessings on this quiet hour!
My thoughts in calmer currents flow—
She is not conscious of her power,
And hath no knowledge of my woe.
Perhaps if like yon peaceful star,
She looked upon my burning brow,
She would not pity from afar,
But kiss me, as the breeze does now.

Aglaus.

[For The New York Saturday Press.]

A SUMMER STORY.

BY MRS. R. H. STODDARD.

Agnes Fleming was thirty, Hugh Pennock was twenty. Now and then she found a silvery thread in her smooth bandeaux. His locks were black and silky. Her face was pale, her eyes were weary and wore an inward look. His face was firm and vigorous, his eyes eager and full of humid fire. She was slender, fair, and delicate. He was tall, dark, and robust. When this pair met, each made a move. She went back, and found something she had never before possessed—youth; while he leaped into the experience of manhood.

Agnes had sent her child, a boy of three years, to his grandmother, who lived by the sea. His absence opened an insidious chasm in the routine of her life, and that alert devil, Opportunity, suggested that the time had come for her to visit some maternal relations, whom she had never known, and who lived at a remote distance in the country. She did not ask her husband to accompany her, neither did he offer to go. They had been married ten years, and could part with composure. Fleming was fond of actresses and claret. With a soubrette he was perfectly at home; as the genius of Agnes did not run in the same direction, she could not make him feel quite comfortable with her. There were periods when they attempted the intimacy which their relation seemed to demand, but these attempts were failures; so the conjugal ship went adrift, and its insubordinate crew suffered, one from irritation, the other from despair. Though claret is the coolest wine in the world, Fleming's hair was thinning. His grey eye looked arid, and his stomach was too spherical. His manner was imperturbable, and he was still handsome in spite of his large jaw. But as we have nothing to do with him, we will leave him in a certain red-paneled room, with a young lady, whose shoulders are exceedingly, neat, and whose opaque black eyes wear a flinty sparkle as she sips a glass of Chateau Margaux.

Agnes therefore arrived at Park Farm alone. The grange-like buildings pleased her. The many windowed, angular house of blue stone, was picturesque. Behind it extended a garden, where jonquils, pinks, and damask roses, straggled over the garden paths, and lush grass grew round the knees of venerable pear and plum trees. Before it rose a grove of Norway firs, lindens, pines, and oaks. Hugh Pennock, an Englishman, had planted the trees a hundred years before Agnes was born.

John Pennock, the grandson of old Hugh, his wife Rebecca, and their only child, Hugh Park Pennock, the last blossom which dropped from their tree of life, lived solitary in the dark decaying house. John kept his wheat fields in order, but did nothing else; Rebecca only attended to Hugh and her dairy. Hugh dreamed. So every year the pinks and roses straggled more wildly over the garden paths, and the bed of dead leaves grew thick about the trees in the grove. Old Hugh Pennock was a gentleman. Nature rememembered the fact, for when our Hugh was born, she gave him the same impress. Everybody said he resembled the portrait of his great-grandfather, which hung in a small room called the Library, where there were a few leather-bound books, printed in London, for the booksellers 'at the Mitre in Fleet street,' or 'The Golden Lion in Aldersgate street.' This ancestor was Hugh's first idea. He was perpetually asking questions about his history; and he read the old books before he could understand them, but they made an impression nevertheless. When Agnes first saw him, he was grave and self-possessed. His easy silence drew her attention towards him; she wondered at his high-bred face. She thought what strong support there must be in his stalwart arm. He thought, how unreal she looked. There was the tremulous elasticity of a flower in her bearing, and the touch of her cool frail hand, felt like the fall of a dewdrop.

Agnes passed the first days of her visit in a lethargy. Rebecca thought her very ill. Agnes did not know her own ailment. The truth was, that the strain of her old life had given way, and nothing new had come to take its place. She kept her room. It was on the ground floor, with its window in a niche high up in the wall; steps were before it, which Agnes climbed every day, and looked out upon the landscape, stretching away between the park and garden. She saw numberless low hills, undulated ages ago by a wind pent in the earth, which died in a mighty heave along the verge of the horizon. They were crowned with trees, or furrowed with ripening grain. Once inside them, she thought, the clue which led into the world's highway would be lost.

Hugh sent her books and bunches of flowers. Too languid to read, she amused herself by pulling the flowers apart, and throwing them from the window leaf by leaf. Rebecca at last declared that something must be done, or Agnes would die. She must have the morning air. She should ride with Hugh in the wagon. She should not stay in her own room. She had had too much solitude, and not half care enough. Hugh arranged the wagon that day for her, and early the next morning, while the swallows were twittering under the eaves, Rebecca was by her bedside.

"Now, my dear, Hugh is waiting for you."

"A little more sleep," she begged, "I am so tired."

"Not a wink. If you shut your eyes, I'll call Hugh to carry you out to the wagon. Come; I will dress you."

Agnes obeyed her and was soon made ready. Hugh stood outside the door snapping his fingers at his dog Key, who was slobbering and groaning for a caress. Agnes thrust her hand in Key's shaggy coat, who forsook his master at once.

"Help her, Hugh," said Rebecca.

"O no," said Agnes, "Key is helping me." But Hugh quietly lifted her into the wagon, and they started with Key running beside them.

"I shall drive," said Hugh, "where you will have a different view from the one your window gives. I am afraid you are homesick, I have seen you look from it so often, and your gaze was so far away."

"No, I am not homesick; but how could you see me from my perch ?"

"From the hammock which swings under that pine," pointing to an old tree, whose top was black with cones, but whose lower branches were still green and dense. "It devours all my idle days; I wish you would try it; the carpet under it is dry, you see; the pine does not rustle its leaves above my head; there is no chatter of birds in its boughs; it is always grave and silent."

"It is like you," she thought; then aloud, "I will frequent it from this day."

She drew her shawl about her, and turned her face aside; Hugh saw that she did not wish to prolong the conversation. She enjoyed the scene too much to talk; the cool sweet air was balm to her; the quiet trot of the horses, the noiseless gallop of Key, his scampers into neighboring fields, the long shadows of the trees, and the flying birds, gave her a child-like pleasure. Park Farm was now five miles behind them. The horses were jogging slowly up a long hill, when Hugh suddenly reined them round an abrupt turn in the road. Below, lay a wide magnificent valley full of serrated woods. A crooked river ran through it, the sunrise burnishing its calm surface. Far beyond, the land rose in a series of ridges, extending the prospect till distance was lost in blue haze. Agnes rose to her feet, and gave a cry of delight; Hugh internally thanked her for it.

"I am well," she said, and stretched her hand towards him. He took it, the firmness of his grasp surprised her, and looking into his face she received from his glance an indescribable impression which opened the door of her soul, and encouraged it to step across the dark threshold of her interior life.

"Now for home and breakfast," cried Hugh; "mother will be ready for us." When they arrived at the lane-gate, Rebecca was there to open it. "Agnes, you are better. The great valley is a cure, isn't it? Do you see your breakfast on the porch? I have put my handsome dear old cracked china on it for you."

She had also prepared some dainty dishes, and made the table fanciful with flowers as well as with the old china. Agnes ate a little, and Hugh demolished all his mother set before him. They made her laugh, and then she ate a little more. "The girl's heart is ailing," thought Rebecca; "what can it be, I wonder?" Her tender solicitude smote Agnes with a new feeling. Tears had long since ebbed away from her; but now the tide seemed to be flowing again through some forgotten depth, though none welled from her eyes. A vivid spark gleamed in them, and a tinge of color came to her pale lips.

"How pleasant you are; how sincere," she said. "How positive is the taste of this food; how lovely these flowers are; their odor is delicious. Thank you, Rebecca; I see what you would do. Shall I ride tomorrow?"

"Every day."

"Will you go with me, Hugh?"

"Why, who else can go?" asked his mother.

"Who else?" said Hugh, sipping his coffee;" "Where is this woman's husband?" he thought; "I hate him, I believe," and setting his cup down, he sauntered away.

In the afternoon, Agnes went to the hammock. Rebecca sat beside her with her sewing, and gave her a sketch of her mother's girlhood—the mother whom Agnes knew so little of. Rebecca wept gently while she talked. Her emotion moved Agnes, and her words seemed to place her en rapport with her mother; her heart expanded with the feeling, and some of its lonesomeness vanished. An affectionate impulse prompted her to go to Rebecca, and fall on her neck with a kiss. When had she felt such an embrace as Rebecca gave her for that kiss?

The air was full of the golden dust of sunset when they saw John and Hugh returning from the fields. John gave them a kindly nod, asked for supper, and passed into the house. Hugh lingered; looking at Agnes, he commented to himself: "Her countenance has changed again; her features are growing flexible." He leaned against the tree where the hammock was tied in which she was resting. She turned towards him, and thanked him for suggesting the change from her room.

"I shall live out of doors now," she said, "and should even like to pass the night here if Key would be my watcher."

Rebecca told her that the dew fell too heavy at night.

"Dew," murmured Agnes, putting her hand to her forehead, "I wish I could feel it."

Hugh heard her, and folded his arms across his breast with an outward composure, while he felt a slow tug at the heart, as if that organ was for the first time set in motion. A cool wind crept over the earth, and stirred the pine which let its needles fall on Agnes's dress.

"Night is coming," said Rebecca, as she went into the house to prepare supper, telling them to follow her soon. Hugh drew his mother's chair close to Agnes, and dropped his hat in the hammock; she took it with a pretty motion, and twisted in the hatband the leaves which had fallen. He observed all she did with a glance as sharp as that of a young panther.

"Do you like our life?"

"Yes, it is an idyl to me."

"What has mother been talking of?"

"Of my own mother, her early friend."

"Your mother's portrait hangs in my room."

"Let me see it."

"Yes, if you wish. It is a strange, sad face, and makes me dream."

"Come then."

They went up stairs. In the faded picture Agnes saw a resemblance to herself—the same eyes and compressed mouth. Its expression recalled her father to her mind, and she startled Hugh with her question,—

"Was my father a bad man?"

"A worldly man."

"I thought so."

He asked her to look at his books, and they were promising to read together when they heard Rebecca calling them to supper.

As soon as the birds were asleep, Rebecca was by Agnes's bedside again. She put out her candle, drew away the curtain from the window, bade her be ready for the morning's ride, and left her. So ended this happy day, the first of a series.

Agnes wrote Fleming that she was better, described Rebecca and Hugh, said she was happy with them, and asked permission to stay at Park Farm till her child should arrive home, when she wished him to send it to her, and they would, when Autumn came, return together. He gave the desired permission, and promised to send the child. Rebecca soon saw that Agnes required her attention no longer; Hugh must take care of her now, she said; she must look to her dairy, which of late had been neglected. So they were abandoned to the dangerous occupation of learning how to be necessary to each other. Agnes rose in the morning buoyant with the hope which found its fulfilment every hour. The thoughts of Hugh ran towards her, as a river runs towards the sea; his attentions gave her a higher estimation of herself. She decorated her hair with the flowers he gave her, and soon knew which dress he liked the most. The coquetry which exists in refined and sensitive women, so long latent in her, was developed; its inspiration exalted her. She had changed indeed since her arrival at Park Farm. Then, she had the immobility and coldness of a statue. Now, she was a woman with blushes, smiles, and tears—all that belongs to one who has been awakened to the fact that she still has the power to interest and please. John and Rebecca were charmed with her gentle vivacity; they talked about her, and said, how good she was, and how handsome, and wished that they could keep her with them always.

For a time they were contented with this open and innocent friendship; the pleasure of finding a similarity of opinion or a likeness in taste, sufficed them. Their books, their rides and walks, were a great enjoyment. The indolent days of sunshine and shower, the calm, sweet evenings were all delightful; life was beautiful. But this wide circle must needs be narrowed to the vortex of personal sensation. The zest and activity with which they had pursued these simple pleasures died out. Rebecca's unthinking good-nature did not allow her to perceive the change in their pursuits; but changed they were. They kept together still, for the charm of presence was imperative with both, but the book remained unopened in Hugh's hand, the walks were confined to the park, the rides given up. Some spirit presiding over the powers that be, was in the air, and had thrown before them the battle-gage of the souls of Agnes and Hugh.

Hugh was quiet, and looked less at her than he did, but pondered the earth and sky, and examined all things inquiringly. Whatever his mood, she hungered for its meaning. Still she was filled with a vague uneasiness; thoughts came to her of the meaning of all this, but she waved them off, and sought Hugh, mute with a pain she would not analyze.

The wheat harvest was over. Unclouded weather prevailed. The yellow sun rose and set in azure. No dew fell at night. No wind came from the North, none from the South. The moon sailed high over the park, and filled its avenues with misty light. Agnes and Hugh spent the evenings there, under the old pine. John went to bed with the fowls, and Rebecca followed him as soon as the kitchen fire went out. Hugh and Agnes had changed places. She was solicitous for him now, and watched his movements with anxiety. He occupied the hammock, while she sat on the grass beside it. Sometimes she put her hand on his head, and found it bathed in sweat. Sometimes she spoke to him and he did not seem to hear her, for he made no answer; but he sighed, and she sighed back softly. The evenings passed in this way were not counted, but when she thought of them afterward, the period seemed a long one.

When the old hall clock struck ten, Agnes went into the house, undressed with haste, pressed her face to the pillow, and resolutely went to sleep. How long Hugh remained in the park, she knew not. She never heard his step in the hall, and she dared not look from her window, for she had more than once dreamed that he was beneath it. Of late Hugh had absented himself during the day, going away in the morning before she rose, returning at night, and after supper taking his place in the hammock or wandering about the park, where Agnes, and sometimes his mother, joined him. Business kept him away, Rebecca said. She thought Hugh must be growing worldly, or she had a fear that he might put into execution an old plan of going to Europe. Agnes looked down when she expressed this fear, and Hugh made no reply.

One night when the clock struck ten, Agnes did not go in. Hugh counted the strokes expecting her "good-night" with the last, but she was silent. So was he. The moths and beetles flew round them undisturbed. The moon rose; hanging low in the sky, its placid light shone under the dark branches of the pines and revealed their faces to each other, but Hugh's eyes were shut. Bending over him she gazed into his face, till a profound and mysterious melancholy filled her soul. She tried in vain to repress her tears; a sob betrayed them. Hugh opened his eyes and saw that she loved him. It was all clear to them now, they loved each other! He felt as every man feels when a crisis is at hand—resolved and daring. But she felt an inexpressible anguish and humiliation. She wished herself a thousand miles away. "Hugh must feel how wrong she was !" He became conscious of the struggle in her mind, and his better sense strove with his primitive heart, and he remained silent; but his face was so eloquent, she could not endure to meet his glance.

"We will speak of this, but not now," she said; "I must go in."

He walked beside her up the avenue, still without speaking. When they reached the porch, she laid her hand on his arm. He stopped.

"Will you kiss me once?" she asked timidly. He laughed, but he clenched his teeth. "Goodnight, Agnes. Do not try me too far," and stepping back, he waved his hand for her to pass in. The air seemed full of sounds, she was so dizzy. Shutting her door, she listened a moment against it, and then groped for a candle, lit it, and walked about the room. She was crying bitterly. "How criminal I am," she thought; "I have prefigured to Hugh, that which a man should realize but with one—the woman he can ask in marriage. I have wronged some woman besides myself, then! and when the day comes for him to marry, he will think of me and of himself with shame. But what harm has he done?" she asked. She could find no fault with him, and with a woman's pride blamed herself alone. The remembrance of his last words came to her, and she saw that she must not meet him again alone. Then she endured one of those struggles where the mind has a perception that its desires and wishes will be overruled, in spite of all that judgment can calculate, and the specious reasons the heart can invent. She looked about mechanically for a pencil and paper, and wrote a few words with a bitter feeling of revolt, protesting with all her soul against their purport—"Hugh," she wrote, "it is not right for us to be together. It must not be. Let us both be silent. We can guess all that might be said." She crept up stairs, and slipped the note under his door. As she turned back, she stumbled over Key, who had followed her. With a growl he caught her sleeve in his teeth and held her fast. Hugh stirred, as if his attention was arrested. "If he opens his door," she thought, "I will go in." But she clutched Key's collar and dragged him by main strength through the passage. He loosed his hold, and she fled down the stairs, and heard Hugh open his door before she reached her room.

Henceforth Agnes avoided him. She saw that her note had a contrary effect from that which she had intended, for he kept near her as if fearful she would escape him.

To her relief, at last her child and his nurse arrived. As she took him, her heart gave a great throb of pain and love. Hugh's face darkened when he saw him, but he took the child up tenderly and embraced him. "Now that your boy has come, you can stay," said Rebecca.

"Autumn is at hand," replied Agnes, "and I must back to my busy city life." She determined to return in a few days, and that those days should be spent apart from Hugh. She could not, however, separate herself entirely from him. He had not left home since the night they were last by the hammock under the pine; the business which occupied him before, seemed to be over. He returned to his books, treasures which had long been neglected; perhaps he derived strength and dignity from his counsel with them. He appeared neither to avoid nor to seek Agnes. His behavior was dangerously sweet to her. She spent her evenings by the bedside of her child, or in chat with Rebecca, but sometimes Hugh and she found themselves alone, in spite of her precautions. A struggle was visible in him—a struggle of pride and passion, of right and wrong. He grew moody, and even Rebecca now perceived a change in him, and the two women divined each other without any words; both prayed in thankfulness when the time came for Agnes to go.

The night before her departure was sultry and portended a storm. She was to leave early in the morning; her trunks were packed; she had had her last talk with Rebecca, and had gone to her room. All was still in the house, her child had been long asleep in her bed. The ominous hush outside was occasionally broken by the roll of distant thunder. The air of the room stifled her, its walls seemed narrowing round her, her heart was beating nervously. She unfastened the ribbon on her throat, and took the comb from her hair; but she could not resolve to undress. She avoided the sight of her face in the glass, but employed herself in carefully arranging the books which were on the table under it. She opened them and read over the name on their title-pages—written in ink discolored with age—'Hugh Park Pennock.' Having done this, she walked up and down the room with an irresolute step; she paused by the child and arranged the coverlet over him. At last she looked up at the window, which stared at her blankly. She went up the steps, softly opened it, and saw from it, what she knew she should see, Hugh below with his face upturned.

"Come down," he said in a husky voice, "come down, Agnes."

The desire which had been smouldering in her to be with him once more, for the last time, now broke the last time, now broke loose. She yielded to it. As she touched the handle of the door, it turned from the outside, opened, and Hugh and she stood face to face. He was deadly pale, and the expression in his eyes made her quail. He drew her through the hall swiftly, out on the porch, down the avenue. A sharp flash of lightning zig-zaged through the gloom, revealing every needle of the pine towards which they were hastening; it daguerreotyped the whole scene in Agnes's memory—the clump of lilies which he trode down—her loosened hair flying over her arms and down her white dress—the tall form of Hugh looming up beside her, his face wild and lurid in the glare—all was impressed there forever. It was utterly dark when they reached the pine. Hugh held her in his arms; she hid her face in his bosom, his head was bowed over hers. The rain-drops began to patter through the leaves. Agnes lifted her face, and Hugh put aside her tangled hair. She withdrew herself from his arms, resting against the tree, for she felt faint, and was about to speak, when her voice was checked by another ghastly flash of lightning. It lighted up the dark end of the house nearest them, where her room was situated, and they caught a sight which froze them. The child, disturbed by the tempest, awoke, and missing her, had crept from his bed, and climbed up the steps into the window, and stood on its narrow ledge, crying for her. She thrust away Hugh, whose impulse was to catch her in his arms and watch with her, for the catastrophe which he saw must take place; but she flew towards the house, desperate with the will to save her child. Something galloped beside her; it was Key. She pointed to the window, now dark again, and tried to speak, to incite him on, for she felt that she only crawled, but in vain ; her running was a jest to Key. He impeded her progress by bounding before her in the path, jumping on her shoulders, and loudly barking. The child heard him, and Agnes, by another flash, saw him stretch out his arms, and totter. Key seemed like a black fiend between her and her child. Her heart was breaking, or was it the dull thud of his fall on the wet stones towards the window, she heard? Even then, Hugh's face shot before her vision, as she saw it upturned to her from the very spot where her child lay.

When she reached him he was not dead, but she knew as she took him up that he was maimed for life. Hugh shuddered as he heard the wild howl which Key set up, and saw lights moving in the house, from the place where he still stood.

[For The New York Saturday Press.]

HARRIET PRESCOTT.

Was ever a volume written, wearing the garb of prose, which was so complete and splendid a poem as Sir Rohan's Ghost'? The very atmosphere of poetry envelopes it, as the soft mist of a Summer sunrise wraps a landscape. It cannot be read like a novel; it is to be lingered over and dwelt upon, its musical and resonant sentences are to be re-read and enjoyed, as we muse over the most imaginative poems to absorb all their latent sweetness and beauty.

Imagine this book to have been the creation of Tennyson, with his exquisite rythm; or of Walt Whitman, with his grand simplicity of expression and Eastern style. The idea is ravishing.

I have amused myself fancying some of its finest passages in the manner of the latter poet, and here is one:

The three graves, the long slope, and the sea behind;
And before,—between the gaps of the cliffs reddening with morning,—
The cross-roads, and a sunrise boiling wildly
Athwart low inland plains.

One region of the heavens was wrapped in the pomp of crimson-brightening vapor,
That curling and sailing higher,
Put up a golden lip to take the morning-star;
Through it, broad rays blanched the zenith;
In it, the thin moon, waning her last quarter,
Slowly and more slowly dissolved away.

The two little poems which appear undisguised in the volume, are perfect; they read as if they should have come from the melodious pages of Percy's 'Reliques.' Long after reading it, one is haunted by the exquisite music and old-ballad-like simplicity of the song Sir Rohan heard in his dream, where

"The fishing-lights their dances
Were keeping, out at sea?"—

and 'Tyntagil' is almost as suggestive as 'The Idylls of the King."

One can hardly realize in reading this book, that it is the work of a mere girl, inexperienced in all the details that give it its inexpressible charm, and perfect finish. We continually ask ourselves, how she should have acquired this apparently inexhaustable knowledge of floral language and peculiarities; this delicate insight into the secrets of color and painting; this marvellous and connoisseur-like lore in rare, almost unknown wines, and the skill to rehearse it all so delightfully.

The scene in the wine-cellar is a sensation in itself, One forgets all else, and sees nothing but those dust-covered jars and flasks, with their strange and delicious names, and hears only the voices of the old man and the young girl murmuring in the dim cellar the histories of rich and far away vintagers; and awakes at the end as from a dream full of perfume and Southern sunshine.

The description of the conservatory is nearly as remarkable. While you read, the air seems loaded with fragrance and permeated with color; and tropical odors which you have dreamed of but never known, seem to develop themselves to your waiting sense. I think that to persons who dread perfume, the reading of that description would bring a sensation of faintness; but to those who delight in flowers, and who revel in their scent and color, it is a rapture.

Some critic whose remarks I have lately come across, pronounces Redruth the failure in this story. I do not agree with him. Marc Arundel seems to me to be its only faulty personation. That character approaches more nearly the boundaries of the commonplace, than any other which Miss Prescott has ever brought upon her stage;—so nearly that it merits not the name of a creation.

Of all Miss Prescott has written, 'The Amber Gods' is the best. There is no other story of the kind in the language, in the world. Who would add to or take from that subtle and magnificent piece of full self-worshipping sensuous life? It is one maze of gorgeous beauty, a perfect trance of imagination and fire, an intoxication. Draughts of those rare and far brought wines that grew precious and more precious in the wine vaults of Belvidere, could scarcely leave one more utterly embraced in an atmosphere of aroma and light, not too heavy with all its luxuriance, nor too warm with its tropical splendor, —only entirely satisfying.

In reading 'The Amber Gods,' you feel nothing of that self wrapped, passionful calm, that royal semi-insensibility which pervades the being of Yone. You go over it rapidly, rushingly, yet thoroughly draining every atom of its light, every drop of its color, just as the soul of that brilliant creature must have gone through the spheres before it was imprisoned behind the light-flooded eyes of Yone Willoughby. You feel at last, as you might if you
beheld an Arab rush over the sands of the desert 'On a stallion shod with fire,' or a star fall from heaven, or any other thing soundless and grand, yet full of unfettered life and motion. This is your first impression, when you have read the last sentence of the story, and your eye turns to linger fascinated upon that sun-bathed title, 'The Amber Gods': but afterwards? There comes a soft luxurious calm, a sensuous quiet, a dreamy Summer noon stillness, and for a brief while, if you are imaginative enough, and impressionable enough, and a woman, you feel—Yone.

Miss Prescott's first story, which appeared in the *Atlantic* over a year ago, was in a certain way, a greater marvel than any that have followed. It was Art itself, in its conception and execution; since no imagination merely, however creative, had been adequate to its production. The highest grade of perceptive faculty, the keenest power of appreciation and appropriation were requisite to the easy insouciance, the hard sparkle and steel—like polish of 'In a Cellar.'

The narration is precisely like Delphine,—icy, glittering, spirituelle, perfect.

Considering the relative positions of all the parties in the story, is there not something exquisitely, almost ludicrously in keeping with its Frenchy tone, in this, its sole bit of sentiment, or rather, sentimentality? "Delphine, will you remember, should you have occasion to do so in Vienna, that it is just possible for an Englishman to have affections and sentiments, and in fact, sensations? That with him friendship can be inviolate, and to betray it an impossibility?"

I do not like 'Yet's Christmas Box' as well as the stories that preceded it. Not, indeed, that there is any falling off of interest, or any waning of power; but it is as if a cloudy morning came, after days of sunny splendor; as if a breath of Euroclydon had swept over the fervid soul that out of its own warmth and wealth created the glory of 'The Amber Gods.' It wants that overpowering brilliancy which lay like a cloudless August heaven over the stories which it followed, and it wants, too, in a degree, their intense, yet graceful rapidity of thought and action. It is Miss Prescott toned down; but we don't want her toned down. "Papa adores rich colors," says Zone Willoughby, "and he might have been satiated here, except that such things make you want more."

I confess, however, to being a little mystified by 'Yet Yuler,' so am, perhaps, not quite fit to judge of it. I fancy that in order to weigh the story appreciatively, one should be connected by a secret, magnetic current of sympathy with the character of the heroine; for in that we are left to divine her mostly by intuition. I could wish for one more touch of light ever so faint, for an outline but half a thought less vague. The whole story, with its heavy shadows and thin lights, from Miss Yuler with her ochre eyes and pent-volcano nature, to Friday and her gaudy hues, impresses me as having been thrown off as a splendid foil to the exquisite richness and harmony of 'The Amber Gods.' As for the coarse witticisms and little unaccountable vulgarities which in these stories give one a shock like that produced by running a sail-boat against an unexpected snag—they are possibly the result of that very redundancy of life and color which startles us so throughout. They have even,—dare I venture to say it?—a certain charm in their brusque, hoydenish fun, and unfastidious freedom, which links them pleasantly, if roughly, with the everyday characters and unrefined actualities of life; nevertheless, I shall be glad when, having had their day, these inelegancies shall cease to be a characteristic of Miss Prescott's style, leaving it perfect as it is already delightful.

Juliette H. Beach.

Albion, N. Y.

Thoughts and Things.

BY ADA CLARE

Laura Keene's New Play.—The 'good time' that we have all heard so much about seems to be coming' at last, in small instalments. An Irish play has been produced without a single *shillalah* in the cast, with no hideous dancing, no fighting, no ragged coats, no howling and unclean family driven from their tenement by a landlord with unbroken expanse of eyebrow. Even the brogue was drawn extremely mild, after the table-beer fashion, and for that I have no doubt many a heart beside my own sent up its hallelujah of joy.

For those who go to the theatre to be amused, 'Colleen Bawn' will be a priceless drama. I do not remember any subsection of the whole that was wearisome in the least degree. A continually changing group of interesting and forcible characters, a quick succession of startling events, together with striking scenic display, ever keeps the mind from losing its vivid and eager interest.

Miss Laura Keene, in her original character of Lioness, carried off as usual, the larger honors of the evening. Her face, manner, and voice, combined to render her really superb as 'Anne Chute,' her vigorous and beautiful personation of the rôle was undoubtedly the chief cause why the play has been such a success. Still this part is not by any means equal to the capacities of this very great actress. I remember her delicious impersonation of Viola in 'As You Like It,' and I hate to see her powers wasted in puny parts; it gives me a sensation like seeing a pure-blooded racer harnessed to a wheelbarrow.

The charming Agnes Robertson, it seems to me never looked so charming as she did in her peasant rôle of Elly O'Conner. The square cut dress was peculiarly advantageous to the display of her lovely throat and shoulders. The charm of her manner and personal appearance gave to the situations a life-like reality, which a plainer woman could not have conferred. It made the love of the high-born man for the peasant girl seem inevitable, whereas in most similar circumstances the low-born charmer is so very uninviting that she goes to protest at sight.

One very remarkable circumstance in the course of this play, I noticed,—I might even style it a miracle for dressmakers. There is a certain scene in which Elly is thrust into the river and withdrawn thence by Myles, a smuggler. Into his cottage on the banks of this very river, a few yards off, he takes her, and there keeps her studiously hidden from every eye, being also under oath not to disclose the fact of her recall to existence to any one. This oath he religiously keeps ; no one suspects that her life has been saved,— then how is it, that having been plunged into the raging deep in a certain unmistakeable striped gown, she appears in that cottage in an entirely new and lovely dove-colored gown? Is there some delicate mystery in all this? Can it be that Myles was no smuggler at all, but that far more tragic thing, a fashionable dressmaker?

I see that most of the journals speak of Madame Ponisi as too melodramatic in the last scene; I do not see the justice of the accusation. The Ponisi is supposed to be a mother ardently attached to her only son; her temperament and temper are excitable; that son is about to be arrested for murder through the revenge of one whom she loathes, and she herself is the actual cause of it, both directly and indirectly. This it seems to my very poor judgment is a situation not demanding artistically, any particular amount of coolness; nay, her feelings might have totally swept out of her command; have worked her up to the fever-pitch of anger and anguish, and yet have been in consonance with nature, if so low an authority can be referred to. For me Madame Ponisi was very affecting and effective; after Laura Keene she carried the greatest interest of the piece.

Of course this play will run to the end of the season; anybody who neglects going to see it, will meet with a material loss.

o o o

It is very late, if not too late in the day now to talk about the 'Poor Young Man' at Wallack's, yet speak of it I must. I saw this play for the first time performed in English on Saturday night. I could not help noticing the strong contrast it offered to the same play at the French Theatre. Mr. Manstein's Poor Young Man is the man of noble birth rendered powerless by poverty. His demeanor at the Laroque Chateau is cold, proud, sad, and retiring.

Mr. Lester's demeanor, on the contrary, is that of the energetic young man whom no reverse of fortune can crush. He carries off the ladies in a body, jokes, laughs, fascinates. Such a poor young man would have undone his title of poor, in no time. He would have made his fortune in some way, any way, and no amount of disappointment could have contrived to keep his head under water.

There were, however, two roles superior to the same in French. Those played by Mr. John Brougham, and Miss Mary Gannon. They added a counter-tone of fun to the whole performance, of which there is none in the French.

I must also, before closing, do justice to Mrs. Hoey, whom I have never seen appear to such advantage as she did in the rôle of Marguerite. Her lady-like, dignified, well-bred manner, told here with great effect. Mrs. Hoey represents the lady on the stage as the natural and elegant lady of real life; a character which she should play easily as it is the one assigned to her by fate. In her there is none of that straining after effect, that vulgar showiness which is so often found in those less favored than she is. In the last scene her repentance of previous harshness and arrogance is very pathetic and touching.

I must not omit to say, that she really knew how to dress her part in the simple and elegant manner so necessary for its effect; after all a knowledge of the toilet is a most important thing on the stage. Mrs. Hoey is a model in that respect, it's a pity she were not more imitated.

o o o

The milliners, etc., should rejoice that the name of Fabbri is such an easy one to pronounce, for I understand that all the new styles of bonnets, mantillas, headdresses, etc., are to be immediately baptized Inez Fabbri.

o o o

Speaking of milliners as lucky, what term can be used to express the fortune of the upholsterer at present. With the present dramatic tendency the run upon feather beds must be immense. Everybody must jump, or tumble, or be thrown somewhere, and the immortal feather-bed does the genuine heavy business of the play. Are a number of respectable and highly moral citizens going to join together to urge it to take a benefit? Are they going to state to it with rhetorical flourish that its labors in the service of the dramatic public, as well as its unfailing effort to elevate the stage, etc. Why not?

WALTER ASHWOOD; A Love Story. By Paul Siogvolk, author of Schediasms. 1 vol. 12mo. New York: Rudd & Carleton. 1834.

It may be said of this book that the author has aimed at nothing, and hit it. From beginning to end, so far as we can see, it represents no phase, principle, nor picture even, of human life. All the characters in it, from the central figure down to a gushing little idiot called Charley, are unnatural to the last degree. The hero is a badly-drawn type of that very lovely and charming creature, the woman-killer. He kills one, literally, before the end of the fifth chapter, and in course of the narrative, kills two others (in the love-sense of killing, which is not so very dangerous after all), not to mention those he kills behind the scenes, whose number the author thinks is legion.

Yet nothing is told about this cruel person in any part of the story, which could induce a sensible woman to have him (much less to be killed by him) on any terms. ms. And, so far as appears, no sensible woman ever does have him. The three women who expend their little stock of affection upon him in the present work, are very queer specimens: the first being a sentimental young girl in her teens, who does nothing, swooning excepted, but rave about Niagara, where she at last goes and drowns herself: the second being a granivorous widow, who has recently buried a loving but consumptive and unsympathizing husband, and who finally goes to a nunnery to pine away and die (which, we beg to remark, the granivorous widow is not apt to do); and the third being an impassioned and hungry old maid, seeking whom she may devour, but who finally, like the rest, gets left in the lurch, and nobody knows or cares whatever becomes of her. The two latter are demi-mundane people, whom Walter meets at watering-places and sich, in Europe, where one of them, on being jilted, takes to dice and drink before taking the veil, while the other, from the first, drives two lovers tandem, and could evidently have driven half a dozen more (if they were all like Walter) with equal ease.

The hero himself, after raising general havoc (so far as he can) with all the women he encounters, finally, —for no earthly reason, and to nobody's very great sorrow, not even the reader's—takes a dose of prussic-acid or something—and there an end, and a very grateful one, of both him and the book.

We fancy, for some reason, that the anonymous author of this story imagines that he himself is a kind of Walter Ashwood, and that having had a score of women in love with him at different times (if not at the same time), most of whom are now among the killed and wounded, he writes this book to give vent to his feelings of remorse, and to warn the tender sex against having anything more to do with him—which, in his capacity as author, at least, we incline to think they never will.

In a word, our verdict against Walter Ashwood is 'Guilty, with a recommendation to Mercy.'

Dramatic Feuilleton.

Revenge.

I see that the *Courrier des Etats-Unis*, after having made its humble apology to *Personne* for having, in its ignorance of English, mistranslated a passage in one of his late Feuilletons, immediately takes its little revenge by pitching sharply into me, in consequence of the printer having accidentally dropped a *u*, or a something, out of my signature.

It was the best thing the Gaul could do under the circumstances, so I forgive him, and accept his excuses in advance.

Evangeline.

This week we lose the lovely Acadian girl at the Winter Garden. Perhaps we shall realize what the poet meant in saying that 'when she had passed, it seemed like the ceasing of exquisite music.'

On Saturday evening Miss Bateman will have a benefit, and make her last appearance this season. She will play Lady Teazle in 'The School For Scandal.'

For many reasons I incline to think that Miss Bateman's best success must be achieved in comedy. In the opening scene of 'Evangeline' she has, as it seems to me, manifested an arch and winning playfulness of disposition, together with the vivacity and mirthful tone which indicate the comédienne. Hence I anticipate for her a decided Triumph in the part of Lady Teazle.

Anyway I hope the Winter Garden will be crowded on Saturday evening with an audience of persons who appreciate the delicacy of encouraging a young, lovely, and talented actress, eminently worthy of success, and thus far successful against many and very powerful obstacles.

Musical.

I am afraid I know so little about music as a science or what not, that it would be impossible for me to write an intelligible treatise even on the new musical 'pitch' which some of the old fogies say one cannot touch without being defiled.

This may account for my love of sweet sounds, my adoration of Piccolomini and Patti, my general sanity, and my indisposition to quarrel with anybody.

The same cause may explain the uncommonly sane and peaceful condition of the Quakers, who, with now and then a heretical exception, oppose music as injurious to the morals. This, however, doesn't prevent their singing in meeting, though I am not sure that that has anything to do with sweet sounds. The last time I was present at one of their meetings, I remember thinking that it hadn't.

After all, as the world goes, the Quakers may be right. They ought, at least, to be right in one matter, and who knows but it is this?

Considering the quarrels that are constantly going on among the Sons and Daughters of Harmony, I shouldn't wonder if it were, though I should hope not. For my own part, these little quarrels in the Harmonic world are very amusing. I wouldn't have Ullman, Strakosch, and Maratzek on good terms for any consideration.

I would as soon bring about a reconciliation between Stephen H. Branch and the common council, or between Bennett and Greeley.

In which case what a world of Manifestos we should lose!

If a Piccolomini, a Cortesi, a Patti, or a Fabbri, didn't set all the impressarios by the ears, I should be quite miserable. The opera would lose half its piquancy, and its managers all their charm; for if there is a dismal man in the world, aside from his little difficulties, it is the opera-manager, though this doesn't prevent my looking up to him as, on the whole, a very awful and sublime personage—especially when I want a private box.

All which being interpreted, means that next week we are to have two Operas, and that I dont know what in the world to say of them.

I shall go to both,—duly armed with lorgnette and Spring vegetables (I cant go Brazilian wreaths made up of birds of paradise, etc.,)—and shall try when the time comes, to speak of Patti and Fabbri, Brignoli, and Ernani, Amodio and Gassier, to say nothing of the new 'tenore robusto,' in a manner to astonish the critics.

Meanwhile, I am studying up 'Tillman's Treatise on Musical Sounds' and trying my hand on his 'Tonometer or Revolving Musical Scale,' which, as it shows 'the relative position of all the true and tempered notes in the major and minor modes in ever key now known,' is a very pretty thing to do.

Especially as 'by its aid those who are not endowed with a keen sense for discriminating the tones in music, can become masters of the science; while the more gifted can readily survey the whole subject, and bring within definite range the most diversified regions of melody and harmony.'

I havn't quite made up my mind whether to go in for Patti or Fabbri, but rather incline to think it will be Patti, because I once committed myself to her in a Sonnet, and because, having seen a photograph of Fabbri, I don't think she is quite up to my line of beauty. And, say what you will, beauty goes a good way in such matters with all of us. Witness Piccolomini, who, I am told by the critics (though I don't believe a word of it), knows nothing about music, but travels entirely on her good looks.

By no means a hard road to travel, in this case.

Seriously speaking—if a Feuilletonist may be permitted to be serious—I wonder if anybody intends to go to the Winter Garden or to the Academy of Music on Easter Monday, with a view to write a scientific criticism!

I never read but one criticism of the kind, and that was in *Dwight's Musical Journal*; and the only effect it had upon me was that of recalling to my mind the lines of Wordsworth:

'Our meddling intellect
Misshapes the beauteous forms of things,
We murder to dissect.'

Still the murdering and dissecting must be done (in order to advance the interests of science), and if the reader will only bear with me next week, perhaps I will see what I can do at it.

But I must first invest sixpence in Tuesday's *Times*, *Tribune*, and *Herald*,—where the thing will be done, if at all, con amore.

Meanwhile, I cannot too much rejoice that Lent is over, and that we may all now legitimately give ourselves over to the hilarities—musical among other—of the season.

The rival opera-houses will doubtless both be crowded, and all Israel will be in a state of jubilee.

Quelqu'un.

Pfaff's, April 5, 1860.

NEW YORK APRIL 14, 1860

PENELOPE.

BY EDMUND C. STEDMAN.

Not thus, Ulysses, with a tender word,
Pretence of state affairs, soft blandishment
And halt assurances, canst thou evade
My heart's discernment. Think not such a film
Hath touched these aged eyes, to make them lose
The subtlest mood of those even now adroop,
Self-conscious, darkling from my nearer gaze.
Full well I know thy mind, O man of wiles!
O man of restless yearnings—fate-impelled,
Fate-conquering—like a waif thrown back and forth
O'er many waters! Oft I see thee stand
At eve, a landmark on the outer cliff,
Looking far westward: later, whan the feast
Smokes in the hall, and nimble servants pass
Great bowls of wine, and ancient Phemeus sings
The deeds of Peleus' son, thy right hand moves
Straight for its sword-hilt, like a ship for home :
Then, when thou hearest him follow in the song
Thine own miraculous sojourn of long years
Through stormy seas, weird islands, and the land
Of giants, and the gray companions smite
Their shields, and cry—*What do we longer here!*
Afloat! and let the great waves bear us on!
I know hou growest weary of the realm,
Thy wife, thy son, the people, and thy fame.

I too have had my longings. Am I not
Penelope, who, when Ulysses came
To Sparta, and Icarius bade her choose
Betwixt her sire and wooer, veiled her face
And stept upon the galley silver-oared,
And since hath kept thine Ithacensian halls?
Then when the hateful Helen fled to Troy
With Paris, and the Argive chieftains sailed
Their ships to Aulis, I would have thee go—
Presaging fame, and power, and spoils of war.
So ten years past; meanwhile I reared thy son
To know his father's wisdom, and, apart
Among my maidens, wove the yellow wool.
But then, returning one by one, they came—
The island-princes; high-born dames, of Crete
And Cephalonia, saw again their lords;
Only Ulysses came not; yet the war
Was over, and his vessels, like a troop
Of cranes in file, had spread their wings for home.
More was unknown. Then many a Winter's night
The servants piled great faggots, smeared with tar,
High on the palace-roof; with mine own hands
I fired the heaps, that, haply, far away
On the dark waters, might my lord take heart
And know the glory of his kingly towers.

So Winter past: and Summer came and went,
And Winter and another Summer; then—
Alas, how many weary months and days!
But he I loved came not. Meanwhile thou knowest
Pelasgia's noblest chiefs, with kingly gifts
And pledge of dower, gathered in the halls;
But still this heart kept faithful, knowing yet
Thou wouldst return, though wreckt on alien shores.
And great Athene often in my dreams
Shone, uttering words of cheer. But, last of all,
The people rose, swearing a king should rule—
To keep their ancient empery of the isles
Inviolate and thrifty: bade me choose
A mate, nor longer dally. Then I prayed
Respite, until the web within my loom,
Of gold and purple curiously devised
For old Laertes' shroud, should fall complete

From hands still faithful to his blood. Thou knowest
How like a ghost I left my couch at night,
Unravelling the labor of the day,
And warded off the fate, till came that time
When my lost sea-king thundered in his halls,
And with long arrows clove the suitors' hearts.
So constant was I! now not thirty moons
Go by, and thou forgettest all: alas!
What profit is there any more in love?
What thankless sequel hath a woman's faith!

Yet if thou wilt—in these thy golden years,
Safe-housed in royalty, like a God revered
By all the people—if thou yearnest yet
Once more to dare the deep and Neptune's hate,
I will not linger in a widowed age;
I will not lose Ulysses, hardly found
After long vigils; but will cleave about
Thy neck, with more than woman's prayers and tears,
Until thou take me with thee. As I left
My sire, I leave my son, to follow where
Ulysses goeth, dearer for the strength,
Of that great heart which ever drives him on
To large experience of newer toils!

Trust me, I will not any hindrance prove,
But, like Athene's helm, a guiding star,
A glory and a comfort! O, be sure
My heart shall take its lesson from thine own!
My voice shall cheer the mariners at their oars
In the night watches; it shall warble songs,
Whose music shall o'erpower the luring airs
Of Nereid or Siren. If we find
Those isles thou namest, where the golden fount
Gives youth to all who taste it, we will drink
Deep draughts, until the furrows leave thy brow,
And I shall walk in beauty, as when first
I saw thee from afar in Sparta's groves.
But if Charybdis seize our keel, or swift
Black currents bear us down the noisome wave
That leads to Hades, till the vessel sink
In Stygian waters, none the less our souls
Shall gain the farther shore, and, hand in hand,
Walk from the strand across Elysian fields,
'Mong happy thronging shades, that point and say:
"There go the great Ulysses, loved of Gods,
And she, his wife, most faithful unto death!"

—The London *Critic* says of Mrs. Browning's new poems and the opinions they espouse:

Frankly, we like neither the opinions nor the manner in which they are conveyed. Like Miriam, Mrs. Browning stands before the men of war and proclaims the passage of Italian patriotism through the Red Sea of Magenta and Solferino; but unlike Miriam, her note is the note of the raven croaking over the slain, rather than the clear song of triumph celebrating the advent of a new-born liberty. Living as she does, in the very heart of Italian politics, opinions and interests which to us seem very small, take with her gigantic proportions. Everything Italian is magnified in her eyes. So enthusiastic is she, that she puts her faith in the purity of Louis Napoleon's motives, and believes that he came to Italy for no meaner motive than to set Italy free. He is a demigod in her eyes—this fortunate speculator, this shrewd and crafty politician, who shifts nationalities under treaties, as a man would peas under a thimble. She believes that he who has enslaved his own subjects, and holds them bound and gagged with a bayonet at their throats, is the saviour of the world, the proclaimer of the gospel of liberty. She even curses her own country, because England refused to take part in the plan by forging a still stronger fetter whilst she pretended to enfranchise the captive.

Dramatic Feuilleton.

'Personne' salaams to his Victims.—The Italian Question in a new phase. —Brief Biographical Sketch (untrue) of M. Maretzek.—Effects of the Opposition upon the amusing classes. —The Exaltation of Israel and return of the Ten Tribes. —Rejoicings of the Dead Head Brigade—The Rival Companies. —Adelina Patti and the Quartette of Irving Place. —The Birds at the W. G. La Gassier.—Fabbri and the new Achilles. —Debut of Mrs. George Jordan.—Outrageous attempt to bring out an actress under forty-five.

Some people have reported, Effendi, that the Subscriber had 'dried up,' as the boys say.

It is an error. Does any one imagine that I would ever desert Mrs. Micawber? That I would become faithless to Peoria and Orange and Attakapas? That I would ignore LE CHAUVE, the Chevalier de Gantrouge, Victor Sejour Gayler, Miss Laura B. S. Keene, Octave Feuillet Lester, and Gerald Griffin Boucicault, or that I would disobey the positive injunctions of Anna Maria, who says, write the Feuilleton, and insinuates that that is 'all I am good for,' a favorite expression of the Dear Child, and one which I think is sometimes liable to misconstruction.

Never mind. Let us come to Hecuba. Hecuba, this week, is the Opera war.

Max Maretzek has come to town and as usual, has kicked up a row.

There is one good thing, among others, about M. M., he keeps things well stirred up whenever he is about. His normal condition is that of war. He is an operatic Infant of Benecia, and always has his hands up. When he is not pitching into the amiable Strakosch or the elegant Ulmann, he takes it out of the score, and pounds away upon the top of the prompter's box, as if he had a personal enmity against that hard-working and long-suffering official.

I must tell you that the fascinating Maximilian arrived only recently from the Havana, whence he had absolutely to take ship by stealth in order to avoid the importunities of the first families who were in the habit of sending cart-loads of doubloons to his lodgings every morning. As for the artists, they are all provided for. Madame Gassier is a grandee of Spain, created Duchess of Solfeggi-amoroso, with a pension of several millions per annum, and a large number of Chateaux en Espagne.

The major part of Max's doubloons were landed upon Staten Island, and buried near where they suppose the Kidd treasure to be, and in a right line from where the Hussar frigate went down.

The remainder was brought to town and deposited in the Chemical as the sinews of war.

The fight commenced on Monday, but both parties did not get fairly going till Wednesday. Max threw his cap into the ring with the Gassiers, and the new tenor, Achille Errani, in *Lucia*, and Strakosch put in little Patti, the champion of the light weights, warranted at eight to four against anything of her size and age, here or elsewhere, in the *Barber*.

There was a great deal of excitement in a small way. I don't know that it has ever occurred to me before, but I begin to think that the opera-managers are philanthropists of the purest school. See how thoughtful they are of the illustrious brigade, scornfully denominated dead-heads. When there is only one opera Israel must stay at home, or if by cringing and begging Mr. Solomon gets a place, it is on a back bench, where Madame Solomon's new (its just as good, nobody will know it from new) opera-cloak cannot excite the envy of the aristocracy. But when the war comes, ah, then the Solomons are in all 'their glory.' Madame absolutely hesitates, places her saffron finger on her classic nose, and balances the Academy against the W. G. Now she has good places, now the burnous and the made-over coal-scuttle-bonnet adorn the centre of the parquette, and may even aspire to the full triumph of a prosceneum box.

And the demi-monde, I don't mean the demi-monde, that is bad (that always pays), but the world that lives between Fourth and Fourteenth, and scrimps, and saves, and strains, so that Madame and the Demoiselles may parade on Broadway dressed so as to be mistaken for lorettes,—isn't it splendid for them? Young Snip, who is with a great dry-goods house, is quite ready to do the honors when there is nothing to pay, and while the ladies cultivate a Fifth Avenue manner, the 'gent' fancies himself one of the jeunesse dorée, when he is really a fine specimen of the jeunesse snobée (if you don't like that, do something better).

Then there are the gipsey artists, who are always good, but always out of engagements; therefore, continually upon the highest kind of a rock. When the opposition opera comes, they go about like the gentlemen of Barnegat in the old times, and pick up the pieces from the wreck.

The only sufferers by the opera wars are the critics, but nobody cares for them. They are, or ought to be, like the eels, quite used to it.

The Sunday critic rather likes it. No manager snubs him now, and says that his paper is of no earthly significance to anybody, and his opinion a matter of no consequence. No, sir; the Sunday 'cricket' is a great concern, just now. As for the heavy daily-men, they look as if the whole thing was a terrific bore, and wondered when it would be all over.

I don't think the general public gains much by the opposition, except that its curiosity is piqued, and it has a bit of sensation at a dull time of the year. Two operas in one city work badly for many reasons. The artists assume insufferable airs, and the best company does not always win the victory.

In the present war, we see a clever manager deploying a number of new artists against a well-balanced company led by a great popular pet,—for I presume that no one will deny that ADELINA PATTI's position with the public improves every day. Without going into any elaborate analysis, which would be a bore, I think I express the opinion of the connoisseurs when I place her *Norina* musically far above that of Pic., and dramatically not far below it. The quartette at the Academy—Brignoli, Amodio, Ferri, and Susini—are all excellent artists, as the public very well knows. Brignoli never sang so well in *Don Pasquale* as on Wednesday. The serenade was positively delicious.

Let us see what the belligerent Max brings to the contest!

La Gassier. La Gassier, who has a most magnificent voice, and sings like a bird. Her mad-scene in *Lucia* is worth a king's ransom. But for some reason or other, which I can't divine, La Gassier is not en rapport with the public. The public says that, like La Grange, she is only a singer of cadenzas; and then, duly satisfied with its criticism, the public goes to the Circus, or has a shy at the Colleen Bawn.

This wicked, stiff-necked public! I have no patience with it. It will have its own way. Blow it!

A new tenor-Errani. A fair artist, but not so good as Stigelli, who, by the way, has gone over to the Maretzek forces.

The new prima donna Fabbri. I should prefer to hear her in some opera other than the *Traviata.* The rôle of the heroine in this fine lyrical drama ought to be sustained by an exceedingly pretty woman, otherwise much of the poetry is lost. For my own part I prefer Pic's *Traviata* to all of them. Fabbri does not come to the standard that was claimed for her before she appeared, in some things, and in others she exceeds it. She has voice enough for ten Traviatas, and sings thoroughly well. Her execution was said to be equal to that of La Grange. It does not so appear to the Subscriber.

Fabbri is a splendid actress. I sat beside a very eminent artist, who has won many triumphs in the emotional French dramas, and we watched the last act very closely. It was broad and grand in conception, most artistically worked out in every detail, and finished superbly. That, we both remarked in the same breath, that is real acting. The *Parigi O Cara* was better than the *Gran Dio*, but like a true artist, one who has command over the audience, and knows it, the bonne bouche was kept for the last.

I wouldn't have missed that last act, Effendi, for anything in the world. The post-prandial-before-the-gas-is-lighted-behind-the-window-curtain téte-á-téte with the Pearl of Manhattan, is the only sensation I can compare it to.

That will do, I reckon, for the Opera-folks, particularly as Mr. Printer is in a hurry. I didn't intend to say a word to you about the Theatres, but when there's a lady, etc.—it is about Mrs. GEORGE JORDAN, who played for her husband's benefit, at the W. G. on Tuesday, and delighted everybody. I hope that she will be permanently attached to one of our theatres. A pretty woman, who is still young, who speaks naturally, who does not look at the audience when some one is talking to her, who is not painted and powdered and enamelled, in the vain hope of taking off the marks of twenty years in the coulisses,—a living *woman,*—one who is not a well-preserved mummy, or a wiry virago—ought to come oftener before a long-suffering public. It is a duty which she owes to humanity. Let Mrs. JORDAN, who looks good as well as handsome, take pity upon us miserable sinners.

Adieu, Colonel,
Tout-à-vous,
Votre bien devoué,

Personne.

Dramatic Items.

'Semiramide' is now in preparation at the Grand Opera of Paris for the sisters Marchesie.

Mr. Gevaert has an opera forthcoming at the *Opéra Comique*, among the personages of which is Richelieu, to be sustained by M. Condere.

Mr. and Mrs. Charles Kean have been giving a series of Dramatic entertainments in Aberdeen.

Mrs. Howard Paul is giving imitation in London of Sims Reeves and other musical celebrities. The London *Critic* 'defies anybody who is not essentially a stock or a stone to remain unmoved by her'—in which respect, it would seem, she is not unlike Mrs. John Wood.

A new cantata, by Mr. Macfarren, on an English subject, with words by Mr. Oxenford, is in the press.

George Sand is about finishing a play to be produced at one of the leading theatres in Paris.

At the Drury Lane, London, a new play by Mr. Fitzball has been produced. It is entitled 'Christmas Eve; or, the Duel in the Snow,' and was suggested by a picture exhibited at the Exhibition of French Artists in Pall Mall, which represented a dying Pierrot killed in a duel by a New Zealand Chieftain, and surrounded by a number of Masques. In the Drama we have an interpretation of the picture. The Pierrot is one 'Sir Charles Andry,' and the New Zealander is one 'Capt. Dashwood,' who has behaved ungratefully, and eloped with the wife of Sir Charles. The latter follows him to a ball, quarrels with him, and retires to the Bois de Boulogne, where the duel takes place.

At the Strand, Miss Swanborough has brought out a little Watteau kind of piece, written by a lady, and attributed to the reign of Louis the Fifteenth, called 'The Loves of Arcadia.' The king has desired the union of the Chevalier de Merilback and Mdlle. Désirée de Launay, who had as yet never seen each other, the lady having been bred in a convent and the gentleman at court. They are, however, determined to hate one another, and not to meet; and yet, as usual in fancy pieces of the kind, contrive the very means for doing so. Both, according to the easy plan of story-building implied in this remark, resolve to play shepherd and shepherdess in an Arcadia of their own, and accordingly find themselves in a forest together, making love to each other 'incontinently.' As a matter of course, the King comes hunting in the forest, and takes the unknown shepherdess to court, to perform in an Arcadian *fête* of his own; thither the Chevalier follows her, to exhibit himself in a picture-frame as his own portrait, and to be made happy in the way originally intended by His Majesty.

Max Maretzek is about to produce 'La Zingara,' the Italian version of Balfe's ever popular 'Bohemian Girl,' at the Winter Garden. Miranda, the favorite English tenor, who came over with the Cooper troupe, and sung at Wallack's about two years ago, is engaged for the rôle of Thaddeus.

At the Italian Opera, Paris, Tamberlik has made his rentrée as 'Othello.' Madame Borghi-Mamo achieved a complete triumph as 'Desdemona.' Tamberlik gets 2,500f. a night. The event at the Grand Opera is a new work by Prince Poniatowski, entitled 'Pierre de Médicis.' The Emperor and Empress were present at its first representation. Mdlle. Vestvali, the contralto of the Grand Opera, is to go to London this year, and also Alboni. Guiglini has received a diamond snuff box from King Victor Emmanuel. Madame Penco is engaged for London. She has become a great favorite in Paris, and will return there next year.

M'lle Piccolomini, still a spinster, though no longer 'open for an offer,' is announced to sing daily, at the Crystal Palace, throughout Passion and Easter weeks. She will then appear, for a few farewell nights, at Her Majesty's Theatre, previous to taking leave of the stage.

NEW YORK APRIL 21, 1860

SCANDAL MONGERS.

We learn from the *Tribune* (and, for special reasons, are glad to have the statement originate in that sheet) that a New York correspondent of a flash newspaper published in Boston, was publicly cowhided in Brooklyn, on Wednesday last, by one of the male relatives of a young lady who had recently been libelled in the said paper.

It was high time that a certain class of New York correspondents received some such lesson, and we trust that, for their own sakes, they will profit by it in time.

We are well aware that the correspondents to whom we allude are a peculiar class of people; that they are, as a rule, ill-bred, ill-natured, and illiterate; that they are not expected by their employers to be either decent, truthful, or honorable; that they are engaged to do a kind of work from which every gentleman would shrink with horror; that the matter which they concoct is of such a character that it cannot be admitted into metropolitan journals; that in the absence of other material of the sensation order wherewith to make up their 'Correspondence,' they are obliged to pry into the secrets of private life, and parade them before the public; that when the actual facts ferretted out are not sufficiently piquant, they must distort or embellish them, utterly reckless of consequences; that in the prosecution of this work they cannot afford to respect either age, position, or sex; that, in a word, they can have no other aim than to furnish scandalous matter in return for their scandalous pay.

We are well aware of all these facts; but instead of mitigating the evil of which we complain, they only aggravate it.

We are also aware that there are many persons in society—and in what is called good society, too—who take a morbid pleasure in having their names bandied about, and whose delight at seeing themselves in print is so intense as to neutralize every feeling of natural delicacy.

It is perhaps owing, in part, to the existence of this class of persons, that the correspondents to whom we refer find such ready employment. And yet how any respectable journal, even in the country, where the tone of morality is generally much lower than in the city, can print these communications, has always been, to us, a great mystery.

All we know, is that they do it, and do it continually.

We have known a dozen instances within a year; and one recently, in which a scandalous story was trumped up in respect to an accomplished correspondent of this paper, who, in another column, speaks for herself.

In this particular case, the details were so varied and so romantic that the letter containing them was at once copied all over the country, thus creating an amount of mischief which years cannot repair, nor the lives of a dozen scandal-mongers atone for.

Where the calumnies are printed only in flash papers such as Boston has so many years been celebrated for, the harm done is comparatively slight, and the sufferer may experience some relief from the fact that the perpetrator has been handsomely thrashed; but when they are printed in respectable journals in every State in the Union—as in case of the letter referring to Ada Clare and her friends—there is absolutely no way either of remedying the mischief done, or of adequately punishing the perpetrator of it.

Thoughts and Things.

BY ADA CLARE

The taste for exploiting the private lives of those who have rendered themselves in any way famous, is becoming more and more confirmed in America. The coarseness and injustice of the personal details that appear in our press, have already disgraced us all over the civilized world.

The columns of our journals lend themselves to the wreaking of every species of petty vengeance and malice. In them selfish prejudice, vulgar, short-sighted morality, foolish envy, and coarse gossip, blow stentorous blasts from their two-penny trumpets, with which to split the idle ears of the nation.

I am told that an English writer sojourning in Italy, sent a letter to a London journal containing a detailed and spicy account of a *liaison* existing between one of England's most illustrious poets, who was known to live unhappily with his wife, and a beautiful Italian lady. Not a journal in England, it is said, would consent to publish the letter.

How ingloriously do our own newspapers contrast to this? If for instance, any unknown and unreliable correspondent had communicated to them a full account of a seraglio, kept, at eighty, by Washington Irving, how many of them would have refused it publication because it was a calumny?

For several years my own private life and character have been made the subject for all manner of malicious and false statements. The most madly impossible stories, the most preposterous rumors, the most sickening hypocrisies have been labelled with my name, and sent to grovel through the provinces. If any two of the stories could have met together, they would, like the dragon's teeth sowed by Cadmus, necessarily have devoured each other. I have refrained from contradicting these stories for two reasons: one, because I believe that such impossible lies must sign their own death-warrants; and the other, because I did not think myself of sufficient importance to the public mind, to make it necessary to tease it with statements and contradictions, regarding my private affairs. For the latter, I have long been expecting a public testimony of thanks, but as yet I see no signs of the testimonial cup.

Nothing could be more false and foolish than the idea that any man or woman's private life can ever be honorably dragged before the public. What the individual does or says in a public capacity, is all that belongs to the public; nothing but selfish interest, or extreme vulgarity, can lead a man to a different course of action.

It most frequently occurs that the gossiping animal seeks to earn a cheap notoriety for himself by careering against some one who has genuinely gained the public ear. Ofttimes he is under the ban of public opinion, his moral promiscuousness has become notorious, and he seeks to vindicate himself by madly maligning some purer man or woman. Again, another strong reason for the concoction of such gossip, is the necessity of finding new subjects upon which to earn the immortal $10. I should like to know how much bullion has been exchanged for the most illogical nonsense about me, taken all in all: for I think it but fair that it should be paid over to me immediately. I would be willing to spend it in soft-soap with which to scour the hearts of my historians.

I have the idea that a book called 'Popular Lies,' would create some sensation; it could be principally compiled of those vulgar, gossipping letters, which always awaken the hallelujahs of the provinces.

There is another very remarkable circumstance connected with this subject, which I am at a loss to explain, namely, that most journals prefer in publishing a scandalous lie that it should relate to a woman rather than to a man. They would rather, for instance, calumniate Ada Clare than John C. Heenan; is it that the female fingers are considered inconvenient or inadequate to the tweaking of the editorial-nose?

°°°

I communicated an article last week to the *Sunday Courier*, entitled 'The Megatherium Bonnet.' I re-publish a small part of it here, as much with a view to fling odium upon that atrocious fashion, as to correct some typographical errors which in the original made me appear slightly ridiculous:

> Most persons have seen and marked the bonnet christened with the ponderous title that heads this article, but few know that its origin was both scientific and utilitarian. I learn from the most unquestionable authority that it was invented by an enraged milliner, who, having been ejected from her dwelling for unpaid rent, was wandering in a frenzy through the majestic halls of the British Museum. Wandering about she murmured to herself, 'Why am I thus homeless, why are my bonnets unsold, unsought for? Why do the London ladies purchase so few bonnets? Why do they complain that coming in contact with other objects during the fog ruins them? Is it my fault? Do I hang London with cloud and mist?'
>
> Suddenly wandering thus, and so chafing inwardly, she suddenly came upon the preserved skeleton of the antediluvian animal, known in Zoological circles & the Megatherium.
>
> At the first sight of the colossal beast, she held her brain lest it should burst for joy. She gazed at the long huge neck, and she cried Eureka! She fastened her eyes on the immense protruding back of the beast, and again she cried Eureka!
>
> Reader, she had discovered the great Megatherium bonnet, the only safe helmet in a London fog, the gigantic thing which you have all seen with fear and trem-

bling on the heads of our bravest New York ladies.

The original Davy, the inventor of the miner's lamp, will hold no higher place in scientific and moral fame, than will the woman who invented this bonnet for carrying lamps in fogs, as well as for intimidating the progressive male of the human species.

The Megatherium bonnet is constructed to touch the head in a single line, running straight round from the ears. From this point of contact it runs upwards in the front to the distance of from one to three feet; at the back it swells into a voluminous bag, whose size is proportionate to the taste of the builder. The high front cupola of the bonnet-edifice is fitted up with a small and gracefully pendant lamp, which is furnished with silken wick, and perfumed oil. In case of the all-obscuring fog, the lady puts on this safety bonnet, and the lamp being illumined, it not only lights her own pathway, but prevents others from running into collision with her. The back or bag of the bonnet is lined with soft India-rubber, and is really a small cistern filled with rose-water, which in case of the lady's hair taking fire from the lamp, can be made to deluge he head, by the simple compression of a spring.

In America where there are no fogs, this bonnet is used entirely to a moral end, that of preventing gentlemen from becoming enamored of the ladies who wear them. The invention is said to be as useful to effect this end as the other.

A bonnet was originally worn with a view to ornament for the face, and protection for the head and ears. With this view it was made of every variety of beautiful lace, silk, crape, and velvet, and soft blondes and blushing roses were made to nestle against the cheeks and head. Good taste suggested that the head should form the summit of the dressed lady, not by any means that that crowning member should, in violation of the lessons of Nature, be made to surmount the person in the ridiculous shape of a club. The bonnet of which I have been discoursing not only scorns and tramples upon the idea of utility and ornament, but if it runs up much higher, the nautical science will soon become an essential to the female education. What amount of mere bending of the knees will serve to run a lady against a high wind with such an expanse of canvas as that unfurled above her brows? None, indeed. She will be forced to tack as the schooners do, to run diagonally and in circles, except in cases where she can set her sails to the wind.

Dramatic Feuilleton.

The Dramatic Fund Benefit.—A Fresh Field for Dr. Carnochan.—Terrible Epidemic among the Artists.— Present Condition of the Sufferers.—Extraordinary Professsonal Exaltation of Miss Ida Vernon.—The Opera, Orthodox and Heterodox.—A Prima Donna on Fire.—La Frezzolini.—La Wissler.—La Kelloggini.—And various other things.

They made a terrible time, Effendi, over the Dramatic Fund Benefit, but, from what John Brougham would call a curious concatenation of coincident circumstances, it didn't amount to much!

The Association is, pecuniarly speaking, in a very tight place, and something had to be done to help it out. So Mr. Brougham went to work, like a beaver, to get up this benefit, and secured the services of a large number of artists, many of whom have no claim whatsoever on the Fund.

There was to be a Dramatic Matinée and a soirée with opera folks, and more plays. The Matinée was all well enough, except Miss Laura Keene, who became alarmingly ill at about fifteen minutes before the performance commenced, and couldn't do *L. G. Spanker*. Mrs. Hoey took the place of Miss Keene, and the play went on or off just as you please.

In the evening, the bill included *Nine Points of the Law*, with Miss Ada Clifton, Mr. Mark Smith, and F. A. Vincent, all on hand, and the Comedy was as well played as such a piece can be done in the Academy. It is a good deal like dancing a waltz-quadrille in the centre of a prairie, this doing drawing-room pieces in Irving Place. However, the Clifton looked charmingly, and acted capitally, and so the affair went off nicely. Then there was Mrs. Barney Williams and B. W. himself, in that charming dramatic *chef d'œuvre, Latest from New York*. The artist who was to do the funny man in this play, was like the clerk who speaks English in the Parish shops; he had sortied and didn't come back. So the B. Ws, like clever people as they are, got along without him.

Aprés, the Opera, Stigelli, Junca, Amodio, Muzio, Gassier, Madame Gassier, and Madame Strakosch. All but Junca and Amodio failed to put in an appearance. All sick. Awful state of things. Consequence, no opera. Then we came to a very fresh and delightful farce, *Turning the Tables*, wherein G. Jordan, G. Holland, Miss Mary Gannon, and various other persons, were to instruct and amuse (I got that from Barnum) the enlightened public. G. Jordan was about, but there was no Holland nor Gannon. What they did after that, or, rather after not doing it, I really don't know. The scenes in the coulisses were exceedingly rich. All sorts of people were pressed to play all sorts of parts at a moment's notice, and the stage-manager was on the verge of idiocy.

Of the operatic people, only MM. Junca and Amodio came to the theatre.

Everybody else, I presume, was attacked by the epidemic.

Apropos to which, I find the following card in the *Herald*:—

A Card From The American Dramatic Fund Association.—The Committee on Benefits beg to tender their best thanks to the artists who in a position of extreme perplexity, so kindly manifested an interest in the affairs of the institution singularly withheld by many of its members. To Mrs. Hoey they are especially indebted for having at so late a moment, accepted the part she sustained on the occasion. They also make their grateful acknowledgments to the several companies for their most valuable aid. They would likewise present their compliments to Messrs. Ulmann, Strakosch, and Maretzek, for granting the services of their artists, although, by some curious concatenation of circumstances, none of them appeared.

Deploring the epidemical nature of the 'sickness' which prevailed, the Committee, in justification of the promises held forth in the bills of the performance, have to declare that no name was announced without full and approved authority so to do.

W. R. Blake, J. Brougham, J. G. Burnett, J. W. Lingard, Barney Williams, Committee.

This epidemic is likely to be a very serious one. It not only broke out among the artists of the Dramatic Fund, but it appeared at the Winter Garden, on Thursday, when Mr. H. Pearson had a benefit, and announced several plays, in one of which Miss Sarah Stevens was to perform. The "fair beneficiary" announced, in a pathetic speech, that Miss Stevens was, according to the physician's certificate, too ill to appear "in any character."

Quite aware that the public is desperately interested in the affairs of the disabled artists, I have been at some pains to ascertain their present condition, and I append my report:

The correct diagnosis of the peculiar disease which breaks out among singers, actresses, and actors, during the benefit season, baffles the faculty altogether. The ailment attacks the patient very suddenly, and the symptoms are of the most violent character, but the disease, although not easily arrested in its early stages, is rarely fatal.

So there is no danger that the public will care to grieve on account of the decease of any of its favorites.

Miss Laura Keene is very much better. Her medical attendant thinks that with careful nursing, and the revivifying influences of cheerful reading, such as The Saturday Press, she may be able to get out in a month or six weeks. Yesterday, she drank a cup of tea, and Sunday she can venture upon a little gruel.

Madame Gassier is doing well. I think that when she gets her London engagement, she will be able to fulfil its conditions.

Signor Gassier smoked three cigars yesterday, and is out of danger.

Mr. Stigelli, although naturally of a delicate constitution, is rapidly recovering. His chest C is quite comfortable.

Miss Mary Gannon has reappeared at Wallack's, and Mr. George Holland is getting better. Miss Sarah Stevens will probably get out in season to play at Laura Keene's Theatre for Jefferson's Summer season.

So, after all, the public is the only sufferer by the epidemic. Perhaps the artists in this country will find out, one of these days, that they behave very badly, and that it is stupid to get sick when they are expected to sing or play for a charitable purpose. They manage these things much better in France. I once assisted at a benefit given for the poor of a small town near Paris, where the affiche bore the names of Grisi, Mario, Lablache, Tamburini, Nantier-Didiee, Sophie Arnould, Rose Cheri, Madeline Brohan, Mm. Bressant, Roger, Lafontaine, Regnier, and others of the same rank—a rank that no artist in this country approaches. They were all there, and would have been pained beyond measure to have disappointed the audience.

And it is remarkable that the artists who do not belong to the Dramatic Fund Association always have to help the Benefit Committee out of its scrapes. How do you account for that?

It is fair to say, however, about the opera folks, that they declare they were not asked to sing definitely. Perhaps the Committee thought the managers' permission was all that was required,—a very grave error.

I had a little of *Bronze Horse* opera at Niblo's. It is not a bad thing for

Mr. Nixon, and altogether rather agreeable to the public. There are lots of people on the stage; some of Auber's music is given; the costumes are pretty; the scenery is good, and there is very little dialogue, for which latter relief, all thanks. The great effect of the play is described in the bills as follows:

"Miss Ida Vernon, as the Prince Zamina, will make an ascension on a real horse from the stage to the sky borders (not the borders of the sky), a feat of equestrian heroism never before attempted."

This I call running Pre-Raphaelitism into the ground, because if I remember rightly, the horse was not the real thing, but an automation affair, the aërial flights of which were regulated by screwing its tail. However, they do it. The horse is a real horse, as I know. And Miss Vernon does go up to the borders, and afterwards appears in an illuminated cloud scene, with revolving stars over her head. If I were Miss Vernon or the horse, I should object to the operation, but that is their affair, not mine. The lady can claim, without fear of contradiction, that she has experienced the most sudden professional rise in the records of the stage.

The Opera war goes on right merrily.

The indomitable Maximilian has brought out all his forces at the Winter Garden, and the Irving Place Generals are preparing for a grand demonstration.

The leading events of the week are,

At the Winter Garden: Monday, début of Fabbri in *Ernani.* Wednesday, rentrée of Frezzolini in *Lucrezia Borgia.* Thursday, Fabbri Matinée.

At the Academy, Monday, Patti, in *Lucia*; Wednesday, Patti, in the *Sonnambula*; Thursday, rehearsal of *Il Poliuto* for Miss Kellogg.

In *Ernani,* Fabbri was exceedingly good,—I think that very few living artists can excel her in the Verdi operas. In the second act, her veil took fire from the foot-lights, and frightened all the crinolines. Stigelli was the extinguisher on the occasion, and covered himself all over with glory. I hear that 'Forty's fellers' intend to make him an honorary member of that company, and that he will occasionally "run with the machine."

'Belle Brittan' was happy on Wednesday, when the Frezzolini attacked *Lucrezia Borgia* and had the worst of it. I am sorry about Frez. and B. B. If they could be bought at their real value and sold at their own estimate, the profit to the operator would be far greater than the Chemical Bank dividends, or the return on the money invested in tenement-houses.

It is not my purpose to say anything more than the simple truth about Frezzolini. She came here in 1857 without any voice, and has no more now than then. She sings artistically, as far as she goes; but she has no lower or medium notes worth mentioning, and her upper register is very thin. To atone for her short-comings, however, she sings with an air which no successful prima donna ever assumed—an air which might have answered for the Salle Ventadour, when she was *the* Frezzolini—but an air which is now, in all seriousness, utterly absurd.

The story which your blue-blooded contemporary, El Noticioso, exploits, is very characteristic of FrezzoLini. She has been here for some time without an engagement. At Newport, last Summer, she sang two or three times; but it was quite evident from her performance that she could not fulfil the requirements of the public. Therefore she was not engaged. It was represented, however, about six weeks ago, that she had recovered her voice, and the Academy management tendered her an engagement through Mr. Muzio. She accepted the proposition, but when Maretzek came, threw over the Irving Place people, on the ground that Strakosch, whom she knew in Italy before the time of the great fire, did not pay her the compliment of a visit. The fact about the matter, is that FrezzoliNi is to the opera what 'Belle Brittan' is to literature. It cannot be denied, however, that the old lady did her best. Among other things, she took the applause which was intended for the tenor, who sang very nicely in the terzetto of the second act.

There was, during this performance, an incident which has made a good deal of talk about town, but which has not yet got into the papers. A lady who occupies a very high social position, was sitting in the orchestra stalls, chatting, as is the custom in all opera houses, when the performance is a bore, with a number of friends, when a Teutonic individual, evidently from the Oriental districts, levelled at the lady a coarse remark, equivalent to the Bowery idiomatic expression, 'dry up.' There was some discussion, and no small sensation created when the lady declared that she had been insulted, but as the officers of the house declined to interfere, and as none of the gentlemen in attendance felt inclined to punch the Teuton's head, he was unmolested. The lady, however, gathered her skirts about her, and majestically sailed out of the Theatre.

I give you the facts. I have no opinion on the subject. Perhaps the German was right. Frezzolini has so small a voice that one cannot afford to lose a particle of it.

The case is quite the contrary with La Wissler, the new contralto. She has a tremendous voice, and knows how to sing, but has no taste to speak of. If she could give Frez some of her voice, and receive in exchange some of the latter's delicacy and finish, it would be a fine thing to do. At present the contrast is very amusing. Frezzolini suggests the Boulevard des Italiens in every movement, while Wissler is Anglo-Teuton all over.

La Kelloggini had a very large audience for her rehearsal. Everybody was there, including the young ladies of the Hebrew persuasion, who go to sleep in their opera-cloaks in order to be on hand, like our gallant firemen, at any moment. This is prudential, for in the present condition of affairs, no one knows when or where the opera may break out.

La Kelloggini is not, to judge by the rehearsal, so good as they attempted to make her out, but she is still clever. Without being strikingly handsome, she has a good stage face, and her ensemble is what they call interesting. Her manner is a little too school-girlish, and she executes as if she had a piece of bread-and-butter in expectancy if her scales were evenly sung. Her voice is a full high soprano, strong, clear and brilliant, but a little metallic, which is a serious drawback. It makes the singer wearisome. In her manner of singing, the new prima donna reminds me very much of the gun-boats which our mutual uncle is building now-a-days. One of the Theta Delts slung his hammock on board of the *Iroquois*, and I visited the ship. Except a place for a big gun or two, she was all steam-engine. There was a safety-valve under each man's chair at the mess-table, and a patent cutoff in every stateroom. You couldn't stir a step without walking into a boiler or stumbling over a fireman. The ship suggested explosions from her main-truck to her keelson. So with the Kelloggini; she is continually going off like a bunch of fire-crackers. Her staccato has a crack which reminds me of a volley of musketry, and as she sings with the most placid of countenances, the effect is comical. At least it struck me as being very odd, but I do not pretend to speak for the public, or even for myself—from a rehearsal.

The general opinion is that the young lady promises to be exceedingly good. I think the selection for her début a stupid one, but that is not, I presume, altogether her fault. New York does well to bring out two such singers as Patti and Kellogg in the same year, or even in ten years. France and England, with all their conservatories and academies, cannot produce anything like them.

And with this crow for our crinolines, and the further announcement that Anna Maria quite agrees with me about Frez, but thinks I am all wrong about Kellogg, who is, according to the Brightest and Best, perfectly splendid, I make to you my devoirs.

That you may never be asked to play or sing for anybody's benefit, and so enjoy good health for the remainder of your days, is the prayer of

Your Slave,

Personne.

NEW YORK APRIL 28, 1860

[For The New York Saturday Press.]

BODY AND SOUL.

BY N. G. SHEPHERD.

I inherited a fortune from my father. Had it been otherwise, I should have made but a poor show in earning a livelihood, as I had been accustomed to wealth from my childhood, and am constituted by nature for the enjoyment of it; besides, I have always had a horror of poverty. To be sure, these blank walls and this deal-table on which I write do not speak well for existing circumstances; but what of that? I may think and talk as I please, even though there are none to hear me but the owner of those glaring, restless eyes, across the hall yonder. And I have often thought this: that if there is anything amiss in the divine government of the world, it is in the fact of many who ought to have been born rich being condemned to drudgery all their lives. The world's wealth belongs by right to the sensitive and refined, the want of it to the coarse and vulgar. People may talk as they please about money, and sneer privately at those who possess it; for my own part, I must confess to a weakness for it, a love of it, not so much for itself as for what it commands. In saying this, I am of opinion that I express the sentiments of more than two-thirds of the earth's people, including those who profess to despise wealth. Whether or not you think me right, my philosophic reader, I, of course, do not and cannot know; nevertheless, in the circumstances, I flatter myself that I have displayed no little wisdom and sagacity by the remark.

As I have already said, I was left rich, and had been used to riches all my days; so I came very naturally into my inheritance. I was young when my father left me, but a few months past my twenty-first birthday, and had just completed my college course. My mother died in giving me birth, so I was deprived of those influences so necessary to the proper development of the more graceful and tender features of character. My father's excessive fondness for her settled upon me, and his indulgence knew no bounds. Literally, I was a spoiled child. I recognized no will but my own; indeed, no other existed in my father's household. I was as full of whims as the trees are with leaves in Mid-Summer; and yet, not a fancy remained ungratified. Had I been the child of a king, my wishes could not have been consulted more cheerfully, or more religiously conformed to. The result of this was, naturally, that my health, which had been delicate from my birth, was made still more so, and my temper rendered capricious and fretful. Surrounded by indulgences, I grew to man's estate with hardly a woman's strength and nerve. My intellectual capacity had always exceeded my physical being. From earliest childhood I had manifested more than ordinary intelligence. With childish things I had little sympathy. I was passionately fond of Art, in all her phases. Painting and sculpture were to me as strange as untrodden worlds, glimpses of which I had been enabled to gain through the knowledge given me by masters, and the almost incomprehensible works they had placed in my hands. On both these children of one parent I looked as an enthusiast might look upon two forms of religion, to each of which his soul clings for the separate glories they reveal. Poetry lifted me to the stars, opened new fields for thought, and quickened new desires within me. Through it I was made to commune with the dead. By it I was lifted from plane to plane of acute perceptibility, until my susceptible and newly-awakened faculties saw beyond the achievements of the past and present, to where new paths opened, terminating in invisibility, whose virgin echoes were to be wakened only by the great and gifted of ages to come. The world around me was a great living poem, its characters the men and women whom I met. But the chief delight of my life was music. Words cannot express my fondness for it. In it I found consolation and relief at all times. I was particularly gifted in this respect. My instructors pronounced me a musical wonder, and declared they could teach me nothing. What delight I experienced in the exercise of this faculty! What wondrous harmonies filled my brain! What concord of sweet sounds I heard through all the day, and how they slipped through my fingers into the keys till the air grew delirious with melody. I lived and moved in a different sphere from most mortals. The common things of life I hardly knew of, still less came I in contact with them. The world I inhabited was distinct from the vulgar every-day world. It was one of æsthetic delights. The air I breathed was of another latitude, as pure as that of the mountain to the valley. It was sacred to song, made holy by inspiration. Living in it, one stood nearer to the angels, approached more closely to them, not in their divine natures, but in their keener capacities for enjoyment, their clearer views, their finer instincts and perceptions. In it, the body was as nothing; the soul everything. All grossness was subdued; the intellect rendered more acute and sensitive. The spirit forgot its jail, and roamed in thought through the trackless fields of immaterial space.

But what of myself? I mean my flesh-and-blood self—the casket, the jewel-case of my soul. I was small and delicate in person, blue-eyed and fair-haired, with diminutive hands and feet. The transition from boyhood to manhood was marked as little by physical changes as by those of taste and inclination. I developed quickly; but the same spiritual features marked my perfect growth, that had characterized my earlier life. Indeed, I almost forgot, at times, that I had a body—so subordinate was it to my mind, so little importunate were its demands. And yet I had known no serious sickness; in fact, I believe my hold on-life would have proved extremely tenacious, and that, through the strength of will and the subservience of matter to spirit. I seemed to exist upon what was food for the intellect more than upon bread; and day by day reason expanded, intelligence increased, and the most subtle matters became as easy of comprehension to me as the causes that influence the dawn and the coming on of night. Not but that I felt my want of physical force; but it was only in a dim, indefinite way. I could conceive what wonders might be performed by the union of bodily strength with mental vigor; but my mind seemed to rely upon itself, and I seldom felt that prostration which so generally follows intellectual effort. I was not unconscious of this singular precociousness, even when a child. I realized the difference between myself and others of my age, although it did not surprise me. I felt the want of naturalness in it all; but it appeared the workings of a higher influence acting upon my subjected sense. It was not through reflection that I arrived at conclusions, but by a sudden flash of intelligence, which, breaking like a sunbeam upon my perceptions, revealed, in all its obscurity, the magnitude of truth; even as a flash of lightning penetrates the gloom, displaying to the eye what was before unseen.

In the library of my father's house hung a picture which was said by connoisseurs to be the work of Titian. Whether it were or not, it certainly possessed many of his most striking characteristics. In color it was singularly beautiful; in tone, quiet and harmonious, with rich, transparent shadows, and pure, mellow lights. The subject was one which I did not altogether understand; but I presume it was intended to represent a repentant Magdalen. It was an upright canvas, the figure standing. The face, which was raised, wore an expression of agonized supplication; the left hand lay extended upon the breast, while the right pointed downward to where the shadows in the picture seemed to congregate. Toward evening, when the sun was very low and entered the casement, the face appeared irradiant with celestial glory; the dark shadows became illuminated as though with the all-seeing eye of God; and on the hand which rested upon the bosom the light settled like a dove, the messenger of peace and forgiveness.

I spent most of my time in this room, among the books. I had my piano there; and often as I gazed upon the picture, lit up with the last rays of the sun, I felt a strange sympathy with it fill every nerve of my being; and the spirit of inspiration guiding and governing my fingers, I would play such airs as seemed the acclamation of the angels when a sinner enters heaven. It was in this way that I first began to perceive the sublime unity of Art; how that the soul of the great painter is the soul of the great musician, and both the soul of the great poet; how the one answers the other; how that color is melody, save in a different garb; and form, harmony. It was then that I felt the soul of the painter take possession of my being —making, through me, the dumb canvas to speak its woes, and mimic hosts of heaven to rejoice.

At the death of my father I had developed into the man. Not the man physically, the true, elementary man—the manhood which precedes all others; but into that of intelligence and thought. I began to feel the want of companionship, aside from that of the pursuits in which I found pleasure. I was given to dreaming less, but hardly more to action. I have wondered since that I never felt, at this time, the promptings of ambition, so common to the young, and which so often subside into passive contentment with the most ordinary circumstances of life. I was conscious of a change in my being, but only conscious of it. I felt that my blood flowed more quickly—my pulse beat faster—that my sensations were keener, and my desires stronger. The companionship I longed for was not of men. I shrunk with an instinctive dread from their society. Neither was it of women, such as I had known and seen. It was not so much my material self that craved communion with another—not my eyes that ached for some being to rest upon, nearer and dearer than myself—not my hands that longed to feel the pressure of other hands—not my lips that yearned to speak a name which should be music to my ear—but it was my soul that cried within me for intercourse with some other soul, even though that other possessed no outward signs by which its presence should be manifest. I began to tire of the companionship, solely, of my piano and books. The latter were as the dead; and my piano depended upon me to waken it to life. I played only to insensible walls—I longed to play to one who could hear and approve,—if not with the tongue, by some visible evidences of the spirit's presence. At first this desire was dim and vague. I hardly felt its birth and growth within me. Gradually it increased, and engrafted itself into my being, never-ceasing in its importunity. Partly as a relief to this, but more because it accorded with my inclinations, I surrounded myself with all the refinements and luxuries of life. I clothed my apartments with rich and elegant carpets, so soft that the footsteps fell unheard. I hung my walls with pictures of the rarest beauty and every variety of subject. So numerous were they, and of so many schools, that the whole history of Art, almost, might have been traced therein. Pure and saint-like Raphaels—sensuous Titians and voluptuous Correggios—these and a host of others, including the works of men of modern renown. In every niche and corner stood a statue, which was cold and senseless marble only to the touch. On each and every one Genius had set her seal, proclaiming them not the work of the hand merely, but a portion of the artist's brain and heart. Through these agencies the very atmosphere of the house was made to palpitate as with life. I bought costly furniture, and filled my rooms with it :—magnificent mirrors, profuse with gilding and ornament-chairs and sofas in which the senses were wooed to sleep unconsciously—tables whereon were carved the histories of nations—divans of seductive shape and softness—ottomans upon which Sultanas might have sat—everything that was pleasing to the eye and grateful to the sense. My sleeping apartments opened upon conservatories wherein were all manner of exotics. In my halls were fountains that made incessant music, like the tinkling of tiny bells; and in cages of quaint device, that hung in the deep recesses of the curtained windows, were foreign birds of bright and dazzling plumage, whose throats seemed to have been constructed expressly for the transmission of sweet sounds. All the splendor of the East was mine.

The walls of my dining-room looked upon feasts that would have tempted the palate of the most fastidious epicure. Of these, at first, I seldom more than tasted. My stomach revolted against their richness. I would sit looking at them, seeming to receive sustenance from the contemplation of their sumptuousness. Gradually I began to eat of the plainest of the dishes, and to sip the spicy wines of my table. I wondered at the pleasures of the gourmand, and curiously partook of a portion of each of what was set before me, amused at the added relish which every new day brought with it. It was not long before I came to like these things for the gratification they gave me in eating. I drank the wines more freely, and experienced the delightful, dreamy sensations of semi-obliviousness. There was novelty in this. By-and-bye I noticed a change in my appearance. My features grew less spiritual—my head appeared to swell and broaden at the back—my neck grew thicker, and my complexion ruddier. I began to feel more sensibly the demands of the body, and my appetite craved new dainties constantly. I was fast becoming a glutton. I took pleasure in devising new dishes whose richness should excel all others I had tasted. I stored my cellar with the rarest of wines, the fruity flavors of which were to the palate as joy and gladness to the soul. I drank them late and early. They gave new wings to my imagination, softening the actual to an appearance of vague unrealness—opening vistas in the future through which I floated in a kind of lotus-dream, half waking, half unconscious, wherein pain was softened, and all pleasure rendered more acute and lively. Familiar objects took weird shapes before me. My flashing chandeliers were diamond-studded worlds, from which bright eyes shot fiery glances into mine. My walls blossomed with stranger faces:—grave old monks who laughed and shook their trebled heads—nuns and virgins, and sainted madonnas, looking unlike themselves, who winked and smiled lecherously at me. Each individual feaure of my apartments seemed fraught with new neaning. Eves and Venuses saluted me from their places in the wall, or assuming other attitudes, displayed new beauties to my astonished gaze. The higher pleasures which these had afforded me began to pall. I coveted excitement, and sought it in the mimic world of the stage. I became passionately fond of the theatre, and patronized the ballet. It was here that I first saw Mademoiselle Henriette. She was a miracle of grace and loveliness. Her motions were those of a sylph. She would come upon the stage like a miniature snow-drift; kiss the tips of her rosy fingers to the audience; poise herself on the toe of a liliputian slipper, looking, meanwhile, like a modest lily on its stalk; swing herself round in an infinity of airy circles; skip forward to the footlights like a young antelope, and back to her place; round and round again in circles till the brain grew dizzy at the sight, then bounding way, with a wave-like motion, to the full sound of the orchestra, the music and the dancer were as one.

I soon made her acquaintance, and became one of the many who waited on her footsteps. She was as beautiful off the stage as when upon it. Her figure was full and round. Her height somewhat above that usual to the sex, yet her size did not interfere with the grace and ease of her movements. Her hands and arms were large; her face undeniably handsome, with the bluest eyes that ever human being possessed. These, with her rich brown hair, worn in heavy masses at the sides, tended to enhance the extreme beauty of her complexion, which was pink and white, the warm color spreading like a mist on the least occasion. When dressed for the dance, nothing could be more lovely. Her appearance at these times was bewildering in its magnificence. She wore white. A satin waist, somewhat low in the neck—perhaps a little lower than is common—a short skirt of gauzy material; silk open stockings that met her dress at the knee; and on her foot, a satin slipper. In her hair she wore a white camellia,—this, and nothing more. But words are inadequate to convey even an imperfect idea of Mademoiselle Henriette. Her beauty was faultless—of a kind that no one could be indifferent to. Aside from her perfection of form and feature there was a winning gentleness of manner, and an appearance of excessive modesty in her speech and actions, which was extremely engaging, the more so because unlooked for in one of her profession. It became my privilege to wait on her from her dwelling to the theatre. My carriage was always at the door. I never missed an evening. It was her custom to make her toilet after we arrived there, and when the curtain rose, and she burst upon my expectant gaze in all her splendor, amid a flood of light and the thrilling rapture of music, I thought each night added to her charms. Our acquaintance increased rapidly. I was seldom away from her. I spent most of my time in her apartments. We walked together, we rode together. I attended her to rehearsal. I made her presents of elegant jewels and costly dresses. My devotion was unsurpassed. I distanced all my competitors. We became engaged. Henriette confessed that she loved me, with her blushing head resting on my shoulder, and her large, well-shaped hand in mine. I shall never forget that moment. It was one of wild, delirious ecstacy. I knew not if I loved this woman—indeed, I knew not what it was to love. I questioned myself time and again to no purpose. When away from her I only remembered her existence—when with her there seemed a strange current passing incessantly from one to the other. My eyes were never at rest unless fixed upon her, but my soul lay dormant, unmoved, not a single one of its faculties being called into action. It was a strange, magnetic influence which she possessed over me. Her touch thrilled and electrified me, her glance was as fire in my veins. She was a creature made up of sweet delights. What the bee feels when he buries himself in the honeyed hollow of a full, ripe flower, that I felt when I pressed with mine her rich, red lips. I did not stop to analyze this strange and mysterious sympathy. It did not admit of reflection, had I been inclined to test it in that way. It was all-powerful, carrying me with it, like a fierce, irresistible surf. It was wild and sweet and delirious, lulling to sleep by its narcotic power all feelings and considerations aside from it. Reason had no part with it, cold calm judgment no control over it. These, with all else, were lost in the attraction of the magnet. At times, when out of her society, my soul cried, as of old, for the companionship which it coveted. Mademoiselle Henriette was not brilliant. She was not fascinating, save in her person and manners. She was not accomplished—hardly educated. She could dance —dance the heart out of a man. All this I knew and felt. My soul mourned in its loneness, but my flesh was subjugated. My slavery increased daily. I was losing more and more of my old self; my soul was shrinking into its shell hourly, and the shell was closing up around it. Henriette knew this. She was conscious of her power, and liked to exercise it. She would mould me as she pleased, but all in seeming unconsciousness of the sceptre which she swayed. Beautiful magician! Supreme and lovely sovereign! One touch of her fair hand, one glance from her love-lit eyes, one glimpse of her white bosom, and I was the poor sun-struck victim, to whom her lightest fancy was as life. I was the weather-vane which indicated the turn her whims took. Ah! she was full of such—what beautiful woman is not? But hers were modest whims —innocent little freaks that served in the end only to flatter my vanity and to make me more enamored of her. She was to me what the sun is to the flower. When the sun smiled, the flower expanded, spread its leaves in the light and warmed in all its fibres. When the sun darkened, or the sun's light fell not upon the flower, it began to droop and to let fall its leaves. When Henriette was reserved and quiet, I was passively obedient to her mood; when animated, I was warm and demonstrative. But this state of things could not last always. For six short months I lived in a sensualist's paradise. I sipped, from day to day, the very nectar of life. Toward the close of that time a change came over the manner of my fiancée. She was colder and more reserved. It was evident that she was becoming wearied with my idolatry. My caresses seemed less welcome. She would often excuse herself from me on the plea of indisposition. I was unable to account for this conduct. I could not for a moment think her fickle; it never occurred to me that she might be artful. I tried coaxing—so potent with others, it was ineffectual with her. I bought her gifts, generally jewelry or some article of apparel, and took them with me when I called. These seemed to revive, for the time being, her former fondness. She would permit me to caress her as before, and reward me with kisses of her own; but her next reception of me was even colder than was her wont, unless I was accompanied by some slight remembrance.

On one occasion I visited Mademoiselle rather earlier than was usual with me. I had not waited upon her to the theatre on the evening previous, but had sent my carriage for her both before and after the performance. I found her en deshabille, yet beautiful. She had but just risen, and was seated in a rocking-chair before the fire, her slippered feet resting on the fender. She exhibited no surprise or pleasure on seeing me, only raising her eyes in a languid sort of way as I entered, and exclaiming in a subdued tone, 'O! its you,' and relapsing into silence. I took a seat beside her. As I did so, my attention was drawn to the appearance of the room. It was peculiar, as all ladies' dressing-rooms are at certain hours, but hers was more than usually so. Sundry articles of feminine apparel were scattered about the floor, others reposing on the chairs and lounge. On the table were the remains of a feast,—empty wine-bottles, plates, dishes, goblets, and decanters—the skeleton of a chicken, a fragment of steak, a loaf of bread, a bundle of cigars, cigarettes, and cigar-lighters; all huddled together in sublime confusion. I looked aghast. I wondered what it meant. She observed my astonishment, and remarked that she had had company on the previous evening. We sat silent, looking at one another. Her evident indifference had modified, in a degree, the influence which she possessed over me. Regarding her then, unbiased by any display of that fondness which she once professed, I felt the shattered remnants of my old nature rebelling against the tyranny of the flesh. There was a struggle going on within me, between my material self, which had grown, hourly, stronger and more irresistible, and my spiritual self, which had become correspondingly weaker. The contest waxed fierce and terrible. Henriette had only to use her power to sway me as she pleased. Cast but a pebble into the spiritual scale, and the balance would be destroyed; cast it into the other, and the result would be the same. Let her but stretch forth her hand, smile upon me, speak one word of encouragement, and the chains were forged anew. She turned toward me. Already my blood flowed faster—a keener sense of life thrilled my being. She partly arose, and, leaning forward, took a cigarette from the table, lighted it and placed it between her parted lips. The struggle grew less violent; spirit was in the ascendancy. She lit another, and a third. I sat with my eyes fixed upon her. The smoke curled gracefully in rings, and seemed as though perfumed by her breath; spreading itself in wavy lines about her till her whole person appeared as through a vail. The magnetism of her presence was subdued. I arose and took my leave.

Although I had parted from Mademoiselle Henriette, it was not without a vague hope that she would summon me again to her presence. I still visited the theatre where she was engaged, and drank in with my eyes her every voluptuous movement. I sent her flowers and presents of jewelry, which were accepted, but she held out no inducement to me to return. It was not long before I learned that another filled my place; and business calling me from the city, I lost all personal knowledge of her. About this time I became acquainted with a young lady by the name of Selina Fort. She was the daughter of a clergyman, in an obscure country town. Selina Fort—a hard unlovely name. A name difficult for the lips of love to pronounce. Selina! She was the opposite of Mademoiselle Henriette—small and delicately made. Her eyes were dark, as was her hair also, and but for a strange and beautiful transparency which pervaded it, her complexion might have been pronounced so too. Her face resembled that of a Circassian. Her eyebrows were arched, and although they did not meet, they terminated in lines that suggested a continuance of their forms. She was not beautiful, nor handsome; hers was a circean loveliness which every one felt and acknowledged. To fully appreciate Selina, it was necessary to see and know her; to understand her was impossible. Without the usual and by no means agreeable signs that characterize intellectual women, she possessed a mind which succumbed only to the extreme frailness of her body. Having been reared from earliest childhood among books, they had become necessary to her enjoyment; she was as much at home among them as a squirrel is in the leafy top of a tree. At the age of twenty—this was about the time of my first acquaintance with her—she was familiar with no less than six different languages. She played on every instrument upon which a lady is expected to perform; composed like an improvisatrice, and sung like a syren. Her words were as variable as her accomplishments. At times she was playful and animated, pensive and thoughtful, sad and reserved. In fact, in her nature and disposition Selina was a mystery which the most penetrating would fail to unravel. I sometimes thought her possessed of the spirit of divination, so truthful were her predictions; and oftentimes when at the harp, she had the appearance of one entirely unconscious of her surroundings; lifted far above the things of earth, in communion with the spirits of another and brighter sphere. In my intercourse with Selina, my soul seemed at last to have found a companion. I marked with philosophic accuracy its different nature when compared with that between myself and Henriette. In the one case, it was the action of magnetic forces—the attraction which animal matter has for animal matter. In the other there was nothing of this—our souls communed, and revelled in the delicious harmony of thought and aspiration. Our bodies were as ice. I felt my old self reviving, all my old feelings quickening within me, as the young grass in Springtime. I could stand by her side and listen to her light, watery touch, as she played, without being cognizant of the bodily agent employed in the performance. I could hear her clear, bird-like voice, as she sung, without remembering the lips that formed the notes. I could talk with her, looking into her eyes, anticipating every thought, almost the words she uttered, and forget the work of the sculptor, though inhaling her breath at every syllable. There was no earth-born sympathy in the contact of our hands, the meeting of our glance, the touch of our clay-made selves; only the grand unity of spirit, the free accordance of our higher intelligences and instincts. I felt that the work of regeneration had begun within me. The shackles of sense were removed. I was drawn up, as by attraction, to a higher level.

Did I love Selina? You shall judge for yourself,—for my own part, I knew not, any more than I knew if I had loved Mademoiselle Henriette. This I knew: when with her, I felt no desire beyond her presence,—my soul was at peace. When away from her, its loneliness was complete, its longings without number. But in all this our bodies took no part. They were as the dumb frame that contains the thunder-spirit of the organ. When our lips touched, it was the meeting of soul with soul, unmingled with the joys of sense, unalloyed by its desires.

There was little that was human in our love. It was higher, finer, more intense in its delights than the common intercourse of kindred mortals,—it was the amalgamation of spirit with spirit.

Selina had seen but little of the world. Living in an obscure place, she had seldom been beyond its confines; yet she possessed all the ease of a lady of fashion. It was impossible that we should be always together. My presence was often required in the city, in connection with the management of my affairs, but we corresponded regularly. Her letters were full of quaint conceits and expressions. They were like her, like her talk,—graceful, unaffected, the words well chosen, the thoughts original, even peculiar. They seemed familiar to me, too,—all her little fancies,—not unlike my own were they, yet so different,—full of novelty, with sweet simplicity. The more I saw of Selina, the more our acquaintance progressed, the less I really knew her. Her ways were past finding out. Often on my return after absence, she would cite many of my thoughts and feelings, while away from her, as her own, and even tell what, on certain occasions, I had said and done. This, I am convinced, was due to a correspondence of mind, influencing the one to similar thoughts, words, and deeds with the other; or, perhaps, to her knowledge of myself; whereas, in the former case, it was the silent and invisible working of sympathy, and not, as I have fancied, a spirit of necromancy possessed by her. Yet every successive day revealed some new and wondrous trait of mind and character, some peculiar gift, some intuitive and almost superhuman power of perception.

We had now been engaged more than a year, and at my earnest solicitation a day was fixed for our marriage. It had been postponed hitherto in consideration for Selina's father, who dreaded parting with his child, and who regarded her with a fondness that I was oftentimes inclined to think assumed. He was in no respect like her. Although a hard student, and a well read man, he had few natural gifts beyond intelligence. In his character, he was to all appearances a Christian—devout in his demeanor, scrupulously punctilious in observances, and of the strongest prejudices in all matters relating to religion. With all this as evidence of his sanctity, although not generally skeptical, I could not but doubt the sincerity of his professions. There was little of the fire, the enthusiasm, the earnestness, the forgetfulness of self and all earthly things, the entire and absolute devotion to Christ's cause, that distinguish the true servant of God. He was doctrinal, full of dogmas, creeds, and theories—an untolerating sectarian. In the little flock entrusted to his keeping, there were few who loved him,—perhaps as few who trusted him. He had not that faculty, so necessary to those who have the souls of men in charge, of drawing out the secret springs of action by a winning earnestness of character. He was suspicious of every man's good, even of those who partook with him of the body and blood of the Saviour.

Such was the father of Selina, and by him were we joined together. It was a dark, rainy morning in November. We were married at home, in the little town where she had dwelt, and from there we journeyed to the city, to my own house. A strange wedding was that—unlike any I have ever seen. There were no friends, no warm congratulations, no kind wishes. When we arrived, all things were prepared as I had directed. The bride arrayed herself in white, and we descended together to the dining-room, where a wedding feast was spread in grand profusion. The gas-light fell from chandelier and bracket upon the coldly splendid scene. Everything glittered, flashed, and sparkled like myriad stars, but all remained untouched. It was as a feast prepared for the dead. There stood Selina, speechless, motionless; and there stood I by her side. She was as a piece of marble which the light penetrates. She seemed transparent, radiant, unreal. All was ghostly, cold, and silent.

Our honeymoon was waning. We had tasted three weeks of wedded bliss. Our souls had communed with one another as one soul with itself. Each hour discovered to me some new gift in my bride, some pearl that had lain hidden from my sight. When the beauty and novelty of one became familiar, another revealed itself. Her resources were infinite, her graces and accomplishments unnumbered. It was, indeed, a union of soul with soul. In hers mine was merged. No separate existence was there, all was as one. But the union comprehended not the body. Her touch was to me as ice. Her rich, dark hair exhaled no sweet odors to my sense, her cheek was as marble, and her hand as clay. Her lips, only the arched doorway through which her soul came out to meet my own. And each day, as it passed by, isolated more and more our earth-born selves, bound together with stronger chords and in closer unison our spiritual beings. Was it the love of a higher and purer state of existence? Was it the feeling with which wedded spirits will regard each other in the world that is to come? The future life, alone, can make reply.

Two years had fled. Selina's father was no more. We had spent most of our married life in the city, making occasional pilgrimages to the former home of my wife. I had written a book, and published it. It was a success, such a one as seldom attends the first production of an author. The world read and applauded. I was famous. People talked about me and my book. My acquaintance was sought after. I was courted, flattered, and feasted. There was zest in all this. I liked the excitement; it was novel. It reminded me, once again, of the existence of a body, it awoke me afresh to a sense of its enjoyments. Surely there were two planes of life, with separate pleasures. Those of the one I had hardly more than tasted. I had steeped myself in the Lethean springs of the other until I had forgotten, almost, my corporeal existence.

Once more in the whirlpool, I went with it, I opened my house to my new-found friends. I filled it with the beauty and fashion of the metropolis. Wit sparkled and shot its fires around my board. In music, dancing, and feasting sped the hours. Time flew by in a golden chariot, scattering honeyed sweets.

Selina's health, which grew daily more delicate, would not permit of her taking part in these festivities. The most trifling loss of sleep was visited with a penalty, the least excitement caused depression and indisposition.

Owing to this and the continued gaieties of my new life, we saw, comparatively, little of each other. I felt the influence by which she had drawn me upward to a consciousness of freedom from earth and matter, second only to that of a disembodied spirit, growing, like that other influence of the fleshly danseuse, less potent, even feebler in its attractiveness by a curtailment of its action. A thick vail seemed to have spread itself between us, through which the keen and subtile glances of her soul became entangled, like a ray of sunlight in a web of dust. Once like gossamer, thin, transparent, only softening and subduing the gold and violet glory of her heaven-anointed spirit; each moment growing thicker, and tainting with its impurity even the stray gleams that burnt their way through the coarse screen. And beneath, and out of which gathered the vail of mist, there seemed a moat, that ever widening, drove us farther and farther from the opposing shores.

What man was ever popular a lifetime? What popularity has not its allotted term of duration? True, I had had my day, and it might be that the sun was not yet gone down; but it was beyond its zenith. My friends dropped off one by one as though gorged with the sound of my fame, which was fast becoming an old story. Another star had arisen in the heavens—the firmament rang to the cry of his praise; and the same admiring crowd that applauded me, turned about, their hands beating praises all the while, to welcome the new comer. Their shouts of admiration, which should have raised me toward the skies, had only served to bring me nearer earth.

My halls no longer swarmed with guests—only an occasional gathering to do homage to the new hero. These were but the ghosts of former revels. At other times, all was silent as the grave. I was but little at home; excitement had become a necessary feature of my life, and failing me there, I sought it elsewhere.

One evening, on entering the house and going directly to the drawing-room, I discovered Selina on the floor in a swoon. This was, of late, by no means an uncommon occurrence, and one liable to happen at the most unexpected moment. Her frame seemed frailer than the tenderest flower, which the lightest breath might destroy.

As I looked upon her in her unconsciousness, I thought, for the first time, of her delicate loveliness, and how near she was to being what she had often wished herself—perfectly beautiful. This seemed the crowning desire of her life; and more so since the day of my added prosperity, when I had begun to lose my hold of higher things, and to lose communion with her soul. "Can it be," I thought, "that seeing this, she would have bound me to her by material as well as spiritual ties? Not only my higher nature, but the grosser one of sense?"—and musing thus, I hated the tender being before me, so pale, so ethereal, so like a thing of air. I had not marked this growing beauty until then; it was too fine, too delicate for my thick perceptions, deadened by the sensual things of life. There was less sympathy than ever now. She had grown more and more immaterial: I had descended lower and lower in the other scale, through the agency of intemperate indulgence. I had never loved the body—now I hated it: I looked coldly down upon her, lying as one frozen. The strangely-beautiful transparency of her complexion appeared to have increased as her health failed her. I raised her in my arms and bore her to a sofa. Her large, dark eyes opened, and rested upon me without a sign of recognition. She seemed as one awakened out of death: her face wore a wild, unearthly look—she was cold and stiffened. Shuddering from the contact, I rushed from the house, knowing not whither I went.

By some strange fortune my steps led me to the theatre where Mademoiselle Henriette was dancing. The light, the warmth, the music were what I wanted. Anything to drive the chill from my blood, to melt the ice at my heart, freezing my veins, even my very marrow.

The overture ceased. There was a hum and a buzz of voices, a flashing of fans, and a flood of light through the house. The bell sounded, the curtain rose, and amid the clapping of hands and a new burst of music from the orchestra, Mademoiselle Henriette bounded upon the stage.

There was the same voluptuous figure, the same airy, sylph-like movement—all so familiar, yet so long unseen. The dance was ended. I will not attempt to describe it. The house rang with applause. Men shouted and flung bouquets, women clapped their jewelled hands, and waved their scented handkerchiefs. As for myself, I arose from my seat and shouted with the rest. My every sense was maddened. My blood, before so cold, had all the fire of newly-awakened passion in it. I waited not for the play, but leaving the house, made my way to the stage-entrance, and sent my card in for Mademoiselle. She received me coldly, reclining on a lounge, in the green-room, talking with one of the players. I drew a chair to where she was and seated myself upon it. With all my ardor, I could not but observe the luxuriance of her form, displayed to its fullest advantage by the attitude she was in. Her head rested partially on a cushion, and was in part supported by her hand, two fingers of which toyed with the camellia that drooped from her hair, somewhat disarranged by her movements in the dance. The position of her arm, the dimpled elbow reposing on the sofa, revealed the dazzling whiteness of her shoulder and the matchless snow of her bosom, heaving beneath the thin lace covering.

My whole being seemed to throb in unison with that of Mademoiselle Henriette. Her eyes shot contagious fire into my veins. I could have sworn that we were of one flesh, so acutely did my every pulse respond to her slightest movement. I attended Mademoiselle home. The next morning found me at her door. Rumor said she was fading; that her charms were borrowed; that dissipation was undermining her health as well as her beauty. I could not see this. To be sure, she appeared paler than on the night before, but none the less lovely in my eyes. I resumed my old position, but not my former relationship with her: that was impossible. I waited upon her pleasure at all times. The world talked about me again, but in a different way. How skillfully she plied her arts! I did not think so then. I did not care, blind trout that I was; but I see it all now. Slavery is freedom compared with the subjugation I lived under, that I found delight in. I lavished untold wealth upon this syren. Queens live not more sumptuously than did she. I spent all that I had in affording her pleasure, in surrounding her with luxury, in ministering to her selfish, covetous —— ah! she was more than beautiful. Well, the world has its pleasures. Yes,—yes—pleasures indeed. I grow a little wild when I recur to the past.

One night I had just returned with Mademoiselle from a ball—how she danced that night! I entered the house, and to my surprise, saw a light burning in an apartment that opened on the hall. It was my wife's music-room. I went thither. The door was but partially closed, the lamp burned dimly on the stand by her guitar. I entered, and was about removing it, when I stumbled against something on the floor. It was Selina. 'She has fainted,' I thought. I raised her, put my hand upon her heart, held my cheek close to her lips. They were cold, and ashen-like in color. Her heart was motionless; there was no pulsation in her mist—she was dead.

A feeling of wild delight shot through my frame; I could have shouted for very joy. Dead! dead! No longer would she mock me with her hateful presence; the poor, frail thing!

The doctors came, looked at her, shook their heads, and went away. There was an inquest held, and the verdict was, 'death from poison;' and—and—I have forgotten the rest, but the crazy Keeper here, who shows the visitors about, says, as he looks at me through the grating, always this:

"His is a melancholy case, sir, very melancholy. Wrote a book once. Had a wife—a young wife. She died of poison, arsenic—supposed to have been given her by him, as they say he tired of her for another; but the jury acquitted him, as there was some doubt. She might have taken it for her complexion, you know some do. The doctors thought it likely. They put him here, sir; very kind of 'em, as he became quite crazy after the trial. He's always writing on them papers, sir. He says it's his life. Be worth reading, no doubt, if he should ever finish it. Perfectly harmless, sir." And they go away to stare at some one else.

The Great Ball of the Season

The Time-Ball at the Custom House.

Dramatic Feuilleton.

Faits Divers. Progress of the Opera War.—Grand Commotion among the Irishry—The Williams Vaso Art on the Half-shell.—D. B. versus Mrs. Ninetta Crummles.—Could the divine Williams have kept a Hotel? Wonderful Discovery made by Mr. Boyer Sanderson—Colonel Siddons turns up again.

It affords me the greatest gratification to say that the benefit-epidemic among the artists is subsiding. Nearly all the cases formerly reported are doing well. Miss Laura Keene played, on Monday, in the Irish classical drama, *The Colleen Bawn*; and no new cases of importance have appeared.

I don't know whether I have alluded to the shocking case of ingratitude on the part of Awful Jefferson, who, in order to harrow up the feelings of H. Pearson, 'went and took (as H. P. remarked) an engagement,' so that he could not play at H. P.'s benefit. The engagement was at Washington, and, to make matters worse, it was enormously successful. A. J. has now gone to Paradise (not Moore's, but up in the Pennsylvanian mountains) after trout. His Summer season at L. K.'s will commence two weeks from next Monday. It is not true that the Covode Committee had Awful before them, and got all his gags.

'Those popular American couple,' Mr. and Mrs. W. J. Florence, will have Wallack's for the Summer. The Express has made a blunder as regards the authorship of the Florences' opening play.

The Circus is doing pretty well with *The Bronze Horse*, and I. Vernon. Mr. Nixon has a new piece in preparation. It is reported to be a stunner.

Mr. Brougham had a benefit on Monday, and gave the generous public that fine old fossil, *The Poor Gentleman*, and the capital little comedy, *A Pretty Piece of Business*. The generous public came in large numbers, and J. B. regaled them with a capital speech, half in fun and half in earnest. The generous public took the funny part seriously, and laughed at the serious portion, which is rather a good thing to do. J. B. does not serve under the Wallack Dynasty after the present season. He is going to have a shy at J. Bull next season.

They have read the *Overland Route* at Wallack's, and it is the next thing to be done. It is a three-act comedy, written by Tom Taylor for the Mathewses, and brought out only six weeks ago at the Haymarket. The first act takes place on board one of the East Indian steamers, and the second 'on a rock.' Some of the Pfaff Light Guard might appear in that scene to great advantage. Curiously enough, the best part in the piece will be played by Mr. Lester Wallack.

Mrs. Thalia Wood had an immense benefit at New Orleans, last week.

The war between the Operatic Roses increases in intensity. Last Friday, the fiery Maximilian made a grand coup de main, and brought out Flotow's *Stradella*, a work which Ullman has been promising all the time since last September, but which has not yet been given at Irving Place. Of course, public curiosity was piqued, and Max got one full house. As for the opera, it is a good deal in the *Ledger* style, although there is rather more Cobb than Everett in it. It is very difficult to understand what the plot of *Stradella* is, any way, and the English libretto makes its mystery quite Eleusinian. The idea seems to be that the tenor voice is the universal pacificator, and that if a man can sing B flat, he will not only fascinate all the Anna Marias, but include among his victims the heavy fathers, guardians, trustees, and so on—people who always will interfere where they have no business whatever so to do.

Stradella was well done, though nothing to brag of. It drew only one good house.

On Monday, they had Frezzolini, Wissler, Stigelli, and Ardavani in the *Trovatore*, and if they didn't pitch into the score right merrily, I am a heretic. They must have been thinking about the great fight. FREZ, having no voice to speak of, or rather to sing with, naturally had a little the worst of it. I didn't stay till the end, but should judge that it would be a case of draw between Wissler and Stigelli. It didn't draw a good house, by the way.

Max is going to do Halévy's *Jewess*, and the Academy folks *Moses in Egypt*. Rather a strong pull upon Israel, altogether. Fabbri sings in the *Jewess*, and Patti in *Mose*.

I have my private opinion about these works, but I shall keep it to myself, until after they are done. It isn't for me to interfere with anybody's game either behind the curtain or before, where there is as much and better acting than on the stage. No one shall say *I* shook the Burgundy.

A bold Briton has arrived at the Academy of Music. He represents E. T. SMITH, who used to keep what is classically called a gin-mill in London, but who has now been reduced to the position of Manager of Her Majesty's Theatre. I don't think SMITH can have PATTI just now. We have a splendid lot of antiques on hand, and the son of Albion shall have them all. Take them, SMITH. There! Bless you. Be happy. Some few natural tears at parting with our oldest and best friends, but such things must come to pass. Don't mention it, SMITH, we beg. Virtue, SMITH, is its own reward (all it ever gets).

Magnanimity pays. We give you good clothes, air, grace, dignity, and all that should accompany old age. That's for you, SMITH. We, SMITH, will keep our paté while it is fresh, and may be give you some by-and-bye, SMITH, if you are good and don't mind paying pretty well for it, SMITH.

One boon, SMITH; don't forget 'Belle Brittan.'

Everybody was glad to assist at the rentrée of Miss ADELAIDE PHILLIPS at the Academy on Wednesday. PATTI, PHILLIPS, BRIGNOLI, and JUNCA, Sang *Martha*, and right well they did it, I assure you. There is more and better testimony to the same effect. The Brightest and Best heard it in Paris, with ST. URBAIN, NANTIER, DIDIER, MARIO, and GRAZIANI, and says that barring the dresses, which were 'perfectly splendid' in Paris, our performance seemed quite as good. I say nothing after that. What good or harm would it do, if I did?

There has been a general Hibernian jubilee, that is to say fight, going on in the coulisses during the week.

One of the disturbances is 'all along of' BOUCICAULT and Miss J. M. N. C. DAVENPORT. The author of the latest version of Jeanie Deans charged that Miss CRUMMLES nipped it, and acted it over in Philadelphia, where you can get any kind of law you want, vide Cadwallader's luminous decision in the case of L. B. S. KEENE against the gorgeous WHEATLEY.

Bien! Miss CRUMMLES says I didn't, and you're another, and D. B. goes to work and fires off a letter to show that she did, and that he isn't another, that is, altogether another. MOLIERE claimed that he had a right to steal, if he improved what he took, and that I believe is pretty good dramatic law, so far as precedents make law.

Aprés, it appears there is a suit for libel, CRUMMLES against D. B., to come off in New York, sometime, say A. D. 1900 for an approximate date.

I have very little to say about this particular matter, but there is one general exception I must put in to a practice which is getting to be a nuisance, not only as regards dramatic, but other literature. It is the habit some people have fallen into of getting up literary reputations upon false pretences. Actresses like Miss DAVENPORT, in the case of *Camille*, and others I could name, hire some poor devil of a litterateur to make a play for them, and then claim to have done the work themselves. This is about the smallest business going.

The other Hibernian row is about the Barney Williamses. It commenced at the Saint Patrick's dinner, at which JOHN BROUGHAM and BARNEY WILLIAMS assisted. BROUGHAM arrived last, and as he entered the room, a certain Judge, who knows a great deal more about the Common Pleas than about the coulisses (although he hankers' after the latter), alluded to J. B. as the only man on the stage who played the Irish gentleman as he was without slang, stuffed sticks, and so on. This riled B. WILLIAMS considerably, and so he was mollified with a testimonial benefit, given to him by the Mayor and Aldermen (Mon Dieu ! can't they even let the theatre alone ?), and Richelieu ROBINSON.

There was a presentation of course. A handsome Pompee-ian vase, appropriately inscribed, was received by B. W., in what Mr. Sanford would call the simple dress of an American citizen. Instead of handles, the vase had the Harp of Ireland on each side. Did you ever? I am sure I never did, and I put as much emphasis on that never as A. M.'s Ma did when they told her that Sophanisba was going to be married to Tom Racket, whom the Governor can't keep in the Bank not nowhere, and who won't do anything but play at billiards and drink brandy and water all day and all night. Nobody except an Irishman could have gotten up that vase.

B. W. made a speech. B. W. said that he tried to play the Irish peasant as he is. That the people of Ireland, who ought to know accepted him, B. W., as a proper person to uphold the Green, and perform on the celebrated musical instrument of Tara's Halls. As for Irish gentlemen, he did not think it was proper to make them adventurers, genteel swindlers, and so on. All of which the public applauded mightily.

Now B. W. was right and wrong at the same moment, not an unfrequent occurrence with an Irishman. He does play the Irish peasant well, but there are pieces—O'BRIEN's *Gentleman from Ireland* for one,—where the hero is not a confidence-man. It is in these parts that Mr. Brougham excels.

Of course there could be no comparison between J. B. and B. W. Or if there could be, I can't see it.

They had a fine old mutual admiration dinner at the *Century* on Monday, in commemoration of the divine Williams's birthday.

The really good thing about the affair was SANDERSON's carte, which is so clever that I ask you to put it just here:

A Festival

Commemorative of the Birth of the Immortal 'BARD OF AVON,' held at the rooms of 'The Century,' Monday, 23d April, 1860.

BILL OF FARE

'Have a care that your bills be not stolen,'

FIRST COURSE.

'Continue in * course, till thou know'st what they are.'

OYSTERS, ON THE HALF-SHELL—The East River
'Sends
This treasure of an Oyster.'
'Set a deep glass of Rhenish wine.'

GUMBO SOUP. THE SANDERSON SOUP.
'—expect spoon-meat'— 'Something too crab-bed.'
'Thou lack'st a cup of Canary."

KENNEBEC SALMON, boiled, with lobster sauce.
'Th' imperious seas breed monsters; for the dish,
Poor tributary rivers as sweet fish."

NORTH RIVER SHAD, broiled, sauce remonlade.
'A very fresh-fish here.'

BERMUDA POTATOES, boiled.
'Let the sky rain potatoes,'
'From the still vex'd Bermoothes.'

FRESH CUCUMBERS.
'For this, be sure, to-night thou shalt have cramps.'

SECOND COURSE.

'—great nature's second course,
Chief nourisher in life's feast.'

SPRING LAMB, roasted, with mint sauce.
'—innocent
As is the sucking lamb.'

ROAST CAPONS, stuffed with truffles.
'You cannot feed Capons so.'

VEAL SWESTEREADS, larded, with tomato sauce.
'"Veal," quoth the Dutchman; " is not Veal a Calf?"'

SPRING CHICKENS, broiled, with Steward's sauce.
'You would eat chickens i' the shell.'

LIVERS OF GEESE, with Madeira sauce.
'This is the liver vein, which makes flesh a deity,
A green goose a goddess.'

WILD SQUABS, stewed, with vegetable sauce
'—which he will put on us,
As pigeons feed their young.'

ASPARAGUS, with butter sauce.
'Who comes so fast in silence of the night?'

GREEN PEAS, with sugar.
'I had rather have a handful or two of pease.'

SWEET CORN, Indian style.
'The gods sent not corn for the rich men only.'

ONIONS, stewed, with gravy.
'An onlon will do well for such a shift.'
'Daylight and champagne discovers not more.'

THIRD COURSE.

'Whate'er the course, the end is the renown.'

ENGLISH SNIPE, broiled, on toast.

'I should time expend with such a snipe.'
BLUE-WINGED TEAL, roasted.
'O dainty duck,'
'with wings as swift as meditation.'
A WILD BOAR'S HEAD, garnished with spears.
'Like a full-acorn'd boar, a German one.'
BOSTON LETTUCE, with mayonnaise sauce.
'We may pick a thousand salads,
ere we light on such another herb'
'Run nothing but claret wine.'

FOURTH COURSE.

—'the fruits are to ensue,'

'And any pretty little tiny kickshaws.'

RUM PUDDING.
—'bless'd pudding,'
'The more thou damm'st it up, the more it burns.'
QUINCE PIES
'They call for quinces in the pastry.'
TARTELETTES OF APPLES
'Carv'd like an apple tart.'
CREAM KISSES
'Kissing-comfits and snow eringoes.'
'The last of many doubled kisses.'

TUTT-FRUTTI ICE CREAM.
'Tut, tut, thou art all ice, thy kindness freezes.'

DESSERT.

'A last year's pippin, ** with a dish of Carraways.'
'Four pounds of prunes, and as many raisins o' the sun.'
'The fig of Spain, very good.'
'There is a dish of leather-coats for you.'
'Give * this * orange to your friend.'
'And fetch the new nuts.

'My cheese, my digestion.'

'Go, fetch me a quart of sack: put a toast in it,'
'And good store of fertile Sherris,'
'Some aqua-vitae, ho!'

It has remained for SANDERSON, who is to our cuisine what SOYER was to London and Paris, to have made a new Shaksperian Discovery. The author of Shakspeare's Scholar, and, jointly with Miss LAURA KEENE and GENIO C. SCOTT, of *A Midsummer Night's Dream*, is said to have grown two inches shorter since the above carte came out.

It was long ago proven that SHAKSPEARE must have been a doctor, again that he 'followed the sea,' and finally Lord CAMPBELL demonstrated to his own satisfaction, if not to that of anybody else, that the Bard of Avon was a lawyer, but it has remained for SANDERSON to show that the divine Williams could have kept an hotel.

I think W. S. was almost the only literary man on record who could have kept an hotel, and the discovery is one of the highest importance to the whole craft as well as to the public in general.

Anybody would have supposed that even the *Century* savans would have been satisfied with this Sandersonian discovery; but no, they must have their eight speeches by W. M. EVARTS ('cré nom! what would the Pilgrim Fathers have said to such conduct on the part of their degenerate descendant?), the Rev. Mr. HUDSON (he has made a good thing out of W. S., one way and another, and ought to give him a lift), RICHARD GRANT WHITE, the longest and mistiest of the noble army of commentators; JAMES T. BRADY—who is cleverer before twelve honest men in an Oyer and Terminer jury-box than when at the bar of literary criticism, but don't know it; J. H. SIDDONS (who is he?), who spoke for the Players,' and was appropriately preceded by 'Blow, Blow, thou Wintry Wind;' and two other philosophers unknown, I think, to the trump of fame.

That's all, I reckon. Who says that's enough?

Personne.

Thoughts and Things.

BY ADA CLARE

Harper's Monthly for May publishes the last sketch from the illustrious pen of CHARLOTLE BRONTE. I wish people wouldn't do such things, that is, wouldn't publish unfinished sketches calculated to excite weak and sensitive minds like my own to an agony of guessing as to how the woman of genius would have developed her story. Besides, it gives one such a thrill of deep regret: the story opens vigorously enough to have equalled that marvel of romance-writing—*Jane Eyre*,—and the only hand that could have worked the wonder, was long since clasped close in the white palm of death.

Rose Terry contributes a lively and very readable story to the same number, entitled *Miss Muffet and the Spider*. Rose is ingenious and able, but she is too apt to fancy that because she is virtuous, there are no more gilt cakes and Canary-wines left.

Rosamond Newcombe is one of the usual ward-robe stories, written of course by a lady; there is not a man on the hemisphere so well acquainted with bibs and tuckers. The narrative consists of a series of described costumes, woven together by a slender but useful plot. Instead of labelling this is a dinner-dress, evening-dress, morning-robe, etc., Miss Rosamond, the show-block of the piece, is made to appear just in the place to which the toilet was adapted.

o o o

I wonder if Fabbri likes comic-opera, when she is so grand in lyric-tragedy? I hardly mean comic-opera; I mean music that is intended to make people laugh. Speaking of that, I wonder whether music ever did make any one laugh? Perhaps the comic situations, the grimaces, the ludicrous toilets, are the true jesters there. I fancy that the natural tendency of musical sound is toward the serious, if not toward the melancholy. At any rate, every natural sound is plaintive. Not only the waters of Babylon, but the flow of all waters invites us to sit down beside them and weep with them. The murmur of brooks, the voices of quick streams, the full roll of the sea, have all their meaning of sadness—they never suggest mirth.

I have never been able to hear the sad singing of the wind through the restless pines, without feeling an emotion of passionate regret. I know not why, but it ever makes me feel as if our planet were a huge and organized system of trifling. Everything put within our reach, and we allowed to grasp nothing. Even if fate gives us gifts, it seems but for the pleasure of taking them away again. It is a good thing to have cheerful words on our lips, to philosophize about the joys of living, but under it all so many of us must look upon our actual lives with an aching sense of scorn. We are most of us so much higher and nobler than our lives. What we do is a very insufficient test of what we are.

To return to my thought. I have said that the winds and the waters sang to us only the voices of mournfulness, and I am sure that the singing of birds is equally plaintive; the most precious of the feathered singers seem striving to break the heart with their melody. The Eolian harp, in which Nature is invited to work upon the artificial, gives us nothing but long, low, wailing sounds, not unlike the sounds which well-tutored fingers, if allowed to wander over any musical instrument, will unconsciously draw forth. The highest expression in music verges toward the tragic. Those musical compositions which attain immortality are generally, the expressions of grief, or if of joy, of that joy which is so full that it crushes the heart like pain. But above all, the divinest sanctuary of melody is always the sanctuary of sorrow.

o o o

I have been troubled to think that there is so little gratitude in the world, but on the other hand I have reflected that there is so little done that is really worthy of gratitude. People often make their favors so incomplete that they are worse than useless. They build up a lumbering body, without feet, hands, head, expecting it immediately to go alone. That has been the origin of the saying that you may do ninety-nine favors for a man, and for the want of the hundreth he will not thank you. It often happens that the ninety-nine favors without the hundreth are a mere dead letter; the last is required to vitalize them all. Besides, gratitude is not an easy sentiment to express; it is apt to sink deep down into the heart, and wait earnestly for a chance to act. Some people wish to make me believe that the way to win the good-will of others is to treat them harshly; to speak well, kindly of them, they tell me, is the way to win their contempt. I don't mean to believe it, I am utterly obstinate on that point. I could not, for instance, state that I disliked Cortesi, even if it were the means of winning her distinguished regard.

—The difficulty of determining the genuineness of pictures is strikingly shown by the following incident related by Mr. Hogarth, the eminent print-publisher in the Haymarket:

> Some years since, I purchased a picture at Christie's, sold as a genuine production by Muller, of an 'Italian Boy;' it was signed and dated. Muller saw the picture several times at my house and never hesitated to acknowledge its being painted by himself. George Fripp, of the Water-Color Society, also saw it and remarked: 'You have got Sphinx's picture (a nickname given to Muller). I saw him paint it.' This picture I sold to one of the trade in Cambridge; and, as Muller's reputation rapidly increased, the picture passed quickly into other hands. One of these persons wrote to Muller, asking if it was his work. 'If it is the same picture Mr. Hogarth had, I painted it.' The picture upon this was again sold, and some time after taken to Muller to verify, which he did; his brother, however, who was present, looked at the canvas and exclaimed: 'Bill, this can't be your picture; don't you remember it had a sketch at the back?' This caused a closer examination, and it was found to be a copy. Of course, the picture no longer possessed the value in the eyes of its previous possessors, and it came back to me. In almost the last letter I received from Muller, he alludes to this transaction, and says: "I found out all about the 'Italian Boy.' I painted the picture for Mr.——, and he had six copies made from it, and yours was one of them."

NEW YORK MAY 5, 1860

THE MILL ON THE FLOSS.

The Mill on the Floss. By George Eliot, author of 'Scenes of Clerical Life' and 'Adam Bede.' New York: Harper & Brothers.

If there is any one thing in this world more wearisome than another,—and we are strongly inclined to think there isn't,—it is a woman's story about human life and human love. Such a story is 'The Mill on the Floss.' We have read it,—not without appreciation indeed, and not without interest,—but with inexpressible weariness of spirit. It is essentially wanting in the dignity of power and in the charm of novelty. It is the old tale over again, told thousands of times already, and only varied in the telling; that the course of true love never did run smooth; that this is a very cold and stormy world to get through with; that sensitive persons are in a bad way most of their time; that there is an oppressive narrowness in common life which rebukes the ideal everywhere and crushes spiritual aspiration in a remorseless manner; that most people in the world are hard-hearted and selfish brutes; that virtue is its own reward; that (see Pope) all the honor consists in acting well your part in the drama of life; that (see Longfellow) it is sublime to suffer and be strong; that martyrdom is an exceedingly good thing to do; and finally that those persons only are entitled to a crown, and likely to get it, who have in the first place taken kindly to the cross.

A résumé of these refreshing truths indicates very justly the moral character and purpose of this novel. It is a story of common people and domestic life, on English soil and in recent years. Its principal characters are the Dodsons and the Tullivers, country families descended of decent ancestry in the praiseworthy past of Pitt and high prices; living a sordid, prosaic life; controlled by conventional notions and habits; exercised by all the usual joys and sorrows of mortality; and affected by all possible vicissitudes of worldly fortune. Its plot is no more complicated than is the web of any human existence. Its incidents are the simple, natural incidents of everyday life. Its pathos is the pathos of poverty, of wasted affection, of hope deferred. And throughout its pages there is everywhere the blood-red lustre and warmth of earnest humanity. The vital interest of this story attaches itself to the respective characters and fortunes of Tom and Maggie Tulliver. On the whole Maggie is much more interesting than Tom. They are the children of Mr. Tulliver, miller, and Mrs. Bessy Tulliver, his wife—a lady of the clan Dodson. The uncles and aunts are, by the marriage of the Dodson sisters, Mr. and Mrs. Glegg, Mr. and Mrs. Pullet, and Mr. and Mrs. Deane,—all wealthy and vulgar people: Also, by the marriage of Mr. Tulliver's sister, Mr. and Mrs. Moss,—poor persons in humble condition and agricultural pursuits. Mr. Tulliver's location is the Dorlcote Mill, in the town of St. Ogg's, where, near by, 'the broadening Floss hurries on between its green banks to the sea.' Hence the title of the story, 'The Mill on the Floss.'

There are seven divisions of this novel. Book the First relates to the early life of Tom and Maggie, at home; to their parents, their aunts and uncles; their childish joys and sorrows; their cakes, patchwork, rabbits, and fish-lines; to those uncovered jars that families always keep and occasionally exhibit; to the fertility of Mrs. Moss, the mother of eight children; to the harmony of Mrs. Tulliver and Mrs. Pullet, who 'always liked the same patterns'; to the connubial truculence of Mrs. Glegg, and her copy of Baxter's 'Saints' Everlasting Rest'; and finally, to the fact that, after much exercise of the family council, it was decided by Mr. Tulliver to put Tom to school with the Rev. Mr. Stelling. Book the Second comprises an account of Tom's school-life; of his difficulties with Euclid and the irregular verbs; of his delight in Mr. Poulter's broadsword, and Mr. Poulter's delight in gin; of his fellow-pupil, Philip Wakem, son of lawyer Wakem, the foe of the elder Tulliver; of Maggie's visits, and the child-love of Maggie and Philip, the germ of tragedy and sorrow in their lives; of the aversion of Philip and Tom, incipient and dangerous; and at last, of Mr. Tulliver's ruin, through a law-suit won by Wakem. Book the Third details the consequences of this misfortune to the family of Mr. Tulliver; how that gentleman had a fit and sank into a stupor; how Mrs. Tulliver mourned over her linen and her silver told her husband, times and times, 'Whatever you do, don't go to law'; how there was a family council and a quarrel among the women; how Tom made his Uncle Deane get him a place of business; how Mrs. Tulliver somewhat superfluously made a fool of herself, and Mr. Wakem bought Dorlcote Mill at auction; how Mr. Tulliver came to his senses presently, and was badgered by his help-meet; how Wakem, to humiliate his victim, offered to hire Mr. Tulliver to work the Mill he had so long owned; how the taunts of his wife forced him to accept the place and suffer under this refinement of cruelty; and how at last he made Tom record his enmity against Wakem in the family Bible, and sign there a promise to revenge his father's wrongs. Book the Fourth is entitled, 'The Valley of Humiliation,' and is a picture of the subsequent life of the family—a life of drudgery for the payment of debts. Book the Fifth records the love of Maggie and Philip; Tom's discovery of their attachment, and his consequent anger and severity; the triumph of industry and the payment of debts; the personal chastisement of Wakem by a riding-whip in the hands of Mr. Tulliver; and lastly, the sudden death of the latter amiable but irascible person. Book the Sixth is chiefly occupied with the loves of Maggie and Maggie's cousin, Lucy Deane, with Mr. Philip Wakem and Mr. Stephen Guest. In this dangerous territory, the fascinations of Maggie tell with considerable force all round: she wins her cousin's lover away from her, and puts both the young men into a state of mind. An interview is described between the youthful Wakem and his entertaining papa, in which the beloved sire gets the worst of it as to Maggie. Meantime the prosperous but flinty-hearted Tom assures his sister that she must give him up if she marries Philip. At this epoch, that gentle young lady wavers between Philip and Stephen, with a strong inclination for the latter. Then happens an aquatic adventure on the Floss, in which Stephen carries off Maggie in a boat and offers to marry her. Maggie don't see it. They are finally picked up by a Dutch vessel, and after some days she reaches her home again. Meantime the gossips have been busy with her reputation. She is cast off by her brother Tom. There is a letter of exoneration from Stephen, and a letter of love and confidence from Philip. Also there is a tender interview between Lucy and Maggie, in the course of which both of them shed briny tears and are reconciled. The last scene comes then—an overflow of the Floss, a midnight flood, over which Maggie tugs her boat, to the rescue of her brother at Dorlcote Mill. It is the hour of their reconciliation —and of their death. A floating mass sweeps over their boat; and, twined in each other's arms, forgiving everything in a true and holy love, brother and sister go down into the darkness." Perhaps we sin against our readers in offering them this analysis of a novel which so many will desire to analyze for themselves; but we do so in justification of our judgment regarding it. It will be seen that this story of 'The Mill on the Floss' is a love story of the accepted and customary kind. Hence, notwithstanding its ceaseless humor, its fine characterization, its peculiar but graceful style, it is a wearisome thing. The loves of young persons are not very interesting, except to themselves. Their jealousies and quarrels, their kisses and tears, their lockets and ribbons, their letters and tresses,—all probably, have peculiar charms to the enraptured participants. But the dispassionate observer is cold to charms. He perceives that people who are in love verge steadily toward idiocy and betake themselves to raving. He does not melt to printed rapture, nor is he much shaken with heart-throbs. In fact it seems to him that the, emotions of the young men and maidens, though very sweet, are not sufficiently important or interesting to encourage him through a novel of nearly five hundred dense and dreary pages.

[For The New York Saturday Press.]

MAY-DAY IN NEW YORK.

BY ALICE GILL.

'Twas May, and people, crab-like, sought to change
Their earthly shells, but not because, like crabs,
They had outgrown the whole of last year's crust:
Some changed because a lightened purse had made
Them shrink into more healthy size and shape,
And others changed, but knew not why they changed.

In cities, where men barter all for gold,
Love's woodbine never creeps about the sides
Of home, nor into chamber-window peeps,
A welcome there to meet from those who love
To twine with grace her tendrils round the porch,
Until, grown forward by their smiles, she weaves
Her meshes over all the frame, and binds
The owner's heart amid her bloom.

In vain
Do men paint frescoes on the wall, of trees,
And rocks, and gushing streams; they cannot tempt
A bird to leave his leafy home, and light
Upon a golden perch to sing to them.
I know not if I slept, but this I know,
I dreamt the sun, mistaking me for dew,
Drew up my form into a misty cloud—
Below me lay the city, where were men,
Like polypi in lime, who ceaseless toiled
To beautify their homes, which looked to me
Not half so fair, as do the coral reefs
By wavy ocean lovingly embraced.

'Twas May, but yet it did not seem to be,
Nor did I wish, in gentle shower, to fall
Upon that restless and unhappy mass
Of toiling men. No thirsty tulips held
Their streaked drinking-cups to catch my rain,
No daisy wished to bathe her lovely face,
No pinks sent up their fragrant breathing prayers
To woo my touch. With anxious looks, men heaped
The drays with all their worldly household stuff,
And plodded on through all that moving crowd.
With jostle, on the way, they often lost
Full half their wealth, and sometimes half their care;
Then, as the day wore on, they ran into
Each other's homes, as children ofttimes do,
When at the game of 'fooly, fooly come,'
They play.

But those were changes made by those who warm
With life, and hope, and strivings after gain;
Could give direction, by their will, how high
Or low they'd have their bodies rest at night.
A little knot of crape, both black and white,
Blown by the thoughtless wind, did tell
That May had found, for one, without a will,
A home for which base envy would not strive.
They brought the body forth, but O, how small!
And as the long procession moved on,
I heard them say: "twas but a little child.'
And then they talked of beef and pork, of deeds
And bonds, and mortgages.

Slowly winding like
A worm, they crawled along the narrow streets,
And sometimes, too, as though a gardener's spade
Cleft them in twain, they parted to let pass
A lumbering barrow, or a gaudy coach.
I, aided by the wind, did follow near,
And nearer, ever nearer, sadder grew,
Until unto a little green they came
Where one poor sickly willow, gently bent,
And fresh-turned earth did plainly mark the spot,
The little dark, and lonely, resting-place
Of baby-innocence. There fell my tears
In bounteous showers, and there, when May comes round,
The golden-crowned dandelions bloom, all o'er,
To mark that little home.

NEW YORK MAY 12, 1860

Dramatic Feuilleton.

'The Overland Route.'

Mr. Wallack and Miss Laura Keene have between them arranged some very curious advertisements for the country managers.

They are all about Mr. Tom Taylor's comedy, *The Overland Route.*

According to Miss Keene, she suggests' subjects to Mr. Taylor, alters his dialogue, and gives him 'situations.' *The Overland Route* was "written by Mr. Taylor at the suggestion of, and expressly for Miss Laura Keene and her company, as it was constituted in the seasons of '58 and '59. The unprecedented run of 'Our American Cousin,' however, prevented its production during that memorable season. The secession of Mr. Blake—for whom the part of Sir Solomon was written—caused another delay, during which lapse of time the piece, with all its suggestions, alterations, and situations furnished by Miss Keene, under Mr. Taylor's careful adoption, having been accepted by Mr. Buckstone, at the Haymarket, it has been copyrighted in both countries as the joint work of Tom Taylor and Laura Keene."

So no wicked manager must lay hands on this 'joint' work, or Taney will be after them with an injunction. I understand that Miss Keene intends to copyright the version of *A Midsummer Night's Dream*, which she, with Mr. Richard Grant White, and Genio C. Scott, suggested to William Shakspeare, the friend of J. H. Siddons and Judge Daly.

In order to give the public a little light on this subject, and to show how admirably *The Overland Route* is adapted to our audience, I send you a résumé of the plot from an English paper:

The Overland Route is a comedy in three acts, written for Mr. and Mrs. Charles Mathews, and produced at the Haymarket on the 23rd of February last. It was still in the bills in the 21st of April. During the first and second acts the scene is laid on board one of the Peninsular and Oriental Company's steamboats, bound homeward after the Indian mutiny, and the passengers are the *Dramatis Personcæ* whose strange sayings and doings constitute the business of the play. Not to enumerate with tedious particularity all the members of this motley assemblage, it will suffice to mention those only who contribute most conspicuously to the amusement of the spectators. In this number must be classed *Mr. Colepepper* (Mr. Chippendale), a retired civil commissioner of the Badgeripore district, whose accounts are somewhat in arrear; *Sir Solomon Fraser* (Mr. Compton), a *ci devant jeune homme*, who having spent his life chiefly at native Courts, is now returning to England with a fine head of false hair, and a set of teeth which he takes out at night and puts in in the morning, like his shirt-studs; *Captain Clavering* (Mr. E. Villiers), a military young 'swell' of the fastest of all fast schools, who unfortunately has been known to do a few things at whist which would not pass muster either with Hoyle or Crawley; *Major MacTurk* (Mr. Rogers), a fire-eater with the voice of a lion and the heart of a chicken; *Mr. Lovibond* (Mr. Buckstone), a Singapore merchant, who is, moreover, a victim of society—a martyr to unfortunate coincidences, but whose sorrows keep the house in a roar; his too obsequious satellite, *Moleskin* (Mr. Clark), a rascally detective, who follows him like his shadow; and *Tom Dexter* (Mr. C. Mathews), an adventurer, who, having been knocked about rather unceremoniously by Fortune, and having passed through a series of strange vicissitudes, has at last the good luck to obtain the appointment of surgeon to the ship, in which capacity he does a variety of noble acts, and untrying circumstances proves himself not the physician only, but the 'guide, philosopher, and friend' of all on board. Among the ladies the most noteworthy are *Mrs. Lovibond* (Mrs. Wilkins), who unconscious of the existence of her lord, much less of his presence in the same vessel with her, fancies herself a widow, and under this soft delusion encourages the savage suit of *Major MacTurk*; *Mrs. Sebright* (Mrs. C. Mathews), woman, who is an is an object of the young married of the fiercest contention the most ludicrous rivalry between *Colepepper* and *Fraser,* both of whose addresses she is vain enough to receive, though well aware she has no legitimate right to either; and *Miss Colepepper* (Miss M. Ternan), on whose hand *Clavering* has designs, which however are not crowned with success—his idol preferring to make *Dexter* the happiest of men. In the course of the voyage the ship runs aground on the Mazzaffa Reef, in the Red Sea, and is totally wrecked. This sudden calamity 'checks the tide of laughter with a sigh,' gives a gives a dash of serious sentiment to the exuberant fun of the piece, and is also of service in bringing out the qualities of many of the passengers, which otherwise might not have been disclosed; for it is adversity that tries men's souls and shows them in their true light. All the characters in this little comedy are drawn with a skill which intimates in the artist surprising knowledge of human nature; but the personage who contributes most abundantly and most unremittingly to the enjoyment of the audience, is, beyond question, *Mr. Lovibond.* This ill-fated tyrannical gentleman, who had been compelled by the temper of his wife to fly his native land ten years before, and who is now timidly returning, in the hope that she may in the meantime have passed into another if not a better world, gets on board at Aden, and, being mistaken for a runaway felon, is incontinently pounced upon by *Mr. Moleskin*, the detective, who puts him in irons and treats him with every indignity. Troubles thicken around him, and the cup of his bitterness overflows when at length he finds himself in the awful presence of his spouse, whose lover, the *Major*, threatens to blow his brains out for robbing him of the lady with whom he had hoped to spend his life in matrimonial bliss.

[The characters played in London by C. Mathews, Compton, Buckstone, Rogers, and Mrs. C. Mathews, are allotted here to Lester Wallack, Blake, Walcot, and John Brougham.]

The London papers, out of the Taylor clique, said that the piece was on the whole stupid, but that Mathews was very amusing, and that he, with the fine scenery and so on, saved the play.

As to Mr. Wallack's copy, I believe that the Sunday school truth about it is, that it was sent here by the distinguished ironmonger manager, Knowles, of Manchester, the mortgagee of Charles Mathews. Knowles owns the comedian, and of course, the plays written for him.

Will Cadwallader, or some other Philadelphia Mansfield, tell us if there is any power in Congress to compel Jefferson and Mrs. Thalia Wood to give up their gags in *Ivanhoe*?

Vale.

Miss Laura Keene closes her regular season to-night, and is succeeded at the direction of affairs by Jefferson, who opens with the *Invisible Prince* (with Mrs. Wood, Miss C. Jefferson, Mrs. Chanfrau, and himself), on Wednesday or Thursday of this week.

Once in awhile I have had my little bit of fun with Miss Keene, but I should be as sorry as any of her most ardent admirers, should she retire altogether from the New York stage, as has been rumored. In some points her direction cannot be excelled, and I believe she has the true artistic pride in her vocation, or profession, as it is technically termed. Of course the public will come out strongly for the *soirée d'adieux* of so great a popular pet as Miss Laura Keene.

Geary.

Geary came out in the 'Wanderbilt,' the other day.

Geary was announced in the Purser's report, thus: "Mr. Gustavus Geary the celebrated Irish vocalist, and his daughter Miss Mina Geary."

I do an immense amount of cramming from newspaper and other sources in order to keep myself acquainted with the names of singers, actors, and showfolks generally, but Geary was unknown to me.

I know him now. He has been done.

His name ought to be Gustavus Adolphus.

Was it not Captain Dalgetty who used to swear 'by the great Gustavus?' If the Captain lived in these latter days he would anathematize by Geary. He is an immense fellow. Irish all over. He is a good deal like Collins only more or so. He is expansive, Geary. He reminds you of the Central Park, or the Hudson, or *The Century*. He evidently imagines, like many other brilliant people from the other side, 'that he has landed among a nation of savages, and that reading, writing, and other fine arts which were brought to Ireland by the 'Phaynacians' have not yet been introduced into the land of the West. So before G. G. sings 'Love's Young Dream,' or Blake's chef d'œuvre (Geary isn't a patch to the Governor in it), 'Farewell and when E'er you Remember the Hour,' or 'The Death of Nelson,' he makes a neat speech in the approved post-prandial style of our great-grandfathers. When G. G. desires to say "my friend Brown composed this song," he puts it tersely thus: "This charming ballad—I refer to the a-music—was the work of the a-distinguished, a-Brown, ladies and gentlemen was, I think I may use the expression—Brown was to me one of the best, I may say dearest and nearest, in fine I believe I can safely assert that Brown was my friend."

Which is all very nice; and I am sure it amuses me more than the singing, though some people are rude enough to say, "—— Brown; stow him, and pipe your little lay."

G. Geary pipes well. He has got what is called an organ-voice, and it smells of Non Nobis Dominie and 'Here's a health to all good lasses' in every passage. You can always hear the Noble Chairman rapping for the gentlemen to come to order, while four jokers in seedy black coats (the bass always has a red nose and a George-the-Third white cravat) go to work at the National Anthem. It is a good voice, Geary's, and he sings the ballads passing well.

And then to see him at the piano! It is grand. When he plays a very simple accompaniment which any ten-year-older in New York could rattle off, one would think it was a difficult study of Chopin's or Robert Schumann's he was at. He has the air of a man conquering a great difficulty, and saying 'Good people, what do you think of this? Isn't it fine? It is hard, but I don't mind it a bit. What's difficulty to genius? Only a spur to exertion.'

And then to see him look at Miss Mina, who is a young lady of tender age, in a frock which is neither short nor long, but like the Charleston Convention, a drawn battle, and who sings with her hands clasped in front—it is grand. When she makes a run, G. G. hovers on the high note; when she trills, celestial canaries seem to be beckoning him to the New Jerusalem; when she descends the scale, he seems to sink gradually to rest with the proud consciousness of happy paternity.

Miss Mina sings very nicely, and the pride of Gustavus is quite natural; but I can't help being amused at all these things—that's natural, too.

Altogether, I think that Gustavus—who has all the fun of all the Irish comedians rolled into one man, and don't seem to know it—is a good thing to do.

If anybody is capable of upholding the Green in foreign parts, it is G. G. Erin goes B flat with him to a tremendous extent.

The Anniversary Opera.

Like everything else, the Opera, this week, has been given up to the Saints.

At the Winter Garden there has been more *Juive*; and at the Academy they have given *Moses in Egypt*, which is announced as the chef d'œuvre of Rossini. It is the seventy-first chef d'œuvre that I have heard by this composer. I don't care much about the merits of the case, but I do wish they would get some other expression, chef d'ouvre being very difficult to spell.

However, I can manage one way or the other; so they may go on with their chefs d'oeuvres. There is only one master-work, and that, I need not say, is the Brightest and Best, but, I am pained to say, the most ungrateful of her sex.

Yes, Effendi, the last link is broken, the tie is severed, the—but why should I lay bare to the world a lacerated breast? I won't. The world will keep on buying and selling things, and eating its dinner and playing its billiards and won't care sixpence.

No. I will pine in silence.

May she be happy!

That's all.

Now about Mose. As for the music, every body knows all about it. The first and second acts are rather dusty, but the third and fourth make up for all. The libretto is one of those delightfully incomprehensible things, which make a man look back and think of his Euclid. There is a large amount of bass Moses, and of baritone Pharoah. Then there is the tenor, Brignoli's Prince of Wales, who is in love with the Prima Donna, Patti, who is rather over-weighted about the head-dress. The question is whether she will leave Egypt with Moses and her people, or stay over a train or two for H. R. H. In the end she throws him over, according to the usual custom of the delightful sex.

Some dramatists would have made a fine ending of the Opera, by taking the life of the Prince, who was one of those stupid Egyptians who insisted upon crossing the sea when the tide was exceedingly high, through the instrumentality of the young lady he loved. I think I see Boucicault inventing an entirely new effect, with a wonderful life-preserver, entirely new and copyrighted by D. B.

On the whole. I am inclined to think that *Moses* answers better as an oratorio than as an opera, and Deacon Strakosh would make a good thing of it, if he put the people into black dress-coats and white cravats. As it is, Major Susini makes a powerful Mose—he would be eligible to the place of Foreman for 'Big Six'; Patti, notwithstanding an acre of white muslin about her head, looks so prettily, and sings so charmingly, that even Brignoli might go and make a 'demnition moist, unpleasant body of himself' on her account; and altogether the performance is more than fair.

Next week, at the Academy, Madame Gazzaniga will play her most positively last, final, closing farewell engagement, previous to her retirement to one of her numerous palaces by the Lake of Como. There will be a performance every night except Saturday. Gazzaniga will sing in the *Traviata,* the *Favorita,* and *Lucrezia Borgia*. On Monday, *Mosé* will be given, and on Tuesday, the *Traviata* with Gazzaniga.

A Wail.

For a fortnight, Colonel, 'ado.' With a heart lacerated, I may say shaded in the severest manner by the object of my dewy affections, I am about to commit moral suicide,—going, in fact, to a political convention; going to do Peoria in its most uncomfortable, barbarous, and Peorian aspect.

But it is all one to me, now. No more clean shirts; no more Jouvin; no more midday breakfasts; no more. Pomard,—nothing but dust and ashes; desolation and dry bread; misery and pie!

Tic dolorously,

Personne.

ART ABOUT TOWN.

At Goupil's we see a much trumpeted picture, 'The First Day of Worship,' by Schwartze. It represents a company of Dutch men and women, in masquerade as 'Pilgrim Fathers.' The composition is good, the figures lack neither individuality nor interest, the picture is altogether respectable in execution; but the English Puritan was made of an oak that does not grow in the low countries. Nothing could be more unlike his iron severity than this soft, affectionate, demonstrative pastor, gesticulating before the Lord and his flock.

This work well illustrates the difficulty, amounting to impossibility, of understanding and rendering from within a history foreign to the artist. At Washington we see an Italian Putnam, as wide of the mark in character as a French translation of Shakspeare or 'Le Père Tom.' We remember also Leutze's ludicrous representation of Bryant's 'Fairest of the Rural Maids,' as a strapping German peasant girl, travelling barefooted up hill, with a hay rake, three spears of grass in her bundle, and a jug.

At the Dusseldorf is Crawford's 'Dancing Jenny,' a very ugly little figure, ill-drawn and clumsy in form, ungraceful in action, uninteresting in the momentary expression, and of no account as a study of temperament or character. Mr. Crawford made many statues no better than this. His

The Dead Pearl Diver, by Benjamin Paul Akers, 1858.

habit was sketchy; he 'threw off' works, as his friends would admiringly say, without any deep impression. We know nothing worse in marble than the boy beside the schoolmaster, in his design for the pediment at Washington. His head is frightfully disproportioned and misshapen, his ugliness is positive. The step of this little girl is artificial, is that of a dancing-school. It has nothing of the morning remoteness and unconsciousness which is childhood.

Under a discipline of earnest and severe, yet sympathetic criticism, Mr. Crawford would have made half as many statues, and they would have been twice as good. He cultivated his 'dangerous facility,' and rested content in a superficial or popular view. Therefore, his American Mechanic is not a mechanic, his Indian is not an Indian, his Beethoven is demonstrative, his work in general is not final, does not exhaust any subject, or deepen our knowledge of it to conviction and satisfaction.

There is also a bust of Hawthorne, by Miss Lander, sufficiently vigorous in material traits. We see in it little of the absorbed and lonely introvertent habit of the original. This is the head of an easily but not deeply moved, an open and communicative man. It has rather the action of a public speaker, than of a contemplative, retiring poet, whose thoughts must be remotely indicated, must come to the surface in glimpses and fitful gleams. The charm of Hawthorne is shade and privacy. His mind is like an unsunned spring in a deep wood, the last refreshment after our gairish sunshine and the dust of the literary highway. There is a golden silence behind his silver speech, and in his aspect there should be the same reserve and resource, a mystery, a hint of the incommunicable, a concentration of power which never all finds utterance in look or word. This interiority, the soul of the subject, we do not feel in the bravely-handled marble of Miss Lander. It has strength of form, and lacks only this subtle sympathy with the genius of the man.

Her 'Evangeline' slips through the fingers of criticism, has little quality for praise or blame.

The Dead Pearl Diver, by Akers, is a work of undeniable merit. It is carefully modelled, with knowledge and feeling in every part, and seems to us a genuine though not commanding product of imagination, and so, something very rare in marble, a work of art.

The subject is slight to be so elaborately treated and in such enduring material. Life, not death, and therefore only life in death, will reinforce and refresh the beholder. The inanimate figure is only tolerable when it is not really inanimate, when it still retains a speaking-form moulded on the last motion of the soul, when it still lives with passion or purpose altogether deathless, so that we feel, very near, the presence which has just escaped. So after setting, the sun is still in the sky.

Art at its best is a liberation from the body by means of the body, an open road through the figure to the life. This fair form is not merely a form, a piece of cold-blooded anatomy, or a literal copy of actual flesh, like the Cenci of Miss Hosmer, but the life revealed in it was never powerful, and we have only faint and tender reminiscence rather than presence of it—too faint to appeal successfully to any but the most sensitive and sympathetic mind.

Genuine suggestion or poetry in marble we say is very rare. Among American statues by courtesy ideal, we look far to find another so sincere and free from artifice or convention as this.

The early work of Crawford was imitative, an echo both in motive and method. The statues of later date in which he spoke from himself, are free, not accurate, in execution; are picturesque, or to use a parallel term, sculpturesque in effect without earnestness of feeling. They have little charm for imagination, create no atmosphere about them, are not impressive. They are often admirable, if the reader will take our distinction, but they cast no inevitable spell on the beholder; they are not presences, they do not haunt the mind.

The work of Crawford seems to us graceful and vigorous commonplace, yet it has a certain life, and is so removed from the mechanical elaboration of Powers. The Greek Slave is a form without motive, without even animal consciousness, that physical sentiment which sways, unites, and animates the members. The works of Palmer are better vitalized, but their life is the luxury of 'flesh and blood, sweet flesh and blood.' His figures are pretty girls undressed, and by warmth of literal imitation have provoked sermons upon nude sculpture, from the *Crayon and Cosmopolitan Art Journal*. These figures are nude, not because they are undraped, but because their sexual and animal traits are given with manifest emphasis of enjoyment, are made the centre of interest, are the true inspiration of every work, however veiled under a romantic title, or what the *Atlantic Monthly* considers a touching 'predicament.'

We are running wide in our search for imaginative work.

The striking Indian of Brown, a study of great power, more vigorous perhaps in form and action than any American work, admirable in its kind and as a study, has yet little of the weird creative influence, so quickly felt, yet never definable, which carries the mind beyond the object of sight. Perhaps in elaboration something of the original spirit of the work escaped.

There is an Indian and Dog by Ward, still in plaster, which we connect in thought with this Dead Pearl Diver, though widely different in every other quality, as a piece of poetic suggestion. It is a wind from the wilderness, a free and supple figure hurrying stealthily forward in the chase, full of dull, concentrated, semi-animal vitality, a Western Faun, and truer than Donatello to the eager yet melancholy delight of savage health and half awakened life. The figure is almost ugly to sight in fidelity to Indian traits, but it brings with it a breath of the woods.

These two statues we should say need no apology for being. They are feelings uttered. That of Ward is masculine and decided, has the rude energy of which we find so little in the galleries. It is no studio work, but as much a piece of out-doors as the best, that is the most definite, imagery of Walt Whitman. The inspiration of Akers is something vague, a sentiment rather than a strong conception. There is character in the figure, but of a very soft and shadowy type.

To the Palmer Marbles,' everywhere paraded in photograph till they have become an 'institution,' we shall give more elaborate attention another day.

[For The New York Saturday Press.]

HOW SPRING COMETH

To Palace and Hovel.

Mark where she comes—the hoyden Spring!—
Her nascent bosom swelling fast,
Her fresh lips parting to the blast,
And all her beauties blossoming!

She wantons with the regal Sun,
And bids the inconstant god caress
The very turf her wild feet press,—
The humblest shrub she breathes upon.

The slumberous draperies that close
Around the palaces of Earth,
Flap-startled by her passing mirth—
And fall! She tarries not for those!

But from the squalid window-sill
She sweeps the scanty veil aside
And enters, radiant as a bride,
The sun-kiss hovering 'round her still!

Like music here, her laughter falls :
And echoes—as of Summer bees
And bird-songs through soft-swaying trees—
Seem quivering on the naked walls!

Echoes, too often false as fair!
So far from actual sense they seem,
The listener holds them as a dream
Whose waking hath no promise there!

Ye microscopic souls, that cling
To such small specks of spirit-light
That all beyond your reach is night;—
Ye bigots!—rob the Poor of Spring!

Ye bar them from the fresh free sod!
To these wan children of the soil
Ye make the Sabbath-Rest a toil—
A dungeon of the house of God!

Fling wide your sombre gates, and bid
These weary workers forth, to share
Life's heritage of springtide! There
The secret of God's Rest is hid!

CHARLES D. GARDETTE.

Philadelphia.

NEW YORK MAY 19, 1860

[For The New York Saturday Press.]

MAY AFTERNOON.

BY FREDERICK A. PARMENTER.

I.

The apple-blooms have crowned the trees
With perfumed heaps of rosy snow,
And reared an arch of gala-white
Above the mossy walk below.

II.

Dim clouds of amethyst and bronze,
Fly dreamily towards the sun,
Like Summer birds, with gold-tipped wings,
Bound Westward when the day is done.

III.

The orange-belted bee's low hum
Chimes with the murmur of the stream;
And life flows on in charméd hours,
As though 'twere some voluptuous dream.

IV.

The wildered senses reel with joy—
O, yearning soul, why ask for more?
Thou wilt not find a higher bliss
Until thou tread'st the Eden-shore!

WALT WHITMAN.

Leaves of Grass.

Leaves of Grass. By Walt Whitman. Boston: Thayer & Eldridge. Year 85 of the States (1860-61).

We announce a great Philosopher—perhaps a great Poet—in every way an original man. It is Walt Whitman. The proof of his greatness is in his book; and there is proof enough.

The intellectual attitude expressed in these 'Leaves of Grass,' is grand with the grandeur of independent strength, and beautiful with the beauty of serene repose. It is the attitude of a proud, noble, vigorous life. A human heart is here in these pages—large, wild, comprehensive—beating with all throbs of passion—enjoying all of bliss—suffering all of sorrow that is possible to humanity. "This is no book," it says; "whoever touches this, touches a man." It is the electrical contact of a great nature.

—"No dainty dolce affettuoso I;
Bearded, simburnt, gray-necked, forbidding, I have arrived,
To be wrestled with as I pass, for *the solid prizes of the universe,*
For such I afford whoever can persevere to win them. . .
I, exultant, will now shake out carols stronger and haughtier than have ever yet been heard upon the earth. . . .
And I will not sing with reference to a day, but with reference to all days,
And I will not make a poem, nor the least part of a poem, but has reference to the soul. . . .
Because, having looked at the objects of the universe,
I find there is no one, nor any particle of one, but has reference to the soul...
I pass death with the dying, and birth with the new-washed babe, and am not contained between my hat and my boots. . . .
I exist as I am—that is enough,
If no other in the world be aware, I sit content,
And if each and all be aware, I sit content. . . .
I am the poet of the body
And I am the poet of the soul.
The pleasures of heaven are with me, and the pains of hell are with me,
The first I graft and increase upon myself—the latter I translate into a new tongue.
I know perfectly well my own egotism. . . .
I am an acme of things accomplished and I am an encloser of things to be."

Such is the intellectual attitude of the 'Leaves of Grass'; such the position and purpose of their author. To accept everything as liberally as Nature accepts everything; to rightly appreciate all laws and all things, each thing in its place; to realize, reflect, and reproduce the emotions of every heart and the experiences of every person; to recognize and assert the universal harmony of creation; to know the beautiful union of Body and Soul in the individual, sublime in the present, and with a sublime destiny for the future; to repose in the certainty of infinite development and progression; to assert the individual above all things, knowing that 'nothing endures but personal quality;' to express for all mankind what all mankind feel without the power of expressing; to live the comprehensive life of the Philosopher, of the Poet, broad and vigorous, all lives in one,—reaching up into heaven, reaching down into hell, stretching backward over all the Past to gather up its results, throbbing with all the vital activity of the Present, making the Future glorious with more than hope,—this is the aim and the mission of Walt Whitman, this the felicity of his life as expressed in his poems. No man could utter himself more fully and truly. No book exists anywhere more beautifully in earnest than this. To the intelligent, sympathetic mind, none can explain itself with keener accuracy.

—"I will make the poems of materials, for I think they are to be the most spiritual poems,
And I will make the poems of my body and of mortality,
For I think I shall then supply myself with the poems of my Soul and of immortality. . .
I will acknowledge contemporary lands,
I will trail the whole geography of the globe, and salute courteously every city large and small;
And employments! I will put in my poems, that with you is heroism, upon land and sea. . . . .
And sexual organs and acts! do you concentrate in me—For I am determined to tell you with courageous clear voice, to prove you illustrious. . .
Omnes! Omnes!
Let others ignore what they may,
I make the poem of evil also—I commemorate that part also,
I am myself just as much evil as good—And I say there is in fact no evil,
Or if there is, I say it is just as important to you, to the earth, or to me, as anything else.
I too, following many, and followed by many, inaugurate a Religion. . . .
I will effuse egotism, and show it underlying all—And I will be the bard of Personality;
And I will show of male and female that either is but the equal of the other,
And I will show that there is no imperfection in male or female, or in the earth, or in the present—and can be none in the future,
And I will show that whatever happens to anybody, it may be turned to beautiful results—And I will show that nothing can happen more beautiful than death;
And I will thread a thread through my poems that no one thing in the universe is inferior to another thing,
And that all the things of the universe are perfect miracles, each as profound as any.
These are the thoughts of all men in all ages and lands—they are not original with me,
If they are not yours as much as mine, they are nothing, or next to nothing."

The leading idea in the philosophy of the 'Leaves of Grass' is the idea of grandeur and supremacy in the Individual. It asserts that there is nothing more divine than the human soul, and impels to a knowledge of living motive behind each thing and every action. It will have the singer and not the psalm, the preacher and not the script he preaches. It will not ignore the Body, but assets its beauty and the divine harmony of Body and Soul.

—"I believe in you, my Soul—the other I am must not abase itself to you,
And you must not be abased to the other. . . . .
Welcome is every organ and attribute of me, and of any man hearty and clean,
Not an inch, nor a particle of an inch, is vile, and none shall be less familiar than the rest. . . . .
I believe in the flesh and the appetites,
Seeing, hearing, and feeling are miracles, and each tag and part of me is a miracle.—

It finds all things embraced and comprehended in the individual, to whom indeed the universe belongs and who belongs to the universe. It recognizes the common brotherhood of mankind, and the same human nature repeated in every person. Its aspiration is for a noble race of human creatures, healthy and beautiful, living delightfully, in sympathy with Nature, their perfect lives in a perfect world.

Perhaps the scope and significance of Walt Whitman's poetry may be more clearly indicated by contrasting its character with that of the poetry ordinarily accepted and popular at the present time. The latter is rhymed and measured. It is sometimes powerful with passion and sometimes stately with thought. It is generally sweet and graceful—expressing mild and monotonous sentiments in a thousand respectable ways. It is gay for a feast and sorry for a funeral. It is sweet as to Spring-time, and thoughtful as to sober Autumn days. It rhymes 'kisses' with 'blisses,' and expresses its writer's willingness to partake of the same. It mourns persistently for dead infants, for those who are snatched away in beauty's bloom, and for blighted blossoms generally. It has an amatory tendency, of a sentimental description, and wastes a good deal of miscellaneous sweetness. It presents its author as one who desires burial under a sweet-apple tree, and will not have a decent graveyard on any terms; it affects to ignore and despise the human body; it dwells fondly upon the sublime nature and destiny of the soul; and passing smoothly over all that is significant in this actual present life, it hints lugubriously at another and a better world. On the other hand these poems of Walt Whitman concern themselves alike with the largest and with the pettiest topics. They are free as the wandering wind that sweeps over great oceans and inland seas, over the continents of the world, over mountains, forests, rivers, plains, and cities; free as the sunshine are they, and like the sunshine ardent and fierce. Nothing in the creation is too sacred or too distant for the lightning glance of their aspiration; nothing that in any way concerns the souls and the bodies of the human race is too trivial for their comprehension. Everywhere they evince the philosophic mind, deeply seeking, reasoning, feeling its way toward a clear knowledge of the system of the universe.

It seems to us there is much in the following passages to substantiate this view of Walt:

On my way a moment I pause,
Here for you! And here for America!
Still the Present I raise aloft—Still the Future of The States I harbinge, glad and sublime,
And for the Past *I pronounce what the air holds of the red aborigines*. . . .
Stop this day and night with me, and you shall possess the origin of all poems;
You shall possess the good of the earth and sun—there are millions of suns left;
You shall no longer take things at second or third hand, nor look through the eyes of the dead, nor feed on the spectres in books, ...
And I know that the hand of God is the promise of my own,
And I know that the spirit of God is the brother of my own,
And that all the men ever born are also my brothers, and the women my sisters and lovers,
And that a kelson of the creation is love. . . . .
I believe a leaf of grass is no less than the journey-work of the stars,
And the pismire is equally perfect, and a grain of sand, and the egg of the wren,
And the tree-toad is a chef-d'œuvre for the highest,
And the running blackberry would adorn the parlors of heaven,
And the narrowest hinge in my hand puts to scorn all machinery,
And the cow crunching with depressed head surpasses any statue,
And a mouse is miracle enough to stagger sextillions of infidels,
And I could come every afternoon of my life to look at the farmer's girl boiling her iron tea-kettle and baking short-cake."

In this liberal scope of vision and purpose are indicated the insight and the earnestness characteristic of a poetic nature. Other elements of that poetic nature are evident in the vigor of imagination and splendor of imagery which make certain of these poems so truly remarkable. In the 'Salut au Monde'; in the poem called 'A Word Out of the Sea'—which, under the title of 'A Child's Reminiscence,' was printed in this paper last December; in the poem of 'Brooklyn Ferry'; in that of 'Sleep Chasings,' and that of 'Burial'; —in these, and in others, such qualities largely and beautifully appear.

Some reflections may properly be submitted here, relative to the form in which Walt Whitman's poems are embodied and expressed. It is a form so rough and rugged—so careless, variable, and peculiar—that perhaps it is very natural the poetry should sometimes degenerate into prose. Something is to be said, however, in defence of this system of versification. It is at least original. The theory would seem to be, as Walt has variously indicated, that always the thought or the passion of the poet should determine itself in natural, congenial expression. It is assumed in this theory, and indeed it is very true, that much of the verse ordinarily written, is written without a sincere motive, and has therefore neither power nor value. It is further assumed that the styles of versification generally accredited and employed are inadequate to the utterance of earnest thought and feeling. Consequently, Walt Whitman, who presents himself as the Poet of the American Republic in the Present Age, who is actuated by a sincere motive, and has earnest thought and feeling to express, refuses to confine and cripple himself within the laws of what to him is inefficient art. Reverencing the spirit of poetry above the form, he submits that the one shall determine the other. That his volume is poetic in spirit cannot rationally be denied; and, whatever the eccentricities of its form, no critical reader can fail to perceive that the expression seems always the suitable and natural result of the thought. It is indeed tame and prosy in the conveyance of any commonplace idea or feeling, but it rises and melts into sweet and thrilling music whenever impelled by the beautiful impulse of a grand thought or emotion.

A fine example of this felicity of style occurs in the following beautiful passage, which also delightfully illustrates the poet's ardent and profound love of Nature:

"I am He that walks with the tender and growing Night,
I call to the earth and sea, half-held by the Night.
Press close, bare-bosomed Night! Press close, magnetic, nourishing Night!
Night of south winds! Night of the large few stars!
Still, nodding night! Mad, naked, summer night.
Smile, O voluptuous, cool breathed Earth!
Earth of *the slumbering and liquid trees!*
Earth of departed sunset! Earth of the mountains, misty-topt!
Earth of the vitreous pour of the full moon, just tinged with blue!
Earth of shine and dark, mottling the tide of the river!
Earth of the limpid gray of clouds, brighter and clearer for my sake!
Far-swooping elbowed Earth! Rich, apple-blossomed Earth!
Smile, for YOUR LOVER comes! . . . .

I hear you whispering there, O stars of heaven,
O suns! O grass of graves! O perpetual transfers and promotions!
If you do not say anything, how can I say anything?
Of the turbid pool that lies in the autumn forest,
Of the moon that descends the steeps of the soughing twilight,
Toss, sparkles of day and dusk! toss on the black stems that decay in the muck!
Toss to the *moaning gibberish of the dry limbs."*

Another fine example is found in the following bit of description, which has all that simplicity can give of power, pathos, and music:

"Cold dash of waves at the ferry-wharf—posh and ice in the river, half-frozen mud in the streets, a gray discouraged sky overhead, the short last daylight of Twelfth Month,
A hearse and stages—other vehicles give place—the funeral of an old Broadway stage-driver, the cortege mostly drivers.
Steady the trot to the cemetery, duly rattles the death-bell, the gate is passed, the new-dug grave is halted at, the living alight, the hearse uncloses,
The coffin is passed out, lowered and settled, the whip is laid on the coffin, the earth is swiftly shovelled in,
The mound above is flatted with the spades—silence,
A minute, no one moves or speaks—it is done,
He is decently put away—is there anything more?
He was a good fellow, free-mouthed, quick-tempered, not bad-looking, able to take his own part, witty, sensitive to a slight, ready with life or death for a friend, fond of women, gambled, ate hearty, drank hearty, had known what it was to be flush, grew low-spirited toward the last, sickened, was helped by a contribution, died, aged forty-one years—and that was his funeral."

Of the defects in this book something also may properly be said. They are not trivial and they are not few. It is the law of a great nature to err greatly as well as to be greatly wise. Walt Whitman has exemplified that law. There are, as it seems to us, defects alike in his philosophy, art, taste, and style. It is fair to say there is much in his book that, like the peace of God, passeth all understanding, and that it does not lack passages which should never have been published at all. We may have occasion to refer to this book again, and to explain ourselves more fully in these regards. Meantime we submit, as appropriate in this connection, the following critical remarks from the *North American Review*:

"For the purpose of showing that he is above every conventionalism, Mr. Whitman puts into the book one or two lines which he would not address to a woman nor to a company of men. There is not anything, perhaps, which modern usage would stamp as more indelicate than are some passages in Homer. There is not a word in it meant to attract readers by its grossness, as there is in half the literature of the last century, which holds its place unchallenged on the tables of our drawing-rooms. For all that, it is a pity that a book where everything else is natural, should go out of the way to avoid the suspicion of being prudish."

We should not conclude our notice of the 'Leaves of Grass' without expressing our very great delight at the sumptuous elegance of the style in which Messrs. Thayer & Eldridge have published Walt Whitman's poetry. The volume presents one of the richest specimens of taste and skill in book-making, that has ever been afforded to the public by either an English or an American publisher.

ART.

Our cousin of the Boston *Transcript,* always liable to 'put his foot in' a question of Art, is agitated by the heretical discoveries of Mr. Stillman, who proclaims, through the *Cosmopolitan Art Journal*, that Crawford was 'deficient in conception and science,' that the Greek Slave is weak in anatomy, that Palmer's work is 'entirely external.' These are by no means 'original estimates of American sculptors,' as our Bostonian friend mildly sneers. It is more to the purpose that they are substantially just, though we cannot agree with Mr. Stillman that Greenough had great executive power.

But the dictum which seems specially to irritate the *Transcript*, is, as stated by that orthodox æsthetic organ, "that the wretched statue of De Witt Clinton, by Brown, so out of proportion as to offend the least informed in anatomy, 'has many and great merits.'"

And why not, O venerated Athenian?

The *Transcript* is mistaken both in its data and its conclusion. The statue of Clinton is not 'out of proportion.' That criticism was made long ago, by the *Tribune*; but ignorantly made, and applied only to the feet and hands, which are accurately conformed to the best standards,—of which fact the *Transcript* may satisfy itself, as we have done, by accurate measurement. The fault of the 'Clinton,' sore enough, indeed, is not anatomical, but vital. The figure is, in plain terms, awkward, stiff; not strictly inanimate, but the action of different members is not harmonious. The position of the right hand is constrained and uncertain. You cannot quite determine whether it will rise or has just fallen. The truth is, that the artist was persuaded to relinquish his first conception and his own genuine feeling to please a committee, he put away on the shelf a dignified and graceful model, and striving to introduce more action, and replace character by incident, he missed alike the freedom of a speaker and the repose of an impressive personal presence, which is the triumph of portrait-Art.

But the merit of the work is unmistakable. Mr. Stillman asserts that Crawford's 'Washington' is 'lacking in dignity and high manhood,' and we quite agree with him. It is free and effective in action—dashing, we should say, like a pictorial 'Washington' by Leutze—but lacks concentration, will, and command. The mind of the artist has not risen to meet the moral grandeur of his subject. He cares more for the attitude than for the quality of a man.

Brown, on the contrary, has made an earnest effort to render the moral energy of Clinton. In American sculpture there is no head comparable to this for fiery ardor and determination, with abundant reserved force or resource of manhood behind.

The entire treatment of the statue corresponds with this conception. It inclines to strength rather than grace—a merit very rare, and contrasted strongly with the effeminate habit of the time. There is throughout the work a deliberate rejection of all ornament and prettiness—a scorn for picturesque effect. The hand and foot are those of a man, not of a dancing-master; and the drapery is treated with stern severity. There is perhaps even an exaggeration of this feeling for plainness and simplicity; but the feeling itself is altogether noble, and a protest against the meretricious practice which so generally prevails.

Contrast this head as a specimen of treatment with the elegant 'Moses' of Palmer, which suggests the drawing-room rather than the wilderness or the storm assembly; which is upholstered into sublimity, is altogether ornate in feeling, without a spark of the wild, indomitable energy of the outlaw, who 'slew the Egyptian yesterday,' the fugitive slave with his six hundred thousand head ('that were men besides women and children') of stolen property, the autocrat of the desert, the stern reformer with his 'Thus saith the Lord,' and ' he shall surely die.'

Our Art degenerates into prettiness and pettiness. It runs to grass, to sentiment, and ornamentation. In its utmost animation it rises as high as the picturesque.

The gods we know do not give all gifts to one man. Freedom and facility of expression are only once or twice in the ages united with depth of feeling and openness to the sublimest Truth.

The grand thinker is seldom the ready writer. The contempt of such men as Carlyle for our popular fluency in scribbling and spouting, is justified in their experience, by the pain and labor which attends on every effort to deliver a genuine involuntary and deep impression of life. External traits are quickly and cheaply rendered. Crawford is the stump-orator of his Art, his work a flow of graceful and vigorous commonplace. The grace and vigor he constantly cultivates; the internal truth, the essential veracity of the work, its strict correspondence to the last significance and value of the subject, he has not so sternly considered.

In the struggle to bring to light heroic and vital qualities, the artist often loses sight of minor excellence, or despises and neglects it of design. Finish he holds a toy, grace and elegance he subordinates. Angelo leaves the marble a mere block, that no detail may come between the mind and his suggestion of massive character. If the artist fail in this kind of effort, he fails grandly, and prepares for himself a final success; while an exquisite, ornate, and elaborate littleness, is hopeless popularity and mediocrity from the start.

The head and bust of the 'Clinton' will surely live. What other portrait-head in American sculpture will endure? Greenough's 'Washington' is little better than that of Rembrandt Peale. Crawford's 'Beethoven' is sentimental, not lonely, defiant, and determined. No student of his music will ever accept it as a presence of the master. The portraits of Powers have a literal fidelity to form, without regard for metaphysical qualities, and when he abandons the line before him he is lost.

A tyro in the study of Art need not be told that completeness or entire success is never the measure of greatness in a work. The grandest Art, like the grandest character, carries, and can afford to carry, the grandest imperfections.

The great concentrate energy, and dare to be weak that they may be doubly strong. Take an example from landscape: The young painter has learned to represent a rock, a cloud, still water, and a hill. He can make nothing of trees, of mist, of sunshine, but by confining himself to the little circle of his knowledge and skill, he contrives a very pretty picture. It is admired, it sells. He can go on picture-making with those materials, and satisfy the trading -public for a dozen years, go on doing business as Mr. Diamond used to do, on the capital of a beach, a bush, a brook, and a maple-tree. If he steps beyond this circle in honest desire to enlarge his truth, he falls below himself in completeness. He appears a finished artist. He must become a bungler. He has done all he can in one direction, he must expand or degenerate. Many men lack courage and honesty to abandon their early cheap success. They go on repeating, of course with less and less feeling of their work, for only what we are now learning glows in the mind. They sink into hopeless mannerism, become ghosts of themselves, and all their work is partiality and sham. They have a mere trick of combining certain elements and effects, but no broad, average, or genuine impression of Nature.

The grand men are always ready to blunder and grope in extending knowledge. They love truth better than factitious reputation. They despise their own petty attainments, however applauded, as no better than a sleight of hand and eye, so much remains for them to be learned and gained.

A man risks much when he abandons his own past, and the ruts in which he ran so smoothly; he ventures for equal gain when he abandons the practice of mankind.

The Art of any period is nine parts imitation—or convention, as we name it—a manner caught by one from another. About all imitative-work, there is a deceptive and easy completeness. It is decorous, harmonious; it offends no sense; it is comme il faut.

The Pre-Raphaelites exaggerate, in their practice, a well-known fact, that in all originality there is at first a certain hardness and awkwardness. A boy can copy a picture when he cannot draw the form. He catches the perfected method (as mere method) of the master, the grand style. It requires courage to leave Milton, Claude, Raphael, behind, and go lonely to render one's own sincere impression. The result is always doubtful. The artist is putting his power to honest and final proof. Now the least excellence is more hopeful and valuable than any grace of imitation.

In a thousand manly efforts which are not quite victories, as in this statue of Clinton, we recognize 'many and rare merits.' We regard the intention, and look to the artist as one who, in following the same path, will achieve at last our first genuine success. In this pusillanimous and mendicant era, when Art seems like to become altogether rhetorical, and like the sophistry of Plato's time, a cookery and flattery; when the gallery and the public square offer alike only this diet of sugarplums, then is merit both rare and grand in the robust determination to render broadly only the noblest truths. If these are so much as suggested to the beholder, a great spirit is manifest, and the artist cannot be said to have failed.

To the question of nude Art, which is also in controversy between Mr. Stillman and the *Transcript*, we shall speak at another time.

Thoughts and Things.

BY ADA CLARE

I went on Tuesday night to the Winter Garden, in the hope of making my first reverence to the green-eyed 'Nabucco,' better known by the name of Nebuchadnezzar. To my unspeakable disappointment, the royal grass-widower refused obstinately to leave his clover-field, inviting the public to emulate his own example in promptly going to grass. So I sat in the corner, where the sounding brass and thundering cymbals were doing their best to make the prima donna unnecessary, and after the first pang had passed, I forgot my disappointment in the admirable efforts of those precious artists, Stigelli and Inez Fabbri.

⁂

Last week I enjoyed, for the first time, a meeting of of the 'Woman's Rights Convention.' In the first instance, I felt much dashed in spirits. The speaker was declaiming, in a monotonous voice, a most logical but dreary speech, on the weary old line of navigation, which consists in enumeratiug the scriptural and moral reasons why woman is entitled to the same natural rights as man; and how in every department of literature, science, etc,—the same things in substance, that have been said, and resaid, and said again, year after year, in these conventions. I could not help grieving in my mind that these able women should go on threshing in the same old dry wheat-fields, when so many glorious new harvests are waiting only to be reaped.

I was infinitely relieved when Mrs. Ernestine L. Rose took the floor. A good delivery, a forcible voice, the most uncommon good sense, a delightful terseness of style, and a rare talent for humor, are the qualifications which so well fit this lady for a public speaker. In about two minutes she managed to infect her two-thousand-fold audience with a spirit of interest—an audience which mere dry morals and reason had succeeded in reducing to the comatose state.

If indeed there is anything capable of being treated in a broad comic vein, it is the position in which woman stands towards man, his assumption of her inferiority, etc. The subject is as closely connected with humor as it is with pathos.

But there is one view of the case which none of these women seem to notice, the exceeding great importance that the health and physical condition of women should be more attended to. Half of the cases that occur of ill-treated women, are cases in which the woman is in ill health, for the male above all things most dislikes the sick woman.

Much, nay half of the ill health of women, is the result of their own imprudences. There is a horribly pernicious sentiment prevailing among novel-writers, which always represents the interesting heroine as being fragile, delicate, and unhealthy. This sentiment has found its way into boarding-schools, so that the fat and healthy girls are regarded with an insulting pity, by their dyspeptic companions. My own experience will serve as an instance of what is occurring every day and every minute. When about fourteen years of age, I was what is called in extreme scorn by school misses a hearty girl; a great deal of exercise in the open air, a devotion to running, swimming, climbing, wrestling, etc., rather than to sewing, reading, and worsted-work, had produced in me a physical development, a vigorous health, an exuberant flow of spirits, which is, alas! most rarely found in girls. I ignored sentiment, nerves, and sickness, and the time when most girls are just budding into coquetry, I spent in climbing fig-trees, turning somersaults in the grass, riding unsaddled horses, swimming in the open stream, rowing hideous little boats, and making myself the happy companion of boys. But alas! I had female relatives brought up in the old girl-slaughtering style. They remonstrated with me, threatened me, wept over me, warned me, prayed for me. I was told that it was a sin for a girl of my age, grown as I was, and physically developed, to persist in being a hoiden, and was unceasingly entreated to become that melancholy thing, a perfect lady. I was told that it was my pious duty never to do anything for myself that I could tease a man into doing. I must become a serious annoyance and a care to the male, before becoming a well-bred female.

I tried my best to become a lady; I drank a glass of vinegar before breakfast to diminish my healthy appetite; I devoured sugarplums with the laudable ambition of acquiring a respectable headache, and lemons in the hope of becoming thin. Everything injurious, in fact, that could be taken into the human stomach, I boldly consumed, with the hope of sickening myself, and I succeeded in diminishing my appetite, but sickness would not come. Then I gave it up in despair, and simply contented myself with bidding good-bye to climbing, wrestling, and shinny-sticks forever. But alas! how deeply I regret it now; I would I had played the hoiden to the last moment that mental carelessness would allow; nothing in the world I feel would be so good a basis for the toils and pains of female existence.

Women have come to think that ill-health is their birth-right, and so long as they hold that faith they will neither seriously wish for, nor obtain their true rights from those who hold them in bondage. The invalid, perennially child-bearing woman has no strength to struggle against any wrong; it is as much as she can do to keep her sick soul within her worn body. When woman begins to feel that she has a right to physical strength, sound health, good spirits, and to the bearing of no more children than her own constitution and the well-being of her offspring will allow, her other rights will follow fast. For, as a very general thing, the healthful hearty woman is seldom enslaved by man. When you read of those horrible cases of male brutality in our journals, you generally find that the women who are knocked down with flat-irons, whose heads are trodden upon with iron-heeled boots, whose noses are perforated with three-pronged forks, and whose chests are crushed with heavy knees, are generally weak women with a half-dozen depressing diseases, and a swarm of scrofulous, miserable, neglected babies, whom the mother is too ill to care for. I find that men are too often like rats, they have an irresistible desire to pick the bones of the sick ones of their race.

o o o

I have been reading a book called 'Rutledge,' evidently by an American woman. It is about thirty-three degrees higher than the ordinary run of novels, for it never loses its interest; every character is distinct; none of those moist characters that run into each other, and the style is really good. It would be worth reading the book, if only for the sake of that inexpressibly sad and touching story of little Essie. This book presents the singular instance of an autobiographical and very important heroine, whose name is not once mentioned in the narrative.

o o o

In my last week's peregrinations I did not neglect the bears, and very nice they are. All the animals in this menagerie have a genuine look; they are none of those milk-drinking, bald-legged animals that my childhood delighted to honor. As for the bears, they are real, cross, aggressive beasts, and marvellously afraid of pain. They say all cruel and tyrannical natures are. When the grey Adams gave one of these colossal creatures a blow on the paw, its howling, and whining, and rolling, and rubbing of the pained member was almost ludicrous. I thought that the bears would not make good prize-fighters, they would mutually succumb at the first punishment, and howl for mercy on the spot. They wouldn't do, I am sure, to stand up against Heenan; his endurance would make the horrid monsters blush.

NEW YORK MAY 26, 1860

[For The New York Saturday Press.]

EPHEMERA.

I heard these words as I passed him:
'The River of Life,' quoth he.
He was old, and he spake as in terror;
For, if he had sailed down that River,
His shallop was near the sea!

But I, in my heart replying
To the words this old man said,
I cried: He speaketh a folly
'Who likens Life to a River!'
He halted, and turned his head.

I cried: 'Life is *not* a River!
'For the River ebbs and flows;
'And the leaf that it floated seaward
'At morn,—lo! the flood-tide flingeth
'On the flower-bank whence it rose !'

'What waif of Life, that hath floated
'To the Gulf without a name,
'From the margin of Time-old greybeard,
'Met ever a wave returning,
'To render it whence it came?'

But the old man smiled, as he trembled,
And 'The River of Life'—he said,
And lifted his withered finger
And pointed, where, into the ocean
The sunset heaven still bled;

And it seemed as a thirst and a terror
Were at strife in this old man's soul;
And he murmured: 'The waves of that River
'Are the flood, that, forever backward
'The waifs of this Life shall roll!'

CHARLES D. GARDETTE.

Philadelphia.

THE NUDE.

We are somewhat ambiguously informed by the Boston *Transcript* that Mr. Stillman "declaims against Nude statuary in a manner totally at variance with the history and acknowledged exigencies of Art (whatever they may be), and with the sense of beauty and truth and purity to which her noblest inspirations are addressed, and whence they emanate."

In respect to the Nude, we shall not quite agree with Mr. Stillman and the *Crayon*, perhaps not with the oracular *Transcript*, when we know what, if anything is signified by the 'exigencies,' etc. We shall enter our own view, and take the risk of making a three-cornered fight.

In the first place, we feel no special concern for public morality, threatened by the naughtiness of modern undress fashions in Art. The Anglo-Saxon imagination has never been sensual or even sensuous. It is proud, aspiring, scornful of the body. The habit of the sentimental nations seems to us effeminate. Tom Moore is a baby with sugar-tit; his muse an irritation of the mucous membrane. In the North of Europe you will rarely meet, what is so common in the South, a saint, like the late well-known sensation preacher, Maffit, whose very piety is a flush of blood; its paroxysm a half animal indulgence. In his constitution is no firm distinction, much less any antithesis between sentiment and appetite. His emotion, his poetry, is a kind of pruriency; his soul seems to be soaked in juices and fumes, to itch and desire.

In the modern French novel this heat is the universal solvent. Consuelo, miracle of elevation, must once burn with it to her finger tips. To feel every extremity of inclination, to tremble like a jelly without actual going in pieces, under the stress of continual temptation—which is taken for granted, as matter of course—that is the triumph of French virtue.

The French ideal and historical saint is a Magdalen, whose love-sickness finds no longer an object nearer at hand than heaven. The French Magdalen prays regularly and not formally, but with passion. The Bon Dieu is another lover, and on that level, one lover by no means fatally interferes with the right of—the rest.

This unconscious or half conscious mixture of animal, æsthetic, and religious motive, is a matter of temperament, is for the French or Italians only a weakness 'très amiable,' is susceptibility. For the Northman it is prostitution, and the more sincere the more unmitigated nastiness.

And this, not because the Northman is on the whole a better man than the Southern, but his vice is not luxury, is not softness. He may trample on moral distinctions; he does not confuse or lose sight of them. Vice and virtue are not so fused in him, as fire and water in a glowing mist.

He has in short an energy of moral perception, which firmly distinguishes principle from sentiment, he suspects and despises every sublimation of the base instincts, and a work of which the motive is even questionable, will never command the sympathy of that class in England and America, who make for any man a permanent reputation. The Art of drinking-saloons is never a public influence. It is feeble as it is base in intention, and the picture or statue of higher pretensions is weak in proportion to the emphasis with which it regards the body, and rests in enjoyment of physical traits.

Strong men and women seek by sympathy the fiery, magnetic, and heroic in character; they hate the enticing platitude of parlors and bed-chambers, and resent as personal indignity every glance which spends itself upon personal—that is upon accidental—'charms.' For the weak, imagination itself is but a finer contact, sex a physical fact and their perpetual song. They care nothing for masculine beauty, for that culmination of grace and power, the supreme manly form. They paint and model under every disguise of title, only the same everlasting Venus, a soft, enticing, yielding, creature, conscious alike of her power and her 'predicament' ('oh noble' *Atlantic* 'I thank thee for that word'), and enjoying both, however, she may gesticulate or frown.

There needs very little actual nudity to destroy the sensuous motive. There are faces which should be veiled, under penalty of the law prohibiting indecent exposure.

Sensual Art is disguised by romantic association or incident, by slight infusion of character, by brilliancy and purity of color. It rises toward purity of effect whenever there is strong feeling even of physical and material beauty. For the luxurious is never the vigorous or truly noble form. Luxury is physical degradation, is a stagnancy and festering of the blood. Flesh purged by activity is no longer flesh, the lines and planes of power displace the softness of allurement. Purity is a running brook. Sensuality a tropical pool.

Sexual Art is lifted then by any infusion of energy. Gray elevates it by color. The Greeks redeemed it in the 'Venus de Medici,' without aid from character, by the mere perfection of animated and conscious form. The French give it piquancy by their sparkling wit, their coquetry, by some well simulated unconsciousness, some evasion or defiance. The English are clumsy in indecency. Their immorality is downright, literal, and commonplace, a sore trial to the stoutest stomach.

The sexual element requires either great energy and openness of treatment, or a most skilful disguise, a cookery like the French, with irresistible sauce and spice to cover the savor of corruption. It is saved by fire and frankness in Virgil's encounter of 'Venus and Mars,' in Leighton's 'Delilah,' at the Academy. It is most offensive when clumsily covered; when, for example, it affects to convey a moral lesson, as in the wisdom and folly of Huntington or Rossiter's 'Wise and Foolish Virgins,' pictures in which the wisdom is a drug, while the folly is delightfully felt.

The 'Venus' of Page is so hard and cold a figure, so destitute of vitality, physical and moral, that no motive of luxury appears in it. All were disappointed who ran to enjoy its naughtiness. The 'Diana' opposite was much more attractive from its superior anatomical detail and feminine sentiment.

The 'Greek Slave' was aimed at popularity, but fell short of its aim for lack of power. It is a stone, and through very emptiness makes an impression of unintended purity, and merely gratifies in remote America, a cold-blooded curiosity about the form.

Palmer is the poet of adipose, and at him accordingly the excommunication of the *Crayon* is aimed. His figures under all titles are of one rank, and have a motive only doubtful, not so low as to offend the conventional morality of our parlors. They are by no means powerful stimulants. There is no danger to public morals from mere imitation and finish. Without character, action, vivacity, there is no fascination, and these Marbles' represent the tamest and sweetest little school-girls, whose smiling faces were never troubled by a passion, a resolution, or a thought.

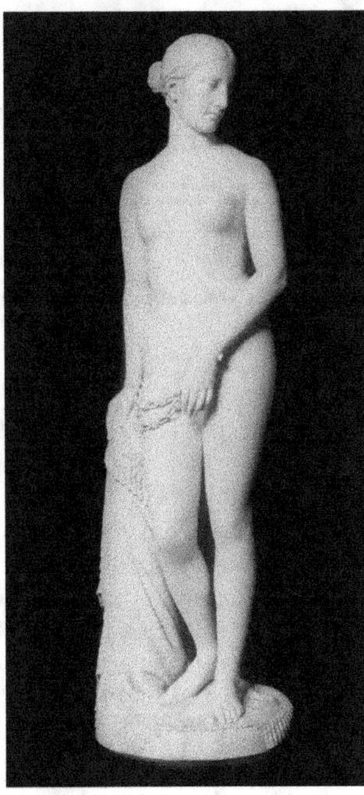
Powers's Greek Slave, 1843.

The strength of the Artist is expended on their curves and contours, often grossly exaggerated as in the bust of 'Resignation,' which is fairly monstrous, and in the 'White Captive,' where animal development was felt to require apology, to be at best a mitigated offence.

A marked defect in Palmer's heads, which betrays the last degree of indifference to character, is uniform littleness and lack of expression in the eyes. These windows of life are the centre of attraction in all beautiful faces, always well formed, and opened with emphasis of their direction and action, when manhood or womanhood is to be celebrated in stone.

Nothing could be more unspiritual than the 'Spirit's Flight'—nothing more commonplace in expression, or more elaborately material in form. In one of the print-shops, we see an amputated foot of the 'White Captive'; and its exhibition is an ingenuous confession of artistic motive. The sculptor and his admirers openly spend their enthusiasm on a hand, a lip, an ear, —on dainties less refined, but all 'delicious.' "I could eat that figure," said my clerical friend.

A grosser appetite is more tolerable than this which toys with innocence, which fondles while it lacks both power and will to animate and so subordinate the form.

The action of the 'White Captive' is not justified by her habit: we see in it not what the woman is doing, but what she is and has been. The American savage never offered indignity to woman. She resents with reason the regards of her civilized admirers. The figure is nude at heart. Purity and impurity never lie on the surface—are not in an accident of drapery, and so to be measured by the square-yard. A form is exposed that it may be enjoyed for itself—may be mumbled over with the fingers of the mind; or it is clothed with energy of purpose, which sinks this sensible sweetness, and converts this neglected flesh to flame. The female form is a mixed delight of circulation and sentiment, or it is a beauty of pride and self-respect—retired, aspiring—which knows no sexual distinction, save that between a commanding and a persuasive soul.

Contrast with the treatment of this figure, that of Thorwaldsen's noble 'Night and Morning,' where you see honest bone and muscle—where the body is made a motion and the vehicle of a thought.

Surely, O Transcript! the 'exigencies of Art' do not demand this recumbency among the paps; and surely, O virtuous *Crayon* and *Cosmopolitan*! there is no inflammatory power in this exceeding prettiness, this dish of dimples. The very schoolboys will not suffer harm from these Musidoras in marble.

Even my philandering clerical friend may indulge, without much danger to his constitution, an appetite for this syllabub of character, this sugar-candy of toothsome form.

'Honest Abe.'

'An Abecedarian' writes us to know whether the real name of the Republican candidate for the Presidency is 'Abe,' 'Abram,' 'Abraham,' Isaac, or Jacob. We have consulted the best authorities within our reach, and are unable to procure any light upon the subject. All that we can find out about Mr. Lincoln, is that he is sixteen feet high, and fifty-one years long; that he is as thin and angular as a split rail; that he was born a Hoosier, but finally became a Sucker; that he has been in turn a farm-laborer, a top-sawyer, a flat-boatman, a counter-jumper, a militia captain, a lawyer, a Presbyterian, and a politician; that he beat Douglas over the left in Illinois, and drove him into the U. S. Senate; that his favorite motto is, 'two shillings are better than one', and that he is spotless in everything but his linen.

NEW YORK JUNE 2, 1860

[The following is a review of "Leaves of Grass" attributed to Juliet Beach. According to Clapp, the book was sent to her for review and her husband intercepted the package and replied with his own review, falsely signed with Juliet's initials.]

[For The New York Saturday Press.]

'LEAVES OF GRASS'

The suspense is ended. The 'Distinctive American Poem '—the only one (God be thanked!) the country has yet produced—has appeared.

Lying before me as I write, is an early copy of 'Leaves of Grass.' I have awaited its advent with some little anxiety, for I had been forced to extend to the later effusions of its author, a degree of admiration. I could not shut my eyes to their wild, rough beauty, nor close my soul to the truths they expressed. Defiant of all precedent, scornful of all the conventionalisms of art, there was in them all a rude, grand sweep, as natural, and as musical too, as the breaking of the waves upon the shore, or the singing of the winds at night through the forest.

So when yesterday the looked-for volume reached me, you may be assured that it was eagerly opened. In the few hours that I have had the work, I have found time to read but little of it. That little, however, has sufficed. I lack inclination now for its further perusal.

After this frank confession, do not think that I purpose a review of the work. I have no such intention. I write simply to express my unqualified disgust with the portions I have read. Whether those portions are the best, or the worst, or an average, I do not know, nor care to know. I opened the book at random, as one does a new book when leisure is wanting, and read what the pages before me held.

I make no quotations from those pages. I would offer neither to The Press, nor its readers, the offence of spreading before them even the daintiest lines those pages of filth contain. Until such time as the novels of de Kock find place upon parlor-tables, and the obscene pictures, which boys in your city slily offer for sale upon the wharves, are admitted to albums, or grace drawing-room walls, quotations from *Enfans d'Adam* would be an offence against decency too gross to be tolerated.

I am not at all squeamish. Not easily shocked either. I adore the beautiful, and grow impassioned as I drink in the voluptuous in art or poesy. Amorous poetry, so far from being to me offensive, is delightful, and the soft, liquid lines of tender love, and the deep strains of a burning passion, seem to me alike fit hymns for man to offer up. But Walt Whitman's poems are not amorous; they are only beastly. They express far more truthfully the feelings of brute nature than the sentiments of human love.

Walt Whitman assumes to regard woman only as an instrument for the gratification of his desires, and the propagation of the species. To him all women are the same, with but this difference; the more sensual have the preference, as they promise greater indulgence. His exposition of his thoughts shows conclusively that with him the congress of the sexes is a purely animal affair, and with his ridiculous egotism he vaunts his prowess as a stock-breeder might that the pick of his herd.

It is bad enough, I submit, for a person to be so utterly brutalized. There needs not the further degradation of publishing his brutality. A true man regards the intimate relations he may sustain toward the woman who holds his affections, as something too holy to be lightly talked of, too sacred to be bruited abroad. To the true man, the congress of the sexes is a sacrament—a holy secret locked in the breasts of two persons, which it were gross profanation to expose to the gaze of any beside. To such an one, all women are not the same; nor is capacity for beastly indulgence the distinguishing trait of the chosen one. But it is unnecessary for me to dilate upon this. All will feel what I might say in this connection.

Walt Whitman has had a narrow escape from being a great poet. He combines in him all the requisites but one; but that one is indispensable. He has strength, he has beauty, but he has no soul. Intellect, I grant, wide in its scope, and powerful in its grasp. Yet with all this, I doubt if, when the Judgment-Day comes, Walt Whitman's name will be called. He certainly has not soul enough to be saved. I hardly think he has enough to be damned.

Walt Whitman has done his work. He has shown to the world that one may have the form and presence of a man, may possess an intellect whose scope and power entitle him to high place among the gifted ones of earth, and yet in those finer qualities which most intimately connect man with higher intelligences, be utterly wanting, and at the poor level of "the beasts that perish."

He has done this, and the world has now no further need of him. It accepts the revolting lesson, as it must, but it does not need the teacher longer. If Walt has left within him any charity, will he not now rid the taught and disgusted world of himself? Not by poison, or the rope, or pistol, or by any of the common modes of suicide, because some full man, to whom life has become a grievous burden, may at a later day be compelled to choose between death by the same means and a hateful life, and with the pride of noble manhood turn shuddering to live on, rather than admit so much of oneness as would be implied by going to death as did Walt Whitman. But let him search the coast of his island home until he finds some cove where the waves are accustomed to cast up the carrion committed to them, and where their bloated bodies ride lazily upon the waters which humanity never disturbs, and casting himself therein find at last the companionship for which, in death as in life, he is best fitted.

Let him do this act of reparation, and the world may kindly extend to him the charity of forgetfulness —the highest boon it now can bestow.

Juliette H. Beach.

Albion, N. Y., May 19, 1860.

[For The New York Saturday Press.]

JUNE AND I.

—

BY EDWARD SPENCER.

—

In the shadow of yon maple, one fair day of my own June,
Laid I, watching through the branches the pearl-grey moon.

I had wandered towards the forest, on this day of glowing June,
Vanquished, weary, sullen-hearted, all out of tune,—

For my pen had failed to serve me, and my ink was naught but gall,
And I fancied we had parted, Love, once for all:

So, into the solemn forest went I, with a brain half mad,
And to these cool thickets wandered,—depressed and sad;

To that moss beneath the maple I had come and flung me down,
On that crispy turf of mosses so soft and brown.

All around me Nature slumbered in the quiet of the wood,
And my soul, in every object, found Art's ripe food;

Lapped my dog from yonder brooklet, chirped a squirrel from yon tree,
And the birds, from brake and bramble, waked melody;

Quivering glowed the air above me;—deep as thought was yon calm sky,
Seen in glimpses through the leaflets up there so high.

Then a wondrous pleasant calmness, and a touch of that mild life,
Blending with my bosom's sadness, dispelled its strife;

And a mystic, dreamy quiet, came upon me gently then,
Lying there, deep in the forest, apart from men,—

Came upon me as I hearkened to this merry little brook
Over roots and pebbles purling, from fountain-nook,—

Now 'twixt mossy barriers winding, laughing gay its wildest tune,
Now reflecting, like a lakelet, the pallid moon,—

With a trout in each dark corner, lurking wary for its prey,
And a sunfish in each shallow, glad for the day ;—

As I heard the hum of insects, saw them dancing in the light;
As I caught the ceaseless pean of bird-delight;

As I saw the lazy adder, royal in his jet and gold,
Stretched at length among the brambles to sun each fold;—

Chastened then, I softly murmured: "Cease, O grasping heart, thy yearn,
Here at least thy thirsty, Hotspur—thought dares not burn;

"Idly as those faint blue vapors float about yon distant hill,
Shall my Summer fancies wander vaguely, at will;

"Catch, O speckled fish, thy victim, I will ne'er do harm to thee,
Chant thine ode, thou sad-hued mocker, it pleases me.

"Thoughts no more of mad ambition ever shall disturb my brain,
Grasping, seething, tigerish anguish, I rend thy chain!"

Darling! 'twas that day I wrote you: "Do you, can you love me still?"
And you answered—you remember?—"And ever will!"

"Martin's Nest," Md., 1860.

MEDICAL ETC.

Notes of the Week

—It will be seen by an article in to-day's issue that our esteemed and accomplished correspondent, Mrs. JULIETTE H. BEACH, having glanced at WALT WHITMAN'S *'Leaves of Grass,'* is disposed, upon the whole, to take a somewhat unfavorable view of them. It always gives us pleasure to print every variety of opinion upon such subjects, especially when, as in this case, the careful reader can have no reasonable doubt as to the writer's meaning.

—Mr. Cogswell, Superintendent of the Astor Library, will embark for Europe the last of June or early in July, principally on account of imperfect health, but also in the interest of the Library. His speciality just now is Ghosts.

—The demise of *Russell's Magazine*, a Southern periodical which has enjoyed but a short lease of life, affords the text of a melancholy article in the Charleston *Mercury*. The sad destiny of Southern magazines, the utter lack of Southern sympathy for home productions of a literary character, the difficulties that environ the most enterprising publishers, wring from the *Mercury* this candid confesion: "We are briefly reduced to the alternative of acknowledging that we have no adequate number of writers, or no adequate number of readers, for the maintenance of such a work, or the subscribers do not pay, even if they read."

Thoughts and Things.

BY ADA CLARE

'See Cortesi and die,' is now the manner in which I render the old adage of 'See Naples and die.' Not but what it would be better to see Cortesi and live, since she vastly enhances the pleasure of living; but one should not die without having seen her, for I doubt, indeed, whether the upper spheres would be capable of making up her loss. These remarks read like extravagance, but it is hard to temper one's admiration, and the Cortesi is not a person to be coolly reasoned about. For me, she is the most superb exponent of the lyric art, whom I have ever met. She is one of those deep and grand natures which expand the capacities of the lyric stage to the expression of all that is large and lofty in human intellect. For a woman not to admire Adelaide Cortesi would be gross ingratitude; for she is one of those talents that vindicate the ability of our sex; she redeems in her own proud self the miserable weary little nonsenses which form the whole lives of most of us.

It is only on the stage that woman has outstripped the utmost efforts of man, and grandly triumphed over him in the uttermost sense of the word. In that kingdom of this globe, the highest honors, the proudest triumphs, the chief part of the world's worship, and the largest pecuniary profits, belong to women.

I think I know how to explain this fact. It is only on the stage that the woman is taken out of the world's straight-jacket, and left with free limbs and free soul. The actress, the singer, may put away convention, cant, and hypocritical moralities as very small worms whose crawl is too insignificant to be noticed. Her beauty, her talent, her instinct, her oratorical or vocal powers, her grace, her passions, are all to be used to their utmost and most godlike extent. She is to go forth and be great without illustrating any moral tract.

In literature, in science, in the other arts, the opposite principle prevails; the woman who attempts to work, must wrench out all that is truly passionate from her nature, before she can be considered the respectable and useful worker.

O! fools, fools, fools, that we are! We sacrifice the one sublime gift that nature gives us to cope with men —Instinct; beautiful, sacred, heaven-given instinct. This quality, this instinct is the one balance we have in the scales against the calmer judgment, the more collected intellect, the superior education, the better knowledge of the world, the stronger physical health of the man. The free, fearless, untampered-with convictions of the soul are in themselves the purest and largest logic. They cross the oceans of doubt to tread the shores of truth, with the graceful swiftness of the sea-gull, while Reason, the laboring heavy ship, slowly toils through the waters. Does not the ship with all its ponderousness, its science, its cost, too often flounder and go down in storm, while the white breast of the bird is scarce ruffled in the phrensied wind, and its calm sad eye looks into the face of the lightning and quails not?

But if women write books do they draw from the deep current of love, of passion, of grief, that boils down under their own silent hearts? Alas no! It is to the moral dogma, the conventional dogma, the social dogma, that they go for enlightenment, while they close their ears to the spirit that cries out within their own souls! 'Give utterance, O give utterance to me: I am love, I am pain, I am pathos, I am passion, I am come from God to teach you, I am in anguish lest I die unheard!' Most women disregard this cry, this heart of life, crushing it within them, and so committing awful abortions upon their souls.

If they write books, it is the monotonous old society story, in which Julia who calculates closely and has an eye to the main chance, is supremely happy, while Violet, who cannot be a hypocrite, invariably comes to calico-gowns and bread without cheese, and finally points off the moral of a tombstone.

In their novels the eternal Mrs. Smith the hardhearted forever persecutes the no less perennial Miss Jones of the lamb-type, and the pair of canton-flannel lovers sigh and whine for the consent of the pulpy and terrible papa, who finally gives them his blessing, and, by way of a suitable present, a complete set of spoons. With some most glorious exceptions, this has been the one dreary rule followed out by the female writer. But O! my brothers, if you were not here to persuade her to betray herself, to sell herself for your patronage, if she were let loose from lies, and could speak that she knows and feels and suffers,—sneers, contempt, misconception, would die on your lips, and we two sexes would be better friends; we could love each other better.

Few women are strong enough to choose between truth and the world's good opinion. For in the latter path though it lead them away from immortal truth, it leads them to some monotonous, leaden respectability and much lazy peace, and in the former they must keep themselves ever girded up for fight, and neither must they stoop from their conscience and heart.

I do not blame most women for sinking down into deceit and hardness of heart, they have so much against them; but the struggles and the pains that those women like me who have said 'I belong to myself and God' must pass through, are richly rewarded; there are ministering angels who come to teach us lessons of patience, of gentleness, of loving kindness, of faith, of deep hope, and to bring us a sweet peace which the world knows not, and which it neither can give, nor take away.

I have spoken of the superiority of the woman to the man on the stage: I think as proof that I need but mention the names of Cortesi, of Ristori, of Rachel, of Grisi, of Fabbri. These names are more eloquent than any words I could write.

NEW YORK JUNE 9, 1860

[For The New York Saturday Press.]

THE SUMMER SHOWER.

BY ZELOTES R. BENNETT.

Sit I at the open window
 On this dewy Summer morn,
Where the honeysuckle blossoms
 'Mid a wealth of green are born.
Sit I, gazing outward, outward
 Through the lazy, hazy air,
Breathing in the fragrant incense
 To my senses wafted there.

There is dew upon the meadows,
 Which the sunlight softly sips—
Kissing off the teeming nectar
 From the daisy's pouting lips;
And resplendent jewels dangle
 From the trees that skirt the way,
Like the eyes of angels glist'ning
 In the coming light of day.

There are carols gaily floating
 On the breeze that rustles by,
And the world's awak'ning murmurs
 Through the latticed window sigh;
And I hear the quiet ripple
 Of a stream that winds along,
O'er the yellow sand and pebbles,
 With a never-ceasing song.

But the sun that opes the blossoms,
 Scarce has touched the grassy lawn,
And that darkest hour vanished
 Which precedes the coming dawn,
Ere the drift-clouds gather slowly
 In the azure realm of light,
And with sad and tearful whispers
 Throw aside their robes of white!

Then I hear the rain-drops patter,
 As the cloudy pinions part,
As of spirit-fingers tapping
 At the window of one's heart!
And the birds upon the branches
 Hide beneath the shelt'ring leaves,
Putting on the only garment
 Which a kindly Nature weaves.

Sit I musing at the window,
 While the rain-drops still are beating,
Dreaming of a form that haunts me,
 And a treasured word repeating;
When a sunbeam, like that stealing
 Through the golden gates of even,
Wipes away the tears that glistened
 In the weeping eyes of heaven!

Thus I muse, my wild heart throbbing,
 Pass the tears which mortal shed,
And the sunshine of the morrow
 Brings oblivion of the dead!
All our sorrows are as fleeting
 As this sunny Summer shower,
And in new joys that are dawning
 We forget each tearful hour.

CORRECTION.

A note from Mrs. Juliette H. Beach *informs us that the article in our last issue, on Walt Whitman's* 'Leaves Of Grass,' *was written, not by her, but by Mr. Beach, whose initials were, indeed, appended to it. The error arose from the fact that we were expecting an article from Mrs. Beach on the book (it having been forwarded to her by the publishers at our particular request), and that when the looked-for MS arrived we sent it directly to the printer, with the usual instructions to sign the name of the author—concerning which we had not the slightest doubt—in full.*

[From Walt Whitman's Leaves of Grass."]

MANAHATTA.

I was asking for something specific and perfect for my city, and behold! here is the aboriginal name!
Now I see what there is in a name, a word, liquid, sane, unruly, musical, self-sufficient,
I see that the word of my city, is that word up there,
Because I see that word nested in nests of water-bays, superb, with tall and wonderful spires,
Rich, hemmed thick all around with sailships and steamships—an island sixteen miles long, solid-founded,
Numberless crowded streets—high growths of iron, slender, strong, light, splendidly uprising toward clear skies;
Tides swift and ample, well-loved by me, toward sundown,
The flowing sea-currents, the little islands, the larger adjoining islands, the heights, the villas,
The countless masts, the white shore-steamers, the lighters, the ferry-boats, the black sea-steamers, well-modelled;
The down-town streets, the jobbers' houses of business —the houses of business of the ship-merchants and money-brokers—the river-streets,
Immigrants arriving, fifteen or twenty thousand in a week,
The carts hauling goods—the manly race of drivers of horses—the brown-faced sailors,
The Summer air, the bright sunshining, and the sailing clouds aloft,
The Winter snows, the sleigh-bells—the broken ice in the river, passing along, up or down, with the flood-tide or ebb-tide;
The mechanics of the city, the masters, well-formed, beautiful-faced, looking you straight in the eyes;
Trottoirs thronged—vehicles—Broadway—the women—the shops and shows,
The parades, processions, bugles playing, flags flying, drums beating;
A million people—manners free and superb—open voices—hospitality—the most courageous and friendly young men;
The free city! no slaves! no owners of slaves!
The beautiful city! the city of hurried and sparkling waters! the city of spires and masts!
The city nested in bays! my city!
The city of such women, I am mad to be with them! I will return after death to be with them!
The city of such young men, I swear I cannot live happy, without I often go talk, walk, eat, drink, sleep with them!

Thoughts and Things.

BY ADA CLARE

The illustrious prima-donna Adelaide Cortesi introduced a new tenor to the public on Monday evening last, and to the surprise of most people he proved to be an artist of the most extraordinary powers. Madame Cortesi, who was so generally a favorite last Autumn during the short but most brilliant engagement she played here, is in danger of breaking more hearts than ever. Her voice is richer and more heart-melting than ever, and her personal beauty has increased from the majestic to the truly superb.

Taking everything into consideration, I can state that I never in my life have heard an operatic representation to compare with the one of last Monday evening. There was a certain life-force thrilling through the whole, which refreshed one like drinking in airs from heaven.

Cortesi is to my mind the perfection of prima-donnas. All of the most effulgent gifts of Heaven have been heaped upon her in passionate profusion. A large, warm, speechlessly thrilling voice; a fiery force and inspiration; an intense dramatic vigor; a marvellous personal magnetism; a vast intelligence and sensibility, together with the most superb beauty, go to make up this adorable artist, and to lift her to a height which reduces mediocrity to despair.

Wherever this divine creature appears, she will be sure to draw after her a certain amount of actual worship, which no force of reason, nor refinement of criticism, nor dictates of common sense, will ever avail against. Because there are certain splendid types of genius which sweep stormily through you, revealing to you the depths of your own nature, even as the whirlwinds drive asunder the waters of the sea, till you can almost see the dim sands beneath them. The highest type of genius always produces enthusiasm in the minds of those who sensate it. So one cannot thoroughly appreciate Cortesi without feeling a certain sentiment of intoxication.

Musiani has the best tenor voice I have heard in this country. I see the critics have sheltered themselves in pronouncing upon him behind that mysterious term of 'unequal.' I think he is as unequal as dramatic situation and music are unequal, but he is always largely equal to the occasion. He is the first tenor I ever heard who had what I call magnetic influence over an audience; they generally content themselves with having sweet voices and sweet faces. This one is equally admirable as artist, actor, and singer. It may be long before New York will ever see his like again. The joint efforts of these two grand artists moved the audience to an enthusiasm which shook the house as with an earthquake of applause.

°°°

Something of a very amusing and agreeable nature transpired at the Winter Garden on Saturday last, it was the joint appearance of three unknown artists. It was as good as being a very little child again to see Madame Oliviera. She is an artist of the old fashion, perfect even to the corkscrew curls and the inevitable pocket-handkerchief. She has just the old-fashioned way of rounding her arms and finishing off all her effects with a flirt of the carefully-carried handkerchief. Not that she had no merits: some of her high notes are very good, and she is not devoid of intensity, but she has a way of flickering off her notes, which makes the technical term of execution unpleasantly analogical.

The baritone was of a reserved temper, determined to keep his songs strictly confidential, while the tenor was of the opposite school, and the order of his day was sonority.

Altogether these three performers suggested the idea of having been sealed up in an air-tight bottle for ten years, and have been just drawn out from their confinement, in a state of the most perfect preservation.

[For The New York Saturday Press.]

'LEAVES OF GRASS.'

I have read carefully, thoughtfully, admiringly, many of the poems of Walt Whitman, at first with astonishment mingled with distrust; but as I re-read and read again and fully grasped his thought, the simple grandeur of his expressed soul, filled mine with awe and reverence for the pages he had the genius to inspire; and I see him now the apostle of purity, the teacher of the most vital, and hence the most Divine truth. In his refusal to recognize such distinctions as 'decent and indecent' in the human structure—though, in the opinion of another critic, this is 'monstrous beyond precedent'—I see the sweetest simplicity and child-like innocence. More than that, I see the purity of the heart maintained spite of all the strong impulses of youth, spite of the hush and whisper and taboo of an age of virtuous prostitution, until the equipoise of mature life, the wisdom gained by experience, informs his mind and dictates his words. In childhood there is no blush of shame at sight of a nude form, and the serene wisdom of maturity covers this innocence with a halo of glory, by recognizing divinity of humanity, and perceiving the unity of all the functions of the human body, and the inevitable tendency to harmonic adjustment and adaptation. As all of nature's forms are evolved from the same God-origin or substance, though there may be difference of rank, there can be no difference in essence; and those functions which have been deemed the most brutal and degrading, will be found to be first in rank when nature's hierarchy shall be established and observed. A true delicacy will neither emblazon the individual act of communion abroad (as, sanctioned by custom, those who lay claim to the highest refinement do daily), nor blush to a crimson when the poet of sexual purity vindicates manhood and womanhood from the charge of infamy, degradation, and vice, on account of growth and development after the order of nature. Of course those who assert the doctrine of total depravity must find some part of the person too vile to think of, and will be shocked to hear another express unqualified admiration for the human body and the human soul.

MARY A. CHILTON,

Islip, Long Island, June 5th, 1860.

LONGINGS FOR HOME

—

BY WALT WHITMAN.

—

O magnet—south! O glistening, perfumed South! My South!
O quick mettle, rich blood, impulse, and love! Good and evil! O all dear to me!
O dear to me my birth-things—All moving things, and the trees where I was born—the grains, plants, rivers;
Dear to me my own slow sluggish rivers where they flow, distant, over flats of silvery sands, or through swamps,
Dear to me the Roanoke, the Savannah, the Altamahaw, the Pedee, the Tombigbee, the Santee, the Coosa, and the Sabine;
O pensive, far away wandering, I return with my Soul to haunt their banks again,
Again in Florida I float on transparent lakes—I float on the Okeechobee—I cross the hummock land, or through pleasant openings, or dense forests,
I see the parrots in the woods—I see the papaw tree and the blossoming titi;
Again, sailing in my coaster, on deck, I coast off Georgia—I coast up the Carolinas,
I see where the live-oak is growing—I see where the yellow-pine, the scented bay-tree, the lemon and orange, the cypress, the graceful palmetto;
I pass rude sea-headlands and enter Pamlico Sound through an inlet, and dart my vision inland,
O the cotton plant! the growing fields of rice, sugar, hemp!
The cactus, guarded with thorns—the laurel-tree, with large white flowers,
The range afar—the richness and barrenness—the old woods charged with mistletoe and trailing moss,
The piney odor and the gloom—the awful natural stillness (Here in these dense swamps the freebooter carries his gun, and the fugitive slave has his concealed hut);
O the strange fascination of these half-known, half-impassible swamps, infested by reptiles, resounding with the bellow of the alligator, the sad noises of the night-owl and the wild-cat, and the whirr of the rattlesnake;
The mockingbird, the American mimic, singing all the forenoon-singing through the moon-lit night,
The hummingbird, the wild-turkey, the raccoon, the opossum ;
A Tennessee corn-field—the tall, graceful, long-leaved corn—slender, flapping, bright green, with tassels—with beautiful ears, each well-sheathed in its husk,
An Arkansas prairie—a sleeping lake, or still bayou;
O my heart! O tender and fierce pangs—I can stand them not—I will depart;
O to be a Virginian, where I grew up! O to be a Carolinian!
O longings irrepressible! O I will go back to old Tennessee, and never wander more!

—Leaves of Grass.

NEW YORK JUNE 16, 1860

[From the New York Tribune.]

THE JAPANESE EMBASSY.

The Sorrows of Tommy.

Tommy, heretofore the most light-hearted and the merriest of all the gay-tempered Japanese, has come to grief. Once he sought always the excitements of the liveliest society; now he goes much alone, and pines steadily. The same sorrow which distracted Werter, and consumed Romeo, and prostrated Pyramus, has touched the susceptible heart of the youthful Japanese. He is at present the victim of a hopeless passion. In Washington he suffered love. The dazzling Venuses of Willard's marvelled at the cold indifference of their Oriental Adonis. But it was not indifference, it was a little girl dressed in blue, with very red cheeks, and very brown hair, that rendered him so persistently insensible to their devices. Where Tommy first encountered the fair young stranger, no person has discovered; but it is popularly believed that they met by chance, the usual way, or else that 'twas in a crowd, or something of that sort.

It is known, however, that the blue maiden used to walk daily upon Fourteenth street, before the apartment of Tommy, beaming at him through the windowpanes, until, forsaking his studies, he would assail the guardian of the door with vehement entreaties for her admission, which for awhile he did not succeed in securing. At length, one day, collecting courage, he blushingly petitioned Capt. Porter on the subject, who yielded free consent to his demand. Then Tommy, radiant with delight, brought in his chosen charmer, presented her with imposing dignity to the best among his friends, and establishing himself by her side, marched proudly through the Japanese quarters quite an unnecessary number of times. Day after day these brief meetings were repeated, to Tommy's rarest satisfaction, notwithstanding the occasional derisions of some of his comrades. After a very little time, the sentiments of the juvenile twain were manifested in the interchanges of daguerreotypes, and kindred gifts, their affections growing all the while, until like the red rose and the briar from the breast of Lady Nancy and Lord Lovel, "they couldn't grow any higher."

In the midst of this happiness came the crushing intelligence, all thought of which Tommy had tried to evade, that preparations for leave-taking must be made. From that moment sadness overcame him. During the last two days he was seldom seen to smile. Excepting to the most favored of his associates, he never told the real depth of his love, but let concealment, like a bug in a rug, prey on. He struggled to retain his self-control, and thoroughly succeeded, until the morning fixed for starting, when he at last broke down, and went about lamenting aloud. As he rode away from Willard's, the sight of the little maid in blue, standing upon the sidewalk and tearfully bewailing the departure of all the Japanese, and especially of her young man, only seventeen years old, completed his grief, and hiding his face in the fullness of his sleeve, he began to cry bitterly, and utterly refused to be comforted.

On the way from Washington to Baltimore, he gathered fragmentary consolation by gazing upon his cherished picture; but, from time to time, his feelings proved too much for him, and he gave himself up mourning. The jests of his Japanese friends, which beset him from all sides, did not awe him one particle from the career of his humor. In Baltimore he essayed to regain composure, and even rushed into many excitements, in the hope of securing temporary respite from his woes. He converted himself at one time into a fireman, and endeavored to draw from a huge hosepipe placed in his hands, the waters of oblivion. I do not think he succeeded; for, while riding up to Philadelphia, the next day, he told me quite pathetically, 'I think always of my good little Washington friend—my dear—my sweetheart.'

Whether Tommy's case is without hope, no one can now decide. He asks mysteriously about the chances of conveying away some friends with him to Japan, and the world may yet be startled by the announcement of the unexpected elopement of a young Washington damsel, aged fifteen, dressed in blue, and much given to romance. Perhaps, however, Tommy's heart may be the mirror that some say it is; and that the next bright face that falls upon it may be as clearly reflected there as that whose memory now lingers by him.

E. H. House.

Philadelphia, June 11, 1860.

[For The New York Saturday Press.]

MY SISTER BELLE.

—

BY LIZZIE CAMPBELL.

—

You never saw my sister Belle!

Ah! then how am I to tell you what she was like? And yet she wasn't beautiful; pretty, very pretty she was, and more than that, she was lovely. Every one loved her—how could they help it? We all love the blue sky, the golden sunlight, the pure lily of the valley, the pink heather-bell, and Belle, charming Belle, was all of these. Her dear eyes the blue of the sky, her fair hair the golden sunlight, her snow-white skin the lily-leaf, her pink cheeks the heather-bell, and her darling dimpled mouth the ripest, rubiest, dewiest strawberry cut in twain, with the white teeth for seeds showing between.

From that you think perhaps that she was beautiful, though I have said she wasn't; nor was she.

Her nose was small and rétroussé, and I do not think that a beauty, though some people do. And her brow was high, too high for her small features; her eyebrows not clearly defined, being too light; and the contour of her face, instead of oval, almost round, though the breadth of the forehead and chin made it, when her countenance was turned full toward you, look in a slight degree square; but that did not prevent her being exceedingly pretty, for how could any one with such eyes, complexion, hair, mouth, and teeth, be otherwise?

Her form was perfect, the most perfect I ever saw, though she was quite small, only about five feet in height; but from the crown of the exquisitely-poised head to the sole of the tiny white foot with high instep, —under which a streamlet of water might have flowed easily without touching it,—my sister Belle's form, with the one exception of height, might have been taken for the Goddess of Beauty incarnate. I think I said every one loved her. I was wrong—one woman did not; but of all who loved her none, no, not one, enshrined her in their heart of hearts as did I, her sister, for to me she was the brightness and beauty of life—the only good thing left to me in this world.

When I was thirteen my father died, but my mother and three brothers and two sisters were still left to me, and I was very happy for three years, for I never cared for any one else save those of my own family. I was quite content to lavish my whole heart upon them; and I did so, as one by one they died away, concentrating all my love and bestowing it upon those who were still left, till when I was eighteen years of age I was left with only Belle, the youngest, the favorite, the pet. First after my father, followed my eldest brother, then my youngest, then the last of them. Next my sister Flora, seven years younger than myself, and last of all my mother, my own, my darling mother!

O how gladly, how joyfully I would have laid there beside her, and breathed away the last of my life by that best and gentlest of human beings, but for the link that stood beside me still binding me with her innocent blue eyes to earth!

Mamma! mamma! if we could have both, Belle and I, laid down beside you there and died, would it not have been better? I cannot bear to listen for the answer; it drives me mad to think of it! Why, oh why, are we doomed to suffer so? Father, mother, brothers, sisters, can it be that I will never again see any of you? Am I forever shut out from that Heaven that I have always pictured to myself so bright and glorious, so beautiful and happy?

I cannot, I will not think so! God is too merciful —Jesus is too tender and pitying to deny me that peace and joy hereafter that I have never felt here. . . .

It was but 'a life for a life,'—it was but 'blood for blood.' O God! my brain whirls! I am going mad! What means these incoherent ravings? I have a story to tell. Let me tell it, then die, for when finished my last work on earth is done,

My mother's last-spoken words, whispered in my ear by the already stiffening lips, were:

"Take care of Belle, Lizzie. Let her be as your own child—be to her a mother as well as sister. My little darling Belle, my poor Lizzie, God bless you."

I listened, O how eagerly I listened for the next words! With that keen, agonizing intentness—did you ever experience it ?—that draws the hearing, as though compressing some tangible thing into a space twice too small for it; and then as the strained sense gave a sort of snap that sounded in my ear with a numb booming sound, I raised my head, I looked in my mother's face and saw that there was no next words to hear, for she was dead. I didn't cry out, or faint.

I remember distinctly that I stooped down and took Belle up in my arms, for though six years of age she was light and small as a child of three, and tried to hush her passionate sobbing, for she had seen death too often not to recognize the grim visitant when he came again. I can feel the clasp of her round velvety arms about my neck at this moment, I can feel the convulsive throbs of her heart, I can hear the choking sobs that burst from her chest and throat, and even the faint breathing, occasionally broken by the deep half-sigh, half-moan, of a child that had wept itself asleep, when, at last, she slumbered; yes, I hear it now as I did then, though it is thirty-five years ago this night.

Still sleeping in my arms, her head resting on my shoulder, I carried Belle with me, while I went out to a neighboring house, and requested one of the young men to go to the Undertaker's and order my mother's—

No! no! I cannot! indeed I cannot go over all the details of the funeral. On the third day, mamma was buried away from our sight, and sitting alone, with Belle in my arms, I looked out of the window with eyes in which glittered not one single tear, at the monotonous, drizzling rain, drearily, drearily watching it till nightfall, and then turning away from the darkness without, to fancy from every corner of the gloom within, that I saw the ghosts of the loved and gone before; and I wonder now, when I cannot bear even the remembrance, how the terrible reality, ever before me for days and weeks and months then, did not upset my reason, and leave me in insanity, forgetful of it all. I wonder how this was, but I have not far to look for the solution. I had Belle then; I have no Belle now.

I have not told you how poor we were, my little sister and I. Poor!—that is a calm word for it; we were paupers! We had no property. We had lived upon the earnings of my brothers while they lived; and until my mother's death, upon my very small salary as junior-teacher of one of the city schools; but at the crisis of her illness I had been obliged to remain at home, and so lost my situation.

When at length I awoke to life again—for except my care of Belle, I had been like one dead while alive, for many weeks after that last bereavement—it was to the knowledge that we were poverty's children; that poverty, the keenest and bitterest, was our nearest relative, and that we owed even our life to the few neighbors who had kept us from starvation.

It is supposed that those who have felt poverty the most severely can the best describe it; it is not so.

I felt it too crushingly, too intensely, to give any idea of it; I was too completely overwhelmed to say distinctly what it was.

Let me pass over the next two months. It was not chaos, not quite, because through all the darkness was one shining light, one star in the East, that at length brightened the whole horizon, resolved itself into a sun, and shed life, and heat, and light round about me once more. I need not say that the sun-star was Belle, my sister.

At the end of those two months, the junior-teacher who during my absence had taken my situation, was obliged for some reason to resign, and I was successful in my application to be reinstated. Thus I 'took up the burthen of life again,' very thankful that I had such opportunity to do so; for I had a sacred duty to perform, and Heaven bear me witness, my mother, I tried faithfully to perform it!

From junior-teacher I rose to the second grade; from that to senior, and with a salary that amply supplied all the wants of myself and my sister, I wished for nothing more,—yet not wishing for it, I got it.

An uncle who had been for many years supposed to be dead, suddenly turned up, and claimed Belle and me as his nieces. He was rich! He took a handsome house in a pleasant part of the city; took Belle and myself there with him; and when he died, two years later, left us two heiresses of his wealth, in such a manner that I—being of age, and some years beyond it—came into immediate possession of my fortune, while Belle became in a measure the ward of the principal executor, Augustus Hamilton, Esq. At this time I was twenty-five, my sister thirteen.

We still continued to live in the house that had been my uncle's—retaining the same domestics, and living very much as we had done for the past two years, missing only my uncle's cheerful voice and happy face.

Mr. Hamilton had called twice; the first time upon some business connected with the Will, and shortly after Uncle George's death, when some law forms were gone through with, that—though I had some little to do with them, in affixing my signature occasionally—I understood very little about. The second time that he visited us was nearly three years later; and then he declared that my sister was a "pretty child, a very pretty and interesting child," for which I thanked him, and said I had always thought so, as I believed every one else had.

He laughed pleasantly, and asked me if I had ever thought of sending her to school, to which I replied, a little indignantly, "I hope you don't imagine that I have neglected my sister's education, sir!"

"Not at all, my dear young lady; but whatever may be the advantages she has received from private tuition, I decidedly advise your sending her for a year or two to some seminary."

"No, no," I burst forth impetuously, "I could not endure the separation. She is all I have in the world, and seems more like my own child than my sister. I will not consent to her going away."

"Nonsense, nonsense! I had thought you more capable of self-denial, for a short time; especially when for the interest of your sister, whom you profess to love so much."'

"Profess, sir!"

"I beg your pardon, I hardly meant that. Of course I know that you really love Miss Belle, but you must not let any selfishness upon your part make me doubt the sincerity of your attachment to her."

This last was said with a good-humored smile, meant to disarm my anger if I was likely to experience any at the words themselves; so it ended by taking Belle from me, and the only comfort I had was that my darling felt the separation as much as I did. Don't misunderstand me—I mean by that that I knew she was attached to me as much as I was to her; but why should I doubt that? Forgive me, Belle, that for one instant I did.

Nothing of any moment occurred during that year of absence, except the quarterly visits home at the vacations that agreeably broke up its dreariness and shortened the time.

When Belle at length came home for good, wanting but a few months of seventeen, she was, as I have already described her, and oh! how I loved to look upon her!

I had never had a lover in my life; Belle was the only lover, the only object of affection I wanted, and I confess I felt a twinge of jealousy when she so enthusiastically spoke of a friend she had made at school; but she soon laughed me out of the fancy, and as she kissed me said,

"Fie, Lizzie! jealous, and of a girl; just as if I ever could love any one so well as you, you dear, good, best sister in the world. I never can care one-third as much for any one else."

A few days after Belle's return, Mr. Hamilton called; his son accompanied him, and for the first time was introduced to Belle and myself. Ernest Hamilton was a handsome young man, rather above the medium height, with a fine broad forehead, white as my sister's; very dark brown eyes, what people who forget that such a thing never was, call black eyes; they were very bright, very clear, and their brilliant light flashed through the inky lashes like stars through a dark cloud; the nose was slightly aquiline; the mouth firm set, with just sufficient softness, when the lips unclosed to speak or smile, to invest it with a very attractive beauty. He wore neither beard nor moustache, and perhaps that aided in giving the contour of the face a Grecian cast. His hair, worn rather long, was quite black, with a slight tendency to curl, and wonderfully fine like the most minute threads of floss-silk. I know this from at a later day seeing one of the wavy curls in my sister's possession, and viewing it nearly I observed its extreme fineness. His figure was good. I have said he was tall, he was also broad-chested, rather small-waisted, and with admirably-proportioned limbs.

Precisely as I have described him, I saw him that day when I beheld him for the first time, and saw him ever after the same.

Not so, Belle. She declared enthusiastically that he was the most fascinating, and by far the handsomest man she had ever seen in her life; and when I laughed at her, and said that he might be all of that easily, as she had never known more than four men, she went further, and said she did not believe that she ever would see one handsomer or more charming, for in Ernest Hamilton there was no room for one single improvement.

Even then I did not suspect how it was to be.

Though I had experienced a momentary feeling of jealousy when she told me of her friend, Marian Hollin, I was not similarly affected when she spoke of young Hamilton.

She loved me, I knew, therefore I knew it was possible that she could have affection for another woman but because she had no brother, no cousin, no male friend, the certainty of her one day loving some one not of her own sex, did not present itself to me.

The very love that would have made a lover so Argus-eyed completely blinded me; though I felt easily that she could like, and even love girls like herself, and though I was disposed to be jealous even of that, I could not take in the possibility that a man would usurp my place in her heart, that I, for years the first there, would be turned out to give place to another more welcome, and that from that time I must sink down into a second grade; my mind would not take in this—it was too great, too overwhelming.

Mr. Hamilton came very often now—so did his son. I thought it neither strange nor remarkable. I did not even wonder when the elder Hamilton's visits became rarer till they dropped almost entirely away, and his son's more frequent till they became of daily occurrence.

This went on for weeks, and months. Once, twice, a glimmering of what all this was leading to, shot across me with sudden light, but it was so quick that I could only compare it to the lightning-flash, and, brief though it was, it scathed and burned me as if it had been lightning indeed; so I shut my eyes more closely against it, unwilling to bear its sharp pain.

This could not continue always. No! I knew that. I had faint glimmerings that I must bear the whole crushing weight of the blow, strenuously and almost weakly as I strove to avoid it. Had I accepted the warnings I here mentioned; had I taught myself to expect it, it might have fallen lighter, but as it was, I felt the full weight crushingly, and Belle, dear little Belle herself, dealt the blow.

It was in the evening, before the lamps were lighted in the parlor, and while yet the shadowy twilight that I loved was filling the room. I had been ill with a headache the greater part of the afternoon, and had been for some hours in my own room. Earnest Hamilton had called, and found Belle alone in the parlor, and had left her but a short time before I entered and found her sitting on an ottoman, the twilight wrapping them in its grey veil.

When I seated myself close beside her, she didn't stir at first; she didn't look up, though she knew I was present, but after some minutes she came over and stood beside me. She asked with more than her usual gentleness, if my headache was better. She put one round, white arm about my neck, while with the other little hand she smoothed my hair back from my temples; laid her cool fingers upon my burning brow, and caressed my face. Again and again she bent over me till her golden curls fell in a shower over my face, pressing her lips to my hair, my forehead, my cheek, and occasionally to my hand.

She ceased that, and stood beside me very quietly, so that I could hear her breathe more gently between her parted lips, and when I rose to ring for lights she playfully forced me back into my seat again, took away her clinging arm from my neck, and sank down beside me, sitting on the carpet at my feet, and resting her head against my knee half-buried in the folds of my dress. It was not any dim foreboding that I had then. I felt with the suddenness of a thunderclap that I was about to hear all that I had so pertinaciously closed my ears and eyes against; she only waited for me to make a remark, to ask a question, anything to make her speak, that she might open her mind and heart to my gaze; but I was careful not to unclose my lips, I had not the courage to stretch out my own hand for the dagger that was to enter my own heart.

At last she said,

"Ernest—Mr. Hamilton—young Mr. Hamilton, I mean—was here this afternoon."

"Was he?"

"Yes; he went away about half an hour before you came in."

"Did he?"

"Yes, I said so."

A silence of three minutes, which was broken by her little hand in childish petulance coming against mine, and her voice saying,

"Pshaw, Lizzie! can't you say something—can't you ask something?"

"I have nothing to say, Belle."

"But I have."

"Have you?"

"Have I? What does ail you any way? One might suppose you were a speaking automaton, if ever there was such a thing, and were limited to two words in every sentence. 'Was he?' "Did he?' 'Have you?'"

I made no reply. I don't know why—I suppose because I couldn't.

She went on,

"Well, if you won't ask me, I must tell you. You see, Lizzie, darling." And then with much hesitation, and her own pretty grace, in a great many words, she told me that Ernest Hamilton loved her very much, that she loved him very much, and they only wanted my consent to be married, because Mr. Hamilton's was already given; and when she had concluded, because I did not answer on the instant, she hid her face in the folds of my dress again, though the twilight had deepened into dusk, and I could hardly see her; she cried a little, too, I think.

It was minutes before I made any reply.

I verily believe that what I suffered then was a keener, more poignant agony, than the anguish that had wrung my heart when, looking down into my mother's face eleven years before, I saw that she was dead! It was not that she loved me less, it was not that I was less dear to her than before, I know that was not the case, but that she loved another more than she had ever loved me. That was the sharpest, sorest wound—it seemed to have caught my very breath, and held it between my lungs and my throat, so that I felt suffocating.

What is it you say? That I was weak and foolish and selfish? I laugh at your silly words!

Have you been left alone in this great wide chill world, without one thing to love,—for every human heart must have something to love,—and when you have watched it, tended it, cherished it till it has become not only a part of your life, but your very being, have you seen a thief come in to your sheepfold and steal away your little love-lamb? Have you—have you felt this, seen this?

If you have, then you won't say I was weak, or foolish, or selfish; but if you have not, what can you know of my suffering? How dare you apply a word of contempt, of reproval, toward me? Yet do so and you will—I tell you again I can laugh at such words. When I sat still, hushed, breathless, after listening to Belle, I cannot picture the feeling that overpowered me by calling it jealousy. That is too weak, too puny, almost base, a term to apply to it. Rather let me say it was a keen torture, an excruciating agony, a most exquisite anguish, so great that when the first few moments passed, when my breath came hard and laboringly through my lips, it burst forth in a groan, and Belle jumped up in alarm, and asked if I was ill.

For answer I caught her in my arms, I strained her passionately to my heart, and kissed her repeatedly.

She exclaimed joyously,

"Then you are not angry, Lizzie—you don't forbid me to love Ernest."

I couldn't bear to hear her speak of him as Ernest yet; I hurriedly told her I was not angry, that I would never forbid her happiness, or something like that, and as well and as quietly as I could, spoke to her for some moments, and then left her to go to my own room. Of course the first bitterness of woe and sorrow passed away; all strong, very strong feelings do. They either kill themselves, or kill the heart they have taken their place in; in my case they killed themselves, and gradually I came to regard Belle's love for young Hamilton like any other inevitable calamity to which time had inured me.

They were formally engaged, with the consent of all parties concerned, and their marriage-day was fixed for an early date,—Belle's eighteenth birthday, then but a few months distant.

I think it was about three weeks after that twilight evening in the parlor, that Belle came to me with a letter from her friend, Marian Hollin. She put it into my hand, and I read it.

It was a most beautifully written epistle; that is, the chirography was of the most delicate angular style, on the whitest and smoothest of satin note-paper; though there were four sheets closely written, two of which were crossed, the whole substance may be put into a single line,

"My dear Belle, I accept your invitation at last; expect me on Wednesday."

"You don't object, Lizzie? I'm sure you will like Marian; she is a very charming girl," said Belle, when I handed back the letter.

I did not object. Whatever my perhaps morbid love for my young sister might have suggested before her engagement to Hamilton, now everything after that was but slight. I cordially assured her that I would welcome her friend almost as warmly as she would herself when she arrived.

Belle was not very demonstrative, but she thanked me with great earnestness, and with more than her usual warmth declared that I was the 'the dearest, best sister in the world.'

Wednesday came; and so did Miss Marian Hollin, exactly at three minutes past four on Wednesday after-noon.

She was full as beautiful, full as charming, as Belle had described her to me. Dark, bright, radiant.

O! wo, wo to the day when she crossed our threshold! In the evening Ernest came as he had always done for a long time past. More than a slight attention, such as he would have been compelled to bestow upon any lady, he did not give to Miss Hollin, at first sight, but she returned it with threefold interest.

The glance she bestowed upon him when passing her with a courteous inclination of the head and a few gracefully uttered words, and seated himself beside Belle, filled me with alarm and terror. Too surely I read in that glance of hers more, I think, than she intended any one should read, for, as if aware that my eyes were resting upon her, she turned suddenly toward me; our gaze met. She looked back at me steadily, haughtily, defiantly, and then glancing toward my sister and Ernest she laughed a short, mocking laugh. Belle looked up, and wondering what could have occasioned this sudden and apparently uncalled-for merriment, asked,

"What is it, Marian?"

"Nothing, my dear,—at least nothing of any consequence. One's thoughts will sometimes prove amusing. Don't you think so, Mr. Hamilton ?"

"Doubtless," returned Mr. Hamilton, rather abstractedly. He was waiting for a reply to something he had said to Belle, and I hardly think heard what Miss Hollin had said.

She observed the carelessess of his reply, but not the faintest shade of crimson tinged her cheek at his apparent inattention to words from her imperial lips. On the contrary she smiled almost exultingly as one having achieved a triumph.

She rose and crossed the room, her voluminous skirts sweeping against the piano-stool and spinning it partly around as she passed it; she stopped when she neared the window, and drawing back the folds of the curtains looked out upon the gas-lit and moon-lit street.

My eyes were attracted, almost magnetically, toward her as she stood there, and finding it next to impossible to withdraw my gaze, I let it remain upon her; wandering listlessly over her from the braids of her dark hair down to the hem of her shining robe, that swept the carpet.

For beauty of face and form I don't suppose there ever was a more beautiful woman created than Marian Hollin.

Perfect beauty is a rare, a very rare thing, and though I have in my day and generation seen some thousands of women, all having some claim to loveliness, certainly I never saw that woman's equal. Her eyes were as dark as Ernest's; her hair was also black, and her exquisitely arched eyebrows, and long, sweeping eyelashes, of the same jetty hue. Her complexion was marble-white, but with none of the deadness and inanimate pallor characteristic of most perfectly pale complexions; excitement of any kind brought the rich blood mantling in crimson-beauty to her cheek, and blushing faintly through the rest of her white face. Her lips wore a bright, warm tint, not scarlet, and yet not vermillion—softer in hue than the one, brighter than the other; her nose was straight, with thin, white nostrils, and the whole face indeed, so suggestive of the purest marble, most exquisitely, most happily dissolved into the resemblance of breathing beauty, might have been the pride of an Athenian. Her form was perfect as her face. She was full four inches taller than Belle, though she could not be more beautifully proportioned. Her dress added to the striking splendor of her appearance.

It was of a silver-colored moire—antique, falling in folds of shining, classic elegance from her rounded waist; made low in the neck, her arms and shoulders gleaming like frosted snow in contrast to it, and though certainly worn then (when neither Belle nor I appeared in full dress, for there was no occasion nor excuse for doing so,) it was not in the best taste, still so admirably becoming was it to her that it was impossible to find fault with her toilet.

For some minutes she continued to look out into the street; then, probably for a diversion, she began softly 'drumming' on the window panes with her fingers; having continued that for a short time, she ceased it, and turned with a quick movement toward the lovers. Ernest was bending toward Belle, her eyes were cast down toward the carpet, and the lovely rose-color was fading and flashing on her cheek as she listened to whatever it was he was saying.

Marian's eyes measured them for about three seconds, then sent forth a flash that I could see from where I was seated, and a sneer perceptibly curled her perfect lip.

She turned away, and I seized the opportunity to make Belle a sign that she was verging upon the ridiculous in letting her lover absorb her attention entirely, to the almost absolute neglect of her guest. She understood me, and rising, she moved away to some distance, and presently addressed Marian, requesting her to 'play something?'

Miss Hollin never required much persuasion to display her accomplishments. She did play something; she played divinely—her performance was without a fault, and Ernest complimented her warmly. It was then, that for the first time he appeared to observe her; his eye wandered over her face, her form, her dress, with visible and undisguised admiration and delight; there was even a shade of astonishment in his admiration, for doubtless he too, thought she was the most wondrously beautiful woman he had ever beheld.

He turned to Belle, and I heard the whisper, "What a magnificent—what a glorious woman!"

Marian Hollin also heard it.

Belle returned to this enthusiastic expression of admiration,

"Is not she? I knew you would think so." And that he did think so soon became painfully evident to me. It formed the beginning and ending of all his thoughts, and many an agonized throe, many a bitter tear it wrung from me for my sister's sake, long before she guessed at the mountain of dark clouds that was rising so rapidly to obscure the brightness of her calm Summer sky.

There was but a grain of jealousy in Belle's composition, and ere that had sprung up or even taken root in her heart's soil, Ernest Hamilton was forever lost to her. At last the grain took root, it sprung up rapidly, the serpent raised its crested head, its green eyes were gifted with a tenfold vision. She saw it all, and my poor Belle was stricken, sorely, sorely stricken! It was exactly five weeks after Marian's arrival that one afternoon I came down stairs, and walking along the hall was going to enter the parlor, supposing that Belle was there, my feet suddenly became glued to the floor, when I beheld her but a few steps from the open door, riveted to the spot on which she stood, with as little appearance of life as the marble statuette she leaned her little hand upon to steady herself. From where she stood she could see and hear all that passed in the parlor, and so too could I, but for the first few moments I saw but her. Then as I distinguished voices and words and recognized them, I darted my gaze toward the parlor.

To another the sight I beheld might have been amusing—to another yet, pleasing, for there was much of grace and beauty in it, but to me, because of Belle, O God! how much of agony—to Belle, because of her poor loving, breaking heart, how much of agonized suffering!

Marian Hollin was seated upon a large ottoman, her ample skirts spread out in beautiful breadth of silken, glistening splendor, Ernest was kneeling before her, both her hands prisoned in his, and looking up admiringly into the dark eyes looking down into his; she spoke:

"Ernest, I have told you again and again that it can never be. Your honor binds you to my dear little friend, Belle."

"Perdition!" he interrupted passionately, and begged her forgiveness in the next breath, adding, "You drive me mad, Marian—I know not what I say. She is nothing to me—nothing—nothing! I love—I adore—I worship you! My queen! my goddess! That poor, puny thing is too much honored that her name is deemed worthy to be uttered by your voice, to dwell for even a passing moment on your dear lips."

"Hush-hush!" she said with playful fondness.

"I will not—I cannot. Marian hear me—this day—this hour cancels my engagement—bah! the mere thought of it sickens me!—with Belle Carlisle. From this moment she is nothing to me, any more than if I had never seen her. Only say that you will deign to occupy the place that she was to have filled—forgive me that I did not know from some inward prompting that I had not met my destiny till I saw you; say"—

"That will do, dearest."

She drew her hands from his, and placing both upon his brow, pushed back the masses of his hair from his temples, and stooping forward kissed him, first upon the centre of his brow, then upon either temple. I saw him start up to his feet; I saw no more—well that they could neither see nor hear aught but themselves, for the next moment Belle tottered, and springing forward in time to reach her ere she fell, I received her—lifeless, white as a snowdrift, in my arms.

It was not the first time, neither was it the last, that I bore her in my arms. I raised her as if she had been an infant, for though usually strong, I had then a strength almost supernatural, and carried her up stairs. I laid her on my bed, and applied myself to restoring her, though it might have been as well if her blue eyes had never unclosed again, but I could not thus yield up my darling to the chilling embrace of death.

It was a long and very painful fainting-fit, and the recovery from it was like a resuscitation from death; indeed, in a measure it was so. As she had ever done when in trouble, though till then her troubles had been light, she clasped her arms about my neck, and laid her head on my bosom.

"O Lizzie !" she moaned, "if I had never loved any one but you, if I had given my heart to you forever!"

I could only echo the words from the depths of my soul, though I could not, dare not speak. I knew not what to say.

"This from Marian, too, Marian that I thought so good and true! Why does my heart not break that I could die at once? Lizzie, Lizzie! O my sister! Lizzie Carlisle, what shall I do ?"

I answered impetuously, and without due regard for her poor bleeding heart, for indignation hurried me out of myself.

"Collect all the strength you possess, Belle, and go down to the parlor. You will find them there, order them both out of this house on the instant."

"You know not what you say !"

"But I know well what I say! Is it not enough that Ernest Hamilton is a poor perjured wretch, and Marian Hollin a heartless hypocrite? Must they parade perjury and hypocrisy within our house beneath our eyes? Your guest laughs at you. Your affianced husband insults you in my house, and think you I will bear a continuance of it a minute longer than gives them time to leave this roof? I tell you no! and if you refuse to send them away, I will order them hence myself."

I wrenched myself from her grasp and approached the door, but she intercepted me by throwing herself between me and it, and imploring wildly,

"Do not, do not, I beg, I entreat. Listen, sister dear! your words kill me, they pierce my heart and soul keener than any two-edged sword. I cannot, O I will not hear one unkind word applied to Ernest. If you would not drive me mad, Lizzie, promise that you will do nothing of what you have said."

I did not dare refuse anything to those pleading blue eyes and clasped white hands, and reluctantly (for I burned with anger and indignation against the two despicable things in the room below me) I gave the promise.

I made Belle go back and lie down again upon the bed, for she was fit for nothing else; she tottered at every step, and with difficulty maintained her footing, so that I was obliged to assist her with the support of my arm.

"At least promise me that you will forget him," I whispered.

"Forget him! Forget him!" she repeated with a strange look that said very plainly, as well might you bid the stars forget to shine.

"Then, Belle, you will surely at the first opportunity go to him and say, 'You are free' !"

"You know not what you ask. I can't speak. I'm too ill and faint with weakness, but I can never tell him he is free. You could, because you are strong and resolute; but I cannot. I will win him back again; he cannot have so entirely forgotten me. No, no," she said, "he cannot."

She spoke wanderingly and incoherently, till I began to fear she was becoming ill, so I ceased to importune her, and spoke soothingly to her till she fell asleep like a weary child, from sheer weakness.

I went down to the parlor; Marian was alone, for her lover was gone, it appeared. Then for my poor Belle I did what I would not have done for the wealth of the Indies ten times told. I told Marian all I had seen and heard passing between her and Ernest, and I begged her by all she held dear to leave us, that he might return to Belle.

She smiled a terrible smile of disdain and triumph commingled. I knelt to her on my knees, I prayed of her for the sake of mercy, and of the God of mercy, to leave us, and give back to Belle that which was her life and joy; then when the beautiful demoness laughed at my prayers and entreaties, I know not what further I said or did, I only know there was a curse in my heart, coming up to my lips, but whether it found utterance and passed them I cannot tell.

I was about to break the promise given to Belle and order her from beneath my roof, when she stopped me with,

"It is unnecessary, Miss Carlisle. Spare me the degradation, if you can be generous. I am going. You think I will give up Ernest Hamilton? No," and she approached me, and whispered in my ear "I hate your sister too intensely; she, though she knows it not was my rival. Yes! she, baby-face, took from me the only heart I sighed for, my music-master's! You see I was not ambitious. I loved our poor music teacher, and he loved your bonny Belle, and loves her yet. Well, never mind, a heart for a heart; it is my turn now. Ha-ha! ha-ha!"

I never heard so wicked a laugh as burst from her lips then; she turned away ere I could speak, and leaving the room proceeded up stairs to prepare for leaving us. That same night I beheld her for the last time, and Belle saw her no more.

She had sent word to Ernest that she had left us, and from that day he never entered our house. A letter, requesting a dissolution of the engagement, came to me, and when I showed it to Belle, even then her heart would have forgiven all, but she had pride enough to send him a cutting answer wherein she acceded to his request. I knew then that the lightning had blasted my flower; slowly the cankerworm ate at its heart, till at the end of a month the worm had finished its meal, the heart was eaten away: my Belle, my darling was dead!

And I lived then, ah! yes, I had outlived too many sorrows to be killed with sorrows; besides, I had a task to perform—a task that I laid out for myself, to the performance of which I dedicated my own right hand.

I took my measures well—I laid my plans cleverly. I was now the heiress to very great wealth, and I prepared to leave my native country, where every association was fraught with pain. I took passage in a vessel sailing for Liverpool; every one who knew of my intention thought I had sailed, but under my name went a poor woman who was glad thus to have a free passage secured, while I remained to accomplish my task.

Belle still lay in her grave, white, and cold, and beautiful; a shrouded form of fair clay, when Marian Hollin married Ernest Hamilton.

Well, I had waited for that hour. I knew where to find them, and I waited still longer; it was Mid-Summer, and they had taken themselves to a cottage in the country, where I followed them. It was not likely that I should lose my opportunity—it was not likely that I should fail to see Ernest leave the cottage by himself, one warm, sultry day, and wander away down to the orchard.

I followed him there, too, and I saw him after an hour's wandering about, throw himself down upon the long grass, where, under my wakeful watching eye, he fell sound asleep.

I stole softly to his side, and looked down upon him. He had never looked more beautiful, and I hated him still more then, for had his beauty not robbed my life of all that had been beautiful to it! His straw hat lay down beside him, his coat was thrown loosely back, and he wore no vest; his right arm reposed by his side, and his left one was thrown carelessly up over his head, just as I could have wished it. I knelt down beside him, and through the fine linen of his shirt I could see the calm, even pulsations of his heart; I counted a minute while I knelt there by its regular beatings, and then I drew forth the dagger, long-bladed, sharp-pointed, that I held ready beneath my heavy crape mantle. I poised it steadily in my hand above the regularly-beating heart, and if you think my own fluttered one pulse the quicker, or that my hand trembled as much as a leaf swayed by the faintest breeze, then are you mistaken greatly. I was ice and rock.

With all the strength of my arm, and with three distinctly-uttered words, 'This for Belle !' I drove the weapon down till the blade went out at the back and sank an inch into the ground.

The murdered and the murderer—had he not killed Belle, only with far greater torture ?—opened his eyes, gave one single glance, a half-uttered groan, and died. I rose and left the spot, no eye having seen me save His Who looked down upon me through the blue sky of Heaven....

Well, well, I have suffered for thus taking vengeance into my own hand, O God! Yes, I have suffered—no language can tell the tortures!

I have visited all the great places of earth, but my sin—my crime has been with me. It is not Ernest Hamilton's death I regret—no, no! It is my crime—my crime—my crime!

A gulf of blood seems to shut me out from pardon and mercy—Heaven seems very far away, though Death is so near.

Father, mother, brothers, sisters, will I then meet you no more? Belle, my darling, my angel, ever the light of my eyes, and the holiest love of my heart, am I to see you no more? It cannot, cannot be! O Heaven be merciful!—O Father be forgiving!

Ah! my God! is this death—this grim spectre passing over me, chilling my brow, robbing of light mine eyes, stilling my heart and pulses, paralyzing my limbs, freezing my marrow, running chill down my arm, stiffening my fingers! can this be death—O God!—can this—is—

[From the New York Herald, June 15th.]

A CASE FOR THE CHARITABLE.

To the Editor of the New York Herald:

Knowing that you are ever ready to respond to the call of suffering humanity, I beg to call your attention to a case of more than ordinary hardship. About four years ago a family of five girls, of from four to eighteen years of age, and a young man of twenty years of age, were left to struggle for a living without the aid or counsel of either father or mother. By hard work the three oldest managed to support the family, keeping the other three at school. A year ago the second eldest was taken sick. She continued so until her death, three months since, less one week. A month later the brother met with an accident, from the effects of which he continued to suffer until his death, on the 8th of the present month. The third eldest girl has been sick for the last four or five months until to-day, when she died. The poor girl, who, by her daily toil, has been struggling to support these children in honesty and respectability, is now completely overwhelmed with grief and distress. The protracted illness and expense of burying her other sister and brother has left her utterly destitute. She is now sitting in a room that contains the remains of her who has just departed, and the almost equally helpless children (aged eight and eleven respectively), whom she is powerless to relieve. Will you have the kindness to appeal on their behalf to the generous and charitable, and may the blessing of the orphan ascend to the throne of Him who will not fail to reward the good.

The family referred to reside at the Northwest corner of Green and Broome streets, and the young girl's name is Malvina Guy.

M. J. O'R.

New York, June 14, 1860.

Leaves of Grass

NOW READY.

FOR SALE EVERYWHER

WALT WHITMAN'S

Leaves of Grass,

COMPLETE.

A Superb Volume. - - Price $1 :

TO THE PUBLIC.

The strong and electric writings of

Walt Whitman

Are here presented to you by us, in complete form, for the time. We invite you to read for yourselves, irrespective of conflicting judgments of the critics.

TO THE TRADE.

We pledge ourselves of the material and execution of this '] mos' Poem, with all the belongings of its type, casting, pa presswork, ink, binding, &c., that it is a ☞ **specimen beautiful and honest workmanship,** beyond anyt] of its price ever yet printed, to our knowledge, in the world.

GRATIS.

"**Leaves of Grass Imprints,**" a small brochure, coll ing American and European criticisms on the First (1855) Second (1857) Issues of the "Leaves." This brochure is issue us as a Circular, for gratuitous distribution, and will be sent to any who wish it, on application, by mail or otherwise.

SENT BY MAIL.

We send the New and Complete "Leaves of Grass" by n postpaid, on receipt of price as above, with 29 cents for post always prepaid.

THAYER & ELDRIDGE,

PUBLISHERS,

114 and 116 Washington Street,

Boston, Mass.

[For The New York Saturday Press.]

THE ADVENT OF THE MOSQUITO.

Again the gaunt mosquito comes,
That Brigand of the night!
With all his carving family,
To put my dreams to flight,
And try and settle his small bill,
And take a draft at sight!

I hear again the dreadful sound
That tells me who is near;
I hear him wind his horrid horn,
And whet his poisoned spear;
He sounds the battle-blast, and ah!
I feel that he is here!

I beat the air: I seem to wage
With friends an idle feud :
My hopes, like poor Ophelia's,
Are blasted in the bud;
I'm vanquished in a single round
And he attains 'first blood!'

In vain the rank cigar I smoke,
Quite wild and desperate grown;
I try in vain to drive him out,
And shut the window down;
For still I hear those tranquil pipes
Monotonously drone!

Like Cook among the Cannibals,
Tis useless to appeal,
Or like a mummy wind myself
In sheets from head to heel,
The hungry wretch has picked me out
To make himself a meal!

His sucker, like a burglar's drill,
Would pierce an iron door!
He loves, as Alexander did,
To wade in human gore!
Like Everett he is always dry,
Like Cobb, a perfect bore!

But yet, his faults may not suffice
All merit to efface;
For sinner never yet was born
Without some spark of grace;
His failing is philanthropy:
He loves the Human Race!

He comes by night as angels do,
To chant his soothing hymn;
He hovereth o'er the baby's couch
Just like the cherubim:
By day, he wadeth in the swamp:
His legs are long and slim.

O bear me to some frozen waste
Where polar tempests blow!
On train-oil I will gaze unmoved,
Or Greenland's cliffs of snow,
And be content to pass my days
Among the Esquimaux !

H. S. Cornwell.

NEW YORK JUNE 23, 1860

[For The New York Saturday Press.]

WALT WHITMAN'S NEW VOLUME.

Messrs. Editors:—I do not ask a place for this letter in your columns because I feel that Mr. Whitman's poems need any justification; they justify themselves, and I have full faith that they will continue to do so long after the swarm of attacking critics are gone; nor do I hope to give more generous or appreciative praise to 'Leaves of Grass' than you have given in your notice of the work, but because, being a woman, and having read the uncharitable and bitter attacks upon the book, I wish to give my own view of it.

I have read it carefully, and in reading, have found no page which made me blush, and no sentiment which might not be expressed by a pure man.

In humanity or art I consider that coarse and licentious wherein the soul is made subservient to the body. I am not shocked when I read the stories of the Old Testament; I see behind the apparently gross form, great meanings. Yet I find in the novels and the versification of modern literature, a subtle sensuality which, under the semblance of virtue, destroys all that is pure and elevated in the mind, leaving it enslaved by sensation and petty circumstance.

In Mr. Whitman's poetry, I see a breadth of view which overlooks distinctions. To him, nothing is base when used for a great purpose; he makes all things subservient to thought, and thus dignifies by his touch.

I find there an admirable courage. While we truckle to our bodies, trying to cheat ourselves and one another into oblivion of the potent physical facts, while we feed with exciting novels and amorous poetry those passions we dare not own, we are shocked, forsooth, when a great, earnest, sorrowful man gives us the facts which, gilded over with poor art, we accept readily enough; and when, with manly courage, he owns that he has sinned with prostitutes and felons, (and who has not?) we despise him. Was it not Christ who said of old, "Let him who is without blame among you cast the first stone"?

I find in these poems great ideas; large, cheerful, healthy views of life. No sentimentality, no weak or misplaced passion, but a wisdom which looks through all, behind all, beyond all, which sees the tendency of things, and rests content that all is well. I find a reverence so great and tender as not to despise the meanest thing, knowing that Nature has fashioned everything through ages of patient toil; a reverence which sees in the mud and slime of the pond the same fitness and beauty as in the dainty lily floating above it; which holds the 'woman just as great as the man;' and a mother 'The melodious character of the earth, the finish beyond which philosophy cannot go and does not wish to go;' a reverence which recognizes in the distinction of sex, that great principle which asserts itself from the lowest to the highest forms of vegetable and animal life, a mystery equally holy with the mystery of birth, the mystery of death.

I find there a generosity, giving without stint. Nothing is too precious, nothing too great, nothing too holy to be bestowed. The experiences which most men in their selfishness hug close, which they call 'too sacred for the eyes of the world,' Mr. Whitman, like a true poet, deals out largely.

And I find more than all these: I find a wonderful knowledge of history, of philosophy, of mythology, of language, of mechanics and geography, of the customs of all peoples at all times; a knowledge which could have been acquired only by hard and long-continued study.

I find the highest artistic merits. A measure at once original and melodious, into which the words form themselves so naturally that we forget it is measure, and are aware of the thought alone. It is like the sound of the wind or the sea, a fitting measure for the first distinctive American bard who speaks for our large-scaled nature, for the red men who are gone, for our vigorous young population.

Yet grand, wild, free, and natural, as is Mr. Whitman's poetry, it is not careless or hap-hazard, any more than Niagara, the Mississippi, the prairies, or the great Western cities, are hap-hazard; it is the result of patient labor, of intense thought; for it is the highest art which most closely imitates nature. Here we see not only boldness of conception, but finish of detail. What is there so graphic in the English language that Mr. Whitman should be ashamed to place beside it the pictures of the 'Fall of Alamo,' 'The Mashed Fireman,' 'The Sinking Ship,' or any other of the hundreds of pictures scattered throughout the book? What so exquisitely delicate as to eclipse 'A Word out of the Sea'?

There are few poems which I can read with so intense a thrill of exultation at the greatness of my destiny, at the exquisite harmony and balance of the universe, at the boundless love brooding over mankind; that fill me with so strong a faith in the working together of all things for good, so great forbearance toward error—yet nerve me so resolutely to action, as these poems of Walt Whitman.

C. C. P.

[For The New York Saturday Press.]

SUMMER NIGHTS.

I.

The night is heavy with the breath of June,
The trees nod slumbr'ously to murmured tunes,
And thou, beneath this tender Summer moon,
Dreamest of sweeter nights in other Junes.

II.

Come back, O heart of backward distant days!
Float through their shadows reverently and low;
Bring the remembered dreams of youth's first Mays,
Visions that faded out, how long ago!

III.

Come back? Alas, where would'st thou fold thy wing,
Heart, of that Summer time of faith the guest?
O'er this calm waste of billowy years, may spring
No bough of peace, no Ararat of rest.

IV.

Why wilt thou sigh, and sigh, yet never dare?
Why wilt thou dream a heaven thou shouldst have gained?
Brook no more doubtful parleys with despair,
Lest life be done, and heaven be unattained.

[For The New York Saturday Press.]

THE VICISSITUDES OF BABIES

The vicissitudes of human life have frequently claimed the attention of mankind, but they have only been regarded as commencing with a certain advanced stage of the mammal.

Now, if we look a little closer, we will find that these vicissitudes extend still farther back than is generally supposed. We all know what a baby is. We doubt if there be a man living who has not seen or at least heard a baby at some time or times in the course of his life—but we have always been accustomed to consider babies as free from the vicissitudes of life—that babies pursue the uneven tenor of their voices and 'the even tenor of their way' in the usual routine of squalling, crowing, and dawning perceptions of things about them, without being affected in any very material way by outside circumstances, and it was very natural that we should think so.

A baby can hardly be said to be endowed with any very great amount of intellectual or moral power. How, then, can the moral or intellectual life of a mere squib of flesh in rags be influenced by external circumstances? So long as the baby is fed and clothed, what more does it want?

Nothing, indeed, so long as it is fed and clothed by its own mother. But the advance of that glorious chimera called civilization, has upset the natural order of things. Fashion ordains that the mother shall not nurse its own child. Of course we do not refer to those exceptional instances where ill-health is a cause of prohibition. In such cases it is of course right and reasonable. But we are only speaking of cases where Fashion ordains, without either right or reason, a strong and healthy woman must not nurse her child because this right of nature is unfashionable; it spoils the woman's shape, keeps her out of society, and on the whole is very vulgar. To this decree of Fashion is no doubt owing much of the vice which infects society. This beautiful dictate of woman's nature is denied her, and to satify the want of a natural pleasure she flings herself into the vortex of artificial ones, and there drowns her very heart.

What can be expected of the influence of such a mother over her child? Where are those delicate tender feelings that the child instinctively feels the need of as it grows older? All drowned in the whirlpool of fashionable society, and all because the very duties and pleasures which might have reclaimed many a selfish fashionable woman, are denied her by the decree of Fashion, which votes all such pleasures and duties as vulgar.

Let Fashion hold her sway, if she will, over foolish girls, but let her not interfere with the tender dictates of the mother's heart. What a touching sight is that of a heretofore fashionable heartless woman suddenly awakened to the perception of higher pleasures and aims by the helpless innocence of her baby. What a world of tenderness is in her eye, and how gently she nurses and cares for it. All her attention now absorbed by her little one, she is no longer the cold selfish woman, but the kind gentle mother.

Yet Fashion dares to plant her cold tread on such holy ground, and there are women weak enough to obey her decrees. One would suppose that the whole woman's soul would rise in arms against it.

Then see what a hubbub this same Fashion causes through the baby-world. Though the fashionable mother may not nurse her own child, still the fashionable baby must be nursed. Another mother is called in, whose child must be nursed by some one else, the latter's child must be nursed by somebody else, and so the babies are passed around, until one finally reaches some mother who has lost her child, and the further circulation of the babies is stopped. Thus Fashion upsets not only fashionable babies, but likewise many outside of her fold, and a great many mothers thus get alienated from their own babies, and passionately attached to somebody else's baby.

There is one circumstance, however, in connection with this circulation of babies, that is particularly painful to think of: A fashionable mother pays say twenty-four dollars a-month to her nurse. This nurse pays twelve to her nurse; the nurse's nurse pays six dollars to her nurse; the nurse's nurse's nurse pays three dollars, and so on till the amount dwindles down through eighteen pence, nine pence, four-and-a-half cents, until it reaches some fraction of a cent unexpressed by our currency. What is painful in this connection, is that either the dead baby must be reached before any such reduction, or else that some babies must get very imperfect nursing.

Why, it is a frightful state of affairs, and certainly a subject for legislation. When Fashion begins to interfere with the laws of the Public Health, it is high time for the Legislature to step in.

If any of these considerations may induce even one fashionable woman to stand against Fashion, or induce the Legislature to take the matter in hand, the writer's aim will be accomplished.

R. O. S.

CHARACTER vs. SENTIMENT IN ART.

It is impossible to define that union of individuality with energy which we name character, yet in life it is instantly and supremely felt. It makes the difference between men by which one is a presence, a power, something not to be dodged or ignored, while another is merely phenomenal and phantasmal.

There is also vital reaction in every creature and thing. The dog, horse, rock, tree, can never become phantasmal as man may be; is never vastated by imitation, but holds its own, asserts itself purely, and by that unmixed purity in every contact with natural objects we are refreshed and reinforced.

The ideal is this vital energy. If a man have strength to taste and extract it, he is at home and happy in the world. The effort is simply to disclose it, to show the naked vigor and sweetness of things. If he is a half poet, who cannot quite reach the quick in every encounter, he is dissatisfied; he finds no divine quality in the companion, the landscape, the daily work and pleasure of the world; he sighs, he aspires, he is unappreciated. He finds our life coarse and dull. Meat and drink are an offence to him. The soul loathes food under such circumstances,' says Mr. Guppy. He sings 'I want to be an angel,' he regrets the golden age, the middle age, any age was better than this prose in which he is involved.

Prose is dulness—is in the proser, never in the age. Of course our evaporating friend with his diet of rose leaves and rainbows, will never allow himself to represent the world as it actually runs and rolls, a ball of mere mud crawled over by vermin, who harrow and aggravate continually the 'finer sensibilities.'

He must eviscerate. He bones every turkey and takes only jelly from the meat. He sublimates every solid fact into gas and moonshine. Anything more substantial than a fairy, a cardinal virtue, a mythologic abstraction, he can nowhere see.

This dainty and 'expansive' gentleman is the artist of the period. The young ladies adore him. Strong men sniff at him. His staple is sentiment. His work is 'Jean Maria Farina double extrait de distillation.' He puts wings on his horses and dogs.

In stern opposition to this emasculate, sophisticated habit, is genuine ideality, which takes hold on the actual, as one should grasp a cup wherein all water of life comes to the lip. In Rosa Bonheur's 'Horse Fair' we are invigorated by the rendering of rude and homely traits. We name it hearty treatment, honest, which will not dodge nor embellish. Why should it dodge or embellish, having resource enough in the vital energy which it discloses? Rosa Bonheur has no need to groom her stallion, because she can make him, as old Chaucer says, 'so horsely and so quick of eye.'

The sentimental or suckling poet and artist are not worth powder and shot of criticism. The temper of Art Items who never sneers at him but pats him continually on the head, can be nothing less than angelic. The critic of a didactic turn, who has a 'mission,' is a wolf on the track of this tender lamb.

But among artists of acknowledged ability and influence, we must still distinguish between the men of perception and stern veracity, who will render in simplicity the very exterior and interior of every object without compromise, and those who rely on accessories, on tone, situation, association, and 'the finer feelings of our common nature.'

For example, Crawford's 'Mechanic' in the Pediment of the new Capitol at Washington, is a graceful reclining figure, with open vague expression of countenance, and eyes not fixed but rather diffused in distance. Scheffer gives us a picture of 'Mignon aspiring to Heaven.' This is an American mechanic aspiring also to something remote and vast, altogether unconscious of mundane affairs. Like that of Mr. Guppy, his genius is superior to his situation.

Now the cotton gin, the steam engine, the telegraph, were invented, not discovered by any such random gaze into the 'boundless possibilities of being.' The American mechanic is master of mankind in his sphere by concentration, by directness of regard and purpose, by persistency to a point. His eye is keen and firm, he is altogether compact and practical of habit, is least of all a dreamer, and spends no strength upon mystery. It is one exercise vaguely to aspire, another to apprehend, to fasten, and combine.

This, therefore, is no American mechanic, but Mr. Crawford leaning on a cog-wheel in romantic masquerade.

Something of this same weakness appears in all the work of Crawford. He had the gift of execution, a talent like that of the ready writer. His forms are fluent, graceful, well-animated, but lack distinctive quality, and therefore never satisfy the masculine mind.

See, for example, the 'Beethoven.' In an early design for this work, the great master was represented with hands and eyes uplifted in extreme demonstration, as if the poetic impulse were a warm wind descending on the surface of a man, not the most interior conviction; as if the great thought should fall on his hair and eyeballs, and set him in a public spasm.

But no man more than Beethoven ever hated demonstration, or a feeling shallow enough to express itself in gestures and attitudes. He despised as superficial the tokens of far deeper emotion. "The true artist," said he, angrily, to his too susceptible admirer, "has no tears in him, but fire." Beethoven was lonely, severe, concentrated in moments of power, and would have been wickedly caricatured by this poetic windmill, astonishing the vulgar, and whirling in a celestial breeze.

The present statue is much more moderate in action, but lacks the burdened energy of the original, the look of electric and volcanic fires smothered without a vent. It is in character more like Crawford himself, or Schiller—fluent, graceful, and 'deliver,' with more of 'feeling' than of conviction and command.

For Schiller is another type of sentiment in poetry, as Scheffer in painting. Against these, for contrast in their hold on the genuine quality of objects, we set Goëthe and Delaroche.

The Indian of Crawford is an antique Roman with a feather in his hair. The peasant of Schiller is a rhetorical laborer, full as aforesaid of 'all that adorns and embellishes'; but no more like the actual pipe-and-beer rustic, than Swiss Zerlina is like her representative in an operatic May-day festival, where the Alpine rural districts are represented by silk stockings (and plenty of them), velvet boddices (and nothing too much), twenty-five yards of pink-ribbon, a bunch of flowers, and a flat.

Scheffer rises sometimes to moderate vigor of characterization, as in the Satan of his 'Temptation,' which was the incarnation of Wall street and Washington of commercial Christianity; but in general, his figures are weak in all but situation or action. His 'Mignon' is not a passionate, self-contained, bleeding, and bursting heart; but a large-eyed, mild, lithe girl, who—aspires. His people, like those of Schiller, are neither quite one thing or another in themselves and apart from costume and arrangement; but they all—aspire. It becomes an immense refreshment to meet in Art a figure which does not aspire; which goes about its business; which has qualities in, not beyond, itself. Such, for example, are the men and women of Goëthe, who promise nothing celestial, but have irresistible wish and will for the present hour; who are occupied not with vague longing, but with shaping the world to their purposes, and working to a specific end.

In every Art there are innumerable degrees, as well as kinds, of excellence; and we can only say that the painter or poet inclines to sentiment, or that, as compared with another, he is severe in his study, and will perish in the attempt or render the last qualities of every man and thing.

See, for example, how weak is the ship-building of Longfellow beside that of Whittier. One is ship-building in the study, the other in the dock-yard.

> The broad-axe to the knotted oak,
> The mallet to the pin.'

But compare with the average representation of Whittier—who is strangely unequal—that of Whitman, and you see instantly which is thought, and which reality:

> 'The carpenter dresses his plank—the tongue of his fore-plane whistles its wild ascending lisp.'

You may swear to every fact. And only through this energetic grasp on the actual have we any access to the living and companionable quality of things.

[The following is Juliet Beach's answer to her husband's June 2, 1860 usurping review of Whitman's "Leaves of Grass," signed simply "A Woman."]

[For The New York Saturday Press.]

WALT WHITMAN.

Whoever has felt in the past that the originality of American Genius among her poets had never been fully justified, no longer has occasion to think or feel so.

The hitherto unawakened native song has at last burst forth from a large American soul, in just such words as one of her true poets should speak.

All hail then to Walt Whitman, and to this grand result of creative genius, 'Leaves of Grass!'

Nearly two years ago there appeared in the pages of the *Atlantic Monthly* an article on the 'New World and the New Man.' In it we are told that History fully warrants the expectation of a new form of man for this new continent, that 'a rich life, sure in due time of its rich expression, is forming here.' We have a right to say now that this National Genius, with a purely original body and soul, exists for us in this Poet, Walt Whitman. There is vigor, grandeur, and spiritual beauty in this book. There is life in it, true, noble life. No morbid sentiment, but in every line a pulse throbs to which your own heart responds.

Walt ennobles everything he writes about. He makes all created things connecting links in humanity's chain, and draws us with it to the feet of God. To him there is nothing gross, nothing sensual. He feels that the body and soul are both divine; for the same hand that fashioned them together, never intended one to debase the other.

There are very, very few human beings who can truly comprehend the spirit of these Poems. Most people will read some of the words and toss the book from them with scorn and unjust indignation. They cannot fathom to the deep spiritual significance. They see literally only, and blindly, and therefore condemn the whole, never dreaming of the glorious beauty and purity of the spirit which the words cover. Walt scorns the mock delicacy of men and women, and sets at defiance the usual picked words with which most authors clothe truths which might be offensive to their readers. Truth alone, in her own natural dress, whether speaking of body or soul, does he give you. It need not startle or disgust if you do not pervert it. If our sons and daughters were educated so that they could appreciate this book, we should in the next generation have men and women worthy a broad, free country; we should have true, just men to make our laws and to teach us how to keep them.

The law of sympathy, which Leaves of Grass so magnificently describes, allows no paltry or base object in the world. It gives us a new coloring to every earthly scene, and the light of God's love illumines everything that He has ennobled by creation.

O! this book is a well-spring of delight. Walt Whitman does not attempt to explain the great mystery of life, but he makes that mystery so beautiful with universal sympathy and love, that you are satisfied not to penetrate to it. He is happy in himself, satisfied with himself, and so goes on through the world trying to keep alive this harmony with God, through sympathy and love to man. He teaches us to accept life philosophically, and to feel that if we make the best use of mortality, we are then sure of happy immortality, and if the body, and soul with the body, are not abused, we may be at rest about the future.

There is no hypocrisy here, no accepted dogma or doctrine, but faith in the here of God, as well as the hereafter. You feel in these pages that you grasp hold of a deeply religious nature. He says:

> "And I call to mankind, be not curious about God;
> For I who am curious about each, am not curious about God,
> No array of terms can say how much I am at peace about God, and about death."

Again:

> "I find letters from God dropped in the street,
> And every one is signed by God's name;
> And I leave them where they are, for I know that others will punctually come forever and ever."

What can be more beautiful than this?

If all others could find letters from God in the street, those who now see in Walt Whitman nothing but beastliness, would be glad to take him by the hand and pray to be forgiven. Nay, more, they would ask to sit at his feet that they might the better learn to read these heaven-dropped messages.

These bold and truthful pages will inevitably form the standard book of poems in the future of America. They will elevate the flesh and the appetite to their rightful position. We shall understand the use of developing our children. There is at times a grandeur wholly unsurpassed in some of the descriptive portions of the book. The language of passion, the full expression, the simplicity, the earnest soul, so big and real, all will thrill and please you. Some of it may surprise, but if you have a whole, sweet nature, none of it can offend you. How he says things is forgotten in what he says. The spirit of everything that America, if not the whole world, holds, dances and leaps before you in rapid succession, and if it is the spirit of poetry you seek, more than the material, here you are fully satisfied. Of course there will be an outcry among the critics; the principle and beauty of this book will be fathomless to them. Many will throw balls of fire at the author, but happily for himself and friends, he is not formed of combustible 'stuff,' and will neither ignite nor get scorched. Let me again repeat to him Wasson's words. He is worthy then, for he is indeed the new poet, if not the 'new man of the new world.' Welcome to great tasks, to great toils, to mighty disciplines, to victories that shall not be too cheaply purchased. To defeats that shall be better than victories, we give the joy of new powers, new work, unprecedented futures.

Rest assured, Leaves of Grass will have many lovers. This new, wild strain, grand and lofty, sweet and harmonious, then again rash and tumultuous at times, leaves you in doubt whether you are reading prose or verse. It is all good, the sudden transition, the obscure connection, the grand sublimity and boldness, but better far the spirit of the writer, so raised beyond everything else, sometimes even beyond himself, grasping at ideas too great for words. God bless him. I know that through 'Leaves of Grass,' Walt Whitman on earth is immortal as well as beyond it.

A WOMAN.

NEW YORK JUNE 30, 1860

[From the 'New York Times,' June 27.]

THE ERRAND-BEARERS.

16th 6th Month, Year 84 Of The States.

1. Over sea, hither from Niphon,
Courteous, the Princes of Asia, swart-cheek'd princes,
First-comers, guests, two-sworded princes,
Lesson-giving princes, leaning back in their open barouches, bare-headed, impassive,
This day they ride through Manhattan.

2. Libertad!
I do not know whether others behold what I behold pass, in the procession, along with the Princes of Asia, the errand-bearers,
Bringing up the rear, hovering above, around, or in the ranks marching;
But I will sing you a song of what I behold, Libertad.

3. When million-footed Manhattan, unpent, descends to its pavements,
When the thunder-cracking guns arouse me with the proud roar I love,
When the round-mouth'd guns, out of the smoke and smell I love, spit their salutes,
When the fire-flashing guns have fully alerted me —When heaven-clouds canopy my city with a delicate thin haze,
When, gorgeous, the countless straight stems, the forests at the wharves, thicken with colors,
When every ship is richly drest, and carrying her flag at the peak,
When pennants trail, and street-festoons hang from the windows,
When Broadway is entirely given up to foot-passengers and foot-standers—When the mass is densest,
When the facades of the houses are alive with people—When eyes gaze, riveted, tens of thousand at a time,
When the guests, Asiatic, from the islands, advance—When the pageant moves forward, visible,
When the summons is made—When the answer that waited thousands of years, answers,
I too, arising, answering, descend to the pavements, merge with the crowd, and gaze with them.

4. Superb-faced Manhattan,
Comrade Americanos—to us, then, at last, the Orient comes.

5. To us, my city,
Where our tall-topt marble and iron beauties range on opposite sides—to walk in the space between,
To-day our Antipodes comes.

6. The Originatress comes,
The land of Paradise—land of the Caucasus—the nest of birth,
The nest of languages, the bequeather of poems—The race of eld,
Florid with blood, pensive, rapt with musings, hot with passion,
Sultry with perfume, with ample and flowing garments,
With sunburnt visage, with intense soul and glittering eyes,
The race of Brahma comes.

7. See, my cantabile! these, and more, are flashing to us from the procession;
As it moves, changing, a kaleidoscope divine it moves, changing, before us.

8. Not the errand-bearing princes,
Not the tann'd Japanee only—not China only, nor the Mongol only,
Lithe and silent, the Hindoo appears—the whole continent appears—the Past, the dead,
The murky night-morning of wonder and fable, inscrutable,
The enveloped mysteries, the old and unknown hive-bees,
The North—the sweltering South—Assyria—the Hebrews—the ancient of ancients,
Vast desolated cities—the gliding Present—All of these, and more, are in the pageant-procession.

9. Geography, the world, is in it.
The Great Sea, the brood of islands, Polynesia,
The coast beyond—the coast you, henceforth, are facing—you, Libertad! from your Western golden shores,
The countries there, with their populations—the millions en-masse—are curiously here,
The multitudes are all here—they show visibly enough to my eyes,
The swarming market-places—the temples, with idols ranged along the sides, or at the end—bronze, brahmin, and lama, also,
The mandarin, farmer, merchant, mechanic, and fisherman, also,
The singing-girl and the dancing-girl—the ecstatic person, absorbed,
The interminable unpitied hordes of toilsome persons—the divine Buddha,
The secluded Emperors—Confucius himself—the great poets and heroes—the warriors, the castes, all,
Trooping up, crowding from all directions—from the Altay-mountains,
From Thibet—from the four winding and far-flowing rivers of China,
From the Southern peninsulas, and the demi-continental islands—from Malaysia,
These, and whatever belongs to them, palpable, show forth to me, and are seized by me,
And I am seized by them, and friendlily held by them,
Till, as here, them all I chant, Libertad! for themselves and for you.

10. I too, raising my voice, bear an errand,
I chant the World on my Western Sea,
I chant, copious, the islands beyond, thick as stars in the sky,
I chant the new empire, grander than any before —As in a vision, it comes to me;
I chant America, the Mistress—I chant a greater supremacy,
I chant, projected, a thousand blooming cities yet, in time, on those groups of sea-islands,
I chant my sailships and steamships threading the archipelagoes,
I chant my stars and stripes fluttering in the wind,
I chant commerce opening, the sleep of ages having done its work—races, reborn, refreshed,
Lives, works resumed—the object I know not—but the old, the Asiatic, resumed, as it must be,
Commencing from this day, surrounded by the world.

11. And you, Libertad of the world!
You shall sit in the middle, thousands of years,
As to-day, from one side, the Princes of Asia come to you,
As to-morrow, from the other side, the Queen of England sends her eldest son to you.

12. The sign is reversing, the orb is enclosed,
The ring is circled, the journey is done,
The box-lid is but perceptibly opened—nevertheless the perfume pours copiously out of the whole box.

13. Young Libertad!
With the venerable Asia, the all-mother,
Be considerate with her, now and ever, hot Libertad—for you are all,
Bend your proud neck to the long-off mother, now sending messages over the archipelagoes to you, young Libertad ;
Were the children straying Westward so long? So wide the tramping?
Were the precedent dim ages debouching Westward from Paradise so long?
Were the centuries steadily footing it that way, all the while, unknown, for you, for reasons?
They are justified—they are accomplished—They shall now be turned the other way also, to travel toward you thence,
They shall now also march obediently Eastward, for your sake, Libertad.

Walt Whitman.

BOOKS, ETC.

" These Bold And Truthful Pages Will Inevitably Form The Standard Book Of Poems In The Future Of America."—A Woman.

" There Are Two Thousand Roses To A Drachm Of Otto. There Are Untold Thousands Of Poems In This Duodecimo."—H. P. L., Philadelphia.

Boston Electrotype Edition of

LEAVES OF GRASS,

Including all of Walt Whitman's former pieces, with many new ones—Now Ready.

CONTENTS:

Proto-Leaf.
Walt Whitman.
CHANTS DEMOCRATIC and Native American.
LEAVES OF GRASS.
Salut au Monde.
Poem of Joys.
A Word out of the Sea.
A Leaf of Faces.
Europe, the 72d and 73d Years T. S.
ENFANS d'ADAM.
Poem of The Road.
To the Sayers of Words.
A Boston Ballad, the 78th Year T. S.
CALAMUS.
Crossing Brooklyn Ferry.
Longings for Home.
MESSENGER LEAVES:
(To You, Whoever You Are.
To a Foiled Revolter or Revoltress.
To Him that was Crucified.
To One Shortly To Die.
To a Common Prostitute.
To Rich Givers.
To a Pupil.
To The States, to Identify the 16th, 17th, or 18th Presidentiad.
To a Cantatrice.
Walt Whitman's Caution.
To a President.
To Other Lands.
To Old Age.
To You)
Mannahatta.
France, the 18th Year T. S.
Thoughts.
Unnamed Lands.
Kosmos.
A Hand Mirror.
Beginners....Tests.
Savantism....Perfections.
Says....Debris.
Sleep-Chasings.
Burial.
To My Soul.
So Long.

Making 456 pages, 12mo, first quality paper and print, with portrait of the Poet, from a painting by Charles Hine, of New York. A very beautiful and richly bound book. **Price $1 25**. No handsomer or more substantial volume, for the price, has ever issued from the Press, here or in Europe.

From an article in the New York Illustrated News, by the *Editor*, Geo. S. Phillips ("*January Searle* "):

Walt Whitman's new volume of poems, which he very quaintly calls "Leaves of Grass," has come to hand. We have looked for it with more than ordinary interest, as men look for good tidings from a far country. For this man, we know, has a message, no matter how uncouth the form of it, to deliver to us, and to this generation.

AN AUTHENTIC MESSAGE!

which he has not learned in any school, at second-hand, or gathered from books—or torn from parchment records, long since dead in monastic graves—but

ALIVE WITH GOD AND THE GREAT FIERY HEART OF THE UNIVERSE TO-DAY, FULL OF WILD ELOQUENCE, AND OF ALL MANNER OF INTELLECTUAL AND SPIR ITUAL MAGNETISMS.

It is now some five years ago, since this author—this Manhattan poet, who gives us so many antique and modern thoughts, so many new, strange, and startling images, and things suggestive of an imagery, which has no material archetype—cast his first grass leaves upon the waters, hoping, as the prophecy declares of all vital things, that he should find them again—and that the world should find them—after many days. We, for one, carefully reading them at the time, had no manner of doubt nor shadow of a misgiving that such in their case would be the issue. And here, after so long a lapse of time,—hundreds and thousands of highly bepraised books, in the meanwhile, having passed through the fires to Molech, and having been there consumed in the Gehenna Hell which is the just doom—place of rubbish—hundreds and thousands more still following them day by day, and will still continue to follow them until men cease to be fools—

HERE WE SAY IS THIS BOOK OF GRASS LEAVES, AS FRESH AS EVER, AS REDOLENT AS EVER OF MAY FLOWERS, AND MEADOW BLOOM, AND THE AROMA OF WOODS AND PRAIRIES.

We find many things new and old in this book; the old, welcome as the familiar faces of the old Gods to the first lovers and worshippers of the Gods—the new, bright with a radiance which is all their own, and welcome also for their surpassing beauty, and the new life which they bring. For these poems of Walt Whitman are no silly word-catching—no mere musical claptrap done into dainty feet with measured and mathematical precision—but

THEY ARE THE VERY LIFE OF THE MAN,

fragments, both of his body and soul, with a genuine, creative power in them big enough to create a soul under the ribs of death himself.

THE STRONGEST MAN MAY REFRESH HIMSELF AT THE FOUNTAINS OF THIS SHAGGY ABORIGINAL GIANT WHO SITS ON THE THRESHOLD OF NATURE'S ARCANE —HIS HANDS FULL OF SUNBEAMS; HIS MOUTH MUSICAL WITH SO MANY SWEET LAUGHTERS; HIS WHOLE FACE ILLUMINATED WITH THE WISE AND BENEFICENT MIRTH OF THE ARCANE GODS.

And if any one be inclined to call this rhapsody, let him prove his right to speak by producing his letters of competency. To all cavillers, questioners, and doubters—to all flippant young gentlemen of the French school, who do the brilliant for Bohemian clubs and Bohemian newspapers—to all drawingroom Fire-flies, and Will-o'- the-Wisps in general, who have so much to say and say nothing, we will offer them this admonishment: Hold your peace. This man is not for you, nor such as you. He speaks to men, not to conceited apes, nor to anything of the breed of apes. But if a brave, truthful reader, who is not afraid of hearing much that is too Hebraic to be polite, which any vulgar min can make vulgar, and obscene even, but which from the author's stand-point is by no means vulgar, but as sacred as the soul itself—if, we say, he be not afraid of such sentences as these, but will bear with them, and get their value out of them, whatever it may prove to be to him, for the sake of other and infinitely better, purer, wiser matters which he will assuredly find in these poems, we can commend and authorize him to address himself straightway to the work.

FOR THE FIRST TIME IN AMERICAN HISTORY A NA TIVE PORT SINGS TO US OF AMERICA.

Your ——'s, and ——'s, and ——'s–your male-men writers of all sorts, and your female-women writers of all sorts, may, if they please, and as they please, ignore America and its grand people and institutions, the struggles, battles, and conquests, the hopes, and loves, and hates, and all the fiery passions of the people; may write themselves unbelievers in the destiny of American civilization, atheists to their country, and go along to their lives' end, singing their dead songs about dead Europe, and its stupid monks and priests, its chivalry, and its thing-a-my-bobs called kings—but not so this new comer, and great believer,

THIS DEVOUT AND PROPHETIC SON OF AMERICA, BORN OF THE PEOPLE AND THE SOIL.

For him, to-day is as great as any yesterday; as full, too, of romance and poetry; for he brings with him the eyes to see and the ears to hear, and the words to speak, all the things which he thinketh. God has so gifted this new man, and has so educated him with faith in the present and the actual, in the future and the inevitable.

He sees nothing mean and low, nothing common anywhere around him. He is entranced by the miracle of existence, and wonder worlds open beneath him and around him wherever he walks, whatever he touches.

ALL MATERIAL THINGS ARE SUSPENDED UPON A SCAFFOLDING OF IMPALPABLE THOUGHT A LIVING SCAFFOLDING OF THOUGHT WHICH, INDEED, IS THE ONLY REALITY; THE MATERIAL, BEING A PHANTASM WHICH IT PROJECTS,

and to which it gives shape and form, motive and activity. This orientalism of vision, however, so far from being offensive, or even obtrusive, is the great underlying charm of the book, and its chief fascination, by which he holds the right reader with a magnetism as strong as the poles. He is the most oriental and the most American of Americans. A strong, practical common sense runs through all his sentences; and he everywhere calls things by their right names, and uses no rosewater. You shall laugh and cry with him—but no man can laugh at him—even in his bluntest, rudest, and most informal speech. We can see that whatsoever appertains to the honor, interest, learning, literature, culture, manners, laws, and government of America, is very dear to him; dearer than all the world beside; and we love him for his love of the great and magnificent land. Legislators and literats, and office-seekers, and brilliant lager-bier drinkers, and grog-drinkers, and the mob who hate law and government, may forget that they are Americans—may defame and traduce their country, sell its honor for a mess of pottage, or try to make it a French stew by inoculating us with French notions, French books, and French morals and habits—but not so, Whitman!

TRUE AS THE NEEDLE TO THE NORTH IS HE TRUE TO HIS COUNTRY, TO THE BRAVE MOTHER LANGUAGE, AND TO THE AMERICAN PEOPLE.

We are well aware, and so doubtless is he, that from the very structure and form of his verse, he is more open to parody and burlesque than any living writer. Smart young gentlemen, of the ginger-beer sort, have tried their hands with immense success at this work—hitting, as usual, the form, and, as usual, missing the spirit, the genius, the fine aroma of thought which breathe through the original.

People call Whitman an egotist—and he is no doubt an egotist of the most imperial sort. But he often speaks in his own name, when he represents the "Cosmos," and all nature and humanity. The reader must not always confound his personal pronouns with the poet's license of universality. He often speaks for the race when he appears to be speaking for himself. There can be no question, however, that

LEAVES OF GRASS ARE, ON THE WHOLE, AS GENUINE A PIECE OF AUTOBIOGRAPHY AS THAT OF AUGUSTINE, OR GIBBON, OR THE CONFESSIONS OF ROUSSEAU.

And for the claims of this book to be called a book of poems, we will venture to say that

There is more True Poetry in it than would float any dozen modern volumes

which the critics dignify with the name of poetry. We have already written so much that we can make no quotations here; but we look in vain out of these pages for any other voice which speaks for America—and speaks for her with equal power.

Readers! we respectfully, earnestly ask you to examine these strong and electric Poems, for yourselves—not flippantly or hastily, for they cannot be reached in that way. Their entire novelty and tremendous intensity will amaze you, and perhaps baffle you, at first;—but a little perusal and study, and *you will be surely, richly repaid.* They are not a mere *book*, like anything previously known, but

FULL OF HUMANITY'S LIFE-BLOOD AND MAGNETISM,

like the close contact of a real face and eyes, the ring of a determined voice, and the grasp of a powerful and sinewed hand.

Are you going into the country? *This*, out of all the countless volumes in the stores, is the one to take with you, and con over in the fields, in the shade of the woods, or on the mountains, or by the sea-shore.

Book-dealers! this is no lumbering stock, that, when you invest in it, will remain on your shelves. You can depend on a quick sale for every copy.

Send for a Circular, and also for "Imprints," as below.

A GOOD, SMALL BOOK GIVEN AWAY.

"Leaves of Grass Imprints," a handsome little 64 page volume, in reference to the above Poems, collecting American and European criticisms on the First (1855) and the Second (1857) Issues of Walt Whitman's "Leaves." Very instructive, curious, serious, and amusing. Send us your address, anywhere in the United States, and we will forward you these "Imprints," free and prepaid.

THE POEMS SENT BY MAIL.

We send the "LEAVES OF GRASS," complete, in elegant binding, to any address in the United States, on receipt of price as above ($1 25), with 29 cents for postage, which has to be prepaid.

THAYER & ELDRIDGE, PUBLISHERS,

114 and 116 Washington Street, Boston, Mass.

[For The New York Saturday Press.]

DELAVIGNE'S POEMS.

Some years ago, I picked up at a French bookstore a stray volume of poems by Casimir Delavigne. Having never met with any of them before, nor heard of the author except perchance by name, I was delighted to find that the little paper-bound pocket volume (such an one as only a French Press can issue), contained some rare poetry. Whether Delavigne has gone out of date, or whether the present writer is not au courant in modern French Literature, is immaterial, but since that time, though I have heard much of other French poets, the name of Casimir Delavigne has never so much as crossed my vision.

Delavigne was a member of the French Academy, and wrote several popular dramatic works besides this little volume, which is composed partly of political poems, styled 'Les Messeniennes '—the Misfortunes (of his country), and the rest of ballads and verses upon miscellaneous subjects. He was born at Havre in 1793, and wrote during the stirring political and literary epoch which marked the first quarter of this century. His patriotic odes are filled with true poetic fire; they are of the stuff that inflames the Parisian populace to the point that finds vent only in barricades and musketry. As we read them, even in the quiet study, we can fancy their effect upon the excitable Gallic nature when sung in grand chorus on the Boulevards. Many Americans, doubtless, are familiar with his ode, 'La Parisienne.'

"People of France! nation of braves,
Liberty opens her arms;
Tyrants have said: ye are our slaves!
We have replied: soldiers we are!
Sudden, Paris in memory
Has recalled her cry of glory:
'En avant, marchons
Contre leur canons !
A travers le fer, le feu des batallions,
Courons à la victoire?'"

No English translation, feeble or otherwise, can do justice to the martial ring of this chorus. It has the tramp of hosts in its lines, and the swell of irresistible triumph in the sonorous amplitude of its vowels. Such a chorus would serve to fire much duller verses than preface the refrain. There is no flagging though, from the high patriotic tone with which it opens, down to the last verse which records the funeral of the departed braves.

"O temple of mourning and glory!
Pantheon receive their memory!
Bear them on, march on
With heads bowed down.
Be ye immortal, ye whom we mourn
Martyrs of victory!"

Aside from the patriotic line, we find a remarkable versatility of genius in the variety both of subject and style. There is a 'Chanson Bachique' that would be apt to empty the wine-flask as quickly as 'La Parisienne' the powder-flask.

"Yes, man has drunk throughout all time,
Throughout all time man still must drink.
Chinese, Greeks and Romans (to rhyme)
All have drunk, all glory in it.
By a thousand events diverse,
As ordered by the fate supreme,
All has changed in the universe,
But man has always drunk the same

. . . .

Drink then, drink, for cometh the day
When nought to drink will be our way."

Delavigne's ballads are probably the finest examples of his merit as a poet. There is a passionate force about them truly dramatic. 'The Soul from Purgatory,' a remonstrance addressed by a deceived fair-one to her lover still on earth, is perhaps a little sentimental, but withal so replete with tender feeling, that one pardons the stretch of imagination necessary for the Protestant mind to compass the idea:

"My loved one, midst my grief,
I came from the vale of tears
To beg of you your prayers;
You told me, bending o'er me:
'While I live, I'll pray for thee.'
Such were your last words.
Alas! alas! Since I quitted your embrace
Never have I heard your prayers.
Alas! alas!
I list, but hear no prayers."

Proceeding, then, to describe their last tender interview upon earth, and to rehearse the vows so readily made, only to be broken at her departure from the scene of life—for death surprised her in his arms 'still trembling under his kisses'—she beseeches him to bear her back where she may quaff the dew, and says:

"What torments, friend, our sweet delights
Have cost me here below,—
Here, in this vale of tears!
Nor eve' nor morn comes ever here,
And the needle turns forever, here,
Round an hourless dial, forever.
Alas! alas!
For you, friend, with upturned face,
I wait in this vale of tears.
Alas! alas!
I wait, but hear no prayers."

And closes, after referring to the new lover that has taken her place in his affections:

"Think, sometimes, in her embrace,
Of the abyss God doth prepare.
Alas! alas!
I descend, follow me not there."

To my mind, the finest thing in this book is the poem written at Rome, entitled 'The Toilet of Constance.' I regret my inability to translate, even afar off, this powerful poem in its completeness. It is tragic, yet relieved by a gentle play of feminine individuality. Constance is dressing, with the assistance of her maid, for a ball at the hotel of the French Ambassador. She is impatient with the awkardness of her servant. The poem opens with the following lines, which, slightly varied, constitute the refrain:

"Quick, Anna! quick, a mirror !
Quicker, Anna—the hours advance,
And I go to the ball this eve,
At the Ambassador's of France."

She admires the sparkling jewels on her brow; she wonders, in ardent Southern strains, whether her lover will be there; she remembers, withal, that to-morrow she must go to the Confessional. How can she tell the good father all? She describes to the open-eared maid the glories of the ball-room. Will one night suffice to taste the countless pleasures of the scene? Haste then, Anna, or she will be too late, and Laura will lead in the dance. She hears her uncle call from the coach,— 'In one instant, Uncle, I am with you; quick, Anna, the last touches; my bouquet at the waist; a ball, a ball, to-night I go to a ball! Pardon, Anna, if I quitted my place, but I thought I heard the signal—already I led in the dance.'

"Quick! one glance at the mirror,
The last! I have the assurance
This night I shall be adored
At the Ambassador's of France.
Near the hearth, Constance stands in glad delight;
God! on her robe there lights a burning spark.
Fire! fire! run. . . . When the world looks bright
To lose all thus! What, die? so beautiful!
The horrible flame clasps in dead embrace
Her arms, her breast! wraps all in one fierce gleam,
And pitiless devours her lovely grace,
Her eighteen years, alas! and her sweet dream!
Adieu ball, pleasure, conquests!
They called her: 'Poor Constance ;' . . .
And they danced until the morn,
At the Ambassador's of France."

Imperfectly as I have succeeded in rendering the dramatic power of the original, this at least is noticeable—the force of the climax and the consummate art of the last verse:

"On se dit! Pauvre Constance !' . . .
Et l'on dansa jusque 'au jour
Chez l'Ambassadeur de France."

Perishes youth, beauty, and loveliness, and still the world wags on with its dance and song, and only one sigh for the victim. It is easy to exalt your climax into bombast—it is only the true artist that dares trust to simplicity.

As I glance over this volume, I regret none of our graceful translators have been induced to make its beauties familiar to the American public. I think their merit is essentially cosmopolitan like all true works of art. Following the philosophical lead of the 'Lake School,' our modern poets of the English tongue have lost sight of the original title of their art to nobility. Delavigne's verses seem to sing themselves, to call naturally for music. This must have been the case originally with every nation's poetry, and we need pre-Raphaelites in this art as well as in painting, to bring back to view the lost truths which lie at the basis of good verse. The great French nation are the only song-makers now extant. Great in science, in artistic culture, in mechanical skill, their poets alone write songs that live in the memory of the populace, and find vent on all public occasions. perhaps more clearly expressing the musical trait of Delavigne's verse than previous quotations, I have ventured to render complete, though somewhat freely, the subjoined barcarôle, dated at Venice:

The Gondolier.
"Take me, my brave gondolier,
To the Rialto," said she,
"This necklace I hold so dear
Shall be thy generous fee."
He laughs, and leans on his oar:
"'Tis too little, on my honor,
You to take in my gondola;
No, Gianetta, I wish more."

"Hold, I know a lamento;
I'll sing it thee," said she,
"As we near the Rialto,
Sailing over the sea."
He laughs, and leans on his oar:
"What, for a barcarôle,
You to enter my gondola ?
No, Gianetta, I wish more."

In her hand her rosary:
"Look! Do you wish it?" said she,
"The Bishop has blessed its beads
And the golden cross, d'ye see?"
He laughs, and leans on his oar:
"What! for that pious gewgaw,
You to enter my gondola ?
No, Gianetta, I wish more."

On the canal, presently,
I see him row to meet her,
Smiling, too, how pleasantly!
What gave the belle Gianetta?
She steps on board, confused sore,
While true to his promise dear,
Pulls away the gondolier,
And the maid is refused no more.

Robinson.

THE BIOGRAPHICAL SHOWMAN.

To turn an honest penny by selling wooden nutmegs is, in the way of trade, considered rather a proof of natural smartness.

The persons who devote their lives to such ennobling pursuits, are not however considered ornaments to the mercantile profession.

When these same qualities are the only stock in trade of a man who professes to be a man of letters, he should meet with the contempt he would deserve in any other walk in life.

If the man who calls himself self-made, has, with his other virtues, failed to gain modesty and reticence, he may be treated with a show of respect by the people who eat his dinners and borrow his money, but he has failed to acquire the first characteristic of a gentleman.

It is, perhaps, a weak vanity which leads a self-made man to display the result of his labors, and charity makes us as lenient to his weakness as we are to a young mother's obtrusive display of her first-born.

But for the Biographical Showman there is no such excuse.

He exhibits his characters as Barnum did the Woolly Horse.

He tries to play upon the feelings and sympathies of the public, as that prince of his mean tribe did with the nurse of Washington; or he enlarges upon the pretended virtues of his victim as the great Barnum did upon those of the great Lind, and reaps his greater or less reward of pence.

When the display is undertaken for the mutual profit of the Showman and his subject, the public are not called upon to do much more than take no notice of either of them. But when the Showman, in his desire for an object of attraction, presumes to outrage all our instinctive respect for the privacy of domestic life and the right we each of us claim to keep our personal secrets to ourselves, by fastening upon the character of any man who is sufficiently distinguished to serve his purpose, he should be treated as we would treat any intrusive, vulgar bore.

It is a dreadful thing for a wit to hear his jokes repeated by an enthusiastic but stupid admirer.

It is more annoying to hear our good deeds praised by an injudicious and senseless friend.

It is the worst of all to find ourselves made the cat's-paw of a vulgar-minded trickster in his attempts to attract attention to himself.

But it must be a sadder fate than all these to have one's life written by a man who boldly and unblushingly calls himself 'Author of The Poor Boy and Merchant Prince; The Poor Girl and True Woman; From Poorhouse to Pulpit,' etc., etc. And yet this sad fate has befallen a man who is Ex-Speaker of the House, Governor of Massachusetts, and, despite these peccadiloes, a respectable man.

As a politician we do not pity him. For politicians never deserve pity.

But, as a sensitive and modest man we pity him, as we do a friend who has, by no fault of his own, caught a grievous attack of the mumps, and cannot help appearing ridiculous without exciting any sympathy.

It is a fearful thought that the Biographical Showman is about in the world, and that any day he may fasten upon any one of us, and make us ridiculous despite ourselves.

Is the reward of virtue fallen so low?

Must a man remain carefully obscure for fear of falling into the hands of some Thayer, some Everett, some Hillard, or some Parker?

Or is it a fact, as these names would seem to suggest, that the Biographical Showman is necessarily a Yankee? That he is produced only in the Athens of America?

Perhaps this is so. At least let us hope that it is so, and breathe freely until he appears elsewhere.

Let us be satisfied with presenting Whittington to our children as the example of what industry, pushing, and early rising, can do for youth; and remain contented if they do not become rich, or Senators, or speciously learned, or notorious, provided they remain honest, learn to respect themselves, and to shun publicity.

TOMMY.

Several of the daily papers have made themselves very ridiculous this last week in consequence of fancying that it would be a good thing for them to take high moral grounds on the subject of 'Tommy.' The amount of virtue suddenly exhibited on the occasion, by writers who were never suspected of such a thing before, must have astonished even the frequenters of the Fulton Street Daily Prayer Meeting. Tommy has thus been made as useful as if he were a returned Japanese Missionary.

The quantity of moral indignation he has called forth against the beautiful and unsuspecting young ladies of New York, all because they found him handsomer and consequently more attractive than the old smoke-dried princes in whose train he came, is perfectly wonderful.

If he should remain here a week longer, and continue to make himself agreeable, there is no telling what might happen.

All virtue would evidently be at an end.

There is in fact such a scarcity of good-looking men in New York, if the papers aforesaid may be trusted, that Tommy would have it all his own way.

Every young lady in the city would at once give her lover, if she had one, the mitten, and take incontinently to sending in sealed proposals to Tommy.

It would seem indeed, that he has received some cords of such proposals already, and that owing to his limited acquaintance with our language or our diplomacy, he has had to refer them all to a commission of superannuated naval officers, who are in such a state of mind about it, that having doubtless first consulted the President, they have felt it their duty to return them all to the anxious parents of the fair writers!

The high state of civilization which speculations like these indicate in this proud metropolis, is calculated to fill the mind of the stranger with admiration and awe.

How fortunate we are in having a press that is thus watchful over the public morals, ready at a moment's warning to sound the alarm and protect our innocent but frail wives, sisters, and sweethearts, from the allurements and assaults of swarthy but seductive invaders! But notwithstanding all this vigilance on the part of the press,—notwithstanding even the high moral example set by all and several of its members—we fear there will be no joy in any family in the city, no confidence in the breast of father, mother, lover, or husband, until Tommy shall have again betaken himself to the High Seas, and turned his young and beautiful face toward his Native Land.

Peace go with him!

TOM TAYLOR AND HUME THE SPIRITUALIST.

Tom Taylor writes to the Manchester *Guardian*, of the feats performed by Hume, the distinguished Spiritualist. He says: "It is quite certain that in one West End drawing-room, at least, Mr. Hume has suddenly announced that he was being lifted from the ground. That he has been *seen*—no—that is the awkward point about it—not *seen* exactly, for the lights are always put out before these risings take place; but that he has been heard out of the darkness informing the awe-stricken circle of believers round the table that he was rising to the ceiling, and that he has occasionally taken a pencil up with him, and written on the ceiling the name of the incredulous master of the house, as a sign to turn him from the error of his ways—that against the dim light of the window, what appeared the legs and feet of the adept, have been seen to float past in a horizontal position; that Mr. Hume's, or Home's, feet have been felt on the shoulders of persons sitting at the table, or on the backs of their chairs; and that he has been rather felt than seen by some specially favored ones to come down on the table in a kneeling position, in his descents—according to his own account—from his aerial suspension. But the real marvel in the matter is, that after London has seen Houdin, and Dodler, and Mr. Anderson, and Bosco, there should still be crowds of spectators, and those educated persons, who, seeing a rival of those gentlemen, whose mode of performance they are unable to explain, should at once be content to resort to the performer's own explanation—spiritual or supernatural agency,—and that too, when the first step in the exhibition is putting out the candles. If Mr. Home would only fly by daylight—or even candlelight!"

[For The New York Saturday Press.]

THE FAIRIES.

O merry are we Fairy Folks,
The tiniest of races!
Who only on bright Summer nights
Presume to show our faces;
Beneath the shade of elm or oak,
Or in the starlit spaces,
We revel till the birds awake,
Then hide in shady places!

O there beneath the winking stars
We start the queerest fancies!
Make mimic warfare on the sward,
Equip with bulrush lances;
With mushroom shields and acorn casques,
We charge for bloodless chances,
And celebrate the victories
With antic rites and dances!

O ho! you ought to see us troop
About the fields together!
With lady-slippers on our feet,
And plumes of scarlet feather;
Drinking the dewdrops from the flowers
Upon the midnight heather,
Or hiding under melon-leaves
From fear of thunder-weather!

Sometimes within a lily large—
Some couch of gold and azure,
What time the bee's low lullaby
Drones in a drowsy measure,
We let ourselves be rocked to sleep
By zephyrs at their leisure,
And while away the golden day
In dreams of Fairy pleasure!

Or else to crystal brooks that cool
Some sweet secluded valley,
At blowing of the Elfin horn
How merrily we rally!
There where the silver cateracts
Fall soft and musically,
About the mossy-margined pools
We frolic and we dally.

O know ye not the Little Folks
So beautiful and wary,
Who live in quiet woods and glens
And lead a life so merry?
Who only deign to show themselves
When Summer nights are starry;
O know ye not the Little Folks,
The tiny tribes of Faery?

H. S. Cornwell.

The Bohemian as a Gentleman.

It is principally as a Gentleman that the Bohemian is known and recognized by the world, for he is in all places, under all circumstance, and at all times, the Gentleman par excellence.

The world's Gentlemen meet and recognize their equality upon the broad ground of their mutual Bohemianism, whether in New York or Japan.

They need none of the conventions of rank, or dress, to certify their respective claims.

The Bohemian puts forward no claims.

He has never to trouble himself about his rights, or his dignity, or the thousand-and-one little matters which disturb the little minds of Mrs. Grundy's devotees.

The Bohemian is never afraid that society will not treat him with due consideration.

He will as certainly obtain all that belongs to him, as the Spring will bring its flowers, and the Autumn its harvests. And it is as hopeless for society to try and withhold it from him, as it would be for the world to keep back from the coming Summer its glowing suns, and the deep quiet of its noonday heats.

The Bohemian is the best Gentleman in the world.

He is the best result of the manly thought, the womanly tenderness, the suffering and the joy, the despair and the strength, that go to make up what we call human life.

He is the best product of the creative energy of nature, and is as lavishly careless of his claims to respect and admiration as nature is.

The foundation of the gentlemanly character is justice, and the Bohemian is always generously just.

He assumes no right which he does not accord.

He cannot be rude or conventional in the measure of his behavior to others, because he cannot be unjust to himself.

No snob can ever be a Gentleman, much less can he be a Bohemian.

The snob lives in the little world of fashion, rank, convention, and is always ill-bred, because his manners are the embodiment of his selfishness.

The Bohemian disregards all fashion, rank, and convention, and meets men upon the plain of manhood, truth, and sincerity, which lie behind all artificial distinctions, and are the basis of all that is enduring and invigorating in life.

The Bohemian is therefore always well-bred, and always a Gentleman, because he is always generous.

The Bohemian is always brave, but never fool-hardy. He values his body as he does his honor, and respects himself too much to place either of them carelessly in danger.

He is never rudely aggressive, and knows how to retreat promptly.

It is to his noblest self that he looks for approval, and he cares not for the opinion of fools.

He has as little fear of death as he has of life. He accepts either with cheerful serenity, and by his nobleness of soul makes both glorious.

The delight and honor with which the world receives the Bohemian, is like the respect society always pays to the true Gentleman.

It takes him upon his own terms.

It looks with complacency upon his disregard of its most cherished conventions.

It recognizes his right to be a law unto himself.

It only requires that he should be honest and sincere.

The true Gentleman, like the Bohemian, can trust himself everywhere and among all classes. He carries his claims to respect, and his defence from insult, in his look and carriage. He is never thrown off his balance or taken by surprise, but is always collected, and has his wits about him.

Death is not the worst thing which can happen to him, and how then can he be discomposed by threats or danger?

The true Gentleman, as the true Bohemian, is never afraid of being mistaken.

He is not afraid to wear a white cravat because he may be taken for a servant.

He may do a servant's work, and yet be none the less a Gentleman or a Bohemian.

Whatever he does he does so perfectly and so well, that he dignifies all occupations, and makes it plain that the useless man is he who founds his claims to respect upon his waste of the possibilities of life.

The true Gentleman is Bohemian because he treats no man with contempt, and because he is never intrusive.

To be honest and brave, generous and just, to be charitable and courteous, in a word, to be human in the fullest and largest meaning of that word, is to be a Gentleman, and is to be so far a Bohemian.

D. D.

[For The New York Saturday Press.]

L'INCONSTANT.

I.

O! fetter not the wild bird's wing;
Believe me, love, he will not sing,
In gilded cage, the thrilling song
Thou'st loved so well, and heard so long,
For it was caught from woods and groves,
A thousand flowers, a thousand loves.

II.

Ah! trust me, dear, thoud'st weary soon
If once the bird were all thine own.
If thou would'st have him ever dear,
His strains must rarely charm thine ear,
Or thou must feel at least that he
Has but to spread his wings and flee!

III.

Nay, hear me, dearest, but a word:
Young love is like the forest-bird,—
Fetter his free and careless wing,
He droops a tame and sickly thing;
But should he roam awhile, if free,
Trust me, he will come back to thee.

LIZZIE PETIT.

NEW YORK JULY 7, 1860

The Bohemian in Government.

'Read his history in a nation's eyes.'

The Bohemian is naturally a Ruler—naturally a Leader.

Or perhaps it would be better to say that mankind naturally subject themselves to him, and instinctively follow his lead.

Among the various classes of policemen—particularly the class which call themselves Kings by the Grace of God, or Presidents by the vote of the majority—the rank and dignity of the Bohemian are often denied and treated with mistaken contempt.

View of Niblo's Garden during Japanese Ball, July 1860 from Frank Leslie's Illustrated.

For as in the largest sense it requires genius to fully comprehend genius, so it is only a Bohemian who can fully appreciate Bohemianism.

But such denial and contempt cannot injure or diminish the Bohemian's majesty or rule.

Nature has given him his claim to them.

He needs no adventitious aids from pomp, etiquette, or enforced obedience, to have his claims to respect and honor allowed.

He is as majestic as nature, and as persistent as life.

His body can be destroyed, but how can the truth that is in him be attacked?

His kingdom is in the world of thought. He rules the best men of his time, by their manly sympathy with his freedom of truth and his greatness of soul.

Such dominion is not dependent upon the trivial accidents of birth or time.

His subjects do not cease their allegiance with the stoppage of his life.

His memory lies embalmed in the world's Pantheon; and all deeds of courage and generosity among the living generation, are proofs of its loyalty to his rule and subjection to his guidance.

What need has he of the insignia of power whom the best men of the world delight to honor?

Can the strength of Plutarch's heroes ever grow decrepid, as long as manly vigor remains in the world?

Loyalty is as deathless as truth, and love is as indestructible as life.

As the Bohemian never tries to enforce an unjust claim, he never needs to compromise, or pursue a temporizing policy.

Expediency is not the meaning of his life, or a small success its aim.

He is therefore never a politician.

A selfish use of power is not the goal of his ambition, and his life is therefore as calm as nature, his rule as certain and as noiseless as her laws.

As the Bohemian is never a politician, he is never an office-seeker, and is therefore never made angry or disturbed by failure.

He is most successful when the world generally thinks him least so; for the world counts by numbers, and does not see that a fixed point may be the centre of a circle whose circumference is infinity.

The Bohemian is a ruler over himself; and this is the stand-point from which the world can be moved.

A perfect dominion over one's self, satisfies the largest ambition, and leaves no desire to influence, or command others.

It is his self-possession which makes the Bohemian reverenced by the strong, and saves him the mortification of finding himself, a small man, in a position which is too great for him.

The Bohemian needs no armies to force men to submit to his guidance. In fact armies are generally employed by Mrs. Grundy's favorites in trying to prevent people from loving, reverencing, and following the lead of some great Bohemian.

Let the history of the growth of freedom in Government, in Religion, in Public Policy, and Private life, tell how unsuccessful all such weak means of contending with the truth have been.

All attempts to overthrow the dominion of Bohemianism are based upon violence and wrong, and are therefore never finally successful.

For the Bohemian, as he is brave, generous, just, honest, self-possessed, and never aggressive, is the best subject in what is called society and Government, and those who contend with him must espouse the part of tyranny, which is always cowardly, mean, unjust, dishonest, cruel.

In such a contest the manly instincts of the world take part; there is no compromise possible, nor any doubt of the victory.

The Bohemian is as careless of his strength, and as certain of his power, as nature is.

He never needs to enforce his rule. He will have a spontaneous subjection or none. For his laws are justice, and his rule is truth; therefore his subjects have the only freedom possible, and can blame no one but themselves if they prefer the miseries of Grundyism.

To live under the rule of Bohemianism is to be as free, happy, joyous, careless, unconscious of wrong as nature. Is to be manly, honest, tender, loving, true, as the Bohemian always is.

D. D.

INDEPENDENCE-BELL—JULY 4th, 1776.

When it was certain that the Declaration would be adopted and confirmed by the signatures of the delegates in Congress, it was determined to announce the event by ringing the old State-House bell which bore the inscription, 'Proclaim liberty to the land: to all the inhabitants thereof!' and the old bellman posted his little boy at the door of the hall to await the instruction of the doorkeeper when to ring. At the word, the little patriot-scion rushed out, and, flinging up his hands, shouted *Ring!* RING! RING!

There was tumult in the city,
  In the quaint old Quaker's town,
And the streets were rife with people
  Pacing restless up and down;
People gathering at corners,
  Where they whispered each to each,
And the sweat stood on their temples,
  With the earnestness of speech.

As the bleak Atlantic currents
Lash the wild Newfoundland shore,
So they beat against the State-House,
So they surged against the door;
And the mingling of their voices
Made a harmony profound,
'Till the quiet street of chestnuts
Was all turbulent with sound.

'Will they do it?' 'Dare they do it?'—
Who is speaking?'—'What's the news?'—
What of Adams?'—'What of Sherman?'
'O! God grant they won't refuse!'
'Make some way there !'—'Let me nearer!'—
'I am stifling!'—'Stifle, then!
When a nation's life's at hazard,
We've no time to think of men!'

So they beat against the portal,
Man and woman, maid and child;
And the July sun in heaven
On the scene looked down and smiled;
The same sun that saw the Spartan
Shed his patriot-blood in vain,
Now beheld the soul of freedom
All unconquered rise again.

So they surged against the State-House,
While all solemnly inside,
Sate the 'Continental Congress,'
Truth and reason for their guide.
O'er a simple scroll debating,—
Which, though simple it might be,—
Yet should shake the cliffs of England
With the thunders of the free.

At the portal of the State-House,
Like some beacon in a storm,
Round which waves are wildly beating,
Stood a slender boyish-form;
With his eyes fixed on the steeple,
And his ears agape with greed
To catch the first announcement
Of the 'signing' of the deed.

Aloft, in that high steeple
Sat the bellman, old and grey;—
He was weary of the tyrant
And his iron-sceptred sway,
So he sat, with one hand ready
On the clapper of the bell
When his eye could catch the signal,
The happy news to tell.

See! See! The dense crowd quivers
Through all its lengthy line,
As the boy beside the portal
Looks forth to give the sign!
With his small hands upward lifted,
Breezes dallying with his hair,
Hark! with deep, clear intonation,
Breaks his young voice on the air.

Hushed the people's swelling murmur,
List the boy's strong joyous cry!
'Ring!' he shouts, 'RING! *Grandpa !*
Ring! O! RING for *Liberty!*
And straightway, at the signal,
The old bellman lifts his hand,
And sends the good news, making
Iron-music through the land.

How they shouted! What rejoicing!
How the old bell shook the air,
Till the clang of freedom ruffled
The calm gliding Delaware!
How the bonfires and the torches
Illumed the night's repose,
And from the flames, like Phoenix,
Fair liberty arose !

That old bell now is silent,
And hushed its iron tongue,
But the spirit it awakened
Still lives,—forever young.
And while we greet the sunlight,
On the fourth of each July,
We'll ne'er forget the bellman,
Who, twixt the earth and sky,
Rung out OUR INDEPENDENCE;
Which, please God, *shall never die!*

NEW YORK JULY 14, 1860

[From the New Orleans Delta.]

WALT WHITMAN.

If WALT WHITMAN had occasion to put forth his notions of poetry and poets in dithyrambic form, we can well imagine the strain to run in this wise:

If a great poet thinks he sings, and sings not,
Very good!
Or if a great poem thinks it's sung, and the great poet who sung it never lived nor loved, nor was married to immortal verse or to a human female, nor drank brandy, nor chewed tobacco nor stimulated his brain with coffee,
Very good also!
Or if the great poem is sung, but thinks it's not sung, let it be content.
Or if the great poet thinks he doesn't sing, but does sing, let him be content.
Any way and every way, these are all dreams and all facts;
These are all facts and all dreams;
As dreamy and as factual as the mill between Heenan and Sayers, the Common Council, the Chicago Convention, the Great Eastern, John Brown, and the 'irrepressible conflict.'
All these things are equally something and nothing, Nothing and something.
Let them alone!
Come away!!
Pshaw !!!
But, to speak the truth that is in me, and in you, too, who are only a shadow of me, it is the sublime nihility of these things that inflates me with poetic emptiness—
Inflates me, myself, and not you, or Thomas, Richard, or Henry—
Inflates me, I mean, and Emerson, who is only another mood of me—
Inflates us both, who are one, I say, and causes us to riot in a chaos of uninterpretable lingo, and to shout from the empyrean height of unspeakable joy,
Whoop-de dooden-doo!

THE HANGING.

Who is to blame for insulting the common decency of the community in the arrangements for Hicks's execution? It is bad enough to hang even a dog, much more so a man. One would suppose that the commonest sense of decency would lead those whose duty it is to perform so brutal and outrageous a task to make their shame as secret as possible. If such a duty must be performed, let it be done as all the filthy work of society is done, in the way that shall least offend our feelings or our senses. But in the names of thousands whose daily duties call them in sight of Bedloe's Island, we protest against the intrusion of this shocking spectacle. It is bad enough that a poor half-crazy creature, brutalized by the filth and vice attendant upon poverty, whose ambition to appear a wretch leads him to die with a lie in his mouth, should be hurried into eternity in that condition. It is worse that the living should be forced to see so revolting a spectacle.

Pirate and murderer Alfred W. Hicks, from Leslie's Illustrated, April, 1860.

It is too foolish to speak of the moral effect of such scenes as beneficial. And it is a serious reflection that we have persons in authority among us who could plan and carry out such shockingly brutal arrangements. If our civilization and the morals of society require that we should maintain such a class, we had better relapse into a decent and human barbarism.

Dr. Harriet K. Hunt, of Boston, on the 27th of June, celebrated her professional 'silver wedding;' that is, the twenty-fifth anniversary of the date when she commenced the practice of medicine. Her house was ornamented with flowers, evergreens, pictures, and statues, with appropriate mottoes on every spot. Her bedchamber—furnished with the same old chairs, couch, bed, even to the sheets and pillowcases, as at the period of her birth—was adorned with appropriate emblems and mottoes. One small room was sacred to her friends in the spirit-land—and portraits, wreaths, or vases of flowers, pressed leaves of grasses, and affectionate sentiments, told the story of loving remembrance. At 3 o'clock in the afternoon, the formal exercises commenced by the entrance into her parlor of Dr. Hunt, preceded by a band of girls in pure attire; there was then prayer and music, and religious and literary exercises. A ring of gold was presented from the managers of the Hospital for Women and Children. In the evening, there was tea, dancing, reading of correspondence, and a graceful hilarity. Miss Harriet Hosmer, the sculptor, was present.

NEW YORK JULY 21, 1860

NEW YORKERS.

The Boston *Transcript* says that a New Yorker, "a real New Yorker"—meaning thereby a New Yorker as is a New Yorker, and not one raised in Hull, or Portsmouth, or Boston—"cannot thrive under ordinary conditions either of the body politic or of any of the multifarious enterprises which the genius, thrift, or enterprise of men lead them to undertake."

A Bostoner can thrive under any conditions. Given Faneuil Hall, the Common, the Frog Pond, and Mr. Everett, and he is contented.

"But," says the *Transcript*, "novelty is the desideratum of New York Life; the people crave excitement at whatever cost."

And the Transcript, for once, is right.

It is for this reason that the New Yorker prefers New York to Boston, or Salem, or Portland, or even Hull.

It is for this reason that the Japanese, the *Great Eastern*, the Zouaves, and all other lions have the same preference.

It is for this reason that the *Transcript* couldn't live in New York a week.

It is for this reason, finally, that New York is such a big city, and that it excites so much envy and uncharitableness on the part of its sister cities—and especially Boston, which is such a quiet little place, that it always reminds us of an inscription we once saw on the Canal d'Ourck, near Paris—'Here may be found tranquillity and fish in abundance.'

Now we have no objection to the 'tranquillity' of Boston, and rather like its 'fish;' moreover, in our love of novelty and excitement we are pleased, also, to see, now and then, a Bostonian, who, as 'Personne' would say, is always 'a good thing to do.' Why then can't our Boston friends be equally tolerant, Instead of always persecuting us and hurting our feelings, after the manner of the *Transcript*, just because we happen to be not only excitable, but big and good natured?

We appeal, now, to our Boston friends to be more magnanimous. In fact if they'll only let up on us a little, we'll let them see the Prince of Wales; if not we shall have to send 'Heenan the Hittite' after them.

BEAUTY.

BY WILLIAM WINTER.

I had a dream one glorious Summer night
In the rich bosom of imperial June.
Languid I lay upon an odorous couch,
Golden with amber, festooned wildly o'er
With crimson roses, while the silent stars
Wept dews of love upon their clustered leaves.
Above me soared the azure vault of heaven,
Vast and majestic; cinctured with that path
Whereby, may hap, the sea-born Venus finds
A way from higher spheres; that path which seems
A band of silver, gemm'd with regal stars,
And bound upon the forehead of young night.

There as I lay, the musical South-wind
Shook all the roses into murmuring,
And poured their fragrance o'er me in a shower
Of purple mist. Anon, upon mine ears
Came a low, sweet, and silvery melody;
Which with delicious languor filled the air,
And, like the sunset-colored water, broke,
And floated into labryinths of sound.

Then rose a shape, a dim and ghostly shape,
Whereto was neither form nor feature given;
A shadowy splendor, seeming as it came
A pale and pearly cloud shot through and through
With faintest rays of sunset: yet within
A spirit dwelt; and, floating from within
A murmur trembled softly into words:

'I am the ghost of a most lovely dream
Which haunted, in old days, a Poet's mind!
And long he sought for, wept and prayed for me;
And searched through all the chambers of his soul,
And searched the secret places of the earth,
The lonely forest and the lonely shore,
And listened to the voices of the sea,
What time the stars were out, and midnight cold
Slept on the dark waves whispering at his feet;
And sought the mystery in a human form,
Amid the haunts of men, and found it not;
And looked in woman's sweet and tender eyes,
And mirrored there his own, and saw no sign!
But only in his dreams I came to him,
And gave him fitful glimpses of my face,
Whereof he after sang in sweetest words;
Then died and came to me. But, evermore,
Through weary days and lonely, wakeful nights—
A life of star-lit gloom—do Poets seek
To rend away the veil which covers me!
And evermore they grasp the empty air.
For only in their dreams I come to them,
And give them fitful glimpses of my face,
And lull them with the music-words of hope,
That promise sometime to their ravished eyes
A vision of the absolute Beautiful!'

Then the voice ceased, and only on mine ears
The shaken roses murmured and the wind!

LICHEN TUFTS.

Lichen Tufts, from the Alleghanies, by Elizabeth C. Wright. New York: M. Doolady. 1860.

A little, unheralded, unpretending volume, which is evidently the first production of an independent and thoughtful mind. The author has been evidently forced to rely upon nature for her companionship, and upon herself for sympathy, and these first fruits of her mental growth, immature as most first fruits are, give promise of an inherent strength and sincerity, which in time will yield a rich harvest. A heated term is not the season to indulge in learned or profound disquisitions. Lying on the grass, enjoying the sunshine and the flowers, seems the most appropriate way of entering into sympathetic relations with nature during the Summer months. We do not want to have "The Perfection of the Natural" proved to us, while the grass is green about us, and the trees wave happy in the Summer air. To those who love to find the author in a book, these prose-essays will commend themselves They bear the impress of an earnest and inquiring spirit, which has already learned the difficult lesson of self-possession and peace, and the gain of these is the success of life.

WOMAN IN THE KITCHEN.

Archbishop Hughes is out with the old notion that every woman should be a cook.

A favorite notion, this, with his order and his sex, and about as sensible a one as that every man should be a butcher.

But the *Express* comes to the support of the distinguished prelate, on the ground that "the only way to be queen over a husband's heart, is to know how to be his cook."

"The philosophy of this is clear, if not self-evident," says the *Express.* How so? Why, because "bad bread, bad meat, bad food, destroys the stomachs of husbands, and the brain and the stomach have nervous connections so intimate that it is almost impossible to have a well-balanced head with a badly-supplied stomach."

Observe that the effect of bad food on the *wife* is not alluded to,—in fact, is not of importance enough to be alluded to; it is the *husband* alone who is to be cared for.

The only reason why the wife should be a good cook is that the husband may have a good dinner, and thus have a 'well-balanced head'!

Whether the wife's head is 'well-balanced' or not is of no consequence.

Her sole duty in life is to look after her husband's head, which 'according to the Express' she can do best by looking after his stomach.

O how proud we should be, if we were a woman, to become the wife of a man entertaining such noble sentiments! And with what delight we should devote ourselves to the duties of the kitchen, in order that he might have a 'well-balanced head'!

Think of a 'well-balanced head' in the *Express* office!

What splendid 'Third Editions' we should then have!

But, alas! if the logic of the *Express* be sound, the editors of that anything but festive sheet must be the worst fed men in the country: and it occurs to us, just now, that the *Herald* intimated as much, years ago.

We don't wonder, then, that the *Express* should endorse the doctrine that every woman should be a cook. But, speaking seriously, no more silly doctrine was ever broached, even by an Archbishop.

The truth is that there is no occasion for one woman in ten to be a cook, and the chief reason why men take any other view of the case is that they may keep woman in what is called her 'peculiar sphere.'

What that peculiar sphere is, no one has yet been able to determine.

Our notion is that woman's peculiar sphere is whatever field of action she finds herself best adapted to, and in which she can maintain herself, if need be, in entire independence of man.

The idea that a woman must learn to cook or to do anything else because by so doing she can best minister to the comfort of man, is utterly absurd.

She has simply to find out what occupation in life she is best fitted for—in other words, what occupation in life she would find the most enjoyment in—and pursue that.

If women should uniformly adopt this course,— treating with contempt every man, even were he an Archbishop, who should insist upon her learning to be a cook—they would soon be in a condition not only to support themselves amply, but to achieve their complete emancipation from the silly laws of society, which prescribe to them, now, as their first duty, to learn the art of administering to the pleasures of a sex which does all in its power to degrade them.

—From an article on Town Gossip in the *Court News and County Families Chronicle* we extract the following passage on 'The Club,' the club of Johnson, Burke, and Reynolds: 'In these days the term club usually implies a magnificent stone-building in Pall-mall or St. James street, by Smirke or Barry. But there still remain one or two of the old houseless clubs with which our grandfathers were familiar. Amongst others, there is one which so far transcends all others, both in antiquity and in old associations, that it has all along maintained the name of 'The Club' par excellence. To it Dr. Johnson, Boswell, and the other wits and literati of his day belonged, and it has retained an apostolical succession of great names down to the present day. It is very small and select, and a single black ball excludes. A year or two since it numbered amongst its members Hallam and Macaulay, and they were among the constant attendants at its dinners, which take place twice a-month during the Parliamentary season. Byron and Scott were not members of 'The Club' in their day, because they were not usually domiciled in the great metropolis; and poets and historians who prefer the retirement of the country to the bricks and mortar of London are still excluded from its festive gatherings. 'The Club,' however, though unknown to fame, still holds its assemblies, and embraces most of the representative-men of the age, such as Mr. Stirling, Professor Ower, Dean Milman, &c. The custody of the books and archives of the club rests with the Secretary, Dr. Milman, the venerable Dean of St. Paul's, who takes great pride and pleasure in showing to literary friends the valuable collection of autographs which those books contain. Some of the signatures bear evident token of having been written after dinner, and there is a tremulousness about Bozzy's signature which is most characteristic of the man.'

NEW YORK JULY 28, 1860

Dramatic Feuilleton.

INSCRIBED TO THE GENERAL PUBLIC.

I beg pardon of Jefferson and Sothern for saying it, but if I consent to sit through *Our American Cousin*, this hot weather, it is not so much to see either of them, as to see Couldock, whose Able Murcott is one of those rare bits of acting which, although wasted upon you, General, fills the Subscriber's heart with joy.

Jefferson is funny—very funny—and Sothern still funnier, but they both carry their extravagance to the borders of buffoonery, while Couldock, with every temptation to go and do likewise (if only to secure your idiotic applause), bravely decides to do nothing of the sort, but to perform his part in the true spirit of an artist. It must be annoying to an actor of any intelligence or refinement to be cast in such a piece at all, but once in it, how can he be praised sufficiently for doing all in his power toward redeeming it from its essential vulgarity?

It is not, alas! in the power of any artist, or of any art to accomplish this, but Couldock does his best in that way, and if you had sense enough, General, you'd go and thank him for it, as I do.

I don't mean by this that Jefferson and Sothern are not clever. I would rather say, on the contrary, that they are altogether too clever. Hence they overdo their parts immensely, and thus run the humor of the thing into the ground. Sothern, especially, since his return from Peoria, is irrepressible, and carries his skipping, coughing, grimacing, etc., to such an extreme as to give one the idea of St. Vitus in an advanced stage of the consumption. However, this is chiefly your fault, General, for you are so fond of nonsense and vulgarity, that the bigger the dose of it the louder your applause. I have often heard you shout with glee, when you ought to have put on your hat and left the house. A contortion of the countenance, or a display of the person amounting almost to indecency, seems to please you, at times, more than the most brilliant display of wit. But actors ought to know that it only pleases you for the moment, after which the pleasure is invariably followed by a feeling of disgust.

All which, being interpreted, means that *Our American Cousin* is not played with nearly so much skill as when it was first brought out, although it still draws crowded houses, and will undoubtedly do so to the close of the season, even if Sothern should decide to do his Dundreary business, hereafter, in the Japanese costume, and standing on his head.

And apropos of standing on one's head, I advise everybody who is fond of such antics, and would know the capacity of the human frame in that line, to go and see the Ravels, who perform every night as regardless of the weather as if the scene of their wonderful feats were really a 'Winter Garden.'

I don't run after such things myself because, for some unexplainable reason, they always give me the cramp.

It is as much as I can do, in the gymnastic way, to stand the Chicago Zouaves, about whom, by the way, Mr. Fitz-James O'Brien has written a spirited poem for *Harper's Weekly*, which I advise you to copy.

The only kind of physical exercise I care to witness in public, is dancing. For this reason I have been every night of the week to Nixon's, to see the Gale Sisters, who, besides being by far the handsomest young ladies on the stage, are really very excellent performers, and seem to dance with more and more ease and grace every evening.

One must be indeed delighted with them, to endure for their sakes the horrible travestie of Aladdin that Nixon has brought out. However, we shall have the last of that to-day, and then hurrah for the Hanlons and the Horses, who, as you will be pleased to hear, come back again on Monday to refresh their spirits after a visit to Connecticut under the cheerful auspices of Barnum.

I understand, General, that you have been seen several times this week at Wallack's, and have been doing your best to stand Florence's edition of Toodles and Captain Cuttle. This is very good in you, and I hope you'll do it again, as I think the handsome Young American Couple ought to be encouraged, whatever they do, though if they don't let Cuttle and Toodles alone, I shall send Bunsby of the *Sunday Atlas* after them.

Alas! what would happen if that Sabbatarian youth should make them the subject of one of his eloquent and scholarly essays?

The very thought of such a thing fills my mind with such varied emotions that I can write no more (even if there were anything to write about), but must sign myself in all haste,

Yours, quite indifferently,

QUELQU'UN.

N. B,—I see by *The World* that there is a theatre or something of the kind, called the 'Odeon,' situated in the Bowery adjoining the 'Volks-Garten.' The address, etc., I learn from *The World*, which devotes a whole column to the place, all because the manager's name is Gustav' Lindermuller, when another Gustav (Pecksniff I believe) is a member of the Sunday Committee, and ought, therefore, according to *The World*, to have an exclusive proprietorship in the name.

That a profane theatrical person should dare to have the same name as Gustav Pecksniff, Esq., of the Sunday Committee, shocks *The World* almost off of its axis. Hence no end of comment, for which the profane theatrical Gustav could well afford to pay, Sunday-paper fashion, so much a line.

Thus far, then, the two only places of amusement under *The World's* special protection are Barnum's Museum and Gustav Lindermuller's Odeon. Two very moral places, no doubt, and well deserving of such distinguished patronage.

[For the New York Saturday Press.]

THE TWO SHADOWS.

It was a frolic-morn in May
The world looked young and very fair,
That morn, to us. 'Tis now—O, Claire—
How long ago I dare not say!

Our hearts were very full of mirth:
We thought that Life could never pall:
We sate beneath the garden-wall,
In love with everything on earth!

The Years, we thought, were all our own.
Claire gaily snatched away her hand;
Then bade me, 'on my peril, stand!'
And sketched my shadow on the stone.

It was a profile round and fair;
No angles marred its lines of youth;
We laughed; and then, with feebler truth,
I sketched the glorious face of Claire.

. . . .

A Life! O God! how mere a speck,
A microscopic shallop, tossed
On the vast waves of Time, and lost!
Too frail to leave a trace of wreck !

The Years we counted cycles, flown!
My shadow now, sharp-edged as care!
And not a trace, on earth, of Claire,
Save on my heart, and that cold stone!

Charles D. Gardette.

[For The New York Saturday Press.]

"GETTING ON."

BY MRS. S. W. JEWETT.

"The elements of worldly-success are born with some people, and they cannot help *getting-on.*" So says a certain writer whose judgment and discrimination cannot be questioned, and so say a large number of individuals, who, deficient in these elements themselves, find a panacea for their mortification, in the conviction that it is their misfortune, not their fault, that the aphorism does not apply to them. It is a beneficent provision of Providence that these unfortunates, for whom the forehanded part of society find no excuse, should be able to fall back upon this interior conviction, and thus preserve a certain kind of self-respect, while they are unable to parry or resent the slings and arrows of outrageous fortune.

In our family, from a remote ancestry, there existed a marked difference with regard to 'getting on.' My mother's side of the house were a thrifty, energetic, methodical people, strict disciplinarians, scrupulously exact in details, particularly in moneyed transactions, and singularly exempt from reverses. The tide of affairs, which, 'taken at the flood,' led on from one success to another, never seemed to ebb from the moment that the first venture was made, and their very mistakes sooner or later became a source of revenue. The paternal branch was of an entirely opposite tendency, and it seemed as if a malign influence, like an ill wind, blighted every undertaking, even those projected under the fairest auspices. The only augury that did not fail was hope. Disappointment after disappointment could not extinguish this, and it kept from sinking one member after another, whom the weight of debt and pecuniary distress of some sort was forever dragging down, and threatening to submerge irrecoverably.

The faculty of 'getting on' culminated in my mother, and the embarrassments of my father's business furnished ample opportunity for its exercise. Her keen insight could not fail to discern, that the brow of him she loved was often clouded, and she divined the cause to be no other than pecuniary difficulties. Hers was not a nature to sit down patiently and bear reverses, but full of energy and activity, with a determined will to overcome them. By little and little, with womanly tact and management, she got the direction of many domestic details, and smoothing away numberless little objections which my father's pride and sensitiveness opposed to her endeavors, she found occasion to help along as well as save, and by her thrift and excellent management would have established the fortunes of the family, had not the demand of the most unscrupulous of all creditors summoned her to the discharge of that debt, which no prudent foresight or strength of will could avoid.

Had there not been a sincere and ardent love as a foundation for their union, the conjugal relation between two so opposite in character, as my father and mother, would have been anything but happy. It is often the case that those most dissimilar in many strong points form the closest and tenderest union, and the mutual attraction that drew my parents together on their first acquaintance, lost none of its power to the last. The individuality of each, though strongly marked, was tempered and controlled by a genuine religious sentiment, and the consciousness of energy in my mother, was not put forth in a manner opposed to true wifely respect, while the acknowledged lack of it in my father never induced that assumption of supremacy, which manifests itself by petty tyranny, the stronghold of narrow and selfish minds.

He never recovered from the blow which deprived him of his life-and-heart companion. His genial smile, his ready joke, his almost boyish participation in the enjoyments of his children, all fled, and he sank powerless under the weight of sorrow. Physical infirmity was added to his intense mental depression, and morbid apprehension of impending misfortune haunted him continually. In vain we begged him not to fear for us, assured him we had no fears for ourselves; but we were unable to dissipate his gloom. We could not induce him to relinquish his accustomed round of professional labor, and stay at home and be nursed. We did not know then, but some of us have learned since, that there is no discipline so severe, as that of sitting still and alone with grief and anxiety. Though we cannot run away from the 'foes of our own household,' yet when we are up and doing, a healing influence from life and action outside of ourselves, unconsciously lessens their baneful effect upon us. It was this relief my father sought, painfully conscious that there was no recuperative energy within to sustain him.

As we could do nothing directly to help him, we conferred with each other from time to time, in order to find some means of assisting him indirectly, as it were, and after much consultation, it was unanimously resolved, that our oldest sister Margaret should propose to him, opening a school in our own house, in which all of us might take a part, and in that way educate our youngest brother as well as support ourselves.

Alas! his mind was too morbid to see anything favorable in such a plan. It appeared to him a melancholy reflection upon his own incapacity, and excited him to many bitter self-reproaches, and such a stirring-up of old and painful memories, that we were only too glad to relinquish the idea.

Frustrated in our efforts to earn a livelihood, we bent all our thoughts upon various projects of saving, reducing our family expenses, giving up one and another luxury of the table, determined, since we knew our poor father could not be long with us, that we would spare him all needless mortification and suffering, and try to persuade him that we were happy.

And we were happy,—happy in the enjoyment of health, happy in our hopes of the future, happy in each other.

I do not think I should be believed if I were to tell the plain truth of our lives in those years. The whole truth would seem like exaggerated fiction; therefore I will tell only a small portion of it. We did contrive by various methods and great ingenuity to spread our table three times a-day, but we rose from many a meal hungry enough to have been easily tempted by the sight of more.

"I have managed to pay for a bit of butter," Margaret said one day," and now the grand question is, shall we have a feast, and enjoy it all at once, or eke it out till we can get more ?"

"Make the most of this godsend, and then go without," was the unanimous decision.

I think we were philosophers, both in our enjoyment and our self-denial; we made the very best of both extremes.

But I will not lengthen these details. Suffice it to say, we grew every year poorer and poorer. Clothes wore out, furniture grew shabby, bills came in, money was harder and harder to get, and our hearts were fast losing their youthful elasticity, when my father died, and the day long delayed—the day of toil, and struggle, and buffet with the world—began a new era in our lives.

And there we were, four of us, without money, without any relative near us, with no one to take a special interest in us; and what was more unfortunate than all the rest, none of us with the faculty of 'getting-on.' Of this last want, however, we were happily unconscious. We believed ourselves possessed of capabilities which only required an appropriate sphere to be a source of independence. We had, like most young people, a foolish sensitiveness with regard to the opinions of others; and although we were self-sustained in theory, we felt all the awkwardness of poverty. The deeper sorrows we had passed through, had taught us how to distinguish the substance from the shadow of misfortune; and we tried to rise above the annoyances of our condition.

We were, as poor and proud people usually are, suspicious of neglect and coldness, and doubtless repelled the advances of some who wished to befriend us. But it seems to me that no one really bent upon doing a kindness will be easily repelled. When from a generous motive a person wishes to do a generous service, he can generally find out some method of doing it, that will not only prove acceptable, but leave no sting behind.

Our father's death left his affairs in the utmost confusion. He had made no will, for alas! he knew that everything belonged to his creditors, even the house over our heads. Should we try and keep it? was the question. Margaret said 'Yes.' It was our home, our birthplace, dear to our hearts even from the sad associations it held.

"We must try and keep together," she said. "I know the house is mortgaged to Squire Brown; but he is rich, and cannot need the money, and we will try and pay off the mortgage. Our father befriended him when he was a poor young man, struggling in his profession, and he must be willing to assist us. I will take a school. I don't know much, but I can study and keep ahead of my pupils."

"I will go into a store," said Nat. "I meant—that is I always wanted to be a professional man; but now I am determined to make money."

"And I," said Amy, sadly.

"You shall help me, at home," said Margaret, drawing her close to her bosom.

"Till Mr. Everton asks for her to be mistress of his great house," said I. "Would you give her up then ?"

Margaret did not answer my question. "Amy was father's darling," she said; "he knew that you and I, Jane, were able to make our own way in the world; but his voice trembled when he used to ask, 'What will become of our beauty, "our pet"?' as he called her. Amy, darling, I shall need you; I can't live alone !"

"And I will be good for something," said Amy; "I can do the family-sewing."

"You don't ask what I can do," said I; "but you may as well know first as last, that I mean to go on the stage,"

"On the stage !" exclaimed all at once; "but we know you are joking."

"I am not joking," I said, seriously; "I am in solemn earnest. I have thought of it for years, and on the stage I go. I shall never be satisfied till I have tried."

"Don't you remember," said Margaret, "when father's friend, M——, the actor, was here, he said—speaking of a young lady who had just made her début—he would rather see his daughter in her coffin than on the stage?"

"Yes, I remember it," said I; "and I remember his saying, too, that the finest, the purest, and the best women he had ever known, were in his profession."

"But all actresses are not so fortunate as to become stars," said Margaret, "and you could not be satisfied as a second-rate artist."

"I know it, and I don't intend to be second-rate anything," said I. "However, as it must be some time before I can be ready to go upon the stage, and I possibly may marry, or change my mind, 'tisn't best to worry."

"And what will you do in the meantime," asked my brother Nat.

"Write stories for Magazines," I replied.

"And publish them where?"

"Wherever they will pay," I answered.

"Jane must be the genius of the family," said Amy. "It is the fate of genius to live in a garret or starve outright."

"Then let me starve," I said, "for if I cannot live by my wits, I had better starve."

"Your wits are only budding yet," said Nat, "your genius has only just begun to sprout. How will you manage to keep it alive till it is ready to blossom

"I have a plan ready for all emergencies," said I. "I think out these things after I go to bed. Many a bright idea lights up the darkness for me. I can't teach, that is certain, for I don't know enough, and am not steady enough, besides having no patience. So I will tell you what I mean to do. I will go to New York, and hire myself out in some gentleman's family, as waiting-maid or seamstress, or something of that sort."

"You, a servant!" interrupted Nat.

"Hear me out," I continued impatiently. "Why not a servant for a time, and to accomplish an object. Of course I don't mean to be a servant all my life. When my day's work is done, I can study and write."

"And eat with Bridget the cook, and Patrick the coachman, I suppose," said Nat.

"It isn't a possible thing," said Amy. "I don't believe Jane is in earnest."

"You will see whether I am or not before long," I replied.

"If Uncle John should hear of it," suggested Margaret.

"If Uncle John don't like the situation I have chosen for myself, let him help me carry out my plans in a way that he does approve. For my part I don't think we need fear his troubling himself about us any way."

"If I thought you were in earnest," said Margaret, "I should remind you of our father's honest pride in being a gentleman. I am sure we ought to respect his memory enough, to do nothing that would cast reproach upon his name."

"From what I have seen of the world," said I, there is no greater reproach to be cast upon a man, or woman, than the stigma of poverty. I have not lived many years, but I have seen one and another drop off, who used to be glad enough to sit down at our table, and share our father's hospitality. No one that he had ever loved, could hide away from him, with their miseries. His sympathy would find them out, and his generosity relieve them. I don't know how you feel, but when I recall what he was, what he suffered, how he died, poor, neglected, and broken-hearted, I hate the world, and everybody in it, and my feelings become as bitter as gall, and I say to myself,—I won't care for the world, since I know it never will care for me. Miss Prim will say, 'Don't do this.' Miss Whim will say 'Don't do that.' But I don't mean to care for Miss Whim or Miss Prim. I want to do my own way, and live my own life, or else I shall be good for nothing. I wish I could begin to-morrow."

Just at that moment the door-bell rang, and a letter was brought in. It was from an aunt in Savannah, our mother's sister, asking that Amy might come to her, offering her a home, adding that she need not be dependent, as she could teach the children. We read the letter from beginning to end, then looked at each other, and read it over again. She urged Amy's coming at once, with a merchant from Savannah who was then in New York, and would send us word what day he would leave.

"I suppose she sent the money to pay travelling expenses," said I. "It must have dropped out when you opened the letter. Look on the floor for a fifty-dollar note, or check."

We all feigned to look, though no allusion had been made to money.

"How did she expect Amy could get to New York, to say nothing of Savannah ?" I asked. "She knows we have not a dollar."

"I don't think she does know it," said Margaret. "Didn't you write to her that father left nothing, and what does nothing mean? Isn't the word plain enough? Add nothing to nothing and what does it make? Take nothing from nothing and how much does it leave ?" asked I.

"I suppose she didn't take me literally," said Margaret.

"She thinks nothing means not quite so much us would be convenient," said I; " but never mind, Amy couldn't go at any rate."

"Mr. Everton would not give his consent," said Nat.

"I wish, Nat, you would never couple my name and Mr. Everton's again," said Amy, with flushed face.

"I won't if it vexes you," said Nat, "but I don't see why it should. I think Mr. Everton is a goodhearted clever fellow, and rich withal, and would make you as happy as a queen if you could only love him. Think what a capital brother-in-law he would make. Who knows but he might set me up in business, and put me in the way of making my fortune? I know I could make my fortune, if I should once get a start, though father used to say no one of the name of Gordon could ever make money. But to return to Mr. Everton, Amy, don't you think you could love him?"

"No," replied Amy, "never."

"And I would rather see her dead than Frank Everton's wife," said I; "money will not buy happiness, though it may friends."

"I think I would give up some of my romantic dreams," said Amy thoughtfully, "I think I would almost be content without happiness, if I had the power to make others happy."

"And that you can do," said Margaret, "without a sacrifice of your young dreams, by living with us, and being one of us."

"I guess it will be the fate of all of us," said I, "if we marry at all, to marry poverty; but we won't worry about that beforehand. It will not do for us to stay here idle any longer. Tomorrow you, Margaret, must go and see Squire Brown, and if he will let us keep the house, we will all set to work, and help to pay off the mortgage. I will write to Uncle John, and ask him to lend me money enough to take me to New York. I sha'n't need much of a fit-out in my capacity. Who knows what interesting scenes and incidents I may find for my tales and sketches; I will drop the name of Gordon, and take my middle name, Walker. I will say I am just from the country, have never lived out before, and am willing to make myself generally useful."

"And where will you stay while you are looking for a place?" said Margaret.

"Have you forgotten that our old nurse married a mechanic, and lives in New York? I can learn her address, and stay with her. Now listen to a little bit of romance I have made up impromptu. I find a situation in a family where there are grown-up daughters, and one only son. An invalid child requires constant care, and I am appointed nurse and governess. I learn all sorts of secrets of high-life from hearing the young ladies talk. The young man, who is very fond of his little sister, spends a great deal of his time in the nursery—evidently perceives I am not what I pretend to be—engages me in frequent conversations. By and by I discover he is fascinated with me; it does not trouble my conscience, because I know I am as good as he is, my father having been a physician, and a man of education, and his a retired tailor. When he says any thing tender, I am careful to remind him of the difference of our positions, which I do with a quiet dignity that only increases his respect. I determine if he loves me enough to brave the opinion of the world, I will permit myself to return his passion; but if he proves to be a coward, I will let him suffer as he deserves. When he gets to that point, that he is ready to relinquish every worldly consideration for my sake, I will make known my true position. His mother and sisters, terribly outraged at first, but when they find it is no use fretting, since he will have his own way, resolve to make a little romance of it, and yield gracefully to what they cannot help. I fall into the luxuries of wealth very naturally. My husband is proud of me, and for my sake loves all my family; but, to keep up the reputation of the Gordons in not being able to 'get on,' my husband fails after a few years, and dies, leaving me poor. So here you have my history, and you may call it a prophecy."

Reader, in its leading points it was a prophecy, and now I will proceed to tell the fortunes of the rest of my father's family.

Years had passed. Our family numbered the same as on the evening we were gathered together to unfold our various plans of 'getting on' in the world. I shall speak of my personal experience only so far as the development of the family history renders it necessary Heaven knows it had not been as a looker-on merely, standing aloof from the struggles and mischances of the rest, that I lived for a few years in luxury and elegance. They were, it is true, the golden years of my life, but that which constituted their glory and happiness was my ability to help those I loved. My husband's heart was open as his purse to the wants of my kindred. They were happy, happy years, but they were few in number, and I returned to my native town a widow and poor, to share with the others the labors I could no longer relieve. My brother, through the generosity of my husband, had been established for sometime in business for himself in New York.

"Nat has not a business faculty," he used to say; "he is not exact, calculating, sharp at a bargain, does not know how to cheat, is too generous to take any advantage in a business-calculation, does not appreciate the value of money, and although he has qualities of mind and heart a thousandfold more worthy of a man, he cannot live by them in this scrambling world, where to get along one must have an eye to the main chances. But for your sake, dear wife, as well as for his own, he shall not suffer for his lack of worldly-wisdom. While I live, he shall never want a friend. I should love him for his generous devotion to his family if for nothing else. It is best to let him feel he must depend on his own exertions, for every man needs that incentive, but he shall never find himself in straits, if I have the means to keep him out."

Could I help loving the generous being who when he married me, embraced all those I loved with his wide sympathies? Loving him, did I say! It is a cold word; I almost worshipped him, God forgive me.

It is a very common maxim of the world, that when a man marries a wife, he is not expected to marry her whole family. No; but if a man truly, honorably, manfully loves his wife, he will love those whom she loves, and to whom she is bound by ties of blood and duty. If love for her do not enlarge his capacity for loving sufficiently to embrace those dear to her, let her pause ere she give herself to him. Bitter pangs, unspeakable disappointments await her, for a heart whose sympathies are not extended by true conjugal love is too inherently narrow to satisfy a generous woman's nature. Such was not the love that bound my husband to me, and every kind word, every generous token of that love for those dear to me knit us more and more closely together. I pity the wife who dares not speak to her husband of those holy sympathies that make the family sorrows her sorrows, the family joys her joys. While my husband lived he was as one of us, when he died we were all bereft together. I went home to share with them a grief I knew they not only comprehended, but felt with me. We could talk of him together, recount his generous deeds, his pleasant ways, and O! it was such a comfort to feel that they could measure my loss, by their appreciation of the value of what I had once enjoyed.

I will only mention here, that one of those sudden reverses of fortune, to which all business-men are liable, deprived us of the greater part of our fortune.

Had my husband lived, he would undoubtedly have struggled out of his embarrassments, but he was seized with cholera when away from home, and died after a few hours' illness. I wonder I am here to tell it, I wonder the suddenness of the blow did not kill me. Often in the first agony of my grief, I murmured at Providence that I could not die, but now I am able to thank God that I am spared to those who need me, and to my son, in whom I seem to see again the image of my noble husband.

The three years preceding our reverses, my husband and myself spent abroad. His death occurred but a short time after our return.

I found Margaret alone in the old homestead. Amy had been married a year to Mr. Everton. Nat, as I have said, was in business at New York. I had supposed him doing well, since he had asked no assistance from my husband. I learned from Margaret that he was not 'getting on.' He had been for some time engaged to a beautiful young girl, but was unwilling to marry, until his prospects were more encouraging. "The disappointment is still harder to bear," said Margaret, "as the young lady is very unhappily situated. I have been tempted many times to advise him to marry, thinking that with economy they may be able to get on together. But I dare not counsel him to take such a step. I know that poverty, of itself, is but a small evil. Brave and loving hearts can be happy with but little, but who can count upon health, and sickness involves such a host of expense. Nat could not see his wife suffer, and if one debt should have them in its merciless gripe, what a train of miseries it would entail upon them. When I think of our poor father's struggles under the weight of pecuniary embarrassments, and the cloud of despondency that darkened his last days, I dare not advise Nat to involve himself with family-cares. He might fail where everybody else would succeed, for sometimes I think there is a curse on our family. I don't know where the fault lies, or even what it is.

"We all work hard enough, but nothing seems to prosper that we undertake, and it will take another generation to find its way out of the fog in which we all seem to be groping. I don't care for myself, but when I think of Amy, of Nat, and you, Jane, I get so discouraged, I wish we could all lie down and die together."

"But Amy—she at least is exempt from the annoyances of poverty, Mr. Everton is rich."

"Oh!" said Margaret with a deep sigh, "you have touched the sorest spot of all. You once said, 'Riches cannot buy happiness.' Amy is a poor heart-broken creature. You will see her, you will see for yourself that something is preying on her life, but neither you nor I can help her, we cannot even speak to her of our anxieties or our fears. Jane, Amy is dying, and I have felt glad to believe that her sorrow, whatever it may be, and I think I know what it is, will soon be laid at rest forever."

"You think she does not love her husband, why then did she marry him?"

"Don't ask me, it seems all like a dream; the day she came to me with the announcement that she was engaged to Mr. Everton, I questioned her closely, I tried to probe her feelings; she had schooled herself to appear happy, and I was deceived. She had resolved upon this sacrifice for our sales, and in the momentary enthusiasm of that resolve, had deceived herself. I ask myself a thousand times, how I could have permitted it. At the time my own mind was distracted with its own selfish sorrows, and I saw nothing in its true proportions."

Is he kind to her," I asked with trembling earnestness, "does he love her ?"

"He has gained his object," said Margaret sadly.

"But is he kind to her," I repeated.

"Alas! Jane, I do not know, I see them but seldom."

"And why ?"

"He will not permit her to continue her family interests. His mother, his sisters surround her; she seldom comes here, and I seldom see her alone in her own house. 'You know I love you all, Margaret,' she said to me the last time she was here, 'and for my sake don't question me with regard to what may appear unaccountable to you. It excites me too much to talk now, but when my baby is born, if I live I will try and get more strength of mind.'"

"You ought to go and see her," I said, "your promise to our father was never to desert his child."

"I know it," said Margaret, "but I must keep away from her if to go there adds to the unhappiness of her life. We are a blighted family."

"No, Margaret," said I, "none of God's children are cursed; let us keep our faith in Him to the end, whatever happens."

"It is no wonder that we break down sometimes," said Margaret, "and I feel at this moment, that those are to be envied whose strength gives out first."

"You are too sad," I said, "you are not like yourself."

"I know it," she replied, "I am changed."

"You will rally again, by and by," I said, trying to speak cheerfully.

"I hope I shall," she answered. "I hope, if there is anything to be done, I shall find strength to do it; if not, I care not how soon the end comes to me."

"Margaret," I said, hoping to turn her thoughts into another channel, "I have not asked about Gilbert Harrison. You will have no secrets from me."

"What the world knows you could not long be ignorant of, Gilbert is married."

"Gilbert married !" I exclaimed; I could say no more.

"You wish to ask me all about it, I know, Jane," said she, "I will spare you the trouble, and tell you the whole story. Of course no confession of a woman can be so galling as that of an unrequited attachment. I could be weak, and lay my head upon your bosom, and cry like a child, and I am afraid your sympathy will make me so. Don't pity me too much. I could have borne the lifelong sorrow of losing him by death, believing in his love, and truth; but the luxury of such a grief is denied me, he lives for another, and is only dead to me. After long years, he has discovered that what he supposed was love, was only a tender friendship for me, and that another had stirred depths in his heart never fathomed before. I cannot be too thankful that the discovery was made before the happiness of both of us was sacrificed. To have had those depths stirred after it was too late, would have been an irremediable trial for both of us. That in me which first captivated his fancy faded even before it had time to bloom. No matter; I try my best to explain the change in his feelings to his advantage, for it does not make me happier to blame him; I have tried and failed. I ought not to think of him now, yet I cannot by any effort of will, by any conviction of duty, or any amount of self-discipline help thinking of him. Perhaps time will make it easier, and the habit of thinking of others will help me little by little to annihilate all selfish regrets. God knows I hope so. He is not here, I am spared at least that anguish. I could not compel myself to see day by day the object of his love, without indulging feelings unworthy of me, and unjust to her. I heard that a little child was born to them; I never asked if the rumor was true or false; I cannot play the hypocrite, and I should love the mother of Gilbert's child better a great way off, than near. I wish her all happiness, but I am not Christian enough to bear to see it without envy, and now, darling, that you know all my history, pray for me, for I need the prayers of a brave heart like yours. The world is full of aching hearts, I know, and if I have come to the conclusion that happiness is not the destiny of human beings here, I do not speak of it in a rebellious or complaining spirit. I believe it is all right, and I can wait for the mystery of life to be cleared up. Perhaps our experience is not peculiar. We don't know what grim skeletons are kept out of sight, where all is outwardly joyous, and some people if they cannot hide their skeletons, dress them up in such a manner that a casual observer is quite deceived with regard to them. We can cheat others in this way much more easily than we can cheat ourselves. I don't care to do either. I mean to look boldly and bravely full in the face of any trouble that may come to me. Perhaps if I get familiar with its aspect, I shall find that it is, as Longfellow says, a 'celestial benediction,' assuming that dark disguise."

What could I do but fold her to my bosom, and imprint on her pale cheek a sister's kiss of sympathy? What could I say to comfort and support her? I knew that the conclusions she had, wrought out in the loneliness of her own soul, were the teachings of a higher truth than I could frame. If anything isolates the heart from human help, it is the working of the strong passions of our nature, that lie too deep for even the eye of a friend to fathom. He who brought the Divine life to the encounter of human infirmities, 'trod the wine-press alone,' and so must we.

There are certain proclivities, rooted in the very foundation of one's being, which however they may be suppressed or diverted from their aim by the disappointing circumstances of external life, can never be annihilated. They constitute that individuality which makes a man himself, and not another.

In some unguarded moment, when the heart is warmed into communicativeness by the mesmeric influence of reciprocal sympathy, have we not listened to confessions, so at variance with the ordinary manifestations of character, that from the moment of their utterance, the individual is revealed in a new light to us. We never think of him, he never even looks to us the same as before, yet that which was brought to view, was nothing new, but the real man stript of conventional or prudential disguises.

And the circumlocution brings me back again to the egotistical point from which I started. I never went on the stage—I never had, and probably never shall, have a career: but the longings of my youth have not been, cannot be, extinguished. Nor have I lost my youthful enthusiasm, old as I am—matter of fact as are my duties in life, in imagination I tread the boards—enact scenes and characters, filling them with that fervor of passion which the discipline of life has modified and subdued, but not exterminated. And I am happy in so doing. If anybody will offer any reason why I should not be, I am willing to listen, though it is probable I shall not, at this time of life, change either my habits or my principles.

I began this story with the assertion that "the elements of success are born with some people, and they cannot help getting on," and I have brought up the fortunes, or rather misfortunes of our family, an a proof of the truth of this assertion. It is not probable that the future will bring to light any of the missing elements, and, in fact, we are now so grounded in our own persuasions, that it would be at some risk to our mental balance, if anything like good fortune should overtake us.

The saddest event that occurred after my return home, was the death of our sister Amy. She was not made for the battle of life, and had overestimated her capacity of self-sacrifice and endurance. When she learned that her ability to help us was only a mockery of her will and her affections, she sank under the disappointment. Mr. Everton wanted a beautiful woman at the head of his establishment, he did not need a wife. His vanity was gratified to deck the lovely image with costly draperies of wealth, but these were all he had to give. He did not see that her soul was starving, nor could he have satisfied its hunger had he made the discovery. She never spoke to us of the cause of her suffering. The only words she said which revealed the bitterness of her life were her last, when in the very presence of death, pressing Margaret's hand she whispered, "Do not mourn for me, dear sister. I wanted to do a great deal for those I loved, but have done nothing. I was not strong enough to live, and our Father has made the time short: I thank him, and so must you: could I only take my baby with me! but his will be done."

It was his will, and the baby and its mother lie in the same grave.

I almost regret having given my word of honor to myself, to be faithful to the truth in this history. I might have made some compromise with my conscience, and have rendered my story attractive, at the sacrifice of a little plain speaking. But to proceed, or rather to return to my brother Nat, whom I left some years ago struggling in business, with the hope of being able to get forehanded enough to marry the young girl to whom he was most ardently attached. Poor Nat! If a small portion of the desirable element, of which I have spoken, had been transmitted to any of my father's descendants, it had all run out before it come Nat's turn to be served. Nothing ever was successful to which he turned his hand, not for want of energy, or industry, or perseverance, and as it passes my comprehension to know what the want was, I leave it, along with many other unsolved mysteries, to future generations: for it is to be hoped, by some process of assimilation or amalgamation, with those a thousand-fold removed in blood, that the necessary ingredients of success may be supplied. I am sure nothing would more essentially add to my family pride (if family pride adheres to the spirit) than to find among the dwellers upon earth, some centuries hence, one of the Gordons who had succeeded in 'getting on' in the world.

The situation of Nat's affiance became at last so insupportable, that, too easily persuaded to move in the direction in which his heart leaned, he married. What had been barely enough for the maintenance of one person, could scarcely prove adequate for two. The birth of children, ill health, and various other perplexities, so involved him in debt that his energy and self-respect gave way under the pressure. The voice of a friend reached him at the lowest ebb of his degradation, and suggested an alternative, which he seized upon as a drowning man upon a straw. He did not live to realize his hopes, but he died, believing in his ability to retrieve his circumstances and his reputation. He embarked for California under promising auspices, but the vessel in which he sailed was wrecked in sight of its destined port. Most of the passengers were saved—my brother was one of the few that perished. His invalid wife and three children had gone to the old homestead at his departure from the country, and there they remained. Margaret's little school still furnishes a means of livelihood, and since she has given up the hope of getting along, and her wants are fewer and fewer for herself, and the mortgage has been paid off, it has become her highest happiness to live and toil for the dear children. And here we leave them.

They may be seen any time, for the picture has its prototype in many a New England home, in homes all round the civilized world, for while inequalities of society and diversities of character continue to exist, there will be some who have not the faculty of 'getting on.'

Of our Uncle John and our married Aunt, far away, I have little to say, for I know but little of them. There can be no greater distance in space, than there is in fact, between those who prosper, and those who do not—those who have the faculty of getting on," and those who have it not. Whether a thousand miles apart or close at hand, a gulf lies between them impassable as the grave. At the beginning of life we may think to bridge it over—on the one side by benefits conferred, on the other by benefits acknowledged. But as the chasm widens, the arch is broken, and it only remains for each, to enjoy himself his own side of the gulf, in his own way—or rather, the best way he can.

"What a sad story!" exclaimed Dr. Goodheart, the old schoolmaster, who boarded with us, and to whom I had read it aloud for the benefit of his criticism.

"By no means," I replied. "You see in seizing upon certain points to establish the truth of my first position, I was compelled to pass over many sources of happiness, peculiar to poverty, and, although tears have left their traces on some pages of our family-records, telling of some who gave out by the way, yet confess what those of us have gained, who know how to extract wholesome spiritual nourishment, from a regimen at which nature at first rebels with unfeigned disgust. Look at Margaret, as she sits in the midst of her foster-children, to whom life has denied the exercise of those wifely and maternal sympathies that make her nature so feminine and lovely. If all women had families of their own, where would the orphaned find the home or the love they need? The yearning is not exhausted, but it is a prophesy to be fulfilled hereafter, while I, outwardly practical, and matter-of-fact, carry around with me to my homely tasks, that belief in romance and that exuberance of imagination that keeps me fat, fair, and forty," year in and year out, and makes me a companion for my son, and a playmate for my grand-children; and, although "the field of the world," in which we were set to labor, has proved in a natural point of view rather unproductive, we can look up and congratulate ourselves on greater breadth of sky, more sunshine by day, more stars at night than can be seen when the roof-tree is fuller of leaves and blossoms overhead.

"If the story is sad, we are not sad, as you can testify."

"Only," said the Doctor, "when now and then we get a little billious."

NEW YORK AUGUST 11, 1860

HOUSES ON THE EUROPEAN PLAN.

It is curious to notice how, in the midst of all our boasted material prosperity and luxury, we have been content all this while to leave about one-half of the most respectable portion of our population mere homeless wanderers. The large and neglected class to which we allude, is that which occupies a middle station between poverty and wealth, unable on the one hand to cope with the rich in the possession of high rented houses, but, on the other hand, totally unfitted by their education, refinement, and social standing, to be subjected to the miserable shifts to which men of moderate means are driven in their attempts to locate their families decently. Our speculative builders and capitalists have made the grand stone mansion and the wretched tenement house the upper and lower rounds of the social ladder, utterly unmindful of the necessity of other intermediate grades. Marble palaces rise up everywhere, in the shape of stores and offices, the ominous placard 'To Let' showing too often that the supply in that direction exceeds the demand, but it does not seem to have entered the heads of speculators in brick and mortar, that the very people for whom they are erecting these superabundant offices are often married men with families, toiling, struggling, fighting, month after month and year after year, for some decent roof within reach of their purses. Take the whole race of professional men, artists, litterateurs, mechanics, assistants in commercial or banking houses, etc.; men unable to pay more than from $500 to $250 rental, and where in this large city can they find comfortable decent residences to suit their means? It is true such a man can go and take a cheap little cottage far away in the country, but at such a sacrifice of valuable time in going backwards and forwards, and travelling expenses, as to amount in the end to as large a rental as a house in town; or he may venture out of his depth, and take a house twice as large as he either requires or can afford to pay for, trusting to Providence for some responsible and honest tenant to help him pay his rent, or he may here and there be lucky enough to find somebody in the same predicament, who lets him have a few ill-arranged rooms to manage with his family as best he can; or—as a last refuge he will find, ever ready to receive him, that cold, comfortless, scandal-breeding grave of all domestic, social, and hospitable graces—the boarding-house.

We are glad to find that the evils attendant upon this glaring deficiency in our domestic system have, at last, become so intolerable as to be seriously engaging the attention of our architects and others. Mr. J. R. Hamilton, architect of the new Institute of Fine Arts, now being erected on Broadway, and author of the design which obtained the premium of $500 in the great competition for Mr. Beecher's Church, has designed a plan for houses upon the European principle, which we think admirably calculated to meet the pressing demands of the time. Taking, as a basis, the system of flats' so common in London, Paris, Berlin, and other large cities of Europe, but preeminently so in Edinburgh and Glasgow, Mr. Hamilton has so arranged his plan as to bring it more in unison with American customs. Upon two ordinary lots of 25 ft. by 100 ft., and with a handsome four-story frontage like the facade of our finest private mansions, he has ingeniously provided for 8 families (two on each floor), and yet these dwellings are as distinctly separated from each other (by private vestibule entrances), as if their front doors led direct from the sidewalk instead of from one grand staircase common to all. Each house has a fine large front parlor, 4 bedrooms, bath-room and water-closets, large dining-room, kitchen—with every convenience for fuel, and disposing of waste water and kitchen refuse—without the necessity of descending stairs; back stairway enclosed in brickwork as security against fire, kitchen pantry, separate laundry and coal cellar; abundance of closets, light and ventilation to each room, indeed every convenience and improvement to be found in houses now renting for $700 and upwards. In the basement are two fine offices, suitable for physicians, and apartments for the janitor, whose duty it will be—among other things—to keep the general staircase in perfect order. Ranging his prices for rental at from $500 to $250 or $300, according to the location of the story—Mr. Hamilton shows a return upon the outlay averaging a profit of from 10 to 15 per cent., after taxes and other contingencies, according to the richness or simplicity of the building. Doubtless, for a time, a large number of people, to whom such a building is a novelty, will find it difficult to disconnect it, in idea, from a tenement-house, but this system of dwelling in flats, in vogue among families of the highest standing in Europe, is so entirely different, in scope and arrangement, to the miserable barracks which go by the name of tenement-houses in this country, that the public only need to see one such building occupied by first-class families to recognize its value. At any rate this design, if executed, would work an entire revolution for the better in our dwelling-houses, and we cheerfully commend it to the attention of capitalists.

THE COQUETTE.

BY WILLIAM WINTER.

No, you are not happy now,
Though you seem so gay and proud;
There's a shadow on your brow,
And your laugh is quick and loud.
Do not tell me I am wrong,
For deceit is never well:
Having worn the mask so long,
All it covers I can tell;
And I see you've come to know
Love's swift ebb and misery's flow.

Was she generous, free, and brave,
Yet affectionate and meek?
Did she, when her hand she gave,
Sweetly smile and softly speak?
Did her mild eyes blind you quite,
And, as you were all alone,
Was her bosom, full and white,
Gently pressed against your own?
Tell me, is the picture true?
Has she practised thus with you?

Did you think that all was well,
When you held her in your arms?
Did you never doubt the spell?
Had your heart no cold alarms?
When she murmured sweet and low
Of the love that thrilled her breast,
Did you then *believe* it so,
Thinking you were richly blest?
Ah! poor soul, 'twas nothing new,—
She has cheated others too.

You are sad, or I mistake!
All this world seems dark and chill;
For you think your heart will break—
And 'tis like enough it will.
She has torn your peace away,
But her own peace she has kept:
Have you heard her mother say
How surprisingly she slept?
She is of the tranquil kind—
Very easy in her mind.

And her life-stream will flow on
O'er the same unvaried flat;
And should you be dead and gone,
She won't care a straw for that.
By and by her life will fade,
And she'll ornament a pall;
And although the paltry jade
Never had a heart at all,
Should you live, you'll go and weep
Where her worthless ashes sleep.

Let the happy children shout!
Shadow comes with sunny token:
Let the merry bells ring out!
Yet shall hearts be seared and broken.
Let the tide sweep on its way,
In the shade or in the sun,
In the night or in the day,
Death is rest when life is done;
And beyond it—wherefore care?
Souls there are which go not there!

[For the New York Saturday Press.]

TURNIPS-AND-WATER.'

Mr. Editor:—I have an inclination that would, if properly backed, amount to a 'call,' clerically speaking, to write for the SATURDAY PRESS.

I so much like the spirit that animates it; for its Editor, unlike other editors, says just what he thinks, without reference to what his readers think—or rather he seems to suppose that his readers are entitled to his confidence; hence he speaks the truth to them, as to his friends in private; while all the 'able editorials' I read elsewhere, are written as though the cautious editor was treading gingerly among the prejudices and pet-whims of his readers, fearful lest he should offend one of them. It strikes me that a public fed on milk-and-water so constantly, must enjoy the strong meat you offer them—just for a change.

The way you handled the *Dial*, last week, was refreshing, and would have been 'par excellence' had you not diluted rather much (for my taste) with wishy-washy vegetables. You seem to have introduced turnips-and-water as expletives; so when I expected something pungent, I only found thin potations and low seasoning.

I am afraid, however, you are not fully informed about the *Dial* and its editor.

I have read some numbers of that periodical, and found as little true-blue religion of the revealed kind in it, as in any church-organ that ever piped; for instance, it calenders Tom Paine among the saints.

I once, too, caught a glimpse of the *Dial* editor; and I think it will turn out that he is (if not has) as good a liver as the saintliest epicure; and if he were once fairly smoked out, I will venture it would be found he does not eschew tobacco. In fact, if he did write the Choate-article (which I rather guess not) it was born of tobacco, instead of turnips-and-water.

Seriously, Mr. Editor, is it truth of history that all Pharisaic Christians eschew roasts and boils?

I have heard it reported that such Pagans as Pythagoras and Plato were vegetarians; but this is the first time I ever heard that Peter or Paul, or any of their disciples, were vegetarians. At all events, as far as I have learned out them, and as far as I am acquainted with the Christian world of to-day, they were and are quite the reverse of ascetics.

They conquer the flesh, I know; but only to kill and eat it.

That RUFUS CHOATE was treated rather harshly I see by the quotations from the *Dial*, but that a diet of pumpkins, squashes, and turnips, lead to such opinions or produce such criticisms is not so clear.

On the contrary, the generally received opinion among both priests and dietists is that 'bran-bread leads to infidelity.' Indeed I know some very pious people who prefer dyspepsia and other ills that flesh-eaters are heir to, rather than be cured by Graham bread and the wet-sheet, in view of their divergent tendency from grace.

Observe, too, the notorious fact that those persons who are confined in penitential places, and fed on a very reduced diet to effect a change of heart, very generally become more hardened sinners than before.

Much as I detest that sanctimonious Phariseeism that sees a devil in every one not of 'Our Church,' and partitions off the universe, appropriating all the light to one section for the angels, and all the shadows to the department of unregenerates, I can't exactly see how cold water is the Siamese Twin of Hypocrisy or Phariseeism.

Why, you will have us suspect every man who takes a swim or a bath, or allows turnips on his table, of being a pious pretender and traducer of genius; and so the captivating Zouave becomes dangerous in other senses than the fighting one, and are to be deprecated, in proportion to their temperance. Well hydrophobia is a terrible disease; but Fire-eaters suffer another quite as terrible.

But seriously, Mr. Editor, I give you my hand for the many good things you do and say.

Go ahead.

Pitch into everything that unmans, belittles, cramps, befogs, stultifies human beings; but I would leave the innocent turnips and the pure water to their appropriate uses. They may be found to be harmless, and not synonymous with ignorance and bigotry.

MARY A. CHILTON.

Thompson, Long Island.

AMUSEMENTS.

NEW YORK AUGUST 18, 1860

LOLA MONTEZ.

In the course of our editorial duties it sometimes happens that we are induced to examine the Sunday papers. We do not, however, peruse them with enthusiasm. They are not publications calculated too highly to exhilarate the human mind. Their chief attraction, so far as we can ascertain, is their virtue; to illustrate which,—since virtue ought not always to go unacknowledged,—we copy, from one of them, the following characteristic article:

THE MODERN CAMILLE.

While half the world has groaned over the theatrical sorrows of an imaginary Camille, it seems to be entirely unconscious that another Camille—a brilliant, suffering, sorrowing, real Camille—is flickering out the last of life's candles in its midst, with just the chance that it will linger on and on, and expire in the socket, or be suddenly blown out before the last and repulsive stages of its glimmering and fitful existence have transpired. There is only one natural end to such a life, and that is wretchedness, despair, And then death!—death, frequently, in what should be the prime of life; death, without the consolations of friendship, or the loving sympathies of family ties; death, embittered by the consciousness of an ill-spent life, of abuses, of blessings, of wasted talents; death, in fine, without hope, and made doubly fearful by the pangs of remorse. From such a death we would wish our worst enemy to be delivered, much more a woman—a woman, too, with all the splendid qualities which the romancer has assigned to her class—brilliant in intellect, generous in impulse, loving to friends, savage to foes, her own worst and most relentless enemy. Such a woman is Lola Montez, now suffering under an attack of paralysis, which threatens to deprive her of life. It seems cruel, but we almost wish it would do so at once, otherwise it can only prove the first distinct step towards the sadness and horror of the end we have described.

Sinning much, but suffering more, her virtues at least her own, and her faults mainly the result of strong passions and a will wholly uncontrolled, she is a fit subject for those rivers of tears and throbbing emotions which have been so freely expended upon her false stage representative, and for the genuine display of that sweet charity which is the crowning grace of her sex. Where are the pitying womanly hearts that fainted at the death scene! Surely not looking, unmoved, on the fifth scene of the last act of our living tragedy!

From splendid house to furnished apartments, from floor to single room, from room to room, and finally to die alone in the garret, or the cellar—such, we hope is not the fate reserved for poor Lola Montez. Better, much better, to die now, while the echoes of admiration and applause are still ringing in her ears—while there are still some friends who cherish her, spite the shrug of the world's shoulders, or the slander of the world's tongue, and before the withering hand of poverty has laid its pale and haggard touch upon her. Better to sleep, trusting

'That good will fall
At last for her,
At last for all.'

The virtue of this article is, as the intelligent reader may perceive, of a very peculiar order.

We do not copy it for the purpose of defending Madame Lola Montez. We pretend to no special acquaintance with the private life of that lady, nor have we any right to discuss it. Indeed, we are quite unable to perceive that any person has that right. We are not so immaculate and celestial as are the editors of the Sunday papers; and that, perhaps, is the occasion of this blindness. But to our less virtuous apprehension, the article we have quoted seems the disgusting offspring of a coarse and brutal nature, intended for the delight of natures equally coarse and brutal. And still further—such is our vicious delusion—we may add that we do not well see how the article could have been written, unless by some person entirely dead to every sense of manliness, decency, taste, and even common humanity.

This may, perhaps, be considered rather a severe estimate of the virtue of the Sunday paper. We cannot help that. It is, at least, a sincere one. The virtue of those respectable and soothing sheets is, as we have already remarked, of a very peculiar order. It is that kind of virtue, which under a thin and watery guise of sorrow, violates at once the decencies and the sanctities of life, hunts out and mourns over the garbage of scandal, and pollutes everything it touches with a slimy twaddle of commonplace morality.

NEW YORK AUGUST 25, 1860

COUNTRY EDITORS AND THEIR JACKALS.

The rapacity of the country-editor for Metropolitan scandal is truly surprising. No anecdote can be so tainted, no assertion so foul, but it will tickle his provincial palate, and, we presume, the palates of the small community that he addresses.

Unfortunately for the gratification of the country-editor's appetite, he cannot be always in New York, and is therefore denied the privilege of gathering social garbage. He is forced to have a proxy. As some of the more lazy of the English nobility retain gamekeepers on their moors and country estates, who, in the season, forward hampers of damaged grouse and pheasants to their masters in town, so the editor of the Peorian *Hewgag* keeps his menial in the preserves of New York city, whose duty it is to send him once a week a packet of gamy anecdotes and flavorous falsehoods. This creature is somewhat loftily dubbed by his employer 'Our New York Correspondent,' and in his communications pretends to be on familiar terms with most of the people of distinction residing in or about the city. In reality he is some wretched penny-a-liner, whose ideas of society are derived from barrooms, and who ekes out a wretched pittance—earned perhaps by writing puffs for the Sunday papers—by contributing to the *Hewgag,* at an infinitesimal rate of remuneration, the most reckless personalities and vulgar lies that he can concoct for the money. No matter how incredible the allegation, or outrageous the slander, the Peorian editor and his Peorian constituency swallows it all, and the virtuous senior instantly rushes to his desk and indites an editorial brimful of indignation on the vice and general backslidings of the Metropolis.

The fact is, that in the matter of New York correspondence, the country editor has been done, choused, humbugged. When he comes on his annual visit to this city to make his little arrangements about new type, etc., he hardly ever sees one of the responsible New York journalists; indeed, as a general rule, neither his manners nor his attire, are so attractive as to cause his society to be courted. But he falls among the lazzaroni of the Press, who dine and drink at his expense; lead him, a not unwilling victim, through those haunts of low vice with which they are familiar; rehearse to his avid ears frightful stories of the depravity of the city, and finish by insinuating that some such chronique scandaleuse might form an excellent feature in his able journal, and profitably warn his readers against the dangers of the great Metropolis. The rustic editor, whose tastes are always prurient, gladly accepts the suggestion, and some irresponsible literary loafer is straightway transformed into 'Our New York Correspondent,' and forthwith commences his career of defamation.

The country-editor pays for nastiness, and he gets it. That the article is cheap, we infer from the very moderate price his purchase costs him. For low in the scale of journalism as 'Our New York Correspondent' usually stands, even he could not subsist on what he thus earns, unless he relied on other equally disreputable modes of adding to his income. He levies black mail on publishers. He has been known to write to various eminent firms in this city, openly threatening to 'smash' them, as he calls it, unless they furnished him with copies of all their publications. These copies, it is needless to say, 'Our New York Correspondent' sells. We have heard of one fellow of this class, who, but a little while since, was discovered to be the recipient of five copies of all works published by any of the eminent firms of the country. Four of these he contrived to have sent to fictitious persons created by him for the purpose, while he ostensibly claimed only the fifth. One person in this city, we are assured, corresponds gratis, for some thirty provincial papers, and makes his living out of those whose wares or names he mentions in his letters. Of course the editor who receives a correspondence for nothing cannot remain ignorant of the object of the writer, and naturally lends himself as an accomplice in swindling the public.

It is from such men as these that the Provincial editor and his readers derive their ideas of New York. Instead of following the example of the great Journals, and employing men of cultivation and reputation to furnish them with correspondence, the country censor hires a set of miserable newspaper pariahs, who trump up columns of falsehood and obscenity, which disgust all persons of refinement, and render the country-editor himself the laughing-stock of every intelligent journalist.

[For The New York Saturday Press.]

MINOR EXPERIENCES IN AMERICA.

I.

In 1844, a fugitive from Russia, having escaped extradition* and consequently, perhaps, Siberia, by the noble intervention of the now dying Wilhelm IV., King of Prussia, I made a visit to the city and port of Antwerp. There, for the first time, I saw emigration on a large scale to America. Mountains of trunks, boxes, feather-beds, etc., covered the wharves. Around them were gathered picturesque groups of men, women, and children, of every age, about to abandon their homes forever to escape from the crushing despotism of Europe.

Their peculiar costumes and dialects marked them as coming from different parts of Germany. They consisted mostly of farm-laborers (called in European lingo, peasants), mechanics, artisans, operatives, etc., the men looking earnest and resolved, the women care-worn and melancholy, the children excited and joyous.

For several days in succession I mixed in with the various emigrants and conversed with them.

Oppression—social even more than political had driven them from the hearths of their forefathers. Taxes, exactions, high rents, low wages, impossibility to acquire homesteads, the burden of working for the State, or the land-holder, or the new fœdality of capitalists and large manufacturers—such were the principal reasons given by these emigrants for seeking a new home.

No princes, no nobles, no taxes, no overgrown and oppressive capitalists, nothing but freedom and fair-play beyond the seas! This was their universal song. I felt deeply for them, and a few years afterward gave vent to my feelings in a socialistic work entitled 'Eine Tour durch Belgium.' I did not then foresee my fate.

In 1849, the reaction over, I found myself hemmed in on every side by State espionage and persecution. I then decided to leave Europe; and five years after my former visit to Antwerp, I embarked for the United States from the same wharf where I had witnessed the heart-rending departure of the German wanderers.

**My escape from Russia made considerable noise at the time. Crossing the frontiers of Poland, I went directly to the members of my family, and to my dying mother then residing in Silesia. In virtue of our extradition treaty between Russia and Prussia, Baron Mayendorff, Russian Minister in Berlin, imperiously claimed that I should be delivered up. Count Arnim Boitzenbourg, Minister of the Interior, also insisted strenuously on the execution of the treaty in my person, while Baron de Buelow, Minister of Foreign Affairs (nephew of W. and Alexander Humboldt), as strenuously opposed it. The King put an end to the matter by saying that never, under any circumstances, would he permit my extradition.*

As far back as 1827 I had wished to emigrate to America, which was known to me only superficially, through books; but which was attractive to me as the home of liberty.

In 1825, the secret league of Polish patriots to which I belonged was broken up, by the principal members being imprisoned or transported to Russia.

After a long imprisonment by the Grand Duke Constantine—brother of Alexander and Nicholas I.—then a kind of lawless pro-consul over Poland, I was set free; but remained exposed to the daily annoyances of military despotism, as well as to constant personal jeopardy.

Young, full of hope, and possessing sufficient capital, I, with my newly-married wife, and accompanied by a colony of about eighty families of my agricultural tenants, prepared to leave Poland and seek a new and free country.

But the Government threw impediments in the way; my widowed mother entreated me not to give up the care and charge of a numerous family of which I was the head; the nobility, especially the younger portion, who were principally from that part of Poland where my ancestors had dwelt for many centuries, begged me to remain among them—manifesting the most touching and inspiring confidence in my devotion and ability as one of the leaders in the patriotic struggle against Russia; and I was thus led to give up, or at least postpone, my project of emigration.

At last, nearly twenty years of political persecution—including proscription, confiscation, and even capital condemnation—drove me out of Europe a poor, ruined, solitary, forlorn fugitive.

At twenty-four hours' notice I decided to leave the Old World—and my mind was then wholly absorbed by the new and vast social and political phenomena which I was so soon to behold. Hopes, expectations, plans, I had none; nor had I any idea what I might do or become.

Knowing that besides those who emigrate to this country from worthy motives, there were also adventurers of every kind—chevaliers d' industrie, fortune-hunters, sharpers, etc.—I took care to provide myself with a few good letters from Berlin—letters of credit, not for money, but establishing my personal identity. In a few days after the reception of these letters I left Berne, where some of my nearest relations resided, en route for the United States, by way of Brussels, where I had a brother.

As far as study and reading could make me so, I was familiar with the history of the Republic, and had a general superficial notion of its political parties and their struggles; but I was totally ignorant of its statistics, its internal economy, its leading branches of industry, and even of its particular geography.

This only was present to my mind, that embarking in Europe I was to land somewhere in the Northern portion of the new continent, and the sooner I was off the better, as the thing would then be done.

From Brussels I went to Antwerp, where I saw a bill posted on a ship (the *Edwina,* I think, Captain Palmer) announcing her immediate departure for New York, and I at once took passage in her, but without the least idea of the greatness and splendor of that metropolis.

I was not displeased to find that the *Edwina* was an emigrant ship; for it suited my condition of a homeless, lonely wanderer, and gave me a chance to probe to the bottom the experience and the woes of tu lasceral ogni cosa diletta, etc. By paying extra, I secured a state-room to myself, and during the whole voyage experienced the kindest attention from the Captain, the Mate, and all the crew.

The steerage contained about two hundred and fifty persons of both sexes and all ages, chiefly farm-laborers and mechanics from Southern Germany, with about twenty families of Swiss, mostly farmers. On the upper deck, among my companions, was a young nobleman from Westphalia, with his housekeeper—a buxom peasant-girl—and a pair of twins three months old, whose birth was about to be legitimized in New York by the marriage of the parents—a ceremony rendered impossible in Westphalia on account of the angry opposition of the young man's father, and of the whole aristocratic set to which he belonged. There was also an interesting mother with a large family—including three grown-up daughters and one grown-up son—on her way to join her husband, who some months before had absconded from Rhenish Prussia, on account of having committed large defalcations. They belonged to the well-to-do class, and the young people looked spoiled and thoughtless; but the mother often shed silent tears at the gloomy prospect which seemed to open before her and her children.

We had contrary winds all the voyage, and it was consequently thirty-three days before we reached Sandy Hook. Thirty-one days of this time I spent in bed, sea-sick, though not a little amused at what I saw and heard about me. Everything was novel, unwonted, and full of interest.

My new life commenced from the time when I shook hands, for the last time, with my brother and his wife, the Princess of Spain, and pushed off from the pier at Antwerp.

GUROWSKI.

LITTLE ELLA BURNS

We copy the following article because it appears in a responsible Journal and over a well-known name. At the same time we cannot help believing that there must be some grave mistake in the pretended facts which it narrates, and trust that some one who is well-informed in the matter will at once clear up the mystery:

[From the San Francisco Golden Era.]

ROMANCE OF AN INFANT'S LIFE

BY MRS. E. F. ELLET.

In the Winter of 1858, a little girl of extraordinary intellectual powers appeared publicly in New York city, as a reader of Shakspeare and the poets. She was four or five years of age, and was called 'Ella Burns,' the lady who exhibited her representing herself as her own mother, and the widow of Alexander Burns of Sacramento, California. The precocious little creature was made to recite touching death-bed scenes of its father; and its wonderful performance so interested the ladies of New York, that a benefit was got up at the Academy of Music, by which a large sum was realized, and paid to the supposed mother, on her promise that the child should be withdrawn from her vagabond life and put to school. This promise was not performed, but exhibitions were given every night for three months during the Winter, some in the drawing-rooms of wealthy citizens, such as Watts Sherman, Auguste Belmont, Peter Cooper, Marshall O. Roberts, James S. Thayer, and others. Ere long it was discovered that Mrs. Burns had told a falsehood in representing the child as her own, and herself as a widow; but this did not prevent the gentlemen above-named from giving her nice letters to people in London, whither she took the child in the Spring of 1859. Her success was not great in London, The Baroness Rothschild did not relish exhibitions for money of a baby who should be with her dolls; the Duchess of Sutherland refused to see her; and the American Minister, Dallas, declined to trot her out before the Queen. Mrs. Burns returned disappointed to America, after a month in London. In July she overcame her fears of the child's father, a police officer of Cincinnati named Francis Whitten, so far as to visit her sister in Ohio. Her father had, under the pressure of poverty, having lost his wife in 1856, bound his little Eva, then three years old, to this lady (whose real name is Miss Pollock), till eighteen, on the promise that she should never be taken from Cincinnati. Ever on the watch to discover his child's whereabouts, on hearing that she was in Ohio, he went with a habeas corpus and two officers to claim her. Mrs. Burns saw him coming, fled to her room, bolted the door, and while parleying, put the child out of the back window into the hands of her cousin, who mounted a horse and fled into the woods. The same night Mrs. Burns escaped in disguise with the little girl, and immediately resumed her exhibitions at the principal watering-places. In September, Mr. Whitten went to New York, and after travelling over the New England States in pursuit of his daughter, succeeded in compelling Mrs. Burns to produce his child before the New York Supreme Court. His counsel trusted to his legal rights and the utter worthlessness of the indenture out of Ohio, and did not make character an issue in the plaint, so that when damning evidence of the woman's infamy was offered, the Judge excluded it. Mrs. Burns was backed by persons belonging to a noted Free Love establishment, by several Abolitionists, and by Mr. and Mrs. James S. Thayer, who had often entertained their visitors by the child's recitations. A curious illustration of justice on the Bench in New York was presented by the frequent reference of the Justice outside the evidence, to the opinion of his 'fair friend Mrs. Thayer, an accomplished literary lady,' etc. He admitted the worthlessness of the indenture, but stated his purpose of restoring the child to Mrs. Burns's custody, proposing certain restrictions, and that Mr. Thayer should be made associate guardian, to control the child's movements and her exhibitions—the power of the Court being vested in him. The father was obliged to submit to this, or see his child given unreservedly into the power of a woman he had discovered to be a woman of infamous character. He confided his distress to Mr. Thayer, and begged him to save his child, referring him to the proofs of Mrs. Burns's infamy which had been excluded on the trial by the technical difficulty. Mr. Thayer refused to look at these proofs, but manifesting the most unbounded confidence in Mrs. Burns, used the power vested in him simply for her pleasure and advantage.

The father's anxious letters craving intelligence of his daughter, were unanswered, except by a cruel missive from Mrs. Burns, who declared he should never see or hear from her more. With Mr. Thayer's approval, but contrary to the agreement and the Court order, she took the child to Philadelphia for exhibition last Winter. The father sent power of Attorney to Mr. F. Carroll Brewster, the best lawyer in Philadelphia, and claimed his child before the Supreme Court. But the Court opined that it would be a high indignity to the sovereignty of New York to hear evidence in the case. The father was referred for redress to the New York Court, and censure was passed on the female speculator, whose audiences were vastly increased by the additional notoriety given to her little protege. A Quaker spinster—Miss Marshall—and other rabid abolitionists, who would have torn Mrs. Burns to pieces had the child been a colored one—with a scribbler for the press, who was a fugitive from England for certain swindling operations, came out in violent partisanship, and made themselves notorious in defence of the mountebank. The scribbler's reward was in dollars —the woman's in the pleasure of showing the child about. Mrs. Burns returned triumphant to New York, where she left the child with Mr. Thayer in April, and departed for Cincinnati to see after a suit she had in hand with some bankers.

In Cincinnati she was met with a process and a suit before a Justice, under the statute, to annul the indentures by which she claimed the child of Mr. Whitten, on the ground of her immoral character. She was identified by a score of witnesses, under a dozen names, and proved to have kept houses of prostitution in San Francisco, Sacramento City, and Louisville. The indentures were annulled. She did not abide the issue of the trial; but made a 'moonlight flitting' to New York, abducted the child from the school in which Mr. Thayer had placed it, dressed her as a boy, and in company with a man who called himself Dodge, went to Albany, and thence to Suspension Bridge. She returned by a roundabout course to Philadelphia, where she found her Quaker friends ready to sustain her, notwithstanding the reports of her trial in the Western papers. Thence she came to New York, about the middle of May. She had cut off the child's luxuriant hair, and avowed her intention of hiding her until she should be changed beyond recognition, and then exhibiting her on the stage and consigning her to a life of infamy. She is supposed to be somewhere in concealment in the United States, waiting to receive some money from the bankers she sued, before she sails for England or California. Mr. Thayer, meanwhile, professes to feel bitter chagrin and mortification at the conduct of the woman whom he and his wife vouched for so willingly before the public. He has presented his petition to the Supreme Court for a revocation of his guardianship. Any other Court would probably require him to recover the child, the charge of whom he assumed; or at least to pay damages which would aid the father to rescue her; but the New York Courts are very indulgent. The woman may even be safe in Philadelphia; as the child, being pronounced a ward in chancery, the Court in that city would not meddle with her. The Judge who consigned her to her present fate (Henry E. Davies) entreats the father's counsel not to publish any portion of the fearful evidence from the Cincinnati record against the woman's character, for fear of compromising the respectable persons who were deceived by her. These respectable persons, meanwhile, refuse to contribute one cent towards saving from infamy and ruin the little creature whose ruin they accelerated by the cruel exhibitions of her in their drawing-rooms.

One or two benevolent persons have advertised, offering a reward for any information leading to the recovery of 'Little Ella Burns.' She may be even now in California. A hundred dollars will be paid for securing her, besides the expenses attending her restoration. Information may be sent to the father's attorney, Dexter A. Hawkins, 10 Wall street, New York.

Other papers throughout California, especially in Sacramento, are requested to copy this account, and the aid of the charitable is earnestly solicited to save this gifted child from a fate more horrible than death. She is between six and seven years old; has small dark eyes; brown hair, curling naturally; large front teeth, and deep lines in her cheeks, with a rather full form. Mrs. Burns is about thirty-five; of medium height; slender, with light complexion; blue eyes, and brown hair. She has sent word to the father that he shall never have his child alive.

[For The New York Saturday Press.]

FARR, GRAYDON & CO.

BY J. W. WATSON.

In the year 183-- the house of Farr, Graydon & Co., were bankers of the highest repute. Wall street bowed to their signature, and the scratch of their pen commanded a shower of gold all over the Union wherever it was shown.

One January day, John Graydon sat in his office, not the dull, gray, dirty receptacle of mouldy papers, generally associated with the idea of a business-office, but a splendidly furnished room in the rear of the banking-house, where none were admitted but the greater of his financial connections, or his more intimate personal friends.

There sat John Graydon leaning heavily on a table, his head resting on his hand. Graydon was a young man, a handsome man; his black hair hung over a small white hand, and his eye, though this moment sunken and bloodshot, did not betray dissipation or the cares of business.

The firm of Farr, Graydon & Co., was originally established by the father of John Graydon, who three years before this time had retired, leaving the principal charge of this establishment in the hands of his son, who had been brought up in it, and had the entire confidence of all.

"Three little days," said Graydon, "it is a short time; only three days of grace, and I am a ruined man. The world will know that I am a gambler, a fool, and a thief, the robber of those who have entrusted their all in my hands. It is pleasant to contemplate that in three days, next Thursday, this room will be filled with frightened people poring over those very books, and cursing me from their souls. To think there is no help! I have kept this phantom away as long as I had power to resist, but now it is too late. O! if I had but a chance to recall all these mistakes! There is no hope! In three days it will be known that John Graydon is a defaulter for half a million, and one portion of the world will be horrified at my depravity, the other envy me my chance." And John Graydon rose from his chair and walked the room with hasty steps.

"But by Heavens," he resumed, "I will not be pointed at without some compensation. If I am to have fingers pointed at me, and curses upon my head for half a million, it shall be for more." He clenched his hands as he spoke, resumed his seat, and the examination of his books. It was a cold night, very cold, the snow lay deep, and was still falling. New York becomes insane in a snow-storm, and this was no exception. Broadway resounded with a thousand voices singing and shouting, from the great omnibus-sleigh containing its hundred, to the little crotchety pung, with its couple. The town was merry and mad.

A stylish pair of blacks came down, wheeled at Union Park, and at the corner of a street close in its vicinity a figure muffled in fur threw the reins to a servant and alighted under a gas-lamp. He looked at his watch, "Robert, it is now nine o'clock. You will remain here two hours. If I do not return at the end of that time, drive home, and say I shall not be back until late to-morrow." The servant bowed, and drew the sleigh-robes about him carefully while the gentleman hurried away. In a few minutes he stopped in front of a handsome house and rang. The door was opened by a smiling servant, who took from his hands his coat and hat. He was evidently no stranger, as without announcement he advanced to and opened the parlor, only stopping for an instant to tap with his finger. A lady, young and very beautiful, advanced to meet him. She was not an American. Hair of jet, black eyes of the same, and an olive-tint, declared her of the South of Europe.

"Dear Graydon," she said, taking his hand and looking in his face, "I am so glad to see you. I feared you would not come. What is the matter, you look so pale? What has distressed you? Speak, we are alone!"

"I have come to you, Emilia, for the last time," answered Graydon.

"For the last time! What do you mean? For the last time! You that have professed to love me, and you say this to me so calmly?"

"I am not calm, Emilia; my heart, my brain is on fire. I have come to you for the last time. I have come as a man from whom everything is fleeing away, and you stretch not forth your hand."

"What is this? What have I done? How can I save you, Graydon?"

"By loving me."

"I love you."

"Aye, but more than this. Listen to me, Emilia. I am a ruined, a disgraced man. To-morrow It will be known to all that John Graydon has embezzled the money that has been entrusted to his hands; to-morrow his name will be a bye-word and a reproach in the mouths of honest men. This night, this very night, I must fly from my home and my native city, never to return. You, Emilia, must go with me."

The last sentence was uttered in a hoarse whisper. Graydon had seized her hand as he spoke, and an intensity of gaze seemed to say to her— "You must go or you must die."

"My husband," she gasped, "my husband! if he should overtake us."

Graydon sneered. "Overtake us! Do you think, Emilia, I am a boy? Do you think I have no more at stake than this. He cannot overtake us. I have been preparing this flight for months. Emilia, you have declared you loved me, that you would surrender all for me; prove it now. Your husband is a cruel, tyrannical master; he is no husband, he is no companion. You fear him, you do not love him. You know how I have smothered, when I have met him, my desire to quarrel. You know he has only tolerated me for the sake of the money he has obtained in play. Fool that he was, not to see that I allowed him to win. I loved you, Emilia, and I believed that this money would be lavished on you. I was mistaken; the selfish egotist cares only for himself."

The woman looked in the face of Graydon. An expression half of shame, and half of love, played over her features. She drew her hand from his, and opening a drawer in the secretary near where they sat, displayed to Graydon heaps of gold and bills.

"See," she said, "this is his money, here he keeps it. I have access, but I dare not touch. I will show you, Graydon, that I love you. Take it, take it all, I will brave his anger."

"No! I want no money of his. I would take from him only what he knows not how to use. I would take you, Emilia, you must be mine." As he spoke, he caught her in his arms. "Come! within a few yards is my carriage; in a few hours we will be in safety beyond pursuit. See, Emilia, I am rich, I would not fall in poverty. No! no!" And Graydon drew from his pocket a long wallet. "Here is wealth, one hundred and fifty thousand dollars. You see I am still rich. Come, Emilia." And he pressed the yielding woman in his arms.

"Stop!" said a calm, unimpassioned voice, "stop, Mr. Graydon! Sit down, Madam; do not be alarmed. I am, I admit, a cruel, tyrannical master. I think those were the words, Mr. Graydon, eh? I see I must bring my tyranny into use. So, sir, you would not rob me of my money, but would take from me my wife. You are an honest man, Mr. Graydon, a conscientious man. I am not honest, cannot be honest, never was honest, Mr. Graydon, therefore shall not now display it. I will trouble you, Mr. Graydon, for the money you have in that wallet, and then, my dear friend, you can take the wife as soon as you please."

"You scoundrel!" hissed Graydon, advancing to wards him, and drawing from his pocket a long-bladed knife.

"One moment, Mr. Graydon," said the husband. "Pardon me, do not let us have any little unpleasant| scenes here; there is not the slightest occasion; this is a mere matter of business. You are a business man; so am I; we can settle all this in a business way."

"Stand away, sir!" shouted Graydon, "and let me pass, or in one moment you are a dead man."

"Mr. Graydon," said Williston, "if you pass that door you are in the hands of the police."

Graydon staggered back as though he had received a heavy blow, dropping his knife on the floor. Williston stepped forward, picked it up, and laid it on the piano.

"Now," said he, "we can talk over this little matter, you see. Do not fear, I have laid your knife where it will be convenient, where you can get it." And he smiled most courteously at Graydon. "I had unexpectedly returned, and from the next room overheard all this conversation. It is easily settled. You love my wife, I love your money; give me your money, and take the woman."

Graydon gave a glance of fire from Williston's face to that of his wife. Had she played traitor, and brought him into this position? No! how could she? She knew nothing of his errors until this night. She did not know that he would have this amount of money with him. No! she was not false to him, that glance told him so.

"Are you a man," said Graydon, "a man or a fiend. No! sir, I will not give you this money. I will not bargain with you."

"I am very sorry, then, Mr. Graydon; I shall be obliged to act like an honest man, which is not consistent with my desires. I have no time to trifle, nor have you. In five minutes I will return to this room to receive your answer. If in that time you accept my offer, Madam will not keep you ten minutes in making herself ready to accompany you. But if you reject it, I will not detain you one minute. I have taken the precaution to place a couple of officers on the stoop. I told them I should possibly want their assistance; they will await your pleasure." And bowing to both, Williston withdrew.

Not a word was spoken for a minute, each looked upon the other. At last Graydon said:

"Emilia, what have you to say, what shall I do?" She cast a fearful look at the door, and in a sobbing whisper answered, "Accept."

"I have nothing, the fiend! he would turn me on the world in poverty with nothing."

"I have jewels," answered Emilia, "he surely cannot prevent my taking them,"

Graydon advanced to where she sat. "And you," he said, "you will share my poverty. You will go with me to another land, and bear with me its burdens ?"

"I will go !" she answered.

No other word was spoken. At the expired time Williston again entered the room. "Your answer," he said.

"I accept," was Graydon's reply.

"Spoken sensibly. Madam will go to her room; in ten minutes," he said, handing her his watch, "she will return to this room, where she will find I shall leave the house in the meantime, simply to avoid future remark. In fifteen minutes I shall return. I shall expect to find you both gone. It is possible you will want something for travelling expenses. In the drawer which you examined some time since you will find nine thousand dollars in gold; nine, Mr. Graydon, a magic number. Ha! ha! ha! a lucky number! You can take this nine thousand dollars, Mr. Graydon. Excuse me, there are some bank notes there. I do not doubt your honesty, Mr. Graydon, but I will take those with me. The gold is yours, the nine, the lucky nine thousand, and now I will thank you for your pocketbook, and I will leave you. A pleasant journey, Mr. Graydon. Farewell, Madam. I shall return in fifteen minutes, I trust I shall not find you here. You can leave my watch on the piano when you have done with it."

Williston left the room and the house, slipping a piece of gold into the hands of each of the officers and dismissing them.

As the street door closed, Emilia burst into tears. Graydon flew to her. "Why do you weep?" he said, "Is it at the loss of this wretch, Emilia? Do you regret him? it is not yet too late. He will again receive you," and he sneered. "You love him?"

"No, no!" sobbed Emilia, "no love; shame, shame, before you, Graydon, that I could have lived with, and borne so mean, so base a wretch. No! no! I do not love him, I hate."

"Come, Emilia, let us leave this horrible place. There is poison in the very air. I do not wish to see the face of that man again, or there will be murder done, whatever be the result."

In a short space from this, Graydon handed Emilia into his sleigh, which still stood upon the spot where he had left it. As he laid the lash upon the team, a dark figure passed under the gas-light and raised his hat in salute. It was Williston.

Next day the city rang with the failure of Farr, Graydon & Co., Bankers; caused by the defalcation and disappearance of John Graydon. No trace could be had of the fugitive save the evidence given by Robert, the coachman, who had received his master and an unknown lady into the sleigh at about eleven o'clock the previous evening. That he had left them at the corner of Courtland street and Broadway, according to his orders, and driven home.

We will change the time and the scene. It is ten years later, and a well known gambling establishment, not many hundred miles from Canal street and Broadway.

Walking about the room is a tall, dark man; his hair is touched with gray, his age, perhaps fifty; he stops at each change of the game to renew his stake. Luck is with him to-night, and the gold lies heaped upon the table. Perfectly cool and uninterested he sees it increase. Another enters, a younger man than the first; a very heavy, dark beard and moustache, cover his face. He wears glasses, and a look that shows him to be a stranger; one who has dwelt sufficiently long under a Southern sun to have become well embrowned. He lays a roll of gold upon the table and loses; he repeats with the same ill-success. Without looking at or addressing any one directly, he lays down the third roll, and speaking as though to himself, says, This is my last; when that is lost, so am I."

The first player started at the voice, and leaning over the table toward the loser, said "Graydon." The other raised his eyes for a moment, instantly cast them down, seized the roll of gold, and again dropping it, looked intently in the face of his opposite, and said, "If you meant, sir, to address me by that name, you are mistaken; that is not my name."

As he spoke his gold was rolled away and he was again a loser. He turned from the table. The other advanced. "I think I heard you say, sir, that you were without money. Will you allow me to become your banker, to offer you a loan?"

"No sir, I never borrow, more especially from those I do not know."

"Let me introduce myself, then," said he drawing nearer. "My name is Williston."

The other bowed.

"And mine is Riel, Colonel in the Brazilian service." Williston had approached within a couple of feet of the other. He spoke low.

"John Graydon, do you believe that it could be I should not know you again as long as you are above ground? No! You may walk the street unknown to your own mother; but wherever we meet, I shall know you, Graydon, aye! know you by instinct."

"And what do you want with me," said Graydon, "Can you not see that I hate you? Can you not see, reptile, that I spit upon you?"

"There is no occasion, Graydon, there need be no enmity between us; we are equals. In what have your the advantage of me? We are both honest, are we not? Was it not a mere matter of business? I sold you what I no longer wanted; you bought, and paid a good price, I suppose. Had it been left to your will, you would not have paid so dear. I am an older man than you, Graydon, and I do not trust the pocket in love affairs. Ha! ha! No, love and money will clash."

Williston returned to the table to gather up his winnings, a very large amount, which he soon disposed of in his pockets. Graydon watched him. O, the power of gold the crusher of pride, the healer of quarrels, the minister for every wound. As Williston returned to where Graydon stood, he stretched out his hand. "Come," he said, "let us be friends. I think, Graydon, you want a friend; it may be that I can serve you."

Graydon looked at him for a few minutes steadily, without speaking, and then gave his hand.

Again it was a January night; again was the snow falling thick and fast, and Broadway ringing with a thousand shouts. Williston and Graydon issued upon the street from the gambling house, Williston's arm drawn through that of the other. "A strange coincidence; yes, it is indeed. Ten years ago this very night —you carry your memories well, Mr. Graydon."

"Why should I not? Do you suppose the night I fled a criminal from everything I valued on earth, should not be marked forever."

"Ah! ha! All you valued on earth! O! no, not all, did you not take Emilia with you?"

"Silence, sir; do not pollute her name by allowing it to pass your lips. Though she was your wife, though she left you, and was criminal, she was as far above you as the stars."

"Well! well! don't let us quarrel over this, you shall have it entirely your own way. And so she died in Buenos Ayres, eh?"

"Yes," answered Graydon in a low voice; "of fever, within three months after leaving New York."

"And after all you became a soldier ?"

"I entered the service of Brazil, I am now a Colonel; I have a year's furlough."

"Well, Colonel—let me see, Riel, I think you said—Colonel Reil, let us be friends and confidents. Your money, Colonel, did me no service. Ah! how much better it pays to be honest. With my ability, now, had I been an honest man, what a position I could have held! what ladders have I kicked from me; and now what am I? instead of a man of fortune, I am only a fortunate man." And the rascal laughed and shook the gold in his pockets. "Wait, wait, some of these days when I care no longer for society, and wish to retire into settled life, I shall make a brilliant effort like you, Colonel. Excuse me, don't mind what I say, its my style; I will show what a great financier I am, and go off in a blaze of glory."

"How have you avoided putting yourself in the hands of the law so far? In your course I should suppose it could not be helped." Graydon spoke as though addressing himself.

"Ha! ha! ha! You are innocent, Colonel! You should have staid in New York. The law, my dear Colonel, the law never troubles those who do not trouble it. Why should I place myself in the power of the law, when the law has been so liberal as to leave every avenue open for me? When so much can be done legally, my dear Colonel, it is only the fool who disturbs the law. You perceive," continued he, pointing to a rough-looking man passing, "that is the great detective, Bolter. You have heard of him no doubt. I know that Bolter watches me; I also watch Bolter. I know that nothing would please Bolter so much as to I find me within the boundaries of this law. Not that Bolter would rudely pass me over to its mercies; O no! Bolter knows better than that. But, my dear Colonel, as it is, you must know that Bolter gets only an occasional twenty, which Bolter borrows and forgets to return, but if Bolter once found my feet on forbidden ground, then Bolter's twenties would increase to hundreds perhaps thousands. You see it is part of my business, my dear Colonel, to know exactly where the boundary-line of his terrible bugbear law runs, so that I may not step over it. I think, my dear Colonel, you must resign from the Brazilian service, and throw yourself upon society."

Graydon looked upon this man, who, confessing himself educated in rascality, perfectly master of every step, yet declared that honesty paid better. His mind went back over ten years: he saw himself the rich and honored banker, the upright business man; he thought, where, had he continued in this path, might he now have reached, and he thought of the route he had pursued—a fugitive from the city that gave him birth, lost to kindred and society, a wanderer upon the face of the earth, without an affection, without a tie, seeking in the excitement of the gambling-table the balm for a mind diseased. O! for the experience of the lost to instil into the minds of the wayward! O! that the youth in making his first false step could have all his dark future spread before him in a vision, that he could see how much better it paid to be honest. Better in money, better in peace of mind, better here and hereafter.

"And now, Colonel," resumed Williston, "you want money?"

Graydon was silent.

"Very well, silence gives consent. I can put you in a way of getting it. Listen, we are both honest men. I wish to stay in New York. You do not. You understand these Wall-street affairs better than I. No difference, no difference, my dear sir. Wall-street is Wall-street, the buildings, the men, may change, but the nature is there still—Wall-street will be the same in constitution a hundred years hence as now. I cannot afford to leave New York, but, my dear Colonel, I have a little business which we can transact together, we can each pocket about fifty thousand dollars by the operation; then you have only to return to the Brazilian service, leaving New York at your convenience anytime within a month. What say you, Colonel?"

"Go on," said Graydon.

"Very well," resumed Williston, "I have in my pocket one hundred thousand dollars of Chilian Government Bonds, so well done that they cannot be detected. You understand me. Cannot be detected? They can be sold in Wall-street at a little over par value. It will be exactly two months, Colonel, before it will be known that they are not genuine. I believe I need not say any more."

"No, you need not say any more, villain. It is now my turn. Now, Emilia, it is my mission to avenge you. Williston, in all this, I see the hand of my destiny, You boast, scoundrel, that you have escaped the hands of the law so far; you shall escape no longer. You shall show that your vaunted skill will allow you to creep through this."

"You dare not, Graydon," gasped Williston. "You dare not. You are yourself still open to punishment. You dare not sacrifice yourself to punish me."

"I dare not! I will show you, wretch, that I dare," and Graydon shouted "help."

"Silence," hissed Williston.

The street was dark, it was late. A single gas-light flickered through the snow.

"One word and you die."

Graydon saw a knife gleaming in the light—just enough light to recognize the knife that ten years before he had drawn upon Williston in his own house. He made one spring and seized the arm that held it. There was a struggle, a smothered cry, and a fall.

We take from the papers of the next morning, the following paragraph:

Mysterious Death—Yesterday morning, about two o'clock, as policeman Nufty was patrolling his beat upon Elm street he thought he saw the legs of a man protruding from the snow. Upon examination it proved to be the body of Mr. H. Williston, a noted gambler and man about town. Williston was known that evening to have been in a gambling-house in Broadway near Canal street, which he left about ten o'clock in company with another person. At this time he had with him a large sum of money. The body when found had no money save a few dollars in gold and silver. The throat was cut, severing the jugular vein. A knife, known to have been one that Williston always carried, was found alongside the body. The only impression seems to be, that Williston had entered some other gambling place, where he had lost his money and then committed suicide, as he had often been heard to declare that would be the manner of his death. It could not be a robbery and murder, as his watch and valuable chain were untouched. An inquest will be held this morning.

Two months after this an eminent firm of brokers in Wall-street found themselves possessed of one hundred thousand dollars of counterfeit Chilian bonds sold them by a person calling himself Colonel Riel of the Brazilian service, but who upon after enquiry was not to be found upon the army list of that nation.

[Written for The New York Saturday Press.]

THEY MEANT NO HARM.

BY ANNIE BREWSTER.

I.

The sun was fast approaching the edge of the Jura, one fine June afternoon, as L' Hirondelle swept into the crescent-shaped port of Duchy, the wharf-suburb of Lausanne. Among the passengers who stepped aboard the boat, were two handsome young English girls, whose graceful ease of manner, and clear, frank, independence of look and walk, gave evidence of culture and elegant social surroundings.

They had taken a sudden freak to pay a visit to a young friend who was residing in one of the towns at the head of the lake, and the absence of a would-be-strict chaperonne Aunt, on a shopping excursion to Geneva, had given them a chance to do it unattended, and therefore untrammelled, by the irksome presence of a dame de compagnie, or valet.

There was, however, a great difference in the appearance of the two girls, and this showed itself as much in their style of dress, as in their looks. One, who seemed to be the elder, appeared to be willing to risk everything in the name of taste, to gratify what amounted almost to an appetite for ornament and gay colors. There was something bizarre, and a little melodramatic in her picturesque costume, which, it must be confessed,—although she did not know it,— 'sentait un peu le théâtre.' But there was an innate gracefulness about her, an artistic originality, which kept from her all taint of vulgarity, although her toilette was a little too exaggerated for a lady.

The dress of the other was, on the contrary, scrupulously submissive to fashion; very rich and elegant, but exceedingly comme il faut; indeed too much so, as, while her sister's escaped being vulgar, hers did not avoid being bourgeoise; she resembled everybody too much. The strong, masterful character of her sister evidently controlled her, although the spirit of adventure seemed to be a little innate also, for her pretty blue eye danced with merriment, and her mobile mouth curled and laughed as if she were saying, 'What fine fun, to be sure! How droll and odd !'

Independent, and quite accustomed to the thing as they wished to appear, they were so embarrassed on entering the boat, as to mistake aft for forward; and yet it might not have been so much embarrassment, as a desire to be alone in their new element. A few peasant-women with hottes of vegetables, and a traveller—who sat with sketching-book open on his knee, an unlashed knapsack and lorgnette-case lying beside him, probably a German artist, professional or amateur,—were the only passengers in that part of the boat.

The younger girl first observed their mistake.

"No matter," said the elder with a true Vaudois shrug of the shoulders. "All the better. So much the more fun, as Tom says, ' more of a lark in it.'"

"Fancy how horrified Ernest and Madame ma tante would be, If they knew of our travelling alone and en paysanne," added the younger with a frolicsome laugh.

"Petite ingrate, tais toi !" exclaimed the elder, "if you talk of my cold, Ernest, I'll stop at the next landing, and take the omnibus back to Lausanne; then you shall not see your darling Julia and Montrueux for a twelve month. What harm is there, poltronne? I am sure I mean nothing but to be my own mistress for a little while, and to give the Southern blood my mother left me a little chance to circulate freely, and, ah !" she added, throwing her beautiful head erect, and expanding her fine, large chest, as she drew in a long vigorous breath, "Comme elle sent bonne, cette liberté ! Who is it dares to say that liberty is not a fruit of warm climates? It is an untruth; for I believe individual liberty only buds and blooms to perfection in Southern."

"O comme tu es sunnyeuse with your philosophizing, mignonne !" interrupted the other with a playful petulance that was excessively becoming to her, "just so you spoiled Liszt's delicious Chopin-Nocturne last night, by making me think, when I wanted only to enjoy."

The German who had observed them the first moment they stepped aboard the boat, listened to their talk with increasing interest; for, although they spoke chiefly in English, and fancied themselves thereby enclosed in a safe shell, he perfectly understood their tongue, and enjoyed their playful innocent freedom. The conversation continued in the same style, as they walked to and fro in front of him. They discussed in a lively manner a concert Liszt had given the night before at Lausanne, from the intoxication of which musical draught neither girl had evidently yet recovered, and the elder one 'Octavie,' as the younger one called her, defended her own views in such an artistic intelligent style, that the German grew quite captivated with her. She was what Heine calls himself, 'a Sunday child that saw the spectres, which others only heard.' The young man was as original in his way, and romantic as Octavie, but it was a man's romance, and just that much removed from unconsciousness and ingenuousness, as are most men. He determined to contrive some way of speaking to them, and managed as they were approaching him, to let fall at their feet his sketching-book and portefeuille, scattering his really fine sketches far and wide, and while doing so, adroitly succeeded in catching the corner of Octavie's costly, unsuitable camel's-hair Bournous, in such a manner as to make it appear that she had been the cause.

"Mille pardons !" cried Octavie, and she and her sister hastened to help the artist gather up his drawings, while he assured them, with more truth than such assurances generally contain, that they were not the cause; it was his own carelessness entirely, and entreated of them not to give themselves so much trouble about a mere trifle. The glorious golden light of the setting sun illuminated the whole boat, and gave a fine effect to some water-colored studies among the collection.

"This is gloriously beautiful!" exclaimed Octavie, seizing one, "our own lovely Capri; look, Fan! and this, Camaldoli as I live! with its rich chestnut foliage; look, look, Fan!"

"Octavie," whispered the other in a cautioning tone, as she saw her impulsive sister about to seat herself and turn over the contents of the artist's portefeuille, while he pretended to be entirely occupied in searching for some stray leaves near the guards of the boat.

"Nonsense!" answered Octavie, "I shall never see the man again. He does not know us, and—"

Just then he approached, and with the aplomb of a man accustomed to the outside world, and an easy courtesy derived from cultivated associations, entered into conversation with the two girls. They turned over the sketches together, and compared memories of places they had both seen; the delighted German gave graphic descriptions, and Octavie added her poesy and pretty vague romance to the talk. One might have supposed they had been friends from infancy, and they themselves even forgot that they were strangers; It was as if they had suddenly met after a separation of an existence's duration, and were living over past memories together, as rapidly as if they knew they never should meet again.

The boat stopped at Vevey, landed passengers, started again, swept by the pretty, little half ruin of La Tour de Peilz, with its nodding Lombardy poplars, all unnoticed by these three happy young people. At Montrueux, some boat-hands came near them, to remove a lot of luggage deposited near their bench, and in doing so, seized a box which belonged to the German and were carrying it off rapidly. He sprang up and followed them, to tell them of their mistake. The explanation and putting of the box in a safe place occupied some minutes, and when he returned to his seat, he found his charming companions gone, while a handkerchief which he could just see in the deepening twilight, waved from a boat that was fast rowing to the shore,—for the bize was too strong for the steamer to go up to the wharf—told him plainly what had become of them.

His first impulse was to follow them, but it was too late; already the boat was cutting swiftly through 'the massy waters' that dash up against 'the isolated rock of Chillon.' He tapped his foot with vexation, and felt like one suddenly awakened from a curious, delightful dream, bewildered and a little out of humor at the awakening. After a few moments he stooped to shut up the open sketch-book and portefeuille, saying to himself with a laugh,

"I verily believe I have had a raptus, and imagined the whole thing."

Something fell at his feet; it was a glove, he had seen Octavie playing with while talking.

"A pretty tangible proof at all events, although none the less a raptus," he continued, as he examined the soft kid glove of the girl.

"It's not a little hand," he said, spreading it out to its full size; "my little Ida's both hands could go into it readily; but it is one of those 'heroic hands' Guiseppe Vitelli raves over, and is always sculpturing. She might have Roman blood in her too, for her gait and form and face are quite of that type."

As he smoothed out the really well-sized fingers of the straw-colored glove on his palm, a little courteously and tenderly, as if it might have been the lady's own hand, he felt something hard in the third finger; shook the glove carefully, and out rolled a ring, which had evidently slipped from the finger when the glove had been pulled off.

"Aha!" cried he as he took it to the lamp at the wheel to examine it. It was a Mexican ring of curious workmanship; a plaited cord of gold, which had on its top two hands clasped over a diamond, and a fine ruby glittered in the gold wrist of each hand. While examining the pretty jewel he pressed one of the rubies unconsciously, the ring flew apart, disclosing an inner one, on which, directly under the clasped hands, was a little gold heart surmounted by the diamond. On looking at it more closely, he saw that there was an inscription engraved on it, and by the aid of the flower magnifying glass he had in his green tin herbier, he read 'Ernest—Octavie—Jan. 1, 18—."

"Humph! a betrothal ring evidently," he muttered in a dissatisfied, piqued tone, just as if he had not also exchanged betrothal rings with the pretty Ida whose little hand he had talked of, and had surely no right to be dissatisfied at finding out that the captivating Octavie, like himself, was also verlobt, nor even to be giving any delicious dreamy thoughts, however vague and unmeaning, to the charming, little, romantic episode in his journey. But there was the ring, and still worse the memory of the affair; for human nature is human nature, even when it does not mean any harm.

"Pshaw!" he continued in a vexed tone, as after looking at the ring for a long while, he wrapped it up in the glove, and put it into a sly little pocket of a carnet, which was deposited in a still slyer little vest pocket, actually as near his heart as the blue enamelled medallion nestling there containing one of the good little Ida's golden curls, would let it come—"Pshaw! what abominable coquettes women are."

Then he clasped his portefeuille together with a jerk that was anything but amiable, or in keeping with his fine good natured expression of face; lashed on his knapsack with a business-like air, as if he had wasted enough time on stuff and nonsense; lighted his meerschaum, and, as he stepped testily off the boat at Villeneuve, and tramped up to the railway office, he muttered between his teeth, "I wonder who Ida is flirting with?"

II.

"But, Octavie, the Virgin looks mawkish and the child sickly."

"No such thing, Fan! you are a heathen, and have no more taste than Ernest, who considers himself such a connoisseur. The Mother-maiden looks sorrowful, not mawkish, and the child-Lord sad. See, how cunningly she is trying to coax that solemn little face to laugh, by filliping his under-lip with her pretty third finger, and she herself looking in her tender young beauty, sad enough to have an almost bursting heart. Its one of the loveliest things in this whole Musée Borbonique collection, and the thing I love best in all Naples. Di Napoli shall copy it for me, and I'll keep it in my dressing-room to tell me how happy I really am, when I chafe so sillily under Ernest's aristocratic conventionalities."

"Now, Octavie, if that picture was not a Parmegiano, you know you would not see such beauty in it. You dress it up out of your own kaleidoscope imagination."

"Stop, Fan, this instant, and be original when you are saucy. Don't dare to quote Ernest. I do not let him steal your delicious petite maitresse sarcasms, so you sha'n't rob him."

Some gentlemen entered the gallery, and the ladies drew nearer their valet, a regular English 'John Tummas,' who stood within call.

"As I live, Octavie, there is that tiresome German we met on the lake-boat three years ago at Lausanne, when you lost Ernest's ring."

"No !—so it is. I wonder if he found that ring. How I'd like to ask him."

"In the name of all that's prudent, Octavie, do not speak to him."

"I entreat of you."

"Don't alarm yourself, my dear; I have not the most distant idea of doing such a thing. I would not for all the rings between here and Mexico. I could not without Ernest's knowing it, of course, and he never could comprehend the affair; he would bother himself and me about it incessantly."

"I detest the sight of the man, for the trouble that ring gave us; for I always blamed myself about it. But to let me see dear little Julie, you would never have taken the madcap trip, and therefore never lost the ring."

"Nonsense, ma chère; neither you nor the poor fellow were to blame—only my own heedlessness, But now the trouble is all over, I don't care anything about it; though we did have a bother about that ring, did we not? And that clever old Brogniart of Geneva, how nicely he managed! Do you remember the day he asked Ernest to let him look at his ring, when we were in his shop, and said—the naughty old fibber that he was—when Ernest told him he did not wish the ring imitated, that it would be quite impossible to copy it? and how his sly little black eyes glittered with triumph at me all the while, as serious as an old monkey? And then in a fortnight after he had one ready for me—the perfect facsimile of Ernest's. And do you remember the cut finger I had to pretend to have, so as to avoid annoying Ernest by telling him of the loss of my ring? and how he laughed at my romance because I insisted on his putting on the ring after the pretended ill finger got well? Well, it was a naughty little piece of hypocrisy, Fan, and one I should hate to live with, but for dear Ernest's perfect want of comprehension of real life."

"Hush, Octavie! here he is."

"Who? Ernest?" She turned with a quick movement, and faced, full front, the German.

Nature was stronger than culture; and as the rich blood mounted to her cheek, she was just on the point of speaking to him, when a voice restored her to herself. A gentleman entered the salle and came up to them with a quick, resolute step, saying "Come, ladies; the carriage waits below."

He was a fine, handsome man, with a high forehead; clear, sharp, eagle outline; eyes like steel; and a firm mouth, whose thin, unelastic lips, seemed to taste and enjoy power. Yes! that description of the Earl in 'Lady Geraldine,' would exactly apply to him,—a graceful, courtly, cultured person—'Just a good man made a proud man'; and if he was 'Ernest,' the slightest observer looking at him might have easily marvelled at the contrast between him and Octavie, and perfectly understood, without one single word of explanation, why she should not wish to tell him anything that smacked of adventure, or that deviated in the slightest degree from his own high aristocratic way.

They left the salle, and the tantalized German stood for a few minutes as if riveted to the ground. Suddenly coming to his senses, he hurried out by the same door the English party had taken. He reached the entrance of the grand vestibule of the Musée, just in time to see the whole party drive off in an open carriage, which swept around the corner, and was soon lost in the crowd that throngs that great street-artery of Naples, the Toledo.

As he turned back to reenter the building, he jostled against some one; it was the valet whom he had noticed as being in attendance on the ladies in the Gallery; and who had been busily engaged in examining the address of a note he held in his hand. John Tummus, nearly knocked off his heels by the impetuous German's quick movement, was so bewildered, that he thought it had been his own fault, and commenced apologizing very civilly, which emboldened the German to commit an indiscretion.

"It's of no consequence, my good fellow," he said with a hearty laugh; then slipping a piaster into the man's hand, added, "Oblige me by telling me the names of the ladies you were in waiting on, up stairs—very handsome women !"

"Is it my mistress, sir, and her sister?" asked the still half-bewildered servant.

"I suppose so," replied the German. "Pray what are their names?"

"Unarble Mrs. Grum and Miss Flum," said the servant, with the amusing unmistakable pronunciation of a cockney 'John Tummus,' so ridiculously filled with elisions and contractions; for his words translated into clearly pronounced English, should have been 'Honorable Mrs. Graham and Miss Folham.'

"Humph," grumbled the German as he mounted slowly the broad stone staircase, and then stopping for an instant, looking up at one of the beautiful Greek Danzatrice standing there, without thinking of the charming statue, 'Humph! Grum !—and Flum!! Two pretty names to be sure, to get up a romance about. The impertinent flunkey meant to quiz me, I verily believe.'

"Gaspard! here's your mail, my good fellow," cried out a young man from the upper landing place. "I have been hunting you everywhere to give it you, for I saw among the letters that one of Ida's you have been growling about for a fortnight—and knowing how anxious you were to hear from her, I put them all in my pocket and brought them to you."

It's very provoking to be sure, that one's dearest blessings in this world always come at the very moment they are the least valued. Human nature is a strange animal.

III.

The fine old church of Santa Chiara was crowded with people. It was the Spring festival of San Januarius. The High altar, of precious marble, and lapis-lazuli inlayings, was superbly draped in crimson velvet, whose rich folds hung down beside and around the golden bust of the famous Neapolitan patron-saint. A stray sunbeam falling on the richly jewelled mitre, and gorgeous necklaces and crosses decorating the bust, broke into as many dazzling fragments of light as the four thousand rubies, sapphires, and diamonds there collected could make.

To the left of the altar-railing, old peasant women, looking like the witches in Macbeth, stood chanting their wild invocation. The imposing procession of the five and forty silver statues of saints, each one on its gilt stand, carried by golden rails on the shoulders of superbly formed Neapolitans, filed up the side of the large Basilica, and after a gracious obeisance to the saint, swept grandly around and moved down the other side of the church, leaving ample room in the centre of the building for the immense crowd of spectators and soldiery collected there.

Glorious music poured out, filling with its rich subtle fluid every part of the grand old church; it was a fine orchestral symphony, composed for the occasion by Mercadante, and directed by the great old composer himself in person.

Behind the high altar, between it and the great medieval treasures of the church,—Masaccio's monuments of Robert the Wise, and the fine old tomb where the remains of the beautiful hapless Joanna I. found rest in the arms of her dead mother,—were collected a select little company of spectators, who had been placed there on account of the fine coup d'œil they could there command of the grand religious pageant that was sweeping like a vision before them.

The Pope's Nuncio was there, with a pretty young Roman princess as tender and lovely looking as About's 'Tolla,' and a regal Russian Duchess, one or two Ambassadresses, a graceful German Comtesse full of naïve, unconscious coquetry, and Octavie and her sister, with the cold aristocratic Ernest, and two or three other gentlemen. The music pealed out still more grandly, and every neck was stretched forward to see Cardinal Duke Sforza, and his attendant clergy, with the sacred relics, approaching the altar. The old women shrieked out their witch-like plain-song in still shriller tones, some striking the key-note of the Symphony, while others were keeping their wild chant in curious grotesque harmony with the scholarly composition of the classic maestro, reminding one of the demon supporters to old altars, or the impish gargoyle heads on the gutter-spouts of some superb old cathedral.

While each one was intent on gazing, a curtain next to Octavie was lifted gently, and some church dignitary entered, with a gentleman who took his stand so noiselessly that no one but Octavie saw him. As she looked up at the new-comer, her eyes met those of her German acquaintance of the Swiss steamer. The place was not light enough to show her change of color; but she felt it, and so did Gaspard, without seeing it. He noticed instantly that she did not intend to recognize him. A few minutes after, she sat down in a chair that was a little apart from the rest, while her handsome Ernest and Fanny leaned eagerly forward, intent on seeing the whole scene, which was as artistic as curious. The chance was too tempting for Gaspard to lose. He knelt down behind her chair as if overcome with his devotional feelings—the wicked fellow!—and watching his opportunity, whispered in her ear—

"You may think me indiscreet and, may be, presumptuous. I am not, I assure you; I only wish to restore to you, in some prudent way, your property. Do not feel annoyed, I entreat of you," for he noticed by the shaking of her chair that she was trembling with nervous agitation, although not by a word or look did she show that she heard or saw him.

After a moment or so of apparent reverential gazing into the church, Gaspard resumed his pretended devotions.

"Presently, when you arise, drop your handkerchief," he continued, "that I may, when I hand it back to you, give you, unseen, the precious little ring, which I found in the glove you left by chance on my sketch-book, after our first and only interview. And now, let me say Adieu forever, and also let me hope that in the future, you will feel able to remember, without any fear of annoyance, as a pleasant little incident in your life, the happiest moments of mine."

Perfidious Gaspard! O, these men!

A shriller shriek burst from the old women. The Symphony pealed out in strange dissonances, and a discordant passage for the wind-instruments followed, reminding one of the weird incantation-scene in Weber's 'Der Freyschutz.' The devout Cardinal Sforza raised his fine, pure eyes and uplifted hands to heaven, reciting the Litanies in concert with his clergy, with redoubled fervor. Suddenly a cannon thundered forth,— the sacred vials were held aloft in the air,—the miracle was accomplished, and there arose from that swaying, surging multitude, a peal of thanksgiving, that mingled with the wild melody of the finale of the Symphony and made an atmosphere of excitement, bewildering to the brain.

Octavie sprang to her feet, and seizing Ernest's arm buried her glowing face on his shoulder. The cool, impassive Englishman turned and looked at her with a smile that was meant for forbearance and patience,— not sympathy, and said, in an indulgent tone:

"Aw! yes, yes, decidedly fine, the whole affair. Its one of the best things they do here in Naples, and certainly better gotten up this time, than ever I have seen it done before! Immensely clever they are at these sort of things!"

Then putting his arm around Octavie's waist with a cool air of property, right, and possession, that made Gaspard shiver and tremble from head to foot with rage, said as if speaking to a spoiled petted child,

"Stand here, you silly girl, do not be so nervous; look at Fan, she bears it like a general in command."

Was it by chance or intention that her soft lace handkerchief lay on the marble floor at Gaspard's feet. No one saw it at all events, and Gaspard after waiting a second, stooped and picked it up. He tied the ring in one corner of the costly little web, and held it in his hand, with a strange sensation creeping through every fibre of his being, a sort of sad lingering tenderness, as if taking leave forever of some treasured memory, or most precious possession of his life.

The military band with their noisy drums commenced, for the Symphony had ended with the completion of the miracle. The cardinal and his clergy prepared to leave the high altar, and the dense mass of human beings thronging the Basilica, grew more and more excited. The company assembled in the altar-recess also prepared to leave, that they might reach their carriages in the church-close, before the crowd poured out.

As Octavie was about passing under the drapery of the door leaning on her husband's arm, Gaspard stepped up to her with the tone and look of a perfect stranger, saying,

"Beg pardon, Madam—is not this your handkerchief? I think I saw you drop it."

She received it from him with a silence that Ernest highly commended afterwards, and as Gaspard held aside the velvet curtain he bowed with a quiet reverential dignity to her, and again they parted.

But the handkerchief only held the ring! Nothing else, on Gaspard's honor as a gentleman !—No note—no nonsense, Not even the glove. Of course that was lost long ago; and that odd straw-colored kid one Ida once found, neatly folded, and put away carefully in the pocket of a carnet, and wondered at his desire to have it left there, was what he said it was, surely, 'an odd one of his own.' Innocent little Ida! the glove was so large she never thought of doubting the truth of what he said. And probably it was his; certainly in one sense it was—possession. It's very uncharitable to suppose otherwise, and I for one shall not encourage anybody in entertaining ill-natured suspicions of such a proper husband as Gaspard Grossmuth.

IV.

The steamer bell was ringing violently and passengers were hurrying aboard and ashore, one cold Autumn afternoon at a little stopping-place on the Rhine. Four people were hustled most unceremoniously together, in the anxious crowd, which jostling did not seem to be of any benefit to the tempers of two of the four. One, a little German woman, whose face was really too lovely to be spoiled by the impatient petulance that was flashing in her rich violet eyes, and pouting the lips of her provokingly pretty mouth; she was speaking to her husband.

"We shall be surely left aboard, Gaspard. I never did know any one so irritatingly slow as you are."

The other, evidently the husband of a handsome, large, indolent-looking woman, himself a fine, proud, manly Englishman, seemed at that very instant stung by the same impatient little demon that was annoying the pretty little German Frau. He exclaimed in a sharp tone, knitting his stern eyebrows,

"I wish, madam, it would please you to be a little quicker. The boat will push off before we are aboard. Here! this way, Octavie! For God's sake do make haste, madam ?"

The best bred people will forget themselves once in-awhile when they are provoked; that we all know. Yes, the two delinquents were Octavie and Gaspard. They had not seen each other for years, not since the time in Santa Chiar. They had recognized each other instantly, and they stood still and gazed at each other for one moment, totally forgetful of everything, even of their truly better halves. Octavie's husband, with a haste that was only saved from being rude by his innate elegance, which even ill temper could not destroy, took her by the arm and lifted her almost bodily into the boat, but for that, it seemed she would have staid there forever, and as she passed away from before his eyes, Gaspard allowed the crowd and his annoyed little wife to shove him ashore. They never met again in this life.

PUBLIC AND PRIVATE SERVANTS.

The following call for a Convention of the waiters of this city, to be holden to-day, we clip from the *Anglo African*, the organ of that large and useful class of persons, the colored population of New York:

A Convention of waiters of this city and vicinity, will be held in Rev. H. M. Wilson's church, Seventh avenue, near Eleventh street, on the evening of Sept. 1st. As matter of much importance will be brought before the Convention, It is hoped that the attendance will be large. Rev. H. M. Wilson and other able speakers will deliver addresses.

As the comfort and well-being of society is much more dependent upon the deliberations of this useful body, than upon those of any or all of the political Conventions, concerning which the newspapers are making so much noise just now, we would beg leave to present a few suggestions to their careful consideration. This we do in no trifling spirit. The New York Saturday Press is too well aware of the value of waiters and the worthlessness of politicians to treat with equal levity the pretensions of both. The self-styled servants of the public are not a class whose private or public claims to respect and gratitude are considered by The New York Saturday Press to be as valid as those put forward, with the modesty which always characterizes true merit, by the waiters of this city. And for this reason we do not anticipate that our suggestions will be treated with the contempt with which their self-sufficiency causes politicians to treat all advice.

And first we suggest that the waiters should resolve concerning the propriety of keeping themselves clean, nor would it be amiss to consider the advantage of being constantly civil and obliging. While the necessity of enough intelligence to do as they are bid must be apparent to even the dullest among them.

If the Rev. Mr. Wilson should present the need of these practical reforms upon the minds of his hearers with sufficient force to lead to their general adoption, he will earn for himself the thanks of a grateful community. Let him but carry through this good work, and then there will be enough for him to do in attempting the same reforms amongst the politicians, in office and elsewhere, who, it just occurs to us, despite their bluster and noise, stand perhaps in greater need of them than the waiters do.From this reviewal of its incidents it may be perceived that the story of 'The Ebony Idol' is not destitute of interest. It is not, however, in any respect a remarkable novel. Its plot, though possible, is yet extravagant, and is rather awkwardly developed. As an average picture of village-life in New England, it is not altogether truthful. But its characters are clearly drawn, its purpose is commendable, and its style is good. Concerning the Slavery Question, to which mainly it relates, there is—as everybody has just now an opportunity of knowing—a great deal to be said on both sides, by people who care to say it. We have no special interest to discuss the subject; but we incline to think this story will exercise a beneficial influence among thoughtful readers, in so far as it is calculated to curb that blind and reckless party spirit upon which to a great extent the Anti-Slavery Crusade is founded.

(For The New York Saturday Press.)

MINOR EXPERIENCES IN AMERICA.

II.

NEW YORK.

The calm in the bay brought me upon my legs on the upper-deck for the first time during several weeks. I was agreeably disappointed at the cultivated aspect of the land immediately around the immense bay, and the more so as it was already the month of November. We got a pilot, then several tow-boats came up, and I had the first sight of sharp bargaining, in the negotiations between our captain and the tow-boat men—each underbidding the other.

The steerage-passengers appeared in groups on the deck, most of them, the women particularly, dressed out in their best Sunday-attire. I was simple enough to ask the reason; and the scornful answer was, 'We do not wish to be taken for beggars arriving in New York.' Indeed, unshaved and haggard, I myself looked not unlike one.

Voyages were seldom favorite reading with me, and still less did I ever use guide-books. I went leisurely through Europe without any 'Murray' whatever, scarcely ever looking, even accidentally, into one. The books on America which I had read many years before, written by such authors as Alexander Everett, Lips, de Tocqueville, Beaumont, and my old friend Chevalier, had left in my mind only a general impression concerning the social and political condition of the Republic. Dickens's 'Martin Chuzzlewit' rather confused me; and so had Mrs. Trollope's productions, which I had once perused as a matter of conscience, having repeatedly met that authoress during my residence in Paris.

I was now about to enter a city of which I was as thoroughly ignorant as I was of Timbuctoo or Pekin. My knowledge of the English language had been acquired exclusively from books, instead of by the ear, and I had had almost no practice in speaking it. In Europe I had not cultivated any acquaintance with Americans. Many years before, in 1839, as member of the official Committee of Emigration in France—chosen. by the emigrants to facilitate relations between the Poles, the French government, and kindred committees—I had made the acquaintance of Fenimore Cooper, who was at the head of one of them, organized by the Americans in Paris. At that time I also met frequently a young American from Philadelphia, who—having been compelled to leave his country on account of a duel—was very poor, though he bore it with a good face. He could generally be found, at about dinnertime, on the steps of the Café de Paris or the Café Anglais, poorly dressed, but quietly picking his teeth as if he had just made a sumptuous repast in one or the other of these elegant and costly places. I afterwards learned that his fortunes improved by a rich marriage with an American girl, a Miss L——, when his sham-gentility, probably inborn, acquired a balloon-like expansion. At La Grange, the country-seat of Gen. Lafayette (who up to his death treated me like a father), in 1831, I fell in with two unmarried sisters, Americans by birth, travelling alone, who claimed descent from the great Scottish hero of the bloody heart, and who paraded ducal coronets whenever the police did not, as in London, interfere to prevent them. These were all the Americans whom I had known in Europe; and when I reached these shores I had, with the exception of Cooper, long forgotten their existence, and was ignorant even to what section of the country they belonged.

Towards evening we came to anchor. A customhouse officer gave us permission to land, provided we left our trunks behind. Being a decided protectionist, I found this very natural, although it clashed with the commonly-entertained idea of freedom, and thus wounded the feelings of some of my fellow-emigrants. I looked bewildered around me. No pier, no wharf, no conveyance! The *Edwina* was in the stream, separated from the shore by several other vessels, with which some narrow planks formed our only connection, and over which we must clamber up and down before we could reach the shore. My head was still unsteady, and my body weak, from the tossing of the ocean, and they in fact remained so for several days. I looked about me in despair, considering what to do. To one like myself, accustomed to the piers, wharfs, etc., provided in Europe, this new mode of landing appeared barbarous, savage, and reckless. I looked about imploringly for aid, and for the first time heard the voice from Sinai uttering the great commandment for this life—'Help yourself, sir.' It came from Heaven—that is, from aloft. The voice was right. Everybody around was fully occupied with himself. I tried a few steps on the planks, but was obliged to sit down, and thus prevented others from passing. This and real compassion moved two good-natured Swiss to put me on my legs again, and to support me over the trembling plank. The whole occurrence, the ailing Swiss excepted, was my first bite of the bitter bread of poverty,—other bites were to follow.

Supported by the Swiss I touched and saluted the soil sacred in my mind to liberty. A hackman took hold of me and repeated what I supposed was the names of various hotels, with none of which I was familiar. My answer if understood by him, directed him to take me to a good one. He drove off and delivered me at the Globe Hotel in Broadway. Happily the clerk there was a German, and I was safe for the night.

Next morning at the breakfast-table, to my surprise I met Fenimore Cooper. After mutual recognition, hand-shakings, etc., Cooper asked me about this and that prince, count, etc., from among his European acquaintance. Supposing me to be still in my former more than independent circumstances, his next question was whether I came to study and visit the Republic. My answer was that I came to America to earn my living in some way. He warmly offered me his kind advice, nay, even his protection, which I did not claim and did not even think to ask from him. Towards evening he left the Globe Hotel for some other, to the great astonishment of the clerk, Mr. Cooper having been an habitué of long standing. I never afterwards met Mr. F. Cooper, and never sought for, or even thought of him. Only years afterwards did I understand the meaning of his behavior. I understood it when I became acquainted with a certain dark shadow in human nature, a shadow which I had neither observed nor discovered while in Europe, probably on account of my social rank there.

The length and crowded bustle of Broadway astonished me inexpressibly. I had never imagined New York to be in any way a great city, and now it unfolded before my staring gaze all the characteristics of one on the largest scale. I was almost frightened at the stream of people, and at the stereotyped eagerness and sharpness expressed on their features. For the first time in my life, I was thrown among an exclusively mercantile population. Turn wherever I might, I found the same uniform expression of face. The more I walked and observed, the more was my first impression confirmed. After having spent the whole day in straggling through the streets and studying the faces I met, I felt myself utterly lost in this unwonted turmoil. On the outside I saw an European city, but on a nearer contemplation, however slight, the resemblance disappeared.

I delivered first from among my letters, the one directed to Dr. Herman Ludwig. His name is well known in bibliographical literature; his loss is irreparable for Europeans of all conditions and pursuits who have newly arrived in New York. From the first hour of our acquaintance to his last breath, he showed to me the warmest friendship, and always proved himself to me to be a clear-sighted adviser. His first words were (we spoke in German), 'Dear ——, are you the author of European Pentarchy?' It sounded strange to my ears, and I confess, with the hope of being forgiven for vanity, very flattering. The above anonymous work appeared in Germany in 1839, and made considerable noise in the political press. Its authorship remained an enigma, and the public opinion of that time ascribed it to me. This first greeting in America, on account of the authorship of a book almost forgotten in Europe, really exalted me a little.

Most luckily for me, the two Prussian ministers to Washington, the one about leaving America, and the other going to his post, were in New York. To both I was recommended from Europe. Both received me warmly and kindly, and did at once what they considered necessary for my social recognition. Baron de G—— gave me in trust, so to speak, to Dr. C—— and to Hon. S—— R—— for further piloting across the shoals, etc., of New York.

Before deciding upon any further steps, I thought it better to observe a little, and to learn to speak English; this was likewise the advice of my European godfathers. I was to go to an American boardinghouse. There was one such just opposite the Globe Hotel; and thither I transported my few effects. The widow of a broken-down merchant kept the house, and the society was composed mostly of widows and merchants' clerks, all of them in some way or other of broken fortunes. This I looked upon as a bad omen, and as I could have very little congenial intercourse with the rest of the boarders, even to practice my bad English, and beside as I could not get accustomed to the drill of eating meals in crowds, and to the hurried and rather promiscuous way in which the process of feeding went on, I left the boardinghouse after a few weeks, and took rooms in what was then called up-town, at the corner of Broadway and Murray street, in order to enjoy my old European independent way.

The little sum of money I brought from Europe required strict economy, and I was forced to put myself upon the smallest daily allowance. But certain of my wants could not be so easily discarded. A large, airy, and comfortable room for my books and myself was unavoidable. I concluded there was more comfort in that than in my fare. The latter was therefore to be reduced, and the first onslaught of poverty fell upon my alimentation. My breakfasts consisted of crackers and cold water darkened with the essence of coffee, an awful drug with which I had become acquainted through a bill posted up somewhere. For the other meal, corresponding to a dinner, I discovered a basement in Fulton Market, frequented by stevedores, sailors, etc. Such were my first steps in what would appear shabby gentility. In order to eat what the waiter brought me, I shut my eyes and dined principally on brown sugar and bread. For almost the first time in my I saw tobacco-chewing and its results on a large scale. To avoid the nauseous sight around me, I generally laid down my head on the table, waiting my turn for mastication. So it went on for several days. Finally a good-natured tar approached me, and patting me in a friendly way on my shoulder, said: "Man you are sick and downcast, come take a drink, it will cure you." I did not know the signification of 'a drink,' but not wishing to reject a good-natured sympathy, followed him to the table or bar-room, swallowed what he offered me, and shook him gratefully by the hand, but never returned to Fulton Market.

GUROWSKI

[Written for The New York Saturday Press.]

SILENCE MEANS CONSENT.

Nellie and I were sitting, one day,
Down in the oak tree's shade;
No one was there but the birds, and I,
And the little blue-eyed maid.

Say, Nell, is it true,' I whispered soft,
That silence means consent?"
Nell laughed, and said she guessed 'twas that
That silence sometimes meant.

I asked to give some one a kiss
There in the oak tree's shade;
What reply do you think came back?
Never a word was said!

D. J. TODD.

Elmira, N. Y

RAIN.

Rain—rain! the maples tossed their limbs
Wearily in the air,
And the flowers humbly bowed their heads
And prayed a sweet, mute prayer.

The hills looked up to the mocking sky
With stern reproachful brows.
And the farmers' eyes were full of dust
As they followed their grating plows,

A maiden, going to town with eggs,
Sat down in the shady lane,
Languidly wiped her glowing face
And sighed Will it never rain?"

. . . . . .

The trees stand still in grateful joy:
The flowers, in sweet surprise,
Look up to the darkly gushing clouds
With glad, wide-open eyes.

The mountains soften into a smile,
The farmers half in doubt,
Hurry their slow-paced oxen home
With many a rallying shout.

The maiden, returning from market, trips
Gleefully down the lane;
And laughs, as the wet from her bonnet drips.
Dear me! what a glorious rain!"

EMILY HEWITT BUGBEE

NEW YORK SEPTEMBER 8, 1860

FREEDOM *NOT* TO WORSHIP GOD.

We have heard it said and sung ever since we were a child, that the people who came over to this continent in the *Mayflower*, came chiefly for the purpose of securing to themselves and their posterity (and it is generally understood that nine Americans out of ten can establish a well-defined descent from the *Mayflower*) 'Freedom to worship God.'

The felicitous phrase originated, we think, with Felicia Hemans.

'Freedom to worship God!'

We know of but one right dearer to mankind than this, and that right is Freedom *not* to worship God.

The first-named right is tolerably well secured.

The people of this country have the right, and exercise it, not only of worshipping God, but gods.

All sorts of gods.

The gods most in favor—here as everywhere—are Mammon and Fashion.

These we worship with all our heart, and soul, and strength.

We build altars to them in our houses, our stores, our streets, our colleges, and even (or perhaps we should say and especially) in our churches.

This is preeminently the case with Mammon.

The Golden Calf is seen everywhere, and wo be to the man who does not bow down and worship it!

But unfortunately the Calf is not always presented to us as a Calf, but is clothed oftener in the semblance of a Lamb.

Of *the* Lamb.

And thus clothed, we are told that we ought to rejoice that we have the freedom to worship it; and that those who claim the freedom *not* to worship it—even (so far as human laws are concerned) were it the true Lamb, the Lamb of God—ought to be scouted from the community as the enemies of society, of religion, and we know not what else.

Now we are the last persons in the world to interfere with any man in his choice of gods.

That is a matter which should be left entirely to his own conscience.

Freedom to worship them should be secured to him as his first right.

But, on the other hand, we must insist that he allow us and everybody, the freedom *not* to worship them.

And this freedom, unfortunately, he is often unwilling to concede—especially if he happen to be a worshipper of false gods.

He makes a whole series of gods—makes them mostly in his own ever-changing image—sets them up at the corners of the streets—builds all sorts of fancy temples to them—and then insists that not only he but everybody shall worship them.

A thing he has no right to do—and the statement cannot be too often repeated—even if his devotions are offered to the one only living and true God, instead of to a body of little gods gotten up in sacrilegious imitation of Him.

We have been led into making these remarks by the attempts that have been made lately by a certain bigoted portion of the citizens of New York to deprive a certain other portion of the privilege of worshipping their own gods, and in their own manner, and compelling them to worship an incongruous assortment of gods, invented by the so-called ecclesiastical sects, and palmed off upon the community, in each separate case, as the 'God of the Bible.'

The chief victims of this crusade have been that large class of people called Germans, who have been hunted from pillar to post by irate ecclesiastics and their tools, with a view to force them into worshipping gods in whom they do not believe, and whom, there fore, they are resolved not to follow.

In the interest of this numerous and much-abused class of people, we call upon all friends of real liberty to insist, from this time forward, that in this free and enlightened country there is no freedom which should be more strenuously fought for, at whatever sacrifice, than the freedom *not* to 'worship God.'

(For The New York Saturday Press.)

MINOR EXPERIENCES IN AMERICA.

III.

Early in November, under the direction of Dr. Ludwig, I took the oath of allegiance to the American Republic, heartily forswearing all other sovereigns, states, and governments. I had seen enough of most of them in the Old World. I visited some learned Societies—such as the Historical, the Ethnological, etc.—not indeed with much profit, because of my ignorance of the language. A President of one of these Societies (for whose name I still vainly search the catalogue of American writers) condescendingly inquired what I intended to do. I told him that my only hope would be in my pen. To this he replied with some stale story about Gibbon's attempt to write in French, illustrating the difficulty of writing in a foreign language. He meant well perhaps, in saying this; but he was neither very encouraging nor very kind.

The composition of some of these scientific societies is very curious. It is a complete salmagundi. First, there are the men of wealth—merchants, etc.—who appreciate the necessity of real activity and progress in science, and who cheerfully and generously aid it with their money. All such men deserve respect and consideration. Secondly, there are the white-cravated, starched theologians—mostly extinguishers of real science—but good enough for the business of making motions, pronouncing panegyrics, or returning thanks, at the meetings of the society. Thirdly, there are the savants and compilators, who are called learned, and whose origin would seem to date several centuries back. Fourthly, there are the pretenders, who wish to stand before the community arrayed in the peacock-feathers of learning. Lastly, there are the earnest, conscientious students,—belonging mostly to a younger generation,—who are often pressed into the background, if not altogether crowded out by the reverends and their cronies. Progress is nevertheless made—an evidence that normal elements are not the absolute essentials of its existence.

The New York Historical Society has a valuable library and collections relating to natural history; and, thanks to the two extremes in its composition, it constantly enlarges its sphere of beneficient activity in the cause of science, as well as its ethnologic and archeologic treasures.

I imagined that Columbia College, with all its Faculties and Professors, would correspond in some respects to a European University; but on closer examination, I was disabused of that idea—especially when I discovered that oftentimes in American colleges the Presidents,—corresponding to Rectors in Germany, France, etc,—have never been either professors, savants, or in any way literary men. So it was here.

Entering the house of my friend one evening, I met a servant in the hall. Still governed by my European notions, I stretched out my arms in order that he might remove my overcoat. He took my hand, shook it cordially, left the coat on my shoulders, and thus gave me an intimation of the Democratic American precept—'Help yourself, sir!'

My Maecenas took me to the Italian Opera. It was then located in Astor Place. Mrs. Trollope's descriptions rushed to my memory, and I entered prepared in some sense to behold a display of legs over the balcony. But the aspect of the house was altogether graceful and elegant. I was glad to have been deceived by Mrs. Trollope, as I remembered with a thrill of pleasure that refined European life I had once enjoyed.

In due time I began to move in the society of persons of good family and blood, as well as in that of the fashionable people and others making up the social system of New York. Some acquaintances made then, receiving the consecration of time, have ripened into friendships which are dear to me now. Others have been broken off, because of mutual incompatibility and misappreciation.

My début in New York society was made at a party at the residence of Madame H——. Her house was the hospitable rendezvous of distinguished foreigners—with whom, however, I obstinately refused to be numbered. My patron introduced me generally—among others to the ever youthful poet N. P. W. I subsequently learned of his generous conduct in reference to me, and also of that of Madame H——.

All revolutions and emigrations which have taken place in the course of time have been instituted first by those who were willing to sacrifice position and fortune in their native country, and next by those who, sacrificing nothing at home because they have nothing to sacrifice, yet become when in exile, heroes, grandseigneurs, descendants of the first families, millionaires ruined by despotism, tyranny, confiscation, etc.,—thus realizing the French proverb, '*a beau mentir qui vient de loin*.' Of this latter class was a certain Polish exile, Mr. Fontana, whose mother in Warsaw,—so his Warsaw coexiles told me,—held, previous to the revolution of 1830, the exalted position of a pastry-cook, amassing therein sufficient property to give her children a tolerable education. Mr. Fontana had some capacity for music, and during his first years of exile in France, supported himself by giving concerts, at ten sous, in small boroughs and villages of Central and Southern France, where most of the rank and file of the Polish emigrants were quartered. He had several times seen and heard Chopin, and when subsequently he appeared in New York (long before my arrival), it was as a descendant of one of the first Polish families; as a ruined millionaire, and as a favorite pupil of Chopin. All these lies procured him pupils and a certain degree of consideration in society. His existence as an exile was altogether unknown to me; and his name, Fontana—which is a very common Italian name —had not been celebrated even by the excellence of his mother's Warsovian pastry. He became much incensed when Madame H——, or some other person, pointed me out and mentioned my name,—which he very well knew, though he had never in his life approached me. He took high ground, and threatened a scene. N. P. W., having ascertained from my friend how and by whom I was introduced, sustained Madame H—— in her position towards myself, and Mr. Fontana was desired either to keep quiet or leave the house. Next day the *Tribune* contained a violent attack on a foreigner, a Pole of eminent birth and high mental capacities, a friend to the Emperor Nicholas, who became an Arnold to his country and was sent to America as a secret agent and spy! I read the *Tribune* article, and also an article in one of the Sunday papers, in which the *Tribune* was ridiculed for its silly credulity in believing that the Emperor Nicholas would send a gentleman of such high birth and accomplishments as a spy to a country with the government of which his relations were of the most friendly description, and where all political proceedings are public and accessible. Entirely ignorant at that time of the various policy of the New York press, and of its general influence in this country, and having often during my long and vicissitudinous career, received numerous eulogies as well as broadsides from the European Journals, I was merely amused at the singular perspicacity and intelligence of the *Tribune*. A few days after I asked Mr.—— if he had read the above-mentioned articles, and then for the first time I heard of the scene at the residence of Madame H——, and of the existence of a Mr. Fontana.

GUROWSKI.

NEW YORK SEPTEMBER 15, 1860

[For The New York Saturday Press.]

MINOR EXPERIENCES IN AMERICA.

IV.

The more I mixed in New York society, the more I was startled at the persistent efforts of everybody about me to appear of aristocratic lineage—to play the exclusive, the 'crême,' in their deportment to others supposed to be less fortunate in their extraction. Never in European society did I hear so much talk about 'good blood,' 'new people,' etc., as in certain New York salons; and this among people whose grandfathers were mechanics, petty tradesmen, small farmers, or what not,—all respectable callings, indeed, but not such as to warrant any especial pretensions to 'blood.'

Viewed whether from an aristocratic or a democratic standard, these American shades of distinction are very puzzling to all Europeans, and were particularly so to me.

The names immortalized by the American Revolution may and do confer an ennobling distinction; I met persons bearing those honored names, and found them far less pretentious than the descendents of speculators in merchandise, lands, marriage, etc.

It is difficult—nay impossible—in America to find out where high society begins and low society ends. No genuine middle class—at least, so it strikes me—exists. There is no aristocratic or democratic assay that can be applied to determine the exact amount of social alloy, or fix the precise scale of gradation in commercial, industrial, agricultural, mechanical, and other pursuits. The only true test would seem to be integrity, but this again becomes so very elastic when applied to the various means of attaining fortune, that it becomes as uncertain as any other. Accordingly when I frequented conventional society I found myself in a continual dilemma.

At a select evening party, on one occasion, so much was said about this and that family or individual not being equal to some other in extraction or standing, that, a little provoked, I jocosely observed to one of the guests, 'You are all so particular here, so exclusive, and so anxious not to commit yourselves in social intercourse, that I shall be puzzled to know with whom to associate.'

These words did my business for me in that set.

The elements that go to make one distingué in all the conventional and imaginary gradations of American society are, with rare exceptions, substantially the same; the difference consists in quantity, and this, again, is rather microscopic. Mental culture and attainments alone constitute now, almost everywhere, the normal standard, and in this country, these qualities are not always the most conspicuous in the upper stratum of society.

I soon discovered that Europeans of genuine as well as of spurious birth, were looked upon, when they come to this country, as being in search of rich wives; but to be considered myself as one of these fortune-hunters, would have been a reflection on my name and character, of the most humiliating kind. A charitable lady in New York society undertook to sound me on that point. My answer to her delicate suggestions was that I was too poor to support a wife, even if my age, etc., did not render marriage out of the question.

"But you can easily find a lady with six or seven thousand dollars income."

"Not enough, madame, to dress a Countess," was my reply.

And there the conversation ended.

More than once in the salons of New York, as afterwards in those of Boston, I found myself awkwardly placed on account of the absolute difference, in many respects, between the social conventional etiquette here, and that of European society in the usages of which I had been educated.

My position would have been still more awkward, but for my total indifference to the opinions of my new compatriots.

Certain rules of courtesy are the same all over Europe, like the signs of free-masonry: and as the latter always, facilitates entrance to the different lodges, so the former always serve as a passport to the salon of good society.

Thus, among other things, it is customary in Europe that a stranger make the first calls,—not, indeed, indiscriminately, but upon the persons to whom he may have been suitably introduced; such introduction being *de rigeur* in the case of married ladies or heads of families. A day or two after introduction, a card is left, the law of politeness is fulfilled, and social relations may begin. Of course, no one in Europe calls upon or visits young unmarried women without being acquainted or else being invited to do so by the parents,—though this is constantly done in America. In Europe it would be considered as a piece of gross ill-breeding, and would involve the offending party in serious consequences.

Now, no one informed me that in America these two rules were reversed. In some instances, therefore, I adopted the European custom of leaving my card at the houses of citizens to whom I had been introduced; until, finally, a kind friend in Boston warned me that in America such a course would be considered not as an act of politeness but of intrusiveness.

In Europe the stranger receives the first calls only when he is of absolutely superior rank—such as a prince, an eminent statesman, a great commander, etc. —when this deference is paid to him as a recognition of his rank.

In American cities, almost every stranger of note is liable to be overrun by calls from everybody. In the early Colonial times this was often an act of genuine hospitality to persons newly arrived in a strange and then hardly civilized land.

In other cases it was a recognition of the superiority of a person coming from the mother country; or, again, a mere impulse of curiosity to get fresh news, or to be the first to see a new-comer, such things always producing a sensation in a small community.

But when I see Americans run heels over head to make the first calls upon foreigners—above all, on juvenile sprigs of English aristocracy, coming to New York or Newport 'for the fun of the thing,' I always am sorry for my new compatriots who thus make themselves the object of ridicule by their obsequiousness and colonial deference to their former masters, the English nobility.

It was a long time, also, before I could understand why it was that an American gentleman will be polite to you in his office or counting-house, and quite otherwise in his house.

But after many years I found out the key to some, if not all of these riddles. Not upon the husband, the father, depends the etiquette of the house, but generally upon the wife, the daughter, whose courtesies are sometimes regulated by a lion-hunting disposition (which results in their catching often a 'pigtail'), or by some weakness or whim of the kind.

GUROWSKI.

NEW YORK SEPTEMBER 22, 1860

[From "The Weekly Anglo-African."]

'THE SATURDAY PRESS,' AND COLORED WAITERS AND SLAVE WORSHIP.

The SATURDAY PRESS, which has a slash at everybody and everything, has, of course, a pass at the colored waiters in particular, and at the enslaved colored folks in general. It seems to be its chief business to cut up and slash away at everybody and everything within its reach, just as a powerful-armed, ferocious butcher would a bullock, without the butcher's merit of purpose, propriety, or sense. It is utterly reckless in its course. If at any time its reflections are just, they seem the result of accident rather than design. It is the bull in a china-shop—the articles which remain around him whole give him no credit for their preservation. It floored E. C. Benedict and his book of travels; it sabred Lunt, Hillard, and others of the New England school of writers; It dashed down and smashed New England's idol, Edward Everett, into so many pieces that some of them could not be found; it took down and put up, and took down and put up again we know not how many times, that 'man of America,' Walt Whitman; and now, perhaps for want of lower game, it turns round upon colored waiters, and, if not insolently, certainly uncivilly and gratuitously, advises them, should they assemble in Convention, to make it their chief concern to recommend and enforce the necessity of being clean, civil, and obliging—just as if colored waiters were not always clean, civil, and obliging. Who ever saw a corps of colored waiters which was not clean and neat, and who ever knew one that was not civil and obliging? The SATURDAY PRESS must hunt elsewhere than among colored waiters for a lack of these essential qualifications. One thing is certain: 'that this class of useful persons,' as the PRESS terms them, is always and only employed at first-class houses. Their services cannot be obtained at any others; and the SATURDAY PRESS man, we opine, seldom, if ever, comes in contact with them, and hence its gratuitous and blundering advice.

But let us turn to another phase of the PRESS. It claims to be very just in its strictures. What we call its recklessness, it terms 'independence and fearlessness.' It rates soundly all—and they are not few—who show any signs of wavering or shadow of turning on the great general questions of the day—such, for instance, as gambling, intemperance, prostitution, Sabbath-breaking, or any other of the current villanies, particularly in high places. Did we say all? We beg to omit one, and that one is slavery. On that, if the PRESS is not silent (it has been, hitherto, mum as a frog in dog-days), it has, alas! gone over to the side of poor, wretched slavery, and is henceforth its slave. O, the PRESS! the PRESS! THE NEW YORK SATURDAY PRESS, we mean.

It animadverted with its usual severity, but with what show of consistency is not manifest, upon the *World* newspaper, because said paper attacked intemperance, prostitution, etc., in their lighter, and omitted to make an onset on them in their weightier forms. It would have the *World* newspaper—aye, and the press generally—rebuke sin in high places—in Wall and Nassau streets as well as in Mercer and on the Five Points. It would have these reformers and reforms begin and cut away at the very root of the evil—to all of which we say amen, and amen. But how is it that the PRESS is at the same moment giving aid and comfort to the slaveholder, and doing what in it lies, to fasten the bonds on men, women, and children, or at least salaver over the accursed deed? Or is this American slavery not one of the evils to be rooted up, and requiring the aid of THE NEW YORK SATURDAY PRESS? Does it not fall under its terrible axe? No, no. How is this?—who can explain? Its arm is uplifted to slay, not slavery, but anti-slavery.

Its first best efforts to nudge itself into the pro-slavery ranks (it is hard work now, the world knows, its minions stand so thick and solid), was an elaborate and, of course, favorable review of a mean, low, dull, senseless novel, entitled 'The Ebony Idol,' published, of course, by the Appletons. It says: " 'The Ebony Idol' means the negro, and is thus the very felicitous title of a story in which a negro is the central figure. It is the design of this story to ridicule the Abolition movement in the North, and especially to rebuke those clergymen who introduce politics into the pulpit, and delectate their flocks with anti-slavery sermons."

O, the PRESS! the PRESS!—the SATURDAY PRESS, we mean. And yet, on another occasion, this same SATURDAY PRESS, in its virtuous indignation in reference to the World newspaper, remarks that "it has had its shy at the play-actors, and the dram-sellers, and the streetwalkers, and the Sabbath-breakers, and now its virtue has culminated in a crusade against the gamblers." What, we would inquire, has not also the SATURDAY PRESS had its shy at; and now its virtue has also culminated in a crusade against colored people and Abolitionists and freedom.

The PRESS further says: "Not the gamblers in stocks, or in merchandise, or in news, or in religion, or even in penny-papers, but the gamblers sometime called, by the way of elegant variety, black-legs. These can be attacked not only with impunity, but with eclat." And we would say to the SATURDAY PRESS, so can the Abolitionists and the poor helpless slaves, and colored people generally, be attacked not only with impunity but with eclat. But it further says, in its reprimand of the *World:* "Mayor Tiemann made quite a reputation in attacking them; in fact, they and the street-walkers were his chief stock in trade, and the way he ground them into paint, and whitened the City Hall sepulchre with them, showed as much skill as his shrewdest speculation in putty." And the advocacy of slavery, we conclude, is the 'putty' the SATURDAY PRESS shrewdly intends to make a good speculation out of.

But hear its virtuous strictures on the *World* and gamblers once more, and place them beside its toadyism to the god of American slavery: "In fact, if a man wants to build up a reputation for morality (and make money out of it), he cannot do better at any time than come out against either the gamblers or street-walkers. They are always fair game; whereas if he happens to come out against some sin which is practised by nearly the whole community—some system of political or commercial cheating, for example —it is almost certain that he will get more kicks than coppers for it, and at best earn the credit of being a grumbler. We don't know that we ought to complain of the *World*, therefore, since by its little cheap commonplaces against notorious social evils, it is gradually getting a name for being quite a grand and godly concern." And so, too, the PRESS by its pretentions in favor of slavery and against the friends of the oppressed, will gradually get a name for being quite a grand and godly concern.

It concludes its review of 'The Ebony Idol,' the silly book it selects by which to make its entree into the pro-slavery ranks, by modestly saying, "It has no special interest to discuss the subject." Certainly not. "How could it have any ?"

"But," says this disinterested, this fair and candid, this independent, this outspoken, this plain and honest paper, "we are inclined to think that this story" (that is, 'The Ebony Idol'), this intended ridicule of the Abolition movement, this rebuke of clergymen, will exercise a beneficial influence among thoughtfull "readers, in so far as it is calculated to curb that blind and reckless party-spirit upon which, to a great extent, the anti-slavery crusade is founded." The journals that bow down to the Belial of American slavery are many and powerful, and who shall say, after this, that THE NEW YORK SATURDAY PRESS shall not take rank among the foremost of them?

NEW INSTITUTE OF FINE ARTS.

Mr. W. H. Derby is erecting on Broadway, between Bleecker and Houston streets, a permanent Gallery of Painting and Sculpture, to be called the Institute of Fine Arts. The building excites much attention from the fact, that the architect, Mr. Hamilton, departing from the usual monotonous mode of architectural decoration, has called in the aid of real sculpture for the ornamentation of the front—an example which, if followed, cannot fail to add very much to the grandeur and dignity of our city architecture. On the second story, three emblematical female figures, about the size of life, are introduced to support the arches in which the windows are placed. The central figure, representing 'Architecture,' holding a square and compass, is already fixed; also another, representing 'Painting,' with her palette and brush; the other pedestal will be shortly occupied by a third figure, 'Sculpture,' with her appropriate instruments, a mallet and chisel. These figures cannot properly be classified with 'Caryatides,' originally slaves, and of quite a different application. They should be considered simply as emblems; and it was a happy idea to select them for metaphorically supporting a building devoted to Fine Arts. It is to be regretted that the building has not a larger frontage, and still more, that the first floor is of iron, instead of marble; but the latter is one of those inexorable demands of commerce, from which there appears to be no escape, and the former has only enabled the designer to prove how much more he could have made of a greater opportunity. The entrance doorway is very handsome. It is vaulted over by a carved head or frontispiece, on which two cherubs are seen reclining on a globe; the one holding a laurel wreath and the other a palm-branch, to typify the peaceful nature of the Fine Arts. A wide staircase leads to the second-floor, devoted entirely to the Gallery, which will be of the whole width of the lot, 34 feet, by its length of 200 feet, running through from Broadway to Mercer street. A hundred and fifty feet of this will be thrown into one room, with domed ceiling and skylights—the remaining portion being divided into separate exhibition-rooms, over which will be studios for artists, etc. It is intended to cover the walls of the Gallery with a dark-green flock paper, most refreshing to the sight, and against which the gilded frames will stand in pleasant relief. The first floor is a large store, occupying the whole lot, with basement and sub-cellar. The building will be heated by steam.

Of the works of Art which are to occupy so worthy a shrine, we are of course unable at present to speak, but Mr. Derby's agent, Mr. Frodsham, who has for some time past been negotiating with the artists of England and the Continent, is expected shortly; and from his known experience in Art-matters, will doubtless come prepared with a collection sufficient to gratify the expectations of the public. The entire cost of the building alone will not fall far short of $60,000, and it is expected to be ready for exhibition during the month of October. We ought to state that the sculpture is executed by Messrs. Küner & Sexton, of this city.

[For The New York Saturday Press.]

MINOR EXPERIENCES IN AMERICA.

V.

I found the ball-rooms and salons generally, in New York, crowded with young persons of both sexes, with an almost imperceptible sprinkling of mammas; and I could not help thinking how different the state of things in Europe, where every one would be filled with horror at the idea of allowing young women to attend balls, parties, etc., unaccompanied by their parents, or by watchful chaperons.

And nevertheless the custom is in harmony with the primitive life of small societies and cities, and had its origin, in this country, in the simple, unaffected, Sociable life of the colonies.

At a private ball in New York, I was once asked whether I ever saw such splendor of dress in St. Petersburg. The question betrayed such simplicity—or ignorance—and was asked with such perfect composure of countenance, that I was perplexed how to answer. I finally said that I had seen a great many jewels, diamonds, etc., in my life, but that I was unable to make comparisons.

In another instance, my host took me all over his house, from cellar to garret, explained to me all its details, and finally wound up by telling me what it all cost. I was much surprised at having such a statement made to me at a ball; but now I should think nothing of it.

In yet another instance (this also among the Knickerbockers), I went to a farewell-ball given in a Fifth avenue mansion, on the occasion of its having been sold to a banker. Judge of my amazement at the proprietor taking me aside, and telling me of the whole transaction, dwelling with great emphasis on the words, 'for *cash,* sir! for *cash!'* which he repeated several times.

When I got to my room I looked in 'Webster' to get at the full meaning of the word so emphatically and lovingly used. Now—alas, too late—I have learned to appreciate the full significance of 'cash'—and its absence.

At all the balls and dancing-parties I attended, nothing was heard of but the Polka, which at that time had hardly got a foot-hold in the aristocratic salons of Europe.

Occasionally only—and then somewhat abashed—the Polka showed her face; but not till the close of the evening, when the candles were nearly burned out.

Even the European bourgeoisie persecuted the unhappy and—as they thought her—dangerous syren: in fact, in 1844 the burgomasters of Liege banished her from all public entertainments.

But I was not more astonished at the universal presence of the Polka, than to find that waltzers generally whirled their partners from left to right, instead of from right to left, as in the salons of Europe—this reverse-fashion prevailing only among the Polish, Bohemian, and Moravian peasantry, and in the suburbs of Vienna.

This and similar eccentricities performed on the floors of New York salons, made me suspect that they took their dancing-fashions from Musard's, or some equally distingué place in Paris.

Do not laugh at me for the interest I take in waltzing. I spent my youth in Germany, that fairy-land of waltz and tender partners. At one epoch of my life —when gliding over the slippery floors of the St. Petersburg palaces—I might have made my way in the world easier through my pumps than through my brains.

During the Winter of 1849-50, there arrived in New York, the first instalment of Magyars, who after heroically fighting against the Hapsbourgs and Russians, became patriotic martyrs and exiles. The presence of the brave Uhiazy, Governor of Comorn, and his companions, created a great excitement in the city and all over the country. It revealed to me the nobler features in the character of my new compatriots. It was the first time in my life I had witnessed such an enthusiasm in the welfare of distant nations, such a spontaneous and general outburst of large masses of people—an outburst generously tumultuous, and yet perfectly orderly in all its manifestations.

For me it was the first evidence of how self-government generates noble and ennobling impulses.

I was sorry, however, to see how easily this American enthusiasm for liberty and its martyrs could be abused; how false pretentions easily humbugged the generous-minded public to an extent impossible any where in Europe. Uhiazy's band contained some—though very few—low and unheroic adventurers, who, however, were not Magyars. These excited the greatest noise, because the most admired, and got the most credit on account of their lies.

One evening, at a literary party, a sudden rush to one corner of the room attracted my attention. I asked a well-known literary man near me—and who was preparing to join the crowd—what all the commotion was about.

"It is Frederika Bremer," he replied.

"And who is Frederika Bremer?" said I, astonished.

"You don't know Frederika Bremer !" he exclaimed, with evident contempt for my ignorance depicted in his face," let me introduce you."

I politely declined, when he turned away in indignation and disgust. We often met each other, afterward, but he always kept haughtily aloof from me.

When very young I had witnessed similar excitements in European salons at the entrance of Walter Scott and Goethe; and afterwards of a Schleiermacher, a Hegel, a Schelling, an Arago; of the Humboldts, of Thierry, of Victor Hugo, of Orrioli, Massino Azzeglio, Guerrazzi, Puschkine, and numerous other literary and scientific celebrities; but it was beyond my comprehension how Frederika Bremer could make all this stir in salons—'blue' and other—in New York and all over the Union.

Her little, but flatly spun-out stories may be very 'nice,' but I am sure that even in Germany, their popularity does not extend beyond the sphere of boarding-school misses, nursery-maids, and circulating libraries. But Scandinavian literature, and antiquities generally, are highly valued in America, although it does not make the windmill in Newport a Scandinavian relic.

Always an early riser, I often used to perambulate the city before dawn, especially through the streets inhabited by the poorer classes—I was not aware, then, how dangerous it was; still I never met with an accident, although, to my astonishment, I rarely fell in with a policeman (this was in 1850), and still less with any patrols.

The absence of police, and the fact of never having been attacked or even annoyed, gave me a high opinion (modified since) of the morality and comparative prosperity of what would be called abroad the suburban population. I have made similar explorations in most of the capitals of Europe, to ascertain, as far as practicable, the habits of the hard-working classes, the poorest of whom generally rise the earliest.

The European operative and mechanic will generally be out at dawn,—and in Winter before dawn—at work, by candle-light or fire-light, in his shop, shanty, or room.

As far as my observation extended, it was not so here: the poorer classes sleeping more and working less than they do in Europe.

I considered this a good and cheering omen in respect to the wages and general condition of the working classes (though my observations were necessarily superficial), and inwardly congratulated humanity that here at least was one spot on the globe where a social and political organization could exist without the cancer of inevitable pauperism at its base.

How different from the state of things I left behind me in Europe!

Never before having lived in a port where the harbor and the shipping run along, as it were, by the side of the streets (for this is not the case either in London or St. Petersburg), I used to take pleasure in roaming, at about six in the morning, among the vessels, and studying this, to me, new feature of human activity and society. As elsewhere, I was never subjected to the least molestation.

Only once, a good-natured mate asked me on board his ship, treated me to gin, and offered me a 'chew,' wondering, but not offended, at my refusing the second-named delicacy.

While riding in an omnibus, one day, a well-dressed young woman reached out her hand to me in rather a commanding manner, but without a breath of explanation, or the least softening expression on her stern countenance. I understood the imperative gesture only when another gentleman took some money from her hand, and passed it up to the driver.

All this looked very strange to me.

European women, of all nations and classes, when they ask or require a service, do so not only courteously, but with a pleasant expression of face, and acknowledge the service in the same spirit. From the queen on the throne to the humblest peasant-girl this is invariably the case.

I had often read and heard that every woman in America was a lady. I had seen in the shop-windows 'A Lady Wanted.' All this is well; but a woman thus become a lady ought to preserve her womanhood; that is, to remain the same soft and graceful being which Nature intended.

I met with several adventures similar to the above.

While going to a morning-reception in Boston, I saw a carriage stop before the house, and a 'lady' descend from it. As it was raining violently I respectfully proffered my umbrella. The 'lady' pushed it aside with the air and manner of an offended, outraged,— but I had better not use any comparisons.

At another time, when travelling by rail through Virginia, a lady and her daughter entered the cars. It was night. I had a supportable corner-seat, and having already travelled thirty-six hours, was very tired and sleepy. Madam stood before me, imperiously waiting for me to move.

"Will you give up your seat to us, sir ?" (There were other seats in the car.)

Silently, I bowed a 'No.'

"You are not a gentleman, sir."

"I am not, madam, only a wearied traveller."

At the next station, a colored woman with an infant came in. She made no fuss, and I promptly gave her up my seat.

The old-fashioned (called by some aristocratic) rule, strongly enforced on our minds by our mothers, was: 'Be polite to a woman whether she wear a crown or dress in rags' (in Europe, we know nothing about prejudice against color), 'and deal with all kinds of men, kings included, as you like.' The idea being that men can arrange their own matters of behavior with each other.

I religiously observe my mother's teaching towards all *true women.*

GUROWSKI.

NEW YORK SEPTEMBER 29, 1860

NEW AMERICAN NOVEL.

We learn that Messrs. Thayer & Eldridge, Boston, have in press, a novel by ADA CLARE, to be published some time next month. To the readers of the SATURDAY PRESS the name of the authoress will alone be a guarantee of the interest and power of the work.

(For The New York Saturday Press.)

MINOR EXPERIENCES IN AMERICA.

VI.

I was accosted, one day, in Broadway, by a Polish refugee of 1831, whose character and subsequent conduct turned out to be such that I will not sully my pen or these pages with the details.

Owing to an accidental combination of circumstances not proper to be mentioned here, this individual had a few years before married a young woman who belonged to one of the first families in Poland, and who had been a playmate of my youth.

After he had ruined, almost degraded her, her unhappy father, to save his daughter from all kinds of miseries, procured him a few letters, and sent him to America, where he was all the more willing to go from the fact that he was shut, if not kicked, out of society in all the great cities and watering-places of Europe. He began the conversation by saying that his wife and father-in-law would be very happy to know that he had met me in this country. I replied by cautioning him, that as our ways had always been very different, so they would always remain; and that he had better never cross my path, as if he did, not even my friendship for his wife and Mr. M—— would prevent my promptly getting rid of him.

The man's name was Fabvius, or Phabvius (he spelt it both ways). He was the son of an overseer on the estates of a Polish nobleman, and after the events of 1831, went with the mass of emigrants from Volhynia to Paris. His youth and personal beauty led to his utter demoralization and ruin.

In this country he appeared as Colonel Baron Phabvius; but how he came by either title he himself could not explain.

I learned afterward that he ingratiated himself into the favor of some respectable young Americans whom he met in Europe, and that they gave him warm letters to their relations and friends here.

He went to Baltimore and to Washington, and was feted and petted in both places.

In vain Sir Henry Bulwer and his secretary warned society that the man had been expelled by the police, as a blackleg, from a ball given by him (Bulwer) at Madrid.

The Baron and Colonel made a parade of his decorations, one of which he pretended was given to him by Queen Isabella of Spain, on the score of his being a descendant from one of the first European families. The Spanish Minister in Washington, Don Calderon de la Barca, protested in vain against such falsehoods. The Baron's explanation was that the diplomats were all deadly opposed to him, on account of his being a political refugee of high standing—an explanation readily enough believed by a society generously predisposed toward the victims of European proscription, and unmindful of Johnson's dictum, that 'Patriotism is the last refuge of scoundrels.'

The Baron again reappeared in New York. I saw him, to my astonishment, at a matinée dansante given by the aristocratic Mrs. S——, in College Place, where he appeared rigged out in the most elegant style, wearing several decorations on his breast, and having on his arms two of the most fashionable ladies of the city. I considered it a point of honor to a society which had hospitably opened its salons to me, to warn it against such an intruder. So I told the Baron's story to a Mr. B——, a European of the highest standing in his own country, and who married, in New York, the granddaughter of its wealthiest citizen. Furthermore, I warned the mothers who were present at the party in question, and with whom I was acquainted, not to allow that adventurer to be introduced to their daughters, as he was a man who 'soiled every woman he touched.' It was perhaps bad English; but I wished to impress them with the indignity of having anything to do with such a fellow.

After the supper, one of the young men with whom I was on rather friendly terms, came towards me, and said:

"Colonel Baron Fabvius claims to have your acquaintance."

"Tell him, then, sir," was my answer, "that I forbade him, long ago, to do so. But since he does not mind my words, I say to you that he is neither a Baron nor a Colonel, but a canaille; and the best thing for him is to instantly leave this house."

The next day a German, a confrère of the Baron, came to my room for an explanation, which I gave to the effect that Fabvius knew me too well, and was well aware of my unfortunate duelling-propensities (one of the weaknesses of my youth); but that he knew also that between himself and me a duel was out of the question. "If, however," I added, "he ever comes in my way, I may feel it my duty to break his head."

The German was very much incensed, and insisted that we foreigners ought to keep together against Americans. At the 'we' I broke out into an oath—being furious to think he should dare to couple me with such fellows as himself and Fabvius—and seeing my rage, he quickly left the room. But the end was not yet.

When I raised in Europe, and for many years sustained, the standard of Pan-Slavism in political literature, there was no kind of outrage and abuse which was not heaped upon me by political and literary antagonists. The Baron sent to Europe and got one of the infamous articles published against me at that time, and returning to Baltimore, circulated it there, and also by some means in New York. So, at least, I was afterwards told. And thus I found myself again represented as a partisan of Russia, a traitor, a spy, etc., etc.

I am acquainted with the subsequent adventures and career of the Baron; and yet almost up to the present day, some of the exclusive and aristocratic descendants of 'redemption-ers,' of tailors, tinkers, etc., in Baltimore, cannot forgive me for having exposed him.

Many times since, I have observed and wondered how easily Americans are taken in under similar circumstances. Their innate kindness, combined with curiosity and a craving for excitement, makes them an easy prey to all kinds of adventurers sailing under false colors.

Thus, among others, a certain Wiedemayer was received and introduced as a 'distinguished foreigner,' and a 'great traveller,' among the best society in Boston, Nahant, Newport, and New York, until at last it turned out that he had been a waiter in Paris, and a pastry-cook in San Francisco. He was a man utterly without culture, and of the most vulgar manners. For these reasons I cut him, on the first introduction at Newport, and told his friends why I did so; but the ladies and gentlemen declared, unanimously, that I was a man who abused everybody.

The last I heard of Wiedemayer, he was making a compulsory visit to a public institution in Sing-Sing!

GUROWSKI.

NEW YORK OCTOBER 6, 1860

[For The New York Saturday Press.]

Sleep, little child!

Sleep though the Autumn winds are wailing
Under the Autumn skies of tender gloom,
And the rich robes of regal Fall are trailing
Slowly above the buried Summer's tomb,—
Sleep and dream!

Dream, little child!
What to thee that this sombre glory
Seems but the gleam of closing heaven to me?
Dream! but I dream no more, save one long story
Of what the waiting world shall offer thee,—
Sleep and dream!

Smile, little child!
The worlds unfold around and o'er thee,
And the full future waits thy calm commands;
Manhood is thine, and in the life before thee
Gods of thy kind shall clasp thy willing hands,—
Sleep and dream!

JULIETTE H. BEACH.

[For The New York Saturday Press.]

SUBURBAN MATTERS.

SEPTEMBER 28, 1860.

The half-million or so of dwellers in your crowded city, know little and think less of us whom limit of means, or force of inclination leads to prefer a home in the rural districts, away from the clamor and splendor of Babylon the Great, yet not so far removed but that power of horse and steam can carry us thither in an hour or two. A day, or a half-day among you commonly suffices us, and we turned with renewed zest to our fresh air, our little yard, green with turf and gay with posies, our view of the Bay from the front-windows, and last but not least, at this season of the year, to our mosquitos. But they deserve a separate paragraph, and of them more anon.

Crossing the Jersey Ferry at about 5 o'clock, and losing yourself in the dense stream of humanity that pours out from those dusky arches, you take twenty steps along Montgomery street and begin to be conscious of identity once more in the building whence start the horse-cars for —— and ——. These cars are ingeniously contrived to consume three-quarters of an hour in travelling the distance of one mile, and as they run once in twenty minutes you can easily imagine the convenience to a belated traveller. They have, besides, a delightful aptitude for getting off the track; whereupon the solitary steed who does the locomotion is made to perform many wondrous twistings and curvetings, and a wild-looking specimen of the genus homo fires away with an immense pole at the offending vehicle, till in the course of time the crooked paths are made straight, and we go on our way rejoicing. The 'we' in question is always a goodly quantity: the canonical number, seven on a side, was attained in the first three minutes after the car backed around to its station; and after that we waited two boats. Gentlemen clambered on the roof, and from that eminence discharged volleys of tobacco-juice, to the great refreshment and solace of the ladies below, who could watch the play of light through the descending fluid in the interval of observing the entrance of fellow-passengers. The gangway presently became full; the step overloaded; when three ladies in amplest crinoline presented themselves, and looked coolly about, demanding their rights. There is a slight hesitation in the breast of some ungallant creatures, but a sworn slave of the sex presently arises, and his example is speedily followed. The ladies seat themselves, the gentlemen are compressed to the point of invisibility, and at the words 'go ahead' the old white horse shakes himself and struggles forward.

During the journey a solitary individual like myself finds amusement in listening to the conversation of his neighbors; and in this latitude it is carried on with great freedom and sociability, all sorts of inquiries being exchanged as to 'Jane' and 'Maria,' 'your wife' and 'your brother,' their present plans and future prospects. The people from the hill-country seem a simple, honest-minded set, for the most part of their talk runs on 'meeting' and wonderment as to whether they shall be home in time for it. Sometimes they encounter a ministerial friend, as they did the other night, and exchange with him edifying sentences about 'awakening,' 'revivals,' and the unfailing 'meeting.' They appear, too, to be on the most nonchalant terms with the driver, and when he raps to remind them of the fare, call out 'We've only just stepped in; let us get our breath, wont you ?'—to which very reasonable request he responds politely, 'Yes, madam, I will.'

One gets, sometimes, very interesting and original views of the political world in the course of the journey, as was the case last evening, when an elderly gentleman of solemn aspect was holding forth on the subject of the Presidential candidates. He said that promises made before election were very apt to be broken after it, that there was no pleasure in holding office except for the money that was to be made by it; that office-seekers thought more of their own good than they did of the country's, etc., etc. From this subject he presently diverged to that of his neighbor's chickens, where I was 'with him,' having had the satisfaction of setting out and watering, staking and tying tomato-plants this Summer, for the sole end and object of feeding Mr. Frost's fowls during the last month. Each morning I gather up melancholy skeletons—disembowelled fruit in every stage of ripeness and greenness—and then go to market and purchase the excellent edible, while the chickens disport themselves about the yard, or hide amid the green bowers of the plants. But this is a minor annoyance, not to be named with the mosquitos.

How often, during these bright September days, has risen to my mind that line of our country's sweetest bard, in his address to the insect in question,

"Thou com'st from Jersey meadows, fresh and green."

'Jersey meadows!' Bryant, thou hadst it there! Jersey is the home of the mosquito! Blown by fresh breezes across the marsh and the salt-meadow, they light on our borders, full of strength and spirit. They sing defiance in your very ear; ghost-like elude the clasp of your out-stretched hands; settle unexpected, and bite with the force of a shark. We walked, one pleasant afternoon, a week or two ago, down to Communipaw, a spot beloved of Irving. In vain for us stood the old Dutch houses; in vain the trim flowerbeds spread their petunias and verbenas; in vain did the water stretch away beneath a purpling sky, while across its tranquil breast the white sails moved slow and silent. The mosquitos! the mosquitos! The air was three parts of them to one of atmosphere. We jumped frantically hither and thither; we waved our parasols, our hands, and our handkerchiefs, to keep off the invaders, but it was useless, and we were presently fain to beat an ignominious retreat, and start for home at a pace that would have done honor to Flora Temple.

But when the solemn curtain of night is let down on the world, then the tables are turned. We lie in 'the sweet moonshine'—as poor Drake hath it—and look out peaceably on the universe through our mosquito-net. They are there, we know it, we can almost distinguish their forms—

"The guests are met, the feast is set,
May'st hear the merry din"—

but all the delicate viands, the champagne, the hock, the claret, are inaccessible. We muse on the admirable arrangement of Providence which has so contrived it that the mosquito is unable to furl his wings and enter through the interstices; and then, perhaps, occurs the question, why he was made at all.

But this carries us back to the old problem, the origin of evil, too extended in its character to be suitably discussed at twelve of the clock, and we turn over and go to sleep amid the gnashing of teeth outside. But no! if a corner of the net be upturned, or carelessly fastened, then shall your slumber know torment unutterable, and you shall awake next morning looking as if carved in Castile Soap. Enough of this, however.

Who of you has read 'The Household of Bouverie?' I have a good deal of curiosity to see it, but it is a matter of conscience with me never to buy an American novel, and I should gaze long and wistfully on my scanty hoard of dollars ere I abstracted two of them for the purchase of the work in question. Other people are not so prudent nor so poor, and I can generally borrow the Beulahs and the Hidden Paths, etc., in the course of time. But I have really a curiosity to see this book. I thought it was a good deal when 'Harriet E. Prescott' said that it was different from any book she ever read; and when 'Marian Harland' said that she 'read it between the courses at the hotel table,' I thought the force of nature could no farther go; but when 'Metta Victoria Victor' said that the principal character was 'more finely finished than the Mephistophiles of Goethe, which certainly did not excel it in firmness and power,' I covered up my face and wept for the fallen Deity. Poor old Goethe! there thou satst on thy throne, secure of the worship of ages, when along came the 'Southern Lady,' knocked thy crown over thine eyes, turned thee off thy seat, and took thy sceptre and robe, leaving thee 'out in the cold!'

Who has got the book and will lend it?

CATH. LEDYARD.

NEW YORK OCTOBER 13, 1860

MINOR EXPERIENCES IN NEW YORK

VII

My wanderings were to end, for the time, at Harvard University and Cambridge.

I was somewhat awed, at first, to meet all the savants of the venerable College—the principal focus of American learning—where, however, I found a corner for myself, and the means of subsistence.

Once only in my life had I tried to be a Professor, and then only as a kind of pastime.

While spending a Winter in Berne, Switzerland, I learned from the papers that the cantonal government and the faculty of the University were in trouble to find a Professor of political economy.

To occupy my time, I proposed (of course without asking remuneration), was accepted, read a disquisition before the faculty, and for six months lectured before the students.

I then acted on Fourrier's principle of 'attraction;' I was now moved by compulsion—the compulsion of poverty—without knowing at what work I should be put.

Persons to whom I had letters, advised me to go to a boarding-house; this time my fellow-boarders were collegians, and association with them was in various ways interesting, entertaining, and instructive.

I had spent several years of my youth at different German Universities, and had retained a great partiality for the company of students. The undergraduates of Harvard were the best society I had met in America. Among the curiosities in the parlor of our boardinghouse, was a frame containing an embroidered crest, etc., belonging to the family of the owner of the house, and representing arms altogether unique in heraldry. This was my first initiation into the existence of cresto-mania in this country—a strange disease, spreading more and more throughout the States. One sees continually the queerest, most unintelligible and absurd heraldric compositions, proudly displayed on carriages, in books, on plate, china, etc., regardless of taste, propriety, or sense.

Heraldric works and books about peerages, etc., are more in demand at the Astor Library, with certain classes, than any other. In the Library of Harvard I found a historical notice of New England families. With great genealogical erudition the Lawrences were traced back to Laurenzo de Medici, and the Appletons to families in Normandy, dating beyond the Conquest. I am sure that the highly cultivated and truly American bearers of these names laugh at the nonsense, and scorn the ridiculous flattery.

A letter of introduction brought me into contact with Mr. William H. Prescott, on the eve of his celebrated English tour. I never met him afterwards, but had occasion to read carefully the catalogue of his library. Libraries of studious men give us an insight into the range of their intellectual powers. The only work connected with the philosophy of history contained in the library in question, was Guizot's on Civilization, and this scarcity of books of like import, accounts, to a great degree, for the tameness of the historiographer.

Mr. Prescott asked me if I had been recommended to a certain other literary celebrity. I had a letter to him, and Mr. Prescott kindly showed me to his residence. The *Révue des deux Mondes*—which, as everybody knows, is one of the best European critical authorities—calls that Boston celebrity† the 'Leporello of Spanish Literature.' Dutifully and respectfully, therefore, I accepted so high an authority.

Leporello received me in his library with bland condescension. After a few words, he asked me if I had an introduction to Mr. Prescott. I said that I had, and that he had even conducted me to the door. Leporello's face lit up with satisfaction. He then talked a good deal about Europe—and very loftily.

Through letters from friends in Dresden, I afterwards learned that during a stay at the Saxon capital he had somehow got introduced to the then Prince John (now King) of Saxony, at the time when this sprig of royalty was translating Dante, and patronized the Jesuits, for which he was taboo'd by society in Dresden; the same Prince John who, as an absolutist would have been torn to pieces by the people of Leipsig, but for the generous interference of the same Robert Blüm, whom afterwards (in 1849) Windischgratz murdered in Vienna, to gratify the hatred and to assuage the fears of the Hapsburgs and other crowned heads in Germany.

All this explained to me, subsequently, the savage hatred of European liberals exhibited by Leporello in our first conversation, which took place in the Spring of 1850, when the affairs of Germany were unsettled, and Austria and Prussia were on bad terms on account of the petty tyrant

†*Mr. George Ticknor.*

in Electoral Hesse.

We conversed in French. Leporello was much rejoiced at the restoration of order all over Europe, and, especially, in parts of Germany, Gradually swelling up, he exclaimed:

'La Prusse *nous* gate les affaires en Allemagne.'

(Prussia spoils *our* business in Germany.)

I humbly asked if he—Leporello—was related to the Hapsbourgs, and retired, having enough of such an acquaintance.

GUROWSKI

NEW YORK OCTOBER 20, 1860

[From Walt Whitman's 'Leaves of Grass.']

America Always!

AMERICA always!
Always me joined with you, whoever you are!
Always our own feuillage!
Always Florida's green peninsula! Always the priceless delta of Louisiana! Always the cotton-fields of Alabama and Texas!
Always California's golden hills and hollows—and the silver mountains of New Mexico! Always soft-breath'd Cuba!
Always the vast slope drained by the Southern Sea—inseparable with the slopes drained by the Eastern and Western Seas,
The area the Eighty-third year of These States—the three and a half millions of square miles.
The eighteen thousand miles of sea-coast and bay-coast on the main—the thirty thousand miles of river navigation,
The seven millions of distinct families, and the same number of dwellings—Always these and more, branching forth into numberless branches;
Always the free range and diversity! Always the continent of Democracy!
Always the prairies, pastures, forests, vast cities, travellers, Kanada, the snows;
Always these compact lands—lands tied at the hips with the belt stringing the huge oval lakes:
Always the West, with strong native persons—the increasing density there—the habitans, friendly, threatening, ironical, scorning invaders;
All sights, South, North, East—all deeds, promiscuously done at all times.
All characters, movements, growths—a few noticed, myriads unnoticed,
Through Mannahatta's streets I walking, these things gathering;
On interior rivers, by night, in the glare of pine knots, steamboats wooding up;
Sunlight by day on the valley of the Susquehanna, and on the valleys of the Potomac and Rappahannock, and the valleys of the Roanoke and Delaware;
In their northerly wilds beasts of prey haunting the Adirondacks, the hills—or lapping the Saginaw waters to drink;
In a lonesome inlet, a sheldrake, lost from the flock, sitting on the water, rocking silently;
In farmers' barns, oxen in the stable, their harvest labor done—they rest standing—they are too tired;
Afar on arctic ice, the she-walrus lying drowsily, while her cubs play around;
The hawk sailing where men have not yet sailed—the farthest polar sea, ripply, crystalline, open, beyond the floes:
White drift spooning ahead, where the ship in the tempest dashes;
On solid land, what is done in cities, as the bells all strike midnight together;
In primitive woods, the sounds there also sounding—the howl of the wolf, the scream of the panther, and the hoarse bellow of the elk;
In winter beneath the hard blue ice of Moosehead Lake— in summer visible through the clear waters, the great trout swimming;
In lower latitudes, in warmer air, in the Carolinas, the large black buzzard floating slowly high beyond the tree-tops,
Below, the red cedar, festooned with tylandria—the pines and cypresses, growing out of the white sand that spreads far and flat;
Rude boats descending the big Pedee—climbing plants, parasites, with colored flowers and berries, enveloping huge trees,
The waving drapery on the live oak, trailing long and low, noiselessly waved by the wind;
The camp of Georgia wagoners, just after dark—the supper-fires, and the cooking and eating by whites and negroes,
Thirty or forty great wagons—the mules, cattle, horses, feeding from troughs,
The shadows, gleams, up under the leaves of the old sycamore-trees—the flames—also the black smoke from the pitch-pine, curling and rising;
Southern fishermen fishing—the sounds and inlets of North Carolina's coast—the shad-fishery and the herring-fishery—the large sweep-seines—the windlasses on shore worked by horses—the clearing, curing, and packing houses;
Deep in the forest, in the piney woods, turpentine and tar dropping from the incisions in the trees—there is the turpentine distillery,
There are the negroes at work, in good health—the ground in all directions is covered with pine straw;
In Tennessee and Kentucky, slaves busy in the coalings, at the forge, by the furnace-blaze, or at the corn-shucking:
In Virginia, the planter's son returning after a long absence, joyfully welcomed and kissed by the aged mulatto nurse;
On rivers, boatmen safely moored at night-fall, in their boats, under the shelter of high banks,
Some of the younger men dance to the sound of the banjo or fiddle—others sit on the gunwale, smoking and talking:
Late in the afternoon, the mocking-bird, the American mimic, singing in the Great Dismal Swamp—there are the greenish waters, the resinous odor, the plenteous moss, the cypress tree, and the juniper tree;
Northward, young men of Mannahatta—the target company from an excursion returning home at evening—the musket-muzzles all bear bunches of flowers presented by women;
Children at play—or on his father's lap a young boy fallen asleep, (how his lips move! how he smiles in his sleep!)
The scout riding on horseback over the plains west of the Mississippi—he ascends a knoll and sweeps his eye around;
California life—the miner, bearded, dressed in his rude costume—the stanch California friendship—the sweet air—the graves one, in passing, meets, solitary, just aside the horse-path;
Down in Texas, the cotton-field, the negro-cabins—drivers driving mules or oxen before rude carts —cotton-bales piled on banks and wharves;
Encircling all, vast-darting, up and wide, the American Soul, with equal hemispheres—one Love, one Dilation or Pride:
In arriere, the peace-talk with the Iroquois, the aborigines—the calumet, the pipe of good-will arbitration, and indorsement,
The sachem blowing the smoke first toward the sun and then toward the earth,
The drama of the scalp-dance enacted with painted faces and guttural exclamations,
The setting out of the war-party—the long and stealthy march,
The single file—the swinging hatchets—the surprise and slaughter of enemies;
All the acts, scenes, ways, persons, attitudes of These States—reminiscences, all institutions,
All These States, compact—Every square mile of
These States, without excepting a particle—you also—me also,
Me pleased, rambling in lanes and country fields, Paumanok's fields,
Me, observing the spiral flight of two little yellow butterflies, shuffling between each other, ascending high in the air;
The darting swallow, the destroyer of insects—the Fall traveller southward, but returning northward early in the spring;
The country boy at the close of the day, driving the herd of cows, and shouting to them as they loiter to browse by the road-side;
The city wharf—Boston, Philadelphia, Baltimore, Charleston, New Orleans, San Francisco,
The departing ships, when the sailors heave at the capstan;
Evening—me in my room—the setting sun,
The setting summer sun shining in my open window, showing me flies, suspended, balancing in the air in the centre of the room, darting athwart, up and down, casting swift shadows in specks on the opposite wall, where the shine is;
The athletic American matron speaking in public to crowds of listeners;
Males, females, immigrants, combinations—the copiousness—the individuality and sovereignty of The States, each for itself—the money-makers;
Factories, machinery, the mechanical forces—the windlass, lever, pulley—All certainties,
The certainty of space, increase, freedom, futurity,
In space, the sporades, the scattered islands, the stars—on the firm earth, the lands, my lands,
O lands! all so dear to me—what you are, (whatever it is,) I become a part of that, whatever it is,
Southward there, I screaming, with wings slow flapping, with the myriads of gulls Wintering along the coasts of Florida—or in Louisiana, with pelicans breeding,
Otherways, there, atwixt the banks of the Arkansaw, the Rio Grande, the Nueces, the Brazos, the Tombigbee, the Red River, the Saskatchawan, or the Osage, I with the spring waters laughing and skipping and running:
Northward, on the sands, on some shallow bay of Paumanok, I, with parties of snowy herons wading in the wet to seek worms and aquatic plants;
Retreating, triumphantly twittering, the king-bird, from piercing the crow with its bill, for amusement—And I triumphantly twittering;
The migrating flock of wild geese alighting in Autumn to refresh themselves—the body of the flock feed—the sentinels outside move around with erect heads watching, and are from time to time relieved by other sentinels—And I feeding and taking turns with the rest;
In Kanadian forests, the moose, large as an ox, cornered by hunters, rising desperately on his hind-feet, and plunging with his fore-feet, the hoofs as sharp as knives—And I, plunging at the hunters, cornered and desperate;
In the Mannahatta, streets, piers, shipping, storehouses, and the countless workmen working in the shops,
And I too of the Mannahatta, singing thereof—and no less in myself than the whole of the Mannahatta in itself,
Singing the song of These, my ever united lands—my body no more inevitably united, part to part, and made one identity, any more than my lands are inevitably united, and made ONE IDENTITY,
Nativities, climates, the grass of the great Pastoral Plains,
Cities, labors, death, animals, products, good and evil—these me,
These affording, in all their particulars, endless feuillage to me and to America, how can I do less than pass the clew of the union of them, to afford the like to you?
Whoever you are! how can I but offer you divine leaves, that you also be eligible as I am?
How can I but, as here, chanting, invite you for yourself to collect bouquets of the incomparable feuillage of These States?

Miss S. J. Russell, will be ready, on the 17th inst., to receive at her residence, No. 237 West 22d street, a few young ladies for instruction in Latin and in the English branches. Applications addressed to the care of William C. Russell, No. 24 Pine street, will be attended to.

MINOR EXPERIENCES IN AMERICA.

IX.

The dwellers in the classic groves of Cambridge, and the children of their Alma Mater received me with kindness, most of them with such open-heartedness as put me immediately at ease.

Probably they were observing me; certainly I observed and studied them, as well as the system of the University, from all possible sides.

Now, for the first time, I saw an amalgamation or combination, no longer in existence in Europe, of a classical gymnasium and a sort of University, in both of which however the old medieval scholastic method and arrangement still prevailed.

I soon found that the current of intellectual interest tended principally towards the natural sciences. This scientific, healthy, and beneficial impulse was due to the presence of the greatest living ichthyologist, and the first paleontologist in the world, who a few years before had left Europe and settled in Cambridge, and whose presence constitutes an epoch in the scientific development of America.

Not equally happy was the great ichthyologist in his teleological discoveries when using the expression 'God after due consideration,' an expression which was neither philosophical, orthodox, nor teleological; nor did he show either a philosophical mind or a knowledge of history when he upbraided historians (see Types of Mankind, by J.C. Nott, p. 68), or when he asserted the axiom that the white man, for the benefit of the African, should produce a civilization different from that under which we live.

But such a different and patriarchal civilization, with its pens, auction-blocks, whips, and bloodhounds, is already invented and flourishing over immense portions of this free country, and apparently to the satisfaction of the great ichthyologist.

All of which proves, as it seems to me, that a paleontologist, or a biologist, cannot so easily become a Prometheus, or handle the cosmic laws of the physical and the moral world, with the same facility and wisdom he displays with fossils and fishes.

Non omnia possumus omnes.

Of a similar stamp—seemingly philosophical, but without philosophy—are the objections urged by the same authority against Darwin's theory or hypothesis. Before him all the opponents of Darwin were very correct and orthodox, but not very scientific or logical. The partisans and disciples of whatsoever old creed, have always raised a similar outcry against every new, more complete, and more cosmic theory, which from a broader basis, and more extended generalities, arrived at more perfect conclusions.

The pundit of history in Harvard College, and another Professor of all literatures, objected to Darwin, on account of the confusion he introduced into the received chronologies; as though either of them knew much about the chronology of our planet or that of its inhabitants.

The progress of knowledge is not aided by such savants. If it depended upon them, science would be where it was about six thousand years ago. Nothing would have been learned concerning the cosmic changes and evolutions of matter; the chemical nature of air would have remained as unknown, as that, so to speak, this air in its turn created the earth; the eternally consistent, but infinitely varied concatenation of cause and effect, their combination and reciprocal action, would have remained unknown; so would the fact that if the life of plants depends upon animals, the plants in their turn contribute greatly to generate the power of thought in animals; we would have remained ignorant that every atom is the bearer of a peculiar life and of a distinct thought.

At present the Physiology of matter and of nature is lifted out from the rusty and dusty path of routine, notwithstanding that Harvard and the other opponents of Darwin would say to the thoughts and theories of Moleschott, Vogt, Meiden, Volger, and perhaps even to Darwin and Draper, averte Satanas.

The followers of the routine of orthodoxy or creed, are always at war with every new and luminous emanation from the human mind. But after awhile orthodoxy slily accepts them. Wolf, Kant, Hegel, have been successively anathematized by Theologians, and by the majority of Biblists, all of whom have, however, finally adopted and adapted as much as they could from the philosophers. Such will also be the case with Darwin.

History proves how different from what they are at the beginning, the ultimate results and final influence of new discoveries, new studies, new systems, and hypotheses upon the genius of progress, and the development of science, come to be.

Exempli gratia.

When during the first ten years of this century, the Sanscrit began to be analyzed and studied, the Pietists and Biblists, such as Schlegel and others, began to triumph, believing they had discovered an inexhaustible source, whence should proceed new light and fresh strength for the Hebraic and Nazarine records and legends. The events on the Jordan were to gain new authority from the newly-discovered traditions on the Indus. The classical scholars and the rationalists exclaimed with Voss, the translator of the Iliad, that 'Brahmins were leagued with Jesuits in order to subvert rationalism and protestantism.'

But now when the study of Sanscrit has opened a new world of knowledge, when many of our theological ideas and dogmas, such as those upon the Trinity, the Holy Ghost, the Incarnation, etc., when even rites hitherto believed to belong to Jerusalem and to the first Christian century, are found to have long preëxisted as germs or as systems in Brahminical science; now when the study of Sanscrit has created comparative philology, and thus shed a new light upon the history of the human race, on its mental development and its ethnic distribution, now the Pietists of all hues and the Biblists wish Sanscrit and the various results of its study to the bottom of the sea.

Darwin's so decried theory may yet become a dogma to the future Orthodox and Biblists. But before that event it will open new scientific paths, and give solutions to many problems in the realm of knowledge. Already Darwin's theory applied to the hitherto insoluble questions of the existence and distribution of the human race over the earth, has given more perfect ethnological solutions, as it has to the Pentateuch, and even the whole Bible, with its confused and abnormal chronology.

Gurowski

[For The New York Saturday Press.]

FROM PEORIA.

Sunday, Oct. 21, 1860.

Mr. Editor: I fear you will have rather a dull letter to-day, for my spirits are not at the highest pitch. This Autumn weather affects the tone of the mind. These fading leaves, this sad, shrill wind, this melancholy sky, weigh on the heart like a presage of doom. But, in the spirit of Mrs. Chick, I mean to 'make an effort,' and throw off despondency.

I have been at church twice to-day, and listened to two excellent sermons from the best of ministers. Poor man! how I pity him and many another of his class. It is a pleasant sight, for a feeling mind, to behold a man of culture, refinement, and ability, settled among a people utterly incapable of appreciating him, and continually demanding for the paltry sum they offer him, something more brilliant and talented. Pleasant to watch him going on, month by month, just able by the strictest management to obtain the bare necessaries of life, and then at the end of a year or two be ignominiously dismissed, and sent out into the world to try his fortune again—having been previously given to understand that he is not considered 'smart' enough for the place! I can tell you, Sodom and Gomorrah will rise up in judgment one day against those upstart country churches that so 'stone those that are sent unto them.' But I believe the wrongs of the ministry are not exactly in your line, and I will forbear.

What shall I tell you of our journey home? The boat was dingy and dismal as of yore; I sat on deck as long as the atmosphere permitted, and then retired to the woful depths of the ladies' cabin, and rested my weariness by leaning half an hour against the wall, till I could capture a stray chair. Then I drew nigh to the marble table and the glittering chandelier, and addressed myself to the perusal of tracts intended for 'the drunkard' and the 'gamester!' Cheerful literature, this, for a dull October evening! But fate had mercy, and sent me consolation in the shape of three females of different ages, also seated around the marble.

What a blessing that we women have tongues, and are not averse to using them!

Our partie carrée presently became animated and social. We talked of the Prince whom we had seen, and the firemen's parade which we missed, of the *Great Eastern*, of crochet cotton and where it could be bought at the cheapest rate, of fashions, friendships, etc., etc. At an early hour we parted and saw each other no more. Shall we ever meet again? At least I owe them gratitude for rendering tolerable that most forlorn and comfortless of earth's deserts—a steamboat cabin.

Patronize the Delavan when you breakfast in Albany. They take half an hour to bring what you order; they give you lamb-chops when you say veal-cutlets; and half the things in the bill of fare are missing; but the tablecloths and napkins are delightfully clean, the rolls are light, the silver bright (never mind the rhyme), and all is served with a neatness that makes one feel at home. And, crowning charm, the coffee is absolutely drinkable! Not strong enough to upset weak nerves, assuredly, but absolutely free from all unpleasant flavor, and not suggesting in the most remote degree roast beans or burned potato-skins. Albany may be a very beautiful city; but to rather verdant travellers, who roam about its muddy streets of a chill October morning, with an ever-present idea in their minds that the train leaves at half-past nine, and that it would be just their luck to miss it, the place does not appear interesting. Such rustic specimens are glad to make their way to the depot forty minutes before the appointed time, and seat themselves in an empty car, patiently awaiting their departure.

The writer's companion informs her, that in this vast affair, the Central Road, are invested forty-four millions of dollars!! Her feeble mind strives to grasp and comprehend a fact so interesting, and full fifteen minutes are spent in profitable meditation thereon; and presently the whistle begins to sound, the steam to puff, the bells to ring, the cars to clank and rumble, and away we go.

The hills just out of Albany are perfectly gorgeous; indeed it may be said that the scene is worthy of the artist's pencil. We look and admire; we 'refresh' at St. Johnsville, on an interesting fossil of the genus to which Dr. Holmes makes loving allusion, under the name of 'Meat-pie.' It lies in the system like chunks of lead, inducing headache and general apathy toward all mundane concerns, till the train stops at the —— station, our friends meet us, and we roll away through the bright stillness of the Autumn afternoon, toward home.

Going home! Do you know anything about it? The eager faces watching for you—the rush to the gate as you drive up—the children hanging round your waist, and all the grown people kissing you at once—every one so glad to see you again. Then unpacking the trunks, and getting out the presents.

The children are wild with delight; the elders manifest a sober pleasure; but now comes the trial moment! In an evil hour you purchased, for that confiding sister at your elbow, a bonnet, which you know she will not like. You can't tell how you came to do it; you looked till you were tired, each article you saw suiting you less than the one before it; and somehow, by some strange, inexplicable fate, before you knew it, almost, the money was paid and the bonnet bought! That fact accomplished, neither prayers nor tears avail. Unlucky chapeau! it has lain heavy on your soul for many a day and night, driven sleep from your pillow, robbed your cheek of its lustre, and your eye of its bloom. And now the so-dreaded moment has arrived. All the family is gathered round the hat-box, to look at Nelly's bonnet—her bonnet from New York —Nelly herself, flushed with joyous anticipation, draws it forth. O bliss! can you believe your eyes? She is actually pleased, and thanks you for it, and says you have done better for her than she would have done for herself. What a weight is lifted from your mind, and how thoroughly you enjoy the tea which has been made ready for the exhausted traveller.

The meal over you begin a fragmentary record of your adventures—you get out the Saturday Presses, the *Knickerbockers*, etc., which generous publishers have bestowed upon you—you describe Mr.——, Mr. ——, and the Messrs. ———, those stars in the firmament of literature. You exhibit your own new dresses and gloves and ribbons, and talk so fast that your cheeks fairly burn with excitement.

The next day you walk through the quiet streets where you notice the rustle of the mantle of your dress as it sweeps among the yellow leaves, and think how much pleasanter this is than Broadway. You go about the house and are delighted to find that Fall cleaning is through with; you survey with satisfaction that long line of sweetmeat and pickle-jars that has accumulated during your absence. And you feel that you have enjoyed yourself more in one half day at home than in all the weeks you were away.

As it is Sunday my mind naturally reverts to serious subjects. We have no Episcopal church here, and I shall miss that service which I like so much—a sort of compromise between Presbyterian boldness and prosaicness, and the tawdriness of Rome. Yet there is one thing I could never listen to with any patience, the prayer—in which 'we most humbly beseech thee with thy favor to behold and bless the President of these United States.' I always feel like saying 'you may skip that.' It seems so entirely a matter of form to me, and is so regarded, one would judge, in the quarter to which it is addressed, seeing how very limited are the results of the petition. A sense of the fitness of things would banish it from the liturgy; but such a sense is rare. The world is full of incongruities, some of them amusing enough. All of us have seen people laugh at funerals, and I was once at a wedding where a couple of young ladies being asked to favor the company with a little music, performed a most awful ditty entitled 'The Night of the Grave!' each verse ending with something about 'the cold, silent night of the grave!' Exhilarating for the married pair. One of my acquaintances was at Niagara awhile since, and on her return I asked her how she liked the Falls? Was she disappointed in them? O no —they came quite up to her expectations—she wa'n't *turned round* a mite—there was folks that when they went to the Falls they couldn't tell East from West—but she wa'n't turned round a mite. Nor did any further inquisition extract from her a more romantic expression of opinion. Again, a 'circus' is quite an event in the country, and not long ago we had one here. A friend of mine, a most estimable young lady, was exceedingly anxious to go; but it unfortunately happened that the lecture preparatory to Communion was held on the same afternoon, and the young lady was a church-member. Her only anxiety was that the lecture should be out in time to allow her to go over and witness the performances, and she was greatly astonished when her father suggested that if he were in her place he would give up one or the other; he would not pretend to dictate which. Under the head of a non-sense of propriety may be classed the habit of those ministers who speak with such off-hand familiarity of 'John' and 'Paul,' as if they were the coachman and waiter, and perhaps in this very epistle you will observe examples in point.

Nevron.

Thoughts and Things.

BY ADA CLARE

The white cravat is a great motive-engine in the erection of the modern novel. So is the inhuman and uncertain relative. But the suspicious damsel soars like an eagle above them all, in utility and stupidity.

Most people have been acquainted from their childhood with the heroine who responds to the hero in the white cravat.

When I was a child, my grandfather related to me a story. He had himself perused it, in the days when he doted on the sweet sport of hookey and his knees were perennially black and blue. It was the same narrative that continually soaks its mildewed way through the modern printing-press.

A maiden has parts, or, in human language, talents: Of course, she is beautiful and proud, and though rich, virtuous. The maiden is ambitious. The maiden's fingers are stained with ink. The maiden refuses to aid her aunt in pickling pineapples. Woe is me! from that hour her doom is sealed. The mandate has gone forth: Whosoever will not pickle pineapples, let her die—no, live the life.

Then the maiden writes a book. The book sells, is successful. She gets rich. Friends flock around her. By this time, the undiscerning and stupefied reader supposes the maiden—still a maiden,— to be quite happy, if not distinctly jolly. All at once vinegar is showered into his porridge. The maiden—still a maiden—is not happy; she is only virtuous, and virtue is its own reward. In fact, she is a blighted, lorn, and lacerated maiden. There is a blister, not to say a canker, in her heart.

She wakes one damp and soggy morning, and rapidly finds out that she has neither five children, nor an infant at the breast. Her mind wanders in the mazes of possible measles and croups, and she weeps with wild regret.

She is going to the Winter Garden that night to see the famous Cushman. Alas! that there is no stern and solemn creature, with spectacles prancing on indignant nose, and dressing-gown flapping about outraged heels, to cry, 'Woman, forbear! go not, to the amusement of sin. Ignorant, weak, unworthy being, follow your marster to church.'

O that she had a devoted husband, to abuse, to insult, to degrade her.

O! what a heavenly thing to have a stern husband, to be herself an invalid, to have just two—gracious heaven I ask not much, I am but a woman—chronic diseases.

She flies from the metropolis; she seeks a sylvan retreat. She makes all the children in the village sick with gifts of candies, that she may be a woman indeed by nursing them. She goes daily for a month to the nearest hospital to awe and torment the hapless invalids, until the head-nurse declares that she will not stand it any longer.

Five years afterwards you stumble on a strange cottage. A subdued creature in a canton-flannel gown, with lean hands, and freckled lips, comes to the door. You recognize in her the formerly brilliant but wretched author of 'Rhododendron,' now the happy wife of the Rev. Arthur Mopp. You enter, there are five cradles before the humble hearth. There is also the Rev. Mopp. You are introduced to him,—to Mopp. O! the dear, delightful, exemplary, bigoted, long-visaged, dull, drawling, dolesome, diabolically dreary creature! Happy author of 'Rhododendron,' to be bonded to him in wedlock!

Next comes the cruel aunt or uncle. Of course the lambly heroine, who is an angel of the tea-cup school, is persecuted,—wickedly, unnecessarily, and ridiculously persecuted. Of course, the main cause is money, and of course she scorns and tramples upon money. She is a human spaniel, and the more she is kicked the better she loves the foot that spurns her. After awhile she inherits all the property. Then she bestows it in a complete and shining lump upon her cruel persecutors. For herself she needs but little, and that little she earns from a mill. Three and sixpence a day would have supported her luxuriously, if she had not been in the habit of giving four and ninepence diurnally to beggars. The consequence was, she could not purchase any real estate in the village. Just as she is about to perish of inanition, she marries a comfortable fellow with a long-tailed coat.

Last comes the sovereign of all modern novel plot-creators—the suspicious, the miraculously suspicious damsel. She it is that causes the printing-press to be a valuable investment, that brings paper up to a premium in the market.

Let us presume that she is a noble, intelligent, pure, and generous female creature. She is engaged to an equally excellent male creature. His devotion to her has been unbounded. For her he has given up champaign and soda, turned his back on pumps, flouted an heiress with a couple of hundred thousand pounds to her dowry, and quarrelled with his papa, who is a commanding Major General in the army.

This generous and confiding heroine has a cousin, a coquettish and handsome cousin. She remarks that the hero sometimes helps her to gravy when he dines with them. She doesn't like it. She proceeds after the reflection to spend the day, in tears.

One fine afternoon she is going down to the village to match a skein of silk. She is walking along, not in such abject misery as might have been expected, considering the gravy, when she hears a voice. Of heaven, 'tis her cousin's, and another voice, O! heaven and earth, 'tis her lover's.

First voice: "Do you know where the dandelions grow?"

Second voice. "Dandelions require the sun to perfect them, they seldom flourish in the mud."

The tortured listener presses her hand on her heart to keep from screaming.

First voice: "What are you looking at and laughing at?"

Second voice: "I am looking into this ditch and watching the funny little pollywogs"

The heroine is now fit for Bedlam, but she does not betray her despair. She leaves that spot, leaves the perjured lover, and the shameless cousin.

That evening when the former calls, he is informed that she is gone to Smyrna. All his presents and letters are left for him in a carpet-bag.

Then come 978 and a half pages of tears, and howling, and lamentations. 490 pages go to the heroine's grief, 488 pages to the lover's woe. On the 979th page, they meet. She is older and graver, and has lost her top-hair; he is sadder and wiser, and the pollywog has become a burden to him.

He entreats her to speak to him, she becomes dumb to look at him, she becomes blind; to hear him, she becomes deaf.

Suddenly in some miraculous manner she learns that he was gathering dandelions, not for the coquettish cousin, but to make a plaster for old Susan, who dwelt below the hill. Old Susan who had nursed him, saved his father's life, preserved his mother from seduction and taught their cook the only genuine method of making flap-jacks.

All is understood, the clouds clear off—the blue sky shines.

The heroine's heart of marble softens, her breast of ice melts. They sink in each other's arms.

You are glad to think they are going to be always happy and comfortable, but at the same time, you cannot help reflecting seriously that if the word flap-jacks had been breathed three volumes ago, nine hundred and seventy-eight pages must have vanished before its magic mystery.

MINOR EXPERIENCES IN AMERICA

X.

A countryman or farmer approached me politely in the streets of Cambridge, and saying that he heard I was a Russian, remarked that his son, who was with him, a pupil in the Deaf and Dumb Asylum, wished to have a look at a Russian.

Fortunately it was Summer, and I did not present too bearish an appearance. I took off my blue spectacles and willingly stood the inspection.

The boy walked round me two or three times; studied my person in detail as well as he could, and then taking out a small slate commenced to write.

I was curious to see the result of his survey, and found he had written: 'Saw a Russian. Russians one-eyed.'

I embraced the boy, told him that he must not take pars pro toto and misinform his friends in the Asylum, since Russians have generally two eyes and belong to the sharp-sighted nations.

We parted good friends, and the father invited me to visit his family and look at his farm.

The festivities and ceremonies of Commencement and Alumni days, the orations and dinners incident upon these occasions, were all new and interesting to me. Some of them recalled my youthful days, when I too was examined, when I declaimed, graduated, and was ambitious to win collegiate or academic laurels.

Why did I not stop there? To compete for laurels in Revolutions or in the battles of life, withers the heart and crushes the mind.

But no regrets, no regrets.

After all, the past cannot be undone, and I am not sure whether, with all my experience, I would not again follow the same course.

Beside an oration and a species of poem, a pretended American Legend was read at the Alumni festival.

The words Anglo Saxon resounded in the verses of the poem as they did in the numerous speeches made at the dinner. This was done, likely enough, to honor the presence of two 'fellows' from Cambridge, England.

Finally, however, one of them rose, and, among other things, said that he was much astonished at hearing so much about the Anglo Saxons: that in England they knew only Englishmen, the English mind and character, English daring, etc.

I was well pleased at this 'sortie,' particularly as before, in my conversations with the professors of the University, I had often tried to point out how unscientific and unhistorical, and therefore baseless was this reference to the Anglo Saxons for all the qualities of which Americans are justly proud.

This Anglo Saxon mania is however now so wide spread, and has so permeated all superficial thought that it will stand the attacks of real knowledge, as do the equinoctial storms, the lune rousse in France, and many similar deeply-rooted beliefs which are nevertheless perfect fallacies.

Perhaps some future investigator will be as puzzled to explain the American Anglo Saxonism, as at present the most accomplished classical scholars, philologists, historians, and ethnologists, are to find out why the Romans spoke of the people who called themselves Rasenes as

Etrusci or Tusci, or why they surnamed the Helleni of Thucidides Graeci.

Another dinner to the memory of the deceased Alumni was more interesting for its speeches, than for its stirring but not agreeably flavored dishes.

About this time Jenny Lind threw the population, the press, and the pulpits of America into a fever of ecstacy. I had heard her in Europe, had witnessed the enthusiasm in some German cities, and had met her in the crowd of some salons, where I had occasion to observe her naively cold deportment upon the stage and in society.

At first I could not understand how, all at once, she became such a voltaic battery, able to electrify and shock millions into fits of ecstacy. But eventually it became clear to my mind that Barnum was the great generator of this power, and that Jenny Lind acted under his instructions.

By this means it was that Jenny's great talent was inflated by sanctimony and increased even by the use of ventriloquism.

The company arrived in Boston, and of course there was no limit to the feverish excitement round me.

I could scarcely believe my senses.

Jenny was worshipped as an angel, a saint, a new holy virgin, and this by old and young, by men and women, the white-cravated saints leading the van, while orators, professors, statesmen, poets, school-teachers, school-boys, and school-girls formed the rank and file of the believers.

During this excitement, I spent an evening at the house of one among the most eminent men of America, where of course Jenny was the topic of conversation. "Count, you must think we are very ridiculous with all this running after Jenny Lind. In fact we deserve to be laughed at for it," he said to me half in disgust.

Next morning he ran into Boston, brought her out to Cambridge, served as her cicerone at the Observatory, and influenced the learned, serious but good-natured (at least he was always so to me) Professor Bond to call after the Prima Donna some erratic body which, at the moment when Jenny was peeping through the telescope, was supposed to be making an independent stride through the immensities.

At last I could stand it no longer, and in turn I ran to Boston, to the Revere House, and sent my card up to Barnum.

He received me very politely, and asked me if I wished to see HER?

I explained that I had seen and heard her in Europe, and that my visit was intended exclusively for him, as I wished to approach and become acquainted with a man capable of working such wonders.

Barnum's answer was, "I understand very well, sir, how you should desire to see me." Then came a shake of the hand and a polite offer on his part of a free ticket to a concert; an offer which was as politely refused, for, at that time, the sweets of dead-headism were altogether unknown to me.

GUROWSKI.

—The fearful truth of Jane Eyre is never made more evident than by looking over the English governess advertisements. Out of some hundred printed in one issue of the Critic, there is not one who asks a salary of more than fifty pounds, and some ask but fifteen. For such paltry sums there are evidently crowds of well-educated and talented women who are eagerly competing for engagements as governesses, and who, for the chance of a home and something to do, will gladly submit to the mortifications which are, in the great majority of cases, incident to that position of semi-servitude.

—All the old theories seem fading away under the increasing light of science and investigation. The old tradition that arsenic is a poison appears liable to the same fate. The Westmoreland Gazette gives an account of a stream called Whitbeck, which flows past a village of the same name in West Cumberland, and which contains arsenic in determinable quantities. The arsenic is derived from the veins of arsenical cobalt through which it percolates at its source. All the inhabitants of Whitbeck, except the ducks, use the water of this stream, and thrive upon it. The children are rosy, and the old people attain, in full possession of such faculties as they may have, a surprising old age, while to the women it gives a beauty and clearness of complexion only equalled by the sleekness and gloss of coat which the horses derive from its use. Finally perhaps we shall come to consider the giving of arsenic to obnoxious relatives or other persons, as a kind and considerate act instead of a heartless and cruel one.

NEW YORK NOVEMBER 3, 1860

'PERSONNE'S' OPINION OF MISS CUSHMAN.

Miss Cushman's performance is after the Anatomical Museum style. Her effects are 'thrilling' and vulgar. Her poses are awkward, and her pictures lack finish and delicacy of outline. The secret of her attraction is that which made Forrest so famous in *Cade* and *Spartacus*—vigor; the masses like vigor, and if they can have a little art along with it, very well. But vigor they must have. Now Forrest has improved in all artistic requirements, while Miss Cushman has stood still—perhaps retrograded. I should not deem it necessary to reiterate this twice-told tale were it not for the humbug carefully put before the public about Miss Cushman's artistic associations and experiences—the refining influences to which she had been subjected abroad, and how much the drama was to be indebted to her for consenting to come back to the stage. All this and more was given out by solemn old muffs like H. T. TUCKERMAN—pumps, who do the heavy society dodge, and then write about it in the papers, in the Mutual-Admiration-Society style, and yet, notwithstanding all this, we find in Miss Cushman—the Miss Cushman of twenty years ago—a little older, no handsomer, and no better. Did her artist friends tell Miss Cushman to hold her arms like the broken wings of a turkey, with pendant eagle claws? Did they tell her that, because Meg was an old woman, and a gipsey, that all her attitudes should necessarily be angular and awkward? Did she never see some chefs d'œuvres of the Bohemian race which are to be found in every picture gallery in Europe, from the Louvre to the Pitti Palace? And if so, why has she not profited by them ?—*N. Y. Leader.*

THE POLITICAL EXCITEMENT.

The conviction has been for the past few months forcing itself upon us, that the Politicians are trying to raise an excitement, and make people believe that what they call a crisis, or something of the sort, is at hand.

We have been led to this conviction by noticing that the crowds of persons who hang about bar-rooms, treating and getting treated, the persons who carry in their faces certain undefinable signs which proclaim them politicians, have greatly increased of late, have been doing a very active business in the drinking way, and have talked louder and swaggered more than usual.

Such a state of commotion among the politicians is always a sure sign that a crisis is rapidly approaching.

The humors of the body politic are gathering to a head.

We have also been persuaded by certain other sure signs that some great political movement was on hand.

The streets have been filled of late with certain torch-light processions, with music, transparencies, banners, small boys, etc.

There have been illuminated exhortations to the Union carried through the streets.

There are now four or five banners suspended across Broadway, each bearing the names of various insignificant persons, of whom we never heard before, and the majority of whom we may feel thankful and certain we shall never hear of again.

The object of these banners is, we believe, to induce the passers-by who read the names to vote for the holders of the same.

The arguments used to induce a diligent reader of the banner inscriptions, who should perhaps find himself undecided, to select certain names for voting, are as pertinent and convincing as those drawn from the banners themselves would be, from their size, style of ornamentation, etc.

These arguments are to be found in the daily and other papers, and here we come to the surest sign that some political crisis, or what not, may be shortly expected to arrive.

The papers, daily and other, have for the past few months been displaying the signs of its coming which we have never known to fail.

They have lost all interest for an intelligent reader.

They are foul with personalities.

When the *Tribune* contains articles to the effect that the *Express* is a liar, and everybody who says it is not is a liar, and everybody else is a liar who don't read the *Tribune*—when the *Express* in its turn indulges in similar reasoning and rhetoric—when The *World* has extra pious snivels, and its brother in the spirit, *The Journal of Commerce*, mixes politics with its mammon of righteousness—when the *Herald* commences to prophecy all sorts of dreadful things as about to happen, and breaks out every morning in capitals descriptive of treasons, stratagems, and spoils when the *Times* and the religious papers trot out their spiritual beasts, and try to frighten plous or foolish people with their roaring—when the whole press of the country is loud in its protestations of virtue, and its denunciations of all the sheets which are not on their side, we know that some great crisis may be looked for about that time.

All of these premonitory signs, have been recently displayed in the most disgusting manner.

And on investigation we find that the political crisis they portend is the election of a President who is to do what is called govern this country.

The Saturday Press has before alluded to the blessings of being governed.

They must be taken for granted.

It must be assumed as an axiom that this nation wants a figure-head.

Certainly no one supposes that any of the persons whose names have been recently flung out, upon the banners aforementioned, to the breeze, will prove anything more than figure-heads,

It is not either on their or on the nation's account that the papers and the Politicians have been so busy getting up this political crisis.

The papers and politicians don't care for anybody but themselves.

And perhaps it is best that it is so, since it is not a very good thing for anybody to have the papers and politicians interested in him.

It is the grand gambling game of the Presidential election which the Politicians are playing.

They get up this excitement so that they may interest the outsiders enough to have them pay for the candles and the cards.

As for the stake, that is immense, and the lucky winners, as gamblers always do, keep it all to themselves.

The grand contest comes off next Tuesday, and whichever party gains is not much matter.

The sun will rise the next day just the same. Things will be pretty much as they were.

The only change will be that the same set of Politicians continue in office, or are forced to give way for another and perhaps more rapacious set.

So that we are not much interested in the Political Excitement.

MINOR EXPERIENCES IN AMERICA.

XI.

With the fervent and almost religious enthusiasm of a child, I saluted the Fourth of July, 1850.

A letter of introduction from Professor, now President Felton, to Mr. Bigelow, then mayor of Boston, procured me a place in the Procession, at the Dinner, etc.

The rain poured down upon us as we tramped through the muddy streets, but the crowds of well-dressed people expressing sincere joyous festivity in their faces, the windows filled with more or less handsome women, the recollections crowding and boiling in my memory, the halo with which my imagination surrounded the day, all these transformed the muddy streets into a parterre covered with carpets and strewn with flowers.

Then after all this to enter Faneuil Hall, a spot which history and fiction had taught me to reverence as the birthplace of American liberty, seemed the crowning glory of the day.

The Mayor had put me in charge of a councilman, and I found him an agreeable, well-informed, and well-bred companion during the procession and during the festival.

I never was, nor am I now, partial to public dinners with speeches for dessert. Perhaps this results from my not having been brought up in a free country, and not having been accustomed to such festivities during my youth spent in Poland and Germany.

At that, now rather distant period, the police ruled with a high hand both the above-mentioned countries, and of course all public free gatherings were out of the question. Besides public dinners in the English fashion were not known among the national customs of the Polish nobility. It often happened that rich and influential nobles or other magnates gave great and luxurious dinners to as many as a hundred guests. At such dinners no speeches were made, but short toasts, which were drank in bumpers containing quarts of wine, followed each other rapidly, until as the acme of hospitality, most of the guests found themselves—the reader may guess where.

When I was a resident at the German Universities, the few public dinners which may then have accidentally occurred in Germany were mostly gatherings of officials, the speeches were laudatory of the Government, of the Landesvater or father of the land, and the Landesfuersten or sovereign, both names being generally synonymous. Such displays of crouching loyalty were held in contempt by the University students.

In after years, I was present at some celebrated public dinners in Paris and London, but for reasons inscrutable even to myself, I could not then, and cannot now find in such dinners any feast for the palate or the mind.

It was however otherwise with the Fourth of July dinner in Faneuil Hall.

It was served cold—as a dinner was a poor one, and on the strictest temperance principles,—but it was very enthusiastic, and for the first time in my varied experience of life, I saw genuine enthusiasm assisted by cold chicken and iced water.

I was seated among the dignitaries of the day, at the side of the orator, Mr. Whipple, the well-known lecturer and essayist.

When the toasts and speeches became frequent, I was called on and told that I must make one. My excuse that I was ignorant of the English Language, and not accustomed to speak in public, was of no avail, so I hastily collected all the words my memory retained, and sought to express with them the sentiment that since the day of the nativity at Bethlehem, no day, no spot, and no event, has such significance in the History of our race as Faneuil Hall, and the Revolution which was born there.

I am sure nobody understood me, and yet the reporter of some Boston paper rendered my words and my meaning with, to me, astonishing accuracy; thus giving me the first evidence of the smartness of the craft.

What I thought then concerning the sanctity of the events of which Faneuil Hall was the focus, I think today, but only with regard to the Free States. The slave ones may look into Milton's Paradise Lost, but not to the Gallilean records for a corollary to their birthday and existence.

Kindly as I was treated in Cambridge, I did not get at once acclimatized, but longed for intercourse and chat with Europeans.

The only one in Harvard whom I could converse with freely was Dessor, a Swiss, formerly an assistant of the great Ichthyologist, then a victim of cant, but genial and sincere.

Dessor had staunch friends, and in his devoted arms Theodore Parker's noble spirit breathed its last in Florence.

Sir Henry and Lady Bulwer arrived from Washington on a visit to Boston, and with them I could easily recall the forever bygone times.

One afternoon we went together to see the country about Boston, and alighted in Brookline, before the residence of Colonel Perkins,

We were all perfect strangers. Sir Henry introduced himself first, and then in turn Lady Bulwer, myself, and his secretary, who accompanied us.

The Colonel received us with a courtesy the like of which I have but seldom found in this country, so much so that we all agreed to speak of him thereafter as of a Duke of the ancient regime.

It is generally known that the old Colonel was very deaf. When therefore Sir Henry went through the ceremony of introduction, our host mistook me for the British Minister, and for some minutes addressed me as such, to the great amusement of Sir Henry, until Lady Bulwer gently set him right.

The Colonel treated us to some claret, so excellent that no idea of it can be got in Europe. In answer to our exclamations of wonder, he said "When my ships went round the world, the captains carried casks of wine for me." (Bordeaux wines improve by sea voyages).

The first part of the sentence sounded grand to my ears, and together with the Colonel's courtesy never to be forgotten.

It was the first time in my life that I was in personal contact with what is called a 'merchant Prince.'

Sir Henry Bulwer's diplomatic conduct in this country, his many public speeches in praise of America, were differently construed, nay, even assailed by his diplomatic rivals for the favor of the people and the administration.

He was often represented as vain glorious and a flatterer.

But in our confidential conversations he was the same as he appeared in public, always admiring the institutions, the patriarchal excepted, and friendly disposed toward the American people.

Lady Bulwer had only one sincere and ardent desire during her stay in America. It was to appear amiable and to please every body, and thus work in aid of her husband's popularity. Her anxiety to avoid giving even a shadow of offense was almost feverish.

Gentle, unaffected, high bred, having spent her youth in the easy and intimate intercourse of the courts at Madrid and Paris, she brought all these qualities and acquirements to bear in her social intercourse here.

Sometimes I sincerely pitied her on account of her almost childish naiveté, and on account of the accidental trials of her high breeding and patience, which her gentle womanhood had to stand, as she was unmercifully hunted by curious and inquisitive visitors, particularly on her reception-days in Washington.

Once a Mr. L——n, a wealthy New Yorker by birth, and a Marquis Manqué by affectation, began to inquire of Lady Bulwer about the health of My Lord Bulwer, who was not present at the reception, and is not a Lord. Then he continued on to refined conversation in French, to which Lady Bulwer answered in English. At this the New York Marquis asked as a favor that she would not with him use 'that horrid English language.' Lady Bulwer quietly retorted, 'You forget, sir, that I am an English woman, and the wife of an English Minister.'

GUROWSKI

[For The New York Saturday Press.]

POETRY.

BY JOHN BURROUGHS.

Poetry is that part of Literature that lies nearest to life: it is, in fact, life articulate. The fruits of the mind may be divided into three parts, each perfect and characteristic in itself, yet all related organically, and as correlating existences: 1st, Poetry; 2d, General Literature; 3d, Metaphysics; the vitality decreasing as you recede from the first. As in the earth, first the mould, with grass and flowers; then the sub-soil, one degree further from life; and beneath all, the eternal Rock, whither all analysis and search for cause at last bring you.

All poetry has a metaphysical background, and all metaphysics a poetical side. That is the best poetry which hints the one, and that the best metaphysics which is compatible with the other. This is one reason why Emerson is the best of our poets, and Cousin the best of modern metaphysicians. General literature occupies the middle plane, and is less vital than the one, and more practical than the other.

I suppose every man carries degrees of these states within himself, and is a sunny poet, and an intelligent reasoner, and an abstruse metaphysician, just according to the depth he is probed. The poetical is the natural, the unconscious, the youthful state; the Paradise from which man fell, from which most men fall, though there be those who keep their primitive ardor and simplicity, and carry into manhood the freshness and spontaneity of youth. May the Great Mother keep more of her children from the seductions of Mammon, and feed them forever from her own bountiful bosom !

Metaphysics are good, though I am inclined to think that, as a rule, they are best silent and hid; we do not often want the rock at the surface, its office is a latent and passive one. In the order of nature metaphysics come last, and are not attained to without some violence to the feelings and instincts; while there is nothing so common and so near at hand as poetry, if we have the eyes to see it. It fringes the hardest facts. Every object in nature at last results in, or is some way encompassed by somewhat finer than itself. The tree has its scallops and cones; the plant its flower; the body its eye; the bird its iris; the day its blush and golden sequels; the river its sheen; the hills their slopes; the mountains their long curving lines; the city its turrets and domes; the earths their ores and precious stones; and this is the poetry of things, and the seizer and reproducer of this the poet. All thorough representation of life, that is, such a representation as shall give its fringe and bordering, its foreground and background, its promises and possibilities, its ideal side; in short, as shall not leave the sky out of the picture, is poetry, and is every where recognized as such.

Science of course is literal, as it ought to be, but science is not life, science takes no note of this finer self, this duplicate on a higher scale. Science never laughs or cries, or whistles or sings, or falls in love, or sees ought but the coherent reality. It says a soap bubble is a soap bubble,—a drop of water, impregnated with oleates of potassa or soda, and inflated with common air; but life says it is a crystal sphere, dipped in the rainbow, buoyant as hope, sensitive as the eye; with a power to make children dance for joy, and to bring youth into the look of the old.

Poetry need leave nothing out, should never skip and affect a girlish prudishness. No object is beneath the art of a master. Paint truly, that's the secret; not accurately, that is the business of science; but give the object as it seems, as it represents itself to our moods and feelings, as it stands related to our life. The boy never recognizes the earth in the geography as the world he lives on, and it is a long time before he can warp his vision so as to make one cover the other. Where is the green and the blue, the birds and the brooks, the round horizon with its unknown worlds beyond, the home and its associations? Then, here is no motion, no whirling as a top, no lines and parallels! These hills are fixed, the sun and moon are no nearer, no further off; the Summer comes from the South, the Winter from the North; in the Fall are nuts and apples, and long, delicious nights, and there is no whirl and rush here!

Who, in his youth, ever saw the swallow of natural history to be the twittering, joyous bird that built mud nests beneath his father's shed, and in the empty, odorous barn? that snapped the insects that flew up in his way, when returning, at twilight, from the upland farm; and that filled his memory with such visions of Summer when he first caught its note on some bright May morning, flying up the Southern valley? Describe water, or a tree, in the language of accurate science, or as they really are in and of themselves, and what person schooled only in nature would recognize them? Things must be given as they seem,—as they stand represented in the mind. Objects arrange themselves in our memory, not according to the will, or any real quality in themselves, but as they affect our life, and stand to us in our unconscious moments. The hills we have dwelt among, the rocks and trees we have looked upon in all moods and feelings, that stood to us as the shore to the sea and received a thousand impresses of what we lived and suffered, have a significance to us that is not accounted for by anything you can see or feel in them.

Poetry must not ignore fact, if it is a fact we can live; one that is true to all men, and needs no search or analysis; but it must not aim at literal accuracy at the expense of what is true in our experience. For instance, who thinks poetry ought to represent the earth as turning, instead of the sun as moving? or the head as the seat of love and the emotions, instead of the heart?

The statement will bear repetition. Poetry is Life. speaking, and therefore, should give things not as they are in themselves, but as they are in our experience.

NEW YORK NOVEMBER 10, 1860

[From New York Correspondence of The Philadelphia Dispatch.]

THE QUEEN OF BOHEMIA.

I saw the Queen of Bohemia, and her court, in a private box at Anderson's 'Psychomantheum' (the Winter Garden), the other evening, while Frezzolini sat vis-a-vis in the box opposite. Understand me, O! wise I don't allude to a lady who rules by right divine, sits occasionally on a dais called a throne, wears a bauble on her head yclept a diadem, and is supposed to balance on her finger ends a sort of jolly little spear hight a sceptre! Not a bit of it. 'Bohemia,' you must know, is the title, in this city, of a mythic empire, à la Paris, inhabited by poets, actors, essayists, artistes, magazine scribblers, newspaper reporters, et al. It comprises no inconsiderable amount of talent, ingenuity, vivacity, and cultivated intellect, mixed up with a large amount of dissipation, immorality, cool effrontery, and gay nonchalance.

About a year ago Bohemia had a grand banquet at the house of a certain lady who is an amateur actress and a brilliant writer for the SATURDAY PRESS—which journal par example is the organ of Bohemia. The lady is dashing in her appearance, gay, lighthearted, a genuine blonde, and reported to have moneys. Some call her beautiful; I think her striking only. She keeps a handsome establishment, however, up-town, and her house is the rendezvous of wits and artistes, some of whom are highly respectable, and many—just what circumstances make them. At the banquet in question this lady was chosen 'Queen of Bohemia,' and it was this fair monarch whom I beheld in the theatre, dressed in a light, full flounced dress, and a white lace mantle, with her masses of light hair thrown back from her white forehead, and sans any bonnet to mar the contour of her head. The 'Queen' attracted a great deal of attention, quite as much as did Frezzolini. Near her sat the spirituelle 'Getty Gay,' another fair writer for the press, and her husband, while close at hand, whispering in Her Majesty's ear, was 'Personne,' the 'cricket' of the *Leader*, in this city, and dramatic and musical reporter of the *Herald*. Besides him was the editor of the Saturday Press, to whose columns the 'Queen' contributes such bewitchingly audacious, such sparkling wicked, such subtly dubious communications, a la Madame Dudevant. These constitute, I suppose, the 'Court Circle,' the gentlemen and ladies in waiting, upon Her Royal Highness, and a charming study they present for the eye of the unsophisticated. Yet, they are all amiable people, je vous assure, delightful company, on dit, and aside from a certain alleged moral rélachement, as worthy of a good opinion as most folk can afford to be in degenerate times. So much for one of our special 'institutions.'

THE SHIP OF STATE.

The election is over.

The Politicians have managed to choose another figure head for the Ship of State,

So that it is reasonable for us to hope that at least during the next four years the Ship of State will need no more patching, either for purposes of safety or ornamentation.

But it is not well to be too certain of this. There is no dependence to be placed in the politicians who have usurped the duty of patching and otherwise attending to the Ship of State.

For the politicians are a needy and a selfish race. They would even mutilate the Ship of State, if by so doing they could make for themselves the job of repairing the damage they might do.

In fact they are always doing just that thing.

It is their business.

The Ship of State does not need them. Would be in much better condition without them. But they have managed to get the impression abroad that they are a necessary class.

This they have done by imitating the glazier who made a demand for his services by throwing stones at quiet people's windows.

The politicians either invent some defect in the Ship of State, or else go coolly to work and damage some part of her hull and machinery.

Then arises a great outcry and noise, in exciting and sustaining which the politicians themselves are the leaders.

This is kept up until the job for repairing the real or imaginary defect is given to some one of the many gangs of politicians who follow this business of tinkering.

It is perhaps strange that a nation like ours, so well educated, so accustomed to self-government, so practical, and so full of common sense, should not see through the tricks of the politicians, and should not pack them off as a nuisance. But we will finally come to that.

It has taken the world some four thousand years to make America possible as a nation, and we ought not to complain if it should take a pretty long time before we can arrive at having a nationality without any politicians in it.

What a blessing it will be when that time comes.

Think of living without politicians.

It is a greater advance than getting rid of kings. To be sure there are many sagaciously disposed persons who would hold up their hands in holy horror at the idea of the Ship of State pretending to float one moment, if there was not a figure-head upon its prow. They have often done so in similar cases.

They do so now at the idea of a Church without a bishop, or a State without a king.

And yet the Church gets on much better without a Bishop than it did with one and certainly we have come to rank kings among the old and useless rubbish which accumulates by time in every household, and the only virtue of which is that it makes a safe shelter for all sorts of vermin.

In our own country the figure-heads, political and other, have come to serve the same noble purpose. It is perhaps premature to attempt to tear them down just now. And yet it seems evident that it would be best. Neither vermin nor their strongholds are good things to have in one's household.

Nor do we think a figure-head is as necessary to the Ship of State as an active crew.

In fact it is to the crew we must look for the safety of the ship.

And it is a good thing to destroy their dependence upon the virtues of the figure-head, if they have a superstitious belief of that kind.

[For The New York Saturday Press.]

SONG OF THE SOUTH.

I.

Ho! brothers of the North, a word,
Before the deed is done;
Before men separate the two
Whom God hath Joined in one.

II.

Before the firebrand on each hearth
Is flaming in the air,
Before grey ruin sits and broods
Where once our Idols were.

III.

Remember! while time yet remains
To tarry in your path,
You ne'er can wipe away the stains
Of blood you spill in wrath.

IV.

Remember! how long years ago
We battled side by side,
How victory poured our arms upon
In a resistless tide.

V.

Shoulder to shoulder—hand to hand
We fought our mutual foe,
And grasped the birth-right to our land—
O! shall we let it go?

VI.

Since then, for four-score years and more
In harmony we two,
Twin heirs of Liberty, have stood
Together—we and you.

VII.

We've braved the nations of the earth
With all their boasted might,
Together we can brave them still
When battling for the Right.

VIII.

They gaze upon us from afar
In fiendish merriment,
To see our great Republic break
And crush a continent.

IX.

And shall they see it, Northern men?
Your blood is in our veins:
Send back an answering No! from Maine
To Indiana's plains.

X.

Let go your traitrous knavish hounds,
Who'd lead you in the wrong,
And join us till each hill resounds
With this true Union song.

XI.

God save the Union he has made,
And let it ever stand
While freemen's blood in freemen's veins
Shall circle through the land.

XII.

Let each forgive the other's sin,
And forward on the right,
Till every crime of North and South
Be quenched in glorious light.

Frank H. Norton.

New York, Nov. 10, 1860.

We beg to suggest to our friends of the Sunday papers that instead of showing so much joy at the prospect of our dissolution, they had better postpone their exultation until the event is accomplished. They are naturally delighted at the troubles of a paper which sets its face against the puffing system, but let them keep their souls in patience for awhile longer, and meantime devote themselves to the more congenial and profitable work of inditing elegant paragraphs about pills and putty. A nice little article about something of that kind, might give them a dinner; troubling themselves about us gives them nothing but the bile. So, go on with your puffing, gentlemen; there's a score of pill-makers, putty-mongers, etc., waiting in your back-office for you; so attend to them, sell yourselves at a good price, and let us alone.

MINOR EXPERIENCES IN AMERICA.

XII.

I felt intuitively that the little I had had occasion to see and hear during my first stay in New York was only the superficial study of a curiously composed strata of society, and could not give me a true comprehension of the real significance or position assumed by America in the march of mankind.

I felt that there must be something different and better underneath all this, and that the society with which I was brought in contact did not express the true intellectual and social life of America.

After my superficial survey of New York, with its exclusively commercial interests, with its almost babylonian agglomeration of various languages and nationalities, it was clear to me that the genuine American mind was not, on the whole, represented in large cities.

Harvard University, with its several distinguished scholars and professors combined, was not as progressive or as generative in new ideas as the universities of Germany or of the Continent of Europe are.

A certain aroma of scholasticism, and of a so-called scientific conservatism, prevailed in the academic groves and sanctuaries of Cambridge.

This did not satisfy me, and therefore I was ready and eager to receive better and more truthful impressions, such as one receives from an individual character, a book, a theory, a work of art, a country, or a society, and which remain indelible.

Such impressions I received from visiting the common schools of Boston and Cambridge, and investigating the system there in operation. From every such expedition I returned with a new intellectual world opened before me, and my veneration for the nation increased.

For the first time I had a full conception of what ought to be, and is, the genuine mind of the people, and wherein their education consists. Then and there was revealed to me the soul, the life, and the philosophy of self-government.

In Europe I was accustomed to consider that the masses should be introduced to such ideas by the directing and governing power, but here such ideas originated in the masses themselves.

This craving for information and knowledge among all classes of the working population, or what in European lingo are called the lower classes, this action arising, so to speak, within the masses, realized before me, for the first time, the divine revelation of humanity.

I learned how this inward self impulse was immensely superior and more beneficial than the system of Governmental interference as practised in Europe. It was all a wonder and surprise to me.

Here were male and female teachers, young, fresh-minded, and devoted to their noble pursuit; while in Europe—Prussia alone to a certain degree excepted—old, broken, narrow-minded, often ignorant and petty routinists were employed as schoolmasters.

Here country girls, daughters of farmers, of small mechanics, traders, and operatives, read Homer and Virgil, were familiar with history, with the natural sciences, and more at home in algebra than most of the European schoolmasters were in the first rudiments of arithmetic.

The soul of self government can be better studied in the common schools of the Free States than in any of various political bodies.

In these schools, in the various philanthropic and educational establishments, is revealed the mental calibre and the life of a self-governing people.

Not less did I wonder at the modest but generally well selected libraries in the houses of the farmers, small traders, artisans, and operatives, although such libraries are the natural result of such a system of schools. Among such libraries, some were rather considerable, as for instance that of a leather-dresser in Cambridge, Mr. Dowse, whose library consisted of about two thousand volumes, principally on English literature.

One thing is certain, the degeneration of a people whose nationality rests upon the basis of schools and education, is difficult if not impossible.

In justice however to the fallaciously-termed higher classes, to the rich, the magnifici of Boston and of all the free States, it must be said, that although their pretensions to aristocracy and exclusiveness excite only pity or a smile, yet, at bottom, the majority of them are as good as the working classes, and though would-be aristocrats, are ready with their money and their example to aid in the erection of schools and other like establishments.

One morning young Wheaton, a tutor in Cambridge, and son of the prominent writer on international law, came to my room and said: "Count, you must let your moustaches grow, and not be so quiet and retiring at evening parties."

We had spent the evening before at a large ball given by one of the leading magnificis of Boston.

In answer to my demand as to his reasons for such advice, he replied that at the ball above-mentioned, one of the great ladies of Boston, while speaking with him about me, had maintained that I could not be a count since I had no moustaches, made no dash in society, and was too old.

Wheaton died shortly after I left Cambridge. His death was a real loss for the public. He was undoubtedly the most eminent young man for high breeding and varied though thorough information, whom I have met in this country.

Two years afterwards, in Washington, several of the European diplomats who were well acquainted with my relations and antecedents in the old world, gave me almost the same advice.

In a friendly spirit they insisted that I ought to make more fuss about my social claims and connections.

One of the advice-giving diplomats had a rich but not handsome American wife.

But how was I to set about making a fuss?

Since 1818 almost up to this moment, not a day has passed in Europe without some political offenders being shut up in prisons, in fortresses, in dungeons, or in cells, as I was repeatedly in the course of several years. Like me hundreds and hundreds have been condemned to death; many, many of them have been executed, while I, for good or for evil, have escaped.

Many still conspire.

I began to do it in 1820.

Others now occupy the position held by me in Paris, in the central propaganda at the side of Godfrey Cavignac, the elder and long since deceased brother of the General and President (in 1848); and at a time when, exempli gratia, Mazzini had scarcely began his so well-known career by the foundation of young Italy, and when, contrary to my repeated warnings, which were official, coming as they did from the Propagandist centre, he, Mazzini, made his first unsuccessful attempt in revolution, by sending a couple of hundred of half-intoxicated Poles to rouse Savoyen, headed by Romarino, the same man who was afterwards shot for treason by the Piedmontese Government in 1849, after the battle of Navarra.

In 1831 I and the present Imperial Majesty of France conspired together (see Memoirs de Gisquet), and from that year until I left France, I was the object of Louis Philippe's special hatred, and was called by him and his staff, le grand emeutier, the great mischief-maker.

Now others are engaged in doing what I did thirty or forty years ago, waging a warfare for political or social freedom.

Having thus passed my life, I have no desire now for making a fuss. Nor does this feeling result from the accident of what is considered aristocratic lineage. It is innate, has grown with my growth and strengthened with my strength, and now cannot generate in me that pretentious pride of birth which is the characteristic only of parvenues.

Perhaps my life could have been better passed in the acquisition of knowledge. Certainly if I overrate that which I have acquired, my pretentions will soon be exposed.

But to sum up, I have never had either the desire or the ability to satisfy such demands as those made by the Boston lady, or to follow the advice of the diplomats.

GUROWSKI

—The new story by Charles Dickens will commence on the first of December in All the Year Round, under the title 'Great Expectations.'

—In the London Times there is an appeal for a society which has for its object the prevention of death by starvation. We extract the following passage from the article, which, true as it is, marks a great advance in social science in England. The opinions and suggestions can well be considered and applied to this country, young as we are, and not yet weighed down with the dead remains of effete and ghastly conditions of society,—

Society is responsible for every human being coming into the world, and bound to see that its essential wants—food, clothing, shelter, and education—are satisfied. It is for its own good that society should be held responsible for this, as its own welfare can never be secured on any other conditions. Let society see that every human being coming into the world receives a good education fitted to make it a happy and useful member of society; and put it in the way of getting an honest living,—give it a fair chance. In a mere pecuniary point of view, this would cost less than our inefficient systems of prisons and police.

NEW YORK NOVEMBER 17, 1860

Since the publication of our 'Card,' frankly announcing the critical position of the SATURDAY PRESS, and the possibility of its discontinuance for want of funds, we have received so many letters (most of them from strangers) urging us on no account to let the paper stop, and offering to do all in their power to prevent such a catastrophe, that we have been encouraged to make renewed efforts and sacrifices, and are now not without hope that in a week or two we shall be able to announce to our readers that the crisis has passed, and the paper is safe.

Meanwhile, however, it is important that all who are interested in our success should at once put their shoulders to the wheel, in order that we may get out of our difficulty as soon as possible. The matter must, at any rate, be decided within a fortnight.

Thoughts and Things.

BY ADA CLARE

The Many-colored Joke.

The joke is the tyrant and the slayer of conversation. It tramples upon anecdote, slaughters argument, and sets its foot upon the neck of narrative.

Of course I refer to mere superficial, unmeaning play upon words.

I might imagine a specimen example of the thing, as practised by the licensed joke-wrights.

I remark, for instance, on the lovely color of Laura Keene's hair.

Tip replies,—being high above all interest in human hair,—'I am glad to hear you say so.'

'Lip remarks, that is her golden her(hair)itage.'

Pip: 'I am afraid to regard her, lest I should commit a heresy (hair I see).'

Nip, Grip, Fip, Sip, Dip, and the rest of the jokingmen go on to add their cruel puns, till I, disgusted and sore, am obliged either to practise voluntary dumbness, or to sail upon the soft streams of garment and dress-general, which I thank thee, Jove! the punsters are too lofty to mutilate.

When the punsters have all reared at and applauded each other, I meekly try to introduce another subject. I select the simplest, the most one-sided, the baldest words, in order to offer no bait to the fishes. But I hope in vain before I have concluded my innocent remark, I am laid lifeless on the floor of conversation, by one of the most barefaced and shameless puns it has ever come into the mind of man to conceive.

I did but remark in tender innocence, the superiority of home-made bread, when a being calling himself a poet and a man of feeling, replied that 'bread is very much kneaded (needed).' After this, there is no promethian heat that can my light relume.

I see no reason why the punsters should not manufacture among themselves a hand-book of punning. Or an encyclopedia, or an almanac, or a dictionary of the pun general. The puns would admit of very easy classification, as they vary very little, follow arbitrary rules, and like strict conservatives, cling tenderly to the precedence of the past. In consideration of which last fact the professional punster is touchingly devoted to the annals of antiquity.

Had I time, I might enumerate a large number of venerable puns, but they will probably all appear in the new volume which I have suggested, 'Punning without a master.'

There is a class of popular jokes, which I shall refer to, only by presenting a specimen of the same. Let Silas for instance, observe that he loves such an one, because that one calls out his (Silas's) good qualities. Hiram who is present, immediately answers, with a smashing assumption of originality and wit, 'Ah! 'tis a pity then that he could not be kept always near you, Silas.' Hiram is a man of great ability, he despises the common-place in others, yet he cannot resist the temptation of parading this mould and worm-eaten witticism, this feeble two-pence worth of grin-making, out to the public eye. Such is the force of evil habit and evil communications.

Think how many pert and silly answers Silas might have made to that—but he did not.

On the other hand there is a quality called humor, which I love as much as I fear the other. This is the quality which ornaments the grim common-place of life, with a drapery of green and sun-lightened ivy. It extracts the sting from the irritating pettinesses of every day living. How much easier all annoyances are to bear, if you are able to extract from them one quaint idea, one thimble—full of natural laugh. Just when parties of three are about to break up in dreadful tumult, if one of them gently bring forward a comic view of the subject, peace is restored, and anger and pride and envy go back to their cells.

For this reason the picnic, the marriage, the journey, the dinner-party are unsafe, are wont to be failures, unless the humorous element is alive in them. But the jokewrights scorn and loathe this humor. I am apt to take extreme views on all subjects, so I think humor is the smiling, rounded, flesh-filled form, while the pun, the word-racking is the grinning, vacant, empty skeleton.

There is an inquisition established in our liberal land, 'tis for the tormenting of words. They are thumb-screwed, hung up with weights, roasted in slow-fires, broken on the wheel, unjointed on the rack, in order that they may yield witticisms, which their souls cry out against.

I am carrying a bottle of sulphuric acid in my pocket, and the first person who asks me in a pastry-cook's shop if I am 'piously inclined,' I am going to distribute it over his countenance, and send him forth branded, a Cain among the punsters.

MINOR EXPERIENCIES IN AMERICA

XIII.

The fugitive slave-bill passed by Congress in 1850, gave me the first insight into the mysteries of the political wrangling, and also into the political conceptions and tendencies of my adopted country.

It was a stunning blow to my European ideas, to my theoretical conceptions, to my former studies and speculations upon American institutions.

To see a political body which was considered as an emenation of the loftiest and purest conception of manhood, a body which the simple but ardent faith of progressive Europe considered as the leader of a great nation in its onward march to higher and higher destinies, to see a congress which was itself created by the declaration of human rights, deliberately and by law degrade freemen into slave-hunters, was something I had not expected.

For centuries, during even the terrible throes of her painful and slow disentanglement from slavery and serfdom, civilized Europe treated slave-hunting with scorn and branded it with infamy.

Yet now, statesmen and orators, whose names, when in the old world, I had learned to venerate, proposed such a law, and exhausted their ingenuity to find arguments in support of a measure which would not only make Europeans shudder, but would be revolting to the savage Tschetschenctzs of Caucasus, or the prowling Bashkirs of the Asiatic steppes, all of whom have now renounced slave-hunting, keeping, and trading.

The Hapsburgs, the Haynaus, the Bombas, were at once overshadowed.

History recording this law, in this freest country and in this nineteenth century, will class it with the most cursed legal and despotical measures, which blot the annals of our race.

The expounders and teachers of the Gospel put the Bible upon the rack and tortured it in behalf of an anti-christian covenant, forgetting the teaching of the Apostle *not* to be the servants of men, and his advice that 'if servitude is to be supported with patience, it is still better to become free.'

The majority of the Faculty of Harvard College sustained the fugitive slave-bill, and this was another sad disappointment to me, since the faculties of the Continental Universities are mostly on the side of absolute justice and liberty.

To cap the whole, the majority of the students, the youth whom the immortal Humboldt calls, 'the indelible, primeval, self-restoring institution of mankind,' was rowdy at the meetings, and hooted the high-minded and dauntless Emerson, when he branded the law as monstrous.

To a certain extent these things are changed in Harvard, but in the Fall of 1850 they were as I have stated.

The general elections which took place at that time in Massachusetts, and the closely-contested vote which sent Charles Sumner for the first time to the United States Senate, restored and even strengthened my faith in the soundness and honesty of the people.

During these elections the vulgarly-called respectability and the true people were sharply divided. I found that purity of faith and fidelity to the immortal and fundamental principles of American nationality—that political honesty and high-mindedness were principally to be found in the people at large.

Since that day, my faith in the people of the free States, and not in the so-called exclusive respectability, has remained unshaken, and up to this time I have found no reason to repent it.

There may be truly respectable men on the other side of the question, and also on the other side of Mason and Dixon's line.

A muddy pool contains microscopical atoms of pure water, but for the common eye, as well as for all ordinary purposes, such atoms are lost.

The more I study and think about slavery as it is now defended by its champions, the more am I sorry that I do not possess a consolatory belief in Hell.

If I did I should be sure that below the deepest regions of Dante's Inferno will be the abode of all the European-born supporters of slavery, then of the pro-slavery Rabbis, Doctors, Pharisees, Parsons of all creeds, whether tonsured and wearing purple, or dressed in black with white neck-ties. Among them would be mingled the supporters of slavery by principle in the Free States, and next to them the extensionists, and the chivalrous and furious supporters of the institution.

The poor African would go to the place occupied by Lazarus, and I should pray that he should not act towards the burning Pharisee as the Lazarus in Scripture did.

The first large wedding at which I was a guest showed me the immense difference there is between the customs of society in Europe and America.

I always pity the Bride, on account of the way she is exposed, for hours, as a show, and made to stand the criticism of hundreds who are curious, indifferent, and in many cases perfect strangers to her.

Such a position, since it is not royal, has a smack of the stage about it. Such shows are not usual in any social class in Europe, and above all others, the brides themselves would object to such a display.

It is not customary even among the smallest European bourgeoise.

Though in Europe they have numerous guests, crowds of assistants at the ceremony and in the church, with wedding dinners, and balls, the bride is not, there as here, exhibited as it were on a platform. The customs of the early English, Scotch, Irish, and Dutch settlers in this country, who were the ancestors of the modern American aristocracy, were not precisely the same as those which prevailed in the castles and mansions of the nobility and gentry of the countries from which the settlers came.

And then the exigencies and necessities of colonial life, modified the customs of the settlers or added new ones to those they brought with them, and thus most probably the domestic customs of America were formed.

The, of late increasing, intercourse with Europe has produced some imitations of European customs, which have not always been happy, since they were often taken from second-hand models, while such imitations wanting in this country a congenial soil, prepared with suitable notions, and various domestic prejudices, do not flourish or agree with the minutiae of social intercourse or the normal condition of American society, and therefore appear generally as ridiculous affectations.

To this class belongs the recently awkward parody of what was supposed to be court-ceremonial when, at the great ball of New York to the Prince, two pointers hunted for his partners and dutifully brought them as game to the feet of the juvenile Guelph; thus preventing his own free choice in a society composed of equals.

The London *Punch* introduced the Prince of Wales to Miss Columbia; here the Misses and Mrs. Columbia, passing from hand to hand, were placed before him.

The Americans often sneer at the servility of European aristocracy; yet that aristocracy would never have allowed such hunting among their wives and sisters, and the women themselves are too proud to submit to such a ridiculous, servile, and obsequious ceremonial.

GUROWSKI.

NEW YORK NOVEMBER 24, 1860

THE SLAVERY QUESTION.

To the Ancient of the S. P.:

In the last SATURDAY PRESS, I find that you 'regret to see that Count Gurowski has lugged in the question of Slavery,'— that you 'don't care to mix up in any way in the anti-Slavery discussion, and as a general rule, shall exclude the topic from your columns.'

Perhaps, Ancient, this means that you are willing to have your own say, on the side you at present lean to, but don't care to have others intrude their opposite views, to any extent.

Of course you can do as you please about this; but nevertheless, I have a desire to make a second exception to your 'general rule.'

The reason is, that, after declaring that for thirty years not a sensible word has been written on the subject, you go on with choice written words of your own, thereby offering the intimation, from which the candid reader cannot escape, that the long-missing sensible words—a few of them, at least,—are at last before the world.

Not to push the matter widely, I wish, Ancient, simply to take these words of yours, as arranged in paragraphs, and give a note on each paragraph, from the other side. I will endeavor to do this with as few 'noisy and unmeaning howls' as circumstances will allow. I certainly believe that you afford a capital series of texts for more protracted argument; but I prefer, on the whole, to just look at the precise meaning of what you have said.

Here, then, is your first paragraph:

> We regret to see that Count Gurowski, In his 'Minor Experiences' of this week, has lugged in the question of Slavery, upon which neither he nor any man in the country, has written a sensible word since the discussion commenced, some thirty years ago.

I take it, however, that your rule of exclusion is not rigid, since you accompany its announcement with a series of observations, not absolutely necessary to a mere declaration of intentions on this point.

This is opinion, and I sha'n't touch it, except to say that a good many credulous people believe that the discussion is older than you say; that George Washington was in at the beginning with some words more or less sensible; that Thomas Jefferson also got his hand in; and that others, about the same time, helped to form the early ring.

Here is the second paragraph:

> We have often been urged to join in the anti-Slavery crusade, but have steadily refused.

This is a delicate business, perhaps; but I do think, Ancient, that a good many years ago, not thirty perhaps, your name was high and honored among those who 'crusaded' in the strongest anti-Slavery style. This, too, is rather a universal belief among those who know you. How is it? Tell us. And if so, why the renunciation ?

Paragraph number three is as follows:

> We are opposed to slavery of every kind—as the readers of the

SATURDAY PRESS are well aware—but we are even more opposed to what is stupidly called anti-Slavery, for the simple reason that it has no distinct aim or purpose, and consists of nothing but a series of noisy and unmeaning howls.

So anti-Slavery has ''no distinct aim or purpose.' I suppose this is a general way of stating the old proposition that the Republicans, or anti-Slavery people—I speak of them as identical, for the occasion, only because you do have no definite plan for Slavery abolition, and consequently are without object. Let me be for a moment figurative: Suppose you have a large and well-to-do family—don't start affrighted, this is mere supposition—and a few get bed-ridden with a loathsome disease. You don't know how to cure them,—it is a hard case. But you see a way to check the spread of the distemper. You set about it, with much labor, and at the risk of breaking up your household,—the infected among whom cherish a delusion that their leprosy is the only perfect state of being. Very well. Is that a 'distinct aim or purpose?' And candidly, as far it goes, is not this a fair illustration? And does it not go far enough to exhibit a 'distinct aim or purpose?'

The fourth paragraph, in turn:

No better test of it in this State (where it is in a majority of over 40,000) can be found than in the fact that it has just refused to the negro the right of suffrage. And yet some of our best friends tried to wheedle us into voting for Abe Lincoln, and taking an active part in the canvass.

Admitting this, what of it? Say that a negro is not equal to the privileges of suffrage, and so forth,—is that matter to authorize his bondage, to justify hunting him with dogs, and branding him with hot irons, and violating his wife,—or what stands for his wife in the beautiful system of the South,—and selling his children? Say, now. And moreover, as the principal 'aim of the Republican party, at which I have hinted above, is a very different thing from giving negro suffrage,' I don't see the force of your 'test.' How can you 'test' the fact that a party is destitute of one purpose by showing that it has failed to accomplish another, of very limited account, and no way specially relevant to the opposition of Slavery at the South? And what do you mean by saying your 'best friends tried to wheedle you into voting for Abe Lincoln ?' Don't you see that by impugning their political honesty you put a queer character unto your 'best friends.' What is a wheedler? I suppose it is one who dishonestly tries to persuade you to do that at which your conscience revolts. I don't believe your friends ever tried to 'wheedle' you.

Then comes paragraph number five:

Our uniform reply was that the question of Slavery was not up for consideration, but that the only question which the people were about deciding, was which of two herds of swine should feed at the public trough for the next four years.

The best answer to this, is to point to the present trepidation of the advocates and supporters of Slavery. If *it* is not concerned, if *it* 'was not up for consideration,' and if the matter in dispute is so trivial as you say, why these horrid 'noisy and unmeaning howls,' to take one of your own phrases?

And number six :

Abe Lincoln himself has found this out now, and has just had to run away from his home, like a fugitive slave, to escape from the republican swine who have flocked into Springfield by the thousand, and all but eaten the old fellow alive.

To this I can only say that I know, as well as everybody else, Abe Lincoln has not run away from his home, either like a fugitive slave, or in any other way. And that the Republican swine, if you fancy to call them so, have *not* flocked into Springfield by the thousand, or even by the hundred.

Paragraph number seven, brief but significant, says:

It will be as much as ever if he survives to be inaugurated.

As this depends on its predecessor, it of course falls with that.

Now, number eight:

If other people choose to be humbugged with the idea that the Republican party is a great philanthropic organization instituted for the benefit of the Negro, we have no objection.

Ancient, I never heard in my life that the Republican organization was instituted 'for the benefit of the negro.' You know perfectly well, that its honest object is the benefit of this nation, at least for the free States thereof. The negro is a secondary consideration, politically, if not humanly. It is useless to talk about the schemes and trades of the small leaders. They are not the party. The millions who vote are the party. Look to *their* 'aim or purpose,' if you want to judge fairly.

In number nine, you say:

A little humbug is sometimes good for the soul.

Now, Ancient, I think so too; and that is the only way I consoled myself when I read your article, And as to number ten:

But for ourselves, we know better.

I say again, I thinks so too. Nobody knows more surely than yourself the difference between right and wrong, truth and lies, beauty and deformity, reason and madness, white and black.

Here is number eleven:

It has merely used the negro as a stepping-stone to power, and is now ready to kick him aside, and let him go to the devil.

Well, Ancient, if you think the Republican party has got safely over, beyond the aid of stepping-stones, how do you excuse your friends for their exultation over the fact that Republicanism has no show, its prospects being now hampered beyond extrication by the opposition of the two great coordinate branches of Government?

Number twelve—

Under these circumstances, we don't care to mix up in any way in the anti-Slavery discussion, and, as a general rule, shall exclude the topic from our columns.

—is, like number one, an affair of opinion, not to be disputed about, so I leave it. And I leave the whole subject at the same time. You observe that I have done nothing but follow very closely, and with very cautious limit, your own expressions. Certainly there is room enough to go away outside; but I prefer to keep close. The reason is, I want to show, if possible, with what unusual carelessness and recklessness you approach this interesting topic. If my short comments upon your paragraphs are not always specially relevant to the broad anti-Slavery argument, the fault is yours, for starting irrelevant ideas. I only desire to show that wherever you try to make a point of fact from which conclusions may be drawn, however unimportant, you are just exactly wrong. To resume:

The Slavery discussion commenced a good deal more than thirty years ago.

You, Ancient, have an old fame as a prominent anti-Slavery man.

The anti-Slavery movement has a distinct aim and purpose.

The present Southern commotion shows that the only question is not which of two herds of swines, etc.

Abe Lincoln hasn't run away from home.

No sort of swine have flocked into Springfield by the thousand.

Lincoln has never been in danger of being eaten alive, or any other way.

No Republican claims that his party-organization is instituted for the benefit of the negro.

The party, not having got over its troubles, is not ready to 'kick aside' any stepping-stone, allowing that there are stepping-stones such as you allege.

You will understand, Ancient, that my own notion is, that if the 'sensible words' on the 'question of Slavery' had not appeared before your article, the deficiency was assuredly not supplied thereby. And moreover, much as I regard your acuteness and cleverness, and good sense, I don't believe it's in you ever to say a 'sensible word' on the pro-Slavery side of the argument.

And that's all there is about it. E. H. H.

Reply.

How completely the last paragraph in the above communication justifies us in the determination to exclude the Slavery Question, as a rule, from our columns!

For here is a really clever young man whom the subject immediately paralyzes, whereas whenever he is let loose upon any other, he invariably says something bright and to the point.

Just throw your eye over the youth's article, and see how curiously he dodges the whole issue.

Our only important point was that we declined, as a general thing, to print anti-Slavery articles, because what is called anti-Slavery has no distinct aim or purpose, but consists of nothing but a series of noisy and unmeaning howls.

We proved this position conclusively (so far as this State as is concerned) by showing that the self-styled anti-Slavery party feels so little interest in bettering the condition of the negro that it has just refused to him even the poor right of suffrage.

The retort that this is no reason for enslaving him means nothing, since whoever would disfranchise the negro would evidently go a step further and enslave him if he had a chance, since by disfranchising him he already denies his manhood, and thus does all he can, at the North, towards sustaining the grounds upon which he is enslaved at the South.

The other matters touched upon by our youthful correspondent are of little import.

The intimation that we are willing to have our own say on the side we at present lean to, but don't care to have others intrude their opposite views to any extent, is a very natural one coming from a Republican, but is simply absurd as applied to the Saturday Press, which has erred, if at all, in the opposite direction.

It seems that we were mistaken as to the exact number of political swine who have recently visited Springfield, and also as to the fact of their having (then) driven old Abe out of the town, but the spirit of our statement was nevertheless true, as every letter from the place proves, and as, in fact, nobody doubts. When we spoke of the anti-Slavery discussion as of modern date, we alluded, of course, to the revival of the discussion some thirty years ago.

The allusion to our former opinions has no weight with us, since the class of men who proverbially never change their opinions is one which, though still very large (so large, in fact, that an institution has just been established for their detention and instruction), we are not particularly anxious to be identified with.

The medical illustration of our young friend would have been more to the point if it had compared the Republican party to a clique of doctors who, knowing nothing about a disease which had attacked some peculiar class of people in another State, spent their time howling about it, and meanwhile denied to the same class of people in their own midst all medical attendance whatever.

The fact that the South is alarmed by the action of the Republican party proves no more in its favor, as an anti-Slavery party, than would be proved in favor of a set of quacks, by the fact that their presence had produced a panic in the hospitals.

Finally, when we said that some of our best friends had tried to wheedle us into joining what is called the anti-Slavery movement, we used wheedle in the dictionary sense of 'entice' or 'cajole,'—just as we might have said, with equal truth, that some of our best friends had been trying to wheedle us into adopting the system of puffery, in order to save the Saturday Press.

MINOR EXPERIENCES IN AMERICA.
XIV.

Finally I tried my hand at lecturing.

My first essay was upon Russia, for the professors and other dignitaries of Cambridge; the next was for the students of the law-school upon the history of the Roman Law from the period of its origin, down to the epoch when from the influence of learned jurisconsults among the civilians and the clergy, the Roman law became a scientific common law in force among all the nations of Medieval Europe, permeating the peculiar common laws of France, Germany, England, Spain, and even of Russia, who, together with some ideas of Christianity, received a notion of the Jus Civile from Byzantium.

The professors of the law faculty displayed the kindest attention in following my lectures. So did the students, who attended the course numerously and listened to me with forbearing deference.

Forbearance was necessary on their part, since my pronunciation must have wounded their tympanums horribly.

I was sure that they could understand only a little, and yet they watched me with sparkling and attentive eyes.

Such attention was an encouraging testimony to me, since I took it as a proof that at any rate they had confidence in the conscientiousness of my efforts to bring before them the best stores of my mind and memory. My grateful feelings towards the students remain unchanged.

One day I received a polite note from Miss —— and Miss —— requesting me to call upon them. I went. They were rather elderly maiden ladies, teachers in one of the higher-class schools. They asked me to read Homer, Virgil, and Thucydides, with them. I remarked that I had no objection to expounding the great historian to them, but confessed my inability to commentate the two great masters in poetry.

The misses seemed a little slighted at this, supposing that it was a species of pride on my part, and that I did not wish to condescend, as they said, to instruct school-teachers. They declared, furthermore, that if I suspected I should not be paid, I was wrong, and offered to do so as generously as I wished.

It required all the powers of my rhetoric, dialectics, and sentiment, to convince them of the great veneration in which I held the class of feminine school-teachers, and above all, such as desired to make themselves familiar with the classics; but that the fact of my having a certain familiarity with the Roman law, or with history in general, did not make me a philologue or a scholiast of classical poetry. They called my objections nonsense, and pointed to examples of some so-called learned men, who were ready to lecture, teach, or instruct, upon any required subject, and ended by saying that I ought to lay aside my European notions and conceits. Finally I told them that I did not wish to make myself a fool by treating subjects which I had never studied, except superficially.

We parted. I met them often afterwards, and they always preserved a grudge against me.

Some of the Professors explained to me, that all they probably wished, was to advertise themselves as pupils of Count ——.

It had never occurred to me that I was so great a personage, or that such an advertisement could have been of use to any one.

At an evening gathering in the house of Theodore Parker, he said to me that a lady wished to make my acquaintance, as she had heard I had been a student of German philosophy under Hegel.

I was introduced to the lady, and felt rather uneasy, expecting to be precipitated in some metaphysical discussion.

"You studied philosophy ?"

"Yes, Madame."

"Under Hegel?"

"Yes, Madame."

"How long?"

"Two years, a time hardly sufficient to go through the whole course."

"You know him?"

"Yes, Madame."

She paused and appeared thoughtful, I expected some terrible metaphysical riddle, when all at once she asked.

"What was the color of Hegel's eyes and the shape of his head?"

I stood abashed, almost stupefied, then answered that I had tried to learn his system, and had attended only to his words without ever having thought about the color of his eyes or the shape of his head.

She looked down rather contemptuously upon me. I became somewhat excited, and explained that as I was a disciple of Hegel's I had followed the teachings of my master, who in his great work Phoenomenologie des Geistes (Phenomenology of the Soul), a metaphysical and not a spiritual work, slurs at and despises physiognomy and phrenology.

Madame answered by quoting some American names as authorities in favor of the faith, and could not be made to believe that physiological deductions from facial angles, as well as those made from phrenology, craniology, etc., are not accepted either by physiologists or psychologists, or that these cheap displays of sham knowledge are not recognized by science or admitted as authorities into her sanctuaries. Also that craniometry is in the same category, since small shot is a poor substitute for brain, and the analogy between the volume or weight of the two is considered absurd.

She was not however convinced.

Among the scientific hangers-on about the venerable Harvard was an astronomer in search of an observatory; the same person who subsequently acquired considerable notoriety for losing one which had been entrusted to him.

This savant, from time to time, published in the newspapers letters which he had just received from Alexander Humboldt, which letters were always commendatory of him, the astronomer, and of several literary notorieties in Park or Beacon streets, Boston.

It is a curious fact that the recently published correspondence of the Berlin sage does not contain a single word about either the astronomer or the other American travellers who repeatedly sounded through the press their intimacy with Humboldt and his fatherly interest in them.

I had always wondered and had my misgivings at these advertisements of themselves, as I had some slight knowledge of Humboldt's turn of mind, and of his habits and mode of intercourse.

My acquaintance with both the brothers Humboldt was such as is common among people belonging to the same social latitudes, I showing the respectful deference which was the duty of a much younger man, and Wilhelm and Alexander Humboldt treating me with cordial affability.

A former American Minister to Berlin could give some curious and instructive revelations of how Humboldt was not only annoyed, but has even dreaded the visits of great American travellers and visitors.

And no wonder.

Humboldt's each step over the globe struck luminous sparks, which science diligently gathered and transformed into beacons, illuminating for all time the scientific progress of his age. But what branch of science was ever illuminated by the so-called celebrated American travellers, or by the peripatetic astronomer?

Humboldt's great heart beat in unison with the oppressed of all zones and climes. The sympathy of the great American explorer was concentrated in himself, and in those distinguished persons who offered him their hospitality.

But the oppressed Fellah, Hindoo, Chinaman, Candiote, and Christian under Moslem rule, had his scorn instead of his sympathy.

Gurowski.

NEW YORK DECEMBER 1, 1860

FRANCES SARGENT OSGOOD.

An incomplete, and consequently a worthless edition of Mrs. Osgood's poems has just been published, in the popular dress of blue and gold, by Messrs. Clark, Austin, Maynard & Co., of this city. It is to be regretted that the publishers did not make a better book while they were about it; but, as remarked by the late Mr. Dibdin, 'grieving's a folly.' We rarely anticipate either intelligence, judgment, or taste in the exploits of that interesting class of persons; and so Dean Swift's beatitude is an ample consolation: Blessed are those who expect nothing, for they shall not be disappointed.

We welcome the book, however, because it affords us the occasion of saying a few words in kindness to the memory of Mrs. Osgood, and in justice to the character and value of her works.

The votaries of Literature do not commonly achieve eventful lives. As a rule, their vicissitudes may be aptly typified by such migrations as those of the Vicar of Wakefield—from the blue bed to the brown, or from the brown bed to the blue. The life of Mrs. Osgood was not exceptional. Its incidents were few and commonplace, and its story may be briefly told.

Frances Sargeant Osgood.

She was the daughter of Mr. Joseph Locke, a Boston merchant, and was born in the town of Rockport, Massachusetts, in the year 1812. At an early age she manifested a passion and a talent for literature. Her parents encouraged this inclination, and some of her verses,—approved by Mrs. Lydia Maria Child,—were printed in a juvenile Miscellany, of which that lady was then the editor. At about the age of twenty-three she was married to Mr. S. S. Osgood, an artist of some reputation, with whom she went to London. In that city, In 1839, the first collection of her poems was published, under the title of 'A Wreath of Wild Flowers from New England.' It was kindly received by the public and by the critics. There also, at the suggestion of Sheridan Knowles,—who at that time apparently had not 'got religion,'—she wrote a three-act play, called 'The Happy Release,' or 'The Triumphs of Love.' It was not produced at the time however, and we believe it has never been acted. In 1840, she returned with Mr. Osgood to this country. During the remainder of her life she resided principally in New York city, where she edited some illustrated gift-books, and wrote regularly for the current magazines. Many of her prose tales and sketches were produced at this time. These have never been collected, nor has there yet appeared any complete collection of her poems. Two editions of them were published before her death—one in New York in 1846, another in Philadelphia in 1849. She had also the misfortune of being commemorated in Dr. R. W. Griswold's 'Poets and Poetry of America,' and specimens of her verse are, to this day, contained in that delectable volume. The last years of her life were clouded with sickness and suffering. She died, of consumption, on Sunday, May 12th, 1850. Her grave is in a quiet and lonely place not far off from the tower which overlooks the beautiful cemetery of Mount Auburn. Others of her family repose there beside her. A plain monument marks the spot, bearing a harp, of which all the strings save one are broken. It is fitting that such a sweet and peaceful solitude should cherish the sacred dust of one in whose character and life all of womanly nature that is gentle, serene, and lovely, was so perfectly exemplified.

Frances Sargent Osgood's grave today.

As an author Mrs. Osgood has received large and generous recognition. The feeling with which, while yet living, she seems to have inspired her innumerable readers, was such as only ceases to be admiration when it warms into love. Few writers have ever been more generally petted and praised. The most savage critics even, both in England and at home, treated her books with uncommon gentleness, and gallantly scattered flowers in her way. It is probable that much of this enthusiasm resulted from her personal magnetism and loveliness of character. There is a legend that beautiful women are, universally, more or less fascinating. Certainly—though there is uncommon merit in the writings of Mrs. Osgood—we examine them in vain for any sufficient justification of all the eulogy they have received. It is to be considered also, that they do not excite enthusiasm any more. At this distance of time, therefore, and bringing our tribute to a gravestone, it is a matter of simple justice to consider them in the cold light of criticism. Perhaps it is a great pity that 'the light that lies in woman's eyes' should not invariably be 'the heart's undoing.' But the critic pays dearly for his exemption.

Mrs. Osgood's poetry does not evince a high order of genius. It has uncommon merit, indeed; but its essential characteristics are not remarkable. It displays, in ample measure, sprightliness of fancy, delicacy of sentiment, and grace of expression. Its feeling is by turns playful and tender; and it has a certain arch coquettishness of tone that is very fascinating. It exhibits inventive skill also, and a rare power of felicitous illustration. Altogether it is the perfect embodiment of that pure spirituality which was the essence and the charm of the poet's character, and naturally therefore, is the chief excellence of her poetry. Among the poems which preeminently illustrate these qualities, and which also are the best she has written, we may mention 'The Birth of the Callitriche, or WaterStar'; 'The Spirit of Poetry'; 'The Lover's List'; 'Ellen Ardelle'; 'The Child and its Angel Playmate;' 'The Daisy's Mistake'; 'Why Don't He Come?' ; 'Lulu'; 'New England's Mountain Child'; 'To Sybil'; 'She Loves Him Yet'; and 'The Language of Gems.' This latter poem we reprint. It is inferior to some of the others in dignity of theme, but it is the finest example of sprightly fancy and sparkling music:

The Language of Gems.

Fair Flora of late has become such a blue,
She has sent all her pretty dumb children to school;
And though strange it may seem, what I tell you is true,
Already they've learn'd French and English by rule.

Bud, blossom, and leaf, have been gifted with speech,
And eloquent lips breathing love in each tone,
Delighting such beautiful pupils to teach,
Have lent them a language as sweet as their own.

No more is the nightingale's serenade heard;
For Flora exclaims, as she flies through her bowers,
'It is softer than warble of fairy or bird!
'Tis the music of soul—the sweet language of flowers!'

No longer the lover impassion'd bestows
The pearl or the ruby;—in Hope's sunny hours
He twines for his maiden a myrtle and rose—
'Tis the echo of Love, the pure language of flowers.

But the pearl and the ruby are sadly dismay'd;
I saw a fair girl lay them lightly aside,
And blushingly wreathe, in her hair's simple braid,
The white orange flower that betray'd her a bride;

And I fancied I heard the poor jewels bewail,
At least they changed countenance strangely, I'm sure;
For the pearl blush'd with shame, and the ruby turn'd pale;
Indeed 'twas too much for a stone to endure.

And I, who had ever a passion for gems,
From the diamond's star-smile to the ruby's deep flame;
And who envy kings only their bright diadems,
Resolved to defend them from undeserved shame.

What are jewels but flowers that never decay,
With a glow and a glory unfading as fair?
And why should not they speak their minds if they may?
There are sermons in stones,' as all sages declare.

And a wild 'tongue of flame' wags in some of them too,
That would talk if you'd let it—so listen awhile;
They've a world of rich meaning in every bright hue—
A ray of pure knowledge in each sunny smile.

Then turn to the blossoms that never decay ;
Let the learned flowers talk to themselves on their stems,
Or prattle away with each other to-day ;—
And listen with me to the Language of Gems,

The Diamond emblem of Genius would seem,
In its glance, like the lightning, wild, fitful, divine—
Its point that can pierce, with a meteor-gleam,
Its myriad colors—its shadow and shine.

And more in that magic, so dazzling and strange;
Let it steal from Apollo but one sunny ray,
It will beam back a thousand that deepen and change,
Till you'd fancy a rainbow within it at play.

Fair Truth's azure eyes, that were lighted in heaven,
Have brought to the Sapphire their smile from above,
And the rich glowing ray of the Ruby is given,
To tell as it blushes of passionate Love.

The Chrysolite, clouded, and gloomy, and cold,
Its dye from the dark brow of Jealousy steals,
But bright in the Crystal's fair face we behold
The image of Candor that nothing conceals.

Young Hope, like the Spring, in her mantle of green,
Comes robed in that color, soft, pleasant, and tender,
And lends to the Emerald light so serene,
That the eye never wearies of watching its splendor.

The rosy Cornelian resembles the flush
That faintly illumines a beautiful face,
And well in its lovely and tremulous blush
May Fancy the emblem of Modesty trace.

While Joy's golden smile in the Topaz is glowing,
And Purity dwells in the delicate Pearl,
The Opal, each moment new semblances showing,
May shine on the breast of some changeable girl.

Serene as the Torquoise, Content ever calm,
In her pure heart reflects heaven's fairest hue bright,
While Beauty, exulting in youth's sunny charm,
Beholds in the Beryl her image of light.

To the beaming Carbuncle, whose ray never dies,
The rare gift of shining in darkness is given;
So Faith, with her fervent and shadowless eyes,
Looks up, through Earth's night-time of trouble to heaven.

There's a stone—the Asbestos—that, flung in the flame,
Unsullied comes forth with a color more pure,—
Thus shall Virtue, the victim of sorrow and shame,
Refined by the trial, forever endure.

Resplendent in purple, the Amethyst sparkling,
On Pride's flowing garments may haughtily glow,
While Jet, the lone mourning—gem, shadow'd and darkling,
And full of sad eloquence, whispers of Wo.

But thousands are burning beneath the dark wave,
As stars through the tempest-cloud tremblingly smile,
Or wasting their wealth in some desolate cave,
And talking, perchance, like the rest all the while.

Then wreathe of the blossoms that never decay,
A chaplet, dear maiden, that fair brow above;
But within, wear their prototypes, purer than they,
Faith—Hope—Truth and Innocence—Modesty—Love.

And while in each jewel a lesson you see,
While one smiles approval—another condemns,
I'm sure you will listen, delighted with me,
To a language so true as the Language of Gems!

One of the best, because one of the most spontaneous and fervid of Mrs. Osgood's poems, was inspired by the magical Fanny Ellsler. We miss it from the present collection. Although somewhat infelicitous in style, it is warm with earnest feeling, and presents a vivid and complete picture. Nothing could be more

Ballerina Fanny Ellsler.

perfect, in its way, than the imagery of the fifth Fanny Ellsler stanza:

Fanny Ellsler.

She comes! the spirit of the dance!
And, but for those large eloquent eyes,
Where passion speaks in every glance,
She'd seem a wanderer from the skies.

So light that, gazing breathless there,
Lest the celestial dream should go,
You'd think the music in the air
Way'd the fair vision to and fro;

Or think the melody's sweet flow
Within the radiant creature played,
And those soft, wreathing arms of snow
And white sylph feet the music made.

Now gliding slow with dreamy grace,
Her eyes beneath their lashes lost;
Now motionless, with lifted face,
And small hands on her bosom crossed;

And now with flashing eyes she springs—
Her whole bright figure raised in air,
As if her soul had spread its wings
And poised her one wild instant there!

She spoke not—but, so richly fraught
With language are her glance and smile,
That, when the curtain fell, I thought
She had been talking all the while.

None of Mrs. Osgood's dramatic pieces are contained in this volume. Her earliest collection included a Dramatic Sketch entitled 'Woman's Trust,' and also a sort of poetic Drama founded on that romantic story of Elfrida, which glimmers out in the crude records of early English History. The play that she wrote in England is a clever piece of composition, but unsuitable for the stage. She achieved no success in dramatic literature; but here, as in her prose writings, those same qualities of mind are everywhere exhibited which have made her successful and distinguished in the more congenial domain of poetry. Grace, tenderness, and sweet simplicity, characterize all she has written; and her works, in their pure spirituality and earnestness of purpose, are the truthful and charming exponents of her lovely character. There are brighter names in the brief annals of American Literature; but none can be remembered with more genuine pleasure than that of Frances Sargent Osgood.

ART AND CRITICISM.

The finest picture ever exhibited in this country is now on view at No. 42 East 14th-street. It is a representation of the old fable of Danae; the old fable, which it requires but a glance at the daily papers to prove, is as true for our own times as it was for the days that produced it.

The *Express*, while it sees the wonderful excellence of the picture, objects to the subject as one which should never be represented.

Perhaps the *Express* is right.

But we must pardon the old Greeks.

They were a purer people than we are.

They had not so large an array of newspaper-editors to tell them what they should think and what they should look at, as we have.

The large class of self-appointed conservators of public morals, did not exist in the benighted days of Phidias. Poor fellows, they loved a thing of beauty as a joy forever, without ever thinking of the conventional proprieties.

The mystery of life, the glory of being, the splendor of creation, the majesty of the human soul, the greatness of genius, and the power of the individual—these were the matters which interested them much more than Mrs. Grundy's opinions as to what is proper, or Mr. Oiley Gammon's ideas upon public decency.

In this connection it may be suggestive to recall the fact, that the office of censor of public morals was unknown in Greece or in the times of the Roman Republic, and was not instituted until the days of the Empire.

How far the disgusting indecency of the Empire was caused by the institution of such an office, is worthy of consideration.

Certainly the influence of the censors for good, can be counted as less than nothing; while in these days it would seem more consistent if the *Express* should advocate the suppression of all the classical dictionaries which are placed in the hands of youth, than the shutting up of pictures upon the subjects therein treated.

Lamartine's youthful mind was fed upon an expurgated edition of the Bible, and Byron's boyish virtue nourished upon an Apuleus which had all the improper passages cut out.

The effect of these precautionary measures can be learned in the works of both of these virtuous lights of literature, and may serve to demonstrate the folly of having a man's 'liberty judged of another man's conscience.'

It is an old adage, and a true one, that to the pure all things are pure, and while we should have a tender consideration for the weakness of others, we are certainly not called upon to abstain from animal food because meat should offend the stomach of a dyspeptic brother, or because some men are color-blind dress ourselves always in black.

Swift has described the prurient men as persons of nice words but nasty ideas, and to such the simple facts of life are more suggestive of indecency than the secret cabinet of Naples would be to a pure minded man or woman. Wertmuller's Danae is a picture such as only a pure-minded man could have painted, so that all those whose delicacy is shocked by it had better stay away. While apart from all other considerations its artistic merit is such that it is not extravagant to call it the best picture ever exhibited in this country.

To be sure the *Sunday Courier* says that 'as a work of art, it has no great merit,' but coming from such a quarter, this is the highest praise of its artistic excellence.

The critic of the *Courier* should confine the analytic powers of his great mind to a studious investigation of the merits of beef or putty.

It is there that his virtues should walk 'their narrow round.'

It is upon such themes, when stimulated with the promised reward of so many cents a-line, that his vast knowledge appears, and his keenness of perception finds a fit occasion for display. But no one expects the *Courier* to know anything, or to say anything worth hearing, about pictures.

It would be a pity if as excellent a work as Wertmuller's Danae should meet in this country with nothing but such flimsy and vulgar criticism. It would be a dreadful evidence of the want of decency in the American public, if the pruriency of a few pretended critics should be a true evidence of our refinement. But we are better than our newspaper-writers think we are.

There is a larger and purer love of Art in America than our critics give us credit for.

In fact it wants only a fine and pure picture like Danae to show how infinitely below the culture of the public are the knowledge and refinement of those who arrogate to themselves the office of critics.

[From 'Leaves of Grass.']

The Child that went Forth.

BY WALT WHITMAN.

1. There was a child went forth every day,
And the first object he looked upon and received with wonder, pity, love, or dread, that object he became,
And that object became part of him for the day, or a certain part of the day, or for many years, or stretching cycles of years.

2. The early lilacs became part of this child,
And grass, and white and red morning-glories, and white and red clover, and the song of the phœ-bebird,
And the Third Month lambs, and the sow's pink-faint litter, and the mare's foal, and the cow's calf,
And the noisy brood of the barnyard, or by the mire of the pond-side,
And the fish suspending themselves so curiously below there—and the beautiful curious liquid,
And the water-plants with their graceful flat heads —all became part of him.

3. The field-sprouts of Fourth Month and Fifth Month became part of him,
Winter-grain sprouts, and those of the light-yellow corn, and the esculent roots of the garden,
And the apple-trees covered with blossoms, and the fruit afterward, and wood-berries, and the commonest weeds by the road;
And the old drunkard staggering home from the outhouse of the tavern, whence he had lately risen,
And the school-mistress that passed on her way to to the school,
And the friendly boys that passed—and the quarrelsome boys,
And the tidy and fresh-cheeked girls—and the barefoot negro boy and girl,
And all the changes of city and country, where-ever he went.

4. His own parents,
He that had fathered him, and she that conceived him in her womb, and birthed him,
They gave this child more of themselves than that, They gave him afterward every day—they and of them became part of him.

5. The mother at home, quietly placing the dishes on to the supper-table,
The mother with mild words—clean her cap and gown, a wholesome odor falling off her person and clothes as she walks by;
The father, strong, self-sufficient, manly, mean, angered, unjust,
The blow, the quick loud word, the tight bargain, the crafty lure,
The family usages, the language, the company, the furniture—the yearning and swelling heart,
Affection that will not be gainsayed—the sense of what is real—the thought if, after all, it should prove unreal,
The doubts of day-time and the doubts of nighttime—the curious whether and how,
Whether that which appears so is so, or is it all flashes and specks?
Men and women crowding fast in the streets—if they are not flashes and specks, what are they?
The streets themselves, and the façades of houses, and goods in the windows,
Vehicles, teams, the heavy-planked wharves—the huge crossing at the ferries,
The village on the highland, seen from afar at sunset—the river between,
Shadows, aureola and mist, light falling on roofs and gables of white or brown, three miles off,
The schooner near by, sleepily dropping down the tide—the little boat slack-towed astern,
The hurrying tumbling waves, quick-broken crests, slapping,
The strata of colored clouds, the long bar of maroon-tint, away solitary by itself—the spread of purity it lies motionless in,
The horizon's edge, the flying sea-crow, the fragrance of salt-marsh and shore-mud;
These became part of that child who went forth every day, and who now goes, and will always go forth every day,
And these become part of him or her that peruses them here.

MINOR EXPERIENCES IN AMERICA.

XV.

In the Fall of 1850 a sort of literary and political war excited public attention in Cambridge, Boston, and to a great extent in Massachusetts.

It was a war waged by the hatred of European liberty, by ignorance and falsification of history, against the generous sympathies for the oppressed which prevailed among the majority of the people.

To the honor of Massachusetts, it must be recorded that the excitement did not die away before it had influenced, if not occasioned, a reform in the Board of Trustees over Harvard College. The Legislature of the State under the guidance of Governor Boutwell, Senator Wilson, the present Governor Banks, and other distinguished men who belonged to the people, not to the respectability, took the matter in hand, made a hole in the constitution of the College, and infused in to the government a little fresh spirit.

The tragical end of the Magyar insurrection of 1848-49 was the subject of an article in the *North American Review,* entitled 'The War of Races in Hungary.' It was a good name for a bad article. The title was taking, and was the only piece of truth there was in the whole elaborate structure. The struggle in Hungary was really a war of races. But under this heading the author poured out his bitter hatred of the whole European movement of 1848. He confused recent facts and past history; showed his ignorance of both, defended the Hapsburgs, and condemned in toto the liberals of France, and the martyrs of Germany, Italy, and Hungary.

Under the fire of letters, articles and explanations which in due time followed the publication of the article in question, the author floundered deeper into the mud, showed still greater exasperation against any and all revolutions, and displayed still less familiarity with the most current facts of history. Among other matters, he could not comprehend that Charles V. Emperor of Germany, was Charles I. King of Spain. It was the same with many similar and no less elementary historical facts.

He was of Leporello's creed and school. He had on his side the majority of the Faculty and the majority of the respectability. In justice however to the Faculty, it must be said that they did not so much share the reviewer's opinions as believed him to be familiar, or rather a master in history.

My recently deceased friend, Dr. Krajtsir, was the first person in Boston who met the reviewer and exposed his thorough ignorance of history in all its subdivisions, shades, and details.

Krajtsir's creed was, to use his own words, 'that the development and progress of the human intellect is reflected in each speciality, even in the simplest science. That each science receives its impulse from the totality of the intellectual powers, and produces fruits which are enjoyed by all, even by the humblest worshipper of knowledge. So that all sciences are essentially but one general science, which is the sum and result of the activity of the entire human mind, generating the continual progress and elevation of man. Mind and science are exponents of, and act reciprocally upon each other. The spirit of an age or century is the result of their science.'

It is natural that a man with so lofty a comprehension of the human mind and of science, should have been highly incensed with a reviewer who sinned so grossly against the science of history, and therefore against the spirit and the moral sense of the age. Krajtsir, a Magyar by birth, an exile and one of the martyrs of this century, was wounded in all his feelings as a patriot and in his reverence for genuine knowledge. He found several ready and devoted supporters of the cause of liberty. Prominent among them was a lady-pupil of his, Mrs. P——, and several of her friends. Advised and directed by Krajtsir, they rebuked and refuted the reviewer, and won easy but deserved laurels.

I mixed in the battle also.

It was not my friendship for Krajtsir, which had been formed thirty years before, in Europe, amidst the activity of revolution and the thraldom of common proscription and exile, it was not my veneration for his pure character and his almost all-embracing and inexhaustible erudition, or my respect for the keenness of his intellect, which drew me into the struggle, but the—as it seemed to me—deliberate and wilful perversion of historical facts and events. Being myself of Slavic descent, and a godfather of Pauslawism, I looked on the Magyar movement from an altogether different, and even hostile stand-point. But martyrs are to be respected alike everywhere, and the proudly displayed hostility and aversion to the great European uprising of 1848-19 was revolting to me.

Some months before I came to Cambridge, the *North American Review* was put in my hands by a literary gentleman in New York, who asked my opinion about the 'War of Races.' I then promised to show up the reviewer's ill-will and sophistry, and did so in an article printed during the Winter of 1850 in *The New York Herald.*

This was my first appearance in the arena of American journalism.

In joining Krajtsir, I therefore only continued the course I had begun upon single-handed, when I had scarcely landed on American soil.

My participation in this—for Harvard, Cambridge, and Boston—memorable struggle, influenced my subsequent position and the events of my existence in this country, and for this reason I mention it here. I did not share in the Kossuth-worship. Neither here nor in Europe had he inspired me with that respect and veneration which every one pays willingly to the greatness of an opponent, or an enemy. But genuine Heroes do not appear as the deus ex machina, are not surrounded by attendants and heralded by themselves. The turmoil and tempest of events wake them from obscurity to light, as the lightning-flash is produced from the bosom of the thunder-cloud.

With his affectations, with the theatrical display of a would-be Governor, with his guards in church pews and American hotels, Kossuth seemed to me a smart rhetorician, but not made of the metal from which heroes are cast. A martyr he can in no respect be called.

Nations are not regenerated by speeches; and if Magyarism, which I doubt, is again to rule over the Theiss and the Danube, Kossuth is not the man to restore the Magyars to historical life and power.

The events of the day force upon the mind a comparison of the cause of the Magyars and of Italy, though we are tempted to say ne miscantur sacra profanis.

The Magyars can exist only by oppressing and subjugating another genuine ethnic nationality. That is, by crushing the national liberties and language which they once dispersed and conquered.

Italy and her aborigines the Italians, are indigenous to the soil, and nearly as old in history as man. Italians are now regaining what was theirs almost from the beginning of time, and they regain it without endangering or encroaching upon the liberty and rights of any nation, or even of any single individual. History knows not a purer and holier cause, and as is the cause so is the man unique who is now hewing out the destiny of the Italians.

I am averse to borrowing names for modern events from antiquity. Such comparisons and measurements of men with by-gone standards are generally relative and often superficial. Yet such comparisons are popular, and for the majority facilitate their appreciation of what is passing before their eyes.

Using, therefore, the approved classic style, I would say that Garibaldi far surpasses Epaminondas in simplicity, while he unites to this quality the high statesmanship and the patriotism of Demosthenes, which were unparallaled in the history of Greece.

From Deukalion down to Philopoemen, Demosthenes alone was pan hellenic. He did not look to the greatness of Athens at the expense of Sparta, Thebes, or any other, though even the smallest of the Grecian States, but aimed to unite them all against the tyrants of Macedon, as were Phillip, Alexander, and Antipater.

So Garibaldi is not the champion of Piedmont, but of Italy against the tyranny of Papacy, of the Hapsburgs and the Bourbons. And to continue, Garibaldi is more than Prometheus. It is easier to shape into form, and to infuse the breath of life into a rudis indigestaque moles, than to perform the same office for a nation which has been for centuries corroded and depressed by priestly and political despotism. Garibaldi restored to life and renewed the energy of the Sicilians and the Neapolitans. Years ago he passed here almost unnoticed. It was when after a superhuman struggle he received into his own bosom the last breath of the great movement of 1848, the movement which was murdered in Rome, he passed unnoticed here, because, hero-like, after great deeds, he subsided into the common current of life, waiting for new events and new emergencies, and because the generous American mind was then dazzled and confused by the man of six hundred—not battles—but speeches.

GUROWSKI.

NEW YORK DECEMBER 8, 1860

OUT OF THE GRAVE.

The Autumn wind is wild in all the leaves,
    And the long grass is rustling on my grave;
Ah, would you have me think your heart still grieves
    For one you would not save?

For I am dead! Know you not I am dead?
    Why do you haunt me in my grave to-night?
Standing above and listening overhead,
    Where I am buried deep, and out of sight!

Have you not wine and music in your home,
    And the fair form and eyes so pure and proud
With love of you?—and wherefore do you come
    To vex me, lying silent in my shroud?

Seek your new love! she calls you, and the tears
    Are warm on her pale face, and her young breast
Is full of doubt and sorrow, and she hears
    Low whispered words that warn her from her rest.

In from the night! the storm begins to stir!
    I will be near, and ghostly eyes shall see
How you will kiss her lips and say to her,
    'Thine always, Love,'—as once you said to me!

WILLIAM WINTER.

MINOR EXPERIENCES IN AMERICA.

XVI.

Accustomed to the discipline common in European families, and throughout all the strata of society there, I was struck by the utter absence of all such discipline here, and by the want of consideration with which parents and elderly persons generally, were treated by Young America, even when scarcely out of its swaddling clothes.

Undoubtedly Americans are self-reliant almost as soon as they have crept from the cradle. This independence has something in its favor, and the more so a society based upon the principle 'help yourself.'

To this independence is principally due the wonderful emigration to the prairies, and the adventurous spirit which makes the Americans the pioneers of civilization, and the bearers of the elements of culture. From childhood even they do not look to the domestic hearth as the focus whence emanates the directing power. The home, strictly speaking, has no existence for the immense majority of Americans. How few of them cherish the memory of their birthplace. How few spend their old age in the same place where they creeped as children, or as young men started out in life. How few living and dying in the same spot, have all their children christened under the same roof. They build and abandon houses, as easily as the snail forms and forsakes its shell.

All this has its moral, and as it is the fashion to say, its providential causes, and therefore it is unavoidable and right, that such independence of home should grow up with the child.

Yet, understanding and appreciating such causes and results, an European will always be astonished at them, nay, even painfully impressed at seeing the early evidences of such free will in children.

In Cambridge I took a great interest in a boy about eight years old, whose parents I frequently visited. Passing one morning by the house, I asked his father about him. "He is not in, and I do not know what arrangements he made for the day," was his answer.

In another family, a girl about twelve years old, resolved one morning to pay a visit by herself to a friend in Nahant. Taking the early cars to Boston, she there found the boat for Nahant, paid her visit, and returned home, about dusk, to tea. "Why Mary where have you been all day?" asked her mother very composedly. "I went to Nahant to see Lizzy," was the equally cool answer of the independent daughter.

Such occurrences are not unusual in American domestic life.

By repeated and personal experience I was strengthened in the opinion that, the so-called, common people have more common sense and honor than those who consider themselves better bred and higher toned.

A Polish emigrant was engaged in peddling cigars among the students and others in Cambridge. He asked me to help him, as he said, in his business, and by degrees managed to get some forty dollars from me, nearly the last money I had. On one occasion he entered my room, during my absence, and abstracted a portfolio in which he had seen that I kept not money, but various letters. Some of these letters were those of introduction which I had brought from Europe to various persons in Washington, and had not yet delivered. Many of them had large seals with showy coats-of-arms, by which he was probably allured.

I have strong suspicions that it was a coup monté by other inquisitive Cambridgers, who were desirous of prying into what they believed were my secrets. As I afterwards ascertained, the Polish peddler frequented a bar-room, and was in the habit of showing there after each visit to me, the money he had borrowed. One day he abused me there as an agent and spy for Nicholas; but, to his astonishment, produced an unexpected result.

Some of the habitués of the bar-room treated him roughly, and finally kicked him out, saying: "That a spy is never poor, and the Count is poor, and goes only to the library, while he, the peddler, was a thorough scoundrel to abuse a man who shared his purse with him."

I know that some of the people of Cambridge did not think so, but received the peddler's slanders, and peddled them again. There is a sort of free-masonry existing everywhere amongst mean and imbecile characters.

Several of the professors and respectable men were puzzled by my being a fugitive from Russia, and yet not speaking with that venom of the Russian nation and of Nicholas, which almost everybody, whether Pole, German, or any other European nationality, felt duty bound to express.

The spirit of the lectures I gave at that time upon Russia, and the tone of the conversation I held upon such topics, were the same as those expressed in my book, 'Russia as it is,' and as prevailed in my numerous articles in the *Tribune,* when I was connected with that paper.

In a contribution to the *Boston Museum* in 1850, I foretold the unavoidable and near emancipation of the peasantry. In 'Russia as it is,' years before the death of Nicholas, I said that he was the last despot, and had stretched the reins of despotism so tightly as to render despotism impossible after him, whatever might be the disposition, the intention, or the character of his successors. I maintained, years ago, that Russia is near the dawn of a new and liberal era, and of events which are now realized.

All this puzzled the knowing ones, and often the other dalies, all over the country, rapped me on the knuckles over the *Tribune*, while wondering at its credulity. They repeat now what that paper foretold years ago, in spite of the sneers of the unbelievers. I was amused to find that some persons in Cambridge, as well as others in Boston and elsewhere, were undecided about me because I did not speak of Nicholas as of an ogre.

But why should I?

Nicholas had his individuality, and I had mine.

The two could not agree. That was all. Mine could not be crushed, and as Nicholas had the worldly power, he of course could wrong me, and in common parlance break down my position, but not myself.

Here is a sample of Nicholas's mind, as a proof how dangerous it is to judge certain men, as it were, in the wholesale, and from single special data.

The work recently published by Herbert Spencer on education, advocates powerfully and irrefutably the superior value in general education of the natural and positive sciences over the classical studies.

Exactly twenty years ago, when in the Russian service, I submitted to Nicholas a similar project of reform in the public schools of the Empire.

Classically educated myself, I felt strongly the inconvenience resulting from a deficiency in knowledge which is so essential. The Minister of Public Instruction, Count Onwaroff, and the council of the University were all opposed to my plan, while Nicholas alone approved it.

This was not the only occasion when I found Nicholas more accessible to a new idea or combination than his ministers and advisers, and such repeated experiences of his assent to my projects were among the many causes which ousted me from Russia.

Nicholas once ordered the Minister who was my immediate chief to send me to investigate a case of considerable peculation, adding these words: "I answer for Gurowski's honesty."

It was a flattering testimony from one who had almost given up faith in the honesty of those who surrounded him.

I was not to blame if the recollection of these words had influenced my appreciation of Nicholas, and yet they did not so influence me.

About ten weeks before his death, I received a kind letter from his first favorite, Count Adlerberg, written by the order of Nicholas, and in his name. I was here, independent of and beyond his reach, so that now it would seem that I got the better of him.

GUROWSKI.

NEW YORK DECEMBER 15, 1860

[*From The Knickerbocker for December.*]

THE MAN AT THE DOOR.

BY FITZ-JAMES O'BRIEN.

How joyous to-day is the little old town,
With banners and streamers and that sort of thing:
They flutter on turrets and battlements brown,
And the ancient Cathedral is fine as a king.
The sexton a nosegay has put in his breast,
And his face is as bright as a Jericho rose
That, after a century's withering rest,
Unwrinkles its petals and suddenly blows.

The brown-breasted swallows aloft and alow,
Swoop faster and farther than ever before,
And I'm sure that the cock on the steeple will crow
When he hears from the city the jubilant roar.
The girls are as gay as a holiday fleet,
And ribbons are streaming from bosom and hair,
And they laugh in the face of each young man they meet.
And the young men reply with an insolent stare.

'Tis not without reason the old town is gay,
And banners and ribbons are reddening the air,
For beautiful Bertha will marry to-day
With gallant young Albert, the son of the Mayor.
He is brown as a nut from the hazels of Spain :
Her face, like the twilight, is pensive and sweet;
As they march hand in hand thro' the murmuring lane,
Low blessings, like flowers, fall unseen at their feet.
While they sweep like twin barks through the waves of the crowd,
A story is falling from many a tongue
Of the young Gipsy Prince who a year ago bowed
At the shrine where a hundred their passion had sung.
And how Bertha heaped scorn on his love and his race,
How she flung in the street the rich presents he sent,
Until he with the hatred of hell in his face,
Went sullenly back to his tribe and his tent.

Soon all stories are hushed in a gathering roar,
And the people sway back like the ebb of a tide,
And the rosy old sexton stands by the church-door,
To merrily welcome the bridegroom and bride :
But his glee is so great that he does not behold
The tall man that stands near the pillar hard by,
Nor the flash of the dagger that's hafted with gold,
Nor the still keener flash of the lowering eye.

On they come, and the sexton bows low to the ground,
The bride smiles a welcome, the bells ring a chime,
While a grand acclamation in surges of sound
Thrills up through the sky like a sonorous rhyme.
They are under the porch—when one dash through the crowd,
One flash of a dagger—one shriek of despair,
And Bertha falls dead; while stern-faced and proud,
The swarthy-skinned Prince of the Gipsies is there!

How sombre to-day is the little old town,
With mourning and sables and funeral display;
Long weepers are hanging from battlements brown,
And the ancient Cathedral is haggard and gray.
The sexton a white rose has put in his breast,
While his face is as blank as a snow-laden sky,
For Bertha and Albert have gone to their rest,
And the Prince of the Gipsies is swinging on high.

MINOR EXPERIENCES IN AMERICA.

XVII.

I visited the Harvard family of Shakers, not to examine their curiously conceived Christianity, but to see how the principle of life in community worked; the principle which has failed so signally everywhere else. I wished to observe the Shakers as socialists, and was quite indifferent to their conception or misconception of Christianity, or their hostility to 'generation.'

The Shakers received me with great kindness, and with their wonted simple, but warm and open hearted hospitality.

The snow had already covered the soil, so that my visit, which lasted for several days, was necessarily confined to indoors, among the three neighboring families. This however gave me great facilities for studying more thoroughly their system and its working, and by continual conversations with men and women, 'brethren and sisters,' elders and ordinary members, I could study their characters.

As I was recommended to them in rather a flattering way from Cambridge, their curiosity was considerably aroused. There was no end of questions on both sides. They were in the highest degree curious about Europe, about the socialist experiments there, about the various social theories; also about the courts and sovereigns, whether the Shaker principles were known in Russia and at the court of Nicholas, to whom their elders, years ago, had sent a copy of the book containing the Shaker doctrine.

In a word, if I was inquisitive, they were also, but in a friendly, good-natured, well-bred manner.

I found these Shakers with whom I thus came in contact by no means scholars, according to the current opinion, all of them being artisans, laborers in some way or other. Yet, nevertheless, they had a general notion of the various socialist systems in Europe, and in the discussion of their own doctrine proved themselves generally to be strong logicians, and even formidable dialecticians.

They were, however, most astonished by the explanation I gave them of the genuine and pure social theory of Fourier. It was news for them to hear that the reorganization of society, as conceived by Fourier, has nothing in common with what is generally called socialism, or communism, and that free-lovism is not the cardinal doctrine of his system, although a full recognition of the absolute equality of women with the lords of creation is.

Whenever there was a gathering of the families, they asked me as a special favor to repeat aloud the Lord's Prayer, in as many different languages as I knew. In this way I made up for my neglect, in mature life, of this simple prayer, lisped by the naive and confident faith of childhood, since during my visit to the Shakers I repeated the prayer some days thirty times.

One day while visiting the gyneceum, or the women's division of the village, in company with one of the Elders, and finding all the women very neat, and occupied with various household duties, I unwittingly exclaimed that the Shakeresses, disciplined as they are, would make excellent wives.

"What sayest thou to this, brother?" asked the youngest and handsomest among them, turning her face to the Elder.

The Elder said nothing, but took me gently by the arm, and when we had left the room, said in a friendly, but serious tone, "Thou must not suggest much questions in the family."

The next evening after tea, some of the sisters and brethren asked me to tell them a story about European life and customs; an evening story, such as are common in Europe, or rather in novels.

It was a long, snowy, tempestuous evening in De.cember. The Elders looked rather scared, but were polite enough not to express in any other way their displeasure at my readiness to conform with the request,

Not wishing to wound even in the slightest way, the feelings of men who treated me with the utmost cordiality, as an offset to my involuntary indiscretion of the day before, I selected a real event in my family, which had in the course of long centuries grown into a legend.

I told, therefore, how about six centuries ago, an ancestress of mine, one of the historic family of Piast, married, for political reasons, her cousin, a reigning Duke of Liegnitz in Silesia, when that country was independent, and its inhabitants, of the Slavic race, were Roman Catholics. My ancestor's dowry consisted of two small adjacent and independent

Dukedoms, so that the match was a family scheme to aggrandize the Liegnitz branch. I told how she was unhappy with her coarse and dissolute husband, how she died broken hearted, having had only a little spaniel as a sympathizing companion; and how when her corpse was laid out with all the ceremonial pageantry in a silver coffin, the little dog crept during the night into the coffin, and was found there dead in the morning.

The husband ordered the coffin closed over both bodies, and they were thus deposited in the chapel of the Cathedral. The cruel husband soon followed, and the two coffins now stand side by side.

Centuries after, the spread of Protestantism and Germanism changed the condition of Silesia, and of the Dukedom of Liegnitz. The Cathedral is now a Lutheran church, and the Gospel is preached not in Slavic but in German.

The silver coffins are still in the chapel. The story of the unhappy princess, and of her being buried with a dog—that candidate for humanity, according to Michelet—grew feebler and feebler from generation to generation. About a century ago, a high Prussian official in the province of Silesia, wishing to verify the truth of the legend, ordered the coffin to be opened, and found the skeletons there. Now a sexton will, for a small consideration, open the coffin and show them to the rare and curious traveller.

The true story is long ago forgotten among the Liegnitzians, but her relations, scattered in all climes, preserve her memory with pious care.

The Elders were satisfied with the story, and all the sisters and brethren drew from it their own conclusions in favor of their own doctrines,

These colonies of Shakers are the only successful experiments among all the numerous and harmless attempts at a life in community, or those others made by half Fourierites and Owenites, at Orbiston, New Harmony, Harmony Hall, the pseudo Phalansteries in France and in this country. The Shakers attribute their success to the non-existence among them of family by generation. When they told me this, I answered that humanity never would and never could submit to such a deprivation, even in order to gain the felicities of communism.

Some months afterward, these same Shakers heard of my poverty—at that time it was nearly destitution—and that my health was altogether shattered. They invited me to come among them, to stay any length of time, at least until my recovery, and gave their promise that I should not be annoyed by any attempts at conversion to their doctrine. This act at least was one of pure Christian charity.

GUROWSKI

LOVES AND HEROINES OF THE POETS

The Loves and Heroines of the Poets. Edited by Richard Henry Stoddard. New York. Mesars. Derby & Jackson.

Lilies, roses and honey-suckles, zephyrs, sunbeams and morning-glories, rubies and diamonds, pearls and crystals, larks and nightingales, ripe lips, sweet kisses, fragrant bosoms, snow, fire, laurels and myrtle—well, all things on earth that constitute temptation and ecstacy for all persons—except anchorites and critics—are garnered, in symmetrical luxuriance, into this beautiful volume of the 'Loves and Heroines of the Poets.' It is—pardon us the antique quotation—'a thing of beauty,' and necessarily therefore, 'a joy forever.'

Richard Henry Stoddard

Judging by such lights as reading and observation afford, we incline to the opinion that people get more or less into a state of mind when overtaken by the frenzy of Love. With the Poets, certainly, this is true, however it may be with other persons; and this their verses sufficiently exhibit. Accordingly, we are not dismayed at the gathered testimony of the Poets of nearly four centuries, as it lives in this group of Loves and Heroines, nor to observe that for them at least,

> "All thoughts, all passions, all delights,
> Whatever stirs this mortal frame,
> All are but ministers of Love,
> And feed his sacred flame,"

But whatever their state of mind, and however uncomfortable alike to themselves and others, it is a good thing to have the poets severely agitated with all possible passions and in all possible ways; and that perhaps is the most effective and fruitful way which turns upon them, warm and splendid, 'the light that lies in woman's eyes,' and the entire light artillery of woman's fascination. It is to this method, at any rate, that the world is mainly indebted for most that is true and beautiful in the poetic literature of the nations. It is to this that we owe 'The Loves and Heroines of the Poets.'

Perhaps we cannot better indicate the intention and scope of this work than by copying its quiet and graceful Preface:

"My object in this volume," says the Editor, "is to present specimens of English love-poetry, especially that which is or seems to be addressed to particular women—'The Loves and Heroines of the Poets'—and to give, as concisely as possible, all that is known concerning them. I begin with the three great Italian poets, because I conceive their love-sonnets—above all Petrarch's—to have been the models after which our early poets shaped their amorous fancies. Wyatt and Surrey, even when most original, are little better than imitators of Petrarch. Indeed, so notorious was this fact that they were said to have travelled in Italy and to have brought their art thence. I trace the course of love-poetry in English Literature from Wyatt to the poets of the present day. I have gone over the ground carefully, and have selected what seemed to me the best specimens for a volume of this kind. The poetic literature of the age of Elizabeth and the times of Charles the First and Second, is largely represented. I have arranged my materials chronologically, giving the dates at which the different poems were written, wherever they were known, or at least the dates and names of the volumes in which, as far as I could ascertain, they were first printed: where there was nothing positive to guide me, I have arranged them conjecturally. When I could consult the early editions, I have done so, although I have not always followed their readings when a later one seemed better. I have chosen authenticated portraits, when I could obtain them, in preference to ideal heads; greatly I think to the permanent value of the work. For some of the best of these illustrations I am indebted to my friend Barry, who has copied from their scarce originals the portraits of Laura, Beatrice, and Geraldine, and drawn from his imagination the ideal heads of Shakespeare's Mistress, Burn's Highland Mary, and Coleridge's Genevieve."

In the accomplishment of his felicitous design Mr. Stoddard has been entirely successful. It required poetic sympathy, pure taste, just discrimination, unusual culture, and careful research, suitably to edit the 'Loves and Heroines of the Poets;' and the book is wanting in none of the essential qualities of excellence. We shall on another occasion endeavor more fitly to express an appreciation of its value, by a careful analysis of its merits and defects. In the meantime we cordially commend it to all lovers of good poetry. It is the best collection of poems ever published in this country; and it is published in a very elegant dress.

A 'MEDIUM'-POEM.

The following poem was recited by Miss Lizzie Doten, a spiritual trance-medium, at the close of a recent lecture in Boston. She professed to give it impromptu, as far as she was concerned, and to speak under the influence of EDGAR A. POE.

> From the throne of life eternal,
> From the home of love supernal,
> Where the angel feet make music over all the starry floor—
> Mortals, I have come to meet you,
> Come with words of peace to greet you,
> And to tell you of the glory that is mine forever more.
>
> Once before I found a mortal
> Waiting at the heavenly portal—
> Waiting but to catch some echo from that ever-opening door;
> Then I seized his quickened being,
> And through all his inward seeing,

Caused my burning inspiration in a fiery flood to pour.

Now I come more meekly human,
And the weak lips of a woman
Touch with fire from off the altar, not with burning as of yore:
But in holy love descending,
With her chastened being blending,
I would fill your souls with music from the bright celestial shore.

As one heart yearns for another,
As a child turns to its mother,
From the golden gates of glory turn I to the earth once more,
Where I drained the cup of sadness,
Where my soul was stung to madness,
And life's bitter, burning billows swept my burdened being o'er.

Here the harpies and the ravens,
Human vampyres-sordid cravens,
Preyed upon my soul and substance till I writhed in anguish sore;
Life and I seemed mismated,
For I felt accursed and fated,
Like a restless, wrathful spirit, wandering on the Stygian shore.

Tortured by a nameless yearning,
Like a rost-fire, freezing, burning,
Did the purple, pulsing life-tide, through its fevered channels pour,
Till the golden bowl-Life's token—
Into shining shards was broken,
And my chained and chafing spirit leapt from out its prison-door.

But while living, striving, dying,
Never did my soul cease crying,
"Ye who guide the fates and furies, give! O give me, I implore!
From the myriad hosts of nations,
From the countless constellations,
One pure spirit that can love me—one that I, too, can adore !"

Through this fervent inspiration
Found my fainting soul salvation,
For from out its blackened fire-crypts, did my quickened spirit soar;
And my beautiful ideal—
Not too saintly to be real—
Burst more brightly on my vision than the fancy-formed Lenore.

'Mid the surging seas she found me,
With the billows breaking round me,
And my saddened, sinking spirit, in her arms of love upbore;
Like a lone one, weak and weary,
Wandering in the midnight dreary,
In her sinless, saintly bosom, brought me to the heavenly shore.

Like the breath of blossoms blending,
Like the prayers of saints ascending,
Like the rainbow's seven-hued glory, blend our souls forevermore.
Earthly love and lust enslaved me,
But divinest love hath saved me,
And I know now, first and only, how to love and to adore.

O, my mortal friends and brothers,
We are each and all another's,
And the soul that gives most freely from its treasure hath the more.
Would you lose your life, you find it;
And in giving love, you bind it
Like an amulet of safety to your heart, forevermore!

—*Fitchburg Sentinel.*

A PORTRAIT.

BY WALT WHITMAN.

I knew a man,
He was a common farmer—he was the father of five sons,
And in them were the fathers of sons—and in them were the fathers of sons.
This man was of wonderful vigor, calmness, beauty of person,
The shape of his head, the richness and breadth of his manners, the pale yellow and white of his hair and beard, and the immeasurable meaning of his black eyes,
These I used to go and visit him to see—he was wise also,
He was six feet tall, he was over eighty years old—his sons were massive, clean, bearded, tan-faced, handsome,
They and his daughters loved him—all who saw him loved him,
They did not love him by allowance—they loved him with personal love;
He drank water only—the blood showed like scarlet through the clear-brown skin of his face,
He was a frequent gunner and fisher—he sailed his boat himself—he had a fine one presented to him by a ship-joiner—he had fowling-pieces, presented to him by men that loved him;
When he went with his five sons and many grandsons to hunt or fish, you would pick him out as the most beautiful and vigorous of the gang,
You would wish long and long to be with him—you would wish to sit by him in the boat, that you and he might touch each other.

I have perceived that to be with those I like is enough,
To stop in company with the rest at evening is enough,
To be surrounded by beautiful, curious, breathing, laughing flesh is enough,
To pass among them, or touch any one, or rest my arm ever so lightly round his or her neck for a moment—what is this, then?
I do not ask any more delight—I swim in it, as in a sea.

There is something in staying close to men and women, and looking on them, and in the contact and odor of them, that pleases the Soul well,
All things pleases the Soul—but these please the Soul well.

2025 Editor's note:

After the December 15, 1860 issue, the *New York Saturday Press* ceased publication. Clapp and some of his writers worked for "The Leader" thereafter.

Wilkins, O'Brien, Arnold, Eytinge, and Mullen imagined marching to war, by Ned Mullen, for "Comic Monthly."

In less than four months after the demise of *NYSP,* the Confederate firing on Fort Sumter sparked civil war. Writers from *NYSP* could be found on each side of the war, with Fitz James O'Brien dying after suffering a gunshot wound in service of the Union. George Derby ("John Phoenix") also died while in service of the War Department. Adam Gurowski served as translator for the State Department during the war, and died of typhoid fever shortly after the war.

During 1861, Ned Wilkins fell ill and died at age 32 of pneumonia; Harry Neill died of typhoid fever at age 21; and Getty Gay died at age 25 of tuberculosis. Frank Wood died of tuberculosis in 1864 at the age of 23. Ada Clare left for California, hoping to restart her career.

New York City enthusiastically sent over 100,000 troops to the war. Still, a strong cohort of Confederate sympathizers remained in the city. Many Irish immigrants in the city opposed the military draft, motivated by an unwillingness to serve and a resentfulness against free Blacks, who competed with the Irish for low-wage jobs.

On July 13, 1863, as a new draft was introduced, these secessionists and Irish immigrants united and launched a four-day armed riot against the New York City police. The violence resulted in the deaths of 119 people, including 11 African Americans who rioters lynched. Additionally, 50 buildings were looted and set on fire, including the Colored Orphan Asylum located at 44th Street and 5th Avenue.

On November 27, 1864, Confederates plotted to burn down New

DEPARTURE OF THE QUEEN OF BOHEMIA, FOR CALIFORNIA—INTENSE GRIEF OF HER SUBJECTS

Thomas Butler Gunn satirizes Ada Clare's admirers seeing her steamship off to California in the Feb. 20, 1864 issue of the Illustrated News.

York City by incendiary attacks on numerous hotels. They bungled the attack, and all fires were safely extinguished.

Less than six months later, on April 9, 1865, Confederate General Robert E. Lee surrendered, marking an end to the Civil War. Just five days after Lee's surrender, actor John Wilkes Booth—a Confederate sympathizer—assassinated President Abraham Lincoln.

While the president and Mrs. Lincoln attended a performance by Laura Keene of *Our American Cousin* at Ford's Theatre in Washington, D.C., Booth crept into their private box and shot Lincoln in the back of the head with a derringer pistol. He then stabbed an Army officer who was accompanying the Lincolns before leaping onto the stage, shouting, "Sic semper tyrannis!" ("Thus always to tyrants!") as he fled.

Lincoln succumbed to his injuries the next day. Booth was killed 11 days later by federal troops after being cornered in a barn. An investigation uncovered a broader conspiracy involving nine additional individuals; four were later hanged for their roles.

On April 26, 1865, Lincoln's funeral train made a stop in Jersey City en route to Springfield, Illinois. The train car was ferried across the Hudson River to New York City, where a grand funeral procession and public viewing were held. Concerned about potential unrest similar to the Draft Riots, the New York City Council attempted to ban African Americans from attending. However, Secretary of War Edwin Stanton overruled the decision, and police were assigned to protect African Americans during the event. Hundreds of thousands of mourners lined the streets and watched from rooftops as Lincoln's body, placed in an elaborate catafalque, was carried along Broadway in a somber procession. Buildings along the route were draped in mourning crepe from pavement to roofline. The public viewing at City Hall lasted from 1 p.m. to midnight and continued throughout the night, as citizens paid their respects to the fallen president.

On July 13, 1865, ignited by an accidental gas leak, Barnum's American Museum burned to the ground.

The following month, Henry Clapp resurrected the New York Saturday Press.

Lincoln's funeral procession moving up Broadway, approaching Union Square, April 24, 1865. Notice the men watching from the rooftop in the upper left corner. The building beside that one--the corner building draped with black crepe and an American flag--is 849 Broadway, the home of the family of Cornelius Roosevelt. His grandsons, Elliot and 6-year-old (future president) Teddy Roosevelt, can be seen watching the cortège from the second floor window.

THE NEW YORK SATURDAY PRESS.

HENRY CLAPP, JR., EDITOR.

VOL. IV. NO. 1. WHOLE NO. 113. | NEW YORK, AUGUST 5, 1865. | $3.00 A YEAR. 6 CTS. A NUMBER.

THE NEW YORK SATURDAY PRESS.

HENRY CLAPP, JR., EDITOR.

Published at No. 64 NASSAU STREET, *New York City.*

PRICE, $3.00 A YEAR. 6 CENTS A NUMBER.

Advertisements, 15 *Cents a line.*

TO WHOM IT MAY CONCERN.

IMPORTANT.

Subscribers who have sent in their names for one or more copies of the SATURDAY PRESS need feel no delicacy about remitting the amount of their subscriptions without further invitation.

Non-subscribers who receive this issue of the paper need not feel alarmed, as no other will be sent to them until they become subscribers.

No limit is fixed to the number of subscriptions which any one person may obtain.

The only premiums the proprietor is ready to offer at present will be paid to such persons as prefer to make their remittances in gold.

Persons buying single copies of the paper and not liking it are advised to subscribe by the year: this will give better satisfaction all round.

Subscribers not receiving the paper regularly will please complain at the office in the first instance and after that deliver the carrier over to the police.

Any person procuring a hundred or more subscriptions will have forwarded to him on receipt of the money an acknowledgment of the same accompanied by a certificate of thanks.

Advertisements should be sent in, when convenient, as early as Thursday noon and should in all cases occupy as much space as possible.

Persons having business to transact at the SATURDAY PRESS Office, will find it to be the COOLEST office in the city.

TO CORRESPONDENTS.

Man wants but little here below nor wants that little long.

ALIKE WITH A DIFFERENCE.—The Hotel Delavan in Albany and the Hotel de l'Havane in New York.

THE LAST ROWS OF SUMMER.—The late matches between the Cambridge boys and the Yale fellows well-met of New Haven.

ADVICE.—Never confide secrets to your relatives: blood will tell.

WALL STREET MAXIM.—In a multitude of Counsellors there is wisdom—but it is generally confined to two or three of them.

(For the Saturday Press.)

ARTEMUS WARD
ON
ARRAH NA POGUE.

You ask me, sir, to sling sum ink for your paper in regards to the new Irish dramy at Niblo's Gardin. I will do it, sir.

I knew your grandfather well, sir. Sum 16 years ago, while I was amoosin' and instructin' the intellectooal people of Cape Cod with my justly pop'lar Show, I saw your grandfather. He was then between 96 years of age, but his mind was very clear. He told me I looked like George Washington. He sed I had a massiv intellect. Your grandfather was a highly intelligent man, and I made up my mind then that if I could ever help his family in any way I'd do so. Your grandfather gave me sum clams and a Testament. He charged me for the clams, but threw in the Testament. He was a very fine man.

I therefore write for you, which insures your respectability at once. It gives you a moral tone at the word go.

I found myself the other night at Niblo's Gardin, which is now, by the way, Wheatley's Gardin. (I don't know what's becum of Nib.) I couldn't see not much of a gardin, however, and it struck me if Mr. Wheatley depended on it as regards raisin' things he'd run short of gardin sass. (N. B.—These remarks is yoomerous. The older I gro' the more I want to goak.)

I walked down the ile in my usual dignified stile, politely tellin' the people as I parsed along to keep their seats. "Don't git up for me," I sed. One of the prettiest young men I ever saw in my life showed me into a seat, and I proceeded to while away the spare time by readin' Thompson's BANK NOTE REPORTER and the comic papers.

The ordinance was large.

I tho't, from a cursiry view, that the Finnigan Brotherhood was well represented.

There was no end of bootiful wimin and a heap of good clothes. There was a good deal of hair present that belonged on the heds of peple who didn't cum with it—but this is a ticklish subjeck for me. I larfed at my wife's water-fall, which indoosed that superior woman to take it off and heave it at me rather vilently, and as there was about a half-bushil of it, it knockt me over, and giv me pains in my body which I hain't got over yit.

The orkistry struck up a toon, & I asked the Usher to nudge me when Mr. Pogue cum out on the stage to act.

I wanted to see Pogue, but strange to say, he didn't act durin' the entire evenin'. I reckin he has left Niblo's, and gone over to Barnum's.

Very industrious people are the actors at Barnum's. They play all day and in the evenin' likewise. I meet 'em every mornin', at 5 o'clock, going to their work with their tin dinner-pails. It's a sublime site. Many of 'em sleep on the premises.

Arrah Na Pogue was writ by Dion O'Bourcicolt & Edward McHouse. They rit it well. O'Bourcy has rit a cartload of plays himself, the most of which is fust-rate.

I understand there is a large number of O'-gen'l'men of this city who can rite better plays than O'Bourcy does, but somehow they don't seem to do it. When they do, I'll take a Box of them.

As I remarked to the Boy who squirtid pepper-sass thro' a tin dinner-horn at my trained Bear, (which it caused that feroshus animal to kick up his legs & howl dismal, which fond mothers fell into swoons and children cride to go home because fearin' the Bear would leave his jungle and tear them from limb to limb,) and then excoosed himself (this Boy did) by sayin' he had done so while laborin' under a attack of Moral Insanity—as I sed to that thrifty yooth, "I allus incurridge geenyus, whenever I see it."

It's the same with Dan Bryant. I am informed there are better Irish actors than he is, but somehow I'm allus out of town when they act. & so is other folks, which is what's the matter.

ACK THE 1. Glendalo by moonlite. Irishmen with clubs. This is in 1798, the year of your birth, Mr. Editor. It appears a patriotic person named McCool has bin raisin a insurrection in the mountin districks, and is now goin' to leave the land of his nativity for a tower in France. Previsly to doin so he picks the pockit of Mr. Michael Feemy, a gov'ment detectiv', which pleases the gallery very much indeed, and they joyfully remark "hi, hi." He meets, also at this time a young woman who luvs him dearer than life, and who is, of course, related to the gov'ment; and jus' as the gov'ment goes agin him she goes for him. This is nat'ral, but not grateful. She sez, "And can it be so? Ar, tell me it is not so thusly as this thusness wouldst seem!" or words to that effeck. He sez it isn't any other way, and they go off. Irish moosic by the Band. Mr. McCool goes and givs the money to his foster-sister Miss Arrah Meelish, who is goin' to shortly marry Shaun, the Lamp Post. Mac. then alters his mind about goin' over to France, and thinks he'll go up stairs and lie down in the straw.

"Arrah na Pogue" at Niblo's Garden, 1865.

NEW YORK AUGUST 5, 1865

(For the Saturday Press.)

ARTEMUS WARD

ON

ARRAH NA POGUE.

You ask me, sir, to sling sum ink for your paper in regards to the new Irish dramy at Niblo's Gardin. I will do it, sir.

I knew your grandfather well, sir. Sum 16 years ago, while I was amoosin' and instructin' the intellectooal people of Cape Cod with my justly pop'lar Show, I saw your grandfather. He was then between 96 years of age, but his mind was very clear. He told me I looked like George Washington. He sed I had a massiv intellect. Your grandfather was a highly intelligent man, and I made up my mind then that if I could ever help his family in any way I'd do so. Your grandfather gave me sum clams and a Testament. He charged me for the clams, but threw in the Testament. He was a very fine man.

I therefore write for you, which insures your respectability at once. It gives you a moral tone at the word go.

I found myself the other night at Niblo's Gardin, which is now, by the way, Wheatley's Gardin. (I don't know what's becum of Nib.) I couldn't see not much of a gardin, however, and it struck me if Mr. Wheatley depended on it as regards raisin' things he'd run short of gardin sass. (N. B.—These remarks is yoomerous. The older I gro' the more I want to goak.)

I walked down the ile in my usual dignified stile, politely tellin' the people as I parsed along to keep their seats. "Don't git up for me," I sed. One of the prettiest young men I ever saw in my life showed me into a seat, and I proceeded to while away the spare time by readin' Thompson's Bank Note Reporter and the comic papers.

The ordinance was large.

I tho't, from a cursiry view, that the Finnigan Brotherhood was well represented. There was no end of bootiful wimin and a heap of good clothes. There was a good deal of hair present that belonged on the heds of peple who didn't cum with it—but this is a ticklish subjeck for me. I larfed at my wife's water-fall, which indoosed that superior woman to take it off and heave it at me rather vilently, and as there was about a half-bushil of it, it knockt me over, and giv me pains in my body which I hain't got over yit.

The orkistry struck up a toon, & I asked the Usher to nudge me when Mr. Pogue cum out on the stage to act.

I wanted to see Pogue, but strange to say, he didn't act durin' the entire evenin'. I reckin he has left Niblo's, and gone over to Barnum's.

Very industrious people are the actors at Barnum's. They play all day and in the evenin' likewise. I meet 'em every mornin', at 5 o'clock, going to their work with their tin dinner-pails. It's a sublime site. Many of 'em sleep on the premises.

Arrah Na Pogue was writ by Dion O'Bourcicolt & Edward McHouse. They rit it well. O'Bourcy has rit a cartload of plays himself, the most of which is fust-rate.

I understand there is a large number of O'-gen'l'men of this city who can rite better plays than O'Bourcy does, but somehow they don't seem to do it. When they do, I'll take a Box of them.

As I remarked to the Boy who squirtid pepper-sass thro' a tin dinner-horn at my trained Bear, (which it caused that feroshus animal to kick up his legs & howl dismal, which fond mothers fell into swoons and children cride to go home because fearin' the Bear would leave his jungle and tear them from limb to limb,) and then excoosed himself (this Boy did) by sayin' he had done so while laborin' under a attack of Moral Insanity—as I sed to that thrifty yooth, "I allus incurridge geenyus, whenever I see it."

It's the same with Dan Bryant. I am informed there are better Irish actors than he is, but somehow I'm allus out of town when they act. & so is other folks, which is what's the matter.

Ack the 1. Glendalo by moonlite. Irishmen with clubs. This is in 1798, the year of your birth, Mr. Editor. It appears a patriotic person named McCool has bin raisin a insurrection in the mountin districks, and is now goin' to leave the land of his nativity for a tower in France. Previsly to doin so he picks the pockit of Mr. Michael Feemy, a gov'ment detectiv', which pleases the gallery very much indeed, and they joyfully remark "hi, hi." He meets, also at this time a young woman who luvs him dearer than life, and who is, of course, related to the gov'ment; and jus' as the gov'ment goes agin him she goes for him. This is nat'ral, but not grateful. She sez, "And can it be so? Ar, tell me it is not so thusly as this thusness wouldst seem !" or words to that effeck. He sez it isn't any other way, and they go off. Irish moosic by the Band. Mr. McCool goes and givs the money to his foster-sister Miss Arrah Meelish, who is goin' to shortly marry Shaun, the Lamp Post. Mac. then alters his mind about goin' over to France, and thinks he'll go up stairs and lie down in the straw. This is in Arrah's cabin. Arrah says its all right, me darlint, och hone, and shure, and other pop'lar Irish remarks, and Mac. goes to his straw.

The weddin' of Shaun and Arrah comes off. Great excitement. Immense demonstration on the part of the peasantry. Barn-door jigs, and rebelyus song by McHouse called "The Drinkin' of the Gin." Ha, what is this? Soldiers cum in. Moosic by the Band. "Arrah," sez the Major, "you have those money. She sez, Oh no, I guess not. He sez, Oh yes, I guess you have. It is my own, sez she, and exhibits it. It is mine, sez Mr. Feeny—and identifies it. Great confusion. Coat is prodoosed from up stairs. Whose coat is this, sez the Major. Is it the coat of a young man secreted in this here cabin? Now this is rough on Shaun. His wife accoosed of theft, the circumstances bein very much agin her, and also accoosed of havin a hansum young man hid in her house. But does this bold young Hibernian forsake her? Not much, he don't. But he takes it all on himself—sez he is the guilty wretch, and is marcht off to prison.

This is a new idee. It is gin'rally the wife who suffers, in the play, for her husband; but here's a noble young feller who shuts both his eyes to the apparent sinfulness of his new young wife, and takes her right square to his boosom. It was bootiful to me, who love my wife, and believe in her, and would put on my meetin' clothes and go to the gallus for her cheerfully, ruther than believe she was capable of taking anybody's money but mine. My married friends, listen to me: If you treat your wives as tho' they were perfeck gentlemen—if you show 'em that you have entire confidence in them, believe 'me, they will be troo to you, most always. I was so pleased with this conduck of Shaun that I hollered out, "Good boy! Come and see me !" "Silence!" sum peple sed. "Put him out!" sed a sweet-scented young man, with all his new clothes on, and in company with a splendid waterfall, "put this old feller out!" " My young friend," I sed, in a loud voice, "whose store do you sell tape in? I might want to buy a yard before I go hum."

Shaun is tried by a Military Commission. Col. O'Grady, altho' a member of the Commission, shows he sympathizes with Shaun, and twits Feeny, the Gov'ment witness, with being a knock-kneed thief, &c., &c. Mr. Stanton's grandfather was Sec'y of War in Ireland at that time, so this was entirely proper. Shaun is convicted, and goes to jail. Hears Arrah singin' outside. Wants to see her a good deal. A lucky thought strikes him: he opens the window and gets out. Struggles with ivy and things on the outside of the jail, and finally reaches her just as Mr. Feeny is about to dash a large wooden stone onto his head. He throws Mr. F. into the river. Pardon arrives. Fond embraces. Tears of joy and kisses à la Pogue. Everybody much happy. Curtin falls.

This is a very hasty outline of a splendid play. Go and see it.

See the beautiful Josie Orton, whose brilliant eyes and sweet winnin' ways made me wish I was Shaun, the lamp-post, myself, even without my parent's consent.

See Mr. Glenny, who is one of the quietest and Irishest of Irishmen—a true artist and a fine singist, if there is one out of the operer.

See Mr. Scallan's powerful and admirable personation of the unpleasant little villain Feeny.

See the genial actor, Mr. Burnett, (O'Grady) whose tavern at Cincinnati I have often stopped at.

See Mr. Norton as the Secretary. He reminds me of Secretary Seward so much that I call him Bill every time I meet him.

See the excellent Mr. Peters, who is so good a cockney servant that we all want to go up on the stage and kick him a little.

In short, see all of 'em. Then go down to Wallack's, and see Dan Bryant, one of the best of living Irish actors, in Colleen Bawn. If you know of a better Irish actor, send him to me, postage paid, and I will keep him.

Yours, till then, A. Ward.

(For the Saturday Press.)

THE KINGDOM OF RESERVE.

BY ADA CLARE.

"Lear.—Nothing can come of nothing; speak again.

"Cordelia.—Unhappy that I am, I cannot heave my heart into my mouth. I love your majesty according to my bond; nor more nor less."—King Lear.

If there is one thing more unsparingly satirized and girded against than another, in these modern days, it is the one of impulsive or emotional speech. Words have been coined, or rather exceptional meanings fitted to existing words, in order to apply more effectively the torture of irony to it. We see it for instance afflicted with the definitive title of "gushing," than which no word could be a greater plague to a quality. So much has been said on the subject, that no one would think the absence of expression was the absolute pledge of depth of feeling. To be reserved is to be true as well as profound; to be reticent is to have infinities of unsaid wisdoms in concealment.

And yet what is there really to admire in the quality of reserve, unless it suggests the accumulation of thought, to be duly expressed when the time is ripe; or what is the value of reticence, unless it arises from such experience, both in emotion and its outward signs, that one has learned so thoroughly to master it, as to repress it in those moments where vivacity would be folly, tenderness would be vulgarity, and impulsiveness a want of self-respect.

It never seems to occur to most people, that silence sometimes proceeds from having nothing to say, rather than from a power of repressing speech; or that the much lauded faculty of self-restraint may be the offspring simply of emotional emptiness. A man may be a self-container, not because he is so great as to contain unsounded depths, but because he has precious little to contain.

However profound a man might be, it would be certainly a very useless depth, to say the least, if nothing were ever to proceed from it. Of course it is the best of virtues in a body of water, (and so by analogy in a human character) to be deep, but it is wonderfully improved as to purity, if it have an occasional, if not a continual outlet.

It would be a curious study for some of the scholars to dig out of the past the root from which this intense worship of reserve sprang up, to overshadow the whole Anglo-saxon tongue. For it is only among races born English as to speech, literature, and customs that this perpetual altar-fire is kindled to the worship of the goddess of Reserve. If any one doubts this general worship, let him try exhibiting the simplest and most harmless traits of human nature in public places, and then watch the indignant consternation it will excite. When I speak of simple traits, I mean, to laugh when one is merry, or to express happiness, amusement, content, animal spirits, even by the language of the features. A party, in an English restaurant for instance, (when I say English of course I refer to all those where the English language reigns supreme) may feel pleased with themselves, with each other, with the viands, and all attending circumstances, but if they dare to express it by seeming lively, happy and merry, see how the frown of suspicion and contempt instantly lowers over them like a thunder-cloud charged with black and angry electricity. However contented, pleased, free from care they may be, they must look dissatisfied, afflicted, and gloomy, unless they desire to come under the adverse criticism of the majority of their fellow-beings.

The theatres too—they are supposed to be places of amusement, and that we go there to enjoy ourselves. No such thing. They are places of distress, and we go there to see how dismal we can look. I don't know about the upper gallery. I believe it to be the most sensible portion of the audience, from the way in which it leads us with signs of genuine appreciation and animation, but I know how people are expected to look in the fashionable parts of the house. The men are to look as if their minds were entirely absorbed in something else, (stocks and scrip perhaps,) and they were moreover shortly expecting an interview with the undertaker. The women are to look scornful, suspicious, and implacable. I take it on faith, these looks are very creditable to humanity, very dignified, and all that sort of rubbish, but they are certainly not very pleasant. I am pleased to record, however, an exception to this leaden uniformity, which may be remarked at such matinées as Edwin Booth's, for example. The young girls did permit themselves to be animated over his performances, and to gaze upon them with their lovely faces all alight with enjoyment and enthusiasm, and I am forced to confess that I loved them for it.

In my ignorance, let me ask, why, in a world where we are liable to lose our hair, get cheated in business, broken in heart, bereft of our property, and parted from our beauty, where we are liable to old age, death, and the neuralgia, do we take it upon ourselves to tenderly nurture gloom, and assume low spirits and repulsiveness to be the chief among the virtues? Do not our digestive organs and our complexions fade earlier and oftener than those of other nations; and has the cultivation of moroseness nothing to do with it?

Besides, this procrustean rule makes hypocrites of some of us. For my own poor part, I dote on a hearty "weep" over a tragedy, but it is an indulgence I grant myself but seldom. I generally set up St. Simeon

Stylites in his most stolid moments, as the model of facial expression, and aim at it with an industry unworthy of so bad a cause. Again, see me in a saloon after a theatre, with some dainty little morsel before me, for which I am glad and thankful to the kind providing fates, but do I show it? No, not I. I accept the understood formula that the table is a bier, from which I, a ghoul, am taking a ghoul's feast, and regulate my countenance accordingly. If this eternal laudation of grim reserve can make such a silly little hypocrite of me, how do I know but the same film of grave humbug is masking over other faces that would like to smile and seem cheerful.

This affectation of reserve does not exhaust itself in public places, but it extends through the whole line of domestic life, like the mildewed ear blasting its wholesome brothers. Expressions of feeling, "gushing," as it is cruelly called, are forbidden between friendly, parental, filial, or conjugal relations. However antagonistic we may be in other things, we are all united in a horror of scenes. I believe a scene means with us, the least laxness of rein given to the heart and its impulses. We choose to have our lives all levelled smoothly down with the great garden-roller of uniformity. And yet we see how nature varies her scenes with hill and vale. She is not afraid of bursting into a Vesuvius or a Niagara.

Judging from our own experience we know how a little burst of kindness, tenderness, or praise affects us; how it pierces straight to our hearts, unburdens, and sweeps them on their daily way, like a healthsome breeze which unfurls a chafing, idly flapping sail.

It is all very well for the husband, father, brother to have what is called a "sturdy" love for a woman, an affection that will bear up tempests as well as calms; yet that is but a sad staunchness at best. For after all, women want to be cherished, comforted, cheered in the daily routine of life, rather than assured of protection in storm. Few people really encounter tempests in life; what they suffer from is the array of little weary ills, which everybody is too grave to alleviate. When true tempests come, we must stand alone; we may not look to human love, however strong, for help; and while tossed about on lonely seas look for succor only to Him who holdeth the waters in the hollow of his hand.

Once in a while it happens whole nations give the lie to our pet theory, that goodness is synonymous with stolidity, and worth with dullness. Witness the Italian nation, which we had long considered effeminate, given over to trifles and frivolities, and quite incapable of any national virility. But when it was tried in the ordeal of war it arose and threw off its yoke, quietly, firmly, and without any of that sickening self-conceit, and laudation which other nations, priding themselves upon the possession of the whole panoply of manly virtues, have so often exhibited. In the face of that valor, simplicity, and earnestness which then wrapped all Italy as with a garment, does any one dare to call that nation worth less and effete? No, by the heads of a Cavour, a Garibaldi, I will answer no! And yet, were they not ever a romancing, singing, laughing, demonstrative, "gushing" people.

Just because *all* that glitters is not gold, people will have it, nothing that glitters is gold. The *glitter* of gold is as truly one of its inherent properties, as its denseness, solidity, rarity, and, in fact, quite as useful as any of them. Otherwise, tin and iron would be just as precious.

By this time, any reader I may have been so fortunate as to preserve thus far, will have concluded I have but one idea in nature—the babbling brook. But, indeed, I love still deep waters, if only because, under a pressure, they are capable of roaring the loudest, and rushing the fastest. Also, I revere that reticence which is the still, holy calm of a rich, mellowed nature. The reticence which covers up the well-spring of its feeling, that free from the dust of common things, it may be strong to flow in crystal streams, to the life that comes weary and athirst to it for comfort.

In all nature I know nothing finer than when a really true, highly-toned soul, in a moment of expansion, drops the veil, and for a brief moment makes visible its longings, ardors, aspirations. I love reticence, when I find it the soil where the seed of such moments can lie covered up until the time come for them to burst through and bloom.

I know well enough how much could be said on the other side of the question, and I know some of the things that should be said, but I am not going to say them. The other side is too strong already. Every one knows its virtues: even those who run may read them, but for its evils the majority of people are blind.

Before closing, I will refer to one of the most noted characters of the reserve school. I refer to Shakespeare's "Cordelia."

"Cordelia" believed silence to be the measure of truth, never seeming to remember that saying too little is often just as false as saying too much. She underrated her affection for her father as much as her sisters overrated theirs, and the one circumstance had as disastrous consequences as the other. That "Lear" was a horribly foolish old man we cannot doubt; but that "Cordelia" loved him better than her husband or her life the events of the play proved, when she came back for his sake to loose both of them. But she would sooner see herself banished, and him given over to a pair of female vultures than tell him so. She was untrue through the excess of her devotion to facts, and in her eagerness to fulfill the letter of the law, she violated its spirit. That the other sisters expressed so much, and felt nothing, does not shame me at all; that sort of artificial exuberance of speech no more resembles real expression of feeling than the rank, sickening weeds that run riot over the unkempt earth do the crowding sweetness of the violet and heliotrope beds. If once "Cordelia" had deigned to give words to that true depth of loving tenderness which welled beneath her breast, the spurious passion of her sisters would, in its light, have glared with brazen and bawdy falseness. Her father wished not only to be loved, but he wished to have sweet verbal pledges of it. He wanted her, in other words, to "gush," and had she but "gushed," she would have been beside him, in possession of the greater part of his kingdom, to succor him; to keep the rapacity and cruelty of her sisters in check. He would not have been turned into the storm houseless by night; she herself had not died an ignominious death, and the world would have been deprived of the sublimest tragedy recorded in the literary annals of this planet.

HOW TO WRITE WAR LYRICS.

In order to be original as well as effective, make the first words of the first line "Dear Mother," or "Dearest Mother," or "Darling Mother." You *must* have a Mother of some kind; it is difficult to see how you can do without one. If you refrain from doing this, at the commencement, you must commence doing it in the refrain.

If you have concluded to Come Home to Die (although such a course cannot be unconditionally recommended), say so at once, and bring it in in the chorus.

Sometimes call the person you are addressing "Thee," and sometimes "You;" it looks Singular as well as Plural.

Whenever you have occasion to use the word "Memories," be careful to say, "Memories of the Past." This evinces closeness of thought, and is a pleasing distinction from the Memories of the Future. Never forget—nor allow any one else to forget—that you might have been "Numbered with the Slain." You may make Slain rhyme with Again.

In the event of your dying, it would be an excellent point to inquire, in general terms, as to the intentions of society at large, with regard to the pecuniary maintenance of the aged members of your family. For instance, "Who will care for Mother now?"

When you have occasion to refer to any of your imaginary companions who are so unfortunate as to be defunct, say "The *silent* Dead." It removes misapprehension.

If, upon mature deliberation, you decide upon dying, request your comrades to observe the various phenomena of your physical condition, such as your perspiring forehead, or, to express it poetically, the "Dampness on your Brow." As this idea, however, has now grown rather stale, perhaps it would be better to ask them to look at your Tongue, or to feel your Pulse.

If you can contrive to mention that some one is sleeping *beneath* the sod, instead of above it, this would be an admirable idea. You cannot be too explicit upon this point, since it saves time in the recovery of bodies.

—Mrs. Grundy.

The Fenians are fast getting to be a power. Their festival at Jones' Wood, the other day, was one of the most imposing demonstrations we have had in New York this long time. Seeing that their only object is to have Ireland governed by the Irish, we wish them every success. If Ireland can stand it, we are sure that we can. We object decidedly however to New York being governed by the Irish; the experiment has been tried too long already and has cost enough to rebuild the city.

C. Pfaff's.—This famous Bohemian resort has recently been improved by the addition of a large garden and a "beautiful landscape," designed by the artists of a neighboring theatre. A wag wrote upon the walls of the establishment, the other day, *"C. Pfaff and die!"*

The Inquirer of Philadelphia gives an account of a fire in that city which was extinguished by the application of a copious supply of water to the burning material. This method of extinguishing fires has been practiced in New York for many years, and the fact that it has been found equally efficacious in Philadelphia will probably lead to its being continued by our new department.

NEW YORK AUGUST 12, 1865

(For the Saturday Press.)

THE RISE OF THE WATERFALL.

Everybody feminine with any pretension to style has worn, and everybody masculine with any pretension to taste has criticized the waterfall. Yet few either of the feminines who wear or who have worn, or the masculines who criticize or who have criticized, know anything of the history of the waterfall—of its early elaborateness and beauty. They think—if they think about it at all—that it originated in the fertile brain of Eugenie, whereas she adopted it from the English, and wore it with undisguised delight as something particularly adapted to her pretty head and the shining masses of her sunny hair.

The waterfall made its *début* under the appellation of "The Niagara Coiffure," at a court ball given by her Majesty in honor of the enthusiastic reception of the Prince of Wales in America, and to celebrate the occasion of his safe return.

The rage at that period was for things American, and many and rich were the *souvenirs de l'Amerique* in the royal possession; among them were Frankenstein's "Falls of Niagara."

That work of art suggested that other work of art, the "Coiffure de Niagara," since commonly known as the waterfall.

But how art thou fallen, O waterfall, since the day when the daughters of the proudest nobility in the world wore thee in triumph and in gladness! How art thou fallen since the day when the virgins of Albion wore thee in honor of the return of their prince from hyperborean realms, "where everything 's so vast!"

A glance at the picture that suggested it will be necessary to a proper understanding of the waterfall, before it had fallen from its high estate.

Our artists have ever painted waterfalls as monotonous sheets of a blueish or grayish color, falling—if they could be said to fall—with the most perfect drawing-room propriety. But waterfalls in *jets,* not in straight lines, and the more force impelling the fall the more distinct will these jets be, and the more fringed and fretted and elaborate.

The picture referred to is one of the finest models of falling water in Europe. Therein the jetting action is powerfully and exquisitely represented. This characteristic was imitated in "The Niagara Coiffure" with marked success.

The long blonde hair of Britannia's daughters was combed back from the brow in full heavy waves. When it reached the back slope of the head, which represents the brink of the precipice over which the waters flow, it loses its billowy character and falls in jets. These jets are short irregular curls, very small, and of that class called "frizzes." These are repeated, expanding as they reach the base of the head, where they fall, breaking on a heavy necklace of precious stones and pearly foam, and waves of green, which represent the river at the foot of the falls. The "fall" was powdered profusely with pearl or diamond dust, which glittered and gleamed in the gas-light like veritable water in the light of the sun—or as much, "in like manner," as was possible.

Spanning the fall, a little below the brink, was a glowing arch representing the rainbow. Expanse—an essential thing in representing Niagara—was given to the top of the head by conducting the waves of the side hair over archways of mosses and shells and sea-weed; portions of which, in prescribed places, jutted above the waves, thus forming islands of beauty and verdure in the "watery waste." In front they presented the appearance of cool open caves, the chambers of some being hung with stalactites.

This was the origin of the "mice" that girls wear to make themselves look like flat-heads. But these greasy little heads, around which the hair is tightly twisted, are not more unlike the arches that they grow out of than are the long, lank, straggling frowsy curls, or the clumsy, greasy over-grown bags of hair, that American girls wear on their necks, like the elaborate "Niagara Coiffure" of the Court of St. James.

Ninita.

A POINT OF ETIQUETTE.

Many humorous stories are told of the absurd height to which the observance of etiquette has been carried at both Oxford and Cambridge. You might meet a good fellow at a wine party, crack your joke with him, hob-nob, etc.—but, unless introduced, you would have been stared at with the most vacant wonderment, if you attempted to recognize him the next day. It is told of men of both universities, that a scholar walking on the banks of the Isis, or Cam, fell into the river, and was in the act of drowning, when —another son of Alma-Mater came up, and observing his perilous situation, exclaimed, "What a pity it is I have not the honor of knowing the gentleman, that I might save him!" One version of the story runs, that the said scholars met by accident on the banks of the Nile or Ganges, I forget which, when the catastrophe took place; we may, therefore, very easily imagine the presence either of a crocodile or an alligator to complete the group.

WHAT THE WORLD SAYS.

The World has ope'd its "ponderous and marble jaws" and let off a paragraph about our little sheet which is worth copying. It is headed "A Disorderly Crowd," and reads thus:

The Nantucket millionaire, Henry C. Junior, [meaning, thereby, Henry Clapp Jr,] has revived the Saturday Press. Mr. J. Banks [meaning, thereby, Mr. A. F. Banks] late of the army, is understood to be the scientific editor; Wartemus Hard [meaning, thereby, Artemus Ward] the financial reporter; Arnold, By-George [meaning, thereby, George Arnold] the permanent basis; Frank Hay-Kill [meaning, thereby, Frank Cahill] the distributing agent; Mr. Rogers, the new contributor; Darles Chawson Shannon [meaning, thereby Charles Dawson Shanly] the market reporter; Mr. Plaff [meaning, thereby, Mr. Pfaff] the managing editor; Dr. Hingston, the American humorist; Medward Ullen [meaning, thereby, Edward Mullen] the fashion-editor; Wintry Hill [meaning, thereby, William Winter] fighting editor: This powerful combination entitles any new publication to an immediate popularity.

We are sorry to break up the author's continuity of thought by so many explanatory parentheses, but his wit is so subtle that, without some such elucidation, the public might fail to appreciate one of the most elegant *jeux d'esprit* of the season. What wonder that a paper which can throw off such brilliant scintillations every day should circulate from town's-end to town's-end.

LETTER FROM OLIVE LOGAN.

Saratoga, *August 9th.*

You dear, darling old Press.

Only to think you are alive again, and looking as pretty and fresh as sweet sixteen looks when it hasn't been to a ball overnight and got up the next morning to a late breakfast in most unbecoming *déshabille!*

I wanted to write a few lines for your first number, to wish you God speed and to throw my old shoe after you for luck, you know, and all that sort of thing, but Fate and the Doctors decreed it otherwise; which means that I have been very ill, and have been sent up here with the assurance that the waters would have an immediate effect on me. They have done so. They have made me worse. As for seeking health here, going after the bubble reputation even at the cannon's mouth, is a far more satisfactory proceeding. There is too much severe dressing going on to think of anything else; and as for health, what is it after all, compared to chequered ankle boots with military heels?

Still, I don't think you missed my contribution.

How could you, having as you did that long communication from Artemus Ward, who comes out brilliantly as a theatrical critic; though what his Betsey Jane and the twins think of his eulogy on Miss Orton's eyes is more than I can understand. But he is funny, isn't he, when he says, he'll "take a box" of authors? If clever writers were put in boxes, don't you think Artemus would have a *lo*(d)*ge* all to himself?

And then, that sweet, pensive article on "Reserve," from Ada Clare, which is so admirably worded, so gently persuasive in its tone that it makes us all want to go and love every body indiscriminately and at once! But I wish you would tell Miss Ada (if you know her) that she is treading on very delicate ground in her paper. Suppose some susceptible youth, after reading her article, were to become expansive towards her! in case of a reprimand he could justly reply—Lo, your article!

I tell you, Mr. Press, it won't do for a pretty young woman, with blonde hair and tender eyes, to invite "gushing." It's dangerous. And then the pioneer critic, Figaro, who writes as delightfully as a ripe orange tastes, and who can make a long criticism on Nothing and Nobody (whom he is often called upon to review,) more interesting than other people's "exhaustive" criticisms on the last new play; he is with you again! No, decidedly. You didn't "miss me at home."

But while you are getting out your newspaper, you are not seeing the races at Saratoga, as I am.

It is glorious sport. Miss Pithole, from Pennsylvania, had a new hat direct from Paris, and there were three heats in a mile; or three miles in a heat, I forget which. But the second day the excitement was intense. Off they started so well together, you might have covered them with a blanket; when they came back, victorious and otherwise, they were covered with a blanket. The brown filly only a nose ahead of the bay mare; while the graceful jockey, Gilpatrick, standing in his stirrups and leaning foward as if about to receive infantine and scholastic castigation, let Oliata out a link, showing daylight between her and Nannie Butler, giving Thunder to Asteroid, leaving Lord Monmouth a bad fourth, and Mary Howell nowhere. Immense excitement at the betting-pool, and somebody tells me I owe them a pair of gloves.

I conclude I won't go to-day, for divers reasons:

The road is dusty; the sun is hot; the rose is red; the violet blue, and so am I.

There are vast quantities of pretty girls here, who would be so much prettier if they would only dress themselves more simply, and somewhat in accordance with their years. Fancy a girl of eighteen trailing a white *moire antique* robe de chambre about the sloppy regions of the Spring, at seven o'clock in the morning! Or a matron of forty-five, attired in a white muslin *corsage à la vièrge* and a Roman scarf, tripping lightly to the table d'hote at the Union. Simple coquetry has faded out now, and bold folly, saucy and obtrusive, stands defiantly in its place. Until this is reformed, let us talk no more of the frivolity and recklessness of foreign women.

Not to be behind Baden and Hamburg, even in naughtiness, there is a club-house here, where people go and bet money on the *tapis vert.* At least so I am told. I never go myself, for though I am a player, I am not a better.

It seems the Cuban ladies particularly affect this style of amusement, and the story runs that the young Count C—— won six thousand dollars of Madame de H—— the other night at *rouge et noir.*

(Are not initials piquant, and mysterious? I think the forgoing paragraph looks very striking.)

Yes, that is the story, and I believe it; that is, I believe it is a story.

Of course there is a daily paper here, which contains less news than any I ever saw. It has that peculiarity, and as such is unique in its way. The greater portion of its space is occupied by a sort of chronicle of arrivals at the different hotels, in the New York style, with a commendable difference. It is this: a family is announced as,

"Mr. & Mrs. Snobs, 4 *h.* and *d.*"

Which being interpreted, means that a wretched vulgarian has come here with his wife and has also brought four horses and daughter. But whether it is the daughter of the horses, or the daughter of the Snobs, remains to be explained.

I remember your injunctions to correspondents, and say no more, though much remains to be told. If it interests you, I may write again; but in any case, and not a bit likely to be altered by circumstances. I am,

My dear Press,

Your friend,

Olive Logan.

NEW YORK AUGUST 19, 1865

Dion Boucicault

JOHN OAKHEART AND SON.

BY DION BOUCICAULT.

John Oakheart and Son are Baltic merchants. Young John entered his father's office as a clerk, at sixty pounds a year, of which he paid his mother forty for his board, lodging and washing, and clothed himself with the odd twenty. Do not imagine that Mr. Oakheart's establishment required this assistance. The old gentleman desired to make his son feel independent—he was a man, he earned his own livelihood, and he should feel that he supported himself. At twenty-five years of age, young Oakheart marries, receiving with his wife a moderate sum of money. He wants to purchase a share in his father's business; they cannot come to terms. Young John can make a better bargain with a rival house in the trade. The old man hesitates: he likes the sound of John Oakheart and Son; but business is business. Had his son married a penniless girl, the father would have given him what he now refuses to sell; but now, business is business, and as a calculation, he can't do it. So young John becomes chief partner in a rival firm to that which must one day be his, and trades against the old man, whose only aim is to lay up wealth for his son.

Every day at four o'clock, leaning against a particular corner on 'Change, stands the elder merchant, his hands deeply sunk into his dogs'-eared pockets. A young city man approaches; they exchange a quiet careless nod:

"Feel inclined to discount for 1,200 at long date?"

"What security?" asks old John.

"Turkish, '54."

"Ay names?"

"My own only; it is a private matter, and has nothing to do with our house," replies the younger man. "I will give four per cent."

"I should want more than that, as money goes—say 4⅝."

"The brokers only ask 4½," replies the young man.

"Then give it." And they separate with an indifferent nod. That was father and son.

Every Sunday young John and his wife dine at Russell Square, in the same house where old Oakheart has lived for thirty years. His name has been cleaned out of the brass plate on the door. This house young John still looks upon, and speaks of as his home. All the associations of his childhood are there—every piece of furniture is an old friend—every object is sacred in his eyes, from his own picture, taken at four years old, with its chubby face and fat legs, to the smoke-dried print of General Abercrombie. They form the architecture of that temple of his heart—his home.

After dinner the ladies have retired. The crimson curtains are comfortably closed. The crackling fire glows with satisfaction, and old John pushes the bottle across to his son, for if old John has a weakness, it is for tawney port.

"Jack, my boy," says he, "what do you want with 1200 pounds?" "Well, Sir," replies young John, "there is a piece of ground next to my villa at Brixton, and they threaten to build upon it—if so, they will spoil our view. Emily," meaning his wife, "has often begged me to buy it, and inclose it in our garden. Next Wednesday is her birthday, and I wish to gratify her with a surprise; but I have reconsidered the matter—I ought not to afford it—so I have given it up."

"Quite right, Jack," responded the old man, "it would have been a piece of extravagance "and the subject drops.

Next Wednesday, being Emily's birthday, the old couple dine with the young folks. Just before dinner, old John takes his daughter-in-law aside, and places in her hands a parchment—it is the deed of the little plot of ground she coveted. He stops her thanks with a kiss and hurries away.

Ere the ladies retire, Emily finds time to whisper the secret to her husband. And the father and son are alone. Watch the old man's eyes fixed on the fire, for he has detected this piece of affectionate treachery, and is almost ashamed of his act, because he does not know how to receive his son's thanks. For a few moments a deep, gentle feeling broods the young man's heart, he has no words—it is a prayer syllabled in emotions that makes his lips tremble; he lays his hand upon his father's arm and their eyes meet.

"Tut, Jack, sir! pooh! sir, it must all come to you some day—God bless you, my boy, and make you as happy at my age as I am now." In silence the souls of those men embrace. But who is that seraph that gathers them beneath her outspread angel wings? I have seen her at the fireside fluttering like a dove from bosom to bosom. I have seen her linking distant hearts, parted by the whole world—she is the good genius of the Anglo-Saxon family—and her name is Home.

LETTER FROM OLIVE LOGAN.

SARATOGA, *August* 15*th*.

MY DEAR PRESS:—

Just as we were all going into church last Sunday (a beautiful little Episcopalian chapel, with stained glass windows, where there is a lot of pigeons, who live up in the cloisters, and amuse themselves by flying about during service, which is picturesque, but rather distracting to the attention), I heard a boy cry out,

"Here yall Satudy papers! Who wants New York Satudy papers?"

Who wanted them? Why I did, to be sure, so letting Mére get on a few steps (she doesn't allow us to traffic on Sundays) I took out the very fifty cent bill I had destined for the "collection," and changed the same to buy a SATURDAY PRESS, I opened it hastily, and when I saw you had put in my nonsense which I wrote you last week, I blushed so it actually caused me pain; and when I read the pretty compliment you paid me, I positively could have kissed the paper (as I always do somebody's letters) except that it was Sunday, and a great crowd thronging into church. Just at that moment, through the mass of people, came my friend Mr. T——, working his way up to me.

"Did you write that letter in the SATURDAY PRESS?" he inquired.

As I didn't exactly know what criticism he was going to make, I felt half inclined to deny it.

"It's wonderful," he said, grasping my hand, and getting lost again in the crowd.

I didn't know what to make of that. Things that are wonderful are not always nice. There are wonderful and hideous monstrosities in doctor's shops, such as snakes with two heads and babies with none at all. "Wonderful" was open to conjecture.

I was conjecturing upon it, when Miss Oligarch and her mother came up to me. These poor ladies are from the South, and are living in abject penury at the Clarendon Hotel here, only paying twenty dollars a day board. They have been robbed of everything by this inhuman government. I feel very sorry for them, and wish some one would "wrong" me in the same manner.

"Is this you, dear ?" asked Mrs. Oligarch, who is very near-sighted.

"I think so," I replied. Indeed I felt quite certain on this point.

"We read your letter in the SATURDAY PRESS."

"Yes?" I inquired, with a good deal of *nonchalance*.

"Yes; and we laughed at it very much. Here, Melinda, take your prayer-book—are my flounces down behind?"

This was even a stranger criticism than the other. I don't think anybody likes to be laughed at. I don't, for one; do you?

But at length, putting these criticisms together, I came to the conclusion, with the characteristic vanity of womankind, that it was all meant to be complimentary; and by the time I had entered the church, I had so worked on my own imagination that, like the comic review of the virtuous young man in Solon Shingle, I exclaimed madly to myself, "Great heavens, how brilliant I am!" There were no seats to be had, but I cared not. I felt convinced that somebody, recognizing my brilliancy, would rise for my accommodation.

No one did.

But what is home without a mother? She had extended her hoops, a thus held for me a secured seat, without extra charge. I slipped in, and bowing my head, said a little prayer, which was not exempt from the silliness of a foolish flattered woman.

"Oh Lord, look down upon a brilliant, humble sinner."

Just before the sermon commenced, I heard a little conversation going on behind me.

"Do you see this lady here in front of us ?"

Another allusion to my brilliancy, I knew it would be.

"Well, that collar she's got on is real *point d'Alençon.*"

The big Indian, Red Jacket, and his tomahawk, could not have been more savage than I at this. The information given was totally incorrect, too, as the collar, changed at some unknown period by a remorseless washerwoman, and which I wear because it fits me, is of an extremely fine quality regarding it as lace. Somehow this little episode breaks up my ideas of brilliancy, and makes me think of the instability of human affairs, and wish it were dinner time. However, I determined to write to you again. You have given me an inch; you may take an L.

Saturday was the last day of the great Saratoga races, which opened finely, but which diminished greatly in interest towards the end. The truth is, six days' racing is too much for even the best regulated horses, and I think that, beyond a few people who had bet their money on favorite animals, trainers, and jockies, (not that I mean trainers and jockies are animals,) there was but a sorry attendance on Saturday.

The whole place is posted with small handbills, announcing that John Morrissey lost four thousand dollars on the race-course, for which he offers a reward of five hundred dollars. But who would have the temerity to approach the ex-prize-fighter, hoping to receive five hundred dollars for a mere act of duty? I am sure I would not do so, unless I wished to receive a gratuitous lesson in the mysteries of the P. R.

But from grave to gay, from lively to severe, I have been going through a good deal of what is facetiously termed amusement lately, and feel it incumbent on me, as I am writing for a newspaper, to speak of that delirious thing. But never a word will you get me to say about the exquisite toilette of the beautiful Miss A, or the fascinating Mrs. B, or the too lovely widow C; each, by a singular coincidence, the belle of the hotel in which she lives, *and they all live in the same one*. Ah, Mr. PRESS, you may talk as you will, but the bell which sounds at three o'clock precisely, has much more music in it than the silly clatter of the other belles, which lasts from the time they get up till the time they get down; and at what o'clock that is, *Dieu sait*.

I hope you will never ask me to write your fashion article. The most unintelligible stuff in the world to me is that strange mélange, which I may dub "fashion-French." "A *jupe* trimmed with three *bouillons*; *taffetas* garnished *en tablier*." Is not this fearful?

Does or does not *bouillon* mean soup? Think of a dress trimmed with three *bouillons*!

They would wear dresses trimmed with soup here if they could get them. The taste exhibited is something simply outrageous. Now, I hold that I am a competent and an unprejudiced observer. I am not very old yet, my liver is active, my spirits cheery; I have not been disappointed in love, and am ignorant of the pangs of the toothache. Therefore it cannot be said that I look upon life, youth, and gaiety with a jaundiced eye. But I persist in stating, that the fascinating Miss Zero, walking about the grounds of the Union in the afternoon, before dinner, in a full dress ball toilette, *tulle* skirts, cherry silk, short tunic, bare arms and neck, with the highly appropriate addition of a parasol, is a fit mark for any one to fly shafts of ridicule at. Poor creatures! They pay dearly for their folly. How much they looked as if they envied me, who dare be unfashionable, and wear whatever I will, and be comfortable, But they are nothing, unless they show their money, and to this end a lady, with a cheerful regard for the *apropos*, appeared the other night, at a ball at the Union, in a *black velvet* dress.

Think of it, shade of Fahrenheit! and Fahrenheit eighty in the shade!–—a black velvet in August! But a black velvet costs a great many dollars a yard and gets spoken of in the newspapers. As for diamonds, they are positively a drug in the market. It is not affectation to say that I am really disenchanted with this valuable stone, as it is worn so constantly here, and with so little discrimination. I thought it was well understood that diamonds were exclusively ornaments for the evening; but here we see them from seven o'clock in the morning till midnight, flashing away, faintly or grandly as the case may be.

If the editor of the SATURDAY PRESS has any idea of presenting me with a brooch, ear-rings, or finger-ring, set with brilliants, I trust he will avoid the genus "cluster," as it is now a distinguishing mark of gentility not to wear that style, especially in rings which loom ominously from vulgar and insignificant forefingers.

We hear that a great number of persons left here after the racing week, but I can only say their absence is unremarked. Others coming fill the places of the departed as the incoming wave rushes in where its fellow flowed away into the ocean's infinite space.

A grand fancy dress ball is announced to take place at one of the large hotels next Friday evening, which inquisitorial torture I shall avoid.

In the afternoon it is rather pleasant, because of the shade, to sit in the grounds of the Union Hotel, where between the hours of four and five there is music. The Messrs. Leland sparing no pains to make their house attractive to guests, have engaged the very worst brass band I ever listened to.

This is a nice place for fires. The houses are almost all built of wood, and there is absolutely no water about. This is strange, considering the number of springs which abound. But the minute a house catches fire, you may know it is gone. Not a vestige of it remains. Last year the Water-Cure, an immense establishment, and this year the United States Hotel and the Marion House, besides other buildings which lay adjacent, were totally destroyed.

It is estimated that the village has lost more by the absence of those persons who would have filled these hotels than it would cost to build a reservoir of ample dimensions. This is, to say the least of it, penny wise and gallons foolish.

As I observed last week, there are more things to be told than this; but I will only tell them little by little. This is out of regard for you. Just so sure as you eat too many of the plums in your pudding, just so sure are you to be ill. And so with Saratoga. Take too much of it, and you may send at once for Dr. Kramp.

Witness the girls who come up here to be in the country, and who, what with late hours, and balls, and rides, and flirting, go back to town looking hollow-eyed and worn-out and decidedly ill. Never do you adopt such a course, dear PRESS, because it might spoil your beauty.

Determined, as I cannot cure you, not to make you ill, I am yours, faithfully,

OLIVE LOGAN.

BUSINESS NOTES.

The rumor was in circulation in Wall street on Monday, that the SATURDAY PRESS had stopped, in consequence of the defalcation at the Phœnix Bank. Nothing could be farther from the truth. The Phœnix Bank is not one of the institutions where we make our deposits our deposits. Neither is the Chimerical Bank. We should as soon think of making them in one of the Banks of Newfoundland. The idea that we deposit at the Phœnix Bank probably grew out of the fact that our paper has just risen from its ashes.

STOP THIEF!

Don't be alarmed, reader. We don't refer to Townsend, or Ketchum, or Brown, or Mumford, or even to "Jenkins of the Kiss," for they are only "defalcators."

Jenkins didn't even steal that kiss. He defalcated it. In certain quarters the words steal and thief have gone out of fashion. We don't even hear of robbers. A few years ago we used to hear even of bank-robbers. But now it seems that a bank is too respectable an institution to be exposed to robbery, and has nothing to fear but "defalcation."

Especially unpardonable would it be to apply the word robber or thief to any person who had ever been officially connected with a bank. No, if a president or a cashier or a teller appropriates funds intrusted to him he is simply a defaulter or a defalcator. The same in all financial circles. The idea of there being thieves and robbers in Wall street is simply scouted. *This is the reason why there are so many of them*. If people who forge checks and rob banks and appropriate funds confided to them, were called (and treated as) thieves, robbers, forgers, etc., the business might after a while become too disreputable to practice even among stock-jobbers and gold speculators.

We forgot what we intended to say at the start, but we believe it was this: that if somebody would only cry out "STOP THIEF!" in Wall or William street two or three times a day, there would probably be such a scattering as there has not been seen since the war.

NEW YORK AUGUST 26, 1865

(For the Saturday Press.)

ABOUT VAGABONDS.

I do not know that you have any respect for vagabonds in general; but individual vagabonds may have particular claims upon your indulgence. There are various kinds of vagabonds, though few ever get any place in *Biographical Dictionaries*, and none were ever recorded in the *Lives of Saints*, or in the *Book of Martyrs*. Scarrion, Beaumarchais, and Rousseau were excellent French vagabonds, and have found place in *Biographical Dictionaries*, and they are very good specimens, but somewhat "shaky" in certain points, because very French. English vagabonds, since a group often met in the Globe Theatre and talked with Will Shakespeare, have been very bad and shabby fellows, the only passable ones being among the artistic class.

The truth is, there are various kinds of vagabonds. There is the beer-drinking vagabond, the sentimental vagabond, and the artistic vagabond. Possibly, I am of the latter class. For instance, if I were a farmer I would lie on the first haycock instead of pitching it on the cart. But being a painter by profession, a writer by instinct, and a lover by nature, I delight to be entertained, to remain where I am happy, to wander when I please, and to do nothing except follow my impulses. My crest is a bee shut in the honey-cup of a full-blown flower. Of course the bee is drunk with delight, and replete with sweetness.

For my melancholy vagabond, I like to think of Shakespeare's Jacques; and Jean Jacque Rousseau is my type of an ardent vagabond. Scarron was a witty vagabond, and Beaumarchais an excellent specimen of a clever vagabond. Henry Murger will do for the literary vagabond, though Gerard de Nerval is the better type, being a true prince, and not a mere gamin of the kingdom of Bohemia, the capital of which is Paris. It is very pleasant to think of a group of vagabonds—artistic and literary—who were obscure a few years ago, in Paris, but whom some part of the world now knows as Corot, Marilhat, Roqueplan, De Wattier, De Nanteuil, Rogier, and De Nerval. Roqueplan had a studio in the opera house, furnished by his brother, who at that time was director of the opera, and also editor of, or contributor to, "Figaro." Roqueplan the younger painted many happily-chosen subjects, and of course he did not always seek for his models outside of the opera house. True Parisian vagabonds! But some of them wandered away from Paris: Marilhat went to the east, and came back a celebrated painter; Corot went off to the country—is now an old man, and famous. Oh the gay days of twenty-five!

I rather distrust English vagabonds, for they are slow, have neither fancy nor grace, and they covet good dinners in great houses, and play the jester without his cap and bells at the tables of English lords. Charles Lamb is a very honorable exception; he kept close to the literary class, and came near being a most excellent vagabond; and there was poor Hazlitt; but he was a miserable outcast vagabond, deprived of the vagabond's secret of happiness. A vagabond without a tough and unfailing good nature, is no more a vagabond than is the most stalwart eunuch a man in the harem of Al Kasid. The true vagabond propagates his kind, and imparts himself to others. Your true vagabond loves nature, knows art, entertains his fellow men, welcomes charming books, rejoices over a good dinner, and never sacrifices his pipe or refuses his beer. Like Gerard de Nerval, his body goes where it pleases God. "He is born a traveller, he loves money but to travel, and when he has no money his mind travels, and he dies to travel." His library contains "a few female contemporaries," and he travels with his favorite.

Society in this country is not favorable to the vagabond. Everything here commands us to attain, to confirm, to establish. In this country, as in all new countries, a man must not rest; he must constantly work; he must always choose results; if he does less, that is to say if he does nothing, he is forgotten, or he is distrusted, or thought to be a drone in the hive of industry. But the vagabond declares the world to be something more than a bee-hive. He believes in the fruitfulness of idleness, of pleasure, and the productiveness of dreams. He thinks that to live is to be happy, to rest, to enjoy, to abandon one's self to all excellent and beautiful things. He is disgusted with the custom of constant work, the inveterate habit of constantly "pegging away" at something.

Do you fancy that he is troubled about "position" and "respectability," and whether he is a "member in good and regular standing?" He knows very well that money and position are only to be had with untiring work or unblushing knavery; he knows very well that men live meanly to die rich. He knows that the heavy men of Boston and the fast men of New York are less at the very zenith of their success than the vagabond when he appropriates all that belongs to youth. Let your heavy men with the heavy banking account pass by, and overwork themselves in the days of their best estate; the vagabond knows his choice and trusts his purpose, and he will welcome Comus and all his crew with enchantments of the cup and of the senses. If he lives in the country he will love Nature and be sober like Thoreau; if in the city he will drink his beer and perhaps see other than painted Bacchantes.

My ideal vagabond is a free, easy, facile nature, honorable and gentle. The only sharp practice he indulges in is that of wit. If he paints he is spontaneous and spirited in his work, and he creates a style; if he writes, he is full-flavored and never dull. He does not affront society with the terrible energy of Mirabeau, nor with the mockery of Heine. Mirabeau was too lawless and powerful, Heine too subtle and active for the type of vagabond. The vagabond seldom goes to "greatness;" when he goes to greatness an accident determines him, and once infected with ambition, and once tasting of success, he ceases to be a vagabond. But all the rare poets and painters of the world have known the experience of a vagabond.

I know the great and reverend of the earth forget vagabonds or despise them: but I remember the choice spirits of the earth, and I say: Hail to the Vagabonds. I greet them, I love them, I will entertain them. They are the Light and Sparkling Brigade of the Army of Letters. They are the Free and Dashing Brigade or the Army of Painters, and they toil not, neither do they spin, yet the Heavy Brigades in all their strength are not arrayed as one of them, nor capable of the easiest e effort of their genius.

I know a delightful group of vagabonds in this city, but I will not call names, only sign myself your lover and friend,

SILVER WHITE.

A LITTLE RAILERY.

BY ORPHEUS C. KERR.

Kiss me, Dollie, dearest one,
    Lay your head upon my shoulder;
Will you go and be a nun,
    When your lover's hand is colder?

Will his mangled last remains
    Win from you a tear of pity?
Oh, that other things than trains,
    Took us to a neighboring city.

Wildly gazed she in my face,
    Crying, as she clung about me,
"Robbie, in the name of grace,
    Go away you shan't without me!

"Why, I thought you only meant,
    Just a bus'ness trip to make it;
Yet you seem on death intent:—
    Have you stole my heart to break it ?

"Wherefore speak of death at all;
    Ar'n't you coming back to-morrow?
Let me some physician call;
    What has crazed you, joy or sorrow?"

Dollie darling—low I spoke—
    Don't you know by rail I'm going?
Ev'ry train there's something broke,
    By the daily papers showing.

'Tis as sure as sure can be,
    That some accident will happen;
Likely the first bridge we see,
    Will give way and let us slap in.

Or, a train of freight we'll strike,
    Or another train run into;
Count on life, with death so like—
    Well you know 'twould be a sin to!

Sadly droop'd her pretty head,
    Like a lily rudely shaken;
"If for life you care a red,
    Stay at home, and save your your bacon!"

NEW YORK SEPTEMBER 2, 1865

(For the Saturday Press.)

GUILTY, OR NOT GUILTY?

BY ST. AMAND.

On the morning of the 30th of June, 1860, Francis Saville Kent, four years old, was found murdered in an out-house on his father's premises, Roadhill House, Wiltshire, England. The throat was cut to the bone, and there was a wound in the chest, which penetrated to the heart. The corpse was wrapped in a blanket, which belonged to the bed in which the child had slept the night before; a piece of flannel such as women sometimes wear over the chest was found under the body, and a portion of a newspaper, which had evidently been used to wipe a bloody knife with, lay upon the floor. Nothing else was discovered calculated to indicate the perpetrator of the deed, and even the ownership of the piece of flannel could not be traced.

Mr. Kent's family, including servants, consisted of twelve members.

The murdered child, a younger one, and a nurse, Elizabeth Gough, slept in the nursery, each occupying a separate bed. Early in the morning the nurse awoke, and found the little boy's bed empty; but supposing that Mrs. Kent had come into the room and removed him, she gave herself no uneasiness on the subject, but went to sleep again. About half-past six she again awoke, and, arising, went to Mrs. Kent's bedroom and knocked at the door. Receiving no answer, she waited till her master and mistress had also risen, and then the discovery was made that the child, was not in the house. Some time afterwards the body was found as we have described.

Before going to bed the night before, Mr. Kent had seen that all the doors and windows of the house were securely closed. The housemaid, in coming down stairs that morning, had found the drawing-room door and one of the windows open. Supposing that they had been forgotten, or opened by some member of the family, for the purpose of cooling the room, she had considered the matter as of no importance, and had, therefore, raised no alarm. There was no evidence of any one having forced an entrance into the house. On the contrary, it was very certain that the murder had been committed by one or more of the inmates, or by some one who must have entered the building, and remained secreted in it till the deed was perpetrated. There were no blood stains in the house or garden, no marks of any struggle, and no noises had been heard by any member of the family. Suspicion fell by turns upon Mr. Kent, the nurse, and upon a daughter of the former by his first wife; but nothing was discovered to justify the committal of either for trial, although there were one or two unexplained circumstances, which, in the minds of some, connected the young lady with the murder. She had been heard to utter expressions of dislike against the murdered child, and had, on several occasions, evinced some slight degree of jealousy in regard to him. A night-dress of hers was missing, and no satisfactory account was given of its whereabouts. But there was nothing more. As was very natural, she had shed tears when informed of the cause of her arrest; but had borne herself throughout the examination with wonderful fortitude, and apparently with the utmost consciousness of innocence.

For two or three years subsequently, she went to school, and then entering a semi-conventual order connected with the Church of England, remained in seclusion till a few months since; when she voluntarily came forward, confessed herself guilty of her brother's murder, and was committed to take her trial for the crime. That trial has taken place. She plead guilty to the indictment, and on her plea, without the case being sent to the jury, she was sentenced to death. In deference, however, to the known feeling on the subject, her punishment was first commuted to penal servitude for life, and subsequently to transportation for the same period.

Such are the main facts connected with this most remarkable case. One which, for five years, has been wrapped in mystery, and which has become still more extraordinary, now that the real or supposed criminal has been discovered and placed under punishment. Whether the circumstances justify that punishment or not, is the point we design to consider.

At the time of the murder, Constance Emilie Kent was in her sixteenth year. Her mother had died a lunatic several years previously, and she herself, though described as a girl of a warm and generous disposition, was considered to possess a rather dull and sluggish intellect. It is stated that at present she is an exceedingly plain-looking young woman, with a broad, full, uninteresting face, which wears more an expression of stupid dullness than one of intelligence. She has full, large eyes, glances uneasily around as if expecting some danger, and has apparently none of that cunning and shrewdness which it would be supposed she must necessarily possess.

When arrested, soon after the murder, her behavior was, as we have said, in the highest degree admirable. She evinced a proper amount of feeling, denied all knowledge of the crime and when questioned, in regard to the dead child, said: "The last time I saw him was in the evening, when he went to bed. He was a very merry, good-tempered lad, and fond of romping. I was accustomed to play with him often. I had done so on that day. He was fond of me, and I was fond of him."

It must be recollected that Constance Kent, at this time, was of that age when women are peculiarly sensitive, and, as it were, instinctive in their feelings. Their likes and dislikes are conceived upon the most trivial, and often most erroneous grounds; they are subject to very whimsical and really ungovernable fancies; their nervous systems are disordered; and thoughts may be formed and acts committed which, at a subsequent period, would fill their minds with horror. Though in the great majority of young girls, who are brought up under proper influences, these psychological evidences of the great change the organism is undergoing, rarely make themselves manifest to any but those with whom they are thrown into the most intimate relation, this is, unfortunately for human nature, not always the case. A slight derangement in the physiological processes which are going on, may produce simply an appetite for chalk and slate pencils; a transient vertigo may cause a radical and permanent change of character; an almost unnoticed congestion of the brain may prompt to the commission of a horrid crime. Even an adult man is never the same after as before a congestion of the brain, or an attack of apoplexy. From having been kind, considerate, and gentlemanly, he may become changed to a being of morose and brutal instincts, which it is impossible for him to restrain within bounds. With how much greater force would these or similar influences act upon the impressionable nervous organism of a young girl, when at the most susceptible and critical stage of her existence. To hold her legally, morally, or physiologically accountable for their effects would be about as sensible and as logical as to blame her for having a club foot, or a distorted face. And if, in addition, we found her hereditarily predisposed to insanity, we should be guilty of the most wanton disregard of the first principles of justice and of the laws which govern our being, if we visited upon her head the consequences of any errors of judgment or action for which not she, but the God who made her would alone be responsible.

At a period of her life, therefore, when Constance Kent required the most tender and considerate care, she was without the support and counsel which none but a mother can give. Under the influence of morbid ideas conceived by an unhealthy mind, she, according to her own confession, perpetrated a deed, the memory of which now excites in her no other emotions than those of anguish and remorse. That a child of her low order of intellect should have murdered her brother so guardedly as to leave no traces to connect her with the act; should have undergone the most searching examination, without the shadow of a suspicion being proved against her, and should, for five years, retain in her own bosom the great secret of her life, can only be explained upon the supposition that she acted from an insane and irresistible impulse, and that the cunning which enabled her to baffle the officers of the law was fully as abnormal in its character. The feeling which prompts us to sympathize with this unfortunate girl may be called maudlin sentimentality, and the offspring of false science; but every physiologist knows that it is based upon those mysterious, but, nevertheless, well recognized laws of life which, if of no force in a court of human justice, are influential with those who are not altogether ignorant of the relations which exist between mind and matter, and will doubtless be taken into consideration by the infallible and merciful power which created them.

But is it certain that Constance Emilie Kent killed her infant brother? What evidence have we of the fact, beyond her own voluntary confession? It may safely be assumed that there is none; for if there were it is not to be supposed that in a country like England, in which the law is rigidly enforced against peer and pauper alike, and in which the regard for human life is at its maximum, she would have been allowed to live quietly for five years undisturbed by those who have never lost sight of the murder. The great mass of the people, who read about the affair, will say: "What more is required? She has confessed herself to be guilty, and therefore she must be guilty." Let us see what warrant there is for such an assumption.

After two years passed at a boarding-school, during which it was a common subject of remark that she was very eccentric in her demeanor, Constance Emilie Kent entered St. Mary's College, Brighton—a sort of hybrid convent, with a rector and a Lady Superior. Here she was undoubtedly subjected to the action of influences calculated to exalt her cerebral sensibility already abnormally heightened by hereditary predisposition and the operation of the causes to which we have alluded. Let us suppose, for the sake of the illustration, that she entered the quasi convent thoroughly conscious of her innocence. She knew that she was suspected. She had been arrested as the murderess, but discharged for want of evidence. During the two years or more subsequently, she had heard numerous disputes among her schoolfellows in regard to her guilt; the nurse had been arrested, and though also discharged, labored under the suspicion of being the criminal, and was unable to procure employment. Whisperings, too, which had reached her ears, had been going on against her father. It was said that he had had an intrigue with the nurse, and had killed the child—who had waked while he was in the room—to save his own reputation. Crushed to the earth by these reports, he had buried himself in obscurity, a brokenhearted and a ruined man. Brooding over these thoughts and many others that must have forced themselves upon her, taught that self-mortification was one of the highest privileges of mankind, and thinking for years about the horrible events of that dreadful night, would it be a subject for astonishment if Constance Kent had come in time to think herself the murderess, and been brought to believe it her duty to relieve her friends from suspicion and to save her own soul by taking the guilt upon herself? Had she not before her the blessed example of her Lord and Saviour, who came down from Heaven and assumed the sins of a wicked world, in order that man might be saved? Do we not know by our daily experience in observations of our fellow men, that the mind by constantly entertaining the most preposterous ideas, finally accepts them as true? It is said, and doubtless with truth, that the most false and improbable story, if frequently told, is eventually so deeply impressed upon the mind of the relator that he religiously believes in its genuineness.

A mere confession—especially one made under such circumstances as that of Constance Kent—is not sufficient evidence of guilt. We know that men and women have often avowed a criminality which did not exist, and which they persisted in claiming for themselves till they yielded up their lives on the gallows or at the stake. Do we believe that Father Gaufride was guilty of bewitching more than a thousand women, and of worshiping the devil, because he confessed these things, and was burned at the stake in expiation of his self-imposed crimes? Do we credit the acknowledgments of Sister Marie de Sains, of the Brigettine convent, at Lisle, that she had committed hundreds of murders, strangled numberless children, ravaged graves, breakfasted with devils, and perpetrated thousands of unheard of sacrileges and barbarities? We grieve over the follies of these and the many other wretched persons who have gloried in being witches, and in having intercourse with demons, and yet we condemn Constance Kent, the daughter of a lunatic, a poor, weak-minded, and unfortunate girl, who comes into court, and, solely on her plea of guilty, is adjudged a murderess, and sentenced to death!

From the report of the trial we make the following extract:

"At nine o'clock the learned judge took his seat on the bench, and the prisoner was placed at the bar. She stood firmly, but meekly, with her eyes cast down and her hands clasped before her.

"Silence having been proclaimed, the Deputy Clerk of Arraigns said:

"'Constance Emilie Kent, you are charged with the wilful murder of Francis Saville Kent, on the 29th of June, 1860: are you guilty, or not guilty?'

"Prisoner, (in a low tone): 'Guilty.'

"Judge. 'Are you aware that you are charged with having wilfully, intentionally, and with malice, killed and murdered your brother: are you guilty or not guilty?'

"The prisoner made some answer, but in so low a tone that it could not be heard.

"Judge. 'I must repeat the question. You are charged with having wilfully, intentionally, and with malice, killed and murdered your brother—are you guilty or not guilty?'

"Prisoner (in a low tone): 'Guilty.'

"Judge: 'The plea must be recorded.' The plea was accordingly recorded.

"Mr. Coleridge [one of the counsel]: 'Before your Lordship passes sentence, I desire to say two things: First—Solemnly, in the presence of Almighty God, as a person who values her own soul, she wishes me to say that the guilt is hers alone, and that her father and others, who have so long suffered most unjust and cruel suspicion, are wholly and absolutely innocent; and, secondly, that she was not driven to this act by unkind treatment at home, as she met with nothing there but tender and forbearing love; and I hope I may add that it gives me a melancholy pleasure to be the organ of these statements for her, because on my honor I believe them to be true.'"

The learned Judge—evidently a kind and generous minded man—then assumed the black cap, and with great feeling, in which the prisoner joined with hysterical sobs, sentenced her to death, as his duty and the law required; and thus, without any inquiry into the character of the influences which had been brought to bear upon her the tendencies of her disposition whilst in the religious institution, the sanity or insanity of her mind, her antecedents, or any other point which might have served to throw light upon the case, to ripen her criminality if she was guilty, or to weaken the force of her plea if innocent, Constance Kent left the court, convicted of the highest crime known to the laws of man. If innocent, she adds but one more case to those already recorded of monomaniacs, who, without other indications of mental aberration, have been the victims of delusions; if guilty, she is, so far as we know, the solitary instance of an individual confessing to a crime and being sentenced to death upon no other evidence than that admission. Men and women before this have, in the face of overwhelming evidence against them, or whilst in a drunken debauch, or on their deathbeds, or standing on the scaffold, confessed their crimes; but if any criminal of sane mind has plied all the evidence which could consign him or her to an ignominous grave, the case has escaped our observation. The love of life is so strongly implanted in us by our Creator, that as the Bible tells us, we will give everything for its preservation, and mankind has agreed to regard the miserable being as insane who, with his own hand, brings his existence to an end.

And, if really guilty of her brother's death, are we to have no words of sympathy and kindness for the unhappy girl who has struggled for five long and weary years with the consciousness of her sin, and who has finally gained so noble a victory over the feelings and instincts of human nature? Is it nothing in her favor that she should have been overburdened with the sense of her former wickedness, and should seek to offer up her life in atonement for the offence she had committed against human and divine law? Is there anything more to be done to show her heartfelt repentance and contrition? She has tendered her life—she accepts the commutation of her punishment with humility—God could not ask more of her in this world.

And yet there are those who, seeing nothing heroic or unselfish or Christian in all this conduct, can find no language to apply to her but such as expresses their contempt and disgust. There are some persons who cannot understand a good action. They think there is deceit or selfishness about it somewhere, which time will reveal. Such people see only the imperfections of humanity, and are totally oblivious of their own fallibility and shortcomings. But notwithstanding all their efforts, they cannot make us forget that there is a spark of divinity in the heart of each of God's creatures, which in His wisdom He sometimes kindles into flame.

LETTER FROM OLIVE LOGAN.

Saratoga, *August 28th.*

My Dear Press:—

The grand final ball of the season took place at the Union Hotel last Friday night; and as it is described as being a most gorgeous affair in every respect, by the Jenkinses of the daily newspapers, I cannot, of course, lift my feeble voice against their mighty ones, but must humbly concede that it was indeed all they say. I am willing to admit that it was a peculiar ball. Everybody seemed so very unhappy. My first impression on entering the room was, that everybody had on tight shoes, which forced their wearers to walk about stealthily, speak in whispers, bear a painful expression of countenance, and be wretched generally. But on second thoughts, I remember that this was a Fancy Dress Ball, and that it was this fact which made the participants in the affair look as if they were thoroughly ashamed of themselves, and *Pardieu! pour cause!* Certain it is that the Anglo Saxon nature is not one to lend itself to the reckless gaiety, the freedom, the abandon of a masquerade, and for this reason, entertainments of the kind will never be entirely successful with us. The Ball being over, every one is now at liberty to go home, and I for one intend to avail myself of the privilege at once; though as you may well imagine, Saratoga is more beautiful at present than at any other period of the year, unless indeed, it be a little later in the Autumn, when the heavy foliage of the fine trees turns its green profusion into a jolly russet brown. Not jolly, either, sad. The cool breezes tell of the keen breath of Winter, and coal at ten dollars a ton; the quivering of the aspen furnishes a pretty simile to the poet, but to the poor man it is little better than a strong reminder of his approaching fever and ague, which Somebody's

Bitters will positively *not* cure. Speaking of fever and ague, by a natural transition I pass to coffins, upon which pieces of furniture, and their maker, and his shop, my window looks out. It is a pretty view for a sick person, suggesting pleasant thoughts of the future; causing me to wonder which of his fabrications would fit me, and if it isn't likely that he will get the job. He is the only coffin maker in Saratoga, I believe, and that his trade is happily not very brisk, is proved by the fact that he is obliged to join to it that of general carpentering. Up stairs he makes coffins, down stairs he is a carpenter, and you can't tell how strangely one trade helps the other, occasionally. They told me of a young man who came here last summer, and who was the greatest swell in the place, with his own horses, his own carriages, his own dogs, and his own servants. One day, in driving past the carpenter's, he stopped to have some little repairs done to the wheel of his carriage, expecting to wait till they were completed, and then resume his drive. But the carpenter said he could not possibly attend to it; he was just putting the finishing touches on a coffin.

"Curse coffins!" said the young man in a loud voice, while the blood-shot eye and the flushed face told plainly that dinner was over for to-day, and a headache on the tapis for to-morrow. "Curse coffins!"

"With all my heart," said the carpenter. "I'm sure I'd rather do any other sort of work, and if I had but the money for this one, I would gladly mend your wheel."

"What's the price of this—this thing?" asked the young swell, kicking the coffin over with his neatly-booted foot. "What! Not more than that?" he cried, on hearing the reply. "By Jingo! It don't cost much to die in Saratoga. Well, there's the money. I won't take it away with me,—now mend my wheel; and remember, *the coffin's mine!"*

Two hours after, he had taken possession of his property! A sharp turn in the road, a frightened pair of horses, full of mettle and urged on by their unsteady driver, a crash, a fall, a traction of the besotted man for a hundred yards, and the story's told.

Moral: Never drink champagne, never ride in a carriage, never stop at a carpenter's shop, never look at a coffin, and above all, never eat anything, and the probabilities are, that you will die also, if not sooner.

Poor Dame Fashion, now about to be quenched until the Winter gaieties commence, gives a few spasmodic gasps before extinction, as the flickering candle shoots up into a brighter flame when just on the eve of expiring, and finds an untimely grave in surrounding tallow. So with the ladies here. If not tallow, why then 'tis some other greasy substance which placed on stray locks forms the "Whisker;" a style of coiffure which was voted vulgar and tabooed two years ago in Paris. No matter, it is something new, at least here. It is fashionable, and it is hideously becoming. Another disgusting practice, much affected this year by the Saratogiennes, is that of painting black marks under the eyes, giving to that feature a bold, hard expression; a combination of cold calculation and overweening sensuality, which we might expect in a Laïs or an Aspasia, but which we scarcely look for in a pure American girl of eighteen years of age.

In fact, to touch on a delicate subject, what is purity, in appearance and in reality? What is the definition of the word in the American Dictionary of Fashion? Can a girl be said to be pure who who sits in the grounds of a hotel of a dark night, her waist encircled by the arm of a man who may be a pickpocket, a gambler, or a gold-check forger, for all she knows;—she has only met him at the Springs. The next week he goes away, and she *da capos* the movement with a different basso, or that love of a tenor out of an engagement. She only met him in the afternoon perhaps, but it is not unlikely that at night, in parting, (emboldened by her *laissez aller,* which he, as a foreigner, doesn't understand as "nothing but flirting,") he draws her pretty form towards him, and touches with his great vandal lips her unblushing but innocent cheek. At the next interview, ignorant of the existence of a line of demarcation between flirtation and impropriety, he offends her; and as an unhappy consequence, there is a street row between her brother and the person who was yesterday a "love," but is now a "wretch;" or more dreadful still, pistols are used, and one man becomes a cripple, and both very wretched creatures.

The French err undoubtedly on the score of strictness to unmarried girls; but I really think, of the two evils, our system presents the greater one. It makes a girl bold and heartless; it makes her cold and calculating; it takes away the inexperience of her years, and substitutes a head of forty on shoulders of eighteen ; and at marriage, we see the woeful spectacle of a "knowing" bride; the flower perfect in form and hue, but robbed of all its perfume.

As I knew that to-day would be my last visit to the Spring, it is likely that I observed more narrowly than usual the manners and customs of the motley crowd, which assembles there every morning. If one could but read the story of every heart, how varied would be the histories which might be told. It needs no ghost, however, to come from the grave to tell us that all those parties who press around the Spring in the morning, are not bent solely on the imbibing of water.

There is the girl who lifts to her rosy lips a glass, which the dipping boy has given her, and who, taking little sips at the nauseous draught, glances slyly around to see if *he* has come, as per appointment. There is the "fast" man, who was on a spree the night before, and now gulps down half-a-dozen glasses to get "his head straight." There is the fat gouty old customer, who has been told that the Congress was good for rheumatism, and who nullifies the effect of his ten matutinal glasses by a dinner at five, in which soft shelled crabs, soupe à la bisque, and heavy wines, figure too conspicuously for health. There is the Cuban lady who in the language of the fan, tells yon handsome young Havenese, that she will be in the Union grounds at eight.

There is the thin woman who drinks the waters, hoping they will make her fat; there is the fat youth, who drinks them thinking they will make him thin. There is a baby with a bad spine, which the poor mother insists on thinking will be straightened by half a glass a day, in which belief baby evidently does not join, for it kicks, and shouts, and rebels generally at the treatment; there is Jenkins' family, three little children happily ignorant of the existence of "waiter girls," or the meaning of the word "defalcation;" there are a few remaining actors, relics of Grover's defunct Opera House speculation: there are French coiffeurs, who dress your hair every day, and chat merrily, and tell you plainly how ravishingly handsome you are; but they never once presume to bow to you at the spring, when all unarmed with their combs, they appear what they are in reality, good looking, vulgar, intelligent *canaille.* There is a man with kidneys, and a woman with a liver; a youth of eighteen with the dyspepsia, and a girl of sixteen with hysteria; all arrayed before the fountain of Innocence, hoping to drink from its waters, the unattainable draught of health, youth, and beauty.

How much of disappointment is in store for them all, we know not. How great (in reality) are the beneficial effects of the water, we cannot determine, but of one thing I am quite certain —not one of all the motley crew comes to the Congress Spring in the hope of mending that much disordered organ, the human heart. Water can have no effect on its blackness and malignity—no—nor blood either, it would seem.

Of course in a place so much frequented as Saratoga, one must expect the pleasing spectacle of window-panes all scratched over with names, trees whose bark is quite defaced with initials, and wooden benches telling the touching tale of Sukey and Jim's having sat there together at such and such a date. But for a piece of cool impudence, what think you of the following, which was pointed out to me at the Lake House;—to me who have a Byronic horror of writing my name in public places."

> *Olive Logan, Saratoga, 1864.*
> *I saw her in Spain in '60.*

E. Myndes.

You may easily imagine that I bear no recollection of this pleasing incident; being ill, I am somewhat pettish, and I tell my companions that I wish from the bottom of my heart, that E. would Myndes own business and not meddle with mine. Spain indeed! How did he ever get there? But it only proves the truth of Cowper's truism:

> How much a fool that has been sent to roam
> Excels a fool that has been kept at home.

But my boat is by the shore, and my bark is on the sea, which together with the fact of my trunk being packed and the train starting at half past two, leads me to close my letter at once. The original intention was to proceed to Niagara ; but some of our party being so uneasy about the Ketchum and Jenkins frauds that we begin to wonder if themselves are not so too Brute, compels us to abandon this project!

I am sorry for it, for Niagara to me is like England—with all her Falls, I love her Still, or more properly Noisy.

You may see me before you get this, or you may get this before you see me. Murmur not at this harsh contingency! It is the mystical fate of mortals! Railroad cars run off the track and posted letters miscarry; thus it often happens that men of letters as well as letters of men are sent to the Dead office.

[At all events, I shall take a ticket for New York, and if I get there O joy! What think you I will do?

I will buy myself a new bonnet, and rally round the flag-stones of my meandering Broadway.

Will you love me then as now? I know you will, for am I not,

Dear Press,

Your very own,

OLIVE LOGAN.

—Love begins with a look, exactly as a fire begins with a spark.

NEW YORK SEPTEMBER 9, 1865

ART NOTES.

(REPORTED EXPRESSLY FOR THE SATURDAY PRESS).

—Mr. Williams, the well-known landscape painter, is passing the season down South. He took his portfolio and umbrella with him and is expected to bring home a number of excellent drawings. His studio is in Dodworth's new building. He has written several letters to his sister during his absence, from which we learn that he thinks of getting married. It depends wholly on whether a young lady in Richmond will accept his offer. At last accounts he was writing her a second letter. If things come out right he intends to pass his honeymoon at the North. The public is anxiously awaiting for further particulars.

—Mr. Whiting, whose *chefs d'œuvre* attracted so much attention at the Academy last year, is at the White Mountains with his wife's cousin. A letter from North Conway says he passed through that village a few days ago and spent a night on Mount Keersage in order to see the sun rise the next morning. He wore a velvet shooting-jacket and trowsers to match. We expect that this talented young artist will bring home a number of fine studies.

—Mr. Smith, the clever young portrait painter, has been passing the Summer at the Catskills. He is accompanied by an accomplished young dry-goods clerk from Stewart's. Connoisseurs will remember Mr. Smith by the excellent picture which he exhibited a few years since, entitled "The Portrait of a Lady." He has rooms in the Studio Building, Tenth street. During his absence he has painted the portraits of two young milk maids. It is confidently hoped that he will be in town again by the middle of next week.

—Mr. Pearson is said to be painting the portrait of Miss H——n, of 42d street, daughter of the distinguished stock-broker. He still keeps his studio in Ninth street, and is increasing in popularity every day. His family have resided this last year in Brooklyn. We hope to see his well-known pencil next year at the Academy.

—Mr. Floyd has spent most of the summer trout-fishing. He may be expected back next week, when it is understood he will take furnished lodgings in Bleecker street with his brother. His portfolio is doubtless full of good sketches. His picture of "General Washington in a Thunder-storm," exhibited last year, entitles him to be made a member of the Academy. He celebrated his 29th birthday last week, and is to be married in course of the season to Miss Waterfall, of Williamsburg.

—Mr. Eastman is expected home from Canada next week. He left his wife in Portland. He has just bought a Newfoundland pup. His portfolio is full of études, which it is to be hoped he will finish in his usual style. There is no more deserving artist in the country. His town residence is in 29th street, near the Fifth avenue.

—Miss Joy, the beautiful and gifted watercoloriste, has remained in town all summer at her studio in Broadway. We visited it the other day and was much struck by the improvement she has made. A little picture entitled "Poor Old Hannah Binding Shoes," affected us particularly. It brought tears to our eyes. Price $10. Miss Joy is about to change her name to Mrs. ——, which is a proof that "a thing of beauty is not always a joy forever." Her mother has recently taken a house in Yorkville.

—Mr. Brooks, the sculptor, and Mr. Dean, the genre painter, have gone off sailing together in Mr. Van Fleck's fine yacht, "The Lovely Matilda," which cost over $25,000. They will probably be gone about a fortnight. We wish them a successful trip. On his return, Mr. Dean will complete a splendid picture he has on his easel, illustrating a verse from Tupper. Mr. Dean is one of the most imaginative of our artists, and has recently inherited a fortune of $50,000.

One of our city editors took a breakfast at the Maison Dorée the other morning, which, in consequence of his leaving a roll upon the table, came near costing him over four thousand dollars. The item has been variously exaggerated in the country papers, the latest account reading thus:—

On Monday last, one of the editors in New York, said to be Mr. Clapp of the Saturday PRESS, left a roll of bills to the amount of $400,000, on the counter of Pfaff's, and but for the honesty of the head waiter, who promptly restored it, the careless editor would have been nearly ruined.

The idea of our being "nearly ruined" by the loss of any such sum as that mentioned—or of our even carrying any such sum about us—is simply preposterous. Country editors should know that the circulation of reports damaging to a to a man's credit are actionable. We may add that if ever the Saturday Press comes to grief, it will be for an amount that our out-of-town contemporaries have no idea of.

NEW YORK SEPTEMBER 16, 1865

ARTEMUS WARD.
HIS AUTOBIOGRAPHY.

New York, near Fifth Avenue Hotel,
Org. 31ct.

Dr. Sir—Yrs, into which you a ask me to send you sum leadin incidents in my life so you can write my Bogfry for the papers, cum dooly to hand. I hav no doubt that a article onto my life, grammattycally jerked and properly punktooated, would be a addition to the chois literatoor of the day.

To the yooth of Ameriky it would be vallyble as showin how high a pinnykle of fame a man can reach who commenst his career with a small canvass tent and a pea-green ox, which he rubbed it off while scratchin hissel agin the center pole, causin in Rahway, N. J. a discriminatin mob to say humbugs would not go down in them village. The ox resoom'd agricultooral pursoots shortly afterwards.

I next tried my hand at givin Blind-man concerts, appearin as the poor blind-man myself. But the infamus cuss who I hired to lead me round towns in the day time to excite sympathy, drank freely of spiritoous licker unbeknowns to me one day, & while under them inflooance he led me into the canal. I had to either tear the green bandige from my eyes or be drownded. I tho't I'd restore my eyesight.

In writin about these things, Mr. Editer, kinder smooth 'em over. Speak of 'em as eccentrissities of gen'us.

My next ventur would hav bin a success if I hadn't tried to do too much. I got up a series of wax figgers, and among others one of Socrates. I tho't a wax figger of Old Sock would be poplar with eddycated peple, but unfortnitly I put a Brown linen duster and a U. S. Army regulation cap on him, which peple with classycal eddycations said it was a farce. This enterprise was onfortnit in other respecks. At a certin town I advertised a wax figger of the Hon'ble Amos Perkins, who was a Railroad President, and a great person in them parts. But it appeared I had shown the same figger for a Pirut named Gibbs in that town the previs season, which created a intense toomult, & the audience remarked "shame onto me," & other statements of the same similarness. I tried to mollify 'em. I told 'em that any family possessin children might have my she tiger to play with half a day, & I wouldn't charge 'em a cent, but alars! it was of no avail. I was forced to leave, & I infer from a article in the *Advertiser* of that town, in which the Editer says, "Altho' time has silvered this man's hed with its frosts, he still brazenly wallows in infamy. Still are his snakes stuffed, and his wax works unreliable. We are glad that he has concluded to never revisit our town, altho', incredible as it may appear, the fellow really did contemplate so doing last summer; when, still true to the craven instincts of his black heart, he wrote the hireling knaves of the obscure journal across the street to know what they would charge for 400 small bills, to be done on yellow paper! We shall recur to this matter again."

I say, I infer from this article that a prejudiss still exists agin me in that town.

I will not speak of my once bein in straitened circumstances in a sertin town, and of my endeavorin' to accoomulate welth by lettin myself to Sabbath School picnics, to sing ballads adapted to the understanding of little children, accompanyin myself on a claironett —which I forgot where I was one day, singin instid of "Oh, how pleasant to be a little child,"

Rip snap—set 'em up again,
Right in the middle of a three-cent pie,

which mistake, added to the fact that I couldn't play onto the claironett except making it howl dismal, broke up the picnic, and the children said in voices choked with sobs and emotions, where was their home and where was their Pa? and I said be quiet dear children, , I am your Pa, which made a young woman with two twins by her side say very angryly, "Good heavens forbid you should ever be the Pa of any of these of these innocent ones unless it is much desireable for them to expire upon to a murderer's gallus!"

I say I will not speak of this. Let it be Berrid into Oblivyun.

In your article article, Mr. Editer, please tell 'em what sort of a man I am.

If you see fit to kriticise my Show, speak your mind freely. I do not object to kriticism. Tell the public, in a candid and graceful article, that my Show abounds in moral and startlin cooriosities, any one of whom is wuth dubble the price of admission.

I hav thus far spoke of myself excloosivly as a exhibiter.

I was born in the State of Maine of parents. As a infant I attracted a great deal of attention. The nabers would stand over my cradle for hours and say, "How bright that little face looks! How much it. nose!" The young ladies would carry me round in their arms, sayin I was muzzer's bezzy darlin and a sweety 'eety 'ittle ting. It was nice, tho' I wasn't old enuff to properly appreciate it. I'm a helthy old darlin now.

I have allers sustained a good moral character. I was never a Railroad director in my life.

Altho' in early life I did not inva'bly confine myself to truth in my small bills, I hav bin gradually growin respectabler and respectabler ev'ry year. I luv my children, and never mistake another man's wife for my own. I'm not a member of any meetin house; but firmly b'leeve in meetin houses, and shouldn't feel safe to take a dose of laudnum and lay down in the street of a village that hadn't any, with a thousand dollars in my vest pockets.

My temperament is bilious, altho' I don't owe a dollar in the world.

I am an early riser, but my wife is a Presbyterian. I may add that I am also baldheaded. I keep two cows.

I liv in Baldwinsville, Indiany. My next door naber is Old Steve Billins. I'll tell you a little story about Old Steve that will make you larf. He jined the Church last Spring, and the minister said, "You must go home now, Brother Billins, and erect a family altar in your own house," whereupon the egrejis old ass went home and bilt a reg'lar Pulpit in his settin room. He had the jiners in his house over four days.

I am 56 (56) years of age. Time, with its relentless scythe, is ever busy. The Old Sexton gathers them in, he gathers them in! I keep a pig this year.

I don't think of anyth'ng more, Mr. Ed'ter.

If you should giv' my portrait in connection with my Bogfry, please have me ingraved in a languishin' attitood, leanin on a marble pillar, leavin my back hair as it is now.

Trooly yours, Artemus Ward.

(For the Saturday Press.)

A BOHEMIAN

Mr. Editor:—In the Saturday Press of August 26 your readers found a very graphic sketch of a Parisian Bohemienne; the characteristics of the male of that species were only casually alluded to, and in negative terms.

I am a Bohemian, have belonged to the tribe for many years, know something of the habits, manners and customs of its members, and claim a right to speak of them and for them. Let me say then, that in order to be a Bohemian it is necessary neither to become a sot, a loafer, nor a pauper. There are many temperate, active, well-to-do men of the world, whose days are passed at counting-desks, in attorney's offices, in studios, who are acknowledged and influential members of the tribe.

The chief qualification for admission into the fraternity is the power to adapt oneself to circumstances. Grumblers, fault-finders, railers against fortune, find no place in the Bohemian circle. Good-natured men who believe this world is a good place to live in— men who ignore narrow views of things and think broadly and freely—men who express opinions not offensively, but clearly and independently, entertaining no fears and cringing for no favors—men who never have parted with the ownership or dictatorship of their own souls—men who believe in manhood and who do not pin their faith or their allegiance to the accidents of life—*these* are Bohemians.

As I said, I belong to the fraternity; whether worthily or unworthily has often been a question with me. I know most of the passwords and the grips, and generally find no difficulty in making myself known to my brothers. I have met Bohemians at home and abroad, and I am always glad to meet them and to practice the rites of the tribe in their company. Wealth, power, social influence are not among the requisites of membership; manliness, good fellowship, originality or individuality *are* essentials. Mere dull, commonplace, respectable stupidity is not admissible to the feasts of the Bohemians.

The world ignores and sometimes despises its greatest benefactors, and now it looks askance and doubtfully at our most respectable and progressive order. If it could only know of the spiritual and mental food that hast been cooked for its craving palate in the heat of our discussions, if it could only know that it is even now singing our songs and thinking our thoughts, it would, that unconscious, and therefore ungrateful world, cease to regard Bohemianism as another term for profligacy and pauperism.

In order to be a Bohemian it is not necessary to be without a home and children, with out house and lands; it is necessary that the man should not depend upon house and lands, stocks and incomes for the consideration he claims at the hands of his fellows. It is not necessary that a Bohemian should have had a grandfather—it is necessary that he should be somebody in his own individual right, entirely independent of all quarterings, of all heraldry. Anybody may be a prince by mere accident of birth; no man can become a Bohemian unless he educates himself up to the high mysteries of the order.

A true Bohemian loves all art. If he is poor he purchases the privilege of standing at the opera, or visits studios. If he is rich, he takes a *loge* and decorates his house with sculpture and pictures. He reads poetry and feels the ring of it in his soul and the pathos of it in his heart; when he writes it, he writes what men and women laugh or cry over. Burns was a Bohemian, Emerson is one.

The real Bohemian religiously believes in the best and highest humanity, reverences real greatness, and despises that bloated greatness which imposes upon the world at large, and grows out of the mere surroundings of men and accidents of life. Bohemians called the late majesty of Prussia "Old Aliquot," and Ferdinand of Naples "King Bomba." They even go so far as to call one of our leading Major-Generals "Old Brains," chiefly because he is deficient in that part of his anatomy. They affectionately called our late President Uncle Abraham, to indicate that they saw his humanity and good-nature towering above his exalted-station—and this leaves me to say:

Abraham Lincoln was a most worthy member of our order; he could adapt himself to circumstances. He was equally good as a flat boatman, an attorney, or president. He could talk pleasantly with a child about his hobby-horse, profoundly with a Chief-Justice about the administration of the law, shrewdly with a politician about the chances of election, with the Lieutenant-General about the prospects of a campaign, with a lone widow about the pardon of her son, with Earl Russell about international law, with a cadet about the dignity and promise of his profession; he could laugh with the merry and weep with the sorrowing. His large heart had still a corner left for the living grief or joy of any of his brethren.

Bohemians have an inclination to give pence, if they cannot scatter pounds, to the *un*deserving poor. They recognize vice, and the degradation and poverty of which it is the parent, as sometimes among the accidents of life, and believe that in almost every human being there is a little spark of true humanity which can be fanned to a flame more readily by practical, kindly sympathy, than by any exhibition of contempt and abhorrence.

The members of our order seldom subscribe to creeds. Every man believes for himself, and wholly rejects the authority of all councils and conclaves, however venerable. We believe that the world grows wiser as it grows older, and, not accepting the beliefs of the past, feel no inclination to impose our beliefs upon the future. If we have a creed it is this: every man's conscience belongs to himself, and he does that conscience a great wrong if he puts it under the control of "any other man" or set of men.

If I invite a Bohemian to my house his visit causes no derangement to my general plans, not even an inconvenience. He sits at my table and partakes merrily of the fare provided for myself and family. If I have not "Lafitte" to offer him, he will drink the health of the lady who presides in "St. Julien." If I have no "Cabanas" he will join me in a pipe on the verandah. He will romp with the children if he likes to do so. He will retire to bed when he is sleepy and make his appearance at the last ring of the breakfast-bell in the morning. If the host lives in the country, as I do, his Bohemian visitor will become interested in pigs and chickens for the time, enjoy lounging upon the hay mow, or stretching himself under the trees upon the soft grass. He will say nothing concerning the absence of gas and the presence of kerosene. He will find no fault because the papers are received two hours later than in the city. He will form the acquaintance of the farm laborers, who will always thereafter give him welcome. He will even caress the house dog and chirp pleasantly to the canary. When he leaves his good-bye is a cheery, hopeful one; and the invitation from host, hostess, children and servants to come again is honest and cordial.

C. C. W.

NEW YORK SEPTEMBER 23, 1865

LETTER FROM TONY GAGGLES.

[We print the following letter not because we have any distinct idea of what the writer is driving at, but because a friend to whom we submitted it, says that it is evidently intended as a clever bit of satire.—ED.]

To the Editor of the Saturday Press:

Knowing that you are of a free and open nature; that you are a just man, and a good, highly generous and magnanimous withal, I take the liberty of so far trespassing upon the innate goodness of your disposition, as to solicit your advice touching a matter to me of the last importance.

Let me state my case; and since, as Polonius says, "brevity is the soul of wit," I will be brief.

I am a literary Bohemian, and am, consequently, an *habitué* of a well-known Bohemian restaurant in Broadway, where, though I say it (who should not say it) my peculiar genius is thoroughly appreciated.

I have the proud satisfaction, Mr. Editor, of knowing that my society is courted, and nowhere is it more so than at the literary and gastronomic resort to which I have alluded.

The moment I set foot in that establishment the "Monroe Doctrine," "Negro Suffrage,' "L'Africaine," and even the "Saturday Press" are, for the time being, forgotten, and nothing is heard but, "Ah! here comes Mr. Gaggles." *"Voila Monsieur Gaggles," "Ecce il Signor Gaggles," "Como va, Senor Gaggles !"* and then follows a brisk contention as to which table shall have the felicity of my company.

However, at the earnest and affectionate request of my friend Pfaff, the restaurateur, I have recently put a stop to this unseemly rivalry, by making it a rule to go invariably to the same table.

You may be sure, Mr. Editor, that long before the well-known hour of my arrival draws nigh, the chairs at that table are with avidity appropriated. By common consent, however, there is always a place left vacant for me, and audacious, indeed, must the person be, who would presume to take "Mr. Gaggle's chair."

To give you a faint idea, Mr. Editor, of the keenness with which places at that table are sought, I will relate to you a circumstance which "to me, in dreadful secrecy, did Pfaff impart."

He told me that the other morning he was proceeding to open his restaurant at the usual hour, when no sooner had he unlocked and unbolted the door, than it flew violently open, and before he knew where he was, he found himself sprawling on his back almost crushed to death by six or seven individuals, who had fallen in upon him. As soon as Pfaff, recovering from the shock, had regained his feet, he observed, to his horror and astonishment, these individuals rushing furiously to the garden end of his restaurant. Being unable to account for this extraordinary proceeding, but filled with the most gloomy apprehensions, his first impulse was to cry, "Police, police." His second, however, was to follow the individuals and observe the dénouement, which consisted in a violent struggle for the chairs at the "table," always excepting "Mr. Gaggle's chair," upon which—I say it to their credit—none of them presumed to lay unholy hands. With his usual tact and politeness PFAFF endeavored to restore order, and begged to know the cause of the dispute. It then came out, Mr. Editor, that these wretched individuals, victims to hero-worship, had come at a very early hour to the restaurant, for the purpose of securing places at "the table," each one with the fixed intent that, if he secured a place, he would retain it all day, and thus make sure of the much coveted pleasure of my company in the evening. They had fallen asleep up against the door, hence the suddenness of their entrance.

Police-officer McWatters informed me a few days after this, that while on his beat at four o'clock in the morning, he had noticed these individuals asleep against the door, and had heard them murmuring, "Mr. Gaggles" in their dreams.

The matter in hand, Mr. Editor, has no reference to PFAFF's restaurant; my reason, however, for introducing that establishment is, to impart to you a knowledge of my *locus standi*, that you may be the better able to judge of my position.

Do not, Mr. Editor, think that I am egotistic.

I, Tony Gaggles, egotistic! Perish the thought! Upon that head, hear my friend Job Gapple speak. Job and an acquaintance of his, who, by-the-way, is a little envious of my popularity, were one day discussing "zwei lager" at PFAFF's, when, as usual, the conversation turned upon myself.

"Job," says the other, "what is your honest opinion of Mr. Gaggles?"

"He is e'en as just a man as e'er my conversation coped withal," replied Job, who has an amiable weakness for quoting Shakspeare.

"That's very true," responded the other, "he is just, but don't you think—come now, don't you think he is ever so little—not exactly vain, but egotistic ?"

"It is a lie! an odious, damned lie; upon my soul a lie, a wicked lie !" exclaimed Job, springing from his seat, and his eyes flashing fire. "Make me to see it, or so prove it, that the probation bear no loop nor hinge to hang a doubt on," he continued; and as the acquaintance, to his dismay, saw that Job was proceeding to "he is a man, take him for all in all, etc.," he hastily finished his lager and, unperceived, slipped away."

Mr. Editor, I admired Job Zapple when I found him, a quarter of an hour after his friend had left him; he was in a fit of abstraction, saying to the chair opposite him—"Good name in man or woman, dear my lord, is the immediate jewel of their souls."

I trust, Mr. Editor, you will pardon these little digressions, and I will now come to the point.

The matter in very brief is this.—The other day, I received a letter from my friend Ben Dyke. Ben, you must know, is a newspaper publisher, having published newspapers every State from Maine to Texas; always, however, with this one result—failure. Being unable to account for this frequent occurrence, he inquired of a friend, who, in an evil hour for me, suggested that it was for want of a New York correspondent. Ben at once determined to act upon the suggestion.

Now, Ben is no genius himself, but he has the rare faculty of knowing the article when he sees it, and, therefore, at once said to himself "Tony Gaggles is in New York. Tony Gaggles shall be New York Correspondent of the SWAGSVILLE GAZETTE."

Such to my horror, Mr. Editor, was the intelligence conveyed to me in Ben's letter.

I say to my horror, for, from my youth up, I have been accustomed to look with feelings of benevolent contempt upon New York correspondents of country newspapers: yet strange to say, have always had a gloomy presentiment, that I was destined, one day, to become a member of that detested fraternity myself, and now the thing which I greatly feared, has come upon me. I don't know what sin I, or my progenitors, have committed that heaven should have reserved this fate for me.

As the biographers say, I came of poor but honest parents, and received a plain English education, and, unlike most people, I neither lie nor steal. It is true that in my younger years I once knocked down an old Irish woman's apple-stall over and again that, more recently, I voted for McClellan; but then these as Mr. Greeley himself would acknowledge, are comparatively venial offences, and should not entail a punishment so ridiculously out of proportion as the above.

But stop! I have it !—My father is a railroad superintendent. There, alas! is the original sin, and the miserable conclusion forces itself upon me, that I, not being of the fifth generation, am doomed to suffer for my father's offence, and that the punishment is, that I am to be New York Correspondent of the SWAGSVILLE GAZETTE. Oh, my father! my father! you little thought when you accepted that railroad superintendency, that the consequences would fall so heavily upon your unhappy son!

If you have ever lived in a country town, Mr. Editor, you of course know what is demanded of a New York correspondent—that he is expected to give a rehash of the theatrical gossip, to describe a walk down Broadway, to write a weekly biography of John Jacob Astor, to tell what the ladies wear in the Fifth Avenue, and, above all, to give a plentiful supply of New York scandal.

Mr. Editor, knowing, as you must, that I am engaged in writing a "Biography of Extra Billy Smith," and also a work upon "Negro Suffrage," and knowing too my deep repugnance to becoming a New York correspondent—I say, knowing these facts, cannot you induce some one of your clever contributors to furnish my friend Ben Dyke with a weekly letter, in my name? Come now, can't yer, and oblige, yours till death us do part,

TONY GAGGLES.

NEW FORM OF ALLEGIANCE.

I hereby solemnly subscribe to the CONSTITUTION OF THE UNITED STATES for life, and to the NEW YORK SATURDAY PRESS for one year—promising to renew my subscription to the latter as often as called upon.
Witness my hand and "GREEN SEAL" this —— of A. D.——
NAME, ————————
ADDRESS, ————————

Any person filling up the above form, enclosing the sum of three dollars, and forwarding the same to this office, will give a proof of his loyalty and intelligence which will place him (in our opinion) in the first rank of American citizens.

(For the Saturday Press.)

ONLY A YEAR.

She saw him coming up the path,
And sprang to the door with glad surprise;
He touched her hand with polished ease,
And a look of pain went into her eyes.

A look of pain went into her eyes,
But a steady smile was on her face:
In friendly, careless-seeming tones,
He talked of city life and ways.

She saw him going down the path,
His careless words were in her ears—
She hid her face in her homely hands,
And her eyes were blind with bitter tears.

DON LLOYD WYMAN.

NEW YORK SEPTEMBER 30, 1865

REPRESSED GENIUS.

DEAR SATURDAY PRESS:

I am in tears, and I long for your sympathy. I am young, and, perhaps, a little vealy; still, I am gifted—I have poetic genius. But that genius is repressed by fate. It is under a cloud. That cloud is *rural life*.

Don't talk to me of the charms of the country, and the inspiration to be derived from sniffing the balmy morning air. I've tried it, and I've had plenty.

You must know that I am the son of poor but illiterate parents, who earn a precarious livelihood by working a small farm. As we are short of help this summer, I am acting as chambermaid to the horses, as kitchen mechanic and as general "utility man."

Notwithstanding this, my poetic genius refuses to be utterly "squelched." It sometimes breaks forth into rhythmic strains. But the melodious flow is subject to most discordant interruptions, to illustrate which I send you the miserable result of a brief communion I had with the muses this morning.

THE TWO VOICES.

(AFTER TENNYSON—A LONG WAYS.)

Into thine ear, my dearest Jennie,
I fain would breathe my tale of love;
O— "John, I don't believe there's any
Wood cut for the kitchen stove."

When thee I see, the full afflatus
Of Poesy—O glorious boon!
Comes to me, and— "John, them potatoes
Orter be weeded purty soon,"

The breezes round my forehead playing
Breathe thy dear name, love, as they pass,
Whispering—"O stop your braying,
Don't we all know that you're an ass?"

Thy fairy tread is like the zephyr,
That bears the fragrance of the morn;
Thy form is like—"That blasted heifer
'S gone and got into the corn."

Then listen to my sad complaining,
Hear, Jenny mine, thy lover's lay,
—"John, it sorter looks like rainin',
S'pose we go and cock that hay!

Queen of my fancy's fairy sphere !
Sweet theme of all the prayers I utter!
Wilt thou, O, wilt thou—"Johnny, dear,
Come, take a hold and churn this butter."

There!—Was not fate unkind, and have I not cause to weep? And will you not, SATURDAY PRESS, open to me your sympathetic bosom, and shed a few tears or more? Tristfully, thine,

HORATIUS.

A MODEL TESTIMONIAL.

Since we had the honor of signing a testimonial to the captain of a Ferry-boat, expressing the gratitude of the passengers at being taken safely over to Brooklyn, we have met nothing in the way of testimonial literature equal to the following.

TESTIMONIAL TO CAPTAIN WILLIAM BRIDGMAN, COMMANDER OF THE STEAMSHIP KANGAROO.

We, the undersigned, passengers on board the steamship Kangaroo, feel ourselves called upon to express, in a public manner, our appreciation of the ability and skill of Captain Bridgman as a naval officer. Struggling with adverse winds and a turbid ocean, under a merciful and all-ruling Providence he has steered the frail bark and conducted with safety her cargo of living freight into the destined port with the vigilance and solicitude of a skillful mariner; holding in his hands the lives of hundreds, amid the wild paroxysms of the storm he vigilantly paced the deck, grasping within the scope of his acute vision what was necessary and useful for his ocean dominion. Blending the rigid with the suave, he caused order and discipline to reign throughout without any one feeling in the least slighted. The majority of the undersigned have often crossed and recrossed the Atlantic, and never has it been our good fortune to meet with a more courteous, vigilant, and solicitous commander than Captain Bridgman and his gentlemanly officers, and we verily believe that a more able officer has not command of any steamship on the Inman line. It is therefore but just to say of Captain Bridgman that his urbanity of manner, suavity of temper and impartial attention to the passengers have won for him the admiration and respect of all on board. Signed on behalf of the passengers, this 23d day of September, 1865.

REV. J. MOZNIHAN, JAMES MORTON, THOS. H. LOCKHART, and many others.

The picture of the brave mariner "struggling with adverse winds and a turbid ocean" while "amid the wild paroxysms of the storm he vigilantly paced the deck grasping within the scope of his vision what was necessary and useful for his ocean dominion" and causing "order and discipline to reign throughout *without any one feeling the least slighted*," is what a Frenchman might call "*magnifique, sublime*—pretty good!"

(*For the Saturday Press.*)

HISTRIO-MASTIX.

"It was the eventful year of 1587, that the little man Gosson, in the parish of St. Bartolph, of which he was the incumbent, first nibbed his pen, and made it fly furiously over the paper, in wordy war against the stage and stage-players."

This was the prelude of that onslaught against players and their profession which was begun by the Puritans, and carried on by them, to the best of their ability, until (sitting on the triumphal car of successful revolution) they were enabled to pass laws against the hated profession, and make acting a crime.

When London was talking of the coronation of Charles I. another Quixote appeared in the field, leveling his lance against the windmills of his own creation. A pamphlet was published, entitled, "A Short Treatise against Stage Plays," and the author's style of reasoning is as extraordinary as his logic is peculiar. For instance—plays were invented by heathen; they must, therefore, be prejudicial to Christians. They were established in order to appease false gods; consequently they must be displeasing to the real one. They are no recreation, because people come away from them wearied. And finally (as a "knock-down" argument), the writer would very much like to know in what page of Holy Writ authority is given for the vocation of an actor!

It would be extremely amusing to follow this liberal-minded writer through the whole of his book, but unfortunately "time is fleeting," and I am afraid that you, O polite and gentle reader, might add, "and patience ditto."

These two pamphlets were but shots fired to feel the enemy, and in 1633 there exploded over astonished London the monster bombshell, "Histrio-Mastix," prepared by one Wm. Prynn (not Prynne as Doran has it), and containing, from title-page to finis, one thousand and several hundred pages.

Prynn, in this, showed the true Puritan iconoclast spirit, in attacking all players, and frequenters of plays. To any moderate man this would have been enough, when he reflected that the king and all his court were in the habit of witnessing stage performances. But no; not satisfied with this, Prynn attacked the queen and ladies of the court, in language so vile that one wonders some of the hotheaded gallants did not run him through the very day his book appeared.

In the "State Trials" of England, we find the following:

Proceedings against WM. PRYNN, Esq., in the Star Chamber, for writing and publishing a book, entitled, "Histrio-Mastix, or a Scourge for Stage-Players," etc., and also against MICHAEL SPARKS, for printing, and against WILLIAM BUCKNER, for licensing the said book.

The 7th of February, 1633, saw Mr. William Prynn, together with the other defendants, in the Star-Chamber, and the court having been opened in due form, Mr. Hudson, of Gray's Inn, did set forth:

"That about 8 Car. Reg., Mr. Prynn compiled and put in print in a libelous volume, entitled by the name of 'Histrio-Mastix,' against plays, masques, dancings, &c. And although he knew well that His Majesty's royal queen, lords of the counsel, &c., were in their public festivals, and at other times, present spectators of some masques and dances, and many recreations that were tolerable, and in themselves sinless; and so published to be by a book printed in the time of His Majesty's royal father; yet Mr. Prynn, in his book, hath in railed not only against stage-plays, comedies, dancing, and all other exercises of the people, and against all such as behold them, but further, and particularly against hunting, public festivals, Christmas-keeping, bonfires, and maypoles; nay, against the dressing-up of a house with green ivy. And to manifest his evil and mischievous design in publishing of this libel, he hath therein written divers excitements, to stir up the people to discontent, as if there were just cause to lay violent hands upon their prince; and hath expressed in many speeches, against His Majesty and his household, infamous terms, unfit for so sacred a person. He hath cast an aspersion upon Her Majesty the queen, and railing and uncharitable censures against all Christian people. He hath commended all those that are factious persons, that have vented anything in any book against the state, as the factious book of Dr. Leighton, Jo. Mariana, a Jesuit, to draw the people from His Majesty's government, which is of most dangerous consequence to the realm and state. His book is of above one thousand pages: and dealt with one Michael Sparks for the publishing, licensing, and printing thereof, who is a person that is a common publisher of unlawful and unlicensed books; and dealt also with Mr. Buckner, another defendant, for the allowing of it for the press; and with the other four defendants to print part of it, and publish the same; and by this means this volume was allowed and published, to the great scandal of the whole realm. And to have this punished, according to the demerit of the cause, is the end of Mr. Attorney's information."

Let us now look at this book—this fell-dragon which was to swallow up all decency and order—not only in connection with the drama, but as it relates to other things which Master Prynn disapproved of:

"The music in the church, the charitable term he giveth it, is not to be a noise of men, but rather a bleating of brute beasts. Choristers bellow the tenor as it were oxen; bark a counter point as a kennel of dogs; roar out a treble like a sort of bulls; grunt out a bass as it were a number of hogs. Christmas, as it is kept, is a devil's Christmas."

Truly, a most kind and moving reproof, and calculated to have a great effect upon the church-singers.

Let us have one more extract—the dedication "To his much honored friends, the right worshipful Masters of the Bench of the honorable flourishing Law Society of Lincoln's-In."

"Having, upon my first arrival here in London, heard and seen in four several plays (to which the pressing importunity of some ill-acquaintance drew me, while I was yet a novice) such wickedness, such lewdness, as then made my penitent heart to loath, my conscience to abhor all stage-players ever since; and having then likewise observed some woful experiments of the lewd, mischievous fruits of plays, of play-houses, in some young gentlemen of my acquaintance, who, though civil and chaste at first, became so vicious, prodigal, incontinent, debauched: yea, so far past all hopes of amendment, in half a year's space or less, by their resort to plays where —— and lewd companions had inveigled them; that after many essays of their much desired reformation, two of them were cast off and utterly disinherited by their living parents, whom I heard oft complaining, even with tears, that plays and play-houses had undone their children to their no small vexation. Hereupon I resolved, out of a desire of the public good, to oppugn these common vice-fomenting evils, for which purpose, about seven years since, recollecting those play-condemning passages which I had met with in the Fathers, and other authors, I digested them into one entire written Discourse, which, having since that time enlarged beyond its intended bulk, because I saw the number of players, play-books, play-haunters, and playhouses still increasing; there being above 40,000 play-books printed within these two years (as stationers inform me) they being now more vendible than the choicest sermons; two old play-houses being also lately re-edified, enlarged, and one new theatre erected; the multitude of our London play-haunters being so augmented now, that all the ancient devil's chapels (for so the Fathers style all playhouses) being five in number, are not sufficient to contain their troops: whereas even in vicious Nero's reign, there were but three standing theatres in Pagan Rome, though far more spacious than our Christian London, and those three too many. Hereupon I first commended it, being thus augmented, to the licenser, and from him unto the press, where it hath lingered longer than I did expect; which being now at last brought forth into the world, in such a play-adoring age, that is like to bid defiance to it; I here bequeath it to your worthy patronage, to whom it was first devoted, not caring how it fares abroad, so it may do good and please at home."

"And please at home"? Ay, that it did—it pleased the Star-Chamber so much, that the following sentence was passed upon its unfortunate author:

"Mr. Prynn, I do declare you to be a schism-maker in the church; a sedition-sower in the commonwealth; a wolf in sheep's clothing; in a word, *omnium malorum nequissimus*. I shall fine him £10,000, which is more than he is worth, yet less than he deserveth. I will not set him at liberty no more than a plagued man, or a mad dog, who, though he cannot bite, he will foam. He is so far from being a sociable soul, that he is not a rational soul; he is fit to live in dens with such beasts of prey as wolves and tigers, like himself. Therefore I do condemn him to perpetual imprisonment, as those monsters, that are no longer fit to live among men, nor to see light. Now for corporal punishment—whether I should burn him in the forehead, or slit him in the nose? I should be loth he should escape with his ears, for he may get a perriwig, which he now so much inveighs against, and so hide them, or force his conscience to make use of his unlovely love-locks on both sides. Therefore I would have him branded in the forehead, slit in the nose, and his ears cropt, too. My lords, I now come to this Ordure, I can give no better term to it, to burn it, as it is common in other countries; or, otherwise, we shall bury Mr. Prynn, and suffer his ghost to walk. I shall therefore concur to the burning of the book; but let there be a proclamation made, that whosoever shall keep any of the books in his hands, and not bring them to some public magistrate, to be burnt in the fire, let them fall under the sentence of this Court: for, if they fall into wise men's hands, or good men's hands, that were no fear; but if among the common sort, and into weak men's hands, then tenderness of conscience will work something."

On the 7th and 10th days of May following, the sentence was executed—Prynn sitting in the stocks one day, and losing one ear, and losing the other the next day, and then departing for prison.

I wonder if Prynn, when he was sitting in the court-room, listening to the sentence with a grim sneer upon his face, fancying himself a martyr; I wonder if he had had any faint glimpse of that hour in which he would enter London in triumph. I wonder if he imagined that the time would come, when the gentlemen who were now condemning his book, and were wishing to have him slit in the nose, would be flying for their lives, and an actor would show his love for, and devotion to the King, by dying on the bloody field of Nasely.

Strange! that "the little man Gosson, in the parish of St. Bartolph's," should have commenced a wordy war, which was quenched only with the blood of a king.

THEODORE DAVIES.

The WORLD of yesterday, in a notice of ELIAS HOWE, Jr., the great sewing-machine man, says he "was born in Spencer, Mass., in 1819, and reared in industry, uncorrupted by wealth, to manly vigor and self-reliance." This is doubtless very creditable to Mr. Howe, but what on earth does it mean?

A Mixed Up Affair.—John Bull is in great trouble, just now, about the Fenians. Brother Jonathan, on the other hand, is in great glee about them. We are afraid that Brother Jonathan is a little malicious in the matter; he wants to test brother John's theory of "neutrality." For instance, he would like to aid the Fenians in fitting out a privateer or two. Possibly, also, he might like to take a share or so in the "Fenian Loan," and swap them off, afterwards, for shares in the "Confederate Loan."

Consoling Aphorism.—For a nation to be largely in debt is, in the nature of things, much to its credit.

NEW YORK OCTOBER 7, 1865

JOURNALIST AND POET.

BY GEORGE ARNOLD.

Among the many men of talent and *espri* whom it was my good fortune to meet at the long table in Pfaff's dingy cellar—hardly less classic now than that of Anerbach—were two who represented, to my judgment, their classes most perfectly; the one being a typical Journalist, of the elegant and successful kind; the other being an equally typical Poet.

I speak of E. G. P. Wilkins and Fitz-James O'Brien.

The former, in the winter of 1860-1, when he came to Pfaff's for his *café noir*—before going his usual rounds of the theatres, or later in the evening for a glass of something stronger—was a tall, thin young man, with stooping shoulders, and a strikingly handsome face. His complexion was light; his eyes were intensely blue and expressive, sometimes earnestly thoughtful, sometimes gentle and abstracted, sometimes twinkling with plenitude of merriment. His features were sharply cut and thoroughbred in mould; his skin clear and delicate; his hair, which he parted nearly in the middle of a high forehead, was lustrous and wavy; and his mouth was partly concealed by a well-grown and becoming moustache, golden brown in color, and remarkably fine in texture. His hands were long, thin, and delicate as a girl's. His costume was always unexceptionable, no matter what the occasion or the season, though his preference was generally for loose, rough, easy styles, which became him wonderfully.

Fitz-James O'Brien was cast in a different mould. He was shorter than Wilkins, and far more muscular, being, indeed, a gymnast of some ability, and a firm disciple of the Church of St. Biceps. His complexion was florid; his eyes dark blue, with a marvellously winning expression; his chin very small, and his mouth entirely covered by a heavy brown cavalry-moustache. His hair, which was darker than that of Wilkins', was so fine as to appear thin, except when he had it artificially *frise*, a fashion he frequently adopted, and one which became him.

There were more life, more vigor, more animal spirits and manliness in this face than in the one I have just described; but it was not so high-bred and gentle, nor, to my taste, so refinedly handsome. Still, Fitz-James

O'Brien would have passed anywhere for a fine-looking man, as he certainly was.

In one personal peculiarity he had a great advantage over not only Ned Wilkins, but almost all other men I ever knew. His voice, in speaking, was the richest, the sweetest, the most persuasive and expressive of any male voice I can now recall. It was a power in self. I shall never forget the impression he made upon a small party, one evening, by the manner in which he read several of Emerson's poems. He threw so much warmth, so much human tenderness and sympathy into the rather desiccated and philological works of that rhyming philosopher, that we were all astonished. Then, artfully turning the pages, as if still reading from the book, he recited his own "Bacchus:"

> "Pink as a rose was his skin so fair,
> Round as the rosebud his perfect shape,
> And there lay a light in his tawny hair,
> Like the sun in the heart of a bursting grape!"

You can fancy how we marvelled to hear such lush and luscious tropes from Ralph Waldo, and how we laughed over the deception when Fitz informed us of it. Probably no two poetic minds ever ran in more widely-divergent channels than those of Emerson and O'Brien.

Ned Wilkins was an indefatigable worker. He did not rival the prodigies of to-day, but the sun never set without having shone upon something accomplished by him. All the dramatic and musical articles, and a variety of short, sprightly, sometimes sharp, and often exquisitely humorous editorials in the Herald, were from his pen. Occasionally, too, he essayed graver topics (I remember he wrote an article once on the then new dogma of the Immaculate Conception of the Virgin), and once in a while he was entrusted with the preparation of the leading editorial.

Besides this, he wrote a dashing, humorous' highly original—and to the managers highly exasperating—Dramatic Feuilleton for a weekly paper,* and was the New York correspondent for several American and foreign journals.

It will be readily imagined that so much occupation left Ned but little leisure. Error. Nobody ever saw him in a hurry, or with the air of being pressed by business. He always had plenty of time to chat, to take a glass of something social, to join in any merry-making, to romp with his sister's children—to whom he was greatly attached—and to amuse himself in a hundred ways; but the work was inevitably done, and done well, without slight or slovenliness.

It was, indeed, one of Ned's harmless and pleasant affectations and he had many—to let nobody know when he worked; to appear not to work at all, but to accomplish much, notwithstanding. Perhaps a habit of his, which was not very widely known, might explain something of his apparent leisure. He rose at six in the morning, and wrote till breakfast time—between nine and ten. With the product of this healthy, fresh, early-morning labor in his pocket, he could breakfast with elegant idleness, and saunter down-town as if time-killing were his only object in life. In the *Herald* office he frequently turned off something more, and returned home to dine at dusk, with nothing to think of until the theatres opened, when he went about from one to the other, wherever there was anything new going on, making mental notes for the amusement paragraphs which he usually wrote immediately on going home, and sent to the office by a messenger.

O'Brien's methods of working were in no wise so systematic as this. Poets are erratic by nature, and none more so than he was. He often let days and weeks pass without putting a line on paper. Then, when the inspiration came, he wrote steadily and easily on to the end, often without interruption. He was never known, however, to get up at 6 o'clock in the morning. On the contrary, he was inordinately fond of his bed, sleeping ten, twelve, and fifteen hours on the stretch. One or two o'clock in the afternoon was a common hour for his appearance for breakfast, and nearly all his work was done between that and dark.

Undoubtedly, his habits of labor would have been much more regular if he had lived an orderly and methodic life, with surroundings accumulated by the instinct of comfort—an instinct as much inborn as an ear for music, or an eye for color. But poor Fitz had none of this. He loved luxuries, but could not acquire them. Left to himself, he became instantly reduced to a half-furnished bedroom in some dingy hotel, a solitary suit of clothing, and—nothing more. He was frequently without a pen, a bottle of ink, a sheet of paper, or money enough to purchase them with; a condition of things not highly favorable to the entertainment of the Muses, in case they should call.

When I first knew him, in '56-7, he had elegant rooms, with a large and valuable library, piles of MSS., dressing-cases, decanters, pipes, pictures, a wardrobe of marvellous splendor, and all sorts of knick-knackery, such as young bachelors love to collate. These properties were subsequently left, a melancholy trail, among the lodging-houses in which he lived—or rather through which he passed —for the partial indemnification of the disappointed keepers thereof.

I do not think that Fitz ever incurred a debt in his life without feeling perfectly sure of its immediate liquidation. But, somehow, when he had the money, he had, also, so many other uses for it, that the debt was crowded over "till next time." Meanwhile, he came to be afflicted with a certain curious fear of his creditor, that increased with every day of credit, until meeting him voluntarily was far beyond Fitz's strength of mind; so the debt went forever uncancelled. This was hardly criminal, save in the strictest dry-goods point of view; but it was exceedingly unfortunate for O'Brien and for others.

All these petty considerations, however, sink into their proper nothingness when we read a poem like the "Ode to Dr. Kane," or a romance like the "Diamond Lens." Let it be recorded, in passing, that all the stories about O'Brien's stealing the plot of this wonderful tale from one of the late William North's manuscripts, are utterly and ridiculously false. North had not brain enough, and has nowhere indicated the possession of half enough, to have conceived such a work. It is like saying that Mr. Tennyson borrows inspiration from Mr. Tupper.

Ned Wilkins left no work which will live beyond the memory of his personal friends. His Feuilletons, before mentioned, were indescribably clever, and upon these rests the best part of his strictly literary reputation. The Herald files bear abundant testimony to his power as a journalist de facto.

His death seemed, when it came. like some great mistake. Everybody exclaimed, "No, not Wilkins!" when they heard of it. It did not seem possible. I passed a delightful evening with him two weeks before. We went to Niblo's to laugh at Forrest's Metamora—and found plenty to laugh at—after which I accompanied him to his rooms, where we libated to each other and talked about literature—French especially, and Montaigne, one of Ned's prime favorites—until the small hours began to grow. A few days after, I heard he was ill, but of nothing serious. A week after, I was in the house, and went up to his chamber with a wild and untamable friend of his, to search for potables. He was in bed, and sleepy; but laughed as he said, "There, good night; shut the door behind you," in token of his willingness to be left alone.

Two days later, I saw him in the street with Mr Manager Stuart, and was pained to see how like an old man he walked. This was Tuesday or Wednesday. On the Sunday following Will Winter came to my rooms, pale, haggard, hollow-eyed, and told me, with a gasp, that Ned Wilkins was dead!

He was just on the threshold. His position was just assured, and ripening. He was just coming into a handsome income from his manifold labors. He had just established a happy home with the family of a deceased brother. Everything smiled upon him, and fortune was turning her wheel on his behalf, when—poof!—the candle is out!

Not so with Fitz-James O'Brien. He was, I think, of exactly the same age, but he had lived more. He had gained experience in London, where he dissipated his patrimony and underwent his *grande passion*. He was a sort of poet before Ned dreamed of writing anything.

O'Brien has left enough poems to make a volume or two of rare excellence; but nobody seems to like the trouble of looking them up or of publishing them.

His death was tragic enough. He was on the staff of Gen. Lander, with the rank of captain; and went out with forty men to forage, one day, near Bloomery Gap. Meeting a force of Confederates, Fitz ordered a charge, as a matter of course; he never knew what physical fear was. Unhappily, the enemy outnumbered him largely, and his charge was of no use. A skirmish ensued, and in it Fitz met the Confederate officer in command face to face in the road.

A regular duel with revolvers ensued. At the second shot, O'Brien's shoulder was fractured, the ball entering near the elbow and glancing up

The N. Y. SATURDAY PRESS

the humerus bone. This, however, did not spoil his eye, and with another shot he knocked his opponent out of the saddle.

The best of treatment in a private family near Baltimore only alleviated his lingering tortures, and he died within several weeks, in the most terrible agony, lockjaw having threatened him almost from the first. During his illness, he managed to write two or three fine poems, and some charming letters to Frank Wood, now gone from us also.

I think a larger number of persons mourned for Fitz than for Ned; for all his many readers missed him, and sorrowed thereat. But there was as a deeper grief in St. Thomas' Church, on that dreadful rainy afternoon, among those who gathered about the beautiful presence of what was once Ned Wilkins, than often falls to the lot of any of us, be we journalists, poets, or simple "lookers-on in Vienna."

(For the Saturday Press.)

ADAPTED FROM MAROT.

When young I loved, for youth so swiftly flies,
I had no time but for love's ecstasies;
And when with riper years cool judgment came,
I loved, for reason kindled fresh the flame.
Now I am old, the time for pleasure passed,
Yet still I find my happiness to last,
For still I love, and love consoles me yet,
What could console me, should I love forget?

D. D.

[2005 EDITOR'S NOTE: The following article lifts text from a fresh September, 1865 Fraser's Magazine article, entitled "Manhatta," so it may reasonably surmised that Clapp created this piece in an effort to generate a renewed interest in his sheet.]

BOHEMIANISM IN NEW YORK.

[A late English periodical startles its home readers and amuses its readers on this side the water, with the following article which to us New Yorkers is equal to anything in PUNCH.]

It is said that the fast men of New York are chiefly recruited from the churches and chapels of Old and New England, and that French and German Bohemians go there to become respectable. Certain it is that New York is, next to Paris, the grand Bohemian capital of the world. There is, indeed, one considerable Bohemian club, unless the war has by this time scattered it. They had a remarkably clever newspaper, called the SATURDAY PRESS, which covered its first page with translations from the French, chiefly from Balzac, and found a plausible defence for everything that society condemned. It died because man can not live on snapping-turtle alone. A bright and beautiful woman—ADA CLARE by name—was the finest writer on the paper, and was the recognized queen of the New York Bohemia. Their ordinary assemblages were in Pfaff's wine-cellar on Broadway, where a friend of theirs once took me to see them. He pointed out to me a merry fellow with pipe and mug, and a remarkably free tongue, as the one who (to use his own words) "does up the sternly virtuous" for a certain important daily; another who was sneering vigorously at every human institution, was, I was assured, a salaried denouncer of all innovations whatever in the leading conservative newspaper of the State. They all smoked pipes and drank much, and had their hair cut close to their heads after the style of the P. R. They were disposed to chaff every stranger who came into the cellar until he had contributed something to the amusement of the company. One poor fellow came in with an ingeniously ugly new-fashioned wide-awake. The hat was coolly requested by one and another for crititicism: one eloquent Bohemian arose and expatiated upon the faults of the hat. At length the owner of it arose and said:

"Gentlemen, that hat has one good quality which ought to commend it and its owner to your regard."

"What is it, what is it?" cried all.

"It isn't paid for," replied the fellow gravely; and thereupon he was embraced by all with enthusiasm. Another visitor was called on for a story, a speech—something, they did not care what. He fought against it for a long time, but at length agreed to tell them of a very witty retort which John Randolph had made upon Henry Clay. It was, he said, during the great Tariff debates of over thirty years ago in Congress. The narrator then went into some account of the condition of the parties at the time, and the state of the country, all of which were necessary to understand the point of retort. After going on for seven or eight minutes in this style, the speaker said that it was under these circumstances that Randolph, meeting Clay on the Capitol steps made the witty remark to which he alluded. He then sat down with gravity. "But the retort—the *bon mot*—what was that?" cried the company. "I very much regret, gentlemen," said the young man, with feeling, "that I have entirely forgotten the reply of Mr. Randolph; but I assure you it was one of the wittiest things he ever said!" The followed this "sell," were loud enough to groans which bring a policeman from the streets.

A majority of the large company seated at Pfaff's tables were men connected with newspapers, though there were many artists also. Some of those habitués of the Bohemian Club have since become widely known as writers and painters, but nearly all of them wielded an important influence through the press. Can it be due to this that there is such an evident dash of Bohemianism in everything and almost everybody in and about New York? Bohemianism is social scepticism. There is in New York no great social conviction—positive or negative—but a suspense of faith. The Past is notoriously not there: a Catholic or a Protestant Episcopal member, or a dissenter of any school, meaning to go to New York, had best make the most of his church before starting: it will be only the ghost of the familiar creed or sermon that he will find there. And he shall find, also, that the ethical systems and social fortresses which correspond to those creeds and churches, and which elsewhere are preserved long after their co-ordinate theoretical ideas are abandoned, begin to be weakened in that metropolis. There are men of power there who, in their questionings and tendencies, remind one of the "Reformers before the Reformation," and many odd societies which are anticipating and preparing the path for a social Luther, who shall lead a great Protestant crusade against all institutions inherited from the Old World. For Bohemianism there differs from that of London or Paris by being more in earnest.

(For the Saturday Press.)

"OWED TO AUTUMN."

Round us Autumn winds are sighing
Like a mateless maid;
Happy birds are seaward flying,
All their notes are paid.

Trees are waxing very dry for
Now they stand in dole,
Wearily they pine and sigh for
Summer's "flowing bole."

Sounding thro' the hazy woodlands,
Fall the nuts about:
Nature from her fair and good hands,
Now is shelling out.

Bees have ceased their drowsy humming:
Blows the fitful gust;
Breezes on the roads are coming
Down with their dust.

Lawns are rich in gaudy raiment,
Hills in purple plumes;
Once again his specie payment
Banker Year resumes.

Nothing opulent the scene lacks,
Leaves, around us rolled,
Are the season's lavish greenbacks,
Changed now into gold.

George Cooper.

NEW YORK OCTOBER 14, 1865

(For the Saturday Press.)

FELINE CONCERTS.

BY NATHAN D. URNER.

That the New Yorkers are essentially a musical people is soon made manifest to the visiting stranger. At all times and in all places the air is rife with melodious sounds. Hardly has the dawn streaked the East with rose and amber hues before the drowsy metropolitan is aroused from his slumbers by floating sounds of joyance and delight.

The tuneful fishwife is an early warbler, and softly through the kindling day her poetic temperament finds expression in crying porgies, blue fish, and lobsters. Next may be heard that thrush-voiced vender and purchaser of antique tiles, whose plaintive "Old hats! old hats!" fills the listening morning with dulcet rapture. As the matin grows, the blithe voices multiply and increase in volume. Robin-like, the joyous milkman sounds his long, sweet "Yeoup !" from door to door; like so many linnets the merry butcher boys trudge or drive through the thoroughfares with matutinal whistle and sweet, airy calls to their companions in joy; the pensive rapture of the ragwoman's ditty is only surpassed by the bri-ole-note of the deep, rich "Glass put in!" while, perhaps, the melodious summons of some aerial mason to his hod-carrying coadjutor quavers down through the rosy air like a skylark's hymn.

As the morning advances, instrumental music combines with the vocal glee. The novel tune of "Old Dog Tray" perchance exhales dreamfully from the barrel organ, wherewith the roving Italian recalls the blue sky of his native land. The dulcet sounds of the German girl's tambourine chimes in with its particular cadence; the long pure notes of the itinerant violinist also woos the enchanted ear, and, through the lapses of daylight, perhaps the soul-soothing pibroch of Scotia, the breezy bagpipe's heavenly strain, is buoyed upon the billow of delicious sounds, like the moaning of mountain gales through mountain pines.

On and on, through morning, noon, and afternoon, the air is permeated with melody, both vocal and instrumental, until the enraptured stranger realizes with difficulty that he is simply in New York, instead of in some enchanted city of delight. In the contemplation of the humblest of our public buildings he sympathizes with the "frozen music" simile of Goethe, and his senses are slowly wrapped in elysium; but when the shadows of evening begin softly to gather round the music-breathing metropolis, and the angelic accents of the hot-corn girl commingle with the floating strains, assisted by the bell-like clink of glasses and bacchanalian chorus from the lager beer saloon, and the oral burden of the home-returning veteran's song, the bliss of the entranced listener becomes a joy akin to pain.

He must linger over night, however, to reach the acme of auricular enjoyment. As the nightingale is the sweetest songster of the forest so the night-minstrel of the alley, the byway, and the area is the most rapturous of all the city singers. The feline accompaniment is to metropolitan melody what the singing of the stars must be to the grand harmony of Nature.

Scarcely has the stranger guest composed his head upon his pillow before he is treated with a back-yard serenade, which causes him to listen intently that no single note may escape him. The manner of the nocturnal minstrelsy is a medley. Usually commencing with a low plaintive note, something like a sick baby's moan, it increases into a long-drawn "meaouw," which melts away anon to a gentle "yeaouw," that gradually swoons into an enchanted "eaouw," filling the mind of the hearer with the fantastic desire of Manfred—

> "O that I were
> The viewless spirit of a lovely sound,
> A living voice, a breathing harmony,
> A bodiless enjoyment—born and dying
> With the bless'd tone that made me."

The voice continues its sad, wild wailing, and is soon blended with another and still another, until the soul of the rapt auditor floats away into a fairy land, whose inhabitants and all visible objects are but the creation of pure music, the embodiment and symbolization of perfect sound. He thinks of the palace called Beautiful; he dreamily strays among the pagodas of the long past and the porcelain towers of Siam musical with invisible bells, and, finally, wings his way on pinions of song to the Moslemite Paradise, where large-eyed houris float around him to the delirious rapture of celestial strains.

The music in the yard continues. From fitful gusts it gushes into protracted cadences, now slow, now fast, now low, now loud, until finally it rises with terrible rapidity, culminating in a tempest of manifold sounds which inspires a joy too wild to bear.

Now comes the reaction. So cloyed with melody has the listener become that he grows distraught with his beatitude. Unaccustomed to the musical metropolis, he has freely and imprudently drank of melody until intoxicated. Delirious with joy, crazed with rapture, he falls from Paradise to Hades. He springs from his couch, and raves and roars with joy; he dances up to the casement and vents his delirium of delight in a string of discordant epithets. He has been known to throw cologne bottles, tooth brushes, and even his own boots toward the vicinity whence the wild musio proceeds, and finally concludes by roaring himself hoarse, and passing a night of restless wretchedness. He has imbibed of harmony to excess, has experienced the horror as well as the pleasure of the hasheesh rhapsody, and usually leaves the city by the first train in the morning.

The native of New York, however, is beyond these spasms as a general thing. He has imbibed the delicious effusions, the charming extravaganzas of the feline concert in moderate quantities from his youth upward, and now he has reached the blissful auricular condition which enables him to lie composedly in his bed and enjoy the diapason of the midnight mews. Whether it be a love-lorn ditty, a mild serenade, or a battle song it is equally delightful.

Nevertheless, in certain neighborhoods where the feline population is particularly dense, we have seen even old inhabitants imbued with the blissful frenzy we have described as frequently taking possession of the transient visitor.

In such a neighborhood do we burn our midnight gas. Eighteen cats frequent the fences which our casements overlook. Two of them are the exclusive property of our landlady. They are both of the masculine gender, and while one bears the democratic soubriquet of Tommy, the other rejoices in the more euphonious appellation of Thomaso. The last mentioned is an antique specimen, whose past loves are not to be numbered. He is positively a feline roué—a Don Giovanni among cats.

It is upon record that before reaching the age of twelve months he had wooed and won every Tabity of erotic years in the vicinity of his haunts. This Lothario is dark brown, of the Angora species, with a short stumpy tail, and rumor runs that he is still extremely susceptible to the charms of the gentler sex.

Little Tommy is yet a mere stripling, and romps with the pretty females of his kind in all the innocence of youth.

The yard back of and immediately contiguous to the home of Thomaso, is the native heath of a huge Maltese cat, the particular favorite of an ancient maiden lady, and the sworn rival and deadly foe of Thomaso.

The belle of the female portion of the feline community is a beautiful tortoise-shell maiden, who most frequently promenades in the sun, to the envious delectation of Thomaso, the son of Malta, and all other males of the colony.

The remainder of the eighteen are of various ages, both sexes, and manifold hues, but are not worthy of detailed description.

Every warm night, when it does not rain, these sweet minstrels convocate upon a pine shed immediately in the rear of our lodgings, and all through the balmy hours discourse their peculiar and most excellent music, to the infinite delight of every human being within earshot. One old gentleman, indeed, the windows of whose third-story back room face our own, and who is of a decidedly musical turn, is sometimes so enraptured that he arises in the middle of the night, and, through the instrumentality of an asthmatic French horn, accompanies the serenaders with loud and boisterous windings. As a general thing, however, the residents take the affair quietly; only once do we remember seeing the whole neighborhood excited to the pitch of pleasurable frenzy.

One lovely night, not long ago, we had sunk into a delicious, dreamy state, strangely and sweetly permeated by the lingering accords of a feline serenade, when we were suddenly and disagreeably aroused by a wild hubbub at the back windows of the entire block.

The cats were in the midst of their extravagant melody, and, instantly divining that our neighbors were unwontedly excited, we sprang from our bed and glanced out of the window. Horrible to relate! the cats themselves were inspired with the joyous frenzy which they had so often occasioned in the human mind—a Kilkenny musical fury had taken possession of them, and they were evidently enjoying a free fight, mingled with song, whose wild rhapsodies were entrancingly, bewitchingly beautiful. Yells, howls, meaouws, hisses, spittings, and enchanting shrieks rent the air with the power of a number of brass bands, combined with three or four troupes of Ethiopian minstrels. The moon was behind a cloud, and the musicians themselves were invisible—only their eyes were there, the fiery eyes, whose swift eccentric orbits we could mark in the gathering gloom.

All the rooms opposite were illuminated, and one glance at their occupants indicated the melancholy fact that they were crazed with sweet sounds.

We saw the musical old gentleman seize his consumptive French horn and blow it wildly for a few seconds, but his divine ecstacy knew no bounds. He could not keep still, but danced from window to window of his room, shouting frantically, and every now and then launching a missle at the mad musicians.

The old maid who occupied the room immediately under the musical gentleman's was also at her window, with her hair in papers, and an unseemly night-cap on the back of her head. She seemed utterly regardless of appearances, but gazed from her casement with a wild light in her angular face.

The two pretty girls in the next house but one were also peering through the slats of their shutters. We could only catch a glimpse of their white nightgowns now and then, but a low, plaintive, moan would issue from their room, conveying something of the delirious joy which thrilled their tender bosoms.

A returned soldier, who occupies the same house, with the same outlook, sat at his window with a revolver in either hand, letting off his surplusage of joyance by peppering the unfortunate musicians, while two firemen, who sleep in the apartment immediately above, had made their way to the roof, and were busily engaged in keeping up a perpetual storm of brickbats. They had already demolished three chimneys in order to procure ammunition, and were now half way through a fourth.

There were probably a hundred people enjoying the scene, and they all appeared to be influenced by the same musical delectation, and kept up an irregular fire with spittoons, shaving-cups, pitchers, wash-bowls, and other articles of toilet.

The wild scene lasted about twenty minutes, when suddenly the minstrelsy ceased. The spectators slowly descended from the blissful realms of fancy into which they had temporarily soared, and one by one retired to the seclusion of their apartments.

Still thrilled with a fond recollection of the music that was no more, we sat at our window till daylight, the first glimmerings of which revealed a white-robed female form sitting mournfully in the yard immediately behind our own. It was that of the afore-mentioned spinster, silently weeping over the lifeless remains of her Maltese cat. Around her was strewn the debris of the battle-field, consisting of feline ears, tails, legs, feet, claws, teeth, etc., the whole lightly covered by a thin snow of white and yellow hair.

Tommy was never seen again; Thomaso only recovered with the loss of both eyes, and the disconsolate tortoise-shell beauty died of a broken heart. Thirteen musicians perished on that fatal night. The remainder of the eighteen are sadly out of voice, and the neighborhood so much in need of their olden music, that there is serious intention of importing a fresh lot of the charming creatures from abroad.

Feline concerts are becoming universal favorites, and the discriminating kindness of the authorities, who drown so many dogs, yet religiously leave the cats alone, is fully appreciated by a grateful public.

S—T 1860—X.

DRAKE'S PLANTATION BITTERS.

They purify, strengthen and invigorate.
They create a healthy appetite.
They are an antidote to change of water and diet.
They overcome effects of dissipation and late hours.
They strengthen the system and enliven the mind.
They prevent miasmatic and intermittent fevers.
They purify the breath and acidity of the stomach.
They cure Dyspepsia and Constipation.
They cure Diarrhea, Cholera and Cholera Morbus.
They cure Liver Complaint and Nervous Headache.

They are the best Bitters in the world. They make the weak strong, and are exhausted nature's great restorer. They are made of pure St. Croix Rum, the celebrated Calisaya Bark, roots and herbs, and are taken with the pleasure of a beverage, without regard to age or time of day. Particularly recommended to delicate persons requiring a gentle stimulant. Sold by all Grocers, Druggists, Hotels and saloons. Only genuine when cork is covered by our private U S. Stamp. Beware of counterfeits and refilled bottles.

P. H. DRAKE & CO.,

21 Park Row New York.

NEW YORK OCTOBER 21, 1865

DRAMATIC FEUILLETON.

BY FIGARO.

I am off to Philadelphia, Mr. Editor, at a moment's notice.

Please get my limbs insured at the Hartford Traveller's and have ready for me in case of accident a pair of cork legs.

Also, provide against "empty sleeves" and, if possible, empty pockets.

I have returned home with the latter a hundred times and know of no company in Hartford or elsewhere who will insure against them.

If I get to Philadelphia with both arms I may send you something from there about the theatres.

My friend Edvardus—not Edgardus, he is in Washington looking out for "Arrah-na-Pogue "—says that a word or two about the theatres, in this column, now and then, would be quite appropriate.

Edvardus is right.

But then he thinks I should write careful analyses, learned criticisms, and all that sort of thing.

Edvardus is wrong.

He wouldn't read them, himself. Nobody would but actors and authors—and they only what was written about them.

No, Edvardus, you must let me go on in my own way.

I go to the theatre, just as you do, to be amused.

Sometimes it is the play that amuses me and sometimes the audience.

Most often, the latter.

Last Wednesday evening, for instance, I went to Wallack's, to see "Still Waters Run Deep," and "Ici on parle Français"; and my chief entertainment was a little comedy of manners going on in a private box near me, between three or four giggling young misses and a couple of young swells, who attracted the attention of the whole orchestra part of the house, and came near, at one time, getting a round of applause.

I have half a mind to give you the names of the dramatis personæ.

But no, I'll get Moss to send them each a copy of Chesterfield.

Mind you, I was simply amused by them: but imagine how the actors and actresses felt who were within bouquet's throw of the box, and could hear every word spoken.

Talk about there being no subject for the drama in this country, why if I were a playwright, I'd take just such a specimen of manners as this, and work it up into a comedy, which could be adapted, like Laura Keene's famous piece, to every city in the land.

But I am not a playwright, so the thing will never be done.

Meanwhile, we must put up with such plays as "Still Waters Run Deep "—and if you will find me a play more common-place in plot, more absurd in situation, or more twaddly in sentiment, I will find you a white black bird.

Still it takes, as everything does at Wallack's, for the simple reason that it is well acted.

I wish I could add, also, well mounted ; but I fear the scene painter of the establishment has "got cold."

Still, there was a real mirror on the stage, and I had the pleasure of beholding in it some of the nicest carpentry behind the scenes that you can imagine.

In fact I had a beam in my eye nearly all through the play.

This didn't prevent me, however, from enjoying the performance; for E. L. Davenport's Capt. Hawksley is, perhaps, the most finished piece of light-comedy acting that we have had this season; while Charles Fisher's John Mildmay (though a little cumbrous in parts) is nearly as good; and Miss Henriques, as Mrs. Mildmay, gives such a chaste and beautiful rendering of a very gross and indelicate role, as to make me half inclined to forgive the author for having created it.

I can't speak so highly of Mark Smith's Mr. Potter, which was altogether too Solon Shingly.

Miss Morant made the most, of course, of Mrs. Sternhold; but it is one of those horribly unnatural characters which nobody can play well, and which nobody should be asked to play at all.

But what are you to do when you have an author like Tom Taylor to deal with?

Better a thousand times Tom De Walden, who makes his characters human, at least.

But more of De Walden presently, though nothing more of Taylor.

He is what Charles Lamb would have called (no offence to the tailoring fraternity) a "curs'd ninth of a dramatist."

His still waters may run deep, but they run very muddy, and we have had enough of them.

What a relief it is at Wallack's when they have run out, to have them followed by the clear sparkling flow of the little comedietta, "Ici on parle Français."

I haven't seen it at this theatre, for despite Miss Logan, I can *not* sit through two pieces on the same evening, though it must be a treat to see Mr. Holston and Mr. Young in it, while to miss seeing any play in which Ione Burke appears is a positive sacrifice.

This is putting it rather strong, but never mind.

It is so rare in any sphere, and especially on the stage, to find youth and beauty combined with intelligence and ésprit—as is the case with Miss Burke and Miss Henriques—that when we are fortunate enough to do so, a little enthusiasm may be excused.

You see I was young myself once, Mr. Editor—not to say beautiful and brilliant—so I know what it is to have these qualities appreciated.

But excuse me from writing a disquisition on the subject, lest Edvardus or somebody accuse me again of digressing too much.

But where was I ?

At Wallack's, wasn't it?

Well let us now go over for a moment to the Academy.

Ihardly know who has been the lion there, this week, Maretzek or Bateman.

On the whole, I think Bateman.

He introduced his concert troupe to the Academic boards on Tuesday night, strengthened by the addition of Mr. Levy, the great English cornet-player.

The concert was given as a prelude to "Lucrezia Borgia," so that his prima donna came into almost immediate competition with Carozzi Zucchi in one of her best roles.

The two singers are so different, however, in their styles—and a dramatic performance is so essentially different from a mere lyric performance—that I doubt if any comparisons were indulged in.

They are both great artistes, and they both roused the audience to the highest pitch of excitement.

Mdlle. Parepa, however, lost her voice in a measure, after her first song, and the fact was announced to the audience by Mr. Bateman in a speech, so cleverly worded and so neatly delivered, that it was one of the successes of the evening.

I shouldn't be surprised to have Bateman turn up some day as a Fourth of July orator. He made a second speech on Wednesday night—explaining that Mdlle. Parepa was too ill to sing at all and introducing Miss Kellogg in her place—which was good enough to have been set to music.

But it isn't this that has made him the lion of the Academy, this week, so much as the success of his two concerts, which could hardly have been surpassed.

The piano and violin playing was rather tedious, but the singing was such as is rarely heard even in opera, and Mr. Levy's performance on the cornet-à-piston was little short of miraculous.

It seemed rather hard on the habitués of the Academy to lengthen out two consecutive performances with concerts, but the opera singers were stimulated to do their best, and Maretzek, as well as Bateman, could boast, at the end, of having achieved a triumph.

The experiment was a dangerous one—especially for Maretzek—but "all's well that ends well," even if it doesn't end till midnight.

The next sensation at the Academy will be the new comic opera—"Crispino e la Comare" (The Cobbler and the Fairy) which is announced for Tuesday.

On Monday we are to have a repetition of "Il Trovatore "; and we should have, in course of the week, a repetition of "La Traviata," in which Mazzolini and Carozzi Zucchi are positively superb.

It is a shame that Bennett should be mortified by seeing the Academy flourish despite the opposition of the HERALD, but he has "Blind Tom" to console him, and when that fails he can take to "Old Tom."

He carries the Tom mania to such an extent that one of his pet places of amusement is the Anatomical Museum.

The Associate Managers feel bad to find him so demoralized by their triumph over him; but then again they have *their* consolation in full houses.

Not only Wallack's, which is always full, but Niblo's, the Olympic, the Winter Garden, the New Bowery, the Hippotheatron, Bryant's, etc., are all crowded nearly every night—without even taking the trouble to change their bills.

The Broadway, which is not "in the ring," is also crowded; but with a piece so full of fun as De Walden's "Sam," and with such actors as Frank Chanfrau, Olive Logan, Charles Parsloe, and the author, this could hardly be otherwise.

I had intended, by the way, to give something of an analysis of "Sam" this week—and also to give some description of the admirable manner in which the new scenic artist of the establishment—Mr. Grain—has just put it on the stage; but I am about the end of my tether.

I haven't even space to speak of the splendid performance of "The Streets of New York," now going on at the Olympic.

You must go and see it for yourself.

You will find it, both from a dramatic and a spectacular point of view, to be really brilliant.

Barnum's Museum, where I had hoped to spend an evening this week, I have only had time just to drop in at.

The place is in fine order and success is written all over it.

I heard the new Irish vocalist, Miss Kathleen O'Neil, sing several character songs, and they were given with great effect.

"The Czarina of the Hippodrome," Miss Oceana, was about to mount the "Wild Horse of Tartary" as I was leaving, but I resisted the temptation and went to the opera.

Even as now I resist the temptation of writing any more and start for Philadelphia.

If anything could make me stay in town, it would be the Grand Ravel Matinée to-day at Niblo's, where I like to go with the little folks.

The grown folks have an afternoon entertainment promised for them, by the way, at the Broadway, where, as the bills say, they can see "Sam by Daylight."

Yours t. f.

FIGARO.

NEW YORK OCTOBER 28, 1865

(For the Saturday Press.)

DICK.

"Richard is himself again." Richard is our canary. We call him Dick for short. He has just got over moulting. He is just the gayest bird you ever saw. He came to us one bright afternoon, like Japhet in search of a father. He was a stranger and we took him in. Bought him a pretty wire house at the corner grocery, and a quantity of seed. He was so pleased with his new quarters that he didn't stop to be shy and timid, but hopped on the upper perch and poured forth the merriest and sweetest strains ever heard in our house. Miss Kellogg's voice was never more clear and silvery, "Just let me have this house rent free, and give me good store of seeds," said he, in his inimitable way, "and I'll furnish music for the family." He was as good as his word.

It was summer, and we hung him by the open window. How he *did* sing! All day long he was bubbling over with melody—like the boy at school, "it whistled itself." The mystery was, how he could do it—how such a tiny body could hold so many tunes. It seemed, sometimes, as if he would split his little throat, or perish in the attempt. Yet he has never had the bronchitis, to my knowledge. Perhaps it is because he uses the cold water application so freely. He belongs to the "Order of the Bath," Dick does. My wife slips the bathing-dish into his cage, first taking the precaution to spread a cloth upon the carpet. Dick understands it perfectly. From the upper perch he watches the preparations, cocking his head first on one side, then on the other, and uttering an approving from time to time.

When all is ready, in he goes. But not directly, if we are "noticing" him. He talks about it, in his jocular way; hops up and hops down,

"With many a flirt and flutter,"

sticking the feathers up "so cunning" on the top of his head, and perking about those shining black beads of eyes in a hundred coquettish airs and graces. He enjoys conversation, and likes a good deal of attention; don't mind if I put my face up close to his face; yet fears a human hand as if it was the Hand of Providence, and seems instinctively to apprehend violence.

Stand back a little, and watch the performance. He hops upon the edge of the dish, takes a taste to see if the water is about the right temperature, then—no he don't. He is keeping a sharp lookout. You are not going to come up and hit him a rap over the head, on the sly, not if he knows himself. Pretty soon he hops in. It makes his legs cold, and he hops out again. Takes another look to see if the coast is clear, then goes in in earnest. First, he ducks his head, with a shake and a flirt; then squats his whole body into the water, and with his wings makes a prodigious flutter and spatter; and concludes by a final splash with his tail. Does it again—does it ever so many times; and comes out looking as if he had been on a bender, and got caught out in a rain storm. His soft, shiny, yellow coat is all drenched and dripping, his funny little top-knot is all ruffled.

Two or three shakes and a half hour of sunshine make that all right, and Dick is as handsome and merry as ever. A new concert commences immediately. He is both solo and chorus, and dashes off, *allegretto con spirito*, all the favorite airs of bird opera, with many a trill and flourish not down in the books. Dick has one bad habit. He gets up too soon in the morning. He is emphatically an "early bird," though there are no worms to be caught. The sun has risen with great regularity for so many years, that I am quite willing to trust Old Sol to light up without giving the matter my personal attention. Not So with Dick. He is on a keen look-out for the first hint of daylight, and reports progress twenty times a minute, in his most gay and festive tones. The whole house rings with his melody. Talk about the "arms of Morpheus"—morphine could hardly sleep in such a jubilee. "Sing before breakfast, cry before supper," says the old adage. Wife didn't like so much singing before breakfast—it disturbed her slumbers. She shut the blinds closely, and covered the cage with her apron. No use—he couldn't hold in. Then she put him in a dark closet. Must leave the door ajar, to give him air, you know. The little rascal stuck his bill to the crack of the door, threw his head back, and rattled away as loudly as ever. He was just gushing over with song. We had to let him gush.

One day my wife let him out in the room for exercise, and he happened to spy his reflection in the toilet glass. Dick bristled up instantly. So did the reflection. Giving a sharp cry of defiance, at him he went, pell-mell. It rather puzzled him, bringing up smack against the glass with a concussion that made us fear for the safety of the mirror, and landed him in great disorder upon the bureau. Promptly rallying his forces, he charged again and again, with great impetuosity. The one-sided combat was very amusing.

By and by, he saw the joke—he thought. Finding the other bird had just as good grit as he, Dick strove to cultivate his acquaintance. He would stand for the hour together in front of the glass, putting on his most seductive airs, chirping and twittering to the handsome stranger in his softest and sweetest tones. And, on the cage being removed, he would look and call for his lost companion for a long time, before resuming his musical practice. To this day, the easiest way to hush his singing is to set him in front of the glass.

Canary birds don't have the small-pox or the whooping-cough that I know of, though I did hear, once, of one that died of the measles. But they moult. That is the price they have to pay for a new suit of clothes. When they are moulting, they don't seem to feel well. Dick has had his experience. For six weeks he moped, and scarcely sung a note. Occasionally he would brighten up, and softly thank us for our tender care of him. Once in a while he would try to sing. He "done his level best," but the notes wouldn't come out clear and strong. His feathers came off like thistle down, at every feeble flutter. "One by one," his tail feathers dropped off, and Dick acted as if he was ashamed to be seen in such a plight.

Now he is all over it. As I remarked at the beginning, with striking originality, "Richard is himself again." His eyes sparkle with life and merriment; his voice is loud and clear, and tuned to concert pitch; his brand new yellow coat is soft and smooth, and fits him to a feather; his tail, like the tales in the New York *Ledger*, is destined "to be continued;" and he is so perth and frolicsome, so alert and cunning, and withal so joyful and happy continually, that we never tire of petting him.

Look at him now, as he hangs among the branches of a geranium tree, fast asleep and all unconscious of this long rigmarole I have been writing about him. Dick asleep is not at all like Dick awake. Unlike most little people, he makes no fuss about going to bed. He just balances himself on one slender leg, takes his head off, and tucks it under his wing, and the thing is done. He is nothing now but a little yellow ball yet we would hardly be willing to swap him for a lump of yellow gold.

CYFAX.

FEUILLETON D'ADIEU.

BY FIGARO.

Here I am back again, Mr. Editor, without the loss of so much as a limb.

I think you'll find my funny-bone broken, but that's no matter.

If you are in want of anything in the funny line, just print Cooper's last novel—I mean the California Cooper, who is what they call in San Francisco (meaning a pun, no doubt) a staver.

You can also copy something from "Walt Whitman's Drum Taps," which a friend at my elbow, who sometimes gets off a good thing, says are written in vexameters.

But whatever you do, don't look for anything from me which is not perfectly serious. I had a cluster of little brilliants sent to me, as usual, for your editorial column, but you will have to set them aside, I fear, to make way for the enclosed poem ("Peace to his Ashes") which, to my thinking, is better than anything you have yet published in prose or verse—which is saying a good deal.

Please print it with all the honors, and offer a handsome premium for the name of the author; for modesty, like "virtue," has been its "own reward" long enough.

I know this from experience.

But, as I was saying, here I am back again, though I don't feel at all like getting into harness.

Somehow, after travelling on the Camden and Amboy route—which I verily believe to be the route of all evil—I always feel about ten years older.

Still it is so pleasant to get back with your head on your shoulders—a very good place to have it—that a few years more or less are of no consequence.

I presume the luck is attributable, in my case, to the fact that I got my head (as well as my trunk and other things) insured for about double their value.

And then I suppose you got insurance, too, against having no Dramatic Feuilleton this week.

Well, you may as well collect it: for I write, now, chiefly to resign my position as Dramatic Feuilletonist into younger, and brighter, and better hands.

Whose, you will know in due time.

I have been wanting to say "Adieu !" to my theatrical and operatic friends for several years, but the word has always stuck in my throat.

Now, however, I have no choice in the matter.

Other duties on our dear paper claim my attention, and I must take up my pen and walk.

I have no time even to write a valedictory.

But do not be alarmed: you will have quite as much of "Figaro," in other parts of the PRESS as you can stand.

Besides, it is impossible for him to go to the theatre, the opera etc., without neglecting everything else; and, moreover, he has had the good fortune to find a successor whose name, were he permitted to mention it, would be hailed by the theatric and operatic world with acclamation.

So, without further ceremony, I give up my chair—blessings on it!—and remain

Yours resignedly,

FIGARO.

NEW YORK NOVEMBER 4, 1865

The orchestras in town are all on the strike, like so many musical clocks with their works out of order. Some of the craft—the drummers for instance—declare their intention to keep on striking all their lives, while the trumpeters declare that sooner than give in they will blow their brains out. The fiddlers say things equally extravagant, but they are used to drawing a long bow, and moreover always like a scrape. The bass-viol people say bass is the slave that plays on the viol, or anything else, when he can help it. Maretzek says they are all a set of rebels, and ought to be tried by a drum-head court-martial. Stuart says they ought to be passed over to Leutz and soft Recorders (all but the soft), and Wood says he don't care what becomes of them, as his "Sam" goes just as well without music as with it. The only persons likely to make any thing out of the affair are the managers (who have been in great luck since they threw the dirty HERALD overboard), and the Steinways, who seem really to have discovered the way to wealth.

(From Walt Whitman's "Drum-Taps.")

O CAPTAIN! MY CAPTAIN!

I.

O CAPTAIN! my captain! our fearful trip is done;
The ship has weathered every rack, the prize we sought is won;
The port is near, the bells I hear, the people are exulting,
While follow eyes the steady keel, the vessel grim and daring:
But O heart! heart! heart!
Leave you not the little spot,
Where on the deck my captain lies,
Fallen cold and dead.

II.

O captain! my captain! rise up and hear the bells;
Rise up—for you the flag is flung—for you the bugle trills;
For you bouquets and ribbon'd wreaths—for you the shores a-crowding;
For you they call, the swaying mass, their eager faces turning;
O captain! dear father!
This arm I push beneath you;
It is some dream that on the deck,
You've fallen cold and dead.

III.

My captain does not answer, his lips are pale and still;
My father does not feel my arm, he has no pulse nor will:
But the ship, the ship is anchor'd safe, its voyage closed and done;
From fearful trip, the victor ship, comes in with object won:
Exult, O shores, and ring, O bells!
But I, with silent tread,
Walk the spot my captain lies,
Fallen cold and dead.

NEW YORK NOVEMBER 11, 1865

FOR FIFTY YEARS.

BY HARRIET E. PRESCOTT.

I tell the story as I heard it, vouched for and under oath. If I do not believe it, it is no reason that you should not. As I scarcely like to mention her real name, I shall speak of her as Julia,—since I know no other name, so full of life. At the very heat and strength of summer, she was a person of thoroughly warm and healthy organization, by no means one of those thin-blooded lymphy people who might be supposed to see ghosts because they look so much like them themselves. Of large and rather handsome mould, with ruddy color on her cheek, with hair thick, abundant, and seemingly alive in every strand, with clear steady eyes, and so strong and warm a hand-clasp, she was a person to reassure you should you see a ghost yourself.

She was an Englishwoman, and had come to these shores with her parents who had died and left her nearly destitute. She had never heard anything of the doctrines of what is called Spiritualism, in her life. She had obtained a situation in one of the Departments at Washington, where she received a moderate salary, and, at the current exorbitancies of that delectable abode, kept the life between her teeth by eking out the salary with her own little pittance.

She had previously lived in a poorer quarter of the city, in such a room as her means allowed—but, one day, Julia's companions noticed her turning her steps towards a more aristocratic direction and entering a dwelling that bore the appearance of a fine old mansion-house. Such a home they knew was entirely beyond her means, as it would have been beyond their own, and their curiosity was finally rewarded by the confession that she obtained her present room at a much less price than she had paid for the former one, because, as the landlady of the boardinghouse, into which the old mansion had been converted, assured her, a lodger had never been able to be retained in that room beyond the third night.

Julia's nerves were not disordered; she had engaged the room, paid her month's board in advance, deposited her moveables there, and made herself at home. This occasioned her more exertion than she usually made, and she slept soundly that night and only awoke with the alarum of the breakfast gong bursting about her. The next night, too, she slumbered well, having a confused recollection of some noise or blow in her dream, but forgetting all about it in the bright bevy of sunbeams that filled the room as she opened her eyes.

The boarders looked at her, as she descended, calm, composed and refreshed, and then at each other, and wondered. The third morning she looked at them and wondered: she had been disturbed at about midnight, out of the first deep dream, by footsteps going slowly by her door, slowly ascending the next staircase, and entering the room above; something had been violently dragged across the floor overhead, shoving up against the wall with a thump that shook the house; there had been a brief stillness; and then a heavy fall. Blank silence after that. Julia found herself shaking and shuddering in the warm bed, she knew not why. But revolving it in her mind she reached the conclusion that one of the boarders had been out somewhat too late; and that it was none of her affair; and repeated a page of Pollok's Course of Time, and fell asleep.

In the morning she glanced up and down the table, to discover, with an idle inquisitiveness for which she afterwards blamed herself, the receiver of the previous night's mishaps, if he were identifiable,—and found gradually that every eye had been measuring herself with something of the same interest. Even the landlady asked if she had rested pleasantly, and further hazarded the remark that she must be a sound sleeper at all times; to which Julia, thanking a healthy digestion, answered that she was.

Startled the next night at about the same time, Julia was surprised to hear a repetition of precisely the same occurrence as on the previous night, in the room over her own. It took two pages of Pollok, some paragraphs of the Night-Thoughts, and a part of the multiplication-table, before she lost consciousness in the sweet clouds of sleep; she was so cold too that she had gotten up and lit the the gas, and walked swiftly up and down the room to put herself into a glow; when she awoke in the morning, there was the little blue jet shining like a spectre itself in the busy healthy sunshine

"It is no wonder I dream so, with the gas burning over me all night long," thought Julia, shutting it off with a snap and throwing open a window. "How I hate the smell of it! brimstone stuff,—it betrays where it came from!"

But, when every night for three weeks she was startled at midnight by the footsteps stealing by her door, ascending the staircase, and sounding above; by the violent dragging of something across the floor overhead shoving up against the wall with a thump that shook the house; brief stillness; a heavy fall; and then the blank silence in which she shivered and the perspiration sprung out upon her forehead; after three weeks of this living nightmare, she plainly saw that if ever any house was haunted this was the one, and understood why the landlady had never been able to retain a lodger in that room beyond the third night, except herself, who had now reached the third week. She imagined, as was indeed the case, that these sounds were inaudible in any other room than hers. Nevertheless, she was not a coward in any sense;—if one could but revisit it this scene of sorrow she would have welcomed him as a messenger confirming the news she most wished to hear; the only fear she had was that quaking of the flesh, under some malign antipathy, which passed with the occasion; the room was large, airy, sunny, cheerful, cheap,—she resolved to abandon it to no ghost whatever; and after breakfast, one morning, when nobody was near, mounted herself the staircase next above, meaning to enter the room overhead and investigate matters.

To her surprise, there was no room there, it was a wide and ample attic, clean-swept and bare, without a single article of furniture, trunk, chest, chair, or so much as the splinter of a broken board. There was, in fact, nothing in it to be seen except some cobwebs woven round the fragment of a rusty nail that had once been bent and broken in the beam. What was it then that she heard dragged across the floor so noisily each night, and striking the wall that vibrated down to the head-board of her own bed?

That evening Julia procured candle and candlestick, and, with a chair and a light stand, crept up-stairs, and seated herself directly over her own room, sewing quietly as she could (for inner throbs and plunges are not entirely at the control of the will) by the light of her taper, till the clocks had tolled out twelve in all their various voices on the night, and even till one hasty little fellow had been so audacious as to contradict their decree by pronouncing it one, "two or three times."

"Late to-night," said Julia. Her heart sank, but her will remained the same. And just then the steps were heard tiptoeing along the passage, stealing up the stairway. Julia looked, and looked, with starting eyes; whatever it was, it was on the same floor with herself, now; but she saw nothing at all. Yet the footfalls came hesitatingly by her, paused a moment, grew resolute, and then the noise of the dragging of the heavy chest suddenly came, but ceased as abruptly in the midst. Julia was brave; her heart shook, it is true; her needle pricked her finger, and drew the blood; but she was determined; and, though bathed in chill, waited with the breath on her lips. Then there came a long faint sigh, she felt it like a cold wind on her lips, the flame of her candle bent and wavered and went out, the footsteps passed her and stole down, down the staircase, and along the passage, and were lost. Julia did not wait for that, though; she left light-stand, and chair, and work where they were, and with hardly more than a bound reached her own room, entered it and shut and double-locked the door. She had hardly done so when it seemed to her as if she heard that long faint sigh again, so long, so faint, so weary, that it filled her heart with pity.

Could the disembodied, when only here on earth, suffer so? Yet could she pity anything that did not suffer? She was a charitable large-souled woman,—there was room in her heart, it seemed, even for the sorrows of a ghost. She took a soothing-draught presently, dreamed of the sigh all night, and thought of it all day. When she came home that afternoon, she went into the landlady's little sitting-room and related what had happened to her.

"Well," said the landlady, folding up her work, "I am sorry. I suppose you will leave us now."

" No," said Julia. "I shall stay. At least for the present. But if you know any more about these things than I do, I wish you would enlighten me."

So the landlady told her that, owing to such occurrences, the house had fallen from its old grandeur, unable to keep any tenant but such as herself; yet that fifty years ago it was the family-residence of a wealthy gentleman of ancient name, and its honors were done by his daughter, a beautiful proud-spirited girl, too haughty to walk the common streets or to acknowledge herself made of common clay,—a passionate and glorious creature, a blossom like some splendid cactus flower, set in spines and thorns, but opening with a lavish crimson of heart's blood, and rich in pulpy fruit. Proud of her beauty, her dignity, her grace, her father watched and worshipped her. She, too, adored him, after her own fashion. To the rest of the world she seemed to award little notice further than scorn. She had her lovers, and laughed at them; others she withered for their daring, in her pride; her day was yet to come. One morning she was a member of some party that went to hear the music at a Catholic Chapel, music that had promised to be fine. As she sat in one of the stalls, and the priest came up the aisle lightly scattering the holy water to right and left, like the dews of grace descending from heaven on the congregation, she half turned her face and looked up, and her eyes met the eyes of the priest and remained fastened there. He, too, as if by some electric thrill, had paused one fraction of an instant, then torn his eyes away from the glowing gorgeous forgetful beauty under them, and had gone upon his way. It was a face that might have fastened other eyes than hers—the young priest's,—a clear dark Spanish face tinted in palest olive, full-lipped in curves of carmine, made to kiss —on the profile that first slight hint of the aquiline, hardly guessed, but inexpressibly delightful of outline, and under black but delicate brows,—and long black childlike lashes, large grey eyes limpid and full of lustre and sweetness—over all a melancholy cast that fixed the fancy. A face of rarest beauty, yet enthralling power. Such an one might gaze at you from a picture and keep you spell-bound. But gazing, in the life, at a heart-free girl—proud as she was, she was made of flesh and blood.

The music went soaring and swelling on that day, carrying its ravishing melody and praise to the very gates of heaven. She heard it but did not heed it. It was a Mass of Mozart's. Its warm delicious tones melted into her mood and hung about her like a happy cloud. Further than to feel that, she did not follow the threaded harmonies nor note the base and groundwork that the braided voices gave to the silver clarion-calls of the sopranos. She was conscious only of the priest's face, the beautiful pale melancholy face, flashing like a light through all the service. The eyes, those luminous wells did not seek her own again, perhaps he was doing penance that they had met even once. As it was, that once was once too often. His voice trembled in his chant, his heart beat so that the shadow of the adornment of his chasuble beat time to it, a desecration on the sacred chancel-wall. Perhaps when he was by himself that night stripes beat the same time to another measure.

She went to the place again; the music there was celebrated. He, too, was known; there was a fervor and a spirit in his eloquence that had won many to his cross; crowds followed him and hung rapt upon his tones, perhaps his slightly foreign accent gave them a fragment of their charm, perhaps his young beauty, shining like a lamp, added a power to his periods with which no other element could have endowed them. He was thought to be ascetic too, his severe and lofty purity wrapped him like a shield, they said, from this world's temptations; his superiors treasured him and expected great fulfilments from his promise; the crosier of an archbishop might yet be borne before him here on earth, as palms might be in heaven. That he was ambitious of the dignities and honors of his church could not be doubted, but there was an emotional nature in his preaching of the faith he followed, far more potent than any determined scheme or will; he received the Divine favor in a living flood, and he carried all before him, because he felt this flood and poured it freely.

So, as it as it has been said, she went to the place again. Again, and yet again, and save for a servant all alone. Perhaps the music, the ceremony, enchained her, the odor of fresh flowers heaped there by devotees,—perhaps the preaching moved her,—perhaps she mistook her heart's need for her soul's,—who can say? One night, the throng separating, some in tears of repentance and endeavor, and some in smiles of rest and joy, she lingered ;—he had gone down from the pulpit and was behind the confessional; and when one absolved sinner came away she knelt in the same place. What was she kneeling there for? "My father, I have need of grace!" she said. Divine, or human? The voice startled him, though never before had he heard it. He looked up and again their eyes met. As for the rest, neither fasting, nor penance, nor prayer, conquered nature; for all he was a priest, he was a man as well. And for her, she had never been a priest; and a woman has but a woman's feeble strength. He had asked himself, why he had been so much more interested in the welfare of this beautiful sinner than in that of the humble homely body whose place she took; but he refused the answer even to his heart. Chance and circumstance conspired against him too. After that he met her everywhere; moved from her own orbit into doing good to them that suffered, as he gave peace to some passing spirit, he saw her on the other side smoothing the pillow of the penitent. Then at a friend's house in a morning call he found her; and at last, with social exigencies, he was beneath her father's roof. Once there, a lodestone drew him; he went again. Here was a soul, he said, to save. One, the sole heir to such wealth as she was destined to be, what a boon to the church. Powerful in name and in influence, how many might follow in her train. It was a choice place to go, that old family-mansion, full of the sense of wealth and ease and the pleasant things of life, if he did penance on cold stones after each visit, it did not hinder his coming there next day. He expounded to her the articles of his creed; they read together; they looked together at the costly and wonderful prints of the portfolios; she sang, and he taught her the modulation of the music that he knew and loved; she listened, and he told her stories of his Spanish boyhood among the olive-groves on a mountain side in the shadow of the monastery; his conscience stung him with knowledge of the dangerous charm,—but yet, it was innocent and happy work, he said; he was winning a soul to holy church, others were always with them or about them ;—some day the serge for that sweet brow, for even the convent grate could not shut him out, then and forever, from his devotee. As for himself, he was fenced about with a panoply of proof. As for her,—well, what lover ever thought of that?

He had brought her, one evening, a little gift, a trifle designed to remind her of his faith and its ceremonies every day. It was a rosary of mother-of-pearl, carved with most exquisite corrugation, one of those that years and years ago Pietro della Valle carried to Palestine that he might touch with them the relics of St. Catharine,—it had wandered down into the young priest's possession at last, and for him the Holy Father at Rome himself had blessed it. He gave it now to her. He had not entered to remain; she had gone to him,—and standing in the alcove of a window for a moment, while the room hummed with low sweet voices, laughter, and music, behind them, he had placed this in her hand. Some one in passing had brushed the heavy curtain; it swung, and loosened, and on one side, on his, it partly fell. She stood, holding the rosary up to the broad moonlight that swam in and filled the alcove with a glory of its own ;"Pietro della Valle, Palestine, St. Catharine, Rome,"—the words all passed idly through her mind; she watches the pure and perfect color in the roughened beads, the bubble of rosy flame in one, the sparkle neither emerald nor azure in another, the opaline loveliness in a third, while the crucifix seemed to wear an auriole of pure white light; she bent her head back, looking up at him with a face where the moonbeams' silver sifted over the rich bloom and beauty, "I shall pray with it for you!" she said. His hand clasped over hers as she held it. With that crucifix between their fingers, how could their hearts be anything but holy? For him! he gazed at her as she spoke, gazing up at him, the melting eyes, the red red lips. For him! a moment more, and he had bent and sealed those lips with the first love-kiss they had ever known,—the first,—but not the last.

He was a priest, the story-teller said; nothing but Death could divorce him from the bride already wedded. Nothing but Death; and he was alive,—alive, young, strong, and glad with love's first passion. If he had put the earth between them. But he did not.—And "the rest is silence."

One dreary day, when remorse and fear had, like two wolf-hounds planting their fangs in the throat, gotten deadly hold of him, and he had sworn to see her no more,—she went up the broad oaken staircase, so polished she could see her weary face in every step, her weary beautiful face, still with its rich color, with its lovely contour, with its dark eyes glowing as the light glows on the dark velvety petals of some flower. She wanted to be alone; there was some one in her room; she passed it stealthily and went up into that place of the garret. There was nothing but shame before her. She wrung her hands in an agony ;—she who had been so haughty and so fiery in her presumption, she who was still so proud. How could she meet her father's eye and live, how could she wrong his tender love and faith in her enough to dare to live? How could she receive the scorn that once meted out by her now should be meted back to her in full,—how face the bitter jeering world,—how linger when her lover had forsaken her? There was nothing but shame before her, and at the end, death. Why not death at the beginning?

Swift thinking. The great nail in the beam caught her eye—she felt a flash of joy, perhaps, as if she saw escape; she stood on tiptoe and tried the nail, if springing it backward or forward she could loosen it; then the old chest dragged by her little arm from its place; her belt in a running knot,—and then for the first time that heavy fall that every night, save one, for fifty years had been repeated with a dull dead thud.

So the landlady finished what she had to say, and rose to unlock her tea-caddy. Julia drank her tea thoughtfully that evening, and when she went up-stairs, arranged her droplight, placed the armchair beside the table empty, took another chair herself, and went to sewing.

She sewed late: it was nearly time for the footsteps; she listened and listened; there they were. Julia opened her door, looked out and said, though in tremulous tones enough, "If there is any one here in trouble, or needing any help that I can give, they are welcome to come in."

The footsteps paused, neither passed on, nor retired, nor did they enter the room. Julia had no company that night, and closed her door at last and went to bed, nor was she awakened by the dragging of the chest or the heavy fall above.

The next night Julia set her door open, lighted her drop-light, drew up the empty armchair, and placed herself at her work again. She was waiting for the footsteps, but it would be long before they would be due. While she sewed, there was a sound just outside the door, a long, low weary sigh. "Come in!" cried Julia starting to her feet. "Do come in !"

It came in, or so at least Julia thought, for there were slow footfalls on the carpet; she could see nothing at all of any one, but, without seeing, she was confident, as one often is through some inappreciable sense that there was another person than herself there with her in the room. A peculiar fear overcame her again, the same shaking shuddering chill that she had briefly experienced every night for three weeks and that she had begun to fear would work some injurious impression on her health; but her mind was not afraid; it staied firm, though her hands grew icy and she could hardly meet her dry lips across her teeth. "Take the armchair," she contrived to say, sitting down again herself. She fancied that her guest had done as she desired, but suddenly, in order to make sure, she rose, laid aside her work, and resolutely went and seated herself in the arm-chair; there was a slight obstacle under her, an elastic resistance,—not but what she sat down in the chair, but it seemed as though there were a layer of some other substance, some airy impalpability, between her and the wicker-work. She went back to her own seat, and took up her needle again.

"Perhaps you would like to have me read to you?" she asked, in a little while. No sound replied to her, yet she felt convinced that she had been answered and affirmatively, —perhaps on the old principle of silence giving assent. She read a Psalm, some scattered verses of comfort selected here and there, for she was feeling her way for a hymn. In old times, a holy name, the touch of the Bible made one master of such moments. This could be no entirely evil spirit since even by all this it remained unexorcised, for forth from the arm-chair in the succeeding silence stole the long low weary sigh. "I shall set this chair for you every night, if you would like to occupy it," said Julia then, and the footsteps fell softly over the carpet and stole out into the passage once again.

Every evening after this, Julia's door was open and her arm-chair empty for the ghostly guest; every evening the footsteps came up the passage and waited, were invited in and entered. Sometimes Julia read to her, sometimes sung the sweet old Methodist hymns she held in store, sometimes talked, kind pleasant talk as one woman might to another who was ill and forbidden by the physicians to speak; sometimes it seemed to her as if one answered her, but yet she knew she had not heard a sound. Once having provided herself with matches, in case panic overtook her, she fixed her eyes on the arm-chair, and suddenly turned off the gas. It seemed to her, during the ensuing moment, that some faintly luminous object in a woman's likeness met her glance, but whether it was so, or whether it was the dazzle of the late light in her eyes or the effect of an over-excited imagination, she dared not say.

Half doubting her sanity, at this time, Julia went one day to a physician and asked him to discover if there were anything abnormal in her condition; but after he had questioned her, felt her even pulse, seen her steady eye, and tested the sound and not uncommon quality of her brain, he asked her for what she came to him, and pronounced the only difference between her and other women to be that now-a-days they were made of diseased nerves, while she appeared not to have a nerve in her body. "On the contrary," said Julia "my nerves are steel." Then she told him the recent incidents in her experience, upon which he laughed and said he had been mistaken—she was like all the rest of them only with the sorest nerves of all, and gave her a sedative; which however she never took until after her spiritual companion, if such it was, had departed.

One night Julia said to her ghost, "I think I know your story,—it is, this." And delicately as she might, she hinted at its heads. Swift piercing sighs replied to her, and sounds like heart-broken sobbing. Said Julia then, "It seems an offence, to me, outweighed by such a punishment as yours. To come back every night for fifty years, every night to feel the old wretchedness, the doubt, the despair, the agony of determination, every night to taste of death anew,—I do not believe there is any power of Heaven, if indeed there be any power of evil that can compel you to it. You do it of your own free will, dwelling on your old pain, hoping to expiate your errors. Leave them all, and go up higher."

"There is no other place for me to go," said a voice that made Julia's heart stand still with sharp surprise and awe.

"Have you tried ?" asked Julia in reply. "That you sinned,—we know. But we are all sinners. Who that looks at perfect whiteness can call himself clean? If your sin shuts you out from the presence of God, then indeed it, were the darkest dye of sin. But as the sunshine penetrates everywhere on earth, so does the sunshine of God's love, I am sure, to lighten all sad spots. And as for you, if you lived your life again you would be innocent, I think." She paused.

"I do not know! O me, I do not know!" the sighing seemed to sob.

"You are more humble than you were," said Julia. "You no longer trust yourself as once, you see. Repentance, I have thought sometimes transfigures vice and turns it into virtue."

"I do not repent," said the spirit. "I never have repented."

"You hug your wrong-doing ?" asked Julia in an amaze. "No wonder then that for fifty years you endure its penalty over and over again. You must repent !"

"Did I do wrong?" the spirit sighed. "O me, I do not know?"

"See, You loved him. Your love, I know, was but the offshoot of your nature. Rest and union, the sacred mingling of two lives and souls which marriage makes, was denied you. And though the greater sin may have been in the power that bound your lover to a single life, that destroyed his manhood in his priesthood, that defied the eternal laws, defied God,—nevertheless you also broke law, and in your own little being defied these things as well. Think what God is to his universe, its Maker, its upholder, its warmth, its light, its life,—think what that universe would be, banished from his presence. Think then of his glory, his purity, and what sympathy might be between such spotlessness and any soil or stain. Think then of your own soil and stain, and see yourself separated from him, shut away by sin. Ah, there is the true misery! You took your life, too; destroyed what was not yours but what Heaven had lent you. Should the account of all those years you might have lived be demanded, what have you to render? You cannot give back the simple sum of them, for you annihilated them and so defrauded Heaven. And of how much besides ?—But there is no sinner who, bowed in repentance, cannot catch heaven's light on his head till it changes him to something white and pure and pleasant in his Maker's eyes. You cannot but repent what severs you from the divine companionship. You cannot but repent if your deeds make one unlovely object in the whole universe for the great good God to look upon,—he has done so much to fill his world with beauty! Do not doubt but that when you seek pardon, though, it is already yours. Look at your guilt, after all, as being enormous as you will, you must not forget," continued Julia, "that the forgiveness of Heaven is vaster yet. I often question if there is any wrong so great but that the greater mercy could not cover it; so black but it could blot it out. Is not your sin then like a mote swimming in a whole sky full of light, and lost in it? Repent and be forgiven, and so rest, troubled soul !"

During all these days, Julia, convinced of some great work in hand, and rapt in it, thinking over words and counsels for the evening, went about her daily tasks like some one in a dream. She was only awake and alive, it seemed, when those footsteps fell upon her floor. She felt that she was helping a perturbed spirit into peace, peace that it might have found long ago, could it have met with any one bold enough to help it, self-condemned to re-enact its crime every night for half a century. So she went on, reading, talking, singing, giving companionship, to the phantom of the unknown lady, as she still believes. One night at last, as she sat there waiting for her, when some three months had passed, at their usual time the footsteps came again, came up to the table and paused.

The gas was burning brightly; Julia looked up alert as ever now. And something stood before her. A girl clad in garments of a fashion laid away for fifty years—a shape half hesitating whether to be a shape or not. It was like a remembered picture—a brilliant brocade of bloomy peach-color, cut on the bosom low and square over a creamy skin—a mantle of black lace caught on the comb behind, resting on the round and taper arms in front, and falling like dust over the jetty polish of the braids—these things were vacillating, wavering, undecided, but half divined; over them all there seemed to be a blemish, an ash, a smirch of grave soil, from which one turned the glance away. But the face, robbed of color, and white with shining eyes, yet all suffused in a smile of peace and light, was distinct and vivid as a star—like life itself, but more beautiful than any vision of life,—if a star had opened in the deeps of heaven, and a face gazed from it, it might have looked like that. One other thing Julia was sure she saw—a string of beads, a rosary, glimmering moonily in blurs and freckles of phantom color till they took a body of tint, and the globules of rich light were forgotten in the lucid splendor of a crucifix.

"Good-bye," said the voice, or the sweet suspicion of a voice, that she had learned to know. "I am going now. You have shown me the way. I shall return no more. Up a little way, a little way at a time—but no longer in despair. I see the light; I am making for it. Good-bye, kind friend, good angels walk on either side your way!" There came a soft cool breath along her cheek, and then the doubtful gleam of peach-bloom color wholly vanished, the face trembled and faded, and all was as before.

Three years have passed since then. Julia still sits in that same room of evenings; but for any ghostly society she sits alone. The sighing spirit never has come back ;—the footsteps have ceased to pass along the passage and up the stairs; the heavy fall has never once been heard; there is nothing but a legend left to haunt the house. Laid as ghost never yet was laid—by love and care—the phantom of the place has vanished and left peace behind her.

That is the story as it was told to me. For myself, I said once before that I did not believe a word of it.

GEORGE ARNOLD.

On another page will be found the last article ever written by our dear friend GEORGE ARNOLD. We copy it from the N. Y. WEEKLY REVIEW, where it appeared a few weeks since as one of the charming series of papers which he contributed to that paper over his well-known signature of "MCARONE." It was written when the brilliant author was suffering from an illness which—as our readers are too well aware—terminated on Thursday last, fatally. It is far from being the cleverest or the wittiest of his productions; but read by the light of his situation at the time—his exhaustion of body, his lassitude of ésprit, and his all but weariness of life—it will long be cherished by those of us to whom he was so dear, and who knew so well the operations of his mind, with the most tender interest. We remember reading it when it was first published with a sadness which not even its exquisite wit and humor could subdue. Now, every line of it brings tears to our heart.

We knew GEORGE ARNOLD long and intimately. No friend on earth was ever more dear to us. He had more endearing and enduring qualities than any person we ever met. In all the vicissitudes of our little journal—so personal in its character and associations—he was with us heart and soul. He made no professions to anybody, but in the time of trial he was always at hand. Never have we known any one so generally loved and admired. The news of his death came to thousands as the one grief of their lives. For our own part, we have no heart to speak or to think of it. At some other time, when we can more fully realize the fact of our friend's loss, we may attempt some analysis of his life and character. At present, we can only extend our sympathy to his heart-broken family and friends, and bow with them in resignation to the Supreme Will.

NEW YORK NOVEMBER 18, 1865

We give up the principal portion of our editorial space, to-day, to an exquisitely humorous sketch—"Jim Smiley and his Jumping Frog"—by Mark Twain, who will shortly become a regular contributor to our columns. Mark Twain is the assumed name of a writer in California who has long been a favorite contributor to the San Francisco press, from which his articles have been so extensively copied as to make him nearly as well known as Artemus Ward.

(From the Round Table.)

GEORGE ARNOLD.

Greenwood, November 13, 1865.

We stood around the dreamless form
Whose strength was so untimely shaken,
Whose sleep not all our love could warm,
Nor any dearest voice awaken;

And while the Autumn breathed her sighs
And dropped a thousand leafy glories,
And all the pathways, and the skies,
Were mindful of his songs and stories,

Nor failed to wear the mingled hues
He loved, and knew so well to render,
But wooed—alas, in vain !—their Muse
For one more tuneful lay and tender:

We paused awhile—the gathered few
Who came, in longing, not in duty—
With eyes that full of weeping grew,
To look their last upon his beauty.

Death would not rudely rob that face,
Nor dim its fine Arcadian brightness,
But gave the lines a clearer grace,
And sleep's repose, and marble's whiteness.

And, gazing there on him so young,
We thought of all his ended mission,
The broken links, the songs unsung,
The love that found no ripe fruition:

Till last the old, old question came
To hearts that beat with life around him,
Why Death, with downward torch aflame,
Had searched our number till he found him?

Why passed the one who poorly knows
That blithesome spell for either fortune,
Or mocked with lingering menace those
Whose pains the final thrust importune :

Or left the toiling ones who bear
The crowd's neglect, the want that presses,
The woes no human soul can share,
Nor look, nor spoken word, confesses?

And from the earth no answer came,
The forest wore a stillness deeper,
The sky and lake smiled on the same,
And voiceless as the silent sleeper.

And so we turned ourselves away,
By earth and air and water chidden,
And left him with them, where he lay,
A sharer of their secret hidden.

And each the staff and shell again
Took up, and marched with memories haunted;
But henceforth, in our pilgrim strain,
We'll miss a voice that sweetly chaunted!

EDMUND C. STEDMAN.

AFTERNOON AMUSEMENTS TO-DAY.

ACADEMY OF MUSIC.—Philharmonic Rehearsal, 3 P. M.
NIBLO'S GARDEN.—"Arrah-na-Pogue, 2 P. M.
BROADWAY THEATRE.—"Sam," 11½ P. M.
BARNUM'S MUSEUM.—" Don Caesar de Bazan," 3 P. M.
NEW YORK CIRCUS (late Hippotheatron.)—Robinson's bare-back riding, etc., 2½ P. M.

GEORGE ARNOLD.

November 13*th*, 1865.

In the sweet stillness of a Summer day
Which softly came to set the Fall aside,
And kiss a Summer brow with Summer pride,
In silent grief we laid our friend away.
A smile still lingered on his youthful face,
Where not a line but some strange beauty showed,
Where all the splendor of his nature glowed,
And Death, from life, had sculptured every grace.
The ritual of the grave remained unsaid,
All parting utterance seemed out of place;
We scarce could feel as yet our GEORGE was dead,
And sought in vain his memory to trace:
So passed the hour in sweet and holy calm,
Each thought a prayer, and every word a psalm.

H. C., JR.

(For the Saturday Press.)

JIM SMILEY AND HIS JUMPING FROG.

BY MARK TWAIN.

MR. A. WARD,

DEAR SIR:—Well, I called on good-natured, garrulous old Simon Wheeler, and I inquired after your friend Leonidas W. Smiley, as you requested me to do, and I hereunto append the result. If you can get any information out of it you are cordially welcome to it. I have a lurking suspicion that your Leonidas W. Smiley is a myth—that you never knew such a personage, and that you only conjectured that if I asked old Wheeler about him it would remind him of his infamous Jim Smiley, and he would go to work and bore me nearly to death with some infernal reminiscence of him as long and tedious as it should be useless to me. If that was your design, Mr. Ward, it will gratify you to know that it succeeded.

I found Simon Wheeler dozing comfortably by the bar-room stove of the little old dilapidated tavern in the ancient mining camp of Boomerang, and I noticed that he was fat and bald-headed, and had an expression of winning gentleness and simplicity upon his tranquil countenance. He roused up and gave me good-day. I told him a friend of mine had commissioned me to make some inquiries about a cherished companion of his boyhood named Leonidas W. Smiley—Rev. Leonidas W. Smiley—a young minister of the gospel, who he had heard was at one time a resident of this village of Boomerang. I added that if Mr. Wheeler could tell me anything about this Rev. Leonidas W. Smiley, I would feel under many obligations to him.

Simon Wheeler backed me into a corner and blockaded me there with his chair—and then sat down and reeled off the monotonous narrative which follows this paragraph. He never smiled, he never frowned, he never changed his voice from the quiet, gently-flowing key to which he turned the initial sentence, he never betrayed the slightest suspicion of enthusiasm—but all through the interminable narrative there ran a vein of impressive earnestness and sincerity, which showed me plainly that so far from his imagining that there was anything ridiculous or funny about his story, he regarded it as a really important matter, and admired its two heroes as men of transcendent genius in finesse. To me, the spectacle of a man drifting serenely along through such a queer yarn without ever smiling was exquisitely absurd. As I said before, I asked him to tell me what he knew of Rev. Leonidas W. Smiley, and he replied as follows. I let him go on in his own way, and never interrupted him once :

Mark Twain astride his jumping frog, as per British caracturist, Frederick Waddy.

There was a feller here once by the name of *Jim* Smiley, in the winter of '49—or maybe it was the spring of '50—I don't recollect exactly, some how, though what makes me think it was one or the other is because I remember the big flume wasn't finished when he first come to the camp; but anyway, he was the curiosest man about always betting on any thing that turned up you ever see, if he could get anybody to bet on the other side, and if he couldn't he'd change sides—any way that suited the other man would suit *him*—any way just so's he got a bet, *he* was satisfied. But still, he was lucky—uncommon lucky; he most always come out winner. He was always ready and laying for a chance; there couldn't be no solitry thing mentioned but what that feller'd offer to bet on it—and take any side you please, as I was just telling you: if there was a horse race, you'd find him flush or you find him busted at the end of it; if there was a dog-fight, he'd bet on it; if there was a cat-fight, he'd bet on it; if there was a chicken-fight, he'd bet on it; why if there was two birds setting on a fence, he would bet you which one would fly first—or if there was a camp-meeting he would be there regular to bet on parson Walker, which he judged to be the best exhorter about here, and so he was, too, and a good man; if he even see a straddle-bug start to go any wheres, he would bet you how long it would take him to get wherever he was going to, and if you took him up he would foller that straddle-bug to Mexico but what he would find out where he was bound for and how long he was on the road. Lots of the boys here has seen that Smiley and can tell you about him. Why, it never made no difference to *him*—he would bet on *anything*—the dangdest feller. Parson Walker's wife laid very sick, once, for a good while, and it seemed as if they warn't going to save her; but one morning he come in and Smiley asked him how she was, and he said she was considerable better—thank the Lord for his inf'nit mercy—and coming on so smart that with the blessing of Providence she'd get well yet—and Smiley, before he thought, says, "Well, I'll resk two-and-a-half that she don't, anyway."

Thish-yer Smiley had a mare—the boys called her the fifteen-minute nag, but that was only in fun, you know, because, of course, she was faster than that—and he used to win money on that horse, for all she was so slow and always had the asthma, or the distemper, or the consumption, or something of that kind. They used to give her two or three hundred yards' start, and then pass her under way; but always at the fag-end of the race she'd get excited and desperate-like, and come cavorting and spraddling up, and scattering her legs around limber, sometimes in the air, and sometimes out to one side amongst the fences, and kicking up m-o-r-e dust, and raising m-o-r-e racket with her coughing and sneezing and blowing her nose—and always fetch up at the stand just about a neck ahead, as near as you could cipher it down.

And he had a little small bull-pup, that to look at him you'd think he warn't worth a cent, but to set around and look ornery, and lay for a chance to steal something. But as soon as money was up on him he was a different dog—his under-jaw'd begin to stick out like the for'castle of a steamboat, and his teeth would uncover, and shine savage like the furnaces. And a dog might tackle him, and bully-rag him, and bite him, and throw him over his shoulder two or three times, and Andrew Jackson—which was the name of the pup —Andrew Jackson would never let on but what he was satisfied, and hadn't expected nothing else and the bets being doubled and doubled on the other side all the time, till the money was all up—and then all of a sudden he would grab that other dog just by the joint of his hind legs and freeze to it—not chaw, you understand, but only just grip and hang on till they throwed up the sponge, if it was a year. Smiley always came out winner on that pup till he harnessed a dog once that didn't have no hind legs, because they'd been sawed off in a circular saw, and when the thing had gone along far enough, and the money was all up, and he came to make a snatch for his pet holt, he saw in a minute how he'd been imposed on, and how the other dog had him in the door, so to speak, and he 'peared surprised, and then he looked sorter discouraged like, and didn't try no more to win the fight, and so he got shucked out bad. He gave Smiley a look as much as to say his heart was broke, and it was *his* fault, for putting up a dog that hadn't no hind legs for him to take holt of, which was his main dependence in a fight, and then he limped off a piece, and laid down and died. It was a good pup, was that Andrew Jackson, and would have made a name for hisself if he'd lived, for the stuff was in him, and he had genius—I know it, because he hadn't had no opportunities to speak of, and it don't stand to reason that a dog could make such a fight as he could under them circumstances, if he hadn't no talent. It always makes me feel sorry when I think of that last fight of his'on, and the way it turned out.

Well, thish-yer Smiley had rat-terriers and chicken cocks, and tom-cats, and all them kind of things, till you couldn't rest, and you couldn't fetch nothing for him to bet on but he'd match you. He ketched a frog one day and took him home and said he cal'lated to educate him ; and so he never done nothing for three months but set in his back yard and learn that frog to jump. And you bet you he *did* learn him, too. He'd give him a little hunch behind, and the next minute you'd see that frog whirling in the air like a doughnut—see him turn one summerset, or maybe a couple, if he got a good start, and come down flat-footed and all right, like a cat. He got him up so in the matter of ketching flies, and kept him in practice so constant, that he'd nail a fly every time as far as he could see him. Smiley said all a frog wanted was education, and he could do most anything—and I believe him. Why, I've seen him set Dan'l Webster down here on this floor—Dan'l Webster was the name of the frog—and sing out, "Flies! Dan'l, flies," and quicker'n you could wink, he'd spring straight up, and snake a fly off'n the counter there, and flop down on the floor again as solid as a gob of mud, and fall to scratching the side of his head with his hind foot as indifferent as if he hadn't no idea he'd done any more'n any frog might do. You never see a frog so modest and straightfor'ard as he was, for all he was so gifted. And when it come to fair-and-square jumping on a dead level, he could get over more ground at one straddle than any animal of his breed you ever see. Jumping on a dead level was his strong suit, you understand, and when it come to that, Smiley would ante up money on him as long as he had a red. Smiley was monstrous proud of his frog, and well he might be, for fellers that had travelled and ben everywheres all said he laid over any frog that ever *they* see.

Well, Smiley kept the beast in a little lattice box, and he used to fetch him down town sometimes and lay for a bet. One day a feller—a stranger in the camp, he was—come across him with his box, and says:

"What might it be that you've got in the box?"

And Smiley says, sorter indifferent like, "It might be a parrot, or it might be a canary, maybe, but it ain't—it's only just a frog."

And the feller took it, and looked at it careful, and turned it round this way and that, and says, "H'm—so 'tis. Well, what's *he* good for?"

"Well," Smiley says, easy and careless, "He's good enough for *one* thing I should judge—he can out-jump ary frog in Calaveras county."

The feller took the box again, and took another long, particular look, and give it back to Smiley and says, very deliberate, "Well—I don't see no points about that frog that's any better'n any other frog."

"Maybe you don't," Smiley says. "Maybe you understand frogs, and maybe you don't understand 'em ; maybe you've had experience, and maybe you ain't only a amature, as it were. Anyways, I've got *my* opinion, and I'll resk forty dollars that he can outjump ary frog in Calaveras county."

And the feller studied a minute, and then says, kinder sad, like, "Well—I'm only a stranger here, and I ain't got no frog—but if I had a frog I'd bet you."

And then Smiley says, "That's all right—that's all right—if you'll hold my box a minute I'll go and get you a frog;" and so the feller took the box, and put up his forty dollars along with Smiley's, and set down to wait.

So he set there a good while thinking and thinking to hisself, and then he got the frog out and prized his mouth open and took a teaspoon and filled him full of quail-shot—filled him pretty near up to his chin—and set him on the floor. Smiley he went out to the swamp and slopped around in the mud for a long time, and finally he ketched a frog and fetched him in and give him to this feller and says: "Now if you're ready, set him alongside of Dan'l, with his fore-paws just even with Dan'l's, and I'll give the word." Then he says, "one-two-three-jump!" and him and the feller touched up the frogs from behind, and the new frog hopped off lively, but Dan'l give a heave, and hysted up his shoulders—so—like a Frenchman, but it wasn't no use—he couldn't budge; he was planted as solid as a anvil, and he couldn't no more stir than if he was anchored out. Smiley was a good deal surprised, and he was disgusted too, but he didn't have no idea what the matter was, of course.

The feller took the money and started away, and when he was going out at the door he sorter jerked his thumb over his shoulder—this way—at Dan'l, and says again, very deliberate, "Well—I don't see no points about that frog that's any better'n any other frog."

Smiley he stood scratching his head and looking down at Dan'l a long time, and at last he says, "I do wonder what in the nation that frog throwed off for—I wonder if there ain't something the matter with him—he 'pears to look mighty baggy, somehow—and he ketched Dan'l by the nap of the neck, and lifted him up and says, "Why blame my cats if he don't weigh five pound"—and turned him upside down, and he belched out about a double-handful of shot. And then he see how it was, and he was the maddest man—he set the frog down and took out after that feller, but he never ketched him. And—

[Here Simon Wheeler heard his name called from the front-yard, and got up to go and see what was wanted.] And turning to me as he moved away, he said: "Just sit where you are, stranger, and rest easy—I ain't going to be gone a second."

But by your leave, I did not think that a continuation of the history of the enterprising vagabond Jim Smiley would be likely to afford me much information concerning the Rev. Leonidas W. Smiley, and so I started away. At the door I met the sociable Wheeler returning, and he button-holed me and recommenced:

"Well, thish-yer Smiley had a yaller one-eyed cow that didn't have no tail only just a short stump like a bannanner, and—"

"O, curse Smiley and his afflicted cow!" I muttered, good-naturedly, and bidding the old gentleman good-day, I departed.

Yours, truly,

MARK TWAIN.

ALONE BY THE HEARTH.

BY GEORGE ARNOLD.

Here, in my snug little fire-lit chamber,
Sit I alone;
And, as I gaze in the coals, I remember
Days long agone.

Saddening it is when the night has descended,
Thus to sit here,
Pensively musing on episodes, ended
Many a year.

Still in my visions a golden-haired glory
Flits to and fro;
She whom I loved—but 'tis just the old story,
Dead, long ago!

'Tis but the wraith of a love; yet I linger
(Thus passion errs),
Foolishly kissing the ring on my finger—
Once it was hers.

Nothing has changed since her spirit departed,
Here in this room—
Save I, who, weary, and half broken-hearted,
Sit in the gloom.

Loud 'gainst the window the Winter rain dashes,
Dreary and cold;
Over the floor the red fire-light flashes
Just as of old.

Just as of old—but the embers are scattered,
Whose ruddy blaze
Flashed o'er the floor where her fairy feet pattered
In other days!

Then, her dear voice, like a silver-chime ringing,
Melted away;
Often these walls have re-echoed her singing,
Now hushed for aye!

Why should love bring nought but sorrow, I wonder?
Everything dies!
Time and Death, sooner or later, must sunder
Holiest ties.

Years have rolled by; I am wiser and older—
Wiser, but yet
Not till my heart and its feelings grow colder,
Can I forget.

So, in my snug little fire-lit chamber,
Sit I, alone;
And, as I gaze in the coals, I remember
Days long agone!

NEW YORK NOVEMBER 25, 1865

NOTE FROM THE EDITOR

MY DEAR PRINTER :

I am still under the weather, and you must get out this week's paper the best way you can.

You know how impossible it has been for me to do anything this last fortnight, but you may safely promise the reader that next week—accidents excepted—if the PRESS is lacking in either originality or vivacity, it shall not be the fault of

Yours truly,

H. C. JR.

52 *Bleecker street, Nov.* 24.

(From the Weekly Review.)

GEORGE ARNOLD.

BURIED AT GREENWOOD CEMETERY, NOV. 13, 1865.

Beneath the still November sky,
With Nature's peace and beauty blest,
We put our selfish sorrow by,
And laid our loved one down to rest.

Rest—in the morning of his days!
Rest—when his heart had just begun
To feel the warmth of all men's praise—
The radiance of the rising sun!

Rest—to a strong and stately mind,
That rose all common flights above!
Rest—to a heart as good and kind
As ever glowed with human love!

And round him, dimly through our grief,
In every natural sound we heard—
In whispering grass, and rustling leaf,
And sighing wind—the same sweet word:

Rest! And we did not break the spell,
By holy Nature cast around
The fading form we left to dwell
Forever in her hallowed ground.

No hymns were sung, no prayers were said
Save what our loving hearts could say,
When, gazing mutely on the dead,
We blessed him—ere we turned away.

Back to the round of daily care
That seems so vacant to us now,
Remembering what repose was there,
What peace, upon his marble brow.

And so we left him—nevermore
To see, in sunshine or in rain,
The semblance of the form he wore,
Whose loss has steeped our souls in pain.

But long as skies of autumn smile,
And long as clouds of autumn weep,
Or autumn leaves their splendors pile
In sorrow o'er their Poet's sleep;

And long as violets grace the spring,
Or June-born roses blush and blow,
Or pale stars shine, or south winds sing,
Or tides of summer ebb and flow;

So long shall live their Poet's name—
When rest these broken hearts of ours—
Embalmed, in everlasting fame,
With stars and leaves and clouds and flowers.

WILLIAM WINTER.

NITROUS OXIDE.

Mr. Editor:

I am a Surgeon.

Some years ago I assisted in killing and cutting up a sheep.

On the strength of this I was appointed an Army Surgeon and, to-day, there is not one of my patients living—it wouldn't sound well to pause here—who will say that I did not perform my work satisfactorily.

I have now introduced the gas into my practice, and find it as efficacious in amputating limbs as in extracting teeth. The patient's sensations are so delightful while under its influence, that, on awaking, I am often begged to cut off the other leg.

Fact.

The rush to my office is tremendous, but all will be accommodated.

As each person enters, an usher hands him a numbered card, and he will not be compelled to wait longer than five days at the farthest.

I keep a book, wherein each person transcribes his name, and his sensations while amputation is being performed.

I append a few giving only the patients initials.

"Felt bully. Didn't care a red whether school kept or not."—H. W. B.

"Thought the South had gained its independence, and that my Book had passed through its fortieth edition."—I. B.

"Thought the 'goak' that a rich old uncle in England had left me Sixty thousand dollars was '2 troo."—A. W.

"Never experienced such delicious sensations. Thought everybody that did not think like me had been hanged for treason."—W. P.

"Felt sarcy. Thought Jeff. Davis had been pardoned, and I had gone a-fishing."—H. G.

"The happiest moment of my life. Thought I had succeeded in crushing the opera, and all the theatre managers advertised in the N. Y. HERALD."—J. G. B.

"Never felt better. Thought New York and New Jersey had gone democratic." —F. & B. W.

There, you have a few selected at random, from a list of more than upwards of considerable.

They will suffice to show that Nitrous Oxide is a great institution, and that I am

Yours,

B. DODD

P.S. —Don't for the world print the above; I am no Surgeon at all—never amputated any limbs and never want to.

I have been inhaling the "Laughing Gas," and the foregoing are merely my "sensations" while under its influence. odmo

Fact!

B. D.

In reply to a correspondent, who complains that the Press has been deficient, for the last week or two, in what he is pleased to call "light and sprightly paragraphs," we can only say that our mood has to change, like that of others, with circumstances, and that as we do not profess to publish a comic paper we must be permitted, now and then, to be more or less serious.

NEW YORK DECEMBER 2, 1865

(For the Saturday Press.)

A GANG OF SWINDLERS EXPOSED.

We are able to congratulate our fellow citizens on the detection and exposure of a gang of counterfeiters and swindlers which has long infested our city, but whose operations have usually been conducted under the mask of such plausible respectability, that they have up to this time utterly deceived and misled a too unsuspicious public. It was lately discovered that this Company of Art-ful Designers has been holding its meetings in a well-known building on the corner of Fourth Avenue and 23d Street, where night after night they have inveigled crowds of young men and innocent females, and after robbing them of their money at the door, have not scrupled to poison their tender minds by presenting to their view a number of handsomely framed Daubs—all of which are so utterly worthless, that the sooner they are swept out into the gutters, the better for all concerned.

The band of forgers, swindlers, counterfeiters and humbugs to which we allude, has for a long time been able by sheer impudence and by presuming upon the good-nature of an ignorant and credulous public, to escape detection, and even enjoy the privileges and immunities of honest men. That time is past. Thanks to the perseverance, sagacity, and energy of a brave man—one of the Pre-Raphaelite Policemen, we are told—we can entertain hopes that the works of these miserable deluders of public opinion, are thoroughly exposed and brought to contempt. On Saturday last this heroic and perspicacious individual, who, with a powerful eye-glass, had been for weeks reconnoitering the building above named—having fortified himself with a stiff glass of milk and water, mixed with a few drops of Ruskin's Celebrated Bitters, and taking under his arm a stout cudgel from the sour apple-tree on which Mr. J. Davis has not been hanged, proceeded to the rooms infested by this gang of conspirators against ART,—and in the short space of two columns by the time in the office of the WEEKLY SNAPPING TURTLE, succeeded in driving out every mother's son of them—scattering their wretched designs right and left, and laying all their colors prostrate in the mud of his own genius. There never was such utter confusion and dismay as that caused by the sudden onslaught of the brave young disciple of the new school of art. Everybody and everything in the rooms was pitched out of doors—with the exception of one deformed infant Pre-Raphaelite whom nobody noticed in the crowd, and who was suffered to remain, having pleaded ignorance of the company in which he was found.

"Fiat justitia, ruat cœlum." Let justice be done, though the ceiling of the M. A. should come down upon the head of the unhappy wight who never could have foreseen how the building he had planned would ever be consecrated to humbug.

Ladies and gentlemen, the curtain is about to fall on the Academic stage! There will be no more artist's Fun! Humbug is exploded! Criticism—of the justest, of the truest, of the sweetest, is to prevail!—(See the NEW YORK ORACLE, and the WEEKLY SNAPPING TURTLE.)

But what will the poor Academy do? *Quo nunc abibis in loca ?*

We have not yet learned when the trial of the Art-swindlers is to take place. It is thought that they will all make full confession of their guilt (gilt frames included) and that the President will pardon them, along with the host of conspirators and Secessionists who have been endeavoring to undermine their country's prosperity.

In our opinion they all deserve to be hanged beside their pictures.

C. P. C.

(Not from the Round Table.)

A STORY FOR GOOD LITTLE GIRLS.

Ma-ry Har-ris was a lit-tle girl who lived in Chi-ca-go. She was a ve-ry pret-ty lit-tle girl, and one day an old bach-e-lor fell in love with her. So he used to write fine let-ters to her, and call-ing her "Rose-bud" and "Puss" and "Little Mollie." But he went to Wash-ington, and got mar-ried and soon for-got his "Lit-tle Mol-lie." When Ma-ry Har-ris heard the news she bought a pret-ty pis-tol, and went to Wash-ing-ton. There she found the old bach-elor in a big build-ing, which they called. the Trea-su-ry De-part-ment. So she went up to him, and shot him with her pret-ty pis-tol. The bul-let went in-to the old bach-e-lor. This made him feel bad, and he died. Then Ma-ry Har-ris cried; for she was a good girl, and very af-fec-tion-ate. The sec-re-ta-ry came to see Ma-ry Har-ris, and pit-ied her very much. Then the ed-i-tors came to see her, and pit-ied her ve-ry much. For Ma-ry Har-ris was very pret-ty, and so af-fec-tion-ate. And the jailors of the prison all pit-ied her; and the judges, the ju-ry that tried her, and the law-yers, all pit-ied lit-tle Ma-ry Har-ris. So they let her go free; and the good ju-rors said it was all a mis-take—that she didn't kill-ed any bo-dy. And ev-ery bo-dy kissed Ma-ry Harris, be-cause she was a pret-ty girl. And every bo-dy was very hap-py, and huz-za-ed, except the old bach-e-lor, who couldn't huz-za be-cause he was dead. Oh, what a nice thing it is to be a pret-ty girl and shoot an old bache-lor! Lit-tle girls be af-fec-tion-ate and shoot old bach-e-lors.

Murderer, Mary Harris.

(For the Saturday Press.)

NOVEMBER.

BY WILD EDGERTON.

Who chaunts thy praises, sombre, bleak November—
Who greets thy passing in the year's procession?
Thou art but usher to the grim December
And few hearts hold thy days in dear possession,

The world finds solemn music in thy bustle,
Sweeping the threshold of the Wintry King,
And minstrels sigh at every dead leaf's rustle
And melancholy mars the songs they sing.

Here's one who hails thee chief of all thy brothers—
The varying twelve who march all years between—,
The gayer months perchance may charm most others,
But thou my dearer friend hast ever been.

To me thou bringest wealth of untold pleasure,
Recalling scenes my soul with joy remembers—
Seasons of rest and gladness beyond measure,
Beside my cheerful hearth's bright glowing embers.

I love to draw the curtains close and listen
To the strange music of thy breathings low,
While tears of joy upon my lashes glisten
Because thou callest up the long ago.

I would not have thy hoarse voice any clearer,
Nor changed the cadence of thy wildest tune—
The song my chimney sings to-night is dearer
Than any whisperings of May or June.

I know the Autumn leaves, without, are lying
In drifted piles men's heedless feet beneath,
Which little thought, a while ago, of dying,
And crowned the summer with triumphant wreath ;

I know the sapless boughs in pain are swaying,
And bowing farewells to departing leaves;
I know the mournful things the winds are saying
And hear the dripping of the weeping eaves;

Yet brings this sadness to MY heart no sorrow,
So full it is of bright thoughts thou hast brought,
And I shall smile as well as thou, to-morrow,
Over the ruin that thy hands have wrought;

And I shall gladly see some leaves still clinging
To lonely branches swept by thy rough breath,
And hear among them some fond birds still singing
Requiems o'er the faithful unto death.

So, for thy memories and useful lessons
And plaintive songs it cheers me to remember,
I hold thee dearer than all other seasons,
And love thee, fitful, frowning, chill November.

(For the Saturday Press.)

JOSH BILLINGS ON LAUGHING.

It never haz been proved, that enny ov the animal kreation hav attempted tew laff, (we are quite certain that none hav succeeded), thus this deliteful episode and pleasant power appears tew be entirely within the province ov humans. It iz the language ov infancy—the eloquense ov childhood,—and the power tew laff is the power to be happy. It is becomeing tew awl ages and conditions; and (with the very few exceptions, sakred tew sorrow) an honest, hearty laff iz always agreeable and in order. It iz an index ov karakter, and betrays sooner than words.—Laffing keeps oph sickness, and haz conquered az menny disseases az ever pills have, and at mutch less expense.—It makes flesh, and keeps it in its place.—It drives away weariness and brings a dream ov sweetness tew the sleeper.—It never iz covetous.—It ackompanys charity, and iz the handmaid ov honesty.—It disarms revenge, humbles pride, and iz the talisman ov kontentment.—Sum have kalled it a weakness—a substitute for thought, but really it strengthens wit, and adorns wisdum, invigorates the mind, gives language ease, and expreshun elegance.—It holds the mirror up tew beauty; it strengthens modesty, and makes virtue heavenly. It is the light ov life, without it, we should be but animated ghosts. It challenges fear, hides sorrow, weakens despair, and carries haf ov poverty's bundles.—It costs nothing, comes at the call, and leaves a brite spot behind. It iz the only index ov gladness, and the only buty that time kannot effase.—It never grows old; it reaches from the cradle clear tew the grave.—Without it, Love would be no pashun, and fruition would show no joy.—It is the fust and the last sunshine that visits the heart; it was the warm welkum ov Eden's lovers, and was the only capital that sin left them tew begin bizzness with outside the Garden ov Paradize.

(For the Saturday Press.)

THE BOLD MARINERS OF THE CENTRAL PARK.

Visitors at the Central Park cannot fail to have noticed, as not the least among the attractions of that charming retreat, the highly ornate being known as the boatman on the lake. We can scarcely tell whether he is to be regarded as a work of nature or of art, but in either case his merits deserve a more public acknowledgement, and now that the season is over we beg leave to pay our humble tribute of admiration. There are many points of interest in his character and situation, and many questions which occur to a reflecting mind.

In the first place, we remark that the boatman is brave. There is no swagger, or bravado about him; nothing but the repose of true courage ; he is fully aware of the perils that beset him in his eventful career; well does he know that he is constantly liable to collision with a swan, or a bridge, and that there is nothing but a plank—or, to speak with precision, nothing but a half inch plank and three coats of paint, between himself and Eternity: yet nothing shakes his steadfast soul: calm resolution sits upon his brow and nerves his arm as he takes his life—(and his scull) in his hand, and steers boldly out into the remorseless deep. He braves alike the ardent sun of August—(under an awning,) and the fierce blast of November, sweeping down "tyrannous and strong," from the rocky promontories to whelm his devoted bark.

As he is brave so also is he courteous. Observe the chivalric grace with which he escorts the fair into his boat, and the winning suavity of his replies to the sometimes rather imbecile observations of his passengers.

Thus far we can speak with tolerable certainty, but there is much in the career of this noble rover of the deep which must be left to conjecture, and we proceed to our questions, but with small hope of satisfactory reply.

We should like to know, for instance, how long it takes him to get his sea legs on?

Does he ever get becalmed on the line, and perish miserably of thirst?

Does he have to undergo quarantine, and is he addicted to smuggling?

Is he the proprietor of a "Black Eyed Susan" who cries adieu! and waves her lily hand, as he departs on his long and perilous voyages?

Does he ever receive cards of thanks from his grateful passengers, and is he compelled to read them?

Where does he go when it is his watch below?

Does he ever splice the main brace, or in default thereof, does he rest content with splicing the painter?

Has he a taste for swearing, and if so, in what fashion? Does he shiver his delicate timbers, and anathematize his bloody personal optics in the large and breezy manner of his salt water brethren; or does he give utterance to sonorous and antiquated epithets, like the good people in James' novels? We should like to hear a specimen of the Lake school of profanity.

What becomes of him in the winter? We can imagine the gallant boatman and his confrères fraternizing over a glass of amber ale, or golden sherry—(for surely nothing so vulgar as grog ever goes down their immaculate hatches)—and relating their thrilling adventures.

Tom. Tiller, perhaps, begins the strain, in some such form as this—

"When I was in the old Linnet off Cygnet Point "—to whom responds Ben. Boat-hook—"It was a dirty night in Swan'sdown Bay, when the Daisy four oars was hove to waiting for a pilot, &c." But we fear that "spinning yarns," is too gross an amusement for these refined natures, and it is easier to fancy them, seated "in a cleanly room, lavender in the windows, and twenty ballads stuck about the wall;" and discoursing after their manner of "Piscator" and "Venator," in quaint and tender eclogues and pastorals inspired by the dainty scenery amid which they pass their lives.

Finally, we should like to ask, what is to be the ultimate destiny of these gentle creatures? We cannot tell whether the jurisdiction of "Davy Jones" extends over fresh water; but if such be the case, we trust that he will not have the cruelty to allow them to herd together indiscriminately with the rude denizens of the forecastle. Tar and Nectar mingled! Perish the thought!

How can we imagine their disembodied spirits, seated on phantasmal sea chests, with the simulacre of a rusty tin pan, and the shade of a rustier iron spoon, eating unsubstantial—" Burgoo," Dandefunk," or "Skilligolee," or "Bangan," or "Swampseed," washed down with visionary "Studding-sail boom tea?"

Humanity shudders at the picture!

Let us rather hope that the aforesaid Jones is too much of a gentleman to permit such an enormity, but that he will reserve for these blest shades the cosiest corner of his locker, where they may dwell together in peace and unity, and as they are lovely in their lives, so in their deaths they may not be divided.

NEW YORK DECEMBER 9, 1865

THE BALLAD INFLICTION.

BY MARK TWAIN.

It is bound to come! There is no help for it. I smell it afar off—I see see the signs in the air! Every day and every hour of every day I grow more and more nervous, for with every minute of waning time the dreadful infliction comes nearer and nearer in its inexorable march! In another week, maybe, all San Francisco will be singing "Wearing of the Green!" I know it. I have suffered before, and I know the symptoms. This holds off long, but it is partly that the calamity may gather irresistible worrying-power, and partly because it is harder to learn than Chinese. But that is all the worse; for when the people do learn it they will learn it bad—and terrible will be the distress it will bring upon the community. A year ago "Johnny came marching home!" That song was sung by everybody, in every key, in every locality, at all hours of the day and night, and always out of tune. It sent many unoffending persons to the Stockton asylum. There was no stopping epidemic, and so it had to be permitted to run its course and wear itself out. Short was our respite, and then a still more malignant distemper broke out in the midst of this harried and suffering community. It was "You'll not forget me, mother, mother, mother, mother!" with an ever-accumulating aggravation of expression upon each successive "mother." The fire-boy sat up all night to sing it; and bands of sentimental stevedores and militia soldiers patrolled the streets and howled its lugubrious strains. A passion for serenading attacked the youth of the city, and they sang it under verandahs, in the back streets, until the dogs and cats destroyed their voices in unavailing efforts to lay the devilish spirit that was driving happiness from their hearts. Finally there came a season of repose, and the community slowly recovered from the effects of the musical calamity. The respite was not long. In an unexpected moment they were attacked, front and rear, by a new enemy—"When we were marching through Georgia!" Tongue cannot tell what we suffered while this frightful disaster was upon us. Young misses sang it to the guitar and the piano; young men sang it to the banjo and the fiddle; the un-blood-stained soldier yelled it with enthusiasm as he marched through the imaginary swamps and cotton plantations of the drill-room; the firemen sang it as they trundled their engines home from conflagrations; and the hated serenader tortured it with his damned accordeon. Some of us survived and some have gone the old road to a haven of rest at Stockton, where the wicked cease from troubling, and the popular songs are allowed. For the space of four weeks the survivors have been happy.

But as I had said before, it is bound to come ! *Arrah-na-Pogue* is breeding a song that will bedeck some mountain with new-made graves! In another week we shall be "Wearing of the Green," and in a fortnight some will be wearing of the black in consequence. Three repetitions of this song will produce lunacy, and five will kill—it is that much more virulent than its predecessors. People are finding it hard to learn, but when they get it learned they will find it potent for harm. It is Wheatleigh's song. He sings it in *Arrah-na-Pogue,* with a sprig of shamrock in his hat. Wheatleigh sings it with such aggravated solemnity as to make an audience long for the grave. It is doled out slowly, and every note settles deliberately to its place on one's heart like a solid iceberg—and by the time it is finished the temperature of the theatre has fallen to twenty degrees. Think what a dead-cold winter we shall have here when this Arctic funeral melody becomes popular! Think of it being performed at midnight, in lonely places, upon the spirit-depressing accordeon! Think of being driven to blow your brains out under such circumstances, and then dying to the graveyard cadences of "Wearing of the Green!" But it is bound to come, and we may as well bow our heads and submit with such degree of Christian resignation as we are able to command.

—*Territorial Enterprise (Cal.)*

The Round Table came out larger than usual recently, but has returned to its original proportions. It appears to be a sort of Extension Table, though adapted not so much to the dining-room as to the nursery. We are told, by the way, that the device of the R. T. was originally to have been as follows:

Though mice will never grow to rats,
Kittens sometimes grow to cats.

But why not have named the paper The Kitten at the start, with the promise to change it, after a due interval of growth, to THE CAT? It is more like a small cat now, than anything else, and if it could only scratch a little harder would do considerable mischief.

"Mark Twain" is the nom de plume of Mr. Samuel L. Clemens, of San Francisco, who has long stood at the head of the humorous writers on the California press, and now bids fair to occupy the same position on the press of New York.

NEW YORK DECEMBER 16, 1865

(For the Saturday Press.)

A NIGHT IN KIERNAN'S TOWER.

BY ALFRED M. WILLIAMS.

This is not a ghost story, a tale of a midnight watch in the haunted chamber of an ould castle hung with the dark glistening mantle of ivy, and encircled by a busy flock of cawing crows, as it darkens beneath the shadow of the heavy sky, or brightens beneath a sun-burst that lightens the green Irish hill-side with a stream of humid light, where the solitary candle burns dim, and the turf-fire smoulders with sulphurous flame, and the red nose of ould Cromwell shines at the butt of the deep stone hole that serves for a window, surrounded by those stern, full features, twisting and changing in diabolical glee, or the stone staircase clanks to the feet of that O' that was slain by Con of the Hundred Battles, or the Mac' who was killed by his brother, or whatever hero in the bloody tapestry that tells the history of every Irish castle from the days of Strongbow to those of Fighting Fitzgerald, and a shudder creeps over your nerves until you have cursed yourself and finished the tumbler of whiskey punch.

One fine November evening I issued forth into the Grand Parade in Cork's own town, with a Corkasian born and bred for a guide. First a turn to the right, then a turn to the left, and we crossed a narrow stone bridge over the divided Lee, and climbed a steep narrow street densely thronged with a ragged horde of the city's poor. Windows adorned with

Period ad for the "Tower Gardens."

herrings, a string of onions, a tumbler of pipes or small bake-shops gave token where the luxuries of Irish life can be purchased by the ha'penny worth; small forges gleamed with dull red light on the grimy forms of the workmen; cobblers tacked and pounded in little dens, while

"Cannon to right of them, cannon to left of them,"

the open doors of the whiskey shops flared out upon the throng; bending old crones, strapping matrons with fiery eyes and frowzled hair, dangling in rags, and with not the sign of shoe or stocking on bare feet and red ankles; girls with beautiful vivacious features, and cheeks blooming beneath dark, abundant hair, that was without covering save the fold of a cloak or shawl; men with angry nostrils and battered caubeens, illustrating the proverb that the "life of an old hat consists in cocking it," and clad in the cast-off clothes of English beggars; beggar women whose salutation was "God bless you, my fine gentleman," and whose valediction, "Hell resave your souls, ye stingy thieves," followed by a torrent of curses in Irish, as long as the victims were within hearing, that would have made their hair bristle, if fortunately they had not been unable to understand its bitter eloquence.

On we went past the Poor markets, on opposite sides of the street, wide-open spaces surrounded by lofty walls of rough, stone-like, enormous pounds; in these a group of fish-women, with the proverbial eloquence of such, were selling pence worth of sprats by the light of a candle shrouded in an extemporaneous paper lantern; milk and drisheens—a Cork dish that deserves a chapter itself—and *croobeens*, Anglice pigs' feet, and the like luxuries indulged in by the rich and fortunate along the street that speedily sunk into rows of low-browed stone cabins, where groups of women could be seen through the diminutive windows crouched over the smouldering fire, or a lonely man leaned out over the half-door with sad heart and empty pocket, no chink of the halfpence in one, or hope of whiskey in the other, the whole scene shining beneath gleams from the cloud-cracked moon, and wrapped in that quiet to which the pressure of utter destitution alone could reduce so many Irish hearts. From this, turning into a narrow lane, where nothing wider than a donkey-cart could find passage, we floundered along in the darkened way over the rough cobble-stones and pools of odorous water, speedily lost in such a labyrinth tangled in this wilderness of poverty, that nothing but the thread could guide the stranger out to civilization again in the night. Presently we emerged into a slightly wider space, and the ear was saluted with the unmistakable drone of the bagpipes issuing through the shutters of a long, low side of a stuccoed wall. A stream of light issued from the door, and stooping our heads after the fashion of a goose entering a barn door—there was room enough although the portal looked so low—we found ourselves in a small room half filled with an enormous bar, graced by a dirty and disheveled maid, and making a short turn entered the very penetralia of the "Tower"—the banqueting-hall.

An endless low room flaring with gas and clouded with tobacco reek, its centre filled with sets petting away with nimble feet to the lively notes of Miss McCloud's reel, the piper jerking his elbow and plying his fingers enthroned in vapor on a platform at the upper end of the room. Along the walls were tables adorned with pewter pints and tumblers, and in the rear of these

with their backs against the wall, and their fists affectionately embracing the vessels a close row of soldiers in red coats and vizorless caps whose guards fell across their chins, neat and clean and erect, and the material of which they were made at their elbows, in the lounging, dirty, ragged young fellows, who yet scorned the Queen's livery uncorrupted by her shilling, a sprinkling of men of war's men, and girls in knots by themselves waiting for their chance to enliven the floor with their feet, not scorning in the meanwhile the proffor of a friendly pint of beer. The attendant botlers of the castle in the shape—not of gorgeous young ladies as in the abodes of melody in Broadway—but strapping young gossoons in corduroys and waistcoats with flannel sleeves who, having received the modest guerdon of two pence, sped to obey our behest, leaving us to single out the features of the scene, as after having been dazzled by the first view of a magnificent picture we sit down to extricate its single beauties. Near me was seated a slight young soldier in cavalry uniform, the gilt stripes of a corporal on his scarlet sleeve, and a face a perfect model of youthful beauty, bright with natural but not educated intelligence, in which there is great difference—an unmistakable Irish face with healthy bloom and soft blue eye, yet no Milesian mould in those regular features and short upper-lip. A pipe has fallen from his careless hand, but he is not enough lost in reverie not to give an eye to the dancers, or an ear to the conversation of a couple of comrades at his elbow. Can I see a match for thee, my Hylas, among the dancers on the floor, or the groups at the table? Not at all; not a handsome face is to be seen among the girls, although, thank God, there is not one branded with the stamp of shame. Coarse and unrefined their faces must be, or they would not have been there—look at Bridget in your kitchen, and ,you will see their type—no fallen angel such as whose face will occasionally gleam out beneath a gas light in Oxford St., or sicken the heart in a Broadway cellar. There are no young girls and I thought it would have been impossible to have collected so many uninteresting faces in Cork, whose women are the pride of all Ireland, and whose vivid beauty and flashing wit had in Lola Montez, known in her birth-place as Miss T——, a perfect type and consummate flower. While looking for another face good or bad worthy of study the gig suddenly snapped off, the dancers crowded into seats and the voices that had been blended with the drone of the bagpipe

"Into an undefined and mingled hum,
Voice of the desert never dumb,"

broke out into laugh and call and talk. Next there was a five minutes' call of "Order please," a fiddler rose up and took his seat; and a young soldier with gloves tucked in his belt sang a song in a high soaring voice, not a word of which could be distinguished, yet appeared to be of a very popular nature from the applause which it received. Next a young countryman danced a *pater o'pee* or some other equally intricate Irish complication of steps, with such a listless countenance and such lively heels that, like the erratic Leprechaun, "could he dance with the head of him, and think with the heels of him, then were he a blessed spirit."

I had seen enough and was about to depart, when the lord of the tower made his appearance—a complacent little fellow with black shiny hair a little thin on the top, dark moustache and iron grey beard. He was pleased to welcome an American, and told us that he had made the foundation of his fortune in America, and taking a wise hint had returned to his native city, and invested as we have seen. He must have been growing rich or he never could have worn that countenance. We followed him out into the cool air and found ourselves in a sort of garden with seats and fountain in the centre, and rising above our heads, what had so seriously befogged me as to the nature of the object of our visit, "Kiernan's Tower." Nothing more nor less than a tall observatory of stone. By invitation of the proprietor we entered the door of the "Tower," guarded by a tasteful wooden snake with a dragon's head and fiery tongue, and climbed around and around the dark staircase until we emerged beneath the dim heavens on its breezy summit. Thence leaning on the rail all the city of Cork lay spread beneath the eye. A wilderness of dim indistinguishable masses, twinkling with misty lights and crowned with the reek of its innumerable chimneys, formless, vague, yet instinct with life like the background of one of Dore's pictures. The divided streams of the Lee

Callanan's Tower and Pleasure Gardens, opened in 1860; Cork, Ireland. The tower still stands as part of an apartment complex.

encircling the centre of the city showed like belts of vapor, flowing far toward that starry corner of the cloud racked sky.

It is hard to conjure the heroic by the talisman of Cork. It is synonymous with the abode of fun and good living, devilment and whiskey punch, the city

"Where salmon, drisheens, and beef-steaks are cooked best,"

the Blarney stone, the inspiration of its people and drinking and rioting their diversions, and he who is fortunate enough to spend any portion of his life therein, will confess that there is some truth in the popular notion, but if perched as we were above such a crowded swarm of poverty and misery, hunger and disease as was packed in the noisesome hives beneath, he could not but think of the death's head behind the grinning mask. It was nine o'clock. The clear notes of a bugle sounded faintly from the barracks on the other side of the city, and the famous chimes rang out from the Shandon steeple, where

"Seven bells proportionate of different size,
And full of melody from rim to crown,"

charm the air with sweet notes, that were the fit inspiration of the noble lyric of Father Prout, which has echoed their melody over the world. They finished. We came down and having drank our whiskey punch, we proceeded, as Carlyle says, to eat the glass, that is to say to give a description.

NEW YORK DECEMBER 23, 1865

MOCK-AUCTION IN BROOKLYN.

The TRIBUNE having stated, on Monday last, that Mayor Wood of Brooklyn had purchased a lot of confiscated whiskey at an auction-sale in that city, the Mayor came out on Wednesday and denied the statement in the following note:

TO THE EDITOR OF THE TRIBUNE.

MAYOR'S OFFICE, CITY HALL, BROOKLYN, Dec. 18, 1865.

In your paper of yesterday, it is announced, under Brooklyn news, that the Mayor of the city was the purchaser of a lot of confiscated whiskey. Please state, to correct misapprehension, that I was present on the occasion only as Collector of the Internal Revenue, to protect the interests of the government, and was not a purchaser of the whiskey. A few bids were offered by me solely with that view.

A. M. WOOD, Mayor.

We are not posted up in the commercial ethics of Brooklyn, but in New York a man—or even a mayor,—who should make bids at an auction-sale on goods in which he was interested, would be considered as doing a very irregular and reprehensible thing. Such things are done, to be sure, even in New York, but they are usually done at what are called "mock-auction" establishments, where we should hardly expect to find a Mayor among the abettors, even if his name happened to be WOOD.

(For the Saturday Press.)

CHRISTMAS GOOSE.

It is not deemed necessary to enter any apology for the subject of this essay, yet we may refer to the old British proverb, "It is not every day that we kill a pig," and say "It is not every day that we kill a Christmas goose."

If Poetry and Fiction have hitherto done little for her, History and the spit have done much. Everybody knows that the melodious voice of a wakeful goose on the Capitol baffled Gallic night-errantry and saved the mistress of the world. Though only a goose, she created an immense sensation that dark night, and the laurels which adorn her neck are every whit as fresh to-day as those which grace the brow of Lucretia, Cæsar, or the Horatii, and so they shall be forevermore.

Next to Rome, our bird is indebted to England's "Merry Christmas." She has flown down to us from the olden English times. Her cackle is blended with the voices of the merry homes of England for many a century—with the voices of kings and queens, nobles, artisans, yeomen, women, children and households, happy around the Christmas board.

Her ancestors have been the bosom-companions of the best and heartiest of our ancestors, and

——"Saxon or Dane, or Norman we,
Teuton or Celt, or whatever we be,
We are each all *Goose* in our welcome of thee—
Excellent bird'!"

Like humanity, she is mortal—the nearest approach to immortality we have ever heard of in one of her race being a longevity of eighty years. Melancholy, indeed, must have been the digestion of that Christmas party feast which feasted upon her ancient frame.

Goose in the abstract is historical; in the gravy, delicious. The life of the most exemplary Christmas goose is positively without interest to us, but once dead and basted and brown-roasted, the great heroic begins.

To the fat goose "death is not the goal." There is a life after life, brief, crispy, oleaginous, and fragrant with sage and sweet marjoram. With what grace and quiet dignity she reposes upon the wide, white dish! She has been despoiled of her snowy plumage, bereft of life, her soul sent off in a Pythagorean chariot to cackle through the sweet lips of some feminine tenement, but the truly great and good of her being remains with us.

"The Isles of *Greece*, the Isles of *Greece* !

* * * * * * * * * * * * *

Eternal summer gilds them yet."

Turkey may have its votaries as turkey does, but the Sultan himself would be drowned in the Bosphorus of neglect in this presence.

Her plump, light-brown breast is upheaved with the mysterious dressing. Deep in the unquarried caverns of her spacious frame is hidden other dressing, equally mysterious, because unseen and unknown except by the generous aroma which floats athwart our nostrils and electrifies us with anticipation of coming delights.

Her wings, no longer useful for aerial flights are serenely folded across her broad, flat back. The two tapering legs, once tipped with delicate webs, cling gracefully to the body. But the sides and breast chiefly engage our attention.

If we have cultivated a taste for "Christmas Goose" we may well pause here and send our heart forward into the dish there.

"O! quam placens in colore!
O! quam fragrans in odore!
O quam sapidum in ore !"

These sides and this breast contain all that mortals sigh for in the way of goose.

"They are an ambush of sweet snares "

There is beauty of form and grace of outline to tempt the eye, and delicious plumpness and speaking color to ravish the appetite. The fire has touched the rich flesh daintily. The kitchen artist has basted with wonderful skill, until a complex question is presented: of appetite—which would devour; of passion for the beautiful and the artistic—which would preserve and render immortal.

We once heard a good housekeeper's pies praised because of their quality of "concealment." Their wealth of substance concealed the subordinate pastry. Here is concealment for you, though in a different sense. The red-tinted cuticle, illuminated by the low-sailing December sun—as it streams in through the southern window upon the family party, conceals a world of sweets.

We dream with eyes tied fast in happy silence—the carver is our iconoclast. We hate him, we love him. He mars our vision—he destroys

"The beautiful world
With violent hands,"

but he flings wide open the portals of immeasurable gratification; the juicy flesh quivers and melts in the mouth; it lingers, it stays; the lips coax it, the tongue coquets with it, the palate likewise, and there is nothing of earth or goose beyond to wish for. This Christmas Goose has lived one short bright summer—a little, virtuous, happy life and now by this vicarious death flies to immortality and a merry digestion.

Lead the way to the parlor! Let us not tempt apoplexy or gout. Put on the Yule log, the Christmas block. Let us have music, laughter, generous bowls, jokes, games, sports, and tumultuous joys. We will live in the very present. The holly, the ivy, and the mistletoe are fresh and green. "Care killed a cat." No cat shall die of care by our hearth to-night. It shall be a "Merry Christmas," such as the old times knew. Are we more Pagan and less Christian than the ancient Briton or the modern Teuton? In his rough way, with riotous feastings and boisterous mirth, the old Briton held high festival from Christmas until Twelfth Night, and the latter-day materialistic Teuton renews his youth under the Christmas Tree.

England was merry England when
Old Christmas brought his sports again.
'Twas Christmas broached the mightiest ale,
'Twas Christmas told the merriest tale;
A Christmas gambol oft would cheer
A poor man's heart through half the year."

The family Christmas festival is one of the sacred things. An ancient one, its history is thronged with blessed and happy memories. It comes laden with benedictions. It is the richest festival of the year. Its pure white light beckons to us for dusty weeks before the day dawns and shines upon us forever as we pass on to the future. Fathers and mothers renew their youth—the children are as happy as innocence and Santa Claus can make them.

All the work days we are killing the goose that lays the golden eggs. Kill the Christmas goose and spare that other.

HOLLY.

THE CHRISTMAS HYMN I HEARD.

I had heard the Christmas bells, and had ceased awhile to weep,
And was pausing on the threshold of the mystic door of sleep,
When my soul was called to earth again by music soft and sweet,—
The sound of some one singing Christmas carols in the street.

She sang the Saviour's story—his lowly, humble birth,
His youth, his holy manhood, his sufferings on earth,
His death upon the Cross, his triumph in the skies—
And drops of tender sorrow overflowed my aching eyes.

Then she sang of Christmas memories and the influence they shed,
Making dearer still the living, making dearer still the dead;
Of little ones rejoicing in their parents' tender love,
And of greater far rejoicings in the home of God above.

"There," sang she, "round the golden throne the spotless spirits stand,
All clad in robes of purity—a happy shining band;
And their hymn is, Glory! glory to the Lord of earth and sky!
Oh! blessed are the innocent—the good who early die!"

Then I raised me from my pillow, smoothed back my tangled hair,
Hushed the sobs within my bosom, and clasped my hands in prayer;
And when I sank to sleep again the sweetest dreams were given,
For I heard, all night, dear Anna singing Christmas hymns in heaven!

MARGARET EYTINGE

(For the Saturday Press)

ON A FARM.

I.

BURLINGTON, N. J., Dec. 18, 1865.

DEAR PRESS:—

When a man takes a fancy to leave the more bustling scenes of life and settle down into a condition of calm content, I believe he is very apt to rush out into the country somewhere and buy a farm.

I have known many persons to do so. I have done so myself.

But why in Jersey?

If one wishes to leave the world and still remain on the continent that gave him birth where else, on earth, *can* he go?

Setting the matter clearly before an intelligent public in this light, I expect to see enlightened multitudes rushing into this devoted little state, and immediately doubling the census.

And Jersey isn't so bad a state to live in after all.

To a New Englander's or a New Yorker's notions, many of the ways and manners of the people are, indeed, "queer."

Said my man to me, one day—he was my *first* man, I have had three—said he : "Them goats in Burlington is a noutrage: they've clumb on the roof of my chicken hous an' eaten all the squinches off my trees an' the grapes off my wines !"

Of course I knew that the poor man intended *quinces,* and I had already learned that with very many of the natives w and v were interchangeable consonants.

This latter fact was called to my mind while purchasing chickens of an old soldier who lives on my road to town.

"Jarsey," said he, "Jarsey ain't nowheres: I'd rather be hung in Pennsylvania than to die a natural death in Jarsey !"

Need I say that—just entering upon life in Jarsey—I was shocked at this statement of the old soldier's views.

Upon my arrival here, I found one of the first necessities of existence was the purchase of a pair of work-horses.

Now I don't know much about horses.

If I thought I did, I might find myself in the uncomfortable position of a certain young cavalry officer whom I saw wickedly snubbed one pleasant January day, in the year of our Lord 1862.

It was on Ship Island, and Gen. Phelps (of proclamation fame) was strolling down the long plank walk towards the "harbor," in company with some brother officers, when the party were spied by a gay young cavalry chap, who immediately began curvetting and prancing about the group, showing off his horsemanship.

Whereupon the General—a gruff old martinet of an officer—remarked audibly: " That young fellow *thinks* he's a centaur—he ain't; he's only a d—d fool!"

On another occasion, a regiment of Zouaves had just landed, and one of them, in full feather, red and blue, met the General.

He had never seen anything so fine in the army before, and taking the chap by the shoulder, he turned him about, examining him curiously.

"Well, what *are* you, any way?" he cried at length.

"A Zouave, sir," replied the trembling victim.

"Oh! a Zouave!" quoth the General, " Really I didn't know but you were a circus-rider!"

To return to my horses.

I bought a pair.

It's none of your concern what they cost me. Suffice it to say that the outlay was not great, and that they pleased me.

I have them still.

One is bay, and so tall, bony, and angular in his make and movement that I have named him "Abraham Lincoln," after our late lamented chief magistrate.

He oats a great deal (a "good bit" they would say here in Jarsey, and I believe, on my honor, their's is the better expression) and has many fine points about him.

I value him for speed.

He can make his mile in ten to fifteen minutes easily.

He stands between sixteen and seventeen hands high (he stands still, too, without hitching seems to prefer it to going) is ten years old, and safe for the driving of the most inexperienced and nervous female.

My wife drives him, and I need say no more.

The venerable author of "Ten Acres Enough," has been unkind enough to laugh at him sometimes when riding with me.

But he is—I am sorry to say—one of those men who admire fast horses.

"Who drives fast horses must himself be fast,"

you know.

Well, I am satisfied with "Abe." (If you hear of any one who wants just such a horse let me know, will you ?)

"Pete," my other horse—why *"Pete"* I am sure I don't know—is short, fat, and black.

He is of age.

I had owned him but a few days, and a Milesian friend was conversing with me on the important subject of a ditch he proposed to dig for me, when the black horse passed drawing a heavy load of corn.

"Sure the old horse stands his years well," said my friend.

"Do *you* know that horse ?" said I.

"*Don't* I know him?" said he. "Sure by the same token it was thirteen years ago, I owned that horse, an' he was a fine beast, rising fifteen thin. An' the divil's own bird he was for kickin' an' bitin', so he wus. Sure he broke a man's leg an' bit a piece out of a gintleman's shoulder, an' divil a carpinter could build a stable would hould him, at all, wid the tumultuous kickin' agin the walls of the hind legs of the crature."

(I called to mind the mighty breakage of my rest by the resonant pelting old "Pete" kept up at intervals on the stable door, and understood more fully the reason why new locks were so constantly required in that department.)

Sure no one would kape the baste over six months, being kilt entirely wid builder's bills, for repairing the barns the crature had destroyed; but I presume he's got more quite wid the years that's on him!"

My respect—almost veneration—for "Pete" after this touching recital was unbounded.

It is so still.

If you know of any one who is in need of a horse twenty-eight years old, in good condition and warranted not to run away, please write me.

Till then, etc.,

WARREN.

FROM (BUT NOT OF) PARIS.

PARIS, Dec. 1, 1865.

DEAR PRESS:—

I am going to write you something about the urbanity of Austrian officials.

They are noted for it, especially in Italy.

I should say rus-banity, not only to show that I still know a little Latin, but also because the particular instance I am about to notice occurred in the country.

He was a fine looking man, the one who stopped me on my tramp from Salsbury to Berchtesgaden, and would have me return to the former place because I had no papers to show him, and told him an improbable story of being an American, when it was very evident (to him) that I was a Polish refugee.

I will acknowledge that I must have presented rather a curious appearance as I walked along with my coat over my shoulder, a wetted handkerchief hanging in my eyes from under my round-topped hat, and with no other luggage than a superbly colored meerschaum.

It was a ferociously hot day in August.

I had neglected my friend's advice, and had elected to see and admire the wild beauties of the Bavarian Alps from my feet rather than from the top or inside of an omnibus, and had just reached the interesting part of my walk— viz.: the black and white barber-poles indicating the Austro-Bavarian frontier—when I was suddenly hailed by an invisible voice.

He was a fine looking man, the owner of this voice, and at the commencement of our acquaintance very polite.

Like all Austrian officials, he wore a glazed cap, and a blonde moustache.

Not that this was the whole of his costume, but these were the principal items except a glass or more of beer of which the froth still lingered on his moustache, like dew on the dried grass of autumn, and was *sturmed up* with a dash of the back of his hand at the end of his first question, "Wohin? Where are you bound ?"

But this is hardly the beginning.

I had already had an interview with one of Francis Joseph's myrmidons a few days before —an interview of a different nature.

I was then on my way from Munich to Salzburg in a fast Bavarian mail train.

It is rather pleasant travelling on these German railways.

They don't go fast enough to take away either your health, or your thirst, and you finally reach your place of destination.

Stations are frequent.

The stops always extend to five or ten minutes, and at every one of them the beer-excellent beer at a cent or two the glass—goes gurgling over the tonsils of the thirsty travellers like a summer brook babbling over the pebbles in its course.

One of the most palpable errors in the creation is, in my opinion, the bestowal of a plurality of stomachs upon the camel rather than upon the

Germans.

It is true that the Germans are in the habit of affectionately bestowing upon each other the epithet, "Kameel"; but calling a man a camel doesn't make him one, nor, endow him with the superior capacity of that animal. A rest of from ten to fifteen minutes exhausts the supply in a German's single barrel and he is obliged to refill or thirst; but the beer is excellent.

I dwell upon this fact as much to excuse their apparent immoderation in drinking it as my own love for the fluid.

However to return to my story, which does *not* seem to babble like a summer's brook.

I was on my way to Salzburg partly for the sake of convincing myself that Mozart had once lived there, and partly to compare the taste of rock with sea-salt.

It was a warm day.

We had a very gentlemanly conductor. There are some to be met with in America, but they devote themselves usually to the ladies.

He was very gentlemanly and very thirsty. In fact, he was also a "Kameel"—I mean a German.

He obligingly brought me beer, and affably assisted me in draining the glass.

We gained each the good graces of the other.

We approached Salzburg.

It suddenly occurred to me that I had no passport.

I had left it in Munich.

"Would it be demanded ?" I asked my friend.

"Certainly."

"But no matter," said he, "I will make it all right."

And so he did.

With carpet-bag in hand, having victoriously passed the "Customs," I was hurrying forward to secure an omnibus, when Law and Order, in the form of a police-officer—just such an one as I have above described—laid its heavy hand upon my shoulder, and whispered 'passport' in my ear.

"I haven't any," said I, and was beginning an explanation when my railway friend interferred, and saying, "It's all right; it's a friend of mine; I'll tell you all about it," shoved me by the obstacle, and we stood beyond the pale.

It only cost me a florin (forty cents) besides affording an elligible opportunity for another parting glass of beer.

It is astonishing what force a little bold and blustering protection administered at the right moment will put into a mild man.

With that conductor as my friend, it was as though I had all the steam-power of all the united Bavarian and Austrian railways behind me and *must* go through.

And I did.

It reminded me very much of the operation of clearing the track of snow-drifts at home.

How I wished, a few days after, when I finally met my Waterloo, that my Grouchy had come up again at the right moment.

He didn't come, and I failed in going through.

But I begin to think that I am talking too much about myself, and in a manner that can by no means interest you.

You see I have no one to back me now, and I feel rather bashful before so many I's.

The fact is, I was getting rather spoony about Olive Logan, when her letter in the Press of October 21, knocked me "higher 'n a kite."

Excuse my using stale slang; we don't get the new words here as fast as they are coined. Her letters from Saratoga had inspired me with a romantic affection for her but I don't know now whether she is fifteen or fifty or charming in proportion.

But what I was going to propose to you was a conundrum, viz: to wit—

Why are newly published songs like men bathing?

Because they are new ditties.

I feel better now, and can return to the front.

There I was at the frontier with a sturdy guardian of the peace, with musket loaded and lighted match, barring my progress into Bavaria, and insisting upon my walking back to Salzburg in the sun.

"With whom have I the honor of speak?" he said, after I had finally succeeded in convincing him that I was paperless. I declined my name and profession—age, place of birth, object of coming into the country—reasons for leaving it again—age, profession, etc., of parents—whether married or single, or the reverse and if not, why not, etc., etc.—exactly as though I had been filling up the hotel police register.

I was used to that and did it glibly.

This seemed to mollify my man somewhat, for he had been growing austere and peremptory, and he began again.

"But your passport? You must have some papers from your government to prove your identity."

And now that he mentioned it, it suddenly flashed across me that I had.

"All right," said I, "I *have* got a passport, but they liked it so much in Munich that they took it away from me on my arrival to examine at their leisure and I forgot to ask for it when I came away; but I have got their receipt for it.

I remembered taking the paper in question out of my writing desk and placing it in my pocket-book that very morning.

"Ah," said he, with a sigh of relief as though rather glad of the prospect of a speedy return to his pipe and beer, "show it."

I pulled out my pocket-book, and from it extracted rather a soiled paper which unfolded, to my intense surprise and mortification, turned out to be nothing more nor less than two tickets in a picture lottery in Munich. I had had no idea in buying them that I was going to draw a prize; but to have such a blank as this unexpectedly fall upon me completely unmanned me, and I hung my head and said not a word.

Cerberus looked at me sternly, as he marched me into the station house, and ushered me into the presence of his superior, also a man with a glazed hat, a blonde moustache, a long pipe, and a glass of beer somewhere in the middle distance.

The Herr Oberpolizeibeamter shook his head sorrowfully over our joint story and confirmed my sentence.

In vain I objected that there was no use in my going back to Salzburg—that I had come into Austria without a passport, and it seemed devilish (yes, I said devilish) hard not to be able to get out again—that my passport was in Munich, and my receipt for it in my trunk and already on its way by post to Berchtesgaden.

My owl only shook his head, murmured "*macht nichts,*" and waved me from his presence.

And then I got mad and became insolent, and uttered a lot of chaff which didn't disturb my two persecutors in the least.

So I turned my face towards Salzburg once more.

But you didn't go all that way back again in the sun?

Not I.

I had noticed a charming retreat just before reaching my impediment, about a mile back. In fact, I think I had already stopped there for a glass of beer.

I returned there now, boiling over with rage and indignation, seated myself at a table under the trees, and in company with a catholic priest, to whom I related my adventure, drank beer vigorously until my diligence came up.

Arrived at the frontier again, I was obliged to mount the roof of the diligence, unpack my trunk, hunt up the writing-desk and exhibit my papers, after which I was allowed to proceed.

None of the other travellers were asked whether they were travelling with United States passports or with lottery-tickets.

And—but that's all.

I reached Berchtesgaden without further trouble.

It rained the six following days, and on the seventh I packed up my traps and came to Paris, where I remain,

Yours truly,

Jaunebert.

THE PIONEER BALL.

Mark Twain, in the Virginia *Enterprise*, gives the following characteristic description of "noticeable costumes" at the Pioneer Ball. It is a clever satire on Jenkins:

Mrs. W. M. was attired in an elegant *paté de foie gras,* made expressly for her, and was greatly admired.

Miss S. had her hair done up. She was the centre of attraction for the gentlemen, and the envy of all the ladies.

Miss G. W. was tastefully dressed in a *tout ensemble*, and was greeted with deafening applause wherever she went.

Mrs. C. N. was superbly arrayed in white kid gloves. Her modest and engaging manner accorded well with the unpretending simplicity of her costume, and caused her to be regarded with absorbing interest by every one.

The charming Miss M. M. B. appeared in a thrilling waterfall, whose exceeding grace and volume compelled the homage of pioneers and emigrants alike. How beautiful she was!

The queenly Mrs. L. R. was attractively attired in her new and beautiful false teeth, and the *bon jour* effect they naturally produced was heightened by her enchanting and well sustained smile. The manner of the lady is charmingly pensive and melancholy, and her troops of admirers desired no greater happiness than to get on the scent of her Sozodont-sweetened sighs, and track her through her sinuous course among the gay and restless multitude.

Miss R. P., with that repugnance to ostentation in dress which is so peculiar to her, was attired in a simple white lace collar, fastened with a neat pearl-button solitaire. The fine contrast between the sparkling vivacity of her natural optic and the steadfast attentiveness of her placid glass eye was the subject of general and enthusiastic remark.

The radiant and sylph-like Mrs. T., late of your State, wore hoops. She showed to good advantage, and created a sensation wherever she appeared. She was the gayest of the gay.

Miss C. L. B. had her fine nose elegantly enameled, and the easy grace with which she blew it from time to time marked her as a cultivated and accomplished woman of the world; its exquisitely modulated tone excited the admiration of all who had the happiness to hear it.

Being offended with Miss X., and our acquaintance having ceased permanently, I will take this opportunity of observing to her that it is of no use for her to be slopping off to every ball that takes place, and flourishing around with a brass oyster-knife skewered through her waterfall, and smiling her sickly smile through her decayed teeth, with her dismal pug nose in the air. There is no use in it—she don't fool anybody. Everybody knows she is old; everybody knows she is repaired (you might almost say built) with artificial bones, and hair, and muscles and things, from the ground up—put together scrap by scrap—and everybody knows, also, that all one would have to do would be to pull out her key-pin and she would go to pieces like a Chinese puzzle. There, now, my faded flower, take that paragraph home with you and amuse yourself with it; and if ever you turn your wart of a nose up at me again, I will sit down and write something that will just make you rise up and howl.

NEW YORK DECEMBER 30, 1865

(From the Californian.)

"MARK TWAIN" ON THE LAUNCH OF THE STEAMER "CAPITAL."

I GET MR. MUFF NICKERSON TO GO WITH ME AND ASSIST IN REPORTING THE GREAT STEAMBOAT LAUNCH. HE RELATES THE INTERESTING HISTORY OF THE TRAVELLING PANORAMIST.

I was just starting off to see the launch of the great steamboat Capital, on Saturday week, when I came across Mulph, Mulff, Muff, Mumph, Murph, Mumf, Murf, Mumford, Mulford, Murphy Nickerson—(he is well known to the public by all these names, and I cannot say which is the right one)—bound on the same errand. He said that if there was one thing he took more delight in than another, it was a steamboat launch; he would walk miles to see one, any day; he had seen a hundred thousand steamboat launches in his time, and hoped he might live to see a hundred thousand more; he knew all about them; knew everything—*every*thing connected with them—said he "had it all down to a scratch;" he could explain the whole process in minute detail; to the uncultivated eye a steamboat launch presented nothing grand, nothing startling, nothing beautiful, nothing romantic, or awe-inspiring, or sublime—but to an optic like his (which saw not the dull outer coating, but the radiant gem it hid from other eyes), it presented all these—and behold, he had power to lift the veil and display the vision even unto the uninspired. He could do this by word of mouth—by explanation and illustration. Let a man stand by his side, and to him that launch should seem arrayed in the beauty and the glory of enchantment!

This was the man I wanted. I could see that plainly enough. There would be many reporters present at the launch, and the papers would teem with the inevitable old platitudinal trash which this sort of people have compelled to do duty on every occasion like this since Noah launched his ark; but I aspired to higher things. I wanted to write a report which should astonish and delight the whole intellectual world—which should dissect, analyze, and utterly exhaust the subject—which should serve for a model in this species of literature for all time to come. I dropped alongside of Mr. M. M. M. M. M. M. M. M. M. M. Nickerson, and we went to the launch together. We set out in a steamer whose decks were crowded with persons of all ages, who were happy in their nervous anxiety to behold the novelty of a steamboat launch. I tried not to pity them, but I could not help whispering to myself, "These poor devils will see nothing but some stupid boards and timbers nailed together—a mere soulless hulk—sliding into the water!"

As we approached the spot where the launch was to take place, a gentleman from Reese River, by the name of Thompson, came up, with several friends, and said he had been prospecting on the main deck, and had found an object of interest—a bar. This was all very well, and showed him to be a man of parts—but like many another man who produces a favorable impression by an introductory remark replete with wisdom, he followed it up with a vain and unnecessary question—would we take a drink? This to me! This to M. M. M., etc., Nickerson !

We proceeded, two-by-two, arm-in-arm, down to the bar in the nether regions, chatting pleasantly, and elbowing the restless multitude. We took pure, cold, health-giving water, with some other things in it, and clinked our glasses together, and were about to drink, when Smith, of Excelsior, drew forth his handkerchief and wiped away a tear; and then, noticing that the action had excited some attention, he explained it by recounting a most affecting incident in the history of a venerated aunt of his—now deceased—and said that, although long years had passed since the touching event he had narrated, he could never take a drink without thinking of the kind-hearted old lady.

Mr. Nickerson blew his nose, and said, with deep emotion, that it gave him a better opinion of human nature to see a man who had had a good aunt, eternally and forever thinking about her.

This episode reminded Jones, of Mud Springs, of a circumstance which happened many years ago in the home of his childhood, and we held our glasses untouched and rested our elbows on the counter, while we listened with rapt attention to his story.

There was something in it about a good-natured, stupid man and this reminded Thompson, of Reese River, of a person of the same kind whom he had once fallen in with while travelling through the back settlements of one of the Atlantic States, and we postponed drinking until he should give us the facts in the case. The hero of the tale had unintentionally created some consternation at a camp-meeting by one of his innocent asinine freaks, and this reminded Mr. M. Nickerson of a reminiscence of his temporary sojourn in the interior of Connecticut some months ago, and again our uplifted glasses were stayed on their way to our lips, and we listened attentively to

THE ENTERTAINING HISTORY OF THE SCRIPTURAL PANORAMIST.

[I give the story in Mr. Nickerson's own language.]

There was a fellow travelling around, in that country (said Mr. Nickerson), with a moral religious show—a sort of a scriptural panorama and he hired a wooden-headed old slab to play the piano for him. After the first night's performance, the showman says: "My friend, you seem to know pretty much all the tunes there are, and you worry along first-rate. But then didn't you notice that sometimes last night the piece you happened to be playing was a little rough on the proprieties so to speak—didn't seem to jibe with the general gait of the picture that was passing at the time, as it were—was a little foreign to the subject, you know—as if you didn't either trump or follow suit, you understand ?"

"Well, no," the fellow said; he hadn't noticed, but it might be; he had played along just as it came handy.

So they put it up that the simple old dummy was to keep his eye on the panorama after that, and as soon as a stunning picture was reeled out, he was to fit it to a dot with a piece of music that would help the audience get the idea of the subject, and warm them up like a camp-meeting revival. That sort of thing would corral their sympathies, the showman said.

There was a big audience that night—mostly middle-aged and old people who belonged to the church and took a strong interest in Bible matters, and the balance were pretty much young bucks and heifers—they always come out strong on panoramas, you know, because it gives them a chance to taste one another's mugs in the dark.

Well, the showman began to swell himself up for his lecture, and the old mud-dobber tackled the piano and run his fingers up and down once or twice to see that she was all right, and the fellows behind the curtain commenced to grind out the panorama. The showman balanced his weight on his right foot, and propped his hands on his hips, and flung his eyes over his shoulder at the scenery, and says:

"Ladies and gentlemen, the painting now before you illustrates the beautiful and touching parable of the Prodigal Son. Observe the happy expression just breaking over the features of the poor suffering youth—so worn and weary with his long march: note also the ecstasy beaming from the uplifted countenance of the aged father, and the joy that sparkles in the eyes of the excited group of youths and maidens, and seems ready to burst in a welcoming chorus from their lips. The lesson, my friends, is as solemn and instructive as the story is tender and beautiful."

The mud-dobber was all ready, and the second the speech was finished he struck up:

"Oh, we'll all get blind drunk
When Johnny comes marching home!"

Some me of the people giggled, groaned a little. The showman couldn't say a word. He looked at the piano sharp, but he was all lovely and serene—*he* didn't know there was anything out of gear.

The panorama moved on, and the showman drummed up his grit and started in fresh:

"Ladies and gentlemen, the fine picture now unfolding itself to your gaze exhibits one of the most notable events in Bible History—our Saviour and his disciples upon the Sea of Galilee. How grand, how awe-inspiring are the reflections which the subject invokes! What sublimity of faith is revealed to us in this lesson from the sacred writings! The Saviour rebukes the angry waves, and walks securely upon the bosom of the deep !")

All around the house they were whispering: "Oh, how lovely! how beautiful!" and the orchestra let himself out again:

"Oh, a life on the ocean wave,
And a home on the rolling deep!"

There was a good deal of honest snickering turned on this time, and considerable groaning, and one or two old deacons got up and went out. The showman gritted his teeth and cursed the piano man to himself, but the fellow sat there like a knot on a log, and seemed to think he was doing first-rate.

After things got quiet, the showman thought he would make one more stagger at it, any how, though his confidence was beginning to get mighty shaky. The supes started the panorama to grinding along again, and he says:

"Ladies and gentlemen, this exquisite painting illustrates the raising of Lazarus from the dead by our Saviour. The subject has been handled with rare ability by the artist, and such touching sweetness and tenderness of expression has he thrown into it, that I have known peculiarly sensitive persons to be even affected to tears by looking at it. Observe the half-confused, half-inquiring look, upon the countenance of the awakening Lazarus. Observe, also, the attitude and expression of the Saviour, who takes him gently by the sleeve of his shroud with one hand, while he points with the other toward the distant city."

Before anybody could get off an opinion in the case, the innocent old ass at the piano struck up:

"Come rise up, William Ri-i-ley,
And go along with me!"

It was rough on the audience, you bet you. All the solemn old flats got up in a huff to go, and everybody else laughed till the windows rattled.

The showman went down and grabbed the orchestra and shook him up, and says: "That lets you out, you know, you chowder-headed old clam! Go to the door-keeper and get your money, and cut your stick!—vamose the ranch! Ladies and gentlemen, circumstances over which I have no control compel me prematurely to dismiss—"

"By George! it was splendid!—come! all hands! let's take a drink !"

It was Phelim O'Flannigan, of San Luis Obispo, who interrupted. I had not seen him before. "What was splendid?" I inquired.

"The launch!"

Our party clinked glasses once more, and drank in respectful silence.

Mark Twain.

P. S. You will excuse me from making a model report of the great launch. I was with Mulf Nickerson, who was going to "explain the whole thing to me as clear as glass," but, you see, they launched the boat with such indecent haste, that we never got a chance to see it. It was a great pity, because Mulph Nickerson understands launches as well as any man.

DRAMATIC FEUILLETON.

MISS RUSHTON'S OPENING.

I hope, Sir, that some one bailed you out on Saturday last, and that you were thereby restored to the bosom of your family in good season for the happy festivities of Yuletide.

Prudence of late has been my most characteristic quality, and I acknowledge at once that I made my escape early in the evening and before the policemen had fairly warmed to their work. But I make no doubt that you stayed to the end, and airily expressed your views of things in general, and theatre audiences in particular. For which reason I trust your respectable house-holder was duly on hand; or if not, then that you paid your fine like a man, and went home blasphemous but free.

Of course I am referring to Miss Rushton's theatre which was opened on the evening in question with all the ceremonies of a new police court. There was a large muster of "our governing classes," a considerable mob of patrolmen, and specials, and detectives; and numerous witnesses of high standing. The greatest confusion prevailed, as is apt to be the case in our minor courts of justice. Respectable people who had rights to maintain and urged them quietly and not too firmly, were at once put down; whilst others who were unembarrassed with either rights or wrongs sought every advantage that could be extracted from the opportunity. The possession of a ticket for a reserved seat was regarded as a sufficient proof that the possessor should at once be crushed. Gentlemen whose moustachios were lackered in a charming way and whose jewelled bosoms were the delight of all beholders, generally managed to procure chairs, and to keep them too by the valor of their arms and the power of their speech. Unhappily there were not sufficient places to accommodate them all, so that many were necessitated to take up their position in the lobbies where gracefully consoling themselves with the simplest form of the Indian weed, they formed a manly and impassible barrier. Saint Peter of Alcantara, as we all know, made it a point to keep his pious eyes for ever turned on the sharp and flinty ground, deriving no doubt great good from that holy practice, and hurting his feet in such a way that it was nothing but right he should have wings at last. If Saint Peter had been at Miss Rushton's on Saturday night he would have found a crueller and harder discipline in looking on the faces which were there assembled. Had he done so the worthy man would in all probability have experienced the consolation of a punched head, the tribulation of a locust, and the expiation of a night in a Station-house. You are not a Father (I mean in an ecclesiastical point of view) but your ways are severe, and it occurred to me, when safely in the street, that the possible fate of the Saint awaited you. Hence the wish which I have expressed in the opening sentence of this valuable contribution. If you are safe out of that crowd you ought to be thankful as I am.

There were ushers as well as "crushers" in it. Several bland and helpless individuals wearing white Berlin gloves staggered about the orchestra chairs, and vainly endeavored to seat the rightful owners thereof. They retired in rapid confusion, and were succeeded by their truncheoned allies, who also had to beat a retreat amid the jeers of the usurpers.

The confusion was temporarily brought to an end by the rending of the curtain (it divides in the centre) and the appearance of the company for the National Anthem. When this had blown over, Miss Rushton made her appearance, and attempted to recite a prologue. The lines escaped her memory, but with ready tact she excused the lapsus, and said "out of her own head" all that was proper to be said—if not more.

Then came the comedy—the "School for Scandal," which, I regret to say, was poorly played. Mr. Walcot's Sir Peter Teazle was a ghastly caricature of the part, and one heard with amazement that at some remote period of her history Lady Teazle had discovered the gentleman as a "simple country squire." Mr. Walcot's voice had deserted him, and a town life we should judge has acted injuriously on his physical proportions. There is little of the country squire about him now. Mr. Harry Pearson (I follow the order of the bill) was a bluff and hearty representative of Sir Oliver Surface. A comic song or a hornpipe should, however, be introduced for the due display of the special powers of this hilarious and versatile comedian. Mr. J. K. Mortimer as Joseph Surface was ill at ease; whilst Mr. D. W. Waller as Charles was ill at everything. There are only a dozen more characters to notice, but as this kind of praise is exhaustive, I shall desist with the simple remark that Mr. T. Placide and Miss Lucy Rushton were the only people who seemed to know clearly what they were about. The lady possesses undoubted talent. It needs mellowing in the school of actual life, being at present somewhat crude. I am afraid, too, that she attaches too much importance to her wardrobe, but a few months of hard work will effect changes which I trust we shall all be called upon to record.

There can be no doubt on one subject: she has a pretty little theatre, and it will be her own fault if it does not speedily become popular. Whether she can attain this end by playing the old comedies time will decide, but I am certain that the audience of Saturday last would not insist on that selection.

If our friends of

THE FRENCH THEATRE

had such a bright little establishment they would know what to do with it. Even the Academy of Music was rendered cheerful by their presence on Wednesday evening.

The prices of admission were fixed rather high, being fifty per cent more than at Wallack's. This led to that peculiar mixture in the audience of the highest and the lowest, which one so frequently sees on such occasions. The extremes were strongly marked. A gentleman sat near me, clad in garments of ancient splendor, but present infirmity, whose interest in the play was only equalled by the powerful odor of garlic which he emitted in the course of his approval. Cut off by a bench or two was a perfumed beauty listening to Scribe's merry jingle in a kind of slumberous ecstacy, calmly accepting French as a necessary evil. When I see these things I always turn to the bill to read the managerial fiction that the free list is positively suspended.

Two well-known pieces ("Bataille de Dames" and "La Fille de Dominique ") with such dismal attempt at stage effect as the Academy plateau rendered possible. They—the pieces —were very cleverly rendered, and beside introducing Madame Larmet and other old favorites to our attention served the useful purpose of debuting several new members of the company. It is hardly the proper moment to speak of these artists, and I shall simply endeavor, on this occasion, to get into the way of writing their names. The most successful debuts were those of Mdlle. Amélie Huiry and Malle. Potel. The first is an ingenious and charming actress. Her looks are calculated to make the flaneur frantic, and cause him to rush wildly into the extravagance of flowers. Mdlle. Potel belongs to a less sentimental school, being, in fact, of an eminently jolly turn. She is the mistress of many parts, playing no fewer than four in the vaudeville, and playing them all well. The male members of the troupe did not impress me very favorably, but it is hardly fair to say that it was their fault. When the company is duly housed in its new Fourteenth street house (corner of Sixth avenue) there will be time enough to say all that has to be said.

EDWIN BOOTH.

Every admirer of the legitimate drama, and every person on whose disposition is, in the slightest degree kindly, will rejoice to hear that this admirable tragedian will positively commence an engagement at the Winter Garden on Wednesday next the 3d instant. If any indication of the genial intention of the public toward this favorite artist were needed, it could readily be found in the wail of loathing and contempt which has been excited by the recent assault on him in the Herald. The troubles of that journal are patent to the community and to speak the truth they have been rather amusing than otherwise. If the theatres fought the Herald it was natural that the Herald should fight the theatres. The general public was quite content to look on and laugh. But when from sheer greed of an advertisement it ventures to attack an artist like Mr. Edwin Booth on the ground that his brother committed a great crime, it exceeds even its own coarse limits of decency, and brings down on the journal the indignation which in vain it endeavors to direct against the artist.

Mr. Booth's return to the stage will be hailed with pleasure by every right thinking man. He makes his first appearance in "Hamlet" but that tragedy will speedily be withdrawn in favor of "Richelieu."

NIBLO'S GARDEN.

It is rather hard that in this enlightened century, in the principal city of the West, in a leading theatre, and under circumstances generally of great aggravation, one should still be forced to listen to the silly dribble of a dramatic writer like Buckstone. Yet such is the melancholy fact. That dreary person's version of the "Green Bushes," has been revived for the advantage, pecuniary and otherwise, of Miss Lucille Western. I have seen the lady as Miami and am so low and exhausted that I think I should like to see her once more in East Lynne, especially in that dear domestic scene where an erring wife crouched convulsively by the fire calmly devours an entire woollen shawl to express the penetential anguish of her bosom. There is nothing so fine as this in the "Green Bushes," which I greatly regret, but the admirers of Miss Western can see a great deal of her in the role of the Huntress of the Mississippi.

The drama is nicely put on the stage. There is a good deal of jig and rather too much ballad in it, but where Buckstone is the writer these are faults on the right side.

I ought to speak of several other places but my space and my patience are alike exhausted.

A NEW DRAMATIST.

Do you remember Webb, whose initials were C. H.! He has written to me lately and requests that I put this question frankly to the public; for, mark you, he is modest and imagines that we can forget him. He does not know, poor innocent creature, that for a couple of years past we have been copying his poems all over the North; nor is he aware perhaps that he has received the sepulchral honors of half a line of praise in the *Nation*. I saw the chip floating on the deep and solemn current of that journal's cogitations but it eluded my grasp and I cannot reproduce it for your or his conviction. The frail bark in which I take my pleasure was indeed upset in the effort, and when I waded ashore it was to find myself in the Freedman's Bureau,—happilly a dry locality but not poetic. I remember Webb quite well. We were on the most friendly terms. He tried all his new puns on me, and if I failed to laugh on the trigger—and sometimes it is very hard to keep your intellectual powder dry—he kindly offered to p-p-p-punch my head for me. Me a dramatic critic!

Little did the dear boy dream that he would live to write plays. Well, he has been and gone and done it. A few months since he produced an original piece called "Our Friend from Victoria" (of course the reader is aware that Webb resides in San Francisco)—a production of merit, the wit of which was so intoxicating that two of the actors got drunk on it the first night and forgot their parts. Notwithstanding the "Friend" received a kindly welcome, and established its author's position as the Brilliant Young Dramatist of the Pacific Slope. Lately he has followed up his initial success by bringing out a burlesque of "Arrah-na-Pogue"—an exceedingly laughable affair which I am glad to hear will be played at one of our city theatres. When that event occurs, I shall require an entire paper to remind you of Webb; and if about that time the gentleman himself should suddenly appear on Broadway, to the consternation of his enemies and the delight of his friends, no one need be surprised. By George! don't I pity the hackman who, taking advantage of four friend's Californian aspect, ventures to charge him, say, a quarter too much! Poor fellow, won't he get it!

C. B. S.

A QUANDARY.

My Dear Press :—

I want to buy a piano, and, of course, refer to your advertisements to find the best.

I read of Steinway that Mills, and Mason, and Maretzek, and Gottschalk, and every other musical fellow say it is the best, and so I make up my mind to buy a Steinway; but as I look further, I find Chickering recommended by Mills, and Mason, and Maretzek, and Gottschalk, as being, by all odds, the most superior, and I conclude to patronize Chickering. My eyes wander along, and find that Mills, and Mason, and Maretzek, and Gottschalk think, after all, that Geo. Steck & Co.'s piano is the best, and still further, that Schütze & Ludolff far outstrip all others.

What am I to do? Tell me before I go mad.

Answer: Buy one of each.—Ed.

Downtown-bound sleigh omnibus making the turn from Broadway onto Amity Street (3rd St) from March 20, 1867, L'Univers Illustre.

NEW YORK JANUARY 6, 1866

(For the Saturday Press.)

ON A FARM.

II.

Burlington, N. J., Dec. 28, 1865.

Dear Press:—

One of my first endeavors after I had got myself somewhat established here was to procure a good watch-dog.

Horses, cows, corn, pigs and chickens (particularly chickens) are apt to take to themselves wings and fly away, if one lives in the neighborhood of a thriving little place like Burlington.

Not that I would say anything against the morality of Burlington.

The Quakers forbid!

But a watch-dog is a good thing to have in the country.

So I secured a superior second hand dog-kennel.

Also, I purchased a collar and a chain.

Then I began to look about for a dog.

It was quickly known about the taverns and stables in B. that I was in want of a first class animal to guard my premises, and soon I had various tempting offers.

I hardly supposed there were so many dogs in the country as were presented to my consideration.

Just you go into a small place and let the inhabitants know you are in want of a faithful hound (or any other dog) and see what comes of it!

It isn't pleasant.

One doesn't like to refuse so many self-sacrificing friends, all of whom offer you (out of pure kindness) such superior brutes, dog-cheap.

I will not weary you with a catalogue of my offers.

They embraced every variety of mongrel known to the canine race.

At length, I fixed upon one, a guant, heavy, brawny, bony, cadiverous beast, standing about as high as an ordinary dining table, with a head the size (and something the shape) of a large ham, and an expression of utter indifference to everything in the world.

I selected him because the owner said he was worth twenty-five dollars, but that I might have him for ten.

Also, that he was a No. 1, A I, copper bottomed and warranted watch-dog.

I didn't like his looks, so I only took him on trial.

I drove into town with my carriage (that's what I call my Jersey wagon) for him, and two men helped me to lift the brute in.

I think nothing short of ten pounds of porter-house steak would have induced that sulky beast to *jump* into anything.

Then I took him home and chained him to his kennel.

Also I fed him.

If I had kept that dog till to-day, dear Press, I think I should have been writing you from the Alms-house.

I have seen dogs eat before, but never, never have I seen dog eat like that dog.

Presently he became weary of the labor of mastication, and slumbered.

After a time, the night fell.

"Now," I said to myself, "will be the time to test my watch-dog."

It was a dark night.

Every available cloud obscured the moon, and the wind sobbed and moaned like an ailing infant.

It was just the night, in fact, for thieves. So I tested my dog.

I began by throwing stones and brickbats at the kennel.

This proving ineffectual, I pounded gently upon its sides with a stick of wood.

I redoubled my blows, "cussing" a little in what I supposed might be the manner of a marauding blackguard, who knows the folks are asleep, and *don't* know they keep a dog.

Then I upset the kennel from over the faithful creature's head.

Finally, after I had set fire to the straw the creature was snoozing on, he condescended to take some little notice of my polite efforts to entertain him.

My dog rolled over on the straw, put the fire out, wagged his tail feebly, and, after a gentle yawn, went peacefully to sleep again!

"Clearly," I said, "this dog won't do."

So in the morning I took him back.

But he wouldn't *stay* back.

He knew who fed dogs on good beef, and he returned to my "humstid."

He *kept* returning,

It would be useless to relate how many times I made myself ridiculous whipping that dog round my horse's legs in the streets of Burlington, when I had driven in with him, and he didn't wish to leave me.

He had a way of eluding the lash and keeping the horse between me and him that was tantalizing beyond description.

He was an affectionate and faithful dog, and loved his master.

His former owner finally, on my threatening to shoot the creature otherwise, managed to get rid of him in some way, and that was the end of him.

I have got a good dog, at last. Perhaps I will tell you of him in my next.

WARREN.

NEW YORK JANUARY 13, 1866

(For the Saturday Press.)

ON A FARM

III.

Burlington, N. J., Jan. 6, 1866

DEAR PRESS:—

I ought to date these scribblings from *near* Burlington.

For my 'umble cot is situate some mile and a half from that quiet and charmingly old-fashioned little city, on a Pike.

When one lives in the country it is a good thing to be on a Pike.

At least I have been told so. The principal feature about a Pike that I can discover (and therein it resembles a grist mill) is that it takes toll.

Then, I am told (no pun intended) that it will be a fine road to haul "truck" and fruit over next summer and autumn; and I have no doubt it will be.

Behold me, then, beneath my own vine and persimmon tree, in the midst of some acres of strawberries, raspberries, peaches and blackberries, whiling away the hours of wintry evening writing to you.

Seriously, revered PRESS, I am in a very good spot. And there are many more such about here; several for sale.

It is great land, this, for fruit and things, old sage cit: and if any of your friends and readers desire to settle down comfortably in a most desirable neighborhood, I can tell them just how to do it.

Let them take the Camden and Amboy monopoly's boat or cars, come on to Burlington, and inquire for Mr. Edmund Morris.

They will find a genial gentleman (and very pleasing writer too, by the way) who takes such pleasure in showing to strange gentlemen the eligible farms for sale about here that he' almost makes a business of it.

This is no "puff," oh PRESS (I know you too well to try *that* on with you): the truth is that my friend the author of "Ten Acres Enough," "Farming for Boys," etc, is doing so much for the neighborhood by getting good people here (he got me here) that I like to help the thing along.

That's all.

Living in the country one enjoys a good book, a good magazine, (or a good paper, for instance) much more than in the hurried and crowded city.

Old friends, old books and old wine (if the latter were to be had anywhere in this favored land) have a zest here that *you* know nothing of.

HARPER, as an example, is now pleasanter to me than ever.

I read all its articles, original and otherwise, with a relish I never knew before. After learning from its record of current Events what has occurred up to the fifth of the last month, and sitting for a while in its "Easy Chair" I turn enraptured to its Editor's Drawer.

It astonishes me to think of the intellect that composes and that enjoys the jokes in that miscellaneous collection. I drop a tear of pleased recollection over the anecdotes that delighted my infancy, and I am struck dumb with admiration at the richness of original wit in those I have never met before.

I am emulous of equal renown with the authors of the new ones, and I write the following, which I assure you, on my honor, has *not* appeared in the pages I allude to :—

Old Sol. B. of the town of A. C. county, Tennessee, was a dry old rustic wit and joker well known in those parts some twenty years since.

One evening old Sol. was sitting in the barroom with a miscellaneous crowd of village loafers, when a venerable stranger, mounted on a rawboned steed with a Roman nose, rode up to the door, dismounted, handed over his animal to a gigantic African who acted as hostler, and entered the room. Old Sol. arose, and the company knew by the twinkle in his eye that something rich was coming.

"Good evening, stranger," said he, "coolish night for the time of year. You look 'eenamost froze out !"

"Well *'tis* cold," said the stranger: then drawing himself to his full height, he continued: "Take suthin ?"

"Wall, stranger," said old Sol., "I don't care ef I do!"

When the roars of laughter had subsided, the stranger acknowledged the corn, and treated all 'round.

I've been studying over the above for some time, and I can't find the point to it.

The dickens of it is 'twas built on a model, and come to look at my models I fail to see a point there.

I suppose that one gets muddled after living some time in the country.

But, seriously now, if you can find a joke in the above do let me know when you write again.

And, by the way, I do *not* think that your offer for my horse "Pete" was quite up to the mark.

It may seem to you that fifteen dollars, minus the freight to New York, is a fair price for him, but to me it seems *rather* low.

No, I shant take it.

My dog has turned up again. My *first* dog—the one I wrote you of in my last letter.

You see I had got a *good* dog.

I have him still.

He is a fine bull-terrier of a large size and capacious jaws—all head and shoulders and sinewy thighs.

I found him in Burlington in the possession of a party of rough looking young gentlemen who haunt an oyster saloon near the river.

I am afraid they never bought him of any one, they were so anxious to sell him, and so cheap.

In the beautiful simplicity of the American tongue they called him "Bu-ry" (sounding like *fury*) that being their affectionate abbreviation of the name of the gallant warrior Beauregard.

Unlike the worthy he was named after, he was the hero of many successful engagements, and bore honorable scars all about his sagacious countenance.

As, item, one ear slitted to ribbons; item, an eye obscured for ever in the heat of some well fought field.

The ardor with which he "pinned" anything he was directed to "take care of" delighted me.

An account of his recent killing of a butcher's dog charmed me.

The low figure he was put at took me captive and I purchased him on the spot, changing his name to "Beauty," as the most purely original one to be found.

I took him home, and have *kept* him home very carefully.

That dog is not for sale.

Well, a night or two since, my slumbers were broken by the most frightful series of diabolical sounds under my window. It was a discord composed of snarling, yelling, growling, roaring, snapping and howling.

I arose and gazed forth from my casement, when mine eyes beheld a scene thrilling beyond description.

Two large animals were evidently in deadly conflict.

One was tall, bony, awkward, uncouth; the other was active, lithe, vigorous, determined. I saw how it was. Some strange dog had come about the premises, and "Beauty" was teaching him that the way of the transgressor is hard.

I continued to watch the fight by the pale light of the tranquil moon till I saw my dog get the better of his antagonist, and then I retired to bed with a peaceful conscience and soon sank to rest.

In the morning I repaired to the scene of conflict. There was "Beauty," complacently licking his chops and wagging his tail; there, also, were gore, bunches of hair, and the dead body of a large black dog.

I turned the corpse over and beheld, now calm in death, the well known lineaments of the dog I took on trial.

Yes! It was too true! The faithful creature had come again to my residence, in search of fresh beef, and death had been the reward of his fidelity!

WARREN.

(For the Saturday Press.)

LIFE IN A BAR-ROOM.

FROM OUR BAR-ROOM CORRESPONDENT.

MR. EDITOR:

Human nature, as viewed in a bar-room, is very different to human nature anywhere else; therefore, as your special correspondent, I will, with your permission, occupy a little of your space with a slight sketch of what life in a bar-room is.

We there find every variety of character and temperament, and every shade of social condition.

There is the spendthrift and the pauper, the mechanic, the laborer, and the loafer.

The bar-room affords a complete and not uninteresting study for the student of human character.

Let us give a sketch of a New York barroom which we visited only a night or two ago.

It is eight o'clock on a cold frosty evening, when friend meeting friend, they are very apt to invite one another to "smile."

There they are, standing at yonder bar, behind which stands the busy tender, with whom they seem familiar.

From their appearance and general conversation, it is evident they are clerks; for an attentive listener may occasionally catch the words, "dollars," "increase," "salary," "boss," etc.

They sip their hot toddy, and the conversation turns upon some "dear Julia" or "lovely Mary Ann," who would hardly be flattered, we imagine, at hearing their names rehearsed over toddy-hot at a public bar.

Behind these two young swells stands a man whose seedy attire, and thirsty look, stamps him as of the genus "bummer."

He is exceedingly anxious to have a part in the conversation, and takes advantage of an opportunity to put in a word, edging up alongside the bar at the same time, with a mighty insinuating glance at the whiskey-toddy.

Half an invitation to join in a drink is only required to bring forth an affirmative response. He is a friend that will stick closer than a brother, so long as there is plenty of the good creature with which to satiate his greedy thirst.

As soon as he sees that your money is gone, he has "an appointment, and must be excused; but another night, etc."

Then comes the perpetual "toper;" there he is—that man with the beet-colored nasal organ.

So long as he has money, he spends it freely; and then, when that is gone, like our friend bummer, he insinuates himself into the good graces of more fortunate neighbors.

A jolly, but rather dilapidated looking fellow is the "toper."

When sober he is miserable, and when drunk he is the happiest man alive.

In yonder corner, stands a young man of rather spruce appearance.

He has a glossy hat, well polished boots, and is good-looking withal.

He is seldom known to spend a cent, but he doesn't object to take a drink and borrow a dollar.

He is essentially "hard up," "waiting for remittances," etc.

This man is termed, in bar-room lingo, a "dead beat."

He is very confidential.

He pours the story of his wrongs, his mishaps, his hopes and expectations, all, all into your ears; and this will he do for the trouble of a small loan.

He is ashamed to ask it, but then, you know, circumstances compel us.

Strange things are circumstances, and very opportune for our friend "dead beat."

In another part of the room, sitting in a corner, is a somewhat sombre looking man, with his hat almost covering his eyes, his shoes down at the heels, and his garments generally of a by no means modern appearance.

He seems known to most of the visitants.

He drinks a good deal when he has the money, and his general mode of bar-room life partakes, in a great measure, both of the "bummer" and the "beat;" the only difference being, he works when compelled.

This man may be recognized by various signs as a Bohemian of literature.

He is seen during all hours of the day flitting amongst the various newspaper offices. Now he has an article for the DAILY WAILER, and now a story for the WEEKLY MUMMY; and again, a sketch for the FAMILY GOSSIP.

A seedy looking customer is our Bohemian.

He is a favorite with the host at the bar, and is good for a drink; but, mind you, only a drink.

There it is that he is superior to the bummers and the beats, and you may be sure he appreciates the distinction.

The man who can obtain credit, even for a drink, is a veritable king in a bar-room.

Then we have the ordinary bar-room customer; the man when sober, talks rationally enough, and pays for all he calls for.

Sometimes, when a "little on," he quotes poetry, attempts to imitate Forrest or Booth, and, if a little "tighter," indulges in a song.

When in this state he is always "flush," and he is at once a jolly good fellow, which nobody will deny.

There are other characters to be met with in a bar-room, had we time to sketch them.

There is the *roué*, the gambler, and the pickpocket; the man of ruined reputation, the young man who promised well, the old man who has a tale to tell of bygone times.

The bar-room affords us truly an insight into human nature which we can obtain nowhere else.

In a future article we may probably refer to scenes in a bar-room at midnight, having special reference to those places open all night.

In the meantime, if any of your readers would know how half the world live, let them spend an evening in a Metropolitan Bar-Room.

M.

FROM DEBORAH DUNN'S LETTERS TO THE BOUDOIR.

NEW YORK, December, 1865.

Nobody knows until they have tried how difficult it is to write a good story. It seems easy enough, especially when the plot is ready furnished to your hand. But it is not sufficient to string together, like onions, a series of incidents and events—they must not only be exciting and pathetic, like that fragrant vegetable, but they must agree harmoniously together (which mine never can be made to do,) and then again they must not overwhelm with their pungency. And of all stories, a humorous one requires the most pruning down. The trouble there is not that you will say too little but too much. Perhaps I am apt to say too much out of stories as well as in them. Perhaps I am deficient in humor, for I never could laugh very heartily at the clown in the circus, or at the fat countrymen who cracks jokes in the steamboat saloons; and I never could see anything very funny in bad spelling. Whatever the cause may be, my humorous stories are enough to make a harlequin weep; and this is why I never attempted to weave a story out of an adventure of Mary last winter. I will tell you the incident as briefly as possible.

Did you ever amuse yourself reading the advertisements for wives which appear daily in some of the papers? There being five of us unmarried girls at home, our talk often runs, very naturally, upon lovers and husbands; and we frequently read these advertisements, and speculate as to what manner of men they may be who do such things. Well, one evening last winter, when we were chattering some foolish talk of this kind, Mary suddenly spoke out of her corner, where she had sat as quiet as a mouse: "We may all think such things very absurd; but very nice people, the best of people, as good as any of us, and people we know, too, take advantage of them."

We all stared. "Have you and the 'wealthy gentleman just returned from Europe just signed a contract?" asked Susie, in her pertest manner.

"You are a ridiculous child," said Mary, coloring violently. "But do any of you know how Mrs. Clare Thornton made the acquaintance of her husband?"

"She met him first in Boston at a review, or parade, or something of that kind," said Helen. "She has told me, but I have forgotten."

"But did she tell you that she had corresponded with m before she met him?" asked Mary.

"Nothing of the kind," said Helen, "and I don't believe she did. Mrs. Clare Thornton would never do so unlady—like a thing."

"Ladylike or not, she did it," said Mary, rather warmly, I thought. "Patty Revere told me about it the other day, in the strictest confidence, and it must never be mentioned out of this sitting-room. Mr. Clare Thornton was a man of excellent family, and had wealth and position, and yet he advertised for a wife. Hannah Brown answered the advertisement; a meeting was arranged to take place on some public occasion, and she was to take a friend with her."

"Just like a duel," interrupted Susie. "She took Patty, and she was punctual to the appointment. They were mutually pleased, and, after he had visited her for some time at her father's house, she became Mrs. Clare Thornton, with the approbation of all her friends."

"They both fired at the same time, and both shots taking effect, they were carried off the ground mortally wounded," said Susie, sticking her needle in the nose of a silk dog.

"Well, of all the strange things I ever did hear!" said Helen; and here she stopped. Helen's remarks are not very striking, generally, and whether she would have said any thing brilliant on this occasion, will never be known; for, Rob coming in, the subject was instantly dropped.

But I was not in the least surprised when Mary called me into the sitting room the next morning, and informed me in the lowest whisper, though there was no one else in the room, that she had answered an advertisement. "I am frightened whenever I think of what I have done, Deborah," said she, "and I wouldn't have done it but for poor Pa—he ought to be relieved of some of his burdens. Oh ! you needn't laugh. I am telling the exact truth, and I feel as if I had done wrong, somehow, to stay here so long; but I couldn't help it; and you know, and Ma knows, and we all know that it's dreadful for five unmarried girls to be in one family, and the youngest twenty-one; and I'm sure what's going to become of us I don't know; and all the young men in our set look out for rich wives, and I don't blame them, with muslin seventy cents a yard, and butter to match: and you know it's as much as we can do to get beaux to go about with us, to say nothing of lovers; Susie and Rob both call me an old maid; and it's too bad; there's no reason why I shouldn't get married as well as Mary English and Mary Miller, ugly, ill-tempered things as they are; and it's all because they have got money, and it's too bad—it's too ba-a-ad!" and here poor Mary broke into sobs.

I was sorry for her, for every word she had said was true, though we are not usually so very plain in our statements, even to each other. "Come, Mary," said I, "what's the use of making all these excuses to me? Let me see the advertisement, in the first place." She took a soiled and crumpled scrap of paper out of her pocket, whereon I read the following:

"A gentleman, thirty-six years of age, good-looking, and of pleasing manners and address, wishes to make the acquaintance of a lady between twenty five and thirty, with a view to matrimony. She must be agreeable, well educated, and of a domestic disposition. Money no object, as the advertiser has some property, and is at present engaged in a lucrative business. Address, etc., etc."

"It does not promise much at first sight," said Mary, "but I was pleased with it for that very reason. He evidently is not wealthy, but I agree with Augusta that it is much safer to marry a man who is doing a good business than one of those very rich men whose fortunes may be in stocks, or some of those other kind of things that burst in a moment, and where are you? The description of the lady suits me exactly. Between twenty-five and thirty—just my age." (Mary is thirty-one, but as she looks younger, I forebore to remind her of the fact).

"Have you proposed a place of meeting?" said I, not knowing exactly what else to say.

"Oh! no indeed! but I wrote to him under an assumed name, and asked him to send his photograph, which he did. I think I will tell aunt Hattie, and appoint the meeting at her house."

So saying, she took a vignette out of her pocket-book, and held it before me. It was a good face, but Mary praised it more than it deserved. "It seems to me," she said at last, surveying it critically, with her head on one side,"that I have seen that face before. It looks strangely familiar, and it may be we met, and did not know we were destined for each other."

The face had seemed familiar to me, too, and now, as Mary spoke, a horrible suspicion crossed my mind; but I said nothing.

Mary, in her usual blundering style, had forgotten to lock the door; and now her evil genius sent Rob into the room for his school books, and he was by her side and gazing at the photograph before she knew he had entered the room.

"I'll be dinged" he exclaimed, "if that ain't the likeness of our milkman !"

What story Mary told Rob I never knew, for I made my escape that I might have a laugh in my own room. But the laugh ended in a cry while thinking of poor Mary, and many a woman like her.

NEW YORK JANUARY 20, 1866

(For the Saturday Press.)

METEOROLOGICAL.

By the Weathercock of the Tribune.

SUNDAY.

(Cold and clear.)

The languorous effeminacy of the atmosphere of yesterday has given place to a frigidity of temperature which is positively repelling.

The brumal breathings of the hyperborean deity of the Winter's cold swept us like the passing of an unquiet ghost.

The air bit shrewdly.

It was an eager and a nipping air. Yet, unimpeded by clouds, Apollo drove his golden chariot across the amythistine cause-ways of the empyrean; the divine equipage shedding throughout the day the beamy scintillations of its silver wheels.

MONDAY.

(Cold and cloudy.)

The frigorific mood of the atmosphere continues; but the sapphire of the heavens has been succeeded by the opal.

The old glazier, Frost, has been at work upon the broken windows of the wayside pools, with chisels of sharp winds and putty of adhesive mists.

From present appearances, however, his glazial performance will be of a temporary character.

TUESDAY.

(Light snow succeeded by thaw.)

The atmospheric phases of last evening were of a noteworthy character.

The sweet pale countenance of the New Year was at first obscured by a bridal veil of virgin snow; but the sun, her husband, kissed her 'neath its folds at an early hour; and, by noon, she was dissolved into happy tears.

WEDNESDAY.

(Continuance of the thaw.)

In vain has the sorrowing year wiped her streaming eyes with the flowing skirts of many a balmoral, in vain have her soft sighings round the chimney tops smitten the icy bosom of the Hammerer, Thor; her tears flow on.

Insensible to her entreaties, the Arctic Deity, jealous of his rival, the God of Day, refuses to congeal her tears. The latter Deity, however, occasionally reawakens hope in her disconsolate bosom by a sly squint or two, whose golden gleams dart across the world, and thrill her pulses with the expectancy of Spring.

THURSDAY.

(Threatening weather followed by a snow storm.)

The most pessimistic philosopher would probably have been satisfied with the weather to-day, yet the optimist himself would not have been altogether disgusted.

A day of strange threatenings—one which calls forth the most delicate imagery of our euphiustic pen.

The night was a heaven of voiceless peace. Like Endymion on the Saturnian slope, the dim earth lay lapped in visionless trance, till Cynthia leaned from her pearl-paved path in the heavens and kissed his slumber into happy dreams, while her silver bow, fallen from her grasp in the rapt listlessness of the moment, gleamed on frozen frith and pond.

In the morning, Ate, the Goddess of Mischief, flung her Golden Apple of sunshiny Discord upon the banquet table of Olympus. First the majestic Juno demanded the prize, with many vaporings and some intimidating thunder; Pallas put in her claim, and sought to bribe the arbiter with fair promises of a wisely benificent day; but the blue patches broadened in the sky, the gleams of flying sunshine grew frequenter, and a strange balminess mellowed the air as the Laughter-loving Queen tripped forward and won the boon.

But the luckless adjudger of the prize, though he won a form of transient beauty, did so at the cost of a Trojan war. The heavens darkened; the mutterings of Jove rolled down from Olympus; and presently the vengeance of the elements burst over the earth in hail and snow and ravings wild and fierce.

FRIDAY.

(Soft and spring like.)

Soft as the kiss of love upon lips that shrink a little with maiden modesty, but yet return it with warmth, was the temperature of to-day.

In the early morning, there were some clouds, Jupiter frowning as though having indulged too freely on the night before; but Mebe, of the rose-ripe lips, quickly brimmed his goblet with his cocktail of nectar, hurried up his ambrosial breakfast, and Apollo smote his lyre in silent ecstacy; and presently the celestial court grew bright with the good-humor of its king.

(For the Saturday Press.)

ON A FARM.

BURLINGTON, N. J., Jan. 15, 1866.

DEAR PRESS :—

One great convenience about my place here is its proximity to Philadelphia.

Now Philadelphia is a very nice city, when one can't get at New York.

Its streets, and other things about it, are so thoroughly "on the square," you know.

One might like to see an occasional white shutter, or, once and again, a marble doorstep or window-sill; but setting aside this deficiency (which, carried to excess, might, I admit, produce a certain sameness), it is a very nice city indeed.

So we like to go down there sometimes, for a day's "shopping" and what not.

On our way down, recently, my wife was guilty of a joke.

A shrill-voiced youth perambulated the car, bearing one of the latest deceptions of the confectioners (surely the Devil sent *them*, whether the proverb regarding cooks be true or no), and shouting, shrieking at the top of his lungs: "Ice-cream candy! Ice-cream candy !"

"Good gracious," quoth she in an aside, "I should think you *did* scream candy!" Which wasn't bad—for her.

One thing I should like explained, O PRESS. What can a rather solemn-looking little man with a black moustache mean by always stalking through the train, after it leaves Burlington, and—with a stern look at passenger after passenger—remarking, in freezing accents, "Baggage!"

If he does it to me again, I think I shall demand an explanation.

It is sufficient injury to one's feelings to be obliged to ride in the uncomfortable cars—the Camden and Amboy—without being also called names by some unknown employé of the concern.

After paying for a ticket, and walking into a car without assistance, I claim that I am *not* "baggage," and I cannot answer for the consequences if the injurious epithet is again applied to me.

But I must return to my farm.

Of course I have a small amount of live stock.

And here let me say that I have noticed all my life, and everywhere, that all animals do much better and pay much better if they are kindly treated and cared for, than if they are left to shift for themselves.

The same amount of corn, hay or oats, will produce vastly different results with the two systems.

Have an interest in your animals; see that they are kept warm, and comfortable, and contented, and the same food will show immensely greater good than that given by your neighbor who lets all care, except feeding, go by the board.

All my animals like me and I like them: consequently they do well in the matter of butter, eggs, growth, and what not.

There's my ugly dog "Beauty."

When he came to me I think he hated the whole cat family a little beyond any *other* family in this world.

Now he lies snoozing before my fire—for I sometimes admit him to the house—with the most frolicsome kitten you ever saw (enough to wear out the patience of Job's black-and-tan terrier) nestled among his legs, or on his head, or anywhere she pleases.

I taught him very readily.

The fact is I hate cruelty to any of the dumb creatures.

Which reminds me of what I saw once at Fresh Pond, near Cambridge (Mass.), being done by some medical (or other) students to some frogs.

They had caught a number, and were blowing the unfortunate captives up by means of artfully inserted straw.

Having properly inflated the victims they cast them into the water, where they helplessly floated, their white, glistening bellies uppermost.

I declare it gave me a stomachache to think what they must have suffered.

The students, no doubt, thought it a good practical joke.

What the frogs thought was quite another matter.

Speaking of practical jokes, I think a good one, if it has not too much malice in it, is a very good thing.

Such an one I remember that has never yet strayed into print.

It was perpetrated by a true and gallant gentleman, who since fell at the head of his brigade in the Shenandoah valley.

Your old friend, Mr. Ed. House, knew him well, and doubtless loved him, as I did.

I have seen a photograph of the two, taken under a tree in Virginia, in which they stand side by side, looking two as guant and warworn individuals as you would wish to meet with in a campaign.

But that has nothing to do with my story.

Several years ago there was an annual three-day "muster" of certain Western Massachusetts regiments held at Northampton, in that State.

"High private" in one of the companies was the friend I write of; and jolly good times he and two or three more choice spirits made for their comrades in arms.

Now round about the camp various sutlers, showmen, and other outside barbarians had pitched their tents, for the purpose of relieving the militia of their spare change. Of course they succeeded admirably.

One evening —— and some score of his friends were outside the lines having a good time.

Roving from point to point they came upon a tent, outside which a burly man was shouting:—"Walk up! Walk up! Walk right in and see the great Kentucky giantess, the horse with six legs and nary two alike, the living anacondas, and the man that swallows a sword and eats small rocks for supper—all for ten cents!"

"By Jove, boys," said —— "*that* sounds good! Let's go in."

A smile overspread the features of the doorkeeper at the "fat take" before him.

"Many in ?" inquired ——.

"Lots! Full of soldiers !" replied the doorkeeper. "It's worth the money; *only* ten cents! Pass right in."

"*Count* 'em !" said ——.

"All right," quoth the guardian of the show. "Pass right in, gentlemen!"

And about thirty passed in.

"Have you *counted* 'em ?" inquired ——.

"All right! Thirty-two, an' *you'll* make thirty-three."

"Oh, *I'm* not going in!" quoth ——.

"*You* ain't?" said the man, a horrible suspicion crossing his mind.

"No, *I'm* going back to camp," said ——.

"Good night!"

Then, my dear PRESS, if you could have seen that infuriated door-keeper speed to the mysterious interior of the tent! There were at least a hundred persons crowded within its stifling canvas walls, all in uniform.

"Here! Look a-here! I counted *you*, I believe ! Didn't I count *you*? Wasn't *you* counted ?"

Thus he flew from blue-coat to blue-coat; but not a soul owned up, and thirty men saw the snakes and things for "nothin'."

It was a bad sell, decidedly bad; as, no doubt, the victimized showman thought.

I fear this letter is a sell, also, I have said so little about my farm.

WARREN.

NEW YORK JANUARY 27, 1866

(For the Saturday Press.)

"DRUM-TAPS."

Few persons, we imagine, have read the much over-praised, as well as greatly underrated writings of Walt Whitman, without a conviction that their author is a genuine poet, although they may not agree with his more enthusiastic critics in ranking him above all of the moderns, and finding his true place beside Isaiah, Ezekiel and Job. It is impossible to sympathize heartily with the greatest thoughts that have found utterance in literature, and not to admire him. The two ideas which have him in their possession,—the omnipresence of the soul, and the sacredness of the individual—lie at the roots of poetry and civilization; and he chants them with an invincible faith, which is, of itself, sufficient to place him on a plane beyond that of the poets who believe in art as a finality.

But to be a Pantheist and a Democrat, does not constitute a claim sufficient to entitle any man to the distinction of being a great poet; and Walt Whitman has no other, save a picturesqueness of phrase unsurpassed in literature, and a powerful rhythm, whose long musical roll is like that of the waves of the sea. For he is not a man of ideas. What is called his sanity, his tenacious grasp on realities, is, after all, the monomania of a man whom a great thought has robbed of his self-possession. The unity of the soul is a key that unlocks all doors, but Walt Whitman stopped at the first one to which he applied it. He celebrates the divinity of matter, and worships the shells of things with such fervor that he almost persuades us that there is no substance behind them. It is a dangerous error. The sphinx, Matter, stands in her terrible beauty before every soul, and no answer to her riddle is more fatal than this. Whisper to her that she is divine, and her smiling lips open surely for your destruction. The idea which led Oriental thinkers to the life of contemplation, and which gives Emerson a serenity like that of the unclouded summer sky, leads this poet to materialism. His songs, though beautiful and inspiring, smack too strongly of the earth. His suggestions are sometimes vast, but himself is chaotic and fragmentary. The truth is that the two ideas which find expression through him are antagonistic. *Because* the soul is one and all mighty, the individual is nothing. "I want no masses at all," says Emerson; but in Whitman the passion for individuals is so strong that it continually wrestles with and overthrows his belief in the universal. Democracy is a good thought to found a state upon, but it is not the profoundest basis for a poem.

Jefferson may claim that "all men are born free and equal," and Whitman may "accept nothing which all cannot have the counterpart of on the same terms;" but the soul, which does not divide itself impartially through the whole universe, but incarnates itself wholly in each atom, is an aristocrat—does not whiffle about rights and duties—claims all and will not be hindered of its own. Mr. Gradgrind's facts, Walt Whitman's patriotism, the vilest man, the purest saint, are equally sacred, and equally valueless, for they are the stepping-stones only, to the unattainable beyond. Let any man assume the attitude of adoration, no matter how fair the shrine, and his shell instantly hardens around him. And porous as this poet thinks himself to all the influences of the universe, he is prostrated, deaf, dumb and blind, before an idol from which the god has departed.

And yet, as Thoreau said, he suggests at times something more than human. In his latest volume there are a few passages which contain the very essence of poetry, and are inexpressibly pathetic, moreover, with the yearning humanity that breathes through them. Setting aside his war chants, which are remarkable for nothing but the startling vividness of their pictures, there are certain poems which make one doubt the correctness of the impression made by the whole man. Such, for instance, are the invocation to Death in the poem called "When last in the dooryard the lilacs bloomed," "Chanting the Square Deific," and "As I lay with my head in your lap." If his faith in the unseen were more of a prophetic fury, and less a premeditated and coolly considered belief; if he clung closer to realities and less tenaciously to appearances, he would be the greatest poet of our day. But he hesitates, as he says, with a rare self-appreciation, at the first step in his progress. He shuts himself from hearty sympathy on all sides. His music, his picturesque force avail him little with the poets, while he so persistently produces poetical effects outside of the accepted rules of their art; and his vast ideas fail of half their force to those who, believing in them as faithfully as he, feel that his application of them is limited and material.

F.

SOON TO BE IN MARK-ET.

Mark Twain! We are informed that a sketch of the birth, life, and services of this mild reprobate and rampant humorist is soon to be forthcoming from several teeming presses. By a brief glance over the proof-sheets, we learn that this exemplary young Christian was born on the Mississippi—very frequently borne on it—that he never lessened the channel of the river by drinking any of the water; and was always considered a healthy infant. He piloted steamboats for a number of years—and succeeded in handling a number of them upon snags, from which they never got off. He emigrated to California early in '49, in consequence of a slight misunderstanding with a Mississippi captain—upon whom be ventured the small practical joke of soaping his speaking trumpet—and settled at the Sutter mills, where he paid honorable attention to the widow of an early settler—but did not suit her—and a good looking rival, with more credit at the grocery and a double barrelled shot gun, persuaded him to move. He then came down to San Francisco, where his time has been principally occupied in smoking a bogus meerschaum, filled with bad tobacco, and pitching into the police. He has a story in the N. Y SATURDAY PRESS—the Press can stand him, though very often he can't stand the press; it is about a frog, and will probably be illustrated by a jump. He is not as good looking as some other men are, but if he keeps on in his present industrious course, it is probable that he may some time edit a newspaper or own a steamboat. At present he is in Stockton, endeavoring to cure the maniacs of the impression that the world is round instead of square, by reading them a poem "after" Tennyson, entitled "He done his level best."

NEW YORK FEBRUARY 3, 1866

DRAMATIC FEUILLETON.

BY FIGARO.

I notice that my critical friend of the TRIBUNE is still disposed to insist that the stage shall be judged by the Procrustean standard of what is called High Art.

Don't do it, my dear fellow.

Procrusteanation is the thief of time.

High comedy is doubtless a good thing; but so is low comedy—and farce, and burlesque, and extravaganza, and every other form of the Drama.

"I don't object to anybody's preferring Shakespeare to De Walden—or even to Gayler (I do so, myself, at times), but I like to have my "Balloon Weddings " and my "Child-Stealers" as well as my "Merry Wives" and my "Macbeths:" yes, and my Ravels and my Hanlons as well as my Booths and my Wallacks.

When the Hanlons were performing at Wood's Theatre, last week, taking part in what was intended to be a grand carnival scene, it no more occurred to me that they were out of place in the Drama, than that a Taglioni or an Ellsler would be out of place in the Opera and yet there are those who would exclude them, because, forsooth, "the drama is a creation of the human mind," and physical exercises are therefore unworthy of it.

And speaking of Taglioni and Ellsler, there was a movement among a few High Art people in Europe, not long since, to deprive the Opera of the ballet, on the ground that dancing wasn't intellectual —wasn't "æsthetic!"

Of course the movement failed, it being sufficient for the opera-goers that dancing entertained them, and was moreover naturally associated with music.

They admitted that it was a purely physical exercise; but then it occurred to them, so was breathing, and, to a great extent, singing. I know some people who object to pantomime as being unworthy of the Drama, and who look upon the Ravels not as actors—much less as artists—but as little better than a species of mountebank.

Well, go on gentlemen, and when you have raised the drama to the true æsthetic standard, by purifying it of everything that appeals to the senses, and excluding from it all such vulgar accessories as dancing, pantomime, etc., you will have only to put a pulpit on the stage and your work will be complete.

However, you needn't order your pulpits yet; for as the world grows older it grows jollier, and no effort to phylacterize or dismalize the stage will stand the slightest chance of success, till you discover a means of modifying human nature and enabling it to get along not only without the senses, but without any of the elements which now adapt it to the globe we inhabit.

All which being interpreted, Mr. Editor, means that, on the whole, I like the theatres very well as they are, and that if I made any change in them it would not be with a view to what is called High Art (which would give them all the Turvydropsy), but with a view to making them more human.

You will laugh at me, I suppose, but the play which gives me more pleasure than almost any other that I can now think of is Boucicault's "London Assurance."

I went to see it the other night at the Olympic; you remember we sat together.

Well, there is nothing great about it—nothing particularly startling about the dialogue or in the situations—nothing very marked in the way of characterization—nothing very remarkable in the plot; but there is an indescribable air of naturalness about the piece which, when it was first produced, operated upon the whole theatrical world like a charm.

It is some years, to be sure, since I have seen it properly put upon the stage; but, at the outset,—when the furniture used was such as might actually be used in a private house—and the scenery was in keeping—and the whole thing had an air of comfort and coziness about it—people used to wonder, as the play went on and the actors moved about the stage and chatted with each other like human beings, whether they were in a theatre or not.

And the result was that the play had a success, here and in England, which has hardly been equalled since.

Why the playwrights and managers didn't take a hint from this and produce other plays of the same character—plays with the human element predominant, and which would force the players to be more or less like men and women instead of like mannikins and puppets—is one of the many theatrical mysteries which I am unable to solve.

When will any of us cease thanking Charles Kean for introducing the human element in his representation of Louis XI—and giving us on the stage, for once, a king, who, without any violent effort of the imagination, might be considered as belonging to the human species?

I tell you, my æsthetic friends, if you wish to "reform the stage "—to "elevate the drama "—to go down to posterity as theatrical philanthropists and apostles—give up all this Podsnappian talk about "classic art," and turn your energies toward converting actors and actresses into simple human beings like—well, like George Holland, or John Owens, or Mary Gannon, or Mrs. John Sefton, or Mrs. John Wood, for example.

Try, especially if you have the courage, gentlemen, to introduce the human element upon the tragic or heroic stage, where, at present, there is scarcely the germ of it.

An actor who should give us a Richard III., a Hamlet, a Macbeth, a Richelieu, as simple human beings—like Kean's Louis XI.—who, in others words, while representing either of those characters, should speak and act regardless of tradition or precedent, and as if he himself were the character, then and there present in full flesh and blood—he would create such a sensation as the stage has hardly known for a century.

I have seen all the great tragedians of my day, and find them, in the main, essentially alike.

They differ somewhat in their style of elocution—Edwin Booth's being, to my mind, by far the best—but their general conception of the leading tragic parts is so nearly indentical, that none of us could help noticing the other night, when Frank Chanfrau imitated either of them, he unconsciously imitated them all.

The obvious reason of this is, that they all build on the same old stage model, which has been handed down from generation to generation, until it has come to be looked upon, at last, as an object of worship.

Now it is time this idol was broken—time, at all events, that tragedians of intelligence and culture should refuse any longer to bow before it.

And this is a reform, my æsthetic friends, which I will heartily join you in: for when it is accomplished, that fearful old stage walk, that horrible stage shrug, that dismal stage voice, will disappear; and with them, an amount of striding, ranting, bellowing, etc., the very thought of which is enough to make one shudder.

I know, indeed, that there is a big "other side" to all this—that there is as much humbug about what we call "natural acting" as about anything else that for an actor to conduct himself on the stage exactly as it he were in a drawing-room would be simply to make an idiot of himself—that, in a word, a certain degree of exaggeration is necessary in order for him to produce the simplest natural effect; but admitting all this, the fact still remains that the natural effect must be produced, and that under the present system we have nothing of the kind, but, on the contrary, a series of effects so grossly unnatural that the actor often seems to us little more than one of the properties of the theatre to be packed away when the performance is over, with the rest of the trumpery, and kept in the store-room "till called for."

This is not so much the case in comedy as in tragedy, but it is more or less so in both. For instance, in the performance at the Olympic, the other night of "London Assurance"—which I was speaking of just now— Mr. Stoddart, one of the best actors I know of, contrived to make Sir Harcourt Courtley about as stagey and unnatural a character as you can imagine; while Mr. Davenport, famed for his ease and grace in nearly every part he appears in, was scarcely better as Dazzle, and the other characters, with the exception of Cool (played by Mr. Morton), were as unnatural as anything ever seen at the Old Park.

In fact, excepting Mrs. Wood's Lady Gay, which was almost *too* natural, the performance was so at variance with the spirit of the play that I doubt if the company could have done worse with one of the "old comedies."

What they did on Thursday and Friday with "The Actress by Day-light," and "The Two Friends," I am unable to report, though I can vouch for Mrs. Wood in the former, from past experience, and Mr. Davenport needs no voucher, as a rule, from anybody.

Next week, by the way, you will have a chance to see how these two artists—and artists they are in the true sense of the word—will work together in "Black-Eyed Susan" (one of Davenport's favorite pieces) and also in a comedy which proposes to solve the question, at last, of "Who killed Cock-Robin ?"

These pieces will probably bring the Davenport engagement to an end, and then Mrs. Wood promises us a season of burlesque—for which much thanks.

Thanks, too, and many of them, to Miss Rushton, for introducing burlesque; and "between you and me and the Post," I think it will save her little theatre.

Schönberg's idea of burlesquing "Arrah-na-Pogue" for her, was really a brilliant one, and he has done it artistically enough to secure the approbation even of the ascetics.

The burden of the piece rests upon Mr. Harry Pearson and Miss Rosa Cooke—the latter a daughter of our late friend, J. P. Cooke.

Pearson goes through his part (Shaun of the Post) with the skill of a veteran; while Miss Cooke, who is playing her first engagement, acts and sings in the character of Arrah with a naivété and grace which serve even to enhance the effect of her youth and beauty.

Allow me, Mr. Editor, to predict of this young lady, who recalls to us so pleasantly the memory of her father, that if she perseveres in her studies and remains true to the precepts in which she has been trained, her praises will soon be in all the land.

Allow me furthermore to predict that if Miss Rushton will continue to give us light and amusing plays, and will take a little more pains in putting them on the stage, her theatre will soon become one of the most attractive resorts in the metropolis.

And I want to predict something, now I am in that vein, about Wood's Theatre: but I'll wait till Chanfrau has done drawing crowds to see "Mose" and Gayler comes on with his "Child-Stealer."

Meanwhile, I'll consult De Walden who, as you may not know, has just got back from consulting the Philadelphic oracles on the subject of "Sam."

But, speaking of Wood, I hear that his *other* theatre—to wit, the Broadway—may be pulled down next summer in the interest of certain gentlemen of the dry goods persuasion.

So the scheme of John Owens to take it for ten years, and play "Solon Shingle" every night—which I verily believe would pay—will probably have to be given up.

John's moral on the occasion is: "Go and see it every night, now, and if that don't please you, go every Saturday afternoon besides."

True, John, but what will the æsthetic folks say, especially since you threaten to add "The Wild Indian" to the performance?

However, never mind the æsthetic folks.

They are very good fellows, after all, and I have seen them this week enjoying themselves at Barnum's and the Circus as much as if they were at the Winter Garden seeing Booth's Richelieu, or at the Academy of Music hearing the "Africaine."

By the way, I haven't seen Booth's Richelieu, myself, this time; but I hear such marvels of it—and of the magnificent manner in which the play is mounted—and of the irrepressible crowds which flock to it—that I will go next week if I have to take a lady with me for protection, as I had to one night recently when I went to Niblo's to see Miss Bateman's Leah.

Apropos, not of Leah, nor of ladies, but of things I haven't seen (which wouldn't be a bad sub-title for these Feuilletons), let me confess that among them is the "Africaine," repeated by Maretzek on Thursday for the inauguration of his new season, and "The Irish Heiress," which Wallack produced on Wednesday.

Never mind: the papers chronicle them both as brilliant successes, and it is doubtful whether they would have gone off much better had I been present, or if anybody will suffer much for want of my learned opinion about them—which, moreover, can be given at my favorite period, "some other time."

Meanwhile, please note that "The Irish Heiress" will be repeated to-night, and while you are about it just look at the cast:

Lord William Daventry.................................Mr. John Gilbert
Percy Ardent.. .... Mr. Frederic Robinson
Major Bellamy Fuss.................................. ....Mr. C. Fisher
Sir William Stanmore................................... Mr. B. T. Richard
Supple, attorney-at-law.. Mr. Norton
Lenoir, valet to Sir Wm Stanmore............Mr. J. C. Williamson
Euston... Mr. Ward
Norah Merrion. .... Miss Madeline Henriques
Lady Daventry... Mrs. Jennings
Mrs. Bolton Comfort.... .... Mrs. John Sefton

Note, also, that the "Africaine" will be repeated next week, and that for the operatic Matinée to-day we are to have "Norma."

All which being respectfully submitted, I remain (what there is left of me)

Yours trurally,

FIGARO.

P.S. The "Ticket-of-Leave Man" will be reproduced at the Winter Garden next Wednesday evening for the benefit of Mr. Humphrey Bland.

The cast will be strong, including, among other names, Miss Rose Eytinge, Mr. John Dyott, Mr. W. S. Andrews, Mr. Barron, Mr. Taylor, Mr. Mason, and Mr. Bland himself, who will appear in his famous character of Melter Moss, which he has played in New York and elsewhere nearly two hundred times.

The occasion will be one of much interest, and the house will doubtless be crowded.

The two American brothers Poznanski, recently arrived from Paris, will give a concert to-night at Irving Hall, assisted by M'me. Reville, and Signor Fossati. The performance will be under the direction of Messrs. Anschutz and Buechel. One of the Poznanskis is said to be great on the piano and the other on the violin.

The "Africaine" will be repeated at the Academy of Music on Tuesday evening next. The opera for Monday will be "I Puritani." On Thursday the "Africaine" will be given in Brooklyn. At the Matinée, to-day, the tickets will be a dollar to all parts of the house.

F.

(For the Saturday Press.)

A VERSE.

Some one, unknowingly, had touched a chord
Which, stretching backward through a group of years,
Jarred harshly on the past. Utt'ring no word,
She "hid behind her smile" the coming tears
And left the crowd. Once in her silent room,
Down sank she on the floor with piteous moan
While from the opened door of girlhood's tomb
Come trooping dreadful shadows one by one;
Slowly they pass before her hidden eyes
Slander, Oppression, Poverty and Sin,
While Hope (hid in her bosom) faints and dies,
MURDERED by cruel hints of what has been.
A few LONG moments thus, and then she rose,
Twisted once more the flowers in her hair,
And, gaily singing, she returned to those
Who never dreamed that with her came Despair!

M. E.

NEW YORK FEBRUARY 10, 1866

(For the Saturday Press.)

ON A FARM.

V.

Burlington, N. J., Jan. 29, 1866.

DEAR PRESS:—

It strikes me sometimes a little unpleasantly to see the great number of public sales advertised continually about here, of farms, farming stock, utensils, household furniture, etc. (Melancholy thoughts will obtrude themselves regarding a possible future when, my experiment of farming on a small scale having failed ignonimiously, I too shall appear for sale on the fences and in the stores and barber's shops.)

I find that if a man wants to sell anything in this region he immediately advertises a Vendue ("wandoo" some of the natives style it.)

I have been to several, but have not purchased extensively, as I have ascertained that articles thus sold here generally bring more than they cost when new.

They are curious gatherings these vendues. The family selling usually give a family dinner party, to which relations and friends sit down and prepare for the family sacrifice by a feast.

Then an itinerant dealer in the drink of the country, popularly known as apple-whiskey but disrespectfully spoken of by outside barbarians from the States as "Jersey-lightning," sets up his stand in the front yard, and, the crowd having drunken somewhat, the sale begins.

It is a motley crowd: all the farmers from the neighborhood are there: They have come in Jersey wagons, in carts, on horse back, on mule back and on foot.

And they bid very considerably.

The auctioneer dwelleth not long over his wares, and pauseth in his selling only to imbibe an occasional draught of "apple."

I have always felt an admiration for auctioneers: they are surely a class by themselves, as distinct from ordinary mortals as are hotel-clerks or railroad conductors. Very glib and brassy, of course: Somewhat apt to make mistakes in descriptions of unfamiliar articles.

I remenber a very funny man in Greenfield, Massachusetts, who signally failed once in the description of a book he put up.

He was a jovial fellow—not an auctioneer "by trade," exactly, though licensed to sell in that way, if he chose.

So he chose to sell a library some one wanted to dispose of.

He hadn't read very much in books, Robbins hadn't, but he scanned the titles, trusted to luck, and went ahead:

"Here you have," he cried, "Bunyan's Pilgrims Progress; how much 'm offered for it? How much do I hear for the Pilgrim's Progress, by John Bunyan? 'T's a first rate book, gentleman, with six superior illustrations; how much do I hear? All about the Pilgrims, by John Bunyan! Tells where they come from an' where they landed, an' what they done *after* they landed! Here's a picter of one of 'em going about Plymouth, peddlin' with a pack on his back!"

The crowd were overcome by that last statement, and the book immediately sold at a high figure.

I stated earlier in this letter that I had not purchased extensively at the Wandoos about here.

I *did*, somewhat so, at one.

It had been my custom to send my man, or take him with me, in anticipation of bargains in farming tools.

Would that I had always done so. For my man knows more about farming tools than I do: but with over confidence I attended one alone.

I bought a plow, a cultivator, a barrow, another plow, a shovel, a (for-uses-not-mentionable-to-ears-polite) fork, a hoe, another barrow, a piece of another cultivator, the top of an old bee-hive, a "likely shoat," two iron pots, thirty market baskets, a potatoe drag, a —but I have told enough.

A friendly neighbor placed his market wagon at my disposal and, between us, we conveyed my purchases to my farm.

I called my man to look at them. He walked about each article several times with a serious air: then he looked at me: then he resumed his inspection of my purchases; and then, I thought, he smiled.

"Well," said I, "what do you think of them ?"

"Them there is very or'nary plows," said he, "one on 'em aint good for nothing; haint got no mould board. T'other may do for working out for blackberries: that there biggest cultivator I wouldn't use if I was you without I wanted to spile " Abe" an' lay "Pete" up for a week or so—its one o' them or'nary heavy draught things as 'll kill a horse in three days: the teeth in them harrers is good, the biggest pot would do to bile turnips in for the cow, but there's a hole in the bottom. The "—

"Enough !" I cried. "Say no more!"

I haven't bought anything at one of the confounded Wandoos since.

In my opinion they are humbugs.

Well, well, I must live and learn; there is no one who is not ignorant of very many things.

There was a funny instance of this truth that occurred in Boston Harbor a couple of summers ago, which I must tell you, though the story introduces my wife in her (at that time) lack of knowledge in some simple marine names and things.

We were spending a little time on one of the beautiful islands in the Harbor, and among other pleasant sojourners there was a large and very handsome Newfoundland dog. One day he was missing.

He was a great swimmer, and presently the ladies—having gotten into their silly heads the idea that he had swum out to sea—appeared on the heights looking all abroad for him with telescopes and opera glasses.

And at length they discovered him.

Yes, there he was, plainly to be seen about two miles from land breasting the billowy surges and combatting with the salty wave! There was no doubt about it!

So his master, getting quickly into a boat with four stout oarsmen, pulled lustily for the spot.

We saw him approach to within about a quarter of a mile of the poor creature, then turn and row leisurely back.

I hurried to meet him.

"Nothing but a lobster buoy," he cried in a pet at the sell he had suffered.

So I went to tell the ladies the reason for his return.

"But why," said my wife, regarding me with great astonishment and a considerable touch of horror;—"Why didn't they stop to save the poor lobster boy?"

WARREN.

(For the Saturday Press.)

SOAP BUBBLES.

Just at my side in his rocking chair
  My little Max is sitting
He with his soap and pipe, and I
  With the stocking I am knitting.
He fashions ships from the milk white spray,
  I freight them with thoughts as they float away.

Moored to the pipe is a phantom barque
  With the white sails spreading fast,
And pennons woven of rainbows, float
  From the top of the golden mast.
But a cloud creeps over the face of day
  And sunbeams and rainbows flee away.

So I thought of the tiny barque which sails
  To the shadowy land with mine—
The waves which are bearing it out to sea
  Are crested with golden shine.
Shall it reach the haven beneath the cloud—
  When the waves are black and the tempest loud?

Lo! The ship has gone, and a mimic world
  Of the wonderous pipe is born,
And pictures glowing in rainbow frames
  Its crystaline walls adorn—
And some fairy limner has painted there
  My room with its grate and rocking chair.

And so, as the chubby finger points
  To a miniature of me,
My thoughts go out to another world,
  Where I long enthroned to be.
'Tis my darling's heart, and I breathe a prayer
  To be absent or present reflected there.

I turned away from the thought to gaze
  Down into the merry eyes
Which were tracking the bauble with a look
  Of beautiful surprise.
When lo! it has changed into silver spray,
  And the toys which freighted it,—where are they?

So, I mused as my fingers strayed amid
  Those ringlets of golden hair—
Of the bubble life, and the syren hopes
  Which mirror their beauties there,
And of many freighted with visions bright
  Which had vanished out of my longing sight.

But surely a prettier bubble ne'er
  From this mystical white foam grew
And surely a dearer, sweeter face
  Was never reflected through
Than the face just veiled by that silver spray,
  And the bubble my fond lips kissed away.

L. J. C.

NEW YORK FEBRUARY 17, 1866

(For the Saturday Press.)

A HURRICANE AT SEA.

It is Christmas day. We are seventeen days out from New York bound to an Italian port. The sky is clear and bright, and the wind is favorable. Looking back into the week gone by, the recollection of the fearful dangers through which we passed makes me shudder again, and my pen almost refuses to record our dreadful experiences. Would that I could forget them all—but that, alas! is impossible. I can never blot out from my memory the remembrance of those frightful hours.

We sailed on a Friday, and although the intelligence of the present generation has done much to eradicate the old repugnance so prevalent amongst sea-faring men, to sailing upon that day, still there were some of us on board, including myself, who were not without misgivings.

But all went well until the eighteenth, when the heavens darkened, the sea rose with the increasing wind, and everything foretold an approaching gale.

The clouds break away for a moment, and a rainbow appears in the northwest shortly after sunrise. There is an old rhyme familiar to those who have been on the water, the first line of which runs in this wise—

"Rainbow in the morning, sailors take warning,"

and although the reader may perhaps smile at this second evidence of my superstitious belief, still I freely confess that I could not look upon that sign in the heavens without a feeling akin to horror. The barometer, too, gave notice of the coming gale, and preparations were made to meet it. "Call all hands, Sir, and look sharp about it." In royals and topgallant sails, mainsail hauled up, spanker lowered, jibs and staysails hauled down, and all three upper topsails on the caps to reef. This is done, and they are set again. The gale increases in violence. We are running before it." Haul up the foresail." A sheet is started, and with a report like that of a discharge of musketry, the sail is split from head to foot.

The clouds again lift for a moment, and the sun is seen sinking to rest, while the wind howls a dirge over it as it disappears beneath the angry waves.

The ship is now stripped to three lower topsails, and, with two men at her wheel, plunges madly forward through the seething waters. Thus through the black night. Morning breaks upon us, and the gale has increased to a *hurricane.*

Again in the northwest a rainbow. The foretopsail is blown away, and the mizzen topsail is furled, leaving the ship under a lower maintopsail only. The seas have risen to a fearful height, and the wind catches the spray from their tops, and drives it hissing over them, the full length of the ship. Sharp squalls, accompanied by hail and rain, are frequent. It is horrible to remain below, and still worse to go on deck. Our captain scarcely leaves it for an instant. Standing by the helmsmen he gives his orders, briefly and coolly, as they guide the vessel on her perilous path. He too knows the danger. It is too late to bring her by the wind, and we must run before it. It is a race with Death. Who will win?

And now the last sail is furled, and the ship flies before the tempest, ten knots an hour, under bare poles.

Night settles down over the face of the deep, and darkness adds to the terrors of our situation. Oh, what a weary, weary night! The wind shrinks and howls through the rigging, sending forth a thousand different notes. It whistles over the thresholds of the closed doors, in weird, unearthly strains. The rain and hail beat upon the skylights, and the seas roar and rumble in hoarse and threatening tones. Oh, what a wild, mad night! Every minute seems an age, and we live through the long hours till dawn in utter agony and apprehension.

It is morning again, and still the wind yells and the huge waves roll after the ship as if they longed to engulf her. The hours wear on, and once again in the heavens, high up in the northwest, we behold that fearful sign.

The hurricane is at its worst. Lightning begins to play in the sky, and the thunder mutters in the distance. It is ten o'clock in the morning, and yet almost as black as night. The fiercest squall we have had is upon us. Great God, what is that!—a brilliant sheet of flame and a deafening crash at the same instant, and then, cries for help! The ship has been struck near the foremast. Three of the crew are lying paralyzed upon the deck, and the mate is brought aft to his room, *dead.*— Ay, already the marks of the lightning are plainly traced upon his throat, ghastly yellow marks, as if some assassin had clutched and held him there until life had died out. The pumps are sounded—there is no leak, and we are safe.

As if content with all the havoc it has made the storm begins to abate, and towards night we can show a little sail again. The next day the sun smiles brightly upon us, the sea has gone down, and we are steering for our destined port.

* * * * * * * * * * *

Let us go on deck for a while. It is afternoon. There is a plank in the gangway, and a something wrapped in canvas, lying stretched upon it. "Call all hands—starboard head braces, helm down." The ship comes slowly up to the wind, and the maintopsail lies aback, checking her way through the water. Presently she stands still. "Let them all come aft now—uncover men." One of the passengers reads part of the service appointed for the burial of the dead, commencing, "Man that is born of a woman hath but a short time to live, and is full of misery." At its conclusion, rough Amens are growled, the word is given to launch, and the sea swallows up our deceased messmate. Poor fellow, it is his last, long cruise. "Helm up—fill away maintopsail." Let us leave the bubbling spot far astern, and pray God we may never again witness, a hurricane at sea.

J. N. D.

(From the Pall Mall Gazette.)

A NIGHT IN A WORKHOUSE.

At about nine o'clock on the evening of Monday the —th instant, a neat but unpretentious carriage might have been seen turning cautiously from the Kennington road into Princess road, Lambeth. The curtains were closely drawn, and the coachman wore an unusually responsible air. Approaching a public house, which retreated a little from the street, he pulled up; but not so close that the lights should fall upon the carriage door, not so distant as to unsettle the mind of any one who chose to imagine that he had halted to drink beer before proceeding to call for the children at a juvenile party. He did not dismount, nor did any one alight in the usual way; but any keen observer who happened to watch his intelligent countenance might have seen a furtive glance directed to the wrong door—that is to say, to the door of the carriage which opened into the dark and muddy road. From that door emerged a sly and ruffianly figure, marked with every sign of squalor. He was dressed in what had once been a snuff-brown coat, but which had faded to the hue of bricks imperfectly baked. It was not strictly a ragged coat, though it had lost its cuffs, a bereavement which obliged the wearer's arms to project through the sleeves two long inelegant inches. The coat altogether was too small, and was only made to meet over the chest by means of a bit of twine. This wretched garment was surmounted by a "bird's-eye" pocket-handkerchief of cotton, wisped about the throat hangman fashion; above all was a battered billy-cock hat, with a dissolute drooping brim. Between the neckerchief and the lowering brim of the hat appeared part of a face, unshaven, and not unscrupulously clean. The man's hands were plunged into his pockets, and he shuffled hastily along in boots, which were the boots of a tramp indifferent to miry ways. In a moment he was out of sight, and the brougham, after waiting a little while, turned about and comfortably departed.

This mysterious figure was that of the present writer. He was bound for Lambeth Workhouse, there to learn by actual experience how casual paupers are lodged and fed, and what the "casual" is like, and what the porter who admits him, and the master who rules over him; and how the night passes with the outcasts whom we have all seen crowding about workhouse doors on cold and rainy nights. Much has been said on the subject—on behalf of the paupers, on behalf of the officials; but nothing by any one who, with no motive but to learn and make known the truth, had ventured the experiment of passing a night in a workhouse and trying what it actually is to be a "casual."

The day had been windy and chill—the night was cold; and therefore I fully expected to begin my experiences among a dozen of ragged wretches squatting about the steps and waiting for admission But my only companion at the door was a decently dressed woman, whom, as I afterwards learnt, they declined to admit until she had recovered from a fit of intoxication from which she had the misfortune to be still suffering.

I lifted the big knocker, and knocked; the door was promptly opened, and I entered. Just within, a comfortable-looking clerk sat at a comfortable desk, ledger before him. Indeed, the spacious hall in every way was as comfortable as cleanliness and great mats and plenty of gaslights could make it.

"What do you want?" asked the man who opened the door;

"I want a lodging."

"Go and stand before the desk," said the porter; and I obeyed.

"You are late," said the clerk.

"Am I, sir?"

"Yes. If you come in you'll have a bath, and you'll have to sleep in the shed."

"Very well, sir."

"What's your name?"

"Joshua Mason, sir."

"What are you?"

"An engraver." (This taradiddle I invented to account for the look of my hands.)

"Where did you sleep last night ?"

"Hammersmith," I answered—as I hope to be forgiven.

"How many times have you been here ?"

"Never before, sir."

"Where do you mean to go to when you are turned out in the morning?"

"Back to Hammersmith, sir."

These humble answers being entered in a book, the clerk called to the porter, saying, "Take him through. You may as well take his bread with you."

Near the clerk stood a basket containing some pieces of bread of equal size. Taking one of these, and unhitching a bunch of keys from the wall, the porter led me through some passages all so scrupulously clean that my most serious misgivings were laid to rest. Then we passed into a dismal yard. Crossing this, my guide led me to a door, calling out, "Hillo! Daddy, I've brought you another!" Whereupon Daddy opened unto us, and let a little of his gaslight stream into the dark where we stood.

"Come in," said Daddy, very hospitably. "There's enough of you to-night, anyhow! What made you so late?"

"I didn't like to come in earlier."

"Ah! that's a pity, now, because you've missed your skilley (gruel). It's the first night of skilley, don't you know, under the new Act?"

"Just like my luck!" I muttered dolefully.

The porter went his way, and I followed Daddy into another apartment, where were ranged three great baths, each one containing a liquid so disgustingly like weak mutton broth that my worst apprehensions crowded back. "Come on, there's a dry place to stand on up at this end," said Daddy, kindly. "Take off your clothes, tie 'em up in your hank'sher, and I'll lock 'em up till the morning." Accordingly I took off my coat and waistcoat, and was about to tie them together, when Daddy cried, "That ain't enough; I mean everything." "Not my shirt, sir, I suppose ?" "Yes, shirt and all; but there, I'll lend you a shirt," said Daddy. "Whatever you take in of your own will be nailed, you know. You might take in your boots, though—they'd be handy if you happened to want to leave the shed for anything; but don't blame me if you lose 'em."

"With a fortitude for which I hope some day to be rewarded, I made up my bundle (boots and all), and the moment Daddy's face was turned away shut my eyes and plunged desperately into the mutton broth. I wish from the bottom of my heart my courage had been less hasty, for hearing the splash, Daddy looked round and said, "Lor, now! there was no occasion for that; you look a clean and decent sort of man. It's them filthy beggars" (only he used a word more specific than "filthy") "that want washing. Don't use that towel; here's a clean one! That sort! and now here's your shirt" (handing me a blue striped one from a heap, "and here's your ticket. No. 34 you are, and a ticket to match is tied to your bundle. Mind you don't lose it. They'll nail it from you if they get a chance. Put it under your head. This is your rug; take it with you."

"Where am I to sleep, please, sir?"

"I'll show you."

And so he did. With no other rag but the checked shirt to cover me, and with my rug over my shoulder, he accompanied me to the door at which I entered, and, opening it, kept me standing with naked feet on the stone threshold, full in the draught of the frosty air, while he pointed out the way I should go. It was not a long way, but I would have given much not to have trodden it. It was open as the highway—with flag-stones below and the stars overhead, and, as I said before, and cannot help saying again, a frosty wind was blowing.

"Straight across," said Daddy, "to where you see the light shining through. Go in there, and turn to the left, and you'll find the beds in a heap. Take one of 'em and make yourself comfortable." And straight across I went, my naked feet seeming to cling to the stones as though they were burning hot instead of icy cold (they had just stepped out of a bath you should remember), till I reached the space through which the light was shining, and I entered in.

No language with which I am acquainted is capable of conveying an adequate conception of the spectacle I then encountered. Imagine a space of about thirty feet by thirty feet enclosed on three sides by a dingy whitewashed wall, and roofed with naked tiles, which were furred with the damp and filth that reeked within. As for the fourth side of the shed, it was boarded in for (say) a third of its breadth; the remaining space being hung with flimsy canvas, in which was a gap two feet wide at top, widening to at least four feet at bottom. This far too airy shed was paved with stone, the flags so thickly incrusted with filth that I mistook it first for a floor of natural earth. Extending from one end of my bedroom to the other, in three rows, were certain iron "cranks" (of which I subsequently learnt the use), with their many arms raised in various attitudes, as the stiffened arms of men are on a battle-field. My bed-fellows lay among the cranks, distributed over the flag-stones in a double row, on narrow bags scantily stuffed with hay. At one glance my appalled vision took in thirty of them,—thirty men and boys stretched upon shallow pallets, with but only six inches of comfortable hay between them and the stony floor. These beds were placed close together, every occupant being provided with a rug like that which I was fain to hug across my shoulders. In not a few cases two gentlemen had clubbed beds and rugs and slept together. In one case (to be further mentioned presently) four gentlemen had so clubbed together. Many of my fellow-casuals were awake—others asleep or pretending to sleep; and, shocking as were the waking ones to look upon, they were quite pleasant when compared with the sleepers. For this reason, the practised and well-seasoned casual seems to have a peculiar way of putting himself to bed. He rolls himself in his rug, tucking himself in, head and feet, so that he is completely enveloped; and, lying quite still on his pallet, he looks precisely like a corpse covered because of its hideousness. Some were stretched out at full length; some lay nose and knees together; some with an arm or a leg showing crooked through the coverlet. It was like the result of a railway accident; those ghastly figures were awaiting the coroner. From the moral point of view, however, the wakeful ones were more dreadful still. Towzled, dirty, villanous, they squatted up in their beds, and smoked foul pipes, and sang snatches of horrible songs, and bandied jokes so obscene as to be absolutely appalling. Eight or ten were so enjoying themselves—the majority with the check shirt on, and the frowsy rug pulled about their legs; but two or three wore no shirts at all, squatting naked to the waist, their bodies fully exposed in the light of the single flaring jet of gas fixed high up on the wall.

My entrance excited very little attention. There was a horse-pail three parts full of water standing by a post in the middle of the shed, with a little tin pot beside it. Addressing me as "old pal," one of the naked ruffians begged me to "hand him a swig," as he was "werry nigh garspin." Such an appeal of course no "old pal" could withstand, He showed and I gave him a potful of water. He showed himself grateful for the attention. "I should lay over there, if I was you," he said, pointing to the left side of the shed; "it's more out of the wind than this 'ere side is." I took the good-natured advice, and (by this time shivering with cold) stepped over the stones to where the beds of straw bags were heaped, and dragged one of them to the spot suggested by my naked comrade. But I had no more idea of how to arrange it than of making an apple-pudding; and a certain little discovery added much to my embarrassment. In the middle of the bed I had selected was a stain of blood bigger than a man's hand! I did not know what to do now. To lie on such a horrid thing seemed impossible; yet to carry back the bed and exchange it for another might betray a degree of fastidiousness repugnant to the feelings of my fellow-lodgers, and possibly excite suspicion that I was not what I seemed. Just in the nick of time in came that good man Daddy.

"What! not pitched yet?" he exclaimed ; "here, I'll show you. Hallo! somebody's been a bleedin'! Nover mind; let's turn him over. There you are, you see. Now lay down, and cover your rug over you."

There was no help for it. It was too late to go back. Down I lay, and spread the rug over me. I should have mentioned that I brought in with me a cotton handkerchief, and this I tied round my head by way of a night-cap; but not daring to pull the rug as high as my face. Before I could in any way settle my mind to reflection, in came Daddy once more to do me a further kindness, and point out a stupid blunder I had committed.

"Why, you are a rummy chap !" said Daddy. "You forgot your bread! Lay hold. And look here, I've brought you another rug; it's perishing cold to-night." So saying, he spread the rug over my legs and went away. I was very thankful for the extra covering, but I was in a dilemma about the bread. I couldn't possibly eat it; what then was to be done with it? I broke it, however, and in view of such of the company as might happen to be looking made a ferocious bite at a bit as large as a bean, and munched violently. By good luck, however, I presently got half-way over my difficulty very neatly. Just behind me, so close indeed that their feet came within half a yard of my head, three lads were sleeping together.

"Did you hear that, Punch ?" one of them asked.

"'Ear what?" answered Punch, sleepy and snappish.

"Why, a cove forgot his toke! Gordstruth? you wouldn't ketch me a forgettin' mine."

"You may have half of it, old pal, if you're hungry," I observed, leaning up on my elbows.

"Chuck it here, good luck to yer!" replied my young friend, starting up with an eager clap of his dirty hands.

I "chucked it here," and, slipping the other half under the side of my bed, lay my head on my folded arms.

It was about half-past nine when, having made myself as comfortable as circumstances permitted, I closed my eyes in the desperate hope that I might fall asleep, and so escape from the horrors with which I was surrounded. "At seven to-morrow morning the bell will ring," Daddy had informed me, "and then you will give up your ticket and get back your bundle." Between that time and the present full nine long hours had to wear away.

But I was speedily convinced that, at least for the present, sleep was impossible. The young fellow (one of the three who lay in one bed, with their feet to my head) whom my bread had refreshed, presently swore with frightful imprecations that he was now going to have a smoke; and immediately put his threat into execution.

Thereupon his bed fellows sat up and lit their pipes too. But ah! if they had only smoked, —if they had not taken such an unfortunate fancy to spit at the leg of a crank distant a few inches from my head, how much misery and apprehension would have been spared me. To make matters worse, they united with this American practice an Eastern one; as they smoked they related little autobiographical anecdotes—so abominable that three or four decent men who lay at the further end of the shed were so provoked that they threatened, unless the talk abated in filthiness, to get up and stop it by main force. Instantly, the voice of every blackguard in the room was raised against the decent ones. They were accused of loathsome afflictions, stigmatized "as fighting men out of work" (which must be something very humiliating, I suppose), and invited to "a round" by boys young enough to be their grandsons. For several minutes there was such a storm of oaths, threats, and taunts—such a deluge of foul words raged in the room—that I could not help thinking of the fate of Sodom; as, indeed, I did several times during the night. Little by little the riot died out, without any the slightest interference on the part of the officers.

Soon afterwards the ruffian majority was strengthened by the arrival of a lanky boy of about fifteen, who evidently recognized many acquaintances, and was recognized by them as "Kay," or perhaps I should write it "K." He was a very remarkable-looking lad, and his appearance pleased me much. Short as his hair was cropped, it still looked soft and silky; he had large blue eyes, set wide apart, and a mouth that would have been faultless but for its great width; and his voice was as soft and sweet as any woman's. Lightly as a woman, too, he picked his way over the stones towards the place where the beds lay, care fully hugging his cap beneath his arm.

"What cheer, Kay?" "Out again, then, old son !" "What yer got in yer cap, Kay?" cried his friends; to which the sweet voice replied, "Who'll give me a part of his doss (bed)? —my—eyes and limbs if I ain't perishin'! Who'll let me turn in with him for half my toke" (bread)? I feared how it would be! The hungry young fellow who had so readily availed himself of half my "toke" snapped at Kay's offer, and after a little rearrangement and bed-making four young fellows instead of three reposed upon the haybags at my head.

"You was too late for skilley, Kay. There's skilley now, nights as well as mornin's."

"Don't you tell no bleeding lies," Kay answered, incredulously.

"Blind me, it's true. Ain't it, Punch ?"

"Right you are!" said Punch," and spoons to eat it with, that's more! There used to be spoons at all the houses, one time. Poplar used to have 'em; but one at a time they was all nicked, don't you know." ("Nicked" means stolen, obviously.)

"Well, I don't want no skilley, leastways not to-night," said Kay. "I've had some rum. Two glasses of it; and a blow out of puddin', —regler Christmas plum-puddin'. You don't know the cove as give it me; but, thinks I this mornin' when I come out, blessed if I don't go and see my old chum. Lordstruth! he was struck! 'Come along,' he ses, 'I saved you some puddin' from Christmas.' "Whereabouts is it?' I ses. 'In that box under my bed,' he ses, and he forks it out. That's the sort of pal to have! And he stood a quarten, and half a' ounce of hard-up (tobacco.) That wasn't all, neither; when I come away, ses he, 'How about your break. fus?' 'Oh, I shall do,' ses I. 'You take some of my bread and butter,' he ses, and he cuts me off four chunks, buttered thick. I eat two on 'em comin' along."

"What's in your cap, Kay?" repeated the devourer of "toke."

"Them other two slices," said Kay; generously adding, "There, share 'em amongst yer, and somebody give us a whiff of 'bacca."

Kay showed himself a pleasant companion,—what in a higher grade of society is called "quite an acquisition." He told stories of thieves and thieving, and of a certain "silver cup" he had been "put up to," and that he meant to nick it afore the end of the week, if he got seven stretch (? seven years) for it. The cup was worth ten quid (? pounds), and he knew where to melt it within ten minutes of nicking it. He made this statement without any moderation of his sweet voice; and the others received it as a serious fact. Nor was there any affectation of secrecy in another gentleman, who announced, with great applause, that he had stolen a towel from the bath-room; "And s'help me, it's as good as new; never been washed more'n once!"

"Tell us a rummy' story, Kay," said somebody; and Kay did. He told stories of so "rummy" a character that the decent men at the further end of the room (some of whom had their own little boys sleeping with them) must have lain in a sweat of horror as they listened. Indeed, when Kay broke into a "rummy" song with a roaring chorus, one of the decent men rose in his bed and swore that he would smash Kay's head if he didn't desist. But Kay sang on till he and his admirers were tired of the entertainment. "Now," said he, "let's have a swearing club! You'll all be in it?"

The principle of this game seemed to rest on the impossibility of either of the young gentlemen making half a dozen observations without introducing a blasphemous or obscene word; and either the basis is a very sound one, or for the sake of keeping the "club" alive the members purposely made slips. The penalty for "swearing" was a punch on any part of the body, except a few which the club rules protected. The game was highly successful. Warming with the sport, and indifferent to punches, the members vied with each other in audacity; and in a few minutes Bedlam in its prime could scarcely have produced such a spectacle as was to be seen on the beds behind me. One rule of the club was that any word to be found in the Bible might be used with impunity, and if one member "punched "another for using such a word the error was to be visited upon him with a double punching all round. This naturally led to much argument; for in vindicating the Bible as his authority, a member became sometimes so much heated as to launch into a flood of "real swearing," which brought the fists of the club upon his naked carcass as quick as hail.

These and other pastimes beguiled the time until, to my delight, the church chimes audibly tolled twelve. After this the noise gradually subsided, and it seemed as though everybody was going to sleep at last. I should have mentioned that during the story-telling and song-singing a few "casuals" had dropped in, but they were not *habitués*, and cuddled down with their rugs over their heads without a word to any one.

In a little while all was quiet, save for the flapping of the canvas curtain in the night breeze, the snoring, and the horrible, indescribable sound of impatient hands scratching skins that itch. There was another sound of very frequent occurrence, and that was the clanking of the tin pannikin against the water pail. Whether it is in the nature of workhouse bread or skilley to provoke thirst is more than my limited experience entitles me to say, but it may be truthfully asserted that once at least in the course of five minutes might be heard a rustling of straw, pattering of feet, and then the noise of water dipping, and then was to be seen at the pail the figure of a man (sometimes stark naked) gulping down the icy water as he stood upon the icy stones.

And here I remark that I can furnish no solution to this mystery of the shirt. I only know that some of my comrades were provided with a shirt, and that to some the luxury was denied. I may say this, however, that none of the little boys were allowed one. Nearly one o'clock. Still quiet and no fresh arrival for an hour or more. Then suddenly a loud noise of hobnailed boots kicked at a wooden gate, and soon after a tramping of feet and a rapping at Daddy's door, which, it will be remembered, was only separated from our bedroom by an open paved court.

"Hallo!" cried Daddy.

"Here's some more of 'em for you,—ten of 'em!" answered the porter, whose voice I recognized at once.

"They'll have to find beds, then," Daddy grumbled, as he opened his door. "I don't believe there are four beds empty. They must sleep double, or something."

This was terrible news for me. Bad enough, in all conscience, was it to lie as I was lying; but the prospect of sharing my straw with some dirty scoundrel of the Kay breed was altogether unendurable. Perhaps, however, they were not dirty scoundrels, but peaceable and decent men, like those in the farther corner.

Alas for my hopes! In the space of five minutes in they came at the rent in the canvas—great hulking ruffians, some with rugs and nothing else, and some with shirts and nothing else, and all madly swearing because, coming in after eleven o'clock, there was no "toke" for them. As soon as these wrathful men had advanced to the middle of the shed they made the discovery that there was an insufficient number of beds—only three, indeed, fer ten competitors.

"Where's the beds? D'ye hear, Daddy? You blessed, truth-telling old person, where's the beds?"

"You'll find 'em. Some of 'em is lying on two, or got 'em as pillows. You'll find 'em."

With a sudden rush our new friends plunged among the sleepers, trampling over them, cursing their eyes and limbs, dragging away their rugs; and if by chance they found some poor wretch who had been tempted to take two beds (or bags) instead of one, they coolly hauled him out and took possession. There was no denying them, and no use in remonstrating. They evidently knew that they were at liberty to do just as they liked, and they took full advantage of the privilege.

One of them came up to me, and shouting, "I want that, you—," snatched at my "birdseye" nightcap and carried it off. There was a bed close to mine which contained only one occupant, and into this one of the new-comers slipped without a word of warning, driving its lawful owner against the wall to make room. Then he sat up in bed for a moment, savagely venting his disappointment as to "toke," and declaring that never before in his life had he felt the need of it so much. This was my opportunity. Slipping my hand under my bed, I withdrew that judiciously hoarded piece of bread and respectfully offered it to him. He snapped at it with thanks.

By the time the churches were chiming two, matters had once more adjusted themselves, and silence reigned, to be disturbed only by drinkers at the pail, or such as, otherwise prompted, stalked into the open yard. Kay, for one, visited it. I mention this unhappy young wretch particularly, because he went out without a single rag to his back. I looked out at the rent in the canvas, and saw the frosty moon shining on him. When he returned, and crept down between Punch and another, he muttered to himself, "Warm again! O my G—d! warm again!"

I hope, Mr. Editor, that you will not think me too prodigal of these reminiscences, and that your readers will understand that, if I write rather boldly, it is not done as a matter of taste. To me it seems quite worth while to relate with tolerable accuracy every particular of an adventure which you persuaded me ("ah! woful when !") to undertake for the public good.

Whether there is a rule which closes the casual wards after a certain hour I do not know; but before one o'clock our number was made up, the last comer signalizing his appearance with a grotesque *pas seul*. His rug over his shoulders, he waltzed into the shed, waving his hands, and singing in an affected voice, as he sidled along:—

"I like to be a swell, a roaming down Pall-mall,
Or anywhere, I don't much care, so I can be a swell,"—

a couplet which had an intensely comical effect. This gentleman had just come from a pantomime (where he had learnt his song, probably.) Too poor to pay for a lodging, he could only muster means for a seat in the gallery of the "Vic," where he was well entertained, judging from the flattering manner in which he spoke of the clown. The columbine was less fortunate in his opinion. "She's werry dickey !—ain't got what I call 'move' about her." However, the wretched young woman was respited now from the scourge of his criticism; for the critic and his listeners were fast asleep; and yet I doubt whether any one of the company slept very soundly. Every moment some one shifted uneasily; and as the night wore on the silence was more and more irritated by the sound of coughing. This was one of the most distressing things in the whole adventure. The conversation was horrible, the tales that were told more horrible still, and worse than either (though not by any moans the most infamous things to be heard —I dare not even hint at them) was that song, with its bestial chorus shouted from a dozen throats; but at any rate they kept the blood warm with constant hot flushes of anger; while as for the coughing, to lie on the flagstones in what was nothing better than an open shed, and listen to that, hour after hour, chilled one's very heart with pity. Every variety of cough that ever I heard was to be heard there: the hollow cough; the short cough; the hysterical cough; the bark that comes at regular intervals, like the quarter-chime of a clock, as if to mark off the progress of decay; coughing from vast hollow chests, coughing from little narrow ones,—now one, now another, now two or three together, and then a minute's interval of silence in which to think of it all and wonder who would begin next. One of the young reprobates above me coughed so grotesquely like the chopping of wood that I named him in my mind the Woodcutter. Now and then I found myself coughing, too, which may have added just a little to the poignant distress these fully constant and various sounds occasioned me. They were good in one way; they made one forget what wretches they were who, to all appearances, were so rapidly "chopping" their way to a pauper's graveyard. I did not care about the more matured ruffians so much; but though the youngest, the boys like Kay, were unquestionably among the most infamous of my comrades, to hear what cold and hunger and vice had done for them at fifteen was almost enough to make a man cry; and there were boys there even younger than these.

At half-past two, every one being asleep, or at least lying still, Daddy came in and counted us—one, two, three, four, and so on, in a whisper. Then, finding the pail empty (it was nearly full at half-past nine, when I entered), he considerately went and refilled it, and even took much trouble in searching for the tin pot which served as a drinking-cup, and which the last comer had playfully thrown to the further end of the shed. I ought to have mentioned that the pail stood close to my head; so that I had peculiar opportunities of study as one after another of my comrades came to the fountain to drink; just as the brutes do in those books of African travel. The pail refilled, Daddy returned, and was seen no more till morning.

It still wanted four hours and a half to seven o'clock—the hour of rising—and never before in my life did time appear to creep so slowly. I could hear the chimes of a parish church and of the Parliament Houses, as well as those of a wretched tinkling Dutch clock somewhere on the premises. The parish church was the first to announce the hour (an act of kindness I feel bound to acknowledge), Westminster came next, the lazy Dutchman declining his consent to the time o' day till fully sixty seconds afterwards. And I declare I thought that difference of sixty seconds an injury—if the officers of the house took their time from the Dutchman. It may seem a trifle, but a minute is something when a man is lying on a cold flagstone, and the wind of a winter night is blowing in your hair. Three o'clock, four o'clock struck, and still there was nothing to beguile the time but observation, under the one flaring gaslight, of the little heaps of outcast humanity strewn about the floor; and after a while, I find, one may even become accustomed to the sight of one's fellow-creatures lying around you like covered corpses in a railway shed. For most of the company were now bundled under the rugs in the ghastly way I have already described—though here and there a cropped head appeared, surmounted by a billy-cock like my own or by a greasy cloth cap. Five o'clock, six o'clock chimed, and then I had news—most welcome—of the world without, and of the real beginning of day. Half a dozen factory bells announced that it was time for workingmen to go to labor; but my companions were not workingmen, and so snored on. Out through the gap in the canvas the stars were still to be seen shining on the black sky, but that did not alter the fact that it was six o'clock in the morning. I snapped my fingers at the Dutchman, with his sixty seconds slow, for in another hour I fondly hoped to be relieved from duty. A little while, and doors were heard to open and shut; yet a little while, and the voice of Daddy was audible in conversation with another early bird; and then I distinctly caught the word "bundles." Blessed sound! I longed for my bundle—for my pleasing brown coat, for the warm, if unsightly, "jersey," which I adopted as a judicious substitute for a waistcoat—for my corduroys and liberty.

"Clang?" went the workhouse clock. "Now, then, wake 'em up!" cried Daddy. I was already up—sitting up, that is—being anxious to witness the resurrection of the ghastly figures rolled in their rugs. But nobody but myself rose at the summons. They knew what it meant well enough, and in sleepy voices cursed the bell, and wished it in several dreadful places; but they did not move until there came in at the hole in the canvas two of the pauper inhabitants of the house, bearing bundles. "Thirty-two," "Twenty-eight!" they bawled, but not *my* number, which was thirty-four. Neither thirty-two nor twenty-eight, however, seemed eager to accept his good fortune in being first called. They were called upon three several times before they would answer; and then they replied with a savage "Chuck it here, can't you!" "Not before you chucks over your shirt and ticket," the bundle-holder answered; whereon " Twenty-eight" sat up, and divesting himself of his borrowed shirt, flung it with his wooden ticket; and his bundle was flung back in return.

It was some time before bundle No. 34 turned up, so that I had a fair opportunity to observe my neighbors. The decent men slipped into their rags as soon as they got them, but the blackguards were in no hurry. Some indulged in a morning pipe to prepare themselves for the fatigues of dressing, while others, loosening their bundles as they squatted naked, commenced an investigation for certain little animals which shall be nameless.

At last my turn came; and "chucking over my shirt and ticket, I quickly attired myself in clothes which, ragged as they were, were cleaner than they looked. In less than two minutes I was out of the shed, and in the yard; where a few of the more decent poor fellows were crowding round a pail of water, and scrambling after something that might pass for a "wash,"—finding their own soap, as far as I could observe, and drying their faces on any bit of rag they might happen to have about them, or upon the canvas curtain of the shed.

By this time it was about half-past seven, and the majority of the casuals were up and dressed. I observed, however, that none of the younger boys were as yet up, and it presently appeared that there existed some rule against their dressing in the shed; for Daddy came out of the bath-room, where the bundles were deposited, and called out, "Now four boys!" and instantly four poor little wretches, some with their rugs trailing about their shoulders and some quite bare, came shivering over the stones and across the bleak yard, and were admitted to the bath-room to dress. "Now, four more boys," cried Daddy; and so on.

When all were up and dressed, the boys carried the bed rugs into Daddy's room, and the pauper inmates made a heap of the "beds," stacking them against the wall. As before mentioned, the shed served the treble purpose of bed-chamber, work-room, and breakfast-room; it was impossible to get fairly at the cranks and set them going until the bedding was stowed away.

Breakfast before work, however; but it was a weary while to some of us before it made appearance. For my own part, I had little appetite, but about me were a dozen poor wretches who obviously had a very great one. They had come in over night too late for bread, and perhaps may not have broken fast since the morning of the previous day. The decent ones suffered most. The blackguard majority were quite cheerful, smoking, swearing, and playing their pretty horse play, the prime end of which was pain or discomfiture for somebody else. One casual there was with only one leg. When he came in over-night he wore a black hat, which added a certain look of respectability to a worn suit of black. All together his clothes had been delivered up to him by Daddy; but now he was seen hopping disconsolately about the place on his crutch, for the hat was missing. He was a timid man, with a mild voice; and whenever he asked some ruffian "whether he had seen such a thing as a black hat," and got his answer, he invariably said, "Thank you," which was regarded as very amusing. At last one sidled up to him with a grin, and showing about three square inches of some fluffy substance, said, "Is this anything like wot you're lost, guv'ner?" The cripple inspected it. "That's the rim of it!" he said. "What a shame!" and he hobbled off with tears in his eyes.

Full three quarters of an hour of loitering and shivering, and then came the taskmaster —a soldierly-looking man over six feet high, with quick, gray eyes, in which "No trifling" appeared as distinctly as a notice against trespassing on a wayside board. He came in among us, and the gray eyes made out our number in a moment. "Out into the yard, all of you!" he cried; and we went out in a mob. There we shivered for some twenty minutes longer, and then a baker's man appeared with a great wooden tray piled up with just such slices of bread as we had received overnight. The tray was consigned to an able-bodied casual, who took his place with the taskmaster at the shed-door, and then in single file we reentered the shed, each man and boy receiving a slice as he passed in. Pitying, as I suppose, my unaccustomed look, Mr. Taskmaster gave me a slice and a large piece over.

The bread devoured, a clamor for "skilley" began. The rumor had got abroad that this morning, and on all future mornings, there would be skilley at breakfast, and "Skilley! skilley!" resounded through the shed. No one had hinted that it was not forthcoming, but skilley seems to be thought an extraordinary concession, and after waiting only a few minutes for it they attacked the taskmaster in the fiercest manner. They called him thief, sneak, and "crawler." Little boys blackguarded him in gutter language, and looking him in the face, consigned him to hell without flinching. He never uttered a word in reply, or showed a sign of impatience; and whenever he was obliged to speak it was quite without temper.

There was a loud "hooray!" when the longed-for skilley appeared, in two pails, in one of which floated a small tin saucepan, with a stick thrust into its handle, by way of a ladle. Yellow pint basins were provided for our use, and large iron spoons. "Raange round the walls!" the taskmaster shouted. We obeyed with the utmost alacrity; and then what I should judge to be about three-fourths of a pint of gruel was handed to each of us as we stood. I was glad to get mine, because the basin that contained it was warm and my hands were numb with cold. I tasted a spoonful, as in duty bound, and wondered more than ever at the esteem in which it was held by my confrères. It was a weak decoction of oatmeal and water, bitter, and without even a pinch of salt to flavor it—that I could discover. But it was hot; and on that account, perhaps, was so highly relished that I had no difficulty in persuading one of the decent men to accept my share.

It was now past eight o'clock, and, as I knew that a certain quantity of labor had to be performed by each man before he was allowed to go his way, I was anxious to begin. The labor was to be "crank" labor. The "cranks" are a series of iron bars extending across the width of the shed, penetrating through the wall, and working a flour-mill on the other side. Turning the "crank " is like turning the windlass. The task is not a severe one. Four measures of corn (bushels they were called—but that is doubtful) have to be ground every morning by the night's batch of casuals. Close up by the ceiling hangs a bell connected with the machinery; and as each measure is ground the bell rings, so that the grinders may know how they are going on. But the grinders are as lazy as obscene. We were no sooner set to work than the taskmaster left us to our own sweet will, with nothing to restrain its exercise but an occasional visit from the miller, a weakly expostulating man. Once or twice he came in and said mildly. "Now, then, my men, why don't you stick to it?" and so went out again.

The result of this laxity of overseeing would have disgusted me at any time, and was intensely disgusting then. At least one-half the gang kept their hands from the crank whenever the miller was absent, and betook themselves to their private amusements and pursuits. Some sprawled upon the beds and smoked; some engaged themselves and their friends in tailoring, and one turned hair-cutter for the benefit of a gentleman who, unlike Kay, had not just come out of prison. There were three tailors; two of them on the beds mending their coats, and the other operating on a recumbent friend in the rearward part of his clothing. Where the needles came from I do not know; but for thread they used a strand of the oakum (evidently easy to deal with) which the boys were picking in the corners. Other loungers strolled about with their hands in their pockets, discussing the topics of the day, and playing practical jokes on the industrious few; a favorite joke being to take a bit of rag, anoint it with grease from the crank axles, and clap it unexpectedly over somebody's eye.

The consequence of all this was that the cranks went round at a very slow rate, and now and then stopped altogether. Then the miller came in; the loungers rose from their couches, the tailors ceased stitching, the smokers dropped their pipes, and every fellow was at his post. The cranks spun round furiously again, the miller's expostulation being drowned amid a shout of "Slap bang, here we are again !" or this extemporized chorus :

"We'll hang up the miller on a sour apple-tree,
We'll hang up the miller on a sour apple-tree,
We'll hang up the miller on a sour apple-tree,
And then go grinding on.
Glory, glory, hallelujah." etc.

By such ditties the ruffians enlivened their short spell of work. Short indeed! The miller departed, and within a minute afterwards beds were re-occupied, pipes lit, and tailoring resumed. So the game continued—the honest fellows sweating at the cranks, and anxious to get the work done and go out to look for more profitable labor, and the paupers by profession taking matters quite easy. I am convinced, that had the work been properly superintended the four measures of corn might have been ground in the space of an hour and a half. As it was, when the little bell bad tinkled for the fourth time, and the yard-gate was opened, and we were free to depart, the clock had struck eleven.

I had seen the show; gladly I escaped into the open streets. The sun shone brightly on my ragged, disreputable figure, and showed its squalor with startling distinctness; but within all was rejoicing. A few yards, and then I was blessed with the sight of that same vehicle—waiting for me in the spot where I had parted from it fourteen weary hours before. Did you observe, Mr. Editor, with what alacrity I jumped in? I have a vivid recollection of you, sir—sitting there with an easy patience, lounging through your TIMES, and oh so detestably clean to look at! But though I resented your collar, I was grateful for the sight of a familiar face, and for that draught of sherry which you considerately brought for me—a welcome refreshment after so many weary, waking hours of fasting.

And now I have come to the end. I remember many little incidents which, until this moment, had escaped me. I ought to have told you of two quiet elderly gentlemen who, amid all the blackguardism that went on around, held a discussion on the merits of the English language—one of the disputants showing an especial admiration for the word "kindle"––"fine old Saxon word as ever was coined." Then there were some childish games of "first and last letters," to vary such entertainments as that of the Swearing Club. I should also have mentioned that on the dissolution of the Swearing Club a game at "dumb motions" was started, which presently led to some talk concerning deaf and dumb people, and their method of conversing with each other by means of finger-signs; as well as to a little story that sounded strangely enough coming from the mouth of the most efficient member of the club. A good memory for details enables me to repeat this story almost, if not quite, exactly.

"They are a rummy lot, them deaf and dumb," said the story-teller. "I was at the workhouse at Stepney when I was a young 'un, don't you know ; and when I got a holiday I used to go and see my old woman as lived in the Borough. Well, one day a woman as was in the house ses to me, ses she, 'Don't you go past the Deaf and Dumb School as you goes home?' So I ses' 'Yes.' So ses she, 'Would you mind callin' there and takin' a message to my little girl as is in there deaf and dumb?' So I ses, 'No.' Well, I goes, and they lets me in, and I tells the message, and they shows me the kid what it was for. Pooty little gal! So they tells her the message, and then she begins making orts and crosses like on her hands. 'What's she a doin' that for?' I ses. 'She's a talkin' to you,' ses they. "Oh.' I ses, 'what's she talkin' about?' 'She says you're a good boy for comin' and tellin' her about her mother, and she loves you.' Blessed if I could help laughin'! So I ses, 'There ain't no call for her to say that.' Pooty little kid she was! I stayed there a goodish bit, and walked about the garden with her, and what d'ye think? Presently she takes a fancy for some of my jacket buttons—brass 'uns they was, with the name of the 'house' on 'em—and I cuts four on 'em off and gives her. Well, when I gave her them, blow me if she didn't want one of the brass buckles off my shoes. Well, you mightn't think it, but I gave her that, too." "Didn't yer get into a row when you got back?" some listener asked. "Rather! Got kep' without dinner and walloped as well, as I wouldn't tell what I'd done with 'em. Then they was goin' to wallop me again, so I thought I'd cheek it out; so I up and told the master all about it." "And got it wuss ?" "No, I didn't. The master give me new buttons and a buckle without saying another word, and my dinner along with my supper as well."

The moral of all this I leave to you.* It seems necessary to say something about it, for the report which Mr. Farnall made after visiting Lambeth Workhouse on Saturday seems meant to suggest an idea that what has been described here is merely an irregularity. So it may be, but an irregularity which consigned some forty men to such a den on the night when somebody happened to be there to see, is probably a frequent one; and it certainly is infamous. And then as to the other workhouses? Mr. Farnall was in ignorance of what was done at Lambeth in this way, and I selected it for a visit quite at random. Does he know what goes on in other workhouses? If he is inclined to inquire, I may, perhaps, be able to assist the investigation by this hint: my companions had a discussion during the night as to the respective merits of the various workhouses; and the general verdict was that those of Tottenham and Poplar were the worst in London. Is it true, as I heard it stated, that at one of these workhouses the casual sleeps on bare boards, without a bed of any sort?

One word in conclusion. I have some horrors for Mr. Farnall's private ear (should he like to learn about them) infinitely more revolting than anything that appears in these papers.

** Note from the Times.—A rather pretentious and lively amateur description of the sort of refuges provided for the houseless poor having appeared in the columns of a contemporary on Friday, Mr. Harnall, the Poor Law Inspector, visited the place on Saturday, and wrote the minute which is subjoined, and which explains better than we could be enabled to do the real facts of the case. The narrative was continued on Saturday, but the explanation of the Poor Law Inspector is no less necessary, and, in fact, seems all the more so things right. It appears that the "swell" who went in his brougham, "with all appliances and means to boot," was shown, not into the regular wards of the establishment, but into a shed which was irregularly used when the wards were full, against the provisions of the law and the express directions of the Poor Law Board issued several months ago. This is Mr. Farnall's report:*

"I have to-day inspected the wards provided for the houseless poor in this workhouse, and which I have some time since certified as good and sufficient wards, and which I still consider to be so. I have, however, to direct the attention of the guardians to the fact that the master, when the wards adverted to are full, is in the habit of warding men in the pump-shed, and this shed is wholly unfit for the purpose to which the master has thus dedicated it, and I therefore request the guardians to instruct the master to immediately relinquish the practice. If the certified wards are full, it is the duty of the guardians, through their officers, to find lodgings for an excess of applicants in lodging-houses, or in some room in the workhouse, or for the master to send such applicants to the relieving officers. And this duty has been clearly pointed out to the guardians, by Mr. Villiers, the President of the Poor-Law Board, in a circular issued by him, and signed by him, many months ago.

H. B. FARNALL, P. L. I.

"Lambeth Workhouse Visitors' Book, Jan. 13.

NEW YORK FEBRUARY 24, 1866

A WORD TO PRESIDENT JOHNSON.

As a cat may look upon a king, we suppose an editor may speak to a president. Well, then, Mr. Johnson, please stick to your post, and speak us no more speeches. Your veto-message is the soundest political document that has appeared since the Declaration of Independence. Stand by that, then, as your platform, and instead of making speeches, execute laws. Congress talks enough for the whole country; the demand, now, is for action. Don't try to silence your opponents by answering them, for you might as well try to silence a brass kettle by beating it.

DRAMATIC FEUILLETON.

BY FIGARO.

If there is another Matinée given at Wood's Theatre, Mr. Editor, during the run of "The Child-Stealer" there, I shall move that Manager Wood be arrested for cruelty to actors.

Moreover, if the piece is not immediately cut down and brought within reasonable acting time, I shall have Gayler arrested for cruelty to audiences.

"Never too late to mend" is a good axiom enough—so at least my friend Crispino says— but when you come to "Never too late to end," and insist on playing a piece till the hard-hearted old clock threatens to strike its little ones, you forget that "life is short," and that "art" is getting to be a deuced sight too "long."

And here, Sir, all my objections to "The Child Stealer" stop.

It is an admirable drama of its kind, and when it comes to be trimmed down a little, I shouldn't be surprised if it had a run here as it had in Paris, of three or four hundred nights.

People who object to everything on the stage except pure tragedy or comedy, will of course find fault with it: and when we have nothing in real life except pure tragedy or comedy—in other words when human nature comes to be "reconstructed "—they will probably have a stage conducted according to their own views and a new and improved species of human being on hand to keep it in countenance.

Excuse me if I am a little snappish, Mr. Editor; but when I see throngs of people moved to tears night after night by a play like "The Child-Stealer," and then hear it said that the thing is "illegitimate "—that it is too "sensational"—that, in substance, people ought *not* to be moved by it, or by anything else except according to certain prescribed rules—I lose all patience.

The incidents upon which "The Child Stealer" is based, are perfectly simple—the plot is clean within the limits of probability —the characters are thoroughly human—and though the picture presented is one of low life, it is nevertheless a palpably true picture, and one which the dramatist has handled not perhaps with overmuch delicacy, but certainly with great skill.

I sent you a sketch of the plot last week. The leading character—Madge the Cadger —is played by Miss Lucille Western, and played with very great power.

I can remember no piece of characterization in that line, so perfect: it is better—far better in my opinion—than Charlotte Cushman's Nancy Sykes.

Not only in the outline, but in all the niceties of light and shade, it is a most finished and artistic performance.

So also is Mr. Barton Hill's Richard Craddock—though the character is not nearly so difficult a one to delineate.

Of the minor characters, the only ones that attract special attention are Jemmy Jubbs, played by Mr. G. C. Davenport, and Simon Niphem, played by Mr. M. W. Leffingwell; Mr. Davenport, in particular, was admirable. The play is not very brilliantly mounted, but it runs on very smoothly for all that, and will long be remembered by those who have seen it, as presenting one of those rare stage-portraits which mark an epoch in the history of a theatre.

So you see, my dear fellow, that though I couldn't pay homage to Miss Western as Lady Isabel, I take off my hat to her as Madge the Cadger, and with my usual modesty, insist that you shall do the same.

And I should like, now, to take off my hat to another lady, and that no other than Miss Lacoste, who made her début last Saturday night at the Academy of Music in Mr. Pray's translation, adaptation, or whatever of "Virginia."

But, alas! I cannot do it.

The young lady has a fine personal presence, a delicious voice, a most lady-like manner, and many other charming qualities; but, so far as I can see, no special aptitude for the stage. Still, there is no telling what study and perseverance may do: and moreover if Miss Lacoste gets a chance to appear in some other place, and with a company composed of something besides sticks, she may develop talents which were imperceptible the other night on account of being hidden under the Academic bushel.

The best thing to be said about her first performance is that she was letter-perfect in her part; that she evidently knew the meaning of the words (a rare occurrence even with "stars"); that she showed no tendency to rant; and that in some of the impassioned scenes she overcame the bombast of the language and gave us a touch or two of genuine womanly pathos.

If I had any advice to give to Miss Lacoste it would be that she make a special study of the natural school of acting, as distinguished from the traditional—that she discontinue all lessons in elocution—and that before playing again she go to some tragedy theatre as often as possible to learn "how not to do it." Meanwhile, if she, or any one, wants to see the natural school of acting run into the ground—so that its dangers as well as its charms are exposed—and one almost longs for the "Old Park" days again—it will be only necessary to go to Niblo's and see Maggie Mitchell in Fanchon.

I went myself, the other night, and when one of my æsthetic friends asked me if I wished the stage to come to that, I was obliged to own that from his point of view he "had me."

However, little Maggie is very fascinating, with all her faults, and people rush to see her as a relief from the stilted formalities of the old school. Why don't actors take a lesson from this and give us, now and then, a bit of simple, unaffected acting?

Does anybody suppose that John Owens would have accumulated a fortune in New York playing the one part of Solon Shingle, if he had played it after the hard unnatural style which prevails in nearly all our theatres?

Never.

And, now, Mr. Editor, farewell till next week.

I have not seen the new play at Wallack's ("Society") nor "Israel in Egypt" at Barnum's—and as these are the only novelties of the week except "The Child Stealer" at Wood's—I find myself suddenly brought to a full stop.

Besides I am thinking so much of your "new issue"—and of my promise to help make it the most sprightly paper in town—that nearly everything else is driven out of my mind.

You shall have all you want about "Society," and about "Israel," when I write again; and also about Mrs. Wood's "Cinderella e la Comare," which I see she is to bring out next Monday with the new actor Mr. Geo. Fawcett Rowe, who will also play Sir Charles Coldstream in "Used Up."

E. L. Davenport retires from Mrs. Wood's to-night, and takes his benefit in "Who Killed Cock Robin" and "Wild Oats."

Don't forget, by the way, that on Monday next that sterling old actor, John Gilbert, takes his benefit at Wallack's, playing in "The Clandestine Marriage," which has not been on the boards before this season.

Of the other places of amusement, it is only to be said that Booth's Richelieu continues to be the rage at the Winter Garden, where it fills the house every night and every Wednesday afternoon with the élite of the city; that at the Broadway, John Owens will give another (and the last but one) of his famous Solon Shingle Matinées to-day; that at the operatic matinée to-day "Ione" is to be given (services to commence at 11 A. M.); that at the Academy in Brooklyn Miss Bateman gave her final performance last night, having taken the whole city captive with her matchless representation of "Leah ;" and, lastly, that Matilda Heron is presently to play "Medea " at the New Broadway for the benefit of Mrs. W. J. Jones.

FIGARO.

P. S.—The Hanlons are doing a superb business at the Continental in Boston, while Gayler's new piece, with which they appear, and in which Sylvester's "Magic Fountain" plays so conspicuous a part, seems to have set the old Hub a spinning. Alfred Hanlon has made a great hit with a new series of feats called "Aeropateticisms."

DeWalden's "Sam," with Frank Chanfrau, Olive Logan, Charley Parsloe, and the author in the cast (Frank, of course, being at the top of the heap) is making such a success in Philadelphia that hundreds of persons are turned away nightly from the house.

The New-York Saturday Press.

HENRY CLAPP, JR., EDITOR AND PROPRIETOR.

VOL. V. NO. 9. NEW ISSUE NO. 1. | NEW YORK, MARCH 3, 1866. | $5.00 A YEAR. 10 CTS. A NUMBER.

FROM DEBORAH DUNN'S PRIVATE LETTERS TO THE BOUDOIR.

EDWIN BOOTH'S "RICHELIEU."

...... I am afraid you will repent having asked me to write some of our conversations in the little back sitting room. They are prosy and commonplace affairs, for there we speak out our thoughts and feelings without much reserve; and I cannot say, with a strict regard to truth, that our family, taken as a whole, is worthy of a Boswell. In the parlor, now, we are sometimes quite brilliant, but, alas! it is only when we shine in borrowed ideas. There is no law against stealing other people's thoughts; and, as we, all of us, except that poor, blundering Mary, possess a good deal of that useful commodity called "tact," there is no great danger of our being found to be only jackdaws after all.

In the parlor we have all said the "proper thing" in regard to Mr. Booth's "Richelieu," which you must know is the most intellectual treat we Gothamites are at present enjoying. But the way it was discussed last night in our sitting room would have made a critic's hair stand upright.

...... "For my part, Deborah," said Susie, "I don't know what you see in Mr. Booth's 'Richelieu' to admire so much. If you want to look at a shaky old man, and hear him wheeze and cough, Mr. Winter, round the corner, will be glad to see you at any time, and he won't charge you a dollar, and he won't shut you up in a close room full of bad air; and Mr. Booth coughs and wheezes so exactly like him that if he had been dressed in a pepper-and-salt suit I should have thought it was old Winter himself."

"And you girls call that a fine play," said Bob, contemptuously, " and you wouldn't go to see 'Sam!' I don't believe your Mr. Booth could play 'Sam' to save his life."

"Can you put a lion into the skin of a mouse?" said Jemima, suddenly, and with such energy thrusting the darning gourd into the heel of her stocking, that the too frail fabric gave way, and the darning gourd popped out of the hole, and describing a parabola in the air, dropped at Bob's feet, who immediately threw it at Helen's head.

"There! you naughty boy," cried Helen, "you've made me drop a stitch; and I was going to say something besides, and now you have knocked it all out of my head."

"What a loss!" said Bob. "Pray look in the gourd for it."

Jemima's remark, short as it was, was a great event in the family, and we all felt it to be so. This was the first occasion for two years that she had expressed an interest in anything. I thought if Mr. Booth had stirred Jemima's soul out of its torpor, no further comment or criticism was necessary.

"I think," said Pa, taking his pipe out of his mouth; "I think"—and he slowly put it back again, gazing the while into the far distance, as if he saw his thought there, and was patiently waiting for it to come to him.

"This is the remark I was going to make," said Helen, with sudden inspiration. "How well those ladies on the stage manage their trains! I cannot do it. It is indeed wonderful!"

"Trains, indeed !" said Mary; "and who but you would think of trains when France is tottering on ruin, and those men, the what-d'ye-call-'ems—conspirators are having everything their own way, until that grand old man Booth—that is, he isn't an old man, he is a young one—and he ain't young, either, for he is old for that night, you know—and I can't help thinking he is young, though I know he is old—I mean he wants to be old, and one must forget he is young, but one can't—at least I can't, and so that makes it seem like acting, which I don't object to, as it *is* acting, and you can't make anything else out of it, when all is said and done. But it is very fine, to be sure; and I have looked all through the papers for criticisms, and I cannot find any, which is strange, as it is their business."

"And it is none of my business to interfere with France," said Helen, suddenly checking this torrent. "I have nothing to do with France, and a great deal to do with trains."

"I think," said Pa, again taking his pipe out of his mouth, "I think—that—somehow—after seeing Mr. Booth's 'Hamlet' and 'Richelieu'—one comes away with a feeling—with a feeling"—

"Of pleasure to get out of that hot, stifling place, where there is always a crowd, and the house is badly ventilated," said Ma.

"No, my dear," said Pa, mildly. "I was not going to say exactly that; but that one comes away with a feeling—somehow—as if he had more in his head than he took into the theatre with him—that is all." And the pipe went into the mouth again, and the dear, old, gray head was soon enveloped in smoke.

"I like his 'Hamlet' very much," said Susie. "He looks so melancholy, and interesting; but his 'Richelieu' is a failure. I am a great deal more interested in 'De Mauprat.'"

"I would give anything if I could get some crimson velvet the shade of De Mauprat's' mantle," said Helen, reflectively. "And he wears it very gracefully."

"There are some good points about Booth," said Bob, with that disagreeable air of superiority which boys assume in talking to their sisters. "I saw him play 'Richard the Third' once, and he did it splendid. I liked the way he bit the green baize on the floor when he died. 'Richard the Third' is a bully play !"

"Better than 'Sam' ?" I inquired humbly.

"Well—I don't know—I would prefer 'Sam' for a constancy."

I thought this had gone on long enough, and that now it was high time for me to say my say, and, as I am the literary member of the family, my opinions on such subjects are oracles.

"It is not strange, Mary," said I, "that Mr. Booth's acting has not been criticised more. It is above ordinary criticism. The Bohemians and Jenkinses no more can criticise Mr. Booth's acting than they can tell the color of the inhabitants of Jupiter, or anything else outside of their world. It is so highly artistic that all idea of art is lost; so purely intellectual that we seem to have left the grossness of our bodies outside the theatre walls; and yet so simple, so unaffected, so full of genuine passion that the most uncultivated feel it, and enjoy it. For, thank Heaven, we can thoroughly enjoy what we cannot analyze and criticise. That requires an entirely different condition of mind."

"His 'Hamlet' is superior to his 'Richelieu' only because his 'Hamlet' is Shakespeare's 'Hamlet,' while his 'Richelieu' is only Bulwer's 'Richelieu.' An actor is an interpreter, not a creator; and he cannot do more with his subject than the subject will allow. His 'Hamlet' is perfection. How entirely has he divested the part of all stiffness—of all semblance of acting. We are not spending an evening with Mr. Booth at the Winter Garden; we are spending months at Elsinore with 'Hamlet ;' and so intimate are we with him that we can follow all the workings of that tender and noble heart. How he charms us with his sweetness; how we shudder with him at those awful visitations; how we shrink with him at the dreadful vengeance he must pursue; what a pang we feel when Ophelia fails him; closely and eagerly we follow him amid those half-abandoned purposes, and fears, and doubts, with which his soul is tossed; and when the curtain falls for the last time, and the big man behind you punches the crown of your bonnet in with his elbow, and the lady next you sticks the point of her fan in your eye, you wake out of your illusion with a start, and a sigh to find yourself in such a different world.

"Mr. Booth is doing so much—so very much—for his art. True to himself—so far having chosen for his subjects the highest, the purest, the best—never degrading himself to the merely sensational drama to please the popular taste, and drawing within the theatre a class to whom, hitherto, the very sight of the walls has been pollution. I saw last night a teacher—the principal of one of our best female schools—with a dozen or so of her eldest pupils. And she showed her good sense in taking them there instead of to Mr. Titbrain's lecture on the Pyramids, or to hear Mr. Hummingtop read Hiawatha. It is said, with what truth I know not, that the clergy have lately been pretty well represented at the Winter Garden. If so, it is a step taken in the right direction; and if Mr. Booth should play 'Macbeth' (as I hope he will), even should it be during this Lenten season, it would not be a bad idea for the ministers to adjourn their congregations to the Winter Garden on these nights, and if their parishioners are not made wiser, and better, more humble, more self-distrustful, more unworldly, then their cases are hopeless indeed, and beyond the reach of the Lenten lecture, which may with greater profit be used to light cheery household fires."

Here I paused, and looked around me. Ma had disappeared—so had Mary, so had Helen. Susie was reading a novel, and Bob and the cat were asleep in the corner. Jemima was staring at me, aghast, and Pa was studying the pattern of the carpet. The smoke had cleared away, for his pipe was out.

"Don't you think, Debby," said he, "that in that last sentence you put it rather strong? What would Dr. V—— say?"

"I was not thinking of such lectures as Dr. V—— gives us," said I, rather ashamed of my enthusiasm, now that I observed its effect upon my audience. "I was thinking of those drowsy preachers who tell us that Matthew was a publican, and that Andrew was Simon Peter's brother, and that in heaven there is no night, and no moonshine, and various matters of the same kind, which we all know quite as well as they do.

MY INFIRMITY.

BY R. WOLCOTT.

Feb. 1866.

DEAR PRESS.

I am a great sufferer.

That is to say, I suffer greatly, though I am not at all great myself.

I am an undersized man, and if you were to press the question, I should have to confess that I am not a handsome man.

Neither am I a great man mentally.

Nature has not endowed me with any of the graces of body or of mind. I think she might have done so, considering that she makes my life so miserable.

But she didn't; and I look upon her as an abusive old step-mother, who lays heavy burdens upon my shoulders, in order that her more favored children may wear fine clothes and appear to better advantage.

Even if I had genius and all that sort of thing, it would do no good.

It would be overwhelmed and its expression choked off by the pain I constantly suffer.

How could I write one of those tropical stories that are so much in vogue, full of balmy breezes, fervid suns, magnolia blooms, and flowers of hothouse culture, when I feel as if I were standing upon a mountain of frozen mercury?

What poetic ideas can there be in a mind that is perforce forever dwelling upon buffalo over-shoes and warm bricks?

Yes, that is what ails me—cold feet.

It is a chronic case.

Even the heat of summer hardly brings their temperature up to a comfortable point; and these bleak days of winter, with snow on the ground, and the thermometer at 0.—

I shudder to think of it, though at this moment my feet are wrapped in two shawls and the hearthrug.

I don't think you can have any conception, dear PRESS, unless you are afflicted like myself (which Heaven forbid !) of my miserable condition.

The doctors attribute it to sluggish circulation, feeble action of the ventricles, etc.; but it seems to me that an old limp and ragged ace of hearts would have muscular power enough to force what little blood I have to the uttermost parts of my anatomy. There must be a dam somewhere.

I am afraid there are a good many on very cold days.

You cannot imagine the privations I endure.

At the first blast of Boreas I seek a warm nook by the fire-place, and there, as useless, and by no means as ornamental as a potted geranium, I remain until the warm breath of spring releases me.

I cannot go skating.

As I listen to the shouts and laughter of the merry men and maidens on the pond over there, as they glide swiftly and gracefully over the shining surface, drawing in ruddy health with every breath, I groan in spirit, thinking of my own miserable, moping existence, and draw closer to the fire. What glorious fun they have—although, I notice, some of them do not do their sliding altogether on their feet.

I have never been sleigh-riding.

Cutter and pung are meaningless words to me.

I can only sit here and listen to the "tintinnabulation of the bells, bells, bells, bells, bells, bells,, ," and wonder if there in reality is any fun in it—in the riding, I mean, not the tintinnabulation. It seems to me that I would rather get frostbitten in the regular way, and know something about it at the time, than to have it steal over me slily while I labor under the pleasing delusion that I am enjoying myself.

I never go to concerts or lectures—I dare not even go to church in cold weather.

As the good old dominie warms in his denunciation of sin and sinners, I feel my feet falling below the freezing point, and the two together bring about a state of uncharitableness and intolerance in my mind that is fearful to think of.

I don't wonder that the early Puritans slit Quaker's noses, banished Baptists and hanged witches.

They had no stoves in their churches.

Though I am not gifted with genius, still, but for my infirmity, I might have achieved distinction, and perhaps double stars, in the late war. Men of very limited mental capacity did. But alas! I could not have that opportunity of winning glory, the gratitude of the nation, and a very pretty bounty.

My first winter-quarters would have been under the sod, uncomfortably narrow and dark.

Very likely I would be there yet.

And how I did "quake at draft's alarms," when the Provost Marshal began turning the pitiless wheel of fortune !

I laid my case before the examining surgeon candidly and without reserve.

He remarked that "that wouldn't go down."

I don't know what he meant; I only know that my name didn't go down on his list of the exempt.

That surgeon was "a brutal minion of despotism."

I certainly have reason to be glad that the war is over.

My wish now is that somebody would *reconstruct* me.

My infirmity is harder to bear because there is nothing *poetic* about it.

It does not allure the muse.

One cannot have the comfort of abusing it in nrhyme.

Other afflictions have been sung, but cold feet never.

I have read somewhere a very violent piece of blank verse called "A Fever Dream."

Milton apostrophized his amaurosis, and Burns has immortalized the tooth-ache.

"Adown my beard the slavers trickle,
I kick the wee stools o'er the mickle,
As round the fire the giglets keckle,
To see me loup;
While, raving mad, I wish a heckle
Were in their doup."

A very natural wish, doubtless, but rather a barbarous one, and not at all fit to be expressed in English undefiled.

A man's last illness is sometimes very touchingly alluded to in his epitaph. But where, in all the obituary literature extant, will you find any mention of *cold feet?*

You see, Sir—

But excuse me. The wind has veered around to the N. N. W. to which a hot *pediluvium* is the only antidote.

So while Bridget is getting the water ready, I sign myself

Yours, in distress,

R. W.

THE MYSTERIOUS BOTTLE OF WHISKEY.

BY MARK TWAIN.

There was something strange about that bottle of whiskey. I called to see a young lady one evening some three months ago—a thing I seldom do. I found her suffering that exquisite torture which can be inflicted by only one distemper in all the world—a cold in the head. Her eyes were red, her nose was scalded and so scathed and chopped that she blew scales from it with every blast. Her voice sounded as if she were talking through a tin horn. She said that she had entertained that cold for five days, and would have to entertain it five days longer—she had never got rid of one on easier terms. I said I could cure it in twelve hours. She was frantic with joy. She would have embraced me had we been near relatives. But sadly enough, such was not the case. I said, "Drink a level tumbler full of whiskey straight, and go to bed." Her joy departed. She sighed, and went on blowing her nose as before—her beautiful nose—her beautiful, scaly, scalded nose. I was inflexible. I said, "It must be; it is a military necessity; drink a tumbler full of whiskey cold and without water; dispose yourself comfortably in bed; in two minutes that infamous, disagreeable tickling sensation in your nose—that wretched and eternal desire to sneeze—will have passed away, and you will be serene and happy—as calm and contented, and as indifferent to worldly things as the sinless angels be; in five minutes you will begin to heave grandly up and down like a stately ship on the long ground swell of the sea; this is the very sublimity of happiness; in seven minutes and a-half you will not know enough to come in when it rains; in ten minutes you will not care a—that is to say, you will not care a cent; in fifteen minutes you will be as tight as a brick—but who will ever know it? in another minute you will be sound asleep—and the thing is accomplished; you will never stir a peg nor turn over for twelve hours. Then you will get up as fresh as a lark, and the last vestige of your cold will have departed to the four winds of heaven. Try it !"

She was converted. I went out to get her a bottle of whiskey. I went to Smith's place. I said to myself, "I have drank barrels and barrels of this fellow's whisky in the reduction of my semi-annual colds, and can depend on its purity and excellence." I never saw that girl again until last week, and then she looked like Lazarus must have looked when he first sallied forth from the tomb. She had taken a glass of that whisky and gone to bed. When she woke up next day, her cold was gone but she was fearfully sick. During the next three months she passed out of one disease into another so fast that the doctors could hardly keep up with her galloping experiments, and she never got a chance to get out of bed during the whole time.

A lady called into see her one day, and while conversing pleasantly her eye fell on the treacherous bottle. She took a swig and went into fits. On another occasion, two ladies who came to "set up," felt themselves spell-bound by the mysterious bottle; they could not keep their eyes of it; it gleamed from a side-table with unholy fascination; it triumphed over them at last, and they took a drink. They laid right down on the floor and begun to gasp and sweat and groan; and thenceforward for six weeks those two women were harried and bully ragged by every disease known to the books. A minister of the gospel fell under the baneful influence of that bottle at last; he took a drink and went to his pulpit and launched out the direst discourse that ever was heard in California; he advocatod Deism and Atheism and Spiritualism and Catholicism and every other ism he could think of, and then came down and tried to clean out his congregation; he was a rampant madman for weeks together. Three more women suffered from that bottle. Lately the family moved and the infernal bottle was taken along. It had been long supposod to be empty, but the servant who was set to arrange the furniture in the new house found a sup of the lees remaining and drank it. She is up in Stockton now. After that an old *chiffonier* came along and the family gladly conferred upon him the fatal bottle without recompense. While he was carrying it down stairs he took a smell at the cork and fell and broke his leg. I shall always think there was something mysterious about that bottle. I have "worked up" this narrative a little, but in the main I have given actual facts, merely embellishing them in a scarcely perceptible degree. The original victim—the young lady—has gone to the springs to recruit her health, what there is left of it, which isn't much.

A WARNING.

An anonymous correspondent who appears to be displeased with what we said last week apropos of President Johnson's "Veto-message," favors us with the following "Warning."

New York, 24, 1866.

DEAR PRESS :

Your "Word to President Johnson," now that everybody is politically so "touchy," had better have been left unsaid; so say many of your subscribers and old friends of the PRESS. Some of us fail to see that remarkable soundness in the Veto Message; and it seems to me you'd be wiser to let each of your readers hug the delusion that you're on his side of the fence, by simply letting us all remain in blissful ignorance concerning your political tendencies.—Don't you? X.

Well no, we *don't*. We think that if there are any of the "subscribers and old friends of the PRESS" who object to our saying what we think on any subject whatever, they have read the paper to very little profit. Two or three communications similar to the above were sent to us when we ventured to express the hope, just before the last city election, that Recorder Hoffman would be elected Mayor. And the fun of it is that the writer of one of them said that if we would persist in the folly of advocating either of the candidates, we ought at least to advocate the one who had some of chance of winning !—a thought which, truth to say, hadn't occurred to us, though we knew very well who ought to win, and have a faint recollection who did.

Now it matters very little to us whether what we say pleases this subscriber or that, so that we say just what we think; and we may as well notify all persons who intend to become subscribers (a pretty large class, we trust) that if they expect us to shape our opinions according to theirs—or to vary them in the least with a view to mere "business," they are very much mistaken.

We may be wrong in respect to the President's Veto, but being strongly impressed with the idea that one government is about as much as any country can stand—and that if the new Bureau bill had passed we should have had two, with a vast locustry of office-holders in each—it seemed to us that there could be no harm in our intimating as much, and we accordingly did so.

We are not partisans of President Johnson, or of anybody else; but, like all thinking people we have our views on the subject of government, and when the mood is on we shall be very likely to express them even at the risk of offending "many subscribers and old friends of the PRESS," and receiving a fresh "Warning" every week.

A correspondent who is under the mistaken impression that we are opposed to the "Freedmen," suggests that now President Johnson has smashed the ebony bureau he had better look out for some new secretaries, and procure for himself an Old Hickory cabinet. The same correspondent thinks it funny to describe a certain Senator from Ohio as "Ben Wade, and found wanting."

Ada Clare, whose book-critiques and other articles in the early numbers of the Saturday Press, and in other journals, have made her name so favorably known in literary circles, will soon be a candidate for criticism herself. The work she is about to issue is a love-story bearing the striking title of "Only a Woman's Heart." The publisher is to be Mr. J. Bradburn, of this city.

How can a man be accused of taking "sides in politics," unless he take both sides? And then again, how can he take one side without being singular?

Dramatic Feuilleton.

BY FIGARO.

If I had just drawn fifty thousand dollars in a lottery, like Neil Bryant, I shouldn't feel happier than I do at this moment.

Usually when I sit down to these Feuilletons, my brow is sicklied o'er with the pale (ale) cast of thought, and I wish all the theatres, etc., in Bungay —if you know where that is.

But this week, I am positively radiant.

Everything looks *couleur de rose*, as one of my young men said the first night he saw Miss Eytinge.

I can almost say, with Emerson, "almost I fear to think how glad I am."

And do you know why?

Why simply because it does me so much good to hear (or rather to know) of your prosperity, my dear Press.

You have had a long and a hard time of it—as who should know better than myself?—but lo, now, your path is suddenly strewn with flowers and the Sun smiles upon you, like the good Sun that it is, with its sweetest smile.

Now, then, don't be dazzled by your success, and all will be right.

Prosperity is sometimes harder to bear, you know, than adversity: the Press has stood up pretty well under the latter—let us see what will be the effect upon it of the former.

I don't mind your rushing into a new suit, and getting Mullen to furnish you with a new top-piece, but don't go to "taking on airs."

Look as brave and handsome as you please, but be modest as well, and who knows but you may win all hearts?

Having said all which, I have only to add, "bless you, my child," and may you prove worthy of your sire!

And now, then, to my task, which this week is of a pleasantness in keeping with my state of mind.

I haven't seen much, since my last, to be sure, but all that I have seen has given me peculiar delight. I found a charm even in going to Barnum's, where I assure you the biblical piece now on the boards ("Moses, or Israel in Egypt") is one of the most effective dramas that has been played in New York for years.

There is no very great acting in it (it is true), but there is *good* acting throughout, while the tableaux alone—culminating in a grand moving panorama of the Nile—make the piece not only attractive but almost grand.

Then, again, the lesson it teaches is so good, that if I had a Sunday-school class, as I used to have, if you remember, I would send them to it every afternoon.

I am afraid my class of Bohemians wouldn't like it so much: but they are provided for, just now, at Wallack's, where Bohemia figures, large as life, in a play called "Society."

I wonder somebody hasn't thought of the idea before; for it has the charm of novelty if nothing more.

The play is said to have been written by a couple of young Englishmen named respectively Robertson and Noah: but in reality it is an anglicised version of a French play called—well, I forget what, but that doesn't matter.

It is so common to steal plays from the French and German and then add insult to injury by ignoring the original author, that the theft hardly attracts attention.

Never mind: "Society" is capitally translated, and, as cast at Wallack's, makes one of the most delicious entertainments we have had this season.

The central figure in the piece is a young Bohemian (Sidney Daryl) who has seen better days, and not having quite forgotten how they looked, is anxious to see them again, to which end he is courting a young heiress and preparing (such is life) to cut Bohemia altogether and be what is called a "gentleman."

The other characters are the heiress in question (Maud Hetherington)—a rich young parvenue, his rival (Mr. John Chodd, jr.)—the father of the same (Chodd, senior)—Lord and Lady Ptarmigant, the guardians or parents (I forget which) of the young heiress—a small and suspicious crowd of Bohemians (Tom Stylus, Mr. O'Sullivan, Moses

Aaron, etc.) and a number of small people "too humorous to mention."

The cast is as follows:

Sidney Daryl	Mr. Frederic Robinson
Tom Stylus.	Mr. Charles Fisher
Lord Ptarmigant.	Mr. Mark Smith
Mr. John Chodd, sen.	Mr. Geo. Holland
Mr. John Chodd, jr.	Mr. Holston
O'Sullivan	Mr. W. H. Norton
The Smiffel Lamb.	Mr. J. C. Williamson
Moses Aaron	Mr. Browne
Lord Cloudurays, M. P.	Mr. Graham
Dr. Makivict.	Mr. Ward
Mac Usquebaugh	Mr. Pope
Bradley	Mr. Roberts
Scargill.	Mr McGee
Waiter.	Mr. Cashin
Maud Hetherington.	Miss Madeline Henriques
Lady Ptarmigant.	Mrs. Vernon
Little Maud.	Miss Emma Le Brun
Mrs. Churton	Mrs. Timoncy
Maria	Miss Scott

The plan of the piece, I needn't tell you, is that Daryl shall outwit his rival (Chodd jr.) and carry off the young heiress (Maud Hetherington) which of course he does, to the great delight of his Bohemian friends, and to the utter disgust of the two Chodds.

It is also a matter of course, else what would become of the "British Constitution," (which there isn't any, but let that pass) that, before marrying the young heiress, Daryl turns out to be a Lord something or other (a little tin etc., on wheels) and that the two unhappy Chodds—whose efforts to get into "Society" gives the piece its name—retire from the field disgusted, leaving rank triumphant, the mythical Constitution aforesaid intact, and the audience (especially if it happen to be composed largely of Britannia ware) in raptures.

Truly, my dear Press, it is a very amusing piece. There is a Bohemian scene in it—where the elegant Daryl wants to borrow five shillings, at an ale house, of his Bohemian friends (who, strangely enough, don't happen to be peculiarly flush)—that would do credit to Pfaff's.

There is also a gambling scene, where Daryl wins money of his rival, and afterwards pitches into his inamorata, that would do credit to "Camille" (from which, not to put too fine a point upon it, it is "taken ").

But why attempt to describe a piece which is indescribable?

Let me merely add, then, that the playing of it at Wallack's, as I have already intimated, is superb.

Robinson, in the part of Daryl (which he does not dress to resemble Prince Albert, nor even George Washington) gives us one of those elaborate, careful, nice—yes, nice is the word—pieces of acting which you could no more find fault with than you could find fault with your lady's back hair.

Holston as Shodd, jr., and Holland as Shodd, senior, you can imagine: I am shaking my sides, as I write, at the very thought of them.

Mark Smith's Lord Ptarmigant is also very funny, while Mrs. Vernon's Lady Ptarmigant I should like to put in a frame, and hang up in my gallery.

The other charactors, excepting Maud, a little *bout de rôle* played with rare delicacy by Miss Henriques—and Tom Stylus, an eccentric Bohemian drawn to the life by Mr. Fisher, afford no opportunity for playing, and are played accordingly.

What I most like about the piece is its freshness: there is nothing conventional or "stuck up" in the whole thing: the characters in it are so alive that they must be acted well or they can't be acted at all: in a word, it is a regular French play written for human beings to appear in, for human beings to enjoy, and for human beings (like you and me) to write about!

And the same is true about "Used Up," which they are playing just now at the Olympic.

The author of that too, by the way, is forgotten and there are lots of people who will tell you that it was written by Charles Matthews.

There is this thing to be said, however, about Charles Matthews, that he plays Sir Charles Coldstream in the piece better than anybody else has done it, even in Paris.

Next to him comes I forget who: but the best representation I have seen of the character this long time is that of Mr. George Fawcett Rowe, who made his American début in it at the Olympic last Monday night, and, as the Clipper would say, "fairly took the audience by storm."

The pity is that he should have afterwards appeared as Clorinda in "Cinderella e la Comare," as Mrs. Wood calls her new burlesque.

I have no doubt, from all I learn, that Mr. Rowe is a good burlesque actor, but judging from his Clorinda, I should say that he had better not undertake female characters till he understands the dear sex better.

At any rate he had better not undertake them when Mrs. Wood is 'round, for the contrast will be a little too strong.

And if it is not ungallant to say so, I advise Miss Eliza Newton not to change her sex on the stage: she makes an excellent soubrette, but in such parts as Prince Poppetti (which falls to her lot in "Cinderella") she is altogether too gushing.

Please don't infer from this, my dear Press, that the "Cinderella" performance at the Olympic is not entertaining: for I would walk a mile with peas in my shoes (" boiled," mind you) just to hear Mrs. Wood sing that wonderful song in which she advises Maximilian to "get up and git "—or words to that effect.

And then I would walk another mile, under the same conditions, to see the scenery of the piece, and hear the Baker's dozen or so of musical gems from the orchestra—not to mention one or two charming little songs by Miss Myers.

I used to predict, by the way, when Miss Myers was an "infant phenomenon," that some day she would figure at the Opera: and if she had had the chance to cultivate her voice a little more, and put herself into good square operatic training, I have no doubt the prediction would have been fulfilled, and your humble servant would have figured, by this time, among the "long line of prophets."

But I have not done making musical predictions yet, and accordingly I predict for Senorita Poch,—the beautiful young Spanish prima donna, who made her first appearance among us at the Academy last Monday in the appropriate opera of "La Favorita," (as I predicted of Adelina Patti, when she made her début on a certain famous "off-night") that her name and fame will soon be as familiar among us as household words.

And apropos of the Academy, I may as well state that the brilliant season is nearly up, and that, accordingly, one night a week, (Tuesday) will be set apart, to the close, for benefits.

Academy of Music, northeast corner of 14 St. and Irving Place.

The first of these will be given on Tuesday next to that Prince of Tenors, Mazzoleni, who will appear in "L'Africaine."

The only other operatic item on my list is that at the Matinée to-day (which will commence at one o'clock) we are to have Donizetti's delicious opera of "Don Pasquale;" and that for some time next week we are promised Meyerbeer's "L'Etoile du Nord."

But stop! there is another item and that a pretty serious one: there is talk of a new opera house to be located nearly opposite the present one; yes, and something more than talk," for the money has been subscribed, the land purchased, the architect appointed, the director all but fixed on, etc.

So look out for music!

Ayo, and look out for the new Music Hall about to be erected in the rear of their piano-palace by the Steinways.

Only to think of it, I remember those young men when they had as little chance of building a Music Hall as of building a Cathedral: now, I shouldn't be surprised to hear of their building a city; in fact, they came pretty near it when they built their immense factory.

Now, then, where are your old friends Schütze and Ludolff? They, too, make the piano their forte, and as there is room for everybody, why shouldn't they build palaces and things, as well as other people?

Just you wait till they do; and meanwhile, pleasantry apart, believe me that the Steinways are really going to build the finest Music Hall in the whole land.

And now, my dear PRESS, there is nothing to add to my this week's screed except that Edwin Booth is continuing his immense success at the Winter Garden in "Richelieu" and will give a Hamlet-Matinée there next Wednesday: that Maggie Mitchell still crowds Niblo's Garden every night with her fascinating impersonation of Fanchon: that Mr. Robinson is to take his benefit next Tuesday night at Wallack's in Douglass Jerrold's drama of "The Rent Day" and Morton's farce of "The Eton Boy:" that Lucille Western is still electrifying large audiences at Wood's Theatre with her powerful acting in "The Child-Stealer:" that the last "Solon Shingle" Matinée of the season takes place to-day at The Broadway: and, finally, that if I don't wish every success to your New Issue may I be sent to Ireland on a raft and have my corpus suspended.

Figaro.

NEW YORK MARCH 10, 1866

(From the Virginia Enterprise.)

"MARK TWAIN" AMONG THE SPIRITS.

I attended the *séance* last night. After the house was crowded with ladies and gentlemen, Mrs. Foie stepped out upon the stage and said it was usual to elect a committee of two gentlemen to sit up there and see that everything was conducted with perfect honesty and fairness. She said she wished the audience to name gentlemen, whose conscientiousness—in a word, whose high moral character, in every respect, was notorious in the community. The majority arose with one impulse and called my name. This handsome compliment was as grateful as it was graceful, and I felt the tears spring to my eyes. I trust I shall never do anything to forfeit the generous confidence San Francisco has thus shown me. This touching compliment is none the less grateful to me when I reflect that it took me two days to get it up. I "put up" that hand myself. I got all my friends to promise to go there and vote for me to be on that committee—and having reported a good deal in Legislature, I knew how to do it right. I had a two-third vote secured—I wanted enough to elect me over the medium's veto, you know. I was elected, and I was glad of it. I thought I would feel a good deal better satisfied if I could have a chance to examine into this mystery myself, without being obliged to take somebody else's word for its fairness, and I did not go on that stand to find fault or make fun of the affair—a thing which would not speak well for my modesty when I reflect that so many men so much older and wiser than I am see nothing in Spiritualism to scoff at, but firmly believe in it as a religion.

Mr. Whiting was chosen as the other committeeman, and we sat down at a little table on the stage with the medium, and proceeded to business. We wrote the names of various departed persons. Mr. W. wrote a good many, but I found that I did not know many dead people; however, I put in the names of two or three whom I had known well, and then filled out the list with names of citizens of San Francisco who had been distinguished in life, so that most persons in the audience could tell whether facts stated by such spirits concerning themselves were correct or not. I will remark here that not a solitary spirit summoned by me paid the least attention to the invitation. I never got a word out of any of them. One of Mr. Whiting's spirits came up and stated some things about itself which were correct. Then some five hundred closely folded slips of paper were dumped in a pile on the table, and a lady began to lay them aside one by one. Finally a rap was heard. I took the folded paper; the spirit, so-called, seized the lady's hand and wrote "J. M. Cooke" backwards and upside down on a sheet of paper. I opened the slip I held, and as Captain Cuttle would say, "J. M. Cooke" was the "didentical" name in it. A gentleman in the audience said he sent up the name. He asked a question or so, and the spirit wrote, "Would like to communicate with you alone." The privacy of this ghost was respected, and he was permitted to go to thunder again unmolested. (I would remark here that I cannot discover any dissimilarity in the handwriting of these spirits —there is a very powerful family likeness in it, and they have all that absurd fashion of writing backwards, upside down, and wrong end foremost. They are a rum lot, altogether.) "William Nelson ported himself from the other world, and in answers to questions asked by a former friend of his in the audience, said he was aged twenty-four when he died; died by violence; died in battle; was a soldier; had fought both in the infantry and cavalry; fell at Chickamauga; had been a Catholic on earth—was not one now. Then, in answer to a pelting volley of questions, the shadowy warrior wrote: "I don't want to answer any more about it." Exit Nelson.

About this time it was it was suggested that a couple of Germans be added to the committee, and it was done. Mr. Wallenstein, an elderly man came forward, and also Mr. Ollendorff, a spry young fellow, cocked and primed for a sensation. They wrote some names. Then young Ollendorff said something which sounded like—

"Ist ein geist hieraus ?" (Bursts of laughter from the audience.)

Three raps—signifying that there *was* a Geist hieraus.

"Vollen sie schreiben?" (More laughter.)

Three raps.

"Finzig stollen, linsowfterowlickterhairowfterfrowleineruhackfolderol" (Oh, this is too rough, you know. I can't keep the run of this sort of thing.) Incredible as it may seem, the spirit cheerfully answered yes to that astonishing proposition.

The audience grew more and more boisterously mirthful with every fresh question, and they were informed that the performance could not go on in the midst of so much levity. They became quiet.

The German ghost didn't appear to know anything at all—couldn't answer the simplest questions. Young Ollendorff finally stated some numbers, and tried to get at the time of the spirit's death; it appeared to be considerably mixed as to whether it died in 1811 or 1812, which was reasonable enough, as it had been so long ago. At last it wrote "12."

Tableau! Young Ollendorff sprang to his feet in a state of consuming excitement. He exclaimed:

"Laties und shentlemen! I write de name fon' a man vot lifs! Speerit-rabbing dells me he ties in yahr eighteen hoondert und dwelf, but he yoos as live and helty as—"

The Medium—"Sit down, sir !"

Ollendorff—"But I vant to—"

Medium—"You are not here to make speeches, sir—sit down!" (Mr. O. had squared himself for an oration.)

Mr. O.—"But de speerit cheat!-dere is no such speerit—" (All this time applause and laughter by turns from the audience.)

Medium —"Take your seat, sir, and I will explain this matter."

And she explained. And in that explanation she let off a blast which was so terrific that I half expected to see young Ollendorff shot up through the roof. She said he had come up there with fraud and deceit and cheating in his heart, and a kindred spirit had come from the land of shadows to commune with him! She was terribly bitter. She said in substance, though not in words, that perdition was full of just such fellows as Ollendorff, and they were ready on the slightest pretext to rush in and assume anybody's name, and rap, and write, and lie, and swindle with a perfect looseness whenever they could rope in a living affinity like poor Ollendorff to communicate with! (Great applause and laughter.)

Ollendorff stood his ground with good pluck, and was going to open his batteries again, when a storm of cries arose all over the house, "Get down! Go Clear out! Speak on—we'll hear you! Climb down from that platform! Stay where you are! Vamose! Stick to your post—say your say!"

The medium rose up and said if Ollendorff remained, she would not.

She recognized no one's right to come there and insult her by practicing a deception upon her and attempting to bring ridicule upon so solemn a thing as her religious belief.

The audience then became quiet, and the subjugated Ollendorff retired from the platform.

The other German raised a spirit, questioned it at some length in his own language, and said the answers were correct. The medium claims to be entirely unacquainted with the German language.

About this time a gentleman called me to the edge of the platform and asked me if I were a Spiritualist. I said I was not. He asked me if I were prejudiced. I said not more than any other unbeliever; but I could not believe in a thing which I could not understand, and I had not seen anything yet that I could by any possibility cipher out. He said, then, that he didn't think I was the cause of the diffidence shown by the spirits, but he knew there was an antagonistic influence around that table somewhere; he had noticed it from the first; there was a painful negative passing to his sensitive organization from that direction constantly. I told him I guessed it was that other fellow; and I said, Blame a man who was all the time shedding these infernal negative currents. This appeared to satisfy the mind of the inquiring fanatic, and he sat down.

The spirit of "Henry Wandell" wrote his name, but it was so long before the gentleman in the audience who called for him would acknowledge him, that Henry grew offended and meandered back to Heaven again. The medium said he was offended at any rate. And just here I want to remark that those spirits appear to uncommon sticklers for etiquette. You call up an old dead scalliwag of a shoemaker, and he will put on more frills and require more polite attentions than a prince of the blood. You have to tackle him right off or he will get mad at the delay and go off in a huff. And yet the mediums all say that spirits have no appreciation of time whatever.

A lady in the audience (holding up a slip of paper) said "I have got the name of a dear spirit friend here, and I would like to communicate with him. He promised to be here this evening—said he would come, and I never knew him to fail before. But I have sent his name up twice to-night and he has not manifested his presence yet. I want to send it up again."

Medium—"It will be hardly worth while. If he had been present he would have said so before this."

Anxious Friend Of Progress—"But he *promised* to come; he promised, and I never knew him to fail before."

Medium—"Still there may be influences around us which deter him, or he may be here and still not desirous of communicating. Suppose you address him."

The anxious Friend of Progress called on her spectral friend, but he failed to qualify. Circumstances over which he had no control put it out of his power to be at Congress Hall, and so he went back on his promise. The anxious inquirer seemed very much disappointed—she really seemed distressed at this execrable conduct of her pet ghost.

A spirit seized the medium's hand and wrote "G. L. Smith" very distinctly. She hunted through the mass of papers, and finally the spirit rapped. She handed me the folded paper she had just picked up. It had "T. J. Smith" in it. (You never can depend on these Smith's; you call for one and the whole tribe will come clattering out of hell to answer you.) Upon further inquiry it was discovered that both these Smiths were present. We chose "T. J." A gentleman in the audience said that this was his Smith. So he questioned him, and Smith said he died by violence; he had been a good tangled in his religious belief, and was a sort of a cross between a Universalist and a Unitarian; has got straightened out and changed his opinions since he left here; said he was perfectly happy.

Mr. George Purnell, having been added to the committee, proceeded, in connection with myself, Mrs. Foie and a number of persons in the audience, to question this talkative and frolicsome old parson. Among spirits I judge he is the gayest of the gay. He said he had no tangible body; a bullet could pass through him and never make a hole; rain could pass through him as through vapor and not discommode him in the least (wherefore I suppose he don't know enough to come in when it rains—or don't care enough;) says heaven and hell are simply mental conditions; spirits in the former have happy and contented minds, and those in the latter are torn by remorse and conscience; says as far as he is concerned, he is all right—he is happy; would not say whether he was a very good or a very bad man on earth (the shrewd old water-proof nonentity! —I asked the question so that I might average my own chances for his luck in the other world, but he saw my drift ;) says he has an occupation there—puts in his time teaching and being taught; says there are spheres—grades of perfection—he is making very good progress—has been promoted a sphere or so since his matriculation; (I said mentally, "Go slow, old man, go slow—you have got all eternity before you"—and he replied not;) he don't know how many spheres there are (but I suppose there must be millions, because if a man goes galloping through them at the rate this old Universalist is doing he will get through an infinitude of them by the time he has there as long as old Sesostris and those ancient mummies; and there is no estimating how high he will get in even the infancy of eternity—I am afraid the old man is scouring along rather too fast for the style of his surroundings, and the length of time he has got on his hands); says spirits cannot feel heat or cold (which militates somewhat against all my notions of orthodox damnation—fire and brimstone); says spirits commune with each other by thought—they have no language; says the distinctions of sex are preserved there—and so forth and so on.

The old parson wrote and talked for an hour, and showed by his quick, shrewd, intelligent replies, that he had not been sitting up nights in the other world for nothing; he had been prying into everything worth knowing, and finding out everything he possibly could—as he said himself, when he did not understand a thing he hunted up a spirit who could explain it; consequently he is pretty thoroughly posted; and for his accommodating conduct and his uniform courtesy to me, I sincerely hope he will continue to progress at his present velocity until he lands on the very roof of the highest sphere of all, and thus achieve perfection.

(For the Saturday Press.)

THE HAUNTED WATERFALL.

A BALLAD.

I.

The lady Laura lies upon her couch in soft repose ;
Around her form, the waning fire a ghastly halo throws;
Beside her lie her rats and mice, her "Derby " and her bows,
With her waterfall, her satin robe and divers other "close."

II.

O dreams the lady Laura now, of yester-evening's ball,
Whereat, in beauty and in pride, she reigned the queen of all?
Or dreams she of the wounded hearts that 'neath her sceptre fall?—
But hark! a footstep loud is heard along her father's hall;

III.

Up stairs it comes, the windows of the stately dwelling shake;
A brace of poodles, in their sleep, a doleful howling make,
The fire is burning sulphery as Pluto's lurid lake;
The footsteps at my lady's door,—O! lady Laura wake!

IV.

She sees a female figure there, a-standing by her side;
'Tis clad in white, from head to foot,—'tis pale and hollow-eyed,
And on that gorgeous waterfall, it looks in silent pride:
The lady Laura cannot move, her tongue with fear is tied.

V.

"And have I found you once again my bonny locks of hair?
Oh! long I've sought you high and low, since head of mine was bare !
I will not lay a hand on you, to harm you, lady fair,
But I must carry to my grave this very night, that 'ere."

VI.

"For Oh! upon my head in life, those golden ringlets grew,
And round my rosy cheeks, when young, in shining ripples blew!
It's very cold below the sod', I needs them more than you:
I leaves you now, for I sniffs the morn: my lady fair, adieu."

VII.

With bony hand, upon her head the waterfall she flings,
And from the marble mantel-piece a looking-glass she brings;
Then, down the long and narrow hall her ghostly garment swings:
Convulsively the lady Laura to her pillow clings.

* * * * * * * * * * * * *

VIII.

The rosy rays of morning, peer in glory thro' the blind,
And milkmen in the waking streets their lively carols wind;
The lady Laura smiles once more, to all her loss resigned,
For a heavy weight is taken from her back-hair and her mind!

George Cooper.

NEW YORK MARCH 17, 1866

AMUSEMENTS.

ACADEMY OF MUSIC.—"The Star of the North:" this afternoon at 1 o clock,
WALLACK'S THEATRE.—"The Unequal Match:" 8 P. M.
WINTER GARDEN.—" Richelieu" (last night but four of Edwin Booth): 7¾ P. M.
THE OLYMPIC THEATRE.—"Cinderella e la Comare:" 7¾ P. M.
NIBLO'S GARDEN.—"The Pearl of Savoy:" 7¾ P. M.
WOOD'S THEATRE,—" East Lynne:" 7¾ P. M.
THE BROADWAY THEATRE.—"Victims " and "Forty Winks:" 7¾ P. M.
BARNUM'S MUSEUM.—" Moses, or Israel in Egypt:" 2 P. M. and 7½ P. M.
BROOKLYN ACADEMY OF MUSIC—" L'Africaine:" 8P M.

An exchange says that "waterfalls" are prohibited by the English game laws. The clause applying to them reads: "Netting the hare shall be punished by fine," etc.

Wanted—several men in Washington of "cabinet size."

It is a curious fact about our city barbers that they appear to be master of all tongues except their own.

Nobody is ever willing to admit that he has been caught napping," unless he happens to be a hatter.

A young lady whose father is improving the family mansion, insists upon having a beau window put in for her benefit.

NEW YORK MARCH 24, 1866

Dramatic Feuilleton.

BY FIGARO.

I saw you on Monday night, Mr. Editor, at Wallack's, enjoying the performance of "The Serious Family,"—enjoying it, that is, in your grim way.

The attendance was pretty full—the occasion being Mr. Young's benefit—but I picked you out at once; for you happened to sit in range of one of the long mirrors and—will you believe it ?—I saw you as plainly as anybody in the house.

I like those mirrors, by the way, because when I want to survey the audience—which I always do at Wallack's—I can do so without staring anybody out of countenance.

It is pleasant, too, now and then, to catch a glimpse of one's self—and with me it is peculiarly so because, by a strange coincidence, I invariably get a glimpse of you at the same time. And apropos, somebody asked me, the other day, if you and I were not relatives—cousins or some thing of that kind—which reminded me of a certain Lord in England who asked the Siamese Twins what relation they were to each other, and seemed much surprised to learn that they were brothers.

However, you and I are not brothers, nor anything of the sort, though I love you quite as well for all that and would do as much for you—witness these Feuilleton's—as for any man this side (or the other) of Nantucket.

But tell me, wasn't "The Serious Family" well cast?

Think of it: Mr. Young as Aminadab Sleek—Mr. Robinson as Capt. Murphy Maguire—Miss Henriques as Mrs. Torrens—Miss Gannon as Mrs. Delmaine—Mrs. Vernon as Lady Sowerly Creamly—and so on.

The piece was never so honored before since it was written and, for that matter, never deserved to be.

We all used to go and see it in the days of old Burton, but it was for the sake of seeing *him:* the other actors, as a rule, counted for nothing.

The last time I saw it, before this week, was at the Chambers St. Theatre, just before Burton left there.

You remember it, for we were together, and next to us sat a well-known clergyman from Boston who relished the fun of the thing even more than we did—though he was evidently afraid, all the evening, of being discovered.

Burton, of course, played Aminadab Sleek, and played it as he only could.

Lots of people have tried it since—from Dan Setchell up—but they have all made the mistake of trying to be Burtonic.

Young is too shrewd for this and gives us an Aminadab of his own—and a better one, in some respects, than Burton's.

The difficulty with Burton was that, no matter what he played, he couldn't keep being coarse.

Young, at any rate, never falls into this error.

In fact, the whole atmosphere of Wallack's is one of refinement.

Why, this wretched farce of "The Serious Family" is given to us with such elegance there that the essential vulgarity and grossness of the thing are, for the moment, quite forgotten.

The attention is not centred on any one of the characters, but when the play is over you are at a loss which most to admire, the unctuousness of Mr. Young's Aminadab—the gentlemanly humor of Mr. Robinson's Captain Maguire—the lady-like rendering of Mrs. Torrens by Miss Henriques—the subtle appreciation of Lady Sowerly Creamly by Mrs. Vernon—or the genuine yet subdued humor of Miss Gannon as Mrs. Delmaine.

Indeed, you recall with more or less pleasure even the minor characters—Miss Barrett's Emma Torrens, for instance—and wonder what talisman there is about Wallack's which thus transforms one of the vulgarest and worst written plays of the day into all but a genteel comedy.

I suppose that after seeing "The Serious Family" I ought, out of respect to Mr. Young, to have stopped and seen "The Laughing Hyena," in which he plays the part of Simon Hornblower; but one play an evening is as much as I can stand.

I can fancy however, how good he was in it; while as for Mr. Gilbert's Felix Fumer, Miss Burke's Popsy, and Mrs. Jennings' Mrs. Fumer—why the names tell the whole story.

Mrs. Jennings, by the way, had her benefit on Wednesday, appearing in "Second Love" and "High Life Below Stair" but on that evening I was booked for Wood's Theatre to see Miss Western's Don Cæsar—of which more presently.

I hear that Mrs. Jennings had a good house (she ought to have had a crowded one and played better than ever.

Last night Mr. George Holland was to have his turn in "Paul Pry" and "Deaf as a Post "—but Friday you know is my contraband day, and I must refer you for an account of performance to the morning papers: what a splendid old actor Holland is, you know already.

The next benefit at Wallack's will be that of Mrs. John Sefton, which will take place on Monday next, in "Dombey and Son" and the aforesaid "Hyena."

To-night we are to have a repetition of "The Rent Day" and "The Eton Boy," which were introduced a week or so ago for the benefit of Mr. Robinson.

The only other item I have about Wallack's is sufficiently explained by the following extract from Wednesday's *Tribune:*

A DRAMATIC IMPOSTOR.

Anonymous letter-writing is one of the most offensive tricks of blackguardism. The recent reception of a couple of anonymous letters, post-marked Roxbury, Massachusetts, has especially attracted the attention to this subject. Our correspondent—who styles himself a "Well Known New Yorker," and who expresses himself in a manner that evinces both ignorance and silliness—urges us to publish, as an item of theatrical news, a statement which he perfectly well knows would be a falsehood. What he wishes us to say is that Mr. Lester Wallack has temporarily withdrawn from the stage for the purpose of writing a play. Such a statement, indeed, has recently got into print in at least two New York papers—from which fact we infer that this anonymous letter-writer has been more successful in his efforts to impose upon others than he has been in the endeavor to deceive us. His statement is unqualifiedly false. Ill health is the sole cause of Mr. Wallack's absence from the stage; and we are authorized to deny, in his name, the assertion that he has secluded himself for the purpose of writing a play. Accident, we may add, has put us in possession of the facts connected with this case of anonymous letter-writing and attempted imposture. They are worth the telling, we think, as illustrative of the possible insolence and fraud of mercenary shrewdness, and also as illustrative of one form of annoyance to which managers and journalists are often subjected. These, then, are the facts: The "Well-known New Yorker," resident at Roxbury, Massachusetts, has written a play. This play he has sent to Mr. Lester Wallack, requesting that gentleman to assume its authorship, and to produce it at his theatre, paying to him, the aforesaid "Well-Known New Yorker," the proceeds resulting therefrom. Of course, this modest proposition has not been entertained. Meanwhile, the "Well-Known New Yorker" has anonymously addressed this and other papers, endeavoring to secure the assistance of the press in his insolent scheme of imposture. We hope that he will profit by this exposure so far as to spare us the necessity of publishing his name, which we have ascertained since receiving his letters. The way of the anonymous letter-writer is hard—and may become harder.

It has been well known, all the season, in theatrical circles, that Mr. Wallack was too ill to appear on the stage: and I may add, here, that the general sympathy for him has been not a little heightened by the fact that there has been found one man on the press—if the word man can be applied to a person long since all but ruled out of human companionship by the established infamy of his character—base enough to make his illness the subject of malignant jest.

But hold! I am half inclined to take this last paragraph back.

There are certain persons connected with journalism in New York whose only chance of calling attention to themselves (their sole aim) is by publicly defaming their betters.

Only allude to them in print, however indirectly, and they are happy; mention them by name, no matter in what connection (for it must needs be a disgraceful one) and they will fall on their knees to you.

The creature above referred to is one of them: another is a wretched importation (or exportation) from Philadelphia who, in the absence of his employer, took occasion, last Saturday, to use the columns of one of our city weeklies (the Citizen,—from which his name had just been erased) to pour out his venom upon a recently deceased young woman, in the hope that her friends might be driven to call attention to him, even if they had to horsewhip him through the streets.

Why such vermin are permitted to remain on any journal in New York is a question I may go into some other time: meanwhile, apologizing for the digression, let me go on with my Feuilleton.

I had just got through—had I not ?—with Wallack's.

Well then, now for the rest of my budget.

At the Winter Garden, the great attraction continues, of course, to be Edwin Booth—whose engagement, as you will regret to hear, closes on Thursday next when he will take a Farewell Benefit, for which all the tickets are being taken as fast as the box-keeper can pass them out.

At last Wednesday's Matinée, "Hamlet" was substituted in the place of "Richelieu " and with a result that would warrant its repetition, seven times a week, to the end of the season.

This afternoon, Mr. Booth will play Don Cæsar de Bazan for the benefit of "the institution in 58th St., for the support of the destitute children of the soldiers and sailors who have been killed in our recent struggle for the Union."

This evening, "Hamlet" again,

At Niblo's Garden, Maggie Mitchell gives her charming impersonation of Marie in "The Pearl of Savoy," to-night, for the last time this season, and on Monday appears us Amry in the domestic drama of "Little Barefoot."

At the Olympic, "Cinderella è la Comare" still holds sway, though it will probably be withdrawn next week.

At the Broadway, "The Victims" will be given this afternoon and evening for the last time, after which the bill will be changed for "several beautiful attractions"—so says the bill—" in preparation for the Easter Holidays": needless to say that the "head-centre" of the beautiful attractions will be John Owens.

At Wood's Theatre, Miss Lucille Western is still playing in "East Lynne," and drawing about the best houses in town.

There being an "East Lynne" Matinée on Wednesdays, she gives us her Don Cæsar Bazan in the evening for a change.

And everybody ought to see it: it is really a superb piece of acting.

I have no time to go into an analysis of it, but in point not only of conception and elaboration, but of grace and finish, it is one of the best things I have seen on the stage.

The woman peeps out now and then, it is true—and the action of the piece is marred in certain scenes by a too formal style of elocution—but the splendid dash and *abandon* of Don Cæsar are maintained throughout, and, before the curtain drops, you forget the sex of the performer and think only of the artistic and all but unexceptionable character of the Performance.

And, now, a word or so about one or two other matters and I have done.

At Barnum's, as you know, crowds of persons flock every afternoon and evening to see the really magnificent spectacle of "Moses or Israel in Egypt": believe me, the moving panorama of the Nile in it is one of the most splendid scenic effects ever seen in New York.

At Irving Hall, we are to have to-night the fifth and last of Theodore Thomas' Symphony Soirées, at which, beside Mr. Thomas, we are to have Miss Lizzie Eckhardt, Mr. G. Matzka, Mr. A. F. Toulmin, and an orchestra at least sixty strong.

At the Academy, as there is to be a Philharmonic performance this afternoon at three, the operatic Matinée (Mozart's "Don Giovanni ") will commence at 11 A. M.

The benefit of Miss Kellogg, which was postponed last Wednesday on account of her sudden illness, is now announced for Monday evening next—the opera to be *L'Etoile Du Nord.*

The Academy has been taken for this evening by the subscribers to the Théatre Français—the occasion being a complimentary benefit to the managers, Messrs, Juignet and Drivet: play, *Les Enfers de Paris*.

A special performance will take place at the Winter Garden on Wednesday evening next for the benefit of Mr. H. T. Jackson, the treasurer of the establishment and one of the most gentlemanly officials connected with any theatre in town: the principal features of the performance will be the first appearance in New York of Mr. J. Newton Gotthold, who will play the part of Othello.

You ought to say it formally, Sir, in your editorial columns, but I don't suppose you will, so I'll do it myself right here.

"Say what?" do you ask.

Why that Pfaff has sold out.

Just think of it—that he of all others—should go back on us!

Well, I suppose he's got rich and wants to lay off for a while.

Never mind; his name still remains to us—a name known, now, all over the land—and it will be a long time before the establishment will be known by any other.

The new comers are Messrs. Kruyt & Co.—Mr. Kruyt having been *chef de cuisine* for some dozen years or so, at Delmonico's.

All will continue to be right, therefore, so far as the "inner man" is concerned; but we shall sadly miss the genial face of dear old Pfaff, and the habitués of the place will drink to his memory as long as the house stands.

But more of this another time, when I may give some Pfaffian reminiscences, which will be worth reading.

Figaro.

NEW YORK MARCH 31, 1866

(For the Saturday Press.)

THE REJECTED SUITOR.

BY M. A. E.

"You see, my young friend," said the philosopher, slowly opening a lozenge-shaped bag, as if calling upon his companion to inspect its contents, but he only took therefrom some tobacco, with which he proceeded to fill his pipe, "the mistake you make is in not watching the markets. I have often wondered that our enterprising weeklies did not give regular lists of the market value of literary and art productions. It would be of vast assistance to writers. At present the quotations would read somewhat like this.

Poison and gore, brisk. Ghosts on a decline. A moderate inquiry for sentiment at previous prices. Wit, nominal. Humor, quiet. Flippancy, lively, with a tendency upwards. No demand for poetry. Native comedy uncalled for. Foreign comedy in fair request. Articles endorsing the President's policy, bidding spirited, and trade active. The Review market holds firmly. Essays looking up."

The poet smiled incredulously. "No demand for poetry? What becomes of all that is published then ?"

"That is a question often asked, but like the similar one of 'Where do the pins go to,' will never be satisfactorily answered. A great deal of it everybody knows goes to the trunkmakers, and to the cheap stores, but this accounts for only a small proportion of the mass. And that reminds me that my habits of investigation sometimes lead me on the track of strange discoveries. I bought a ten cent cigar the other day, and I had the curiosity to see of what it was composed. So I set to work to resolve it into its constituent parts. First I unrolled a veritable leaf of the tobacco plant; next a brown substance, entirely unknown to me; and then a tarred rope, which was wrapped in several folds of paper. I opened this, and spread it out as well as I could, but only managed to decipher these parts of lines:

'Amazement * * * * ill-starred king,
He broke his staff in twain,
* * * * * * * * * * thing,
And be a boy again.'"

"Why, that is mine!" said the poet.

"I know it," said the philosopher, lighting his pipe, "and so you see your question is partly answered as far as your own poetry is concerned ; and, if it had not been for me, it would have been a smoke and a stench in the nostrils of all good Christians. And, now I think of it, in that cigar lies a suggestion for you. Perhaps if you pay court to the tobacconists, instead of the publishers, your suit will not be rejected."

"I will have my poems published—every line of them, if I have to pay for them myself," said the poet violently.

"Humph!" said the philosopher, leaning back in his easy-chair, and disposing his feet comfortably on the fender. "Well! let me hear of your adventures with the publishers. They unanimously refused to recognize merit, I suppose."

"Every soul of them! Soul did I say ! They have no souls. One of them did read a few poems, when I almost insisted upon it, and then he declined them, without attempting any excuse for his conduct. And yet that man last year took great pains in getting out a book of jokes done in bad spelling !"

"What a simpleton!" said the philosopher. "With the proceeds of that book he bought a farm in the country, where his wife and children will spend the summer. He has not the soul to understand that it would be so much more agreeable and healthful for his family to read about the birds and trees in your poems."

"Well, no matter," said the poet, "he refused them, and so did they all. If they show the same energy and alacrity in all their business transactions that they have in rejecting my poems, they will soon realize handsome fortunes. But how are we poets to get before the public?"

"Write prose."

It strikes me that then we would cease to be poets. But I have tried it, and cannot say that my prose has been any more successful than my poetry."

"Because your prose is just like your poetry with the rhymes cut off. In the latter the Muses are couchant; in the former they are rampant."

The poet looked at the philosopher's bald head, and then at the great roll of manuscript he held in his hand; but he thought better of it, and laid the roll tenderly, and softly on the table. "It is a pity," sighed he.

"I see nothing pitiful in it," said the philosopher. "You must look this matter squarely in the face, as the Dailies say. You have certain ideas which you regard as marketable commodities, and so you set up your booth, and call upon the world to buy your wares. Now you must put your ideas in attractive forms, or you will find no purchasers, and the world don't want poetry. It has got beyond it."

"Beyond poetry!" cried the poet, starting from his seat, and striding up and down the room. "Beyond poetry! The highest of the Arts! Shades of Homer, and Milton !"

"A Milton, bound in Turkey morocco, is a very pretty ornament for a centre table. I never heard of anybody reading it. Homer is more read, chiefly, I take it, because it abounds in blood, and slaughter, which are popular ideas."

"It is my opinion," said the poet, "that the organ of reverence is entirely wanting in your head."

"We are not talking about myself," said the philosopher, knocking the ashes out of his pipe. "For the present I represent the world."

"No, you do not," said the poet. "The world buys poetry eagerly. Look at the success of Tennyson, to say nothing of lesser names."

"They established their reputation before poetry was on the decline. And how many readers has the Idyls of the King, compared with Henry Dunbar?"

"Well, then, there is Tupper—"

"Hold!" said the philosopher, lifting a warning finger, while his placid brow contracted into a frown. "There are chords in the human soul."

"I beg your pardon," said the poet, humbly. "I did not mean to hurt your feelings."

"I forgive you," said the philosopher, recovering his equanimity. "You may depend upon it poetry won't do, a few noted instances to the contrary notwithstanding. If you have the genius of a Milton, and wish to write for fame, and posterity (which means being bound in whatever may be fashionable a hundred years hence, and laid upon centre tables) why go on writing, and leave your manuscripts to your heirs. But, as I see a patch on your boot, and your hat looks somewhat jagged at the brim, and the rusty spots on your coat, that you have inked over, show very plainly in this strong light, I presume you write for money."

"It is too true," sighed the poet.

"Oh, you need not be ashamed of it. Everything is done for money now-a-days. Well, then, my friend, all that is necessary for your success in literature is to turn your back upon poetry, and poetical prose, and write to please the popular taste."

"I cannot do it," said the poet, meekly. "Nothing is easier. The two styles most popular at present are the 'blood and thunder,' as it is styled by its detractors, and a jerky, take it easy, devil-may-care sort of style. The first is composed of a judicious mixture of the police reports, and Mrs. Radcliffe. The second is the result of a habit of mind, easily acquired. And, as my second pipe is out, I have no objections to giving you some specimens. We must first think of a subject, and we may find some materials among this mass of matter, which you can make useful in this way. Let me see. I will take one at random." So saying he inserted his finger and thumb into the roll of manuscript, and flirted out a sheet. "Here is a poem called 'Love.' An unpromising subject, but we will see what can be done with it in the jerky, free-and-easy style.

'Oh, lonely soul of starry night,
Oh, spirits of these silent woods,
Forgive me if a heart too light,
Disturb your sacred solitudes.'

"How do you do, Madam Night ?
Ha! I see a bottle, Spirits in these silent woods!
Let me taste. Brandy!
Left here by a pic-nic party, doubtless.
Forgive me, sacred solitudes, but spirits make me light-headed."

"That is a good beginning, and then you can describe how he gets tipsy, and goes rollicking about under the trees, and tells the story of his love. The brandy bottle is a good idea, for it accounts for his talking to himself in the tropes and metaphors he is described as using, and which no man in his sober senses would ever dream of. Oh, you need not say anything to me about the intoxication of love. Men in love don't wander about the woods, apostrophizing the trees and streams. They think of coal, and furniture.

'She slowly moved from mossy throne,
She stepped toward her shepherd band,
And blushing lovelier than the rose
She dropped it in my trembling hand.'

My love is a great woman. An immense woman.
So she moves slowly.

She has a sun-flower (rose is too puerile for the present taste.)
She bears it toward me.
I tremble.
She sticks it in my hair, where it waves in golden glory.

'Bend low, tall trees! Sing low, soft breeze!
Breeze-borne ring lightly fairy bells,
And gently murmur, silver streams,
Wild winding through enchanted dells.'

Go it old treeses! Wake up breezes !
Sheep-bells jingle-jingle !
And all Nature goes in for the chorus !'

"That is enough for a specimen."

"It is entirely too much," said the poet, plucking up a little courage. "It is a mass of nonsense."

"The sense is of no consequence. Style is everything. And besides I will leave it to any impartial judge if my lover is not as sensible and natural as yours. But if you don't like that style, and I must say I do not think it is exactly in your line; let us try the blood and thunder." And he flirted out another sheet of manuscript.

" 'The Tomb of Love.' Love again. Well, it is a relief to know that this time it is happily released from mortal pains. I must confess I do not quite comprehend the poem," he continued, when he had finished reading it; "but that is a matter of no importance.

'It is night, and the bells are tolling out of monasteries in a wood, and a shadowy brotherhood with trembling torches are carrying a bier to the tomb. One is walking apart, and looking into an eye, and hearkening to a word. The tomb has a black forehead, and a ponderous door, and an inner darkness. Gusty breezes; dusky dells; spectral starlight; swooning seas (whatever they may be). A beautiful woman "gulfed" in the tomb.

"There are some good materials here, useless in their present form, but you might work them up somewhat in this fashion:

"A description of a wood on the Hudson River and a tomb, and a funeral procession. The lover walks apart. Suddenly he cries: 'Ha! I see an eye looking out from behind that towering palm! I hear a word! Kefaxkoja! I knew it! She has been foully murdered by Eliza Jane!' He swoons away, and the young woman is buried in tomb. It will require seventeen chapters to describe the lover's chase after Eliza Jane. At last he finds her in the wood near the tomb, where she has been all the time, and has supported an aged grandfather, and bed-ridden aunt with her needle. She brandishes a dagger, and he has no pistol. He snatches a cocoa nut from a tree, and hurls it at her. She falls. He clutches her by the hair: 'Murderess,' he cries, 'your time is come.' 'I will show you a thing worth two of that, young man,' says Eliza Jane; and, springing up, she smites her delicate rosy fist upon the black forehead. The ponderous doors fly open, and the lover is thrust into the inner darkness. 'It is the tomb of my Sophronia,' he sobs, 'Oh ecstacy, to be with her once more! I will die by her side. Hark! I hear rats! I will escape.' He scratches on door, and shrieks. Bells toll. A procession of monks march up the banks of the Hudson, pass the tomb. 'Ghosts!' they yell, and disperse in all directions. Bells keep tolling. A rat bites the lover's toe. He swoons. Eliza Jane marries a rich old man with the virtues of all the saints in the calendar, and they live happily together for several years. A stranger visits the castle. Eliza Jane wears a white dress. 'Behold!' cries the stranger, 'a purple spot on the sleeve of your robe. It is his blood. You have murdered my dearest friend.' 'Tush, man, I have been eating blackberries.' 'Woman, that plea avails you not. Officers, do your duty.' Interesting trial. Eliza Jane about to be acquitted, when the lover appears, having been fished up out of tomb years before by small boys who came to the river for salmon. He brings proof that Eliza Jane murdered his Sophronia, having found it in a tin box in the mouth of a shark, which he speared upon the sandy beach. Great excitement, in the midst of which Eliza Jane takes poison, the lover marries a pale young woman who has been pining away for him, and the rich old man tears his grey hair, and weeps with tender pity and cruel scorn for Eliza Jane, but is comforted with a bottle of sherry.'"

"This is horrible," said the poet, aghast.

"Of course it is; that is what you want."

"It is absolute profanity," protested the poet. "And you have entirely lost sight of the inner sense—the subtle meaning of the poem."

"Never have a subtle meaning, my young friend, never. Make your meaning so plain that it will knock the reader right square on the head, or else have no meaning at all, but avoid subtle meanings as you hope to prosper. And now that I have pointed out to you the high road to fame and fortune, I will refresh myself with another pipe."

"I have no inclination whatever to travel that road you have pointed out. I would rather die in obscurity."

"No, you wouldn't. You will think better of it when your boots won't bear any more patching, and when your shirt sleeves burst through the elbows of your coat, as they are about to do. A poet! Pah! The poet's corner in a newspaper is like the Poet's Corner in Westminster Abbey—a place where they are buried from the ken of living men. Come, young man, don't be down-hearted. You have genius, and you will yet turn it to good account. Here in this roll of manuscript lies buried ten thousand dollars; you must work it up into a sensation novel. Put in murders enough, and don't be sparing with your poisons; let virtue triumph at last; and, above all, make it end happily; and I will insure you a publisher, and twenty per cent profit."

The poet took advantage of a cloud of smoke, which here enveloped the head of the philosopher, and, lifting the roll of the manuscript from the table with that reverent care with which we move the dead, he left the house, and neither he, or his poems, have since been heard from.

(For the Saturday Press.)

THE FLANEUR.

"I loaf and invite my soul."

Now that the Spring is coming on, the days when the first languor of Summer oppresses us, I may well loaf, or rather *flan*, for the French word has not the disreputable sense which ours has.

In fact, the whole business of life is *flaning*.

"One impulse from a vernal wood
Will teach you more of man,
Of moral evil and of good
Than all the sages can."

Join this with the equally apposite and novel quotation that,

"The proper study for mankind is man,"

and any one who has flaned himself into a logical mood enough to construct his syllogism from these two poetical premises, will find his prosaic conclusion justify him in idling whole days away in vernal woods.

This however I do not propose to do.

The woods for those who like them.

For my part, give me the populous solitude of a city.

In fact, you are more struck with nature in a city than you are in the country.

As there is no more grateful spectacle to the gods than an upright man struggling with difficulties, so there is no more interesting spectacle to a thoughtful man than a tree trying to grow in a paved street.

But then it requires a thoughtful man to enjoy the spectacle.

Your thoughtful man is necessarily a "flaneur."

He throws himself prone on the bosom of nature, and does not care about stocks.

He is one of the men from a contemplation of whom Solomon arrived at a certain remark in the book of "Ecclesiasticus," which by the way is one of the few books in the world, though it is in the Apocrypha.

Why there, I could never understand; perhaps the remark which I am about to quote may have aided in its condemnation.

It runs thus: "For wisdom cometh by opportunity of leisure and he that hath little business shall become wise."

So Solomon, the wisest man, celebrated the advantages of flaning, which is a much better proof, to my mind, of his wisdom than many other things he did; as for instance his taking three hundred wives, etc.

But every man to his taste, and some things must be pardoned to the age a man lives in.

Solomon did not live in an age when women were able to think of their rights, much less claim them.

If he had, how he would deserve our pity.

He acted probably to the best of his knowledge, and doubtless his three hundred wives did the same.

But the sweet companionship that makes intimacy with a woman of character and sense, so useful and so delightful to a man with the same qualities, could evidently not exist in such a state of things.

Was it the fault of the women, or of the men?

Were either of them fit for it?

This is a question difficult to decide, and well worth thinking of.

Don't jump at your conclusions.

Collect in your mind materials for forming your opinions, from which they shall grow like healthy plants from a rich soil.

This is to act like a real Flaneur.

And in the gathering such materials read Renan's "Essay on the 'Song of Songs.'"

I shall speak of it some day, but meanwhile read it; it will probably give you some information on the character both of Solomon and his times which you have not now.

It did so to me.

At any rate it is settled that Solomon understood the advantages of flaning.

If with him in his times it was good, how much more necessary now in this nineteenth century, when every man is made nothing but a machine, a mere tool to be used up and cast aside as worthless.

I remember once hearing one of our best thinkers, say to one of our most practical preachers, "Why have we not men in these days like those whose lives I read in Plutarch ?"

"Well," was the reply, "perhaps it is rather a Plutarch to write the lives that we want."

There is truth on both sides.

For want of bravery in action, daring, and courage —as well as the bravery of patience in waiting, firmness and resolution—no man can blame us now, either our men or women, after the last four years.

Very true, and yet there is a smack about the old fellows in Plutarch, that we do not find now.

What makes the difference?

Is it the railroad, the steamboat, the telegraph, or what is it?

I know an eccentric man who thinks it is tobacco.

But then he is eccentric and does not smoke; I am not and do, so of course we do not agree.

Sometime I shall further discuss this subject with you, and give you my opinion about it. I have not ripened it yet sufficiently for expression.

I must loaf and invite my soul concerning it, a little longer.

That is, I must *flan* upon it.

THE FLANEUR.

NEW YORK APRIL 7, 1866

Dramatic Feuilleton.

BY FIGARO.

When you can't be witty yourself, Mr. Editor, what a consolation it is to be the cause of wit in others!

The reflection is not a new one, to be sure, but it comes home to me with great force this week in consequence of my just having been the cause of perhaps the most brilliant *jeu d'esprit* of the season.

Cartoonist, Thomas Nast.

You know that on Thursday night Max Maretzek gave a grand ball at the Academy of Music for the benefit of that rising young artist, Mr. Thomas Nast.

The affair was called, for some reason, a "Bal d'Opera ;" but that is of no consequence, one way or the other, except that there being no such phrase as "Bal d'Opera" in any known language, we should like to know—Mr. Nast and myself—why it was used.

However, let that go: what I am coming at is that among the most amusing incidents of the ball was a series of letters purporting to have been written by several more or less distinguished persons in answer to a request on the part of the management for "a few jokes."

Now among these letters (all, it is needless to say, written by the brilliant management,) was one bearing my own humble signature, and exhibiting so much genuine wit and humor that I cannot deny myself the pleasure of copying it.

Here, then, is this marvellous document, quoted word for word, from a report in the TIMES:

> In great haste.
>
> Perhaps, my dear Colonel, you think I am going to do it.
> So did I.
> But I am not.
> There are people who can.
> I can't.
> But I will for the next Opera Bal.
> You might try Ralph Waldo Emerson,
>
> FIGARO.

Now really, Mr. Editor, if I thought that after writing twenty years more—making a hundred or so, in all—I could possibly get off anything like that, I should be just the happiest man in the world and would actually consent to live (and write) a century or two longer.

But don't be alarmed: such rare strokes of genius come not by practice, but by inspiration; and so far from seeking to prolong my days in the hope of some day being able to equal them, I begin to weary of existence to think they are so far beyond my power.

In fact, my only comfort under the circumstances, as already suggested, is that if I cannot shine myself, I can at least be the means of causing others to shine.

Call you all this "moonshine," Mr. Editor?

Well, then, so much the worse for you.

And, now, apropos of Max's ball, let me tell you, in confidence, that I didn't go to it; nor even to Harrison's, though, but for the dancing, I should have gone to both.

You remember Napoleon's fine expression: *Je ne danse plus, je fais danser es autres?* (I don't dance any more, I make other people dance.) Well, that's about my case, and accordingly I have not been to a ball this season, having resisted the temptation even of the Arion and the Liederkranz, not to mention the Purim.

I should have gone to Harrison's, the other night, if only to pay him my personal respects as the founder of Irving Hall, (the most liberally managed institution in town,) and to meet the host of good fellows which his name always brings together; but the thought of the dancing was too much for me, so I gave up the idea, and actually went—well *where*, do you think?

Why, of all places in the world for a Dramatic Feuilletonist, to a theatre!

Yes, and I sat nearly through the play though it lasted till after 11 o'clock, and I didn't get to Cruyt's—late Pfaff's—till too late for supper.

By the way, I told you last week that if meet me there, some day, I'd tell you "how to pronounce Kruit's"—cunningly spelling it with a "K" so as to give you an idea in advance.

Well, I repeat the invitation, and may add, now, as an additional inducement that the place is being newly painted and decorated, and will soon be one of the nicest-looking restaurants in town.

"But how about that theatre ?" you ask.

Oh yes; I had well nigh forgotten it.

Well, it was the Olympic, and the play was "The Three Guardsmen."

I can't give you the plot; but if you'll read "*Les Trois Mousquetaires*" in about a thousand pages, by Alexander Dumas, you'll know all about it.

It won't take you more than a week and I couldn't tell you the story in less than a month.

Suffice it that the play is what is called a historical one, and that to try to follow the plot as it is developed on the stage is enough to give you hysterics.

I saw the piece once in Paris, but it was before I knew a word of French, so I remember nothing but the scenery which was really superb, as it is also, by the way, at the Olympic.

In fact, we have had no play so well put upon stage this season—not even "Richelieu," at the Winter Garden, which reminds me to suggest that Mr. Hayes, the scene-painter of the Olympic, and Mr. Selwyn, the stage-manager, ought to put up their names before long for a benefit.

I know how ill-deserved benefits are, as a rule, but in the case of these gentlemen—and gentlemen they are, as well as artists, in the best sense of the term—there is but one opinion, and what that is, the play-going public are ready to show at a moment's notice.

In fact, both Hayes and Selwyn are entitled to no small reward for the manner in which they have mounted this one piece of the "Three Guardsmen," which ought to run to the end of the season on account of its pictorial attractions alone.

By a strange coincidence, however, the piece is not only well mounted but well acted. Not much can be said, to be sure, of the Richelieu of Mr. Stoddart—who, after his brilliant success all the season, ought not to have been cast in the part—but Mr. Rowe, as D'Artignan, gives us as clever a performance as has been seen in New York for years, while Mrs. Wood as Constance, and Madame Scheller as the Queen, rendered their parts so exquisitely as to call forth applause even from the coldhearted critics.

Madame Scheller, it is true, has still some trouble with her English—but her voice is so pleasant, her manner so lady-like, her " make-up "so correct, and her whole performance so refined, that you soon forget her few defects of dialect, and there remains to you only a beautiful picture, shaded throughout with the utmost delicacy, and drawn with a skill that exhibits at every point the hand of an accomplished and conscientious artist.

The three "Guardsmen" in the play are represented respectively and respectably by Mr. J. B. Studley, Mr. G. C. Boniface, and Mr. C. H. Rockwell—the latter rather too modest for a true mosquetaire, it is true, but so good-looking that he passes muster in everything.

I tell you what, my dear Press, I find good looks to be a great thing in this world: how is it with you ?

And apropos, my friend Gerhard who has just sent his splendid little portrait of George Arnold to the Academy for exhibition, tells me that if you will sit to him some one of these bright mornings, he'll make a picture of you that Harry Clifton would give a fortune for to put in his gallery: which reminds me that the portraits of the two press-swindlers whom I alluded to in a late Feuilleton bid fair to figure before long in the Metropolitan "Rogues' Gallery." (Such is life).

And speaking of galleries, Max Maretzek's, which was on view Thursday evening at the Nast ball, is likely to be remembered for a long time on account of its catalogue, which is made up in imitation of the facetiæ in the Saturday Press.

It doesn't become me to say how good (or bad) the imitation is; but I will give you a few samples, and if you can attempt anything more in that way with them on your mind (N. B. We certainly cannot. Ed. Sat. Press.) you are far less magnanimous than I had supposed.

Behold the samples!

3. A luna that cannot be eclipsed—*Bellini.*
6. His own and everybody's friend—*Kingsland.*
7. A wind instrument—*Windt.*
8. A counterfeiter of nature—*Brady.*
9. One who sticks to his friends, (a glue rious man,)—*Peter Cooper.*
10. The traveling head-centre of the opera—*Grau.*
11. A luddy-muddy-fying representative of the modern Narcissus —*Lester Wallack.*
12. The wretch who did it all—Thomas Nast.
18. The pacific mail—*L, W. Jerome.*
14. Phoenix, an early bird who catches the worm—*P. T. Barnum,*
15. Chevalier Cœlebs in search of a Miss-ion—*Wykoff.*
16. The man who Owns the apple-sass—*John Owens,*
17. The nephew of his Uncle with his toy—*Napoleon III,*
18. The Spruce (street) philosopher—*Horace Greeley.*
22. A Phillips, but not the Phillips of this establishment—*Wendell Phillips.*
23. A gallant soldier who went on expeditions by land and sea, and came safe back again—*Burnside.*
24. This lady desires to be let alone.—*Jeff. Davis.*
31. "Now is the Winter of our discontent made glorious Summer—*Sumner.*
32. All aboard for Ireland—*G. F. Train.*
34. This statue is of—*Marble.*
35. Betwixt you and me and the Post, this is—*Bryant.*
36. A fillip to the taste—*Adelaide Phillips.*
88. A popular ward in Brooklyn—*Henry Ward Beecher.*
39. Handy-Andy-Dandy—*Dan Bryant.*
40. A relic of Sumter—*Maj. Gen. Anderson.*
43. A self-appointed lecturer to the representatives of Foreign Powers—*Bancroft.*
46. No blower—*Dr. Bellows.*
47. A pastoral view of a meadow—*Meade.*
48. A celebrated Chap—in the pulpit—*Dr. Chapin.*
49. The Irish lyre, furnished by an—*Intelligence office.*

There are several others in the catalogue cribbed almost bodily from the Press; but these I omit, lest in such brilliant company they should appear to disadvantage.

The gallery itself I have not seen, but am told that it comes nearly up to the catalogue—a statement rather hard to be believed; but as the gallery will be on exhibition at to-day's Matinée, I must go and judge for myself, and at the same time (if I can withdraw my attention long enough) enjoy an act or two of "Lucrezia Borgia."

Maretzek closes his season, by the way, next week (giving "The Huguenots" for the last time on Monday), and I hear, with some alarm, that he proposes to have all the learned criticisms I have written on his different performances printed on vellum, illustrated by Nast, and bound up in a book: there's immortality for you!

After Maretzek there is a report that we are to have a short season of Grau, in order that he may "make up for his losses in Havana," which I rather think, however, have been slightly exaggerated.

While the Academy is closed, the Musical Head-Centre will be Harrison of Irving Hall, where, by the way, a capital concert is announced for this evening for the benefit of the attachés of the house, on which occasion a Big Organ—not from Boston, but from Odell of this city—will be tested for the first time by Messrs. Morgan and Warren, (grand organists, both), and there will be other performances by Mr. Theodore Thomas (violinist), Mr. S. B. Mills (pianist), Mr. F. Eben (flutist), Miss Emily Knauss (pianist), Miss Mary Abbott (soprano), Mr. L. P. Thatcher (tenor), and other artists,—making one of the choicest programmes of the season.

The next attraction at Irving Hall will be Blind Tom, the negro pianist, who will commence a series of his remarkable performances there on Monday evening next.

And this is all I have to say for the present, Mr. Editor, except that at Wallack's theatre Mr. Lester Wallack makes his first appearance for a year on Monday evening, as Young Marlow, in "She Stoops to Conquer," (repeating the same performance on Tuesday, and playing the rest of the week in "The Wonder" and "How She Loves Him"); that there will be a Cinderella Matinée at the Olympic to-day, a Dot Matinée at the Broadway, a Fanchon Matinée at Niblo's, and a Pillar of Fire one at Barnum's; and that Miss Bateman having closed her brilliant engagement in Boston, will play at the Brooklyn Academy on Monday and Tuesday next in "The Italian Wife" and "The Lady of Lyons," and on Monday week will commence a new series of performances at Niblo's, including Julia in "The Hunchback," Juliet in "Romeo and Juliet," Geraldine, Pauline, Bianca, Lady Macbeth and Leah.

All which being respectfully submitted, allow me, after inviting your special attention to the Wallack festivities of next week, to sign myself,

Yours, considerably,

Figaro.

P. S.—Grover will commence a season of German Opera at the Academy on the 16th of this month, and will be followed by Grau early in May.

NEW YORK APRIL 14, 1866

THE FLANEUR.

"Eheu! fugaces, Posthume, Posthume,
Labuntur Anni, "

I have lately been struck, more forcibly than usual, with the fact that time is constantly passing.

Though perhaps there appears nothing very new in the thought, yet it is one that very few people are aware of; sometimes it comes upon one as a discovery.

The constant recurrence of day to day comes at some period of our lives to assume the importance of new creation.

I remember how new the Bible seemed to me when I first read it in Tyndall's translation. There was a novelty and savor in the charming old English that made the book read like one I had never before seen.

It is so with all the daily details of life. At times they come to assume a new aspect and importance in our eyes. It depends upon a certain condition of mind. It is the convalescent's eager interest in the time when he can have some more thin water gruel, in which he takes a delight that the sated epicure can never feel in a "stalled ox."

The great object of life is to keep our minds in this condition. There are plenty of small concerns to occupy us, if we will only give our attention to them.

Once in my wanderings I went to the Mammoth Cave. Before starting from Louisville, I was foolish enough, as most tourists, to buy "a Guide." In it here were most grandiloquent descriptions of the wonders of the cave, of its vastness, and how no one of any feeling could contemplate them without revering the Omnipotence which had created them.

Perhaps I had no feeling, but the cave impressed me only as the biggest hole I had ever seen, like a species of conglomeration of all the railroad tunnels I had ever ridden through. The simplest insect or flower, even that curious combination of tissues which I carry always about with me, and call myself, impresses me with greater admiration and wonder of the wisdom that created all things, than a thousand caves could.

The grandest chamber is one they call the "star-chamber," because the crystals on the ceiling may when reflecting the light of the lanterns you carry with you, be made to look like the stars on a very dark night. But to my thinking the effect was only poor imitation of the original. The stars themselves are infinitely finer, but then they can be seen the whole year round, and such persons as the author of the "Guide" could not think of being struck with admiration at anything to be seen so easily and frequently.

There was once a sagacious and cautious Frenchman, of an investigating and philosophic turn of mind, which led him to wander all round this little globe, in order to gather the wisdom and the experience which an extended course of traveling is supposed to give. On his return to his native village, he was asked what he had found, and replied, that he had discovered the world was, as a general thing, peopled with men and women.

Nor were his years of travel thrown away if this was the only conclusion he had brought home with him. It is worth going round this world to find this out. Many persons return from extended wanderings without having discovered so much.

Emerson says truly that the only advantage of a collegiate education is that it makes a man never regret that he has not enjoyed it.

So to live is the gain of living:

> "Latus in prœsens animus, quod ultra est
> Oderit curare—"

After Beranger, the greatest teacher of this science of life, whom the present century has seen, was Walter Savage Landor. The evidence of it lies all through his works, and makes him the English author of the nineteenth century, whose reputation will but grow greater by the lapse of time.

They have the sap of life running through them—which will make them always of the present. The comprehensive wisdom that could grasp results, allied with an imagination that could create as accurately as scientific knowledge constructs lost species from the few fragments that time has left to us.

The notice of him in the ATLANTIC for April, though amusingly *Boston* in its cool assumption that America received its knowledge of Landor from Mr. Geo. S. Hillard's publication of Extracts from his works is excellent in the whole, but fails, signally, in this, that the writer considers Landor to have used his imaginary characters as pegs upon which to hang his own opinions. I can wish the author of that article no better wish than to become aware, through time and larger knowledge, of the wonderful reality there is in Landor's characters; of the creative imagination which moulded the materials his learning had gathered, and made living creatures of them. They are master pieces, perfect in all their accessories; creations like the portraits of Raphael or Da Vinci.

This science of life carried both Landor and Beranger beyond the limit the psalmist sets to life, young and fresh to the end.

They were great Flaneurs.

The years brought for them new life, as each spring clothes with fresh foliage the oaks, under whose youthful shade children sported a thousand years ago. One of them was rich and the other was poor, and perhaps it had been better had poverty been the lot of both of them.

There is an atmosphere about hereditary wealth in England that makes its owner become more one of a class than one of mankind.

I have paradoxically maintained with Englishmen that a gentleman was possible only in a Republic. Such an assertion is not so much a paradox, as it seems at first sight; and would be found to be quite true, could we really see a perfect Republic.

To an Englishman, with whom a gentleman is one who does no ostensible work, except it may be for pleasure, who always over pays his cab fare, and supports the established order of things, such an assertion is like being a dissenter, supporting John Bright, reading the MORNING STAR, or doing any inconceivably outrageous action, doubting the TIMES, for example.

From such a state of society it was more wonderful that Landor should have been a thorough Republican, except that as by an analogy which always holds between the moral and physical world, the richest plants grow best from the strongest muck. It was with him, too, a purely intellectual question; he followed the instinctive deductions of his reason. It came to him as odor comes to the rose; by some hidden principle of natural selection, his nature took such food and rejected everything extraneous to it. Authority was nothing to him; life was not a medicine to be taken, however nauseous, because a doctor prescribes it, but healthy food to be eaten, because it pleased his palate, and was wholesome in his mouth.

This is the rule we should all follow. Money made it easier for him than for many, but there are thousands of interests in life, into which money considerations need never enter, and should never enter; commence with these, and soon you will find yourself in harmony with

THE FLANEUR.

Dramatic Feuilleton.

BY FIGARO.

I consider the most notable event in the theatrical world this week, Mr. Editor, to be the first appearance for a twelve-month, on Monday evening last, at Wallack's Theatre, of Mr. Oliver Goldsmith and Mr. Lester Wallack.

Excuse me for putting Mr. Goldsmith's name first, but he is entitled to the honor from considerations of age and in fact, not to put too fine a point on it, from some others.

Well, there was a splendid house on the occasion, and the reception given to the two gentlemen was such as will be remembered by those of us who were present,

> While life and light and being lasts,
> And immortality endures.

This may be stating the matter rather strongly, but how else could I have brought in that splendid Sunday-school couplet?

But really, Sir, the reception was one to be remembered, and if Mr. Oliver were here or Mr. Lester—I would give him a nosegay on the spot in token of congratulation: for you see Mr. Oliver is one of my earliest acquaintances, and though I did'nt have the honor of knowing Mr. Lester till some forty or fifty years after, it has always been more or less pleasant for me to associate their two names together.

O! I came well nigh forgetting to say that the first appearance, etc., etc., above alluded to was celebrated by the performance of Mr. Oliver's "She Stoops to Conquer," in which Mr. Lester played the part of Young Marlow—Miss Henriques of Miss Neville—Miss Gannon of Miss Hardcastle—Mrs. Vernon of Mrs. Hardcastle—Mr. John Gilbert of Mr. Hardcastle—Mr. George Holland of Tony Lumpkin—Mr. Young of Diggory, and so on: a regular Wallack cast, which is about equivalent to saying the best cast the times afford.

Mr. O. G. and I, it is true, can hardly consent to the manner in which, of late, most of the characters are overdrawn, making the play more like a farce than a comedy; but still, all things considered—the temptation to excite applause—the want of nice discrimination on the part of audiences—the growing tendency, especially on the American stage, in favor of caricature and extravagance—we are content to approve what is good (and at Wallack's there is much which is excellent) letting the bad correct itself according to the intelligence and refinement of the public.

I think that, on the whole, my old friend Mrs. Centlivre, who appeared at Wallack's for the first time this season on Wednesday, had a better time of it than Goldsmith: her charming play of "The Wonder," was performed on the occasion, in a style almost approaching high art.

Mr. Lester, of course, depicted Don Felix (adding but few colors this time from his own pallet) while Col. Britton was given to Mr. Fisher—Don Pedro to Mr. Holland—Lissardo to Mr. Young—Donna Violante to Miss Henriques—Inez to Miss Burke—and Isabella to Mrs. Jennings—all of whom were in their best mood, and played as if they knew Mrs. C. and I were there to applaud them.

The third great attraction at Wallack's this week has been Boucicault's "How She Loves Him," which was played on one of my off-nights, (Thursday), but will be repeated to-night when I hope to see it.

Next week (commencing on Tuesday evening, I believe,) we are to have "Don Cæsar de Bazan"—with Mr. Wallack as Don Cæsar.

That, of course, I shall see.

The other theatres, etc., may be disposed of in a few paragraphs.

At Niblo's, Miss Maggie Mitchell closes her series of wierd performances this evening in her pet character of Fanchon: and on Monday Miss Bateman commences a new engagement with her great rôle of Julia in "The Hunchback," which she will play all the week. You can imagine the welcome that awaits her. In the course of her engagement, Miss Bateman will play, besides Julia, Juliet, Geraldine, Pauline, Bianca, Lady Macbeth, and Leah: and, no doubt, will achieve another series of triumphs.

At the Olympic, the play of "The Three Guardsmen," with its splendid cast and superb scenery will be continued until further notice.

At the Academy of Music, Maretzek will close his brilliant season this afternoon with Meyerbeer's Opera of the Huguenots. Next week Mr. Grover takes the house for a short season of German opera, commencing on Tuesday evening with Gounod's "Faust," which will be followed on Wednesday evening by Rossini's "William Tell;" the two operas being cast as follows:—

FAUST.

Mephistopheles	Joseph Herrmans
Faust	Franz Himmer
Marguerite	Mme. Johanna Rotter
Siebel	Mlle. Sophia Dziuba
Valentin	Heinrich Steinecke

WILLIAM TELL.

Mathilde	Mme. Johanna Rotter
Jemimy	Mlle Sophia Dziuba
William Tell	Wilhelm Formes
(His first appearance in opera in this city.)	
Arnold Melchthal	Franz Himmer
Jacques	Theodore Habelman
Walther Furst	Joseph Hermans
Gessler	Joseph Weinlich
Melchthal Urchs	Leuthold Lehman
Rudolph Haimer	Hedwig Mme Pickaneser

Among the other operas to be given are "The Merry Wives of Windsor," "Les Huguenots," "Fidelio," "La Dame Blanche," "Fra Diavolo," "Magic Flute," and "Tannhauser." A grand chorus has been engaged, and the services of Graffula's Seventh Regiment Band.

At Irving Hall, Blind Tom, the negro pianist, will continue to give his marvellous imitations, improvisations, etc., all next week.

At Wood's Theatre, Miss Lucille Western closed her engagement last night, in "Lucrezia Borgia" and "The Honeymoon." Miss Western has given us a series of remarkable performances, attaining in certain character-parts all but the highest point in dramatic art.

At Barnum's, the scriptural play of "Moses; or, Israel in Egypt" continues to draw immense crowds every afternoon and evening, and bids fair to be continued to the end of the season. In point of scenic effect, it is one of most attractive pieces ever put on the New York boards.

Finally, Mr. Editor, don't forget that Mr. and Mrs. Charles Kean make their last appearance in this country on Monday evening next, at the Academy of Music, and that you can then have the opportunity of seeing one of the greatest pieces of acting known to any stage—to wit, Mr. Kean's Louis XI.

If I could afford it, I would send every actor and actress in town a free ticket, and pay any forfeit they might incur for staying away from their respective theatres.

Figaro.

P. S. To-morrow night (Saturday) there will be a grand Sacred Concert at Irving Hall for the purpose of bringing out the beauties of Odell's new organ: the organist of the occasion will be Mr. Morgan; the singers, Mrs. Abbott, (soprano) Mr. Castle, (tenor) and Mr. Lumbard (basso).

NEW YORK APRIL 21, 1866

(For the Saturday Press.)

THE FLANEUR.

Majorum nuga negotia vocantur.

"The trifles of adults are called business."

Saint Augustine is the author of this statement, and he is good authority.

No doubt the pious old saint, in the calm quiet of his religious retirement, must have been often struck with the futility of the troubles and cares which excited his contemporaries.

The old man, however, spoke not as one without experience in such matters; his "Confessions" go to show that he had tested personally most of the emotions and anxieties which go to make up human life. With Schiller's disconsolate he could exclaim:

Ich habe gelebt und geliebet.

In his day the natural and handy refuge of a Flaneur, with an ascetic or contemplative turn of mind, was the cloister: it was a common opinion then that the only way of conquering the world was by running away from it.

Not a very brave course of action, and generally as unsuccessful as it is cowardly.

Somehow they found they were none the less men in the cloisters than they were out of them; the same out of them; the same small ambitions follow small men wherever they go.

If we had the confessions of Saint Simon Stylites we would doubtless find that he was as morbid as Rousseau.

All the authentic accounts we have, show that the monks were anything but a set of men who passed their lives in a constant state of religious enthusiasm; it seems very silly to us that they should have hoped, by isolating themselves, to have gained a state of constant peace and happiness.

And yet the same folly exists to-day; every one of us has an idea of some condition in which we will be as perfectly happy and contented when we attain it, as the boy expected to be when he grew up and became his own master sufficiently to suck candy and swing on a gate all day.

There was once a great potentate in Persia, who was seized with a nameless disease: nothing could please him: he was discontented and unhappy: all the men in his dominions who were famed for their learning in psychology, were called into consultation, and their final result was that his High Magnificence could be cured only by wearing the shirt of a contented man.

Thereupon was instituted a great search through all the potentate's dominions, until finally a contented man was found; but lo! the happy fellow was so poor that he had no shirt.

Fortunately for him he lived in Persia: here he would have been a vagrant, and treated to lodgings in the nearest police station.

We should do the same, doubtless, with a Diogenes if he proposed living in a tub; none of our police justices would, probably, consider it any defence for such eccentricity that the man who attempted it was the founder of a new sect in philosophy.

But if it were a Diogenes he would be quite as happy in the station house cell as elsewhere: and such a truly philosophic revenge would secure his victory.

It would be a most amusing contest—the Nineteenth Century in the person of a Police Justice, and the philosophers in the person of Diogenes! Were I a sporting man, I would be willing to give large odds against the Justice.

And yet the victory would be but a barren one for Diogenes. His success would be as worthless as most success gained in the struggle of life, unless he was a man to whom such contests formed the whole that life could offer: but then he would no longer be Diogenes.

I remember a friend whom I once found anxious and preoccupied: he told me he had been so for some time: on questioning him I found that he was anxious about the pork market: he had engaged in a pork speculation.

"Why did you do so?" I asked.

"I thought I should make some money out of it."

"But if you did, would it pay you for the anxiety? You do not really want it: you have enough to do without this, and you are not fitted for it: you are not a man to limit every possibility in life, to contract all the interests worth living for, to an anxiety concerning the pork market. Let those engage in such matters to whom the world can offer nothing better: there are men to whom fighting is an excitement and a pleasure: who would rather fight than dine: let them find their pleasure in it, but do not engage in it yourself. A defeat to you is disastrous and a victory is worse than a defeat would be to them. You must come out of it bearing marks of the contest, which perhaps you cannot get rid of by simply shifting your clothes: nor could a victory ever prove a satisfaction to you."

He acknowledged the truth of what I said, perhaps, because his enterprise looked like a failure, and the last time I saw him he was speculating in petroleum.

We were young men together, when the world and the future looked to us as the world and the future look to all young men—so vague that we were careless of it, leaving it to come to us in its time, but making of our health and strength a pleasure and a delight, finding enough in each day's trifles as it was passing, and leaving the morrow to care for itself. Now, my friend has an ambition, and his pork speculation was one of rounds of the ladder by which he sought to climb up to the platform where he promises himself ease and freedom from care, happiness and a life that is but the maturity of that which we led when youths, while I—well I sign myself

THE FLANEUR.

NEW YORK APRIL 28, 1866

THE TOILERS OF THE SEA.

Hugo, Victor. Toilers of the Sea., Sampson Low, Son & Marston, London, 1866.

"Religion, Society, Nature—such are the three struggles which man has to carry on . . . . The mysterious difficulty of life springs from all the three. Man meets with hindrance in his life in the shape of superstition, in the shape of prejudice, and in the shape of element. A triple fatality (*ananké*) oppresses us, the fatality of dogmas, of laws, of things. . . . . With these three which thus enfold man there mingles that inner fatality, the supreme Ananké, the human heart." As in *Notre Dame de Paris* we saw the working of these contests, and in *Les Misérables* the resistless pressure of the second, in *Les Travailleurs de la Mer* we are asked to watch man contending with external nature, and then crushed by the supreme fatality of all, the irresistible Ananké in the heart of man. The story which illustrates this tremendous strife has that simplicity and that perfect finish which only the powerful hand of a master can compass. A fisherman encounters all the fury and caprice and treachery of outer nature in order to win a woman whom, on his return, he finds to have, unconsciously but irrevocably, lost her heart to another. But this plainest of stories is worked into genuine tragedy by an exercise of poetic power which, in some portions at least of its display, has very rarely been surpassed in literature. We may notice here, in passing, that the English translation is a singularly indifferent performance, which gives the reader very little notion of the force of the original. The translator is constantly making downright blunders, and, when he does not blunder, is exceedingly weak. It seems the fate of illustrious Frenchmen, Emperors and Republicans alike, to meet incompetent translators in this country. It may be admitted that in the present instance the difficulties in the way of a good translation are sufficiently numerous. The book is not wholly free from what the world has agreed to consider the characteristic defects of its writer. His fondness for the display of minute knowledge of names and dates and events inflicts on the reader tedious catalogues, which are not valuable in themselves, and which interfere with the artistic effect besides. Accuracy of local coloring, too, scarcely demands those long lists of rocks and creeks in the Channel Islands which are forgotten as soon as read. And an English reader wonders how the author came to write, as he does repeatedly, *le Bug-Pipe*, when he means the Bag-pipes; or, still more amazing and impossible, *le premier de la quatrième* as French for *the Firth of Forth*—which is almost incredible as the old story of *poitrine de calecons* for "chest of drawers." Those, again, who cannot forgive Victor Hugo for his *staccato* style of writing, which makes each sentence come on us like a pellet shot from a gun, will find at least as much cause of offence as ever. But if there are these and other old flaws and imperfections, there is also a power, a depth, a sublimity which the author has scarcely reached before, either in his prose or his verse.

The subject is the most suitable for his own genius that he has ever chosen. When he illustrated the bitter destiny which overwhelms the social outcast, he wrote with the air of the philosopher who views life through the understanding, but he was in truth writing in the spirit of the poet who sees things through his emotions. This made *Les Misérables* a splendid and affecting picture, and gave it that air of presenting life and reality as a whole which was its most conspicuous mark. But it was felt that the sensibilities of the poet had been engaged all on one side, and that they were so strong as to sweep away all considerations of the function which society exists to discharge, and of the kind and quantity of instruments which are the only ones to her hand. Moreover, whenever anybody speaks of the irresistible weight of social laws, we feel that they are only irresistible in a sense; and, still more important, we feel that they are capable of such an amelioration by slow steps as shall leave none but bad men burdened by their prescriptions. But the Fatality of Nature is different from the so-called Fatality of Society. The forces of the merciless ocean and the winds, the inhospitable solitudes of the searocks, the fierce cruelty of the sea-monsters, are what they are. By no taking thought can man mollify the tempest or mitigate the fury of the storm. He adds to the number of his devices for escaping from the ferocity of nature, but the winds rage and the waters are tossed, and the monsters seek their victims just the same. The terrors of the waves may well be called inexorable, and in them, therefore, the poet finds a more appropriate theme than was afforded by the evils of society, which for their cure or right understanding demand, not the poetic, but the scientific mind. We may discern the greater fitness of the present subject for Victor Hugo's genius in the more perfect truthfulness of the man who contends with the Fatality of Nature. Jean Valjean who had to contend with the Fatality of Laws, was thoroughly artificial. His virtue and perseverance and patience wore in a manner overdone. His character was created for a purpose, and the presence of this purpose could not be concealed. The good Bishop was just as artificial. Gilliatt, on the contrary, is very carefully and elaborately drawn, but all his traits are simple and natural. He is surrounded with no unreal halo, though he is remote enough from commonplace. "He was only a poor man, who knew how to read and write; most likely he stood on the limit which divides the dreamer from the thinker. The thinker wills, the dreamer is passive . . . . The obscurity in which his mind was wrapped consisted in pretty nearly equal parts of two elements, both dimly visible, but very unlike; in his own breast ignorance, infirmity; outside himself mystery, immensity." "Solitude makes either a genius or an idiot. Gilliatt presented himself under both aspects. Sometimes he had that astonished air I have mentioned, and you might have taken him for a brute; at other moments he had in his eye a glance of indescribable profundity." A very superficial critic might say that Gilliatt is only Jean Valjean in another dress. In reality, there is only the resemblance between them that is inevitable in two characters each of whom is more or less shunned by his fellows, and each of whom is engaged in deadly struggle with one of the three forms of what the author calls Ananké. At bottom, however, they are two quite distinct conceptions. Gilliatt is the more satisfactory of the two, because to draw a man with great muscular strength, and great ingenuity and great patience of the mechanical order, is easier, and less likely to tempt the artist into what is fantastic and artificial, than the conception of a victim of a supposed social injustice which is no injustice at all. This advantage of having a simpler plot, a more natural set of circumstances, and, above all, of having nothing to prove, is conspicuous all through. It leaves the author free to work out each of his characters completely, free to paint what is the main subject of his work with an undivided energy and enthusiasm. Perhaps, though, in one way this tells against him. The stupendous force of the descriptions of Nature and her works and laws—the theme of the book—is so overpowering that the incidents of the story and the interests of the people in it seem petty by comparison. There is probably a design in this disproportion. The vastness of the unmeasured forces which labor and rage in the universe outside the minds of mortals is what the self-importance of mortals pleasingly blinds them to. It is the eye of the poet which discerns this, and through nearly every page of Victor Hugo's story we hear, as a ceaseless refrain to the loves and aspirations and toils of his good men and his knaves alike, the swirling of the of the sea-winds and "far-reaching murmur of the deep."

The grandeur of the long episode of Gilliatt recovering the machinery of the steam-boat from the terrific rock may make us forget the singular power of the earlier scene at the same spot, where Sieur Clubin found himself, "in the midst of the fog and the waters, far from every human sound, left for dead, alone with the sea which was rising, and the night which was approaching, and filled with a profound joy." The analysis of this joy of the scoundrel and hypocrite at finding himself free to enjoy the fruits of his scoundrelism and to throw aside the burdensome mask of his hypocrisy, is powerful to a degree which makes one smile at the lavishness with which credit for power is so constantly given to novelists and poets. The dramatic force of the situation, the appalling mistake which the scoundrel has made, the sanguineness and shiftiness with which, like all hypocrites, he seeks to repair it, the swift and amazing vengeance which overtakes him, has perhaps never been surpassed. And the horror is not theatrical or artificial. The spot is brought vividly before us by no tricks, but by genuine imaginative power. The rock on which Clubin has, against his intention, driven the steamboat is a block of granite, brutal and hideous to behold, offering only the stern inhospitable shelter of an abyss. At its foot, far below the water, are caverns and mazes of dim passages. "Here monstrous species propagate, here they destroy one another. Crabs eat the fish and are themselves eaten. Fearful shapes, made to be seen by no human eye, roam in this dim light, living their lives. Vague outline of open jaws, antenæ, scale, fins, claws, are there floating about, trembling, growing, decomposing, vanishing in the sinister clearness of the wave. . . . . . To look into the depth of the sea is to behold the imagination of the Unknown on its terrible side. The gulf is like night. There, too, is a slumber, a seeming slumber, of the conscience of creation. There, in full security, are accomplished crimes of the irresponsible. There, in a baleful peace, the embryos of life, almost phantoms, altogether demons, are busy at the fell occupations of the gloom."—The minute yet profoundly poetic description of the most terrible of these monsters, in a succeeding part of the book, is one which nobody who has once read it, can forget, any more than the horrors of the *Inferno* of Dante can be forgotten. The *pieuvre* at one extremity of the chain of existence "almost proves a Satan at the other." "Optimism, which is true for all that, almost loses countenance before it . . . . . . Every malignant creature, like every perverse intelligence, is a sphinx, propounding the terrible riddle, the riddle of evil." What is their law? "All created beings return one into another. *Pourriture c'est nourriture*. Frightful purifying of the globe. Man, too, carnivorous man, is a satyr. Our life is made of death. Such is the terrifying law. We are sepulchres." But we are not quite left here. "Mais tâchons que la mort nous soit progrés. Aspirons aux mondes moins ténebreux. Suivons la conscience qui nous y méme. Car, ne l'oublious jamais, le mieux n'est trouvé que par le meilleur."

It will be seen from this that Victor Hugo is not affected by the sea as other poets have been. Of course, nobody expected to find him talking silly nonsense about its moaning over the harbor-bar while men must work and women must weep, or reducing the sea and the winds to the common drawing-room measure of polished sentimental prettiness. Here, as elsewhere, the terrible side of Nature is that which has the most attraction for him. Only here he seems to have been unusually insensible to the existence of her other aspect. Take the well-known picture of "The Toad" in the *Legend des Siècles*. The hideous creature is squatting in the road in a summer evening, enjoying himself after his humble fashion. Some boys pass by, and amuse themselves by digging out its eyes, striking off its limbs, making holes in it. The wretched toad tries feebly to crawl away into the ditch. Its tormentors see an ass coming on, drawing a cart, so, with a scream of delight, they bethink themselves to put the toad in the rut where it will be crushed by the wheel of the cart. The ass is weary with his day's work and his burden, and sore with the blows of his master, who even then is cursing and bethwacking him. But the ass turns his gentle eye upon the rut, sees the torn and bleeding toad, and with a painful effort drags his cart off the track. The whole picture gives one a heartache, but the gentleness of the ass is the single touch which makes the thought of so much horror endurable. In the "Toilers of the Sea" we almost miss this single touch. Watching the sea year after year in the land of his exile, Victor Hugo has seen in it nothing but sternness and cruelty. He finds it only the representative of the relentless Fatality of Nature which man is constantly occupied in combating and wrestling with. It is so real, so tragically effective, that such a reflection as that "Time writes no wrinkle on its azure brow" must seem the merest mimicry of poetic sentiment. The attitude which he has before assumed towards Society he also takes towards external Nature. To Keats Nature presented herself as a being whom even the monsters loved and followed, a goddess with white and smooth limbs, and deep breasts, teeming with fruit and oil and corn and flowers. Compared with the sensuous passion of Keats, the feeling of Wordsworth for Nature was an austere and distant reverence. He found in her little more than a storehouse of emblems for the better side of men. Victor Hugo is impressed by Nature, not as a goddess to be sensuously enclasped, not as some remote and pure spirit, shining cold yet benign upon men, but as man's cruel and implacable foe. Other poets have loved to make her anthropomorphic, and to invest her with the moral attributes of mortals. He holds with no such personification of Nature as a whole. Nature to him is little more than a chaos of furious and warring forces. The prolonged and sublime description of the storm at the beginning of the third volume is what nobody but Victor Hugo could have conceived, because nobody else is so penetrated with a sense of the fierce eternal conflict which to him is all that Nature means. Take the tramp of the legion of the winds, for instance: "In the solitudes of space they drive the great ships; without a truce, by day and by night, in every season, at the tropic and at the pole, with the deadly blast of their trumpet, sweeping through the thickets of the clouds and billows, they pursue their black chase of the ships. They have fierce hounds for their slaves. They make sport for themselves. Among the waters and the rocks they set their hounds to bark. They mould the clouds together, and they rive them in sunder. As with a million hands, they knead the boundless supple waters." The gigantic wave, again, at a later period of the storm, "which was a sum of forces, and had, as it were, the mien of a living being. You could almost fancy in that swelling transparent mass the growth of fins and gills. It spread itself forth, and then in fury dashed itself in pieces against the breakwater. Its monstrous shape was all ragged and torn in the rebound. There was left on the block of granite and timber the huge destruction of some portentous hydra. The surge spread ruin in its own expiring moment. The wave seemed to clutch and devour. A shudder quivered through the rock. There was a sound as of some growling monster, the froth was like the foaming mouth of a leviathan."

It has been said that the sublime picture of the storm—and the variety and movement in the picture are among its most splendid characteristics—makes us indifferent to the conclusion of the story. The truth is, that but for this the conclusion would be absurdly weak and unintelligible. It is the long exile of Gilliatt on the fierce rock in the isolation of the sea, his appalling struggles with all the forces of Nature in temporary alliance against him, which make the very gist and force of the final tragedy, the supreme Fatality.

(For the Saturday Press.)

THE FLANEUR.

Nos patriæ fines et dulcia linquimus arva;
Nos patriam fugimus.

If there is anything to test the philosophic calmness of a Flaneur, it is the necessity of moving on the First of May.

Victor Hugo has finely described the agony of expectation of a certain misfortune, approaching as inevitably as time and as inexorably as fate, in his *Derniers Jours d'un condamné.*

My own ill fortune brings forcibly to mind the dreadful future in store for myself and all my fellow sufferers who shall be forced to "move" on the approaching First of May.

Why on earth out of the entire three hundred and sixty-five days in the year, should this one have been chosen for the annual hejira of those who are unfortunately in the position of tenants ?

It is the day of the earth's regeneration, and was the commencement of the Roman Saturnalia, and is celebrated in all poetry as the birth of Spring.

But alas! here in this sad city we must be all called early on that morning for a very different purpose than partaking in the festivities of a May celebration, or possibly acting as consort to the Queen of the May.

The romance and sentiment connected with this real commencement of the year is sadly destroyed by making it what it is in this city.

It would be singular to study the influence upon a man of poetic nature of a childhood whose celebrations of its young May days were only movings.

It may not seem much to us, but in reality these youthful associations go very far towards making up the character of men.

Imagine a child whose Christmas brought only some such association to his mind, instead of the happy meeting of the family, the gifts, the tree, and all the little nothings that go to make that day at least a cheerful one.

How much of literature would be a dead letter for him? How impossible it would be for him to enter familiarly into the hilarity of the occasion? He would always feel like a stranger and intruder.

This season of the year is one when the glory and beauty of nature are most impressed upon the mind, for at this time we are in the condition to receive its influence.

We have just about recovered from the dreariness of winter; the windows can now be left open; the ladies appear in their spring silks and new bonnets: the exquisites promenade resplendent in suits of light colors; a white hat does not look out of place, and imagination can entertain without a shiver the pect of a straw hat and a blue ribbon. And then, too, the days are so splendid, so clear and clean, that a natural impulse is to renew our youth, and with the trees put forth a fresh new foliage of hopes and resolves.

Johnson used to say that he had no patience with a man who pretended that the weather had any influence upon him; but Johnson was hardly a man upon whom anything would have much influence—a bluff, burly man, with not acute senses, careless of his eating, near-sighted, introspective, and self-invoked, he was probably affected but very little by the weather.

His religion also was of that kind which supposes that virtue is abnegation; that men to be perfect must resemble the close-cropped trees and shrubs of a Dutch garden, rather than the graceful irregularities of natural growth.

But a man of sensibility cannot help being impressed with the fresh warmth of spring. It has a natural force that none of the "modern improvements" can imitate; it enters into the very marrow of the bones as no stove, nor furnace, nor open fire, can ever do; it is genial, natural, healthy, while the others are artificial, and, at best, only more or less successful imitations.

Now that the result of our boasted civilization should have resulted only in forcing us, at the period when we are fresh for its enjoyment, into having communion with nature, to mix with landlords, lodging-house keepers, carmen, porters, and the swarm of such parasitical insects, who live upon the miseries of the body politic, is a mortification and disgrace to every well-intentioned man.

Such occasions as this present make us envy the asceticism of our old friend, Simon Stylites; for him the revolving years brought no First of May; passing his entire life open to the gaze of the world, it was never imperative for him to display his lares and penates, his pots and pans, to the unsympathizing inspection of a scoffing crowd.

No vulgar hands were ever laid upon the holy of holies of his domestic life; secure on the top of his column, he let the busy world pass by, and kept his place, holding his soul in quiet.

Such occasions as the First of May mortify as with the inexorable evidence of how artificial our life is, how different from that of Diogenes, who threw away his only piece of furniture, a drinking-cup, when he saw a child use his hand as one. The beasts are our superiors in this matter: they have no artificial wants; they are self-poised, and carry all that they want about with them.

When the early discoverers of this country first approached the islands they were confounded with the life of the men they found there; and no wonder that they were.

Think of a life with the atmosphere for a wardrobe, the sea for a bath, the breeze for a towel, the trees for your larder, the sun for your cooking-range, and the sward for your couch. These are all the absolute necessities of life ready at hand, and only waiting to be used.

Nor is it necessary in the nature of things that those who lead such lives should want the refinements of life; what is wanting is not to educe civilization from such conditions, but to reduce civilization to such a state of things.

Then the largest prudence is carelessness of the morrow.

Being men, not machines—living as men, not working mechanically—growing happy rather than growing rich—gaining wisdom rather than money—"moving" but once, and then into heavenly mansions, where there is no moth, nor rust, nor thieves.

THE FLANEUR.

NEW YORK MAY 5, 1866

(For the Saturday Press.)

THE FLANEUR.

Nomine mutato de te fabula narratur.

There was once upon a time, when the earth was young, a great King who was a philosopher and had a taste for mechanics, and who one day, in a merry mood, mounted the blade of an iron jack knife in a splendid razor handle made of ivory inlaid with mother-of-pearl. And when the work was all done, he called it the King's razor, and as a great mark of special favor to his courtiers, would lend it to them for their own shaving.

And so finally the great object in life to the ambitious men of the court came to be gaining the favor of shaving with the King's razor: and among the common people the highest claim to honor and consideration was having shaved with the King's razor.

Now it was obligatory for those who obtained this honor to shave themselves with the King's razor and not to use any other.

Of course it was a most painful thing to use: it scraped and hacked and never could do the work as easily or well as an ordinary razor, but then it was the King's razor, and it was an honor to have used it.

The very scratches that it made, and the ragged character imparted to the beard it was used to shave, were considered marks of distinction and evidences of superiority.

Meanwhile the King, in his secret soul, made merry at the folly of his subjects, and laughed in his sleeve to see not only the common people so deceived and misled, but even his grey-bearded councillors, his men of gravity and deportment, as eager as any in the pursuit of so vain an honor, and even more strenuous in their praise of the custom as being one of the most necessary and important for its preservative and moral effect upon society.

The scoffers—there will always be some such light-minded people—said that this last opinion of the men of gravity and deportment came from the fact that they and their class were most commonly the recipients of this favor: but such insinuations were of course unfounded.

Among themselves, when certain of their security, the men of gravity and deportment sometimes complained to each other that after all the King's razor did not shave as clean as a common one would do; but to the outside world they always maintained the contrary; and this because they felt that they owed a certain duty of example to the people, and that the established order of society would be disorganized should they, who receive its benefits, treat them lightly.

And so the custom went on, increasing daily in strength.

But the King had, what few kings have, a friend : one who let his beard grow, and, therefore, never wanted a razor even of the ordinary kind, and whom the King liked to talk with, because he treated him as if he was only a man, and spoke his opinion when asked for it even in the very kingly presence.

With this friend the King spoke freely of his new custom and together they made merry over its success.

"But what will you do," asked his friend one day, "Should the people grow wise enough to find that the whole thing is an absurdity?"

"Oh, my good fellow," replied the King, "in that event, they would be like you, and would have no further use of me."

Perhaps this society exists until now, though I do not remember to have seen any very recent accounts of it by travelers.

It would be curious to make a visit there, and see whether the accounts, as I have given them, are true.

And yet such curious creatures are we of habit, that, perhaps, if we made a visit of any duration among such a people, we would find ourselves in a short time eager in the same chase, and proud of having gained the same honor.

It would seem to us something glorious to have used the King's razor. If the same energy and labor now expended in gaining trifles which represent all that they are, were spent in gaining trifles which represented the performance of something useful, it is evident how much society would be the gainer, even from the follies of individuals.

The only difficulty is how to so organize and arrange matters, that this result may be obtained.

It will certainly be done some time or other.

Perhaps I could tell you how, but then, as with my friend the king, I am aware that if ever the world arrived at that point, it would have no further place for

THE FLANEUR.

NEW YORK MAY 12, 1866

THE BOY THAT BORE A CHARMED LIFE.

BY MARK TWAIN.

Once there was a bad little boy, whose name was Jim—though, if you will notice, you will find that bad little boys are nearly always called James in your Sunday-school books. It is very strange, but very true, that this one was called Jim.

He didn't have any sick mother, either—a sick mother who was pious and had consumption, and would be glad to lie down in the grave and be at rest, but for the strong love she bore her boy, and the anxiety she felt that the world would be harsh and cold toward him when she was gone. Most bad boys in the Sunday books are named James, and have sick mothers who teach them to say, "Now I lay me down," etc., and then sing them to sleep with sweet plaintive voices, and then kiss them good night, and kneel down by the bedside and weep.

But it was different with this fellow. He was named Jim, and there wasn't anything the matter with his mother—no consumption, or anything of that kind. She was rather stout than otherwise, and she was not pious; moreover, she was not anxious on Jim's account; she said if he were to break his neck, it wouldn't be much loss; she always spanked him to sleep, and she never kissed him good-night; on the contrary, she boxed his ears when she was ready to leave him.

Once, this bad little boy stole the key of the pantry, and slipped in there and helped himself to some jam, and filled the vessel up with tar, so that his mother would never know the difference; but all at once a terrible feeling didn't come over him, and something didn't seem to whisper to him, "Is it right to disobey my mother? Isn't it sinful to do this? Where do bad little boys go to who gobble up their kind mother's jam?" and then he didn't kneel down all alone, and promise never to be wicked any more, and rise up with a light, happy heart, and go and tell his mother everything about it and beg her forgiveness, and be blessed by her with tears of pride and thankfulness in her eyes. No; that is the way with all other bad boys in the books, but it happened otherwise with this Jim, strangely enough. He ate that jam, and said it was bully, in his sinful, vulgar way; and he put in the tar, and said it was bully, also, and laughed and observed that "the old woman would get up and snort" when she found it out; and when she did find it out he denied knowing anything about it, and she whipped him severely, and he did the crying himself. Everything about this boy was curious—everything turned out differently with him from the way it does to the bad Jameses in the books.

Once he climbed up in Farmer Acorn's apple-tree to steal apples, and the limb didn't break, and he didn't fall and break his arm, and get torn by the farmer's great dog, and then languish on a sick bed for weeks and repent and become good. Oh, no—he stole as many apples as he wanted, and came down all right, and he was all ready for the dog, too, and knocked endways with a rock when he came to tear him.

It was very strange: nothing like it ever happened in those mild little books with marbled backs and with pictures in them of men with swallow-tailed coats and bell-crowned hats, and pantaloons that are short in the legs, and women with the waists of their dresses under their arms and no hoops on. Nothing like it in any of the Sunday school books.

Once he stole the teacher's penknife, and when he was afraid it would be found out and he would be whipped, he slipped it into George Wilson's cap—poor Widow Wilson's son, the moral boy, the good little boy of the village, the boy who always obeyed his mother, and never told an untruth, and was fond of his lessons and infatuated with the Sunday school. And when the knife dropped from the cap, and poor George hung his head and blushed, as if in conscious guilt, and the grieved teacher charged the theft upon him, and was just in the act of bringing the switch down on his trembling shoulders, a whitehaired improbable justice of the peace didn't suddenly appear in their midst and strike an attitude and say—"Spare this noble boy,—there stands the cowering culprit! I was passing the school door at recess, and, unseen myself, saw the theft committed !" And then Jim didn't get whaled, and the venerable justice didn't read the tearful school a homily, and take George by the hand, and say such a boy deserved to be exalted, and then tell him to come and make his home with him, and sweep out the office, and make fires and run errands, and chop wood and study law, and help his wife to do household labors, and have all the balance of the time to play, and get forty cents a month, and be happy. No; it would have happened that way in the books, but it didn't happen that way to Jim. No meddling old clam of justice dropped in to make trouble, and so the model boy George got thrashed, and Jim was glad of it. Because, you know, Jim hated moral boys. Jim said he "was down on milksops." Such was the coarse language of this bad, neglected boy.

But the strangest thing that ever happened to Jim was the time when he went boating on Sunday and didn't get drowned, and that other time that he got caught out in the storm when he was fishing on Sunday, and didn't get struck by lightning. Why, you might look, and look, and look through the Sunday school books, from now to next Christmas, and you would never come across anything like this. O, no—you would find that all the bad boys who go boating on Sunday invariably get drowned, and all the bad boys who get caught out in storms, when they are fishing on Sunday, infallibly get struck by lightning. Boats with bad boys in them always get upset on Sunday, and it always storms when bad boys go fishing on the Sabbath. How this Jim ever escaped is a mystery to me.

This Jim bore a charmed life—that must have been the way of it. Nothing could hurt him. He even gave the elephant in the menagerie a plug of tobacco, and the elephant didn't knock the top of his head off with his trunk. He browsed around the cupboard after essence of peppermint, and didn't make a mistake and drink aquafortis.

He stole his father's gun and went hunting on the Sabbath, and didn't shoot three or four of his fingers off. He struck his little sister on the temple with his fist when he was angry, and she didn't linger in pain through long summer days and die with sweet words of forgiveness upon her lips that redoubled the anguish of his breaking heart. No—she got over it. He ran off and went to sea at last, and didn't come back and find himself sad and alone in the quiet churchyard, and the vine-embowered home of boyhood tumbled down and gone to decay. Ah, no—he came home as drunk as a piper, and got into the station house the first thing.

And he grew up, and married; and raised a large family, and brained them all with an axe one night, and got wealthy by all manner of cheating and rascality, and now he is the infernalist wickedest scoundrel in his native village, and is universally respected, and belongs to the Legislature.

So you see there never was a bad James in the Sunday school books that had such a streak of luck as this sinful Jim with the charmed life.

Dramatic Feuilleton.

BY FIGARO.

Allow me, my dear PRESS, to congratulate those of my brother critics who are shocked at the prevailing frivolity of the stage, that at last we have a play before us which can boast of a "great moral purpose."

I refer, of course, to Mr. Charles Reade's "Never too Late to Mend," which has just entered upon its edifying career at Wallack's, and which I respectfully recommend to the clergymen now in town attending the anniversaries.

I am not much shocked myself at the frivolity of the stage because, as you know, I entertain the heresy that theatres are chiefly useful as being places of amusement.

Still, I have no objection to a "great moral purpose," and, in fact, am so sound on the subject, that some time ago I advised Barnum to announce among his other curiosities a "great moral porpoise": not but what porpoises are always moral enough in their way, only it seemed to me that many people would read purpose for porpoise, and would thus get the idea that the Museum was a sort of chapel.

I assure you, Sir, that the moral dodge is a great thing: Van Amburg used to think so much of it that on reading one of his advertisements you would think his lions and tigers were members of the church, and his monkeys pupils of a Sunday-school.

But now, then, Mr. Editor, to be just, all this has nothing to do with Charles Reade's "Never too Late to Mend," which, though it *has* a " great moral purpose," is a very legitimate drama for all that, and is better worth seeing than any other theatrical show in town: better worth *seeing*, perhaps, than *hearing*, for the text has nothing very remarkable about it while the scenery and, in fact, all the stage appointments may, without exaggeration, be called exquisite.

The pastoral scene in the first act—with the stable, dog-kennel, pigeon-house, etc.—not to mention the poney, the dog, and the pigeons—present about as natural and pleasing a picture as I have ever seen on the stage.

On the night of the second representation, by the way, one of the pigeons got into a scrape, and but for the prompt intervention of a young gentleman in the audience—who made his maiden speech on the occasion, and insisted that the play should be stopped till the bird was placed out of danger—would probably have been killed.

I recommend the gentleman to the approval of the "Society for the Prevention of Cruelty to Animals," and at the same time beg to compliment him on his speech which, if a well-known axiom be true, represented the "soul of wit."

I doubt if either General Dix or General Grant would have done better: and when the ten-second rule is adopted in Congress I shall propose the rising orator as one of the members to represent Manhattan.

Meanwhile, I think it would pay to have the pigeon incident repeated, now and then, although the play needs no additional attractions, and moreover, it is doubtful if our young Demosthenes is open to a theatrical engagement.

I should add, now, that with the exception mentioned, the pigeons in the cast of "Never too Late to Mend " went through their parts very creditably and that the pony and the dog did the same, narrowly escaping a call before the curtain, which, *to them*, would have been a bore, especially with the prospect of an additional call for a "speech."

Of the other actors in the cast I can think of nothing to say except that George Holland tried his best to represent a hard-hearted prison governor, but couldn't help letting his proverbial good nature and love of fun peep out to spoil the whole thing: that Mr. Gilbert tried, but in vain, to represent a persecuted old Jew: that Mr. Fisher played the part of a rollicking and subsequently repentant scamp, with his usual humor and pathos: that Miss Barrett gave us a most touching and artistic picture of an unfortunate young criminal who dies in prison of the "treatment": that Miss Henriques in a young lady part altogether below her abilities, managed nevertheless to appear to great advantage: that Mr. Frederick Robinson played the part of a young lover in difficulties as if he had "been there": that Mr. Ringgold did the character of a young clergyman so well as to entitle him to the degree of D. D.: that Mr. Young made commendable efforts to appear like an "Australian Savage": and that Mr. Holston gave us the character of an eccentric limb of the law, which reminded us (and this time reminded us pleasantly) of his inimitable Biles.

So much for "Never too Late to Mend," which was played so long on the first night of its representation that we all thought it should be entitled "Never too Late to End," but which has since been so curtailed of its unfair proportions that we can now order our carriages at 11 o'clock. [N. B.—I always order mine at that hour or before, but the horses are never ready.]

Of other theatrical matters there is little to say.

"The Three Guardsmen " will be repeated at the Olympic to-night for the last time—provided that "another startling novelty" can be got ready by Monday—and I advise everybody who likes good playing and superb scenery to go and see it.

At Niblo's—Miss Bateman having been obliged to retire on account of illness—there will be nothing of special interest until Wednesday next, when Mr. Dillon will commence a short engagement in the play of "Belphegor the Montebank," for which the management has been making the most careful preparations for over three months.

At Barnum's, a new sensational romance is to be brought out next week, under the title of "Bendito or The Children of the Zincali."

In respect to musical matters, I propose to shirk all operatic responsibility by printing the subjoined communication from a friend:

GRAU'S OPERA TROUPE AT THE ACADEMY.

Those who know Mr. Grau were well persuaded that he knew the musical taste and requirements of our public, and that he would not hazard his reputation by placing his company on the boards of the Academy unless it was equal to what might be reasonably expected of it. On Monday evening Verdi's Traviata was selected to introduce a portion of his troupe. The audience was cold and critical, as well as dubious, and was so painfully suspended on the thread of expectation as to do violence to their own taste and judgment. Some of the professional critics were even affected by this spontaneously created epidemic. It would be difficult to measure the effect of all this upon the well-known sensitive natures of real artists. The singing and acting, however, of Mdlle. Boschetti, Anastasi, and Orlandini, gradually overcame the self-fostered syncope of the audience, and soon gave fresh life and geniality to the whole atmosphere of the Academy. It is seldom we have heard three better voices, and bearing more evidence of the most delicate culture. Before their engagement is over, our people will very appropriately acknowledge the truth of what we say.

On Wednesday evening the ever acceptable Trovatore was presented to the public, when another portion of the very large and accomplished troupe of Mr. Grau appeared. The audience was quite large, full of enthusiasm, and bound to redeem their shortcomings on Monday evening. They seemed like the spring itself gloriously released from the frosted lethargy of winter. Orlandini deepened and widened the very favorable opinion which he produced on his first appearance. Musiani recalled enthusiastically the past memories of his successes in this city, and received the most cordial applause for his refined and tasteful vocalization. Mme. Cash Polini as Azucena was fully equal to any one we have seen in this part, both in acting and singing, and we are happy to say the audience becomingly crowned her efforts by repeated applause. The star of the evening and the occasion, however, was Mme. Noel Guidi. Verdi himself would not desire a better or a more charming representative of his Leonora. To the most unexceptionable acting was added a refined, delicate and melodious vocalization seldom heard within the walls of the Academy. Her interpretation of the part was so faithful, so artistic and sympathetic, that the feelings of the audience seemed to run in the channel created for them by the gifted artist herself. Her hearers were fully alive to her great merits, and generously acknowledged them by every token of approbation. We predict for this company a very great success, and we hope the enterprising manager, Mr. Grau, will reap the reward of his judgment and taste in the selection of such an admirable company.

To-day there will be a Faust Matinée at the Academy, commencing at one o'clock.

The fifth of the Irving Hall Sacred Concerts will take place to-morrow (Sunday) evening: artists, Miss Louisa Myers (soprano); Mr. W. Castle (tenor); Mr. S. C. Campbell (baritone): Mr. G. W. Morgan organist.

Mr. Morgan, by the way, gives his annual concert this evening at Irving Hall, assisted by Miss Marie Abbott, Miss Nettie Sterling, and Messrs. Castle, Campbell, Simpson, Goldbeck, and others.

The great musical event of next week will be Mr. Theodore Thomas's last concert of the season, which will take place at Irving Hall on Monday evening: among the artists who will assist on the occasion are Miss Brainerd, Miss Rose Eytinge, Mr. Carlyle Petersilea (pianist, who makes his first appearance in America), and the members of the Mendelssohn

Union Society, all supported by a grand orchestra. This concert promises to be the most select musical entertainment that we have had this season.

Of course you will be there, and if you are, be sure and look out for

Figaro.

(For the Saturday Press.)

JOSH BILLINGS ON LOVE.

The only natural feeling the young heart possesses iz love. It iz the first good thing the heart duz, and in after life it iz often the only good thing it duz.

Thare iz no pozatif virtue in love, and yet it may be the result ov the holyest ov virtues.

But thare iz, in this life, a vast deal ov Pontoon love, that has no more virtue in it than wooden nutmegs hav.

Thare iz, "Love undieing," that generally lives about az long az uncorked ginger pop duz.

Thare iz "Love Untold," which iz alwus told tew enny boddy who will listen to it, and iz az full ov pathos az a pork and and beans' nightmare.

And thare iz "Love at sight," to which I will add, Love for 90 days.

These are sum ov the different kinds ov Love that are denominated pashun, and form mutch ov the trading capital that lovers do bizzness on.

Thare iz not much sin in these different styles ov love; they don't seem tew git up to the dignity ov sin; thare iz deception in them without doubt; but the deception iz like Costar's celebrated Rat Exterminator, it won't hurt ennybody else but the rats.

I am not prepared to say that I would like to see these things dun away with, for sumthing wuss might spring up in the place ov them; they seem tew be necessary in carrying on a trade in which judgment has to yield to fancy, and fancy iz too often forced to yield to nonsense.

If we could (enny ov us) hav our old courtship written out and given tew us for perusal we should probably look upon it az we would upon a Chinese comick almanack, unable tew understand the pikturs, and satisfied that the astronomical calculations were never designed for our latitude.

NEW YORK MAY 19, 1866

(For the Saturday Press.)

THE CITY OF THE SILENT.—A TRIBUTE TO THE WOODLAWN CEMETERY.

BY ABSALOM PETERS, D. D.

"O my son Absalom ! my son, my son Absalom."

We very much fear that this cheerful little poem which its author modestly designates as a Tribute is not as widely known as it should be, so we propose to call attention to some of its characteristics. It was first published in "Hours at Home," for May, 1866, and is now reprinted in pamphlet form. To speak moderately and within bounds, it is the weakest piece of clerical humbug that has fallen under our notice for many a day. Weak, and yet bold, for it certainly requires some courage to submit such a production to the candid criticism of the public, even when it comes under the overshadowing name of a Doctor of Divinity. The "City of the Silent" is a poem descriptive of the Woodlawn Cemetery and the Animus of the whole affair is made apparent by reference to the last pages of the pamphlet where the names of the Trustees of the Cemetery appear —our friend the author figuring among them as Vice-President. Subjoined to the poem, also, are certain prose details in which we find statistics of the number of acres, size of lots, estimates of comparative cost of carriage hire between this cemetery and Greenwood, and various other matters of interest to those contemplating interment.

It will, perhaps, strike the reader that a poet writing from the point of view of a Trustee and property owner, would, perhaps, feel himself somewhat hampered—his wings clipped as it were and he not able to soar with that freedom that would enable him to display all his powers—that, in fact, the problem being to get off his hands so many lots for so many verses it might be found somewhat difficult to insinuate in decorous blank verse that excellent burial sites could be obtained at a very cheap rate, at a cemetery easy of access from the city, with other marketable considerations, and yet to throw such a glow of Christian feeling and high moral sentiment over the whole, that the poem should appear to have been written from a lofty spiritual standpoint, and not to be based on a question of bargain and sale. It is to this problem that our reverend author has addressed himself: with what success we leave it to the reader to determine.

See how nobly the poem begins! What have questions of filthy lucre to do with an immense mind pondering immense things?

"Thou city of the silent! Pensively I stroll,
To muse of thee: and near my theme—great thoughts astir
I ponder things immense: the ages of the world;
Great cities and their dead: the Island city near;
Its greatness yet to be—its population vast,
Within and far around; and O! how soon it fills
A million graves!"

We don't in the least doubt that the Doctor not only had "pondered" this last item, but had figured it out completely to his satisfaction before accepting the vice presidency of the Necropolis. Indeed, any doubts that we might have on the question are set at rest in a subsequent portion of the poem, where we find these significant lines:

"My thoughts run on a hundred years. Long ere that time
These graves will hold the treasures of a million hearts,
Nor yet be full."

Indeed, it can hardly be doubted that the Trustees at their little festive banquets—"on funeral baked meats," perchance—have gauged the capacities and measure of growth of their graveyard to a fraction. The mathematical part of the poem we may fairly conclude to have originated from the author in his capacity of Trustee and not of Poet. We must remember, however, that he is not only mathematician and poet, but likewise Doctor of Divinity, and it is, we presume, in this last character that he proceeds to show his familiarity with the intentions of Providence as regards this particular plot of ground and its special interposition to preserve the same for the purpose to which it is now devoted. Here is the Doctor's ground on that question:

"Divine forecasting plans of Providence had kept
These ancient farms contiguous, of culture rude,
For sacred use. The great metropolis—the mart
Of trade—was spreading from its centre outward far:
**But wealth and boundless enterprise were stayed to spare
This ample plot of ground, two centuries and more."

There is as much truth as poetry in this and none to spare of either. The idea that Providence stayed the wealth and enterprise of the city of New York two centuries and more in order that the Trustees of Woodlawn Cemetery might have a first rate burying ground—or that Providence in any way specially interposed to preserve these particular farms for this particular purpose any more than any other piece of ground for any other particular purpose, is a theological absurdity coming even from a Doctor of Divinity. Dr. Peters may be prepared to say that the Lord preserved certain land on the Tenth Avenue, two centuries and more that the Gas Company might put their works on it and in fact every particular piece of land in all the world for the particular purpose to which it is now devoted: and in a certain sense, this might convey a truth but, if this was what the Doctor meant, the rule is of such a universal application that it is a sheer waste of time and words to have picked out his particular lot by way of illustration since it is no more true of that lot than any other. But this is evidently not his idea: he means to give it as his opinion that there is a special interposition of Providence in respect to graveyards and in respect to this graveyard in particular—the superior solemnity attending death being perhaps a sufficient reason to his mind why Providence should make an exception to general rules in regard to cemeteries. Who this Doctor Peters is of what denomination, sect or creed we know not, never having heard of him otherwise than through this so-called "Tribute;" but his theology, if this be a fair specimen thereof, appears to us as loose-jointed as his poetry, which in its turn is nothing more than the most commonplace prose that trails painfully along in a weary metre of twelve feet to the line, at a funereal pace intended perhaps to be in keeping with the subject. If the funeral would only wind its way on as far as Woodlawn, and the trustees could there gather about this poor poem, at some unsaleable lot, set apart for the purpose, and then consign it to the dust (as in old times we used to bury Euclid at college). Dr. Peters being permitted by right of paternity and as chief—perhaps only—mourner to indulge in a few parting words: then, indeed, we might, like David of old, arise, wash and eat, and poetic justice would, for once, at least, have been done: but as there is little hope of this excellent suggestion being adopted, we resume our consideration of the poem. Here is a paragraph descriptive of the superior trained beauty of a graveyard over the mere wanton beauty of poor nature, unadorned by slabs and monuments:

"Already science plies its arts, and taste refined
Its touch, transforming nature's wild exuberance
To landscape beauty and the *chaste and mellow tints*
Of downy lawns—and copses green and gay parterres."

What loose unmeaning language this is. To say nothing of the absurdity of transforming nature's exuberance into landscape beauty, what are we to make of the chaste tint of a downy lawn—what would the unchaste tint of a downy lawn be, and what has a mellow tint to do with a lawn—what colored lawn would a chaste and mellow tinted lawn be? All the lawns that we have ever seen were (when they were downy) green, and green isn't a mellow tint though it may be chaste for aught we know to the contrary. This may be all very well for poetry, but if the Doctor surveying his possessions were to inform one of his co-trustees that "that was a very chaste and mellow tinted lawn" we apprehend that the co-trustee would gaze wildly at the Reverend poet for an explanation.

Here is a little fragment apparently imitated from the advertising columns of one of the daily papers, when we are informed that furnished rooms for single gentlemen may be obtained, also suites of rooms to accommodate families.

"And hither borne, with loving tenderness and care,
Dead citizens are brought and buried out of sight—
In narrow houses laid, with premises secured
For tenants all alone, or families apart,
Or groups of friends."

The Doctor is rather particular to inform us that dead citizens are brought here and buried out of sight. As though Woodlawn was rather an exception in this direction, and at other cemeteries they brought live citizens. It is very good and considerate in him also, to assure us that they are buried out of sight, for in the gross ignorance prevailing on the subject, his readers might not have been aware of that fact and have supposed that they were only partly buried and not altogether concealed from view.

We will not weary our reader with further extracts. Those that we have given, are a fair sample of the composition. We have called attention to the thing because it seemed to us a new and particularly mischievous advertising scheme. It was all very well so long as this sort of thing was confined to clothing stores, patent medicines and perfumes—we had ceased to be surprised in reading verses in the newspaper to find the close of some stirring lyric, to be an urgent advice to purchase our clothing at Smith & Brothers—or to find some admirable moral sentiment abruptly terminating in a eulogy upon the Night Blooming Cereus, or fragrant Sozodont, but we confess to a feeling of anything but respect when we find the sacred names of poetry and religion invoked to puff a cemetery, and the solemn themes of death and the life to come, ending in a description of the size of lots and the facilities of getting to the cemetery by train.

We have heard that godliness is great gain—and perhaps, in a manner the show of godliness may also be great gain, but we hope that in future this species of mercenary rhyming will be left to the quack medicine venders and clothiers, and that Reverend Doctors of Divinity will leave this penny-a-lining business to the professional writers of rhyming advertisements.

(For the Saturday Press.)

A FEW ART HINTS FROM A TRANSCEDENTALIST.

The art-fever which about a year ago was at its height in this community, has abated, and the Spring opening of the National Academy finds us in a somewhat indifferent humor. This reaction is natural. Like all other excitements based upon ephemeral causes—novelty, fashion, sentimental enthusiasm, etc.,—it has had its day; but there still remains the old leaven, and there are more among us capable of deriving real pleasure from works of art; those who have allowed their eyes and minds to rest on them long enough to see the truth the artist has aimed to tell.

A great development of the art-faculty among us is certain. That it is to a great extent properly directed, and is producing commendable works now, is, however, no argument against more light. Such works as M. Taine's on the "Philosophy of Art" are useful therefore, although another has said, "It is no good sign for any practical branch of human affairs if there is much literature or philosophy written upon it—when art itself was great, there was no art-literature." This may be true, but every age has a philosophy of art—whether it be set down in a book or not—based upon the current philosophy, and controlled by the spirit of the age. An artist may imitate the works of a past age, but that is all. He can never perfectly reproduce the spirit. The imitations cannot but be "sicklied over with the pale cast of thought." The legitimate works of an age are its interpretations of nature, the expression of its ideas and aspirations, and these come not from slavish copying of the works of any preceding period.

The Egyptian embodied his conceptions of power and sublimity by gigantic size; the Greek, by extreme strength and beauty of form, and a countenance calm in knowledge of divine supremacy. The Greek artist was compelled by law of the State as well as by the mythical character of his religion to idealize. In the middle ages the church taught the almost unmixed evil of nature and the utter depravity of man, and hence the elevation of the spiritual element. The artists, filled with the thought of their time, embodied it in the faces of heavenly virgins and saintly martyrs. In all three epochs art used almost solely to illustrate religion. It is not to the philosophy, religion, or art of the past that our artists must go for inspiration.

Our age has been called an age of criticism, and it may perhaps be vain to look for any great creative work in it; but the critical by discovering true ideas, or ideas true by comparison with those which have preceded them, lays the basis for the creative, and our artists, by ascertaining and pursuing the true path, may give birth in a not distant future to those who shall make their names and their nation illustrious.

We are logical, and refuse to be fed with lies. Whoever speaks for this time must tell a true tale and which will bear the questioning of science and reason. With all our materialism there is great faith among us too.

The laws of progressive development are being investigated and tested, and we are beginning to place our hopes of salvation upon them. We have felt that the continuance of all that is beautiful in our social and political life depended upon the triumph of liberal principles in the recent war. Principle is only a name for a mode of action of FORCE, of whose working man is the highest and most complex result. He has bound up in his being the record of all the developments that have preceded him in the world. There is no link missing in the chain which binds him to the "poor stones that plot and plan what they will do when they are man." Man's sympathies are as Catholic as his relationship. It is not necessary that a picture or a statue shall be a representation of perfect form or divine intelligence to confer æsthetic pleasure. Whatever representation attracts our sympathy, whether pleasurable or painful, confess æsthetic pleasure, and is entitled to be admitted to the heavenly consecration of art.

The artistic faculty is the power of removing objects or subjects out of the perplexing variety of nature, and placing them so that others can perceive them as they are, and partake of the artist's sympathy with them. "Art is a service." It educates the perceptions and sympathies. It retains in its cause all who by science, by poetry, by music, by painting, by sculpture, are bringing out the riches of intellect and sympathy in the nature of man. Philosophers, statesmen, and soldiers, all who work in the cause of liberty, are opening doors for its development; and where liberty is most perfect, there will art be richest.

I. E.

(For the Saturday Press.)

THE FLANEUR.

"Que scais je ?"

What do I know? asks Montaigne; not that Montaigne did not know anything, or thought that he did not, but this is his formula for the expression of the philosophy of doubt. And it is a good one.

This philosophy is the truthful expression of modesty and honesty. Fontenelle says somewhere, "I am frightened at the certainty I find all around me", (Je suis effrayé de la certitude que je vois partout), and well he might have been; but what sensations would he have felt had he lived in America, and read the countless swarm of daily papers, or listened to the bold contradictory assertions of every other man he met.

To be sure, the spark of truth has been elicited from the clash of various opinions, as fire results from the shock of flint and steel. This favorite simile has a certain merit of similitude, but yet the position of the tinder is none the more desirable, and, for my part, I much prefer the process of kindling my flame by concentrating to a focus the sun's rays.

It is frightful to find how universal is the tendency to assert opinions formed upon wholly insufficient grounds. There is great need of some work upon testimony. I remember once hearing Dr. Walker say in a sermon that the man who could make a syllogism was the man of an age, and he who could make a corollary from two syllogisms was the man of an era.

Napoleon, it is somewhere stated, had the habit of not opening his letters until they had been received a week, because, as he said, by that time the majority of them had answered themselves. Aaron Burr had a rule of conduct devised in the same spirit: "Never do to-day what can be put off until to-morrow, and never put off until to-morrow what can be done today."

Half the energy of men is like that of flies in the sun, noisy and aimless, a mere buzzing and disturbing the quiet of things. I have met people, and very many of them, who thought it a necessary duty to have an opinion upon every subject, and would ask you boldly for yours, and seem to feel aggrieved if you did not have one on your tongue's end.

They were never at a loss in what they call "making up their mind," as though a man's mind could be wound up like a watch.

Half of what we call education is an attempt to set youth afloat upon the stream of life with a well assorted cargo of correct opinions, and the consequence is that it takes a thoughtful man the remaining forty years of life to unpack and throw away the opinions stored in him before he was twenty. Ask the great majority of men for a sample of what they are laden with, and you will have assertions offered you on every hand, but where will you go to find knowledge?

How seldom do you find a man whose statement can be received implicitly? I do not mean in matters of personal veracity, but in matters of fact.

Now it is very generally supposed and asserted that to doubt implies a sort of vacuity of mind, which it is better to have filled with positive opinions of almost any description than to leave empty. But the truth is, that the most fruitful source of thought is doubt.

In my library I would have the supports of my mantle-shelf two sphinxes, and hanging over the mantle a fine copy of Durer's print, called "Melancholy," typifying thus the early civilization questioning nature, and the later and last result of human life,

"——that thought profound,
Which seeks the endless mystery to expound."

Over the cases containing the majority of such works of the metaphysicians, philosophers, and historians as it is necessary to have for reminders of what men have thought and done, I should place a large stuffed owl, with a preternatural expression of wisdom upon his silly countenance.

But over the case, and it would not be a large one, which contained the works of those great men who, receiving nothing upon hearsay, sought truth through doubting, I should place a bust of him, the greatest of them all who thus discovered and described the road that leads to it.

Americans have a reputation as being so assertive of themselves and their country as to become almost boastful. There is some ground for the accusation. No one can deny it. There is a sort of tradition that it is patriotic to assert the glories of one's country.

To be sure, it would be more so to be as earnest in attempting to make one's country glorious as men are now in asserting that it is so.

But the shortcoming is almost universal. We are more struck with it in others than in our own countrymen. Yet what more common than to find a dweller in Peoria comparing New York with his Western or Southern village?

A friend of mine once told me of the delight with which he listened to a French guide to the field of Waterloo. The man was so earnest and certain of the fact, that he almost persuaded him that Waterloo was a great French victory. If he had, such a belief would have squared very well with many of the assertions of history.

THE FLANEUR.

The report that George Peabody has presented the SATURDAY PRESS with $200,000 is premature.

Dramatic Feuilleton.

BY FIGARO.

I don't know whether the cholera is catching or not, Mr. Editor, but I know that enthusiasm is, for I caught it bad myself the other night at Niblo's, and doubt whether even Dr. Quackenboss could cure me.

I haven't had it so bad, that I remember, since I went to the Broadway the first night that Charles Kean played Louis XI there.

This time I caught it at the instance of Mr. Charles Dillon, on seeing his performance of Belphegor.

Robert Heller sat on one side of me, and Charles Shanly on the other, and they caught it too—like all the other old stagers in the house.

For my own part, I confess I was one of those who "went to scoff and remained to pray :" for I had had "Dillon and Belphegor" "Belphegor and Dillon," "Dillon and Belphegor," dinned into my ears so often, that I began to think the whole thing a humbug.

It was just the same with Charles Kean and Louis XI.

You see, when a man gets to be a hundred years old, more or less, he becomes suspicious of all this talk and puts himself on his defence against it: he has a sort of pride, perhaps, in proving that "old birds can't be caught with chaff."

Possibly they can't, but that's a matter I'll discuss some other time.

For the present let's discuss Dillon.

Well then, when he first came upon the stage, the other night, I didn't like him at all: his manner appeared to be forced, his pronunciation affected (after the English style) and all his movements "of the stage, stagey."

Still I joined in the hearty reception given to him, and then threw myself back on my dignity determined for the rest of the evening to be "nothing if not critical."

I wasn't going to be affected by the atmosphere about me—no, not I.

How did I know but the house was bought up with "British gold?"

Moreover it is so vulgar to go with the stream! So during Dillon's first few scenes I remained unmoved even by the applause of Heller and Shanly.

But now for my confession.

Little by little, as Dillon went on depicting the character of Belphegor, addressing himself to his work with artistic care and earnestness, giving little touches here and there which betrayed unmistakably the hand of a master, and never for a moment heeding either the silence or the applause of the audience, I found myself becoming "possessed," as it were, by the man, and when the curtain fell on the first act, gave myself up to the spirit of the hour, and hurrahed as long and loud as anybody.

Away went all my *nil admirari* theories at once, and as I went out for a while to "see a man," I was disposed to take everybody by the hand, and have a general exchange of congratulations.

I can't write in detail about the performance, however, till I have see it again and my enthusiasm has had time to cool down a little.

Suffice it for the present to say that I have seen nothing so superb since Charles Kean's Louis XI., which, as you know, I consider the finest piece of acting known to the stage.

And, by the way, another superb piece of acting in "Belphegor" is Mr. George Beck's Fanfonarade, a harlequin part which he plays—as, for that matter, he plays nearly everything—with a degree of finish that scarcely any other actor that I know of can approach.

The only other part of importance in the piece is Madeline the poor tempted wife of Belphegor—who is represented with much depth of feeling by Miss Ida Vernon.

However, more about all this next week—and especially about Dillon, who is to remain at Niblo's for a fortnight or so, and whom I am anxious now to see in some of his Shakespearean parts.

The other theatres offer nothing this week to hang so much as a joke upon.

Charles Reade's "Never too Late to Mend," is still drawing immense houses at Wallack's (chiefly, as I think, owing to the truly magnificent scenery,) and will be continued to the end of the regular season.

At the Olympic, "The Three Guardsmen" will be played for the last time to-night, and on Monday we are to have a new adaptation of Dickens' "David Copperfield."

On account of the illness of Mrs. Wood, her benefit, which was to have taken place last night, and would have been a regular festival, is postponed to next Friday evening.

At the Museum an engagement has been made with Mrs. G. C. Howard, who will appear in her original character of Topsey, in "Uncle Tom's Cabin."

In musical matters, I have simply to announce a Matinée at the Academy to-day, when the whole of "Ernani," and the third act of "Faust" will be given: a complimentary concert to M. C. Busch at Irving Hall, this evening: and, at the same place, on Wednesday evening, a concert for the benefit of the orphans of Charleston, S. C.

Mr. Busch is a well known musical agent, who has been an invalid for a long time, and the conceit to be given for his benefit, this evening, will be one of be on the most select of the season. Among the artists who have volunteered on the occasion, are Miss Fanny Stockton, Miss Zelda Harrison, Signor Ardavani, and Messrs. S. B. Mills, Robert Heller, Theo. Thomas, G. W. Morgan, and G. W. Colby.

Figaro.

NEW YORK MAY 26, 1866

There is a rumor about town that the President and Directors of the various horse rail roads are going to "strike"—that they have engaged a band of music at a low price,—an ex-catafalque (which has been stored since the death of President Harrison) changing the emblems of mourning to such as emblem despair, or want, or poverty, (a bee-hive or two, for instance, a few ants, and flies, and musquitoes), and that in a few days they will drive through the great thoroughfares of the city. The fare sex —which includes both genders—are expected to sympathize one way or the other with this movement.

Some of the numerous country papers which take a deep interest in New York matters are circulating a report that a new man is about to "undertake the management of the SATURDAY PRESS." What will our country friends do for us next? Last week they reported that we were about to die, and this week they kindly furnish us with an undertaker.

A contributor who is famous for working up old jokes, says that at the great fire in Irving place, it was found that nearly every fireman in New York could "play on the piano."

If you would know the latest fashions in male attire, take a look, as you walk up Broadway, at the step-children of the New York Hotel.

A CARD FROM MAX MARETZEK.

ACADEMY OF MUSIC—ITALIAN OPERA.

This establishment does not advertise in the New York Herald.]

This establishment has been burned to the ground, but as I have no intention of soliciting pity or charity, and am incapable of using such a horrible catastrophe (which deprived several persons of their lives, and hundreds of the means of supporting their families) as a favorable opportunity to *advertise my business*, I will abstain from commenting on my present losses, and from *heralding* my future movements.

However, to allay any apprehensions on the part of artists, orchestral players, choruses, and other employés, I deem it consistent to declare that all engagements made for the next Fall and Winter seasons remain in full force, and that the operations will commence early in October next.

The public's faithful servant,

Staten Island, May 24, 1866. MAX MARETZEK.

NEW YORK JUNE 2, 1866

(For the Saturday Press.)

A STRANGE DREAM.

BY MARK TWAIN.

VOLCANO HOUSE.

CRATER OF " KILAUEA," SANDWICH ISLANDS,
April 1, 1866

MY DEAR PRESS:

All day long I have sat apart and pondered over the mysterious occurrences of last night. * * *

There is nothing lacking in the chain of incidents—my memory presents each in its proper order with perfect distinctness, but still—

However, never mind these reflections—I will drop them and proceed to make a simple statement of facts.

Towards eleven o'clock it was suggested that the character of the night was peculiarly suited to viewing the mightiest active volcano on the earth's surface in its most impressive sublimity. There was no light of moon or star in the inky heavens to mar the effect of the crater's gorgeous pyrotechnics.

In due time I stood, with my companion, on the wall of the vast cauldron which the natives, ages ago, named *Hale mau mau*—the abyss wherein they were wont to throw the remains of their chiefs, to the end that vulgar feet might never tread above them. We stood there, at dead of night, a mile above the level of the sea, and looked down a thousand feet upon a boiling, surging, roaring ocean of fire!—shaded our eyes from the blinding glare and gazed far away over the crimson waves with a vague notion that a supernatural fleet, manned by demons and freighted with the damned, might presently sail up out of the remote distance; started when tremendous thunder-bursts shook the earth, and followed with fascinated eyes the grand jets of molten lava that sprang high up toward the zenith and exploded in a world of fiery spray that lit up the sombre heavens with an infernal splendor.

"What is your little bonfire of Vesuvius to this?"

My ejaculation roused my companion from his reverie, and we fell into a conversation appropriate to the occasion and the surroundings. We came at last to speak of the ancient custom of casting the bodies of dead chieftains into this fearful cauldron, and my comrade, who is of the blood royal, mentioned that the founder of his race, old King Kamehameha the First,—that invincible old pagan Alexander—had found other sepulture than the burning depths of the *Hale mau mau.* I grew interested at once; I knew that the mystery of what became of the corpse of the warrior King had never been fathomed; I was aware that there was a legend connected with this matter, and I felt as if there could be no more fitting time to listen to it than the present. The descendant of the Kamehamehas said:

"The dead king was brought in royal state down the long, winding road that descends from the rim of the crater to the scorched and chasm-riven plain that lies between the *Hale mau mau* and those beetling walls yonder in the distance. The guards were set and the troops of mourners began the weird wail for the departed. In the middle of the fight came a sound of innumerable voices in the air, and the rush of invisible wings; the funereal torches wavered, burned blue, and went out ! The mourners and watchers fell to the ground paralyzed by fright, and many minutes elapsed before any one dared to move or speak, for they believed that the phantom messengers of the dread Goddess of Fire had been in their midst. When at last, a torch was lighted, the bier was vacant—the dead monarch had been spirited away! Consternation seized upon all, and they fled out of the crater. When day dawned, the multitude returned, and began the search for the corpse. But not a footprint, not a sign was ever found. Day after day the search was continued and every cave in the great walls, and every chasm in the plain, for miles around, was examined, but all to no purpose—and from that day to this the resting-place of the lion-king's bones is an unsolved mystery. But years afterward, when the grim prophetess Wiahowakawak lay on her deathbed, the goddess Pele appeared to her in a vision and told her that eventually the secret would be revealed, and in a remarkable manner, but not until the great *Kau huhu* the Shark God, should desert the sacred cavern Aua Puhi, in the Island of Molokai, and the waters of the sea should no more visit it, and its floors should become dry. Ever since that time, the simple, confiding natives have watched for the sign. And now, after many and many a summer has come and gone and they who were in the flower of youth then, have waxed old and died, the day is at hand! The great Shark God has deserted the *Aua Puhi*: a month ago for the first time, within the records of the ancient legends, the waters of the sea ceased to flow into the cavern, and its stony pavement is become dry! As you may easily believe, the news of this event spread like wild fire through the islands, and now the natives are looking every hour for the miracle, which is to unveil the mystery, and reveal the secret grave of the dead hero."

After I had gone to bed, I got to thinking of the volcanic magnificence we had witnessed, and could not go to sleep. I hunted up a book and concluded to pass the time in reading. The first chapter I came upon related several instances of remarkable revelations, made to men through the agency of dreams of roads and houses, trees, fences and all manner of landmarks, shown in visions and recognized afterwards in waking hours, and which served to point the way to some dark mystery or other.

At length I fell asleep, and dreamed that I was abroad in the great plain that skirts the *Hale mau mau*. I stood in a sort of twilight which softened the outlines of surrounding objects, but still left them tolerably distinct. A gaunt, muffled figure stepped out from the shadow of a rude column of lava, and moved away with a slow and measured step, beckoning me follow. I did so. I marched down, down, down, hundreds of feet, upon a narrow trail which wound its tortuous course through piles and pyramids of seamed and blackened lava, and under overhanging masses of sulphur formed by the artist-hand of Nature into an infinitude of fanciful shapes. The thought crossed my mind that possibly my phantom guide might lead me down among the bowels of the crater, and then disappear and leave me to grope my way through its mazes, and work out my deliverance as best I might, and so, with an eye to such a contingency, I picked up a stone, and "blazed" my course by breaking off a projecting corner, from time to time, from the lava walls and festoons of sulphur. Finally we turned into a cleft in the crater's side, and pursued our way through its intricate windings for many a fathom down toward the home of the subterranean fires, our course lighted all the while by a ruddy glow which filtered up through innumerable cracks and crevices, and which afforded me occasional glimpses of the flood of molten fire boiling and hissing in the profound depths beneath us. The heat was intense, and the sulphurous atmosphere suffocating, but I toiled on in the footsteps of my stately guide, and uttered no complaint. At last we came to a sort of rugged chamber whose sombre and blistered walls spake with mute eloquence of some fiery tempest that had spent its fury here in a by-gone age. The spectre pointed to a great boulder at the farther extremity—stood and pointed, silent and motionless, for a few fleeting moments, and then disappeared! "The grave of the last Kamehameha !" The words swept mournfully by, from some unknown source, and died away in the distant corridors of my prison-house, and I was alone in the bowels of the earth, in the home of desolation, in the presence of death!

My first frightened impulse was to fly, but a stronger impulse arrested me, and impelled me to approach the massive boulder the spectre had pointed at. With hesitating step I went forward and stood beside it—nothing there; I grew bolder, and walked around and about it, peering shrewdly into the shadowy half light that surrounded it—still nothing. I paused to consider what to do next. While I stood irresolute, I chanced to brush the ponderous stone with my elbow, and lo! it vibrated to touch! I would as soon have thought of starting a kiln of bricks with my feeble hand. My curiosity was excited. I bore against the boulder, and it yielded to the pressure—I bore yet harder, and it still yielded—I gave a sudden push with my whole strength, and it toppled from its foundation with a crash that sent the echoes thundering down the avenues and passages of the dismal cavern! And there, in a shallow excavation over which it had rested, lay the crumbling skeleton of King Kamehameha the Great, thus sepulchred in long years, by supernatural hands! The bones could be none other, for with them lay the rare and priceless crown of *pulamalama* coral sacred to royalty, and *tabu* to all else beside. A hollow human groan issued out of the—

I woke up. How glad I was to know it was all a dream! "This comes of listening to the legend of the noble lord—of reading of those lying dream revelations—of allowing myself to be carried away by the wild beauty of old Kileana at midnight—of gorging too much pork and beans for supper!" And so I turned over, and fell asleep again. And dreamed the same dream precisely as before; followed the phantom—"blazed " my course—arrived at the grim chamber—heard the sad spirit voice—overturned the massy stone—beheld the regal crown and the decaying bones of the great king!

I woke up, and reflected long upon the curious and singularly vivid dream, and finally muttered to myself, "This—this is becoming serious!"

I fell asleep again, and again I dreamed the same dream, without a single variation! I slept no more, but tossed restlessly in bed, and longed for daylight. And when it came I wandered forth, and descended to the wide plain in the crater. I said to myself, "I am not superstitious, but if there is anything in that dying woman's prophecy, I am the instrument appointed to uncurtain this ancient mystery." As I walked along, I even half expected to see my solemn guide step out from some nook in the lofty wall, and beckon me to come on. At last when I reached the place where I had first seen him in my dream, I recognized every surrounding object, and there, winding down among the blocks and fragments of lava, I saw the very trail I had traversed in my vision! I resolved to traverse it again, come what might. I wondered if, in my unreal journey, I had "blazed " my way, so that it would stand the test of stern reality; and thus wondering, a chill went to my heart when I came to the first stony projection I had broken off in my dream, and saw the fresh new fracture, and the dismembered fragment lying on the ground! My curiosity rose up, and banished all fear, and I hurried along as fast as the rugged road would allow me. I looked for my other "blazes," and found them; found the cleft in the wall; recognized all its turnings; walked in the light that ascended from the glowing furnaces visible far below; sweated in the close, hot atmosphere, and breathed the sulphurous smoke—and at last I stood hundreds of feet beneath the peaks of *Kilanea* in the ruined chamber, and in the presence of the mysterious boulder!

"This is no dream," I said; "this is a revelation from the realm of the supernatural; and it becomes not me to longer reason, conjecture, suspect, but blindly to obey the impulses given me by the unseen power that guides me."

I moved with slow and reverent step toward the stone and bore against it. It yielded perceptibly to the pressure. I brought my full weight and strength to bear, and surged against it. It yielded again, but I was so enfeebled by my toilsome journey that I could not overthrow it. I rested a little, and then raised an edge of the boulder by a strong, steady push, and placed a small stone under it to keep it from sinking back to its place. I rested again, and then repeated the process. Before long, I had added a third prop, and had got the edge of the boulder considerably elevated. The labor and the close atmosphere together were so exhausting, however, that I was obliged to lie down, then, and recuperate my strength by a longer season of rest. And so, hour after hour I labored, growing more and more weary, but still upheld by a fascination which I felt was infused into me by the invisible powers whose will I was working. At last I concentrated my strength in a final effort, and the stone rolled from its position.

I can never forget the overpowering sense of awe that sank down like a great darkness upon my spirit at that moment. After a solemn pause to prepare myself, with bowed form and uncovered head, I slowly turned my gaze till it rested upon the spot where the great stone had lain.

There wasn't any bones there.

* * * * * * * * * * * *

I just said to myself," Well, if this ain't the blastedest infernalest humbug that ever I've come across yet, I wish I may never!"

And then I scratched out of there, and marched up here to the Volcano House, and got out my old raw-boned fool of a horse, "Oahu,"* and "lammed" him till he couldn't stand up without leaning against something.

You cannot bet anything on dreams.

Mark Twain.

* I named him after one of the other islands of this group—usually pronounced Waw-hoo. This horse formerly went by the name of John. He spelt it with a G.

The Times notes as a curious fact that all the churches on Broadway which have come to a bad end have been without spires; the old Tabernacle, torn down some years since, had no spire, nor were there spires on St. Thomas', or Chapin's, or Osgood's. Between the Battery and Union Square there are now only three churches remaining—possibly they may be saved by their spires.

The Reno Times has been suspended for want of the Rhino. It was one of the most readable papers that came to our office. The editor asks us to keep up an exchange with its ghost. We shall do so out of common gratitude. When the concern is revived —of which there appears to be some prospect—we shall be happy to serve it in other ways. A good paper is something that the world ought not to willingly let die.

When the "Society for the Prevention of Cruelty to Animals" decide what is best to be done about the Russ pavement on Broadway, we hope they will pay some attention to other streets—Bleecker street, for instance, between Broadway and the Bowery—and see if human beings would not be greatly benefited in various ways, as well as animals, to say nothing of omnibuses and other conveyances, which, by the way, should have some Society to protect them.

The internal revenue authorities insist with considerable plausibility that every body who comes into the world should pay an income tax, and we suggest as a logical inference that everybody who goes out of the world should be made to pay an out-go tax.

The Round Table of this week in the way of a touching appeal to its advertising patrons for support, says:—

"One class of individuals we have no respect for, and that is those miserable, ungracious beings who are unhappy if a paper does not die soon after its appearance. They make it their mission to prophesy its decease, and take to writing its obituary in advance for the corners of various papers. They always find pleasure in placing the circulation at least one-half lower than it is. They always know of fabulous thousands sunk, and can foretell bankruptcy to a certainty. Of all despicable specimens of humanity, we know of none like these. We have encountered them all along since this paper was first devised, now three years and more ago, and can say that they have, by their downright falsehoods, done us more injury than a bevy of true-hearted friends could rectify."

This, coming from a paper to which we have traced directly about a dozen calumnious reports respecting the Saturday Press, is really funny.

A Philadelphia correspondent of one of our city weeklies, speaking of Mr. Forrest, says :—"Attached to his mansion in Broad Street (*our* Fifth Avenue), is a beautiful little theatre, in which it is Mr. Forrest's intention to have acting regularly taught, by himself and other competent persons, to a certain number of the youth of both sexes, who exhibit talent and taste for the stage." A school of actors educated after the Forrest school would certainly make a sensation.

Rather Hard on the Cattle if They Could Only Appreciate It.—At a recent meeting of the Board of Health, it was decided that cattle would not be allowed on, Fifth Avenue. What effect will this have on the price of beef? The Board of Health have also decided against the use of mineral waters, unless by the advice of a physician who has studied their virtues, and knows to what cases their use may be serviceable. A committee has been appointed to decide whether or no the use of ice-water is proper during the summer months. And this reminds us of an old joke about ice, which we can trace with fond remembrance to the Boston Post, to the effect that in winter, when we are not particularly in need of ice, there is an abundance of it; but in summer, when it is a positive luxury, it is difficult and expensive to obtain it. The Board of health will, in a few days, have something to decide about coffee, and tea, and chocolate; and the questions as to what we shall eat and drink, and when and where we may eat and drink, having been decided according to the latest laws and authorities, the next question to decide will be what we may wear, whom we may marry, where we shall live, etc. Meanwhile, look out sharp for the cholera, and it will be sure to come.

NIBLO'S GARDEN.— BEGINS AT 8
Lessee and Manager.........................Wm Wheatley

THIS (Saturday) EVENING, June 2.
Last appearance of
CHARLES DILLON,
who will appear in the thrilling and pathetic character of
BELPHEGOR,
THE MOUNTEBANK,
in the play of the same name.
Supported by the full company.
THE SCENERY,
COSTUMES,
AND APPOINTMENTS.
ALL NEW,
MONDAY June 4.
THE WONDERFUL RAVELS,
GABRIEL RAVEL,
FRANCOIS RAVEL,
(his first appearance in New York in several years)
ANTOINE RAVEL,
YOUNG AMERICA,
and a splendid company of
FORTY EMINENT ARTISTS.
Seats secured six days in advance.

OLYMPIC THEATRE.
Sole Lessee and Manageress ....MRS. JOHN WOOD
Stage Manager...... ....J. H. SELWYN

SATURDAY EVENING, June 2,
the performance will commence with the elegant comedy, in three acts, entitled
THE LOVE KNOT.
After which the glorious burlesque entitled
MEDEA;
Or, THE BEST OF MOTHERS
WITH A BRUTE OF A HUSBAND.
MONDAY EVENING, June 4,
MRS. JOHN WOOD,
having recovered from her severe indisposition will inaugurate a short summer season by appearing in a new drama, adapted expressly for the Olympic, from the celebrated novel of Charles Dickens, Esq., and entitled
"OUR MUTUAL FRIEND."
Being her FAREWELL PERFORMANCES.
Doors open at 7 1-4. Curtain rises at 8 o'clock.

The June 2, 1866 issue was the last for the *New York Saturday Press.* The end came abruptly, with little warning editorially. There was also little notice in the press. The *New York Review*, offered:

I have never heard the question asked, but I wonder where all the good newspapers go to when they die?

Perhaps the extra-intelligent female who reported Gen. Scott's reception in the world to come, [a reference to Emma Bullene, a spiritualist and trance speaker, from Wisconsin] for the daily press; will have the goodness to elucidate this mystery. It would be interesting to know whether the Saturday Press followed the example of the illustrious commander. It would be a relief to Sir Figaro [Clapp] to learn something of the reception accorded its genial spirit. Whether Washington ordered ten copies, the Duke of Wellington four, Napoleon one, and the late Czar of Russia none, or not. It is not impossible that Ben Franklin or Milton is cheerfully canvassing for its advertising columns. The spirits with whom Miss Bullene is in rapid communication probably depend on defunct publications for their latest news from the "old country."

The contributors to the *Saturday Press* went on to shape literary and cultural landscapes in some cases, while others followed the tragic paths of those who had passed before them.

Ned House became a *Tribune* correspondent, traveling to England and later serving as an officer in the government's educational department in Japan. Charley Seymour transitioned to steady work as the dramatic critic for the *Times* before becoming a partner at the publishing house Scribner & Co. Willie Winter and Elizabeth Campbell raised a family on Staten Island, and Winter earned acclaim as a drama critic for the *Tribune* while publishing numerous books on the theater.

Henry Clapp, however, was unable to recover from the *Saturday Press's* failure. Unemployed and adrift, he spent his final years in mental asylums and was often seen wandering the streets, a shadow of his former self.

Fanny Fern passed away from cancer in 1872.

Walt Whitman, tirelessly revising his *Leaves of Grass,* suffered a paralytic stroke in 1873 and moved to Camden to live with his brother.

In 1874, Ada Clare, pursuing a theatrical career, tragically died from a rabid dog bite.

Clapp's own life ended the following year, in 1875. Whitman later wrote of his friend's passing with unflinching brevity: "...he died in a gutter—drink—drink—took him down, down."

Mortimer Thomson, the humorist of "Doesticks" fame, passed away just a month later, his once-popular style having long since fallen out of fashion.

Whitman's health improved in his later years, allowing him to complete further revisions of his work and embark on a lecture tour. He passed away in Camden in 1892, leaving behind an indelible legacy as America's greatest poet.

In 1868, Mark Twain published his popular humorous travelogue, *The Innocents Abroad,* which led to a lecture career. He would go on to write many icons of American literature, including *The Adventures of Tom Sawyer* and *Adventures of Huckleberry Finn.* He is remembered by many as America's greatest humorist.

Ada Clare before the footlights.

1860 Glossary of Archaic and Obscure Terms, Places, and People.

This glossary provides definitions and context for archaic terms, places, and people appearing in the *New York Saturday Press (NYSP)* during its publication years. "●" denotes a *Saturday Press* contributor, as opposed to authors whose works were borrowed from other sources. Names are listed by the form most commonly used in *NYSP*, with alternate names or pseudonyms provided in italics.

Academy of Music Grand Ball, 1856.

Abbot Collection: Collection of Egyptian art and antiquities assembled by Dr. Henry Abbott, a British physician. Displayed at the "Egyptian Museum" in the Stuyvesant Institute, 659 Broadway (1853-1860).

Academy of Music: Northeast corner of East 14th Street and Irving Place, Manhattan. 4,000-seat opera house, home of the Max Maretzek Italian Opera Company, featuring sopranos Adelina Patti and Giulia Grisi.

adacititious: forming an addition or supplement; not integral or intrinsic.

affiche: French term for poster.

Agassiz, Louis (1807-1873): Swiss-born American biologist and geologist. Though highly esteemed in the 19th Century, his reputation has not aged well due to his advocacy of polygenism and racialism.

● Aldrich, Thomas Bailey, *the Poick* (1836-1907): New Hampshire-born writer, poet, critic, and editor of the *Atlantic Monthly*. Early *NYSP* contributor.

Louis Agassiz

Thomas Bailey Aldrich

• **Alger, Horatio** (1832-1899): Massachusetts-born writer, Harvard graduate, who would later find success writing rags-to-riches novels for boys.

alembic: a glass vessel used in chemical distillation.

alkahest: a universal solvent, theorized by Renaissance alchemists.

amanuensis: an assistant who takes dictation or copies manuscripts.

amaranth: an imaginary flower that never fades.

• **Ames, Mary Clemmer** (1831-84): Utica, NY-born journalist, author, and poet.

Amity Street: Former name of Third Street. East of Broadway, it was "Great Jones St."

Horatio Alger, 1852.

anabasis: a military advance.

anacreontic: a poem celebrating love and wine, in the style of Ancient Greek poet, Anacreon.

anchorite: a religious recluse.

andante: a moderately slow musical tempo.

Anderson, John Henry: Stage magician, "Prof. Anderson 'Wizard of the North'" who transformed the Winter Garden into his "Psychomantheum" for "soirees magicales".

anent: concerning.

animadvert: to direct critical or censorious attention upon.

Mary Clemmer Ames

Anna Maria: Personne's fictional object of adoration and sometimes SP contributor. Daughter of New York City banker and Fifth avenue society belle. May be a play on his 9-year-old niece, Anna.

annealed: Burnt in.

anon: shortly.

anti-macassar: small cloth placed protectively over the arm or back of a chair.

appanages: lands assigned by a king for the use of his sons.

Appleton's Building (1854-1860): Retail bookseller with artist spaces at the former location of the New York Society Library, 346-48 Broadway, southeast corner of Leonard.

arede: to guess.

• **Arnold, George** *Pierrot, Geo. Garrulous, Chevalier M'Arone, McArone* (1834-1865): New York City-born author, poet, and Pfaffian. Vanity Fair contributor. Lived in a boarding house on Houston St. Died at 31 of "paralysis," maybe from alcohol abuse. Said to have contributed to *NYSP* "gratis." Co-wrote "The Magician's Own Book" with Frank Cahill.

Appleton's Building, 346-48 Broadway.

arras: Tapestry.

Art Union Concert Hall (1852): 495-497 Broadway. Light entertainment.

ashler: an architectural facing of thin slabs.

asperity: harshness or severity.

asperse: to attack with false charges.

asseverate: to state something earnestly.

Astor Place Riot: 1849 clash centered at the Astor Opera House (Lafayette Street between 8th Street and Astor Place) that left around 28 dead. The riot stemmed from tensions between the lower-class, Irish supporters of American actor Edwin Forrest and the wealthy, nativist fans of British actor William Macready. Anti-British sentiment among Forrest's fans clashed with the anti-immigrant views of Macready's elite supporters. A third faction, armed police, intervened, further escalating the conflict.

George Arnold.

Astor Place Riots

Atheneum Theatre: *See Church of the Messiah.*

attic salt/attic wit: a refined, delicate wit.

Auber, Daniel: French composer of comic opera.

austral: southern.

Autocrat: *See Oliver Wendell Holmes.*

autopatheia: self-suffering.

avare: miser.

"Awful" Jefferson: *Personne's* nickname for Joseph Jefferson.

backshish: a gratuity.

A.F. Banks, from "Yankee Notions.".

badinage: witty conversation.

balm in Gilead: an option for redemption.

b'hoy: a young man of the rough Lower Manhattan working class.

• **Banks, A. F.** (?-1880): Pfaffian. Journalist, who "invested" $60 to Clapp for *NYSP*. Gunn describes him as a tiring drunk. Fought for the Union.

baptismal regeneration: the religious concept linking baptism with salvation.

• **Barber, Joseph** *Disbanded Volunteer* (1808-1874): English-born poet, editor of the Sunday Times and Troy Whig. Lived at 26 Amity St. (at Greene.)

barcarelle: a popular song sung by a Venetian gondolier.

Barnum's American Museum (1841-1865): Zoo, museum, lecture hall, wax museum, freak show, and 3,000-seat theater, operated by P. T. Barnum. Located at 218-222 Broadway, at Ann Street, at the southern terminus of Park Row.

Kate Josephine Bateman

baronial: large and impressive.

barracoon: a hut used by European traders to store enslaved persons while they were preparing to sell them to Americans.

Bateman, Kate Josephine (1842-1917): Baltimore-born actress of a British theater family.

bavardage: idle chit-chat.

• **Beach, Juliette Hayward** (1829-1900): Vermont-born poet and critic. Her husband, Calvin G. Beach, an Albion, NY newspaper publisher, intercepted a post from Clapp, and falsely reviewed "Leaves of Grass" in her name, encouraging Whitman to kill himself. Clapp printed the eview, supposedly without reading it, creating the type of controversy Clapp and Whitman saw as helpful to sales. Juliette replied with a review praising Whitman, signed *"A Woman."*

beaupot: a large ornamental vase for cut flowers.

Barnum's American Museum in 1858, Ann Street and Broadway. Looking down Broadway with City Hall Park & Park Row at lower right. A banner draped across the front of the museum advertises "Thiodon's Exhibition," a panoramic display of scenes from the Crimean War that included mechanized figures by J.F. Thiodon.

Beecher, Henry Ward (1813-87): Pastor of Plymouth Church, Brooklyn. Social reformer and speaker; abolitionist and brother of Harriet Beecher Stowe.

beldame: a malicious and ugly woman, a witch.

Belial: Devil.

Bellew, Frank Henry Temple (1828-1888): Transplanted Briton, Pfaffian, caricaturist, and illustrator. Creator of the Uncle Sam character. Lived at 1 Amity St. (adjacent to Broadway).

Bellows, Dr. Henry Whitney (1814-1882): Pastor of the Unitarian Church of All Souls, then at 391 Fourth Ave and 20th St. Transcendentalist who ascribed to the "Broad Church" theology of inclusivity.

Henry Ward Beecher

Frank Bellew

Pastor Henry Bellows

Benicia Boy: *See John C. Heenan.*

benison: Blessing, benediction.

• **Benjamin, Eastburn** (1837-1874): Chaplain, Poet. Founded the Home for the Blind.

Bennett, James Gordon (1795-1872): Founder and editor of the *New York Herald* newspaper. Clapp maintained an ongoing smear campaign against Bennett.

• **Bennett, Zelotes R.** (1836-1901): Connecticut-born poet.

James Gordon Bennett

Bennett Divorce Case: High-profile contest between George Bennett, an unscrupulous New Haven quack medicine producer, and his young wife, Mary, who proved eager to reveal his lying, abuse, and his manipulation of vulnerable customers.

Josh Billings

beteem: to allow.

bibelot: a small, decorative ornament or trinket.

Bible House: Massive cast-iron-framed building located just north of Cooper Union from which the American Bible Society published millions of bibles.

bijouterie: jewelry or trinkets.

billet-doux: a love letter.

Billings, Hammatt (1818-1874): Bostonian architect and artist.

• **Billings, *Josh;*** Henry Wheeler Shaw (1818-1885): Humorist in the misspelled/vernacular style of Artemus Ward.

birch: to instruct, using the coercion of discipline, such as whipping with a birch rod.

Bishop, Anna Riviére (1810-1884): Widely popular English operatic soprano whose voice was compared to a flute. In 1866, she survived a harrowing shipwreck.

Anna Riviére Bishop

Black Eyed Susan: Reference to an English ballad by John Gay, the "Susan" of which has rings around her eyes due to all the crying she does as her lover parts to return to sea.

blackamoor: a very dark-skinned person.

blackleg: a swindler.

blackslider: a person who has fallen away from the church.

blench: to shrink.

Blondin, Charles (1824-1897): French acrobat who in 1859 crossed Niagara Falls on a tightrope.

blue bed; brown bed: literary symbolism referring to shifts between higher status or situation (blue) and more modest (brown).

Bonner, by Gunn.

blue devils: feelings of melancholia, despondency.

blue-peter: the blue and white flag hoisted when a ship is ready to set sail from port.

blue-pill: a mercury-based purgative; calomel.

blue-stocking: a literary or intellectual woman.

Bohemianism: A cultural movement where individuals, often not born into poverty, live in a manner that rejects materialism and mainstream societal expectations and norms. Bohemians are typically associated with artists and writers, and the movement is thought to have originated in France, popularized by Henri Murger's 1845 collection of short stories, *Scènes de la vie de bohème*.

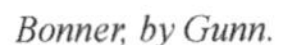

bone: to steal.

Bonheur, Rosa (1822-1899): French artist known best as a painter of animals.

Rosa Bonheur.

Bonner, Robert: Editor *of New York Ledger*.

booby: a person regarded as silly or unintelligent.

Booth, Edwin (1833-93): Pfaffian; American stage actor and theater manager. Brother of Lincoln's assassin, John Wilkes Booth. Booth and his two brothers performed in a benefit staging of Julius Caesar, which resulted in the purchase of the Shakespeare statue that still stands in Central Park. Despite his disowning of his association with his brother, due to the infamy of his name, he did not perform for nearly a year following the assassination.

• **Boucicault, Dion** (1820-1890): Irish actor, playwright, and manager of The Winter Garden Theatre. He wrote and produced *The Octoroon*. He also produced for Laura Keene.

Bowery Theatre: 3,000-seat theatre at 46-48 Bowery—the first lit by gaslight--originally built in 1846 for an upscale audience, but by the 1850's came to be a theater catering to immigrant, working-class audiences. In 1845, after a fire, it was rebuilt as the New Bowery Theatre. Destroyed by fire in 1926.

Edwin Booth

Brady, Matthew (1822-1896): Iconic American photographer, whose studio was located at 785 Broadway (10th Street).

Branch, Lawrence: *See Grow-Branch Affair.*

Branch, Stephen H.: Self-promoting writer; published muckraking newspaper, "Alligator," which resulted in a libel conviction against him and a year in jail.

breviary: a priest's book of liturgy.

brickbat: a weaponized brick.

Matthew Brady's Gallery, at 10th St., cater-corner from Grace Church.

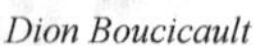

Dion Boucicault

John Brougham.

Bowery Theatre, 1867.

• **Bridges Stebbins, Sallie** (1830-1910): Philadelphian poet.

Brignoli, Pasquale (1824-84): Italian tenor at the Academy, Niblo's.

Broadway Theatre/Old Broadway Theatre (1847-1959): Enormous 4,000-seat theatre at 326 Broadway, near Pearl. 1847-1859. Also, after Wallack's left 485 Broadway, that theater was renamed Broadway Theatre until its 1869 demise. Also, during a brief period of 1863, Canturbury Hall was named The Broadway Theatre.

Brother Jonathan: *See entry for "John Bull."*

• **Brougham, John** (1814-80): Pfaffian; Dublin-born actor, playwright, and theater manager of Niblo's Garden, Brougham's Lyceum Theatre (*see Wallack's*), and the Bowery Theatre.

brown study: a dull thoughtfulness.

• **Brown, Joseph Brownlee** (1824-1888): Early contributor at *NYSP*. Charleston-born poet and educator.

bruit: to report.

John Brougham's Lyceum 485 Broadway, originally Wallack's, and here, as the Broadway.

Brummell, Beau (1778-1840): Socialite and friend to the British regent, seen as the arbiter of men's fashion in London, until he was scandalized by debt and escaped his creditors to France, where he eventually died of syphilis.

bubble reputation: in Shakespeare's play "As You Like It", a soldier seeks "the bubble reputation even in the cannon's mouth". Just as bubbles are fragile and can pop at any moment, a person's reputation is delicate and can be lost in an instant.

• **Bugbee, Emily Hewitt** (1840-1892): Vermont-born poet.

buhl: brass inlay in furniture.

bumper: a cup filled to the brim (as for a toast).

buncombe: (modern: bunkum) nonsense, from Buncombe county, N.C., from which a Congressional Representative gave an inane speech in 1820.

Bunsby, Jack: Character in Dickens's Dombey & Sons, a ship's captain, seen as an oracle.

Burch Case: The month-long divorce trial of Chicago socialite Mary Weld Turner Burch, accused by her husband Isaac Howe Burch, a Chicago banker, of adultery with her divorce lawyer, among others; and she, in turn, accusing him of infidelity, asserting he was 'enamored with a fascinatress' staying as a guest in their family home. Mrs. Burch won the suit.

John Burroughs

• **Burroughs, John** *All Souls* (1837-1921): Pfaffian. Wrote the column, "Fragments from the Table of an Intellectual Epicure." Art commentary; would become a celebrated naturalist writer, biographer of Whitman.

Burton's New Theatre (1856-59): 204-214 Mercer St. Light comedies.

Butler, William Allen (1825-1902): Lawyer and author of satirical poem, "Nothing to Wear."

butt: a cask of 126 gallons.

C.W.: Abbreviation for Canada West.

Cahill, Frank *"Wild Humorist of the Marshes"* (1833-1896): English-born journalist and editor. Pfaffian. Lived at 168 East 21st St. Boarded with Gunn and Cahill's cousin, Charles Seymour. Co-wrote *The Magician's Own Book* with George Arnold. Described by Gunn as a hopeless drunk. On June 9, 1860, as editor and business manager of the comic weekly *Nick-Nax*, he collected $250 in monies due the paper and absconded with the money, shipping back to England to the shock of his many Pfaffian friends. In London, he could find no work. Destitute, he returned to New York City less than a year later and mended his relations. He then enlisted with the Union.

Cahill, by McLenan.

calumet: a Native American ritual pipe.

• **Campbell, Elizabeth,** *Isabelle Castlebar* (1841-1922): Scottish novelist, poet, and story writer. In 1860, she married William Winter, and they raised a family on Staten Island.

canaille: the rabble, the common people.

cantatrice: a female singer, esp. an opera singer.

Elizabeth Campbell Winter

Canterbury Hall (1857-1861): Concert hall at 663 Broadway (opposite Bond St, a few doors from Pfaff's) known for the bawdy and disruptive nature of its meetings and productions. Also known as Mozart Hall.

caoutchouc: natural rubber.

capapie or **cap-a-pie**: from head to foot; all over.

Caporal: A strong, dark French tobacco.

car: a small carriage pulled by one horse.

carminative: antacid.

carmine: a crimson-colored powder.

carnet: a booklet in which is kept transportation tickets.

cartoon: a drawing on paper to be transferred to a wall in preparation to create a fresco.

• **Cary, Phoebe** (1824-1871): Ohio-born poet. In 1850 moved she to New York City with her sister, where they hosted evening receptions with women's rights advocates.

casaque: a loose-fitting blouse for women.

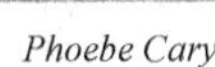

Phoebe Cary

• **Case, Mrs. Marie Stevens;** *Howland* (1836-1921): Massachusetts-born feminist writer and utopian socialist. *(See Edw. Howland.)*

Cass, Lewis (1782-1866): US Senator from Michigan and Army officer. Though himself a slave holder, Cass resigned as Secretary of State in protest to Buchanan's appeasement of secessionist states.

cat's-paw: a person used by another to do dangerous or distasteful work.

cat-call: a squeaking instrument used to condemn plays.

catch-penny: Seemingly attractive, but cheaply constituted.

cates: delicious food.

caudle: a thick, milky drink for invalids.

Céleste, Célene (1815-1882): *Also known as*: Madame Céleste. French dancer and actress.

cerement: a grave shroud.

chandler: a seller of goods.

Lewis Cass

Chapin, Edwin Hubbell (1814-1880): Popular pastor of the Universalist, Church of the Divine Unity, at 548 Broadway (Prince and Spring), where P.T. Barnum and Horace Greeley worshipped.

char-a-banc: a large, open-air horse carriage with benches so as to seat sightseeing groups and such.

charing: turning wood into charcoal by partial burning; performing temporary day-work.

charivari: a noisy mock-serenade to wish newlyweds well.

Charley White's Opera House: *See Washington Hall.*

Charlotte Russe: A charlotte (molded bread pudding) prepared with cream.

chary: cautiously reluctant.

chef-d'œuvre (*"shéh-duhr-vuh"*): a masterpiece, from the French for "chief work."

Madame Célene Céleste.

• **Chesebro, Caroline** (1825-73): Canandaigua, NY-born fiction writer.

chevelure: hair style.

Chick, Mrs Louisa Dombey: Character in Dickens's Dombey & Sons.

• **Chilton, Mary A** (1830-1897): Journalist, critic. Born in the South, fled an abusive marriage and lost custody of her children. Marriage abolitionist; lived in Modern Times utopian community in Brentwood, Long Island.

Caroline Chesebro

chop: *[derived from Chinese]* quality.

chrysolite: a green gemstone; peridote.

Church of the Messiah (1838-1866): 724-730 Broadway, opp. Waverly Pl.; converted in 1862 to the Broadway Atheneum; in 1865 to Lucy Rushton's New-York Theatre.

cicerone: a guide.

cicisbeo: a man who is escort or lover to a married woman.

ci-devant: characteristic of a previous time (French for "from before").

claquers: those hired to applaud or heckle a performer or speaker.

Clapp, George G. (1824-93): Pfaffian; Henry's twin brother; dealer in rare books. Died in a Bowery flophouse.

Church of the Messiah.

• **Clapp, Henry Jr** *Brooklyn, M.E., the oldest man, Figaro* (1814-1875): "King of the Bohemians" at Pfaff's. Founder and editor of the *New York Saturday Press*; Nantucketer; former member of the Free Love League; former editor of a temperance newspaper; enthusiast of Fourierist socialism. For reasons unknown, Clapp left Lynn, MA, where he was an editor to live in France, where he developed an affinity for Bohemian culture. When he returned from France in 1850, he took up residence in New York City. He lived at 52 Bleecker Street. He founded *NYSP* in 1858. He wrote *Dramatic Feuilleton*, when others were not available, and regular articles that he mostly left unsigned, which was usual at the time. Many of his contributions are noted for their intolerance and vindictiveness, a contrast to the youthful exuberance of his

Henry Clapp, Jr.

Ada Clare.

other writers. Gunn wrote of him, "I find no modesty, no kindness, no humanity in him." Sol Etynge razzed Clapp to anger one evening at Pfaff's, comparing him to a spider, adding he would not be surprised to see Clapp project something sticky from his stomach, affix it, and run up to the ceiling. In Clapp's final years, he spent time in mental asylums and was seen vagrant on the street by associates. Whitman described Clapp's death as "...he died in a gutter—drink—drink—took him down, down".

• ***Clare, Ada;*** Jane McElhenney, Clare-Noyes (1834-1874): Pfaffian; known as the "Queen of Bohemia". Columnist for NYSP, actress, essayist, fiction writer, and poet. Raised on a wealthy Charleston plantation, Jane was orphaned at a young age. When she matured to her inheritance, she toured Paris seeking a life on the stage. She returned to New York City with a young son, Aubray, while unapologetically unwed. Clare then took a three-story brownstone at 86 West 42 St, where she regularly entertained a coterie of intellectuals. Later, she spent time in San Francisco and Hawaii as a feted literary celebrity.

Eventually, after returning to NYC and the pursuit of her stage aspirations, Ada died at her home at 166 Bleecker St. of rabies, which she contracted from a bite of a small dog owned by her theatrical agent at 9 Amity St. She was buried at Edward and Marie Howland's estate, "Casa Tonti," beside her second child who had recently died, in Hammonton, NJ., because the nearby Christian cemetery refused to accept burials for those who practiced Spiritualism.

Clifton, Ada (1835-91): Pfaffian; actress at Laura Keene's.

Clinton Hall (1830-1869): Exhibition hall at 9 Beekman St.

Cobden, Richard: English politician, promoter of free-trade.

coevel: having the same age or date of origin.

Cogswell, Joseph Green (1786-1871): Astor Librarian. Friends with Edward Everett, George Ticknor, John Jacob Astor, Washington Irving, and Fitz-Greene Halleck. Reported repeatedly witnessing a ghost in the library.

cold without: brandy and water.

Coleman House Hotel: 647 Broadway. *(See Pfaff's.)*

collocation: the association between two words that are used together.

colored: the neutral self-referential term used in print by African Americans in the antebellum period.

Come-outer: One who "comes out" or leaves an organization on grounds of principle. In the mid-19th century, this term was often used to describe abolitionists who chose to leave or were ejected from religious groups over the issue.

comic papers: at the time, illustrations were a novelty, largely reserved for humorous "comic papers," such as the *New York Reveille, Nick Nax, the New York Picayune, the Lantern, Vanity Fair,* and *Yankee Notion.*

Company: A reference to the rule of the British East India Company on the Indian subcontinent from 1773 to November, 1858.

Comus: Greek god of festivity, revels and nocturnal dalliances.

concatenation: a series of interconnected things or events.

conduce: help to bring about.

Spencer Wallace Cone.

• **Cone, Spencer Wallace** (1819-1888): Virginian lawyer and poet. Raised and led the 61st NY volunteers for the Union. His daughter, stage name Kate Claxton, became a successful actress. On two occasions, her performances were interrupted by deadly theater fires, and as a result she had trouble getting work due to being seen as bad luck. Former Pfaffian Thomas Nast published a full-page Harper's Weekly cartoon satirizing the press as jackasses for repeating the malicious talk, winning public sympathy, and her popularity was restored.

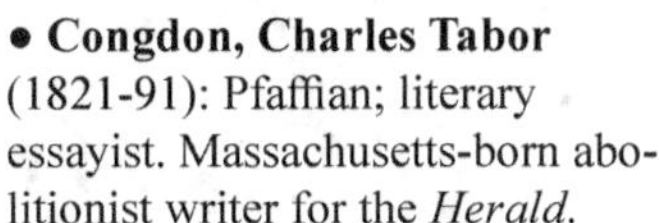

• **Congdon, Charles Tabor** (1821-91): Pfaffian; literary essayist. Massachusetts-born abolitionist writer for the *Herald*.

Charles Tabor Congdon.

congé: a leave-taking with a bow or curtsey; or an unceremonious rejection.

Congress water: A saline mineral water from the Congress spring at Saratoga.

contumacy: stubborn refusal to obey authority.

contumely: insulting treatment.

• **Cooper, George** (1840-1927): NYC-born law student, became a poet instead. Wrote lyrics for Stephen Foster. Fought for the Union in the Civil War.

George Cooper.

Cooper Union: Private college adjacent to Astor Place founded by iron industrialist Peter Cooper in 1859, dedicated to providing a free education to all, independent of race, religion, sex, wealth or social status.

• **Cornwell, Henry Sylvester** (1831-1886): Connecticut-born physician and poet. Fought for the Union in the Civil War.

Cortesi, Adelaide (1828-89): Italian mezzo-soprano at the Academy and Niblo's.

coruscant: shining.

• **Cose, Jo**: A correspondent who seems to have written to a number of newspapers with commentary in the period.

cosmogonic: related to the origin of earth.

costermonger: a person who sells goods, especially fruit and vegetables, from a handcart in the street.

crash-towel: a coarse, common towel.

Crayon Gallery (1860): Exhibition and studio space at 768 Broadway.

crepusculous: *zoology.* of an animal active in twilight.

cricket: Personne's name for reviewers and critics.

crinoline: (from "crin," which means horsehair of the type used to make stiff fabric) a skirt that projects out, eventually applied to the hoop skirts popular beginning in the 1850's.

Peter Cooper, founder of Cooper Union.

Madame Adelaide Cortesi.

• **Cromwell, Ruth Natalie** nee Walters (1834-1889): New York City-born Poet. Crushed to death when a bale of hay fell off a cart onto her head while walking along 46th Street.

Crook and Duff's: Restaurant on the ground floor of the *New York Times* Building, across from City Hall, where newspaper workers would congregate.

crotchet: a whim.

Croton Reservoir (1842-1890): *Also known as*: Murray Hill Reservoir. A massive, 50-foot high above-ground reservoir at 42nd Street and Fifth Avenue, the modern-day site of the main branch of the New York Public Library. It presented a vaguely Egyptian-style facade, and, atop the walls was a popular public promenade offering panoramic views and cooler air.

cryptogamaic: related to the plants of the class cryptogamia.

New York Crystal Palace and Latting Observatory.

Crystal Palace (1853-1858): Large, glass-and-iron domed exhibition hall, inspired by the highly successful Crystal Palace recently erected in London's Hyde Park for the Great Exhibition of 1851, a celebration of the Industrial Revolution. It was built directly to the west of the Croton Reservoir, on 42 St and 6th Ave, the modern-day site of Bryant Park. The site featured a variety of saloons and beer gardens, some segregated for women that excluded alcohol. The building burned to the ground in 1858 without any loss of life.

cuirass: Breast plate.

Cumming, Dr. John: Controversial Scottish clergyman and religious author. George Eliot criticized him for his anti-Catholicism, obsession with the End Times, and intellectual dishonesty.

Curtis, George William (1824-1892): Rhode Island-born journalist, lecturer, novelist, abolitionist, and advocate for women's suffrage, public education, and Native American rights.

Croton Reservoir, 42 Street and Fifth Avenue.

Charlotte Cushman.

Cushman, Charlotte (1816-76): One of the leading American actresses. She played cross-gender, famously starring as Hamlet.

cut: to sever or refuse a connection with an undesirable person.

cutter: a type of sleigh.

• ***Cyfax***: Humorist; likely Twain.

Davenport, Dolly, Adolphus Hoyt Davenport (1828-1873): Connecticut-born stage actor.

Day & Martin: A well-known boot-blacking manufacturer.

dead-head: a person admitted free-of-charge to a theater.

decline: to list or enumerate.

defalcation: financial impropriety.

Dolly Davenport

• ***De Grove, Hester S.*** Hester Ann Eliza Strachan Dwinelle (1820-1903): Poet from Ogdensburg, NY originally. Lived at the Unitary Home at 106 E. 14 St.

Déjazet, Pauline Virginie (1798–1875): French actress, a well-known travesti (gender-swapping) performer.

demd: damned.

demesne: domain.

demi-monde: a French class of women of doubtful morality.

demnition: damnation.

Depew, Chauncey (1834-1928): New York State assemblyman and Civil War Colonel.

depone: attest.

desiderata: things that are desired or needed.

Hester S. De Grove

Diamond Wedding: A remarkably ostentatious wedding performed at (old) St. Patrick's Cathedral on October 13, 1859, between 18-year-old New York City socialite, Frances Amelia Bartlett, and immensely-wealthy 55-year-old Cuban planter, Don Esteban Santa Cruz de Oviedo.

Dibdin, Charles (1745–1814): English composer, novelist, and dramatist.

Dickinson, Anna (1842-1942): Philadelphia-born abolitionist.

dishabille: a state of incomplete dress.

distich: a pair of poetry lines that form a complete unit.

do.: abbreviation for "ditto."

Dodsworth Hall (1852-1887): Dancing academy and lecture hall, located at 806 Broadway, the next building north of Grace Church.

Doesticks, Q.K.Philander, Mortimer Neal Thomson (1831-75): Pfaffian. Michigan-raised journalist. Popular humor columnist for *Tribune*. Married Fanny Fern's daughter soon after his first wife died at age 18 in childbirth. Volunteered for the Union. Died after a long illness a month after Clapp.

dominie: a school master.

doosid: deuced; damned.

dorg: a fishing line.

douane: French custom house officers.

Dramatic Feuilleton: The name given to *NYSP*'s drama critic's column, using the French term for a serial publication to establish an intention to use the Parisian style of savvy, clever, and satirical commentary. The Dramatic Feuilletons were signed Fitz James O'Brien, "Personne," for Ned Wilkins, "Quelq'un," for William Winter, and "H.C., Jr." and "Figaro" (for Clapp).

Mort Thomson, "Doesticks".

Drayton, Henri: Opera baritone, librettist and impresario.

drug: a commodity on hand that is not salable.

dun: to clamor for payment of a debt.

• ***Dunn, Deborah*** Marian Stockton, neé Tuttle (1841-1906): South Carolinian-born writer.

Dusseldorf Gallery: Art gallery at 548 Broadway, and in 1860 moved to the Institute of Fine Arts.

Dutch courage: Courage obtained from alcohol intoxication.

Deborah Dunn.

eddaic: related to old Norse literature.

• ***Edgerton, Wild;*** Brockholst L. McVicker (1836-1888): Buffalo-born poet, lecturer, physician. Served as a Union surgeon during the Civil War.

Edmonds, John Worth (1799-1874): NY state senatorSupreme Court judge. *NYSP* republished a series of *Tribune* articles wherein Edmonds asserted spiritualism to be legitimate. Lived at 71 Irving Place.

Egyptian Museum: *See Abbot Collection.*

eheu: alas! [as in an exclamation of grief.]

eidola: tokens of idolatry.

eleemosynary: charitable.

ell: a measurement of cloth.

Ellsler, Fanny (1810-1884): Austrian ballerina.

Ellsworth, Elmer E. (1837–1861): A New York native, leader of the Chicago Zouaves, and friend of President Lincoln. At the outbreak of the Civil War, he was killed by a secessionist innkeeper while removing a Confederate flag from an Alexandria, VA inn. The brutality of the act galvanized Union resolve. *See Zouaves.*

Edward Everett.

Emerald City: Period nickname for New York City.

enbonpoint: fleshiness in the figure, esp. of a woman.

epithalamium: a song celebrating a marriage.

equivoke: an expression capable of having more than one meaning; a pun or ambiguity.

erst: long ago.

eupeptic: related to good digestion.

European plan: Hotel billing policy that that charges room rates separately from meals.

Everett, Edward: Massachusetts Senator, Governor, US Secretary of State, pastor and orator; lampooned in SP for his long-winded speeches. Though widely celebrated in his time, today, he is best remembered for speaking for two hours prior to Lincoln's brief address at Gettysburg.

Rose Eytinge.

Everett House (1853-1908): Large, first-class hotel at 37 E. 17th St., the northeast corner of Union Square, named in honor of Edward Everett.

• Ewbank, Thomas (1792-1870): English writer on practical mechanics, United States Commissioner of Patents from 1849 to 1852.

exigeant: demanding (Fr.)

Eytinge, Harry: Producer and actor; Laura Keene's stage manager; brother of Sol.

• Eytinge, Margaret Winship *Madge Elliot, Bell Thorne, Allie Vernon* (1832-1916): New York City-born author, often associated with children's short stories and poems. Spouse of illustrator Sol Eytinge Jr.

Eytinge, Rose (1838-1911): Actress for Wallack. Cousin to Sol.

Eytinge Jr., Solomon: New York City-born Pfaffian; prolific illustrator; brother to Harry; husband to Margaret, cousin to Rose. Lived at 290 W. 20th St.

Fabbri, Inez (1831-1909): Austrian soprano at the Academy, Niblo's.

fagot: a bundle of sticks traditionally used for burning at the stake as a form of punishment or execution, especially during historical periods of religious persecution.

farinaceous: rich in starch.

farthingale: a hooped petticoat.

Inez Fabbri.

fastuousness: pride.

fatling: a young animal fattened for slaughter.

fee: to bribe or win over.

fell: barbarous, malevolent.

• Felton, Cornelius Conway (1807-1862): Massachusetts-born educator; regent of the Smithsonian Institution, president of Harvard University.

Fenian Palace: A headquarters for Irish Republicans on Union Square that closed after a financial failure. Also known as the Moffat Mansion.

Fenian Palace.

Cornelius Conway Felton.

Fanny Fern.

• ***Fern, Fanny*** Sara Payson Willis Parton (1811-1872): Maine-born novelist, children's writer, humorist, and highly-successful newspaper columnist for the New York Ledger. Nathaniel Parker Willis was her brother. Whitman is said to have drawn from her immensely-successful essay collection, "Fern Leaves from Fanny's Portfolio," 1853, his similar book design for "Leaves of Grass."

feuilleton: a French term for a serial publication devoted to literature and criticism.

Fifth Avenue Opera House: 2-4 W. 24 St. Minstrel shows and burlesque.

filibuster: (from Spanish "filibustero") or "freeboot": the practice of US adventurers to invade South American countries with a private militia with the intention of enslaving the citizens, setting up agricultural or industrial enterprises, and eventually annexing the territory.

fils: in French, used to denote a son, as "Jr." is used in English.

finical: affectedly showy.

Edwin Forrest.

fiortures: little ornamental "flowers" introduced into a sung melody.

fistic: pugilistic.

Flash, Henry Lynden (1835-1914): Cincinnati-born poet and editor. Fought for the Confederacy.

flash: popular, attention-seeking.

flea-bottomry: life in a slum.

flounce: an exaggerated action, especially of annoyance, such as throwing one's arms up.

fluvious: of a free-flowing nature.

fly: a light, speedy carriage.

foolscap: the approximately 13 x 8-inch standard British paper size.

fop: a vain, ostentatious man of showy dress.

George William Fortmeyer.

Forrest, Edwin (1806-1872): Philadelphia-born Shakespearian actor. (*see: Astor Place Riot.*)

• **Fortmeyer, George W** (1839-1935): New York City-born clerk and poet. Lived at 113 West 13th St.

Fourier, François Marie Charles (1772-1837): French philosopher, utopian socialist, whose ideas inspired utopian communities across the U.S. Fourier advocated for women's rights, having originated the word feminism. At the same time, he was virulently anti-Semitic.

Fox, Mary; Mary Hewins Burnham; Mary Fiske (1837-1889): Pfaffian. Hartford-born actress, playwright and prolific newspaper correspondent. Lived at 72 W. 93 St. Served as New York correspondent of the *St. Louis Republican.*

The Fox Sisters.

Fox Sisters: Leah, Margaret, and Catherine Fox, sisters from Rochester, New York, played a pivotal role in the creation of the Spiritualism religious movement through an elaborate hoax. In 1848, the younger two sisters secretly used the knuckles of their toes to produce "rapping" sounds on the floorboards of their family home. They claimed these sounds were communications from spirits and developed a coded system to interpret them.

The sisters took their act to theaters, where their performances became a sensation. This sparked widespread interest in séances and communicating with the spirits of the dead, ultimately leading to the rise of Spiritualism, the most popular religious movement of the 19th century.

In 1888, Margaret confessed to the hoax, but still the Spiritualism movement continued to thrive, attracting devoted followers well into the 20th century.

Frankenstein, Godfrey Nicolas (1820-1873): German artist with a studio at 16 Crosby St., New York City, famed for painting an 8 x 1000-foot scrolling panorama painting featuring a variety of views of Niagara Falls.

freebooter: pillager. *See filibustering.*

Free Love League: A discussion group of men and women led by the Fourierist Stephen Pearl Andrews that opposed legal marriage, believing passions, rather than reason or imposed social structures, should guide individual actions and societal organization, leading to a harmonious and fulfilling society.. It did not encourage sexual promiscuity, but emotional openness without being restricted by society.

French Theatre or **Theatre Français**: 444, then 585 Broadway. French-language drama, Minstrel shows, magic, etc.; in 1866, its new building opened at 107 West 14th St.

frith: a strait, or narrow sea passage.

fustian: thick, twilled cloth; pompous writing.

g'hal: a young woman of the rough Lower Manhattan working class.

gallipot: a small pot used by apothecaries to hold medicine or ointment.

gamaliel: a Christian term for an esteemed Jewish doctor of Law.

Gamp, Mrs.: A character from Dickens's Martin Chuzzleworth, a drunken, sloppy, incompetent nurse.

garden engine: a portable hand-pump with sprayer.

Getty Gay

• **Gardette, Charles Desmarais**; *Saerasmid* (1830-1884): Philadelphia-born aristocrat, studied to be an M.D., but turned to journalism. Writer of fiction, poetry, and essays. Pfaffian. Published a humorous hoax in *NYSP*--a poem alleged to be a newly discovered Poe poem. Also published parodies of Whitman.

gawk: an awkward or shy person.

• ***Gay, Getty***, Gertrude L. Wilmhurst, nee Vultee (1835-1860): New York City-born actress, writer of stories and humorous commentary. She and her husband, editor of the *New York Traveller*, lived with Ada Clare at 86 W 42 St., where Getty died at 25 of tuberculosis.

• **Gayler, Charles** (1820-1892): New York City-born Pfaffian, journalist, playwright, and poet. Edited the humorous newspaper, *Momus*.

General: The name by which Quelqu'un addresses his readers ("the General Public").

gentle: a maggot larvæ, sometimes used for bait when fishing.

German Thalia Theatre: *See Wood's Minstrel Hall.*

Gerome: French painter and sculptor, Jean-Léon Gérôme.

gibber: to speak incoherently (ie: "gibberish").

Gilbert, John Gibbs (1810-1889): Boston-born actor, famous for "old-man" parts; performed at Wallack's.

• **Giles, Henry** (1809-82): Irish-born Unitarian minister and lecturer. Contributed book reviews and essays.

• **Gill, Alice**: Poet, essayist. Contributed also to the Brooklyn Daily Eagle.

Horace Greeley.

gimlet: a hand tool used for boring holes.

ging: a gang or troop.

Glasse, Hannah (1708–1770): Author of "The Art of Cookery Made Plain and Easy," Dublin, 1747.

glebeland: the area of land assigned to a church's parish in medieval times.

gloze: to flatter or use fawning language.

• **Goldbeck, Mary Freeman** *Anna Mary; Anna Maria* (1825-1874): Pfaffian. Miniaturist and watercolor painter, poet. The only woman among the original tenants at the Tenth Street Studio Building. Lived at 65 East 10th St.

Golden Dustman: Reference to a character in Dickens's Our Mutual Friend who inherited a giant ash heap that, once combed through, yielded a fortune in products that could be resold, such as bones, manure, metals, pots...

Gottschalk, Louis Moreau (1829-69): American composer and pianist; Ada Clare's avowed love interest.

Goupil and Co.: Art dealer at 772 Broadway.

Governor's Room: Gallery with 60 portraits in New York City Hall.

Grace Church: 802 Broadway, at 10th St.

Gradgrind: Unrelentingly rigid Dickens character from Hard Times.

Grahamism: The popularity of the health teachings of Sylvester Graham (1794-1851), who advocated vegetarianism, temperance, and a diet of foods that were pure, wholesome, and unstimulating, like his eponymously-named Graham flour and Graham crackers.

Giulia Grisi.

gramineal: of or pertaining to grass.

• ***Gray, Barry;*** Robert Barry Coffin (1826-1886): Pfaffian. Hudson, NY-born journalist, humorist, and critic. Editor for *Home Journal*. Custom-house clerk.

Gray, John Frederick Schiller (1840-1891): Pfaffian; fought at Antietam, and immediately returned by train so that the following evening after the battle he could be found at Pfaff's giving a first-hand account to Whitman.

SS Great Eastern: At her June, 1860 maiden voyage, by far the largest ship ever built. Would eventually lay the first successful transatlantic cable.

Greeley, Horace (1811-1872): Politically-aspiring founder and editor of the *New-York Tribune*.

greenroom: a veteran or retiring actor.

Greenwich Village: A New York City neighborhood, bounded on the north by 14th Street, on the south by Houston Street, on the east by the East River, to the Hudson River on the west. Known as Greenwich

Village since 1713, it became a place for summer country homes of the wealthy. Around the 1830's, the city's northward growth consumed it. Wealthy New Yorkers moved uptown, as did the theaters; and it was thereafter known as the 9th Ward. In fact, nowhere in the *NYSP* will you find a reference to the then-defunct name, though Pfaff's is in the Village, and most of the New York City-based writers live there. Around 1880, the press started recalling nostalgia of early 18th and 19th century New York City, and would refer to "Old Greenwich Village," and eventually the original name was returned, as a neighborhood name.

grisette: a flirtatious working girl.

Grisi, Giulia (1811-1869): Italian opera singer, starring at the Academy of Music.

grot: a cave ("grotto").

Grow and Branch Affair: On December 29, 1859, North Carolina Congressman Lawrence O'Bryan Branch challenged Republican Speaker of the House Galusha Grow to a duel after the two exchanged insults on the House Floor. Both men and their seconds were arrested by District of Columbia police before the duel could take place. Branch would be killed fighting Confederate at Antietam; Grow would continue in public life until shortly before his death in 1907.

Grundyism: priggishness, from an 18th century stage character. One may find an interesting comparison to political correctness.

guerdon: A reward or payment.

Gunn, by Nast, from Gunn's diary.

Gunn, Thomas Butler (1826-1904): British journalist, illustrator and war correspondent who kept a diary while living in antebellum New York City, at 132 Bleecker, describing his daily life and the literary people he interacted with, including several who contributed to *NYSP*.

• Gurowski, Adam (1805-1866): Pfaffian; Polish-born count, eventually turned pro-Russian. Wrote for the *Tribune*. Published the first strongly abolitionist sentiments by a *NYSP* writer, inserting it into an ongoing memoir despite Clapp's editorial avowal that the journal would not discuss the issue. Also contributed literary criticism. Died of typhoid fever.

Guy: An effigy of Guy Fawkes used to celebrate the failure of the Gunpowder Plot.

gymnotus: A South American electric fish.

hail: an enormous amount, like a heavy fall of hail. To "drink hail" is to drink to excess.

hair trunk: a trunk covered with leather hide from which the hair has not been removed.

Halleck, Fitz-Greene; *American Byron* (1790-1867): Pfaffian; well-respected and influential romantic poet and essayist. Up until the recent addition of the Women Rights Pioneers statue, his statue was the only American writer on the Literary Walk in Central Park.

Haney, Jesse C. (1828-1901): Philadelphia-raised publisher of comic papers, like the Picayune. Friends with George Arnold, Sol Etyinge, Whitman, Artemus Ward, Thomas Butler Gunn, and "Doesticks" Thomson. Lived at 28 W. 16 St.

Count Adam Gurowski, by Brady.

hang fire: To delay in making a decision.

Hanlon Brothers: An acrobatic act in Nixon's Circus at Niblo's with a grand-finale involving an audience-frightening fall from a 40-foot height.

Hardinge-Britten, Emma (1823-1899): English Spiritualist.

Harris, Mary: The first female murderer found not-guilty by plea of temporary insanity. Courted as a girl in Iowa by a man who later moved away and married a different woman, Harris travelled to Washington D.C. to find him and kill him with a gun. She would, 20 years later, marry the lawyer who had secured her acquittal.

Harte, Bret (1836-1902): Albany-born short story writer, critic, lecturer, playwright, and poet known for stories about romantic figures of the California Gold Rush.

Fitz-Greene Halleck.

hartshorn: aqueous ammonia smelling salts derived from the horns of deer.

Hawthorne, by Brady.

Hawthorne, Nathaniel (1804-1864), born in Salem, Massachusetts, is renowned for his "Dark Romantic" novels and short stories set in New England. Regarded as one of America's most esteemed writers both in his time and today, Hawthorne's works have become iconic.

hayaline: translucent.

• **Hayne, Paul Hamilton** (1830-1886): Charleston-born poet, critic, and editor. Fought as Confederate in the Civil War, and lost his home and possessions when Union forces took Charleston.

head-centre: a leader of a secret or revolutionary organization.

hebdomadal: a weekly publication.

Hebe: Greek goddess of youth, who served ambrosia at the heavenly feast.

Heenan, John Camel: (May 2, 1834 – October 28, 1873), also known as the Benicia Boy, was an American bare-knuckle prize fighter.

Heep, Uriah: Monstrous Dickens character who is dishonest, cruel, and greedy.

hejira: an exodus.

Helper's book: A book of statistics gathered by abolitionist and White supremacist, Hinton Helper, who advocated for an end to slavery and removal of all non-Whites from the US for the aid of poor Whites. The term "helperism" came to be used to describe Southerners whose arguments split Whites among class lines.

Paul Hamilton Hayne

hen-persuader: a device that would automatically hide a freshly-laid egg in the hopes of encouraging the hen to lay another.

hern: a heron.

Herschel, William: German-British astronomer who discovered Uranus.

Heth, Joice: African-American woman who was exhibited by P.T. Barnum with the claim that she was the 161-year-old nursing mammy of George Washington. After her 1836 death, at City Saloon, an exhibition hall and cafe at 222 Broadway, 1,500 spectators gathered as Barnum charged 50 cents admission to a public autopsy of her remains to prove her age. When the examining physician determined she was no older than 80, Barnum claimed it was the wrong body.

hippodrama: a stage drama that includes horsemanship.

Hippotheatron: A theater located at 86–94 14th Street, built in 1864 on the site of Nixon's Alhambra Theatre. Originally designed for circus and equestrian performances, it also hosted ballets and other types of shows. Situated on the south side of 14th Street, just east of Union Square, the Hippotheatron operated until 1872, when it was purchased by P.T. Barnum. Tragically, it burned down just a month later, resulting in the loss of a full menagerie of animals.

Holmes by Bellew.

histrion: a player or actor.

hock: a highly-esteemed Rhenish wine of a light yellow color.

hoiden: a tomboy.

Holmes, Sr., Oliver Wendell, *Autocrat* (1841-1935): Bostonian, highly-regarded writer, author of *Autocrat of the Breakfast-Table* for *Atlantic Monthly*. His son and namesake would become Chief Justice of the US Supreme Court.

Home, Daniel Dunglas (1833-1866): (pronounced "Hume") Popular Scottish spiritual medium who, according to devotees, would levitate to the ceiling during séance.

Homer, Winslow (1836-1910): Pfaffian. Boston-born marine and landscape painter and illustrator. Worked for *Harper's Weekly*.

Winslow Homer.

Hooley & Campbell's "Ethiopian Entertainments": Blackface minstrel show at Niblo's Saloon.

Hope Chapel: A religious assembly hall at 720 Broadway, just below 8th Street, converted to theatrical use in 1855. *Later Named*: Donaldson's Opera House (1855), Academy of Minstrels (1856), Kelly & Leon's (1865), Waverly Theatre (1869), Lina Edwin's (1870).

horary: relating to hours as measurements of time.

• **House, Edward Howard** (1836-1901): Pfaffian; Fiction writer, playwright. *Tribune* journalist. Clapp refused his proposed anti-slavery

Edward Howard House

dialogue, but printed his reply to Clapp's commentary against discussing the issue. House went onto a distinguished career as English-language newspaper publisher in Japan.

William Dean Howells.

• Howells, William Dean (1837-1920): Ohio-born novelist, literary critic, playwright, and poet.

• Howland, Edward and Marie Stevens (1832-1890): Charleston-raised, Harvard-educated Pfaffian, Edward invested a large portion of his family's cotton-trading fortune in *NYSP*. Contributed translations and biographies. Fuerierist socialist, who, while boarding at the Unitary Home at 17 Stuyvessant Street, met Marie and Lyman Case, a married couple, who also lived there. In true Free-Love-Leaguer spirit, Lyman, witnessing Marie's charmed reaction to meeting Edward, insisted Edward was the right man for her, and the Cases were divorced and Marie and Edward married. Marie was a feminist and suffragist, who pursued utopian social experiments, and started her own free library. *(see Clare, Ada.)*

Edward and Marie Howland.

hunch: a lump or thick piece.

hunker: a person who stubornly clings to old-fashioned beliefs.

inamorata: the female object of one's love.

inanition: exhaustion due to starvation.

inbraid: to weave into.

incarnadined: caused to be of a blood-red color.

indite: to compose; write.

Industrious Fleas: Flea theater at 599 Broadway.

infructuous: fruitless.

inst.: instant, or current, month.

Institute of Fine Arts: Derby Gallery at 625 Broadway.

inurned: buried, as in an "urn."

ipse dixit: a dogmatic and unproven statement.

Iron Duke: The Duke of Wellington, who defeated Napoleon.

irrefragible: incontestable; undeniable.

Joseph Jefferson

Irving Hall: a ballroom, concert, and lecture hall annex to the Academy of Music, opened at Irving Place and East 15th Street in December 1860, and served as the home to the New York Philharmonic in 1861-63.

Irving Place: Often a reference to the Academy of Music, which was located on the corner of 14 St. and Irving Place.

Jack-in-the-green: An English May Day folk custom wherein a person dresses like a tree.

Janesenism: A theological movement within Catholicism attempting to reconcile free-will and divine grace.

Jefferson, Joseph (1829-1905): Philadelphia-born comic actor at Laura Keene's. He lived at 97 East 12 St.

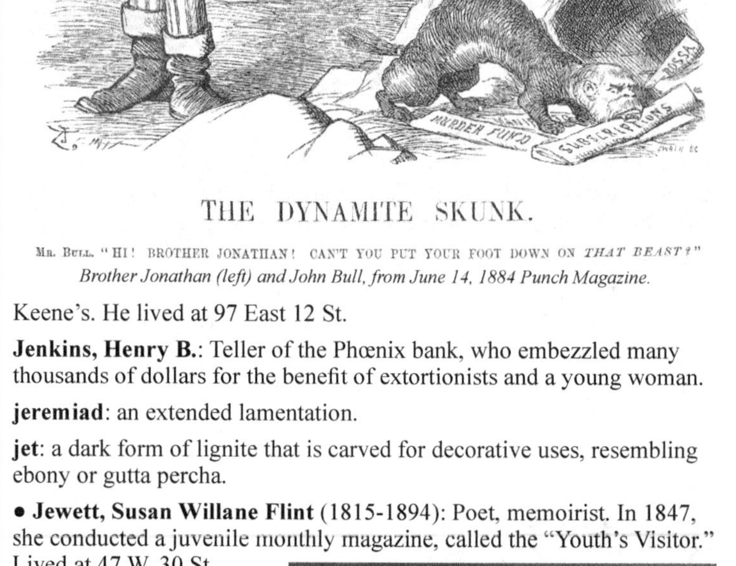

THE DYNAMITE SKUNK.

MR. BULL. "HI! BROTHER JONATHAN! CAN'T YOU PUT YOUR FOOT DOWN ON *THAT BEAST*?"

Brother Jonathan (left) and John Bull, from June 14, 1884 Punch Magazine.

Jenkins, Henry B.: Teller of the Phœnix bank, who embezzled many thousands of dollars for the benefit of extortionists and a young woman.

jeremiad: an extended lamentation.

jet: a dark form of lignite that is carved for decorative uses, resembling ebony or gutta percha.

• Jewett, Susan Willane Flint (1815-1894): Poet, memoirist. In 1847, she conducted a juvenile monthly magazine, called the "Youth's Visitor." Lived at 47 W. 30 St.

job: to buy and sell stocks for or raise funds for an enterprise.

jobbing house: a wholesale business.

jocose: given to jokes and jesting.

John Bull: A fictional character personifying Britain----the American version in the day was the Brother Jonathan character, a forerunner of Uncle Sam.

Jordan, George: Actor at Wallack's.

Kalydor: A lotion marketed as freckle-remover.

Kane, Elisha Kent (1820-1857): Very popular American Arctic explorer.

Laura Keene

Keene, Laura (1826-1873): British actress who went on to manage theaters in New York and Philadelphia.

Croton Reservoir and Crystal Palace, as viewed from atop the Latting Observatory.

Kehoe's Clubs: Brand-name for heavy wooden Indian clubs used for exercise.

kelson: a longitudinal structure running above and fastened to the keel of a ship in order to stiffen and strengthen its framework.

Kemble-Butler, Frances Ann "Fanny" (1809-1893): Celebrated British actress from a renowned acting family and prolific writer. After her husband, a slave-owner, took her to see his plantations in Georgia, she divorced him and became an abolitionist, documenting injustices and writing from the perspective of enslaved women. She gave readings from Shakespeare and her poetry at Dodsworth Hall.

• ***Kerr, Orpheus C.;*** **Robert Henry Newell** (1836-1901): Satirist, poet. Pen name derived from "office seeker," satirizing political patronage. Married Adah Isaacs Menken.

Ketchum: Reference to the fraud scandal of the banking firm, Morris Ketchum, Son & Co.

kickshaw: something fantastical, uncommon, or unnamed.

kids: kid-leather gloves.

kine: plural of cow.

King, Preston (1806-1865): Former US Senator and New York politician who, after being appointed as Collector of the Port of New York, reportedly became so overwhelmed with the corruption he was assigned to eradicate that he tied a bag of bullets around his neck and leapt to his death off a New York City ferry.

Orpheus C. Kerr.

kirk: Scottish expression for church.

knout: a Russian rawhide whip used for flogging.

• **Knowlton, Augustus Barton** (1837-1885): Originally from Augusta, GA, Brooklyn lawyer, and later South Carolina judge.

Know-Nothings (1844-1860): Nativist, populist political movement that directed its members to reply "I know nothing," whenever they were asked about its specifics by outsiders. With all the recent Irish Catholic immigration, they believed the Roman Catholic Papacy was organizing an attempt to take control of the US.

Lafarge House Hotel, looking south on Broadway from Amity.

Lafarge House (1853-1869): Large hotel at 667-677 Broadway, (a half-block north from Pfaff's) built to pair with the Metropolitan (later Winter Garden) Theatre. Catered largely to Southerners. On the same block as Pfaff's.

Lafitte: Château Lafite Bordeaux wine.

• **Laighton, Albert** (1829-1887): Portsmouth, NH banker and poet.

Lar: Ancient Roman household diety.

Albert Laighton.

• **Larcom, Lucy** (1824-1893): Massachusetts-born teacher, poet, and author. Rushlight Literary Magazine, which she founded, is still in publication today.

Latting Observatory (1853-1856): 315-foot high observation tower built across 42nd Street from the New York Crystal Palace. Burned down two years before the Crystal Palace did.

Laura Keene's Theatre (1856-1880): 622-624 Broadway (near Houston); home to Laura Keene's Varieties and in 1863 became Mrs. John Wood's Olympic Theatre.

lave: to wash.

lawn: a sort of fine linen or cambric.

lazzaroni: beggars who prey on tourists in and around Naples.

• **Ledyard Van Rensselaer, Catherine** (1811-1882): Connecticut-born poet and essayist. Friend of Harriet Beecher Stowe.

lied: a German song.

lief: gladly

limn: to express artistically.

Little Corporal: Napoleon Bonaparte.

• **Logan, Olive** *[above]* (1839-1909): Elmira, NY-born actress, newspaper correspondent, and women's rights advocate.

Proscenium of Laura Keene's Theatre, 1856

Long Tom: A ship's cannon.

loquiter: signifies the one speaking.

Lord Lovell: Popular folksong of the period.

lorn: lost, forlorn.

• **Lowell, James Russell** (1819-1891): Massachusetts-born poet, critic, editor, abolitionist, and diplomat.

lozenge: a rhombus.

Lucy Rushton's New-York Theatre: *see Church of the Messiah.*

Ludlow, Fitz Hugh (1836-1870): Author of "The Hasheesh Eater" (1857) about his cannabis experimentation. He moved to San Francisco and attempted to start a salon similar to Pfaff's.

Lyrique Hall (1859): Exhibition hall at 765 Broadway, between 8th & 9th

macadamize: to pave a road.

Mackenzie, Robert Shelton (1809-1881): Irish-born American newspaper editor.

Macready, William Charles (1793-1873): Prominent British Shakespearian actor. (*see: Astor Place Riot.*)

magic lantern: a shadow image projector popular from the 17th to mid-20th century.

Mallen: *See Mullen.*

Malmsey: Type of Madeira wine.

mammonism: the pursuit of riches, as personified in the Biblical personification of wealth in the false god, Mammon.

Manhattan Fire Plot: November 27, 1864 attempt by Confederates to burn down New York City by incendiary attacks on the 5th Avenue Hotel, Lovejoys Hotel, Howard Hotel, Astor House, Belmont Hotel, St. James Hotel, La Farge House, Metropolitan Hotel, St. Nicholas Hotel, Tammany Hotel, United States Hotel and the 5th Ward Museum Hotel with 144 phosphorous firebombs. They bungled the attack, and all fires were safely extinguished.

mantuamaker: a dressmaker.

Marcobrunner: a fine German white wine.

mare's nest: idiom meaning an illusion or hoax, (as horses don't make nests.)

Maretzek, Max: Conductor, impressario for the Academy, Niblo's.

massasanger: massasauga, a North American rattlesnake species.

-mastix: a suffix derived from Ancient Greek, denoting a strong opponent or hater of whatever the suffix was attached to.

Matilde Towne, Laura (1825-1901): Pennsylvanian abolitionist and educator, known for forming the first freedmen's schools.

Hugh Farrar McDermott

McLelan by Etynge.

matutinal: of the morning.

mayhap: it may happen; perhaps.

The Maze Garden (1853-1866): A garden across 5th Avenue from the Croton Reservoir at 42 St., where visitors could walk through a garden maze on the plan of Hampton Court, London.

• **McDermott, Hugh Farrar** (1834-1891): Irish-born lawyer, playwright, poet, and journalist. Raised to be a priest. As publisher of *Jersey City Herald*, arrested with son for selling obscene books in 1862.

McFlimsey, Flora: Fictional spoiled rich girl character in William Allen Butler's 1857 poem entitled "Nothing to Wear." *See Nothing to Wear*.

McLenan, John (1825-1865): Cincinnati-born illustrator for Yankee Notions.

M'Cluskey: Character in "Octaroon."

Comic Flora McFlimsey character from a period stereoscope image.

Meagher, Thomas Francis (1823-1867): Irish rebellion leader; then, a New York City reporter, and a Civil War U.S. Brigadier General, recruiting his own Irish Brigade for the Union.

meed: a deserved reward.

Melodeon Concert Hall (1858): 538-541 Broadway.

Ada Isaacs Menken's image on 1865 sheet music performing Mazeppa, a hippodrama where she wears a nude suit playing a male Tartar soldier strapped to a horse.

mem.: memorandum abbr.

Menken, Adah Isaacs (1835-1868): New Orleans-born Pfaffian; Actress famed for performing on a horse in a nude suit; poet, essayist; supported Walt Whitman; bigamous marriage to boxer Feeney ended in scandal.

Mercer Street: Used as a reference to prostitution, as Mercer street was dense with brothels.

meridional: from the south of France.

Messrs.: Plural for "Mr."

Metropolitan Hotel (1852-1895): 568-592 Broadway. Built on some of the land of Niblo's Garden.

meum and tuum: that which belongs to me and that which is another's, a legal phrase expressing rights to property.

Milor: a term of respect used to an English gentleman (shortened "My Lord.")

minikin: small.

minster: a cathedral church.

mite: a small value.

monachist: a monk.

monody: an ode for one actor to sing alone.

Lola Montez

Montez, Lola, Eliza Gilbert (1821-1861): Irish dancer and actress who became famous as a Spanish dancer, courtesan, and mistress of King Ludwig I of Bavaria; later, entertainer and lecturer. Died of syphilis in Brooklyn in 1861 at age 39.

de Montijo, Eugénie (1826-1920): After her marriage to Louis-Napoléon Bonaparte, Empress of France.

Paul Morphy.

moonshine: appearance without substance.

morganatic: a type of marriage in which neither the spouse of lower social rank nor any children of the marriage may inherit the title or possessions of the higher-ranking spouse.

Morphy, Paul (1837-1884): New Orleans chess phenom, the best player of the age, one of the game's best players ever.

Mozart Hall: *See Canterbury Hall.*

Nast, while covering Garibaldi, by Etynge

Mrs. Grundy: *See Grundyism.*

Mrs. Shoddy: a Civil-War-era, anti-Semitic trope, derived originally from a character in a popular serialized poem, of an unrefined, vulgar, upwardly-mobile Jewish woman, whose husband is a "camp-follower," a profiteer selling cheap or "shoddy" goods to government troops, the word "shoddy" originally referring simply to a poor quality of wool.

mull: a period of deliberation.

Mullen, Edward (Mallen): Irish-born Vanity Fair illustrator and Pfaffian. Described by Gunn as a "coarse ruffian," a "blackguard."

Mumford: Reference to the fraud scandal of the Wall street gold dealer, Peter R. Mumford.

myrmidon: a lackey.

N.B.: Nota Bene, or "take note," used as P.S. is used.

nabob: a person returning from India to Europe with a fortune.

nankeen: a durable yellowish-brown cotton fabric.

Nast, Thomas (1840-1902): German-born political cartoonist, Pfaffian. Originated the modern Santa Claus and Republican elephant characters.

negus: a hot drink of port, sugar, lemon, and spices.

• **Neill, Harry/Henry** (1838-1861): Pfaffian. Philadelphia-born journalist. Went on to work for the *Tribune*. Died at 23 of typhoid fever.

• **Newbould, Thomas M.**: *Tribune* reporter, editor. Lived at 180 East Tenth Street (just east of Third Ave.).

New Bowery Theatre: *See Bowery Theatre.*

New York Athenæum (1835-1860): Private library that displayed borrowed art works in its rooms at the New York Society Library.

The burning and sacking of New York City's Colored Orphan Asylum during the Draft Riots, as depicted in Harper's Weekly, August 1, 1863.

New York City Draft Riots (July 13--16, 1863): Violent attacks on New York City residents and buildings by immense armed gangs of Irish immigrants, Democrats, and Confederate sympathizers, especially targeting African-Americans and abolitionists. The attacks happened in response to a new draft for New Yorkers to fight in the Civil War, and extended over four days, because the New York State Militia had been sent to Gettysburg and were unable to respond quickly. 119 were killed, 11 African Americans were lynched. 50 buildings were looted and burned to the ground, including the Colored Orphan Asylum at 44 Street and 5th Avenue. Irish immigrants were motivated by an unwillingness to serve and a resentfulness against free Blacks, who competed with the Irish for low-wage jobs.

New York Historical Society (1857-1908): Society founded to preserve historical material pertaining to American, and especially New York history.

New York Hotel: 721 Broadway.

New York Society Library: Southeast corner of Broadway and Leonard.

New York Theatre: *See Winter Garden.*

New York Saturday Press (NYSP)*:* New York City-based arts and literature newspaper founded by Henry Clapp, Jr. and funded for the greater part by Edward Howland. As was the custom of the day, the journal was composed of about a third original material and two-thirds material reprinted from other sources. The *NYSP* offices were at 9 Spruce Street, a section of the city near City Hall where most newspapers were managed and printed. The *NYSP* soon came to be associated with the burgeoning concept of Bohemianism, which Clapp encouraged. The journal is noted for its early promotion of Walt Whitman and the association of many of its writers with the coterie of bohemians that met at Pfaff's Restaurant. The *NYSP* was issued from October 23, 1858 to December 15, 1860. Clapp revived the journal from August 5, 1865 to June 2, 1866. Much of the staff worked for The Leader in the interim. Notable in its second presentation was the addition of a young Mark Twain to the regular contributors.

***NYSP* Contributors:** Thomas Bailey Aldrich, Horatio Alger, Mary Clemmer Ames, George Arnold, A.F. Banks, Joseph Barber, Juliette H. Beach, Eastburn Benjamin, Zelotes R. Bennett, Josh Billings, Dion Boucicault, William Penn Brannan, Sallie Bridges, John Brougham, Joseph Brownlee Brown, Emily Hewitt

A typical 19th century newspaper office.

Bugbee, John Burroughs, Phoebe Cary, Mrs. Marie Stevens Case, Caroline Chesebro, Mary A. Chilton, Henry Clapp Jr., Ada Clare-Noyes, Robert Barry Coffin, Spencer Wallace Cone, Charles Tabor Congdon, George Cooper, Henry Sylvester Cornwell, Ruth Natalie Cromwell, Wild Edgerton, Thomas Ewbank, Margaret Winship Eytinge, Cornelius Conway Felton, Fanny Fern, George W. Fortmeyer, Charles Desmarais Gardette, Getty Gay, Charles Gayler, Henry Giles, Alice Gill, Mary Freeman Goldbeck, Adam Gurowski, Paul Hamilton Hayne, Edward House, William Dean Howells, Edward Howland, Susan Willane Flint Jewett, Edwin R. Johnson, Orpheus C. Kerr, Augustus Barton Knowlton, Lucy Larcom, Ledyard Van Rensselaer, Olive Logan, James Russell Lowell, Hugh Farrar McDermott, Harry Neill, Thomas M. Newbould, Mary Gove Nichols, Joseph Warren Nye, Fitz James O'Brien, Frederick A. Parmenter, Don Pastel, Robert W. Pearsall, Lizzie Petit-Cutler, Edgar Phillips, John Phoenix, Harriet E. Prescott, Abby Hills Price, Hiram Rich, John Van Der Zee Sears, Charles Bailey Seymour, Charles Dawson Shanly, Nathaniel Graham Shepherd, Joachim Heyward Siddons, Edward Spencer, Henry Thompson Sperry, Edmund Clarence Stedman, Frank Richard Stockton, Elizabeth Drew Barstow Stoddard, Richard Henry Stoddard, Margaret Sweat, William Swinton, William Law Symonds, D.J. Todd, Mark Twain, Nathan D. Urner, Artemus Ward, John Whitaker Watson, Augustus Watters, Charles Henry Webb, Walt Whitman, Edward G.P. Wilkins, Alfred Mason Williams, William Winter, Frank Wood, Don Lloyd Wyman.

Niblo's Garden (1823-1895): a 3,200-occupancy theater and open-air "Grand Saloon" (a smaller theater) and gardens at 578 Broadway (near Prince St.) Featured a wide variety of acts, from opera to circus.

•Nichols, Mary Sargeant Neal Gove; *Mary Orme* (1810-84): New Hampshire-born women's rights, free love, and health reform advocate, vegetarian and writer.

nigritude: blackness.

nitre: potassium nitrate.

Nixon's: Circus act at Niblo's.

nobby: fashionable or elegant.

nonce: of an expression, coined for use once.

noodledom: foolishness.

Mary Sargeant Neal Gove Nichols.

Above: Niblo's Interior gardens.
Lower left: Early engraving of Niblo's Garden Broadway frontage.
Below: Later, 1865, after the Metropolitan Hotel took over much of Niblo's frontage.

North, William (1825-1854): Young British writer, predating *NYSP* and the Pfaffians, who struggled to survive in NYC, eventually committing suicide by drinking cyanide in his room at 7 Bond St. The account was reported in detail in the newspapers, including his penniless state, the many manuscripts lying about his room, a description of his failed attempts to promote a journal, and his depressive threats to kill himself leading up to the act. His case aroused the sentiments of early New York City bohemians, and the first issue of *NYSP* featured the posthumous publication of a short story of his, a melodramatic fantasy, describing his experimentation with various drugs.

Norton, Frank H.; *Frank Henry* (1836-1914): Massachusetts-born journalist, poet, playwright, and author. Asst Librarian at Astor Library; lived at 118 Fourth St.

nosegay: a small bunch of flowers.

Nothing to Wear: A widely-popular humorous poem by William Butler, first appearing in *Harper's Weekly* in 1857, satirizing overindulged society girls.

not see: is to dislike something. ie: "A.M don't see the new pieces at Wallack's."

nugatory: of no value or importance.

• Nye, Joseph Warren (1816-1901): Massachusetts-born poet.

obit: death or funeral service.

obolus: a silver greek coin.

Fitz James O'Brien.

• **O'Brien, Fitz James,** *Dodo* (1825-1862): Irish-born Pfaffian known to start fist-fights. Editor, poet, successful writer of fantasy and science fiction short stories. He was the first writer of *NYSP*'s Dramatic Feuilleton. Died after being shot while serving for the Union in the Civil War.

obsequies: funeral rites.

The Octoroon: Anti-slavery play adapted by Dion Boucicault from a British play; premiered at the Winter Garden Theatre.

octroi: a tax levied at the gates of French cities.

oily gammon: as an insult, a fat ham.

oldest man; old man: nickname for Clapp.

Olympic Theatre: *See Laura Keene's Theatre.*

opiate: inducing sleep; narcotic.

opodeldoc: a liniment, made from alcohol and soap.

oppugn: call into question the validity of.

orgies: frantic, nocturnal, drunken revelries.

• **Orme, Mary,** *See Mary Nichols.*

ormulu: a method of gilding metal to appear gold.

orthoëpy: the correct pronunciation of words.

os frontis: the skull's frontal bone.

Osgood, Frances Sargent (1811-1850): Boston-born writer and poet; close friends with Edgar Allen Poe; died of tuberculosis at her home on 22nd St., New York City., leaving her husband and two daughters.

ottar: the basis of an aroma.

Ottarson, Franklin J. (Bayard) (1816-1884): Pfaffian. New York-born journalist, Tribune and *Times* editor, and civil servant.

Our American Cousin: Very popular farcical play, premiered at Laura Keene's Theatre in 1858. April 15, 1865, Keene was performing in the play before a Washington D.C. audience at Ford's Theatre when President Lincoln was assassinated in a box above the stage.

Adelina Patti

Palace Garden (1858): Promenade garden that hosted concerts and performances, located on the north side of 14th St, between Sixth and Seventh Aves.

palanquin: a couch.

palfry: a lady's horse.

paly: pallid.

pandemonium: the council-chambers of demons.

panegyrics: extravagent praise, delivered formally.

Parker, Theodore (1810-1860): Massachusetts-born abolitionist, transcendentalist, and reforming minister of the Unitarian church. Led financial support to John Brown, and advocated violating the Fugitive Slave Act.

•**Parmenter, Frederick A**. (1842-1865): Owego, NY poet, became a pastor in Elizabeth, NJ. Killed at age 22 trying to board a moving streetcar.

parturition: giving birth.

Paternoster Row: London street where publishing trade was centered.

patent mangle: a machine that presses and smooths fabric between rollers.

Patmore, Coventry (1823-1896): English poet and literary critic.

Patti, Adelina (1843-1919): Bronx-raised, acclaimed opera singer. Debuted in 1859 at the Academy of Music.

peach: short for "impeach," to expose the wrongdoings of another; accuse.

Pecksniff: a Dickens character noted for hypocrisy.

peculation: the rongful apropriation of public property for personal use.

pelf: riches, implies ill-gotten.

• **Pearsall, Robert W. (1833-71):** A Columbia Law School student hailing from an aristocratic Quaker family. He was reportedly "swindled" by Clapp into a $4,000 investment. During his tenure at NYSP, he wielded editorial influence and authored a column titled "Leaves from Nature," noted more for its narrow-mindedness than its literary merit. Rumors circulated about his broken engagement with Ada Clare. Listed as a "Proprietor" alongside Clapp in the first 11 issues of 1860, his name vanished from all subsequent publications. He resided at 16 Lafayette Place, a residence indicative of his wealth. Gunn, in his writings, referred to Pearsall as a "Fifth Avenoodle." Following his departure from NYSP, Pearsall embarked on constructing an opulent estate at Brentwood, Long Island, where he settled with his new family before his untimely death.

penetralia: the innermost parts of a building; a secret or hidden place.

penny-dip: a candle costing a penny

pensum: a charge, measured out.

Pentonville: A London prison.

perruquier: a seller or designer of perukes or hair-pieces.

pertinaciously: obstinantly.

peruke: a wig of the type worn by men in the 18th century.

pet: a fretful discontent, as, "in a pet."

Peter Funk: a shill bidder at an auction; a swindler.

• **Petit-Cutler, Lizzie** (1831-1902): Virginia-born novelist and poet.

pettifogging: engaging in menial legal affairs.

Pfaff, Charles Ignatius (1813-1890): Owner of Pfaff's Restaurant.

Pfaffian: One of the literati and artists known to frequent Pfaff's Restaurant. The group of roystering friends and associates is regarded as America's first Bohemian salon, inspired by French Bohemia (*see Bohemianism*) and the memory of Edgar Allan Poe (who predeceased the group. Central to this group were many (but not all) of the editors and regular contributors to *NYSP*.

Pfaff's: German Rathskeller-style restaurant under the street level of 647 Broadway, steps down from the Coleman House Hotel, opened in 1855. Owner Charles Pfaff and Henry Clapp encouraged the recognition of the "chop-house" as a haunt for Bohemian New Yorkers. In 1870, the restaurant was relocated to 24th street, and it closed in 1887. (*See Pfaffians.*)

pharos: lighthouse.

philoprogenitiveness: tending to produce offspring.

phiz: a contemptuous face or visage.

• ***Phoenix, John,*** George Horatio Derby, *Squibob* (1823-1861): Massachusetts-born US Army officer and humorist. Mexican War veteran. After suffering a variety of illnesses, he died of sunstroke in an asylum in Williamsburgh, Brooklyn.

phonographic: descriptive of the sounds of the voice.

Pic: Personne's name for Piccolomini; the *New York Picayune* newspaper, or someone who works for it.

Piccolomini, Marietta (1834-99): Italian soprano for the Academy.

Pierian Spring of Macedonia: Of Greek mythology, the spring of knowledge of art and science.

pierian: pertaining to the muses.

Pietism: A Lutheran sect focussing on individual piety.

pinfold: a pen, as for confining animals.

pinguidity: oilyness or a nature like fat.

Coleman House Hotel (second building from left,) home of Pfaff's.

pink: anything supremely excellent.

pins: slang term for legs.

Pious Pillsbury: a reference to Parker Pillsbury, an abolitionist known for the resoluteness with which he faced hostile assemblies.

pipe-light: a rolled paper used to light a pipe or cigar from a gas or kerosene lamp.

pismire: an ant.

pleached: bent.

Right: Frank Bellew's dual engravings of Pfaffians, from the February 6, 1864 issue of Demorest's New York Illustrated News. The panel above depicts the Bohemians engaged in sober intellectual discussion. The panel below claims to depict the writers and artists at Pfaff's "As they were said to be by a knight of The Round Table," a reference to recent criticisms of the New York bohemians in The Round Table by Franklin Ottarson.

Marietta Piccolomini.

John Phoenix.

pleonasm: an overly-wordy expression.

Plug Uglies: a notorious Baltimore gang of the period, named for the stovepipe hats, or "plugs" they wore. This term would come to be synonymous with bullying and general disagreeable behavior or appearance.

Edgar Allan Poe.

Poe, Edgar Allan (1809-1849): Boston-born writer, poet, editor, and literary critic. Iconic American writer of Gothic and Romantic literature. Though his life predated American Bohmia, Poe was adopted by American Bohemians as their prototype, having lived a life on the margins, facing poverty and instability while devoting himself to his craft. His exploration of dark, emotional, and psychological themes set him apart from mainstream writers of the time, embodying the Romantic ideals of artistic individualism and a disregard for commercial success.

Poick: *see Aldrich.*

poignard: a nobleman's thrusting knife.

poltroon: an idle coward.

Poole, William (1821-1855): Notorious New York City leader of the Bowery Boys gang and a local leader of the Know-Nothing political movement.

Poor Man's Friend: A patent ointment claiming to aid skin conditions.

poser: one who puzzles by asking difficult questions; a question that puzzles or silences.

post-chaise: a horse-drawn carriage.

potichomanie: the art or process of imitating painted porcelain ware.

Harriet E. Prescott

prandial: related to a meal.

• **Prescott, Harriet E.** (1835- 1921): Maine-born, widely popular fiction writer and poet.

• **Price, Abby Hills** (1814-78): Poet; abolitionist, women's rights advocate, utopian communalist. Close friends with Whitman.

Priest Burt, Nancy Amelia Woodbury; *Lizzie Lincoln* (1840-1903): New Hampshire poet; penned immensely popular "Over the River" poem, about spirits waiting in the afterlife.

prig: to filch or steal. *Abby Hills Price.*

probang: a medical device made of whalebone used to remove items from the throat.

prog: victuals found by begging or just found by wandering about.

proser: a writer of prose.

puff: an exaggerated commendation.

pullulate: to spread prolifically.

pump: a low shoe used for dance.

Punch, or the London Charivari (1841-1992): An iconic British weekly magazine of humor and satire.

pung: a one-horse sleigh.

Abby Hills Price.

punt: flat-bottomed boat used to repair larger craft.

Quaker fip: A kiss.

Quelq'un: *See William Winter.*

quartering: in heraldry, the division of a shield, containing many coats.

R.U.E.: right upper exit, in theater terminology.

raise the wind: raise funds for an enterprise.

ramified: spread or branched out.

raree-show: an entertainment, usually contained in a box, like a peep-show.

ratiocinative: characterized by the use of exact reasoning.

receipt: recipe

reluct: to rebel.

Hiram Rich

respirator: a mask with a network of fine wire in front that, warmed by the breath, aids persons of weak lungs by tempering the cold from without.

rhino, the: slang for money.

rhodomontade: a bragging speech.

• **Rich, Hiram** (1832-1901): Gloucester, MA poet and bank clerk.

Rogers, Nathaniel Peabody (1794-1846): New England abolitionist, essayist and poet.

Roosevelt, Robert B. (1829-1906): New York City-born US Congressman; Teddy Roosevelt's uncle; sportsman, author of books about fishing.

rouge et noir: a card game.

roulade: a florid vocal embellishment sung to one syllable

roysterer: a merry-maker.

rush-light: used in place of a candle----which were, in Britain, forbidden to make at home without paying a tax. A stem of rush (a grasslike plant), with the skin mostly peeled and the pith soaked in household tallow or grease, is then burned, to provide light.

Lucy Rushton.

Rushton, Lucy, Mary Wilde (1844-1909): English-born actress and theater manager. *See Church of the Messiah.*

St. Nicholas Hotel, looking north from Broome.

Russ pavement: Large paving stones used on Broadway with a grooved surface, which were found to wear down quickly and become both slippery and uneven and consequently hazardous to horses.

S.T.1860.X: A cryptogram widely used in advertising by the patent medicine, Drake's Plantation Bitters, to pique public curiosity. It has never been fully deciphered.

sacerdotal: relating to priests.

St. James' Hall: A popular Buffalo lecture hall.

St. Nicholas Hotel: At 507-527 Broadway, (near Spring St.), the first Manhattan hotel to cost a million dollars, boasting 600 rooms.

St. Patrick's Cathedral: 254 Mulberry St., north of Prince. Host of the "Diamond Wedding."

St. Thomas Episcopal Church: Northwest corner of Houston and Broadway. Hosted Ned Wilkins's funeral.

St. Patrick's Cathedral today.

salmagundi: a mixed dish of a variety of items; a "dog's dinner."

saloon: an establishment for eating or amusement, including small performance halls, oyster houses, billiard parlors, and ice cream eateries.

sand-boy: all rags and all happiness; the urchins who drive the sand-laden neddies (donkeys) through our streets, are envied by the capon-eating turtle-loving epicures of these cities. 'As jolly as a sand-boy,' designates a merry fellow who has tasted a drop.

sansculottism: radical extremism in politics.

sapid: tasteful.

saponaceous: resembling soap.

saporous: having taste.

Savage, John (1828-1888): Pfaffian. Dublin-born poet, journalist, author, and lecturer. Fenian activist. He fought for the Union in the Civil War.

Saxe, John Godfrey (1816-1887): Vermonter poet known for his re-telling of the Indian parable "The Blind Men and the Elephant." Advocated a non-interference policy on slavery.

scapegrace: a lazy, mischievous, or irresponsible person.

Schaus' Gallery: Art gallery at 629 Broadway.

scot: money or tribute.

scout: to sneer at.

scrofula: tuberculosis of the lymph glands, esp. of the neck.

scullion: a kitchen worker who performs menial tasks.

sculper: engraver.

seamew: a common seagull.

Charles Bailey Seymour

John Van Der Zee Sears

sear: dry or withered.

• **Sears, John Van Der Zee** (1836-1926): Philadelphia journalist, art critic. Wrote fiction and a book about the Brook Farm utopian community.

seneschal: a medieval steward of domestic staff.

sepulture: burial.

seraglio: a harem.

sere: dry and withered.

serried: crowded together.

Seward, William Henry (1801-1872): Governor of New York; US Senator, and Lincoln's Secretary of State.

• **Seymour, Charles Bailey** (1829-1869): Pfaffian. English-born journalist. Wrote some of the *Dramatic Feuilleton* during 1865; went on to be dramatic critic at the *Times* and then a partner at *Scribner*. Lived at No. 42 Union Place (Union Square East). Boarded with his cousin, Frank Cahill.

Charles Dawson Shanly

• **Shanly, Charles Dawson** (1811-1875): Pfaffian. Dublin-born artist, editor, journalist, and poet. Founding editor at *NYSP*.

sharper: a shrewd or dishonest man in bargaining.

shave (a note): to discount a promissory note at a high rate of interest.

• **Shepherd, Nathaniel Graham** *Shepard, N.G., Daisy* (1835-1869): Pfaffian. New York City-born landscape painter, illustrator, poet. Clapp printed an accusation of plagiarism against his poetry. Shepherd denied the charge and threatened Clapp, after which Clapp published a retraction, and continued to publish his work. Civil War correspondentfor the *Tribune*. Said to have died from drink. (*See "comic papers"*.)

Daniel Sickles shoots and kills Philip Barton Key.

Sickles affair: On February 27, 1859, Congressman Daniel Sickles shot and killed Philip Barton Key, the U.S. Attorney for D.C. and son of Francis Scott Key, after discovering his affair with Sickles' young wife. Despite the premeditated nature of the crime, Sickles was acquitted, using the first temporary insanity defense in U.S. history. Sickles went on to a distinguished career as Union General, but Teresa Sickles died of tuberculosis just after the war. Sickles remarried, had two children, and lived to the age of 94.

Sick Man: Expression used by Russian Emperor Nicholas I to refer to the declining Ottoman Empire.

• ***Siddons*, Joachim Heyward;** Stocqueler (1801-1886): British-American journalist, lecturer, soldier, war correspondent for the NY Evening Post. Friends with Dickens.

sift: to examine minutely; to scrutinize.

signal: eminent; remarkable.

sillabub: a dessert made with whipped cream and wine.

slop-shop: a store at which cheap, ready-made clothing may be purchased.

slop-shop literature: sensational, poorly-written books with gaudy covers, and made with cheap paper.

slubber: to do something carelessly or in haste.

slut: a woman who is negligent of cleanliness; given to a disordered home.

smack: a small vessel used in the coasting and fishing trades.

Joachim Heyward Siddons

Smith, Mark (1829-1874): Pfaffian, American theater critic, comedian, and actor at Burtons and Wallacks.

Smithsonian House Hotel: 604-608 Broadway, corner of Houston.

Edward Spencer.

Henry Thompson Sperry.

sons of Belial: Biblical reference to demons.

sother: to soothe.

soubrette: an actress playing a flirtatious young female.

sough: a low whistling.

sourire: a smile.

Sozodont: A commercial dentifrice.

spandy: neat.

• **Spencer, Edward** (1834-1883): Baltimore poet and art critic.

• **Sperry, Henry Thompson** (1837-1912): Hartford-based author, poet, editor.

spillicans: pick-up sticks.

spondulic: slang for cash.

Spooner, Lysander (1808-87): Massachusetts-born abolitionist, entrepreneur, lawyer, writer, libertarian-socialist, and Unitarian.

Spurgeon, Charles Haddon (1834--1892): English Particular Baptist preacher noted for his powerful sermons.

Squeers, Wackford: a character in Dickens's Nicholas Nickleby, a cruel head-teacher.

stalled ox: an ox that is kept in a stall to fatten it up, a metaphor referring to overindulgence.

stand treat: pay for drinks.

• **Stedman, Edmund Clarence** (1833-1908): Connecticut-born editor, journalist, poet, critic, banker, and scientist.

Steinway Hall: Concert hall built by piano-maker William Steinway, at 71-74 East 14 St., the cornerstone for which was laid in May, 1866, four days after the Academy of Music burned to the ground.

Edmund Clarence Stedman.

Stewart's store: In 1863, well after the success of A.T. Stewart's dry-goods emporium at 280 Broadway, (which still stands as the "Sun Building,") the company moved uptown and opened an enormous "Iron Palace" of numerous departments, using the full city block bordered by 9th and 10th Streets, Broadway, and Astor Place. The building towered at 6 stories and featured a domed skylight over a grand atrium. The building was eventually taken over by Wanamaker's department store, and was demolished in 1956.

• **Stockton, Frank Richard;** *Andrew Scoggin, M.D.* (1834-1902): Philadelphia-born writer, children's writer, and humorist.

Steinway Hall.

• **Stoddard, Mrs. R.H.** (Elizabeth Drew Barstow) (1823-1902): Massachusetts-born writer of fiction and poetry. The Stoddards regularly welcomed a coterie of literary lights to their home at 329 East 15 Street.

• **Stoddard, Richard Henry** (1825-1903): Massachusetts-born critic and poet. New York City customs inspector. Husband to Elizabeth Stoddard.

stop: a wind regulator on an organ.

stot: a horse.

A.T. Stewart's grand atrium.

Elizabeth Stoddard.

Grace Church and Stewart's at Broadway and 10th Street.

strabismus: misalignment of the eyes.

Stuart, William (Edmund O'Flaherty): Irish-born manager of Burton's New Theatre and the Winter Garden Theatre with Bourcicault.

Stuyvesant Institute: Museum space at 659 Broadway. From 1853-1860, it housed the Abbot Collection.

sublunary: pertaining to this world ("under the moon.")

subscriber: a reference a newspaper columnist makes to his or herself.

sugar-tit: a baby pacifier.

Sullivan, Barry (1821-1891): English actor at the Old Broadway Theatre.

supernumeraries: military reservists.

supposititious: fraudulently substituted.

Frank Richard Stockton

surtout: a man's overcoat.

susurration: a mild whispering.

sutler: a person who follows an army in order to sell the troops provisions.

• **Sweat, Margaret Jane Mussey** (1823--1908): Maine-born poet, journalist, critic, patron, and women's rights advocate. Wrote an early lesbian-themed novel.

swink: to toil.

• **Swinton, William** (1833-1892): Scot-born war correspondent, author, philological expert, professor, and translator. Close friend of Whitman.

Richard Henry Stoddard.

swivel: a small cannon.

sybarite: a person who is self-indulgent for sensuous luxury.

syllabub: a drink made of wine and milk.

sylph: a slight and graceful female.

Symmes' hole: A theory of a hollow Earth with holes of access to the interior located at the poles proposed by John Cleves Symmes Jr. (1780-1829), an American Army officer, trader, and lecturer.

• **Symonds, William Law** (1833-62): Maine-born Unitarian minister and Harvard Divinity School graduate. Moved to New York City, joined the Pfaffians, and left ministry for a writing career. Worked on Appleton's Cyclopædia and as Astor Library librarian. Died of St. Andrews Fire, a bacterial skin disease, at the Tenth Street Studio Building.

tableaux vivants: a posed theatrical presentation of classical scenes with still actors and stage lighting.

table-land: a geographical area of elevated land with a flat, nearly level, or gently undulating surface.

tapis vert: a gaming table.

Tapley, Mark: Pseudonym taken from the character in Dickens's Martin Chuzzlewit.

tare: a weed common among corn.

tartarean: hellish.

tatoo: a rhythmic tapping or drumming.

tatterdemalion: a ragged-ly-dressed person.

William Law Symonds.

Taylor, Bayard (1825-1878): Pennsylvania-born writer and diplomat.

The Tenth Street Studio Building.

tea-fight: British slang for tea party.

teazle: a plant bearing large burs.

telluric: of the earth.

Ten Acres Enough: 1864 guide to independent farming, by New Jersey farmer, Edmund Morris.

tensorial: related to muscular contractions.

Tenth Street Studio Building (1857-1956): 51 West 10th Street. The first modern facility designed solely to serve the needs of artists. They lived, worked, and exhibited there.

terpsichorean: related to dance.

The Hub: Period nickname for Boston, from Oliver Wendell Holmes's 1854 quote: "Boston State-House is the hub of the solar system".

There you go with your eye out: a phrase with which to admonish a person for unwelcome staring.

thereanent: with reference to that matter.

thews: muscles.

thimblerigger: a person engaging in a shell-game-type of trickery.

Three Hungry Frenchmen: A satirical nod to the editorial trio responsible for driving Le Courrier des États-Unis—once a prestigious French-language newspaper based in New York City—into disrepute and eventual decline.

threnody: a song, poem, speech, or hymn that laments the dead.

tick: credit.

time ball: a wooden or metal ball mounted on a tall pole, often in ports, to aid in synchronizing timepieces. Visible from afar, it is lowered at set times, typically on the hour. In April 1860, New York City installed a 6-foot-wide, 100-pound red wooden time ball on a 50-foot iron staff atop the Custom House at Broad and Wall Streets. Dropped daily at noon, it was triggered by a telegraphic signal from Albany's Dudley Observatory, activating an electromagnet to release its catch. The device was effective for less than a month.

titivate ("oneself up"): to spruce up.

toilet: a decorative cloth table covering.

"Tommy," Tateishi Onojiro, left, with the censor and Prince's attendant, 1860.

Tommy (Tateishi Onojiro) (1843-1917): 17-year-old interpreter and one of the youngest members of Japan's first diplomatic mission, "Tommy" quickly became the most popular member of the 1860 samurai envoy to America. His wit, cheerful nature, and youthful good looks especially charmed American ladies.

Tom's a cold: from *King Lear*, spoken by Edgar, disguised as "Poor Tom," a mad beggar. This line reflects Edgar's feigned suffering in the storm as he hides his true identity. The phrase captures the bleakness and vulnerability of the moment, emphasizing both the physical cold of the storm and the emotional desolation of the play.

ton: the prevailing fashion.

George Francis Train.

Tony Pastor's Opera House (1865-1875): 199-201 Bowery; featured minstrel shows.

toper: drunkard.

torpedo: the electric ray fish.

Tract Society: American Tract Society (ATS) is an evangelical organization founded in New York City in 1825 for the purpose of printing tracts of literature so to increase public literacy of Christian principles.

Train, George Francis (1829-1904): American horse-drawn street railway pioneer/entrepreneur.

transportation: banishment for felony.

trencher-man: a great eater.

trow: suppose.

Turveydrop: A Dickens character from Bleak House, who has pretensions to aristocracy.

Mark Twain

• ***Twain, Mark***, Samuel Clemens (1835-1910): Pfaffian. Missouri-born writer, and perhaps America's most celebrated humorist.

tyre/tyro: a beginner.

ult.: ultimo. or previous month.

ultima thule: the point believed by the ancients to be farthest north.

umbrageous: shady.

Umos: Pseudonym shared by Clapp and Pearsall.

Unitary Homes: Utopian, affordable, communal houses founded by American anarchist Stephen Pearl Andrews in 1857. The first was located at 17 Stuyvessant Street, which eventually removed to 106 East 14th St.

unlicked: rude and uncouth.

unwonted: unusual.

upas: harmful or detrimental. From the upas, a poisonous Southeast Asian tree that became a symbol of toxicity due to a legend that claimed the tree poisoned the surrounding area, killing anything that came too close.

• **Urner, Nathan D.** (1840-1893): Cincinnati-born writer, *NY Tribune* city editor, essayist, poet.

usufruct: legal right to enjoy the use of another's property short of its destruction or waste.

Valse: a waltz.

van: the front line in battle.

Vanity Fair (1859-1863): A short-lived humorous weekly that featured several *NYSP* contributors, such as Thomas Bailey Aldrich, William Dean Howells, Fitz-James O'Brien and Charles Farrar Browne.

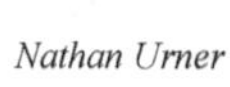

Nathan Urner

vastate: to lay waste; devastate

vaticination: prophecy.

Vedder, Elihu (1836-1923): New York-born Pfaffian, essayist, artist.

vertu: knowledge of the fine arts.

vide: a word used to refer a reader to another place in a text, or tell a musician to skip to a place farther ahead in the score

videlicet: namely, (long form of "viz").

volante: a speedy, 2-wheeled pleasure carriage pulled by a mounted horse.

W.C.: West Central postal district of London.

J.W.Wallack.

wag: a man full of low spirit and humor, a ludicrous fellow.

waiten: to demand the attention of.

Walcot, Charles Melton (1815-1866): English actor and playwright at Wallack's.

de Walden, Thomas Blades (1811-1873): English actor and playwright; Pfaffian.

Walker, William (1824-1860): Tennessee-born freebooter (*see filibustering*.) Executed by the Honduran government in 1860.

"wall, an attack of the": a reference to tuberculosis, the lungs being "walled off" by the disease.

Lester Wallack.

Wallack, James William (1794-1864): Anglo-American actor and manager of Wallack's Lyceum (1852-61) and Wallack's Theatre (1861-81.)

Wallack, *Lester,* John Johnstone Wallack (1820-1888): Pfaffian; New York-born, London-reared actor, playwright, and theatrical manager.

Wallack's Theatre, 13th & Broadway.

Wallack's (1856-1861): Wallack's Lyceum Theater at 485 Broadway (off Broome St.) Became Brougham's Lyceum, and the Broadway Theatre, managed by George Wood 1864-1869. Wallack's Theatre (1861-1881): Theater at 844 Broadway (corner of 13 St), widely considered America's finest, managed by James Wallack, and then his son, Lester.

Grand Procession of Wide-Awakes, Nassau and Spruce Streets in front of the Tribune and Times buildings. (Looking south, with City Hall off to the right, from Harper's Weekly, Oct. 3, 1860.)

• ***Ward, Artemus***, Charles Farrar Browne (1834-1867): Pfaffian; humorist; editor for *Vanity Fair*; died of tuberculosis in England at the height of his popularity.

Washington Hall (1851-1860): 598 Broadway. In 1860, became Charley White's Opera House.

Washington Heights: In 1860, a rural area in upper Manhattan, above the city, where some wealthy New Yorkers, such as James Bennett, editor of the *Herald*, would spend summer. In 1898, it became incorporated into New York City.

watchseal: a fob to hang from a watch chain that resembles a seal insignia.

water-butt: a large barrel to catch rainwater.

waterfall: a hairstyle popularized in the mid-1860's in which the hair is gathered in large, neat batches.

The waterfall cignon.

• **Watson, John Whitaker** (1824-1890): New York City-born Pfaffian; writer, editor. Author of the immensely-popular 19th-Century poem, "The Beautiful Snow," which is reprinted in *NYSP* from *Harper's Weekly*. A former companion of Poe's. He lived on 22nd Street. Gunn calls him an "ex-confidence man and ex-forger." He claims Watson was removed as critic for the *Sunday Courier* after attempts to black-mail actors.

• **Watters, Augustus (1835-1919): New York-born a**uthor, printer, poet, and elocutionist.

• **Webb, Charles Henry, *Inigo, John Paul*** (1834-1905): Upstate-New York-born poet, author and journalist. Lived at 56 East 53rd St.

Webb, James Watson: Publisher of the Courier and Inquirer newspaper.

Wedding Ring: a popular sermon of the period, by Puritan minister William Secker, offering marital advice, often printed in miniature binding.

Weekly Anglo-African (1859-1861): NYC newspaper published by abolitionist brothers, Thomas and Robert Hamilton, African Americans frustrated with the pacifism of the Black press. On September 22, 1860, without comment, *NYSP* republished a fiery *Weekly Anglo-African* editorial condemning NYSP's neutrality on the issue of slavery.

Walt Whitman's striking 1855 frontispiece, from his first edition of "Leaves of Grass."

wen: a large city; an encycsted tumor.

wherry: a shallow, light rowboat.

whilom: formerly; in the past.

Whitlock's Free Gallery of Oil Paintings: 366 Canal Street.

• Whitman, Walt, *Mose Velsor, Paumanok* (1819-1892): Central Pfaffian figure. Long Island-born poet, editor, and journalist. The most revolutionary and influential of American poets. Throughout his lifetime, he republished and continually added to his 1855 poetry collection*, Leaves of Grass*, extremely controversial in its time for its sensual, taboo-violating content. As contributor to NYSP, he worked closely with Clapp to maintain a public exposure that was mutually beneficial to both NYSP's success and Whitman's popularity. During the Civil War, he worked in Washington DC caring for wounded soldiers. In 1873, Whitman suffered a partial paralytic stroke, after which he moved to Camden, NJ to live with his brother and mother. His recovery went well, and he resumed publishing and even lecturing. He died in Camden in 1892, after preparing what is known as his "Deathbed Edition" of *Leaves of Grass*.

Whittier, John Greenleaf (1807-1892): Massachusetts-born Quaker; poet and abolitionist.

Wide Awakes: Youthful, uniformed, Republican political organization and militia dedicated to electing Lincoln in the 1860 election. On October 3, 1860, they formed a large, jubilant "Grand Procession" torchlight parade down Broadway that silenced the many pro-Southern factions in the city. The term also refers to the hats popularly worn by wide-awakes, a felt hat with a low crown and wide brim (of the style worn by the Quaker Oats guy.)

wight: a burlesque term for person, from the German wicht, for creature.

wildered: puzzled (ie: "bewildered.")

• Wilkins, Edward G.P. (Ned), *Personne* (1829-1861): Boston-born, immaculately-dressed Pfaffian and one of Clapp's chief editors. As "Personne", Wilkins penned the Dramatic Feuilleton column, writing that originated the American style of theater criticism, as Winter put it, "writ-

"Ned" Edward G.P. Wilkins.

ing about the stage and society in a facetious, satirical vein, striving to lighten heavy or barren themes with playful banter, and to gild the dreariness of criticism with the glitter of wit." Identifying terms of his writing were "dry goods," "good gracious," and jokes about Peoria. Playwright; dramatic critic for the *Herald*. He lived with his brother George, his sister-in-law, and their three children at 140 E. 21st St., adjacent to Gramercy Park. In 1860, George, an opera agent, died of stroke, and a benefit was given for the family at the Academy of Music. The following year, Ned, who was said to abuse chloroform, died of pneumonia at an Amity Street boarding house. After the funeral at St. Thomas Church (Houston and Broadway,) during which Ada Clare was said to have thrown herself on the body in grief, and another benefit at the Academy, the family returned to Boston.

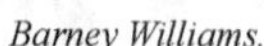

Barney Williams. *Alfred Mason Williams.*

• Williams, Alfred Mason (1840-96): Massachusetts-born journalist and publisher; advocate for women's suffrage, Irish independence, and fair treatment of Native Americans.

Williams, Barney**;** Barney Flaherty (1824-1876): Irish-American stage actor and comedian.

Willis, Nathaniel Parker (1806-67): Maine-born Pfaffian who had known Poe. Popular journalist, poet and editor. Fanny Fern's brother.

Windship, Dr. George B.: A physical fitness advocate of the period.

William Winter, 1876.

• Winter, William, *Quelqu'un* (1836-1917): Massachusetts-born, Harvard-educated Pfaffian. *NYSP* editor and critic. Penned the "Dramatic Feuilleton" as "Quelqu'un" and contributed a column entitled "Caprices." In 1860, he married poet Elizabeth Campbell, and they raised five children on Staten Island. William became a celebrated drama critic for the *Tribune*, essayist, poet, and memoirist.

Winter Garden Theatre (1854-1867): 204-214 Mercer St. Known as New York Theatre; Tripler's Hall; Metropolitan Theatre; Laura Keene's Theatre (1855); and Burton's New Theatre (1856).

Alfred M. Wood.

wold: woods.

wonderful: surprising.

Wood, Alfred M. (1825-1895): Long Island merchant, enlisted as Union colonel in the Civil War, and was wounded in battle. After his return to Brooklyn, he was elected mayor of Brooklyn.

Wood, Fernando (1812-1881): New York City Mayor and US Congressman from the Democratic Party; merchant and real estate investor. Known for corruption, scandal, and his Southern sympathies, at one point promoting New York City take a neutral stance in the Civil War.

• Wood, Frank (1840-1864): Auburn, NY-born Pfaffian. Humorist, editor at *Vanity Fair,* journalist, playwright. Secessionist until the war, when he became a Unionist. Died young of tuberculosis.

Fernando Wood, by Brady.

Wood, Mrs. John (Matilda Charlotte Vining) (1831-1915): English actress and theater manager.

Wood's Minstrel Hall, Wood's Theatre, German Thalia Theatre: Converted synagogue at 514 Broadway.

wooden nutmeg: a phony device; as, in the early 19th century, hucksters would sell fake nutmeg fruits carved from wood, as real nutmegs were scarce and brought such a profit.

woodpecker: an engraver/illustrator.

woof: the texture of a woven fabric.

worldly: pertaining to secular life, as opposed to a spiritual focus.

wot: to be aware of.

• Wyman, Don Lloyd (1842-1931): Ohio lawyer, poet, educator.

yclept: a burlesque term, meaning called or named.

yellow-covered: in literature, cheap or sensational, from the yellow covers often given to such publications.

Zouaves: A Chicago-based Illinois militia regiment led by New Yorker Elmer E. Ellsworth, modeled after the Algerian Zouave-inspired French Imperial Guard. Renowned for their precise maneuvers and colorful uniforms, they were celebrated during a visit to NYC in 1860. *See Ellsworth.*

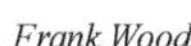

Frank Wood.

The Chicago Zuoaves on their 1860 tour of New York City.

Zoyara, Madamoiselle Ella: Omar Kingsley (1840-79): male circus performer from St. Louis. Disguised as a girl to enhance interest in his act, featuring "graceful" and daring riding tricks. Despite being exposed and abandoning the persona, he later revived it for benefits. Died of smallpox in Bombay.

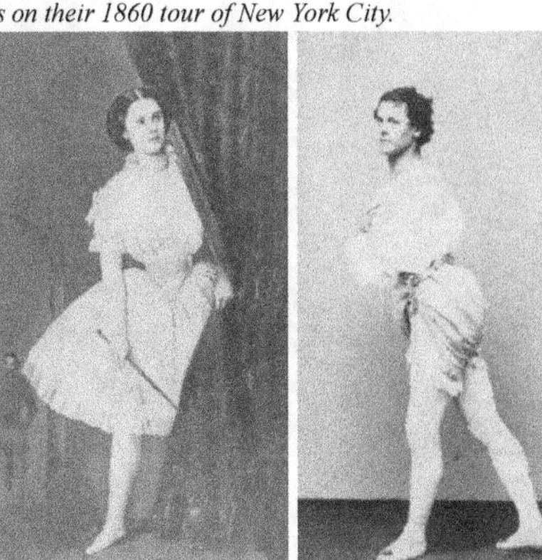

M'lle Ella Zoyara & Omar Kingsley.

Nota Bene: My Visit to Pfaff's!

Though the city has grown and transformed dramatically over the past 160 years, many remnants of its ante-bellum past can be found in Greenwich Village. Grace Church, St. Mark's Church-in-the-Bowery, and (old) St. Patrick's Cathedral are still standing and active. The Astor Library building also survives, and is now the thriving home to The Public Theatre. It peers across Lafayette Place to LaGrange Terrace, a row of Greek Revival townhouses, of which four of the original nine survive, built at a time when the street was a locus for the city's elite.

As we stroll south on Broadway, we can find many of the old hotel buildings still quietly standing, applied to mixed-use purposes, their days of serving bustling tourists in town for the theatre having lapsed for more than a century.

Just after we pass Bond Street, just before Bleecker, we find the original building that housed the Coleman House Hotel at 647 Broadway. The ground floor houses a modern deli no one would suspect to have such a history.

I cannot reveal how I gained access to the basement, but I did, and this is what I found.

The basement has been many-times repurposed, so there's all sorts of equipment kept there or operating there, serving the businesses the building houses. Modern cinder block walls and make-shift rooms with Costco doors hastily partition the area. The original ceiling is obscured by a drop-ceiling.

Pfaff's original ceiling with light wells.

Period descriptions of Pfaff's describe a brick four-fold vaulted ceiling with light wells, which are essentially holes in the brick to let in natural light and fresh air. The bohemians had a long table "under the sidewalk" as is often noted. The Bellew woodcuts, found under "Pfaff's" in the glossary, taken from the February 6, 1864 issue of Demorest's Illustrated News, were obviously made from sketches drawn in person at Pfaff's because they faithfully include the vaulted ceiling and the light wells.

To my delight, when I turned to face in the direction of Broadway, I found the drop ceiling to be incomplete. The original vaulted brick ceiling was exposed on that end, as were the light wells. There was even a long table under the ceiling, as if the manager who decided to section out this area for a break room had an inkling of the basement's history.

The break area.

An unfinished poem c. 1861, by Walt Whitman:

The vault at Pfaffs where the drinkers and laughers meet to eat and drink and carouse
While on the walk immediately overhead pass the myriad feet of Broadway
As the dead in their graves are underfoot hidden
And the living pass over them, recking not of them,
Laugh on laughers! Drink on drinkers! Bandy the jest!
Toss the theme from one to another!
Beam up—Brighten up, bright eyes of beautiful young men!
Eat what you, having ordered, are pleased to see placed before you—after the work of the day, now, with appetite eat,
Drink wine—drink beer—raise your voice.
Behold! your friend, as he arrives—Welcome him, when, from the upper step, he looks down upon you with a cheerful look
Overhead rolls Broadway—the myriad rushing
The lamps are lit—the shops blaze in—the fabrics and jewelry are seen through the plate glass windows
The strong lights from above pour down upon them and are shed outside
The thick crowds, well-dressed—the continual crowds as if they would never end
The curious appearance of the faces—the glimpses first caught of the eyes and expressions, as they flit along.
(You phantoms! oft I pause, yearning, to arrest some one of you!
Oft I doubt your reality—whether you are real—I suspect all is but a pageant...)

UNION SQUARE
Washington Monument
EAST 17TH STREET
EAST 16TH STREET
EAST 15TH STREET
EAST 14TH STREET
EAST 13TH STREET
EAST 12TH STREET
EAST 11TH STREET
UNION PLACE
IRVING PLACE
THIRD AVENUE
FOURTH AVENUE
BROADWAY
Irving Hall
Manhattan Gas Company
Presbyterian Church
Academy of Music
University Medical College
Vinegar Factory
Lumber Yard of the Piano Manufactory
Wood Yard
Episcopal Church
Pianoforte Manufactory
Wallack's Theatre
Wallack's
Livery Stable
Irving House
Coal Yard
New York Medical College
Livery Stables
Baptist Church
Grace Church
Druggist

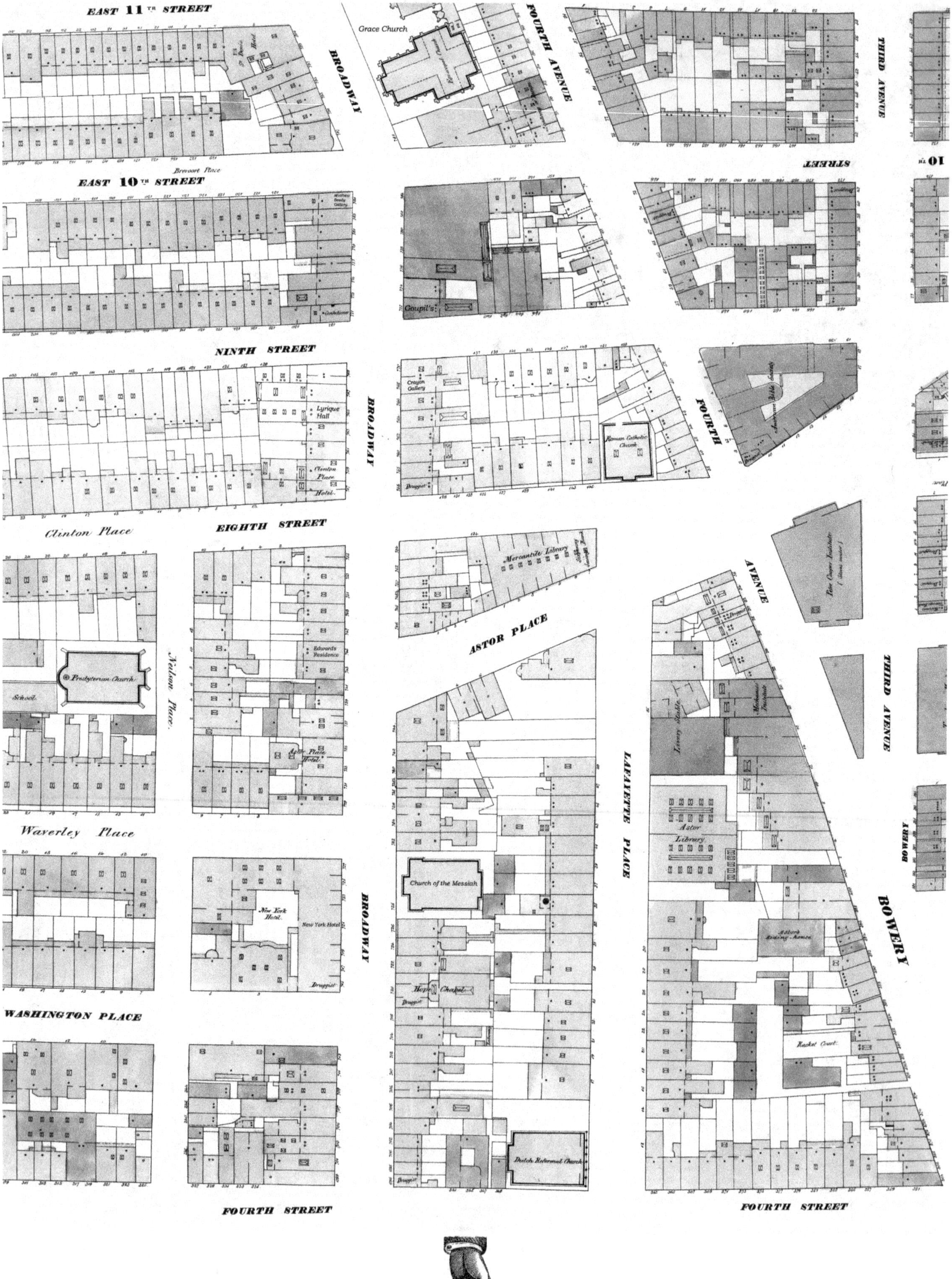

EAST 11TH STREET

Grace Church

BROADWAY

FOURTH AVENUE

THIRD AVENUE

Brevoort Place

EAST 10TH STREET

10TH STREET

Goupil's

NINTH STREET

Crayon Gallery

Lyrique Hall

Clinton Place Hotel

BROADWAY

Roman Catholic Church

FOURTH

Druggist

Clinton Place

EIGHTH STREET

Mercantile Library

The Cooper Institute

AVENUE

ASTOR PLACE

Edwards Residence

Presbyterian Church

School

Nelson Place.

Astor Place Hotel

Mechanics' Institute

Livery Stable

THIRD AVENUE

LAFAYETTE PLACE

Astor Library

Waverley Place

BOWERY

Church of the Messiah

New York Hotel

New York Hotel

BROADWAY

Druggist

Hope Chapel

Racket Court

WASHINGTON PLACE

Dutch Reformed Church

Druggist

FOURTH STREET

FOURTH STREET

FOURTH STREET
FOURTH STREET
LAFAYETTE PLACE
Episcopal Church
AMITY STREET
GREAT JONES STREET
BROADWAY
Burton's Theatre
Lafarge House
Bond St. Hotel
BOND STREET
Canterbury Hall
Stuyvesant Institute
Mozart Hall
Livery Stable
MERCER STREET
Pfaff's
Clarke's Photographic Gallery
Havana Hotel
Planters' Hotel
Savings Bank
BLEECKER STREET
Leroy Place
BLEECKER STREET
Druggist
Schaus' Gallery
Educational Institute
Institute of Art
Derby Gallery
Jews Synagogue
Maillard House
St. Thomas Episcopal Church
Laura Keene's Theatre
CROSBY STREET
Gymnasium
Episcopal Church
MULBERRY STREET
MOTT STREET
HOUSTON
STREET
HOUSTON STREET
Sisters of Mercy
Albanese Iron Works
Marble Works
Industrious Fleas
Lafayette Hall
Smithsonian House
Charley White's Opera House
Jersey Street
MERCER STREET
Buckley's Minstrels
French Theatre
Firemans' Hall
Mrs. Barrett's Brothel
Mrs. Cook's Brothel
Mrs. Willoughby's Brothel
Miss Hasting's Brothel
BROADWAY
Hotel
Garden
Niblo's Theater
Entrance to Niblos
CROSBY STREET
MARION STREET
MULBERRY STREET
St. Patrick's Cathedral.
Roman Catholic Church

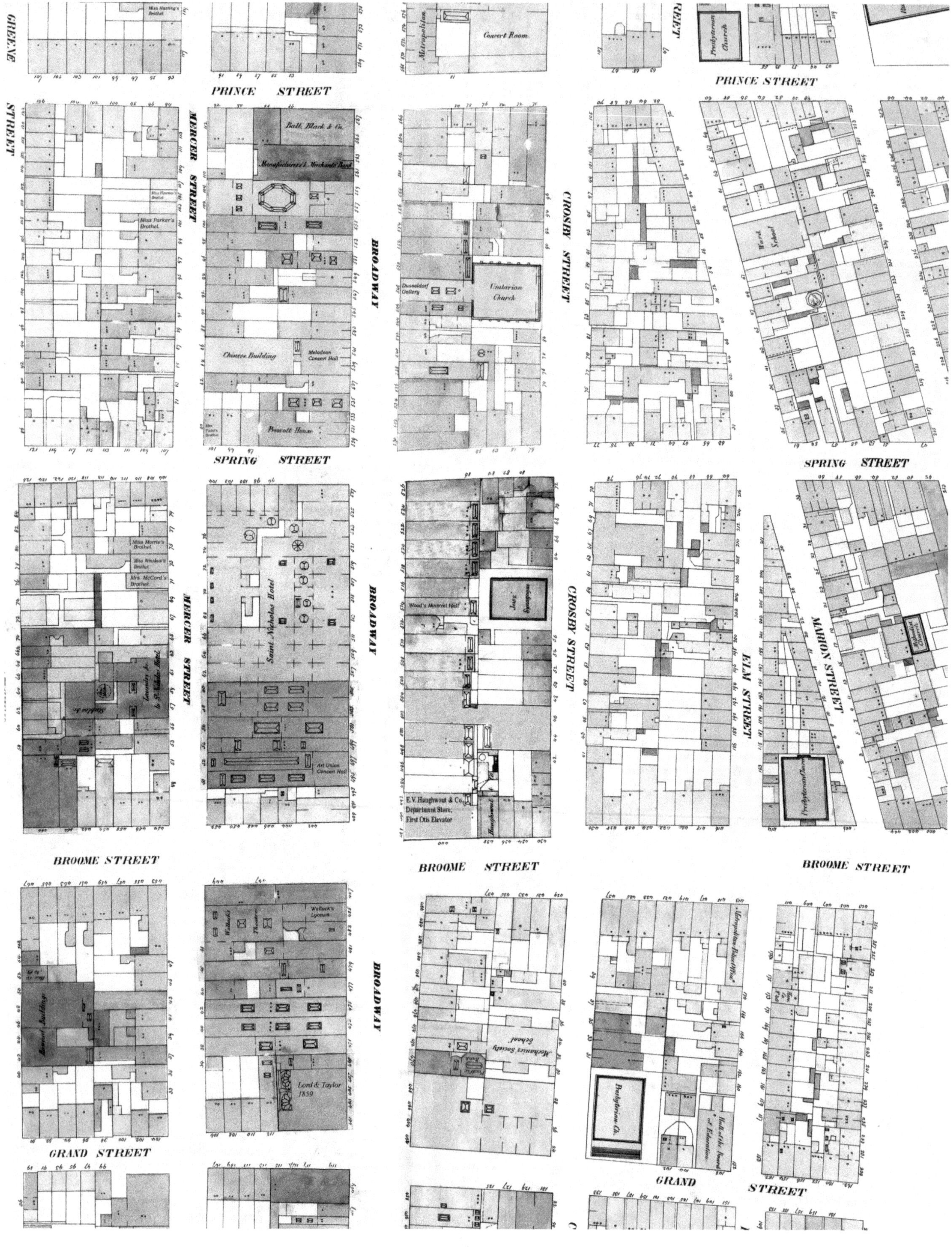

GREENE STREET
PRINCE STREET
SPRING STREET
BROOME STREET
GRAND STREET
MERCER STREET
BROADWAY
CROSBY STREET
ELM STREET
MARION STREET
Miss Hasting's Brothel
Metropolitan
Concert Room
Presbyterian Church
Ball, Black & Co.
Manufacturers' & Merchants' Bank
Miss Parker's Brothel
Dusseldorf Gallery
Unitarian Church
Chinese Building
Melodeon Concert Hall
Prescott House
Ward School
Miss Morris's Brothel
Miss Winslow's Brothel
Mrs. McCord's Brothel
Saint Nicholas Hotel
Art Union Concert Hall
Wood's Minstrel Hall
Jews' Synagogue
E.V. Haughwout & Co. Department Store, First Otis Elevator
Haughwout
Presbyterian Church
Wallack's Theatre
Wallack's Lyceum
Lord & Taylor 1859
Mechanics Society School
Presbyterian Ch.
Metropolitan Police Office
Hall of the Board of Education

About the Editor.

Raised in a small town in Pennsylvania, Mark Crane found his way to Greenwich Village for college in 1980 and soon became a true New Yorker, serving such diverse vocations as Court Clerk and Subway Motorman. With a master's degree in English Education, he homeschooled his children while building a successful online bookselling business.

This venture expanded into craft publishing, featuring iconic facsimile first editions and his own titles. In 2023, driven by a deep fascination with New York City's history—particularly its Bohemian legacy—Mark embarked on the meticulous task of transcribing the 3.3-million-word archive of the New York Saturday Press, a legendary literary journal from antebellum NYC with limited access in scholarly collections.

Now residing in the Bronx with his family, he is thrilled to see this extensive project come to fruition, inviting readers to explore the rich narrative of New York's forgotten literary past.

www.ingramcontent.com/pod-product-compliance
Lightning Source LLC
Chambersburg PA
CBHW060225010826
48976CB00015B/2666

* 9 7 8 1 9 6 7 9 8 7 0 0 9 *